# Pronunciation table

| CONSONANTS | | VOWELS | |
|---|---|---|---|
| These symbols are used for both the British and American pronunciations: | | | |
| Symbol | Key Word | Symbol | Key Word |
| p | pack | e | bed |
| b | back | æ | bad |
| t | tie | iː | sheep |
| d | die | ɪ | ship |
| k | class | ɑː | calm |
| g | glass | ɒ | pot |
| tʃ | church | ɔː | caught, horse |
| dʒ | judge | ʊ | put |
| | | uː | boot |
| f | few | ʌ | cut |
| v | view | ɜː | bird |
| θ | throw | ə | better |
| ð | though | eɪ | make |
| s | soon | əʊ | boat |
| z | zoo | aɪ | bite |
| ʃ | shoe | aʊ | now |
| ʒ | measure | ɔɪ | boy |
| m | sum | ɪə | here |
| n | sun | eə | hair |
| ŋ | sung | ʊə | poor |
| h | hot | eɪə | player |
| l | lot | əʊə | lower |
| r | rod | ɔɪə | employer |
| j | yet | aɪə | tire |
| w | wet | aʊə | flower |
| These additional symbols are used for the American pronunciations: | | ɑ | hot, father |
| | | ɔ | horse, long |
| | | ɝ | bird |
| | | o | hoarse, court |

# СЛОВАРЬ АКТИВНОГО УСВОЕНИЯ ЛЕКСИКИ АНГЛИЙСКОГО ЯЗЫКА

**Специальное издание**

**ЛОНГМАН ГРУП ЛИМИТЕД, ХАРЛОУ**

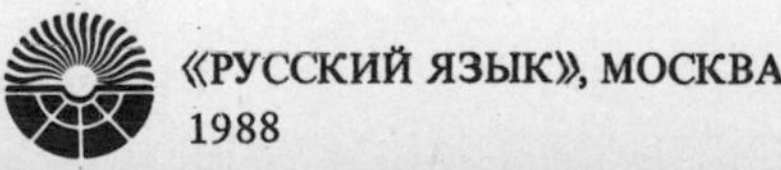

**«РУССКИЙ ЯЗЫК», МОСКВА**

1988

ББК 81.2 Англ–4
С48

**Словарь** активного усвоения лексики английского языка – С48 М.: Рус. яз., 1988 – 710 с.

Данный словарь – переиздание в СССР словаря, впервые выпущенного в 1983 г. английским издательством «Лонгман». Он включает в себя около 38 тыс. слов и словосочетаний, снабженных 55 тыс. примеров для активного использования учащимися в речи. В словаре даны иллюстрации, помогающие расширению словарного запаса. Дается грамматическая информация, некоторые правила правописания, указаны английские и американские варианты произношения.

Словарь окажет большую помощь изучающим английский язык на среднем этапе изучения.

Распространяется только на территории СССР.

С $\frac{4602020000-66}{015(01)-88}$ 179–88 ББК 81.2 Англ–4

ISBN 5–200–00011–4

This book was first published in the English language by Longman Group Limited of London.

С целью ускорения выпуска словаря, актуального для лиц, изучающих английский язык, словарь отпечатан способом фотоофсета с английского издания. Издательство надеется, что отдельные недочеты печати не послужат серьезной помехой при пользовании книгой.

Зав. редакцией
Л. П. Попова

Технический редактор
И. В. Богачева

Художественный редактор
В. С. Голубев

ИБ 5330

Подписано в печать 04.08.88. Формат 60x90/16. Бумага книжно-журн. Гарнитура таймс. Печать офсетная (фотоофсет). Усл. печ. л. 46,0. Усл. кр.-отт. 46,25. Уч.-изд. л. 96,84. Тираж 100 000 (I з-д 1–60 000 экз.). Зак. № 960. Цена 3 руб. Издательство „Русский язык" В/О „Совэкспорткнига" Государственного комитета СССР по делам издательств, полиграфии и книжной торговли. 103012 Москва, Старопанский пер., 1/5. Можайский полиграфкомбинат В/О „Совэкспорткнига" Государственного комитета по делам издательств, полиграфии и книжной торговли. 143200 Можайск, ул. Мира, 93.

# Contents

# Guide to the dictionary

## Spelling

| | | |
|---|---|---|
| Different spelling | **judg·ment, judgement** /ˈdʒʌdʒmənt/ *n* **1** the ability to decide correctly: *I can't make that decision for you. You'll have to use your judgment. . . .* | Different spellings are shown here –see page 10a |
| British and American spelling | **col·our**[1] *BrE* ‖ **color** *AmE* /ˈkʌlər/ *n* **1** [U] the quality which allows one to see the difference between (for example) a red flower and a blue flower when both are the same size and shape | American spellings are shown like this –see page 11a |
| Irregular plurals | **po·ta·to** /pəˈteɪtəʊ/ *n* **-toes** [C;U] a roundish root vegetable with a thin brown or yellowish skin, that is cooked and served in many different ways | Is the plural **-os** or **-oes**? We show the correct spelling here –see page 21a |
| Irregular verbs | **hope**[1] /həʊp/ *v* **hoped**, **hoping** [I;T +*to-v*/ (*that*)/*for*] to wish and expect; desire in spite of doubts: *We're hoping to visit England this year.* | Does the spelling change? We show it here if it does –see page 23a |

## Sound/pronunciation

| | | |
|---|---|---|
| Sound | **ap·ple** /ˈæpəl/ *n* a hard round fruit with white juicy flesh, and a red, green, or yellow skin | The pronunciation of each word is shown like this –see page 11a |
| Stress | **a·bil·i·ty** /əˈbɪləti/ *n* **-ties** [C;U] power and skill, esp. to do, think, make, etc.: *She has the ability to go to university, but she doesn't want to.* | Do you say **a̲bility** or **abi̲lity**? –see page 13a |

For more information on pronunciation turn to the inside of the back cover of this dictionary.

# Meaning

Clear and simple explanations

**egg** /eg/ *n* **1** [C] a rounded object with a hard shell, which comes out of a female bird, snake, etc., and which contains a baby animal before it is born (HATCHED) **2** this when eaten as food: *I had a boiled egg for breakfast.*

Word meanings are simply explained and easy to understand. Words that you may not know are written in large letters like THIS. You can find all these words in the dictionary –see page 14a

More than one mea ing

**a·cute** /ə'kju:t/ *adj* **1** (of the mind or the senses) able to notice small differences, esp. of meaning or sound; working very well; sharp: *Dogs have an acute sense of smell.* | *She has very acute hearing.* **2** severe; very great: *an acute lack of water* **3** (of a disease) coming quickly to a dangerous condition –compare CHRONIC **4** *tech* (of an angle) being less than 90 degrees –compare OBTUSE

Many words have more than one meaning. The first meaning is the most common one, but don't forget to check the others too –see page 16a

Examples of use

**flinch** /flɪntʃ/ *v* [I *from*] to move back a little when shocked by pain or fear: *Jane didn't flinch once when the doctor cleaned the cut in her arm.* | *He flinched when I raised my hand suddenly. He thought I was going to hit him.*

Many helpful examples show you how to use the word –see page 15a

# Grammar

Parts of speech

**age**[1] /eɪdʒ/ *n* **1** [C;U] the period of time a person has lived or a thing has existed: *He is ten years of age.*
**age**[2] *v* **aged, aging** *or* **ageing** [I;T] to (cause to) become old: *After his wife's death he aged quickly.*

These letters tell you if the word is a noun or a verb –see page 20a

Word families

**a·brupt** /ə'brʌpt/ *adj* **1** sudden and unexpected: *The train came to an abrupt stop, making many passengers fall off their seats.* . . . **–abruptly** *adv*: *The train stopped abruptly.* **–abruptness** *n* [U]

Words which are part of the same word family and which have different parts of speech are often shown like this

Grammar codes: countable and uncountable nouns

**ac·tion** /'ækʃən/ *n* **1** [U] movement using force or power for some purpose; doing things: *We must take action* (=begin to act) *before it is too late.* **2** [C] something done; deed: *Actions are more important than words.*

These letters tell you if you can use the noun in the plural. [C] means you can, and [U] means you cannot use this meaning in the plural –see page 20a

Transitive and intransitive verbs

**ar·rive** /ə'raɪv/ *v* **-rived, -riving** [I] **1** to reach a place, esp. at the end of a journey: *We arrived safely.*

**ar·rest**[1] /ə'rest/ *v* [T] **1** to seize in the name of the law and usu. put in prison: *The policeman arrested the thief.*

These letters tell you if the word is followed by a direct object. [I] means you cannot use this verb with an object. [T] means you must use this verb with an object –see page 22a

Verbs followed by a preposition or adverb

**ac·cuse** /ə'kjuːz/ *v* **-cused, cusing** [T *of*] to charge (someone) with doing wrong or breaking the law; blame: *The police accused him of murder.*

This means that the verb is often followed by the preposition *of* –see page 24a

Verbs followed by another verb

**en·joy** /ɪn'dʒɔɪ/ *v* **-joyed, -joying** [T] **1** [+*v-ing*] to get happiness from; like: *I always enjoy going to the cinema.*

**want**[1] /wɒnt/ *v* **1** [T +*to-v*] to have a strong desire to or for; feel a strong desire to have: *I want to go to the cinema tonight.*

These letters tell you that *enjoy* is often followed by a verb in the *-ing* form, and that *want* is often followed by a verb in the infinitive form –see page 25a

Phrasal verbs

**account for** sthg. *v prep* [T +*v-ing*] to give an explanation or reason for: *How do you account for all these mistakes?*

**thrash** sthg. ↔ **out** *v adv* [T] to reach agreement about (a problem) or produce (a decision) by much talk and consideration: *After a long discussion we were able to thrash out a plan.*

These letters tell you that the object always follows the preposition when you use *account for*. The arrow ↔ means that you can say *thrash the plan out* or *thrash out the plan* –see page 26a

# Choosing the right word

Formal and informal

> **kid**[1] /kɪd/ *n* **1** [C] *infml* a child: *There were three kids playing in the street.*

Would it be correct to use this word in a school essay? –see page 16a

British and American words

> **pave·ment** /ˈpeɪvmənt/ *n* **1** *BrE* ‖ **sidewalk** *AmE*– a hard surface or path at the side of the street for people to walk on

Shows the American word with the same meaning –see page 19a

Usage notes

> **a·lone** /əˈləʊn/ *adv,adj* [F] **1** without others: *He lives alone.* | *The house stands alone on a hill. . . .*
>
> USAGE **Alone** is neither good nor bad: *She reads a lot when she's* **alone. Solitary** and **lone,** when used of things, mean that there is only one: *a* **solitary/lone** *tree in the garden,* but when used of people they may show sadness, like **lonely** or **lonesome** (esp. *AmE*): *Come over and see me, I'm feeling a bit* **lonely.**

Usage note explains the meaning and use of similar words –see page 18a

Synonyms

> **ab·surd** /əbˈsɜːd/ *adj* against reason or common sense; clearly false or foolish; RIDICULOUS: *It's absurd not to wear a coat in such cold weather.*
>
> **foot·ball** /ˈfʊtbɔːl/ *n* **1** [U] also **soccer**– a ball game between two teams of 11 players, using a round ball which is kicked but not handled

This shows another word you can use with the same meaning –see page 17a

Opposites

> **hap·py** /ˈhæpi/ *adj* **-pier, -piest 1** feeling, giving, or showing pleasure or contentment: *She is a happy child.* | *They have a happy marriage.* –opposite **unhappy**

Shows a word with the opposite meaning –see page 19a

Related words

> **home·work** /ˈhəʊmwɜːk/ *n* [U] schoolwork, such as essays, which is done outside the classroom, esp. at home, in a library, etc. –see also HOUSEWORK

Shows a word which is related or which might be confused –see page 17a

# Using your dictionary

This dictionary tells you a lot about English words and how to use them – in writing and speaking English, as well as in reading. Like any dictionary, it tells you the meaning of words and how to spell them, but it can also help you with word-building, grammar, pronunciation, and other important parts of the language.

To use your dictionary properly, you need to know how to find all the information in it. It is easy to do this once you understand how the dictionary works. These exercises will help you to learn how to use the dictionary and to understand the most important language points that you need to know. You can work through them either by yourself or with your teacher in class. You will find the answers to the exercises on pages 702–703.

# Spelling

The words in this dictionary are listed in alphabetical order. Here is the alphabet:

a b c d e f g h i j k l m n o p q r s t u v w x y z

A B C D E F G H I J K L M N O P Q R S T U V W X Y Z

Here are some exercises to help you to find words in alphabetical order:

**Exercise 1** Can you put these words in order? We have done the first three:

| | |
|---|---|
| **fight** | arm |
| **end** | bend |
| **arm** | car |
| **car** | ........................ |
| **date** | ........................ |
| **bend** | ........................ |

**Exercise 2** Now do the same with these words:

| | |
|---|---|
| **wind** | under |
| **under** | ........................ |
| **zoo** | ........................ |
| **yellow** | ........................ |
| **Xmas** | ........................ |
| **visit** | ........................ |

## Finding a word quickly

Because the words in this dictionary are listed in alphabetical order, this means that words beginning with **a** are listed at the front of the dictionary, words beginning with **z** are listed at the back, and words beginning with **m** are listed around the middle. So if you want to find the word **menu** you can turn straight to the middle of the dictionary. You don't have to start at the front and look through all the pages.

To help you to find words quickly, in the top corner of each page you can see the first or the last word on that page. So you can work through the dictionary quickly just looking at these words until you find one which begins with the same letters as the word you are looking for. You can then read down the page to find the word you want. So you'll will find the word **braces** on the page with **bracelet** on the top.

**bracelet**

**bracelet** *n* a band or ring, usu. of metal, worn round the wrist or arm as a decoration
**braces** *BrE*||**suspenders** *AmE*– *n* [P] elastic cloth bands worn over the shoulders to hold up trousers –see PAIR[1] (USAGE)
**bracing** *adj apprec* (esp. of air) fresh and health-giving: *I love this bracing sea air!*

## Two-word entries

Sometimes words are joined together with a hyphen, like **middle-aged**, and sometimes they are written as two words, like **ice cream** and **right angle**. All these expressions are listed alphabetically as though they were only one word, so **ice cream** is listed after **icebox** and before **icicle**:

**icebox** *n* **1** a box where food is kept cool with blocks of ice **2** *AmE* for FRIDGE
**ice cream** *n* a sweet mixture which is frozen and eaten cold, usu. containing milk or other fat products: *chocolate ice cream*
**icicle** *n* a pointed stick of ice formed when water freezes as it runs or drips down: *icicles hanging from the roof*

EXERCISE 3 Put these two-word expressions in the correct place in the lists.

**ice cream** **absent-minded** **all right** **power station**

| | | | |
|---|---|---|---|
| **ice** | **absent** | **allowable** | **power** |
| ...................... | ...................... | ...................... | ...................... |
| **iceberg** | **absently** | **alloy** | **powerless** |
| ...................... | ...................... | ...................... | ...................... |
| **icicle** | **absolute** | **all-round** | **power point** |
| ...................... | ...................... | ...................... | ...................... |

## Phrasal verbs

In English there are many two- or three-word verbs. These verbs (PHRASAL VERBS) have a different meaning from the main verb on its own, so they are listed separately, under the main verb, like this:

> **add** *v* to put together with something else so as to increase the number, size, importance, etc.
> **add to** *v prep* to increase
> **add up** *v adv* to make sense; seem likely . . .
> **addendum** *n* something added . . .

**EXERCISE 4** Put these words and phrasal verbs in alphabetical order:

| | |
|---|---|
| **add up** | act ........................ |
| **act** | ........................ |
| **actual** | ........................ |
| **addition** | ........................ |
| **add** | ........................ |
| **act out** | ........................ |
| **act up** | ........................ |

## Abbreviations

Abbreviations, like **BBC**, **RAF**, **a.m.**, and **e.g.** are listed in the dictionary in the usual way, so you will find **a.m.**, and **AM**, listed between **am** and **amalgamate**:

> **am** *1st person sing. present tense of* BE
> **AM** *abbrev. for* amplitude modulation, . . . .
> **a.m.** *abbrev. for Latin* ante meridiem (=before midday) . . .
> **amalgamate** *v* (esp. of businesses, societies, groups, etc.) to join

## Different spelling

If you look up the word **judgment** in the dictionary, you will see that there are two different spellings for this word. Both of them are correct, but **judgment** is the more common spelling, so it is written first:

> **judgment, judgement** *n* **1** the ability to decide correctly: *I can't make that decision for you; you'll have to use your judgment.* **2** an opinion: *to form a judgment* **3** an official decision given by a judge of a court of law: *He passed judgment on the accused man.*

**EXERCISE 5** Find these words in the dictionary. Put a tick (✓) by the most common spellings:

| | | | | | |
|---|---|---|---|---|---|
| **judgment** | .......... | **generalise** | .......... | **enroll** | .......... |
| **judgement** | .......... | **generalize** | .......... | **enrol** | .......... |

## British and American spellings

If you look up the word **colour**, you will see that there are two spellings for this word, and that **colour** is used in British English (*BrE*), while **color** is used in American English (*AmE*).

> **colour** *BrE* || **color** *AmE* n the quality which allows one to see the difference between (for example) a red flower and a blue flower when both are the same size and shape

In this dictionary British and American spelling differences are always shown with the sign ||; the British spelling is on the left of this sign, with the label *BrE* and the American spelling is on the right, with the label *AmE*.

**Exercise 6** Look up these words in the dictionary. Which spelling would a British person use? Which spelling would an American use?

| | | | |
|---|---|---|---|
| **theatre** | ........................ | **rumour** | ........................ |
| **theater** | ........................ | **rumor** | ........................ |

---

# Pronunciation

The dictionary also tells you how to pronounce words.

We use a special alphabet to show pronunciation. It is written after the word between sloping lines /...../, like this: **apple** /ˈæpəl/.

> **apple** /ˈæpəl/ n a hard round fruit with white juicy flesh, and a red, green, or yellow skin

## Vowels and consonants

Here is a list of all the phonetic letters:

vowels: e æ iː ɪ ɑː ɒ ɔː ʊ uː ʌ ɜː ə

consonants: p b t d k g tʃ dʒ f v θ ð s z ʃ ʒ m n ŋ h l r j w

If you turn to the inside back cover, you will see a list of all these letters, with some common words to show you how they are pronounced. For example:

| CONSONANTS | | VOWELS | |
|---|---|---|---|
| These symbols are used for both the British and American pronunciations: | | | |
| Symbol | Key Word | Symbol | Key Word |
| p | pack | e | bed |
| b | back | æ | bad |

This means that the phonetic letter /p/ is said like the **p** at the beginning of the word **pack**, and that the phonetic letter /b/ is said like the **b** at the beginning of the word **back**. /e/ is said like the **e** in **bed**, and /æ/ is said like the **a** in **bad**. You don't have to learn all of the phonetic letters. Just remember to look at the list on the inside back cover when you're not sure how to pronounce them.

**EXERCISE 7** All the words below have one of these vowel sounds:

/iː/ as in **team** /e/ as in **bed** /ɒ/ as in **pot** /uː/ as in **do**.

Put each word in one of the lists under the correct vowel sound. Use your dictionary for any words you don't know how to pronounce:

**bed, blue, boot, bread, bury, cough, do, field, friend, group, key, move, people, pot, said, scene, sheep, shoe, team, watch**

| /iː/ | /e/ | /ɒ/ | /uː/ |
|---|---|---|---|
| team | bed | pot | do |
| ...................... | ...................... | ...................... | ...................... |
| ...................... | ...................... | ...................... | ...................... |
| ...................... | ...................... | ...................... | ...................... |
| ...................... | ...................... | ...................... | ...................... |
| ...................... | ...................... | ...................... | ...................... |

Now check the sounds with the list on the inside back cover, and practise saying the words in the lists.

Did you notice that the words **bed**, **bread**, **bury**, **friend**, and **said** all contain the same /e/ sound, even though they are spelt differently?

## Spelling notes

Because many different letters can have the same sound in English, it is often difficult to know how to spell a word that you have never seen, but only heard. To help you to find these words, the dictionary contains a number of Spelling Notes, like the one shown here. This tells you that if you have heard a word that begins with the sound /f/, it may actually be spelt **ph-**, like **photograph**. If you don't find the word you are looking for at **f-**, you should look at **ph-**.

**F, f**

**SPELLING NOTE**
Words beginning with the sound /f/ may be spelt **ph-**, like **photograph**

**F, f** /ef/ the 6th letter of the English alphabet

**fable** /ˈfeɪbəl/ *n* a short story that teaches a lesson (a MORAL) or truth, esp. one in which animals or objects speak

# Stress

Most of the words in the exercises so far have been very short, and contain only one vowel sound. But many words consist of more than one SYLLABLE. Words like **about**, **afraid**, and **alone** have two syllables, or parts:

**about** /ə'baʊt/ **afraid** /ə'freɪd/ **alone** /ə'ləʊn/

If you look at the pronunciation guides for these words, you will see that they each have a /'/ sign, like the one in front of the /'b/ in **about**. This means that when we say these words we put more force (or STRESS) on the second syllable of the word:

**about** **afraid** **alone**

Look at the pronunciation guides for **able**, **almost**, and **angry** below:

**able** /'eɪbəl/ **almost** /'ɔːlməʊst/ **angry** /'æŋgri/

With these words, the /'/ sign is at the beginning of the word, and so we put more stress (force) on the first syllable of the word:

**able** **almost** **angry**

Practise saying the words **about**, **afraid**, and **alone**, and then say **able**, **almost**, and **angry**. Can you hear the difference? Remember to look for the /'/ sign when you look up a new word in the dictionary.

EXERCISE 8 Look up the pronunciation guides for the words below. All of them have more than one syllable, so look for the /'/ sign. Underline the part of the word that has the stress put on it:

| **ability** | **advantage** | **afternoon** | **afterwards** |
|---|---|---|---|

# Nouns and verbs with different stress

Read these sentences aloud:

*I bought a new* **record** *today.*
*The band went to the studio to* **record** *their new song.*

Did you say **record** correctly in the two sentences? The pronunciation guide in the dictionary will show you that the noun **record** is pronounced **record**, but the verb is pronounced **record**.

EXERCISE 9 Many words in English like **record** can be stressed in two different ways. Look up the words **increase** and **permit** in the dictionary, and underline the part of the word that is stressed in each example:

*The number of students at the school will* **increase** *next year.*
*There will be an* **increase** *in the number of students next year.*

*This card will* **permit** *you to enter the building.*
*You need a* **permit** *to enter the building.*

More information about stress is given on page 710.

## Syllables and hyphenation

It helps to learn the sound of a long word if you start by saying it one syllable at a time. If you look at the entry for **ability**, you will see that the word is divided into four parts by little dots:

**a·bil·i·ty** /ə'bɪlə̦ti/

This means that the word **ability** has four syllables, and you can learn to say it one syllable at a time:

**a bil i ty**
/ə 'bɪl ə̦ ti/

Now say it right through. Remember to put the stress on /'bɪl/:

**abil ity**

The dots in the word also show you where you can break a word at the end of a line of writing:

*Jane shows a lot of* **abil-**
**ity** *at school*

*Jane shows a lot of* **abili-**
**ty** *at school*

But don't leave only one letter at the beginning or the end of a line.

# Meaning

One of the main reasons that you need a dictionary is to find out the meaning of a word – its DEFINITION. In this dictionary, the definitions have been written using a limited defining vocabulary of only 2000 common words, the same as in the *Longman Dictionary of Contemporary English.* This means that the definitions of even the most difficult words are simply explained and easy to understand.

For example, look at the entry for **egg** shown here. Because there are no difficult words used in these definitions, you don't have to look up other words to understand what **egg** means.

**egg** *n* **1** a rounded object with a hard shell, which comes out of a female bird, snake, etc., and which contains a baby animal before it is born **2** this when eaten as food: *I had a boiled egg for breakfast.*

**Exercise 10** Use your dictionary to answer these questions by looking up the words shown in **dark type** and reading their definitions.

1. What would you write an **address** on?

Answer: a letter, envelope, or parcel

> **address** *n* the number of the building, name of the street and town, etc., where a person lives or works, esp. when written on a letter, envelope, or parcel

2. When you **abridge** something, do you make it longer or shorter?

Answer: ..........

3. If two things are **adjacent**, are they close together or far apart?

Answer: ..........

4. What can be **ajar**?

Answer: ..........

5. What kinds of animals are **poultry**?

Answer: ..........

6. Is an unmarried man a **spinster** or a **bachelor**?

Answer: ..........

7. What might cause you to **flinch**?

Answer: ..........

> **flinch** *v* to move back a little when shocked by pain or fear: *Jane didn't flinch once when the doctor cleaned the cut in her arm.* | *He flinched when I raised my hand suddenly. He thought I was going to hit him.*

The entry for **flinch** shown here has two examples after the definition, *written like this*. These examples give you more information about what the word means and how to use it. So to answer question 7 you could have said "pain or fear", or you could have said "a doctor cleaning a wound", or "thinking that someone is going to hit you". In this way you can use the examples, as well as the definitions, to answer the questions.

8. What can be said to **act up**?

Answer: ..........

9. What is sometimes called "an **addition** to the family?"

Answer: ..........

10. What two things might **adjoin** each other?

Answer: ..........

## More than one meaning

When you looked at the entry for **addition** to answer question 9, you probably saw that it has two different meanings, numbered **1** and **2**. When an entry has more than one meaning like this, you should always read through all the meanings until you find the one that correctly explains the use of the word you are looking for.

EXERCISE 11 In the sentences below, the words in **dark type** all have more than one meaning. Look them up in the dictionary and decide which meaning correctly explains the use of the word in these sentences, and write the number here:

1. *She is a very* **able** *teacher.* ........
2. *I can't pay you, I have no money in my bank* **account**. ........
3. *John just won't listen to* **reason** *any more.* ........
4. *Janet was over the* **moon** *when she passed her driving test.* ........

When you answered question 3, did you see the phrase **listen to reason** at **reason** (definition **3**)? This phrase is in dark type to show that it is a very common expression.

**Over the moon** (question 4) is listed in the dictionary as a separate definition because it is an IDIOM. It is difficult to guess the meaning of an idiom because it is different from the meanings of the words in the idiom. We show idioms in the dictionary in **dark type**, and we list them under the first important word, so **over the moon** is in the dictionary at **moon**, **pull someone's leg** is at **leg**, and **take on board** is at **board**.

# Choosing the right word

## Formal and informal

Most of the words in this dictionary can be used by people in all parts of the world, and in any situation. But some words you will hear only on very formal occasions, or see when you are reading government or legal papers, for example; and some words are used only in informal speech or when writing to a close friend. Words which are suitable only for formal occasions are marked *fml* in the dictionary, and words which are suitable only for informal use are marked *infml*:

**destitute** *adj fml* without food, clothing, shelter, etc., or the money to buy them; very poor

**kid** *n infml* a child: *There were three kids playing in the street.*

**Exercise 12** Some of the words in the list below would not be suitable for a school essay, because they are too formal (*fml*), or too informal (*infml*). Tick (✓) the words that you could use in your essay:

| | | | |
|---|---|---|---|
| **adorn** | …….. | **seek** | …….. |
| **begin** | …….. | **succinct** | …….. |
| **commence** | …….. | **telly** | …….. |
| **erroneous** | …….. | **television** | …….. |
| **look for** | …….. | **wrong** | …….. |

If you look at the entry for **advertisement**, you'll see that it tells you that both **ad** and **advert** are other words for **advertisement**, but these words are used only in informal situations.

> **advertisement** *n* also **ad, advert** *infml*– a notice of something for sale, job to be filled, room to rent, etc, as in a newspaper, on television, or pasted on a wall

In English you can sometimes use two different words to mean the same thing. For example, you can say:

*John plays* **football** *for the school team.*
or:
*John plays* **soccer** *for the school team.*

We show this in the dictionary by writing:

> **football** *n* also **soccer**– a ball game between two teams of 11 players, using a round ball which is kicked but not handled

## See also/Compare

**Homework** and **housework** are two words that are often confused with each other:

> **homework** *n* schoolwork, such as essays, which is done outside the classroom, esp. at home, in a library, etc –see also HOUSEWORK

> **housework** *n* work done to keep the inside of a house clean and tidy –see also HOMEWORK

When you look up a word that is easily confused with another word, such as **homework** and **housework**, the dictionary tells you to look at the other one so that you can be sure that you have chosen the right word for the meaning you want.

## Usage notes

Look at the entry for **kill** here. After the definitions there is a USAGE note which tells you the different meanings and uses of this and other words which all mean "kill".

**kill** *v* **1** to cause to die: .....
USAGE **kill** is a general word meaning to cause (anything) to die, but **murder** means to kill a person on purpose: *My uncle was* **killed** *in a plane crash.* | *The cold weather* **killed** *our tomato plants.* | *She was sent to prison for* **murdering** *her husband.* ..... To **assassinate** means to kill an important political figure: *an attempt to* **assassinate** *the President*

EXERCISE 13 Read through the USAGE note at **kill**, and use one of the words **kill**, **murder**, and **assassinate** to complete the sentences below.

*There was an election after the President was .......................*

*The boy was ...................... in a car accident.*

## Study notes

The Study Notes, like the Usage notes bring together a lot of words to tell you something about their meaning, use, or grammar. Turn to the Study Notes on **pairs of verbs** on page 429. This tells you the differences between **lend** and **borrow**, **bring** and **take**, and **say** and **tell**.

EXERCISE 14 Read the Study Note on **pairs of verbs** on page 429. Then put **bring** or **take** in each sentence:

*Please ....................... some wine when you come to the party.*

*Next week my father is going to ....................... my young sister to the cinema.*

## Pictures

In the dictionary you will find pictures of a shop, a station, an airport, and other things. You can easily see the names of things in the pictures, and underneath you will find more useful words and expressions.

Many of the pictures have questions about the names of things in the picture, or about the words and expressions that are used underneath. Turn to the picture of a shop on page 563. Look at the picture and read the text underneath, then answer the questions here:

EXERCISE 15 Fill in the gaps with the correct words from the shop picture text:

**a** This dress is too big. It doesn't .............. me.
**b** When you buy clothes in a .............. they are cheaper.
**c** I like this dress. Can I .............. it on?

## British and American words

We have already seen that words are sometimes spelt differently in British and American English, and there are some word differences too. For example a British speaker would use the word **pavement** where an American would use the word **sidewalk**. In the dictionary, words which are used only by British speakers are marked *BrE*, and words which are used only by American speakers are marked *AmE*. They are separated by the sign ||, like this:

**pavement** *BrE* || **sidewalk** *AmE*– *n* a hard surface or path at the side of a street for people to walk on

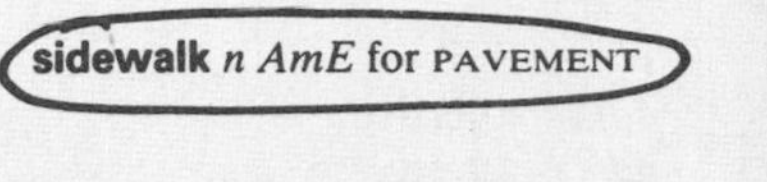
**sidewalk** *n AmE* for PAVEMENT

This means that **sidewalk** is the American word for **pavement**, and that you can find the meaning of **sidewalk** at **pavement** in the dictionary.

## Opposites

When you look up a word, the dictionary also shows you words with the opposite meaning, like this:

**happy** *adj* feeling, giving, or showing pleasure or contentment: *She is a happy child.* | *They have a happy marriage.* –opposite **unhappy**

This means that **unhappy** has the opposite meaning to **happy**, and we can say:

*Is she* **happy** *in her new job? No, she's very* **unhappy**.

Opposites like **unhappy** are often formed by adding a small group of letters to the beginning of a word. So we have:

**accurate** opposite **inaccurate** **allow** opposite **disallow**

EXERCISE 16 Look up the words below in the dictionary, and write down their opposites.

| | | | |
|---|---|---|---|
| **agree** | ...................... | **relevant** | ...................... |
| **adaptable** | ...................... | **inflate** | ...................... |
| **allow** | ...................... | **logical** | ...................... |
| **adequate** | ...................... | **mature** | ...................... |

Sometimes the opposite is not formed by adding letters, but is a completely different word. For example the opposite of **heavy** is **light**, and the opposite of **hard** is **soft** or **easy**. These opposites are shown in the same way:

**hard** *adj* **1** firm and stiff; not easily broken or bent: *hard stone* | *hard skin* | *The snow has frozen hard.* –opposite **soft** **2** difficult (to do or understand): *This question is too hard, I can't answer it.* –opposite **easy**

# Grammar

## Parts of speech

This dictionary tells you a lot about the grammar of words and how to use them in sentences. The first thing it tells you is whether a word is a noun, verb, adjective, etc. This information is shown like this:

*n* = noun
*v* = verb
*adj* = adjective
*adv* = adverb
*prep* = preposition

**action** *n* .....
**add** *v* .....
**afraid** *adj* .....
**afterwards** *adv* .....
**at** *prep* .....

**Exercise 17** Choose the correct noun (*n*) from the list to complete these sentences:

**active** **activity** **advice** **advise**

*The market was very busy and there was a lot of* ..................................

*My brother wanted to buy a car so he asked for my* .............................

**Exercise 18** Now choose an adjective (*adj*) to complete these sentences:

**height** **high** **heat** **hot** **afraid** **fear**

*That huge building is over 200 feet* ..................................

*My little brother is* .................................. *of dogs.*

*He burned his hand because he didn't know that the pan was* ................

## Countable [C] and uncountable [U] nouns

If the word you look up is a noun, the dictionary shows you whether it has a plural or not. Nouns that don't have a plural are UNCOUNTABLE nouns, and are shown with a [U]; nouns that do have a plural are COUNTABLE nouns. We show these with a [C], or with no sign at all if they are only countable in all of their meanings (see Study Notes on page 494)

**bar** *n* **1** a piece of wood, metal, etc. that is longer than it is wide: *an iron bar | a bar of soap/chocolate/gold* **2** a length of wood or metal across a door, gate, or window that keeps it shut and prevents movement through it: *There were bars across the windows of the prison.*

**child** *n* **children** a young human being: *We've got five children* (= sons and/or daughters) *but one's still a baby.*

**EXERCISE 19** Tick (✓) the nouns in the list below that you can use in the plural:

| | |
|---|---|
| **attack** | ........................................ |
| **rice** | ........................................ |
| **apple** | ........................................ |
| **furniture** | ........................................ |
| **information** | ........................................ |
| **adventure** | ........................................ |

You will find more information on countable and uncountable nouns in the Study Notes on page 494.

## Irregular plurals

If you look at the entry for **child** above, you will see that it has a special plural form, **children**. Most nouns make plural forms by adding **-s** or **-es**. If a noun has a different plural form or where there is some doubt (as with nouns ending **-o** or **-y**) then the dictionary shows the plural like this:

**baby** *n* babies a very young child, esp. one who has not learnt to speak

**monkey** *n* -keys a small tree-climbing animal with a long tail, and part of the class of animals most like man

**potato** *n* -toes a roundish root vegetable with a thin brown or yellowish skin, that is cooked and served in many different ways

**radio** *n* -os an apparatus made to receive sound broadcast through the air by means of electrical waves

**foot** *n* feet the movable part of the body at the end of the leg, on which a person or animal stands

**sheep** *n* sheep a grass-eating animal that is farmed for its wool and its meat

**EXERCISE 20** What is the plural of these nouns?

| | | | |
|---|---|---|---|
| **donkey** | ........................ | **mouse** | ........................ |
| **tomato** | ........................ | **car** | ........................ |
| **ox** | ........................ | **fish** | ........................ |

## Nouns for groups of people [C;U +*sing./pl. v*]

There is a small set of nouns, like **team** and **committee**, that usually represent a group of people, and which can be used with either a singular or a plural verb when the noun is singular or uncountable [U]. For example:

*The football* **team is going** *to Europe next month.*
*The football* **team are going** *to Europe next month.*

When the noun is plural, however, it always has a plural verb:

*Both the football* **teams are going** *to Europe next month.*

These nouns all have the sign: [C +*sing./pl. v*] or [U +*sing./pl. v*] and are shown in the dictionary like this:

> **team** *n* [C +*sing./pl. v*] a group of people who work, act, or esp. play together

## Nouns that are only singular [S] or only plural [P]

Look at the entries for **clatter** and **cattle** here:

> **clatter** *n* [S] a number of rapid short knocking sounds, as when a number of things fall to the ground: *There was a clatter of dishes in the kitchen.*

> **cattle** *n* [P] large four-legged farm animals, esp. cows, kept for their meat or milk: *The cattle are in the shed.*

The [S] means that **clatter** is usually used only in the singular, with a singular verb. It has no plural.

The [P] means that **cattle** is used only in the plural, with a plural verb. It has no singular form. Many of these [P] nouns end in **-s** or **-es**, like **scissors**, but some do not, like **cattle**

## Transitive [T] and intransitive [I] verbs

If the word you look up is a verb, the dictionary tells you a lot about how to use it in a sentence. First, it tells you whether the verb is TRANSITIVE OF INTRANSITIVE (–see Study Notes on page 647). Transitive verbs are followed by a noun or noun phrase as a direct OBJECT, and are shown with a [T]; intransitive verbs don't have a direct object, and are shown with an [I]:

> **kick** *v* [T] to hit with the foot: *She kicked the ball.*

> **pause** *v* [I] to stop for a short time before continuing: *He walked to the end of the road and paused before he crossed over.*

But many verbs can be both [T] and [I]. For example, **smell** can be [T], as in:

*He stopped to* **smell** *the flower.*

or it can be [I], as in:

*The flower* **smells** *nice.*

> **smell** *v* 1 [I] to have or use the sense of the nose: *The flower smells nice.* 2 [T] to notice, examine, or recognize by this sense: *He stopped to smell the flower.*

**EXERCISE 21** Which of these are complete sentences, and which must have an object to complete the sentence?

| |
|---|
| *He* **abandoned** .............................................................. |
| *The storm* **abated** .............................................................. |
| *They* **amazed** .............................................................. |
| *The train* **arrived** .............................................................. |

For information on the objects of phrasal verbs, turn to the Study Notes on page 447.

## Verbs like *be* and *seem*

Some verbs, like **seem**, do not have an [I] or a [T] after them. These verbs are followed by another word which tells us something about the subject of the sentence. For example:

*John* **seems** *happy today.* *This bag* **seems** *heavy, what's in it?*

You will find more information on verbs in the Study Notes on page 647.

## Irregular verbs

Most verbs add **-ed** for the past tense and past PARTICIPLE, and **-ing** for the present PARTICIPLE, like **help:**

**help helped helping**

But look at the sentences below, with the verbs **break** and **fly**:

*Be careful or you'll* **break** *the glass.*
*Who* **broke** *the window?*
*Somebody* **has broken** *the clock.*
*You're always* **breaking** *things.*

*Birds can* **fly**.
*The aeroplane* **flew** *past.*
*I've never* **flown** *in an aeroplane.*
*Do you like* **flying?**

**Break** and **fly** are examples of irregular verbs, and to help you use them we list the different parts of the verb, like this:

**break** *v* **broke, broken, breaking** [I;T] to (cause to) separate into parts suddenly or violently, but not by cutting or tearing: *I dropped the glass and it broke.* | *Somebody has broken the chair.*

**broken** *v past participle of* BREAK

**fly** *v* **flew, flown, flying** [I] to move through the air by means of wings or a machine: *A bird flew in through the window.* | *I have never flown in an aeroplane.*

**flew** *v past tense of* FLY

There is a list of irregular verbs with their different parts on page 708.

**Exercise 22** This list contains some irregular verb past forms. Look them up in the dictionary to find the present:

| | | | |
|---|---|---|---|
| **awoke** | ...................... | **drank** | ...................... |
| **chosen** | ...................... | **rode** | ...................... |

## Verbs not used in the *-ing* form [not *be* + *v-ing*]

With most verbs we can say:

*I go to London every week.* or *I am going to London tomorrow.*

Other verbs we do not usually use in the **-ing** form. For example:

*I* **know** *John quite well.* NOT– **I am knowing John quite well.*
*I can* **see** *the book on the shelf.* NOT– **I am seeing the book on the shelf.*

Verbs like **know** and **see** are shown in the dictionary like this. Other verbs used like this include **like**, **love**, **want**, **wish**, **believe**, **mean**, **understand**, **appear**, **seem**, etc.

> **know** v [not *be* + *v-ing*] to have information in the mind: *I know he's there because I saw him.*

## Verbs followed by prepositions and adverbs [*of, from*]

Look at the sentences below:

*The police accused John of stealing the money.*
*She accused me of breaking her watch.*

You can see that both of these sentences use the verb **accuse**, and follow it with a direct object and then the preposition **of** (accuse someone of something). This is how we show this pattern in the dictionary:

> **accuse** v [T *of*] to charge (someone) with doing wrong or breaking the law; blame: *The police accused him of murder.*

**Exercise 23** Complete the sentences below by writing in the correct preposition:

*He* **absconded** .................................. *the bank with a lot of money.*

*I* **abstained** .................................. *voting at the meeting.*

*We* **adapted** .................................. *the cold weather very quickly.*

*I went to* **apply** .................................. *the job, but it had already gone.*

## Verbs followed by a clause beginning with *that*

The sentences below all show verbs which are often followed by a clause beginning with the word **that**:

*I* **think that** *he will be late.* *I* **believe that** *we will win.*

**think** and **believe** are often used with **that**, so we show it in the dictionary:

**think** *v* 2 [T +*that*] to believe; consider: *I think (that) he's wrong, don't you*?

Note that the word **that** is in brackets (.......) here, because you can sometimes miss it out. We could also say, for example: *I think he's wrong, don't you*?

## Verbs followed by another verb in the *-ing* form

**enjoy** and **like** are often followed by another verb in the **-ing** form:

*I* **enjoy riding** *my bicycle.* *I* **like going** *to the cinema.*

This is how we show this in the dictionary. If you read the examples you can see that you can use a noun after **enjoy**, but if you do use a verb it must be in the **-ing** form.

**enjoy** *v* [T +*v-ing*] to get happiness from; like: *I enjoyed the film.* | *I always enjoy going to the cinema.*

## Verbs followed by another verb in the infinitive [+*to-v*]

**want** and **tell** are examples of verbs that can be followed by the INFINITIVE form of another verb with **to**:

*I* **want to go** *to the library.* *I* **told** *you* **to finish** *your homework.*

These verbs are shown in the dictionary like this. The examples tell you that you don't have to use a verb after **want**, but if you do the verb must be in the infinitive form with **to**.

**want** *v* [T +*to-v*] to have a strong desire to or for; feel a strong desire to have: *I want a drink.* | *I want to have a drink.*

When you look up a verb, check to see if it is followed by a word or phrase like the verbs above. Turn to the inside front cover for a full list.

EXERCISE 24 Make complete sentences using the words and verbs below:

| | |
|---|---|
| *I* **enjoy** ...................... *football.* | (play) |
| *I* **want** ...................... *home.* | (go) |
| *I have* **given up** ...................... | (smoke) |
| *We* **hope** ...................... *you again.* | (see) |

## Objects of Phrasal Verbs

The dictionary helps you to decide the correct position of the object when you are using a phrasal verb. Sometimes the object comes after the phrasal verb, and sometimes the object comes between the parts of the phrasal verb. Here are two examples:

| **look after** (sbdy) *v prep* [T] | **push** (sbdy) **around** *v adv* [T] |
|---|---|

*I* **looked after** *the sick man.*

*The older boys were always* **pushing** *the young boys* **around**.

You can see that the dictionary also tells you if the object is a person (sbdy.) or a thing (sthg.). The Study Note on phrasal verbs (page 447) tells you more about how the dictionary helps you to use and understand phrasal verbs correctly.

**Exercise 25** Use the dictionary to put the object of these phrasal verbs in the correct position. The object is always somebody (sbdy.) or something (sthg.):

| | |
|---|---|
| **look after** | ........................................................................ |
| **push around** | ........................................................................ |
| **reckon on** | ........................................................................ |
| **call on** | ........................................................................ |
| **throw around** | ........................................................................ |

## Adjectives

Most English adjectives can be used either before a noun or after a verb, like this:

*It's a* **long** *way into the city.* *The journey was quite* **long**.
*He told us an* **interesting** *story.* *His story was* **interesting**.

But some adjectives can be used in only one of these positions, and these adjectives are shown with the sign [A] or [F]. Turn to the Study Notes on page 9 for an explanation of these signs, and some examples.

If you turn to the Study Notes on page 119, you will find more information on COMPARATIVE and SUPERLATIVE adjectives.

# A, a

**A, a** /eɪ/ **A's, a's** *or* **As, as** the first letter of the English alphabet
**A** (in Western music) a musical note
**a** /ə; *strong* eɪ/ also (*before a vowel sound*) **an**– *indefinite article, determiner* **1** one: *a* THOUSAND *pounds|a* DOZEN *eggs|I caught a fish yesterday.|He's a friend of mine.* (=one of my friends) **2** (before some words of quantity): *a few weeks|a little water|a lot of people* **3** (after *half, so, such, what, how, rather, too*): *rather a nice girl|What a nice girl (she is)!|I've never met such a nice girl.* **4** any; every; the thing called: *A bicycle has two wheels.* **5** a kind of: *Médoc is a very good wine.* **6** a container or UNIT (1) of: *I'd like a coffee, please.|I'd like a beer, please.* **7** (used before [S] nouns. Some of these words are actions): *You need a wash.* **8** each; every; PER: *Six times a day|£2 a* DOZEN
**ab·a·cus** /'æbəkəs/ *n* **-cuses** a frame holding wires on which small balls can be moved, used for counting
**a·ban·don** /ə'bændən/ *v* [T] **1** to leave completely and for ever; desert: *He abandoned his wife and went away with all their money.* **2** to give up, esp. without finishing; stop: *The search was abandoned when night came.* –**abandonment** *n* [U]
**a·base** /ə'beɪs/ *v* **-based, -basing** [T] *fml* to make (someone, esp. oneself) have less self-respect; make humble: *He would not abase himself by showing fear.* –**abasement** *n* [U]
**a·bashed** /ə'bæʃt/ *adj fml* uncomfortable and ashamed, esp. in the presence of others: –see also UNABASHED
**a·bate** /ə'beɪt/ *v* **-bated, -bating** [I] *fml* (of storms, pain, sounds, etc.) to become less fierce; decrease: *The ship waited in the harbour until the storm abated.* –see also UNABATED –**abatement** *n* [U]
**ab·at·toir** /'æbətwɑːʳ/ *n BrE* for SLAUGHTERHOUSE
**ab·bess** /'æbɪ̵s, 'æbes/ *n* a woman who is the head of a religious establishment for women (CONVENT) –compare ABBOT
**ab·bey** /'æbi/ *n* (esp. formerly) a building in which Christian men (MONKS) or women (NUNS) live and work; MONASTERY or CONVENT –compare PRIORY
**ab·bot** /'æbət/ *n* [A;C] a man who is the head of a religious establishment for men (MONASTERY) –compare ABBESS
**ab·bre·vi·ate** /ə'briːvieɪt/ *v* **-ated, -ating** [T] to make (a word, story, etc.) shorter
**ab·bre·vi·a·tion** /əˌbriːvi'eɪʃən/ *n* a shortened form of a word, often one used in writing (such as *Mr*)
**ab·di·cate** /'æbdɪkeɪt/ *v* **-cated, -cating** [I;T *from*] *fml* to give up (a position or right): *The King abdicated (from) the* THRONE.*|He abdicated all responsibility for the care of the child.* –**abdication** /-'keɪʃən/ *n* [C;U]
**ab·do·men** /'æbdəmən, æb'dəʊ-/ *n tech* a main part of the body in animals, between the chest and legs –**abdominal** /æb'dɒmɪ̵nəl‖-'dɑ-/ *adj*
**ab·duct** /æb'dʌkt, əb-/ *v* [T] to take away (a person) unlawfully, often by force; KIDNAP: *The police think the missing boy has been abducted.* –**abduction** *n* [U]
**a·bet** /ə'bet/ *v* **-tt-** [T] **aid and abet** *law or humor* to help (someone) in a plan, esp. a crime
**a·bey·ance** /ə'beɪəns/ *n fml* the condition of not being in force or in use, at or for a certain time: *an old custom that has* **fallen into abeyance***|Your plan is* **in abeyance**.
**ab·hor** /əb'hɔːʳ, æb-/ *v* **-rr-** [T] to feel great hatred for; DETEST: *Most people abhor cruelty to children.*
**ab·hor·rent** /əb'hɒrənt‖-'hɔr-/ *adj* [*to*] hateful; DETESTable: *The idea of killing animals for food is abhorrent to many people.* –**abhorrence** *n* [U]
**a·bide**[1] /ə'baɪd/ *v* **-bided, -biding** [T +*to-v/v-ing*] (*usu. not in simple statements*) to bear; TOLERATE: *I can't abide people who keep me waiting.* –see BEAR[2] (USAGE)
**abide by** sthg. *v prep* **-bided, - biding** [T *no pass.*] to obey (laws, agreements, etc.): *If you join the club you must abide by its rules.*
**abide**[2] *v* **-bode** /'bəʊd/, **-bided, -biding** [I] *lit and old use* to stay; remain; live (in or at a place)
**a·bil·i·ty** /ə'bɪlɪ̵ti/ *n* **-ties** [C;U] power and skill, esp. to do, think, make, etc.: *She has the ability to go to university, but she doesn't want to.|a job more suited to his abilities* –see GENIUS (USAGE)
**ab·ject** /'æbdʒekt/ *adj* **1** (of a condition) as low as possible; deserving great pity: *abject poverty* **2** not deserving respect; showing lack of self-respect: *an abject beggar|an abject apology* –**abjectly** *adv*
**a·blaze** /ə'bleɪz/ *adj* [F] on fire: *The wooden house was quickly ablaze.|*(fig.) *ablaze with anger*
**a·ble** /'eɪbəl/ *adj* **1** [F +*to-v*] having the power, skill, knowledge, time, etc., necessary to do something: *Will you be able to come?|I was able to reach the handle.* –opposite **unable;** see COULD (USAGE); see Study Notes on page 386 **2** clever; skilled: *a very able student/teacher*
**a·bly** /'eɪbli/ *adv* in an able manner: *She controlled the meeting very ably.*
**ab·norm·al** /æb'nɔːməl‖-'nɔr-/ *adj* not NORMAL; different (usu. in a bad sense) from what is ordinary or expected; unusual; peculiar: *Is the child abnormal in any way?* –**abnormally** *adv* –**abnormality** /ˌæbnɔː'mælɪ̵ti‖-nər- / *n* **-ties** [C;U]
**a·board** /ə'bɔːd‖ə'bord/ *adv,prep* [F] on or into (a ship, train, aircraft, bus, etc.): *The boat is ready to leave. All aboard!|They went aboard the ship.*
**a·bode** /ə'bəʊd/ *n lit, fml, or humor* place where one lives; home: (*law*) *a person* **of/with no fixed abode**
**a·bol·ish** /ə'bɒlɪʃ‖ə'bɑ-/ *v* [T] to bring to an end by law; stop: *Slavery was abolished in England in the*

*19th century.*|*There are many bad customs and laws that ought to be abolished.* –**abolition** /ˌæbəˈlɪʃən/ *n* [U]: *the abolition of slavery* –**abolitionist** *n*

**a·bom·i·na·ble** /əˈbɒmənəbəl, -mənə-‖əˈbɑ-/ *adj* causing great dislike; hateful; DETESTable: *The judge said it was the most abominable crime he had ever heard of.*|*(infml) The food in this hotel is abominable.* –**abominably** *adv*

**ab·o·rig·i·ne** /ˌæbəˈrɪdʒəni/ *n* a member of a group, tribe, etc., that has lived in a place from the earliest times, esp. in Australia –**aboriginal** *adj,n*

**a·bort** /əˈbɔːt‖-ɔrt/ *v* **1** [T] to end (a PREGNANCY), or cause (a child) to be born too soon so that the child cannot live: *The doctor had to abort the baby/the pregnancy.* **2** [I;T] to give birth too early to (a dead child) –compare MISCARRY (1) **3** [I;T] to end or cause (a plan, job, etc.) to end before the expected time because of some trouble: *The space flight had to be aborted because of difficulties with the computer.*

**a·bor·tion** /əˈbɔːʃən‖əˈbɔr-/ *n* [C;U] (an example of) the act of giving birth or causing to give birth before the baby is properly developed so that the child cannot live, esp. when done intentionally –compare MISCARRIAGE (1)

**a·bor·tive** /əˈbɔːtɪv‖əˈbɔr-/ *adj* coming to nothing; not developing; unsuccessful: *an abortive attempt by the army to get rid of the government*

**a·bound** /əˈbaʊnd/ *v* [I] to exist in large numbers or great quantity: *Wild animals abound here/in this park.*

**abound in / with** sthg. *v prep* [T] to have in large numbers or great quantity: *The country abounds in valuable minerals.*

**a·bout**[1] /əˈbaʊt/ *prep* **1** on the subject of: *a book about stars* **2** in; through:|*They walked about the streets.*|*books lying about the room*|*He's somewhere about the house.* **3** *fml* on the body of: *He had a gun hidden* **about his person.** (=in his clothes) **4 what/how about: a** what news or plans have you concerning: *What about Jack? We can't just leave him here.* **b** (making a suggestion): *How about a drink?*

**about**[2] *adv* **1** here and there; in all directions or places; on all sides; around: *They go about together most of the time.*|*We sat about on the floor.* **2** somewhere near: *Is there anybody about?* **3** a little more or less than: *about five miles*|*about ten years* **4** so as to face the opposite way **5 be about to** to be just ready to; be going to: *We were about to leave when it started to rain.*

**a·bove**[1] /əˈbʌv/ *prep* **1** higher than; over: *We flew above the clouds.*|(fig.) *There's nothing in this shop (at/for) above £5.* –compare OVER **2** more than: *The company values hard work above good ideas.* **3** higher in rank or power than: *The captain of a ship is above a seaman.* –opposite **below** (for **1, 3**) **4** too good, proud, or honest to: *He wouldn't steal; he's above that.*|*He's above stealing.* **5 above all** most important of all

**above**[2] *adv* **1** [F] in or to a higher place; higher: *The clouds above began to get thicker.* **2** more; higher: *20 and above*|*children of six and above* (=six or older)|*a military meeting for captains and above* (=of higher rank) **3** on an earlier page or higher on the same page: *the facts mentioned above* –opposite **below**

**a·bove·board** /əˌbʌvˈbɔːd◂, əˈbʌvbɔːd‖əˈbʌvbord/ *adj* [F] without any trick or attempt to deceive; honourable: *His part in the affair was quite (open and) aboveboard.*

**a·bra·sive** /əˈbreɪsɪv/ *adj* **1** causing the wearing away of a surface **2** tending to annoy; rough: *She has an abrasive way of treating people.* –**abrasively** *adv*

**a·breast** /əˈbrest/ *adv* [F] **1** side by side, on a level, and facing the same direction: *lines of soldiers marching five abreast* **2 keep/be abreast of** to know the most recent facts about (something): *She reads the papers to* **keep abreast of the times.**

**a·bridge** /əˈbrɪdʒ/ *v* **-bridged, -bridging** [T] to make (something written or spoken) shorter –see also UNABRIDGED

**a·bridg·ment, abridgement** /əˈbrɪdʒmənt/ *n* something, such as a story, book, or play, that has been made shorter: *an abridgment for radio in five parts*

**a·broad** /əˈbrɔːd/ *adv* [F] **1** to or in another country: *He lived abroad for many years.* **2** *fml* over a wide area; everywhere: *The news of his death soon spread abroad.*

**a·brupt** /əˈbrʌpt/ *adj* **1** sudden and unexpected: *The train came to an abrupt stop, making many passengers fall off their seats.* **2** (of behaviour, character, etc.) rough and rather impolite –**abruptly** *adv*: *The train stopped abruptly* –**abruptness** *n* [U]

**ab·scess** /ˈæbses/ *n* a swelling on or in the body where a thick yellowish poisonous liquid (PUS) has gathered

**ab·scond** /əbˈskɒnd, æb-‖æbˈskɑnd/ *v* [I *from, with*] *fml* to go away suddenly and secretly because one has done wrong: *He absconded from the bank with all the money.*

**ab·sence** /ˈæbsəns/ *n* **1** [U] the state of being away or of not being present: *Please look after my house during my absence.* –opposite **presence 2** [C] an occasion or period of being away **3** [U] non-existence; lack: *The police were delayed by the absence of information about the crime.*

**ab·sent**[1] /ˈæbsənt/ *adj* **1** not present: *Four students are absent today.* **2** [A] showing lack of attention to what is happening: *an absent look on his face*

**ab·sent**[2] /əbˈsent, æb-‖æb-/ *v* [T *from*] *fml* to keep (oneself) away: *He absented himself from the meeting.*

**ab·sen·tee** /ˌæbsənˈtiː/ *n* a person who ought to be present but who stays away: *There were many absentees from the meeting.*

**ab·sen·tee·is·m** /ˌæbsənˈtiːɪzəm/ *n* [U] regular absence without good cause, esp. from work or duty

**ab·sent·ly** /ˈæbsəntli/ *adv* in a manner showing lack of attention

**absent-mind·ed** /ˌ·· ··◂/ *adj* so concerned with one's thoughts as not to notice what is happening, what one is doing, etc. –**absent-mindedly** *adv* –**absent-mindedness** *n* [U]

**ab·so·lute** /ˈæbsəluːt/ *adj* **1** complete; perfect: *That's absolute nonsense!* **2** having complete power; without limit: *An absolute ruler can do just as he pleases.* **3** not depending on or measured by comparison with other things: *In absolute terms, wages have risen, but not in comparison with the cost of living.* –compare RELATIVE –**absoluteness** *n* [U]

**ab·so·lute·ly** /'æbsəlu:tli, ˌæbsə'lu:tli/ *adv* **1** completely: *It's difficult to cross the desert by car, but not absolutely impossible.*|*I'm absolutely* BROKE. (=completely without money) –see Study Notes on page 389 **2** *infml* certainly: *"Do you think so?" "Absolutely!"* –compare RELATIVELY

USAGE The adverbs **absolutely** and **altogether** are pronounced /'····/ when they come before the word they describe: *I* **absolutely** *refuse.*|**altogether** *different.* They are pronounced /ˌ··'··/when they come after the word they describe, or when they stand alone: *different* **altogether**|"**Absolutely!**"

**ab·so·lu·tion** /ˌæbsə'lu:ʃən/ *n* [U] (esp. in the Christian religion) forgiveness for a SIN

**ab·solve** /əb'zɒlv‖-ɑlv/ *v* **-solved, -solving** [T *from*] to free (someone) from fulfilling a promise or a duty, or from having to be punished for a wrong

**ab·sorb** /əb'sɔ:b, əb'zɔ:b‖-ɔrb/ *v* [T] **1** to take or suck in (esp. liquids): *Use the cloth to absorb the ink.*|*The walls of the house absorb heat during the day.*|(fig.) *She's a good student and absorbs new ideas quickly.* **2** [*in, by; usu. pass.*] to fill completely the attention, interest, time, etc., of: *I was absorbed in a book and didn't hear you call.* –compare ENGROSSED **–absorption** *n* [U]

**ab·sor·bent** /əb'sɔ:bənt, -'zɔ:-‖-ɔr-/ *adj* able to ABSORB (1)

**ab·sorb·ing** /əb'sɔ:bɪŋ, -'zɔ:-‖-ɔr-/ *adj* very interesting; ENGROSSING

**ab·stain** /əb'steɪn/ *v* [I *from*] to keep oneself from drinking, voting, etc.; REFRAIN[1] (from something) **–abstainer** *n*

**ab·sten·tion** /əb'stenʃən/ *n* [C;U] the act or an example of keeping oneself from doing something, esp. from voting: *50 votes for, 35 against, and 7 abstentions*

**ab·sti·nence** /'æbstɪ̟nəns/ *n* [U] the act of keeping away from pleasant things, esp. from alcoholic drink **–abstinent** *adj*

**ab·stract**[1] /'æbstrækt/ *adj* **1** thought of as a quality rather than as an object or fact; not real or solid: *an abstract argument about justice*|*The word "honesty" is an* **abstract noun.** –compare CONCRETE[1]; see Study Notes on page 494 **2** (in art) connected with or producing ABSTRACTS[2] (2)

**abstract**[2] /'æbstrækt/ *n* **1** a shortened form of a statement, speech, etc. **2** (in art) a painting, drawing, etc., that does not try to represent an object as it would be seen by a camera

**ab·stract**[3] /əb'strækt, æb-/ *v* [T *from*] to remove by drawing out gently; separate: *to abstract the most important points from a long report*

**ab·stract·ed** /əb'stræktɪ̟d, æb-/ *adj* not noticing what is happening; deep in thought **–abstractedly** *adv*

**ab·strac·tion** /əb'strækʃən, æb-/ *n* **1** [U] the state of not attending to what is going on; ABSENT-MINDEDness **2** [C] an idea of a quality as separate from any object: *A good judge must consider all the facts of a case as well as the abstraction "justice".*

**ab·struse** /əb'stru:s, æb-/ *adj fml* difficult to understand **–abstrusely** *adv* **–abstruseness** *n* [U]

**ab·surd** /əb'sɜ:d, -'zɜ:d‖-ɜrd/ *adj* against reason or common sense; clearly false or foolish; RIDICULOUS: *It's absurd not to wear a coat in such cold weather.* **–absurdly** *adv* **–absurdity** /əb'sɜ:dɪ̟ti, -'zɜ:-‖-ɜr-/ *n* **-ities** [C;U]

**a·bun·dance** /ə'bʌndəns/ *n* [S;U] a great quantity; plenty: *At the party there was food and drink* **in abundance.**|*The country has an abundance of skilled workers, but not enough jobs.*

**a·bun·dant** /ə'bʌndənt/ *adj* more than enough: *The country has abundant supplies of oil.* **–abundantly** *adv*

**a·buse**[1] /ə'bju:z/ *v* **-bused, -busing** [T] **1** to say cruel or rude things to or about **2** to put to wrong use; use badly: *to abuse one's power*

**a·buse**[2] /ə'bju:s/ *n* **1** [U] unkind, cruel, or rude words: *He greeted me with* **a stream of abuse. 2** [C;U] wrong use: *the abuse of power/of drugs*

**a·bu·sive** /ə'bju:sɪv/ *adj* using or containing unkind, cruel, or rude language: *an abusive letter* **–abusively** *adv*

**a·bys·mal** /ə'bɪzməl/ *adj* very bad: *The food was abysmal.*

**a·byss** /ə'bɪs/ *n* a great hole which appears to have no bottom: (fig.) *an abyss of despair*

**AC** *abbrev. for* alternating current; a flow of electricity that changes direction with regularity, and at a very rapid rate –compare DC

**a·ca·cia** /ə'keɪʃə/ *n* **-cias** *or* **-cia** a tree, found mainly in hot countries, from which a GUM[2] (1) is obtained

**ac·a·dem·ic**[1] /ˌækə'demɪk/ *adj* **1** concerning teaching or studying, esp. in a college or university **2** concerning those subjects taught to provide skills for the mind rather than for the hand **3** *derog* not concerned with practical examples: *The question of how many souls exist in heaven is academic.*

**academic**[2] *n* a college or university teacher

**a·cad·e·my** /ə'kædəmi/ *n* **-mies 1** a society of people interested in the advancement of art, science, or literature **2** a school for training in a special art or skill: *a military academy*|*an academy of music*

**ac·cede** /ək'si:d, æk-/ *v* **-ceded, -ceding** [I *to*] *fml* **1** to agree to a suggestion, plan, demand, etc., often after disagreeing: *to accede to a request* **2** to take a high post or position after someone has left it –see also ACCESSION

**ac·cel·e·rate** /ək'seləreɪt/ *v* **-rated, -rating** [I;T] to (cause to) move faster –opposite **decelerate**

**ac·cel·e·ra·tion** /əkˌselə'reɪʃən/ *n* [U] the act of increasing speed; rate at which speed is increased –opposite **deceleration**

**ac·cel·e·ra·tor** /ək'seləreɪtə[r]/ *n* the piece of apparatus in a car, etc., which is used to increase speed –see picture on page 85.

**ac·cent**[1] /'æksənt‖'æksent/ *n* **1** a particular way of speaking, usu. connected with a country, area, or class: *He speaks with a strong Welsh accent.* **2** importance given to a word or part of a word by saying it with more force: *The accent in the word "important" is on the second syllable.* **3** the mark used, esp. above a word or part of a word, in writing or printing to show what kind of sound is needed when it is spoken

**ac·cent**[2] /ək'sent‖'æksent/ *v* [T] to pronounce (a word or a part of a word) with added force

**ac·cen·tu·ate** /ək'sentʃueɪt/ *v* **-ated, -ating** [T] to give more importance to; direct attention to: *The dark frame accentuates the brightness of the picture.* **–accentuation** /-'eɪʃən/ *n* [U]

**ac·cept** /ək'sept/ *v* **1** [I;T] to take or receive (something offered or given), esp. willingly: *The police aren't allowed to accept rewards.|He asked her to marry him and she accepted (him).* **2** [T +*that*] to believe; admit; agree to: *Did she accept your reasons for being late?|For a long time she could not accept that her husband was really dead.* –compare REJECT

**ac·cep·ta·ble** /ək'septəbəl/ *adj* **1** good enough: *Your work is not acceptable; do it again.* **2** worth receiving; welcome: *The gift is very acceptable.* –opposite **unacceptable** **–acceptability** /əkˌseptə'bɪlȷ̇ti/ *n* [U] **–acceptably** /ək'septəbli/ *adv*

**ac·cept·ance** /ək'septəns/ *n* **1** [C;U] the act of accepting or of being accepted **2** [U] favour; approval: *She won acceptance by her husband's family only through great patience.*

**ac·cess** /'ækses/ *n* **1** [C] means of entering; way in; entrance: *The only (means of) access to that building is along a muddy track.* **2** [U] means or right of using, reaching, or entering: *Students need easy access to books.*

**ac·ces·si·ble** /ək'sesəbəl/ *adj* easy to get or get into, to, or at: *The island is accessible only by boat.* –opposite **inaccessible** **–accessibility** /-ə'bɪlȷ̇ti/ *n* [U]

**ac·ces·sion** /ək'seʃən/ *n fml* [U *to*] the act of acceding (ACCEDE) or coming to a high position, office, etc.

**ac·ces·so·ry** /ək'sesəri/ *n* **-ries** **1** [*usu. pl.*] something which is not a necessary part of something larger but which makes it more useful, effective, etc.: *car accessories including the roof rack and radio|a black dress with matching accessories* (=hat, shoes, etc.) **2** also **accessary**– *law* a person who is not present at a crime but who helps another in doing something criminal

**ac·ci·dent** /'æksȷ̇dənt/ *n* [C;U] **1** something, esp. something unpleasant, undesirable, or damaging, that happens unexpectedly or by chance: *I had an accident in the kitchen and broke all the glasses.|We got back without accident.* **2** **by accident** by chance

**ac·ci·den·tal** /ˌæksȷ̇'dentl/ *adj* not happening by plan or intention; happening by chance **–accidentally** *adv*

**accident-prone** /'···· ·/ *adj* (of a person) more likely to have accidents than most people

**ac·claim¹** /ə'kleɪm/ *v* [T *as*] to greet or publicly recognize: *The new drug has been acclaimed (as) the most important discovery for years.*

**acclaim²** *n* [U] strong expressions of approval and praise: *The book received considerable acclaim.*

**ac·cla·ma·tion** /ˌæklə'meɪʃən/ *n* [C;U *usu. pl.*] loud sounds of approval and praise; ACCLAIM

**ac·cli·ma·tize**||also **-tise** *BrE* /ə'klaɪmətaɪz/ *v* **-tized, -tizing** [I;T *to*] to (cause to) become accustomed to the conditions of weather in a new part of the world: *We lived in Africa for five years, but never really acclimatized (to the hot weather).* **–acclimatization** /əˌklaɪmətaɪ'zeɪʃən||-tə-/ *n* [U]

**ac·co·lade** /'ækəleɪd/ *n* strong praise and approval: *His new book received accolades from the papers.*

**ac·com·mo·date** /ə'kɒmədeɪt||ə'kɑ-/ *v* **-dated, -dating** [T] **1** to provide with room in which to live or stay **2** to have enough space for **3** [*to*] *fml* to change (oneself, one's habits, etc.) to fit new conditions: *I can accommodate you/your wishes.*

**ac·com·mo·dat·ing** /ə'kɒmədeɪtɪŋ||ə'kɑ-/ *adj* willing to help; ready to change to suit new conditions –opposite **unaccommodating** **–accommodatingly** *adv*

**ac·com·mo·da·tion** /əˌkɒmə'deɪʃən||əˌkɑ-/ *n* [U] a place to live; room, flat, house, hotel room, etc.: *The high cost of accommodation makes life difficult for students in London.*

**ac·com·pa·ni·ment** /ə'kʌmpənimənt/ *n* **1** something which is usually or often found with something else **2** music played to support singing or another instrument

**ac·com·pa·nist** /ə'kʌmpənȷ̇st/ *n* a person who plays a musical ACCOMPANIMENT

**ac·com·pa·ny** /ə'kʌmpəni/ *v* **-nied, -nying** [T] **1** to go with, as on a journey **2** to happen or exist at the same time as: *Lightning usually accompanies thunder.* **3** to make supporting music for –see also UNACCOMPANIED

**ac·com·plice** /ə'kʌmplȷ̇s||ə'kɑm-, ə'kʌm-/ *n* a person who helps someone to do wrong

**ac·com·plish** /ə'kʌmplɪʃ||ə'kɑm-, ə'kʌm-/ *v* [T] to succeed in doing; finish successfully: *We tried to arrange a peace but accomplished nothing.*

**ac·com·plished** /ə'kʌmplɪʃt||ə'kɑm-, ə'kʌm-/ *adj* skilled; good at something, though not professional

**ac·com·plish·ment** /ə'kʌmplɪʃmənt||ə'kɑm-, ə'kʌm-/ *n* **1** [U] the act of ACCOMPLISHing or finishing work completely and successfully **2** [C] a skill; something in which one is ACCOMPLISHED: *Being able to play the piano well is just one of his accomplishments.*

**ac·cord¹** /ə'kɔːd||-ɔrd/ *v* [I *with*] *fml* to agree: *What you have just said does not accord with what you told us earlier.*

**accord²** *n* [U] **1** agreement: *The two governments are completely in accord on the question of preserving peace.* **2** **of one's own accord** without being asked; willingly **3** **with one accord** with everybody agreeing

**ac·cord·ance** /ə'kɔːdəns||-ɔr-/ *n* [U] agreement: *I sold the house,* **in accordance with** *your orders.*

**ac·cord·ing·ly** /ə'kɔːdɪŋli||-ɔr-/ *adv fml* **1** in a suitable manner: *Please inform us if you are not satisfied with the car, and we will act accordingly.* (=by giving you another one) **2** therefore; so –see Study Notes on page 128

**according to** /·'·· ·/ *prep* **1** as said or shown by: *According to my watch it is 4 o'clock.|According to George, she's a really good teacher.* **2** in a way that agrees with: *We will be paid according to the amount of work we do.*

**ac·cor·di·on** /ə'kɔːdɪən||-ɔr-/ *n* a musical instrument played by pressing the middle part together to force air through holes opened and closed by KEYS¹ (3) worked by the fingers –compare CONCERTINA

**ac·cost** /ə'kɒst||ə'kɔst, ə'kɑst/ *v* [T] to go up to and speak to (esp. a stranger), often in a threatening manner: *A strange man accosted him and asked for money.*

**ac·count¹** /ə'kaʊnt/ *n* **1** [C] a written or spoken report; description; story: *Give us an account of what* *happened.*|*He is a great footballer,* **by all accounts.** (=according to what everyone says) **2** [U] consideration; thought: *You must* **take into account** *the boy's long illness.* **3** [U] advantage; profit: *He* **put/turned** *his knowledge* **to (good) account.** **4** [C] a record or statement of money received and paid out, as by a bank or business: *The accounts show that business is beginning to improve.* **5** [C] an arrangement which allows one to buy goods and pay for them later: *I'll pay for the shirt now, but please put the shoes on my account.* **6** [C] a statement of money owed: *Please settle your account immediately.* (=pay what you owe)|(fig.) *I have an account to settle with you for calling me a thief.* **7** [C] a sum of money kept in a bank which may be added to and taken from: *My account is empty, I have no money in it.* –see also CURRENT ACCOUNT, DEPOSIT ACCOUNT, SAVINGS ACCOUNT **8 of great/no account** of great/no importance **9 on account of** because of –see Study Notes on page 128 **10 on no account** also **not on any account**– not for any reason: *On no account must you go there.*

**account²** *v* → ACCOUNT FOR

**ac·coun·ta·ble** /ə'kaʊntəbəl/ *adj* [F *to, for*] responsible; having to give an explanation: *I am not accountable to you for my actions.*

**ac·coun·tan·cy** /ə'kaʊntənsi/‖also **accounting** *AmE*– *n* [U] the work or job of an ACCOUNTANT

**ac·coun·tant** /ə'kaʊntənt/ *n* a person whose job is to keep and examine the money accounts of businesses or people

**account for** sthg. *v prep* [T +*v-ing*] to give an explanation or reason for: *How do you account for all these mistakes?* –see also UNACCOUNTABLE

**ac·cu·mu·late** /ə'kjuːmjʊleɪt‖-mjə-/ *v* **-lated, -lating** [I;T] to make or become greater in quantity or size; collect or grow into a mass: *to accumulate a large fortune* –**accumulation** /-'leɪʃən/ *n* [C;U]: *an accumulation of work while I was ill*

**ac·cu·ra·cy** /'ækjərəsi/ *n* [U] the quality of being ACCURATE; exactness or correctness –opposite **inaccuracy**

**ac·cu·rate** /'ækjərət/ *adj* careful and exact; exactly correct: *Give me an accurate report of what happened.*|*Is the station clock accurate?* –opposite **inaccurate** –**accurately** *adv*

**ac·cu·sa·tion** /,ækjʊ'zeɪʃən‖-kjə-/ *n* [C;U] (a) charge of doing wrong: *The accusation was that he had murdered a man.*

**ac·cuse** /ə'kjuːz/ *v* **-cused, -cusing** [T *of*] to charge (someone) with doing wrong or breaking the law; blame: *The police accused him of murder.*|*The angry man gave her an accusing look.*|*The judge asked the accused man to stand.* –**accuser** *n* –**accusingly** *adv*

**ac·cus·tom** /ə'kʌstəm/ *v* [T *to*] *fml* to make used to: *He had to accustom himself to the cold weather.*

**ac·cus·tomed** /ə'kʌstəmd/ *adj more fml than* **used**– **1** [F *to*] in the habit of: *I'm not accustomed to getting up so early.* **2** [A *no comp.*] regular; usual: *The director took her accustomed place at the end of the table.*

**ace** /eɪs/ *n* **1** a playing card that has a single mark or spot and usu. has the highest or the lowest value **2** *infml* a person of the highest class or skill in something: *She's an ace at cards*/*an ace card-player.*

**ache¹** /eɪk/ *v* **ached, aching** [I] to have or suffer a continuous dull pain: *I ache all over.*|*My head aches.*|(fig.) *She was aching to go to the party, but her parents wouldn't let her.*

**ache²** *n* a continuous dull pain: *an ache in the arm*|*headache*|(fig.) *heartache*

USAGE Nouns formed from **ache** are often treated as [U] when they mean a condition or state: *Chocolate gives me* **toothache**. When they mean a single attack of pain, they are either [C] or [U]: *to get* **stomachache** or *a* **stomachache**. But **headache** is always a [C] noun: *a nasty* **headache**.

**a·chieve** /ə'tʃiːv/ *v* **-chieved, -chieving** [T] **1** to finish successfully (esp. something, anything, nothing): *He will never achieve anything if he doesn't work.* **2** to gain (an aim, etc.) as the result of action: *As a result of advertising, we've achieved a big increase in sales this year.* –**achievable** *adj*

**a·chieve·ment** /ə'tʃiːvmənt/ *n* **1** [U] the successful finishing or gaining of something **2** [C] something successfully finished or gained esp. through skill and hard work

**ac·id¹** /'æsɨd/ *n* **1** [C;U] a type of chemical substance containing HYDROGEN which may destroy things it touches: *The acid burnt a hole in the carpet.* –opposite **alkali** **2** [U] *infml* for LSD (1) **3 acid test** a test or trial which will prove whether something is as valuable as it is supposed to be

**acid²** *adj* **1** having a sour or bitter taste like that of unripe fruit or VINEGAR **2** hurtful in speech –compare SARCASTIC

**a·cid·i·ty** /ə'sɪdɨti/ *n* [U] the quality of being acid; sourness

**ac·knowl·edge** /ək'nɒlɪdʒ‖-'nɑ-/ *v* [T] **-edged, -edging 1** [+*v-ing*/*that*] to accept or recognize (as); recognize the fact or existence (of): *When the election results were made known, the Prime Minister acknowledged defeat*/*that she was defeated.*|*She is acknowledged as*/*to be their best tennis-player.* **2** to state that one has received (something): *We must acknowledge his letter.* **3** to show that one recognizes (someone) as by smiling, or waving: *He walked right past me without even acknowledging me.*

**ac·knowl·edg·ment, -edgement** /ək'nɒlɪdʒmənt‖-'nɑ-/ *n* **1** [U] the act of acknowledging (ACKNOWLEDGE): *He was given a gold watch in acknowledgment of his work for the business.* **2** [C] something given, done, or said as a way of thanking, showing that something has been received, etc.: *I wrote to them three weeks ago, and I haven't had an acknowledgment yet.*

**ac·ne** /'ækni/ *n* [U] a disease (common among young people) in which spots appear on the face and neck

**a·corn** /'eɪkɔːn‖-ɔrn, -ərn/ *n* the nut of the OAK tree

**a·cous·tics** /ə'kuːstɪks/ *n* **1** [U] the scientific study of sound **2** [P] the qualities of a place, esp. a hall, which make it good, bad, etc., for hearing music and speeches: *The acoustics of the hall are so good that you can hear everything even from the cheapest seats.*

**ac·quaint** *v* → ACQUAINT WITH

**ac·quaint·ance** /ə'kweɪntəns/ *n* **1** [C] a person whom one knows, esp. through work or business, but who may not be a friend **2** [S;U *with*] information or knowledge, as obtained through personal experience rather than careful study

**ac·quaint** sbdy. **with** sthg. /ə'kweɪnt/ *v prep* [T] **1** *fml* to tell; make known to: *I am already acquainted with the facts.* **2 be acquainted (with)** to have met socially

**ac·qui·esce** /ˌækwi'es/ *v* **-esced, -escing** [I *in*] *fml* to agree, often unwillingly but without raising an argument **–acquiescence** *n* [U] **–acquiescent** *adj*

**ac·quire** /ə'kwaɪəʳ/ *v* **-quired, -quiring** [T] **1** to gain or come to possess by one's own work, skill, action, etc.: *He acquired a knowledge of the language by careful study.*|*The company has recently acquired a new office building in central London.* **2 acquired taste** something that one must learn to like: *Some alcoholic drinks are an acquired taste and are not liked at first.*

**ac·qui·si·tion** /ˌækwə̇'zɪʃən/ *n* **1** [U] the act of acquiring (ACQUIRE) **2** [C] something ACQUIRED: *This car is my latest acquisition.*

**ac·quis·i·tive** /ə'kwɪzə̇tɪv/ *adj often derog* in the habit of acquiring (ACQUIRE) or collecting things **–acquisitiveness** *n* [U]

**ac·quit** /ə'kwɪt/ *v* **-quitted, -quitting** [T] **1** to give a decision as in a court of law that (someone) is not guilty of a fault or crime: *They* **acquitted** *him* **of** *murder.* –opposite **convict 2** *fml, usu. apprec* to cause (oneself) to act in the stated (usu. favourable) way: *She acquitted herself rather well.*

**ac·quit·tal** /ə'kwɪtl/ *n* [C;U] the act of declaring or condition of being found not guilty, as in a court of law –opposite **conviction**

**a·cre** /'eɪkəʳ/ *n* a measure of land; 4,840 square yards or about 4,047 square metres

**a·cre·age** /'eɪkərɪdʒ/ *n* [S;U] the area of a piece of land measured in ACRES

**ac·rid** /'ækrə̇d/ *adj* (of taste or smell) bitter; causing a stinging sensation: *the acrid smell of burning wood*|(fig.) *an acrid remark*

**ac·ri·mo·ny** /'ækrə̇məni‖-məuni/ *n* [U] bitterness, as of manner or language **–acrimonious** /ˌækrə̇'məunɪəs/ *adj* **–acrimoniously** *adv*

**ac·ro·bat** /'ækrəbæt/ *n* a person skilled in walking on ropes or wires, balancing, walking on hands, etc., esp. at a CIRCUS **–acrobatic** /-'bætɪk/ *adj*

**ac·ro·bat·ics** *n* /ˌækrə̇'bætɪks/ [P;U] the art or tricks of an ACROBAT

**a·cross** /ə'krɒs‖ə'krɔs/ *prep,adv* **1** from one side to the other (of): *The stream is six metres across.*|*a bridge across/over the river*|*Can you swim across?* –see Study Notes on page 474 **2** [F] on the opposite side (of): *They live across (the road) from us.* **3** so as to cross: *The two lines cut across each other.*

**act¹** /ækt/ *v* **1** [I *on, for, as*] to take action: *The council must act before more people are killed on that dangerous road.*|*She acted on our suggestion.*|*In this case I'm acting for* (=in the interests of) *my friend Mr Smith.*|*A trained dog can* **act as** (=fulfil the purpose of) *a guide to a blind person.* **2** [I] to behave as stated: *The report said that the doctor had acted correctly.* **3** [I;T] to represent (a part) or perform by action, esp. on the stage: *Olivier is acting ("Macbeth") tonight.* **4** [I *on, upon*] to produce an effect; work: *Does the drug take long to act (on the pain)?*

**act** sthg. ↔ **out** *v adv* [T] to express (thoughts, unconscious fears, etc.) in actions and behaviour rather than in words

**act up** *v adv* [I] *infml* to cause trouble or suffering to someone; behave badly: *The children have been acting up again.*|*This old car is always acting up.*

**act²** *n* **1** *fml* a thing done; deed (of the stated type): *a foolish act*|*an act of cruelty* **2** (*often cap.*) a law: *Parliament has passed an Act banning the drug.* **3** (*often cap.*) one of the main divisions of a stage play: *Hamlet kills the king in Act 5 Scene 2.* **4** one of a number of short events in a theatre or CIRCUS performance: *The next act will be a snake charmer.* **5** *derog infml* an example of insincere behaviour used for effect (often in the phrase **put on an act**): *He doesn't really mean it, it's just an act.* **6 get in on the/someone's act** *infml* to get a share of an/someone's activity, and esp. any advantages that may come as a result

USAGE When **action** is used as a [C] noun it means the same thing as **act**: *a kind* **act/action**. Certain fixed phrases use **act** and not **action**: *an* **act** *of cruelty/of mercy*|*caught in the* **act** *of stealing*. **Action**, unlike **act**, is also used as a [U] noun: *the* **action** *of a runner/of a medicine* (=the way or effect of doing something) or in other fixed phrases: *to take (quick)* **action** (=to act (quickly))

**act·ing¹** /'æktɪŋ/ *adj* [A *no comp.*] appointed to carry out the duties of (an office or position) for a short time: *Our director is in hospital, but the acting director can see you.*

**acting²** *n* [U] the art of representing a character, esp. in a play or film

**ac·tion** /'ækʃən/ *n* **1** [U] movement using force or power for some purpose; doing things: *We must take action* (=begin to act) *before it is too late.* **2** [C] something done; deed: *Actions are more important than words.* –see ACT² (USAGE) **3** [C *usu. sing.*] the way in which something moves or works: *Today we'll study the action of the heart.* **4** [C] effect: *Photographs are made possible by the action of light on film.* **5** [C *usu. sing.*] the main events in a play or book rather than the characters in it: *The action took place in a mountain village.* **6** [C;U] a military fight or fighting: *Many were killed in action.* **7** [C;U] a charge or a matter for consideration by a court of law: *If he doesn't pay us soon we will have to bring an action against him.* **8 in/into action** in/into operation or a typical activity: *He is a very good tennis player: you ought to see him in action.* **9 out of action** out of operation; no longer able to do a typical activity: *Can I borrow your car –mine's out of action.*

**ac·tiv·ate** /'æktə̇veɪt/ *v* **-ated, -ating** [T] to cause to be active; bring into use: *This button activates the heating system.* **–activation** /-'veɪʃən/ *n* [U]

**ac·tive¹** /'æktɪv/ *adj* **1** doing things or always ready to do things; able or ready to take action: *Although he is over 70 he is still active.*|*an active member of the club who goes to every meeting* **2** able to produce the typical effects or act in the typical way: *Be careful! That dangerous chemical is still active!* –opposite **inactive** (for **1, 2**) **3** *tech* (of a verb or sentence) having as the subject the person or thing doing the action (as in *The boy kicked the ball.*) –compare PASSIVE[1] (2) –**actively** *adv*

**active**[2] also **active voice** /ˌ·· ˈ·/– *n* [S] *tech* the ACTIVE[1] (3) part or form of a verb: *"The boy kicked the ball" is in the active.* –compare PASSIVE[2]

**ac·tiv·ist** /ˈæktɪvɪ̈st/ *n* a person taking an active part, esp. in a political movement

**ac·tiv·i·ty** /ækˈtɪvɪ̈ti/ *n* **-ties 1** [U] movement; action; the state of being active: *There's been a lot of activity in the town centre today.* –opposite **inactivity 2** [C *often pl.*] something that is done or is being done: *She has many activities that take up her time when she's not working.*

**ac·tor** /ˈæktəʳ/ *n* a person who acts in a play or film

**ac·tress** /ˈæktrɪ̈s/ *n* a woman who acts in a play or film

**ac·tu·al** /ˈæktʃuəl/ *adj* [A *no comp.*] existing as a real fact: *The actual cost of the repairs was a lot less than we had expected.*

**ac·tu·al·ly** /ˈæktʃuəli, -tʃəli/ *adv* **1** really: *The people who actually have power are the owners of big industries.|Actually, you owe me more than this.* **2** strange as it may seem: *He not only invited me into his house but he actually offered me a drink.*

**ac·u·men** /ˈækjumən, əˈkjuːmən‖əˈkjuː-/ *n* [U] *fml* ability to think and judge quickly and well: *Her business acumen has made her very successful.*

**ac·u·punc·ture** /ˈækjuˌpʌŋktʃəʳ/ *n* [U] the method of stopping pain and curing diseases by pricking certain parts of the body with needles, used esp. in China

**a·cute** /əˈkjuːt/ *adj* **1** (of the mind or the senses) able to notice small differences, as of meaning or sound; working very well; sharp: *Dogs have an acute sense of smell|She has very acute hearing.* **2** severe; very great: *an acute lack of water* **3** (of a disease) coming quickly to a dangerous condition –compare CHRONIC **4** *tech* (of an angle) being less than 90 degrees –compare OBTUSE –**acutely** *adv* –**acuteness** *n* [U]

**AD** *abbrev. for: Latin* Anno Domini; (in the year) since the birth of Christ: *1649 AD* –compare BC

**ad** /æd/ *n infml* for advertisement

**ad·age** /ˈædɪdʒ/ *n* an old wise phrase; PROVERB

**ad·a·mant** /ˈædəmənt/ *adj* [+*that*] *fml* (esp. of a person or behaviour) hard, immovable, and unyielding: *I've tried to persuade him to change his mind, but he's adamant.* –**adamantly** *adv*

**Ad·am's ap·ple** /ˌædəmzˈæpəl‖ˈ·· ··/ *n* that part at the front of the throat that is seen to move when a person, esp. a man, talks or swallows

**a·dapt** /əˈdæpt/ *v* [I;T *to, for*] to change so as to be or make suitable for new needs, different conditions, etc.: *He adapted an old car engine to drive his boat.|When we moved to France, the children adapted (to the change) very well.* –compare ADOPT

**a·dap·ta·ble** /əˈdæptəbəl/ *adj often apprec* able to change or be changed so as to be suitable for new needs, different conditions, etc. –opposite **unadaptable** –**adaptability** /-əˈbɪlɪ̈ti/ *n* [U]

**ad·ap·ta·tion** /ˌædæpˈteɪʃən/ *n* [C;U] the state of being ADAPTed or thing adapted: *a new adaptation (of a book) for television*

**a·dapt·er, -or** /əˈdæptəʳ/ *n* something that ADAPTS esp. an apparatus (PLUG) that makes it possible to use more than one piece of electrical machinery from a single supply point (SOCKET)

**add** /æd/ *v* **1** [T *to*] to put together with something else so as to increase the number, size, importance, etc.: *Add a few more names to the list.* **2** [I;T *to, up*] to join (numbers, amounts, etc.) so as to find the total: *If you add 5 and/to 3 you get 8.|Add up these figures, please.* –compare SUBTRACT **3** [T+*that*] to say also: *I should like to add that we are pleased with the result.* **4 add insult to injury** to make matters even worse, esp. by causing annoyance as well as harm

**add to** sthg. *v prep* [T] to increase: *The rise in electricity costs has added to our difficulties.*

**add up** *v adv* [I not *be+v-ing*] *infml* to make sense; seem likely: *The various facts in the case just don't add up.*

**ad·den·dum** /əˈdendəm/ *n* **-da** /də/ *tech* something added or to be added, as at the end of a speech or book

**ad·der** /ˈædəʳ/ *n* a small poisonous snake found in northern Europe and northern Asia

**ad·dict** /ˈædɪkt/ *n* a person who is unable to free himself from a harmful habit, esp. of taking drugs

**ad·dict·ed** /əˈdɪktɪ̈d/ *adj* [*to*] dependent on; unable to stop having, taking, etc.: *addicted to* HEROIN|(fig.) *The children are addicted to television.* –compare DEVOTED

**ad·dic·tion** /əˈdɪkʃən/ *n* [C;U] (an example of) the state of being ADDICTED: *Smoking can be a dangerous addiction.*

**ad·dic·tive** /əˈdɪktɪv/ *adj* (of drugs, etc.) causing ADDICTION; habit-forming –opposite **non-addictive**

**ad·di·tion** /əˈdɪʃən/ *n* **1** [U] the act of adding, esp. of adding numbers together **2** [C] something added: *A newly born child is often called an addition to the family.* **3 in addition (to)** as well (as) –see Study Notes on page 128

**ad·di·tion·al** /əˈdɪʃənəl/ *adj* [*no comp.*] in addition; added: *An additional charge is made for heavy bags.* –**additionally** *adv*

**ad·di·tive** /ˈædɪ̈tɪv/ *n* a substance added in small quantities to something else, as to improve the quality, or add colour, taste, etc.

**ad·dress**[1] /əˈdres/ *v* [T] **1** to write a name and ADDRESS[2] on (an envelope, parcel, etc.) **2** to direct speech to (a person or group): *The Queen addressed the crowd.* **3** [*to*] *fml* to put (oneself) to work at: *He addressed himself to the main difficulty.*

**ad·dress**[2] /əˈdres‖əˈdres, ˈædres/ *n* the number of the building, name of the street and town, etc., where a person lives or works, esp. when written on a letter, envelope, or parcel: *I can't read the address on this letter.*

**ad·dress**[3] /əˈdres/ *n* a speech, esp. one that has been formally prepared

**ad·ept** /ˈædept, əˈdept‖əˈdept/ *adj* [*at, in*] highly skilled: *very adept at cheating* –**adeptly** *adv*

**ad·e·quate** /ˈædɪkwɪ̈t/ *adj* **1** [*for*] enough for the purpose, and no more: *The city's water supply is no longer adequate.* –compare AMPLE **2** [F *to*] having the necessary ability or qualities: *I hope he will be adequate to the job.* –opposite **inadequate** –**adequately** *adv* –**adequacy** /ˈædɪkwəsi/ *n* [U *for*]

**ad·here** /ədˈhɪəʳ/ *v* **-hered, -hering** [I *to*] to stick firmly (to another or each other): *The two surfaces adhered (to each other), and we couldn't get them apart.*

**adhere to** sthg. *v prep* [T] *often fml* to favour strongly; be faithful to (an idea, opinion, belief, etc.): *She adhered to her plan to leave early.*

**ad·her·ence** /əd'hɪərəns/ *n* [U *to*] the act or condition of sticking to something firmly: (fig.) *adherence to one's religious beliefs*

**ad·her·ent** /əd'hɪərənt/ *n* a person who favours and remains with a particular idea, opinion, or political party

**ad·he·sion** /əd'hiːʒən/ *n* [U] the state or action of sticking together

**ad·he·sive** /əd'hiːsɪv/ *n,adj* (a substance, such as GLUE) that can stick or cause sticking

**ad hoc** /ˌæd 'hɒk, -'həʊk‖-'hɑk, -'həʊk/ *adj Latin* made, arranged, etc., for a particular purpose: *an* **ad hoc committee** *specially established to deal with a particular subject*

**a·dieu** /ə'djuː‖ə'duː/ *interj,n* **adieus** *or* **adieux** /ə'djuːz‖ə'duːz/ goodbye

**ad·ja·cent** /ə'dʒeɪsənt/ *adj* [*to*] *fml* very close; touching or almost touching; next: *The two families live in adjacent streets.*

**ad·jec·tive** /'ædʒɨktɪv/ *n* a word which describes a noun (such as *black* in *a black hat*) –**adjectival** /ˌædʒɨk'taɪvəl/ *adj: an adjectival phrase* –see Study Notes on page opposite

**ad·join** /ə'dʒɔɪn/ *v* [I;T] *fml* to be next to, very close to, or touching (one another): *Our house adjoins theirs.|Our two houses adjoin.|the adjoining room*

**ad·journ** /ə'dʒɜːn‖-ɜrn/ *v* [I;T *for, till, until*] (of a meeting, trial, etc.) to bring to or come to a stop for a particular period or until a later time: *This trial has been adjourned.|The committee adjourned for an hour.* –**adjournment** *n* [C;U]

**ad·ju·di·cate** /ə'dʒuːdɪkeɪt/ *v* **-cated, -cating** [I;T *on*] *fml or tech* to act as a judge –**adjudicator** *n*

**ad·junct** /'ædʒʌŋkt/ *n* something added or joined to something else but not as a necessary part of it

**ad·just** /ə'dʒʌst/ *v* [I;T] to change slightly, esp. in order to set right or make suitable for a particular job or new conditions: *I must adjust my watch, it's slow.|He adjusted (himself) very quickly to the heat of the country.* –**adjustable** *adj* –**adjustment** *n* [C;U]: *to make adjustments*

**ad lib** /ˌæd 'lɪb/ *adv* [F] *infml* spoken, played, performed, etc., without preparation: *The best joke in the play was ad lib.* –**ad-lib** *adj* [A]

**ad-lib** /ˌ·'·/ *v* **-bb-** [I;T] *infml* to invent and deliver (music, words, etc.) without preparation: *The actress forgot her lines but ad-libbed very amusingly.*

**ad·min·is·ter** /əd'mɪnɨstəʳ/ *v* [T] *fml* **1** to direct or control (the affairs of a person or group): *The courts administer the law.* **2** [*to*] to give: *She administered the medicine to the sick woman.*

**ad·min·is·tra·tion** /ədˌmɪnɨ'streɪʃən/ *n* **1** [U] the control or direction of affairs, as of a country or business: *You will need some experience in administration.* **2** [*the* C] *esp. AmE (often cap.)* the national government: *the Kennedy Administration*

**ad·min·is·tra·tive** /əd'mɪnɨstrətɪv‖-streɪtɪv/ *adj* [*no comp.*] of or concerning the control and direction of affairs, as of a country or business: *administrative responsibilities* –**administratively** *adv*

**ad·min·is·tra·tor** /əd'mɪnɨstreɪtəʳ/ *n* a person who controls or directs the affairs, as of a country or business

**ad·mi·ra·ble** /'ædmərəbəl/ *adj* worthy of admiration; very good: *an admirable meal* –**admirably** *adv*

**ad·mi·ral** /'ædmərəl/ *n* [A;C] (an officer who holds) a very high rank or the highest rank in a navy

**Ad·mi·ral·ty** /'ædmərəlti/ *n BrE* [S;U *+sing./pl.v*] the government department which controls the navy; this department's building

**ad·mi·ra·tion** /ˌædmɨ'reɪʃən/ *n* [U] a feeling of pleasure and respect: *I was filled with admiration for his courage.*

**ad·mire** /əd'maɪəʳ/ *v* **-mired, -miring** [T *for*] to regard or look at with pleasure and respect; have a good opinion of: *We all admired her for the way she saved the children from the fire.|Stop looking in the mirror admiring yourself!* –see WONDER[1] (USAGE) –**admirer** *n: He is one of her many admirers.*

**ad·mis·si·ble** /əd'mɪsəbəl/ *adj* able to be allowed or considered: *an admissible excuse|admissible* EVIDENCE –opposite **inadmissible** –**admissibility** /-ə'bɪlɨti/ *n* [U]

**ad·mis·sion** /əd'mɪʃən/ *n* **1** [U] allowing or being allowed to enter or join a school, club, building, etc.: *Admission to the concert costs £5.* **2** [C] a statement saying or agreeing that something is true (usu. something bad); CONFESSION (1): *His admission of guilt surprised everyone.*|**By/On his own admission**, (=as he himself admitted) *he is a bad driver.*

USAGE In the meaning "permission to go in" **admittance** is more formal than **admission**, which is the more ordinary word. The entrance price is **the admission**, not ***the admittance**. **Admittance** could not be used in an expression like *his* **admission** *of guilt.*

**ad·mit** /əd'mɪt/ *v* **-tt- 1** [I;T *+v-ing/(that)/to*] to state or agree to the truth of (usu. something bad); CONFESS (1): *He never admits his mistakes/that he is wrong.|He admitted to the murder.|John has admitted (to) breaking the window.* –compare DENY **2** [T] to permit to enter; let in: *He was admitted to (the) hospital suffering from burns.* **3** [T *of*] *fml* to allow: *The facts admit of no other explanation.*

**ad·mit·tance** /əd'mɪtəns/ *n* [U] allowing or being allowed to enter; right of entrance: *As the theatre was full I was unable to gain admittance.* –see ADMISSION (USAGE)

**ad·mit·ted·ly** /əd'mɪtɨdli/ *adv* it must be admitted (that): *Admittedly, he is rather foolish.*

**ad·mon·ish** /əd'mɒnɪʃ‖-'mɑ-/ *v* [T *against, for*] *fml* to scold or warn gently –**admonishing** *adj* –**admonishingly** *adv* –**admonition** /ˌædmə'nɪʃən/ *n* [C;U]

**a·do** /ə'duː/ *n* **without much/more/further ado** with no further delay or FUSS[1] (1)

**ad·o·les·cent** /ædə'lesənt/ *adj,n* (of) a boy or girl in the period between being a child and being a grown person; young TEENAGER of about 13–16 –see CHILD (USAGE) –**adolescence** *n* [S;U]

**a·dopt** /ə'dɒpt‖ə'dɑpt/ *v* [T] **1** to take (someone else's child) into one's family and to take on the full responsibilities in law of a parent –compare FOSTER (2) **2** to take and use as one's own: *We adopted the new method of making wine.* **3** to approve formally;

## STUDY NOTES adjectives

### position of adjectives

Most English adjectives can come either before a noun or after a verb in a sentence. For example, we can say:

*She lives in a* **beautiful** *house.*
or
*Her house is* **beautiful.**

But some adjectives are different, and can be used in only one position.

For example:

**single** and **main** are used only before a noun. We can say:

*There was a* **single** *tree in the middle of the garden.*
*The* **main** *reason I came home was to see my parents.*

In the dictionary, adjectives like this are marked [A], to mean "only before a noun":

> **single** *adj* [A] only one: *A single tree gave shade from the sun.* | *His single aim was to make money.*

**asleep** and **unwell** are used only after a verb. We can say:

*Is he* **unwell**?
*No, he's* **asleep.**

In the dictionary, adjectives like this are marked [F], to mean "only after a verb":

> **asleep** *adj* [F] sleeping: *He was* **sound/fast asleep.** (=completely asleep) –opposite **awake**

Some adjectives, esp. when used in expressions of measurement, are always used after a noun. We can say:

*The hole is three metres* **deep.**

*The cupboard is two feet* **high** *and four feet* **wide.**

There are not many adjectives like this. In the dictionary they are marked [after *n*], to mean "only after a noun":

> **thick** *adj* **2** [after *n*] measuring in depth or width: *ice five centimetres thick*

Some adjectives have an [A], [F], or [after *n*] for just one of their meanings, like **thick**.

When you find an adjective like this in the dictionary, write it here to remind you how to use it. We have started the list for you:

[A]

medium, very

[F]

afraid, sure

[after *n*]

ago

accept: *The committee adopted her suggestions.* –compare ADAPT

**a·dop·tion** /ə'dɒpʃən‖ə'dɑp-/ *n* [C,U] (an example of) the act of ADOPTing: *If you cannot have children of your own, why not consider adoption?*

**a·dop·tive** /ə'dɒptɪv‖ə'dɑp-/ *adj* [*no comp.*] *fml* having ADOPTed (esp. a child): *her adoptive parents*

**a·dor·a·ble** /ə'dɔːrəbəl‖ə'dor-/ *adj* **1** worthy of being loved deeply **2** *infml* charming or attractive: *What adorable curtains!*

**ad·o·ra·tion** /ˌædə'reɪʃən/ *n* [U] **1** religious worship **2** deep love and respect

**a·dore** /ə'dɔːʳ‖ə'dor/ *v* **-dored, -doring** [T not *be +v-ing*] **1** to worship; love deeply and respect highly: *He adores his elder brother.* **2** [*+v-ing*] *infml* to like very much: *She adores going to the cinema.*

**a·dorn** /ə'dɔːn‖-ɔrn/ *v* [T *with*] *fml* to add beauty or decoration to: (fig.) *He adorned his story with a lot of lies.* –see DECORATE (USAGE) **–adornment** *n* [U]

**a·dren·a·lin** /ə'drenəl$\frac{1}{2}$n/ *n* [U] a chemical substance (HORMONE) made by the body during anger, fear, anxiety, etc., causing quick or violent action

**a·drift** /ə'drɪft/ *adv,adj* [F] (esp. of boats) not fastened, and driven about by the sea or wind; loose

**a·droit** /ə'drɔɪt/ *adj* [*at, in*] having or showing ability to use the skills of mind or hand, esp. quickly **–adroitly** *adv* **–adroitness** *n* [U]

**ad·u·la·tion** /ˌædʒʊ'leɪʃən‖ˌædʒə-/ *n* [U] *fml* praise that is more than is necessary or deserved, esp. to win favour

**ad·ult** /'ædʌlt, ə'dʌlt/ *adj,n* (of) a fully grown person or animal, esp. a person over an age stated by law, usu. 18 or 21

**a·dul·ter·ate** /ə'dʌltəreɪt/ *v* **-ated, -ating** [T *with*] to make impure or of poorer quality by the addition of something of lower quality –see also UNADULTERATED **–adulteration** /-reɪʃən / *n* [U]

**a·dul·ter·y** /ə'dʌltəri/ *n* [U] sexual relations between a married person and someone outside the marriage **–adulterous** *adj* **–adulterer adulteress** /-tr$\frac{1}{2}$s/ *fem.– n*

**ad·vance¹** /əd'vɑːns‖əd'væns/ *v* **-vanced, -vancing** [I;T *on, upon, against*] to (cause to) move forward: *Napoleon's army advanced on Moscow.*|*A month has passed and the work has not advanced.*|*(fml) The report advances* (=introduces) *the suggestion that safety standards should be improved.* –compare RETREAT **–advancement** *n* [U]

**advance²** *n* **1** [C] forward movement: *You cannot stop the advance of old age.*|(fig.)*There have been great advances* (=developments) *in medicine in the last 50 years.* –compare RETREAT **2** [C *of*] money that is paid before the proper time or lent: *I was given an advance of a month's pay.* **3** [A] going or coming before **4 in advance** before in time: *We always pay the rent in advance.*

**ad·vanced** /əd'vɑːnst‖əd'vænst/ *adj* far on in development: *advanced studies*|*the advanced industrial nations of the world*|*an advanced child*

**ad·vanc·es** /əd'vɑːns$\frac{1}{2}$z‖əd'væn-/ *n* [P] efforts made to become friends with or to gain favourable attention from: *She refused his advances.*

**ad·van·tage** /əd'vɑːntɪdʒ‖əd'væn-/ *n* **1** [C *over*] something that may help one to be successful or to gain a desired result: *He had the advantage (over other boys) of being born into a rich family.* **2** [U] profit; gain; BENEFIT¹ (1): *Is there any advantage in getting there early?* –opposite **disadvantage** (for **1, 2**) **3 Advantage X** (in tennis) (said when X has won the point after DEUCE): *Advantage Miss Austin.* **4 take advantage of** to make use of, e.g. by deceiving someone

**ad·van·ta·geous** /ˌædvən'teɪdʒəs, ˌædvæn-/ *adj* helpful; useful; bringing a good profit –opposite **disadvantageous –advantageously** *adv*

**ad·vent** /'ædvent/ *n* **the advent of** the arrival or coming of (an important event, period, person, etc.): *People are much better informed since the advent of television.*

**ad·ven·ture** /əd'ventʃəʳ/ *n* **1** [C] a journey, activity, experience, etc., that is strange, exciting, and often dangerous: *I told them of my adventures in the mountains.* **2** [U] excitement, as in a journey or activity; risk: *He lived for adventure.* –see VENTURE (USAGE)

**ad·ven·tur·er** /əd'ventʃərəʳ/ **adventuress** /-r$\frac{1}{2}$s/ *fem.– n* a person who has or looks for adventures

**ad·ven·tur·ous** /əd'ventʃərəs/ *adj* eager for or providing adventure: *an adventurous person/life* –opposite **unadventurous –adventurously** *adv*

**ad·verb** /'ædvɜːb‖-ɜrb/ *n* a word which describes or adds to the meaning of a verb, an adjective, another adverb, or a sentence, and which answers such questions as *how? when?* or *where?* (as in "He ran *slowly.*" "It was *very* beautiful." "Come *tomorrow.*" "Come *here.*") **–adverbial** /əd'vɜːbɪəl‖-ɜr-/ *n,adj*

**ad·ver·sa·ry** /'ædvəsəri‖'ædvərseri/ *n* **-ries** *fml* an opponent or enemy

**ad·verse** /'ædvɜːs‖-ɜrs/ *adj fml* not in favour of; going against; opposing: *The judge gave us an adverse decision.*|*in adverse conditions* –compare AVERSE **–adversely** *adv*

**ad·ver·si·ty** /əd'vɜːs$\frac{1}{2}$ti‖-ɜr-/ **-ties** *n* [C;U] (an example of) bad fortune; trouble: *a time of adversity*|*to meet with adversities*

**ad·ver·tise** /'ædvətaɪz‖-ər-/ *v* **-tised, -tising 1** [I;T] to make (something for sale, services offered, room to rent, etc.) known to the public, as in a newspaper, or on television: *I advertised my house in the "Daily News".* **2** [I *for*] to ask (for someone or something) by placing an advertisement in a newspaper, shop window, etc.: *We should advertise for someone to look after the garden.* **–advertiser** *n*

**ad·ver·tise·ment** /əd'vɜːt$\frac{1}{2}$smənt‖ˌædvər'taɪz-/ *n* also **ad, advert** *infml–* a notice of something for sale, job to be filled, room to rent, etc., as in a newspaper, on television, or pasted on a wall

**ad·ver·tis·ing** /'ædvətaɪzɪŋ‖-ər-/ *n* [U] the business of making known to the public what is for sale and encouraging them to buy, esp. by means of advertisements

**ad·vice** /əd'vaɪs/ *n* [U] opinion given by one person to another on how that other should behave or act: *I asked the doctor for her advice.*|*a piece of advice*

**ad·vi·sab·le** /əd'vaɪzəbəl/ *adj* [F] sensible; wise: *It is advisable always to wear a safety belt when you're driving.* –opposite **inadvisable –advisability** /-ə'bɪl$\frac{1}{2}$ti/ *n* [U]

**ad·vise** /əd'vaɪz/ *v* **-vised, -vising 1** [I;T *+to-v*/

v-ing/(*that*)/*on*] to tell (somebody) what one thinks should be done; give advice to (somebody): *I advise waiting till the proper time.*|*I will do as you advise.*|*The doctor advised me to take more exercise.* **2** [T] *fml* to give notice to; inform: *We wish to advise you that you now owe the bank £500.* **3** **well-advised/ill-advised** wise/unwise: *You would be well-advised to stay at home today.*

**ad·vis·er**||also **advisor** *AmE* /əd'vaɪzə^r/ *n* a person who gives advice, esp. to a government or business: *the government's special adviser on foreign affairs*

**ad·vi·so·ry** /əd'vaɪzəri/ *adj* giving advice; having the power or duty to advise

**ad·vo·cate¹** /'ædvəkeɪt/ *v* **-cated, -cating** [T +*v-ing*] to speak in favour of; support (esp. an idea or plan): *The opposition party advocates an immediate reduction in transport costs.*

**ad·vo·cate²** /'ædvək½t, -keɪt/ *n* **1** *law* a person, esp. a lawyer, who speaks in defence of or in favour of another person **2** a person who speaks for or supports an idea, way of life, etc.: *He is a strong advocate of prison reforms.*

**aer·i·al¹** /'eərɪəl/ *n* a wire, rod, or framework put up, often on top of a house or on a car, to receive radio or television broadcasts –see picture on page 297

**aerial²** *adj* [A *no comp.*] of, from, or concerning the air; happening in the air: *an aerial battle*

**aer·o·drome** /'eərədrəum/ *esp. BrE*||**airfield** *esp. AmE*– *n* a small airport

**aer·o·dy·nam·ics** /ˌeərəudaɪ'næmɪks/ *n* **1** [U] the science that studies the forces that act on bodies moving through the air **2** [P] the qualities necessary for movement through the air –**aerodynamic** *adj* –**aerodynamically** *adv*

**aer·o·plane** /'eərəpleɪn/ *BrE*||**airplane** *AmE* –*n* a flying vehicle that is heavier than air, that has wings, and is driven by at least one engine –see picture on page 16

**aer·o·sol** /'eərəsɒl||-sɑl/ *n* a small container from which liquid can be forced out in the form of a fine mist

**aes·thet·ic**||also **esthetic** *AmE* /iːs'θetɪk, es- ||es-/ *adj* of, concerning, or showing a sense of beauty: *The building is aesthetic, but not very practical.* –**aesthetically** *adv*

**aes·thet·ics**||also **esthetics** *AmE* /iːs'θetɪks, es-||es-/ *n* [U] the study, science, or PHILOSOPHY (1) of beauty, esp. beauty in art

**a·far** /ə'fɑː^r/ *adv lit* at a distance; far off

**af·fa·ble** /'æfəbəl/ *adj* easy to talk to; ready to be friendly; pleasant –**affability** /ˌæfə'bɪl½ti/ *n* [U] –**affably** /'æfəbli/ *adv*

**af·fair** /ə'feə^r/ *n* **1** a happening; event; action: *The meeting was a noisy affair.* **2** [*often pl.*] something that has been done; something needing action or attention; business: *The minister deals with important affairs of state.* **3** a sexual relationship between two people not married to each other, esp. one that lasts for some time

**af·fect¹** /ə'fekt/ *v* [T] **1** to cause some result or change in; influence: *Smoking affects health.* **2** to cause feelings of sorrow, anger, love, etc., in: *She was deeply affected by the news of his death.*

USAGE Compare **affect** and **effect**: *Will government policy be* **affected** (=changed) *by the appointment of a new minister?*|*The new minister hopes to* **effect** (=produce) *changes in the government's policy.*

**affect²** *v* [T +*to-v*] *fml, often derog* to pretend to feel, have, or do: *He affected illness so that he did not have to go to work.* –see also UNAFFECTED

**af·fec·ta·tion** /ˌæfek'teɪʃən/ *n* [C;U] *derog* (an example of) behaviour which is AFFECTED: *She is sincere and quite without affectation.*

**af·fect·ed** /ə'fekt½d/ *adj derog* not real or natural; pretended: *She showed an affected interest in his work.* –opposite **unaffected**

**af·fec·tion** /ə'fekʃən/ *n* [U] gentle, lasting love or fondness

**af·fec·tion·ate** /ə'fekʃən½t/ *adj* showing gentle love –**affectionately** *adv*

**af·fil·i·ate** /ə'fɪlieɪt/ *v* **-ated, -ating** [I;T *with, to*] (esp. of a society or group) to join or connect: *Our club is affiliated to a national organization of similar clubs.* –opposite **disaffiliate** –**affiliation** /-'eɪʃən/ *n* [C;U]

**af·fin·i·ty** /ə'fɪn½ti/ *n* **-ties** **1** [C;U *between, with*] a relationship, close likeness, or connection **2** [C *for, to, between*] strong attraction: *He feels a strong affinity for/to her.*|*a strong affinity between them*

**af·firm** /ə'fɜːm||-ɜrm/ *v* [T +*that*] *fml* to declare (usu. again, or in answer to a question): *The minister affirmed the government's intention to reduce taxes.* –compare DENY (1) –**affirmation** /ˌæfə'meɪʃən||ˌæfɜr- / *n* [C;U]

**af·fir·ma·tive** /ə'fɜːmətɪv||-ɜr-/ *n,adj often fml* (a word) declaring "yes": *The answer was in the affirmative.* –opposite **negative** –**affirmatively** *adv*

**af·fix¹** /ə'fɪks/ *v* [T *to*] *fml* to fix, fasten, or stick: *Please affix a stamp.*

**af·fix²** /'æfɪks/ *n* a group of letters or sounds added to the beginning of a word (PREFIX) or at the end of a word (SUFFIX) to change its meaning or its use (as in "*un*tie", "*mis*understand", "kind*ness*", "quick*ly*")

**af·flict** /ə'flɪkt/ *v* [T *usu. pass.*] to cause to suffer in the body or mind; trouble: *afflicted with blindness*

**af·flic·tion** /ə'flɪkʃən/ *n* [C;U] *fml* something causing suffering or grief

**af·flu·ent** /'æfluənt/ *adj* having plenty of money or other possessions; wealthy –**affluence** *n* [U]

**af·ford** /ə'fɔːd||-ord/ *v* [T] **1** [+*to-v*] (*usu. with can, could, able to*) to be able to do, spend, buy, bear, etc., esp. without serious loss or damage: *Can you afford £35,000 for a house?*|*I can't afford three weeks away from work.* **2** *fml & lit* to provide with; supply with; give: *The tree afforded us shelter from the rain.*

**affront** /ə'frʌnt/ *n* an act, remark, etc., that is rude to someone or hurts his/her feelings, esp. when intentional or in public

**a·field** /ə'fiːld/ *adv* **far afield** far away, esp. from home: *Don't go too far afield or we might lose you.*|*We get a lot of tourists from Europe, and some from even further afield.*

**a·flame** /ə'fleɪm/ *adv,adj* [F] on fire

**a·float** /ə'fləut/ *adv,adj* [F] floating; at sea

**a·foot** /ə'fut/ *adv,adj* [F] *often derog* being prepared, made ready, or in operation: *There is* **a plan afoot** *to pull down the old building.*

**a·fraid** /ə'freɪd/ *adj* [F] **1** [+*to-v*/(*that*)/*of*] full of fear; FRIGHTENED: *Don't be afraid of the dog.*|*He was* *afraid that he would lose.*|(fig.) *Don't be afraid of asking for help.* **2** [+ *(that)*] *polite* sorry for something that has happened or is likely to happen: *I am afraid I've broken your pen.*|*"Are we late?" "I'm afraid so."*|*"Are we on time?" "I'm afraid not."*

**a·fresh** /ə'freʃ/ *adv fml* once more; again: *I've spoiled the painting and must start afresh.*

**Af·ri·can** /'æfrɪkən/ *adj,n* of, from, or about Africa; a person from Africa

**af·ter**[1] /'ɑːftər||'æf-/ *prep* **1** following in time; later than: *We'll leave after breakfast.* (Compare *We'll leave in an hour.*) **2** following continuously: *Year after year went past.* **3** following in place or order; behind: *He entered the room after his father.*|*Your name comes after mine in the list.*|*Shut the door after you.* **4** because of: *After the way he treated me I never want to see him again.* **5** in spite of: *After all my care in packing it, the clock arrived broken.* **6** in search of (esp. in order to punish); looking for: *The police are after me.* **7** with the name of: *The boy was named after his uncle.* **8 after all: a** in spite of everything: *So you see I was right after all!* **b** it must be remembered (that): *I know he hasn't finished the work, but, after all, he is very busy.* –*compare* BEFORE[2]

**after**[2] *adv* [F or after *n*] later; afterwards: *John came last Tuesday, and I arrived the day after.* –compare BEFORE[1]

**after**[3] *conj* at a later time than (when): *I found your coat after you had left the house.* –compare BEFORE[3]

**af·ter·ef·fect** /'ɑːftərɪ̵fekt||'æf-/ *n* [*often pl.*] an effect (usu. unpleasant) that follows some time after the cause or after the main effect

**af·ter·life** /'ɑːftəlaɪf||'æftər-/ *n* **-lives** /laɪvz/ [*usu. sing.*] the life that is thought by some people to follow death

**af·ter·math** /'ɑːftəmæθ||'æftər-/ *n* [*usu. sing.*] the result or period following a bad event such as an accident, storm, war, etc.: *Life was much harder in the aftermath of the war.*

**af·ter·noon** /ˌɑːftə'nuːn||ˌæftər-/ *adj,n* (of) the period between midday and sunset: *I'll sleep in the afternoon.*|*I'll have an afternoon sleep.*

**af·ter·wards** /'ɑːftəwədz||'æftərwərdz/ ||also **afterward** *AmE*– *adv* later; after that: *She had her supper and went to bed soon afterwards.*

**a·gain** /ə'gen, ə'geɪn||ə'gen/ *adv* **1** once more; another time: *Please say that again.*|*Never do that again!*|*He told the story yet again.* **2** back to the place or condition as before: *She was ill but now she is well again.*|*He's home again now.* **3** besides; further: *That wasn't much; I could eat as much again.* **4** but; on the other hand: *He might go, but there again he might not.* **5 again and again** very often; repeatedly: *I've told you again and again not to play there.*

**a·gainst** /ə'genst, ə'geɪnst||ə'genst/ *prep* **1** in the direction of and meeting: *The rain beat against the windows.* **2** in opposition to: *We will fight against the enemy.*|*Stealing is* **against the law**. **3** in an opposite direction to: *We sailed against the wind.* **4** as a defence or protection from: *We are all taking medicine against the disease.* **5** having as a background: *The picture looks good against that light wall.* **6** touching, esp. for support –see Study Notes on page 474

**age**[1] /eɪdʒ/ *n* **1** [C;U] the period of time a person has lived or a thing has existed: *What is your age?*|*He is 10 years of age.*|*At your age you should know beter.*|*What ages are your children?* **2** [U] one of the periods of life: *At the age of 40 a person has reached* **middle age**. **3** [U] the state of being old: *His back was bent with age.* **4** [U] the particular time of life at which a person becomes able or not able to do something: *People who are either* **under age** *or* **over age** *may not join.* **5** [C *usu. sing.*] (*usu. cap.*) a particular period of history: *The period in which man learnt to make tools of iron is called the Iron Age.* **6** [C *often pl.*] *infml* a long time: *It's been ages/an age since we met.* **7 (be/come) of age** (to be or reach) the particular age when a person becomes responsible in law for his own actions, is allowed to vote, get married, etc.

**age**[2] *v* **aged, aging** *or* **ageing** [I;T] to (cause to) become old: *After his wife's death he aged quickly.* –**ageing, aging** /'eɪdʒɪŋ/ *n,adj* [U]

**aged**[1] /'eɪdʒd/ *adj* [F] being of the stated number of years: *My son is aged 10 years.*

**ag·ed**[2] /'eɪdʒɪ̵d/ *adj* very old: *an aged man*|*The sick and the aged need our help.*

**age·less** /'eɪdʒlɪ̵s/ *adj* never growing old or never showing signs of growing old: *an ageless song*

**a·gen·cy** /'eɪdʒənsi/ *n* **-cies** a business that makes its money esp. by arranging for people to meet others or to learn about the products of others: *I got this job through an employment agency.*

**a·gen·da** /ə'dʒendə/ *n* **-das** a list of the business or subjects to be considered at a meeting

**a·gent** /'eɪdʒənt/ *n* **1** a person who acts for another, esp. one who represents the business affairs of a firm: *Our agent in Rome deals with all our Italian business.*|*a secret agent* (=a political SPY) **2** a person or thing that works to produce a result: *Rain and sun are the agents which help plants to grow.*|*Soap is a cleansing agent.*

**ag·gra·vate** /'ægrəveɪt/ *v* **-vated, -vating** [T] **1** [U] to make more serious; make worse: *The lack of rain aggravated the serious lack of food.* **2** to annoy: *If he aggravates me any more I shall hit him.*|*an aggravating delay* –**aggravation** /-'veɪʃən/ *n* [U]

USAGE Although **aggravate** is commonly used to mean "annoy", this is thought by teachers to be incorrect: a *difficulty* is **aggravated;** a *person* is **irritated** or **annoyed.** –see ANGRY (USAGE)

**ag·gre·gate** /'ægrɪgɪ̵t/ *n* [C;U] a total: *a low goal aggregrate last season* –**aggregate** *adj* [A]

**ag·gres·sion** /ə'greʃən/ *n* [U] the starting of a quarrel, fight, or war, esp. without just cause –see also NONAGGRESSION

**ag·gres·sive** /ə'gresɪv/ *adj* **1** *derog* always ready to quarrel or attack; threatening **2** *apprec* not afraid of opposition: *If you want to be a success in business you must be aggressive.* **3** (of weapons) made for use in attack –**aggressively** *adv* –**aggressiveness** *n* [U]

**ag·gres·sor** /ə'gresər/ *n fml derog* a person or country that begins a quarrel, fight, war, etc., with another, esp. without just cause

**ag·grieved** /ə'griːvd/ *adj fml* suffering from a personal offence, showing hurt feelings, etc.

**a·ghast** /ə'gɑːst||ə'gæst/ *adj* [F *at*] suddenly filled with surprise, fear, and shock: *aghast at the sight of blood on the floor*

**ag·ile** /'ædʒaɪl‖'ædʒəl/ *adj* able to move quickly and easily; active –**agility** /ə'dʒɪlˌti/ *n* [U]

**ag·i·tate** /'ædʒˌteɪt/ *v* **-tated, -tating 1** [T] to shake or move (a liquid) about **2** [T] to cause anxiety to; worry **3** [I *for*] to argue strongly in public for or against some political or social change

**ag·i·ta·tion** /ˌædʒˌ'teɪʃən/ *n* [U] **1** painful excitement of the mind or feelings; anxiety **2** [*for*] public argument, action, unrest, etc., for or against political or social change

**ag·i·ta·tor** /'ædʒˌteɪtəʳ/ *n* a person who excites and influences other people's feelings, esp. towards political change

**a·glow** /ə'gləʊ/ *adj* [F *with*] bright with colour or excitement: *Her face was aglow as she met him.*

**ag·nos·tic** /æg'nɒstɪk, əg-‖-'nɑ-/ *n,adj* (a person) who believes that nothing can be known about God or life after death –compare ATHEIST –**agnosticism** /-sɪzəm/ *n* [U]

**a·go** /ə'gəʊ/ *adv,adj* [after *n* or *adv*] back in time from now; in the past: *He left 10 minutes ago.|He died long ago.|How long ago did he leave?*

USAGE 1 **Ago** is not used with verbs formed with *have*. Compare *I came here a year* **ago** and *I have been here* **for** *a year*/**since** *1981*. 2 **Before** shows the difference between a distant and a nearer point in the past: *My grandfather died five years* **ago**; *my grandmother had already died three years* **before**. (=eight years ago)

**a·gog** /ə'gɒg‖ə'gɑg/ *adj* [F *with*] *infml* excited and expecting something to happen: *The children were all agog (with excitement) at the circus.*

**ag·o·nize**‖also **-nise** *BrE* /'ægənaɪz/ *v* **-nized, -nizing** [I *over*] *infml* to suffer great pain or anxiety: *He agonizes over every decision|an agonized cry*

**ag·o·niz·ing** ‖also **-nising** *BrE* /'ægənaɪzɪŋ/ *adj* causing great pain or anxiety: *an agonizing decision/delay* –**agonizingly** *adv*

**ag·o·ny** /'ægəni/ *n* **-nies** [C;U] very great pain or suffering of mind or body: *He lay in agony until the doctor arrived.|in agonies of doubt*

**a·grar·i·an** /ə'greərɪən/ *adj* of land, esp. farmland or its ownership: *agrarian reforms*

**a·gree** /ə'griː/ *v* **-greed, -greeing 1** [I;T +*to-v*/(*that*)/ *on, about, with*] to have or share the same opinion, feeling, or purpose: *She agreed with me.|We agreed to leave at once.|They agreed that they should ask him.|We agreed on a price for the car.* –opposite **disagree**; see REFUSE (USAGE) **2** [I *to*] to say yes to an idea, opinion, etc., esp. after unwillingness or argument; accept; approve: *He agreed to my idea.|We met at the agreed place.*

**agree with** sbdy./sthg. *v prep* [T *no pass.*] **1** to be in accordance with: *Your story agrees with his in everything except small details.* **2** (usu. used in NEGATIVES²) *infml* to suit the health of: *The fruit did not agree with me–now I've got a pain in my stomach.* –opposite **disagree with 3** *tech* (of nouns, adjectives, verbs, etc.) to have the same number, person, CASE¹ (6), etc., as (the subject)

**a·gree·a·ble** /ə'griːəbəl/ *adj* **1** to one's liking; pleasant: *agreeable weather* –opposite **disagreeable 2** [F *to*] ready to agree; willing: *Are you agreeable (to my suggestion)?*

**a·gree·a·bly** /ə'griːəbli/ *adv* pleasantly: *I was agreeably surprised.* –opposite **disagreeably**

**a·gree·ment** /ə'griːmənt/ *n* **1** [U] the state of having the same opinion, feeling, or purpose: *We are in agreement with their decision.|The two sides were unable to reach agreement.* –opposite **disagreement 2** [C] an arrangement or promise of action, as made between people, groups, businesses, or countries: *You have broken our agreement.*

**ag·ri·cul·ture** /'ægrɪˌkʌltʃəʳ/ *n* [U] the art or practice of farming, esp. of growing crops –**agricultural** /ˌægrɪ'kʌltʃərəl/ *adv* –**agricultur(al)ist** *n*

**a·ground** /ə'graʊnd/ *adv,adj* [F] (of a ship) on or onto the shore or bottom of a sea, lake, etc. (esp. in the phrase **run aground**)

**ah** /ɑː/ *interj* (a cry of surprise, pity, pain, joy, dislike, etc.): *Ah! I hurt my foot.|Ah, there you are!*

**a·ha** /ɑː'hɑː/ *interj* (a cry of surprise, satisfaction, amused discovery, etc.): *Aha, so there you are!*

**a·head** /ə'hed/ *adv,adj* [F] **1** in front; forward; in advance: *One man went ahead to see if the road was clear.|The road ahead was full of sheep.* **2** in or into the future: *to plan ahead* **3** in advance of; succeeding better: *Our company is ahead of other makers of soap.* **4 get ahead** to do well; succeed

**a·hoy** /ə'hɔɪ/ *interj* (a cry of greeting made by sailors, esp. from one ship to another)

**aid¹** /eɪd/ *v* [T] to give support to; help –see HELP (USAGE)

**aid²** *n* **1** [U] support; help: *He went to the aid of the hurt man.|What is the money* **in aid of?** **2** [C] a person or thing that supports or helps: *A dictionary is an important aid in learning a new language.*

**aide** /eɪd/ *n* a person who helps, esp. a person employed to help a government minister

**ail** /eɪl/ *v* [I] to be ill and grow weak: (fig.) *the country's ailing* ECONOMY¹ (2)

**ail·ment** /'eɪlmənt/ *n* an illness, esp. one that is not serious: *He's always complaining of some ailment.*

**aim¹** /eɪm/ *v* **1** [I;T *at, for*] to point or direct (a weapon, shot, remark, etc.) towards some object, esp. with the intention of hitting it: *He aimed the gun carefully.|He aimed it at the bottles.|My remarks were not aimed at you.* **2** [I +*to-v*/*at, for*] to direct one's efforts (towards doing or obtaining something); intend (to): *I aim to be a writer.|The factory must aim at increased production/at increasing production.*

**aim²** *n* **1** [U] the act of directing a weapon, remark, etc.: *The hunter took aim at the lion.|His aim was very good.* **2** [C] the desired result of one's efforts; purpose; intention: *What is your aim in life?*

**aim·less** /'eɪmlˌs/ *adj* without any purpose; lacking intention –**aimlessly** *adv* –**aimlessness** *n* [U]

**ain't** /eɪnt/ *v nonstandard* short for *am not, is not, are not, has not,* and *have not*: *We ain't coming.|They ain't got it.*

**air¹** /eəʳ/ *n* **1** [U] the mixture of gases which surrounds the earth and which we breathe: *breathing in the fresh morning air|a hot* **airless** *room* **2** [U] the sky or the space above the ground: *He jumped into the air.|It's quicker* **by air** *than by sea.* **3** [C] the general character of, or feeling caused by, a person or place: *There was an air of excitement at the meeting.* **4 into thin air** *infml* completely out of sight **5 on/off the air** broadcasting/not broadcasting –compare WIND[1] (1); see also AIRS

**air²** *v* **1** [I;T] to (cause to) dry in a place that is warm or has plenty of dry air: *If the sheets aren't aired properly, they won't be dry; put them in the* **airing cupboard**. **2** [I;T] to (cause to) become fresh by letting in air: *We aired the room by opening the windows.* **3** [T] to make known to others (one's opinions, ideas, complaints, etc.), often in an unwelcome way: *He's always airing his knowledge.* –**airing** *n* [C;U *usu. sing.*]: *to give the room/one's ideas a good airing*

**air·borne** /ˈeəbɔːn‖ˈeərborn/ *adj* **1** (esp. of seeds) carried about by the air **2** (esp. of aircraft) in the air; in flight

**air·bus** /ˈeəbʌs‖ˈeər-/ *n* an aircraft for carrying large numbers of passengers on short flights

**air-con·di·tion·ing** /ˈ· ·ˌ···/ *n* [U] the system that uses one or more machines (**air-conditioners**) to keep air in a building or room cool –**air-conditioned** *adj*

**air·craft** /ˈeəkrɑːft‖ˈeərkræft/ *n* **aircraft** a flying machine of any type, with or without an engine

**aircraft car·ri·er** /ˈ·· ˌ···/ *n* a warship that carries aircraft and has a large flat surface where they can take off and land

**air·field** /ˈeəfiːld‖ˈeər-/ *n* a place where aircraft may land and take off but which need not have any large buildings –compare AIRPORT

**air force** /ˈeəfɔːs‖ˈeərfors/ *n* the part of the military organization of a country that is concerned with attack and defence from the air

**air·host·ess** /ˈeəˌhəustɪ̈s‖ˈeər-/ *n* a woman who looks after the comfort and safety of the passengers in an aircraft

**air·i·ly** /ˈeərɪ̈li/ *adv* in a light manner; not seriously

**air·lift** /ˈeəˌlɪft‖ˈeər-/ *n* the carrying of large numbers of people or amounts of supplies by aircraft, esp. to or from a place that is difficult to get to –**airlift** *v* [T]

**air·line** /ˈeəlaɪn‖ˈeər-/ *n* a business that runs a regular service for carrying passengers and goods by air

**air·lin·er** /ˈeəˌlaɪnəʳ‖ˈeər-/ *n* a large passenger aircraft

**air·lock** /ˈeəlɒk‖ˈeərlɑk/ *n* **1** a bubble in a tube or pipe that prevents the passage of a liquid **2** an enclosed space or room into which or from which air cannot accidentally pass, as in a spacecraft or apparatus for working under water

**air·mail** /ˈeəmeɪl‖ˈeər-/ *n* [U] **1** letters, parcels, etc., sent by air **2** the system of sending things by air

**air·man** /ˈeəmən‖ˈeər-/ **airwoman** /ˈeəˌwumən‖ˈeər-/ *fem.*– *n* **-men** /mən/ *BrE* a person of low rank in an air force

**air·plane** /ˈeəpleɪn‖ˈeər-/ *n AmE* for AEROPLANE

**air·port** /ˈeəpɔːt‖ˈeərport/ *n* a place where aircraft land and take off, which has several buildings, and which is regularly used by paying passengers –see picture on page 16

**air raid** /ˈ· ·/ *n* an attack by military aircraft

**airs** /eəz‖eərz/ also **airs and graces** /ˌ· · ˈ··/– [P] *derog* unnatural manners or actions intended to make people think one is more important than one really is (esp. in the phrases **give oneself airs, put on airs**)

**air·ship** /ˈeəˌʃɪp‖ˈeər-/ *n* (esp. formerly) an aircraft without wings, containing gas to make it lighter than air, with an engine to make it move

**air·sick** /ˈeəˌsɪk‖ˈeər-/ *adj* sick because of the movement of an aircraft –**airsickness** *n* [U]

**air·space** /ˈeəspeɪs‖ˈeər-/ *n* [U] the air or sky above a country, regarded as the property of that country

**air·strip** /ˈeəˌstrɪp‖ˈeər-/ *n* a stretch of land used by aircraft to take off and land, esp. in war or time of trouble

**air·tight** /ˈeətaɪt‖ˈeər-/ *adj* not allowing air to pass in or out: *airtight containers*

**air·wor·thy** /ˈeəˌwɜːði‖ˈeərˌwɜrði/ *adj* (of aircraft) in proper and safe working condition –**airworthiness** *n* [U]

**air·y** /ˈeəri/ *adj* **-ier, -iest 1** of, in, or having plenty of air: *The large window makes the room seem airy.* **2** *derog* having little substance; empty: *Nothing results from his airy plans.*

**aisle** /aɪl/ *n* a passage between rows of seats, as in a cinema or theatre, or esp. a church –see picture on page 463

**a·jar** /əˈdʒɑːʳ/ *adv,adj* [F] (of a door) not quite closed; slightly open

**a·kin** /əˈkɪn/ *adj* [F *to*] having the same appearance, character, etc.; like

**à la carte** /ˌælə ˈkɑːt, ˌɑːlɑː-‖-ɑrt/ *adj,adv* (of food in a restaurant) according to a list (MENU) where each dish has its own separate price –compare TABLE D'HÔTE

**a·lac·ri·ty** /əˈlækrɪ̈ti/ *n* [U] *fml* quick and willing readiness

**a·larm¹** /əˈlɑːm‖əˈlɑrm/ *n* **1** [U] sudden fear and anxiety, as caused by the possibility of danger **2** [C] a warning of danger, as by ringing a bell or shouting: *I* **raised the alarm** *as soon as I saw the smoke.* **3** [C] any apparatus, such as a bell, noise, flag, etc., by which a warning is given

**alarm²** *v* [T] to excite with sudden fear and anxiety

**alarm clock** /·ˈ· ·/ also **alarm**– *n* a clock that can be set to make a noise at any particular time to wake up sleepers

**a·larm·ist** /əˈlɑːmɪ̈st‖əˈlɑr-/ *n derog* a person who always expects danger, often without cause, and says so to others

**a·las** /əˈlæs/ *interj lit* (a cry expressing grief, sorrow, or fear)

**al·be·it** /ɔːlˈbiːɪ̈t/ *conj fml* even though; although: *It was a very important albeit small mistake.*

**al·bi·no** /ælˈbiːnəu‖ælˈbaɪ-/ *n* **-nos** a person or animal with a pale milky skin, very light hair, and eyes that are pink because of a lack of colouring matter

**al·bum** /ˈælbəm/ *n* **1** a book used for collecting photographs, stamps, etc. **2** → LP

**al·bu·men** /ˈælbjumɪ̈n‖ælˈbjuː-/ *n* [U] the white or colourless part of an egg

**al·che·my** /ˈælkəmi/ *n* [U] (esp. in the MIDDLE AGES) the science concerned with finding a way to turn all metals into gold –**alchemist** /-ɪ̈st/ *n*

**al·co·hol** /ˈælkəhɒl‖-hɔl/ *n* [U] **1** the colourless liquid present in wine, beer, and SPIRITS[1] (7) that can make one drunk **2** the drinks containing this

**al·co·hol·ic¹** /ˌælkəˈhɒlɪk‖-ˈhɔ-/ *adj* of, caused by, or containing alcohol –opposite **non-alcoholic**

**alcoholic²** *n* a person who cannot stop the habit of drinking too much alcoholic drink

**al·co·hol·is·m** /ˈælkəhɒlɪzəm‖-hɔ-/ *n* [U] the

diseased condition caused by the continued drinking of alcohol in great quantities

**al·cove** /'ælkəuv/ *n* a small partly enclosed space in a room or wall, for a seat, bed, etc.

**al·der·man** /'ɔːldəmən‖-dər-/ *n* **-men** /mən/ a local government officer having any of various duties

**ale** /eɪl/ *n* [U] any of various types of beer, esp. one that is pale in colour

**a·lert**[1] /ə'lɜːt‖-ɜrt/ *adj* quick to see and act; watchful **–alertness** *n* [U]

**alert**[2] *n* **1** a warning to be ready for danger: *to sound the alert* –compare ALL CLEAR **2 on the alert (for)** in a state of watchfulness for danger, as after a warning

**alert**[3] *v* [T] **1** to put (esp. soldiers) on the ALERT[2] (2) **2** to warn: *The policeman alerted me to the danger.*

**A lev·el** /'eɪ ˌlevəl/ also **advanced level**– *n* [C;U] (the higher of the two standards of) examination in the British GCE, necessary for entrance to a university or college –compare O LEVEL

**al·gae** /'ældʒiː, -gi/ *n* [P] very simple, usu. very small plants that live in or near water

**al·ge·bra** /'ældʒ$\frac{1}{3}$brə/ *n* [U] a branch of MATHEMATICS in which signs and letters are used to represent numbers and values **–algebraic(al)** /-'breɪ-ɪk(əl)/ *adj* **algebraically** *adv*

**al·go·rith·m** /'ælgərɪðəm/ *n* a list of instructions, esp. to a computer, which are carried out in a fixed order to find the answer to a question or esp. to calculate a number **–algorithmic** /-'rɪðmɪk/ *adj*

**a·li·as**[1] /'eɪlɪəs/ *adv* (esp. of a criminal) also known as; also called: *The thief's real name was John Smith, alias Edward Ball.*

**alias**[2] *n* **-ases** a name other than the usual or officially recognized name, used esp. by a criminal; false name

**al·i·bi** /'æl$\frac{1}{3}$baɪ/ *n* **-bis** an argument or defence that a person who is charged with a crime was in another place when the crime was done and that he/she therefore could not have done it: *His wife gave Jim an alibi by saying that he was at home with her on the night of the robbery.*

**a·li·en**[1] /'eɪlɪən/ *adj* **1** [*no comp.*] belonging to another country or race; foreign **2** [*to*] different in nature or character, esp. so different as to be opposed: *Their ideas are quite alien to our own.*

**alien**[2] *n* a foreigner who has not become a citizen of the country where he/she is living –compare CITIZEN, NATIONAL

**a·li·en·ate** /'eɪlɪəneɪt/ *v* **-ated, -ating** [T] to cause to stop being or feeling friendly: *to alienate one's family/someone's affections*

**a·li·en·a·tion** /ˌeɪlɪə'neɪʃən/ *n* [U *from*] a feeling of not belonging to or being part of one's surroundings: *The increasingly dull nature of many industrial jobs has led to the alienation of many workers.*

**a·light**[1] /ə'laɪt/ **alighted** *or* **alit** /ə'lɪt/, **alighting** *v* [I *from*] *fml* to get off or down from something, esp. at the end of a journey

**alight on/upon** sthg. *v prep* [T] **1** to come down from the air onto **2** *fml becoming rare* to find unexpectedly; HAPPEN **on**

**alight**[2] *adj* [F] on fire; in flames

**a·lign**‖also **aline** *BrE* /ə'laɪn/ *v* [I;T] to come, bring, form, or arrange into a line

**align** sbdy./sthg. **with** *v prep* [T] **1** to cause to come into the same line as: *to align a picture with one next to it* **2** to cause to come into agreement with: *They aligned themselves with the army.* –see also NON-ALIGNED

**a·lign·ment**‖also **aline-** *BrE* /ə'laɪnmənt/ *n* [U] **1** the act of forming or arranging into a line: *to bring into/move out of alignment (with)* **2** (of people or countries with the same aims, ideas, etc.) the act of forming into groups, as in a war –opposite **nonalignment** (for 2)

**a·like** /ə'laɪk/ *adj,adv* [F] like one another; the same: *The two brothers are very much alike.*

**al·i·men·ta·ry** /ˌæl$\frac{1}{3}$'mentəri/ *adj tech* concerning food and the way it is treated (DIGESTed[1] (1)) in the body

**al·i·mo·ny** /'æl$\frac{1}{3}$məni‖-məuni/ *n* [S;U] money that a man or woman has been ordered to pay regularly to his/her former partner after they have been SEPARATED[1] (4) or DIVORCED[2] (1)

**a·live** /ə'laɪv/ *adj* [F] **1** [*no comp.*] having life; not dead; living **2** full of life; active: *Although old he is still very much alive.*|(fig.) *The argument was kept alive by the politicians.* **3 alive to** having full knowledge of: *He was alive to the dangers of the work.* **4 alive with** covered with or full of (living things): *The dead tree is alive with insects.*

**al·ka·li** /'ælkəlaɪ/ *n* **-lis** *or* **-lies** [C;U] *tech* any of various substances that form chemical salts when combined with acids –opposite **acid –alkaline** /-laɪn‖-l$\frac{1}{3}$n/ *adj*

**all**[1] /ɔːl/ *determiner, predeterminer* **1** the whole of: *He ate all his food.*|*He ate it all.*|*We walked all the way.*|*We worked hard all last year.* **2** every one (of): *We're all hungry.*|*All children like toys.*|*Please answer all the questions.*|*Answer them all.*|*We bought* **all kinds of** *things.* (=lots of different things) –see Study Notes on page 494 **3 all in** *infml* very tired **4 all-in** with everything included: *I'll sell you the car, tyres, and radio for* **an all-in price. 5 all out, all-out** *infml* using all possible strength and effort: *We* **went all out/made an all-out effort** *to climb the mountain.* –see also ALL RIGHT, ALL-ROUND

**all**[2] *adv* **1** [*+adj/adv/prep*] completely; wholly: *She sat all alone.*|*I got all dirty.*|*He got mud all over the seat.* **2** for each side: *The result of the match was three all; neither side won.* **3 all but** almost; nearly: *It's all but impossible.* **4 all over: a** everywhere (on an object or surface): *Paint it green all over!* **b** *esp. AmE* everywhere in a place: *We've been hunting for her all over.* **c** right across; to every part of (a place): *to travel all over India* **d** finished: *Our hopes are all over.* **e** *infml* very like; thoroughly like: *He's always late; that's Billy all over.* **5 all the same** *infml* even so; in any case: *You say the bridge isn't safe; all the same I shall go over it.*

**all**[3] *pron* **1** everybody, everything, or everyone: *He gave all he had.*|*I brought all of them.* **2 (not) at all** (only used in questions, NEGATIVES[2], etc.) (not) in any way: *I do not agree with you at all.*

USAGE **All** is sing. with [U] nouns: **All** *the money is spent.* It is pl. with pl. nouns: **All** *the people have gone.*

**Al·lah** /'ælə/ *n* (the Muslim name for) God

**al·lay** /ə'leɪ/ *v* **-layed, -laying** [T] *fml* to make (fear, anger, doubt, etc.) less

Pat arrived at the **airport** two hours ago to **catch** her **plane** to Tokyo. At the **check-in counter**, a ticket agent looked at her **ticket** and her **passport**, and her **baggage** was **checked in**/weighed on the scales. Pat's **suitcases** were very heavy, so she had to pay an **excess baggage charge** (amount of money for additional weight). Next she was given a **boarding pass** (a ticket that allows her to get on the plane). The boarding pass has a seat number written on it, and Pat was given a window seat in the **non-smoking section.** Her suitcases were labeled and sent off to be **loaded** into the **hold** of the **airplane.**

While waiting for the **flight** to be **called,** Pat goes to the **newsstand** to buy a newspaper. Then she goes through the **security check,** where her **carry-on luggage** (the bags she is keeping with her on the plane) is searched. Then Pat goes into the **duty-free shop** where she has a chance to buy some things cheaply. The goods she buys here are cheap because they are not taxed.

In the **departure lounge,** Pat joins the other passengers who are sitting and waiting until it is time for their flight to depart. After a few minutes Pat hears the **announcement**: 'Flight 156 to Tokyo now **boarding** at **Gate Three**", and she goes to **board** (get on) her plane.

**Questions** (Answers on page 702)

**a** When you arrive at the airport you first go to the . . . . . . . . . . counter.
**b** You have to have a . . . . . . . . . . pass so that you can get on the plane.
**c** After the security check, you wait in the . . . . . . . . . . lounge.
**d** You can buy many things cheaply at the . . . . . . . . . . shop.
**e** When you hear the announcement, you go to the . . . . . . . . . . to board your plane.

aeroplane/plane
tail
wing
Gate 2
Gate 3
Café
seat
stool
ashtray
EXIT
Duty Free
ENTRANCE

**all clear** /ˌ· ˈ·/ *n* a signal (such as a whistle or loud cry) that danger is past –compare ALERT² (1)

**al·le·ga·tion** /ˌælɪˈgeɪʃən/ *n fml* a statement that charges someone with doing something bad or criminal but which is not supported by proof: *allegations of cruelty*

**al·lege** /əˈledʒ/ *v* **-leged, -leging** [T +*that*] *fml* to state or declare without proof or before finding proof: *The police allege that the man was murdered but they have given no proof.* **–allegedly** /əˈledʒɪdli/ *adv*

**al·le·giance** /əˈliːdʒəns/ *n* [C;U] loyalty, faith, and dutiful support to a leader, country, idea, etc.: *allegiance to the King*

**al·le·go·ry** /ˈælɪgəri‖-gori/ *n* **-ries** [C;U] (the style of) a story, poem, painting, etc., in which the characters and actions represent good and bad qualities **–allegorical** /ˌælɪˈgɒrɪkəl‖-ˈgɔ-, -ˈgɑ-/ *adj*

**al·le·lu·ia** /ˌælɪˈluːjə/ *n,interj* → HALLELUJA

**al·ler·gic** /əˈlɜːdʒɪk‖-ɜr-/ *adj* [*to*] related to or suffering from an ALLERGY: *He is allergic to the fur of cats.*|*an allergic reaction to cats*

**al·ler·gy** /ˈælədʒi‖-ər-/ *n* **-gies** a condition of being unusually sensitive to something eaten, breathed in, or touched, in a way that causes pain or suffering

**al·le·vi·ate** /əˈliːvieɪt/ *v* **-ated, -ating** [T] to make (pain, suffering, anger, etc.) less **–alleviation** /-ˈeɪʃən/ *n* [U]

**al·ley** /ˈæli/ *n* **-leys** a narrow street or path between buildings in a town –see also BLIND ALLEY

**al·li·ance** /əˈlaɪəns/ *n* **1** [U] the act of allying or the state of being allied (ALLY) (esp. in the phrase **in alliance (with)**) **2** [C] a close agreement or connection between countries, groups, families, etc.: *We are hoping for an alliance between government and industry.* **3** [C +*sing./pl.v*] a group or association, esp. of countries, formed to look after the interests of its members

**al·lied** /ˈælaɪd, əˈlaɪd/ *adj* [*to*] related or connected, esp. by common qualities: *painting and allied arts*

**al·li·ga·tor** /ˈælɪgeɪtəʳ/ *n* **-tors** *or* **-tor** a large cold-blooded fierce animal (like the CROCODILE) that lives on land and in lakes and rivers in the hot wet parts of America and China

**al·lit·er·a·tion** /əˌlɪtəˈreɪʃən/ *n* [U] the appearance of the same sound or sounds at the beginning of two or more words that are next to or close to each other (as in "*R*ound the *r*ocks *r*uns the *r*iver") **–alliterative** /əˈlɪtərətɪv‖-təreɪtɪv/ *adj*

**al·lo·cate** /ˈæləkeɪt/ also **allot**– *v* **-cated, -cating** [T] to set apart for somebody as a share or for some purpose: *That space has already been allocated for building a new hospital.*

**al·lo·ca·tion** /ˌæləˈkeɪʃən/ *n* **1** [U] the giving of shares or places **2** [C] a share, as of money or space

**al·lot** /əˈlɒt‖əˈlɑt/ *v* **-tt-** [T] → ALLOCATE

**al·lot·ment** /əˈlɒtmənt‖əˈlɑt-/ *n* **1** [C] a share, as of money or space **2** [C] (in Britain) a small piece of land rented out, esp. by a town council, to people who will grow vegetables on it

**al·low** /əˈlaʊ/ *v* [T] **1** [+*v-ing*] to let (somebody) do something; let (something) be done; permit: *They do not allow it/smoking/you to smoke.* –opposite **disallow** **2** to permit to be or to come: *They won't allow dogs in the house.* **3** [*of*] to permit as possible; admit: *The facts allow (of) no other explanation.* **4** to provide (esp. money or time): *You'll have to allow three days for that job.*

**allow for** sbdy./sthg. *v prep* [T +*v-ing*] to take into consideration: *Allowing for the train being late, we should be back by 10.30.*

**al·low·a·ble** /əˈlaʊəbəl/ *adj* that may be allowed or permitted

**al·low·ance** /əˈlaʊəns/ *n* **1** [C] **a** something, esp. money, provided regularly: *an allowance of £5,000 a year*|*a travelling allowance* **b** *AmE* for POCKET MONEY (2) **2** [C;U] the taking into consideration of facts that may change something, esp. an opinion (esp. in the phrase **make allowance(s) for**)

**al·loy** /ˈælɔɪ‖ˈælɔɪ, əˈlɔɪ/ *n* a metal made by mixing together two or more different metals

**all right** /ˌ· ˈ·/ *adv,adj* [F *no comp.*] **1** safe, unharmed, or healthy: *Is the driver all right after the accident?* **2** *infml* satisfactory but not very good; acceptable; in a satisfactory or acceptable manner: *His work is all right (but he could be faster).* **3** (*in answer to a suggestion, plan, etc.*) I/we agree; yes: *"Let's go now." "All right."* –see ALRIGHT (USAGE)

**all-round** /ˈ· ·/ *adj* [A] having ability in many things, esp. in various sports **–all-rounder** /ˌ· ˈ··/ *n*

**al·lude to** sbdy./sthg. /əˈluːd/ *v prep* **-luded, -luding** [T +*v-ing*] *fml* to speak of but without going straight to the point: *She did not say Mr Smith's name, but it was clear she was alluding to him.*

**al·lure¹** /əˈlʊəʳ/ *v* **-lured, -luring** [T] to attract by the offer of something pleasant; TEMPT: *an alluring look*

**allure²** *n* [S;U] attraction; charm

**al·lu·sion** /əˈluːʒən/ *n* [C;U *to*] *fml* the act of speaking of something in an indirect manner, or something spoken of without directness, esp. while speaking about something else **–allusive** /əˈluːsɪv/ *adj*

**al·lu·vi·al** /əˈluːvɪəl/ *adj* being, concerning, or made of soil put down by rivers, lakes, floods, etc.

**al·ly¹** /əˈlaɪ‖əˈlaɪ, ˈælaɪ/ *v* **-lied, -lying** [I;T *with, to*] to join or unite, as by political agreement or marriage

**ally²** /ˈælaɪ‖ˈælaɪ, əˈlaɪ/ *n* **-lies** a person or country that helps or supports one, esp. in war

**al·ma·nac** /ˈɔːlmənæk‖ˈɔl-, ˈæl-/ *n* a book giving a list of the days of a year, together with the times of sunrise and sunset, changes in the moon, the rise and fall of the sea, etc.

**al·might·y** /ɔːlˈmaɪti/ *adj* **1** (*often cap.*) having the power to do anything; OMNIPOTENT: *God Almighty*|*(God,) the Almighty* **2** *infml* very big, strong, great, etc.: *an almighty crash*

**al·mond** /ˈɑːmənd‖ˈɑ-, ˈæ-, ˈæl-/ *n* **1** a fruit tree whose seeds are eaten as nuts **2** the nut of this tree

**al·most** /ˈɔːlməʊst‖ˈɔlməʊst, ɔlˈməʊst/ *adv* very nearly but not quite: *I almost dropped the cake.*|*She said almost nothing.*|*almost everybody* –see Study Notes on page 389

**alms** /ɑːmz‖ɑmz, ɑlmz/ *n* [P] *old use* money, food, clothes, etc., given to poor people

**a·loft** /əˈlɒft‖əˈlɔft/ *adv* [F] high up, as in the air or among the sails of a ship: *The flag was flying aloft.*

**a·lone** /əˈləʊn/ *adv,adj* [F] **1** without others: *He lives alone.*|*The house stands alone on a hill.* **2** only: *You alone can do it.* (=you are the only person who can do it) **3 leave/let alone: a** to allow to be by oneself

**b** to allow to remain untouched or unchanged: *Leave that alone: it's mine.* –see also LET **alone**

USAGE **Alone** is neither good nor bad: *She reads a lot when she's* **alone**. **Solitary** and **lone**, when used of things, mean that there is only one: *a* **solitary/lone** *tree in the garden*, but when used of people they may show sadness, like **lonely** or **lonesome**(*esp. AmE*): *Come over and see me; I'm feeling a bit* **lonely.**

**a·long**[1] /ə'lɒŋ‖ə'lɔŋ/ *prep* **1** from one end of to the other: *We walked along the road. –see Study Notes on page 474* **2** in a line next to the length of: *Trees grew along the river bank.* **3** at a point on the length of: *His room is along this passage.*

**along**[2] *adv* **1** forward; on: *She bicycled along, singing loudly.* **2** with others or oneself: *When we went to Paris I took my sister along (with me).* **3** [F] here or there; over; across: *I'll be along soon.|Come along and visit us next week.* **4 all along** all the time: *I knew the truth all along.*

**a·long·side** /ə,lɒŋ'saɪd‖ə,lɔŋ-/ *prep,adv* close to and in line with the edge of (something); along the side: *We brought our boat alongside (their boat).*

**a·loof** /ə'lu:f/ *adj,adv* apart; distant in feeling or interest; RESERVED (1): *He held/kept himself aloof from the others.* **–aloofness** *n* [U]

**a·loud** /ə'laʊd/ also **out loud** *–adv* in a voice that may be heard: *The teacher asked him to read the poem aloud.|The pain caused him to cry aloud.*

**al·pha** /'ælfə/ *n* the first letter (A, α) in the Greek alphabet

**al·pha·bet** /'ælfəbet/ *n* the set of letters used in writing any language, esp. when arranged in order

**al·pha·bet·i·cal** /,ælfə'betɪkəl/ *adj* [*no comp.*] of, belonging to, or in the order of the alphabet: *In a dictionary the words are arranged in alphabetical order.* **–alphabetically** *adv*

**al·pine** /'ælpaɪn/ *adj* of or concerning **the Alps** or other high mountains

**al·read·y** /ɔ:l'redi/ *adv* **1** by or before a particular time; even before expected: *He had already gone (when I arrived).|She's here already; she's early.* **2** before: *I've been there already and don't want to go again.*

USAGE Note the difference between **already** and **all ready**: *We're* **all ready** means either that all of us are ready or that we are completely ready; **already** could not be used here. –see JUST[2] (USAGE)

**al·right** /,ɔ:l'raɪt/ *adv* [*no comp.*] all right

USAGE **Alright** is very common now, but teachers prefer **all right**.

**al·so** /'ɔ:lsəʊ/ *adv* **1** as well; besides; too: *The weather was* **not only** *cold,* **but also** *wet.* (=both cold and wet) –see Study Notes on page 128

**al·tar** /'ɔ:ltə^r/ *n* a table or raised level surface used in a religious ceremony, esp. in the Christian service of COMMUNION

**al·ter** /'ɔ:ltə^r/ *v* [I;T] to (cause to) become different: *This shirt must be altered; it's too large. |You have altered since I last saw you.*

**al·ter·a·tion** /,ɔ:ltə'reɪʃən/ *n* **1** [U] the act of making or becoming different **2** [C] a change; something changed: *The alterations to your coat will take a week.*

**al·ter·ca·tion** /,ɔ:ltə'keɪʃən‖-tər-/ *n fml* a noisy disagreement; quarrel

**al·ter·nate**[1] /ɔ:l'tɜ:nɨt‖'ɔltɜr-, 'æl-/ *adj* **1** (of two things) happening by turns; first one and then the other: *a week of alternate rain and sunshine* **2** one of every two; every second: *He works on alternate days.* –compare ALTERNATIVE **–alternately** *adv*

**al·ter·nate**[2] /'ɔ:ltəneɪt‖-ər-/ *v* **-nated, -nating** [I;T *with, between*] to (cause to) follow by turns: *My life alternated between work and sleep.* **–alternation** /-'neɪʃən/ *n* [C;U]

**al·ter·na·tive**[1] /ɔ:l'tɜ:nətɪv‖ɔl'tɜr-, æl-/ *adj* [*no comp.*] (of two things) that may be used, had, done, etc., instead of another; other: *We returned by an alternative road.* –compare ALTERNATE **–alternatively** *adv*

**alternative**[2] *n* [C;S *to*] something, esp. a course of action, that may be taken or had instead of one or more others: *We had to fight: there was no (other) alternative.|There are several alternatives to your plan.*

USAGE Sentences such as: *We have several* **alternatives** *to choose from.* are quite common, but this is thought by teachers to be incorrect, because there should be only *two* **alternatives.**

**al·though** /ɔ:l'ðəʊ/ *conj* in spite of the fact that; though: *They are generous although they are poor.* –see Study Notes on page 128

**al·ti·tude** /'æltɨtju:d‖-tu:d/ *n* **1** [*usu. sing.*] height, as of a mountain above sea level: *The plane flew at an altitude of 30,000 feet.* –compare ELEVATION **2** [*usu. pl.*] a high place or area: *At high altitudes it is difficult to breathe.*

**al·to** /'æltəʊ/ *n* **-tos** (a person with) a singing voice between SOPRANO and TENOR

**al·to·geth·er** /,ɔ:ltə'geðə^r◂/ *adv* **1** completely; thoroughly: *It is not altogether bad.|That's altogether different.* **2** considering all things; on the whole: *It was raining, but altogether it was a good trip.* –see ABSOLUTELY (USAGE)

**al·tru·is·m** /'æltru-ɪzəm/ *n* [U] consideration of the happiness and good of others before one's own; unselfishness –compare EGOISM

**al·tru·ist** /'æltru-ɨst/ *n* a person who is habitually good to others **–altruistic** /-'ɪstɪk/ *adj*

**al·u·min·i·um** /,ælju'mɪnɪəm, ,ælə-/ *BrE*‖**alu-minum** /ə'lu:mɪnəm/ *AmE– n* [U] a silver-white metal that is a simple substance (ELEMENT (1)) light in weight, and easily shaped

**al·ways** /'ɔ:lwɨz, -weɪz/ *adv* **1** at all times; at each time: *The sun always rises in the east.|We've always lived here.* **2** for ever: *I will love you always.* **3** (used with the *-ing* form of a verb) all the time and often in an annoying way: *He's always asking silly questions.* –compare FOREVER[2]; see NEVER (USAGE)

**am** /m, əm; *strong* æm/ *1st person sing. present tense of* BE: *I am (living) here now.|Here I am!* –see AREN'T (USAGE)

**AM** amplitude modulation; a system of broadcasting in which the strength of the sound waves varies: *an AM radio* –compare FM

**a.m.** /,eɪ 'em/ *abbrev. for Latin*: ante meridiem (=before midday) (*used after numbers expressing time*): *the 8 a.m. (train) from London* –see also P.M.

**a·mal·gam·ate** /ə'mælgəmeɪt/ **-ated, -ating** *v* [I;T *with*] (esp. of businesses, societies, groups, etc.) to join; unite; combine –**amalgamation** /-'meɪʃən/ *n* [C;U]

**a·mass** /ə'mæs/ *v* [T] to gather or collect (money, goods, power, etc.) in great amounts

**am·a·teur** /'æmətəʳ, -tʃʊəʳ, -tʃəʳ, ˌæmə'tɜːʳ/ *adj,n* **1** (of, by, or being) a person who performs plays, takes part in sports, takes photographs, etc., for enjoyment and without being paid for it: *an amateur photographer/footballer|Only amateurs may compete in the Olympic Games.* –compare PROFESSIONAL² **2** (typical of) a person without experience or skill in a particular art, sport, etc.: *We made a rather amateur job of painting the house.*

**am·a·teur·ish** /'æmətərɪʃ, ˌæmə'tjʊərɪʃ, -'tɜːrɪʃ‖ˌæmə'tʊʳ-, -'tɜr-/ *adj derog* lacking skill; not good; poor –**amateurishly** *adv* –**amateurism** *n* [U]

**a·maze** /ə'meɪz/ *v* **-mazed, -mazing** [T] to fill with great surprise; cause wonder in: *I was amazed by the news.|It amazed me to hear that you were leaving.* –**amazement** *n* [U]

**a·maz·ing** /ə'meɪzɪŋ/ *adj usu. apprec* causing great surprise or wonder because of quantity or quality: *What an amazing film!* –**amazingly** *adv* –see Study Notes on page 389

**am·bas·sa·dor** /æm'bæsədəʳ/ **ambassadress** /-drɪ̀s/ *fem.* – *n* a minister of high rank representing his/her country in the capital city of a foreign country either for a special occasion or for a longer period in an EMBASSY –compare CONSUL –**ambassadorial** /æmˌbæsə'dɔːrɪəl‖-'do-/ *adj*

**am·ber** /'æmbəʳ/ *n* [U] (the colour of) a yellowish brown hard clear substance used for jewels, ornaments, etc.

**am·bi·dex·trous** /ˌæmbɪ'dekstrəs/ *adj* able to use either hand with equal skill

**am·bi·ence** ‖also **ambiance** *AmE* /'æmbɪəns/ *n* [U] the character, quality, feeling, etc., of a place: *The little restaurant has a pleasant ambience.*

**am·big·u·ous** /æm'bɪgjʊəs/ *adj* able to be understood in more than one way; of unclear meaning: *an ambiguous reply* –opposite **unambiguous**; compare AMBIVALENT –**ambiguously** *adv* –**ambiguity** /ˌæmbɪ̀'gjuːɪ̀ti/ *n* **-ties** [C;U]: *Her reply was full of ambiguities.*

**am·bi·tion** /æm'bɪʃən/ *n* **1** [U] strong desire for success, power, riches, etc.: *That politician is full of ambition.* **2** [C] that which is desired in this way: *One of her ambitions is to become a minister.*

**am·bi·tious** /æm'bɪʃəs/ *adj* **1** having a strong desire for success, power, riches, etc.: *an ambitious man* **2** demanding a strong desire for success, great effort, great skill, etc.: *an ambitious attempt to climb the dangerous mountain* –**ambitiously** *adv*

**am·biv·a·lent** /æm'bɪvələnt/ *adj* [*towards, about*] having opposing feelings towards, or opinions about, something or someone –compare AMBIGUOUS –**ambivalence** *n* [U]

**am·ble** /'æmbəl/ *v* **-bled, -bling** [I *about, around*] to walk at an easy gentle rate –see WALK (USAGE) –**amble** *n* [S]

**am·bu·lance** /'æmbjʊləns‖-bjə-/ *n* a motor vehicle for carrying sick or wounded people, esp. to hospital

**am·bush¹** /'æmbʊʃ/ *v* [T] to attack from a place where one has hidden and waited

**ambush²** *n* [C; *in* U] a surprise attack from a place of hiding; the place where the attackers hide

**a·me·li·o·rate** /ə'miːlɪəreɪt/ *v* **-rated, -rating** [I;T] *fml* to make better or less bad; improve –**amelioration** /-'reɪʃən/ *n* [U]

**a·men** /ɑː'men, eɪ-/ *interj* (*used at the end of a prayer or* HYMN) may this be true; so be it

**a·me·na·ble** /ə'miːnəbəl/ *adj* [*to*] able to be guided or influenced (by): *She is amenable to reason.*

**a·mend** /ə'mend/ *v* [T] to make changes in the words of (a rule or law)

**a·mend·ment** /ə'mendmənt/ *n* [C;U] (the act of making) a change, made in or suggested for a statement, etc.: *So many amendments were made to the law that its original meaning was completely changed.*

**a·mends** /ə'mendz/ *n* [P] **make amends** to repair or pay for some harm, unkindness, damage, etc.: *I'm sorry I crashed your car – how can I make amends (for what I did)?*

**a·me·ni·ty** /ə'miːnɪ̀ti‖ə'me-/ *n* **-ties** [*often pl.*] a thing or condition in a town, hotel, place, etc., that one can enjoy and which makes life pleasant: *Parks and swimming baths are just some of the town's* **local amenities.**

**A·mer·i·can** /ə'merɪ̀kən/ *adj,n* (a person) belonging to North, Central, or South America, esp. the United States of America

**American foot·ball** /·ˌ··· '··/ *BrE*‖**football** *AmE*– *n* [U] an American game (rather like RUGBY) played by two teams of 11 players each

**A·mer·i·can·is·m** /ə'merɪ̀kənɪzəm/ *n* a word, phrase, speech sound, etc., of English as spoken in America, esp. in the United States

**am·e·thyst** /'æmɪ̀θɪ̀st/ *n* [C;U] (the colour of) a purple stone, used in jewellery

**a·mi·a·ble** /'eɪmɪəbəl/ *adj* of a pleasant nature; good-tempered; friendly –**amiability** /ˌeɪmɪə'bɪlɪ̀ti/ *n* [U] –**amiably** /'eɪmɪəbli/ *adv*

**am·i·ca·ble** /'æmɪ̀kəbəl/ *adj* suitable between friends; friendly: *We reached an amicable agreement.* –**amicably** *adv*

**a·mid** /ə'mɪd/ also **amidst** /ə'mɪdst/– *prep fml & lit* in the middle of; among: *He felt strange amid so many people.*

**a·mi·no ac·id** /əˌmiːnəʊ 'æsɪ̀d, əˌmaɪ-/ *n* a substance coming from, found in, and necessary to living matter

**a·miss** /ə'mɪs/ *adj,adv* [F *no comp.*] *fml* **1** wrong(ly) or imperfect(ly): *Is something amiss?* **2 take something amiss** to be angry at something, esp. because of a misunderstanding

**am·mo·ni·a** /ə'məʊnɪə/ *n* [U] a strong gas with a sharp smell, used in explosives, in chemicals (FERTILIZERS) to help plants grow, etc.

**am·mu·ni·tion** /ˌæmjʊ'nɪʃən‖ˌæmjə-/ *n* [U] bullets, bombs, explosives, etc., esp. things fired from a weapon: (fig.) *The recent tax increases have provided the government's opponents with plenty of ammunition.*

**am·ne·si·a** /æm'niːzɪə‖-ʒə/ *n* [U] loss of memory, either in part or completely

**am·nes·ty** /'æmnəsti/ *n* **-ties** [C;U] (a) general act of forgiveness, esp. as allowed by a state to political criminals

**a·mok** /ə'mɒk‖ə'mɑk/ also **amuck**– *adv* **run amok** to run wild and out of control, esp. with a desire to kill people

**a·mong** /ə'mʌŋ/ also **amongst** /ə'mʌŋst/– *prep* **1** in the middle of; surrounded by: *Their house is hidden among trees.|I was among the crowd.* **2** in the group of; being one of: *He is among the best of our students.|She's very keen on sport: among other things, she plays tennis twice a week.|They talked about it among themselves.* (=together) **3** (when things are shared by more than two people): *Divide the money among the five of them.* (Compare *Divide the money between the two of them.)* –see BETWEEN (USAGE)

**a·mor·al** /eɪ'mɒrəl, æ-‖eɪ'mɔ-, -'mɑ-/ *adj* having no understanding of right and wrong: *Young children are amoral.* –see also IMMORAL, MORAL **–amorality** /ˌeɪmɒ'rælɪ̈ti, ˌæ-‖ˌeɪmə-/ *n* [U]

**am·o·rous** /'æmərəs/ *adj* of love; easily moved to love, esp. sexual love: *amorous looks|an amorous girl* **–amorously** *adv* **–amorousness** *n* [U]

**a·mor·phous** /ə'mɔːfəs‖-ɔr-/ *adj* having no fixed form or shape: *I can't understand his amorphous plans.* **–amorphously** *adv*

**a·mount** /ə'maʊnt/ *n* a quantity or sum: *Large amounts of money were spent on the bridge.*

USAGE **Amount** is used with [U] nouns: *the* **amount** *of money.* With plurals it is better to use **number**: *the* **number** *of mistakes.*

**amount to** sthg. *v prep* [not *be* +*v-ing*] to be equal to: *Your words amount to a refusal.|His debts amount to over £1,000.*

**amp** /æmp/ *n* **1** also **ampere** /'æmpeəʳ‖'æmpɪər/ *fml–tech* the standard measure of the quantity of electricity that is flowing past a point –compare VOLT **2** *infml* for →AMPLIFIER

**am·phet·a·mine** /æm'fetəmiːn, -mɪ̈n/ *n* [C;U] a drug used in medicine and by people wanting excitement

**am·phib·i·an** /æm'fɪbɪən/ *n* an animal (such as a FROG) that is able to live both on land and in water **–amphibious** /æm'fɪbɪəs/ *adj: an amphibious animal|an amphibious vehicle* (=one which can travel both on land and in water)

**am·phi·the·at·re** *BrE*‖**amphitheater** *AmE* /'æmfɪ̈θɪətəʳ/ *n* an open building with rows of seats all around a central area, used for competitions and plays, esp. in ancient Rome

**am·ple** /'æmpəl/ *adj* **1** (more than) enough: *We have ample money for the journey.* **2** large **–amply** *adv*

**am·pli·fi·er** /'æmplɪ̈faɪəʳ/ also **amp** *infml– n* an instrument, as used in radios and RECORD PLAYERS, that makes electrical current or power stronger, music louder, etc.

**am·pli·fy** /'æmplɪ̈faɪ/ *v* **-fied, -fying 1** [I;T *on, upon*] to make larger, esp. to explain in greater detail: *He amplified (on) his remarks with drawings and figures.* **2** [T] to increase the strength of (something, esp. sound from electrical instruments) **–amplification** /-fɪ̈'keɪʃən/ *n* [S;U]

**am·pu·tate** /'æmpjʊteɪt‖-pjə-/ *v* **-tated, -tating** [I;T] to cut off (part of the body), esp. for medical reasons: *Her leg was so badly damaged that the doctors had to amputate (it).* **–amputation** /-'teɪʃən/ *n* [C;U]

**a·muck** /ə'mʌk/ *adv* → AMOK

**a·muse** /ə'mjuːz/ *v* **-mused, -musing** [T] **1** to cause laughter in; excite the sense of humour of: *an amused expression on one's face|an amusing story* **2** to cause to spend time in a pleasant manner: *The children amused themselves by playing games.*

**a·muse·ment** /ə'mjuːzmənt/ *n* **1** [U] the state of being amused; enjoyment: *To everybody's amusement the actor fell off the stage.* **2** [C] something that causes one's time to pass enjoyably: *Big cities have theatres, films, football matches, and many other amusements.*

**an** /ən; *strong* æn/ *indefinite article, determiner* (*used when the following word begins with a vowel sound*) a: *an elephant, not a dog|an R.A.F. officer*

USAGE When putting **a** or **an** before a set of letters like R.A.F. (an ABBREVIATION) one must know how they are said in speech. R.A.F. begins with the consonant "r", but the name of the consonant begins with the vowel sound /ɑː/; one says **an R.A.F.** *officer* but **a BBC** *broadcaster.*

**a·nach·ro·nis·m** /ə'nækrənɪzəm/ *n* a person, thing, or idea that is or appears to be in the wrong period of time: *It is an anachronism to say Julius Caesar looked at his watch.* **–anachronistic** /əˌnækrə'nɪstɪk/ *adj* **–anachronistically** *adv*

**a·nae·mi·a**‖also **anemia** *AmE* /ə'niːmɪə/ *n* [U] the unhealthy condition of not having the proper number of red cells in the blood **–anaemic** /ə'niːmɪk/ *adj*

**an·aes·the·si·a**‖also **anesthesia** *AmE* /ˌænɪ̈s'θiːzɪə‖-ʒə/ *n* [U] the state of being unable to feel pain, etc., as produced by an ANAESTHETIC

**an·aes·thet·ic**‖also **anesthetic** *AmE* /ˌænɪ̈s'θetɪk/ *n* [C;U] a substance that produces an inability to feel pain, either in a limited area (**local anaesthetic**) or in the whole body, together with unconsciousness (**general anaesthetic**) **–anaesthetist** /ə'niːsθɪ̈tɪ̈st‖ə'nes-/ *n*: *The anaesthetist gave the patient an anaesthetic.*

**a·naes·the·tize**‖also **-tise** BrE, also **anesthetize** *AmE* /ə'niːsθɪ̈taɪz‖ə'nes-/ *v* **-tized, -tizing** [T] to make unable to feel pain by giving an ANAESTHETIC

**an·a·gram** /'ænəgræm/ *n* a word or phrase made by changing the order of the letters in another word or phrase: *"Silent" is an anagram of "listen".*

**a·nal** /'eɪnəl/ *adj* of, concerning, or near the ANUS

**an·al·ge·sic** /ˌænəl'dʒiːzɪk/ *n,adj* [C;U] (a substance) which makes one unable to feel pain

**a·nal·o·gous** /ə'næləgəs/ *adj* [F *to, with*] *fml* like or alike in some ways: *Your suggestion was analogous to/with one that was made earlier.*

**a·nal·o·gy** /ə'nælədʒi/ *n* **-gies 1** [C] a degree of likeness or sameness: *There is an analogy between the way water moves in waves and the way light travels.* **2** [U] the act of explaining by comparing something with another thing that is like it in some way

**an·a·lyse**‖also **analyze** *AmE* /'ænəlaɪz/ *v* **-lysed, -lysing** [T] to examine (something) carefully in order to find out about (it): *He analysed the food and found it contained poison.*

**a·nal·y·sis** /ə'nælɪ̈sɪ̈s/ *n* **-ses** /siːz/ [C;U] (an) examination of something together with thoughts and judgments about it: *His analysis of the accident showed what had happened*.

**an·a·lyst** /'ænəl¦st/ *n* **1** a person who makes an ANALYSIS, esp. of chemicals **2** *AmE* for PSYCHO-ANALYST

**an·a·lyt·ic** /,ænə'lɪtɪk/ also **analytical**– *adj* of, concerning, or using ANALYSIS –**analytically** *adv*

**an·ar·chis·m** /'ænəkɪzəm‖-ər-/ *n* [U] the political belief that society should have no government, laws, police, etc. –**anarchist** *n*

**an·ar·chy** /'ænəki‖-ər-/ *n* [U] (lawlessness and disorder caused by) absence of government or control –**anarchic** /æ'nɑːkɪk‖-ar-/ *adj*

**a·nath·e·ma** /ə'næθ¦mə/ *n* [S;U *to*] something hated: *Those terrible ideas are (an) anathema to me.*

**a·nat·o·my** /ə'nætəmi/ *n* **-mies 1** [U] the scientific study of the bodies of living things, esp. by cutting up dead bodies **2** [C *usu. sing.*] the way a living thing works or is built: *to study the anatomy of insects/plants* –**anatomical** /,ænə'tɒmɪkəl‖-'tɑ-/ *adj* –**anatomist** /ə'nætəm¦st/ *n*

**an·ces·tor** /'ænsəstəʳ, -ses-‖-ses-/ *n* a person, esp. one living a long time ago, from whom another is descended: *My ancestors came from Spain.* –compare DESCENDENT –**ancestral** /æn'sestrəl/ *adj* [A]: *one's ancestral home*

**an·ces·try** /'ænsəstri, -ses-‖-ses-/ *n* **-tries** [C;U] a person's ANCESTORS considered as a group

**an·chor¹** /'æŋkəʳ/ *n* a heavy piece of metal, usu. hooked, at the end of a chain or rope, for lowering into the water to keep a ship from moving

**anchor²** *v* **1** [I] to stop sailing and lower the ANCHOR **2** [I;T] to (cause to) be fixed firmly

**an·chor·age** /'æŋkərɪdʒ/ *n* a place where ships may ANCHOR² (1)

**an·cho·vy** /'æntʃəvi‖'æntʃəʊvi/ *n* **-vies** *or* **-vy** a small strong-tasting fish

**an·cient** /'eɪnʃənt/ *adj* **1** in or of times long ago: *ancient Rome and Greece* **2** *often humor* very old –see OLD (USAGE)

**an·cil·la·ry** /æn'sɪləri‖'æns¦leri/ *adj* [*to*] *fml or tech* providing help, support, or additional service

**and** /ənd, ən, *strong* ænd/ *conj* **1** (*joining two things, esp. words of the same type or sentences of the same importance*) as well as; also: *a knife and fork*|*John and I*|*He was cold and hungry.*|*He started to shout and sing.* –see Study Notes on page 128 **2** then; afterwards: *I woke up and got out of bed.* **3** (used to express a reason or result): *She was sick and took some medicine.* (=because she was sick) Compare *She took some medicine and was sick.* (=because she took the medicine) **4** (used instead of *to* after *come, go, try*, etc.): *Come and have tea with me.*|*Try and get here before 4 o'clock.*

**an·ec·dote** /'ænɪkdəʊt/ *n* a short interesting or amusing story about a particular person or event –**anecdotal** /-'dəʊtəl/ *adj*

**a·ne·mi·a** /ə'niːmɪə/ *n AmE* for ANAEMIA –**anemic** *adj*

**a·nem·o·ne** /ə'neməni/ *n* **1** a plant with quite large red, white, or blue flowers **2** also **sea anemone**– a simple sea animal with a jelly-like body and brightly coloured flower-like parts that can often sting

**an·es·the·si·a** /,æn¦s'θiːzɪə‖-ʒə/ *n AmE* for ANAESTHESIA –**anesthetic** /,æn¦s'θetɪk/ *adj* –**anesthetist** /ə'niːsθ¦t¦st‖ə'nes-/ *n* –**anesthetize** /ə'niːsθ¦taɪz‖ə'nes-/ *v* [T]

**a·new** /ə'njuː‖ə'nuː/ *adv lit* in a new or different way; again

**an·gel** /'eɪndʒəl/ *n* **1** a messenger and servant of God, usu. represented as a person with wings and dressed in white **2** a person who is very kind, beautiful, etc. –**angelic** /æn'dʒelɪk/ *adj*

**an·ger¹** /'æŋgəʳ/ *n* [U] a fierce feeling of displeasure, usu. leading to a desire to hurt or stop the person or thing causing it

**anger²** *v* [T] to make angry –see ANGRY (USAGE)

**an·gle¹** /'æŋgəl/ *n* **1** the space between two lines or surfaces that meet or cross each other, measured in degrees that represent the amount of a circle that can fit into that space: *An angle of 90° is called a* **right angle**.|*The plant was growing* **at an angle**. (=not upright) **2** *infml* a point of view: *Looked at from another angle the accident was very funny.*

**angle²** *v* **-gled, -gling** [T] **1** to turn or move at an angle **2** *often derog* to represent (something) from a particular point of view: *She angles her reports to suit the people she is speaking to.*

**angle³** *v* [I] to fish with a hook and line: *He loves (to go) angling.* –**angler** *n: a keen angler* –**angling** *n* [U]

**angle for** sthg. *v prep* [T] *often derog* to try to get, esp. by tricks or questions which are not direct: *to angle for an invitation to a party*

**An·gli·can** /'æŋglɪkən/ *n,adj* (a member) of a branch (CHURCH OF ENGLAND) of the Christian religion –**Anglicanism** *n* [U]

**an·gli·cize**‖also **-cise** *BrE* /'æŋgl¦saɪz/ *v* **-cized, -cizing** [I;T] to (cause to) become English in appearance, sound, character, etc.

**An·glo-Sax·on** /,æŋgləʊ'sæksən/ *adj,n* **1** [C] (of or concerning) a member of the people who lived in England in early times, from about 600 to 1066 AD **2** [U] (of or concerning) their language

**an·gry** /'æŋgri/ *adj* **1** filled with anger: *I was angry (with him) for keeping me waiting so long.* **2** (of the sky or clouds) stormy –**angrily** *adv*

USAGE **Bother** means "displease" or "trouble": *Will it* **bother** *you if I put the radio on?* Things, people, or events can **annoy** or **irritate** one without being bad enough to make one **angry** (=to **anger** one) or (*AmE infml*) **mad:** *He has an* **annoying/irritating** *habit of biting his nails.*|*I was* **angered** *by his refusal to help.*|*The teacher was* **angry** *because the children wouldn't stop talking.* To make someone **furious** (to **infuriate** someone) or drive someone into a **rage** are stronger expressions still.

**an·guish** /'æŋgwɪʃ/ *n* [U] very great pain and suffering, esp. of mind –**anguished** *adj*: *anguished cries*

**an·gu·lar** /'æŋgjʊləʳ‖-gjə-/ *adj* **1** having sharp corners **2** (of a person) with the bones able to be clearly seen; thin: *her sharp angular face* –**angularity** /-'lær¦ti/ *n* [U]

**an·i·mal¹** /'æn¦məl/ *n* **1** a living creature, having senses and able to move itself when it wants to: *Snakes, fish, and birds are all animals.*|*Of all the animals, man is the cleverest.* **2** all this group except human beings **3** → MAMMAL

**animal²** *adj* **1** of, concerning, or made from animals **2** *usu. derog* concerning the body, not the mind or the spirit: *animal desires*

**an·i·mate¹** /'ænəmət/ *adj* (of plants and animals) alive; living –opposite **inanimate**

**an·i·mate²** /'ænəmeɪt/ *v* **-mated, -mating** [T] to give life or excitement to: *Laughter animated his face.*

**an·i·ma·ted** /'ænəmeɪtəd/ *adj* full of spirit and excitement; lively: *an animated argument*/DEBATE

**an·i·ma·tion** /,ænə'meɪʃən/ *n* [U] **1** excitement; spirit; life: *They were full of animation as they talked of their holiday.* **2** the making of CARTOONS (2)

**an·i·mos·i·ty** /,ænə'mɒsəti‖-'mɑ-/ *n* **-ties** [C;U *against, towards, between*] (an example of) powerful, often active, hatred

**an·i·seed** /'ænəsi:d/ *n* [U] the strong-tasting seeds of a plant (**anise**), used esp. in alcoholic drinks

**an·kle** /'æŋkəl/ *n* **1** the joint between the foot and the leg **2** the thin part of the leg just above the foot -see picture on page 299

**an·nals** /'ænəlz/ *n* [P] *fml* a history or record of events, discoveries, etc., produced every year, esp. by societies for the advancement of learning or science: (fig.) *one of the most interesting periods in the annals* (=history) *of modern science*

**an·nex** /ə'neks‖ə'neks, 'æneks/ *v* [T *to*] to take control and possession of (land, a small country, etc.) esp. by force –**annexation** /,ænek'seɪʃən/ *n* [C;U]

**an·nexe, annex** /'æneks/ *n* a building joined or added to a larger one: *a hospital annexe*

**an·ni·hi·late** /ə'naɪəleɪt/ *v* **-lated, -lating** [T] to destroy completely: –**annihilation** /-'leɪʃən/ *n* [U]

**an·ni·ver·sa·ry** /,ænə'vɜ:səri‖-ɜr-/ *n* **-ries** a day which is an exact year or number of years after something has happened: *a wedding anniversary* –compare BIRTHDAY

**An·no Dom·i·ni** /,ænəʊ 'dɒmənaɪ‖-'dɑ-/ *fml* for AD

**an·no·tate** /'ænəteɪt/ *v* **-tated, -tating** [T] *fml* to add notes to (a book) to explain certain parts–**annotation** /-'teɪʃən/ *n* [C:U]

**an·nounce** /ə'naʊns/ *v* **-nounced, -nouncing** [T] **1** to state in a loud voice: *Everyone was silent as he announced the winner of the competition.* **2** [+*that*] to make known publicly: *The government announced that they would pay their debts.* –see also UNANNOUNCED –**announcement** *n*

**an·nounc·er** /ə'naʊnsəʳ/ *n* a person who reads news or introduces people, acts, etc., esp. on radio or television

**an·noy** /ə'nɔɪ/ *v* **-noyed, -noying** [I;T] to cause (someone) trouble; make a little angry: *These flies are annoying me.* –see ANGRY (USAGE)

**an·noy·ance** /ə'nɔɪəns/ *n* **1** [U] the state of being annoyed **2** [C] something which annoys: *The noisy traffic is a continual annoyance.*

**an·nu·al¹** /'ænjʊəl/ *adj* (happening, appearing, etc.) every year or once a year; for one year: *an annual event*|*his annual salary* –**annually** *adv*

**annual²** *n* **1** a plant that lives for only one year or season –compare BIENNIAL **2** a book produced once each year having the same title but containing different stories, pictures, information, etc.

**an·nu·i·ty** /ə'nju:əti‖ə'nu:-/ *n* **-ties** a fixed sum of money paid each year to a person for a stated number of years or until death

**an·nul** /ə'nʌl/ *v* **-ll-** [T] *tech* to cause (a marriage, agreement, law, etc.) to cease to exist –**annulment** *n* [C;U]

**an·ode** /'ænəʊd/ also **positive pole**– *n tech* the part of an electrical instrument (such as a BATTERY (1)) which collects ELECTRONS, often a rod or wire shown as (+) –compare CATHODE

**a·noint** /ə'nɔɪnt/ *v* [T *with*] to put oil on (a person, head, or body), esp. in a religious ceremony –**anointment** *n* [C;U]

**a·nom·a·ly** /ə'nɒməli‖ə'nɑ-/ *n* **-lies** *fml* a person or thing that is different from the usual type: *A cat with no tail is an anomaly.* –**anomalous** /ə'nɒmələs‖ə'nɑ-/ *adj*: *in an anomalous position* –**anomalously** *adv*

**a·non¹** /ə'nɒn‖ə'nɑn/ *adv old use or lit* soon

**anon²** *abbrev. for* (esp. at the end of a poem, letter, etc.) ANONYMOUS

**a·non·y·mous** /ə'nɒnəməs‖ə'nɑ-/ *adj* with name unknown; without the writer's name: *It is unpleasant to receive anonymous letters.* –**anonymity** /,ænə'nɪməti/ *n* [U] –**anonymously** *adv*

**an·o·rak** /'ænəræk/ also **parka**– *n* a short coat with a HOOD (1),which keeps out wind and rain

**an·oth·er** /ə'nʌðəʳ/ *determiner,pron* **1** (being) one more of the same kind: *Have another drink and another of these cakes.* **2** a different one; some other: *He lost his book and borrowed one from another boy*/*from another of the boys.* –see OTHER (USAGE)

**an·swer¹** /'ɑ:nsəʳ‖'æn-/ *n* **1** [C;U *to*] what is said or written when one is asked a question, sent a letter, etc.; reply: *I've had no answer to my letter yet.*|*I said good morning to him but he gave no answer.*|**In answer to** *my shouts people ran to help.* **2** [C] something which is discovered as a result esp. of thinking, using figures, etc.; SOLUTION (1): *The answer was 279.*|(fig.) *I'm getting too fat–the only answer is to eat less.*

**answer²** *v* [I;T] **1** [*with*] to give an answer (to); reply (to): *You didn't answer his question.*|*Why didn't you answer?*|*I telephoned, but nobody answered (the telephone).* –see TELEPHONE (USAGE) **2** [*to*] to be as described in; equal; fit: *He answers (to) the description of the criminal.* **3** [*for*] to be satisfactory (for)

USAGE **Answer** and **reply** are the usual verbs for answering questions; **respond** (*fml*) means the same thing but is much less common: *He* **answered/replied to** *the question/his mother.*|*"Are you coming?" "Yes", he* **answered/replied.**|*I spoke, but he didn't* **answer/reply/respond.**|*He* **answered/replied** *that he was coming.* **Retort** or (*rare*) **rejoin** are angrier: *"Are you ready?" "Why should I be ready when you're not?" she* **retorted**.

**answer** (sbdy.) **back** *v adv* [I;T *no pass.*] *infml* (esp. of children talking to grown-ups) to reply rudely (to): *Don't answer (me) back: it's not polite.*

**answer for** sbdy./sthg. *v prep* [T *to*] **1** to be or become responsible for: *I will answer for his safety.* **2** to act, pay, or suffer as a result of: *You will have to answer for your violent behaviour in court.*

**an·swer·a·ble** /'ɑ:nsərəbəl‖'æn-/ *adj* **1** [F *to, for*] responsible: *I am* **answerable to** *the government* **for**

*any decision I make.* **2** able to be answered

**ant** /ænt/ *n* a small insect living on the ground and famous for hard work

**an·tag·o·nis·m** /æn'tægənɪzəm/ *n* [C;U] (an example of) active opposition or hatred between people or groups –**antagonist** /æn'tægən$\frac{1}{2}$st/ *n* –**antagonistic** /-'nɪstɪk/ *adj* –**antagonistically** *adv*

**an·tag·o·nize**‖also **-nise** *BrE* /æn'tægənaɪz/ *v* **-nized, -nizing** [T] to cause to become an enemy: *His rudeness only antagonizes people.*

**ant·arc·tic** /æn'tɑːktɪk‖-ɑr-/ *adj,n* [*the* S] (*often cap.*) (of or concerning) the very cold most southern part of the world –compare ARCTIC

**an·te·ced·ent** /ˌænt$\frac{1}{2}$'siːdənt/ *n,adj* [*to*] *fml* (a thing, event, etc.) coming or being before

**an·te·date** /'æntɪdeɪt, ˌæntɪ'deɪt/ *v* **-dated, -dating** [T] to be earlier in history than: *This old carriage antedates the invention of the car.* –see also POSTDATE

**an·te·lope** /'ænt$\frac{1}{2}$ləʊp‖'æntəl-/ *n* **-lopes** *or* **-lope** a graceful animal like a deer, able to run very fast

**an·te·na·tal** /ˌæntɪ'neɪtl/ *BrE*‖also **prenatal** *AmE*– *adj* [A] *tech* of or for the time before a birth: *An* **antenatal clinic** *is a place where women who are expecting babies go for medical examinations and exercises.* –compare POSTNATAL

**an·ten·na**[1] /æn'tenə/ *n* **-nae** /niː/ a long thin sensitive hairlike organ, usu. in pairs, on the heads of some insects and animals that live in shells, and used to feel with

**antenna**[2] *n* **-nas** *AmE* for AERIAL

**an·ter·i·or** /æn'tɪərɪəʳ/ *adj* [*to; no comp.*] **1** *fml* earlier in time **2** *usu. tech* nearer the front –opposite **posterior**

**an·them** /'ænθəm/ *n* an esp. religious song of praise –see also NATIONAL ANTHEM

**an·thol·o·gy** /æn'θɒlədʒi‖æn'θɑ-/ *n* **-gies** a collection of poems, or of other writings, often on the same subject, chosen from different books or writers –compare OMNIBUS (1)

**an·thrax** /'ænθræks/ *n* [U] a serious disease which attacks cattle, sheep, and sometimes humans

**an·thro·poid** /'ænθrəpɔɪd/ *adj,n* (an animal) like a man

**an·thro·pol·o·gy** /ˌænθrə'pɒlədʒi‖-'pɑ-/ *n* [U] the scientific study of the human race, including its different bodily types, its beliefs and social habits, etc. –compare SOCIOLOGY, ETHNOLOGY –**anthropological** /ˌænθrəpə'lɒdʒɪkəl‖-'lɑ-/ *adj* –**anthropologically** *adv* –**anthropologist** /ˌænθrə'pɒlədʒ$\frac{1}{2}$st‖-'pɑ-/ *n*

**an·ti·bi·ot·ic** /ˌæntɪbaɪ'ɒtɪk‖-'ɑ-/ *n,adj* (a medical substance, such as PENICILLIN) produced by living things and able to stop the growth of, or destroy, harmful bacteria that have entered the body

**an·ti·bod·y** /'æntɪˌbɒdi‖-ˌbɑ-/ *n* **-ies** a substance produced in the body which fights disease

**an·tic·i·pate** /æn'tɪs$\frac{1}{2}$peɪt/ *v* **-pated, -pating** [T] **1** [+*v-ing/that*] to expect: *We are not anticipating (that there will be) trouble when the factory opens again.* **2** to do something before (someone else): *We anticipated our competitors by getting our book into the shops first.* **3** [+*that*] to see (what will happen) and act as necessary, often to stop someone else doing something: *We anticipated that the enemy would cross the river and so we destroyed the bridge.*|*We're trying to anticipate what questions we'll be asked in the examination.* –**anticipatory** /ænˌtɪs$\frac{1}{2}$'peɪtəri‖æn'tɪsəpətori/ *adj*

USAGE Although **anticipate** is commonly used to mean "expect", this is thought by teachers to be incorrect.

**an·tic·i·pa·tion** /ænˌtɪs$\frac{1}{2}$'peɪʃən/ *n* [U +*that/of*] the act of anticipating (ANTICIPATE), esp. with hope: *We waited at the station* **in anticipation of** *her arrival.*

**an·ti·cli·max** /ˌæntɪ'klaɪmæks/ *n* something unexciting coming after something exciting: *To be back in the office after climbing mountains for a week was an anticlimax for him.* –see also CLIMAX –**anticlimactic** /-klaɪ'mæktɪk/ *adj*

**an·ti·clock·wise** /ˌæntɪ'klɒkwaɪz‖-'klɑk-/ *BrE*‖ **counterclockwise** *AmE*– *adj,adv* in the opposite direction to the movement of hands of a clock –opposite **clockwise**

**an·tics** /'æntɪks/ *n* [P] strange or unusual behaviour, esp. with odd, amusing, or foolish movements: *Everyone laughed at his foolish antics.*

**an·ti·cy·clone** /ˌæntɪ'saɪkləʊn/ *n tech* a mass of air that is heavy, causing calm weather, either hot or cold, in the area over which it moves –see also CYCLONE

**an·ti·dote** /'æntɪdəʊt/ *n* a substance to stop a poison working inside a person, or to prevent the effects of a disease

**an·ti·freeze** /'æntɪfriːz/ *n* [U] a chemical substance put in water to stop it from freezing in very cold weather, used esp. in car engines

**an·tip·a·thy** /æn'tɪpəθi/ *n* **-thies** [C;U *to, towards, against, between*] (an example of) a fixed dislike or hatred –**antipathetic** /ˌæntɪpə'θetɪk/ *adj*

**an·ti·quat·ed** /'ænt$\frac{1}{2}$kweɪt$\frac{1}{2}$d/ *adj often derog* old and not suited to present needs or conditions; not modern; old-fashioned –see OLD (USAGE)

**an·tique** /æn'tiːk/ *n,adj* (a piece of furniture, jewellery, etc., that is) old and therefore becoming rare and valuable

**an·tiq·ui·ty** /æn'tɪkw$\frac{1}{2}$ti/ *n* **-ties 1** [U] the state of being very old; great age: *a building of great antiquity* **2** [C;U] (a building, work of art, etc., remaining from) the ancient world, esp. of Rome or Greece

**an·ti-Sem·i·tis·m** /ˌæntɪ 'sem$\frac{1}{2}$tɪzəm/ *n* [U] hatred of Jews –**anti-Semitic** /-s$\frac{1}{2}$'mɪtɪk/ *adj*

**an·ti·sep·tic** /ˌænt$\frac{1}{2}$'septɪk/ *n,adj* (a chemical substance) able to prevent disease in a wound, etc., esp. by killing bacteria

**an·ti·so·cial** /ˌæntɪ'səʊʃəl/ *adj* **1** not social; causing damage to the way in which people live together peacefully: *Playing music so loudly that it annoys everyone else in the street is antisocial.* **2** not liking to mix with others: *Jane's very friendly, but her husband's rather antisocial.*

**an·tith·e·sis** /æn'tɪθ$\frac{1}{2}$s$\frac{1}{2}$s/ *n* **-ses** /siːz/ [*of, to*] the direct opposite: *The antithesis of death is life.*

**ant·ler** /'æntləʳ/ *n* either of the pair of branched horns of a male deer (STAG)

**an·to·nym** /'æntənɪm/ *n tech* a word opposite in meaning to another word: *"Pain" is the antonym of "pleasure".* –opposite **synonym**

**a·nus** /'eɪnəs/ *n tech* the hole in the body through which solid food waste leaves the bowels

**an·vil** /'ænvḷl/ *n* a shaped iron block on which metals are hammered to the shape wanted

**anx·i·e·ty** /æŋ'zaɪəti/ *n* **-ties** [C;U] **1** fear and worry, esp. as caused by uncertainty about something: *After hearing their advice he had no more anxieties.* **2** [+*to-v/that*] a strong wish to do something; eagerness: *anxiety to please*

**anx·ious** /'æŋkʃəs/ *adj* **1** [*for, about*] feeling or causing anxiety; troubled: *I was anxious about the children when they didn't come home from school.* **2** [+*to-v/that/for*] having a strong wish to do something; eager: *He was anxious to please his guests.* –see NERVOUS (USAGE) **–anxiously** *adv*

**an·y**[1] /'eni/ *determiner,pron* **1** every; no matter which (of more than two): *They're all free–take any you like.|Any child would know that.* **2** (used only in NEGATIVES[2], questions, etc.) some; even the smallest number or amount: *Have you got any money?|He hasn't got any imagination.|Are there any letters for me? I never seem to get any.* (Compare *There are* **some** *(letters) for you.*)|*Come and see me if you have any time.* –see EITHER[1] (USAGE); see Study Notes on page 494 **3** as much as possible; all: *He will need any help he can get.* **4 in any case: a** also **at any rate**– whatever may happen: *We may miss the next bus, but in any case we'll be there before midday.* **b** besides; also: *I don't want to go out tonight, and in any case we can't afford it.*

**any**[2] *adv* (used only in NEGATIVES[2], questions, etc.) in the least; at all: *I can't stay any longer.|Do you feel any better?*

**an·y·bod·y** /'eni,bɒdi, 'enibədi‖-,bɑdi/ also **anyone**– *pron* **1** all people; no matter who: *Anybody can cook–it's easy.|He's cleverer than anybody else.* **2** (used only in NEGATIVES[2], questions, etc.) any person: *Is anybody listening?|There isn't anybody listening.|If anybody is listening, I hope he/they will say so.*

**an·y·how** /'enihaʊ/ *adv infml* **1** carelessly; without any regular order: *His clothes were thrown down just anyhow.* **2** also **anyway**– in spite of that; in any case: *He told me not to buy it, but I bought it anyhow.* **3** also **anyway**– (used when going on with a story): *"Well, anyhow, I rang the bell..."*

**an·y·one** /'eniwʌn/ *pron* anybody

USAGE Compare **anyone** and **any one**: *Don't let* **anyone** *in.|There are three possible answers–***any one** *of them will be accepted.*

**an·y·thing** /'eniθɪŋ/ *pron* **1** (used only in NEGATIVES[2], questions, etc.) any one thing; something: *Is there anything in that box?|You can't believe anything she says.* **2** no matter what: *He will do anything for a quiet life.|Anything will do to keep the door open.* **3 anything but** not at all; far from: *That little bridge is anything but safe.* **4 anything like** at all like; at all: *It isn't anything like as cold as it was yesterday.* **5 as easy/fast/strong, etc., as anything** *infml* very easy/fast/strong, etc. **6 like anything** *infml* (used to add force to a verb): *We ran like anything.* (=very fast/hard) **7 or anything** (suggests that there are other possibilities): *"If Bernard wants to call me or anything, I'll be here all day."* (SEU S.)

**an·y·way** /'eniweɪ/ *adv infml* → ANYHOW (2, 3)

**an·y·where** /'eniweə^r/ *adv* **1** in, at, or to no matter what place: *Sit anywhere you like.* **2** (only in NEGATIVES[2], questions, etc.) (in, at, or to) any place at all: *Did you go anywhere yesterday?* –see SOME (USAGE)

**a·part** /ə'pɑːt‖-ɑrt/ *adv* **1** [after *n*] separate by a distance: *The two buildings are three miles apart.|We planted the trees wide apart.|He and his wife are living apart.* **2** into parts: *He took the clock apart to repair it.* **3 apart from** also **aside from**– **a** without considering; except for: *good work, apart from a few slight faults* **b** as well as: *Apart from being too large, the hat doesn't suit me.* **4 tell/know apart** to be able to see the difference between: *I can't tell the two boys apart.*

**a·part·heid** /ə'pɑːtheɪt, -teɪt, -taɪt, -taɪd‖-ɑr-/ *n* [U] the separation of races in one country, esp. of blacks and whites in South Africa

**a·part·ment** /ə'pɑːtmənt‖-ɑr-/ *n* **1** [*often pl.*] a room, esp. a large or splendid one: *the Royal Apartments* **2** *AmE* for FLAT[4] –see HOUSE (USAGE)

**ap·a·thet·ic** /,æpə'θetɪk/ *adj* without feeling or interest; lacking desire to act **–apathetically** *adv*

**ap·a·thy** /'æpəθi/ *n* [U] lack of feeling or interest in something or everything; lack of desire or ability to act in any way: *We lost the election because of the apathy of our members.*

**ape**[1] /eɪp/ *n* a large man-like animal without a tail or with a very short tail (such as a GORILLA or CHIMPANZEE)

**ape**[2] *v* **aped, aping** [T] to copy (a person or a person's behaviour, manners, speech, etc.); IMITATE

**a·per·i·tif** /ə,perḷ'tiːf/ *n* a small alcoholic drink drunk before a meal

**ap·er·ture** /'æpətʃə^r‖'æpərtʃʊər/ *n* a hole, crack, or other narrow opening, esp. one that admits light into a camera

**a·pex** /'eɪpeks/ *n* [*usu. sing.*] the top or highest part of anything: *the apex of a* TRIANGLE

**aph·o·ris·m** /'æfərɪzəm/ *n* a true or wise saying or principle expressed in a few words; MAXIM

**aph·ro·dis·i·ac** /,æfrə'dɪziæk/ *n,adj* (a medicine, drug, etc.) causing sexual excitement

**a·piece** /ə'piːs/ *adv* to, for, or from each person or thing; each: *The apples cost six pence apiece.*

**a·pol·o·get·ic** /ə,pɒlə'dʒetɪk‖ə,pɑ-/ *adj* expressing sorrow for some fault or wrong **–apologetically** *adv*

**a·pol·o·gize**‖also **-gise** *BrE* /ə'pɒlədʒaɪz‖ə'pɑ-/ *v* **-gized, gizing** [I *to, for*] to say one is sorry, as for a fault or for causing pain: *I apologized (to her) (for stepping on her foot).*

**a·pol·o·gy** /ə'pɒlədʒi‖ə'pɑ-/ *n* **-gies** a statement expressing sorrow for a fault, for causing trouble or pain, etc.: *I must offer her an apology for not going to her party.|I must make an apology to her.|Please accept my apologies.*

**ap·o·plex·y** /'æpəpleksi/ *n* [U] the sudden loss of the ability to move, feel, think, etc.; STROKE[2] (3) **–apoplectic** /,æpə'plektɪk/ *adj*

**a·pos·tle** /ə'pɒsəl‖ə'pɑ-/ *n* any of the 12 followers of Christ chosen by him to spread his message

**a·pos·tro·phe** /ə'pɒstrəfi‖ə'pɑ-/ *n* the sign (') used in writing **a** to show that one or more letters or figures have been left out of a word or figure (as in *don't* and *'47* for *do not* and *1947*) **b** before or after *s* to show possession (as in *John's hat, James' hat, lady's hat, ladies' hats, children's hats*) **c** before *s* to show the plural of letters and figures (as in *There are 2 f 's in off* and *Your 8's look like S's*)

**a·poth·e·ca·ry** /ə'pɒθǝ̇kəri‖ə'pɑθǝ̇keri/ *n* **-ries** *old use* a person with a knowledge of chemistry who mixed and sold medicines; PHARMACIST (2)

**ap·pal** *BrE*‖**appall** *AmE* /ə'pɔːl/ *v* **-ll-** [T] to shock deeply; fill with fear, hatred, terror, etc.: *We were appalled when we heard she had been murdered.*

**ap·pal·ling** /ə'pɔːlɪŋ/ *adj* **1** causing fear; shocking; terrible **2** *infml* very bad: *an appalling waste* –**appallingly** *adv: an appallingly bad driver*

**ap·pa·ra·tus** /,æpə'reɪtəs‖-'ræ-/ *n* **-tuses** *or* **-tus** [C;U] a set of instruments, machines, tools, materials, etc., needed for a particular purpose: *sports apparatus|a piece of apparatus*

**ap·par·el** /ə'pærəl/ *n* [U] *lit & old use* clothes, esp. of a fine or special sort: *priestly apparel*

**ap·par·ent** /ə'pærənt/ *adj* **1** [*to*] easily seen or understood; plain: *Her anxiety was apparent to everyone.* **2** not necessarily true or real; seeming: *Their apparent grief soon turned to laughter.*

**ap·par·ent·ly** /ə'pærəntli/ *adv* it seems (that); as it appears: *I wasn't there, but apparently she tried to drown him.* –compare EVIDENTly, OBVIOUSLY

**ap·pa·ri·tion** /,æpə'rɪʃən/ *n* the spirit of a dead person moving in bodily form; GHOST[1] (1): *He saw the apparition of his dead wife.*

**ap·peal**[1] /ə'piːl/ *n* **1** [C;U] (a) strong request for help, support, money, mercy, etc.: *an appeal for money to build a new hall* **2** [U] power to move the feelings; attraction; interest: *Films of that sort have lost their appeal for me.|sex appeal* **3** [C;U] a call to a higher court to change the decision of a lower court: *the right of appeal|a court of appeal*

**appeal**[2] *v* [I] **1** [+*to-v*/*to, for*] to make a strong request for help, support, money, mercy, etc.; beg: *The government is appealing to everyone to save water.* **2** [*to*] to please, attract, or interest: *Does the idea of working abroad appeal to you?* **3** to call on a higher law court to change the decision of a lower court

**appeal to** sbdy./sthg. *v prep* [T *for*] to look for support in: *By appealing to his better nature, we persuaded him to give some money to the school.*

**ap·peal·ing** /ə'piːlɪŋ/ *adj* **1** able to move the feelings: *an appealing photograph* **2** attractive or interesting: *What an appealing little baby!* –opposite **unappealing** (for 2) –**appealingly** *adv*

**ap·pear** /ə'pɪə^r/ *v* **1** [I] to become able to be seen; come into sight: *In this disease spots appear on the skin.|If I fail to appear* (=come) *by 7 o'clock, I will not be coming at all.|Her new book will appear in the shops very soon.* –opposite **disappear** **2** [+*to-v*/*(that)*; not *be* +*v-ing*] to seem; look: *He appears to want to leave.|You appear well this morning.|So it appears.|It appears so/not.* **3** [I] to be present officially, as in a court of law: *He had to appear before the committee to explain his behaviour.*

**ap·pear·ance** /ə'pɪərəns/ *n* **1** [C] the act of appearing, as to the eye, mind, or public: *My appearance at the party was not very welcome.|He* **put in an appearance**, *but didn't stay long.* –opposite **disappearance** **2** [C;U] that which can be seen; outward qualities; look: *They changed the whole appearance of the house just by painting it.|Don't judge by appearances.*

**ap·pease** /ə'piːz/ *v* **-peased, -peasing** [T] to make calm or satisfy, esp. by yielding to demands or by giving or doing something: *The angry man was appeased by their apology.* –**appeasement** *n* [C;U]

**ap·pend** /ə'pend/ *v* [T *to*] *fml* to add (esp. something written onto the end of a letter or other piece of written material): *I append a list of those shops which sell our products.* –compare ENCLOSE (2)

**ap·pend·age** /ə'pendɪdʒ/ *n* something added, joined to, or hanging from something, esp. something larger

**ap·pen·di·ci·tis** /ə,pendǝ̇'saɪtǝ̇s/ *n* [U] the diseased state of the APPENDIX (1)

**ap·pen·dix** /ə'pendɪks/ *n* **-dixes** *or* **-dices** /-dǝ̇siːz/ **1** a short wormlike organ leading off the bowel, and having little or no use **2** something added, esp. additional information at the end of a book

**ap·per·tain to** sthg. /,æpə'teɪn‖-ər-/ *v prep* [T *no pass.*] *fml* to belong to: *the responsibilities appertaining to the chairmanship*

**ap·pe·tite** /'æpǝ̇taɪt/ *n* [C;U] a desire or wish, esp. for food: *Don't eat anything that will spoil your appetite for dinner.*|(fig.) *He had no appetite for hard work.|sexual appetites* –see DESIRE (USAGE)

**ap·pe·tiz·er**‖also **-tiser** *BrE* /'æpǝ̇taɪzə^r/ *n* something small and attractive eaten at the beginning of a meal to increase the desire for food

**ap·pe·tiz·ing**‖also **-tising** *BrE* /'æpǝ̇taɪzɪŋ/ *adj* causing desire, esp. for food –opposite **unappetizing** –**appetizingly** *adv: food appetizingly cooked*

**ap·plaud** /ə'plɔːd/ *v* [I;T] **1** to praise (a play, actor, performer, etc.), esp. by striking one's hands together (CLAPping) **2** to express strong approval of (a person, idea, etc.): *We all applauded the council's decision not to close the hospital.*

**ap·plause** /ə'plɔːz/ *n* [U] loud praise for a performance or performer, esp. by striking the hands together (CLAPping)

**ap·ple** /'æpəl/ *n* **1** a hard round fruit with white juicy flesh and a red, green, or yellow skin **2 apple of someone's eye** *infml* the person or thing most liked

**ap·pli·ance** /ə'plaɪəns/ *n* an apparatus, instrument, or tool for a particular purpose –see MACHINE (USAGE)

**ap·plic·a·ble** /ə'plɪkəbəl, 'æplɪkəbəl/ *adj* [*to*] suitable (for), concerning, or able to have an effect (on): *The new law is applicable to everybody from next Monday.* –opposite **inapplicable**

**ap·pli·cant** /'æplɪkənt/ *n* a person who makes a request, esp. officially and in writing, for a job, etc.

**ap·pli·ca·tion** /,æplɪ'keɪʃən/ *n* **1** [C;U] (the act of making) a request, esp. in writing: *Tickets may be bought on application to the theatre.|I wrote five applications for jobs but got nothing.* **2** [C;U *of, to*] the putting to use: *The application of new scientific discoveries to industrial production methods usually makes jobs easier to do.|the application of a medicine (onto the skin)* **3** [U] careful and continuous attention or effort: *He worked with great application.*

**ap·plied** /ə'plaɪd/ *adj* (esp. of a science) able to be put to practical use: *applied* MATHEMATICS –opposite **pure**

**ap·ply** /ə'plaɪ/ *v* **-plied, -plying** **1** [I *to, for*] to request something, esp. in writing: *I'll apply for the job today.* **2** [T *to*] to bring or put into use: *Apply as much force as is necessary.*|*to apply a new method*|*Apply some medicine to his wound.* **3** [I;T *to*] to (cause to) have an effect; be directly related: *This rule does not apply.* **4** [T *to*] to cause to work hard or carefully: *He applied himself/his mind to the job.*

**ap·point** /ə'pɔɪnt/ *v* [T] **1** to choose for a position, job, etc.: *We must appoint a new teacher soon.*|*They appointed him (to be) chairman.* –see HIRE (USAGE) **2** *fml* to arrange; fix; decide: *The committee has appointed a day in July for your case to be considered.*|*She wasn't there at the appointed time.*

**ap·point·ment** /ə'pɔɪntmənt/ *n* **1** [U] the agreement of a time and place for meeting: *He will only see you by appointment.* **2** [C] a meeting at an agreed time and place: *I have an appointment with the doctor.* **3** [C;U *of, as*] the choosing of someone for a position or job: *We were all pleased about his appointment as chairman.*|*a teaching appointment*

USAGE When you arrange to see someone at a fixed time you **make an appointment**. If you then actually see the person as arranged, you **keep your appointment**. If you cannot come, you write or telephone to **cancel the appointment**. –see also JOB (USAGE)

**ap·por·tion** /ə'pɔːʃən‖-or-/ *v* [T *between, among(st)*] *fml* to divide and share out: *It was difficult to apportion the blame for the accident.*

**ap·praise** /ə'preɪz/ *v* **-praised, -praising** [T] *fml* to judge the worth, quality, or condition of; find out the value of –**appraisal** *n*

**ap·pre·cia·ble** /ə'priːʃəbəl/ *adj* enough to be felt, noticed, or considered important: *an appreciable difference* –**appreciably** *adv*

**ap·pre·ci·ate** /ə'priːʃieɪt/ **-ated, -ating 1** [T] to understand and enjoy the good qualities or value of: *to appreciate good wine*|*I appreciate your help.* **2** [I *in*] (of property, possessions, etc.) to increase in value: *Houses in this area have all appreciated (in value) since the new road was built.* –**appreciation** /-'eɪʃən/ *n* [C;U]

**ap·pre·cia·tive** /ə'priːʃətɪv/ *adj* **1** grateful; thankful **2** feeling or showing understanding or admiration –opposite **unappreciative** –**appreciatively** *adv*

**ap·pre·hend** /ˌæprɪ'hend/ *v* [T] *fml* to sieze (a person who breaks the law); ARREST[1] (1)

**ap·pre·hen·sion** /ˌæprɪ'henʃən/ *n* [U] anxiety, esp. about the future; fear: *We waited for their decision with a great deal of apprehension.*

**ap·pre·hen·sive** /ˌæprɪ'hensɪv/ *adj* [*for, about,* etc.] worried; anxious: *He looked apprehensive as he waited for the result.* –**apprehensively** *adv*

**ap·pren·tice**[1] /ə'prentɨs/ *n* a person who is under an agreement to serve, for a number of years and usu. for low wages, a person skilled in a trade, in order to learn that person's skill: *an apprentice electrician*|*He was apprentice to an electrician.*

**apprentice**[2] *v* **-ticed, -ticing** [T *to*] to make or send as an APPRENTICE: *He's apprenticed to an electrician.*

**ap·pren·tice·ship** /ə'prentɨsʃɪp/ *n* [C;U] (the condition or period of) being an APPRENTICE

**ap·proach**[1] /ə'prəʊtʃ/ *v* **1** [I;T] to come near or nearer (to): *We approached the camp.*|*The time is approaching when we must leave.* **2** [T *about*] to speak to in order to make an offer or request for the first time: *Did he approach you about lending him some money?* **3** [T] to begin to consider or deal with: *There are several ways of approaching this problem.*

**approach**[2] *n* **1** [U] the act of APPROACHing: *The approach of winter brings cold weather.* **2** [C] a means or way of entering: *All approaches to the town were blocked.* **3** [C] a manner or method of doing something: *a new approach to teaching English* **4** [C] speaking to someone for the first time: *I'm not very good at making approaches to strangers.*

**ap·proa·cha·ble** /ə'prəʊtʃəbəl/ *adj* **1** easy to speak to or deal with; friendly: *You'll find the director a very approachable person.* –opposite **unapproachable 2** able to be reached

**ap·pro·ba·tion** /ˌæprə'beɪʃən/ *n* [U] *fml* praise; approval –opposite **disapprobation**

**ap·pro·pri·ate**[1] /ə'prəuprɪ-ɨt/ *adj* [*for, to*] correct or suitable: *His bright clothes were not appropriate for a funeral.* –opposite **inappropriate** –**appropriately** *adv* –**appropriateness** *n* [U]

**ap·pro·pri·ate**[2] /ə'prəuprieɪt/ *v* **-ated, -ating** [T *for*] **1** *fml* to set aside for some purpose: *The government appropriated a large sum of money for building hospitals.* **2** *euph* to take for oneself; steal: *The minister was found to have appropriated government money.* –**appropriation** /-'eɪʃən/ *n* [C; U]

**ap·prov·al** /ə'pruːvəl/ *n* [U] **1** the act of approving: *We can't start the job until we have the director's approval.* –opposite **disapproval 2 on approval** *BrE infml* (of goods taken or sent from a shop) to be returned without payment if not found satisfactory

**ap·prove** /ə'pruːv/ *v* **-proved, -proving** [T] to agree officially to: *The minister approved the building plans.* –see also DISAPPROVE

**approve of** sbdy./stthg. *v prep* [T + *v-ing*] to consider good, right, wise, etc.: *I don't approve of smoking/of people who smoke.* –**approvingly** *adv*

**ap·prox** *written abbrev. said as*: APPROXIMATE(ly)[1]

**ap·prox·i·mate**[1] /ə'prɒksɨmɨt‖ə'prɑk-/ *adj* [*no comp.*] nearly correct but not exact: *The approximate number of boys in the school is 300.* –**approximately** *adv: approximately 300*

**ap·prox·i·mate**[2] /ə'prɒksɨmeɪt‖ə'prɑk-/ *v* **-mated, -mating** [I *to*] to come near to: *Your story only approximates to the real facts.* –**approximation** /-'meɪʃən/ *n* [C;U *to, of*]

**a·pri·cot** /'eɪprɨkɒt‖'æprɨkɑt/ *n* [C] a round soft orange or yellow fruit with a furry outside like a PEACH and a single large stone

**A·pril** /'eɪprɨl/ also **Apr.** *written abbrev*– *n* the 4th month of the year

**April fool** /ˌ·· '·/ *n* a person who has been deceived or made fun of by a trick played on the morning of April 1st (**April Fools' Day, All Fools' Day**)

**a·pron** /'eɪprən/ *n* a simple garment worn over the front part of one's clothes to keep them clean, e.g. while cooking

**apt** /æpt/ *adj* **1** [F +*to-v*] having a tendency to do something; likely: *This kind of shoe is apt to slip on wet ground.* **2** exactly suitable: *an apt remark* –**aptly** *adv* –**aptness** *n* [U]

**ap·ti·tude** /'æptɨtjuːd‖-tuːd/ *n* [C;U *for*] natural

ability or skill, esp. in learning: *He showed great aptitude/an aptitude for learning languages.|an aptitude test* –see GENIUS (USAGE)

**a·quar·i·um** /əˈkweərɪəm/ *n* **-iums** *or* **-ia** /ɪə/ **1** a glass container for fish and other water animals **2** a building (esp. in a zoo) containing many of these

**A·quar·i·us** /əˈkweərɪəs/ *n* see ZODIAC

**a·quat·ic** /əˈkwætɪk, əˈkwɒ-‖əˈkwæ-, əˈkwɑ-/ *adj* living or happening in or on water: *aquatic plants/animals*

**aq·ue·duct** /ˈækwɪ̈dʌkt/ *n* a bridge, pipe, or CANAL that carries a water supply, esp. one that is built across a valley

**aq·ui·line** /ˈækwɪ̈laɪn‖-laɪn, -lɪ̈n/ *adj* of or like an EAGLE: *an* **aquiline nose** *like an eagle's beak*

**Ar·ab** /ˈærəb/ *n* a person who speaks ARABIC, esp. one from North Africa or the Arabian PENINSULA

**A·ra·bi·an** /əˈreɪbɪən/ *adj* of Arabia, esp. the PENINSULA containing Saudi Arabia and several other countries: *the Arabian desert*

**Ar·a·bic** /ˈærəbɪk/ *adj,n* [U] (of or concerning) the language or writing of the ARABS: *Arabic literature*

**Arabic nu·me·ral** /ˌ··· ˈ···/ *n* any of the signs most commonly used for numbers in the English and many other alphabets (such as 1, 2, 3, 4, etc.) –compare ROMAN NUMERAL

**ar·a·ble** /ˈærəbəl/ *adj* (of land) suitable or used for growing crops

**ar·bi·tra·ry** /ˈɑːbɪ̈trəri‖ˈɑrbɪ̈treri/ *adj often derog* **1** decided by or based on chance or personal opinion rather than reason: *I didn't know anything about any of the books so my choice was quite arbitrary.* **2** typical of power that is uncontrolled and used without considering the wishes of others: *arbitrary decisions taken without thought for others* **–arbitrarily** /ˈaːbɪtrərəli‖ˌɑrbɪˈtrerəli/ *adv* **–arbitrariness** /ɑːbɪtrərɪnɪ̈s‖ˈɑrbɪtrerinɪ̈s/ *n* [U]

**ar·bi·trate** /ˈɑːbɪ̈treɪt‖ˈɑr-/ *v* **-trated, -trating** [I;T *between*] to act as a judge in (an argument), esp. at the request of both sides: *Someone must arbitrate (between them).* **–arbitration** /-ˈtreɪʃən/ *n* [U]: *The men agreed to* **go to arbitration** *to settle their pay claim.* **–arbitrator** /ˈɑːbɪ̈treɪtəʳ‖ˈɑr-/ *n*

**arc** /ɑːk‖ɑrk/ *n* part of a circle or any curved line

**ar·cade** /ɑːˈkeɪd‖ɑr-/ *n* a covered passage, esp. one with an arched roof, often with shops on one or both sides: *a shopping arcade*

**arch¹** /ɑːtʃ‖ɑrtʃ/ *n* **1** the top curved part over a doorway, window, bridge, etc.: *The bridge had seven arches.* **2** something with this shape, esp. the middle of the bottom of the foot

**arch²** *v* [I;T] to form (into) an arch: *The cat arched her back in anger.|The trees arched over the path.*

**ar·chae·ol·o·gy, archeology** /ˌɑːkiˈɒlədʒi‖ˌɑrkiˈɑ-/ *n* [U] the study of the buried remains of ancient times, such as houses, pots, tools, and weapons **–archaeological** /ˌɑːkɪəˈlɒdʒɪkəl‖ˌɑrkɪəˈlɑ-/ *adj* **–archaeologically** *adv* **–archaeologist** /ˌɑːkiˈɒlədʒɪ̈st‖ˌɑrkiˈɑ-/ *n*

**ar·cha·ic** /ɑːˈkeɪ-ɪk‖ɑr-/ *adj* belonging to the past; no longer used

**arch·bish·op** /ˌɑːtʃˈbɪʃəp◂‖ˌɑrtʃ-/ *n* (in the Christian church) a priest of very high rank in charge of the churches and BISHOPS (1) in a large area

**ar·cher** /ˈɑːtʃəʳ‖ˈɑr-/ *n* a person who shoots arrows from a piece of bent wood (BOW³ (1))

**ar·cher·y** /ˈɑːtʃəri‖ˈɑr-/ *n* [U] the art or sport of shooting arrows

**ar·chi·pel·a·go** /ˌɑːkɪ̈ˈpeləgəʊ‖ˌɑr-/ *n* **-goes** *or* **-gos** (an area of sea containing) a group of small islands

**ar·chi·tect** /ˈɑːkɪ̈tekt‖ˈɑr-/ *n* a person who plans new buildings and sees that they are built properly

**ar·chi·tec·ture** /ˈɑːkɪ̈tektʃəʳ‖ˈɑr-/ *n* [U] **1** the art and science of building, including its planning, making, and decoration **2** the style or manner of building: *the architecture of ancient Greece* **–architectural** /-ˈtektʃərəl / *adj* **–architecturally** *adv*

**ar·chives** /ˈɑːkaɪvz‖ˈɑr-/ *n* [P] (a place for storing) old papers, such as records, reports, and letters of a particular group, country, etc., kept esp. for historical interest

**arc·tic** /ˈɑːktɪk‖ˈɑr-/ *adj,n* [*the* S] *(often cap)* (of or concerning) the very cold most northern part of the world –compare ANTARCTIC

**ar·dent** /ˈɑːdənt‖ˈɑr-/ *adj* strongly active; eager; fierce: *an ardent supporter of the government* **–ardently** *adv*

**ar·dour** *BrE*‖**ardor** *AmE* /ˈɑːdəʳ‖ˈɑr-/ *n* [C;U] *fml* strong excitement; burning eagerness: *His political ardour led him into many arguments.*

**ar·du·ous** /ˈɑːdjʊəs‖ˈɑrdʒʊəs/ *adj* needing much effort; difficult: *an arduous climb|arduous work* **–arduously** *adv* **–arduousness** *n* [U]

**are** /əʳ; *strong* ɑːʳ/ *v present tense pl. of* BE

**ar·e·a** /ˈeərɪə/ *n* **1** [C;U] the size of a flat surface measured by multiplying the length by the width: *What's the area of your garden?* –compare VOLUME **2** [C] a place; a part or division of the world, a country, etc.; REGION: *There aren't any big shops in this area (of the town).* **3** [C] a space or surface with a particular purpose: *There's a parking area behind the cinema.* **4** [C] a subject, specialist field, or activity: *new developments in the area of language teaching*

**a·re·na** /əˈriːnə/ *n* an enclosed area used for sports, public amusements, etc.: *a sports arena*

**aren't** /ɑːnt‖ˈɑrənt/ *v short for*: **1** are not: *They aren't here.* **2** (in questions) am not

USAGE There is no natural short form of "**am** *I not?*" Compare: 1 *(fml) I am your friend, am I not?* 2 *(infml) I'm your friend, aren't I?*

**ar·gu·a·ble** /ˈɑːgjʊəbəl‖ˈɑr-/ *adj* **1** [*that*] able to be supported with reasons: *It is arguable that we should destroy all weapons.* **2** doubtful in some degree: *an arguable decision* **–arguably** *adv*

**ar·gue** /ˈɑːgjuː‖ˈɑr-/ *v* **-gued, -guing 1** [I *with, against, about*] to disagree in words; fight with words; quarrel: *Do what you are told and don't argue (with me).|They're always arguing about money.* **2** [I;T +*that*] to provide reasons for or against (something), esp. clearly and in proper order: *He argues well.|It could be argued that sending men to the moon is a waste of money.* **3** [I;T *against, over,* etc.] to reason strongly in defence of (one's wishes or opinions), esp. in opposition to others: *Her speech argued the case against atomic weapons very effectively.*

**ar·gu·ment** /ˈɑːgjʊmənt‖ˈɑrgjə-/ *n* **1** [C] a disagreement, esp. one that is noisy; quarrel **2** [C +*that/for,* *against*] a reason given to support or disprove something: *There are many arguments against smoking.* **3** [U] the use of reason to decide something: *We should try to settle this by argument, not fighting.*

**ar·gu·men·ta·tive** /ˌɑːgjuˈmentətɪv‖ˌɑrgjə-/ *adj derog* (of a person) liking to ARGUE (1)

**a·ri·a** /ˈɑːrɪə/ *n* a song that is sung by only one person in an OPERA

**ar·id** /ˈærɪ̵d/ *adj* (of land or a country) having so little rain as to be very dry and unproductive

**Ar·ies** /ˈeəriːz, ˈæri-iːz/ *n* see ZODIAC

**a·rise** /əˈraɪz/ *v* **arose** /əˈrəʊz/, **arisen** /əˈrɪzən/, **arising** [I] **1** to come into being or to notice; happen; appear: *Some unexpected difficulties have arisen.* **2** *old use or lit* to get up –see RISE (USAGE)

**ar·is·toc·ra·cy** /ˌærɪ̵ˈstɒkrəsi‖-ˈstɑ-/ *n* **-cies** [C +*sing./pl. v*] the people of the highest social class, esp. people from noble families and with titles of rank –see also UPPER CLASS

**ar·is·to·crat** /ˈærɪ̵stəkræt, əˈrɪ-‖əˈrɪ-/ *n* a member of an ARISTOCRACY –**aristocratic** /-ˈkrætɪk/ *adj*

**a·rith·me·tic**[1] /əˈrɪθmətɪk/ *n* [U] the science of numbers; calculation by numbers –compare MATHEMATICS

**ar·ith·met·ic**[2] /ˌærɪθˈmetɪk/ also **-ical**– *adj* of or concerning ARITHMETIC –**arithmetically** *adv*

**arm**[1] /ɑːm‖ɑrm/ *n* **1** either of the two upper limbs of a human being or other animal that stands on two legs: *She carried the box under her arm.*|*She welcomed them* **with open arms.** (=gladly)|*They walked down the road* **arm in arm.** (=with arms joined) –see picture on page 299 **2** something that is shaped like or moves like an arm: *the arm of the chair* **3** the part of a garment, such as a coat, that covers the arm **4** a part or division of the armed forces: *the air arm* **5 keep somebody at arm's length** to keep a safe distance away; avoid being friendly with somebody –**armless** *adj*

**arm**[2] *v* [I;T *with*] to supply or fit with weapons or armour: *I warn you that I am armed.* (=have a gun)|*He was charged with armed robbery.* (=done using a gun)|(fig.) *He was armed with many facts and figures to prove his case.* –opposite **disarm**; see also UNARMED

**ar·ma·da** /ɑːˈmɑːdə‖ɑr-/ *n* [C +*sing./pl. v*] *lit* a collection (FLEET) of armed ships: *The Spanish Armada sailed to England in 1588.*

**arm·band** /ˈɑːmbænd‖ˈɑrm-/ *n* a band of material worn round the arm to show official position, as a sign of MOURNING, etc.

**arm·chair** /ˈɑːmtʃeəʳ, ˌɑːmˈtʃeəʳ‖ˈɑrm-, ˌɑrm-/ *n* a chair with supports for the arms –see picture on page 355

**arm·ful** /ˈɑːmfʊl‖ˈɑrm-/ *n* all that a person can hold in one or both arms: *an armful of fresh flowers*

**ar·mi·stice** /ˈɑːmɪ̵stɪ̵s‖ˈɑrm-/ *n* an agreement made during a war to stop fighting, usu. for a limited period of time

**ar·mour** *BrE*‖**armor** *AmE* /ˈɑːməʳ‖ˈɑr-/ *n* [U] **1** strong protective metal or leather covering as worn formerly in battle by fighting men and their horses **2** strong protective metal covering on fighting vehicles, ships, and aircraft

**ar·moured** *BrE*‖**armored** *AmE* /ˈɑːməd‖ˈɑrmərd/ *adj* covered with or protected by armour: *an* **armoured car**

**ar·mour·y** *BrE*‖**armory** *AmE* /ˈɑːməri‖ˈɑr-/ *n* **-ies** a place where weapons are stored

**arm·pit** /ˈɑːmˌpɪt‖ˈɑrm-/ *n* the hollow place under the arm at the shoulder –see picture on page 299

**arms** /ɑːmz‖ɑrmz/ *n* [P] **1** weapons of war **2**→ COAT OF ARMS **3 up in arms** *infml* very angry and ready to argue or fight: *The women are up in arms over/about their low rate of pay.*

**arms race** /ˈ· ·/ *n* a struggle between unfriendly countries in which each tries to produce more and better weapons of war than the other

**ar·my** /ˈɑːmi‖ˈɑr-/ *n* **-mies 1** the military forces of a country, esp. those trained to fight on land **2** any large group, esp. one that is united for some purpose: *an army of workers/ants*

**a·ro·ma** /əˈrəʊmə/ *n* a strong usu. pleasant smell: *the aroma of fresh coffee* –**aromatic** /ˌærəˈmætɪk/ *adj: Aromatic plants are often used in cooking.*

**a·rose** /əˈrəʊz/ *v past tense of* ARISE

**a·round**[1] /əˈraʊnd/ *adv* [*no comp.*] *esp. AmE* **1 a** here and there; about: *They travel around together.* **b** somewhere near; about: *Is there anybody around?* **2** a little more or less than; about: *around five miles/around 30 years* **3** so as to face the other way; round: *He turned around when he heard a noise behind him.* **4 a** moving in a circle; measured in a circle; round: *turning around and around*|*a tree three metres around* **b** on all sides; all round: *The children gathered around to hear the story.*

**around**[2] *prep* **1** on all sides of; all round: *We sat around the table.*|*He put a fence around the garden.* **2 a** here and there in; about: *They walked around the streets.*|*books lying around the room* **b** near to: *He lives somewhere around London.* **3** so as to get past; round: *Let's go around the town, not through it.*

**a·rouse** /əˈraʊz/ *v* **-roused, -rousing** [T] **1** to cause to wake; ROUSE (1) **2** to cause to become active; cause (a feeling) to exist: *His strange behaviour aroused the* SUSPICIONS *of the police.*

**ar·range** /əˈreɪndʒ/ *v* **-ranged, -ranging** [T] **1** to set in a good or pleasing order: *to arrange flowers in a* VASE **2** [+*to-v/v-ing/that/about, for, with*] to plan or agree in advance: *I have arranged a taxi (for us).*|*We arranged to meet them at 10 o'clock.* **3** [*for*] to set out (a piece of music) in a certain way, as for different instruments: *a piece of music arranged for the piano*

**ar·range·ment** /əˈreɪndʒmənt/ *n* **1** [C;U +*to-v/about, for, with*] (the act of making) an agreement or plan; something arranged: *She's in charge of all the arrangements for the royal wedding.*|*I have an arrangement with my bank by which they let me have money before I have been paid.*|*We made an arrangement to meet at 10.* **2** [C] something that has been put in order: *a beautiful flower arrangement* **3** [C;U] (an example of) the setting out of a piece of music in a certain way, as for different instruments

**ar·ray**[1] /əˈreɪ/ *v* **-rayed, -raying** [T] *fml or lit* **1** to set in order for battle, show, etc. **2** to dress, esp. finely

**array**[2] *n* **-rays 1** a fine show, collection, or ordered group: *a beautiful array of dress materials*|*The crowd were met by an array of policemen.* –see also DISARRAY **2** *lit* fine clothes, esp. for a special occasion

**ar·rears** /ə'rɪəz‖-ərz/ *n* [P] **1** money that is owed from the past and should have been paid: *He was two weeks* **in arrears** *with the rent.* (=he owed rent for two weeks) **2** work that is still waiting to be done

**ar·rest¹** /ə'rest/ *v* [T] **1** to seize in the name of the law and usu. put in prison: *The policeman arrested the thief.* **2** *fml* to bring to an end; stop: *The treatment arrested the growth of the disease.* **3** to catch and fix (esp. somebody's attention): *an arresting statement*

**arrest²** *n* [C;U] the act of ARRESTing¹ (1) or of being ARRESTed: *The police made several arrests.*|*He was quickly* **put/placed under arrest.**

**ar·riv·al** /ə'raɪvəl/ *n* **1** [C;U] the act of arriving: *The arrival of the aircraft has been delayed.*|*On (my) arrival home I was greeted by my parents.* –compare DEPARTURE **2** [C] a person or thing that has arrived: *The new arrival was a large healthy baby.*

**ar·rive** /ə'raɪv/ *v* **-rived, -riving** [I] **1** to reach a place, esp. at the end of a journey: *We arrived safely.*|*What time does the plane arrive in New York?*|(fig.) *He felt he had really arrived* (=won success) *when he made his first record.* –compare LEAVE, DEPART **2** to happen; come: *At last our holidays arrived.*|*Her baby arrived* (=was born) *yesterday.*

**arrive at** sthg. *v prep* [T] to reach; come to: *After many hours' talk, the committee arrived at a decision.*

**ar·ro·gant** /'ærəgənt/ *adj* proud and self-important in a rude way that shows no respect for other people: *an arrogant official*|*arrogant manners* **–arrogantly** *adv* **–arrogance** *n* [U]: *His arrogance made him unpopular.*

**ar·row** /'ærəʊ/ *n* **1** a thin straight stick with a point at one end and feathers at the other, which is shot in fighting or sport from a long piece of bent wood (BOW³ (1)) **2** a sign like an arrow (→) used to show direction or the position of something

**ar·se·nal** /'ɑːsənəl‖'ɑr-/ *n* a building where weapons and explosives are made or stored

**ar·se·nic** /'ɑːsənɪk‖'ɑr-/ *n* [U] a very poisonous substance used in medicine, for killing rats, etc.

**ar·son** /'ɑːsən‖'ɑr-/ *n* [U] the crime of setting fire to property in order to cause destruction **–arsonist** *n*

**art¹** /ɑːt‖ɑrt/ **1** [U] the making or expression of what is beautiful or true, as in music, literature, or esp. in painting and SCULPTURE **2** [U] things produced in this way: *Japanese art*|*modern art*|*The painting was a* **work of art.** **3** [C;U] fine skill in the making or doing of anything: *The art of painting well is not easily learnt.*|*the art of making friends*|*Driving a car in central London is quite an art!* (=needs great skill) –see also ARTS

**art²** *v* **thou art** *old use or bibl* (when talking to one person) you are

**ar·te·ry** /'ɑːtəri‖'ɑr-/ *n* **-ries** **1** a blood vessel that carries blood from the heart to the rest of the body –compare VEIN (1) **2** a main road, railway, river, etc. **–arterial** /ɑː'tɪərɪəl‖ɑr-/ *adj* [A]: *Arterial blood is bright red.*|*arterial roads leading into London*

**art·ful** /'ɑːtfəl‖'ɑr-/ *adj* clever; skilful, often in a bad way; CUNNING: *He's very artful and usually succeeds in getting what he wants.* –see also ARTLESS **–artfully** *adv* **–artfulness** *n* [U]

**ar·thri·tis** /ɑː'θraɪtɪ̵s‖ɑr-/ *n* [U] a disease causing pain and swelling in the joints of the body **–arthritic** /ɑː'θrɪtɪk‖ɑr-/ *adj,n*

**ar·ti·choke** /'ɑːtɪ̵tʃəʊk‖'ɑr-/ *n* [C;U] **1** also **globe artichoke**– a plant with a leafy kind of flower that may be eaten as a vegetable **2** also **Jerusalem artichoke**– a plant with a potato-like root that may be eaten as a vegetable

**ar·ti·cle** /'ɑːtɪkəl‖'ɑr-/ *n* **1** a particular or separate thing or object, esp. one of a group: *I am wearing several articles of clothing.* **2** a piece of writing on a particular subject in a newspaper, magazine, etc.: *an article on new industries* **3** *tech* the words "a" or "an" (**indefinite article**) and "the" (**definite article**)

**ar·tic·u·late¹** /ɑː'tɪkjʊlɪ̵t‖ɑr'tɪkjə-/ *adj* **1** *apprec* expressing or able to express thoughts and feelings clearly, esp. in words: *one of the most articulate supporters of this political party* **2** (of speech) having clear separate sounds or words –opposite **inarticulate** **–articulately** *adv* **–articulateness** *n* [U]

**ar·tic·u·late²** /ɑː'tɪkjʊleɪt‖ɑr'tɪkjə-/ *v* **-lated, -lating** **1** [I;T] to speak, esp. clearly and effectively: *He articulated (each word) carefully.* **2** [T *usu. pass.*] to unite by joints that allow movements: *The bones of our fingers are articulated.*|*In an* **articulated vehicle/lorry** *the driver's part is attached to the main part in such a way as to make turning corners easier.* **–articulation** /-'leɪʃən/ *n* [U]

**ar·ti·fact, arte-** /'ɑːtɪ̵fækt‖'ɑr-/ *n* anything made by humans, esp. something useful

**ar·ti·fi·cial** /ˌɑːtɪ̵'fɪʃəl◂‖ˌɑr-/ *adj* **1** made by man; not natural: *artificial flowers*|*artificial silk* –compare NATURAL **2** insincere; unreal: *She welcomed me with an artificial smile.* **–artificially** *adv* **–artificiality** /ˌɑːtɪ̵fɪʃi'ælɪ̵ti‖ˌɑr-/ *n* [U]

**artificial res·pi·ra·tion** /ˌ····· ··'··/ *n* [U] the attempt to make a person who is nearly dead (esp. through drowning) breathe again, as by pressing the chest, moving the arms, and blowing air into the mouth –see also KISS² (2)

**ar·til·le·ry** /ɑː'tɪləri‖ɑr-/ *n* [U +*sing./pl. v.*] (the part of the army that uses) large guns

**ar·ti·san** /ˌɑːtɪ̵'zæn‖'ɑrtɪ̵zən/ *n* a person who does skilled work with his/her hands

**art·ist** /'ɑːtɪ̵st‖'ɑr-/ *n* **1** a person who practises or works in one of the FINE ARTS, esp. painting **2** → ARTISTE

**ar·tiste** /ɑː'tiːst‖ɑr-/ also **artist**– *n* a professional singer, actor, dancer, etc.

**ar·tis·tic** /ɑː'tɪstɪk‖ɑr-/ *adj* **1** [*no comp.*] of, concerning, or typical of art or artists **2** having or showing imagination and skill in art: *He's very artistic.*|*an artistic flower arrangement* –opposite **inartistic** (for 2) **–artistically** *adv*

**art·ist·ry** /'ɑːtɪ̵stri‖'ɑr-/ *n* [U] *apprec* inventive imagination and ability; artistic skill

**art·less** /'ɑːtlɪ̵s‖'ɑr-/ *adj* not trying to deceive; simple, almost foolish; natural: *an artless village girl* –see also ARTFUL **–artlessly** *adv* **–artlessness** *n* [U]

**arts** /ɑːts‖ɑrts/ *n* [P] **1** those subjects or fields of study that are not considered to be part of science, esp. as taught at a university: *History is an arts subject.* –compare **the** SCIENCES, HUMANITIES **2** → FINE ARTS: *Should the government provide money to support the arts?*

**art·y** /'ɑːti‖'ɑrti/ *adj* **-ier, -iest** *often derog* making a show of being interested in art –**artiness** *n* [U]

**as**[1] /əz; *strong* æz/ *adv,prep* **1** (*used in comparisons*) equally; like: *He's as old as me.|She's clever, but her brother is just as clever/not as clever/not so clever.* **2** in the condition of; when considered as being: *He works as a farmer.|As a writer, she's wonderful, but as a teacher she's not very good.|This is regarded as* (=thought to be) *his best film.|She was dressed as a man.* **3 I thought as much!** *infml* I thought so!

**as**[2] *conj* **1** (used in comparisons): *He's as old as I am.|She doesn't run as/so fast as she used to.* **2** in the way or manner that: *Do as I say!* **3** while; when: *He saw her as she was getting off the bus.* **4** because: *As she has no car, she can't get there easily.* –see Study Notes on page 128 **5** though: *Tired as I was, I tried to help them.* **6 as it is** in reality; in fact: *I hoped things would get better, but as it is they are getting worse.* **7 as it were** so to speak; in a certain way: *He is my best friend, my brother, as it were.* –see also SO **as to,** SUCH **as**

USAGE **As** can be used in comparisons with or without "not": *He's* **as** *old/not* **as** *old* **as** *me.|He's* **as** *old/not* **as** *old* **as** *I am.* **So** can be used only with "not": *He's not* **so** *old* **as** *me/not* **so** *old* **as** *I am.* –see also LIKE[3] (USAGE)

**as for** /'· ·/ *prep* (*used when starting to talk about a new subject, connected with what came before*) with regard to; concerning: *You can have a bed, but as for the children, they'll have to sleep on the floor.*

**as if** /· '·/ also **as though**– *conj* **1** as it would be if (something were true): *I couldn't move my legs–it was as if they were stuck to the floor.|Why doesn't she buy us a drink–it isn't as if she had no money!* (=she has plenty of money) **2** in a way that suggests that (something is true): *He shook his head as if to say no.|The bus has gone–it looks as if we'll have to walk.*

**as of** /'· ·/ also **as from**– *prep* starting from (the time stated): *As of today you are in charge.*

**as re·gards** /· ·'·/ *prep* **1** *(esp. in business letters)* on the subject of; regarding: *As regards your recent enquiry . . .|As regards (doing) that, I haven't decided yet.* **2** according to: *correctly placed as regards size and colour*

**as to** /'· ·/ *prep* **1** *(used esp. when speaking of arguments and decisions)* with regard to; concerning: *As to (doing) that, I haven't decided yet.|He's very uncertain as to whether it's the right job for him.* **2** according to; AS **regards** (2): *correctly placed as to size and colour*

**a.s.a.p.** *written abbrev. said as:* as soon as possible

**as·bes·tos** /əs'bestɒs, æs-/ *n* [U] a soft grey material that is made into clothes or solid sheets that protect against fire or heat

**as·cend** /ə'send/ *v* [I;T] *often fml* to climb; go, come, or move from a lower to a higher level: *The stairs ascended in a graceful curve.|He ascended the stairs.* –opposite **descend**

**as·cen·dan·cy, -dency** /ə'sendənsi/ *n* [U] governing or controlling influence; power: *He slowly gained ascendancy over/in the group.*

**as·cent** /ə'sent/ *n* **1** [C;U] the act of going, moving, or climbing up; act of rising: *We made a successful ascent of the mountain.|*(fig.) *the ascent of man from his original state to modern civilization* **2** [U] a way up; upward slope, path, etc.: *a steep ascent*–opposite **descent**

**as·cer·tain** /ˌæsə'teɪn‖ˌæsər-/ *v* [T +*that*] *fml* to discover (the truth about something); get to know for certain: *The police are trying to ascertain exactly who was at the party.*

**as·cet·ic** /ə'setɪk/ *n,adj* (of) a person who does not allow himself/herself bodily pleasures, esp. for religious reasons –**asceticism** /ə'set½sɪzəm/ *n* [U]

**as·cribe** sthg. **to** sbdy./sthg. /ə'skraɪb/ *v prep* **-cribed, -cribing** [T]→ ATTRIBUTE TO: *He ascribes his success to skill and hard work.*

**ash**[1] /æʃ/ *n* [U] the soft grey powder that remains after something has been burnt: *cigarette ash|The house burnt to ashes.*

**ash**[2] *n* [C;U] (the hard wood of) a forest tree

**a·shamed** /ə'ʃeɪmd/ *adj* [F +*to-v/that/of*] feeling shame, guilt, sorrow, or unwillingness: *You should be ashamed (of yourself/your behaviour)!*–**ashamedly** /ə'ʃeɪm½dli/ *adv*

**ash·en** /'æʃən/ *adj* of (the colour of) ashes; pale grey: *His ashen face showed how shocked he was.*

**ash·es** /'æʃ½z/ *n* [P] the remains of a dead body after it has been burnt (CREMATED): *Her ashes were scattered over the sea.*

**a·shore** /ə'ʃɔːʳ‖ə'ʃor/ *adv* [F] on, onto, or to the shore or land: *We came ashore from the boat.*

**ash·tray** /'æʃtreɪ/ *n* a small dish for cigarette ash –see picture on page 355

**Ash Wednes·day** /ˌ· '··/ *n* the first day of LENT

**A·sian** /'eɪʃən, 'eɪʒən‖'eɪʒən, 'eɪʃən/ *n,adj* (a person) of Asia

**a·side**[1] /ə'saɪd/ *adv* **1** to the side; out of the way: *She stepped aside to let them pass.|He put his work aside for a time.|I've put some money aside* (=saved it) *for my holiday.* **2 aside from** →APART **from**

**aside**[2] *n* a remark in a low voice not intended to be heard by everyone present

**ask** /ɑːsk‖æsk/ *v* **1** [I;T +*to-v/that/for*] to call on (a person) for an answer (to); make a question or request: *Ask him who he is/where to go/if he'd like a drink.|If you need any help, just ask.|He asked (her) a question.|She asked him to wake her at six o'clock.|She asked (for) his advice.* **2** [T *for, of*] to demand; expect: *He is asking a lot of money (for his house).|You're asking too much (of them) if you expect them to work at the weekend.* **3** [T *for, to*] to invite: *I have asked some friends (to come) (for/to tea).|I asked her in/up/down for a drink.*

USAGE 1 **Ask** is the usual verb for questions: *He* **asked** *a question.|He* **asked** *(them) where they lived.|"Where do you live?" he* **asked**.*|If you don't know, you must* **ask**. **Inquire** (also **enquire**) is more formal but has the same meaning and could be used in the 3rd and 4th of these sentences, or in the 2nd without "them": *He* **inquired** *where they lived.* To **demand** means to ask for (something) very strongly: *I* **demand** *an explanation!|I* **demand to** *know the truth!* To **question** a person means to ask him/her many questions, and to **interrogate** suggests that the person being questioned is unwilling to answer, and force may be used: *The police* **questioned/interrogated** *the prisoner.* 2 Compare **ask** and **ask for** (*fml* **request**): *I saw the teacher and* **asked for** (*fml* **requested**) *a book.*|*I* **asked** *the teacher to give me a book.* –see also ORDER (USAGE)

**ask for** sthg. *v prep* [T] *infml* to behave so as to cause oneself (trouble or difficulty): *If you park on those yellow lines, you're (really)* **asking for it/ trouble!** –see also HEAD **for**

**a·skew** /ə'skjuː/ *adj,adv* [F] not straight or in the proper manner: *He wore his hat askew.*

**a·sleep** /ə'sliːp/ *adj* [F] **1** sleeping: *He was* **sound/fast asleep** (=completely **asleep**) –opposite **awake 2** (of an arm or leg that has been in one position too long) unable to feel; NUMB **3 fall asleep** to go to sleep

**as·par·a·gus** /ə'spærəgəs/ *n* **-gus** [C;U] a plant whose young green stems are eaten as a vegetable

**as·pect** /'æspekt/ *n* **1** a particular side of a many-sided state of affairs, idea, plan, etc.: *You have only considered one aspect of the problem, but there are many.* **2** the direction in which a window, room, front of a building, etc., faces: *The house has a south-facing aspect.*

**as·per·sion** /ə'spɜːʃən, -ʒən‖-ɜr-/ *n fml or humor* an unkind remark or unfavourable judgment: *Are you* **casting aspersions on** (=raising doubts about) *my ability to drive?*

**as·phalt** /'æsfælt‖'æsfɔlt/ *n* [U] a black sticky material that is firm when it hardens, used for the surface of roads: *an asphalt road (surface)*

**as·phyx·i·ate** /æ'sfɪksieɪt, ə-/ *v* **-ated, -ating** [I;T] *fml* to (cause to) be unable to breathe; esp. to (cause to) die in this way; SUFFOCATE **–asphyxiation** /æˌsfɪksi'eɪʃən, ə-/ *n* [U]

**as·pi·rant** /ə'spaɪərənt, 'æspɪrənt/ *n* [*for, after*] *fml* a person who hopes for and tries to get something important

**as·pi·ra·tion** /ˌæspɪ'reɪʃən/ *n* [C;U] (a) strong desire, esp. to do something great or important: *She has aspirations to become a great writer.*

**as·pire** /ə'spaɪər/ *v* **-pired, -piring** [I +*to-v/to, after*] to direct one's hopes and efforts to some important aim: *He aspired to the leadership of the party.*

**as·pi·rin** /'æsprɪn/ *n* **-rin** *or* **-rins** [C;U] (a TABLET (1) of) a medicine that lessens pain and fever

**ass** /æs/ *n* **1** an animal like a horse but smaller and with longer ears, e.g. a donkey **2** *infml* a stupid foolish person: *Be quiet, you silly ass!*

**as·sail** /ə'seɪl/ *v* [T] *fml* to attack powerfully, either physically or with words, feelings, etc.: *I was assailed with doubts/worries.*

**as·sai·lant** /ə'seɪlənt/ *n fml* an attacker

**as·sas·sin** /ə'sæsɪn/ *n* a person who murders (a ruler or politician) for political reasons or reward

**as·sas·sin·ate** /ə'sæsɪneɪt‖-səneɪt/ *v* **-ated, -ating** [T] to murder (a ruler, politician, etc.) for political reasons or reward –see KILL (USAGE) **–assassination** /əˌsæsɪ'neɪʃən‖-sən'eɪ-/ *n* [C;U]

**as·sault¹** /ə'sɔːlt/ *n* [C;U] a sudden violent attack: *He led an assault against the castle.*|*an assault on* (=attempt to climb) *Mount Everest.*|*sent to prison for assault* (=an attack on another person)

**assault²** *v* [T] to attack suddenly and violently

**as·sem·ble** /ə'sembəl/ *v* **-bled, -bling 1** [I;T] to gather or collect together: *If we can assemble (everybody) quickly then we can leave.* **2** [T] to put together: *to assemble cars/machines*

**as·sem·bly** /ə'sembli/ *n* **-blies** [C;U] (the meeting of) a group of people, esp. one gathered together for a special purpose: *School assembly will begin at nine o'clock.*

**as·sent** /ə'sent/ *v* [I +*to-v/to*] *fml* to agree to a suggestion, idea, etc. –see also CONSENT **–assent** *n* [U]: *We're waiting for the director to give his assent.* –opposite **dissent**

**as·sert** /ə'sɜːt‖-ɜrt/ *v* [T] **1** [+*that*] to state or declare forcefully: *She asserted (her belief) that he was not guilty.* **2** to make a claim to; show, esp. forcefully, the existence of: *He asserted his* AUTHORITY (1) *by making them be quiet.* **3 assert oneself: a** to act in a way that shows one's power, control, etc. **b** to behave in a way that attracts notice

**as·ser·tion** /ə'sɜːʃən‖-ɜr-/ *n* [C;U +*that*] (the act of making) a forceful statement or claim: *He repeated his assertion that he was not guilty.*

**as·ser·tive** /ə'sɜːtɪv‖-ɜr-/ *adj* forceful; expressing or tending to express strong opinions or claims; showing CONFIDENCE: *Her assertive manner has made her a success.* **–assertively** *adv* **–assertiveness** *n* [U]

**as·sess** /ə'ses/ *v* [T *at*] **1** to calculate or decide on the value of (property) or an amount for some special purpose: *They assessed the house (at £90,000).*|*to assess the amount of damage caused by a storm* **2** to judge the quality or worth of: *He's so lazy that it's difficult to assess his ability.* **–assessment** *n* [C;U]

**as·set** /'æset, 'æsɪt/ *n* something such as a building or furniture, that has value and that may be sold to pay a debt: *The company's assets were being sold.*|(fig.) *A sense of humour is a great asset.* –compare LIABILITY (3)

**as·sid·u·ous** /ə'sɪdjuəs‖-dʒuəs/ *adj* having or showing careful and continued attention **–assiduously** *adv*

**as·sign** /ə'saɪn/ *v* [T] **1** [*to*] to give as a share or for use: *They have assigned me a small room.* **2** [*for, to*] to appoint; decide on: *I've been assigned to take notes.*|*We assigned a day for our meeting.*

**as·sign·ment** /ə'saɪnmənt/ *n* **1** [C] a job which one is given or to which one is being sent: *He's going to India on an assignment for his newspaper.* **2** [U] the act of ASSIGNING

**as·sim·i·late** /ə'sɪmɪleɪt/ **-lated, -lating** *v* **1** [I;T *to, into*] to (cause to) become part of: *America has assimilated many people from Europe.*|*They assimilated quite quickly into their new country.* **2** [I;T] **a** to take (food) into the body after eating; DIGEST¹ (1) **b** (of food) to be taken into the body; be DIGESTED¹ (1) **3** [T] to learn and understand properly: *You have to assimilate the facts, not just remember them.* **–assimilation** /-'leɪʃən/ *n* [U]

**as·sist** /ə'sɪst/ *v* [I;T *in*] to help or support: *A team of nurses assisted the doctor in performing the operation.* –see HELP¹ (USAGE)

**as·sist·ance** /ə'sɪstəns/ *n* [U] help; support: *Can I be* **of any assistance?**|*She* **came to my assistance.**

**as·sis·tant** /ə'sɪstənt/ *n* a person who helps another, as in a job, and is under that person's direction: *When the shop is busy he employs an assistant.*|*He is an assistant cook.* –see picture on page 563

**assoc.** *written abbrev. said as:* **1** ASSOCIATED¹ **2** association

**as·so·ci·ate¹** /ə'səʊʃieɪt, ə'səʊsi-/ *v* **-ated, -ating 1** [I;T *with*] to (cause to) join as friends or business partners: *I don't think you should associate with people like that!* **2** [T *with*] to connect, esp. in the mind, with something or someone else: *What do you associate with summer?* –opposite **dissociate**

**as·so·ci·ate²** /ə'səʊʃiˌt, -ʃˌt/ *n* a person connected with another, esp. in work: *He is not a friend but a business associate.*

**as·so·ci·a·tion** /əˌsəʊsi'eɪʃən, əˌsəʊʃi-/ *n* **1** [C+ *to-v/of*] a society of people joined together for a particular purpose: *an association to help blind people* **2** [U *with*] joining or being joined with somebody or something: *I am working* **in association with** *another person.* **3** [U] the act of connecting things, esp. in the mind –opposite **dissociation** (for **2, 3**)

**Association Foot·ball** / ·ˌ···· '··/ *n* [U] *BrE fml* for FOOTBALL

**as·sort·ment** /ə'sɔːtmənt‖-ɔr-/ *n* a group of mixed things or of various examples of the same type of thing; mixture: *This tin contains an assortment of sweets.* **–assorted** *adj: a bag of assorted sweets*

**as·sume** /ə'sjuːm‖ə'suːm/ *v* **-sumed, -suming** [T] **1** [+(*that*)] to take as a fact or as true without proof; suppose: *If he's not here in five minutes, we'll assume he isn't coming.|Assuming it rains tomorrow, what shall we do?* **2** to begin to use or perform (sometimes without the right): *The army assumed control of the government.* **3** to pretend to have or be **–assumption** /ə'sʌmpʃən/ *n* [C;U]: *our wrong assumption that we would win*

**as·sur·ance** /ə'ʃʊərəns/ *n* **1** [U] also **self-assurance**– strong belief in one's ability and powers: *The new teacher lacked assurance in front of his class.* **2** [C +*that/of*] a firm statement; promise: *You have my assurance that the job will be finished on time.* **3** [U] *BrE* for insurance: *life assurance*

**as·sure** /ə'ʃʊəʳ/ *v* **-sured, -suring** [T] **1** [+*that/of*] to try to cause (someone) to believe or trust in something; make (someone or oneself) sure or certain: *He assured us that the police were doing all they could.|You can* **rest assured** (=feel certain) *that your money is safe with us.* **2** *tech* to INSURE, esp. against death

**as·sured** /ə'ʃʊəd‖-ərd/ *adj* having or showing certainty, esp. of one's own abilities: *an assured manner* **–assuredly** /ə'ʃʊərˌdli/ *adv*

**as·te·risk** /'æstərɪsk/ also **star**– *n* a starlike mark (*) **a** used to call attention to something written or printed **b** used in this dictionary to show that a word or phrase is wrong

**as·te·roid** /'æstərɔɪd/ also **minor planet**– *n* one of many small PLANETS between MARS and JUPITER

**asth·ma** /'æsmə‖'æzmə/ *n* [U] a diseased condition which makes breathing very difficult at times **–asthmatic** /æs'mætɪk‖æz-/ *adj,n: He is (an) asthmatic.*

**as·tig·ma·tis·m** /ə'stɪgmətɪzəm/ *n* [U] the inability of the eye to see properly or clearly because of its shape

**as·ton·ish** /ə'stɒnɪʃ‖ə'stɑ-/ *v* [T] to produce great surprise or wonder in (someone): *We were astonished to hear that he had passed his driving test.|an astonished look|an astonishing price*

**as·ton·ish·ment** /ə'stɒnɪʃmənt‖ə'stɑ-/ *n* [U] great surprise or wonder: **To my astonishment** *he was early.*

**as·tound** /ə'staʊnd/ *v* [T] to surprise very much: *He was astounded when he heard he had won.*

**a·stray** /ə'streɪ/ *adj,adv* [F] off the right path or way: (fig.) *The attractions of the big city soon* **led** *the young man* **astray.** (=into bad ways)|*to* **go astray**

**a·stride** /ə'straɪd/ *adv,prep* [F] with a leg on each side (of): *He rode astride the horse.*

**as·trin·gent** /ə'strɪndʒənt/ *adj* **1** able to tighten up the skin or stop bleeding **2** severe; bitter: *an astringent remark*

**as·trol·o·gy** /ə'strɒlədʒi‖ə'strɑ-/ *n* [U] the art of understanding the supposed influence on events and character of the stars and PLANETS **–astrological** /ˌæstrə'lɒdʒɪkəl‖-'lɑ-/ *adj* **–astrologically** *adv* **–astrologer** /ə'strɒlədʒəʳ‖ə'strɑ-/ *n*

**as·tro·naut** /'æstrənɔːt‖-nɔt, -nɑt/ *n* a person who travels in a spacecraft

**as·tro·nom·i·cal** /ˌæstrə'nɒmɪkəl‖-'nɑ-/ *adj* **1** of or concerning (the study of) the stars **2** *infml* very large: *Astronomical sums of money will be needed for this plan.* **–astronomically** *adv*

**as·tron·o·my** /ə'strɒnəmi‖ə'strɑ-/ *n* [U] the scientific study of the sun, moon, stars, etc. **–astronomer** *n*

**as·tute** /ə'stjuːt‖ə'stuːt/ *adj* clever and able to see quickly something that is to one's advantage **–astutely** *adv* **–astuteness** *n* [U]

**a·sy·lum** /ə'saɪləm/ *n* **1** [C;U] (a place which offers) protection and shelter, esp. as given by one country to people who have left another for political reasons **2** [C] *becoming rare* for MENTAL HOSPITAL

**at** /ət; *strong* æt/ *prep* **1** (shows a point in space): *at my house|at the bottom of a hole|He stood at the door.|We arrived at the airport.* (Compare *in London, in France, an island in the Atlantic*) –see Study Notes on page 474 **2** (shows a point in time): *at 10 o'clock|at midnight|at Christmas|at the moment* (Compare *on Tuesday, on July 1st, in the morning, in 1984*) **3** (*shows an intended aim or object*) in the direction of: *He shot at the bird, but missed it.* (Compare *He shot the bird.* (=he did not miss it)|*He threw a stone at me.* (=to hurt me) (Compare *He threw the ball to me.* (=he wanted me to catch it)|*He shouted at the boy.* **4** (used when one acts or feels in answer to something): *I was surprised/amused/pleased at* (=by) *his behaviour.|I laughed at his joke.* **5** (shows that somebody does something well, badly, etc.): *He's good/clever/bad at arranging things.|He's good/bad at football.|She's a* GENIUS (1) *at chemistry.* **6** (shows what one is doing or the state one is in): *at work|at school|at rest |at war* **7** (used to measure a cost, rate, degree, level, age, speed, etc.): *bought at (a price or cost of) 10 cents each|The temperature stood at 40°.|to stop working at (the age of) 60|to drive at 100 kilometres an hour* **8 at a/an** as a result of only one; in only one: *to reduce prices at a stroke|two at a time*

**ate** /et, eɪt‖eɪt/ *v past tense of* EAT

USAGE The usual British pronunciation is /et/, though some people say /eɪt/. Most Americans say /eɪt/, and /et/ is thought to be nonstandard by many Americans.

**a·the·is·m** /'eɪθi-ɪzəm/ *n* [U] disbelief in the existence of God

**a·the·ist** /'eɪθi-ᵻst/ *n* a person who does not believe in the existence of God –compare AGNOSTIC **–atheistic(al)** /ˌeɪθi'ɪstɪk(əl)/ *adj*

**ath·lete** /'æθliːt/ *n* a person who practises bodily exercises and games that need strength and speed (**athletics**) –see picture on page 592

**ath·let·ic** /æθ'letɪk, əθ-/ *adj* **1** of or concerning ATHLETES or ATHLETICS **2** (of people) strong in body, with plenty of muscle

**ath·let·ics** /æθ'letɪks, əθ-/ *n* [U] the practice of bodily exercises and of sports demanding strength and speed, such as running and jumping –see picture on page 592

**at·las** /'ætləs/ *n* a book of maps

**at·mo·sphere** /'ætməsfɪəʳ/ *n* **1** the mixture of gases that surrounds any heavenly body, esp. the earth **2** the air, as in a room: *a smoky atmosphere* **3** the general character or feeling of a place: *Ever since their quarrel, there has been an unpleasant atmosphere in the office.*

**at·mo·spher·ic** /ˌætməs'ferɪk◂/ *adj* [A] of or concerning the earth's ATMOSPHERE (1)

**at·om** /'ætəm/ *n* the smallest piece of a simple substance (ELEMENT (1)) that still has the same qualities and can combine with other substances (to form MOLECULES)

**atom bomb** /'·· ·/ also **atomic bomb** /·ˌ·· '·/– *n* a bomb whose very powerful explosion is caused by splitting an atom and setting free its force

**a·tom·ic** /ə'tɒmɪk‖ə'tɑ-/ *adj* **1** of or concerning an atom or atoms **2** working on or moving by ATOMIC ENERGY: *an atomic ship* **–atomically** *adv*

**atomic en·er·gy** /·ˌ·· '···/ also **nuclear energy**– *n* [U] the powerful force that is given out when an atom is split. It is used to make electricity, to drive large ships, in ATOM BOMBS, etc.

**a·tone** /ə'təʊn/ *v* **-toned, -toning** [I *for*] to make repayment (for some crime, etc.): *He tried to atone for his rudeness by sending her flowers.* **–atonement** *n* [U]

**a·tro·cious** /ə'trəʊʃəs/ *adj* **1** very cruel, shameful, shocking, etc.: *atrocious behaviour* **2** *infml* very bad: *an atrocious meal* **–atrociously** *adv*

**a·troc·i·ty** /ə'trɒsᵻti‖ə'trɑ-/ *n* **-ties** (an act of) great evil, esp. cruelty: *the atrocities of war*

**at·tach** /ə'tætʃ/ *v* [T *to*] to fix; fasten; join: *The picture is attached to the wall by a nail.* –see also UNATTACHED (1)

**attach** sbdy. **to** sbdy./sthg. *v prep* **1** [T] to cause (oneself) to join as a member of, esp. for a short time: *I was attached to the naval college as a special instructor for six months.* **2 attach importance to** to consider important **3 be attached to** to be fond of: *I am very attached to that old car.*

**at·tach·ment** /ə'tætʃmənt/ *n* **1** [U *to*] the act of attaching or of being attached (ATTACH; ATTACH **to** (1)) **2** [C] something that is fixed to something else **3** [C *for, to*] fondness or friendship: *I felt an attachment for him.*

**at·tack¹** /ə'tæk/ *v* **1** [I;T] to use violence (on), esp. with weapons: *The enemy attacked (us) at night.* **2** [T] to speak or write strongly against: *a powerful speech attacking government policy* **3** [T] to harm, spoil, trouble, damage, etc., esp. by a continuing action: *The disease attacked the crops.* **4** [T] to begin with eagerness: *He attacked the difficulties at once.* **–attacker** *n*

**attack²** *n* **1** [C;U] (an act of) violence intended to harm: *The city came* **under attack** *during the night.* **2** [C *on*] writing or words intended to hurt or damage: *an attack on government spending* **3** [C *of*] a sudden and severe period of (esp. serious) illness: *an attack of* MALARIA|*a* HEART ATTACK|*a sudden attack of nerves*

**at·tain** /ə'teɪn/ *v* [T] to succeed in arriving at, esp. after effort; reach: *He attained the position of minister.* **–attainable** *adj* **–attainment** *n* [C;U]

**at·tempt¹** /ə'tempt/ *v* [T *+to-v/v-ing*] to make an effort at; try: *I attempted to leave but was stopped.*

**attempt²** *n* [C *+to-v/at, on*] an effort made to do something: *We failed in our attempt (to climb the mountain).*|*an attempt on her life* (=to kill her)|*I passed the test at the second attempt.* (=the second time I tried)

**at·tend** /ə'tend/ *v* **1** [T] to be present at; go to: *I shall be attending the meeting.* **2** [I *to*] *fml* to give one's attention; listen: *Are you attending (to what is being said)?* **3** to look after; serve: *I have a good doctor attending me.* **4** [T] *fml* to go with; be connected with: *Danger attended everything he did.*

USAGE People who **attend** a play or concert are the **audience;** people who **attend** a church service are the **congregation;** people who **attend** a game, such as football, are **spectators.** But an **attendant** is someone who is employed to look after a public place or the people who use it: *a swimming-pool* **attendant.** Someone who works in a shop is an **assistant** (or **shop assistant**).

**attend to** sbdy./sthg. *v prep* [T] to direct one's efforts and interest towards: *I have an urgent matter to attend to.*

**at·tend·ance** /ə'tendəns/ *n* **1** [U] the act of attending: *The doctor is* **in attendance on** *the sick man.* **2** [C;U *at*] the act of being present, esp. regularly: *Attendance at school is demanded by law.* **3** [S *at*] the number of people present: *a large attendance at the meeting*

**at·tend·ant** /ə'tendənt/ *n* a person who looks after a place or person: *a* MUSEUM *attendant*

**at·ten·tion** /ə'tenʃən/ *n* [U] **1** the act of fixing the mind on something, esp. by watching or listening; full thought and consideration: *You must* **pay attention to** *the teacher.* –opposite **inattention 2** particular care, notice, or action: *Old cars need a lot of attention.* **3 at/to attention** in a military position in which a soldier stands straight and still

**at·ten·tive** /ə'tentɪv/ *adj* taking careful notice: *He was very attentive to the old lady and did everything for her.* –opposite **inattentive –attentively** *adv* **–attentiveness** *n* [U]

**at·tic** /'ætɪk/ *n* the space in a building just below the roof, and above the top room

**at·tire** /ə'taɪəʳ/ *n* [U] *fml* dress; clothes

**at·ti·tude** /'ætᵻtjuːd‖-tuːd/ *n* **1** a way of feeling, thinking, or behaving: *She had an unfriendly attitude.*|*What is the company's attitude to this idea?* **2** *fml* a position of the body

**at·tor·ney** /ə'tɜːni‖-ɜr-/ *n* **-neys** *AmE* for LAWYER

**at·tract** /ə'trækt/ *v* [T] to cause to like, admire,

notice, or turn towards: *She was attracted by his smile.|Flowers attract bees.|His new book is attracting a lot of attention.*

**at·trac·tion** /ə'trækʃən/ *n* **1** [U] the ability to attract; act of attracting: *The idea of living in the city has little attraction to me.* **2** [C] something which attracts: *The city's bright lights, theatres, films, etc., are great attractions.*

**at·trac·tive** /ə'træktɪv/ *adj* **1** having the power to attract: *The idea is very attractive.* **2** pretty or HANDSOME: *an attractive girl/young man* –opposite **unattractive**; see BEAUTIFUL (USAGE) –**attractively** *adv* –**attractiveness** *n* [U]

**at·tri·bute** /'ætrǝbjuːt/ *n* a quality forming part of the nature of a person or thing: *Kindness is just one of his many attributes.*

**at·trib·ute** sthg. **to** sbdy./sthg. /ə'trɪbjuːt‖-bjət/ *v prep* **-uted, -uting** [T] to believe (something) to be the result or work of: *Jim attributes his success to hard work/to working hard.|This song is usually attributed to Bach.* –**attribution** /ˌætrǝ'bjuːʃən/ *n* [U]

**at·trib·u·tive** /ə'trɪbjʊtɪv‖-bjə-/ *adj* (of an adjective, noun, or phrase) describing and coming before a noun: *In "a major success", "major" is an attributive adjective.* –compare PREDICATIVE

**at·tune** sbdy./sthg. **to** sthg. /ə'tjuːn‖ə'tuːn/ *v prep* **-tuned, -tuning** [T *usu. pass.*] to cause to become used to or ready for: *I'm not really attuned to his way of thinking.*

**au·ber·gine** /'əʊbəʒiːn‖-bər-/ *n* [C;U] *BrE* for EGGPLANT

**au·burn** /'ɔːbən‖-ərn/ *adj,n* [U] (esp. of hair) reddish-brown

**auc·tion¹** /'ɔːkʃən/ *n* [C;U] a public meeting to sell goods to the person who offers the most money: *a furniture auction|I shall sell my house* **by auction.**

**auction²** *v* [T *off*] to sell by AUCTION

**auc·tio·neer** /ˌɔːkʃə'nɪəʳ/ *n* a person who is in charge of an AUCTION

**au·da·cious** /ɔː'deɪʃəs/ *adj* **1** (foolishly) daring; brave **2** daringly impolite; CHEEKY –**audaciously** *adv*

**au·dac·i·ty** /ɔː'dæsǝti/ *n* [U] daring, boldness, or daring rudeness

**au·di·ble** /'ɔːdǝbəl/ *adj* able to be heard –opposite **inaudible** –**audibility** /ˌɔːdǝ'bɪlǝti/ *n* –**audibly** /'ɔːdǝbli/ *adv*

**au·di·ence** /'ɔːdɪəns‖'ɔ-, 'ɑ-/ *n* **1** [+*sing./pl. v*] the people listening to or watching a performance, speech, television show, etc.: *The audience was/were very excited by the show.* –see ATTEND (USAGE); see picture on page 463 **2** a formal meeting with somebody powerful or important: *an audience with the Pope*

**au·di·o** /'ɔːdi-əʊ/ *adj* [A] *tech* connected with or used in the broadcasting or receiving of sound radio signals –compare VIDEO (1)

**audio-vis·u·al** /ˌ··· '···◂/ *adj* [*no comp.*] of, for, or concerning both sight and hearing: *The school's audio-visual apparatus includes films and records.*

**au·dit** /'ɔːdǝt/ *v* [T] to make an official examination of (the accounts) of a business, etc., usu. done once each year. –**audit** *n: The yearly audit takes place each December.* –**auditor** *n*

**au·di·tion¹** /ɔː'dɪʃən/ *n* a test performance requested of a singer, actor, etc., by the people from whom he/she hopes to get employment

**audition²** *v* [I;T] to give or cause (someone) to give an AUDITION

**au·di·to·ri·um** /ˌɔːdǝ'tɔːrɪəm‖-'to-/ *n* the space in a theatre, hall, etc., where people sit when listening to or watching a performance –see picture on page 463

**aug·ment** /ɔːg'ment/ *v* [I;T] *fml* to (cause to) become bigger, more valuable, better, etc.: *He augments his income by teaching in the evenings.*

**au·gur** /'ɔːgəʳ/ *v* **augur well/ill (for)** also **bode well/ill (for)**– *lit* to be a sign of good things/bad things in the future (for): *This rain augurs well for the farmers.*

**au·gust** /ɔː'gʌst/ *adj lit* causing feelings of great respect; noble and grand

**Au·gust** /'ɔːgəst/ also **Aug.** *written abbrev.*– *n* the 8th month of the year

**aunt** /ɑːnt‖ænt/ also **auntie, aunty** /'ɑːnti‖'ænti/ *infml*– *n* [A] the sister of one's father or mother or the wife of one's uncle: *Hello, auntie!|Aunt Jane has just got married again.* –see picture on page 217

**au pair** /ˌəʊ'peəʳ/ *n* a young foreigner, esp. a girl (an **au pair girl**), who lives with a family in return for doing light work in the house, usu. to learn the language

**au·ra** /'ɔːrə/ *n* an effect or feeling that seems to surround and come from a person or place: *an aura of decay in the empty village*

**au·ral** /'ɔːrəl/ *adj tech* of or received through hearing
USAGE **aural** is sometimes pronounced /'aʊrəl/ to show a difference with **oral** /'ɔːrəl/.

**aus·pic·es** /'ɔːspǝsǝz/ *n* [P] *fml* help, support, and favour: *This concert has been arranged* **under the auspices of** *the Queen.*

**aus·pi·cious** /ɔː'spɪʃəs/ *adj fml* giving, promising, or showing signs of future success –**auspiciously** *adv: The year began auspiciously with good trade figures for January.* –opposite **inauspicious**

**aus·tere** /ɔː'stɪəʳ, ɒ-‖ɔ-/ *adj* **1** lacking comfort; hard: *We led an austere life in the mountains.* **2** self-controlled; serious: *an austere person/manner* –**austerely** *adv* –**austerity** /ɒ'sterǝti, ɔː-‖ɔ-/ *n* **-ties** [C;U]

**au·then·tic** /ɔː'θentɪk/ *adj* known to have been made, painted, written, etc., by the person who is claimed to have done it; GENUINE: *Is that an authentic Roman* STATUE, *or a modern copy?* –**authentically** *adv* –**authenticity** /ˌɔːθen'tɪsǝti/ *n* [U]

**au·then·tic·ate** /ɔː'θentɪkeɪt/ *v* **-ated, -ating** [T] to prove (something) to be AUTHENTIC –**authentication** /-'keɪʃən/ *n* [U]

**au·thor** /'ɔːθəʳ/ **authoress** /'ɔːθərǝs/ *fem. sometimes derog*– *n* the writer of a book, newspaper article, play, poem, etc.

**au·thor·i·tar·i·an** /ɔːˌθɒrǝ'teərɪən‖ɔˌθɑ-, əˌθɔ-/ *adj,n* (a person) favouring or demanding obedience to rules and laws whether or not they are right: *an authoritarian teacher|authoritarian government* –**authoritarianism** *n* [U]

**au·thor·i·ta·tive** /ɔː'θɒrǝtətɪv, ə-‖ə'θɑrəteɪtɪv, əˌθɔ-/ *adj* **1** having or showing AUTHORITY (1); demanding or deserving respect or obedience: *an* *authoritative voice* **2** able to be trusted: *an authoritative dictionary* –compare DEFINITIVE –**authoritatively** *adv*

**au·thor·i·ty** /ɔːˈθɒrɪ̇ti, ə-‖əˈθɑ-, əˈθɔ-/ *n* **-ties 1** [C;U] (a person or group with) the ability, power, or right to control and command: *Who is in authority here?|What authority have you for entering this house?|The government is the highest authority in the country.|The authorities at the town hall are slow to deal with complaints.* **2** [U] power to influence: *Although she has no official position in the party, she has a lot of authority.* **3** [C] a person, book, etc., whose knowledge or information is dependable, good, and respected: *an authority on plants*

**au·thor·ize** ‖also **-ise** *BrE* /ˈɔːθəraɪz/ *v* **-ized, -izing** [T] to give formal permission to or for: *I authorized Mr Jones to act for me while I was away.|I authorized the payment of this bill.* –**authorization, -isation** /-ˈzeɪʃən/ *n* [C;U]

**au·to·bi·o·graph·i·cal** /ˌɔːtəbaɪəˈgræfɪkəl/ also **autobiographic** /-ˈgræfɪk/– *adj* of or concerning the facts of one's own life, esp. as written in a book –**autobiographically** *adv*

**au·to·bi·og·ra·phy** /ˌɔːtəbaɪˈɒgrəfi‖-baɪˈɑ-/ *n* **-phies** a book written by oneself about one's own life –compare BIOGRAPHY

**au·toc·ra·cy** /ɔːˈtɒkrəsi‖ɔˈtɑ-/ *n* **-cies** [C;U] rule by one person with unlimited power

**au·to·crat** /ˈɔːtəkræt/ *n* **1** a ruler with unlimited power **2** a person who gives orders to others without considering their wishes –**autocratic** /-ˈkrætɪk/ *adj* –**autocratically** *adv*

**au·to·graph**[1] /ˈɔːtəgrɑːf‖-græf/ *n* a person's name in his/her own writing (SIGNATURE), esp. the signature of someone famous: *The little boys asked the footballer for his autograph.*

**autograph**[2] *v* [T] (esp. of a famous person) to sign (a letter, statement, book, etc.) with one's own name: *an autographed copy of a book*

**au·to·mate** /ˈɔːtəmeɪt/ *v* **-mated, -mating** [I;T] to make (something) work by machinery with little or no work by people

**au·to·mat·ic** /ˌɔːtəˈmætɪk◂/ *adj* **1** (esp. of a machine) able to work or move by itself without needing the operation of a person: *The heating system here has an automatic temperature control.* **2** done without thought, esp. as a habit: *The movements needed to ride a bicycle soon become automatic.* **3** certain to happen: *an automatic increase in pay every year* –**automatically** *adv*

**au·to·ma·tion** /ˌɔːtəˈmeɪʃən/ *n* [U] the use of machines that need little or no human control, esp. in place of workers

**au·to·mo·bile** /ˈɔːtəməbiːl‖-məʊ-/ *n AmE* for car

**au·ton·o·mous** /ɔːˈtɒnəməs‖ɔˈtɑ-/ *adj* governing itself: *an autonomous country* –**autonomously** *adv*

**au·ton·o·my** /ɔːˈtɒnəmi‖ɔˈtɑ-/ *n* [U] the condition of self-government, esp. of an area or group within a country

**au·top·sy** /ˈɔːtɒpsi‖-tɑp-/ *n* **-sies** → POSTMORTEM

**au·tumn** /ˈɔːtəm/‖also **fall** *AmE*– *n* [C;U] the season between summer and winter –**autumnal** /ɔːˈtʌmnəl/ *adj*

**aux·il·i·a·ry** /ɔːgˈzɪljəri, ɔːk-‖ɔgˈzɪljəri, -ˈzɪləri/ *adj* offering or giving help; adding support: *auxiliary workers/machinery* –**auxiliary** *n* **-ries**

**auxiliary verb** /·ˌ···· ˈ·/ *n tech* a verb that goes with another verb to show person, tense, etc. (such as *am, didn't,* and *have* in *"I am running", "I didn't climb", "they have heard"*)

**av.** *written abbrev. said as:* AVERAGE

**a·vail**[1] /əˈveɪl/ *n* [U] advantage; use: *We tried and tried, but it was all* **of/to no avail**: *we just couldn't open the door.*

**avail**[2] *v* → AVAIL OF

**a·vai·la·ble** /əˈveɪləbəl/ *adj* able to be got, obtained, used, seen, etc.: *I'm sorry, those shoes are not available in your size.|The doctor is (not) available now.* –opposite **unavailable** –**availability** /-ˈbɪlɪ̇ti/ *n* [U]

**avail** sbdy. **of** sthg. *v prep* [T] *fml* to give (oneself) the advantage of; make use of: *You should avail yourself of every chance to improve your English.*

**av·a·lanche** /ˈævəlɑːnʃ‖-læntʃ/ *n* a large mass of snow and ice crashing down the side of a mountain: (fig.) *an avalanche of letters*

**a·vant-garde** /ˌævɔːŋ ˈgaːd‖ˌævaŋ ˈgard/ *adj* being, or produced by, one of the people who produce the most recent and original ideas, esp. in the arts: *avant-garde painters/painting*

**av·a·rice** /ˈævərɪ̇s/ *n* [U] *fml* too great eagerness and desire to get or keep wealth; GREED –**avaricious** /ˌævəˈrɪʃəs/ *adj*

**a·venge** /əˈvendʒ/ *v* **-venged, -venging** [T *on, upon*] *esp. lit* to get satisfaction for (a wrong) done to (someone) by punishing those who did it: *I shall avenge my brother: the man who killed him shall die.* –see REVENGE (USAGE) –**avenger** *n*

**av·e·nue** /ˈævɪ̇njuː‖-nuː/ *n* **1** a road or way between two rows of trees, esp. one that leads to a house **2** also **Ave.** *abbrev.*– (part of the name of) a wide street in a town: (fig.) *They explored every avenue* (=tried every possible method) *but could not do it.* –see ROAD (USAGE)

**av·e·rage**[1] /ˈævərɪdʒ/ *n* **1** [C] the amount found by adding together several quantities and then dividing by the number of quantities: *The average of 3, 8, and 10 is 7.* **2** [C;U] a level or standard regarded as usual or ordinary: *He is* **above/below average** *in his lessons.|On average we receive five letters each day.* –**average** *adj* [*no comp.*]: *What is the average rainfall for July?|an average film –see picture on page 494*

**average**[2] *v* **-raged, -raging 1** to do, get, or come to an average: *My mail averages 20 letters a day.* **2** [T] to calculate the average of (figures)

**average out** *v adv* [I] *infml* to come to an average or ordinary level or standard, esp. after being higher or lower: *Months of high and low sales average out over the year.*

**a·verse** /əˈvɜːs‖-ɜrs/ *adj* [F *to*] *fml or humor* opposed: *I am not averse to a good meal.* –compare ADVERSE

**a·ver·sion** /əˈvɜːʃən‖əˈvɜrʒən/ *n* [C;U *to*] (an object of) strong dislike; hatred: *She has an aversion to cats.|Cats are an aversion of hers.*

**a·vert** /əˈvɜːt‖-ɜrt/ *v* [T] **1** to prevent happening; avoid: *Accidents can be averted by careful driving.* **2** [*from*] *fml* to turn away (one's eyes, thoughts, etc.)

**a·vi·a·ry** /ˈeɪvɪəri‖ˈeɪvieri/ *n* **-ries** a large cage or enclosure for keeping birds in

**a·vi·a·tion** /ˌeɪviˈeɪʃən‖ˌeɪ-, ˌæ-/ *n* [U] **1** the science or practice of the flight of aircraft **2** the aircraft industry

**a·vi·a·tor** /ˈeɪvieɪtəʳ‖ˈeɪ-, ˈæ-/ *n old use* an aircraft pilot

**av·id** /ˈævɪd/ *adj* [*for*] eager; keen: *an avid reader* –**avidly** *adv*

**av·o·ca·do** /ˌævəˈkɑːdəʊ◂/ also **avocado pear** /ˌ···· ˈ·/– *n* **-dos** *or* **-does** a green tropical fruit with a large stone and smooth oily flesh

**a·void** /əˈvɔɪd/ *v* [T +*v-ing*] to miss or keep away from, esp. on purpose: *She avoided answering my questions.*|*To avoid the city centre, turn right here.* –**avoidable** *adj* –**avoidance** *n* [U]

**av·oir·du·pois** /ˌævədəˈpɔɪz, ˌævwɑːdjuːˈpwɑː‖ˌævərdəˈpɔɪz/ *n,adj* [U] the system of weights in which the standard measures are the OUNCE (1), pound, and TON (1): *16* OUNCES *avoirdupois* –compare METRIC

**a·vow** /əˈvaʊ/ *v* [T +*that*] *fml* to state openly; admit: *He avowed that he would never return.* –opposite **disavow** –**avowal** *n* [C;U]

**a·vowed** /əˈvaʊd/ *adj* [A] openly declared or admitted: *an avowed supporter of a political party* –**avowedly** /əˈvaʊɪdli/ *adv*

**a·wait** /əˈweɪt/ *v* [T] *fml* to wait for: *I am awaiting your reply.*|*A warm welcome awaits you.*

**a·wake**[1] /əˈweɪk/ *adj* [F] not asleep; having woken: *The children are still* **wide awake.** (=not at all sleepy)|(fig.) *He is* **awake to** (=conscious of) *the problem.*

**awake**[2] also **awaken** /əˈweɪkən/– *v* **awoke** /əˈwəʊk/ *or* **awaked, awaked** *or* **awoken** /əˈwəʊkən/, **awaking** [I;T +*to-v*/*to*] to (cause to) stop sleeping; wake: *The noise awoke me.*|(fig.) *People must be awakened to the danger of these weapons.*

**a·wak·en·ing** /əˈweɪkənɪŋ/ *n* **1** the act of waking from sleep **2 rude awakening** a sudden consciousness of an unpleasant state of affairs: *We had all been enjoying ourselves, but the rude awakening came when our firm started to lose money.*

**a·ward**[1] /əˈwɔːd‖əˈwɔrd/ *v* [T] to give, esp. as the result of an official decision: *He was awarded the prize for being the fastest runner.*|*The judge awarded a large sum of money to those hurt by the explosion.*

**award**[2] *n* something, esp. a prize or money, given as the result of an official decision: *an award of £5,000 to those hurt in the explosion*|*The award for the year's best actor went to Jack Nicholson.*

**a·ware** /əˈweəʳ/ *adj* [+*that*/*of*] having knowledge or understanding: *He doesn't seem to be aware of the problems/aware that there are any problems.*|*I'm quite aware (of) how you must feel.*|*She is politically/artistically aware.* –opposite **unaware** –**awareness** *n* [U]

**a·wash** /əˈwɒʃ‖əˈwɔʃ, əˈwɑʃ/ *adj* [F] level with the water and washed over by the waves: *The river overflowed till the streets were awash.*

**a·way**[1] /əˈweɪ/ *adv* **1** [F] from here; from there; in another direction: *Go away!*|*He swam away from the ship.*|*They're away on holiday*|*He lives far away.* –see picture on page 474 **2** [after *n*] at a stated distance: *He lives three miles away.* **3** in a safe place: *He put the food away (in the cupboard).* **4** so as to be all gone or used up: *The sounds died away.*|*The water boiled away.*|*He gave all his money away.*|*He worked his life away.* **5** all the time; continuously: *They worked away all day.*

**away**[2] *adj* [A] (of a sports match) played at the place, sports field, etc., of one's opponent: *an away match* –opposite **home**

**awe** /ɔː/ *n* [U] a feeling of respect mixed with fear and wonder: *We looked with a sense of awe at the enormous ancient buildings.*

**awe-in·spir·ing** /ˈ· ·ˌ··/ *adj* causing feelings of AWE

**awe·some** /ˈɔːsəm/ *adj* expressing or causing feelings of AWE (esp. when fear is present): *an awesome account of the terrors of war*

**awe·struck** /ˈɔːstrʌk/ also **awestricken** /ˈɔːstrɪkən/– *adj* filled with, made silent by, or showing AWE: *We sat in awestruck silence after hearing the truth at last.*

**aw·ful** /ˈɔːfəl/ *adj* **1** terrible; shocking: *The pain was awful.* **2** *infml* very bad; very great: *awful weather*

**aw·ful·ly** /ˈɔːfəli/ *adv infml* very: *awfully cold* –see picture on page 389

**a·while** /əˈwaɪl/ *adv esp. lit* for a short time: *We rested awhile at the side of the road.*

**awk·ward** /ˈɔːkwəd‖-ərd/ *adj* **1** lacking skill in moving the body or parts of the body easily; CLUMSY (1): *The child was awkward with a knife and fork.* **2** not well made for use; causing difficulty: *an awkward tool to use* **3** difficult to deal with; inconvenient; EMBARRASSING: *Our visitors came at an awkward time.*|*Don't be awkward: we have to get this finished by five o'clock.*|*a long awkward silence after their quarrel* –**awkwardly** *adv* –**awkwardness** *n* [U]

**aw·ning** /ˈɔːnɪŋ/ *n* a (CANVAS) covering, used to protect shop windows, ships' decks, etc., from sun or rain

**a·woke** /əˈwəʊk/ *v past tense of* AWAKE[2]

**a·wok·en** /əˈwəʊkən/ *v past participle of* AWAKE[2]

**axe**[1] ‖also **ax** *AmE* /æks/ *n* **axes** /ˈæksɪz/ a tool with a heavy metal blade on the end of a long handle, used to cut down trees, etc.

**axe**[2] ‖also **ax** *AmE v* **axed, axing** [T] *infml* to remove suddenly and usu. without warning from a job, a list of plans for completion, a system of services, etc.: *750 jobs were axed by the government.*

**ax·i·om** /ˈæksɪəm/ *n* a statement that is generally accepted as true –**axiomatic** /ˌæksɪəˈmætɪk/ *adj*

**ax·is** /ˈæksɪs/ *n* **axes** /ˈæksiːz/ **1** the usu. imaginary line around which a spinning body moves **2** a fixed line used as a reference point, esp. the HORIZONTAL and VERTICAL lines around a GRAPH

**ax·le** /ˈæksəl/ *n* a bar with a wheel on either end, around which the wheels turn, as on a car

**aye** /aɪ/ *adv dial or lit* (used esp. by sailors) yes: *Aye, aye, sir.*

**az·ure** /ˈæʒəʳ, ˈæʒjʊəʳ, ˈæzjʊəʳ‖ˈæʒər/ *adj,n* [U] bright blue, as of the sky

# B, b

**B, b** /biː/ **B's**, **b's** *or* **Bs**, **bs** the second letter of the English alphabet

**b.** *written abbrev. said as:* born: *b. 1885*

**BA** *abbrev. for:* Bachelor of Arts; (a title for someone who has) a first university degree in an ARTS subject: *Susan Potter, BA|He has a BA.* –compare BSc

**baa** /bɑː/ *v* **baaed, baaing** [I] to make the sound that a sheep or lamb makes –**baa** *n*

**bab·ble**[1] /'bæbəl/ *v* **-bled, -bling 1** [I;T] to talk quickly and foolishly or in a way that is hard to understand: *During his fever he babbled without stopping.|He babbled the secret (out) to his friends.* **2** [I] to make continuous sounds like a stream: *a babbling stream|The baby babbled (away/on) for hours.* –compare BURBLE

**babble**[2] *n* **1** [S] a confused sound of many people talking at the same time: *a babble of voices* **2** [U] a sound like that of water running gently over rounded stones: *the babble of running water*

**babe** /beɪb/ *n* **1** *lit* a baby **2** *AmE infml* a (usu. young) woman

**ba·boon** /bə'buːn||bæ-/ *n* a large doglike monkey of Africa or S. Asia

**ba·by** /'beɪbi/ *n* **babies 1** [A;C] a very young child, esp. one who has not learnt to speak –see CHILD (USAGE) **2** [A;C] a very young animal or bird: *a baby monkey* **3** [A;C] the youngest or smallest of a group: *the baby of the class* **4** [C] *AmE infml* a person, esp. a girl or woman

**baby car·riage** /'·· ˌ··/ *n AmE* for PRAM

**ba·by·hood** /'beɪbihʊd/ *n* [U] the period of time when one is a baby

**ba·by·ish** /'beɪbi-ɪʃ/ *derog* like a baby: *They told him it was babyish to cry.*

**baby-mind·er** /'·· ˌ··/ also **child-minder** *n BrE* a person whose job is to take care of babies or children while their parents are away working –compare BABY-SITTER

**baby-sit** /'·· ·/ *v* **-sat, -sitting** [I *for*] to take care of children while their parents are out –**baby-sitter** *n* –compare BABY-MINDER

**bach·e·lor** /'bætʃələʳ/ *n* **1** an unmarried man –compare SPINSTER **2** a person who holds a first university degree, such as **Bachelor of Science** (BSc)/**Arts** (BA)

**back**[1] /bæk/ *n* **1** [C] the part of a person's or animal's body that is the side opposite the chest and goes from the neck to the bottom of the SPINE or the tail: *The woman was carrying the baby on her back.|If we really* **put our back into** *the job* (=work very hard at it) *we can finish it today.*|(fig.) *He's always been kind to me; I can't just* **turn my back on** (=desert) *him now he's ill and poor.* **2** [*the* S] the part opposite the front: *You can't hear the speaker from the back of the hall.|There's a lot of useful information at the back of the dictionary.* **3** [C] the part of a chair that one leans against when sitting **4 back of beyond** a very distant place: *They live on a farm somewhere in the back of beyond.* **5 be glad to see the back of** *infml* to be glad when someone goes away **6 behind someone's back** unknown to the person concerned: *This decision was taken behind my back.* **7 have/with one's back to/against the wall** *infml* (to be) in the greatest possible difficulties, so that one must try very hard **8 in back of** *AmE* at the back of **9 on/off someone's back** causing (or not causing) someone annoyance: *I wish they'd get off my back!* (=stop annoying me) **10 put someone's back up** *infml* to annoy someone –compare FRONT –**backless** *adj*

**back**[2] *adv* **1** where someone or something was before: *Put the book back on the shelf when you've finished it.|Back in Nigeria (where I come from) we used to play a lot of tennis.|She came back for her keys.* **2** towards or at the back; away from the front: *Sit well back or you won't be able to fasten your seat belt.* **3** away from the speaker: *Stand back! My dog is dangerous.* **4** towards or in an earlier time: *back in 1968|to put the clock back* (=so that it shows an earlier time) **5** in return; in reply: *Telephone me back when you know the answer.*

**back**[3] *adj* [A] **1** at the back: *the back door/back yard* **2** (of money) owed from an earlier time: *back pay/rent*

**back**[4] *v* **1** [I;T] to (cause to) go backwards: *She backed the car through the gate.|The dog* **backed away** *as the man raised his whip.* **2** [T *up*] to support and encourage, often with money: *The bank refused to back our plan.* **3** [T] to put money on the success of in a race or competition; BET on: *The horse I backed came in last, so I lost my money.*

**back down**||also **back off** *AmE* –*v adv* [I] to yield in argument, opinion, or claim; admit that one was wrong: *I saw that she was right, so I had to back down.*

**back onto** sthg. *v prep* [T] (of a place or building) to be near to at the back: *The house backs onto the river.*

**back out** *v adv* [I *from, of*] to fail to fulfil (a promise, contract, etc.): *I hope I can depend on you not to back out at the last moment.*

**back** sbdy./sthg. **up** *v adv* [T] to support: *The policeman wouldn't have believed me, if you hadn't backed me up.* –see also BACKUP

**back·biting** /'bækbaɪtɪŋ/ *n* [U] *derog* unkind talk about someone who is absent: *I didn't enjoy working there–there was too much backbiting.*

**back·bone** /'bækbəʊn/ *n* **1** [C] → SPINE (1) **2** [*the* S] someone or something providing the main support for a group, plan, etc.: *The small local groups are the backbone of the party.* **3** [U] firmness of mind; strength of character: *"No backbone," said the old man. "That's the trouble with young people today!"*

**back·break·ing** /'bækbreɪkɪŋ/ *adj* (of work) very

hard to do: *a backbreaking job/load*

**back·date** /ˌbækˈdeɪt/ *v* **-dated, -dating** [T] to make effective from an earlier date: *The increase in pay agreed in June will be backdated to January.* –see also POSTDATE

**back·drop** /ˈbækdrɒp‖-drɑp/ also **backcloth**– *n* → BACKGROUND (2): *The events of the 1930s provided the backdrop for the film.*

**back·er** /ˈbækəʳ/ *n* someone who supports a plan, a political party, etc., with money

**back·fire** /ˌbækˈfaɪəʳ‖ˈbækfaɪəʳ/ *v* **-fired, -firing** [I] **1** (of a car, etc.) to make a loud noise as a result of an explosion in the engine which comes too soon **2** to have an effect opposite to the effect intended: *His plan backfired (on him), and he lost all his money.*

**back·gam·mon** /ˈbækgæmən/ *n* [U] a game for two players, using round wooden pieces and DICE on a special board

**back·ground** /ˈbækgraʊnd/ *n* **1** the scenery or ground behind the main object or event: *There are some mountains in the background of the picture.|She has a lot of power, but likes to remain* **in the background.** –see also FOREGROUND **2** the conditions existing when something happens or happened: *I'll need a bit more background (information) before I can help you.* **3** a person's family, experience, and education: *a young man of excellent background*

**back·hand** /ˈbækhænd/ *n* (the ability to make) a stroke (as in tennis) with the back of the hand turned in the direction of movement: *He's got an excellent backhand.* –compare FOREHAND

**back·hand·ed** /ˌbækˈhændɪ̣d‖ˈbækhændɪ̣d/ *adj, adv* **1** using or made with a BACKHAND **2** using, made, or done with the back of the hand: *a backhanded blow* **3 backhanded compliment** a remark that might cause either pleasure or displeasure

**back·ing** /ˈbækɪŋ/ *n* **1** [U] help or support, esp. with money: *The plan has plenty of backing, and will probably succeed.* **2** [C;U] something that is used to form the back of an object: *(a) backing of cardboard* **3** [C] (esp. in popular music) the sound made by the instruments that support the main singer or player

**back·lash** /ˈbæklæʃ/ *n* **1** a sudden violent backward movement **2** a strong feeling against a growing belief or practice, esp. against a political or social development

**back·log** /ˈbæklɒg‖-lɔg, -lɑg/ *n* [C *usu. sing.*] a group of things to be done that were not done at the proper time: *a backlog of work after the weekend*

**back num·ber** /ˈ· ˌ··/ also **back issue** /ˈ· ˌ··/ *n* a newspaper, magazine, etc., earlier than the most recent one

**back·ped·al** /ˌbækˈpedl‖ˈbækˌpedl/ *v* **-ll-** *BrE*‖**-l-** *AmE* **1** to PEDAL² backwards, as on a bicycle **2** *infml* to take back a statement; change an earlier opinion

**back seat** /ˌ· ˈ·◂/ *n* **1** [C] a seat at the back of a car **2** [S] a less important position: *After five years as a director, she won't take a back seat now.*

**back·side** /ˈbæksaɪd/ *n infml* the part of the body on which one sits

**back street** /ˈ· ·/ *n* a street away from the main streets, esp. in a poor area of a town

**back·stroke** /ˈbækstrəʊk/ *n* [S;U] a swimming stroke done on one's back

**back·track** /ˈbæktræk/ *v* [I] **1** to go back over the same path **2** → BACKPEDAL (2): *The government is backtracking from its more expensive plans.*

**back·up** /ˈbækʌp/ *n* a thing or person ready to be used in place of or to help another –see also BACK **up**

**back·ward** /ˈbækwəd‖-ərd/ *adj* **1** [*no comp.*] directed towards the back, the beginning, or the past: *a backward look* **2** late in development: *a backward country|a backward child* –compare FORWARD¹ (2) **–backwardly** *adv* **–backwardness** *n* [U]

**back·wards** /ˈbækwədz‖-ərdz/ also **backward** *AmE*– *adv* **1** towards the back, the beginning, or the past: *Can you say the alphabet backwards?* (=from Z to A) **2** with the back part in front: *to walk backwards|You've put your hat on backwards.* **3 backwards and forwards** first in one direction and then in the opposite direction **4 know something backwards** to know something perfectly: *All the actors know the play backwards.* –compare FORWARD²

**back·wa·ter** /ˈbækwɔːtəʳ/ *n* a place not influenced by outside events or new ideas: *There aren't any good shops in this village; it's just a backwater.*

**back·yard** /ˌbækˈjɑːd◂‖-ˈjɑrd◂/ *n* **1** *BrE* a yard behind a house, covered with a hard surface **2** also **yard** *AmE*– a yard behind a house, usu. covered with grass

**ba·con** /ˈbeɪkən/ *n* [U] salted or smoked meat from the back or sides of a pig

**bac·te·ri·a** /bækˈtɪərɪə/ *n* [P] very small living things (related to plants), some of which cause disease. They exist in water, soil, air, plants, and the bodies of people and animals –compare GERM (1), VIRUS

**bad** /bæd/ *adj* **worse** /wɜːs‖wɜrs/, **worst** /wɜːst‖wɜrst/ **1** not good: *a very bad performance* (=not of acceptable quality)|*The recent rain has had a bad* (=unfavourable) *effect on the crops.|This fish has* **gone bad.** (=has become unfit to eat)|*Play in the cricket match was stopped because of bad light.* (=because it was too dark)|*Smoking is bad for you/your health.|bad* (=incorrect) *grammar|I felt bad* (=ashamed or sorry) *about not being able to come last night.|My leg's bad again.* (=is hurting)|*I'm rather* **bad at** *sums.* (=can't do them very well) **2** serious; severe: *a bad cold|a bad defeat* **3 bad debt** a debt that is unlikely to be paid **4 have/get a bad name** to lose or have lost people's respect: *That kind of car has a bad name among motorists.* **5 in a bad way** very ill or in serious trouble **6 (It's/That's) too bad** *infml* I'm sorry: *Too bad you couldn't come last night.* **7 make the best of a bad job** to do as well as one can in a difficult position **8 not (so) bad** *infml* really rather good/well **–badness** *n* [U]

**bade** /bæd, beɪd/ *v past tense and participle of* BID¹

**badge** /bædʒ/ *n* a piece of metal or other material worn to show a person's employment, rank, membership of a group, etc.

**bad·ger¹** /ˈbædʒəʳ/ *n* **-ger** *or* **-gers** an animal which has black and white fur, lives in holes in the ground, and is active at night

**badger²** *v* [T] to ask again and again; PESTER: *The children badgered me into taking them to the cinema.*

**bad·ly** /ˈbædli/ *adv* **1** in a bad manner: *badly made clothes|to play badly* –opposite **well 2** very much: *to*

*want help badly|be badly in need of help*
**badly-off** /ˌ·· ˈ·/ *adj* **worse-off, worst-off** [F] poor –opposite **well-off**; compare OFF[1] (7)
**bad·min·ton** /ˈbædmɪntən/ *n* [U] a game similar to tennis played by two or four people who hit a small feathered object (SHUTTLECOCK) over a high net
**baf·fle** /ˈbæfəl/ *v* **-fled, -fling** [T] to confuse so much that action is impossible: *The question baffled me completely and I couldn't answer it.* **–bafflement** *n* **–baffling** *adj: a baffling question*
**bag**[1] /bæg/ *n* **1** a container made of cloth, paper, leather, etc., opening at the top: *a shopping bag* –see pictures on pages 501 **2** also **bagful**– the amount held in a bag **3 in the bag** *infml* certain to be won, gained, etc.: *We're sure to win. The match is in the bag.*
**bag**[2] *v* **-gg- 1** [T] to put (material or objects in large quantities) into a bag or bags **2** *infml* to kill or catch (animals or birds): *We bagged a rabbit.*
**bag·gage** /ˈbægɪdʒ/ also **luggage**– *n* [U] all the bags, etc., with which a person travels
**baggage room** /ˈ·· ·/ *n AmE* for LEFT LUGGAGE OFFICE
**bag·gy** /ˈbægi/ *adj* **-gier, -giest** *infml* hanging in loose folds; not tight: *His trousers were baggy at the knees.*
**bag·pipes** /ˈbægpaɪps/ *n* [P] a musical instrument in which air stored in a bag is forced out through pipes to produce the sound: *to play the bagpipes*
**bags** /bægz/ *n* [P] *BrE infml* lots (of): *She has bags of money!*
**bah** /bɑː/ *interj* (shows a low opinion of someone or something)
**bail**[1] /beɪl/ *n* [U] **1** money left with a court of law so that a prisoner may be set free until he/she is tried **2 stand/go bail for someone** to pay money so that someone may be set free in this way
**bail**[2] *n* (in cricket) either of two small pieces of wood laid on top of the STUMPS[1] (2)
**bail**[3] *v* →BAIL OUT
**bai·liff** /ˈbeɪlɪf/ *n BrE* **1** *law* an official, esp. one who takes possession of goods or property when money is owed **2** a person who looks after a farm or land for the owner
**bail out** *v adv* **1** [T] (**bail** sbdy.↔ **out**)] to obtain freedom for (someone) by paying money (BAIL[1]) to ensure appearance in court at a future date: *He was bailed out for £500.* **2** [I;T (=**bail** sthg.↔ **out**)] also **bale out** *BrE*– to remove water from (a boat) **3** [T] (**bail** sbdy./sthg.↔ **out**) to help (esp. a business) out of difficulties by providing money **4** [I] *AmE* for BALE OUT
**bait**[1] /beɪt/ *v* [T] **1** to put BAIT[2] (1) on (a hook) to catch fish, or in (a trap) to catch animals **2** to make angry intentionally: *At school they baited the boy mercilessly because of the way he talked.*
**bait**[2] *n* [S;U] food or something like food used to attract and catch fish, animals, or birds: (fig.) *The shop used free gifts to attract new customers.*
**baize** /beɪz/ *n* [U] thick woollen cloth, usu. green, used esp. to cover tables on which certain games (esp. BILLIARDS) are played
**bake** /beik/ *v* **baked, baking** [I;T] **1** to (cause to) cook in an OVEN: *to bake bread|The bread is baking.* **2** to (cause to) become hard by heating: *In former times, bricks were baked in the sun.* –see COOK[2] (USAGE)
**bak·er** /ˈbeɪkəʳ/ *n* a person who bakes bread and cakes, esp. professionally
**bak·er·y** /ˈbeɪkəri/ *n* **-ies** a place where bread and sometimes cakes are baked and/or sold
**bal·ance**[1] /ˈbæləns/ *n* **1** [S;U] a state of steadiness in which all parts are of equal or proper weight; EQUILIBRIUM: *I found it hard to* **keep my balance** *on the icy path.|He* **lost his balance** *and fell over.*|(fig.) *We try to* **strike a** *proper* **balance** *between justice and mercy.* –opposite **imbalance 2** [C] an instrument for weighing things by seeing whether the amounts in two hanging pans are equal: (fig.) *The nation's future* **hangs in the balance.** (=is uncertain) **3** [C *usu. sing.*] something which is left over: *My bank balance isn't very large.* (=I haven't got very much money in the bank)|*May I take the balance of my holidays* (=the holidays I have not yet taken) *next month?* **4 on balance** (with) all things considered; taking everything into consideration
**balance**[2] *v* **-anced, -ancing 1** [I;T] to (cause to) be in a state of balance: *The dog balanced a ball on its nose.|The company accounts did not balance.* (=show money spent to be equal to money received) **2** [T] to consider or compare: *You have to balance the advantages of living in the country against the disadvantages.*
**balance of pay·ments** /ˌ·· · ˈ··/ also **balance of trade** /ˌ·· · ˈ·/– *n* [S] the amount of money coming into a country compared with the amount going out
**balance of pow·er** /ˌ·· · ˈ··/ *n* [*the* S] a position in which power, esp. political or military power, is evenly balanced on all sides: *The growth of the new political party* **upset the balance of power.**
**bal·co·ny** /ˈbælkəni/ *n* **-nies 1** a place for people to stand or sit on, built out from the upstairs wall of a building: *You can see the sea from our balcony.* –compare VERANDA; see picture on page 297 **2** also **circle**– the seats upstairs in a theatre.
**bald** /bɔːld/ *adj* **1** with little or no hair (on the head) **2** with little or no decoration; plain: *a bald statement* **–baldness** *n* [U]
**bald·ing** /ˈbɔːldɪŋ/ *adj* becoming BALD (1)
**bald·ly** /ˈbɔːldli/ *adv* spoken plainly, even cruelly: *The doctor told him baldly that if he didn't stop smoking he'd be dead in a year.*
**bale**[1] /beɪl/ *n* a large tightly tied mass of esp. soft goods or material ready to be taken away: *a bale of cotton*/STRAW
**bale**[2] *v* → BALE OUT
**bale·ful** /ˈbeɪlfəl/ *adj* (of appearance and behaviour) full of hate and desire to do harm; evil: *a baleful look* **–balefully** *adv*
**bale out** *v adv* **baled, baling 1** [I *of*] *BrE*‖**bail out** *AmE*– to escape from an aircraft by PARACHUTE[1] **2** [I;T (=**bale** sthg.↔ **out**)] *BrE* for BAIL OUT (2)
**balk**‖also **baulk** *BrE* /bɔːk, bɔlk/ *v* **1** [T] to stop or get in the way of on purpose **2** [I *at*] to be unwilling to face or agree to something difficult or unpleasant: *I wanted to buy the dress, but I balked at the high price.*
**ball**[1] /bɔːl/ *n* **1** a round object used in play; anything of like shape: *to throw a ball|The Earth is like a ball.|a snowball* **2** a rounded part of the body: *the ball*

*of the foot*|EYEBALL **3 on the ball** *infml* showing up-to-date knowledge and the ability to think and act quickly: *That writer is really on the ball.* **4 play ball** *infml* for COOPERATE **5 start/keep the ball rolling** to begin/continue something

**ball²** *n* **1** a large formal occasion for social dancing **2** *infml* a very good time: *They all* **had a ball** *at the party.*

**bal·lad** /ˈbæləd/ *n* a simple song or a short story in the form of a poem

**bal·last** /ˈbæləst/ *n* [U] heavy material which is **a** carried on a ship to keep it steady **b** put down under a road or railway

**ball bear·ing** /ˌ· ˈ··/ *n* (one of the) metal balls moving in a ring round a bar in a machine so that the bar may turn more easily

**ball·cock** /ˈbɔːlkɒk‖-kɑk/ *n* an apparatus for opening and closing a hole through which water passes, worked by a hollow floating ball which rises and falls with the level of the water

**bal·le·ri·na** /ˌbæləˈriːnə/ *n* a female BALLET dancer

**bal·let** /ˈbæleɪ‖bæˈleɪ, ˈbæleɪ/ *n* **1** [C] a kind of dance with music in which a story is told **2** [S;U] the art of doing such dances: *She has studied (the) ballet for six years.* **3** [C +*sing./pl. v*] a group of ballet dancers who work together: *the Bolshoi Ballet*

**bal·lis·tics** /bəˈlɪstɪks/ *n* [U] the scientific study of the movement of objects that are thrown or forced through the air, such as bullets fired from a gun

**bal·loon¹** /bəˈluːn/ *n* **1** a bag of strong light material filled with gas or heated air so that it can float in the air: *He flew hundreds of miles in a balloon.* **2** a small rubber bag that can be blown up, used as a toy

**balloon²** *v* [I esp. *out*] to get rounder and rounder, like a BALLOON¹ being blown up: *Her skirt ballooned out in the wind.*

**bal·lot** /ˈbælət/ *n* **1** [C] a sheet of paper used to make a secret vote: *They are counting the ballots now.* **2** [C;S] the action or system of secret voting: *We put it to the ballot* (=had a vote) *to decide on the new leader.*

**ball·point** /ˈbɔːlpɔɪnt/ also **biro** *BrE*– *n* a pen which has a ball at the end that rolls thick ink onto the paper

**ball·room** /ˈbɔːlrʊm, -ruːm/ *n* a large room for a BALL² (1)

**balm** /bɑːm‖bɑm, bɑlm/ *n* [C;U] (an) oily liquid with a strong but pleasant smell, often from trees, used as medicine or to lessen pain

**balm·y** /ˈbɑːmi‖ˈbɑmi, ˈbɑlmi/ *adj* **-ier, -iest** *apprec* (of air) soft and warm; MILD (2)

**bal·us·trade** /ˌbæləˈstreɪd‖ˈbæləstreɪd/ *n* a row of upright pieces of stone or wood with a bar along the top, guarding the outer edge of any place from which people might fall

**bam·boo** /ˌbæmˈbuː◂/ *n* **-boos** [C;U] a tall plant of the grass family, or its hard, hollow, jointed stems, used e.g. for making furniture

**bam·boo·zle** /bæmˈbuːzəl/ *v* **-zled, -zling** [T *into/out of*] *infml* to deceive; trick

**ban¹** /bæn/ *v* **-nn-** [T] to forbid, esp. by law

**ban²** *n* [*on*] an order BANning something: *There's a ban on smoking in theatres.*

**ba·nal** /bəˈnɑːl, bəˈnæl/ *adj derog* uninteresting because very common: *a banal remark* **–banality** /bəˈnælǝ̇ti/ *n* [C;U]

**ba·na·na** /bəˈnɑːnə‖-ˈnæ-/ *n* a long curving tropical fruit, with a yellow skin and a soft sweet inside

**band¹** /bænd/ *n* **1** a thin flat narrow piece of material, **a** for fastening things together, or for putting round something to strengthen it **b** forming part of an article of clothing: *neckband*|*wristbands* **2** a line of a different colour or pattern that stands out against a background: *There was an orange band on the snake's back.* **3** one of the parts into which a larger whole can be divided: *a band of radio waves*

**band²** *v* → BAND TOGETHER

**band³** *n* [C +*sing./pl. v*] a group of people formed for some common purpose and often with a leader: *a band of robbers*|*The musicians played in a dance band.*

**ban·dage¹** /ˈbændɪdʒ/ *n* a long narrow piece of material, esp. cloth, for binding round a wound or round a part of the body that has been hurt

**bandage²** *v* **-daged, -daging** [T *up*] to tie up or bind round with a BANDAGE¹: *The doctor bandaged (up) his broken ankle.*

**ban·dit** /ˈbændǝ̇t/ *n* a robber, esp. one of an armed band

**band·stand** /ˈbændstænd/ *n* a raised place, open at the sides but with a roof, for a band when playing music outside, usu, in a park

**band to·geth·er** /ˌ· ·ˈ··/ *v adv* [I] to unite, usu. for some special purpose

**band·wa·gon** /ˈbændˌwægən/ *n* **jump on the bandwagon** to do or say something just because a lot of other people are doing or saying it

**ban·dy¹** /ˈbændi/ *v* **-died, -dying** [T] **bandy words (with)** to quarrel (with)

**bandy** sthg. **about** *v adv* [T] to spread (esp. unfavourable or untrue ideas) by talking: *The news of the murder was quickly bandied about.*

**bandy²** *adj* **-dier, -diest 1** (of legs) curved outwards at the knees **2 bandy-legged** /ˌ·· ˈ·‖ˈ·· ·/ – having such legs

**bane** /beɪn/ *n* **the bane of one's existence/life** a cause of continual trouble

**bang¹** /bæŋ/ *v* **1** [T] to strike sharply; BUMP¹ (1): *He fell and banged his knee.* **2** [I;T] (to cause to) knock, beat, or push forcefully, often with a loud noise: *She banged the chair against the wall.* **3** [I] to make loud noise or noises: *There is someone banging about upstairs.*

**bang²** *n* **1** a sharp blow **2** a sudden loud noise: *The door shut with a bang.*

**bang³** *adv* [*adv + prep/adv*] *infml* right; directly: *Your answer's* **bang on.** (=exactly correct)|*The lights went out bang* (=exactly) *in the middle of the performance.*

**bang·er** /ˈbæŋəʳ/ *n BrE infml* **1** a SAUSAGE **2** an old car in poor condition **3** a noisy FIREWORK

**ban·gle** /ˈbæŋgəl/ *n* a metal band worn round the arm or ankle as a decoration

**ban·ish** /ˈbænɪʃ/ *v* [T] to send away, usu. from one's own country, as a punishment: *She was banished by the government for political reasons.* –compare EXILE² **–banishment** *n* [U]

**ban·is·ter** /ˈbænǝ̇stəʳ/ *n* a row of upright pieces of

wood or metal with a bar along the top guarding the outer edge of stairs

**ban·jo** /ˈbændʒəʊ/ *n* **-jos** *or* **-joes** a stringed musical instrument with a long neck, and a body like a drum, used esp. to play popular music

**bank**[1] /bæŋk/ *n* **1** land along the side of a river, lake, etc. –see SHORE[1] (USAGE) **2** a raised area or heap, esp. of earth or mud **3** a mass of snow, clouds, etc.: *The banks of dark cloud promised rain.* **4** → SANDBANK: *The Dogger Bank in the North Sea can be dangerous for ships.*

**bank**[2] *n* **1** a place in which money is kept and paid out on demand **2** a place where something is stored, esp. ORGANIC (1) products of human origin for medical use: *Hospital bloodbanks have saved many lives.*

**bank**[3] *v* [T] to put or keep (money) in a bank

**bank on** sbdy./sthg. *v prep* [T *no pass.*] to depend on; trust in: *I'm banking on you to help me.*

**bank up** *v adv* [I;T (=**bank** sthg.↔ **up**)] to form into a mass or heap: *The wind banked the snow up against the wall.*|*At night we bank up the fire.*

**bank·er** /ˈbæŋkəʳ/ *n* a person who owns, works in, or controls a BANK[2] (1): *Who are your bankers?* (=which bank do you use)

**bank hol·i·day** /ˌ· ˈ···/ *n BrE* an official public holiday, not a Saturday or Sunday, when the banks are closed

**bank note** /ˈ· ·/ *n* a piece of paper money printed by the national bank of a country for public use

**bank·rupt**[1] /ˈbæŋkrʌpt/ *adj* unable to pay one's debts: *The company* **went bankrupt** *because it couldn't sell its products.*|(fig.) **morally bankrupt** (=completely without morals)

**bankrupt**[2] *v* to make BANKRUPT or very poor

**bank·rupt·cy** /ˈbæŋkrʌptsi/ *n* **-cies** [C;U] (an example of) the state of being BANKRUPT

**ban·ner** /ˈbænəʳ/ *n* **1** *lit* a flag **2** a long piece of cloth on which a sign is painted, usu. carried between two poles: *The marchers' banners said "We want work."*

**banns** /bænz/ *n* [P] a public declaration, esp. made in church, of an intended marriage

**ban·quet** /ˈbæŋkw½t/ *n* a formal dinner for many people, esp. one at which speeches are made

**ban·tam** /ˈbæntəm/ *n* a small variety of farm chicken

**ban·ter** /ˈbæntəʳ/ *v* [I] to speak or act playfully or jokingly –**banter** *n* [U]: *The actress exchanged banter with reporters.*

**bap·tis·m** /ˈbæptɪzəm/ *n* [C;U] a Christian religious ceremony in which a person is touched or covered with water to make him/her pure and show that he/she has been accepted as a member of the Church –**baptismal** /bæpˈtɪzməl/ *adj*

**Bap·tist** /ˈbæpt½st/ *n* a member of a branch of the Christian church which believes that BAPTISM should be only for people old enough to understand its meaning

**bap·tize**‖also **-tise** *BrE* /bæpˈtaɪz/ *v* **-tized, -tizing** [T] to perform the ceremony of BAPTISM on

**bar**[1] /bɑːʳ/ *n* **1** a piece of wood, metal, etc. that is longer than it is wide: *an iron bar*|*a bar of soap/chocolate/gold* –see picture on page 449 **2** a length of wood or metal across a door, gate, or window that keeps it shut or prevents movement through it: *There were bars across the windows of the prison.*|(fig.) *His bad English is a bar to* (=prevents) *his getting a job.* **3** a bank of sand or stones under the water, parallel to a shore, at the entrance to a harbour, etc. **4** a group of notes in music: *She sang the first three bars of the song, and then stopped.* **5** (a place with) a COUNTER[1] where alcoholic drinks or food and drinks are sold: *a coffee bar* **6 behind bars** in prison **7 prisoner at the bar** the person being tried in a court of law

**bar**[2] *v* **-rr-** [T] **1** to block or close firmly with or as if with a bar: *to bar the door*|*Military vehicles barred all the roads out of the city.* **2** to keep in or out by barring a door, gate, etc.: *They barred themselves in.* **3** to forbid or prevent: *He has been barred from playing for two weeks because of bad behaviour.*

**bar**[3] *prep* except: *The whole group was at the party, bar John.*

**barb** /bɑːb‖bɑrb/ *n* the sharp point of a fish hook, arrow, etc., with a curved shape which prevents it from being easily pulled out –**barbed** *adj: a barbed hook*|(fig.) *a barbed remark* (=unkind; sharp)

**bar·bar·i·an** /bɑːˈbeərɪən‖bɑr-/ *n derog* an uncivilized person, esp. one who is rough and wild in behaviour: *The barbarians conquered Rome.* –**barbaric** /bɑːˈbærɪk‖bɑr-/ *adj: barbaric people/customs*|*a barbaric punishment* (=very cruel) –**barbarically** *adv* –**barbarism** /ˈbɑːbərɪzəm‖ˈbɑr-/ *n* [C;U] –**barbarous** /ˈbɑːbərəs‖ˈbɑr-/ *adj* –**barbarously** *adv*

**bar·bar·i·ty** /bɑːˈbær½ti‖bɑr-/ *n* **-ties** *derog* [C;U] (an example of) cruelty of the worst kind: *The barbarities of the last war must not be repeated.*

**bar·be·cue**[1] /ˈbɑːbɪkjuː‖ˈbɑr-/ *n* **1** a large framework on which to cook esp. meat over an open fire, usu. outdoors **2** a party at which food is cooked in this way and eaten

**barbecue**[2] *v* **-cued, -cuing** [T] to cook food on a BARBECUE (1)

**barbed wire** /ˌ· ˈ·/ *n* [U] wire with short sharp points in it: *a barbed-wire fence*

**bar·ber** /ˈbɑːbəʳ‖ˈbɑr-/ *n* a person (usu. a man) who cuts men's hair and SHAVES them –compare HAIRDRESSER

**bar·bi·tu·rate** /bɑːˈbɪtʃʊr½t‖bɑrˈbɪtʃər½t,-reɪt/ *n* [C;U] *tech* a drug that calms the nerves and puts people to sleep

**bard** /bɑːd‖bɑrd/ *n lit* a poet

**bare**[1] /beəʳ/ *adj* **1** uncovered; empty; without: *bare skin*|*bare fields*|*a room bare of furniture* **2** [A *no comp.*] not more than; only: *I killed him with my bare hands.* –**bareness** *n* [U]

**bare**[2] *v* **bared, baring** [T] to take off a covering; bring to view: *The animal bared its teeth in anger.*

**bare·back** /ˈbeəbæk‖ˈbeər-/ *adj,adv* [A] riding, esp. a horse, without a SADDLE: *a bareback rider*

**bare·faced** /ˌbeəˈfeɪst◂‖ˈbeərfeɪst/ *adj derog* shameless: *a barefaced lie*

**bare·foot** /ˈbeəfʊt‖ˈbeər-/ *adj,adv* without shoes or other covering on the feet

**bare·head·ed** /ˌbeəˈhed½d◂‖ˈbeərhed½d/ *adj,adv* without a hat

**bare·ly** /ˈbeəli‖ˈbeərli/ *adv* **1** only just; hardly: *We have barely enough money to last the weekend.* –see HARDLY (USAGE) **2** in a bare way: *The room was* *furnished barely.* (=with very little furniture)

**bar·gain**[1] /ˈbɑːgᵻn‖ˈbɑr-/ *n* **1** an agreement, esp. one to do something in return for something else: *He made a bargain with his wife: "You do the shopping and I'll cook."* **2** something bought or offered cheaply: *These shoes are a real bargain at such a low price.* **3 drive a hard bargain** to get an agreement in one's own favour **4 into the bargain** in addition: *She had to look after four children –and her sick mother into the bargain.*

**bargain**[2] *v* [I] to talk about the conditions of a sale, agreement, or contract: *If you bargain with them they might reduce the price.*

**bargain for** sbdy./sthg.‖also **bargain on** sbdy./sthg. *AmE– v prep* [T] to take into account; consider: *I had not bargained for rain, and I got wet.*

**barge**[1] /bɑːdʒ‖bɑrdʒ/ *n* a large low flat-bottomed boat used mainly for carrying heavy goods on a CANAL or river

**barge**[2] *v* **barged, barging** [I;T] to move in a heavy ungraceful way, often hitting against things: *He barged his way onto the bus before everyone else.*

**barge in** *v adv* [I] to rush in rudely; interrupt: *The door burst open and the children barged in.*

**bar·i·tone** /ˈbærᵻtəʊn/ *n* (a man with) the male singing voice lower than TENOR and higher than BASS[2]

**bark**[1] /bɑːk‖bɑrk/ *v* **1** [I *at*] to make the sound that dogs make: *The dog always barks at the postman.* **2** [T *out*] to say (something) in a sharp loud voice: *The officer barked (out) an order.* **3 bark up the wrong tree** *infml* to go to the wrong place or have a mistaken idea: *"You're barking up the wrong tree!" he told the policeman.*

**bark**[2] *n* **1** (a sound like) the sound made by a dog **2 His bark is worse than his bite** *infml* He sounds worse than he is

**bark**[3] *n* [U] the strong outer covering of a tree

**bar·ley** /ˈbɑːli‖ˈbɑrli/ *n* [U] a grasslike grain plant grown for food and also used in the making of beer and SPIRITS[1] (7)

**bar·man** /ˈbɑːmən‖ˈbɑr-/ **barmaid** /ˈbɑːmeɪd‖ˈbɑr-/ *fem.– n* **-men** /mən/ a man who serves drinks in a BAR[1] (5)

**barn** /bɑːn‖bɑrn/ *n* a farm building for keeping animals or for storing crops and food for animals

**bar·na·cle** /ˈbɑːnəkəl‖ˈbɑr-/ *n* a small SHELLFISH which collects in large numbers on rocks and on the bottoms of ships, and which is hard to remove

**barn·yard** /ˈbɑːnjɑːd‖ˈbɑrnjɑrd/ *n* a yard on a farm, usu. enclosed by a fence, with BARNS and perhaps other buildings round it

**ba·rom·e·ter** /bəˈrɒmᵻtəʳ‖-ˈrɑ-/ *n* an instrument for measuring the air pressure in order to help to judge probable changes in the weather or to calculate height above sea level **–barometric** /ˌbærəˈmetrɪk/ *adj* **–barometrically** *adv*

**bar·on** /ˈbærən/ *n* **1** [A;C] **baroness** /ˈbærənᵻs/ *fem.–* (in Britain) (the title of) a nobleman with the lowest rank in the House of Lords **2** [C] someone in a position of great power or influence, esp. in business: *an oil baron|trade union barons*

**bar·on·et** /ˈbærənᵻt, -net/ *n* (in Britain) (the rank of) a KNIGHT[1] (2) whose title passes on to his son when he dies

**ba·ro·ni·al** /bəˈrəʊnɪəl/ *adj* **1** of, like, or about a BARON **2** large, rich, and noble: *a baronial hall*

**bar·rack** /ˈbærək/ *v* [I;T] *BrE & AustrE infml* to interrupt by shouting or pretended cheering: *They barracked (the speaker) during the meeting.*

**bar·racks** /ˈbærəks/ *n* **barracks** a building or group of buildings that soldiers live in

**bar·rage**[1] /ˈbærɑːʒ‖ˈbɑrɪdʒ/ *n* a manmade BAR[1] (3) built across a river usu. to provide water for farming

**bar·rage**[2] /ˈbærɑːʒ‖bəˈrɑʒ/ *n* the firing of a number of heavy guns at once: (fig.) *a barrage of questions*

**bar·rel** /ˈbærəl/ *n* **1** a round wooden container with curved sides and a flat top and bottom: *a beer barrel* **2** also **barrelful** /-fʊl/– the amount of liquid contained in a barrel **3** a part of something that serves as a container and has the shape of a tube or CYLINDER: *a gun barrel*

**bar·ren** /ˈbærən/ *adj* **1** (of female animals) not able to REPRODUCE **2** (of trees or plants) bearing no fruit or seed **3** (of land) unable to produce a good crop **4** useless; empty; which produces no result: *a barren argument* –compare FERTILE **–barrenness** *n* [U]

**bar·ri·cade**[1] /ˈbærᵻkeɪd, ˌbærᵻˈkeɪd/ *n* a quickly-built wall of trees, earth, bricks, etc., put across a way or passage to block the advance of the enemy

**barricade**[2] *v* **-caded, -cading** [T] **1** to block off or close off with a BARRICADE **2** to defend a given place by means of a BARRICADE: *to barricade oneself in one's room*

**bar·ri·er** /ˈbærɪəʳ/ *n* something placed in the way in order to prevent or control the movement of people or things: *The police put up barriers to control the crowd.*|(fig.) *The colour of one's skin should be no barrier to success in life.* –see picture on page 521

**bar·ring** /ˈbɑːrɪŋ/ *prep* except for: *The whole group was at the party, barring John.|We shall return at midnight, barring accidents.* (=if there are no accidents)

**bar·ris·ter** /ˈbærᵻstəʳ/ *n* (esp. in England) a lawyer who has the right of speaking and arguing in the higher courts of law –compare SOLICITOR

**bar·row** /ˈbærəʊ/ *n* **1** a small cart, usu. with two wheels **2** → WHEELBARROW

**bar·ter** /ˈbɑːtəʳ‖ˈbɑr-/ *v* [I;T *for, with*] to exchange goods for other goods: *They bartered farm products for machinery.|bartering for food* **–barter** *n* [U]

**base**[1] /beɪs/ *n* **bases 1** the part of a thing on which the thing stands; the bottom: *We camped at the base of the mountain.|Draw a square with the line "xy" as its base.* **2** the part from which something originates or from which other things develop: *the base of the thumb* (=where it joins the hand)|*Many languages have Latin as their base.* **3** a centre from which something is controlled, plans are made, etc.: *Our company's base is in London, but we have branches all round the world.|a London-based firm* **4** *tech* a chemical substance which combines with an acid to form a salt **5** a centre for military operations, stores, etc. **6** any of the four points which a BASEBALL player must touch in order to make a run

**base**[2] *adj derog esp. lit* (of people, actions, etc.) low; dishonourable: *base conduct* (=very bad behaviour) **–basely** *adv* **–baseness** *n* [U]

**base**[3] *v* → BASE ON

**base·ball** /'beɪsbɔːl/ *n* [U] a game played with a BAT and ball (**baseball**) between two teams of nine players each on a large field of which the centre is four BASES[1] (6): *a baseball player/team*

USAGE In **baseball** the **batter** tries to hit the ball thrown by the **pitcher**

**base·ment** /'beɪsmənt/ *n* a room or rooms in a house which are below street level: *She lives in a basement flat.* –compare CELLAR

**base** sthg. **on** sthg. also **base** sthg. **upon** sthg.– *v prep* **based, basing** [T] to form or do (something) using (something else) as the starting point or reason: *His ideas are based on the teachings of Buddha.*|*You should base your opinions on facts, not on hearsay.*

**bash**[1] /bæʃ/ *v* [T] *infml* to hit hard, so as to break or hurt in some way: *He bashed his finger (with a hammer).*

**bash**[2] *n usu. infml* **1** a hard or fierce blow: *He gave me a bash on the nose.* **2 have a bash (at)** *BrE* to make an attempt (at): *I've never rowed a boat before, but I don't mind having a bash (at it).*

**bash·ful** /'bæʃfəl/ *adj* unsure of oneself; made nervous or unhappy by attention; SHY: *The bashful child felt uncomfortable with strangers.* **–bashfully** *adv* **–bashfulness** *n* [U]

**ba·sic** /'beɪsɪk/ *adj* on which everything else depends or is built; being the main or most important part: *the basic principles of mathematics*|*my basic* SALARY (=before any additional payments)

**ba·sic·al·ly** /'beɪsɪkəli/ *adv* with regard to what is most important and BASIC; FUNDAMENTALLY: *Basically, he's a nice person, but he doesn't always show it.*|*He's basically nice.*

**ba·sics** /'beɪsɪks/ *n* [*the* P] *often infml* the simplest but most important parts of something: *The basics of education are reading, writing, and simple calculations.*

**ba·sin** /'beɪsən/ *n* **1** a round hollow vessel for holding liquids or food; bowl **2** also **basinful**– the contents of a basin **3** → WASHBASIN **4** a circular or egg-shaped valley; all that area of country from which water runs down into a river: *the Amazon Basin*

**ba·sis** /'beɪs$\frac{1}{2}$s/ *n* **bases** /'beɪsiːz/ that from which something is made, started, built, developed, or calculated: *The main basis of this drink is orange juice.*|*What is the basis of/for your opinion?*|*His ideas have no basis in reality.*

**bask** /bɑːsk‖bæsk/ *v* [I *in*] to sit or lie in enjoyable heat and light: *We basked in the sunshine.*| (fig.) *He basked in* (=enjoyed) *his employer's approval.*

**bas·ket** /'bɑːsk$\frac{1}{2}$t‖'bæ-/ *n* **1** (the contents of) a container which is made of bent sticks or other such material: *They were carrying several baskets of fruit.* –see picture on page 615 **2** an open net fixed to a metal ring high up off the ground, through which players try to throw the ball in the game of BASKETBALL

**bas·ket·ball** /'bɑːsk$\frac{1}{2}$tbɔːl‖'bæs-/ *n* [C;U] (the ball used in) a usu. indoor game between two teams of five players, in which each team tries to throw a large ball through the other team's BASKET (2)

**bass**[1] /bæs/ *n* **bass** *or* **basses** a fresh-water or salt-water fish that has prickly skin and can be eaten

**bass**[2] /beɪs/ *n* **1** (a man with) the lowest male singing voice –compare TENOR **2** the lowest part in written music –compare TREBLE **3** → DOUBLE BASS –sounds like **base**

**bas·soon** /bə'suːn/ *n* a wooden musical instrument, played by blowing through a double REED (2), that makes a deep sound

**bas·tard** /'bæstəd, 'bɑː-‖'bæstərd/ *n* **1** a child of unmarried parents **2** *infml* a person, esp. that one strongly dislikes: *The lucky bastard!*

**baste**[1] /beɪst/ *v* **basted, basting** [I;T] to join (pieces of cloth) together in long loose stitches; TACK[2] (3)

**baste**[2] *v* **basted, basting** [I;T] to pour melted fat over (meat that is cooking)

**bat**[1] /bæt/ *n* **1** a specially shaped wooden stick used for hitting the ball in games such as cricket, BASEBALL, and table tennis **2** → BATSMAN: *one of the best bats in the game* **3 off one's own bat** *infml* through one's own efforts; without being told or forced to: *Have you done all this work off your own bat?*

**bat**[2] *v* **-tt- 1** [T] to strike or hit with a BAT[1] (1): *to bat a ball* **2** [I] (in cricket and BASEBALL) to have a turn to bat: *Who's batting now?* **–batter** *n* –compare BATSMAN

**bat**[3] *n* **1** a flying mouselike animal that usu. eats insects or fruit and is active at night **2 as blind as a bat** *infml* not able to see well

**bat**[4] *v* **not bat an eyelid** *infml* to show no sign of one's feelings or surprise: *She heard the news without batting an eyelid.*

**batch** /bætʃ/ *n* [C +*sing./pl. v*] a quantity of material or number of things to be dealt with at one time: *a batch of bread/loaves*|*several batches of letters*

**bat·ed** /'beɪt$\frac{1}{2}$d/ *adj* **with bated breath** hardly breathing at all (because of fear, excitement, etc.): *He waited for the news with bated breath.*

**bath**[1] /bɑːθ‖bæθ/ *n* **baths** /bɑːðz, bɑːθs‖bæðz, bæθs/ **1** also **bathtub** *AmE*– a container in which one sits to wash the whole body **2** an act of washing one's whole body at one time: *to have (BrE)/take (AmE) a bath* –see also BATHS

**bath**[2] *v BrE* **1** [T] to give a bath to: *He's bathing the baby.* **2** [I] to have a bath: *She baths every day.*

USAGE One **baths** to get clean: *He* **baths** *every morning.*|*When does she* **bath** *the baby?* We can also say *He has a* **bath** (*BrE*) or *takes a* **bath** *(AmE) every morning*. One **bathes** something to make it clean in a medical way: *to* **bathe** *a wound*/**bathe** *one's eyes*. **Bathe** is also the word for swimming: *to* **bathe** *in the sea*|*to have a* **bathe** *in the river*. (Note the spelling of **bathing, bathed**. When they are formed from **bath** they are pronounced /'bɑːθɪŋ, bɑːθt|'bæ-/ but when they are formed from **bathe** they are pronounced /'beɪðɪŋ, beɪðd/.) The large container in which one **baths** is a **bath** (usu. **bathtub** *AmE*).

**bathe**[1] /beɪð/ *v* **bathed, bathing 1** [I] *esp. BrE* to go into a body of water or swimming pool for pleasure; go swimming: *I like to bathe in the sea.* **2** [T] to pour water or other liquid over; place in water or other liquid, esp. for medical reasons **3** [I] *AmE* for BATH[2] (2) **4** [T] to spread over with (or as if with) light, water, etc.: *The fields were bathed in sunlight.* –see BATH[2] (USAGE) **–bather** *n*

**bathe²** *n* [S] *BrE infml* the act of going into a body of water or swimming pool to bathe or swim: *Let's go for a bathe.*

**bath·ing** /ˈbeɪðɪŋ/ *n* [U] the act or practice of going into water to bathe or swim: *Mixed bathing* (=by men and women) *is allowed in this swimming pool.*

**bathing suit** /ˈ·· ·/ also **swimsuit, swimming costume**– *n BrE* the type of clothing worn by women for swimming

**bath·robe** /ˈbɑːθrəʊb‖ˈbæθ-/ *n* **1** a loose garment worn before and after bathing, esp. by men **2** *AmE* for DRESSING GOWN, esp. as worn by men

**bath·room** /ˈbɑːθrʊm, -ruːm‖ˈbæθ-/ *n* a room containing a BATH¹ (1) and/or a TOILET (1) –see picture on page 297

**baths** /bɑːðz, bɑːθs‖bæðz, bæθs/ *n* **baths** a place with a swimming pool or baths for public use: *the public baths*

**bat·man** /ˈbætmən/ *n* **-men** /mən/ *BrE* (in the armed services) an officer's personal servant

**bat·on** /ˈbætɒn‖bəˈtɑn, bə-/ *n* **1** a short thin stick used esp. by a leader of music (CONDUCTOR) to show the beat of the music **2** a short thick stick used as a weapon by a policeman

**bats·man** /ˈbætsmən/ *n* **-men** /mən/ the player in cricket who tries to hit the ball with a BAT¹ (1)

**bat·tal·i·on** /bəˈtælɪən/ *n* [+ *sing./pl. v*] a group of 500–1,000 soldiers made up of four or more companies (COMPANY (5)): *The second battalion is/are going abroad.*

**bat·ten** /ˈbætn/ *n* a long board used for fastening other pieces of wood

**batten down** sthg. *v adv* [T] (on ships) to fasten with boards of wood: *There's a storm coming, so let's* **batten down the hatches.** (=entrances to the lower parts of the ship)

**bat·ter¹** /ˈbætəʳ/ *v* [I;T] to beat hard and repeatedly, esp. causing damage, wounds, or loss of shape: *The police battered at the door.|a battered old hat|There has been an increase in* **baby-battering.** (=violence by parents against their small children)

**batter²** *n* [U] a mixture of flour, eggs, and milk, beaten together and used in cooking

**bat·ter·ing ram** /ˈ··· ·/ also **ram**– *n* (in former times) a large heavy log, used in war for breaking through the doors and walls of castles and towns

**bat·ter·y** /ˈbætəri/ *n* **-ies** **1** a piece of apparatus for producing electricity, consisting of a group of connected electric CELLS **2** a number of big guns, as on a warship or fort **3** a line of small boxes in which hens are kept and specially treated so that they will lay eggs frequently: *battery hens* **4** a group of similar things that are kept together: *They've got a battery of cooking pots in their kitchen.*

**bat·tle¹** /ˈbætl/ *n* an esp. short fight between enemies or opposing groups; a struggle: *the Battle of Waterloo|a battle for power in the government|They died in battle.* –compare WAR

**battle²** *v* **-tled, -tling** [I] to fight or struggle: *The firemen battled to control the flames.*

**bat·tle·field** /ˈbætlfiːld/ also **battleground** /-graʊnd/ *n* a place at which a battle is or has been fought

**bat·tle·ments** /ˈbætlmənts/ *n* [*the* P] a low wall round the flat roof of a castle or fort, with spaces to shoot through

**bat·tle·ship** /ˈbætlˌʃɪp/ -*n* the largest kind of warship, with the biggest guns and heaviest armour

**bau·ble** /ˈbɔːbəl/ *n* a cheap jewel

**baulk** /bɔːk, bɔːlk/ *n,v* → BALK

**baux·ite** /ˈbɔːksaɪt/ *n* [U] the clay (ORE) from which the metal ALUMINIUM is made

**bawd·y** /ˈbɔːdi/ *adj* **-ier, -iest** concerned with sex in a rude or funny way: *bawdy jokes* –**bawdily** *adv*

**bawl** /bɔːl/ *v* [I;T] to shout or cry in a loud, rough, ugly voice: *He bawled at me/for his dinner.|The captain bawled (out) an order.*

**bay¹** /beɪ/ *adj,n* (a horse whose colour is) reddish-brown

**bay²** also **bay tree**– *n* a tree like the LAUREL, whose leaves may be used in cooking

**bay³** *n* a part of a building; built-out part of a room: *In the library, the books on history are all kept in one bay.*

**bay⁴** *n* **hold/keep at bay** to keep someone or something some distance away: *He kept me at bay with a knife.*

**bay⁵** *n* a part of the sea or of a large lake enclosed in a curve of the land: *the Bay of Biscay*

**bay·o·net¹** /ˈbeɪənɨt, -net/ *n* a long knife fixed to the end of a soldier's gun (RIFLE)

**bayonet²** *v* **-neted** *or* **-netted, -neting** *or* **-netting** [T] to drive a BAYONET into

**ba·zaar** /bəˈzɑːʳ/ *n* **1** (in Eastern countries) a marketplace or a group of shops **2** (in English-speaking countries) a sale to get money for some good purpose: *a church/hospital bazaar*

**BBC** *n abbrev. for:* British Broadcasting Corporation; the British radio and television broadcasting company that is paid for by public money: *She works for the BBC.|It's on BBC tonight.* –compare ITV

**BC** *abbrev. for:* (in the year) before the birth of Christ: *Rome was begun in 753 BC.* –compare AD

**be¹** /bɪ; *strong* biː/ *v* [used as a helping verb with another verb]

| *present tense* | |
|---|---|
| *singular* | *plural* |
| *I* **am,** *I'm* | *We* **are,** *we're* |
| *You* **are,** *you're* | *You* **are,** *you're* |
| *He/She/It* **is** *he's/she's/it's* | *They* **are,** *They're* |
| *past tense* | |
| *singular* | *plural* |
| *I* **was** | *We* **were** |
| *You* **were** | *You* **were** |
| *He/She/It* **was** | *They* **were** |
| *past* PARTICIPLE | **been** |
| *present* PARTICIPLE | **being** |
| NEGATIVE *short forms* | **aren't, isn't, wasn't, weren't** |

For the pronunciation of these forms look them up in the dictionary at their own place.

**1** [+*v-ing*] (forms the continuous tenses of verbs): *I'm working now.|She was reading.|We're leaving tomorrow.* (=it is arranged) **2** (used with the past participle to form the passive of verbs): *Smoking* *is not permitted.|The money was found.|The house is being painted.* **3** [+*to-v*] **a** (shows what must happen): *All prisoners are to be* (=must be) *in bed by 10 o'clock.|You are not to smoke here.* (=you must not smoke) **b** (shows arrangements for the future): *We are to be married next week.|We were to be married last week, but I was ill.|What am I to do?* (=what should I/can I do?) **c** (shows possible future happenings): *If I were to go home what would you say?* –see also BEEN –SEE STUDY NOTES ON PAGE 386

**be²** *v* [used as a connecting verb] **1** (shows that something or someone is the same as the subject): *January is the first month of the year.* **2** (shows position or time): *The book is on the table.|The concert was last night.|Their party is* (=will take place) *on Saturday.* **3** to belong to a group or have a quality: *She's a doctor.|Horses are animals.|A knife is for cutting with.|You're right/wrong.* –see also BEEN

**be³** *v* [I] to exist: *There is the possibility that he will arrive late.|Once upon a time there was a beautiful princess.* –see also BEEN

**beach¹** /biːtʃ/ *n* a shore of an ocean, sea, or lake covered by sand, smooth stones, or larger pieces of rock –see SHORE¹ (USAGE)

**beach²** *v* [T] to run or drive (a boat, etc.) onto the shore

**beach ball** /'· ·/ *n* a large light ball, filled with air, for use at the BEACH

**beach·comb·er** /'biːtʃˌkəʊməʳ/ *n* a person who lives on or near the BEACH, and sometimes earns money by selling things found there

**bea·con** /'biːkən/ *n* **1** a signal fire on a hill, tower, or pole **2** a (flashing) light, to act as a guide or warning to sailors or airmen

**bead** /biːd/ *n* a small ball of glass or other material with a hole through it for a string or wire, worn with others on a thread, esp. round the neck, for decoration: *She was wearing a string of green beads.*|(fig.) *beads of blood/of* SWEAT¹ (1)

**bead·y** /'biːdi/ *adj* **-ier, -iest** (esp. of an eye) small, round, and shining, like a BEAD

**bea·gle** /'biːgəl/ *n* a smooth-haired dog with short legs and large ears, used esp. in the hunting of HARES

**beak** /biːk/ *n* the hard horny mouth of a bird

**bea·ker** /'biːkəʳ/ *n* **1** a drinking cup with a wide mouth and usu. no handle **2** a small glass cup shaped for pouring, as used in a chemical LABORATORY

**beam¹** /biːm/ *n* a large long heavy piece of wood, esp. as used in the framework of a building

**beam²** *n* **1** a line of light shining out from some bright object: *the bright beam of the car's front lights*|(fig.) *She opened the door with a beam* (=a bright look) *of welcome.* **2** radio waves sent out along a narrow path in one direction only, often to guide aircraft

**beam³** *v* **1** [I] (of the sun or other shining objects) to send out light (and heat) **2** [I] to smile brightly and happily: *beaming with satisfaction* **3** [T] to send out (esp. radio or television signals) in a certain direction using special apparatus: *The news was beamed to East Africa by* SATELLITE.

**bean** /biːn/ *n* **1** a seed of any of various upright climbing plants, esp. one that can be used as food **2** a plant bearing these seeds **3** a long container of these seeds (a POD), itself used as food when not yet fully grown **4** a seed of certain other plants, from which food or drink can be made: *coffee beans* **5 full of beans** *infml* full of active bodily strength and eagerness **6 spill the beans** *infml* to tell a secret, usu. unintentionally

**bear¹** /beəʳ/ *n* **bears** *or* **bear** a usu. large and heavy animal with thick rough fur that eats fruit and insects as well as flesh

**bear²** *v* **bore** /bɔːʳ‖bor/, **borne** /bɔːn‖born/, **bearing 1** [T] *fml* to carry from one place to another: *The bird seized the mouse and bore it off to its nest.*|(fig.) *He didn't do the job very well, but you must* **bear in mind** (=not forget) *that he was ill at the time.* **2** [T] to support: *Will the ice on the lake bear your weight?*|(fig.) *All the costs of the repairs will be borne* (=paid) *by our company.* **3** [T] to have or show: *The letter bears her signature.|What he says* **bears no relation** *to the truth.* (=it is very different from the truth) **4** [T+*to-v*/*v- ing*] to suffer without complaining: *She bore the pain with great courage.*|(fig.) *I can't bear* (=greatly dislike) *the smell of tobacco smoke.* –see USAGE **5** [T] to give birth to: *She bore/has borne three children.* –see BORN² (USAGE) **6** [I;T] to produce (a crop, fruit, or other product): *The tree is bearing a lot of apples this year.* **7** [I] to move in the stated direction: *Cross the field, bear left, and you'll soon reach the village.*

USAGE Compare **abide, bear, endure, stand, tolerate.** 1 **abide, bear, stand,** and **endure** are all used with "can" in questions and with NEGATIVE¹ (1) words to express great dislike, but **endure** is usu. only used about something really serious: *I can't* **abide/bear/stand** *strong coffee.|I can't* **endure** *talking to people who are* RACISTS. 2 **bear, endure,** and **stand** are also used for great bodily hardship; **endure** suggests pain that lasts a long time: *He* **bore/stood** *the pain as long as he could.|She had* **endured** *great pain for a number of years.* 3 **tolerate** is used of people or behaviour, but usu. not of suffering: *I find it hard to* **tolerate** *your rudeness.*

**bear down on/upon** sbdy./sthg. *v adv prep* [T] to come near threateningly: *The enemy ship bore down on our small boat.*

**bear on** sthg. also **bear upon** sthg.– *v prep* [T] to show some connection with: *How does your news bear on this case?* –see also BEARING (2)

**bear** sthg.↔ **out** *v adv* [T] to support the truth of: *The prisoner's story was borne out by his wife.*

**bear up** *v adv* [I] **1** [*under*] to show courage or strength by continuing (in spite of difficulties) **2** *BrE* for CHEER **up**

**bear with** sbdy./sthg. *v prep* [T] to show patience towards; PUT **up with**: *You must bear with his bad temper: he is very ill.*

**bear·a·ble** /'beərəbəl/ *adj* that can be borne or suffered: *The pain was just bearable.* –opposite **unbearable –bearably** *adv*

**beard** /bɪəd‖-ərd/ *n* hair on the lower parts of a man's face: *a tall man with a beard* –compare MOUSTACHE, WHISKERS; see picture on page 299 **bearded** *adj: a tall, bearded man|a grey-bearded old man*

**bear·er** /'beərəʳ/ *n* **1** a person who bears or carries: *Please help the bearer of this letter.|the flagbearer* **2** a person who helps to carry the body at a funeral

**bear·ing** /ˈbeərɪŋ/ *n* **1** [S;U] manner of holding one's body or way of behaving: *upright, proud bearing* **2** [S;U] connection with or influence on something: *What you have said has no bearing on the subject.* **3** [C] *tech* the part of a machine in which a turning rod is held, or which turns on a fixed rod –compare BALL BEARING **4** [C] *tech* a direction or angle as shown by a compass: *to take a (compass) bearing*|(fig.) *In all this mass of details I'm afraid I've rather* **lost my bearings.** (=become confused)

**beast** /biːst/ *n* **1** a four-footed (farm) animal **2** *derog* a person (or sometimes a thing) that one doesn't like: *a beast of a job*|*Her husband was a real beast.*

**beast·ly** /ˈbiːstli/ *adj* **-lier, -liest** *derog* that one does not like; very nasty or unpleasant: *a beastly person* –compare BESTIAL –**beastliness** *n* [U]

**beat**[1] /biːt/ *v* **beat, beaten** /biːtn/ *or* **beat, beating 1** [I;T] to hit repeatedly: *His father beat him/gave him a beating for being disobedient.*|*The police beat the door down in order to get into the house.*|(fig.) *The sun beat down all day.* **2** [T] to mix with regular blows of a fork, spoon, etc.: *Beat the eggs, then add the flour.* **3** [I;T] to move regularly: *You can hear its heart beating.*|*The bird beat its wings rapidly.* **4** [T] to defeat; do better than: *She beat her brother at tennis.*|(fig.) **It beats me** *how he can have done it.* (=I can't understand it) **5 beat about the bush**||also **beat around the bush** *AmE*– to delay talking about or considering the most important part of a subject **6 beat time** to make regular movements or noises by which the speed of music can be measured

**beat** sbdy.↔ **down** *v adv* [T] *infml* to persuade to reduce a price: *He wanted £5 for the dress, but I beat him down to £4.50.*

**beat** sthg.↔ **out** *v adv* [T] **1** to sound by beating: *The drummers beat out their music, and we all danced.* **2** to put out (a fire) by beating

**beat** sbdy.↔ **up** *v adv* [T] *infml* to wound severely by hitting: *The boys beat the old man up.*

**beat**[2] *n* **1** [C] a single stroke or blow, esp. as part of a group: *one beat of the drum every 60 seconds*|(fig.) *a heartbeat* **2** [S] a regular sound produced by or as if by repeated beating: *the beat of the drum* **3** [C; *the* S] the regular pattern of time in music: *Every member of the band must follow the beat.* **4** [C] the usual path followed by someone on duty (esp. a policeman)

**beat**[3] *adj* [F *no comp.*] *infml* very tired: *I'm (dead) beat after all that work!*

**beat·en** /ˈbiːtn/ *adj* [*no comp.*] **1** (of metal) made to take a certain shape by beating with a hammer: *a plate made of beaten gold* **2** given shape by the feet of those who pass along it: *We followed a well-beaten path through the forest.*|*Let's go somewhere* **off the beaten track** (=not well-known) *this summer.*

**beat·er** /ˈbiːtəʳ/ *n* **1** a tool or instrument used for beating: *an egg beater* **2** a person who drives wild birds or animals towards the guns of those waiting to shoot them

**be·at·i·fy** /biˈætʲ̥faɪ/ *v* **-fied, -fying** [T] (in the ROMAN CATHOLIC church) to declare (a dead person) officially blessed and holy –**beatification** /-fʲ̥keɪʃən/ *n* [C;U]

**beau·ti·cian** /bjuːˈtɪʃən/ *n* a person who gives beauty treatments (as to skin and hair)

**beau·ti·ful** /ˈbjuːtʲ̥fəl/ *adj* having beauty –**beautifully** *adv*

USAGE When used to describe a person's appearance, **beautiful** is a very strong word meaning "giving great pleasure to the senses". Its opposite is **ugly** or, even stronger, **hideous; plain** is a less *derog* way of saying **ugly. Pretty, handsome, good-looking,** and **attractive** all mean "pleasant to look at"; but **pretty** is only used of women and children, and **handsome** (usually) only of men. **Good-looking, handsome,** and **plain** are normally only used of people, but the other words can also be used of things: *a* **pretty** *garden*|*a* **hideous** *dress*

**beau·ti·fy** /ˈbjuːtʲ̥faɪ/ *v* **-fied, -fying** [T] to make beautiful

**beau·ty** /ˈbjuːti/ *n* **-ties 1** [U] qualities that give pleasure to the senses or lift up the mind or spirit: *a woman/a poem of great beauty* **2** [C] someone (usu. female) or something beautiful: *She is a great beauty.*|*the beauties of our city* **3** [C] *infml* something very good or fine: *That apple is a real beauty.* **4 the beauty (of something)** the advantage (of something): *The beauty of my idea is that it is so simple!*

**beauty spot** /ˈ·· ·/ *n* a place known for the beauty of its scenery

**bea·ver** /ˈbiːvəʳ/ *n* **-ver** *or* **-vers** [C;U] (the valuable fur of) a type of water and land animal of the rat family, which builds DAMS across streams

**be·calmed** /bɪˈkɑːmd/ *adj* (of a sailing ship) unable to move forward because of lack of wind

**be·cause** /bɪˈkɒz, bɪˈkəz||bɪˈkɔz, bɪˈkəz/ *conj* for the reason that: *I was angry because he was late.*|*"Why can't I go?" "Because you're too young."* –see REASON[1] (USAGE); see Study Notes on page 128

**because of** *prep* by reason of: *I came back because of the rain.* –see Study Notes on page 128

**beck** /bek/ *n* **at someone's/one's beck and call** always ready to do everything someone/one asks

**beck·on** /ˈbekən/ *v* [I;T] to make a silent sign, as with the finger, to call (someone): *She's beckoning (to) me.*|*She beckoned me to follow her.*

**be·come** /bɪˈkʌm/ *v* **-came** /bɪˈkeɪm/, **-come, -coming** /bɪˈkʌmɪŋ/ **1** to come to be: *He became king.*|*The weather became warmer.* **2** [T] *fml* to be right or fitting for: *Those words do not become a person in your position.*

**become of** sbdy./sthg. *v prep* [T] to happen to, often in a bad way: *Whatever will become of the boy if he keeps failing his examinations?*

USAGE Compare **become, come, go: Become** is the most formal, and can be used of people or things: *Mary* **became** *famous.*|*The sky* **became** *cloudy.*|*It* **became** *clear that he was lying.* People can **go** or **become** mad, blind, LAME[1] (1), brown (=from the sun) or grey (=have grey hair) but one cannot say **He* **went** *famous/angry.* One can use **go** to mean **become** about things: *The meat* **went** *bad.*|*Everything's* **going** *wrong.*|*The sky* **went** *cloudy.* Note also the use of **come** in the phrases: *Her dream* **came true.**|*Everything will* **come right** *in the end.* –see GET[1] (USAGE).

**be·com·ing** /bɪˈkʌmɪŋ/ *adj fml* **1** *apprec* (of colour, clothes, etc.) looking very well on the wearer: *Blue always looks very becoming on her.* **2** proper; suitable; right: *His behaviour during the meal was not very becoming.* –opposite **unbecoming** –**becomingly** *adv*

**bed**[1] /bed/ *n* **1** [C;U] an article of furniture to sleep on: *a room with two beds|It's time for bed/It's bedtime.|He helped me to* **make the bed.** (=make it ready for sleeping in) **2** [C] a surface that forms the base or bottom of something: *the bed of the river|the seabed* **3** [C] a piece of ground prepared for plants: *a flowerbed* **4** [C] a band of rock of a certain kind lying above or below others; STRATUM (1): *There's a bed of rock a few feet below the surface.* **5 a bed of roses** *infml* a happy comfortable state **6 get out of bed on the wrong side** *infml* to be in a bad temper

**bed**[2] *v* **-dd-** [T] **1** to fix on a base (or beneath the surface); EMBED: *The machine is bedded in cement.* **2** to plant in a bed of soil: *These young plants will soon be ready for bedding (out).*

**bed down** *v adv* **1** [T] (=**bed** sbdy./sthg. **down**) to make (a person or animal) comfortable for the night **2** [I] to make oneself comfortable for the night: *I'll bed down on these chairs.*

**bed and board** /ˌ· · '·/ *n* [U] lodging and food

**bed·clothes** /'bedkləuðz, -kləuz/ *n* [P] the sheets, covers, etc., put on a bed

**bed·ding** /'bedɪŋ/ *n* [U] **1** materials on which a person or animal can sleep: *This dried grass will make good bedding for the animals.* **2**→ BEDCLOTHES

**be·deck** /bɪ'dek/ *v* [T *with*] *fml* to decorate: *The cars were all bedecked with flowers for the ceremony.*

**be·dev·il** /bɪ'devəl/ *v* **-ll-** *BrE*||**-l-** *AmE* [T] to trouble greatly: *The committee's work was bedevilled by arguments.* –**bedevilment** *n* [U]

**bed·lam** /'bedləm/ *n* [S;U] *infml* a wild noisy place or activity

**bed·pan** /'bedpæn/ *n* a low wide vessel used by a sick person for emptying the bowels without getting out of bed –compare POT[1] (3)

**be·drag·gled** /bɪ'drægəld/ *adj* with the clothes and hair in disorder: *a bedraggled appearance*

**bed·rid·den** /'bedˌrɪdn/ *adj* unable to get out of bed because of illness or old age

**bed·room** /'bedrum, -ruːm/ *n* a room for sleeping in –see picture on page 297

**bed·side** /'bedsaɪd/ *n* the side of a bed: *He was called to the bedside of his sick father.|a bedside lamp*

**bed·sit·ter** /ˌ· '··/ also **bed-sitting room** /ˌ· '·· ·/ *fml*, **bed-sit** /'· ˌ·/ *infml*– *n BrE* a room used for both living and sleeping in –see HOUSE (USAGE)

**bed·spread** /'bedspred/ *n* a decorative cloth spread over a bed

**bee** /biː/ *n* **1** a stinging insect that makes HONEY and lives in groups **2 a bee in one's bonnet** *infml* a fixed idea: *He has a bee in his bonnet about health foods.*

**beech** /biːtʃ/ *n* [C;U] (the wood of) a tree with a smooth grey trunk, spreading branches, and dark green or copper-coloured leaves –sounds like **beach**

**beef**[1] /biːf/ *n* [U] the meat of farm cattle –see MEAT (USAGE)

**beef**[2] *v* [I *about*] *infml often derog* to complain (about): *Stop beefing (about pay) and do some work!*

**beef·y** /'biːfi/ *adj* **-ier, -iest** *infml* (of a person) big, strong, and perhaps fat

**bee·hive** /'biːhaɪv/ *n*→ HIVE

**bee·line** /'biːlaɪn/ *n* **make a beeline for** *infml* to go quickly along a straight direct course for: *The hungry boy made a beeline for his dinner.*

**been** /biːn, bɪn||bɪn/ *v* **1** *past participle of* BE **2** (to have) gone and come back from: *Have you ever been to India?* **3** *BrE* (to have) arrived and left: *I see the postman hasn't been yet.* –see GO[1] (USAGE)

**beer** /bɪəʳ/ *n* **1** [C;U] (a glass of) a bitter alcoholic drink made from grain: *Do you like beer?|We had several beers.* **2** [U] (*in comb*) any of several kinds of drink, usu. non-alcoholic, made from roots or plants: GINGER[1] *beer* –**beery** *adj: a beery smell*

**bees·wax** /'biːzwæks/ *n* [U] wax made by bees, used for making furniture polish, candles, etc.

**beet** /biːt/ *n* **1** also **sugar beet**– a plant which grows under the ground and from which **beet sugar** is obtained **2** *AmE* for BEETROOT

**bee·tle** /'biːtl/ *n* an insect with hard wing coverings –compare BUG[1] (1)

**beet·root** /'biːtruːt/ *BrE*||**beet** *AmE*– *n* **beetroot** *or* **beetroots** [C;U] a plant with a large round red root, which is cooked and eaten as a vegetable: *a beetroot* SALAD

**be·fall** /bɪ'fɔːl/ *v* **-fell** /bɪ'fel/, **-fallen** /bɪ'fɔːlən/, **-falling** [I;T] *fml* (usu. of something bad) to happen (to), esp. as if by fate: *Some misfortune must have befallen them.*

**be·fore**[1] /bɪ'fɔːʳ||bɪ'for/ *adv* [*no comp.*] at an earlier time: *Haven't I seen you before?* –compare AFTER[2]; see AGO (USAGE)

**before**[2] *prep* **1** earlier than: *before 1937|the day before yesterday* (=two days ago)|*He got there before me.* **2** in front of; ahead of: *Your name comes before mine in the list.|You will have to swear before the judge.* **3** in a more important position than: *to put quality before quantity* –compare AFTER[1]

**before**[3] *conj* **1** earlier than the time when: *Say goodbye before you go.* –compare AFTER[3] **2** more willingly than; rather than: *I will die before I tell you what you want to know.*

**be·fore·hand** /bɪ'fɔːhænd||-'for-/ *adv* [*no comp.*] before something else happens: *We knew they were coming, so we bought some food beforehand.*

**be·friend** /bɪ'frend/ *v* [T] *fml* to act as a friend to (someone younger, poorer, or weaker): *He befriended me when I was young.*

**beg** /beg/ *v* **-gg- 1** [I;T +*that/to-v/of, for*] to ask humbly for (food, money, etc.): *He lives by begging (for money).|to beg a favour (of someone)|to beg that one (should/may) be allowed to go|He begged me to stay.* **2** [T +*to-v*] *fml* to allow oneself: *I beg to point out that your facts are incorrect.*

**beg·gar**[1] /'begəʳ/ *n* **1** a person who lives by BEGging (1) **2** *infml* a fellow: *He's a cheerful little beggar, your son!* **3 Beggars can't be choosers** *infml* If you are asking for help, you must take what you are offered

**beggar**[2] *v* [T] *fml* to make very poor: *He was beggared by spending so much on drinking.*

**beg·gar·ly** /'begəli||-ərli/ *adj* much too little; MISERLY

**be·gin** /bɪ'gɪn/ *v* **began** /bɪ'gæn/, **begun** /bɪ'gʌn/, **beginning** [I;T +*to-v/v-ing*] to start; take the first step: *She began working here in 1962.|to begin by dancing/with a story/on a new book/at the beginning|It began to rain.|We can't go. To begin with,* (=the first reason is) *it's too cold. Besides, we've no money.* –see START[1] (USAGE)

**be·gin·ner** /bɪ'gɪnəʳ/ *n* a person who has very little experience of some activity –compare STARTER

**be·gin·ning** /bɪ'gɪnɪŋ/ *n* [C;U] the start; starting point; origin: *She knows that subject from beginning to end.* (=completely)|at/*in the beginning*

**be·grudge** /bɪ'grʌdʒ/ *v* **-grudged, -grudging** [T +*v-ing*] → GRUDGE[1]

**be·guile** /bɪ'gaɪl/ *v* **-guiled, -guiling** [T] *fml* **1** [*into, out of*] to deceive; cheat: *He beguiled me into lending him my bicycle.* **2** to charm: *Her eyes and voice beguiled me.* **–beguiling** *adj*

**be·half** /bɪ'hɑːf||bɪ'hæf/ *n* **on behalf of someone/on someone's behalf** also **in behalf of someone/in someone's behalf** *AmE*– (acting, speaking, etc.) for someone; in the interests of someone: *The President is ill, so I'm speaking on his behalf.*

**be·have** /bɪ'heɪv/ *v* **-haved, -having** [I] **1** to act; bear oneself: *She behaved with great courage.*|(fig.) *My car has been behaving well since it was repaired.* **2** [I;T] to bear (oneself) in a socially-acceptable or polite way: *Behave (yourself)!|a well-behaved/badly-behaved child*

**be·hav·iour** *BrE*||**behavior** *AmE* /bɪ'heɪvɪəʳ/ *n* [U] **1** way of behaving **2 be on one's best behaviour** to try to show one's best manners

**be·head** /bɪ'hed/ *v* [T] to cut off the head of, esp. as a punishment; DECAPITATE

**be·hind**[1] /bɪ'haɪnd/ *adv* [*no comp.*] **1** towards or at the back: *a house with a garden behind* –compare FRONT[1] **2** where something or someone was before: *I can't unlock the car because I've left the keys behind.|They went for a walk but I stayed behind to look after the baby.* **3** late; slow; BEHINDHAND: *We're a month behind with the rent.* (=we should have paid it a month ago)

**behind**[2] *prep* **1** towards or at the back of: *She ran out from behind a tree.* –see Study Notes on page 474 **2** less good than; below: *We're three points behind the team in first place.* **3** in support of; encouraging: *We're all behind you* (=we all agree with you) *in this decision.*

**behind**[3] *n euph infml* the part of the body that a person sits on; BUTTOCKS: *a kick in the behind*

**be·hind·hand** /bɪ'haɪndhænd/ *adj,adv* [*with, in*] *fml* late; slow: *We're a month behindhand with the rent.*

**be·hold** /bɪ'həʊld/ *v* **-held** /bɪ'held/, **-holding** [T] *lit & old use* to have in sight; see **–beholder** *n: Beauty is in the eye of the beholder.*

**beige** /beɪʒ/ *n,adj* [U] a pale dull yellowish brown

**be·ing** /'biːɪŋ/ *n* **1** [U] existence; life: *When did the club first come into being?* **2** [C] a living thing, esp. a person: *a human being*

**be·lat·ed** /bɪ'leɪtɪ̣d/ *adj* delayed; arriving too late **–belatedly** *adv*

**belch** /beltʃ/ *v* **1** [I] (of a person) to pass wind noisily from the stomach out through the throat **2** [T *out*] to throw out with force or in large quantities: *Chimneys belch (out) smoke.* **–belch** *n: He gave a loud belch.*

**bel·fry** /'belfri/ *n* **-fries** a tower for a bell, esp. on a church

**be·lie** /bɪ'laɪ/ *v* **-lied, -lying** [T] *fml* to give a false idea of: *Her smile belied her real feelings of displeasure.*

**be·lief** /bɪ̣'liːf/ *n* **1** [S;U *in*] the feeling that something is true or that something really exists: *(a) belief in God|my belief that he is right|His story is* **beyond belief.** (=too strange to be believed) **2** [S;U *in*] trust; a feeling that someone or something is good or able to be depended on: *The failure of the operation has shaken* (=made less strong) *my belief in doctors.* **3** [C] something believed; an idea which is considered true, often one which is part of a system of ideas: *my religious beliefs*

**be·lie·va·ble** /bɪ̣'liːvəbəl/ *adj* capable of being believed –see also UNBELIEVABLE **–believably** *adv*

**be·lieve** /bɪ̣'liːv/ *v* **-lieved, -lieving** [T not *be +v-ing*] **1** to consider to be true or honest: *to believe someone* –see also DISBELIEVE **2** [+*(that)*] to hold as an opinion; suppose: *I believe him to have done it/believe that he did it.*

**believe in** sbdy./sthg. *v prep* **1** [T] to accept as true the existence of: *Do you believe in fairies?* **2** to have faith or trust in: *Christians believe in Jesus.* **3** to consider (something) to be of worth: *Jim believes in going for a run every morning.*

**be·lit·tle** /bɪ'lɪtl/ *v* **-tled, -tling** [T] *fml* to cause to seem small or unimportant: *Don't belittle yourself/your efforts.*

**bell** /bel/ *n* a round hollow metal vessel, which makes a ringing sound when struck

**bell-bot·toms** /'· ˌ··/ *n* [P] trousers with legs that become wider at the bottom –see PAIR[1] (USAGE)

**belle** /bel/ *n* a popular and attractive girl or woman: *the belle of the* BALL (=the prettiest girl at the dance)

**bel·li·cose** /'belɪkəʊs/ *adj fml* warlike; ready to quarrel or fight

**bel·lig·er·ent** /bɪ̣'lɪdʒərənt/ *adj* having or showing anger and readiness to fight: *You said some very belligerent things–were you trying to start a fight?* **–belligerency** *n* [U]

**bel·low** /'beləʊ/ *v* **1** [I] to make the loud deep hollow sound typical of a BULL (1) **2** [I;T] to shout (something) in a deep voice: *to bellow (out) with pain|to bellow (out) orders* **–bellow** *n*

**bel·lows** /'beləʊz/ *n* **bellows** an instrument used for blowing air into a fire, ORGAN (3), etc. –see PAIR[1] (USAGE)

**bel·ly** /'beli/ *n* **-lies 1** *infml* the part of the human body, between the chest and the legs, which contains the stomach and bowels **2** a surface or object curved like this part of the body: *the belly of the plane* **3 -bellied** having a BELLY of the stated type: *fat-bellied*

**bel·ly·ache** /'beli-eɪk/ *v* **-ached, -aching** [I *about*] *infml often derog* to complain, esp. without good cause: *Stop bellyaching and get on with the job!*

**belly but·ton** /'·· ˌ··/ *n infml* for NAVEL (1)

**bel·ly·ful** /'belifʊl/ *n* [S] *infml* too much: *I've had a bellyful of your complaints.*

**be·long** /bɪ'lɒŋ||bɪ'lɔŋ/ *v* [I] to be in the right place: *That chair belongs in the other room.*

**belong to** sbdy./sthg. *v prep* [T *no pass.*] **1** to be the property of: *That dictionary belongs to me.* **2** to be a member of; be connected with: *What party do you belong to?*

**be·long·ings** /bɪ'lɒŋɪŋz‖bɪ'lɔŋ-/ *n* [P] those things which belong to one, which are one's property: *She lost all her belongings in the fire.*

**be·loved** /bɪ'lʌvd/ *adj,n* [S] (a person who is) dearly loved: *beloved by/of her friends|His beloved (wife) died.*

**be·low**[1] /bɪ'ləu/ *adv* [*no comp.*] **1** in a lower place; lower: *I live on the fifth floor; he lives on the floor below.|the rank of captain and below* (=of lower rank)|*children of seven and below* (=younger) –opposite **above**; compare UNDERNEATH **2** under the surface: *miners working below* (=under the earth)|*The captain told the sailors to go below.* (=to a lower DECK (1) of the ship) **3** on a later page or lower on the same page: *See p. 85 below.* –opposite **above**

**below**[2] *prep* lower than; under: *below the knee|a mile below the village|children below the age of seven* (=younger than seven)|*A captain is below a general.* (=lower in rank)|*below the surface of the water* –opposite **above**; compare UNDER[2], BENEATH[2] –see Study Notes on page 474

**belt**[1] /belt/ *n* **1** a band worn around the waist: *a leather belt* **2** a long circular piece of leather or other such material used for driving a machine or for carrying materials –see also FAN BELT **3** an area that has some special physical quality: *the Green Belt* (=an area of farms and parks around a city) **4 hit below the belt** *infml* to give an unfair blow (to) or attack unfairly **5 tighten one's belt** *infml* to try to live on less money: *Because of unemployment many people had to tighten their belts.*

**belt**[2] *v* **1** [T] to fasten with a belt: *She belted (up) her raincoat.* **2** [T] to hit with a belt: *Jones really belted his son!* **3** [T] *infml* to hit very hard, esp. with the hand: *I belted him in the eye.* **4** [I] *infml* to travel fast: *really belting along/down the* MOTORWAY

**be·moan** /bɪ'məun/ *v* [T] *fml* to feel very sorry for oneself because of: *He bemoaned his fate.*

**be·mused** /bɪ'mju:zd/ *adj* having or showing inability to think properly: *a bemused expression|bemused by/with all the questions*

**bench** /bentʃ/ *n* **1** [C] a long usu. wooden seat for two or more people: *a park bench* **2** [S] a judge or his seat in court: *The bench declared....|to speak from the bench* **3** [*the* U +*sing./pl.v*)] judges as a group: *What does/do the bench feel about this?* **4** [C] a long worktable

**bend**[1] /bend/ *v* **bent** /bent/, **bending 1** [I;T] to (cause to) move or be shaped in a curve or angle: *to bend the wire|*(fig.) *She is very firm about it: I cannot bend her into changing her mind.* **2** to (cause to) slope or lean away from an upright position: *to bend over/down/forward/back|bent down with age* –see picture on page 669 **3** [T] to direct (one's efforts): *He bent his mind to the job.* –see also BENT[2], BENT ON

**bend**[2] *n* **1** the act or action of bending or the state of being bent **2** something that is bent: *a bend in the road/river* **3 round the bend** *infml, often humor* mad: *He really drives me round the bend!*

**be·neath**[1] /bɪ'ni:θ/ *adv* [*no comp.*] *fml* below; underneath: *He looked down from the mountain to the valley beneath.* –compare BELOW[1], UNDER[1]

**beneath**[2] *prep* **1** below; so as to be covered or sheltered by: *The ship sank beneath the waves.* **2** *fml* not worthy of: *Such behaviour is beneath you.* –compare BELOW[2], UNDER[2]

**ben·e·dic·tion** /ˌbenˈdɪkʃən/ *n* (a prayer or religious service giving) a blessing

**ben·e·fac·tion** /ˌbenˈfækʃən/ *n* [C;U] doing good or giving money for a good purpose; money so given

**ben·e·fac·tor** /'benˌfæktəʳ/ *n* a person who does good or who gives money for a good purpose

**be·nef·i·cent** /bɪ'nefsənt/ *adj fml apprec* doing good; kind –**beneficence** *n* [U]

**ben·e·fi·cial** /ˌbenˈfɪʃəl/ *adj* (of non-living things) helpful; useful: *His holiday has had a beneficial effect.* –**beneficially** *adv*

**ben·e·fi·cia·ry** /ˌbenˈfɪʃəri‖-'fɪʃieri/ *n* **-ries** the receiver of a BENEFIT (1), esp. a person who receives money or property left by someone who has died

**ben·e·fit**[1] /'benfɪt/ *n* **1** [U] advantage; profit; good effect: *She had the benefit of a good education.|I've done it for his benefit.|It is of great benefit to everyone.* **2** [C;U] money provided by the government as a right, esp. to people who are sick or unemployed: *collecting unemployment benefit|sickness benefits* **3 benefit of the doubt** favourable consideration in the absence of complete proof of wrongness or guilt: *We must give him the benefit of the doubt until we are certain he's guilty.*

**benefit**[2] *v* **-fited, -fiting** [T] *fml* (of non-living things) to be useful or profitable to: *Such foolish behaviour will not benefit your case.*

**benefit from/by** sbdy./sthg. *v prep* [T] to gain advantage from; receive BENEFIT from: *Who will benefit from the old man's death?*

**be·nev·o·lent** /bˈnevələnt/ *adj* having or showing the desire to do good and help others –see also MALEVOLENT –**benevolence** *n* [U] –**benevolently** *adv*

**be·nign** /bɪ'naɪn/ *adj* having or showing a kind or harmless nature: *A benign* TUMOUR *will not cause you harm.* –compare MALIGNANT (2) –**benignly** *adv*

**bent**[1] /bent/ *adj BrE infml* **1** dishonest; allowing oneself to be influenced by money or gifts (BRIBES): *a bent* COPPER (=policeman) **2** → HOMOSEXUAL –opposite **straight**

**bent**[2] *n* [*for*] special natural skill or cleverness (in): *She has a natural bent for art.*

**bent**[3] *v past tense and participle of* BEND

**bent on** also **bent upon**– *adj* [F +*v-ing*] with one's mind set on; determined on: *She seems bent on becoming a musician.*

**be·queath** /bɪ'kwi:ð, bɪ'kwi:θ/ *v* [T *to*] *fml* to give or pass on to others after death: *They bequeathed him a lot of money.* –**bequest** /bɪ'kwest/ *n: a bequest of £5,000 to his children*

**be·reave** /b'ri:v/ *v* **bereaved** *or* **bereft** /b'reft/, **bereaving** [T *of*] *fml* to take away, esp. by death: *He was bereaved (of his wife) last year.|a bereaved mother* (=one whose child has died) –**bereavement** *n* [U]: *Bereavement is often a time of great grief.*

**be·reft** /b'reft/ *adj* [F *of*] completely without: *bereft of all hope*

**be·ret** /'bereɪ‖bə'reɪ/ *n* a round usu. woollen cap with a tight headband and a soft full flat top

**ber·ry** /'beri/ *n* **-ries** a small soft fruit

**ber·serk** /bɜːˈsɜːk, bə-‖bɜrˈsɜrk, ˈbɜrsɜrk/ *adj* [F] mad with violent anger: *My husband will go berserk if he finds you here.*

**berth¹** /bɜːθ‖bɜrθ/ *n* **1** a place where a ship can stop and be tied up, as in a harbour **2** a sleeping place in a ship or train **3 give someone/something a wide berth** *infml* to stay at a safe distance from someone or something dangerous or unpleasant

**berth²** *v* [I;T] **a** (of a ship) to come into port to be tied up **b** to bring (a ship) into port to be tied up

**be·seech** /bɪˈsiːtʃ/ *v* **besought** /bɪˈsɔːt/ *or* **beseeched, beseeching** [T] *fml or lit* to ask eagerly and anxiously: *He besought a favour of the judge.*

**be·set** /bɪˈset/ *v* **beset, besetting** [T *usu. pass.*] to trouble from all directions; attack without ceasing: *The plan was beset with difficulties.*

**be·side** /bɪˈsaɪd/ *prep* **1** by the side of; next to: *a town beside the sea* **2** compared with: *This year's profits don't look very good beside last year's results.* **3 beside oneself (with)** almost mad (with): *The children were beside themselves with excitement.* **4 beside the point** having nothing to do with the main point or question: *How much it costs is beside the point.* –see BESIDES² (USAGE)

**be·sides¹** /bɪˈsaɪdz/ *adv* [*no comp.*] in addition; also: *I don't want to go; (and) besides, I'm tired.*|*This car belongs to Mrs Smith; she has two others besides.*

**besides²** *prep* as well as; in addition to: *There were three other people at the meeting besides Mr Day.* –see Study Notes on page 128

USAGE **Besides** means "as well as" but **except** means "leaving out; but not". So *All of us passed* **besides** *John* means that John passed too, but *All of us passed* **except** *John* means that John did not pass.

**be·siege** /bɪˈsiːdʒ/ *v* **-sieged, -sieging** [T] to surround with armed forces: (fig.) *The crowd besieged the minister with questions about their taxes.*

**be·sot·ted** /bɪˈsɒtɪ̇d‖bɪˈsɑ-/ *adj* [F *with*] made dull or foolish: *besotted with drink/love/power*

**be·sought** /bɪˈsɔːt/ *v past tense and participle of* BESEECH

**best¹** /best/ *adj* (SUPERLATIVE² *of* GOOD) **1** the highest in quality; the most good: *the best tennis-player in the world*|*She's my best friend.* –compare WORST¹ **2 the best part of** most of: *the best part of a year*

**best²** *adv* (SUPERLATIVE² *of* WELL³) **1** in the best way; most well: *The one who does best will get the prize.* **2** to the best degree; most: *the best-loved singer*|*Tuesday will suit me best.* **3 as best one can** as well as one can **4 had best**‖also **would best** *AmE*–→ **had** BETTER² (3) –compare WORST²

**best³** *n* [S] **1** the most good thing or part; the greatest degree of good: *Only the best is good enough.* **2** one's best effort or state: *He did his best/tried his best to finish it.*|*to look one's best*|*I'm never* **at my best** *early in the morning.* **3 one's (Sunday) best** one's best clothes **4 All the best!** (*used when saying good-bye*) I wish you success and happiness! **5 at (the) best** if the best happens: *At best the company will lose money this year–at worst it may have to close down.* –compare WORST³ **6 make the best of** to do as well as one can with (something not very good): *to make the best of a bad job*

**bes·ti·al** /ˈbestɪəl‖ˈbestʃəl/ *adj derog* **1** (of human beings and their behaviour) like a wild animal **2** very cruel; BRUTAL: *bestial cruelty* –compare BEASTLY –**bestially** *adv* –**bestiality** /ˌbestɪˈælɪ̇ti‖ˌbestʃɪ-/ *n* [U]

**best man** /ˌ· ˈ·/ *n* (at a marriage ceremony) the friend and attendant of the man who is to be married (BRIDEGROOM) –compare BRIDESMAID

**be·stow** /bɪˈstəʊ/ *v* [T *on, upon*] *fml* to give: *Several gifts were bestowed on the royal visitors.* –**bestowal** *n* [U]

**best·sel·ler** /ˌ· ˈ··/ *n* something (esp. a book) that sells in very large numbers

**bet¹** /bet/ *n* **1** an agreement to risk money on the result of a future event: *I've made a bet that my party will win the next election.*|*to win/lose a bet* **2** a sum of money so risked: *a £5 bet*

**bet²** *v* **bet** *or* **betted, betting** [I;T +(*that*)/*on*] **1** to risk (money) on the result of a future event: *I bet (you) (£5) that they'll win the next election.*|*I bet on the wrong horse–it lost the race!* **2 I bet** *infml* I'm sure: *I bet it rains/will rain tomorrow!*

**be·tide** /bɪˈtaɪd/ *v lit* **Woe betide (you, him,** etc.) you, he, etc., will be in trouble: *Woe betide him if he's late!*

**be·tray** /bɪˈtreɪ/ *v* **-trayed, -traying** [T] **1** [*to*] to be disloyal or unfaithful to: *I thought he would be too loyal to betray his friends!* **2** [*to*] *fml* to give away or make known (esp. a secret): *He betrayed the secret to his friends.* **3** [+*that*/*to*] to show the real feelings or intentions of: *Her face betrayed her nervousness/betrayed (the fact) that she was nervous/betrayed what she was thinking.* –**betrayer** *n*

**be·tray·al** /bɪˈtreɪəl/ *n* [C;U] (an example of) the act of BETRAYing: *a betrayal of my principles*

**be·troth** /bɪˈtrəʊð, bɪˈtrəʊθ/ *v* [T *to*] *becoming rare* to promise to give (oneself) in marriage –**betrothal** /bɪˈtrəʊðəl/ *n* [U]

**bet·ter¹** /ˈbetəʳ/ *adj* **1** (COMPARATIVE² *of* GOOD²) higher in quality; more good: *Their house is better than ours.*|*I'm worse at sums than Jean, but better at history.* **2** (COMPARATIVE² *of* WELL⁵) **a** improved in health: *I'm feeling a little better today.* **b** [*no comp.*] completely well again after an illness: *Now that he's better he can play football again.* **3 one's better half** *infml humor* one's wife or husband **4 the better part of** more than half: *I haven't seen him for the better part of a month!* –compare WORSE¹

**better²** *adv* (COMPARATIVE² *of* WELL³) **1** in a better way: *He swims better than he used to.* **2** to a greater degree: *She knows the story better than I do.* **3 had better** ought to; should: *You'd better go home now.*|*I'd better not tell him.* –compare WORSE²

**better³** *n* **1 a change for the better** a change with good results **2 get the better of** to defeat (someone) or deal successfully with (a difficulty): *to get the better of one's opponents* –compare WORSE³

**better⁴** *v* [I;T] to (cause to) improve (on): *He wants to better his record for running the mile.*|*Living conditions have bettered a great deal.* –compare WORSEN

**be·tween¹** /bɪˈtwiːn/ *prep* **1** (used to show that two things are separated): *between five and six o'clock*|*You shouldn't eat between meals.*|*There's a regular air service between London and Paris. –see Study Notes on page 474* **2** (used when things are shared by two or more): *Divide the money between the two of them.*|*Between us we can finish the job in* *an hour.* **3 between you and me** without anyone else knowing; privately: *Between you and me, (I think) he's rather dishonest.*

USAGE Compare **among** and **between: Between** should only be followed by two people, things, etc., and **among** by three or more: *Divide it* **between** *the two children*/**among** *all the children.* However, we always use **between,** not **among,** when we speak of an exact position in the middle of several things: *Ecuador lies* **between** *Colombia, Peru, and the Pacific Ocean.*

**between²** *adv* **1** in or into a space, or period of time, that is between: *I ate breakfast and dinner but nothing between.* **2 few and far between** *infml* rare and infrequent

**bev·el** /ˈbevəl/ *v* **-ll-** *BrE*‖**-l-** *AmE* [T] to make a sloping edge on (wood or glass) **–bevel** *n*

**bev·er·age** /ˈbevərɪdʒ/ *n fml* a liquid for drinking: *We sell hot beverages.* (=tea, coffee, etc.)|*an alcoholic beverage*

**be·wail** /bɪˈweɪl/ *v* [T] *fml* to express deep sorrow for, esp. by or as if by weeping

**be·ware** /bɪˈweəʳ/ *v* [I;T *of*] to be very careful

USAGE **Beware** is only used in giving or reporting warnings, and its form does not change: **Beware** *of the dog.*|*You must* **beware of fast traffic.**

**be·wil·der** /bɪˈwɪldəʳ/ *v* [T] to confuse: *Big city traffic bewilders me.*|*a bewildering mass of details* **–bewilderment** *n* [U]

**be·witch** /bɪˈwɪtʃ/ *v* [T] **1** to have a magic effect, often harmful, on **2** to charm as if by magic: *a bewitching smile* –compare ENCHANT

**be·yond¹** /bɪˈjɒnd‖bɪˈjɑnd/ *adv* on or to the further side; further: *I will go with you to the bridge, but not a step beyond.*|(fig.) *"...to prepare for the changes of the 1970s and beyond"* (SEU W.)

**beyond²** *prep* **1** on or to the further side of: *What lies beyond those mountains?* **2** past the limits of: *The fruit was beyond my reach.*|*It's quite beyond me* (=too hard for me to understand) *why she married him.* **3** besides; except for: *I own nothing beyond the clothes on my back.*|*I can't tell you anything beyond what you know already.*

**bi·as¹** /ˈbaɪəs/ *n* **-ases** [C;U] **1** a tendency to be in favour of or against something or someone; PREJUDICE¹ (1, 2): *a bias towards/against the government* **2** a tendency of mind: *Her scientific bias showed itself in early childhood.*

**bias²** *v* **-s-** *or* **-ss-** [T] to cause to form favourable or unfavourable opinions without enough information to judge fairly; PREJUDICE² (1): *His background biases him against foreigners.* –see also UNBIASED

**bib** /bɪb/ *n* a cloth or plastic shield tied under a child's chin to protect its clothes when eating

**bi·ble** /ˈbaɪbəl/ *n* [C; *the* S] (*usu. cap.*) (a copy of) the holy book of the Christians and the Jews **–biblical** /ˈbɪblɪkəl/ *adj*

**bib·li·og·ra·phy** /ˌbɪbliˈɒgrəfi‖-ˈɑg-/ *n* **-phies** a list of writings on a subject, esp. a list of all writings used in the preparation of a book or article

**bi·car·bon·ate** /baɪˈkɑːbənət, -neɪt‖-ˈkɑr-/ also **bicarbonate of soda** /·ˌ··· ·ˈ··/ also **bicarb** /ˈbaɪkɑːb‖-kɑrb/ *infml*– *n* [U] a chemical substance used esp. in baking and as a medicine

**bi·cen·te·na·ry** /ˌbaɪsenˈtiːnəri‖-ˈtenəri, -ˈsentəneri/ *n* **-ries** the day or year exactly 200 years after a particular event: *The company's bicentenary was in 1974.*

**bi·cen·ten·ni·al** /ˌbaɪsenˈtenɪəl/ *n AmE* for BICENTENARY

**bi·ceps** /ˈbaɪseps/ *n* **biceps** the large muscle on the front of the upper arm

**bick·er** /ˈbɪkəʳ/ *v* [I *about, over*] to quarrel, esp. about small matters: *The two children were always bickering (with each other) (over/about their toys).*

**bi·cy·cle¹** /ˈbaɪsɪkəl/ also **cycle, bike** *infml*– *n* a two-wheeled vehicle which one rides by pushing its PEDALS with the feet: *She goes to work on her bicycle/***by bicycle**. –see TRANSPORT (USAGE)

**bicycle²** also **cycle, bike** *infml*– *v* **-cled, -cling** [I] to travel by bicycle

**bid¹** /bɪd/ *v* **bid, bidding** [I;T] **1** to offer (a price) whether for payment or acceptance, as at an AUCTION: *She bid £5 for the book.*|*What am I bid for this old book?* (=what will people bid for it?) **2** (in card games) to make a BID² (3): *I bid two* SPADES³. **–bidder** *n*

**bid²** *n* **1** an offer to pay a certain price, esp. at an AUCTION : *a bid of £5 for that old book* **2** an offer to do some work at a certain price; TENDER³ (1): **Bids** *for building the bridge* **were invited** *from British and American firms.* **3** (a chance or turn to make) a declaration of the number of games (TRICKS) a cardplayer says he/she intends to win: *a bid of two* SPADES³ **4** an attempt to get or win: *The criminal made* **a bid for freedom** *by trying to run away.*

**bid³** *v* **bade** /bæd, beɪd/ *or* **bid, bidden** /ˈbɪdn/ *or* **bid, bidding** *old use or lit* **1** [T *to*] to say (a greeting or goodbye to someone): *He bid me good morning as he passed.* **2** [T] to order or tell (someone to do something): *She bade him come.*

**bid·ding** /ˈbɪdɪŋ/ *n* [U] **1** order; command (esp. in the phrases **at one's bidding, do someone's bidding**) **2** the act or action of making BIDS

**bide** /baɪd/ *v* **bode** /bəʊd/ *or* **bided, bided, biding**: **bide one's time** to wait, usu. for a long time, until the right moment: *He seems to be doing nothing, but really he's just biding his time.*

**bi·det** /ˈbiːdeɪ‖bɪˈdeɪ/ *n* a kind of small low bath on which one sits to wash the lower parts of the body

**bi·en·ni·al** /baɪˈenɪəl/ *adj* **1** (of events) happening once every two years: *a biennial art show* **2** (of plants) living for two years and producing seed in the second year –compare ANNUAL **–biennially** *adv*

**bier** /bɪəʳ/ *n* a movable frame like a table, for supporting a dead body or COFFIN

**bi·fo·cals** /baɪˈfəʊkəlz‖ˈbaɪfəʊ-/ *n* [P] eyeglasses having an upper part made for looking at distant objects, and a lower part made for reading –see PAIR¹ (USAGE) **–bifocal** *adj*

**big** /bɪg/ *adj* **-gg- 1** of more than average size, weight, force, importance, etc.: *a big box*|*How big is it?*|*bigger than a house*|*That child is big for her age.*|*The big question is what to do next.*|(fig.) *big-hearted* (=generous; unselfish)|(fig.) *John is a big spender.* (=spends money freely)| *a big eater* –see LARGE (USAGE); see Study Notes on page 494 **2** [F] *infml* very popular, successful, or important: *She's very big*/**a big name**/**in the big time** *in the music world.* **3 too big for one's boots** *infml* believing oneself to be more important than one really is **4 that's big of (you, him, etc.)** *infml* that's generous of (you, him, etc.) –**bigness** *n* [U]

**big·a·my** /'bɪgəmi/ *n* [U] the state of being married to two people at the same time: *Bigamy is considered a crime in many countries.* –see also MONOGAMY, POLYGAMY –**bigamist** *n* –**bigamous** *adj*

**big broth·er** /ˌ· '··/ *n (usu. caps)* an organization or leader that has complete power and allows no freedom

**big·head** /'bɪghed/ *n infml* a person who thinks too highly of his/her own importance

**big·ot** /'bɪgət/ *n derog* a person who thinks unreasonably that other opinions and beliefs than his own are wrong, esp. on religion, race, or politics –**bigoted** *adj derog: bigoted people/opinions*

**big·ot·ry** /'bɪgətri/ *n* [U] *derog* acts or beliefs typical of a BIGOT

**bike** /baɪk/ *n,v* **biked, biking** [C;I] **1** *infml* for BICYCLE **2 on your bike**! *infml* (an expression used to indicate that what someone is saying or doing is unacceptable and that he/she should leave at once)

**bi·ki·ni** /bə̇'kiːni/ *n* a very small two-piece bathing suit for women

**bi·lat·er·al** /baɪ'lætərəl/ *adj* of, on, or with two sides; between or concerning two parties: *a bilateral agreement* –see also MULTILATERAL, UNILATERAL –**bilaterally** *adv*

**bil·ber·ry** /'bɪlbəri‖-ˌberi/ *n* **-ries** (the blue-black fruit of) a low bushy plant growing in Northern Europe –compare BLUEBERRY

**bile** /baɪl/ *n* [U] **1** a bitter green-brown liquid formed in the LIVER[1] to help the DIGESTION of food **2** *fml* bad temper

**bilge** /bɪldʒ/ *n* **1** [C;U] (dirty water in) the bottom of a ship **2** [U] *infml* foolish talk: *Don't give me that bilge!*

**bi·lin·gual** /baɪ'lɪŋgwəl/ *adj* **1** of, containing, or expressed in two languages: *a bilingual French-English dictionary* **2** able to speak two languages equally well

**bil·i·ous** /'bɪlɪəs/ *adj* having sickness from too much BILE (1) in the body: *Fatty food makes some people bilious.* –**biliousness** *n* [U]

**bill**[1] /bɪl/ *n* **1** a list of things bought and their price: *She paid the bill (for the meal).* **2** a plan for a law, written down for the government to consider **3** *AmE* a piece of paper money; NOTE[2] (6): *a five-dollar bill* **4** a printed notice: *Stick No Bills* (a public warning on a wall, fence, etc.) **5 foot the bill (for)** *infml* to pay (for): *Who's going to foot the bill for the new library?*

**bill**[2] *n* the beak of a bird

**bill·board** /'bɪlbɔːd‖-ord/ *n AmE* for HOARDING (2)

**bil·let** /'bɪlə̇t/ *n,v* [C;T] (to provide) a house for lodging soldiers in, esp. for a short time: *The soldier was billeted on Mrs Smith.* (=in Mrs Smith's house)

**bil·li·ards** /'bɪljədz‖-ərdz/ *n* [U] a game played on a cloth-covered table (**billiard table**) with balls knocked with long sticks (CUEs) into pockets at the corners and sides

**bil·li·on** /'bɪljən/ *determiner,n,pron* **billion** *or* **billions 1** (the number) 1,000,000,000 or $10^9$ **2** *BrE* (the number) 1,000,000,000,000 or $10^{12}$ –see Study Notes on page 494 –**billionth** *determiner,n,pron,adv*

**bil·low**[1] /'bɪləʊ/ *n* a wave, esp. a very large one: (fig.) *a great billow of smoke* –**billowy** *adj*

**billow**[2] *v* [I] to rise in waves; swell out: *billowing sails/skirts*

**billy goat** /'···/ *n (used esp. by or to children)* a male goat –compare NANNY GOAT

**bi·month·ly** /baɪ'mʌnθli/ *adv,adj* (appearing or happening) **a** every two months: *a bimonthly magazine* **b** twice a month

**bin** /bɪn/ *n* a large wide-mouthed container (esp. one with a lid) for bread, flour, coal, etc., or for waste –see also DUSTBIN

**bi·na·ry** /'baɪnəri/ *adj tech* **1** consisting of two things or parts; double: *A* **binary star** *is a double star, consisting of two stars turning round each other.* **2** using the two numbers, 0 and 1, as a base: *A binary system of numbers is used in many computers.*

**bind** /baɪnd/ *v* **bound** /baʊnd/, **binding 1** [T] to tie: *Bind the prisoner (to his chair) with rope.*|*Bind the prisoner's arms (together).*|(fig.) *He stood there, bound by the magic of the music.* **2** [T] BANDAGE[2]: *to bind (up) wounds* **3** [T] to strengthen or decorate with a cover or a band of material: *to bind a book* **4** [I;T] to (cause to) stick together: *This flour mixture isn't wet enough to bind properly.* **5** [T] to cause to obey, esp. by a law or a solemn promise: *I am bound by my promise.*|*a* **binding agreement**

**bind** sbdy.↔ **over** *v adv* [T] *Br law* to declare it necessary for (someone) to cause no more trouble under threat of punishment: *The judge* **bound over** *the two criminals* **to keep the peace** *for a year.*

**bind·er** /'baɪndə[r]/ *n* **1** a machine or person that binds, esp. books: *Your book is still at the binder's.* **2** a usu. removable cover, esp. for holding sheets of paper, magazines, etc.

**bind·ing** /'baɪndɪŋ/ *n* **1** [C] a book cover: *The binding of this book is torn.* **2** [U] material sewn or stuck along the edge of something, such as a dress, for strength or decoration

**bin·go** /'bɪŋgəʊ/ *n* [U] a game played for prizes by covering rows of numbered squares on a card

**bi·noc·u·lars** /bɪ'nɒkjʊləz, baɪ-‖-'nɑkjələrz/ *n* [P] a pair of glasses like short TELESCOPEs for both eyes, used for looking at distant objects: *I watched the racing through my binoculars.* –see PAIR[1] (USAGE)

**bi·o·chem·is·try** /ˌbaɪəʊ'kemə̇stri/ *n* [U] (the scientific study of) the chemistry of living things

**bi·o·de·gra·da·ble** /ˌbaɪəʊdɪ'greɪdəbəl/ *adj* able to decay or DISINTEGRATE naturally: *Plastic is not biodegradable.*

**bi·og·ra·phy** /baɪ'ɒgrəfi‖-'ɑg-/ *n* **-phies** [C;U] (the branch of literature that deals with) a written account of a person's life: *Boswell wrote a famous biography of Dr Johnson.* –**biographer** *n* –**biographical** /ˌbaɪə'græfɪkəl/ *adj* –**biographically** *adv*

**biological war·fare** /ˌ·····'··/ also **germ warfare**– *n* [U] methods of fighting a war in which living things such as bacteria are used for harming the enemy

**bi·ol·o·gy** /baɪ'ɒlədʒi‖-'ɑl-/ *n* [U] the scientific study of living things –**biologist** *n* –**biological** /ˌbaɪə'lɒdʒɪkəl◄‖-'lɑ-/ *adj* –**biologically** *adv*

**bi·on·ic** /baɪ'ɒnɪk‖-'ɑn-/ *adj infml* having greater

than human powers (such as speed, strength, etc.)
**bi·par·tite** /baɪ'pɑːtaɪt‖-'pɑr-/ *adj* being in two parts; shared by two parties: *a bipartite agreement*
**bi·ped** /'baɪped/ *n tech* a two-footed creature
**bi·plane** /'baɪpleɪn/ *n* an aircraft with two sets of wings, one above the other –compare MONOPLANE
**birch¹** /bɜːtʃ‖bɜrtʃ/ *n* **1** [C;U] (wood from) a tree, common in northern countries, with smooth wood and thin branches **2** [C] a rod made from this wood, used for punishing
**birch²** *v* [T] to whip or hit, esp. with a BIRCH¹ (2), esp. as a punishment
**bird** /bɜːd‖bɜrd/ *n* **1** a creature with wings and feathers, which can usu. fly in the air **2** *BrE infml* a woman **3 early bird** *infml* a person who gets up or arrives early **4 kill two birds with one stone** *infml* to get two results with one action
**bird of prey** /ˌ··'·/ *n* any bird that kills other birds and small animals for food
**bird's-eye view** /ˌ··'·/ *n* a view seen from high up; (fig.) a general view: *a bird's-eye view of Rome*
**biro** /'baɪərəʊ/ *n* **biros** [C;U] *tdmk* → BALLPOINT: *written with a biro/in biro*
**birth** /bɜːθ‖bɜrθ/ *n* **1** [C;U] the act or time of being born, of coming into the world esp. out of the body of a female parent: *the birth of a child|She weighed eight pounds at birth.*|(fig.) *the birth of a new political party|She* **gave birth to** *a fine healthy baby.* –compare DEATH **2** [U] family origin: *of noble birth|French by birth*
**birth con·trol** /'··ˌ·/ *n* [U] various methods of limiting the number of children born –compare CONTRACEPTIVE
**birth·day** /'bɜːθdeɪ‖'bɜr-/ *n* **1** the date on which someone was born: *When is your birthday?* **2** the day in each year when this date falls: *Let me wish you a happy birthday!*
**birth·mark** /'bɜːθmɑːk‖'bɜrθmɑrk/ *n* an unusual mark on the body at birth
**birth·rate** /'bɜːθreɪt‖'bɜr-/ *n* the number of births for every 100 or every 1000 people during a given time: *a birthrate of 3 per 100*
**bis·cuit** /'bɪskɪ̵t/ *n* **1** *BrE*‖**cookie** *AmE*– a flat thin dry cake, sweetened or unsweetened, usu. sold in tins or packets **2** *AmE* for SCONE **3 take the biscuit** *BrE infml* to be very surprising; be the best/worst
**bi·sect** /baɪ'sekt‖'baɪsekt/ *v* [T] *tech* to divide into two usu. equal parts –**bisection** /baɪ'sekʃən‖'baɪsek-/ *n* [U]
**bi·sex·u·al** /baɪ'sekʃʊəl/ *adj* **1** possessing qualities of both sexes: *a bisexual plant* **2** sexually attracted to people of both sexes: *a bisexual person* –see also HETEROSEXUAL, HOMOSEXUAL –**bisexuality** /baɪˌsekʃʊ'ælɪ̵ti/ *n* [U]
**bish·op** /'bɪʃəp/ *n* **1** [A;C] (*often cap.*) (in some branches of the Christian church) a priest in charge of the churches and priests in a large area **2** [C] one of the powerful pieces in the game of CHESS
**bish·op·ric** /'bɪʃəprɪk/ *n* → DIOCESE
**bi·son** /'baɪsən/ *n* **bison** *or* **bisons** a large wild cowlike animal formerly very common in Europe and North America
**bis·tro** /'biːstrəʊ/ *n* **-tros** (esp. in France) a small or simple BAR¹ (5) or restaurant

**bit¹** /bɪt/ *n* **1** [C *of*] a small piece or quantity: *every bit of the food|"I did a bit of Christmas shopping."* (SEU S.) –see picture on page 449 **2** [S] a short time: *I'm just going out for a bit.* **3** [S] some (in the phrases **a bit of luck/advice/news**) **4 a bit (of)** *infml* to some degree; rather: *a bit tired|That's a bit (too) much to pay.|"He's* **not a bit** *like that really."* (SEU W.) (=he's not at all like that) –see USAGE **5 bits and pieces** *infml* small things of various kinds: *Let me get my bits and pieces together.* **6 bit by bit** also **a bit at a time**– *infml* a little at a time; gradually **7 every bit as** *infml* just as; quite as: *He's every bit as clever as you are.* **8 to bits** into small pieces: *The bridge was blown to bits by the explosion.*|(fig.) *My nerves have gone (all) to bits lately.*
USAGE Use **a bit** before adjectives: *I'm* **a** *(little)* **bit** *tired;* and **a bit of** before nouns: **a bit of** *money*|**a bit of** *a problem.*
**bit²** *n* **1** a metal bar, part of a BRIDLE, that is put in the mouth of a horse and used for controlling its movements **2** a part of a tool for cutting or making holes
**bitch¹** /bɪtʃ/ *n* **1** a female dog **2** *derog* a woman, esp. when unkind or bad-tempered: *You bitch!*
**bitch²** *v* [I *about*] *infml* to complain
**bitch·y** /'bɪtʃi/ *adj* **-ier, -iest** having a tendency to make nasty jokes about other people and find fault with everything –**bitchily** *adv* –**bitchiness** *n* [U]
**bite¹** /baɪt/ *v* **bit** /bɪt/, **bitten** /'bɪtn/, **biting 1** [I;T] to cut, crush, or seize (something) with the teeth or to attack (someone or something) with the teeth: *Be careful; my dog bites.|The boy bit into the piece of cake.|He bit a large piece out of it.|The fierce dog bit me on the leg/bit a hole in my trousers.* **2** [I;T] (of insects and snakes) to prick the skin (of) and draw blood: *He was bitten by a mosquito.* **3** [I] (of fish) to accept food on a fisherman's hook (and so get caught): (fig.) *I wanted to interest her in my plan, but she didn't bite.* (=express any interest) **4** [I] to take hold of something firmly: *The car wheels would not bite because of the ice.* **5** [I] to have or show an effect, unpleasant to some: *The government's new higher taxes are really beginning to bite.* **6 bite someone's head off** *infml* to speak to or answer someone rudely and angrily **7 bite the dust** *infml* to fall to the ground (esp. in a fight)
**bite** sthg.↔ **back** *v adv* [T] *infml* to control; prevent from being expressed: *Peter was about to tell the secret, but he bit his words back.*
**bite²** *n* **1** [C] (something removed or caused by) an act of biting: *He took a bite out of the apple.|Her face was covered with insect bites.|He sat by the river for hours without (getting) a bite.* (=without catching a fish)| (fig.) *There's a bite* (=sharpness) *in this cold wind.* **2** [S] *infml* something to eat: *He hasn't had a bite (to eat) all day.*
**bit·ing** /'baɪtɪŋ/ *adj* painful; cruel: *a cold and biting wind|He said some biting things about my homework.* –**bitingly** *adv: a bitingly cold wind*
**bit·ter¹** /'bɪtəʳ/ *adj* **1** having a sharp, biting taste, like beer or black coffee without sugar –opposite **sweet 2** (of cold, wind, etc.) very sharp, cutting, biting, etc.: *a bitter winter wind* **3** filled with or caused by hate, anger, sorrow, or other unpleasant feelings: *bitter enemies|bitter tears|Losing the race was a bitter dis-*

appointment to him. **4 to the bitter end** *infml* to the end in spite of all unpleasant difficulties –**bitterly** *adv* –**bitterness** *n* [U]

**bitter²** *n* [U] *BrE* a type of bitter beer: *a pint of bitter*

**bit·ty** /ˈbɪti/ *adj* **-tier, -tiest** *often derog* consisting of or containing little bits: *a rather bitty collection of short stories*

**bi·tu·men** /ˈbɪtʃʊmə̇n‖bə̇ˈtuː-/ *n* [U] a sticky substance (such as ASPHALT or TAR), esp. as used in road-making –**bituminous** /bə̇ˈtjuːmə̇nəs‖bə̇ˈtuː-/ *adj*

**biv·ou·ac¹** /ˈbɪvʊ-æk/ *n* a soldiers' camp without tents

**bivouac²** *v* **-ck-** [I] (esp. of soldiers) to spend the night in the open without tents: *They have/are bivouacked behind those trees.*

**bi·week·ly** /baɪˈwiːkli/ *adv,adj* **1** appearing or happening every two weeks: *a biweekly magazine* **2** appearing or happening twice a week

**bi·zarre** /bə̇ˈzɑːʳ/ *adj* (esp. of appearance or happenings) strange; peculiar; odd –**bizarrely** *adv*

**blab** /blæb/ *v* **-bb-** [I] *infml* to tell a secret

**black¹** /blæk/ *adj* **1** of the colour of night; without light; having the colour black: (fig.) *I like my coffee black.* (=without milk or cream)|(fig.) *Your hands are black!* (=very dirty) **2** (of feelings, behaviour, news, etc.) very bad: *Things looked very black for us when we heard the news.*|(fig.) *He gave me a black* (=very angry) *look.* **3** [*no comp.*] (of a person) of a black-skinned race –compare WHITE¹ (2) **4 black and blue** (darkly) discoloured (BRUISED² (2)) as the result of a blow: *After the fight he was black and blue all over.* **5 in black and white** in writing: *I want this agreement in black and white.* **6 black sheep** a worthless member of a respectable group: *He was the black sheep of the family after he had been to prison.* –**blackness** *n* [U]

**black²** *n* **1** [U] the darkest colour: *After her husband died, she dressed in black for six months.* **2** [C] a person of a black-skinned race **3 in the black** having money in a bank account: *Our account is (nicely) in the black this month.* –opposite **in the red**

**black³** *v* [T] **1** to make black, as with a blow or by covering with a black substance: *to black someone's eye* **2** *BrE* (esp. of a trade union) to refuse to work with (goods, a business firm, etc.): *They blacked a firm that refused to pay proper wages.*

**black out** *v adv* **1** [T (=**black** sthg.↔ **out**)] to darken so that no light is seen: *During the war we had to black out all our windows.* **2** [I] to faint: *After the accident he blacked out and couldn't remember what had happened.* –compare BLACKOUT

**black·ber·ry** /ˈblækbəri‖-beri/ *n* **-ries** the fruit of a type of BRAMBLE

**black·bird** /ˈblækbɜːd‖-ɜrd/ *n* a European and American bird of which the male is completely black

**black·board** /ˈblækbɔːd‖-ord/ *n* a dark smooth surface (usu. black or green) used esp. in schools for writing or drawing on, usu. with chalk –see picture on page 105

**black·cur·rant** /ˈblæk,kʌrənt‖-ˈkɜr-/ *n* a European garden fruit with small round blue-black berries

**black·en** /ˈblækən/ *v* [T] to (cause to) become black or dark: (fig.) *Don't blacken my good name by spreading lies.*

**black eye** /,·ˈ·/ *n* darkening of the skin round someone's eye by a blow: *He had a black eye after the fight.*

**black·head** /ˈblækhed/ *n* a kind of spot on the skin with a black centre

**black hole** /,·ˈ·/ *n* an area in outer space into which everything near it, including light itself, is pulled

**black·jack** /ˈblækdʒæk/ *n* **1** [U] → PONTOON **2** [C] *AmE* for COSH¹

**black·leg** /ˈblækleg/ *n BrE derog* a person who continues to work when others are on STRIKE² (1); SCAB¹ (3)

**black·list** /ˈblæk,lɪst/ *v* [T] to put on a list of usu. people who have done something wrong or who are to be punished: *blacklisted for non-payment of debts* –**blacklist** *n*

**black mag·ic** /,·ˈ··/ *n* [U] magic that is used for evil purposes –compare WHITE MAGIC

**black·mail¹** /ˈblækmeɪl/ *n* [U] the obtaining of money etc. by threatening, usu. to make known unpleasant facts about a person or group

**blackmail²** *v* [T *into*] to obtain money etc. from (someone) by BLACKMAIL¹: *Don't think you can blackmail me (into doing that).* –**blackmailer** *n*

**black mar·ket** /,·ˈ·· ◂/ *n* [*usu. sing.*] the illegal buying and selling of goods, foreign money, etc.: *They bought butter on the black market during the war.* –**black marketeer** *n*

**black·out** /ˈblækaʊt/ *n* **1** a period of darkness enforced during wartime or caused by the failure of the electric power supply: *The streets were not lighted at night during the blackout.* **2** a loss of consciousness for a short time: *He had had a blackout after the accident.* –compare BLACK **out**

**black pow·er** /,·ˈ··/ *n* [S] (*usu. cap.*) the belief that black people should have equality of political and ECONOMIC power

**black·smith** /ˈblæk,smɪθ/ also **smith**– *n* a person who makes and repairs things made of iron, esp. horseshoes, usu. by hand

**blad·der** /ˈblædəʳ/ *n* **1** a bag of skin inside the body of human beings or animals, in which waste liquid collects **2** a bag of skin, leather, or rubber which can be filled

**blade** /bleɪd/ *n* **1** the flat cutting part of a knife, sword, etc. **2** the flat wide part of an OAR, a PROPELLER, etc. **3** a long flat leaf of grass

**blame¹** /bleɪm/ *v* **blamed, blaming** [T *for, on*] to consider (someone) responsible for (something bad): *They blamed the failure on George.*|*They blamed George (for the failure).*|*The children* **were (not) to blame for** (=(not) guilty of) *the accident.*

**blame²** *n* [U] responsibility for something bad: *The judge* **laid/put the blame** *for the accident on the driver of the car.*|*We were ready to* **take/bear the blame for** *what had happened.*

**blame·less** /ˈbleɪmlə̇s/ *adj* free from blame; guiltless: *a blameless life* –**blamelessly** *adv*

**blame·wor·thy** /ˈbleɪm,wɜːði‖-ɜr-/ *adj fml* deserving blame

**blanch** /blɑːntʃ‖blæntʃ/ *v* **1** [T] to make something colourless, as by removing the skin or keeping out of the light: *blanched* ALMONDS **2** [I +*to-v*/*with, at*] to become pale with fear, cold, etc.: *Her face blanched* with fear at the news.

**blanc·mange** /blə'mɒnʒ, -'mɒndʒ‖-'mɑ-/ *n* [C;U] a cold, solid mixture of CORN FLOUR, sugar, milk, and other sweet materials

**bland** /blænd/ *adj* **1** (of food) without much taste **2** (of people and behaviour) not giving offence or being unusual in any way **–blandly** *adv* **–blandness** *n* [U]

**blank**[1] /blæŋk/ *adj* **1** without writing, print, or other marks: *a blank page*|*Write your name in the blank space at the top of the page.* **2** expressionless; without understanding: *I tried to explain, but he just gave me a blank look.* **–blankly** *adv* **–blankness** *n* [U]

**blank**[2] *n* **1** an empty space: (fig.) *When I tried to remember his name,* **my mind was a complete blank.** **2** → BLANK CARTRIDGE **3 draw a blank** *infml* to be unsuccessful

**blank car·tridge** /ˌ·ˈ··/ *n* a CARTRIDGE (1) that contains an explosive but no bullet

**blank cheque** *BrE*‖**check** *AmE* /ˌ·ˈ·/ *n* a cheque signed and given to someone to write in whatever amount he/she wishes to receive

**blan·ket** /'blæŋk$\frac{1}{3}$t/ *n* **1** [C] a thick woollen covering used on beds to protect from cold: (fig.) *The valley was covered with a blanket of snow.* **2** [A] including all conditions or possible happenings: *a blanket rule*

**blank verse** /ˌ· ˈ·/ *n* [U] poetry which does not RHYME: *Shakespeare's plays are written in blank verse.*

**blare** /bleəʳ/ *v* **blared, blaring** [I;T *out*] (of a horn or other loud sound-producing instrument) to produce (sounds or words) loudly, and unpleasantly: *The radio blared out (the news).* **–blare**

**bla·sé** /'blɑːzeɪ‖blɑ'zeɪ/ *adj* without further interest or enjoyment: *The pop star is blasé about money now.*

**blas·pheme** /blæs'fiːm/ *v* **-phemed, -pheming** [I;T *against*] to speak without respect of or use bad language about (God or religious matters): *blaspheming (against) God* **–blasphemer** *n* **–blasphemous** /'blæsf$\frac{1}{3}$məs/ *adj* **–blasphemously** *adv*

**blas·phe·my** /'blæsf$\frac{1}{3}$mi/ *n* **-mies** [C;U] (an example of) disrespectful or bad language about God or holy things: *Their conversation was full of blasphemy/blasphemies.*

**blast**[1] /blɑːst‖blæst/ *n* **1** [C] a sudden strong movement of wind or air: *the icy blast(s) of the north wind* **2** [C;U] the very powerful rush of air caused by an explosion **3** [C] a very loud usu. unpleasant sound of a brass wind instrument: *He blew several loud blasts on his horn.*

**blast**[2] *v* [I;T] to break up (esp. rock) by explosions: *The road is closed because of blasting.*|*They're trying to blast away the face of this rock.*

**blast off** *v adv* [I] (of a space vehicle) → TAKE **off**

**blast·ed** /'blɑːst$\frac{1}{3}$d‖'blæst$\frac{1}{3}$d/ *adj* [A] *euph* for DAMN[3] (1): *Make that blasted dog keep quiet!*

**blast fur·nace** /'·ˌ··/ *n* a steel container where iron is separated from iron ORE by the action of heat and air blown through at great pressure

**blast-off** /'· ·/ *n* (of a space vehicle) → TAKE-OFF

**bla·tant** /'bleɪtənt/ *adj* shameless; offensively noticeable: *his blatant disregard for the law* **–blatantly** *adv*

**blaze**[1] /bleɪz/ *n* [*usu. sing.*] **1** the sudden sharp shooting up of a flame; a very bright fire: *The fire burned slowly at first, but soon burst into a blaze.*|(fig.) *a blaze of anger* **2** a big dangerous fire: *The firemen were unable to control the blaze.* –see also ABLAZE

**blaze**[2] *v* **blazed, blazing** [I *with*] to (begin to) burn with a bright flame: (fig.) *Lights blazed in every room.*|(fig.) *Her eyes blazed with anger.* **–blazing** *adj*

**blaze**[3] *v* **blaze a/the trail** to make marks along a path (TRAIL) for others to follow: (fig.) *Our company has blazed a trail in new methods of advertising.*

**blaz·er** /'bleɪzəʳ/ *n* a JACKET sometimes with the sign of a school, club, etc., on it

**bleach**[1] /bliːtʃ/ *v* [I;T] to (cause to) become white or whiter: *The bones were bleached by the sun.*

**bleach**[2] *n* [U] a substance used in BLEACHing: *My shirt was so dirty that I had to use bleach on it.*

**bleak** /bliːk/ *adj* cold, cheerless, and uninviting: *The weather in December was bleak and unpleasant.*|(fig.) *The future of this firm will be very bleak indeed if we keep losing money.* **–bleakly** *adv*

**blear·y** /'blɪəri/ *adj* **-ier, -iest** (esp. of eyes) red and unable to see well because of tiredness, tears, etc.: *A bad cold has made him* **bleary-eyed.** **–blearily** *adv*

**bleat** /bliːt/ *v* **1** [I] to make the sound of a sheep, goat, or CALF[1] (1a) **2** [I;T] *infml* to speak or say (something) in a weak, shaking voice **–bleat** *n* [*usu. sing.*]

**bleed** /bliːd/ *v* **bled** /bled/, **bleeding** **1** [I] to lose blood: (fig.) *My heart bleeds for* (=I feel very sorry for) *those poor children.* **2** [T] to make (someone) pay too much money: *He bled them for every penny they had.*

**bleep**[1] /bliːp/ *n* a high, usu. repeated, sound sent out by a machine to attract someone's attention

**bleep**[2] *v* [I;T] to send out one or more BLEEPS: *The machine bleeped.*|*They're bleeping (for) you, doctor.*

**blem·ish**[1] /'blemɪʃ/ *v* [T] to spoil the beauty or perfection of: *a face blemished by spots*

**blemish**[2] *n* a mark that spoils beauty or perfection: (fig.) *a blemish on his character*

**blend**[1] /blend/ *v* **1** [I;T *together, with*] to (cause to) mix; produce by mixing: *Blend the flour and eggs (together).* **2** [I *with*] to go well together; HARMONIZE (3): *These houses blend (in) well with the trees.*

**blend**[2] *n* a product of BLENDing[1]: *a blend of coffee*|*His manner was a blend of friendliness and respect.*

**blend·er** /'blendəʳ/‖also **liquidizer** *BrE*– *n* a small electric machine used in the kitchen for making solid foods into liquid-like forms, such as soups or juices

**bless** /bles/ *v* **blessed** *or* **blest** /blest/, **blessing** [T] **1** to ask God's favour for: *The priest blessed the new ship.* **2** to make or call holy: *Bless the name of the Lord!* –compare DAMN **3 be blessed with** to be fortunate enough to have: *blessed with good health*

**bless·ed** /'bles$\frac{1}{3}$d/ *adj* holy; favoured by God: *"Blessed are the peacemakers."* **–blessedness** *n* [U]

**bless·ing** /'blesɪŋ/ *n* **1** [C] an act of asking or receiving God's favour, help, or protection: *The blessing of the Lord be upon you all.* **2** [U] approval; encouragement: *The government has given its blessing to the new plan.* **3 a blessing in disguise** something not very pleasant, which however is really a good thing after all

**blew** /bluː/ *v past tense of* BLOW[1]

**blight**¹ /blaɪt/ **1** [U] a disease of plants **2** [C;U *usu. sing.*] something that spoils, or the condition of being spoilt: *The accident* **cast a blight on** *the family.*
**blight**² *v* [T] to spoil with or as if with BLIGHT¹: *Her life was blighted by ill health.*
**blind**¹ /blaɪnd/ *adj* **1** unable to see: *blind in one eye|The blind do not always need our help.*|(fig.) *The pilot made a blind landing in the mist.* (=using his instruments only and not looking outside) **2** of poor judgment or understanding: *He is blind to the probable results of his behaviour.|I have a blind spot where modern art is concerned.* (=I don't understand it) **3** uncontrolled: *blind haste/anger|the blind forces of nature* **4** at or in which one cannot see: *a dangerous blind corner* **5 turn a blind eye (to)** to pretend not to notice (something): *The teacher turned a blind eye to their bad behaviour.* –**blindly** *adv* –**blindness** *n* [U]
**blind**² *v* [T] to make unable to see: *a blinding flash of light*|(fig.) *His desire to do it blinded him to all the difficulties.*
USAGE **Blinded** and **deafened** are used only concerning the event itself: **blinded** *in the war.|The music* **deafened** *me.* For describing a state, use the adjectives **blind** and **deaf**: *He became* **blind.**|*a* **deaf** *child.*
**blind**³ *n* **1** [*usu. sing.*] also **window shade** *AmE*– cloth or other material pulled down from a roller to cover a window –see picture on page 337 **2** also **blinds** →VENETIAN BLIND
**blind al·ley** /ˌ·ˈ··/ *n* a narrow street that does not lead anywhere: *trapped in a blind alley*
**blind date** /ˌ·ˈ·/ *n infml* a social meeting (DATE¹ (3)) between a boy and a girl who have not met before
**blind drunk** /ˌ·ˈ·/ *adj* [F] *infml* very drunk
**blind·fold**¹ /ˈblaɪndfəʊld/ *v* [T] to cover (the eyes) with a piece of material
**blindfold**² *n* a piece of material that covers the eyes to prevent seeing
**blink**¹ /blɪŋk/ *v* **1** [I;T] to shut and open (the eyes) quickly, once or several times: *She blinked (her eyes) at the bright light.* **2** [I] (of distant lights) to go rapidly on and off –compare WINK
**blink**² *n* an act of BLINKing¹
**blink·ers** /ˈblɪŋkəz||-ərz||/ also **blinders** *AmE*– *n* [P] flat pieces of leather fixed beside a horse's eyes to prevent sight of objects at his sides –**blinkered** *adj:* (fig) *blinkered opinions*
**blip** /blɪp/ *n* a very short regular sound or image, produced by an electrical machine –compare BLEEP¹
**bliss** /blɪs/ *n* [U] complete happiness –**blissfully** *adv*
**blis·ter**¹ /ˈblɪstəʳ/ *n* **1** a thin swelling under the skin, caused by rubbing, burning, etc.: *His new shoes raised blisters on his feet.* **2** a swelling on the surface of things such as painted wood or a rubber tyre
**blister**² *v* [I;T] to (cause to) form BLISTERS¹ (on): *His hands blister easily.|The heat blistered the paint on the building.*
**blithe** /blaɪð||blaɪð, blaɪθ/ *adj* (of behaviour, language, spirits, etc.) happy; free from care –**blithely** *adv: She continued blithely on in spite of all difficulties.*
**blitz** /blɪts/ *n* a (period of) sudden heavy attack, esp. from the air: (fig.) *an advertising blitz*
**bliz·zard** /ˈblɪzəd||-ərd/ *n* a long severe snowstorm –see WEATHER (USAGE)
**bloat·ed** /ˈbləʊtɪ̵d/ *adj* unpleasantly swollen: *the bloated body of a drowned animal*
**blob** /blɒb||blɑb/ *n* a drop or small round mass: *a blob of paint on the floor*
**bloc** /blɒk||blɑk/ *n* **1** a group of people, political parties, or nations that act together: *the* COMMUNIST *bloc* **2 en bloc** /ˌɒn ˈblɒk||ˌɑn ˈblɑk/ all together; all at once: *Let's consider all the difficulties en bloc.*
**block**¹ /blɒk||blɑk/ *n* **1** a solid usu. straight-sided mass or piece of wood, stone, etc.: *a block of ice* –see picture on page 449 **2** a large building divided into separate parts: *a block of flats|an office block* –see picture on page 297 **3** (the distance along one of the sides of) a building or group of buildings built between two streets: *The office is four blocks from here.* **4** a quantity of things considered as a single whole: *a block of seats in a theatre|a block of shares in a business* **5** something that stops movement or activity: *a block in the water pipe|He has a memory block.* (=he can't remember anything) **6** *AmE* for BRICK (3)
**block**² *v* [T] to prevent (the movement, activity, or success of or through something): *Something's blocking the pipe/the flow of water through the pipe.|The door was blocked.|My nose is all blocked up and I can't breathe.* –see also UNBLOCK
**block·ade**¹ /blɒˈkeɪd||blɑ-/ *n* the preventing of people or goods coming into or going from a place by warships and soldiers –compare EMBARGO
**blockade**² *v* **-aded, -ading** [T] to put under a BLOCKADE¹: *The ships blockaded the harbour.*
**block·age** /ˈblɒkɪdʒ||ˈblɑ-/ *n* something that causes a block: *a blockage in the pipe*
**block·head** /ˈblɒkhed||ˈblɑk-/ *n infml* a stupid person
**block let·ters** /ˌ·ˈ··/ also **block capitals** /ˌ·ˈ···/– *n* [P] *BrE* the writing of words with each letter in its big (CAPITAL) form: *Please write your name in block letters.*
**bloke** /bləʊk/ *n BrE infml* a man; fellow
**blond** /blɒnd||blɑnd/ *adj,n* **1** (of hair) light-coloured (usu. yellowish) **2** (**blonde**/same pronunciation/*fem.*) (a person) with light-coloured hair and skin –compare BRUNETTE
**blood** /blʌd/ *n* [U] **1** red liquid which flows through the body: *His cruelty to his children* **makes my blood boil.** (=makes me very angry)|*The sound of footsteps in the dark* **made his blood run cold.** (=made him very afraid) **2** family relationship: *a woman of noble blood|Farming* **runs in their blood,** *their family have been farmers for 200 years.* **3 fresh/new blood** a new person or new people (in a firm, group, etc.): *We need some fresh blood with new ideas.* **4 in cold blood** cruelly and on purpose: *They killed the old man in cold blood!* **5 -blooded: a** having a certain kind of blood: *Fish are cold-blooded creatures.* **b** showing a certain character: *a hot-blooded young man* (=showing strong feelings)
**blood·bath** /ˈblʌdbɑːθ||-bæθ/ *n* the killing at one time of many men, women, and children
**blood·cur·dling** /ˈblʌdˌkɜːdlɪŋ||-ɜr-/ *adj* causing a feeling of fear to run through the whole body: *bloodcurdling cries of pain*
**blood group** /ˈ··/ also **blood type**– *n* any of the four

classes into which human blood can be separated: *What is your blood group?*

**blood·hound** /ˈblʌdhaʊnd/ *n* a large hunting dog with a very sharp sense of smell, used for tracking people or animals

**blood·less** /ˈblʌdlǝ̇s/ *adj* without blood; without killing or violence: *a bloodless victory* –see also BLOODY[1] **–bloodlessly** *adv*

**blood poi·son·ing** /ˈ··ˌ···/ also **septicaemia** *tech– n* [U] a condition in which an infection spreads from a part of the body through the BLOODSTREAM

**blood pres·sure** /ˈ·ˌ··/ *n* [C;U] the measurable force with which blood travels through the BLOODSTREAM: *Your blood pressure is a little high.*

**blood·shed** /ˈblʌdʃed/ *n* [U] killing, usu. in fighting: *There was a lot of bloodshed during the war.*

**blood·shot** /ˈblʌdʃɒt‖-ʃɑt/ *adj* (of the eyes) having the white part coloured red: *His eyes were bloodshot after too much drinking.* (=of alcohol)

**blood sport** /ˈ··/ *n* [*usu. pl.*] the hunting and killing of birds and animals for pleasure: *She is against all blood sports, especially foxhunting.*

**blood·stain** /ˈblʌdsteɪn/ *n* a mark or spot of blood: *There were bloodstains on the floor where they had been fighting.* **–bloodstained** *adj:* (fig.) *This castle has a bloodstained history.*

**blood·stream** /ˈblʌdstriːm/ *n* [S] the blood as it flows through the blood vessels of the body: *an infection of the bloodstream*

**blood·thirst·y** /ˈblʌdˌθɜːsti‖-ɜr-/ *adj* having or showing eagerness to kill or too much interest in violence **–bloodthirstily** *adv* **–bloodthirstiness** *n* [U]

**blood type** /ˈ··/ *n* → BLOOD GROUP

**blood ves·sel** /ˈ·ˌ··/ *n* any of the tubes of various sizes through which blood flows in the body

**blood·y**[1] /ˈblʌdi/ *adj* **-ier, -iest 1** covered with blood: *a bloody nose* **2** with much wounding and killing: *a bloody battle* –see also BLOODLESS **–bloodiness** *n* [U]

**bloody**[2] *adj,adv* [A] *BrE infml not polite* (used for giving force to a value judgment): *Don't be a bloody fool!*|*It's bloody wonderful!*

**bloody-mind·ed** /ˌ··ˈ··◂/ *adj BrE infml derog* showing an unreasonable desire to oppose the wishes of others **–bloody-mindedness** *n* [U]

**bloom**[1] /bluːm/ *n* **1** *apprec* a flower: *What beautiful blooms!*|*The roses are* **in full bloom. 2 in the bloom of** at the best time of: *in the bloom of youth*

**bloom**[2] *v* [I] to produce flowers, come into flower, or be in flower: *The roses are blooming.*|(fig.) *Jane is blooming with health and beauty.* –compare BLOSSOM

**bloom·ers** /ˈbluːmǝz‖-ǝrz/ *n* [P] (esp. formerly) a woman's garment of short loose trousers gathered at the knee –see PAIR[1] (USAGE)

**blos·som**[1] /ˈblɒsǝm‖ˈblɑ-/ *n* **1** [C] the flower of a tree or bush: *apple blossoms* **2** [U] many such flowers on a single plant or tree: *a tree (covered) in blossom*

**blossom**[2] *v* [I] **1** (of a tree or bush) to produce or yield flowers; BLOOM[2]: *The apple trees are blossoming.* **2** [*out, into*] to develop: *a blossoming friendship* –compare BLOOM

**blot**[1] /blɒt‖blɑt/ *n* **1** a spot or mark that spoils or makes dirty, esp. as of ink: *a blot of ink on the paper* **2** a fault or shameful act: *a blot on one's character*

**blot**[2] *v* **-tt-** [I;T] **1** to make one or more BLOTS[1] (on): (fig.) *He blotted his driving record by having an accident.* **2** to dry with BLOTTING PAPER **3 blot one's copybook** *infml* to spoil one's record: *She blotted her copybook when she arrived late for work.*

**blot** sthg.↔ **out** *v adv* [T] to cover; hide: *The mist blotted out the sun.*

**blotch** /blɒtʃ‖blɑtʃ/ *n* a large spot or mark on the skin, one's clothes, etc. **–blotchy** *adj*

**blot·ter** /ˈblɒtǝʳ‖ˈblɑ-/ *n* **1** a large piece of BLOTTING PAPER on which writing paper can be pressed face down to dry the ink **2** *AmE* a book where records are written every day

**blotting pa·per** /ˈ··ˌ··/ *n* [U] special thick soft paper which is used to dry wet ink on paper after writing

**blouse** /blaʊz‖blaʊs/ *n* **blouses** /blaʊzǝ̇z/ a usu. loose garment for women, reaching from the neck to the waist –see picture on page 563

**blow**[1] /blǝʊ/ *v* **blew** /bluː/, **blown** /blǝʊn/, **blowing 1** [I] to send out a strong current of air: *The wind's blowing hard tonight.*|*She blew on her food to make it cool.* **2** [I;T] to move by the force of a current of air: *The wind has blown my hat off.*|*Several trees were blown down in the storm.* **3** [I;T] to (cause to) sound by blowing: *to blow a horn*|*The horn blew (loudly).* **4** [I] to take short quick breaths, usu. because of effort: *He was (*PUFF*ing and) blowing as he climbed the stairs.* **5** [I;T] **a** (of an electrical FUSE[2]) to suddenly stop working because a part has melted **b** to cause (a FUSE[2]) to do this: *The radio's not working–the fuse has blown.* **6** [T] *infml* to lose (money or a favourable chance) as the result of foolishness: *I blew £10 at cards the other night.*|*I've blown it!* **7** [T] *euph infml* for DAMN[1] (7): *Well, I'm blowed! He's won again!* **8 blow hot and cold (about)** *infml* to be favourable (to) at one moment and unfavourable (to) at the next **9 blow off steam** *infml* to show one's anger or excitement **10 blow one's mind** *infml* to fill one with strong feelings of wonder or confusion –see also MIND-BLOWING **11 blow one's nose** to clean the nose by sending a strong breath through it into a handkerchief **12 blow one's own trumpet/horn** *infml* to say good things about oneself to others, usu. immodestly **13 blow one's top/stack** *infml* to become violently angry

**blow out** *v adv* **1** [I;T (=**blow** sthg.↔ **out**)] to (cause to) stop burning by blowing: *Jane blew the candle out.* **2** [I] (esp. of a tyre) to burst: *The tyre blew out on my way to work.* **3** [I;T (=**blow** sthg.↔ **out**)] to (cause to) be driven out by the force of air etc.: *The explosion blew the windows out.* –see also BLOWOUT

**blow over** *v adv* [I] (of bad weather) to stop blowing; cease: *The storm has blown over.*|(fig.) *I hope your troubles will soon blow over.*

**blow up** *v adv* **1** [I;T (=**blow** sthg.↔ **up**)] to (cause to) explode or be destroyed by exploding: *to blow up the bridge*|(fig.) *My father blew up* (=was very angry) *when I arrived home late.* **2** [I;T (=**blow** sthg.↔ **up**)] to (cause to) become firm by filling with air: *Be sure to blow up the tyres before you drive off.* **3** [T (**blow** sthg.↔ **up**)] to enlarge (a photograph): (fig.) *The argument was blown up by the newspapers.* **4** [I] (of bad weather) to start blowing; arrive: *There's a storm blowing up.*

**blow**[2] *n* an act or example of blowing: *Give your nose* a good blow.

**blow³** *n* **1** a hard stroke with the open or closed hand, a weapon, etc.: *a blow on the head|The children* **came to blows.** (=started fighting) **2** a shock or misfortune: *It was a great blow to her when her mother died.* **3 a blow-by-blow account** an account describing all the events in the order in which they happened

**blow·fly** /ˈbləʊflaɪ/ *n* **-flies** a fly that lays its eggs esp. on meat or in wounds

**blow·lamp** /ˈbləʊlæmp/ also **blowtorch** /-tɔːtʃ‖-tɔrtʃ/– *n* a lamp (or gas-pipe) from which a mixture of gas and air is blown out under pressure to give a small, very hot flame

**blown** /bləʊn/ *v past participle of* BLOW¹

**blow·out** /ˈbləʊaʊt/ *n* the bursting of a container (esp. a tyre): *He had a blowout and crashed his car.*

**blow·pipe** /ˈbləʊpaɪp/ also **blowgun** /-gʌn/– a tube used for blowing small stones or poisoned arrows (DARTS), used as a weapon

**blub·ber** /ˈblʌbəʳ/ *n* [U] the fat of sea creatures, esp. WHALES, from which oil is obtained

**blue¹** /bluː/ *adj* **1** having the colour blue: *The sky is deep blue.|He painted the door blue.|Your hands are* **blue with cold. 2** [F] *infml* sad and without hope: *I'm feeling rather blue today.* **3 till one is blue in the face** unsuccessfully for ever: *You can telephone her till you're blue in the face but she'll never come.* **–blueness** *n* [U] **–bluish** *adj*

**blue²** *n* [C;U] **1** the colour of the clear sky or of the deep sea on a fine day: *dressed in blue* **2 bolt from the blue** *infml* something unexpected and unpleasant: *His death came as a bolt from the blue.* **3 out of the blue** unexpectedly: *John arrived out of the blue.*

**blue·bell** /ˈbluːbel/ *n* a blue bell-shaped flower

**blue·ber·ry** /ˈbluːbəri‖-beri/ *n* **-ries** (the fruit of) a small bush which grows in North America –compare BILBERRY

**blue blood** /ˌ·ˈ·‖ˈ··/ *n* [U] the quality of being a nobleman or noblewoman by birth **–blue-blooded** /ˌ·ˈ··/ *adj*

**blue·bot·tle** /ˈbluːˌbɒtl‖-bɑtl/ *n* a large blue fly

**blue-col·lar** /ˌ·ˈ··◂/ *adj* [A] of or relating to workers who do hard or dirty work with their hands: *blue-collar workers|a blue-collar union* –compare WHITE-COLLAR

**blue film** /ˌ·ˈ·/ *n* a cinema film about sex, esp. one that is shown at a private club

**blue·print** /ˈbluːˌprɪnt/ *n* a copy of a plan for making a machine or building a house: *These are the blueprints of the new engine.*

**blues** /bluːz/ *n* [U +*sing./pl. v*] **1** a type of slow, sad music from the Southern US: *a blues concert|a well-known blues singer* **2** *infml* the state of being sad: *a sudden attack of the blues*

**bluff¹** /blʌf/ *v* **1** [I] to deceive by pretending to be stronger, cleverer, surer of the truth, etc., than one is: *He says he'll win the race, but he's only bluffing.* **2** [T *through, out of*] to find or make (one's way) by doing this: *He could bluff his way through any difficulty.* **3 bluff it out** *infml* to escape trouble by continuing a deception: *Here come the police; do you think we can bluff it out?*

**bluff** sbdy. **into** sthg. *v prep* [T +*v-ing*] to persuade into (doing something) by BLUFFing¹ (1): *He bluffed me into thinking that his stick was a gun.*

**bluff²** *n* [S;U] **1** the action of BLUFFing¹ (1): *He threatened to dismiss me from my job, but it's all (a) bluff.* **2 call someone's bluff** to tell someone to do what he/she threatens to do

**bluff³** *adj* (of a person or his/her manner) rough, plain, and cheerful: *He has a bluff way of speaking, but a kind heart.* **–bluffly** *adv* **–bluffness** *n* [U]

**blun·der¹** /ˈblʌndəʳ/ *n* a stupid or unnecessary mistake

**blunder²** *v* [I] **1** to make a BLUNDER¹ **2** to move awkwardly or unsteadily, as if blind: *He blundered through the dark forest.* **–blunderer** *n*

**blun·der·buss** /ˈblʌndəbʌs‖-ər-/ *n* an old kind of gun with a wide mouth to the barrel

**blunt¹** /blʌnt/ *adj* **1** (of a knife, pencil, etc.) not sharp: (fig.) *Too much alcohol makes your senses blunt.* **2** (of a person or his/her speech) rough and plain, without trying to be polite or kind: *a blunt man|a few blunt words* **–bluntness** *n* [U]

**blunt²** *v* [T] to make BLUNT¹ (1)

**blunt·ly** /ˈblʌntli/ *adv* roughly and plainly: *To speak bluntly, you are sure to fail.*

**blur¹** /blɜːʳ/ *n* [S] something whose shape is not clearly seen: *The houses appeared as a blur in the mist.|*(fig.) *My memory of the accident is only a blur.*

**blur²** *v* **-rr-** [T] to make difficult to see (through or with) clearly: *His eyes were blurred with tears.*

**blurt** sthg.↔ **out** /blɜːt‖blɜrt/ *v adv* [T] to say (something which should not be said) suddenly and without thinking: *Peter blurted out the news.*

**blush¹** /blʌʃ/ *v* [I *at, with*] to become red in the face, from shame or because people are looking at one: *He blushed with shame.* **–blushingly** *adv*

**blush²** *n* a case of BLUSHing¹: *His remark brought a blush (in)to my cheeks.*

**blus·ter¹** /ˈblʌstəʳ/ *v* [I] **1** to speak loudly and roughly, with noisy threats, often to hide lack of real power **2** (of wind) to blow roughly

**bluster²** *n* [U] **1** noisy threatening talk **2** the noise of rough wind or waves: *the bluster of the storm*

**blus·ter·y** /ˈblʌstəri/ *adj* (of weather) rough, windy, and violent: *a blustery winter day*

**b o** /ˌbiː ˈəʊ/ *n* [U] *abbrev. (often caps.) for:* body odour; an unpleasant smell from a person's body, esp. as caused by SWEAT² (1): *He's got B O.*

**bo·a** /ˈbəʊə/ also **boa constrictor** /ˌ···ˈ·· /– *n* a large non-poisonous South American snake that kills creatures by crushing them

**boar** /bɔːʳ/ *n* **boar** *or* **boars 1** a male pig on a farm that is kept for breeding (=is not CASTRATED) –compare HOG¹ (1), SOW¹ **2 →** WILD BOAR

**board¹** /bɔːd‖bord/ *n* **1** [C] a long thin flat piece of cut wood; PLANK¹ (1) **2** [C] a flat piece of hard material used for a particular purpose: *She pinned the list up on the* NOTICE BOARD.*|He wrote the date on the* BLACKBOARD. **3** [U] (the cost of) meals: *I pay £15 a week for* **board and lodging**/*for* **bed and board. 4** [C +*sing./pl. v (often cap.)*] a committee of company directors, government officials, etc., with special responsibility: *He has joined/been elected to the board of the company.|Mary is now on the Board.|The Board is/are meeting in the* **boardroom. 5 above board** completely open and honest **6 across the**

board including all groups or members, as in an industry: *a wage increase of £10 across the board* **7 go by the board** (of plans, arrangements, etc.) to come to no result; fail completely **8 on board** in or on (a ship or public vehicle): *They got on board the train.|She enjoys life on board ship.* –compare ABOARD **9 sweep the board** to win nearly everything: *Our party swept the board in the election.* (=won nearly all the seats in Parliament) **10 take on board** *infml* to consider and accept (an idea, suggestion, plan, etc.): *The unions could not take on board the idea of a pay freeze.*

**board**² *v* **1** [T *up, over*] to cover with BOARDS¹ (1): *Board the windows up.* **2** [T] to go on BOARD¹ (8) (a ship or public vehicle): *Passengers should board the train now.* –see TRANSPORT (USAGE) **3** [I] (of an aircraft) to take on passengers: *Flight 387 for New York is now boarding at Gate 15.* **4** [I;T *at, with*] to get or supply with meals and usu. lodging for payment: *I'm boarding with a friend.*

**board·er** /ˈbɔːdəʳ‖ˈbor-/ *n* **1** a schoolchild who lives at the school **2** a person who pays to live and to receive meals at another person's house; lodger

**board·ing·house** /ˈbɔːdɪŋhaus‖ˈbor-/ *n* **-houses** /ˌhauzɨz/ a private lodging house (not a hotel) that supplies meals

**boarding school** /ˈ···/ *n* [C;U] a school at which children live instead of going there daily from home

**boast**¹ /bəust/ *n* [C *that*] **1** *usu. derog* an expression of self-praise: *His boast that he was the strongest man in the village turned out to be untrue.* **2** *not derog* a cause for pride: *It is one of their proudest boasts that nobody is sent to prison without trial.*

**boast**² *v* **1** [I;T *that/about, of*] *usu. derog* to say or talk (too) proudly: *She boasts that her car is faster than mine.|He boasted of/about the big fish he had caught.|He's only boasting.* **2** [T] *not derog* (usu. not of people) to be lucky enough to own: *This little village boasts three shops.*

**boast·ful** /ˈbəustfəl/ *adj derog* (of a person or his/her words) full of self-praise **–boastfully** *adv* **–boastfulness** *n* [U]

**boat** /bəut/ *n* **1** a small open vessel for travelling across water: *a small fishing/sailing/rowing boat|They crossed the river* **by boat**/*in a boat.* **2 in the same boat** in the same unpleasant conditions; facing the same dangers: *If you lose your job I'll lose mine, so we're both in the same boat.* **3 rock the boat** *infml* to make matters worse for a group by expressing differences of opinion

USAGE **Boats** are usually smaller than **ships**: *a fishing* **boat**. However, the word may be used informally of a large passenger vessel: *We went to Australia by* **boat.** Large naval vessels are always called **ships:** *How many* **ships** *are there in the navy?* –see TRANSPORT (USAGE)

**boat·swain** /ˈbəusən/ *n* → BOSUN

**boat train** /ˈ··/ *n* a train that takes people to or from ships in port

**bob**¹ /bɒb‖bɑb/ *v* **-bb-** [I;T] to move (something) quickly and repeatedly up and down, as on water

**bob**² *n* **bob** *infml* a former British coin, the SHILLING (=5p): *It'll cost you four bob.*

**bob·bin** /ˈbɒbɨn‖ˈbɑ-/ *n* a small roller on which thread is wound, as in a sewing machine –compare REEL¹

**bob·by** /ˈbɒbi‖ˈbɑbi/ *n* **-bies** *BrE infml* a policeman

**bob·sleigh** /ˈbɒbsleɪ‖ˈbɑb-/ also **bobsled** /-sled/– *v,n* [C;I] (to ride in) a small vehicle that runs on metal blades, and is used for sliding down snowy slopes (TOBOGGANing)

**bode**¹ /bəud/ *v* **boded, boding**[I *well/ill*] *lit* for AUGUR

**bode**² *v past tense of* BIDE

**bod·ice** /ˈbɒdɨs‖ˈbɑ-/ *n* the (usu. close-fitting) upper part of a woman's dress or undergarment above the waist

**bod·i·ly**¹ /ˈbɒdɨli‖ˈbɑ-/ *adj* [A] of the human body: *He likes his bodily comforts.* –see also PHYSICAL (4)

**bodily**² *adv* by taking hold of the body; completely: *He carried the child bodily to bed.*

**bod·y** /ˈbɒdi‖ˈbɑdi/ *n* **bodies 1** [C] the whole of a person or animal as opposed to the mind or soul: *Her whole body was covered from head to toe in painful red spots.|He was there in body but not in spirit.* (=he wished he was somewhere else)|*Where did you bury the body?* (=of the dead person or animal) **2** [C] a body without the head or limbs: *He had a wound on his leg and two more on his body.*|(fig.)*We sat in* **the body of** *the hall.* (=in the main part) **3** [C *of*] a (large) amount: *The oceans are large bodies of water.* **4** [C +*sing./pl. v* (*sometimes cap.*)] a number of people who do something together in a planned way: *The House of Commons is an elected body.|the Governing Body of the College|They marched* **in a body** (=all together) *to the minister's house.* **5** [C] *tech* an object; piece of matter: *The sun, moon, and stars are* **heavenly bodies.**|**a foreign body** (=something that ought not to be there) *in one's eye* **6** [C] the part (of a car) in which people sit as opposed to the engine, wheels, etc. **7** [U] (of wine) full strong quality **8 -bodied** having a certain kind of body: *a big-bodied man*

USAGE One's **figure** is the shape of one's **body,** considered as to whether it is sexually attractive or to its relation to clothes: *She has a nice* **figure**. **Body** used here would be considered impolite. **Figure** is usually used of women; to talk about a man's body, the usual word is **physique**: *He has a powerful* **physique. Build** could be used of either a man or woman: *a man/woman of small* **build**.

**bod·y·guard** /ˈbɒdigɑːd‖ˈbɑdigɑrd/ *n* [+*sing./pl. v*] a man or group of men whose duty is to guard an important person: *The Queen's bodyguards stopped a man who was carrying a gun.|The President's bodyguard is/are waiting in the hall.*

**bod·y·work** /ˈbɒdiwɜːk‖ˈbɑdiwɜrk/ *n* [U] the main outside parts of a motor vehicle, as opposed to the engine, wheels, etc.: *We repainted the bodywork of the bus.* –compare BODY (6)

**bog** /bɒg‖bɑg, bɔg/ *n* [C;U] (a large area of) soft wet ground containing a great deal of decaying vegetable matter: *Don't walk across that field; it's a bog.* **–boggy** *adj*

**bog down** *v adv* **-gg-** [I;T (=**bog** sthg.↔ **down**) *usu. pass.*] to (cause to) sink (as if) into a BOG: (fig.) *The talks with the workers (got) bogged down on the question of working hours.*

**bo·gey, bogy, bogie** /ˈbəʊgi/ *n* **1** also **bogey man** /ˈ··,·/– (used by or to children) an imaginary evil spirit **2** an imaginary fear

**bog·gle** /ˈbɒgəl‖ˈbɑ-/ *v* **-gled, -gling** [I *at*] to make difficulties (about something) esp. owing to fear or surprise: **The/My mind boggles** *(at the idea)!* (=I can't imagine it) –see also MIND-BOGGLING

**bo·gus** /ˈbəʊgəs/ *adj derog* pretended; false

**bo·he·mi·an** /bəʊˈhiːmɪən, bə-/ *adj,n becoming rare* (a person) that does not follow the usual rules of social life, though obeying the law: *That writer is a bohemian/leads a bohemian life.*

**boil¹** /bɔɪl/ *v* [I;T] **1 a** to cause (a liquid or the vessel containing it) to reach the temperature at which liquid changes into a gas: *Peter boiled the* KETTLE.|*I'm boiling the baby's milk.* **b** (of a liquid or the vessel containing it) to reach this temperature: *Is the kettle/the milk boiling yet?|The pot/the water is boiling away* (=is continuing to boil) *on the fire.*|(fig.) *boiling with anger|Injustice* **makes my blood boil.** (=makes me very angry) **2** to cook in water at 100°C: *Boil the potatoes for 20 minutes.|Shall I boil you an egg?|The potatoes have been boiling (away) for 20 minutes.* **3 boil dry: a** (of a liquid) to disappear by changing into a gas: *The water all boiled dry.* **b** to become dry because the liquid has disappeared in this way: *Don't let the pot/the vegetables boil dry.* –see also HARD-BOILED; see COOK² (USAGE)

**boil away** *v adv* [I] to be reduced to nothing (as if) by boiling: *The water had all boiled away and the pan was burned.*

**boil down to** sthg. *v adv prep* [T] infml to be or mean, leaving out the unnecessary parts: *It all boils down to a question of money.*

**boil over** *v adv* [I] (of a liquid) to boil and flow over the sides of a container: *Turn off the gas, the milk is boiling over.*

**boil up** *v adv* [I] (of troubles) to reach a dangerous level: *Trouble is boiling up in the Middle East.*

**boil²** *n* [S] **1** an act or period of BOILing (2): *Give the dirty clothes a good boil.* **2** → BOILING POINT: *The water is on the boil.|Bring the soup to the boil.*

**boil³** *n* a painful infected swelling under the skin, which bursts when ripe

**boil·er** /ˈbɔɪləʳ/ *n* a container for boiling, as in a steam engine, or to make hot water in a house

**boiler suit** /ˈ···/ *n* a garment made in one piece, worn for dirty work; OVERALLS

**boiling point** /ˈ···/ *n* **1** [C] the temperature at which a liquid boils: *Water has a boiling point of 100°C.* **2** [S] the point at which high excitement, anger, etc., breaks into action

**bois·ter·ous** /ˈbɔɪstərəs/ *adj* (of a person or his/her behaviour) noisily cheerful and rough **–boisterously** *adv* **–boisterousness** *n* [U]

**bold** /bəʊld/ *adj* **1** (of a person or his/her behaviour) daring; courageous; adventurous **2** *derog* (of a person) without respect or shame; rude: *She's* **as bold as brass. 3** (of the appearance of something) strongly marked; clearly formed: *a drawing done in a few bold lines* **–boldly** *adv* **–boldness** *n* [U]

**bol·lard** /ˈbɒləd‖ˈbɑlərd/ *n* a short thick post

**bol·shy** /ˈbɒlʃi‖ˈbəʊlʃi, ˈbɔl-, ˈbɑl-/ *adj BrE infml derog* (of a person or his/her behaviour) against the established social order; showing unwillingness to help in a common aim: *I asked her to help me but she's being a bit bolshy about it.*

**bol·ster** /ˈbəʊlstəʳ/ *n* a long round PILLOW

**bolster** sbdy./sthg.↔ **up** *v adv* [T] to give necessary support and encouragement (to a person or his/her feelings or beliefs): *to bolster up someone's pride*

**bolt¹** /bəʊlt/ *n* **1** a screw with no point, which fastens onto a NUT¹ (2) to hold things together **2** a sliding metal bar that fastens a door etc. –compare LATCH¹ **3** → THUNDERBOLT

**bolt²** *v* **1** [I] (esp. of a horse) to run away suddenly, as in fear: *My horse bolted and threw me in the mud.|The thief bolted when he saw the policeman.* **2** [T] to swallow hastily: *She bolted (down) her breakfast.* **3** [I;T] to (cause to) fasten with a BOLT¹ (1, 2): *She bolted the door.|This door bolts on the inside.* –opposite **unbolt** (for 3)

**bolt³** *adv* straight and stiffly: *He made the children sit* **bolt upright.**

**bolt⁴** *n* [S] an act of running away: *The prisoner* **made a bolt for it.** (=tried to run away)

**bomb¹** /bɒm‖bɑm/ *n* **1** [C] a hollow metal container filled with explosive: *They planted a bomb in the post office.* **2** [*the* S] the atomic bomb: *Has that country got the bomb now?* **3 (go) like a bomb** *infml* (to go) very well: *My new car goes like a bomb.*

**bomb²** *v* [I;T] to attack with bombs, esp. by dropping them from aircraft

**bom·bard** /bɒmˈbɑːd‖bɑmˈbɑrd/ *v* [T] to keep attacking heavily (as if) with gunfire: *The speaker was bombarded with questions.* **–bombardment** *n*

**bomb·er** /ˈbɒməʳ‖ˈbɑ-/ *n* an aircraft that carries and drops bombs –compare FIGHTER (2)

**bomb·shell** /ˈbɒmʃel‖ˈbɑm-/ *n* [*usu. sing.*] *infml* a great and often unpleasant surprise: *The news of the defeat was a bombshell to us.*

**bo·na fi·de** /ˌbəʊnə ˈfaɪdi‖ˈbəʊnə faɪd/ *adj,adv Latin law* real(ly); in good faith: *The hotel car park is only for bona fide guests.* (=only for people staying at the hotel)

**bo·nan·za** /bəˈnænzə, bəʊ-/ *n* something very profitable

**bond¹** /bɒnd‖bɑnd/ *n* **1** [C] an agreement, feeling, likeness, etc., that unites people or groups: *two countries united in the bonds of friendship* **2** [C] a paper in which a government etc. promises to pay back with interest money that has been lent (INVESTed) **3** [S] a state of being stuck together: *This new paste makes a firmer bond.*

**bond²** *v* [I;T *together, to*] to (cause to) stick together as with paste: *These two substances won't bond (together).*

**bond·age** /ˈbɒndɪdʒ‖ˈbɑn-/ *n* [U] *lit* the condition of being a slave, or any state which seems like this

**bonds** /bɒndz‖bɑndz/ *n* [P] *lit* chains, ropes, etc., used for tying up a prisoner: *to escape from one's bonds*

**bone¹** /bəʊn/ *n* [C;U] **1** (one of) the hard parts of the body, which protect the organs within and round which are the flesh and skin: *He broke a bone in his leg.* –see also SKELETON (1) **2 bone of contention** something that causes argument **3 cut to the bone** to reduce (costs, services, etc.) as much as possible:

*The bus service has been cut to the bone.* **4 feel in one's bones** to believe strongly though without proof: *I'm going to fail the examination! I can feel it in my bones.* **5 have a bone to pick with someone** to have something to complain about to someone: *I've got a bone to pick with you. Why did you take my bicycle?* **6 make no bones about (doing) something** to feel no doubt or shame about (doing) something: *She made no bones about telling me the truth.* **–boneless** *adj*

**bone²** *v* **boned, boning** [T] to take the bones out of: *Will you bone this piece of fish for me?* **–boned** *adj*

**bone-dry** /ˌ·ˈ·◂/ *adj infml* perfectly dry

**bone-i·dle** /ˌ·ˈ··◂/ also **bone-lazy**– *adj derog* very lazy

**bon·fire** /ˈbɒnfaɪəʳ‖ˈbɑn-/ *n* a large fire built in the open air

**bon·go** /ˈbɒŋgəʊ‖ˈbɑŋ-/ also **bongo drum** /ˈ···/– *n* **-gos** *or* **-goes** either of a pair of small drums played with the hands

**bon·ho·mie** /ˈbɒnəmiː‖ˌbɑnəˈmiː/ *n* [U] cheerfulness; easy friendliness

**bon·kers** /ˈbɒŋkəz‖ˈbɑŋkərz/ *adj* [F] *BrE infml humor* mad: *You're completely bonkers.*

**bon·net** /ˈbɒnʲ̣t‖ˈbɑ-/ *n* **1** a round head-covering tied under the chin, worn by babies –compare CAP, HAT **2** *BrE*‖**hood** *AmE*– a metal lid over the front of a car –see picture on page 85

**bon·ny** /ˈbɒni‖ˈbɑni/ *adj* **-nier, -niest** *apprec* pretty and healthy: *a bonny baby*

**bo·nus** /ˈbəʊnəs/ *n* **1** an additional payment beyond what is usual, necessary, or expected, e.g. to those who work for a business: *The workers got a Christmas bonus.* **2** *infml* anything pleasant in addition to what is expected: *We like our new house, and it's a real bonus that my mother lives so near.*

**bon·y** /ˈbəʊni/ *adj* **-ier, -iest 1** very thin so that the bones can be seen **2** (of food) full of bones: *bony fish*

**boo¹** /buː/ *interj,n* **boos** a shout of disapproval or strong disagreement

**boo²** *v* **booed, booing** [I;T] to express disapproval (of) or strong disagreement (with), esp. by shouting "BOO": *The crowd booed (the speaker).*

**boob** /buːb/ *v* [C;I] *infml* (to make) a foolish mistake

**boobs** /buːbz/ *n* [P] *infml* a woman's breasts

**booby prize** /ˈbuːbi praɪz/ *n* a prize given (esp. as a joke) for the worst performance in a competition

**booby trap** /ˈ·· ·/ *n* **1** a hidden bomb which explodes when some harmless-looking object is touched **2** any harmless trap used for surprising someone

**book¹** /bʊk/ *n* **1** a collection of sheets of paper fastened together as a thing to be read, or to be written in **2** [*usu. pl.*] written records of money, names, etc.: *How many names have you on your books?* **3** any collection of things fastened together, esp. one with its own covers: *a book of stamps/tickets* **4 by the book** according to the rules **5 in someone's good/bad books** *infml* in favour/disfavour with someone **6 take a leaf out of someone's book** to behave as someone else does or has done **7 throw the book at (someone)** (esp. of the police or a judge) to make all possible charges against (someone)

**book²** *v* **1** [I;T *up*] to arrange in advance to have (something); RESERVE²: *to book seats on a plane/a table in a restaurant* **2** [T] *infml* to enter charges against, esp. in police records: *He was booked on a charge of speeding.*

**book in** *v adv BrE* **1** [I;T (=**book** sbdy. **in**)] to (cause to) have a place kept for one at a hotel: *I've booked you in at the Grand Hotel.* **2** [I] to report one's arrival, as at a hotel desk, an airport, etc.; CHECK **in** (1): *We booked in at 3 o'clock.*

**book** sthg.↔ **up** *v adv* [T *usu. pass.*] to keep (a place or time) for people who have made arrangements in advance: *The hotel is (fully) booked up.* (=full)

**book·a·ble** /ˈbʊkəbəl/ *adj* that can be BOOKED² (1) in advance: *bookable seats in a theatre*

**book·case** /ˈbʊk-keɪs/ *n* a piece of furniture consisting of shelves to hold books –see picture on page 355

**book·end** /ˈbʊkend/ *n* [*usu. pl.*] one of a pair of supports to hold up a row of books

**book·ing** /ˈbʊkɪŋ/ *n* [C;U] *BrE* **1** a case or the act of BOOKING² (1), esp. a seat; RESERVATION: *All bookings must be made by post.*|*She bought a ticket at the* **booking office.** –see picture on page 501 **2** a case or the act of BOOKING² (2)

**book·keep·ing** /ˈbʊkˌkiːpɪŋ/ *n* [U] the act of keeping the accounts of money of a business company, a public office, etc. **–bookkeeper** *n*

**book·let** /ˈbʊklʲ̣t/ *n* a small book, usu. with a paper cover; PAMPHLET

**book·mak·er** /ˈbʊkˌmeɪkəʳ/ also **bookie** /ˈbʊki/ *infml*, **turf accountant**– *n* a person who takes money (BETS¹ (2)) risked on the results of competitions, esp. horse races

**book·mark** /ˈbʊkmɑːk‖-ɑrk/ also **bookmarker**– *n* something put between the pages of a book to keep a place in it

**book·stall** /ˈbʊkstɔːl/ *n* a table or small shop open at the front, where books, magazines, etc., are sold, esp. on railway stations

**book to·ken** /ˈ·ˌ··/ *n* a small card that can be exchanged for books at a bookshop: *a £5 book token*

**book·worm** /ˈbʊkwɜːm‖-ɜrm/ *n often derog* a person who is very fond of reading and study

**boom¹** /buːm/ *v* **1** to make a deep hollow sound; RESOUND (1): *The guns boomed.* **2** to grow rapidly, esp. in value: *Business is booming.*

**boom out** *v adv* [I;T (=**boom** sthg.↔ **out**)] to (cause to) come out with a deep hollow sound: *He boomed out his answer.*|*His answer boomed out.*

**boom²** *n* **1** a BOOMING¹(1) sound or cry **2** a rapid growth increase: *There has been a boom in* EXPORTS *this year.*

**boom³** *n* **1** a long pole, esp. on a boat, to which a sail is fastened, or as part of an apparatus for loading and unloading **2** a heavy chain fixed across a river to stop things (esp. logs) floating down or prevent ships sailing up

**boo·mer·ang** /ˈbuːməræŋ/ *n* a curved stick which makes a circle and comes back when thrown, used by Australian ABORIGINES as a hunting weapon

**boon** /buːn/ *n* something favourable; a help: *A car is a real boon when you live in the country.*

**boor** /bʊəʳ, bɔːʳ‖bʊr/ *n derog* a rude ungraceful person **–boorish** *adj* **–boorishly** *adv* **–boorishness** *n* [U]

**boost¹** /buːst/ *v* **1** [*up*] to push up from below **2** to increase; raise: *to boost prices*|(fig.) *We need a holiday to boost our spirits.*

**boost²** *n* **1** a push upwards **2** an increase in amount **3** an act that brings help or encouragement

**boost·er** /'bu:stəʳ/ *n* **1** a person or machine that BOOSTS¹ **2** a substance that increases the effectiveness of a drug or medicine: *This medicine will last for a time, but after six months you'll need a booster.*

**boot¹** /bu:t/ *n* **1** [C *usu. pl.*] a covering of leather or rubber for the foot and ankle, usu. heavier and thicker than a shoe: *army boots* –see picture on page 563 **2** [C] *BrE*‖**trunk** *AmE*– an enclosed space at the back of a car for bags and boxes –see picture on page 85 **3** [C] *infml* a blow given by or as if by a foot wearing a boot **4** [*the* S] *infml* the act of sending someone away rudely, esp. from a job: *He got the boot for coming late.* –compare SACK¹ (2) **5 the boot is on the other foot** *infml* the state of affairs has changed to the opposite **6 lick someone's boots** *infml derog* to try to gain someone's favour by being too obedient **7 put the boot in** *BrE infml* to kick someone, usu. when he/she is already on the ground **8 too big for one's boots** *infml* too proud

**boot²** *v infml* [T] to kick: *He booted the ball away.*

**boot** sbdy.↔ **out** *v adv* [T] *infml* to send away rudely and sometimes with force, esp. to dismiss from a job: *They booted him out for being drunk at work.*

**boot³** *n* **to boot** *fml or humor* besides; in addition: *He is dishonest, and a coward to boot.*

**boot·ee** /'bu:ti:, bu:'ti:/ *n* [*usu. pl.*] a baby's woollen boot

**booth** /bu:ð‖bu:θ/ **booths** /bu:ðz/ *n* **1** (at a market or FAIR³) a tent or small building where goods are sold or games are played **2** a small enclosed place for one person: *a telephone booth|a voting booth*

**bootleg** /'bu:tleg/ *v* **-gg-** [I;T] to make, carry, or sell (alcoholic drink) illegally –**bootlegger** *n*

**boot·y** /'bu:ti/ *n* [U] goods stolen by thieves or taken by a victorious army

**booze¹** /bu:z/ **boozed, boozing** *v* [I] *infml* to drink alcohol, esp. too much alcohol: *He spends every night boozing with his friends.*

**booze²** *n* [U] *infml* alcoholic drink

**booz·er** /'bu:zəʳ/ *n infml* **1** a person who BOOZES, esp. habitually **2** *BrE* for PUB

**booze-up** /'··/ *n BrE infml* a party at which a lot of alcohol is drunk

**bor·der¹** /'bɔ:dəʳ‖'bɔr-/ *n* **1** (land near) the dividing line between two countries: *soldiers guarding the border|over the border* **2** edge: *a border of flowers*

**border²** *v* [T] **1** to be a border to: *fields bordered by woods* **2** to have a common border with: *France borders Germany along parts of the Rhine.*

**border on/upon** sthg. *v prep* [T] to be very much like: *His remarks bordered on rudeness.*

**bor·der·line¹** /'bɔ:dəlaɪn‖'bɔrdər-/ *n* [C *usu. sing.*] (a line marking) a border: *the borderline between France and Germany/between sleeping and waking*

**borderline²** *adj* [A *no comp.*] that may or may not belong to a certain type: *I'm not sure whether to pass him or fail him; he's* **a borderline case.**

**bore¹** /bɔ:ʳ‖bor/ *v* [I;T] to make a round hole or passage (in something): *This machine can bore through solid rock.|to bore a hole/a well* –**borer** *n*

**bore²** *v past tense of* BEAR²

**bore³** *n* **1** [C] *derog* a person who causes others to lose interest in him/her, by continual dull talk **2** [S] *BrE infml* something which one does not want to do: *It's a bore having to go to school.*

**bore⁴** *v* [I;T] to make (someone) uninterested, e.g. by continual dull talk: *The lesson was boring.|The students were bored (by it).* –**boredom** *n* [U]

**bore⁵** *n* a measurement of the width of the hollow inside a gun barrel or pipe: *12-bore|small-bore*

**born¹** /bɔ:n‖bɔrn/ *adj* [*no comp.*] **1** [F] brought into existence by birth: *Shakespeare was born in 1564.*|(fig.) *The new political party was born at the meeting/***born of** *the disagreement between the parties.* **2** [F] at birth; originally: *Carlos Gardel was born French, but grew up in Argentina.* **3** [+*to-v*] having a stated quality from or as if from birth: *a born leader|born to succeed* **4 born and bred** having grown up from birth: *She was born and bred in Yorkshire.* **5 -born** born as stated: *new-born|first-born|still-born* (=born dead) –see also UNBORN

**born²** *v past participle of* BEAR²

USAGE This is one of the two past participles of **bear** when it means "to give birth to". Compare: *He was* **born** *in 1950.|She has* **borne** *three children.*

**borne** /bɔ:n‖bɔrn/ *v* **1** *past participle of* BEAR² –see BORN² (USAGE) **2 -borne** carried as stated: *Some plants have windborne seeds.*

**bo·rough** /'bʌrə‖-rəʊ/ *n* a town, or a division of a large town, with powers of government: *the London Borough of Camden|the Borough of Brooklyn*

**bor·row** /'bɒrəʊ‖'bɑ-, 'bɔ-/ *v* [I;T] **1** to take or receive (something) for a certain time, intending to return it: *to borrow (£5) from a friend* –compare LEND, LOAN¹·²; see Study Notes on page 429 **2** to take or copy (esp. ideas, words, etc.) –**borrower** *n*

**bos·om** /'bʊzəm/ *n often euph or lit* the front of the human chest, esp. the female breasts: *She held the child to her bosom.*|a **bosom friend** (=a very close friend)

**boss¹** /bɒs‖bɔs/ *n infml* a master; employer; person having control over others: *to ask the boss for more money|Who's (the) boss?* (=who's in charge?)

**boss²** *v* [I;T *about, around*] *infml* to give orders (to); act in a BOSSY way: *Tom likes bossing people (about).*

**boss·y** /'bɒsi‖'bɔsi/ *adj* **-ier, -iest** *infml derog* having or showing too much liking for giving orders: *a bossy person/manner* –**bossiness** *n* [U]

**bo·sun, boatswain** /'bəʊsən/ *n* a chief seaman on a ship: *Are we ready to sail, bosun?*

**bot·a·ny** /'bɒtəni‖'bɑ-/ *n* [U] the scientific study of plants –**botanical** /bə'tænɪkəl/ *adj* [A] –**botanist** /'bɒtənɪst‖'bɑ-/ *n*

**botch** /bɒtʃ‖bɑtʃ/ *v infml* [T *up*] to do (something) badly, esp. to repair (something) badly: *I'm afraid I've rather botched (up) dinner tonight.|a botched job* –**botch,** also **botch-up** /'··/– *n: I've* **made a botch/botch-up of** *repairing the car.*

**both** /bəʊθ/ *predeterminer, determiner, pron* **1** the two together; the one as well as the other: *Both children/Both of the children/Both the children won prizes.|She and her husband both like dancing.|Both (of them) like dancing.* –see EACH (USAGE) **2 both ... and ...** not only ... but also ... : *We visited both New York and London.|She both speaks and writes Swahili.*

**both·er**[1] /ˈbɒðəʳ||ˈbɑ-/ *v* **1** [T] to cause to be nervous; annoy or trouble, esp. in little ways: *I'm busy: don't bother me.*|(polite) *I'm sorry to bother you, but can you tell me the time?* **2** [I +*to-v*/*with, about*] to cause inconvenience or trouble to oneself: *Don't bother with/about it.*

**bother**[2] *n* [C;U] trouble, inconvenience, or anxiety (usu. caused by small matters and lasting a short time): *We had a lot of bother finding our way here.*|*I don't want to be a bother, but could I stay here tonight?*

**bot·tle**[1] /ˈbɒtl||ˈbɑtl/ *n* **1** a container for liquids, usu. made of glass or plastic, with a narrow neck or mouth and usu. no handle –see picture on page 615 **2** the quantity held by a bottle: *He drank a whole bottle/bottleful of wine!* **3 the bottle** alcoholic drink, esp. when drunk too much: *Poor John's* **on the bottle/hitting the bottle** *again!*

**bottle**[2] *v* **-tled, -tling** [T] to put into bottles: *a machine for bottling beer*|*to bottle fruit*

**bottle** sthg.↔ **up** *v adv* [T] to control in an unhealthy way: *Tell us what's worrying you; don't bottle it up!*

**bot·tle·neck** /ˈbɒtlnek||ˈbɑ-/ *n* a narrow part of a road which slows down traffic: (fig.) *a bottleneck in production*

**bot·tom**[1] /ˈbɒtəm||ˈbɑ-/ *n* **1** [C] the base on which something stands; the lowest part: *at the bottom of the stairs*|*The glasses all had wet bottoms.*|*some tea left at/in the bottom of your cup* **2** [*the* S *of*] the ground under the sea, a lake, or a river: *They sent the enemy ship to the bottom (of the sea).*|*the river-bottom* **3** [*the* S *of*] the least important or least worthy part of anything: *always at the bottom of the class* (=always getting low marks)|*He started life* **at the bottom of the ladder** *and worked his way up (to success).* **4** [*the* S *of*] the far end: *I'll walk with you to the bottom of the road.* **5** [C] the part of the body on which one sits: *to fall on one's bottom* **6** [*the* S *of*] *often derog* the starting point; the cause: *Who is* **at the bottom of** *all this trouble?*|*I intend to* **get to the bottom of it.** (=find the cause) **7** [A] lowest; last: *in the bottom row* **8 bet one's bottom dollar** *infml* to be completely sure: *You can bet your bottom dollar that she'll win.* **9 from the bottom of one's heart** truly; with real feeling: *I said from the bottom of my heart I was sorry.* –compare TOP[1]

**bottom**[2] *v* → BOTTOM OUT

**bot·tom·less** /ˈbɒtəmləs||ˈbɑ-/ *adj* with no bottom or limit; very deep

**bottom out** *v,adv* [I] to reach the lowest point before rising again: *House prices bottomed out in April.*

**bough** /baʊ/ *n* a main branch of a tree

**bought** /bɔːt/ *v past tense and participle of* BUY[1]

**boul·der** /ˈbəʊldəʳ/ *n* a large stone or rock

**boule·vard** /ˈbuːlvɑːd||ˈbuːləvɑrd, ˈbʊ-/ *n* (part of the name of) a broad street, often having trees on each side: *Sunset Boulevard* –compare AVENUE (1, 2)

**bounce**[1] /baʊns/ *v* **bounced, bouncing 1** [I;T] **a** (of a ball) to spring back or up again from something solid **b** to cause (a ball) to do this: (fig.) *She bounced the baby (on her knee).* **2** [I] *infml* (of a cheque) to be returned by a bank as worthless

**bounce**[2] *n* [C;U] the act or action of bouncing (BOUNCE[1]): *The ball gave a high bounce.*|*The ball has plenty of bounce.*

**bounc·ing** /ˈbaʊnsɪŋ/ *adj* [A *no comp.*] *apprec* (esp. of babies) healthy and active

**bounc·y** /ˈbaʊnsi/ *adj* **1** full of life and eager for action: *a bouncy manner* **2** that BOUNCES well: *a bouncy ball* **–bouncily** *adv* **–bounciness** *n* [U]

**bound**[1] /baʊnd/ *adj* intending to go (to); going (to): *bound for home*|*homeward-bound*

**bound**[2] *v* [T *usu. pass.*] to mark the edges of; keep within a certain space: *The US is bounded on the north by Canada and on the south by Mexico.*

**bound**[3] *adj* **1** [F *to*] fastened by or as if by a band; kept close to: *bound to one's job*|*bound to a post*|*housebound* (=not often or ever leaving one's house)|*The airport was fogbound, so no aircraft could take off.* **2** [F+*to-v*] certain; sure: *It's bound to rain soon.* **3** [F+*to-v*] having to, by law or morally: *I felt bound to tell you.* **4** (of a book) fastened within covers: *a leather-bound book* **5 bound up in** busy with; very interested in: *She is bound up in her work.* **6 bound up with** dependent on; connected with: *His future is closely bound up with that of his company.*

**bound**[4] *n* a jump or LEAP[2]: *With one bound, he was over the wall.*

**bound**[5] *v* **1** to jump or LEAP[1]: *He bounded away.* **2** to spring or BOUNCE[1] back from a surface

**bound·a·ry** /ˈbaʊndəri/ *n* **-ries 1** the dividing line between surfaces, spaces, countries, etc.; border: *A river forms the boundary (line) between the two countries.* **2** the outer limit of something: *the boundaries of human knowledge* **3** (in cricket) the line which marks the limit of the field of play: *A ball hit to or over the boundary is worth four or six runs.*

**bound·less** /ˈbaʊndləs/ *adj* without limits: *boundless wealth/imagination* **–boundlessly** *adv* **–boundlessness** *n* [U]

**bounds** /baʊndz/ *n* [P] **1** the limits or edges of something; the limits beyond which one may not go: *His foolishness went beyond the bounds of reason.* **2 out of bounds (to)** forbidden to be visited (by): *This area is out of bounds (to soldiers).* –see also BOUNDLESS

**boun·te·ous** /ˈbaʊntɪəs/ also **bountiful**– *adj fml or lit* given or giving freely: *bounteous gifts*|*a bounteous giver* **–bounteously** *adv* **–bounteousness** *n* [U]

**boun·ty** /ˈbaʊnti/ *n* [U] generosity: *a rich lady famous for her bounty to the poor*

**bou·quet** /bəʊˈkeɪ, buː-/ *n* **1** a bunch of flowers carried by a BRIDE, given at a formal occasion, etc. **2** the smell of a wine: *a rich bouquet*

**bour·geois** /ˈbʊəʒwɑː||bʊəˈʒwɑ/ *adj* **1** of, related to, or typical of the MIDDLE CLASS **2** *derog* too interested in material possessions and one's social position

**bour·geoi·sie** /ˌbʊəʒwɑːˈziː||-ər-/ *n* [*the* U +*sing./pl. v*] the MIDDLE CLASS: –compare PROLETARIAT

**bout** /baʊt/ *n* a short period of fierce activity or illness: *a bout of drinking* (=drinking alcohol)|*several bouts of fever*

**bou·tique** /buːˈtiːk/ *n* a small shop that sells up-to-date clothes and other fashionable personal articles

**bo·vine** /ˈbəʊvaɪn/ *adj* of or like a cow or ox

**bow**[1] /baʊ/ *v* **1** [I;T *down, to*] to bend forward the upper part of the body, or the head, to show respect, yielding, etc.: *The guilty man bowed his head in shame.*|*He stood with bowed head at the funeral.*|(fig.) *trees bowed down with snow* –compare CURTSY **2 bow and scrape** *usu. derog* to behave to someone with too much politeness

**bow out** *v adv* [I *of*] to leave, or stop doing something: *The singer bowed out of the competition.*

**bow to** sbdy./sthg. *v prep* [T] to yield to; obey: *I don't agree but I bow to your greater experience.*

**bow**[2] /baʊ/ *n* **1** a bending forward of the upper part of the body, or the head, to show respect or yielding **2 take a bow** to come on stage to receive praise (APPLAUSE) at the end of a performance

**bow**[3] /bəʊ/ *n* **1** a piece of wood held in a curve by a tight string and used for shooting arrows –see also CROSSBOW, LONGBOW **2** a long thin piece of wood with a tight string fastened along it, used for playing musical instruments that have strings **3** a knot formed by doubling a line into two curved pieces, and used for decoration in the hair, in tying shoes, etc.: *She tied the ribbon in a bow.*

**bow**[4] /baʊ/ *v* [I] to bend or curve

**bow**[5] /baʊ/ *n* the forward part of a ship –compare STERN

**bow·els** /'baʊəlz/ *n* [P] **1** a system of pipes from the stomach which carries the waste matter out of the body –compare INTESTINE **2** the inner, lower part (of anything) (esp. in the phrase **the bowels of the earth**)

**bowl**[1] /bəʊl/ *n* **1** a deep round container for holding liquids, etc.: *a washing-up bowl*|*a sugar bowl* –see picture on page 337 **2** the contents of a bowl: *a bowl/bowlful of sugar*

**bowl**[2] *v* **1** [I;T] to throw or roll (esp. a ball) as in some games, esp. (in cricket) to throw the ball at the BATSMAN **2** [I] to play the game of BOWLS or BOWLING: *He goes bowling every Saturday.*

**bowl along** *v adv* [I] *infml* to move smoothly (and often quickly) along: *The car bowled along.*

**bowl** sbdy.↔ **over** *v adv* [T] **1** to knock down: *Someone ran round the corner and nearly bowled me over.* **2** to give a great, esp. pleasant, surprise to: *Your news has quite bowled me over.*

**bow-legged** /'bəʊ,legd, -,legɪ̈d/ *adj* (esp. of people) having the legs curving outwards at the knee; BANDY[2] (2)

**bowl·er**[1] /'bəʊləʳ/ *n* a person who BOWLS[2] esp. in cricket –see CRICKET[2] (USAGE)

**bowler**[2] also **bowler hat** /,·· '·/ *BrE*||**derby** *AmE*– *n* a man's round hard hat, usu. black: *He wears a bowler to go to his office.*

**bowl·ing** /'bəʊlɪŋ/ *n* [U] a game in which balls are rolled at an object or objects: **tenpin bowling**

**bowls** /bəʊlz/ *n* [U] an outdoor game in which one tries to roll a big ball as near as possible to a small ball called "the JACK"

**bow tie** /,bəʊ taɪ/ *n* a TIE fastened at the front with a knot in the shape of a BOW[3] (3)

**box**[1] /bɒks||bɑks/ *n* **1** a container for solids, usu. with stiff sides and often with a lid: *a wooden box*|*a shoebox* –see picture on page 615 **2** the contents of a box: *He's eaten a whole box/boxful of chocolates.* **3** a small room or enclosed space: *a box at the theatre*|*the witness box in a law-court*|*the signal box on a railway line* –see picture on page 463 **4 the box** *BrE infml* television: *What's on the box tonight?*

**box**[2] *v* [T] to put in a box or boxes: *The oranges were boxed and sent off quickly.*

**box** sbdy./sthg.↔ **in/up** *adv* [T] to enclose in a small space: *She feels boxed in living in that small flat.*

**box** sbdy./sthg.↔ **off** *v adv* [T] to separate by putting into an enclosed space: *We are each boxed off (from the others) in our own little offices.*

**box**[3] *v* [I;T *with, against*] **1** to fight (someone) with tightly closed hands (FISTS) esp. as a sport –compare WRESTLE; see BOXING (USAGE) **2 box someone's ears** *infml* to hit someone on the ears

**box·er** /'bɒksəʳ||'bɑk-/ *n* **1** a person who BOXES[3] (1) **2** a largish short-haired dog of German origin, usu. light brown in colour

**box·ing** /'bɒksɪŋ||'bɑk-/ *n* [U] the sport of fighting with tightly closed hands (the FISTS)

USAGE One **boxes** in a **ring** wearing special **gloves** and wins on **points**, by winning more **rounds** than the other man, or by a **knockout**.

**Boxing Day** /'·· ·/ *n* a public holiday in England and Wales, on the first day after Christmas that is not a Sunday

**box num·ber** /'·,··/ *n* a number used as a mailing address, esp. in replying to newspaper advertisements

**box of·fice** /'· ,··/ *n* a place in a theatre, concert hall, etc., where tickets are sold: *The play was a* **box-office success.** (=made a large profit)

**boy**[1] /bɔɪ/ *n* **1** a young male: *Our new baby is a boy.* **2** a son, esp. young **3 -boy** a boy or man working at a certain job: *a cowboy*|*a delivery boy*

**boy**[2] *interj AmE infml* (expressing excitement): *Boy, what a game!*

**boy·cott** /'bɔɪkɒt||-kɑt/ *v* [T] to refuse to do business with, attend, or take part in: *They're boycotting the shop because the people who work there are on* STRIKE.|*to boycott a meeting* –**boycott** *n*

**boy·friend** /'bɔɪfrend/ *n* a girl or young woman's usual male companion; to whom she is not married –see also GIRLFRIEND

**boy·hood** /'bɔɪhʊd/ *n* [C;U *usu. sing.*] the state or period of being a boy: *a happy boyhood* –see also GIRLHOOD, CHILDHOOD

**boy·ish** /'bɔɪ-ɪʃ/ *adj often apprec* of or like a boy: *boyish laughter* –**boyishly** *adv* –**boyishness** *n* [U]

**boy scout** /,·'·||'··/ **girl guide** *fem. BrE*||**girl scout** *fem. AmE* also **scout**– *n* (*often cap.*) a member of an association (the **Boy Scouts**) for training boys in character and self-help

**Br** also **Brit**– *written abbrev. said as:* British

**BR** *abbrev. for:* British Rail (the British railway system)

**bra** /brɑː/ also **brassiere** *fml*– *n* a woman's undergarment worn to support the breasts

**brace**[1] /breɪs/ *n* **1** something used for supporting, stiffening, or fastening **2** a wire worn inside the mouth, usu. by children, to straighten teeth

**brace**[2] **braced, bracing** *v* [T] **1** to make stronger; support with a brace: *We had to brace the walls when* *we put the new roof on.* **2** to prepare (oneself), usu. for something unpleasant or difficult: *Brace yourself for a shock!*

**brace·let** /ˈbreɪslǝ̇t/ *n* a band or ring, usu. of metal, worn round the wrist or arm as a decoration

**brac·es** /ˈbreɪsǝ̇z/ *BrE*‖**suspenders** *AmE*– *n* [P] elastic cloth bands worn over the shoulders to hold up trousers –see PAIR[1] (USAGE)

**brac·ing** /ˈbreɪsɪŋ/ *adj apprec* (esp. of air) fresh and health-giving: *I love this bracing sea air!*

**brack·en** /ˈbrækən/ *n* [U] a plant (a FERN) which grows in forests, etc., and becomes rich red-brown in autumn

**brack·et**[1] /ˈbrækǝ̇t/ *n* **1** a piece of metal or wood put in or on a wall to support something: *a lamp bracket* **2** [*usu. pl.*] **a** also **square bracket**– either of the pair of signs [ ] used for enclosing a piece of information: *The information about the grammar of this word is in brackets.* **b** → PARENTHESIS **3** [*+sing./pl. v.*] a group of people who share some quality: *the upper income bracket|the 16–25 age bracket*

**bracket**[2] *v* [T] to enclose in BRACKETS[1] (2): *to bracket (off) some words*|(fig.) *to bracket two people (together) because they seem similar*

**brack·ish** /ˈbrækɪʃ/ *adj* (of water) not pure; a little salty –**brackishness** *n* [U]

**brag** /bræg/ *v* **-gg-** [I;T *+that/of, about*] *derog* to speak in praise of oneself, often falsely; BOAST[2] (1): *Don't brag!|He bragged of having won first prize/bragged that he had won first prize.|Untidy work is* **nothing to brag about.**

**Brah·man** /ˈbrɑːmən/ also **Brahmin** /ˈbrɑːmǝ̇n/– *n* a Hindu of the highest rank (CASTE)

**braid** /breɪd/ *v* [T] *esp. AmE* for PLAIT[2] –**braid** *n*

**braille** /breɪl/ *n* [U] (*sometimes cap.*) (a way of) printing with raised round marks which blind people can read by touching

**brain**[1] /breɪn/ *n* **1** [C] the organ of the body in the upper part of the head, which controls thought and feeling: *The brain is the centre of higher nervous activity.|I've got that song* **on the brain**. (=I'm thinking about it continually) **2** [C;U] the mind; INTELLIGENCE (1): *She's got a good brain.* **3** [C] *infml* a person with a good mind: *Some of the best brains in the country are here tonight.*

**brain**[2] *v* [T] *infml* to hit (someone) on the head very hard

**brain·child** /ˈbreɪntʃaɪld/ *n infml* somebody's idea or invention, esp. if successful: *This brainchild of mine has saved us a lot of money.*

**brain·less** /ˈbreɪnlǝ̇s/ *adj derog* foolish; silly; stupid –see also BRAINY –**brainlessly** *adv*

**brains** /breɪnz/ *n* [U] **1** the material of which the brain consists **2** *infml* the ability to think: *She's got brains.* **3 pick someone's brains** *infml* to find out someone's knowledge, e.g. by asking questions **4 rack/beat one's brains** *infml* to think very hard so as to find an answer

**brain·storm** /ˈbreɪnstɔːm‖-stɔrm/ *n infml* **1** *BrE* a sudden great disorder of the mind **2** *AmE* for BRAINWAVE

**brain·wash** /ˈbreɪnwɒʃ‖-wɔʃ, -wɑʃ/ *v* [T *into*] *infml derog* to cause (someone) to obey, change his/her beliefs, etc., by very forceful persuasion: *People today are brainwashed by advertising.* –**brainwashing** *n* [U]

**brain·wave** /ˈbreɪnweɪv/ *n BrE infml* a sudden clever idea: *I've just had a brainwave; I know the answer!* –see also BRAINSTORM

**brain·y** /ˈbreɪni/ *adj* **-ier, -iest** *infml* clever –see also BRAINLESS –**braininess** *n* [U]

**braise** /breɪz/ **braised, braising** *v* [T] to cook (meat) slowly in liquid in a covered dish

**brake**[1] /breɪk/ *n* an apparatus for slowing or reducing movement and bringing a wheel, car, etc., to a stop: (fig.) *The government* **put the brakes on** *all our plans by giving us less money.*

**brake**[2] *v* **braked, braking** [I;T] to (cause to) slow or stop by or as if by using a BRAKE: *I braked suddenly.*

**bram·ble** /ˈbræmbəl/ *n* a common wild prickly bush of the rose family, esp. the wild BLACKBERRY

**bran** /bræn/ *n* [U] the crushed skin of wheat and other grain separated from the flour

**branch**[1] /brɑːntʃ‖bræntʃ/ *n* an armlike part or division of some material thing, esp. a tree: *a branch of a tree|a branch railway*|(fig.) *a branch of knowledge/of a family|Our firm has branches in many cities.*

**branch**[2] *v* [I *off*] to become divided into or form branches: *Take the road that branches (off) to the right.*

**branch out** *v adv* [I *into*] to add to the range of one's activities: *The bookshop has decided to branch out into selling music and records.*

**brand**[1] /brænd/ *n* **1** a class of goods which is the product of a particular firm or producer: *What is your favourite brand of soap?|The* **brand name** *of this soap is "Flower".*|(fig.) *He has his own brand of humour.* **2** a mark made (as by burning) usu. to show ownership **3** *fml* a piece of burnt or burning wood

**brand**[2] *v* [T] to mark by or as if by burning, esp. to show ownership: *Our cattle are branded with the letter B.*|(fig.) *His unhappy childhood has branded him for life.|He is* **branded as** *a thief.*

**bran·dish** /ˈbrændɪʃ/ *v* [T] to wave (something, esp. a weapon) about: *He brandished a newspaper at me and said, "Have you read the good news?"*

**brand-new** /ˌ·ˈ·◂/ *adj apprec* new and completely unused

**bran·dy** /ˈbrændi/ *n* **-dies** [C;U] a strong alcoholic drink usu. made from wine

**brash** /bræʃ/ *adj* **1** *derog* rudely disrespectful and proud **2** hasty and too bold, esp. from lack of experience –**brashly** *adv* –**brashness** *n* [U]

**brass** /brɑːs‖bræs/ *n* [U] **1** a very hard bright yellow metal, a mixture of COPPER[1] (1) and ZINC: *a brass band* (=a band consisting mostly of brass musical instruments) **2 (get down to) brass tacks** *infml* (to come to) the important facts or business

**bras·siere** /ˈbræzjəʳ‖brəˈzɪər/ *n fml* for BRA

**brass·y** /ˈbrɑːsi‖ˈbræsi/ *adj* **-ier, -iest 1** like brass in colour **2** like brass musical instruments in sound **3** shameless and loud in manner

**brat** /bræt/ *n derog* a child, esp. a bad-mannered one

**bra·va·do** /brəˈvɑːdəʊ/ *n* [U] the (often unnecessary) showing of courage or boldness

**brave**[1] /breɪv/ *adj apprec* courageous, fearless, and ready to suffer danger or pain: *brave* *soldiers/actions|Fortune favours the brave.* **–bravely** *adv* **–bravery** /ˈbreɪvəri/ *n* [U]

**brave²** *v* **braved, braving** [T] to meet (danger, pain, or trouble) without showing fear: *She braved her parents' displeasure by marrying him.|The director wants to see me about the mistake I made; I'd better go and* **brave it out.**

**bra·vo** /ˈbrɑːvəʊ, brɑːˈvəʊ/ *interj,n* **-vos** well done!

**brawl** /brɔːl/ *n* a noisy quarrel or fight, often in a public place **–brawl** *v* [I] **–brawler** *n*

**brawn** /brɔːn/ *n* [U] muscle; MUSCULAR strength: *He's got more brawn than brains.* (=he's strong but not very clever) **–brawny** *adj: His brawny arms are very strong* **–brawniness** *n* [U]

**bray** /breɪ/ *v,n* [C;I] (to make) the sound that a donkey makes: (fig.) *He brayed with laughter.*

**bra·zen** /ˈbreɪzən/ *adj* shameless; immodest: **–brazenly** *adv*

**brazen out** *v adv* **brazen it out** to face trouble or blame with shameless daring, even when wrong

**bra·zier** /ˈbreɪzjəʳ‖-ʒər/ *n* a container for burning coals

**breach** /briːtʃ/ *n* **1** [C;U] an act of breaking, not obeying, or not fulfilling a law, promise, custom, etc.: *a breach of our agreement|You are* **in breach of** *your contract.|He was sent to prison for a* **breach of the peace.** (=fighting in public) **2** [C] an opening, esp. one made in a wall by attackers **–breach** *v* [T]

**bread** /bred/ *n* [U] **1** a common food made of baked flour: *a loaf of bread|bread and butter* (=bread spread with butter)|*bread and cheese* **2** food as a means of staying alive: *our daily bread|Who is the* **breadwinner** *in your family?* (=who works to supply the money, food, etc.?) **3** *infml* money **4 bread and butter** *infml* way of earning money: *He doesn't just write for fun: writing is his bread and butter.* **5 know which side one's bread is buttered** *infml* to know who or what will be of most gain to oneself **6 on the breadline** very poor

**bread·crumb** /ˈbredkrʌm/ *n* a very small bit of the inner part of a loaf of bread: *breadcrumbs to feed the birds*

**breadth** /bredθ, bretθ/ *n* [C;U] **1** *fml* (the) distance from side to side; width: *What is the breadth of this river?|The breadth is 16 metres./It's 16 metres in breadth.|a breadth of 16 metres* –compare LENGTH (1) **2** a wide stretch: *His book showed the great breadth of his learning.|breadth of mind/opinions*

**break¹** /breɪk/ *v* **broke** /brəʊk/, **broken** /ˈbrəʊkən/, **breaking 1** [I;T] to (cause to) separate into parts suddenly or violently, but not by cutting or tearing: *I dropped the glass and it broke.|Somebody has broken the chair.|to break a window/a leg|The rope broke when they were climbing.|The window broke into pieces.|to break a branch off a tree|A large piece of ice broke away from the main mass.*|(fig.) *You'll* **break your neck** (=kill yourself) *if you aren't more careful!* **2** [I;T] to (cause to) become unusable by damage to one or more parts: *He broke the clock by dropping it.|This machine is broken and must be repaired.* **3** [I;T] to (cause to) become, suddenly or violently: *The prisoner broke free/loose.|The box broke open when it fell.|They broke the door down.* **4** [T] to disobey; not keep; not act in accordance with: *to break the law/a promise* **5** [I] to force a way (into, out of, or through): *He broke into the shop and stole £100.* **6** [T] to bring under control: *to break a horse/a person's spirit* **7** [T] to do better than: *to break a record (in sports, business, etc.)* **8** [I;T] to (cause to) be destroyed: |*He may break under continuous questioning.* **9** [I;T] to interrupt (an activity): *We broke our journey to Rome at Venice.|The bushes broke my fall.|Let's break for a meal and begin again afterwards.* **10** [I;T] to (cause to) come to an end: *to break the silence with a cry|The cold weather broke at the end of March.|The visit was* **broken short** *because there was talk of war.* **11** [I;T] to (cause to) come esp. suddenly into being or notice: *as day breaks|The storm broke.|The news broke.|Break the bad news gently.* **12** [T] to discover the secret of: *She broke their* CODE. (=she was able to understand their secret writing)| **13 break the back of** *infml* to finish the main or the worst part of: *It took them all day to break the back of the job.* **14 break cover** (of an animal) to run out from a hiding place –see also UNBREAKABLE

USAGE One cannot **break** soft things like cloth or paper, but one can **tear** them, which means "pull apart so as to leave rough edges", or **cut** them, which means "divide by using a sharp edge": *He* **tore** *the paper into pieces.|I* **cut** *the cake with a knife.* Things made of glass and CHINA may **break** (or be broken) or **smash**, which means "break suddenly into small pieces": *The dish* **smashed** *on the floor.* **Crack** means "break without the parts becoming separated": *You've* **cracked** *the window, but luckily you haven't* **broken** *it.* **Burst** means "break suddenly by pressure from inside": *She blew up the paper bag until it* **burst**.

**break away** *v adv* [I] to escape (from someone): *The criminal broke away from the policemen who were holding him.*|(fig.) *Modern music has broken away from the old rules.* –see also BREAKAWAY

**break down** *v adv* **1** [I;T (=**break** sthg.↔ **down**)] to destroy; reduce or be reduced to pieces: *They broke the door down.|The old cars were broken down for their metal and parts.*|(fig.) *I tried to break down his opposition to our plan.|His opposition broke down.* **2** [I] (of machinery) to fail; stop working: *The car broke down.*|(fig.) *The peace talks have broken down.* **3** [I] (of a person) to lose control of one's feelings: *Peter broke down and wept when his mother died.* **4** [I;T (=**break** sthg.↔ **down**) *into*] to (cause to) separate into different kinds or divide into types: *Chemicals in the body break our food down into useful substances.* –see also BREAKDOWN

**break even** *v adv* [I] to make neither a loss nor a profit in doing business

**break in** *v adv* **1** [I] to enter a building by force: *He broke in and stole my money.* –see also BREAK-IN **2** [I] to interrupt: *She broke in with some ideas of her own.|She broke in on/upon my thoughts when she called me.* **3** [T] (**break** sthg.↔ **in**) to bring under control; make accustomed to something: *to break new shoes in* (=wear them to make them comfortable)

**break into** sthg. *v prep* [T] **1** to enter by force: *to break into a house* **2** to interrupt **3** also **burst into** sthg.– to begin suddenly to sing, laugh, etc.: *to break* *into song/laughter* **4** to begin suddenly: *break into a run* **5** to use part of, unwillingly: *to break into money one has saved*

**break** sbdy. **of** sthg. *v prep* [T] to cure of (a bad habit): *Doctors keep trying to break him of smoking/of his dependence on the drug.*

**break off** *v adv* [I;T (=**break** sthg.↔ **off**)] **1** to (cause to) end; interrupt: *Those two countries have broken off relations (with each other).* **2** to (cause to) become separated from the main part with suddenness or violence, but not by cutting: *He broke off a branch.|A branch broke off (the tree).*

**break out** *v adv* [I] **1** (esp. of something bad) to begin suddenly: *War/A fire broke out.* –see also OUTBREAK **2** [*in*] to show or give voice to, suddenly: *His face broke out* (=became covered) *in spots.|She broke out in curses.* **3** [*of*] to escape (from): *to break out of prison*

**break through** *v adv prep* [I;T (=**break through** sthg.)] **1** to force a way through: *The sun broke through (the clouds).* **2** to make a new discovery in (something), esp. after a long time: *The doctors broke through in their fight against heart disease.* –see also BREAKTHROUGH

**break up** *v adv* **1** [I;T (=**break** sthg.↔ **up**)] to (cause to) divide into smaller pieces: *The ice will break up when the warm weather comes.* **2** [I;T (=**break** sthg. ↔ **up**)] to (cause to) come to an end: *The police broke up the fight.|Their marriage broke up.* **3** [I] also **split up**– to separate: *What will happen to the children if Jim and Mary break up?|The crowd broke up.* **4** [I;T (=**break** sbdy. **up**)] to (cause to) suffer severe anxiety and pain: *He may break up under all this pressure.* –see also BREAK **down,** BREAKUP

**break with** sbdy./sthg. *v prep* [T] to end (a friendship, etc.): *to break with one's former friends/with old ideas*

**break²** *n* **1** an opening made by breaking or being broken: *a break in the clouds* **2** a pause for rest; period of time between activities: *a coffee break|We've worked 24 hours* **without a break.** (=continuously) **3** a change from the usual pattern or custom: *a break from/with the past* **4** the time of day before sunrise when daylight first appears: *the break of day|at break of day|at daybreak* **5** *infml* a chance (esp. to make things better); piece of luck: *Give him a break and he'll succeed.*

**break·age** /ˈbreɪkɪdʒ/ *n* [C;U] (the action of causing) a broken place or part; the (value of the) articles broken: *a breakage in the gas pipes*

**break·a·way** /ˈbreɪkəweɪ/ *n* [C; A] an act or example of BREAKing **away** (as from a group or custom): *A* **breakaway group** *within the old political party formed a new one.*

**break·down** /ˈbreɪkdaʊn/ *n* **1** a sudden failure in operation; a stop: *Our car had a breakdown.|a breakdown of talks between workers and employers|a* **nervous breakdown** (=being unable to continue one's usual way of life because of anxiety, etc.) **2** a division into smaller groups; explanation in detail: *a breakdown of the report* –see also BREAK **down,** BREAKUP

**break·fast** /ˈbrekfəst/ *n* [C;U] the first meal of the day: *He has breakfast at seven o'clock.|It happened at/during breakfast.|She likes eggs for breakfast.* –**breakfast** *v* [I *on*]: *We breakfasted early.*

**break-in** /ˈ··/ *n* the illegal, forcible entering of a building: *a break-in at the bank* –see also BREAK **in**

**break·neck** /ˈbreɪknek/ *adj* [A] very fast or dangerous: **at breakneck speed**

**break·through** /ˈbreɪkθruː/ *n* (the action of making) an important discovery (often after earlier failures): *Scientists have made a breakthrough in their treatment of that disease.* –see also BREAK **through**

**break·up** /ˈbreɪkʌp/ *n* **1** (esp. of a relationship or association) a coming to an end: *the breakup of a marriage* **2** a division into smaller parts: *the breakup of the large farms* –see also BREAK **up,** BREAKDOWN

**break·wa·ter** /ˈbreɪkˌwɔːtəʳ‖-ˌwɔ-, -ˌwɑ-/ *n* a thick wall built out into the sea to lessen the force of the waves near a harbour

**breast** /brest/ *n* **1** either of the two parts of a woman's body that produce milk, or the smaller part like this on a man's body: *a baby still at its mother's breast/at the breast* –see picture on page 299 **2** *lit* the upper front part of the body where the feelings are supposed to be: *a* **troubled breast** –compare HEART (2), BOSOM **3 make a clean breast of** to tell the whole truth about (something, esp. something bad that one has done)

**breast·stroke** /ˈbrest-strəʊk/ *n* [S;U] a way of swimming with one's chest downwards, and one's arms pulling backwards HORIZONTALly from in front of one's head

**breath** /breθ/ *n* **1** [U] air taken into and breathed out of the lungs: *After all that running I have no breath left.* **2** [C] a single act of breathing air in and out once: *Take a deep breath.|*(fig.) *Let's go out for a breath of fresh air.|She claimed not to like the place, but* **in the next breath** *said she was taking her holiday there.* **3** [S *of*] a sign or slight movement of (something): *There was hardly* **a breath of air.** (=there was very little wind) **4 get one's breath (back) (again)/catch one's breath** to return to one's usual rate of breathing: *I need time to get my breath after running.* **5 hold one's breath** to stop breathing for a time: (fig.) *The country held its breath* (=waited anxiously) *to see who would win the election.* **6 out of breath** breathing very rapidly (as from tiring exercise); BREATHLESS (1) **7 take one's breath away** to make one unable to speak (from surprise, pleasure, etc.): *The picture took my breath away.* **8 under one's breath** in a low voice or a whisper

**breath·a·lyse** /ˈbreθəl-aɪz/ *v* **-lysed, -lysing** [T] *infml* to test (a driver) with a BREATHALYSER

**breath·a·lys·er** /ˈbreθəl-aɪzəʳ/ *n infml* an apparatus used by the police in Britain to measure the amount of alcohol that the driver of a car has drunk

**breathe** /briːð/ *v* **breathed, breathing 1** [I;T] to take (air, gas, etc.) into the lungs (and send it out again): *If you stop breathing you'll soon become unconscious.|The doctor told him to breathe in deeply* (=take air in) *and then breathe out.|He became ill after breathing coal dust for many years.|*(fig.) *breathing words of love into her ear* **2** [T *into*] to give or send out (a smell, a feeling, etc.): *The new general was able to breathe courage/new life* *into the army.*|(fig.) *He really* **breathes fire** *when he gets angry!* **3 (be able to) breathe again** to stop feeling anxious: *He's gone; you can breathe (freely) again.* **4 breathe down someone's neck** *infml* to keep too close a watch on what someone is doing

**breath·er** /ˈbriːðəʳ/ *n infml* a short pause for a rest: *Let's have/take a breather for a few minutes.*

**breath·less** /ˈbreθlǝs/ *adj* **1** breathing with difficulty; needing to breathe rapidly: *By the time I got to the top I was completely breathless.* **2** causing one to stop breathing (because of excitement, fear, etc.): *a breathless silence during the last game of the tennis match*|*breathless haste/hurry/speed* –**breathlessly** *adv* –**breathlessness** *n* [U]

**breath·tak·ing** /ˈbreθˌteɪkɪŋ/ *adj* **1** very exciting: *a breathtaking horse race* **2** very unusual: *breathtaking beauty* –**breathtakingly** *adv*

**breech·es** ‖also **britches** *AmE* /ˈbrɪtʃǝz/ *n* [P] short trousers, esp. for men, fastened at or below the knee: *riding breeches* –see PAIR[1] (USAGE)

**breed**[1] /briːd/ **bred** /bred/, **breeding** *v* **1** [I] (of animals) to produce young: *Rabbits breed very quickly.* **2** [T] to keep (usu. animals or fish) for the purpose of producing and developing young in controlled conditions: *These horses were bred in Ireland.* **3** [T] to cause or be the beginning of: *Dirt is the* **breeding-ground** *of disease.* (=the place where it can develop) –**breeding** *n* [U]: *a person of fine breeding* (=trained in polite social behaviour)

**breed**[2] *n* a kind or class of animal (or plant), usu. developed under the influence of man: *a breed of dog*|*The islanders are a strong breed of people.*

**breed·er** /ˈbriːdəʳ/ *n* a person who BREEDS[1] (2) animals, birds, or fish

**breeze**[1] /briːz/ a light gentle wind –see WEATHER[1] (USAGE)

**breeze**[2] *v* **breezed, breezing** [I] *infml* to move swiftly or without care: *He just breezed in and smiled.*

**breeze/sail through** sthg. *v prep* [T] *infml* to go through or pass easily: *She breezed through the examination with no trouble at all!*

**breez·y** /ˈbriːzi/ **-ier, -iest** *adj* **1** of or having fairly strong BREEZES **2** quick, cheerful, and bright in manner: *His breezy manner made him popular.* –**breezily** *adv* –**breeziness** *n* [U]

**breth·ren** /ˈbreðrǝn/ *n* [P] (used as a form of address to people in a church service) brothers

**brev·i·ty** /ˈbrevǝti/ *n* [U] (of non-material things) shortness: *the brevity of his writing/his life*

**brew** /bruː/ *v* [I;T] **1** to make (beer) **2** [*up*] **a** to mix (tea or coffee) with hot water and prepare for drinking **b** (of tea or coffee) to become ready for drinking after being mixed with hot water: (fig.) *Trouble/a storm was brewing.* –**brew** *n*

**brew·er** /ˈbruːəʳ/ *n* a person who makes beer

**brew·er·y** /ˈbruːəri/ **-ies** *n* a place where beer is made

**bri·ar** /ˈbraɪəʳ/ *n* [C;U] → BRIER

**bribe**[1] /braɪb/ *v* **bribed, bribing** [T *with, into*] to influence unfairly (esp. someone in a position of trust) by favours or gifts: *He bribed the policeman (to let him go free/into letting him go free).*

**bribe**[2] *n* something offered or given in bribing (BRIBE): *The official took bribes from people who wanted favours.*

**brib·er·y** /ˈbraɪbəri/ *n* [U] giving or taking of a BRIBE[2]

**bric-a-brac** /ˈbrɪk əˌbræk/ *n* [U] small decorations in a house

**brick**[1] /brɪk/ *n* **1** [C;U] (a hard piece of) baked clay used for building: *They used yellow bricks to build the house.*|*The house is made of brick.* **2** [C] something in the shape of a brick: *a brick of ice cream* **3** [C] *BrE*‖**block** *AmE*– a small building block as a child's toy **4 beat/run one's head against a brick wall** *infml* to waste one's efforts by trying to do something impossible **5 like a ton of bricks** *infml* with sudden crushing weight or force or in sudden anger: *He came down on me like a ton of bricks when I arrived late.* **6 drop a brick** *BrE infml* to make a foolish remark which hurts someone's feelings

**brick**[2] *v*→ BRICK UP

**brick·lay·er** /ˈbrɪkˌleɪəʳ/ *n* a workman who lays bricks (=puts bricks in place) –**bricklaying** *n* [U]

**brick** sthg.↔ **up/in** *v adv* [T] to fill completely with bricks: *They've bricked up the door opening.*

**bride** /braɪd/ *n* a girl or woman about to be married, or just married: *The bride wore a beautiful white dress.* –see also BRIDEGROOM –**bridal** *adj*

**bride·groom** /ˈbraɪdgruːm, -grʊm/ also **groom**– *n* a man about to be married, or just married –see also BRIDE

**brides·maid** /ˈbraɪdzmeɪd/ *n* an unmarried girl or woman who attends the BRIDE on the day of the marriage ceremony –compare BEST MAN

**bridge**[1] /brɪdʒ/ *n* **1** something that carries a road or railway over a valley, river, etc. **2** the raised part of a ship on which the captain or officer stands when controlling the ship **3** the bony upper part of the nose

**bridge**[2] *v* **bridged, bridging** [T] to build a bridge across: *to bridge a river*

**bridge**[3] *n* [U] a card game for four players

**bri·dle**[1] /ˈbraɪdl/ leather bands put on a horse's head for controlling its movements

**bridle**[2] *v* **bridled, bridling** **1** [T] to put a BRIDLE on: *to bridle a horse* **2** [I *at*] to show anger or displeasure: *He bridled (with anger) at my request.*

**brief**[1] /briːf/ *adj* short, esp. in time: *a brief look at the newspaper*|*a brief letter*|**In brief** (=in as few words as possible) *he says "No".* –**briefly** *adv: She spoke briefly.*

**brief**[2] *n* a short spoken or written statement, esp. one giving facts or arguments about a law case

**brief**[3] *v* [T] to give last instructions or necessary information to: *Before the meeting, let me brief you on what to expect.* –see also DEBRIEF –**briefing** *n* [C;U]: *Before the meeting, let me give you a briefing.*

**brief·case** /ˈbriːfkeɪs/ *n* a flat, usu. soft leather case for carrying papers or books, which opens at the top –see picture on page 16

**briefs** /briːfs/ *n* [P] men's UNDERPANTS or women's PANTIES without legs –see PAIR[1] (USAGE)

**bri·er, briar** /ˈbraɪəʳ/ *n* [C;U] (a) wild bush covered with prickles (THORNS), esp. the wild rose bush

**bri·gade** /brɪˈgeɪd/ *n* [+*sing./pl. v*] **1** a part of an army, of about 5,000 soldiers **2** an organization formed to carry out certain duties, such as putting out fires: *the Fire Brigade*

**brig·a·dier** /ˌbrɪgəˈdɪəʳ/ *n* an officer of high rank in an army

**bright** /braɪt/ *adj* **1** full of light; shining; giving out or throwing back light very strongly: *The sun is brighter than the moon.|What a bright sunny day!|*(fig.) *one of the brightest moments in our country's history|a face bright with happiness* **2** (of a colour) strong, clear, and easily seen: *bright red/yellow* **3** clever; quick at learning: *a bright child/idea* **4** showing hope or signs of future success: *You have a bright future ahead of you!* **5 look on/at the bright side (of things)** to be cheerful and hopeful in spite of difficulties **–brightly** *adv* **–brightness** *n* [U]

**bright·en** /ˈbraɪtn/ *v* [I;T *up*] to (cause to) become bright: *She brightened when she heard the good news.*

**bril·liant** /ˈbrɪlɪənt/ *adj* **1** very bright, splendid, or showy in appearance: *a brilliant sun/sea|brilliant blue* **2** very clever; causing great admiration or satisfaction: *a brilliant scientist|a brilliant piece of music* **–brilliance, –cy** *n* [U] **–brilliantly** *adv*

**brim**[1] /brɪm/ *n* **1** the top edge of a cup, glass, bowl, etc., esp. with regard to how full it is: *The glass was full to the brim.* **2** the bottom part of a hat which turns outwards to give shade, or protection against rain –compare CROWN[1] (3) **3 -brimmed** (of hats) having a brim of the stated kind: *a wide-brimmed hat*

**brim**[2] *v* **-mm-** [I *over*] to be full to the top and nearly overflowing: *His eyes brimmed (over) with tears.|a brimming cup of coffee*

**brim over** *v adv* [I *with*] to express a lot of (usu. a good feeling): *brimming over (with joy)* –compare BUBBLE[2]

**brim·ful, -full** /ˈbrɪmˌfʊl/ *adj* [F *of, with*] full to the top; overflowing: *to fill the bowl brimful with sugar|eyes brimful of tears*

**brine** /braɪn/ *n* [U] water containing quite a lot of salt, used for preserving food **–briny** *adj*

**bring** /brɪŋ/ *v* **brought** /brɔːt/, **bringing** [T] **1** [*to, for, over, across,* etc.] to come with, carry, or lead (to or towards): *Bring (me) the book.|Bring your friend to the party.|The prisoner was brought before the judge.|The beauty of the music brought tears to her eyes.* –see Study Notes on page 429 **2** to cause or lead to: *Old age brings happiness.|He could never bring himself to kill an animal or bird.* **3** to be sold for: *This old car will bring about £10.* **4** [*against*] *law* to make officially: *The policeman brought a charge against the fast driver.* **5** to cause to come (to a certain place or state): *His cries brought the neighbours (running).|Bring them in/out/back/together.|That brings the total (up) to £200.|to* **bring** *something* **to an end**|*to* **bring** *someone* **to his knees** (=to defeat)

**bring** sthg.↔ **about** *v adv* [T] to cause: *Science has brought about many changes in our lives.*

**bring** sbdy. **around/over/round** *v adv* [T] to persuade into a change of opinion: *We must bring him around to our point of view.*

**bring** sbdy./sthg.↔ **back** *v adv* [T *to*] **1** to cause to return: *If I go with you in your car, will you be able to bring me back?|Bring us back our books, please.|That old song certainly brings back memories!|They want to bring back hanging as a punishment.* (=hanging isn't used as a punishment now) **2** to obtain and return with: *When you go to the post office, will you please bring me back some stamps?/bring me some stamps back?/bring some stamps back for me?*

**bring** sbdy./sthg.↔ **down** *v adv* [T] to cause to fall or come down: *The pilot brought the plane down gently.|*(fig.) *to bring down prices|to bring someone down to your own level|to* **bring down** *trouble* **on** *the family*

**bring** sthg.↔ **forward** *v adv* [T] **1** to introduce; suggest: *The director brought forward a new plan for the company.* **2** also **put** sthg.↔ **forward**– to bring nearer to the present time: *The election will be brought forward to June instead of July.*

**bring** sbdy./sthg.↔ **in** *v adv* [T] **1** to introduce: *to bring in a* BILL[1] (2) *(in Parliament)|to bring in a new fashion|to bring in experienced people to help* **2** to produce as profit or earnings; earn: *The sale brought (us) in over £200.|She's bringing in £150 a week.* **3** to give a decision in court: *to bring in a* VERDICT *of guilty or not guilty* **4** to bring to a police station: *The policeman brought in the criminal.*

**bring** sthg. **into** sthg. *v prep* [T] to cause (an activity or condition) to start: *to bring a new system into being/into play/into force*

**bring** sthg.↔ **off** *v adv* to succeed in doing (something difficult): *It was a very difficult job but Anne was able to bring it off successfully.*

**bring** sthg.↔ **on** *v adv* [T] to cause, help (to grow), or improve: *Going out in the rain brought on a fever.|This warm weather should bring on the crops.*

**bring** sthg. **on/upon** sbdy. *v prep* [T] to cause (something, usu. unpleasant) to happen to (esp. oneself): *You've brought this trouble on yourself.*

**bring** sbdy./sthg.↔ **out** *v adv* [T] **1** to produce: *to bring out a new kind of soap|*(fig.) *to bring out the worst in someone* **2** also **draw** sbdy.↔ **out**– to encourage, esp. to talk: *Bill is very quiet: try to bring him out.* **3** to cause to stop working for a purpose (STRIKE[1] (5))

**bring** sbdy.↔ **round/to** *v adv* [T] to cause to regain consciousness: *Peter has fainted: try to bring him round.*

**bring/carry** sbdy. **through** sthg. *v prep* [T] to save (someone) from (an illness, etc.): *The doctor brought Mother through a serious illness.|The people's courage brought them through the war.*

**bring** sbdy./sthg.↔ **up** *v adv* **1** [T] to educate and care for in the family until grown-up: *to bring up children* **2** [T] to raise or introduce (a subject): *to bring up the question of your holidays* –compare COME **up** (1) **3** [T] *esp. BrE* to be sick; VOMIT (one's food) **4** bring sbdy. **up short** to cause to stop suddenly: *John was about to leave, when he was brought up short by a loud noise.*

**brink** /brɪŋk/ *n* [*usu. sing.*] an edge at the top of a cliff, at the side of water, etc.; VERGE: (fig.) **on the brink of** DISASTER|*His failures brought him* **to the brink of** *ruin.*

**brisk** /brɪsk/ *adj* quick and active: *a brisk walker/walk|*(fig.) *a brisk wind* (=pleasantly cold and strong) **–briskly** *adv* **–briskness** *n* [U]

**bris·tle**[1] /ˈbrɪsəl/ *n* [C;U] (a) short stiff coarse hair: *His chin was covered with bristles.*

**bristle**[2] *v* **-tled, -tling** [I *up, with*] (esp. of hair, fur, etc.) to stand up stiffly: *The animal's fur bristled (up) with anger.|*(fig.) *The castle* **bristled with** (=was full of) *guns.*

**bris·tly** /ˈbrɪsli/ *adj* **-tlier, -tliest** like or full of BRISTLES[1]: *a bristly face*

**britch·es** /ˈbrɪtʃɨz/ *n* [P] *AmE* for BREECHES

**Brit·ish** /ˈbrɪtɪʃ/ *adj* of Britain (or the British COMMONWEALTH)

**brit·tle** /ˈbrɪtl/ *adj* hard but easily broken or damaged: *brittle glass*|(fig.) *a brittle nature*

**broach** /brəʊtʃ/ *v* [T] to introduce as a subject of conversation: *At last he broached the subject of the new contract.*

**broad** /brɔːd/ *adj* **1** large (or larger than usual) measured from side to side; wide: *broad shoulders*|*a broad river* –compare NARROW **2** [after *n*] (*after a measurement*) in width; across: *4 metres broad* **3** not limited; generous in thought: *a broad imagination*|*broadminded* **4** [A] general; not particular: *Give me a broad idea of your plans.* **5** [A] full and clear (esp. in the phrase **broad daylight**) **6** (of a way of speaking) strongly marked; showing clearly where the speaker comes from: *She spoke broad Scots.*|*a broad* ACCENT[1] (1) –**broadly** *adv: Broadly (speaking), I agree with you.* –**broadness** *n* [U]

**broad bean** /ˌ·ˈ·‖ˈ··/ *n* a large flat kind of bean

**broad·cast**[1] /brɔːdkaːst‖-kæst/ *n* a single radio or television presentation: *She made/gave an interesting broadcast about modern art.*

**broadcast**[2] *v* **-cast**‖also **-casted** *AmE*, **-casting 1** [I;T] to send out or give (radio or television presentations): *The BBC broadcasts to all parts of the world.*|(fig.) *to broadcast* (=make widely known) *the news to all one's friends* **2** [I] to speak or perform on radio or television –**broadcaster** *n* –**broadcasting** *n* [U]

**broad·en** /ˈbrɔːdn/ *v* [I;T *out*] to (cause to) become broad or broader: *Travel broadens the mind.*|*The river broadens (out) at this point.* –compare WIDEN, NARROW[2]

**broad·mind·ed** /ˌbrɔːdˈmaɪndɨd◂/ *adj* willing to respect the opinions (and actions) of others even if very different from one's own –opposite **narrow-minded** –**broadmindedness** *n* [U]

**broad·side** /ˈbrɔːdsaɪd/ *n* a forceful spoken or written attack: *She delivered a broadside* (=made a strong attack) *against the government's action.*

**bro·cade** /brəˈkeɪd‖brəʊ-/ *n* [U] decorative cloth with a raised pattern of gold or silver threads

**broc·co·li** /ˈbrɒkəli‖ˈbrɑ-/ *n* a vegetable similar to CAULIFLOWER whose young green flower heads are eaten

**bro·chure** /ˈbrəʊʃəʳ, -ʃʊəʳ‖brəʊˈʃʊər/ *n* a small thin book (BOOKLET; PAMPHLET), esp. one giving details of a service offered for money: *a holiday brochure*|*an advertising brochure*

**brogue**[1] /brəʊg/ *n* [*usu. pl.*] a strong thick shoe, esp. one with a pattern made in the leather –see PAIR[1] (USAGE)

**brogue**[2] *n* [*usu. sing.*] a way of speaking, esp. the way in which the Irish speak English

**broil** /brɔɪl/ *v* [I;T] *AmE* for GRILL[1] (1) (esp. chicken, meat, or fish): (fig.) *It's really broiling* (=it's very hot) *today.* –see COOK (USAGE)

**broil·er** /ˈbrɔɪləʳ/ *n* **1** a young small chicken bred esp. to be cooked by BROILing (or GRILLing) **2** *infml* a very hot day: *Yesterday was a real broiler!*

**broke**[1] /brəʊk/ *adj* [F *no comp.*] *infml* completely without money: *I'm* **(flat/stony) broke.**|*His firm has gone broke.*

**broke**[2] *v past tense of* BREAK

**bro·ken**[1] /ˈbrəʊkən/ *adj* **1** violently separated into smaller pieces; damaged: *a window broken by a ball*|*a broken clock/leg*|(fig.) *broken dreams*|*a broken spirit*|*a broken man*|*a broken-down car* (=a car in a state of disrepair) **2** not kept to; destroyed: *a broken law/promise*|*a broken marriage/home* **3** imperfectly spoken or written: *broken English*

**broken**[2] *v past participle of* BREAK

**broken-heart·ed** /ˌ··ˈ··◂/ *adj* filled with grief: *He was broken-hearted when his wife died.* –**broken-heartedly** *adv*

**bro·ker** /ˈbrəʊkəʳ/ *n* a person who buys and sells (shares in business or foreign money, etc.) for another

**brol·ly** /ˈbrɒli‖ˈbrɑli/ *n* **-lies** *BrE infml* for UMBRELLA (1)

**bron·chi·tis** /brɒŋˈkaɪtɨs‖brɑŋ-/ *n* [U] an illness (INFLAMMATION) of the **bronchial tubes** (=the two branches connecting the WINDPIPE with the lungs), which causes coughing –**bronchitic** /-ˈkɪtɪk/ *adj*

**bron·to·sau·rus** /ˌbrɒntəˈsɔːrəs‖ˌbrɑn-/ *n* **-ri** /raɪ/ a very large four-footed plant-eating DINOSAUR

**bronze**[1] /brɒnz‖brɑnz/ *n* [U] (the dark reddish-brown colour of) a hard mixture (ALLOY[1]) mainly of copper and tin

**bronze**[2] *v* **bronzed, bronzing** [T] to give the appearance or colour of BRONZE to: *bronzed by the sun*

**brooch** /brəʊtʃ/ *n* a decoration worn on women's clothes, fastened on by means of a pin

**brood**[1] /bruːd/ *n* [C +*sing./pl.v*] a family of young creatures, esp. young birds: *a brood of ducks*

**brood**[2] *v* [I] **1** to sit on eggs as a hen does **2** [*over, about*] to continue to think (about something, often bad): *Don't just sit there brooding about your problems.*|*She was brooding over what to do.* **3** [*over*] to hang closely over: *Dark clouds were brooding over the city.* –**broody** *adj* –**broodily** *adv* –**broodiness** *n* [U]

**brook** /brʊk/ *n* a small stream

**broom** /bruːm, brʊm/ *n* a large sweeping brush, usu. with a long handle

**broom·stick** /ˈbruːmˌstɪk, ˈbrʊm-/ *n* the long thin handle of a BROOM

**broth** /brɒθ‖brɔθ/ *n* [C;U] soup in which meat, fish, rice, or vegetables have been cooked: *chicken broth*

**broth·el** /ˈbrɒθəl‖ˈbrɑ-, ˈbrɔ-/ *n* a house of PROSTITUTES, where sex can be had for money

**broth·er** /ˈbrʌðəʳ/ *n* **1** a male relative with the same parents: *John and Peter are brothers.*|*John is Peter's brother* –see picture on page 217 **2** a male member of the same group: *a brother doctor* **3** [*often cap.*] (a title for) a male member of a religious group, esp. a MONK: *a Christian Brother* –compare SISTER –**brotherly** *adj: brotherly love* –**brotherliness** *n* [U]

**broth·er·hood** /ˈbrʌðəhʊd‖-ər-/ *n* **1** [U] the quality or state of being brothers **2** [C *usu. sing.*] the whole body of people in a business, profession, or association: *the medical brotherhood* –compare SISTERHOOD

**brother-in-law** /ˈ···ˌ·/ *n* **brothers-in-law 1** the brother of one's husband or wife **2** the husband of one's sister **3** the husband of the sister of one's husband or wife –see picture on page 217

**brought** /brɔːt/ *v past tense and participle of* BRING

**brow** /braʊ/ *n* **1** [*usu. pl.*] → EYEBROW **2** → FOREHEAD **3** the top of a steep slope or a hill

**brow·beat** /ˈbraʊbiːt/ *v* **-beat, -beaten** /biːtn/, **-beating** [T *into*] to force to obey by using fierce looks or words: *to browbeat someone (into doing something)*

**brown**[1] /braʊn/ *n,adj* [C;U] (of) the colour of earth: *brown shoes|dark brown|a dark brown*

**brown**[2] *v* [I;T] to (cause to) become brown or browner: *browned by the sun|First brown the meat in hot fat.*

**browse** /braʊz/ *v* **browsed, browsing** [I] **1** to feed on young plants, grass, etc.: *cows browsing in the fields* **2** to read parts of books, without purpose: *to browse through/among books* **–browse** *n* [*usu. sing.*]: *I had a browse through the books on the shelf.*

**bruise**[1] /bruːz/ *n* a discoloured place where the skin of a human, animal, or fruit has been INJURED by a blow but not broken

**bruise**[2] *v* **bruised, bruising 1** [T] to cause one or more BRUISES on: *She fell and bruised her knee.|a bruised knee* **2** [I] to show one or more BRUISES: *The skin of a soft fruit bruises easily.*

**brunch** /brʌntʃ/ *n* [C;U] *infml* a late breakfast, an early LUNCH, or a combination of the two

**bru·nette** ||also **brunet** *AmE*– /bruːˈnet/ *n* a woman with dark hair –compare BLOND (2)

**brunt** /brʌnt/ *n* **bear the brunt of** to suffer the heaviest part of (an attack)

**brush**[1] /brʌʃ/ *n* **1** an instrument for cleaning, smoothing, or painting, made of sticks, stiff hair, nylon, etc.: *a clothesbrush|a toothbrush|a hairbrush|a paintbrush* **2** an act of brushing: *I'll just give my coat/hair a quick brush.*

**brush**[2] *v* [I;T] **1** to clean or smooth with a brush: *to brush one's coat/the floor/one's teeth/one's hair*|(fig.) *She brushed* (=moved lightly or carelessly) *past me.* **2** to remove with or as if with a brush: *to brush away a fly (with one's hand)|to brush dirt off* **3** to put into the stated condition with or as if with a brush: *to brush a piece of paper off a table*

**brush** sbdy./sthg.↔ **aside/away** *adv* [T] to refuse to pay attention to: *to brush difficulties/opposition aside*

**brush** sbdy. **off** *v adv* [T] to refuse to listen to or have a relationship with –see also BRUSH-OFF

**brush/polish** sthg.↔ **up** *v adv* [T *on*] to improve one's knowledge of (something known but partly forgotten) by study: *I must brush up (on) my French before going to Paris.* **–brush-up** *n*

**brush**[3] *n* [U] **1** also **brushwood**– small branches broken off from trees or bushes **2** (land covered by) small rough trees and bushes

**brush-off** /ˈ· ·/ *n* **brush-offs** *infml* a clear refusal to be friendly or to listen: *I wanted to speak to her, but she* **gave** *me* **the brush-off.** –see also BRUSH **off**

**brusque** /bruːsk, brʊsk||brʌsk/ *adj* quick and rather impolite: *a brusque person/manner|brusque behaviour* **–brusquely** *adv* **–brusqueness** *n* [U]

**brus·sels sprout** /ˌbrʌsəlz ˈspraʊt/ also **sprout**– *n* [*usu. pl.*] a small tight bunch of leaves, used as a vegetable, which grows in groups on the sides of a high stem

**bru·tal** /ˈbruːtl/ *adj* having or showing no fine or tender human feeling; cruel: *a brutal lie/person|a brutal attack/attacker*|(fig.) *the brutal* (=unpleasantly correct) *truth* **–brutally** /ˈbruːtəli/ *adv* [C;U]: *the brutality/brutalities of war*

**bru·tal·ize**||also **-ise** *BrE* /ˈbruːtəlaɪz/ *v* **-ized, -izing** [T] **1** to make BRUTAL or unfeeling **2** to treat in a BRUTAL manner **–brutalization** /ˌbruːtəlaɪˈzeɪʃən||-lə-/ *n* [U]

**brute**[1] /bruːt/ *n* **1** *often derog* an animal, esp. a large one: (fig.) *Her husband is an unfeeling brute.* **2** an unfortunate animal: *The horse broke its leg when it fell and the poor brute had to be destroyed.*

**brute**[2] *adj* [*no comp.*] like an animal in being unreasonable, cruel, or very strong: **brute force/strength**

**brut·ish** /ˈbruːtɪʃ/ *adj derog* suitable for or typical of animals rather than people: *The poor people lived in brutish conditions.|brutish behaviour* **–brutishly** *adv*

**BSc** /ˌbiːes ˈsiː/ *BrE*||**BS** *AmE*– *abbrev. for:* Bachelor of Science; (a title for someone who has) a first university degree in a science subject: *He is/has a BSc in Chemistry|Mary Jones, BSc* –compare BA

**bub·ble**[1] /ˈbʌbəl/ *n* a hollow ball of liquid containing air or gas: *bubbles on a boiling liquid|soap bubbles*

**bubble**[2] *v* **-bled, -bling 1** [I] to form, produce, or rise as bubbles: *The gas bubbled to the surface of the water.*|(fig.) *She was* **bubbling over with** *joy.* (=showing great happiness) –compare BRIM **over 2** to make the sound of bubbles rising in liquid: *We could hear the pot bubbling (away) quietly on the fire.*

**bub·bly** /ˈbʌbli/ *adj* **-blier, -bliest 1** full of bubbles **2** showing good feelings freely: *bubbly people at a party*

**buck**[1] /bʌk/ *n* **1 bucks** *or* **buck, doe** *fem.*– the male of certain animals, esp. the deer, the rat, and the rabbit **2 bucks** *or* **buck** → ANTELOPE **3** *infml* responsibility: *I don't know enough about it to decide, so I'll* **pass the buck** *(to you).* **4** *AmE infml* an American dollar

**buck**[2] *v* **1** [I] (esp. of a horse) to jump up with all four feet off the ground **2** [T] to throw off (a rider) by doing this: *The wild horse bucked its first rider off.*

**buck up** *v adv infml* **1** [T] (**buck** sthg.↔ **up**) to try to improve: *You'd better buck up your ideas.* **2** [I] → HURRY **up:** *You'd best buck up or we'll be late.* **3** [I;T] (=**buck** sbdy. **up**)] → CHEER **up:** *Buck up! Lots of people fail their driving test first time.*

**buck·et**[1] /ˈbʌkɪ̈t/ *n* **1** an open metal, plastic, or wooden container with a handle for carrying liquids; PAIL **2** its contents: *a bucket/a bucketful of water*|(fig.) *The rain came down* **in buckets.** (=it rained very hard) **3 kick the bucket** *humor infml* to die

**bucket**[2] *v* [I *down*] *BrE infml* to rain very hard: *It's been bucketing (down) all day.*

**buck·le**[1] /ˈbʌkəl/ *n* a metal fastener used for joining the ends of a belt, or two leather bands (STRAPS), or for decoration

**buckle**[2] *v* **-led, -ling** [I;T] **1** [*up, together*] to (cause to) fasten or stay in a stated place with a BUCKLE[1]: *He buckled (up) his belt tightly.|The belt buckled (up) easily.|The two ends buckle (together) at the back.|He buckled on his sword.* –opposite **unbuckle 2** to (cause to) become bent or wavy through heat, shock, pressure, etc.: *The accident buckled the wheel of my* *bicycle.*|*The wheel buckled.*|(fig.) *to buckle* (=yield) *under the attack and run away*

**buckle down** *v adv* [I *to*] *infml* to begin to work seriously (at): *to buckle down to work/working*

**bud¹** /bʌd/ *n* [C;U] a young tightly rolled-up flower (or leaf) before it opens: *The plant will* **come into bud** *in spring.*

**bud²** *v* **-dd-** [I] to produce BUDS

**Bud·dhis·m** /ˈbʊdɪzəm‖ˈbuː-, ˈbʊ-/ *n* [U] a religion of east and central Asia growing out of the teaching of Gautama Buddha that pureness of spirit is the answer to suffering **–Buddhist** *n*

**bud·ding** /ˈbʌdɪŋ/ *adj* [A *no comp.*] beginning to develop: *a budding poet*

**bud·dy** /ˈbʌdi/ *n infml* **1** (esp. of a man) friend; partner: *We're good buddies.* **2** *esp. AmE* (used as a form of address, often in anger) fellow: *Get out of my way, buddy!*

**budge** /bʌdʒ/ *v* **budged, budging** [I;T] to (cause to) move a little: *I can't budge this rock.*|(fig.) *She won't budge from her opinions.*

**bud·ger·i·gar** /ˈbʌdʒərigɑːʳ/ also **budgie** /ˈbʌdʒi/ *infml*– *n* a small bright-coloured bird of Australian origin, often kept as a cage bird in British houses

**bud·get¹** /ˈbʌdʒ¹ɜt/ *n* **1** a plan of how to arrange private or public income or spending: *a family budget*|*the government's efforts to* **balance the budget** (=make sure that no more money is being spent than is being earned) **2** the quantity of money stated in these plans: *a budget of £10,000,000*

**budget²** *v* [I] to plan private or public spending within the limits of a certain amount of money: *She budgeted for* (=planned to save enough money for) *a holiday.* **–budgetary** *adj* [*no comp.*]

**buff¹** /bʌf/ *n,adj* [U] a faded yellow colour: *buff yellow*

**buff²** *v* [T *up*] to polish (metal) with something soft

**buff³** *n infml* a person who is very interested in and knowledgeable about the stated subject: *a film buff*

**buf·fa·lo** /ˈbʌfələʊ/ *n* **-loes** *or* **-lo 1** any of several kinds of very large black cattle with long flattish curved horns, found mainly in Asia and Africa **2 →** BISON

**buff·er** /ˈbʌfəʳ/ *n* a spring put on the front and back of a railway vehicle to take the shock when it runs into anything: (fig.) *A little money can be a useful buffer in time of need.* –see picture on page 501

**buf·fet¹** /ˈbʌf¹ɜt/ *v* [T] to strike sharply or repeatedly: *We were buffeted by the wind and the rain.*|*We were buffeted about* (=thrown from side to side) *during the rough boat ride.*

**buf·fet²** /ˈbʊfeɪ‖bəˈfeɪ/ *n* (a place, esp. a long table, where one can get) food, usu. cold, to be eaten standing up, or sitting down somewhere else –see picture on page 501

**buf·foon** /bəˈfuːn/ *n* a rough and noisy fool: *to play the buffoon at a party* **–buffoonery** *n* [U]

**bug¹** /bʌg/ *n* **1** *AmE* any small insect, creeping or flying –compare BEETLE **2** *infml* a small living thing causing disease; GERM (1): *I'm not feeling well: I must have picked up a bug somewhere.* **3** *infml* an apparatus for listening secretly to other people's conversations: *The police tested the room for bugs.* **4** [*the* S] *infml* an eager but sometimes foolish or not lasting interest in something: *bitten by the travel bug*

**bug²** *v* **-gg-** [T] *infml* **1** to fit with a secret listening apparatus: *The police have bugged my office.* **2** *AmE* to annoy (someone) continually: *Stop bugging me!*

**bug·ger¹** /ˈbʌgəʳ/ *n esp. BrE infml not polite* **1** (used in expressions of good or kind feeling) fellow or animal: *Poor bugger!* **2** something that causes a lot of trouble or difficulty: *a bugger of a job*

**bugger²** *interj BrE infml not polite* (used for adding force to expressions of displeasure): *Oh, bugger it! I've missed my train!*

**bu·gle** /ˈbjuːgəl/ *n* a brass musical instrument, played by blowing, like a TRUMPET but shorter, used esp. for army calls **–bugler** *n*

**build¹** /bɪld/ *v* **built** /bɪlt/, **building** [I;T *for, out of*] to make (one or more things) by putting pieces together: *That house is built of brick(s).*|*a brick-built house*|*They're building (houses) in that area now.*|(fig.) *Hard work builds (up) character.*|*Reading builds* (=develops) *the mind.* **–builder** *n*

**build up** *v adv* [I;T (= **build** sthg.↔ **up**)] to (cause to) form steadily, become larger, or develop: *to build up one's strength*|*The clouds are building up.*|*She gradually built up a good business.* –see also BUILDUP

**build²** *n* [C;U] shape and size, esp. of the human body: *a powerful build*|*We are of the same build.* –see BODY (USAGE)

**build·ing** /ˈbɪldɪŋ/ *n* **1** [C] something, usu. with a roof and walls, that is intended to stay in one place and not to be moved or taken down again: *Houses and churches are buildings.* **2** [U] the art or business of making buildings

**building so·ci·e·ty** /ˈ·· ·ˌ···/ *n* (in Britain) an association into which people put money which is then lent to those who want to buy or build houses

**build·up** /ˈbɪld-ʌp/ *n* increase: *the buildup of our military forces*|*the buildup of traffic on the road* –see also BUILD **up**

**built-up** /ˌ·ˈ·◂/ *adj* covered with buildings: *a built-up area*

**bulb** /bʌlb/ *n* **1** a round root of certain plants **2** any object of this shape, esp. the glass part of an electric lamp: *a light bulb*

**bul·bous** /ˈbʌlbəs/ *adj often derog* shaped like a BULB (1); fat and round: *a bulbous nose*

**bulge¹** /bʌldʒ/ *n* a swelling of a surface caused by pressure from within or below: (fig.) *the* **population bulge** (=sudden unusual increase, which does not last) **–bulgy** *adj* **–bulginess** *n* [U]

**bulge²** *v* **bulged, bulging** [I *with, out*] to swell out: *His pockets were bulging with money.*

**bulk** /bʌlk/ *n* **1** [U] great size, shape, mass, or quantity **2** [C *usu. sing.*] an unusually large, fat, or shapeless body: *The elephant lowered its great bulk.* **3** [*the* S *of*] the main or greater part (of): *The bulk of the work has been done.* **4 in bulk** in large quantities; not packed in separate parcels: *to buy/sell in bulk*

**bulk·y** /ˈbʌlki/ *adj* **-ier, -iest 1** having BULK (1) esp. if large of its kind or rather fat **2** having great size or mass in comparison with weight: *a bulky woollen garment* **–bulkiness** *n* [U]

**bull** /bʊl/ *n* **1** the male form of cattle, kept on farms to be the parent of young cattle **2** the male of certain other large land or sea animals: *a bull elephant* –compare cow[1] **3 a bull in a china shop** *infml* a rough, careless person in a place where skill and care are needed **4 take the bull by the horns** *infml* to face difficulties in spite of fear

**bull·dog** /ˈbʊldɒg‖-dɔg/ *n* a fierce dog of English origin, with a short neck and short thick legs

**bull·doze** /ˈbʊldəʊz/ *v* **-dozed, -dozing** [T] to force (objects, earth, etc. out of the way) with a special heavy machine (**bulldozer**) used when a level surface is needed: *to bulldoze the ground before building*|(fig.) *He bulldozed his plan through Parliament.*|*They bulldozed him into agreeing.*

**bul·let** /ˈbʊlə̇t/ *n* a type of shot fired from a gun, usu. long and with a rounded or pointed end: *A* **bullet-proof** *car/garment stops bullets from passing through it.* –compare SHOT[1] (6), SHELL[1] (3)

**bul·le·tin** /ˈbʊlətə̇n/ *n* **1** a short public usu. official notice or news report intended to be made public without delay: *Here is the latest bulletin about the President's health.* **2** a short printed newspaper, esp. one produced by an association or group

**bull·fight** /ˈbʊlfaɪt/ *n* a ceremonial fight between men and a BULL (1), esp. as practised as a sport in Spain, Portugal, and Latin America –**bullfighter** *n* –**bullfighting** *n* [U]

**bul·lion** /ˈbʊljən/ *n* [U] bars of gold or silver: *gold bullion*

**bul·lock** /ˈbʊlək/ *n* a young BULL which cannot breed, often used for pulling vehicles –compare STEER[2]

**bull·ring** /ˈbʊlˌrɪŋ/ *n* a circular place (an ARENA) for BULLFIGHTS, surrounded by rows of seats

**bull's-eye** /ˈ··/ *n* the circular centre of a TARGET (1) that people try to hit when shooting: *That shot was a bull's eye.* (=it hit the centre and had the highest value)|(fig.) *Your last remark really* **hit the bull's-eye***: it was exactly right.*

**bul·ly** /ˈbʊli/ *v* **-lied, -lying** [I;T *into*] to use one's strength to hurt (weaker people); make them afraid: *He was always bullying smaller boys (into doing things).* –**bully** *n* **-lies**

**bul·rush** /ˈbʊlrʌʃ/ *n* a tall grasslike waterside plant

**bul·wark** /ˈbʊlwək‖-ərk/ *n* a strong wall built for defence or protection: (fig.) *That country is a bulwark of freedom.*

**bum[1]** /bʌm/ *n infml not polite, esp. BrE* the part of the body on which a person sits; BUTTOCKS

**bum[2]** *v* **-mm-** [T] *infml* to ask for (something) with no intention of returning it: *Can I bum a cigarette?*

**bum·ble** /ˈbʌmbəl/ *v* **-bled, -bling** [I *on, about*] *infml* to speak so that the words are hard to hear clearly: *He kept bumbling on about something.*

**bum·ble·bee** /ˈbʌmbəlbiː/ *n* a large bee which makes a loud noise when flying

**bump[1]** /bʌmp/ *v* **1** [I;T] to strike or knock with force or violence: *The car bumped (into) the tree.*|*The two cars bumped (together/each other).*|*I've bumped my knee (against/on the wall).*|*Something bumped against me.* **2** [I] to move (along) with much sudden shaking, as of a wheeled vehicle over uneven ground: *We bumped along/up and down.*

**bump into** sbdy. *v prep* [T] *infml* to meet by chance

**bump** sbdy.↔ **off** *v adv* [T] *infml* to kill; murder

**bump** sthg.↔ **up** *v adv* [T] *infml* to increase; raise: *You need more high marks to bump up your average.*

**bump[2]** *n* **1** (the sound of) a sudden forceful blow or shock: *We heard a bump in the next room.* **2** a raised round swelling, often as caused by a blow: *a bump on his knee* –**bumpy** *adj* **-ier, -iest** –**bumpiness** *n* [U]

**bump[3]** [*adv +prep*] suddenly; hard; with a sudden BUMP[2] (1): *He wasn't looking, and ran bump into a tree.*

**bum·per[1]** /ˈbʌmpər/ *n* **1** a bar fixed on the front or back of a car to protect the car when it knocks against anything: *The traffic was* **bumper-to-bumper**. (=very close together) –see picture on page 85 **2** *AmE* for BUFFER

**bumper[2]** *adj* [A] very full or large: *a* **bumper crop**

**bun** /bʌn/ *n* **1** a small round sweet cake **2** hair fastened into a tight round shape, usu. at the back of the head: *She wears her hair in a bun.*

**bunch[1]** /bʌntʃ/ *n* [*of*] a number of things (usu. small and of the same kind) fastened, held, or growing together at one point: *a bunch of flowers/fruit/keys*|(*infml*) *This bunch of* (=group of) *girls enjoys/enjoy swimming.*|*John is* **the best of the bunch**. (=the best person in a group)

**bunch[2]** *v* [I;T *up*] to (cause to) form into one or more bunches: *Bunch (up) together and you'll keep warm.*|*This cloth bunches up.* (=gathers into folds)

**bun·dle[1]** /ˈbʌndl/ *n* **1** [C *of*] a number of articles tied, fastened or held together, usu. across the middle **2** [S *of*] *infml* a mass (of): *I'm so anxious I'm just* **a bundle of nerves.**|*She's* **a bundle of fun/laughs.**

**bundle[2]** *v* **-dled, -dling** [I;T] **1** to (cause to) move or hurry in a rather quick and rough manner: *The police bundled him into a car.*|*We all bundled into a car.*|*They bundled the children off (to school).* **2** [T] to put together or store in a disordered way: *Don't bundle all the clothes up like that/into that bag so carelessly.*

**bung[1]** /bʌŋ/ *n* a round piece of wood or other such material used to close the hole in a container

**bung[2]** *v* [T] *BrE infml* to put, push, or throw, esp. roughly: *He picked up a stone and bunged it over the fence.*|*Bung me a cigarette, will you?*

**bung** sthg.↔ **up** *v adv* [T] *infml* to block; stop up: *to bung up a hole*|*My nose is bunged up with a cold.*

**bun·ga·low** /ˈbʌŋgələʊ/ *n* a house which is all on one level –see HOUSE (USAGE); see picture on page 297

**bun·gle** /ˈbʌŋgəl/ *v* **-gled, -gling** [I;T] to do (something) badly: *to bungle a job* –**bungler** *n* –**bungle** *n*

**bun·ion** /ˈbʌnjən/ *n* a painful swelling on the big toe

**bunk** /bʌŋk/ *n* a bed usu. fixed to the wall (as on a ship) and that is often one of two placed one above the other: **Bunk beds** *are useful for children.*

**bun·ker** /ˈbʌŋkər/ *n* **1** a place to store coal, esp. on a ship or outside a house **2** a strongly-built shelter for soldiers, esp. one built underground

**buoy[1]** /bɔɪ‖ˈbuːi, bɔɪ/ *n* a floating object fastened to the bed of the sea, e.g. to show where there are rocks

**buoy[2]** *v* [T *up usu. pass.*] to keep floating: (fig.) *Her spirits were buoyed up by hopes of success.*

**buoy·an·cy** /ˈbɔɪənsi‖ˈbɔɪənsi, ˈbuːjənsi/ *n* [S;U] **1** the tendency of an object to float, or to rise when pushed down into a liquid: *the buoyancy of light* *wood*|(fig.) *a buoyancy of spirit that keeps her happy* **2** the power of a liquid to force upwards an object pushed down into it: *the buoyancy of water* –**buoyant** *adj* –**buoyantly** *adv*

**bur·ble** /ˈbɜːbəl‖ˈbɜr-/ *v* **-bled, -bling** [I] to make a sound like a stream flowing over stones: (fig.) *He burbled on/away* (=talked) *for hours.*

**bur·den¹** /ˈbɜːdn‖-ɜr-/ *n fml* a heavy load: (fig.) *the burden of duty/responsibility*

**burden²** *v* [T] *fml* to load or trouble: *I will not burden you with a lengthy account of what happened.*|*burdened with heavy taxation* –see also UNBURDEN

**bu·reau** /ˈbjʊərəʊ/ *n* **bureaux** /ˈbjʊərəʊz/ **1** *BrE* a large desk or writing-table with a wooden cover which slides over the top to close it **2** *AmE* a chest of drawers for bedroom use **3** a government department **4** a business office, esp. one that collects and/or keeps facts: *an information bureau*

**bu·reauc·ra·cy** /bjʊˈrɒkrəsi, bjʊə-‖-ˈrɑ-/ *n* **-cies** *usu. derog* **1** [S] a group of government, business, or other officers who are appointed rather than elected **2** [C;U] government by such officers, often supposed to be ineffective and full of unnecessary rules –**bureaucratic** /ˌbjʊərəˈkrætɪk/ *adj: too many bureaucratic rules* –**bureaucratically** *adv*

**bu·reau·crat** /ˈbjʊərəkræt/ *n usu. derog* a member of a BUREAUCRACY

**bur·glar** /ˈbɜːgləʳ‖ˈbɜr-/ *n* a thief who breaks into houses, shops, etc., esp. during the night –see THIEF (USAGE)

**bur·glar·y** /ˈbɜːgləri‖ˈbɜr-/ *n* **-ies** [C;U] (an example of) the crime of entering a building (esp. a home) by force with the intention of stealing

**bur·gle** /ˈbɜːgəl‖ˈbɜr-/ also **burglarize** /ˈbɜːgləraɪz‖ˈbɜr-/ *AmE*– *v* **-gled, -gling**‖**-ized, -izing** [I;T] to break into a building and steal from (it or the people in it): *Help! I've been burgled.*

**bur·i·al** /ˈberɪəl/ *n* [C;U] the act, action, or ceremony of putting a dead body into a grave

**bur·ly** /ˈbɜːli‖ˈbɜrli/ *adj* [*no comp.*] (of a person) strongly and heavily built –**burliness** *n* [U]

**burn¹** /bɜːn‖bɜrn/ *v* **burnt** /bɜːnt‖bɜrnt/ *or* **burned, burning 1** [I] to be or become on fire: *The whole city's burning!*|*Coal of this quality doesn't burn very easily.*|(fig.) *He's burning with fever/desire.* –see USAGE **2** [I;T] to (cause to) suffer the effects of fire or heat: *I've burnt my hand.*|*You should burn all those old papers.*|*The house was burnt to the ground.*|*I've burnt a hole in my shirt.*|*Turn the heat down on the cooker; you'll burn the potatoes.*|*The potatoes have burnt; we can't eat them.* **3** [T] to use for power, heating, or lighting: *lamps that burn oil*|*a coal-burning ship* **4** [I] *old use* to produce light; shine: *A light was burning in the window.* **5** [I] to produce or experience an unpleasant hot feeling: *the burning sands*|*My ears were burning after being out in the cold wind.* **6** [I +*to-v*] to be very eager: *She's burning to tell you the good news.* **7 burn one's boats/bridges** *infml* to destroy all means of going back, so that one must go forward

USAGE In *BrE,* the past tense and participle **burned** is usually only used when the verb is INTRANSITIVE: *The fire* **burned** *brightly.*

**burn away** *v adv* [I;T (=**burn** sthg.↔ **away**)] to destroy or disappear by burning: *The roof of the house was burnt away.*

**burn down** *v adv* [I;T (=**burn** sthg.↔ **down**)] to destroy (usu. a building) or be destroyed by fire: *The building (was) burnt down and only ashes were left.* –compare BURN **out,** BURN **up**

**burn** sthg. **into** sthg. *v prep* [T] to fix (as a mark) by burning, so that removal is impossible: *The owner's mark was burnt into the animal's skin.*

**burn** sthg.↔ **off** *v adv* [T] to destroy by burning: *The farmers are burning off the* STUBBLE *from the fields.*

**burn out** *v adv* **1** [T *usu. pass.*] (**burn** sthg. **out**) to make hollow by fire: *The building was burnt out and only the walls remained.* –compare BURN **down 2** [I,T (=**burn** sbdy./sthg. **out**)] to stop burning because there is nothing left to burn: *That small fire can be left to burn (itself) out.*|(fig.) *You'll burn yourself out if you work too hard.* **3** [I;T (=**burn** sthg. **out**)] to stop working through damage caused by heat: *The engine has/is burned out.*|*a* **burnt out** (=worn out) *machine*

**burn up** *v adv* **1** [I] to flame more brightly or strongly **2** [T] (**burn** sthg.↔ **up**) to destroy completely by fire: *All the wood has been burnt up.* –compare BURN **down**

**burn²** *n* [C;U] a hurt place (INJURY) or mark, produced by burning: *burns on her hand/her coat*

**burn·ing** /ˈbɜːnɪŋ‖ˈbɜr-/ *adj* [A] **1** being on fire: *a burning house*|(fig.) *burning cheeks* (=cheeks that are hot and red)|*a burning* (=very strong) *interest in science* **2** producing (a sensation of) great heat or fire: *a burning fever*|*a burning sensation on the tongue* **3** having very great importance; urgent: *Mass unemployment is one of the burning questions of our time.*

**bur·nish** /ˈbɜːnɪʃ‖ˈbɜr-/ *v* [T] to polish (esp. metal), usu. with something hard and smooth

**burnt** /bɜːnt‖bɜrnt/ *v past tense & participle of* BURN

**burp** /bɜːp‖bɜrp/ *v infml* **1** [T] to help (a baby) to get rid of stomach gas, esp. by rubbing or gently striking the back **2** [I] →BELCH (1) –**burp** *n*

**bur·row¹** /ˈbʌrəʊ‖ˈbɜrəʊ/ *n* a hole in the ground made by an animal, esp. a rabbit, in which it lives

**burrow²** *v* **1** [T] to make by or as if by digging: *to burrow a hole in the ground* **2** [I] to move ahead by or as if by digging: *to burrow into/through the sand* **3** [I;T] to (cause to) move as if looking for warmth, safety, or love: *She burrowed her head into my shoulder.*

**bur·sar** /ˈbɜːsəʳ‖ˈbɜr-/ *n* a person in a college or school who has charge of money, property, etc.

**burst¹** /bɜːst‖bɜrst/ *v* **burst, bursting** [I;T] **1** [+*to-v*] to (cause to) break suddenly, esp. by pressure from within: *The bottle/tyre burst.*|*He burst a blood vessel.*|*The storm burst and we all got wet.*|(fig.) *That bag is* **bursting with** (=filled very full with) *potatoes.*|(fig.) *My heart was* **bursting with** (=filled with) **grief/joy.**|*He is* **bursting to** (=very eager to) *tell you the news.* **2** to (cause to) come into the stated condition suddenly, often with force: *He burst free (from the chains).*|*The police burst open the door.*

**burst in on/upon** sbdy./sthg. *adv prep* [T] to interrupt, usu. noisily: *They burst in on me while I was working.*

**burst into** sthg. *v prep* [T] **1** to enter hurriedly (usu. a room) **2** → BREAK **into** (3)

**burst out** *v adv* **1** [I +*v-ing*] to begin suddenly (to use the voice without speaking): *They burst out laughing/crying/into song.* **2** [T] to say suddenly: *"I don't believe it!" burst out the angry old man.* –see also OUTBURST

**burst**[2] *n* a sudden outbreak of effort: *a burst of laughter/of speed*

**bur·y** /ˈberi/ *v* **-ied, -ying** [T] **1** to put into the grave: *to bury a dead person*|(fig.) *to bury a quarrel and forget the past* **2** to hide away esp. in the ground: *The dog has buried a bone.*|(fig.) *They've buried themselves in the country.*|*The facts are buried in a few old books.*|*with one's head buried in a newspaper*|*He buried his head in his hands.* **3 bury the hatchet** *infml* to become friends again after a quarrel

**bus**[1] /bʌs/ *n* a large passenger-carrying motor vehicle, esp. one which carries the public on payment of small amounts: *to travel* **by bus**|*I saw him on the bus.*|*to catch/miss the bus*

**bus**[2] *v* **-ss-** [I;T] to carry (or travel) by bus: *The village children are bussed to the school in the nearest town.*

**bush** /bʊʃ/ *n* **1** a small low tree: *a rose bush* –see picture on page 297 **2 the bush** uncleared wild country, esp. in Australia or Africa **3 beat about the bush** *infml* to avoid coming to the main point: *Tell me the truth: don't beat about the bush.*

**bush·y** /ˈbʊʃi/ *adj* **-ier, -iest** (of hair) growing thickly: *a bushy beard/tail* –**bushiness** *n* [U]

**busi·ness** /ˈbɪznǝ̇s/ *n* **1** [C;U] one's work or employment: *I'm in the insurance business.*|*I'm here on business, not for pleasure.* **2** [U] trade and the getting of money: *"How's business?" "Business is good."*|*It's a pleasure to do business with you.* **3** [C] a particular money-earning activity or place, such as a shop: *to sell one's/the business* **4** [S] a duty: *It's a teacher's business to help children learn.* **5** [S] an affair; event; matter; thing: *I don't understand this business.*|*a strange business* **6 have no business to do something** also **have no business doing something**– to have no right to do something **7 Mind your own business** *infml* Don't ask about things that don't concern you **8 none of your business** *infml* nothing that concerns you

**busi·ness·like** /ˈbɪznǝ̇s-laɪk/ *adj* having the ability to succeed in business or to do things calmly and with common sense: *a businesslike person/manner*

**busi·ness·man** /ˈbɪznǝ̇smən/ **businesswoman** /-ˌwʊmən/ *fem.*– *n* **-men** /mən/ a person who works in business, e.g. the owner of a business firm

**bus stop** /ˈ··/ *n* a fixed place where buses stop for passengers: *I saw him waiting at the bus stop.*

**bust**[1] /bʌst/ *v* **busted** *or* **bust, busting** [T] *infml* to break, esp. with force: *I bust(ed) my watch this morning.* –**bust** *adj* [*no comp.*]: *My watch is bust; I must get it repaired.*|*The business will* **go bust** (=fail) *soon.*

**bust**[2] *n* **1** the human head, shoulders, and chest, esp. as shown in a SCULPTURE **2** *euph* a woman's breasts; BOSOM **3** a measurement round a woman's breasts and back: *rather big round the bust*

**bust**[3] *v* [T] *infml* **1** (of the police) to take to a police station; ARREST[1] (1): *He was busted for having* MARIJUANA. **2** (of the police) to enter without warning to look for something illegal; RAID: *The police busted his house this morning and took some drugs away.* –**bust** *n*

**bus·tle** /ˈbʌsəl/ *v* **-tled, -tling** [I] to be busy, often with much noise: *He bustled about the house.*|*The city* **bustles with** (=has lots of) *life.* –**bustle** *n* [S]: *the bustle of the big city*|*a bustle of activity*

**bust-up** *n infml* **1** a quarrel, noisy and sometimes with fighting: *There was quite a bust-up last night outside the cinema.* **2** *AmE* for BREAKUP (1): *the bust-up of their marriage*

**bus·y**[1] /ˈbɪzi/ *adj* **-ier, -iest 1** doing a lot of things, esp. working; not free: *She is busy now and cannot see you.*|*He is busy writing.*|*to be busy with some important work*|*a busy man* **2** full of work or activity: *a busy day/town* **3** *AmE* (of telephones) in use; ENGAGED (2): *I'm sorry, sir, the (telephone) line is busy.* –**busily** *adv*

**busy**[2] *v* **busied, busying** [T *with*] to make or keep (esp. oneself) busy: *To forget his troubles, he busied himself with answering letters/in his garden.*

**bus·y·bod·y** /ˈbɪziˌbɒdi‖-ˌbɑdi/ *n derog* a person who takes too much interest in the affairs of others

**but**[1] /bət; *strong* bʌt/ *conj* **1** instead: *not one, but two!* **2** yet at the same time; in spite of this: *He would like to go, but he can't.*|*It's not cheap, but it's very good.* **3** except that: *We were coming to see you, but it rained (so we didn't).*|*There's no doubt/no question but he's guilty.* –see Study Notes on page 128 **4** (shows disagreement): *"I'll give you £5." "But that's not enough!"* **5** (shows surprise) *"She's won first prize." "But that's wonderful!"* **6** (introduces a new subject): *But now to our next question ...*

**but**[2] *prep* **1** (after **no, all, nobody, who, where,** etc.) other than; except: *There's no one here but me.*|*Who but George would do such a thing?*|*everywhere but in Scotland*|**But for** *her, I would have drowned.* **2 the first/next/last but one, two, etc.** *esp. BrE* one, two, etc., from the first/next/last: *His house is the last but one in this street.*

USAGE Compare **but, except,** and **save**. In this sentence we can use all three: *We're all here* **but/except/**(*fml*) **save** *Mary.* But in this sentence **but** cannot be used: *The window is never opened* **except/save** *in summer.* Use **but** only after words like *no, all, nobody, anywhere, everything,* or after question-words like *who?, where?, what?* It is usually followed by a noun or PRONOUN: *everywhere* **but** *in Scotland*|*Who* **but** *John would say that?*

**butch·er**[1] /ˈbʊtʃəʳ/ *n* a person who kills animals for food or one whose shop sells meat: *I bought this chicken at the new butcher's (shop).*

**butcher**[2] *v* [T] to kill (animals) and prepare for sale as food: (fig.) *The soldiers butchered their enemies.* –see KILL[1] (USAGE) –**butchery** *n* [U]

**but·ler** /ˈbʌtləʳ/ *n* the chief male servant of a house, in charge of the others

**butt**[1] /bʌt/ *v* [I;T] to strike or push against (someone or something) with the head or horns: *He butted (his head) against the wall.* –**butt** *n*: *The goat gave me a butt in the stomach!*

**butt in** *v adv* [I *on, to*] *infml, often derog* to interrupt, usu. by speaking: *I wish you wouldn't keep* *butting in on our conversation!*

**butt²** *n* a person (or perhaps thing) that people make fun of: *Poor John was* **the butt of all their jokes.**

**butt³** *n* a large, thick, or bottom end of something: *a cigarette butt* (=the last unsmoked end)

**but·ter¹** /ˈbʌtəʳ/ *n* [U] **1** yellow fat made from milk, spread on bread, used in cooking, etc. **2 Butter wouldn't melt in his/her mouth** *infml* He/She pretends to be kind and harmless but is not really so! –**buttery** *adj*

**butter²** *v* [T] to spread with or as if with butter

**butter** sbdy.↔ **up** *v adv* [T] *infml* to FLATTER (1) (someone), esp. to gain something in return: *She buttered him up by saying he was a skilled footballer.*

**but·ter·cup** /ˈbʌtəkʌp‖-ər-/ *n* a yellow wild flower

**but·ter·fly** /ˈbʌtəflaɪ‖-ər-/ *n* **-flies 1** any of several insects that fly by day and often have large beautifully-coloured wings **2 have butterflies in one's stomach** *infml* to feel very nervous before doing something

**but·ter·scotch** /ˈbʌtəskɒtʃ‖-ərskɑtʃ/ *n* [U] a sweet food made from sugar and butter (and perhaps sweet SYRUP) boiled together

**but·tock** /ˈbʌtək/ *n* [*usu. pl.*] either of the two fleshy parts on which a person sits: *the left/right buttock* –see picture on page 299

**but·ton¹** /ˈbʌtn/ *n* **1** a small usu. round or flat thing that is fixed to a garment or other object and usu. passed through an opening (BUTTONHOLE¹ (1)) to act as a fastener: *a row of buttons down the front of his shirt|a button nose* (=a small broad flattish nose) **2** a button-like part, object, or piece of apparatus, esp. one pressed to start a machine: *I pressed the button, and a bell rang.* **3** *AmE for* BADGE: *wearing a button saying "Make Love Not War"*

**button²** *v* [I;T *up*] to (cause to) close or fasten with buttons: *to button (up) one's shirt|My shirt doesn't button (up) easily.*

**buttoned up** /ˌ·· ˈ◂/ *adj infml* successfully completed: *The new contract is all buttoned up now.*

**but·ton·hole¹** /ˈbʌtnhəʊl/ *n* **1** a hole for a button to be put through to fasten a shirt, coat, etc. **2** *BrE* a flower to wear in a buttonhole or pinned to one's coat or dress: *He wore a beautiful buttonhole.*

**buttonhole²** *v* **-holed, -holing** [T] *infml* to stop and force to listen: *She buttonholed me outside the Minister's office, and asked me about my plans.*

**but·tress** /ˈbʌtrɪ̵s/ *n* a support for a wall –**buttress** *v:* (fig.) *Buttressed by its past profits, the company stayed in business through a difficult period.*

**bux·om** /ˈbʌksəm/ *adj apprec* (of a woman) attractively fat and healthy-looking

**buy¹** /baɪ/ *v* **bought** /bɔːt/, **buying 1** [I;T *for, from, with*] to obtain (something) by giving money (or something else of value): *She bought me a book from them for £5.|He bought a new car.|When prices are low, I buy.* –opposite **sell 2** [T] *infml* to accept; believe: *I don't buy that nonsense.* **3 buy time** *infml* to delay an action or decision that seems to be coming too soon: *He tried to buy time by talking.*

**buy** sbdy./sthg.↔ **off** *v adv* [T] → BRIBE¹

**buy** sbdy./sthg.↔ **out/up** *adv* [T] **1** to gain control of by buying the whole of: *to buy out a business* **2** to buy the business of: *We bought out the owners.*

**buy** sthg.↔ **up** *v adv* [T] **1** to buy all the supplies of: *to buy up all the sugar in London* **2** → BUY **out**

**buy²** *n infml* **1** an act of buying **2** something of value at a low price; BARGAIN¹ (2): *It's a good buy at that price!*

**buy·er** /ˈbaɪəʳ/ *n* a person who buys, esp. the head of a department in a firm or large store

**buzz** /bʌz/ *v* **1** [I] to HUM, as bees do: (fig.) *The crowd/room* **buzzed with** *excitement.* **2** [I;T *for*] to call (someone) by using an electrical signalling apparatus (**buzzer**): *She buzzed (for) her secretary (to come).* –**buzz** *n* –**buzzer** *n: Come in when you hear the buzzer.*

**buzz off** *v adv* [I] *infml BrE* (in giving orders) to go away: *Buzz off, you nasty little boy!*

**buz·zard** /ˈbʌzəd‖-ərd/ *n* **1** (in Britain) a heavy slow-flying bird that kills and eats other creatures (a HAWK) **2** (in America) a heavy slow-flying black bird that eats dead flesh (a VULTURE)

**by¹** /baɪ/ *prep* **1** near; beside: *standing by the window|Sit by me.* –see Study Notes on page 474 **2** past: *He walked/passed by me without noticing me.* **3** through the use of; through: *to enter by the door|to travel by train|to earn money by writing|to take the hammer by the handle|I did it by mistake.|What do you mean by that?* **4** (shows the person or thing that does the action): *a play by Shakespeare|struck by lightning* **5** not later than: *Be here by four o'clock.|Will you finish it by tomorrow?* **6** in accordance with: *to play by the rules* **7** to the amount of: *They* OVERCHARGED *me by £3.|It's better by far.* (=much better) **8** (in expressions of strong feeling and solemn promises): *By God he's done it!|to* SWEAR *by heaven* **9** (in measurements and numbers): *a room 15 feet by 20 feet|to divide 10 by 5|to multiply 10 by 5* **10** (often with plurals or *the* +singular) (showing a measure or a rate): *paid by the hour/by result(s)* **11** (showing the size of groups that follow each other): *little by little|The animals went in two by two.* **12** during: *Cats sleep by day and hunt by night.* **13** with regard to: *a doctor by profession|French by birth* **14 (all) by oneself** (completely) alone: *She was by herself.|He did it all by himself!* **15 by the way** *infml* (introducing a new subject or one that has not been mentioned earlier): *By the way, what happened to all the money I gave you?*

**by²** *adv* **1** past: *Please let me (get) by.|A lot of time has gone by since then.* **2** near: *some people standing by* **3** *AmE infml* at or to someone's home: *Stop/Come by for a drink after work.* **4 by and by** *infml* before long; a bit later: *I'll do it by and by.* **5 by and large** on the whole; in general: *By and large, your plan is a good one.* **6 lay/put/set (something) by** to keep or store (something, esp. money) for the future

**bye** /baɪ/ also **bye-bye** /ˌ·ˈ·‖ˈ··/, also **bye now** *AmE*– *interj infml* goodbye

**by-e·lec·tion** /ˈ··ˌ··/ *n* a special election held between regular elections to fill a position whose holder has left it or died

**by·gone** /ˈbaɪgɒn‖-gɔn/ *adj* [A *no comp.*] gone by; past: *in bygone days of long ago*

**by·gones** /ˈbaɪgɒnz‖-gɔnz/ *n* **let bygones be bygones** *infml* to forget (and forgive) the bad things in the past

**by·pass**[1] /'baɪpɑːs||-pæs/ *n* a road round something, esp. round a busy town

**bypass**[2] *v* [T] to avoid: *If we bypass the town we'll miss all traffic.*

**by-prod·uct** /'·,··/ *n* **1** something additional formed when making or doing something: *Silver is often obtained as a by-product during the separation of lead from rock.* **2** an additional result, sometimes unexpected or unintended

**by·stand·er** /'baɪ,stændəʳ/ *n* a person standing near, but not taking part in, what is happening; ONLOOKER: *The police asked some of the bystanders about the accident.*

**by·way** /'baɪweɪ/ also **byroad** /baɪrəʊd/– *n* a smaller road or path which is not much used or known

**by·word** /'baɪwɜːd||-ɜrd/ *n* (the name of) a person, place, or thing that is taken as representing some quality: *The soldier's name was a byword for bravery.*

# C, c

**SPELLING NOTE**
Words with the sound /k/, like **cut**, may be spelt **k-**, like **key**, or **qu-**, like **queen.**
Words with the sound /s/, like **city**, may be spelt **s-**, like **soon**, or **ps-**, like **psychology.**

**C, c** /siː/ **C's, c's** *or* **Cs, cs**– **1** the third letter of the English alphabet **2** the ROMAN NUMERAL (number) for 100

**c** *written abbrev. said as:* **1** cent **2** CIRCA: *c 1834*

**C** *written abbrev. said as:* CENTIGRADE (=CELSIUS): *100°C*

**cab** /kæb/ *n* **1** a taxi: *Shall we walk or take a cab/go* **by cab? 2** (in former times) a horse-drawn carriage for hire **3** the part of a bus, railway engine, etc., in which the driver sits or stands

**cab·a·ret** /'kæbəreɪ||,kæbə'reɪ/ *n* [C;U] (a) performance of popular music and dancing while guests in a restaurant have a meal, usu. at night

**cab·bage** /'kæbɪdʒ/ *n* [C;U] a large round vegetable with thick green leaves which are used (usu. cooked) as food –compare LETTUCE

**cab·in** /'kæb$^{\text{!}}_{\text{ə}}$n/ *n* **1** a small room on a ship usu. used for sleeping **2** a small roughly built usu. wooden house: *They lived in a little log cabin in the mountains.* **3** the room at the front of an aircraft in which the pilot sits

**cab·i·net** /'kæb$^{\text{!}}_{\text{ə}}$n$^{\text{!}}_{\text{ə}}$t, 'kæbn$^{\text{!}}_{\text{ə}}$t/ *n* **1** a piece of furniture, with shelves and doors, or drawers, used for showing or storing things: *a* FILING CABINET|*I put my collection of old glasses in the cabinet.* **2** [*+sing./pl. v*] (in various countries) the most important ministers of the government, who meet as a group to make decisions or to advise the head of the government

**ca·ble**[1] /'keɪbəl/ *n* **1** [C;U] (a length of) thick heavy strong, esp. wire, rope used on board ships, to support bridges, etc. –compare WIRE **2** [C;U] a set of wires put underground or under the sea which carry electricity or telegraph and telephone messages **3** [C] also **cablegram** /-,græm/ *fml*– a telegram

**cable**[2] *v* **-bled, -bling** [I;T + *to-v/(that)*] to send (someone) (something) by telegraph: *I cabled (him) (some money).*|*She cabled him (to come).*

**ca·ca·o** /kə'kɑːəʊ||kə'kaʊ/ *n* **-os** (the South American tree which produces) a seed from which COCOA and chocolate are made

**cack·le** /'kækəl/ *v* **-led, -ling** [I] **1** to make the noise made by a hen **2** to laugh loudly and unpleasantly with a sound like this –**cackle** *n*

**cac·tus** /'kæktəs/ *n* **-tuses** *or* **-ti** /taɪ/ a desert plant protected by sharp prickles, with thick fleshy stems and leaves

**ca·dav·er** /kə'deɪvəʳ, kə'dæ-||kə'dæ-/ *n fml* a dead human body

**ca·dence** /'keɪdəns/ *n* **1** a regular beat of sound; RHYTHM **2** the rise and fall of the human voice esp. in reading poetry

**ca·det** /kə'det/ *n* a person studying to become an officer in one of the armed forces or the police

**cadge** /kædʒ/ *v* **cadged, cadging** [I;T] *infml derog* to get or try to get (something) by asking, often seeming to be taking advantage of someone: *He cadged 50p for cigarettes (from me) yesterday.* –**cadger** *n*

**cae·sar·e·an, ce-, -ian** /s$^{\text{!}}_{\text{ə}}$'zeərɪən/ *n* an operation in which a woman's body is cut open to allow the baby to be taken out, when an ordinary birth may be difficult: *Our first baby was born by caesarean.*

**ca·fe, café** /'kæfeɪ||kæ'feɪ, kə-/ *n* a small restaurant where light meals and drinks (in Britain only non-alcoholic drinks) are served –compare RESTAURANT

**caf·e·te·ri·a** /,kæf$^{\text{!}}_{\text{ə}}$'tɪərɪə/ *n* a restaurant where people collect their own food and drink, often in a store, factory, college, etc. –see also CANTEEN (1)

**caf·feine** /'kæfiːn||kæ'fiːn/ *n* [U] a chemical substance found in coffee and tea, often used in medicines as a STIMULANT

**cage**[1] /keɪdʒ/ *n* an enclosure made of a framework of wires or bars, esp. for keeping animals or birds in

**cage**[2] *v* **caged, caging** [T] to put into a cage: *caged birds*|(fig.) *Mothers of young children often feel* **caged in** *staying at home all day.*

**cag·ey** /'keɪdʒi/ *adj* **cagier, cagiest** *infml* careful; secretive; unwilling to talk or to be friendly: *She's very cagey about her past life.* –**cagily** *adv* –**caginess** *n* [U]

**ca·jole** /kə'dʒəʊl/ *v* **-joled, -joling** [T *into, out of*] to persuade by praise or deceit: *She's always cajoling people (into doing things for her).*

**cake**[1] /keɪk/ *n* **1** [C;U] (a piece of) a food made by baking a (usu. sweet) mixture of flour, eggs, etc.: *a birthday cake*|*Would you like some cake?* **2** [C] a round flat shaped piece of something, esp. food: *a* *fish cake|a cake of soap* **3 (be) a piece of cake** *infml, esp. BrE* (to be) very easy **4 (sell/go) like hot cakes** (to be sold) very quickly **5 have one's cake and eat it** *infml* to have the advantages of something without the disadvantages that go with it

**cake²** *v* **caked, caking** [T *with/on*] to (cause to) cover thickly: *After walking through the field, my boots were caked with mud.* –compare ENCRUSTED

**ca·lam·i·ty** /kəˈlæmǰti/ *n* **-ties** a terrible or very bad event; serious misfortune –**calamitous** *adj*

**cal·ci·um** /ˈkælsiəm/ *n* [U] a silver-white metal that is a simple substance (ELEMENT (1)) and is found in bones, teeth, and chalk

**cal·cu·late** /ˈkælkjʊleɪt, -kjə-‖-kjə-/ *v* **-lated, -lating 1** [I;T +*(that)*] to work out or find out (something) by using numbers; COMPUTE: *Have you calculated the result?|I calculated that we would arrive at 6.00 p.m.|The scientists calculated when the spaceship would reach the moon.* **2** [T +(*that*)] to plan; intend: *a calculated threat*

**cal·cu·lat·ing** /ˈkælkjʊleɪtɪŋ, -kjə-‖-kjə-/ *adj usu. derog* coldly planning and thinking about future actions, esp. whether they will be good or bad for oneself; SHREWD (1)

**cal·cu·la·tion** /ˌkælkjʊˈleɪʃən, -kjə-‖-kjə-/ *n* [C;U] the act or result of calculating: *The calculations are based on these* STATISTICS.*|He lied with cold calculation.*

**cal·cu·la·tor** /ˈkælkjʊleɪtəʳ, -kjə-‖-kjə-/ *n* a small machine which can carry out number operations and which usu. has a MEMORY (5) –see picture on page 415

**cal·cu·lus** /ˈkælkjʊləs, -kjə-‖-kjə-/ *n* [U] (in MATHEMATICS) a way of making calculations about quantities which are always changing, e.g. the speed of a falling stone or the slope of a curved line

**cal·en·dar** /ˈkælǰndəʳ/ *n* a list showing the days and months of the year: *I used the calendar to count how many days it was until my birthday.|From January 1st to February 1st is one* **calendar month.**

**calf¹** /kɑːf‖kæf/ *n* **calves** /kaːvz‖kævz/ the young of the cow or of other large animals such as the elephant –see MEAT (USAGE)

**calf²** *n* **calves** the fleshy back part of the human leg between the knee and the ankle –see picture on page 299

**cal·i·brate** /ˈkælǰbreɪt/ *v* **-brated, -brating** [T] to mark degrees and dividing points on (the scale of a measuring instrument) –**calibration** *n* [C;U]

**cal·i·bre** ‖also **caliber** *AmE* /ˈkælǰbəʳ/ *n* **1** [S;U] the quality of something or someone: *This work's of a very high calibre.* **2** [C] the size of a bullet

**cal·i·co** /ˈkælɪkəʊ/ *n* [U] a type of heavy cotton cloth

**call¹** /kɔːl/ *v* **1** [I;T *to, for, out*] to shout; speak or say in a loud clear voice: *He called for help.|"Hello" she called.|I've been calling for five minutes; why doesn't she answer?* **2** [T] to name: *We'll call the baby Jean.* **3** [T] to (try to) cause to come by speaking loudly or officially or by sending an order or message: *Mother is calling me.|He called me over to his desk.|The minister called the union leaders to a meeting.|Call a doctor!* **4** [I] **a** to make a short visit to someone: *Let's call (in) on John for ten minutes.|She called (on me) (on Tuesday).|He called to collect the money.|Do you think we should call at Bob's when we go to London?* **b** (of people esp. selling things) to make regular visits: *The milkman calls every day.* **5** [I;T] to (try to) telephone or radio (to): *I called him this morning but he was out.|The office called to find out where you were.* –see TELEPHONE (USAGE) **6** [T] to cause to happen: *The president called an election.* **7** [T] to say or consider that (someone or something) is (something): *She called me a coward.|I don't call that a good painting.|How can you still call yourself my friend?|Did you hear what he called me?* **8** [I;T *to*] (of an animal) to make the usual cry to (another animal): *The birds are calling (each other).*

**call back** *v adv* **1** [T] (**call** sbdy.↔ **back**) to cause to return: *Mrs Jones was about to leave when her secretary called her back.* **2** [I] to pay another visit: *The salesman will call back later.* **3** [I;T (= **call** sbdy. **back**)] to return a telephone call: *I'll call (you) back.* –see also CALL² (3): see TELEPHONE (USAGE)

**call by** *v adv* [I] *infml* to visit when passing: *I'll call by at the shops on the way home.*

**call for** sbdy./sthg. *v prep* [T] **1** to demand: *to call for the waiter|The opposition called for an inquiry.* **2** to need; deserve: *Your unkind remark was* **not called for.**|*It was* **uncalled-for. 3** to collect: *I'll call for you at nine o'clock.*

**call** sbdy./sthg.↔ **in** *v adv* [T] **1** to ask to come to help: *Call the doctor in.* **2** to request the return of: *The makers have called in some cars with dangerous faults.*

**call** sthg.↔ **off** *v adv* [T] **1** to cause not to take place: *The football match was called off because of the snow.* **2** to order to keep away: *Call off your dog; it tried to bite me!*

**call on/upon** sbdy. *v prep* [T] **1** to visit: *We can call on Mary tomorrow.* **2** *fml* to ask (someone) to do something: *The Prime Minister called on everyone to work hard for national unity.*

**call** sbdy.↔ **out** *v adv* [T] **1** to order (someone) officially to come to one's help: *Call out the army.* **2** to cause to stop work (to STRIKE¹ (5)): *The miners' leader called out his men.*

**call up** *v adv* **1** [T] (**call** sthg.↔ **up**) to bring back to memory; RECALL¹ (1) **2** [T] (**call** sbdy.↔ **up**) *BrE infml*‖**draft** *AmE*– to order to join the armed forces: *He was called up in 1917.* **3** [I;T (**call** sbdy.↔ **up**)] to telephone: *I'll call you up this evening.*

**call²** *n* **1** a shout; cry: *They heard a call for help.|The call of this bird is very loud.* **2** [+ *to-v/to*] a command to meet, come, or do something; SUMMONS: *The minister waited for a call to the palace.* **3** an attempt to ring someone on the telephone; conversation over the telephone: *I have a call for you from London.|I gave my wife a call but she was out.|Ask him to* **return my call** *when he arrives home, please.* **4** a short usu. formal visit: *The President is* **making/paying a call on** *the king.* **5 close call/shave/thing** something bad that nearly happened, but didn't: *That was a close call! We nearly hit the other car!* **6 no call for** no need for: *There's no call for office workers now; try again next month.* **7 on call** not working but ready to work if needed: *The nurse is on call tonight.* **8 within call** near enough to hear a call

**call box** /ˈ· ·/ *n BrE* for TELEPHONE BOOTH

**call·er** /ˈkɔːləʳ/ *n* **1** a person who makes a short visit: *John's a regular caller.* **2** a person making a telephone call, esp. as addressed by the OPERATOR: *I'm sorry, caller, the number is* ENGAGED (2).

**call girl** /ˈ· ·/ *n* → PROSTITUTE

**call·ing** /ˈkɔːlɪŋ/ *n* **1** [+*to-v, for*] a strong desire or feeling of duty to do a particular job; VOCATION: *My son had a calling to become a priest.* **2** *fml* profession; trade

**cal·li·pers** ||also **calipers** *AmE* /ˈkælǝ̣pəz||-ərz/ [P] **1** an instrument with two legs used for measuring thickness, the distance between two surfaces, and inner width (DIAMETER) –see PAIR¹ (USAGE) **2** metal supports fixed to the legs to help a person with weak legs to walk

**cal·lous** /ˈkæləs/ *adj* unkind; without feelings for the sufferings of other people –compare CALLUS **–callously** *adv* **–callousness** *n* [U]

**cal·low** /ˈkæləʊ/ *adj derog* (of a person or behaviour) young and without experience; IMMATURE

**cal·lus** /ˈkæləs/ *n* an area of thick hard skin: *calluses on his hands* –compare CALLOUS

**calm¹** /kɑːm||kɑm, kɑlm/ *adj* **1** free from excitement; quiet; untroubled: *Even when the car crashed she was calm.* **2 a** (of weather) not windy: *After the storm it was calm.* **b** (of water) not rough; smooth; still: *The sea was calm* **–calmly** *adv*

**calm²** *n* [S;U] **1** a time of peace and quiet; absence of excitement or worry **2** (of weather) an absence of wind or rough weather

**calm³** *v* [T] to make calm: *She calmed her child by giving it some milk.*

**calm down** *v adv* [I;T (=**calm** sbdy.↔ **down**)] to become or make calm: *The excited girl quickly calmed down.|It was difficult to calm my brother down.*

**cal·o·rie** /ˈkæləri/ *n* **1** a measure used when stating the amount of heat or ENERGY (2) that a food will produce: *One thin piece of bread has 90 calories.|I can eat only 1,500 calories a day on this diet.* **2** a measure of heat

**calves** /kɑːvz||kævz/ *n plural of* CALF

**ca·lyp·so** /kəˈlɪpsəʊ/ *n* **-sos** or **-soes** a type of West Indian song

**cam·ber** /ˈkæmbəʳ/ *n* [C;U] a slight upward curve in the shape of a road or other surface which causes water to run off

**came** /keɪm/ *v past tense of* COME

**cam·el** /ˈkæməl/ *n* a large long-necked animal with one or two large HUMPs on its back, used for riding or carrying goods in desert countries

**ca·mel·li·a** /kəˈmiːlɪə/ *n* the large roselike sweet-smelling flower of an East Asian bush

**cam·e·o** /ˈkæmi-əʊ/ *n* **-os** a piece of women's jewellery consisting of a raised shape or figure on a darker background

**cam·e·ra** /ˈkæmərə/ *n* **1** an apparatus for taking photographs or moving pictures **2 in camera** *fml* in secret; privately: *The court met in camera.*

**SPELLING NOTE**

Words with the sound /k/, like **cut**, may be spelt **k-**, like **key**, or **qu-**, like **queen.**

Words with the sound /s/, like **city**, may be spelt **s-**, like **soon**, or **ps-**, like **psychology.**

**cam·ou·flage** /ˈkæməflɑːʒ/ *v* **-flaged, -flaging** [T] to make (esp. a military object) difficult to see or find esp. by the use of branches, paint, nets, etc. **–camouflage** *n* [C;U]

**camp¹** /kæmp/ *n* a place where people live in tents or huts usu. for a short time: *a military camp|When we went to the coast we stayed in a* **holiday camp.**|*The climbers had a camp near the top of the mountain.|Let's go back to camp.*

**camp²** *v* [I] to set up (PITCH¹ (1)) or live in a camp: *The hunters camped near the top of the mountain.|We go camping every summer.|We* **camped out** (= outdoors) *last night.*

**cam·paign¹** /kæmˈpeɪn/ *n* a connected set of military, political, or business actions intended to obtain a particular result: *The campaign succeeded and she won the election.|an advertising campaign*

**campaign²** *v* [I] to lead, take part in, or go on a CAMPAIGN: *Joan is campaigning for equal rights for women.* **–campaigner** *n*

**cam·phor** /ˈkæmfəʳ/ *n* [U] a strong-smelling white substance, used esp. in medicine to prevent unconsciousness, and to keep insects away

**cam·pus** /ˈkæmpəs/ *n* **-puses** [C;U] the grounds of a university, college, or school

**can¹** /kən; *strong* kæn/ *v* **could** /kəd; *strong* kʊd/, *3rd person sing. present tense* **can**, NEGATIVE *contraction* **can't** /kɑːnt||kænt/ *or* **cannot** /ˈkænət, -nɒt||-nɑt/, *past tense* NEGATIVE *contraction* **couldn't** /ˈkʊdnt/ [I +*to-v*] **1** to be able to; know how to: *She can speak French.|I can't remember where I put it.|Can you swim?|everything that money can buy|It can be* (= sometimes it is) *very cold in Scotland.* **2** to be allowed to; have permission to; may: *You can't play football here.|Can we go home now, please?* (This use of **can** is now more common than **may.**) **3** (used when asking someone to do something): *Can you help me (to) lift it, please?* –compare COULD (4); see Study Notes on page 386

USAGE **Can** is often used with verbs which are marked [not *be* +*v-ing*], such as **see, hear,** and **believe**: *I'm looking at him and I* **can** *see him.|I'm listening hard but I* **can't** *hear it.|I* **can** *smell something burning.|I* **can** *believe that.|I* **can't** *imagine why.|***Can** *you guess the answer?|* **Can** *you remember where they live?* –see also COULD (USAGE)

**can²** /kæn/ *n* **1** a small closed metal container in which foods or drinks are preserved without air; TIN¹ (2): *He opened a can of beans/a can of beer.* –see picture on page 615 **2** a usu. round metal container with an open top or removable lid and sometimes with handles, used for holding milk, coffee, oil, waste, ashes, etc. **3** the contents of such a container: *Add a can/canful of juice to the mixture and it will taste better.* **4 carry the can** *infml, esp. BrE* to take the blame: *Why do I always have to carry the can when something goes wrong?*

**can³** /kæn/ *v* **-nn-** [T] to preserve (food) by putting in a closed metal container without air: *The fish is canned in this factory.|canned fruit*

**ca·nal** /kəˈnæl/ *n* a waterway dug in the ground, esp. to allow ships or boats to travel along it: *The Panama*

*Canal joins two oceans.|The goods are sent here by canal.*

**ca·nar·y** /kə'neəri/ *n* **-ies** a small yellow bird usu. kept as a pet for its singing

**can·cel** /'kænsəl/ *v* **-ll-***BrE*||**-l-** *AmE* [T] **1** to give up or call off (a planned activity, idea, etc.): *She cancelled her trip to New York as she was ill.|She cancelled her order for a new car.* **2** [*out*] to balance; equal: *The increase in the strength of their navy is cancelled by that in our army.* **3** to cross out (writing, e.g. on a cheque) by drawing a line through it

**can·cel·la·tion** /ˌkænsə'leɪʃən/ *n* [C;U] (an example of) the act of CANCELling (1): *The cancellation of the order for planes led to the closure of the factory.|Because there have been cancellations you can now have tickets.*

**can·cer** /'kænsəʳ/ *n* [C;U] (a) diseased growth in the body, which may cause death: *He's got a cancer in his throat.|He's got cancer of the throat.* –compare CANKER **–cancerous** *adj: a cancerous growth*

**Cancer** *n* [S] see ZODIAC; see also TROPIC

**can·did** /'kændɨd/ *adj* directly truthful, even when telling the truth is uncomfortable or unwelcome **–candidly** *adv*

**can·di·date** /'kændɨdɨt||-deɪt, -dɨt/ *n* **1** a person who wants, or whom others want, to be chosen for a position, esp. in an election: *Jean was the best candidate for the job.|He was a candidate in the presidential election.* **2** a person taking an examination

**can·dle** /'kændl/ *n* a usu. round stick of wax containing a length of string (the WICK) which gives light when it burns

**can·dle·stick** /'kændlˌstɪk/ *n* a holder for usu. one candle

**can·dour** *BrE*||**candor** *AmE* /'kændəʳ/ *n* [U] the state or quality of being sincerely honest and truthful (CANDID)

**can·dy¹** /'kændi/ *n* **-dies** [C;U] *esp. AmE* (a shaped piece of) various types of boiled sugar, sweets, or chocolate –compare SWEET² (1)

**candy²** *v* **-died, -dying** [T] to preserve (food) by cooking in sugar: *candied fruit*

**cane¹** /keɪn/ *n* [C;U] (a length of) the hard smooth thin often hollow stem of certain plants (tall grasses such as BAMBOO): *cane furniture|The teacher hit him with a cane/gave him the cane for fighting in school.*

**cane²** *v* **caned, caning** [T] to punish (someone) by striking with a CANE: *When I was young, teachers used to cane us when we behaved badly.*

**ca·nine** /'keɪnaɪn, 'kæ-||'keɪ-/ *adj,n tech* (of, for, typical of) a dog or related animal

**can·is·ter** /'kænɨstəʳ/ *n* a usu. metal container used for holding a dry substance or a gas

**can·ker** /'kæŋkəʳ/ *n* [C;U] a sore or area of soreness caused by a disease which attacks the wood of trees and the flesh (esp. the mouth and ears) of animals and people –compare CANCER **–cankerous** *adj*

**can·na·bis** /'kænəbɨs/ also **dope, pot, grass** *infml*– *n* [U] the drug produced from a particular type of HEMP plant (the **Indian hemp**), sometimes smoked in cigarettes to give a feeling of pleasure, leading to sleepiness –see also HASHISH, MARIJUANA

**can·ni·bal** /'kænɨbəl/ *n* an animal or person that eats the flesh of its own kind **–cannibalism** *n* [U] **–cannibalistic** /-'ɪstɪk/ *adj*

**can·non¹** /'kænən/ *n* **cannons** *or* **cannon** a big gun, often fixed to the ground or onto a usu. two-wheeled carriage: *In this castle there are cannons from the 15th century.|Our fighter planes are all armed with cannon.* –compare CANON¹, ²

**cannon²** *v* [I] to strike forcefully; knock: *He came running round the corner, cannoned into me, and knocked me over.*

**can·not** /'kænət, -nɒt||-nɑt/ *v fml* can not: *Mr Smith is sorry that he cannot accept your kind invitation to dinner.* –compare CAN'T

**can·ny** /'kæni/ *adj* **-nier, -niest** clever; not easily deceived, esp. in money matters

**ca·noe¹** /kə'nuː/ *n* a long light narrow boat, pointed at both ends, and moved by a PADDLE¹ (1) held in the hands: *We crossed the lake by canoe/in a canoe.*

**canoe²** *v* **-noed, -noeing** [I] to travel by CANOE **–canoeist** *n*

**can·on¹** /'kænən/ *n* **1** an established law of the Christian Church **2** *fml* a generally accepted standard of behaviour or thought: *His behaviour offends against the canons of good manners.* –compare CANNON **–canonical** /kə'nɒnɪkəl||kə'nɑ-/ *adj*

**canon²** *n* [A;C] a Christian priest with special duties in a CATHEDRAL

**can·on·ize**|| also **-ise** *BrE* /'kænənaɪz/ *v* **-ized, -izing** [T] to declare (a dead person) a SAINT (1)

**can·o·py** /'kænəpi/ *n* **-pies** a cover usu. of cloth fixed above a bed or seat: (fig.) *a canopy of branches*

**canst** /kənst; *strong* kænst/ **thou canst** *old use or bibl* (when talking to one person) you can

**cant** /kænt/ *n* [U] *derog* insincere talk about oneself, esp. about one's religious practices; HYPOCRISY

**can't** /kɑːnt||kænt/ *v short for:* can not: *I can't come with you: I'm busy.|You can swim, can't you?* –compare CANNOT

**can·tan·ker·ous** /kæn'tæŋkərəs/ *adj infml* bad-tempered; quarrelsome **–cantankerously** *adv*

**can·teen** /kæn'tiːn/ *n* **1** a place in a factory, military camp, etc., where people may buy and eat food, meals, drinks, sweets, etc. **2** a small usu. leather container in which water or other drink is carried **3** *BrE* a set of knives, forks, and spoons (CUTLERY) usu. for 6 or 12 people

**can·ter** /'kæntəʳ/ *n* [*usu. sing.*] (of a horse) a movement which is fast, but slower than a GALLOP **–canter** *v* [I;T]

**can·vas** /'kænvəs/ *n* [C;U] (a piece of) strong rough cloth used for tents, sails, bags, etc.: *We spent the night* **under canvas.** (=in a tent)|*The artist showed me his canvases.* (=pictures painted on pieces of canvas)

**can·vass, -vas** /'kænvəs/ *v* [I;T *for*] to go through (an area) or to (people) to ask for (esp. political support) or to find out (people's opinions)

**can·yon** /'kænjən/ *n* a deep narrow steep-sided valley usu. with a river flowing through –see VALLEY (USAGE)

**cap¹** /kæp/ *n* **1** a soft head-covering, esp. a flat closely fitting one, e.g. worn by nurses and soldiers: *a schoolboy's cap|an officer's cap* –compare HAT (1) **2** a protective covering for the end or top of an object: *Put the cap back on the bottle.* **3** also **Dutch cap,**

**diaphragm**– a small round object fitted inside a woman to allow her to have sex without having children –see CONTRACEPTIVE **4 cap in hand** humbly

**cap**[2] *v* **-pp-** [T] **1** to put a cap on (someone or something); cover with a cap: (fig.) *Clouds capped the hills.* **2** to improve on (what someone has said or done): *He capped my story by telling a better one.* **3 to cap it all** lastly; on top of everything else: *His wife left him, his car was stolen, then to cap it all he lost his job!*

**ca·pa·bil·i·ty** /ˌkeɪpəˈbɪl$\frac{1}{3}$ti/ *n* **-ties** [C;U] the quality of being CAPABLE (1): *The child has great capabilities.*|*She has great capability as a singer and should be trained.*|NUCLEAR (1) *capability* (=the ability to fight a NUCLEAR (1) war)

**ca·pa·ble** /ˈkeɪpəbəl/ *adj* [F *of*] **1** having the ability of doing or being, or the power to do or be: *She's capable of any crime.*|*a very capable doctor* (=a good doctor)|*My son's very capable* (=skilful) *as a driver.* **2** able to be; ready for; open to: *That remark is capable of being misunderstood.* –opposite **incapable** –**capably** *adv*

**ca·pac·i·ty** /kəˈpæs$\frac{1}{3}$ti/ *n* **-ties 1** [S;U] the amount that something can hold or produce: *The seating capacity of this theatre is 500.*|*working at full capacity* (=producing the greatest amount possible)|*The theatre was* **filled to capacity.** (=completely full) **2** [C;U *for*] ability; power: *He has a capacity for enjoying himself.*|*Understanding this book is beyond my capacity.* –see GENIUS (USAGE) **3** [C] character; position: *I'm speaking in* **my capacity as** *minister of trade.*

**cape**[1] /keɪp/ *n* a loose outer garment without SLEEVES, fastened at the neck and hanging from the shoulders and usually quite short: *A bicycle cape will protect you in wet weather.* –compare CLOAK

**cape**[2] *n* (often in names) a piece of land joined to the coast and standing out into the sea: *the Cape of Good Hope*

**ca·per** /ˈkeɪpə$^r$/ *v* [I] to jump about in a joyful manner: *The lambs were capering in the fields.* –**caper** *n*

**ca·pil·la·ry** /kəˈpɪləri‖ˈkæpəleri/ *n* **-ries** a very fine hairlike tube, e.g. one of the smaller blood vessels in the body

**cap·i·tal**[1] /ˈkæp$\frac{1}{3}$tl/ *n* **1** [C] a town where the centre of government is: *Paris is the capital of France.* **2** [S;U] wealth, esp. money used to produce more wealth or for starting a business; the machines, buildings, and goods used in a business: *This business was started with a capital of £10,000/with £10,000 capital.* **3** [C] a CAPITAL[2] (2) letter, esp. one at the beginning of a word: *The word* DICTIONARY *is printed here in capitals.* –compare LOWER CASE

**capital**[2] *adj* [A] **1** punishable by death: *Murder can be a capital offence.*|CAPITAL PUNISHMENT **2** (of a letter) written or printed in its large form (such as A, B, C) rather than in its small form (such as a, b, c)

**cap·i·tal·is·m** /ˈkæp$\frac{1}{3}$tl-ɪzəm/ *n* [U] the type of production and trade based on the private ownership of wealth –compare COMMUNISM, SOCIALISM

**SPELLING NOTE**

Words with the sound /k/, like **cut**, may be spelt **k-**, like **key**, or **qu-**, like **queen.**
Words with the sound /s/, like **city**, may be spelt **s-**, like **soon**, or **ps-**, like **psychology.**

**cap·i·tal·ist**[1] /ˈkæp$\frac{1}{3}$tl-$\frac{1}{3}$st/ *n* a person who owns or controls much wealth (CAPITAL[1] (2)) and esp. who lends it to businesses, banks, etc., for INTEREST[1] (5)

**capitalist**[2] *adj* practising or supporting CAPITALISM: *the capitalist countries of the West*

**cap·i·tal·ize on** sthg. /ˈkæp$\frac{1}{3}$tl-aɪz/ *v prep* **-ized, -izing** [T] to use to one's advantage: *She capitalized on his mistake and won the game.*

**capital pun·ish·ment** /ˌ··· ˈ···/ *n* [U] punishment by death according to law; the death PENALTY

**ca·pit·u·late** /kəˈpɪtʃʊleɪt‖-tʃə-/ *v* **-lated, -lating** [I] *fml* to yield to the enemy, usu. on agreed conditions; SURRENDER –**capitulation** /-ˌpɪtʃʊˈleɪʃən/ *n* [C;U]

**ca·price** /kəˈpriːs/ *n* [C;U] (a) sudden often foolish change of mind or behaviour usu. without any real cause; sudden wish to have or do something; WHIM

**ca·pri·cious** /kəˈprɪʃəs/ *adj* often changing; untrustworthy; caused by CAPRICE: *We can't go camping while the weather is so capricious.* –**capriciously** *adv* –**capriciousness** *n* [U]

**Cap·ri·corn** /ˈkæprɪkɔːn‖-ɔrn/ *n* see ZODIAC; see also TROPIC

**cap·si·cum** /ˈkæpsɪkəm/ *n* [C;U] *tech* for PEPPER[1] (2)

**cap·size** /kæpˈsaɪz‖ˈkæpsaɪz/ *v* **-sized, -sizing** [I;T] **a** (esp. of a boat) to turn over **b** to turn (esp. a boat) over: *The boat capsized in the storm, but luckily it didn't sink.*

**cap·sule** /ˈkæpsjuːl‖-səl/ *n* **1** a measured amount of medicine inside an outer covering, the whole of which is swallowed **2** the part of a spaceship in which the pilots live and work and from which the engine is separated when the takeoff is completed

**cap·tain**[1] /ˈkæpt$\frac{1}{3}$n/ *n* **1** the leader of a team or group **2** the person in command of a ship or aircraft: *Are we ready to sail, Captain?* **3** an officer of middle rank in the armed forces

**captain**[2] *v* [T] to be captain of; command; lead

**cap·tion** /ˈkæpʃən/ *n* words written above or below a picture, newspaper article, etc., to say what it is or give further information

**cap·ti·vate** /ˈkæpt$\frac{1}{3}$veɪt/ *v* **-vated, -vating** [T] to charm, excite, and attract (someone or something): *the city's captivating beauty*

**cap·tive**[1] /ˈkæptɪv/ *adj* **1** taken prisoner, esp. in war: *We were* **held captive** *for three months.* **2** not allowed to move about freely; imprisoned: *captive animals* **3 a captive audience** one who cannot easily leave and must therefore listen: *Lying in my hospital bed, I was a captive audience to her uninteresting stories.*

**captive**[2] *n* a person taken prisoner esp. in war

**cap·tiv·i·ty** /kæpˈtɪv$\frac{1}{3}$ti/ *n* [U] the state of being CAPTIVE[1]: *Many animals do not breed when* **in captivity.**

**cap·tor** /ˈkæptə$^r$/ *n usu. fml* a person who has CAPTURED[1] (1) someone or something: *I soon escaped from my captors.*

**cap·ture**[1] /ˈkæptʃə$^r$/ *v* [T] **1** to take (a person or animal) prisoner: *He was captured trying to escape from the country.* **2** to take control of (something) by force from an enemy; win; gain **3** to preserve on film, in words, etc.: *In his book he tried to capture the* beauty of Venice.

**capture²** *n* [U] the act of taking or being taken by force

**car** /kɑːʳ/ *n* **1** also **motor car** *BrE fml*||also **automobile** *AmE*– a vehicle with wheels, driven by a motor, and used for carrying people: *She goes to work* **by car.** –see picture on page 85 **2** *esp. AmE* a carriage or vehicle for use on railways or CABLES¹ (1), esp. of a stated kind: *This train has a restaurant car/a sleeping car.*

**car·a·mel** /ˈkærəməl/ *n* **1** [U] burnt sugar used for giving food a special taste and colour **2** [C;U] (a piece of) sticky boiled sugar containing this and eaten as a sweet

**car·at** ||also **karat** *AmE* /ˈkærət/ *n* a division on the scale of measurement for expressing the amount of gold in golden objects, or the weight of a jewel: *a 22-carat gold ring*

**car·a·van** /ˈkærəvæn/ *n* **1** *BrE*||**trailer** *AmE*– a vehicle which can be pulled by car, which contains apparatus for cooking and sleeping, and in which people live or travel for holidays **2** *BrE*||**wagon** *AmE*– a covered horse-drawn cart in which people such as gipsies (GIPSY) live or travel **3** a group of people with animals or vehicles travelling together for protection through unfriendly areas, esp. in the desert

**car·bo·hy·drate** /ˌkɑːbəʊˈhaɪdreɪt, -drət||ˌkɑr-/ *n* [C;U] any of various types of substance, such as sugar, which consist of oxygen, HYDROGEN, and CARBON, which provide the body with heat and power (ENERGY (2)) and if eaten too much make one fat

**car·bon** /ˈkɑːbən||ˈkɑr-/ *n* **1** [U] a simple substance (ELEMENT (1)) found in a pure form as diamonds, etc., or in an impure form as coal, petrol, etc. **2** [C;U] also **carbon paper**– (a sheet of) thin paper with a coat of coloured material on one side used between sheets of writing paper for making one or more copies **3** [C] also **carbon copy** /ˌ·· ˈ··/– a copy made by using this paper; DUPLICATE: (fig.) *John is a carbon copy of his father.*

**carbon di·ox·ide** /ˌ·· ·ˈ··/ *n* [U] the gas produced when animals breathe out or when CARBON (1) is burned in air

**carbon mo·nox·ide** /ˌ·· ·ˈ··/ *n* [U] a poisonous gas produced when CARBON (1) (esp. petrol) burns in a small amount of air

**car·bun·cle** /ˈkɑːbʌŋkəl||ˈkɑr-/ *n* a large ugly BOIL³

**car·bu·ret·tor** *BrE*|| **-retor** *AmE* /ˌkɑːbjʊˈretəʳ, -bə-||ˈkɑrbəreɪtəʳ/ *n* an apparatus, esp. used in car engines, for mixing the necessary amounts of air and petrol to produce the explosive gas which burns in the engine to provide power

**car·cass, -case** /ˈkɑːkəs||ˈkɑr-/ *n* the body of a dead animal, esp. one which is ready to be cut up as meat

**card** /kɑːd||kɑrd/ *n* **1** [C] also **playing card** *fml*– one of a set (PACK) of 52 small sheets of stiffened paper marked to show class (SUIT) and number and used for various games –see CARDS (USAGE) **2** [C] a small sheet of plastic or stiffened paper usu. with information printed on it and having various uses: *a membership card|Let me give you my business card.|A* **banker's card** *states that a bank will pay the owner's cheques up to a stated amount.* **3** a piece of stiffened paper, usu. with a picture on the front and a message inside, sent to a person by post on special occasions (e.g. a birthday, Christmas, etc.): *I sent her a* **get-well card** *when she was in hospital.|a* **postcard** *from Italy* **4** [U] stiffened paper –compare CARDBOARD **5 have a card up one's sleeve** *infml* to have a secret, usu. effective, plan or intention

**card·board** /ˈkɑːdbɔːd||ˈkɑrdbɔrd/ *n* [U] a thick stiff paperlike usu. brownish or greyish material used for making boxes, the backs of books, etc. –compare CARD (4)

**car·di·ac** /ˈkɑːdi-æk||ˈkɑr-/ *adj* [A] *tech* connected with the heart or with heart disease

**car·di·gan** /ˈkɑːdɪgən||ˈkɑr-/ *n* a short KNITted coat with SLEEVEs (1), fastened at the front with buttons or a belt –see picture on page 563

**car·di·nal¹** /ˈkɑːdənəl||ˈkɑr-/ *n* [A;C] a priest with one of the highest ranks of the ROMAN CATHOLIC church

**cardinal²** *adj* [*no comp.*] *fml* most important; chief; main: *a cardinal* SIN

**cardinal num·ber** /ˌ··· ˈ··/ *n* one of the numbers 1, 2, 3, etc. –compare ORDINAL NUMBER

**card in·dex** /ˈ· ˌ··/ *n* (a case containing) a number of cards each carrying a particular piece of information and arranged in a special order

**cards** /kɑːdz||kɑrdz/ *n* [P] **1** also **playing cards** *fml*– a set (PACK) of 52 CARDs¹ **2** games played with such a set; card playing: *Let's* **play cards** *tonight.* **3 lay/put one's cards on the table** to be completely honest; say openly what one intends to do **4 on the cards** *infml* probable: *They say war's on the cards.*

USAGE The **cards** used in card games come in two red **suits**, **hearts** and **diamonds**; and two black ones, **clubs** and **spades**. Each **suit** has an **ace**, a **king**, a **queen**, and a **jack**; and nine other cards numbered two to ten: *the* **ace** *of* **hearts**|*the* **king** *of* **clubs**|*the* **queen** *of* **diamonds**|*the* **jack** *of* **spades**

**care¹** /keəʳ/ *n* **1** worry; anxiety; sorrow; grief; suffering of the mind: *free from care* **2** [C] an anxiety; worry; cause of sorrow, grief, etc. **3** [U] charge; keeping; protection; responsibility: *under the doctor's care|We left the baby in the care of our neighbour.* **4** [U] serious attention; effort: *You must do your work with more care.* **5** [U] carefulness in avoiding harm, damage, etc.: *Glass; handle with care!* |*Cross the road with care.*|**Take care.** (=be careful) **6 care of** →c/o **7 take care of** to be responsible for: *Take care of the baby while I'm out.*

**care²** *v* **cared, caring 1** [I;T *about*] to be worried, anxious, or concerned (about); mind: *When his dog died Alan didn't seem to care at all.|John said he didn't really care whether we won or lost.* **2** [T +*to-v*] to like; want: *Would you care to visit us this weekend?*

**care for** sbdy./sthg. *v prep* [T] **1** to nurse or attend; look after: *He's very good at caring for sick animals.* **2** [*used only in questions and* NEGATIVEs² (1); *no pass.*] to like; want: *I don't really care for tea; I like coffee better.*

**ca·reer¹** /kəˈrɪəʳ/ *n* **1** a job or profession for which one is trained and which one intends to follow for the whole of one's life **2** (a part of) the general course of a person's working life: *She spent most of her career as a teacher in London.* –see JOB (USAGE)

**career²** *adj* [A] professional; intending to make a job one's CAREER (1): *He's a career teacher; it's the only job he's ever done.*|*a career soldier*

**career³** *v* [I] to go at full speed; rush wildly: *The car careered uncontrollably down the hill.*

**care·free** /'keəfriː||'keər-/ *adj apprec* free from anxiety; happy; without sorrow or fear: *On a fine spring day like this I feel quite carefree.* –see also CARELESS, CAREFUL

**care·ful** /'keəfəl||'keər-/ *adj* **1** [+*to-v*/(*that*)] taking care (with the intention of avoiding danger): *Be careful not to fall/that you don't fall off the ladder.*|*Be careful what you say.*|*You should have been more careful when you crossed the road.* **2** showing attention to details: *He's a careful worker.* **3** done with care; showing care: *The doctor made a careful examination.* –see also CARELESS, CAREFREE **–carefully** *adv* **–carefulness** *n* [U]

**care·less** /'keələs||'keər-/ *adj* **1** not taking care; inattentive: *He's a very careless driver: he never thinks about what he's doing.* **2** [A] not showing care: *This is careless work; do it again!* Compare: *After we finished our examinations we all felt happy and* **carefree.**|*He failed his examination because his work was* **careless** *and full of mistakes.* **–carelessly** *adv* **–carelessness** *n* [U]

**ca·ress¹** /kə'res/ *n* a light tender touch or kiss showing one's love for someone

**caress²** *v* [T] to give a CARESS to (someone): *She caressed his cheek lovingly.*

**care·tak·er** /'keəteɪkər||'keər-/ **1** [C] also **janitor** *esp. AmE* – a person employed to look after a school or other usu. large public building and to be responsible for small repairs, cleaning, etc. **2** [A;C] a government or person in charge for a usu. short time until another is elected: *a caretaker government*

**car·go** /'kɑːgəʊ||'kɑr-/ *n* **-goes** [C;U] (one load of) the goods carried by a ship, plane, or vehicle: *We sailed from Sweden with a cargo of paper.*

**car·i·ca·ture** /'kærɪkətʃʊər/ *n* [C;U] (the art of making) a representation of a person, esp. in literature or art, made so that parts of his appearance or character seem more noticeable, odd, or amusing than they really are: *Newspapers often contain caricatures of well-known politicians.* **–caricature** *v* **-tured, -turing** [T] **–caricaturist** *n*

**car·nage** /'kɑːnɪdʒ||'kɑr-/ *n* [U] *fml* the killing and wounding of many animals or esp. people: *The battlefield was a scene of great carnage.*

**car·nal** /'kɑːnl||'kɑrnl/ *adj* [A] *usu. derog* of the flesh, bodily, or esp. sexual: *carnal pleasures/desires*

**car·na·tion** /kɑː'neɪʃən||kɑr-/ *n* (a garden plant with) a sweet-smelling white, pink, or red flower

**car·ni·val** /'kɑːnəvəl||'kɑr-/ *n* **1** [U] public rejoicing with feasting, dancing, drinking, and often processions and shows: *carnival time in Rio de Janeiro* **2** [C] a period when this takes place esp. in ROMAN CATHOLIC countries in the weeks before LENT

**car·ni·vore** /'kɑːnəvɔːr||'kɑrnəvor/ *n* a flesh-eating animal: *Lions are carnivores; rabbits are not.* **–carnivorous** /kɑː'nivərəs||kɑr-/ *adj*

**car·ol** /'kærəl/ *n* a religious song of joy and praise esp. sung at Christmas

**car·ou·sel, carr-** /ˌkærə'sel/ *n AmE* for MERRY-GO-ROUND

**carp¹** /kɑːp||kɑrp/ *v* [I *on*] *derog infml* to find fault and complain continuously and unnecessarily: *Please stop carping (on) about the way I dress.*

**carp²** *n* **carp** *or* **carps** a large FRESHWATER fish that lives in lakes, pools, and slow-moving rivers

**car·pal** /'kɑːpəl||'kɑr-/ *adj* [A] *tech* of the wrist or the bones in the wrist

**car park** /'· ·/ *n BrE* **1** also **parking lot** *AmE*– an open place where cars and other vehicles may be parked, sometimes for a small payment **2 parking garage** *AmE*– an enclosed place used for this purpose: *My car is on the third floor of a* MULTISTOREY (=with many floors) *car park.*

**car·pen·ter** /'kɑːpəntər||'kɑr-/ *n* a person who is skilled at making and repairing wooden objects –compare JOINER

**car·pen·try** /'kɑːpəntri||'kɑr-/ *n* [U] the art or work of a CARPENTER

**car·pet¹** /'kɑːpət||'kɑr-/ *n* **1** [U] heavy woven often woollen material for covering floors or stairs **2** [C] a shaped piece of this material, usu. fitted to the size of a particular room: (fig.) *a carpet of flowers* –see picture on page 355 **3 sweep (something) under the carpet** *BrE*/**rug** *AmE infml* to keep (something) secret

**carpet²** *v* [T] to cover with or as if with a CARPET

**car·riage** /'kærɪdʒ/ *n* **1** [C] a wheeled vehicle, esp. a private horse-drawn vehicle **2** *BrE*||**car** *AmE*– [C] a railway passenger vehicle: *I'll be sitting in the third carriage from the front of the train.* –see picture on page 501 **3** [U] (the cost of) the act of moving goods from one place to another **4** [C] a wheeled support for moving a heavy object, esp. a gun **5** [C] a movable part of a machine: *A* TYPEWRITER *has a carriage which holds and moves the paper.* **6** [C;U] the manner of holding one's head and body when standing or walking; DEPORTMENT

**car·ri·er** /'kærɪər/ *n* **1** a person or thing that carries, esp. a business that carries goods or passengers from one place to another for payment **2** a person or thing that carries and passes diseases to others without himself or itself suffering from the disease

**carrier bag** /'··· ·/ *BrE*||**shopping bag** *AmE*– *n* a cheap strong paper or plastic bag, esp. with handles, for carrying goods away from a shop –see picture on page 563

**carrier pi·geon** /'···ˌ··/ also **homing pigeon**– *n* a PIGEON (a type of bird) that has been trained to carry messages from one place to another

**car·rot** /'kærət/ *n* **1** [C;U] (a plant with) an orange-red pointed root eaten as a vegetable: *Have some more carrots/carrot.* **2** [C] *infml* a promised reward or advantage for doing something

**carry** /'kæri/ *v* **carried, carrying 1** [T] to move while supporting, containing, or taking: *She carried her child on her back.*|*Pipes carry oil across the desert.*|*In*

**SPELLING NOTE**

Words with the sound /k/, like **cut**, may be spelt **k-**, like **key**, or **qu-**, like **queen.**
Words with the sound /s/, like **city**, may be spelt **s-**, like **soon**, or **ps-**, like **psychology.**

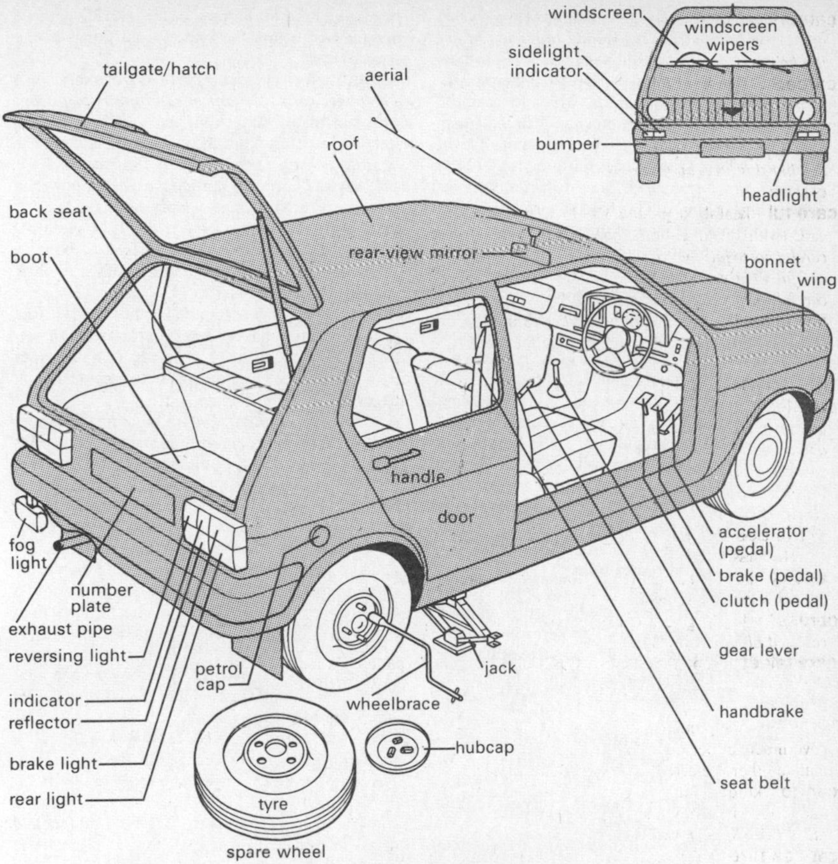

windscreen
windscreen wipers
sidelight
indicator
bumper
headlight
tailgate/hatch
aerial
roof
back seat
boot
rear-view mirror
bonnet
wing
handle
door
fog light
number plate
exhaust pipe
reversing light
petrol cap
indicator
reflector
brake light
rear light
accelerator (pedal)
brake (pedal)
clutch (pedal)
gear lever
jack
wheelbrace
handbrake
hubcap
seat belt
tyre
spare wheel

mileometer
heater controls
fuel gauge
speedometer
temperature gauge
indicator switch
glove compartment
light switch
choke
ignition
key
radio
windscreen wiper switch
horn
steering wheel

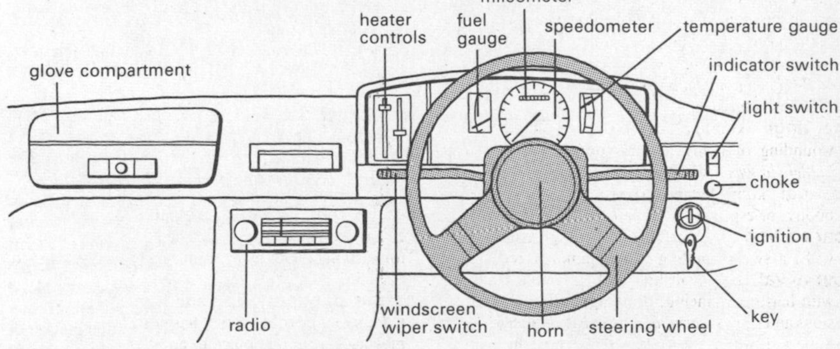

**driving a car**
to get into a car
to fasten the seat belt
to start the car/engine
to take off/release the handbrake
to drive off/pull away
to change gear
to overtake
to accelerate
to brake
to slow down
to park
to have a breakdown/a puncture
to change a tyre

**at the garage**
running low (on petrol)
to fill up (with petrol)
to check the oil
to top up with oil
to check the tyres/tyre pressures
to check the battery level

*Britain the police don't usually carry* (=wear) *guns.*|(fig.) *Her ability carried her to the top of her profession.* –see picture on page 669 **2** [T] to pass from one person to another; spread: *Many serious diseases are carried by insects.* **3** [T] to bear the weight of; support without moving: *This pillar carries the whole roof.*|(fig.) *His opinion* **carries** *a lot of* **weight** *with her.* (=influences her greatly) **4** [T] to contain: *All the newspapers carried articles about the government's plans.* **5** [T] to have as a usual or necessary result: *Such a crime carries a serious punishment.* **6** [I] to be able to reach a certain distance; cover space: *We couldn't hear her at the back of the hall because her voice doesn't carry (very well).* **7** [I;T *usu. pass*] **a** (esp. of a law or plan) to be approved **b** to cause (esp. a law or plan) to be approved: *The law was carried by 310 votes to 306.* **8** [T *no pass.*] to win the sympathy, support, or agreement of: *The government carried the country and won the election.* **9** [I;T] to put (a number) into the next upright row to the left as when doing addition: *9+5? Write 4 and carry 1.* **10 be carried away** to be excited: *She got carried away by the music at the concert and started to sing it herself.* **11 carry the day** to win; be completely successful **12 carry (something) too far** to do (something) for too long or to too great a degree

**carry** sthg.↔ **forward/over** *v adv* [T] (when adding up accounts) to move a total from the bottom of one row of figures to the next row for further addition

**carry** sthg.↔ **off** *v adv* [T] **1** to perform or do (a part, action, duty, etc.) easily and successfully: *She carried off her part in the plan with no difficulty.* **2** to win (the prize, honour, etc.): *Jean carried off all the prizes.*

**carry on** *v adv* **1** [I;T (=**carry** sthg. **on**) +*v-ing*] to continue, esp. in spite of an interruption or difficulties: *We'll carry on (with) our discussion tomorrow.* **2** [I] *infml* to behave in a very excited and anxious manner: *Stop carrying on!*

**carry on with** sbdy. *v adv prep* [T *no pass.*] *infml* to have a love affair with

**carry** sthg.↔**out/through** *v adv* [T] to fulfil; complete: *to carry out a plan, order, duty, etc.*

**carry through**[1] *v adv* **1** [T] (**carry** sthg.↔ **through**) →CARRY **out:** *In spite of a long struggle we succeeded in carrying most of our plans through.* **2** [I] to continue to exist: *feelings that carry through to the present*

**carry** sbdy. **through**[2] *v adv; prep* [T] to help to continue in an effective way during (an illness, difficult period, etc.): *His courage carried him through (his illness).*

**car·ry·cot** /'kærikɒt||-kɑt/ *n esp. BrE* a small boxlike object which can be easily carried, and in which a baby can sleep

**cart**[1] /kɑ:t||kɑrt/ *n* **1** a usu. two-wheeled wooden vehicle pulled by an animal, esp. a horse, or by hand, and used for farming or for carrying goods **2 put the cart before the horse** to put things in the wrong order

> **SPELLING NOTE**
> Words with the sound /k/, like **cut**, may be spelt **k-**, like **key**, or **qu-**, like **queen.**
> Words with the sound /s/, like **city**, may be spelt **s-**, like **soon**, or **ps-**, like **psychology.**

**cart**[2] *v* [T *off, away*] to carry in or as if in a cart: (fig.) *The police carted the prisoners off/away to prison.*

**carte blanche** /ˌkɑ:t 'blɑ:nʃ||ˌkɑrt-/ *n* [U +*to-v*] full freedom, esp. in politics and in spending money: *The minister gave me carte blanche in this matter.*

**cart·horse** /'kɑ:thɔ:s||'kɑrthɔrs/ *n* a heavy powerful horse, esp. used for heavy work and pulling carts

**car·ti·lage** /'kɑ:təlɪdʒ||'kɑr-/ *n* [C;U] (a piece of) strong elastic substance found instead of bone in young animals and, esp. round the joints, in older animals: –compare GRISTLE

**car·tog·ra·phy** /kɑ:'tɒgrəfi||kɑr'tɑ-/ *n* [U] the science or art of making maps **–cartographer** *n*

**car·ton** /'kɑ:tn||'kɑrtn/ *n* a box made from stiff paper (CARDBOARD) used for holding goods –see picture on page 615

**car·toon** /kɑ:'tu:n||kɑr'-/ *n* **1** a humorous drawing, often dealing in an amusing (SATIRICAL) way with something of interest in the news **2** also **animated cartoon**– a cinema film made by photographing a set of drawings –see also COMIC STRIP **–cartoonist** *n*

**car·tridge** /'kɑ:trɪdʒ||'kɑr-/ *n* **1** a usu. metal or paper tube containing explosive and a bullet for a gun **2** (in a record player) a small case containing the needle (STYLUS) that picks up sound signals from a record **3** a container holding recorded MAGNETIC TAPE used esp. with a TAPE RECORDER –compare CASSETTE (1)

**cart·wheel** /'kɑ:t-wi:l||'kɑrt-/ *n* a circular movement in which a person turns over by putting the hands on the ground and moving the legs sideways in the air –compare SOMERSAULT **–cartwheel** *v* [I]

**carve** /kɑ:v||kɑrv/ *v* **carved, carving 1** [T] to cut (a special shape) out of (a piece of usu. wood or stone): *The artist carved an interesting decoration from/out of this piece of wood.*|(fig.) *She carved herself (out) a good position in the business.* **2** [I;T] to cut (cooked meat) into (pieces or SLICES), esp. at a meal: *He carved me a nice piece from the chicken.*

**carve** sthg.↔**up** *v adv* [T] to divide, esp. in a way favourable to oneself

**carv·ing** /'kɑ:vɪŋ||'kɑr-/ *n* **1** [C] something made by carving (CARVE (1)) **2** [U] the work, art, or skill of a person who CARVES (1)

**cas·cade**[1] /kæ'skeɪd/ *n* **1** a steep high usu. small waterfall, esp. one part of a bigger waterfall **2** anything that seems to pour or flow downwards: *Her hair fell over her shoulders in a cascade of curls.*

**cascade**[2] *v* **-caded, -cading** [I;T] to (cause to) pour in quantity: *rainwater cascading down the window*

**case**[1] /keɪs/ *n* **1** [C] a particular occasion or state of affairs: *They might not offer me much money.* **In that case,** *I won't work for them.* **2** [C] a single example: *It was a case of stupidity, not dishonesty.*|*Several cases of fever have been reported.* **3** [C] a combination or set of events needing police or other inquiry or action: *a police case*|*a case of robbery with violence* **4** [C] a question to be decided in a court of law: *The case against Mr Smith will be heard* (=judged) *today.* **5** [C *usu. sing.*] the facts and arguments supporting one side in a disagreement or in a question brought before a court of law: *The police have a clear* *case against the prisoner.* **6** [C;U] (*in grammar*) (changes in) the form of a word (esp. of a noun, adjective, or PRONOUN) showing its relationship with other words in a sentence: *"Me" is the* **object case** *of "I".|"Mine" is the* **possessive case** *of "I".* **7 in any case** whatever happens: *In any case, you'll need to be at the station by nine.* **8 (just) in case** so as to be safe if (something happens): *Take your coat in case it rains/it should rain.* **9 in case of** if or when something happens: *In case of fire, ring the bell.*

**case²** *n* **1** a large box in which goods can be stored or moved: *A* **suitcase** *is used to take your clothes with you on holiday.* |*a case of wine* (=12 bottles) **2** the amount such a box holds: *a case/caseful of money* **3 lower case** (of letters of the alphabet) small: *The letter "e" is lower case.* **4 upper case** (of letters of the alphabet) large (CAPITAL² (2)): *The letter "E" is upper case.*

**case³** *v* **cased, casing** [T] to enclose or cover with a case

**case·ment win·dow** /ˌkeɪsmənt 'wɪndəʊ/ also **casement**– *n* a window that opens like a door –compare SASH WINDOW

**cash¹** /kæʃ/ *n* [U] **1** money in coins and notes, rather than cheques: *I've no cash on me, can I pay by cheque?* **2** *infml* money in any form: *The business has a* **cash flow** *of £50,000 a month.* (= the flow of money payments to or from a firm or business) **3 cash on delivery** →C.O.D.

**cash²** *v* [T] to exchange (a cheque or other order to pay) for CASH: *Can you cash this postal order for me?*

**cash in** *v adv* [I *on*] to take advantage or profit (from): *Let's cash in on the fine weather and go out.*

**cash crop** /'· ·/ *n* a crop produced for sale rather than for use by the grower

**cash desk** /'· ·/ *n* the desk in a shop where payments are made

**ca·shew** /'kæʃu:, kə'ʃu:/ *n* (a tropical American tree with) a small curved nut

**cash·ier** /kæ'ʃɪəʳ/ *n* a person in charge of money receipts and payments in a bank, hotel, shop, etc.

**cash·mere** /'kæʃmɪəʳ||'kæʒ-, 'kæʃ-/ *n* [U] fine soft wool used esp. for KNITted clothes

**cash reg·is·ter** /'· ˌ···/ *n* a business machine used in shops for calculating and recording the amount of each sale and the money received, and sometimes for giving change –see picture on page 615

**cas·ing** /'keɪsɪŋ/ *n* a protective covering: *This wire has a rubber casing.*

**ca·si·no** /kə'si:nəʊ/ *n* **-nos** a building used for social activities, esp. playing games for money

**cask** /kɑ:sk||kæsk/ *n* (the amount contained in) a barrel-shaped container for storing liquids

**cas·ket** /'kɑ:skʲ̇t||'kæs-/ *n* **1** a small box for holding jewels, letters, and other small valuable things **2** *AmE* for COFFIN

**cas·sa·va** /kə'sɑ:və/ [C;U] (flour made from the thick fleshy roots of) a tropical plant

**cas·se·role** /'kæsərəʊl/ [C;U] (the food cooked in) a deep usu. covered dish in which food, esp. meat, may be cooked and served: *Would you like some more casserole?*

**cas·sette** /kə'set/ *n* **1** a container holding MAGNETIC TAPE, which can be fitted into a TAPE RECORDER or VIDEO: *Put another cassette in the* **cassette recorder.** –compare CARTRIDGE (3) –see picture on page 105 **2** a container with photographic film already in it which can be fitted complete into a camera

**cast¹** /kɑ:st||kæst/ *v* **cast, casting** [T] **1** *often lit* to throw or drop: *The fishermen cast their nets into the sea.*|(fig.) *The evening sun casts long shadows.*|(fig.) *This misuse of public money has* **cast doubts on** *the actions of the whole government.* **2** [*off*] to throw off; remove: *Every year the snake casts (off) its skin.* **3** to give an acting part to (a person) in (a play): *The director cast me as a mad scientist.* **4** to make (an object) by pouring (hot metal or plastic) into a specially shaped container (MOULD): *to cast* BRONZE **5** to make (a vote, SPELL², etc.): *She cast her vote against the new tax.*|*In the story, the* WITCH **cast a spell** *on him, and made him ill.*

**cast** sbdy./sthg.↔ **aside** *v adv* [T] to get rid of; DISCARD: *As soon as she became rich she cast aside all her old friends.*

**cast** sbdy.↔ **away** *v adv* [T *usu. pass.*] to leave somewhere as the result of a shipwreck: *We were cast away on an island without food or water.* –see also CASTAWAY

**cast off** *v adv* **1** [I;T (=**cast** sthg.↔ **off**)] **a** (of a boat or ship) to be set free on the water by a rope being untied **b** to set (a boat or ship) free by untying a rope **2** [T] (**cast** sthg.↔ **off**) to give or throw away (clothes no longer wanted) –see also CASTOFF

**cast** sbdy./sthg.↔ **out** *v adv* [T *of*] *lit* to drive out or away; EXPEL: *to cast out the devil*

**cast²** *n* **1** [C +*sing./pl. v*] the actors in a play, film, etc.: *The cast is/are ready to start the play.* **2** [C] an act of throwing (esp. a fishing line) **3** [C] a hard stiff protective covering for holding a broken bone in place while it gets better **4** [S] general shape or quality: *an inquiring cast of mind*

**cas·ta·nets** /ˌkæstə'nets/ *n* [P] a musical instrument made from two shells of hard wood, plastic, etc., which are hit together repeatedly

**cast·a·way** /'kɑ:stəweɪ||'kæst-/ *n* a person who escapes from a shipwreck and reaches the shore of a strange country or lonely island –see also CAST **away**

**caste** /kɑ:st||kæst/ *n* [C;U +*sing./pl. v*] (a group resulting from the) division of society based on class differences of wealth, rank, rights, profession, or job: *The caste system is still strong in India.*

**cast·er, -or** /'kɑ:stəʳ||'kæs-/ *n* a wheel fixed to the base of a piece of furniture so that it can be easily moved

**cast·i·gate** /'kæstʲ̇geɪt/ *v* **-gated, -gating** [T] *fml* to punish or scold severely in order to correct

**cast·ing** /'kɑ:stɪŋ||'kæstɪŋ/ *n* **1** [C] a usu. metal or plastic object shaped by having been CAST¹ (4) **2** [U] the act of CASTing¹ (3), esp. of actors for a play

**casting vote** /ˌ·· '·/ *n* a deciding vote (usu. by a chairman) used when both sides have an equal number of votes

**cast-iron** /ˌ·'·· ◂/ *adj* **1** made of CAST IRON **2** *infml* hard; strong; unyielding: *She has a cast-iron stomach; she can eat anything.*|*a cast-iron excuse*

**cast i·ron** /ˌ· '··/ *n* [U] a hard but easily breakable type of iron

**cas·tle** /'kɑ:səl||'kæ-/ *n* **1** a large strongly-built building or set of buildings made in former times to be defended against attack **2** also **rook**– one of the powerful pieces in the game of CHESS

**cast·off** /ˈkɑːstɒf‖ˈkæst-/ *n infml* an unwanted article of clothing: *She gave her castoffs to her younger sister.* –see also CAST **off** –**cast-off** *adj*

**castor**/ˈkɑːstəʳ‖ˈkæs-/*n* →CASTER

**castor oil** /ˌ·· ˈ·◂/ *n* [U] a yellowish medicinal oil used esp. as a LAXATIVE

**cas·trate** /kæˈstreɪt‖ˈkæstreɪt/ *v* **-trated, -trating** [T] to remove all or part of the sex organs of (a male animal or person) –**castration** /kæˈstreɪʃən / *n* [C;U]

**cas·u·al** /ˈkæʒuəl/ *adj* **1** resulting from chance; not happening intentionally: *a casual meeting* **2** informal: *casual clothes* **3** [A] not serious or thorough: *The casual newspaper reader wouldn't like articles on politics every day.* **4** [A] (of workers) employed for a short period of time –**casually** *adv* –**casualness** *n* [U]

**cas·u·al·ty** /ˈkæʒuəlti/ *n* **-ties 1** [C] a person hurt in an accident: *There were ten serious casualties in the train crash.*|(fig.) *The new school was never finished: it was a casualty of the recent spending cuts.* **2** [C] a military person lost through death, wounds, or illness **3** [S] also **casualty ward, department**– a place in a hospital where people hurt in accidents are taken for treatment: *They rushed her to casualty after the accident.*

**cat** /kæt/ *n* **1** a small animal with soft fur, sharp teeth, and CLAWS often kept as a pet or in buildings to catch mice and rats: *A young cat is called a* **kitten. 2** any of various animals related to this, such as the lion or tiger **3 let the cat out of the bag** *infml* to tell a secret (often unintentionally) **4 rain cats and dogs** *infml* to rain very heavily

**cat·a·clys·m** /ˈkætəklɪzəm/ *n fml* a violent and sudden change or event, esp. a serious flood or EARTHQUAKE –**cataclysmic** /-ˈklɪzmɪk / *adj*

**cat·a·comb** /ˈkætəkuːm‖-kəum/ *n* [ *usu. pl.*] an underground burial place made up of many passages and rooms

**cat·a·logue¹** ‖also **-log** *AmE*–/ˈkætəlɒg‖-lɔg,-lɑg/*n* a list of places, names, goods, etc. (often with information about them) put in a special order so that they can be found easily

**catalogue²** ‖also **-log** *AmE v* **-logued** *or* **-loged, -loguing** or **-loging** [T] **1** to make a CATALOGUE of goods, places, names, etc.): *Can you catalogue the furniture you sell and send me a copy?* **2** to enter (a book, place, name, etc.) into a CATALOGUE

**cat·a·lyst** /ˈkætl-ɪ̇st/ *n* [C;U] a substance which, without itself changing, causes chemical activity to quicken: (fig.) *The workers' demand for better conditions was a catalyst for social change.*

**cat·a·pult¹** /ˈkætəpʌlt, -pult/ *n* **1** *BrE*‖**slingshot** *AmE*– a small Y-shaped stick with a rubber band fastened between the forks, used by children to shoot small stones at objects **2** a machine for throwing heavy stones, balls, etc., used as a weapon in former times

**SPELLING NOTE**

Words with the sound /k/, like **cut**, may be spelt **k-**, like **key**, or **qu-**, like **queen.**
Words with the sound /s/, like **city**, may be spelt **s-**, like **soon**, or **ps-**, like **psychology.**

**catapult²** *v* [I;T] to fire from a CATAPULT: (fig.) *The car stopped suddenly and I was catapulted through the* WINDSCREEN.

**cat·a·ract** /ˈkætərækt/ *n* **1** a large waterfall **2** a diseased growth on the eye causing a slow loss of sight

**ca·tarrh** /kəˈtɑːʳ/ *n* [U] a disease, esp. of the nose and throat, causing discomfort and a flow of thick liquid, as when one has a cold

**ca·tas·tro·phe** /kəˈtæstrəfi/ *n* a sudden, unexpected, and terrible event that causes great suffering, misfortune, or ruin: *The flood was a terrible catastrophe in which many people died.* –**catastrophically** *adv*

**catch¹** /kætʃ/ *v* **caught** /kɔːt/, **catching 1** [T] to get hold of (something moving in the air): *The dog caught the ball in its mouth.* –see picture on page 669 **2** [T] to trap (esp. an animal) after chasing or hunting; take: *Cats like to catch mice.* **3** [T] to find unexpectedly; discover suddenly or by surprise: *The police caught him stealing a car.* **4** [T] to be in time for: *We had to drive very quickly in order to catch the train.* –opposite **miss 5** [T] to get (an illness); become infected with: *You'll* **catch (a) cold** *if you don't put a coat on.* **6** [I;T] to (cause to) become hooked, held, fastened, or stuck: *I caught my dress on a nail.* **7** [T] to attract (esp. interest or attention): *I'd like another drink; try to* **catch** *the waiter's* **eye.** (=look at him to attract his attention) **8** [T not *be+v-ing*] to get or notice for a moment: *I* **caught sight of** *my old friend in town today.* **9** [T not *be+v-ing*] to hear; understand: *I didn't catch what you said. Could you say it again please?* **10** [I;T] to start to burn: *The wood* **caught fire.**

**catch on** *v adv* [I] **1** to become popular: *The new song caught on really quickly.* **2** [*to*] to understand: *He's always the last to catch on.*

**catch** sbdy.↔ **out** *v adv* [T] to show to be at fault

**catch up** *v adv* **1** [I;T *with*] to come up from behind; draw level (with): *Will we catch up with Japan in industrial production?*|*You walk on and I'll catch up with you later. (BrE* also *catch you up later)* **2** [I *on*] to bring or come up to date: *I have to catch up on my work so I can't come out.* **3 caught up in** included in, often against one's wishes; INVOLVED in: *The government seems to have got caught up in the argument between Russia and America.*

**catch²** *n* **1** an act of seizing and holding a ball **2** (the amount of) something caught: *The boat brought back a big catch of fish.* **3** a hook or other apparatus for fastening something or holding it shut: *The catch on this door seems to be broken. It won't open.* **4** *infml* a hidden or awkward difficulty: *That house is very cheap; there must be a catch in it somewhere!*

**catch·ing** *adj* [F] *infml* (of a disease) infectious

**catch·word** /ˈkætʃwɜːd‖-ɜrd/ *n* a word or phrase repeated so regularly that it becomes representative of a political party, newspaper, etc.; SLOGAN

**catch·y** /ˈkætʃi/ *adj* **-ier, -iest** easy to remember: *a catchy song*

**cat·e·chis·m** /ˈkætɪ̇ˌkɪzəm/ *n* a set of questions and

answers, often in the form of a small book, used for religious instruction in some branches of the Christian church

**cat·e·gor·i·cal** /ˌkætəˈgɒrɪkəl‖-ˈgɔ-, -ˈgɑ-/ *adj* unconditional; wholly fixed; made without any doubt in the mind of the speaker or writer: *a categorical statement* **–categorically** *adv: I asked her several times to come, but she categorically refused.*

**cat·e·go·rize**‖also **-rise** *BrE* /ˈkætəgəraɪz/ *v* **-rized, -rizing** [T *as*] to put in a CATEGORY

**cat·e·go·ry** /ˈkætəgəri‖-gori/ *n* **-ries** a division or class in a system for dividing objects into groups according to their nature

**ca·ter** /ˈkeɪtəʳ/ *v* [I] to provide and serve food and drinks, usu. for payment, at a public or private party rather than a restaurant **–caterer** *n*

**cater for** sbdy./sthg. *BrE*‖**cater to** sbdy./sthg. *AmE– v prep* [T] to provide with what is necessary: *Our magazines try to cater for all opinions.*

**cat·er·pil·lar** /ˈkætəˌpɪləʳ‖-tər-/ *n* a small long many-legged wormlike creature (LARVA of the BUTTERFLY and other insects) which feeds on the leaves of plants

**ca·the·dral** /kəˈθiːdrəl/ *n* the chief church of a DIOCESE (an area with a BISHOP)

**cath·ode** /ˈkæθəʊd/ also **negative pole**– *tech n* the part of an electrical instrument (such as a BATTERY (1)) from which ELECTRONs leave, represented by the sign [-] –compare ANODE

**cathode ray tube** /ˌ·· ˈ· ·/ *n* a glass instrument in which streams of ELECTRONs from the CATHODE (**cathode rays**) are directed onto a flat surface where they give out light, as in a television receiver

**cath·o·lic** /ˈkæθəlɪk/ *adj fml* (esp. of likings and interests) general; widespread; broad: *catholic opinions/taste*

**Catholic** *adj,n* (a member) of the ROMAN CATHOLIC church: *Catholic children|Catholic schools|Is he (a) Catholic or (a)* PROTESTANT? **–Catholicism** /kəˈθɒləsɪzəm‖kəˈθɑ-/ *n* [U]

**cat·nap** /ˈkætnæp/ *n infml* a very short light sleep

**cat's eye** /ˈ· ·/ *n* a small object fixed in the middle of a road which shines when lit by car lights in the dark

**cat·tle** /ˈkætl/ *n* [P] large four-legged farm animals, esp. cows, kept for their meat or milk: *The cattle are in the shed.*

**cat·ty** /ˈkæti/ *adj* **-tier, -tiest** *derog infml* (esp. of a woman or her behaviour) marked by hatred or anger that is not openly expressed; SPITEful **–cattiness** *n* [U] **–cattily** *adv*

**caught** /kɔːt/ *v past tense & participle of* CATCH

**cau·li·flow·er** /ˈkɒlɪˌflaʊəʳ‖ˈkɔ-, ˈkɑ-/ *n* [C;U] (the white part of) a garden vegetable with green leaves around a large white head of undeveloped flowers

**cause¹** /kɔːz/ *n* **1** [C] something which produces an effect; a person, thing, or event that makes something happen –see REASON¹ (USAGE); see Study Notes on page 128 **2** [U] reason: *Don't complain without (good) cause.* **3** [C] a principle or movement strongly defended or supported: *She fought for the cause all her life.*

**cause²** *v* **caused, causing** [T] to lead to; be the cause of: *What caused his illness?|His illness caused him to miss the game.|He often causes trouble to/for people.|This car has caused me a lot of trouble.*

**cause·way** /ˈkɔːzweɪ/ *n* a raised road or path esp. across wet ground or water

**caustic** /kɔːstɪk/ *adj* able to burn or destroy by chemical action; able to CORRODE: (fig.) *caustic remarks*

**cau·tion¹** /ˈkɔːʃən/ *n* **1** [U] great care; the act of paying attention or of taking care **2** [C] a spoken warning usu. given by a policeman, judge, etc., when a person has broken the law

**caution²** *v* [T *about*] to warn officially: *The policeman said, "I must caution you that anything you say may be used against you (at your trial)."*

**cau·tion·ar·y** /ˈkɔːʃənəri‖-neri/ *adj* [*no comp.*] *fml or humor* giving advice or a warning: *cautionary* TALEs (=stories) *intended to warn us*

**cau·tious** /ˈkɔːʃəs/ *adj* careful; paying attention; having or showing CAUTION¹ (1) **–cautiously** *adv* **–cautiousness** *n* [U]

**cav·al·cade** /ˌkævəlˈkeɪd, ˈkævəlkeɪd/ *n* [*+sing./pl. v*] a ceremonial procession of riders, carriages, vehicles, etc.

**cavalier** /ˌkævəˈlɪəʳ/ *derog adj* thoughtless; in an ARROGANT manner: *I'm annoyed at your cavalier treatment of him.*

**cav·al·ry** /ˈkævəlri/ *n* [*the* U *+sing./pl.v*] (esp. in former times) soldiers who fight on horseback –compare INFANTRY

**cave** /keɪv/ *n* a deep natural hollow place either underground, or in the side of a cliff or hill

**cave in** *v adv* [I] (of a roof or the covering over a hollow place) to fall in or down: *The roof of the old house caved in.*

**cave·man** /ˈkeɪvmæn/ *n* **-men** /men/ a person who lived in a cave in very ancient (PREHISTORIC) times

**cav·ern** /ˈkævən‖-ərn/ *n* a large deep cave **–cavernous** *adj: a cavernous hole*

**cav·i·ar, -are** /ˈkæviɑːʳ/ *n* [U] the salted eggs (ROE) of various large fish, esp. the **sturgeon**, highly regarded as food

**cav·i·ty** /ˈkævəti/ *n* **-ties** a hole or hollow space in a solid mass: *a cavity in a tooth*

**ca·vort** /kəˈvɔːt‖-ɔrt/ *v* [I] *infml* (esp. of a person) to jump or dance about noisily –compare CAPER

**caw** /kɔː/ *n, v* [C;I] (to make) the loud rough cry of various large birds (such as CROWs¹)

**cay·enne pep·per** /ˌkeɪen ˈpepəʳ/ also **cayenne** /ˌkeɪˈen◂/– *n* [C;U] (a powder made from) a type of PEPPER¹ (2) with long thin very hot-tasting red fruit

**CB** *abbrev. for:* Citizens' Band; a system of radio communication by which people, esp. drivers, can send messages to one another, esp. over short distances

**CBI** *abbrev. for:* Confederation of British Industry: an organization that represents the views of employers in industry –compare TUC

**cease** /siːs/ *v* **ceased, ceasing** [I;T *+to-v/v-ing*] *fml* to stop (esp. an activity): *Cease fire!* (=Stop shooting!)| *At last they ceased work(ing).* –see also CEASELESS

**cease-fire** /ˈ··/ *n* an act of stopping fighting for a long or short period –compare TRUCE

**cease·less** /ˈsiːsləs/ *adj fml* unending; continuous; without ceasing: *ceaseless activity* **–ceaselessly** *adv*

**ce·dar** /ˈsiːdəʳ/ *n* [C;U] (the reddish sweet-smelling wood of) a tall EVERGREEN tree

**cede** /siːd/ *v* **ceded, ceding** [T *to*] *fml* to yield (usu. land or a right) to (another country or person), esp. after losing a war

**cei·ling** /ˈsiːlɪŋ/ *n* **1** the inner surface of the top of a room –compare ROOF[1] (1) **2** a usu. official upper limit on wages, rents, etc.

**cel·e·brate** /ˈseləbreɪt/ *v* **-brated, -brating 1** [I;T] to mark (an event or special occasion) with public or private rejoicings: *We celebrated the New Year with a party.* **2** [T] to praise in writing, speech, etc. **3** [T] (of a priest) to perform (esp. the MASS) solemnly and officially

**cel·e·brat·ed** /ˈseləbreɪtəd/ *adj* [*for*] well-known; famous: *celebrated for her beauty*

**cel·e·bra·tion** /ˌseləˈbreɪʃən/ *n* **1** [U] the act of celebrating (CELEBRATE) **2** [C] an occasion of celebrating

**ce·leb·ri·ty** /səˈlebrəti/ *n* **-ties** a famous person

**cel·e·ry** /ˈseləri/ *n* [U] (the greenish-white stems of) a small plant eaten as a vegetable: *He was eating a stick of celery.*

**ce·les·ti·al** /səˈlestɪəl‖-tʃəl/ *adj fml* of or belonging to the sky or heaven: *The sun, the stars, and the moon are celestial bodies.*

**cel·i·bate** /ˈseləbət/ *adj,n* (a person, esp. a priest or NUN, who is) unmarried and without sexual activity or experience, esp. as the result of a religious promise –**celibacy** *n* [U] /-bəsi/

**cell** /sel/ *n* **1** a small room **a** in a prison for one person or a small number of people **b** in a MONASTERY or CONVENT for one person **2** one small part of a larger whole **3** a very small division of living matter, with one centre of activity (NUCLEUS (1)), able alone or with others to perform all the operations necessary for life **4** an apparatus for making a current of electricity by chemical action

**cel·lar** /ˈseləʳ/ *n* an underground room, usu. used for storing goods: *a wine cellar* –compare BASEMENT

**cel·list** /ˈtʃeləst/ *n* a person who plays the CELLO

**cel·lo** /ˈtʃeləʊ/ also **violoncello** *fml*– *n* **-los** a four-stringed musical instrument, like the VIOLIN but larger and producing a deeper sound, that is held between the knees and played with a BOW[3] (2)

**cel·lo·phane** /ˈseləfeɪn/ *n* [U] *tdmk* thin transparent material used for wrapping goods

**cel·lu·lar** /ˈseljʊləʳ‖-jə-/ *adj* consisting of CELLS (3)

**cel·lu·loid** /ˈseljʊlɔɪd‖-jə-/ *n* [U] *tdmk* a plastic substance made mainly from CELLULOSE, formerly used for making photographic film

**cel·lu·lose** /ˈseljʊləʊs, -əʊz‖-jə-/ *n* [U] the material from which the cell walls of plants are made, used in making paper, plastic, many man-made materials, etc.

**Cel·si·us** /ˈselsɪəs/ *n,adj* [A or after *n*] CENTIGRADE

**Cel·tic** /ˈkeltɪk, ˈseltɪk/ *adj* of (the languages of) the Celts, a European people who include the Welsh

> **SPELLING NOTE**
> Words with the sound /k/, like **cut**, may be spelt **k-**, like **key**, or **qu-**, like **queen.**
> Words with the sound /s/, like **city**, may be spelt **s-**, like **soon**, or **ps-**, like **psychology.**

**ce·ment**[1] /səˈment/ *n* [U] **1** a grey powder, made from a burned mixture of lime and clay, which becomes hard like stone after having been mixed with water and allowed to dry **2** a thick sticky hard-drying chemical liquid (ADHESIVE) used for filling holes, as in the teeth, or for joining things together

**cement**[2] *v* [T] to join together or make firm with or as if with CEMENT: (fig.) *Our holiday together cemented our friendship.*

**cem·e·tery** /ˈsemətri‖-teri/ *n* **-teries** an area of ground, usu. not belonging to a church, set aside for the burial of dead people –compare CHURCHYARD, GRAVEYARD

**cen·sor** /ˈsensəʳ/ *n* an official who examines printed matter, films, or (esp. in war) private letters with the power to remove anything offensive or (in war) helpful to the enemy –**censor** *v* [T] –**censorship** *n* [U]

**cen·sure**[1] /ˈsenʃəʳ/ *n fml* [U] the act of blaming, unfavourably judging, or expressing strong disapproval: *The opposition passed a* **vote of censure** *on the government.*

**censure**[2] *v* **-sured, -suring** [T] *fml* to express strong disapproval of; judge severely and unfavourably

**cen·sus** /ˈsensəs/ *n* **-suses** an official count of a country's total population, with other important information about the people

**cent** /sent/ *n* 0·01 of certain money standards, such as the dollar

**cen·te·na·ry** /senˈtiːnəri‖-ˈte-, ˈsentəneri/ ‖also **centennial** *AmE*– *n* **-ries** the day or year exactly 100 years after a particular event

**cen·ten·ni·al** /senˈtenɪəl/ *n AmE* for CENTENARY

**cen·ter** /ˈsentəʳ/ *n,v AmE* for CENTRE

**Cen·ti·grade** /ˈsentəgreɪd/ also **Celsius**– *n* a scale of temperature in which water freezes at 0° and boils at 100° –compare FAHRENHEIT

**cen·ti·me·tre** *BrE*‖**centimeter** *AmE* /ˈsentəˌmiːtəʳ/ *n* (a measure of length equal to) 0·01 metres or about 0·4 inches

**cen·tral** /ˈsentrəl/ *adj* **1** [A *no comp.*] being the centre: *This is the central city of the whole area.* **2** at, in, or near the centre: *The shops are in a central position in the city.* **3** [A *no comp.*] chief; main; of greatest importance: *The central aim of this government is social equality.* **4** [F] convenient; easily reached: *Our house is very central for the shops.*

**central heat·ing** /ˌ·· ˈ··/ *n* [U] a system of heating buildings in which heat is produced and controlled at a single point and carried by pipes to the various parts of the building in the form of hot air or water

**cen·tral·ize** ‖also **-ise** *BrE* /ˈsentrəlaɪz/ *v* **-ized, -izing** [T] to gather (esp. the controlling power of government) under central control –see also DECENTRALIZE –**centralization** /-ˈzeɪʃən/ *n* [U]

**cen·tre**[1] *BrE*‖**center** *AmE* /ˈsentəʳ/ *n* **1** [C] a middle part or point; point equally distant from all sides; the exact middle, esp. the point around which a circle is drawn: *Although London is Britain's capital it is not at the centre of the country.* **2** [C] a point, area, person, or thing that is the most important to an interest, activity, or condition: *a shopping centre*|*He likes to be the centre of attention.* **3** [A; *the* S] a middle

(MODERATE[1] (2)) position, esp. in politics: *The centre parties are hoping to win the next election.*

**centre²** *BrE*||**center** *AmE v* **-tred,** *or* **-tered, -tring** *or* **-tering 1** [I;T *on, upon, round, around*] to (cause to) gather to a centre; (cause to) have a centre: *Our thoughts centred on the girl who had died.* **2** [T] to place in or at the centre

**centre of grav·i·ty** /ˌ·· · '···/ *n* that point in any object on which it will balance

**cen·tri·fu·gal** /ˌsentrɪ'fjuːgəl◂/ *adj* tending to move in a direction away from the centre: *centrifugal force*

**cen·tu·ri·on** /ˌsen'tʃʊərɪən||-'tʊ-/ *n* an army officer of ancient Rome, commanding about 100 men

**cen·tu·ry** /'sentʃəri/ *n* **-ries 1** a period of 100 years **2** (*sometimes cap.*) one of the 100-year periods counted forwards or backwards from the supposed year of CHRIST's birth: *the twentieth century*

**ce·ram·ics** /sǝ'ræmɪks/ *n* [P;U] (articles produced by) the art or practice of making bricks, pots, etc., by shaping bits of clay and baking until hard **–ceramic** *adj* [A]

**ce·re·al** /'sɪərɪəl/ *n* **1** [C] (a plant which is grown to produce) grain for food, such as wheat, rice, etc. **2** [C;U] (a) food made from grain, esp. eaten at breakfast

**cer·e·bral** /'serǝbrəl||sə'riː-, 'serǝ-/ *adj tech* (often of illnesses) of or connected with the brain

**cer·e·mo·ni·al** /ˌserǝ'məʊnɪəl/ also **ceremonious**– *adj* marked by or done according to ceremony **–ceremonially** *adv*

**cer·e·mo·ni·ous** /ˌserǝ'məʊnɪəs/ *adj* **1** fond of ceremony and formal behaviour; formally polite –see also UNCEREMONIOUS **2** →CEREMONIAL **–ceremoniously** *adv*

**cer·e·mo·ny** /'serǝməni||-məʊni/ *n* **-nies 1** [C] a formal, solemn, and well-established action or set of actions used for marking an important esp. public, social, or religious event: *the wedding ceremony* **2** [U] the special order and formal behaviour demanded by custom on particular occasions: *The queen was crowned with proper ceremony.*

**cer·tain¹** /'sɜːtn||'sɜrtn/ *adj* **1** sure; having no doubt: *I'm certain she saw me yesterday.|There's no certain cure for this illness.* **2** [+*to-v/that*] sure to happen: *It's almost certain that the government will lose the next election.* **3** [F +*to-v/(that)*] (of people) sure: *She's certain to do well in the examination.|Are you certain that you'll get there in time?* **4 make certain** to do something in order to be sure: *Make certain (that) you know what time the train goes.* –see also UNCERTAIN; see SURE[1] (USAGE)

**certain²** *determiner,pron* **1** (used like **some,** when something is not clearly known or described): *There are certain reasons why I must say no.* (=I am not going to tell you what my reasons are) **2** some but not a lot: *He makes a certain amount of profit from his business, but he'll never be rich.*

**cer·tain·ly** /'sɜːtnli||'sɜr-/ *adv* **1** without doubt; surely **2** (used as a polite or strong way of answering a question) yes; of course: *"Will you help me?" "Certainly I will."* **3 certainly not** (as a strong way of answering a question) no; of course not: *"Will you lend me some money?" "Certainly not!"* –see SURE[1] (USAGE)

**cer·tain·ty** /'sɜːtnti||'sɜr-/ *n* **-ties 1** [U] the state of being certain; freedom from doubt: *I can't say with certainty what my plans are.* –opposite **uncertainty 2** [C] a clearly established fact: *It's a certainty that this horse will win the race.*

**cer·tif·i·cate** /sə'tɪfɪkət||sər-/ *n* an official sheet of paper (DOCUMENT) on which is written or printed a statement made by an official person that a fact or facts are true: *a birth/marriage/death certificate*

**cer·ti·fy** /'sɜːtǝfaɪ||'sɜr-/ *v* **fied, -fying** [T] **1** to declare that (something) is correct or true: *The bank certified my accounts.* **2** [+*that*] to declare, esp. after some kind of test: *The doctor certified the prisoner mad.* **3** to give a CERTIFICATE to (someone) declaring successful completion of a course of training for a particular profession: *a certified teacher*

**cer·ti·tude** /'sɜːtǝtjuːd||'sɜrtǝtuːd/ *n fml* [U +*that*] the state of being or feeling certain; freedom from doubt

**cer·vix** /'sɜːvɪks||'sɜr-/ *n* **-vices** /vɪsiːz/ *or* **-vixes** *tech* a narrow necklike opening into an organ of the body, esp. into the WOMB **–cervical** *adj*

**ce·sar·e·an, -ian** /sǝ'zeərɪən/ *n* →CAESAREAN

**ces·sa·tion** /se'seɪʃən/ *n fml* a short pause or a stop; act of ceasing: *a cessation of hostilities* (= fighting with an enemy)

**cess·pit** /'sesˌpɪt/ also **cesspool** /'ses-puːl/– *n* an underground container or hole, in which the waste from a house, esp. body waste (SEWAGE), is collected

**cf.** *written abbrev. said as:* compare

**chafe** /tʃeɪf/ *v* **chafed, chafing 1** [I;T] to (cause to) become sore, painful, or uncomfortable by rubbing: *Her skin chafes easily.|Her shoes chafed the skin on her feet.* **2** [I] to become or be impatient, or annoyed: *He chafed at the delay.*

**chaff** /tʃɑːf||tʃæf/ *n* [U] the outer covers (HUSKS) of seeds, separated from the grain

**chaf·finch** /'tʃæˌfɪntʃ/ *n* a small bird, with a cheerful song, common in Europe

**chain¹** /tʃeɪn/ *n* **1** [C;U] (a length of) usu. metal rings, connected to or fitted into one another, used for fastening, supporting, decorating, etc.: *The bridge was supported by heavy iron chains hanging from two towers.|a lot of chain* **2** [C] a number of connected things, such as events, shops, restaurants, mountains, etc.: *a* **chain store** (=group of shops under one ownership)|*chain of events* **3 in chains** kept in prison or as a slave

**chain²** *v* [T *up*] to limit the freedom of with or as if with a chain: *It's time the dogs were* **chained up** *for the night.* –opposite **unchain**

**chain mail** /'· ·/ also **chain armour** /'· ˌ··/– *n* [U] armour made by joining small metal rings together to form a protective garment worn formerly in battle

**chain re·ac·tion** /ˌ· ·'··/ *n* a number of events or chemical changes so related to each other that each causes the next

**chain-smoke** /'· ·/ *v* **smoked, smoking** [I;T] to smoke (cigarettes) continually **–chain-smoker** *n*

**chair¹** /tʃeəʳ/ *n* **1** a piece of furniture on which one person may sit, which has typically a back, seat, usu. four legs, and sometimes arms –see also ARMCHAIR, WHEELCHAIR; see pictures on pages 105, 415, 521 **2**

the office, position, or official seat of someone, such as a chairman, in charge of a meeting **3** the position of PROFESSOR (1): *She holds the chair of chemistry in that university.*

**chair**[2] *v* [T] to be chairman of (a meeting)

**chair·man** /'tʃeəmən‖'tʃeər-/ also **chairperson, chairwoman** (*fem.*)– *n* **-men** /mən/ a person **a** in charge of a meeting: *one of our most experienced chairmen* **b** who directs the work of a committee, department, etc.: *He was elected (the) chairman of the education committee.*

**chair·man·ship** /'tʃeəmənʃɪp‖'tʃeər-/ *n* [*usu. sing.*] the rank, position, or period in office of chairman

**chair·per·son** /'tʃeəˌpɜːsən‖'tʃeərˌpərsən/ *n* **-persons** a CHAIRMAN or CHAIRWOMAN

**chair·wom·an** /'tʃeəˌwʊmən‖'tʃeər-/ *n* **-women** /ˌwɪmɪn/ a woman in charge of a meeting

**chal·et** /'ʃæleɪ‖ʃæ'leɪ/ *n* **1** a usu. wooden house with a steeply sloping roof, esp. common in Switzerland **2** a small house (BUNGALOW) or hut, esp. as in a holiday camp

**chal·ice** /'tʃælɪ̇s/ *n* a gold or silver decorated cup, used esp. to hold wine in Christian religious services

**chalk**[1] /tʃɔːk/ *n* **1** [U] a type of soft white rock, used for making lime and various writing materials **2** [C;U] (a piece of) this material, white or coloured, used for writing or drawing: *The teacher wrote on the (black)board with a piece of chalk/with chalk.* –see picture on page 105 **3 as different as chalk and cheese** *infml* completely unlike each other –**chalky** *adj* **-ier, -iest**

**chalk**[2] *v* [I;T] to write, mark, or draw with chalk

**chalk** sthg.↔ **up** *v adv* [T] *infml* to succeed in getting (esp. points in a game): *Our team has chalked up another victory.*

**chal·lenge**[1] /'tʃælɪ̇ndʒ/ *v* **-lenged, -lenging** [T] **1** [*to*] to call (someone) to compete against one, esp. in a fight, match, etc.: *I challenged him to a game of tennis.*|(fig.) *a challenging* (=difficult) *problem* –compare DARE **2** to question the legality or rightness of –**challenger** *n*

**challenge**[2] *n* **1** [C +*to-v*] an invitation to compete in a fight, match, etc.: *He accepted his friend's challenge to swim across the river.* **2** [C;U] (something with) the quality of demanding competitive action, interest, or thought: *To build a bridge in a month was a real challenge.*

**cham·ber** /'tʃeɪmbə^r/ *n* **1** *old use* a room, esp. a bedroom **2** [*the* S] (the hall used for meetings of) a usu. elected law-making body: *In Britain the upper chamber or parliament is the* **House of Lords**, *the lower the* **House of Commons. 3** [*often pl.*] a room set aside for a special purpose: *Cases not heard* (= dealt with) *in court are sometimes heard in the judge's chambers.* **4** an enclosed space, esp. in a body or machine: *The heart has four chambers.*

**cham·ber·lain** /'tʃeɪmbəlɪ̇n‖-bər-/ *n* (esp. formerly) an important official who directs the housekeeping affairs of a king, etc.

**SPELLING NOTE**
Words with the sound /ʃ/, like **chauffeur**, may be spelt **sh-**, like **shop**.

**cham·ber·maid** /'tʃeɪmbəmeɪd‖-ər-/ *n* a female servant employed to clean and tidy bedrooms, esp. in a hotel

**chamber mu·sic** /'·· ˌ··/ *n* music written for a small group of instruments and suitable for performance in a private home or small hall

**cha·me·le·on** /kə'miːlɪən/ *n* a small LIZARD which can change its colour to match its surroundings

**cham·pagne** /ʃæm'peɪn/ *n* [U] a French white wine containing a lot of bubbles, usu. drunk on special occasions

**cham·pi·on**[1] /'tʃæmpɪən/ *n* **1** also **champ** /tʃaemp/ *infml*– a person or animal who has won competitions of courage, strength, or skill: *a tennis champion* **2** a person who fights for, supports strongly, or defends a principle, movement, person, etc.: *a champion of women's rights/of the poor*

**champion**[2] *v* [T] to fight for, support strongly, or defend (a principle, movement, person, etc.)

**cham·pi·on·ship** /'tʃæmpɪənʃɪp/ *n* **1** a competition held to find the CHAMPION[1] (1) **2** the position, title, rank, or period of being CHAMPION[1] (1)

**chance**[1] /tʃɑːns‖tʃæns/ *n* **1** [U] the force that seems to make things happen without cause or reason; luck; good or bad fortune: *Chance plays an important part in many card games.*|*It happened quite* **by chance. 2** [C;U *of*] (a) possibility; likelihood that something will happen: *You'd have more chance of catching the train if you got a bus to the station instead of walking.*|*Is there any chance of the team winning this week?*|(*infml*) **Chances are** (=it is likely) *he has already heard the news.* **3** [C+*to-v*/*of*] a favourable occasion; OPPORTUNITY: *I never miss a chance of playing/to play football.* **4** [C] a risk: *The rope might break but that's a chance I'll have to take!* **5 on the (off) chance** in view of the (unlikely) possibility; in the hope: *We went to the cinema on the (off) chance of seeing Paul there.*

USAGE Compare **chance** and **opportunity**: You can have a **chance** or **opportunity** to do something/of doing something, which means that luckily it is possible for you at a favourable moment: *I had the* **chance/opportunity** *of visiting Paris.*|*I had no* **opportunity/chance** *to see him.* But we can also say *There is a* **chance** (=possibility) *that I will see him*, and **opportunity** could not be used here.

**chance**[2] *v* [not *be*+*v-ing*] **1** [I+*to-v*] *fml* to take place by chance; happen by accident: *She chanced to be in the park when I was there.* **2** [T+*v-ing*] to take a chance with; risk: *You shouldn't chance all your money at once.* **3 chance it** *infml* to take a chance of success, though failure is possible

**chance on/upon** sbdy./sthg. *prep* [T] *fml* to meet by chance; find by chance

**chance**[3] *adj* [A] accidental; unplanned: *a chance meeting*

**chan·cel·lor** /'tʃɑːnsələ^r‖'tʃæn-/ *n* (*often cap.*) a state or law official of high rank: *In Britain the* **Chancellor of the Exchequer** *deals with taxes and government spending.*

**chanc·y** /'tʃɑːnsi‖'tʃænsi/ *adj* **-ier, -iest** *infml* risky; uncertain as to the result: *That was a chancy thing to do; you could have been killed.*

**chan·de·lier** /ˌʃændəˈlɪəʳ/ *n* a usu. large decorated holder for electric lights or candles, usu. hanging from the CEILING (1)

**change¹** /tʃeɪndʒ/ *v* **changed, changing 1** [I;T] to make or become different: *In autumn the leaves change from green to brown.|Nothing will change him; he will always be the same.|The weather's changing; I think it's going to rain.* **2** [T *for*] to give, take, or put something in place of (something else, usu. of the same kind); exchange: *His new shoes didn't fit so he took them back to the shop and changed them (for another pair).|She changed her books at the library.|She's changed her job.* (=got a new job)|*He changed trains* (=left one and entered another) *at Birmingham.|Would you mind* **changing places** (=exchanging positions) *with me so that I can be nearer the fire?* **3** [I;T *into, out of*] to put (different clothes) on oneself: *She changed her dress.|I'm just going to change.* **4** [T] to put (fresh clothes or coverings) on (a baby, child, bed, etc.): *Did you change (the sheets on) your bed this week?|The baby needs changing.* **5** [T] to give (money) in exchange for money of a different type: *Where can I change my English money (for dollars)?|Can you change a pound (for me)?* (=give me CHANGE² (5) for a pound note) –compare EXCHANGE²

**change into** *v prep* **1** (**change into** sbdy./sthg.) to become (something different): *The next morning, the water had changed into ice.* **2** [T] (**change** sbdy./sthg. **into** sbdy./sthg.) to cause to become (something different): *The scientist tried to change iron into gold.*

**change over** *v adv* [I *from, to*] to make a complete change: *In 1971 Britain changed over from pounds, shillings, and pence to the new decimal money system.* –see CHANGEOVER

**change²** *n* **1** [C;U] (an example of) the act or result of changing: *a change of government|The doctor said the girl had taken a* **change for the worse** *and was seriously ill.|a change in the weather* **2** [C *usu. sing.*] something different done for variety, excitement, etc.: *Let's go to a restaurant* **for a change.**|*She's on holiday; she needed a change (from work).* **3** [C *of*] something new and fresh used in place of something else: *He took a change of clothes with him, because he was going to stay until the next day.|Your car needs an oil change.* **4** [U] the money returned when the amount given is more than the cost of the goods being bought: *If it costs 25 pence and you give her a pound you should get 75 pence change.* **5** [U] **a** coins of low value: *How much have you got* **in change? b** money in low-value coins or notes exchanged for a coin or note of higher value: *Can you give me change for a 50-pence piece?*

**change·a·ble** /ˈtʃeɪndʒəbəl/ *adj* (esp. of the weather) likely to change; variable –**changeability** /-əˈbɪləti/ *n* [U]

**changeover** /tʃeɪndʒˌəʊvəʳ/ *n* a change from one activity or system of working to another; an important change –see also CHANGE **over**

**chan·nel¹** /ˈtʃænl/ *n* **1** a narrow sea passage connecting two seas or oceans: *The English Channel separates England and France.* **2** the deepest part of a river, harbour, or sea passage **3** a way, course, or passage for liquids: *There's a channel in the middle of the old street to help rainwater flow away.* **4** a band of radio waves used for broadcasting television; a television station: *Turn to the other channel, I don't like this show.* **5** a course or way along which information travels: *You should go through the official channels to get help.*

**channel²** *v* **-ll-** *BrE*‖**-l-** *AmE* [T] **1** to direct: *I decided to channel my abilities into something useful* **2** to form a CHANNEL¹ (1,2,3) in

**chant¹** /tʃɑːnt‖tʃænt/ *v* [I;T] **1** to sing (words) to a CHANT **2** to continuously repeat (words) in time: *The crowd chanted "Down with the government".*

**chant²** *n* [C;S] **1** an often-repeated tune, often with many words sung on one note, esp. used in religious services **2** words continuously repeated in time: *The crowd's chant was "More jobs! More money!"*

**cha·os** /ˈkeɪ-ɒs‖-ɑs/ *n* [S;U] a state of complete disorder and confusion: *After the failure of electricity supplies the city was in chaos.*

**cha·ot·ic** /keɪˈɒtɪk‖-ˈɑtɪk/ *adj* in a state of complete disorder and confusion: *The traffic in the city was chaotic.* –**chaotically** *adv*

**chap¹** /tʃæp/ *n infml esp. BrE* a man or boy; FELLOW

**chap²** *v* **-pp-** [I;T] to (cause to) become sore, rough, and cracked: *chapped hands*

**chap·el** /ˈtʃæpəl/ *n* **1** [C] a place, such as a small church, a room in a hospital, prison, etc., used for Christian worship **2** [U] the religious services held in such a place

**chap·er·one¹, -on** /ˈʃæpərəʊn/ *n* (esp. formerly) an older person (usu. a woman) who goes with a young unmarried woman in public, and is responsible for her behaviour

**chaperone², -on** *v* **-oned, -oning** [I;T] to act as a CHAPERONE to (a person or people)

**chap·lain** /ˈtʃæpl¦n/ *n* a priest or other religious minister responsible for the religious needs of a club, a college, a part of the armed forces, etc. –see PRIEST (USAGE)

**chap·ter** /ˈtʃæptəʳ/ *n* one of the main divisions of a book or long article, usu. having a number or title

**char¹** /tʃɑːʳ/ *v* **-rr-** [I;T] to (cause to) become black by burning: *There was nothing left but a few charred remains.*

**char²** *n BrE infml* for CHARWOMAN

**char·ac·ter** /ˈkær¦ktəʳ/ *n* **1** [C;U] the qualities which make a person, thing, place, etc., different from another; nature: *a man of good character|When they pulled down the old houses in the centre of the town, the whole character of the place was changed.* –compare PERSONALITY (1), CHARACTERISTIC², REPUTATION **2** [U] moral strength; honesty; INTEGRITY (1): *a woman of great character* **3** [C] a person in a book, play, etc.: *I find all the characters in his new play very real.* **4** [C] *infml* a person as stated: *He's a strange character.* **5** [C] *infml* an odd or humorous person: *She's a real character, she makes everyone laugh.* **6** [C] a letter, mark, or sign used in writing and printing: *The characters in Chinese writing look like small pictures.* **7 in/out of character** like/unlike one's usual nature

**char·ac·ter·is·tic¹** /ˌkær¦ktəˈrɪstɪk/ *adj* typical; representing a person's or thing's usual character:

*characteristic generosity* –**characteristically** *adv*

**characteristic²** *n* [*of*] a special and easily recognized quality of someone or something: *A characteristic of this animal is its ability to live for a long time without water.* –compare CHARACTER (1), REPUTATION

**char·ac·ter·ize**‖also **-ise** *BrE* /ˈkærǝktəraɪz/ *v* **-ized, -izing** [T] **1** to be typical of: *This kind of behaviour characterizes the criminal mind.* **2** [*as*] to describe the character of: *She characterized him as lazy and selfish.* –**characterization** /-ˈzeɪʃən/ *n* [C;U]

**cha·rade** /ʃəˈrɑːd‖ʃəˈreɪd/ *n* an act or position which is easily seen to be false or foolish

**char·coal** /ˈtʃɑːkəʊl‖ˈtʃɑr-/ *n* [U] the black substance made by burning wood in a closed container with little air, used as FUEL or for drawing with

**charge¹** /tʃɑːdʒ‖tʃɑrdʒ/ *v* **charged, charging 1** [I;T] to ask in payment: *How much do you charge for your eggs?*|*The hotel charged me £15 for a room for the night.* –see COST² (USAGE) **2** [T] to record (something) to someone's debt: *Don't forget to charge the money to my account.* **3** [I;T *at, towards,* etc.] to rush in or as if in an attack: *Suddenly the wild animal charged at us.*|*The children charged out of school.* **4** [T *with*] to bring a CHARGE² (4) against; ACCUSE: *He was charged with stealing the jewels.*|*He was charged last night.* **5** [T+*to-v*] *fml* to command; give as a responsibility: *She charged me to look after her son.* **6** [I;T] to (cause to) take in the correct amount of electricity: *Does your car* BATTERY *charge easily?*

**charge²** *n* **1** [C] the price asked or paid for goods or a service: *The charge for a front-row seat is £5.*|*What are the charges in this hotel?* **2** [U *of*] care; control; responsibility: *I'm* **in charge of** *your class tomorrow so you must do as I tell you.*|*She* **took charge of** *the family business when her father died.*|(*fml*) *He* **has charge of** *the children while his wife is at work.* **3** [C] *fml* a person or thing for which one is responsible: *I became my uncle's charge after my father's death.* **4** [C] a spoken or written statement blaming a person for breaking the law or for doing something morally wrong: *He was arrested* **on a charge of** *murder.*|*The police* **brought a charge** *of murder* **against** *him.* **5** [C] a rushing forceful attack **6** [C] the amount of explosive to be fired at one time **7** [C;U] (a quantity of) electricity put into a BATTERY or other electrical apparatus: *The battery is* **on charge.** (= is having a charge put into it)

**char·i·ot** /ˈtʃæriət/ *n* a two-wheeled horse-drawn vehicle with no seats, used in ancient times in battles and races –**charioteer** /-ˈtɪəʳ/ *n*

**cha·ris·ma** /kəˈrɪzmə/ *n* [U] the special charm or personal qualities which cause a person to win and keep the interest and attention of other people –**charismatic** /ˌkærǝzˈmætɪk/ *adj*: *a charismatic figure*

**char·i·ty** /ˈtʃærǝti/ *n* **-ties 1** [U] sympathy and kindness; the feeling of generosity, esp. towards poor people: *She did it* **out of** (=because of) **charity. 2** [C] a society or organization that gives help to the poor: *The Red Cross is an international charity.* –**charitable** *adj*: *a charitable act/organization* –see also UNCHARITABLE

**SPELLING NOTE**
Words with the sound /ʃ/, like **chauffeur**, may be spelt **sh-**, like **shop**.

**char·la·tan** /ˈʃɑːlətn‖ˈʃɑr-/ *n derog* a person who deceives others by falsely claiming to have a special knowledge or skill: *That charlatan! I lost hundreds of pounds because I followed his advice.*

**charm¹** /tʃɑːm‖tʃɑrm/ *n* **1** [C;U] the power or ability to please or delight: *She has a lot of charm; she's very likeable.*|*This town has a charm you couldn't find in a big city.*|*He needed all his charm to persuade her he was right.* **2** [C] an object worn to keep away evil or bring good luck **3** [C] an act, expression, or phrase believed to have magical powers **4 work like a charm** to happen or take place with complete success

**charm²** *v* [T] **1** to please; delight: *The child charms everyone.* **2** to control (something) as if by magic: *It seemed as if he had* **a charmed life**; *nothing bad ever happened to him.* –**charmer** *n*

**charm·ing** /ˈtʃɑːmɪŋ‖-ɑr-/ *adj* very pleasing; delightful: *What a charming young man!* –**charmingly** *adv*

**chart¹** /tʃɑːt‖tʃɑrt/ *n* **1** (a sheet of paper with) information written or drawn in the form of a picture, GRAPH, etc.: *a weather chart* **2** a map, esp. a detailed map of a sea area

**chart²** *v* [T] to make a map or CHART of; show or record on a chart: (fig.) *The book charts her rise to fame as an actress.*

**char·ter¹** /ˈtʃɑːtəʳ‖-ɑr-/ *n* **1** [C] a written or printed signed statement from a ruler, government, etc., giving rights, freedoms, etc., to the people, an organization, or a person: *The rights of our citizens are governed* **by charter. 2** [A;U] the practice of hiring or renting cars, buses, planes, etc., for special use: *This travel firm specializes in charter flights.*

**charter²** *v* [T] **1** to give a CHARTER¹ (1) to (a country, firm, organization, etc.) **2** to hire or rent (a plane, train, bus, etc.) for a special use –see HIRE¹ (USAGE)

**chartered ac·coun·tant** /ˌ·· ·ˈ··/ *n BrE* an ACCOUNTANT who has successfully completed his/her training

**char·wom·an** /ˈtʃɑːˌwʊmən‖ˈtʃɑr-/ also **charlady**, also **char** *infml*– *n* **-women** /ˌwɪmɪn/ *esp. BrE* a woman who works as a cleaner in a house, office, or public building

**char·y** /ˈtʃeəri/ *adj* **-ier, -iest** [F *of*] *fml* careful; unwilling to take risks; CAUTIOUS –**charily** *adv*

**chase¹** /tʃeɪs/ *v* **chased, chasing 1** [I;T] to follow rapidly in order to catch: *The cat chased the mouse but could not catch it.*|(fig.) *He's always chasing new jobs.* **2** [T] to cause to leave or run away: *They chased the dog away.* **3** [I] to run; hurry: *The children are always* **chasing in and out/chasing about.**

**chase²** *n* **1** an act of chasing something: *There was a long chase before the criminal was caught.* **2 give chase** to chase someone

**chas·m** /ˈkæzəm/ *n* a very deep crack or opening in the surface of the earth or ice

**chas·sis** /ˈʃæsi/ *n* **chassis** /ˈʃæsiz/ the framework on which the body and working parts of a vehicle, radio, etc. are fastened or built

**chaste** /tʃeɪst/ *adj* pure in word, thought, and deed,

esp. without sexual activity –**chastely** *adv*

**chas·ten** /'tʃeɪsən/ *v* [T] *fml* to cause (a person or behaviour) to improve by punishment or suffering: *He was chastened by the accident; he had nearly died.*

**chas·tise** /tʃæ'staɪz/ *v* **-tised, -tising** [T] *fml* to punish or blame severely, esp. by beating –**chastisement** *n* [C;U]

**chas·ti·ty** /'tʃæstǝ̇ti/ *n* [U] (esp. of young women) the state of being sexually pure: *Chastity before marriage is still demanded in some societies.* –compare VIRGINITY

**chat¹** /tʃæt/ *v* **-tt-** [I *about, away*] to talk in a friendly familiar informal manner: *The two friends sat in a corner and chatted (away) about the weather.*

**chat** sbdy.↔ **up** *v adv* [T] *BrE infml* (esp. of men) to try to make friends with by talking to (esp. a woman): *He's always chatting up the office girls.*

**chat²** *n* a friendly informal conversation

**chât·eau, chat-** /'ʃætəʊ‖ʃæ'təʊ/ *n* **-teaus** *or* **-teaux** /'ʃætəʊz‖ʃæ'təʊz/ *French* a castle or large country house in France

**chat·tel** /'tʃætl/ *n tech or fml* an article of movable property (esp. in the phrase **goods and chattels**)

**chat·ter¹** /'tʃætəʳ/ *v* [I] **1** [*away, on, about*] (of people) to talk rapidly and at length, usu. about something unimportant: *The teacher told the children to stop chattering in class.* **2** (of the teeth or machines) to knock together, esp. through cold or fear: *I was so cold my teeth were chattering.* –**chatterer** *n*

**chatter²** *n* [U] **1** rapid informal unimportant conversation **2** a rapid knocking sound made by teeth, machines, etc.: *the chatter of the* MACHINEGUN

**chat·ter·box** /'tʃætəbɒks‖-tərbɑks/ *n infml* a person, esp. a child, who talks a lot

**chat·ty** /'tʃæti/ *adj* **-tier, -tiest** *infml* fond of talking: *He's a friendly, chatty sort of person.*

**chauf·feur** /'ʃəʊfəʳ, ʃeʊ'fɜːʳ/ **chauffeuse** /ʃəʊ'fɜːz‖-ɜrz/ *fem.– n* a person employed to drive someone's car –**chauffeur** *v* [I;T]

**chau·vin·is·m** /'ʃəʊvǝ̇nɪzəm/ *n* [U] **1** very great and often blind admiration of one's country; proud belief that one's country is politically, morally, and militarily better than all others **2** unreasoned belief that the sex to which one belongs is better than the other sex: *People who support equal rights for women fight against* **male chauvinism.**

**chau·vin·ist** /'ʃəʊvǝ̇nǝ̇st/ *n,adj* (a person or organization) favouring, feeling, or showing CHAUVINISM: *Her husband's such a chauvinist that he tries to tell her how to vote.* –**chauvinistic** /ˌʃəʊvǝ̇'nɪstɪk/ *adj* –**chauvinistically** *adv*

**cheap¹** /tʃiːp/ *adj* **1** low in price; costing little: *Fresh vegetables are very cheap in the summer.|Bread is cheap in this shop because they bake it themselves.* –compare DEAR **2** charging low prices: *This is the cheapest restaurant in town.* **3** of poor quality; SHODDY (1): *Her shoes looked* **cheap and nasty** *to me.* **4** needing little effort: *a cheap victory* **5 feel cheap** *infml* to feel ashamed: *I felt cheap because I'd lied to my friend.* –**cheaply** *adv* –**cheapness** *n* [U]

**cheap²** *adv* **1** at a very low price: *I was very lucky to get it so cheap.* **2** *infml* in a way that lowers one's worth: *I wish she wouldn't act so cheap.*

**cheap·en** /'tʃiːpən/ *v* [T] to make (esp. oneself) less popular or good: *By your rudeness you've cheapened yourself in everyone's opinion.*

**cheat¹** /tʃiːt/ *v* **1** [I *at*] to act dishonestly or deceitfully to win an advantage esp. in a game: *He always cheats at cards; I never play with him.* **2** [T *of, out of*] to take from (someone) unfairly, dishonestly, or deceitfully: *He cheated the old woman ((out) of her money) by making her sign a paper she didn't understand.* **3** [T] *lit* to avoid or escape as if by deception: *The swimmers cheated death in the stormy seas.*

**cheat²** *n* a person who cheats; dishonest person

**check¹** /tʃek/ *n* **1** [C *on*] an examination to make certain that something is correct: *a check on the quality of all goods leaving the factory* **2** [S] a stop; control: *We've kept the disease* **in check** *for a year now.* **3** [C] *AmE* for TICK² (2) **4** [C] a receipt; ticket or object for claiming something: *I've lost the check for my coat.* **5** [C] *AmE* a bill at a restaurant **6** [C;U] a pattern of squares **7** [U] (in CHESS) the position of the king when under direct attack from an opponent's piece(s) **8** [C] *AmE* for CHEQUE

**check²** *v* **1** [I;T +*that*] to test, examine, or mark to see if something is correct; make sure; VERIFY: *Have you checked the examination papers yet?|When I checked my shopping list I found I'd forgotten to buy eggs.|"Is the baby asleep?" "I'll just go and check."* **2** [T] to find out and note: *He checked the temperature every morning before leaving home.* **3** [T] to stop; control; hold back; RESTRAIN: *A change of wind checked the fire.* –see also UNCHECKED **4** [T] (in CHESS) to move one's pieces so as to put (the opponent's king) under direct attack **5** [T] *AmE* for TICK² (2)

**check in** *v adv* [I *at, to*] to report one's arrival, as at a hotel desk, an airport, etc.: *You must check in at the airport an hour before your plane leaves.* –compare CHECK **out** (1)

**check out** *v adv* **1** [I *of*] to leave a hotel after paying the bill –compare CHECK **in 2** [I;T (=**check** sbdy./sthg. ↔ **out**)] *infml* **a** to find out whether something is true or correct by making inquiries: *to check out his story* **b** to be found to be true after inquiries have been made: *How does his story check out with the facts?* –see also CHECKOUT

**check** sthg.↔ **over** *v adv* [T] to examine: *Please check over your work and correct any mistakes.*

**check up on** sbdy./sthg. *v adv prep* [T] *infml* to make thorough inquiries about: *The police were checking up on what the man had told them.*

**checked** /tʃekt/ *adj* having a pattern of squares (CHECKS¹ (6)): *Do you like these checked curtains?*

**check·ers** /'tʃekəz‖-ərz/ *n* [U] *AmE* for DRAUGHTS

**checking ac·count** /'·· ·ˌ·/ *n AmE* for CURRENT ACCOUNT

**check·list** /'tʃekˌlɪst/ *n* a complete list of books, goods, voters, etc., so arranged as to provide an easy means of finding information about these things; CATALOGUE

**check·mate¹** /'tʃekmeɪt, ·'·/ *n* [C;U] **1** (in CHESS) the position of a king when under direct attack from an opponent's pieces so that escape is impossible **2** (a) complete defeat

**checkmate**[2] *v* **-mated, -mating** [T] **1** (in CHESS) to win the game with a CHECKMATE **2** to stop; completely defeat

**check·out** /ˈtʃek-aʊt/ *n* a desk in a self-service shop where one shows the goods one has chosen and pays for them –see also CHECK **out**

**check·point** /ˈtʃekpɔɪnt/ *n* a place where a CHECK[1] (1) is made on people, traffic, goods, etc.: *There are a number of checkpoints on the border between East and West Berlin.*

**check·up** /ˈtʃek-ʌp/ *n infml* a general medical examination: *You look tired and ill; why don't you have a checkup?*

**ched·dar** /ˈtʃedəʳ/ *n* [U] (*often cap.*) a firm smooth usu. yellowish cheese

**cheek**[1] /tʃiːk/ *n* **1** [C] the part of the face below the eye, esp. in human beings: *Her cheeks were red after she ran up the stairs.* –see picture on page 299 **2** [U] *infml* bold disrespectful rude behaviour **3 -cheeked** having cheeks of the stated kind: *red-cheeked*

**cheek**[2] *v* [T] *infml, esp. BrE* to behave boldly, disrespectfully, or rudely towards

**cheek·bone** /ˈtʃiːkbəʊn/ *n* the bone above the cheek, just below the eyes

**cheek·y** /ˈtʃiːki/ *adj* **-ier, -iest** *infml* disrespectful; rude –compare IMPERTINENT **–cheekiness** *n* [U]

**cheep** /tʃiːp/ *v,n* [I;S] (to make) the weak high noise made by young birds

**cheer**[1] /ˈtʃɪəʳ/ *n* **1** [C] a shout of praise, encouragement, etc.: *I heard the cheers of the crowd, and I knew that our team was winning.* **2** [U] happiness of mind; good spirits; gaiety

**cheer**[2] *v* **1** [I] to shout in praise, approval, or support: *The crowd cheered as the teams arrived.* **2** [T *on*] to encourage by shouting approval or support: *The crowd cheered their favourite team (on).* **3** [T] to give encouragement or hope to: *The trapped miners were cheered when they heard the rescue party.*

**cheer up** *v adv* [I;T (=**cheer** sbdy. **up**)] *infml* to (cause to) become happier or more cheerful: *Cheer up! The news isn't too bad.*

**cheer·ful** /ˈtʃɪəfəl‖-ər-/ *adj* happy; in good spirits: *a cheerful person* **–cheerfully** *adv* **–cheerfulness** *n* [U]

**cheer·ing** /ˈtʃɪərɪŋ/ *adj* encouraging; gladdening: *the cheering news of his return*

**cheer·i·o** /ˌtʃɪəriˈəʊ/ *interj BrE infml* goodbye

**cheer·lead·er** /ˈtʃɪəˌliːdəʳ‖-ər-/ *n* (esp. in the US) a person who calls for and directs cheering, as at a football match

**cheer·less** /ˈtʃɪələ̇s‖-ər-/ *adj* dull; without comfort; saddening: *a cheerless rainy day*

**cheers** /tʃɪəz‖tʃɪərz/ *interj BrE infml* **1** (when drinking with someone) good health **2** (esp. on the telephone) good-bye: *"Goodbye." "Cheers!"*

**cheer·y** /ˈtʃɪəri/ *adj* **-ier, -iest** bright; cheerful: *a cheery greeting.* **–cheerily** *adv* **–cheeriness** *n* [U]

**cheese** /tʃiːz/ *n* [C;U] a soft or firm solid food made from pressed and sometimes ripened milk solids (CURDS): *cheese made from the milk of cows, sheep, or goats|a very good cheese*

**SPELLING NOTE**
Words with the sound /ʃ/, like **chauffeur**, may be spelt **sh-**, like **shop**.

**cheese·cake** /ˈtʃiːzkeɪk/ *n* [C;U] a cake made from a mixture containing soft or unripe cheese

**chee·tah** /ˈtʃiːtə/ *n* a spotted African animal of the cat family, able to run very fast

**chef** /ʃef/ *n* a skilled cook, esp. the chief cook in a hotel or restaurant –compare COOK

**chem·i·cal**[1] /ˈkemɪkəl/ *adj* of, connected with, used in, or made by chemistry: *A chemical change takes place in paper when it burns.* **–chemically** *adv*

**chemical**[2] *n* any substance used in or produced by chemistry, esp. an ELEMENT (1) or COMPOUND[2] (1)

**chem·ist** /ˈkemə̇st/ *n* **1** a scientist who specializes in chemistry **2** also **pharmacist** *BrE fml & AmE*– a person who owns or runs a shop (**chemist's, pharmacy** *fml BrE*‖**drugstore** *AmE)* where medicines and sometimes COSMETICS are sold –compare PHARMACIST

**chem·is·try** /ˈkemə̇stri/ *n* [U] the science which studies the substances (ELEMENTS (1)) which make up the earth, universe, and living things: *a chemistry student*

**cheque** *BrE*‖**check** *AmE* /tʃek/ *n* **1** (a written order on) a small printed sheet of paper supplied by a bank used to pay someone a stated sum of money: *I'd like to pay* **by cheque**, *please.|Can you please let me have (a* **chequebook** *of) 30 cheques?* **2 a blank cheque** *infml* full freedom to do something, esp. to spend money: *I had/was given a blank cheque to make any changes I wanted.*

**chequ·er·ed** *BrE*‖**checkered** *AmE* /ˈtʃekəd/ *adj* marked by changes of good and bad luck; varying: *He'd had a chequered past but was now determined to be successful.*

**cher·ish** /ˈtʃerɪʃ/ *v* [T not *be +v-ing*] *fml* to care for tenderly; love: (fig.) *He cherished the memory of his dead wife.*

**cher·ry**[1] /ˈtʃeri/ *n* **-ries 1** [C] a small soft fleshy red, yellow, or black round fruit with a hard seed in the middle –compare GRAPE **2** [C;U] (the wood of) the tree on which this fruit grows

**cherry**[2] *adj,n* [U] (having) a red colour like a CHERRY[1] (1)

**cher·ub** /ˈtʃerəb/ *n* **-rubs, -ubim** /əbɪm/, **-ubims 1** a beautiful and usu. winged child in paintings; ANGEL (1) **2** a beautiful child **–cherubic** /tʃəˈruːbɪk / *adj*

**chess** /tʃes/ *n* [U] a game for two players, each of whom starts with 16 pieces (**chessmen**) which can be moved according to fixed rules across a **chessboard** in an attempt to trap (CHECKMATE) the opponent's king

**chest** /tʃest/ *n* **1** the upper front part of the body enclosing the heart and lungs –see picture on page 299 **2** a large strong box in which valuable objects are kept, goods packed, etc.: *a chest of tea|a* **chest of drawers** (=a piece of furniture with several drawers) *for her clothes* **3 get (something) off one's chest** to bring (a worry) out into the open by talking **4 -chested** having a chest of the stated kind: *flat-chested*

**chest·nut**[1] /ˈtʃesnʌt/ *n* **1** [C] a smooth reddish-brown nut that stays enclosed in a prickly case until ripe, eaten raw or cooked **2** [C;U] (the wood of) the tree on which this nut grows **3** [C] a reddish-brown horse

**chestnut**[2] *adj, n* [U] (having) a deep reddish-brown colour

**chest·y** /ˈtʃesti/ *adj* **-ier, -iest** *infml* sounding as if coming from the chest: *away from work because of* **a chesty cough** **–chestily** *adv*

**chew**[1] /tʃuː/ *v* [I;T *up,on*] **1** to crush (food) with or as if with the teeth: *You must chew your food well before you swallow it.* **2 bite off more than one can chew** *infml* to attempt more than one can deal with or succeed in finishing

**chew** sthg.↔ **over** *v adv* [T] *infml* to think about (a question, problem, etc.): *I'll chew it over for a few days and then let you have my answer.*

**chew**[2] *n* **1** [S] the act of CHEWing **2** [C] a sweet or piece of tobacco made to be CHEWed but not swallowed: *a chew of tobacco|a penny chew* (=a sweet bought for a penny)

**chew·ing gum** /ˈ·· ·/ also **gum**– *n* [U] a type of sweet usu. having a special taste, made to be CHEWed but not swallowed

**chic** /ʃiːk/ *adj,n* [U] (showing) good style: *I think your hat is rather chic.* **–chicly** *adv*

**chick** /tʃɪk/ *n* **1** the young of any bird, esp. of a chicken **2** *infml* a young woman

**chick·en**[1] /ˈtʃɪkɨn/ *n* **1** [C;U] (the meat of) a hen: *He keeps chickens in his garden.|Do you like boiled chicken?|A young chicken is called a* **chick.** –see MEAT (USAGE) **2** [C] *infml* a person who lacks courage; COWARD **3 count one's chickens before they're hatched** to make plans depending on something which has not yet happened

**chicken**[2] also **chicken-hearted** /ˌtʃɪkɨnˌhɑːtɨd‖-ar-/– *adj* [F] *infml* lacking courage

**chicken**[3] *v* →CHICKEN OUT

**chick·en·feed** /ˈtʃɪkɨnfiːd/ *n* [U] *infml* a small unimportant amount of money: *The bank offered to lend us £1000 but it's chickenfeed compared to what we need.*

**chicken out** *v adv* [I *of*] *derog infml* to decide not to do something because of being afraid: *I wanted to tell the director what I thought, but I chickened out at the last minute.*

**chicken pox** /ˈ·· ·/ *n* [U] a disease, caught esp. by children, that is marked by a slight fever and spots on the skin

**chic·o·ry** /ˈtʃɪkəri/ also **endive** *AmE*– *n* [U] **1** a plant whose leaves are eaten raw as a vegetable **2** a powder made from the dried crushed roots of this plant and added to coffee to give a special taste

**chide** /tʃaɪd/ *v* **chided** *or* **chid** /tʃɪd/, **chid** *or* **chidden** /ˈtʃɪdn/, **chiding** [I;T *for, with*] *lit* to scold

**chief**[1] /tʃiːf/ *n* [A;C] **1** a leader; ruler; person with highest rank; head of a party, organization, etc.: *The president is chief of the armed forces.|an* INDIAN (2) *chief* **2 -in-chief** /ˌ· ˈ·/ having the highest rank: *commander-in-chief*

**chief**[2] *adj* [A] highest in rank; most important: *the chief clerk|Rice is the chief crop in this area.*

**chief·ly** /ˈtʃiːfli/ *adv* **1** mainly; mostly but not wholly: *Bread is chiefly made of flour.|The accident happened chiefly because you were careless.* **2** above all; especially: *Chiefly, I ask you to remember to write to your mother.*

**chief·tain** /ˈtʃiːftɨn/ *n* the leader of a tribe or other such group; chief

**chif·fon** /ˈʃɪfɒn‖ʃɪˈfɑn/ *n* [U] a soft thin silky material used for scarves (SCARF), dresses, etc.

**chil·blain** /ˈtʃɪlbleɪn/ *n* a red painful swelling or sore usu. on the toes, ears, or fingers, caused by coldness and poor blood CIRCULATION (1)

**child** /tʃaɪld/ *n* **children** /ˈtʃɪldrən/ **1** a young human being: *We've got five children* (=sons and/or daughters) *but one's still a baby.|Our first child died a month after he was born.*|(fig.) *Peter's a child* (=inexperienced) *in money matters.*|(fig.) *The atomic bomb is* **the child of** (=a product of) *20th-century science.* –see picture on page 217 **2 child's play** something very easy to do: *Riding a bicycle is child's play when you've had some practice.* **3 get someone/be with child** *lit* to make someone/be PREGNANT (1)

USAGE A very young **child** is a **baby** or (more formal) an **infant.** A child who has just learned to walk is a **toddler.** Children aged 13 to 19 are **teenagers** and younger **teenagers** may also be called **adolescents.** A **youth** is an older, usually male, **teenager,** but this word often shows disapproval: *The police arrested several* **youths** *who were fighting.*

**child·bear·ing** /ˈtʃaɪldˌbeərɪŋ/ *n* [A;U] the act of giving birth to children: *a woman of childbearing age*

**child·birth** /ˈtʃaɪldbɜːθ‖-ɜrθ/ *n* [U] the act of giving birth to a child

**child·hood** /ˈtʃaɪldhʊd/ *n* [C;U] **1** the time or condition of being a child: *He had a happy childhood in the country.* **2 second childhood** weakness of mind caused by old age; DOTAGE

**child·ish** /ˈtʃaɪldɪʃ/ *adj* **1** of, typical of, or for a child: *The little girl spoke in a high childish voice.* **2** *derog* having a manner unsuitable for a grown up; IMMATURE: *a childish remark* –compare CHILDLIKE **–childishly** *adv* **–childishness** *n* [U]

**child·like** /ˈtʃaɪldlaɪk/ *adj often apprec* of or typical of a child, esp. having a natural lovable quality: *childlike trust* –compare CHILDISH (2)

**chill**[1] /tʃɪl/ *v* [I;T] to (cause to) become cold, esp. without freezing: *chilled beer*|(fig.) *a chilling* (=frightening) *murder story*

**chill**[2] *n* **1** an illness marked by coldness and shaking of the body: *I think I've* **caught a chill. 2** [*usu. sing.*] a certain coldness: *There was a chill in the air this morning.*

**chill**[3] *adj* cold: *a chill wind*|(fig.) *a chill greeting*

**chil·li** ‖also **chile, chili** *AmE* /ˈtʃɪli/ *n* **chillies** *or* **chiles** *or* **chilies** [C;U] (a powder made from) the seed case of the PEPPER[1] (2) plant, used to give a hot taste to food

**chill·y** /ˈtʃɪli/ *adj* **-ier, -iest** rather cold; cold enough to be uncomfortable: *It grew chilly when the fire went out.|I feel chilly without a coat.*|(fig.) *The minister was given a chilly welcome when he arrived at the factory.* **–chilliness** *n* [S;U]

**chime**[1] /tʃaɪm/ *n* the sound made by or as if by a set of bells: *The chime of the clock woke him up.*

**chime**[2] *v* **chimed, chiming** [I;T] to make musical bell-like sounds; show (the time) in this way: *The clock chimed one o'clock.*

**chime in** *v adv* [I;T +*that/with*] *infml* to interrupt or join in a conversation by expressing (an opinion): *He's always ready to chime in with his opinion.*

**chim·ney** /'tʃɪmni/ *n* **-neys 1** a hollow passage often rising above the roof of a building, which allows smoke and gases to pass from a fire: *The factory chimneys poured smoke into the air.* –see picture on page 297 **2** a glass tube often wide at the centre and narrow at the top, put around a flame as in an oil lamp

**chim·ney·pot** /'tʃɪmnipɒt‖-pɑt/ *n* a short EARTHENWARE or metal pipe fixed to the top of a chimney –see picture on page 297

**chim·ney·sweep** /'tʃɪmni-swi:p/ also **sweep** *infml– n* a person whose job is cleaning the insides of chimneys, esp. by pushing brushes up them

**chim·pan·zee** /ˌtʃɪmpæn'zi:, -pən-/ also **chimp** /tʃɪmp/ *infml– n* a large dark-haired African monkey-like animal (APE) smaller and less fierce than a GORILLA

**chin** /tʃɪn/ *n* **1** the front part of the face (esp. of a human being) below the mouth –see picture on page 299 **2 (Keep your) chin up!** *infml* Don't stop trying to succeed or be cheerful!

**chi·na** /'tʃaɪnə/ *n* [U] **1** a hard white substance made by baking fine clay at high temperatures –compare PORCELAIN **2** plates, cups, etc., made from this or a substance like this; CROCKERY: *Please put the china away carefully.*

**chink** /tʃɪŋk/ *n* a narrow crack or opening: *He watched them secretly, through a chink in the wall.*

**chintz** /tʃɪnts/ *n* [U] cotton cloth printed with brightly coloured patterns, used for making curtains, furniture covers, etc.

**chip¹** /tʃɪp/ *n* **1** a small piece of brick, wood, paint, etc., broken off something: *a chip of wood* –see picture on page 449 **2** a crack or mark left when a small piece is broken off or knocked out of an object: *I was annoyed to find a chip in my new table.* **3** [*usu. pl.*] *BrE*‖**French fry** *AmE*– a long thin piece of potato cooked in deep fat: *fish and chips* **4** [*usu. pl.*] *AmE* for CRISP² **5** a flat plastic object (COUNTER² (1)) used for representing money in certain games **6** *infml* for MICROCHIP **7 a chip off the old block** *infml often apprec* (usu. said by and about males) a person very like his father in character **8 have a chip on one's shoulder** *infml* to be quarrelsome, as a result of feeling badly treated: *He's got a chip on his shoulder about not having gone to university.*

**chip²** *v* **-pp- 1** [I;T] to (cause to) lose a small piece from the surface or edge: *This rock chips easily.*|*Someone's chipped my best glass.*|*I've chipped (a piece out of) your table, I'm afraid.* **2** [T] *esp. BrE* to cut (potatoes) into small pieces ready to be cooked as CHIPS¹ (3)

**chip away** *v adv* **1** [T] (**chip** sthg.↔ **away**) to destroy (something) bit by bit, by breaking small pieces off: *He chipped away the old brick and replaced it with a new one.* **2** [I *at*] to (try to) break small pieces off something: *He was chipping away at the rock with a hammer.*

**chip in** *v adv* [I;T (=**chip in** sthg.)] *infml* **1** [+*that*/*with*] to enter a conversation suddenly with an opinion: *John chipped in that it was time to go home.* **2** to add (one's share of money or activity): *I could only afford to chip in a few pounds.*

**SPELLING NOTE**
Words with the sound /ʃ/, like **chauffeur**, may be spelt **sh-**, like **shop**.

**chip·munk** /'tʃɪpmʌŋk/ *n* a small American SQUIRREL-like animal with a long bushy tail and bands of black and white colour along its back

**chi·rop·o·dist** /k½'rɒpədist,ʃ½-‖-'rɑ-/ *n* a person who cares for and treats the human foot –**chiropody** *n* [U]

**chirp** /tʃɜ:p‖tʃɜrp/ also **chirrup** /'tʃɪrəp‖'tʃɪ-, 'tʃɜ-/– *v,n* [C;I *away, out*] (to make) the short sharp sound(s) of small birds or some insects

**chirp·y** /'tʃɜ:pi‖'tʃɜrpi/ *adj* **-ier, -iest** *infml, esp. BrE* (of people) in good spirits; cheerful: *You seem very chirpy today.* –**chirpily** *adv* –**chirpiness** *n* [U]

**chis·el¹** /'tʃɪzəl/ *n* a metal tool with a sharp cutting edge at the end of a blade, used for cutting into or shaping wood, stone, etc.

**chisel²** *v* **-ll-** *BrE*‖**-l-** *AmE* [I;T *away, into/out of*] to cut or shape with a CHISEL: *He chiselled a hole in the door to fit a new lock.* –compare CARVE (1)

**chit** /tʃit/ *n* a short letter, esp. a signed note showing a sum of money owed (for drinks, food, etc.)

**chit·chat** /'tʃɪt-tʃæt/ *n* [U] *infml* informal conversation

**chiv·al·rous** /'ʃɪvəlrəs/ *adj* (esp. of men) marked by politeness, honour, generosity, and good manners –opposite **unchivalrous** –**chivalrously** *adv*

**chiv·al·ry** /'ʃɪvəlri/ *n* [U] **1** (in the MIDDLE AGES) the beliefs or practices of noble soldiers (KNIGHTS) as a group **2** (when speaking of a man) good manners, esp. towards women

**chive** /tʃaɪv/ *n* a plant related to the onion, with narrow grasslike leaves, used for giving a special taste to food

**chlo·ri·nate** /'klɔ:r½neɪt‖'klo-/ *v* **-nated, -nating** [T] to disinfect by putting CHLORINE into (esp. water): *Water is usually chlorinated in public swimming baths to keep it pure.* –**chlorination** /-'neɪʃən/ *n* [U]

**chlo·rine** /'klɔ:ri:n‖'klori:n/ *n* [U] a gas that is a simple substance (ELEMENT (1)), greenish-yellow, strong-smelling, and used to DISINFECT things and places

**chlor·o·form** /'klɒrəfɔ:m‖'klorəfɔrm/ *n* [U] a colourless strong-smelling poisonous chemical liquid, used as an ANAESTHETIC

**chlo·ro·phyll** /'klɔ:rəfɪl‖'klor-/ *n* [U] the green-coloured substance in the stems and leaves of plants

**chock** /tʃɒk‖tʃɑk/ *n* a shaped piece of wood placed under something, such as a door, boat, barrel, or wheel to prevent it from moving –**chock** *v* [T]

**chock-a-block** /ˌtʃɒk ə'blɒk◄‖'tʃɑk əˌblɑk/ *adj, adv* [F *with*] *infml* very crowded; packed tightly: *The road was chock-a-block with cars again today.*

**chock-full** /ˌ· '·◄/ *adj* [F *of*] *infml* completely full: *The train was chock-full of travellers.*

**choco·late** /'tʃɒkl½t‖'tʃɑkəl½t, 'tʃɔk-/ *n* **1** [U] a solid sweet usu. brown substance made from the crushed seeds of a tropical American tree (CACAO), eaten as a sweet: *Would you like a piece of chocolate?* **2** [C] a small sweet made by covering a centre, such as a nut, with this substance: *a box of chocolates* **3** [U] a sweet brown powder made by crushing this substance, used for giving a special taste to sweet foods and drinks: *drinking chocolate* **4** [C;U] (a cupful of) a drink made from hot milk (and water) mixed with this powder: *A hot chocolate, please.*

**choice**[1] /tʃɔɪs/ *n* **1** [C] the act or result of choosing: *What influenced you when you made your choice?|She is the people's choice for president.* **2** [U] the power, right, or chance of choosing: *I* **have no choice;** *I must do as he tells me.* **3** [C] a variety from which to choose: *There was a big choice of shops in the small town.*

**choice**[2] *adj* (esp. of food) worthy of being chosen; of high quality: *choice apples* –**choiceness** *n* [U]

**choir** /ˈkwaɪəʳ/ *n* [C +*sing./pl. v*] a group of people who sing together esp. during religious services: *The church choir is/are singing tonight.*

**choke**[1] /tʃəʊk/ *v* **choked, choking 1** [I;T] to (cause to) struggle to breathe or (cause to) stop breathing because of blocking of or damage to the breathing passages: *Water went down his throat and he started to choke.|I choked him to death.*| (fig.) *plants choked by long grass* **2** [T *up, with*] to fill (a space or passage) completely: *The roads were choked up with traffic.|The pipe was choked with leaves.*|(fig.) *I was choked up (with anger), and unable to speak.*

**choke** sthg.↔ **back** *v adv* [T] to control (esp. violent or very sad feelings) as if by holding in the throat: *to try to choke back one's anger/one's tears*

**choke**[2] *n* **1** the act of choking (CHOKE[1] (1)) **2** an apparatus that controls the amount of air going into a car engine, esp. to help a cold engine start –see picture on page 85

**chol·e·ra** /ˈkɒlərə‖ˈkɑ-/ *n* [U] an infectious disease of tropical countries which attacks esp. the stomach and bowels, and often leads to death

**cho·les·te·rol** /kəˈlestərɒl‖-rol/ *n* [U] a substance found in all cells of the body, which helps to carry fats

**choose** /tʃuːz/ *v* **chose** /tʃəʊz/, **chosen** /ˈtʃəʊzən/, **choosing** [I;T] **1** [ +*v-ing/between, from*] to pick out from a greater number; show (what one wants) by taking: *Have you chosen a hat yet?|Will you help me choose myself a new coat?|Who did you choose to be/as your new member of parliament?|Have you chosen where to go?|There are ten to choose from.|I had to choose between staying with my parents and going abroad.* **2** [ +*to-v/that*] to decide: *He chose not to go home until later.* **3 There's little/not much to choose between them** they are very much alike

**choos·y, choosey** /ˈtʃuːzi/ also **picky** *AmE*– *adj* **-ier, -iest** careful in choosing; hard to please: *Jean's very choosy about what she eats.*

**chop**[1] /tʃɒp‖tʃɑp/ *v* **-pp- 1** [I;T] to cut by repeatedly striking with a heavy sharp-ended tool, such as an axe: *She chopped the block of wood in two with a single blow.|to chop down a tree* **2** [T *up*] to cut into very small pieces: *Chop the onions up, please.* **3 chop and change** to keep changing (direction, one's opinion, plans, etc.): *I wish you wouldn't keep chopping and changing like this; make up your mind!*

**chop**[2] *n* **1** a quick short cutting blow as with an axe **2** a small piece of meat, esp. lamb or PORK, usu. containing a bone **3 get the chop** *infml* **a** to be dismissed from work: *He got the chop for always being late.* **b** to be stopped suddenly: *Our plans got the chop.*

**chop·per** /ˈtʃɒpəʳ‖ˈtʃɑ-/ *n* a heavy sharp-ended tool for cutting wood or meat; axe

**chop·py** /ˈtʃɒpi‖ˈtʃɑpi/ *adj* **-pier, -piest** (of water) with many short rough waves: *The sea was choppy today because of the wind.* –**choppiness** *n* [U]

**chop·stick** /ˈtʃɒp-stɪk‖ˈtʃɑp-/ *n* [*usu. pl.*] either of a pair of narrow sticks held between the thumb and fingers and used in East Asian countries for lifting food to the mouth: *When we go to a Chinese restaurant we always use chopsticks instead of a knife and fork.*

**cho·ral** /ˈkɔːrəl‖ˈko-/ *adj* [A *no comp.*] of, related to, or sung by a CHOIR or CHORUS: *a choral group/society/dance*

**chord**[1] /kɔːd‖kɔrd/ *n* a combination of two or more musical notes sounded at the same time

**chord**[2] *n* a straight line joining two points on a curve

**chore** /tʃɔːʳ‖tʃor/ *n* a small bit of regular work, quickly and easily done; necessary, but uninteresting job, esp. in a house: *Each morning I get up and do the chores before I go out.|It's such a chore to do the shopping every day!*

**chor·e·og·ra·phy** /ˌkɒriˈɒgrəfi, ˌkɔː-‖ˌkoriˈɑg-/ *n* [U] the art of dancing or of arranging dances for the stage –**choreographer** *n*

**chor·tle** /ˈtʃɔːtl‖ˈtʃɔrtl/ *v,n* **-tled, -tling** [C;I] (to give) a laugh of pleasure or satisfaction; CHUCKLE

**cho·rus**[1] /ˈkɔːrəs‖ˈkorəs/ *n* **1** [C +*sing./pl. v*] a group of people who sing together: *The chorus was/were very good today.* **2** [C] a piece of music played or sung after each group of lines (VERSE) of a song **3** [S *of*] something said by a lot of people together: *The actor's speech was greeted by a chorus of laughter.*

**chorus**[2] *v* [I;T *that*] to sing or speak at the same time: *The papers all chorused the praises of the president.*

**chose** /tʃəʊz/ *v past tense of* CHOOSE

**cho·sen** /ˈtʃəʊzən/ *v past participle of* CHOOSE

**Christ** /kraɪst/ *n* also **Jesus Christ**– the man who established Christianity, considered by Christians to be the son of God

**chris·ten** /ˈkrɪsən/ *v* [T] to make (someone, esp. a child) a member of a Christian church by BAPTISM and, usually the giving of a name: *The baby was christened by the priest.|We christened our baby John.*|(fig.) *The ship was christened the Queen Mary.*

**Chris·ten·dom** /ˈkrɪsəndəm/ *n* [U] *old use* all Christian people in general

**chris·ten·ing** /ˈkrɪsənɪŋ/ *n* [C;U] the Christian ceremony of BAPTISM or of naming a person, usu. a child

**Chris·tian**[1] /ˈkrɪstʃən, -tɪən/ *n* a person who believes in the teachings of Jesus Christ

**Christian**[2] *adj* **1** believing in or belonging to any of the various branches of Christianity: *the Christian church* **2** of or relating to CHRIST, Christianity, or Christians: *Christian ideas|He behaved in a Christian* (=kind and generous) *way to his enemies.*

**Chris·ti·an·i·ty** /ˌkrɪstiˈænʒti/ *n* [S] the religion based on the life and teachings of CHRIST: *to believe in Christianity*

**Christian name** /ˈ·· ·/ *n* the FIRST NAME of a Christian

**Christ·mas** /ˈkrɪsməs/ *n* [C;S] **1** also **Christmas Day** /ˌ·· ˈ·/– a Christian holy day held on December 25th (or in some churches January 6th) in honour of the birth of Christ, usu. kept as a public holiday **2** the period before and after this: *Did you have a nice Christmas/a nice time at Christmas?*

**Christmas Eve** /ˌ·· ˈ·/ *n* the day, and esp. the evening, before Christmas: *I always go to my parents' house on Christmas Eve.*

**Christmas tree** /ˈ·· ·/ *n* a real or man-made tree decorated with candles, lights, coloured paper, etc., and set up in the home at Christmas

**chrome** /krəum/ *n* [U] a hard metal combination (ALLOY) of CHROMIUM with other metals, esp. used for covering objects with a thin shiny protective metal plate: *There is a lot of chrome on that car.*

**chro·mi·um** /ˈkrəumɪəm/ *n* [U] a metal that is a simple substance (ELEMENT (1)) found only in combination with other chemicals, used for covering objects with a thin shiny protective plate: *chromium-plated*

**chro·mo·some** /ˈkrəuməsəum/ *n tech* a threadlike body found in all living cells, which passes on and controls the nature, character, etc., of a young plant, animal, or cell

**chron·ic** /ˈkrɒnɪk‖ˈkrɑ-/ *adj* **1** (of a disease) continual; lasting a long time: *a chronic cough* –compare ACUTE **2** [A] suffering from a disease or illness over a long period: *a chronic alcoholic* **3** *BrE infml* very bad; terrible: *a chronic example of bad work* –**chronically** *adv*

**chron·i·cle¹** /ˈkrɒnɪkəl‖ˈkrɑ-/ *n* a record of historical events, arranged in order of time

**chronicle²** *v* **-cled, -cling** [T] to make a CHRONICLE of (events)

**chron·o·log·i·cal** /ˌkrɒnəˈlɒdʒɪkəl‖ˌkrɑnəˈlɑ-/ *adj* [*no comp.*] arranged according to the order of time: *We'll talk about the causes of the war in chronological order.* –**chronologically** *adv*

**chro·nol·o·gy** /krəˈnɒlədʒi‖-ˈnɑ-/ *n* **-gies** *fml* **1** [U] the science which measures time and gives dates to events **2** [C] a list or table arranged according to the order of time: *a chronology of the events of last year*

**chrys·a·lis** /ˈkrɪsəlʒs/ *n* **-lises** /-siːz/ a hard case-like shell in which a PUPA is enclosed –compare COCOON

**chry·san·the·mum** /krɪˈsænθʒməm, -ˈzæn-/ *n* a garden plant with large brightly-coloured flowers in autumn

**chub·by** /ˈtʃʌbi/ *adj* **-bier, -biest** *infml* (of animals or people) having a full round usu. pleasing form; slightly fat –see THIN (USAGE) –**chubbiness** *n* [U]

**chuck** /tʃʌk/ *v* [T] *infml* to throw (something), esp. with a short movement of the arms: *Let's chuck all these old papers away!*|(fig.) *Don't be so noisy, or the driver will chuck us off (the bus).*|(fig.) *He's decided to* **chuck in/up** (=leave) *his job.*

**chuck** sbdy./sthg.↔ **out** *v adv* [T] *infml* **1** to force (a person) to leave: *The owner threatened to chuck us out (of the pub) if we got drunk.* **2** to throw out; throw away

**chuck·le¹** /ˈtʃʌkəl/ *v* **-led, -ling** [I] to laugh quietly: *I could hear him chuckling to himself as he read his book.*

**chuckle²** *n* a quiet laugh: *He gave a quiet chuckle.*

**chug** /tʃʌg/ *v* **-gg-** [I] (of an engine) to make a repeated knocking sound while moving: *I heard the engine chugging away/along.* –**chug** *n* [S]: *the chug of the engine*

**chum** /tʃʌm/ *n infml* a good friend, esp. among boys

**chum·my** /ˈtʃʌmi/ *adj* **-mier, -miest** *infml* friendly

**chump** /tʃʌmp/ *n infml* a fool: *He's a real chump.*

**chunk** /tʃʌŋk/ *n* a thick piece or lump; a large part or amount: (fig.) *That new car took quite a chunk out of her salary.* –see picture on page 449

**chunk·y** /ˈtʃʌŋki/ *adj* **-ier, -iest** rather thick and solid; (of people) short and rather fat: *a chunky little man*

**church** /tʃɜːtʃ‖tʃɜrtʃ/ *n* **1** [C] a building made for public Christian worship: *I'm going to church today.* **2** [*the* S;U] the profession of the CLERGY (priests and people employed for religious reasons) of a religious body: *When he was 30 he joined the church and became a priest.*|*Do you agree with the separation of church* (=religious power) *and state?* **3** [*usu cap.*] the organization of Christian believers: *the Church of England*|*the Catholic Church*

**Church of Eng·land** /ˌ· · ˈ··/ *n* [*the* S] the state church which is established by law in England and was separated from the ROMAN CATHOLIC church in the 16th century. Its priests and BISHOPS may marry, and its head is the King or Queen

**church·yard** /ˈtʃɜːtʃjɑːd‖ˈtʃɜrtʃjɑrd/ *n* an open space around and belonging to a church, in which dead members of that church are buried –compare CEMETERY, GRAVEYARD

**churl·ish** /ˈtʃɜːlɪʃ‖-ɜr-/ *adj lit derog* bad-tempered; rude –**churlishly** *adv* –**churlishness** *n* [U]

**churn¹** /tʃɜːn‖tʃɜrn/ *n* **1** a container in which milk is beaten until it becomes butter **2** *BrE* a large metal container in which milk is stored or carried from the farm

**churn²** *v* [I;T] **1** to make butter by beating (milk) **2** to (cause to) move about violently: *The ship churned the water up as it passed.*|(fig.) *My stomach started to churn when I thought about the examination.*

**churn** sthg.↔ **out** *v adv* [T] *infml* to produce a large quantity of, as if by machinery: *That writer churns out about three new books every year.*

**chute** /ʃuːt/ *n* a sloped passage along which something may be passed, dropped, or caused to slide: *a waste/rubbish chute*

**chut·ney** /ˈtʃʌtni/ *n* [U] a mixture of various fruits, hot-tasting seeds, and sugar, which is eaten with other dishes, such as meat or cheese

**CIA** *abbrev. for:* Central Intelligence Agency; the group of people in the US who gather information about other countries, esp. in secret

**CID** *abbrev. for:* Criminal Investigation Department;

**SPELLING NOTE**

Words with the sound /ʃ/, like **chauffeur**, may be spelt **sh-**, like **shop**.

the branch of the UK police force made up of DETECTIVES –see also SCOTLAND YARD

**ci·der, cyder** /'saɪdəʳ/ *n* [C;U] (a glass or bottle of) an alcoholic drink made from apple juice: *Two ciders and a beer, please.*

**ci·gar** /sɪ'gɑːʳ/ *n* a tightly-packed tube-shaped roll of tobacco leaves for smoking –compare CIGARETTE

**cig·a·rette** ‖also **cigaret** *AmE* /ˌsɪgə'ret/ *n* finely cut tobacco rolled in a narrow tube of thin paper for smoking –compare CIGAR

**cinch** /sɪntʃ/ *n* [S] *infml* **1** something done easily: *My examination was a cinch; I passed easily.* **2** something certain: *That horse is a cinch to win the next race.*

**cin·der** /'sɪndəʳ/ *n* a small piece of partly burned wood, coal, etc., that is not yet ash and that can be burned further but without producing flames

**cin·e·ma** /'sɪnᵻmə/ *n* **1** [C] *BrE*‖**movie theater** *AmE*– a theatre in which moving pictures are shown **2** [*the* S] also **pictures** *BrE infml*‖**movies** *AmE*– a showing of a moving picture: *Let's go to the cinema tonight.* **3** [*the* S] also **movies** *AmE*– the art or industry of making moving pictures

**cin·na·mon** /'sɪnəmən/ *n* [U] a sweet-smelling powder made from the strong outer covering (BARK) of a tropical Asian tree, used for giving a special taste to food

**ci·pher, cypher** /'saɪfəʳ/ *n* **1** (a system of) secret writing; CODE: *The government uses a special cipher so that official messages are kept secret.* –see also DECIPHER **2** *lit* the number 0; zero

**cir·ca** /'sɜːkə‖'sɜr-/ *prep fml* (used esp. with dates) about: *She was born circa 1060 and died in 1118.*

**cir·cle¹** /'sɜːkəl‖'sɜr-/ *n* **1** (a flat round area enclosed by) a curved line that is everywhere equally distant from one fixed point **2** something having the general shape of this line; ring; group: *a circle of trees*|(fig.)*a large circle of friends*|(fig.)*In political circles there is talk of war.* **3** an upper floor in a theatre, usu. with seats set in curved lines: *Are we going to sit in the circle or in the* STALLS? –see picture on page 463 **4 come full circle** to go through a set of developments that lead back to the starting point

**circle²** *v* **-cled, -cling** [I;T] to draw, form, or move in a circle: *The teacher circled the pupils' spelling mistakes in red ink.*|*The plane circled the airport before landing.*|*The birds were circling around in the air.*

**cir·clet** /'sɜːklᵻt‖'sɜr-/ *n lit* a narrow round band of gold, silver, jewels, etc., worn (esp. by women) on the head, arms, or neck as decoration

**cir·cuit** /'sɜːkᵻt‖'sɜr-/ *n* **1** a complete ring: *She ran three circuits of the track.* **2** (the establishments on) a regular journey from place to place: *The judge is* **on circuit** *for most of the year.* (=visits different courts)|*the tennis circuit* **3** the complete circular path of an electric current: *A break in the circuit had caused the lights to go out.*

**cir·cu·i·tous** /sɜː'kjuːᵻtəs‖sɜr-/ *adj fml* going a long way round instead of in a straight line: *the river's circuitous course*|*a circuitous route* **–circuitously** *adv*

**cir·cu·lar¹** /'sɜːkjʊləʳ‖'sɜrkjə-/ *adj* **1** round; shaped like or nearly like a circle **2** forming or moving in a circle: (fig.) *a circular argument that doesn't lead anywhere*

**circular²** *n* a printed advertisement, paper, or notice intended to be given to a large number of people for them to read: *Did you see that circular from the new local theatre?*

**cir·cu·late** /'sɜːkjʊleɪt‖'sɜrkjə-/ *v* **-lated, -lating 1** [I;T] to (cause to) move or flow along a closed path: *Blood circulates round the body.*|*The heart circulates blood round the body.*|(fig.) *The government has started to circulate false stories about the union.* **2** [I] *infml* to move about freely: *He circulated at the party, talking to lots of people.* **–circulatory** /-lətəri‖-tori/ *adj*

**cir·cu·la·tion** /ˌsɜːkjʊ'leɪʃən‖ˌsɜrkjə-/ *n* **1** [C;U] the flow of liquid around a closed system, esp. the movement of blood through the body: *Bad circulation can cause tiredness.* **2** [U] the movement of something such as news or money from place to place or from person to person: *The government has reduced the number of £5 notes* **in circulation.** –compare TRAFFIC (1) **3** [C] the average number of copies of a newspaper, magazine, book, etc., sold or read over a certain time: *This magazine has a circulation of 400,000.*

**cir·cum·cise** /'sɜːkəmsaɪz‖'sɜr-/ *v* **-cised, -cising** [T] to cut off the loose fold of skin (FORESKIN) at the end of the sex organ of (a man) or part of the sex organ (CLITORIS) of (a woman): *circumcised at birth* **–circumcision** /'sɪʒən/ *n* [C;U]

**cir·cum·fer·ence** /sə'kʌmfərəns‖sər-/ *n* the length round the outside of a circle; distance round a round object: *The earth's circumference is more than 40,000 kilometres.*

**cir·cum·spect** /'sɜːkəmspekt‖'sɜr-/ *adj fml* (of a person or an action) done or acting after careful thought; CAUTIOUS **–circumspectly** *adv* **–circumspection** /'spekʃən / *n* [U]

**cir·cum·stance** /-'sɜːkəmstæns, -stəns‖'sɜr-/ *n* **1** [*usu. pl.*] a fact, condition, or event concerned with and influencing another event, person, or course of action: *We can't judge what he did till we know all the circumstances.*|*Circumstances forced me to accept a very low price when I sold the house.* **2 in/under no circumstances** never; whatever happens **3 in/under the circumstances** because of the conditions or facts: *I wanted to leave quickly but under the circumstances (my uncle had just died) I decided to stay another night.*

**cir·cum·vent** /ˌsɜːkəm'vent‖ˌsɜr-/ *v* [T] *fml* to avoid by or as if by passing round: *The company has opened an office abroad in order to circumvent our tax laws.* **–circumvention** /-'venʃən/ *n* [U]

**cir·cus** /'sɜːkəs‖'sɜr-/ *n* **1** a public performance by a group of performers of various acts of skill and daring, often using animals and usu. travelling to different places **2** the tent-covered place where this performance happens,with seats round a ring in the middle **3** *BrE* a round open area where a number of streets join together: *Oxford Circus*

**cis·sy** /'sɪsi/ *n* **-sies** →SISSY

**cis·tern** /'sɪstən‖-ərn/ *n* a container for storing water, esp. in a house for a TOILET (1)

**cit·a·del** /'sɪtədl, -del/ *n lit* a strong heavily-armed fort, usu. commanding a city, built to be a place of safety and defence in time of war –compare STRONGHOLD (1)

**cite** /saɪt/ *v* **cited, citing** [T] *fml* **1** to mention, esp. as an example in a statement, argument, etc.; QUOTE[1] (2): *The minister cited the latest crime figures as proof of the need for more police.* **2** to call (someone) to appear before a court of law; give a SUMMONS[1] to: *He was cited in a* DIVORCE *case.*

**cit·i·zen** /ˈsɪtᵢ̣zən/ *n* **1** a person who lives in a particular city or town, esp. one who has certain voting or other rights in that town **2 a** a person who is a member of a particular country by birth or by being NATURALIZED (=being officially allowed to become a member) **b** a person who belongs to and gives his/her loyalty to a particular country and who expects protection from it: *She's a British citizen but lives in India.* –compare SUBJECT[1] (1)

**cit·i·zen·ship** /ˈsɪtᵢ̣zənʃɪp/ *n* [U] the state of being a citizen: *After eight years in the country he gained his citizenship.* –compare NATIONALITY

**cit·rus** ||also **-trous** *BrE* /ˈsɪtrəs/ *adj* [*no comp.*] (of fruits) with thick skins and juicy flesh with a sour or sour-sweet taste: *Oranges and lemons are citrus fruits.*

**cit·y** /ˈsɪti/ *n* **-ies 1** a usu. large and important group of houses, buildings, etc., esp. with a centre where amusements can be found and business goes on. It is usu. larger and more important than a town, and in Britain it usually has a CATHEDRAL –compare TOWN, VILLAGE **2 the City** the centre for money matters in London

**civ·ic** /ˈsɪvɪk/ *adj* of a city or its citizens: *The president's visit was the most important civic event of the year.*|*civic duties*

**civ·ics** /ˈsɪvɪks/ *n* [U] a social science dealing with the rights and duties of citizens, the way government works, etc.

**civ·il** /ˈsɪvəl/ *adj* **1** [*no comp.*] of, belonging to, or consisting of the general population; not military or religious: *We were married in a civil ceremony, not in church.* **2** [*no comp.*] (of law) dealing with the rights of private citizens; concerned with judging private quarrels between people rather than with criminal offences: *Civil law is different to criminal law.* **3** polite enough to be acceptable, esp. if not friendly: *Try to be civil to him, even if you don't like him.*|**Keep a civil tongue in your head!** (=stop speaking rudely) –opposite **uncivil** (for **3**); see also CIVILLY

**ci·vil·i·an** /sᵢ̣ˈvɪlɪən/ *n,adj* [*no comp.*] (a person) not of the armed forces: *civilian government*

**ci·vil·i·ty** /sᵢ̣ˈvɪlᵢ̣ti/ *n* **-ties** [C;U] *fml* (an act of) politeness; the quality of having good manners; helpfulness; COURTESY –opposite **incivility**

**civ·i·li·za·tion** ||also **-sation** *BrE* /ˌsɪvəl-aɪˈzeɪʃən|| -vəl-ᵢ̣ˈzeɪ-/ *n* **1** [U] a stage of human social development, esp. one with a high level of art, religion, science, government, etc., and a written language **2** [C] the type of advanced society of a particular time or place: *the civilization of ancient China*

> **SPELLING NOTE**
> Words with the sound /k/, like **cut**, may be spelt **k-**, like **key**, or **qu-**, like **queen.**
> Words with the sound /s/, like **city**, may be spelt **s-**, like **soon**, or **ps-**, like **psychology.**

**civ·i·lize** ||also **-lise** *BrE* / sɪvəl-aɪz/ *v* **-lized, -lizing** [T] **1** to (cause to) come from a lower stage of development to a more highly developed stage of social organization: *The Romans hoped to civilize all the tribes of Europe.* **2** *infml* to (cause to) improve in education and manners

**civ·il·ly** /ˈsɪvəl-i/ *adv* politely; in a CIVIL (3) manner

**civil rights** /ˌ·· ˈ·/ *n* [P] rights such as freedom, equality before the law, etc., which belong to all citizens without regard to their race, religion, colour, or sex

**civil ser·vant** /ˌ·· ˈ··/ *n* a person employed in the CIVIL SERVICE –see OFFICER (USAGE)

**civil ser·vice** /ˌ·· ˈ··/ *n* **1** [*the* S] all the various departments of the national government except the armed forces and law courts: *She works in/for the civil service.* **2** [U +*sing./pl. v*] all the people who are employed in this: *The civil service has/have too much power.*

**civil war** /ˌ·· ˈ·/ *n* [C;U] (a) war between opposing groups of people from the same country, fought within that country

**clack** /klæk/ *v* [I;T] to (cause to) make one or more quick sharp sounds –**clack** *n* [S]

**clad** /klæd/ *adj* [F *in; no comp.*] *lit* covered; clothed: *The mountain was clad in mist.*|*an armour-clad ship*

**claim**[1] /kleɪm/ *v* **1** [I;T *on, for*] to ask for, demand, or take (a title, property, money, etc.) as the rightful owner, or as one's right: *Did you claim on the insurance after your car accident?*|(fig.)*The flood claimed hundreds of lives.* **2** [T +*to-v*/*(that)*] to declare to be true; state esp. in the face of opposition; MAINTAIN (4): *He claims to be rich/claims that he is rich but I don't believe him.*

**claim**[2] *n* **1** [*for, on*] a demand for something as one's own by right: *The government would not even consider his claim for money.* **2** [*to, on*] a right to something: *He has a rightful claim to the property; it was his mother's.*|*The town's* **claim to fame** *is that it has the country's oldest church.* **3** [+*to-v*/*that*] a statement of something as fact: *His claim about the number of people killed in the war was clearly mistaken.* **4** something claimed, esp. an area of land or sum of money

**clair·voy·ant** /kleəˈvɔɪənt||kleər-/ *adj,n* (of or related to the powers of) a person who can see what will happen in the future –**clairvoyance** *n* [U]

**clam**[1] /klæm/ *n* a small soft-bodied sea animal with a double shell, that lives in sand or mud and is eaten

**clam**[2] *v* →CLAM UP

**clam·ber** /ˈklæmbəʳ/ *v* [I *over*] to climb using both feet and hands, usu. with difficulty or effort: *Tell the children to stop clambering (about) over my new furniture.*

**clam·my** /ˈklæmi/ *adj* **-mier, -miest** unpleasantly sticky, slightly wet, and usu. cold: *clammy hands/weather* –**clammily** *adv* –**clamminess** *n* [U]

**clam·our**[1] *BrE*||**clamor** *AmE* /ˈklæməʳ/ *n* a loud continuous usu. confused noise or shouting, esp. of people complaining: *a clamour of voices*|*public clamour for lower taxes* –**clamorous** *adj*

**clamour**[2] *BrE*|| **clamor** *AmE v* [I;T +*to-v*/*that*/*for*] to express (a demand) continually, loudly, and strongly: *The children were clamouring to be fed.*

**clamp¹** /klæmp/ *n* an apparatus for fastening or holding things firmly together

**clamp²** *v* [T *together*] to fasten with a CLAMP: *Clamp these two pieces of wood together.*

**clamp down** *v adv* [I *on*] *infml* to become more firm; make limits: *The police are going to clamp down on criminal activity in this area.* –see also CLAMPDOWN

**clamp·down** /'klæmpdaʊn/ *n infml* a sudden usu. official limitation or prevention of doing or saying something: *The government has decided to have a clampdown on building roads.* –see also CLAMP **down**

**clam up** *v adv* **-mm-** [I] *infml* to become silent: *She clammed up when I mentioned the police.*

**clan** /klæn/ *n* [C +*sing./pl. v.*] **1** (esp. in Scotland) a group of families, all originally descended from one family; tribe **2** *humor* a large family

**clan·des·tine** /klæn'destɪn/ *adj* done secretly or privately often for an unlawful reason: *a clandestine meeting* –**clandestinely** *adv*

**clang** /klæŋ/ *v* [I;T] to (cause to) make a loud ringing sound, such as when metal is struck: *The metal tool clanged when it hit the wall.* –**clang** *n* [S]

**clang·er** /'klæŋəʳ/ *n BrE infml* a very noticeable mistake or unfortunate remark: *She* **dropped a clanger** *when she mentioned the broken window.*

**clank** /klæŋk/ *v* [I;T] to (cause to) make a short loud sound, like that of a heavy moving metal chain: *The prisoner's chains clanked as he walked.* –**clank** *n* [S]

**clan·nish** /'klænɪʃ/ *adj often derog* (of a group of people) tending to keep together as a group, esp. supporting each other against those from outside –**clannishly** *adv*

**clap¹** /klæp/ *v* **-pp-** **1** [I;T] to strike (one's hands) together with a quick movement and loud sound, esp. to show approval of a performance: *The teacher clapped her hands to attract the class's attention.*|*The people in the theatre enjoyed the play and clapped loudly.* **2** [T *on*] to strike lightly with the open hand usu. in a friendly manner: *He clapped his son on the back.* **3** [T *in*] *infml* to put, place, or send usu. quickly and effectively: *The judge clapped her in prison before she had had time to explain.*

**clap²** *n* **1** [C] a loud explosive sound: *a clap of thunder* **2** [S] an act of CLAPping¹ (1): *The people liked the singer and gave him a clap.* –compare CLAPPING, HAND¹ (5) **3** [S *on*] a light friendly hit, usu. on the back, with an open hand

**clap·per** /'klæpəʳ/ *n* the hammerlike object hung inside a bell which strikes the bell to make it ring

**clap·ping** /'klæpɪŋ/ *n* [U] the sound of hands being CLAPped¹ (1); APPLAUSE: *The people enjoyed the singer so much that the clapping continued for a long time.*|*the sound of clapping* –compare CLAP² (2)

**clap·trap** /'klæptræp/ *n* [U] *infml* empty, insincere, and worthless speech or writing; nonsense

**clar·i·fy** /'klærɪfaɪ/ *v* **-fied, -fying** [I;T] to (cause to) become clearer and more easily understood: *When will the government clarify its position on equal pay for women?* –**clarification** *n* [C;U]: *He asked for (a) clarification of the government's position.*

**clar·i·net** /,klærɪ'net/ *n* a long tubelike usu. wooden musical instrument, played by blowing

**clar·i·ty** /'klærɪti/ *n* [U] clearness: *clarity of thinking/speech*

**clash¹** /klæʃ/ *v* **1** [I *with*] to come into opposition: *The two armies clashed* (=fought) *near the border.*|*This shirt clashes with my trousers.* (=the colours don't match)|*Her wedding* **clashed with** (=was at the same time as) *my examination so I couldn't go.* **2** [I;T *together*] to (cause to) make a loud confused noise

**clash²** *n* **1** [S] a loud confused noise **2** [C] an example of opposition or disagreement: *a clash of interests*|*a border clash* (=fight at a border)

**clasp¹** /klɑːsp‖klæsp/ *n* **1** a usu. metal fastener for holding two things or parts of one thing together: *the clasp on a belt* **2** [*usu. sing.*] a tight firm hold, esp. by the hand; GRIP –compare CLINCH²

**clasp²** *v* [T] **1** to take or seize firmly; enclose and hold, esp. with the fingers or arms: *He clasped the money in his hands.* **2** [*together*] to fasten with a CLASP¹ (1) –opposite **unclasp**

**class¹** /klɑːs‖klæs/ *n* **1** [U] the fact that there are different social groups with different social and political positions and points of view: *Class differences can divide a nation.* **2** [C +*sing./pl. v*] a social group whose members have the same political, social, and ECONOMIC (1) position and rank: *the ruling class*|*lower-class life*|*the upper classes* –see also MIDDLE CLASS, WORKING CLASS **3** [C] a group of pupils or students taught together **4** [C;U] a period of time during which pupils or students are taught: *What time does the next class begin?* **5** [C] a division of people or things; a kind: *What class (of degree) did you get: first, second, or third?* **6** [C] a level of quality of travelling conditions on a train, plane, boat, etc.: *(A) first-class (ticket) to Birmingham, please.*

**class²** *v* [T *as*] to put into a CLASS¹ (5); CLASSIFY

**clas·sic¹** /'klæsɪk/ *adj* [A *no comp.*] **1** having the highest quality; of the first or highest class or rank **2** belonging to an established set of standards; well known, esp. as the best example: *a classic style of dress/building*|*a classic example/case* –compare CLASSICAL

**classic²** *n* a piece of literature or art, a writer, or an artist of the first rank and of lasting importance: *That book is one of the classics of English literature.*|(fig.)*That joke's a classic; it really is funny.*

**clas·si·cal** /'klæsɪkəl/ *adj* **1** (*sometimes cap.*) in accordance with ancient Greek or Roman models in literature or art: *classical literature*|*a classical education* **2** [*no comp.*] (of music) written and arranged (COMPOSED) with serious artistic intentions: *Bach and Beethoven wrote classical music.* **3** of or related to a form or system established before modern times: *Classical scientific ideas about light were changed by Einstein.* –compare CLASSIC¹

**clas·si·fi·ca·tion** /,klæsɪfɪ'keɪʃən/ *n* **1** [U] the act or result of CLASSIFYing, esp. plants, animals, books, etc. **2** [C] a group, division, class, or CATEGORY into which something is placed

**clas·si·fied** /'klæsɪfaɪd/ *adj* **1** divided or arranged in classes; placed according to class: *a classified list of books in a library* **2** (of government, esp. military, information) officially secret: *This information is classified; only a few people can see it.* **3 classified ad**

also **small ad** *BrE*– a usu. small advertisement placed in a newspaper by a person wishing to sell or buy something, offer or get employment, etc.

**clas·si·fy** /'klæsǝ̀faɪ/ *v* **-fied, -fying** [T] to arrange or place (animals, plants, books, etc.) into classes or groups; divide according to class: *People who work in libraries spend a lot of time classifying books.*

**class·room** /'klɑːs-rʊm, -ruːm‖'klæs-/ *n* a room in a school, college, etc., in which a class meets for a lesson –see picture opposite

**class·y** /'klɑːsi‖'klæsi/ *adj* **-ier, -iest** *infml* stylish; fashionable; of high class or rank

**clat·ter¹** /'klætǝʳ/ *v* [I;T] to (cause to) move with a number of rapid short knocking sounds: *The metal dish clattered down the stone stairs.*

**clatter²** *n* [S] a number of rapid short knocking sounds, as when a number of things fall to the ground: *There was a clatter of dishes in the kitchen.*

**clause** /klɔːz/ *n* **1** (in grammar) a group of words containing a subject and a verb, usu. forming only part of a sentence. In *"She came home when she was tired", She came home* and *when she was tired* are two separate clauses –compare PHRASE, SENTENCE **2** a separate part or division of a written agreement or DOCUMENT

**claus·tro·pho·bi·a** /ˌklɔːstrǝ'fǝʊbɪǝ, ˌklɒ-/ *n* [U] fear of being enclosed in a small closed space –**claustrophobic** *adj*

**claw¹** /klɔː/ *n* **1** a sharp usu. curved nail on the toe of an animal or bird **2** a limb of certain insects and sea animals, such as CRABS, used for attacking and holding objects

**claw²** *v* [I;T] to tear, seize, pull, etc., with or as if with CLAWS: *The cat clawed at the leg of the table.|It clawed a hole in my stocking.*

**clay** /kleɪ/ *n* [U] heavy firm earth, soft when wet, becoming hard when baked at a high temperature, and from which bricks, pots, EARTHENWARE, etc., are made –**clayey** /'kleɪ-i / *adj*

**clean¹** /kliːn/ *adj* **1** free from dirt: *Are your hands clean?* **2** not yet used; fresh: *clean clothes|a clean piece of paper* **3** morally or sexually pure: *He led a clean life.|(infml) a clean joke* (=not rude)*|a clean (=fair) fight |(infml) She is clean/has a clean record.* (=is not a criminal) **4** having a smooth even edge or surface; regular: *a clean cut|the aircraft's clean lines* **5 come clean** *infml* to admit one's guilt; tell the unpleasant truth: *Why don't you come clean and tell us your plans?* –**cleanness** *n* [U]

**clean²** *v* [I;T] to (cause to) become clean: *Please clean the windows as I can hardly see out.|These pots clean easily.* –**clean** *n* [S]: *I must give the windows a good clean.*

**clean** sbdy./sthg.↔ **out** *v adv* [T] **1** to make (the inside of a room, box, drawer, etc.) clean and tidy **2** *infml* **a** to take all the money of (someone) by stealing or by winning: *I got cleaned out playing cards.* **b** to steal everything from (a place): *The thieves cleaned out the store.* –**cleanout** *n* [S]: *I've just given my room a good cleanout.*

**SPELLING NOTE**

Words with the sound /k/, like **cut**, may be spelt **k-**, like **key**, or **qu-**, like **queen.**
Words with the sound /s/, like **city**, may be spelt **s-**, like **soon**, or **ps-**, like **psychology.**

**clean up** *v adv* **1** [I;T (=clear sthg.↔ **up**)] to make clean or tidy: *It's your turn to clean (the bedroom) up.|Clean up the pieces of broken bottle.* **2** [I;T (=**clean up** sthg.)] *infml* to gain (money) as profit: *He really cleaned up* (=made a lot of money) *at the races today.* –**cleanup** *n* [S]: *I'm going to give the house a good cleanup.*

**clean³** *adv infml* [+ *prep/adv; no comp.*] completely: *The bullet went clean through (his arm).|I'm clean out (of food) and the shops are shut.*

**clean·er** /'kliːnǝʳ/ *n* **1** a person whose job is cleaning offices, houses, etc. **2** a machine, apparatus, or substance used in cleaning

**clean·er's** *n* a place where clothes, material, etc., can be taken to be cleaned –see also DRY-CLEAN

**clean·li·ness** /'klenlinǝ̀s/ *n* [U] habitual cleanness

**clean·ly¹** /'klenli/ *adj* **-lier, -liest** careful to keep clean; always clean

**clean·ly²** /'kliːnli/ *adv* in a clean manner

**cleanse** /klenz/ *v* **cleansed, cleansing** [T] to make (usu. a cut, wound, etc.) clean or pure: *The nurse cleansed the wound before stitching it.*

**cleans·er** /'klenzǝʳ/ *n* [C;U] a substance, such as a chemical liquid or powder, used for cleaning

**clear¹** /klɪǝʳ/ *adj* **1** easy to see through: *clear glass* **2** free from anything that marks or darkens: *a clear sky* (=with no clouds)*|clear eyes|clear skin* **3** (esp. of sounds, people, writing, etc.) easily heard, seen, read, or understood: *a clear speaker|a clear article/style of writing* **4** (esp. of the mind or a person) thinking without difficulty; understanding clearly: *a clear thinker* **5** [F +*(that)/about*] (of a person) certain; showing CONFIDENCE (1): *She seems quite clear about her plans/what to do.* **6** open; empty; free from blocks or dangers, not OBSTRUCTed: *a clear view|The road's clear of snow now.* **7** [*of*] free from guilt or blame; untroubled: *a clear conscience* **8** plain; noticeable; OBVIOUS: *a clear case of murder|It's clear from his actions that he loves her.* **9 in the clear** *infml* free from danger, blame, guilt, etc. –see also CLARITY –**clearness** *n* [U]

**clear²** *adv* **1** in a clear manner: *Speak* **loud and clear.** **2** [*no comp.*] out of the way; so as to be no longer inside or near: *She jumped clear (of the train).* **3** [*adv +prep/adv; no comp.*] completely; all the way: *The prisoner got clear away.*

**clear³** *v* **1** [I;T] to make or become clear: *After the storm the sky cleared.|This soap should help clear your skin (of spots).* **2** [T *away, of, from*] to remove (something) from (an area); take away; get rid of: *I'll just clear the plates away, then we can use the table.|Whose job is it to clear snow from the road?|Please clear the table of all these papers.* **3** [T *of*] to show or declare to be free from blame: *The judge cleared the prisoner of any crime and set him free.* **4** [T] to give official permission to or for: *The plans for the new school have not yet been cleared by the council.* **5** [T] to pass by or over (something) without touching: *The horse easily cleared every fence.* **6** [T] to repay (a debt) in full **7 clear the air** to remove doubt and bad feeling by honest explana-

It is the beginning of **term**. Before each **lesson** begins, Stephen has to look at his **timetable** to see which **subject** he has next. There are lessons in mathematics, English, geography, history, and science; they are the subjects on the **curriculum** for this year.
The teacher first makes sure that the class have done their **English homework**, and she **goes through** the **answers** with them. The **syllabus** for this year includes practice in listening, and this week the class listens to a **cassette** of a policeman talking about his job. The teacher writes the new **vocabulary** on the **board** for the students to **copy down**. Then the students do an **exercise** in their **workbooks**. They **fill in** the **answers**, and the teacher tells them that they can also **look up** words that they don't know in their **dictionary**. For homework this week, the teacher tells the class to read a passage from their **textbook/ coursebook**.
At the end of this **term**, Stephen will **leave school** and start looking for a job.

tion, usu. by having an argument: *We had been annoyed with each other for weeks before we cleared the air by talking about it.*

**clear** sthg.↔ **away** *v adv* [T] to make an area tidy by removing (plates from a table, toys from a floor, etc.)

**clear off** *v adv* [I] *infml* to leave a place, often quickly: *When the two boys saw the policeman they cleared off as quickly as they could.*

**clear out** *v adv* **1** [I *of*] *infml* to leave esp. a building or enclosed space, often quickly: *When the police arrived the thieves quickly cleared out of the house.* **2** [T] (**clear** sthg.↔ **out**) to collect and throw away (unwanted objects): *I decided to clear out all the old clothes that we never wear.* **3** [T] (**clear** sthg. ↔**out**) to clean thoroughly: *I'm going to clear out my bedroom today.* –**clearout** *n* [S] *infml esp BrE: We gave the house a good clearout today.* (=cleaned and tidied everything)

**clear up** *v adv* **1** [T] (**clear** sthg.↔ *up*) to find an answer to; explain: *to clear up the mystery* **2** [I;T (=**clear** sthg.↔ **up**)] to put in order; tidy up; finish: *I've lots of work to clear up by the weekend.|Would you clear up (this room) before our visitors arrive?* **3** [I] to become less bad or come to an end: *I hope the weather clears up before Sunday.*

**clear·ance** /ˈklɪərəns/ *n* [C;U] **1** the act or result of CLEARING[3]: *The ship sailed as soon as it got clearance from the port* AUTHORITY. **2** the distance between one object and another passing beneath or beside it: *There was a clearance of only ten centimetres between the bridge and the top of the bus.*

**clear-cut** /ˌ· ˈ·◂/ *adj* **1** having a smooth regular neat shape (OUTLINE) **2** clear in meaning; DEFINITE: *a clear-cut plan*

**clear-head·ed** /ˌ· ˈ··◂/ *adj* having or showing a clear understanding; sensible –**clear-headedly** *adv* –**clear-headedness** *n* [U]

**clear·ing** /ˈklɪərɪŋ/ *n* an area of land cleared of trees but surrounded by other trees

**clear·ly** /ˈklɪəli‖ˈklɪərli/ *adv* **1** in a clear manner: *He spoke very clearly; I could hear every word.* **2** undoubtedly; OBVIOUSLY: *That's clearly a mistake.| Clearly, he's a very stupid person.*

**clear-sight·ed** /ˌ· ˈ··◂/ *adj* able to see clearly and make good judgments –**clear-sightedly** *adv* –**clear-sightedness** *n* [U]

**cleav·age** /ˈkliːvɪdʒ/ *n* [C;U] **1** (the act of making) a division or break caused by splitting **2** *infml* the space between a woman's breasts, esp. that which can be seen when she is wearing a low-cut dress

**cleave** /kliːv/ *v* **cleaved** *or* **cleft** /kleft/ *or* **clove** /kləʊv/, **cleaved** *or* **cleft** *or* **cloven** /ˈkləʊvən/, **cleaving** [T] *becoming rare* to divide or make by a cutting blow

**cleav·er** /ˈkliːvə^r/ *n* an axelike tool, used esp. for cutting up large pieces of meat

**SPELLING NOTE**

Words with the sound /k/, like **cut**, may be spelt **k-**, like **key**, or **qu-**, like **queen.**
Words with the sound /s/, like **city**, may be spelt **s-**, like **soon**, or **ps-**, like **psychology.**

**clef** /klef/ *n* a sign put at the beginning of a line of written music to show the height (PITCH[1] (3)) of the notes

**cleft** /kleft/ *v past tense of* CLEAVE

**clem·en·cy** /ˈklemənsi/ *n* [U] mercy, esp. when shown in making punishment less severe

**clem·ent** /ˈklemənt/ *adj* (esp. of the weather) not severe; MILD –opposite **inclement** –**clemently** *adv*

**clench** /klentʃ/ *v* [T] to close or hold tightly: *She clenched her teeth.|He clenched his money in his hand.*

**cler·gy** /ˈklɜːd·i‖-ɜr-/ *n* [P] the members of esp. the Christian priesthood who are allowed to perform religious services: *a member of the clergy*

**cler·gy·man** /ˈklɜːdʒimən‖-ɜr-/ *n* **-men** /mən/ a Christian priest or MINISTER –see PRIEST (USAGE)

**cler·i·cal** /ˈklerɪkəl/ *adj* [*no comp.*] **1** of or concerning a clerk: *clerical work in an office* **2** of or concerning the CLERGY: *wearing a clerical collar* –**clerically** *adv*

**clerk** /klɑːk‖klɜrk/ *n* **1** a person employed in an office, shop, etc., to keep records, accounts, etc., and to do written work **2** an official in charge of the records of a court, town council, etc.: *town clerk* **3** also **salesclerk** *AmE*– a person who works in a shop, esp. selling things

**clev·er** /ˈklevə^r/ *adj* **1** quick at learning and understanding; having a quick, skilful, and able mind or body: *a clever student|a clever worker|clever with his hands* **2** being the result of a quick able mind; showing ability and skill: *a clever idea* –**cleverly** *adv* –**cleverness** *n* [U]

**cli·ché** /ˈkliːʃeɪ‖kliːˈʃeɪ/ *n derog* an idea or expression used so commonly that it has lost much of its meaning

**click**[1] /klɪk/ *n* a slight short sound, such as the noise of a key turning in a lock

**click**[2] *v* **1** [I;T] to (cause to) make a slight short sound: *The door clicked shut.* **2** [I *with*] *infml* to fall into place; be understood: *Her joke suddenly clicked (with us) and we all laughed.* **3** [I *with*] *infml* to be a success: *That film's really clicked (with young people); it's very popular.*

**cli·ent** /ˈklaɪənt/ *n* **1** a person who pays a professional person, esp. a lawyer, for help and advice **2** → CUSTOMER –see CUSTOMER (USAGE)

**cliff** /klɪf/ *n* a high very steep face of rock, esp. on a coast: *the white cliffs of Dover|He stood on the* **clifftop** *looking out to sea.*

**cliff·hang·er** /ˈklɪfˌhæŋə^r/ *n infml* a story or competition of which the result is in doubt until the last moment: *The game was a real cliffhanger.*

**cli·mac·tic** /klaɪˈmæktɪk/ *adj* of or forming a CLIMAX –compare CLIMATIC

**cli·mate** /ˈklaɪm$\frac{1}{2}$t/ *n* the average weather conditions at a particular place: *a warm climate*|(fig.) *the present political climate* (=political opinions)

**cli·mat·ic** /klaɪˈmætɪk/ *adj* [*no comp.*] of or related to CLIMATE –compare CLIMACTIC –**climatically** *adv*

**cli·max**[1] /ˈklaɪmæks/ *n* **1** the most powerful or interesting part of a book, film, etc., usu. happening near the end of the story –see also ANTICLIMAX **2** → ORGASM

**climax**[2] *v* [I *in, with*] to reach a CLIMAX[1] (1)

**climb**[1] /klaɪm/ *v* **climbed, climbing 1** [I;T] to move, esp. from a lower to a higher position, up, over, or through, esp. by using the hands and feet: *Do you think you can climb that tree?|to climb a ladder|The old lady climbs (up) the stairs with difficulty.|The child climbed into/out of the car.* **2** [I] to rise to a higher point; go higher: *It became hotter as the sun climbed in the sky.|The plane climbed quickly.|The road climbed steeply up the hill.*

**climb down**[1] (sthg.) *v adv; prep* [I;T] to go down, esp. by using the hands and feet: *We easily climbed down (the side of the cliff).*

**climb down**[2] *v adv* [I] *infml* to admit that one has been wrong, has made a mistake, etc., esp. in order to make a difficult state of affairs easier; BACK[4] **down**

**climb**[2] *n* [*usu. sing.*] **1** a journey upwards made by climbing; act of climbing: *After a climb of two hours, they reached the top of the mountain.|The minister's climb to power had taken 20 years.* **2** a place to be climbed; very steep slope: *There was a steep climb on the road out of town.*

**climb·er** /ˈklaɪməʳ/ *n* a person or thing that climbs: *a famous mountain climber|*(fig.)*He's always been a* **social climber.** (=tried to reach a higher social position)

**clinch**[1] /klɪntʃ/ *v* [T] *infml* to settle (a business matter or an agreement) firmly: *The two businessmen* **clinched the deal** *quickly.|The offer of more money clinched it for her. She accepted the job.*

**clinch**[2] *n* [S] the position of two people when holding each other tightly with the arms; EMBRACE: *The fighters/lovers were* **in a clinch.** –compare CLASP[1] (2)

**cling** /klɪŋ/ *v* **clung** /klʌŋ/, **clinging** [I *to*] to hold tightly; stick firmly; refuse to let go: *The wet shirt clung to his body.|The child was clinging to its mother.|*(fig.) *She still clings to the belief that her son is alive.*

**cling·ing** /ˈklɪŋɪŋ/ *adj* **1** (esp. of clothes) tight-fitting; sticking tightly and closely to the body **2** too dependent upon the presence of another person: *a clinging child that will not leave its mother*

**clin·ic** /ˈklɪnɪk/ *n* a building or part of a hospital where usu. specialized medical treatment and advice is given: *The clinic is near the station.|an eye clinic|the ear, nose, and throat clinic* –compare SURGERY (2)

**clin·i·cal** /ˈklɪnɪkəl/ *adj* **1** of or connected with a CLINIC or hospital **2** cold; not showing much personal feeling: *He seemed to have a rather clinical view of the breakup of his marriage.* **–clinically** *adv*

**clink** /klɪŋk/ *v* [I;T] to (cause to) make a slight knocking sound like that of pieces of glass or metal lightly hitting each other **–clink** *n* [S]

**clip**[1] /klɪp/ *n* a small variously-shaped plastic or usu. metal object for holding things tightly together or in place: *Fasten these sheets of paper together with a clip, please.|a paper clip|a hair clip*

**clip**[2] *v* **-pp-** [I;T *on, to, together*] to (cause to) fasten onto something with a CLIP: *Clip these sheets of paper together please.|Does your jewellery clip on?* –opposite **unclip**

**clip**[3] *v* **-pp-** [T] **1** to cut with scissors or another sharp instrument, esp. to cut small parts off something: *I'm going to clip this picture out of the paper.|We clipped 50 sheep today.* (=cut off the wool)|*The guard on the train clipped our tickets to show we'd used them.* **2** *infml* to strike with a short quick blow: *I'll* **clip your ears** *if you don't behave!*

**clip**[4] *n* **1** the act or result of CLIPPING[3] **2** *infml* a short quick blow: *a clip round the ears*

**clip·pers** /ˈklɪpəz‖-pərz/ *n* [P] a usu. scissor-like tool used for CLIPPING[3] (1): *nail clippers* –see PAIR[1] (USAGE)

**clip·ping** /ˈklɪpɪŋ/ *n* **1** a piece cut off or out of something: *nail clippings* **2** *AmE* for CUTTING[1] (2)

**clique** /kliːk/ *n derog* [C +*sing./pl. v*] a small closely united group of people who do not allow others easily to join their group

**clit·o·ris** /ˈklɪtərɪ̌s/ *n* a small front part of the female sex organ which becomes bigger when the female is sexually excited

**cloak**[1] /kləʊk/ *n* a loose outer garment, usu. without arm-coverings (SLEEVES), which is sometimes worn instead of a coat

**cloak**[2] *v* [T] to hide, keep secret, or cover (ideas, thoughts, beliefs, etc.): *cloaked in secrecy*

**cloak-and-dag·ger** /ˌ· · ˈ··/ *adj* [A] (esp. of plays, films, stories, etc.) dealing with adventure and mystery

**cloak·room** /ˈkləʊkrʊm, -ruːm/ *n* **1** also **checkroom** *AmE*– a room, as in a theatre, where hats, coats, bags, etc., may be left for a short time **2** *esp. BrE euph* a room containing a LAVATORY (1), esp. in a public building

**clob·ber** /ˈklɒbəʳ‖ˈklɑ-/ *v* [T] *infml* to strike or attack severely and repeatedly: (fig.) *We were clobbered* (=severely defeated) *at the last election.*

**clock**[1] /klɒk‖klɑk/ *n* **1** an instrument (not worn like a watch) for measuring and showing time: *According to the station clock, the train was an hour late.* –see picture on page 355 **2 around/round the clock** all day and all night: *We worked around the clock to finish the job.* **3 put the clock back/on/forward**/*AmE* **ahead**– (in countries which officially change the time at the beginning of winter and summer) to move the hands of a clock back/forward one or two hours: *In Italy they put the clock back two hours every October.|In Britain they put the clock on an hour in spring.* **4 put the clock back** to set aside modern laws, ideas, plans, etc., and return to old-fashioned ones: *The government's plans for education will put the clock back 20 years.* **5 watch the clock** *derog infml* to think continually of how soon work will end **6 work against the clock** to work very quickly in order to finish a job before a certain time –see also O'CLOCK

USAGE If a **clock** or **watch** says 11.50 at 12 o'clock, then it is (10 minutes) **slow**; if it says 12.05, it is (5 minutes) **fast**. If it gets faster every day, it **gains** (time); if it gets slower every day, it **loses** (time). When one puts it to the right time one **sets** it: ***I* set my watch** *by the radio* (=by listening to the radio time signal).

**clock**[2] *v* [T] →TIME[2] (2): *I clocked him while he ran a mile.*

**clock up** sthg. *v adv* [T] *infml* to record (a distance travelled, points won, etc.): *We clocked up 1,000 miles coming here.*

**clock·wise** /ˈklɒk-waɪz‖ˈklɑk-/ *adj,adv* [*no comp.*] in the direction in which the hands of a clock move:

*Turn the lid clockwise if you want to fasten it tightly.|a clockwise movement of the lid* –opposite **anticlockwise**

**clock·work** /'klɒk-wɜːk||'klɑk-wɜrk/ *n* [A;U] **1** machinery that can usu. be wound up with a key, and that is used esp. in clocks and toys: *clockwork toys* **2 like clockwork** *infml* smoothly; easily; regularly; without trouble

**clod** /klɒd||klɑd/ *n* a lump or mass, esp. of clay or earth

**clog**[1] /klɒg||klɑg/ *n* [*usu. pl.*] a kind of shoe **a** with a thick usu. wooden bottom **b** completely made from one piece of wood –see PAIR[1] (USAGE)

**clog**[2] *v* **-gg-** [I;T *up*] to (cause to) become blocked: *The pump won't work. It's clogged (up) with dirt.*

**clois·ter** /'klɔɪstəʳ/ *n* [*usu. pl.*] a covered passage, which has open archways on one side facing into a garden or courtyard, and which usu. forms part of a church, college, MONASTERY, or CONVENT

**cloistered** /'klɔɪstəd/ *adj* shut away from the world in or as if in a CONVENT or MONASTERY: *a cloistered life*

**clone** /kləʊn/ *n tech* the descendant of a single plant or animal, produced nonsexually from any one cell, and with exactly the same form as the parent

**clop** /klɒp||ɒp/ *v,n* **-pp-** [I;S] (to make) a sound like horses' feet (HOOFS)

**close**[1] /kləʊz/ *v* **closed, closing 1** [I;T] to (cause to) shut: *Close the windows and keep out the cold air.|When does the shop close?|The firm has decided to close (down) its London branch.* –opposite **open 2** [T] to bring to an end: *She closed her speech with a funny joke.* –see OPEN[2] (USAGE)

**close in** *v adv* [I] **1** [*on, upon*] to surround gradually and usu. from all sides: *The people were trapped when the enemy army closed in.|*(fig.) *Night is closing in.* **2** to have fewer hours of daylight: *The days are beginning to close in now that it's autumn.*

**close up** *v adv* **1** [T] (**close** sthg.↔ **up**) to close completely; block: *The old road has now been closed up.* **2** [I] to come nearer each other: *The teacher told the children to close up to each other.*

**close**[2] /kləʊz/ *n* the end, esp. of an activity or of a period of time: *As the evening* **came/drew to a close** *the guests went home.|She* **brought** *the meeting* **to a close.**

**close**[3] /kləʊs/ *n* **1** [C] an enclosed area or space, esp. the area around a large important church (CATHEDRAL); COURTYARD **2** [S *usu. cap.*] (part of the name of) a street in a town: *12 Fern Close*

**close**[4] /kləʊs/ *adj* **1** near: *The church is close to the shops.* **2** [A] near in relationship: *He's one of my closest relatives/one of my closest friends.* –opposite **distant 3** tight; with little space: *When she sewed she always used close stitches.* **4** thorough; careful: *We kept a close watch on the prisoners.|She made a close study of the subject.* **5** without fresh air, and perhaps too warm: *It's very close in here; open the window.* **6** decided by a very small difference: *a close result/game* –compare NARROW[2] (3) **7** [F] secretive: *She's always been very close about her past life.* **8 a close call/shave/thing** *infml* something bad that nearly happened but did not: *That was a close shave! We nearly hit that car!* –see also NEAR[1] (USAGE) **–closely** *adv* **–closeness** *n* [U]

**SPELLING NOTE**

Words with the sound /k/, like **cut**, may be spelt **k-**, like **key**, or **qu-**, like **queen.**
Words with the sound /s/, like **city**, may be spelt **s-**, like **soon**, or **ps-**, like **psychology.**

**close**[5] /kləʊs/ *adv* [F] **1** near: *We live close to the church/close by the church.|to sit close together|to follow close behind|Don't come too close!* **2 close on** *infml* almost: *It happened close on 50 years ago.*

**closed** /kləʊzd/ *adj* **1** [*to*] (esp. of a shop or public building) not open to the public: *The shop is closed on Thursdays.|a club with a closed membership* **2 closed book** something of which one knows nothing: *Fishing is a closed book to me.*

**closed shop** /ˌ· '·◂/ *n* a factory or other establishment in which the employer hires only members of a particular trade union

**close-knit** /ˌkləʊs 'nɪt◂/ also **closely-knit**– *adj* tightly bound together by social, political, religious, etc., beliefs and activities: *a close-knit family*

**close-set** *adj* set close together: *close-set houses/eyes*

**clos·et** /'klɒzɪ̆t||'klɑ-, 'klɔ-/ *n esp. AmE* a cupboard built into the wall of a room and going from floor to CEILING (1)

**close-up** /'kləʊs ʌp/ *n* a photograph taken from very near

**clo·sure** /'kləʊʒəʳ/ *n* [C;U] (an example of) the act of closing: *Lack of money forced the closure of the company.* –compare OPENING[1] (1)

**clot**[1] /klɒt||klɑt/ *n* **1** a half-solid mass or lump, usu. formed from a liquid, esp. blood: *a blood clot in his leg* **2** *esp. BrE infml* a stupid person; fool: *You've broken that cup, you clot!*

**clot**[2] *v* **-tt-** [I;T] to (cause to) form into CLOTS[1] (1)

**cloth** /klɒθ||klɔθ/ *n* **cloths** /klɒθs||klɔðz, klɔθs/ [C;U] (a piece of) material made from wool, hair, cotton, etc., by weaving, and used for making garments, coverings, etc.: *I need a lot of cloth if I'm going to make a long dress.|a tablecloth|Clean the windows with a cloth.* –see CLOTHES (USAGE)

**clothe** /kləʊð/ *v* **clothed**||also **clad** /klæd/ *AmE*, **clad**||also **clothed** *AmE*, **clothing** [T] to provide clothes for: *They have to work hard to feed and clothe their family.*

**clothes** /kləʊðz, kləʊz/ *n* [P] garments, such as trousers, dresses, shirts, etc., worn on the body

USAGE Compare **clothes, cloth, clothing,** and **dress**: **Clothes** is the usual word for all the garments that one wears (such as shirts and dresses), and these are made from various kinds of **cloth** or **material** (such as wool and cotton): *He spends a lot of money on* **clothes.**|*She's got some beautiful* **clothes.**|*How much* **cloth/material** *will I need to make a pair of trousers?* **Clothing** is a more formal word for **clothes.** A **dress** is a kind of outer garment worn by women and girls, but in certain expressions **dress** [U] can mean a particular type of **clothing;** *What a pretty* **dress** *she's wearing today!|My parents had to wear formal evening* **dress** *to go to the company dinner.*

**clothes·horse** /'kləʊðzhɔːs,'kləʊz-||-ɔrs/ *n BrE* a framework on which clothes are hung to dry, usu. indoors

**cloth·ing** /ˈkləʊðɪŋ/ *n* [U] *often fml* the garments, such as trousers, dresses, shirts, etc., worn together on different parts of the body: *warm winter clothing|food, clothing, and shelter* –see CLOTHES (USAGE)

**cloud¹** /klaʊd/ **1** [C;U] (a usu. white or grey mass of) very small drops of water floating high in the air: *When there are black clouds you can tell it's going to rain.|There's more cloud today than yesterday.*|(fig.) *Clouds of smoke rose above the bombed city.*|(fig.) *a cloud of insects* **2** [C] something that causes unhappiness or fear: *The clouds of war were gathering.* **3 under a cloud** out of favour; looked on with distrust: *He left his job under a cloud.*

**cloud²** *v* [I;T *over*] to (cause to) become covered with or as if with clouds: *The sky clouded over: we could see it was going to rain.*|(fig.) *Age clouded his memory.*

**cloud·burst** /ˈklaʊdbɜːst‖-ɜr-/ *n* a sudden very heavy fall of rain

**cloud·y** /ˈklaʊdi/ *adj* **-ier, -iest 1** full of clouds; OVERCAST: *a cloudy day/sky* **2** not clear or transparent: *cloudy beer* **–cloudiness** *n* [U]

**clout¹** /klaʊt/ *n* **1** [C] *infml* a blow or knock esp. given with the hand **2** [U] *esp. AmE infml* influence

**clout²** *v* [T] *infml* to strike, esp. with the hand

**clove¹** /kləʊv/ *n* the dried flower of a tropical Asian plant, used usu. whole for giving a special taste to food

**clove²** *n* any of the smallest pieces into which the root of the GARLIC plant can be divided

**clove³** *v past tense of* CLEAVE

**clo·ven** /ˈkləʊvən/ *v past participle of* CLEAVE: *Cows, sheep, and goats have* **cloven hoofs.** (=each foot divided into two parts)

**clo·ver** /ˈkləʊvəʳ/ *n* [C;U] **1** a small usu. three-leafed plant with pink, purple, or white flowers, often grown as food for cattle **2 in clover** *infml* living in comfort

**clown¹** /klaʊn/ *n* a performer, esp. in the CIRCUS, who dresses funnily and makes people laugh by his/her jokes, tricks, or actions

**clown²** *v* [I *about, around*] *often derog* to behave like a CLOWN; act stupidly or foolishly

**club¹** /klʌb/ *n* **1** (a building for) a society of people who join together for a certain purpose, esp. sport or amusement: *a working-men's club|a cricket club|a golf club* **2** a heavy stick, suitable for use as a weapon **3** a specially shaped stick for striking a ball in certain sports, esp. GOLF: *a golf club* **4** a playing card with one or more three-leafed figures printed on it in black –see CARDS (USAGE)

**club²** *v* **-bb-** [T] to beat or strike with a heavy stick (CLUB): *clubbed to death*

**club together** *v adv* [I] to share the cost of something with others: *We clubbed together to buy her a present.*

**cluck** /klʌk/ *v,n* [C;I] (to make) the noise that a hen makes

**clue** /kluː/ *n* **1** something that helps to find the answer to a question, difficulty, etc.: *Have any clues been found that can help the police find the criminal?* **2 not have a clue** *infml* to be unable to understand; know nothing: *"Do you know the time of the next train?" "I haven't a clue".*

**clued up** *adj infml* very well-informed; knowing a lot: *He's quite clued up about music.*

**clump¹** /klʌmp/ *n* **1** [C] a group of trees, bushes, plants, etc., growing together **2** [C] a heavy solid lump or mass of dirt, soil, mud, etc. **3** [S] a heavy slow sound, as made by slow footsteps

**clump²** *v* [I] to walk with slow heavy noisy footsteps

**clum·sy** /ˈklʌmzi/ *adj* **-sier, -siest** *derog* **1** awkward and ungraceful in movement or action; without skill or grace: *He's a terrible dancer: he's too clumsy, and keeps stepping on my feet.*|(fig.) *a clumsy remark* **2** difficult to handle or control: *You shouldn't wear such clumsy shoes.* **–clumsily** *adv* **–clumsiness** *n* [U]

**clung** /klʌŋ/ *v past tense and past participle of* CLING

**clus·ter¹** /ˈklʌstəʳ/ *n* a number of things of the same kind growing or being close together in a group: *a cluster of stars*

**cluster²** *v* [I;T *around, round, together*] to (cause to) gather or grow in one or more CLUSTERS: *The boys clustered together round the fire and sang songs.*

**clutch¹** /klʌtʃ/ *v* [T] to hold tightly: *The mother clutched her baby in her arms.|He* **clutched at** (=tried to hold) *the branch but could not reach it.*

**clutch²** *n* **1** [*usu. sing.*] the act of CLUTCHing; a tight hold: *His clutch was not tight enough and he fell from the branch.* **2** an apparatus, esp. in a car, which allows working parts of an engine to be connected or disconnected –see picture on page 85 **3 in the clutches of** in the control or power of: *Once he was in the clutches of the enemy he knew he'd never escape.*

**clut·ter¹** /ˈklʌtəʳ/ *v* [T *up*] to make untidy or confused: *The room was cluttered (up) with furniture.*

**clutter²** *n* [C;U] (a collection of) things scattered about in a disorderly manner: *a room full of clutter*

**cm** *written abbrev. said as:* CENTIMETRE(*s*)

**c/o** *written abbrev. said as:* care of; (esp. used when writing addresses) to be held or looked after by: *Send it to John Smith c/o Dorothy Smith.*

**Co.¹** *written abbrev. said as:* COUNTY: *Darlington, Co. Durham*

**Co.²** /kəʊ/ *abbrev. for:* COMPANY (1): *James Smith & Co.*

**coach¹** /kəʊtʃ/ *n* **1** *BrE*‖**bus** *AmE*– a bus used for long-distance travel or touring: *We went* **by coach. 2** also **carriage** *BrE*‖**car** *AmE*– a railway passenger carriage **3** a person who trains sportsmen and sportswomen for games, competitions, etc.: *a football coach* **4** a large enclosed four-wheeled horse-drawn carriage, used esp. in former times or in official ceremonies

**coach²** *v* [I;T *for, in*] to train or teach (a person or a group of people); give instruction or advice to (a person or a group of people): *I coach people for English examinations.*

**co·ag·u·late** /kəʊˈægjʊleɪt‖-gjə-/ *v* **-lated, -lating** [I;T] to (cause to) change from a liquid into a solid or nearly solid mass: *Blood coagulates when it meets air.* **–coagulation** /-ˈleɪʃən/ *n* [U]

**coal** /kəʊl/ *n* **1** [C;U] (a piece of) a black or dark brown mineral which is dug (MINEd) from the earth, which can be burned to give heat, and from which gas and many other products can be made: *a coal fire* **2 haul over the coals** *infml* to scold (someone) for doing something wrong

**co·a·lesce** /ˌkəʊəˈles/ *v* **-lesced, -lescing** [I] to grow together or unite so as to form one group, body, mass, etc. **–coalescence** *n* [U]

**co·a·li·tion** /ˌkəʊəˈlɪʃən/ *n* a union of political parties for a special purpose, usu. for a limited period of time: *a coalition government*

**coal·mine** /ˈkəʊlmaɪn/ ‖also **coal pit** /ˈ· ·/, **pit** *BrE– n* a mine from which coal is obtained

**coarse** /kɔːs‖kors/ *adj* **1** not fine or smooth; lumpy; rough: *a coarse woollen garment* **2** rough in manner; not delicate: *coarse behaviour|a coarse joke* **–coarsely** *adv* **–coarseness** *n* [U]

**coast[1]** /kəʊst/ *n* [*usu. sing.*] **1** the land next to the sea; seashore: *a trip to the coast* –see SHORE[1] (USAGE) **2 the coast is clear** *infml* all danger has gone: *"Come on. The coast is clear!"*

**coast[2]** *v* [I *along*] to keep moving, esp. down a hill, without any effort: *The children were enjoying coasting along (on their bicycles).*

**coast·guard** /ˈkəʊstgɑːd‖-ɑrd/ *n* a person serving in the COAST GUARD

**coast guard** /ˈ· ·/ *n* [U +*sing./pl. v*] (*often caps.*) a naval or police organization intended to watch for ships in danger and prevent illegal activity at sea

**coast·line** /ˈkəʊstlaɪn/ *n* the shape (OUTLINE) of a coast, esp. as seen from the sea

**coat[1]** /kəʊt/ *n* **1** an outer garment with long SLEEVES, often fastened at the front with buttons, and usu. worn to keep warm or for protection –see picture on page 563 **2** → JACKET (1): *a coat and skirt* **3** an animal's fur, wool, hair, etc. **4** also **coating**– a covering spread over a surface: *a coat of paint/of dust*

**coat[2]** *v* [T *in, with*] to cover with a COAT[1] (4): *The table was coated in/with dust.*

**coat of arms** /ˌ· · ˈ·/ *n* **coats of arms** a group of patterns or pictures, usu. painted on a shield, used by a noble family, town council, university, etc., as their special sign

**coax** /kəʊks/ *v* [T] **1** [*into, out of, to*] to persuade (someone) by gentle kindness or patience: *I coaxed him into going to school, although I had to promise to go with him.* **2** to obtain (something) by gently persuading **–coaxingly** *adv*

**cob** /kɒb‖kɑb/ also **corncob**– *n* the long hard central part of an ear of CORN[1] (2)

**cob·bled** /ˈkɒbəld‖ˈkɑ-/ *adj* (of a road) covered (PAVED) with COBBLESTONES: *old cobbled streets*

**cob·bler** /ˈkɒbləʳ‖ˈkɑ-/ *n old use* a person who repairs shoes

**cob·ble·stone** /ˈkɒbəlstəʊn‖ˈkɑ-/ also **cobble**– *n* [*often pl.*] a naturally rounded stone, used for covering the surface of roads in former times

**co·bra** /ˈkɒbrə, ˈkəʊ-‖ˈkəʊ-/ *n* an African or Asian poisonous snake

**cob·web** /ˈkɒbweb‖ˈkɑb-/ *n* a very fine network of sticky threads made by a SPIDER to catch insects

**SPELLING NOTE**

Words with the sound /k/, like **cut**, may be spelt **k-**, like **key**, or **qu-**, like **queen.**
Words with the sound /s/, like **city**, may be spelt **s-**, like **soon**, or **ps-**, like **psychology.**

**Co·ca-Co·la** /ˌkəʊkə ˈkəʊlə/ also **coke** /kəʊk/– *n* [C;U] *tdmk* (a small bottle or glass of) a popular non-alcoholic dark-coloured bubbly drink of American origin

**co·caine** /kəʊˈkeɪn/ also **coke** /kəʊk/ *infml– n* [U] a drug used for preventing pain, or taken (illegally) for pleasure

**cock** /kɒk‖kɑk/‖also **rooster** *AmE– n* a fully-grown male bird, esp. a chicken

**cock·a·too** /ˌkɒkəˈtuː‖ˈkɑkətuː/ *n* **cockatoos** *or* **cockatoo** an Australian bird (PARROT) with a lot of large feathers (CREST) on the top of its head

**cock·crow** /ˈkɒk- krəʊ‖ˈkɑk-/ *n* [U] *lit* early morning; sunrise

**cock·e·rel** /ˈkɒkərəl‖ˈkɑ-/ *n* a young COCK

**cock·eyed** /ˌkɒkˈaɪd◂‖ˌkɑk-/ *adj infml* turned or twisted to one side; CROOKED (1): *That picture's not hanging straight; it's cockeyed.*

**cock·le** /ˈkɒkəl‖ˈkɑ-/ *n* a very small European soft-bodied sea animal used for food –compare SCALLOP

**Cock·ney** /ˈkɒkni‖ˈkɑkni/ *n* a person from London, esp. one from the industrial area near the sea-port (**East End**)

**cock·pit** /ˈkɒkˌpɪt‖ˈkɑk-/ *n* the part of a plane or racing car in which the pilot or driver sits

**cock·roach** /ˈkɒk-rəʊtʃ‖ˈkɑk-/ *n* a large black insect which lives esp. in dirty or old houses

**cock·tail** /ˈkɒkteɪl‖ˈkɑk-/ *n* **1** a mixed alcoholic drink **2** a small quantity of specially prepared SEAFOOD eaten as part of a meal: *a shrimp/prawn cocktail|a fruit cocktail* (a mixture of small pieces of different fruits)

**cock-up** /ˈ· ·/ *n BrE infml* a confused state of affairs; example of complete lack of order

**cock·y** /ˈkɒki‖ˈkɑki/ also **cocksure** /kɒkˈʃʊə -ˈʃɔːʳ‖ˌkɑk-/– *adj* **-ier, -iest** *infml derog* too sure of oneself: *I don't like him; he's far too cocky.* **–cockiness** *n* [U]

**co·coa** /ˈkəʊkəʊ/ *n* **1** [U] a dark brown powder, used in making chocolate **2** [C;U] (a cupful of) a drink made from this powder

**co·co·nut** /ˈkəʊkənʌt/ *n* [C;U] (the hard white flesh of) a very large nut with a hollow centre filled with a milky juice

**co·coon** /kəˈkuːn/ *n* a protective case of silky threads in which a PUPA is enclosed –compare CHRYSALIS

**cod** /kɒd‖kɑd/ also **codfish** /ˈkɒdˌfɪʃ‖ˈkɑd-/– *n* **cod** *or* **cods** [C;U] (the flesh of) a large North Atlantic fish

**C.O.D.** *abbrev. for*: cash on delivery; with payment to be made when something is delivered

**code[1]** /kəʊd/ *n* **1** [C;U] a system of words, letters, numbers, etc., used instead of ordinary writing, esp. to keep messages secret: *a message written* **in code** |*a computer code* **2** [C;U] a system of signals used instead of letters and numbers in a message that is to be broadcast, telegraphed, etc.: *a telegraphic code* **3** [C] a system or collection of social customs or laws: *a code of behaviour*

**code[2]** also **encode** *fml– v* **coded, coding** [T] to translate into a CODE[1] (1,2) –see also DECODE

**co·ed** /ˌkəʊˈed◂‖ˈkəʊed/ *n AmE infml* a female student in a college or university open to both sexes

**co·ed·u·ca·tion** /ˌkəʊedʒʊˈkeɪʃən‖-dʒə-/ *n* [U] the system of educating boys and girls together

–**coeducational** *adj*

**co·erce** /kəʊ'ɜːs‖-'ɜrs/ *v* **-erced, -ercing** [T] *fml* to make (an unwilling person or group of people) do something, by using force, threats of punishment, etc.: *The terrorists coerced the government into paying them a million pounds.* –**coercion** *n* [U]: *The terrorists got what they wanted by coercion.* –**coercive** *adj*

**co·ex·ist** /ˌkəʊɪg'zɪst/ *v* [I *with*] to exist together at the same time: *The war started because the two countries couldn't coexist peacefully.*

**C of E** /ˌsiː əv 'iː/ *abbrev. for:* CHURCH OF ENGLAND

**cof·fee** /'kɒfi‖'kɔfi, 'kɑfi/ *n* **1** [U] a brown powder made by crushing **coffee beans** **2** [C;U] (a cupful of) a hot brown drink made from this powder: *Would you like a (cup of)/some coffee?|Two coffees, please!*

**coffee table** /'·· ·/ *n* a small long low table, usu. used in a LIVING ROOM –see picture on page 355

**cof·fer** /'kɒfəʳ‖'kɔfər, 'kɑ-/ *n lit* or *humor* a large strong chest for holding money, jewels, or other valuable objects

**cof·fin** /'kɒfɪ̈n‖'kɔ-/ *n* the box in which a dead person is buried

**cog** /kɒg‖kɑg/ *n* any of the teeth round the edge of a wheel (**cogwheel**) that cause it to move or be moved by another wheel in a machine

**co·gent** /'kəʊdʒənt/ *adj* able to prove, CONVINCE, or produce belief; forceful in argument: *a cogent argument* –**cogently** *adv* –**cogency** *n* [U]

**cog·i·tate** /'kɒdʒɪ̈teɪt‖'kɑ-/ *v* **-tated, -tating** [I *about, upon*] *fml* to think carefully and seriously about something –**cogitation** /-'teɪʃən/ *n* [U]

**co·gnac** /'kɒnjæk‖'kəʊ-, 'kɑ-/ *n* [C;U] (a glass of) a fine strong alcoholic drink (BRANDY) made in France

**co·hab·it** /ˌkəʊ'hæbɪ̈t/ *v* [I *with*] *fml* (of two unmarried people) to live together as though married –**cohabitation** /-'teɪʃən / *n* [U]

**co·here** /kəʊ'hɪəʳ/ *v* **-hered, -hering** [I] *fml* **1** to stick together; be united **2** to be reasonably and naturally connected, esp. in thought

**co·her·ent** /kəʊ'hɪərənt/ *adj* (esp. of speech, thought, ideas, etc.) naturally or reasonably connected; easily understood; CONSISTENT –opposite **incoherent** –**coherently** *adv* –**coherence** *n* [U]

**co·he·sion** /kəʊ'hiːʒən/ *n* [U] the act or state of sticking together tightly: *We need more cohesion in the party if we're going to win the next election.* –**cohesive** *adj* : *cohesive forces in society*

**coif·fure** /kwɒ'fjʊəʳ‖kwɑ-/ *n fml* a style of arranging and combing a woman's hair –**coiffured** *adj*

**coil¹** /kɔɪl/ *v* [I;T *up*] to (cause to) wind or twist into a ring or continuous circular shape (SPIRAL): *Coil the rope up, please.|The snake coiled (itself) around the tree.* –opposite **uncoil**

**coil²** *n* **1** [C] (any of) a connected set of rings or twists into which a rope, wire, etc., can be wound: *a coil of rope|a loose coil of hair* **2** [C] *tech* an apparatus made by winding wire into a continuous circular shape, used for carrying an electric current **3** [C; *the* S] → I.U.D.

**coin¹** /kɔɪn/ *n* [C;U](a piece of usu. flat and round) metal made by a government for use as money: *I changed a pound note at the bank, because I needed some coins for the ticket machine.*

**coin²** *v* [T] **1** to make (coins) from metal: *The government has decided to coin more 50-pence pieces.* **2** to invent (a word or phrase): *Who coined the word "nuke"?*

**co·in·cide** /ˌkəʊɪ̈n'saɪd/ *v* **-cided, -ciding** [I *with*] **1** to happen at the same time **2** (of ideas, opinions, etc.) to be in agreement: *My religious beliefs don't coincide with yours.*

**co·in·ci·dence** /kəʊ'ɪnsɪ̈dəns/ *n* [C;U] (a) combination of events, happening by chance, but in such a way that it seems planned or arranged: *What a coincidence that I was in London at the same time as you!*

**co·in·ci·den·tal** /kəʊˌɪnsɪ̈'dentl/ *adj* resulting from a COINCIDENCE: *a coincidental meeting* –**coincidentally** *adv*

**coke¹** /kəʊk/ *n* [U] the solid substance that remains after gas has been removed from coal by heating, burnt as a FUEL

**coke²** *n infml for:* **1** [C;U] *tdmk* →COCA-COLA **2** [U] → COCAINE

**col·an·der** /'kʌləndəʳ, 'kɒ-‖'kʌ-, 'kɑ-/ also **cullender** /'kʌ-/– *n* a bowl-shaped pan with many small holes in the bottom, used for separating liquid from food

**cold¹** /kəʊld/ *adj* **1** having a low or lower than usual temperature; not warm: *a cold wind|It's a cold day for July, isn't it?|I'm (feeling) cold today.* **2** (of people or their actions) showing a lack of (friendly) feelings; unkind **3** (of food) cooked but not eaten hot **4 (out) cold** unconscious, esp. as the result of a severe blow to the head –**coldly** *adv* –**coldness** *n* [U]

**cold²** *n* **1** [*the* S] the absence of heat; low temperature; cold weather: *Don't go out into the cold without a coat!* **2** [C;U] an illness of the nose and/or throat which causes headaches, coughing, slight fever, and general discomfort (esp. in the phrases **catch/have (a) cold, the common cold**) **3 (out) in the cold** *infml* not considered; as if unwanted: *He was left out in the cold at school because he didn't like sports.*

**cold-blood·ed** /ˌ· '··◂/ *adj* **1** [*no comp.*] having a body temperature that changes according to the temperature of the surroundings: *Snakes are cold-blooded.* –compare WARM-BLOODED **2** *derog* showing complete lack of feeling; cruel: *a cold-blooded murder* –opposite **hot-blooded**

**cold-heart·ed** /ˌ· '··◂/ *adj* lacking sympathy or feeling; unkind –compare WARM-HEARTED –**cold-heartedly** *adv* –**cold-heartedness** *n* [U]

**cold war** /'· ·/ *n* (*sometimes caps.*) a severe political struggle, without actual fighting, between states with opposed political systems

**col·ic** /'kɒlɪk‖'kɑ-/ *n* [U] a severe pain in the stomach and bowels (esp. of babies)

**col·lab·o·rate** /kə'læbəreɪt/ *v* **-rated, -rating** [I *with*] **1** to work together or with someone else, esp. for a special purpose: *The police and the army collaborated to catch the terrorists.* **2** *derog* to help an enemy country which has taken control of one's own: *Anyone who collaborated was shot.* –**collaborator** *n* –**collaboration** /-'reɪʃən/ *n* [U]: *The two companies are working* **in collaboration** *with each other.*

**col·lage** /'kɒlɑːʒ‖kə'lɑːʒ/ *n* a picture made by sticking various materials or objects onto a surface

**col·lapse¹** /kə'læps/ *v* **-lapsed, -lapsing** **1** [I;T] to (cause to) fall down or inwards suddenly: *The bridge collapsed under the weight of the train.*|(fig.) *All opposition to the government collapsed because of the war.* **2** [I] to fall helpless or unconscious: *He collapsed at the end of the five mile race.* **3** [I;T] to fold into a shape that takes up less space: *This table collapses, so I can store it easily when I'm not using it.*

**collapse²** *n* **1** [S;U] (an example of) the act of falling down or inwards: *The storm caused the collapse of the roof.*|(fig.) *The collapse of the peace talks caused more fighting.* **2** [C;U *usu. sing.*] (an example of) the act of suddenly and completely losing strength and/or will: *He suffered from a nervous collapse.*

**col·lap·si·ble** /kə'læpsəbəl/ *adj* that can be COLLAPSED¹ (3) for easy storing

**col·lar¹** /'kɒləʳ||'kɑ-/ *n* **1** the part of a shirt, dress, or coat that fits round the neck –see picture on page 563 **2** a leather or metal band put round an animal's neck –see also BLUE-COLLAR, WHITE-COLLAR

**collar²** *v* [T] *infml* to catch and hold (someone): *The police collared him as he was getting on the boat.*

**col·lar·bone** /'kɒləbəʊn||'kɑlər-/ *n* either of a pair of bones joining the RIBS to the shoulders

**col·lat·e·ral** /kə'lætərəl/ *n* [S;U] *fml* property or something valuable promised to a person if one is unable to repay a debt: *He used his house as (a) collateral for the loan.* –compare SECURITY (3)

**col·league** /'kɒliːg||'kɑ-/ *n* a fellow worker, esp. in a profession

**col·lect** /kə'lekt/ *v* **1** [I;T] to bring or gather together: *Collect the books and put them in a pile on my desk.*|*A crowd of people collected to see the new school.*|*I collect foreign coins.* (=as a HOBBY)|*The government could save money by improving the way it collects taxes.*|(fig.) *I tried to* **collect my thoughts** *but I was too excited.* **2** [T] to call for and take away: *He collected the children from school.*

**col·lect·ed** /kə'lektɨd/ *adj* having control of oneself, one's thoughts, senses, etc.; calm: *How can you stay so* **cool, calm, and collected** *after an argument?*

**col·lec·tion** /kə'lekʃən/ *n* [C;U] the act of collecting, or set of things collected: *Janet has a very good collection of foreign stamps.*|*What does the church do with the money it gets from collections?*

**col·lec·tive¹** /kə'lektɪv/ *adj* [*no comp.*] of, by, or related to a number of people or groups of people considered or acting as one: *the collective opinion of the governments of Western Europe*|*collective ownership*|*In a system of* **collective bargaining**, *a small group of people represent the views of a larger group, esp. the workforce in a factory, office, etc., to the managers of the company.* **–collectively** *adv*

**collective²** *n* [C +*sing./pl. v.*] a business or firm owned and controlled by the people who work in it

**col·lec·tor** /kə'lektəʳ/ *n* **1** a person employed to collect taxes, tickets, debts, etc. **2** a person who collects stamps, coins, etc., as a HOBBY

**SPELLING NOTE**
Words with the sound /k/, like **cut**, may be spelt **k-**, like **key**, or **qu-**, like **queen**.
Words with the sound /s/, like **city**, may be spelt **s-**, like **soon**, or **ps-**, like **psychology**.

**col·lege** /'kɒlɪdʒ||'kɑ-/ *n* **1** [C;U] a school for higher and professional education; part of a university: *The college is next to the station.*|*He starts college in January.* **2** [C] *fml* a body of people with a common profession, duties, or rights: *She's a member of the Royal College of Nursing.*

**col·lide** /kə'laɪd/ *v* **-lided, -liding** [I *with*] to crash (together) violently: *Many people were hurt when the two buses collided.*

**col·lie·ry** /'kɒljəri||'kɑl-/ *n* **-ries** *esp. BrE* a coalmine and the buildings, machinery, etc., connected with it

**col·li·sion** /kə'lɪʒən/ *n* [C;U] (an example of) the act of colliding (COLLIDE): *Many people were hurt in the collision between the bus and the car.*

**col·lo·qui·al** /kə'ləʊkwɪəl/ *adj* (of words, phrases, style, etc.) of or suitable for ordinary, informal, or familiar conversation **–colloquially** *adv* **–colloquialism** *n*

**col·lu·sion** /kə'luːʒən/ *n* [U] *fml* secret agreement between two or more people with the intention of cheating or deceiving others

**co·lon** /'kəʊlən, -lɒn/ *n* a mark (:) used in writing and printing to introduce a statement, example, etc.

**colo·nel** /'kɜːnəl||'kɜr-/ *n* [A;C] an officer of middle rank in an army or air force

**co·lo·ni·al** /kə'ləʊnɪəl/ *adj* [A *no comp.*] of or related to colonies (COLONY (1)): *The African people have successfully fought against colonial rule.*

**co·lo·ni·al·is·m** /kə'ləʊnɪəlɪzəm/ *n* [U] the having or keeping of colonies (COLONY (1)) abroad: *British colonialism led to the establishment of a large empire.* –compare IMPERIALISM **–colonialist** *adj,n*

**col·o·nize** ||also **-ise** *BrE* /'kɒlənaɪz||'kɑ-/ *v* **-nized, -nizing** [I;T] to make (a country, area, etc.) into a COLONY **–colonization** /ˌkɒlənaɪ'zeɪʃən||ˌkɑlənə-/ *n* [U] **–colonist** *n*

**col·on·nade** /ˌkɒlə'neɪd||ˌkɑ-/ *n* a row of pillars with equal spaces between

**col·o·ny** /'kɒləni||'kɑ-/ *n* **-nies** **1** a country or area under the control of a distant country and often settled by people from that country **2** a group of people from the same country or with the same interests, living together: *the French colony in Saigon* **3** a group of the same kind of animals or plants living or growing together: *a colony of plants*

**co·los·sal** /kə'lɒsəl||kə'lɑ-/ *adj* very large: *a colossal building/debt* –see Study Notes on page 494

**co·los·sus** /kə'lɒsəs||kə'lɑ-/ *n* **-suses** *or* **-si** /saɪ/ a person or thing of very great size: *a colossus of a man*

**col·our¹** *BrE*||**color** *AmE* /'kʌləʳ/ *n* **1** [U] the quality which allows one to see the difference between (for example) a red flower and a blue flower when both are the same size and shape **2** [C] red, blue, green, black, brown, yellow, white, etc.: *"What colour is this paint?" "It's red."*|*What colour did you paint the door?* **3** [C;U] (a) paint; DYE: *The artist painted in watercolours.* **4** [U] the general appearance of the skin; COMPLEXION: *As she became more annoyed Jean's colour changed.*|*You look a little* **off colour** (=a little ill) *today.* **5** [U] details or behaviour of a place, thing, or person, that interest the mind or eye and excite the imagination: *She loved the life, noise, and colour of the market.*

USAGE When asking questions about colour, say *What* **colour** *is it?* (not **What* **colour** *has it?*) When answering, say *It's red.* (not **a red* **colour**).

**colour²** *BrE*||**color** *AmE v* **1** [T *in*] to cause (something) to have colour, esp. with a CRAYON or pencil rather than a brush: *The child is colouring the picture.* **2** [I] to take on or change colour: *The leaves start to colour in autumn.* **3** [T] to give a special effect or feeling to (a person, event, etc.): *Personal feelings coloured* (=influenced) *his judgment.* **4** [I] to become red in the face; BLUSH: *He coloured with annoyance.* –compare DISCOLOUR

**colour bar** /'·· ·/ ||also **color line** *AmE– n* the set of customs or laws in some places which prevent people of different colours from mixing freely

**colour-blind** /'·· ·/ *adj* unable to see the difference between certain colours –**colour blindness** *n* [U]

**col·oured¹** *BrE*||**colored** *AmE* /'kʌləd||-ərd/ *adj* **1** *euph* belonging to a race that does not have a white skin: *Many coloured people live in Bradford.* **2** of the stated colour: *She wore a cream-coloured dress.*

USAGE Many non-whites now prefer to be called **black**, and think that **coloured** is offensive.

**coloured²** *BrE*||**colored** *AmE n often derog* a person belonging to a race that does not have a white skin

**col·our·ful** *BrE*||**colorful** *AmE* /'kʌləfəl||-ər-/ *adj* **1** showily coloured; full of colour or colours; bright: *a bird with colourful wings* **2** exciting the senses or imagination; rich in expressive variety or detail: *a colourful period of history*

**col·our·ing** *BrE*||**coloring** *AmE* /'kʌlərɪŋ/ *n* **1** [C;U] a substance used for giving a special colour to another substance, esp. food; DYE: *This tin of beans contains no artificial colouring.* **2** [U] (healthy or ill appearance as expressed by) skin colour: *People always think I'm ill because of my colouring.*

**col·our·less** *BrE*||**colorless** *AmE* /'kʌlələs||-ər-/ *adj* **1** without colour: *Water is a colourless liquid.* **2** dull; lacking variety, interest, excitement, etc.

**col·ours** *BrE*||**colors** *AmE* /'kʌləz||-ərz/ *n* [P] **1** the official flag of a country, ship, part of an army, etc. **2** a dress, cap, piece of material, etc., worn as a sign of one's club, school, team, etc. **3 with flying colours** with great success: *She passed her examination with flying colours.*

**colt** /kəʊlt/ *n* a young male horse –compare FILLY

**col·umn** /'kɒləm||'kɑ-/ *n* **1** a pillar used in a building as a support or decoration or standing alone as a MONUMENT **2** anything looking like a pillar in shape or use: *a column of smoke|to add up a column of figures|a column of soldiers marching down the road* **3** an article by a particular writer, that regularly appears in a newspaper or magazine

**col·umn·ist** /'kɒləməst, -ləmnəst||'kɑ-/ *n* a person who writes a regular article for a newspaper or magazine

**co·ma** /'kəʊmə/ *n* a state of long unnatural deep unconsciousness, from which it is difficult to wake up, caused by disease, poisoning, a severe blow, etc.: *After she drank the poison she* **went into a coma.**

**co·ma·tose** /'kəʊmətəʊs/ *adj tech* in a COMA; deeply unconscious

**comb¹** /kəʊm/ *n* **1** [C] a toothed piece of bone, metal, plastic, etc., used for tidying and straightening the hair **2** [S] an act of combing: *Your hair needs a good comb.*

**comb²** *v* [T] **1** to tidy, straighten, or arrange with a comb: *If you combed your hair more often you wouldn't look so untidy.* **2** to search (a place) thoroughly: *The police combed the woods for the missing boy.*

**com·bat¹** /'kɒmbæt, kəm'bæt||kəm'bæt, 'kɑmbæt/ *v* **-tt-** *BrE*|| **-t-** *or* **-tt-** *AmE* [I;T] *fml* to fight or struggle against: *to combat evil|The doctor spent his life combatting disease.*

**com·bat²** /'kɒmbæt||'kɑm-/ *n* [C;U] (a) struggle between two people, armies, ideas, etc.: *These soldiers have just been* **in combat**. (=fighting)

**com·ba·tant** /'kɒmbətənt||kəm'bætənt/ *n* a person playing a direct part in fighting: *In the last war as many noncombatants as combatants were killed.*

**com·bi·na·tion** /ˌkɒmbə'neɪʃən||ˌkɑm-/ *n* **1** [U] the act of combining or state of being combined **2** [C] a number of people or things that are combined or united in a common purpose: *A combination of parties formed the new government.* **3** [C] the list of special numbers or letters needed to open a special lock, SAFE, etc.

**com·bine¹** /kəm'baɪn/ *v* **-bined, -bining** [I;T] to (cause to) come together, unite, or join together: *The two parties have combined to form a government.*

**com·bine²** /'kɒmbaɪn||'kɑm-/ *n* a group of people, businesses, etc., joined or acting together

**com·bus·ti·ble** /kəm'bʌstəbəl/ *n,adj* (a substance) that can catch fire and burn easily: *Petrol is highly combustible so don't smoke while you're handling it.*

**com·bus·tion** /kəm'bʌstʃən/ *n* [U] the act of catching fire and burning

**come** /kʌm/ *v* **came** /keɪm/, **come, coming** [I] **1** [+*v-ing*] to move towards the speaker or a particular place: *I recognized him as soon as he came towards me through the door.|The little girl came running to me for sympathy.|The train came slowly into the station.* **2** to arrive: *I've been waiting for hours and he still hasn't come!|Darkness comes at six o'clock.|Christmas is coming soon.* **3** to reach: *The water came (up) to my neck.|Her hair comes (down) to her waist.* **4** to be in a particular place or position: *In this list of goods the price comes next to the article.|A comes before B.|Monday comes after Sunday.|Your family should always* **come before** (=be more important than) *your job.* **5** [+*to-v*] to happen: *How did Jean come to be invited to this party?|No good will come of* (=happen as a result of) *all this.* **6** [+*to-v*] to begin: *Later you may come to enjoy school.* **7** to become: *The buttons on my coat came unfastened.|The door came open.* –compare COME **away**, COME **off** –see BECOME (USAGE) **8** to be offered, produced, etc.: *Shoes come in many shapes and sizes.|Milk comes from cows or other animals.* **9 come and go** to pass or disappear quickly; change: *Fashions come and go but this dress is always popular.* **10 come unstuck** to meet with difficulties or failure: *The government's going to come unstuck if prices keep rising.* **11 how come?** *infml* how did it happen (that): *How come you got that job at the factory?* **12 to come** in the future: *the years/days to* *come* –compare GO[1]

**come about** *v adv* [I +*that*] to happen: *How did this dangerous state of affairs come about?*

**come across[1]/upon** sbdy./sthg. *v prep* [T *no pass.*] to meet or discover, esp. by chance: *I've just come across an old friend I haven't seen for years.*

**come across[2]** *v adv* [I] *infml* to be effective and well received: *Your speech came across very well; everyone liked it.*

**come along** *v adv* [I] **1** also **come on**– to advance; improve, esp. in health: *How's your work coming along?|Mother's coming along nicely, thank you.* **2** to happen; arrive by chance: *I got the job because I came along at the right time.* **3 Come along!** also **Come on (now)!**– *infml* Try harder!; Hurry up!

**come apart** *v adv* [I] to break into pieces without the need of force: *I picked up the old book and it just came apart in my hands.*

**come at** sbdy./sthg. *v prep* [T *no pass.*] to advance towards in a threatening manner: *She came at me with a knife.*

**come away** *v adv* [I *from*] to become disconnected without being forced: *I only touched the handle; it came away in my hands.*

**come back** *v adv* [I] **1** to return **2** [*to*] to return to memory: *It's suddenly come back to me where I met you.* **3** to become fashionable or popular again: *Do you think long dresses will ever come back?* –see also COMEBACK

**come between** sbdy./sthg. *v prep* [T *no pass.*] to interrupt (two people or things); cause trouble between (two people or things): *John lets nothing come between himself and his work.*

**come by** sthg. *v prep* [T] to obtain or receive: *Jobs are* **hard to come by** (=difficult to find) *with so many people out of work.|How did you come by that wound in your arm?*

**come down** *v adv* [I] **1** to fall: *The roof came down during the night.*|(fig.) *I don't think meat will come down* (=fall in price) *this year, do you?*|(fig.) *Since Julia lost her job, she has really* **come down in the world.** (=fallen to a humbler standard of living) **2** to be passed on from one period of history to another: *This song comes down to us from the 10th century.* **3 come down in favour of/on the side of** to decide to support: *The industrial court came down on the side of the unions.* **4 come down to earth** to return to reality –compare COMEDOWN

**come down on** sbdy./sthg. *v adv prep* [T *no pass.*] to punish: *The courts are going to come down heavily on young criminals.*

**come down to** sthg. *v adv prep* [T +*v-ing; no pass.*] to be able to be reduced to: *Our choices come down to going or staying.*

**come down with** sthg. *v adv prep* [T *no pass.*] *infml* to catch (an infectious illness): *I think I'm coming down with a cold.*

**SPELLING NOTE**

Words with the sound /k/, like **cut**, may be spelt **k-**, like **key**, or **qu-**, like **queen.**
Words with the sound /s/, like **city**, may be spelt **s-**, like **soon**, or **ps-**, like **psychology.**

**come forward** *v adv* [I] to offer oneself to fill a position, give help to the police, etc.: *No one has come forward with information about the murder.*

**come from** sthg. *v prep* [T *no pass;* not *be +v-ing*] to have as a place of origin: *I come from Newcastle but have spent most of my life in London.|Where do you come from?*

**come in** *v adv* [I] **1** to arrive as expected: *Has the train come in yet?* **2** also **get in**– to be elected; come into power; win: *If the Workers' Party comes in at the next election, there will be a lot of changes.* **3** to become fashionable, seasonal, etc.: *When did the short skirt first come in?* **4** to be: *This material will* **come in useful/handy** *one day, so don't throw it away.*

**come in for** sthg. *v adv prep* [T *no pass.*] to receive (esp. blame): *He came in for a lot of the blame for the accident.*

**come in on** sthg. *v adv prep* [T *no pass.*] *infml* to join; take part in: *Let's ask Alice to come in on the plan.*

**come into** sthg. *v prep* [T] **1** to gain (a sum of money), esp. after someone's death; INHERIT: *He came into a fortune when his mother died.* **2** (*before nouns of type* [U] ) to begin to be in (a state or activity): *to come into fashion/existence/force/consideration|The town came into sight as we turned the corner.*

**come of** sthg. *v prep* [T *no pass.*] **1** to result from: *I don't know if any good will come of your actions.* **2 come of age** to reach an age (usu. 18 or 21) when one is considered by law to be responsible for oneself and for obedience to the law

**come off[1]** *v adv* [I] **1** to become unfastened or disconnected: *A button came off my coat.* **2** to take place; happen, esp. successfully: *The wedding came off as planned.*

**come off[2]** *v prep* **Come off it!** (usu. in giving an order) to stop lying or pretending: *Come off it; tell the truth!*

**come on** *v adv* [I] *infml* **1** to start: *I can feel a cold coming on.* **2** →COME **along** (1, 3)

**come out** *v adv* [I] **1** to appear: *The stars came out as soon as it was dark.|When will John's new book come out?* (=be offered for sale to the public) **2** to become known: *The news came out that the king was very ill.* **3** to be seen, as in a photograph: *Mary always comes out well in pictures.* **4** (of a photograph) to be DEVELOPed: *The pictures I took didn't come out; I'll have to take some more.* **5** (of colour, a mark, etc.) to be removed; disappear: *I've washed this shirt twice and the ink still hasn't come out.* **6** to refuse to work: *Workers in all the factories are coming out in support of the dismissed men.* **7** to end in the stated way: *The answer to the sum came out wrong/right.*

**come out against** sthg. *v adv prep* [T +*v-ing; no pass.*] to declare one's opposition to: *The American government came out against the new British plane.*

**come out in** sthg. *v adv prep* [T *no pass.*] *infml* to be partly covered by (marks caused by an illness or disease): *Jean has come out in spots so she's staying in bed.*

**come out with** sthg. *v adv prep* [T *no pass.*] *infml* to say, esp. suddenly or unexpectedly: *John came out with a foolish remark.*

**come over**[1] *v adv* [I] **1** [*to, from*] to come from a distance: *When did you first come over to England?* **2** to make a short informal visit: *Come over and see us sometime.* **3** [*to*] to change sides or opinions; COME **round** (2) **4** →COME **across**[2]

**come over**[2] sbdy. *v prep* [T *no pass.*] (of a sudden strong feeling) to trouble or annoy (someone): *A feeling of faintness came over me, so I had to lie down.*

**come round** *v adv* [I] **1** also **come to, come around**– to regain consciousness **2** [*to*] to change sides or opinions: *He'll come round to our way of thinking sooner or later.* **3** to happen regularly: *It's coming round to Christmas again.* **4** to travel a longer way than usual: *We came round by the fields as we didn't want to go through the woods in the dark.* **5** →COME **over**[1] (2)

**come through**[1] *v adv* [I] to arrive as expected: *Have your examination results come through yet?*

**come through**[2] *v adv; prep* [I;T *no pass.*] to continue to live after (something dangerous): *John was so ill he was lucky to come through (his operation).*

**come to** sbdy./sthg. *v prep* [T] **1** [*no pass.*] to reach; arrive at: *It has come to my notice* (=I have discovered) *that some money is missing.*|*to come to an end*|*The bill came to* (=amounted to) *£5.50.* **2** [+*v-ing; no pass.*] to concern: *When it comes to politics I know nothing.* **3** [*no pass.*] to enter the mind suddenly: *Suddenly the words of the song came to me.* **4 come to pass** *fml* to happen **5 What is X coming to?** (asked when X is becoming worse) What is going to happen to X?: *What's the world coming to?*

**come under** sthg. *v prep* [T *no pass.*] **1** to be governed or controlled by: *This committee will come under the new Education Department.* **2** to receive: *We came under heavy enemy gunfire.* **3** to be able to be found below or after (a key word, heading, etc.): *What heading does this come under?*

**come up** *v adv* [I] **1** to come to attention or consideration: *Your question came up at the meeting.* **2** to happen: *I'll let you know if anything comes up.* **3** to come near: *He came up and said, "Pleased to see you".* **4 come up in the world** to reach a higher standard of living or social rank –opposite **come down in the world**

**come up against** sbdy./sthg. *v adv prep* [T *no pass.*] to meet (usu. a difficulty or opposition): *They came up against problem after problem.*

**come up to** sthg. *v adv prep* [T] to equal: *Your recent work hasn't come up to your usual high standards.*

**come up with** sthg. *v adv prep* [T *no pass.*] *infml* to think of (a plan, answer, reply, etc.); produce: *He couldn't come up with the answer.*

**come·back** /'kʌmbæk/ *n* a return to a former position of strength or importance: *The old actor made a successful comeback after twenty years.* –see also COME **back**

**co·me·di·an** /kə'mi:dɪən/ *n* **1** an actor whose job is telling jokes or making people laugh **2** *infml* an amusing person: *Paul's a real comedian; he's always very funny.*

**co·me·di·enne** /kəˌmi:di'en/ *n* an actress whose job is telling jokes or making people laugh

**come·down** /'kʌmdaʊn/ *n infml* a fall in importance, rank, or respect: *It's a bit of a comedown to leave school and then not get a job.* –compare COME **down**

**com·e·dy** /'kɒmədi||'kɑ-/ *n* **-dies** [C;U] a (type of) funny play, film, or other work in which the story and characters are amusing and which ends happily –compare TRAGEDY

**come-hith·er** /ˌ·'··◂/ *adj* [A] *infml* purposefully attractive in a sexual way: *a come-hither look*

**come·ly** /'kʌmli/ *adj* **-lier, -liest** *lit* attractive; having a pleasing appearance: *a comely young woman* –**comeliness** *n* [U]

**com·et** /'kɒmət||'kɑ-/ *n* a heavenly body, like a very bright star, that moves round the sun

**com·fort**[1] /'kʌmfət||-ərt/ *n* **1** [U] the state of being free from anxiety, pain, or suffering, and of having all one's bodily wants satisfied: *to live* **in comfort** **2** [C;U] (a person or thing that gives) strength, hope, or sympathy: *My husband was a great comfort to me when I was ill.*|*The priest spoke a few words of comfort to the dying man.* –see also DISCOMFORT

**comfort**[2] *v* [T] to give COMFORT[1] (2) to: *I tried to comfort Jean after her mother's death.* –**comforter** *n*

**com·for·ta·ble** /'kʌmftəbəl, 'kʌmfət-||'kʌmfərt-, 'kʌmft-/ also **comfy, -fier, -fiest** *infml*– *adj* **1** having or providing comfort: *a comfortable chair*|*a comfortable income* **2** [F] not experiencing (too much) pain, grief, anxiety, etc.: *The doctor said that mother was comfortable after her operation.* –see also UNCOMFORTABLE –**comfortably** /-təbli / *adv*

**com·ic**[1] /'kɒmɪk||'kɑ-/ *adj* **1** funny; causing laughter; humorous: *a comic performance* **2** [A] of COMEDY: *a comic actress* –compare TRAGIC

**comic**[2] *n* **1** also **comic book** *AmE*– a magazine for children containing COMIC STRIPS **2** *infml* a person who is funny or amusing, esp. a professional COMEDIAN (1)

**com·i·cal** /'kɒmɪkəl||'kɑ-/ *adj* amusing in an odd way; strange

**comic strip** /'·· ·/||also **strip cartoon** *BrE* /'· ·ˌ·/– *n* a set of drawings telling a short story, often with words showing the speech of the characters in the pictures

**com·ing**[1] /'kʌmɪŋ/ *n* [S] **1** arrival: *With the coming of winter days get shorter.* **2 comings and goings** *infml* acts of arriving and leaving: *We saw the comings and goings of the visitors from our bedroom window.*

**coming**[2] *adj* [A] that is coming or will come: *the coming winter*

**com·ma** /'kɒmə||'kɑmə/ *n* the mark (,) used in writing and printing for showing a short pause

**com·mand**[1] /kə'mɑ:nd||kə'mænd/ *v* **1** [I;T +*that*] to direct (a person or people), with the right to be obeyed; order: *He commanded that we (should) attack at once.*|*The king commands the armed forces.* –see ORDER[2] (USAGE) **2** [T] to deserve and get: *This great man is able to* **command** *everyone's* **respect.**

**command**[2] *n* **1** [C] an order: *All his commands were quickly obeyed.* **2** [U *of*] control: *The army is under the king's direct command.*|*Who is* **in command of** *our navy?* **3** [S;U] the ability to control and use: *He has (a) good command of spoken French.*

**com·man·dant** /ˌkɒmən'dænt||'kɑməndænt/ *n*

[A;C] the chief officer in charge of a military organization

**com·man·deer** /ˌkɒmən'dɪəʳ‖ˌkɑ-/ *v* [T] to seize (private property) for public, esp. military use: *The soldiers commandeered the houses.*

**com·mand·er** /kə'mɑːndəʳ‖kə'mæn-/ *n* [A;C] an officer of middle rank in a navy or air force

**com·mand·ing** /kə'mɑːndɪŋ‖kə'mæn-/ *adj* **1** [A] having command; being in charge: *Who's your commanding officer?* **2** deserving or expecting respect and obedience: *The teacher has such a commanding voice that everyone obeys her.*

**com·mand·ment** /kə'mɑːndmənt‖kə'mænd-/ *n* *(often cap.)* any of the ten laws (**Ten Commandments**) which according to the Bible were given by God to the Jews on Mount Sinai

**com·man·do** /kə'mɑːndəʊ‖kə'mæn-/ *n* **-dos** *or* **-does** (a member of) a small fighting force specially trained for making quick attacks into enemy areas

**com·mem·o·rate** /kə'meməreɪt/ *v* **-rated, -rating** [T] to be in memory of; give honour to the memory of: *This building commemorates those who died in the war.* –**commemoration** /-'reɪʃən/ *n* [U]: *A religious service will be held* **in commemoration of** *those who died in the war.* –**commemorative** *adj*: *a commemorative stamp*

**com·mence** /kə'mens/ *v* **-menced, -mencing** [I;T +*to-v*/*v-ing*] *fml* to begin; start: *The meeting commenced at 8 o'clock.* –**commencement** *n* [U]

**com·mend** /kə'mend/ *v* [T *to*] *fml* **1** to speak favourably of: *Our shop has always been very highly commended.* **2** to put (esp. oneself) into the care or charge of someone else: *The dying man commended his soul/himself to God.*

**com·men·da·ble** /kə'mendəbəl/ *adj* worthy of praise: *commendable efforts* –**commendably** *adv*

**com·men·da·tion** /ˌkɒmən'deɪʃən‖ˌkɑ-/ *n* an official prize or honour given because of one's good qualities: *She was given a commendation for bravery after she saved the children from the fire.*

**com·men·su·rate** /kə'menʃərɪ̇t/ *adj* [*with*] *fml* equal to; fitting; suitable: *He was given a job commensurate with his abilities.*

**com·ment¹** /'kɒment‖'kɑ-/ *n* [C;U] (an) opinion, explanation, or judgment written or spoken about an event, person, state of affairs, etc.: *I asked the minister if she had any comments about the election.*|*No comment!* (=I've nothing to say)

**comment²** *v* [I;T +*that*/*on, upon*] to make a remark; give an opinion: *The teacher refused to comment on the examination results.*

**com·men·ta·ry** /'kɒməntəri‖'kɑmənteri/ *n* **-ries 1** [C] a written collection of opinions, explanations, judgments, etc., on a book, event, person, etc. **2** [C;U] (a number of) opinions or descriptions spoken and usu. broadcast during an event, football match, etc.: *a sports commentary on the radio*

> **SPELLING NOTE**
> Words with the sound /k/, like **cut**, may be spelt **k-**, like **key**, or **qu-**, like **queen.**
> Words with the sound /s/, like **city**, may be spelt **s-**, like **soon**, or **ps-**, like **psychology.**

**com·men·tate** /'kɒmənteɪt‖'kɑ-/ *v* **-tated, -tating** [I *on*] to give a COMMENTARY (2) –**commentator** *n*: *a football commentator*

**com·merce** /'kɒmɜːs‖'kɑmɜrs/ *n* [U] the buying and selling of goods, esp. between different countries; trade: *Our country has grown rich because of its commerce with other nations.*

**com·mer·cial¹** /kə'mɜːʃəl‖kə'mɜr-/ *adj* **1** of, related to, or used in COMMERCE: *Our commercial laws changed when we joined the EEC.* **2** likely to produce profit: *Oil has been found in commercial quantities in the North Sea.* –**commercially** *adv*

**commercial²** *n* an advertisement on television or radio

**com·mer·cial·ize**‖also **-ise** *BrE* /kə'mɜːʃəlaɪz‖kə'mɜr-/ *v* **-ized, -izing** [T] *often derog* to make (something) a matter of profit: *Do you agree that Christmas is too commercialized these days?* –**commercialism** *n* [U]

**commercial ve·hi·cle** /·ˌ·· '···/ *n* a vehicle used for carrying goods from place to place

**com·mie** /'kɒmi‖'kɑ-/ *n infml derog* for COMMUNIST

**com·mis·e·rate with** sbdy. /kə'mɪzəreɪt/ *v prep* **-ated, -ating** [T] to feel or express sympathy, sorrow, or pity for (a person): *I commiserated with my friend after he failed his examination.*

**com·mis·e·ra·tion** /kəˌmɪzə'reɪʃən/ *n* [C;U] (an expression of) sorrow, sympathy, or pity for the misfortune of another

**com·mis·sion¹** /kə'mɪʃən/ *n* **1** [C;U] (an amount of) money, usu. related to the value of goods sold, paid to the salesman who sold them: *He gets 10% commission so if he sells goods worth £100 his commission is £10.* **2** [U] the act of giving special powers or certain duties to a person or group of people **3** [C +*to-v*] the job, duty, or power given in such a way: *The commission for the new theatre was given to a well-known* ARCHITECT. **4** [C +*sing.*/*pl. v*] *(often cap.)* a group of people specially appointed to RESEARCH and write a report on a special subject: *She established a commission to suggest improvements in the educational system.* –compare COMMITTEE **5** [C] (an official paper appointing someone to) any of several high ranks in the armed forces

**commission²** *v* [T] to give a COMMISSION¹ (3,5) to (a person or group of people): *The King commissioned an artist to paint a picture of the Queen.*

**com·mis·sion·aire** /kəˌmɪʃə'neəʳ/ *n esp. BrE* a uniformed attendant at the entrance to a cinema, theatre, hotel, etc.

**com·mis·sion·er** /kə'mɪʃənəʳ/ *n (often cap.)* **1** [A;C] (in some countries) an official in charge of a certain government department: *Commissioner Addo is responsible for education.* **2** [C] a member of a COMMISSION¹ (4)

**com·mit** /kə'mɪt/ *v* **-tt-** [T] **1** to do (something wrong, bad, or illegal): *to commit a crime*|*commit* SUICIDE **2** [*to; usu. pass.*] to order (someone) to be placed under the control of another, esp. in prison or in a MENTAL (3) hospital: *He was found guilty and committed to prison.* **3** [*to*] to promise (esp. oneself, one's property, etc.) to a certain cause, opinion, or course of action: *The government has committed itself to improving the National Health Service.*|*He* *won't* **commit himself on** (=give his opinion on) *women's rights.* **4 commit to memory** *fml* for MEMORIZE: *He committed the address to memory.*

**com·mit·ment** /kə'mɪtmənt/ *n* [C +*to-v*] a responsibility or promise to follow certain beliefs or a certain course of action: *We must honour our commitments to smaller nations.*|*I don't want to get married because I don't want any commitments.*

**com·mit·tal** /kə'mɪtl/ *n* [C;U] (an example of) the act of sending a person to prison or to a MENTAL (3) hospital

**com·mit·ted** /kə'mɪtɪ̠d/ *adj* [*to*] giving one's whole loyalty to a particular aim, job, or way of life: *Jean's a committed nurse/Christian/teacher.*

**com·mit·tee** /kə'mɪti/ *n* [C +*sing./pl. v*] a group of people chosen, esp. by a larger group, to do a particular job or for special duties: *He's on the education committee.*|*The committee meets/meet every week.* –compare COMMISSION (4)

**com·mod·i·ty** /kə'mɒdɪ̠ti‖kə'mɑ-/ *n* **-ties** an article of trade or COMMERCE, esp. a farm or mineral product: *Wine is one of the many commodities that France sells abroad.*

**com·mo·dore** /'kɒmədɔːʳ‖'kɑmədor/ *n* [A;C] an officer of middle rank in the navy

**com·mon¹** /'kɒmən‖'kɑ-/ *adj* **1** found or happening often and in many places; usual: *Rabbits and foxes are common in Britain.* –compare SCARCE **2** [*no comp.*] of no special quality; ordinary: *the common man/woman*|*Common salt is very cheap.*|*the* **common cold 3** [*no comp.*] **a** belonging to or shared equally by two or more; united; JOINT²: *the common desire of France and Britain* **b** of or belonging to society as a whole; public: **The common good** *would best be served by keeping prices from rising too quickly.*|*It is* **common knowledge** *among politicians that an election will soon be called.*|*When it comes to politics, my mother and I are* **on common ground.** (=we share the same beliefs) **4** *derog* coarse in manner; VULGAR: *The way you speak is very common.*|*I don't like him; he's* **as common as muck/dirt.** (=very common) **–commonness** *n* [U]

**common²** *n* **1** (*often in names*) an area of grassland with no fences which all people are free to use: *Every Saturday Jean went riding on the village common.* **2 in common** in shared possession: *John and I have nothing in common.* (=no shared interests, qualities, etc.)

**com·mon·er** /'kɒmənəʳ‖'kɑ-/ *n* a person who is not a member of a noble family; person without a title –compare NOBLE²

**common law** /ˌ·· '·◂/ *n* [U] *tech* the unwritten law based on custom and court decisions rather than on laws made by Parliament **–common-law** *adj* [A]: *She's his common-law wife because she's lived with him for three years without marrying him.*

**com·mon·ly** /'kɒmənli‖'kɑ-/ *adj* **1** usually; generally; ordinarily –compare UNCOMMONLY **2** *derog* in a COMMON¹ (4) manner

**Common Mar·ket** /ˌ·· '··◂/ *n* [*the* S] → EEC

**common noun** /ˌ·· '·/ *n tech* a noun that is not the name of a particular person, place, or thing: *"Book" and "sugar" are common nouns in English.* –see also PROPER NOUN

**common-or-gar·den** /ˌ·· · '··◂/ *adj* [A] *BrE infml* ordinary: *They've got a common-or-garden house just like anyone else.*

**com·mon·place** /'kɒmənpleɪs‖'kɑ-/ *adj* common; ordinary: *Soon it will be commonplace for people to travel to the moon.*

**Com·mons** /'kɒmənz‖'kɑ-/ *n* [*the* S] see HOUSE¹ (3)

**common sense** /ˌ··'·◂/ *n* practical good sense and judgment gained from experience, rather than special knowledge from school or study: *Although he's not very clever he's got lots of common sense.*|*a common sense approach to the problem* –see also SENSIBLE

**Com·mon·wealth** /'kɒmənwelθ‖'kɑ-/ also **Commonwealth of Nations** *fml*– *n* [*the* S] an organization of independent states which were formerly parts of the British Empire, established to encourage trade and friendly relations among its members

**com·mo·tion** /kə'məʊʃən/ *n* [C;U] (an example of) great and noisy confusion or excitement: *The imprisonment of the union leaders caused a commotion in Parliament.*

**com·mu·nal** /'kɒmjʊnəl‖kə'mjuː-/ *adj* [*no comp.*] shared by or used by members of a group or a COMMUNITY: *communal land*|*communal tools*

**com·mune¹** /kə'mjuːn/ *v* **-muned, -muning** [I *with, together*] *esp. lit* to exchange thoughts, ideas, or feelings

**commune²** /'kɒmjuːn‖'kɑ-, kə'mjuːn/ *n* [C +*sing./pl. v*] **1** (esp. in countries practising COMMUNISM) a group of people who work as a team for the general good, esp. in raising crops and animals **2** a group of people who live together, though not of the same family, and who share their lives and possessions

**com·mu·ni·ca·ble** /kə'mjuːnɪkəbəl/ *adj fml* that can be (easily) COMMUNICATED (=passed from one person to another): *a communicable disease*

**com·mu·ni·cate** /kə'mjuːnɪ̠keɪt/ *v* **-cated, -cating** *fml* **1** [T] to make (news, opinions, feelings, etc.) known: *I don't think the teacher communicates his ideas clearly.* **2** [I *with*] to share or exchange opinions, news, information, etc.: *Has the Minister for Foreign Affairs communicated with the American President yet?* **3** [I *with*] (esp. of rooms) to join; connect: *communicating bedrooms*

**com·mu·ni·ca·tion** /kəˌmjuːnɪ̠'keɪʃən/ *n* **1** [U] the act of communicating (COMMUNICATE (1, 2)): *Communication with France was difficult during the telephone and postal strike.*|*Radio and television are important* **means of communication. 2** [C] something COMMUNICATED; message: *I've had a communication from the minister.* –see also COMMUNICATIONS

**com·mu·ni·ca·tions** /kəˌmjuːnɪ̠'keɪʃənz/ *n* [P] the various ways of travelling, moving goods and people, and sending information between places; roads, railways, radio, telephone, television, etc.: *Moscow has excellent communications with all parts of the Soviet Union.*

**com·mu·ni·ca·tive** /kə'mjuːnɪ̠kətɪv/ *adj* readily and eagerly willing to talk or give information; not secretive

**com·mu·nion** /kə'mjuːnɪən/ *n* [U *with*] the sharing or exchange of beliefs, ideas, feelings, etc.

**Communion** also **Holy Communion**– *n* the religious service in Christian churches in which bread and wine are shared in a solemn ceremony; EUCHARIST –compare MASS

**com·mu·ni·qué** /kə'mjuːnɪ̇keɪ‖kə͵mjuːnɪ̇'keɪ/ *n* an official report or declaration, usu. to the public or newspapers: *In its latest communiqué the government suggests that both sides will soon reach an agreement.*

**com·mu·nis·m** /'kɒmjʊnɪzəm‖'kɑmjə-/ *n* [U] a classless social and political system in which the means of production are owned and controlled by the state or the people as a whole –compare SOCIALISM, CAPITALISM

**Communism** *n* [U] the international political movement aimed at establishing COMMUNISM

**com·mu·nist** /'kɒmjʊnɪ̇st‖'kɑmjə-/ *adj,n* (of or related to) a person, group, political party, or nation that favours the principles of COMMUNISM

**com·mu·ni·ty** /kə'mjuːnɪ̇ti/ *n* **-ties 1** [C +*sing./pl. v*] a group of people living together and/or united by shared interests, religion, nationality, etc.: *The Polish community in Britain has/have succeeded in keeping its/their language and way of life alive.* **2** [*the* S] the public; people in general: *The job of a politician is to serve the community.*

**com·mute** /kə'mjuːt/ *v* **-muted, -muting 1** [I] to travel regularly a long distance between one's home and work esp. by train: *She commutes from Cambridge to London/between Cambridge and London every day.* **2** [T] *fml* to make (a punishment) less severe

**com·mut·er** /kə'mjuːtəʳ/ *n* a person who COMMUTES (1)

**com·pact¹** /kəm'pækt/ *adj* **1** firmly and closely packed together; solid: *The trees grew in a compact mass.* **2** arranged in or filling a small space: *a compact little flat* **–compactly** *adv* **–compactness** *n* [U]

**com·pact²** /'kɒmpækt‖'kɑm-/ *n* **1** a small flat usu. round container for a woman's face powder (=a type of COSMETIC¹), usu. with a mirror **2** also **compact car** /͵·· '·/ *esp. AmE*– a small car

**com·pact³** /'kɒmpækt‖'kɑm-/ *n fml* an agreement between two or more parties, countries, etc.

**com·pact·ed** /kəm'pæktɪ̇d/ *adj* pressed, joined together, or united firmly and closely: *a compacted mass of snow*

**com·pan·ion** /kəm'pænjən/ *n* **1** a person who spends time with another, because he/she is a friend or by chance, as when travelling: *He was my only companion during the war.*|*My fellow travellers made/were good companions.* **2** either of a pair or set of things; one thing that matches another **3** (usu. in titles) a book which gives one instructions on how to do something; guide; HANDBOOK: *the Motorist's Companion*

**com·pan·io·na·ble** /kəm'pænjənəbəl/ *adj* friendly; likely to be a good companion

> **SPELLING NOTE**
> Words with the sound /k/, like **cut**, may be spelt **k-**, like **key**, or **qu-**, like **queen.**
> Words with the sound /s/, like **city**, may be spelt **s-**, like **soon**, or **ps-**, like **psychology.**

**com·pan·ion·ship** /kəm'pænjənʃɪp/ *n* [U] the relationship of companions; friendly company; fellowship: *He missed the companionship he'd enjoyed in the navy.*

**com·pa·ny** /'kʌmpəni/ *n* **-nies 1** [C +*sing./pl. v*] a group of people combined together for business, trade, artistic purposes, etc.: *a bus company*|*Which company do you work for?*|*The theatre company make/makes a tour of the country every summer.* **2** [U] companionship; fellowship: *I was grateful for Jean's company when I travelled up to Edinburgh.*|*After two years of marriage they* **parted company.** (=ended their relationship) **3** [U] companions; the people with whom a person spends time: *John isn't very* **good company** (=a good person to be with) *at the moment.* **4** [U] one or more guests: *No, you can't go out tonight; we're expecting company.*|*You shouldn't swear* **in company.** (=when guests are present) **5** [C +*sing./pl. v*] a body of (usu. about 120) soldiers

**com·pa·ra·ble** /'kɒmpərəbəl‖'kɑm-/ *adj fml* that can be compared: *A comparable car would cost far more abroad.* –see also INCOMPARABLE **–comparably** *adv*

**com·par·a·tive¹** /kəm'pærətɪv/ *adj* **1** making a comparison: *a comparative study of European languages* **2** measured or judged by comparison: *the comparative wealth of the south of England* (=its wealth compared with the rest of the country) **3** of or related to the form of adjectives or adverbs expressing an increase in quality, quantity, or degree: *"Bigger" is the comparative form of "big".*|*"Worse" is the comparative form of "bad."* **–comparatively** *adv*

**comparative²** *n tech* the COMPARATIVE¹ (3) form of an adjective or adverb: *"Better" is the comparative of "good".* –see Study Notes on page opposite

**com·par·a·tive·ly** /kəm'pærətɪ̇vli/ *adv* **1** to a certain degree; rather: *Man is a comparatively new creature on the face of the earth.* **2** in a COMPARATIVE¹ (1) way

**com·pare** /kəm'peəʳ/ *v* **-pared, -paring** [T *to, with*] **1** to examine or judge (one thing) against another in order to show the points of likeness or difference: *If you compare British football with American football you'll find many differences.*|*If you compare both of our cars you'll find they're very much alike.* **2** to show the likeness or relationship of (one thing and another): *It's impossible to compare the two towns; they're quite different.*

USAGE **Compare** can be followed by "to" or "with": *London is large,* **compared** *to/with Paris.* **Compare to** usually means to say that one thing is similar to something else; **compare with** usually means to examine the ways in which one thing is similar to or different from another: *The writer of the poem* **compares** *his lover* **to** *a rose.* (=says she is like a rose)|*In today's lesson we will* **compare** *the British system of government* **with** *the American.*

**compare with** sbdy./sthg. *v prep* [T +*v-ing*] to be worthy of comparison with: *Living in a town can't compare with living in the country.*

**com·pa·ri·son** /kəm'pærɪ̇sən/ *n* **1** [U] the act of comparing : *By/In comparison with London, Paris is small.* **2** [C] the result of comparing; a statement of

## STUDY NOTES more and most, -er and -est

The COMPARATIVE and SUPERLATIVE forms of adjectives and adverbs, which are used to show an increase in quality, quantity, or degree, are formed in three ways:

by adding **-er** and **-est** to the end of short words, like this:

*Peter, David, and Stephen are all* **tall**.
*Peter is* **taller than** David.
*Stephen is* **taller than** *both David and Peter.*
*Stephen is* **the tallest** *of the three.*

by adding **more** and **most** before longer words, like this:

*All of these rings are* **expensive.**
*The gold ring is* **more expensive than** *the silver ring.*
*The diamond ring is* **more expensive than** *both the silver ring and the gold ring.*
*The diamond ring is* **the most expensive.**

by using a different word, like this:

All of the girls' work is **good**.
*Mary's work is* **better than** *Anne's.*
*Jane's work is* **better than** *both Anne's and Mary's.*
*Jane's work is* **the best**.

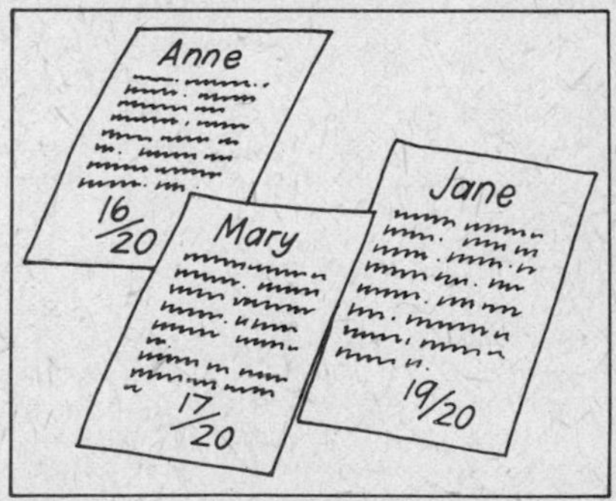


Other words like this are **bad, far, well, badly,** and **little** *adv*. Look these words up in the dictionary to see what their comparative and superlative forms are.

Note that some words, like **foreign** and **main**, have no comparative or superlative forms. These words cannot be used to show an increase in quality, quantity, or degree. They are marked in the dictionary like this [*no comp.*]:

> **main** *adj* [*no comp.*] chief; first in importance or size: *a busy main road*

*the points of likeness* and difference between two things **3** [U] likeness: *There is* **no comparison** *between frozen and fresh food.*

**com·part·ment** /kəm'pɑːtmənt‖-ɑr-/ *n* any of the parts into which an enclosed space is divided, such as **a** one of the small rooms in a railway carriage –see picture on page 501 **b** one of the small box-like containers inside the front of a car: *We sat in a second-class compartment.*|*The driver kept his maps in the* **glove compartment** *in the front of his car.* –see picture on page 85

**com·part·men·tal·ize**‖also **-ise** *BrE* /ˌkɒmpɑːt'mentl-aɪz‖kəmˌpɑrt- / *v* **-ized, -izing** [T] to divide into separate COMPARTMENTS

**com·pass** /'kʌmpəs/ *n* **1** an instrument for showing direction, usu. consisting of a freely-moving needle which always points to the north **2** [*usu. pl.*] a V-shaped instrument used for drawing circles, measuring distances on maps, etc. –see, PAIR[1] (USAGE) **3** [*usu. sing.*] *fml* an area; range; limit: *Finance is not* **within the compass of** *this department.*

**com·pas·sion** /kəm'pæʃən/ *n* [U] pity or sympathy for the sufferings and misfortunes of others, causing a desire to give help or show mercy: *The nurse showed great compassion for her patients.*

**com·pas·sion·ate** /kəm'pæʃənɪ̠t/ *adj* feeling or showing COMPASSION –**compassionately** *adv*

**com·pat·i·ble** /kəm'pætəbəl/ *adj* [F *with*] that can exist or work in agreement together or with another: *Their marriage ended because they were simply not compatible (with each other).* –opposite **incompatible** –**compatibly** *adv*

**com·pat·ri·ot** /kəm'pætrɪət‖-'peɪt-/ *n* a person who was born in or who is a citizen of the same country as another; COUNTRYMAN: *John and Jean are compatriots because they both come from Scotland.*

**com·pel** /kəm'pel/ *v* **-ll-** [T] to make (a person or thing) do something by or as if by force; make necessary: *My father compelled us to stay indoors.*|(fig.) *Her cleverness and skill compel our admiration.* (=compel us to admire her) –**compelling** *adj* –**compellingly** *adv*

**com·pen·di·um** /kəm'pendɪəm/ *n* **-diums** *or* **-dia** /dɪə/ *fml* a short but detailed and complete account of facts, information, a subject, etc.: *a compendium of useful information*

**com·pen·sate** /'kɒmpənseɪt‖'kɑm-/ *v* **-sated, -sating** [T +*v- ing*/*for*] to provide with a balancing effect for some loss or something lacking; make a suitable payment for some loss: *Many firms compensate their workers if they are hurt at work.*|*Nothing can compensate (me) for the loss of my wife/for losing my wife.* –**compensatory** /kəm'pensətəri, ˌkɒmpən'seɪ-‖kəm'pensətori/ *adj: compensatory payments*

**com·pen·sa·tion** /ˌkɒmpən'seɪʃən‖ˌkɑm-/ *n* [S;U *for*] something given to COMPENSATE: *Did you get any compensation* (=any money) *when you were dismissed from your job?*|*She received £10,000 in compensation for her husband's death.* –compare CONSOLATION, RECOMPENSE

> **SPELLING NOTE**
> Words with the sound /k/, like **cut**, may be spelt **k-**, like **key**, or **qu-**, like **queen.**
> Words with the sound /s/, like **city**, may be spelt **s-**, like **soon**, or **ps-**, like **psychology.**

**com·pere** /'kɒmpeəʳ‖'kɑm-/ *n,v* **-pered, -pering** [C;I;T] *BrE* (a person whose job is) to introduce the various acts in a stage or television show: *Who compered last night's show?*|*Who was the compere?*

**com·pete** /kəm'piːt/ *v* **-peted, -peting** [I +*to-v*] to try to win something in competition with someone else: *John competed for a place at the school, but didn't get in.*|*Only four horses competed in the race.*

**com·pe·tence** /'kɒmpɪ̠təns‖'kɑm-/ *n* [U] ability to do what is needed; skill: *Janet drives with competence.* –opposite **incompetence** –see GENIUS (USAGE)

**com·pe·tent** /'kɒmpɪ̠tənt‖'kɑm-/ *adj* **1** having the ability or skill to do what is needed: *a competent swimmer* –opposite **incompetent** **2** very satisfactory: *She did a competent job.* –**competently** *adv*

**com·pe·ti·tion** /ˌkɒmpɪ̠'tɪʃən‖ˌkɑm-/ *n* **1** [U] the act of competing: *He was* **in competition with** *10 others, so he did well to win the race.* **2** [C] a test of strength, skill, ability, etc.: *a dancing competition* **3** [U] the person or people competing: *There was a lot of competition for the job.*

**com·pet·i·tive** /kəm'petɪ̠tɪv/ *adj* of, related to, based on, or decided by competition: *the competitive nature of business* –**competitively** *adv* –**competitiveness** *n* [U]

**com·pet·i·tor** /kəm'petɪ̠təʳ/ *n* a person, team, firm, etc., competing with another or others; RIVAL: *There were 10 competitors in the race.*

**com·pi·la·tion** /ˌkɒmpɪ̠'leɪʃən‖ˌkɑm-/ *n* [C;U] (a report, book, etc. produced by) the act or action of compiling (COMPILE)

**com·pile** /kəm'paɪl/ *v* **-piled, -piling** [T] to make (a report, book, etc.) from facts and information found in various places: *It takes years of hard work to compile a good dictionary.* –**compiler** *n*

**com·pla·cen·cy** /kəm'pleɪsənsi/ also **complacence**– *n* [U] *usu. derog* a COMPLACENT feeling: *With the state of affairs in the North so dangerous I see no reason for the government's complacency.*

**com·pla·cent** /kəm'pleɪsənt/ *adj usu. derog* pleased or contented with oneself, perhaps unreasonably; self-satisfied: *We lost because we became complacent.* –**complacently** *adv*

**com·plain** /kəm'pleɪn/ *v* [I;T +*that*] to express feelings of annoyance, pain, unhappiness, etc.; speak or say in an unhappy, annoyed, dissatisfied way: *Mary is always complaining (about something).*|*He complained that he couldn't find a job anywhere.*|*Our neighbour said he'd complain about us to the police if we made any more noise.*|*Father is complaining of a pain in his chest.* –**complainingly** *adv*

**com·plaint** /kəm'pleɪnt/ *n* **1** [C] a cause or reason for complaining: *The workers made a list of their complaints.*|*He suffers from a chest complaint.* (=an illness) **2** [C] a statement expressing annoyance, unhappiness, pain, dissatisfaction, grief, etc.: *The police received several complaints about the noise from our party.* **3** [U] the act of complaining: *If your neighbours are too noisy then you have* **cause for complaint.**

**com·plai·sant** /kəm'pleɪzənt/ *adj fml* ready and willing to please others; ready to agree –**complaisantly** *adv* –**complaisance** *n* [U]

**com·ple·ment¹** /'kɒmpl̩mənt‖'kɑm-/ *n* **1** something that completes or makes perfect: *A fine wine is a complement to a good meal.* **2** the quantity needed to make something complete: *The school's English department has its* **full complement** *of teachers.* (=has all the teachers it needs) –compare COMPLIMENT¹

**com·ple·ment²** /'kɒmpl̩ment‖'kɑm-/ *v* [T] to make (something) complete; be the COMPLEMENT¹ (1) of: *This wine complements the food perfectly.* –compare COMPLIMENT²

**com·ple·men·ta·ry** /ˌkɒmpl̩'mentəri‖ˌkɑm-/ *adj* serving to complete; supplying what is needed for completion –compare COMPLIMENTARY

**com·plete¹** /kəm'pliːt/ *adj* **1** having all necessary, usual, or wanted parts; lacking nothing: *John's birthday did not seem complete without his father there.*|*We bought a house* **complete with** *furniture.* –opposite **incomplete 2** finished; ended: *When will work on the new railway be complete?* **3** [A] thorough; full: *It was a complete surprise to see you on the bus yesterday.* –**completeness** *n* [U]

**complete²** *v* **-pleted, -pleting** [T] to finish; add what is missing or needed to (something) to form a finished whole: *I need one more stamp before my collection is completed.*

**com·plete·ly** /kəm'pliːtli/ *adv* altogether; totally: *The operation was completely successful.* –see Study Notes on page 389

**com·plex¹** /'kɒmpleks‖ˌkɑm'pleks◂/ *adj* **1** difficult to understand or explain: *a complex problem/idea* **2** consisting of many closely connected parts: *A computer is a complex machine.* –compare SIMPLE –**complexity** /kəm'pleks̩ti/ *n* **-ties** [C;U]

**com·plex²** /'kɒmpleks‖'kɑm-/ *n* **1** a system consisting of a large number of closely connected parts: *The new sports complex has everything needed for many different activities.* **2** a group of unconscious wishes, fears, feelings, etc., which influence a person's behaviour without him/her knowing it: *Andrew's complex about sex made his marriage a failure.*|*an* **inferiority/superiority complex** (a feeling that one is INFERIOR/SUPERIOR to other people)

**com·plex·ion** /kəm'plekʃən/ *n* **1** the natural colour and appearance of the skin, esp. of the face: *a good/dark/fair/pale complexion* **2** [*usu. sing.*] a general character or nature: *the complexion of the government*

**com·pli·ance** /kəm'plaɪəns/ *n* [U *with*] *fml* obedience: *Compliance with the law is expected*

**com·pli·ant** /kəm'plaɪənt/ *adj* readily acting in accordance with a rule, order, the wishes of others, etc.: *I don't respect people who are too compliant.* –**compliantly** *adv*

**com·pli·cate** /'kɒmpl̩keɪt‖'kɑm-/ *v* **-cated, -cating** [T] to make (something) difficult to understand or deal with: *It is a serious problem, complicated by the fact that we have no experience in this area.* –compare SIMPLIFY

**com·pli·cat·ed** /'kɒmpl̩keɪt̩d‖'kɑm-/ *adj* difficult to understand or deal with: *Don't ask me such complicated questions.*|*a complicated machine* –compare SIMPLE –**complicatedly** *adv* –**complicatedness** *n* [U]

**com·pli·ca·tion** /ˌkɒmpl̩'keɪʃən‖ˌkɑm-/ *n* something that adds new difficulties: *The car ran out of petrol, and as an added complication I had no money!*

**com·plic·i·ty** /kəm'plɪs̩ti/ *n* [U] the act of taking part with another person in some wrongful action, esp. a crime –see also ACCOMPLICE

**com·pli·ment¹** /'kɒmpl̩mənt‖'kɑm-/ *n* an expression of praise, admiration, or respect: *He received many compliments on his new suit.*|*She's always ready to pay a compliment.* –compare COMPLEMENT¹

**com·pli·ment²** /'kɒmpl̩ment‖'kɑm-/ *v* [T *on*] to praise with a COMPLIMENT: *John complimented Jean on her new job.* –compare COMPLEMENT²

**com·pli·men·ta·ry** /ˌkɒmpl̩'mentəri‖ˌkɑm-/ *adj* **1** expressing admiration, praise, respect, etc. –opposite **uncomplimentary 2** given free: *complimentary tickets for the theatre* –compare COMPLEMENTARY

**com·pli·ments** /'kɒmpl̩mənts‖'kɑm-/ *n* [P] good wishes: *That was an excellent dinner, Pierre: my compliments to the* CHEF!

**com·ply** /kəm'plaɪ/ *v* **-plied, -plying** [I *with*] *fml* to act in accordance with a demand, order, rule, etc.: *You must comply with the law.*

**com·po·nent** /kəm'pəunənt/ *n* any of the parts that make up a whole (esp. a machine or system)

**com·pose** /kəm'pəuz/ *v* **-posed, -posing 1** [T] *more fml than* **make up**– to make up (something); form (something): *Water is composed of* HYDROGEN *and* OXYGEN. –compare DECOMPOSE; see COMPRISE (USAGE) **2** [I;T] to write (music, poetry, etc.) **3** [T] to make (esp. oneself) calm, quiet, etc.: *Jean was nervous at first but soon composed herself.*

**com·pos·er** /kəm'pəuzəʳ/ *n* a person who writes music –compare MUSICIAN

**com·pos·ite** /'kɒmpəz̩t‖kɑm'pɑ-/ *adj,n* (something) made up of a number of different parts or materials: *The police artist made a composite picture of the criminal.*

**composition** /ˌkɒmpə'zɪʃən‖ˌkɑm-/ *n* **1** [C;U] (an example of) the act of composing (COMPOSE (2)): *a piece of music of her own composition* **2** [C;U] the arrangement of the various parts of which something is made up: *Who decided the composition of the committee?* **3** [C] a short piece of writing (ESSAY) done as an educational exercise **4** [C] a mixture of various substances: *a composition of different chemicals*

**com·post** /'kɒmpɒst‖'kɑmpəust/ *n* [U] a mixture of decayed plant or animal matter, such as cut grass or leaves, used for making the soil richer

**com·po·sure** /kəm'pəuʒəʳ/ *n* [U] complete control over one's feelings; calmness; steady manner or state of mind: *Keep calm: don't lose your composure.*

**com·pound¹** /kəm'paund/ *v* [T] **1** [*by*] to add to or increase (something bad): *Our difficulties were compounded by other people's mistakes.* **2** [*from, of*] to make (a substance or state) by combining various parts, qualities, etc.

**com·pound²** /'kɒmpaund‖'kɑm-/ *adj,n* (something) consisting of a combination of two or more parts –compare ELEMENT, MIXTURE

**com·pound³** /'kɒmpaund‖ 'kɑm-/ *n* a group of buildings enclosed by a wall, fence, etc.

**com·pre·hend** /ˌkɒmprɪ'hend‖ˌkam-/ *v* [I;T] *fml* to understand: *The judge said that it was difficult to comprehend the actions of the police in this matter.*

**com·pre·hen·si·ble** /ˌkɒmprɪ'hensəbəl‖'kam-/ *adj* able to be understood: *You often find a writer's books more comprehensible if you know about his life.* –opposite **incomprehensible** –**comprehensibility** /-sə'bɪləti/ *n* [U]

**com·pre·hen·sion** /ˌkɒmprɪ'henʃən‖ˌkam-/ *n* **1** [U *of*] the act of understanding; ability to understand –opposite **incomprehension** **2** [C;U] (in schools) an exercise to test and improve the pupil's ability to understand language

**com·pre·hen·sive**[1] /ˌkɒmprɪ'hensɪv‖ˌkam-/ *adj* **1** thorough; broad; including much: *The government gave a very comprehensive explanation of its plans for industrial development.* **2** [*no comp.*] *BrE* (of education) teaching pupils of all abilities in the same school –**comprehensively** *adv*

**comprehensive**[2] also **comprehensive school** /ˌ··'·· ·/– *n BrE* a school where pupils of all abilities are taught from the age of 11 –compare GRAMMAR SCHOOL

**com·press** /kəm'pres/ *v* [T] **1** to force (a substance) into less space; press together: *compressed air* **2** to put (thoughts, ideas, etc.) into fewer words

**com·pres·sion** /kəm'preʃən/ *n* [U] **1** the act of COMPRESSing **2** the state of being COMPRESSed

**com·prise** /kəm'praɪz/ *v* **-prised, -prising** [not *be +v-ing*] to consist of; include; be made up of

USAGE Compare **comprise, compose, consist of, constitute,** and **include:** *The United Kingdom* **includes** *Northern Ireland and Wales.* (=these are two of the parts that make up the United Kingdom)|*The United Kingdom* **consists of/is composed of/comprises** *England, Wales, Scotland, and Northern Ireland.* (=these are all the parts that make it up)|*England, Wales, Scotland, and Northern Ireland* **constitute/compose** (=make up) *the United Kingdom.*

**com·pro·mise**[1] /'kɒmprəmaɪz‖'kam-/ *n* [C;U] (an example of) the act of settling an argument by each side taking a middle course acceptable to all sides: *He wanted £10; I wanted to pay £5; we* **reached a compromise,** *and I paid £7.50.*

**compromise**[2] *v* **-mised, -mising 1** [I] to settle an argument or differences of opinion by taking a middle course acceptable to all sides: *We couldn't agree whether to go to the theatre or a restaurant, so we compromised and went to the pub.* **2** [T] to make (someone or something) open to dishonour, danger, etc.: *The minister was compromised by the news of his relationship with the* PROSTITUTE, *and had to leave Parliament.*

**com·pul·sion** /kəm'pʌlʃən/ *n* **1** [U] force or influence that makes a person do something: *I will pay nothing* **under compulsion. 2** [C *+to-v*] a strong usu. unreasonable desire that is difficult to control: *Drinking is a compulsion with her.*

**com·pul·sive** /kəm'pʌlsɪv/ *adj* [A] resulting from a COMPULSION (2): *Compulsive eating is bad for one's health.* –**compulsively** *adv*

**com·pul·so·ry** /kəm'pʌlsəri/ *adj* [*no comp.*] put into force by the law, orders, etc.: *Education is compulsory for all children in Britain.* –compare VOLUNTARY (1) –**compulsorily** /-sərəli/ *adv*

**com·punc·tion** /kəm'pʌŋkʃən/ *n* [U] (*often in* NEGATIVE[1] *sentences*) guilt; shame: *That woman didn't have the slightest compunction about stealing.*

**com·pute** /kəm'pjuːt/ *v* **-puted, -puting** [I;T] to calculate (a result, answer, sum, etc.)

**com·put·er** /kəm'pjuːtər/ *n* an electric calculating machine that can store and recall information and make calculations at very high speeds

**com·put·er·ize**‖also **-ise** *BrE* /kəm'pjuːtəraɪz/ *v* **-ized, -izing** [I;T] to use a computer to control (an operation, system, etc.): *The firm has decided to computerize its wages department.*

**com·rade** /'kɒmrəd, -reɪd‖'kamræd/ *n* **1** [C] a close companion, esp. a person who shares difficult work or troubles **2** [A;C] (esp. used as a title in countries practising COMMUNISM) a citizen; fellow member of a union, political party, etc.

**com·rade·ship** /'kɒmrədʃɪp, -reɪd-‖'kamræd-/ *n* [U] companionship; friendship

**con**[1] /kɒn‖kan/ *n* [C *usu. pl.*] see PRO[1]

**con**[2] *v* **-nn-** [T *into, out of*] *infml* to trick (a trusting person) in order to make money: *They've conned me out of all my money!*

**con·cave** /ˌkɒn'keɪv◂, kən-‖ˌkan'keɪv◂, kən-/ *adj tech* curved inward, like the inside surface of a hollow ball: *a concave mirror* –opposite **convex**

**con·ceal** /kən'siːl/ *v* [T] *more fml than* **hide**– to hide; keep from being seen or known: *He was very unhappy, but nobody knew, because he concealed his feelings.* –**concealment** *n* [U]

**con·cede** /kən'siːd/ *v* **-ceded, -ceding 1** [I;T *+that*] to admit as true, just, or proper, often unwillingly: *The government* **conceded defeat** *as soon as the election results were known.*|*I'm willing to concede that a larger car would have cost more, but I still think we should have bought one.* **2** [T] to give as a right; allow; yield: *After the First World War, Germany conceded her neighbours much valuable land.*

**con·ceit** /kən'siːt/ also **conceitedness**– *n* [U] too high an opinion of one's own abilities, value, etc.: *That man's* **full of conceit.** –**conceited** *adj*

**con·cei·va·ble** /kən'siːvəbəl/ *adj* that can be thought of or believed; imaginable: *It is conceivable that there will be a third world war, but I hope it won't happen.* –opposite **inconceivable** –**conceivably** *adv*

**con·ceive** /kənsiːv/ *v* **-ceived, -ceiving 1** [T +*(that)*] to think of; imagine; consider: *Scientists first conceived the idea of the atomic bomb in the 1930s.* –see PERCEIVE (USAGE) **2** [I;T] *tech or bibl* to become PREGNANT with (a child): *The baby was conceived in March and born in December.*

**conceive of** sbdy./sthg. *v prep* [T *+v-ing*] to think of; imagine: *It's difficult to conceive of travelling to the moon.*

**SPELLING NOTE**

Words with the sound /k/, like **cut**, may be spelt **k-**, like **key**, or **qu-**, like **queen.**
Words with the sound /s/, like **city**, may be spelt **s-**, like **soon**, or **ps-**, like **psychology.**

**con·cen·trate**[1] /ˈkɒnsəntreɪt‖ˈkɑn-/ *v* **-trated, -trating** [I;T] **1** [*on, upon*] to keep or direct (all one's thoughts, efforts, attention, etc.): *You should concentrate on the road when you're driving.|If you don't concentrate more on your work you'll lose your job.* **2** to (cause to) come together in or around one place: *Industrial development is being concentrated in the south of the country.*

**concentrate**[2] *n* [C;U] a CONCENTRATED form of something: *orange juice concentrate*

**con·cen·trat·ed** /ˈkɒnsəntreɪtɪ̣d‖ˈkɑn-/ *adj* **1** increased in strength by the removal of liquid or the addition of more of a substance **2** [A] very strong: *a concentrated effort to improve*

**con·cen·tra·tion** /ˌkɒnsənˈtreɪʃən‖ˌkɑn-/ *n* **1** [U] close attention: *This book will need all your concentration.* **2** [C] a close gathering: *There is a concentration of industry in the south of the country.*

**concentration camp** /ˌ··ˈ·· ·/ *n* a large enclosed area where political prisoners are imprisoned

**con·cen·tric** /kənˈsentrɪk/ *adj tech* having the same centre: *concentric circles*

**con·cept** /ˈkɒnsept‖ˈkɑn-/ *n* [C +*that/of*] a general idea, thought, or understanding: *I understand the concept, but I'm not sure about the details.*

**con·cep·tion** /kənˈsepʃən/ *n* **1** [C;U +*that/of*] (a) general understanding; idea: *You have no conception of how difficult my job is.* **2** [U] the act of forming an idea, plan, etc.: *The conception of the book took five minutes; but writing it took a year.* **3** [C;U] *tech* the starting of a new life by the union of a male and a female sex cell

**con·cep·tu·al** /kənˈseptʃuəl/ *adj* of or based on (the formation of) CONCEPTS: *conceptual thinking* **–conceptually** *adv*

**con·cern**[1] /kənˈsɜːn‖-ɜrn/ *v* [T] **1** [*no pass.*] to be about: *This story concerns a person who lived in Russia a long time ago.* **2** to be of importance or interest to; have an effect on: *The marriage of a queen concerns all the people who live in her country.* **3** [*about, with*] to worry (esp. oneself); interest (esp. oneself): *When she finished working, she concerned herself with looking after the old people in her area.*

**concern**[2] *n* **1** [C] a matter that is of interest or importance to someone: *The fact that you are unemployed isn't my concern.* **2** [U] worry; anxiety: *There is no* **cause for concern***; the storm was not too serious.|a nurse's concern for a sick man* **3** [C] a business; firm: *It was two years before the business was* **a going concern.** (=was making a profit)

**con·cerned** /kənˈsɜːnd‖-ɜr-/ *adj* **1** [+*to-v/about*] anxious; worried: *I was very concerned about my mother's illness.* –see NERVOUS (USAGE) **2** [after *n*] interested; taking part: *All the people concerned enjoyed their afternoon visit to the museum.* **3 as far as I'm concerned** (esp. with an expression of unfavourable feeling or opinion) in my opinion **4 where X is/are concerned** in matters that have an effect on X: *Where work is concerned, I always try to do my best.* –see also UNCONCERNED

**con·cern·ing** /kənˈsɜːnɪŋ‖-ɜr-/ *prep more fml than* **about**– about; with regard to: *Concerning your letter, I am pleased to inform you that ...*

**con·cert** /ˈkɒnsət‖ˈkɑnsərt/ *n* **1** a musical performance given by a number of singers or musicians or both –compare RECITAL **2 in concert** working together; in agreement

**con·cert·ed** /kənˈsɜːtɪ̣d‖-ɜr-/ *adj* **1** planned or done together by agreement; combined: *a concerted effort by all governments to stop crime* **2** *infml* very strong: *This pupil has made* **a concerted effort** *to improve her work.* **–concertedly** *adv*

**con·cer·ti·na** /ˌkɒnsəˈtiːnə‖ˌkɑnsər-/ *n* a small musical instrument of the ACCORDION family, held and played in the hands by pressing in from both ends

**con·cer·to** /kənˈtʃɜːtəʊ‖-ˈtʃertəʊ/ *n* **-tos** a piece of music for one or more SOLO instruments and ORCHESTRA

**con·ces·sion** /kənˈseʃən/ *n* **1** [C;U] (a result of) the act of yielding, esp. after a disagreement: *The firm's promise to increase our pay was a concession to union demands.* **2** [C +*to-v/from*] a right given or yielded by a government, owner of land, etc., to do something special: *oil concessions in the North Sea|He won the food concession for the town hall.* (=he agreed to supply all the food for sale)

**con·cil·i·ate** /kənˈsɪlieɪt/ *v* **-ated, -ating** [T] to remove the anger or distrust of (someone); win the friendly feelings of

**con·cil·i·a·tion** /kənˌsɪliˈeɪʃən/ *n* [U] the act of conciliating (CONCILIATE): *Conciliation is the best way of regaining a person's trust after an argument.*

**con·cil·i·a·to·ry** /kənˈsɪlɪətəri‖-tori/ *adj* tending or intending to CONCILIATE: *He was very conciliatory but I still can't forgive him.*

**con·cise** /kənˈsaɪs/ *adj* short and clear; expressing much in few words: *a concise report* **–concisely** *adv* **–concision** /kənˈsɪʒən/ also **conciseness**– *n* [U]

**con·clude** /kənˈkluːd/ *v* **-cluded, -cluding 1** [I;T] *fml* to (cause to) come to an end: *We concluded the meeting at eight o'clock with a vote of thanks.* **2** [T *with*] to arrange or settle (something): *We concluded an agreement with the enemy and soon made peace.* **3** [T +*that*] to come to believe after consideration of known facts: *The judge concluded that the prisoner was guilty.*

**con·clu·sion** /kənˈkluːʒən/ *n* **1** a judgment or decision: *What conclusions did you come to/draw/reach?|Be careful not to* **jump to conclusions.** (=to form a judgment too quickly) **2** *more fml than* **end**– the end; closing part: *I found the conclusion of her book very exciting.* **3** an arrangement or agreement that introduces a changed state of affairs which is likely to last for some time: *The conclusion of peace is in the interests of both countries.* **4 foregone conclusion** something decided in advance; something very likely to happen **5 in conclusion** as the last thing: *In conclusion, I'd like to say how much I've enjoyed staying here.*

**con·clu·sive** /kənˈkluːsɪv/ *adj* putting an end to doubt or uncertainty: *conclusive proof that he was the murderer* –opposite **inconclusive –conclusively** *adv*

**con·coct** /kənˈkɒkt‖-ˈkɑkt/ *v* [T] to make (something) by mixing or combining parts: (fig.) *John concocted* (=made up) *an excuse for being late and the teacher believed him.* **–concoction** *n: They gave* me a very strange concoction to drink.

**con·com·i·tant** /kən'kɒmɪ̣tənt||-'kɑ-/ *adj,n fml* (something) existing or happening together with something else: *war with all its concomitant sufferings* –**concomitantly** *adv*

**con·cord** /'kɒŋkɔːd||'kɑŋkɔrd/ *n* [U] *fml* friendly relationship; complete peace and agreement –compare DISCORD (1)

**con·course** /'kɒŋkɔːs||-ors/ *n fml* a large hall or open place where crowds of people can gather: *the airport concourse*

**con·crete**[1] /'kɒŋkriːt||'kɑŋ-/ *adj* [*no comp.*] *fml* existing as something real or solid; actual: *Coal is a concrete object; heat is not.*|(fig.) *Have you any concrete suggestions on how to deal with this difficulty?* –compare ABSTRACT[1] –**concretely** *adv*

**concrete**[2] *v,n* **-creted, -creting** [T;U] (to cover with) a building material made by mixing sand, very small stones, cement, and water

**con·cur** /kən'kɜːʳ/ *v* **-rr-** [I *with*] *fml* to agree: *Our opinions on this matter concur.*

**con·cur·rent** /kən'kʌrənt||-'kɜr-/ *adj fml* **1** existing or happening at the same time **2** in agreement –**concurrently** *adv* –**concurrence** *n* [C;U]

**con·cus·sion** /kən'kʌʃən/ *n* [U] damage of the brain caused by a heavy blow, shock, or violent shaking: *He's suffering from concussion after falling off his bicycle.*

**con·demn** /kən'dem/ *v* [T] **1** to express strong disapproval of (someone or some action): *Most people are willing to condemn violence of any sort (as evil).* **2** [ +*to-v*] to state the punishment for (a guilty person): *The prisoner was* **condemned to death.**|(fig.) *His bad leg condemned him to* (=forced him to remain in) *a wheelchair.* **3** to declare (something) officially unfit for use: *Although this house is condemned (as unfit), an old lady still lives here.* –**condemnation** /ˌkɒndəm'neɪʃən,-dem-||ˌkɑn-/ *n* [C;U]

**con·den·sa·tion** /ˌkɒnden'seɪʃən, -dən-||ˌkɑn-/ *n* **1** [U] drops of liquid formed when steam or hot air becomes cool: *There was condensation on the windows.* **2** [C;U] (the act or result of) condensing (CONDENSE (2))

**con·dense** /kən'dens/ *v* **-densed, -densing 1** [T] to put into a smaller or shortened form: *a condensed report* **2** [I;T] to (cause to) become liquid, or sometimes solid, esp. by cooling

**con·de·scend** /ˌkɒndɪ'send||ˌkɑn-/ *v* [I +*to-v*] **1** to do something beneath one's social rank: *The general condescended to eat with the soldiers.* **2** *derog* to make oneself appear of a higher social rank than others: *I don't like Mrs Smith: she's so condescending.* –**condescension** *n* [U]

**con·di·ment** /'kɒndɪ̣mənt||'kɑn-/ *n* [*usu. pl.*] *fml* a powder or liquid used for giving a special taste to food: *Pepper and salt are condiments.*

**SPELLING NOTE**

Words with the sound /k/, like **cut**, may be spelt **k-**, like **key**, or **qu-**, like **queen.**
Words with the sound /s/, like **city**, may be spelt **s-**, like **soon**, or **ps-**, like **psychology.**

**con·di·tion**[1] /kən'dɪʃən/ *n* **1** [C *of*] a state of being or existence: *The* ASTRONAUTS *soon got used to the condition of weightlessness.* **2** [U] the state of general health, fitness, or readiness for use: *Michael is* **out of condition** *because he never takes any exercise.*|*This car is in very good condition.*|*Her condition is improving.* (=she is getting well) **3** [C] something stated as necessary or desirable for something else: *She will join us* **on one condition:** *that we divide all the profits equally.*|*I'll come* **on condition that** (=if) *John is invited too.* –see also CONDITIONS

**condition**[2] *v* [T] **1** to settle; decide; control: *The amount of money I spend is conditioned by the amount I earn.* **2** *derog* to train: *Most people have been conditioned to accept what they see on television.*

**con·di·tion·al** /kən'dɪʃənəl/ *adj* [*on,upon*] depending on a certain condition or conditions: *His agreement to buy our house was conditional on us leaving all the furniture in it.* –opposite **unconditional** –**conditionally** *adv*

**con·di·tions** /kən'dɪʃənz/ *n* [P] state of affairs; CIRCUMSTANCES: *What are housing conditions like in your country now?*|*Even under the best conditions, we couldn't finish in less than three days.* –see also CONDITION[1]

**con·do·lence** /kən'dəʊləns/ *n* [C;U *often pl.*] (an expression of) sympathy for someone who has experienced great sorrow, misfortune, etc.: *Please accept my condolences on your mother's death.*

**con·dom** /'kɒndəm||'kɑn-, 'kʌn-/ *n* a usu. rubber covering worn over the male sex organ during SEXUAL INTERCOURSE, used as a means of birth control and/or a protection against disease

**con·do·min·i·um** /ˌkɒndə'mɪnɪəm||ˌkɑn-/ also **condo** /'kɒndəʊ||'kɑn-/ *infml*– *n AmE* (a flat in) a block of flats in which the people who live in the flats own them

**con·done** /kən'dəʊn/ *v* **-doned, -doning** [T] to forgive (wrong behaviour); treat (a wrong action) as harmless: *I cannot condone the use of violence.*

**con·du·cive** /kən'djuːsɪv||-'duː-/ *adj* [F *to*] *fml* likely to produce: *Plenty of exercise is conducive to good health.*

**con·duct**[1] /kən'dʌkt/ *v* **1** [T] to direct or lead: *She conducts her business very successfully.*|*He conducted (us on) a tour of the castle.* **2** [T] *fml* to behave (oneself): *Your children conduct themselves well.* **3** [I;T] to stand before and direct the playing of (musicians or a musical work) **4** [T] to act as the path for (electricity, heat, etc.): *Plastic and rubber won't conduct electricity, but copper will.*

**con·duct**[2] /'kɒndʌkt, -dəkt||'kɑn-/ *n* [U] **1** *fml* behaviour: *I'm glad to see your conduct at school has improved.* **2** direction of the course of (a business, activity, etc.)

**con·duc·tor** /kən'dʌktəʳ/ *n* **1** a person who directs the playing of a group of musicians **2** a person employed to collect payments from passengers on a public vehicle: *a bus conductor* **3** a substance that readily acts as a path for electricity, heat, etc.: *Wood is a poor conductor of heat.*|*A* **lightning conductor** *protects a building from damage by lightning.*

**cone** /kəʊn/ *n* **1** a solid object with a round base and a point at the top **2** a hollow or solid object shaped like this: *an ice-cream cone* **3** the fruit of a PINE or FIR

**con·fec·tion·e·ry** /kən'fekʃənəri/ *n* [U] sweet foods, cakes, sweets, etc. **–confectioner** *n*

**con·fed·e·ra·cy** /kən'fedərəsi/ *n* **-cies** *fml* an esp. political union of people, parties, or states **–confederate** *adj*

**con·fed·e·rate**[1] /kən'fedərət/ *n* **1** a member of a CONFEDERACY **2** *derog* a person who shares in a crime

**con·fed·e·rate**[2] /kən'fedəreɪt/ *v* **-rated, -rating** [I;T] to (cause to) combine in a CONFEDERACY **–confederation** *n*

**con·fer** /kən'fɜː'/ *v* **-rr-** [I *on, with*] *fml* to talk together; compare opinions: *The ministers are still conferring on this matter.* **–conferment** *n* [C;U]

**con·fe·rence** /'kɒnfərəns‖'kɑn-/ *n* [C;U] a meeting held so that opinions and ideas on a subject, or a number of subjects, can be exchanged: *a conference of West European states|The minister cannot see you now: he is* **in conference.** –see also PRESS CONFERENCE

**con·fess** /kən'fes/ *v* [I;T +*v-ing*/*(that)*] **1** to admit (a fault, crime, something wrong): *The prisoner has confessed her crime.|She confessed (to) stealing the money.|Jean confessed (that) she'd broken the speed limit.|He confessed where he had hidden the money.* **2** *tech* to make (one's faults) known to a priest or God

**con·fessed** /kən'fest/ *adj* not secretive; open; by one's own admittance or declaration: *Mrs Jones is a (self-)confessed alcoholic.* –opposite **unconfessed**

**con·fes·sion** /kən'feʃən/ *n* **1** [C;U] (an example of) the act of admitting one's crimes, serious faults, etc. **2** [U] *tech* a religious service at which a person tells his/her faults to a priest

**con·fet·ti** /kən'feti/ *n* [U] small pieces of coloured paper thrown about at weddings

**con·fi·dant** /'kɒnfɪ̈dænt, ˌkɒnfɪ̈'dænt‖'kɑnfɪ̈ dænt/ **confidante** *fem.*– *n* a person to whom one tells one's secrets or with whom one talks about personal matters

**con·fide** /kən'faɪd/ *v* **-fided, -fiding** [T +*v-ing*/*that*] to tell (secrets, personal matters, etc.) secretly to a person one trusts: *He confided to me that he had spent five years in prison.*

**confide in** sbdy. *v prep* [T] to talk freely to, esp. about one's secrets: *John felt he could confide in his brother.*

**con·fi·dence** /'kɒnfɪ̈dəns‖'kɑn-/ *n* **1** [U] full trust; belief in one's own or another's ability: *She has won his confidence; he trusts her.|Peter lacks confidence in himself.* **2** [C] a secret; some personal matter told secretly to a person **3** **in confidence** privately; secretly: *I told you that in confidence so why did you tell Jean about it?*

**con·fi·dent** /'kɒnfɪ̈dənt‖'kɑn-/ *adj* [F +*that*/*of*] having a belief in one's own powers or ability; feeling or showing CONFIDENCE (1): *a confident smile|The government is confident of winning/that it will win the next election.* **–confidently** *adv*

**con·fi·den·tial** /ˌkɒnfɪ̈'denʃəl‖ˌkɑn-/ *adj* spoken or written in secret; to be kept secret: *confidential information* **–confidentially** *adv*

**con·fid·ing** /kən'faɪdɪŋ/ *adj* trustful: *her confiding nature* **–confidingly** *adv*

**con·fine** /kən'faɪn/ *v* **-fined, -fining** [T *to*] to enclose within limits; keep in a small space: *The animal was confined in a very small cage.|John was* **confined to bed** *for a week with his cold.* **–confinement** *n* [U]: *The prisoner was kept in* **solitary confinement.** (=kept completely alone)

**con·fines** /'kɒnfaɪnz‖'kɑn-/ *n* [P] limits; borders: *within the confines of one country| the confines of human knowledge*

**con·firm** /kən'fɜːm‖-ɜrm/ *v* [T] **1** [+*(that)*] to support; make certain; give proof (of): *Please confirm your telephone message in writing.|The minister confirmed that the election would be on June 20th.|His statement confirmed what we already believed.* **2** *tech* to admit (a person) to full membership of a church

**con·fir·ma·tion** /ˌkɒnfə'meɪʃən‖ˌkɑnfər-/ *n* [C;U] **1** [+*that*] something that CONFIRMS (1): *Your news was really confirmation for my beliefs.* **2** *tech* a religious service in which a person is made a full member of a church

**con·firmed** /kən'fɜːmd‖-ɜr-/ *adj* [A] firmly settled in a particular way of life: *He'll never get married: he's a confirmed* BACHELOR.

**con·fis·cate** /'kɒnfɪ̈skeɪt‖'kɑn-/ *v* **-cated, -cating** [T] to seize (private property) officially and without payment, esp. as a punishment: *The teacher confiscated my radio because she heard me playing it in class.* **–confiscation** /-'keɪʃən / *n* [C;U]

**con·fla·gra·tion** /ˌkɒnflə'greɪʃən‖ˌkɑn-/ *n fml* a very large fire that destroys much property, esp. buildings or forests

**con·flict**[1] /'kɒnflɪkt‖'kɑn-/ *n* [C;U] **1** (a) disagreement; argument; quarrel: *The two political parties have been* **in conflict** *since the election.* **2** (a) war; battle; struggle: *Many people were hurt in the conflict.*

**con·flict**[2] /kən'flɪkt/ *v* [I] to be in opposition (to another or each other); disagree: *Do British laws conflict with any international laws?|My husband and I hold conflicting opinions on this matter.*

**con·flu·ence** /'kɒnfluəns‖'kɑn-/ *n* [C;U] *fml* the flowing together of two or more rivers

**con·form** /kən'fɔːm‖-ɔrm/ *v* [I *to*] *fml* to be obedient to, or act in accordance with established patterns, rules, etc.: *You must conform to the rules or leave the school.* **–conformity** *n* [U]

**con·form·ist** /kən'fɔːmɪ̈st‖-ɔr-/ *adj,n sometimes derog* (of, concerning, or being) a person who acts and thinks in accordance and agreement with the established rules, values, and customs of society –opposite **nonconformist**

**con·found** /kən'faʊnd/ *v* [T] to confuse and surprise (a person or group of people): *The bad election results confounded the government.* **–confounded** *adj*

**con·front** /kən'frʌnt/ *v* [T] to face boldly or threateningly: *When I left the pub I was confronted by two men who asked me for money.*

**confront** sbdy. **with** sthg. *v prep* [T] to bring face to face; cause to meet: *The police confronted her with the* EVIDENCE, *and she admitted that she had stolen the money.*

**con·fron·ta·tion** /ˌkɒnfrən'teɪʃən‖ˌkɑn-/ *n* [C;U] (an example of ) the act of CONFRONTing: *We cannot risk another confrontation with the government.*

**con·fuse** /kən'fjuːz/ *v* **-fused, -fusing** [T] **1** to mislead; cause to be mistaken: *I was confused by all the noise.|They confused the teacher by having the same names.* **2** [*with*] to mix up; fail to tell the difference between (two things): *I'm always confusing John and/with Paul–which one is John?* **–confused** *adj* **–confusedly** /kən'fjuːzᵻdli/ *adv* **–confusing** *adj* **–confusion** /kən'fjuːʒən/ *n* [U]: *There was some confusion as to whether we had won or lost.|To avoid confusion, the teams wore different colours.*

**con·geal** /kən'dʒiːl/ *v* [I;T] to (cause to) become thick or solid: *The liquid congealed.|congealed blood*

**con·ge·ni·al** /kən'dʒiːnɪəl/ *adj fml* pleasant; in agreement with one's nature: *congenial work* –opposite **uncongenial –congenially** *adv*

**con·gen·i·tal** /kən'dʒenᵻtl/ *adj tech* (of diseases) existing at or from one's birth: (fig.) *a congenital liar* **–congenitally** *adv*

**con·ges·ted** /kən'dʒestᵻd/ *adj* (of a street, city, narrow place, etc.) very full or blocked, esp. because of traffic: *Oxford Street is always very congested.|The baby couldn't breathe because its nose was congested.* (=blocked with MUCUS) **–congestion** *n* [U] : *I don't like driving through London because there's too much congestion.*

**con·glom·e·rate** /kən'glɒmərᵻt||-'glɑ-/ *n* a large business firm producing goods of different kinds

**con·glom·e·ra·tion** /kənˌglɒmə'reɪʃən||-ˌglɑ-/ *n* a collection of many different things gathered together: *a strange conglomeration of objects*

**con·grat·u·late** /kən'grætʃʊleɪt||-tʃə-/ *v* **-lated, -lating** [T *on*] to speak to (a person) with praise and admiration for a happy event or something successfully done: *We congratulated her on having passed the examinations.|Let me congratulate you on the birth of your daughter.* **–congratulation** /-'leɪʃən/ *n* [U] **–congratulatory** /kənˌgrætʃʊ'leɪtəri||-'grætʃələtori/ *adj*

**con·grat·u·la·tions** /kənˌgrætʃʊ'leɪʃənz||-tʃə-/ also **congrats** /kənˌgræts/ *infml– interj,n* [P *on*] an expression of joy for someone's success, good fortune, luck, etc.: *It's your birthday today? Congratulations!*

**con·gre·gate** /'kɒŋgrᵻgeɪt||'kɑŋ-/ *v* **-gated, -gating** [I] to gather together: *The crowds congregated in the town square to hear the President.*

**con·gre·ga·tion** /ˌkɒŋgrᵻ'geɪʃən||ˌkɑŋ-/ *n* a group of people gathered together, esp. in a church for religious worship –see ATTEND (USAGE)

**con·gress** /'kɒŋgres||'kɑŋgrᵻs/ *n* **1** (*often cap.*) the elected law-making body of certain countries, esp. the US: *Congress has approved the new education laws.* –compare SENATE **2** a formal meeting of representatives of societies, countries, etc., to exchange information and opinions: *a medical congress* **–congressional** /kən'greʃənəl/ *adj: congressional elections*

**con·i·cal** /'kɒnɪkəl||'kɑ-/ also **conic** /'kɒnɪk||'kɑ-/ *fml– adj* shaped like a CONE (1): *a conical hat|huts with conical roofs* **–conically** *adv*

> **SPELLING NOTE**
> Words with the sound /k/, like **cut**, may be spelt **k-**, like **key**, or **qu-**, like **queen.**
> Words with the sound /s/, like **city**, may be spelt **s-**, like **soon**, or **ps-**, like **psychology.**

**co·ni·fer** /'kəʊnᵻfəʳ, 'kɒ-||'kɑ-/ *n* a tree which bears CONES (3) and usu. keeps its leaves in winter **–coniferous** /kə'nɪfərəs||kəʊ-, kə-/ *adj*

**con·jec·ture** /kən'dʒektʃəʳ/ *n* [C;U] (the formation of) an idea, guess, etc., based on incomplete or uncertain information: *It is* **pure conjecture** *that prices will rise next year.* **–conjectural** *adj*

**con·ju·gal** /'kɒndʒʊgəl||'kɑndʒə-/ *adj* [A] *fml* concerning the relationship between husband and wife: *the conjugal bed|conjugal rights*

**con·ju·gate** /'kɒndʒʊgeɪt||'kɑndʒə-/ *v* **-gated, -gating** [T] *tech* to give the various forms of (a verb) that show number, person, tense, etc.: *Can you conjugate "to have" in all its tenses?* **–conjugation** /-'geɪʃən/ *n*

**con·junc·tion** /kən'dʒʌŋkʃən/ *n* **1** (in grammar) a word such as "but" or "and" that connects parts of sentences, phrases, etc. –see Study Notes on page 128 **2 in conjunction with** in combination with; together with; along with: *The army is acting in conjunction with the police in the hunt for terrorists.*

**con·jure** /'kʌndʒəʳ||'kɑn-/ *v* **-jured, -juring** [I;T] to cause to appear by or as if by magic: *The magician conjured a rabbit out of his hat.*

**conjure** sthg.↔ **up** *v adv* [T] **1** to imagine: *Try to conjure up a picture of life in Ancient Egypt.* **2** to cause to be remembered: *to conjure up memories of the past* **3** to cause (spirits of the dead, etc.) to appear: (fig.) *Jean can conjure up a good meal in half an hour.*

**con·jur·er, -or** /'kʌndʒərəʳ||'kɑn-/ *n* a person who practises magic, esp. to amuse others for payment

**con·nect** /kə'nekt/ *v more fml than* **join– 1** [T *up*] to join; unite; LINK: *They got two connecting rooms in the hotel.|The scientist connected the wires (up).* **2** [T *often pass.*] to think of as related; LINK: *She was connected with the crime.* **3** [T] to join by telephone: *I was connected to the wrong person.* **4** [T] to join to an electricity supply: *Make sure the machine's connected properly.*–opposite **disconnect** (for **1, 2, 3, 4**) **5** [I *with*] (of one or more trains, buses, etc.) to be so planned that passengers can change from one to the other: *The next flight connects with a flight for Paris.*

**con·nect·ed** /kə'nektᵻd/ *adj* **1** joined or related: *connected events* –opposite **unconnected 2** having social, professional, or business relationships of the stated kind: *You must be very* **well-connected**: *you seem to know all the right people.*

**con·nec·tion** ||also **connexion** *BrE* /kə'nekʃən/– *n* **1** [U] the act of connecting: *the connection of the house pipes to the water supply* –opposite **disconnection 2** [C;U] (an example of) the state of being connected; relationship: *Do you know that there's a connection between smoking and heart disease?* **3** [C] a plane, train, bus, etc., planned to take passengers arriving by another one: *There are connections at Paris for all European capitals.* **4** [C] anything that connects or is connected: *excellent road and railway connections with the coast|a bad telephone connection|The machine won't work because of a faulty connection.* **5** [C *usu. pl.*] a person connected to others, e.g. by family or business: *She's English but* has Irish connections.|*We have connections with a firm in Zurich.* **6 in connection with** with regard to: *In connection with your request of March 18th we are sorry to tell you . . .*

**con·nive** /kə'naɪv/ *v* **-nived, -niving** [I +*to-v/with*] *fml* to work together secretly, esp. for some wrong or illegal purpose: *The student connived with her friend to cheat in the examination.* **–connivance** *n* [U *at, with*]: *The criminals could not have escaped without your connivance.*

**con·nois·seur** /ˌkɒnə'sɜːʳ‖ˌkɑ-/ *n apprec* a person with a good understanding of a subject for which knowledge and good judgment are needed: *a connoisseur of fine wines/art*

**con·no·ta·tion** /ˌkɒnə'teɪʃən‖ˌkɑ-/ *n* [*often pl.*] an idea suggested by a word in addition to the formal meaning of the word: *The word "good" sometimes has moral connotations.*

**con·quer** /'kɒŋkəʳ‖'kɑŋ-/ *v* **1** [I;T] to take (land) by force; win (land) by war: *The Normans conquered England in 1066.*|*a conquering army*|*a conquered city* **2** [I;T] to defeat (an enemy); be victorious over (an enemy) **3** [T] to gain control over (something unfriendly or difficult): *After many attempts to climb it, the mountain was conquered in 1982.* **–conqueror** *n*

**con·quest** /'kɒŋkwest‖'kɑŋ-/ *n* **1** [U] the act of conquering: *The conquest of this rare disease has always been her aim.* **2** [C] something conquered, esp. land gained in war: *French conquests in Asia*|(fig.) *Peter is one of Jane's conquests; he's fallen in love with her already.*

**con·science** /'kɒnʃəns‖'kɑn-/ *n* [C;U] an inner sense that knows the difference between right and wrong: *You should act according to your conscience.*|*to have a guilty conscience/a clear conscience*

**con·sci·en·tious** /ˌkɒnʃi'enʃəs‖ˌkɑn-/ *adj* showing great care, attention, or seriousness of purpose: *a conscientious worker*|*a conscientious piece of work* –compare CONSCIOUS **–conscientiously** *adv* **–conscientiousness** *n* [U]

**con·scious** /'kɒnʃəs‖'kɑn-/ *adj* **1** [F] having one's mind and senses working; able to think, feel, etc.; awake: *He hurt his head in the accident, but he is still conscious.*|*Is he conscious enough to answer questions?* –see also UNCONSCIOUS **2** [F +*(that)/of*] knowing; understanding: *Jean's always been very conscious that she annoys many people.* **3** [A] intentional: *a conscious decision to do something* –compare CONSCIENTIOUS **–consciously** *adv*

USAGE The opposite of **conscious** is **unconscious** in all the above meanings: *He's not yet* **conscious**/*still* **unconscious** *after the accident.*|*I was* **conscious/unconscious** *of her presence.* But in PSYCHOLOGY, **conscious** is also compared with **subconscious**: *the* **conscious/subconscious/unconscious** *mind.*

**con·scious·ness** /'kɒnʃəsn$\frac{1}{2}$s‖'kɑn-/ *n* **1** [U] the condition of being able to think, feel, understand what is happening, etc.: *Roger* **lost consciousness** *at four o'clock in the afternoon and died in the night.* **2** [U] all the ideas, opinions, etc., held by a person or a group of people: *the moral consciousness of a country*|*class consciousness* **3** [S;U +*that/of*] knowledge or a feeling, esp. of a not very clear kind; AWAREness: *a consciousness that someone else was in the room*

**cons·cript** /kən'skrɪpt/ ‖also **draft** *AmE*– *v* [T *into*] to make (someone) serve in one of the armed forces **–conscript** /'kɒnskrɪpt‖'kɑn-/ *n*: *He's a conscript.* **–conscription** *n* [U]

**con·se·crate** /'kɒns$\frac{1}{2}$kreɪt‖'kɑn-/ *v* **-crated, -crating** [T] **1** to declare as holy in a special ceremony: *to consecrate a church* **2** to set apart solemnly for a particular purpose **–consecration** /ˌkɒns$\frac{1}{2}$kreɪʃən‖ˌkɑn-/ *n* [C;U]

**con·sec·u·tive** /kən'sekjʊtɪv‖-kjə-/ *adj* following in regular or unbroken order: *The numbers 4, 5, 6 are consecutive.* **–consecutively** *adv*

**con·sen·sus** /kən'sensəs/ *n* [*usu. sing.*] a general agreement; the opinion of a group: *What is the* **consensus of opinion?**

**con·sent**[1] /kən'sent/ *v* [I +*to-v/to*] to agree; give permission: *Jean tried to persuade her mother but she refused to consent (to let Jean go).* –see also ASSENT, DISSENT

**consent**[2] *n* [U] **1** agreement; permission: *Jean's parents refused their consent to her marriage.* **2 age of consent** the age at which one may legally marry or have sex –see also ASSENT, DISSENT

**con·se·quence** /'kɒns$\frac{1}{2}$kwəns‖'kɑns$\frac{1}{2}$kwens/ *n* **1** [C] something that follows from an action or condition; result **2** [U] *fml* importance: *a matter of little/no consequence*

**con·se·quent·ly** /'kɒns$\frac{1}{2}$kwəntli‖'kɑn-/ *adv fml* as a result; therefore: *The rain was heavy, (and) consequently the road was flooded.* –see Study Notes on page 128

**con·ser·va·tion** /ˌkɒnsə'veɪʃən‖ˌkɑnsər-/ *n* [U] **1** the act of conserving (CONSERVE); preservation: *the conservation of wild life* **2** the controlled use of a limited supply of natural things, to prevent waste or loss: *Conservation of water is of great importance in desert areas.* **–conservationist** *n: The conservationists want to give more protection to wild animals.*

**con·ser·va·tis·m** /kən'sɜːvətɪzəm‖-ɜr-/ *n* [U] **1** dislike of change, esp. sudden change: *conservatism in matters of language* **2** the belief that the established order of society should be kept as it is for as long as possible and then changed only slowly

**con·ser·va·tive** /kən'sɜːvətɪv‖-ɜr-/ *adj* **1** favouring the established order of society; not liking change, esp. sudden change: *very conservative in matters of education* **2** not showy; modest: *She dresses in a rather conservative way.* **3** careful; kept within reasonable limits: *He made a conservative guess at the population of London.* **–conservatively** *adv* **–conservative** *n: Aunt Mary's a real conservative. She doesn't like change at all.*

**Conservative** *adj,n* (of, concerning, or being) a member of the Conservative Party (one of the main British political parties) –compare TORY

**con·ser·va·to·ry** /kən'sɜːvətəri‖-'sɜrvətori/ *n* **-ries** **1** a glass enclosed room where plants are grown **2** a school where people are trained in music or acting

**con·serve** /kən'sɜːv‖-ɜrv/ *v* **-served, -serving** [T] to use (a supply) carefully; preserve: *We must conserve water during the drought.*

## STUDY NOTES conjunctions

(words and phrases like **and, but, because,** and **so**, that join two or more nouns, verbs, adjectives, or parts of a sentence)

### ways of saying **and**

There are many words and phrases in English that can be used like **and** to join two or more ideas in a sentence. These ideas are often similar in meaning.

So instead of always saying:

*When we went to town we visited the zoo* **and** *the museum.*
*Peter* **and** *Paul came to the party.*

We can say:

*We went to the zoo. We visited the museum* **as well**.
*We went to the zoo. We went to the museum* **too**.
*We went to the museum* **as well as** *the zoo.*
*We went to the zoo. We* **also** *visited the museum.*
**Not only** *did we go to the zoo, we* **also** *went to the museum.*
**Besides** *going to the zoo, we went to the museum.*
**In addition to** *visiting the zoo, we went to the museum.*

*Paul came to the party. Peter came* **as well**.
*Paul came to the party. Peter came* **too**.
*Peter came to the party with us* **as well as** *Paul.*
*Paul came to the party.* **So** *did Peter.*
*Peter and* **also** *Paul came with us to the party.*
**Not only** *Peter* **but also** *Paul came with us to the party.*
*A lot of people came to the party* **besides** *Peter and Paul.*
*A number of people came to the party* **in addition to** *Peter and Paul.*

If you look up these words in the dictionary, you will find more examples and definitions to help you to learn how to use them.

---

### ways of saying **because**

There are many words and phrases like **because** that can be used to join two or more ideas in a sentence. These words and phrases all answer the question *Why?*

Some of these words and phrases show the *cause* of something:

*She was late for school* **because** *she missed the bus.*
*She was late* **because of** *missing the bus.*
**Since/As** *he has no money he can't buy a bicycle.*
*We stayed inside* **on account of** *the rain.*
*His failure was* **due to** *his lack of work.*
*He failed* **owing to** *his lack of work.*
*We lost the game* **through** *poor play.*
*The dog died* **from** *eating poison.*
*He kicked the door* **out of** *bad temper.*

– see also DUE TO (USAGE)

Some of these words and phrases show the *purpose* of something:

*He only said it* **to** *annoy me.*
*He said it* **in order to** *annoy me.*
*I had a big breakfast* **so (that)** *I wouldn't be hungry later on.*
*I had a big breakfast* **so as** *not to be hungry later on.*
*I went to live in the town* **in order that** *I might get a job.*

## ways of saying **but**

There are many words and phrases like **but** that can be used to join two or more ideas in a sentence. These words often join different ideas, or show that different things may be true. They join verbs, nouns, adjectives, and sentences in various ways.

So we can say:

*My room is small* **but** *comfortable.* (=because my room is small you might not expect it to be comfortable, but it is)

*She drove very fast to the airport,* **but** *she missed the plane.* (=because she drove very fast you might have expected her to get there in time, but she didn't)

We can express this meaning in a number of other ways:

by using **although** and (**even**) **though**, with two verbs, like this:

**Although** *my room is small it is comfortable.*
*My room is very comfortable* **even though** *it is small.*

**Although** *she drove very fast to the airport she missed the plane.*
*She missed the plane* **even though** *she drove very fast to the airport.*

by using **in spite of** and **despite**, with a noun, like this:

*My room is very comfortable,* **in spite of/despite** *its small size.*

*She missed the plane,* **in spite of/despite** *driving very fast to the airport.*

by using **however** and **even so**, with two sentences, like this:

*My room is small. It's very comfortable,* **however/even so.**

*She drove very fast to the airport.* **However/Even so** *she missed the plane.*

by using **although** and **yet**, with two adjectives, like this:

*My room is very comfortable,* **although** *small.*
*My room is small,* **yet** *very comfortable.*

With some of these words and phrases you can change the order of the words in the sentence:

**Even though** *my room is small it's very comfortable.*
**In spite of/Despite** *driving very fast to the airport, she missed the plane.*

If you look up these words and phrases in the dictionary, you'll find more examples and definitions to help you to learn how to use them. Other words that can be used like this are **nonetheless, nevertheless,** and **still.**

---

## ways of saying **so**

Words and phrases like **so** are used to show what happens as a *result* of something.

*I was feeling ill* **so** *I went to bed.* (=because I was feeling ill I went to bed.)
*I was feeling ill.* **That's why** *I went to bed.*

**so** and **that's why** are less formal ways of showing the result of something. More formal ways of expressing a similar meaning are:

*Jane got the highest marks in the exam. She was* **therefore** *chosen to go to college.*
*We do not have enough money.* **Therefore/Thus** *we cannot buy a new car.*
*I've never been to China.* **Consequently/Hence** *I know very little about it.*
*He was asked to leave the meeting and* **accordingly** *he went.*

Note that **thus, consequently, hence,** and **accordingly** are all marked *fml* in the dictionary.

---

**con·sid·er** /kən'sɪdəʳ/ *v* **1** [I;T +*v-ing*] to think about; examine: *I considered changing my job, but then decided not to.* **2** [T not *be* +*v-ing*] to think of in a stated way: *I consider him (to be) a good musician.|I consider it a great honour to be here with you today.* **3** [T +*that*] to take into account; remember: *If you consider (the fact) that she's only been studying English a year, she speaks it very well.*

**con·sid·e·ra·ble** /kən'sɪdərəbəl/ *adj* fairly large in amount, size, or degree: *a considerable length of time* –see also INCONSIDERABLE **–considerably** *adv: We have a considerably smaller house than theirs.*

**con·sid·er·ate** /kən'sɪdər½t/ *adj apprec* thoughtful of the rights or feelings of others: *to be considerate towards old people* –opposite **inconsiderate –considerately** *adv* **–considerateness** *n* [U]

**con·sid·e·ra·tion** /kən,sɪdə'reɪʃən/ *n* **1** [U *to*] careful thought; attention: *We shall give your request (our) careful consideration.|I've sent my poem to a magazine for (their) consideration.|consideration to detail* **2** [U *for*] thought for the wishes and feelings of others: *John never showed any/had no consideration for anyone.* **3** [C] a fact to be considered when making a decision: *Cost is an important consideration for me when I buy new clothes.* **4 take into consideration** to remember about (something) when making a judgment: *Your teacher will take your recent illness into consideration when judging your essay.*

**con·sid·ered** /kən'sɪdəd||-ərd/ *adj* **1** [A] reached after careful thought: *It is my* **considered opinion** *that you are wrong.* **2 all things considered** when one considers everything

**con·sid·er·ing** /kən'sɪdərɪŋ/ *prep,conj* if one remembers the rather surprising fact (of/that): *He did poorly in his examinations, considering how hard he had studied for them.*

**con·sign** /kən'saɪn/ *v* [T] *fml* **1** [*to*] to send (something) to a person or place for sale: *The goods were consigned to you by railway.* **2** to put into the care of another; hand over

**con·sign·ment** /kən'saɪnmənt/ *n* **1** [U] the act of CONSIGNing (1) **2** [C +*sing./pl. v. of*] a number of goods CONSIGNed together: *One consignment of bananas was/were bad.*

**con·sist** *v* → CONSIST OF

**con·sis·ten·cy** /kən'sɪstənsi/ also **consistence**– *n* **-cies 1** [U] the state of always keeping to the same principles or course of action: *Your actions lack consistency; you say one thing and do another!* –opposite **inconsistency 2** [C;U] the degree of firmness or thickness: *To make this cake you must first mix butter and sugar to the consistency of thick cream.*

**con·sis·tent** /kən'sɪstənt/ *adj* (of a person, behaviour, beliefs, etc.) keeping to the same principles, line of reasoning, or course of action: *This statement is not consistent with what you said yesterday.* –opposite **inconsistent –consistently** *adv*

**SPELLING NOTE**

Words with the sound /k/, like **cut**, may be spelt **k-**, like **key**, or **qu-**, like **queen.**
Words with the sound /s/, like **city**, may be spelt **s-**, like **soon**, or **ps-**, like **psychology.**

**con·sist of** sthg./kən'sɪst/ *v prep* [T not *be +v-ing, no pass.*] to be made up of: *The United Kingdom consists of Great Britain and Northern Ireland.* –see COMPRISE (USAGE)

**con·so·la·tion** /,kɒnsə'leɪʃən||,kɑn-/ *n* [C;U] (a person or thing that gives) comfort during a time of sadness or disappointment: *I got many letters of consolation when mother died.* –compare COMPENSATION

**con·sole¹** /kən'səʊl/ *v* **-soled, -soling** [T *with*] to give comfort or sympathy to (someone) in times of disappointment or sadness: *We tried to console her when her husband died, but it was very difficult.*

**con·sole²** /'kɒnsəʊl||'kɑn-/ *n* a flat surface containing the controls for a machine, electrical apparatus, etc.

**con·sol·i·date** /kən'sɒl½deɪt||-'sɑ-/ *v* **-dated, -dating** [I;T] **1** to make or become strong or firm: *Britain is trying to consolidate her position in the North Atlantic.* **2** to (cause to) combine into fewer or one: *Several small businesses consolidated to form a large powerful company.* **–consolidation** /-'deɪʃən/ *n* [C;U]

**con·som·mé** /kən'sɒmeɪ, 'kɒnsəmeɪ||,kɑnsə'meɪ/ *n* [C;U] (a) clear soup made from meat and/or vegetables

**con·so·nant** /'kɒnsənənt||'kɑn-/ *n* (a letter representing) any of the speech sounds made by partly or completely stopping the flow of air as it goes through the mouth: *All the letters of the English alphabet except* a, e, i, o, *and* u *are consonants.* –compare VOWEL

**con·sort¹** /'kɒnsɔːt||'kɑnsɔrt/ *n* the wife or husband of a ruler

**consort²** *v* → CONSORT WITH

**con·sor·ti·um** /kən'sɔːtɪəm||-ɔr-/ *n* **-tiums** *or* **-tia** /tɪə/ [C +*sing./pl. v*] a combination of a number of companies, banks, businesses, etc., for a particular purpose

**consort with** sbdy. /kən'sɔːt||-ɔrt/ *v prep* [T] *often derog* to spend time in the company of (esp. bad people): *She consorts with all kinds of strange people.*

**con·spic·u·ous** /kən'spɪkjʊəs/ *adj* noticeable; attracting attention: *She's always conspicuous because of her bright clothes.* –opposite **inconspicuous –conspicuously** *adv* **–conspicuousness** *n* [U]

**con·spi·ra·cy** /kən'spɪrəsi/ *n* **-cies** [C;U] (the act of making) a secret plan by two or more people to do something illegal: *a conspiracy to seize control of the government|The men were guilty of conspiracy.*

**con·spi·ra·tor** /kən'spɪrətəʳ/ *n* a person who takes part in a CONSPIRACY **–conspiratorial** /kən,spɪrə'tɔːrɪəl/-'tor-/ *adj*

**con·spire** /kən'spaɪəʳ/ *v* **-spired, -spiring** [I] **1** [+*to-v/with, together*] to plan together secretly (something illegal or bad): *The criminals conspired to rob a bank.* **2** [+*to-v*] (of events) to combine: *Events conspired to produce difficulties for the government.*

**con·sta·ble** /'kʌnstəbəl||'kɑn-/ *n* [A;C] *BrE* a policeman of the lowest rank –compare W.P.C., POLICEMAN, POLICEWOMAN, PATROLMAN

**con·stab·u·la·ry** /kən'stæbjʊləri||-jəleri/ *n* **-ries** [C +*sing./pl. v*] the police force of a particular area or country

**con·stan·cy** /'kɒnstənsi||'kɑn-/ *n* [U] firmness of mind; freedom from change; faithfulness

**con·stant** /'kɒnstənt||'kɑn-/ *adj* **1** unchanging; fixed: *He drove at a constant speed.*|(*lit*) *a constant* (=loyal) *friend* **2** happening all the time: *I dislike these constant arguments.* –**constantly** *adv*

**con·stel·la·tion** /,kɒnst$_5^1$'leɪʃən||,kɑn-/ *n* a group of fixed stars, often having a name, such as the Great Bear

**con·ster·na·tion** /,kɒnstə'neɪʃən||,kɑnstər-/ *n* [U] great shock and fear

**con·sti·pa·tion** /,kɒnst$_5^1$'peɪʃən||,kɑn-/ *n* [U] the (medical) condition of being unable to empty the bowels effectively –**constipated** /'kɒnst$_5^1$'peɪt$_5^1$d|| 'kən-/ *adj*

**con·sti·tu·en·cy** /kən'stɪtʃuənsi/ *n* **-cies 1** [C] an area of a country, represented in Parliament by one or more people **2** [C +*sing./pl. v*] the voters living in such an area

**con·sti·tu·ent**[1] /kən'stɪtʃuənt/ *n* **1** a voter; member of a CONSTITUENCY **2** any of the parts that make up a whole: *the constituents of an atom*

**constituent**[2] *adj* being one of the parts that make a whole: *the constituent parts of an atom*

**con·sti·tute** /'kɒnst$_5^1$tju:t||'kɑnst$_5^1$tu:t/ *v* **-tuted, -tuting** *fml* [T not *be* +*v-ing*] to make up; form: *Seven days constitute a week.* –see COMPRISE (USAGE)

**con·sti·tu·tion** /,kɒnst$_5^1$'tju:ʃən||,kɑnst$_5^1$'tu:-/ *n* **1** [C] the laws and principles according to which a country is governed: *According to the American Constitution, Presidential elections are held every four years.* **2** [C] the general condition of a person's body or mind: *an old man with a weak constitution* **3** [C] the way in which something is made up

**con·sti·tu·tion·al** /,kɒnst$_5^1$'tju:ʃənəl||,kɑnst$_5^1$'tu:-/ *adj* **1** limited or allowed by the CONSTITUTION (1): **2** of a person's CONSTITUTION (2): *a constitutional weakness of the mind* –**constitutionally** *adv: The government must always act constitutionally.*

**con·strain** /kən'streɪn/ *v* [T] *fml* to make (someone) do something by force or by strongly persuading: *I felt constrained to do what he told me.*

**con·strained** /kən'streɪnd/ *adj* awkward; unnatural: *a constrained manner* –opposite **unconstrained**

**con·straint** /kən'streɪnt/ *n* **1** [U] the condition of hiding one's natural feelings and behaviour: *The children showed constraint in the presence of the new teacher.* **2** [C *on*] something that limits one's freedom of action: *lawful constraints on immoral behaviour* **3** [U] the threat or use of force: *We acted under constraint.*

**con·strict** /kən'strɪkt/ *v* [T] to make narrower, smaller, or tighter: (fig.) *a constricted point of view* –**constrictive** *adj* –**constriction** *n* [C;U]: *constriction of the blood vessels*

**con·struct** /kən'strʌkt/ *v* [T] *more fml than* **make**– to build; make by putting together or combining parts: *a difficult sentence to construct*

**con·struc·tion** /kən'strʌkʃən/ *n* **1** [U] the business or work of building: *I work in the construction industry.*|*a construction firm* **2** [U] the act or manner of CONSTRUCTing: *There are two new hotels near here* **under construction**. **3** [C] something CONSTRUCTed, esp. a building –see also DESTRUCTION

**con·struc·tive** /kən'strʌktɪv/ *adj* helping to improve or develop something; helpful: *constructive suggestions* –**constructively** *adv*

**con·strue** /kən'stru:/ *v* **-strued, -struing** [T] *fml* to place a certain meaning on (a statement, etc.); understand; INTERPRET: *You can construe what he said in a number of different ways.* –see also MISCONSTRUE

**con·sul** /'kɒnsəl||'kɑn-/ *n* a person appointed by a government to protect and help its citizens and its interests in trade in a foreign city –compare AMBASSADOR –**consular** /'kɒnsjulə$^r$||kɑnsələ$^r$/ *adj*

**con·su·late** /'kɒnsjul$_5^1$t||'kɑnsəl$_5^1$t/ *n* **1** the official building in which a CONSUL lives or works **2** the rank of a CONSUL

**con·sult** /kən'sʌlt/ *v* [T] to go to (a person, book, etc.) for information, advice, etc.: *Have you consulted your doctor about your illness?* –**consultative** *adj*: *a consultative committee*

**consult with** sbdy. *v prep* [T] to exchange opinions, information, etc., with (a person or people): *Before we can accept the firm's offer we must consult with the workers.*

**con·sul·tant** /kən'sʌltənt/ *n* **1** a person who gives specialist professional advice to others: *an industrial relations consultant*|*a firm of consultants* **2** *BrE* a high ranking hospital doctor who gives specialist advice –**consultancy** *n* **-cies**: *He was appointed to a consultancy.*

**con·sul·ta·tion** /,kɒnsəl'teɪʃən||,kɑn-/ *n* **1** [C] a meeting held to exchange opinions and ideas **2** [C;U] (an example of) the act of CONSULTing: *We made the decision* **in consultation with** *the others on the committee.*

**con·sume** /kən'sju:m||-'su:m/ *v* **-sumed, -suming** [T] **1** to eat or drink **2** to use up: *Paperwork consumed much of the committee's time.* **3** (of a fire) to destroy: *The fire soon consumed the wooden buildings.*|(fig.) *She was consumed by hatred/guilt.*

**con·sum·er** /kən'sju:mə$^r$||-'su:-/ *n* a person who buys and uses goods and services: *The consumers complained about the increase in the price of meat.*

**con·sum·mate**[1] /kən'sʌm$_5^1$t/ *adj fml* perfect; complete: *consummate skill*

**con·sum·mate**[2] /'kɒnsəmeɪt||'kɑn-/ *v* **-mated, -mating** [T] *fml* **1** to make perfect **2** to make (a marriage) complete by having sex

**con·sum·ma·tion** /,kɒnsə'meɪʃən||,kɑn-/ *n* **1** [C *usu. sing.*] the point at which something is made complete or perfect: *the consummation of ten years' work* **2** [U] the act of consummating (CONSUMMATE[2] (2)) a marriage

**con·sump·tion** /kən'sʌmpʃən/ *n* [U] **1** the act of consuming, or amount CONSUMEd: *The nation's consumption of coal increased last year.* **2** *old use* TUBERCULOSIS of the lungs: *She died of/from consumption.*

**cont.** *written abbrev. said as*: continued

**con·tact**[1] /'kɒntækt||'kɑn-/ *n* **1** [U] the condition of meeting, touching, or receiving information from: *Have you been* **in contact with** *your sister recently?*|*to* **make contact with** *the ship by radio* **2** [C] *infml* a social or business connection; person one knows who can help one: *I've got a contact in the tax office. She can help us.* **3** [C] an electrical part that can be moved to touch another part to complete an electrical CIRCUIT (3)

**contact²** *v* [T] to reach (someone) by messages, telephone, etc.

**contact lens** /'·· ·/ also **contact** *infml*– *n* a very small LENS specially shaped to fit closely over the eye to improve eyesight

**con·ta·gious** /kən'teɪdʒəs/ *adj* **1** (of a disease) that can be passed from one person to another by touch: (fig.) *Her laughter is contagious.* **2** [F] (of a person) having a CONTAGIOUS disease –compare INFECTIOUS –**contagiously** *adv* –**contagiousness** *n* [U]

**con·tain** /kən'teɪn/ *v* [T] **1** to hold; have within itself: *This box contains ten bottles.|Beer contains alcohol.* **2** to hold back; keep under control: *Try to contain your anger/yourself!*

**con·tain·er** /kən'teɪnəʳ/ *n* a box, bottle, etc., used for holding something.

**con·tam·i·nate** /kən'tæmɨneɪt/ *v* **-nated, -nating** [T] to make impure or bad by mixing with dirty or poisonous matter: *Don't eat this food: it's been contaminated by flies.|The water was contaminated.* –**contamination** /-'neɪʃən/ *n* [U]

**contd.** *written abbrev. said as:* continued

**con·tem·plate** /'kɒntəmpleɪt||'kɑn-/ *v* **-plated, -plating** [I;T +*v-ing*] to consider with continued attention; think about: *The doctor contemplated the difficult operation he had to perform.|I hope she isn't contemplating coming to stay with us!*

**con·tem·pla·tion** /ˌkɒntəm'pleɪʃən||ˌkɑn-/ *n* [U *of*] deep thought: *She spent an hour in quiet contemplation.* –**contemplative** /kən'templətɪv, 'kɒntəm pleɪtɪv||kən'templətɪv, 'kɑntəmpleɪtɪv/ *adj: a quiet, contemplative nature*

**con·tem·po·ra·ne·ous** /kənˌtempə'reɪnɪəs/ *adj* [*with*] *fml* existing or happening during the same period of time as another or each other –**contemporaneously** *adv*

**con·tem·po·ra·ry¹** /kən'tempərəri, -pəri||-pəreri/ *adj* **1** modern; of the present: *contemporary history/art/morals|a contemporary building* **2** [*no comp.*] of or belonging to the same (stated) time: *Contemporary reports of past events are often more interesting than the modern writer's view of them.* –see NEW (USAGE)

**contemporary²** *n* **-ries** a person living at the same time or of the same age as another: *Susan is my contemporary: we were at school together.*

**con·tempt** /kən'tempt/ *n* [U] a lack of respect; the feeling that someone or something is of poor quality: *I feel nothing but contempt for such dishonest behaviour.*

**con·temp·ti·ble** /kən'temptəbəl/ *adj* deserving to be treated with CONTEMPT: *That was a contemptible trick to play on a friend!* –**contemptibly** *adv*

**SPELLING NOTE**

Words with the sound /k/, like **cut**, may be spelt **k-**, like **key**, or **qu-**, like **queen**.
Words with the sound /s/, like **city**, may be spelt **s-**, like **soon**, or **ps-**, like **psychology**.

**con·temp·tu·ous** /kən'temptʃuəs/ *adj* [*of*] feeling or expressing CONTEMPT: *She gave a contemptuous laugh.* –**contemptuously** *adv* Compare: *His speech was full of* **comptemptuous** *remarks about the queen.|It was* **contemptible** (=very disrespectful) *of him to speak like that about the queen!*

**con·tend** /kən'tend/ *v* **1** [I *against, for, with*] to compete: *She contended for first prize in the race.* **2** [T +*that*] to claim; say with strength: *The lawyer contended that his client was innocent.*

**con·tend·er** /kən'tendəʳ/ *n* [*for*] (esp. in sports) a person who takes part in a competition

**con·tent¹** /kən'tent/ *adj* [F +*to-v/with*] satisfied; happy: *Mary seems content to sit in front of the television all night.* –see also DISCONTENT

**content²** /kən'tent/ *v* [T *with*] to make happy or satisfied: *John contented himself with one glass of wine.*

**con·tent³** /'kɒntent||'kɑn-/ *n* **1** [U] the subject matter, esp. the ideas, of a book, paper, etc.: *I like the style of this book but I don't like the content.* –compare CONTENTS (2) **2** [S] the amount of a substance contained in something: *Oranges have a high water content.*

**con·tent·ed** /kən'tentɨd/ *adj* [+*to-v/with*] satisfied; happy: *Jean seems contented just to sit and drink beer.* –opposite **discontented** –**contentedly** *adv* –**contentment** *n* [U]

**con·ten·tion** /kən'tenʃən/ *n* **1** [U] the act of CONTENDING: *We're in trouble; this is no time for contention.* **2** [C +*that*] *fml* a claim; argument: *My contention is that the plan will never succeed.*

**con·ten·tious** /kən'tenʃəs/ *adj* **1** *fml* likely to cause argument **2** (of a person) tending to argue

**con·tents** /'kɒntents||'kɑn-/ *n* [P] **1** that which is contained in an object: *to drink the contents of the bottle* **2** (a table at the front of a book showing) what a book contains: *Before buying a book, I look at the* **contents page.** –compare CONTENT³ (1), INDEX¹ (1)

**con·test¹** /'kɒntest||'kɑn-/ *n* a struggle or fight; a competition: *a contest of skill|a beauty contest*

**con·test²** /kən'test/ *v* [T] *fml* **1** to compete for; fight for: *How many people are contesting this seat on the council?* **2** to argue about the rightness of (something): *I intend to contest the judge's decision in another court.*

**con·tes·tant** /kən'testənt/ *n* someone competing in a CONTEST: *There are 50 contestants in this competition.*

**con·text** /'kɒntekst||'kɑn-/ *n* **1** the words around a word, phrase, etc., often used for helping to explain the meaning of the word, phrase, etc.: *You should be able to tell the meaning of this word from its context.* **2** the general conditions in which an event, action, etc., takes place –**contextual** /kən'tekstʃuəl/ *adj*

**con·tin·ent** /'kɒntɨnənt||'kɑn-/ *n* **1** any of the seven main large masses of land on the earth: *Africa is a continent.* **2 the Continent** *BrE* Europe without the British Isles: *He's gone for a holiday on the Continent.*

**con·ti·nen·tal** /ˌkɒntɨ'nentl◂||ˌkɑn-/ *adj* **1** of, related to, or typical of Europe without the British Isles **2** related to or typical of a very large mass of land: *The weather in Siberia is typically continental.*

**continental quilt** /ˌ···· '·/ *n BrE* for DUVET

**con·tin·gen·cy** /kən'tɪndʒənsi/ *n* **-cies** a possibility, esp. one that would cause problems if it happened: *We must be prepared for all contingencies.|contingency plans*

**con·tin·gent¹** /kən'tɪndʒənt/ *adj* [F *on, upon*] dependent on something uncertain: *Our arrival time is contingent on the weather.*

**contingent²** *n* **1** [C] a group of soldiers, ships, etc., gathered together to help a larger force: *The army was strengthened by a large contingent of foreign soldiers.* **2** [C +*sing.*/*pl. v*] a group forming part of a large gathering

**con·tin·u·al** /kən'tɪnjuəl/ *adj* repeated; frequent: *He has continual arguments with his father.* **–continually** *adv*

USAGE Compare **continual** and **continuous. Continual** means "happening again and again over a long period of time", and is often used of bad things; **continuous** means "continuing without interruption": **continual** *interruptions|six hours'* **continuous** *driving|The telephone has been ringing* **continually** *all morning.|The telephone rang* **continuously** *for five minutes.*

**con·tin·u·a·tion** /kənˌtɪnju'eɪʃən/ *n* **1** [U] the act of continuing **2** [C] something which continues from something else: *The Baltic Sea is a continuation of the North Sea.*

**con·tin·ue** /kən'tɪnjuː/ *v* **-ued, -uing 1** [I;T +*to-v*/*v-ing*] to (cause to) go on happening: *The fighting continued for two days.* **2** [I;T +*to-v*/*v-ing*] to (cause to) start again after an interruption: *After a short break the play continued.* **3** [I;T +*that*] to go on saying, esp. after an interruption: *The politician continued by saying that he thought taxes should be lowered.* –see also DISCONTINUE

**con·ti·nu·i·ty** /ˌkɒntə'njuːəti‖ˌkɑntə'nuː-/ *n* [U] uninterrupted connection or union

**con·tin·u·ous** /kən'tɪnjuəs/ *adj* continuing without interruption; unbroken: *The brain needs a continuous supply of blood.* –opposite **discontinuous**; see CONTINUAL (USAGE) **–continuously** *adv*

**con·tort** /kən'tɔːt‖-ɔrt/ *v* [I;T *with*] to (cause to) twist violently out of shape: *Her face was contorted with pain.* **–contortion** *n* [C;U]: *contortions of the body caused by poison*

**con·tour** /'kɒntʊəʳ‖'kɑn-/ *n* **1** the shape of the edges of an area: *the contour of the British coast* **2** also **contour line** /'·· ·/– a line drawn on a map to show the different heights of areas

**con·tra·band** /'kɒntrəbænd‖'kɑn-/ *adj,n* [U] (of or concerning) goods which it is illegal to bring into or send out of a country: *Contraband goods were found in his house.|contraband trade*

**con·tra·cep·tion** /ˌkɒntrə'sepʃən‖ˌkɑn-/ *n* [U] birth control; the methods of preventing sex from resulting in a woman becoming PREGNANT: *to practise contraception* –compare ABORTION

**con·tra·cep·tive** /ˌkɒntrə'septɪv‖ˌkɑn-/ *adj,n* (of or concerning) a drug, object, or material used as a means of preventing an act of sex from resulting in a woman becoming PREGNANT –see also CAP; CONDOM; IUD; PILL; SHEATH

**con·tract¹** /'kɒntrækt‖'kɑn-/ *n* **1** [+*to-v*] a formal agreement, having the force of law, between two or more people or groups: *Our shop has entered into/made a contract with a clothing firm to buy 100 coats a week.* **2** a signed paper on which the conditions of such an agreement are written: *We've signed the contract!* **–contractual** /kən'træktʃuəl/ *adj: You have a contractual obligation to finish the building this month.* **–contractually** *adv*

**con·tract²** /kən'trækt/ *v* **1** [I;T] to (cause to) become smaller: *Metal contracts as it becomes cool.|In conversational English "is not" often contracts to "isn't".* –opposite **expand**; compare DILATE **2** [I;T +*to-v*] to arrange by formal agreement: *They have contracted to build a railway across Africa.* **3** [T] to get (an illness): *My son's contracted a severe fever.*

**con·trac·tion** /kən'trækʃən/ *n* **1** [U] the act of CONTRACTING² (1, 3) **2** [C] the shortened form of a word or words: *"Didn't" is a contraction of "did not".* –compare EXPANSION

**con·trac·tor** /kən'træktəʳ‖'kɑntræk-/ *n* a person, business, or firm that provides building materials or labour

**con·tra·dict** /ˌkɒntrə'dɪkt‖ˌkɑn-/ *v* **1** [I;T] to declare to be wrong or untruthful; say the opposite of: *It's difficult to contradict someone politely.|Don't contradict!* **2** [T] (of a statement, action, fact, etc.) to be opposite in nature or character to **–contradictory** *adj* [*no comp.*]: *The prisoner's statement was contradictory to the one he'd made earlier.*

**con·tra·dic·tion** /ˌkɒntrə'dɪkʃən‖ˌkɑn-/ *n* **1** [U] the act of CONTRADICTING (1) **2** [C;U] a statement, action, or fact that CONTRADICTS (2) another or itself: *It is a contradiction to say you know him but he's a stranger.*

**con·tral·to** /kən'træltəʊ/ *n* **-tos** a female ALTO

**con·trap·tion** /kən'træpʃən/ *n infml* a strange-looking machine or apparatus: *I don't understand how this contraption works.*

**con·tra·ry¹** /'kɒntrəri‖'kɑntreri/ *adj* [*to*] **1** completely different; wholly opposed: *contrary suggestions* **2 contrary to** in opposition to: *Contrary to all advice he gave up his job.*

**con·tra·ry²** /'kɒntrəri‖'kɑntreri/ *n* **1** [*the* S] the opposite: *They say he is guilty, but I believe the contrary.* **2 on the contrary** (*used for expressing strong opposition to what has just been said*) not at all; no: *"I hear you like your new job." "On the contrary, it's rather dull."* **3 to the contrary** to the opposite effect; differently: *If you don't hear (something) to the contrary I'll meet you at seven o'clock tonight.*

USAGE Compare **on the contrary, on the other hand, in contrast**: Use **on the contrary** to show complete disagreement with what has just been said: "*Does it rain a lot in the desert?*" "**On the contrary,** *it hardly ever rains.*" Use **on the other hand** when adding a new and different fact to a statement: *It rarely rains in the desert, but* **on the other hand** *it rains a lot in the coastal areas.* Use **in contrast** to show the (surprising) difference between two very different facts: *It is hot in the desert in the day, but* **in contrast** *it is very cold at night.*

**con·trar·y³** /kən'treəri/ *adj* (of a person ) difficult to handle or work with; unreasonable **–contrarily** *adv* **–contrariness** *n* [U]

**con·trast¹** /'kɒntrɑːst‖'kɑntræst/ *n* **1** [U] comparison of unlike objects, esp. to show differences: *In contrast with/to your belief that we shall fail, I know we shall succeed.* –see CONTRARY[2] (USAGE) **2** [C;U *between*] (a) difference or unlikeness: *such a contrast between brother and sister|This artist uses contrast (between light and dark) skilfully.*

**con·trast[2]** /kən'trɑːst‖-'træst/ *v* [*with*] **1** [T] to compare (two things or people) so that differences are made clear: *In this book the writer contrasts Europe with/and America.* **2** [I] to show a difference when compared: *Your actions contrast unfavourably with your principles.*

**con·tra·vene** /ˌkɒntrə'viːn‖ˌkɑn-/ *v* **-vened, -vening** [T] to act in opposition to; break (a law, rule, custom, etc.): *Your behaviour contravened the law of the country.* **–contravention** /-'venʃən/ *n* [C;U]

**con·trib·ute** /kən'trɪbjuːt/ *v* **-uted, -uting 1** [I;T *to, towards*] to join with others in giving (money, help, etc.): *Everybody contributed towards Jane's present when she left the office.* **2** [I *to*] to help in bringing about; have a share in: *Plenty of fresh air contributes to good health.* **3** [I;T *to*] to write and send (a written article) to a magazine, newspaper, etc. **–contributor** *n: a regular contributor to our magazine* **–contribution** /ˌkɒntrə'bjuːʃən‖ˌkɑn-/ [C;U]: *He gave a small contribution of £5.*

**con·trib·u·to·ry** /kən'trɪbjʊtəri‖-jətori/ *adj* helping to bring about a result: *Your carelessness was a contributory cause of the fire.*

**con·trite** /'kəntraɪt‖'kɑn-/ *adj old use or lit* feeling or showing guilt: *contrite tears* **–contritely** *adv* **–contrition** /kən'trɪʃən/ *n* [U]

**con·trive** /kən'traɪv/ *v* **-trived, -triving** [T +*to-v*] to succeed in (doing something), esp. in spite of difficulty: *After much difficulty I contrived to escape.*

**con·trived** /kən'traɪvd/ *adj* unnatural and forced: *the contrived cheerfulness of a worried doctor*

**con·trol[1]** /kən'trəʊl/ *v* **-ll-** [T] to direct; fix the time, amount, degree, etc. of: *The pressure of steam in the engine is controlled by this button.|Control yourself/your temper; don't get angry.*

**control[2]** *n* **1** [U *of, over*] the power to control or direct: *Which political party has control of the town council? George* **took control** *of the business when his father died.|I* **lost control** *(of myself) and hit him.* **2** [U *on, over*] the act of controlling: *government control over industry|price controls* **3** [C *often pl.*] the place from which a machine, etc., is controlled: *He sat at the controls of the aircraft.|the* **control tower** *of an airport* **4 in control** in command; in charge **5 in the control of** controlled by **6 out of control** in(to) a state of not being controlled: *The car went out of control and crashed.* **7 under control** working properly; controlled in the correct way: *It took the teacher months to bring his class under control.*

**con·tro·ver·sial** /ˌkɒntrə'vɜːʃəl‖ˌkɑntrə'vɜrʃəl/ *adj* causing much argument or disagreement: *a controversial speech* **–controversially** *adv*

**SPELLING NOTE**

Words with the sound /k/, like **cut**, may be spelt **k-**, like **key**, or **qu-**, like **queen.**
Words with the sound /s/, like **city**, may be spelt **s-**, like **soon**, or **ps-**, like **psychology.**

**con·tro·ver·sy** /'kɒntrəvɜːsi, kən'trɒvəsi‖'kɑntrəvɜrsi/ *n* **-sies** [C;U] (a) fierce argument about something: *The new law has caused much controversy.*

**con·ur·ba·tion** /ˌkɒnɜː'beɪʃən‖ˌkɑnɜr-/ *n* a number of cities and towns that have spread and joined together into one area, often with a large city as its centre

**con·va·lesce** /ˌkɒnvə'les‖ˌkɑn-/ *v* **-lesced, -lescing** [I] to spend time getting well after an illness

**con·va·les·cence** /ˌkɒnvə'lesəns‖ˌkɑn-/ *n* [S;U] the length of time a person spends getting well after an illness

**con·va·les·cent** /ˌkɒnvə'lesənt‖ˌkɑn-/ *adj,n* (for, related to, or being) a person spending time getting well after an illness: *a convalescent nursing home*

**con·vec·tion** /kən'vekʃən/ *n* [U] the movement in a gas or liquid caused by warm gas or liquid rising, and cold gas or liquid sinking: *a convection heater|Warm air rises by convection.*

**con·vene** /kən'viːn/ *v* **-vened, -vening** [I;T] **a** (of a group of people, committee, etc.) to meet **b** to call (a group of people, committee, etc.) to meet

**con·ve·ni·ence** /kən'viːnɪəns/ *n* **1** [U] fitness; suitableness: *We bought this house for its convenience. It's very near the shops.* –opposite **inconvenience 2** [C] an apparatus, service, etc., which gives comfort or advantage to its user: *This house has all the modern conveniences.* **3** [U] personal comfort or advantage: *Come* **at your** *earliest* **convenience.** (=as soon as is convenient for you) **4** [C] *BrE fml* for PUBLIC CONVENIENCES

**con·ve·ni·ent** /kən'viːnɪənt/ *adj* **1** suited to one's needs: *a convenient house/time/place* **2** [*for*] near; easy to reach: *Our house is very convenient for the shops.* –opposite **inconvenient –conveniently** *adv*

**con·vent** /'kɒnvənt‖'kɑnvent/ *n* a special house in which NUNS live –compare MONASTERY

**con·ven·tion** /kən'venʃən/ *n* **1** [C] a formal agreement: *The countries all agreed to sign the convention.* **2** [C;U] (an example of) generally accepted social behaviour: *It is the convention for men to wear suits.* –see HABIT (USAGE) **3** [C] a group of people gathered together with a shared purpose: *a teachers' convention*

**con·ven·tion·al** /kən'venʃənəl/ *adj* **1** *often derog* following accepted customs and standards, sometimes too closely: *conventional clothes/opinions/ideas* –opposite **unconventional 2** [*no comp.*] (of a weapon) not atomic: *conventional weapons/warfare* **–conventionally** *adv*

**con·verge** /kən'vɜːdʒ‖-ɜr-/ *v* **-verged, -verging** [I *on*] to come together towards a common point: *The roads converge just before the station.|converging lines* –see also DIVERGE **–convergent** *adj* [*no comp.*] **–convergence** *n* [C;U]

**con·ver·sant** /kən'vɜːsənt‖-ɜr-/ *adj* [F *with*] *fml* familiar with: *I'm not conversant with chemistry because I've never studied it.*

**con·ver·sa·tion** /ˌkɒnvə'seɪʃən‖ˌkɑnvər-/ *n* [C;U] (an) informal talk in which people exchange news, feelings, and thoughts: *Conversations with Joan are always interesting.* **–conversational** *adj: conversa-*

*tional French* –**conversationally** *adv*

**con·verse¹** /kən'vɜːs‖-ɜrs/ *v* **-versed, -versing** [I *on, about, with*] *more fml than* **talk**– to talk informally: *I can converse with anyone about anything!*

**con·verse²** /'kɒnvɜːs‖kən'vɜrs/ *adj,n* [*the* S] *fml* opposite: *I believe the converse of what you are saying.* –**conversely** /kən'vɜːsli‖-ɜr- / *adv*

**con·ver·sion** /kən'vɜːʃən‖-'vɜrʒən/ *n* **1** [C;U *of, from, into, to*] the act of CONVERTing¹; a change from one purpose, system, etc. to another: *the conversion of a house into flats|conversion from yards into metres* **2** [C *from, to*] a change in which a person accepts completely a new religion, belief, etc.

**con·vert¹** /kən'vɜːt‖-ɜrt/ *v* [I;T] **1** [*to, into*] to (cause to) change into another form, substance, or state, or from one purpose, system, etc. to another: *Coal can be converted to gas.|This seat converts into a bed.|I want to convert some dollars into pounds.* **2** [*from, to*] (to persuade a person) to accept a particular religion, political belief, etc.: *John has converted to Buddhism.|She converted him to her opinion.*

**con·vert²** /'kɒnvɜːt‖'kanvɜrt/ *n* a person who has been persuaded to accept a particular religion, political belief, etc.

**con·ver·ti·ble¹** /kən'vɜːtəbəl‖-ɜr-/ *adj* **1** that can be CONVERTed: *a convertible bed that changes into a seat* **2** [*into*] (of a type of money) that can be freely exchanged for other types of money

**convertible²** *n* a car with a roof that can be folded back

**con·vex** /ˌkɒn'veks◂, kən-‖ˌkan'veks◂, kən-/ *adj tech* curved outwards, like the outside edge of a circle: *a convex mirror* –opposite **concave**

**con·vey** /kən'veɪ/ *v* **-veyed, -veying** [T] **1** [*from, to*] to take or carry from one place to another: *to convey electricity from power stations to houses* **2** to make (feelings, ideas, thoughts, etc.) known: *I can't convey my feelings in words.*

**con·vey·er belt** /kən'veɪəʳ belt/ *n* an endless moving belt that carries objects from one place to another –see picture on page 16

**con·vict¹** /kən'vɪkt/ *v* [T *of*] to give a decision as in a court of law that (someone) is guilty of a fault or crime: *The criminal was convicted of murder.* –opposite **acquit**

**con·vict²** /'kɒnvɪkt‖'kan-/ *n* a person who has been found guilty of a crime and sent to prison, esp. for a long time: *an escaped convict*

**con·vic·tion** /kən'vɪkʃən/ *n* **1** [C] an occasion on which one has been CONVICTed¹: *This was her third conviction for stealing.* –opposite **acquittal** **2** (a) very firm and sincere belief: *I speak in the full conviction that our cause is just.|speaking from conviction*

**con·vince** /kən'vɪns/ *v* **-vinced, -vincing** [T +*(that)*] to cause (someone) to believe; persuade (someone): *It took many hours to convince me of his guilt.|I was convinced* (=quite sure) *you were here.|It was hard to convince you that we couldn't afford a new car.|a convinced Christian* (=sure of his/her faith)

USAGE Compare **convince** and **persuade**: *The newspaper article has* **convinced** *me* (=made me believe) *that smoking is a dangerous habit.|The doctor* **persuaded** *me to stop smoking.*

**con·vinc·ing** /kən'vɪnsɪŋ/ *adj* able to CONVINCE: *a convincing speaker/speech* –opposite **unconvincing** –**convincingly** *adv*

**con·viv·i·al** /kən'vɪvɪəl/ *adj fml* friendly; with eating, drinking, and good company: *a very convivial party* –**conviviality** /-ˌvɪvi'ælɪ̆ti / *n* [U]

**con·vo·lut·ed** /'kɒnvəluːtɪ̆d‖'kan-/ *adj fml* twisted; curved: (fig.) *convoluted arguments* –**convolution** /ˌkanvə'luːʃən‖ˌkan-/ *n*

**con·voy¹** /'kɒnvɔɪ‖'kan-/ *n* **-voys** [C +*sing./pl. v*] (a group of ships or vehicles travelling with) a protecting force of armed ships, vehicles, etc.: *We decided to travel* **in convoy** *for safety.*

**convoy²** *v* **-voyed, -voying** [T] (of an armed ship, vehicle, soldiers, etc.) to go with and protect (a group of ships, vehicles, etc.)

**con·vulse** /kən'vʌls/ *v* **-vulsed, -vulsing** [T *with*] to shake or upset (a person, society, etc.) violently

**con·vul·sion** /kən'vʌlʃən/ [*usu. pl.*] an unnaturally violent and sudden movement: *Her nervous illness often threw her into convulsions.* –**convulsive** *adj* –**convulsively** *adv*

**coo** /kuː/ *v* **1** [I] to make the low soft cry of a DOVE or PIGEON, or a sound like this **2** [I;T] to speak softly and lovingly: *to coo at a baby*

**cook¹** /kʊk/ *n* a person who prepares and cooks food: *John's a cook in a hotel.|Peter's a good cook, he often makes dinner.* –compare CHEF; see picture on page 521

**cook²** *v* **1** [I;T] to prepare (food) for eating by using heat; make (a dish): *Do you want your vegetables cooked or raw?|I'm going to cook dinner tomorrow.* **2** [I] (of food) to be prepared in this way: *Make sure this meat cooks for at least an hour.*

USAGE A modern gas or electric **cooker** usually has three parts: the **oven**, the **grill** (*AmE* **broiler**), and the **burners** or **hot plates** on top. The **oven** is used for **baking** bread and cakes or **roasting** a large piece of meat. The **grill** is an apparatus for cooking by direct heat, and can be used e.g. for **grilling** (*AmE* **broiling**) meat or **toasting** bread (=making it hard and brown). The gas **burners** or electric **hotplates** can be used for **boiling** food in a pot with water; for **stewing** food (=cooking food slowly in liquid to make a **stew**); or for **frying** (=cooking food in hot fat or oil). **Simmering** is very gentle slow boiling.

**cook** sthg.↔ **up** *v adv* [T] to invent falsely: *I think she's cooked up that excuse. I don't believe it.*

**cook·er** /'kʊkəʳ/ *BrE*‖**stove** *esp. AmE*– *n* an apparatus on which food is cooked; STOVE –see COOK² (USAGE) –see picture on page 337

**cook·e·ry** /'kʊkəri/ *n* [U] the science of preparation of food: *cookery lessons|a cookery book*

**cook·ie, cooky** *AmE* /'kʊki/ *n* **-ies** **1** a BISCUIT **2** *infml* a person, esp. a man: *a clever cookie*

**cool¹** /kuːl/ *adj* **1** neither warm nor cold; pleasantly cold: *a cool day* **2** calm; unexcited: *Even when you argue you should try and keep cool.|John has* **a very cool head.** (=he never gets too excited) **3** [*towards*] (of a person, manner, behaviour, etc.) not as friendly as usual: *Charles seemed very cool towards me today. I wonder if I've offended him.* **4** *infml* good because of living according to one's own standards and being unconcerned about the opinion of other people –**coolly** /'kuːl-li/ *adv* –**coolness** *n* [U]

**cool²** *v* [I;T *down*] to (cause to) become cool: *Open the windows to cool the room.|Let your tea cool (down) a little before you drink it.* –compare WARM²

**cool down/off** *v adv* [I:T (=**cool** sbdy. **down**)] to (cause to) become calmer and less excited: *It took her a long time to cool down after the argument.|I tried to cool her down, but she was too angry.*

**cool³** *n* [*the* S] **1** a temperature that is neither warm nor cold: *the cool of the evening* **2 keep/lose one's cool** *infml* to keep/lose one's calmness and self control: *Ok, ok, don't lose your cool!*

**cool⁴** *adv* **play it cool** *infml* to act in a calm and unexcited way

**coop¹** /kuːp/ *n* a cage for small creatures, esp. hens

**coop²** *v* → COOP UP

**co-op** /'kəuɒp|-ɑp/ *n infml* for COOPERATIVE²

**co·op·e·rate, co-operate** /kəu'ɒpəreɪt||-'ɑp-/ *v* **-rated, -rating** [I +*to-v*/*with, in*] to work or act together for a shared purpose: *The British cooperated with the French in building the new plane.|Let's all cooperate to get the work done quickly.*

**co·op·e·ra·tion, co-op-** /kəu,ɒpə'reɪʃən||-,ɑp-/ *n* [U] **1** the act of working together for a shared purpose **2** willingness to work together; help: *I need your cooperation in this matter.*

**co·op·e·ra·tive¹, co-op-** /kəu'ɒpərətɪv||-'ɑp-/ *adj* **1** helpful: *The teacher thanked her pupils for being so cooperative.* –opposite **uncooperative 2** [*no comp.*] made, done, or worked by people acting together: *a cooperative farm* **–cooperatively** *adv*

**cooperative², co-op-** also **co-op**– *n* a COOPERATIVE¹ (2) firm, farm, shop, etc.: *a farm cooperative*

**co-opt** /,kəu 'ɒpt||-'ɑpt/ *v* [T *into, onto*] (of an elected group) to choose (someone not elected) as a fellow member: *I wasn't elected to the committee: I was co-opted onto it.*

**coop** sbdy./sthg.↔ **up** /kuːp/ *v adv* [T] to enclose; limit the freedom of (a person or animal): *cooped up in prison*

**co·or·di·nate** /kəu'ɔːdəneɪt||-'ɔr-/ *v* **-nated, -nating** [I;T] to (cause to) work together, esp. to increase effectiveness: *We need to coordinate our efforts.*

**co·or·di·na·tion** /kəu,ɔːdə'neɪʃən||-,ɔr-/ *n* [U] **1** the act of coordinating (COORDINATE) **2** the way in which muscles work together when performing a movement: *Dancers need good coordination.*

**coot** /kuːt/ *n* a small grey water bird

**cop¹** /kɒp||kɑp/ *n infml* for COPPER²

**cop²** *v* → COP OUT

**cope** /kəup/ *v* **coped, coping** [I *with*] to deal successfully with something: *I can't cope with (driving in) heavy traffic.*

**co·pi·ous** /'kəupɪəs/ *adj* plentiful: *copious tears|She was a copious writer.* **–copiously** *adv*

**cop out** /kɒp||kɑp/ *v adv* **-pp-** [I *of, on*] *infml often derog* to fail to take the responsibility of making a difficult decision or to do what one thinks right: *You've got to do it: don't try to cop out (of it) by telling me you're too busy!* **–cop-out** *n*

**SPELLING NOTE**

Words with the sound /k/, like **cut**, may be spelt **k-**, like **key**, or **qu-**, like **queen.**
Words with the sound /s/, like **city**, may be spelt **s-**, like **soon**, or **ps-**, like **psychology.**

**cop·per¹** /'kɒpə'||'kɑ-/ *n* **1** [U] a soft reddish metal **2** [C] *BrE infml* a coin of low value made of this or of BRONZE: *He had only a few coppers in his pocket.* **3** [U] a reddish-brown colour **–coppery** /'kɒpəri||'kɑ- / *adj*

**copper²** also **cop**– *n infml* a policeman

**cop·ra** /'kɒprə||'kɑprə/ *n* [U] the dried flesh of the coconut, from which oil is pressed for making soap

**copse** /kɒps||kɑps/ *n* a small wood, usu. with small trees or bushes

**cop·u·late** /'kɒpjuleɪt||'kɑpjə-/ *v* **-lated, -lating** [I *with*] *fml* to have sex **–copulation** /-'leɪʃən/ *n* [U]

**cop·y¹** /'kɒpi||'kɑpi/ *n* **-ies 1** a thing made to be exactly like another: *I asked my secretary to make me four copies of the letter.* **2** a single example of a magazine, book, newspaper, etc.: *Did you get your copy of "The News" today?*

**copy²** *v* **-ied, -ying 1** [T] to make a copy of (something) **2** [T] to follow (someone or something) as a standard or pattern: *Jean always copies the way I dress.* **3** [I;T *from, off*] to cheat by writing exactly the same thing as (someone else): *He never does his homework himself; he just copies his brother's.*

**copy** sthg.↔ **out** *v adv* [T] to write exactly as written elsewhere: *The teacher asked the children to copy out notes from their history book.*

**cop·y·cat** /'kɒpikæt||'kɑ-/ *n infml derog* a person who regularly and without thought copies other people's behaviour, dress, manners, work, etc.

**cop·y·right** /'kɒpiraɪt||'kɑ-/ *n* [C;U] the right in law to be the only producer or seller of a book, play, film, record, etc., for a fixed period of time

**cor·al** /'kɒrəl||'kɔ-, 'kɑ-/ *n* [U] a white, pink, or reddish stonelike or hornlike substance formed from the bones of very small sea animals. It is often used for making jewellery

**cord** /kɔːd||kɔrd/ *n* **1** [C;U] (a length of) thick string or thin rope **2** [C;U] (a piece of) wire with a protective covering, for joining electrical apparatus to a supply of electricity **3** [C] also **chord**– a part of the body, such as a nerve or number of bones joined together, that is like string: *the vocal cords*

**cor·di·al¹** /'kɔːdɪəl||'kɔrdʒəl/ *adj* warmly friendly: *a cordial smile/welcome/invitation* **–cordiality** /,kɔːdi'æləti||,kɔrdʒi'æ-/ *n* [U]

**cordial²** *n* **1** [U] fruit juice which is added to water and drunk **2** [C;U] → LIQUEUR

**cor·di·al·ly** /'kɔːdɪəli||'kɔrdʒəli/ *adv* in a CORDIAL manner: *You are cordially invited to the wedding.*

**cor·don** /'kɔːdn||'kɔrdn/ *n* a line or ring of police, military vehicles, etc., placed around an area to protect or enclose it

**cordon** sthg.↔ **off** *v adv* [T] to enclose (an area) with a line of police, soldiers, military vehicles, etc.

**cords** /kɔːdz||kɔrdz/ also **corduroys** /'kɔːdərɔɪz||'kɔr-/– *n* [P] *infml* trousers made from CORDUROY –see PAIR¹ (USAGE)

**cor·du·roy** /'kɔːdərɔɪ||'kɔr-/ *n* [U] thick strong cotton cloth with thin raised lines on it, used esp. for making outer clothing

**core¹** /kɔː'||kor/ *n* **1** the hard central part containing the seeds of certain fruits, such as the apple: *An*

**apple core** is *the part of an apple left after the outside has been eaten.* **2** the most important or central part of anything **3 to the core** thoroughly; completely: *She's American to the core.*

**core²** *v* **cored, coring** [T] to remove the CORE¹ (1) from (a fruit)

**cor·gi** /ˈkɔːgi‖ˈkɔrgi/ *n* a small dog with short legs and a foxlike head

**cork¹** /kɔːk‖kɔrk/ *n* **1** [U] the outer covering (BARK) of the **cork oak** (=a tree from Southern Europe and North Africa) **2** [C] a round piece of this material fixed into the neck of a bottle to close it tightly

**cork²** *v* [T *up*] to close (the neck of a bottle or other object) tightly with a CORK¹ (2) –opposite **uncork**

**cork·screw** /ˈkɔːkskruː‖ˈkɔrk-/ *n* **1** an apparatus of twisted metal with a handle, used for pulling CORKS¹ (2) out of bottles **2** → SPIRAL¹

**cor·mo·rant** /ˈkɔːmərənt‖ˈkɔr-/ *n* a large black fish-eating seabird with a long neck

**corn¹** /kɔːn‖kɔrn/ *n* [U] **1** *BrE* (the seed of) any of various types of grain plants, esp. wheat **2** *AmE*‖also **maize, sweet corn** *BrE*– (the seed of) a tall plant grown, esp. in America and Australia, for its ears of yellow seeds

**corn²** *n* a painful area of thick hard skin on the foot, usu. on or near a toe

**cor·ne·a** /ˈkɔːnɪə‖ˈkɔr-/ *n* a strong transparent protective covering on the front outer surface of the eye

**cor·ner¹** /ˈkɔːnəʳ‖ˈkɔr-/ *n* **1** (the inside or outside of) the point at which two lines, surfaces, or edges meet: *the bottom corners of the page|the corner of the desk|the corner of a box* **2** the place where two roads, paths, or streets meet: *I'll meet you on/at the corner of Smith Street and Beach Road.* **3** [*often pl.*] a distant part of the world: *People came from all the corners of the world to hear her sing.* **4** also **corner kick** /ˈ·· ·/– (in football) a kick taken from the corner of the field **5 cut corners** *infml* to do something in the easiest or quickest way, by paying no attention to rules, using simpler methods, etc. **6 in a tight corner** in a difficult or threatening position from which escape is difficult

**corner²** *v* **1** [T] to force (a person or animal) into a difficult position: *He fought like a cornered animal.* **2** [T] to gain control of (the buying, selling, or production of goods): *By defeating their main competitor this firm will* **corner the** *wheat* **market.** **3** [I] (of a vehicle, driver, etc.) to turn a corner: *My car corners well even in wet weather.*

**cor·ner·stone** /ˈkɔːnəstəun‖ˈkɔrnər-/ *n* **1** a stone set at one of the bottom corners of a building, often put in place at a special ceremony **2** something of first importance

**cor·net** /ˈkɔːnᵻt‖kɔrˈnet/ *n* **1** a small brass musical instrument like a TRUMPET **2** also **cone** *BrE*– a thin pastry container for ice-cream, pointed at one end, eaten together with its contents

**corn·flakes** /ˈkɔːnfleɪks‖ˈkɔrn-/ *n* [P] small FLAKES made from coarsely crushed corn, usu. eaten at breakfast, often with milk and sugar

**corn flour** /ˈ··/*BrE*‖ **cornstarch** /ˈkɔːnstɑːtʃ‖ˈkɔrnstɑrtʃ/ *AmE*– *n* [U] a fine white flour made from crushed corn, rice, or other grain, used in cooking to thicken liquids

**cor·nice** /ˈkɔːnᵻs‖ˈkɔr-/ *n* a decorative border at the top edge of the front of a building or pillar or round the top inside edges of the walls in a room

**corn·y** /ˈkɔːni‖ˈkɔrni/ *adj* **-ier, -iest** *infml* too common or done too often before to be new or exciting: *a corny joke/film/play|corny acting*

**co·rol·la·ry** /kəˈrɒləri‖ˈkɔrəleri, ˈkɑ-/ *n* **-ries** *fml* a statement that naturally follows from another

**cor·o·na·ry** /ˈkɒrənəri‖ˈkɔrəneri, ˈkɑ-/ *adj* [A] *tech* of or related to the heart

**coronary throm·bo·sis** /ˌ···· ·ˈ··/ also **coronary** *infml*– *n* **-ses** or **-ries** →HEART ATTACK

**cor·o·na·tion** /ˌkɒrəˈneɪʃən‖ˌkɔ-, ˌkɑ-/ *n* the ceremony at which a king, queen, etc., is crowned

**cor·o·ner** /ˈkɒrənəʳ‖ˈkɔ-, ˈkɑ-/ *n* a public official who inquires into the cause of a person's death when it is not clearly the result of natural causes

**cor·o·net** /ˈkɒrənᵻt‖ˌkɔrəˈnet, ˌkɑ-/ *n* a small crown usu. worn by princes or nobles

**cor·po·ral¹** /ˈkɔːpərəl‖ˈkɔr-/ *adj fml* of, on, or related to the body; bodily: *corporal punishment*

**corporal²** *n* [A;C] a person of low rank in an army or air force

**cor·po·rate** /ˈkɔːpərᵻt‖ˈkɔr-/ *adj* **1** of, belonging to, or shared by all the members of a group; COLLECTIVE: *corporate responsibility/effort* **2** of, belonging to, or related to a CORPORATION (2) –**corporately** *adv*

**cor·po·ra·tion** /ˌkɔːpəˈreɪʃən‖ˌkɔr-/ *n* [C +*sing./pl. v*] **1** *BrE* a group of people (COUNCIL) elected to govern a town: *The corporation has/have decided . . .* **2** a large business organization: *John works for a large American chemical corporation.*

**corps** /kɔːʳ‖kor/ *n* **corps** /kɔːz‖korz/ [C +*sing./pl. v*] **1** *(often cap.)* a trained army group with special duties: *the medical corps* **2** *(often cap.)* a branch of the army equal in size to two DIVISIONS (2) **3** a group of people united in the same activity: *the* **press corps**|*the* **diplomatic corps**

**corpse** /kɔːps‖korps/ *n* a dead body, esp. of a person

**cor·pu·lent** /ˈkɔːpjulənt‖ˈkɔrpjə-/ *adj euph* very fat –**corpulence** *n* [U]

**cor·pus** /ˈkɔːpəs‖ˈkɔr-/ *n* **corpora** /ˈkɔːpərə‖ˈkɔr-/ *or* **corpuses** a collection of all the writings of a special kind: *the corpus of Shakespeare's works*

**cor·pus·cle** /ˈkɔːpəsəl, kɔːˈpʌ-‖ˈkɔrpə-/ *n* any of the red or white cells in the blood

**cor·ral** /kɒˈrɑːl, kə-‖kəˈræl/ *n* (esp. in Western America) an enclosed area where cattle, horses, etc., are kept

**cor·rect¹** /kəˈrekt/ *adj* **1** right; without mistakes: *a correct answer|correct spelling* **2** keeping to proper standards of manners, etc.: *correct behaviour* –opposite **incorrect** –**correctly** *adv* –**correctness** *n* [U]

**correct²** *v* to make right or better; mark the mistakes in: *Correct my spelling if it's wrong.*

**cor·rec·tion** /kəˈrekʃən/ *n* **1** [U] the act of CORRECTing **2** [C] a change that corrects something: *Teachers usually make corrections in red ink.* **3** [U] *euph* punishment: *The prisoner was sent to a labour camp for correction.*

**cor·rec·tive** /kəˈrektɪv/ *adj,n* (something) intended to correct: *corrective punishment* –**correctively** *adv*

**cor·re·la·tion** /ˌkɒrᵻˈleɪʃən‖ˌkɔ-, ˌkɑ-/ *n* [*between*] a shared relationship or causal connection: *a high correlation between unemployment and crime*

**cor·re·spond** /ˌkɒrɨ̣ˈspɒnd‖ˌkɔrɨ̣ˈspɑnd, ˌkɑ-/ *v* [I] **1** [*with, to*] to be in agreement; match: *These goods don't correspond with/to the list of those I ordered.* **2** [*with*] to exchange letters regularly: *Janet and Bob corresponded (with each other) for many years.*

**cor·re·spon·dence** /ˌkɒrɨ̣ˈspɒndəns‖ˌkɔrɨ̣ˈspɑn-, ˌkɑ-/ *n* [C;U] **1** agreement between particular things; likeness **2** the act of exchanging letters **3** the letters exchanged between people: *to do/take a* **correspondence course** (=a course of lessons by post)

**cor·re·spon·dent** /ˌkɒrɨ̣ˈspɒndənt‖ˌkɔrɨ̣ˈspɑn-, ˌkɑ-/ *n* **1** a person with whom another person exchanges letters regularly **2** someone employed by a newspaper, television, etc., to report news from a distant area: *a war correspondent*

**cor·re·spon·ding** /ˌkɒrɨ̣ˈspɒndɪŋ‖ˌkɔrɨ̣ˈspɑn-, ˌkɑ-/ *adj* matching; related: *All rights carry with them corresponding responsibilities.* **–correspondingly** *adv*

**cor·ri·dor** /ˈkɒrɨ̣dɔːʳ‖ˈkɔrɨ̣dər, ˈkɑ-/ *n* **1** a passage, esp. between two rows of rooms: *Room 101 is at the end of the corridor.* **2** a narrow piece of land that passes through a foreign country

**cor·rob·o·rate** /kəˈrɒbəreɪt‖kəˈrɑ-/ *v* **-rated, -rating** [T] to support (an opinion, belief, idea, etc.) by fresh information or proof: *A person who saw the accident corroborated the driver's statement.* **–corroborator** *n* **–corroborative** *adj* **–corroboration** /kəˌrɒbəˈreɪʃən‖kəˌrɑ-/ *n* [U]

**cor·rode** /kəˈrəʊd/ *v* **-roded, -roding** [I;T *away*] to (cause to) become worn or be destroyed slowly, esp. by chemical action: *Acid causes metal to corrode.* **–corrosive** *adj*

**cor·ro·sion** /kəˈrəʊʒən/ *n* [U] **1** the act of corroding (CORRODE) **2** a substance, such as RUST[1] (1), produced by this act: *corrosion on the car's body*

**cor·ru·ga·ted** /ˈkɒrəgeɪtɨ̣d‖ˈkɔ-,ˈkɑ- *adj*/ having wavelike folds: *Sheets of* **corrugated iron** *are often used for roofs and fences.*

**cor·rupt**[1] /kəˈrʌpt/ *v* **1** [I;T] to make morally bad; cause to change from good to bad: *He could have been a great man, but he was corrupted by power.* **2** [T] to influence (esp. a public official) improperly; BRIBE: *He was sent to prison for trying to corrupt a policeman (with money).* **3** [T] to change the original form of (a language, set of teachings, etc.) in a bad way **–corruptible** *adj* **–corruptibility** /-təˈbɪlɨ̣ti/ *n* [U]

**corrupt**[2] *adj* **1** immoral; wicked; bad: *a corrupt political system, full of violence* **2** dishonest; open to being BRIBED: *a corrupt judge* **3** containing mistakes; different from the original: *They spoke a corrupt form of French.* **–corruptly** *adv* **–corruptness** *n* [U]

**cor·rup·tion** /kəˈrʌpʃən/ *n* [U] **1** the act of CORRUPTing **2** dishonesty; immoral behaviour; the state of being CORRUPT[2] (2): *the corruption of the government* **3** decay; impurity

**cor·set** /ˈkɔːsɨ̣t‖ˈkɔr-/ *n* a very tight-fitting undergarment worn, esp. by women, to give shape to the waist and HIPS **–corseted** *adj*

**SPELLING NOTE**

Words with the sound /k/, like **cut**, may be spelt **k-**, like **key**, or **qu-**, like **queen.**

Words with the sound /s/, like **city**, may be spelt **s-**, like **soon**, or **ps-**, like **psychology.**

**cor·tege, -tège** /kɔːˈteɪʒ‖kɔrˈteʒ/ *n fml* a procession of attendants, esp. at a funeral

**cosh** /kɒʃ‖kɑʃ/ *v,n* [C;T] *BrE infml* (to strike with) a short heavy metal pipe or rubber tube used as a weapon

**cos·met·ic**[1] /kɒzˈmetɪk‖kɑz-/ *n* [*usu. pl.*] a face-cream, body-powder, etc., intended to make the skin or hair more beautiful: "*Do you use cosmetics?*" "*Yes, I use face-cream and wear* LIPSTICK."

**cosmetic**[2] *adj* **1** of, related to, or causing increased beauty of the skin or hair: *a cosmetic cream* **2** *derog* dealing with the outside appearance rather than the central part of a problem: *They made only cosmetic repairs on the house before they sold it.*

**cos·mic** /ˈkɒzmɪk‖ˈkɑz-/ *adj* of or related to the whole universe **–cosmically** *adv*

**cos·mo·naut** /ˈkɒzmənɔːt‖ˈkɑz-/ *n* a Soviet ASTRONAUT

**cos·mo·pol·i·tan** /ˌkɒzməˈpɒlɨ̣tn‖ˌkɑzməˈpɑ-/ *adj* **1** consisting of people from many different parts of the world: *London is a very cosmopolitan city.* **2** (of a person, belief, opinion, etc.) not narrow-minded; showing wide experience of different people and places

**cos·mos** /ˈkɒzmɒs‖ˈkɑzməs/ *n* [*the* S] the universe considered as an ordered system

**cos·set** /ˈkɒsɨ̣t‖ˈkɑ-/ *v* [T] to pay a great deal of attention to making (a person) comfortable and contented

**cost**[1] /kɒst‖kɔst/ *n* **1** [S] the amount paid or asked for goods or services; price: *The cost of postage stamps is going up again next week.*|*He bought it at a cost of £300.*|(fig.) *She saved him from the fire, but at the cost of her own life.*|*We must avoid war,* **at all costs.** (=whatever might happen) **2** [C] the price of making or producing something: *We cannot lower our prices until we can get our costs down.*

**cost**[2] *v* **cost, costing** [I;T *no pass.*; not *be +v- ing*] to have (an amount of money) as a price: *It will cost you £50 to fly to Paris.*|*what does it cost?* |(fig.) *That mistake* **cost him his life**.

USAGE The **price** of a thing is what it **costs** you, or what the person who is selling it **charges** you for it: *What is the* **price** *of this watch?*|*What does it* **cost?**|*How much did he* **charge** *you for repairing the car?* The **value** of a thing is what it is worth: *He sold it at a* **price** *below its real* **value. Cost,** not **price,** is used **a** for services: *the* **cost** *of having the house painted* **b** for more general things: *the* **cost** *of living.* **Expense** is used like **cost,** esp. when this is thought of as too large: *the terrible* **expense** *of having the house painted.* A person **makes** a **charge, charges** a **price,** or (for professional services) a **fee.** A thing **costs** a sum of money: *This watch* **costs** *£10.*

**cost**[3] *v* [T] to calculate the price to be charged for (a job, someone's time, etc.)

**co-star** /ˈkəʊ stɑːʳ/ *n* a famous actor or actress who appears together with another famous actor or actress in a film or play

**cost·ly** /ˈkɒstli‖ˈkɔstli/ *adj* **-lier, -liest 1** costing a lot of money; EXPENSIVE **2** gained or won at a great loss:

the costliest war in our history –**costliness** *n* [U]

**cost of living** /ˌ· · ˈ··/ *n* [*the* S] the cost of buying the necessary goods and services to provide a person with the average accepted things for living: *As the cost of living goes up, my* **standard of living** (=degree of wealth and comfort) *goes down.*

**cos·tume** /ˈkɒstjʊm‖ˈkɑstuːm/ *n* [C;U] the clothes typical of a certain period, country, or profession, esp. as worn in plays: *actors in strange costumes*

**co·sy**[1] ‖also **cozy** *AmE* /ˈkəʊzi/ *adj* **-sier, -siest** *apprec* warm and comfortable: *a cosy little house* –**cosily** *adv* –**cosiness** *n* [U]

**cosy**[2] ‖also **cozy** *AmE n* **cosies, cozies** a covering put over a boiled egg or teapot to keep the contents warm: *a tea cosy|an egg cosy*

**cot** /kɒt‖kɑt/ *BrE*‖**crib** *AmE*– *n* a small bed for a young child, usu. with movable sides so that the child cannot fall out

**cot·tage** /ˈkɒtɪdʒ‖ˈkɑ-/ *n* a small house, esp. in the country –see HOUSE (USAGE)

**cottage cheese** /ˌ·· ˈ‖ˈ·· ·/ *n* [U] soft lumpy white cheese made from sour milk

**cot·ton** /ˈkɒtn‖ˈkɑtn/ *n* [U] **1** (a tall plant which produces) soft white hair used for making thread, cloth, COTTON WOOL, etc. **2** thread or cloth made from this: *a cotton dress|a* REEL *of white cotton*

**cotton on** *v adv* [I *to*] *BrE infml* to understand: *It was a long time before I cottoned on (to what he meant).*

**cotton wool** /ˌ·· ˈ·/ *n* [U] *BrE* a soft mass of COTTON used for cleaning wounds, etc.

**couch**[1] /kaʊtʃ/ *n* a long piece of furniture, usu. with a back and arms, on which more than one person may sit or lie; SOFA

**couch**[2] *v* [T *usu. pass.*] to express (words, a reply, etc.) in a certain way: *The government's refusal was couched in friendly language.*

**cou·chette** /kuːˈʃet/ *n* a narrow shelf-like bed on which a person can sleep when on a train

**cou·gar** /ˈkuːgəʳ/ also **mountain lion, puma**‖also **panther** *AmE*– *n* **-gars** *or* **-gar** a large powerful brown wild cat from the mountainous areas of western North America and South America

**cough**[1] /kɒf‖kɔf/ *v* **1** [I] to push air out from the throat with a rough explosive noise, esp. because of discomfort in the lungs or throat during a cold or other infection **2** [T *up*] to clear (something) from the throat by doing this: *I knew she was seriously ill when she began to cough (up) blood.* **3** [I] to make a sound like a cough

**cough up** sthg. *v adv* [T] *infml* to produce (money or information) unwillingly.

**cough**[2] *n* **1** [C] an act or sound of coughing: *She* **gave** a *nervous* **cough. 2** [S] a (medical) condition marked by frequent coughing: *John had a bad cough all last week.*

**could** /kəd; *strong* kʊd/ *v negative contraction* **couldn't** /ˈkʊdnt/ [I +to-v] **1** *past tense of* can: *I can't sing now, but I could when I was young.* **2** (used instead of *can* to describe what someone has said, asked, etc.): *He said we could smoke.* (=He said: "You can smoke.") **3** (used to show that something might be possible): *I could come tomorrow (if you would like me to).|I could have bought it, but I didn't.* **4** (used when making a polite request): *Could you help me to lift it, please?* –compare CAN[1] (3) –see Study Notes on page 386

USAGE *I* **managed** *to* or *I was* **able** *to* both mean that I succeeded in doing something difficult: *I* **managed** *to/I was* **able** *to get the tickets yesterday.* (=I could and I did) *I* **could** means only "I had the power". One does not say **I* **could** *get the tickets yesterday,* but one can say *I* **could** *play the piano* (not **I* **managed** *to*) *when I was three.* –see also CAN[1] (USAGE)

**couldn't** / ˈkʊdnt/ *v short for:* could not: *"Couldn't you see?" "No, I couldn't."*

**coun·cil**[1] /ˈkaʊnsəl/ *n* [+*sing./pl.v*] a group of people appointed or elected to make laws or decisions, for a town, church, etc., or to give advice –sounds like **counsel**

**council**[2] *adj* [A] *BrE* (of houses, flats, etc.) owned and controlled by the local government of an area: *He lives in a council house.*

**coun·cil·lor** /ˈkaʊnsələʳ/ *n* [A;C] a member of a council: *What do you think, Councillor Evans?*

**coun·sel**[1] /ˈkaʊnsəl/ *n* [U] **1** *law* the lawyer(s) speaking for someone in a court of law: *The judge asked (the) counsel to explain his argument.* **2** *becoming rare* advice –sounds like **council**

**counsel**[2] *v* **-ll-** *BrE*‖**-l-** *AmE* [T +*v-ing*] *fml* to advise: *the counselling service for new students*

**coun·sel·lor** *BrE*‖**counselor** *AmE* /ˈkaʊnsələʳ/ *n* **1** [C] an adviser: *a marriage guidance counsellor* **2** [A;C] *esp. AmE* a lawyer

**count**[1] /kaʊnt/ *v* **1** [I;T *up, to*] to say or name the numbers in order, one by one or by groups: *He counted (up) to 100 and then came to find us.|Count 20 then open your eyes.* **2** [T] to say or name (objects) one by one in order to find the whole number in a collection; total: *Count how many apples are in this box.|Have the votes been counted yet?* **3** [T] to include: *There are six people in my family counting my parents.* **4** [T] to consider; regard: *Pavlova was counted among the greatest dancers of the century.* **5** [I] to have value, force, or importance: *It is not how much you read but what you read that counts.*

**count down** *v adv* [I] to count backwards in seconds to zero, esp. before sending a spacecraft into space –see also COUNTDOWN

**count** sbdy. **in** *v adv* [T] *infml* to include: *If you're planning a trip to London, count me in.* –opposite **count** sbdy. **out**

**count on/upon** sbdy./sthg. *v prep* **1** [T +*to-v*/*v-ing*] to depend on (someone, something, or something happening): *You can't count on the weather being fine.|You can count on him to come.* **2** [T +*v-ing*] to expect; take into account: *I didn't count on John arriving so early.* –compare RELY ON (USAGE)

**count** sbdy./sthg.↔ **out** *v adv* [T] **1** to put down in turn while counting: *He counted out ten £5 notes.* **2** to declare (a BOXER who fails to rise from the floor after ten seconds) to be loser of a fight **3** *infml* to leave out: *If you're playing football in this weather you can count me out.* –opposite **count** sbdy. **in**

**count**[2] *n* **1** an act of counting; total reached by counting **2 keep/lose count** to know/fail to know the exact number: *I've lost count of how many times that actress has been married.* **3 be out for the count** (in

BOXING) to be COUNTED[1] **out** (2); be unconscious

**count[3]** **countess** *fem.*– *n* [A;C] (*often cap.*) (the title of) a European nobleman with the rank of a British EARL

**count·a·ble** /'kaʊntəbəl/ *adj* that can be counted: *A* **countable noun** *is often marked* [C] *in this dictionary.* –opposite **uncountable** –see Study Notes on page 494

**count·down** /'kaʊntdaʊn/ *n* an act of counting backwards in seconds to zero: *a ten-second countdown before the spaceship takes off: ten, nine, eight, seven ...* –see also COUNT **down**

**coun·te·nance[1]** /'kaʊntənəns/ *n fml* the appearance or expression of the face

**countenance[2]** *v* **-nanced, -nancing** [T +*v-ing*] *fml* to give support or approval to; allow: *We will never countenance violence.*

**coun·ter[1]** /'kaʊntər/ *n* **1** a narrow table or flat surface at which people in a shop, bank, etc., are served –see picture on page 521 **2 under the counter** privately, secretly, and often illegally: *During the war you could only get cigarettes under the counter–at high prices.*

**count·er[2]** *n* **1** *BrE* a small flat object used in some table games instead of money **2** a person or machine that counts

**counter[3]** *v* **1** [T] to oppose; move or act in opposition to (something): *My employer countered my request for more money by threatening to dismiss me.* **2** [I;T] to meet (an attack or blow) with another attack or blow; RETALIATE

**counter[4]** *adv;adj* [F *to*] (in a manner or direction that is) opposed or opposite: *He acted counter to all advice.*

**coun·ter·act** /,kaʊntə'rækt/ *v* [T] to reduce or oppose the effect of (something) by opposite action: *This drug should counteract the snake's poison.* –compare NEUTRALIZE –**counteraction** /-'ækʃən/ *n* [C;U]

**coun·ter·at·tack[1]** /'kaʊntərətæk/ *n* an attack made to stop, oppose, or return an enemy attack

**counterattack[2]** *v* [I;T] to make a COUNTERATTACK (on)

**coun·ter·bal·ance[1]** /'kaʊntə,bæləns‖-tər-/ also **counterpoise**– *n* a weight or force that acts as a balance for another weight or force

**counterbalance[2]** /,kaʊntə'bæləns‖-tər-/ also **counterpoise**– *v* **-anced, -ancing** [T] to oppose or balance with an equal weight or force

**coun·ter·clock·wise** /,kaʊntə'klɒkwaɪz‖-tər 'klɑk-/ *adj,adv AmE* for ANTICLOCKWISE

**coun·ter·feit[1]** /'kaʊntəfɪt‖-tər-/ *v* [T] to copy (something) closely in order to deceive: *It is against the law to counterfeit money.* –**counterfeiter** *n*

**counterfeit[2]** *adj* made exactly like something real in order to deceive: *a counterfeit banknote*

**coun·ter·foil** /'kaʊntəfɔɪl‖-tər-/ *n* a part of a cheque, money order, etc., kept by the sender as a record –compare STUB[1] (2)

**SPELLING NOTE**

Words with the sound /k/, like **cut**, may be spelt **k-**, like **key**, or **qu-**, like **queen.**
Words with the sound /s/, like **city**, may be spelt **s-**, like **soon**, or **ps-**, like **psychology.**

**coun·ter·mand** /,kaʊntə'mɑːnd, 'kaʊntəmɑːnd‖'kaʊntərmænd/ *v* [T] to declare (a command already given) ineffective, often by giving a different order

**coun·ter·pane** /'kaʊntəpeɪn‖-ər-/ *n becoming rare* for BEDSPREAD

**coun·ter·part** /'kaʊntəpɑːt‖-ərpɑrt/ *n* a person or thing that serves the same purpose or has the same position as another

**coun·ter·sign** /'kaʊntəsaɪn‖-ər-/ *v* [T] to sign (a paper already signed by someone else): *They signed the agreement; it was then countersigned by the president.*

**coun·tess** /'kaʊntɪs/ *n* [A;C] (*often cap.*) a woman who holds the rank of EARL or COUNT[3] for herself or because she is married to an EARL or COUNT

**count·less** /'kaʊntlɪs/ *adj* very many; too many to be counted

**coun·try[1]** /'kʌntri/ *n* **-tries 1** [C] a nation or state with its land or population: *Some parts of this country are much warmer than others.* **2** [C] the people of a nation or state: *That country is opposed to war.* **3** [*the* S] the land outside cities or towns; land used for farming or left unused: *We're going to have a day in the country tomorrow.* **4** [U] land with a special nature or character: *good farming country*

**country[2]** *adj* [A] of, in, from, or related to the COUNTRY[1] (3): *country life|a country house*

**country and west·ern** /,·· · '··/ also **country music** /,·· '··/– *n* [U] popular music in the style of the southern and western US

**coun·try·man** /'kʌntrimən/ **countrywoman** /-,wʊmən/ *fem.*– *n* **-men** /mən/ a person from one's own country; COMPATRIOT

**coun·try·side** /'kʌntrisaɪd/ *n* [U] land outside the cities and towns, used for farming or left unused; country areas

**coun·ty** /'kaʊnti/ *n* **-ties** a large area of land divided from others for purposes of local government

**coup** /kuː/ *n* **coups** /kuːz/ **1** a clever move or action that obtains the desired result: *Getting the contract was quite a coup.* **2**→ COUP D'ETAT

**coup d'é·tat** /,kuːdeɪ'tɑː‖-de'tɑ/ also **coup**– *n* **coups d'état** (*same pronunciation*) a sudden or violent seizure of power in a state by a small group that has not been elected

**cou·pé** /'kuːpeɪ‖kuː'peɪ/ also **coupe** /kuːp/– *n* an enclosed car with two doors and a sloping back

**cou·ple[1]** /'kʌpəl/ *n* **1** two things related in some way; two things of the same kind: *I found a couple of socks in the bedroom but they don't make a pair.* **2** a man and a woman together, esp. a husband and wife: *Adam and Pam are a nice couple. Let's invite them to dinner.* **3** [*of*] *infml* a few; several; small number: *I'll just have a couple of drinks.*

USAGE Compare **pair** and **couple**: A **pair** means a set of two things which are not used separately from each other. These may be two things which are not joined together, such as *shoes*, or something made in two parts, such as *trousers*: *a* **pair** *of socks|a* **pair** *of scissors.* Any two things of the same kind can be spoken of as a **couple**: *I saw a* **couple** *of cats in the garden.|Could you lend me a* **couple** *of pounds?* –see also PAIR[1] (USAGE)

**couple²** *v* **-pled, -pling 1** [T *together*] to join together; connect: *They coupled the carriages of the train together.* –opposite **uncouple 2** [I *with*] (of animals) to unite sexually; MATE

**cou·pon** /ˈkuːpɒn‖-pɑn/ *n* **1** a ticket that shows the right of the holder to receive some payment, service, etc.; VOUCHER: *I have a coupon for ten pence off a packet of soap.* **2** a printed form e.g. in a newspaper, on which goods can be ordered, a competition entered, etc.

**cour·age** /ˈkʌrɪdʒ/ *n* [U] **1** the quality of mind that makes a person able to control fear in the face of danger, pain, misfortune, etc.; bravery: *a woman of courage|She showed great courage during the war.* **2 have the courage of one's (own) convictions** to be brave enough to do or say what one thinks is right

**cou·ra·geous** /kəˈreɪdʒəs/ *adj* brave; fearless; marked by courage: *a courageous action/person* –**courageously** *adv* –**courageousness** *n* [U]

**cour·gette** /kʊəˈʒet‖kʊr-/ *n BrE*– a small green MARROW eaten cooked as a vegetable

**cou·ri·er** /ˈkʊrɪəʳ/ *n* **1** someone who goes with and looks after travellers on a tour **2** a messenger, esp. one on urgent or official business

**course¹** /kɔːs‖kors/ *n* **1** movement from one point to another; continuous movement in space or time: *The enemy should be defeated* **in the course of** (=during) *the year.|During the course of the flight we shall be serving drinks.* **2** direction of movement taken by someone or something: *Our course is directly south.|the course of a stream|*(fig.) *Your best* **course of action** *is to complain to the director.|The ship is* **on/off course.** (=moving in the right/wrong direction) **3** a set of lessons or studies: *a French course|an evening course|a four-year history course* **4** *BrE* a set of events of a planned number, as of medical treatment: *a course of drugs/treatment* **5** any of the several parts of a meal: *We had a three-course dinner.|The first course was soup.* **6** an area of land or water on which a race is held or certain types of sport played: *a* GOLF *course* **7 a matter of course** that which one expects to happen; something natural **8 in due course** without too much delay **9 of course** certainly; NATURALLY (3)

**course²** *v* **coursed, coursing** [I] (of liquid) to flow or move rapidly: *Tears coursed down his cheeks.*

**court¹** /kɔːt‖kort/ *n* **1** [C;U] a room or building in which law cases can be heard and judged: *The case was settled out of court.* (=without having to be heard by a judge) **2** [*the* S;U] people gathered together to hear and judge a law case: *The court stood when the judge entered.* **3** [C;U] (a part of) an area specially prepared and marked for various ball games, such as TENNIS: *Are the players on court yet?* –see picture on page 592 **4** [C] a short street enclosed by buildings on three sides: *They lived in Westbury Court.* **5** [C;U] (people attending) the chief royal palace: *The British court is in London.* **6 take (someone) to court** to start an action in law against (someone)

**court²** *v* [T] **1** to pay attention to (an important or influential person) in order to gain favour, advantage, approval, etc. **2** to risk (something bad), often foolishly or without enough thought: *to court danger/defeat/*DISASTER **3** *becoming rare* (of a man) to visit and pay attention to (a woman he hopes to marry)

**cour·te·ous** /ˈkɜːtɪəs‖ˈkɜr-/ *adj fml* polite and kind; marked by good manners and respect for others –opposite **discourteous** –**courteously** *adv* –**courteousness** *n* [U]

**cour·te·sy** /ˈkɜːtɪ̈si‖ˈkɜr-/ *n* **-sies** [C;U] (an example of) polite behaviour or good manners –opposite **discourtesy**

**court·ier** /ˈkɔːtɪəʳ‖ˈkor-/ *n* (in former times) a noble who attended at the court of a king or other ruler

**court-mar·tial¹** /ˌ·ˈ··◂‖ˈ· ˌ··/ *n* **courts-martial** *or* **court-martials** [C;U] (a trial before) a military court of officers appointed to try people for offences against military law

**court-martial²** *v* **-ll-** ‖also **-l-** *AmE* [T] to try (someone) in a military court for an offence against military law

**court·ship** /kɔːt-ʃɪp‖ˈkort-/ *n* [C;U] *becoming rare* (the length of time taken by) COURTING² (3)

**court·yard** /ˈkɔːtjɑːd‖ˈkortjɑrd/ *n* a space enclosed by walls or buildings, next to or within a castle, large house, etc.

**cous·in** /ˈkʌzən/ *n* the child of one's uncle or aunt –see picture on page 217

**cove** /kəʊv/ *n* a small sheltered BAY⁵

**cov·en** /ˈkʌvən/ *n* a gathering of WITCHes

**cov·e·nant** /ˈkʌvənənt/ *n* **1** a formal solemn agreement between two or more people or groups **2** a written promise to pay a regular sum of money to a church, CHARITY (2), etc.

**Cov·en·try** /ˈkʌvəntri, ˈkɒv-‖ˈkʌv-, ˈkɑv-/ *n* **send (someone) to Coventry** (of a group of people) to refuse to speak to (someone) as a sign of disapproval or as a punishment

**cov·er¹** /ˈkʌvəʳ/ *v* **1** [T] to place or spread something upon, over, or in front of (something) in order to protect, hide, etc.: *The noise was so loud that she covered her ears with her hands.* –opposite **uncover 2** [T] to be or lie on the surface of (something); spread over (something): *furniture covered in dust|The town covers five square miles.* **3** [T] to include; consist of; take into account: *The doctor's talk covered the complete history of medicine.* **4** [T] to travel (a distance): *I want to cover 100 miles before it gets dark.* **5** [T] to report the details of (an event), e.g. for a newspaper: *Our best reporter covered the trial.* **6** [T] to be enough money for: *Will £10* **cover the cost of** *a new skirt?* **7** [T *against*] to protect as from loss; INSURE: *I'm covered against all accidents.* **8** [T] to keep a gun aimed at someone: *The policeman covered the criminal with a gun.* **9** [T] (in sport) **a** to guard the play of (an opponent) **b** to defend (an area or position) against attack by the other team **10** [I;T *for*] to act in place of (someone who is absent): *John's ill today so will you cover for him, Jean?*

**cover up** sthg.↔ *v adv* [T] to prevent (something) from being noticed: *She tried to cover up her nervousness.* –see also COVER-UP

**cover up for** sbdy. *v adv prep* [T] *infml* to hide something wrong or shameful in order to save (someone else) from punishment, blame, etc.: *He says he did it, but he's covering up for a friend.*

**cover²** *n* **1** [C] anything that protects by covering, esp. a piece of material, lid, or top: *Put a cover over the hole.*|*a* CUSHION *cover* **2** [C] the outer front or back page of a magazine or book: *the photograph on the cover of the magazine* **3** [U] shelter or protection: *The flat land gave the soldiers no cover from enemy fire.*|*When it started raining we* **took cover** *under a tree.* **4** [U] insurance against loss, damage, etc.: *cover against fire* **5** [C *usu. sing.*] something that hides or keeps something secret: *This business is a cover for illegal activity.* **6 break cover** to come out of hiding **7 under plain/separate cover** in a plain/separate envelope

**cov·er·age** /'kʌvərɪdʒ/ *n* [U] the amount of time and space given by television, a newspaper, etc., to report a particular piece of news or event

**cov·er·ing** /'kʌvərɪŋ/ *n* something that covers or hides: *Put a covering over the hole.*

**covering let·ter** /ˌ··· '··/ *n* a letter or note containing an explanation or additional information, sent with a parcel or another letter

**cov·ert** /'kʌvət||'kəuvərt/ *adj fml* [*no comp.*] secret; hidden; not openly shown: *covert reasons*|*covert dislike* –opposite **overt** –**covertly** *adv*

**cov·er-up** /'·· ·/ *n* an attempt to prevent something shameful or criminal from becoming publicly known –see also COVER **up**

**cov·et** /'kʌv$\frac{1}{3}$t/ *v* [I;T] *bibl & derog* to desire eagerly to possess (something, esp. something belonging to another person): *Never covet wealth and power.* –**covetous** *adj* –**covetousness** *n* [U]

**cow**[1] /kau/ *n* **1** the fully-grown female form of cattle, kept on farms esp. to provide milk: *A young cow is called a* **calf**. **2** the female form of certain other large sea and land animals: *a cow elephant* –compare BULL, CALF –see MEAT (USAGE)

**cow**[2] *v* [T] to conquer or bring under control by violence or threats

**cow·ard** /'kauəd||-ərd/ *n* a person unable to face danger, pain, etc., because he/she lacks courage; a person who shows fear in a shameful way: *You coward! Are you afraid of water?* –**cowardly** *adj*

**cow·ard·ice** /'kauəd$\frac{1}{3}$s||-ər-/ also **cowardliness** /'kauədlin$\frac{1}{3}$s||-ərd-/– *n* [U] lack of courage

**cow·boy** /'kaubɔɪ/ *n* a man, usu. working on horseback, employed to look after cattle, esp. in North America

**cow·er** /'kauəʳ/ *v* [I] to bend low and draw back as from fear or shame; CRINGE

**cowl** /kaul/ *n* a loose head covering (a HOOD), for the whole of the head except the face, worn esp. by MONKS

**cow·pat** /'kaupæt/ *n euph* a lump of cow DUNG

**cow·slip** /'kauˌslɪp/ *n* a wild plant of the PRIMROSE family with yellow flowers

**cox** /kɒks||kaks/ also **coxswain** /'kɒksən, -sweɪn|| 'kak-/ *fml*– *n* a person who guides and controls a rowing boat, esp. in races

**SPELLING NOTE**

Words with the sound /k/, like **cut**, may be spelt **k-**, like **key**, or **qu-**, like **queen.**
Words with the sound /s/, like **city**, may be spelt **s-**, like **soon**, or **ps-**, like **psychology.**

**coy** /kɔɪ/ *adj* (esp. of a woman) pretending to be modest or SHY in the presence of others so as to attract attention –**coyly** *adv* –**coyness** *n* [U]

**coy·ote** /'kɔɪ-əut, kɔɪ'əuti||'kaɪ-əut, kaɪ'əuti/ *n* **coyotes** *or* **coyote** a small WOLF that lives in western North America and Mexico

**coy·pu** /'kɔɪpuː/ *n* **coypus** *or* **coypu** a large water rat of South America, kept for its valuable fur

**co·zy** /'kəuzi/ *adj,n* **-zier, -ziest** *AmE* for COSY –**cozily** *adv* –**coziness** *n* [U]

**crab** /kræb/ *n* **1** [C] a sea animal with a broad flat shell and five pairs of legs **2** [U] the flesh of this animal cooked as food

**crab·by** /'kræbi/ *adj* **-bier, -biest** bad-tempered

**crack**[1] /kræk/ *v* **1** [I;T *open*] to (cause to) break without dividing into separate parts; split: *Don't pour hot water into the glass or it will crack.*|*I don't like drinking from cracked cups.* **2** [I;T] to (cause to) make a sudden explosive sound: *The whip cracked threateningly.* **3** [I;T] to (cause to) strike with a sudden blow: *The boy fell and cracked his head against the wall.* **4** [I *up*] to fail or yield as a result of difficulties; lose control or effectiveness: *Pressure of work caused John to crack (up).* **5** [T] *infml* to tell (a joke) **6** [T] to discover the secret of (esp. a CODE[1] (1)) –see BREAK (USAGE)

**crack down** *v adv* [I *on*] to become more severe: *The military government decided to crack down on all political activity.* –**crackdown** *n: a crackdown on drunken driving*

**crack**[2] *n* **1** a line of division caused by splitting; thin mark or opening caused by breaking: *a crack in the window*|*a crack in the ice*|(fig.)*The door was opened just a crack.* **2** an explosive sound **3** a sudden sharp blow: *a crack on the head* **4** *infml* an attempt: *This is her first* **crack at** *writing a book.* **5** a clever quick joke or remark: *He's always making cracks about my big feet.* **6 crack of dawn** the first light of day

**crack**[3] *adj* [A *no comp.*] of high quality or good ability; skilful: *a crack shot* (=someone who is very good at shooting)

**crack·er** /'krækəʳ/ *n* **1** a small thin unsweetened BISCUIT: *cheese and crackers* **2** a small harmless explosive charge used for making loud noises on special occasions **3** also **Christmas cracker**– a tube of brightly coloured paper, which often contains a small gift, and which makes a loud noise (BANG) when pulled apart from both ends by two people, esp. at Christmas parties

**crack·le** /'krækəl/ *v* **-led, -ling** [I;T] to (cause to) make small sharp sounds: *The fire crackled.* –**crackle** *n* [S]: *the crackle of burning logs*|*a loud crackle*

**crack·ling** /'kræklɪŋ/ *n* [U] **1** the hard easily broken brown skin of baked PORK **2** the sound of crackling (CRACKLE): *the crackling of the fire*

**crack·pot** /'krækpɒt||-pat/ *adj,n* [A;C] *infml & often humor* (of, belonging to, or being) a person with very strange, foolish, or mad ideas

**cra·dle**[1] /'kreɪdl/ *n* **1** a small bed for a baby, esp. one that can be moved gently from side to side **2** the place where something begins; origin: *Greece was the cradle of Western civilization.* **3** a framework used for supporting something being built or repaired, or for doing certain jobs: *Window cleaners are pulled up* and down tall buildings on cradles.

**cradle**[2] *v* **-dled, -dling** [T] to hold gently as if in a CRADLE[1] (1): *John cradled the baby in his arms.*

**craft**[1] /krɑːft‖kræft/ *n* a job or trade needing skill, esp. with one's hands: *the jeweller's craft*

**craft**[2] *n* **craft** a boat, esp. a small one; vessel: *The harbour was full of sailing craft.*

**crafts·man** /ˈkrɑːftsmən‖ˈkræ-/ *n* **-men** /mən/ a highly skilled worker: *furniture made by the finest craftsmen* **–craftsmanship** *n* [U]

**craft·y** /ˈkrɑːfti‖ˈkræf-/ *adj* **-ier, -iest** cleverly deceitful: *The politician was too crafty.* **–craftily** *adv* **–craftiness** *n* [U]

**crag** /kræg/ *n* a high steep rough rock or mass of rocks

**crag·gy** /ˈkrægi/ *adj* **-gier, -giest** steep and rough; having many CRAGS: (fig.) *his craggy face*

**cram** /kræm/ *v* **-mm- 1** [T] to force (a person or thing) into a small space: *to cram people into a railway carriage|Have you seen the way he crams food down (his throat)?* **2** [T] to fill (something) too full **3** [I *for*] to prepare oneself for an examination by working very hard for a short time: *He sat up all night cramming (for his history examination).*

**cramp**[1] /kræmp/ *n* [C;U] severe pain from the sudden tightening of a muscle, which makes movement difficult: *The swimmer had an attack of cramp and had to be lifted from the water.*

**cramp**[2] *v* [T] **1** to keep within limits; prevent the natural growth or development of **2 cramp someone's style** *infml* to prevent someone from showing his/her abilities to the full

**cramped** /kræmpt/ *adj* limited in space: *a cramped little flat*

**cran·ber·ry** /ˈkrænbəri‖-beri/ *n* **-ries** a small red sour-tasting berry

**crane**[1] /kreɪn/ *n* **1** a machine for lifting heavy objects by means of a very strong rope or wire fastened to a movable arm **2** a tall waterbird with very long legs and neck

**crane**[2] *v* **craned, craning** [I;T] to stretch out (one's neck) esp. to get a better view

**cra·ni·um** /ˈkreɪnɪəm/ *n* **-niums** *or* **-nia** /nɪə/ *tech* the bony framework of the animal or human head; part of the SKULL that covers the brain **–cranial** *adj*

**crank** /kræŋk/ *n* **1** an apparatus, such as a handle fixed at right angles to a rod, which changes movement in a straight line into circular movement **2** *infml, sometimes humor* a person with very peculiar ideas: *a food crank*

**crap** /kræp/ *n* [U] *infml* **1** nonsense: *His speech was* **a load of (old) crap. 2** unwanted things: *Clear all this crap off the table.*

**craps** /kræps/ *n* [U] an American game played with two DICE for money: *to shoot* (=play) *craps*

**crash**[1] /kræʃ/ *v* **1** [I;T] to (cause to) have a violent and noisy accident: *The car crashed on the bend, killing its driver and two passengers.* **2** [I;T] to (cause to) fall or strike something noisily and violently: *The plates crashed onto the floor.* **3** [I] to move violently and noisily: *The angry elephant crashed through the forest.* **4** [I] to make a sudden loud noise: *The lightning flashed and thunder crashed.* **5** [I] (in the world of business and money matters) to fail suddenly; come to ruin: *The New York* STOCK EXCHANGE *crashed in 1929.*

**crash**[2] *n* **1** a violent vehicle accident: *All the passengers were killed in the train/plane/car crash.* **2** a sudden loud noise as made by a violent fall, break, etc.: *a crash of thunder|the crash of breaking glass* **3** a sudden severe business failure: *the crash of the New York* STOCK EXCHANGE

**crash**[3] *adj* [A] marked by a very great effort to reach the desired results quickly: *She wanted to lose weight so she went on* **a crash diet.**|**a crash course** *in conversational French*

**crash hel·met** /ˈ· ˌ··/ *n* a very strong protective head covering (HELMET) worn by racing car drivers, MOTORCYCLE riders, etc.

**crash-land** /ˈ· ·/ *v* [I;T] (to cause a plane) to crash in a controlled way so that as little damage as possible is done **–crash landing** /ˌ·ˈ··/ *n* [C;U]

**crass** /kræs/ *adj* **1** stupid; unfeeling; coarse: *crass behaviour* **2** (of stupidity, foolishness, etc.) complete; very great **–crassly** *adv* **–crassness** *n* [U]

**crate** /kreɪt/ *n* a box or framework, esp. made of wood, for holding fruit, bottles, furniture, etc.: *a milk crate|a crate of apples*

**cra·ter** /ˈkreɪtəʳ/ *n* **1** the round bowl-shaped mouth of a VOLCANO **2** a rough round hole in the ground: *a bomb crater|craters on the moon's surface*

**cra·vat** /krəˈvæt/ *n BrE* a wide piece of material worn round the neck by men –compare TIE[1] (1)

**crave** /kreɪv/ *v* **craved, craving** [I;T] to have a very strong desire for (something): *Sometimes I crave for/after a piece of chocolate.*

**cra·ven** /ˈkreɪvən/ *adj derog* completely lacking courage: *a craven bully* **–cravenly** *adv*

**crav·ing** /ˈkreɪvɪŋ/ *n* a very strong desire: *a craving for sweets* –see DESIRE[2] (USAGE)

**crawl**[1] /krɔːl/ *v* [I] **1** to move slowly with the body close to the ground or floor: *The baby crawled across the room.|There's an insect crawling up your back!*|(fig.) *The traffic crawled along at ten miles an hour.* –see picture on page 669 **2** [*with*] to be completely covered by insects, etc.: *The room was crawling with flies.*|(fig.) *The town was crawling with soldiers.* **3** *infml* to try to win the favour of someone by being too nice to them: *She got her job by crawling to the minister.*

**crawl**[2] *n* [S] **1** a very slow movement **2** a rapid way of swimming on one's stomach, moving first one arm and then the other over one's head, and kicking the feet up and down: *Do a/the crawl to the other side of the pool!*

**cray·fish** /ˈkreɪˌfɪʃ/ also **crawfish** ˈkrɔ-/– *n* **-fish** *or* **-fishes** [C;U] (the flesh of) a small LOBSTER-like animal that lives in rivers and streams

**cray·on** /ˈkreɪən, -ɒn‖-ɑn, -ən/ *n* a stick of coloured wax or chalk used for writing or drawing, esp. on paper **–crayon** *v* [I;T]

**craze**[1] /kreɪz/ *n* [*for*] a very popular fashion, usu. for a very short time: *This new toy is the latest craze in America.*

**craze**[2] *v* **crazed, crazing** [T *usu.pass.*] to make very excited, angry, or mad: *a crazed expression*

**cra·zy** /ˈkreɪzi/ *adj* **-zier, -ziest 1** [+*to-v*] mad; foolish: *He's crazy to go out in this weather!|a crazy* idea **2** [F *about*] wildly excited; very fond (of) or interested (in): *She's crazy about dancing.* **3 like crazy** *infml* wildly and/or very actively: *to work like crazy* –**crazily** *adv* –**craziness** *n* [U]

**creak**[1] /kri:k/ *v* [I] to make the sound of a badly-oiled door when it opens: *We must oil this door to stop it creaking.*|(fig.) *creaking with age*

**creak**[2] *n* [C;S] the sound made by a badly-oiled door when it opens

**creak·y** /'kri:ki/ *adj* **-ier, -iest** that CREAKS: *a creaky door* –**creakily** *adv* –**creakiness** *n* [U]

**cream**[1] /kri:m/ *n* **1** [U] the thick fatty yellowish liquid that rises to the top of milk: *Have some cream in your coffee.*|*a cream cake* **2** [C;U] something similar to or containing this: ARTIFICIAL *cream*|*a chocolate cream*|*cream of chicken soup* **3** [C;U] a mixture made thick and soft like CREAM (1): *face cream*|*Put some of this cream on that burn.* **4** [*the* S] the best part of anything: *the cream of society*

**cream**[2] *adj,n* [U] (having) the colour of CREAM; (having) a yellowish-white colour: *a cream dress*

**cream** sbdy./sthg.↔ **off** *v adv* [T] to remove (the best): *We cream off the cleverest pupils and send them to a special school.*

**cream·y** /'kri:mi/ *adj* **-ier, -iest** containing, or similar to, cream: *creamy soap* –**creaminess** *n* [U]

**crease**[1] /kri:s/ *n* **1** a line made on cloth, paper, etc., by folding or pressing: *You've got a crease in your dress where you've been sitting.* **2** a line marked on the ground to show special areas in certain games

**crease**[2] *v* **creased, creasing** [I;T] to make or become pressed into CREASES: *She wanted to wear her black dress but it was too creased.*|*cloth that creases easily*

**cre·ate** /kri'eɪt/ *v* **-ated, -ating** [T] **1** to cause (something new) to exist; produce (something new): *God created the world.*|*They created a new city in the desert.*|*The new plans* **created (quite) a stir**. (=caused excitement) **2** to appoint (someone) to a special rank or position: *The Queen's son was created Prince of Wales.*

**cre·a·tion** /kri'eɪʃən/ *n* **1** [U] the act of creating (CREATE) **2** [C] something CREATED; something produced by invention or imagination **3** [U] the universe, world, and all living things

**cre·a·tive** /kri'eɪtɪv/ *adj* **1** producing new and original ideas and things: *creative thinking* **2** resulting from newness of thought or expression: *useful and creative work* –**creatively** *adv* –**creativity** /ˌkri:eɪ'tɪv$^{\text{I}}_{\text{ə}}$ti/ also **creativeness**– *n* [U] : *Someone with creativity is needed for this job.*

**cre·a·tor** /kri'eɪtəʳ/ *n* a person who CREATES (1)

**Creator** *n* [*the* S] God

**crea·ture** /'kri:tʃəʳ/ *n* **1** an animal or being of some kind: *all God's creatures*|*creatures from outer space* **2** a person when considered in a particular way: *The poor creature had no family at all.*

**crèche** /kreʃ/ *n BrE* a place where babies and young children are cared for while their parents work –compare NURSERY, PLAYGROUP

**SPELLING NOTE**

Words with the sound /k/, like **cut**, may be spelt **k-**, like **key**, or **qu-**, like **queen.**
Words with the sound /s/, like **city**, may be spelt **s-**, like **soon**, or **ps-**, like **psychology.**

**cre·dence** /'kri:dəns/ *n* [U] *fml* acceptance as true; belief: *The newspapers are* **giving** *no* **credence to** *his latest statements.*

**cre·den·tials** /krɪ'denʃəlz/ *n* [P] a letter or other written proof of a person's position, trustworthiness, etc.

**cred·i·bil·i·ty** /ˌkred$^{\text{I}}_{\text{ə}}$'bɪl$^{\text{I}}_{\text{ə}}$ti/ *n* [U] the state or quality of being CREDIBLE

**cred·i·ble** /'kred$^{\text{I}}_{\text{ə}}$bəl/ *adj* that can be believed; trustworthy: *a credible news report* –see also INCREDIBLE –**credibly** *adv*

**cred·it**[1] /'kred$^{\text{I}}_{\text{ə}}$t/ *n* **1** [U] a system of buying goods or services when they are wanted and paying for them later: *You can buy the furniture* **on credit.**|*six months' credit* –compare HIRE PURCHASE **2** [U] the quality of being likely to repay debts: *His credit is good. You can trust him.* **3** [U] (the amount of) money in a person's account, as at a bank: *The account is* **in credit.** (=there is money in it) **4** [U] belief; trust; faith: *I have no credit in this government's abilities.*|*This story is gaining credit.* –see also DISCREDIT[2] (1) **5** [U] public attention; praise; favourable notice or regard: *I got/was given no credit for my invention.* **6** [S;U] a cause of honour: *You're a credit to your team.*|*Our armed forces* **do us credit.** (=are a credit to us) –opposite **discredit 7** [C] (esp. in the US) a measure of work completed by a student, esp. at a university **8 to someone's credit: a** in someone's favour: *It is to the workers' credit that they opposed the establishment of a military government.* **b** as one's property; belonging to one: *She's not yet 30 years old, and already she has five books to her credit!* (=she's written five books)

**credit**[2] *v* [T] **1** to believe: *Do you really credit the government's statement?* –see also DISCREDIT **2** [*with, to*] to record (an amount of money) added to (an account): *Please credit £10 to my account.*|*Credit my account with £10.* –compare DEBIT[2]

**credit** sbdy. **with** sthg. *v prep* [T] to give CREDIT[1] (2) to (a person) for: *Please credit me with some sense!*

**cred·i·ta·ble** /'kred$^{\text{I}}_{\text{ə}}$təbəl/ *adj* deserving praise, honour, approval, etc.: *a creditable effort to establish peace* –opposite **discreditable** –**creditably** *adv*

**credit card** /'·· ·/ *n* a card allowing the holder to obtain goods and services without payment, the cost being charged to his/her account and paid later

**cred·i·tor** /'kred$^{\text{I}}_{\text{ə}}$təʳ/ *n* a person or firm to whom money is owed –compare DEBTOR

**cred·u·lous** /'kredjʊləs‖-dʒə-/ *adj* too willing to believe, esp. without real proof –see also INCREDULOUS –**credulously** *adv* –**credulousness** *n* [U] –**credulity** /krɪ'dju:l$^{\text{I}}_{\text{ə}}$ti‖-'du:-/ *n* [U]

**creed** /kri:d/ *n* a system of (esp. religious) beliefs or principles

**creek** /kri:k/ *n* a small narrow stream or body of water –sounds like **creak**

**creep** /kri:p/ *v* **crept** /krept/, **creeping** [I] **1** to move slowly and quietly, esp. with the body close to the ground: *The cat crept silently towards the mouse.*|*The sea crept up the shore.* **2** to grow along the ground or a surface: *a creeping plant*

**creep in** *v adv* [I] to begin to happen: *Mistakes are*

*creeping in which could have been avoided.*

**creep into** sthg. *v prep* [T *no pass.*] to begin to happen in: *You must stop these mistakes creeping into your work!*

**creep·er** /ˈkriːpəʳ/ *n* a plant which climbs up trees and walls or grows along the ground

**creeps** /kriːps/ *n* [*the* P] *infml* an unpleasant sensation of fear: *The old castle* **gives me the creeps.**

**creep·y** /ˈkriːpi/ *adj* **-ier, -iest** *infml* causing or feeling an unpleasant sensation of fear: *a creepy old house/man* –**creepily** *adv* –**creepiness** *n* [U]

**cre·mate** /krɨ̵ˈmeɪt||ˈkriːmeɪt/ *v* **-mated, -mating** [T] to burn (a dead person) at a funeral ceremony –**cremation** /krɨ̵ˈmeɪʃən/ *n* [C;U]

**crem·a·to·ri·um** /ˌkreməˈtɔːrɪəm||ˌkriːməˈto-/ also **crematory** /ˈkremətəri||ˈkriːmətori/– *n* **-riums** *or* **-ria** /rɪə/ a building in which dead people are CREMATED

**cre·ole** /ˈkriːəʊl/ *n* (*often cap.*) **1** [C;U] a language which is a combination of a European language with one or more others and is the native language of its speakers –compare PIDGIN **2** [C] (of, being, or related to) a person of both European and African blood

**cre·o·sote** /ˈkriːəsəʊt/ *n* [U] thick brown oily liquid used for preserving wood

**crepe, crêpe** /kreɪp/ *n* **1** [U] a light soft thin cloth with a slightly rough surface made from cotton, silk, wool, etc. **2** [U] also **crepe rubber** /ˌ· ˈ··/– tightly pressed rubber used esp. for the bottoms of shoes **3** [C] a very thin PANCAKE

**crept** /krept/ *v past tense and participle of* CREEP

**cre·scen·do** /krɨ̵ˈʃendəʊ/ *n* **-dos** a gradual increase of force or loudness, esp. of music

**cres·cent** /ˈkresənt, ˈkrez-/ *n* **1** the curved shape of the moon during its first and last quarters, when it forms less than half a circle **2** something shaped like this, e.g. a curved row of houses or a curved street

**cress** /kres/ *n* [U] a very small plant whose leaves are eaten raw: **Mustard and cress** *is often eaten as part of a salad.* –see also WATERCRESS

**crest** /krest/ *n* **1** a showy growth of feathers on top of a bird's head: (fig.) *the crest of feathers on top of a soldier's* HELMET **2** the top of something, esp. of a mountain, hill, or wave **3** a special picture used as a personal mark on letters, envelopes, etc.

**crest·fal·len** /ˈkrestˌfɔːlən/ *adj* disappointed; low in spirits; sad

**cret·in** /ˈkretɨ̵n||ˈkriːtn/ *n* **1** *infml* a very stupid foolish person **2** *tech* a person whose development of mind and body has stopped in early childhood

**cre·vasse** /krɨ̵ˈvæs/ *n* a deep open crack, esp. in thick ice

**crev·ice** /ˈkrevɨ̵s/ *n* a narrow crack or opening, esp. in rock

**crew** /kruː/ *n* [C +*sing./pl. v*] **1** all the people working on a ship, plane, etc., sometimes except for the officers: *The crew is/are waiting for instructions from the ship's owner.* **2** a group of people working together: *the stage crew for the new play*

**crib¹** /krɪb/ *n* **1** *AmE* for COT **2** an open box or wooden framework holding food for animals; MANGER

**crib²** *v* **-bb-** [I;T *from, off*] *infml* to copy (something) dishonestly from someone else: *I didn't know the answers so I cribbed them off John.*

**crick** /krɪk/ *n* a painful stiffening of the muscles, esp. in the back or the neck, making movement difficult

**crick·et¹** /ˈkrɪkɨ̵t/ *n* an outdoor game played with a ball, BAT, and WICKETS, by two teams of 11 players each –**cricketer** *n*

USAGE One plays **cricket** on a **pitch/wicket**, which is in the middle of a **field.** The **bowler bowls** the ball at the **wicket**, and the **batsman** SCORES² (1) **runs.**

**cricket²** *n* a small brown insect, the male of which makes loud noises by rubbing its wings together

**cried** /kraɪd/ *v past tense and participle of* CRY¹

**cries** /kraɪz/ *v 3rd person sing. present tense of* CRY¹

**crime** /kraɪm/ *n* **1** [C] an offence which is punishable by law: *If you* **commit** (=do) **a crime** *you must expect to be punished.*|(fig.) *It's a crime* (=a shame) *that this food should be wasted.* **2** [U] illegal activity in general: *It is the job of the police to prevent crime.* –compare SIN

**crim·i·nal¹** /ˈkrɪmɨ̵nəl/ *adj* **1** [A] of or related to crime or its punishment: *a specialist in criminal law* **2** of the nature of a crime: *a criminal act*|(fig.) *It's criminal to waste money like that.* –**criminally** *adv*

**criminal²** *n* a person who is guilty of crime: *The judge sent the criminal to prison.*

**crim·son** /ˈkrɪmzən/ *adj,n* [U] (having) a deep slightly purplish red colour

**cringe** /krɪndʒ/ *v* **cringed, cringing** [I] **1** to bend and move back, esp. from fear; COWER **2** [*before, to*] to show too much humbleness to someone

**crin·kle** /ˈkrɪŋkəl/ *v* **-kled, -kling** [I;T] to (cause to) become covered with fine lines: *his crinkled face*|*a crinkled piece of paper* –**crinkle** *n* –**crinkly** *adj* **-klier, -kliest** –compare WRINKLE

**crip·ple¹** /ˈkrɪpəl/ *n* a person unable to use properly one or more of his/her limbs, esp. the legs

**cripple²** *v* **-pled, -pling** [T] to hurt or wound (a person) in such a way that use of one or more of the limbs is made difficult or impossible:(fig.) *His business was crippled by the government's decision.*

**cri·sis** /ˈkraɪsɨ̵s/ *n* **-ses** /siːz/ a turning point in the course of something; moment of great danger or difficulty: *a governmental/political crisis*|*the crisis in Southern Africa*|*He's reached the crisis in his illness.*

**crisp¹** /krɪsp/ *adj* **1** hard; dry; easily broken: *crisp pastry* **2** firm; fresh: *a crisp apple*|*crisp vegetables*|*a crisp new bank note* **3** (of style, manners, etc.) quick; showing no doubts or slowness; clear: *a quick crisp reply* **4** (of the air, weather, etc.) cold; dry; fresh: *a crisp winter day* –**crisply** *adv* –**crispness** *n* [U]

**crisp²** also **potato crisp** *BrE*||**potato chip** *AmE* – *n* a thin piece of potato cooked in very hot fat, dried, and usu. sold in packets

**crisp·y** /ˈkrɪspi/ *adj* **-ier, -iest** → CRISP¹ (1, 2) –**crispiness** *n* [U]

**criss·cross** /ˈkrɪskrɒs||-krɔs/ *n* [A;C] a pattern made by crossing a number of straight lines: *a crisscross pattern* –**crisscross** *v* [I;T]

**cri·te·ri·on** /kraɪˈtɪərɪən/ *n* **-ria** /riə/ *or* **-rions** an established standard or principle on which a judgment is based: *What criteria do you use when judging a student's work?*

**crit·ic** /ˈkrɪtɪk/ *n* **1** a person skilled in forming judgments about something, esp. art, music, etc. **2** a person who finds fault: *He's one of her strongest critics.*

**crit·i·cal** /ˈkrɪtɪkəl/ *adj* **1** [*of*] finding fault; judging severely: *Why are you so critical of the government?* **2** very serious or dangerous: *His condition is reported as being critical.* **3** [A] of or related to the work of a CRITIC (1): *critical writings on art* –**critically** *adv*

**crit·i·cis·m** /ˈkrɪtɪsɪzəm/ *n* [C;U] **1** the act of forming judgments about the good or bad qualities of anything, esp. artistic work; work of a CRITIC (1) **2** (an) unfavourable judgment; disapproval: *The government intends to stop unfavourable criticism by controlling the newspapers.*

**crit·i·cize** ||also **-ise** *BrE* /ˈkrɪtɪsaɪz/ *v* **-cized, -cizing** [I;T *for*] **1** to find fault with; judge severely: *The minister criticized my decision.* **2** to make judgments about the good and bad points of

**cri·tique** /krɪˈtiːk/ *n* an article, book, etc., criticizing (CRITICIZE (2)) the work of esp. a writer

**croak** /krəʊk/ *v* **1** [I] to make a deep low noise such as a FROG makes **2** [I;T] to speak or say with a rough voice as if one has a sore throat –**croak** *n*

**cro·chet¹** /ˈkrəʊʃeɪ||krəʊˈʃeɪ/ *n* [U] **1** a way of making clothes, decorations, etc., with a special hooked needle (**crochet-hook**) **2** examples of work done in this way

**crochet²** *v* **-cheted** /ˈkrəʊʃeɪd/, **-cheting** /ˈkrəʊʃeɪ-ɪŋ/ [I;T] to make by means of CROCHET: *to crochet a dress for a baby* –compare KNIT

**crock·e·ry** /ˈkrɒkəri||ˈkrɑ-/ *n* [U] cups, plates, pots, etc.

**croc·o·dile** /ˈkrɒkədaɪl||ˈkrɑ-/ *n* **crocodiles** *or* **crocodile** **1** [C] a large animal (REPTILE) with a long hard-skinned body and a long mouth with many teeth –compare ALLIGATOR **2** [U] the skin of this animal used as leather

**cro·cus** /ˈkrəʊkəs/ *n* **-cuses** *or* **-ci** /kaɪ, kiː/ a small plant with purple, yellow, or white flowers which open in early spring

**crois·sant** /ˈkrwɑːsɒŋ||krwɑːˈsɔŋ/ *n* a piece of buttery breadlike pastry, shaped like a CRESCENT

**cro·ny** /ˈkrəʊni/ *n* **-nies** *infml & sometimes derog* a friend or companion: *The minister's always doing favours for his cronies.*

**crook¹** /krʊk/ *n* **1** *infml* a thief **2** a bend or curve: *She carried the parcel in the crook of her arm.*

**crook²** *v* [I;T] to bend

**crook·ed** /ˈkrʊkɪd/ *adj* **1** not straight; twisted; bent: *a crooked street* **2** *infml* dishonest –**crookedness** *n* [U]

**croon** /kruːn/ *v* [I;T] to sing gently in a low soft voice

**crop¹** /krɒp||krɑp/ *n* **1** [*often pl.*] a plant or plant product such as grain, fruit, or vegetables grown by a farmer: *Wheat is a widely grown crop in Britain.* **2** the amount of such a product produced and gathered in a single season or place: *We've had the biggest wheat crop ever this year.*|(fig.) *a fine crop of hair*|(fig.) *a whole new crop of students*

> **SPELLING NOTE**
> Words with the sound /k/, like **cut**, may be spelt **k-**, like **key**, or **qu-**, like **queen.**
> Words with the sound /s/, like **city**, may be spelt **s-**, like **soon**, or **ps-**, like **psychology.**

**crop²** *v* **-pp-** [T] **1** (of an animal) to bite off and eat the tops of (grass, plants, etc.) **2** to cut (a person's hair or a horse's tail) short

**crop up** *v adv* [I] *infml* to happen or appear unexpectedly: *A problem has cropped up at work so I'll be late home tonight.*

**cro·quet** /ˈkrəʊkeɪ, -ki||krəʊˈkeɪ/ *n* [U] a game played on grass in which players knock balls through small metal arches (HOOPS) with a wooden MALLET

**cross¹** /krɒs||krɔs/ *n* **1** a mark, (× or +), often used **a** as a sign of where something is or should be **b** as a sign that something is incorrect **2** an upright post with a bar across it near the top on which people were bound or nailed and left to die as a punishment in ancient times: *Christ's death on* **the Cross** **3** [*often cap.*] (an object of) this shape as the sign of the Christian faith or religion: *the sign of the Cross* **4** any of various representations of this, used for decoration, in art, JEWELS, etc.: *a gold cross* **5** a decoration of this shape worn as an honour (a MEDAL), esp. for military bravery: *He won the George Cross during the war.* **6** an example of sorrow or suffering as a test of one's patience or goodness: *Everyone* **has his own cross to bear** *in this life.* **7** a combination of two different things: *The drink tasted like a cross between coffee and hot chocolate.*

**cross²** *v* **1** [T] to go, pass, or reach across: *The soldiers took three days to cross the desert.*|*Be careful when you're crossing the road.* **2** [I;T] to place, lie, or pass across each other: *I'll meet you where the paths cross.*|*Jean crossed her legs.* –opposite **uncross** **3** [T] to oppose (someone or his/her plans, wishes, etc.): *Anne hates being crossed so don't argue with her.* **4** [T] to make a movement of the hand forming a cross on (oneself) as a religious act: *She crossed herself as she left the church.* **5** [T] to cause (an animal or plant) to breed with one of another kind: *Is it possible to cross a tiger with/and a lion?*

**cross** sbdy./sthg. **off** (sthg.) *v adv; prep* [T] to remove (from) by drawing a line through: *If you don't want to come, cross your name off (the list).*

**cross** sthg.↔ **out** *v adv* [T] to draw a line through (writing): *I crossed out the mistakes in my sentence.*

**cross³** *adj* angry; bad-tempered: *The old man was really cross when Jane broke his window.* –**crossly** *adv* –**crossness** *n* [U]

**cross·bow** /ˈkrɒsbəʊ||ˈkrɔs-/ *n* a powerful type of BOW³, used esp. in former times –compare LONGBOW

**cross·breed** /ˈkrɒsbriːd||ˈkrɔs-/ *n* an animal or plant which is a mixture of breeds –**crossbred** /-bred/ *adj*: *a crossbred horse*

**cross·check** /ˌkrɒsˈtʃek||ˌkrɔs-/ *v* [T] to find out the correctness of (a calculation, answer, etc.) by using a different method or information from different places

**cross-coun·try** /ˌ· ˈ·· ◂/ *adj,adv* across the fields or open country: *a cross-country race*

**cross-ex·am·ine** /ˌ· ·ˈ··/ also **cross-question** /ˌ· ˈ··/– *v* **-ined, -ining** [I;T] to question (esp. a witness) very closely, usu. in order to compare the answers with other answers given before –**cross-examination** /ˌ· ···ˈ··/ *n* [C;U]

**cross-eyed** /ˈ· ·/ *adj* having the eyes looking in

towards the nose

**cross·fire** /'krɒsfaɪə^r^||'krɔs-/ *n* [U] one or more lines of gunfire firing across the direction of movement

**cross·ing** /'krɒsɪŋ||'krɔ-/ *n* **1** a journey across the sea **2** a place where two lines, tracks, etc., cross **3** a place at which a road, river, etc., may be crossed

**cross-legged** /ˌkrɒs 'legd◂||ˌkrɔs 'legȷ̈d◂/ *adj,adv* having one leg placed over and across the other when sitting

**cross-pur·pos·es** /ˌ· '···/ *n* **at cross-purposes** with different and opposing purposes in mind: *to talk at cross-purposes*

**cross-re·fer** /ˌ· ·'·/ *v* **-ferred, -ferring** [I;T *from, to*] to direct (the reader) from one place in a book to another place in the same book: *In this dictionary* CAPITAL *letters are used to cross-refer from one word to another.*

**cross-ref·erence** /ˌ·'··||'·ˌ··/ *n* a note directing the reader from one place to another in the same book: *In this dictionary cross-references are shown in* CAPITAL *letters.*

**cross·roads** /'krɒsrəudz||'krɔs-/ *n* **crossroads 1** a place where two or more roads cross **2** a point at which an important decision must be taken

**cross-sec·tion** /'· ˌ··/ *n* (a drawing of) a surface made by cutting across something, esp. at right angles to its length: *a cross-section of a worm/a plant stem*|(fig.) *a cross-section of society* (=a representative example of society)

**cross·word** /'krɒsˌwɜːd||'krɔsˌwɜrd/ also **crossword puzzle** /'·· ˌ··/– *n* a printed game in which words are fitted into a pattern of numbered squares in answer to numbered CLUES (=questions, information, etc. that help one to find the necessary word)

**crotch** /krɒtʃ||krɑtʃ/ also **crutch**– *n* the place between the tops of the legs of the human body

**crotch·et** /'krɒtʃȷ̈t||'krɑ-/ *BrE*||**quarter note** *AmE*– *n tech* a musical note

**crotch·et·y** /'krɒtʃȷ̈ti||'krɑ-/ *adj infml* (esp. of someone

old) bad-tempered; liking to argue or complain

**crouch** /krautʃ/ *v* [I *down*] to lower the body close to the ground by bending the knees and back: *The cat saw the bird and crouched down ready to jump.* –see picture on page 669

**crou·pi·er** /'kruːpɪə^r^/ *n* a person who collects the money lost and pays out the money won at a table where games such as ROULETTE are played

**crow**[1] /krəu/ *n* **1** a large shiny black bird with a low loud cry **2 as the crow flies** in a straight line: *We're twenty kilometres from town as the crow flies, but nearly thirty by road.*

**crow**[2] *v* [I] **1** to make the loud high cry of a COCK (=a fully-grown male chicken) **2** [*about, over*] *infml* to speak proudly: *I wish John would stop crowing about his examination results.*

**crow**[3] *n* [S] the loud high cry of a COCK (=a fully-grown male ckicken)

**crow·bar** /'krəubɑː^r^/ *n* an iron bar used to raise heavy objects off the ground or to force open boxes, etc.

**crowd**[1] /kraud/ *n* [C +*sing./pl. v*] **1** a large number of people gathered together: *a crowd waiting for a bus*|*There were crowds of people at the theatre.* **2** a particular social group: *I don't like the college crowd.* **3** a large number of things in disorder

**crowd**[2] *v* **1** [I] (esp. of people) to come together in large numbers: *People crowded round the scene of the accident.* **2** [T] (esp. of people) to fill: *Shoppers crowded the streets.*

**crowd·ed** /'kraudȷ̈d/ *adj* completely full; filled with a crowd: *a crowded room*|*a crowded street*

**crown**[1] /kraun/ *n* **1** [C] a decoration for the head, usu. made of gold with jewels in it, worn by a king or queen as a sign of royal power **2** [C] a decoration of this shape used in art, etc. **3** [C] the top or highest part of anything, e.g. of the head, a hat, a mountain, etc.: *the crown of a hill* **4** [*the* S] (*usu. cap.*) the governing power of a kingdom: *land belonging to the Crown* **5** [*the* S] a CHAMPIONSHIP title: *He won the boxing crown in 1981.*

**crown**[2] *v* [T] **1** to place a crown solemnly on the head of (a person) as a sign of royal power **2** to cover the top of (something): *Mist crowned the mountain.* **3** to complete worthily: *Success in the peace talks has crowned this government's period in power.* **4 to crown it all** to complete good or bad fortune: *His house burnt down, his car was stolen, and to crown it all he lost his job.*

**crown jew·els** /ˌ· '··/ *n* [P] the crowns, jewels, etc., worn by a king or queen on great state occasions

**crown prince** /ˌ· '·◂/ **crown princess** *fem.*– *n* [A;C] the man who has the lawful right to be king after the death of the present king or ruling queen

**cru·cial** /'kruːʃəl/ *adj* [*to, for*] of the greatest importance: *at a crucial moment*|*Speed is crucial to our success.* **–crucially** *adv*

**cru·ci·fix** /'kruːsȷ̈fɪks/ *n* a cross with a figure of Christ on it

**cru·ci·fix·ion** /ˌkruːsȷ̈'fɪkʃən/ *n* **1** [C;U] (an example of) the act of CRUCIFYing **2** [C] (usu. cap.) (a picture or other representation of) the death of Christ on the Cross

**cru·ci·fy** /'kruːsȷ̈faɪ/ *v* **-fied, -fying** [T] to kill (someone) by nailing or binding to a CROSS[1] (2) and leaving to die: (fig.) *He was crucified by public opinion because his new book offended people.*

**crude** /kruːd/ *adj* **1** in a raw or natural state; untreated: *crude oil*|*crude rubber* **2** lacking grace or sensitive feeling: *crude behaviour*|*crude people* **3** not skilfully made or finished **–crudely** *adv*

**cru·di·ty** /'kruːdȷ̈ti/ also **crudeness** /'kruːdnȷ̈s/– *n* **-ties** [C;U] (an example of) the quality of being CRUDE[1]

**cru·el** /'kruːəl/ *adj* **-ll- 1** liking to cause pain or suffering; taking pleasure in the pain of another; merciless: *Anyone who likes watching people suffer is cruel.* **2** painful; causing suffering: *a cruel punishment/remark* |(fig.) *a cruel wind/disease* **–cruelly** *adv*

**cru·el·ty** /'kruːəlti/ *n* **-ties 1** [U] also **cruelness** /'kruːəlnȷ̈s/– the quality of being cruel: *cruelty to animals* **2** [C] a cruel act, remark, etc.

**cru·et** /'kruːȷ̈t/ *n* a set of containers for pepper, salt, oil, MUSTARD, VINEGAR, etc., standing on a specially shaped holder of glass or metal, for use at meals

**cruise**[1] /kruːz/ *v* **cruised, cruising** [I] **1** to sail in an unhurried way **2** (of a car, plane, etc.) to move at a

fairly high but steady speed, esp. on a long journey: *a cruising speed of 60 miles an hour*
**cruise²** *n* a sea voyage for pleasure
**cruis·er** /ˈkruːzəʳ/ *n* **1** a fairly large pleasure boat, usu. covered and with places to sleep and prepare food **2** a large fast warship
**crumb** /krʌm/ *n* a very small piece of dry food, esp. bread or cake: *Sweep up the crumbs from under the table.*|(fig.) *crumbs of knowledge/information* –see picture on page 449
**crum·ble** /ˈkrʌmbəl/ *v* **-bled, -bling** [I;T] to break into very small pieces: *He crumbled the bread in his fingers.*|*As the years passed, the old church crumbled.* (=became a ruin)
**crum·bly** /ˈkrʌmbli/ *adj* **-blier, -bliest** easily CRUMBLED
**crum·pet** /ˈkrʌmpɪ̈t/ *n* (esp. in Britain) a small thick round breadlike cake with holes in one side
**crum·ple** /ˈkrʌmpəl/ *v* **-pled, -pling** [I;T *up*] to (cause to) become full of irregular folds by pressing, crushing, etc.: *I won't wear a crumpled dress.*|*The front of the car crumpled as he drove it into the wall.*
**crunch¹** /krʌntʃ/ *v* **1** [I;T *on*] to crush (food) noisily with the teeth: *The dog was crunching (on) a bone.* **2** [I] to make a crushing noise: *Our feet crunched on the snow.*|*The stones crunched under the car tyres.* **–crunchy** *adj* **-ier, -iest**
**crunch²** *n* [*the* S] **1** a sound as of CRUNCHing **2** *infml* a difficult moment at which an important decision must be made (esp. in the phrase **when/if it comes to the crunch**)
**cru·sade¹** /kruːˈseɪd/ *n* **1** (*usu. cap.*) any of the Christian wars to win back the Holy Land (Palestine) from the Muslims 800 years ago **2** a united effort for the defence or advancement of an idea, principle, etc.: *a crusade for women's rights*
**crusade²** *v* **-saded, -sading** [I *against, for*] to take part in a CRUSADE: *to crusade for women's rights* **–crusader** *n*
**crush¹** /krʌʃ/ *v* **1** [T] to press with great force so as to destroy the natural shape or condition: *This machine crushes wheat grain to make flour.*|*The tree fell on top of the car and crushed it.*|(fig.) *The government has crushed all opposition.* **2** [I;T] to press tightly; CROWD: *The people crushed through the gates.* **3** [I;T] → CRUMPLE
**crush²** *n* **1** [S] uncomfortable pressure caused by a great crowd of people: *There was such a crush on the train!* **2** [U] a drink made by crushing fruit **3** [C *on*] *infml* a strong foolish and short-lived love for someone: *Ben* **has a crush on** *his music teacher.*
**crust** /krʌst/ *n* [C;U] **1** the hard usu. brown outer surface of baked bread **2** the baked pastry on a PIE **3** a hard outer covering (as of earth or snow): *the earth's crust*|*a thin crust of ice*
**crus·ta·cean** /krʌˈsteɪʃən/ *adj,n* (of, belonging to, or being) any of a group of animals with a hard outer shell: SHELLFISH *are crustaceans.*

**SPELLING NOTE**
Words with the sound /k/, like **cut**, may be spelt **k-**, like **key**, or **qu-**, like **queen.**
Words with the sound /s/, like **city**, may be spelt **s-**, like **soon**, or **ps-**, like **psychology.**

**crust·y** /ˈkrʌsti/ *adj* **-ier, -iest 1** having a hard well-baked CRUST (1): *a crusty loaf* **2** bad-tempered; bad-mannered: *a crusty old man*
**crutch** /krʌtʃ/ *n* **1** a stick with a piece that fits under the arm, for supporting a person who has difficulty in walking: *When he broke his leg he had to walk on crutches.* **2** → CROTCH
**crux** /krʌks/ *n* [S] the central part of a problem: *The crux of the matter is ...*
**cry¹** /kraɪ/ *v* **cried, crying 1** [I;T] to produce (tears) from the eyes as a sign of sorrow, sadness, etc.: *She cried when she heard the news of her friend's death.*|*to* **cry oneself to sleep** (=cry till one falls asleep) –compare WEEP **2** [I *out*] to make a loud sound expressing fear, pain, or some other strong feeling: *The little boy cried out with pain when he burnt his fingers.* **3** [I;T] to call loudly; shout: *The trapped woman cried out for help.*|*"Run, run!" he cried.* **4** [I] to make the natural sound of certain animals and birds: *Listen to the seabirds crying.* **5 cry one's eyes/heart out** to cry very bitterly
**cry off** *v adv* [I] to fail to fulfil a promise or agreement: *He cried off after saying he would help us.*
**cry out against** sthg. *v adv prep* [T +*v-ing*] to express one's disapproval of
**cry out for** sthg. *v adv prep* [T] to be in great need of; demand: *The garden is crying out for rain.*
**cry²** *n* **cries 1** [C *of*] any loud sound expressing fear, pain, etc.: *a cry of anger/pain/fear* **2** [C] a loud call; shout: *a cry of "Stop, thief!"*|*a* **battle cry** (=a cry to show or encourage bravery in a battle)|(fig.) *a national cry for lower taxes* **3** [S] a period of crying: *You'll be better after you've had a (good) cry.* **4** [C] the natural sound of certain animals or birds
**cry·ing** /ˈkraɪ-ɪŋ/ *adj* [A] *infml* (esp. of something bad) that demands attention: *a crying need/shame*
**crypt** /krɪpt/ *n* an underground room, esp. under a church
**cryp·tic** /ˈkrɪptɪk/ *adj* hidden; secret; mysterious: *a cryptic message*|*a cryptic remark* (=with hidden meaning) **–cryptically** *adv*
**crys·tal** /ˈkrɪstl/ *n* **1** [U] a transparent natural mineral that looks like ice **2** [U] colourless glass of very high quality: *a crystal wine glass* **3** [C] a small regular shape formed naturally by a substance when it becomes solid: *sugar and salt crystals*
**crys·tal·lize** ||also **-ise** *BrE* /ˈkrɪstəlaɪz/ *v* **-lized, -lizing** [I;T] **1** to (cause to) form CRYSTALS (3): *At what temperature does sugar crystallize?* **2** to (cause to) become clear or fixed in form: *She's trying to crystallize her ideas into a practical plan.* **–crystallization** /-ˈzeɪʃən/ *n* [U]
**CSE** *abbrev. for:* Certificate of Secondary Education; (in Britain) an examination in one of many subjects taken in schools by pupils aged 15 or over, and at a lower level than the GCE
**cu.** *written abbrev. said as:* CUBIC
**cub** /kʌb/ *n* the young of wild animals such as the lion, bear, etc.: *a fox and her cubs*
**cube¹** /kjuːb/ *n* **1** a solid object with six equal sides: *a sugar cube* **2** the number made by multiplying a number by itself twice: *The cube of 3 is 27.* (3×3×3=27)

**cube**[2] *v* **cubed, cubing** [T] **1** to cut (something) into CUBEs[1] (1) **2** to multiply a number by itself twice: *3 cubed* (written $3^3$) *is 27.*
**cu·bic** /ˈkju:bɪk/ *adj* being a measurement of space when the length of something is multiplied by the width and height of it: *a cubic inch/foot/metre*
**cu·bi·cle** /ˈkju:bɪkəl/ *n* a very small enclosed division of a larger room, e.g. for dressing or undressing at a swimming pool
**cubs** /kʌbz/ *n* [*the* P] a division of the BOY SCOUTs for younger boys
**cuck·oo** /ˈkʊku:‖ˈku:ku:, ˈkʊ-/ *n* **-oos** a grey European bird that has a call that sounds like its name
**cu·cum·ber** /ˈkju:kʌmbə$^r$/ *n* [C;U] a long, thin, round vegetable with a dark green skin and light green watery flesh
**cud·dle**[1] /ˈkʌdl/ *v* **-dled, -dling** [I;T *up*] to hold (someone, something, or each other) lovingly and closely in the arms
**cuddle**[2] *n* [S] an act of cuddling (CUDDLE): *My mother gave me a cuddle before I went to bed.*
**cud·dly** /ˈkʌdli/ *adj* **-dlier, -dliest** lovable; suitable for cuddling (CUDDLE)
**cud·gel** /ˈkʌdʒəl/ *n* a short thick heavy object used as a weapon; short heavy CLUB[1] (2)
**cue**[1] /kju:/ *n* (esp. in a play) a signal for the next person to speak or act: *The actor missed his cue and came onto the stage late.* –sounds like **queue**
**cue**[2] *n* a long straight wooden rod used for pushing the ball in games like BILLIARDS, SNOOKER, etc.
**cuff**[1] /kʌf/ *n* **1** the end of a SLEEVE (=the arm of a garment) –see picture on page 563 **2** *AmE* for TURN-UP **3 off the cuff** without preparation: *I'm afraid I can't answer your question off the cuff.*
**cuff**[2] *n,v* [T] (to give) a light blow with the open hand
**cui·sine** /kwɪˈzi:n/ *n* [U] a style of cooking: *French cuisine*
**cul-de-sac** /ˈkʌl d$^{ɪ}_{ə}$ ˌsæk, ˈkʊl‖ˌkʌl d$^{ɪ}_{ə}$ ˈsæk, ˌkʊl/ *n* **cul-de-sacs** *or* **culs-de-sac** /kʌl-, kʊl-/ *BrE* a street with only one way in or out; BLIND ALLEY
**cul·i·na·ry** /ˈkʌl$^{ɪ}_{ə}$nəri‖ˈkʌl$^{ɪ}_{ə}$neri, ˈkju:l-/ *adj* [*no comp.*] *fml* of, related to, or suitable for the kitchen or cooking
**cull** /kʌl/ *v* [T] to search through (a group of animals) and kill the weakest –**cull** *n*: *a seal cull*
**cul·len·der** /ˈkʌl$^{ɪ}_{ə}$ndə$^r$/ *n* → COLANDER
**cul·mi·nate in** sthg. /ˈkʌlm$^{ɪ}_{ə}$neɪt/ *v prep* **-nated, -nating** [T] *fml* to reach the highest point, degree, or development in: *The battle culminated in total victory.* –**culmination** /-ˈneɪʃən/ *n*
**cul·pa·ble** /ˈkʌlpəbəl/ *adj fml* deserving blame; guilty: *culpable behaviour* –**culpability** /ˌkʌlpəˈbɪl$^{ɪ}_{ə}$ti/ *n* [U] –**culpably** *adv*
**cul·prit** /ˈkʌlpr$^{ɪ}_{ə}$t/ *n* the person guilty of a crime or offence
**cult** /kʌlt/ *n* (the group of people believing in) a particular system of religious worship, principle, fashion, etc.: *When did he join the cult?|an ancient tribal cult|Her books have a* **cult following**. (=are keenly read by a certain group)
**cul·ti·vate** /ˈkʌlt$^{ɪ}_{ə}$veɪt/ *v* **-vated, -vating** [T] **1** to prepare (land) for the growing of crops **2** to plant, grow, and raise (a crop) by preparing the soil, providing with water, etc. **3** to encourage the growth of friendship with (a person): *John always tries to cultivate people who are useful to him.*
**cul·ti·vat·ed** /ˈkʌlt$^{ɪ}_{ə}$veɪt$^{ɪ}_{ə}$d/ *adj* having or showing good education, manners, etc.; CULTURED –opposite **uncultivated**
**cul·ti·va·tion** /ˌkʌlt$^{ɪ}_{ə}$ˈveɪʃən/ *n* [U] **1** the act of cultivating (CULTIVATE): *to bring new land under cultivation* **2** the state or quality of being CULTIVATED
**cul·tu·ral** /ˈkʌltʃərəl/ *adj* of or related to CULTURE (1, 2, 3): *cultural independence|cultural activities* –**culturally** *adv*
**cul·ture** /ˈkʌltʃə$^r$/ *n* **1** [C;U] the particular system of art, thought, and customs of a society: *ancient Greek culture|a tribal culture* **2** [U] artistic and other activity of the mind and the works produced by this: *London is a good city for anyone who is interested in culture.* **3** [U] a state of high development in art and thought: *a man of little culture* **4** [U] the practice of raising animals and growing plants: *bee culture*
**cul·tured** /ˈkʌltʃəd‖-ərd/ *adj* **1** having or showing good education, good manners, sensitivity, etc.; CULTIVATED: *a cultured mind* –opposite **uncultured 2** grown or produced by man: *a cultured* PEARL
**cum·ber·some** /ˈkʌmbəsəm‖-bər-/ *adj* heavy and awkward to carry, wear, etc.: *a cumbersome parcel*
**cu·mu·la·tive** /ˈkju:mjʊlətɪv‖-mjə-/ *adj* increasing steadily in amount by one addition after another: *cumulative interest payable on a debt* –**cumulatively** *adv: At first, the drug does no harm, but cumulatively its effects are bad.*
**cun·ning** /ˈkʌnɪŋ/ *adj,n* [U] (showing or having) cleverness in deceiving; clever: *as cunning as a fox|She showed her cunning in the way she avoided answering the question.* –**cunningly** *adv*
**cup**[1] /kʌp/ *n* **1** a small round container, usu. with a handle, from which liquids are drunk: *to wash the coffee cups* –see pictures on pages 337, 521 **2** also **cupful** /ˈkʌpfʊl/– the amount held by one CUP[1] (1): *Add one cup of flour to half a cup of sugar.* **3** a specially shaped usu. silver vessel given as a prize in a competition: *Which team do you think will win the cup this year?* **4** a small circular object: *the cup of a flower*
**cup**[2] *v* **-pp-** [T] to form (esp. the hands) into the shape of a cup: *She cupped her cold hands round the bowl.*
**cup·board** /ˈkʌbəd‖-ərd/ *n* a set of shelves enclosed by doors, where clothes, plates, food, etc., may be stored –compare CLOSET; see picture on page 337
**cu·pid·i·ty** /kjʊˈpɪd$^{ɪ}_{ə}$ti/ *n* [U] *fml & derog* very great desire, esp. for money and property
**cur** /kɜ:$^r$/ *n* a worthless bad-tempered dog, esp. of mixed breed –compare MONGREL
**cu·rate** /ˈkjʊər$^{ɪ}_{ə}$t/ *n* a priest of the lowest rank appointed to help the priest of a PARISH
**cu·ra·tor** /kjʊˈreɪtə$^r$/ *n* the person in charge of a MUSEUM, library, etc.
**curb**[1] /kɜ:b‖kɜrb/ *n* **1** a controlling influence; CHECK[1] (2): *Keep a curb on your anger.* **2** *AmE* for KERB
**curb**[2] *v* [T] to control (one's feelings, temper, spending, etc.)
**curd** /kɜ:d‖kɜrd/ *n* [C;U] the thick soft substance that separates from milk when it becomes sour –compare WHEY
**cur·dle** /ˈkɜ:dl‖ˈkɜrdl/ *v* **-dled, -dling** [I;T] to (cause

to) form into CURDS; (cause to) thicken: (fig.) *a loud cry in the night which* **made his blood curdle** (=made him very afraid) –see also BLOODCURDLING

**cure¹** /kjʊəʳ/ *v* **cured, curing** [T] **1** [*of*] to bring health to (a person) in place of disease or illness: *This medicine cured me of my cold.*|(fig.) *Parents try to cure their children of bad habits.* **2** to make (a disease, illness, etc.) go away, esp. by medical treatment: *The only way to cure backache is to rest.*|(fig.) *government action to cure unemployment* **3** to preserve (food, tobacco, etc.) by drying, hanging in smoke, covering with salt, etc.

**cure²** *n* **1** a medicine that cures an illness, disease, etc.: *There is still no cure for the common cold.*|(fig.) *Is there a cure for rising prices?* **2** a course of medical treatment: *He went for a cure at a famous hospital.* **3** a return to health after illness: *This drug should bring about a cure.*

**cur·few** /ˈkɜːfjuː||ˈkɜr-/ *n* (a usu. military rule stating) a time during which all people should be indoors

**cu·ri·o** /ˈkjʊərɪəʊ/ *n* **-os** a usu. small object, valuable because of its age, rarity, or beauty

**cu·ri·os·i·ty** /ˌkjʊəriˈɒsəti||-ˈɑs-/ *n* **-ties 1** [S;U +*to-v*] the desire to know or learn: *Curiosity is part of a child's nature.* **2** [C] a strange, interesting, or rare object, custom, etc.

**cu·ri·ous** /ˈkjʊərɪəs/ *adj* **1** [F +*to-v*] eager to know or learn: *A student should always be curious to learn.* **2** showing too much interest in other people's affairs: *Don't be so curious about my affairs!* **3** odd; strange; peculiar: *a curious state of affairs* **–curiously** *adv: Curiously (enough), I had met John's new friend before.*

**curl¹** /kɜl||kɜrl/ *n* **1** a small mass of twisted or waved hair –compare WAVE² (3) **2** something with the shape of the lines on a screw; SPIRAL: *a curl of smoke*

**curl²** *v* [I;T *up*] **1** (esp. of hair) to twist into or form a curl or curls: *I don't like my hair straight so I'm having it curled.*|*The leaves became brown, curled up, and died.*|(fig.) *She curled up in front of the fire with a book.*|*She curled herself/her feet up on the bed.* **2** to (cause to) wind: *The plant's stem curled round the branches of the tree.* –opposite **uncurl**

**curl·y** /ˈkɜːli||ˈkɜrli/ *adj* **-ier, -iest** having curls or tending to curl: *curly hair* **–curliness** *n* [U]

**cur·rant** /ˈkʌrənt||ˈkɜr-/ *n* **1** a small dried seedless GRAPE, esp. used in baking cakes **2** the small black, red, or white juicy fruit that grows in bunches on certain bushes: *a* REDCURRANT

**cur·ren·cy** /ˈkʌrənsi||ˈkɜr-/ *n* **-cies 1** [C;U] the particular type of money in use in a country: *The German currency is very strong now.* **2** [U] the state of being in general acceptance: *Reports about the president's illness are* **gaining currency** *among ministers.*

**cur·rent¹** /ˈkʌrənt||ˈkɜr-/ *adj* **1** belonging to the present time; of the present day: *current fashions/events/prices* **2** commonly accepted; in general use: *That word is no longer in current use.* –see NEW (USAGE) **–currently** *adv*

**current²** *n* **1** [C] a continuously moving mass of liquid or gas: *The current is strongest in the middle of the river.*|*air currents*|(fig.) *the current of public opinion* **2** [C;U] the flow of electricity past a fixed point

**current ac·count** /ˈ·· ·ˌ·/ *BrE*||**checking account** /ˈ·· ·ˌ·/ *AmE*– *n* a bank account which usu. does not earn INTEREST¹ (5) and from which money can be taken out by cheque –compare DEPOSIT ACCOUNT

**cur·ric·u·lum** /kəˈrɪkjʊləm||-kjə-/ *n* **-la** /lə/ *or* **-lums** a course of study offered in a school, college, etc. –compare TIMETABLE

**curriculum vi·tae** /kəˌrɪkjʊləm ˈvaɪtiː, ˈviːtaɪ|| -kjə-/ also **résumé** *AmE*– *n* [*usu. sing.*] *Latin fml* a short written account of one's education and past employment, used esp. when looking for a new job

**cur·ry¹** /ˈkʌri/ *n* **-ries** [C;U] an esp. Indian dish of meat, vegetables, etc., cooked in a thick hot-tasting liquid, usu. eaten with rice: *I like vegetable curry.*

**curry²** *v* **-ried, -rying** [T] to make (meat, vegetables, eggs, etc.) into CURRY: *curried chicken*

**curse¹** /kɜːs||kɜrs/ *n* **1** a word or sentence asking God, heaven, etc., to bring down evil or harm on someone or something **2** a cause of misfortune, evil, etc.: *Insects can be a curse to farmers.* **3** a word or words used in swearing; word or words expressing anger, hate, etc.

**curse²** *v* **cursed, cursing 1** [T] to call down evil or misfortune upon: *She cursed him/his name for ruining her life.* **2** [I;T] to swear (at): *The rider cursed his horse.*|*She cursed terribly.* **3 cursed with** suffering misfortune or great harm because of

**cur·so·ry** /ˈkɜːsəri||ˈkɜr-/ *adj* (of work, reading, etc.) not thorough; done without attention to details **–cursorily** *adv*

**curt** /kɜːt||kɜrt/ *adj* (of a person, his/her manner, etc.) too short in speech to be polite: *a curt reply/answer/manner* **–curtly** *adv* **–curtness** *n* [U]

**cur·tail** /kɜːˈteɪl||kɜr-/ *v* [T] *fml* to cut short; reduce; limit: *The minister had to curtail his visit.* **–curtailment** *n* [C;U]

**cur·tain** /ˈkɜːtn||ˈkɜrtn/ *n* a piece of hanging cloth that can cover a window or door, divide a room in two, etc.: **Draw the curtains** (=pull them across the window); *it's getting dark.*|(fig.) *The castle was hidden behind a curtain of smoke.* –see pictures on pages 355, 463

**curtain** sthg.↔**off** *v adv* [T] to separate or divide off with a curtain: *We can curtain off each bed in the hospital.*

**curt·sy¹**, **curtsey** /ˈkɜːtsi||ˈkɜr-/ *n* **-sies** *or* **-seys** a woman's act of respect to someone of higher rank, done by bending the knees and lowering the head and shoulders –compare BOW¹ (1)

**curtsy²**, **curtsey** *v* **-sied, -sying** [I] to make a CURTSY

**cur·va·ture** /ˈkɜːvətʃəʳ||ˈkɜr-/ *n* [C;U] the degree to which something is curved; state of being curved: *the curvature of the earth's surface*

**curve¹** /kɜːv||kɜrv/ *v* **curved, curving** [I;T] to (cause to) bend in the shape of a curve: *The road curved to the right.*

**curve²** *n* a line of which no part is straight and which

**SPELLING NOTE**
Words with the sound /k/, like **cut**, may be spelt **k-**, like **key**, or **qu-**, like **queen.**
Words with the sound /s/, like **city**, may be spelt **s-**, like **soon**, or **ps-**, like **psychology.**

contains no angles; rounded bend: *a curve in the road*

**cush·ion**[1] /'kʊʃən/ *n* **1** a bag filled with a soft substance on which a person can lie, sit, or rest comfortably: *He lay on the floor with a cushion under his head.* –see picture on page 355 **2** something like this in shape or purpose: HOVERCRAFT *ride on a cushion of air.*

**cushion**[2] *v* [T *against*] to lessen the force of: *Nothing can cushion (us against) the fear of death.*

**cush·y** /'kʊʃi/ *adj* **-ier, -iest** *infml* (of a job, style of life, etc.) needing little effort; easy –**cushiness** *n* [U]

**cus·tard** /'kʌstəd‖-ərd/ *n* [U] *BrE* a thick sweet yellow liquid made of milk and eggs or flour, and poured over sweet foods

**cus·to·di·an** /kʌ'stəʊdɪən/ *n* a person in charge of a public building; keeper of a library, castle, etc.

**cus·to·dy** /'kʌstədi/ *n* [U] **1** the act or right of caring for someone, esp. when this right is given in a court of law: *After his* DIVORCE *the father was given custody of the children.* **2** the state of being guarded, esp. by the police: *The stolen car is now in police custody.*|*The criminal was taken into custody.*

**cus·tom** /'kʌstəm/ *n* **1** [C;U] (an) established socially accepted practice: *Social customs vary greatly from country to country.* **2** [C] the habitual practice of a person: *His custom was to get up early and have a cold bath.* **3** [U] *fml* regular support given to a shop by those who buy goods or services: *We lost a great deal of custom when that new shop opened.* **4** **custom-** (done) in accordance with the wishes of the buyer (CUSTOMER): *a custom-built car*|*custom-made clothes* –see HABIT (USAGE)

**cus·tom·a·ry** /'kʌstəməri‖-meri/ *adj* established by custom; usual; habitual: *It is customary to give people gifts on their birthdays.* **–customarily** /-mərəli‖ˌkʌstə'merəli/ *adv*

**cus·tom·er** /'kʌstəmə^r/ *n* a person who buys goods or services from a shop, esp. regularly: *The new shop across the road has taken away most of my customers.* –see picture on page 563

USAGE When you go out to buy things in the shops, you are a **shopper**; when you buy goods from a particular shop, you are that shop's **customer**: *a busy street full of* **shoppers**|*Mrs Slocombe can't come to the telephone–she's serving a* **customer.** If you are paying for professional services, e.g. from a lawyer, you are a **client**, but in the case of medical services you are a **patient**. If you are staying in a hotel, you are a **guest**.

**cus·toms** /'kʌstəmz/ *n* [P] **1** (*often cap.*) a place where travellers' belongings are searched when leaving or entering a country: *As soon as I'd got through customs I felt at home.* **2** taxes paid on goods entering or leaving a country **3** (*often cap.*) the government organization established to collect these taxes

**cut**[1] /kʌt/ *v* **cut, cutting 1** [I;T] to make a narrow opening in (something) with a sharp edge or instrument, accidentally or on purpose: *He cut his fingers on the broken glass.*|*This knife won't cut. Perhaps it needs sharpening.*|(fig.) *His remark cut me deeply.* (=hurt my feelings) **2** [T *up*] to divide (something) or separate with a sharp edge or instrument: *The boys cut the cake in two and ate half each.* **3** [I] to be able to be divided or marked as with a sharp instrument: *A freshly baked cake doesn't cut easily.* **4** [I;T] to make (something) by using a sharp instrument: *They cut (their way) through the forest with their axes.*|*to cut a hole in a piece of paper* **5** [T *away, off, out*] to remove with a sharp instrument: *Cut the dead wood away from the trees.* **6** [T] to shorten, take away, or lessen with or as if with a sharp instrument: *Your fingernails need cutting.*|*Some violent scenes were cut from the film.* **7** [T *back*] to make smaller, less frequent, etc.: *They're cutting (back) train services and postal deliveries.* **8** [T] to grow (a tooth): *Our baby's cutting her first teeth so she needs something to bite on.* **9** [T *off*] to interrupt (a supply of gas, electricity, etc.): *The water was cut (off) for two hours yesterday while the road was being repaired.* **10** [I;T] to divide (a pile of playing cards) in two before DEALing[1] (1) **11** [T] to cross: *The path cuts the field in two places.* **12** [T] to set free or loose by CUTting[1] (2) a rope, metal, etc.: *I cut myself free with my axe.* **13 cut corners** to do something in a less than perfect way in order to save time, money, etc. **14 cut it fine** to leave oneself little time, money, etc., to do what is needed **15 cut one's losses** to stop taking part in a failing business, firm, etc., before one loses too much money

**cut across** sthg. *v prep* [T] **1** to take a shorter way across (a field, corner, etc.) **2** to go beyond or across the limits of: *a new group of Members of Parliament that cuts across party lines*

**cut back** *v adv* **1** [T] (**cut** sthg.↔ **back**) to cut (a plant) close to the stem; PRUNE[2] (2) **2** [I;T (=**cut** sthg.↔ **back**) *on*] to reduce in size or amount: *We oppose any plans to cut back (on) production.* –see also CUTBACK

**cut down** *v adv* **1** [T] (**cut** sthg.↔ **down**) to bring down by cutting; FELL[2]: *to cut down a tree* **2** [I;T (=**cut down** sthg.) *on*] to reduce in quantity or amount: *I have to cut down (on) smoking.* **3** [T] (**cut** sbdy.↔ **down**) to knock down or kill (someone) esp. by striking with a sharp weapon

**cut in** *v adv* [I *on*] *infml* **1** to interrupt **2** to drive into a space between cars in a dangerous way: *You nearly caused a crash by cutting in (on me) like that!*

**cut off** *v adv* [T] **1** (**cut** sthg. ↔ **off**) to separate by cutting: *Cut me off a piece of cheese, will you?* (=cut off a piece for me) **2** (**cut** sbdy./sthg. **off**) to disconnect: *We were cut off in the middle of our telephone conversation.*|*The water was cut off last week.* **3** (**cut** sbdy. **off**) to take away the right to have one's property when one is dead; DISINHERIT: *If you marry that girl I'll* **cut you off without a penny** (=with no money)! **4** (**cut** sbdy./sthg. **off**) [*from*] to block off or surround so that further movement out or in is impossible: (fig.) *Mary felt cut off from her friends when we moved.*

**cut out** *v adv* **1** [T *of*] (**cut** sthg.↔**out**) to remove by cutting: *She cut the advertisement out of the newspaper.* **2** [T] (**cut** sthg.↔**out**) to make by cutting: (fig.) *The rain and wind have cut out a deep valley.* **3** [T +*v-ing*] (**cut out** sthg.) *infml* to leave out; stop: *I must cut out smoking.* **4** [I] (of a motor) to stop suddenly: *Every time I got my car started the engine cut out.* **5 cut it/that out** *infml* to stop it: *John and Jean were arguing, so their father told them to cut it out or go to bed.* **6 not cut out for something/to do**

**something** not naturally well-suited for something
**cut** sbdy./sthg.↔ **up** *v adv* [T] **1** to cut into little pieces **2** *infml* to cause suffering to (someone): *He was really cut up when his wife left him.*

**cut²** *n* **1** the result of cutting; an opening; wound: *a cut in the cloth|How did you get that cut on your hand?* **2** something obtained by cutting: *cuts* (=pieces) *of fresh lamb* **3** [*in*] a reduction in size, amount, etc.: *cuts in government spending* **4** [*of,in*] *infml* a share: *The government plans to take a 50% cut of oil profits.* **5** the act of cutting (dividing) a pile of playing cards in two before DEALing¹ (2) **6 a cut above** *infml* better than; of higher quality or rank than

**cut-and-dried** /ˌ· · '·◂/ also **cut-and-dry**– *adj* already prepared and unlikely to be changed; fixed or settled in advance: *cut-and-dried opinions*

**cut·back** /'kʌtbæk/ *n* a planned decrease in size or amount –see also CUT **back**

**cute** /kjuːt/ *adj esp. AmE*– delightfully pretty and often small: *What a cute little baby!* **–cutely** *adv* **–cuteness** *n* [U]

**cu·ti·cle** /'kjuːtɪkəl/ *n* hard skin surrounding the lower edges of the nails on the toes and fingers

**cut·lass** /'kʌtləs/ *n* a short sword with a slightly curved blade, esp. as used formerly by a PIRATE¹ (1)

**cut·le·ry** /'kʌtləri/ *n* [U] knives, forks, spoons, and other instruments used for eating

**cut·let** /'kʌtl½t/ *n* a small piece of meat

**cut-price** /ˌ· '·◂/ also **cut-rate**– *adj* [A] (of goods) cheap; sold at reduced prices: *cut-price food/petrol*

**cut·ter** /'kʌtəʳ/ *n* **1** a small fast boat –compare SLOOP **2** an instrument for cutting: *a pair of wire-cutters*

**cut·ting¹** /'kʌtɪŋ/ *n* **1** a stem, leaf, etc., cut from a plant, which can form roots and grow into a new plant **2** *BrE*||**clipping** *AmE*– a piece cut out from a newspaper, magazine, etc. **3** something produced by cutting, esp. a passage cut through higher land so that a road, railway, etc., can pass

**cutting²** *adj* **1** bitter; unkind: *cutting remarks* **2** (esp. of the wind) uncomfortably strong and cold **–cuttingly** *adv*

**cwt** *n written abbrev. said as:* HUNDREDWEIGHT

**cy·a·nide** /'saɪənaɪd/ *n* [U] a very strong poison

**cyc·la·men** /'sɪkləmən/ *n* **cyclamen** a plant with white, purple, pink, or very red flowers

**cy·cle¹** /'saɪkəl/ *n* **1** a number of related events happening in a regularly repeated order: *the cycle of the seasons* **2** the period of time needed for this to be completed: *a 50-second cycle*

**cycle²** *v,n* **-cled, -cling** → BICYCLE

**cy·clic** /'saɪklɪk/ also **cyclical** /-klɪkəl/– *adj* happening in CYCLEs¹ (1) **–cyclically** *adv*

**cy·clist** /'saɪkl½st/ *n* a person who rides a bicycle

**cy·clone** /'saɪkləun/ *n tech* a very violent wind moving rapidly in a circle round a calm central area; TORNADO –see also ANTICYCLONE

**cyg·net** /'sɪgn½t/ *n* a young SWAN

**cyl·in·der** /'sɪl½ndəʳ/ *n* **1** a hollow or solid body with a circular base and straight sides **2** the vessel within which a PISTON moves backwards and forwards as in an engine

**cy·lin·dri·cal** /s½'lɪndrɪkəl/ *adj* having the form of a CYLINDER (1) **–cylindrically** *adv*

**cym·bal** /'sɪmbəl/ *n* either of a pair of round thin metal plates struck together to make a loud ringing noise, used in music **–cymbalist** *n*

**cyn·ic** /'sɪnɪk/ *n sometimes derog* a person who thinks that people act only in their own interests, who sees little or no good in anything, and who shows this by making unkind remarks about people and things **–cynical** *adj: cynical remarks/behaviour* **–cynically** *adv* **–cynicism** /'sin½sɪzəm/ *n* [U]

**cy·press** /'saɪpr½s/ *n* a tree with dark green leaves and hard wood, that does not lose its leaves in winter

**cyst** /sɪst/ *n* an enclosed hollow growth in or on the body, containing liquid matter

**czar** /zɑːʳ/ *n* [A;C] → TSAR

# D, d

**D, d** /diː/ **D's, d's** *or* **Ds, ds 1** the fourth letter of the English alphabet **2** the ROMAN NUMERAL (=number) for 500

**-'d** *short form of* **1** would: *I asked if he'd go.* (=if he would go) **2** had: *I asked if he'd gone.* (=if he had gone)

**d** *written abbrev. said as:* died: *d 1937*

**d'** *short form of* do: *D'you like it?*

**dab¹** /dæb/ *n* a slight or light touch: *He made a few dabs at the fence with the paintbrush, but didn't really paint it.*

**dab²** *v* **-bb-** [I;T] to touch lightly or gently, usu. several times: *She dabbed (at) the wound with a wet cloth.*

**dab³** also **dab hand** /ˌ· '·/– *n BrE infml* a person who is very good: *She's a dab hand at cards.*

**dab·ble** /'dæbəl/ *v* **-bled, -bling** [I *at, in*] *sometimes derog* to work at or study something without serious intentions: *to dabble in politics* **–dabbler** *n*

**dachs·hund** /'dækshʊnd, -sənd/ *n* a small dog with short legs and a long body

**dad** /dæd/ also **daddy** /'dædi/– *n infml* (*used esp. by or to children*) father: *What are you doing, dad?* –compare MUM

**daf·fo·dil** /'dæfədɪl/ *n* a yellow flower of early spring

**daft** /dɑːft||dæft/ *adj esp. BrE infml* silly; foolish: *a daft person|a daft thing to do* **–daftness** *n* [U]

**dag·ger** /'dægəʳ/ *n* a short pointed knife used as a weapon, esp. formerly

**dai·ly¹** /'deɪli/ *adj,adv* every day (or every day except Sunday and perhaps Saturday): *a daily journey|The mail is delivered twice daily.|a daily newspaper*

**daily²** *n* **-lies** a newspaper printed and sold every day except Sunday

**dain·ty**[1] /ˈdeɪnti/ *adj* **-tier, -tiest** small, pretty, and delicate: *a dainty child/movement* **–daintily** *adv* **–daintiness** *n* [U]

**dainty**[2] *lit n* **-ties** an especially nice piece of food, esp. a small cake

**dair·y** /ˈdeəri/ *n* **-ies 1** a place on a farm where milk is kept and butter and cheese are made **2** a shop where milk, butter, cheese, and eggs are sold

**dairy cat·tle** /ˈ·· ˌ··/ *n* [P] cattle kept for milk rather than for meat

**da·is** /ˈdeɪǝs, deɪs/ *n* [*usu. sing.*] a raised part built at one end of a hall, for speakers to stand on

**dai·sy** /ˈdeɪzi/ *n* **-sies** a very common small flower, which is white around a yellow centre

**dale** /deɪl/ *n N EngE & lit* a valley

**dal·ly** /ˈdæli/ *v* **-lied, -lying** [I *about, over*] to be slow or waste time: *Don't dally about or we'll be late.*

**dal·ma·tian** /dælˈmeɪʃən/ *n* (*usu. cap.*) a large dog, which is white with black spots

**dam**[1] /dæm/ *n* a wall or bank built to keep back water, esp. to make a RESERVOIR –compare DIKE: *The Aswan Dam helps to control the River Nile in Egypt.*

**dam**[2] *v* **-mm-** [T *up*] **1** to build a dam across: *to dam (up) the river* **2** to keep back by means of a dam: *to dam (up) the water*|(fig.) *Damming up your anger leads to trouble.*

**dam·age**[1] /ˈdæmɪdʒ/ *n* [U] harm; loss: *The storm caused great damage.*|*This new law has done a lot of damage to the government's popularity.*

**damage**[2] *v* **-aged, -aging** [T] to cause damage to

**dam·ag·es** /ˈdæmɪdʒǝz/ *n* [P] *law* money that must be paid for damage that has been done: *The newspaper was ordered to pay damages to the film star for printing an untrue story about him.*

**dam·ask** /ˈdæməsk/ *n,adj* [U] (a kind of cloth) decorated with a special pattern

**dame** /deɪm/ *n AmE infml* (esp. said by men) a woman: *What a dame!*

**Dame** *n* [A;C] (the title of) a woman who has been given a British rank of honour equal to that of KNIGHT: *Dame Ellen Terry was a famous actress.*

**damn**[1] /dæm/ *v* [T] **1** (esp. of God) to send to punishment without end after death **2** (often used in curses): *(God) Damn it!*|*Damn you!* –compare BLESS **3** to declare to be bad: *The play was bad; the newspapers all damned it.* **4** to ruin: *He damned himself with one stupid remark.*

**damn**[2] also **damned**– *adj,adv* [A] *infml* **1** (used for giving force to an expression, good or bad): *a damn fool*|*damn foolish*|*He ran damn fast.* **2 damn well** (used for giving force to a verb, usu. about something bad): *Don't lie to me–you knew damn well what was happening!*

**damn**[3] also **damnation**– *interj infml* (an expression of anger or disappointment)

**damn**[4] *n infml* (used in NEGATIVES[2], questions, etc.) even the smallest amount: *I don't* **care/give a damn** *what you do.*|*His promise isn't* **worth a damn.**

**dam·na·tion** /dæmˈneɪʃən/ *n* [U] the act of DAMNing[1] (1) or state of being damned

**damn·ing** /ˈdæmɪŋ/ *adj fml* very strongly against: *Some damning information against them was discovered.*

**damp**[1] /dæmp/ also **dampness**– *n* [U] wetness: *The damp in the air makes me feel cold.*

**damp**[2] *adj* rather wet: *damp air*|*a damp room* **–damply** *adv*

**damp** sthg.↔ **down** also **dampen** sthg.↔ **down**– *v adv* [T] to make (a fire) burn more slowly: *Damp down the fire before you go to bed.*

**damp·en** /ˈdæmpən/ *v* **1** [I;T] to (cause to) become DAMP: *The rain hardly dampened the ground.* **2** [T] to make (feelings of happiness, eagerness, etc.) less strong: *Nothing can dampen my spirits today!*

**dam·sel** /ˈdæmzəl/ *n lit* a young unmarried woman of noble birth

**dam·son** /ˈdæmzən/ *n* (the small purple fruit of) a type of PLUM tree

**dance**[1] /dɑːns‖dæns/ *v* **danced, dancing** [I;T *to*] to move to music: *She loves to dance to fast music.*|*She danced the* WALTZ *with me.* **–dancer** *n*

**dance**[2] *n* **1** an act of dancing: *Let's have one more dance before we go home.* **2** (the name of) a set of movements, esp. performed to music: *The* WALTZ *is a beautiful dance.* **3** a social meeting for dancing: *My parents are going to a dance tonight.*

**dan·de·li·on** /ˈdændǝlaɪən/ *n* a small wild bright yellow flower

**dan·druff** /ˈdændrəf, -drʌf/ *n* [U] a common disease in which bits of dead skin form on the head and can be seen in the hair

**dan·ger** /ˈdeɪndʒə^r/ *n* **1** [U] the possibility of harm or loss: *The sign says "Danger! Falling rocks".*|*a danger signal*|*a place where children can play without danger*|*She had been very sick, but now she was* **out of danger.**|*He is* **in** *(great, real,* etc.) **danger of** *losing his job.* **2** [C] a case or cause of danger: *the dangers of smoking*

**dan·ger·ous** /ˈdeɪndʒərəs/ *adj* able to or likely to cause danger: *a dangerous criminal/drug*|*It's dangerous to smoke.* **–dangerously** *adv: Don't drive so dangerously.*|*He is dangerously ill.*

**dan·gle** /ˈdæŋgəl/ *v* **-gled, -gling 1** [I;T] to (cause to) hang or swing loosely: *keys dangling from a chain*|*He sat on the edge of the table dangling his legs.* **2** [T *in front of, before*] to offer as an attraction

**dank** /dæŋk/ *adj* unpleasantly wet and usu. cold: *an unhealthy house with dank stone walls*

**dap·per** /ˈdæpə^r/ *adj* (esp. of small men) (perhaps too) neat in appearance and quick in movements

**dap·pled** /ˈdæpəld/ *adj* marked with spots of colour, or of sun and shadow: *a dappled horse*

**dare**[1] /deə^r/ *v* **dared, daring,** *pres. tense* NEGATIVE *short form* **daren't 1** [I *+to-v*/ *+to-v*;not *be +v- ing*] to be brave or rude enough (to): *I dare not/daren't go.*|*I didn't dare (to) ask.*|*That's as much as I dare spend.*|*How dare you say that?* –see Study Notes on page 386 **2** [T] to (try to) persuade (someone) to do something dangerous: *I dared him to jump.*

**dare**[2] *n* a statement that someone is not brave enough to do something; CHALLENGE

**daren't** /deənt‖deərnt/ *short for* dare not: *I daren't ask him.*

**dare·say** /deəˈseɪ‖ˈdeər-/ *v BrE (only with "I")* [I;T +*(that)*] (I) suppose (that); perhaps: *I daresay you're right.*|*It will come, I daresay.*

**dar·ing**[1] /ˈdeərɪŋ/ *adj* very brave (in a good or bad sense): *a daring attempt to save the children from the* fire|a daring crime

**daring²** *n* [U] bravery: *an act of great daring*

**dark¹** /dɑːk‖dɑrk/ *adj* **1** partly or completely without light: *too dark to read|In winter it gets dark here early.* **2** tending towards black: *dark hair/green/clothes|a tall dark good-looking man|*(fig.) *Don't always look on the dark side of things.|*(fig.) *dark days ahead* **3** secret; hidden: *He kept his plans dark.* **4 dark horse** a person who may be successful although not much is known about him/her –**darkly** *adv: He spoke darkly of trouble to come.* –**darkness** *n* [U]

**dark²** *n* [*the* S;U] **1** the absence of light; darkness: *Can cats see in the dark?|Some children are afraid of the dark.|We don't go out* **after dark.**|*Get home* **before dark. 2 keep someone in the dark** to keep someone without knowledge

**dark·en** /ˈdɑːkən‖ˈdɑr-/ *v* [I;T] to (cause to) become dark: *The sky quickly darkened after sunset.|His face darkened with anger when he heard the bad news.* –compare LIGHTEN¹

**dar·ling¹** /ˈdɑːlɪŋ‖ˈdɑr-/ *n* (usu. used to address someone) a person who is very much liked or loved: *Darling, will you please hurry up!*

**darling²** *adj* [A] dearly loved: *my darling husband/wife/child*

**darn¹** /dɑːn‖dɑrn/ *v* [I;T] to repair (a hole in cloth or a garment with a hole in it) by passing threads through and across: *to darn a sock/the hole in a sock* –**darn** *n*

**darn²** *n,adj,adv,interj euph* → DAMN

**dart¹** /dɑːt‖dɑrt/ *n* **1** a small sharp-pointed object to be thrown, shot, etc., esp. one used as a weapon or in games: *a poisoned dart* **2** [S] a quick movement in a particular direction: *The prisoner* **made a dart for** *the door.* **3** a fold sewn into a garment to make it fit better

**dart²** *v* **1** [I *across, out,* etc.] to move suddenly and quickly: *He darted out/towards the door.* **2** [T] to throw or send out suddenly and quickly: *She darted an angry look at her husband.*

**darts** /dɑːts‖dɑrts/ *n* [U] a game in which DARTS¹ (1) are thrown at a circular board (**dartboard**)

**dash¹** /dæʃ/ *v* **1** [I] to run quickly and suddenly: *I must dash (off) to catch my train.|He dashed across the road.* –see WALK (USAGE) **2** [I;T] to (cause to) strike with great force: *The waves dashed the boat against the rocks.* **3** [T] *esp. lit* to destroy (hopes, spirits, etc.): *The accident dashed John's hopes of playing in the football team.*

**dash²** *n* **1** [S] a sudden quick run: *The prisoners* **made a dash for** *freedom.* **2** [C] a small amount of something: *a dash of pepper/colour* **3** [C] a mark (–) used in writing and printing: *The dash is longer than the* HYPHEN. **4** [U] a combination of bravery and style

**dash·board** /ˈdæʃbɔːd‖-bord/ *n* the instrument board in a car, where many of the controls are

**dash·ing** /ˈdæʃɪŋ/ *adj* having a lot of DASH² (4): *a dashing young officer* –**dashingly** *adv*

**da·ta** /ˈdeɪtə, ˈdɑːtə/ *n* [P;U] facts; information: *The data are/is all ready for examination.|We keep the data in a* **(computer) data bank.**

USAGE Although plural in its Latin form, **data** is now often used as a [U] noun: *This* **data** *is very interesting.*

**date¹** /deɪt/ *n* **1** time shown by one or more of the following: the number of the day, the month, and the year (but not usu. by month alone): *The date on the coin is 1921.|What's the date today? It's the third of August.* **2** an arrangement to meet at a particular time and place: *They made a date to meet soon.* **3** *infml* a special social meeting between a man and woman, or boy and girl: *My mother tries to stop me going out on dates.* –see also BLIND DATE **4** *AmE infml* a person with whom one has such a meeting: *Of course you can bring your date to my party.* **5 out of date: a** not modern; old fashioned: *out-of-date methods* **b** no longer able to be used: *This ticket is out of date.* **6 to date** until today: *To date he has done half the work.* **7 up to date** modern: *It was a modern factory–everything was really up to date.*

**date²** *v* **dated, dating 1** [T] to guess or show the date of: *I can't date the pot exactly, but it must be very old.* **2** [T] to write the date on: *Please date your letters to me in future.* **3** [I;T] to (cause to) seem no longer in fashion: *This type of music is beginning to date.* **4** [I;T] *AmE infml* to go on or have a DATE¹ (3) with (another or each other): *They've been dating (each other) for months.*

**date back to** sthg. *v adv prep* [T *no pass.*] to have lasted since (the date of building or origin): *This church dates back to 1173.*

**date from** sthg. *v prep* [T *no pass.*] to have lasted since: *This building dates from 1626.*

**date³** *n* a small brown sweet fruit with a long stone, from hot countries

**dat·ed** /ˈdeɪtɨd/ *adj* out of DATE¹ (5); no longer in common use: *Those words all seem rather dated: I haven't heard them since about 1965!*

**daub** /dɔːb/ *v* [T *with/on*] to cover with something soft and sticky: *to daub the wall with paint|He daubed paint on the wall.*

**daugh·ter** /ˈdɔːtəʳ/ *n* someone's female child: *Mr and Mrs Jones have three daughters.* –compare SON (1); see picture on page 217 –**daughterly** *adj*

**daughter-in-law** /ˈ·· · ·/ *n* **daughters-in-law** the wife of someone's son –compare SON-IN-LAW; see picture on page 217

**daunt** /dɔːnt/ *v* [T] to cause to lose courage or the will to act: *The examination questions were rather daunting.*

**daunt·less** /ˈdɔːntlɨs/ *adj lit* not DAUNTed; fearless: *dauntless courage/soldiers* –**dauntlessly** *adv*

**daw·dle** /ˈdɔːdl/ *v* **-dled, -dling** [I] *infml* to waste time; be slow: *He dawdled all morning/all the way to school.* –**dawdler** *n*

**dawn¹** /dɔːn/ *n* [C;U] **1** the time of day when light first appears; the first appearance of light in the sky before the sun rises: *The postman has to get up before dawn every day.|*(fig.) *the dawn of civilization* –compare DUSK **2 dawn is breaking** light is just beginning to appear

**dawn²** *v* [I] (of the day, morning, etc.) to begin to grow light just before the sun rises

**dawn on/upon** sbdy. *v prep* [T] to become known by: *It suddenly/gradually dawned on me that I had caught the wrong train.*

**day** /deɪ/ *n* **1** [C] a period of 24 hours: *There are seven days in a week.|Christmas Day was a Wednesday last year.* –see USAGE **2** [C;U] the time between sunrise and sunset: *Call me in the evening as I'm usually out during the day.* –compare NIGHT (1) **3** [C] a period of work within a 24-hour period: *She works an eight-hour day.|They're demanding a four-day week.* **4** [C] a period or point of time: *People don't seem so polite* **these days.** /'··/ (=now, as opposed to in the past)|**In my day** *things were different.*|**One day** (=at some time in the future) *we'll get ourselves a new car.|We've never heard the whole story* **to this day.** (=up to and including now) **5** [S] a period of success or fame: *He was a very fine actor, but I'm afraid he has* **had his day** *now.* (=is no longer good or popular) **6 call it a day** *infml* to finish working for the day: **7 day after day/day in day out** continuously **8 from day to day/day by day** each day; as time goes on **9 make someone's day** *infml* to make someone very pleased or happy **10 the other day** in the recent past: *I saw your friend the other day.*

USAGE If today is Wednesday, then Monday was **the day before yesterday** and Friday will be **the day after tomorrow.** One cannot leave out **the day** in these expressions.

**day·break** /'deɪbreɪk/ *n* [U] → DAWN[1]

**day·dream[1]** /'deɪdriːm/ *n* a pleasant dreamlike set of thoughts while one is awake

**daydream[2]** *v* [I] to have DAYDREAMS: *She's always daydreaming: she never listens to what the teacher's saying.* **–daydreamer** *n*

**day·light** /'deɪlaɪt/ *n* [U] the light of day: *We use less electricity in summer because there's more daylight.*

**days** /deɪz/ *n* [P] life: *He began his days in a village.*

**day·time** /'deɪtaɪm/ *n* [*the* S;U] → DAY (2): *I cannot sleep in the daytime.|daytime flights* –opposite **nighttime**

**day-to-day** /ˌ· · '·◂/ *adj* [A *no comp.*] happening, etc., each day: *life's day-to-day difficulties* –compare EVERYDAY

**daze[1]** /deɪz/ *v* **dazed, dazing** [T] to make unable to think or feel clearly, esp. by a blow: *After the accident John was dazed.*|(fig.) *The news left him dazed.* **–dazedly** /'deɪzɨdli / *adv*

**daze[2]** *n* **in a daze** in a DAZEd condition

**daz·zle** /'dæzəl/ *v* **-zled, -zling** [T] to make unable to see by throwing a strong light in the eyes: *The lights of the car dazzled me.*|(fig.) *She was dazzled by her success.* **–dazzle** *n* [S]: *the dazzle of her smile*

**DC** *abbrev. for:* direct current; a flow of electricity that moves in one direction only –compare AC

**DDT** *n* [U] a chemical that kills insects

**dea·con** /'diːkən/ **deaconess** /-nɨs/ *fem.*– *n* an officer of various Christian churches, below a priest

**dead[1]** /ded/ *adj* **1** no longer alive: *a dead man/plant/leaf|Do the dead ever come back to life?|* (fig.) *His love for you is now dead.|a dead language|dead ideas* –see USAGE **2** without the necessary power: *a dead match/*BATTERY (1)|*The telephone has* **gone dead.** (=is not working) –compare LIVE[2] (2, 3) **3** [A] complete: *a dead stop|dead silence* **4 dead centre** the exact centre **5 dead end** a position or state that leads to nothing further: *We've come to a dead end in our talks.|I want to leave this dead-end job.* **6 dead heat** a race in which two or more people finish at exactly the same time **7 dead wood** useless people or things

USAGE Compare **dead** and **died**: Someone (or something) that is no longer alive *is* **dead** or *has* **died**: *My uncle* **died** *last week.|My grandfather has been* **dead** *for years.|Our old dog has just* **died.**|*These flowers are* **dead.**

**dead[2]** *n* **in the dead of** in the quietest or least active period of: *in the dead of night/winter*

**dead[3]** *adv* **1** suddenly and completely: *She stopped dead.* **2** [*adv* + *adj*] *infml* completely: *dead certain|dead tired* **3** [*adv* + *adv*] *infml* directly: *dead ahead*

**dead·en** /'dedn/ *v* [T] to cause to lose (strength, feeling, brightness): *to deaden the pain|Thick walls deaden noise.*

**dead·line** /'dedlaɪn/ *n* a date or time before which something must be done: *I hope we can finish this before the deadline!*

**dead·lock** /'dedlɒk||-lɑk/ *n* a disagreement which cannot be settled: *The talks about arms control have reached (a) complete deadlock.*

**dead·ly[1]** /'dedli/ *adj* **-lier, -liest 1** dangerous; likely to cause death: *a deadly disease/weapon* **2** highly effective against something or someone: *a deadly remark* **3** [A] aiming to kill or destroy: *a deadly enemy/weapon* **4** *derog* very dull: *a deadly conversation* **–deadliness** *n* [U]

**deadly[2]** *adv* **1** very: *deadly serious|deadly dull* **2** like death: *deadly pale*

**dead·pan** /'dedpæn/ *adj infml* with no show of feeling, esp. when telling jokes: *deadpan humour|a deadpan expression*

**dead·weight** /'dedˌweɪt/ *n* [S] the whole weight of something that does not move

**deaf** /def/ *adj* **1** unable to hear at all or to hear well: *deaf people|a special school for the deaf|He wears a* **deaf-aid.** (=a small electric machine, worn on the body, which makes sounds louder) **2** [F *to*] unwilling to hear or listen: *deaf to all my prayers|She* **turned a deaf ear to** *his request.* **–deafness** *n* [U]

**deaf·en** /'defən/ *v* [T] to make deaf: (fig.) *The music is deafening me!*

**deal[1]** /diːl/ *v* **dealt** /delt/, **dealing 1** [I;T *to, out*] to give out (playing cards) to players in a game **2** [T *to, out*] to give as a share **3** [T] *fml* to strike (a blow): *She* **dealt him a blow** *on the head.*

**deal in** sthg. *v prep* [T] to buy and sell; trade in: *This shop deals in men's clothing.*

**deal with** sbdy./sthg. *v prep* [T] **1** to do business, esp. trade, with: *I've dealt with this store/person for 20 years.* **2** to treat; take action about: *How do you deal with this problem?* **3** to be about: *This new book deals with the troubles in Ireland.*

**deal[2]** *n* **1** [C] an arrangement, esp. in business, to the advantage of both sides: *The car company has* **done/made a deal** *with a Japanese firm, which will supply engines in exchange for wheels.* **2** [S *of*] a quantity or degree, usu. large: *A great deal of money has been spent on the new hospital.|You will have to work a good deal faster.* –see Study Notes on page 494 **3** [*the* S;C] the act of giving out cards to players in a card game: *Who has the deal now?* **4 dirty/raw deal** *infml* bad treatment received

**deal·er** /'diːləʳ/ *n* **1** a person in a stated type of business: *a used-car dealer* **2** a person who deals playing cards

**deal·ing** /ˈdiːlɪŋ/ *n* [U] method of business; manner of behaving: *I'm in favour of plain honest dealing.*

**deal·ings** /ˈdiːlɪŋz/ *n* [P] personal or business relations: *I've had dealings with him, but I don't know him very well.*

**dean** /diːn/ *n* **1** [A;C] (in several Christian churches) an officer in charge of several priests or church divisions **2** [C] (in some universities) an important officer

**dear**[1] /dɪəʳ/ *adj* **1** much loved; precious: *a dear friend* **2** [A] *(usu. cap.)* (used at the beginning of a letter): *Dear Jane|Dear Sir* **3** *BrE* costly: *It's too dear: I can't afford it.* –compare CHEAP

**dear**[2] *n* a person who is loved or lovable: *Did you have a good day at work, dear?*

**dear**[3] *interj* (used for expressing surprise, sorrow, slight anger): *Oh dear! I've lost my pen.|Dear! Dear! I'm sorry to hear that.*

**dear·ly** /ˈdɪəli‖ˈdɪərli/ *adv* **1** with much feeling, usu. good feeling: *He loves his wife dearly.* **2** at a terrible cost in time, effort, pain, etc.: *He paid dearly for his mistake.*

**dearth** /dɜːθ‖dɜrθ/ *n* [S *of*] *fml* a lack (of); SHORTAGE

**death** /deθ/ *n* **1** [C;U] the end of life; time or manner of dying: *He was happy till the day of his death.|His mother's death was a great shock to him.|Car accidents cause many deaths.|*(fig.) *Drinking will* **be the death of** *him.|If you go out without a coat, you'll* **catch your death of cold**. –compare BIRTH **2** [U] the state of being dead: *as still/cold as death* –compare LIFE **3** [*the* S] the end or destruction (of something not alive): *a defeat that meant the death of all my hopes* **4 put to death** to kill, esp. with official permission: *The prisoners were all put to death.* **5 to death** beyond all acceptable limits: *I am sick to death of your complaints.*

**death·blow** /ˈdeθbləʊ/ *n* [*usu. sing.*] an act, action, or event that destroys or ends someone or something

**death du·ty** /ˈ· ˌ··/ *BrE*‖**death tax** /ˈ··/ *AmE*– *n* money that must be paid to a government on property left to a person when the original owner has died

**death·ly** /ˈdeθli/ *adj, adv* **-lier, -liest** like death: *a deathly cold body|a deathly silence*

**death trap** /ˈ· ·/ *n* something or some state that may be very dangerous to life: *That old boat is a real death trap.*

**death war·rant** /ˈ· ˌ··/ *n* a written official order to kill (EXECUTE (1)) someone

**de·bar** sbdy. **from** sthg. /dɪˈbɑːʳ/ *v prep* **-rr-** [T] *fml* to prevent from

**de·base** /dɪˈbeɪs/ *v* **-based, -basing** [T] to lower in quality, esp. in the opinion of others –**debasement** *n* [C;U]

**de·ba·ta·ble** /dɪˈbeɪtəbəl/ *adj* doubtful; perhaps not true: *They say their actions have not caused unemployment, but I think that's debatable.*

**de·bate**[1] /dɪˈbeɪt/ *n* a usu. public meeting in which a question is talked about by at least two people or groups, each expressing a different point of view: *a long debate in Parliament*

**debate**[2] *v* **-bated, -bating** [I;T *about, upon, with*] to talk or argue about (something) with someone, usu. in an effort to persuade other people: *They're debating whether to increase the price of petrol.*

**de·bauch·ed** /dɪˈbɔːtʃt‖dɪˈbɔtʃt, dɪbɑtʃt/ *adj* away from socially approved forms of behaviour, esp. in relation to sex and alcohol: *a debauched man*

**de·bauch·e·ry** /dɪˈbɔːtʃəri/ *n* [U] *derog* behaviour that goes beyond socially-approved limits, esp. in relation to sex and alcohol

**de·bil·i·tate** /dɪˈbɪlǫteɪt/ *v* **-tated, -tating** [T] to make weak: *a debilitating disease|debilitating heat*

**de·bil·i·ty** /dɪˈbɪlǫti/ *n* **-ties** [C;U] *fml* (a) weakness, esp. as the result of disease

**deb·it**[1] /ˈdebǫt/ *n* a record in a book of accounts of money spent or owed –compare CREDIT[1] (6)

**debit**[2] *v* [T *with, from*] to record (an amount of money) taken from an account: *Debit Mr Smith/Mr Smith's account with £10.|The bank debited £10 from Mr Smith's account.* –compare CREDIT[2] (2)

**deb·o·nair** /ˌdebəˈneəʳ/ *adj apprec becoming rare* (usu. of men) cheerful and charming, but also polite and well-dressed: *a debonair manner/young man*

**de·brief** /ˌdiːˈbriːf/ *v* [T] to find out information from (someone on one's own side), by thorough questioning after an action: *We debriefed our pilot after he had flown over the enemy's land.* –see also BRIEF[3]

**deb·ris** /ˈdebri, ˈdeɪ-‖dəˈbriː, deɪ-/ *n* [U] the remains of something broken to pieces or destroyed; ruins: *After the bombing there was a lot of debris.*

**debt** /det/ *n* **1** [C;U] something owed to someone else: *a debt of £10|to pay one's debts|*(fig.) *a debt of* GRATITUDE *for your help* **2** [U] the state of owing; the duty of repaying something: *I'm heavily* **in debt** *at the moment, but hope to be* **out of debt** *when I get paid.|in debt to him for his help* **3 run into debt** to begin to owe money

**debt·or** /ˈdetəʳ/ *n* a person who owes money –compare CREDITOR

**de·bunk** /ˌdiːˈbʌŋk/ *v* [T] *infml* to point out the truth about a wrong idea: *A lot of people used to believe that, but now it's been completely debunked.*

**de·but** /ˈdeɪbjuː, ˈdebjuː‖deɪˈbjuː, dɪ-/ *n* a first public appearance: *The singer made his debut as Mozart's Don Giovanni.*

**deb·u·tante** /ˈdebjʊtɑːnt/ also **deb** *infml*– *n* a girl who is making, or has just made, her formal entrance into upper-class society

**dec·ade** /ˈdekeɪd, deˈkeɪd/ *n* a period of 10 years: *Prices have risen steadily during the past decade.*

**dec·a·dent** /ˈdekədənt/ *adj* marked by a fall from one level (esp. of morals) to a lower level: (fig.) *How decadent to stay in bed all day!* –**decadence** *n* [U]

**de·cant** /dɪˈkænt/ *v* [T] to pour (liquid, esp. wine) from one container into another

**de·cant·er** /dɪˈkæntəʳ/ *n* a container (usu. of glass and decorated) for holding liquid (esp. wine)

**de·cap·i·tate** /dɪˈkæpǫteɪt/ *v* **-tated, -tating** [T] *fml* to cut off the head of (esp. as a punishment); BEHEAD –**decapitation** /-ˈteɪʃən/ *n* [C;U]

**de·cay**[1] /dɪˈkeɪ/ *v* **1** [I;T] to (cause to) go bad: *Sugar can decay the teeth.* **2** [I] to fall to a lower or worse state; lose health, power, etc.

**decay**[2] *n* [U] the action, state, or result of decaying: *The empty house has* **fallen into decay.**

**de·ceased** /dɪˈsiːst/ *n* **deceased** *fml & law* the dead person: *The deceased left a large sum of money to his wife.* –**deceased** *adj*

**de·ceit** /dɪ'siːt/ *n* [U] *derog* the quality of being dishonest

**de·ceit·ful** /dɪ'siːtfəl/ *adj derog* dishonest –**deceitfully** *adv* –**deceitfulness** *n* [U]

**de·ceive** /dɪ'siːv/ *v* **-ceived, -ceiving** [T *in, into*] to cause (someone) to accept as true or good what is false or bad: *I trust him because I know he would never deceive me.|He deceived me–he lied about the money.* –**deceiver** *n*

**De·cem·ber** /dɪ'sembəʳ/ also **Dec.** *written abbrev.*– *n* the 12th and last month of the year

**de·cen·cy** /'diːsənsi/ *n* [U] the quality of being DECENT (1)

**de·cent** /'diːsənt/ *adj* **1** socially acceptable; not causing shame or shock to others: *Those tight trousers of yours aren't very decent!|decent behaviour* –opposite **indecent 2** *infml* rather good: *You can get quite a decent meal there without spending too much money.* **3** *infml* nice; kind: *It's very decent of you to drive me to the station.* –**decently** *adv*

**de·cen·tral·ize**||also **-ise** *BrE* /ˌdiː'sentrəlaɪz/ *v* **-ized, -izing** [I;T] **a** to move (government, a business, etc.) from one central place or office to several different smaller places **b** (of government, a business, etc.) to change in this way –see also CENTRALIZE –**decentralization** /-'zeɪʃən/ *n* [U]

**de·cep·tion** /dɪ'sepʃən/ *n* [C;U] (an) act of deceiving

**de·cep·tive** /dɪ'septɪv/ *adj* tending or having power to deceive; misleading –**deceptively** *adv* –**deceptiveness** *n* [U]

**dec·i·bel** /'desɪ̣bel/ *n tech* a measure of the loudness of sound

**de·cide** /dɪ'saɪd/ *v* **-cided, -ciding 1** [T +*to-v*/(*that*)] to arrive at an answer or an end to uncertainty about: *to decide where to go/where they should go|She decided to go.|I decided (that) it would cost too much to repair the car.* **2** [I] to make a choice or judgment: *I've been waiting all day for them to decide!* **3** [T] to bring to a clear or certain end: *One blow decided the fight.*

**decide on** sthg. *v prep* [T] to decide in favour of: *I've decided on going to America for my holidays.*

**de·cid·ed** /dɪ'saɪdɪ̣d/ *adj fml* **1** very clear and easily seen or understood: *a decided change for the better* **2** having or showing no doubt: *a man of very decided opinions* –**decidedly** *adv* –see also UNDECIDED

**de·cid·u·ous** /dɪ'sɪdʒuəs/ *adj tech* having leaves that fall off in autumn: *deciduous trees* –compare EVERGREEN

**dec·i·mal¹** /'desɪ̣məl/ *adj* based on the number 10

**decimal²** also **decimal fraction**– *n* a number like .5, .375, .06, etc.: *You know 0.6 is a decimal because there's a* **decimal point** *between the 0 and the 6.* –compare INTEGER

**dec·i·mal·ize**||also **-ise** *BrE* /'desɪ̣məlaɪz||'desəmə-/ *v* **-ized, -izing** [I;T] to change to a DECIMAL system of money, counting, etc. –**decimalization** /-'zeɪʃən/ *n* [U]

**dec·i·mate** /'desɪ̣meɪt/ *v* **-mated, -mating** [T] *fml* to destroy a large part of: *Disease decimated the population.* –**decimation** /-'meɪʃən/ *n* [U]

**de·ci·pher** /dɪ'saɪfəʳ/ *v* [T] to read (something difficult, esp. a CODE¹ (1))

**de·ci·sion** /dɪ'sɪʒən/ *n* **1** [C;U] (a) choice or judgment: *Who* **made the decision** *to go there?|Whose decision was it?|They expect to* **reach/come to a decision** *soon.* **2** [U] the quality of being able to make choices or judgments –opposite **indecision**

**de·ci·sive** /dɪ'saɪsɪv/ *adj* **1** showing determination or firmness: *A decisive person acts quickly.* **2** leading to a result: *It was a decisive battle–we won the war because of it.* **3** unquestionable: *a decisive advantage* –opposite **indecisive** –**decisively** *adv* –**decisiveness** *n* [U]

**deck¹** /dek/ *n* **1** the usu. wooden floor of a ship **2** *AmE* a set of playing cards; PACK¹ (4) **3 -decker** having a certain number of levels, floors, or thicknesses: *A double-decker (bus) has two floors.*

**deck²** *v* → DECK OUT

**deck·chair** /'dektʃeəʳ/ *n* a folding chair with a long seat of cloth (usu. CANVAS), used outdoors.

**deck** sbdy./sthg.↔ **out** *v adv* [T *in*] to decorate: *The street was decked out in flags.*

**de·claim** /dɪ'kleɪm/ *v* [T] *often derog* to say (something) loud and clear, with pauses and hand movements to increase the effect of the words –**declamation** /ˌdeklə'meɪʃən/ *n* [C;U] –**declamatory** /dɪ'klæmɪtəri||-tori/ *adj*

**dec·la·ra·tion** /ˌdeklə'reɪʃən/ *n* **1** the act of declaring: *a declaration of war* **2** a statement, giving information in an official manner: *Please make a written declaration of all the goods you bought abroad.*

**de·clare** /dɪ'kleəʳ/ *v* **-clared, -claring** [T] **1** to make known publicly or officially, according to rules, custom, etc.: *Our government has declared war on Ruritania.|Jones was declared the winner.|I declare Mr B. Schiff elected!* **2** [+(*that*)] to state (or show) with great force so that there is no doubt about the meaning: *She declared (that) she knew nothing about the robbery.|He declared himself (to be) a member of their party.* **3** to make a full statement of (property for which tax may be owed to the government): *Have you anything to declare?*

**de·clared** /dɪ'kleəd||-ərd/ *adj* openly admitted as: *It's their declared intention to increase taxes.*

**de·cline¹** /dɪ'klaɪn/ *v* **-clined, -clining 1** [I] to move from a better to a worse position, or from higher to lower: *His power/health/influence has begun to decline now that he is old.* **2** [I;T +*to-v*] *fml* to refuse, usu. politely; be unwilling: *We asked them to come to our party, but they declined (the invitation).|The minister at first declined to make a statement, but later she agreed.* –see REFUSE (USAGE)

**decline²** *n* [C *usu. sing.*;U] a period of declining (DECLINE¹ (1)), esp. as something or someone gets near the end: *There has been a sharp decline in interest in farming.|Interest in sports in our town is* **on the decline.**

**de·code** /ˌdiː'kəud/ *v* **-coded, -coding** [T] to discover the meaning of (something written in a CODE¹ (1, 2)) –see also ENCODE

**de·com·pose** /ˌdiːkəm'pəuz/ *v* **-posed, -posing** [I;T] to (cause to) decay; break up into simple parts –**decomposition** /ˌdiːkɒmpə'zɪʃən||-kɑm- / *n* [U]

**dé·cor** /'deɪkɔːʳ||deɪ'kɔr/ *n* [C;U] the decorative furnishing of a place, esp. a house or stage

**dec·o·rate** /ˈdekəreɪt/ *v* **-rated, -rating 1** [T *with*] to serve as, or provide with, something added because it is beautiful, esp. for a special occasion: *The streets were decorated with flags.* **2** [I;T] to paint or put paper, etc., on the walls of a house: *How much will it cost to decorate the kitchen?* **3** [T *for*] to give (someone) an official mark of honour, such as a MEDAL

USAGE **Decorate, adorn, embellish,** and **garnish** are all verbs meaning "to add something to, so as to make more attractive". **Decorate,** as in def. **1,** is usually used of places, and often of special occasions: *The children* **decorated** *the house for Christmas*; **adorn** is particularly used of things: *She* **adorned** *herself with jewels;* **embellish** is normally used of things: *The door of the church was* **embellished** *with decorations.* and **garnish** is most often used of cooking: *a baked fish* **garnished** *with pieces of tomato.*

**dec·o·ra·tion** /ˌdekəˈreɪʃən/ *n* **1** [U] the act or art of decorating; the state of being decorated **2** [C] an ornament; something that decorates: *decorations for a party* **3** [C] something given as a sign of honour, esp. military; MEDAL

**dec·o·ra·tive** /ˈdekərətɪv‖ˈdekərə-, ˈdekəreɪ-/ *adj apprec* attractive; used for decorating: *a decorative gold table* **–decoratively** *adv*

**dec·o·ra·tor** /ˈdekəreɪtəʳ/ *n* a person who paints houses inside and outside

**dec·o·rous** /ˈdekərəs/ *adj fml* (of appearance or behaviour) correct; properly serious in manner according to the customs of society **–decorously** *adv* **–decorum** /dɪˈkɔːrəm‖-ˈko-/ *n* [U]: *I hope you will behave with decorum at the funeral.*

**de·coy** /ˈdiːkɔɪ/ *n* **-oys** something which is used for getting a person or bird into a trap **–decoy** /dɪˈkɔɪ,ˈdiːkɔɪ/ *v* [T *into*]

**de·crease** /dɪˈkriːs/ *v* **-creased, -creasing** [I;T] to (cause to) become less in size, number, strength, or quality: *Our sales are decreasing.|The company decreased the number of workers.* –opposite **increase** **–decrease** /ˈdiːkriːs/ *n* [C;U *of, in*]

**de·cree¹** /dɪˈkriː/ *n* an official command or decision

**decree²** *v* **-creed, -creeing** [I;T +(*that*)] to order officially, with the force of law

**de·crep·it** /dɪˈkrepɨt/ *adj derog* weak or in bad condition from old age

**de·cry** /dɪˈkraɪ/ *v* **-cried, -crying** [T] *fml* to speak ill of; say bad things about

**ded·i·cate** /ˈdedɨkeɪt/ *v* **-cated, -cating** [T *to*] to give to, or declare for, a cause, purpose, or person: *The doctor dedicated his life/himself to finding a cure.|He dedicated his first book to his mother.*

**ded·i·cat·ed** /ˈdedɨkeɪtɨd/ *adj* (esp. of people) very interested in or working very hard for an idea, purpose, etc.; COMMITTED: *She's very dedicated to her work.|a dedicated doctor*

**ded·i·ca·tion** /ˌdedɨˈkeɪʃən/ *n* **1** [C;U] the act of dedicating (DEDICATE) **2** [C;U] the state of being DEDICATED: *She worked with great dedication to find a cure for the disease.* **3** [C] (esp. in a book) the words used in dedicating (DEDICATE (1))

**de·duce** /dɪˈdjuːs‖dɪˈduːs/ *v* **-duced, -ducing** [T +(*that*)] to determine or decide (something) from general principles: *Because there was no cloud he deduced that it was going to be a cold night.* –see also DEDUCTION **–deducible** *adj*

**de·duct** /dɪˈdʌkt/ *v* [T *from*] to take away (an amount, a part) from a total **–deductible** *adj*

**de·duc·tion** /dɪˈdʌkʃən/ *n* **1** [C +(*that*)] that which is DEDUCED: *Her deduction that he was now dead was correct.* **2** [C;U] the act or action of DEDUCTing **3** [C] that which is DEDUCTed: *She earned less money because of deductions from her wages.*

**deed** /diːd/ *n* **1** *esp. lit* something done on purpose: *good deeds* **2** *law* a written paper that is an official record of an agreement

**deem** /diːm/ *v* [T +(*that*); not *be +v-ing*] *fml* to consider; have the opinion: *Do you deem this plan (to be) sensible?*

**deep** /diːp/ *adj,adv* **1** [*adj, adv +prep/adv*] going far down from the top: *The river is very deep here.|a mine two kilometres deep|ankle-deep in mud|a deep breath* (=filling the lungs) **2** [*adj, adv +prep/adv*] going far in from the outside or the front edge: *a deep wound|a shelf 30 cm deep and 120 cm long|a house deep in the forest|*(fig.) *For some people, smoking is a* **ˌdeep-rooted** (=hard to stop) *habit.* **3** (of a colour) strong and dark: *The sky was deep blue.* –compare LIGHT² (2), PALE¹ (2) **4** difficult to change; strong: *deep sleep|deep feeling* **5** seriously bad or damaging: *in deep trouble|deep in debt* **6** understanding serious matters thoroughly: *a deep mind/thinker* **7** difficult to understand: *deep scientific principles* **8 go off the deep end** *infml* to lose one's temper suddenly or violently **9 in deep water** in serious trouble **10 thrown in at the deep end** suddenly and unexpectedly faced with a difficult piece of work, a new job, etc. –see also DEPTH; compare SHALLOW **–deeply** *adv* **–deepness** *n* [U]

**deep·en** /ˈdiːpən/ *v* [I;T] to (cause to) become deeper: *The colour of the sky deepened as the sun went down.*

**deep freeze** /ˌ· ˈ·‖ˈ· ·/ *n* → FREEZER (1)

**deep-seat·ed** /ˌ· ˈ··◂/ *adj* existing far below the surface: *a deep-seated sorrow*

**deer** /dɪəʳ/ *n* **deer** a large fast four-footed animal, of which the males usu. have wide branching horns (ANTLERS) –sounds like **dear**

**de·face** /dɪˈfeɪs/ *v* **-faced, -facing** [T] to spoil the surface or appearance of, e.g. by writing or making marks on **–defacement** *n* [U]

**de·fame** /dɪˈfeɪm/ *v* **-famed, -faming** [T] *fml* to damage the good name of, usu. by unfair means **–defamatory** /dɪˈfæmətəri‖-tori/ *adj* **–defamation** /ˌdefəˈmeɪʃən/ *n* [U]

**de·fault** /dɪˈfɔːlt/ *v* [I *on*] to fail to fulfil a contract, agreement, or duty, esp. **a** to fail to pay a debt **b** to fail to take part in a competition **–default** *n* [U]: *She won* **by default**, *because her opponent refused to play.*

**de·feat¹** /dɪˈfiːt/ *v* [T] **1** to win a victory over; beat: *Our team/army/political party has defeated our opponents!* **2** to cause to fail; FRUSTRATE (1): *It was lack of money that defeated their plan.*

**defeat²** *n* [C;U] **1** (an example of) the act of defeating: *the defeat of the losing army* **2** the act or state of being defeated: *their defeat by the winning army|*

*After several defeats, the team is now doing well again.* –compare VICTORY, WIN

**de·feat·is·m** /dɪˈfiːtɪzəm/ *n* [U] the practice of thinking or behaving in a way that shows an expectation of being defeated **–defeatist** *n*

**def·e·cate** /ˈdefɪ̇keɪt/ *v* **-cated, -cating** [I] *fml* to pass waste matter from the bowels **–defecation** /-ˈkeɪʃən/ *n* [U]

**de·fect¹** /ˈdiːfekt, dɪˈfekt/ *n* something lacking or imperfect; fault: *The machine is unsafe because of the defects in it.*

**de·fect²** /dɪˈfekt/ *v* [I *from, to*] to desert a political party, group, or movement, esp. in order to join an opposing one **–defection** /dɪˈfekʃən/ *n* [C;U]: *What caused his defection?* **–defector** *n: He's a defector.*

**de·fec·tive** /dɪˈfektɪv/ *adj* lacking something necessary; faulty: *defective machinery/hearing* **–defectively** *adv* **–defectiveness** *n* [U]

**de·fence** ‖also **defense** *AmE* /dɪˈfens/ *n* **1** [U] the act or action of defending: *the defence of one's country|He spoke* **in defence of** *justice.* **2** [C;U] means, methods, or things used in defending: *The government has increased its spending on defence.|Trees are a defence against the wind.* **3** [C *usu. sing.*] arguments used in defending oneself, esp. in a court of law: *The prisoner's defence was rather weak.* **–defenceless** *adj*

**de·fend** /dɪˈfend/ *v* [T] **1** [*from, against*] to keep safe from harm; protect against attack: *The fort can't be defended against an air attack.*|(fig.) (in sport) *They defended very well.* **2** to argue in favour of (something which is being attacked): *to defend one's beliefs* –compare ATTACK **3** to act as a lawyer for (the person who has been charged) –compare PROSECUTE **–defensible** *adj* **–defender** *n* –see picture on page 592

**de·fen·dant** /dɪˈfendənt/ *n law* a person against whom a charge is brought in a court of law –compare PLAINTIFF

**de·fen·sive** /dɪˈfensɪv/ *adj* that defends: *defensive weapons/play|a defensive position* –opposite **offensive** **–defensively** *adv* **–defensiveness** *n* [U]

**de·fer** /dɪˈfɜːʳ/ *v* **-rr-** [T] to delay until a later date; POSTPONE: *Let's defer the decision for a few weeks.* **–deferment** *n* [C;U]

**defer to** sbdy./sthg. *v prep* [T] *fml* to yield to, esp. in opinion: *defer to your advice*

**def·er·ence** /ˈdefərəns/ *n* [U] *fml* regard for another's wishes, opinions, etc., because of the other's higher position or greater power **–deferential** /ˌdefəˈrenʃəl/ *adj*

**de·fi·ant** /dɪˈfaɪənt/ *adj* showing no fear or respect; fearlessly refusing to obey **–defiance** *n* [U] **–defiantly** *adv*

**de·fi·cien·cy** /dɪˈfɪʃənsi/ *n* **-cies** [C;U] (a case of) the quality or state of being DEFICIENT; lack: *The deficiencies in this plan are very clear and it can't possibly succeed.*

**de·fi·cient** /dɪˈfɪʃənt/ *adj* having none or not enough (of); lacking (in): *a deficient supply of water|deficient in skill* **–deficiently** *adv*

**def·i·cit** /ˈdefɪ̇sɪ̇t/ *n* an amount by which something is less than what is needed, (esp.) the amount by which money that goes out is more than money that comes in: *The directors have reported a deficit of £2.5 million.*

**de·file** /dɪˈfaɪl/ *v* **-filed, -filing** [T] *fml* to destroy the pureness of: *The animals defiled the water.* **–defilement** *n* [U]

**de·fine** /dɪˈfaɪn/ *v* **-fined, -fining 1** [I;T] to give the meaning(s) of (a word or idea); describe exactly: *Some words are hard to define.* **2** [T] to show the limits or shape of: *I saw a clearly defined shape outside the window.*

**def·i·nite** /ˈdefɪ̇nɪ̇t, ˈdefənɪ̇t/ *adj* clear; without any uncertainty: *We demand a definite answer.|a definite success* –see also INDEFINITE; compare DEFINITIVE

**def·i·nite·ly** /ˈdefɪ̇nɪ̇tli, ˈdefənɪ̇tli/ *adv* without doubt; clearly: *That was definitely the best play I've seen all year.|He is definitely coming/definitely not coming.|Definitely not!*

**def·i·ni·tion** /ˌdefɪ̇ˈnɪʃən/ *n* **1** [C] an exact statement of the meaning, nature, or limits of something, esp. a word or phrase **2** [U] clearness of shape, colour, or sound: *This photograph lacks definition.*

**de·fin·i·tive** /dɪˈfɪnɪ̇tɪv/ *adj* **1** that provides a last decision that cannot be questioned: *a definitive answer* **2** that cannot be improved as a treatment of a particular subject: *She's written the definitive history of Vienna.* –see also DEFINITE; compare AUTHORITATIVE **–definitively** *adv*

**de·flate** /ˌdiːˈfleɪt, dɪ-/ *v* **-flated, -flating** [I;T] **1** to (cause to) become smaller, esp. by losing air or gas: (fig.) *One sharp remark is enough to deflate him.* **2** to reduce the supply of money (of) or lower the level of prices (of) (esp. a national ECONOMY) –opposite **inflate** **–deflation** /-ˈfleɪʃən/ *n* [C;U]

**de·flect** /dɪˈflekt/ *v* [I;T] to (cause to) turn from a straight course or fixed direction, esp. after hitting something: *Mary threw a stone at John but it was deflected away from him by a tree.* **–deflection** *n* [C;U]

**de·form** /dɪˈfɔːm‖-ɔrm/ *v* [T] to spoil the form or appearance of: *a face deformed by disease/anger* **–deformation** /ˌdiːfɔːˈmeɪʃən,ˌde-‖-ɔr-/ *n* [C;U]

**de·for·mi·ty** /dɪˈfɔːmɪ̇ti‖-ɔr-/ *n* **-ties** [C;U] (an) imperfection of the body, esp. that can be seen: *He's very attractive in spite of his slight deformity.*

**de·fraud** /dɪˈfrɔːd/ *v* [T *of*] to deceive so as to get or keep something wrongly and usu. illegally

**de·frost** /ˌdiːˈfrɒst‖-ˈfrɔst/ *v* [I;T] to remove ice from; unfreeze: *to defrost a* FRIDGE|*Don't let the meat defrost too quickly.*

**deft** /deft/ *adj apprec* effortlessly skilful: *a deft performance/catch* **–deftly** *adv* **–deftness** *n* [U]

**de·funct** /dɪˈfʌŋkt/ *adj fml or law* dead: (fig.) *defunct ideas*

**de·fuse** /ˌdiːˈfjuːz/ *v* **-fused, -fusing** [T] to remove the FUSE (3) from (something explosive) so as to prevent an explosion: *to defuse a bomb*|(fig.) *to defuse a dangerous state of affairs*

**de·fy** /dɪˈfaɪ/ *v* **-fied, -fying** [T] **1** to show no fear of nor respect for; refuse to obey: *These criminals are defying the law.|The child defied his parents and went to the cinema after school.*|(fig.)*This new invention seems to defy the laws of science.* **2** to ask, very strongly, to do something considered impossible; dare: *I defy you to give me one good* *reason for believing you.*

**de·gen·e·rate¹** /dɪˈdʒenərᵻt/ *adj* having become worse in character, quality, etc., in comparison with a former state **–degenerate** *n* **–degeneracy** *n* [U]

**de·gen·e·rate²** /dɪˈdʒenəreɪt/ **-rated, -rating** *v* [I *from, into*] **1** to pass from a higher to a lower type or condition: *Their conversation degenerated into a quarrel.* **2** to sink into a low state of mind or morals **–degeneration** /ˈreɪʃən/ *n* [U]

**de·grade** /dɪˈgreɪd/ *v* **-graded, -grading** [T] to bring down in the opinion of others, in self-respect, or in behaviour: *It was very degrading to be punished in front of the whole class.* **–degradation** /ˌdegrəˈdeɪʃən/ *n* [U]

**de·gree** /dɪˈgriː/ *n* **1** [C] *tech* any of various measures: *Water freezes at 32 degrees* FAHRENHEIT *(32°F) or 0 degrees* CENTIGRADE *(0°C).|an angle of 90 degrees (90°)* **2** [C;U] a point on an imaginary line, which is used for measuring ability, progress, etc.: *The students have different degrees of ability.|He is getting better by degrees.* **3** [C] a title given by a university: *To do the job, you must have a degree in chemistry.*

**de·hy·drate** /ˌdiːhaɪˈdreɪt/ *v* **-drated, -drating** [T] to dry; remove all the water from: *to dehydrate milk to make milk powder* **–dehydrated** /ˌdiːhaɪˈdreɪtᵻd/ *adj* **–dehydration** /ˌdiːhaɪˈdreɪʃən/ *n* [U]

**de·i·fy** /ˈdiːᵻfaɪ, ˈdeɪ-/ *v* **-fied, -fying** [T] *fml* to make a god of; take as an object of worship: *to deify trees and stones* **–deification** /-fɪˈkeɪʃən/ *n* [U]

**deign** /deɪn/ *v* [T +*to-v*] *derog* to lower oneself to act or give something to people one considers unimportant: *Now that she is rich and famous, she doesn't deign to visit her former friends.* –compare CONDESCEND (1)

**de·i·ty** /ˈdiːᵻti, ˈdeɪ-/ *n* **-ties** a god or goddess

**dé·jà vu** /ˌdeɪʒɑː ˈvjuː, -ˈvuː/ *n* [U] the feeling of remembering something that one is in fact experiencing for the first time

**de·jec·ted** /dɪˈdʒektᵻd/ *adj* sad; having or showing low spirits: *a dejected look/person* **–dejectedly** *adv* **–dejection** /dɪˈdʒekʃən/ [U]

**de·lay¹** //dɪˈleɪ/ *v* **-layed, -laying 1** [T +*v-ing*] to do something later than planned; put off: *We decided to delay (going on) our holiday until next month.* **2** [I;T] to stop for a time, move slowly, or cause to be late: *What delayed you?*

**delay²** *n* **-lays** [C;U] the act of delaying or the state of being delayed: *Delays of two hours or more were reported on the roads this morning.*

**de·lec·ta·ble** /dɪˈlektəbəl/ *adj apprec* very pleasing; delightful: *What delectable food you cook!* **–delectably** *adv*

**del·e·gate¹** /ˈdelᵻgᵻt/ *n* a person acting for one or more others, such as a representative to a meeting or an organization

**del·e·gate²** /ˈdelᵻgeɪt/ *v* **-gated, -gating** [T *to*] to give (part or all of one's power, rights, etc.) for a certain time; appoint as one's DELEGATE: *I have delegated him to serve in my place.*

**del·e·ga·tion** /ˌdelᵻˈgeɪʃən/ *n* **1** [U] the act of delegating (DELEGATE) or the state of being delegated **2** [C +*sing./pl. v*] a group of DELEGATES

**de·lete** /dɪˈliːt/ *v* **-leted, -leting** [T *from*] to take, rub, or cut out (esp. words): *Delete his name from the list.* **–deletion** /dɪˈliːʃən/ *n* [C;U]

**de·lib·e·rate¹** /dɪˈlɪbərᵻt/ *adj* **1** intentional; on purpose: *The car crash wasn't an accident; it was a deliberate attempt to kill him!* **2** (of speech, thought, or movement) slow; unhurried: *He stood up in a deliberate way and left the room.* **–deliberately** *adv* **–deliberateness** *n* [U]

**de·lib·e·rate²** /dɪˈlɪbəreɪt/ *v* **-rated, -rating** [I;T *upon, about*] *fml* to consider carefully, often in formal meetings with other people: *The judges are deliberating (the question).* **–deliberation** /-ˈreɪʃən/ *n* [C;U]

**del·i·ca·cy** /ˈdelɪkəsi/ *n* **-cies 1** [U] the quality of being DELICATE **2** [C] something pleasing to eat that is considered rare or costly: *That food is a great delicacy.*

**del·i·cate** /ˈdelɪkᵻt/ *adj* **1** finely made; needing careful handling; easily broken, hurt, or made ill: *The body is a delicate machine.|Be careful with those plates–they're very delicate.* **2** needing careful treatment or TACT; likely to go wrong at any moment: *a delicate affair/position/subject* **3** pleasing but not strong and not easy to recognize: *a delicate taste/smell/colour* **4** sensitive: *That delicate instrument can record very slight changes.* **–delicately** *adv*

**del·i·ca·tes·sen** /ˌdelɪkəˈtesən/ *n* a shop that sells foreign foods, esp. cooked and ready to eat

**de·li·cious** /dɪˈlɪʃəs/ *adj* pleasing to one of the body's senses, esp. those of taste or smell: *What delicious food you've cooked!* **–deliciously** *adv*

**de·light¹** /dɪˈlaɪt/ *v* [I;T] to cause great satisfaction, enjoyment, or joy: *a book that is certain to delight|He delighted them with his performance.*

**delight in** sthg. *v prep* [T +*v-ing*] to take or receive great pleasure in: *She delights in (looking at) pictures.*

**delight²** *n* [C;U] (something that gives) great pleasure or satisfaction; joy: *I read your new book with real delight.|the delights of London's night life*

**de·light·ful** /dɪˈlaɪtfəl/ *adj* highly pleasing: *a delightful little house* **–delightfully** *adv*

**de·lin·quen·cy** /dɪˈlɪŋkwənsi/ *n* [U] (a tendency towards) behaviour, esp. of young people, that is not in accordance with accepted social standards or with the law; the state of being DELINQUENT

**de·lin·quent** /dɪˈlɪŋkwənt/ *adj* having broken a law, esp. one which is not very important; having a tendency to break the law or to do socially unacceptable things: *delinquent behaviour* **–delinquent** *n*

**de·lir·i·ous** /dɪˈlɪərɪəs/ *adj* in an excited dreamy state, esp. caused by illness: *He was so ill he became delirious.* **–deliriously** *adv:* (fig.) *deliriously happy* **–delirium** /-rɪəm/ *n* [U]

**de·liv·er** /dɪˈlɪvəʳ/ *v* [T] **1** [*to*] (in business) to take things to people's houses or places of work: *Letters are delivered every day.|Yes, we deliver newspapers.* **2** [*up, to*] to give; produce; hand over: *We deliver results.* **3** to help in the birth of: *The doctor delivered her baby.* **4** to say; read aloud: *He delivered his speech effectively.* **5** [*from*] *fml* to set free

**de·liv·er·ance** /dɪˈlɪvərəns/ *n* [U *from*] *fml* the act of saving from danger or freeing from bad conditions or the state of being saved from danger

**de·liv·er·y** /dɪ'lɪvəri/ *n* **-ries 1** [C;U *to*] the act of taking something to somebody, or the things taken: *The next postal delivery is at 2 o'clock.*|*the delivery of letters to your house* **2** [C] the birth of a child: *The mother/The child had an easy delivery.* **3** [C;U] the act or style of speaking in public: *a good/slow delivery*

**del·ta** /'deltə/ *n* **1** the fourth letter of the Greek alphabet(Δ, δ) **2** an area of low land shaped like a (Δ) where a river divides into branches towards the sea: *the Nile Delta in Egypt*

**de·lude** /dɪ'lu:d/ *v* **-luded, -luding** [T *with, into*] to mislead the mind or judgment of; deceive; trick: *Don't delude yourself with false hopes.*

**del·uge**[1] /'delju:dʒ/ *n fml* **1** a great flood: (fig.) *a deluge of questions* **2** a very heavy rain

**deluge**[2] *v* **-uged, -uging** [T *with*] *fml* to pour out a great flood of things over: *The minister was deluged with questions/cries/shouts.*

**de·lu·sion** /dɪ'lu:ʒən/ *n* **1** [U] the act of deluding or the state of being DELUDED **2** [C] a false belief, esp. if strongly held: *He is* **under the delusion** *that he is Napoleon.* –see ILLUSION (USAGE)

**de luxe** /də'lʌks||-'lʊks/ *adj* of especially good quality: *The de luxe model costs a lot more.*

**delve** /delv/ *v* **delved, delving** [I *into, among*] to search deeply: *He delved into lots of old books for the facts.*

**dem·a·gogue** /'deməgɒg||-gɑg/ *n derog* a leader who tries to gain, or has gained, power by exciting popular feelings rather than by reasoned argument **–demagogic** /ˌdemə'gɒgɪk||-'gɑ/ *adj*

**de·mand**[1] /dɪ'mɑ:nd||dɪ'mænd/ *n* **1** [C *for*] an act of demanding; claim: *The workers' demand for higher wages seems reasonable.*|(fig.) *This work makes great demands on my time.* **2** [U *for*] the desire of people for particular goods or services: *Is there much demand/a great demand for teachers in this town?* | *Oil is in great demand these days.*

**demand**[2] *v* [T +*to-v/(that)*] to claim as if by right; ask for (something) very strongly: *I demand my rights/an answer.*|*I demanded to know the truth.*|*They demanded that they should get more money.* –see ASK (USAGE)

**de·mand·ing** /dɪ'mɑ:ndɪŋ||dɪ'mæn-/ *adj* needing a lot of effort or attention: *a very demanding baby*

**de·mar·ca·tion** /ˌdi:mɑ:'keɪʃən||-ɑr-/ *n* [U] limitation; separation: *a demarcation line between two jobs in a factory*

**de·mean** /dɪ'mi:n/ *v* [T] *fml* to lower in the opinion of oneself or others: *demeaning behaviour/work*

**de·mea·nour** *BrE*||**demeanor** *AmE* /dɪ'mi:nəʳ/ *n fml* behaviour towards others: *His demeanour has always been that of a perfect gentleman.*

**de·men·ted** /dɪ'mentəd/ *adj* mad; of unbalanced mind **–dementedly** *adv*

**de·mise** /dɪ'maɪz/ *n* [U] *law or euph* death: *Upon his demise his house passed to his son.*

**de·mo·bi·lize** ||also **-lise** *BrE* /di:'məʊbəlaɪz/ **-lized, -lizing** *n* [T] *fml* to send (members of an army or other armed group) back to peacetime life –see also MOBILIZE (2) **–demobilization** /dɪˌməʊbəlaɪ'zeɪʃən|| -bələ-/ *n* [U]

**de·moc·ra·cy** /dɪ'mɒkrəsi||dɪ'mɑ-/ *n* **-cies 1** [U] government by elected representatives of the people **2** [C] a country governed by its people or their representatives **3** [U] social EQUALITY and the right to take part in decision-making: *How much democracy is there in local government?*

**dem·o·crat** /'deməkræt/ *n* a person who believes in or works for DEMOCRACY

**dem·o·crat·ic** /ˌdemə'krætɪk/ *adj* **1** of, related to, or favouring DEMOCRACY **2** favouring and practising social equality **–democratically** *adv*

**de·mol·ish** /dɪ'mɒlɪʃ||dɪ'mɑ-/ *v* [T] to destroy (esp. something large); pull or tear down: *They're going to demolish that old building.*|(fig.)*We've demolished all her arguments.*

**dem·o·li·tion** /ˌdemə'lɪʃən/ *n* [C;U] (an example of) the action of DEMOLISHing

**de·mon** /'di:mən/ *n* an evil spirit: (fig.) *That child is a little demon.* **–demonic** /dɪ'mɒnɪk||dɪ'mɑ-/ *adj*

**de·mon·stra·ble** /dɪ'mɒnstrəbəl, 'demən-||dɪ 'mɑn-/ *adj fml* that can be DEMONSTRATEd: *a demonstrable truth* **–demonstrably** *adv*

**dem·on·strate** /'demənstreɪt/ *v* **-strated, -strating 1** [T+*(that)*] to show clearly: *Please demonstrate how the machine works.* **2** [T +*(that)*] to prove or make clear, esp. by reasoning or giving many examples: *Galileo demonstrated that objects of different weight fall at the same speed.* **3** [I *about, against*] to take part in a public show of strong feeling or opinion, often with marching, big signs, etc.: *They demonstrated against the new law.* **–demonstrator** *n*

**dem·on·stra·tion** /ˌdemən'streɪʃən/ *n* **1** [C;U+ *(that)*] the act of demonstrating (DEMONSTRATE): *She gave us a demonstration of the machine to show us how it worked.* **2** [C] also **demo** /'deməʊ/ *infml*– a public show of strong feeling or opinion, often with marching, big signs, etc.: *a demonstration against the war*

**de·mon·stra·tive** /dɪ'mɒnstrətɪv||dɪ'mɑn-/ *adj* showing feelings openly: *a demonstrative person/action*

**de·mor·al·ize** ||also **-ise** *BrE* /dɪ'mɒrəlaɪz||dɪ'mɔ-, dɪ'mɑ-/ *v* **-ized,-izing** to lessen or destroy the courage and self-respect of: *The army was demoralized by defeat.* **–demoralization** /-'zeɪʃən/ *n* [U]

**de·mote** /dɪ'məʊt/ *v* **-moted, -moting** [T] to lower in rank or position –opposite **promote –demotion** /dɪ'məʊʃən/ *n* [C;U]

**de·mur** /dɪ'mɜ:ʳ/ *v* **-rr-** [I *at*] *fml* to show signs of being against something

**de·mure** /dɪ'mjʊəʳ/ *adj* (esp. of women and children) quiet and serious: *a demure young lady* **–demurely** *adv*

**den** /den/ *n* the home of a usu. large fierce wild animal, esp. a lion: (fig.) *a den of thieves*

**de·ni·al** /dɪ'naɪəl/ *n* **1** [U] the act of DENYing **2** [C] an example or statement of this: *a denial of justice*|*a public denial of the story in the newspaper*

**den·im** /'denəm/ *n* [U] a strong cotton cloth used esp. for JEANS

**den·ims** /'denəmz/ *n* [P] *infml* trousers made of DENIM; JEANS –see PAIR[1] (USAGE)

**de·nom·i·na·tion** /dɪˌnɒmə'neɪʃən||dɪˌnɑ-/ *n* **1** a religious group; a division of a religious body: *Among Christians there are many denominations.* **2** a standard, esp. of value: *coins of many denominations*

**de·note** /dɪ'nəʊt/ *v* **-noted, -noting** to be a name or mark of; mean: *The sign "=" denotes that two things are equal.*|*A smile often denotes pleasure.*

**de·nounce** /dɪ'naʊns/ *v* **-nounced, -nouncing** [T *to, as*] to speak or write against: *The minister's action was denounced in the newspapers.*

**dense** /dens/ *adj* **1** closely packed or crowded together: *a dense crowd*|*dense traffic* **2** difficult to see through: *a dense mist* **3** stupid; difficult to reach with ideas: *a dense mind*|*He's dense.* **–densely** *adv* **–denseness** *n* [U] **–density** *n* [U]

**dent** /dent/ *n* a small hollow place in the surface of something man-made, which is the result of a blow or pressure: *a dent in a car*|(fig.) *a dent in one's pride* **–dent** *v* [I;T]: *I'm afraid I've dented the car.* –compare BUMP

**den·tal** /'dentl/ *adj* of or related to the teeth

**den·tist** /'dentɪ̈st/ also **dental surgeon** /ˌ·· '··/ *fml*– *n* a person professionally trained to treat the teeth **–dentistry** *n* [U]

**den·tures** /'dentʃəz||-ərz/ *n* [P] → FALSE TEETH

**de·nude** /dɪ'njuːd||dɪ'nuːd/ *v* **-nuded, -nuding** [T *of*] *fml* to remove the covering from

**de·nun·ci·a·tion** /dɪˌnʌnsi'eɪʃən/ *n* [C;U] (an example of) the act of denouncing (DENOUNCE)

**de·ny** /dɪ'naɪ/ *v* **-nied, -nying** [T] **1** [+*v-ing*/*(that)*] to declare untrue; refuse to accept as a fact: *Can you deny the truth of his statement?*|*He denied telling me/that he had told me.* –compare AFFIRM, ADMIT **2** to refuse to give or allow: *I was denied the chance of going to university.* **3** *fml* to disclaim connection with or responsibility for: *He has denied his country and his principles!*

**de·o·do·rant** /diː'əʊdərənt/ *n* [C;U] a substance that removes unpleasant smells, esp. those of the human body

**de·part** /dɪ'pɑːt||-ɑrt/ *v* [I *from*] *fml* to leave; go away: *The royal train departed from the capital at 12 o'clock.* –compare ARRIVE (1)

**depart from** sthg. *v prep* [T] *fml* to turn or move away from: *I'd like to depart from the main subject of my speech for a few moments.*

**de·part·ed** /dɪ'pɑːtɪ̈d||-ɑr-/ *adj* gone for ever: *to remember one's departed youth/fame*

**de·part·ment** /dɪ'pɑːtmənt||-ɑr-/ also **dept.** *written abbrev.*– *n* any of the important divisions or branches of a government, business, etc.: *the History Department of a university*|*the toy department of a large store* **–departmental** /ˌdiːpɑːt'mentl||-ɑr- / *adj*

**department store** /-'·· ·/ *n* a large shop divided into departments, in each of which a different type of goods is sold

**de·par·ture** /dɪ'pɑːtʃə^r||-ɑr-/ *n* [C;U] the action of DEPARTing; an act of DEPARTing: *What is the departure time of the flight?*|*The new system is a departure from our usual methods.* –compare ARRIVAL

**de·pend** /dɪ'pend/ *v* **That (all) depends/It all depends** I have certain doubts about that/it

**depend on/upon** sbdy./sthg. *v prep* [T] **1** to trust (usu. a person): *We're depending on you to finish the job by Friday.*|*I depended on the map, but it was wrong.* **2** to be supported by: *His family depend on him.* **3** to vary according to: *Whether the game will be played depends on the weather.*

**de·pen·da·ble** /dɪ'pendəbəl/ *adj* that can be depended on or trusted **–dependably** *adv* **–dependability** /dɪˌpendə'bɪlɪ̈ti / *n* [U]

**de·pen·dant,dependent** /dɪ'pendənt/ *n* a person who depends on another for food, clothing, money, etc.: *Please state on the paper whether you have any dependants.*

**de·pen·dence** /dɪ'pendəns/ *n* [U *on, upon*] **1** the quality or state of being controlled or materially supported by another person **2** the need to have something, esp. certain drugs, regularly

**de·pen·dent** /dɪ'pendənt/ *adj* [*on*] that depends on: *a dependent child*|*The success of the show is dependent on the weather.* –see also INDEPENDENT

**de·pict** /dɪ'pɪkt/ *v* [T] *fml* to represent by a picture or describe: *This painting depicts the Battle of Waterloo.* **–depiction** /dɪ'pɪkʃən / *n* [C;U]

**de·plete** /dɪ'pliːt/ *v* **-pleted, -pleting** [T] *fml* to lessen greatly **–depletion** /dɪ'pliːʃən / *n* [U]

**de·plore** /dɪ'plɔː^r||-or/ *v* **-plored, -ploring** [T] to be very sorry about **–deplorable** *adj*: *deplorable* (=very bad) *behaviour* **–deplorably** *adv*: *She behaved deplorably.*

**de·ploy** /dɪ'plɔɪ/ *v* **-ployed, -ploying** [T] to arrange for esp. military action: *We must deploy our forces correctly to win the battle.* **–deployment** *n* [C;U]

**de·port** /dɪ'pɔːt||-ort/ *v* [T] to send (an undesirable foreigner) out of the country **–deportation** /ˌdiːpɔː'teɪʃən||-por- / *n* [C;U]

**de·port·ment** /dɪ'pɔːtmənt||-or-/ *n* [U] *fml* the way a person, esp. a young lady, stands and walks *(BrE)*/behaves *(AmE)*

**de·pose** /dɪ'pəʊz/ *v* **-posed, -posing** [T] to remove from a high official position, esp. from that of ruler: *The head of state was deposed by the army.*

**de·pos·it**[1] /dɪ'pɒzɪ̈t||dɪ'pɑ-/ *v* [T] **1** to put down (usu. in a stated place): *Where can I deposit this load of sand?*|*A fine soil was deposited by winds carrying desert dust.* **2** to place in a bank or SAFE[2] (1): *He's deposited quite a lot of money recently.* –compare WITHDRAW (2)

**deposit**[2] *n* **1** [C;U] something DEPOSITed: *There are rich deposits of gold in those hills.* **2** [C *usu. sing.*] a part payment of money, which is made so that the seller will not sell the goods to anyone else: *You must pay a deposit to the hotel if you want them to keep a room free for you.*

**deposit account** /-'·· ·ˌ·/ *n* a bank account which earns INTEREST[1] (5) and from which money can be taken out only if advance notice is given –compare CURRENT ACCOUNT

**dep·ot** /'depəʊ||'diːpəʊ/ *n* **1** a storehouse for goods **2** a place where soldiers' stores are kept, and where new soldiers are trained **3** *AmE* a usu. small railway station

**de·prave** /dɪ'preɪv/ *v* **-praved, -praving** [T] to make bad in character: *The judge described the murderer as a depraved character.* **–depravity** /dɪ'prævɪ̈ti/ *n* **-ties** [C;U]

**de·pre·ci·ate** /dɪ'priːʃieɪt/ *v* **-ated, -ating** [I] (esp. of money) to fall in value –opposite **appreciate** **–depreciation** /-'eɪʃən/ *n* [U]

**de·press** /dɪ'pres/ *v* [T] **1** to sadden; discourage: *The bad news depressed me.* **2** to make less active or strong: *The threat of war has depressed business activity.* **3** *fml* to press down: *Depress this button in case of fire.* **–depressing** *adj* **–depressingly** *adv*

**de·pressed** /dɪ'prest/ *adj* **1** low in spirits; sad **2** suffering from low levels of business activity: *depressed areas of the country*

**de·pres·sion** /dɪ'preʃən/ *n* **1** [C;U] a feeling of sadness and hopelessness: *He's suffering from depression.* **2** [C] a period of reduced business activity and high unemployment: *the great depression of the 1930s* **3** [C] a part of a surface lower than the other parts: *The rain collected in depressions on the ground.*

**deprive** *v* → DEPRIVE OF

**de·prived** /dɪ'praɪvd/ *adj* (esp. of people) lacking food, money, etc.; poor: *deprived children*

**de·prive** sbdy. **of** sthg. /dɪ'praɪv/ *v prep* **-prived, -priving** [T] to take away from; prevent from using: *They deprived the criminal of his rights.* **–deprivation** /ˌdeprə̇'veɪʃən/ *n* [C;U]

**dept.** *n written abbrev. said as:* DEPARTMENT

**depth** /depθ/ *n* [C;U] **1** the state of being deep; distance from the surface or front to the bottom or back: *What is the depth of this lake?|a depth of 30 feet|*(fig.)*the depth of her feeling* –compare HEIGHT **2 in depth** done with great thoroughness: *an in-depth study of the problems of unemployment* **3 out of one's depth**: **a** in water that is deeper than one's height **b** beyond one's ability to understand: *I'm out of my depth in this argument.*

**dep·u·ta·tion** /ˌdepjʊ'teɪʃən‖-pjə-/ *n* a group of people who act on behalf of a larger group: *The minister agreed to receive a deputation from the railwaymen's union.*

**dep·u·tize**‖also **-tise** *BrE* /'depjʊtaɪz‖-pjə-/ *v* **-tized, -tizing** [I *for*] to act as DEPUTY (1)

**dep·u·ty** /'depjʊti‖-pjə-/ *n* **-ties 1** a person who has the power to act for another: *Jean will be my deputy while I am away.* **2** a member of the lower house of parliament in certain countries

**de·rail** /ˌdiː'reɪl, dɪ-/ *v* [I;T] to (cause to) run off the railway line: *a derailed train* **–derailment** *n* [C;U]

**de·range** /dɪ'reɪndʒ/ *v* **-ranged, -ranging** [T] to put (esp. the mind) into a state of disorder: *The poor woman's mind has been deranged for many years.|She is deranged.* **–derangement** *n* [U]

**der·e·lict** /'derə̇lɪkt/ *adj* left to decay: *a derelict old house too dangerous to live in*

**de·ride** /dɪ'raɪd/ *v* **-rided, -riding** [T +*v-ing*] *fml* to laugh at or make fun of, e.g. as of no value

**de·ri·sion** /dɪ'rɪʒən/ *n* [U] the act of deriding (DERIDE) or the state of being derided **–derisive** /dɪ'raɪsɪv, -zɪv/ *adj: derisive laughter* **–derisively** *adv*

**de·ri·so·ry** /dɪ'raɪsəri/ *adj* deserving DERISION because useless, ineffective, or not enough: *a derisory offer of £10 for something worth £100* **–derisorily** *adv*

**de·riv·a·tive** /dɪ'rɪvətɪv/ *n,adj* (something) coming from something else: *French is a derivative of Latin.|a rather derivative* (=not original or new) *piece of music*

**de·rive from** /dɪ'raɪv/ *v prep* **-rived, -riving** [T] **1** (**derive** sthg. **from** sbdy./sthg.) to obtain from: *He derives a lot of pleasure from meeting new people.* **2** (**derive from** sthg.) to come from: *The word* "DERIDE" *derives from Latin.* **–derivation** /ˌderə̇'veɪʃən/ *n* [C;U]

**der·ma·ti·tis** /ˌdɜːmə'taɪtə̇s‖ˌdɜr-/ *n* [U] a disease of the skin, marked by redness, swelling, and pain

**de·rog·a·to·ry** /dɪ'rɒgətəri‖dɪ'rɑgətori/ *adj fml* showing or causing lack of respect: *derogatory remarks about the government*

**der·rick** /'derɪk/ *n* a CRANE[1] (1) for lifting and moving heavy weights, for example into or out of a ship

**de·scend** /dɪ'send/ *v* [I;T] *fml* to come, fall, or sink from a higher to a lower level; go down: *The sun descended behind the hills.|She descended the stairs.* –opposite **ascend**

**descend on/upon** sbdy./sthg. *v prep* [T] **1** (of a group of people) to attack: *Thieves descended on the traveller.* **2** to arrive suddenly at: *The whole family descended on us at Christmas.*

**descend to** sthg. *v prep* [T +*v-ing*] to lower oneself to: *He descended to cheating.*

**de·scen·dant** /dɪ'sendənt/ *n* a person or animal that has another as grandfather or grandmother, great-grandfather, etc.: *He is a descendant of Queen Victoria.* –compare ANCESTOR **–descended (from)** *adj: descended from George Washington*

**de·scent** /dɪ'sent/ *n* **1** [C;U] the act or fact of going or coming down: *The road makes a sharp descent just past the lake.|his descent into a life of crime* –opposite **ascent 2** [U] family origins: *She is* **of** *German* **descent.**

**de·scribe** /dɪ'skraɪb/ *v* **-scribed, -scribing** [T] to say what something is like; give a picture (of) in words: *Try to describe exactly what happened.*

**de·scrip·tion** /dɪ'skrɪpʃən/ *n* [C;U] (the act of making) a statement or account that describes: *I recognized the man from the description in the newspaper.* **–descriptive** *adj: descriptive writing* **–descriptively** *adv*

**des·e·crate** /'desɪkreɪt/ *v* **-crated, -crating** [T] to use (something holy, such as a church) for purposes which are not holy **–desecration** /-'kreɪʃən/ *n* [C;U]

**des·ert**[1] /'dezət‖-ərt/ *n* a large sandy piece of land where there is very little rain and not many plants: *the Sahara Desert|a hot desert wind*

**de·sert**[2] /dɪ'zɜːt‖-ɜrt/ *v* **1** [T] to leave empty or leave completely: *the silent deserted streets of the city at night|All my friends have deserted me!* **2** [I;T] to leave (military service) without permission **–desertion** /dɪzɜːʃən‖-ɜr-/ *n* [C;U]

**de·sert·er** /dɪ'zɜːtə[r]‖-ɜr-/ *n* a person who leaves military service without permission

**de·serve** /dɪ'zɜːv‖-ɜrv/ *v* **-served, -serving** [T +*to-v*; not *be* +*v-ing*] to be worthy of; be fit for: *You've been working all morning–you deserve a rest.|She deserved to win.*

**de·serv·ed·ly** /dɪ'zɜːvə̇dli‖-ɜr-/ *adv* rightly: *Rembrandt is a deservedly famous artist.*

**des·ic·cate** /'desə̇keɪt/ *v* **-cated, -cating** [I;T] *fml* to (cause to) dry up

**de·sign**[1] /dɪ'zaɪn/ *v* **1** [I;T] to make a drawing or pattern of; to draw the plans for: *Who designed the Sydney Opera House?* **2** [T] to develop for a certain purpose or use: *a book designed mainly for use in colleges|This weekend party was designed to bring the two musicians together.* **–designer** *n: She's a dress* designer/an aircraft designer.

**design²** *n* **1** [C] a plan **2** [C] a drawing or pattern showing how something is to be made **3** [U] the art of making such drawings or patterns: *She attended a school of dress design.* **4** [C] a decorative pattern

**des·ig·nate** /ˈdezɪgneɪt/ *v* **-nated, -nating** [T] *fml* **1** to point out or call by a special name: *These x-marks on the drawing designate all the entrances to the castle.* **2** [*for*] to appoint (for special work): *I am designating you to act for me while I am away.* **–designation** /-ˈneɪʃən/ *n* [C;U]

**designate** sbdy./sthg. **as** sthg. *v prep* [T] *fml* to name officially as: *She has been designated as the Minister for Education.*

**de·signs** /dɪˈzaɪnz/ *n* [P *on, against*] evil plans: *They have designs on your money/your life.*

**de·sir·a·ble** /dɪˈzaɪərəbəl/ *adj* worth having, doing, or desiring: *a desirable job/house* –opposite **undesirable –desirability** /-əˈbɪlɨti/ *n* [U] **–desirably** *adv*

**de·sire¹** /dɪˈzaɪəʳ/ *v* **-sired, -siring** [T] **1** [+*to-v*/(*that*)] *fml* to wish or want very much: *The minister desires to see you.|She desires you to come at once.* **2** to wish to have sexual relations with

**desire²** *n* [C;U] **1** [+*to-v/that*] a strong wish: *filled with a/the desire to see her family again* **2** [*for*] a strong wish for sexual relations with: *Antony's desire for Cleopatra*

USAGE You can have a **desire** for anything: *his* **desire** *for success|She has expressed a* **desire** *to attend our next meeting.* You have an **appetite** only for things of the body: *The baby has a good/healthy* **appetite** (=likes eating); and a **craving** is a strong desire, esp. for things that are thought to be bad: *I can't cure my* **craving** *for cigarettes.* **Lust** is a very strong and usu. *derog* word: **lust** *for power/sex.*

**de·sir·ous** /dɪˈzaɪərəs/ *adj* [F +*that, of*] *fml* feeling or having a desire: *The president is strongly desirous that you should attend the meeting.*

**de·sist** /dɪˈzɪst, dɪˈsɪst/ *v* [I *from*] *fml* to cease doing: *The judge told the man to desist from threatening his wife.*

**desk** /desk/ *n* a table, often with drawers, at which one reads, writes, or does business –see pictures on pages 105, 415

**des·o·late** /ˈdesələt/ *adj* sad and lonely **–desolately** *adv* **–desolation** /-ˈleɪʃən/ *n* [U]

**de·spair¹** /dɪˈspeəʳ/ *v* [I *of*] to lose all hope (of): *Don't despair: things will get better soon!|Sometimes I despair of ever passing my driving test!*

**despair²** *n* [U] complete loss of hope: *Defeat after defeat filled us with despair.*

**de·spatch** /dɪˈspætʃ/ *n,v* [C;T *to*] → DISPATCH

**des·per·ate** /ˈdespərɨt/ *adj* **1** (of a person) ready for any wild act because of loss of hope: *a desperate criminal|He was desperate for work.* **2** (of an action) wild or dangerous; done as a last attempt: *a last desperate effort to win* **3** (of a state of affairs) very difficult and dangerous: *The country is in a desperate state.* **–desperately** *adv*

**des·per·a·tion** /ˌdespəˈreɪʃən/ *n* [U] the state of being DESPERATE: *He kicked at the locked door in desperation.*

**des·pic·a·ble** /dɪˈspɪkəbəl, ˈdespɪ-/ *adj* that deserves to be DESPISEd: *a despicable act* **–despicably** *adv: You behaved despicably!*

**de·spise** /dɪˈspaɪz/ *v* **-spised, -spising** [T] to regard as worthless, low, bad, etc.; dislike very much

**de·spite** /dɪˈspaɪt/ *prep fml* in spite of: *He came to the meeting despite his illness.* (=though he was ill) –see Study Notes on page 128

**de·spon·dent** /dɪˈspɒndənt‖dɪˈspɑn-/ *adj* feeling a complete loss of hope and courage **–despondently** *adv* **–despondency** *n* [U]

**des·pot** /ˈdespɒt, -ət‖ˈdespət, -ɑt/ *n derog* a person who uses great power unjustly or cruelly **–despotic** /dɪˈspɒtɪk, de-‖-ˈspɑ-/ *adj* **–despotism** /despətɪʒəm/ *n* [U]

**des·sert** /dɪˈzɜːt‖- ɜrt/ *n* [C;U] sweet food served at the end of a meal: *We had cake for dessert.* –compare PUDDING, SWEET

**des·ti·na·tion** /ˌdestɨˈneɪʃən/ *n* a place which is set for the end of a journey or to which something is sent: *The parcel was sent to the wrong destination.*

**des·tined** /ˈdestɨnd/ *adj* [+*to-v/for*] intended for some special purpose; intended by fate: *He was destined by his parents for life in the army.|His work was destined never to succeed.*

**des·ti·ny** /ˈdestɨni/ *n* **-nies** [C;U] fate; that which must or had to happen: *It was the great woman's destiny to lead her country.*

**des·ti·tute** /ˈdestɨtjuːt‖-tuːt/ *adj fml* **1** without food, clothing, shelter, etc., or the money to buy them; very poor **2** [F *of*] completely without: *She was destitute of human feeling.* **–destitution** /-ˈtjuːʃən‖-ˈtuː-/ *n* [U]

**de·stroy** /dɪˈstrɔɪ/ *v* **-stroyed, -stroying** [T] to ruin; put an end to the existence of (something): *The fire destroyed most of the building.|*(fig.)*All hopes of a peaceful settlement were destroyed by his speech.*

**de·stroy·er** /dɪˈstrɔɪəʳ/ *n* **1** a person who destroys **2** a small fast warship

**de·struc·tion** /dɪˈstrʌkʃən/ *n* [U] the act of destroying or state of being destroyed: *the destruction of the forest by fire|The enemy bombs caused death and destruction.* –see also CONSTRUCTION

**de·struc·tive** /dɪˈstrʌktɪv/ *adj* **1** causing destruction: *a destructive storm* **2** wanting or tending to destroy **–destructively** *adv* **–destructiveness** *n* [U]

**des·ul·to·ry** /ˈdesəltəri, ˈdez-‖- tori/ *adj fml* passing from one thing to another without purpose: *a desultory conversation–not serious at all*

**de·tach** /dɪˈtætʃ/ *v* [T *from*] to separate esp. from a larger mass and usu. without violence or damage **–detachable** *adj*

**de·tached** /dɪˈtætʃt/ *adj* **1** separate; not connected **2** (of a house) not connected with any other building –see also SEMIDETACHED –see picture on page 297 **3** (of a person or an opinion) not influenced by personal feelings

**de·tach·ment** /dɪˈtætʃmənt/ *n* **1** [U] the act of DETACHing **2** [U] the state of being DETACHED (3) **3** [C +*sing./pl. v*] a group, esp. of soldiers, sent from the main group on special duty

**de·tail** /ˈdiːteɪl‖dɪˈteɪl/ *n* [C;U] a small point or fact: *Everything in her story is correct (down) to the smallest detail.|He has a good eye for detail; he* notices everything. **–detailed** *adj*: *a detailed account*

**de·tain** /dɪ'teɪn/ *v* [T] *fml* to keep (a person) somewhere for a certain time: *The police have detained two men for questioning at the police station.*

**de·tect** /dɪ'tekt/ *v* [T] to find out; notice: *Poison was detected in the dead man's stomach.* **–detection** /dɪ'tekʃən/ *n* [U]: *His crime escaped detection* (=was not found out) *for many years.*

**de·tec·tive** /dɪ'tektɪv/ *n* a policeman, etc., whose special job is to find out information about criminals

**dé·tente** /'deɪtɒnt, deɪ'tɒnt‖-ɑnt/ *n* [C;U] (a state of) calmer political relations between countries

**de·ten·tion** /dɪ'tenʃən/ *n* [C;U] (an example of) the act of preventing a person from going away for a period of time

**de·ter** /dɪ'tɜːʳ/ *v* **-rr-** [T *from*] *fml* to prevent from acting, esp. by the threat of something unpleasant; DISSUADE: *The storm clouds deterred them from going out.* **–deterrent** /dɪ'terənt‖-'tɜr-/ *adj,n*: *a deterrent weapon*|*a* NUCLEAR (1) *deterrent*

**de·ter·gent** /dɪ'tɜːdʒənt‖-ɜr-/ *n* [C;U] a chemical product used for cleaning esp. clothing and dishes –compare SOAP

**de·te·ri·o·rate** /dɪ'tɪərɪəreɪt/ *v* **-rated, -rating** [I] to become worse: *his deteriorating health* –compare IMPROVE (1) **–deterioration** /-'reɪʃən/ *n* [U]

**de·ter·mi·na·tion** /dɪˌtɜːmə̇'neɪʃən‖-ɜr-/ *n* [U] **1** firmness of intention; strong will (to succeed, etc.): *The police chief spoke of his determination to catch the killers.* **2** the act of determining (DETERMINE (1))

**de·ter·mine** /dɪ'tɜːmə̇n‖-ɜr-/ *v* **-mined, -mining** [T] *fml* **1** to decide; find out: *to determine the rights and wrongs of the case*|*to determine the position of a star* **2** [+*to-v*/(*that*)] to (cause to) form a firm intention in the mind: *He determined to go at once/that he would go at once.*

**de·ter·mined** /dɪ'tɜːmə̇nd‖-ɜr-/ *adj* firm; having a strong will: *a very determined woman*|*I am determined to go.*

**de·ter·min·er** /dɪ'tɜːmə̇nəʳ‖-ɜr-/ *n tech* a word that limits the meaning of a noun and comes before adjectives that describe the same noun: *In the phrase "his new car", the word "his" is a determiner.*

**de·test** /dɪ'test/ *v* [T +*v-ing*] to hate with very strong feeling: *I detest people who deceive and tell lies.*|*They detest war.* **–detestable** *adj* **–detestably** *adv*

**det·o·nate** /'detəneɪt/ *v* **-nated, -nating** [I;T] to (cause to) explode suddenly: *They detonated the bomb and destroyed the bridge.* **–detonation** /-'neɪʃən/ *n*

**de·tour** /'diːtʊəʳ/ *n* a way round something: *They* **made a detour** *to avoid the centre of the town.*

**de·tract from** sthg. /dɪ'trækt/ *v prep* [T] to take something away from; make less the value of: *All the decoration detracts from the beauty of the building's shape.* –compare ADD **to**

**det·ri·ment** /'detrə̇mənt/ *n* [U] *fml* harm; damage: *He smoked a lot,* **to the detriment of** *his health.* **–detrimental** /-'mentl/ *adj*

**deuce** /djuːs‖duːs/ *n* [U] (in tennis) 40–40; 40 points to each player

**de·val·u·a·tion** /diːˌvæljʊ'eɪʃən/ *n* [U] a reduction in the value of something, esp. the exchange value of money

**de·val·ue** /diː'væljuː/ *v* **-ued, -uing 1** [I;T] to reduce the exchange value of (money): *We had to devalue (our money) last year.* –see also REVALUE **2** [T] to cause or be responsible for a DEVALUATION of (e.g. a person or a work of art): *Let's not devalue his work unjustly.*

**dev·a·state** /'devəsteɪt/ *v* **-stated, -stating** [T] to destroy completely; make impossible to live in **–devastation** /-'steɪʃən/ *n* [U]

**dev·a·stat·ing** /'devəsteɪtɪŋ/ *adj* **1** completely destructive: *a devastating storm*| (fig.) *a devastating argument* **2** *infml* very good, attractive, etc.: *You look devastating in that new dress.* **–devastatingly** *adv*

**de·vel·op** /dɪ'veləp/ *v* **1** [I;T *from, into*] to (cause to) grow, increase, or become more complete: *to develop from a seed into a plant*|*to develop a business/one's mind/an idea* **2** [I;T] to (cause to) begin to be seen, become active, or show signs: *Trouble is developing in the cities.*|*He seems to be developing an illness.* **3** [T] to put (something) through various stages of production: *developing the natural* RESOURCES *of a country*|*These photographs should be good when they're developed.*

**de·vel·op·er** /dɪ'veləpəʳ/ *n* a person who hopes to make a profit from developing land or buildings

**de·vel·op·ment** /dɪ'veləpmənt/ *n* **1** [U] the act or action of developing or the state of being developed: *the development of a seed into a plant/of his shop into a big business* **2** [C] a result of developing: *This new rose is a development from a very old kind of rose.* **3** [C] a new event or piece of news: *the latest developments in the murder trial*|*The use of computers in business is an important new development.*

**de·vi·ant** /'diːvɪənt/ also **deviate** /'diːvi-ə̇t/ *AmE– adj,n* (a person or thing) that is different from an accepted standard: *sexually deviant behaviour*|*Deviant children need help.*

**de·vi·ate** /'diːvieɪt/ *v* **-ated, -ating** [I *from*] to be different or move away from an accepted standard

**de·vi·a·tion** /ˌdiːvi'eɪʃən/ *n* [C;U] (a) noticeable difference from what is expected, esp. from accepted standards of behaviour: *sexual deviation*

**de·vice** /dɪ'vaɪs/ *n* **1** an instrument, esp. one that is cleverly thought out: *a device for sharpening pencils* **2** a plan, esp. for a purpose not wholly good

**dev·il** /'devəl/ *n* **1** [*the* S] (*usu. cap.*) the most powerful evil spirit; Satan **2** [C] an evil spirit **3** *infml* (in expressions of strong feeling) fellow; man; boy: *He failed his examination, (the) poor devil.*

**dev·il·ish** /'devəlɪʃ/ *adj* evil; like the devil **–devilishness** *n* [U]

**de·vi·ous** /'diːvɪəs/ *adj* **1** not going in the straightest or most direct way: *a devious path* **2** *derog* not direct and probably not completely honest: *Mary is a devious person and I don't trust her.* **–deviously** *adv* **–deviousness** *n* [U]

**de·vise** /dɪ'vaɪz/ *v* **-vised, -vising** [T] to plan or invent (esp. cleverly): *He devised a plan for winning the game.*

**de·void** /dɪ'vɔɪd/ *adj* [F *of*] *fml* empty (of); lacking (in): *He is devoid of human feeling!*

**de·vo·lu·tion** /ˌdiːvə'luːʃən/ *n* [U] the giving of governmental or personal power to another person or group

**devolve on** sbdy. /di'vɒlv‖dɪ'vɑlv/ also **devolve upon** sbdy.– *v prep* [T] (of power, work, etc.) to be passed to (another person or group): *While he's ill, most of his work will devolve on me.*

**de·vot·ed** /dɪ'vəʊt$^{1}_{3}$d/ *adj* [*to*] loyal; caring a great deal; fond of: *a devoted father/friend|He is very devoted to his wife.|devoted to football/helping others* **–devotedly** *adv* –compare ADDICTED

**dev·o·tee** /ˌdevə'tiː/ *n* [*of*] a person who admires someone or something: *a devotee of Bach* (=Bach's music)

**de·vote** sthg. **to** sbdy./sthg. /dɪ'vəʊt/ *v prep* **-voted, -voting** [T] to set apart for; give wholly or completely to: *He has devoted his life to helping blind people.*

**de·vo·tion** /dɪ'vəʊʃən/ *n* [U *to*] **1** the act of devoting or the condition of being DEVOTED TO: *The devotion of too much time to sports leaves too little time for studying.* **2** great fondness **3** attention to religion; DEVOUTness

**de·vour** /dɪ'vaʊəʳ/ *v* [T] to eat up quickly and hungrily: *The lion devoured the deer.*|(fig.) *She devoured the new book.*

**de·vout** /dɪ'vaʊt/ *adj* **1** (of people) seriously concerned with religion: *a devout Hindu* **2** [A] felt very deeply: *a devout hope* **–devoutness** *n* [U] **–devoutly** *adv*

**dew** /djuː‖duː/ *n* [U] the small drops of water which form on cold surfaces during the night –sounds like **due**

**dew·y** /'djuːi‖'duːi/ *adj* wet (as if) with DEW: *dewy-eyed*

**dex·ter·i·ty** /dek'ster$^{1}_{3}$ti/ *n* [U] *apprec* the quality of cleverness and skill, esp. in the use of the hands: *the dexterity with which she plays the piano* **–dexterous** /'dekstərəs/ also **dextrous** /'dekstrəs/ *adj*

**di·a·be·tes** /ˌdaɪə'biːtiːz, -t$^{1}_{3}$s/ *n* [U] a disease in which there is too much sugar in the blood

**di·a·bet·ic** /ˌdaɪə'betɪk/ *adj,n* (typical of or suitable for) a person suffering from DIABETES

**di·a·bol·i·cal** /ˌdaɪə'bɒlɪkəl‖-'bɑ-/ *adj derog* **1** of or like the devil **2** *infml* very unpleasant and annoying: *What diabolical weather!* **–diabolically** *adv*

**di·ag·nose** /'daɪəgnəʊz‖-nəʊs/ *v* **-nosed, -nosing** [T *as*] to discover the nature of (a disease): *The doctor diagnosed my illness (as a rare bone disease).*

**di·ag·no·sis** /ˌdaɪəg'nəʊs$^{1}_{3}$s/ *n* **-ses** /siːz/ [C;U *of*] (a statement which is the result of) diagnosing (DIAGNOSE): *The two doctors made/gave different diagnoses of my disease.* –see also PROGNOSIS **–diagnostic** /-'nɒstɪk‖-'nɑ-/ *adj*

**di·ag·o·nal** /daɪ'ægənəl/ *n,adj* **1** a straight line joining two opposite corners of a square, or other four-sided figure: *The two diagonals of a square cross in the centre.* **2** (any straight line) which runs in a sloping direction: *a cloth with a diagonal pattern* **–diagonally** *adv*

**di·a·gram** /'daɪəgræm/ *n* a plan or figure drawn to explain an idea; drawing which shows how something works **–diagrammatic** /ˌdaɪəgrə'mætɪk / *adj* **–diagrammatically** *adv*

**di·al**[1] /'daɪəl/ *n* **1** the face of an instrument, such as a clock, which shows measurements by means of a pointer and figures **2** the wheel on a telephone with numbered holes for the fingers, which is moved round when one makes a telephone call

**dial**[2] *v* **-ll-** *BrE*‖**-l-** *AmE* [I;T] to make a telephone call (to): *How do I dial Paris?|Put in the money before dialling.* –see TELEPHONE[1] (USAGE)

**di·a·lect** /'daɪəlekt/ *n* [C;U] a variety of a language, spoken in one part of a country, which is different from other forms of the same language: *the Yorkshire and Lancashire dialects|a poem written in Scottish dialect* **–dialectal** /ˌdaɪə'lektl/ *adj*

**di·a·lec·tic** /ˌdaɪə'lektɪk/ also **dialectics** /ˌdaɪə'lektɪks/ *n* [U] *tech* the art or method of arguing according to certain rules of question and answer **–dialectical** *adj*

**di·a·logue** *BrE*‖**dialog** *AmE* /'daɪəlɒg‖-lɔg, -lɑg/ *n* [C;U] **1** (a) written conversation in a book or play **2** (a) conversation which examines differences of opinion, e.g. between leaders: *At last there can be (a) reasonable dialogue between our governments.* –see also MONOLOGUE

**di·am·e·ter** /daɪ'æm$^{1}_{3}$təʳ/ *n* (the length of) a straight line going from one side of a circle to the other side, passing through the centre of the circle –compare RADIUS

**di·a·met·ri·cally** /ˌdaɪə'metrɪkli/ *adv* completely; directly: *I am* **diametrically opposed to** (=I completely disagree with) *his ideas.*

**di·a·mond** /'daɪəmənd/ *n* **1** [C;U] a very hard, valuable, precious stone, usu. colourless, which is used esp. in jewellery: *a diamond ring|a diamond mine* **2** [C] a figure with four straight sides of equal length that stands on one of its points **3** [C] a playing card with one or more of these figures printed on it in red: *the 4 of diamonds* –see CARDS (USAGE)

**di·a·per** /'daɪəpəʳ‖'daɪpər/ *n AmE* for NAPPY

**di·a·phragm** /'daɪəfræm/ *n* **1** the muscle that separates the lungs from the stomach **2** any thin plate or piece of stretched material which is moved, e.g. by sound **3** → CAP[1] (3)

**di·ar·rhoe·a, -rhea** /ˌdaɪə'rɪə/ *n* [U] an illness in which the bowels are emptied too often and in too liquid a form

**di·a·ry** /'daɪəri/ *n* **-ries 1** (a book containing) a daily record of the events in a person's life: *Mary keeps* (=writes) *a diary.* **2** a book in which one keeps a record of things to be done in the future: *"Can you come on Wednesday?" "I'll just look in my diary to see if I'm free."*

**dice**[1] /daɪs/ *n* **-dice** a small six-sided block of wood, plastic, etc., with a different number of spots from 1-6 on the various sides, used in games of chance: *to throw the dice|a pair of dice*

**dice**[2] *v* **-diced, -dicing 1** [T] to cut (food) into small square pieces: *The meat should be finely diced.* **2** [I *for, with*] to play with DICE **3 dice with death** to take a great risk

**dic·ey** /'daɪsi/ *adj* **-ier, -iest** *infml* risky and uncertain

**di·chot·o·my** /daɪ'kɒtəmi‖-'kɑ-/ *n* **-mies** [*between*] *fml* a division into two (esp. opposite) parts or groups: *the growing dichotomy between opponents and supporters of* NUCLEAR (1) *weapons*

**dic·tate** /dɪk'teɪt‖'dɪkteɪt/ *v* **-tated, -tating** [I;T *to*] **1** to say (words) for someone else to write down or for a machine to record: *She was dictating (a letter) to her secretary.* **2** to state (demands, conditions, etc.) with the power to enforce: *We're now in a position to dictate (our own demands) to our employers.*

**dic·ta·tion** /dɪk'teɪʃən/ *n* **1** [U] the act of dictating or writing down what is DICTATED (1): *a secretary taking dictation* **2** [C] something dictated to test one's ability to hear and write a language correctly: *The teacher gave us two French dictations today.*

**dic·ta·tor** /dɪk'teɪtəʳ‖'dɪkteɪtər/ *n derog* a ruler who has complete power over a country, esp. if he/she has gained the power by force **–dictatorial** /ˌdɪktə'tɔːrɪəl‖-tor-/ *adj*

**dic·ta·tor·ship** /dɪk'teɪtəʃɪp‖-'teɪtər-/ *n derog* **1** [C;U] (the period of) government by a dictator **2** [C] a country ruled by a dictator

**dic·tion** /'dɪkʃən/ *n* [U] the way in which a person pronounces words: *Actors need training in diction.*

**dic·tion·a·ry** /'dɪkʃənəri‖-neri/ *n* **-ries** a book that gives a list of words in alphabetical order, with their meanings in the same or another language: *a German-English dictionary|a science dictionary* (=a dictionary of scientific words)

**did** /dɪd/ *v past tense of* DO

**di·dac·tic** /daɪ'dæktɪk/ *adj fml* (of speech or writing) meant to teach, esp. to teach a moral lesson

**did·n't** /'dɪdnt/ *short for*: did not: *You saw him, didn't you?*

**die**[1] *v* **died, dying** /'daɪ-ɪŋ/ [I] **1** (of creatures and plants) to stop living: *She's very ill and I'm afraid she's dying.|He died in his sleep.*(=while he was sleeping)*|He died of a fever/in an accident/by drowning/from a wound.*|(fig.) *My love for you will never die.*|(fig.) *His secret died with him,* (=was lost when he died) **2 be dying for/to** *infml* to have a great wish for/to: *I'm dying for a cigarette.|We're dying to hear what happened.* –see DEAD (USAGE)

**die away** *v adv* [I] (esp. of sound, wind, light) to fade and become less and less and cease

**die down** *v adv* [I] to become less strong or violent: *The fire is dying down.|The excitement died down.*

**die off** *v adv* [I] to die one by one: *As she got older and older, her relatives all died off.*

**die out** *v adv* [I] (of families, races, practices, and ideas) to disappear completely: *The practice of children working in factories has nearly died out.*

**die**[2] *n* a metal block used for shaping metal, plastic, etc.

**die·sel** /'diːzəl/ also **diesel oil**– *n* [U] a liquid used for producing power in the engine of a train, etc. (**diesel engine**): *We filled up with diesel at the petrol station.*

**di·et**[1] /'daɪət/ *n* **1** [C;U] the sort of food and drink usually taken (by a person or group): *Proper diet and exercise are both important for health.|The Irish used to live on a diet of potatoes.* **2** [C] a limited list of food and drink that one is allowed: *The doctor ordered him to* **go on a diet** *to lose weight.|I mustn't have chocolate–I'm* **on a diet.**

**diet**[2] *v* [I] to eat according to a DIET[1] (2): *No sugar in my coffee, please; I'm dieting.*

**dif·fer** /'dɪfəʳ/ *v* [I] **1** [*from*] to be unlike: *Nylon and silk differ.|Nylon differs from silk in/as to origin and cost.* **2** [*with*] to have an opposite opinion; disagree: *The two brothers often differ.|He differed with his brother about/on/over a political question.*

**dif·fe·rence** /'dɪfərəns/ *n* **1** [C *between*] a way of being unlike: *There are many differences between living in a city and living in the country.* **2** [S;U *between, in, of, to*] (an) amount or manner in which things are unlike: *The difference between 5 and 11 is 6.|Flowers make no/a lot of difference to a room.|It doesn't make much/any/the least difference to me what you do.|When you're learning to drive, having a good teacher* **makes all the difference.** **3** [C] a slight disagreement: *They've* **settled their differences** *and are friends again.*

**dif·fe·rent** /'dɪfərənt/ *adj* **1** [*from, than, to*] unlike; not of the same kind: *Mary and Jane are quite different.|Mary is different from/than/to Jane.* **2** [A] various; several; not the same one or ones: *We make this dress in (three/a lot of) different colours.|This is a different car from the one I drove yesterday.* **–differently** *adv*

USAGE 1 Although **different to** (*BrE*) and **different than** (*AmE*) are commonly used, teachers prefer **different from. Indifferent** can be followed only by **to**: *I am* **indifferent to** *this question.* 2 Compare **different** and **various**: Both mean "not the same" but **various** means "several not the same": *The minister gave* **various** *reasons* (=a number of different reasons) *for the government's decision.|The two ministers gave* **different** *reasons for the government's decision.* (=they did not each give the same reason) Unlike **various, different** can also be used with a singular noun, and it then means that the noun is compared with something else that may or may not be mentioned: *You look* **different** *(from before) with your hair cut.|They each wanted to see a* **different** *film (from each other).*

**dif·fe·ren·tial** /ˌdɪfə'renʃəl/ *n* the amount of difference between things, esp. difference in wages between workers at different levels in the same industry

**dif·fe·ren·ti·ate** /ˌdɪfə'renʃieɪt/ *v* **-ated, -ating** [I;T *from, between*] to see, express, or make a difference (between): *This company does not differentiate between men and women–they employ both equally.* **–differentiation** /-'eɪʃən/ *n* [C;U]

**dif·fi·cult** /'dɪfɪkəlt/ *adj* **1** not easy; taking time or effort to do, make, or understand: *English is difficult/a difficult language to learn.* **2** (of people) unfriendly and always quarrelling; not easily pleased: *a difficult child*

**dif·fi·cul·ty** /'dɪfɪkəlti/ *n* **-ties 1** [U *in*] the quality of being difficult; trouble: *She had/found great difficulty in understanding him.|He did it without much/any difficulty.|He's* **in difficulty** *with his schoolwork.* **2** [C] something difficult; a trouble: *He's having* FINANCIAL (=money) *difficulties.*

**dif·fi·dent** /'dɪfɪdənt/ *adj* [*about*] having or showing a lack of belief in one's own powers or ability, lacking CONFIDENCE: *He is diffident about expressing his opinions.* **–diffidently** *adv* **–diffidence** *n* [U]

**dif·fuse**[1] /dɪ'fjuːs/ *adj fml* **1** widely spread; DIFFUSED[2]: *Direct light is better for reading than diffuse light.* **2** *derog* using too many words and not keeping to the point: *a diffuse speech/writer* **–diffusely** *adv* **–diffuseness** *n* [U]

**dif·fuse**[2] /dɪ'fjuːz/ *v* **-fused, -fusing** [I;T] *fml* to (cause to) spread out freely in all directions: *to* *diffuse knowledge* **–diffusion** /dɪˈfjuːʒən/ *n* [U *of*]

**dig¹** /dɪg/ *v* **-dug** /dʌg/, **digging** [I;T] **1** to break up and move (earth): *We must dig (over) the vegetable garden.|The dog has been digging in that corner for an hour.* **2** to make (a hole) by taking away the earth: *We shall have to dig under the river/through the mountain/into the hill to lay this pipe.|The prisoners escaped by digging an underground passage.*

**dig** sthg. **into** sbdy./sthg. *v prep* [T] to push into

**dig** sthg.↔**out** *v adv* [T *of*] **1** to find by searching: *I dug out these old trousers to give to the boy.* **2** to get out by digging; free from being buried: *He had to dig the car out of the snow.*

**dig** sthg.↔**up** *v adv* [T] **1** to make a hole in by taking away earth, etc.: *They're digging up the road outside our house.* **2** to find or take out of the ground, by digging: *Father dug up an old coin in the garden.*|(fig.) *The newspapers have dug up that unpleasant old story.*

**dig²** *n infml* a quick push: *John's falling asleep; just give him a dig!*|(fig.) *That last remark was* **a dig at** *me.* (=made in order to annoy me)

**di·gest¹** /daɪˈdʒest, dɪ̇-/ *v* **1** [I;T] to (cause to) be changed into a form that the body can use: *Mary can't digest fat.|Cheese doesn't digest easily.* **2** [T] to think over and arrange in the mind: *to digest the contents of a book* **–digestible** *adj* **–digestive** *adj* [A]

**di·gest²** /ˈdaɪdʒest/ *n* a short account (of a piece of writing) which gives the most important facts

**di·ges·tion** /daɪˈdʒestʃən, dɪ̇-/ *n* [C;U] (a) power of DIGESTING¹ (1) food: *Cheese is bad for the digestion.* –compare INDIGESTION

**di·git** /ˈdɪdʒɪ̇t/ *n* **1** any of the numbers from 0 to 9: *The number 2001 contains four digits.* **2** *fml* a finger or toe **–digital** *adj* [A]: *A* **digital watch** *shows the time by electronically lit up numbers, e.g. 12.14.*

**dig·ni·fied** /ˈdɪgnɪ̇faɪd/ *adj* having or showing DIGNITY: *a dignified manner|a dignified old man* –opposite **undignified**

**dig·ni·ta·ry** /ˈdɪgnɪ̇tərі‖-teri/ *n* **-ries** *fml* a person holding a high position: *Many of the local dignitaries attended the funeral.*

**dig·ni·ty** /ˈdɪgnɪ̇ti/ *n* [U] **1** true worth and nobleness of character: *He always acted with great dignity.* **2** calm, formal, and grand behaviour: *The dignity of the occasion was lost when he fell down the steps.*

**di·gress** /daɪˈgres/ *v* [I *from*] *fml* (of a writer or speaker) to stop what one is saying and begin to talk about something else: *I'll tell you a funny story, if I may digress (from my subject) for a moment.* **–digression** /daɪˈgreʃən/ *n* [C;U]

**digs** /dɪgz/ *n* [P] *BrE infml* lodgings: *When his family left London, Tom moved into digs.*

**dike, dyke** /daɪk/ *n* **1** a thick bank or wall built to control water and prevent flooding –compare DAM **2** a narrow passage dug to carry water away; ditch

**di·lap·i·dat·ed** /dɪ̇ˈlæpɪ̇deɪtɪ̇d/ *adj* (of things) broken and old; falling to pieces: *a dilapidated old car/castle* **–dilapidation** /-ˈdeɪʃən/ *n* [U]

**di·late** /daɪˈleɪt/ *v* **-lated, -lating** [I;T] to make or become wider or further open: *Her eyes/*PUPILS² *dilated with terror.* –compare CONTRACT² (1) **–dilation** /-ˈleɪʃən/ *n* [U]

**di·lem·ma** /dɪ̇ˈlemə, daɪ-/ *n* a difficult choice to be made between two courses of action: *She was* **in a dilemma** *as to whether to stay at school or get a job.*

**dil·i·gent** /ˈdɪlɪ̇dʒənt/ *adj* (of people and behaviour) hardworking; showing steady effort: *Though he's not clever he's a diligent worker and should do well in the examinations.* **–diligently** *adv* **–diligence** *n* [U]

**di·lute** /daɪˈluːt/ *v* **-luted, -luting** [T *with*] to make (a liquid) weaker or thinner by mixing another liquid with it: *He diluted the paint with water.* –compare CONCENTRATED (1) **–dilute** *adj*: *dilute acid* **–dilution** /daɪˈluːʃən/ *n* [C;U]

**dim¹** /dɪm/ *adj* **-mm- 1** not bright; not clear: *The light is too dim for me to read easily.* **2** *infml* (of people) stupid **–dimly** *adv* **–dimness** *n* [U]

**dim²** *v* **-mm-** [I;T] to (cause to) become DIM¹ (1): *The lights in the theatre began to dim.*

**dime** /daɪm/ *n* a coin of the US and Canada, worth 10 cents

**di·men·sion** /daɪˈmenʃən, dɪ̇-/ *n* **1** a measurement in any one direction: *Length is one dimension, and width is another.|Time is sometimes called the fourth dimension.*|(fig.) *There is another dimension to this problem which you haven't mentioned.* **2 -dimensional** having the stated number of DIMENSIONS: *A three-dimensional object has length, depth, and height.*

**di·men·sions** /daɪˈmenʃənz, dɪ̇-/ *n* [P] (measurements of) size: *What are the dimensions of this room?* (=its height, length, and width)|*a box of large dimensions|The dimensions of this difficulty have only recently been recognized.*

**di·min·ish** /dɪ̇ˈmɪnɪʃ/ *v* [I;T] *fml* to (cause to) become or seem smaller: *His illness diminished his strength.|the government's diminishing popularity* **–diminution** /dɪ̇mɪˈnjuːʃən‖-ˈnuː-/ *n* [C;U]

**di·min·u·tive** /dɪ̇ˈmɪnjʊtɪv‖-njə-/ *adj fml* very small

**dim·ple** /ˈdɪmpəl/ *n apprec* a little hollow place on the skin, esp. one formed in the cheek when a person smiles

**din** /dɪn/ *n derog* a loud, continuous, confused, and unpleasant noise

**dine** /daɪn/ *v* **-dined, -dining** [I] *fml* to eat dinner: *I'm going to dine with Peter/at Peter's tonight.*

**dine out** also **eat out**– *v adv* [I] to eat dinner away from home, esp. in a restaurant

**din·er** /ˈdaɪnəʳ/ *n* **1** a person who DINES, esp. in a restaurant **2** *AmE* a small restaurant beside the road **3** *AmE* a carriage on a train where food is served

**ding·dong** /ˌdɪŋˈdɒŋ◂‖ˈdɪŋdɔŋ/ *adv,adj,n* [A;S] (like) the noise made by a bell

**din·ghy** /ˈdɪŋgi/ *n* **-ghies** a small open boat

**din·gy** /ˈdɪndʒi/ *adj* **-gier, -giest** (of things and places) dirty and faded: *a dingy little room* **–dingily** *adv* **–dinginess** *n* [U]

**dining room** /ˈ·· ·/ *n* a room where meals are eaten in a house, hotel, etc. –see picture on page 297

**din·ner** /ˈdɪnəʳ/ *n* **1** [C;U] the main meal of the day, eaten either at midday or in the evening: *I'm busy cooking (the) dinner.|It's dinner time/time for dinner.|We're having fish for (our) dinner.* **2** [C] a formal occasion in the evening when this meal is eaten: *The company is giving/holding an important dinner.* USAGE If **dinner** is at midday, the evening meal is called **tea** or **supper.** If **dinner** is in the evening, the midday meal is called **lunch.**

**dinner jack·et** /'·· ,··/ ||also **tuxedo** *AmE*– *n* a man's black or white coat for rather formal evening occasions

**di·no·saur** /'daɪnəsɔːʳ/ *n* a very large long-tailed creature (REPTILE) that lived in very ancient times and disappeared suddenly and without explanation

**di·o·cese** /'daɪəsɪ̆s/ also **bishopric**– *n* (in the Christian religion) the area under the government of a BISHOP –compare SEE²

**dip¹** /dɪp/ *v* **-pp- 1** [T *in, into*] to put (something) in/into a liquid for a moment: *to dip one's hand into the water* **2** [I;T] to (cause to) drop slightly: *The sun dipped below the western sea.|You should dip the car's* HEADLIGHTS (=lights at the front) *when you meet another car at night.|The road dips just around the corner.*

**dip into** sthg. *v prep* [T] **1** to read or study for a short time: *I haven't read that book properly–I've only dipped into it.* **2** to put one's hand into (a place) and take something out: *He* **dipped into his pocket** *and bought drinks for his friends.*

**dip²** *n* **1** a slope down; slight drop in height: *a dip in the road* **2** *infml* a quick bathe in the sea, a lake, etc.

**diph·ther·i·a** /dɪf'θɪərɪə, dɪp-/ *n* [U] a serious infectious disease of the throat which makes breathing difficult

**diph·thong** /'dɪfθɒŋ, 'dɪp-||-θɔŋ/ *n tech* a compound vowel made by pronouncing two vowels quickly one after the other: *The vowel sound in "my" is a diphthong.*

**di·plo·ma** /dɪ̆'pləumə/ *n* an official paper showing that a person has successfully finished a course of study or passed an examination: *She has a diploma in education.*

**di·plo·ma·cy** /dɪ̆'pləuməsi/ *n* [U] **1** the art and practice of establishing and continuing relations between nations **2** skill at dealing with people and getting them to agree: *He needed all his diplomacy to settle their quarrel.*

**dip·lo·mat** /'dɪpləmæt/ *n* a person employed in DIPLOMACY (1)

**dip·lo·mat·ic** /,dɪplə'mætɪk◂/ *adj* **1** [A *no comp.*] of or related to DIPLOMACY (1): *Nigel joined the diplomatic service.* **2** skilled in dealing with people; having TACT: *Try to be diplomatic when you refuse her invitation, so as not to cause bad feeling.* –opposite **undiplomatic** (for **2**) **–diplomatically** *adv*

**dire** /daɪəʳ/ *adj* **1** very great; terrible: *in dire need of food* **2** [A] causing great fear for the future: *a dire warning*

**di·rect¹** /dɪ̆'rekt, daɪ-/ *v* [T] **1** [*to*] to tell (someone) the way to a place: *I'm lost. Can you direct me to the station?* **2** to control and be in charge of (the way something is done): *He directed the building of the new bridge.|Who directed that play on television last night?* **3** [+*to-v*/*that*] *fml* to order: *The policeman directed the crowd to move back.* **4** [*to, at, towards*] to turn or aim (attention, remarks, movement, etc.) in the stated direction: *This warning is directed at you.|We directed our steps towards the house.* see LEAD¹ (USAGE)

**direct²** *adj* **1** straight; going from one point to another without turning aside: *Which is the most direct way to London?|a direct flight from London to Los Angeles* **2** [*no comp.*] leading from one thing to another without anything coming between: *He was asked to leave school as a direct result of his behaviour.* (=and for no other reason) **3** (of people and behaviour) honest and easily understood: *He gave a direct answer to my question.* **4** [A] exact: *He's the direct opposite of his brother.* –see also INDIRECT **–directness** *n* [U]

**direct³** *adv* in a straight line; without stopping or turning aside: *The next flight doesn't go direct to Rome; it goes by way of Paris.*

**di·rec·tion** /dɪ̆'rekʃən, daɪ-/ *n* **1** [U] the action of DIRECTing¹ (2); control: *The singing group is* **under the direction of** *Mr Blair.* **2** [C;U] the course on which a person or thing moves or is aimed: *He drove away* **in the direction of** (=towards) *London.|She has* **a good/poor sense of direction** *and never/always gets lost.* **3** [C] the point towards which a person or thing faces: *What direction does this house face?* **4** [C *usu. pl.*] a set of instructions on what to do or how to get somewhere: *He gave me directions to the station.|You must follow the directions on the packet.*

**di·rec·tive** /dɪ̆'rektɪv, dəɪ-/ *n fml* an official order

**di·rect·ly¹** /dɪ̆'rektli, daɪ-/ *adv* **1** in a direct manner: *He lives directly opposite the church.|She answered me very directly.* –opposite **indirectly 2** at once: *(infml) He should be here directly.* (=very soon)

**directly²** *conj infml* as soon as: *I came directly I got your message.*

**di·rec·tor** /dɪ̆'rektəʳ, daɪ-/ *n* **1** a person who directs an organization or company **2** a person who directs a play or film, instructing the actors, cameramen, etc. –compare PRODUCER (2)

**di·rec·to·ry** /daɪ̆'rektəri, daɪ-/ *n* **-ries** a book or list of names, facts, etc., usu. arranged in alphabetical order: *The telephone directory gives people's names, addresses, and telephone numbers.* –see TELEPHONE¹ (USAGE)

**dirge** /dɜːdʒ||dɜrdʒ/ *n* a slow sad song sung over a dead person

**dirt** /dɜːt||dɜrt/ *n* [U] **1** unclean matter, esp. in the wrong place: *Wash the dirt off the floor/off your hands.|The floor is covered in/with dirt.* **2** soil; loose earth: *The children were outside playing happily in the dirt.* **3 treat someone like dirt** to treat someone as though he/she were worthless

**dirt·y¹** /'dɜːti||'dɜr-/ *adj* **-ier, -iest 1** not clean: *dirty hands|This dress is getting dirty; it needs washing.|Repairing cars is a dirty job.* **2** (of thoughts or words) concerned with sex in an unpleasant way: *They sat drinking and telling dirty stories.* **3 dirty trick** a mean trick **4 (give someone) a dirty look** *infml* (to give someone) a look of great disapproval **–dirtily** *adv*

**dirty²** *v* **-ied, -ying** [I;T] to (cause to) become dirty: *Don't dirty your hands.*

**dis·a·bil·i·ty** /,dɪsə'bɪlɪ̆ti/ *n* **-ties 1** [U] the state of being DISABLEd **2** [C] something that DISABLEs: *He gets money* (a **disability pension**) *from the Government because of his disabilities.*

**dis·a·ble** /dɪs'eɪbəl/ *v* **-bled, -bling** [T *from*] to make (a person) unable to do something, esp. to use his body properly: *He was disabled in the war; he lost his left arm.* –**disablement** *n* [C;U]

**dis·a·bled** /dɪs'eɪbəld/ *n* [*the* P] DISABLEd people: *The disabled are to receive more money.*

**dis·ad·van·tage** /ˌdɪsəd'vɑːntɪdʒ‖-'væn-/ *n* an unfavourable condition or position; anything which makes one less successful than other people: *His bad health is a great disadvantage to him.*|*If you don't speak good English, you'll be* **at a** *big* **disadvantage** *when you try to get a job.* –opposite **advantage** –**disadvantageous** /ˌdɪsædvan'teɪdʒəs,-væn-/ *adj* [*to*]

**dis·a·gree** /ˌdɪsə'griː/ *v* **-greed, -greeing** [I *with*] to have or show different opinions; not agree: *I often disagree with him (about/over/as to what we ought to do).*|*These two reports of the accident disagree.*

**disagree with** sbdy. *v prep* [T *no pass.*] (of food or weather) to have a bad effect on; make ill: *Chocolate always disagrees with me.* –opposite **agree with**

**dis·a·gree·a·ble** /ˌdɪsə'griːəbəl/ *adj* unpleasant; not to one's liking: *a disagreeable job/person* –opposite **agreeable** –**disagreeably** *adv*

**dis·a·gree·ment** /ˌdɪsə'griːmənt/ *n* [C;U] the fact or a case of DISAGREEing: *serious disagreement between the two political parties*|*We have been having a few disagreements lately.*

**dis·al·low** /ˌdɪsə'laʊ/ *v* [T] *fml* to refuse officially to recognize or allow: *to disallow a goal/a claim* –opposite **allow**

**dis·ap·pear** /ˌdɪsə'pɪəʳ/ *v* [I] **1** to go out of sight: *The sun disappeared behind a cloud.* **2** to cease to exist; become lost: *These beautiful birds are fast disappearing.*|*My keys have disappeared off the table.* –opposite **appear** –**disappearance** *n* [C;U]: *Her disappearance was very worrying.*

**dis·ap·point** /ˌdɪsə'pɔɪnt/ *v* [T] to fail to fulfil the hopes of (a person): *I'm sorry to disappoint you, but I can't come after all.*

**dis·ap·point·ed** /ˌdɪsə'pɔɪntɪ̵d/ *adj* [*about, at, in, with*] unhappy at not seeing hopes come true: *Are you very disappointed about/at losing the race?*|*My parents will be disappointed in/with me if I fail the examination.* –**disappointedly** *adv*

**dis·ap·point·ing** /ˌdɪsə'pɔɪntɪŋ/ *adj* causing one to be unhappy at not seeing hopes come true: *Your examination marks are rather disappointing; I hoped you would do better.* –**disappointingly** *adv*

**dis·ap·point·ment** /ˌdɪsə'pɔɪntmənt/ *n* **1** [U] the state of being disappointed: **To his** *great* **disappointment**, *she wasn't on the train.* **2** [C] someone or something disappointing: *The film was a bit of a disappointment; we expected it to be much better.*

**dis·ap·prov·al** /ˌdɪsə'pruːvəl/ *n* [U] the state of disapproving: *He spoke with disapproval of your behaviour.*|*She shook her head* **in disapproval.** (=as a sign of disapproval) –opposite **approval**

**dis·ap·prove** /ˌdɪsə'pruːv/ *v* **-proved, -proving** [I *of*] to not approve (of); have a bad opinion (of): *We strongly disapprove of the firm's new methods.* –**disapprovingly** *adv*

**dis·arm** /dɪs'ɑːm‖- 'ɑrm/ *v* **1** [T] to take the weapons away from: *The police disarmed the criminal.* **2** [I] (esp. of a country) to reduce the size and strength of armed forces –opposite **arm** (for **1,2**); see also REARM **3** [T] *apprec* to drive away anger from: *a disarming smile*

**dis·ar·ma·ment** /dɪs'ɑːməmənt‖-'ɑr-/ *n* [U] the act or principle of DISARMing (2): *new plans for* **nuclear disarmament**

**dis·ar·ray** /ˌdɪsə'reɪ/ *n* [U] *fml* the state of disorder: *She rushed out of the burning house with her clothes* **in disarray**. –see also ARRAY

**dis·as·so·ci·ate** /ˌdɪsə'seʊʃieɪt, -sieɪt/ *v* **-ated, -ating** [T *from*] →DISSOCIATE

**di·sas·ter** /dɪ'zɑːstəʳ‖dɪ'zæ-/ *n* [C;U] (a) sudden great misfortune: *The flood was a terrible disaster; hundreds of people died.*

**di·sas·trous** /dɪ'zɑːstrəs‖dɪ'zæ-/ *adj* very bad; causing a DISASTER: *a disastrous mistake*|*The results were disastrous.* –**disastrously** *adv*

**dis·band** /dɪs'bænd/ *v* [I;T] to break up and separate: *The club has disbanded.* –see also BAND **together**

**dis·be·lief** /ˌdɪsbɪ̵'liːf/ *n* [U] lack of belief: *He listened to my story with/in disbelief.*

**dis·be·lieve** /ˌdɪsbɪ̵'liːv/ *v* **-lieved, -lieving** [T] to refuse to believe: *I was forced to disbelieve him.*

USAGE People usually say: *I don't* **believe** *you.*|*I don't* **believe** *(in) that story.* **Disbelieve** would not be used here. **Disbelieve** is not used as the opposite of **believe** when it means **approve of**. People say: *I don't* **believe** *in letting children do whatever they like.*

**disc** *BrE*‖**disk** *AmE* /dɪsk/ *n* **1** something round and flat: *the disc of the full moon* **2** →(GRAMOPHONE) RECORD² (4) **3** a flat piece of strong bendable material (CARTILAGE) between the bones (VERTEBRAe) of one's back: *The pain was caused by a* **slipped disc.**

**dis·card** /dɪs'kɑːd‖-ɑrd/ *v* [T] to get rid of as useless: *to discard an old coat/one's old friends*

**di·scern** /dɪ'sɜːn‖-ɜrn/ *v* [T +*that*; not *be +v-ing*] *fml* to see, notice, or understand, esp. with difficulty: *He was just able to discern the road in the dark.* –**discernible** *adj* –**discernibly** *adv*

**di·scern·ing** /dɪ'sɜːnɪŋ‖-ɜr-/ *adj apprec* having or showing the power to decide and judge; having good taste: *a discerning man/mind* –**discernment** *n* [U]

**dis·charge¹** /dɪs'tʃɑːdʒ‖-ɑr-/ *v* **-charged, -charging** *fml* **1** [T *from*] to allow or ask (a person) to go: *The judge discharged the prisoner.*|*Although she was still ill, she discharged herself from hospital.* **2** [I;T] to send, pour, or let out (gas, liquid, etc.): *The chimney discharged smoke.* **3** [T] to perform (a duty or promise) **4** [T] to pay (a debt) in full **5** [I;T] to unload: *The ship discharged its cargo of coal.* **6** [T *at, into*] to fire or shoot (a gun, arrow, etc.)

**dis·charge²** /dɪs'tʃɑːdʒ, 'dɪstʃɑːdʒ‖-ɑr-/ *n* [C;U] the action or result of discharging (DISCHARGE): *After my discharge from the army I went into business.*|*the discharge from the chimney*

**di·sci·ple** /dɪ'saɪpəl/ *n* a follower of any great teacher (esp. religious), esp. one of the first followers of Christ

**dis·ci·pli·nar·i·an** /ˌdɪsɪ̵plɪ̵'neərɪən/ *n* a person who can make people obey orders: *He's a good teacher but he's not much of a disciplinarian.*

**dis·ci·pline¹** /'dɪsɪ̵plɪ̵n/ *n* [U] **1** training of the mind and body to produce obedience and self-control: *school/military discipline* **2** control gained as a result of this training: *The teacher can't keep discipline in her classroom.* **3** punishment: *That child needs discipline.* –**disciplinary** /'dɪsɪ̵plɪnəri,

ˌdɪsɨ̍ˈplɪ-‖ˈdɪsɨ̍plɨ̍neri/ *adj*

**discipline²** *v* **-plined, -plining** [T] **1** to keep under control; train: *You must learn to discipline yourself.* **2** to punish: *She never disciplines her children and they are uncontrollable.*

**disc jock·ey** /ˈ· ˌ··/ *n* → DJ

**dis·claim** /dɪsˈkleɪm/ *v* [T +*v-ing*] to say that one does not own or accept; DENY: *He disclaimed all responsibility for the accident.*

**dis·close** /dɪsˈkləuz/ *v* **-closed, -closing** [T] **1** [+ *that*] to make known: *He disclosed that he had been in prison.* **2** to show by uncovering

**dis·clo·sure** /dɪsˈkləʊʒəʳ/ *n* [C;U] the act or result of disclosing (DISCLOSE (1)): *She made several surprising disclosures about her past life.*

**dis·col·our** *BrE*‖ **discolor** *AmE* /dɪsˈkʌləʳ/ *v* [I;T] to (cause to) change colour for the worse: *his discoloured teeth* **–discoloration, -ouration** /dɪsˌkʌləˈreɪʃən/ *n* [C;U]

**dis·com·fort** /dɪsˈkʌmfət‖-ərt/ *n* **1** [U] lack of comfort: *The wound isn't serious, but may cause some discomfort.* **2** [C] something that makes one uncomfortable: *the discomforts of travel*

**dis·con·cert** /ˌdɪskənˈsɜːt‖-ɜrt/ *v* [T] to cause (someone) to feel doubt and anxiety: *She was disconcerted to see that she was being watched.|a disconcerting remark* **–disconcertingly** *adv*

**dis·con·nect** /ˌdɪskəˈnekt/ *v* [T *from*] to undo the connection of: *They disconnected the telephone because I didn't pay the bill.* –opposite **connect –disconnection** *n* [C;U]

**dis·con·nect·ed** /ˌdɪskəˈnektɨ̍d/ *adj* (of thoughts and ideas) badly connected; not well planned: *a few disconnected remarks*

**dis·con·so·late** /dɪsˈkɒnsəlɨ̍t‖-ˈkɑn-/ *adj* [*about, at*] *fml* hopelessly sad, esp. at the loss of something: *The children were disconsolate about/at the death of their mother.* **–disconsolately** *adv*

**dis·con·tent** /ˌdɪskənˈtent/ also **discontentment** /-mənt/ *n* [U *with*] lack of contentment; dissatisfaction **–discontented** *adj* **–discontentedly** *adv*

**dis·con·tin·ue** /ˌdɪskənˈtɪnjuː/ *v* **-ued, -uing** [I;T +*v-ing*] *fml* to stop or end: *The bus service was discontinued because nobody used it.* –see also CONTINUE

**dis·cord** /ˈdɪskɔːd‖ˈdɪskɔrd/ *n* [C;U] **1** *fml* (a case of) disagreement between people: *A good deal of discord has arisen over this question.* –see also CONCORD; compare HARMONY (2) **2** (a) lack of agreement heard when sounds are made or notes played which do not sound well together –opposite **harmony –discordant** /dɪsˈkɔːdənt‖-ɔr-/ *adj*

**dis·co·theque** /ˈdɪskətek/ also **disco** /ˈdɪskəʊ/ *infml*– *n* a club where young people dance to recorded popular music

**dis·count¹** /ˈdɪskaʊnt/ *n* a reduction made in the cost of buying goods in a shop: *a discount of 10 per cent* –compare REBATE

**dis·count²** /dɪsˈkaʊnt‖ˈdɪskaʊnt/ *v* [T] to pay little attention to; believe (a story or piece of news) to be not completely true: *Much of what he says must be discounted; he imagines things.*

**dis·cour·age** /dɪsˈkʌrɪdʒ‖-ˈkɜr-/ *v* **-aged, -aging** [T] **1** to take away courage and spirit from: *If you fail your driving test first time, don't let it discourage you/don't be discouraged.* **2** [+ *v-ing/from*] to try to prevent (an action, or someone from doing something) esp. by showing disfavour: *We discourage smoking in this school.|His mother discouraged him from joining the navy.* –opposite **encourage –discouragingly** *adv n* **discouragement** *n* [C;U]

**dis·course** /ˈdɪskɔːs‖-ors/ *n* [C;U *on, upon*] *fml* (a) serious conversation or speech

**dis·cour·te·ous** /dɪsˈkɜːtɪəs‖-ɜr-/ *adj fml* (of people or their behaviour) not polite –opposite **courteous –discourteously** *adv* **–discourtesy** /dɪsˈkɜːtəsi‖-ɜr-/ *n* **-sies** [C;U]

**dis·cov·er** /dɪsˈkʌvəʳ/ *v* [T] **1** to find (something existing but not known before): *Columbus discovered America in 1492.* –see INVENT (USAGE) **2** [+*to-v/that*] to find out (a fact, or the answer to a question): *Did you ever discover who sent you the flowers?|Scientists have discovered that this disease is carried by rats.* **–discoverer** *n*

**dis·cov·e·ry** /dɪsˈkʌvəri/ *n* **-ries 1** [U] the event of discovering: *The discovery of oil on their land made the family rich.* **2** [C] something discovered: *to make an important scientific discovery*

**dis·cred·it¹** /dɪsˈkredɨ̍t/ *v* [T] to cause people to lack faith in or respect for; stop people believing in: *The idea that the sun goes round the earth has long been discredited.|Much of his work has been discredited because we now know that he used false information.* –see also CREDIT² (1)

**discredit²** *n* **1** [U] loss of belief and trust **2** [S *to*] someone or something that is harmful (to the good name of the stated person or group); a DISGRACE: *That boy is* **a discredit to** *his family.* –opposite **credit** (for **2**)

**dis·cred·i·ta·ble** /dɪsˈkredɨ̍təbəl/ *adj fml* (of behaviour) shameful –opposite **creditable**

**di·screet** /dɪˈskriːt/ *adj* (of people, their behaviour, or speech) careful and polite; showing good sense and judgment: *My friend is very discreet. He won't tell anyone what I said.* –opposite **indiscreet –discreetly** *adv*

**di·screp·an·cy** /dɪˈskrepənsi/ *n* **-cies** [C;U *between*] difference; lack of agreement: *You said you paid £5 and the bill says £3; how do you explain the discrepancy?*

**di·scre·tion** /dɪˈskreʃən/ *n* [U] **1** the quality of being DISCREET –opposite **indiscretion 2** the ability to decide what is most suitable to be done: *I won't tell you what time to leave–you're old enough to* **use** *your own* **discretion.**|*The hours of the meetings will be fixed* **at the chairman's discretion.** (=according to the chairman's decision)

**di·scrim·i·nate** /dɪˈskrɪmɨ̍neɪt/ *v* **-nated, -nating** [I] **1** [*between*] to see or make a difference (between two or more things or people): *You must try to discriminate between facts and opinions.* **2** [*against/in favour of*] *usu. derog.* to treat (a person or group) as worse/better than others: *This new law discriminates against lower-paid workers.*

**di·scrim·i·na·tion** /dɪˌskrɪmɨ̍ˈneɪʃən/ *n* [U] **1** [*against*] *often derog* treating different things or people in different ways: *Pay us all the same wage! There must be no discrimination.* **2** *apprec* ability to choose the best by seeing small differences **–discriminating** /dɪ'skrɪmɪ̣neɪtɪŋ/ *adj*

**di·scur·sive** /dɪ'skɜːsɪv‖-ɜr-/ *adj fml* (of a person, words, or writing) passing from one subject or idea to another in an informal way, without any clear plan: *to write in a discursive style* **–discursively** *adv*

**dis·cus** /'dɪskəs/ *n* **discuses** a heavy plate of wood, metal, or stone, which is thrown as far as possible, as a sport

**di·scuss** /dɪ'skʌs/ *v* [T *with*] to talk about (with someone) from several points of view, esp. formally: *We discussed what to do and where we should go.*

**di·scus·sion** *n* [C;U] a case or the action of DISCUSSing: *to have/hold a discussion about future plans|After much discussion the matter was settled.|Education is* **under discussion** *today.*

**dis·dain¹** /dɪs'deɪn/ *n* [U] *fml* lack of respect; the feeling that someone or something is low and worthless –compare CONTEMPT, SCORN¹ **–disdainful** *adj [of, towards]* **–disdainfully** *adv*

**disdain²** *v* [T not *be +v-ing*] *fml* **1** to regard with DISDAIN –compare DESPISE **2** [*+to-v/v-ing; no pass.*] to refuse (to do an action) because of DISDAIN: *She disdained to answer his rude remarks.*

**dis·ease** /dɪ'ziːz/ *n* [C;U] (an) illness or disorder caused by infection or unnatural growth, not by an accident: *to catch/die of/suffer from/cure a disease| plant diseases|*(fig.) *diseases of the mind/of society* **–diseased** *adj: a diseased bone/plant*

USAGE 1 Though **illness** and **disease** are often used alike, **illness** is really a state, or length of time, of being unwell, which may be caused by a **disease**. It is **diseases** that can be caught and passed on if they are infectious or CONTAGIOUS, and that are the subjects of medical study: *Several children are away from school because of* **illness**.|*a rare heart* **disease** 2 A person who has a **disease** is **ill** or (esp. *AmE*) **sick**. In *BrE* to be or feel **sick** means to VOMIT or feel that one is going to vomit. Although it is sometimes used to mean "to be/feel ill", this is thought by teachers to be incorrect; but **sick** can be used in this meaning before a noun: *a* **sick** *child.*

**dis·em·bark** /ˌdɪsɪ̣m'bɑːk‖-ɑrk/ *v* [I;T *from*] to (cause to) go on shore from a ship–opposite **embark** **–disembarkation** /ˌdɪsembɑː'keɪʃən‖-ɑr- / *n* [U]

**dis·em·bod·ied** /ˌdɪsɪ̣m'bɒdɪd‖-'bɑ-/ *adj* [A *no comp.*] existing as if without a body: *Disembodied voices could be heard in the darkness.*

**dis·en·chant·ed** /ˌdɪsɪ̣n'tʃɑːntɪ̣d‖-'tʃæntɪ̣d/ *adj* (of a person) having lost one's belief (in the value of something): *disenchanted with my job* **–disenchantment** *n* [U]

**dis·en·gage** /ˌdɪsɪ̣ŋ'geɪdʒ/ *v* **-gaged, -gaging** [I;T *from*] *fml* **a** (esp. of parts of a machine) to come loose and separate **b** to loosen and separate (esp. parts of a machine): *Disengage the* GEARS (1) *when you park the car.* **2** (of soldiers, ships, etc.) to stop fighting –opposite **engage**

**dis·en·tan·gle** /ˌdɪsɪ̣n'tæŋgəl/ *v* **-gled, -gling** [I;T *from*] to make or become straight and free from knots –opposite **entangle** **–disentanglement** *n* [U]

**dis·fa·vour** *BrE*‖**disfavor** *AmE* /dɪs'feɪvəʳ/ *n* [U] *fml* **1** dislike; disapproval: *Mary seems to look upon/regard/*VIEW *John with disfavour.* **2** the state of being disliked: *John seems to be/have* **fallen into disfavour** *(with Judy).* –see also FAVOUR

**dis·fig·ure** /dɪs'fɪgəʳ‖-'fɪgjər/ *v* **-ured, -uring** [T] to spoil the beauty of: *The disease left his face disfigured.* **–disfigurement** *n* [C;U]

**dis·grace¹** /dɪs'greɪs/ *v* **-graced, -gracing** [T] **1** to be a DISGRACE² to: *He disgraced himself last night by drinking too much.* **2** to put (a public person) out of favour with DISGRACE²; DISCREDIT: *The dishonest minister was publicly disgraced.*

**disgrace²** *n* [S;U *to*] (a cause of) shame or loss of honour and respect: *Being poor is no disgrace.|Harry is* **in disgrace** (=regarded with disapproval) *because of his behaviour.|Doctors like that are a disgrace to our hospitals.|That old car of yours is a disgrace.* **–disgraceful** *adj* **–disgracefully** *adv*

**dis·grun·tled** /dɪs'grʌntld/ *adj* [*at, with*] annoyed and disappointed

**dis·guise¹** /dɪs'gaɪz/ *v* **-guised, -guising** [T] **1** [*as*] to change the usual appearance, etc. of, so as to hide the truth: *She disguised herself as a man.* **2** to hide (the real state of things): *It is impossible to disguise the fact that business is bad.*

**disguise²** *n* **1** [C] something that is worn to hide who one really is: *Nobody saw through his disguise.*(= nobody recognized him) **2** [U] the state of being DISGUISEd: *He went to the party* **in disguise.**

**dis·gust¹** /dɪs'gʌst, dɪz-/ *n* [U *at*] strong feeling of dislike: *The food/The smell/His behaviour filled her with disgust.*

**disgust²** *v* [T *at, with*] to cause a feeling of DISGUST in: *We're all disgusted at the way his wife has treated him.|What a disgusting smell!*

**dish¹** /dɪʃ/ *n* **1** a large flat (often round or OVAL) vessel from which food is put onto people's plates: *A meat dish is a dish for meat, a wooden dish is a dish made of wood.* **2** (an amount of) cooked food of one kind: *Baked apples are his favourite dish.*

**dish²** *v* → DISH OUT, DISH UP

**dis·heart·en** /dɪs'hɑːtn‖-ɑr-/ *n* [T] to cause to lose hope; discourage: *He's easily disheartened by difficulties.* –opposite **hearten**

**dish·es** /'dɪʃɪ̣z/ *n* [P] all the dishes, plates, cups, knives, forks, etc., used for a meal: *Let's wash/do the dishes.*

**di·shev·elled** /dɪ'ʃevəld/ *adj* (of a person or his/her appearance) untidy

**dis·hon·est** /dɪs'ɒnɪ̣st‖-'ɑ-/ *adj* not honest; deceiving: *a dishonest politician|to get money by dishonest means* **–dishonestly** *adv* **–dishonesty** *n* [U]

**dis·hon·our** *BrE*‖**dishonor** *AmE* /dɪs'ɒnəʳ‖-'ɑ-/ *n* [S;U *to*] *fml* (something or someone that causes) loss of honour: *His desertion from the army brought dishonour on his family.* **–dishonour** *v* [T] **–dishonourable** *adj* **–dishonourably** *adv*

**dish** sthg.↔ **out** *v adv* [T] *infml* to serve out to several people; HAND **out**: *to dish out the examination papers/advice*

**dish** (sthg.↔) **up** *v adv* [I;T] to put (the food for a meal) into dishes: *Help me dish up (the dinner).*

**dish·y** /'dɪʃi/ *adj* **-ier, -iest** *infml* (of a person) having sexual charm: *She's just married this dishy man.*

**dis·il·lu·sion** /ˌdɪsɪ̣'luːʒən/ *v* [T] to free from a wrong idea (ILLUSION): *She doesn't know her father is* a thief, and I don't want to disillusion her. **–disillusionment** *n* [U]

**dis·il·lu·sioned** /ˌdɪsˈluːʒənd/ *adj* [*at, about, with*] feeling bitter and unhappy as a result of having been DISILLUSIONed: *He's very disillusioned with the present government.*

**dis·in·clined** /ˌdɪsɪnˈklaɪnd/ *adj* [F +*to-v/for*] unwilling: *I feel disinclined for exercise/to go out in this weather.* –see also INCLINED **–disinclination** /ˌdɪsɪŋkləˈneɪʃən/ *n* [S;U +*to-v/for*]

**dis·in·fect** /ˌdɪsənˈfekt/ *v* [T] to clean (things and places) with a chemical that can destroy bacteria **–disinfection** /-ˈfekʃən/ *n* [U]

**dis·in·fec·tant** /ˌdɪsənˈfektənt/ *n* [C;U] a chemical used to destroy bacteria

**dis·in·her·it** /ˌdɪsənˈherət/ *v* [T] to take away from (usu. one's child) the lawful right to receive (INHERIT) one's goods after one's death

**dis·in·te·grate** /dɪsˈɪntəgreɪt/ *v* **-grated, -grating** [I;T] to (cause to) break up (as if) into small pieces: *The box was so old it just disintegrated when he picked it up.* **–disintegration** /-ˈgreɪʃən / *n* [U]

**dis·in·terest·ed** /dɪsˈɪntrəstəd/ *adj apprec* willing to judge or act fairly because not influenced by personal advantage: *His action was not disinterested because he hoped to make money out of the affair.* **–disinterestedly** *adv*

USAGE Compare **disinterested** and **uninterested**: *The argument can only be settled by someone who is* **disinterested**. (=who will not gain personally by deciding in favour of one side or another)|*Settle your own argument–I'm quite* **uninterested**! (=your argument doesn't interest me) Although **disinterested** is commonly used to mean "uninterested" this is thought by teachers to be incorrect.

**dis·joint·ed** /dɪsˈdʒɔɪntəd/ *adj* (of words or ideas) not well connected; not following in reasonable order: *He gave a rather disjointed account of his holiday.* **–disjointedly** *adv* **–disjointedness** *n* [U]

**disk** /dɪsk/ *n AmE* for DISC

**dis·like**[1] /dɪsˈlaɪk/ *v* **-liked, -liking** [T +*v-ing*; not *be* +*v-ing*] to consider unpleasant; not to like: *I dislike big cities/being spoken to like that.*

**dislike**[2] /ˌdɪsˈlaɪk◂/ *n* [C;U *of, for*] (a) feeling of disliking (DISLIKE): *to have a dislike of/for cats*|*She* **took a dislike to** *him* (=began to dislike him) *at once.*

**dis·lo·cate** /ˈdɪsləkeɪt‖-ləʊ-/ *v* **-cated, -cating** [T] to put (a bone) out of place: *He dislocated his shoulder.*|*a dislocated shoulder* **–dislocation** /-ˈkeɪʃən/ *n* [C;U]

**dis·lodge** /dɪsˈlɒdʒ‖-lɑdʒ/ *v* **-lodged, -lodging** [T *from*] to force or knock out of a position: *He dislodged the rock and it rolled down the hill* –see also LODGE[1] (3)

**dis·loy·al** /dɪsˈlɔɪəl/ *adj* [*to*] not loyal **–disloyally** *adv* **–disloyalty** *n* [C;U *to*]

**dis·mal** /ˈdɪzməl/ *adj* showing or causing sadness; lacking comfort: *a dismal song*|*dismal weather* **–dismally** *adv*

**dis·man·tle** /dɪsˈmæntl/ *v* **-tled, -tling** [I;T] **a** to take (a machine or article) to pieces **b** (of a machine or article) to be able to be taken to pieces: *This engine dismantles easily.*

**dis·may**[1] /dɪsˈmeɪ/ *v* **-mayed, -maying** [T] to fill with DISMAY

**dismay**[2] *n* [U *in, with*] strong feeling of fear and hopelessness: *They were* **filled with dismay** *by the news.*|**To their dismay**, *the news was bad.*

**dis·mem·ber** /dɪsˈmembər/ *v* [T] to cut or tear (a body) apart, limb from limb: *The young man's dismembered body was found by the police.*

**dis·miss** /dɪsˈmɪs/ *v* [T] **1** [*from*] *fml* to take away (the job of): *If you're late again you'll be dismissed (from your job).* –compare SACK[2] **2** to send away: *The teacher dismissed the class early.*|(fig.) *He just laughed, and dismissed the idea as impossible.* **–dismissal** *n* [C;U]

**dis·mount** /dɪsˈmaʊnt/ *v* [I] to get down (e.g. from a horse or bicycle) –opposite **mount**

**dis·o·be·di·ent** /ˌdɪsəˈbiːdɪənt, ˌdɪsəʊ-/ *adj* [*to*] (of a person or his/her behaviour) failing to obey: *a disobedient child*|*He was disobedient to his mother.* –opposite **obedient** **–disobediently** *adv* **–disobedience** *n* [U *to*]

**dis·o·bey** /ˌdɪsəˈbeɪ, ˌdɪsəʊ-/ *v* **-beyed, -beying** [I;T] to fail to obey: *He disobeyed his mother and went to the party.*

**dis·or·der** /dɪsˈɔːdər‖-ɔr-/ *n* **1** [U] lack of order; confusion **2** [C;U] (a) violent public expression of political dissatisfaction: *public disorder because of the tax increases* **3** [C;U] slight disease or illness: *suffering from (a) stomach disorder*

**dis·or·der·ly** /dɪsˈɔːdəli‖-ɔrdər-/ *adj* **1** untidy; confused **2** violent in public: *disorderly behaviour/youths* –see DRUNK[1] **–disorderliness** *n* [U]

**dis·or·gan·ize** ‖also **-ise** *BrE* /dɪsˈɔːgənaɪz‖-ɔr-/ *v* **-ized, -izing** [T] to throw (arrangements, a system, etc.) into disorder –see also ORGANIZE **–disorganization** /dɪsˌɔːgənaɪˈzeɪʃən‖- ɔrgənə- / *n* [U]

**dis·or·i·en·tate** /dɪsˈɔːrɪənteɪt‖-ˈor-/ also **-disorient** /-rɪənt/ *AmE*– *v* **-tated, -tating** [T *usu. pass.*] to cause (someone) to lose the sense of time, direction, etc.; confuse: (fig.) *Father worked in the same job for 30 years, and has been very disorientated since he stopped working.* **–disorientation** /-ˈteɪʃən / *n* [U]

**dis·own** /dɪsˈəʊn/ *v* [T] to refuse to accept as one's own: *Peter's father disowned him when he was caught taking drugs.*

**di·spar·age** /dɪˈspærɪdʒ/ *v* [T] to make (someone or something) sound of little value or importance: *In spite of your disparaging remarks, I think he did well.* **–disparagingly** *adv* **–disparagement** *n* [C;U]

**di·spar·i·ty** /dɪˈspærəti/ *n* **-ties** [C;U *between, in, of*] *fml* (an example of) difference or INEQUALITY: *There is (a) great disparity between the amount of work that I do and what I get paid for it.* –see also PARITY

**dis·pas·sion·ate** /dɪsˈpæʃənət/ *adj apprec* (of a person or his behaviour) calm and fair; not taking sides in an argument **–dispassionately** *adv*

**di·spatch**[1], **despatch** /dɪˈspætʃ/ *v* [T *to*] to send off: *The parcels were dispatched yesterday.*

**dispatch**[2], **despatch** *n* **1** [U] a message carried by a government official, or sent to a newspaper by one of its writers: *to send/carry a dispatch from Rome to London* **2** [U] *fml* speed and effectiveness

**di·spel** /dɪˈspel/ *v* **-ll-** [T] to drive away (as if) by scattering: *His calm words dispelled our fears.*

**di·spen·sa·ble** /dɪˈspensəbəl/ *adj* not necessary; that can be DISPENSED **with** –opposite **indispensable**

**di·spen·sa·ry** /dɪˈspensəri/ *n* **-ries** a place where medicines are DISPENSED (2), esp. in a hospital or school –compare PHARMACY (2)

**dis·pen·sa·tion** /ˌdɪspənˈseɪʃən, -pen-/ *n* [C;U] (a case of) permission to disobey a general rule or break a promise: *By a special dispensation from the Church, he was allowed to re-marry.*

**di·spense** /dɪˈspens/ *v* **-spensed, -spensing** [T] **1** [*to*] to deal out; give out (to a number of people): *A judge dispenses justice.*|*This machine dispenses coffee.* **2** to mix and give out (medicines) **–dispenser** *n: a coffee dispenser*

**dispense with** sbdy./sthg. *v prep* [T] **1** to do without: *We shall have to dispense with the car; we can't afford it.* **2** to make unnecessary: *This new office machine dispenses with the need for a secretary.*

**di·sperse** /dɪˈspɜːs‖-ɜrs/ *v* **-spersed, -spersing** [I;T] to (cause to) scatter in different directions: *The wind dispersed the smoke.*|*The crowd dispersed.*

**di·spir·it·ed** /dɪˈspɪrɪ̵tɪ̵d/ *adj lit* discouraged

**dis·place** /dɪsˈpleɪs/ *v* **-placed, -placing** [T] **1** to force out of the usual place: *He displaced a bone in his knee.*|*A* **displaced person** *is one who has been forced to leave his/her country.* **2** [*as*] to take the place of –see REPLACE (USAGE) **–displacement** *n* [U]

**di·splay¹** /dɪˈspleɪ/ *v* **-splayed, -splaying** [T] *more fml than* **show**– to show: *to display goods in a shop window*|*He displayed no feelings when they told him the news.*

**display²** *n* [C;U] the act or result of DISPLAYing: *a display of skill*|*The goods were* **on display** *in the shop window.*

**dis·please** /dɪsˈpliːz/ *v* **-pleased, -pleasing** [T] *fml* to annoy, offend, or make angry: *The old lady was displeased with/by the children's noisy behaviour.* –opposite **please –displeasure** /dɪsˈpleʒəʳ/ *n* [U]

**dis·po·sa·ble** /dɪˈspəʊzəbəl/ *adj* intended to be used once and then thrown away: *disposable paper plates*

**dis·pos·al** /dɪˈspəʊzəl/ *n* [U] **1** the act or action of getting rid of; removal: *waste disposal* **2 at someone's disposal** able to be used freely by someone: *During his visit I put my car at his disposal.*

**dispose of** sthg. /dɪˈspəʊz/ *v prep* **-posed, -posing** [T] to get rid of; throw away; finish with: *Dispose of these old papers.*|(fig.) *I can dispose of your argument quite easily.*

**dis·posed** /dɪˈspəʊzd/ *adj* [F +*to-v*] *fml* willing: *I don't feel disposed to help you.* –see also INDISPOSED

**dis·po·si·tion** /ˌdɪspəˈzɪʃən/ *n* [C;U +*to-v*] *fml* a general tendency of character, behaviour, etc.; nature: *He has a happy disposition.*

**dis·pos·sess** /ˌdɪspəˈzes/ *v* [T *of*] *fml* to take property away from

**dis·pro·por·tion·ate** /ˌdɪsprəˈpɔːʃənɪ̵t‖-or-/ *adj* [*to*] unequal; too much or too little: *We spend a disproportionate amount of our money on rent.* –opposite **proportionate –disproportionately** *adv*

**dis·prove** /dɪsˈpruːv/ *v* **-proved, -proving** [T] to prove (something) to be false

**di·spu·ta·ble** /dɪˈspjuːtəbəl, ˈdɪspjʊ-‖dɪˈspjuː-, ˈdɪspjə-/ *adj* not necessarily true; open to question –opposite **indisputable –disputably** *adv*

**di·spute¹** /dɪˈspjuːt/ *v* **-sputed, -sputing 1** [I;T *about*] to argue, esp. angrily and for a long time: *They disputed for hours (about) whether to build a new school.* **2** [T] to call into question; doubt: *He disputed the truth of my statement.*

**dispute²** /dɪˈspjuːt, ˈdɪspjuːt/ *n* an argument or quarrel: *The miners were* **in dispute** *with their employers about pay.*

**dis·qual·i·fy** /dɪsˈkwɒlɪ̵faɪ‖-ˈkwɑ-/ *v* **-fied, -fying** [T] to make or declare unfit, unsuitable, or unable to do something: *He won the game, but was later disqualified because of his cheating.* **–disqualification** /-fɪ̵ˈkeɪʃən/ *n* [C;U]

**dis·quiet** /dɪsˈkwaɪət/ *v* [T] *fml* to make anxious: *disquieted by his long silences*|*a disquieting remark* **–disquiet** *n* [U]

**dis·re·gard** /ˌdɪsrɪˈgɑːd‖-ɑrd/ *v* [T] to pay no attention to; IGNORE **–disregard** *n* [U *for, of*]: *his disregard of my instructions*

**dis·re·pair** /ˌdɪsrɪˈpeəʳ/ *n* [U] the state of being in need of repair: *The old houses had* **fallen into disrepair**.

**dis·rep·u·ta·ble** /dɪsˈrepjʊtəbəl‖-pjə-/ *adj* having or showing a bad character; having a bad REPUTATION: *disreputable people/behaviour* –opposite **reputable –disreputably** *adv*

**dis·re·spect** /ˌdɪsrɪˈspekt/ *n* [U] lack of respect or politeness **–disrespectful** *adj* **–disrespectfully** *adv*

**dis·rupt** /dɪsˈrʌpt/ *v* [T] to bring or throw into disorder: *An accident has disrupted railway services into and out of the city.* **–disruption** /-ˈrʌpʃən/ *n* [C;U] **–disruptive** *adj*: *He has a disruptive influence on the other children.*

**dis·sat·is·fy** /dɪˈsætɪ̵sfaɪ, dɪsˈsæ-/ *v* **-fied, -fying** [T] to fail to satisfy; displease **–dissatisfaction** /dɪˌsætɪ̵sˈfækʃən, dɪsˌsæ-, ˌ···ˈ··/ *n* [U *that*]: *dissatisfaction with her new job*

**dis·sect** /dɪˈsekt, daɪ-/ *v* [I;T] to cut up (esp. the body of a plant or animal) into parts, in such a way as to study the relationship of the parts **–dissection** /-ˈsekʃən/ *n* [C;U]

**dis·sem·i·nate** /dɪˈsemɪ̵neɪt/ *v* **-nated, -nating** [T] *fml* to spread (news, ideas, etc.) widely **–dissemination** /-ˈneɪʃən/ *n* [U]: *the dissemination of ideas*

**dis·sen·sion** /dɪˈsenʃən/ *n* [C;U] (a) disagreement, esp. leading to argument: *His words caused a great deal of dissension.*

**dis·sent** /dɪˈsent/ *n* [U] disagreement; difference of opinion: *When I asked for agreement there was no dissent.* –opposite **assent**; see also CONSENT **–dissent** *v* [I *from*] **–dissenter** *n*

**dis·ser·vice** /dɪˈsɜːvɪ̵s, dɪsˈsɜː‖-ɜr-/ *n* [S;U] harm or a harmful action: *You have done a serious disservice to your country by selling military secrets to our enemies.* –see also SERVICE¹ (3)

**dis·si·dent** /ˈdɪsɪ̵dənt/ *adj,n* (a person) openly and often strongly disagreeing with an opinion or a group: *political dissidents* **–dissidence** *n* [U]

**dis·sim·i·lar** /dɪˈsɪmɪ̵ləʳ, dɪsˈsɪ-/ *adj* unlike; not SIMILAR

**dis·si·pate** /ˈdɪsɪ̵peɪt/ *v* **-pated, -pating** *fml* **1** [I;T] to (cause to) disappear or scatter: *He tried to dissi-*

*pate the smoke by opening a window.* **2** [T] to spend, waste, or use up foolishly: *He dissipated his large fortune in a few years.*

**dis·si·pat·ed** /ˈdɪsɪ̇peɪtɪ̇d/ *adj* (typical of a person) who wastes his/her life in search of foolish or dangerous pleasure

**dis·so·ci·ate** /dɪˈsəʊʃieɪt, -sieɪt/ also **disassociate**– *v* **-ated, -ating** [T *from*] to separate from association or union with something or someone else: *The politician dissociated himself from the decision to close the school.* –opposite **associate** –**dissociation** /dɪˌsəʊ ʃiˈeɪʃən, -siˈeɪʃən / *n* [U]

**dis·so·lute** /ˈdɪsəluːt/ *adj fml* (typical of a person) who leads a bad or immoral life: *a dissolute person/life* –**dissolutely** *adv* –**dissoluteness** *n* [U]

**dis·so·lu·tion** /ˌdɪsəˈluːʃən/ *n* [U] *fml* the ending or breaking up of an association, group, marriage, etc.: *the dissolution of Parliament before a general election*

**dis·solve** /dɪˈzɒlv‖dɪˈzɑlv/ *v* **-solved, solving 1** [I;T] to make or become liquid by putting into a liquid: *Sugar dissolves in water.* **2** [I;T] **a** to cause (an association, group, etc.) to end or break up **b** (of an association, group, etc.) to end or break up **3** [I] to lose one's self-control under the influence of strong feeling: *to dissolve in/into tears/laughter*

**dis·suade** /dɪˈsweɪd/ *v* **-suaded, suading** [T *from*] to advise (somebody) against doing something; persuade not to do: *I tried to dissuade her (from joining the club).* –see also PERSUADE (1) –**dissuasion** /dɪˈsweɪʒən/ *n* [U]

**dis·tance** /ˈdɪstəns/ *n* **1** [C;U] (the amount of) separation in space or time: *What is the distance to London/between London and Glasgow/from London to Glasgow?|The school is some distance* (=quite far) *away.|within (easy) walking distance of home|The dog looked dangerous, so I decided to* **keep my distance** (=stay far away) *from it.*|(fig.) *There has been (a) great distance between us since our quarrel.* **2** [S *of*] a distant point or place: *One can see the ancient ruins* **in the distance.**

**dis·tant** /ˈdɪstənt/ *adj* **1** separate in space or time; far off: *distant lands|the distant sound of a bell|the distant past* **2** [A] not very close: *a distant connection between two ideas|Those two boys are distant relations.* **3** showing social distance or lack of friendliness: *a distant manner* –**distantly** *adv*: *Those two people/ideas are distantly related.*

**dis·taste** /dɪsˈteɪst/ *n* [S;U *for*] dislike; displeasure: *She looked at him with distaste.*

**dis·taste·ful** /dɪsˈteɪstfəl/ *adj* [*to*] causing DISTASTE: *The very idea of cheating him is distasteful to me.* –see TASTELESS (USAGE) –**distastefully** *adv* –**distastefulness** *n* [U]

**dis·tend** /dɪˈstend/ *v* [I;T] *fml* to (cause to) swell: *His stomach was distended because of lack of food.* –**distension** *n* [U]

**dis·til** ‖also **-till** *AmE* /dɪˈstɪl/ *v* **-ll-** [T] to make (a liquid) into gas and then make the gas into liquid, as when separating alcohol from water: *Water can be made pure by distilling it.|distilled water* –**distillation** /ˌdɪstɪ̇ˈleɪʃən/ *n* [C;U]

**dis·til·le·ry** /dɪˈstɪləri/ *n* **-ries** a factory or business firm where SPIRITS[1] (7) are made

**dis·tinct** /dɪˈstɪŋkt/ *adj* **1** [*from*] different; separate: *Those two ideas are quite distinct (from each other).* **2** clearly seen, heard, understood, etc.; noticeable: *a distinct smell of burning* –opposite **indistinct** –**distinctly** *adv*: *He spoke very distinctly.* –**distinctness** *n* [U]

USAGE Anything clearly noticed is **distinct**: *There's a* **distinct** *smell of beer in this room.* A thing or quality that is clearly different from others of its kind is **distinctive**, or **distinct** *from*: *Beer has a very* **distinctive** *smell; it's quite* **distinct** *from the smell of wine.*

**dis·tinc·tion** /dɪˈstɪŋkʃən/ *n* **1** [C;U *between*] difference: *Can you* **make/draw a distinction between** *these two ideas?* **2** [S;U] the quality of being unusual, esp. of being unusually good; worth: *a writer of true distinction* **3** [C] a special mark of honour

**dis·tinc·tive** /dɪˈstɪŋktɪv/ *adj* clearly marking a person or thing as different from others: *She had a distinctive appearance.* –see DISTINCT (USAGE) –**distinctively** *adv* –**distinctiveness** *n* [U]

**dis·tin·guish** /dɪˈstɪŋgwɪʃ/ *v* **1** [T] to hear, see, or recognize: *He is easily distinguished by his uniform.|Can you distinguish objects at a distance?* **2** [I;T *from, between*] *Can you distinguish (between) those two objects/ideas?|to distinguish right from wrong* **3** [T] to set apart or mark as different: *Elephants are distinguished by their long noses* (TRUNKS). **4** [T] to behave (oneself) noticeably well: *He* **distinguished himself** *by his performance in the examination.*

**dis·tin·gui·sha·ble** /dɪˈstɪŋgwɪʃəbəl/ *adj* [*from*] that can be clearly seen, heard, or recognized as different: *Those two objects/ideas are not easily distinguishable (from each other).* –opposite **indistinguishable**

**dis·tin·guished** /dɪˈstɪŋgwɪʃt/ *adj* marked by excellent quality or deserved fame: *a distinguished performance/politician/writer* –see FAMOUS (USAGE)

**dis·tort** /dɪˈstɔːt‖-ɔrt/ *v* [T] to twist out of a natural, usual, or original shape or condition: *a face distorted by/with anger*|(fig.) *He gave a distorted* (=untrue) *account of what had happened.* –**distortion** *n* [C;U]

**dis·tract** /dɪˈstrækt/ *v* [T *from*] to take (a person, a person's mind) off what he/she is doing: *She was distracted by the noise outside.*

**dis·tract·ed** /dɪˈstræktɪ̇d/ *adj* [*by, with*] anxious or troubled about many things: *a distracted look* –**distractedly** *adv*

**dis·trac·tion** /dɪˈstrækʃən/ *n* **1** [C] something or someone that DISTRACTS; amusement: *There are too many distractions here for me to work properly.* **2** [U] an anxious confused state of mind: *The child's continual crying* **drove him to distraction**. **3** [U] the act of DISTRACTing or the state of being DISTRACTed

**dis·traught** /dɪˈstrɔːt/ *adj* [*with*] very anxious and troubled: *distraught with grief/worry*

**dis·tress[1]** /dɪˈstres/ *n* **1** [S;U] (a cause of) great suffering, pain, or discomfort: *The sick man showed signs of distress.|people* **in distress** *because of lack of money* **2** [U] a state of danger or great difficulty: *Send out a* **distress signal**; *the ship is sinking.*

**distress[2]** *v* [T] to cause DISTRESS to

**dis·tress·ing** /dɪˈstresɪŋ/ *adj* causing DISTRESS[1]: *distressing news* –**distressingly** *adv*

**dis·trib·ute** /dɪˈstrɪbjuːt/ *v* **-uted, -uting** [T] **1** [*to,* *among*] to divide among several or many; give out: *to distribute the prizes to/among the winners* **2** [*over*] to spread out; scatter

**dis·tri·bu·tion** /ˌdɪstr$\frac{1}{2}$ˈbjuːʃən/ *n* [C;U] an act of distributing or the state of being DISTRIBUTED: *the distribution of prizes*

**dis·trict** /ˈdɪstrɪkt/ *n* an area of a country, city, etc., esp. made officially for particular purposes: *a postal district|a district council|a poor district in a city*

**dis·trust¹** /dɪsˈtrʌst/ *v* [T] to lack trust in; mistrust: *He distrusts banks so he keeps his money at home.*

**distrust²** *n* [S;U] lack of trust; mistrust: *He regards banks with distrust.* **–distrustful** *adj* **–distrustfully** *adv*

**dis·turb** /dɪˈstɜːb‖-ɜrb/ *v* [T] **1** to break in upon (esp. a person who is working); interrupt: *I'm sorry to disturb you but . . .* **2** to upset; worry: *disturbing news* **3** to change the usual or natural condition of: *A light wind disturbed the surface of the water.*

**dis·turb·ance** /dɪˈstɜːbəns‖-ɜr-/ *n* [C;U] **1** an act of DISTURBing or the state of being DISTURBed: *Those men were charged by the police with* **causing a disturbance** (=making a lot of noise and possibly fighting) **2** something that DISTURBS: *The noise of traffic is a continual disturbance.*

**dis·turbed** /dɪˈstɜːbd‖-ɜr-/ *adj* having or showing signs of an illness of the mind or the feelings: EMOTIONALly *disturbed*

**dis·use** /dɪsˈjuːs/ *n* [U] the state of no longer being used: *That law has* **fallen into disuse**. **–disused** /dɪsˈjuːzd/ *adj esp. BrE*: *a disused mine*

**ditch¹** /dɪtʃ/ *n* a not very deep V- or U-shaped passage cut into the ground, esp. for water to flow through: *The water flows into the ditch at the edge of the field.*

**ditch²** *v* [T] *infml* to get rid of; leave suddenly; ABANDON (1): *His old car stopped working so he decided to ditch it.*

**dith·er** /ˈdɪðəʳ/ *v* [I *about*] *infml* to act nervously or be unable to decide **–dither** *n* [S]

**dit·to** /ˈdɪtəʊ/ *n* **-tos** a mark (··) meaning the same

**dit·ty** /ˈdɪti/ *n* **-ties** a short simple song

**di·van** /dɪˈvæn‖ˈdaɪvæn/ *n* a long soft seat or bed (**divan bed**) on a base, usu. without back or arms

**dive¹** /daɪv/ *v* **dived,**‖also **dove** /dəʊv/ *AmE*, **dived, diving** [I] **1** [*in, off, from, into*] to jump head first into the water: *The boy dived into the swimming pool from the* **divingboard**. –see pictures on pages 592, 669 **2** [*down, for*] to go under the surface of the water; SUBMERGE: *They are diving for gold from the Spanish wreck.* **3** to move quickly, esp. downwards or out of sight: *The bird dived down on the rabbit.|The rabbit dived into its hole.|He dived into the doorway so he wouldn't be seen.*

**dive²** *n* **1** an act of diving (DIVE): *a graceful dive into the pool|When the shots sounded, we made a dive for the nearest doorway.* **2** *infml* a not very respectable place, esp. for meeting, eating, or amusement: *I'm not going to eat in a dive like that.*

**div·er** /ˈdaɪvəʳ/ *n* a person who DIVES, esp. one who works at the bottom of the sea in special dress (a **diving suit** /ˈ··ˌ·/) with a supply of air

**di·verge** /daɪˈvɜːdʒ, d$\frac{1}{2}$-‖-ɜr-/ *v* **-verged, -verging** [I *from*] *fml* to separate and go on in different directions: *I'm afraid our opinions diverge (from each other) on the subject of politics.* –see also CONVERGE **–divergence** *n* [C;U] **–divergent** *adj*

**di·verse** /daɪˈvɜːs‖d$\frac{1}{2}$ˈvɜrs, daɪ-/ *adj fml* different; various: *many diverse interests* **–diversely** *adv*

**di·ver·si·fy** /daɪˈvɜːs$\frac{1}{2}$faɪ‖d$\frac{1}{2}$ˈvɜr-, daɪ-/ **-fied, -fying** [I;T] to make different or various in form or quality; vary: *Our factory diversified several years ago.* (=started to make many different sorts of products)

**di·ver·sion** /daɪˈvɜːʃən, d$\frac{1}{2}$-‖-ɜrʒən/ *n* **1** [C;U] a turning aside from a course, activity, or use: *the diversion of a river to supply water to the farms|The traffic had to follow a diversion because of an accident on the main road.* **2** [C] something that turns someone's attention away from something else that one does not wish to be noticed: *I think your last argument was a diversion to make us forget the main point.* **3** [C] something that DIVERTS or amuses: *Big cities have lots of cinemas and other diversions.*

**di·ver·si·ty** /daɪˈvɜːs$\frac{1}{2}$ti, d$\frac{1}{2}$-‖-ɜr-/ *n* [S;U *of*] the condition of being different or having differences; variety: *Mary has a great diversity of interests: she likes sports, travel, photography, and gardening.*

**di·vert** /daɪˈvɜːt, d$\frac{1}{2}$-‖-ɜr-/ *v* [T] **1** [*from, to*] to cause to turn aside or from one use or direction to another: *They diverted the river to supply water to the town.|diverted traffic* **2** [*from*] to turn (a person or a person's attention) away from something, with good or bad result: *A loud noise diverted my attention.* **3** *fml* to amuse: *a game to divert the children*

**di·vest** sbdy. **of** sthg. /daɪˈvest, d$\frac{1}{2}$-/ *v prep* [T] *fml* to take away (the position, rights, property, etc.) of: *They divested the king of all his power.*

**di·vide** /d$\frac{1}{2}$ˈvaɪd/ *v* **-vided, -viding 1** [T] to share: *Divide the cake (up) between/among you.|He divides his time between reading and writing.* **2** [I;T *into, from*] to (cause to) separate into parts: *This class is too large. We shall have to divide it.|The class divided into groups.|The new road will divide the farm.|(fig.) I hope this quarrel will not divide us.* **3** [I;T *by, into*] to find out how many times one number contains or is contained in another number: *15 divided by 3 is 5.|3 divides into 15 5 times.* –compare MULTIPLY

**div·i·dend** /ˈdɪv$\frac{1}{2}$dənd, -dend/ *n* **1** that part of the money made by a business which is divided among those who own shares in the business: *The company declared a large dividend at the end of the year.* **2 pay dividends** to produce an advantage; be useful in the future

**di·vid·ers** /d$\frac{1}{2}$ˈvaɪdəz‖-ərz/ *n* [P] an instrument for measuring or marking off lines, angles, etc. –see PAIR¹ (USAGE)

**di·vine¹** /d$\frac{1}{2}$ˈvaɪn/ *adj* **1** [*no comp.*] of, coming from, or being God or a god: *the divine right of kings* **2** *infml* very very good: *That play we saw last night was simply divine!* **–divinely** *adv*

**divine²** *v* **-vined, -vining** [I;T] **1** *fml* to discover or guess (the unknown, esp. the future) by or as if by magic **2** to be able to find (water or minerals) underground esp. by using a Y-shaped stick (a **divining rod** /·ˈ·· ˌ·/)

**di·vin·i·ty** /d$\frac{1}{2}$ˈvɪn$\frac{1}{2}$ti/ *n* **-ties 1** [U] the quality or state of being DIVINE¹ (1) **2** [C] (*often cap.*) a god or goddess **3** [U] →THEOLOGY

**di·vis·i·ble** /dǝ̇ˈvɪzǝbǝl/ *adj* that can be divided: *15 is divisible by 3.*

**di·vi·sion** /dǝ̇ˈvɪʒǝn/ *n* **1** [U] separation or sharing: *the division of responsibility among the teachers* **2** [C +*sing./pl. v*] one of the parts into which a whole is divided: *He works in the foreign division of the company.*|*a naval division* (=a number of ships that fight together) **3** [C] something that divides or separates: *The river forms the division between the old and new parts of the city.* **4** [U] disagreement; lack of unity **5** [U] the act or action of finding out how many times one number or quantity is contained in another: *the division of 15 by 3*

**di·vi·sive** /dǝ̇ˈvaɪsɪv/ *adj* tending to divide people; causing disunity or arguments: *He is a divisive influence at meetings.* **–divisively** *adv*

**di·vorce¹** /dǝ̇ˈvɔːs‖-ors/ *n* [C;U] (a case of) the ending of a marriage as declared by a court of law: *She got a divorce after years of unhappiness.*|*He is suing* (SUE) *for divorce.* (=trying to get a divorce) –compare SEPARATION

**divorce²** *v* **-vorced, -vorcing 1** [I;T] to end a marriage between (a husband and wife) or to (a husband or a wife): *The court divorced them.*|*They divorced (each other).* **2** [T *from*] *fml* to separate: *It is hard to divorce love and duty/love from duty in one's mind.*

**di·vor·cée** /dǝ̇ˈvɔːsiː‖dǝ̇ˌvorˈseɪ, -ˈsiː/ *n* a woman whose marriage has ended in DIVORCE –compare WIDOW

**di·vulge** /daɪˈvʌldʒ, dǝ̇-/ *v* **-vulged, -vulging** [T +*that/to*] *fml* to tell (what has been secret): *Newsmen divulged that the President had been ill for some time before he died.*

**diz·zy** /ˈdɪzi/ *adj* **-zier, -ziest 1** having an unpleasant feeling of loss of balance, as if things are going round and round: *The room was so hot that she felt dizzy.* **2** causing this feeling: *a* **dizzy height** **–dizzily** *adv* **–dizziness** *n* [U]

**DJ** *n abbrev. for:* disc jockey; a broadcaster who introduces records of popular music on a radio or television show

**DNA** *abbrev. for: tech* deoxyribonucleic acid; the acid which carries GENETIC information in a cell

**do¹** /duː/ *v*

| *present tense* singular | plural |
|---|---|
| *I* **do** | *We* **do** |
| *You* **do** | *You* **do** |
| *He/She/It* **does** | *They* **do** |
| *past tense* singular | plural |
| *I* **did** | *We* **did** |
| *You* **did** | *You* **did** |
| *He/She/It* **did** | *They* **did** |
| *past* PARTICIPLE | **done** |
| *present* PARTICIPLE | **doing** |
| NEGATIVE *short forms* | **don't, doesn't, didn't** |

For the pronunciation of these forms look them up at their own place in the dictionary.

**1** [I +*to-v*] **a** (used as a helping verb with another verb): *Do you like it?*|*Don't stop.*|*He didn't answer.*|*Doesn't he look funny!*|*Why don't you come for the weekend?* (=please come!) **b** (used to make another verb stronger): *Do be careful!*|*"Why didn't you tell me?" "I did tell you!"* **2** [I] (used instead of another verb): *He likes it, and so do I.*|*He speaks English better than he did.* (=better than he used to speak it)|*"You stepped on my toe." "No, I didn't!"* **3** [T] (used instead of another verb): *"What are you doing?" "(I'm) cooking."*

**do²** *v* **1** [T] (used of actions): *to do a sum*|*to do repairs*|*to do the cooking*|*to do one's teeth* (=clean them)|*to do one's hair* (=arrange it) –see DO **with** (USAGE) **2** [T] (used in certain expressions): *I did my best (to help him).*|*I used to do business with him.*|*This medicine will do you good.*|*I have some work to do.*|*Do me a favour.* **3** [I] to be enough or be suitable: *Will £5 do?*|*This little bed will do for the baby.*|*You needn't use milk–water will do.*|*That will do! Stop!* **4** [I] to behave: *Do as you're told!* **5** [I] to continue or end in the stated way: *They did well in the examination.* **6 do-it-yourself** *infml* (*abbrev.*: **DIY**) the idea of doing repairs and building things oneself, instead of paying workmen: *She's very interested in do-it-yourself.* **7 How do you do?** *polite* (used when one is introduced to someone) **8 make do (with something)** also **make (something) do**– *infml* to use (something) even though it may not be perfect or enough: *We haven't got meat, so we'll have to make do with bread.* **9 What do you do (for a living)?** What is your work? –see MAKE (USAGE)

**do away with** sbdy./sthg. *v adv prep* [T] **1** to cause to end; ABOLISH: *The government did away with free school meals.* **2** *infml* to kill or murder (someone or oneself)

**do in** *v adv* [T] *infml* **1** (**do** sbdy.↔ **in**) to kill: *They did her in with an axe!* **2** [not *be* +*v-ing*] (**do** sbdy. **in**) to tire completely: *That long walk really did me in!*

**do** sbdy. **out of** sthg. *v adv prep* [T] *infml* to cause to lose, by cheating: *I've been done out of my rights.*

**do** sbdy./sthg.↔**up** *v adv* [T] *infml* **1** to fasten: *Do up your buttons/my dress/this knot.* **2** to repair; improve: *to do up the house* **3** to wrap: *to do up a parcel* **4** to make (oneself) more beautiful: *Mary has done herself up for the party.*

**do with** sthg. *v prep* [T] **1** [+*v-ing; no pass.*] (*usu. after* could *or sometimes* can) to need or want: *I could do with a cup of tea.*|*This room could do with (a) cleaning.* **2** to cause (oneself) to spend time doing: *The boys didn't know what to do with themselves when school ended.* **3** (*in questions with* "what") to do with regard to: *"What have you done with my pen?" "I've put it away."* **4 have/be to do with** to have a connection with: *His job has/is to do with the government.* **5 have/be something/nothing/anything/a lot, etc., to do with** to have some/no/any/a lot of, etc., connection with: *His job has nothing to do with the government.*|*Don't have anything to do with those nasty people.*|*What he does at home is nothing to do with* (=does not concern) *his teacher.*

USAGE Compare **do to** and **do with**: *What have you* **done with** *my book?* means "Where is it?" *What have* *you* **done to** *my book?* suggests that you have damaged it.

**do without** (sbdy./sthg.) *v adv; prep* [I;T] to continue to live without; DISPENSE **with:** *I haven't enough money to buy a car, so I'll just have to do without (one).*

**do³** *n* **dos** *or* **do's** /duːz/ *infml* **1** *BrE* a big party **2 dos and don'ts** rules of behaviour: *the dos and don'ts of working in an office*

**do·cile** /'dəusaɪl‖'dɑsəl/ *adj* quiet and easily taught or led: *a docile child/animal* **–docility** /dəu'sɪlʒti‖dɑ-/ *n* [U]

**dock¹** /dɒk‖dɑk/ *n* **1** a place where ships are loaded and unloaded, or repaired **2** the place in a court of law where the prisoner stands

**dock²** *v* [I;T *at*] to (cause to) sail into, or remain at, a DOCK¹ (1)

**dock³** *v* [T] to cut off the end of: *docking a horse's tail*|(fig.) *to dock a man's wages to pay for damage he has caused*

**dock·er** /'dɒkəʳ‖'dɑ-/ *n* a person who works at a DOCK¹ (1), loading and unloading ships

**doc·tor¹** /'dɒktəʳ‖'dɑk-/ *n* **1** [A;C] a person whose profession is to attend to and treat sick people (or animals): *an animal doctor*|*You should see a doctor.*|*Good morning, doctor.* **2** [A;C] a person holding one of the highest degrees given by a university (such as a PhD) **3** [A] *AmE* for DENTIST

**doctor²** *v* [T] *infml* **1** to give medical treatment to **2** *derog* to change, esp. in a dishonest way: *They were charged with doctoring the election results.* **3** *euph* to make (esp. an animal) unable to breed; NEUTER³: *The cat has been doctored.*

**doc·tri·naire** /ˌdɒktrʒ'neəʳ‖ˌdɑk-/ *adj derog* typical of a person who tries to put into action some system of ideas (a DOCTRINE) without considering the practical difficulties: *doctrinaire beliefs*

**doc·trine** /'dɒktrʒn‖'dɑk-/ *n* [C;U] a principle, or set of principles, that is taught: *religious doctrine* –see also INDOCTRINATE **–doctrinal** /dɒk'traɪnl‖dak-/ *adj*

**doc·u·ment¹** /'dɒkjʊmənt‖'dɑkjə-/ *n* a paper that gives information, proof, or support of something else: *Let me see all the official documents concerning the sale of this land.*

**doc·u·ment²** /'dɒkjument‖'dɑkjə-/ *v* [T] to prove or support with DOCUMENTS: *The history of this area is very well documented.* **–documentation** /-men'teɪʃən/ *n* [U]

**doc·u·men·ta·ry¹** /ˌdɒkjʊ'mentəri‖ˌdɑkjə-/ *adj* [A] of or related to DOCUMENTS¹: *documentary proof/*EVIDENCE

**documentary²** *n* **-ries** a film, or television or radio broadcast, that presents facts: *We saw a documentary about Yorkshire coal miners.*|*a documentary film* –compare FEATURE¹ (4)

**dod·der·ing** /'dɒdərɪŋ‖'dɑ-/ also **doddery–** *adj infml* weak, shaky, and slow, usu. from age

**dod·dle** /'dɒdl‖'dɑdl/ *n BrE infml* something that is very easy: *That driving test was a real doddle.*

**dodge** /dɒdʒ‖dɑdʒ/ *v* **dodged, dodging 1** [I;T] to avoid (something) by suddenly moving aside: *He dodged the falling rock and escaped unhurt.*|*He dodged past me.* **2** [T] *infml* to avoid by a trick or in some dishonest way: *tax-dodging* **–dodge** *n* **–dodger** *n*

**dodg·y** /'dɒdʒi‖'dɑ-/ *adj* **-ier, -iest** *BrE infml* **1** not safe; risky; dangerous: *a dodgy plan/car* **2** cleverly and perhaps dishonestly tricky: *a dodgy person/company*

**do·do** /'dəudəu/ *n* **dodoes** *or* **dodos 1** a large bird that could not fly and that no longer exists **2 (as) dead as a dodo** *infml* completely dead

**doe** /dəu/ *n* **does** or **doe** the female of certain animals, esp. the deer, the rat, and the rabbit –compare BUCK

**does** /dəz; *strong* dʌz/ *v 3rd person sing. present of* DO[1,2]

**doesn't** /'dʌzənt/ *short for:* does not: *She likes it, doesn't she?*

**dog¹** /dɒg‖dɔg/ *n* **1** a common four-legged flesh-eating animal, esp. any of the many varieties used by man: *A young dog is called a* **puppy**. **2** the male of this animal and of certain animals like it, esp. the fox and the WOLF **3 lead (someone) a dog's life** *infml* to (cause to) have an unhappy life with many troubles **4 Let sleeping dogs lie** Leave alone things which may cause trouble **5 not have a dog's chance** *infml* to have no chance at all **6 top dog** *infml* the person on top, who has power –compare UNDERDOG

**dog²** *v* **-gg-** [T *by*] to follow closely (like a dog); PURSUE (1): *We were dogged by bad luck during the whole journey.*

**dog-eared** /'· ·/ *adj* (esp. of books and papers) having the corners of the pages bent down with use

**dog·ged** *adj* having or showing a character which refuses to yield or give up in the face of difficulty or opposition **–doggedly** *adv* **–doggedness** *n* [U]

**dog·gy, doggie** /'dɒgi‖'dɔgi/ *n* **-gies** (*used esp. to or by children*) a dog

**dog·house** /'dɒghaus‖'dɔg-/ *n* **in the doghouse** *infml* in a state of disfavour or shame

**dog·ma** /'dɒgmə‖'dɔgmə, 'dɑgmə/ *n* [C;U] an important belief or set of beliefs that people are expected to accept without reasoning: *church dogma*|*political dogma*

**dog·mat·ic** /dɒg'mætɪk‖dɔg-, dɑg-/ *adj* **1** of or based on DOGMA **2** *usu. derog* (typical of a person) who puts forward beliefs expecting other people to accept them without question: *a dogmatic opinion/manner/person* **–dogmatically** *adv*

**dogs·bod·y** /'dɒgzˌbɒdi‖'dɔgzˌbɑdi/ *n* **-dies** *BrE infml* a person in a low position who has to do the least interesting work: *I'm just the dogsbody in this office.*

**do·ing** /'duːɪŋ/ *n* [U] **a** something that one has done: *This must be your doing.* (=you did this) **b** hard work: *That job will take a lot of doing.*

**dol·drums** /'dɒldrəmz‖'dəul-, 'dɑl-, 'dɔl-/ *n* **in the doldrums** *infml* in a sad state of mind

**dole¹** /dəul/ *n* **go/be on the dole** *BrE infml* to (start to) receive money from the government because one is unemployed: *I've been on the dole for six months.*

**dole²** *v* DOLE OUT

**dole·ful** /'dəulfəl/ *adj* causing or expressing unhappiness or low spirits: *a doleful look* **–dolefully** *adv* **–dolefulness** *n* [U]

**dole** sthg.↔ **out** *v adv* **doled, doling** [T *to*] to give (esp. money or food in small quantities) to people in need

**doll¹** /dɒl‖dɑl, dɔl/ *n* **1** a small figure of a person, esp.

of a baby, for a child to play with **2** *infml* a pretty young woman

**doll²** *v* →DOLL UP

**dol·lar** /'dɒləʳ‖'dɑ-/ *n* **1** a standard of money, as used in the US, Canada, Australia, New Zealand, Hong Kong, etc. Its sign is $ and it is worth 100 cents **2** a piece of paper, a coin, etc. of this value

**dol·lop** /'dɒləp‖'dɑ-/ *n* [*of*] *infml* a shapeless mass, esp. of food: *a dollop of mashed potato*

**doll** sbdy.↔ **up** *v adv* [T] *infml* to dress (someone or oneself ) prettily: *all dolled up to go to a party*

**dol·ly** /'dɒli‖'dɑli, 'dɔli/ *n* **-lies** (*used esp. by and to children*) →DOLL¹ (1)

**dol·phin** /'dɒlf¦n‖'dɑl-, 'dɔl-/ *n* a sea-animal two to three metres long, which swims about in groups

**do·main** /də'meɪn, dəʊ-/ *n* **1** land(s) owned or controlled by one person, a government, etc. **2** a subject of activity, interest, or knowledge

**dome** /dəʊm/ *n* a rounded roof on a building or room

**domed** /dəʊmd/ *adj* covered with or shaped like a DOME

**do·mes·tic¹** /də'mestɪk/ *adj* **1** of the house, home, or family: *domestic responsibilities/problems|not very domestic* (=not liking cooking, cleaning, etc.) **2** (of an animal) not wild: *The cat is a domestic animal in many countries.* **3** of one's own country or some particular country; not foreign: *the government's domestic affairs* –**domestically** *adv*

**domestic²** *n* a servant, usu. female, who works in a house

**do·mes·ti·cate** /də'mest¦keɪt/ *v* **-cated, -cating** [T] **1** to make (an animal) able to live with people and serve them, esp. on a farm or as a pet –compare TAME² (1) **2** to cause to be interested in and enjoy home life and duties –**domestication** /-ɪ'keɪʃən/ *n* [U]

**do·mes·tic·i·ty** /ˌdəʊmes'tɪs¦ti/ *n* [U] (a liking for) home or family life

**dom·i·cile** /'dɒm¦saɪl‖'dɑ-, 'dəʊ-/ *n fml* the place where one lives

**dom·i·nance** /'dɒm¦nəns‖'dɑ-/ *n* [U] the fact or state of dominating (DOMINATE); importance, power, or controlling influence: *the director has complete dominance of/over the whole committee* –compare DOMINATION

**dom·i·nant** /'dɒm¦nənt‖'dɑ-/ *adj* dominating (DOMINATE): *My sister had a very dominant nature; we all did what she wanted.|The castle was built in a dominant position on a hill*

**dom·i·nate** /'dɒm¦neɪt‖'dɑ-/ *v* **-nated, -nating** **1** [I;T] to have or exercise controlling power (over): *Her desire to dominate (other people) has caused trouble in her family.* **2** [I;T] to have the most important place or position (in): *Sports, and not learning, seem to dominate (in) that school.|That team has dominated football for years.* **3** [T] to rise or to be higher than; provide a view from a height above: *The church dominated the whole town.*

**dom·i·na·tion** /ˌdɒm¦'neɪʃən‖'dɑ-/ *n* [U] the act or fact of dominating or the state of being DOMINATED: *His domination by his brother made him very angry.* –compare DOMINANCE

**dom·i·neer·ing** /ˌdɒm¦'nɪərɪŋ‖ˌdɑ-/ *adj derog* showing a desire to control others, usu. without any consideration of their feelings or wishes: *a domineering person/manner*

**do·min·ion** /də'mɪnɪən/ *n* **1** [U *over*] *lit* the power or right to rule **2** [C] the land(s) held in complete control by one person, ruler, or government **3** [C] a self-governing nation of the British COMMONWEALTH: *the Dominion of Canada*

**dom·i·no** /'dɒm¦nəʊ‖'dɑ-/ *n* **-noes** one of a set of flat pieces of wood, bone, etc., with a different number of spots on each, used for playing a game (**dominoes**)

**don** /dɒn‖dɑn/ *n* (esp. in the Universities of Oxford and Cambridge) a teacher

**do·nate** /dəʊ'neɪt‖'dəʊneɪt/ *v* **-nated, -nating** [I;T *to*] to make a gift of (something), esp. for a good purpose –see also DONOR

**do·na·tion** /dəʊ'neɪʃən/ *n* [C;U] the act of donating or something DONATED: *She made a donation of £1,000 to the Children's Hospital.*

**done¹** /dʌn/ *v past participle of* DO¹·²

**done²** *adj* [F *no comp.*] **1** finished: *The job's nearly done.* **2** also **done for** /'--/ **done in** /ˌ-'-/ – very tired: *I feel completely done!* **3** cooked enough to eat: *Are the potatoes done yet?* **4 Done!** I agree! I accept!: *"I'll give you £5 for it." "Done!"* **5 not done** not socially acceptable: *It isn't done to call your teachers by their first names.*

**don·key** /'dɒŋki‖'dɑŋki/ *n* **-keys** an animal like a horse, but smaller and with longer ears, used by man to carry loads; ASS¹

**don·key·work** /'dɒŋkiwɜːk‖'dɑŋkiwɜrk/ *n* [U] *BrE infml* the hard uninteresting part of a piece of work: *Why do I always have to* **do the donkeywork?**

**do·nor** /'dəʊnəʳ/ *n* **1** a person who gives or DONATES **2** a person who permits part of his/her body to be put into someone else for medical purposes: *a blood donor|a kidney donor*

**don't** /dəʊnt/ *short for*: do not: *You know him, don't you?*

**doo·dle** /'duːdl/ *v* **-dled, -dling** [I] to draw lines, figures, etc., aimlessly –**doodle** *n*

**doom¹** /duːm/ *n* [C;U] a terrible fate; unavoidable destruction or death: *to meet one's doom*

**doom²** *v* [T *usu. pass.*] to cause to experience or suffer something unavoidable and unpleasant, such as death or destruction: *From the start, the plan was doomed (to failure/to fail).*

**dooms·day** /'duːmzdeɪ/ *n* **till doomsday** *infml* for ever

**door** /dɔːʳ‖dor/ *n* **1** a movable flat surface that opens and closes the entrance to a building, room, piece of furniture, or vehicle: *the kitchen/cupboard door|Most houses have a* **front door** *at the front and a* **back door** *at the back.|Will you* **answer** (=open) **the door**? *There's someone knocking (at it).|Mr Brown is leaving now. Will you* **show him to** (=go with him to) **the door**? –see pictures on pages 85, 297 **2** DOORWAY: *to come through the door* **3** (in certain fixed phrases) a house; building: *My sister lives only two/a few doors away.|He sells books* **(from) door to door**.*|He is a* **door-to-door** *salesman.|My brother lives* **next door** *(to us).* **4 at death's door** *lit* near death **5 be on the door** *infml* to have some duty at the door, such as collecting tickets **6 by the back door** secretly or by a trick **7 out of doors** →OUTDOORS

**door·step** /ˈdɔːstep‖ˈdor-/ *n* a step outside an outer door

**door·way** /ˈdɔːweɪ‖ˈdor-/ *n* an opening for an entrance door into a building or room: *She stood in the doorway, unable to decide whether or not to enter.*

**dope**[1] /dəʊp/ *n infml* **1** [U] a drug whose use is forbidden by law except on the orders of a doctor **2** [C] a stupid person

**dope**[2] *v* **doped, doping** [T *up*] *infml* to give DOPE[1] (1) to or put dope in, esp. to make someone or something sleepy: *to dope a person/a horse/a drink*

**dop·ey, dopy** /ˈdəʊpi/ *adj* **-ier, -iest** *infml* **1** having or showing a dullness of the mind (as if) caused by alcohol or a drug; sleepy and unable to think clearly **2** stupid

**dor·mant** /ˈdɔːmənt‖ˈdɔr-/ *adj* inactive, esp. not actually growing or producing typical effects: *dormant animals asleep for the winter*

**dor·mi·to·ry** /ˈdɔːmɨ̆təri‖ˈdɔrmɨ̆tori/ also **dorm** /dɔːm‖dɔrm/ *infml*– *n* **-ries** a large room for sleeping, containing a number of beds: *a school dormitory*

**dor·mouse** /ˈdɔːmaʊs‖ˈdɔr-/ *n* **-mice** /maɪs/ a small European forest animal with a long furry tail, that looks like a SQUIRREL

**dor·sal** /ˈdɔːsəl‖ˈdɔr-/ *adj tech* [A] of, on, or near the back: *the dorsal* FIN *of a fish*

**dos·age** /ˈdəʊsɪdʒ/ *n* [*usu. sing.*] the amount of a DOSE[1]

**dose**[1] /dəʊs/ *n* a measured amount (esp. of liquid medicine) given or to be taken at a time: *Take one dose, three times a day.*|(fig.) *In the accident, the workers received a heavy dose of* RADIATION.

**dose**[2] *v* **dosed, dosing** [T] to give a DOSE to, esp. to give medicine to

**doss down** /dɒs‖dɒs/ *v adv* [I] *BrE infml* to find a (usu. humble) place to sleep: *It was too late to go home so he dossed down on the floor.*

**dos·si·er** /ˈdɒsieɪ‖ˈdɔsjeɪ, ˈdɑ-/ *n* a set of papers containing detailed information: *The police keep dossiers on all criminals.*

**dot**[1] /dɒt‖dɑt/ *n* **1** a small round mark: *a dot on the letter i*|(fig.) *He watched the train until it was only a dot in the distance.* **2 on the dot** *infml* at the exact point in time (or space): *The 3 o'clock train arrived on the dot.*

**dot**[2] *v* **-tt-** [T] **1** to mark with a dot: *to dot an i* **2** to cover (as if) with dots: *a lake dotted with boats*

**do·tage** /ˈdəʊtɪdʒ/ *n* [U] weakness of the mind caused by old age: *We have to look after grandfather now he's* **in his dotage.**

**dote on/upon** sbdy. /dəʊt/ *v prep* **doted, doting** [T] to have or show too much fondness for (esp. a person): *He dotes on his youngest son.*

**dot·ing** /ˈdəʊtɪŋ/ *adj* [A] having or showing (too) much fondness: *a doting husband* –**dotingly** *adv*

**dot·ted line** /ˌ·· ˈ·/ *n* **1** a line of dots on paper, on which something is to be written, esp. one's name **2 sign on the dotted line** *infml* to agree to something quickly and unconditionally

**dot·ty** /ˈdɒti‖ˈdɑti/ *adj* **-tier, -tiest** *infml* weak-minded, foolish, or mad

**doub·le**[1] /ˈdʌbəl/ *adj* **1** in two parts; two together: *double doors|a double lock on the door|a cloth folded double* (=into two)|*a double meaning|a double* WHISKY (=twice the usual amount) –compare SINGLE[1] (2) **2** made for two: *a double bed|a double room in a hotel* –**double** *adv*: *When you drink too much, you sometimes see double.*

**double**[2] *n* **1** [C;U] something that is twice another in size, quantity, value, etc.: *I paid only £2 for this old book and Mr Smith offered me double* (=£4) *for it.*|*I'll have a double* (SCOTCH), *please.* **2** [C] a person who looks very much like another: *He is my double, though we are not related.* **3 at the double** (esp. of soldiers) at a rate between walking and running **4 on the double** *infml* very quickly –see also DOUBLES

**double**[3] *predeterminer* twice: *I bought double the amount of milk.*|*His weight is double what it was.*

**double**[4] *v* **-led, -ling** [I;T] to make, be, or become twice as great or as many: *If you double five you make ten.*|*Prices doubled in five years.*|*Double the sheet* (=fold it once) *and you'll stay warmer.*

**double as** sbdy./sthg. *v prep* [T] to have as a second use, job, etc.: *This chair doubles as a bed.*

**double back** *v adv* [I] to return along the same path: *He started running towards the street but suddenly doubled back to the house.*

**double up** *v adv* [I;T (=**double** sbdy.↔**up**)] to (cause to) bend at the waist (usu. with pain orlaughter): *They all doubled up (with laughter) when I told my joke.*|*He was doubled up (in pain).*

**double-bar·relled,** *BrE*‖**-reled** *AmE* /ˌ··ˈ··◂/ *adj* **1** (of a gun) having two barrels fixed side by side **2** *BrE infml* (of family names) connected by a HYPHEN (as in Smith-Fortescue)

**double bass** /ˌdʌbəl ˈbeɪs/ also **bass**– *n* the largest stringed musical instrument of the VIOLIN family, with a very deep sound

**double-breast·ed** /ˌ·· ˈ··◂/ *adj* (of a coat or JACKET) made so that one side of the front is brought across the other side of the front and usu. having a double row of buttons

**double-check** /ˌ··ˈ·/ *v* [I;T] to examine (something) twice for exactness or quality

**double chin** /ˌ·· ˈ·/ *n* a fold of loose skin between the face and neck

**double-cross** /ˌ·· ˈ·/ *v* [T] *infml* to cheat by pretended friendship; BETRAY (1) –**double cross** /ˈ··ˌ·/ *n* –**double-crosser** *n*

**double-deck·er** /ˌ·· ˈ··◂/ *n* [C;U] a bus with two levels –compare SINGLE-DECKER

**double-dutch** /ˌ·· ˈ·/ *n* [U] *humor derog* speech or writing that one cannot understand

**double-glaze** /ˌ·· ˈ·/ *v* **-glazed, -glazing** [T] to provide (a window) with an additional sheet of glass –**double-glazing** *n* [U]: *This double-glazing keeps in the heat and keeps out the noise.*

**double-joint·ed** /ˌ·· ˈ··◂/ *adj* having joints that allow movement (esp. of the fingers) backwards as well as forwards: *He's double-jointed.*

**double-quick** /ˌ·· ˈ·◂/ *adj,adv infml* very quick(ly)

**doub·les** /ˈdʌbəlz/ *n* **doubles** a match (esp. of tennis) played between two pairs of players: *Who'll win the men's/women's doubles at Wimbledon this year?* –compare SINGLES

**double-talk** /ˈ·· ·/ *n* [U] *infml* language that appears to be serious and have meaning but in fact is a mixture of sense and nonsense –**double-talk** *v* [I;T]

–**double-talker** *n*

**doub·ly** /ˈdʌbli/ *adv* **1** to twice the degree: *Her life is doubly interesting because she became famous so young.* **2** in two ways: *That family is doubly troubled; they have no money and now their father is ill.*

**doubt**[1] /daʊt/ *v* [T +(*that*); not *be* +*v-ing*] **1** to be uncertain (about): *I doubt whether/if it's true.|I doubt his honesty.* **2** to consider unlikely: *I doubt that John will come.* –**doubter** *n*

USAGE In NEGATIVE[1] (1) statements, **doubt** is always followed by *that*: *I don't* **doubt** *that he's telling the truth.* In simple statements it is often followed by *if* or *that*, but teachers prefer *whether*: *I* **doubt** *whether he's telling the truth.*

**doubt**[2] *n* [C;U +*that/about*] (a feeling of) uncertainty of belief or opinion: *There is some doubt (as to/about) whether John will come on time.|There's no doubt that/***Without doubt** *he'll come on time.|He says he can cure me, but I still have my doubts (about him/it).* **2 in doubt** in a condition of uncertainty: *The whole matter is still in doubt.*

USAGE 1 **Doubt** is followed by *that* after *no* or *not*: *There is some* **doubt** *(as to) whether he is guilty.|There is no* **doubt** *that he is guilty.* 2 **No doubt** and **doubtless** can be used as adverbs simply to mean "I think" or "I agree": **No doubt** *you'll be in the pub tonight* (=I expect you'll be there) But **without doubt** and **undoubtedly** express a stronger sense of knowing the real truth: *There will* **undoubtedly** (=certainly) *be trouble with the unions if she is dismissed.*

**doubt·ful** /ˈdaʊtfəl/ *adj* **1** [*about*] full of doubt; uncertain: *I feel very doubtful about this/about whether to go.|The future is too doubtful for us to make plans.* **2** not probable; unlikely: *It is doubtful if we can get home before midnight.* –**doubtfully** *adv*

**doubt·less** /ˈdaʊtl½s/ *adv* **1** without doubt: *John will doubtless come early as he always does.* **2** probably: *It will doubtless rain on sports day* –see DOUBT[2] (USAGE)

**dough** /dəʊ/ *n* [U] **1** flour mixed with water ready for baking **2** *infml, esp. AmE* money

**dough·nut** /ˈdəʊnʌt/ *n* a small round, often ring-shaped, cake cooked in fat and covered with sugar

**dour** /dʊəʳ||daʊər, dʊər/ *adj* hard and cold in one's nature; unfriendly; unsmiling: *a dour look* –**dourly** *adv*

**douse, dowse** /daʊs/ *v* **doused, dousing** [T *with, in*] to put into water or throw water over

**dove**[1] /dʌv/ *n* a type of PIGEON; soft-voiced bird often used as a sign of peace

**dove**[2] /dəʊv/ *v esp. AmE a past tense of* DIVE

**dow·dy** /ˈdaʊdi/ *adj* **-dier, -diest** *derog* (of clothes, esp. dresses) uninteresting; old-fashioned; (of people) badly, dully dressed –**dowdily** *adv* –**dowdiness** *n* [U]

**down**[1] /daʊn/ *adv* [*no comp.*] **1** from above towards a lower place; to the floor, the ground, or the bottom: *The man bent down to kiss the child.|It gets cold quickly when the sun goes down.|She came down (the stairs) from her bedroom.|The telephone wires were blown down by the storm.* **2** in a low place: *down at the bottom of the sea* **3** from an upright or raised position: *You needn't stand; please sit down.* **4** towards or in the south: *He's travelling down to London from Scotland.* –compare UP[1] (5) **5** along; away from the person speaking: *Will you walk down to the shop with me?* **6** firmly; tightly; safely: *Have you stuck down the back of the envelope?* **7** on paper; in writing: *"Did you write/copy/mark/put down the telephone number?" "I have it down somewhere."|to put one's name down on a list* **8** (showing a lower level or worse condition): *Production has gone down this year.* (=we have produced less)|*Let's mark down the prices.|The temperature's down ten degrees.* **9** (showing less noise, strength, activity, etc.): *Let the fire burn down.|Please turn the radio down* (=lower) *a bit.|They shouted the speaker down.* (=made him stop talking) **10** from the past: *These jewels have been passed down in our family from mother to daughter for 300 years.* **11 down under** *infml* in or to Australia or New Zealand **12 down with** ill with: *Mother has gone/come down with a cold.* **13 Down with** I/We don't want: *Down with the government!*

**down**[2] *adj* [F *no comp.*] sad; in low spirits: *I feel a bit down today.*

**down**[3] *prep* **1** to or in a lower place in; downwards by way of: *He ran down the hill.|The water poured down the pipe.|The bathroom is down those stairs.* –see picture on page 474 **2** along; to or at the far end of: *He looked down the pipe.|They live just down the road.* **3** in the direction of the current of: *to go/be down the river*

**down**[4] *v* [T] **1** to knock to the ground **2** to swallow quickly (esp. a liquid): *He downed his coffee and left.* **3 down tools** *BrE* (of workers) to stop working, esp. to STRIKE[1] (5)

**down**[5] *n* [U] fine soft feathers or hair –**downy** *adj* **-ier, -iest**

**down-and-out** /ˌ· · ˈ·◂/ *adj,n* **down-and-outs** (a person who is) suffering from bad fortune, lack of money and work, etc.

**down·cast** /ˈdaʊnkɑːst||-kæst/ *adj* having or showing low spirits or sadness: *with downcast eyes*

**down·fall** /ˈdaʊnfɔːl/ *n* **1** (something that causes) a sudden fall (esp. from high rank); ruin: *Rising prices were the company's downfall.* **2** a sudden or heavy fall (esp. of rain)

**down·grade** /ˈdaʊngreɪd, daʊnˈgreɪd||ˈdaʊngreɪd/ *v* **-graded, -grading** [T] to lower in rank, position, or importance –opposite **upgrade**

**down·heart·ed** /ˌdaʊnˈhɑːt½d◂||-ɑr-/ *adj* having or showing low spirits or sadness –**downheartedly** *adv*

**down·hill**[1] /ˌdaʊnˈhɪl/ *adv* **1** [after *n*] towards the bottom of a hill: *to run downhill|the road downhill* **2 go downhill** to move towards a lower or worse state or level: *His work has been going downhill recently. I hope it improves again soon.*

**down·hill**[2] /ˌdaʊnˈhɪl◂/ *adj* **1** [A] sloping or going towards the bottom of a hill **2** *infml* easy: *The hardest part of the work is over and the rest is downhill.*

**down·pour** /ˈdaʊnpɔːʳ||-por/ *n* a heavy fall of rain

**down·right** /ˈdaʊnraɪt/ *adv infml* (esp. with something bad) thoroughly; completely: *She was downright rude.* –**downright** *adj* [A]: *a downright cheat*

**downs** /daʊnz/ *n* [P] *BrE* low rounded grassy hills esp. as in the South of England

**down·stairs** /ˌdaʊnˈsteəz‖-ərz/ *adv* [F] on or to a lower floor and esp. the main or ground floor of a house: *to come downstairs|Is anyone downstairs yet?* –see also **upstairs** –**downstairs** /ˌ·ˈ·◂/ *adj* [A]: *a downstairs bedroom* –**downstairs** *n* –see picture on page 297

**down·stream** /ˌdaʊnˈstriːm◂/ *adv,adj* (moving) with the current, towards the mouth of a river, stream, etc. –opposite **upstream**

**down-to-earth** /ˌ· · ˈ·◂/ *adj* practical and honest; saying what one thinks: *a very down-to-earth person*

**down·trod·den** /ˈdaʊnˌtrɒdn‖-ˌtrɑ-/ *adj esp. lit* treated badly by those in positions of power

**down·ward** /ˈdaʊnwəd‖-wərd/ *adj* [A] going down: *a downward movement of prices/of the head* –opposite **upward**

**down·wards** /ˈdaʊnwədz‖-ər-/ also **downward** /-wəd‖wərd/ *AmE*– *adv* **1** going down: *He looked downwards to avoid my eyes.* **2** with a particular side towards the ground: *He lay on the floor face downwards.*

**down·wind** /ˌdaʊnˈwɪnd/ *adj,adv* (going or being) in the direction that the wind is moving –opposite **upwind**

**dow·ry** /ˈdaʊəri/ *n* **-ries** the property that a woman's father gives to her husband when she marries

**dowse** /daʊs/ *v* **dowsed, dowsing** [T] →DOUSE

**doze** /dəʊz/ *v* **dozed, dozing** [I] to sleep lightly –**doze** *n* [S]: *He likes (to have) a doze after dinner.*

**doze off** also **drop off, nod off**– *v adv* [I] to fall asleep unintentionally: *I just dozed off (for a moment).*

**doz·en** /ˈdʌzən/ *abbrev.* **doz.** – *determiner, n* **dozen** *or* **dozens** a group of 12: *a dozen eggs|These eggs are 40p a half dozen.* (=40p for six) –see Study Notes on page 494

**doz·y** /ˈdəʊzi/ *adj* **-ier, -iest 1** sleepy: *a dozy feeling* **2** *BrE infml* stupid; lacking understanding: *a dozy person* –**dozily** *adv* –**doziness** *n* [U]

**Dr** *written abbrev. said as:* Doctor

**drab** /dræb/ *adj* uninteresting; dull: *a drab colour|drab lives* –**drably** *adv* –**drabness** *n* [U]

**drabs** /dræbz/ *n* see DRIBS

**draft¹** /drɑːft‖dræft/ *n* **1** [C;U] the first rough written form of anything or a rough plan: *I've made a first draft of my speech for Friday.|a plan still only* **in draft** **2** [C;U] a written order for money to be paid by a bank, esp. from one bank to another –compare CHEQUE **3** [*the* S;U] *AmE* (a group of people chosen by) CONSCRIPTION **4** [C;U] *AmE* for DRAUGHT

**draft²** *v* [T] **1** to make a DRAFT¹ (1) of **2** [*into*] *AmE* for CONSCRIPT

**drafts·man** /ˈdrɑːftsmən‖ˈdræfts-/ *n* **-men** /mən/ *esp. AmE* for DRAUGHTSMAN

**draft·y** /ˈdrɑːfti‖ˈdræfti/ *adj* **-ier, -iest** *AmE* for DRAUGHTY

**drag¹** /dræg/ *n* **1** [C;U] the action or an act of dragging **2** [C] something that is dragged along over a surface **3** [C *on, upon*] something or someone that makes it harder to advance towards a desired end: *He felt that his family was a drag on his success.* **4** [S] *infml* something dull and uninteresting: *The party was a drag, so we left early.* **5** [C] *infml* an act of breathing in cigarette smoke **6** [U] *infml* woman's clothing worn by a man: *in drag*

**drag²** *v* **-gg- 1** [T] to pull (a heavy thing) along: *dragging a great branch along*|(fig.) *Why must you drag me out to a concert on this cold night!* –see picture on page 669 **2** [I;T *along*] to (cause to) move along while touching the ground: *dragging his feet in the dust* **3** [I] to move along too slowly in space or time: *He dragged behind the others.*

**drag on** *v adv* [I] to last an unnecessarily long time: *The meeting seemed to drag on for hours.*

**drag out** *v adv* **1** [I;T (=**drag** sthg.↔**out**)] to (cause to) last an unnecessarily long time: *They dragged out the meeting with long speeches.* **2** [T *of*] (**drag** sthg.↔ **out**) to force (something) to be told: *The police dragged the truth out of the prisoner.*

**drag** sthg.↔**up** *v adv* [T] *infml* to raise (a subject) unnecessarily: *The newspapers keep dragging up the politician's mistake.*

**drag·on** /ˈdrægən/ *n* an imaginary fire-breathing animal in children's stories: (fig.) *That old woman's a real dragon!*

**drag·on·fly** /ˈdrægənflaɪ/ *n* **-flies** a large harmless brightly-coloured insect

**drain¹** /dreɪn/ *v* [I;T] **1** [*away, off, out*] to (cause to) flow off gradually or completely: *to drain all the water out|The water drained (off/away).|Drain all the oil from/out of the engine.*|(fig.) *The old lady's strength is draining away.* **2** [*of*] to (cause to) become dry (as water or other liquid is removed): *Let the wet glasses drain (dry) before you put them away.|She was so afraid/angry that her face (was) drained of blood.|They want to drain the land to make crops grow better on it.|She drained her glass* (=drank all the contents) *and asked for more wine.*|(fig.) *His recent illness has really drained him.* (=made him weak)

**drain²** *n* **1** (the GRATING over) a ditch or usu. underground pipe which carries esp. waste water away from buildings: *The drains are blocked up.* –see picture on page 297 **2** something that DRAINS¹ (1), empties, or uses up: *All this spending is a drain on the money I have saved.* **3 down the drain** *infml* used wastefully: *(The results of) years of work went down the drain in the fire.*

**drain·age** /ˈdreɪnɪdʒ/ *n* [U] a system or means for DRAINing: *This soil has good drainage.*

**drain·ing board** /ˈ·· ·/ *n* a sloping board, usu. fixed to a SINK², on which dishes are placed after washing to allow them to dry –see picture on page 337

**drain·pipe** /ˈdreɪnpaɪp/ *n* a pipe which carries esp. waste water away from buildings, or from the roof of a building into a DRAIN¹ (2) –see picture on page 297

**drake** /dreɪk/ *n* a male duck

**dram** /dræm/ *n* a small measure of weight

**dra·ma** /ˈdrɑːmə/ *n* **1** [C] a serious work of literature that can be acted or read as a PLAY¹ (2) **2** [U] the art or study of PLAYS¹ (2): *Which do you like better: music or drama?* **3** [U] a group of exciting events: *Their holidays are always full of drama.*

**dra·mat·ic** /drəˈmætɪk/ *adj* **1** [*no comp.*] of or related to the DRAMA (2) or the theatre **2** exciting; catching the imagination: *a dramatic moment when the film star fell from the roof* –**dramatically** *adv*

**dra·mat·ics** /drəˈmætɪks/ *n* [U +*sing./pl. v*] **1** the study or practice of theatrical arts such as acting **2**

*often derog* DRAMATIC (2) behaviour or expression: *Your dramatics isn't/aren't going to change my mind.*

**dram·a·tist** /ˈdræmətəst/ *n* a writer of plays, esp. serious ones; PLAYWRIGHT

**dram·a·tize**||also **-ise** *BrE* /ˈdræmətaɪz/ *v* **-tized, -tizing 1** [T] to change (a book, report, etc.) so that it can be acted or read as a play: *He's dramatizing the book about his life.* **2** [I;T] to present (something) in a DRAMATIC (2) manner: *Don't dramatize–just give us the facts!* **–dramatization** /-ˈzeɪʃən/*n* [C;U]

**drank** /dræŋk/ *v past tense of* DRINK[1]

**drape** /dreɪp/ *v* **draped, draping** [T] **1** [*with, in, round, over*] to cover or decorate (something) with (folds of cloth): *They draped the flag over the soldier's coffin.* **2** [*over, (a)round*] to cause to hang or stretch out loosely or carelessly: *He draped his legs over the arm of the chair.*

**drap·er** /ˈdreɪpəʳ/ *n BrE becoming rare* a person who sells cloth, curtains, etc.

**drap·er·y** /ˈdreɪpəri/ *BrE*||**dry goods** *AmE– n* [U] the trade of or goods sold by a DRAPER: *the drapery department of the store*

**drapes** /dreɪps/ *n* [P] *AmE* for CURTAINS

**dras·tic** /ˈdræstɪk/ *adj* strong, sudden, and often violent or severe: *Drastic changes are necessary to improve the government of the country.* **–drastically** *adv*: *His work has changed drastically this term. It is full of mistakes now.*

**draught** ||also **draft** *AmE* /drɑːft||dræft/ *n* **1** [C] a current of air, flowing through a room, a chimney, etc.: *You may catch (a) cold if you sit in a draught.* **2** [C] an act of swallowing liquid or the amount of liquid swallowed at one time **3** [A;U] the drawing of a liquid from a large container such as a barrel: *Haven't you got beer* **on draught** *here?* |*I want draught beer, not bottled beer!* **4** [C] *BrE*||**checker** *AmE* a small round piece used in playing DRAUGHTS

**draughts** /drɑːfts||dræfts/ *BrE*||**checkers** *AmE – n* [U] a game played by two people, each with 12 round pieces, on a board of 64 squares (**draughtboard**)

**draughts·man** *esp. BrE*||**draftsman** *esp. AmE* /drɑːftsmən||dræfts-/ *n* **-men** /mən/ **1** a person whose job is to make detailed drawings of all the parts of a new building, machine, etc. **2** *fml* a person who draws well

**draught·y**||also **drafty** *AmE* /ˈdrɑːfti||ˈdræfti/ *adj* **-ier, -iest** with cold DRAUGHTS (1) blowing through: *a draughty room*

**draw[1]** /drɔː/ *v* **drew** /druː/, **drawn** /drɔːn/, **drawing 1** [I;T] to make (pictures) with a pencil or pen: *Jane draws very well.*|*to draw a line/a map*|*He drew a house.* **2** [T] to cause to come, go, or move by pulling: *The horse drew the cart up the hill.*|*She* **drew me aside** *and whispered in my ear.*|(fig.) *Don't let yourself get drawn into the argument.*|*He drew the curtains.* (=opened or closed them) **3** [T] to take or pull out: *to draw water from the well.*|*He suddenly drew a knife and threatened me with it.*|*I drew £100 from my bank account today.*|*She drew the winning ticket in the* lottery.|*The insect bit him and* **drew blood** *from his arm.*|(fig.) *After three attempts he* **drew the conclusion** (=decided by reason) *that he would never pass the examination.* **4** [I] *rather lit* to move or go steadily or gradually: *Winter is drawing near.*|*The train drew into/out of the station.* **5** [T] to attract: *The play is drawing large crowds/*AUDIENCES.|*Her shouts drew the attention of the police.* **6** [I;T] to end (a game, battle, etc.) without either side winning: *They drew (the match) 5 points to 5.* (=5 all)|*a drawn game* –compare TIE[1] (5) **7** to take (a breath) in: *She drew a deep breath and then continued.* **8** [I] to produce or allow a current of air, esp. to make a fire burn better: *The chimney isn't drawing very well.* **9 draw the line** to fix a limit of what one will not do or agree to: *to draw the line at stealing*|*I'm sorry but that's where I draw the line; I won't help him to cheat.*

**draw away** *v adv* **1** [I;T (=**draw** sbdy./sthg.↔**away**) *from*] to move (something) away, usu. quickly: *She drew the child away from the fire.* **2** [I *from*] to get further and further ahead (of): *The leader was gradually drawing away from the other runners.*

**draw back** *v adv* [I *from*] **1** to move oneself away from: *The crowd drew back in terror as the building crashed to the ground.* **2** to be unwilling to consider or fulfil (something) –see also DRAWBACK

**draw in** *v adv* [I] **1** to move to one side of the road and stop: *The bus drew in to let the cars pass.* **2** [*on, upon*] →CLOSE **in** (1) –compare DRAW **out** (2)

**draw on/upon** sthg. *v prep* [T] to make use of: *I shall have to draw on the money I've saved.*|*A writer has to draw on his imagination and experience.*

**draw out** *v adv* **1** [T] (**draw** sthg.↔ **out**) to cause to stretch in space or time: *a long-drawn-out speech* **2** [I] to have more hours of daylight: *The days are drawing out now that it's Spring.* –compare CLOSE **in** (1)

**draw up** *v adv* **1** [T] (**draw** sthg.↔ **up**) to form and usu. write: *to draw up a plan/a contract* **2** [I] (of a vehicle) to get to a certain point and stop: *The car drew up (at the gate) and three men got out.* **3 draw oneself up** to make (oneself) stand straight, often proudly: *to draw oneself up to one's full height*

**draw[2]** *n* **1** an act or example of DRAWing[1] (3), esp. in a LOTTERY: *He picked a winning number on the first draw.*|*He won and I lost: that's* **the luck of the draw**. **2** a result with neither side winning: *The game ended in/was a draw.* **3** a person or thing that attracts esp. a paying public: *That new singer is a big draw.*

**draw·back** /ˈdrɔːbæk/ *n* a difficulty or disadvantage; something that can cause trouble: *The only drawback of the plan is that it costs too much.* –see also DRAW **back**

**drawer** /drɔːʳ/ *n* a sliding box-like container with an open top (as in a table or desk): *The paper is in my desk drawer.* –see picture on page 337

**draw·ing** /ˈdrɔːɪŋ/ *n* **1** [U] the art of drawing with lines made with a pen, pencil, etc.: *good at drawing* **2** [C] a picture made by drawing: *a drawing of a cat*

**drawing pin** /ˈ··,·/ *BrE*||**thumbtack** *AmE– n* a short pin with a broad flat head, used esp. for putting notices on boards or walls

**drawing room** /ˈ·· ·/ *n fml* for LIVING ROOM

**drawl** /drɔːl/ *v* [I;T] to speak or say slowly, with vowels greatly lengthened **–drawl** *n*: *She speaks in/with a drawl.*

**drawn[1]** /drɔːn/ *adj* **1** (esp. of the face) changed as if by pulling or stretching: *a face drawn with sorrow* **2** (of games, competitions, etc.) ended with neither side winning: *The match was drawn 5-5.*

**drawn²** *v past participle of* DRAW¹

**dread¹** /dred/ *v* [T +*to-v*/*v-ing*/*that*] to fear greatly: *I dread him coming.*|*I* **dread to think** *what will happen if he comes.*

**dread²** *n* [S] a great fear, esp. of some harm to come: *She suffers from a great dread of heights.*

**dread·ful** /'dredfəl/ *adj* **1** causing great fear or anxiety; terrible: *the dreadful news of the accident*|*dreadful pain* **2** *infml* very unpleasant; unenjoyable; bad: *What a dreadful noise!*

**dread·ful·ly** /'dredfəli/ *adv* **1** *infml polite* very: *I'm dreadfully sorry.* **2** in a DREADFUL manner –see Study Notes on page 389

**dream¹** /dri:m/ *n* **1** a group of thoughts, images, or feelings experienced during sleep or when the mind is not completely under conscious control: *She woke up in the middle of an exciting dream.* **2** [*usu. sing.*] a state of mind in which one does not pay much attention to the real world: *John lives* **in a dream. 3** something imagined and hopefully desired: *It was his dream to play football for his country.* **4** *infml* a thing or person notable for beauty, excellence, or enjoyable quality: *Their new car is a real dream.* **–dreamlike** *adj*

**dream²** *v* **dreamed** /dri:md, dremt/ *or* **dreamt** /dremt/, **dreaming** [I;T +(*that*)/*of, about*] to have a dream (about something): *Do you dream at night?*|*I dreamt he would come.*|(fig.) *I* **wouldn't dream of** (=wouldn't consider) *hurting the child.*

USAGE For both the past tense and the past participle, **dreamed** and **dreamt** are both used in *BrE*, but Americans more often use **dreamed**.

**dream** sthg. ↔ **away** *v adv* [T] to spend (time) in dreaming or inactivity: *to dream away the hours*

**dream** sthg. ↔ **up** *v adv* [T] *infml often derog* to think of or imagine (something unusual or surprising): *They can always dream up some new excuse for the train arriving late.*

**dream·er** /'dri:məʳ/ *n* **1** a person who dreams **2** a person who has ideas or plans that are considered impractical

**dream·y** /'dri:mi/ *adj* **-ier, -iest 1** (of a person) living more in the imagination than in the real world **2** *infml* wonderful; desirable; beautiful **–dreamily** *adv* **–dreaminess** *n* [U]

**dreary** /drɪəri/ *adj* **-ier, -iest** dull; sad; uninteresting: *a dreary day, cold and without sunshine*|*Addressing envelopes all the time is dreary work.* **–drearily** *adv* **–dreariness** *n* [U]

**dredge** /dredʒ/ *v* **dredged, dredging** [I;T *for*] to use a DREDGER (in, on, or for something): *Can we dredge the river to make it deeper?*

**dredg·er** /'dredʒəʳ/ also **dredge**– *n* a machine or ship used for digging or sucking up mud and sand from the bottom of a river, CANAL, etc.

**dregs** /dregz/ *n* [P] bitter bits of matter in a liquid that sink to the bottom and are thrown away: (fig.) *Murderers and thieves are the dregs* (=worthless part) *of society.*

**drench** /drentʃ/ *v* [T] to make (usu. people, animals, or clothes) thoroughly wet: *I am drenched! I had no coat on when the rain started.*

**dress¹** /dres/ *v* **1** [I;T] to put clothes on (oneself or someone else): *I'll be ready in a moment; I'm dressing.*|*Please dress the baby, George.* –opposite **undress** –see USAGE **2** [I;T] to provide (oneself or someone else) with clothes of the stated type: *She dresses well on very little money.*|*She's very well-dressed.*|*an old lady dressed in black* **3** [I] to put on formal clothes for the evening **4** [T] to clean and put medicine and a protective covering on (a wound) **5** [T] to treat (food) so as to make ready for cooking or eating: *He dressed the* SALAD *with oil and* VINEGAR.

USAGE Compare **dress**, **put on**, and **wear**: **Dress** can mean either "to put on clothes" or "to have on or wear clothes of the stated type", but **wear** cannot be used to mean "put on", or **put on** to mean "wear": *She got out of the bath and* **dressed**/*got* **dressed**/**put on** *her clothes.*|*Wait a minute–I'm just* **dressing** *the baby*/**putting** *the baby's clothes* **on**. Compare: *She always* **dresses** *in black*/**wears** *black.*|*He's not* **dressed** *in his uniform*/**wearing** *his uniform*

**dress** sbdy.↔ **down** *v adv* [T] to scold; TELL **off** **–dressing-down** *n*: *The naughty child got a good dressing-down.*

**dress up** *v adv* **1** [I] (usu. of children) to wear someone else's clothes for fun and pretence **2** [T] (**dress** sbdy./sthg.↔ **up**) to make (something or someone) seem different or more attractive: *He dressed the facts up to make them more interesting.*

**dress²** *n* **1** [C] a woman's or girl's outer garment that covers the body from shoulder to knee or below –compare SKIRT; see picture on page 563 **2** [U] clothing, esp. outer clothing: *Do we have to wear evening dress for this party?* –see CLOTHES (USAGE)

**dress³** *adj* [A *no comp.*] **1** of or used for a dress: *dress material* **2** (of clothing) suitable for a formal occasion: *a dress shirt*/*coat*/*suit*

**dress·er** /'dresəʳ/ *n* **1** *esp. BrE* a piece of furniture for holding dishes, with open shelves above and cupboards below **2** *AmE* a chest of drawers, used esp. for clothing, often with a mirror on top

**dress·ing** /'dresɪŋ/ *n* **1** [U] the act or action of a person who dresses: *Dressing is difficult for her since her accident.* **2** [C] material used to cover a wound: *a clean dressing* **3** [C;U] a usu. liquid mixture for adding to food, esp. a SALAD

**dressing gown** /'·· ·/ *n* a garment rather like a long loose coat, worn after rising from bed and before putting on outer clothes

**dressing ta·ble** /'·· ˌ··/ *n* a low table with a mirror, usu. in a bedroom, at which one sits to arrange one's hair, etc.

**dress·y** /'dresi/ *adj* **-ier, -iest** (of clothes) showy or decorative, not for ordinary wear

**drew** /dru:/ *v past tense of* DRAW¹

**drib·ble** /'drɪbəl/ *v* **-bled, -bling 1** [I;T] (of a liquid, esp. SALIVA) to flow or fall out in drops little by little: *The water dribbled from the pipes* **2** [I] to let a liquid, esp. SALIVA, fall or flow out slowly drop by drop: *The baby is dribbling; wipe its mouth.* **3** [I;T] (in ball games) to move (esp. a ball) by a number of short kicks or hits **–dribble** *n*: *a dribble from the pipe*

**dribs** /drɪbz/ *n* **dribs and drabs** *infml* small and unimportant amounts: *He's paying me back in dribs and drabs.*

**dried** /draɪd/ *v past tense and participle of* DRY²

**dri·er** /ˈdraɪəʳ/ *n* →DRYER

**drift¹** /drɪft/ *n* **1** [C;U] the movement or course of something DRIFTING²: (fig.) *We must stop this drift towards war.*|(fig.) *the drift of young people from the country to the city* **2** [C] a mass of matter (such as snow or sand) blown together by wind: *a snowdrift* **3** [S] the general meaning: *I'm sorry; I can't quite* **catch the drift of** *what you're saying.*

**drift²** *v* **1** [I] to float or be driven along by wind, waves, or currents: *They drifted (out to sea).*|(fig.) *She just drifts from job to job.*| (fig.) *They had been married for a long time but gradually drifted apart until they separated.* **2** [I;T] to (cause to) pile up under the force of the wind or water: *The snow was drifting in great piles against the house.*

**drift·er** /ˈdrɪftəʳ/ *n often derog* a person who DRIFTS, esp. one who travels or moves about aimlessly

**drill¹** /drɪl/ *v* [I;T] **1** to use a DRILL² (1) on (something); to make with a drill: *to drill a hole in the wall*|*The workmen have been drilling (the road) all day.* **2** to train and exercise (soldiers, students, etc.) by means of DRILLS² (2): *Let's drill them in English pronunciation.*

**drill²** *n* **1** [C] a tool or machine for making holes: *a road drill*|*a* DENTIST'S *drill* **2** [C;U] training and instruction in a subject, esp. by means of repeating and following exact orders **3** [C] practice in how to deal with a dangerous state of affairs: *a fire drill*

**drill³** *n* **1** a machine used for planting seeds in rows **2** a row of seeds planted in this way

**dri·ly** *adv* see DRY¹

**drink¹** /drɪŋk/ *v* **drank** /dræŋk/, **drunk** /drʌŋk/, **drinking 1** [I;T *up*] to swallow (liquid): *Drink (up) your tea before it gets cold.*|(fig.) *drinking air into his lungs* **2** [I] to take in alcohol, esp. too much: *He doesn't smoke or drink.*|*He drinks like a fish.*

**drink** sthg.↔ **in** *v adv* [T] to take in through the senses, esp. eagerly: *They drank in the sights and sounds of the city.*

**drink to** sbdy./sthg. *v prep* [T] to wish good health or success to; drink a TOAST² (2) to

**drink²** *n* [C;U] **1** a liquid suitable for swallowing: *a drink of water* **2** the habit or an act of drinking alcohol: *Their frequent quarrelling* **drove him to drink.**

**drink·er** /ˈdrɪŋkəʳ/ *n* a person who drinks alcohol, esp. too much: *a heavy drinker*

**drip¹** /drɪp/ *v* **-pp-** [I;T] to fall or let fall in drops: *Water is dripping (down) from the roof.*|*The* TAP¹ *is dripping.* (=water is dripping from the tap)

**drip²** *n* **1** [S] the action or sound of falling in drops: *All night I heard the drip drip drip of the water.* **2** [C] (an apparatus for) liquid put into a blood vessel at a slow rate **3** [C] *infml* a dull and unattractive person

**drip-dry** /ˌ·ˈ·◂/ *adj* (of clothing) that will dry smooth and needs no ironing when hung while wet: *a drip-dry shirt*

**drip·ping** /ˈdrɪpɪŋ/ *n* [U] fat and juices that have come from meat during cooking

**drive¹** /draɪv/ *v* **drove** /drəʊv/, **driven** /ˈdrɪvən/, **driving 1** [I;T] to guide and control (a vehicle): *She drives well.*|*They drove to the station.*|*I never learnt to drive a car.* –see LEAD¹ (USAGE), **2** [T] to take (someone) in a vehicle: *Can you drive me to the station?* **3** [T] to force to go: *The farmer was driving his cattle along the road.*|*The bad weather has driven trade away.* **4** [T] to provide the power for: *The engines drive the ship.* **5** [T] to force (someone) to work hard or to be or act as stated: *He drives his workers very hard.*|*It was her pride that drove her to do it.*|*driven mad with pain* **6** [T] to hit: *He drove the nail into the wood.*|*She drove the ball 150 metres.* **7** [I] (esp. of rain) to fall or move along with great force: *driving rain* **8 drive something home (to)** to make something unmistakably clear (to)

**drive at** sthg. *v prep* [T *no pass.*] *infml* (*in -ing form*) to mean without actually saying; HINT: *What are you driving at?* (=What do you mean?)

**drive** sbdy./sthg.↔ **off** *v adv* [T] to force away or back; REPEL: *He drove off his attackers.*

**drive²** *n* **1** [C] a journey in a vehicle **2** [C] also **driveway**– a road, esp. one through a public park or to a private house –see picture on page 297 **3** [C] an act of hitting a ball forcefully **4** [C] a strong well-planned effort by a group for a particular purpose: *The club is having a membership drive.* (=to get more members) **5** [C] an important natural need which must be fulfilled: *Hunger, thirst, and sex are among the strongest human drives.* **6** [U] a forceful quality of mind or spirit that gets things done: *He's clever but he won't succeed because he lacks drive.* **7** [C;U] the apparatus by which a machine is set or kept in movement: *This car has (a) front-wheel drive.* (=the engine turns the front wheels)

**drive-in** /ˈ· ·/ *n,adj* [A;C] (a place) that people can use while remaining in their cars: *a drive-in restaurant/cinema/bank*

**driv·el** /ˈdrɪvəl/ *n,v* **-ll-** *BrE*‖ **-l-** *AmE* [I;U] (to talk) nonsense: *Don't talk drivel!*

**driv·er** /ˈdraɪvəʳ/ *n* a person who DRIVES: *Who was the driver of the car when the accident happened?*

**driving li·cence** *BrE*‖**driver's license** *AmE* /ˈ·· ˌ··/ *n* a LICENCE (1) to drive a motor vehicle, obtained after success in a **driving test** /ˈ·· ·/

**driz·zle¹** /ˈdrɪzəl/ *v* **-zled, -zling** [*it*+I] to rain in very small drops or very lightly –see WEATHER¹ (USAGE)

**drizzle²** *n* [S;U] a fine misty rain –**drizzly** *adj*

**droll** /drəʊl/ *adj* having a humorously odd or unusual quality: *a droll person/expression* –**drolly** /ˈdrəʊl-li/ *adv*

**drom·e·da·ry** /ˈdrʌmədəri, ˈdrɒm-‖ˈdrɑməderi/ *n* **-ries** a camel with one HUMP¹

**drone¹** /drəʊn/ *v,n* **droned, droning** [I;S] (to make) a continuous low dull sound like that of bees: *the drone of the enemy aircraft*|(fig.) *The politician droned on and on* (=spoke for a long time in an uninteresting manner) *about his new plans.*

**drone²** *n* a male bee

**drool** /druːl/ *v* [I] *derog* to let liquid flow from the mouth: *At the sight of the food he started drooling.*|(fig.) *I don't like the way people drool* (=show pleasure in a foolish way) *about/over that singer.*

**droop** /druːp/ *v* [I] to hang or bend downwards: *His shoulders drooped with tiredness.*|*The flowers drooped and faded.*|(fig.) *His spirits drooped.* (=he became sad) –**droop** *n* [S]

**drop¹** /drɒp‖drɑp/ *n* **1** [C] a small round mass of liquid: *a drop of oil*|*a teardrop*|*Drops of rain fell on* *the window.*|(fig.) "*Would you like some more tea?*" "*Just a drop* (=a little) *please.*" –see picture on page 449 **2** [C] a small round sweet: *fruit drops/chocolate drops* **3** [S] a distance or movement straight down: *a long drop to the bottom of the cliff*|*a drop in temperature/quantity/quality*|*a drop of 10 metres* **4** (**only**) **a drop in the ocean** a small unimportant quantity

**drop²** *v* **-pp- 1** [I;T] to fall or let fall: *The fruit dropped (down) from the tree.*|*to drop one's voice* (=to talk more quietly)|*Prices dropped* (=became lower) *in the first half of the year.*|*The wind has dropped.* (=has become less strong)|(fig.) *They worked until they dropped.* (=from tiredness) **2** [T] *infml* to allow (someone) to get out of a vehicle: *Drop me (off) at the corner.* **3** [T] to stop seeing, talking about, using, or practising: *Let's drop the subject.* (=let's talk about something else)|*I'm going to drop history this year.* (=stop studying it)|*He's dropped all his old friends.* **4** [T] to leave out: *I've been dropped (from the team) for next Saturday's match.* **5** [I *in, by, round* ] to visit unexpectedly or informally: *Drop in (and see us) when you're next in London!*|*Drop round* (=visit me) *one evening next week.* **6** [I *away, behind*] to get further away from a moving object by moving more slowly than it: *Our boat started the race well, but soon dropped away (from the others)/behind (the others).* **7 drop a brick/clanger** *BrE infml* to do or say something that is socially unacceptable **8 drop dead** *infml* (*often used in commands as an* INSULT) to die suddenly **9 drop someone a line/note** to write a short letter to someone

**drop off** *v adv* [I] **1** also **drop away**– to lessen; become fewer: *Interest in the game has dropped off.* **2** *infml* for DOZE **off**

**drop out** *v adv* [I] to stop attending or taking part: *He dropped out of college after only two weeks.* –see also DROPOUT

**drop·out** /'drɒp-aʊt‖'drɑp-/ *n* a person who leaves **a** a school or college without completing the course **b** ordinary society to practise another life-style –see also DROP **out**

**drop·per** /'drɒpəʳ‖'drɑ-/ *n* a short glass tube with a rubber part (BULB) at one end used for measuring out liquids, esp. liquid medicine, in drops

**drop·pings** /'drɒpɪŋz‖'drɑ-/ *n* [P] waste matter from the bowels of animals and birds

**drops** /drɒps‖drɑps/ *n* [P] liquid medicine to be taken drop by drop: *eyedrops*

**dross** /drɒs‖drɑs, drɔs/ *n* [U] waste or impure matter

**drought** /draʊt/ *n* a long period of dry weather, when there is not enough water: *The crops died during the drought.*

**drove¹** /drəʊv/ *n* a large group of people or animals moving or acting together

**drove²** *v past tense of* DRIVE

**drown** /draʊn/ *v* **1** [I;T] to (cause to) die under water because unable to breathe **2** [T] to cover completely with water, esp. by a rise in the water level: *streets and houses drowned by the floods* **3** [T *out*] to cover up (a sound) by making a loud noise: *The band drowned out our conversation so we sat and said nothing.* **4 drown one's sorrows** to drink alcohol in an attempt to forget one's troubles

**drowse** /draʊz/ *v* **drowsed, drowsing** [I *off*] to fall into a light sleep

**drow·sy** /'draʊzi/ *adj* **-sier, -siest 1** ready to fall asleep **2** making one sleepy: *a drowsy summer afternoon* **–drowsily** *adv* **–drowsiness** *n* [U]

**drudge** /drʌdʒ/ *v* **drudged, drudging** [I] to do hard, humble, or uninteresting work **–drudge** *n*

**drudg·e·ry** /'drʌdʒəri/ *n* [U] hard dull humble uninteresting work

**drug¹** /drʌg/ *n* **1** a medicine or material used for making medicines **2** a substance one takes, esp. as a habit, esp. for pleasure or excitement: *Tobacco and alcohol can be dangerous drugs.*|*Is he* **on drugs**? (=Does he take drugs?)

**drug²** *v* **-gg-** [T] to add drugs or give drugs to, esp. so as to produce unconsciousness: *to drug a sick man in pain*|*a drugged cup of coffee*

**drug·gist** /'drʌgɪ̈st/ *n AmE* for PHARMACIST

**drug·store** /'drʌgstɔːʳ‖-stor/ *n esp. AmE* a PHARMACY, esp. one which sells not only medicine, beauty products, film, etc., but also simple meals

**dru·id** /'druːɪ̈d/ *n* (*often cap.*) a member of the ancient CELTIC priesthood of Britain, Ireland, and France, before the Christian religion

**drum¹** /drʌm/ *n* **1** a musical instrument consisting of a skin stretched tight over one or both sides of a hollow circular frame, and struck by hand or with a stick **2** something that looks like such an instrument, esp. a part of a machine or a large container for liquids: *an oil drum*

**drum²** *v* **-mm-** [I] **1** to beat or play a drum **2** to make drum-like noises, esp. by continuous beating or striking: *He drummed on the table with his fingers.*|*the rain drumming against the window*

**drum** sthg. **into** sbdy. *v prep* [T] *infml* to put (an idea) firmly into (someone's mind) by steady effort or continuous repeating: *She drummed into the children that they must not cross the road alone.*

**drum** sthg.↔ **up** *v adv* [T] *infml* to obtain by continuous effort and esp. by advertising: *Let's try to drum up some more business.*

**drum·mer** /'drʌməʳ/ *n* a person who plays a drum

**drum·stick** /'drʌm,stɪk/ *n* **1** a stick for beating a drum **2** *infml* the lower meaty part of the leg of a bird, eaten as food

**drunk¹** /drʌŋk/ *adj* [F] under the influence of alcohol: *The police charged him with being* **drunk and disorderly**.|*He's* **dead/blind drunk**. (=very drunk)|(fig.) *drunk with power* –compare SOBER¹ (1)

**drunk²** also **drunkard** /'drʌŋkəd‖-ərd/– *n often derog* a person who is drunk, esp. often or continually

**drunk³** *v past participle of* DRINK¹

**drunk·en** /'drʌŋkən/ *adj* [A] **1** drunk: *a drunken sailor* **2** resulting from or marked by too much drinking of alcohol: *a drunken sleep*|*a drunken party* **–drunkenly** *adv* **–drunkenness** *n* [U]

**dry¹** /draɪ/ *adj* **drier, driest 1** having no water or other liquid inside or on the surface; not wet: *Don't put your shirt on until it's dry.*|*The well has gone dry.*|*Be careful! The paint isn't dry yet.*|*dry skin* (=without natural liquids) **2** without rain or wetness: *dry weather*|*a dry month*|*dry heat* –compare HUMID **3** having or producing thirst: *I always feel dry in this hot weather.*|*It's dry work digging in the sun.* **4** (of alcoholic drinks, esp. wine) not sweet; not fruity in taste **5** amusing without appearing to be so; quietly IRONIC: *I like his dry humour.* **6** dull and uninteresting: *The book was* **as dry as dust**. (= very uninteresting) **7 (as) dry as a bone** also **bone-dry**– *infml* very dry **–dryly, drily** *adv* **–dryness** *n* [U]

**dry²** *v* **dried, drying 1** [I;T *out, up*] to (cause to) become dry: *Dry your hands.|The wet clothes will soon dry (out) in the sun.* **2** [T] to preserve (food) by removing liquid: *dried fruit/milk*

**dry out** *v adv* [I;T (=**dry** sbdy. **out**)] to (cause to) give up dependence on alcoholic drink

**dry-clean** /ˌ·ˈ·/ *v* [T] to clean (clothes, material, etc.), with chemicals instead of water, in a special shop (**dry cleaner's**)

**dry dock** /ˈ· ·/ *n* a place in which a ship is held in position while the water is pumped out, leaving the ship dry for repairs: *a ship* **in dry dock** *being painted*

**dry·er, drier** /ˈdraɪəʳ/ *n* a machine that dries: *to sit under the hair dryer*

**dry ice** /ˌ·ˈ·/ *n* [U] CARBON DIOXIDE in a solid state, used mainly to keep food and other things cold

**dry rot** /ˌ·ˈ·/ *n* [U] diseased growth in wood (as in wooden floors) which turns wood into powder: *They didn't buy the house because it had dry rot.*

**du·al** /ˈdjuːəl‖ˈduːəl/ *adj* [A] consisting of two parts or having two parts like each other; double: *He has a dual interest in the football team; he's the trainer and his son plays for them.|a dual-purpose instrument* –sounds like **duel**

**dual car·riage·way** /ˌ·· ˈ···/ *n BrE* a main road on which the traffic travelling in opposite directions is kept apart by a central band or separation of some sort

**dub¹** /dʌb/ *v* **-bb-** [T] **1** *lit or old use* to make (someone) a KNIGHT by a ceremonial touch on the shoulder with a sword **2** *humor (or in newspapers)* to name humorously or descriptively: *They dubbed him Fatty because of his size.*

**dub²** *v* [T] to give new or different sound effects to, or change the original spoken language of (a cinema film, radio show, or television show): *Is the film dubbed or does it have* SUBTITLES?

**du·bi·ous** /ˈdjuːbɪəs‖ˈduː-/ *adj* **1** feeling doubt; undecided: *I'm still dubious about that plan.* **2** causing doubt; of uncertain value or meaning: *a dubious suggestion|a rather dubious character* (=a possibly dishonest person) **–dubiously** *adv* **–dubiousness** *n* [U]

**duch·ess** /ˈdʌtʃɨ̤s/ *n* (*often cap.*) (the title of) **a** the wife of a DUKE **b** a woman who holds the rank of DUKE in her own right

**duck¹** /dʌk/ **drake** *masc.*– *n* **ducks** *or* **duck 1** a common swimming bird with a wide beak, sometimes kept for meat, eggs, and soft feathers (**down**): *A young duck is called a* **duckling**. **2 lame duck** a person or business that is helpless or ineffective **3 like water off a duck's back** *infml* having no effect **4 (take to something) like a duck to water** *infml* (to learn or get used to something) naturally and very easily

**duck²** *v* **1** [I;T] to lower (one's head or body) quickly, esp. so as to avoid being hit or seen: *She had to duck to get through the low doorway.|He saw a policeman coming and ducked behind a car.* **2** [T] to push under water: *He ducked his head in the stream to get cool.* **3** [T] *infml* to try to avoid (a difficulty or unpleasant responsibility); DODGE: *Don't try to duck (out of) cleaning up the kitchen!* **–duck** *n*

**duct** /dʌkt/ *n* **1** a thin, narrow tube in the body or in plants which carries liquids, air, etc.: *tearducts* **2** any kind of pipe or tube for carrying liquids, air, electric power lines, etc. –see also AQUEDUCT, VIADUCT

**dud** /dʌd/ *n infml* a person or thing that is worthless or useless: *a dud cheque*

**due¹** /djuː‖duː/ *adj* **1** [F *to*] *fml* owed or owing as a debt or right: *Our grateful thanks are due to you.* –see DUE **to** (USAGE) **2** [A] *fml* proper; suitable; enough: *driving with due care and attention* **3** [F] payable: *a bill due today* **4** [F *+to-v/for*] (showing arrangements made in advance) expected; supposed (to): *The next train to London is due here at 4 o'clock.|I am due to leave quite soon now.|I am due for an increase in pay soon.* **5 in due course/time** in or at the proper time –see also DULY

**due to** *prep* because of; caused by: *His illness was due to bad food.* –see Study Notes on page 128

USAGE Teachers prefer **due to** be used only after the verb **to be**: *His absence was* **due to** *the storm.* However, **due to** is often used in the same way as **owing to** and **because of**: *He arrived late* **due to/owing to/because of** *the storm.*

**due²** *n* something that rightfully belongs to someone, esp. something non-material: *I don't like him, but,* **to give him his due,** *he is a good singer.*

**due³** *adv* (*before* north, south, east, *and* west) directly; exactly: *due north (of here)*

**du·el¹** /ˈdjuːəl‖ˈduːəl/ *n* (esp. formerly) a fight with hand guns or swords between two people, to settle a quarrel: (fig.) *another duel between the company and the union* –sounds like **dual**

**duel²** *v* **-ll-** *BrE*‖ **-l-** *AmE* [I *with*] to fight a DUEL –sounds like **dual –dueller, duellist** *n*

**dues** /djuːz‖duːz/ *n* [P] official charges or payments: *harbour dues*

**du·et** /djuːˈet‖duːˈet/ *n* a piece of music for two performers –compare SOLO¹

**duf·fel coat, duffle coat** /ˈdʌfəl ˌkəʊt/ *n* a loose coat made of a rough heavy woollen cloth (**duffel**), usu. fastened with long tubelike buttons (TOGGLE*s*) and often having a headcovering (HOOD)

**dug** /dʌg/ *v past tense and participle of* DIG¹

**dug·out** /ˈdʌgaʊt/ *n* **1** a small light boat made by cutting out a deep hollow in a log: *a dugout* CANOE **2** [I] a (usu. military) shelter dug in the ground with an earth roof –compare TRENCH

**duke** /djuːk‖duːk/ *n* (*often cap.*) (the title of) a nobleman of the highest rank outside the Royal Family –see DUCHESS

**dul·cet** /ˈdʌlsɨ̤t/ *adj lit* (esp. of sounds) sweet; pleasant; calming: *her dulcet tones* (=of her voice)

**dull¹** /dʌl/ *adj* **1** not bright or shining: *a dress of some uninteresting dull colour|The weather's dull today: we shall have rain.* **2** not clear or sharp: *a dull knocking sound somewhere in the house|The old man's hearing has become dull, so you must speak clearly to him.|a dull pain* **3** slow in thinking and understanding: *He couldn't teach such dull children.* **4** uninteresting; unexciting; lacking in imagination; boring

(BORE[4]): *I slept through his dull speech.* **–dully** *adv* **–dullness** *n* [U]

**dull²** *v* [I;T] to (cause to) become dull: *Give me something to dull* (=ease) *the pain.*

**du·ly** /'dju:li‖'du:li/ *adv* [*no comp.*] *fml* in a DUE manner, time, or degree; properly: *The taxi that we had ordered duly arrived, and we drove off.*

**dumb** /dʌm/ *adj* **1** unable to speak: *dumb animals|The deaf and dumb* (=people unable to hear or speak) *are sent to a special school.|The terrible news* **struck us all dumb**. **2** unwilling to speak; silent **3** *infml* stupid **–dumbly** *adv* **–dumbness** *n* [U]

**dumb·bell** /'dʌmbel/ *n* [*usu. pl.*] a weight consisting of two large metal balls connected by a short bar and usu. used in pairs for exercises

**dumb·found, dumfound** /dʌm'faʊnd/ *v* [T *usu. pass.*] to make unable to speak because of wonder, surprise, or lack of understanding: *He stood there, dumbfounded by the news.*

**dum·my** /'dʌmi/ *n* **-mies 1** an object made to look like and take the place of a real thing: *a dummy gun made of wood* **2** something like a human figure made of wood or wax and used to make or show clothes: *a dressmaker's dummy* **3** *BrE*‖**pacifier** *AmE*– a rubber thing for sucking, put in a baby's mouth to keep it quiet **4** *infml, esp. AmE* a stupid fool

**dump¹** /dʌmp/ *v* [I;T] **1** to drop or unload (something) in a heap or carelessly: *Don't dump that sand in the middle of the path!|They dumped their bags on my floor and left!* **2** *derog* to sell (goods) in a foreign country at a very low price

**dump²** *n* **1** a place for DUMPing something (such as waste material) **2** *derog infml* a dirty and untidy place: *This town's a real dump.*

**dump·ling** /'dʌmplɪŋ/ *n* **1** a lump of boiled DOUGH, often served with meat or having meat inside it **2** a sweet food made of pastry with fruit inside it: *apple dumplings*

**dumps** /dʌmps/ *n* **(down) in the dumps** *infml* sad; DEPRESSED (1)

**dump·y** /'dʌmpi/ *adj* **-ier, -iest** *infml* (esp. of a person) short and fat: *a dumpy little man*

**dunce** /dʌns/ *n* a slow learner; stupid person

**dune** /dju:n‖du:n/ also **sand dune**– *n* a sandhill (often long and low) piled up by the wind on the seashore or in a desert

**dung** /dʌŋ/ *n* [U] solid waste material passed from the bowels of animals (esp. cows and horses); animal MANURE

**dun·ga·rees** /ˌdʌŋgə'ri:z/ *n* [P] trousers with a BIB (2) or work clothes made of heavy cotton cloth (DENIM), usu. blue –compare OVERALLS; see PAIR¹ (USAGE)

**dun·geon** /'dʌndʒən/ *n* a dark underground prison, esp. beneath a castle

**dunk** /dʌŋk/ *v* [T *in*] *infml* to dip (esp. food) into liquid while eating: *to dunk* BISCUITS *in coffee*

**du·o** /'dju:əʊ‖'du:əʊ/ *n* **duos** two musicians who play or sing together

**dupe¹** /dju:p‖du:p/ *n* a person who is tricked or deceived by someone else

**dupe²** *v* **duped, duping** [T *into*] to trick or deceive: *The old lady was duped by the dishonest salesman.*

**du·pli·cate¹** /'dju:plɪ̈kɪ̈t‖'du:-/ *adj,n* [A;C] (something that is) exactly like another in appearance, pattern, or contents: *If you've lost your key, I can give you a duplicate (key).*

**du·pli·cate²** /'dju:plɪ̈keɪt‖'du:-/ *v* [T] to copy exactly: *Can you duplicate this key for me?|Can you duplicate these letters for me and send one to every student?* **–duplication** /-'keɪʃən/ *n* [U]

**du·pli·ca·tor** /'dju:plɪ̈keɪtəʳ‖'du:-/ *n* a machine that makes copies of written, printed, or drawn material

**du·plic·i·ty** /dju:'plɪsɪ̈ti‖du:-/ *n* [U] *fml* deceit; deception

**dur·a·ble** /'djʊərəbəl‖'dʊ-/ *adj* long-lasting: *durable clothing|We must make a durable peace.* **–durability** /- ə'bɪlɪ̈ti / *n* [U]

**du·ra·tion** /djʊ'reɪʃən‖dʊ-/ *n* [U] *fml* the time during which something exists or lasts: *He will be in hospital for the duration of the school year.|an illness of short duration*

**du·ress** /djʊ'res‖dʊ-/ *n* [U] *fml* illegal or unfair threats: *a promise made under duress*

**dur·ing** /'djʊərɪŋ‖'dʊ-/ *prep* **1** all through (a length of time): *He swims every day during the summer.* (Compare *He swam every day for three months.*)|*They lived abroad during the war.* (=while the war was happening) **2** at some moment in (a length of time): *He died during the night.*

**dusk** /dʌsk/ *n* [U] the time when daylight is fading; darker part of TWILIGHT: *The street lights go on at dusk.* –compare DAWN

**dusk·y** /'dʌski/ *adj* **-ier, -iest** darkish in colour; shadowy: *the dusky light of the forest*

**dust¹** /dʌst/ *n* **1** [U] powder made up of very small pieces of waste or other matter: *There was a layer of dust on the books before I cleaned them.|gold dust/coal dust* **2** [U] finely powdered earth: *The car caused a cloud of dust as it went down the dirt road.*

**dust²** *v* **1** [I;T] to clean the dust from; remove dust: *Please dust all the books on the bottom shelf.* **2** [T *with*] to cover with dust or fine powder: *to dust the crops with a substance that will kill insects*

**dust·bin** /'dʌstˌbɪn/ *BrE*‖**garbage can, trash can** *AmE*– *n* a container with a lid, for holding waste materials such as empty tins and bottles until they can be taken away –see picture on page 297

**dust·cart** /'dʌstkɑ:t‖-kɑrt/ *BrE*‖**garbage truck** *AmE*– *n* a LORRY which goes from house to house in a town to collect the contents of DUSTBINs

**dust·er** /'dʌstəʳ/ *n* a cloth for dusting furniture

**dust jack·et** /'· ˌ··/ also **dust cover, jacket**– *n* a loose paper cover put as a protection round the hard cover of a book, often having writing or pictures describing the book

**dust·man** /'dʌstmən/ *BrE*‖**garbage collector** *AmE*– *n* **-men** /mən/ one of the people employed (e.g. by a town) to remove waste material from DUSTBINs

**dust·pan** /'dʌstpæn/ *n* a flat container with a handle into which house dust can be brushed

**dust·up** /'dʌst-ʌp/ *n BrE infml* a quarrel or fight

**dust·y** /'dʌsti/ *adj* **-ier, -iest** dry and covered or filled with dust: *In the summer the town becomes very dusty.*

**Dutch** /dʌtʃ/ *adj* **1** of or related to the people, country, or language of the Netherlands (Holland) **2 go**

Dutch (**with someone**) to share expenses: *Charles and Kate always go Dutch at the restaurant.* –see also DOUBLE-DUTCH

**Dutch cour·age** /ˌ· ˈ··/ *n* [U] *infml* the courage that comes from being drunk

**du·ti·ful** /ˈdjuːtɪfəl‖ˈduː-/ *adj* (of people and their behaviour) having or showing a sense of DUTY (1); with proper respect and obedience –**dutifully** *adv*

**du·ty** /ˈdjuːti‖ˈduːti/ *n* **-ties** [C;U] **1** what one must do either because of one's job or because one thinks it right: *His duties include taking the letters to the post office and arranging meetings.*|*to do one's duty*|*It's my duty to help you.*|**duty bound** (=required by one's conscience) *to visit an old aunt* **2** a tax: CUSTOMS *duties are paid on goods entering the country and death duties on property when the owner dies.* **3 heavy duty** (as of a machine) able to do hard work: *heavy duty tyres* **4 on/off duty** (esp. of soldiers, nurses, etc.) required/not required to work: *When I'm off duty I play tennis.*

**duty-free** /ˌ·· ˈ·◂/ *adj,adv* (of goods) allowed to come into the country without tax: *the duty-free shop at the airport*

**du·vet** /ˈduːveɪ/ also **continental quilt** *BrE*– *n* a large bag filled with feathers, used on a bed to take the place of all the other coverings

**dwarf**[1] /dwɔːf‖dwɔrf/ *n* **dwarfs** *or* **dwarves** /dwɔːvz‖dwɔrvz/ **1** a person, animal, or plant of much less than the usual size: *a dwarf apple tree* **2** a small imaginary manlike creature in fairy stories: *Snow White and the Seven Dwarfs*

**dwarf**[2] *v* [T] to cause to appear small by comparison: *The tall office building dwarfs all the little shops.*

**dwell** /dwel/ *v* **dwelt** *or* **dwelled, dwelling** [I] *fml* **1** to live (in a place): *They dwell in a forest/on an island.* **2 -dweller** a person or animal that lives (in the stated place): *cave-dwellers*|*city-dwellers*

**dwell on/upon** sthg. *v adv* [T] to think, speak, or write a lot about: *Don't dwell so much on your past.*

**dwelling** /ˈdwelɪŋ/ *n fml and humor* a house, flat, etc., where people live

**dwin·dle** /ˈdwɪndl/ *v* **-dled, -dling** [I *away*] to become gradually fewer or smaller: *The number of people who live on the island is dwindling.*

**dye**[1] /daɪ/ *n* [C;U] a vegetable or chemical substance, usu. liquid, used to colour things esp. by dipping –compare PAINT[1]

**dye**[2] *v* **dyed, dyeing** [I;T] to give or take (a stated) colour by means of DYE: *She dyed the dress (red).*

USAGE Compare **die** (verb): **dies, died, dying.**

**dyed-in-the-wool** /ˌ· · · ˈ·◂/ *adj often derog* impossible to change (as to the stated or known quality): *Charles is a dyed-in-the-wool Republican.*

**dyke** /daɪk/ *n,v* →DIKE

**dy·nam·ic** /daɪˈnæmɪk/ *adj* **1** *often apprec* (of people, ideas, etc.) full of or producing power and activity: *a dynamic person*|*a dynamic period in history* **2** *tech* of or relating to force or power that causes movement –compare STATIC –**dynamically** *adv*

**dy·nam·ics** /daɪˈnæmɪks/ *n* [U] the science that deals with matter in movement

**dy·na·mis·m** /ˈdaɪnəmɪzəm/ *n* [U] (in a person) the quality of being DYNAMIC (1)

**dy·na·mite**[1] /ˈdaɪnəmaɪt/ *n* [U] **1** a powerful explosive used esp. in MINING **2** *infml* something or someone that will cause great shock, surprise, admiration, etc.: *That news story/That new singer is really dynamite!*

**dynamite**[2] *v* **-mited, -miting** [T] to blow up with DYNAMITE[1] (1)

**dy·na·mo** /ˈdaɪnəməʊ/ *n* **-mos** a machine (esp. small) which turns some other kind of power into electricity: *the dynamo on my bicycle* –compare GENERATOR

**dyn·a·sty** /ˈdɪnəsti‖ˈdaɪ-/ *n* **-sties** [C +sing./pl. v] a line of rulers all of the same family: *a dynasty of Welsh kings* –**dynastic** /dɪˈnæstɪk‖daɪ-/ *adj*

**dys·en·te·ry** /ˈdɪsəntəri‖-teri/ *n* [U] a painful disease of the bowels that causes them to be emptied more often than usual and to produce blood and MUCUS

**dys·lex·i·a** /dɪsˈleksɪə/ also **word blindness**– *n* [U] *tech* inability to read, caused by difficulty in seeing letter shapes –**dyslexic** *adj*

**dys·pep·si·a** /dɪsˈpepsɪə, -ˈpepʃə/ *n* [U] difficulty in DIGESTING food; INDIGESTION

**dys·pep·tic** /dɪsˈpeptɪk/ *adj* (typical of a person) suffering from DYSPEPSIA

# E, e

**E , e** /iː/ **E's, e's** *or* **Es, es** the 5th letter of the English alphabet

**E** *written abbrev. said as:* east(ern)

**each**[1] /iːtʃ/ *determiner,pron* every single one of two or more separately: *each foot/each of my feet*|*They each want to do something different.*|*She cut the cake into pieces and gave one to each of the children.*

USAGE Compare **each, every,** and **both**: 1 **Both** is used for two people or things taken together; **each** is used for any number of people or things taken separately; and **every** is used for a whole group: **Both** *my children* (=I have two children) *go to the same school.*|**Each** *of my children* (= I have two or more children) *goes to a different school.*|**Each** *child in the class gave a different answer.*|**Every** *child in the class passed the examination.* 2 **Both** always takes a plural verb; **every** always takes a singular verb: **Both** *our children go to the local school.*|**Every** *child in the street goes to the local school.* **Each** usually takes a singular verb, except after a plural subject: **Each** *has his own room.*|*They* **each** *have their own rooms.* 3 **Every** cannot be used in sentences like: **Both/Each** *of the boys...*|*The boys* **both/each**... –see ALL[3] (USAGE)

**each²** *adv* for or to every one: *The tickets are £1 each.*

**each oth·er** /ˌ· ˈ··/ also **one another**– *pron* [*not used as the subject*] (means that each of two or more does something to the other(s)): *Susan and Robert kissed each other.* (=Susan kissed Robert and Robert kissed Susan)

USAGE Some teachers prefer **each other** to be used about two people or things, and **one another** about more than two: *After the tennis match, the two players shook hands with* **each other.**|*After the football match, the players all shook hands with* **one another.**

**ea·ger** /ˈiːgəʳ/ *adj* [+*to-v*/*that*/*for, about*] full of interest or desire; keen: *He listened to the story with eager attention.*|*He is eager for success*/*for you to meet his friends.* **–eagerly** *adv* **–eagerness** *n* [U]

**ea·gle** /ˈiːgəl/ *n* a very large BIRD OF PREY with a hooked beak and very good eyesight

**eagle-eyed** /ˌ·· ˈ·◂/ *adj* having very good eyesight: (fig.) *an eagle-eyed teacher*

**ear¹** /ɪəʳ/ *n* **1** [C] either of the two organs of hearing, one on each side of the head: *Don't shout in my ear!* –see picture on page 299 **2** [S *for*] good recognition of sounds, esp. in music and languages: *Peter can play the most difficult piano music* **by ear.** (=without written musical notes) **3 out on one's ear** *infml* suddenly thrown out of a place because of bad behaviour **4 play it by ear** *infml* to act as conditions change rather than making plans in advance **5 up to one's ears in** *infml* deep in or very busy with: *I'm up to my ears in work*/*debt.* **6 -eared** having ears of a certain kind: *Rabbits are long-eared animals.*

**ear²** *n* the head of a grain-producing plant, used for food: *an ear of corn*/*wheat*

**ear·drum** /ˈɪədrʌm‖ˈɪər-/ *n* a tight thin skin inside the ear, which allows one to hear sound

**earl** /ɜːl‖ɜrl/ *n* [A;C *often cap.*] (the title of) a British nobleman of high rank: *the Earl of Warwick* –compare COUNT³, COUNTESS **–earldom** *n*

**ear·lobe** /ˈɪələʊb‖ˈɪər-/ *n* the fleshy bottom part of the EAR¹ (1)

**ear·ly¹** /ˈɜːli‖ˈɜrli/ *adj* **-lier, -liest 1** [after *n*] arriving, happening, etc., before the usual or expected time: *The train was 10 minutes early.* **2** [A *no comp.*] happening towards the beginning of the day, a period of time, etc.: *She returned in the early morning.*|*All the shops are shut in the afternoon on* **early closing (day).**|*I hope for an early answer to my letter.* –compare LATE¹ (1,2) **3 at the earliest** and not sooner: *The letter will reach him on Monday at the very earliest.* –opposite **at the latest –earliness** *n* [U]

**early²** *adv* **-lier, -liest 1** before the usual, arranged, or expected time: *He always arrives early.* **2** towards the beginning of a period: *The bush was planted early (on) in the season.* –compare LATE²

**ear·mark** /ˈɪəmɑːk‖ˈɪərmɑrk/ *v* [T] to set aside (money, etc.) for a particular purpose

**earn** /ɜːn‖ɜrn/ *v* [T *by*] **1** to get (money) by working: *He earns £3,000 a year (by writing stories).* **2** to get (something that one deserves) because of one's qualities or actions: *She earned her place in the team by training hard.* –see WIN¹ (USAGE)

**ear·nest¹** /ˈɜːnɪ̈st‖ˈɜr-/ *adj* determined and (too) serious: *John is a very earnest young man; he should be more cheerful.* **–earnestly** *adv* **–earnestness** *n* [U]

**earnest²** *n* [U] seriousness: *It soon began to snow* **in (real) earnest.** (=very hard)

**earn·ings** /ˈɜːnɪŋz‖ˈɜr-/ *n* [P] money which is earned by working

**ear·ring** /ˈɪəˌrɪŋ/ *n* a decoration worn on the ear –see PAIR¹ (USAGE)

**ear·shot** /ˈɪəʃɒt‖ˈɪərʃɑt/ *n* **within/out of earshot** within/beyond the distance at which a sound can be heard

**earth¹** /ɜːθ‖ɜrθ/ *n* **1** [*the* S;U] the world on which we live: *They returned from the moon to the earth.*|*the biggest lake on earth* **2** [U] soil in which plants grow: *He planted the seeds in earth.* –see LAND¹ (USAGE) **3** [C *usu. sing.*] *BrE*‖**ground** *AmE* (an additional safety wire which makes) a connection between an electrical apparatus and the ground **4** [C] the hole where certain wild animals live, esp. foxes: (fig.) *After searching everywhere, she* **ran him to earth** (=found him) *in the garden shed.* **5 on earth** *infml* (used for giving force to a question with *what, who,* etc.): *What on earth are you doing?* **6 cost/charge/pay the earth** to ask/pay a lot of money for something

**earth²** *BrE*‖**ground** *AmE v* [T] to make an electrical apparatus safer by connecting it to the ground with a wire

**earth·en·ware** /ˈɜːθənweəʳ, -ðən-‖ˈɜr-/ *n* [U] cups, dishes, pots, etc., made of baked clay

**earth·ly** /ˈɜːθli‖ˈɜrθli/ *adj* [A *no comp.*] **1** of this world as opposed to heaven; material: *earthly possessions* **2** [*used only in questions,* NEGATIVES², *etc.*] *infml* possible: *There's no earthly reason for me to go.*|*He hasn't an earthly (chance)* (=any hope) *of winning.*

**earth·quake** /ˈɜːθkweɪk‖ˈɜrθ-/ *n* a sudden usu. violent shaking of the earth's surface: *The town was destroyed by the earthquake.*

**earth·y** /ˈɜːθi‖ˈɜrθi/ *adj* **-ier, -iest** concerned with things of the body, not of the mind: *Peter has an earthy sense of humour; he likes rude jokes.* **–earthiness** *n* [U]

**ear·wig** /ˈɪəˌwɪg‖ˈɪər-/ *n* an insect with two curved parts on its tail

**ease¹** /iːz/ *n* [U] **1** the ability to do something without difficulty: *He jumped the wall* **with ease.** –compare EASILY (1) **2** the state of being comfortable and without worry or anxiety: *to lead a life of (the greatest) ease*|*Don't worry about meeting my father; I'm sure he'll* **put you at (your) ease. 3 ill at ease** worried and nervous **4 (stand) at ease** (*used as a military command*) (to stand) with feet apart –compare **at** ATTENTION (3)

**ease²** *v* **eased, easing 1** [I;T *off*] to make or become less severe: *I gave him some medicine to ease the pain.*|*The pain has eased (off).*|*I eased her mind by telling her that her children were safe.* **2** [I] to become less troublesome or difficult: *The relationship between the two countries has eased.* **3** [T] to cause (something) to move carefully, esp. slowly and gently: *The thief eased his body through the window.* **4** [T] to make looser: *The coat is too tight; it must be eased under the arms.*

**ease up/off** *v adv* [I *on*] *infml* to do (something) with less force: *It's time my father eased up (on his work) a bit; he's getting old.*

**ea·sel** /'i:zəl/ *n* a wooden frame to hold a BLACKBOARD, or to hold a picture while it is being painted

**eas·i·ly** /'i:zəli/ *adv* **1** without difficulty: *I can easily finish it today.* –see also EASE[1] (1), EASY[1] (1) **2** without doubt: *She is easily the cleverest girl in the class.*

**east[1]** /i:st/ *adv (often cap.)* towards the east: *The room faces East, so we get the morning sun.*

**east[2]** *n [the* S] *(often cap.)* **1** the direction in which the sun rises –compare EASTERN **2** one of the four main points of the compass, which is on the right of a person facing north **3** the eastern part **a** of the world, esp. Asia: *travelling in the Far East*–compare ORIENT **b** of a country: *the east of Britain*

**Eas·ter** /'i:stər/ *n* **1** the yearly feast-day when Christians remember Christ's death and his return to life **2** [A] happening at that time of the year: *the Easter holidays*

**eas·ter·ly** /'i:stəli‖-ərli/ *adj [no comp.]* **1** towards the east: *in an easterly direction* **2** (of a wind) coming from the east

**east·ern** /'i:stən‖-ərn/ *adj (often cap.)* of or belonging to the east part of the world or of a country

**east·ward** /'i:stwəd‖-ərd/ *adj [no comp.]* going towards the east: *an eastward journey* **–eastwards**‖also **eastward** *AmE– adv: to sail eastwards*

**eas·y[1]** /'i:zi/ *adj* **- ier, -iest** [+*to-v*] **1** not difficult: *an easy book*|*John is easy to please.* (=it is not difficult to please him) –opposite **hard**; see also EASE[1] (1), EASILY (1) **2** comfortable and without worry or anxiety: *He has stopped working now, and leads a very easy life.*|*with an easy mind*–see also EASE[1] (2) **3 I'm easy** *infml* I don't mind at all **–easiness** *n* [U]

**easy[2]** *adv* **-ier, -iest 1 easier said than done** harder to do than to talk about: *Passing examinations is much easier said than done.* **2 go easy on** *infml* **a** to be kinder to (someone) **b** not to use too much of (something): *Go easy on the salt in the soup.* **3 take it/things easy** not to work too hard

**easy chair** /'·· ,·/ *n* a big comfortable chair with arms

**eas·y·go·ing** /,i:zi'gəuɪŋ◂/ *adj* taking life easily: *He's an easygoing person; he never gets angry.*

**eat** /i:t/ *v* **ate** /et, eɪt‖eɪt/, **eaten** /'i:tn/, **eating 1** [T *up*] to take (food) into the mouth and swallow it in order to feed the body: *Eat your dinner!*|*Tigers eat meat.*|(fig.) *A big car eats up money.* **2** [I] to have a meal: *What time do we eat?* **3** [I;T *away, into*] to damage or destroy (something), esp. by chemical action: *The acid ate away/ate a hole in/ate into the metal.* **4 be eaten up with** to be completely and violently full of (jealousy, desire, etc.) **5 eat one's words** to admit to having said something wrong **6 eat out of someone's hand** *infml* to be very willing to obey or agree with someone

**eat into** sthg. *v prep* [T] to use part of: *Our holiday has eaten into the money we saved.* –compare EAT (3)

**ea·ta·ble** /'i:təbəl/ *adj* (of food) in a fit condition to be eaten

USAGE Compare **eatable** and **edible**: Something is **edible** if it can be used as food; food is **eatable** if it is fresh, nicely prepared, etc.: *Are these berries* **edible,** *or are they poisonous?*|*The food at my school is so bad it's* **uneatable**/*hardly* **eatable.**

**eat·er** /'i:tər/ *n* a person who eats in a certain way: *He's a big eater.* (=he eats a lot)

**eau de co·logne** /,əu də kə'ləun/ *n* [U] →COLOGNE

**eaves** /i:vz/ *n* [P] the edges of a roof which come out beyond the walls: *birds nesting under the eaves*

**eaves·drop** /'i:vzdrɒp‖-drɑp/ *v* **-pp-** [I *on*] to listen secretly (to other people's conversation) **–eavesdropper** *n*

**ebb[1]** /eb/ *n* [U] **1** the flow of the sea away from the shore; the going out of the TIDE (1): *The tide is on the ebb.* –compare FLOW[2] (5) **2 at a low ebb** in a low state: *Business is at rather a low ebb.*

**ebb[2]** *v* [I *away*] (of the sea) to flow away from the shore: (fig.) *His strength slowly ebbed away.* (=grew less)

**eb·o·ny** /'ebəni/ *n, adj* [U] (having the colour of) a hard black wood

**e·bul·li·ent** /ɪ'bʌlɪənt, ɪ'bu-/ *adj fml or lit* full of happiness and excitement: –compare EXUBERANT **–ebullience** *n* [U]

**ec·cen·tric[1]** /ɪk'sentrɪk/ *adj* (of a person or his/her behaviour) peculiar; unusual; rather strange: *The old lady has some eccentric habits.* **–eccentrically** *adv* **–eccentricity** /,eksen'trɪsəti, -sən-/ *n* **-ties** [C;U]

**eccentric[2]** *n* an ECCENTRIC person

**ec·cle·si·as·ti·cal** /ɪ,kli:zi'æstɪkəl/ also **ecclesiastic**– *adj* connected with a Christian church: *ecclesiastical history/music*

**ech·o[1]** /'ekəu/ *n* **-oes** a sound sent back or repeated, e.g. from a wall or inside a cave

**echo[2]** *v* **-oed, -oing** [I;T *with, to*] to (cause to) come back as an ECHO: *Their voices echoed round the cave.*|*The room echoed with the sound of music.*|(fig.) *She echoes* (=repeats) *everything I say.*

**é·clair** /ɪ'kleər, eɪ-/ *n* a finger-shaped pastry with cream inside

**e·clipse[1]** /ɪ'klɪps/ *n* **1** [C] the disappearance, complete or in part, of the sun's light when the moon passes between it and the earth **2** [C;U] the loss of fame, power, success, etc.

**eclipse[2]** *v* **-clipsed, -clipsing** [T] **1** to cause an ECLIPSE[1] (1): *The moon is partly eclipsed.* **2** to do or be much better than; make (someone or something) lose fame: *She is quite eclipsed by her clever sister*

**e·col·o·gy** /ɪ'kɒlədʒi‖ɪ'kɑ-/ *n* [U] (the scientific study of) the pattern of the natural relations of plants, animals, and people to each other and to their surroundings **–ecologist** *n* **–ecological** /,i:kə'lɒdʒɪkəl‖-'lɑ-/ *adj* **–ecologically** *adv*

**ec·o·nom·ic** /,ek'nɒmɪk, i:-‖-'nɑ-/ *adj [no comp.]* **1** [A] connected with trade, industry, and wealth; of or concerning ECONOMICS: *The country is in a bad economic state.* **2** profitable: *She sold her house at an economic price.* –Compare: *The railway service to our village is no longer* **economic.** (=it is losing money)|*For most people in the village, it is more* **economical** (=it costs less) *to travel by car.* –opposite **uneconomic** (for **2**)

**ec·o·nom·i·cal** /,ekə'nɒmɪkəl, ,i:- ‖-'nɑ-/ *adj* using money, time, goods, etc., without waste: *A small car is more economical than a large one, because it uses less petrol.*

**ec·o·nom·i·cally** /ˌekəˈnɒmɪkli, ˌiː-‖-ˈnɑ-/ *adv* **1** not wastefully: *She cooks very economically.* –compare EXTRAVAGANTly **2** in a way which is connected with ECONOMICS

**ec·o·nom·ics** /ˌekəˈnɒmɪks, ˌiː-‖-ˈnɑ-/ *n* [P;U] the science or principles of the way in which industry and trade produce and use wealth **–economist** /ɪˈkɒnəmɨst‖ɪˈkɑ-/ *n*

**e·con·o·mize** ‖also **-mise** *BrE* /ɪˈkɒnəmaɪz‖ɪˈkɑ-/ *v* **-mized, -mizing** [I;T] to save (money, time, goods, etc.); to avoid waste: *to economize on petrol* –see also ECONOMICAL

**e·con·o·my¹** /ɪˈkɒnəmi‖ɪˈkɑ-/ *n* **-mies 1** [C;U] (an example of) the careful use of money, time, etc.: *economy of effort* –see also ECONOMICAL **2** [C] the ECONOMIC (1) life or system of a country; operation of a country's money supply, industry, and trade

**economy²** *adj* [A] cheap; intended to save money: *An* **economy class** *air ticket costs much less.*|*We had an* **economy drive** (=we all tried to spend less) *in order to save money for our holiday.*

**ec·sta·sy** /ˈekstəsi/ *n* **-sies** [C;U] a state of very strong feeling, esp. of happiness: *in an ecstasy of joy/delight*

**ec·stat·ic** /ɪkˈstætɪk, ek-/ *adj* causing or experiencing ECSTASY, esp. feeling very happy **–ecstatically** *adv*

**e·cu·men·i·cal, oecu-** /ˌiːkjʊˈmenɪkəl‖ˌekjə-/ *adj* favouring, or tending towards, Christian unity all over the world

**ec·ze·ma** /ˈeksɨmə‖ˈeksɨmə, ˈegzɨmə, ɪgˈziːmə/ *n* [U] a red swollen condition of the skin

**ed·dy** /ˈedi/ *n* **-dies** a circular movement of water, dust, smoke, etc.

**E·den** /ˈiːdn/ *n* (in the Bible) the garden where Adam and Eve lived before their disobedience to God

**edge¹** /edʒ/ *n* **1** the thin sharp cutting part of a blade, tool, etc.: **2** the part along the outside of something: *the edge of a plate*|*Can you stand a coin up* **on its edge?**|*the water's edge* –compare LIMIT¹ **3 have the edge on** to be better than; have an advantage over **4 on edge** nervous; EDGY **5 -edged** having a certain kind or number of edges: *a two-edged knife*

**edge²** *v* **edged, edging 1** [T *with*] to place an edge or border on: *a white handkerchief edged with blue* **2** [I;T] to (cause to) move sideways little by little: *He edged (himself/his way) to the front of the crowd.*

**edge·ways** /ˈedʒweɪz/ also **edgewise** /-waɪz/– *adv* **1** in the direction of the edge; sideways **2 get a word in edgeways** (used only in NEGATIVES² questions, etc.) *infml* to get a chance to speak when someone else is speaking

**edg·ing** /ˈedʒɪŋ/ *n* [C;U] something that forms an edge or border

**edg·y** /ˈedʒi/ *adj* **-ier, -iest** *infml* nervous: *She's been a bit edgy lately, waiting for the examination results.*

**ed·i·ble** /ˈedɨbəl/ *adj* fit to be eaten; eatable: *the difference between edible and poisonous berries* –opposite **inedible**; see EATABLE (USAGE)

**e·dict** /ˈiːdɪkt/ *n fml* (in former times) an official public order; DECREE

**ed·i·fice** /ˈedɨfɨs/ *n fml* a large fine building

**ed·i·fy** /ˈedɨfaɪ/ *v* **-fied, -fying** [T] *fml* to improve (the character or mind of): *He read edifying books to improve his mind.* **–edification** /-fɪˈkeɪʃən/ *n* [U]

**ed·it** /ˈedɨt/ *v* [T] to prepare a book, newspaper, film, etc., for printing or showing

**e·di·tion** /ɪˈdɪʃən/ *n* one printing, esp. of a book: *a* **paper-back** *edition* (=in paper covers)|*a* **hard-back** *edition* (=in hard cardboard covers)

**ed·i·tor** /ˈedɨtəʳ/ *n* a person who EDITs

**ed·i·to·ri·al¹** /ˌedɨˈtɔːrɪəl‖-ˈtor-/ *adj* of an EDITOR: *an editorial office* **–editorially** *adv*

**editorial²** ‖also **leader, leading article** *BrE*– *n* a part of a newspaper giving an opinion on a problem or event, rather than news

**ed·u·cate** /ˈedjʊkeɪt‖ˈedʒə-/ *v* **-cated, -cating** [T] to teach; train the character or mind of: *He was educated at a very good school.* **–educated** *adj*

**ed·u·ca·tion** /ˌedjʊˈkeɪʃən‖ˌedʒə-/ *n* [S;U] teaching or the training of mind and character: *She has had a good education.*

**ed·u·ca·tion·al** /ˌedjʊˈkeɪʃənəl‖ˌedʒə-/ *adj* of, about, or providing education: *an educational establishment/film* **–educationally** *adv*

**ed·u·ca·tion·ist** /ˌedjʊˈkeɪʃənɨst‖ˌedʒə-/ also **educationalist**– *n* a specialist in education

**EEC** *abbrev. for:* European Economic Community; a West European political and ECONOMIC organization established to encourage trade and friendly relations between its member countries: *to join the EEC*

**eel** /iːl/ *n* a long snake-like fish

**e'er** /eəʳ/ *adv lit short for:* EVER

**ee·rie** /ˈɪəri/ *adj* causing fear because strange: *walking through the dark, eerie woods* **–eerily** *adv* **–eeriness** *n* [U]

**ef·face** /ɪˈfeɪs/ *v* **-faced, -facing** [T] *fml* to rub out; destroy the surface of –see also SELF-EFFACING

**ef·fect¹** /ɪˈfekt/ *n* [C;U] **1** a result: *the effects of an illness*|*One of the effects of bad weather is a poor crop.* **2 in effect: a** in operation: *The rules will remain in effect until October.* **b** for all practical purposes: *Although he is her employer, she has, in effect, full control.* **3 into effect** into operation: *The rule will come/be brought/be put/go into effect on Monday.* **4 take effect** to come into operation; start to have results

**effect²** *v* [T] *fml* to cause, produce, or have as a result: *She effected several changes in the company.* –see AFFECT¹ (USAGE)

**ef·fec·tive** /ɪˈfektɪv/ *adj* **1** producing the desired result: *His efforts to improve the school have been very effective.* –opposite **ineffective** **2** [*no comp.*] actual; real: *Although there is a parliament, the army is in effective control of the country.* –compare EFFICACIOUS, EFFICIENT **–effectively** *adv* **–effectiveness** *n*

**ef·fects** /ɪˈfekts/ *n* [P] *fml or law* belongings; personal property: *He died poor, and left no (personal) effects.*

**ef·fec·tu·al** /ɪˈfektʃʊəl/ *adj fml* (of actions) producing the results intended; effective –opposite **ineffectual** **–effectually** *adv*

**ef·fem·i·nate** /ɨˈfemɨnɨt/ *adj derog* (of a man or his behaviour) having qualities often thought to be usual in women; soft; weak **–effeminately** *adv* **–effeminacy** *n* [U]

**ef·fer·vesce** /ˌefəˈves‖ˌefər-/ *v* **-vesced, -vescing** [I] *fml or tech* (of a liquid) to have bubbles forming inside; bubble **–effervescence** *n* [U] **–effervescent** *adj*

**ef·fi·ca·cious** /ˌefᵻ'keɪʃəs/ *adj fml* (esp. of medicines) producing the desired effect –compare EFFECTIVE, EFFICIENT **–efficacy** /'efᵻkəsi/ [U]

**ef·fi·cient** /ɪ'fɪʃənt/ *adj* working well, quickly, and without waste: *She is a quick, efficient worker.|This new machine is more efficient than the old one.* –Compare: *an* **efficient** *secretary* (=who does his/her job well)|*an* **effective** *medicine* (=which produces the desired result) –opposite **inefficient** **–efficiently** *adv* **–efficiency** *n* [U]: *attempts to improve efficiency*

**ef·fi·gy** /'efᵻdʒi/ *n* **-gies** *fml* a wooden, stone, etc., likeness of a person: *an effigy of Christ*

**ef·flu·ent** /'efluənt/ *n* [C;U] *tech* (a type of) liquid waste that flows out from a factory, etc.: *Dangerous effluent is being poured into our rivers.*

**ef·fort** /'efət‖'efərt/ *n* [C;U +*to-v*] (an example of) the use of strength; trying hard: *He lifted the heavy box* **without effort.**|*The prisoner* **made no effort** *to escape* (=did not try to escape)

**ef·fort·less** /'efətlᵻs‖'efərt-/ *adj* seeming to need or make no effort, yet very good: *He is a skilful and effortless player.* **–effortlessly** *adv* **–effortlessness** *n* [U]

**ef·fron·te·ry** /ɪ'frʌntəri/ *n* [U +*to-v*] bold rudeness without any sense of shame: *You crashed my car and now you have the effrontery to ask me for my bicycle!*

**ef·fu·sive** /ɪ'fjuːsɪv/ *adj often derog* showing too much feeling: *Her effusive welcome was not sincere.* **–effusively** *adv* **–effusiveness** *n* [U]

**e.g.** /ˌiː 'dʒi/ *abbrev. for:* Latin exempli gratia (=for example): *sweet foods, e.g. cake, chocolate, sugar, and ice cream*

**e·gal·i·tar·i·an** /ɪˌgælᵻ'teərɪən/ *adj* having the belief that all people are equal and should have equal rights **–egalitarianism** *n* [U]

**egg¹** /eg/ *n* **1** [C] a rounded object with a hard shell, which comes out of a female bird, snake, etc., and which contains a baby animal before it is born (HATCHed): *This hen lays beautiful brown eggs.* **2** [C;U] this when eaten as food: *I had a boiled egg for breakfast.|The baby had egg all over his face|A dozen* (=twelve) *eggs, please.* **3** [C] the seed of life inside a female, which joins with the male seed (SPERM) to make a baby –see FERTILIZE, OVUM **4 put all one's eggs in one basket** *infml* to depend completely on the success of one thing

**egg²** *v* →EGG ON

**egg·head** /'eghed/ *n usu. derog* a person who is (too) highly educated; HIGHBROW

**egg** sbdy.↔**on** *v adv* [T] to encourage strongly: *They egged me on to throw a stone through the window.*

**egg·plant** /'egplɑːnt‖'egplænt/ ‖also **aubergine** *BrE– n* [C;U] (a plant having) a large purple fruit that is eaten as a vegetable

**e·go** /'iːgəʊ, 'egəʊ/ *n* **egos** the way in which a person sees and feels about himself/herself: *Success is good for one's ego.*

**e·go·cen·tric** /ˌiːgəʊ'sentrɪk, ˌe-/ *adj derog* selfish; thinking only about (one)self

**e·go·is·m** /'iːgəʊɪzəm, 'e-/ *n* [U] *derog* the quality of always thinking about oneself; selfishness –compare EGOTISM, ALTRUISM **–egoist** *n* **–egoistic** /-'ɪstɪk/ *adj* **–egoistical** *adj*

**eg·o·tis·m** /'egətɪzəm, 'iː-‖'iː-/ *n* [U] *derog* the quality of talking too much about oneself –compare EGOISM **–egotist** *n* **–egotistic** /-'tɪstɪk/ *adj* **–egotistical** *adj*

**ei·der·down** /'aɪdədaʊn‖-dər-/ *n* a thick warm bed covering filled with feathers (DOWN⁵)

**eight** /eɪt/ *determiner,n,pron* (the number) 8 **–eighth** /eɪtθ/ *determiner,n,pron,adv*

**eigh·teen** /eɪ'tiːn◂/ *determiner,n,pron* (the number) 18 **–eighteenth** *determiner,n,pron,adv*

**eigh·ty** /'eɪti/ *determiner,n,pron* **-ties** (the number) 80 **–eightieth** /'eɪtiᵻθ/ *determiner,n,pron,adv*

**ei·ther¹** /'aɪðəʳ‖'iː-/ *determiner,pron* **1** one or the other of two: *There's coffee or tea–you can have either.|Are/Is either of the boys coming?* –compare ANY¹; see also NEITHER¹ **2** one and the other of two; each: *He sat in the car with a policeman on either side of him.*

USAGE When **either, neither, none,** or **any** are used as PRONOUNs and followed by a plural, they usually take a singular verb in formal writing: **None/Neither** *of the boys has passed the examination.|Is* **any** *of these substances safe to eat?* In speech, however, a plural verb is usually used, and this is quite acceptable: *Have* **any/either** *of you seen this film before?|***Neither/None** *of us enjoy getting up early.*

**either²** *conj* (used to begin a list of possibilities separated by *or): The baby will be either a boy or a girl.|Either say you're sorry or (else) get out!|It's either red, blue, or green–I can't remember.*

USAGE **either ... or** and **neither ... nor** are usually followed by a plural verb: *If either David or Janet come, they will want a drink.* It is more formal to use the singular: *If either David or Janet comes, he or she will want a drink.*

**either³** *adv* (*used with* NEGATIVE² *expressions*) also; besides: *I haven't read this book, and my brother hasn't either.* (=both haven't read it)|*"I can't swim!" "I can't, either!"/"Neither can I!"* (=I, too, am unable to swim)

**e·jac·u·late** /ɪ'dʒækjʊleɪt‖-kjə-/ *v* **-lated, -lating** [I;T] **1** *fml* to cry out or say (something) suddenly **2** to throw out suddenly and with force from the body (esp. the male seed (SPERM)) **–ejaculation** /-'leɪʃən/ *n* [C;U]

**e·ject** /ɪ'dʒekt/ *v* [T *from*] *fml* to throw out with force: *The police came and ejected the noisy youths from the restaurant.* **–ejection** /ɪ'dʒekʃən/ *n* [C;U]

**eke** sthg. ↔ **out** /iːk/ *v adv* **eked, eking** [T *with, by*] **1** to cause (a small supply) to last longer: *She eked out her small income by cleaning other people's houses.* **2 eke out a living** to make just enough money to live

**e·lab·o·rate¹** /ɪ'læbərət/ *adj* full of detail; carefully worked out and with a large number of parts: *an elaborate plan/pattern* **–elaborately** *adv*

**elaborate²** /ɪ'læbəreɪt/ *v* **-rated, -rating** [I;T *on*] to add more detail to (something): *Just tell us the facts; don't elaborate (on them).* **–elaboration** /-'reɪʃən/ *n* [C;U]

**e·lapse** /ɪ'læps/ *v* **-lapsed, -lapsing** [I] *fml* (of time) to pass away: *Three months have elapsed since he left home.*

**e·las·tic¹** /ɪ'læstɪk/ *adj* (of material such as rubber) able to spring back into shape after being stretched:

an elastic band|(fig.) *The rules are elastic.* (=not fixed) –**elasticity** /ˌiːlæˈstɪsəti, ɪˌlæ-/ n [U]

**elastic²** *n* [U] (a piece of) ELASTIC material

**elastic band** /ˌ·· ˈ·/ *n BrE* for RUBBER BAND

**e·lat·ed** /ɪˈleɪtəd/ *adj* [+*to-v*/*that*/*at*] filled with pride and joy: *The crowds were elated by the news.* –**elation** *n* [U]

**el·bow¹** /ˈelbəʊ/ *n* the joint where the arm bends, esp. the outer point of this –see picture on page 299

**elbow²** *v* [T] to push with the elbows: *He elbowed his way through the crowd.*

**el·bow·room** /ˈelbəʊrʊm, -ruːm/ *n* [U] space in which to move freely

**el·der¹** /ˈeldəʳ/ *adj* [A] (of people, esp. in a family) older, esp. the older of two: *my elder brother* (=I have one brother, who is older than I am)|*My elder daughter is married.* (=I have two daughters)

USAGE Compare **elder** and **older**: **Older** is used of people or things, but **elder** is only used of people, and can never be used in comparisons: *Jane is Mary's* **elder** *sister.*|*Jane is* **older** *than* (not ***elder** *than*) *Mary.*

**elder²** *n* **1** the older of two people: *Which is the elder (of the two sisters)?*|*Shouldn't we respect* **our elders?** (=older people) **2** a person holding a respected official position: *a Church elder*|*an elder* STATESMAN

**elder³** *n* a small tree with white flowers and red or black berries

**el·der·ly** /ˈeldəli||ˈeldərli/ *adj* [*no comp.*] (of a person) getting near old age

**el·dest** /ˈeldəst/ *adj,n* (a person who is) oldest of three or more: *She has three children, and her eldest has just started school.*

**e·lect¹** /ɪˈlekt/ *v* [T] **1** [*as, to*] to choose (someone) by voting: *They elected Reagan (as) President.*|*to elect a new member to the committee* **2** [+*to-v*] *fml* to decide (to do something important): *She elected to return to work after her baby was born.*

**elect²** *adj* [after *n*] *fml* chosen, but not yet at work: *the president elect*

**e·lec·tion** /ɪˈlekʃən/ *n* [C;U] (an example of) the choosing of representatives for a (political) position by vote: *to call a general election*|*the election results* –**elector** /ɪˈlektəʳ||-tər, -tɔr/ *n* –**electoral** *adj* [A]: *the electoral system*

**e·lec·to·rate** /ɪˈlektərət/ *n* [C +*sing./pl.v*] all the people in a country who have the right to vote: *The British electorate is/are voting today.*

**e·lec·tric** /ɪˈlektrɪk/ *adj* **1** [*usu.* A] producing or worked by electricity: *an electric clock*|*electric power* **2** very exciting: *His speech had an electric effect on the crowd; they all cheered him.* –**electrically** *adv*

USAGE Anything directly worked by or producing electricity is **electric**: *an* **electric** *clock/shock/light/*GENERATOR. Otherwise, the word is **electrical,** which is a more general expression, used of people and their work or of things: *an* **electrical** *engineer/an* **electrical** *apparatus/an* **electrical** *fault in the system.* –see also ELECTRONIC

**e·lec·tri·cal** /ɪˈlektrɪkəl/ *adj* [A] concerned with or using electricity: *an electrical* ENGINEER|*an electrical fault* –see ELECTRIC (USAGE) –**electrically** *adv*

**electric chair** /ˌ·· ˈ·/ also **chair** *infml*– *n* [*the* S] a punishment of death, in some states of the US, in which electricity is passed through a person's body to kill him/her –see also ELECTROCUTE

**el·ec·tri·cian** /ɪˌlekˈtrɪʃən/ *n* a person whose job is to fit and repair electrical apparatus

**e·lec·tri·ci·ty** /ɪˌlekˈtrɪsəti/ *n* [U] the power which is produced by various means (e.g. by a BATTERY (1) or GENERATOR) and which provides heat and light, drives machines, etc.

**e·lec·tri·fy** /ɪˈlektrəfaɪ/ *v* **-fied, -fying** [T] **1** to pass an electric current through (something) **2** to change (something) to a system using electric power: *The national railways have now been electrified.* **3** to excite greatly: *The band gave an electrifying performance.* –**electrification** /-fɪˈkeɪʃən/ *n* [U]

**e·lec·tro·cute** /ɪˈlektrəkjuːt/ *v* **-cuted, -cuting** [T] to kill by passing electricity through the body –**electrocution** /-ˈkjuːʃən/ *n* [C;U]

**e·lec·trode** /ɪˈlektrəʊd/ *n* either of the two points (the TERMINALS² (2)) at which the current enters and leaves a BATTERY (1), or other electrical apparatus

**e·lec·tron** /ɪˈlektrɒn||-trɑn/ *n* one of the parts of an atom; "bit" of NEGATIVE¹ (3) electricity –see also PROTON, NEUTRON

**e·lec·tron·ics** /ɪˌlekˈtrɒnɪks||- ˈtrɑ-/ *n* [U] the branch of industry that makes products like radios, televisions, and recording apparatus –**electronic** *adj*: *an electronic watch*|*electronic music*

**el·e·gant** /ˈelɪgənt/ *adj apprec* having the qualities of grace and beauty; stylish: *an elegant woman*|*elegant manners*|*an elegant piece of furniture* –opposite **inelegant** –**elegantly** *adv* –**elegance** *n* [S;U]

**el·e·gy** /ˈeləd͡ʒi/ *n* **-gies** a poem or song written esp. to show sorrow for the dead –compare EULOGY

**el·e·ment** /ˈeləmənt/ *n* **1** [C] any of certain simple substances that, alone or in combination, make up all substances: HYDROGEN *and oxygen are elements, but water, which is formed when they combine, is not.* **2** [S] a small amount: *There is an element of truth in what you say.* **3** [C] a part of a whole: *Honesty is an important element in anyone's character.* **4** [C] the heating part of a piece of electrical apparatus **5 in one's element** doing what one is most happy doing

**el·e·men·tal** /ˌeləˈmentl/ *adj* of or like a great force of nature: *the elemental violence of the storm* –see also ELEMENTS

**el·e·men·ta·ry** /ˌeləˈmentəri/ *adj* **1** simple and easy **2** concerned with the beginnings, esp. of education and study: *some elementary English exercises for the learner*

**el·e·ments** /ˈeləmənts/ *n* [*the* P] **1** the beginnings; the first steps in a subject **2** *lit* the weather, esp. bad weather: *He walked on even though the elements were against him.* –see also ELEMENTAL

**el·e·phant** /ˈeləfənt/ *n* **-phants** *or* **-phant** a very large animal, with two long curved teeth (TUSKS) and a long nose called a TRUNK

**el·e·vate** /ˈeləveɪt/ *v* **-vated, -vating** [T] **1** to make (the mind, soul, etc.) better, higher, or more educated: *an elevating book* **2** *fml* to raise: *He was elevated to the rank of captain.*

**el·e·va·tion** /ˌeləˈveɪʃən/ *n* **1** [U] *fml* the act of being ELEVATED: *elevation to the rank of a lord* **2** [S] height above sea-level: *Their house is at an elevation of 2,000 metres.* –compare ALTITUDE **3** [C] (a drawing of) a flat upright side of a building: *the front elevation of a house* –compare PLAN[1] (2), PERSPECTIVE

**el·e·va·tor** /ˈeləveɪtər/ *n AmE* for LIFT[2] (3)

**e·lev·en** /ɪˈlevən/ *determiner,n,pron* **1** (the number) 11 **2** [C +*sing./pl.v*] a team of eleven players in football, cricket, etc.: *The school football eleven is/are playing tomorrow.* –**eleventh** *determiner,n, pron,adv*

**elf** /elf/ *n* **elves** /elvz/ a small fairy with pointed ears –**elfin** /ˈelfən/ *adj*

**e·li·cit** /ɪˈlɪsət/ *v* [T *from*] *fml* to get, draw out (facts, information, etc.): *After much questioning, he elicited the truth.* –sounds like **illicit**

**el·i·gi·ble** /ˈelədʒəbəl/ *adj* **1** [F +*to-v/as, for*] having the right (esp. by law) to do, receive, etc. (something): *He will become eligible to vote on his next birthday.|Is she eligible for sickness pay?* **2** suitable to be chosen: *I know an eligible young man who would be an excellent husband for Jane.* –**eligibility** /-ˈbɪləti/ *n* [U] –**eligibly** *adv*

**e·lim·i·nate** /ɪˈlɪməneɪt/ *v* **-nated, -nating** [T *from*] to remove or get rid of: *to eliminate people from the competition* –**elimination** /-ˈneɪʃən/ *n* [U]

**e·lite** /eɪˈliːt, ɪ-/ *n* [C +*sing./pl.v*] *often derog* the most powerful or cleverest people in a group: *a country controlled by an elite*

**e·lit·is·m** /eɪˈliːtɪzəm, ɪ-/ *n* [U] (belief in) leadership or rule by an ELITE –**elitist** *adj,n*

**e·lix·ir** /ɪˈlɪksər/ *n* [C;U] *lit* an imaginary liquid having the power to make life last for ever

**elk** /elk/ *BrE*‖**moose** *AmE n* **elks** *or* **elk** a very large deer, with big flat ANTLERS (branching horns)

**el·lip·tical** /ɪˈlɪptɪkəl/ also **elliptic**– *adj* having the curved shape of a circle when one looks at it sideways; OVAL: *The Earth's path round the sun is elliptical.* –**elliptically** *adv*

**elm** /elm/ *n* [C;U] (the hard heavy wood of) a large tall broad-leaved tree

**el·o·cu·tion** /ˌeləˈkjuːʃən/ *n* [U] the art of good clear speaking in public

**e·lon·gate** /ˈiːlɒŋgeɪt‖ɪˈlɔŋ-/ *v* **-gated, -gating** [T] to make (a material thing) longer: *This picture that you've painted isn't like me. The face is too elongated.* –**elongation** /-ˈgeɪʃən/ *n* [C;U]

**e·lope** /ɪˈləʊp/ *v* **-loped, -loping** [I *with*] (of lovers) to run away secretly usu. with the intention of getting married: *They eloped last week.* –**elopement** *n* [C;U]

**el·o·quent** /ˈeləkwənt/ *adj fml* (of a person or speech) able to express ideas and opinions well, so that the hearers are influenced: *an eloquent speaker/speech* –**eloquently** *adv* –**eloquence** *n* [U]

**else** /els/ *adv* **1** besides; also: *What else* (=what more) *can I say?|There's nothing else to eat.* **2** apart from that; otherwise: *Everybody else but me* (=all the other people) *has gone to the party.|She was wearing someone else's coat.* (=not her own coat)*|He must pay £100* **or else** *go to prison.*

**else·where** /elsˈweər, ˈelsweər‖ˈelsweər/ *adv* in or to another place; somewhere else: *This hotel is full. We must look for rooms elsewhere.*

**e·lu·ci·date** /ɪˈluːsədeɪt/ *v* **-dated, -dating** [T] *fml* to explain or make clear (a difficulty or mystery): *Please elucidate the reasons for your decision.* –**elucidation** /-ˈdeɪʃən/ *n* [C;U]

**e·lude** /ɪˈluːd/ *v* **-luded, -luding** [T] to escape from, esp. by means of a trick: (fig.) *His name eludes me for the moment.* (=I can't remember it)

**e·lu·sive** /ɪˈluːsɪv/ *adj* difficult to catch, find, or remember: *I've been trying all day to reach him on the telephone, but he's very elusive.* –**elusively** *adv* –**elusiveness** *n* [U]

**elves** /elvz/ *n pl. of* ELF

**'em** /əm/ *pron infml* for THEM

**e·ma·ci·at·ed** /ɪˈmeɪʃieɪtəd/ *adj* very thin, as a result of illness or lack of food –see THIN[1] (USAGE) –**emaciation** /ɪˌmeɪsiˈeɪʃən/ *n* [U]

**em·a·nate from** sthg. /ˈeməneɪt/ *v prep* **-nated, -nating** [T *no pass.*] *fml* to come (out) from: *The idea emanated from a discussion we had.* –**emanation** /-ˈneɪʃən/ *n* [C;U]

**e·man·ci·pate** /ɪˈmænsəpeɪt/ *v* **-pated, -pating** [T *from*] to make free socially, politically, and in law –**emancipation** /-ˈpeɪʃən/ *n*: *the emancipation of women*

**em·balm** /ɪmˈbɑːm/ *v* [T] to treat (a dead body) with chemicals, oils, etc., to prevent decay –**embalmer** *n*

**em·bank·ment** /ɪmˈbæŋkmənt/ *n* a wide earth wall, which is built to stop a river overflowing, or to carry a road or railway over low ground

**em·bar·go[1]** /ɪmˈbɑːgəʊ‖-ɑr-/ *n* **-goes** an official order forbidding trade: *to put/lay an oil embargo on an enemy country*

**embargo[2]** *v* **-goed, - going** [T] to put an EMBARGO on (something)

**em·bark** /ɪmˈbɑːk‖-ɑrk/ *v* [I;T] to go, put, or take on a ship: *We embarked at Southampton, and* **disembarked** *in New York a week later.* –**embarkation** /ˌembɑːˈkeɪʃən‖-ɑr-/ *n* [C;U]

**embark on/upon** sthg. *v prep* [T] to start (something new): *to embark on a new way of life*

**em·bar·rass** /ɪmˈbærəs/ *v* [T] to cause to feel ashamed, uncomfortable, or anxious: *I don't like making speeches in public; it's so embarrassing.* –**embarrassment** *n* [C;U]: *a rude child, who was an embarrassment to his parents|He could not hide his embarrassment.*

**em·bas·sy** /ˈembəsi/ *n* **-sies** (the official building of) a group of officers, usu. led by an AMBASSADOR, who are sent by a government to live in a foreign country and keep good relations with its government –compare CONSULATE

**em·bed** /ɪmˈbed/ *v* **-dd-** [T *in, with*] to fix (something) firmly and deeply: (fig.) *That terrible day will be embedded in my memory.*

**em·bel·lish** /ɪmˈbelɪʃ/ *v* [T *with*] to make more beautiful: (fig.) *Tell the truth; don't embellish the story.* –see DECORATE (USAGE) –**embellishment** *n* [C;U]

**em·ber** /ˈembər/ *n* [*usu. pl.*] a red-hot piece of wood or coal, esp. in a fire that is no longer burning with flames

**em·bez·zle** /ɪmˈbezəl/ *v* **-zled, -zling** [I;T] to steal (money that is placed in one's care): *The clerk embezzled a thousand pounds from the bank where he worked.* –**embezzlement** *n* [U] –**embezzler** *n*

**em·bit·ter** /ɪmˈbɪtər/ *v* [T] to fill with painful or bitter feelings

**em·blem** /ˈembləm/ *n* [*of*] an object which is the sign of something: *The national emblem of England is a rose.* –compare SYMBOL –**emblematic** /ˌemblə'mætɪk/ *adj*

**em·bod·y** /ɪm'bɒdi‖ɪm'bɑdi/ *v* **-ied, -ying** [T] **1** to express: *The letter embodied all his ideas.* **2** to contain or include: *The new car embodies many improvements.* –**embodiment** *n*: *The new factory is the embodiment of the very latest ideas.*

**em·boss** /ɪm'bɒs‖ɪm'bɑs, -'bɔs/ *v* [T *on, with*] to decorate (metal, paper, etc.) with a raised pattern: *The name and address of the firm are embossed on its paper.*

**em·brace**[1] /ɪm'breɪs/ *v* **-braced, -bracing 1** [I;T] to take and hold (another or each other) in the arms as a sign of love: *She embraced her son tenderly.*|*The two sisters embraced.* **2** [T] *fml* to contain or include: *a course of study embracing several different subjects* **3** [T] *fml* to become a believer in

**embrace**[2] *n* the act of embracing (EMBRACE[1] (1))

**em·broi·der** /ɪm'brɔɪdə$^r$/ *v* [I;T *with, in, on*] to do decorative needlework on (cloth): *a dress embroidered with flowers in silk thread*

**em·broi·der·y** /ɪm'brɔɪdəri/ *n* [U] the act or result of EMBROIDERing: *embroidery on a dress*

**em·broil** /ɪm'brɔɪl/ *v* [T] to cause (oneself or another) to join in something troublesome: *to get embroiled in an argument*

**em·bry·o** /'embriəʊ/ *n* **-os** the young of any creature in its first state before it is born –compare FOETUS –**embryonic** /-'ɒnɪk‖-'ɑnɪk/ *adj*

**em·e·rald** /'emərəld/ *adj,n* [C;U] (the colour of) a bright green precious stone

**e·merge** /ɪ'mɜːdʒ‖-ɜr-/ *v* **-merged, -merging** [I] **1** [*from, out of*] to come or appear (from/out of somewhere): *The sun emerged from behind the clouds.* **2** [*from*] to become known as a result of inquiry: *It emerged that the driver of the car had been drunk.* –**emergence** *n* [U] *fml*

**e·mer·gen·cy** /ɪ'mɜːdʒənsi‖-ɜr-/ *n* **-cies** an unexpected and dangerous happening which must be dealt with quickly: *Ring the bell in an emergency.*|*an emergency* EXIT[1] (1)

**e·mer·gent** /ɪ'mɜːdʒənt‖-ɜr-/ *adj* [A] beginning to be independent and noticeable: *the emergent countries of Africa*

**e·met·ic** /ɪ'metɪk/ *n,adj* [C;U] *tech* (something, esp. medicine) eaten or drunk to cause a person to throw up food from the stomach

**em·i·grate** /'em$\frac{1}{2}$greɪt/ *v* **-grated, -grating** [I *from, to*] to leave one's own country in order to go and live in another –**emigrant** *n* –**emigration** /-'greɪʃən/ *n* [C;U]

USAGE to **migrate** is to move from one country to another for a limited period; the word is esp. used of birds, and the practice is called **migration**: *the spring* **migration** *of the wild ducks.* To **emigrate** is to leave one country to go and become a citizen of another, and the practice is called **emigration**: *to* **emigrate** *to Australia.* But from the point of view of the country which they enter, people who **emigrate** are **immigrants,** and the practice is called **immigration.** –compare IMMIGRATE

**em·i·nent** /'emɪnənt/ *adj* (of people) famous and admired: *an eminent doctor* –Compare: *We are expecting the arrival of an eminent scientist.*|*The scientist's arrival is imminent.* (=he will arrive very soon) –see FAMOUS (USAGE) –**eminence** *n* [U]

**em·i·nent·ly** /'emɪnəntli/ *apprec* (of qualities or abilities) very; unusually: *Your decision was eminently fair.*

**e·mir** /e'mɪə$^r$/ *n* a Muslim ruler, esp. in Asia and parts of Africa

**e·mir·ate** /e'mɪəreɪt, -r$\frac{1}{2}$t/ *n* the position, state, power, lands, etc., of an EMIR

**em·is·sa·ry** /'em$\frac{1}{2}$səri‖-seri/ *n* **-ries** [*of*] *fml* a person who is sent with an official message or to do special work

**e·mit** /ɪ'mɪt/ *v* **-tt-** [T] *fml* to send out: *The chimney emitted smoke.* –**emission** /ɪ'mɪʃən/ *n* [C;U]

**e·mol·u·ment** /ɪ'mɒljʊmənt‖ɪ'mɑljə-/ *n* [*usu. pl.*] *fml* money received for work; wage –compare SALARY

**e·mo·tion** /ɪ'məʊʃən/ *n* **1** [C] any of the strong feelings of the human spirit: *Love, hatred, and grief are emotions.* **2** [U] strength of feeling; excited state of the feelings: *He described the accident in a voice shaking with emotion.* –**emotionless** *adj* –**emotionlessly** *adv*

**e·mo·tion·al** /ɪ'məʊʃənəl/ *adj* **1** having feelings which are strong or easily moved: *He was very emotional; he cried when I left.* –opposite **unemotional 2** (of words, music, etc.) showing or causing strong feeling **3** concerning the EMOTIONs (1): *The child's bad behaviour is a result of emotional problems.* –**emotionally** *adv*

**e·mo·tive** /ɪ'məʊtɪv/ *adj* causing strong feeling: "*Home*" *is a much more emotive word than* "*house*".

**em·pa·thy** /'empəθi/ *n* [S;U *with*] the power of imagining oneself to be another person, and so of sharing his/her feelings

**em·pe·ror** /'empərə$^r$/ **empress** *fem.*– *n* the head of an empire

**em·pha·sis** /'emfəs$\frac{1}{2}$s/ *n* **-ses** /siːz/ [C;U *on, upon*] special force given to something, to show that it is particularly important: *The dictionary places/lays/puts an emphasis on examples.* –**emphatic** /ɪm'fætɪk/ *adj*: *He answered the question with an emphatic* "*No*". –**emphatically** *adv*

**em·pha·size** ‖also **-ise** *BrE* /'emfəsaɪz/ *v* **-sized, -sizing** [T] to place EMPHASIS on: *I must emphasize the fact that they are only children.*

**em·pire** /'empaɪə$^r$/ *n* (*often cap.*) a group of countries under one government, usu. ruled by an EMPEROR: *the former British Empire*|(fig.) *the industrial empire of Standard Oil*

**em·pir·i·cal** /ɪm'pɪrɪkəl/ *adj* (of people or methods) guided only by practical experience of the world that we see and feel, not by ideas out of books –**empirically** *adv* –**empiricism** /ɪm'pɪr$\frac{1}{2}$sɪzəm/ *n* [U]

**em·ploy** /ɪm'plɔɪ/ *v* **-ployed, -ploying** [T] **1** [*as*] to use (a person) as a paid worker; appoint (a person) to a job: *We're employing three new secretaries from Monday.*|*We employ her as an adviser.* –see also UNEMPLOYED (1) **2** [*as, in*] *fml* to use –see HIRE[1] (USAGE)

**em·ploy·ee** /ɪm'plɔɪ-iː, ˌemplɔɪ'iː/ *n* [*of*] a person who is employed: *a Government employee*

**em·ploy·er** /ɪm'plɔɪə$^r$/ *n* a person or group that

employs others: *The car industry is one of our biggest employers.*

**em·ploy·ment** /ɪm'plɔɪmənt/ *n* [U] **1** the state of being EMPLOYed (1) –opposite **unemployment 2** the act of using: *the employment of force*

**em·pow·er** /ɪm'paʊə^r/ *v* [T] *fml* to give (someone) a power or lawful right: *The new law empowered the police to search private houses.* –compare ENABLE, ENTITLE (2)

**em·press** /'empr½s/ *n* [*of*] **1** a female EMPEROR **2** the wife of an EMPEROR

**emp·ti·ly** /'empt½li/ *adv* in an EMPTY¹ (2) way

**emp·ty¹** /'empti/ *adj* **1** containing nothing: *an empty cup|There are three empty houses in our street.|He drove through streets empty of* (=without) *traffic.* –compare FULL¹ **2** [*of*] *derog* (of words, talk, etc.) without sense or purpose; meaningless; unreal: *empty promises* **–emptiness** *n* [U]

**empty²** *v* **-tied, -tying** [I;T] **1** to make or become EMPTY¹ (1): *They emptied the bottle.* (=drank all that was in it)|*The room emptied very quickly.* –compare FILL¹ (1) **2** [*out, into, onto*] to put or move (the contents of a container) somewhere else: *He emptied out all his pockets onto the table.*

**e·mu** /'iːmjuː/ *n* **emus** *or* **emu** a large Australian bird which has a long neck and cannot fly

**em·u·late** /'emjʊleɪt‖'emjə-/ *v* **-lated, -lating** [T] *fml* to try to do as well as (another person): *You must work hard to emulate your sister's success.* **–emulation** /-'leɪʃən/ *n* [U *of*]

**e·mul·sion** /ɪ'mʌlʃən/ *n* [C;U] a creamy mixture of liquids such as oil and water: *emulsion paint*

**en·a·ble** /ɪ'neɪbəl/ *v* **-bled, -bling** [T] to make able; give the power, means, or right: *The bird's large wings enable it to fly.|The new law enables a person to claim money from the state.|This dictionary enables you to understand English words.* –compare EMPOWER, ENTITLE (2)

**en·act** /ɪ'nækt/ *v* [T] (of the government) to make or pass (a law) **–enactment** *n* [C;U]

**e·nam·el¹** /ɪ'næməl/ *n* [U] **1** a glassy substance which is melted, and put as a decoration or protection onto objects made of metal, etc. **2** a kind of paint which produces a very shiny surface **3** the hard smooth outer surface of the teeth

**enamel²** *v* **-ll-** *BrE*‖**-l-** *AmE* [T] to cover or decorate with ENAMEL (1,2)

**en·am·oured** *BrE*‖**enamored** *AmE* /ɪ'næməd‖-ərd/ *adj* [F *of, with*] *fml* very fond of; charmed by

**en·camp·ment** /ɪn'kæmpmənt/ *n* a large esp. military camp

**en·case** /ɪn'keɪs/ *v* **-cased, -casing** [T *in*] to cover completely: *His body was encased in shining armour.*

**en·chant** /ɪn'tʃɑːnt‖ɪn'tʃænt/ *v* [T] **1** to fill (someone) with delight: *He was enchanted by/with the idea.* **2** to use magic on: *a palace in an enchanted wood* **–enchanter, enchantress** /- tr½s/ *fem.– n* **–enchantment** *n* [C;U]

**en·chant·ing** /ɪn'tʃɑːntɪŋ‖ɪn'tʃæn-/ *adj apprec* delightful: *an enchanting child* **–enchantingly** *adv*

**en·cir·cle** /ɪn'sɜːkəl‖-ɜr-/ *v* **-cled, -cling** [T *by, with, in*] to surround; make a circle round: *The army encircled the airport.*

**en·clave** /'enkleɪv, 'eŋ-/ *n* a part of a country or nation which is completely surrounded by another

**en·close** /ɪn'kləʊz/ *v* **-closed, -closing** [T *by, in*] **1** to surround with a fence or wall so as to shut in or close: *a garden enclosed by a high wall* **2** to put (esp. something sent with a letter) inside: *I enclose a cheque for £50 (with this letter).*

**en·clo·sure** /ɪn'kləʊʒə^r/ *n* **1** a piece of land that is enclosed: *There's a special enclosure where you can look at the horses before the race starts.* **2** something that is put in with a letter

**en·com·pass** /ɪn'kʌmpəs/ *v* [T *with*] *fml* to surround on all sides

**en·core** /'ɒŋkɔː^r‖'ɑŋ-/ *n,interj* (something which is performed again because of) a call (=Please do it again!) which is made by listeners who are pleased with a song or other performance

**en·coun·ter** /ɪn'kaʊntə^r/ *v* [T] *fml* to meet (something unexpected or dangerous): *He encountered many difficulties.* **–encounter** *n* [*with*]: *an unpleasant encounter with a dangerous snake*

**en·cour·age** /ɪn'kʌrɪdʒ‖ɪn'kɜr-/ *v* **-aged, -aging** [T *in*] to give confidence or hope to (someone); urge (someone) on: *The new company has made an encouraging start.* –opposite **discourage –encouragingly** *adv* **–encouragement** *n* [C;U]: *He owed his success to his wife's encouragement.*

**en·croach** /ɪn'krəʊtʃ/ *v* [I *on, upon*] to go beyond, or take more than, what is right or usual: *His new farm buildings encroach on his neighbour's land.* **–encroachment** *n* [C;U]

**en·crust·ed** /ɪn'krʌst½d/ *adj* [*with*] covered in (gold, jewels, etc.): *boots encrusted with mud*

**en·cum·ber** /ɪn'kʌmbə^r/ *v* [T *with*] *fml* to make free action or movement difficult **–encumbrance** *n*

**en·cy·clo·pe·di·a, -paedia** /ɪnˌsaɪklə'piːdɪə/ *n* a book or set of books dealing with every branch of knowledge, or with one particular branch: *an encyclopedia of modern science|A dictionary explains words and an encyclopedia explains facts.* **–encyclopedic** /-'piːdɪk/ *adj*

**end¹** /end/ *n* **1** [*of*] the point where something stops: *the ends of a rope/of a stick|Which end of the box has the opening?|He walked to the end of the road/the garden.|I start work at the end of August.|The year is* **at an end/coming to an end. 2** a little piece that is left over: *cigarette ends* –see also ODDS AND ENDS **3** *fml* an aim or purpose: *He wants to buy a house, and is saving money to/for this end.|to* ACHIEVE *one's ends* **4 at a loose end** *BrE*‖ **at loose ends** *AmE* (restless and) having nothing to do **5 end to end** with the points or the narrow sides touching each other: *We can provide seats for 10 people if we place these two tables end to end.* **6 get (hold of) the wrong end of the stick** to get a completely wrong idea **7 in the end** at last: *He tried many times to pass the examination, and in the end he succeeded.* **8 make (both) ends meet** to get just enough money for one's needs **9 no end of** *infml* a very great deal of: *That car has caused me no end of worry.* **10 on end: a** (of time) continuously: *He sat there for hours on end.* **b** upright: *We had to stand the table on end to get it through the door.* **11 put an end to** to stop from happening any more

**end²** *v* [I;T] to (cause to) finish: *The party ended at midnight.|The war ended in 1975.|He ended his letter* *(off) with good wishes to the family.*

**end in** sthg. *v prep* [T] to result in: *The battle ended in a victory/in everyone dying.*

**end up** *v adv* [I +*v-ing*] to finish in a particular place or way: *He ended up running the firm.*

**en·dan·ger** /ɪn'deɪndʒəʳ/ *v* [T] *fml* to cause danger to: *You will endanger your health if you smoke.*

**en·dear** *v* →ENDEAR TO

**en·dear·ment** /ɪn'dɪəmənt‖ɪn'dɪər-/ *n* [*usu. pl.*] an expression of love

**en·dear** sbdy. **to** sbdy. /ɪn'dɪəʳ/ *v prep* [T] to cause (esp. oneself) to be loved: *His kindness endeared him to everyone.* –**endearing** *adj* : *an endearing smile* –**endearingly** *adv*

**en·deav·our** *BrE*‖**endeavor** *AmE* /ɪn'devəʳ/ *v* [I +*to-v*] *fml* to try: *You must endeavour to improve your work.* –**endeavour** *BrE*‖**endeavor** *AmE n* [C;U]

**en·dem·ic** /en'demɪk, ɪn-/ *adj* [*in, to*] (esp. of diseases) found regularly in a particular place: *a disease of the chest endemic among miners*

**ending** /'endɪŋ/ *n* the end, esp. of a story, film, play, or word: *a happy ending* –compare BEGINNING

**end·less** /'endlɨs/ *adj* never finishing: *The journey seemed endless.* –**endlessly** *adv*

**en·dorse, in-** /ɪn'dɔːs‖-ɔrs/ *v* **-dorsed, -dorsing** [T] **1** to write, esp. one's name, on the back of (esp. a cheque) **2** *BrE* to write a note on (a driving LICENCE) to say that the driver has broken the law **3** *fml* to express approval or support of (opinions, actions, etc.) –**endorsement** *n* [C;U]

**en·dow** /ɪn'daʊ/ *v* [T] to give money to (a school, hospital, etc.) –**endowment** *n* [C;U]

**endow** sbdy. **with** sthg. *v prep* [T *usu. pass.*] *apprec* to make rich in (a good quality or ability) from birth: *She is endowed with great musical ability.*

**en·dur·ance** /ɪn'djʊərəns‖ɪn'dʊər-/ *n* [U] the state or power of enduring (ENDURE (1)): *When the pain was* **beyond/past endurance** (=impossible to bear), *she went to the doctor.*

**en·dure** /ɪn'djʊəʳ‖ɪn'dʊəʳ/ *v* **-dured, -during 1** [T +*to-v*/*v-ing*] to bear (pain, suffering, etc.): *I can't endure that noise a moment longer.* –see BEAR[2] (USAGE) **2** [I] *fml* to last –**endurable** *adj*

**end·ways** /'endweɪz/ also **endwise** /-waɪz/– *adv* with the end forward; not sideways: *The box is quite narrow when you look at it endways (on).*

**en·e·my** /'enəmi/ *n* **-mies 1** [C] a person who hates or dislikes another person: *A politician often has many enemies.* (=many people dislike him)|*John and Paul are enemies.* (=of each other)|(fig.) *Abraham Lincoln was the enemy of slavery.* –compare FRIEND (1) **2** [C + *sing.*/*pl.v*] the army with whom one is fighting: *The enemy is/are advancing.*

**en·er·get·ic** /ˌenə'dʒetɪk‖-ər-/ *adj* full of ENERGY (1): *an energetic tennis player* –**energetically** *adv*

**en·er·gy** /'enədʒi‖-ər-/ *n* [U] **1** (of people) the quality of being full of life and action; power and ability to be active, do a lot of work, etc.: *Young people usually have more energy than the old.*|*to* APPLY/DEVOTE *all one's energies to a job* **2** the power which does work and drives machines: *atomic/electrical energy*

**en·force** /ɪn'fɔːs‖-ors/ *v* **-forced, -forcing** [T] **1** to cause (a rule or law) to be carried out: *The new law about safety belts in cars will be difficult to enforce.* **2** to make (something) happen, esp. by threats or force –**enforceable** *adj* –**enforcement** *n* [U]

**en·fran·chise** /ɪn'fræntʃaɪz/ *v* **-chised, -chising** [T] to give FRANCHISE (the right to vote at elections) to –opposite **disenfranchise** –**enfranchisement** /-tʃɨz mənt/ *n* [U]

**en·gage** /ɪn'geɪdʒ/ *v* **-gaged, -gaging 1** [T *as*] to arrange to employ (someone): *to engage a new secretary* **2** [T] to take up (time, thought, attention, etc.): *The new toy engaged the child's attention.* **3** [I;T *with*] to (cause to) fit into or lock together: *This wheel engages with that wheel and turns it.* **4** [T *in*] *fml* to attack: *They engaged the enemy (in battle).* –see also DISENGAGE

**en·gaged** /ɪn'geɪdʒd/ *adj* [F] **1** [ *in, on*] (of people) busy; spending time on doing something: *"Can you come on Monday?" "No, I'm engaged."* (=I've arranged to do something)|*engaged in politics/trade* **2** *BrE*‖**busy** *AmE* (of a telephone line) in use: *Sorry! The line/the number is engaged.* –see TELEPHONE[1] (USAGE) **3** [+*to-v*/*to*] having agreed to marry: *My daughter is engaged (to a doctor).*|*They're engaged (to be married).*

**en·gage·ment** /ɪn'geɪdʒmənt/ *n* **1** an agreement to marry: *Have you heard that John has broken off his engagement to Mary?* (=said he no longer wishes to marry her) **2** an arrangement to meet someone or to do something, esp. at a particular time: *I can't come out on Monday because I have an engagement.*

**en·gag·ing** /ɪn'geɪdʒɪŋ/ *adj apprec* charming: *an engaging smile* –**engagingly** *adv*

**en·gine** /'endʒɨn/ *n* **1** a piece of machinery with moving parts which changes power from steam, electricity, oil, etc. into movement: *the engine of a car* –see MACHINE[1] (USAGE) **2** also **locomotive** *fml*– a machine which pulls a railway train **3 -engined** having a certain number of engines or kind of engine: *a* DIESEL-*engined car*|*a four-engined aircraft*

**en·gi·neer[1]** /ˌendʒɨ'nɪəʳ/ *n* a person who plans and understands the making of machines, roads, bridges, harbours, etc.: *an electrical*/CIVIL/MECHANICAL *engineer*

**engineer[2]** *v* [T] to cause by secret planning: *His enemies engineered* (=arranged) *his ruin.*

**en·gi·neer·ing** /ˌendʒɨ'nɪərɪŋ/ *n* [U] the science or profession of an ENGINEER[1]

**En·glish[1]** /'ɪŋglɪʃ/ *adj* belonging to England, its people, etc.: *an English village*

**English[2]** *n* **1** [*the* P] the people of England **2** [U] the language of the UK, the US, etc.: *Do you speak English?*|*She's Japanese, but her English is excellent.*

**en·grave** /ɪn'greɪv/ *v* **-graved, -graving** [T *with, on*] to cut (words, pictures, etc.) on wood, stone, or metal –**engraver** *n* –**engraving** *n* [C;U]

**en·gross·ed** /ɪn'grəʊst/ *adj* [F *in*] having one's time and attention completely filled: *He was so engrossed in his work that he forgot to eat.* –compare ABSORB (2)

**en·gross·ing** /ɪn'grəʊsɪŋ/ *adj* very interesting; filling one's attention: *an engrossing film/book*

**en·gulf** /ɪn'gʌlf/ *v* [T] *lit* (of the earth, the sea, etc.) to destroy by swallowing up: *The stormy sea engulfed the small boat.*

**en·hance** /ɪn'hɑːns‖ɪn'hæns/ *v* **-hanced, -hancing**

[T] to increase (good things such as value, power, or beauty): *Passing the examination should enhance your chances of getting a job.|computer-enhanced learning* (=learning in which the student is helped or guided by a computer as well as by a teacher)

**e·nig·ma** /ɪ'nɪgmə/ *n* a mysterious person, thing, or event that is hard to understand **–enigmatic** /ˌenɪg'mætɪk/ *adj* **–enigmatically** *adv*

**en·joy** /ɪn'dʒɔɪ/ *v* **-joyed, -joying** [T] **1** [+*v-ing*] to get happiness from; like: *I enjoyed the film/I always enjoy going to the cinema.* **2** *fml* to possess or use (something good): *He has always enjoyed* (=had) *very good health.* **3 enjoy oneself** to be happy; experience pleasure: *Did you enjoy yourself at the party?* **–enjoyment** *n* [C;U]

USAGE A verb after **enjoy** always ends in **-ing**: *I* **enjoyed** *meeting him*

**en·joy·a·ble** /ɪn'dʒɔɪəbəl/ *adj* (of things and experiences) pleasant: *an enjoyable holiday* **–enjoyably** *adv*

**en·large** /ɪn'lɑːdʒ‖-ɑr-/ *v* **-larged, -larging** [I;T] to (cause to) grow larger or wider: *We're enlarging the vegetable garden to grow more food.|This photograph probably won't enlarge well.* **–enlargement** *n* [C;U]: *I'm sending mother an enlargement of the baby's photograph.*

**enlarge on** sthg. *v prep* [T] to add more length and detail to: *to enlarge on a story/report*

**en·light·en** /ɪn'laɪtn/ *v* [T] to cause to understand; free from false beliefs: *The child thought the world was flat until I enlightened him!* **–enlightened** *adj*: *to hold enlightened opinions* **–enlightenment** *n* [U]

**en·list** /ɪn'lɪst/ *v* **1** [I;T] to (cause to) enter the armed forces or a course of study: *He enlisted when he was 18.* **2** [T *in*] to obtain (help, sympathy, etc.) **–enlistment** *n* [C;U]

**en·liv·en** /ɪn'laɪvən/ *v* [T] to make (people or events) more active, spirited, or cheerful

**en·mi·ty** /'enmɪ̵ti/ *n* [U] the state or feeling of being an enemy or enemies

**en·no·ble** /ɪ'nəʊbəl/ *v* **-bled, -bling** [T] to make better and more honourable

**e·nor·mi·ty** /ɪ'nɔːmɪ̵ti‖-ɔr-/ *n* **-ties 1** [C;U] (an act of) very great evil **2** [U] the quality of being very large; ENORMOUSness: *the enormity of the job of feeding the whole school*

**e·nor·mous** /ɪ'nɔːməs‖-ɔr-/ *adj* very large indeed: *an enormous house/meal/amount of money* –see Study Notes on page 494 **–enormousness** *n* [U]

**e·nor·mous·ly** /ɪ'nɔːməsli‖-ɔr-/ *adv* very much indeed: *enormously rich|He's enormously popular.*

**e·nough**[1] *determiner,pron* [A or after *n; +to-v/for*] as much or as many as is necessary: *We have enough seats for everyone.|There's enough money to buy a car.|She hasn't got enough to do.|I've eaten* **more than enough.** (=too much)

USAGE **Enough** can come either before or after a plural or [U] noun, but the first position is more common: *Are there* **enough** *desks/desks* **enough** *for all the students?|Is there* **enough** *space*/space **enough** *for all the desks?*

**enough**[2] *adv* **1** [+*to-v*] to the necessary degree: *It's warm enough to swim.|He didn't run fast enough (to catch the train).* **2** not very but only rather: *She runs well enough, but she would run very well indeed if she tried harder.|He's lived in France for years, but* **strangely enough** (=although this is rather strange) *he can't speak French.|It's* **fair enough** (=reasonable) *to ask your own brother to help.* **3 sure enough** *infml* as expected: *He said he would come, and sure enough he did.*

**en·quire** /ɪn'kwaɪəʳ/ *v* **-quired, -quiring** [I;T] →INQUIRE –see ASK (USAGE)

**en·qui·ry** /ɪŋ'kwaɪəri‖'ɪŋkwaɪəri, ɪŋ'kwaɪəri, 'ɪŋkwɪ̵ri/ *n* →INQUIRY

**en·rage** /ɪn'reɪdʒ/ *v* **-raged, -raging** [T] to make very angry **–enraged** *adj* [+*to-v/that/at, by*]

**en·rap·ture** /ɪn'ræptʃəʳ/ *v* **-tured, -turing** [T] to fill (someone) with great joy or delight (RAPTURE): *They were enraptured to meet the great singer.*

**en·rich** /ɪn'rɪtʃ/ *v* [T *by, with*] to make rich: *The discovery of oil will enrich the nation.|*(fig.) *Music can enrich your whole life.* **–enrichment** *n* [U]

**en·rol, enroll** /ɪn'rəʊl/ *v* **-ll-** [I;T *as, in*] to make (oneself or another person) officially a member of a group, school, etc. **–enrolment** *n* [C;U *as, in, of*]

**en route** /ˌɒn 'ruːt‖ˌɑn-/ *adv* [F *for, from, to*) on the way: *I met her at the airport when I was en route to New York.*

**en·sconce** /ɪn'skɒns‖ɪn'skɑns/ *v* **-sconced, -sconcing** [T] *fml or humor* to place or seat (oneself) comfortably in a safe place **–ensconced** *adj* [F *on, in*]

**en·sem·ble** /ɒn'sɒmbəl‖ɑn'sɑm-/ *n French* **1** [C] *fml* a set of things that combine with or match each other to make a whole: *Your coat, hat, and shoes make an attractive ensemble.* **2** [C *+sing./pl. v*] a small group of musicians who regularly play together –compare ORCHESTRA

**en·sign** /'ensaɪn, -sən‖'ensən/ *n* **1** [C] a flag on a ship, esp. to show what nation the ship belongs to **2** [A;C] an officer of the lowest rank in a navy

**en·sue** /ɪn'sjuː‖ɪn'suː/ *v* **-sued, -suing** [I *from*] *fml* to happen afterwards (often as a result): *A bomb exploded and I got lost in the ensuing confusion.*

**en·sure** /ɪn'ʃʊəʳ/ *v* **-sured, -suring** [T +*that*] to make (something) certain to happen: *If you want to ensure that you catch the plane, take a taxi.* –see also INSURE

**en·tail** /ɪn'teɪl/ *v* [T] to make (an event or action) necessary: *Writing a book entails a lot of work.*

**en·tan·gle** /ɪn'tæŋgəl/ *v* **-gled, -gling** [T *among, in, with*] to cause (something) to become twisted or mixed (with something else): *The bird became entangled in the net/wire.* –opposite **disentangle**; compare TANGLE, ENTWINE **–entanglement** *n* [C;U]

**en·ter** /'entəʳ/ *v* **1** [I;T] *more formal than* **go/come into**– to come or go into (a room, etc.): *to enter a room/a house|Please do not enter without knocking on the door.* **2** [T] to become a member of: *to enter the medical profession* **3** [T *up, in*] to write down (names, amounts of money, etc.) in a book

**enter** (sbdy.) **for** sthg. *v prep* [T] to put the name (of oneself or another) on a list for: *John entered (himself) for the examination.*

**enter into** sthg. *v prep* [T] **1** [*with*] to begin: *to enter into a contract with a firm* **2** to take part in: *He entered into the spirit of the game*

**en·ter·prise** /'entəpraɪz‖-ər-/ *n* **1** [C] a plan, esp. to do something new or difficult **2** [U] the courage that is needed to do something daring or difficult **3** [U] a way of organizing business: *Do you believe in* **private enterprise**, *or in government ownership of industry?*

**en·ter·pris·ing** /'entəpraɪzɪŋ‖-ər-/ *adj apprec* having or showing ENTERPRISE (2) –opposite **unenterprising**

**en·ter·tain** /ˌentə'teɪn‖-ər-/ *v* **1** [I;T] to amuse and interest: *A teacher should entertain as well as teach.* **2** [I;T] to give a party (for); to provide food and drink (for): *He does most of his entertaining in restaurants.* **3** [T] to be ready and willing to think about (an idea, doubt, etc.)

**en·ter·tain·er** /ˌentə'teɪnəʳ‖-ər-/ *n* a person who ENTERTAINS (1) professionally: *a popular television entertainer*

**en·ter·tain·ing** /ˌentə'teɪnɪŋ‖-ər-/ *adj apprec* amusing and interesting: *an entertaining story* **–entertainingly** *adv*

**en·ter·tain·ment** /ˌentə'teɪnmənt‖-ər-/ *n* **1** [U] the act of ENTERTAINing (2) people; esp. the providing of food and drink **2** [C;U] (a) public amusement: *A cinema is a place of entertainment.*

**en·thral, enthrall** /ɪn'θrɔːl/ *v* **-ll-** [T] to hold the complete attention and interest of: *The boy was enthralled by the soldier's stories.* **–enthralling** *adj*

**en·throne** /ɪn'θrəʊn/ *v* **-throned, -throning** [T] to place on a THRONE (official seat of a king or queen) **–enthronement** *n* [C;U]

**en·thuse** /ɪn'θjuːz‖ɪn'θuːz/ *v* **-thused, -thusing** [I *about, over*] *infml* to show ENTHUSIASM: *He was enthusing about his new radio.*

**en·thu·si·as·m** /ɪn'θjuːziæzəm‖ɪn'θuː-/ *n* [C;U *for, about*] a strong feeling of interest or admiration: *The new teacher is full of enthusiasm.* **–enthusiast** *n* **–enthusiastic** *adj* **–enthusiastically** *adv*

**en·tice** /ɪn'taɪs/ *v* **-ticed, -ticing** [T *away, from, into*] to persuade (someone) to do something usu. wrong: *He enticed me away from work.* **–enticement** *n* [C;U]

**en·tire** /ɪn'taɪəʳ/ *adj* [A] complete: *She spent the entire day in bed.*|*I am in entire agreement with you.* **–entirely** *adv* –see Study Notes on page 389

**en·tir·e·ty** /ɪn'taɪərᵊti/ *n* [U] completeness; wholeness: *Consider the matter* **in its entirety.** (=as a whole)

**en·ti·tle** /ɪn'taɪtl/ *v* **-tled, -tling** [T] **1** to give a title to (a book, play, etc.) **2** [*to*] to give (someone) the right to do something: *This ticket entitles you to travel first class.* –compare ENABLE **–entitlement** *n* [U]

**en·ti·ty** /'entᵊti/ *n* **-ties** something that has a single separate and independent existence: *Since the war Germany has been divided; it is no longer one political entity.*

**en·to·mol·o·gy** /ˌentə'mɒlədʒi‖- 'mɑ-/ *n* [U] the scientific study of insects –compare ETYMOLOGY **–entomologist** *n*

**en·tou·rage** /'ɒntʊrɑːʒ‖'ɑn-/ *n* [C +*sing./pl. v*] all the people who surround and follow an important person

**en·trails** /'entreɪlz/ *n* [P] *old use* the inside parts of an animal, esp. the bowels

**en·trance¹** /'entrəns/ *n* **1** [C] a gate, door, or other opening by which one enters: *Excuse me, where is the entrance to the cinema?* –compare ENTRY (3); see picture on page 297 **2** [C] the act of entering: *to make one's entrance* **3** [U] the right to enter: *the entrance money* (=money which must be paid)|*a school entrance examination*

USAGE Compare **entrance** and **entry**: Both words can be used to mean an act of entering: *to make one's* **entrance** *onto the stage*|*Britain's* **entry** *into the EEC;* or the right to enter: *a school* **entrance** *examination*|*"No* **Entry**" (road sign). In *AmE* both words can also mean the place by which you enter, but in *BrE* only **entrance** is used in this way: *We went into the museum by the front* **entrance** (also **entry** *AmE*).

**en·trance²** /ɪn'trɑːns‖ɪn'træns/ *v* **-tranced, -trancing** [T] *apprec* to fill (someone) with great wonder and delight

**en·trant** /'entrənt/ *n* a person who enters into a profession, race, or competition

**en·treat** /ɪn'triːt/ *v* [I;T +*that/for*] *fml* to beg humbly or very seriously: *She entreated him to forgive her.* **–entreaty** *n* **-ties** [C;U]

**en·trenched** /ɪn'trentʃt/ *adj often derog* (of rights, beliefs, etc.) firmly established

**en·tre·pre·neur** /ˌɒntrəprə'nɜːʳ‖ˌɑn-/ *n* a person who owns and runs a business

**en·trust** /ɪn'trʌst/ *v* [T *with, to*] to give (someone) (something) to take care of: *I entrusted the child to your care.*

**en·try** /'entri/ *n* **-tries 1** [C *into*] the act of coming or going in; ENTRANCE¹ (2): *Britain's entry into the war* **2** [U] the right to enter: *You mustn't drive into a street with a "No Entry" sign.* **3** [C] *AmE* a door, gate, or passage by which one enters **4** [C;U] the act or result of writing something down on a list: *The next entry in this dictionary is the word "entwine".* **5** [C] a person or thing, entered in a race or competition: *This painting is Mrs Smith's entry in the competition.* –see ENTRANCE¹ (USAGE)

**en·twine** /ɪn'twaɪn/ *v* **-twined, -twining** [T *in, (a)round*] to twist together, round, or in: *They walked along with their fingers entwined.* –compare ENTANGLE

**e·nu·me·rate** /ɪ'njuːməreɪt‖ɪ'nuː-/ *v* **-rated, -rating** [T] *fml* to name (things on a list) one by one **–enumeration** /-'reɪʃən/ *n* [C;U]

**e·nun·ci·ate** /ɪ'nʌnsieɪt/ *v* **-ated, -ating** *fml* **1** [I;T] to pronounce (words): *An actor must learn to enunciate clearly.* **2** [T] to express (ideas, opinions, etc.) clearly and firmly **–enunciation** /'eɪʃən/ *n* [C;U]

**en·vel·op** /ɪn'veləp/ *v* [T *in*] to wrap up or cover completely: *The building was soon enveloped in flames.* **–envelopment** *n* [U]

**en·ve·lope** /'envələʊp, 'ɒn-‖'en-/ *n* the paper cover of a letter

**en·vi·a·ble** /'enviəbəl/ *adj* causing ENVY; very desirable: *his enviable good luck*|*an enviable job* –opposite **unenviable –enviably** *adv*

**en·vi·ous** /'enviəs/ *adj* feeling or showing ENVY: *She was envious of her sister's new job.* –see JEALOUS (USAGE) **–enviously** *adv*

**en·vi·ron·ment** /ɪn'vaɪərənmənt/ *n* [C;*the* S] the natural or social conditions in which people live: *We must stop spoiling the environment.* (=the air, water, and land)|*Children need a happy home environment.* **–environmental** /-'mentl/ *adj*: *Those factories are causing a lot of environmental* POLLUTION, *with all*

*their noise and smoke.*
USAGE Compare **environment** and **surroundings: Surroundings** are simply the physical things which surround a place or person: *a hotel set in pleasant* **surroundings.** Your **environment** means all the things around you, esp. as they influence your feelings and development. Compare *to grow up in beautiful* **surroundings/***to grow up in a happy* **environment.**
**en·vis·age** /ɪn'vɪzɪdʒ·/‖ also **envision** /ɪn'vɪʒən/ *AmE*– *v* **-aged, -aging** [T +*v-ing/that*] to see in the mind as a future possibility: *When do you envisage being able to pay back the money?*
**en·voy** /'envɔɪ/ *n* a messenger, esp. one sent by one government to do business with another
**en·vy¹** /'envi/ *n* [U *at, of*] a feeling one has towards someone when one wishes that one had his/her qualities or possessions: *The boy's new toy was* **the envy of** *his friends.* (=it made them feel envy) –see JEALOUS (USAGE)
**envy²** *v* **-vied, -vying** [T] to feel ENVY for or of: *I don't envy you your journey in this bad weather.*
**en·zyme** *n* a chemical substance (CATALYST) produced by certain living cells, which can cause chemical change in plants or animals
**ep·au·let, -lette** /ˌepə'let/ *n* a shoulder decoration, esp. on a military or naval uniform
**e·phem·e·ral** /ɪ'femərəl/ *adj* having a very short life: *Her success as a singer was ephemeral.*
**ep·ic¹** /'epɪk/ *adj usu. apprec* (of stories, events, etc.) full of brave action and excitement, like an EPIC²
**epic²** *n* a long poem about the deeds of gods and great men: *The Odyssey is an epic of ancient Greece.*
**ep·i·cure** /'epɪkjʊəʳ/ *n* a person who takes great interest in the pleasures of food and drink; GOURMET –**epicurean** /ˌepɪkjʊ'riːən/ *adj,n*
**ep·i·dem·ic** /ˌepˌ'demɪk/ *n* a large number of cases of the same infectious disease at the same time: *an epidemic of* CHOLERA/*a* CHOLERA *epidemic* –**epidemic** *adj*: *(fig.) Violence is reaching epidemic levels in the city.*
**ep·i·gram** /'epˌgræm/ *n* a short clever amusing poem or saying –**epigrammatic** /ˌepˌgrə'mætɪk/ *adj*
**ep·i·lep·sy** /'epˌlepsi/ *n* [U] a disease of the brain which causes sudden attacks of uncontrolled violent movement and loss of consciousness
**ep·i·lep·tic** /ˌepˌ'leptɪk/ *adj,n* (being or concerning) a person who suffers from EPILEPSY: *an epileptic child*/ FIT³ (1)
**ep·i·logue** /'epˌlog‖-lɑg/ *n* the last part of a piece of literature, which finishes it off, esp. a speech made by one of the actors at the end of a play –opposite **prologue**
**e·pis·co·pal** /ɪ'pɪskəpəl/ *adj* [A] **1** *fml* of or concerning BISHOPS **2** (*often cap.*) (of a church) governed by BISHOPS
**ep·i·sode** /'epˌsəʊd/ *n* (an account in a play or book of) one separate event: *There was a rather amusing episode in the pub last night.*|*The next episode of this radio play will be broadcast next week.*
**e·pis·tle** /ɪ'pɪsəl/ *n fml or humor* a (long and important) letter
**Epistle** *n* any of the letters written by the first followers (APOSTLES) of Christ, in the Bible
**ep·i·taph** /'epˌtɑːf‖-tæf/ *n* a short description of a dead person, often written on a stone above his/her grave
**ep·i·thet** /'epˌθet/ *n* an adjective or descriptive phrase, esp. used of a person: *He cursed me, using a lot of rude epithets like "bloody".*
**e·pit·o·me** /ɪ'pɪtəmi/ *n* [*of*] a thing or person that shows, to a very great degree, a quality: *My cat is* **the epitome of** *laziness.* (=is very lazy)
**e·pit·o·mize** ‖also –**mise** *BrE* /ɪ'pɪtəmaɪz/ *v* **-mized, -mizing** [T] to be an EPITOME of; be very typical of: *He epitomizes the good qualities of his family.*
**e·poch** /'iːpɒk‖'epək/ *n* a period of historical time, during which certain events or developments happened –compare ERA
**eq·ua·ble** /'ekwəbəl/ *adj* (of temperature, or a person's character) without great changes; even and regular: *I like working with John because he's so calm and equable.* –**equably** *adv*–**equability** /ˌekwə'bɪlˌti/ *n* [U]
**e·qual¹** /'iːkwəl/ *adj* **1** [*in, to; no comp.*] (of two or more) the same in size, number, value, rank, etc.: *Cut the cake into six equal pieces.*|*Women deserve equal pay* (=equal to men) *and to work* **on equal terms** (=as equals) *with men.* **2** [*to*] (of a person) having enough strength, ability, etc. (for): *Bill is quite equal to (the job of) running the office.* –opposite **unequal**
**equal²** *n* a person who is equal (to another or to oneself): *The teacher is popular because he treats the children as (his) equals.*
**equal³** *v* **-ll-** *BrE*‖ **-l-** *AmE* [T not *be* +*v-ing*] **1** (of sizes or numbers) to be the same (as): *"x=y" means that x equals y.* **2** [*in, as*] to be as good, clever, etc. (as)
**e·qual·i·ty** /ɪ'kwɒlˌti‖ɪ'kwɑ-/ *n* [U] the state of being equal: *the equality of man* (=of all people) –opposite **inequality**
**e·qual·ize** ‖also –**ise** *BrE* /'iːkwəlaɪz/ *v* **- ized, -izing** **1** [T] to make equal in size or numbers **2** [I] (in sport) to reach the same total (SCORE¹ (1)) as one's opponent –**equalization** /ˌiːkwəlaɪ'zeɪʃən‖-lə- / *n* [U]
**eq·ual·ly** /'iːkwəli/ *adv* **1** as (much); to an equal degree: *They can both run equally fast.* **2** in equal shares: *They shared the work equally between them.*
**eq·ua·nim·i·ty** /ˌiːkwə'nɪmˌti, ˌekwə-/ *n* [U] *fml* calmness of mind: *He received the bad news with surprising equanimity.*
**e·quate** /ɪ'kweɪt/ *v* **-quated, -quating** [T *with*] to consider or make (two or more things or people) equal: *You can't equate passing examinations with being educated.*
**e·qua·tion** /ɪ'kweɪʒən/ *n tech* a statement that two quantities are equal: *x+2y=7 is an equation.*
**e·qua·tor** /ɪ'kweɪtəʳ/ *n* [*the* S] (*often cap.*) an imaginary line (of LATITUDE (1)) drawn round the world halfway between its most northern and southern points (POLES² (1a)) –**equatorial** /ˌekwə'tɔːrɪəl‖ˌiːkwə'tor-/ *adj*
**e·ques·tri·an** /ɪ'kwestrɪən/ *adj* concerning horse-riding; of a rider on a horse
**e·qui·lat·e·ral** /ˌiːkwˌ'lætərəl/ *adj* (of a TRIANGLE (1)) having all three sides equal
**e·qui·lib·ri·um** /ˌiːkwˌ'lɪbrɪəm/ *n* [U] *fml* a state of

balance: *He lost his equilibrium and fell into the lake.*

**eq·uine** /ˈekwaɪn, ˈiː-/ *adj* of or like horses

**eq·ui·nox** /ˈiːkwɨnɒks, ˈe-‖-nɑks/ *n [the]* one of the two times in the year when all places in the world have day and night of equal length –compare SOLSTICE

**e·quip** /ɪˈkwɪp/ *v* **-pp-** [T *with, for*] to provide (oneself or another) with what is necessary for doing something: *They can't afford to equip their army properly.|Your education will equip you for a job.*

**e·quip·ment** /ɪˈkwɪpmənt/ *n* [U] the things needed for a particular activity: *modern office equipment|photographic equipment*

**eq·ui·ty** /ˈekwɨti/ *n* [U] the quality of being fair and just –opposite **inequity –equitable** *adj*: *an equitable division of the money* –opposite **inequitable –equitably** *adv*

**e·quiv·a·lent**[1] /ɪˈkwɪvələnt/ *adj* [*to*] (of time, amount, number, etc.) same; equal: *He changed his pounds for the equivalent amount in dollars/an equivalent amount of dollars.* **–equivalance** *n* [U]

**equivalent**[2] *n* something that is EQUIVALENT: *Some American words have no British equivalents.*

**e·quiv·o·cal** /ɪˈkwɪvəkəl/ *adj* **1** (of words) having a double or doubtful meaning **2** (of behaviour or events) questionable; mysterious –opposite **unequivocal –equivocally** *adv*

**e·ra** /ˈɪərə/ *n* a set of years which is counted from a particular event or named after an important development: *the era of space travel* –compare EPOCH

**e·rad·i·cate** /ɪˈrædɨkeɪt/ *v* **-cated, -cating** [T] to end; destroy completely: *to eradicate crime/disease* **–eradication** /-ˈkeɪʃən/ *n* [U]

**e·rase** /ɪˈreɪz‖ɪˈreɪs/ *v* **-rased, -rasing** [T] *more fml than* **rub out**– to rub out or remove (something, esp. a pencil mark)

**e·ras·er** /ɪˈreɪzəʳ‖-sər/ *n fml or AmE* for RUBBER[1] (2)

**e·rect**[1] /ɪˈrekt/ *adj* upright; standing straight up on end **–erectly** *adv* **–erectness** *n* [U]

**erect**[2] *v* [T] **1** *fml* to build: This MONUMENT *was erected in honour of the Queen.* **2** to fix or place in an upright position: *to erect a tent* **–erection** *n* [C;U]

**er·mine** /ˈɜːmɨn‖ˈɜr-/ *n* **-mines** *or* **-mine** [C;U] (the white winter fur of) a small animal also called a STOAT

**e·rode** /ɪˈrəʊd/ *v* **-roded, -roding 1** [T *away*] to eat into; wear or rub away: *The sea erodes the rocks.|(fig.) Jealousy is eroding our friendship.* **2** [I] to be or become worn away or rubbed away: *The coast is slowly eroding away.* **–erosion** /ɪˈrəʊʒən/ *n* [U]: *soil erosion by rain and wind*

**e·rot·ic** /ɪˈrɒtɪk‖ɪˈrɑ-/ *adj* of or concerning sexual love and desire: *erotic feelings|an erotic picture* **–erotically** *adv* **–eroticism** /-sɪzəm/ *n* [U]

USAGE Compare **erotic, sexual,** and **sexy: erotic** is used particularly for works of art: *an* **erotic** *film|some* **erotic** *Japanese pictures,* **sexual** simply means connected with or in regard to sex: *the* **sexual** *organs|***sexual** *habits*, and **sexy** means exciting in a **sexual** way: *You look very* **sexy** *in those tight trousers!*

**err** /ɜːʳ/ *v* [I] *fml* to make a mistake; do something wrong: *To err is human.* (old saying)|*It is better to* **err on the side of** mercy. (=to be too merciful, rather than not merciful enough)

**er·rand** /ˈerənd/ *n* a short journey made esp. to buy something: *I've no time to* **go on/run errands for** *you!|I've got a few errands to do* (things to go and get) *in town.*

**er·rant** /ˈerənt/ *adj* [A] *old use or lit* mistaken; ERRing: *An errant husband is one who leaves his wife for other women.*

**er·rat·ic** /ɪˈrætɪk/ *adj* changeable without reason; not regular in movement or behaviour: *an erratic tennis-player* (=sometimes good, sometimes bad) **–erratically** *adv*

**er·ro·ne·ous** /ɪˈrəʊnɪəs/ *adj fml* (of a statement, a belief, etc.) incorrect: *the erroneous belief that the world is flat* **–erroneously** *adv*

**er·ror** /ˈerəʳ/ *n* **1** [C] a mistake; something done wrongly: *an error of judgment* **2** [U] the state of being wrong in behaviour or beliefs: *The accident was caused by* **human error.**|*I did it* **in error**. (=by mistake)

USAGE An **error** is the same as a **mistake** except that **a**: **error** suggests a moral wrong, **mistake** a misjudgment: *It was a* **mistake** *buying that car.|the* **errors** *of his* **youth**; **b**: **error** is a more formal word: *Your work is full of spelling* **mistakes**/(*fml*) **errors**; **c**: in certain fixed phrases only one of them can be used: *an* **error** *of judgement|by* **mistake.** A small unintended mistake is a **slip** or an **oversight**: *I meant to write "son" not "sun"–it was just a* **slip** *of the pen.|By an* **oversight,** *I forgot to post the letter.*

**er·u·dite** /ˈerʊdaɪt‖ˈerə-/ *adj fml* full of learning: *an erudite person/book* **–eruditely** *adv* **–erudition** /-ˈdɪʃən/ *n* [U]

**e·rupt** /ɪˈrʌpt/ *v* [I] (of a VOLCANO) to explode and pour out fire: (fig.) *Violence erupted after the football match.* **–eruption** *n* [C;U]: *a* VOLCANO *in a state of eruption*

**es·ca·late** /ˈeskəleɪt/ *v* **-lated, -lating 1** [T] to make (a war) more serious by stages **2** [I] (of prices and wages) to rise, one after the other: *The cost of living is escalating.* **–escalation** /-ˈleɪʃən/ *n* [U]

**es·ca·la·tor** /ˈeskəleɪtəʳ/ *n* a set of moving stairs in a store, railway station, airport, etc.

**es·ca·pade** /ˈeskəpeɪd/ *n* a wild, exciting, and sometimes dangerous act, esp. one that disobeys rules or causes some trouble

**es·cape**[1] /ɪˈskeɪp/ *v* **-caped, -caping 1** [I;T *from*] to find a way out; get out: *They escaped from the burning house/from prison.|Some gas is escaping from the pipe.* **2** [I;T +*v-ing*] (of a person) to avoid: *He narrowly* (=only just) *escaped being drowned.* **3** [T] (of an event, a fact, etc.) to be unnoticed or forgotten by: *I'm afraid your name escapes me.* (=I've forgotten it)|*Nothing escaped his attention.*

**escape**[2] *n* **1** [C;U *from, of, out of*] (an example or case of) the act of escaping or fact of having escaped: *an escape of gas|The thief jumped into a car and* **made his escape. 2** [S;U] something that frees one from unpleasant or dull reality: *He reads adventure stories as an escape.* –see also ESCAPISM

**es·cap·is·m** /ɪˈskeɪpɪzəm/ *n* [U] *derog* activity intended to provide escape from unpleasant or dull reality: *That story about three beautiful girls in a spacecraft is pure escapism!* **–escapist** *adj,n*

**e·scarp·ment** /ɪˈskɑːpmənt‖-ɑr-/ *n* a long cliff on a mountain-side

**es·cort**[1] /ˈeskɔːt‖-ɔrt/ *n* [C +*sing./pl. v*] a person or people who go with another as a guard, or as a companion: *The prisoner travelled* **under police escort.** (=with some policemen)|*Mary's escort arrived to take her out for the evening.*

**e·scort²** /ɪ'skɔːt||-ɔrt/ *v* [T] to go with (someone) as an ESCORT: *The queen was escorted by the directors as she toured the factory.*

**e·soph·a·gus** /ɪ'sɒfəgəs||ɪ'sɑ-/ *n* →OESOPHAGUS

**es·o·ter·ic** *adj* limited to, or understood by, only a small number of people: *Some words are really too esoteric for this dictionary.* **–esoterically** *adv*

**ESP** *abbrev. for:* extrasensory perception; knowledge which seems to have been gained without the use of the five senses

**es·pe·cial** /ɪ'speʃəl/ *adj* [A] *fml* →SPECIAL¹

**es·pe·cial·ly** /ɪ'speʃəli/ *adv* **1** also **specially**– to a particularly great degree: *"Do you like chocolate?" "Not especially."*|*I love Italy, especially in summer.* **2** →SPECIALLY (1): *especially for you*

**es·pi·o·nage** /'espɪənɑːʒ/ *n* [U] the action of SPYing² (2); work of finding out (a country's) secret information and sending it to enemies

**es·pla·nade** /'espləneɪd||-nɑd/ *n* a level open space for walking, often beside the sea

**Esq.** /ɪ'skwaɪəʳ||'esk-, ɪ'skwaɪər/ *n* [after *n*] *esp. BrE written abbrev. said as:* esquire (used as a title of politeness usu. written after a man's full name): *The envelope is addressed to Peter Jones, Esq.*

**es·say** /'eseɪ/ *n* a usu. short piece of writing on a subject esp. as part of a course of study: *We've got to write an essay on the war with Napoleon.*

**es·sence** /'esəns/ *n* **1** [U *of*] the central or most important quality of a thing, which makes it what it is: *The essence of his religious teaching is love for all men.* **2** [C;U] the best part of a substance, taken out and reduced to a jelly, liquid, etc.: *essence of roses*|*Did you use coffee essence in making this cake?* **3 in essence** in its/one's nature; ESSENTIALLY (1)

**es·sen·tial** /ɪ'senʃəl/ *adj* **1** [*to, for*] necessary: *We can live without clothes, but food and drink are essential to life.* **2** [A] central; most important or most notable: *What is the essential difference between these two political systems?* **–essential** *n*: *The room was furnished with the simplest essentials: a bed, a chair, and a table.*

**es·sen·tial·ly** /ɪ'senʃəli/ *adv* in reality; BASICally: *She's essentially kind.*

**es·tab·lish** /ɪ'stæblɪʃ/ *v* [T] **1** to set up (esp. an organization): *This company/school was established in 1850.*|*The club has established a new rule allowing women to join.* **2** [*as, in*] to place (oneself or another) in a particular (esp. favourable) position: *He quickly established himself as a powerful member of the new government.* **3** [+*that*] to find out or make certain of (a fact, answer, etc.): *to establish the truth of a story* **4** to cause people to accept or recognize (a claim, fact, etc.): *His next film, "Taxi Driver", established his fame as an actor.* **5** to make (a religion) official for a nation: *The established religion of Egypt is Islam.*

**es·tab·lish·ment** /ɪ'stæblɪʃmənt/ *n* **1** [U] the act of ESTABLISHing (1): *the establishment of new industry by the Government* **2** [C +*sing./pl. v*] *fml* a business organization: *The establishment you are looking for is in Oxford Street.*

**Establishment** *n* [*the* U +*sing./pl.v*] the powerful organizations and people who control public life and support the established order of society

**es·tate** /ɪ'steɪt/ *n* **1** [C] *BrE* a piece of land on which buildings (of a stated type) have all been built together in a planned way: *an industrial estate*|*a* **housing estate** **2** [C] a (large) piece of land in the country, usu. with one large house on it **3** [U] *law* the whole of a person's property, esp. after death

**estate a·gent** /·'· ,··/ *BrE*||**real estate agent** *AmE*– *n* a person whose business is to buy and sell houses, property, and land for people

**estate car** /·'· ·/ *BrE*||**station wagon** *AmE*– *n* a private motor vehicle with a door at the back and a lot of room to put bags, cases, etc.

**es·teem¹** /ɪ'stiːm/ *n* [U] *fml* respect; good opinion (of a person): *All David's friends* **held** *him* **in (high) esteem.** –compare ESTIMATION

**esteem²** *v* [T] *fml* **1** to respect and admire greatly: **2** to believe to be (esp. something good): –compare ESTIMATE

**es·ti·ma·ble** /'estɪ̣məbəl/ *adj apprec* (of a person or his behaviour) worthy of ESTEEM¹ –see also INESTIMABLE

**es·ti·mate** /'estɪ̣meɪt/ *v* **-mated, -mating** [I;T +*that*] to calculate (an amount, cost, etc.); form an opinion about (something): *I estimate her age at thirty-five.*|*I asked the building firm to estimate for the repairs to the roof.* (=to tell me how much the repairs would cost) –see UNDER/OVERESTIMATE; compare QUOTE¹ (3) **–estimate** *n* [+*that*/*of*]: *My estimate of her character was wrong.*|*We got three estimates before having the roof repaired, and accepted the lowest.*

**es·ti·ma·tion** /,estɪ̣'meɪʃən/ *n* [U] judgment or opinion: *He has lowered himself in my estimation.* –compare ESTEEM¹

**es·trange** /ɪ'streɪndʒ/ *v* **-tranged, -tranging** [T *from*] to make unfriendly: *His behaviour estranged him from his brother.* **–estrangement** *n* [C;U *from, with, between*]

**es·tu·a·ry** /'estʃʊəri/ *n* **-ries** the wide lower part or mouth of a river, into which the sea enters at high TIDE (1)

**etc.** *adv written abbrev. said as:* etcetera /,et'setərə/ and the rest; and so on: *They bought tea, coffee, sugar, etc.*

**etch** /etʃ/ *v* [I;T *on*] to draw (a picture) by cutting lines on a metal plate with a needle and acid so that one can print from the plate: (fig.) *The terrible event is etched for ever in my memory.* **–etching** *n* [C;U]: *a beautiful etching of a bird*

**e·ter·nal** /ɪ'tɜːnəl||-ɜr-/ *adj* going on for ever; without beginning or end **–eternally** *adv*

**e·ter·ni·ty** /ɪ'tɜːnɪ̣ti||-ɜr-/ **-ties** [S;U] time without end; state of time after death, which is said to last forever: (fig.) *I was so anxious that every moment seemed an eternity.*

**e·ther** /'iːθəʳ/ *n* [U] a light colourless liquid, easily changed into a gas, which is often used as an ANAESTHETIC to put people to sleep before an operation

**e·the·re·al** /ɪ'θɪərɪəl/ *adj* of unearthly lightness and delicacy; like a spirit or fairy **–ethereally** *adv*

**eth·ic** /'eθɪk/ *n* a system of moral behaviour

**eth·i·cal** /'eθɪkəl/ *adj* **1** of ETHICS (2): *The use of animals in scientific tests raises some difficult ethical questions.* **2** (*only used in* NEGATIVES[2] (1), *questions, etc.*) morally good: *The judge said that the doctor's behaviour had not been ethical.* –opposite **unethical** (for **2**) –**ethically** *adv*

**eth·ics** /'eθɪks/ *n* **1** [U] the science which deals with morals **2** [P] moral principles

**eth·nic** /'eθnɪk/ *adj* of or related to a racial, national, or tribal group

**eth·nol·o·gy** /eθ'nɒlədʒi‖eθ'nɑ-/ *n* [U] the science of the different human races –compare ANTHROPOLOGY, SOCIOLOGY

**et·i·quette** /'etɪket‖-kət/ *n* [U] the formal rules of proper behaviour

**et·y·mol·o·gy** /ˌetɪ'mɒlədʒi‖-'mɑ-/ *n* [U] the scientific study of the origins, history, and changing meanings of words –compare ENTOMOLOGY

**eu·ca·lyp·tus** /ˌjuːkə'lɪptəs/ *n* **-tuses** *or* **-ti** /taɪ/ [C;U] (the strong smelling oil produced by) a tall tree, such as the Australian GUM tree

**Eu·cha·rist** /'juːkərɪst/ *n* [*the* S] (the bread and wine taken at) the Christian ceremony based on Christ's last supper on Earth –see also MASS, COMMUNION

**eu·lo·gize** ‖also **-gise** *BrE* /'juːlədʒaɪz/ *v* **-gized, -gizing** [T] *fml* to make a EULOGY about

**eu·lo·gy** /'juːlədʒi/ *n* **-gies** [C;U *on, of*] *fml* (a speech or a piece of writing containing) high praise (usu. of a person or his/her qualities) –compare ELEGY

**eu·nuch** /'juːnək/ *n* a man who has been CASTRATED (=had part of his sex organs removed)

**eu·phe·mis·m** /'juːfɪmɪzəm/ *n* [C;U] (an example of) the use of a pleasanter, less direct name for something thought to be unpleasant: *"Pass away" is a euphemism for "die".* –**euphemistic** /-'mɪstɪk/ *adj*

**eu·pho·ri·a** /juː'fɔːrɪə‖jʊ'forɪə/ *n* [U] a feeling of happiness and cheerful excitement –**euphoric** /juː'fɒrɪk‖jʊ'fɔrɪk, - 'fɑr- / *adj* –**euphorically** *adv*

**Eu·ro·pe·an** /ˌjʊərə'pɪən/ *adj* of or related to Europe

**European Com·mu·ni·ty** /··ˌ·· ·'···/ *n fml* for EEC

**eu·tha·na·si·a** /ˌjuːθə'neɪzɪə‖-'neɪʒə/ *n* [U] the painless killing of incurably ill or old people

**e·vac·u·ate** /ɪ'vækjʊeɪt/ *v* **-ated, -ating** [T] **1** to take all the people away from (a place): *The village was evacuated because of the danger of a flood.* **2** [*from, to*] to move (people) out of danger –**evacuation** /-'eɪʃən/ *n* [C;U]

**e·vac·u·ee** /ɪˌvækjʊ'iː/ *n* a person who has been EVACUATED

**e·vade** /ɪ'veɪd/ *v* **-vaded, -vading** [T] **1** [+ *v-ing*] *derog* to avoid, or avoid doing (something one should do): *He evaded* (=did not answer properly) *the question.* **2** to get out of the way of or escape from: *After his escape he evaded the police/evaded* CAPTURE (2) *for several days.*

**e·val·u·ate** /ɪ'væljʊeɪt/ *v* **-ated, -ating** [T] *fml* to calculate the value or degree of: *The school has only been open for six months, so it's too early to evaluate its success.* –**evaluation** /-'eɪʃən/ *n* [C;U]

**e·van·gel·i·cal** /ˌiːvæn'dʒelɪkəl/ *adj,n (often cap.)* (a member) of certain PROTESTANT Christian churches which believe in the importance of faith and of studying the Bible, rather than in religious ceremonies

**e·van·ge·list** /ɪ'vændʒɪlɪst/ *n* a person who travels from place to place and holds EVANGELICAL religious meetings –**evangelism** *n* [U]

**e·vap·o·rate** /ɪ'væpəreɪt/ *v* **-rated, -rating** [I;T] to (cause to) change into steam and disappear: *The pool of water evaporated in the sun.*|(fig.) *Hopes of reaching an agreement are beginning to evaporate.* (=to disappear) –**evaporation** /- 'reɪʃən/ *n* [U]

**e·va·sion** /ɪ'veɪʒən/ *n* **1** [C;U] *derog* an action, lack of action, or statement which EVADES (1): *George is in prison for tax evasion.*|*a speech full of evasions* **2** [U] the act of evading (EVADE (2))

**e·va·sive** /ɪ'veɪsɪv/ *adj* which EVADES or tries to evade: *an evasive answer*|*If the enemy attacks,* **take evasive action.** –**evasively** *adv* –**evasiveness** *n* [U]

**eve** /iːv/ *n* [S] **1** the night or day before a religious feast or holiday: *a party on New Year's Eve* **2** the time just before an important event: *on the eve of our examination*

**e·ven**[1] /'iːvən/ *adj* **1** level, smooth, regular; forming a straight line (with): *This table isn't very even; one of its legs is too short.*| *an even temperature* **2** [*with*] (of things that can be measured and compared) equal: *She won the first game and I won the second, so now we're even/now I'm even with her.*|*He cheated me, but I'll* **get even with** *him* (=harm him as he has harmed me) *one day!* **3** (of a number) that can be divided exactly by two: *2, 4, 6, 8, etc. are even numbers.* –opposite **odd** (for **3**) –**evenly** *adv* –**evenness** *n* [U]

**even**[2] *adv* **1** (used just before the surprising part of a statement, to make it stronger) which is more than might be expected: *Even the King and Queen experienced hardship during the war.* (=so certainly everyone else did)|*The King and Queen did not experience hardship even during the war.* (=so certainly not at any other time) **2** (used for making comparisons stronger): *It was cold yesterday, but it's even colder today.* **3 even if** no matter if; though: *Even if we could afford it, we wouldn't go abroad for our holidays.* (=because we don't want to) Compare *If we could afford it, we'd like to go abroad for our holidays.* (=but we can't) **4 even so** in spite of that; though that is true: *It's raining. Even so, we must go out.*

**even**[3] *v* → EVEN OUT

**eve·ning** /'iːvnɪŋ/ *n* [C;U] the end of the day and early part of the night: *Are you planning to go out this evening?*

**evening dress** /'·· ·/ *n* **1** [U] special clothes worn for formal occasions in the evening **2** [C] a usu. long dress worn by women for such an occasion

**even out** *v adv* [I;T (=**even** sthg.↔**out**)] to (cause to) become level or equal: *Prices have been rising very fast, but they should even out now.*

**e·vent** /ɪ'vent/ *n* **1** a happening, usu. an important one: *the chief events of 1981*|*I'll probably see you tomorrow, but* **in any event** (=whatever may happen) *I'll telephone.* –see also NON-EVENT; compare FACT (1) **2** any of the races, competitions, etc., arranged as part of a day's sports: *The next event will be* *the 100 metres race.* **3 in the event of (something)** if (something) happens: *In the event of rain, the party will be held indoors.*

**e·vent·ful** /ɪ'ventfəl/ *adj* full of important or interesting events: *an eventful life/meeting* –opposite **uneventful**

**e·ven·tu·al** /ɪ'ventʃuəl/ *adj* [A] (of an event) happening at last as a result: *the eventual success of his efforts* **–eventually** *adv*: *After failing four times, I eventually passed my driving test on the fifth attempt.*

**e·ven·tu·al·i·ty** /ɪˌventʃu'ælɪti/ *n* **-ties** a possible, esp. unpleasant, event: *We must be prepared for all eventualities/for any eventuality.*

**ev·er** /'evəʳ/ *adv* **1** (used mostly in questions, NEGATIVES² (1), comparisons, and sentences with *if*) at any time: *Nothing ever makes him angry.|Have you ever met?|I* **hardly ever** (=almost never) *go to the theatre.|If you ever come to Spain, we must meet.|He ran faster than ever.|It was the best holiday we've ever had.* **2** (used for giving force to an expression): *|He's been here ever since Monday.|Why ever not?* –see USAGE **3** (in some expressions) always: *They lived happily* **ever after.** (at the end of a fairy story)|*Yours ever, John* (at the end of a letter)|*the ever-increasing population* **4 ever so/such** *BrE infml* very: *It's ever so cold.* –compare NEVER

USAGE When ever is used after "how", "what", "when", etc. to show surprise or give force to a question, the two words should be written separately: Compare *What* **ever** *are you doing?* and *Do* **whatever** *she tells you.*

**ev·er·green** /'evəgriːn‖-ər-/ *adj,n* (a tree or bush) that does not lose its leaves in winter –compare DECIDUOUS

**ev·er·last·ing** /ˌevə'lɑːstɪŋ◂‖ˌevər'læ-/ *adj* **1** *fml* lasting for ever; without an end: *He believes in everlasting life/in life everlasting after death.* **2** [A] *derog* happening too often: *I'm tired ofyour everlasting complaints!*

**ev·er·more** /ˌevə'mɔːʳ‖ˌevər'mor/ *adv lit* always: *He swore to love her (for) evermore.*

**ev·ery** /'evri/ *determiner* [A] **1** each or all (of more than two): *I believe every word he says.|I enjoyed every minute of the party.|She's* **every bit as** (=just as) *clever as her sister.* –see Study Notes on page 494 **2** (of things that can be counted) once (in) each: *He comes to see us every day/every three days.|Change the oil in the car every 5,000 miles.* **3** all possible; as much as possible: *She made every attempt to go.* **4 every other** (of things that can be counted) the 1st, 3rd, 5th ... or the 2nd, 4th, 6th ... : *Take some medicine every other day.*

USAGE Compare **every one** and **everyone**: **Everyone** (or **everybody**) can only be used of people and is never followed by "of"; **every one** means each person or thing, and is often followed by "of": **Everyone** *in the class passed the exam.|There are 16 students and* **every one** *of them passed.* –see EACH¹ (USAGE)

**ev·ery·bod·y** /'evribɒdi‖-bɑdi/ also **everyone** /'evrɪwʌn/– *pron* every person: *Everybody else has gone home except me.* –see also NOBODY

USAGE **Anybody**, **every**, **everybody**, and **somebody** always take a singular verb, but they are often followed by a plural PRONOUN, except in very formal speech and writing: *Has* **everybody** *finished their drinks/his or her drink. (fml)?|***Anybody** *can use the library, can't they?|***Somebody** *lost their coat/his coat/her coat (fml).*

**ev·ery·day** /'evrideɪ/ *adj* [A *no comp.*] ordinary, common, and usual: *These are my everyday shoes, not my best ones.*

**ev·ery·thing** /'evriθɪŋ/ *pron* [*used with sing. verb*] **1** each thing; all things: *Everything is ready now for the party.|I've forgotten everything I learnt at school.* **2** all that matters: *Money isn't everything.* –compare NOTHING

**ev·ery·where** /'evriweəʳ/‖ also **everyplace** /-pleɪs/ *AmE*– *adv* in or to every place: *I can't find it, though I've looked everywhere.|She follows me everywhere I go.* –see also NOWHERE

**e·vict** /ɪ'vɪkt/ *v* [T *from*] to take (a person) away from a house or land by law: *If you don't pay your rent you'll be evicted.* **–eviction** /ɪ'vɪkʃən/ *n* [C;U]

**ev·i·dence** /'evɪ̣dəns/ *n* [U +*that/of, for*] **1** words or objects which prove a statement, support a belief, or make a matter more clear: *Can you show me any evidence for your statement?|The police have evidence that the killer was a woman.* **2 in evidence** able to be seen and noticed: *The police were much in evidence* (=very noticeable) *whenever the President made a public appearance.*

**ev·i·dent** /'evɪ̣dənt/ *adj* plain, esp. to the senses; clear because of EVIDENCE: *It's evident that you've been drinking.* **–evidently** *adv*

**e·vil¹** /'iːvəl/ *adj* **-ll-** *BrE*‖ **-l-** *AmE fml* very bad, esp. in thought or behaviour; wicked; harmful: *evil thoughts* –see WICKED (USAGE) **–evilly** *adv*

**evil²** *n* [C;U] *fml* (a) great wickedness or misfortune: *"Deliver us from evil."* (prayer) –opposite **good**

**e·vil·do·er** /ˌiːvəl'duːəʳ/ *n fml* a person who does evil

**e·vince** /ɪ'vɪns/ *v* **-vinced, -vincing** [T] *fml* (of a person or his/her behaviour) to show clearly (a feeling, quality, etc.)

**e·voc·a·tive** /ɪ'vɒkətɪv‖ɪ'vɑ-/ *adj* that produces memories and feelings: *Those toys are evocative of my childhood.*

**e·voke** /ɪ'vəʊk/ *v* **-voked, -voking** [T] *fml* to produce or call up (a memory, a feeling, or its expression): *That old film evoked memories of my childhood.* **–evocation** /ˌevə'keɪʃən, ˌiːvəʊ-/ *n* [C;U]

**ev·o·lu·tion** /ˌiːvə'luːʃən, ˌevə- ‖ˌevə-/ *n* [U] (the scientific idea of) the development of the various types of plants, animals, etc., from fewer and simpler forms: (fig.) *the evolution of the modern motor car* **–evolutionary** *adj*

**e·volve** /i'vɒlv‖ɪ'vɑlv/ *v* **-volved, -volving** [I;T *from*] to (cause to) develop gradually: *The British political system has evolved over several centuries.*

**ewe** /juː/ *n* a fully grown female sheep –compare RAM¹ (1)

**ex·a·cer·bate** /ɪg'zæsəbeɪt‖-ər-/ *v* **-bated, -bating** [T] *fml* to make worse (pain, diseases, problems, etc.) **–exacerbation** /-'beɪʃən/ *n* [C;U]

**ex·act¹** /ɪg'zækt/ *adj* **1** [A] correct and without mistakes; PRECISE: *an exact amount/weight|Your exact height is 1.79 metres.* **2** marked by thorough consideration or careful measurement of small details of fact: *You have to be very exact in this job, because a small mistake can make a big difference.* –opposite **inexact** –**exactness, exactitude** /-ɪtjuːd/ *n* [U]

**exact²** *v* [T *from*] *fml* to demand and obtain by force, threats, etc.: *He exacted obedience from the children.*

**ex·act·ing** /ɪg'zæktɪŋ/ *adj* demanding much care, effort, and attention: *an exacting child/piece of work*

**ex·act·ly** /ɪg'zæktli/ *adv* **1** (used with numbers and measures, and with *what, where, who,* etc.) with complete correctness: *Tell me exactly where she lives.|The train arrived at exactly 8 o'clock.* (=neither earlier nor later) **2** (used for adding force to an expression) just; really; quite: *Our new house is beautiful; exactly what we've always wanted.* **3** (used as a reply to something that has been said) Quite right!: *"So you believe, minister, that we must spend more on education?" "Exactly!"*

**ex·ag·ge·rate** /ɪg'zædʒəreɪt/ *v* **-rated, -rating** [I;T] to make (something) seem larger, better, worse, etc., than in reality: *That new machine is very useful, but he's exaggerating when he calls it the greatest invention ever made!* –**exaggerated** *adj* –**exaggeration** /- reɪʃən/ *n* [C;U]

**ex·alt** /ɪg'zɔːlt/ *v* [T] *fml* **1** to praise highly **2** to raise (a person) to a high rank –compare EXULT

**ex·al·ta·tion** /ˌegzɔːl'teɪʃən, ˌeksɔːl-/ *n* [U] *fml or lit* the joy of success

**ex·alt·ed** /ɪg'zɔːltɪ̵d/ *adj* (of a person or his/her position) of high rank

**ex·am·i·na·tion** /ɪgˌzæmɪ̵'neɪʃən/ *n* **1** [C *in, on*] also **exam** *infml*– a spoken or written test of knowledge: *Did you pass your history exam?|When will we know the examination results?* **2** [C;U] (an act of) examining (EXAMINE (1,2)): *Before we can offer you the job, you will have to have a medical examination.*

**ex·am·ine** /ɪg'zæmɪ̵n/ *v* **-ined, -ining** [T] **1** to look at (a person or thing) closely, in order to find out something: *My bags were examined when I entered the country.* **2** [*in, on*] to ask (a person) questions, in order to measure knowledge or find out something, as in a school or a court of law –compare CROSS-EXAMINE –**examiner** *n*

**ex·am·ple** /ɪg'zɑːmpəl‖ɪg'zæm-/ *n* **1** something which shows a general rule: *Her rudeness was a typical example of her usual bad manners.|This church is a wonderful example of the* GOTHIC *style of building.* **2** [*to*] *apprec* a person, or his behaviour, that is worthy of being copied: *He arrived at the office early, to* **set an example/a good example** *to the others.* **3 for example** also **e.g.** *abbrev.*– here is one of the things or people just spoken of: *The government has reduced spending in several areas, for example education and health.* **4 make an example of someone** to punish someone so that others will be afraid to behave as he/she did

USAGE Compare **set** an **example** and **give** an **example**: When we ourselves are an **example** to be copied, then we **set** it: *Drink your milk and* **set** *a good* **example** *to the other children!* When we invent an example to explain what we mean – *large animals, for* **example,** *elephants* – we are **giving** an **example.**

**ex·as·pe·rate** /ɪg'zɑːspəreɪt‖ɪg'zæ-/ *v* **-rated, -rating** [T] to annoy or make angry: *an exasperating delay* –**exasperation** /-'reɪʃən/ *n* [U]

**ex·ca·vate** /'ekskəveɪt/ *v* [T] to make or uncover by digging: *They've excavated a hole in the road.* –**excavation** /- 'veɪʃən/ *n* [C;U]

**ex·ca·va·tor** *n* a person or machine that EXCAVATES

**ex·ceed** /ɪk'siːd/ v [T] *fml* **1** [not *be* +*v*- *ing*] to be greater than: *The cost will not exceed £50.* **2** to do more than (what is lawful, necessary, etc.): *Don't exceed* (=drive faster than) *the speed limit.*

**ex·ceed·ing·ly** /ɪk'siːdɪŋli/ *adv* very; to an unusual degree: *Susan drove exceedingly fast.*

**ex·cel** /ɪk'sel/ *v* **-ll-** [I;T *as, at, in*; not *be* +*v-ing*] *fml* to be very good; do or be better than: *She excels as a teacher of dancing.*

**Ex·cel·len·cy** /'eksələnsi/ *n* **-cies** (the word used when speaking to or of certain persons of high rank in the state or church): *The King will see you now, (your) Excellency.*

**ex·cel·lent** /'eksələnt/ *adj* very good; of very high quality: *excellent health|Your examination results are excellent.* –**excellently** *adv* –**excellence** *n* [U]: *the excellence of her work*

**ex·cept¹** /ɪk'sept/ also **except for**– *prep,conj* leaving out; not including: *He answered all the questions except the last one.|I know nothing about it except what I read in the paper.|She can do everything except cook.|Except for one old lady, the bus was empty.* (=she was the only person in the bus) –see BESIDES² (USAGE)

**except²** *v* [T] *fml* to leave out; not include: *You will all be punished; I can except no one.*

**ex·cept·ed** /ɪk'septɪ̵d/ *adj* [after *n*] left out; apart from: *the whole family, with John excepted* (=except John)

**ex·cept·ing** /ɪk'septɪŋ/ *prep* leaving out; except: *They were all saved excepting the captain.*

**ex·cep·tion** /ɪk'sepʃən/ *n* [C;U] **1** (a case of) EXCEPTING (2) or being excepted: *You must answer all the questions without exception.|It's been very cold, but today's an exception; it's warm and sunny.|We don't usually accept cheques, but we'll* **make an exception** *in your case.* **2 take exception (to)** to be made angry (by): *I took the greatest exception to his rude letters.* **3 with the exception of** except; apart from: *Everyone was tired with the exception of John.*

**ex·cep·tion·al** /ɪk'sepʃənəl/ *adj often apprec* unusual, often in a good sense: *All her children are clever, but the youngest boy is really exceptional.* –**exceptionally** *adv*

**ex·cerpt** /'eksɜːpt‖-ɜr-/ *n* a piece taken from a book, speech, or musical work

**ex·cess¹** /ɪk'ses, 'ekses/ *n* [S;U *of*] **1** the fact of EXCEEDing, or an amount by which something EXCEEDs (the stated amount): *Never spend* **in excess of** (=more than) *your income.* **2** *derog* more than the reasonable degree or amount: *an excess of anger|to drink* **to excess**

**ex·cess²** /'ekses/ *adj* [A] additional; more than is usual, allowed, etc.: *to pay an excess baggage charge*

**ex·ces·sive** /ɪk'sesɪv/ *adj derog* too much; too great: *The food was bad and the bill was excessive.* –**excessively** *adv*

**ex·change¹** /ɪks'tʃeɪndʒ/ *n* **1** [C;U] (a case of) the act or action of exchanging: *an exchange of political* *prisoners between the two countries|He gave me an apple* **in exchange for** *a piece of cake.* **2** [C] also **telephone exchange**– (*often cap.*) a central place where telephone wires are connected so that people may speak to each other **3** [C] a place where businessmen meet to buy and sell (goods): *They sell shares in companies at the* STOCK EXCHANGE.

**exchange**[2] *v* **-changed, -changing** [T *for, with*] to give and receive (something in return for something else): *The two armies exchanged prisoners.|John exchanged books with Peter.* (=each gave the other his book) –compare CHANGE[1] (2) –**exchangeable** *adj*

**exchange rate** /·'· ·/ also **rate of exchange**– *n* the value of the money of one country compared to that of another country

**Ex·cheq·uer** /ɪks'ʃekəʳ||'ekstʃekər/ *n* (in Britain) the Government department which collects and controls public money, led by the **Chancellor of the Exchequer** –compare TREASURY

**ex·cise**[1] /'eksaɪz/ *n* the government tax on certain goods produced and used inside a country –compare CUSTOMS (2)

**ex·cise**[2] /ɪk'saɪz/ *v* **-cised, -cising** [T] *fml* to remove (as if) by cutting out: *to excise an organ from the body* –compare AMPUTATE –**excision** /ɪk'sɪʒən/ *n* [C;U]

**ex·ci·ta·ble** /ɪk'saɪtəbəl/ *adj* easily excited –**excitability** /-ə'bɪlɪ̣ti/ *n* [U]

**ex·cite** /ɪk'saɪt/ *v* **-cited, -citing** [T] **1** to cause (someone) to lose calmness and to have strong feelings, often pleasant: *The story excited the little boy very much.* **2** *fml* to cause (something to happen) by raising strong feelings: *The court case has excited a lot of public interest.*

**ex·cit·ed** /ɪk'saɪtɪ̣d/ *adj* full of strong, pleasant feelings; not calm: *The excited children were opening their Christmas presents.* –**excitedly** *adv*

**ex·cite·ment** /ɪk'saɪtmənt/ *n* [C;U] (something which causes) the condition of being excited: *As the end of the game grew near, the crowd's excitement increased.*

**ex·cit·ing** /ɪk'saɪtɪŋ/ *adj* that excites one: *an exciting story/football match* –opposite **unexciting**

**ex·claim** /ɪk'skleɪm/ *v* [T +*that*] (*usu. used with the actual words of the speaker*) to say suddenly, because of strong feeling: *"Good heavens!" he exclaimed. "It's 6 o'clock."* –compare EXPLAIN

**ex·cla·ma·tion** /ˌekskləˈmeɪʃən/ *n* the word(s) expressing a sudden strong feeling: *"Good heavens!" is an exclamation (of surprise).*

**exclamation mark** /··'·· ·/ *BrE*||**exclamation point** *AmE*– *n* a mark (!) which is written after the actual words of an EXCLAMATION: *"I'm hungry!"*

**ex·clude** /ɪk'sklu:d/ *v* **-cluded, -cluding** [T] **1** [*from*] to keep or leave out: *They excluded people under 21 from (joining) the club.* –opposite **include 2** to shut out from the mind (a reason or possibility): *We can't exclude the possibility that it will rain.* –**exclusion** /ɪk'sklu:ʒən/ *n* [U *from*]

**ex·clud·ing** /ɪk'sklu:dɪŋ/ *prep* not counting; not including: *There were 30 people in the hotel, excluding the hotel workers.* –opposite **including**

**ex·clu·sive**[1] /ɪk'sklu:sɪv/ *adj* **1** that EXCLUDES (1) people thought to be socially unsuitable and charges a lot of money: *one of London's most exclusive hotels* **2** [A] not shared with others: *This bathroom is for the President's exclusive use.* **3 exclusive of** not taking into account; without; EXCLUDING: *The hotel charges £15 a day, exclusive of meals.* –opposite **inclusive of** –**exclusiveness** *n* [U]

**exclusive**[2] *n* a newspaper story at first given to or printed by only one newspaper

**ex·clu·sive·ly** /ɪk'sklu:sɪvli/ *adv* only; and nothing/no one else: *This room is exclusively for women.*

**ex·com·mu·ni·cate** /ˌekskəˈmju:nɪ̣keɪt/ *v* **-cated, -cating** [T] to punish (someone) by driving him/her out from active membership in the Christian church –**excommunication** /-'keɪʃən/ *n* [C;U]

**ex·cre·ment** /'ekskrɪ̣mənt/ *n* [U] *fml* the solid waste matter passed from the body through the bowels –compare EXCRETA

**ex·cre·ta** /ɪk'skri:tə/ *n* [P] *fml* the solid and liquid waste matter (EXCREMENT, URINE, and SWEAT[1] (1)) passed from the body

**ex·crete** /ɪk'skri:t/ *v* **-creted, -creting** [I;T] *fml* to pass out (EXCRETA) –see also SECRETE[1]

**ex·cre·tion** /ɪk'skri:ʃən/ *n* [C;U] *fml* (the act of producing) EXCRETA

**ex·cru·ci·at·ing** /ɪk'skru:ʃieɪtɪŋ/ *adj* (of pain) very bad: *an excruciating headache* –**excruciatingly** *adv*

**ex·cur·sion** /ɪk'skɜ:ʃən||ɪk'skɜrʒən/ *n* a short journey made for pleasure, usu. by several people together: *to go on a day excursion* (=there and back in a day) *to Blackpool*

**ex·cu·sa·ble** /ɪk'skju:zəbəl/ *adj* (of behaviour) that can be forgiven –opposite **inexcusable** –**excusably** *adv*

**ex·cuse**[1] /ɪk'skju:z/ *v* **-cused, -cusing** [T] **1** [+*v-ing*/*for*] to forgive (someone) for a small fault: *Please excuse my bad handwriting/my lateness.* **2** (*mainly used in* NEGATIVES[2] (1), *questions, etc.*) to make (bad behaviour) seem less bad, or harmless: *Nothing can excuse his violent behaviour.* **3** [*from*] to free (someone) from a duty: *Can I be excused (from) football practice today?* **4 Excuse me: a** (*a polite expression used when starting to speak to a stranger, when one wants to get past a person, or when one disagrees with something he/she has said*) Forgive me: *Excuse me, does this bus go to the station?* **b** *AmE* for SORRY (2): *He said "Excuse me" when he stepped on my foot.* –see SORRY (USAGE)

**ex·cuse**[2] /ɪk'skju:s/ *n* [C;U *for*] the true or untrue reason given when asking to be forgiven for wrong behaviour: *Have you any excuse to offer for coming so late?|Stop making excuses!*

USAGE Compare **reason, excuse,** and **pretext**: *His* **reason** *for leaving early was that his wife was ill.* (=she really was ill)|*His* **excuse** *for leaving early was that his wife was ill.* (=she may or may not have been ill)|*He left early on the* **pretext** *that his wife was ill.* (=she was not ill at all, and he had another reason for leaving early)

**ex·e·cra·ble** /'eksɪ̣krəbəl/ *adj fml* very bad: *What an execrable meal!* –**execrably** *adv*

**ex·e·cute** /'eksɪ̣kju:t/ *v* **-cuted, -cuting** [T] **1** [*for*] to kill (someone) as a lawful punishment: *executed for murder* **2** to carry out (an order, plan, or piece of work): *He asked his brother to execute* (=carry out the orders in) *his* WILL² (4). **3** *fml* to perform (music, dance steps, etc.)

**ex·e·cu·tion** /ˌeksǝˈkjuːʃǝn/ *n* **1** [C;U] (a case of) lawful killing as a punishment: *Executions used to be held in public.* **2** [U *of*] the carrying out (of an order, plan, or piece of work): *This good idea was never* **put into execution.**

**ex·e·cu·tion·er** /ˌeksǝˈkjuːʃǝnǝʳ/ *n* the official who EXECUTES (1) criminals

**ex·ec·u·tive¹** /ɪgˈzekjʊtɪv‖-kjǝ-/ *adj* [A] **1** concerned with making and carrying out decisions, esp. in business: *a woman of great executive ability* **2** having the power to carry out government decisions and laws: *the executive branch of government*

**executive²** *n* **1** a person in an EXECUTIVE¹ (1) position **2** the person or group in the EXECUTIVE¹ (2) position in a government: *The President of the US is the chief executive.*

**ex·ec·u·tor** /ɪgˈzekjʊtǝʳ‖-kjǝ-/ n the person who carries out the orders in a WILL² (4)

**ex·em·pla·ry** /ɪgˈzemplǝri/ *n* [A] suitable as an example or as a warning: *exemplary behaviour* (=very good behaviour)

**ex·em·pli·fy** /ɪgˈzemplǝfaɪ/ *v* **-fied, -fying** [T] to be or give an example of: *The recent oil price rises exemplify the difficulties which the motor industry is now facing.* **–exemplification** /-fǝˈkeɪʃǝn/ *n* [C;U]

**ex·empt¹** /ɪgˈzempt/ *adj* [F *from*] freed (from a duty, service, payment, etc.): *He is exempt from military service, because of his bad health.*

**exempt²** *v* [T *from*] to make EXEMPT: *His bad health exempted him from military service.* **–exemption** *n* [C;U *from*]

**ex·er·cise¹** /ˈeksǝsaɪz‖-ǝr-/ *n* **1** [C;U] (a) use of any part of the body or mind so as to strengthen and improve it: *If you don't take/get more exercise you'll get fat.|Here is a set of exercises which will strengthen your arm muscles.* **2** [C] a question or set of questions to be answered by a pupil for practice **3** [U] the use of a (stated) power or right: *the exercise of one's right to vote* **4** [C] a movement made by soldiers, naval ships, etc., in time of peace, to practise fighting

**exercise²** *v* **-cised, -cising 1** [I;T] to (cause to) take exercise: *You should exercise more.* **2** [T] *fml* to use (a power or right): *You should try to exercise patience.*

**exercise book** /ˈ··· ˌ·/ *n* a book of plain paper in which students write (answers to) EXERCISES¹ (2) –see picture on page 105

**ex·ert** /ɪgˈzɜːt‖-ɜrt/ *v* [T] to use (strength, skill, etc.): *My wife's been exerting a lot of* PRESSURE *on me to change my job.|He never exerts himself* (=makes an effort) *to help anyone.*

**ex·er·tion** /ɪgˈzɜːʃǝn‖-ɜr-/ *n* [C;U] (a case of) EXERTing; (an) effort: *The doctor says he must avoid all exertion.*

**ex·hale** /eksˈheɪl/ *v* **-haled, -haling** [I;T] to breathe out (air, gas, etc.) –opposite **inhale –exhalation** /ˌekshǝˈleɪʃǝn/ *n* [C;U]

**ex·haust¹** /ɪgˈzɔːst/ *v* [T] **1** to tire out: *What an exhausting day!* **2** to use up or deal with completely: *to exhaust the supply of oxygen|I think we've exhausted this subject: let's go on to the next.*

**exhaust²** *n* **1** [C] also **exhaust pipe** /·ˈ· ·/– the pipe which allows unwanted gas, steam, etc., to escape from an engine or machine –see picture on page 85 **2** [U] the gas or steam which escapes through this pipe

**ex·haus·tion** /ɪgˈzɔːstʃǝn/ *n* [U] the state of being very tired: *to suffer from exhaustion*

**ex·haus·tive** /ɪgˈzɔːstɪv/ *adj* thorough: *an exhaustive study* –compare: *The men made an* **exhaustive** *search of the forest, but couldn't find the missing children.|The men have spent an* **exhausting** (=very tiring) *day searching the forest.* **–exhaustively** *adv*

**ex·hib·it¹** /ɪgˈzɪbǝt/ *v* [T] **1** to show in public, as for sale, or in a competition: *to exhibit paintings/flowers/new cars* **2** *fml* to show that one possesses (a feeling, quality, etc.): *to exhibit signs of fear/guilt*

**exhibit²** *n* **1** something that is EXHIBITed¹ (1), esp. in a MUSEUM **2** *AmE* for EXHIBITION (1)

**ex·hi·bi·tion** /ˌeksǝˈbɪʃǝn/ *n* **1** a public show of objects: *an international trade exhibition|The children's paintings are* **on exhibition** (=being shown publicly) *at the school.* **2** [*of*] an act of EXHIBITing¹ (2): *an exhibition of bad temper*

**ex·hi·bi·tion·is·m** /ˌeksǝˈbɪʃǝnɪzǝm/ *n* [U] *often derog* the behaviour of a person who wants to be looked at and admired **–exhibitionist** *n*

**ex·hib·i·tor** /ɪgˈzɪbǝtǝʳ/ *n* a person, firm, etc., that EXHIBITS¹ (1)

**ex·hil·a·rate** /ɪgˈzɪlǝreɪt/ *v* **-rated, -rating** [T] to make cheerful and excited: *We felt very exhilarated after our day at the seaside.* **–exhilaration** /-ˈreɪʃǝn/ *n* [U] **–exhilerating** *adj*

**ex·hort** /ɪgˈzɔːt‖-ɔrt/ *v* [T +*to-v*/*to*] *fml* to urge or advise strongly: *The general exhorted his men to fight hard.* **–exhortation** /ˌeksɔːˈteɪʃǝn/ *n* [C;U]

**ex·hume** /ɪgˈzjuːm, eksˈhjuːm‖ɪgˈzuːm, ɪkˈsjuːm/ *v* **-humed, -huming** [T] *fml* to take (a dead body) out of the grave **–exhumation** /ˌeksjʊˈmeɪʃǝn/ *n* [C;U]

**ex·ile¹** /ˈeksaɪl, ˈegzaɪl/ *n* **1** [S;U] unwanted absence from one's country, often for political reasons: *Napoleon was sent into exile.|to die in exile* **2** [C] a person who has been forced to leave his/her country, esp. for these reasons: *a tax exile* (=a person who lives in another country to avoid paying taxes in his/her own country)

**exile²** *v* **-iled, -iling** [T *to*] to send (someone) into EXILE¹ (1)

**ex·ist** /ɪgˈzɪst/ *v* [I] **1** to live or be real; to have being: *Do fairies exist?|The Roman Empire existed for several centuries.* **2** (of a person) to continue to live, esp. with difficulty: *She exists only on tea and bread.*

**ex·ist·ence** /ɪgˈzɪstǝns/ *n* **1** [U] the state of existing: *a new country which* **came into existence** *in 1918* **2** [S] life; way of living: *Working as a writer can be a very lonely existence.*

**ex·ist·ing** /ɪgˈzɪstɪŋ/ *adj* [A] present: *Food will not get cheaper under existing conditions.*

**ex·it¹** /ˈegzǝt, ˈeksǝt/ *n* **1** (*often written over a door*) a way out, e.g. from a theatre **2** an act of leaving, esp. of an actor leaving the stage: *Make your exit through the door at the back of the stage.*

**exit²** *v* [I] (*used as a stage direction* ) goes out; goes off stage: *Exit Hamlet, bearing the body of Polonius.*

USAGE In stage directions, **exit** comes before its subject and has only one tense.

**ex·o·dus** /'eksədəs/ *n* [S *of, from*] a going out or leaving by a great number of people: *an exodus of cars from the city every evening*

**ex·on·e·rate** /ɪg'zɒnəreɪt‖ɪg'zɑ-/ *v* **-rated, -rating** [T *from*] *fml* to free (someone) from blame: *The report on the accident exonerates the company (from any responsibility).* –**exoneration** /-'reɪʃən/ *n* [U]

**ex·or·bi·tant** /ɪg'zɔːbɪtənt‖-ɔr-/ *adj* (of cost, demands, etc.) much greater than is reasonable: *That hotel charges exorbitant prices.* –**exorbitantly** *adv*

**ex·or·cize,** ‖also **-cise** *BrE* /'eksɔːsaɪz‖-ɔr-/ *v* **-cized, -cizing** [T] to drive out (an evil spirit) from a person or place (as if) by solemn command –**exorcist** *n* –**exorcism** *n* [C;U]

**ex·ot·ic** /ɪg'zɒtɪk‖ɪg'zɑ-/ *adj usu. apprec* strange and unusual; (as if) from a distant country: *exotic flowers/food/smells* –**exotically** *adv*

**ex·pand** /ɪk'spænd/ *v* [I;T] to (cause to) grow larger: *Iron expands when it is heated.*|*The company has expanded its operations in Scotland by building a new factory there.* –opposite **contract** –**expandable** *adj*

**expand on** sthg. *v prep* [T] to make (a story, argument, etc.) more detailed by addition

**ex·panse** /ɪk'spæns/ *n* [*of*] a wide space: *an expanse of grass/of desert*

**ex·pan·sion** /ɪk'spænʃən/ *n* [U] the action of EXPANDing or state of being expanded: *the expansion of metals when they are heated*|*The new factory is large, to allow room for expansion.* –compare CONTRACTION

**ex·pan·sive** /ɪk'spænsɪv/ *adj* **1** (of a person) friendly and willing to talk: *After she'd had a few drinks, Mary became very expansive.* **2** large and splendid –compare EXPENSIVE –**expansively** *adv*

**ex·pat·ri·ate** /ek'spætrɪət, -trieɪt‖ek'speɪ-/ *n* a person living outside his or her own country

**ex·pect** /ɪk'spekt/ *v* [T] **1** [+*to-v*/*(that)*] to think (that someone or something will come or that something will happen): *I expect (that) he'll pass the examination.*|*We expect to make a small profit this year.*|*"Will she come soon?" "I expect so."*|*We're expecting visitors.*|*I expect John home at 6 o'clock.*|*His weakness after the illness is* **to be expected.** (=usual) **2** to believe, hope, and think (that someone will do something): *The train leaves at 8.30 so I'm expecting you all to be at the station on time.* **3** [+*(that)*; not *be* +*v-ing*] *BrE infml* to think (that something is true): *"Who broke that cup?" "I expect it was the cat."* **4 be expecting (a baby)** (of a woman) to be PREGNANT (1) (=carrying a child in her body)

**ex·pec·tan·cy** /ɪk'spektənsi/ *n* [U] hope; the state of expecting: *a feeling of expectancy*

**ex·pec·tant** /ɪk'spektənt/ *adj* [*no comp.*] **1** hopeful: *The expectant crowds waited for the queen to pass.* **2 expectant mother** a PREGNANT (1) woman –**expectantly** *adv: They waited expectantly.*

**ex·pec·ta·tion** /ˌekspek'teɪʃən/ *n* [C;U *of*] the condition of expecting; that which is expected: *We thought Mary would pass and John would fail, but* **contrary to expectation(s)** (=in spite of what was expected) *it was the other way round.*|*I usually enjoy his films, but the latest one didn't* **come up to/live up to** *my* **expectations**. (=was not as good as I expected)

**ex·pe·di·en·cy** /ɪk'spiːdɪənsi/ also **expedience** /-dɪəns/– *n* [U] **1** the quality of being EXPEDIENT **2** *derog* regard only for one's own personal advantage: *All his actions are governed by expediency.*

**ex·pe·di·ent¹** /ɪk'spiːdɪənt/ *adj fml* [F] (of a course of action) useful or helpful for a purpose: *She thought it expedient not to tell her mother where she had been.* –opposite **inexpedient** –**expediently** *adv*

**expedient²** *n fml* an EXPEDIENT plan, idea, or action

**ex·pe·dite** /'ekspɪdaɪt/ *v* **-dited, -diting** [T] *fml* to make (a plan or arrangement) go faster: *The builders promised to expedite the repairs to the roof.*

**ex·pe·di·tion** /ˌekspɪ'dɪʃən/ *n* (the persons, vehicles, etc., going on) a (long) journey for a certain purpose: *an expedition to photograph wild animals in Africa* –see TRAVEL (USAGE)

**ex·pe·di·tion·a·ry** /ˌekspɪ'dɪʃənəri‖-neri/ *adj* [A] of or making up an EXPEDITION of war: *an* **expeditionary force**

**ex·pel** /ɪk'spel/ *v* **-ll-** [T *from*] **1** to dismiss officially (from a school, club, etc.): *He was expelled for smoking in class.* **2** *fml* to force out (from the body or a container): *to expel air from one's lungs*

**ex·pend** /ɪk'spend/ *v* [T *in, upon*] to spend or use up (esp. time, care, etc.): *to expend one's energy*

**ex·pen·da·ble** /ɪk'spendəbəl/ *adj* that may be used up for a purpose: *The officer regarded his soldiers as expendable.* (=did not mind if they were killed)

**ex·pen·di·ture** /ɪk'spendɪtʃə^r/ *n* [S;U *of, on*] spending or using up: *efforts to reduce government expenditure*

**ex·pense** /ɪk'spens/ *n* [U] **1** cost of money, time, effort, etc.: *She* **spared no expense/went to great expense** (=spent a lot of money) *to make the party a success.*|*He finished the job* **at the expense of** (=causing the loss of) *his health.* –see COST² (USAGE) **2 at someone's expense** with someone paying the cost: *He had to repair his car at his own expense.*|(fig.) *He tried to be clever at my expense.* (=to make me seem silly)

**ex·pens·es** /ɪk'spensɪz/ *n* [P] the money used or needed for a purpose: *travelling/holiday/funeral expenses*

**ex·pen·sive** /ɪk'spensɪv/ *adj* costing a lot of money: *an expensive new coat*|*Buying that car was an expensive mistake.* –opposite **inexpensive** –**expensively** *adv*

**ex·pe·ri·ence¹** /ɪk'spɪərɪəns/ *n* **1** [U] (the gaining of) knowledge or skill from practice rather than from books: *a teacher with five years' experience* **2** [C] something that happens to one and has an effect on the mind and feelings: *Our journey by camel was quite an experience.*

**experience²** *v* **-enced, -encing** [T] to feel, suffer, or know, as an experience: *to experience joy/difficulties/defeat*

**ex·pe·ri·enced** /ɪk'spɪərɪənst/ *adj* [*in*] having the right kind of experience: *an experienced doctor/traveller* –opposite **inexperienced**

**ex·per·i·ment¹** /ɪk'sperɪmənt/ *n* [C;U] (a) trial made in order to learn something or prove the truth of an idea: *to make/carry out/perform an experiment*|*to prove by experiment*

**experiment²** *v* [I *on, upon, with*] to make an EXPERIMENT: *They experimented with new materials.*|*Many people disapprove of experimenting on animals.* –**experimentation** /- men'teɪʃən/ *n* [U]

**ex·per·i·men·tal** /ɪkˌsperɪ̆ˈmentl/ *adj* used for or connected with EXPERIMENTS: *an experimental farm* –**experimentally** *adv*

**ex·pert** /ˈekspɜːt||-ɜrt/ *adj,n* [*at, in*] (a person) with special knowledge or training: *She's (an) expert in/at/on teaching small children.* –**expertly** *adv*

**ex·per·tise** /ˌekspɜːˈtiːz||-ɜr-/ *n* [U] skill in a particular field; KNOW-HOW: *business expertise*

**ex·pi·ra·tion** /ˌekspɪ̆ˈreɪʃən/ also **expiry** /ˈekspɪ̆ri, ɪkˈspaɪəri/– *n* [U] the end of (something which lasts for a period of time): *the expiration of a trade agreement between two countries|What is the* **expiry date** *on your library book?*

**ex·pire** /ɪkˈspaɪəʳ/ *v* **-pired, -piring** [I] **1** *more fml than* **run out**– (of something which lasts for a period of time) to come to an end: *Our trade agreement with China will expire next year.* **2** *lit* to die

**ex·plain** /ɪkˈspleɪn/ *v* **1** [I;T +*that/to*] to give the meaning (of something); make (something) clear, by speaking or writing: *I don't understand this, but Paul will explain (it) (to us).|Can you explain what this word means?* **2** [T] to give or be the reason for; account for: *Can you explain your stupid behaviour?|That explains why he's not here.*

**ex·pla·na·tion** /ˌekspləˈneɪʃən/ *n* [C;U *of, for*] **1** (an act of) explaining: *She's giving an explanation of how the machine works.* **2** something that explains: *Can you think of any explanation for his rudeness?*

**ex·plan·a·to·ry** /ɪkˈsplænətəri||-tori/ *adj* (of a statement, a piece of writing, etc.) that explains –see also SELF-EXPLANATORY

**ex·ple·tive** /ɪkˈspliːtɪv||ˈeksplətɪv/ *n* an often meaningless word used to express violent feeling; OATH (2) or curse: "DAMN" *is an expletive.*

**ex·pli·ca·ble** /ˈeksplɪkəbəl||ekˈsplɪ-/ *adj* [F] *fml* (of behaviour or events) that can be explained–opposite **inexplicable** –**explicably** *adv*

**ex·pli·cit** /ɪkˈsplɪsɪ̆t/ *adj* (of statements, rules, etc.) clear and fully expressed: *to give explicit directions* –compare IMPLICIT (1) –**explicitly** *adv*

**ex·plode** /ɪkˈspləud/ *v* **-ploded, -ploding** [I;T] (esp. of a bomb or other explosive) to (cause to) blow up or burst: (fig.) *to explode with/in anger*

**ex·ploit**[1] /ɪkˈsplɔɪt/ *v* [T] **1** *derog* to use (esp. a person) unfairly for one's own profit: *to exploit the poor by making them work for less pay* **2** to use or develop (a thing) fully so as to get profit: *to exploit the undersea oil* –**exploitation** /ˌeksplɔɪˈteɪʃən/ *n* [U]

**ex·ploit**[2] /ˈeksplɔɪt/ *n apprec* a brave, bold, and successful deed

**ex·plore** /ɪkˈsplɔːʳ/ *v* **-plored, -ploring** [T] to travel into or through (a place) for the purpose of discovery: (fig.) *We must explore* (=examine carefully) *all the possibilities.* –**explorer** *n* –**exploration** /ˌeksplәˈreɪʃən/ *n* [C;U]: *a journey of exploration into China* –**exploratory** /ɪkˈsplɒrətəri||-tori/ *adj*

**ex·plo·sion** /ɪkˈspləuʒən/ *n* **1** (a loud noise caused by) an act of exploding: *When she lit the gas there was a loud explosion.|*(fig.) *explosions of loud laughter* **2** a sudden increase: *population explosion*

**ex·plo·sive**[1] /ɪkˈspləusɪv/ *adj* that can explode: *It's dangerous to smoke when handling explosive materials.|*(fig.) *The question of race is an explosive one.* (=causes strong feelings) –**explosively** *adv*

**explosive**[2] *n* an explosive substance

**ex·po·nent** /ɪkˈspəunənt/ *n* [*of*] a person who expresses, supports, or is an example of (a stated belief or idea): *She's an exponent of the opinions of Freud.*

**ex·port**[1] /ɪkˈspɔːt||-ɔrt/ *v* [I;T] to send (goods) out of a country for sale –compare IMPORT[1] –**exportable** *adj*

**ex·port**[2] /ˈekspɔːt||-ɔrt/ *n* **1** [U] also **exportation** /ˌekspɔːˈteɪʃən||-ɔr-/– (the business of) EXPORTing: *the export trade|The export/exportation of gold is forbidden.* **2** [C] something that is EXPORTed: *Wool is one of the chief exports of Australia.* –compare IMPORT[2] (1,2)

**ex·port·er** /ɪkˈspɔːtəʳ||-ɔr-/ *n* a person or country that EXPORTS: *Zambia is the world's largest exporter of copper.* –compare IMPORTER

**ex·pose** /ɪkˈspəuz/ *v* **-posed, -posing** [T] **1** [*to*] to uncover; leave unprotected: *to expose one's skin to the sun* |(fig.) *As a photographer in the war, she was exposed to many dangers.* **2** [*to*] to make known (a secretly guilty person or action): *I threatened to expose him (to the police).* **3** to uncover (a film) to the light, when taking a photograph

**ex·po·sé** /ekˈspəuzeɪ||ˌekspəˈzeɪ/ *n* [*of*] a public statement of the (esp. shameful) facts (about something): *a newspaper exposé of* CORRUPTION

**ex·po·si·tion** /ˌekspəˈzɪʃən/ *n* **1** [C;U] *fml* (an act of) explaining and making clear: *a full exposition of her political beliefs* **2** [C] an international show (EXHIBITION (1)) of the products of industry

**ex·po·sure** /ɪkˈspəuʒəʳ/ *n* **1** [C;U *to*] (a case of) being EXPOSED (1): *We nearly died of exposure on the cold mountain.|much exposure to danger* **2** [C;U *of*] a case of exposing, or the experience of being EXPOSED (2): *I threatened him with public exposure.* **3** [C] the amount of film that must be EXPOSED (3) to take one photograph: *I have three exposures left on this film.*

**ex·pound** /ɪkˈspaund/ *v* [T *to*] *fml* to give an EXPOSITION (1) of: *The priest expounded his religious ideas*

**ex·press**[1] /ɪkˈspres/ *v* [T] to show (a feeling, opinion, or fact) in words or in some other way: *I can't express how grateful I am.|She expressed surprise when I told her you were coming.|He* **expresses himself** (=speaks or writes) *in good clear English.*

**express**[2] *n* **1** [C] also **express train** /·ˈ· ·/– a fast train which stops at only a few stations **2** [U] *BrE* a service given by the post office, railways, etc., for carrying things faster than usual

**express**[3] *adv* by EXPRESS[2] (2): *I sent the parcel express.*

**express**[4] *adj* [A] **1** (of a command, wish, etc.) clearly stated or understood; EXPLICIT: *It was her express wish that you should have her jewels after her death.* **2** going or sent quickly: *an express train*

**ex·pres·sion** /ɪkˈspreʃən/ *n* **1** [C;U] (an example of) the act of expressing: *A government should permit the free expression of political opinion.* **2** [U] the quality of showing or performing with feeling: *She doesn't sing with much expression.* **3** [C] a word or group of words: *"In the family way" is an old-fashioned expression meaning* "PREGNANT". **4** [C] a look on a person's face: *a wise/angry expression*

**ex·pres·sion·less** /ɪkˈspreʃənlɪ̆s/ *adj* (esp. of a voice or face) without EXPRESSION (2) –**expressionlessly** *adv*

**ex·pres·sive** /ɪk'spresɪv/ *adj* [*of*] (esp. of words or a face) full of feeling and meaning –**expressively** *adv*

**ex·press·ly** /ɪk'spresli/ *adv* clearly; in an EXPRESS[4] (1) way: *I told you expressly to lock the door.*

**ex·press·way** /ɪk'spresweɪ/ *n AmE* for MOTORWAY

**ex·pro·pri·ate** /ɪk'sprəuprieɪt/ *v* **-ated, -ating** [T] *fml* to take away (something owned by another), often for public use: *The State expropriated all the oil wells.* –**expropriation** /-'eɪʃən/ *n* [C;U]

**ex·pul·sion** /ɪk'spʌlʃən/ *n* [C;U] (an act of) EXPELling or being expelled: *the expulsion of a child from school*

**ex·pur·gate** /'ekspəgeɪt‖-ər-/ *v* **-gated, -gating** [T] *fml* to make (a book, play, etc.) pure by taking out anything which is considered improper –**expurgation** /-'geɪʃən/ *n* [C;U]

**ex·qui·site** /ɪk'skwɪz½t, 'ekskwɪ-/ *adj apprec* very finely made or done; almost perfect: *an exquisite piece of jewellery* –**exquisitely** *adv*

**ex·tem·po·re** /ɪk'stempəri/ *adj,adv* (spoken or done) in haste, without time for preparation: *an extempore speech*

**ex·tend** /ɪk'stend/ *v* **1** [I] (of space, land, or time) to reach, stretch, or continue: *The hot weather extended into October.* **2** [T] to make longer or greater: *to extend the railway to the next town* **3** [T] to stretch out (a part of one's body) to the limit: *a bird with its wings extended* **4** [T] *fml* to give or offer (help, friendship, etc.) to someone: *to extend a warm welcome to him*|*The bank will extend you* CREDIT[1] (4).

**ex·ten·sion** /ɪk'stenʃən/ *n* **1** [U] the act of EXTENDing or condition of being EXTENDed (2,3,4): *the extension of our foreign trade* **2** [C] a part which is added to make something longer, wider, or greater: *to build an extension onto the house* **3** [C] any of many telephone lines which connect the SWITCHBOARD to various rooms or offices in a large building: *Could I have extension 45, please?*

**ex·ten·sive** /ɪk'stensɪv/ *adj* large in amount or area: *an extensive garden*|*extensive damage from the storm* –see also INTENSIVE –**extensively** *adv*

**ex·tent** /ɪk'stent/ *n* **1** [U *of*] the length or area to which something EXTENDs (1): *The full extent of the desert is not known.*|(fig.) *I was surprised at the extent of his knowledge.* **2** [S;U] (a) (stated) degree: *I agree with what you say to some/a certain extent.* (=partly)

**ex·ten·u·ate** /ɪk'stenjueɪt/ *v* **-ated, -ating** [T] *fml* to lessen the seriousness of, by finding excuses for (bad behaviour): *He stole the money, but there are* **extenuating circumstances.** (=facts that might excuse him)

**ex·te·ri·or**[1] /ɪk'stɪərɪə<sup>r</sup>/ *adj* outer; on or from the outside (esp. of places): *the exterior walls of the prison* –opposite **interior**; compare EXTERNAL

**exterior**[2] *n* the outside; the outer appearance or surface: *the exterior of the house* –opposite **interior**

**ex·ter·mi·nate** /ɪk'stɜːm½neɪt‖-ɜr-/ *v* **- nated, -nating** [T] to kill (all the creatures or people in a place, or all those of a certain kind or race) –**extermination** /-'neɪʃən/ *n* [U]

**ex·ter·nal** /ɪk'stɜːnəl‖-ɜr-/ *adj* on, of, or for the outside: *This medicine is for external use* only. (=for putting on the skin) *not for drinking*|*This newspaper doesn't pay much attention to external* (=foreign) *affairs.* –opposite **internal**; compare EXTERIOR –**externally** *adv*

**ex·tinct** /ɪk'stɪŋkt/ *adj* (esp. of a kind of animal) no longer existing: *The* DODO *is extinct.* (=there are no live DODOs anywhere in the world)|*an extinct* (= no longer active) VOLCANO

**ex·tinc·tion** /ɪk'stɪŋkʃən/ *n* [U] **1** the state of being or becoming EXTINCT: NUCLEAR *war threatens the human race with complete extinction.* **2** the act of EXTINGUISHing or making EXTINCT: *the extinction of his hopes*

**ex·tin·guish** /ɪk'stɪŋgwɪʃ/ *v* [T] *fml* to put out (a light or fire)

**ex·tin·guish·er** /ɪk'stɪŋgwɪʃə<sup>r</sup>/ *n* an instrument for putting out small fires by shooting liquid chemicals at them

**ex·tol** /ɪk'stəul/ *v* **-ll-** [T] *fml* to praise very highly: *He keeps extolling the* MERITS *of his new car.*

**ex·tort** sthg. **from** sbdy. /ɪk'stɔːt‖-ɔrt/ *v prep* [T] to obtain (esp. money) by force or threats: *He's been charged with extorting money from several shopkeepers.* –**extortion** *n* [U]: *money obtained by extortion*

**ex·tor·tion·ate** /ɪk'stɔːʃən½t‖-ɔr-/ *adj derog* (of a demand, price, etc.) much too high; EXORBITANT –**extortionately** *adv*

**ex·tra**[1] /'ekstrə/ *adj,adv* **1** [A] additional(ly); beyond what is usual or necessary: *an extra loaf of bread*|*to work extra hard* **2** [F] as well as the regular charge: *Dinner costs £8, and wine is extra.*|*They charge extra for wine.*

**extra**[2] *n* **1** something added, for which an EXTRA[1] (2) charge is made: *At this hotel a hot bath is an extra.* **2** a film actor who has a very small part, e.g. in a crowd scene

**ex·tract**[1] /ɪk'strækt/ *v* [T *from*] **1** to pull or take out, often with difficulty: *to extract a tooth*|(fig.) *He extracted a promise from me* (=made me promise) *that I'd come to the party.* **2** to take out with a machine or instrument, or by chemical means (a substance which is contained in another substance): *to extract gold from the rocks*

**ex·tract**[2] /'ekstrækt/ *n* **1** [C;U *of*] (a) product obtained by EXTRACTing[1] (2): *meat extract* –compare ESSENCE (2) **2** [C *from*] a passage of written or spoken matter that has been taken from a book; EXCERPT: *She read me a few extracts from his letter.*

**ex·trac·tion** /ɪk'strækʃən/ *n* **1** [C;U *from*] the act or an example of EXTRACTing: *Her teeth are so bad that she needs five extractions.*|*the extraction of coal from a mine* **2** [U] (the stated) origin (of a person's family): *an American of Russian extraction* (=his family came from Russia)

**ex·trac·tor** /ek'stræktə<sup>r</sup>/ *n* an apparatus which sends out impure or smelly air from a kitchen, factory, etc. –see picture on page 521

**ex·tra·cur·ric·u·lar** /ˌekstrəkə'rɪkjʊlə<sup>r</sup>‖-kjə-/ *adj* (esp. of activities such as sports, music, or acting) outside the regular course of work (CURRICULUM) in a school or college

**ex·tra·dite** /'ekstrədaɪt/ *v* [T *from, to*] **1** to send (someone who may be guilty of a crime in another country) back for trial **2** to obtain (such a person) for trial in this way –**extradition** /-'dɪʃən/ *n* [C;U]

**ex·tra·ne·ous** /ɪk'streɪnɪəs/ *adj fml* not belonging or directly connected: *His account of the war includes a lot of extraneous details.* –**extraneously** *adv*

**extra·or·di·na·ry** /ɪk'strɔːdənəri‖ɪk'strɔrdn-eri, ˌekstrə'ɔr-/ *adj* **1** very strange: *What an extraordinary idea!* –see also ORDINARY **2** [A] more than what is ordinary: *a girl of extraordinary beauty*|*Owing to the danger of war, there will be an extraordinary* (=as opposed to regular) *meeting of Parliament tonight.* **–extraordinarily** *adv*

**ex·trap·o·late** /ɪk'stræpəleɪt/ *v* **- lated, -lating** [I;T] *fml* to guess (something in the future) from facts already known

**ex·trav·a·gant** /ɪk'strævəgənt/ *adj derog* **1** wasteful, esp. of money: *an extravagant method of production* **2** (of ideas, behaviour, and the expression of feeling) uncontrolled; beyond what is reasonable: *He makes the most extravagant claims for his new system.* **–extravagantly** *adv* **–extravagance** *n* [C;U]: *Try to shop carefully and avoid extravagance.*|*His latest extravagance is a hand-made silk shirt.*

**ex·treme¹** /ɪk'striːm/ *adj* **1** [A *no comp.*] the furthest possible; at the very beginning or very end: *extreme old age* **2** [A *no comp.*] the greatest possible: *extreme heat/danger* **3** *often derog* (of opinions and those who hold them) going beyond the usual limits: *His political ideas are rather extreme.* –compare MODERATE¹ (2)

**extreme²** *n* **1** an EXTREME¹ (2) degree: *Sometimes he eats too much and sometimes he eats nothing. He goes from one extreme to the other.*|*She has been generous* **in the extreme.** (=very generous) –compare EXTREMITY **2 go/be driven to extremes** to act too violently; to behave in an EXTREME¹ (3) way

**ex·treme·ly** /ɪk'striːmli/ *adv* very: *I'm extremely sorry.* –see Study Notes on page 389

**ex·trem·is·m** /ɪk'striːmɪzəm/ *n* [U] *derog* (esp. in politics) the quality or state of being EXTREME¹ (3) **–extremist** *n,adj*

**ex·trem·i·ty** /ɪk'stremǝ̍ti/ *n* **-ties 1** [S;U *of*] the highest degree (esp. of suffering and sorrow); (a case of) the greatest misfortune **2** [C] the furthest point: *His extremities* (=hands and feet) *were frozen.*

**ex·tri·cate** /'ekstrǝ̍keɪt/ *v* **-cated, -cating** [T *from*] to set free from something that it is difficult to escape from: *I thought he was going to talk for hours, but I extricated myself by saying I had to catch a train.* **–extricable** /ek'strɪkəbəl/ *adj* **–extrication** /-ˌekstrɪ'keɪʃən/ *n* [U]

**ex·tro·vert, extravert** /'ekstrəvɜːt‖-ɜrt/ *n* a person who is cheerful and likes to be with and amuse other people rather than being quiet and alone –see also INTROVERT

**ex·u·be·rant** /ɪg'zjuːbərənt‖ɪg'zuː-/ *adj* overflowing with life and cheerful excitement: *an exuberant child*|(fig.) *the exuberant growth of a tropical rain forest* **–exuberantly** *adv* **–exuberance** *n* [U]

**ex·ude** /ɪg'zjuːd‖ɪg'zuːd/ *v* **-uded, -uding** [I;T] to (cause to) flow out slowly and spread in all directions: (fig.) *He's very popular with all the women here; he simply exudes charm.*

**ex·ult** /ɪg'zʌlt/ *v* [I +*to-v*/*at, in*] *fml or lit* to rejoice; to show delight: *The people exulted in/at the victory.* –compare EXALT **–exultant** *adj* **–exultantly** *adv* **–exultation** /ˌegzʌl'teʃən/ *n* [U *at, over*]

**exult over** sbdy./sthg. *v prep* [T] to rejoice proudly over (esp. a defeated enemy)

**eye¹** /aɪ/ *n* **1** the bodily organ with which one sees: *He lost an eye in an accident, and now he has a glass eye.*|*She has blue eyes.* –see picture on page 299 **2** the power of seeing: *My eye fell upon* (=I noticed) *an interesting article in the newspaper.*|*She has* **a (good) eye for** (=the ability to see, judge, etc.) *fashion.* **3** the hole in a needle through which the thread passes **4** a small ring-shaped or U-shaped piece of metal into which a hook fits for fastening clothes: *Her dress was fastened with hooks and eyes.* **5 in the eyes of** in the opinion of: *In her father's eyes, she can do nothing wrong.* **6 keep an eye on** *infml* to watch carefully: *Please keep an eye on the baby for me.* **7 keep an eye out for** to try to notice and remember; be on the LOOKOUT (1) for **8 keep one's eyes open** (also **skinned** *BrE*‖**peeled** *AmE*) to watch carefully (for) **9 see eye to eye (with)** to agree completely (with): *He and his brother always see eye to eye.* **10 under/before one's very eyes** in front of one, so that one can see with no difficulty: *They stole the jewels under my very eyes.* **11 up to the/one's eyes in** *infml* having more than one can easily deal with: *I'm up to the eyes in work/debt.* **12 with one's eyes open** knowing what may possibly happen: *You married him with your eyes open, so don't complain now!* **13 -eyed** having eyes of the stated kind or number: *blue-eyed*|*one-eyed*|*bright-eyed* **–eyeless** *adj*

**eye²** *v* **eyed, eyeing** *or* **eying** [T] to look at closely, esp. with interest or distrust

**eye·ball** /'aɪbɔːl/ *n* the whole of the eye, including the part hidden inside the head

**eye·brow** /'aɪbraʊ/ *n* **1** the line of hairs above each of the two human eyes –see picture on page 299 **2 raise one's eyebrows (at)** to express surprise, doubt, or disapproval (at): *There were a lot of raised eyebrows/eyebrows raised at the news of the minister's dismissal.*

**eye-catch·ing** /'· ˌ··/ *adj* (of a thing) so unusual that one cannot help looking at it: *an eye-catching advertisement*

**eye·lash** /'aɪlæʃ/ *n* one of the small hairs which grow from the edge of each eyelid –see picture on page 299

**eye·lid** /'aɪˌlɪd/ *n* either of the pieces of covering skin which can move down to close each eye

**eye-o·pen·er** /'· ˌ···/ *n* [S] something surprising, which makes a person see a truth he/she did not formerly believe: *I knew he was strong, but it was an eye-opener to me when I saw him lift that car.*

**eye·sight** /'aɪsaɪt/ *n* [U] the power of seeing: *good/poor eyesight*

**eye·sore** /'aɪsɔːʳ/ *n* something ugly to look at (esp. when many people can see it): *That new shopping centre is a real eyesore.*

**eye·strain** /'aɪstreɪn/ *n* [U] a painful and tired condition of the eyes, as caused by reading very small print

**eye·wit·ness** /'aɪˌwɪtnǝ̍s/ *n* [*to, of*] a person who sees and is able to describe an event: *Were there any eyewitnesses to the crime?*

# F, f

**SPELLING NOTE**
Words with the sound /f/ may be spelt **ph-**, like **photograph.**

**F , f** /ef/ **F's, f's** *or* **Fs, fs** the 6th letter of the English alphabet

**F** *written abbrev. said as:* FAHRENHEIT

**fa·ble** /ˈfeɪbəl/ *n* **1** [C] a short story that teaches a lesson (a MORAL) or truth, esp. one in which animals or objects speak **2** [C;U] a story or stories about great people who never actually lived; LEGEND (1); MYTH

**fab·ric** /ˈfæbrɪk/ *n* **1** [C;U] cloth made of threads woven together **2** [U] the walls, roof, etc., of a building: (fig.) *The whole fabric* (=framework) *of society was changed by the war.*

**fab·ri·cate** /ˈfæbrɪkeɪt/ *v* **-cated, -cating** [T] to make or invent (in order to deceive) **–fabrication** /-ˈkeɪʃən/ *n* [C;U]: *His story was a complete fabrication.* (=was completely untrue)

**fab·u·lous** /ˈfæbjʊləs‖-jə-/ *adj* **1** nearly unbelievable: *a fabulous sum of money* **2** *infml* very good or pleasant; excellent: *We had a fabulous holiday.* **3** existing or told about in FABLES: *fabulous creatures*

**fab·u·lous·ly** /ˈfæbjʊləsli‖-jə-/ *adv* very (rich, great, etc.)

**fa·cade, façade** /fəˈsɑːd, fæ-/ *n* **1** the front of a building **2** a false appearance: *a facade of honesty*

**face¹** /feɪs/ *n* **1** [C] the front part of the head from the chin to the hair: *a round face* –see picture on page 299 **2** [C] an expression on the face: *their happy faces|She* **pulled a long face**. (=looked sad) **3** [C] the front, top, or most important surface of something: *the face of a clock|We climbed the north face of the mountain.|They seem to have disappeared* **off the face of the earth. 4** [C] a rock surface, either above or below ground, from which coal, gold, diamonds, etc., are dug **5** [U] the condition of being respected: *He was afraid of risking failure because he didn't want to* **lose face.**|*England* **saved (their) face** *by getting 3 points in the last minute and drawing the match.* **6 face to face (with)** in the direct presence (of): *I've often talked to him on the telephone, but I've never met him face to face.|She came face to face with death.* **7 in the face of** in opposition to; in spite of **8 on the face of it** judging by what one can see; APPARENTLY **9 to someone's face** openly in someone's presence: *He wouldn't say rude things about her to her face.* **10 -faced** having a certain kind of face or expression: *red-faced|sad-faced*

**face²** *v* **faced, facing 1** [I;T] to have the face or front pointing (towards): *The house faces (towards the) north/faces the park.* **2** [T] to be in the presence of and oppose; CONFRONT: *We're faced with a difficult decision.|I couldn't face another day at work, so I pretended to be ill.* **3** [T *with*] to cover esp. the front part of (something) with a different material: *The brick house was faced with stone.* **4 face the music** to meet and deal with the unpleasant results of one's actions

**face up to** sthg. *v adv prep* [T] to be brave enough to accept or deal with: *to face up to one's responsibilities*

**face·cloth** /ˈfeɪsklɒθ‖-klɔθ/ also **washcloth** *AmE– n* a small cloth (FLANNEL) used to wash the body

**face·less** /ˈfeɪsləs/ *adj* without any clear character: *Crowds of faceless people pour into the city each day.*

**face-lift** /ˈ· ˌ·/ *n* a medical operation to make the face look younger by tightening the skin: (fig.) *to give a room a face-lift* (= to improve its appearance)

**fac·et** /ˈfæsət/ *n* any of the many flat sides of a cut jewel or precious stone: (fig.) *The question had many facets.* (= parts to be considered)

**fa·ce·tious** /fəˈsiːʃəs/ *adj derog* humorous; tending to use unsuitable jokes: *facetious remarks* **–facetiously** *adv* **–facetiousness** *n* [U]

**face val·ue** /ˌ· ˈ··/ *n* [C;U] the value or cost as shown on the front of something, such as a postage stamp: (fig.) *If you take his remarks only* **at (their) face value** (=as they appear at first), *you won't understand his full meaning.*

**fa·cial¹** /ˈfeɪʃəl/ *adj* of or concerning the face: *facial hair* **–facially** *adv*

**facial²** *n* a beauty treatment for the face

**fa·cile** /ˈfæsaɪl‖ˈfæsəl/ *adj derog* **1** [A] easily done or obtained: *facile success* **2** too easy; not deep; meaningless: *facile remarks*

**fa·cil·i·tate** /fəˈsɪləteɪt/ *v* **-tated, -tating** [T] *fml* to make easy or easier; help: *The new underground railway will facilitate the journey to the airport.*

**fa·cil·i·ties** /fəˈsɪlətiz/ *n* [P] means to do things; that which can be used: *The college has excellent sporting facilities.*

**fa·cil·i·ty** /fəˈsɪləti/ *n* **-ties 1** [C;U] *fml* (an) ability to do something easily: *His facility with/in languages is surprising.* **2** [C] an advantage; CONVENIENCE (2): *A free bus to the airport is a facility offered only by this hotel.*

**fac·ing** /ˈfeɪsɪŋ/ *n* [U] **1** an outer covering or surface, as of a wall, for protection, decoration, etc. **2** additional material sewn into the edges of a garment, to improve it, esp. in thickness

**fac·sim·i·le** /fækˈsɪməli/ *n* an exact copy, esp. of a picture or piece of writing

**fact** /fækt/ *n* **1** [C] something that has actually happened or is happening; something known to be, or accepted as being, true: *Certain facts have become known about the materials of the moon.|It is a fact that Alexander Graham Bell invented the telephone.|She didn't answer my letter. The fact is she didn't even read it.* –compare EVENT (1) **2** [U] the truth: *Is this story fact or* FICTION? **3 as a matter of fact, in (actual) fact, in point of fact** really; actually: *He doesn't mind.*

*In fact, he's very pleased.* –compare INDEED (1)

**fac·tion** /'fækʃən/ *n* [C;U] (disagreement in) a group or party within a larger group, esp. one that makes itself noticed

**fac·tor** /'fæktəʳ/ *n* **1** any of the forces, conditions, influences, etc., that act with others to bring about a result: *His friendly manner is an important factor in his rapid success.* **2** (in MATHEMATICS) a whole number which, when multiplied by one or more whole numbers, produces a given number: *2, 3, 4, and 6 are all factors of 12.*

**fac·to·ry** /'fæktəri/ *n* **-ries** a building or group of buildings where goods are made, esp. in great quantities by machines: *factory workers|a car factory*

**facts of life** /ˌ· · '·/ *n euph* the details of sex and how babies are born: *Have you told your child about the facts of life yet?*

**fac·tu·al** /'fæktʃuəl/ *adj* of, concerning, or based on facts: *a factual account of the war* **–factually** *adv*

**fac·ul·ty** /'fækəlti/ *n* **-ties 1** a natural power or ability, esp. of the mind: *the faculty of hearing|He has the faculty to learn languages easily.* **2** a branch or division of learning, esp. in a university: *the law/science faculty* **3** [+*sing./pl. v*] *AmE* all the teachers and other workers of a university or college

**fad** /fæd/ *n* a short-lived interest or practice: *His interest in photography is only a passing fad.*

**fade** /feɪd/ *v* **faded, fading** [I;T] to (cause to) lose strength, colour, freshness, etc.: *The sun has faded the material.|The sound of thunder faded (away) into the distance.|Hopes of a peace settlement are now fading.*

**fade out** *v adv* [I;T (=**fade** sthg.↔ **out**)] (in film or sound mixing) to (cause to) disappear slowly by reducing the sound or strength

**fae·ces** ||also **feces** *AmE* /'fiːsiːz/ *n* [P] *fml & tech* the solid waste material passed from the bowels

**fag¹** /fæg/ *n* [S] *infml* an unpleasant and tiring piece of work: *Grammar lessons are a real fag.*

**fag²** *n infml* **1** *BrE* for CIGARETTE **2** *AmE* for HOMOSEXUAL

**fagged** /fægd/ [F] *BrE infml* very tired

**fag·got** ||also **fagot** *AmE*– /'fægət/ *n* **1** a ball of cut-up meat which is cooked and eaten **2** a bunch of small sticks for burning

**Fah·ren·heit** /'færənhaɪt/ *n* a scale of temperature in which water freezes at 32° and boils at 212° –compare CENTIGRADE

**fail¹** /feɪl/ *v* **1** [I;T] to be unsuccessful (in): *He failed (to pass) his driving test.* **2** [T] to decide that (somebody) has not passed an examination: *The teachers failed me on the written paper.* –opposite **pass** (for 1,2) **3** [I;T +*to-v*] to not produce the desired result; not perform or do: *Last year the crops failed.|When money is in short supply many businesses fail.* (=are unable to continue)|*We waited half an hour, but the bus failed to arrive.* **4** [T] to disappoint: *I've got a lot of faith in the team; I'm sure they won't fail us.* **5** [I;T] to be not enough (for): *His courage failed him in the end.* **6** [I] to lose strength; become weak: *The sick woman is failing quickly.*

**SPELLING NOTE**

Words with the sound /f/ may be spelt **ph-**, like **photograph.**

**fail²** *n* **1** an unsuccessful result in an examination –opposite **pass 2 without fail** certainly: *I shall bring you that book without fail.*

**fail·ing¹** /'feɪlɪŋ/ *n* a fault or weakness: *This machine has one big failing.*

**failing²** *prep* in the absence of; without: *Failing instructions I did what I thought best.*

**fail·ure** /'feɪljəʳ/ *n* **1** [U] lack of success; failing: *His plans ended in failure.* **2** [C] a person, attempt, or thing that fails: *As a writer, he was a failure.* **3** [C;U] the non-performance or production of something expected or desired: *crop failures|(a) heart failure|His failure to explain the noise worried us.*

**faint¹** /feɪnt/ *adj* **1** [F] weak and about to lose conscious ness: *We felt faint for lack of food.* **2** lacking clearness, brightness, strength, etc.: *a faint sound|faint-hearted* (=lacking in courage) **3** very small; slight: *a faint possibility|(infml) I haven't the faintest idea what you're talking about.* **–faintly** *adv* **–faintness** *n* [U]

**faint²** *v* [I] to lose consciousness *n*

**fair¹** /feəʳ/ *adj* **1** free from dishonesty or injustice: *a fair decision|It is not fair to kick another player in football.|There must be* **fair play** (=just and honest treatment of all concerned) *in this competition.|They will win the election* **by fair means or foul.** (=in any way, honest or dishonest) –opposite **unfair 2** fairly good, large, fine, etc.: *Her knowledge of the language is fair.|a fair-sized garden* **3** (of weather) fine; clear **4** (having skin or hair that is) light in colour; not dark **5** having a good clear clean appearance or quality **6** (of women) *esp. old use* beautiful; attractive: **the fair sex** (=women as a group) **–fairness** *n* [U]

**fair²** *adv* **1** in a just or honest manner; fairly: *You must play fair.* **2 fair and square: a** honestly; justly: *It was a good game and they beat us fair and square.* **b** straight; directly: *I hit him fair and square on the nose.*

**fair³** *n* **1** *BrE* for FUNFAIR **2** a market, esp. one held at regular periods for selling farm produce **3** a very large show of goods, advertising, etc.: *a book fair*

**fair·ground** /'feəgraʊnd||'feər-/ *n* an open space on which a FUNFAIR is held

**fair·ly** /'feəli||'feərli/ *adv* **1** in a manner that is free from dishonesty, injustice, etc.: *I felt that I hadn't been treated fairly.* –opposite **unfairly 2** for the most part; rather; quite: *She speaks English fairly well.* –see RATHER (USAGE); see Study Notes on page 389

**fai·ry** /'feəri/ *n* **-ries** a small imaginary figure with magical powers and shaped like a human

**fairy tale** /'·· ·/ also fairy story/'·· ˌ··/– *n* **1** a story about fairies and other small magical people **2** a story or account that is hard to believe

**fait ac·com·pli** /ˌfeɪt ə'kɒmpli||-ˌækɑm'pliː/ *n* **faits accomplis** /ˌfeɪt a'kɒmpliːz||-ˌækɑm'pliːz/ something that has already happened or has been done and that cannot be changed

**faith** /feɪθ/ *n* **1** [U] strong belief; trust: *I'm sure she'll pass the test; I've got great faith in her.* **2** [U] (loyalty to one's) word of honour; promise: *I kept/broke faith with them.|The government has acted* **in good/bad faith.** (=acted sincerely/insincerely) **3** [C;U] (a system of) religious belief; religion

**faith·ful** /'feɪθfəl/ *adj* **1** full of or showing loyalty: *a faithful old dog* **2** true to the facts or to an original: *a* *faithful account* **3** [*to*] loyal to one's (marriage) partner by having no sexual relationship with anyone else –see also UNFAITHFUL, FIDELITY **–faithfulness** *n* [U]

**faith·ful·ly** /ˈfeɪθfəli/ *adv* **1** with faith: *I promised you faithfully.* **2** exactly: *I copied the letter faithfully.* **3 yours faithfully** (the usual polite way of ending a letter written to someone whom one does not know) –compare SINCERELY (2)

**faith·less** /ˈfeɪθləs/ *adj* disloyal; false: *a faithless friend* **–faithlessly** *adv* **–faithlessness** *n* [U]

**fake¹** /feɪk/ *v* **faked, faking** [T] to make or copy (something, such as a work of art) in order to deceive: *She got the money from the bank by faking her mother's handwriting.*|(fig.) *She faked illness so that she did not have to go to school.*

**fake²** *n* a person or thing that is not what he/she/it looks like: *The painting looked old but was a recent fake.* **–fake** *adj*: *a fake painting*

**fal·con** /ˈfɔːlkən‖ˈfæl-/ *n* a bird that kills and eats other animals, and can be trained by man to hunt

**fall¹** /fɔːl/ *v* **fell** /fel/, **fallen** /ˈfɔːlən/, **falling** [I] **1** to descend through the air: *He fell off the ladder.*|*The stone fell 10 metres before reaching the bottom of the well.* **2** to come down from a standing position, esp. suddenly: *She slipped and fell (down/over).*|*Five trees fell over in the storm.* **3** to become lower in level, degree, or quantity: *The temperature fell 4°.*|*Their voices fell to a whisper.* –opposite **rise 4** to hang loosely: *Her hair falls over her shoulders.* **5** (of the face) to take on a look of sadness, disappointment, etc.: *Her face fell when I told her the bad news.* **6** to be killed, esp. in battle: *soldiers who had fallen in the war* **7** to be defeated or conquered: *The government has fallen.* (=lost power) **8** to come or happen as if by descending: *Night fell quickly.*|*A silence fell as he entered the room.*|*Christmas falls on a Friday this year.* **9** to pass into a new condition; become: *She fell ill.*|*He fell in love with her.*|*This old coat of mine is falling to pieces.* **10 fall flat** to fail to produce the desired effect or result: *His jokes fell flat: nobody laughed at them.* **11 fall foul of: a** to be prevented from succeeding by: *Our plans have fallen foul of the new government rules.* **b** to get into a bad relationship with: *I don't want to fall foul of the police.* **12 fall on one's feet** *infml* to come out of a difficult state of affairs without harm **13 fall over backwards/oneself** to be very eager or too eager; do everything one can: *I've fallen over backwards to please you: what more can I do?* **14 fall short** to fail to reach a desired result, standard, etc.: *The government planned to build 10,000 new houses last year, but they fell short (of their aim).*

**fall about** *v adv* [I] *infml* to lose control of oneself (with laughter): *They fell about (laughing/with laughter) when they heard his funny voice.*

**fall back** *v adv* [I] to move or turn back: *The crowd fell back to let the doctor through.*

**fall back on** sthg. *v adv prep* [T] to use when there is failure or lack of other means: *Even if he is not successful as a singer, he has his training as a teacher to fall back on.*

**fall/get behind** *v adv* [I *with*] to fail to produce something on time: *to fall behind with one's work*

**fall for** sbdy./sthg. *v prep* [T] **1** to be cheated by: *Don't fall for his tricks.* **2** *infml* to fall in love with, esp. suddenly: *She fell for him in a big way.*

**fall off** *v adv* [I] to become less in quality, amount, etc.: *Membership of the club has fallen off this year.*

**fall on** sbdy./sthg. *v prep* [T] to attack eagerly: (fig.) *The hungry children fell on the food.*

**fall out** *v adv* [I *with*] to quarrel: *Jean and Paul have fallen out with each other again.*

**fall through** *v adv* [I] to fail to be completed: *The plan fell through.*

**fall²** *n* **1** [C] an act of falling: *He had a bad fall and broke his wrist.*|*It's a fall of 70 metres to the bottom of the cliff.* **2** [C] something that has fallen: *A fall of rocks blocked the road.*|*a fall of snow* **3** [C] a decrease in quantity, price, demand, degree, etc.: *a sudden fall in temperature* –opposite **rise 4** [S *of*] a defeat: *the fall of France/of the government* **5** [*the* S] *AmE* for AUTUMN –see also FALLS

**fal·la·cious** /fəˈleɪʃəs/ *adj fml* containing or based on false reasoning; wrong: *a fallacious argument* **–fallaciously** *adv*

**fal·la·cy** /ˈfæləsi/ *n* **-cies 1** [C] a false idea or belief: *It is a popular fallacy that success always brings happiness.* **2** [C;U] false reasoning, as in an argument

**fall·en** /ˈfɔːlən/ *v past participle of* FALL

**fal·li·ble** /ˈfæləbəl/ *adj* able or likely to make a mistake: *Everybody is fallible.* –opposite **infallible** **–fallibility** /ˌfæləˈbɪləti/ *n* [U]

**fall·out** /ˈfɔːlaʊt/ *n* [U] the dangerous dust that is left in the air after an atomic (or NUCLEAR (1)) explosion: *Many people believe that a* **fallout shelter** (a very strong underground room) *will not protect them from an atomic explosion.*

**fal·low** /ˈfæləʊ/ *adj* (of land) dug (or PLOUGHed) but left unplanted to improve its quality

**falls** /fɔːlz/ *n* [P] → WATERFALL: *Niagara Falls*

**false** /fɔːls/ *adj* **1** not true or correct: *false statements/ideas*|*A* **false start** *in a race is when a runner leaves the starting line too soon.* **2** not faithful or loyal: *a false friend* **3** not real: *false teeth/diamonds* **4** made or changed so as to deceive: *The thieves got into the house* **under false pretences,** *by saying they had come to repair the telephone.* **5 false alarm** a warning of something bad, which does not happen: *Someone shouted "Fire!" but it was a false alarm and there was no danger.* **–falsely** *adv* **–falseness** *n* [U]

**false·hood** /ˈfɔːlshʊd/ also **falsity**– *n* [C;U] (the telling of) an untrue statement; lie

**false teeth** /ˌ· ˈ·/ also **dentures**– *n* [P] a set of teeth made of plastic and worn in the mouth of a person who has lost all or most of his/her natural teeth

**fal·si·fy** /ˈfɔːlsəfaɪ/ *v* **-fied, -fying** [T] **1** to make false by changing something: *to falsify the receipts/facts* **2** to state or represent falsely: *Her speech in Parliament was falsified by the newspapers.* **–falsification** /-fəˈkeɪʃən/ *n* [C;U]

**fal·ter** /ˈfɔːltəʳ/ *v* **1** [I;T *out*] to walk, move, or say (something) unsteadily, as through weakness or fear: *The sick man faltered a few steps then fell.*|*Her voice faltered, and then she lost consciousness.* **2** [I] to lose strength of purpose or action; HESITATE (1): *He faltered and lost his chance.* **–falteringly** *adv*

**fame** /feɪm/ *n* [U] the condition of being well known and talked about: *She hoped to find fame as a poet.*

–**famed** *adj*: *The Scottish mountains are famed for their beauty.*

**fa·mil·i·ar** /fə'mɪlɪəʳ/ *adj* **1** [*to*] generally known, seen, or experienced; common: *a familiar sight* **2** [F *with*] having a thorough knowledge (of): *Are you familiar with the rules of football?* –opposite **unfamiliar** (for **1**, **2**) **3** *derog* too friendly for the occasion: *The man's unpleasant familiar behaviour angered the girl.*

**fa·mil·i·ar·i·ty** /fəˌmɪli'ærɪ̈ti/ *n* [U] **1** [*with*] thorough knowledge (of): *His familiarity with many strange languages surprised us all.* **2** freedom of behaviour usu. only expected in the most friendly relations: *He behaved towards her with great familiarity.*

**fa·mil·i·ar·ize** sbdy. **with** sthg.‖also **-ise** *BrE* /fə'mɪlɪəraɪz/ *v prep* **-ized, -izing** [T] to make (oneself or someone else) informed about: *I spent the first few weeks familiarizing myself with the new job.*

**fa·mil·i·ar·ly** /fə'mɪlɪəli‖-lɪər-/ *adv* in an informal, easy, or friendly manner

**fam·i·ly** /'fæməli/ *n* **-lies 1** [C +*sing./pl. v*] any group of people related by blood or marriage, esp. a group of two parents and their children: *My family is very large.|My family are all tall.|Our family has lived in this house for over a hundred years.* **2** [A] suitable for children as well as older people: *a family film* **3** [S;U] children: *Have you any family?* **4** [C] a group of things, esp. plants or animals, related by common characteristics: *The cat family includes lions and tigers.* **5 run in the family** (of a quality) to be shared by several members of a family

**family plan·ning** /ˌ··· '··/ *n* [U] the controlling of the number of children born in a family by the use of any of various (CONTRACEPTIVE) methods

**family tree** /ˌ··· '·/ *n* a plan of the relationship of the members of a family –see picture on page 000

**fam·ine** /'fæmɪ̈n/ *n* [C;U] (a case of) very serious lack of food for a very large number of people: *Many people die during famines every year.* –compare HUNGER

**fam·ished** /'fæmɪʃt/ *adj* [F] suffering from very great hunger

**fa·mous** /'feɪməs/ *adj* very well known: *a famous actor|France is famous for its fine food and wine.*

USAGE Compare **famous**, **well-known**, **distinguished**, **eminent**, **notorious**, and **infamous**: **1 Famous** is like **well-known**, but is a stronger word and means known over a wide area: *the doctor, the postman, and other* **well-known** *people in the village|A* **famous** *film-star has come to live in our village.* **2 Distinguished** and **eminent** are used esp. of people who are famous for serious work in science, the arts, etc.: *a* **distinguished** *writer|an* **eminent** *scientist.* **3 Notorious** means famous for something bad; **infamous** also means very bad, but not necessarily famous: *Everyone was talking about the* **notorious** *murderer.|the* **infamous** *killing of an unarmed policeman*

**SPELLING NOTE**
Words with the sound /f/ may be spelt **ph-**, like **photograph.**

**fa·mous·ly** *adv infml* very well: *He is doing famously in his new job.*

**fan**[1] /fæn/ *n* an instrument meant to make a flow of (cool) air, such as an arrangement of feathers or paper in a half circle waved by hand, or a set of broad blades turned by a motor

**fan**[2] *v* **-nn- 1** [T] to cause air to blow on (something) (as if) with a FAN: *She fanned her face with a newspaper.* **2** [I;T *out*] to spread like a FAN: *The soldiers fanned out across the hillside.*

**fan**[3] *n* a very keen follower or supporter, esp. of a sport or famous person: *football fans|The famous singer employed two people to answer his* **fan mail.** (=letters sent to him by fans)

**fa·nat·ic** /fə'nætɪk/ also **fanatical**– *adj* showing very great and often unreasoning keenness, esp. in religious or political matters –**fanatic** *n: a health food fanatic* –**fanatically** *adv* –**fanaticism** /fə'nætɪ̈sɪzəm/*n* [C;U]

**fan·ci·er** /'fænsɪəʳ/ *n* a person who has an interest in breeding or training certain types of birds, dogs, plants, etc.: *a dog-fancier*

**fan·ci·ful** /'fænsifəl/ *adj* **1** showing imagination rather than reason and experience: *a fanciful idea* **2** unreal; imaginary –**fancifully** *adv*

**fan·cy**[1] /'fænsi/ *n* **-cies 1** [U] the power of inventing imaginative ideas and expressions in the mind **2** [C] an image, opinion, or idea imagined: *I think he will come but it's only a fancy of mine.* **3** [C] a liking formed without the help of reason: *I have* **taken a fancy to** *that new bicycle.*

**fancy**[2] *v* **-cied, -cying** [T] **1** to form a picture of; imagine: *Fancy having a fool like that for a husband!|Fancy that!* **2** to have a liking for; wish for: *I fancy a swim.|I fancy that girl.* **3** [+(*that*)] *fml* to think: *I fancy I have met you before.* **4 fancy oneself** to have a very high (perhaps too high) opinion of oneself: *He fancies himself (as) a good swimmer.*

**fancy**[3] *adj* decorative or brightly coloured; not ordinary: *fancy goods|fancy cakes|We went to the party in* **fancy dress**: *John was dressed as Julius Caesar and I went as Queen Elizabeth I.* –**fancily** *adv*

**fancy-free** /ˌ·· '·/ *adj* free to do anything or like anyone, esp. because not bound by love –compare FOOTLOOSE

**fan·fare** /'fænfeəʳ/ *n* a short loud piece of music played, esp. on the TRUMPET, to introduce a person or event

**fang** /fæŋ/ *n* a long sharp tooth, as of a dog or a poisonous snake

**fan·tas·tic** /fæn'tæstɪk/ *adj* **1** odd, strange, or wild in shape, meaning,etc.: *fantastic dream/story/fears* **2** (of an idea, plan, etc.) too unrelated to reality to be practical or reasonable **3** *infml* very good; wonderful: *a fantastic meal* –**fantastically** *adv*

**fan·ta·sy** /'fæntəsi/ *n* **-sies** [C;U] (something made by the) imagination: *The story is a fantasy.|He lives in a world of fantasy.*

**far**[1] /fɑːʳ/ *adj* **farther** /'fɑːðəʳ‖'fɑr-/ *or* **further** /'fɜːðəʳ‖fɜr-/, **farthest** /'fɑːðɪ̈st‖'fɑr-/ *or* **furthest** /'fɜːðɪ̈st‖'fɜr-/ **1** distant; a long way off: *Shall we walk? It's not far.|a far country* **2** [A *no comp.*] (of one of two things) more distant: *Can we fish here, or must we*

**grandparents**

grandfather = grandmother

grandfather = grandmother

**parents**

mother-in-law = father-in-law

uncle = aunt

father = mother

cousins

**Helen** = Helen's husband (Helen is his wife)

sister = brother-in-law

brother = sister-in-law

**children**

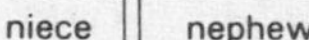

niece

nephew

son-in-law = daughter

son = daughter-in-law

**grandchildren**

grandson

granddaughter

The people shown here are all Helen's relations.
For example: uncle = aunt means Helen's uncle and Helen's aunt.
The sign = means "is married to".
For example: brother = sister-in-law means that the woman who married Helen's brother becomes Helen's sister-in-law.

*cross to the far bank of the river?* **3 a far cry** a long way; very different: *This big house is a far cry from that little flat they used to live in.* –compare NEAR (1)

**far²** *adv* **farther** *or* **further, farthest** *or* **furthest 1** [*adv +adv/prep*] a long way: *We walked far into the woods.*|*How far is it from here?* (=What is the distance?)|*It's not far beyond the church.*|*We worked far into the night.* (=very late)|*His rudeness went too far.* (=He was too rude) **2** very much: *far better*|*far too busy* **3 as/so far as** to the degree that: *So far as I know, they're coming.* **4 far from** rather than; instead of: *Far from being angry, he's delighted.* **5 how far** how much: *I don't know how far to believe him.* **6 so far**: **a** until now: *I've been here three weeks, and so far I've enjoyed it.* **b** up to a certain point: *You can trust him only so far and no further.* –see FURTHER¹ (USAGE)

USAGE **Far** is used in questions or NEGATIVES² (1) about distance: *How* **far** *did you walk?*|*Did you walk* **far**?|*No, we didn't walk* **far**. It is also used in simple statements after *too, as,* and *so*: *Yes, we walked as* **far** *as the river.*|*We walked much too* **far**! (compare *Yes, we walked a long way.* **Far** could not be used here.)

**far·a·way** /ˈfɑːrəweɪ/ *adj* distant: *a faraway place*|*a faraway* (=dreamy) *look in her eyes*

**farce** /fɑːs‖fɑrs/ *n* **1** [C;U] a (type of) light humorous play full of silly things happening **2** [C] an occasion or set of events that is a silly and empty show: *The talks were a farce since the minister had already made the decision.* –**farcical** *adj* –**farcically** *adv*

**fare¹** /feəʳ/ *n* **1** [C] the price charged to carry a person, as by bus, train, or taxi **2** [C] a paying passenger, esp. in a taxi **3** [U] food, esp. as provided at a meal: *good/simple fare*

**fare²** *v* **fared, faring** *fml* to get on; succeed: *I think I fared quite well in the examination.*

**fare·well** /feəˈwel‖feər-/ *n,interj fml & old use* for GOODBYE: *We shall have a farewell party before we leave.*

**far·fetched** /ˌfɑːˈfetʃt‖ˌfɑr-/ *adj* improbable or difficult to believe: *a far-fetched excuse*

**far-flung** /ˌ· ˈ·◂/ *adj* spread over a great distance: *Our far-flung trade connections cover the world.*

**farm¹** /fɑːm‖fɑrm/ *n* **1** an area of land, with its buildings, concerned with the growing of crops or the raising of animals: *a pig farm*|*We work on the farm.* **2** → FARMHOUSE

**farm²** *v* [I;T] to use (land) for growing crops, raising animals, etc.

**farm** sthg.↔ **out** *v adv* [T] to send (work) for other people to do: *We have more work here than we can deal with and must farm some out.*

**farm·er** /ˈfɑːməʳ‖ˈfɑrmər/ *n* a person who owns or plans the work on a farm

**farm·house** /ˈfɑːmhaʊs‖ˈfɑrm-/ also **farm**– *n* the main house on a farm, where the farmer lives

**farm·ing** /ˈfɑːmɪŋ‖ˈfɑrmɪŋ/ *n* [U] the practice or business of being in charge of or working on a farm

> **SPELLING NOTE**
> Words with the sound /f/ may be spelt **ph-**, like **photograph.**

**farm·yard** /ˈfɑːmjɑːd‖ˈfɑrmjɑrd/ *n* a yard surrounded by farm buildings

**far-off** /ˌ· ˈ·◂/ *adj* distant in space or time

**far-reach·ing** /ˌ· ˈ··◂/ *adj* having a wide influence or effect: *far-reaching political changes*

**far·sight·ed** /ˌfɑːˈsaɪtɪ̣d◂‖ˌfɑr-/ *adj* **1** able to see the future effects of present actions –opposite **shortsighted 2** *AmE* for LONGSIGHTED –**farsightedness** *n* [U]

**far·ther** /ˈfɑːðəʳ‖ˈfɑr-/ also **further**– *adv,adj* [*adv +adv/prep*] (COMPARATIVE² *of* FAR) more far: *The Festival Hall is on the farther side of the river.*|*We walked a mile farther/further down the road.*|*We can't go any farther/further ahead with this plan.* –see FURTHER (USAGE)

**far·thest** /ˈfɑːðɪ̣st‖ˈfɑr-/ also **furthest**– *adv,adj* [*adv +adv/prep*] (SUPERLATIVE *of* FAR) most far: *Who can swim farthest/furthest?*|*Our house is the farthest/furthest from the shops.* –see FURTHER (USAGE)

**far·thing** /ˈfɑːðɪŋ‖ˈfɑr-/ *n* (formerly) a British coin worth one quarter of a penny

**fas·ci·nate** /ˈfæsɪ̣neɪt/ *v* **-nated, -nating** [T *with/by*] to charm powerfully; be very interesting to: *I'm fascinated with/by Buddhist ceremonies.* –**fascinating** *adj : Your ideas are fascinating.* –**fascinatingly** *adv* –**fascination** [S;U]: *Old castles have a certain strange fascination for me.*

**fas·cis·m** /ˈfæʃɪzəm/ *n* [U] (*often cap.*) a political system in which all industrial activity is controlled by the state, no political opposition is allowed, nationalism is strongly encouraged, and SOCIALISM violently opposed –**fascist** *n,adj*

**fash·ion¹** /ˈfæʃən/ *n* **1** [C;U] the way of dressing or behaving that is considered the best at a certain time: *Narrow trousers are the latest fashion.*|*Long hair is very much* **out of/in fashion** (=(not) considered very modern) *now.* **2** [U] changing custom, esp. in women's clothing: *to study the history of fashion* **3** [S] *fml* a manner; way of making or doing something: *He behaves in a very strange fashion.* **4 after a fashion** not very well: *John speaks Russian after a fashion, but Jean speaks it much better.*

**fashion²** *v* [T] *fml* to shape or make, usually with one's hands: *He fashioned the clay into a pot.*

**fash·ion·a·ble** /ˈfæʃənəbəl/ *adj* (made, dressed, etc.) according to the latest fashion: *a fashionable hat/woman/restaurant* –opposite **unfashionable**; see also OLD-FASHIONED –**fashionably** *adv*: *fashionably dressed*|*to dress fashionably*

**fast¹** /fɑːst‖fæst/ *adj* **1** quick; moving quickly: *a fast car*|*fast music* **2** firm; firmly fixed: *The colours aren't fast, so be careful when you wash this shirt.*|*He* **made** *the rope* **fast** (=tied it firmly) *to the metal ring.* **3** [F; after *n*] (of a clock) showing a time that is later than the true time: *My watch is fast/is five minutes fast.* –compare SLOW

**fast²** *adv* **1** quickly: *You're learning very fast.*|*He ran faster and faster.* **2** firmly; tightly: *to stick fast in the mud* **3 fast asleep** sleeping deeply

**fast³** *v* [I] to eat no food, esp. for religious reasons: *Muslims fast during Ramadan.*

**fast⁴** *n* an act or period of FASTING³

**fas·ten** /ˈfɑːsən‖ˈfæ-/ *v* [I;T *up, together, to*] to make or become firmly fixed or joined: *He fastened (up) his coat.|The bag won't fasten properly.|The door fastens with a hook.|*(fig.) *She fastened her eyes on him.* –opposite **unfasten**

**fasten on/upon** sthg. *v prep* [T] to seize on; take and use: *The President fastened on the idea at once.*

**fas·ten·er** /ˈfɑːsənəʳ||ˈfæ-/ *n* something that fastens things together: *Please do up the fasteners on the back of my dress.* –compare ZIP

**fa·sten·ing** /ˈfɑːsənɪŋ||ˈfæ-/ *n* something that holds things shut, esp. doors and windows

**fas·tid·i·ous** /fæˈstɪdɪəs/ *adj* difficult to please; disliking anything at all dirty, nasty, or rough: *I knew he wouldn't enjoy his camping holiday, he's too fastidious!* –**fastidiously** *adv*

**fast·ness** /ˈfɑːstnɨs||ˈfæst-/ *n* [U] the quality of being firm and fixed: *the fastness of a colour*

USAGE There is no noun formed from **fast** when it means **quick**. Use instead **speed** or **quickness.**

**fat**[1] /fæt/ *adj* **1** (of creatures and their bodies) having (too) much fat: *fat cattle|You'll get even fatter if you eat all those potatoes.* **2** thick and well-filled; plentiful: *a fat bank account|fat profits* **3 a fat lot of** *infml* no; not any: *A fat lot of good that is!* –**fatness** *n* [U]

**fat**[2] *n* [U] **1** the material under the skins of animals and human beings which helps to keep them warm **2** this substance considered as food or used in cooking: *potatoes fried* (FRY[1]) *in deep fat* –compare LEAN[2] (2) **3 live on/off the fat of the land** to live in great comfort with plenty to eat

**fa·tal** /ˈfeɪtl/ *adj* **1** [*to*] causing or resulting in death: *a fatal accident/illness* **2** very dangerous and unfortunate: *She took the fatal decision to marry Henry.* –compare FATEFUL –**fatally** *adv*: *fatally wounded*

**fa·tal·is·m** /ˈfeɪtl-ɪzəm/ *n* [U] the belief that events are decided by FATE (1) –**fatalist** *n* –**fatalistic** /feɪtl-ˈɪstɪk/ *adj*

**fa·tal·i·ty** /fəˈtælɨti/ *n* **-ties** [C;U] *fml* a violent accidental death: *It was a bad crash, but there were no fatalities.*

**fate** /feɪt/ *n* **1** [S *often cap.*] the imaginary cause beyond human control that is believed to decide events: *He expected to spend his life in Italy, but fate had decided otherwise.* **2** [C] an end or result, esp. death: *They met with a terrible fate.* **3** [C] (a person's) future; what will happen to (one): *I wonder whether the examiners have decided our fate yet?|Now that oil is scarce, the fate of the motor car is uncertain.* –sounds like **fete**

**fat·ed** /ˈfeɪtɨd/ *adj* [F +*to-v*/*that*] caused or fixed by FATE (1): *We were fated to meet.*

**fate·ful** /ˈfeɪtfəl/ *adj* important (esp. in a bad way) for the future: *the fateful night of the accident* –compare FATAL –**fatefully** *adv*

**fa·ther**[1] /ˈfɑːðəʳ/ *n* a male parent: *the fathers and mothers of the schoolchildren|*(fig.) *He was the father of* (=person who began) *modern scientific thought.* –see picture on page 217

**father**[2] *v* [T] *old use or humor* (of a man) to cause the birth of (one's child): (fig.) *to father a plan*

**Father** [A] (a title of respect for) a priest, esp. in the ROMAN CATHOLIC Church

**Father Christ·mas** /ˌ·· ˈ··/ *n esp. BrE* for SANTA CLAUS

**father fig·ure** /ˈ·· ˌ··/ *n* an older man on whom one depends for advice and help

**fa·ther·hood** /ˈfɑːðəhʊd||ˈfɑðər-/ *n* [U] the condition of being a father: *the responsibilities of fatherhood* –see also MOTHERHOOD

**father-in-law** /ˈ·· · ·/ *n* **-s-in-law** the father of one's wife or husband –see picture on page 217

**fa·ther·ly** /ˈfɑːðəli||ˈfɑðərli/ *adj* like or typical of a father: *Let me give you some fatherly advice.* –**fatherliness** *n* [U]

**fath·om**[1] /ˈfæðəm/ *n* a measure (6 feet or 1·8 metres) of the depth of water: *The boat sank in 20 fathoms.*

**fathom**[2] *v* [T *out*] to get at the true meaning of: *I can't fathom your meaning/fathom what you mean.*

**fa·tigue**[1] /fəˈtiːg/ *n* [U] **1** great tiredness: *He was pale with fatigue after his sleepless night.* **2** *tech* the tendency of a metal to break as the result of repeated bending

**fatigue**[2] *v* **-tigued, -tiguing** [T] *fml* to make tired: *a very fatiguing job*

**fat·ten** /ˈfætn/ *v* [T *up*] to make (a creature) fat: *Have some more cake! You need fattening up a bit.*

**fat·ty** /ˈfæti/ *adj* (of food) containing a lot of fat –**fattiness** *n* [U]

**fat·u·ous** /ˈfætʃʊəs/ *adj* very silly without seeming to know it: *What a fatuous remark!* –**fatuously** *adv*

**fau·cet** /ˈfɔːsɨt/ *n AmE* for TAP[1] (1)

**fault**[1] /fɔːlt/ *n* **1** a mistake or imperfection: *a small electrical fault in the motor|Through no fault of her own* (=not because of any mistake she made) *she lost her job.|Which driver was* **at fault** (=in the wrong) *in the car crash?|She's always* **finding fault with** (=complaining about) *the way I do things.* **2** *tech* (in the science of the earth (=GEOLOGY)) a crack in the earth's surface **3 be one's fault** to be something for which one can rightly be blamed: *Whose fault is it (that) we're late? It's not our fault.*

**fault**[2] *v* [T] *(used only in* NEGATIVES[2] (1), *questions, etc.)* to find a FAULT[1] (1) in: *It was impossible to fault her performance.*

**fault·less** /ˈfɔːltlɨs/ *adj* without a fault; perfect: *a faultless performance on the piano* –**faultlessly** *adv* –**faultlessness** *n* [U]

**fault·y** /ˈfɔːlti/ *adj* **-ier, -iest** having FAULTS[1] (1): *a faulty wire in the electrical system|faulty reasoning* –**faultily** *adv*

**fau·na** /ˈfɔːnə/ *n* [C;U] *tech* all the animals living in a particular place, or of a particular age in history: *the fauna of the forest* –compare FLORA

**faux pas** /ˌfəʊ ˈpɑː, ˈfəʊ pɑː/ *n* **faux pas** /ˌfəʊ ˈpɑːz/ a social mistake, in words or behaviour

**fa·vour**[1] *BrE*||**favor** *AmE* /ˈfeɪvəʳ/ *n* **1** [U] active approval: *I'm afraid I'm* **out of favour** *with her* (=she is annoyed with me) *at the moment.|He worked hard to get back* **in the teacher's favour.**|*He did all he could to* **win** *her* **favour**. –see also DISFAVOUR **2** [U] unfairly kind treatment to one person, to the disadvantage of others: *The teacher refused to have his daughter in his class, for fear of showing favour to her.* **3** [C] a kind act: *I want to* **ask a favour** *of you: will you lend me your car?|***Do me a favour** *and turn off that radio!* **4 in favour of** approving of or choosing: *Are you in favour of workers' control of companies?|He refused a job in the steel industry in favour of a university* *appointment.* **5 in one's favour** to one's advantage: *The bank has made an* ERROR (=mistake) *in your favour: we owe you £100.*

**favour²** *BrE*||**favor** *AmE v* [T] **1** to believe in (a plan or idea); regard with FAVOUR¹ (1): *Did he favour your suggestion?* **2** to be unfairly fond of; treat with FAVOUR¹ (2): *A mother mustn't favour one of her children more than the others.*

**favour** sbdy. **with** sthg. *v prep* [T] *fml* to give (someone) (something nice): *She favoured him with a charming smile.*

**fa·vou·ra·ble** *BrE*||**favorable** *AmE* /ˈfeɪvərəbəl/ *adj fml* **1** (of a message, answer, etc.) saying what one wants to hear: *I hear favourable accounts of your work.* **2** [*to*] (of conditions) advantageous: *The company will lend you money on very favourable terms.* –opposite **unfavourable –favourably** *adv*

USAGE Compare **favourable** and **favourite:** Your **favourite** (thing or person) is the one you like the best. Conditions are **favourable** when they are helpful, and words are **favourable** when they express agreement or approval: *Who's your* **favourite** *writer?|John's a great* **favourite** *with me.|The game will be played on Saturday if the weather is* **favourable.**|*a* **favourable** *answer to my letter.*

**fa·vou·rite¹** *BrE*||**favorite** *AmE* /ˈfeɪvərɪ̈t/ *n* **1** something or someone that is loved above all others: *These books are my favourites.* **2** *derog* someone who receives too much FAVOUR¹ (2): *A teacher shouldn't have/make favourites in the class.* **3** (in horse racing) the horse in each race that is expected to win: *The favourite came in second.* –see FAVOURABLE (USAGE)

**favourite²** *BrE*||**favorite** *AmE adj* being a favourite: *Who's your favourite writer?* –see FAVOURABLE (USAGE)

**fa·vou·ri·tis·m** *BrE*||**favoritism** *AmE* /ˈfeɪvərɪ̈tɪzəm/ *n* [U] *derog* the practice of showing FAVOUR¹ (2)

**fawn** /fɔːn/ *n* **1** [C] a young deer **2** [S;U] a light yellowish-brown colour

**fawn on/upon** sbdy. *v prep* [T] **1** (of dogs) to jump on, rub against (someone), etc., as an expression of love **2** to try to gain the favour of (someone) by being insincerely attentive: *They were fawning on their rich uncle.*

**FBI** *n abbrev. for*: Federal Bureau of Investigation; the police department in the USA that is controlled by the central (FEDERAL (2)) government, and is particularly concerned with matters of national SECURITY (4) (=the protection of political secrets)

**fear¹** /fɪəʳ/ *n* [C;U +*that*] **1** the feeling that one has when danger is near; the feeling that something (usu. unpleasant) is likely to happen: *I couldn't move for* (=because of) *fear.|She has a great fear of fire.|The government's fear/fears that the unemployment figures would rise again was/were today proved correct.|There's* **not much fear** (=likelihood) *of snow at this time of year.|We live* **in** *daily* **fear of** *an enemy attack.* **2 No fear!** *infml* (in answer to a suggestion that one should do something) Certainly not!

**SPELLING NOTE**
Words with the sound /f/ may be spelt **ph-**, like **photograph.**

**fear²** *v* [not *be +v-ing*] *fml* **1** [T] to be afraid of: *He has always feared mice.* **2** [I *for*] to be afraid (for the safety of someone or something): *She feared for the lost child.* **3 I fear** (*used when telling bad news*) I'm sorry that I must say: *I fear we'll be late.*

**fear·ful** /ˈfɪəfəl||ˈfɪər-/ *adj* **1** [+*that/of*] *fml* afraid: *He was fearful of her anger.* –opposite **fearless 2** causing fear: *a fearful storm* **3** *pomp* very bad; very great; FRIGHTFUL: *What a fearful waste of time!* **–fearfully** *adv*: *a fearfully cold day* **–fearfulness** *n* [U]

**fear·less** /ˈfɪəlɪ̈s||ˈfɪər-/ *adj* [*of*] without fear: *fearless of what might happen* –opposite **fearful –fearlessly** *adv* **–fearlessness** *n* [U]

**fear·some** /ˈfɪəsəm||ˈfɪər-/ *adj humor* causing fear: *a fearsome sight*

**fea·si·ble** /ˈfiːzɪ̈bəl/ *adj* able to be done; possible: *Your plan sounds quite feasible.* –compare PLAUSIBLE (1) **–feasibly** *adv* **–feasibility** /-əˈbɪlɪ̈ti/ *n* [U]: *a feasibility study (=to see if a job can be done)*

**feast¹** /fiːst/ *n* **1** a splendid esp. public meal: *The king gave/held a feast.* **2** a day kept in memory of a religious event

**feast²** *v* **1** [I *on, upon*] to eat and drink very well **2** [T *on, upon*] *fml* to feed (someone) specially well (on): (fig.) *He feasted his eyes on the beautiful scene.*

**feat** /fiːt/ *n* a clever action, showing strength, skill, or courage: *It was quite a feat to move that piano by yourself.* –sounds like **feet**

**fea·ther¹** /ˈfeðəʳ/ *n* **1** one of the many parts of the covering which grows on a bird's body, like a thin stick with soft hair-like material on each side **2 a feather in one's cap** a deserved honour that one is proud of **3 birds of a feather** people of the same (often bad) kind

**feather²** *v* **feather one's nest** to make oneself rich, esp. dishonestly, while in a trusted position

**fea·ther·y** /ˈfeðəri/ *adj* **1** covered with feathers **2** soft and light: *feathery pastry*

**fea·ture¹** /ˈfiːtʃəʳ/ *n* **1** a (typical or noticeable) part or quality: *Wet weather is a feature of life in Scotland.* **2** any of the noticeable parts of the face: *His nose is his best feature.|to have regular features* **3** a special long newspaper article: *a front-page feature on coalmining* **4** a full-length cinema film with an invented story –compare DOCUMENTARY²

**feature²** *v* **-tured, -turing 1** [T] to include as a special FEATURE¹ (1): *a new film featuring Jack Nicholson* **2** [I] to be present as a FEATURE¹ (1): *Work features largely in her life.*

**Feb·ru·a·ry** /ˈfebruəri||ˈfebjueri/ also **Feb.** *written abbrev.– n* the 2nd month of the year

**feck·less** /ˈfeklɪ̈s/ *adj* (of a person or behaviour) worthless and without plans for the future **–fecklessly** *adv* **–fecklessness** *n* [U]

**fed** /fed/ *v past tense and participle of* FEED –see also FED UP

**fed·e·ral** /ˈfedərəl/ *adj* **1** of or formed into a political FEDERATION (1): *Switzerland is a federal republic.* **2** (in the US) of or relating to the central government of the FEDERATION (1) as opposed to the states that form it: *to pay both federal taxes and state taxes*

**fed·e·ral·is·m** /ˈfedərəlɪzəm/ *n* [U] the belief in

political FEDERATION (1) –**federalist** *n,adj*

**fed·e·rate** /ˈfedəreɪt/ *v* **-rated, -rating** [I;T] to form or become a FEDERATION (1)

**fed·e·ra·tion** /ˌfedəˈreɪʃən/ *n* **1** [C;U] (the action of uniting) a group of states with one government which decides foreign affairs, defence, etc., but in which each state decides its own affairs **2** [C] a group of societies, organizations, etc., that have come together in this way: *the Federation of British Fishing Clubs*

**fed up** /ˌ· ˈ·/ *adj* [F +*that/about, with*] *infml* unhappy, tired, and discontented: *I won't wait any longer; I'm fed up!|I'm fed up with your complaints.*

**fee** /fiː/ *n* a sum of money paid for professional services to a doctor, lawyer, private school, etc. –see PAY² (USAGE)

**fee·ble** /ˈfiːbəl/ *adj* weak; with little force: *Grandfather has been getting feebler lately.|a feeble joke* –**feebly** *adv* –**feebleness** *n* [U]

**fee·ble·mind·ed** /ˌfiːbəlˈmaɪnd½d◂/ *adj euph* with less than the usual INTELLIGENCE (1)

**feed¹** /fiːd/ *v* **fed** /fed/, **feeding 1** [T *on, with*] to give food to: *to feed the dog on meat|The baby will soon learn to feed himself.* |(fig.) *to feed the fire with logs* **2** [I] (esp. of animals or babies) to eat: *The horses were feeding quietly in the field.|Cows feed on grass.* **3** [T] to put, supply, or provide, esp. continually: *to feed the wire into/through the hole|The information is fed into the company's computer.*

**feed²** *n* **1** [C] a meal taken by an animal or baby **2** [U] food for animals: *a bag of hen feed*

**feed·back** /ˈfiːdbæk/ *n* [U] information about the results of a set of actions, passed back to the person (or machine) in charge, so that changes can be made if necessary: *The company welcomes feedback from people who use the goods it produces.*

**feel¹** /fiːl/ *v* **felt** /felt/, **feeling 1** [T] to get knowledge of by touching with the fingers: *The doctor felt my arm to find out if it was broken.|I can't feel where the handle is.* **2** [T] to search with the fingers rather than the eyes: *She felt in her bag for a pencil.* **3** [T] to experience the touch or movement of: *I felt an insect creep(ing) up my leg.* **4** [T] to suffer because of (a condition or event): *He feels the cold in winter.|She felt the death of her father very much.* **5** to have the experience of being, or seeming to oneself to be: *I feel ill.|She felt happy.|Please* **feel free** *to make suggestions.|I felt sure it was him.|I felt such a fool when I arrived three hours early.* **6** to produce the stated sensation: *Your feet feel cold.|This sheet feels wet.|How does it feel to be famous?|I'm holding something that feels like a potato.* **7** [T+(*that*)] to have as an opinion; believe, but not as a result of reasoning: *I feel you haven't been completely honest with me.* **8 feel as if/as though** to have or give the sensation that; seem to be: *My leg felt as though it was broken.* **9 feel in one's bones that** to be certain that **10 feel like** to have a wish for; want: *Do you feel like a beer?|I don't feel like dancing now.* **11 feel one's way: a** to move carefully (as if) in the dark: *They felt their way down the dark passage.* **b** to act slowly and carefully: *He hasn't been in the job long and he's still feeling his way.*

**feel for** sbdy. *v prep* [T] to be sorry for; be unhappy about the suffering of

**feel²** *n* [S] **1** the sensation caused by feeling something: *Its skin has a rough feel.* **2** *infml* an act of feeling: *Let me have a feel in my pocket.* **3 get the feel of** to become used to: *You'll soon get the feel of the new job/car.*

**feel·er** /ˈfiːləʳ/ *n* **1** [*usu. pl.*] the thread-like part on the front of an insect's head, with which it touches things **2 put out feelers** to make a suggestion as a test of what others will think or do: *I'm putting out feelers to see if she'd like to come and work for us.*

**feel·ing** /ˈfiːlɪŋ/ *n* **1** [S *of*] a consciousness of something felt: *a feeling of shame/danger/thirst/pleasure* **2** [S +(*that*)] a belief or opinion, not based on reason: *I have a feeling we're being followed.* **3** [U] the power to feel sensation: *He lost all feeling in his toes.* **4** [U] excitement of mind, esp. in a bad sense: *The new working hours caused a lot of* **bad/ill feeling** *at the factory.* **5** [U *for*] sympathy and understanding: *to play the piano with great feeling*

**feel·ings** /ˈfiːlɪŋz/ *n* [P] **1** sensations of joy, sorrow, hate, etc.; the part of a person's nature that feels, compared to the part that thinks: *She has very strong feelings on this subject.|You'll hurt his feelings* (=make him unhappy) *if you forget his birthday.* **2 no hard feelings** *infml* no feeling of anger, annoyance, hatred, etc. (usu. said to someone after an argument, fight, etc.)

**feet** /fiːt/ *n pl. of* FOOT –sounds like **feat**

**feign** /feɪn/ *v* [T +*that*] *fml* to pretend to have or be: *He feigned death.|a feigned illness*

**feint** /feɪnt/ *n* [*of*] *fml* a false attack or blow, made to draw the enemy's attention away from the real danger –sounds like **faint**

**fe·line** /ˈfiːlaɪn/ *adj,n* (of or like) a member of the cat family: *Lions and tigers are felines.*

**fell¹** /fel/ *v past tense of* FALL¹

**fell²** *v* [T] to cut or knock down: *a felled* OAK|*He felled the man at a* (=with one) *blow.*

**fell³** *n NEngE* high wild rocky country

**fel·low¹** /ˈfeləʊ/ *n* **1** *infml* a man: *See if those fellows want some beer.* **2** [*of*] a member (of a society connected with some branch of learning or of some university colleges): *a Fellow of the Royal Society*

**fellow²** *adj* [A] another (of two or more things or people like oneself): *one's fellow creatures/prisoners/students|I have a lot of/a certain* **fellow feeling** (=sympathy) *for her because we both come from Scotland.*

**fel·low·ship** /ˈfeləʊʃɪp/ *n* **1** [C] a group or society: *Our son is a member of a youth fellowship.* **2** [C] the position of a FELLOW¹ (2) **3** [U] the condition of being friends through sharing or doing something together; companionship

**fel·o·ny** /ˈfeləni/ *n* **-nies** *law* a serious crime: *Murder is a felony.* –compare MISDEMEANOUR (2)

**felt¹** /felt/ *past tense and participle of* FEEL

**felt²** *n* [U] thick firm cloth made of wool, hair, or fur, pressed flat: *a felt hat*

**felt-tip pen** /ˌ· · ˈ·/ *n* a pen with a small piece of FELT at the end instead of a NIB

**fem.** *adj written abbrev. said as*: FEMININE –compare MASC.

**fe·male¹** /ˈfiːmeɪl/ *n* **1** a female person or animal **2**

*esp. derog* a woman –compare MALE²

**female²** *adj* **1** (typical) of the sex that gives birth to young: *a female elephant|the female form* **2** (of plants or flowers) producing fruit

USAGE **Female** and **male** are used to show what sex a creature is. **Feminine** and **masculine** are used of the qualities that are supposed to be typical of the two human sexes. Men can have **feminine** (but not **female**) qualities, and women can have **masculine** (but not **male**) ones: *her loud* **masculine** *voice.|He has a rather* **feminine** *walk.*

**fem·i·nine** /ˈfemᵻnᵻn/ *adj* **1** of or having the qualities suitable for a woman: *He has a very feminine voice.* –see FEMALE² (USAGE) **2** *tech* (in grammar) of a certain class of words: *"Actress" is the feminine form of "actor".* –compare MASCULINE, NEUTER

**fem·i·nin·i·ty** /ˌfemᵻˈnɪnᵻti/ *n* [U] the quality of being FEMININE (1) –compare MASCULINITY

**fem·i·nis·m** /ˈfemᵻnɪzəm/ *n* [U] the principle that women should have the same rights and chances as men –**feminist** *n,adj*

**fen** /fen/ *n* an area of low wet land, esp. in the east of England

**fence¹** /fens/ *n* **1** a wall made of wood or wire, dividing two areas of land: *a garden fence* –see picture on page 297 **2** *infml* someone who buys and sells stolen goods **3 sit on the fence** *usu. derog* to avoid taking sides inan argument

**fence²** *v* **fenced, fencing 1** [I] to fight with a long thin pointed sword (FOIL) as a sport **2** [I] to avoid giving an honest answer –compare HEDGE² (2) **3** [T *around, in*] to put a fence round

**fence** sthg.↔ **off** *v adv* [T] to separate or shut out (an area) with a fence

**fenc·ing** /ˈfensɪŋ/ *n* [U] **1** the sport of fencing (FENCE² (1)) **2** (material for making) fences: *surrounded by wire fencing/by a wire fence*

**fend** /fend/ *v* **fend for oneself** to look after oneself: *I've had to fend for myself since I was 14.*

**fend** sbdy./sthg.↔ **off** *v adv* [T] to push away; act to avoid: (fig.) *He fended off the difficult questions.*

**fend·er** /ˈfendəʳ/ *n* **1** a low metal wall round an open fireplace, to stop the coal from falling out **2** *AmE* for WING (=guard over the wheel of a car)

**fer·ment¹** /fəˈment‖fər-/ *v* [I;T] **1** to (cause to) be in a state of FERMENTATION: *fermented apple juice|The wine is beginning to ferment.* **2 a** to be in a state of political trouble and excitement **b** to cause (this state)

**fer·ment²** /ˈfɜːment‖ˈfɜr-/ *n* [U] (the condition of) political trouble and excitement: *The whole country was in a state of ferment.*

**fer·men·ta·tion** /ˌfɜːmenˈteɪʃən‖ˌfɜrmən-/ *n* [U] the period or event of chemical change caused by the action of certain living substances such as YEAST: *Milk becomes cheese by fermentation.*

**fern** /fɜːn‖fɜrn/ *n* **ferns** *or* **fern** a green plant with feathery shaped leaves and no flowers

**SPELLING NOTE**
Words with the sound /f/ may be spelt **ph-**, like **photograph.**

**fe·ro·cious** /fəˈrəʊʃəs/ *adj* fierce, cruel, and violent: *a ferocious lion|ferocious punishments* –**ferociously** *adv* –**ferocity** /fəˈrɒsᵻti‖fəˈrɑ-/, **ferociousness** *n* [U]

**fer·ret¹** /ˈferᵻt/ *n* a small fierce sharp-nosed animal of the WEASEL family, used for catching rats and rabbits

**ferret²** *v* [I *about, around*] to search for rats and rabbits with FERRETS: (fig.) *I've been ferreting around among my papers for the missing letter.*

**ferret** sthg.↔ **out** *v adv* [T] to discover (something) by searching: *to ferret out the truth*

**fer·rous** /ˈferəs/ *adj tech* related to or containing iron: *ferrous metals* –opposite **nonferrous**

**fer·ry¹** /ˈferi/ *v* **-ried, -rying** [T] to carry (as if) on a FERRY² (1): *ferrying the children to and from school in my car*

**ferry²** *n* **-ries 1** also **ferryboat**– a boat that carries people and things across a narrow stretch of water: *You can cross the river by ferry.* **2** a place from which a ferry leaves: *We waited three hours at the ferry.*

**fer·tile** /ˈfɜːtaɪl‖ˈfɜrtl/ *adj* able to produce or grow many young, fruits, or seeds: *Some fish are very fertile: they lay thousands of eggs.|Wheat grows well on fertile soil.|*(fig.) *a fertile* (=inventive) *imagination* –opposite **infertile**; compare STERILE, BARREN (4) –**fertility** /fɜːˈtilᵻti‖fɜr-/ *n* [U]: *Margaret wants a child so she is taking medicine to increase her fertility.*

**fer·ti·lize**‖also **-ise** *BrE* /ˈfɜːtᵻlaɪz‖ˈfɜrtl-aɪz/ *v* **-lized, -lizing** [T] **1** to start the development of young in (a female creature or plant): *Bees fertilize the flowers.* **2** to put FERTILIZER on (land) –**fertilization** /ˌfɜːtᵻlaɪˈzeɪʃən‖ˌfɜrtələ-/ *n* [U]

**fer·ti·liz·er** /ˈfɜːtᵻlaɪzəʳ‖ˈfɜrtl-aɪzər/ *n* [C;U] (any type of) chemical or natural substance that is put on the land to make crops grow better –compare MANURE

**fer·vent** /ˈfɜːvənt‖ˈfɜr-/ *adj* feeling or showing strong and warm feelings: *a fervent desire to win|He's a fervent believer in free speech.* –**fervently** *adv*

**fer·vour** *BrE*‖**fervor** *AmE* /ˈfɜːvəʳ‖ˈfɜr-/ *n* [U] the quality of being FERVENT

**fes·ter** /ˈfestəʳ/ *v* [I] (of a cut or wound) to become infected and diseased

**fes·ti·val** /ˈfestᵻvəl/ *n* **1** a time of public gaiety and feasting, esp. to mark a religious occasion: *Christmas is one of the festivals of the Christian church.* **2** a group of artistic performances (musical, theatrical, etc.) held usu. regularly in a particular place: *the Cannes Film Festival*

**fes·tive** /ˈfestɪv/ *adj* of or suitable for a FESTIVAL (1): *Christmas is often called the festive season.*

**fes·tiv·i·ty** /feˈstɪvᵻti/ *n* **-ties** [*usu. pl.*] a FESTIVE event: *to stay in London during the festivities*

**fes·toon** /feˈstuːn/ *v* [T *with*] to decorate with chains of flowers, RIBBONS, etc.: *to festoon the room with flowers*

**fe·tal** /ˈfiːtl/ *adj* see FOETUS

**fetch** /fetʃ/ *v* [T] **1** to go and get from another place and bring back: *Run and fetch the doctor!* –see Study Notes on page 429 **2** *infml* to be sold for: *The house'll fetch at least £30,000.*

**fetch·ing** /ˈfetʃɪŋ/ *adj becoming rare* attractive; pleasing: *You look very fetching in that hat.*

**fete**[1] /feɪt/ *n* a day of public gaiety and amusement held usu. out of doors and often to collect money for a special purpose: *Our village is holding a fete to raise money for the building of the new hall.* –sounds like FATE

**fete**[2] *v* **feted, feting** [T *usu. pass.*] to show honour to (someone) with public parties and ceremonies: *The Queen was feted everywhere she went.*

**fet·id** /ˈfiːtɪ̈d‖ˈfetɪ̈d/ *adj* smelling bad: *fetid water*

**fet·ish** /ˈfetɪʃ, ˈfiː-/ *n* **1** an object that is worshipped and thought to have magic power **2** something to which one pays an unreasonable amount of attention, or which one admires to a foolish degree: *Make sure you clean your room before he comes; he* **has a fetish about/makes a fetish of** *tidiness.*

**fet·ter**[1] /ˈfetəʳ/ *n* [*usu. pl.*] a chain for the foot of a prisoner: (fig.) *to escape from the fetters of an unhappy marriage*

**fetter**[2] *v* [T] *fml* to bind with or as if with FETTERS: *fettered by responsibility*

**fet·tle** /ˈfetl/ *n* [U] condition; state of body and mind (in the phrase **in fine/good fettle**)

**fe·tus** /ˈfiːtəs/ *n* → FOETUS

**feud** /fjuːd/ *n* a state of strong dislike and/or violence which continues over a long time as a result of a quarrel, usu. between two families

**feud·al** /ˈfjuːdl/ *adj* [A] of or relating to the system by which people held land, and received protection, in return for giving work to the land owner, as practised in Western Europe from about the 9th to the 15th century –**feudalism** *n* [U]

**fe·ver** /ˈfiːvəʳ/ *n* [S;U] (a medical condition caused by) an illness in which the sufferer suddenly develops a very high temperature: *yellow fever|She is running/has a very high fever.*|(fig.) *in a fever of excitement*

**fe·ver·ish** /ˈfiːvərɪʃ/ *adj* (as if) caused by fever: *in a feverish condition|a feverish dream* –**feverishly** *adv: working feverishly* (=very quickly and excitedly) *to finish the job*

**few** /fjuː/ *determiner,pron,n* **1** [U +*pl. v.*] (*used without* a *to show the smallness of a number*) not many; not enough: *She has very few friends.|So few (members) came that we were unable to hold the meeting.|There were* **no fewer than** (=there were at least) *a thousand cars.|Which of you has made the fewest mistakes?* –compare PLENTY, LITTLE[3] (2) **2** [*always sing. in form but takes a pl. v; no comp.*] (*used with* a) a small number, but at least some: *We need a few eggs and a little milk.|Let's stay a few days longer.|Why not invite a few of your friends?|There are only a few* (=there are not many) *left.* –compare LITTLE[3] (2) –see Study Notes on page 494 **3 few and far between** not happening often: *Holidays are few and far between.* **4 quite a few** also **a good few**– a reasonable number: *Quite a few of us are getting worried.*

USAGE *Only a* **few** and *only a* **little** are the commonest ways to express the idea of "not many" or "not much": *Only a* **few** *of the children can read.|I understood only a* **little** *of his speech.*

**fez** /fez/ *n* **fezzes** *or* **fezes** a round red hat with a flat top and no BRIM, worn by some Muslim men

**fi·an·cé** /fiˈɒnseɪ‖ˌfiɑnˈseɪ/ **fiancée** (*same pronunciation*) *fem.*– *n* a man to whom a woman is ENGAGED (=whom she has promised to marry): *George is my fiancé.|Martha is my fiancée.*

**fi·as·co** /fiˈæskəʊ/ *n* **-cos** *BrE*‖**-coes** *AmE* [C;U] the complete failure of something planned: *The party was a total fiasco/ended in fiasco.*

**fib**[1] /fɪb/ *n infml* a small unimportant lie

**fib**[2] *v* **-bb-** [I] to tell FIBS –**fibber** *n*

**fi·bre** *BrE*‖**fiber** *AmE* /ˈfaɪbəʳ/ *n* **1** [C] one of the thin thread-like parts that form many animal and plant growths such as wool, wood, or muscle **2** [U] a mass of threads, used for making cloth, rope, etc.: *Cotton is a natural fibre; nylon is a man-made fibre.* **3** [U] strength of character: *He lacks moral fibre.* –**fibrous** *adj*

**fi·bre·glass** *BrE*‖**fiberglass** *AmE* /ˈfaɪbəglɑːs‖-bərglæs/ *n* [U] material made from glass FIBRES used for car bodies, furnishing materials, and esp. building light boats

**fick·le** /ˈfɪkəl/ *adj* not loyal in love or friendship; often changing: *He's changed his mind again; he's so fickle!* –**fickleness** *n* [U]

**fic·tion** /ˈfɪkʃən/ *n* **1** [U] stories or NOVELS about things that did not really happen, as compared to other sorts of literature like history or poetry: *a writer of popular fiction||Truth is sometimes stranger than fiction.* –see also NON-FICTION **2** [S;U] an invention of the mind; an untrue story; invented information: *The newspaper's account of what happened was a complete fiction.* –compare FACT

**fic·tion·al** /ˈfɪkʃənəl/ *adj* belonging to FICTION (1); told as a story: *a fictional account of a journey to the moon* –compare FICTITIOUS

**fic·ti·tious** /fɪkˈtɪʃəs/ *adj* [*no comp.*] untrue; invented; not real: *Hamlet was a fictitious character.* –compare: *His account of the bank robbery was completely* **fictitious**. (=the robbery really happened, but his account of it was untrue)|*a* **fictional** *account of a bank robbery* (=a story of an imaginary event)

**fid·dle**[1] /ˈfɪdl/ *n infml* **1** a VIOLIN, or any musical instrument of that family: *Can you play the fiddle?|I'm tired of* **playing second fiddle to** (=taking a less important part than) *George; why can't I run the business?* **2** a dishonest practice **3 (as) fit as a fiddle** perfectly healthy

**fiddle**[2] *v* **-dled, -dling** *infml* **1** [I] to play the FIDDLE[1] (1) **2** [I *with, about, around*] to move or play (with something) aimlessly rather than acting with a purpose: *Stop fiddling (around) with that gun. It might go off!|Well, we'd better get started and stop fiddling about.* **3** [T] to lie about (something) to gain money, etc.: *to fiddle one's income tax* –**fiddler** *n*

**fi·del·i·ty** /fɪˈdelɪ̈ti/ *n* [U] **1** [*to*] *fml* faithfulness; loyalty: *fidelity to one's leader/to one's wife or husband* –see also INFIDELITY; compare FAITHFUL (3) **2** (of something copied or reported) truthfulness; closeness in sound, facts, colour, etc. to the original: –see also HI-FI

**fid·get**[1] /ˈfɪdʒɪ̈t/ *v* [I] to move one's body around in a restless, impatient way: *children fidgeting in class* –**fidgety** *adj*

**fidget**[2] *n infml* someone, esp. a child, who FIDGETS: *Sit still, you little fidget!*

**field**[1] /fiːld/ *n* **1** [C] a stretch of land on a farm marked off in some way and used for animals or crops: *fields of corn* **2** [C] any open area where **a** the stated game or other activity takes place: *a football field|a battlefield|An airfield is a place where aircraft can take off or land.* **b** the stated substance is MINED[3] (1): *a coalfield|an oilfield* **3** [C] a branch of knowledge or activity: *a lawyer famous in his own field|the field ofpolitics/art/Greek history* **4** [*the* S] the place where real operations happen, as compared to places where they are studied: *He studies tribal languages in the field, not from books in the library.* –see also FIELDWORK **5** [C] the area in which the (stated) force is felt: *the moon's* GRAVITATIONAL *field|Our* **field of vision** (= the area within seeing distance) *is limited by that tall building.* **6** [*the* U +*sing./pl. v*] (in horseracing) all the horses in the race: *The rest of the field is/are far behind Shergar.* **7 have a field day** to enjoy oneself very much

**field²** *v* [I;T] (in cricket and BASEBALL) to catch or stop a ball: *Our team is* BATT*ing this morning and will be fielding in the afternoon.* –**fielder** *n*

**field e·vent** /'··,·/ *n* a competitive sports event, such as weight-throwing or jumping

**field glass·es** /'·,··/ *n* [P] → BINOCULARS –see PAIR[1] (USAGE)

**field mar·shal** /'·,··/ *n* [A;C] the officer of highest rank in the British army: *Field Marshal Montgomery*

**field·work** /'fi:ldwɜ:k||-ɜrk/ *n* [U] scientific or social study done in the FIELD[1] (4), such as measuring and examining things or asking people questions

**fiend** /fi:nd/ *n* **1** a devil or evil spirit **2** a person who is very keen on something stated: *a fresh air fiend*

**fiend·ish** /'fi:ndɪʃ/ *adj* **1** fierce and cruel: *a fiendish temper* **2** *infml* very clever; not plain or simple: *a fiendish plan* –**fiendishly** *adv*: *fiendishly cruel|a fiendishly difficult question* –**fiendishness** *n* [U]

**fierce** /fɪəs||fɪərs/ *adj* **1** angry, violent, and cruel: *a fierce dog to guard the house|a fierce-looking man* **2** very great or strong: *Because there is so much unemployment, the competition for jobs is very fierce.* –**fiercely** *adv* –**fierceness** *n* [U]

**fi·er·y** /'faɪəri/ *adj* **-ier, -iest** flaming and violent; looking like fire: *fiery red hair*|(fig.) *a fiery temper*

**fi·es·ta** /fi'estə/ *n* (esp. in ROMAN CATHOLIC countries) a religious holiday with public gaiety and rejoicings

**fif·teen** /fɪf'ti:n◂/ *determiner,n,pron* (the number) 15 –**fifteenth** *determiner,n,pron,adv*

**fifth** /fɪfθ, fɪθ/ *determiner,n,pron,adv* 5th

**fif·ty** /'fɪfti/ *determiner,n,pron* **-ties** (the number) 50 –**fiftieth** *determiner,n,pron,adv*

**fifty-fifty** /,··'··◂/ *adj,adv* [A;F] (of shares or chances) equal(ly): *You have a fifty-fifty chance of winning.* (you have an equal chance of winning or losing)|*Let's* **go fifty-fifty on** (=let's share equally) *the cost of petrol.*

**fig** /fɪg/ *n* (the tree that bears) a soft sweet fruit with many small seeds, growing chiefly in warm countries and often eaten dried

**fig.** *written abbrev. said as:* **1** FIGURATIVE **2** FIGURE[1] (6)

> **SPELLING NOTE**
> Words with the sound /f/ may be spelt **ph-**, like **photograph.**

**fight¹** /faɪt/ *v* **fought** /fɔ:t/, **fighting 1** [I;T] to use violence (against others): *Britain fought against/with the US in the War of Independence.|Did your father fight in the war?*|(fig.) *We must fight the government's action.*|(fig.) *to fight crime/a fire/for equal rights* **2** [I] to quarrel: *He and his wife are always fighting about who will take the car.* **3 fight one's way** to move along by fighting or pushing: *He had to fight his way through the crowd.*

**fight back** *v adv* [I] to defend oneself by fighting

**fight** sthg.↔ **off** *v adv* [T] to keep away with an effort: *to fight off a cold*

**fight on** *v adv* [I] to continue fighting

**fight** sthg. **out** *v adv* [T] to settle (a disagreement) by fighting (esp. in the phrase **fight it out**)

**fight²** *n* **1** [C] a battle; an occasion of fighting: *to have a fight|The police were called to stop a fight outside the school.* **2** [U] also **fighting spirit** /,··'··/– the power or desire to fight: *There's not much fight left in him now.* **3 put up a good/poor fight** to fight well/badly

**fight·er** /'faɪtə^r/ *n* **1** someone who fights, esp. a soldier or BOXER **2** also **fighter plane**– a small fast aircraft, esp. part of an air force, that can destroy enemy aircraft in the air –compare BOMBER

**fig·ment** /'fɪgmənt/ *n* **a figment of one's imagination** something believed but not real

**fig·u·ra·tive** /'fɪgjʊrətɪv, -gə-||-gjə-, -gə-/ *adj* (of words) used in some way to make a word picture or comparison: *"A sweet temper" is a figurative expression, but "sweet coffee" is not.* –compare LITERAL (3) –**figuratively** *adv*

**fig·ure¹** /'fɪgə^r||'fɪgjər/ *n* **1** (the shape of) a whole human body, as shown in art or seen in reality: *a group of figures on the left of the picture* –see BODY (USAGE) **2** the human shape considered from the point of view of being attractive: *doing exercises to improve one's figure|What a* **fine figure of a man/woman**! (=a person with an attractive bodily shape) **3** an important person: *Mahatma Gandhi was both a political and a religious figure in Indian history.* **4** any of the number signs from 0 to 9: *Write the amount in words and in figures.|I'm no good at figures!* (= sums)|*Her income is in five figures/She has a five-figure income.* (=more than £10,000) **5** an amount, esp. of money **6** a numbered drawing, map, or DIAGRAM, used in a book to explain something

**figure²** *v* **-ured, -uring 1** [I *as, in*] to take part: *Roger figured as chief guest at the party.* **2** [I;T +(*that*)] *AmE* to consider; believe: *I figured (that) you'd want to go out.* **3 That figures!** That seems reasonable and what I expected, esp. when bad

**figure on** sthg. *v prep* [T +*v-ing*] *esp. AmE* to plan on; include in one's plans: *I'm figuring on (getting) a pay increase.*

**figure** sbdy./sthg.↔ **out** *v adv* [T] to understand by thinking: *We must figure out how to do it.*

**fig·ure·head** /'fɪgəhed||'fɪgjər-/ *n* **1** the head or chief in name only: *The President is just a figurehead; it's the party leader who has the real power.* **2** a decoration on the front of a ship, often in the shape of a person

**figure of eight** /,·· · '·/ ||also **figure eight** /,·· '·/

*AmE*– *n* anything of the shape of an 8, such as a knot, stitch, or pattern

**figure of speech** /ˌ·· · ˈ·/ *n* an example of the FIGURATIVE use of words: *I didn't really mean my partner is a snake; it was just a figure of speech.*

**fil·a·ment** /ˈfɪləmənt/ *n* a thin thread, such as that inside an electric light BULB

**filch** /fɪltʃ/ *v* [T] *infml* to steal secretly (something of small value)

**file**[1] /faɪl/ *n* a steel tool with a rough face, used for smoothing or cutting hard surfaces

**file**[2] *v* **filed, filing** [I;T] to use a FILE[1] on: *to file one's nails|to file through the bars*

**file**[3] *n* **1** any of various arrangements of drawers, shelves, boxes, or cases for storing papers in an office –see also FILING CABINET **2** [*on*] a collection of papers on one subject, stored in this way: *Here's our file on the Middle East.|I'll keep your report* **on file.** (=stored in a file) –see picture on page 415

**file**[4] *v* [T] **1** to put in a FILE[3]: *Please file this letter (away), Peter.* **2** *law* to send in or record officially: *to file an* APPLICATION (1)

**file**[5] *n* [C +*sing./pl. v*] a line of people one behind the other (often in the phrase **in single file**) –see also RANK[1] (4)

**file**[6] *v* [I] to walk in single FILE[5]: *They filed slowly past the grave of their leader.*

**fil·et** /ˈfɪl$\frac{1}{3}$t, ˈfɪleɪ, fɪˈleɪ/ *n AmE* for FILLET

**fi·li·al** /ˈfɪlɪəl/ *adj fml* of or suitable to a son or daughter: *filial love*

**fil·i·bus·ter** /ˈfɪl$\frac{1}{3}$bʌstəʳ/ *v* [I] *esp. AmE* to try to delay or prevent action in a parliament or other lawmaking body, by being very slow and making long speeches

**fil·i·gree** /ˈfɪl$\frac{1}{3}$griː/ *n* [U] delicate decorative wire work: *silver filigree jewellery*

**filing cab·i·net** /ˈ·· ˌ···/ *n* a piece of office furniture with drawers, for storing papers in –see picture on page 415

**fil·ings** /ˈfaɪlɪŋz/ *n* [P] very small sharp bits that have been rubbed off a metal surface with a FILE[1]: *iron filings*

**fill**[1] /fɪl/ *v* **1** [I;T *with*] to make or become full: *The house soon filled (with children).*|(fig.) *Laughter filled the room.|The thought fills me with pleasure.* **2** [T] to (cause to) enter (a position): *John's the best person to fill this* VACANCY (2). **3** [T] to fulfil; meet the needs or demands of: *Can you fill this* PRESCRIPTION (3), *please?* –compare EMPTY[2]

**fill in** *v adv* **1** [T] (**fill** sthg.↔ **in**) **a** to put in (whatever is needed to complete something): *You draw the trees and I'll fill in the sky.|Fill in your name on this cheque.* **b** also **fill** sthg.↔ **out** *esp. AmE*– to complete by putting in whatever is needed: *to fill in one's income tax* FORM[1] (3) **2** [T *on*] (**fill** sbdy. **in**) to supply the most recent information to: *Please fill me in on what happened at the meeting.* **3** [I *for*] to take someone's place: *Can you fill in for Steve tonight as he's ill?*

**fill out** *v adv* **1** [I] to get fatter: *Her face is beginning to fill out.* **2** [T] (**fill** sthg.↔ **out**) → FILL IN (1)

**fill up** *v adv* [I;T (=**fill** sthg.↔ **up**)] to make or become completely full: *The room soon filled up with people.*

**fill**[2] *n* a full supply; as much as is needed or wanted: *to drink one's fill|John annoys me; I've* **had my fill of** *him for one evening!*

**fil·let**[1] /ˈfɪl$\frac{1}{3}$t, ˈfɪleɪ, fɪˈleɪ/ ||also **filet** *AmE*– *n* a piece of fish or meat with the bones removed: *a fillet* STEAK|*fillets of* SOLE

**fillet**[2] ||also **filet** *AmE*– *v* [T] to remove the bones from (a piece of fish or meat); cut into FILLETS[1]

**fill·ing** /ˈfɪlɪŋ/ *n* **1** (the material put into) a hole in a tooth by a DENTIST to preserve it: *You've got a lot of fillings.* **2** a food mixture folded inside pastry, SANDWICHES, etc.

**filling sta·tion** /ˈ·· ˌ··/ also **petrol station** *BrE*||**gas station** *AmE*– *n* a place (GARAGE) that sells petrol and oil and may also repair motor vehicles –compare SERVICE STATION

**fil·ly** /ˈfɪli/ *n* **-lies** a young female horse –compare COLT

**film**[1] /fɪlm/ *n* **1** [S;U] a thin skin of any material: *a sheet of plastic film|a film of dust* **2** [C;U] (a roll of) the substance on which one takes photographs or makes cinema pictures: *to buy a film/some film for my camera* **3** [C] *esp. BrE*||**movie** *AmE*– a cinema picture: *to* **shoot** (= make) **a film**|*Have you seen any good films lately?*

**film**[2] *v* [I;T] to make a cinema picture (of): *We'll be filming all day tomorrow.*

**film star** /ˈ· ·/ ||also **movie star** *AmE*– *n* a well-known actor or actress in cinema pictures

**film·strip** /ˈfɪlmˌstrɪp/ *n* [C;U] (a length of) photographic film used to show (PROJECT[2] (3)) photographs, drawings, etc., one after the other as still pictures: *a filmstrip on the life of the ant*

**film·y** /ˈfɪlmi/ *adj* **-ier, -iest** fine and thin, so that one can see through it: *a filmy silk dress* –**filminess** *n* [U]

**fil·ter**[1] /ˈfɪltəʳ/ *n* **1** an apparatus through which substances can be passed so as to make them clean: *the oil filter in a car* **2** a (coloured) glass that changes light admitted into a camera

**filter**[2] *v* [I;T] to pass or send (as if) through a FILTER: *to filter the drinking water|Sunlight filtered through the curtains.*|(fig.) *The news slowly filtered through to everyone in the office.*

**filter** sthg.↔ **out** *v adv* [T] to remove by means of a FILTER: *to filter out the dirt/the blue light*

**filth** /fɪlθ/ *n* [U] **1** very nasty dirt: *Go and wash that filth off your hands.* **2** something rude or unpleasant: *I don't know how you can read such filth.* –**filthy** *adj* **-ier, -iest** –**filthily** *adv* –**filthiness** *n* [U]

**fin** /fɪn/ *n* **1** a winglike part that a fish uses in swimming **2** a part shaped like this on a car, aircraft, or bomb

**fi·nal**[1] /ˈfaɪnəl/ *adj* **1** [A] last; coming at the end: *Z is the final letter in the alphabet.|a final cup of coffee before we left* **2** (of a decision, offer, etc.) that cannot be changed: *I won't go, and that's final!|Is that your final offer?*

**final**[2] *n* [*often pl.*] the last and most important test in **a** a set of matches: *the tennis finals* **b** a college course: *When do you take your finals?* (=final examinations)

**fi·na·le** /fɪˈnɑːli||fɪˈnæli/ *n* the last division of a piece of music

**fi·nal·ist** /ˈfaɪnəl-$\frac{1}{3}$st/ *n* one of the people or teams left in the FINAL, after the others have been defeated

**fi·nal·i·ty** /faɪ'næl$\frac{1}{2}$ti, fɪ-/ *n* [U] the quality of being or seeming FINAL[1] (2): *"No!" he said with finality.*

**fi·nal·ize** ||also **-ise** *BrE* /'faɪnəl-aɪz/ *v* **-ized, -izing** [T] to finish and make firm (plans, arrangements, etc.)

**fi·nal·ly** /'faɪnəli/ *adv* **1** at last: *After several long delays, the plane finally left at 6 o'clock.* **2** so as not to allow further change: *It's not finally settled yet.*

**fi·nance**[1] /'faɪnæns, f$\frac{1}{2}$'næns||f$\frac{1}{2}$'næns, 'faɪnæns/ *n* [U] **1** the control of (esp. public) money **2** money, esp. provided by a bank or similar organization, to help run a business or buy something: *Unless we get more finance, we'll have to close the hotel.*

**finance**[2] *v* **-nanced, -nancing** [T] to provide money for: *The repairs to the school will be financed by the local council.*

**fi·nanc·es** /'faɪnæns$\frac{1}{2}$z, f$\frac{1}{2}$'næns$\frac{1}{2}$z||f$\frac{1}{2}$'næns$\frac{1}{2}$z, 'faɪnæns$\frac{1}{2}$z/ *n* [P] the amount of money owned by a person, organization, or government

**fi·nan·cial** /f$\frac{1}{2}$'nænʃəl, faɪ-/ *adj* connected with money: *Mr Briggs is our financial adviser.* –**financially** *adv*

**fi·nan·cier** /f$\frac{1}{2}$'nænsɪəʳ, faɪ'næn-||ˌfaɪnæn'sɪər/ *n* someone who controls or lends large sums of money

**finch** /fɪntʃ/ *n* a small singing bird such as the CHAFFINCH

**find**[1] /faɪnd/ *v* **found** /faʊnd/, **finding** [T] **1** [not *be* +*v-ing*] to discover, esp. by searching: *I can't find my boots!|They found him somewhere to live/found somewhere for him to live.|Did you find what you were looking for?|They found the lost child (hiding) in the cave.|We've found oil under the North Sea.* –compare LOSE (1) **2** [+(*that*)/*out*] to learn or discover (something) by effort, chance, experience, etc.: *Please find (out) what time they're coming.|I find (that) I have plenty of time now.|When I woke up, I found myself* (=I found that I was) *in hospital.|We went to her house but found her out/found that she was out.|I'm finding her (to be) a rather difficult person to work with.|This type of tree* **is found** (=exists) *only in Australia.* –compare FIND **out** (1) **3** *fml* (of things) to reach; arrive at: *The bullet found its mark.* **4** [not *be* +*v-ing*] to obtain by effort: *How ever do you find the time to make cakes?|At last she found the courage to tell him.* **5** [not *be*+*v-ing*] *law* to decide (someone) to be: *"How do you find the prisoner?" "We find him not guilty."|She was found guilty of stealing.*

**find out** *v adv* **1** [I;T (=**find** sthg.↔ **out**)] to learn or discover (a fact that was hidden): *Did you ever find out why he left his last job?* –compare FIND[1] (2) **2** [T] (**find** sbdy. **out**) to discover in a dishonest act: *He was stealing money from the company for years before they found him out.*

**find**[2] *n* something (good) that is found: *This little restaurant is quite a find/is a real find. I didn't know it existed!*

**find·ing** /'faɪndɪŋ/ *n* **1** *law* a decision made by a judge or JURY **2** something learnt as the result of an official enquiry: *the findings of the committee on child care*

> **SPELLING NOTE**
> Words with the sound /f/ may be spelt **ph-**, like **photograph.**

**fine**[1] /faɪn/ *n* an amount of money paid as a punishment: *to pay a £5 fine*

**fine**[2] *v* **fined, fining** [T] to take money from as a punishment: *He was fined £200.*

**fine**[3] *adj* **1** [A] beautiful and of high quality; better than most of its kind: *a fine house/musician/wine/view|I've never seen a finer animal.|We use only the finest materials to make our furniture.* **2 a** very thin: *fine hair/thread/silk|a pencil with a fine point* –see THIN (USAGE) **b** in very small grains or bits: *fine sugar/dust* –opposite **coarse 3** (of weather) bright and sunny; not wet: *It's* **turned out fine** *again.|a fine summer morning* **4** [*no comp.*] (of a person or conditions) healthy and comfortable: *"How's your wife?" "She's fine, thank you."|This flat's fine for two people, but not more.* **5** [A] (of work) delicate and careful: *fine sewing|the finest workmanship|*(fig.) *I missed some of the finer points in the argument.*|**Not to put too fine a point on it** (=to express it plainly), *I think he's mad.* **6** [A] *humor* terrible: *That's a fine thing to say!*

**fine**[4] *adv* **1** also **finely**– so as to be very thin or in very small bits: *Cut up the vegetables very fine.* **2** very well: *It suits me fine.|The machine works fine if you oil it.* **3 cut/run it fine** to allow only just enough time: *You're cutting it a bit fine if you want to catch the 5.30 train!*

**fine arts** /ˌ· '·/ *n* [*the* P] those arts such as painting, music, and SCULPTURE, that are chiefly concerned with producing beautiful rather than useful things

**fine·ly** /'faɪnli/ *adv* **1** closely and delicately: *These instruments are very finely set.* **2** so as to be in small grains or bits: *finely cut vegetables*

**fi·ne·ry** /'faɪnəri/ *n* [U] beautiful clothes and decorations: *the guests in their wedding finery*

**fi·nesse** /f$\frac{1}{2}$'nes/ *n* [U] delicate skill: *Paul handled the meeting with great finesse.*

**fin·ger**[1] /'fɪŋgəʳ/ *n* **1** one of the movable parts with joints, at the end of each human hand (sometimes including the thumb) –compare TOE[1]; see picture on page 299 **2 (have) a finger in every pie** *infml* (to have) a part in everything that is going on **3 keep one's fingers crossed** *infml* to hope for the best: *We must just keep our fingers crossed that the weather will stay fine for tomorrow's game.* **4 lift a finger** (*in* NEGATIVES[2] (1), *questions, etc.*) to make any effort to help: *No one lifted a finger to save the prisoners.* **5 put one's finger on** to find: *I can't quite put my finger on what's wrong.* **6 pull one's finger out** *infml* to start working hard

**finger**[2] *v* [T] to feel or handle with one's fingers: *She fingered the rich silk.*

**fin·ger·nail** /'fɪŋgəneɪl||-ər-/ also **nail**– *n* one of the hard flat pieces that cover the ends of the fronts of the fingers –see picture on page 299

**fin·ger·print** /'fɪŋgəˌprɪnt||-ər-/ *n* the mark of a finger, esp. as used in the discovery of crime: *The police took the man's fingerprints.* (=made a picture of them)

**fin·ger·tip** /'fɪŋgəˌtɪp||-ər-/ *n* the end of a finger: (fig.) *You'd better ask David; he has all the information* **at his fingertips.** (=has a ready knowledge of it)

**fin·i·cky** /ˈfɪnɪki/ *adj* disliking many things; FUSSY: *Eat up your fish and don't be so finicky.*

**fin·ish¹** /ˈfɪnɪʃ/ *v* **1** [I;T +*v-ing/up, off*] to come or bring to an end; complete: *What time does the concert finish?|When do you finish your college course?|I haven't finished reading that book yet.|We took the night train and finished up in Paris.|I must finish (off) this dress I'm making; I'm just giving it the last* **finishing touches.** –compare START **2** [T *up, off*] to eat or drink the rest of: *The cat will finish (up) the fish.|Let's finish (off) the wine.* **3** [T] *infml* to take away all one's strength, hopes of success, etc.: *Climbing all those stairs has really finished me.*

**finish with** sbdy./sthg. *v prep* [T] to have no more use for: *I'll borrow the scissors if you've finished with them.|I've finished with Mary after the way she's treated me.*

**finish²** *n* **1** [S] the end or last part, esp. of a race: *That was a close finish!* (=the competitors were almost level) –compare START **2** [S;U] the appearance or condition of having been properly finished, with paint, polish, etc.: *the beautiful finish of old French furniture*

**fin·ished** /ˈfɪnɪʃt/ *adj* **1** [F] ended; with no hope of continuing: *If the bank refuses to lend us the money, we're finished.* **2** [A] properly made and complete: *the finished product|a beautifully finished old table*

**fi·nite** /ˈfaɪnaɪt/ *adj* having an end or limit: *a finite number of possibilities* –opposite **infinite**

**fi·ord** /ˈfiːɔːd, fjɔːd‖fiːˈɔrd, fjord/ *n* → FJORD

**fir** /fɜːʳ/ also **firtree**– *n* a straight tree that keeps its thin sharp leaves (NEEDLE*s*) in winter, and grows esp. in cold countries. –sounds like **fur**

**fire¹** /faɪəʳ/ *n* **1** [U] burning with flames: *Horses are afraid of fire.|insurance against (destruction by) fire|The pile of papers* **caught fire.** (=started to burn) *Someone must have* **set fire to** *it*/**set** *it* **on fire.** **2** [C] a mass of burning material, lit on purpose for cooking, heat, etc., or lit by accident: *The hunters lit a fire to keep warm at night.|Put some more coal on the fire.|Thousands of trees were lost in the forest fire.* **3** [C] *BrE* a gas or electrical apparatus for warming a room, with the flames or red-hot wires able to be seen –compare STOVE **4** [U] shooting by guns: *We were* **under fire** (=being shot at) *from all sides.* **5 on fire** (of something not meant to burn) burning: *The house is on fire!* –compare FIERY

USAGE You **light** a **fire** or a candle (=make it burn), but you **fire** a gun (=shoot bullets from it), and you can also **fire** clay pots (=bake them in a KILN). If you **light** something that is not intended to burn, you **set fire to** it: *Someone* **set fire to** *the school bus.* When a thing begins to burn, it **catches fire**: *Her dress* **caught fire.**

**fire²** *v* **fired, firing 1** [I *at*] (of a person or a gun) to shoot off bullets: *He's firing at us!* **2** [T *at*] (of a person) to shoot bullets from (a gun): *He ran into the bank and fired his gun into the air.* **3** [T *at*] (of a person, gun, or BOW³ (1)) to shoot (bullets or arrows): *Hinckley fired five shots at the President.* –see SHOOT (USAGE) **4** [T] to bake (clay pots, dishes, etc.) in a KILN **5** [T *with*] to produce (strong feelings) in (someone): *a speech that fired the crowd's imagination* **6** [T] *infml* to dismiss from a job; SACK²: *Get out! You're fired!*

**fire a·larm** /ˈ· ·ˌ·/ *n* a signal, such as a ringing bell, to warn people of fire

**fire·arm** /faɪərɑːm‖-ɑrm/ *n* [*usu. pl.*] a gun

**fire bri·gade** /ˈ· ·ˌ·/ *BrE*‖**fire department** /ˈ· ·ˌ··/ *AmE*– *n* [C +*sing./pl. v*] an organization for preventing and putting out fires: *The fire brigade is/are coming!*

**fire en·gine** /ˈ· ˌ··/ *n* a special vehicle that carries firemen (FIREMAN) and special apparatus to put out fires

**fire es·cape** /ˈ· ·ˌ·/ *n* a set of metal stairs leading down outside a building to the ground, by which people can escape in case of fire –see picture on page 297

**fire·guard** /ˈfaɪəgɑːd‖ˈfaɪərgɑrd/ *n* a protective metal framework put round a fireplace

**fire·man** /ˈfaɪəmən‖-ər-/ *n* **-men** /mən/ a person whose job is putting out fires

**fire·place** *n* the opening for a fire in the wall of a room, with a chimney above it and often a HEARTH and MANTELPIECE around it –see picture on page 355

**fire-rais·ing** /ˈ· ˌ··/ *n* [U] the crime of starting fires on purpose; ARSON

**fire·side** /ˈfaɪəsaɪd‖-ər-/ *n* [*usu. sing.*] the area around the fireplace: *to sit by the fireside*

**fire sta·tion** /ˈ· ˌ··/ *n* a building for firemen (FIREMAN) and their fire-fighting apparatus

**fire·wood** /ˈfaɪəwʊd‖-ər-/ *n* [U] wood cut to be used on fires

**fire·work** /ˈfaɪəwɜːk‖ˈfaɪərwɜrk/ *n* [*often pl.*] a small container filled with an explosive powder that is burnt to produce a show of light, noise, and smoke

**fir·ing squad** /ˈfaɪərɪŋ skwɒd‖skwɑd/ *n* a group of soldiers with the duty of shooting an offender dead

**firm¹** /fɜːm‖fɜrm/ *adj* **1** strong; solid; hard: *Do you think this jelly's firm enough to eat yet?* **2** steady; strong and sure: *firm on one's feet|I don't think that chair's firm enough to stand on.|He kept a firm hold on my hand as he helped me over the fence.* **3** not changing or yielding: *a firm belief/believer in God|The pound stayed firm against the dollar yesterday, but fell a little against the yen.|You will have to be firm with Class Three as they are rather disobedient.* –**firmly** *adv* –**firmness** *n* [U]

**firm²** *n* a business company

**fir·ma·ment** /ˈfɜːməmənt‖ˈfɜr-/ *n* [*the* S] *lit* the sky

**first¹** /fɜːst‖fɜrst/ *n,pron* **1** [+*to-v*] the person or thing before all the others: *He was the first/one of the first to arrive.|Whoever is (the) first to finish will get a prize.* –compare LAST **2** [C] the highest class of British university degree: *She and her husband both got firsts.* **3 at first** at the beginning: *At first I didn't like him but now I do.* –compare **at** LAST¹ **4 from the (very) first** from the beginning

**first²** *determiner,adv* **1** before anything else; before the others: *"Let's go!" "I must put on my shoes first."|George arrived first/was the first person to arrive.* **2** for the first time: *Is this your first visit to London?|I remember when I first met him.* –compare LAST **3** at the beginning: *When we first lived here there were no buses.* **4 first and foremost** most importantly; above all else **5 first of all** as the first thing **6 first thing** at the earliest time in the morning

**first aid** /ˌ· ˈ·/ *n* [U] treatment to be given by an ordinary person to a person hurt in an accident or suddenly taken ill: *She pulled the drowning man from the water and gave him first aid.*

**first class** /ˌ· ˈ·◂/ *n* [U] the best and most expensive method of travel or of sending mail: *If you send your letter first class it will get there quicker.|I like to travel in comfort, so I always go first class on the train.* –see also SECOND CLASS

**first-class** *adj* of the highest or best quality: *Your work is first-class; I'm very pleased with it.*

**first floor** /ˌ· ˈ·◂/ *n* **1** (in Britain) the first floor of a building above ground level –see picture on page 297 **2** (in the US) the floor of a building at ground level –compare GROUND FLOOR

**first·hand** /ˌfɜːstˈhænd◂‖-ɜr-/ *adj,adv* (learnt) directly from the point of origin: *I heard her news firsthand.* (=from her)|*firsthand information* –compare SECOND-HAND[1] (2)

**first la·dy** /ˌ· ˈ··/ *n* [*the* S] (in the US) the wife of the President

**first·ly** /ˈfɜːstli‖-ɜr-/ *adv* → FIRST[2] (1)

USAGE Teachers prefer **first** to **firstly** in sentences like this: *There are three reasons against it:* **first** . . .

**first name** /ˈ· ·/ *n* the name or names that stand before one's SURNAME (=family name); one's personal name: *Smith's first name is Peter.|His first names are Peter George.*

USAGE In English-speaking countries, your **first name** is the one always used by your family and friends. People whose SURNAMES come before their other names, as in Chinese, Hungarian, etc., may prefer to use **given name** rather than **first name.**

**first per·son** /ˌ· ˈ··◂/ *n* [*the* S] **1** a form of verb or word standing for a noun (PRONOUN) used to show the speaker: *"I", "me", "we", and "us" are first person* PRONOUNS.|*"I am" is the first person present singular of "to be".* **2** a way of telling a story in which the teller uses the FIRST PERSON (1): *The story was written in the first person. It began "I was born in. . ."*

**first-rate** /ˌ· ˈ·◂/ *adj* very good: *This beer is first-rate!* –compare SECOND-RATE

**fis·cal** /ˈfɪskəl/ *adj fml* of or related to public money, taxes, debts, etc.

**fish**[1] /fɪʃ/ *n* **fish** *or* **fishes 1** [C] a creature which lives in water and uses its FINS and tail to swim: *We caught three little fishes/several fish.* **2** [U] its flesh when used as food: *We had fish/some fish/a piece of fish for dinner.*

**fish**[2] *v* **1** [I *for*] to try to catch fish; search (for something under water): *Let's go fishing.|to fish for* TROUT|(fig.) *Why are you* **fishing around** *in your pockets?*|(fig.) *I think he's just* **fishing for compliments.** (=trying to attract admiring words) **2** [T] to catch fish in (a piece of water): *This river has been fished too much.*

**fish** sthg.↔ **out** *v adv* [T] to bring out after searching: *to fish out a coin/a handkerchief from one's pocket*

> **SPELLING NOTE**
> Words with the sound /f/ may be spelt **ph-**, like **photograph.**

**fish·er·man** /ˈfɪʃəmən‖-ər-/ *n* **-men** /mən/ a man who catches fish, for sport or as a job –compare ANGLER

**fish·ing** /ˈfɪʃɪŋ/ *n* [U] the sport or job of catching fish: *to do some fishing in the holidays*

**fish·mon·ger** /ˈfɪʃmʌŋgəʳ/ *n esp. BrE* (someone who works in) a shop that sells fish

**fish·y** /ˈfɪʃi/ *adj* **-ier, -iest 1** tasting or smelling of fish **2** seeming false: *the fishiest story I've ever heard*

**fis·sion** /ˈfɪʃən/ *n* [U] *tech* the splitting into parts of certain cells or atoms

**fis·sure** /ˈfɪʃəʳ/ *n fml* a deep crack in rock or earth

**fist** /fɪst/ *n* (the shape of) the hand with the fingers closed in tightly: *She shook her fist angrily.*

**fit**[1] /fɪt/ *v* **-tt- 1** [I;T] to be the right size or shape (for): *This dress doesn't fit (me).* **2** [T] to make suitable for: *Her special abilities fit her well for the job.* –see also FIT **in** (1) **3** [T] to provide and put correctly into place: *We're having new locks fitted on all the doors.* –see also FITTED (2) **4 fit the bill** to be just what one wants **5 fit like a glove** to fit very well and closely

USAGE The usual past tense and past participle of **fit** is **fitted,** but in the first meaning **fit** is also used, esp. in *AmE*: *When he left the shop, the suit* **fit** *him perfectly.*

**fit in** *v adv* **1** [I;T (=**fit** sthg.↔ **in**) *with*] to (cause to) be suitable (to): *to fit my arrangements in with yours|to fit in with his ideas* **2** [T] (**fit** sbdy./sthg.↔ **in**) to find a time to see (someone) or do (something): *Doctor Jones can fit you in on Thursday afternoon.*

**fit** sbdy./sthg.↔ **out** *v adv* [T] to supply with necessary things: *The ship has been newly fitted out.*

**fit**[2] *n* [S] the way in which something fits: *This coat's a beautiful fit.|I'll try to climb through, but it's a tight fit.*

**fit**[3] *n* **1** a period of loss of consciousness, with strange uncontrolled movements of the body: (fig.) *Father will* **have a fit** (=be very angry) *when he hears what you have done.* **2** [*of*] a short attack (of a slight illness or violent feeling): *a fit of coughing|I hit her in a fit of anger.*|(fig.) *She kept them* **in fits (of laughter)** *with her jokes.* **3 by/in fits and starts** continually starting and stopping; not regularly

**fit**[4] *adj* **1** [+*to-v/for*] right and suitable: *She's not fit/not a fit person to be in charge of small children.|a meal fit for a king|The president has* **seen/thought fit** (=has decided) *to let the prisoner go free.* **2** in good health or bodily condition: *He runs three miles every morning; that's why he's so fit.|She goes to* **keep-fit** *classes and does exercises every day.* –opposite **unfit**

**fit·ful** /ˈfɪtfəl/ *adj* restless: *to spend a fitful night* –**fitfully** *adv*

**fit·ment** /ˈfɪtmənt/ *n* a piece of fitted furniture: *bathroom fitments*

**fit·ness** /ˈfɪtnɪ̵s/ *n* [U] **1** the state of being fit in body: *doing exercises to improve their fitness* **2** [+*to-v/for*] the quality of being suitable

**fit·ted** /ˈfɪtɪ̵d/ *adj* **1** [F *with*] having (a part, piece of apparatus, etc.): *Is the car fitted with a radio?* **2** [A] fixed in place: *a fitted* CARPET|*fitted cupboards*

**fit·ter** /ˈfɪtəʳ/ *n* someone whose work is either **a** putting together machines or electrical parts or **b** cutting out and fitting clothes

**fit·ting**[1] /ˈfɪtɪŋ/ *adj fml* right; suitable: *It is fitting that* *we should remember him on his birthday.*

**fitting²** *n* **1** [*usu. pl.*] something necessary that is fixed into a building but able to be moved: *electric light fittings* –compare FIXTURE (1) **2** an occasion of putting on clothes that are being made for one, to see if they fit: *I'm going for a fitting on Tuesday.*

**five** /faɪv/ *determiner,n,pron* (the number) 5 –see also FIFTH

**fiv·er** /'faɪvəʳ/ *n BrE infml* £5 or a five pound note: *It costs a fiver.|I've only got fivers.*

**fix¹** /fɪks/ *v* **1** [T] to fasten firmly: *He fixed the picture in position with a nail.*|(fig.) *Let me fix the address in my mind.*|(fig.) *The rent was fixed at £20.* **2** [I;T +*to-v/up*] to arrange: *If you want to meet them, I can fix it.|We haven't fixed (up) where to stay yet.|We've fixed up to go to Austria.* –compare FIX **on** (1) **3** [T] to arrange the result of unfairly: *The election/race was fixed.* **4** [T] to repair: *I must get the radio fixed.* **5** [T] *esp. AmE* to prepare (esp. food or drink) for (someone): *Let me fix you a drink/Let me fix a drink for you.* **6** [T] *infml* to deal with; get even with (someone): *I'll fix him for calling me a liar!*

**fix on** *v prep* [T] **1** (**fix on** sbdy./sthg.) [+*v-ing*] to decide on: *We've fixed on the 14th of April for the wedding.|We've fixed on starting tomorrow.* –compare FIX¹ (2) **2** (**fix** sthg. **on** sbdy./sthg.) to direct (one's eyes, attention, etc.) steadily at: *She fixed her eyes on the clock.* **3 fix the blame on (someone)** to decide that someone is guilty

**fix** sbdy. **up** *v adv* [T *with*] to provide with; make the arrangements for: *We must fix him up with a job/with a room in the hotel.*

**fix²** *n infml* **1** an awkward or difficult position: *We're in a real fix; there's nobody to look after the baby!* **2** [*of*] (used by drug-takers) an INJECTION (of the stated drug)

**fix·a·tion** /fɪk'seɪʃən/ *n tech* (in PSYCHOLOGY) a strong unhealthy feeling (about) or love (for): *He has a fixation about her|a mother fixation.*

**fixed** /fɪkst/ *adj* fastened; not movable or changeable: *The tables are firmly fixed to the floor.|The date is fixed now.|* (fig.) *He has very fixed ideas.*

**fix·ed·ly** /'fɪksɪ̥dli/ *adv* unchangingly; with great attention (in phrases like **to stare fixedly**)

**fix·ture** /'fɪkstʃəʳ/ *n* **1** something that is fixed into a building and sold with it: *bathroom fixtures* –compare FITTING² (1) **2** a match or sports competition taking place on an agreed date

**fizz¹** /fɪz/ *v* [I] (of a liquid, usu. a drink) to produce bubbles, making the sound typical of this

**fizz²** *n* [S] the sound of FIZZing –**fizzy** *adj* **-zier, -ziest**: *fizzy drinks*

**fiz·zle out** /'fɪzəl/ *v adv* **-zled, -zling** [I] to end in nothing after a good start: *The party fizzled out before midnight.*

**fjord, fiord** /'fiːɔːd, fjɔːd||fiː'ɔrd, fjord/ *n* a narrow arm of the sea between cliffs or steep slopes, esp. in Norway

**flab·ber·gast·ed** /'flæbəgɑːstɪ̥d||-ərgæst-/ *adj* [*at, by*] *infml* very surprised

**flab·by** /'flæbi/ *adj* **-bier, -biest** having too soft flesh; (of muscles) too soft: *I became rather flabby after I stopped playing football regularly.* –**flabbiness** *n* [U]

**flac·cid** /'flæksɪ̥d/ *adj* not firm enough; weak and soft: *flaccid plant stems*

**flag¹** /flæg/ *n* a square or OBLONG piece of cloth, usu. with a pattern or picture on it, fastened by one edge to a pole (**flagpole**) or rope: *to* FLY (=have on a pole) *the national flag of Norway|flags hanging* **at half-mast** (=lower than the top of the pole) *as a sign of sorrow*

**flag²** *v* **-gg-** [I] to become weak and less alive or active: *After walking for three hours we began to flag.|his flagging interest in the subject* –see also UNFLAGGING

**flag** sbdy./sthg.↔ **down** *v adv* [T] to cause (a vehicle) to stop by waving at the driver

**flag³** *n* → FLAGSTONE

**flag·on** /'flægən/ *n* a large container for liquids such as wine, usu. with a lid, a handle, and a lip or SPOUT for pouring

**fla·grant** /'fleɪgrənt/ *adj* (of a bad person or action) open and shameless: *flagrant cheating|a flagrant coward* –**flagrantly** *adv*

**flag·ship** /'flæg,ʃɪp/ *n* the chief ship, on which an ADMIRAL sails, among a group of warships

**flag·stone** /'flægstəʊn/ also **flag**– *n* a flat square of stone for a floor or path

**flail** /fleɪl/ *v* [I;T] to wave violently but aimlessly about: *Her legs flailed in the water.*

**flair** /fleəʳ/ *n* [S;U *for*] the natural ability to do some special thing: *a flair for writing|He shows little flair for this subject.*

**flake¹** /fleɪk/ *n* a light leaf-like little bit: *soap flakes|flakes of snow* –see picture on page 449 –**flaky** *adj* **-ier, -iest**: *flaky pastry*

**flake²** *v* **flaked, flaking** [I *off*] to fall off in FLAKEs: *The paint's beginning to flake (off).*

**flake out** *v adv* [I] *infml* to faint or COLLAPSE¹ (2)

**flam·boy·ant** /flæm'bɔɪənt/ *adj* (of a thing or person) noticeable; showy, and bold: *a flamboyant orange shirt* –**flamboyantly** *adv* –**flamboyance** *n* [U]

**flame¹** /fleɪm/ *n* [C;U] **1** (a tongue of) red or yellow burning gas: *The dry sticks burst into flame(s).|The whole city was* **in flames. 2 old flame** someone with whom one used to be in love

**flame²** *v* **flamed, flaming** [I *out, up*] to become (red, bright, etc.) by or as if by burning: *The candles flamed brighter.|Her cheeks flamed red.*

**fla·men·co** /flə'meŋkəʊ/ *n* **-cos** *or* **-coes** a kind of Spanish dancing and music, very fast and exciting

**flam·ing** /'fleɪmɪŋ/ *adj* [A] burning brightly; bright; strong: (fig.) *I was* **in a flaming temper.**

**fla·min·go** /flə'mɪŋgəʊ/ *n* **-gos** *or* **-goes** a tall tropical water bird with long thin legs and pink and red feathers

**flam·ma·ble** /'flæməbəl/ *adj AmE & tech* → INFLAMMABLE –opposite **non-flammable**

USAGE **Flammable** and **inflammable** are not opposites: they have the same meaning, but **flammable** is used in the US and is also the *BrE tech* word.

**flan** /flæn/ *n* a round flat open PIE made of pastry or cake, with a fruit, cheese, etc. filling

**flange** /flændʒ/ *n* the flat edge that stands out from the main surface of an object such as a railway wheel, to keep it in position

**flank¹** /flæŋk/ *n* the side of an animal, person, or moving army: *The enemy attacked on the left flank.*

**flank²** *v* [T *with, by*] to be placed beside: *a road flanked with tall buildings*

**flan·nel** /ˈflænl/ *n* **1** [U] smooth woollen cloth with a slightly furry surface: *flannel trousers* **2** [C] a piece of cloth used for washing oneself

**flan·nels** /ˈflænlz/ *n* [P] men's FLANNEL (1) trousers, esp. as worn for games like cricket –see PAIR¹ (USAGE)

**flap¹** /flæp/ **1** [C] a wide flat part of anything that hangs down, esp. so as to cover an opening: *to creep under the flap of the tent|the flap on an envelope* **2** [S] the sound of FLAPping² (1): *the slow flap of the sails* **3** [C] *infml* a state of excited anxiety: *Don't get in a flap; we'll soon find it.*

**flap²** *v* **-pp-** **1** [I;T] to move (something large and soft) up and down or to and fro, making a noise: *The large bird flapped its wings.|The sails flapped in the wind.* **2** [I] *infml* to be in a FLAP¹ (3)

**flare¹** /fleəʳ/ *v* **flared, flaring** [I] to burn with a bright flame, but uncertainly or for a short time: *candles flaring in the wind*

**flare up** *v adv* [I] to burn suddenly: (fig.) *Trouble may flare up in the big cities.*

**flare²** *n* **1** [S] a flaring (FLARE) light: *a sudden flare as she lit the gas* **2** [C] something that provides a bright light out of doors, often used as a signal: *As our ship began to sink, we sent out flares to attract attention.*

**flared** /fleəd‖fleərd/ *adj* (of trousers or a skirt) shaped so as to get wider by degrees towards the bottom: *a very flared skirt*

**flash¹** /flæʃ/ *v* **1** [I] (of a light) to appear or shine for a moment: *The lightning flashed.|the flashing lights of the cars|*(fig.) *flashing eyes* **2** [T *at*] to make a flash with; shine for a moment (at): *Why is that driver flashing his lights (at me)?|*(fig.) *She flashed a sudden smile at him.|to flash a message on the cinema* SCREEN¹ (3) **3** [T] to send (a telegraph or radio message): *They flashed the news back to London.* **4** [I] to move very fast: *The days seem to flash by.|*(fig.) *The idea flashed into/across/through my mind.*

**flash back** *v adv* [I *to*] to return suddenly (to an earlier time), as in a FLASHBACK: *My mind flashed back to last Christmas.*

**flash²** *n* **1** [C] a sudden quick bright light: *flashes of lightning|*(fig.) *a sudden flash of* INSPIRATION **2** [C] a short news report, received by telegraph, radio, etc.: *A* **newsflash** *from Beirut says they've been shot.* **3** [C;U] (in photography) the method or apparatus for taking photographs in the dark: *Did you use flash?* **4** **flash in the pan** a sudden success that will not be repeated **5** **in a/like a flash** very quickly; at once

**flash·back** /ˈflæʃbæk/ *n* [C;U] part of a cinema film that goes back in time to show what happened earlier in the story: *The events of his childhood are shown in (a) flashback.* –see also FLASH **back**

**flash·light** /ˈflæʃlaɪt/ *n* **1** *esp. AmE* an electric hand-light (TORCH (1)) **2** also **flash**– an apparatus for taking flash photographs: *Did you bring your flashlight/your flash?*

> **SPELLING NOTE**
> Words with the sound /f/ may be spelt **ph-**, like **photograph.**

**flash·y** /ˈflæʃi/ *adj* **-ier, -iest** over-decorated; unpleasantly big, bright, etc.: *a large flashy car|cheap flashy clothes* –**flashily** *adv: flashily dressed*

**flask** /flɑːsk‖flæsk/ *n* **1** a narrow-necked glass bottle for containing liquids, esp. as used by scientists in the LABORATORY **2** a flat bottle for carrying alcohol or other drinks in the pocket, fastened to one's belt, etc. **3** also **thermos, thermos flask, vacuum flask**– a bottle which is specially made for keeping liquids either hot or cold

**flat¹** /flæt/ *adj* **-tt-** **1** smooth and level: *Find me something flat to write on.|He spread the map out flat on the floor.* **2** broad, smooth, and not very thick or high: *flat cakes* **3** (of a tyre) without enough air in it **4** (of beer and other gassy drinks) no longer fresh because the gas has been lost: *This beer has gone flat.|*(fig.) *Everything seems so flat* (=uninteresting) *since you left.* **5** (of a group of electric cells (BATTERY (1))) having no more electric current left inside **6** [after *n; no comp.*] (in music) lower than the true note. –compare SHARP¹ (10) **7** [A *no comp.*] complete; firm; with no more argument (in phrases like **flat refusal, flat denial**) **8** **that's flat!** *infml* that's my decision –**flatness** *n* [U]

**flat²** *n* **1** [*usu. pl.*] a low level plain, esp. near water: *mud flats* **2** [*of*] the flat part or side (of): *I hit him with the flat of my hand/of my sword.* **3** (the sign, for) a FLAT¹ (6) note in music –compare SHARP¹ (10) **4** *esp. AmE* a flat tyre

**flat³** *adv* **1** completely: *He's flat* BROKE¹. (=without any money) –compare FLATLY (2) **2** (in music) lower than the true note: *You keep singing flat.* –compare SHARP¹ (10) **3** [after *n*] (after an expression of time, showing surprise at its shortness) exactly; and not more: *I got dressed in three minutes flat!* **4** **flat out** at full speed: *working flat out|The car does 100 miles per hour flat out.*

**flat⁴** *BrE*‖**apartment** *AmE*– *n* a set of rooms esp. on one floor, usu. one of many such sets in a building or block: *to divide the house into flats|the people in the top flat* –see HOUSE¹ (USAGE); see picture on page 297

**flat·ly** /ˈflætli/ *adv* **1** in a dull level way: *"It's hopeless," he said flatly.* **2** completely; firmly: *I flatly refuse to come.* –compare FLAT¹ (7)

**flat rac·ing** /ˈ·,··/ *n* [U] the sport of horseracing on flat ground –compare STEEPLECHASE (2)

**flat rate** /ˈ· ·/ *n* one charge including everything: *You can eat as much as you like for a flat rate of £5.*

**flat·ten** /ˈflætn/ *v* [I;T *out*] to make or become flat: *I flattened myself against the wall.|The hills flatten (out) here.*

**flat·ter** /ˈflætəʳ/ *v* **1** [T *about, on*] to praise (someone) too much or insincerely in order to please: *He flattered her (on/about her cooking).* **2** [I;T] (of experiences) to give pleasure to: *She was flattered at the invitation/to be invited/that they invited her.* **3** [I;T] (of a picture or photograph) to make (the person shown there) look too beautiful: *a flattering photograph of George|The picture certainly doesn't flatter you.* **4** **flatter oneself (that)** to have the pleasant though perhaps mistaken opinion (that): *We flatter ourselves that we can do without their help.* –**flatterer** *n*

**flat·ter·y** /ˈflætəri/ *n* **-ies** [C;U] the action of FLATTERing (1), or a flattering remark
**flat·u·lence** /ˈflætjʊləns‖ˈflætʃə-/ *n* [U] *fml* too much gas in the stomach; WIND¹ (3)
**flaunt** /flɔːnt‖flɔnt, flɑnt/ *v* [T] *derog* to show for public admiration (something one is proud of): *to flaunt one's new fur coat* –compare: *She came into school* **flaunting** *her new red dress.*|*She* **flouted** (=purposely broke) *the school rules by not wearing the proper uniform.*
**flau·tist** /ˈflɔːtəst/ *BrE*‖**flutist** *AmE*– *n* someone who plays the FLUTE
**fla·vour¹** *BrE*‖**flavor** *AmE* /ˈfleɪvəʳ/ *n* [C;U] **1** (a) taste; quality that only the tongue can experience: *a strong flavour of cheese* |*Choose from six popular flavours of ice cream!*|(fig.) *a story with an unpleasant flavour* **2 -flavoured** having the stated flavour: *strawberry-flavoured ice cream*
**flavour²** *BrE*‖**flavor** *AmE* *v* [T *with*] to give FLAVOUR to: *I flavoured the cake with chocolate.*
**fla·vour·ing** *BrE*‖**flavoring** *AmE* /ˈfleɪvərɪŋ/ *n* [U] something added to food to give or improve the FLAVOUR: *Add a spoonful of banana flavouring.*
**flaw¹** /flɔː/ *n* a small sign of damage that makes an object not perfect: *a flaw in a plate*|(fig.) *the flaws in a contract* –sounds like **floor**
**flaw²** *v* [T] to make a FLAW in: *The* SCAR (=mark on the skin) *flawed her skin.*
**flaw·less** /ˈflɔːləs/ *adj* perfect; with no FLAW: *flawless beauty*|(fig.) *a flawless performance* **–flawlessly** *adv*
**flax** /flæks/ *n* [U] (the thread made from the stem of) a plant with blue flowers, used for making LINEN
**flax·en** /ˈflæksən/ *adj esp. lit* (of hair) pale yellow
**flea** /fliː/ *n* a small jumping insect without wings, that bites human or animal flesh to live on blood
**flea mar·ket** /ˈ·ˌ··/ *n* a market usu. in the street, where old or used goods are sold
**fleck¹** /flek/ *n* a small mark or spot; a bit (of something): *brown cloth with flecks of red*|*flecks of dust*
**fleck²** *v* [T *usu. pass.*] to mark or cover with FLECKS
**flee** /fliː/ *v* **fled** /fled/, **fleeing** [I;T] *esp. lit* to escape (from) by hurrying away: *They all fled (from) the burning building.*
**fleece¹** /fliːs/ *n* a sheep's woolly coat
**fleece²** *v* **fleeced, fleecing** [T] *infml* to rob by a trick or by charging too much money
**fleec·y** /ˈfliːsi/ *adj* **-ier, -iest** woolly, like a FLEECE: *a coat with a warm fleecy* LINING|*little fleecy clouds*
**fleet** /fliːt/ *n* [C +*sing.*/*pl. v*] **1** a number of ships, such as warships in the navy: *The fleet is/are coming!* **2** a group of buses, aircraft, etc., under one control
**fleet·ing** /ˈfliːtɪŋ/ *adj* (of time or periods) short; passing quickly: *a fleeting look* **–fleetingly** *adv*
**flesh** /fleʃ/ *n* **1** [U] the soft substance including fat and muscle, that covers the bones and lies under the skin **2** [U] the soft part of a fruit or vegetable, which can be eaten **3** [*the* S] (the desires, esp. sexual, of) the human body as opposed to the mind or soul: *the pleasures of the flesh* **4 flesh and blood** relatives; family: *I must help them because they're my own flesh and blood.* **5 in the flesh** in real life
**flesh·y** /ˈfleʃi/ *adj* **-ier, -iest** of or like flesh; fat
**flew** /fluː/ *v past tense of* FLY

**flex¹** /fleks/ *v* [T] to bend and move (one of one's limbs, muscles, etc.) so as to stretch and loosen: *The runners flexed their muscles as they waited for the race to begin.*
**flex²** *n* [C;U] *esp. BrE* (an) electric wire in a protective covering, which connects an electrical apparatus to a supply
**flex·i·ble** /ˈfleksəbəl/ *adj* **1** that can be bent easily **2** that can change or be changed to be suitable for new needs, changed conditions, etc.: *We can visit you on Saturday or Sunday; our plans are fairly flexible.* –opposite **inflexible**; compare RIGID **–flexibility** /ˌfleksəˈbɪləti/ *n* [U]
**flick¹** /flɪk/ *v* **1** [I;T] to (cause to) move with a light quick blow: *to flick the* SWITCH¹ (1)|*The cow flicked the flies away with its tail.* **2** [T] to strike with a light quick blow from a whip, the finger, etc.
**flick²** *n* a short light blow, stroke, or movement as with a whip, finger, etc.: *He hit the ball with just a flick of the wrist.*
**flick·er¹** /ˈflɪkəʳ/ *v* [I] to burn or move unsteadily: *The wind blew the flickering candle out.*|*Shadows flickered on the wall.*
**flicker²** *n* [S] a FLICKERing action: (fig.) *a flicker of hope*
**flick knife** /ˈ· ·/ *BrE*‖**switchblade** *AmE*– *n* a knife with a blade that springs out from inside the handle when a button is pressed
**flies** /flaɪz/ *n* [P] the front opening of a pair of trousers
**flight¹** /flaɪt/ *n* **1** [C;U] the act of flying: *a bird in flight*|*a bird's first flight from the nest*|(fig.) *a flight of the imagination* **2** [C] a trip by plane: *Did you have a good flight?* –see TRAVEL² (USAGE) **3** [C +*sing.*/*pl. v*] a group of birds or aircraft flying together **4** [C] a set of stairs (between floors): *to fall down a flight of stairs*
**flight²** *n* [C;U] (an example of) the act of running away or escaping (FLEEing): *When the police arrived, the thieves* **took (to) flight,** *leaving the jewels.*
**flight·less** /ˈflaɪtləs/ *adj* unable to fly: *The* PENGUIN *is a flightless bird.*
**flight·y** /ˈflaɪti/ *adj* **-ier, -iest** (esp. of a woman or a woman's behaviour) unsteady; often changing **–flightiness** *n* [U]
**flim·sy** /ˈflɪmzi/ *adj* **-sier, -siest** not strong; light and thin: (fig.) *a flimsy argument* **–flimsiness** *n* [U]
**flinch** /flɪntʃ/ *v* [I *from*] to move back a little when shocked by pain or fear: *Jane didn't flinch once when the doctor cleaned the cut in her arm.*|*He flinched when I raised my hand suddenly. He thought I was going to hit him.*
**fling¹** /flɪŋ/ *v* **flung** /flʌŋ/, **flinging** [T] to throw violently or with force: *Don't fling your clothes on the floor; hang them up.*|*The military government flung its opponents into prison.*
**fling²** *n* **1** a spirited Scottish dance: *a* HIGHLAND *fling* **2** a short, often wild time of satisfying one's own desires, (esp. in the phrase **have one's/a fling**)
**flint** /flɪnt/ *n* **1** [C;U] (a piece of) very hard grey stone that makes very small flashes of flame when struck with steel **2** [C] a small piece of metal used in cigarette lighters to light the petrol or gas
**flip¹** /flɪp/ *v* **-pp- 1** [T] to send (something) spinning

into the air with a light quick blow: *to flip a coin* **2** [I;T *over*] to turn over: *to flip the pages over* **3** [I] *infml* to become angry, excited, etc.: *I knew you'd flip when you saw my new car.*

**flip through** sthg. *v prep* [T] to read (a book, paper, etc.) rapidly and carelessly

**flip²** *n* [C] a quick light blow that sends something spinning into the air

**flip·pant** /ˈflɪpənt/ *adj* disrespectful about serious subjects, esp. when trying to be amusing: *flippant remarks* –**flippantly** *adv* –**flippancy** *n* [U]

**flip·per** /ˈflɪpəʳ/ *n* a limb of certain larger sea animals (esp. SEALS), with a flat edge used for swimming

**flirt¹** /flɜːt‖flɜrt/ *v* [I *with*] to behave with a member of the opposite sex in away that attracts his/her attention: (fig.) *I've been flirting with* (=considering, but not very seriously) *the idea of changing my job.* –**flirtation** /-ˈteɪʃən/ *n* [C;U] –**flirtatious** *adj*

**flirt²** *n* a person who generally FLIRTS with members of the opposite sex

**flit** /flɪt/ *v* **-tt-** [I] to fly or move lightly or quickly: *The birds flitted from branch to branch.*

**float¹** /fləʊt/ *v* **1** [I;T] to (cause to) stay at the top of liquid or be held up in air without sinking: *Wood floats on water.* |*A feather floated down on the wind.* **2** [T] to establish (a business, company, etc.) by selling shares **3** [I;T] to allow the exchange value of (a country's money) to vary freely from day to day

**float²** *n* **1** a piece of wood or other light object that floats, esp. as used on a fishing line or net **2** a large flat vehicle on which special shows, ornamental scenes, etc., are drawn in processions –see also MILK FLOAT **3** a sum of money kept for use if an unexpected need arises –compare KITTY² (2)

**float·ing** /ˈfləʊtɪŋ/ *adj* not fixed or settled: *London has a large floating population.*

**flock¹** /flɒk‖flɑk/ *n* [C +*sing./pl. v*] **1** a group of sheep, goats, or birds **2** *infml* a crowd; large number of people **3** the group of people who regularly attend a church

**flock²** *v* [I *to, into*] to gather or move in large crowds: *People flocked to the cinema to see the new film.*

**floe** /fləʊ/ *n* **floes** a large mass of ice floating on the surface of the sea

**flog** /flɒg‖flɑg/ *v* **-gg-** [T] **1** to beat severely with a whip or stick, esp. as a punishment **2** *BrE infml* to (try to) sell **3 flog a dead horse** *infml* to waste one's time with useless efforts

**flog·ging** /ˈflɒgɪŋ‖ˈflɑgɪŋ/ *n* [C;U] a severe beating with a whip or stick, esp. as a punishment

**flood¹** /flʌd/ *n* **1** the covering with water of a place that is usu. dry; great overflow of water: *The town was destroyed by the floods after the storm.*|*The water rose to flood level.* **2** a large flow: *There was a flood of complaints about the bad language used in the show.*

**flood²** *v* [I;T] **1** to (cause to) be filled or covered with water: *Every spring the river floods (the valley).*|*Our street floods whenever we have rain.* **2** to arrive (at) (a place) in large numbers: *Requests for information flooded in after the advertisement.*

> **SPELLING NOTE**
> Words with the sound /f/ may be spelt **ph-**, like **photograph.**

**flood·gate** /ˈflʌdgeɪt/ *n* a gate used for controlling the flow from a large body of water: (fig.) *The new law* **opened the floodgates** *as lots of people applied for government aid.*

**flood·light¹** /ˈflʌdlaɪt/ *n* a large electric light used for lighting football grounds, the outside of buildings, etc., at night –compare SEARCHLIGHT

**floodlight²** *v* **-lighted** *or* **-lit** /lɪt/, **lighting** [T] to light by using FLOODLIGHTS

**floor¹** /flɔːr‖flor/ *n* **1** [C] the surface on which one stands indoors; surface nearest the ground: A **dance floor** *is a level area specially prepared for dancing.* **2** [C] a level of a building; STOREY; *I live on the ground floor* (=the floor level with the street) *of a block of flats.*|*Our office is on the 6th floor.* **3** [*the* S] the part of a parliament or council building where members sit and speak –sounds like **flaw**

**floor²** *v* [T] **1** to provide with a floor: *The room was floored with boards.* **2** *infml* to knock down: (fig.) *The news completely floored me; I hadn't been expecting it at all.*

**floor·board** /ˈflɔːbɔːd‖ˈflorbord/ *n* a board in a wooden floor

**flop** /flɒp‖flɑp/ *v* **-pp-** [I] **1** to move or fall heavily or awkwardly: *He can't swim much; he just flops about in the water.* **2** *infml* (of a plan, a performance, etc.) to fail badly; be unsuccessful: *The new play flopped after only two weeks.* –**flop** *n* [C;S]: *The party was a complete flop; nobody enjoyed it.*

**flop·py** /ˈflɒpi‖ˈflɑpi/ *adj* **-pier, -piest** soft and falling loosely: *a floppy hat*|*This material's too floppy for a coat.* –**floppily** *adv* –**floppiness** *n* [U]

**flo·ra** /ˈflɔːrə‖ˈflorə/ *n* [C;U] *tech* all the plants growing wild in a particular place, or belonging to a particular age in history –compare FAUNA

**flo·ral** /ˈflɔːrəl‖ˈflorəl/ *adj* [*no comp.*] of flowers: *floral patterns*

**flor·id** /ˈflɒr¹₃d‖ˈflɔ-, ˈflɑ-/ *adj* **1** *often derog* having (too) much ornamentation **2** (of a person's face) having a red skin: *a florid* COMPLEXION –**floridly** *adv*

**flor·ist** /ˈflɒr¹₃st‖ˈflo-/ *n* (a person who keeps) a shop for selling flowers

**flo·til·la** /fləˈtɪlə‖fləʊ-/ *n* a group of small ships, esp. warships

**flounce** /flaʊns/ *v* **flounced, flouncing** [I *out, off*] to move violently in a temper: *She refused my advice and flounced out of the house.*

**floun·der** /ˈflaʊndəʳ/ *v* [I] to move about with great difficulty, esp. making violent efforts not to sink: *The child floundered in the water till someone jumped in to save him.*|(fig.) *The nervous speaker floundered and forgot what he was saying.*

**flour** /flaʊəʳ/ *n* [U] grain, esp. wheat, made into powder and used for making bread, pastry, cakes, etc. –sounds like **flower**

**flour·ish¹** /ˈflʌrɪʃ‖ˈflɜrɪʃ/ *v* **1** [I] to grow healthily; be active or successful: *This plant will not flourish without water.*|*The company has really flourished since we moved our factory to Scotland.* **2** [T] to wave in the hand and so draw attention to (something): *"I've passed my examination!" shouted Jane, flourishing a letter.*

**flourish²** *n* a showy fancy movement or manner that

draws people's attention to one: *He opened the door with a flourish.*

**flout** /flaʊt/ *v* [T] *fml* to treat without respect or consideration; go against: *She flouted all my offers of help and friendship.*|*You've flouted my orders.* (=disobeyed them) –compare FLAUNT

**flow¹** /fləʊ/ *v* [I] (of liquid) to run or spread smoothly like a river; pour: *Blood was flowing from his wound.*|*Her tears flowed fast.*|(fig.) *The cars flowed in a steady stream along the main road.*|(fig.) *As they sat around the fire, the conversation began to flow freely.*

**flow²** *n* **1** [S *of*] a pouring out: *A flow of oil poured all over the floor.*|*a flow of meaningless words* **2** [*the* U *of*] (the rate of) a smooth steady movement: *the gentle flow of the river* **3** [*the* S *of*] the rise (of the TIDE (1)) –compare EBB¹ (1)

**flow·er¹** /ˈflaʊəʳ/ *n* **1** the part of a plant, often beautiful and coloured, that produces seeds or fruit: *The roses are* **in flower** (=the flowers are open) *now.* **2** a plant that is grown for the beauty of this part: *We grow vegetables in the back garden, and flowers in the front garden.* –sounds like **flour**

**flower²** *v* [I] (of a plant) to produce flowers: *This bush flowers in the spring.*

**flow·er·bed** /ˈflaʊəbed‖-ər-/ *n* a piece of ground, esp. in a garden, in which flowers are grown for decoration –see picture on page 297

**flow·ered** /ˈflaʊəd‖-ərd/ *adj* [A] decorated with flower patterns: *flowered dress material*

**flow·er·pot** /ˈflaʊəpɒt‖-ərpɑt/ *n* a pot in which a plant can be grown in earth

**flow·er·y** /ˈflaʊəri/ *adj* **-ier, -iest** decorated with flowers: *a flowery pattern*|(fig.) *flowery speech/writing*

**flown** /fləʊn/ *v past participle of* FLY

**flu** /fluː/ also **influenza** *fml*– *n* [U] a disease which is like a bad cold but more serious

**fluc·tu·ate** /ˈflʌktʃueɪt/ *v* **-ated, -ating** [I] *fml* to rise and fall; change from one state to another: *The price of vegetables fluctuates according to the season.*| *His feelings fluctuated between excitement and fear.* –**fluctuation** /-ˈeɪʃən/ *n* [C;U *in*]

**flue** /fluː/ *n* a metal pipe or tube up which smoke or heat passes, usu. to a chimney

**flu·en·cy** /ˈfluːənsi/ *n* [U *in*] the quality or condition of being FLUENT

**flu·ent** /ˈfluːənt/ *adj* **1** [*in*] (of a person) speaking or writing in an easy smooth manner: *He is fluent in five languages.* **2** (of speech, writing, etc.) expressed readily and without pause: *She speaks fluent though not very correct English.* –**fluently** *adv*

**fluff¹** /flʌf/ *n* [U] **1** soft light loose waste from woollen or other materials: *The room hasn't been properly cleaned; there's fluff and dust under the furniture.* **2** very soft fur or hair on a young animal or bird

**fluff²** *v* [T] **1** [*out, up*] to make (something soft) appear larger by shaking or by brushing or pushing upwards: *The bird fluffed out its feathers in the sun.*|*She fluffed up her hair.* **2** *infml* to do (something) badly or unsuccessfully: *The actress fluffed her lines.* (=forgot what she had to say)

**fluff·y** /ˈflʌfi/ *adj* **-ier, -iest** like or covered with FLUFF¹ (2) –**fluffiness** *n* [U]

**flu·id¹** /ˈfluːɪ̈d/ *adj* having the quality of flowing, like liquids, air, gas, etc.; not solid: (fig.) *Our ideas on the subject are still fluid.* (=not fixed or settled) –**fluidity** /fluːˈɪdɪ̈ti/ *n* [U]

**fluid²** *n* [C;U] a liquid

**fluid ounce** /ˌ··ˈ·/ *n* (a measure of liquid equal to) one 20th of a PINT (1) or 0·0284 of a litre

**fluke** /fluːk/ *n* [S] *infml* a piece of accidental good fortune: *She is not usually good at tennis; that winning stroke was a fluke.*

**flum·mox** /ˈflʌməks/ *v* [T] *infml esp. BrE* to confuse and make (someone) uncertain what to say or what action to take: *She was completely flummoxed by the question.*

**flung** /flʌŋ/ *v past tense & past participle of* FLING

**flu·o·res·cent** /flʊəˈresənt‖flʊə-, flo-/ *adj* (of a substance) having the quality of giving out bright white light when electric or other waves are passed through: *fluorescent lighting* –**fluorescence** *n* [U]

**flur·ry¹** /ˈflʌri‖ˈflɜri/ *n* **-ries** **1** [C] sudden sharp rush of wind, rain or snow **2** [S *of* ] a sudden shared feeling: *A flurry of excitement went round the crowd as the film star arrived.*

**flurry²** *v* **-ried, -rying** [T] to confuse and make (someone) have difficulty in thinking clearly of what should be done; make nervous and uncertain

**flush¹** /flʌʃ/ *n* **1** [S *of*] (an act of cleaning with) a sudden flow (of liquid, esp. water): *The pipe is blocked; give it a good flush.*|(fig.) *He felt a flush of anger, and hit her.* **2** [C;S] (a red appearance of the face because of) a flow of blood to the face: *The sick boy had an unhealthy flush and breathed with difficulty.* **3 in the first flush of** in the first part of something pleasant

**flush²** *v* **1** [T *out*] to clean or drive out by a sudden flow of water: *The waste pipe is blocked; try flushing it (out) with hot water.*|(fig.) *The police flushed the criminals out (of their hiding place).* **2** [I;T] to (cause to) become empty of waste matter by means of a flow of water: *The lavatory won't flush; I've tried flushing it several times, but it won't work.* **3** [I;T] (of a person, the skin, or face) to (cause to) become red: *She flushed when she couldn't answer the question.*| (fig.) *He was flushed with excitement when he learned that he had won.*

**flush³** *adj* **1** [*with; no comp.*] exactly on a level (with); even in surface: *These cupboards are flush with the wall.* (=they do not stick out) **2** [F] *infml* having plenty of money: *I've just been paid, so I'm feeling quite flush.*

**flush⁴** *adv* [*adv* +*adv/prep*] in a FLUSH³ (1) way: *The door fits flush into its frame.*

**flus·ter** /ˈflʌstəʳ/ *v* [T] to cause (someone) to be hot, nervous, and confused: *The shouts of the crowd flustered the speaker and he forgot what he was going to say.* –**fluster** *n* [S]: *I got in an awful fluster at some traffic lights, so I failed my driving test.*

**flute** /fluːt/ *n* a pipelike wooden or metal musical instrument with finger holes, played by blowing across a hole in the side

**flut·ist** /ˈfluːtɪ̈st/ *n AmE* for FLAUTIST

**flut·ter¹** /ˈflʌtəʳ/ *v* **1** [I;T] (of a bird, an insect with large wings, etc.) to move (the wings) quickly and lightly without flying: *I can hear a bird fluttering in* *the chimney.* **2** [I] to fly by doing this: *The* BUTTERFLY *fluttered into the room.*|(fig.) *The dead leaves fluttered to the ground.* **3** [I;T] to wave or move quickly up and down or backwards and forwards: *The flag fluttered in the wind.*|*to flutter one's* EYELASHES|(fig.) *His heart fluttered with excitement.*

**flutter**[2] *n* [S] a FLUTTERing[1] movement: *There was a flutter of wings among the trees.*|(fig.) *Everybody was* **in a flutter** *(of excitement) as the queen came in.*

**flux** /flʌks/ *n* [U] *fml* continual change; condition of not being settled: *Our future plans are unsettled; everything is* **in a state of flux.**

**fly**[1] /flaɪ/ *v* **flew** /fluː/, **flown** /fləʊn/, **flying 1** [I] to move through the air by means of wings or a machine: *A bird flew in through the window.*|*I have never flown in an aeroplane.* **2** [I;T] **a** (of an aircraft) to move through the air: *The plane flew to New York.* **b** to cause (an aircraft) to move through the air: *She flew the plane round the world.* **3** [I] to travel by aircraft: *He flew to London yesterday.* **4** [T] to move through the air over: *Powerful aircraft now fly the Atlantic in a few hours.* **5** to move rapidly or suddenly: *The train flew past.*|*She flew up the stairs.*|*The window flew open.*|*The day has simply flown (by).* (=has passed quickly)|(fig.) *He* **flew into a** *(terrible)* **temper.**|(fig.) *I'm late, I must fly.* (=leave quickly) **6** [I;T *from*] to escape (from); FLEE **7 fly off the handle** *infml* to become suddenly and unexpectedly angry **8 let fly (at)** to attack with words or blows

**fly**[2] *n* **flies 1** a small flying insect with two wings, esp. the **housefly 2** any of several other types of flying insect: *a* BUTTERFLY **3 fly in the ointment** a small unwanted thing that spoils the pleasure, perfection, etc. of an occasion **4 there are no flies on someone** someone is not a fool and cannot be tricked

**fly·ing**[1] /ˈflaɪ-ɪŋ/ *adj* [A *no comp.*] **1** (of a jump) made after running for a short distance: *He took a flying* LEAP *and jumped across the stream.* **2 flying visit** a very short visit **3 get off to a flying start** to make a very good beginning **4 pass (something)/come off with flying colours** to succeed at (an examination, a test, etc.) particularly well **5 send/knock flying** to knock (someone) over, backwards, or through the air, esp. with a violent blow

**flying**[2] *n* [U] the action of travelling by aircraft, as a means of getting from one place to another or as a sport: *I don't like flying; it makes me feel sick.*

**flying sau·cer** /ˌ·· ˈ··/ *n* a plate-shaped spaceship which is believed to come from another world

**fly·o·ver** /ˈflaɪ-əʊvəʳ/ *BrE*‖**overpass** *AmE*– *n* a place where roads cross each other and where one passes high over the other by way of a kind of bridge

**FM** *abbrev. for:* frequency modulation; a system of broadcasting, usu. on VHF, in which the signal comes at a varying number of times per second: *an FM radio* –compare AM

**foal** /fəʊl/ *n* a young horse

**foam**[1] /fəʊm/ *n* [U] a whitish mass of bubbles on the surface of a liquid or on skin: *The breaking waves had edges of foam.*|**Foam rubber** *is soft rubber full of small air-bubbles.* –**foamy** *adj* **-ier, -iest**

**foam**[2] *v* [I] to produce FOAM: *The dying animal was found* **foaming at the mouth.**

**fob** sbdy. **off** /fɒb‖fɑb/ *v adv* **-bb-** [T *with*] to take no notice of; wave (someone) aside (by means of): *I asked her for the money she owed me, but she just fobbed me off (with a stupid excuse).*

**fo·cal point** /ˌfəʊkəl ˈpɔɪnt/ *n* [*the* U] → FOCUS[1] (2): *Television is now the focal point of family life in many British homes.*

**fo'c'sle** /ˈfəʊksəl/ also **forecastle** *fml*– *n* the front part of a ship, where the sailors live

**fo·cus**[1] /ˈfəʊkəs/ *n* **-cuses** *or* **-ci** /kaɪ, ki, si/ **1** [C] the point at which beams of light or heat, or waves of sound meet after their direction has been changed **2** [*the* U *of*] the central point; place of greatest activity; centre of interest: *Because of his strange clothes, he immediately became the focus of attention when he entered the room.* **3 in/out of focus** (not) giving a clear picture because the LENS (1) is (not) correctly placed: *This picture of John isn't in focus; I can't see his face clearly.* –**focal** /ˈfəʊkəl/ *adj*

**focus**[2] *v* **-s-** *or* **-ss-** [I;T *on*] to bring or come into (a) FOCUS: *This photograph looks funny; I think you forgot to focus the camera.*|(fig.) *All eyes were focused on him.*|(fig.) *I must try to focus my mind on work.*

**fod·der** /ˈfɒdəʳ‖ˈfɑdər/ *n* [U] food for horses and farm animals

**foe** /fəʊ/ *n lit* an enemy

**foe·tus, fetus** /ˈfiːtəs/ *n* a young human or other creature in the early stages of development inside the mother, esp. before it is recognizable as a baby or able to live separately –compare EMBRYO –**foetal, fetal** /ˈfiːtl/ *adj* [A *no comp.*]

**fog**[1] /fɒg‖fɑg, fɔg/ *n* [C;U] (a state or time of) very thick mist which makes it difficult to see

**fog**[2] *v* **-gg-** [I;T *up*] to (cause to) become difficult to see through because of a misty covering: *My glasses have fogged up in this steamy room.*

**fog·bound** /ˈfɒgbaʊnd‖ˈfɑg-, ˈfɔg-/ *adj* [*no comp.*] prevented by FOG from travelling as usual: *We were fogbound at London Airport for 12 hours.*

**fog·gy** /ˈfɒgi‖ˈfɑgi, ˈfɔgi/ *adj* **-gier, -giest 1** not clear because of FOG; very misty: *Foggy weather has made driving conditions very dangerous.* **2 not have the foggiest (idea)** *infml* not to know at all: *"What are you going to do this evening?" "I haven't the foggiest."* –**foggily** *adv* –**fogginess** *n* [U]

**foi·ble** /ˈfɔɪbəl/ *n fml* a small rather foolish personal habit: *My grandfather always carries his watch in his pocket; it's a foible of his.*

**foil**[1] /fɔɪl/ *v* [T *in*] *fml* to prevent (someone) from succeeding in (some plan): *We foiled his attempt to escape.*

**foil**[2] *n* a light narrow sword with a covered point, used in FENCING (1) –compare SABRE

**foil**[3] *n* **1** [U] (paper covered with) metal beaten or rolled into very thin paperlike sheets: *Milk bottle tops are made of tin foil.*|*Cigarettes are wrapped in foil to keep them fresh.* **2** [C *for, to*] a person or thing that makes more noticeable the better or different quality of another: *In the play, a wicked old uncle*

**SPELLING NOTE**

Words with the sound /f/ may be spelt **ph-**, like **photograph.**

*acts as a foil to the noble young prince.*

**foist** sbdy./sthg. **on** sbdy. /fɔɪst/ *v prep* [T] to cause (an unwanted person or thing) to be suffered for a time by (someone): *They didn't invite him to go out with them, but he foisted himself on them.*

**fold**[1] /fəʊld/ *v* **1** [T *up*] to turn, bend, or press back one part of (something) and lay on the remaining part: *She folded the letter (up/in half).|She folded up the paper to make a toy aircraft.|He folded his arms.* (= crossed them over his chest) –opposite **unfold** **2** [I] to be able to be bent back: *Does this table fold?|a folding bed* **3** [T] to wrap: *He folded the seeds in a piece of paper.* **4** [I *up*] (esp. of a business) to fail

**fold**[2] *n* a folded part or place: *The curtain hung in heavy folds.|the folds in a shirt/in a newspaper*

**fold**[3] *n* a sheltered corner of a field where farm animals, esp. sheep, are kept for protection, surrounded by a fence or wall

**fold·er** /ˈfəʊldəʳ/ *n* a folded piece of cardboard used for holding loose papers –see picture on page 415

**fo·li·age** /ˈfəʊli-ɪdʒ/ *n* [U] *fml* leaves

**folk**[1] /fəʊk/ also **folks** *AmE*– *n* [P] people (of one race or nation, or sharing a particular kind of life): *country folk*

**folk**[2] *adj* [A *no comp.*] (esp. of music) of the ordinary people: *folk music/songs/art*

**folk·lore** /ˈfəʊklɔːʳ‖-lor/ *n* [U] (the study of) all the knowledge, beliefs, habits, etc., of a racial or national group, still preserved by memory, or in use from earlier and simpler times –see also LORE

**folks** /fəʊks/ *n* [P] *infml* **1** relations, esp. parents: *I'd like you to meet my folks.* **2** *AmE* for FOLK[1]

**fol·low** /ˈfɒləʊ‖ˈfɑ-/ *v* **1** [I;T] to come or go after: *You go first and I'll follow (you) later.|The child* **follows** *her mother* **about** *all day.* **2** [T] to go after in order to catch: *I think we're being followed!* **3** [I;T] to come next (after) in order: *The number 5 follows the number 4.|Disease often follows war.|The results were* **as follows.** (=as will now be listed)|*I'll have fish, with fruit* **to follow.** (=as the next dish) **4** [T] to go in the same direction as; continue along: *Follow the road until you come to the hotel.* **5** [T] to listen to carefully: *He followed the speaker with the greatest attention.* **6** [I;T] to understand clearly: *I didn't quite follow (you/what you said); could you explain it again?* **7** [T] to accept and act according to: *Did you follow the instructions on the packet?|These orders must be followed.|He followed his sister's example and went to university.* **8** [I] to be a necessary effect or result: *Just because you are rich, it doesn't follow* (=you cannot reason from this) *that you are happy.* **9** **follow in someone's footsteps** to follow an example set by someone in the past

**follow** sthg.↔ **through** *v adv* [T] to complete; carry out exactly to the end: *to follow through a line of inquiry*

**follow** sthg.↔ **up** *v adv* [T] **1** to act further on (something): *That's an interesting suggestion, and I'll certainly follow it up.* **2** [*with*] to take further action after (something) (by means of something else): *He followed up his letter with a visit the next week.* –**follow-up** /ˈ·· ·/ *n* [A;C]: *a follow-up* (additional) *visit from the doctor*

**fol·low·er** /ˈfɒləʊəʳ‖ˈfɑ-/ *n* an admirer or supporter of some person, belief, or cause

**fol·low·ing**[1] /ˈfɒləʊɪŋ‖ˈfɑ-/ *adj* [*the* A] next (to be mentioned): *The child was sick in the evening, but on the following day he seemed quite well again.|Payment may be made in any of the following ways: by cash, by cheque, or by* CREDIT CARD.

**following**[2] *n* **following** **1** [*the*] the one or ones about to be mentioned: *The following have been chosen to play in tomorrow's match: Duncan Ferguson, Hugh Williams, Robin Sinclair . . .* **2** [*usu. sing.*] a group of supporters or admirers: *This politician has quite a large following in the North.*

**following**[3] *prep* after: *Following the speech, there will be a few minutes for questions.*

**fol·ly** /ˈfɒli‖ˈfɑli/ *n* **-lies** [C;U] *fml* (an act of) foolishness: *To reduce public spending on health would be an act of the greatest folly.*

**fond** /fɒnd‖fɑnd/ *adj* **1** [*of*] loving in a kind, gentle, or tender way: *He signed the letter, "With fondest love, Cyril".|She likes all her grandchildren, but she's especially fond of Peter.|I'm very fond of ice cream.* **2** [A] foolishly loving; yielding weakly to loving feelings: *A fond mother may spoil her child.* **3** [A] foolishly trusting or hopeful: *In spite of his bad results in the examination, he has* **a fond belief** *in his own cleverness.* –**fondness** *n* [C;U *for*]

**fon·dle** /ˈfɒndl‖ˈfɑndl/ *v* **-dled, -dling** [T] to touch gently and lovingly; stroke softly: *The old lady fondled her cat as it sat beside her.*

**fond·ly** /ˈfɒndli‖ˈfɑndli/ *adv* **1** in a loving way: *She greeted her old friend fondly.* **2** in a foolishly hopeful manner: *She fondly imagined that she could pass her examination without working.*

**font** /fɒnt‖fɑnt/ *n* a large vessel in a church, usu. made of stone, that contains the water used for baptizing (BAPTIZE) people

**food** /fuːd/ *n* [C;U] **1** something that living creatures or plants take into their bodies to give them strength and help them to develop and to live: *Milk is the natural food for young babies.|a new sort of liquid plant food* **2** (an example of) something solid for eating: *They gave us plenty of food, but there wasn't enough to drink.*|(fig.) *His father's advice gave the boy* **food for thought.** (=plenty to think about)

**fool**[1] /fuːl/ *n derog* a silly person: *You fool! I asked for water, not wine.|I felt such a fool when I realized I'd got on the wrong bus.|He's always afraid of* **making a fool of himself.** (=doing something silly)|*Are you trying to* **make a fool of me?** (=trick me)

**fool**[2] *v* **1** [T] to deceive; trick: *You can't fool him; he's much too clever for that.* **2** [I *around, about*] to behave in a silly way: *You shouldn't fool about/around with dangerous chemicals.* **3** [I] to speak without serious intention; joke: *I was only fooling.*

**fool·e·ry** /ˈfuːləri/ *n* **-ries** [C;U] *usu. derog* (an example of) silly behaviour

**fool·har·dy** /ˈfuːlhɑːdi‖-ɑr-/ *adj* too bold; taking or needing useless or unwise risks: *a foolhardy attempt|You were very foolhardy to jump off the bus while it was still moving.* –**foolhardiness** *n* [U]

**fool·ish** /ˈfuːlɪʃ/ *adj derog* without good sense; stupid; laughable: *It was very foolish of you to park the car in the middle of the road.|I couldn't answer the teacher's question, and this made me feel rather* *foolish.* **–foolishly** *adv* **–foolishness** *n* [U]

**fool·proof** /ˈfuːlpruːf/ *adj* [*no comp.*] **1** that cannot go wrong: *a foolproof plan* **2** *infml* very simple to understand, use, work, etc.: *a foolproof machine*

**fools·cap** /ˈfuːlskæp/ *n* [U] a large size of paper, esp. writing paper

**foot[1]** /fʊt/ *n* **feet** /fiːt/ **1** [C] the movable part of the body at the end of the leg, below the ankle, on which a person or animal stands: *I stood on a nail, and my foot's very sore.*|*It's nice to sit down after being* **on your feet** (=standing or walking) *all day.*|*He* **got to his feet** (=stood up) *when he heard the bell.*|(*fml*) *She said she wouldn't* **set foot in** (=enter) *the room until it was properly cleaned.* –see picture on page 299 **2** [C] (*pl. sometimes* **foot**) (a measure of length equal to) 12 inches or about ·305 metres: *Three feet make one yard.*|*He's six feet/foot tall.* –see also FOOT[1] (15) **3** [U *of*] the bottom or lower part: *He stood at the foot of the stairs/bed.* –compare HEAD[1] (2) **4 find one's feet** to become used to new or strange surroundings; settle in **5 get/have cold feet** to be too nervous to do something, esp. losing courage just before something **6 have one foot in the grave** to be very old and near death **7 on foot** (by) walking: *My bicycle is broken, so I'll have to go on foot.* **8 put a foot wrong** (*only used in* NEGATIVES[2] (1), *questions, etc.*) to say or do the wrong things: *He's very good at dealing with all kinds of people; he never puts a foot wrong.* **9 put one's best foot forward** to make one's best effort **10 put one's feet up** *infml* to rest by lying down or sitting with one's feet supported on something **11 put one's foot down** *infml* to speak and act firmly on a particular matter: *The father didn't like his son staying out at night, so he put his foot down and forbade him to do it again.* **12 put one's foot in it** *infml* to say the wrong thing or make an awkward mistake **13 be run off one's feet** *infml* to be very busy **14 -footed** having a certain number or kind of feet: *four-footed animals*|*Ducks are web-footed to help them move through the water.* **15 -footer** a person or thing a certain number of feet long, high, or tall: *My brother is a six-footer.*

**foot[2]** *v* [T] *infml* to pay (a bill)

**foot·ball** /ˈfʊtbɔːl/ *n* **1** [U] also **soccer**– a ball game between two teams of eleven players, using a round ball which is kicked but not handled: *They play football at school.*|*a football field*/(*BrE*) PITCH|*football boots* **2** [C] a large ball filled with air, usu. made of leather, used in these games **–footballer** *n*

**football pools** /ˈ·· ·/ *n* [*the* P] → POOLS

**foot·bridge** /ˈfʊtˌbrɪdʒ/ *n* a narrow bridge to be used only by people walking

**foot·hill** /ˈfʊtˌhɪl/ *n* [*of; usu. pl.*] a low hill at the bottom of a mountain or chain of mountains

**foot·hold** /ˈfʊthəʊld/ *n* a space (as on a rock) where a foot can be placed to help one to continue to climb up or down: (fig.) *It isn't easy to get a foothold as a film actor.*

**foot·ing** /ˈfʊtɪŋ/ *n* [S;U] a firm placing of the feet; room or a surface for the feet to stand on: *The roof of the house sloped steeply, so the man who was doing the repairs couldn't get much of a footing on it.*|(fig.) *Is this business* **on a firm footing?** (= properly planned, with enough money to support it)

> **SPELLING NOTE**
> Words with the sound /f/ may be spelt **ph-**, like **photograph.**

**foot·lights** /ˈfʊtlaɪts/ *n* [P] a row of lights along the front edge of the floor of a stage at the theatre, to show up the actors –see picture on page 463

**foot·loose** /ˈfʊtluːs/ *adj* free to go wherever one pleases and do what one likes; having no family or business duties which control one's way of living (often in the phrase **footloose and fancy-free**)

**foot·man** /ˈfʊtmən/ *n* **-men** /mən/ (esp. formerly) a manservant who wears a uniform

**foot·note** /ˈfʊtnəʊt/ *n* a note at the bottom of a page in a book, to explain some word or sentence, add some special remark or information, etc.

**foot·path** /ˈfʊtpɑːθ‖-pæθ/ *n* a narrow path or track for people to walk on: *a footpath across the fields*

**foot·print** /ˈfʊtˌprɪnt/ *n* a footshaped mark made by pressing a foot onto a surface: *Who left these muddy footprints on the kitchen floor?*

**foot·sore** /ˈfʊtsɔːʳ‖-sor/ *adj* having tender, painful, or swollen feet, esp. as a result of much walking

**foot·step** /ˈfʊtstep/ *n* a mark or sound of a person's step: *He heard soft footsteps coming up the stairs.*

**foot·wear** /ˈfʊtweəʳ/ *n* [U] *tech* shoes and boots: *A shopkeeper would say he sold footwear; we would say he sold shoes.*

**foot·work** /ˈfʊtwɜːk‖-ɜrk/ *n* [U] the use of the feet, esp. skilfully in dancing, sports, etc.

**for[1]** //fəʳ; *strong* fɔːʳ/ *prep* **1** meant to be given to, used by, or used in: *I've got a present for you.*|*We bought some new chairs for the office.*|*The doctor gave her some medicine for her cold.* **2** (shows purpose): *This knife is for cutting bread.*|*What's that handle for?* (=What is its purpose?) **3** instead of; so as to help: *Let me lift that heavy box for you.* **4** in favour, support, or defence of: *He plays football for England.* **5** towards; so as to reach: *The children set off for school.*|*This bus is for London.* **6** so as to have, catch, or get: *waiting for a bus*|*He's gone for a swim.*|*Run for your life!* (=so as to save your life)|*It's too early for dinner.* **7** as part of; as being: *She ate it for breakfast.*|*What do you want for a present?*|*I'm warning you for the last time.*|*For one thing, I don't like the colour, and for another, the price is too high.* **8** meaning; as a sign of: *red for danger*|*What's the French word for "dog"?* **9** (shows payment, price, or amount): *You can get a room at the hotel for £20 a day.*|*She paid 50 pence for the book.*|*He punished them for talking.*|*I wouldn't hurt him for anything.* (= whatever I was offered) **10** (shows length of time or distance): *We have been here for a week.* (Compare *We have been here* **since** *last Tuesday/We arrived a week* **ago.**)|*They ran for ten miles.*|*It's the worst accident for months.* (=the worst there has been in several months) **11** at the time of: *We invited our friends for 6 o'clock.*|*She came home for Christmas.* **12** because of: *He was rewarded for his bravery.*|*She couldn't speak for laughing.* **13** in regard to; in connection with: *Eggs are good for you.*|*Italy is famous for its wine.*|*He has great respect for his father.* **14** considered as; considering: *She's* *tall for her age.* (=other girls the same age are not so tall)|*It's cold for April.* **15** (used in sentences like this): *There's no need for you to worry.* (=no reason why you should worry)|*It's dangerous for him to run so fast.* (=that he should run so fast)|*Is there somewhere for me to sleep?* (=where I can sleep) **16 for all: a** in spite of: *For all his efforts, he didn't succeed.* **b** considering how little: *He may be dead, for all I know.* (=I don't know that he isn't dead) **17 if it weren't/if it hadn't been for** if something were not true or had not happened: *If it hadn't been for your help* (=if you had not helped) *we would never have finished it.*

USAGE Verbs like **buy** or **make** can be used without **for**, in the first meaning, if something is bought or made **for** a person or animal: *She bought a present* **for** *her friend* or *She bought her friend a present.*|*He bought a new chair* **for** *the office,* but not **He bought the office a new chair.* –see also AS **for**; see AGO (USAGE)

**for²** *conj fml or lit (used after the main part of a sentence)* and the reason is that: *She doesn't go out now, for she is very old.*

**for·age** /ˈfɒrɪdʒ‖ˈfɑ-, ˈfɔ-/ *v* **-aged, -aging** [I] to wander about looking for food or other supplies: (fig.) *He foraged about in his bag for 10 minutes, but couldn't find the ticket.*

**foray** /ˈfɒreɪ‖ˈfɔ-, ˈfɑ-/ *n* a sudden rush into enemy country, usu. by a small number of soldiers, in order to damage or seize arms, food, etc.:(fig.) *his unsuccessful foray into politics*

**for·bear** /fɔːˈbeəʳ, fə-‖fɔr-, fər-/ *v* **-bore** /ˈbɔːʳ‖ˈbor/, **-borne** /bɔːn‖ˈborn/, **-bearing** [I *+to-v/v-ing/from*] *fml* to make no attempt to do something that one has the right to do (esp. in a generous and merciful way): *The judge said he would forbear (from) sending her to prison, on condition that she promised not to steal again.*

**for·bear·ance** /fɔːˈbeərəns‖for-/ *n* [U] *fml* control of one's feelings so as to show patient forgiveness

**for·bear·ing** /fɔːˈbeərɪŋ‖fɔr-/ *adj apprec* long-suffering; gentle and merciful: *He has a forbearing nature; he accepts trouble with a smile.*

**for·bid** /fəˈbɪd‖fər-/ *v* **-bade** /ˈbeɪd‖ˈbæd/ *(fml) or* **-bad** /ˈbæd/, **-bidden** /ˈbɪdn/ *or* **-bid** /ˈbɪd/, **-bidding** [T] to command not to do something: *I forbade my son to use my car.*|*Smoking is forbidden/You are forbidden to smoke in class.* –compare ALLOW

**for·bid·ding** /fəˈbɪdɪŋ‖fər-/ *adj* having a fierce, unfriendly, or dangerous look: *She has a forbidding manner and is slow in making friends.*|*a forbidding range of mountains* –**forbiddingly** *adv*

**force¹** /fɔːs‖fors/ *n* **1** [U] natural or bodily power: *the force of the explosion*|*He had to use force to get the lid off the tin.* **2** [U] violence: *The thief took the money from the old man by force.* **3** [C;U] someone or something that has a strong influence or great power: *the forces of evil*|*I did it from* **force of habit. 4** [C;U] a power that changes or may produce change of movement in a body on which it acts: *The force of* GRAVITY (2) *makes things fall to earth.* **5** [C] a group of people brought together and trained for special action, esp. fighting: *the* **police force**|*The navy is one of* **the armed forces. 6 in force** in large numbers: *The police were out in force to stop any trouble.* **7 in(to) force** (of a rule, order, law, etc.) in(to) effect

**force²** *v* **forced, forcing** [T] **1** to use bodily force or strong influence on: *I didn't want to give him the information; he forced me (to do it).*|*We had to force our way through the crowd.*|*She forced the window open.*|*The thieves forced the lock.* (=opened it by force) **2** to produce by unwilling effort, with difficulty, or unnaturally: *forced laughter* **3** to hasten the growth of (a plant) by the use of heat **4 force someone's hand** to make someone act as one wishes or before they are ready to

**forced** /fɔːst‖forst/ *adj* [A *no comp.*] done or made because of a sudden happening which makes it necessary to act without delay: *The aircraft made a forced landing because two of its engines were on fire.*

**force·ful** /ˈfɔːsfəl‖ˈfors-/ *adj apprec* (of a person, words, ideas, etc.) strong; powerful: *a forceful speech* –compare FORCIBLE –**forcefully** *adv* –**forcefulness** *n* [U]

**for·ceps** /ˈfɔːseps, -s¦ps‖ˈfɔr-/ *n* [P] a medical instrument used for holding objects firmly: *a pair of forceps* –see PAIR¹ (USAGE)

**for·ci·ble** /ˈfɔːsəbəl‖ˈfor-/ *adj* [A] **1** using bodily force: *The police had to make a forcible* ENTRY (1) *into the house where the thief was hiding.* **2** having power to influence the minds of others: *I haven't yet heard a really forcible argument in favour of the new plan.* –compare FORCEFUL

**for·ci·bly** /ˈfɔːsəbli‖ˈfor-/ *adv* **1** by bodily force, esp. against one's will: *He complained that he's been forcibly held by the police without good reason.* **2** in a strong manner that carries belief: *Her ideas are always forcibly expressed.* **3** strongly: *His manner of speaking reminded me forcibly of his father's.*

**ford¹** /fɔːd‖ford/ *n* a place in a river where the water is not very deep, and where it can be crossed on foot, in a car, etc., without using a bridge –**fordable** *adj*

**ford²** *v* [T] to cross (a river, stream, etc.) by means of a FORD

**fore** /fɔːʳ‖for/ *n* **come to the fore** to become well-known; come to have a leading position

**fore·arm** /ˈfɔːrɑːm‖ˈforɑrm/ *n* the lower part of the arm between the hand and the elbow

**fore·bod·ing** /fɔːˈbəudɪŋ‖for-/ *n* [C;U +*(that)*] *fml* a feeling of coming evil

**fore·cast¹** /ˈfɔːkɑːst‖ˈforkæst/ *v* **-cast** *or* **-casted, -casting** [T +*that*] to say, esp. with the help of some kind of knowledge (what is going to happen at some future time): *forecasting the future*|*Heavy rain has been forecast for tomorrow.* –compare PREDICT

**forecast²** *n* [+*that*] a statement of future events, based on some kind of knowledge or judgment: *Did you listen to the weather forecast on the radio?*|*The newspaper's forecast that the government would only last for six months was quite right.* –compare PREDICTION

**fore·castle** /ˈfəuksəl‖ˈfəuksəl, ˈforˌkæ-/ *n fml* for FO'C'SLE

**fore·court** /ˈfɔːkɔːt‖ˈforkort/ *n* a courtyard in front of a large building: *a garage forecourt*

**fore·fa·ther** /ˈfɔːˌfɑːðəʳ‖ˈfor-/ *n* [*usu. pl.*] a person from whom the stated person is descended; relative in the far past; (male) ANCESTOR

**fore·fin·ger** /ˈfɔːˌfɪŋgəʳ‖ˈfor-/ also **index finger**– *n* the finger next to the thumb, with which one points

**fore·front** /ˈfɔːfrʌnt‖ˈfor-/ *n* [*the* S] the most forward place; leading position: *The brave soldier was* **in the forefront of** *the fighting.*

**fore·ground** /ˈfɔːgraʊnd‖ˈfor-/ *n* [*the* S] the nearest part of a scene in a view, a picture, or a photograph: *This is a photograph of our town, with a church in the foreground.* –compare BACKGROUND (1)

**fore·hand** /ˈfɔːhænd‖ˈfor-/ *n,adj* [A;C] (in tennis) (a stroke) played with the inner part of the hand and arm facing forward –compare BACKHAND

**fore·head** /ˈfɒrɪ̈d, ˈfɔːhed‖ˈfɔrɪ̈d, ˈfɑrɪ̈d, ˈforhed/ *n* the part of the face above the eyes and below the hair –see picture on page 299

**for·eign** /ˈfɒrɪ̈n‖ˈfɔ-, ˈfɑ-/ *adj* [*no comp.*] **1** of a country or nation that is not one's own: *foreign travel|Do you speak any foreign languages?|the minister for* **foreign affairs** (=one who looks after the nation's relations with other countries) –compare NATIVE, DOMESTIC **2** [*to*] having no place (in): *He's a very good person; cruelty is foreign to his nature.*|(fig.) *The swelling on her finger was caused by a* **foreign body** *in it.* (=a small piece of some solid material that had entered it by accident) –compare STRANGE (2)

**for·eign·er** /ˈfɒrɪ̈nəʳ‖ˈfɔ-, ˈfɑ-/ *n* a person belonging to a race or country other than one's own –compare STRANGER (2)

**fore·leg** /ˈfɔːleg‖ˈfor-/ *n* either of the two front legs of a four-legged animal –compare HIND

**fore·man** /ˈfɔːmən‖ˈfor-/ *n* **-men** /mən/ **forewoman** *fem.*– a skilled and experienced worker who is put in charge of other workers –compare SUPERVISOR

**fore·most** /ˈfɔːməʊst‖ˈfor-/ *adj* [*the* A] *apprec* most important; leading

**fore·name** /ˈfɔːneɪm‖ˈfor-/ *n fml* for FIRST NAME

**fo·ren·sic** /fəˈrensɪk, -zɪk/ *adj* [A] *tech* related to or used in the law and the tracking of criminals: *A specialist in* **forensic medicine** *was called as a witness in the murder trial.*

**fore·run·ner** /ˈfɔːˌrʌnəʳ‖ˈfo-/ *n* a person or thing that prepares the way for, or is a sign of the coming of, someone or something that follows: *Mrs Pankhurst, who fought for votes for women, was a forerunner of the modern women's movement.*

**fore·see** /fɔːˈsiː‖for-/ *v* **-saw** /ˈsɔː/, **-seen** /ˈsiːn/, **-seeing** [T +(*that*)] to form an idea or judgment about (what is going to happen in the future); expect: *He couldn't foresee (that) his journey would be delayed by bad weather.*

**fore·see·a·ble** /fɔːˈsiːəbəl‖for-/ *adj* [*no comp.*] that can be FORESEEN: *The house needs a new roof, but we can't afford one* **in the foreseeable future.** (=as far ahead in time as we can see)

**fore·shad·ow** /fɔːˈʃædəʊ‖for-/ *v* [T] *esp. lit* to be a sign of (what is coming); represent or be like (something that is going to happen)

**fore·sight** /ˈfɔːsaɪt‖ˈfor-/ *n* [U] *usu. apprec* the ability to imagine what will probably happen, allowing one to act to help or prevent developments; care or wise planning for the future

**SPELLING NOTE**

Words with the sound /f/ may be spelt **ph-**, like **photograph.**

**fore·skin** /ˈfɔːˌskɪn‖ˈfor-/ *n* a loose fold of skin covering the end of the male sex organ

**for·est** /ˈfɒrɪ̈st‖ˈfɔ-, ˈfɑ-/ *n* [C;U] (a large area of land thickly covered with) trees and bushes: *A large part of Africa is made up of thick forest.* –compare WOOD (2), JUNGLE

**fore·stall** /fɔːˈstɔːl‖for-/ *v* [T] *fml* to defeat (someone or someone's plan) by acting first: *I meant to meet my friend at the station, but she forestalled me by arriving on an earlier train and coming to the house.|She forestalled my plan to meet her.*

**for·est·er** /ˈfɒrɪ̈stəʳ‖ˈfɔ-, ˈfɑ-/ *n* a person who works in, or is in charge of, a forest

**for·est·ry** /ˈfɒrɪ̈stri‖ˈfɔ-, ˈfɑ-/ *n* [U] the science of planting and caring for large areas of trees

**fore·swear** /fɔːˈsweəʳ‖for-/ *v* [T] → FORSWEAR

**fore·tell** /fɔːˈtel‖for-/ *v* **-told** /ˈtəʊld/, **-telling** [T +(*that*)/*to*] to tell (what will happen in the future); PROPHESY

**fore·thought** /ˈfɔːθɔːt‖ˈfor-/ *n* [U] *often apprec* wise planning for future needs; consideration of what is to come: *If I'd had the forethought to bring my raincoat, I wouldn't have got wet in the storm.*

**for·ev·er, for ever** /fəˈrevəʳ/ *adv* **1** for all future time: *He wants to live forever (and ever).* **2** *(used with the* -ing *form of a verb)* all the time and in an annoying way; ALWAYS (3): *He's forever asking silly questions.*

**fore·warn** /fɔːˈwɔːn‖forˈwɔrn/ *v* [T +*that/of, against, about*] to warn (someone) of coming danger, unpleasantness, etc.; advise (that something will happen or be done)

**fore·word** /ˈfɔːwɜːd‖ˈforwɜrd/ *n* a short introduction at the beginning of a book, esp. in which someone who knows the writer and his/her work says something about them –compare PREFACE

**for·feit** /ˈfɔːfɪ̈t‖ˈfɔr-/ *v* [T] to have (something) taken away from one because some agreement or rule has been broken, or as a punishment, or as the result of some action: *If you don't return the article to the shop within a week, you forfeit your right to get your money back.* **–forfeit** *n* [C; *the* U *of*]

**for·gave** /fəˈgeɪv‖fər-/ *v past tense of* FORGIVE

**forge**[1] /fɔːdʒ‖fordʒ/ *v* **forged, forging 1** [I;T] to make a copy of (something) in order to deceive: *He got the money by forging his brother's signature on a cheque.|He was sent to prison for forging.|a forged* PASSPORT **2** [T] to form by heating and hammering: (fig.) *forging a new political party*

**forge**[2] *n* **1** (a building or room containing) a large apparatus with a fire inside, used for heating and shaping metal objects: *Horseshoes are made in a forge.* **2** (a part of a factory containing) a large apparatus that produces great heat inside itself, used for melting metal, making iron, etc.

**forge**[3] *v* **forged, forging** [I] to move with a sudden increase of speed and power: *He forged into the lead just before the end of the race.*|(fig.) *He didn't do very well at school, but he's* **forged ahead** *in the last two years.*

**forg·er** /ˈfɔːdʒəʳ‖ˈfor-/ *n* a person who FORGES[1] (1)

**for·ge·ry** /ˈfɔːdʒəri‖ˈfɔr-/ *n* **-ries** [C;U] (a result of) the act or an action of forging (FORGE[1] (1)): *He was sent to prison for forgery.|When he bought the picture he was told it was by Rubens, but he later found out that it was a forgery.*

**for·get** /fəˈget‖fər-/ *v* **-got** /ˈgɒt‖ˈgɑt/, **-gotten** /ˈgɒtn‖ˈgɑtn/, **-getting** [I;T] **1** [+*to-v*/*v-ing*/(*that*)] to fail to remember: *She asked me to visit her, but I forgot (about it)/I forgot to.|I've forgotten his name.|Don't forget the tickets.* (=remember to bring them)|*I had forgotten that you don't like coffee.|I'll never forget meeting you for the first time.|I forget who it was who said it.* **2** [*about*] to stop thinking (about); put out of one's mind: *Let's forget (about) our disagreements and be friends again.|"I'm sorry I broke your teapot." "Forget it."* **3 forget oneself** to lose one's temper or self-control, or act in a way that is unsuitable or makes one look silly: *The little girl annoyed him so much that he forgot himself and hit her.*

**for·get·ful** /fəˈgetfəl‖fər-/ *adj* [*of*] having the habit of forgetting: *My old aunt has become rather forgetful.* **–forgetfully** *adv* **–forgetfulness** *n* [U]

**forget-me-not** /·ˈ· · ˌ·/ *n* a small plant with blue flowers

**for·give** /fəˈgɪv‖fər-/ *v* **-gave** /ˈgeɪv/, **-given** /ˈgɪvən/, **-giving** /ˈgɪvɪŋ/ [I;T *for*] to say or feel that one is no longer angry about and/or wishing to give punishment to (someone) for (something): *I'll never forgive you for what you said to me last night.|It's best to* **forgive and forget.**

**for·give·ness** /fəˈgɪvnǝs‖fər-/ *n* [U *of*] *fml* the act of forgiving or state of being forgiven: *He asked for forgiveness of his wrong-doings.*

**for·giv·ing** /fəˈgɪvɪŋ‖fər-/ *adj apprec* willing or able to forgive: *She has a gentle forgiving nature.*

**for·go, fore-** /fɔːˈgəʊ‖fɔr-/ *v* **-went, -going, -gone** [T] to give up; (be willing) not to have (esp. something pleasant): *If we are going to finish this today, we'll have to forgo our lunch hour.*

**fork[1]** /fɔːk‖fɔrk/ *n* **1** an instrument for holding food or carrying it to the mouth, having a handle at one end with two or more points at the other –see picture on page 521 **2** a farm or gardening tool having a wooden handle with two or more metal points at the other end **3** a place where something long and narrow divides, or one of the divided parts: *We came to a fork in the road, and we couldn't decide whether to take the left fork or the right.*

**fork[2]** *v* [I] **1** (of something long and narrow) to divide, esp. into two parts: *You'll see our house on the left, just before the road forks.* **2** (of a person) to take the (left or right) FORK[1](3) of a road: *Fork left at the bus station.*

**fork** sthg.↔ **out** *v adv* [I;T *for, on*] *infml* to pay (money) unwillingly: *I had to fork out £200 to get the car repaired!*

**forked** /fɔːkt‖fɔrkt/ *adj* [*no comp.*] **1** having one end divided into two or more points: *Snakes have forked tongues.* **2** that divides into two or more parts at a point: *a forked road|forked lightning*

**fork·lift truck** /ˈfɔːkˌlɪft‖ˈfɔrk-/ *n* a small vehicle with a movable apparatus on the front, used for lifting and lowering heavy goods, moving them about, and placing them on top of each other

**for·lorn** /fəˈlɔːn‖fərˈlɔrn/ *adj esp. lit or fml* **1** (typical of one who is) left alone and unhappy: *a forlorn look on his face* –see ALONE (USAGE) **2 forlorn hope** a plan or attempt that is very unlikely to succeed **–forlornly** *adv* **–forlornness** *n* [U]

**form[1]** /fɔːm‖fɔrm/ *n* **1** [C;U] shape; appearance: *She has a tall graceful form.|a bowl in the form of* (=shaped like) *a boat* **2** [C *of*] a kind; sort: *different forms of government|This disease takes the form of* (=shows itself as) *high fever and sickness.|I dislike any form of exercise.* **3** [C] an official printed paper with spaces in which to answer questions and give other information: *Please fill in/out/up this form, giving your name, age, and address.* **4** [U] condition of skill and fitness for taking part in sport, etc.: *He's been* **in bad form/out of form** *recently, and hasn't won a game for three months.* **5** [U] spirits: *Tom was* **in fine form/on (good) form** *last night; he amused everyone with his stories.* **6** [C] a class in British schools, and in some American schools; *The oldest children are in the sixth form.*

**form[2]** *v* [I;T] **1** to take or make into a shape: *A cloud of smoke formed over the burning city.|She formed the clay into a bowl/formed a bowl from the clay.*|(fig.) *School helps to form a child's character.* **2** to take the shape of: *She tied the two sticks together to form a cross.* **3** to (cause to) come into being: *A plan began to form in his mind.|The king asked him to form a new government.* **4** to be: *Flour, eggs, fat, and sugar form the main contents of a cake.* **5** [*up*] to (cause to) stand or move in (a certain order): *The soldiers formed (up) into a line.*

**form·al** /ˈfɔːməl‖ˈfɔr-/ *adj* ceremonial; according to accepted rules or customs: *a formal dinner party|Formal dress must be worn.|Business letters are usually formal, but we write in an informal way to friends.*|(fig.) *He's always very formal; he never joins in a laugh.* –opposite informal **–formally** *adv*

**for·mal·i·ty** /fɔːˈmælǝti‖fɔr-/ *n* **-ties 1** [C] **a** an act in accordance with law or custom: *There are a few formalities to settle before you become the lawful owner of the car.* **b** an act which has lost its real meaning: *The written part of the examination is just a formality; no one ever fails it.* **2** [U] careful attention to rules and accepted forms of behaviour

**for·mat** /ˈfɔːmæt‖ˈfɔr-/ *n* **1** the size, shape, etc., in which something, esp. a book, is produced **2** the general plan or arrangement of something: *We're trying a new format for our television show this year.*

**for·ma·tion** /fɔːˈmeɪʃən‖fɔr-/ *n* **1** [U] the shaping or developing of something: *School life has a great influence on the formation of a child's character.* **2** [C;U] (an) arrangement of people, ships, aircraft, etc.; order: *The soldiers were drawn up in battle formation.* (=in correct position to begin a battle) **3** [C] a thing which is formed; way in which a thing is formed: *There are several kinds of cloud formation.*

**for·ma·tive** /ˈfɔːmətɪv‖ˈfɔr-/ *adj* [A] having influence in forming or developing: *a child's formative years* (=the time when the character is formed)

**for·mer[1]** /ˈfɔːməʳ‖ˈfɔr-/ *adj* [A *no comp.*] *fml* of an earlier time: *a former President of the United States*

**former[2]** *n* **former** *fml* the first of two people or things just mentioned: *Of Nigeria and Ghana, the former*

(=Nigeria) *has the larger population.*|*Did he walk or swim? The former* (=walking) *seems more likely.* –compare LATTER (2)

**for·mer·ly** /ˈfɔːməli‖ˈfɔrmərli/ *adv* in earlier times: *He formerly worked in a factory, but now he's a teacher.* –compare LATTERLY

**for·mi·da·ble** /ˈfɔːmɨ̥dəbəl, fəˈmɪd-‖ˈfɔr-/ *adj fml* **1** causing fear, doubt, anxiety, etc.: *a formidable voice*|*The king's mother was formidable old lady.* **2** difficult; hard to defeat: *They faced formidable difficulties in their attempt to reach the South Pole.* **–formidably** *adv*

**for·mu·la** /ˈfɔːmjʊlə‖ˈfɔrmjələ/ *n* **-las** *or* **-lae** /ləɪ/ [*for*] **1** *tech* a general law, rule, fact, etc., expressed shortly by means of a group of letters, signs, numbers, etc.: *The chemical formula for water is $H_2O$.* **2** a list of instructions for making something: *Someone has stolen the secret formula for the liquid that fires our new spacecraft.*|(fig.) *The two countries tried to make a peace formula.*

**for·mu·late** /ˈfɔːmjʊleɪt‖ˈfɔrmjə-/ *v* **-lated, -lating** [T] **1** to express in a short clear form **2** to invent and prepare (a plan, suggestion, etc.) **–formulation** /-ˈleɪʃən/ *n* [U]

**for·ni·cate** /ˈfɔːnɨ̥keɪt‖ˈfɔr-/ *v* **-cated, -cating** [I] *esp. law or bibl* to have sexual relations with someone outside marriage **–fornication** /-ˈkeɪʃən/ *n* [U]

**for·sake** /fəˈseɪk‖fər-/ *v* **-sook** /ˈsʊk/, **-saken** /ˈseɪkən/, **-saking** [T] *fml* to desert; leave for ever; give up completely –see also GODFORSAKEN

**for·swear, fore-** /fɔːˈsweəʳ‖for-/ *v* **-swore** /ˈswɔːʳ‖ˈswor/, **-sworn** /ˈswɔːn‖ˈsworn/, **-swearing** *fml* [T +*v-ing*] to make a solemn promise to give up or to stop doing (something)

**fort** /fɔːt‖fort/ *n* **1** [C] a strongly made building used for defence at some important place **2** [A;C] (*usu. cap. as part of name*) a (town containing a) fixed army camp: *In former times the British army kept lots of soldiers at Fort William in Scotland.* **3 hold the fort** to look after everything while someone is away

**for·te** /ˈfɔːteɪ‖fort/ *n* [*usu. sing.*] a strong point in a person's character or abilities: *Games are his forte; he plays cricket and football excellently.*

**forth** /fɔːθ‖forθ/ *adv* **1** *esp. bibl or lit* (*after a verb*) out; forward: *He went forth into the desert to pray.* **2 and (so on and) so forth** etc.; and other like things: *She kept saying that she was sorry for what she'd done, she'd never do it again, it was just a mistake, and so forth.* **3 back and forth** first in one direction and then in the other

**forth·com·ing** /ˌfɔːθˈkʌmɪŋ◂‖ˌforθ-/ *adj* **1** [*no comp.*] happening or appearing in the near future: *On the noticeboard there was a list of forthcoming events at school.* **2** [F *no comp.*] (*often with* NEGATIVES² (1)) ready; supplied; offered when needed: *When she was asked why she was late, no answer was forthcoming.* **3** *infml* (*often with* NEGATIVES² (1)) ready to be helpful and friendly: *I asked several villagers the way to the river, but none of them was very forthcoming.*

**SPELLING NOTE**

Words with the sound /f/ may be spelt **ph-**, like **photograph.**

**forth·right** /ˈfɔːθraɪt‖ˈforθ-/ *adj* direct in manner and speech; expressing one's thoughts and feelings plainly: *His forthright behaviour shows that he's honest, but he seems rude to some people.* **–forthrightness** *n* [U]

**forth·with** /fɔːθˈwɪð, -ˈwɪθ‖forθ-/ *adv esp. lit* at once; without delay

**for·ti·eth** /ˈfɔːtiɨ̥θ‖ˈfɔr-/ *determiner,n,pron,adv* 40th

**for·ti·fi·ca·tion** /ˌfɔːtɨ̥fɨ̥ˈkeɪʃən‖ˌfɔr-/ *n* **1** [C *usu. pl.*] towers, walls, gun positions, etc., set up as a means of defence **2** [U] the act or science of FORTIFYing

**for·ti·fy** /ˈfɔːtɨ̥faɪ‖ˈfɔr-/ *v* **-fied, -fying** [T] to build forts on; strengthen against possible attack: *a fortified city* **–fortifiable** *adj*

**for·ti·tude** /ˈfɔːtɨ̥tjuːd‖ˈfɔrtɨ̥tuːd/ *n* [U] *apprec* firm and lasting courage in bearing trouble, pain, etc., without complaining

**fort·night** /ˈfɔːtnaɪt‖ˈfort-/ *n* [*usu. sing.*] *BrE* two weeks: *I'm going away for a fortnight's holiday.*|*He's coming in a fortnight's time.* (=two weeks after today)|*Her birthday is Tuesday fortnight.* (=two weeks later than next Tuesday)

**fort·night·ly** /ˈfɔːtnaɪtli‖ˈfort-/ *adj,adv BrE* (happening, appearing, etc.) every FORTNIGHT or once a fortnight: *a fortnightly visit*

**for·tress** /ˈfɔːtrɨ̥s‖ˈfɔr-/ *n* a large fort; place strengthened for defence

**for·tu·i·tous** /fɔːˈtjuːɨ̥təs‖fɔrˈtuː-/ *adj fml* happening by chance; accidental: *a fortuitous meeting* **–fortuitously** *adv*

**for·tu·nate** /ˈfɔːtʃənət‖ˈfɔr-/ *adj more fml than* **lucky**– having or bringing good fortune; lucky: *He's fortunate in having a good job.*|*She's fortunate enough to have very good health.*|*It was fortunate for her that she had enough money to repair the car.* –opposite **unfortunate**

**for·tu·nate·ly** /ˈfɔːtʃənətli‖ˈfɔr-/ *adv* by good chance; luckily: *I was late in getting to the station, but fortunately for me, the train was late too.*|*Fortunately, he found the money that he'd lost.* –opposite **unfortunately**

**for·tune** /ˈfɔːtʃən‖ˈfɔr-/ *n* **1** [U] luck: *She had the good fortune to be free from illness all her life.* **2** [C] whatever happens to a person, good or bad: *Through all his changing fortunes, he never lost courage.* **3** [C] that which will happen to a person in the future: *He offered to* **tell** *my* **fortune.** (=to discover what he claims my future will be by using a special method, such as examining my hand) **4** [C] wealth; a large amount of money: *He* **made a fortune** *in* (=became rich by selling) *oil.*|*That new car must have cost you a fortune*/*a* **small fortune.**

**fortune-tell·er** /ˈ·· ˌ··/ *n* a person, usu. a woman, who claims to be able to tell FORTUNES (3)

**for·ty** /ˈfɔːti‖ˈfɔrti/ *determiner,n,pron* **-ties** (the number) 40 –see also FORTIETH

**for·um** /ˈfɔːrəm/ *n* **1** any place where public matters may be talked over and argued about: *The letters page of this newspaper is a forum for public argument.* **2** a meeting for such a purpose: *A group of schoolteachers are holding a forum on new ways* *of teaching history.*

**for·ward¹** /ˈfɔːwəd‖ˈfɔrwərd/ *adj* **1** [A *no comp.*] towards the front, the end, or the future: *a forward movement|the forward part of the train* **2** [A *no comp.*] advanced in development: *a forward child|We aren't very far forward with our plans yet.* **3** too bold; too sure of oneself: *That little girl is rather forward; she's always asking people for sweets.* –compare BACKWARD (2)

**forward²** also **forwards**– *adv* **1** towards the front, the end, or the future; ahead: *The soldiers crept forward under cover of darkness.|They never met again from that day forward.|Even though we have little money, our plans are going forward.* **2** towards an earlier time: *We'll bring the date of the meeting forward from the 20th to the 18th.* **3** into a noticeable position: *The lawyer brought forward some new reasons.* –compare BACKWARDS

**forward³** *v* [T *to*] to send or pass on (letters, parcels, etc.) to a new address: *When we moved house, we asked the people who took our old house to forward all our mail.|The man who left yesterday didn't leave* **forwarding instructions/a forwarding address,** *so I don't know where to send this letter.*

**for·went, fore-** /fɔːˈwent‖for-/ *v past tense of* FORGO

**fos·sil¹** /ˈfɒsəl‖ˈfɑ-/ *n* a hardened part or print of an animal or plant of long ago, that has been preserved in rock, ice, etc.

**fossil²** *adj* [A *no comp.*] **1** being or in the condition of a FOSSIL: *a fossil seashell* **2** being made of substances that were living things in the distant past: *Coal is a fossil* FUEL.

**fos·sil·ize** ‖also **-ise** *BrE* /ˈfɒsəlaɪz‖ˈfɑ-/ *v* **-ized, -izing** [I;T] to (cause to) become a FOSSIL¹: (fig.) *fossilized ideas*

**fos·ter** /ˈfɒstəʳ‖ˈfɔ-, ˈfɑ-/ *v* [T] **1** *fml* to encourage (something) to grow or develop: *We hope these meetings will help foster friendly relations between our two countries.* **2** to care for (a child or young animal) as one's own, usu. for a certain period and without taking on the full lawful responsibilities of the parent: *We fostered the young girl while her mother was in hospital.* –compare ADOPT (1) **3 foster-** giving or receiving parental care although not of the same family: *a foster-parent|a foster-home*

**fought** /fɔːt/ *v past tense & participle of* FIGHT¹

**foul¹** /faʊl/ *adj* **1** bad-smelling and impure: *foul air* **2** (of weather) rough; stormy: *It's a foul night tonight; it's pouring with rain.* **3** evil; wicked: *a foul murder* **4** *infml* very bad; unpleasant: *He has a foul temper.|I've had a foul morning; everything's gone wrong.* **–foully** *adv* **–foulness** *n* [U]

**foul²** *n* (in sport) an act that is against the rules

**foul³** *v* [I;T] **1** to (cause to) become dirty, impure, or blocked with waste matter: *The dog's fouled the path.*|(fig.) *Don't* **foul up** *this chance!* (=spoil this chance) **2** (in sports, esp. football) to be guilty of a FOUL² (against): *Smith ran suddenly into Jones and fouled him just as Jones was kicking the ball.*

**found¹** /faʊnd/ *v* [T] **1** [*on, upon*] to start building (something large); establish: *The castle is founded on solid rock.|The Romans founded a great city on the banks of this river.|This company was founded in 1724.*|(fig.) *This story is founded on/upon fact.* **2** to start and support, esp. by supplying money: *The rich man founded a hospital and a school in the town where he was born.*

**found²** *v past tense & participle of* FIND¹

**foun·da·tion** /faʊnˈdeɪʃən/ *n* **1** [U] the act of starting the building or planning of something large, or starting some kind of organization: *The university has been famous for medical studies ever since its foundation.* **2** [C] (*often cap. as part of name*) an organization that gives out money for certain special purposes: *The Gulbenkian Foundation gives money to help artists.* **3** [U] that on which a belief, custom, way of life, etc., is based; BASIS: *The foundation on which many ancient societies were built was the use of slaves.|The report was completely* **without foundation.** (=was untrue)

**foun·da·tions** /faʊnˈdeɪʃənz/ *n* [P] the base on which something is supported or built: *The workmen are laying the foundations of the new hospital.|He laid the foundations of his success by study and hard work.*

**found·er¹** /ˈfaʊndəʳ/ *n* a person who FOUNDS¹ something: *Mohammed was the founder of the Muslim religion.|He was a* **founder member** (=a member from the start) *of the club.*

**foun·der²** *v* [I] (of a ship) to fill with water and sink: (fig.) *The plan was a good one, but it foundered for* (=because of) *lack of support.*

**foun·dry** /ˈfaʊndri/ *n* **-dries** a place where metals are melted down and poured into shapes to make separate articles or parts of machinery, such as bars, wheels, etc.: *an iron foundry|foundry workers*

**foun·tain** /ˈfaʊntən/ *n* (an ornamental apparatus producing) a stream of water that shoots straight up into the air: *The children played in the fountain in the park.*

**four** /fɔːʳ‖for/ *determiner,n,pron* **1** (the number) 4 **2 on all fours** (of a person) on the hands and knees: *The baby was crawling about on all fours.*

**four·teen** /ˌfɔːˈtiːn◂‖ˌfor-/ *determiner,n,pron* (the number) 14 **–fourteenth** *determiner,n,pron,adv*

**fourth** /fɔːθ‖forθ/ *determiner,n,pron,adv* 4th

**fowl** /faʊl/ *n* **fowl** *or* **fowls** *tech* a bird, esp. a hen –see also WILDFOWL

**fox¹** /fɒks‖fɑks/ **vixen** /ˈvɪksən/ *fem.*– *n* **foxes** *or* **fox** a small doglike European wild animal with reddish fur, which is hunted in Britain and is often said to have a clever and deceiving nature

**fox²** *v* [T] *infml* **1** to deceive cleverly; trick **2** to be too difficult for (someone) to understand: *The second question on the examination paper foxed me completely; I couldn't understand it at all.*

**fox·trot** /ˈfɒkstrɒt‖ˈfɑkstrɑt/ *n* (a piece of music for) a formal dance with short quick steps

**fox·y** /ˈfɒksi‖ˈfɑksi/ *adj* **-ier, -iest** *derog* like a fox, in appearance or nature; not to be trusted: *a foxy character|foxy* FEATURES

**foy·er** /ˈfɔɪeɪ‖ˈfɔɪər/ *n* an entrance hall to a theatre or hotel –see picture on page 463

**frac·as** /ˈfrækɑː‖ˈfreɪkəs/ *n* **fracas** /ˈfrækɑːz/ *BrE*‖ **-ases** /əsəz/ *AmE*– a noisy quarrel in which a number of people take part, and which often ends in a fight

**frac·tion** /ˈfrækʃən/ *n* **1** (in MATHEMATICS) a division or part of a whole number: ⅓ and ⅜ *are fractions.* **2** a very small piece or amount: *She's careful with her money, and spends only a fraction of her earnings.* **–fractional** *adj* [*no comp.*]

**frac·tion·al·ly** /ˈfrækʃənəli/ *adv* to a very small degree: *If your calculations are even fractionally incorrect, the whole plan will fail.*

**frac·tious** /ˈfrækʃəs/ *adj fml* (esp. of a child or an old or sick person) restless and complaining; bad-tempered about small things and ready to quarrel **–fractiously** *adv* **–fractiousness** *n* [U]

**frac·ture¹** /ˈfræktʃəʳ/ *n* [C;U *of*] *tech* (an example of) the act or result of breaking something, esp. a bone: *Fracture of the leg can be very serious in old people.*|*The gas escaped from a fracture in the pipe.*

**fracture²** *v* **-tured, -turing** [I;T] *tech* to (cause to) break or crack: *He fell and fractured his arm.*

**fra·gile** /ˈfrædʒaɪl‖-dʒəl/ *adj* **1** easily broken or damaged: *This glass dish is very fragile.*|(fig.) *a fragile relationship* **2** slight in body or weak in health: *a fragile old lady*|(*usu. humor*) *I'm feeling rather fragile this morning; I must have drunk too much beer last night.* **–fragility** /frəˈdʒɪlʲti/ *n* [U]

**frag·ment¹** /ˈfrægmənt/ *n* a small piece broken off; an incomplete part: *She dropped the bowl on the floor, and it broke into fragments.*

**frag·ment²** /frægˈment‖ˈfrægment/ *v* [I] to break into FRAGMENTS: (fig.) *He could tell only a fragmented account of the story.* **–fragmentation** /ˌfrægmənˈteɪʃən,-men-/ *n* [C;U]

**frag·ment·ary** /ˈfrægməntəri‖-teri/ *adj* made up of pieces; not complete: *His knowledge of the subject is no more than fragmentary.*

**fra·grance** /ˈfreɪgrəns/ *n* [C;U] *apprec* (the quality of having) a sweet or pleasant smell: *This soap is made in several fragrances.*

**fra·grant** /ˈfreɪgrənt/ *adj apprec* having a sweet or pleasant smell (esp. of flowers): *The air in the garden was warm and fragrant.* **–fragrantly** *adv*

**frail** /freɪl/ *adj* weak in body or health: *a frail old woman*|*She's still feeling a bit frail.*

**frail·ty** /ˈfreɪlti/ *n* **-ties** [C;U] (an example of) the quality of being FRAIL

**frame¹** /freɪm/ *v* **framed, framing** [T] **1** to surround with a solid protecting edge; put a border round: *I'm having this picture framed, so that I can hang it on the wall.* **2** *fml* to form (words, sentences, ideas, etc.); express: *An examiner must frame his questions clearly.* **3** *infml* to cause (someone) to seem guilty of a crime by means of intentionally false statements, proofs, etc.: *He was framed by the real criminals and was sent to prison for a crime he hadn't done.*

**frame²** *n* **1** the main supports over and around which something is stretched or built: *In some parts of the world small boats are made of skins stretched over a wooden frame.*|*a bicycle frame*|*This old bed has an iron frame.* **2** (the form or shape of) a human or animal body: *a man with a powerful frame* **3** a firm border or case into which something is fitted or set: *I can't close the door; it doesn't fit properly into its frame.*|*a window frame* **4 frame of mind** the state or condition of one's mind or feelings at a particular time: *In his present frame of mind he shouldn't be left alone.*

> **SPELLING NOTE**
> Words with the sound /f/ may be spelt **ph-**, like **photograph.**

**frame·work** /ˈfreɪmwɜːk‖-ɜrk/ *n* a supporting frame; STRUCTURE: *This building has a steel framework.*|(fig.) *the framework of modern government*

**franc** /fræŋk/ *n* the standard coin of France, Switzerland, Belgium, and many countries that formerly belonged to France

**fran·chise** /ˈfræntʃaɪz/ *n* **1** [*the* U] *fml* the right to vote in a public election, esp. one held to choose a parliament: *In Britain, women were given the franchise in 1918.* **2** [C] a special right given by a company to one person to sell that company's goods or services in a particular place

**frank** /fræŋk/ *adj often apprec* free and direct in speech; plain and honest; truthful: *If you want my frank opinion, I don't think the plan will succeed.*|*Will you be quite frank with me about this matter?* (=tell me the truth, without trying to hide anything) **–frankness** *n* [U]

**frank·ly** /ˈfræŋkli/ *adv* speaking honestly and plainly: *Frankly, I don't think your chances of getting the job are very good.*

**fran·tic** /ˈfræntɪk/ *adj* very anxious, afraid, happy, etc.: *There was a frantic rush to get everything ready for the queen's visit.*|*That noise is driving me frantic.* (=making me mad) **–frantically** *adv*

**fra·ter·nal** /frəˈtɜːnəl‖-ɜr-/ *adj* [A *no comp.*] of, belonging to, or like brothers **–fraternally** *adv*

**fra·ter·ni·ty** /frəˈtɜːnʲti‖-ɜr-/ *n* **-ties** **1** [C +*sing./pl. v*] any association of people having work, interests, etc., in common: *He's a member of the medical fraternity.* (=is a doctor) **2** [U] *fml* the state of being brothers; brotherly feeling

**frat·er·nize**‖also **-nise** *BrE* /ˈfrætənaɪz‖-ər-/ *v* **-nized, -nizing** [I *with*] *fml* to meet and be friendly (with someone) as equals

**fraud** /frɔːd/ *n* **1** [C;U] (an act of) deceitful behaviour for the purpose of gain, which may be punishable by law; dishonesty: *The judge found the man guilty of fraud.* **2** [C] *derog* a person who pretends or claims to be what he/she is not: *He said he was an insurance salesman but later she realized he was a fraud.*

**fraud·u·lent** /ˈfrɔːdjʊlənt‖-dʒə-/ *adj fml* deceitful; got or done by FRAUD (1): *She got the job of science teacher by fraudulent means; she pretended she'd studied at university.* **–fraudulently** *adv* **–fraudulence** *n* [U]

**fraught** /frɔːt/ *adj* **1** [F *with*] *fml* full of (something unpleasant): *The long journey through the forest was fraught with danger.* **2** *infml* worried; troubled by small anxieties: *You're looking very fraught, Jane; is anything wrong?*

**fray¹** /freɪ/ *v* **1** [T] to cause (rope, cloth, etc.) to become thin or worn by rubbing, so that loose threads develop: *This old shirt of mine is frayed at the collar.*|(fig.) *Her nerves were frayed by the noisy children.* **2** [I] (of rope, cloth, etc.) to become thin or worn so that loose threads develop: *The electric wire is fraying and could be dangerous to handle.*|(fig.)

*Tempers began to fray at the meeting.*

**fray²** *n* [*the* S] *lit* a fight, argument, quarrel, etc.: *Are you ready for the fray?*

**freak¹** /friːk/ *n* **1** a living creature of unnatural form: *One of the new lambs is a freak; it was born with two tails.* **2** a peculiar happening: *By some strange freak, a little snow fell in Egypt a few years ago.* **3** *infml* a person who takes a special interest in the stated thing; FAN³: *a film freak*

**freak²** *adj* [A *no comp.*] unnatural in degree or type; very unusual: *The country's been having freak weather; it's been very hot during the winter.*|*a freak storm*

**freak³** *v* → FREAK OUT

**freak·ish** /ˈfriːkɪʃ/ *adj* unusual; unreasonable; strange: *freakish behaviour* –**freakishly** *adv*

**freak out** *v adv* [I;T (= **freak** sbdy.↔ **out**)] *infml* to (cause to) become greatly excited or anxious, esp. because of drugs

**freck·le** /ˈfrekəl/ *n* [*often pl.*] a small flat brown spot on the skin –**freckled** *adj*: *a freckled nose*

**free¹** /friː/ *adj* **1** able to act as one wants; not in prison or under control: *She felt free when she left home and moved to the city.*|*The prisoner will be* **set free** *next week.*|*You are free to do as you wish.*|*This is a free country.* (=the state does not control everything) **2** not limited in any way, esp. by rule or custom: *The people won the right to* **free speech** *and a* **free press.** (=they could express ideas and judgments in public and in newspapers)|*a free translation* (=one in which the general meaning is translated without giving an exact translation of every single word) **3** [*no comp.*] without payment of any kind; costing nothing: *a free ticket for the concert*|*Anyone who buys this breakfast food gets a free gift of a small plastic toy.*|*"Are the drinks free?" "No, you have to pay for them."* **4** [*no comp.*] not busy; without work or duty: *He has little free time.*|*a free afternoon*|*The doctor will be free in 10 minutes; can you wait that long?* **5** [*no comp.*] not being used; empty: *"Is this seat free?" "Yes; no one is using it."*|*She picked it up with her free hand.* **6** [F *from, of*] without (someone or something unwanted); untroubled by: *The old lady is never free from/of pain.*|*She was free from all blame for the accident.* **7** (esp. of bodily action) natural; graceful; not stiff or awkward: *free movement to music* **8** [F *with*] ready to give; generous: *She's very free with her money.*|*He's too free with his advice.* (=gives advice when it isn't wanted) **9** **free and easy** lacking in too great seriousness and ceremony; cheerful and unworried: *She leads a free and easy sort of life and never troubles much about anything.* **10** **-free** free from; without: *People with certain diseases have to eat salt-free foods.*|*a trouble-free journey*

**free²** *adv* **1** in a FREE¹ (1) manner: *Don't let the dog run free on the main road.* **2** without payment: *Babies are allowed to travel free on buses.* **3** so as to become loose or disconnected: *Two of the screws in this old wooden door have worked themselves free.* (=loosened or fallen out as a result of use)

**free³** *v* **freed** /friːd/, **freeing** [T *from*] **1** to set FREE¹ (1): *Free the prisoners!*|*She freed the bird from its cage.* **2** to move or loosen (someone or something that is stuck or trapped): *Can you free this window? It's stuck.* **3** [*of*] to take away something unpleasant from: *I need to go out; can you free me (from duty) for an hour?*

**free·dom** /ˈfriːdəm/ *n* **1** [U] the state of being free; state of not being under control: *The people there are fighting to gain freedom from foreign control.*|*During the school holidays the children enjoyed their freedom.*|*the freedom to choose what to do*|*freedom from fear* **2** [C;U +*to-v*/*of*] the power to do, say, think, or write as one pleases: *Two of the four freedoms spoken of by President Roosevelt in 1941 are freedom of speech and freedom of religion.* –compare LIBERTY

**free-for-all** /ˈ·· ˌ·/ *n infml* an argument, quarrel, etc., in which many people join and express their opinions, esp. in a noisy way: *The discussion about the new road soon became a free-for-all.*

**free·hand** /ˈfriːhænd/ *adj* (of (a) drawing) done by hand, without the use of a ruler or other instrument –**freehand** *adv*

**free·lance** /ˈfriːlɑːns‖-læns/ *n,adj* (done by) a writer or other trained worker who sells his/her work to a number of employers: *a freelance journalist* –**freelancer** *n*

**free·ly** /ˈfriːli/ *adv* **1** willingly; readily: *I freely admit that what I said was wrong.*|*He gives his time freely to help the school.* **2** openly; plainly; without hiding anything: *You can speak quite freely in front of me; I shan't tell anyone what you say.* **3** without any limitation on movement or action: *Oil the wheel; then it will turn more freely.*

**free·way** /ˈfriːweɪ/ *n AmE* for MOTORWAY

**free·wheel** /ˌfriːˈwiːl/ *v* [I] to ride a bicycle or drive a vehicle, esp. downhill, without providing power from the legs or the engine –compare COAST²

**free will** /ˌ· ˈ·/ *n* [U] the ability of a person to decide freely what he/she will do: *She did it* **of her own free will.** (=it was completely her decision)

**freeze¹** /friːz/ *v* **froze** /frəʊz/, **frozen** /ˈfrəʊzən/, **freezing 1** [I;T] to (cause to) harden into or become covered with ice: *Water freezes at 0 degrees* CENTIGRADE.|*The lake has frozen over/up.*|*The milk has frozen solid.*|*the hard frozen ground* –compare MELT, THAW **2** [I;T *up*] to (cause to) be unable to work properly as a result of ice or very low temperatures: *The engine has frozen up.*|*The cold has frozen the lock on the car door.* **3** [I] (of weather) to be at or below the temperature at which water becomes ice: *It's freezing tonight.* **4** [I;T] *infml* to (cause to) be, feel, or become very cold: *It's freezing in this room; can't we have a fire?*|*We nearly froze to death.* (=died of cold)|*I'm frozen stiff after sitting in that cold wind.*|(fig.) *His terrible stories made our blood freeze.* (=made us cold with fear) **5** [I;T] to preserve or be preserved by means of very low temperatures: *frozen beans*|*Not all fruit freezes well.* **6** [I;T] to (cause to) stop suddenly or become quite still, esp. with fear: *The child froze at the sight of the snake.*|*A sudden terrible cry froze him to the spot.*|*A wild animal will sometimes freeze in its tracks when it smells an enemy.* **7** [T] to fix (prices or wages) officially at a given level for a certain length of time

**freeze²** *n* [S] **1** a period of very cold icy weather: *He slipped and broke his leg during the big freeze last* *winter.* **2** a fixing of prices or wages at a certain level: *a wage freeze* –sounds like **frieze**

**freez·er** /ˈfriːzəʳ/ also **deep freeze** /ˌ· ˈ·/– *n* a type of FRIDGE in which supplies of food can be stored at a very low temperature for a long time –see pictures on pages 337, 615

**freez·ing point** /ˈfriːzɪŋ pɔɪnt/ *n* **1** [U] also **freezing**– the temperature (0 degrees CENTIGRADE) at which water becomes ice: *It's very cold today; the temperature has dropped to freezing point/below freezing.* **2** [C] the temperature at which any particular liquid freezes: *The freezing point of alcohol is much lower than that of water.*

**freight** /freɪt/ *n* [U] **1** (money paid for) the carrying of goods by some means of TRANSPORT (1): *This aircraft company deals with freight only; it has no passenger service.|to send something by airfreight/freight train* **2** the goods carried in this way: *This freight must be carefully handled when loading.* –**freight** *v* [T]

**freight·er** /ˈfreɪtəʳ/ *n* a ship for carrying goods

**French¹** /frentʃ/ *adj* belonging to France, its people, etc.: *French wine*

**French²** *n* **1** [*the* P] the people of France **2** [U] the language of France: *We have a French lesson/French every Tuesday.*

**French fries** /ˌ· ˈ·/ *n* [P] *esp. AmE* for CHIPS¹ (3)

**French win·dows** /ˌ· ˈ··/ also **French doors** /ˌ· ˈ·/ *AmE*– *n* [P] a pair of light outer doors made up of squares of glass in a frame, usu. opening out onto the garden of a house

**fre·net·ic, phrenetic** /frəˈnetɪk/ *adj* showing FRANTIC activity; overexcited –**frenetically** *adv*

**fren·zied** /ˈfrenzid/ *adj* full of uncontrolled excitement and/or wild activity; mad; FRANTIC: *The house was full of frenzied activity on the morning of the wedding.* –**frenziedly** *adv*

**fren·zy** /ˈfrenzi/ *n* [S;U] a state of great excitement or anxiety; sudden, but not lasting, attack of madness: *In a frenzy of hate he killed his enemy.|He worked himself up into a frenzy before his exams.*

**fre·quen·cy** /ˈfriːkwənsi/ *n* **-cies 1** [U *of*] the repeated or frequent happening of something: *The frequency of accidents on that road made the council lower the speed limit.|Accidents are happening there with increasing frequency.* **2** [C] *tech* a rate at which something happens or is repeated: *This radio signal has a frequency of 200,000* CYCLES¹ (2) *per second.* **3** [C] a particular number of radio waves per second at which a radio signal is broadcast: *This radio station broadcasts on three different frequencies.* –see also FM, VHF

**fre·quent¹** /ˈfriːkwənt/ *adj* common; found or happening often: *Sudden rainstorms are frequent on this coast.* –opposite **infrequent**; see NEVER (USAGE) –**frequently** *adv*

**fre·quent²** /friˈkwent‖friˈkwent, ˈfriːkwənt/ *v* [T] *fml* to be often in (a place, someone's company, etc.): *She's fond of books, and frequents the library.*

> **SPELLING NOTE**
> Words with the sound /f/ may be spelt **ph-**, like **photograph.**

**fresh** /freʃ/ *adj* **1** (of food) not long gathered, caught, produced, etc., and therefore in good condition: *This fish isn't fresh; it smells!|fresh bread|fresh fruit* (=not tinned or frozen) –compare STALE **2** [A *no comp.*] (of water) not salt; drinkable **3** (of air) pure and cool: *It's healthy to spend time* **in the fresh air**. (=outside) **4** [A *no comp.*] (an) other and different: *Let me make you a fresh pot of tea.|It's time to take a fresh look at this subject.* **5** [*no comp.*] lately arrived, happened, supplied, or added: *There's been no fresh news of the fighting since yesterday.|The new teacher's fresh from university.* **6** (of skin) clear and healthy: *She has dark hair and a fresh* COMPLEXION (1). **7** [F] *infml* (of weather) cool and windy: *It's a bit fresh today.* **8** [F] *infml* (too) bold with someone of the opposite sex: *That girl's not behaving at all well; she's trying to* **get fresh with** *my brother.* –see also AFRESH –**freshness** *n* [U]

**fresh·en** /ˈfreʃən/ *v* [I;T] to make or become fresher: (fig.) *The wind is freshening.* (=becoming stronger)

**freshen up** *v adv* [I;T (**freshen** sbdy./sthg.↔ **up**)] to (cause to) feel more comfortable and attractive by washing: *I must just go and freshen (myself) up before tea.*|(fig.) *She's freshened up the house with a coat of paint.*

**fresh·er** /ˈfreʃəʳ/ also **freshman** /-mən/– *n infml* a student in his/her first year at university

**fresh·ly** /ˈfreʃli/ *adv* (*before a past participle*) just lately; just now; recently: *"This coffee smells good." "Yes, it's freshly made."* |*His shirts have been freshly washed and ironed.*

**fresh·wa·ter** /ˌfreʃˈwɔːtəʳ◂‖-ˈwɔ-, -ˈwɑ-/ *adj* [A] of rivers or inland lakes; not belonging to the sea: *freshwater fish* –opposite **saltwater**

**fret** /fret/ *v* **-tt-** [I] to be continually worried and anxious, dissatisfied, or bad-tempered about small or unnecessary things: *Don't fret; everything will be all right.|The child's fretting for his absent mother.*

**fret·ful** /ˈfretfəl/ *adj* complaining and anxious, esp. because of dissatisfaction or discomfort: *The child was tired and fretful.* –**fretfully** *adv* –**fretfulness** *n* [U]

**fret·work** /ˈfretwɜːk‖-ɜrk/ *n* [C;U] (the art of making) patterns cut in wood with a special tool (**fretsaw**)

**Fri.** *n written abbrev. said as:* Friday

**fri·ar** /ˈfraɪəʳ/ *n* a man belonging to a Christian religious group who, esp. in former times, were very poor and travelled around the country teaching the Christian religion –compare MONK

**fric·tion** /ˈfrɪkʃən/ *n* [U] **1** the natural force which tries to stop one surface sliding over another **2** the rubbing, often repeated, of two surfaces together: *The friction of the rope against the rock made the rope break and the climber fell.* **3** unfriendliness and disagreement caused by two different sets of opinions or natures: *Mary's neat and Jane's careless; if they have to share a room there'll probably be friction.*

**Fri·day** /ˈfraɪdi/ *n* the 6th day of the week: *He'll arrive (on) Friday morning.|Lots of people eat fish on Fridays.* (=every Friday) –see also GOOD FRIDAY

**fridge** /frɪdʒ/ also **refrigerator** *fml*‖also **ice-box** *AmE*– *n* a large box or cupboard, used esp. in the home, in which food or drink can be stored for a short time at a low temperature, but without being frozen –compare FREEZER; see picture on page 337

**friend** /frend/ *n* **1** a person whom one knows well and likes, but who is not related: *Although Peter is* **a close friend** *of mine, David is my* **best** (=closest) **friend**.|*Mary's* **an old friend**; *we've known each other/been friends for 16 years.* –compare ENEMY **2** [*of, to*] a helper; supporter; person showing kindness and understanding: *Vote for Johnson–the people's friend!*|*He only got the job because he had* **friends in high places**. (=people in a position to influence others to help him) **3 make friends (with)** to form a friendship or friendships –see also BEFRIEND

**friend·ly** /'frendli/ *adj* **-lier, -liest 1** [*to, with*] acting or ready to act as a friend: *A friendly dog came to meet us at the farm.* |*a friendly nation* (=not an enemy)|*They quarrelled once, but they're quite friendly with each other now.* –opposite **unfriendly 2** kind; generous; ready to help: *You're always sure of a friendly welcome at this hotel.* **3** not causing unpleasant feelings: *We've been having a friendly argument on politics.*|*Our two teams are playing* **a friendly (game)** *next Saturday. The game isn't part of a serious competition.* **–friendliness** *n* [U]

**friend·ship** /'frendʃɪp/ *n* [C;U] (an example of) the condition of sharing a friendly relationship; feeling and behaviour that exists between friends: *True friendship is worth more than money.*|*His friendships never last very long.*

**frieze** /friːz/ *n* a decorative border along the top of a wall, either outside a building or inside a room –sounds like **freeze**

**frig·ate** /'frɪgǀt/ *n* a small fast-moving warship

**fright** /fraɪt/ *n* [C;U] (an experience that causes) the feeling of (usu. not very great) fear: *I was shaking with fright.*|*You* **gave me a fright** *by knocking so loudly on the door.*|*I got* **the fright of my life** (=the biggest fright I've ever had) *when the machine burst into flames.*|*He* **took fright** *and ran away when he saw the policemen.*

**fright·en** /'fraɪtn/ *v* [T] **1** to fill with fear: *The child was frightened by the big dog.*|*a frightening dream* **2** to cause (someone) to do, go, etc., from fear: *I frightened the bird away by moving suddenly.*|*He frightened the old lady into/out of signing the paper.* **–frighteningly** *adv*

**fright·ened** /'fraɪtnd/ *adj* [+*to-v*/(*that*)/*at, of*] in a state of fear; afraid: *He was frightened at the thought of his coming examination.*|*I was frightened (that)* (=worried that) *you wouldn't come.*|*Some people are frightened of thunder, others of snakes.* –see also AFRAID (1)

**fright·ful** /'fraɪtfəl/ *adj* **1** causing a feeling of shock; very unpleasant **2** *infml, becoming rare* very bad; unpleasant: *We're having frightful weather this week.* **–frightfulness** *n* [U]

**fright·ful·ly** /'fraɪtfəli/ *adv infml, becoming rare* very: *I'm afraid I'm frightfully late.*

**fri·gid** /'frɪdʒǀd/ *adj* **1** (of a woman) having an unnatural dislike of sexual activity **2** *tech* very cold: (fig.) *a frigid* (=rather unfriendly) *welcome* **–frigidly** *adv* **–frigidity** /frɪ'dʒɪdǀti/ *n* [U]

**frill** /frɪl/ *n* **1** a decorative edge on a dress, curtain, etc., made of a band of cloth with a wavy edge **2** [*usu. pl.*] something decorative or pleasant, but not necessary; an EXTRA[1] (1): *I just want an ordinary car without the frills.*

**frill·y** /'frɪli/ also **frilled**– *adj* **-ier, -iest** having many FRILLS (1): *The little girl wore a frilly party dress.* **–frilliness** *n* [U]

**fringe**[1] /frɪndʒ/ *n* **1** a decorative edge of hanging threads on a curtain, tablecloth, garment, etc. **2** a short border of hair cut in a straight line, hanging over a person's forehead: *The girl wore her hair* **in a fringe**. **3** [*of*] the part farthest from the centre; edge: *It was easier to move about on the fringe of the crowd.*|*A* **fringe group** *separated from the main political party.*|*In that factory the company provides free meals as a* **fringe benefit**.

**fringe**[2] *v* **fringed, fringing** [T *with*] to act as a FRINGE[1] (4) to: *A line of trees fringed the river.*

**frisk** /frɪsk/ *v* **1** [I] (of an animal or child) to run and jump about playfully **2** [T] *infml* to search (someone) for hidden weapons, goods, etc., by passing the hands over the body

**frisk·y** /'frɪski/ *adj* **-ier, -iest** overflowing with life and activity; joyfully alive: *frisky lambs*|*The spring weather's making me feel quite frisky.* **–friskily** *adv* **–friskiness** *n* [U]

**frit·ter** sthg.↔ **away** /'frɪtəʳ/ *v adv* [T *on*] *derog* to waste (time, money, etc.): *She fritters away all her money on cheap clothes.*

**fri·vol·i·ty** /frɪ'vɒlǀti‖- 'vɑ-/ *n* **-ties** *derog* **1** [U] the condition of being FRIVOLOUS: *His frivolity annoys the other people in the office.* **2** [C] a FRIVOLOUS act or remark: *A serious political speech should not be full of frivolities.*

**friv·o·lous** /'frɪvələs/ *adj derog* not serious; silly: *He has a frivolous nature and won't take anything seriously.* **–frivolously** *adv* **–frivolousness** *n* [U]

**frizz** /frɪz/ *v* [T *out, up*] *infml* to cause (hair) to go into short wiry curls

**frizz·y** /'frɪzi/ *adj* **-ier, -iest** *infml* (of hair) very curly; with short wiry curls: *Some people have naturally frizzy hair.*

**fro** /frəʊ/ *adv* see TO-AND-FRO

**frock** /frɒk‖frɑk/ *n becoming rare* a woman's or girl's dress

**frog** /frɒg‖frɑg, frɔg/ *n* **1** a small hairless jumping animal without a tail, that lives in water and on land, and makes a deep rough sound (CROAK[1] (1)) –compare TOAD **2 a frog in the/one's throat** *infml* a difficulty in speaking because of roughness in the throat

**frog·man** /'frɒgmən‖'frɑg-, 'frɔg-/ *n* **-men** /mən/ a person skilled at swimming under water, and who wears a special apparatus for breathing, and large flat shoes (FLIPPERS) –compare SKIN-DIVER

**frol·ic** /'frɒlɪk‖'frɑ-/ *v* **-ck-** [I *about*] to play and jump about gaily: *The young lambs were frolicking in the field.* **–frolic** *n*

**from** /frəm; *strong* frɒm‖frəm; *strong* frʌm, frɑm/ *prep* **1** starting at: *the train from London*|*The shop is open from eight till five o'clock.*|*They stayed here from Monday to/till Friday.*|*Where do you come from?* (=Where is your home?)|*Can you translate this letter from French into English?* –see Study Notes on page 474 **2** sent or given by: *a letter from John|She borrowed the money from her sister.* **3** using; out of: *Bread is made from flour.|She played the music from memory.* **4** (shows separation, difference, or taking away): *The village is five miles from the coast.|He needs a rest from work.|A tree gave us shelter from the rain.|She took the matches away from the baby.|Take two from four.|He lives apart from his family.|I don't know one kind of car from another.* **5** because of: *suffering from heart disease|From his appearance, you wouldn't think he was old.|The campers died from/of cold.* –see Study Notes on page 128

**frond** /frɒnd‖frɑnd/ *n* a leaf of a FERN or of a PALM[1]

**front**[1] /frʌnt/ *n* **1** [*the* S *of*] the most forward position, part, or surface, furthest from or opposite to the back: *The teacher called the boy out to the front of the class.|The front of the school faces south. |The front of the postcard shows a picture of our hotel.|This dress fastens at the front.* **2** [S] the manner and appearance a person shows to others: *She was nervous of meeting strangers, but she* **put on a bold front** (=acted as if she wasn't afraid) *and went to the party.|We must show* **a united front** *against the enemy.* **3** [*the* S] a line along which fighting takes place in time of war: *He lost his life at the front.* **4** [C] (*often cap.*) a widespread and active political movement **5** [C] *tech* a line of separation between two masses of air of different temperature: *A cold front is the forward edge of a mass of moving cold air.* **6** [A;C *for*] *infml* a person, group, or thing used for hiding the real nature of a secret or illegal activity: *a travel company used as a front for bringing dangerous drugs into the country|He is* **the front man** *for a criminal gang.* **7 in front: a** ahead: *The grandmother walked slowly, and the children ran on in front.* **b** in or at the part facing forwards: *This dress fastens in front.* **c** in the most forward or important position: *The driver sits in front, and the passengers sit behind.* **8 in front of: a** towards or outside the front of: *I can't read the notice because he's standing in front of it.|a car parked in front of the house* –compare BEHIND[2] **b** in the presence of: *Don't say that in front of the children!* **9 in the front** in FRONT[1] (7b, c) **10 in the front of** in the most forward or important position: *He's sitting in the front of the car with the driver.|In the front of the picture is the figure of a man.*

**front**[2] *v* [I;T] (of a building) to have the front towards; face: *The hotel fronts (onto) the main road.*

**front**[3] *adj* [A *no comp.*] being at the front: *Write your name on the front cover of the exercise book.|his front teeth|front row seats|the front garden* –opposite **back**; see also REAR[2]

**front·age** /ˈfrʌntɪdʒ/ *n* a part of a building or of land that stretches along a road, river, etc.: *The shop has frontages on two busy streets.*

**front·al** /ˈfrʌntl/ *adj* [A *no comp.*] **1** (of an attack) direct; (as if) from the front **2** of, at, or to the front –**frontally** *adv*

**fron·tier** /ˈfrʌntɪəʳ‖frʌnˈtɪər/ *n* a limit or border, esp. where the land of two countries meets: *They were shot trying to cross the frontier.*|(fig.) *The frontiers of medical knowledge are being pushed farther outwards every year.*

> **SPELLING NOTE**
> Words with the sound /f/ may be spelt **ph-**, like **photograph.**

**frost**[1] /frɒst‖frɔst/ *n* **1** [U] a white powdery substance formed on outside surfaces from very small drops of water when the temperature of the air is below freezing point: *The car windows were covered with frost in the early morning.* –compare ICE[1] (1) **2** [C;U] (a period or state of) weather at a temperature below the freezing point of water: *Frost has killed several of our new young plants.|There was a hard frost last night.* (=a severe one)

**frost**[2] *v* **1** [I;T *over*] to (cause to) become covered with FROST[1] (1): *The cold has frosted the windows.|The fields have frosted over.* **2** [T *usu. pass.*] to make the surface of a sheet of (glass) rough so that it is not possible to see through: *a frosted glass door*

**frost·bite** /ˈfrɒstbaɪt/ *n* [U] harmful swelling and colouring of a person's limbs, caused by a great cold –**frostbitten** /-ˌbɪtn/ *adj*

**frost·y** /ˈfrɒsti‖ˈfrɔsti/ *adj* **-ier, -iest** very cold; cold with FROST[1] (2): (fig.) *a frosty greeting* (=not friendly) –**frostily** *adv* –**frostiness** *n* [U]

**froth**[1] /frɒθ‖frɔθ/ *n* [S;U] a white mass of bubbles formed on top of or in a liquid, or in the mouth; FOAM[1]

**froth**[2] *v* [I] to make or throw up FROTH: *The beer frothed as it was poured out.|The horse was frothing at the mouth after its fast run.*

**froth·y** /ˈfrɒθi‖ˈfrɔθi/ *adj* **-ier, -iest** full of or covered with FROTH: *frothy beer* –**frothily** *adv* –**frothiness** *n* [U]

**frown** /fraʊn/ *v* [I] to draw the hair-covered parts above the eyes (BROWS (1)) together esp. in anger or effort, or to show disapproval, causing lines to appear on the forehead: *The teacher frowned angrily at the noisy class.* –compare SMILE –**frown** *n: She looked at her examination paper with a frown.* –**frowningly** *adv*

**frown on/upon** sthg. *v prep* [T +*v-ing*] to disapprove of: *Mary wanted to go to France by herself, but her parents frowned on the idea.*

**froze** /frəʊz/ *v past tense of* FREEZE[1]

**fro·zen** /ˈfrəʊzən/ *v past participle of* FREEZE[1]

**fru·gal** /ˈfruːgəl/ *adj* **1** careful in the use of money, food, etc.: *Although he's become rich, he's kept his frugal habits.* **2** small in quantity and cost: *a frugal supper of bread and cheese.* –**frugally** *adv* –**frugality** /fruːˈgælǝti/ *n* [C;U]

**fruit**[1] /fruːt/ *n* [C;U] **1** (an example or type of) the part of a tree or bush that contains seeds, esp. considered as food: *Apples, oranges, and bananas are fruit.|The potato is a vegetable, not a fruit.|Would you like some more fruit?|a fruit shop* |**the fruits of the earth** (=plants used for food) **2** a/the result: *The old man enjoyed the fruits of* (=rewards of) *his life's work.|Their plans haven't* **borne fruit.** (=had a successful result)

**fruit**[2] *v* [I] (of a tree, bush, etc.) to bear fruit: *The apple trees are fruiting early this year.*

**fruit·er·er** /ˈfruːtərəʳ/ *n* (a person who has) a shop in which fruit is sold (also called a **fruit shop**)

**fruit·ful** /ˈfruːtfəl/ *adj* successful; useful; producing good results: *a fruitful meeting* –opposite **fruitless** –**fruitfully** *adv* –**fruitfulness** *n* [U]

**fru·i·tion** /fruːˈɪʃən/ *n* [U] fulfilment (of plans, aims, desired results, etc.): *After much delay, the plan to build the new hospital came to/was brought to fruition.*

**fruit·less** /ˈfruːtlɪ̆s/ *adj* (of an effort) useless; unsuccessful; not bringing the desired result: *So far the search for the missing boy has been fruitless.* –opposite **fruitful** –**fruitlessly** *adv* –**fruitlessness** *n* [U]

**fruit·y** /ˈfruːti/ *adj* **-ier, -iest 1** *usu. apprec* like fruit; tasting or smelling of fruit: *This red wine is soft and fruity.* **2** *infml* (of a person's voice) rich and deep: *a fruity laugh*

**frus·trate** /frʌˈstreɪt‖ˈfrʌstreɪt/ *v* **-trated, -trating** [T] **1** to prevent the fulfilment of; defeat (someone or someone's effort): *The bad weather frustrated all our hopes of going out.* **2** to cause (someone) to have feelings of annoyed disappointment or dissatisfaction: *I'm feeling rather frustrated in my present job.|After two hours' frustrating delay, our train at last arrived.* –**frustration** /frʌˈstreɪʃən/ *n* [C;U]: *Life is full of frustrations.*

**fry** /fraɪ/ *v* **fried, frying** [I;T] to (cause to) be cooked in hot fat or oil: *The eggs were frying in the pan.|fried rice* –see COOK (USAGE)

**fry·ing pan** /ˈ·· ˌ·/ also **skillet** *AmE*– *n* a flat pan with a long handle, used for FRYing food –see picture on page 337

**ft** *written abbrev. said as:* **1** feet: *4 ft long* **2** foot: *5 ft long* –see FOOT[1] (2)

**fuch·sia** /ˈfjuːʃə/ *n* a garden bush with hanging bell-like red, pink, or white flowers

**fudge** /fʌdʒ/ *n* [U] a soft creamy light brown sweet made of sugar, milk, butter, etc.

**fu·el**[1] /fjʊəl‖ˈfjuːəl/ *n* [C;U] (a type of) material that is used for producing heat or power by burning: *Wood, coal, oil, and gas are different kinds of fuel.|Petrol is no longer a cheap fuel.*

**fuel**[2] *v* **-ll-** *BrE*‖**-l-** *AmE* [I;T] to take in or provide with FUEL[1]: *Aircraft sometimes fuel while in the air.* –see also REFUEL

**fu·gi·tive** /ˈfjuːdʒɪ̆tɪv/ *n* a person escaping from danger, the police, etc.: *a fugitive from justice* –**fugitive** *adj* [A]

**ful·crum** /ˈfʊlkrəm, ˈfʌl-/ *n* **-crums** *or* **-cra** /krə/ the point on which a bar (LEVER) turns or is supported in lifting or moving something

**ful·fil** ‖ also **fulfill** *AmE* /fʊlˈfɪl/ *v* **-ll-** [T] **1** to perform or carry out (an order, duty, promise, etc.): *The doctor's instructions must be fulfilled exactly.|A chimney fulfils the* FUNCTION *of taking away smoke.|If you make a promise, you should fulfil it.* **2** to supply or satisfy (a need, demand, or purpose): *The travelling library fulfils an important need for people who live far from the town.* **3** to make or prove to be true; cause to happen: *If he's lazy, he'll never fulfil his* AMBITION *to be a doctor.* **4** to develop fully the character and abilities of (oneself): *She fulfilled herself both as a mother and as a successful writer.*

**ful·fil·ment** ‖also **fulfillment** *AmE* /fʊlˈfɪlmənt/ *n* [U] **1** the act of fulfilling or condition of being fulfilled: *After many years, his plans have come to fulfilment.* **2** satisfaction after successful effort: *a sense of fulfilment*

**full**[1] /fʊl/ *adj* **1** [*of, with*] (of a container or space) filled completely; holding as much or as many as possible: *You can't put any more liquid into a full bottle.|The drawer was full up with old clothes.|The train's full (up); there are no seats left at all.|a full train|The doctor had a very full day.* (=had work to do all the time)|*It's rude to speak with your mouth full.* (=while you are eating)|(fig.) *a story full of sadness* –compare EMPTY[1] (1) **2** [*of*] (of a container) filled with liquid, powder, etc., as near to the top as convenient: *They brought us out a pot full of steaming coffee.|This bag of flour is only half full.* (=contains half the amount that it can hold)|*Don't fill my cup too full.* **3** [F *of*] containing or having plenty (of): *The field was full of sheep feeding on the new grass.|This work's full of mistakes.* **4** [*up*] *infml* well fed, often to the point of discomfort; satisfied: *I can't eat any more; I'm full up.|a full stomach* **5** complete; whole: *Please write down your full name and address.|She rose to her full height.* (=stood up very straight and proudly)|*He has led a full life.* (=has had every kind of experience) **6** [A] the highest or greatest possible: *He drove the car at full speed through the town.* **7** [F *of*] having the mind and attention fixed only (on): *too full of my own troubles to care about the problems of others|She's always full of herself.* (=thinks she's very important)|*He's full of his visit to America.* (=talks about it a lot) **8** (of a part of a garment) wide; flowing; fitting loosely: *a full skirt* **9** (of a shape or someone's body) *often apprec* round; rounded; fleshy: *a full moon|Her face was full when she was younger; now it's much thinner.* **10** [A] *apprec* (of colour, smell, sound, or taste) deep, rich, and powerful: *wine with a full body* (=having strength and taste)

**full**[2] *adv* [*adv+prep/adv*] **1** straight; directly: *The sun shone full on her face.* **2** very; quite: *They knew* **full well** *that he wouldn't keep his promise.*

**full**[3] *n* **1 in full** completely: *The debt must be paid in full.* **2 to the full** to the greatest degree; very greatly: *We enjoyed our holiday to the full.*

**full-blown** /ˌ· ˈ·◂/ *adj often lit* (of a flower) completely open: (fig.) *We're afraid that the fighting on the border may develop into a full-blown* (=fully developed) *war.*

**full-grown** /ˌ· ˈ·◂/ also **fully-grown** /ˌ·· ˈ·◂/ *BrE*– *adj* (esp. of an animal, plant, or (*tech*) person) completely developed

**full-length** /ˌ· ˈ·◂/ *adj* **1** (of a painting, mirror, etc.) showing a person from head to foot **2** (of a garment) reaching to the ground: *a full-length evening dress* **3** (of a play, book, etc.) not short; not shorter than is usual: *He has written several one-act plays, but only one full-length play.*

**full moon** /ˌ· ˈ·/ *n* [S;U] (the time of the month of) the moon when seen as a circle

**full-scale** /ˌ· ˈ·◂/ *adj* **1** (of a model, drawing, copy, etc.) of the same size as the object represented: *He made a full-scale model of an elephant, but he couldn't get it out of the room.* **2** [A] using all one's powers, forces, etc.: *a full-scale attack*

**full stop** /ˌ· ˈ·/ ‖also **period, point** *AmE*– *n* **1** a point (.) marking the end of a sentence or a shortened form of a word **2 come to a full stop** to stop completely

**full-time** /ˌ· ˈ·◂/ *adj,adv* working for the normal number of hours or days in job, course of study, etc.: *a full-time student|full-time employment|He used to work full-time, but now he only works three days a week.* –see also PART-TIME

**full time** /ˌ· ˈ·/ *n* [U] *BrE* (in some sports, such as football) the end of the fixed period of time during which a match is played –see also HALF TIME

**ful·ly** /ˈfʊli/ *adv* **1** completely; altogether; thoroughly: *I don't fully understand his reasons for leaving.|a fully trained nurse* **2** quite; at least: *It's fully an hour since he left.*

**fully-fledged** /ˌ·· ˈ·◂/ *BrE*||also **full-fledged** *AmE*– *adj* completely trained: *a fully-fledged doctor*

**fum·ble** /ˈfʌmbəl/ *v* **-bled, -bling 1** [I *about, around*] to move the fingers or hands awkwardly in search of something, or in an attempt to do something: *She fumbled about in her handbag for a pen.*|(fig.) *He's not a very good speaker; he often has to fumble for the right word.* **2** [I;T] to handle (something) without neatness or skill; mishandle: *The cricketer fumbled and dropped the ball/fumbled his attempt to catch it.*

**fume** /fjuːm/ *v* **fumed, fuming** [I] to show signs of great anger and restlessness: *"Was he angry?" "Yes, he was really fuming."*

**fumes** /fjuːmz/ *n* [P] heavy strong-smelling air given off from smoke, gas, fresh paint, etc.: *The air in the railway carriage was thick with tobacco fumes.|Petrol fumes from car engines poison the air.*

**fu·mi·gate** /ˈfjuːmʲgeɪt/ *v* **-gated, -gating** [T] to clear of disease, bacteria, or harmful insects by means of chemical smoke or gas: *The man was found to have an infectious disease, so his house had to be fumigated.* –**fumigation** /-ˈgeɪʃən/ *n* [U]

**fun** /fʌn/ *n* [U] **1** playfulness: *The little dog's full of fun.* **2** (a cause of) amusement; enjoyment; pleasure: *There's no fun in spending the evening doing nothing.|Have fun!* (=enjoy yourself)|*He's learning French* **for fun/for the fun of it.** (=for pleasure)|*Swimming in the sea is* **great/good fun. 3 in fun** as a joke; without serious or harmful intention: *I'm sorry I hid your car keys; I only did it in fun.* **4 make fun of/poke fun at** to (cause others to) laugh rather unkindly at

**func·tion¹** /ˈfʌŋkʃən/ *n* **1** a usual purpose (of a thing) or special duty (of a person): *The function of an adjective is to describe or add to the meaning of a noun.|The function of a chairman is to lead and control meetings.* **2** a large or important gathering of people for pleasure or on some special occasion: *This room may be hired for weddings and other functions.|The minister has to attend all kinds of official functions.*

**function²** *v* [I] (esp. of a thing) to be in action; work: *The machine won't function properly if you don't oil it.*

**func·tion·al** /ˈfʌŋkʃənəl/ *adj* made for or concerned with practical use without ornamentation: *functional furniture* –**functionally** *adv*

> **SPELLING NOTE**
> Words with the sound /f/ may be spelt **ph-**, like **photograph.**

**fund¹** /fʌnd/ *n* a supply or sum of money set apart for a special purpose: *government funds|the school sports fund|I'm a bit* **short of funds.** (=without much money)|(fig.) *She's got a fund of amusing jokes.*

**fund²** *v* [T] to provide money for (an activity, organization, etc.): *The search for a cure for this disease is being funded by the government.*

**fun·da·men·tal¹** /ˌfʌndəˈmentl/ *adj* (of a non-material thing) of the greatest importance; deep; being at the base, from which all else develops: *The new government has promised to make fundamental changes.|Fresh air is fundamental* (=necessary) *to good health.* –**fundamentally** *adv: She is fundamentally unsuited to office work.*

**fundamental²** *n* [*of*] a rule, law, etc., on which a system is based; basic part: *If the boys are going to camp for ten days, they'll need to know the fundamentals of cooking.*

**fu·ne·ral** /ˈfjuːnərəl/ *n* [A;C] a ceremony, usu. religious, of burying or burning a dead person: *a funeral service|a funeral procession*

**fu·ne·re·al** /fjʊˈnɪərɪəl/ *adj* heavy and sad; suitable to a funeral

**fun·fair** /ˈfʌnfeəʳ/ *n BrE* a noisy brightly lit show which for small charges offers all kinds of amusements

**fun·gus** /ˈfʌŋgəs/ *n* **-gi** /dʒaɪ, gaɪ/ *or* **-guses 1** [C] a plant without flowers, leaves, or green colouring matter, with a fleshy stem supporting a broad rounded top (MUSHROOMS, TOADSTOOLS, etc.), or in a very small form, with a powderlike appearance (MILDEW, MOULD, etc.) **2** [U] these plants in general, esp. considered as a disease: *roses suffering from fungus*

**fu·nic·u·lar** /fjʊˈnɪkjʊləʳ||-kjə-/ also **funicular railway** /·ˌ··· ˈ··/– *n* a small railway up a slope or a mountain, worked by a thick metal rope

**funk·y** /ˈfʌŋki/ *adj* **-ier, -iest** *apprec infml, esp. AmE* **1** (of JAZZ or similar music) having a simple coarse style and feeling, like the BLUES **2** fine; good: *a funky party*

**fun·nel¹** /ˈfʌnəl/ *n* **1** a tubelike vessel that is wide and round at the top and narrow at the bottom, used for pouring liquids or powders into a vessel with a narrow neck **2** a metal chimney for letting out smoke from a steam engine or steamship

**funnel²** *v* **-ll-** *BrE*||**-l-** *AmE* [I;T] to (cause to) pass through or as if through a FUNNEL¹ (1): *The large crowd funnelled out of the gates after the football match.*

**fun·ni·ly** /ˈfʌnʲli/ *adv* **1** in an unusual or amusing way: *She's been acting rather funnily just recently.* **2 funnily enough** *BrE*||**funny enough** *AmE*– although this is strange: *There were black clouds and loud thunder, but funnily enough it didn't rain.*

**fun·ny** /ˈfʌni/ *adj* **-nier, -niest 1** amusing; causing laughter: *I heard such a funny story this morning.|I don't think that's at all funny.* (=is a fit cause for laughter) **2** strange; unexpected; hard to explain; unusual: *What can that funny noise be? |It's a funny thing, but she put the book on the table five minutes ago, and now it can't be found.|When I saw them* *whispering to each other, I knew there was something funny* (=dishonest) *going on.* **3** [F *no comp.*] *infml* slightly ill: *She always feels a bit funny if she looks down from a height.* –**funniness** *n* [U]

**fur** /fɜːʳ/ *n* **1** [U] the soft thick fine hair that covers the body of some types of animal, such as bears, rabbits, cats, etc. **2** [A;C] a hair-covered skin of certain animals (such as foxes, rabbits, MINK, BEAVERS, etc.), used for clothing; a garment made of one or more of these: *a fur coat* **3** [U] a hard covering on the inside of pots, hot-water pipes, etc. –see SCALE³ (2) –sounds like **fir**

**fu·ri·ous** /ˈfjʊərɪəs/ *adj* **1** [+*to-v*] very angry in an uncontrolled way: *He'll be furious with us if we're late.*|*He'll be furious at being kept waiting.* –see ANGRY (USAGE) **2** wild; uncontrolled: *a furious temper*|*There was a furious knocking at the door.* –**furiousness** *n* [U] –**furiously** *adv*

**furl** /fɜːl‖fɜrl/ *v* [T] to roll or fold up (a sail, flag, FAN, UMBRELLA (1), etc.) –see also UNFURL

**fur·long** /ˈfɜːlɒŋ‖ˈfɜrlɔŋ/ *n* (a measure of length equal to) 220 yards or 201 metres, used mainly in horse racing

**fur·nace** /ˈfɜːn¹̩s‖ˈfɜr-/ *n* **1** an apparatus in a factory, in which metals and other substances are heated to very high temperatures in an enclosed space **2** a large enclosed fire used for producing hot water or steam: *This room's like a furnace.* (=it's much too hot)

**fur·nish** /ˈfɜːnɪʃ‖ˈfɜr-/ *v* [T] **1** to put furniture in (a room or building); supply with furniture: *The new hotel's finished, but it's not yet furnished.*|*They're renting a furnished house.* (=one with furniture already in it) **2** *fml* to supply (what is necessary for a special purpose)

**fur·ni·ture** /ˈfɜːnɪtʃəʳ‖ˈfɜr-/ *n* [U] all large or quite large movable articles, such as beds, chairs, tables, etc., that are placed in a house, room, or other area: *This old French table is a very valuable piece of furniture.*|*garden furniture*

**fu·ro·re** /fjʊˈrɔːri, ˈfjʊərɔːʳ‖ˈfjʊərɔr/ *BrE*‖**furor** /ˈfjʊərɔːʳ‖-rɔr/ *AmE*– *n* [S] a sudden burst of angry or excited interest among a large group of people

**fur·ri·er** /ˈfʌrɪəʳ‖ˈfɜr-/ *n* a person who prepares furs, makes fur garments, and/or sells them

**fur·row¹** /ˈfʌrəʊ‖ˈfɜr-/ *n* a long narrow track, esp. one cut by a PLOUGH in farming land: *The deep furrows made it difficult to walk across the field.*|(fig.) *Worry had caused deep furrows to appear on her forehead.*

**furrow²** *v* [T] to make FURROWS in: (fig.) *She looked at the examination paper with a furrowed* BROW. (=a forehead with lines in it because she was worried)

**fur·ry** /ˈfɜːri/ *adj* **-rier, -riest** of, like, or covered with fur

**fur·ther¹** /ˈfɜːðəʳ‖ˈfɜr-/ *adv,adj* [*adv+adv/prep*] **1** (COMPARATIVE² *of* FAR) also **farther**– more far: *He can swim further/farther than I can.*|*She can't remember further back than 1970.* **2** more: *I have nothing further to say.*|*There will be a further performance* (=another performance) *of the play next week.*

USAGE **Farther** and **farthest** are only used when speaking of real places and distances: **farther/further** *down the road*|*What's the farthest/furthest place you've ever been to?* Otherwise, use **further** and **furthest**: *Nothing was* **further** *from my mind.*|*We'll have to wait a* **further** *two weeks to know the results.*

**further²** *v* [T] *fml* to help (something); advance; help to succeed: *the government's plans to further the cause of peace*

**further ed·u·ca·tion** /ˌ·· ··ˈ··/ *BrE*‖also **continuing education** *AmE*– *n* [U] education after leaving school, but not at a university –compare HIGHER EDUCATION

**fur·ther·more** /ˌfɜːðəˈmɔːʳ‖ˈfɜrðərmɔr/ *adv fml* besides what has been said: *The house is too small, and furthermore, it's too far from the town.*

**fur·ther·most** /ˈfɜːðəməʊst‖ˈfɜrðər-/ *adj* [A] most distant; farthest away

**fur·thest** /ˈfɜːð¹̩st‖ˈfɜr-/ also **farthest**– *adv,adj* [*adv+adv/prep*] (SUPERLATIVE¹ *of* FAR) most far: *Who can swim furthest/farthest?*|*Our house is the furthest away.*|*Our house is the furthest/farthest from the shops.* –see FURTHER (USAGE)

**fur·tive** /ˈfɜːtɪv‖ˈfɜr-/ *adj* secret and/or not direct, as expressing guilty feelings; trying or hoping to escape notice: *The man's furtive manner made the policeman watch him to see what he would do.* –**furtively** *adv* –**furtiveness** *n* [U]

**fu·ry** /ˈfjʊəri/ *n* **-ries 1** [S;U] (a state of) very great anger: *She was filled with fury/in a fury and could not speak.* **2** [U *of*] wild force or activity: *At last the fury of the storm lessened.*

**fuse¹** /fjuːz/ *n* (a container with) a thin piece of wire, placed in an electric apparatus or system, which melts if too much electric power passes through it, and thus breaks the connection and prevents damage: *You'll* **blow a fuse** *if you put the electric heater and the cooker and all the lights on at the same time. Then all the lights will fail.*

**fuse²** *v* **fused, fusing** [I;T] **1** to (cause to) melt in great heat: *Lead will fuse at quite a low temperature.* **2** [*together*] to join or become joined by melting: *The aircraft came down in flames, and the heat fused most of the parts together into a solid mass.* **3** to (cause to) stop working owing to the melting of a FUSE¹: *The lights have fused; the whole place is in darkness.*

**fuse³** *n* **1** a long string or a narrow pipe used for carrying fire to an explosive article and so causing it to blow up **2** an apparatus in a bomb, SHELL¹ (3), or other weapon, which causes it to explode when touched, thrown, etc.

**fu·se·lage** /ˈfjuːz¹̩lɑːʒ‖-səlɑʒ/ *n* the main body of an aircraft, in which travellers and goods are carried

**fu·sion** /ˈfjuːʒən/ *n* [C;U *of*] (a) melting or joining together by melting: *This metal is formed by the fusion of two other types of metal.*|(fig.) *His work is a fusion of several different styles of music.*

**fuss¹** /fʌs/ *n* [S;U] **1** unnecessary, useless, or unwelcome excitement, anger, impatience, etc.: *What a fuss about nothing!*|*Don't make so much fuss over losing a penny.*|*There's sure to be a fuss when they find the window's broken.*|*Aunt Mary always* **makes a great fuss of** (=pays a lot of attention to) *the children* **2 kick up a fuss** to cause trouble, esp. by complaining loudly or angrily

**fuss²** *v* [I *about*] to act or behave in a nervous,

restless, and anxious way over small matters: *Don't fuss; we're sure to catch our train.*

**fuss·y** /ˈfʌsi/ *adj* **-ier, -iest** *usu. derog* **1** (of a person or a person's actions, character, etc.) nervous and excitable about small matters: *small fussy movements of her hands* **2** (of a person) too much concerned about details: *He's fussy about his food; if it isn't cooked just right, he won't eat it.* **–fussily** *adv* **–fussiness** *n* [U]

**fus·ty** /ˈfʌsti/ *adj* **-tier, -tiest** *derog* (of a room, box, clothes, etc.) having an unpleasant smell as a result of having been shut up for a long time, esp. when not quite dry **–fustiness** *n* [U]

**fu·tile** /ˈfjuːtaɪl‖-tl/ *adj often derog* (of an action) having no effect; unsuccessful; useless: *All his attempts to unlock the door were futile, because he was using the wrong key.* **–futility** /fjuːˈtɪlȧti/ *n* [U]: *the futility of war*

**fu·ture** /ˈfjuːtʃəʳ/ *adj,n* **1** [A; *the* S] (in) time yet to come: *You should save some money; it's wise to provide for the future.|in future years|Keep this book for future use.* (=to use at a later time)|*In the future, we may all work fewer hours a day.*|**In the distant future** (=much later) *people may live on the moon.|We're hoping to move to Scotland* **in the near future** (=soon)/**in the not too distant future.** (=quite soon) –compare PAST[1] (1) **2** [A;C] (expected or planned for) a person's life in time yet to come; that which will happen to someone or something: *I wish you a very happy future.|The company has had a difficult year, and its future is uncertain.|He has* **a bright future** *as a painter.* (=will be successful)|*my future husband/wife* (=the man/woman whom I am going to marry)|*We're leaving this town; our future home will be in London.* **3** [A;S] *tech* (in grammar) (being) the tense of a verb that expresses what will happen at a later time: *The future (tense) of English verbs is formed with "shall" and "will".* –compare PAST[1] (2) **4** [U] *infml* likelihood of success: *There's no future in trying to sell furs in a hot country.* **5 in future** (used in giving a warning) from now on: *In future, be more careful with your money.*

**fu·tur·is·tic** /ˌfjuːtʃəˈrɪstɪk/ *adj infml* of strange modern appearance: *a futuristic building/design* **–futuristically** *adv*

**fuzz**[1] /fʌz/ *n* [U] *infml* a soft light substance such as rubs off a woollen article; FLUFF

**fuzz**[2] *n* [U +*sing./pl. v*] *infml* police

**fuzz·y** /ˈfʌzi/ *adj* **-ier, -iest** *infml* **1** (of hair) standing up in a light short mass **2** not clear in shape; misty: *The television picture is rather fuzzy tonight.* **3** (of cloth, a garment, etc.) having a raised soft hairy surface **–fuzzily** *adv* **–fuzziness** *n* [U]

# G, g

**G, g** /dʒiː/ **G's, g's** *or* **Gs, gs** the 7th letter of the English alphabet

**G** *abbrev. for: tech* **1** GRAVITY (2) **2** the amount of force caused by GRAVITY on an object that is lying on the earth, used as a measure

**gab** /gæb/ *n* [U] *infml* **(have) the gift of the gab** (have) the ability to speak well continuously

**gab·ble** /ˈgæbəl/ *v* **-bled, -bling** [I;T] to say (words) so quickly that they cannot be heard clearly **–gabble** *n* [S;U]: *the gabble of excited children*

**ga·ble** /ˈgeɪbəl/ *n* the three-cornered upper end of a wall where it meets the roof

**gad a·bout** (sthg.) /gæd/ *v prep; adv* **-dd-** [I;T] *infml* to travel round (somewhere) to enjoy oneself: *She gads about (Europe) a lot.*

**gad·get** /ˈgædʒȧt/ *n* a small machine or useful apparatus: *a clever little gadget for opening tins* –see MACHINE (USAGE)

**gag**[1] /gæg/ *n* **1** a piece of cloth, etc., put over or into the mouth to prevent the person from talking or shouting **2** *infml* a joke or funny story

**gag**[2] *v* **-gg-** [T] to prevent from speaking by putting a GAG[1] (1) into the mouth of: (fig.) *The newspapers have been gagged, so nobody knows what really happened.*

**gage** /geɪdʒ/ *n,v* **gaged, gaging** *AmE* for GAUGE

**gag·gle** /ˈgægəl/ *n* [+ *sing./pl. v*] a number of geese (GOOSE) together: (fig.) *a gaggle of noisy children*

**gai·e·ty** /ˈgeɪȧti/ *n* **-ties 1** [U] the state of being cheerful **2** [C *usu. pl.*;U] joyful events and activities, esp. at a time of public holiday

**gai·ly** /ˈgeɪli/ *adv* in a cheerful manner

**gain**[1] /geɪn/ *v* **1** [T] to obtain (something useful, necessary, wanted, etc.): *I'm new in the job but I'm already gaining experience.* **2** [I;T] to make (a profit or increase in amount): *The car gained speed as it went down the hill.|My watch has gained ten minutes* (=by moving too fast) *since yesterday.|The People's Party is* **gaining ground** (=becoming stronger, more popular, etc.) *in the country.* –opposite **lose** (for **2**); see also WIN

**gain on/upon** sbdy./sthg. *v prep* [T] to reduce the distance between oneself and (a competitor)

**gain**[2] *n* [C;U] (the act of making) an increase in wealth, amount, weight, etc.: *The baby had a gain of half a pound (in weight) last week.* –opposite **loss**

**gait** /geɪt/ *n* a way or manner of walking; WALK[2] (1) –sounds like **gate**

**ga·la** /ˈgɑːlə‖ˈgeɪlə, ˈgælə/ *adj,n* (of) an occasion of feasting or public amusement: *a gala occasion*

**gal·ax·y** /ˈgæləksi/ *n* **-ies** any of the large groups of stars which make up the universe: (fig.) *a galaxy of film stars* **–galactic** /gəˈlæktɪk/ *adj*

**gale** /geɪl/ *n* a strong wind: *The old tree was blown down in a gale.*|(fig.) *gales* (=sudden bursts) *of laughter* –see WEATHER (USAGE)

**gall** /gɔːl/ *n* [U] **1** *old use* a bitter liquid formed by the LIVER **2 a** a feeling of bitterness or hatred **b** rudeness; bad manners: *They* **had the gall to** *call me fat!*

**gal·lant** /'gælənt/ *adj* **1** courageous: *a gallant deed/soldier* **2** *lit* (of men) attentive and polite to women **–gallantly** *adv* **–gallantry** *n* [U]

**gal·le·on** /'gælıən/ *n* a large sailing ship, formerly used esp. by the Spaniards

**gal·le·ry** /'gæləri/ *n* **-ries 1** a room, hall, or building where works of art are shown and sometimes offered for sale: *an art gallery* **2** an upper floor built out from an inner wall of a hall, from which activities in the hall may be watched **3** a long narrow room, such as one used for shooting practice **4** a level underground passage in a mine **5** the highest upper floor in a theatre

**gal·ley** /'gæli/ *n* **-leys 1** (in former times) a ship which was rowed by slaves, esp. an ancient Greek or Roman warship **2** a ship's kitchen

**gal·li·vant** /'gæl$\frac{1}{2}$vænt/ *v* [I *about*] *infml & derog* to go around amusing oneself; GAD ABOUT: *to go gallivanting about town*

**gal·lon** /'gælən/ *n* (a measure for liquids equal to) 8 PINTS or 4 QUARTS (in Britain 4·54, in America 3·78 LITRES)

**gal·lop**[1] /'gæləp/ *n* **1** [S] the movement of a horse at its fastest speed **2** [C] a ride at this speed: *a long gallop before breakfast*

**gallop**[2] *v* [I *off, away*] (of a horse, or a person riding a horse) to go at the fastest speed

**gal·lows** /'gæləuz/ *n* **gallows** the wooden frame on which murderers used to be killed by hanging from a rope

**Gal·lup poll** /'gæləp pəul/ *n tdmk* a special count of opinions in a country by questioning a number of people chosen by chance (=a POLL[1] (2)), esp. so as to guess the result of a coming election

**ga·lore** /gə'lɔːʳ/ *adj* [after *n*] *apprec* (in) plenty: *money galore|friends galore*

**ga·losh** /gə'lɒʃ‖gə'lɑʃ/ *n* [*usu. pl.*] a rubber shoe worn over an ordinary shoe when it rains or snows –see PAIR[1] (USAGE)

**gal·va·nize**‖also **-nise** *BrE* /'gælvənaız/ *v* **-nized, -nizing** [T] **1** to put a covering of metal, esp. ZINC, over (a sheet of another metal, esp. iron), by using electricity: *galvanized iron* **2** to shock (someone) into action: *The fear of losing his life galvanized him (into fighting back).*

**gam·bit** /'gæmb$\frac{1}{2}$t/ *n* an action made to produce an advantage in the future, esp. an opening move in a game, an argument, or a conversation –compare PLOY

**gam·ble**[1] /'gæmbəl/ *v* **-bled, -bling** [I] to risk one's money on horse races, in (card) games, business, etc.: *to spend the night gambling*|(fig.) *I escaped from the prison at night, gambling on the fact that* (=hoping that) *I wouldn't be seen because of the darkness.* **–gambler** *n*

**gamble** sthg.↔ **away** *v adv* [T] to lose (money) by gambling (GAMBLE[1]): *He's gambled away all his money.*

**gamble**[2] *n* [S] a risky matter or act: *The operation may not succeed; it's a gamble.*

**gam·bol** /'gæmbəl/ *v* [I *about*] **-ll-** *BrE*‖**-l-** *AmE* to jump about in play, as esp. lambs do **–gambol** *n*

**game**[1] /geım/ *n* **1** [C] a form of play or sport, or one example or type of this: *Football is a game which doesn't interest me.*|*Let's have a game of cards.* –see also GAMES; see RECREATION (USAGE) **2** [C] a single part of a set into which a match is divided, as in tennis, BRIDGE[3], etc. **3** [U] wild animals, some birds, and some fish, which are hunted for food and as a sport: *a game bird*|*game laws*|*Lions and elephants are called* **big game** *when they are hunted.* **4** [C] a trick or secret plan: *What's your little game, then?*|*Try not to* **give the game away**. (=let it be known)

**game**[2] *adj* [+*to- v*/*for*] brave and ready (for action): *Even though he's old he's game for anything.* **–gamely** *adv*

**game·keep·er** /'geım,kiːpəʳ/ *n* a man employed to raise and protect GAME[1] (3), esp. birds, on private land

**games** /geımz/ *n* **games 1** [U] *BrE* a school subject, including the playing of team games and other forms of bodily exercise out of doors **2** [*the* C +*sing.*/*pl. v*] (in names) a particular set of games and sports competitions: *The* OLYMPIC GAMES *is/are held every four years.*

**gam·mon** /'gæmən/ *n* [U] *esp. BrE* the meat from a pig (HAM), when it has been preserved by smoke or salt

**gam·ut** /'gæmət/ *n* [*the* S] the whole range of a subject: *He's* **run the whole gamut of** (=experienced all of) *human experience.*

**gan·der** /'gændəʳ/ *n* a male GOOSE

**gang**[1] /gæŋ/ *n* [C +*sing.*/*pl.v*] **1** a group of people working together, esp. criminals, prisoners, or building workers: *The gang were/was planning a robbery.* **2** a group of friends: *Have you seen any of the gang lately?*

**gang**[2] *v* → GANG UP

**gang·ling** /'gæŋglıŋ/ *adj* unusually tall and thin, so as to appear awkward in movement

**gang·plank** /'gæŋplæŋk/ *n* a board of wood which is used to make a bridge to get on or off a ship

**gan·grene** /'gæŋgriːn/ *n* [U] the decay of the flesh of part of the body because blood has stopped flowing there **–gangrenous** /-grınəs/ *adj*

**gang·ster** /'gæŋstəʳ/ *n* (esp. in modern times) a member of a group (GANG) of (armed) criminals

**gang up** *v adv* [I *on, against*] *derog* to work together as a close group (against someone): *You've all ganged up on/against me!*

**gang·way** /'gæŋweı/ *n* **1** an opening in the side of a ship and the movable board (GANGPLANK) which is used to make a bridge from it to the land **2** *BrE* a clear space between two rows of seats in a cinema, theatre, bus, or train; AISLE

**gan·try** /'gæntri/ *n* **-tries** a metal frame which is used to support movable heavy machinery or railway signals

**gaol** /dʒeıl/ *n,v BrE* for JAIL

**gaol·er** /'dʒeıləʳ/ *n BrE* for JAILER

**gap** /gæp/ *n* an empty space between two objects or two parts of an object: *The gate was locked but we went through a gap in the fence.*|(fig.) *There are wide gaps in my knowledge of history.*|(fig.) *I* **bridged a gap** (=filled an empty moment) *in the conversation by telling a joke.*

**gape** /geıp/ *v* **gaped, gaping** [I] **1** [*at*] to look hard in surprise, esp. with the mouth open: *She gaped at the* *tall man, not believing that he was her younger brother.* –compare GAWP **2** to be or come apart or wide open: *a gaping hole/wound*

**gar·age¹** /'gærɑːʒ, -ɪdʒ‖gə'rɑʒ/ *n* **1** a building in which motor vehicles can be kept –see picture on page 297 **2** a place where (petrol can be bought and) cars can be repaired

**garage²** *v* **-aged, -aging** [T] to put in a garage

**gar·bage** /'gɑːbɪdʒ‖'gɑr-/ *n esp. AmE* **1** waste material; RUBBISH: *The street is covered with old tins and other forms of garbage.* **2** *derog* stupid and worthless ideas, words, etc.

**garbage can** /'·· ·/ *n AmE* for DUSTBIN

**gar·bled** /'gɑːbəld‖'gɑr-/ *adj* (of a statement) confused; giving a false idea of the facts: *The nervous man gave a garbled account of the accident.*

**gar·den¹** /'gɑːdn‖'gɑr-/ *n* **1** a piece of land, usu. near a house, on which flowers and vegetables may be grown **2** [*often pl.*] a public park with flowers, grass, paths, and seats **3 lead (someone) up the garden path** to trick (someone) into believing what is not true and acting on it

**garden²** *v* [I] to work in a garden, making plants grow –**gardener** *n* –**gardening** *n* [U]

**gar·gan·tu·an** /gɑː'gæntʃuən‖gɑr-/ *adj* (usu. in connection with food) very big: *a gargantuan meal*/APPETITE

**gar·gle** /'gɑːgəl‖'gɑr-/ *v* **-gled, -gling** [I] to wash the throat with liquid by blowing through it at the back of the mouth –**gargle** *n* [S]

**gar·goyle** /'gɑːgɔɪl‖'gɑr-/ *n* a hollow figure of a person or animal esp. on the roof of a church, through whose mouth rainwater is carried away

**gar·ish** /'geərɪʃ/ *adj* unpleasantly bright: *garish colours|garish light* –**garishly** *adv* –**garishness** *n* [U]

**gar·land** /'gɑːlənd‖'gɑr-/ *n* a circle of flowers, leaves, or both, esp. to be placed round the neck for decoration or as a sign of victory –compare WREATH –**garland** *v* [T]: *garlanded with flowers*

**gar·lic** /'gɑːlɪk‖'gɑr-/ *n* [U] a plant rather like an onion, which is used in cooking to give a strong taste

**gar·ment** /'gɑːmənt‖'gɑr-/ *n fml* (the name used, esp. by the makers, for) an article of clothing: *This garment should be washed carefully.*

**gar·net** /'gɑːnɨt‖'gɑr-/ *n* a type of red jewel

**gar·nish¹** /'gɑːnɪʃ‖'gɑr-/ *v* [T] to add something to (esp. food) as a decoration –see DECORATE (USAGE)

**garnish²** *n* pieces of fruit, vegetable, or any of the things which are used to make food look better

**gar·ret** /'gærɨt/ *n esp.lit* a usu. small unpleasant room at the top of a house; ATTIC

**gar·ri·son¹** /'gærɨsən/ *n* [C +*sing./pl.v*] a group of soldiers living in a town or fort and defending it

**garrison²** *v* [T] (to send soldiers) to guard (something) in a GARRISON: *The government will garrison the coastal towns.*

**gar·ru·lous** /'gærələs/ *adj fml* habitually talking too much –**garrulously** *adv* –**garrulity** /gə'ruːlɨti/ also **garrulousness** *n* [U]

**gar·ter** /'gɑːtə^r‖'gɑr-/ *n* a band of elastic material worn round the leg to keep a stocking up

**gas¹** /gæs/ *n* **1** [C;U] (a type of) substance like air, which is not solid or liquid: *There are several kinds of gas in the air.* **2** [U] a substance of this type which is burnt in the home for heating and cooking **3** [U] *AmE infml* for GASOLINE; petrol

**gas²** *v* **-ss- 1** [T] to poison with gas **2** [I *about*] *infml* to talk a long time about unimportant things

**gas cham·ber** /'· ˌ··/ *n* a room which can be filled with gas so that animals or people may be put to death

**gas·e·ous** /'gæsiəs, 'geɪ-/ *adj* of or like gas

**gash** /gæʃ/ *v* [T] to make a deep cut in –**gash** *n*

**gas·ket** /'gæskɨt/ *n* a flat piece of soft material which is placed between two surfaces so that steam, oil, gas, etc., cannot escape

**gas mask** /'· ·/ *n* a breathing apparatus worn over the face to protect the wearer against poisonous gases

**gas·o·line, -lene** /'gæsəliːn/ also **gas** *infml*– *n* [U] *AmE* for PETROL

**gas·o·me·ter** /gæ'sɒmɨtə^r‖-'sɑ-/ *n BrE infml* a very large round metal container in which gas is stored

**gasp** /gɑːsp‖gæsp/ *v* [I] **1** to breathe quickly, esp. with difficulty, making a sudden noise: *I came out of the water and gasped for breath.* **2** to catch the breath suddenly, esp. because of surprise, shock, etc.: *I gasped with/in surprise at the unexpected news.* –**gasp** *n: He gave a gasp of surprise.*

**gas sta·tion** /'· ˌ··/ *n AmE* for FILLING STATION

**gas·sy** /'gæsi/ *adj* **-sier, -siest** full of (a) gas: *a gassy drink*

**gas·tric** /'gæstrɪk/ *adj* [A] *tech* of or belonging to the stomach: *the gastric juices* (=acids which break down food in the stomach)

**gas·tro·en·te·ri·tis** /ˌgæstrəʊentə'raɪtɨs/ *n* [U] an illness in which the food passages, including the stomach and INTESTINES, are swollen

**gas·tron·o·my** /gæ'strɒnəmi‖gæ'strɑ-/ *n* [U] the art and science of cooking and eating good food –**gastronomic** /ˌgæstrə'nɒmɪk‖-'nɑ-/ *adj* –**gastronomically** *adv*

**gas·works** /'gæswɜːks‖-ɜr-/ *n* **gasworks** a place where gas for use in the home is made from coal

**gate** /geɪt/ *n* **1** a movable frame, often with bars across it, which closes an opening in a fence, wall, etc.: *the garden gate|park gates|*LEVEL CROSSING *gates* –see picture on page 297 **2**→ GATEWAY **3** (the money paid by) the number of people who go in to see a sports event, esp. a football match –sounds like **gait**

**gâ·teau** /'gætəʊ‖gɑ'təʊ/ *n* **-teaux** /təʊz/ [C;U] *BrE* a specially attractive type of large cream cake

**gate·crash** /'geɪtkræʃ/ *v* [I;T] to go to (a party) without having been invited –**gatecrasher** *n*

**gate·post** /'geɪtpəʊst/ *n* a post beside a gate, from which the gate is hung or to which it fastens

**gate·way** /'geɪt-weɪ/ *n* an opening in a fence, wall, etc., across which a gate may be put: (fig.) *Passing examinations is the gateway to* (=the way of finding) *success.*

**gath·er** /'gæðə^r/ *v* **1** [I;T *round*] to (cause to) come together: *Gather round, and I'll tell you a story.|A crowd gathered to see what had happened.* **2** [T] to obtain (information or qualities) bit by bit: *As we came onto the open road we gathered speed.* **3** [T *in, up*] to collect or pick (flowers, crops, etc.): *Gather your toys up.* **4** [T +(*that*)] to understand from something said or done: *I gather she's ill, and that's why* *she hasn't come.* **5** [T] to draw (material) into small folds *a gathered skirt* (=at the waist)

**gath·er·ing** /ˈgæðərɪŋ/ *n* a meeting

**gauche** /gəʊʃ/ *adj* awkward (in social behaviour); doing and saying the wrong things

**gau·dy** /ˈgɔːdi/ *adj* **-dier, -diest** too bright in colour and/or with too much decoration **–gaudily** *adv* **–gaudiness** *n* [U]

**gauge**[1] ||also **gage** *AmE* /geɪdʒ/ *n* **1** an instrument for measuring size, amount, etc., such as the width of wire, the amount of rain falling, etc. **2** a standard measure of weight, size, etc., to which objects can be compared

**gauge**[2] ||also **gage** *AmE v* **gauged, gauging** [T] **1** to measure by means of a GAUGE **2** to judge the worth, meaning, etc., of (something or somebody's actions)

**gaunt** /gɔːnt/ *adj* thin, as if ill or hungry –compare HAGGARD **–gauntness** *n* [U]

**gaunt·let** /ˈgɔːntlɨt/ *n* **1** a long GLOVE covering the hand and wrist, which protects the hand (in certain sports, in industry, or formerly in battle) **2 run the gauntlet** to suffer or experience attack, blame, danger, etc.

**gauze** /gɔːz/ *n* [U] net-like material, sometimes used in medicine to cover wounds, or as a curtain: *cotton gauze*

**gave** /geɪv/ *v past tense of* GIVE

**gaw·ky** /ˈgɔːki/ *adj* **-kier, -kiest** (of a person) awkward in movement **–gawkiness** *n* [U]

**gawp** /gɔːp/ *v* [I *at*] *BrE* to look at something in a foolish way –compare GAPE (1)

**gay** /geɪ/ *adj* **1** cheerful; happy: *We were all gay at the thought of the coming holidays.* **2** bright or attractive: *We're painting the kitchen in gay colours.* **3** *infml* for HOMOSEXUAL

**gay·ness** /ˈgeɪnɨs/ *n* [U] **1** *infml* for HOMOSEXUALity **2** → GAIETY

**gaze**[1] /geɪz/ *v* **gazed, gazing** [I *at*] to look steadily for a long or short period of time: *He sat gazing out of the window.*

**gaze**[2] *n* [S] a steady fixed look: *She turned her gaze from one person to the other.*

**ga·zelle** /gəˈzel/ *n* **-zelles** *or* **zelle** a type of animal (ANTELOPE) like a small deer, which jumps in graceful movements

**ga·zette** /gəˈzet/ *n* an official newspaper esp. one from the government, giving important notices, etc.

**ga·zump** /gəˈzʌmp/ *v* [I;T] *BrE infml* (of the owner of a house) to refuse to sell a house to (someone who thinks he has bought it) and sell instead to someone who has offered more money

**GB** *abbrev. for:* Great Britain

**GCE** *abbrev. for:* (in Britain) General Certificate of Education; an examination in one of many subjects, taken in schools by pupils aged 15 or over: *She's sitting/taking her GCEs next week.* –compare CSE

**gear** /gɪəʳ/ *n* **1** [C;U] an arrangement, esp. of toothed wheels in a machine, which allows power to be passed from one part to another, esp. from the engine of a car to its wheels: *She* **changed gear** *to make the car go up the hill faster.*|*"The car isn't moving!" "That's because you're not* **in gear.**" **2** [C] an apparatus or part of a machine which has a special use in controlling a vehicle: *the landing gear of an aircraft*|STEERing *gear* **3** [U] a set of things collected together, esp. for a particular purpose: *climbing gear*

**gear·box** /ˈgɪəbɒks||ˈgɪərbɑks/ *n* a metal case containing the GEARS (1) of a vehicle

**gear le·ver** /ˈ· ˌ··/ also **gear stick** /ˈ· ˌ·/ *BrE*||**gear shift** also **stick shift** /ˈ· ·/ *AmE– n* the apparatus which controls the GEARS (1) of a vehicle –see picture on page 85

**gear** sthg. **to** sthg. *v prep* [T] to cause (one thing) to depend on or be fixed in relation to (another): *Education should be geared to the children's needs and abilities.*

**geese** /giːs/ *n pl. of* GOOSE

**gei·sha** /ˈgeɪʃə/ also **geisha girl** /ˈ·ˈ· ·/– *n* a Japanese girl who is trained to dance, sing, and perform various arts to amuse men

**gel** /dʒel/ *v* **-ll-** [I] → JELL

**gel·a·tine** /ˈdʒelətiːn||-tn/ ||also **gelatin** *AmE* /ˈdʒelətɨn/– *n* [U] a clear substance from boiled animal bones, used for making jellies

**ge·lat·i·nous** /dʒɨˈlætɨnəs/ *adj tech* like jelly; in a state between solid and liquid

**gel·ig·nite** /ˈdʒelɪgnaɪt/ *n* [U] a very powerful explosive

**gem** /dʒem/ *n* **1** a jewel; precious stone, esp. when cut into a regular shape **2** a thing or person of special value

**Gem·i·ni** /ˈdʒemɨnaɪ||-ni/ *n* see ZODIAC

**gen** /dʒen/ *n* [U *on*] *BrE infml* the correct or complete information: *He gave me all the gen on the new office arrangements.* –see also GENNED-UP

**gen·der** /ˈdʒendəʳ/ *n tech* **1** [U] (in grammar) the state of being MASCULINE, FEMININE, or NEUTER **2** [C] any of these states: *German has three genders.*

**gene** /dʒiːn/ *n* a single part of the material at the centre (NUCLEUS) of a cell, which controls the development of qualities in a living thing which have been passed on (INHERITed) from its parents

**ge·ne·al·o·gy** /ˌdʒiːniˈælədʒi/ *n* **-gies** [C;U] (the study of) the history of the members of a family, often shown in a drawing with lines and names spreading like the branches of a tree **–genealogist** *n* **–genealogical** /ˌdʒiːnɪəˈlɒdʒɪkəl||-ˈlɑ-/ *adj*

**gen·e·ral**[1] /ˈdʒenərəl/ *adj* **1** [A] concerning or felt by everybody or most people: *the general public* (=the mass of ordinary people)|*The general feeling is* (=most people feel) *that it's wrong.*|*Worry about high food prices is now fairly general.*|*It's not* **in the general interest** *to close railways.* (=it's not good for most people) **2** not limited to one thing, place, etc.: *a general university degree* (=in several subjects)|*general education* (=in many subjects) **3** not detailed; describing the main things only: *Give me a general idea of the work.* **4** [after *n*] *(as the second part of an official title)* chief: *Postmaster-General*

**general**[2] *n* [A;C] **1** an officer of very high rank in an army or air force **2 in general: a** also **as a general rule** usually; in most cases: *In general, people like her.* **b** *(after a pl. noun)* most: *People in general like her.* –compare GENERALLY

**general e·lec·tion** /ˌ··· ·ˈ··/ *n BrE* an election in which all the voters in the country choose the Members of Parliament

**gen·e·ral·i·ty** /ˌdʒenəˈrælɨti/ *n* **-ties** **1** [U] the quality of being general **2** [C] a general statement; point for consideration which is not at all detailed: *The President's speech was full of generalities.*

**gen·e·ral·i·za·tion** ||also **-isation** *BrE* /ˌdʒenərəl aɪˈzeɪʃən||-lə-/ *n* [C;U] (the act of making) a general statement, principle, or opinion resulting from the consideration of particular facts

**gen·e·ral·ize** ||also **-ise** *BrE* /ˈdʒenərəlaɪz/ *v* **-ized, -izing** [I] **1** to make a general statement (about): *Our history teacher is always generalizing; he never deals with anything in detail.* **2** to form a general principle, opinion, etc., after considering only a small number of the facts: *Is it fair to generalize from these two accidents and say that all young people are bad drivers?*

**gen·er·al·ly** /ˈdʒenərəli/ *adv* **1** usually: *We generally go to the sea for our holidays.* **2** by most people: *The plan has been generally accepted.* **3** without considering details, but only the main points

**general prac·ti·tion·er** /ˌ··· ·ˈ···/ also **GP**– *n* a doctor who is trained in general medicine and whose work (**general practice** /ˌ··· ˈ··/) is to treat people in a certain local area

**gen·e·rate** /ˈdʒenəreɪt/ *v* **-rated, -rating** [T] *tech* to produce (esp. heat or electricity): *Our electricity comes from a new generating station.*|(fig.) *The teacher's remark generated loud laughter.*

**gen·e·ra·tion** /ˌdʒenəˈreɪʃən/ *n* **1** [C] a single stage in the development of a family, or the average period of time (about 30 years) between each stage: *a family photograph showing three generations* (=myself, my parents, and my grandparents) **2** [C] all people of about the same age: *the younger generation* (=young people in general)|*Most people of my father's generation have experienced war.* **3** [U] the act or action of generating (GENERATE): *Falling water may be used for the generation of electricity.*

**gen·e·ra·tor** /ˈdʒenəreɪtəʳ/ *n* a machine which GENERATES, usu. electricity

**ge·ner·ic** /dʒ½ˈnerɪk/ *adj* **1** of or concerning a GENUS **2** shared by or typical of a whole class of things

**gen·e·rous** /ˈdʒenərəs/ *adj* **1** showing readiness to give money, help, kindness, etc.: *It was very generous of you to lend me your car yesterday.* –compare MEAN[1] (1) **2** larger, kinder, etc., than usual: *a generous meal*|*a generous gift* **–generously** *adv* **–generosity** /dʒenəˈrɒs½ti||-ˈrɑ-/ *n* **-ties** [C;U]

**Gen·e·sis** /ˈdʒen½s½s/ *n* the first book of the Bible, which tells the story of the beginning of the world

**ge·net·ic** /dʒ½ˈnetɪk/ *adj* of or concerning GENES or GENETICS **–genetically** *adv*

**ge·net·ics** /dʒ½ˈnetɪks/ *n* [U] the study of how living things develop according to the effects of those substances passed on in the cells from the parents –see also GENE, HEREDITY

**ge·ni·al** /ˈdʒiːnɪəl/ *adj* kind; pleasant: *a genial person*|*genial weather* **–genially** *adv* **–geniality** /ˌdʒiː niˈæl½ti/ *n* [U]

**ge·nie** /ˈdʒiːni/ *n* **-nies** *or* **-nii** /niaɪ/ a magical spirit in arab fairy stories

**gen·i·tals** /ˈdʒen½tlz/ also **genitalia** /-ˈteɪlɪə/ *fml*– *n* [P] the outer sex organs –see picture on page 299 **–genital** *adj* [A]

**gen·i·tive** /ˈdʒen½tɪv/ *adj,n tech* (in grammar) (a form or a word) showing esp. possession or origin

**ge·ni·us** /ˈdʒiːnɪəs/ *n* **1** [C;U] (a person of) very great ability: *Her latest book is a work of genius.* **2** [S *for*] a special ability: *She has a genius for music.*

USAGE **Genius** is a very strong word, and is only used of a rare ability or the person who has it: *Einstein had* **genius**/*was a* **genius. Talent** also means a special ability (though not the person who has it), but it is not as strong a word as **genius**: *a young actress with a lot of* **talent**|*She has a* **talent** *for music.*|*He is a* **talented** *footballer.* Both **talent** and **genius** are used of powers which a person is born with, but **skill**, which means the ability to do something well, is something that can be learnt: *The minister answered his opponents' questions with great* **skill.**|*a* **skilled** *electrician.* You may be born with a **capacity** or **aptitude** for (doing) something, and this means that you will easily develop **skill** if you are taught: *The child shows a great* **capacity/aptitude** *for learning languages.* **Competence** is a satisfactory but not unusual degree of **skill**: *a test of one's* **competence** *as a driver*/*John's a* **competent** *teacher.*

**genned-up** /ˌ· ˈ·◂/ *adj* [F] *BrE infml* well- informed: *genned-up on/about foreign affairs* –see also GEN

**gen·o·cide** /ˈdʒenəsaɪd/ *n* [U] the act of killing a whole group of people, esp. a whole race

**gen·teel** /dʒenˈtiːl/ *adj* trying to show (unnaturally) polite manners **–genteelly** *adv* **–gentility** /-ˈtɪl½ti/ *n* [U]

**gen·tile** /ˈdʒentaɪl/ *adj,n* [*sometimes cap.*] (a person who is) not Jewish

**gen·tle** /ˈdʒentl/ *adj* not rough or violent in manner or movement; kind; soft: *Be gentle when you brush the baby's hair.*|*a gentle wind*|*a gentle slope* (=not steep) **–gentleness** *n* [U] **–gently** *adv*

**gen·tle·man** /ˈdʒentlmən/ *n* **-men** /mən/ **1** a man who behaves well towards others and who can always be trusted to act honourably **2** *polite* a man –compare LADY

USAGE **Gentlemen** and **lady** are polite and rather old-fashioned words for **man** and **woman**. They are used esp. when speaking about someone in their presence, or when addressing a gathering of people: *Mr Smith, there's a* **gentleman/lady** *here to see you–shall I send him/her in?*|**Ladies** and **gentlemen,** *I'd like to introduce our speaker for tonight.....* Otherwise, **man** and **woman** are the usual words: *Is the director a* **man** *or a* **woman**?|*the first* **woman** *prime minister.* **Man** is also used to mean human beings (men and women) in general: **Man** *is the only animal to use tools.*

**gen·try** /ˈdʒentri/ *n* [*the* P] people of high social class

**Gents, Gents'** /dʒents/ *BrE*|| **men's room** *AmE*– *n* **Gents(')** *infml* a public LAVATORY for men –compare LADIES

**gen·u·ine** /ˈdʒenjʊ½n/ *adj* **1** (of an object) real; really what it seems to be: *a football made of genuine* (=not ARTIFICIAL) *leather* –compare FAKE[3] **2** (of people or feelings) sincere; real, not pretended **–genuinely** *adv* **–genuineness** *n* [U]

**ge·nus** /ˈdʒiːnəs/ *n* **genera** /ˈdʒenərə/ *tech* a division of a FAMILY (4) of living things, which usu. includes several closely related SPECIES (=kinds of animal or plant) –see also GENERIC

**ge·og·ra·phy** /dʒi'ɒgrəfi, 'dʒɒgrəfi‖dʒi'ɑg-/ *n* [U] the study of the countries of the world and of the seas, rivers, towns, etc., on the earth's surface **–geographer** *n* **–geographical** /ˌdʒɪə'græfɪkəl/ *adj* **–geographically** *adv*

**ge·ol·o·gy** /dʒi'ɒlədʒi‖-'ɑlə-/ *n* [U] the study of the materials (rocks, soil, etc.) which make up the earth, and their changes in the history of the world **–geologist** /dʒi'ɒlədʒəst‖-'ɑl-/ *n* **–geological** /ˌdʒɪə'lɒdʒɪkəl‖-'lɑ-/ *adj* **–geologically** *adv*

**ge·om·e·try** /dʒɪ'ɒmətri‖-'ɑm-/ *n* [U] the study in MATHEMATICS of the angles and shapes formed by the relationships of lines, surfaces, and solids in space **–geometric** /ˌdʒɪə'metrɪk/ *adj: geometric patterns* (=of straight lines and regular shapes) *in Muslim art*

**ge·ra·ni·um** /dʒə'reɪnɪəm/ *n* a garden or pot plant with red or white flowers and rounded leaves

**ge·ri·at·rics** /ˌdʒeri'ætrɪks/ *n* [U] the medical treatment and care of old people **–geriatric** *adj* [A]

**germ** /dʒɜːm‖dʒɜrm/ *n* **1** a very small living thing which cannot be seen but may live on food or dirt or in the body, so causing disease –compare BACTERIA, MICROBE **2** a beginning point, esp. of an idea (esp. in the phrase **the germ of**)

**Ger·man mea·sles** /ˌ·· '··/ *n* [U] an infectious disease in which red spots appear on the body for a short time

**ger·mi·nate** /'dʒɜːməneɪt‖'dʒɜr-/ *v* **-nated, -nating** [I;T] **1** (of a seed) to start growing **2** to cause (a seed) to start growing **–germination** /-'neɪʃən/ *n* [U]

**germ war·fare** /ˌ· '··/ *n* [U] → BIOLOGICAL WARFARE

**ger·und** /'dʒerənd/ *n* → VERBAL NOUN

**ges·ta·tion** /dʒe'steɪʃən/ *n* [S;U] the carrying of a child or young animal inside the mother's body before birth

**ges·tic·u·late** /dʒe'stɪkjʊleɪt‖-kjə-/ *v* **-lated, -lating** [I] to make movements of the hands and arms to express something, esp. while speaking **–gesticulation** /dʒeˌstɪkjʊ'leɪʃən‖-kjə-/ *n* [C;U]

**ges·ture**[1] /'dʒestʃər/ *n* **1** [C;U] movement, usu. of the hands, to express a certain meaning: *He made an angry gesture.* **2** [C] an action which is done to show one's feelings: *We invited our new neighbours to dinner as a gesture of friendship.*

**gesture**[2] *v* **-tured, -turing** [I] to make a GESTURE[1] (1)

**get** /get/ *v* **got** /gɒt‖gɑt/, **got** *esp. BrE*‖**gotten** /'gɒtn‖'gɑtn/ *AmE*, **getting 1** [T] to receive or obtain: *I got a letter today.*|*He got three years in prison.*|*I'll get you* (=for you) *that book you wanted.*|*Can you get* (=hear) *London on your radio?* **2** to become: *The food's getting cold.*|*She must have got lost.* **3** [I] to go or arrive: *We got home very late.*|*Where has my hat* **got to**?|*At last we're really* **getting somewhere**. (=arriving at success) **4** [T] to put into a place or state: *I'll get the car started.*|*We couldn't get the table through the door.* **5** [T] to cause to do: *I got him to help me when I moved the furniture.* **6** [T +*to-v*] to succeed in or be allowed: *He's very nice when you get to know him.*|*I never get to drive the car.* **7** [T] to prepare (a meal): *I'm just getting the dinner.* **8** [T] to catch (an illness): *He got a rare tropical disease.* **9** [T] *infml* to understand: *He didn't get the joke.*|*Do you get me/get what I mean?* **10** [T] *infml* to annoy: *His stupid remarks really get me.* **11** [T] *infml* to hit: *One of the stones got him in the eye.* **12 get something done**: **a** to cause something to be done: *I must get my shoes mended.* **b** to experience something that happens to one: *I got my hand caught in the door.* **13 have got** see HAVE[2]

USAGE In formal writing it is better to avoid **get**, and to use **become, receive, obtain, move**, etc., according to the meaning.

**get about/around** *v adv* [I] **1** to be able to move again after an illness **2** *infml* to travel: *She gets about quite a lot, working for an international company.* **3** also **get round**– (of news, etc.) to spread

**get across/over** *v adv* [I;T (=**get** sthg. **across**)] to (cause to) be understood (esp. by a large group): *Our teacher is clever, but not very good at getting his ideas across.* –compare GET **through**[1] (2)

**get ahead** *v adv* [I *of*] to advance (beyond someone or something): *You have to get ahead of your competitors.* –compare FALL **behind**

**get along** *v adv* [I] **1** (of people) to move away; leave: *I must be getting along now.* **2** also **get on**– (of people and activities) to advance; go well: *How is your work getting along?* **3** to continue (often in spite of difficulties): *We can get along without your help.* **4** [*with*] also **get on**– (of people) to have a friendly relationship (with another or each other): *Do you get along well with your aunt?*

**get around** *v adv* [I] → GET **about**

**get around/round to** sthg. *v adv prep* [T +*v-ing*] to find time, or have the time, for: *After a long delay, he got around to writing the letter.*

**get at** sbdy./sthg. *v prep* [T] **1** [*pass. rare*] to reach: *Put the food where the cat can't get at it.*|(fig.) *to get at the truth* **2** [*no pass.*] (*in tenses with the* -ing *form*) to mean: *What are you getting at?* **3** *infml* (*esp. in tenses with the* -ing *form*) to say unkind things esp. repeatedly to: *Stop getting at me!*

**get away** *v adv* [I] to escape, e.g. from the scene of a crime: *The thieves got away (with all our money).*|*I'm sorry I'm late; I was in a meeting and couldn't get away.*|(fig.) *You* **can't get away from** (=you must admit) *the fact that. . .* –see also GETAWAY

**get away with** sthg. *v adv prep* [T +*v-ing*] to do (something bad) and escape punishment: *How did he get away with cheating?*|*You'll never get away with it.*

**get back** *v adv* [I] **1** to return, esp. to one's home: *I heard you were away. When did you get back?* **2** to return to power after having lost it: *Will the Labour Party get back at the next election?* **3** [*to*] *infml* to speak or write to a person at a later time, esp. in order to give a decision or information: *I can't answer your question now, but I'll definitely get back to you tomorrow.* **4 get back at someone** also **get one's own back on someone**– *infml* to punish someone in return for a wrong done to oneself: *I'll get back at him one day!*

**get behind** *v adv* [I] → FALL[1] **behind**

**get by** *v adv* [I] **1** to continue one's way of life: *She can't get by on so little money.* **2** to be good enough but not very good: *Your work will get by, but try to improve it.*

**get down** *v adv* [T] **1** (**get** sthg.↔ **down**) to swallow with difficulty: *Try to get the medicine down.* **2** (**get**

sthg.↔ **down**) to record in writing: *Get down every word she says.* **3** (**get** sbdy. **down**) to make feel nervous, ill, or sad: *This continual wet weather is getting me down.*

**get down to** sthg. *v adv prep* [T +*v-ing*] to begin to give serious attention to: *to get down to work/business*

**get in**[1] *v adv* **1** [I] to arrive (inside a place): *The plane got in late.* **2** [I] → COME **in** (4) **3** [T] (**get** sbdy. **in**) to call (someone) to one's help, esp. in the house: *Get the doctor in.* **4** [T] (**get** sthg. **in**) to say (something), esp. by interrupting a conversation: *May I get a word in?* **5** [I *at, on*] to take part in (something): *to get in at the start*

**get in**[2] (sthg.) *v adv; prep* [I;T] to enter (a vehicle): *They got in and drove off.* –compare GET **on**[2], GET **out**

**get into** *v prep* [T] **1** (**get into** sthg.) → GET **in**[2]: *They got into the car and drove off.* **2** (**get** (sbdy.) **into** sthg.) to put (oneself or someone else) into (a bad condition): *I've got (myself) into trouble/into the habit of smoking.|I'm sorry I got you into trouble with the teacher.* **3** [*no pass.*] (**get into** sthg.) to learn or become accustomed to: *I'll soon get into the way of things.* –compare GET **out of**

**get off**[1] sthg. *v adv; prep* [I;T] **1** to leave (work): *When do you get off (work)?* **2** to leave **a** a public vehicle: *Get off (the bus) at the hospital.* **b** a bicycle, horse, etc.; DISMOUNT (from) –compare GET **on**[2]

**get off**[2] *v adv* [I;T (=**get** sbdy. **off**) *with*] to (cause to) escape punishment: *The two boys got off with only a warning, but the judge sent the man to prison.*

**get off with** sbdy. *v adv prep* [T] *BrE infml* to start a relationship with (someone of the other sex): *She got off with him at the party.*

**get on**[1] *v adv* [I] **1** → GET **along** (2, 4) **2** (*in tenses with the -ing form*) to become later or older: *Time is getting on.* **3** [*with*] to continue, often after interruption: *Get on with your work!* **4** [*in*] to succeed: *All he ever thought about was getting on (in his job).*

**get on**[2] (sthg.) *v adv; prep* [I;T *to*] **1** to seat oneself on (a bicycle, horse, etc.) **2** to enter (a public vehicle): *They got on (the plane) at Cairo.* –compare GET **off**[1] (2), GET **in**[2]

**get on for** sthg. *v adv prep* [T] *BrE* to be almost reaching, in time, age, or distance: *It's getting on for 8 o'clock, we'll have to hurry!*

**get onto** sbdy./sthg. *v prep* [T *no pass.*] **1** to speak or write to; CONTACT[2]: *I'll get onto the director and see if he can help.* **2** to find out about deceit by (someone): *He tricked people for years until the police got onto him.* **3** to begin to talk about or work at: *How did we get onto that subject?* **4** → GET **on**[2] –compare GET **in**[2]

**get out** *v adv* **1** [I;T (=**get** sbdy. **out**) *of*] to (cause to) escape: *Several men got out (of prison) yesterday.* **2** [T] (**get** sthg.↔ **out**) to produce: *We hope to get the report out before the end of the month.* **3** [I] → LEAK[1] **out**: *How did the story get out?*

**get out of** *v adv prep* [T] **1** [+*v-ing*] (**get out of** sthg.) to escape responsibility for: *He tried to get out of helping me.* **2** [*no pass.*] (**get out of** sthg.) to be able to stop or leave: *to get out of a bad habit* –compare GET **into 3** (**get** sthg. **out of** sbdy.) to force from: *The police got the truth out of him.* **4** (**get** sthg. **out of** sthg.) to gain from: *I can't understand why people smoke. What do they get out of it?*

**get over**[1] *v adv* **1** [T *with*] (**get** sthg. **over**) to reach the end of (usu. something unpleasant): *You'll be glad to get your operation over (with).* **2** [I;T (=**get** sthg. **over**)] → GET **across**

**get over**[2] sthg. *v prep* [T] **1** to return to one's usual state of health, happiness, etc., after a bad experience of or with: *to get over an illness|She can't get over the death of her husband.* **2 I can't/couldn't get over** *infml* I am/was very much surprised at

**get round** sbdy./sthg. *v prep* [T] **1** to find a way to deal with (something) to one's advantage: *You can sometimes get round the tax laws.* **2** to persuade (someone) to accept one's own way of thinking: *Father doesn't want to let us go, but I know I can get round him.*

**get round to** sthg. *v adv prep* [T +*v-ing*] → GET **around to**

**get through**[1] *v adv* **1** [I *to*] to reach someone, esp. by telephone: *I tried to telephone you but I couldn't get through.* **2** [I;T (=**get** sthg. **through**) +*that/to*] to (cause to) be understood by (someone): *I can't get (it) through to him that he must rest.* –compare GET **across 3** [I *with*] to finish: *When you get through with your work, let's go out.*

**get through**[2] *v adv; prep* [I;T (=**get** (sbdy.) **through** sthg.)] to (cause to) come successfully to the end of: *to get through an examination*

**get together** *v adv* [I *with*] to have a meeting or party: *When can we get together?* –see also GET-TOGETHER

**get up** *v adv* **1** [I;T (=**get** sbdy. **up**)] to (cause to) rise from bed: *What time do you normally get up?* **2** [I] *BrE* (of a wind, fire, etc.) to arise and increase **3** [T] (**get up** sthg.) to increase the amount of: *get up steam/speed* –see also GETUP

**get up to** sthg. *v adv prep* [T] **1** to reach: *What page have you got up to?* **2** to do (esp. something bad): *The children are very quiet; I wonder what they're getting up to!*

**get·a·way** /ˈgetəweɪ/ *n* [A;S] *infml* an escape: *The thieves* **made a** *quick* **getaway**.|*a getaway car* –see also GET **away**

**get-to·geth·er** /ˈ· ·ˌ··/ *n* a friendly informal meeting for enjoyment: *"the old school get-together that you both went to"* (SEU W.) –see also GET **together**

**get·up** /ˈgetʌp/ *n infml* a set of clothes, esp. unusual clothes –see also GET **up**

**gey·ser** /ˈgiːzəʳ‖ˈgaɪzər/ *n v adv prep* **1** a natural spring of hot water which from time to time rises suddenly into the air from the earth **2** *BrE* an apparatus for heating water by gas, used in the home

**ghast·ly** /ˈgɑːstli‖ˈgæstli/ *adj* **-lier, -liest 1** causing great fear or shock **2** *infml* very bad: *We had a ghastly time at the party.* **3** (of a person) very pale and ill-looking

**gher·kin** /ˈgɜːkɨ̬n‖ˈgɜr-/ *n* a small green vegetable which is usually eaten after being PICKLEd in VINEGAR (=kept in a sour liquid); type of CUCUMBER

**ghet·to** /ˈgetəʊ/ *n* **-tos** a part of a city in which a group of people live who are poor and/or are not accepted as full citizens

**ghost** /gəʊst/ *n* **1** (the spirit of) a dead person who appears again: *Do you believe in ghosts?* (=that they exist) **2 to give up the ghost** to die **3 the ghost of a** the slightest: *the ghost of a chance*

**ghost·ly** /'gəustli/ *adj* **-lier, -liest** like a GHOST (1), esp. having a faint or uncertain colour and shape: *I saw a ghostly light ahead of me in the darkness.* **-ghostliness** *n* [U]

**ghost town** /'· ·/ *n* an empty town, esp. one that was once busy because people came to find gold, and left when it was finished

**ghoul** /gu:l/ *n* **1** a spirit which (in the stories told in Eastern countries) takes bodies from graves to eat them **2** a person who delights in (thoughts of) dead bodies and other nasty things **-ghoulish** *adj*

**GI** *n* **GI's** *or* **GIs** a soldier in the US army, esp. during World War Two

**gi·ant** /'dʒaɪənt/ *n* **1** [C] (in fairy stories) a very big strong man, often unfriendly and very cruel -compare DWARF[1] (1) **2** [C] a man who is much bigger than is usual **3** [A] very large: *The giant (size) packet gives you more for less money!*

**gib·ber·ish** /'dʒɪbərɪʃ/ *n* [U] meaningless sounds or talk

**gib·bet** /'dʒɪbɨt/ *n* (in former times) the GALLOWS or wooden post from which criminals were hanged

**gib·bon** /'gɪbən/ *n* an animal like a monkey (APE) with no tail and long arms

**gibe, jibe** /dʒaɪb/ *n* a remark which makes someone look foolish

**gib·lets** /'dʒɪblɨts/ *n* [P] the parts of a bird, such as the heart and LIVER, which are taken out before it is cooked

**gid·dy** /'gɪdi/ *adj* **-dier, -diest 1** (of a person) feeling unsteady, as though everything is moving round oneself: *The children enjoyed going round and round, but I felt giddy just watching them.* **2** causing a feeling of unsteady movement and/or falling: *a giddy height* **-giddily** *adv* **-giddiness** *n* [U]

**gift** /gɪft/ *n* **1** something which is given freely; present -see Study Notes on page 429 **2** a natural ability to do something: *He has a gift for music.* **3** *BrE infml* something easily done, cheaply obtained, etc.: *At £2 it's a gift!*

**gift·ed** /'gɪftɨd/ *adj* having one or more special abilities; TALENTED: *a gifted painter/child*

**gig** /gɪg/ *n infml* a musician's job or performance: *They're doing a gig in London next month.*

**gi·gan·tic** /dʒaɪ'gæntɪk/ *adj* unusually large in amount or size -see Study Notes on page 494 **-gigantically** *adv*

**gig·gle** /'gɪgəl/ *v* **-gled, -gling** [I] to laugh in a silly, uncontrolled manner **-giggle** *n*

**gild** /gɪld/ *v* **gilded** *or* **gilt** /gɪlt/, **gilding** [T] to cover with a thin coat of gold (paint)

**gill**[1] /gɪl/ *n* one of the organs through which a fish breathes

**gill**[2] /dʒɪl/ *n* a measure equal to ¼ PINT (1) or 0·142 LITRES

**gilt** /gɪlt/ *n* [U] shiny material, esp. gold, used as a thin covering: *The plates have a gilt edge.*

**gim·mick** /'gɪmɪk/ *n infml* a trick or object which is used to draw attention: *The pretty girl on the cover of the book is just a sales gimmick.* (=to encourage people to buy the book) **-gimmicky** *adj*

**gin** /dʒɪn/ *n* [U] a colourless alcoholic drink made from grain and certain berries

**gin·ger**[1] /'dʒɪndʒə^r/ *n* [U] a plant with a root which can be used in cooking to give a hot strong taste

**ginger**[2] *adj,n* [U] (of) an orange-brown colour: *He's called "Ginger" because of his bright ginger hair.*

**ginger ale** /,·· '·‖'·· ·/ also **ginger beer**- *n* [U] a gassy non-alcoholic drink made with GINGER[1]

**gin·ger·ly** /'dʒɪndʒəli‖-ər-/ *adv* carefully and with controlled movements so as not to cause harm: *I reached out gingerly to touch the snake.*

**ging·ham** /'gɪŋəm/ *n* [U] a type of cotton woven with a pattern of squares (CHECKS[1] (6))

**gip·sy** ‖also **gypsy** *esp. AmE* /'dʒɪpsi/ *n* **-sies** a member of a dark-haired race which travels about in covered carts (CARAVANS (2)), earning money as horse dealers, musicians, basket makers, FORTUNE tellers, etc.

**gi·raffe** /dʒɨ'rɑ:f‖-'ræf/ *n* **-raffes** *or* **-raffe** an African animal with a very long neck and legs and orange skin with dark spots

**gir·der** /'gɜ:də^r‖'gɜr-/ *n* a strong beam, usu. of iron or steel, which supports a floor or roof or part of a bridge

**gir·dle** /'gɜ:dl‖'gɜr-/ *n* an undergarment for women, worn around the waist and hips, meant to hold the flesh firm; light CORSET

**girl** /gɜ:l‖gɜrl/ *n* **1** a young female person: *There are more girls than boys in this school.|My little girl* (=my daughter) *is ill.* **2** a woman: *The men have invited the girls to play football against them.|shop/office girls* **3** → GIRLFRIEND: *John's girl* **-girlish** *adj: sounds of girlish laughter* **-girlishly** *adv* **-girlishness** *n* [U]

**girl·friend** /'gɜ:lfrend‖'gɜrl-/ *n* **1** a male's favourite female friend, with whom he spends a lot of time, and to whom he is not married: *He seems to have a new girlfriend every week.* **2** *AmE* a female friend with whom one spends time and shares amusements: *She is always on the phone to her girlfriends.* -see also BOYFRIEND

**girl guide** /,· '·/ *BrE*‖**girl scout** /'· ·/ *AmE*- *n* a member of an association for girls, the **Girl Guides,** who take part in activities like camping, and learn useful skills -compare BOY SCOUT

**girl·hood** /'gɜ:lhʊd‖'gɜrl-/ *n* [U] the state or time of being a young girl -see also BOYHOOD, CHILDHOOD

**gi·ro** /'dʒaɪərəu/ *n* (in Britain) a system of banking by which payments can be made directly from the account of one person/organization to that of another

**girth** /gɜ:θ‖gɜrθ/ *n* [C;U] *fml* the measure of thickness round something: *the girth of a tree*

**gist** /dʒɪst/ *n* [*the* S] the main points (as of an argument): *I haven't time to read this report; can you give me the gist of it?*

**give**[1] /gɪv/ *v* **gave** /geɪv/, **given** /'gɪvən/, **giving 1** [T] to cause (someone) to have, receive or own (something): *She gave him a book for his birthday.|Give me the bags while you open the door.* **2** [T] to allow to have: *Give him enough time to get home before you telephone.|Give me a chance to try the job.* **3** [T] to produce (an effect) on (someone); cause to experience: *The cold wind gave me a pain in the ears.|I hope my son hasn't given you a lot of trouble.|The news gave us a shock.* **4** [T] to produce; supply with:

*Cows give milk.|Can you give me more information?|Does that clock give the right time?* **5** [T *to*] to set aside (time, thought, strength, etc.) for a purpose: *She gives all her time to her family.* **6** [T *for*] to pay in exchange: *How much did you give to have the roof mended?* **7** [T] to do (an action) (to): *She gave a sudden shout of surprise.|Give me a kiss.|to give an order|to give permission|He gave the door a push.* **8** [T] to admit the truth of: *It's not cheap, I give you that, but it's a really good hotel.* **9** [T *often pass.*] to cause to believe because of information one has received: *I was given to understand that he was ill.* **10** [I] to bend or stretch under pressure: *The branch he was sitting on began to give.* **11 give or take** (a certain amount) or (a certain amount) more or less: *It will take an hour, give or take a few minutes (either way).* **12 give way (to): a** to yield, as in an argument: *He refused to give way and admit he was wrong.* **b** to break: *The floor gave way under the weight.* **c** to become less useful or important than: *Steam trains gave way to electric trains.* **d** to allow oneself to show (esp. a feeling) **13 What gives?** *infml* What's going on? –**giver** *n*

**give** sbdy./sthg.↔ **away** *v adv* [T] **1** to make someone a present or prize of (something): *She gave away all her money to the poor.*|(fig.) *Our team just gave the match away by playing so badly.* **2** to deliver or formally hand over (a woman) to the husband at the wedding: *Mary was given away by her father.* **3** to make known (a secret) intentionally or unintentionally: *He tried to pretend that he wasn't worried, but his shaking hands gave him away*/**gave the game away.** (=showed his real feelings) –see also GIVEAWAY

**give** sbdy. **back** sthg. *v adv* [T] to return (something) to the owner or original possessor: *Give me back my pen.|Give me my pen back.* –see Study Notes on page 429

**give in** *v adv* **1** [I *to*] to yield: *The boys fought until one gave in.|Don't give in to him.* **2** [T] (**give** sthg.↔ **in**) to deliver; hand in: *Give your examination papers in (to the teacher) when you've finished.*

**give off** sthg. *v adv* [T] to send out (esp. a liquid, gas, or smell): *to give off steam*

**give out** *v adv* **1** [T] (**give** sthg.↔ **out**) to give to each of several people: *Give out the examination papers.|Give the money out to the children.* **2** [I] also **run out**– *infml* to come to an end: *His strength gave out.*

**give over** *v adv* [I;T (=**give over** sthg.) +*v-ing; often in commands*] *BrE infml* to stop

**give up** *v adv* **1** [T +*v-ing*] (**give up** sthg.) to stop having or doing: *The doctor told me to give up smoking.|I've gave that idea up a long time ago.* **2** [I;T (=**give** sthg.↔ **up**)] to stop working at or trying to do (something): *to give up one's studies|He tried to swim the English Channel, but had to give up halfway.* **3** [T] (**give** sbdy. **up**) to stop believing that (someone) can be saved, esp. from death: *The boy was* **given up for lost/for dead.** **4** [T *to*] (**give** sbdy. **up**) to offer (someone or oneself) as a prisoner: *He gave himself up (to the police).* –compare SURRENDER **5** [T *to*] (**give** sthg.↔ **up**) to deliver or allow to pass (to someone else): *Give your seat up to the old lady.*

**give²** *n* [U] the quality of moving (esp. bending, stretching, or loosening) under pressure: *Shoes get slightly larger after wearing, because of the give in the leather.*

**give-and-take** /ˌ· · ˈ·/ *n* [U] willingness of each person to yield to (some of) the other's wishes: *We can only settle this argument if there is a bit of give-and-take on both sides.*

**give·a·way** /ˈgɪvəweɪ/ *n* [S] something unintentional that makes a secret known: *She tried to hide her feelings, but the tears in her eyes were* **a dead giveaway**. –see also GIVE **away** (3)

**giv·en¹** /ˈgɪvən/ *adj* **1** fixed for a purpose and stated as such: *The work must be done within the given time.* **2** if allowed or provided with: *I'd come and see you in Austria, given the chance.*

**given²** *prep* if one takes into account: *Given their inexperience/Given that they're inexperienced, they've done a good job.*

**given name** /ˈ·· ·/ *n AmE* for FIRST NAME

**giz·zard** /ˈgɪzəd‖-ərd/ *n* the second stomach of a bird, where food is broken into powder

**gla·cial** /ˈgleɪʃəl/ *adj* of or concerning ice or GLACIERS

**gla·ci·er** /ˈglæsɪəʳ‖ˈgleɪʃər/ *n* a mass of ice which moves very slowly down a mountain valley

**glad** /glæd/ *adj* **-dd- 1** [F +*to-v*/(*that*)/*about, of*] (of people) pleased and happy: *I'm glad he's got the job/about his new job.|Thanks for the help; I was very glad of it.|I'll be glad to help you repair the car.* **2** [A] causing happiness: *glad news of victory* –compare SAD –**gladness** *n* [U]

**glad·den** /ˈglædn/ *v* [T] to make glad or happy: *The sight of the child running about after his long illness gladdened his father's heart.* –compare SADDEN

**glade** /gleɪd/ *n lit* an open space without trees in a wood or forest

**glad·i·a·tor** /ˈglædieɪtəʳ/ *n* (in ancient times in Rome) an armed man who fought against men or wild animals in a public place (ARENA)

**glad·ly** /ˈglædli/ *adv polite* very willingly; eagerly: *I'll gladly come and help you.*

**glam·o·rize**‖also **-rise** *BrE* /ˈglæməraɪz/ *v* **-rized, -rizing** [T] to make (something) appear better, more attractive, etc., than in reality

**glam·or·ous, -ourous** /ˈglæmərəs/ *adj* having GLAMOUR: *a glamorous job/girl* –**glamorously** *adv*

**glam·our** *BrE*‖**glamor** *AmE* /ˈglæməʳ/ *n* [U] a special quality of charm and beauty; attractiveness: *the glamour of foreign countries|She added a touch of glamour by wearing a beautiful dress.*

**glance¹** /glɑːns‖glæns/ *v* **glanced, glancing** [I] to give a rapid look: *He glanced at his watch.|She glanced down the list of names.*

**glance off** (sthg.) *v adv; prep* [I;T] to hit and move off (BOUNCE **off**) at once: *The rock fell down and glanced off the car.*

**glance²** *n* **1** a rapid look or movement of the eyes: *One glance at his face told me he was ill.|He gave it an admiring glance.* **2 at a glance** with one look; at once

USAGE Compare **glance** and **glimpse**: *As I waited for John to arrive, I* **glanced at**/*took a* **glance at the clock** (=had a quick look at it) *and saw that he was late.|I caught a* **glimpse** *of the Town Hall clock* (=saw it just for a moment) *as we drove quickly past.* The verb to

**glimpse** has the same meaning as the noun but is not common.

**glanc·ing** /'glɑːnsɪŋ||'glæn-/ *adj* [A] (of a blow) which slips to one side: *a glancing blow on the chin*

**gland** /glænd/ *n* an organ of the body which treats materials from the bloodstream to produce various liquid substances: *a* SWEAT *gland* **–glandular** /'glæn djʊlər||-dʒə- / *adj: glandular fever*

**glare¹** /gleər/ *v* **glared, glaring** [I] **1** *at*] to look in an angry way: *They didn't fight, but stood there glaring at one another.* **2** to shine with a strong light esp. in a way that hurts the eyes

**glare²** *n* [S] **1** an angry look or STARE: *I started to offer help, but the fierce glare on his face stopped me.* **2** a hard, unpleasant effect given by a strong light: *There was a red glare over the burning city.*

**glar·ing** /'gleərɪŋ/ *adj* **1** too bright: *This glaring light hurts my eyes.* **2** (of mistakes) very noticeable: *The report is full of glaring errors.* **–glaringly** *adv*

**glass** /glɑːs||glæs/ *n* **1** a hard transparent solid material made from melted sand: *a glass bottle/window|I cut my hand on some broken glass.* **2** [U] a collection of objects made of this: *glass and* CHINA (2) **3** [C] **a** a drinking vessel made of glass –see picture on page 337 **b** also **glassful**– the amount which this holds: *Would you like a glass of water?* **4** [C] *esp. lit* for BAROMETER:*The glass is falling; it's going to rain.* –see also GLASSES

**glass·es** /'glɑːsɨz||'glæ-/ *n* [P] two pieces of specially-cut glass usu. in a frame and worn in front of the eyes to help a person to see; SPECTACLES: *I have to wear glasses for reading.|some new glasses* (=a new pair of glasses) –see also SUNGLASSES; PAIR¹ (USAGE)

**glass·ware** /'glɑːsweər||'glæs-/ *n* [U] glass objects generally, esp. dishes, drinking glasses, etc.

**glass·y** /'glɑːsi||'glæsi/ *adj* **-ier, -iest 1** like glass, esp. (of water) smooth and shining **2** (of eyes) of a fixed expression, as if without sight or life

**glaze¹** /gleɪz/ *v* **glazed, glazing 1** [T] to cover (esp. window frames) with glass **2** [T] to put a shiny surface on (pots and bricks) **3** [I *over*] (of eyes) to become dull and lifeless: *His eyes glazed (over) and he fell unconscious.*

**glaze²** *n* a shiny surface, esp. one fixed on pots

**gla·zi·er** /'gləɪzɪər||-·ər/ *n* a workman who fits glass into window frames

**glaz·ing** /'gleɪzɪŋ/ *n* [C;U] the piece of glass used to fill a window –see also DOUBLE GLAZING

**gleam¹** /gliːm/ *n* **1** a shining light, esp. one making objects bright: *the red gleam of the firelight* **2** a sudden showing of a feeling or quality for a short time: *A gleam of interest came into her eye.|a gleam of hope* –compare GLIMMER

**gleam²** *v* [I] to give out a bright light: *The furniture gleamed after being polished.*

**glean** /gliːn/ *v* [T] *fml* to gather (esp. information) in small amounts and often with difficulty

**glee** /gliː/ *n* [U] a feeling of joyful satisfaction at something which pleases one:*The child danced with glee when she heard the good news.* **–gleeful** *adj* **–gleefully** *adv*

**glen** /glen/ *n* a narrow mountain valley, esp. in Scotland

**glib** /glɪb/ *adj* **-bb- 1** able to speak well and easily, whether speaking the truth or not: *a glib talker* **2** spoken too easily to be true: *a glib excuse|His answer was just too glib.* **–glibly** *adv* **–glibness** *n* [U]

**glide¹** /glaɪd/ *v* **glided, gliding** [I] **1** to move (noiselessly) in a smooth, continuous manner, which seems easy and without effort: *The boat glided over the river.|The dancers glided across the floor.* **2** to fly in a plane which has no engine (GLIDER) but follows movements of the air currents

**glide²** *n* a gliding movement (GLIDE¹)

**glid·er** /'glaɪdər/ *n* a plane without an engine

**glid·ing** /'glaɪdɪŋ/ *n* [U] the sport of flying GLIDERS

**glim·mer** /'glɪmər/ *v,n* [I] (to give) a very faint, unsteady light: *A faint light glimmered at the end of the passage.*|(fig.) *a glimmer of hope* –compare GLEAM

**glimpse¹** /glɪmps/ *v* **glimpsed, glimpsing** [T] to have a quick view of: *I glimpsed her among the crowd just before she disappeared from sight.* –see GLANCE² (USAGE)

**glimpse²** *n* [*at, of*] a quick look at or incomplete view of: *I only* **caught a glimpse** *of the thief, so I can't really describe him.* –see GLANCE² (USAGE)

**glint¹** /glɪnt/ *v* [I] to give out small flashes of light: *The gold was glinting in the sunlight.*|(fig.) *His eyes glinted when he saw the money.*

**glint²** *n* a flash of light, as from a shiny metal surface: (fig.) *I knew he was angry by the glint in his eye.*

**glis·ten** /'glɪsən/ *v* [I *with*] to shine from or as if from a wet surface: *eyes glistening with tears*

**glit·ter** /'glɪtər/ *v* [I] to shine brightly with flashing points of light: *The diamond ring glittered on her finger.* **–glitter** *n* [S;U]: *the glitter of broken glass*

**glit·ter·ing** /'glɪtərɪŋ/ *adj* [A] splendid; excellent: *a glittering performance*

**gloat** /gləʊt/ *v* [I *over*] to look at something or think about it with satisfaction, often in an unpleasant way: *He gloated over his brother's failure to win the prize.|a gloating look* **–gloatingly** *adv*

**glo·bal** /'gləʊbəl/ *adj* **1** of or concerning the whole earth: *global travel|global changes* **2** taking account of all possible considerations: *The report takes a global view of the company's problems.* **–globally** *adv*

**globe** /gləʊb/ *n* **1** the earth: *She has travelled all over the globe.* **2** an object in the shape of a round ball, esp. one on which a map of the earth is painted **3** a round glass bowl, esp. used as a cover for a lamp (LAMPSHADE)

**globe·trot·ter** /'gləʊbtrɒtər||-trɑ-/ *n* a person who habitually travels round the world

**glob·u·lar** /'glɒbjʊlər||'glɑbjə-/ *adj* **1** in the form of a GLOBULE **2** in the form of a GLOBE (2)

**glob·ule** /'glɒbjuːl||'glɑ-/ *n* a small drop of a liquid or melted solid: *Globules of wax fell from the candle.*

**gloom** /gluːm/ *n* **1** [U] darkness: *He couldn't see the house in the gloom.* **2** [C;U] a feeling of deep sadness: *The news of defeat filled them with gloom.*

**gloom·y** /'gluːmi/ *adj* **-ier, -iest 1** almost dark: *a gloomy day* **2** having or giving little hope or cheerfulness: *gloomy news* **–gloomily** *adv*

**glo·ri·fy** /'glɔːrɨfaɪ||'glo-/ *v* **-fied, -fying** [T] **1** to give glory, praise, or fame to **2** to cause to appear more important than in reality –**glorification** /-fǝ̀ˈkeɪʃən/ *n* [U]

**glo·ri·ous** /ˈglɔːrɪəs‖ˈglo-/ *adj* **1** having, or worthy of, great fame and honour: *a glorious victory* **2** beautiful; splendid: *glorious colours|a glorious day* –**gloriously** *adv*

**glo·ry** /ˈglɔːri‖ˈglori/ *n* **-ries 1** [U] great fame or success; praise and honour: *The minister was* **bathed in glory** *when she arranged a peaceful settlement.* **2** [U] beauty; splendid appearance: *The bright moonlight showed the Taj Mahal* **in all its glory. 3** [C *usu. pl.*] special beauty or cause for pride

**glory in** sthg. *v prep* **-ried, -rying** [T] to enjoy, often in a selfish way: *He gloried in his victory.*

**gloss**[1] /glɒs‖glɔs, glɑs/ *n* [S;U] shiny brightness on a surface: *gloss paint|the gloss on her hair*

**gloss**[2] *v* → GLOSS OVER

**glos·sa·ry** /ˈglɒsəri‖ˈglɔ-, ˈglɑ-/ *n* **-ries** a list of esp. unusual words, with an explanation of their meanings, at the end of a book

**gloss over** sthg. *v adv* [T] to speak kindly of (something bad); hide (faults): *to gloss over his failure*

**gloss·y** /ˈglɒsi‖ˈglɔsi, ˈglɑsi/ *adj* **-ier, -iest** shiny and smooth: *Our cat has glossy black fur.|A* **glossy magazine** *has lots of pictures of fashionable clothes and is printed on good quality paper.*

**glove** /glʌv/ *n* **1** a garment which covers the hand, with separate parts for the thumb and each finger –compare MITTEN; see PAIR[1] (USAGE) **2 fit like a glove** to fit perfectly **3 handle with kid gloves** to treat very gently and carefully

**glow**[1] /gləʊ/ *v* [I *with*] **1** to give out heat and/or light without flames or smoke: *The iron bar was heated till it glowed.|The fire was glowing.|The cat's eyes glowed in the darkness.* **2** to show redness and heat in the face, esp. after hard work or because of strong feelings: *glowing with health and happiness*

**glow**[2] *n* [S] **1** a light from something burning without flames or smoke: *the red glow in the sky above the town|The oil-lamp gives a soft glow.* **2** brightness of colour: *the glow of copper in the kitchen* **3** the feeling and/or signs of heat and colour in the body and face, as after exercise or because of good health: *the glow of health|a glow of happiness*

**glow·er** /ˈglaʊəʳ/ *v* [I *at*] to look with an angry expression: *Instead of answering he just glowered (at me).|a glowering look* –**gloweringly** *adv*

**glow·ing** /ˈgləʊɪŋ/ *adj* showing a favourable picture: *She gave a glowing description of the film, which made me want to see it for myself.* –**glowingly** *adv*

**glow-worm** /ˈ· ·/ *n* an insect, the female of which gives out a greenish light from the end of her tail

**glu·cose** /ˈgluːkəʊs, -kəʊz/ *n* [U] a natural form of sugar found in fruit

**glue**[1] /gluː/ *n* [U] a sticky substance used for joining things together –**gluey** *adj* **-ier, -iest**

**glue**[2] *v* **glued, gluing** *or* **glueing** [T] to join with GLUE[1]: *She glued the two pieces of wood together.|*(fig.) *The children are always glued to* (=always watching) *the television.*

**glum** /glʌm/ *adj* **-mm-** sad; in low spirits, esp. because of disappointment: *Why do you look so glum?* –**glumly** *adv* –**glumness** *n* [U]

**glut**[1] /glʌt/ *v* **-tt-** [T] **1** to supply with too much; overfill **2 glut oneself** to fill oneself (esp. by eating)

**glut**[2] *n* [*usu. sing.*] a larger supply than is necessary: *a glut of eggs (on the market)*

**glu·ti·nous** /ˈgluːtǝ̀nəs/ *adj fml* sticky: *a bowl of glutinous rice*

**glut·ton** /ˈglʌtn/ *n* **1** a person who eats too much **2** [*for*] *infml* a person who is always ready to do more of something hard or unpleasant: *She kept coming to work even when she was ill: she's a real* **glutton for punishment.**

**glut·ton·ous** /ˈglʌtənəs/ *adj* GREEDY, esp. for food

**glut·ton·y** /ˈglʌtəni/ *n* [U] the habit of eating (and drinking) too much

**gly·ce·rine, -rin** /ˈglɪsərɪn/ *n* [U] a sweet sticky colourless liquid used in making soap, medicines, and explosives

**gm.** *n written abbrev. said as:* GRAM

**GMT** *abbrev. for:* GREENWICH MEAN TIME

**gnarled** /nɑːld‖nɑrld/ *adj* rough and twisted, with hard lumps, esp. as a result of age or hard work: *a gnarled tree trunk|the old man's gnarled hands*

**gnash** /næʃ/ *v* [T] **gnash one's teeth** to make a noise with (one's teeth) by biting hard in anger or worry

**gnat** /næt/ *n* a small flying insect that stings

**gnaw** /nɔː/ *v* [I;T *away, at*] to keep biting steadily on (a bone, etc.), esp. until one makes (a hole, etc.): *Our dog likes to gnaw a bone.|*(fig.) *Something's gnawing at* (=worrying) *my mind.*

**gnaw·ing** /ˈnɔːɪŋ/ *adj* [A *no comp.*] painful or worrying in a small but continuous way: *gnawing hunger/anxiety*

**gnome** /nəʊm/ *n* (in fairy stories) a little (old) man who lives under the ground and guards stores of gold

**go**[1] /gəʊ/ *v* **went** /went/, **gone** /gɒn‖gɔn/, **going 1** [I] to leave the place where the speaker is (so as to reach another): *It's late; I must go/be going.|The train goes in 15 minutes.|*(fig.) *The summer is going fast.* –compare COME (1) **2** [I] to move or travel: *We went by bus.|The car's going too fast.|We went to France for our holidays.|His hand went to his pocket.* **3** [I +*v-ing*] to travel somewhere to do (an activity): *to go walking/shopping/swimming* **4** [I] to reach (as far as stated): *Which road goes to the station?|The valley goes from east to west.|The roots of the plant go deep.* **5** [I] to be placed, esp. usually placed: *"Where do the knives go?" "In this drawer."* **6** to become: *Her hair's going grey.|She went red in the face and rushed out angrily.|to go mad/blind* **7** to remain (in a certain state): *Should a criminal go free?|When the crops fail, the people go hungry.* **8** [I] (of machines) to work (properly): *The car won't go.* **9** [I *for*] to be sold: *The car was going cheap.|It went for £300.* **10** [I] to become weakened or worn out: *My voice is going because of my cold.|These old shoes are going.* **11** [T] to have the stated words or make the stated sound: *Ducks go "quack".* **12** [I] to match or fit: *It won't go in the box.|Blue and green don't go (together).|The belt won't go round (my waist).* –compare GO **with** (1), GO **together 13 be going to (do or happen)** (shows the future, esp. for events and actions which are intended, planned, or probable): *He's going to buy her some shoes.* (compare *He will buy her some shoes if she asks him to.*)*|Is it going to rain?|I'm going to be sick!|She's going to have a baby.* –see GONNA

(USAGE) **14 go and: a** to go in order to: *I'll go and get my book.*|*I went and bought* (=I went and I bought) *another one.* **b** *BrE infml* (expresses surprise): *She's gone and bought a new car!* **15 to go** left before something happens: *Only three days to go before/to Christmas!* **16 -goer** a person who goes regularly to a certain place or activity: *church-goers|filmgoers* –see also GOING[1] (4)

USAGE The usual past participle of **go** is **gone,** but if it means "visited" or "arrived (and left)" it is **been.** Compare: *George has* **gone** *to Paris.* (=he's there now, not here)|*George has* **been** *to Paris.* (=he has visited Paris in the past)|*The doctor hasn't* **gone** *yet.* (=he is still here)|*The doctor hasn't* **been** *yet.* (=he has not yet arrived) –see BECOME (USAGE)

**go about[1]** *v adv* → GO[1] **around** (1, 3)

**go about[2]** sthg. *v prep* [T] **1** to perform or do: *to go about one's business* **2** [+*v-ing*] also **set about**– to begin working at: *How do you go about repairing this clock?*

**go after** sbdy./sthg. *v prep* [T *pass. rare*] to try to obtain or win; chase: *to go after a job/a girl/a prize*

**go against** sbdy./sthg. *v prep* [T *no pass.*] **1** to act or be in opposition to: *She went against her mother/her mother's wishes* –compare GO **along** (2) **2** to be unfavourable to: *The case may go against you.*

**go ahead** *v adv* [I *with*] to begin or continue: *The council gave us permission to go ahead with our building plans.*|*Work is going ahead on the new bridge.* –see also GO-AHEAD

**go along** *v adv* [I] **1** to continue: *I like to add up my bank account as I go along.* **2** [*with*] to agree with; support: *We'll go along with you/your suggestion.* –compare GO **against** (1)

**go around/round** *v adv* [I] **1** (*usu. in tenses with the -ing form*) (of an illness) to spread: *There are a lot of colds going around.* **2** [with] to be often out in public (with someone): *Why do you go around with such strange people?* **3** to be enough for everyone: *If there are not enough chairs to go around, some people will have to stand.*

**go at/for** sbdy. *v prep* [T *no pass.*] to attack: *Our dog went at the postman.*

**go back** *v adv* [I] **1** to return: *Let's go back to what the chairman said earlier.* **2** [*to*] to reach backwards in time: *My family goes back to the 18th century.*

**go back on** sthg. *v adv prep* [T *pass. rare*] to break or not keep (a promise, agreement, etc.)

**go by[1]** *v adv* [I] to pass (in place or time): *A car went by.*|*Two years went by.*|*He let the chance go by.*

**go by[2]** sthg. *v prep* [T *no pass.*] **1** to act according to; be guided by; judge by: *to go by the rules/the book*|*You can't go by what he says.*|*Going by her clothes, she must be very rich.* **2 go by the name of** to be called, esp. in addition to one's real name

**go down** *v adv* [I] **1** to become lower: *The floods are going down.*|*The standard of work has gone down.*|*Eggs are going down (in price).* –compare GO **up** (1) **2** to sink: *Three ships went down in the storm.*|*before the sun goes down* **3** to become less swollen: *My ankle has gone down, so I should be able to walk soon.*|*This tyre is going down; I'll pump it up.* **4** [*with*] to be accepted: *He/His speech went down well (with the crowd).* **5** [*in*] to be recorded: *This day will go down in history.*

**go far** *v adv* [I] **1** to be successful; succeed: *She is very clever and will go far (in her new job).* **2** to satisfy many needs: *This food won't go far for ten people.*

**go for** sbdy./sthg. *v prep* [T *no pass.*] **1** → GO **at 2** → GO **after**: *to go for a job/a prize* **3** to like or be attracted by: *I don't go for men of his type.* **4** to concern or be true for (someone or something) in the same manner as for others: *I find this report badly done, and that goes for all the other work done in this office.* **5** to be sold for (esp. in the phrase **go for a song** =to be sold very cheaply)

**go in for** sthg. *v adv prep* [T] **1** to take part in (a test of skill or knowledge): *Several people went in for the race.* **2** [+*v-ing*] to make a habit of (doing), esp. for enjoyment: *I don't go in for sports.*

**go into** sthg. *v prep* [T] **1** [*no pass.*] to enter (a place, a profession, etc.): *to go into town/politics* **2** to examine or concern oneself with: *The police are going into the murder case.*|*Let's not go into details.*

**go off[1]** *v adv* [I] **1 a** to explode **b** to ring or sound loudly: *The* ALARM[1] (3) *went off when the thieves got in.* **2** *BrE* to fall in quality, esp. (of food) to go bad: *This milk has gone off.* **3** to succeed or fail: *The party went off very well/badly.* (=was a success/failure) **4** to fall asleep or lose consciousness: *Has the baby gone off yet?* –compare DROP **off** (2) **5** to cease operation: *The heating goes off at night.* –compare GO **on[1]** (4) **6 go off with** to take away without permission: *He's gone off with my car!*

**go off[2]** sbdy./sthg. *v prep* [T] to lose interest in or liking for: *I've gone off coffee; give me some tea.*

**go on[1]** *v adv* [I] **1** to take place or happen: *What's going on here?* **2** [+*to-v/v-ing/with*] to continue (to behave in a certain way): *He went on talking even though no one was listening.*|*Go on with your work.*|*If he goes on like this he'll lose his job.* **3** (of time) to pass: *As the day went on, it became hotter.* **4** to be put into operation: *The lights went on at six o'clock.* –compare GO **off[1]** (5) **5** [*at*] to keep complaining or scolding: *He's always going on at his wife.* **6** to keep talking: *She does go on so!* **7 go on (with you)!** I don't believe you! **8 to be going/go on with** *infml esp. BrE* (to use) for the moment: *Here's £3 to be going on with. I'll give you some more tomorrow.*

**go on[2]** sthg. *v prep* [T *no pass.*] to use as a reason, proof, or base for further action: *All the police had to go on was a torn letter.*

**go out** *v adv* [I] **1** to leave the house, esp. for amusement: *She's gone out for a walk.*|*We go out three times a week.*|*He's not old enough to go out to work.* **2** [*together, with*] (*usu. in the -ing form*) to spend time regularly (with someone of the other sex): *They've been going out together for two years.* **3** [*to*] to travel (to a distant place): *My friends went out to Africa.* **4** (of a fire, light, etc.) to stop burning or shining: (fig.) *He went out like a light.* (=to sleep, or into unconsciousness) **5** (of the sea or TIDE (1)) to go back to its low level **6** to cease to be fashionable or customary: *Short skirts went out some time ago, but they've come back again.* **7** [*to*] (of feelings) to be in sympathy (with): *Our thoughts go out to our friends.*

**go over[1]** sthg. *v prep* [T] **1** to look at or examine: *We went over the list of names and chose two.* **2** to repeat:

*I'll go over the explanation of how it works.*

**go over**[2] *v adv* [I *from* and/or *to*] to change (one's political party, religion, etc.): *She went over to the Republicans after their election victory.*

**go round** *v adv* [I] → GO **around**

**go through**[1] *v adv* [I] to be approved officially: *Their business arrangements went through.*

**go through**[2] sthg. *v prep* [T] **1** to suffer or experience: *The country has gone/been through too many wars.* **2** → GET **through**[2] **3** to pass through or be accepted by: *The new law has gone through Parliament.* **4** → GO **over**[1] (1)

**go through with** sthg. *v adv prep* [T] to complete (something which has been agreed or planned), often with difficulty: *He promised to sign the contract, but now he doesn't want to go through with it.*

**go to** sthg. *v prep* [T *no pass.*] **1** to cause oneself to experience: *She went to a lot of trouble for me.* **2** to enter or start experiencing (a state) (in phrases like **go to sleep, go to war)**

**go together** *v adv* [I] (of two things) to GO **with** (1) each other; match

**go under** *v adv* [I] (of a ship or floating object) to sink: (fig.) *After he got into debt, his business went under.* (=failed) –compare GO **down** (2)

**go up** *v adv* [I] **1** to rise: *Prices have gone up again.* –compare GO **down** (1) **2** to be built: *How many houses have gone up this year?* **3** to BLOW **up** (1) or be destroyed in fire: *The whole house went up in flames.*

**go with** sthg. *v prep* [T *no pass.*] **1** to match or suit: *Mary's blue dress goes with her eyes.* **2** [+*v-ing*] to be often found with; ACCOMPANY (1, 2): *Happiness doesn't necessarily go with (having) money.*

**go without** (sthg.) *v prep; adv* [I;T +*v-ing*] **1** → DO **without**: *I'm afraid there's no coffee, so we'll just have to go without* (it). **2 it goes without saying** it's clear without needing to be stated

**go**[2] *n* **goes** *infml* **1** [U] the quality of being full of activity: *The children are full of go.* **2** [C] an attempt to do something: *He had several goes at the examination before he passed.* **3** [C *usu. sing.*] one's turn (esp. in a game): *It's my go to hide now.* **4 on the go** working all the time

**goad** /gəʊd/ *n* something which urges a person to action

**goad** sbdy. **into** sthg. *v prep* [T] to cause (someone) to (do something) by strong or continued annoyance: *They goaded him into doing it by saying he was a coward.*

**go·a·head**[1] /'· ·ˌ·/ *n* [*the* S] permission to act: *We're all ready to start the new building, as soon as we get the go-ahead from the council.* –see also GO **ahead**

**go-ahead**[2] *adj* [A] (of people) active in using new methods: *a go-ahead company*

**goal** /gəʊl/ *n* **1** one's aim or purpose; something one wishes to obtain or reach: *His goal is a place at university.*|*The company has* ACHIEVED *all its goals this year.* (=done everything it planned to do) **2** (in games like football) the place, usu. between two posts (**goalposts**) with a net between them, where the ball must go for a point to be gained: *She keeps goal* (=defends the goal) *for the school team.* –see picture on page 592**3** the point gained (SCORED[2] (1)) when the ball is caused to do this

**goal·keep·er** /'gəʊlˌkiːpə^r/ also **goalie** /'gəʊli/ *infml*– *n* (in games like football) the player who is responsible for preventing the ball from getting into his/her team's GOAL (2) –see picture on page 592

**goat** /gəʊt/ *n* a four-legged animal related to the sheep. It has horns and gives milk and a rough sort of wool –see also BILLY GOAT, NANNY GOAT, KID[1] (1)

**gob** /gɒb‖gɑb/ *n BrE infml, not polite* the mouth: *Shut your gob!*

**gob·ble**[1] /'gɒbəl‖'gɑ-/ *v* **-bled, -bling** [I;T *up*] to eat very quickly, and sometimes noisily: *The children gobbled up their food and rushed out to play.*

**gobble**[2] *v,n* (to make) the sound a TURKEY makes

**gob·let** /'gɒblˌ̍t‖'gɑb-/ *n* a drinking vessel, usu. of glass or metal, with a base and stem but no handles, and used esp. for wine

**gob·lin** /'gɒblˌ̍n‖'gɑb-/ *n* a usu. unkind or evil spirit which plays tricks on people

**god** /gɒd‖gɑd/ *n* **goddess** /'gɒdˌ̍s‖'gɑd-/ *fem.*– a being (one of many) which is worshipped, as one who made or rules over (a part of) the world

**God** *n* **1** the being who in the Christian, Jewish, and Muslim religions is worshipped as maker and ruler of the world **2 God forbid that** may it not happen that **3 God (alone) knows** *infml* it's impossible to say: *God knows where he went!* **4 God willing** if all goes well **5 Oh God/My God/Good God** (expressions of surprise, fear, etc.) **6 Thank God** (an expression of gladness that trouble has passed):*Thank God you're safe!*

**god·child** /'gɒdtʃaɪld‖'gɑd-/ *n* (in the Christian religion) the child (**godson** or **goddaughter**) for whom one takes responsibility by making promises at a ceremony (BAPTISM) –see also GODPARENT

**god-fear·ing** /'· ˌ··/ *adj fml* good and well-behaved according to the rules of the Christian religion

**god·for·sak·en** /'gɒdfəseɪkən‖'gɑdfər-/ *adj* (of a place) empty, containing nothing useful or interesting, etc.

**god·less** /'gɒdlˌ̍s‖'gɑd-/ *adj fml* wicked; not showing respect to or belief in God

**god·like** /'gɒdlaɪk‖'gɑd-/ *adj* like or suitable to God or a god: *godlike beauty/calm*

**god·ly** /'gɒdli‖'gɑdli/ *adj* **-lier, -liest** *fml* showing obedience to God by leading a good life

**god·pa·rent** /'gɒdˌpeərənt‖'gɑd-/ *n* the person (**godfather** or **godmother**) who makes promises to help a Christian newly received into the church at a special ceremony (BAPTISM) –see also GODCHILD

**god·send** /'gɒdsend‖'gɑd-/ *n* an unexpected lucky chance or thing: *It was a godsend to have him there just when we needed someone.*

**gog·gle** /'gɒgəl‖'gɑ-/ *v* **-gled, -gling** [I *at*] to look hard with the eyes wide open, as in surprise:*They all goggled at my funny clothes.* –compare STARE

**gog·gles** /'gɒgəlz‖'gɑ-/ *n* [P] (a pair of) large round glasses with an edge which fits against the skin so that dust, water, etc., cannot get near the eyes: *motorcycle goggles* –see PAIR[1] (USAGE)

**go-go** /'· ·/ *adj* of or concerned in a form of fast dancing, usu. performed by one or more girls wearing little clothing: *go-go dancers*

**go·ing**[1] /'gəʊɪŋ/ *n* [U] **1** the act of leaving: *Her going will be a great loss to the company.* **2** the act or speed of travel or work: *We climbed the mountain in three* *hours, which was good going.* **3** the condition or possibility of travel: *The mud made it rough/hard/heavy going for the car.*|(fig.) *This book is very heavy going.* (=very difficult to read)|(fig.) *Let's leave* **while the going's good.** (=while we can) **4 -going** going regularly to a certain place or activity: *theatre going|churchgoing* –see also **-goer** (GO[1] (16))

**going²** *adj* [A] **1** as charged at present: *The* **going rate** *for the job is £4 per hour.* **2** in operation: *a* **going** CONCERN[2] (3) (=an active profitable business) **3 have a lot/plenty/nothing going for one** to have many/no advantages; be in a favourable/unfavourable situation

**going-o·ver** /ˌ·· ˈ··/ *n* **goings-over** *infml* a (thorough) examination and/or treatment: *The car needs a good going-over before we use it again.*

**goings-on** /ˌ·· ˈ·/ *n* [P] activities, usu. of an undesirable kind: *There was shouting, and loud music, and all sorts of goings-on I can't describe!*

**going to** /ˈ·· ˌ·/ → GO[1] (13)

**go-kart** /ˈgəʊ kɑːt‖-kɑrt/ *n* a very small low racing car made of an open framework with little or no BODYWORK

**gold** /gəʊld/ *n* [U] **1** a valuable soft yellow metal (an ELEMENT (1)) used for making coins, jewellery, etc.: *He wore a gold watch.|Gold is found in rock and streams.* **2** the colour of this metal: *gold paint* **3 as good as gold** (esp. of children) very well behaved

**gold·en** /ˈgəʊldən/ *adj* of or like gold: (fig.) *a golden* (=very fortunate) OPPORTUNITY

**gold·fish** /ˈgəʊldˌfɪʃ/ *n* **goldfish** *or* **goldfishes** a small fish which is kept as a pet in glass bowls or in ornamental pools

**gold·mine** /ˈgəʊldmaɪn/ *n* **1** a place where gold is taken (MINED[3] (2)) from the rock **2** a successful business or activity which makes large profits: *With this new invention, we're* **sitting on a goldmine**. (= we possess something very valuable)

**golf¹** /gɒlf‖gɑlf, gɔlf/ *n* [U] a game in which people hit small hard balls into holes, using any of a special set of sticks (**golf clubs**), trying to do so with as few strokes as possible. The piece of land on which the game is played is called a **golf course.**

**golf²** *v* [I] (*esp. in the* -ing *form*) to play GOLF: *to go golfing* **–golfer** *n*

**golf club** /ˈ· ·/ *n* **1** a club for GOLFers[2] with the buildings and land it uses **2** a long-handled wooden or metal stick used for hitting the ball in GOLF

**gon·do·la** /ˈgɒndələ‖ˈgɑn-, gɑnˈdəʊlə/ *n* a long narrow flat-bottomed boat with high points at each end, used only on the waterways (CANALS) which run between the houses in Venice in Italy

**gon·do·lier** /ˌgɒndəˈlɪəʳ‖ˌgɑn-/ *n* a man who guides and rows a GONDOLA

**gone** /gɒn‖gɔn/ *v past participle of* GO –see GO (USAGE)

**gong** /gɒŋ‖gɑŋ, gɔŋ/ *n* a round piece of metal hanging from a frame, which when struck with a stick makes a deep ringing sound

**gon·na** /gɒnə, gənə‖ˈgɑnə,/ going to

USAGE When **going to** is used before another verb, to show the future, it is sometimes pronounced in this way. It may be written **gonna** in stories, to show an informal way of speaking: *You* **gonna** *tell him?* (=are you going to tell him?) But **going to** in *I'm going to Canada* is not pronounced in this way.

**gon·or·rhe·a, -rhoea** /ˌgɒnəˈrɪə‖ˌgɑ-/ *n* [U] a disease of the sex organs, passed on during sexual activity –compare SYPHILIS

**good¹** /gʊd/ *adj* **better** /ˈbetəʳ/, **best** /best/ **1** having the right qualities; satisfactory; enjoyable: *a good play|good weather|Have a good time!* **2** suitable; favourable: *It's a good day for a swim.| a good chance of getting a job* **3** suitable for its purpose: *a good idea|good advice* **4** [*for*] useful to the health or character: *Milk is good for you.|It isn't good (for you) to have everything you want.* **5** morally right: *to do a good deed|to lead a good life* **6** [*of, to*] (of people) kind; helpful: *She's always been very good to me.|It's good of you to help.* **7** (esp. of children) well-behaved: *Be good when we visit your aunt.* **8** [*at*] skilful; having the ability to do something:*a good cook|She's good at languages.* –opposite **bad 9** [A *no comp.*] complete; thorough: *Have a good look.|Their team gave us a good beating.* **10** [A *no comp.*] large in size, amount, etc.: *We waited a good while.* **11** [A *no comp.*] at least or more than: *It's a good five kilometres away.* **12 a good deal** quite a lot: *a good deal of support.* **13 as good as** almost (the same thing as): *We're as good as ruined.* **14 Good!** I agree *or* I'm glad **15 in good time** early

**good²** *n* [U] **1** that which is right and useful in accordance with religious beliefs or moral standards: *You must learn the difference between good and evil.* –opposite **evil 2** that which causes gain or improvement: *I don't want to punish you, but it's* **for your own good.**|*Milk* **does you good**. (=is good for your health)|**It's no good** (=it's useless) *crying now!|Is this new paint* **any good?** (=is it good paint?)|**What's the good of/What good is** *having a car if you can't drive!* –compare HARM[1] (1) **3 for good** for ever: *We thought they'd come for a visit, but it seems they're staying for good.* **4 up to no good** doing or intending to do something wrong or bad

**good af·ter·noon** ˌ··ˈ·/ *interj,n* (an expression used when meeting or leaving someone in the afternoon)

**good·bye** /gʊdˈbaɪ/ *interj,n* (an expression used when leaving, or being left by, someone): *"Goodbye, Mrs Smith."|They said their goodbyes and left.* –compare HELLO

**good eve·ning** /· ˈ··/ *interj,n* (an expression used when meeting or leaving someone in the evening) –compare GOODNIGHT

**good-for-noth·ing** /ˈ· · ˌ··/ *adj,n* [A;C] (a person who is) worthless, who does no work, etc. *Get out of bed, you good-for-nothing (fool)!*

**Good Fri·day** /ˌ· ˈ··/ *n* the Friday before EASTER

**good-hu·moured** *BrE*‖**-humored** *AmE* /ˌ· ˈ·· ◂/ *n* having or showing a cheerful, friendly state of mind **–good-humouredly** *adv*

**good·ish** /ˈgʊdɪʃ/ *adj* [A *no comp.*] **1** quite good, but not very good **2** rather large, long, far, etc.: *Their house was a* **goodish distance** *from the bus-stop.*

**good-look·ing** /ˌ· ˈ·· ◂/ *adj* attractive: *a good-looking man* –see BEAUTIFUL (USAGE)

**good mor·ning** /· ˈ··/ *interj,n* (an expression used when meeting or leaving someone in the morning)

**good-na·tured** /ˌ· ˈ·· ◂/ *adj* naturally kind; ready

to help, to forgive, not to be angry, etc. –opposite **ill-natured –good-naturedly** *adv*

**good·ness** /ˈgʊdnɪ̵s/ *n* [U] **1** the quality of being good –opposite **badness 2** the best part, esp. (of food) the part which is good for the health: *All the goodness has been boiled out of the vegetables.* **3** (used in expressions of surprise and annoyance): **For goodness' sake**, *stop making such a noise!*

**good·night** /gʊdˈnaɪt/ *interj,n* (an expression used when leaving, or being left by, someone at night, esp. before going to bed or to sleep) –compare GOOD EVENING

**goods** /gʊdz/ *n* [P] **1** movable articles (e.g. clothes, food, kitchen materials, etc.) which can be owned, bought, or sold: *This shop sells a variety of goods.* **2** *BrE*‖**freight** *AmE*– heavy articles which can be carried by road, train, etc.: *a goods train*

**good·will** /ˌgʊdˈwɪl/ *n* [U] **1** kind feelings towards or between people: *There is goodwill between the former enemies.* **2** the popularity of a business, usu. included as part of its selling price: *We paid £10,000 for the shop, and £2,000 for its goodwill.*

**good·y¹** /ˈgʊdi/ *n* **-ies** [*usu. pl.*] *infml* something particularly attractive, pleasant, or desirable, esp. something nice to eat

**goody²** *interj* (an expression of pleasure used esp. by children)

**goody-good·y** /ˈ·· ˌ··/ *n* **goody-goodies** *often derog* a person who likes to appear faultless in behaviour so as to please others,not because he or she is really good

**goo·ey** /ˈguːi/ *adj* **-ier, -iest 1** sticky and (usu.) sweet: *gooey cakes* **2** over-sweet; SENTIMENTAL: *a gooey film*

**goof** /guːf/ *v,n* [C;I] *infml esp. AmE* (to make) a silly mistake

**goof·y** /ˈguːfi/ *adj* **-ier, -iest** silly; slightly mad

**goon** /guːn/ *n infml* a silly, foolish person

**goose** /guːs/ **gander** *masc.– n* **geese** /giːs/ a large white bird which looks like a duck and makes a HISsing noise: *A young goose is a* **gosling.**

**goose·ber·ry** /ˈgʊzbəri, ˈguːz-, ˈguːs-‖ˈguːsberi/ *n* **-ries 1** the small, round, green fruit of a bush grown in gardens: *a gooseberry bush* **2 play gooseberry** *BrE* (of a third person) to be present with a man and woman, esp. lovers, who would rather be alone

**goose·flesh** /ˈguːsfleʃ/ *n* [U] a condition in which the skin is raised up in small points, as when a person is cold or frightened

**goose pim·ples** /ˈ· ˌ··/ *n* [P] →GOOSEFLESH

**go·pher** /ˈgəʊfəʳ/ *n* a ratlike animal of North and Central America which makes and lives in holes in the ground

**gore** *v* **gored, goring** [T] (of an animal) to wound with the horns or TUSK

**gorge** /gɔːd·‖gɔrd·/ *n* a narrow valley with steep sides usu. made by a stream running through it –see VALLEY (USAGE)

**gorge** sbdy. **on/with** sthg. *v prep* **gorged, gorging** [T] to fill (oneself) with (food)

**gor·geous** /ˈgɔːd·əs‖ˈgɔr-/ *adj infml* delightful; very beautiful: *gorgeous colours*|*a gorgeous day* (=hot and bright) **–gorgeously** *adv*

**go·ril·la** /gəˈrɪlə/ *n* the largest of the manlike monkeys (APES)

**gorse** /gɔːs‖gɔrs/ *n* [U] a bush with prickles and bright yellow flowers, which grows wild

**gor·y** /ˈgɔːri‖ˈgori/ *adj* **-ier, -iest** full of violence: *a gory film*|*all the gory details of the murder*

**gosh** /gɒʃ‖gɑʃ/ *interj* (an expression of surprise)

**gos·ling** /ˈgɒzlɪŋ‖ˈgɑz-, ˈgɔz-/ *n* a young GOOSE

**go-slow** /ˌ· ˈ·◂/ *n BrE* a decision to work slowly, as a form of STRIKE² (1)

**gos·pel** /ˈgɒspəl‖ˈgɑs-/ also **gospel truth** /ˌ·· ˈ·/ *n* [U] *infml* something which is completely true: *What I'm telling you is gospel/the gospel truth.*

**Gospel** *n* any of the four accounts in the Bible of Christ's life

**gos·sa·mer** /ˈgɒsəməʳ‖ˈgɑ-/ *n* [U] **1** light, silky thread which SPIDERs leave on grass, bushes, etc. **2** a very light thin material

**gos·sip¹** /ˈgɒsɪ̵p‖ˈgɑ-/ *n* **1** [C;U] (an example of) talk or writing, often untruthful, about other people's actions and private lives: *I don't approve of gossip.*|*two neighbours having a gossip in the street*|*I read about it in the* **gossip column**. (= writing in a newspaper about the private lives of well-known people) –compare RUMOUR **2** [C] a person who likes talking about other people's private lives

**gossip²** *v* [I *with, about*] to talk or write GOSSIP¹ (1)

**got** /gɒt‖gɑt/ *v past tense and participle of* GET –see GOTTEN (USAGE)

**Goth·ic** /ˈgɒθɪk‖ˈgɑ-/ *adj* **1** of a style of building common in Western Europe between the 12th and 16th centuries, with pointed arches, arched (VAULTed¹ (1)) roofs, and tall thin pillars (PIERs (3)) **2** of a style of writing in the 18th century which produced stories (NOVELs (1)) set in lonely fearful places: *Gothic novels*

**got·ta** /ˈgɒtə‖gɑtə/ **1** have/has got to **2** have/has a

USAGE **have got to** and **have got a** are sometimes pronounced in this way. They may be written **gotta** in stories to show an informal way of speaking: *I gotta go.* (=I have got to go, I must go)|*Gotta match?* (=Have you got a match?)

**got·ten** /ˈgɒtn‖ˈgɑtn/ *v AmE past participle of* GET –see also ILL-GOTTEN

USAGE In *AmE,* **gotten** is much more common than **got** as the past participle of **get**, except where it means **a** "possess": compare *I've* **got** *a new car.* (=I possess one) and *I've* **gotten** *a new car.* (=I've bought one); or **b** "must": compare *I've* **got** *to go.* (=I must go)|*I've* **gotten** *to go.* (=I've succeeded in going). But Americans often say *I have a new car.*|*I have to go* and avoid using **got** altogether. **Gotten** is not used in *BrE.*

**gouge** sthg.↔ **out** /gaʊdʒ/ *v adv* **gouged, gouging** [T] to press or dig out with force: *to gouge out someone's eyes*

**gou·lash** /ˈguːlæʃ‖-lɑʃ, -læʃ/ *n* [C;U] meat and vegetables cooked together with PAPRIKA, which gives a hot taste

**gourd** /gʊəd‖gord, gʊərd/ *n* a large fruit with a hard shell which is often used as a drinking vessel or dish

**gour·met** /ˈgʊəmeɪ‖ˈgʊər-, gʊərˈmeɪ/ n a person who knows a lot about and enjoys good food and drink; EPICURE

**gout** /gaʊt/ *n* [U] a disease which makes esp. the toes, knees, and fingers swell and give pain

**gov·ern** /ˈgʌvən‖-ərn/ **1** [I;T] to rule (a country, city, etc. and its people): *We have a queen, but it is the* PRIME MINISTER *and* CABINET (2) *who govern.* **2** [T] to control or determine: *The price of coffee is governed by the quantity which has been produced.*

**gov·ern·ess** /ˈgʌvənɪ̈s‖-ər-/ *n* (esp. in former times) a female teacher who lives with a family and educates their children at home

**gov·ern·ment** /ˈgʌvəmənt, ˈgʌvənmənt‖ˈgʌvərn-/ *n* **1** [U] the action, form, or method of ruling: *The country has always had fair government.* **2** [C +*sing./pl. v*] (*often cap.*) the people who rule: *The Government is/are planning new tax increases.* **–governmental** /ˌgʌvənˈmentl‖ˌgʌvərn-/ *adj*

**gov·er·nor** /ˈgʌvənəʳ/ *n* a person who controls a certain type of organization or place: *the governor of the prison/the Bank of England|the governor of California|a school governor* **–governorship** *n* [U]

**gown** /gaʊn/ *n* **1** *old use or AmE* a long dress, esp. one worn on formal occasions: *an evening gown* **2** a (long) loose usu. black outer garment worn for special ceremonies by judges, teachers, lawyers, etc.

**G P** *n abbrev. for:* GENERAL PRACTITIONER

**GPO** *n abbrev. for:* General Post Office; (in Britain) the organization that controls the POST³ (1)

**grab¹** /græb/ *v* **-bb-** [I;T *at*] to seize with a sudden, rough movement, esp. for a selfish reason:*He grabbed the money and ran off.*

**grab²** *n* a sudden attempt to seize something: *The thief* **made a grab at** *my bag but I pushed him away.*

**grace¹** /greɪs/ *n* **1** [U] the quality of being fine, effortless, and attractive in movement, form, or behaviour: *to dance with grace* **2** [U] kindness; willingness to do what is right: *She* **had the grace** *to say that he was right.|He agreed that he was wrong* **with a good/bad grace** (=willingly/unwillingly) **3** [U] favour; mercy: *the grace of God* **4** [U] a delay allowed as a favour for payment, work, etc.: *The bill should be paid by Friday, but they're giving us a week's grace.* **5** [C;U] a prayer before or after meals, giving thanks to God: *Who'll say grace today?* **6** [C *usu. cap.*] a way of speaking to or of a DUKE, DUCHESS, or ARCHBISHOP:*Your/His/Her Grace*

**grace²** *v* **graced, gracing** [T] *fml or humor* to decorate; add a fine quality to by one's presence; HONOUR: *We were graced with the presence of our chairman.*

**grace·ful** /ˈgreɪsfəl/ *adj* **1** (of shape or movement) attractive to see: *a graceful dancer/runner* **2** (of speech and feeling) suitably and pleasantly expressed –see GRACIOUS (USAGE) **–gracefully** *adv*

**grace·less** /ˈgreɪslɪ̈s/ *adj* **1** awkward in movement or form **2** lacking in good manners **–gracelessly** *adv*

**gra·cious** /ˈgreɪʃəs/ *adj fml* **1** polite, kind, and pleasant –opposite **ungracious 2** [A] used in speaking of royal persons: *Her Gracious* MAJESTY *Queen Elizabeth* **3** [A] having those qualities which are made possible by wealth, such as comfort, beauty, and freedom from hard work: *gracious living* **–graciously** *adv* **–graciousness** *n* [U]

USAGE Compare **gracious** and **graceful**. **Graceful** means attractive or pleasant, and is used esp. to describe bodily movements or form, though it can also be used of people's manners: *a* **graceful** *dancer|a deer running* **gracefully** *through the forest|He admitted* **gracefully** *that he was wrong.* **Gracious** is normally used of people's manners and suggests a very grand person being polite to someone less important: *The Queen thanked them* **graciously**.

**gra·da·tion** /grəˈdeɪʃən/ *n* a stage in a set of changes or degrees of development

**grade¹** /greɪd/ *n* **1 a** a degree of rank or quality **b** the members of the group at this level: *This grade of wool can be sold at a lower price.|low-grade apples* **2** *AmE* a class for the work of a particular year of a school course: *She's in the second/eighth grade* –compare FORM¹ (6) **3** *esp. AmE* a mark for the standard of a piece of schoolwork **4** *AmE* for GRADIENT **5 make the grade** to succeed; reach the necessary standard

**grade²** *v* **graded, grading** [T] to separate into levels of rank or quality: *These potatoes have been graded according to size and quality.*

**gra·di·ent** /ˈgreɪdɪənt/ *n* the degree of slope, as on a road: *A gradient of 1 in 4 is a rise or fall of one metre for every four metres forward.*

**grad·u·al** /ˈgrædʒʊəl/ *adj* happening slowly and by degrees; not sudden: *There has been a gradual increase in the number of people owning cars.|a gradual rise in the path* **–gradually** *adv*

**grad·u·ate¹** /ˈgrædʒʊɪ̈t/ *adj,n* [A;C] **1** a person who has completed a university degree course, esp. for a first degree –see also BACHELOR (2), UNDERGRADUATE **2** *AmE* a person who has completed a course at a college, school, etc. **3** *esp. AmE* for POSTGRADUATE: *graduate school|a graduate student*

**grad·u·ate²** /ˈgrædʒʊeɪt/ *v* **-ated, -ating 1** [I *from*] to obtain a degree at a university, esp. a first degree **2** [I *from*] *AmE* to complete an educational course **3** [T] to arrange in order of degree, amount, or quality (GRADE²): *The salary scale is graduated so that you get more money each year.* **4** [T] *tech* to make marks showing degrees of measurement (on)

**grad·u·a·tion** /ˌgrædʒʊˈeɪʃən/ *n* [C;U] the act of graduating with, or ceremony at which one receives, a university degree or American high school DIPLOMA

**graf·fi·ti** /grəˈfiːti/ *n* [U] drawings or writing on a wall, esp. of a rude or political nature

**graft¹** /grɑːft‖græft/ *n* **1** [C] a piece cut from one plant and bound inside a cut in another, so that it grows there **2** [C] a piece of healthy living skin or bone taken from a person's body, and placed on or in another part of the body which has been damaged: *a skin graft on the burnt leg* **3** [U] *esp. AmE* the practice of gaining money or advantage by the dishonest use of political influence **4** [U] *BrE infml* hard work

**graft²** *v* [T *on, onto*] to put (a piece) as a GRAFT (1,2) on a tree or body

**grain** /greɪn/ *n* **1** [C] a seed of rice, wheat, or other such food plants **2** [U] crops from plants which produce such seeds, esp. from wheat **3** [C] a piece of a substance which is made up of small hard pieces: *a grain of sand/salt*|(fig.) *There is not* **a grain of truth** (=there is no truth at all) *in your statement.* –see picture on page 449 **4** [*the* U] the natural arrangement of the threads or FIBRES (1) in wood, flesh, rock, and cloth, or the pattern of lines one sees as a result of this: *It is easiest to cut wood in the direction of the grain.*|(fig.) **It goes against the grain** *for me to* *borrow money.* (=I don't like doing it) **5** [C] the smallest measure of weight, as used for medicines (1/7000 of a pound or ·0648 gram)

**gram, gramme** /græm/ *n* (a measure of weight equal to) 1/1000 of a kilogram

**gram·mar** /ˈgræməʳ/ *n* **1** [U] (the study and use of) the rules by which words change their forms and are combined into sentences: *I find German grammar very difficult.*|*You must try to improve your grammar.* **2** [C] a book which teaches these rules: *This is the best Italian grammar I've seen.*

**grammar school** /ˈ·· ·/ *n* **1** (in Britain, esp. formerly) a school for children over the age of 11, who are specially chosen to study for examinations which may lead to higher education –compare COMPREHENSIVE² **2** *AmE becoming rare* for ELEMENTARY SCHOOL

**gram·mat·i·cal** /grəˈmætɪkəl/ *adj* **1** [A] concerning grammar **2** correct according to the rules of grammar: *That is not a grammatical sentence.* **–grammatically** *adv*

**gram·o·phone** /ˈgræməfəun/ *n BrE becoming rare* →RECORD PLAYER

**gran** /græn/ *n BrE infml* grandmother

**gra·na·ry** /ˈgrænəri‖ˈgreɪ-, ˈgræ-/ *n* **-ries** a storehouse for grain, esp. wheat: (fig.) *The Mid-West is the granary of the US.*

**grand¹** /grænd/ *adj* **1** splendid in appearance; IMPRESSIVE: *There's a grand view of the mountains from this hotel.* **2** (of people) important, or (esp.) thinking oneself so **3** *infml* very pleasant; delightful: *That was a grand party.* **4** [A] complete (esp. in the phrase **the grand total**) **–grandly** *adv* **–grandness** *n* [U]

**grand²** *n* **grand** *infml* 1,000 dollars, pounds, etc.: *He paid fifteen grand for that car.*

**gran·dad, granddad** /ˈgrændæd/ *n infml* a grandfather

**grand·child** /ˈgræntʃaɪld/ *n* **grandchildren** /ˈgrænˌtʃɪldrən/ the child (**grandson** or **granddaughter**) of someone's son or daughter –see picture on page 217

**grand·daugh·ter** /ˈgrænˌdɔːtəʳ/ *n* the daughter of someone's son or daughter –see also GRANDSON; see picture on page 217

**gran·deur** /ˈgrændʒəʳ/ *n* [U] *fml* great beauty or power, often combined with great size:*the grandeur of nature*|*He has* **delusions of grandeur**. (=he thinks he is more important than he really is)

**grand·fa·ther** /ˈgrænˌfɑːðəʳ/ *n* the father of someone's father or mother –see also GRANDMOTHER; see picture on page 217

**grandfather clock** /ˈ···· ·, ˌ··· ˈ·/ *n* a tall clock which stands on the floor, with a wooden outer case and the face at the top

**gran·di·ose** /ˈgrændiəus/ *adj often derog* intended to have the effect of seeming important, splendid, etc.: *He's always producing grandiose plans that never work.*

**grand·ma** /ˈgrænmɑː/ *n infml* grandmother –see also GRANDPA

**grand·moth·er** /ˈgrænˌmʌðəʳ/ *n* the mother of someone's father or mother –see also GRANDFATHER; see picture on page 217

**grand·pa** /ˈgrænpɑː/ *n infml* grandfather –see also GRANDMA

**grand·par·ent** /ˈgrænˌpeərənt/ *n* the parent (**grandfather** or **grandmother**) of someone's father or mother –see picture on page 217

**grand pi·an·o** /ˌ· ·ˈ··/ *n* a large expensive piano, usu. played at concerts

**grand·son** /ˈgrænsʌn/ *n* the son of someone's son or daughter –see also GRANDDAUGHTER; see picture on page 217

**grand·stand** /ˈgrændstænd/ *n* the seats, arranged in rows and sometimes covered by a roof, from which people watch sports matches, races, etc. –compare TERRACE (3)

**grange** /greɪndʒ/ *n* (*often cap. as part of a name*) a ccountry house with farm buildings

**gran·ite** /ˈgrænɪt/ *n* [U] a hard grey rock, used for building and making roads

**gran·ny,** /ˈgræni/ *n* **-nies** *infml* grandmother

**grant¹** /grɑːnt‖grænt/ *n* money given esp. by the state for a particular purpose, e.g. to a university or to support a student during his/her studies: *She finds it difficult to live on her grant.*|*You can get a grant to improve your house.*

**grant²** *v* [T] **1** *fml* to give, esp. what is wanted or requested: *The boys were granted an extra day's holiday.* **2** [+*that*] to admit to (the truth of (something)): *I grant you that the government isn't very popular at the moment, but I think it will win the next election.* **3 granted** yes (but): *"We've been very successful this year." "Granted. But can we do it again next year?"* **4 take something/someone for granted: a** to accept a fact, action, etc., without question: *I took it for granted that you would want to see the play, so I bought you a ticket.* **b** to treat something or someone with no attention or thought; not realize the true value of: *He's so busy with his job that he takes his family for granted.*

**gran·u·lated** /ˈgrænjuleɪtɪd‖-jə-/ *adj* consisting of small bits (GRAINS (3) or GRANULES):*granulated sugar* (=ordinary powdery sugar, not large lumps)

**gran·ule** /ˈgrænjuːl/ *n* a small bit like a fine grain: *a granule of salt* **–granular** /ˈgrænjuləʳ‖-jə-/ *adj*

**grape** /greɪp/ *n* **1** a small round juicy fruit usu. green (called "white") or dark purple (called "black"),which grows on a VINE (1) and is often used for making wine: *a bunch of grapes* **2 sour grapes** the act of pretending to dislike what one really desires, because it is unobtainable: *Since losing the election, John says he never really wanted to become a politician anyway, but I think it's just sour grapes.*

**grape·fruit** /ˈgreɪpfruːt/ *n* **grapefruit** *or* **grapefruits** a large round yellow fruit with a thick skin, like an orange but with a more acid taste

**grape·vine** /ˈgreɪpvaɪn/ *n* **1** [C] the climbing plant that bears GRAPES **2** [*the* S] a secret way of spreading news or RUMOUR: *I heard about your new job* **on/through the** (*office*) **grapevine.**

**graph** /græf, grɑːf‖græf/ *n* a drawing showing the relationship between two changing quantities; for example a line which shows the monthly profits of a business –compare CHART¹ (1)

**graph·ic** /ˈgræfɪk/ *adj* [A] **1** concerned with written signs, usu. letters or drawings: *the graphic arts* **2** which gives a clear and detailed description or lifelike picture, esp. in words: *a graphic description of the accident*

**graph·i·cally** /ˈgræfɪkli/ *adv* **1** in a GRAPHIC (2) manner: *She described the events so graphically that I could almost see them.* **2** *fml* by means of a GRAPH

**grap·ple with** sbdy./sthg. /ˈgræpəl/ *v prep* **-pled, -pling** [T] to seize and struggle with: *He grappled with the bank robber, but was thrown to the ground.*|(fig.) *to grapple with a difficult problem*

**grasp**[1] /grɑːsp‖græsp/ *v* [T] **1** to take or keep a firm hold of, esp. with the hands: (fig.) *to grasp an* OPPORTUNITY **2** to succeed in understanding: *I grasped the main points of the speech.*

**grasp at** sthg. *v prep* [T] to reach for; try to take, seize, or hold: *He grasped at anything that might help him.*

**grasp**[2] *n* [S] **1** a firm hold: *I kept her hand in my grasp.* **2** →REACH[2] (1): *Success is within her grasp.* **3** understanding: *This work is* **beyond my grasp.**|*She has* **a good grasp of** *the English language.*

**grasp·ing** /ˈgrɑːspɪŋ‖ˈgræs-/ *adj derog* eager for more, esp. money: *Don't let those grasping taxi-drivers charge you too much.*

**grass** /grɑːs‖græs/ *n* **1** [U] a common low-growing green plant growing in fields and on hills: *She was lying on the grass.*|*We played football on the grass.* **2** [C] a green plant with tall, straight stems and flat blades: *He hid behind some tall grasses* **3** [U] *infml* →MARIJUANA

**grass·hop·per** /ˈgrɑːsˌhɒpəʳ‖ˈgræsˌhɑ-/ *n* an insect which can jump high and make a sharp noise by rubbing parts of its body together

**grass·land** /ˈgrɑːslænd‖ˈgræs-/ *n* [U] a stretch of land covered mainly with grass,esp. land used for cattle to feed on

**grass roots** /ˌ· ˈ·/ *n* [P] the ordinary people in a country, political party, etc., not the ones with power:*grass roots opinion*|*a grass roots movement*

**gras·sy** /ˈgrɑːsi‖ˈgræsi/ *adj* **-sier, -siest** covered with growing grass

**grate**[1] /greɪt/ *n* the bars and frame which hold the coal, wood, etc., in a fireplace –sounds like **great**

**grate**[2] *v* **grated, grating 1** [T] to rub (usu. food) on a hard, rough surface so as to break into small pieces: *grated cheese* **2** [I *on*] to make a sharp sound, unpleasant to the hearer: *The nails in his boots grated on the stones.*|*His whistling grated on her nerves.* –sounds like **great**

**grate·ful** /ˈgreɪtfəl/ *adj* [*to, for*] feeling or showing thanks to another person: *I was most grateful to John for bringing the books/for his kindness.* –opposite **ungrateful**; see also GRATITUDE –**gratefully** *adv* –**gratefulness** *n* [U]

**grat·i·fy** /ˈgrætɪ̈faɪ/ *v* **-fied, -fying** [T] *fml* to give pleasure and satisfaction to: *It gratified me to know how soon he would be well again.* –**gratification** /-fɪ̈ˈkeɪʃən/ *n* [U] –**gratifying** *adj* [+*to-v*]: *It was gratifying to know of the success of our efforts.*

**grat·ing**[1] /ˈgreɪtɪŋ/ *n* a frame or network of bars, usu. metal, to protect a hole or window: *The coin fell through a grating at the side of the road.*

**grating**[2] *adj* (of a noise or sound) sharp, hard, and unpleasant –**gratingly** *adv*

**grat·is** /ˈgrætɪ̈s, ˈgrɑːtɪ̈s/ *adv,adj* [F] *fml* free; (given) without payment

**grat·i·tude** /ˈgrætɪ̈tjuːd‖-tuːd/ *n* [U *to, for*] the state or feeling of being grateful; kind feelings towards someone who has been kind: *She showed me her gratitude by inviting me to dinner.* –opposite **ingratitude**

**gra·tu·i·tous** /grəˈtjuːɪ̈təs‖-ˈtuː-/ *adj* **1** done freely, without reward or payment being expected **2** *derog* not deserved or necessary: *a gratuitous, rude remark*|*His films are full of gratuitous violence.* –**gratuitously** *adv*

**gra·tu·i·ty** /grəˈtjuːɪ̈ti‖-ˈtuː-/ *n* **-ties 1** a gift of money for a service done; TIP[4] **2** *BrE* a gift of money to a worker who is leaving his/her employment

**grave**[1] /greɪv/ *n* **1** the place in the ground where a dead person is buried: (fig.) *Is there life beyond the grave?* (=after death) **2 make someone turn in his/her grave** to do something which would anger a person now dead: *That use of English would make Shakespeare turn in his grave.*

**grave**[2] *adj* serious or solemn: *His face was grave as he told them about the accident.*|*The sick man's condition is grave.* (=he is seriously ill) –**gravely** *adv*

**grav·el**[1] /ˈgrævəl/ *n* [U] a mixture of small stones with sand, used on the surface of roads or paths

**gravel**[2] *v* **-ll-** *BrE*‖**-l-** *AmE* [T] to cover (a road) with GRAVEL: *a gravelled path*

**grave·stone** /ˈgreɪvstəʊn/ *n* a stone put up over a grave bearing the name,dates of birth and death, etc., of the dead person

**grave·yard** /ˈgreɪvjɑːd‖-ɑrd/ *n* a piece of ground, sometimes near a church, where people are buried; CEMETERY –compare CHURCHYARD

**grav·i·tate towards** sthg. /ˈgrævɪ̈teɪt/ also **gravitate to** sthg.– *v prep* **-tated, -tating** [T] to be drawn towards and move to: *In the 19th century, industry gravitated towards the north of England.*

**grav·i·ta·tion** /ˌgrævɪ̈ˈteɪʃən/ *n* [U] **1** the act of gravitating (GRAVITATE TOWARDS) **2** →GRAVITY (2) –**gravitational** *adj*

**grav·i·ty** /ˈgrævɪ̈ti/ *n* [U] **1** seriousness (as of manner, of a situation, etc.): *He doesn't understand the gravity of his illness.* –see GRAVE[2] **2** the natural force by which objects are attracted to each other,esp. that by which a large mass pulls a smaller one to it: *Anything that is dropped falls to the ground, pulled by the force of gravity.*

**gra·vy** /ˈgreɪvi/ *n* [U] **1** the juice which comes out of meat as it cooks **2** the thickened liquid made from this (with flour, etc., added) to serve with meat and vegetables

**gray** /greɪ/ *adj,n,v AmE* for GREY

**graze**[1] /greɪz/ *v* **grazed, grazing 1** [I] (of animals) to feed on grass: *The cattle are grazing in the field.* **2** [T] to cause (animals) to feed on grass: *We're grazing the sheep in the next field.*

**graze**[2] *v* [T] **1** to break the surface of (esp. the skin) by rubbing against something: *She fell down and grazed her knee.* **2** to touch (something) lightly while passing: *The car just grazed the gate as it drove through.*

**graze**[3] *n* [*usu. sing.*] a surface wound

**grease**[1] /griːs/ *n* [U] **1** animal fat when soft after being melted: *It was difficult to get the* BACON *grease* *off the plates.* **2** a thick oily substance: *He puts grease on his hair to make it shiny.*

**grease²** /griːs, griːz/ *v* **greased, greasing** [T] to put GREASE ON: *If you grease the lock it will turn more easily.|Grease the tin with butter before baking the cake.*

**grease·proof** /'griːs-pruːf/ *adj BrE* [A] (of paper) which does not let GREASE pass through it

**greas·y** /'griːsi, -zi/ *adj* **-ier, -iest** covered with or containing GREASE; slippery: *greasy food/skin/hair|The roads are greasy after the rain.* **–greasily** *adv* **–greasiness** *n* [U]

**great** /greɪt/ *adj* **1** of excellent quality or ability: *the great women of the past|a great king, artist, etc.* **2** [A] important: *a great occasion* **3** large in amount or degree: *Take great care.|It was a great loss to us all.|a great deal|a great many* **4** [A] (of people) unusually active in the stated way: *He's a great talker.|We're great* (=very close) *friends.* **5** [A] (*usu. before another adj of size*) big: *a great (big) tree* **6** *infml* unusually good; very enjoyable: *What a great idea!|This new singer is really great!* **7 great-: a** being the parent of a person's grandparent: *great-grandfather* **b** being the child of a person's grandchild: *great-granddaughter* **c** being the brother or sister of a person's grandparent: *great-aunt* **d** being the child of a person's nephew or niece: *great-nephew* **–greatness** *n* [U]

**great·ly** /'greɪtli/ *adv* (*with verb forms, esp. the past participle*) to a large degree; very:*greatly moved by his kindness|greatly to be feared*

**greed** /griːd/ *n* [U *for*] *usu. derog* strong desire to obtain a lot or more than what is fair,esp. of food, money, or power: *He eats because of greed, not hunger.|greed for gold*

**greed·y** /'griːdi/ *adj* **-ier, -iest** *usu. derog* full of GREED, esp. for food: *The greedy little boy ate all the food at the party.|greedy for power* **–greedily** *adv* **–greediness** *n* [U]

**green¹** /griːn/ *adj* **1** of a colour between yellow and blue; of the colour of leaves and grass: *a green* SALAD|*The country is very green* (= covered in fresh leaves and grass) *in the spring.* **2** unhealthily pale in the face, as though from sickness **3** [F] also **green with envy**– very jealous **4** *infml* young and/or inexperienced and therefore easily deceived and ready to believe anything **5 have green fingers** *BrE*||**a green thumb** *AmE* to have natural skill in making plants grow well **6 the green light** the sign, or permission, to begin an action: *We're ready to rebuild our house. We're just waiting for the green light from the council.* **–greenness** *n* [U]

**green²** *n* **1** [U] the colour which is green: *She was dressed in green.* **2** [C] a smooth stretch of grass, for a special purpose, as for playing a game or for the general use of the people of a town: *They are dancing on the village green.|a* BOWL*ing²* (2) *green|The* GOLF*er² hit his ball onto the green in one stroke!*

**green belt** /'· ·/ *n* [C;U] a stretch of land round a town, where building is not allowed, so that fields, woods, etc., remain

**green·e·ry** /'griːnəri/ *n* [U] green leaves and plants (FOLIAGE), esp. when used for ornament

**green·gage** /'griːngeɪdʒ/ *n* a soft juicy greenish-yellow fruit; kind of PLUM (1)

**green·gro·cer** /'griːnˌgrəusəʳ/ *n esp. BrE* (a person who has) a shop selling vegetables and fruit: *I bought some oranges at the greengrocer's.* –compare GROCER

**green·house** /'griːnhaus/ *n* a building made of glass, used for growing plants which need heat,light, and protection from winds

**greens** /griːnz/ *n* [P] green leafy vegetables that are cooked and eaten

**Green·wich Mean Time** /ˌgrɪnɪdʒ 'miːn taɪm, ˌgre-, -nɪtʃ/ (*abbrev.* **GMT**) *n* the time at a place near London (Greenwich) which is on an imaginary line dividing east from west. Times in the rest of the world are fixed in relation to this: *European time is usually one hour later than Greenwich Mean Time.*

**greet** /griːt/ *v* [T] **1** to welcome on meeting: *She greeted us by shouting a friendly* "HELLO!"|*He greeted her with a loving kiss.*|(fig.) *As we entered the room, we were greeted by complete disorder.* **2** to receive with an expression of feeling: *The speech was greeted by loud cheers.*

**greet·ing** /'griːtɪŋ/ *n* **1** a form of words or an action used on meeting someone:*"Good morning," I said, but she didn't return the greeting.* **2** [*usu. pl.*] a good wish: *We sent a card with birthday/Christmas greetings.*

**gre·gar·i·ous** /grɪ'geərɪəs/ *adj* living in groups; enjoying the companionship of others **–gregariously** *adv* **–gregariousness** *n* [U]

**gre·nade** /gr¹₂'neɪd/ *n* a small bomb which can be thrown by hand or fired from a gun

**grew** /gruː/ *v past tense of* GROW

**grey¹** ||also **gray** *AmE* /greɪ/ *adj* **greyer, greyest 1** of the colour like black mixed with white; of the colour of lead,ashes, rain clouds, etc.: *Her hair is going grey with worry.|a grey coat*|(fig.) *His life in prison seemed grey* (=dull) *and joyless.* **2** having grey hair: *She's gone grey within a few weeks.* **3** (of the skin of the face) of a pale colour because of sudden fear or illness:*His face turned grey as he heard the bad news.* **–greyness** *n* [U]

**grey²** ||also **gray** *AmE n* [C;U] (a) grey colour: *She was dressed in grey.|dull greys and browns*

**grey³** ||also **gray** *AmE v* [I] (of hair) to become grey: *greying hair*

**grey·hound** /'greɪhaund/ *n* a thin dog with long legs, which can runswiftly in hunting and racing

**grid** /grɪd/ *n* **1** a set of bars set across each other in a frame; GRATING¹: *a grid over a drain|a cattle grid* (=to stop cattle leaving a field) **2** a network of electricity supply wires connecting the power stations: *the national grid* **3** a system of numbered squares printed on a map so that the exact position of any place on it may be stated or found

**grid·dle** /'grɪdl/ *n* an iron plate which can be used for baking over a fire or on top of a cooker –see picture on page 521

**grief** /griːf/ *n* [U] **1** great sorrow or feelings of suffering, esp. at the death of a loved person:*She went nearly mad with grief after the child died.|His wild behaviour was a cause of grief to his parents.* **2 come/be brought to grief** to fail, causing harm to oneself: *My plan came to grief, and I was left penniless.* **3 good grief!** (an expression of surprise and some dislike)

**griev·ance** /ˈgriːvəns/ *n* a report of or cause for complaint, esp. of unjust treatment: *a committee to deal with workers' grievances*

**grieve** /griːv/ *v* **grieved, grieving 1** [I *for*] to suffer from grief and sadness, esp. over a loss: *She is still grieving (for her dead husband).* **2** [T] to cause grief to; make very unhappy: *It grieves me to see him in such bad health.*

**griev·ous** /ˈgriːvəs/ *adj* [A] *fml* very seriously harmful; severe: *a grievous mistake|grievous wounds* **–grievously** *adv*

**grill¹** /grɪl/ *v* **1** [I;T] to cook (something) under or over direct heat, not in a SAUCEPAN: (fig.) *He is grilling (himself) under the hot sun.* –compare BROIL; see COOK² (USAGE) **2** [T] *infml* (esp. of the police) to question severely and continuously: *He was grilled for two hours before the police let him go.*

**grill²** *n* **1** an open metal shelf under direct heat in a cooker, or a set of bars which can be put over a hot open fire, so that food can be cooked quickly: *Put the bread under the grill to make the* TOAST² (1) *for breakfast.* –see picture on page 337 **2** meat cooked this way (esp. in the phrase **a mixed grill** =several types together)

**grille** /grɪl/ *n* a framework of usu. upright metal bars filling a space in a door orwindow, esp. in a bank or other place where money is handled and must be protected

**grim** /grɪm/ *adj* **-mm- 1** cruel, hard, or causing fear: *His expression was grim when he told them they had lost their jobs.|the grim news of his death* **2** determined, esp. in spite of fear: *a grim smile* **3** *infml* unpleasant; not cheerful: *What grim weather!* **–grimly** *adv* **–grimness** *n* [U]

**gri·mace** /grɪˈmeɪs, ˈgrɪməs||ˈgrɪməs, / *v* **-maced, -macing** [I *at, with*] to make an expression of pain, annoyance, etc., which makes the face look unnaturally twisted: *The teacher grimaced as he looked at my work.|He grimaced with pain.* **–grimace** *n*: *a grimace of pain*

**grime** /graɪm/ *n* [U] a surface of thick black dirt: *His face and hands were covered with grime from the coal dust.*

**grim·y** /ˈgraɪmi/ *adj* **-ier, -iest** covered with dark dirt or GRIME **–griminess** *n* [U]

**grin¹** /grɪn/ *v* **-nn-** [I *with, at*] **1** to make a wide smile: *They grinned with pleasure when I gave them the sweets.* –compare SMILE,LAUGH **2 grin and bear it** *infml* to suffer what is unpleasant without complaint

**grin²** *n* a smile, esp. a very wide smile: *I knew she was joking because she had a big grin on her face.*

**grind¹** /graɪnd/ *v* **ground** /graʊnd/, **grinding** [T] **1** to crush into small pieces or a powder by pressing between hard surfaces: *Grind up the wheat to make flour.|freshly-ground coffee* **2** to make smooth or sharp by rubbing on a hard surface: *A man came to grind the knives and scissors.* **3** to press upon, or press together, with a strong, twisting movement: *The dirt was deeply ground into the floor.|Some people grind their teeth during their sleep.* **4 grind to a halt** to come slowly and/or noisily to a stop

**grind** sbdy.↔ **down** *v adv* [T]→OPPRESS: *The people were ground down by lack of food and money.*

**grind** sthg.↔ **out** *v adv* [T] *derog* to produce (esp. writing or music of poor quality) continuously, like a machine

**grind²** *n* [S] hard uninteresting work: *He finds any kind of study a real grind.|the daily grind of the housework*

**grind·er** /ˈgraɪndəʳ/ *n* a person or machine that GRINDS¹ (1): *a coffee grinder|a knife grinder*

**grind·stone** /ˈgraɪndstəʊn/ *n* **1** a round stone which is turned to sharpen tools, knives, etc. **2 one's nose to the grindstone** *infml* in a state of hard dull work: *He's got to keep his nose to the grindstone to feed his five children.*

**grip¹** /grɪp/ *v* **-pp-** [I;T] to take a very tight hold (of): *Grip harder.|He gripped my hand in fear.|*(fig.) *The pictures gripped my imagination.*

**grip²** *n* **1** [C *usu. sing.*] a very tight forceful hold: *The policeman would not let go his grip on the thief.|*(fig.) *He keeps a firm grip on his children.* **2** [S] the power of understanding or doing: *I played badly; I seem to be* **losing my grip**. **3** [C] *AmE or old use* a bag or case for a traveller's personal belongings **4** [C] (a part of) an apparatus which GRIPS: *a hairgrip* **5 come/get to grips with** to deal seriously with (something difficult): *The speaker talked a lot, but never really got to grips with the subject.*

**gripe¹** /graɪp/ *v* **griped, griping** [I *at, about*] *infml* to complain continually: *He's griping about his income tax again.*

**gripe²** *n infml* a complaint: *My main gripe is, there's no hot water.*

**grip·ping** /ˈgrɪpɪŋ/ *adj* that holds the attention: *a gripping film* **–grippingly** *adv*

**gris·ly** /ˈgrɪzli/ *adj* **-lier, -liest** unpleasant because of destruction, decay, or death which is shown or described: *the grisly remains of the bodies|a grisly story about people who ate human flesh* –compare GRUESOME

**gris·tle** /ˈgrɪsəl/ *n* [U] the material in meat which is too tough to eat, found near the bones –compare CARTILAGE **–gristly** *adj* **-ier, -iest**

**grit¹** /grɪt/ *n* [U] **1** small pieces of a hard material, usu. stone: *Grit is spread on roads to make them less slippery in icy weather.* **2** *infml* determination; lasting courage; cheerful effort made during difficulty **–gritty** *adj* **-tier, -tiest**

**grit²** *v* **-tt- grit one's teeth** to become determined when in a position of difficulty: *The snow was blowing in her face, but she gritted her teeth and went on.*

**groan¹** /grəʊn/ *v* [I] to make a GROAN²: *The old man who had been in the accident lay groaning beside the road.|*(fig.) *The table groaned with food.* (=there was lots of food on it)|(fig.) *The people groaned under the load of taxes.*

**groan²** *n* a rather loud sound of suffering, worry, or disapproval, made in a deep voice: *There were loud groans when he asked them for money.|*(fig.) *The old chair gave a groan when the fat man sat down on it.*

**gro·cer** /ˈgrəʊsəʳ/ *n* a shopkeeper who sells dry and preserved foods, like flour, coffee, sugar, rice, and other things for the home, such as matches and soap –compare GREENGROCER

**gro·cer·ies** /ˈgrəʊsəriz/ *n* [P] the goods sold by a GROCER: *He brought the box of groceries in from the car.*

**grog·gy** /'grɒgi||'grɑgi/ *adj* **-gier, -giest** [F] *infml* weak because of illness, shock, etc., esp. when not able to walk steadily: *When I left my bed after my long illness I felt too groggy to stand.* **–groggily** *adv*

**groin** /grɔɪn/ *n* the place where the tops of the legs meet the front of the body

**groom**[1] /gru:m, grʊm/ *n* **1** a person who is in charge of horses **2** →BRIDEGROOM

**groom**[2] /gru:m/ *v* [T] **1** to take care of (horses), esp. by rubbing, brushing, and cleaning **2** to take care of the appearance of (oneself), by dressing neatly, keeping the hair tidy, etc.: *a well-groomed look* **3** [*for*] to prepare (someone) for a special position or occasion: *grooming her for stardom* (=to play big parts in plays or films)

**groove** /gru:v/ *n* a long narrow path or track made in a surface, esp. to guide the movement of something: *The needle moves along the groove on a record.|The cupboard door slides open along a groove.*

**grope** /grəʊp/ *v* **groped, groping** [I;T *for*] to search about with the hands in or as if in the dark; feel: *He groped in his pocket for his ticket.|I groped my way to a seat in the dark cinema.*|(fig.) *We are groping after the truth.*

**gross**[1] /grəʊs/ *adj* **1** unpleasantly fat **2** (of people's speech and habits) rough, impolite, and offensive: *She was shocked by his gross behaviour at the party.* **3** inexcusable; FLAGRANT: *gross negligence* (=carelessness) **4** [*no comp.*] total: *The gross weight of the box of chocolates is more than the weight of the chocolates alone.* –compare NET[3] **–grossly** *adv* **–grossness** *n* [U]

**gross**[2] *v* [T] to gain as total profit or earn as a total amount: *The company grossed £2,000,000 last year.* –compare NET[4]

**gross**[3] *determiner,n* **gross** *or* **grosses** a group of 144; 12 DOZEN

**gro·tesque** /grəʊ'tesk/ *adj* strange and unnatural so as to cause fear or be laughable: *The fat old man looked grotesque in tight trousers.* **–grotesquely** *adv* **–grotesqueness** *n* [U]

**grot·to** /'grɒtəʊ||'grɑ-/ *n* **-toes** *or* **-tos** a natural cave, esp. of limestone, or a man-made one in a garden

**grot·ty** /'grɒti||'grɑti/ *adj* **-tier, -tiest** *BrE infml* bad, nasty, unpleasant, etc.: *She lives in a grotty little room with nowhere to cook.* **–grottiness** *n* [U]

**grouch**[1] /graʊtʃ/ *n infml* **1** a bad-tempered complaint **2** a person who keeps complaining

**grouch**[2] *v* [I] *infml* to complain; GRUMBLE[1] (1)

**ground**[1] /graʊnd/ *n* **1** [*the* S;U] the surface of the earth: *The branch broke and fell to the ground.* –compare FLOOR[1] (1)|*They built a bomb shelter below ground/underground.*|(fig.) *The book says nothing new; it just goes over the same old ground/doesn't* **break new ground**.|You're **on dangerous ground** *if you mention modern music to him–he hates it!* **2** [U] soil; earth: *The ground is too dry for planting seeds.* –see LAND (USAGE) **3** [C] a piece of land used for a particular purpose: *a football ground|a playground* **4** [U] an argument or position which one will defend: *He refused to* **give ground** *in the argument.* (= would not admit the point) **5** [C] →BACKGROUND: *The curtains have white flowers on a blue ground.* **6 gain ground** to have more success or become more popular: *The opposition party seems to be gaining ground.* **7 get off the ground** to make a successful start –see also GROUNDS

**ground**[2] *v* **1** [I] (of a boat) to strike against the bottom or the ground **2** [T] to cause (a pilot or plane) to come to or stay on the ground, instead of flying **3** [T *on, in*] to base: *an argument grounded on personal experience*

**ground**[3] *v past tense and participle of* GRIND

**ground floor** ||also **first floor** *AmE* /ˌ· '·◄ /– *n* the part of a building, often the lowest, at ground level: *I live on the ground floor.* –compare FIRST FLOOR; see picture on page 297

**ground·ing** /'graʊndɪŋ/ *n* [S] a complete training in the main points which will enable thorough study or work on some subject: *a good grounding in English grammar*

**ground·less** /'graʊndlǝs/ *adj* (of feelings, ideas, etc.) without base or good reason: *groundless fears/worries* **–groundlessly** *adv*

**ground·nut** /'graʊndnʌt/ *n BrE* for PEANUT

**grounds** /graʊndz/ *n* [P] **1** land surrounding a large building, such as a country house or hospital, usu. made into gardens and enclosed by a wall or fence: *a walk through the grounds* **2** a reason: *We have good grounds for thinking that she stole the money.|He left* **on (the) grounds of** *ill-health.* **3** small bits of solid matter which sink to the bottom of a liquid, esp. coffee

**grounds·man** /'graʊndzmən/ *n esp. BrE* a man employed to take care of a sports field or large gardens

**ground·work** /'graʊndwɜ:k||-ɜrk/ *n* [U] the work which forms the base for some kind of study or skill

**group**[1] /gru:p/ *n* [*+sing./pl. v*] **1** a number of people, things, or organizations placed together or connected in a particular way: *a photograph of a family group|a group of tall trees|School-children are taught according to age groups.|a language group* **2** a usu. small number of players of popular music: *My favourite group is/are playing here tonight.*

**group**[2] *v* [I;T] to form into one or more groups: *We can group animals into several types.*

**group·ie** /'gru:pi/ *n infml* a person, esp. a young girl, who follows POP[4] group players to the concerts they give, esp. to have sex with them

**group·ing** /'gru:pɪŋ/ *n* [*usu. sing.*] a (way of) arrangement into a group: *The new grouping of classes means that there are larger numbers in each class.*

**grouse**[1] /graʊs/ *n* **grouse** a smallish fat bird which is shot for food and sport

**grouse**[2] *v,n* [C;I] *infml* (to make) a complaint; GRUMBLE

**grove** /grəʊv/ *n* **1** *lit* a small group of trees **2** (part of the name of) a road

**grov·el** /'grɒvəl||'grɑ-, 'grʌ-/ *v* **-ll-** *BrE*||**-l-** *AmE* [I *to*] *derog* to lie or move flat on the ground, esp. in fear of or obedience to someone powerful: *The dog grovelled at his feet when he shouted at it.*|(fig.) *I had to grovel to my employer before she would agree to increase my pay.* **–groveller** *n*

**grow** /grəʊ/ *v* **grew** /gru:/, **grown** /grəʊn/, **growing 1** [I] (of (parts of) living things) to increase in size by natural development: *Grass grows after rain.|He's grown six inches (taller).|A lamb grows into a* *sheep.*|*She's letting her hair grow.*|*a growing boy*|*The population is growing* (=increasing in numbers) *too quickly.* **2** [I] (of plants) to exist and be able to develop, esp. after planting:*Cotton grows wild here.*|*Oranges grow in Spain.* **3** [T] to cause to or allow to grow (esp. plants and crops): *Mary grows vegetables.*|*Plants grow roots.*|*He's grown a beard.*|*She's grown her hair long.* **4** [+*to-* *v*] to become (gradually): *She's growing fat.*|*The noise grew louder.*|*It's growing dark; we must go home soon.*|*I think you'll grow to like him when you know him better.*

**grow away from** sbdy. *v adv prep* [T *no pass.*] to have a less close relationship with (esp. one's parents, husband, or wife): *Since she went to university she's grown away from the family.*

**grow into** sbdy./sthg. *v prep* **1** to become: *She's grown into a fine young woman.* **2** [T *no pass.*] to become big enough for (clothes): *The coat is too long, but she'll grow into it.* –compare GROW **out of** (1)

**grow on** sbdy. *v prep* [T] to become gradually more pleasing or more of a habit to:*Modern music is difficult to listen to, but it starts to grow on you.*

**grow out of** sthg. *v adv prep* [T +*v-ing*] **1** to become too big or too old for (esp. clothes, shoes, etc.): *My daughter has grown out of all her old clothes* –compare GROW **into** (2) **2** [*no pass.*] to develop as a result of: *Her political beliefs grew out of her hatred of injustice.*

**grow up** *v adv* [I] **1** (of people) to develop from child to man or woman **2** to arise; develop into something lasting: *The custom grew up of dividing the father's land between the sons.*

**grow·er** /'grəʊəʳ/ *n* a person who grows plants, fruit, etc., for sale

**growl** /graʊl/ *v,n* [C;I] (to make) a deep rough sound in the throat, or a sound like this: *Our dog always growls at visitors.*|*the growl of distant thunder*

**grown** /grəʊn/ *adj* [A] of full size or development; ADULT:*A grown man like you shouldn't act like that.*

**grown-up** /,· '·◂/ *adj* fully developed; ADULT: *She has a grown-up daughter who lives abroad.* –**grown-up** /'··/ *n* : *infml: Go to bed now and let the grown-ups have a little time to themselves.*

**growth** /grəʊθ/ *n* /grəʊv/ **1** [U] the act or rate of growing and developing: *the slow growth of world* LITERACY **2** [S;U] increase in numbers or amount: *the growth of large companies*|*a sudden growth in the membership of the club* **3** [C] something which has grown: *Nails are growths at the ends of the fingers.* **4** [C] a lump produced by an unnatural and unhealthy increase in the number of cells in a part of the body –compare TUMOUR

**grub¹** /grʌb/ *n* **1** [C] an insect in the wormlike form it has when just out of the egg **2** [U] *infml* food

**grub²** *v* **-bb-** [I] to turn over the soil; dig: *The dog was grubbing (about) under the bush, looking for a bone.*

**grub·by** /'grʌbi/ *adj* **-bier, -biest** dirty

**grudge¹** /grʌd·/ also **begrudge**– *v* **grudged, grudging** [T +*v-ing*] to give or allow (something) unwillingly: *He grudged paying so much for such bad food.*

**grudge²** *n* [*against*] **1** a cause for dislike, real or imagined, esp. of another person: *I always feel he has a grudge against me, although I don't know why.* **2** **bear a grudge/grudges** to continue to have feelings of anger about someone's past actions: *He bears a grudge against me because I took his place in the team.*

**grudg·ing** /'grʌd·ɪŋ/ *adj* ungenerous; unwilling (to give): *She was very grudging in her thanks.* –**grudgingly** *adv*

**gru·el** /'gru:əl/ *n* [U] a thin liquid food, esp. for sick people

**gru·el·ling** *BrE*‖**grueling** *AmE* /'gru:əlɪŋ/ *adj* very hard and tiring

**grue·some** /'gru:səm/ *adj* (esp. of something connected with death or decay) terrible to the senses; shocking and sickening –compare GRISLY –**gruesomely** *adv* –**gruesomeness** *n* [U]

**gruff** /grʌf/ *adj* (of a person's voice or way of speaking) rough and unfriendly: *Although he has a gruff manner, he is really very kind.* –**gruffly** *adv* –**gruffness** *n* [U]

**grum·ble¹** /'grʌmbəl/ *v* **-bled, -bling** [I] **1** [*about*] to express discontent or dissatisfaction; complain, not loudly, but angrily:*He has everything he needs: he has nothing to grumble about.* **2** (of thunder and certain noises) RUMBLE –**grumbler** *n*

**grumble²** *n* a complaint or expression of dissatisfaction

**grump·y** /'grʌmpi/ *adj* **-ier, -iest** bad-tempered, esp. because of low spirits: *You're very grumpy today –what's the matter?* –**grumpily** *adv* –**grumpiness** *n* [U]

**grunt** /grʌnt/ *v,n* [C;I] (to make) a short deep rough sound in the throat, as if the nose were closed: *a grunting pig*|*He didn't say anything–he just gave a grunt of agreement.*

**guar·an·tee¹** /,gærən'ti:/ *n* [+*to-v*/*that*/*of*] **1** a formal declaration that something will be done, esp. a written agreement by the maker of an article to repair or replace it if it is found imperfect within a period of time: *The radio has a two-year guarantee.*|*The car is less than a year old, so it is still* **under guarantee**.|(fig.) *Clear skies are no guarantee that the weather will stay fine.* **2** an agreement to be responsible for the fulfilment of someone else's promise, esp. for paying a debt **3** something of value given to someone to keep until the owner has fulfilled a promise, esp. to pay:*He gave them the papers which proved his ownership of the land, as a guarantee that he would repay the money.* –compare SECURITY (3)

**guarantee²** *v* **-teed, -teeing** [T] **1** to give a promise of quality, payment, or fulfilment (a GUARANTEE) about: *The watch is guaranteed for three years.*|*They have guaranteed delivery within a month.* **2** [+*to-v*/*that*] to promise (that something will certainly be so): *I guarantee that you'll enjoy yourself.*

**guar·an·tor** /,gærən'tɔ:ʳ/ *n law* a person who gives a GUARANTEE¹ (2)

**guar·an·ty** /'gærənti/ *n* **-ties** *law* a GUARANTEE, esp. of payment

**guard¹** /gɑ:d‖gɑrd/ *n* **1** [U] a state of watchful readiness to protect or defend: *There are soldiers* **on guard** *at the gate, to prevent anyone getting in or out.*|*They are keeping/standing guard over the house.* **2** [U] a position for defence, esp. in a fight: *He hit him* **when his guard was down.** (= when he was not ready to defend himself) **3** [C] a person, esp. a soldier, policeman, or prison officer, who guards someone or something: *The camp guards are changed every night.* **4** [C +*sing./pl. v*] a group of people, esp. soldiers, whose duty it is to guard someone or something:*The prisoner was brought in* **under** *armed* **guard.**|*The guard is/are changed every hour.* **5** [C] *BrE*||**conductor** *AmE*– a railway official in charge of a train –see picture on page 501 **6** [C] an apparatus which covers and protects: *A fireguard prevents children getting near the fire.*|*a mudguard over the wheel of a bicycle* **7 on/off one's guard** ready/not ready to deal with a sudden trick or attack: *Be on your guard against* PICKPOCKETS.

**guard²** *v* [T] **1** [*against, from*] to defend; keep safe, esp. by watching for danger: *The dog guarded the house (against strangers).*|*The soldiers were guarding the bridge.* **2** to watch (a prisoner) in order to prevent escape

**guard against** sthg. *v prep* [T +*v-ing*] to (try to) prevent by special care: *You should wash your hands when preparing food, to guard against spreading infection.*

**guard·ed** /'gɑːdȝd||'gɑr-/ *adj* (of speech) careful; not saying too much –**guardedly** *adv*

**guard·i·an** /'gɑːdɪən||'gɑr-/ *n* **1** a person or place that guards or protects: *The Bank of England is the guardian of our wealth.*|*A* **guardian angel** *is believed to be a good spirit which protects a person or a place.* **2** *law* a person who has the responsibility of looking after a child not his/her own, esp. after the parents' death –compare WARD (3)

**gua·va** /'gwɑːvə/ *n* (a small tropical tree bearing) a round fruit with pink or white flesh and seeds in the centre

**guer·ril·la, guerilla** /gə'rɪlə/ *n* a member of an unofficial fighting group which attacks the enemy in small groups unexpectedly: *guerrilla warfare*

**guess¹** /ges/ *v* **1** [I;T +(*that*)/*at*] to form (a judgment) or risk giving (an opinion) without knowing or considering all the facts: *Can you guess (at) the price?*|*Guess how much/what it cost.*|*I guess her age as 35.* **2** [T] to get to know by guessing: *She guessed my thoughts.* **3** [T +(*that*)] *infml esp. AmE* to suppose; consider likely: *I guess you don't have time to go out now you have young children.* **4 keep someone guessing** to keep someone uninformed and uncertain about what will happen next

**guess²** *n* **1** an attempt to guess: *Have a guess at the answer.* **2** an opinion formed by guessing: *My guess is that he didn't come because he was angry with us.* **3 at a guess** by guessing, without being certain or exact: *At a guess, I'd say she was 35.*

**guess·work** /'geswɜːk||-ɜrk/ *n* [U] the act of guessing, or the judgment which results

**guest** /gest/ *n* **1** a person who is in someone's home by invitation, for a short time (as for a meal), or to stay (one or more nights): *I can't come out now; we have guests.* –compare VISITOR **2** a person who is invited out and paid for at a theatre, restaurant,etc.: *They are coming to the concert as my guests.*|*a* **guest artist** (=actor or singer who is invited to perform) **3** a person who is lodging in a hotel, or in someone's home: *She takes in* **paying guests. 4 be my guest!** *infml* I would not mind if you did so;please feel free to do so: *"May I borrow your pen?" "Be my guest!"* –see CUSTOMER (USAGE)

**guest·house** /'gesthaʊs/ *n* **-houses** /haʊzȝz/ a private house where visitors may stay and have meals for payment

**guf·faw** /gə'fɔː, 'gʌfɔː/ *v,n* [C;I] (to make) a loud and perhaps rude laugh

**guid·ance** /'gaɪdəns/ *n* [U] help; advice

**guide¹** /gaɪd/ *n* **1** something or somebody that shows the way, esp. someone whose job is to show a place to tourists: *You need a guide to show you the city.* **2** something which influences or controls a person's actions or behaviour: *It may not be a good thing to take your friend's experience as a guide.* **3** [*to*] also **guide book** /'· ·/– a book which gives a description of a place, for the use of visitors, or which teaches something **4** →GIRL GUIDE

**guide²** *v* **guided, guiding** [T] to act as a guide to: *She guides people around the city.*|*The light guided them back to harbour.*|(fig.) *The government will guide the country through the difficulties ahead.* –see LEAD (USAGE)

**guide·lines** /'gaɪdlaɪnz/ *n* [P] the main points about something which is to be dealt with (esp.something official)

**guild** /gɪld/ *n* an association of people who share the same interests or (esp. in former times) the same skills or profession: *the guild of tailors*

**guile** /gaɪl/ *n* [U] deceit, esp. of a clever, indirect kind –compare CUNNING –**guileful** *adj*

**guile·less** /'gaɪl-lȝs/ *adj* (appearing to be) lacking in any deceit: *She gave him a guileless look, but he knew he couldn't really trust her.*

**guil·lo·tine¹** /'gɪlətiːn/ *n* **1** [C; *the* S] a machine used in France for cutting off the heads of criminals, which works by means of a heavy blade sliding down between two posts **2** [C] a machine for cutting paper

**guillotine²** *v* **-tined, -tining** [T] to use a GUILLOTINE¹ (1) as punishment on: *Many members of noble families were guillotined in France in the late 18th century.*

**guilt** /gɪlt/ *n* [U] **1** the fact of having broken a law: *There can be no doubt about the guilt of a man who is found with stolen money in his pockets.* –opposite **innocence 2** responsibility for something wrong; blame: *The children behave badly,but the guilt lies with the parents, who don't care about their behaviour.* **3** the knowledge or belief that one has done wrong; shame: *His face showed guilt, though he said he had done nothing wrong.* –**guiltless** *adj* –**guiltlessness** *n* [U]

**guilt·y** /'gɪlti/ *adj* **-ier, -iest 1** [*of*] having broken a law or disobeyed a moral or social rule:*guilty of murder*|*He was found* (=declared) *guilty.* –opposite **innocent 2** [A] having or showing a feeling of guilt: *I have a* **guilty conscience** *about forgetting to post your letter.* –**guiltily** *adv* –**guiltiness** *n* [U]

**guin·ea** /'gɪni/ *n* the sum of one pound one shilling (now £1·05), used formerly in fixing professional charges, prices of certain valuable goods (like paintings), etc.

**guinea pig** /'·· ·/ *n* **1** a small roundish furry animal rather like a rat without a tail, which is often kept by children as a pet, and is sometimes used in scientific tests **2** a person who is the subject of some kind of test: *I must try my cooking out on someone. Will you be my guinea pig?*

**guise** /gaɪz/ *n* [*usu. sing.*] *fml* an outer appearance, often one which is intended to deceive: *The thieves came into the house* **in/under the guise of** *television repair men.*

**gui·tar** /gɪˈtɑːʳ/ *n* a musical instrument with six or more strings, a long neck, and a wooden body like a VIOLIN but larger, played by PLUCKING[1] (3) the strings with the fingers

**gulch** /gʌltʃ/ *n esp. AmE* (esp. in the western US) a narrow stony valley with steep sides formed by a rushing stream

**gulf** /gʌlf/ *n* **1** a large deep stretch of sea partly enclosed by land: *the Gulf of Mexico* **2** a deep hollow place in the earth's surface: *The ground trembled,and suddenly a great gulf opened before us.* **3** a great area of division or difference, esp. between opinions: *a huge gulf between them*

**gull** /gʌl/ also **seagull**– *n* a largish flying seabird with a loud cry

**gul·let** /ˈgʌl$^{\text{l}}_{\text{ɔ}}$t/ *n infml* the (inner) throat; foodpipe from mouth to stomach

**gul·li·ble** /ˈgʌl$^{\text{l}}_{\text{ɔ}}$bəl/ *adj* easily tricked, esp. into a false belief: *He's so gullible you could sell him anything.* **–gullibility** /ˌgʌl$^{\text{l}}_{\text{ɔ}}$ˈbɪl$^{\text{l}}_{\text{ɔ}}$ti/ *n* [U] **–gullibly** /ˈgʌl$^{\text{l}}_{\text{ɔ}}$bli/ *adv*

**gul·ly**, **-ley** /ˈgʌli/ *n* **-lies 1** a small narrow valley cut esp. into a hillside by heavy rain **2** a man-made deep ditch or other small waterway

**gulp** /gʌlp/ *v* **1** [T *down*] to swallow hastily: *Don't gulp your food.* **2** [I] to make a sudden swallowing movement as if surprised or nervous **–gulp** *n*

**gulp** sthg.↔**back** *v adv* [T] to prevent the expression of feeling by or as if by swallowing: *She gulped back her tears.*

**gum**[1] /gʌm/ *n* [*usu. pl.*] either of the two areas of firm pink flesh in which the teeth are fixed,at the top and bottom of the mouth

**gum**[2] *n* **1** [U] sticky substance obtained esp. from the stems of some trees and bushes, used for sticking things together **2** [C] also **gumdrop** *AmE*– a hard transparent jelly-like sweet: *a fruit gum* **3** [U] →CHEWING GUM

**gum**[3] *v* **-mm-** [T] to stick (something somewhere) with GUM[2] (1): *He gummed the labels on the boxes.*

**gump·tion** /ˈgʌmpʃən/ *n* [U] *infml* common sense

**gun** /gʌn/ *n* a weapon from which bullets or larger metal objects (SHELLS[1] (3))are fired through a metal tube (BARREL) –compare CANNON

**gun·boat** /ˈgʌnbəʊt/ *n* a small but heavily armed naval warship

**gun** sbdy.↔ **down** *v adv* [T] to shoot, causing to fall to the ground dead or wounded

**gun·fire** /ˈgʌnfaɪəʳ/ *n* [U] the sound or act of firing one or more guns

**gun·man** /ˈgʌnmən/ *n* **-men** /mən/ a criminal armed with a gun

**gun·ner** /ˈgʌnəʳ/ *n* [A;C] a soldier in a part (REGIMENT) of the British Army which uses heavy guns (ARTILLERY)

**gun·point** /ˈgʌnpɔɪnt/ *n* **at gunpoint** under a threat of death by shooting: *We were robbed*

**gun·pow·der** /ˈgʌnˌpaʊdəʳ/ *n* [U] an explosive material made of various substances,in the form of a powder

**gun·run·ner** /ˈgʌnˌrʌnəʳ/ *n* a person who unlawfully and secretly brings guns into a country,esp. for the use of those who wish to fight against their own government **–gunrunning** *n* [U]

**gun·shot** /ˈgʌnʃɒt‖-ʃɑt/ *n* **1** [C] the act or sound of firing a gun: *a gunshot wound* **2** [U] the distance reached by a shot from a gun: *We were careful not to come* **within gunshot** *of the enemy.*

**gur·gle** /ˈgɜːgMl‖ˈgɜr-/ *v,n* **-gled, -gling** [C;I] (to make) a sound like water flowing unevenly, as out of an opening: *The baby lay gurgling in her bed.|The water gurgled out of the bottle.*

**gu·ru** /ˈgʊruː/ *n* **-rus** [A;C] an Indian priest or teacher of religious practices that produce peace of mind: (fig.) *Mr Brown is the President's guru on all matters concerning defence.*

**gush**[1] /gʌʃ/ *v* [I] **1** (of liquids) to flow or pour out in large quantities, as from a hole or wound: *Oil gushed out from the broken pipe.|Blood gushed from his wound.* **2** [*over*] to express too much admiration, pleasure, etc., in a great flow of words, foolishly or without true feeling **–gushing** *adj*: *a gushing spring| gushing praise* **–gushingly** *adv*

**gush**[2] *n* [S] a (sudden) flow (of liquid): *There was a gush of blood as the wound re- opened.*|(fig.) *a gush of interest*/ENTHUSIASM

**gust** /gʌst/ *n* [*of*] a sudden strong rush of air, rain, smoke, etc.,carried by wind: *A gust of wind blew the door shut.* –compare PUFF[2] (2) **–gusty** *adj* **-ier, -iest:** *gusty weather*

**gus·to** /ˈgʌstəʊ/ *n* [U] eager enjoyment (in doing or having something):*He started painting* **with great gusto.**

**gut**[1] /gʌt/ *n* **1** [C;U] the foodpipe which passes through the body **2** [U] strong thread made from this part of animals:*The fishing line is made of gut.*

**gut**[2] *v* **-tt-** [T] **1** to take out the inner organs (esp. GUTS (1)) of (a dead animal) **2** to destroy completely the inside of (a building), esp. by fire: *The huge factory was gutted in minutes.*

**gut**[3] *adj* [A] *infml* arising from or concerning one's strongest feelings and needs, not from thought:*a gut feeling that something terrible would happen|a* **gut reaction** *against the new government*

**guts** /gʌts/ *n* [P] *infml* **1** the bowels or INTESTINES **2** bravery; determination: *She has a lot of guts; she went on arguing even though no one agreed with her.*

**gut·ter** /ˈgʌtəʳ/ *n* **1** [C] a small hollow or ditch beside a street, or an open pipe fixed to a roof, to collect and carry away rainwater –see picture on page 297 **2** [*the* S] the lowest poorest social conditions, as in a dirty part of a city: *The* **gutter press** *is those newspapers which are full of shocking stories about people's private lives.*

**gut·tur·al** /ˈgʌtərəl/ *adj* of or in the throat: *He made a few guttural sounds.*

**guy** /gaɪ/ *n infml* a man; fellow: *a nice guy*

**guz·zle** /ˈgʌzəl/ *v* **-zled, -zling** [I;T] to eat or drink eagerly and greedily (GREEDY): *Pigs guzzle their food.|He's been guzzling beer all evening.* **–guzzler** *n*

**gym** /dʒɪm/ *n infml* **1** [C] → GYMNASIUM **2** [U] →

PHYSICAL TRAINING: *a gym class*

**gym·kha·na** /dʒɪm'kɑːnə/ *n esp. BrE* a local sports meeting, esp. horse racing, jumping etc.

**gym·na·si·um** /dʒɪm'neɪzɪəm/ *n* a hall with wall bars, ropes, and other such things, for climbing, jumping, etc.

**gym·nast** /'dʒɪmnæst, -nəst/ *n* a person who trains and is skilled in certain bodily exercises

**gym·nas·tics** /dʒɪm'næstɪks/ *n* [U] the art of training the body by means of certain exercises, often done in competition with others –**gymnastic** *adj* [A]

**gym·slip** /'dʒɪm,slɪp/ *n BrE* a sort of dress without arms, formerly worn by girls as part of a school uniform

**gy·nae·col·o·gy** /,gaɪnɨ'kɒlədʒi‖- 'kɑ-/ *n* [U] the study in medicine of the workings of the female sex organs, esp. in child-bearing, and the study and treatment of their diseases –**gynaecological** /-kə 'lɒdʒɪkəl‖-'lɑ- / *adj* –**gynaecologist** /,gaɪnɨ'kɒlədʒɨst‖-'kɑ- / *n*

**gyp·sy** /'dʒɪpsi/ *n* **-sies** *esp. AmE* (*sometimes cap.*) →GIPSY

**gy·rate** /dʒaɪ'reɪt‖'dʒaɪəreɪt/ *v* **-rated, -rating** [I] to swing round and round a fixed point, in one direction or with changes of direction: *The dancers gyrated quickly to the strong beat of the music.* –**gyration** /-'reɪʃən/ *n* [C;U]

**gy·ro·scope** /'dʒaɪərəskəʊp/ also **gyro** /'dʒaɪərʊ/ *infml*– *n* a heavy wheel which spins inside a frame, used for keeping ships and aircraft steady, and also as a children's toy –**gyroscopic** /,dʒaɪərə'skɒpɪk/ *adj*

# H, h

**H, h** /eɪtʃ/ **H's, h's** *or* **Hs, hs** the 8th letter of the English alphabet

**ha** /hɑː/ *interj* a shout of surprise, interest, etc.

**hab·er·dash·er** /'hæbədæʃəʳ‖-bər-/ *n* **1** *BrE* a shopkeeper who sells pins, sewing thread, and other small things used in dressmaking **2** *AmE* a shopkeeper who sells men's clothing, esp. hats, GLOVES, etc.

**hab·er·dash·er·y** /'hæbədæʃəri‖- bər-/ *n* **-ies** [C;U] (the goods sold in) a HABERDASHER's shop or department in a department store

**hab·it** /'hæbɨt/ *n* **1** [C;U] (an example of) customary behaviour: *It was her habit to go for a walk before lunch.*|*I smoke* **out of habit,** *not for pleasure.* **2** [C] a special set of clothes, esp. that worn by MONKs and NUNs in religious ORDERS[1] (10)

USAGE A **habit** usually means something done regularly by a single person, and a **custom** usually means something that has been done for a long time by a whole society: *He has an annoying* **habit** *of biting his nails.*|*the* **custom** *of giving presents at Christmas.* **Practice** is like **custom** but is often *derog: the* **practice** *of eating one's enemies.* The **conventions** of a society are its generally accepted standards of behaviour: *As a matter of* **convention,** *people attending funerals wear dark clothes.*

**hab·i·ta·ble** /'hæbɨtəbəl/ *adj* which can be lived in (INHABITed) –opposite **uninhabitable**

**hab·i·tat** /'hæbɨtæt/ *n* the natural home of a plant or animal: *plants in their natural habitat*

**hab·i·ta·tion** /,hæbɨ'teɪʃən/ *n fml* [U] the act of living in (INHABITing): *a house unfit for human habitation*

**ha·bit·u·al** /hə'bɪtʃʊəl/ *adj* [A *no comp.*] **1** usual; customary: *She gave her habitual greeting.* **2** (done) by habit: *He's a habitual smoker–he always has a cigarette after dinner.* –**habitually** *adv*: *habitually late*

**hack**[1] /hæk/ *v* [I;T *at, away*] to cut (up), esp. roughly or in uneven pieces: *He hacked away (at the trees) all night.* |*They hacked their way through the forest.*

**hack**[2] *n* **1** an old tired horse **2** a light horse for riding **3** a writer who does a lot of poor quality work

**hack·ing cough** /'·· ·,·· '·/ *n* a cough with a rough unpleasant sound

**hack·neyed** /'hæknid/ *adj* (of a saying) meaningless because used and repeated too often

**hack·saw** /'hæksɔː/ *n* a tool (SAW (1)) that has a fine-toothed blade and is used for cutting metal

**had** /d, əd, həd; *strong* hæd/ *v* **1** *past tense and participle of* HAVE **2 be had** *infml* to be tricked or made a fool of: *I've been had! The camera I bought doesn't work.*

**had·dock** /'hædək/ *n* **haddock** *or* **haddocks** [C;U] a common fish found in northern seas, used as food

**had·n't** /'hædnt/ *v short for:* had not: *They'd arrived, hadn't they?*

**hag** /hæg/ *n* an ugly or unpleasant woman, esp.one who is old and is thought to be evil

**hag·gard** /'hægəd‖-ərd/ *adj* having lines on the face and hollow places around the eyes as if through tiredness: *a haggard look* –compare GAUNT

**hag·gis** /'hægɨs/ *n* **-gises** *or* **-gis** [C;U] a food eaten in Scotland, made from the heart and other organs of a sheep cut up and boiled inside a skin made from the stomach

**hag·gle** /'hægəl/ *v* **-gled, -gling** [I *over/about* and/or *with*] to argue over something, esp. over fixing a price: *He haggled over the price of the horse.*

**ha-ha** /,· '·/ *interj* (a shout of laughter)

**hail**[1] /heɪl/ *n* [U] frozen rain drops which fall as little hard balls: (fig.) *a hail of bullets* –see WEATHER (USAGE)

**hail**[2] *v* [*it* I] (of HAIL) to fall: *It's hailing.*

**hail**[3] *v* [T] to call out to (someone) in greeting or to gain attention: *She hailed a taxi.*

**hail** sbdy./sthg. **as** sthg. *v prep* [T] to recognize as (something good): *They hailed it as a work of art.*

**hail from** sthg. *v prep* [T *no pass.*] to come from; have as one's home: *She hails from Liverpool.*

**hail·stone** /'heɪlstəʊn/ *n* a small ball of HAIL

**hail·storm** /ˈheɪlstɔːm‖-ɔrm/ *n* a storm when HAIL falls heavily

**hair** /heəʳ/ *n* **1** [C] a fine threadlike growth from the skin of a person or animal: *The cat has left her loose hairs all over my clothes.* –see picture on page 299 **2** [U] a mass of such growths, such as that on the head of human beings: *My hair has grown very long.* –compare FUR **3 let one's hair down** *infml* to do as one likes; behave wildly, esp. after one has had to be controlled in behaviour, as after a formal occasion **4 make someone's hair stand on end** to make someone very afraid; TERRIFY **5 not turn a hair** *infml* to show no fear or worry (when in difficulty) **6 split hairs** *derog* to be too concerned with unimportant differences, esp. in arguments –see also HAIR-SPLITTING **7 -haired** having a certain kind of hair: *long-haired|fair-haired*

**hair·brush** /ˈheəbrʌʃ‖ˈheər-/ *n* a brush used for the hair to get out dirt and to make the hair smooth

**hair·cut** /ˈheəkʌt‖ˈheər-/ *n* **1** an occasion of having the hair cut **2** the style the hair is cut in

**hair·do** /ˈheəduː‖ˈheər-/ *n* **-dos** *infml* **1** an occasion of a person esp. a woman having his/her hair shaped into a style **2** the style a person's hair is shaped into: *Do you like my new hairdo?*

**hair·dress·er** /ˈheəˌdresəʳ‖ˈheər-/ *n* a person who shapes the hair (esp. of women) into a style by cutting, SETTING[1] (14), etc., or who changes its colour –compare BARBER –**hairdressing** *n* [U]

**hair·grip** /ˈheəgrɪp‖ˈheər-/ *n BrE* a flat HAIRPIN with the ends pressed close together

**hair·line** /ˈheəlaɪn‖ˈheər-/ *n* **1** the place on the forehead where the hair starts growing **2** also **hairline crack** /ˌ·· ˈ·/ –a narrow crack

**hair·net** /ˈheənet‖ˈheər-/ *n* a net (worn esp. by women) which stretches over the hair to keep it in place

**hair·piece** /ˈheəpiːs‖ˈheər-/ *n* a piece of false hair used to make one's own hair seem thicker

**hair·pin** /ˈheəˌpɪn‖ˈheər-/ *n* a pin made of wire bent into a U-shape to hold the hair in position on the head

**hairpin bend** /ˌ·· ˈ·/ *n* a narrow U-shaped curve in a road, as when going up a steep hill

**hair-rais·ing** /ˈ· ˌ··/ *adj* that makes one very afraid: *a hair-raising experience*

**hair's breadth** /ˈ· ·/ also **hairbreadth** /ˈheəbretθ‖ˈheərbredθ/– *n* a very short distance: *We missed the other car by a hair's breadth*

**hair-split·ting** /ˈ· ˌ··/ *n* [U] too much interest in unimportant differences and points of detail, esp. in argument

**hair·y** /ˈheəri/ *adj* **-ier, -iest 1** (when used of people, not usu. describing the hair on the head) having a lot of hair: *a hairy chest* **2** *infml* exciting in a way that causes fear, or dangerous: *It was rather hairy driving down that narrow road.* –**hairiness** *n* [U]

**hal·cy·on** /ˈhælsɪən/ *adj* [A *no comp.*] *lit* calm or peaceful (esp. in the phrase **halcyon days**)

**hale** /heɪl/ *adj* **hale and hearty** /ˌ· · ˈ··/ very healthy –sounds like **hail**

**half**[1] *n,pron* **halfs, halves** /hɑːvz‖hævz/ **1** either of two equal parts of something; ½: *the bottom half of the class|the first half of the football match|Half of it was broken.|Half of them are already here.|a kilo and a half* (=1½ kilos) *of rice|Cut it* **in half**. (=into two halves) –compare WHOLE[2] (1,2) **2** a coin, ticket, drink, etc. of ½ the value or amount: *Three halves of beer, please.|One and two halves to Oxford Circus please.* (=tickets for one adult and two children) **3** the number ½: *3 halves make 1½* **4 go halves (in/on something) (with someone)** *infml* to share (the cost of something) (with someone)

**half**[2] *predeterminer,adj* ½ in amount: *Half the car was damaged.|Half the boys are already here.|half a minute|half a mile/a half mile|a half smile* (=not quite complete)

**half**[3] *adv* **1** partly; not completely: *half cooked|She's half French and half English.* **2 half and half** /ˌ· · ˈ·/ half of one and half of the other; two equal parts of two things: *"Is it made with milk or water?" "Half and half."* **3 not half** *BrE infml:* **a** very; very much: *"Are you busy?" "Not half!"* (=I'm very busy) **b** not at all: *The food's not half bad.* (=quite good)

**half a doz·en** /ˌ· · ˈ··/ also **(a) half dozen** /ˌ·ˌ· ˈ··/– *determiner,n* **half dozens** six; a set of six: *half a dozen eggs |I'll have two half dozens.* (= two groups of half a dozen) –see also DOZEN

**half·back** /ˈhɑːfbæk‖ˈhæf-/ also **half**– *n* (in games like football) a player or position between the centre players (ATTACKERS) and the DEFENDERS

**half-baked** /ˌ· ˈ·◂/ *adj* (of ideas) stupid; not sensible

**half-broth·er** /ˈ· ˌ··/ *n* a brother related through one parent only

**half-caste** /ˈ· ·/ also **half-breed**– *n,adj sometimes derog* (a person) with parents of different races

**half-heart·ed** /ˌ· ˈ··◂‖ˈ· ˌ··/ *adj* showing little effort and no real interest: *a half-hearted attempt to mend the window* –see also WHOLE-HEARTED –**half-heartedly** *adv* –**half-heartedness** *n* [U]

**half-mast** /ˌ· ˈ·/ *n* a point near the middle of a flagpole where the flag flies as a sign of sorrow: *All the flags were* **at half-mast** *when the king died.*

**half·penny** /ˈheɪpni/ *n* **halfpennies** *or* **halfpence** /ˈheɪpəns/ also **half p** *infml*– (in Great Britain) a very small BRONZE coin, two of which make a penny; ½p –see PENNY (USAGE)

**half-sis·ter** /ˈ· ˌ··/ *n* a sister related through one parent only

**half term** /ˌ· ˈ·◂/ *n* (in Britain) a short holiday, usu. two or three days, in the middle of a school TERM[1] (1)

**half time** /ˌ· ˈ·◂‖ˈ·· / *n* [U] the period of time between two parts of agame, such as a football match –see also FULL TIME

**half·way** /ˌhɑːfˈweɪ◂‖ˌhæf-/ *adj,adv* **1** at the midpoint between two things: *halfway between London and Birmingham* **2** by an incomplete amount: *You can't go halfway when you're painting the walls–once you've started you have to finish the job.* **3 meet someone halfway** to make an agreement with someone which partly satisfies the demands of both sides: *You want to pay £1 but I want £2. Meet me halfway and make it £1.50.*

**half-wit** /ˈ· ·/ *n usu. derog* a person of weak mind –**half-witted** /ˌ· ˈ··◂/ *adj*

**hal·i·but** /ˈhælɪbət/ *n* **-but** *or* **-buts** [C;U] a very large fish used as food

**hall** /hɔːl/ *n* **1** a large room in which meetings,

dances, etc., can be held **2** the passage just inside the entrance of a house, from which the rooms open –see picture on page 297 **3** (in a university, etc.) the room, where the members live or eat together: *I live in a* **hall of residence**.

**hal·le·lu·ja** /ˌhælǽˈluːjə/ also **alleluia**– *interj,n* (a song, cry, etc., that is an expression of) praise, joy, and thanks to God

**hall·mark¹** /ˈhɔːlmɑːk‖-ɑrk/ *n* the mark made on objects of precious metal to prove that they are silver or gold: (fig.) *Clear expression is the hallmark of a good writer.* (=the sign which shows that the writer is good)

**hallmark²** *v* [T] to make a HALLMARK on (something)

**hal·lo** /həˈləʊ, he-, hæ-/ *interj, n* **-los** *BrE* for HELLO

**hal·low** /ˈhæləʊ/ *v* [T *usu. pass.*] to make holy: (fig.) *the hallowed memories of great people*

**Hal·low·e'en** /ˌhæləʊˈiːn/ *n* the night of October 31, when children play tricks and dress up in strange clothes

**hal·lu·ci·nate** /həˈluːsǽneɪt/ *v* **-nated, -nating** [I] to see things which are not there

**hal·lu·ci·na·tion** /həˌluːsǽˈneɪʃən/ *n* [C;U] (the experience of seeing) something that is not really there, often as the result of a drug or illness

**hall·way** /ˈhɔːlweɪ/ *n esp. AmE* for HALL (2)

**ha·lo** /ˈheɪləʊ/ *n* **-loes** *or* **-los** a golden circle representing light around the heads of holy people in religious paintings

**halt¹** /hɔːlt/ *v* [I;T] *fml* to (cause to) stop: *The train was halted by work on the line ahead.*

**halt²** *n* [S] a stop or pause: *The car came to a halt just in time to prevent an accident.*

**hal·ter** /ˈhɔːltəʳ/ *n* a rope or leather band fastened round a horse's head, esp. to lead it

**halt·ing** /ˈhɔːltɪŋ/ *adj* stopping and starting as if uncertain: *a halting voice* **–haltingly** *adv*

**halve** /hɑːv‖hæv/ *v* **halved, halving** [T] **1** to divide into halves: *Let's halve the work between the two of us.* **2** to reduce to half

**halves** /hɑːvz‖hævz/ *n pl. of* HALF

**ham** /hæm/ *n* **1** [C;U] preserved meat from the upper part of a pig's leg **2** [C] *infml* an actor, speaker, etc. whose performance is unnatural **3** a person who receives and/or sends radio messages using his/her own apparatus

**ham·burg·er** /ˈhæmbɜːgəʳ‖-ɜr-/ *n* a flat circular cake of very small pieces of meat, esp. eaten in a ROLL¹ (2) of bread

**ham-fist·ed** /ˌ· ˈ·· ◂/ also **ham-handed**– *adj* awkward in using the hands; CLUMSY

**ham·let** /ˈhæmlǽt/ *n* a small village

**ham·mer¹** /ˈhæməʳ/ **1** a tool with a heavy head used esp. for driving nails into wood **2** a heavy metal ball on the end of a wire used for throwing as a sport –see picture on page 592 **3** something made to hit something else, as in a piano, or part of a gun **4 be/go at it hammer and tongs** (of two people) to fight or argue violently

**hammer²** *v* **1** [I;T] to strike (something) with a hammer: *Hammer the nails in.*|(fig.) *The police hammered* (= knocked hard) *at the door.* **2** [T] *infml* to conquer (someone) by fighting, or in a game: *We hammered the other team.*

**hammer** sthg. ↔ **out** *v adv* [T] to talk about in detail and come to a decision about: *The government tried to hammer out an agreement with the workers.*

**ham·mock** /ˈhæmək/ *n* a long piece of sailcloth (CANVAS) or net which can be hung up by the ends to form a bed

**ham·per¹** /ˈhæmpəʳ/ *v* [T] to cause difficulty in movement or activity

**hamper²** *n* a large basket with a lid, often used for carrying food

**ham·ster** /ˈhæmstəʳ/ *n* a small animal with pockets (POUCHES) in its cheeks for storing food, kept as a pet

**ham·string¹** /ˈhæmˌstrɪŋ/ *n* a cordlike TENDON at the back of the leg, joining a muscle to a bone

**hamstring²** *v* **-strung** /strʌŋ/, **-stringing** [T] to cut the HAMSTRING of, destroying the ability to walk

**hand¹** /hænd/ *n* **1** [C;U] the movable parts at the end of the human arm, including the fingers: *She had a book in her hand.*|*I can't carry you; my hands are full.* (=I'm holding things in both hands)|*I can't come today; I've* **got my hands full**. (=I'm very busy)|*It was written* **by hand**. (=not printed) –see picture on page 299 **2** [C] a pointer or needle on a clock or machine: *The minute hand is bigger than the hour hand.* **3** [C] a set of playing cards held by one person in a game **4** [C] a worker who uses his/her hands, esp. a sailor: *All hands on* DECK! (=a call for all sailors to come up to the DECK)|*a factory hand*|*She's* **a good hand at** *making bread.*|(fig.) *I'm* **an old hand** (=an experienced person) *at this game; you can't trick me.* **5** [S] encouragement or approval given to a performer by striking the hands together; APPLAUSE: *They gave the singer* **a big hand.** –compare CLAP² (2) **6** [S] help: *Could you* **give/lend** *me* **a hand** *to move this box, please?* **7** [U] control: *The meeting is* **getting out of hand**–*can we have just one speaker at a time.*|*Don't worry; I have the matter well* **in hand**. (=I'm dealing with it) **8 at first hand** by direct experience of oneself or another person: *I found out about it at first hand.* **9 at hand** *fml* near in time or place: *Election day is at hand.* **10 at second/third/fourth hand** as information passed on through one, two, or three people –see also FIRSTHAND, SECOND-HAND **11 change hands** to go from the possession of one person to that of another: *The car had changed hands five times* (=had six owners) *before I bought it.* **12 get/keep one's hand in** to become/stay used to an activity by practising **13 give somebody a free hand** to allow somebody to do things in his/her own way **14 hand in glove (with)** closely connected (with someone), esp. in something bad **15 hand in hand: a** holding each other's hand: *They walked down the street hand in hand.* **b** always happening together: *Dirt and disease go hand in hand.* **16 have a hand in** to share (an activity); be partly responsible for: *I had a hand in arranging the party.* **17 on hand** ready for use or to take part **18 on the one/other hand** (used for comparing different things or ideas): *On the one hand this job doesn't pay very much, but on the other (hand) I can't get another one.* **19 play into (someone's) hands** to do something which gives (one's opponent) an advantage **20 to hand** within reach: *I don't have my diary to hand, so I'll have to check later.* **21 turn one's hand to** to begin to practise (a skill) **22 wait on (somebody) hand and foot** to do everything for somebody, as if they were unable to look after themselves **23 -handed** having or using a certain kind of hand or hands: *right-handed|heavy-handed* –see also HANDS

**hand²** *v* [T] **1** to give from one's own hand into that of (someone else): *Hand me that book, please.|She handed the book back to him.|Please hand the sweets round.* (= offer them to everyone) **2 (have to) hand it to (someone)** to (have to) admit the high quality or success of (someone): *You have to hand it to her, she's a good talker.*

**hand** sthg.↔ **down/on,** also **pass** sthg.↔ **down**– *v adv* [T] to give or leave to people who are younger or come later: *This ring was handed down from my aunt.*

**hand** sthg.↔ **in** *v adv* [T] to deliver; give by hand: *Please hand in your books at the end of the lesson.*

**hand** sthg.↔ **on** *v adv* [T] to give from one person to another (esp. something which can be used by many people one after the other): *Please read this notice and hand it on.*

**hand** sthg.↔ **out** *v adv* [T *to*] to give, esp. one of (a set of things) to each member of a group of people: *Hand out the pencils.* –see also HANDOUT

**hand** sbdy./sthg.↔**over** *v adv* [T *to*] to give into someone else's care, control, etc.: *The thief was handed over to the police.*

**hand·bag** /'hændbæg/ *n* a small bag for a person, usu. a woman, to carry money and personal things in –see picture on page 85

**hand·book** /'hændbʊk/ *n* a short book giving all the most important information about a subject –compare MANUAL²

**hand·brake** /'hændbreɪk/ *n* an apparatus (BRAKE) *that stops a vehicle,* worked by the driver's hand, not foot –see picture on page 85

**hand·cuff** /'hændkʌf/ *v* [T] to put HANDCUFFS on

**hand·cuffs** /'hændkʌfs/ *n* [P] metal rings joined together, for fastening the wrists of a criminal –see PAIR¹ (USAGE)

**hand·ful** /'hændfʊl/ *n* **1** an amount which is as much as can be held in the hand: *I picked up a handful of letters and began to open them.* **2** a small number (of people): *We invited thirty people, but only a handful of them came.* **3** a living thing which is so active that it is difficult to control: *That child is quite a handful.*

**hand·i·cap¹** /'hændikæp/ *n* **1** a disability or disadvantage: *Blindness is a great handicap.* **2** (in a race or other sport) a disadvantage given to the stronger competitors, such as carrying more weight or running further than others

**handicap²** *v* **-pp-** [T] **1** to cause (someone) to have a disadvantage: *Lack of money handicapped him badly.* **2** [*usu. pass.*] (of a disability of mind or body) to prevent (someone) from acting and living normally: *physically handicapped*

**hand·i·craft** /'hændikrɑːft‖- kræft/ *n* [*usu. pl.*] a skill needing careful use of the hands, such as sewing, weaving, etc.

**hand·i·work** /'hændiwɜːk‖-ɜrk/ *n* [U] **1** work demanding the skilful use of the hands **2** action, usu. showing some sign of the person who has done it

**hand·ker·chief** /'hæŋkətʃɪ̵f‖-kər-/ *n* **-chiefs** a piece of cloth or thin soft paper for drying the nose, eyes, etc.

**han·dle¹** /'hændl/ *n* a part of an object which is specially made for holding it or for opening it –see picture on page 85

**handle²** *v* **-dled, -dling** [T] **1 a** to feel in the hands **b** to move by hand: *Handle with care!* **2** to deal with; control: *He handled a difficult argument skilfully.|Ms Brown handles the company's accounts.|A good teacher must know how to handle children.* **3** to use (goods) in business; DEAL **in**: *We don't handle that sort of book.* **–handleable** *adj*

**han·dle·bars** /'hændlbɑːz‖-ɑrz/ *n* [P] the bar above the front wheel of a bicycle or motorcycle, which controls the direction it goes in

**han·dler** /'hændləʳ/ *n* a person who controls an animal

**hand lug·gage** /'· ,··/ *n* [U] a traveller's light or small bags, cases, etc., which can be carried by hand

**hand·out** /'hændaʊt/ *n* **1** something given free, such as food, clothes, etc., esp. to someone poor **2** information given out, esp. a printed sheet: *Please read the handout carefully.* –see also HAND **out**

**hand·picked** /,hænd'pɪkt/ *adj* chosen with great care

**hands** /hændz/ *n* [P] possession: *A valuable book has* **come into my hands**.|I know the child's **in good hands** (=being well cared for) *with her aunt.|Where can I* **lay my hands on** (=get possession of) *a cheap bicycle?|Now the children are* **off my hands** (=I am no longer responsible for them). –see also HAND

**hand·shake** /'hændʃeɪk/ *n* an act of taking each other's right hand when two people meet or leave each other

**hand·some** /'hænsəm/ *adj* **1** (esp. of men) good-looking; of attractive appearance –see BEAUTIFUL (USAGE) **2** generous; plentiful: *a handsome reward* **–handsomely** *adv*

**hand·stand** /'hændstænd/ *n* a movement in which the legs are kicked into the air so that the body is upside down and supported on the hands

**hand-to-mouth** /,· · '· ◂/ *adj,adv* (of a way of life) spending one's money as soon as it comes in

**hand·writ·ing** /'hænd,raɪtɪŋ/ *n* [U] (a particular person's style of) writing done by hand

**hand·y** /'hændi/ *adj* **-ier, -iest 1** useful and simple to use: *This is a handy little box.|A few more traveller's cheques may* **come in handy** (=may be useful) *on holiday.* **2** clever in using the hands **3** *infml* near; **at** HAND: *The shops are quite handy.* **–handily** *adv*

**hand·y·man** /'hændimæn/ *n* **-men** /men/ a person who does repairs and practical jobs well, esp. in the house

**hang¹** /hæŋ/ *v* **hung** /hʌŋ/, **hanging 1** [I;T] to fix or be fixed at the top so that the lower part is free: *to hang curtains|Hang your coat (up) on the hook.|The curtains hang well.* **2** [T] to fix (wallpaper) on a wall

**hang about** *v adv;prep infml* **1** [I;T (=**hang about** sthg.)] also **hang around**– to wait or stay near (a place) without purpose or activity: *I hung about/around (the station) for an hour but he didn't come.* **2** to delay or move slowly; DAWDLE: *Don't hang about–we have a train to catch!*

**hang back** *v adv* [I] to be unwilling to act or move:

We all hung back when we saw how old the car was.

**hang on** *v adv* [I] *infml* **1** [*to*] to keep hold of; keep possession of : *Hang on (to the* STRAP (1)). *The bus is starting.* **2** to wait: *Hang on a minute: I'm just coming.*|*I'm afraid the line* (=telephone line) *is busy, would you like to hang on?* –compare HANG **up** (1) **3** to keep doing something: *You must be tired, but try to hang on till all the work's finished.*

**hang onto** sthg. also **hold onto** sthg.– *v prep* [T] to try to keep: *We should hang onto the house until prices are higher.*

**hang up** *v adv* [I] **1** to finish a telephone conversation by putting the RECEIVER (1) back: *I was so angry I hung up on her.* (=while she was talking) –compare HANG **on** (2); see TELEPHONE (USAGE) **2 be hung up on/about** *infml* to be anxious or have a fixed idea about –see also HANGUP

**hang²** *v* **hanged** /hæŋd/, **hanging** [I;T] to (cause to) die, esp. in punishment for a crime, by dropping with a rope around the neck: *He was hanged for murder.*

**hang³** *n* **get/have the hang of something** *infml* to develop the skill of doing something, or an understanding of how something works: *Press this button when the light goes on–you'll soon get the hang of it.*

**han·gar** /ˈhæŋəʳ/ *n* a big building where planes are kept

**hang·er** /ˈhæŋəʳ/ also **coat hanger, clothes hanger**– *n* a hook and crosspiece to fit inside the shoulders of a dress, coat, etc., to keep the shape of the garment when it is hung up

**hanger-on** /ˌ·· ˈ·/ *n* **hangers-on** *usu. derog* a person who tries to be friendly with another person or group, esp. for his/her own advantage

**hang glid·ing** /ˈ· ˌ··/ *n* [U] the sport of GLIDING using a large KITE (2) instead of a plane

**hang·ing** /ˈhæŋɪŋ/ *n* [C;U] death by hanging (HANG²): *Are you in favour of hanging?*

**hang·man** /ˈhæŋmən/ *n* **-men** /mən/ the person whose work is hanging criminals

**hang·o·ver** /ˈhæŋəʊvəʳ/ *n* **1** the feeling of headache, sickness, etc., the day after drinking too much alcohol **2** a condition or effect resulting from an earlier event or state: *His cough is a hangover from a bad illness he had.*

**hang·up** /ˈhæŋʌp/ *n infml* something which a person gets unusually worried about: *a hangup about women* –see also HANG **up** (2)

**han·ker af·ter** sthg. /ˈhæŋkəʳ/ also **hanker for** sthg.– *v prep* [T] *infml* to have a strong wish for (usu. something one cannot have); LONG⁴ for: *He's lonely and hankers for friendship.* **–hankering** *n* [*for, after*]: *a hankering after fame and wealth*

**han·kie, -ky** /ˈhæŋki/ *n* **-kies** *infml* a handkerchief

**hank·y-pank·y** /ˌhæŋki ˈpæŋki/ *n* [U] *infml* deceit or improper behaviour of a not very serious kind

**hap·haz·ard** /ˌhæpˈhæzəd◂‖-ərd/ *adj* happening in an unplanned disorderly manner: *The town grew in a haphazard way.* **–haphazardly** *adv*

**hap·pen** /ˈhæpən/ *v* **1** [I *to*] to take place: *A funny thing happened yesterday.*|*Did you hear what happened to Peter last night?* **2** [I +*to-v*; not *be+v-ing*] to have the good or bad luck (to): *I happened to see him yesterday.* **3** [*it*+I+*that*; not *be+v-ing*] to be true by or as if by chance (note the phrases **as it happens/happened**): *It (so) happened that I saw him yesterday.* (=I saw him yesterday, as it happens)

USAGE People or things **become** something, in the meaning of passing from one state to another: *Mervyn* **became** *an engineer* (not ***became** *engineer*).|*The horse* **became/got** *thirsty.*|*This idea is* **becoming/getting** *fashionable.* Events **happen** (usually by accident) or **take place** (usually by arrangement): *When did the explosion* **happen**? |*When will the wedding* **take place**?

**happen on/upon** sbdy./sthg. also **chance (up)on** sbdy./sthg.– *v prep* [T *no pass.*] to find or meet by chance: *I happened on an old country hotel.*

**hap·pen·ing** /ˈhæpənɪŋ/ *n* something which happens; event

**hap·pi·ly** /ˈhæpəli/ *adv* **1** in a happy manner: *laughing happily* **2** fortunately: *Happily, the accident was prevented.*

**hap·pi·ness** /ˈhæpinəs/ *n* [U] the state of being happy

**hap·py** /ˈhæpi/ *adj* **-pier, -piest 1** feeling, giving, or showing pleasure or contentment: *She is a happy child.*|*They have a happy marriage.* –opposite **unhappy 2** (of behaviour, thoughts, etc.) suitable: *That was not a very happy remark.* **3** [F+*to-v*/*that; no comp.*] *polite* pleased; not finding it difficult (to): *I'll be happy to meet him when I have time.* **4** [A] (of wishes) joyful: **Happy New Year**|**Happy Birthday**

**happy-go-luck·y** /ˌ··· ˈ··◂/ *adj usu. not derog* (of people or their acts) showing a lack of careful thought or planning; CAREFREE

**ha·rangue** /həˈræŋ/ *v,n* **-rangued, -ranguing** [C;T] (to attack or try to persuade with) a long often loud and scolding speech

**har·ass** /ˈhærəs‖həˈræs, ˈhærəs/ *v* [T] to make (somebody) worried by causing trouble, esp. on repeated occasions: *I felt harassed by all the work at the office.* **–harassment** *n* [U]

**har·bour¹** *BrE*‖**harbor** *AmE* /ˈhɑːbəʳ‖ˈhɑr-/ *n* [C;U] an area of water which is sheltered from rough waters, esp. the sea, so that ships are safe inside it

**harbour²** *BrE*‖**harbor** *AmE v* [T] to give protection and shelter, usu to something/someone bad: *Harbouring criminals is an offence in law.*|(fig.) *He harbours* (=keeps in his mind) *a wish to be a singer.*

**hard¹** /hɑːd‖hɑrd/ *adj* **1** firm and stiff; not easily broken or bent: *hard stone*|*hard skin*|*The snow has frozen hard.* –opposite **soft 2** [+*to-v*] difficult (to do or understand): *This question is too hard; I can't answer it.* –opposite **easy 3** needing or using force of body or mind: *Give it a hard push, then it will move.* |*We must take a long hard look at this plan.* (=examine it very carefully) **4** full of difficulty and trouble; not pleasant: *a hard life*|*It's been a hard winter.* (=very cold and snowy)|*The police gave him a hard time.* (=hurt him physically and/or mentally) **5** [*on*] showing no kindness; severe: *Don't be too hard on him; he didn't mean to do it.*|*He* **takes a hard line** *on the question of punishing young criminals.* –see also HARDLINE **6** (of water) containing lime, that prevents soap from mixing properly with the water **7** [A *no comp.*] (of a drug) being one on which a user can become dependent (ADDICTed) in such a way that he/she is ill without it **8** [*no comp.*] (in English pronunciation): **a** (of the letter *c*) pronounced as /k/ rather than /s/ **b** (of the letter *g*) pronounced as /g/ rather than /dʒ/: *The letter "g" is hard in "get" and soft in "gentle".* –opposite **soft** (for 1,6,7,8); see also HARD UP; see HARDEN (USAGE) **–hardness** *n* [U]

**hard²** *adv* **1** with great effort: *Push hard!|She's working hard.|I had to think long and hard before I could find the answer.* **2** in large amounts; heavily: *It's raining harder than ever.* **3 be hard hit (by)** to suffer loss because of (some event): *The farmers were hard hit by the bad weather.* **4 be hard put (to it) to (do something)** to have great difficulty (in doing something) **5 hard done by** *BrE* unfairly treated: *I felt very hard done by when I got less money than anybody else, and I'd worked twice as long.* **6 hard at it** *infml* working with great effort **7 take (it) hard** to suffer deeply: *She's taking her father's death very hard.*

**hard-and-fast** /ˌ· · '·◂/ *adj* [A] (of rules) fixed and unchangeable

**hard·back** /'hɑːdbæk‖'hɑrd-/ *n* a book with a strong stiff cover (BINDING) –compare PAPERBACK

**hard·board** /'hɑːdbɔːd‖'hɑrdbord/ *n* [U] a heavy thick strong cardboard made out of fine pieces of wood pressed into sheets

**hard-boiled** /ˌ· '·◂/ *adj* (of eggs) boiled until the yellow part is hard –see also SOFT-BOILED

**hard cash** /ˌ· '·/ *n* [U] coins and notes, not a cheque: *I offered him a cheque, but he demanded hard cash.*

**hard-core** /ˌ· '·◂/ *adj* [A *no comp.*] *often derog* refusing to change, yield, or improve: *hard-core opposition to the government's plans*

**hard core** /ˌ· '·/ *n* [U +*sing./pl. v*] *often derog* the people most concerned at the centre of an activity, esp. when opposed to some other group: *The hard core in the party make|makes all the decisions.*

**hard·en** /'hɑːdn‖'hɑrdn/ *v* [I;T] to (cause to) become hard or firm: *The snow hardened until ice was formed.|My hands hardened when I was working on the farm.|*(fig.) *Don't harden your heart against* (=don't be hard and unkind towards) *him.* –compare SOFTEN

USAGE **Harden** means "to make or become hard", but should only be used when hard means "firm and stiff" or "unkind and severe". Otherwise, use **get harder.** Compare: *Leave the jelly in a cool place to* **harden**. (=become firm)|*to* **harden** *one's heart* (=show unkindness),and *The exercises in this book gradually* **get harder**. (=become more difficult)|*Life seems to be* **getting harder** (=becoming more troublesome) *for everyone.*

**harden** sbdy. **to** sthg. *v prep* [T +*v-ing; usu. pass.*] to make (someone) less sensitive to (something or doing something): *I'm quite hardened to the cold weather here now.*

**hard·head·ed** /ˌhɑːd'hedᵻd◂‖ˌhɑrd-/ *adj* tough and practical: *a hardheaded businesswoman*

**hard-heart·ed** /ˌ· '··◂/ *adj* having no kind feelings; HARD¹ (5) –opposite **soft-hearted –hard-heartedly** *adv* **–hard-heartedness** *n* [U]

**hardline** /ˌhɑːd 'laɪn ◂/ *adj infml* unwilling to move from a fixed, usu. strict, position; UNCOMPROMISING: *hard line supporters of the government's policies* **–hardliner** *n*

**hard luck** /ˌ· '·◂/ also **tough luck**, also **hard lines** *BrE– interj,n* [U] *infml* (sorry about your) bad luck: *You failed your examination? Hard luck!*

**hard·ly** /'hɑːdli‖'hɑrdli/ *adv* **1** almost not: *I could hardly wait to hear the news.|I was so angry that I could hardly speak.|I* **hardly ever** (=almost never) *go out these days.* **2** only just: *I hardly know the people I work with.|Hardly had we started our journey* (=we had only just started) *when the car got a flat tyre.|We'd hardly arrived before we had to go back.* **3** not at all; not reasonably: *This is hardly the time for buying new clothes–I've only got just enough money for food.*

USAGE Compare **hardly, scarcely, barely,** and **no sooner** : **1 Hardly, scarcely,** and **barely** are followed by *when,* but **no sooner** is followed by *than,* in sentences like these: *The game had* **hardly/scarcely/barely** *begun when it started raining.|The game had* **no sooner** *begun than it started raining.* **2** The word order in all these sentences can be changed like this: **Hardly/barely/scarcely** *had the game begun when it started raining.|* **No sooner** *had the game begun than it started raining.* **3 Hardly, scarcely,** and (less commonly) **barely** can be followed by *any, ever,* and *at all,* to mean "almost no", "almost never", and "almost not": We've **hardly/scarcely/barely** *any money left.|He's* **hardly/scarcely** *ever late for work.*

**hard of hear·ing** /ˌ· · '··/ *adj* [F] *euph* unable to hear properly; (rather) DEAF

**hard·ship** /'hɑːdʃɪp‖'hɑrd-/ *n* [C;U] (an example of) difficult conditions of life, such as lack of money, food, etc.

**hard up** /ˌ· '·◂/ *adj* [F *for*] in need (of); not having enough esp. money: *We were very hard up when I lost my job.|The company is hard up for new ideas.*

**hard·ware** /'hɑːdweəʳ‖'hɑrd-/ *n* [U] **1** goods for the home and garden, such as pans, tools, etc. –compare IRONMONGERY **2** machinery which makes up a computer –compare SOFTWARE

**hard·wear·ing** /hɑːd'weərɪŋ‖ˌhɑrd-/ *BrE*‖**long-wearing** *AmE– adj* (esp. of clothes, shoes, etc.) that last for a long time, even when used a lot

**hard·wood** /'hɑːdwʊd‖'hɑrd-/ *n* [U] strong heavy wood from trees like the OAK, used to make good furniture –opposite **softwood**

**har·dy** /'hɑːdi‖'hɑrdi/ *adj* **-dier, -diest 1** (of people or animals) strong; able to bear cold, hard work, etc. **2** *tech* (of plants) able to live through the winter above ground **–hardiness** *n* [U]

**hare¹** /heəʳ/ *n* **hares** *or* **hare** an animal rather like a rabbit, but usu. larger, with long ears,a short tail, and long back legs which make it able to run fast –sounds like **hair**

**hare²** *v* **hared, haring** [I *off*] *BrE infml* to run very fast: *He hared off down the road.* –sounds like **hair**

**hare·brained** /'heəbreɪnd‖'heər-/ *adj* (of people or plans) very impractical; quite foolish

**hare·lip** /ˌheə'lɪp‖ˌheər-/ *n* the top lip divided into two parts, because it did not develop properly before birth **–harelipped** /ˌheə'lɪpt◂‖ˌheər- / *adj*

**har·em** /'heərəm, hɑː'riːm‖'hɑrəm/ *n* **1** the place in a Muslim house where the women live **2** [+*sing./pl. v*] the women who live in this place

**hark back** /hɑːk‖hɑrk/ *v adv* [I *to*] *infml* to mention things which happened in the past: *You're always* *harking back to how things were 50 years ago.*

**har·lot** /'hɑːlət||'hɑr-/ *n old use* →PROSTITUTE

**harm¹** /hɑːm||hɑrm/ *n* [U] **1** damage; wrong: *He means no harm* (=doesn't intend to do anything hurtful) *by saying what he thinks.|It wouldn't* **do** *him* **any harm** (=it would be good for him) *to work a little harder.|The ship was caught in a bad storm, but it* **came to no harm.** (=it wasn't harmed)*|He spilled wine on the carpet but there was* **no harm done**. –opposite **good 2 out of harm's way** safe from danger –**harmful** *adj* –**harmfully** *adv* –**harmfulness** *n* [U]

**harm²** *v* [T] to hurt; spoil; damage: *There was a fire in our street, but our house wasn't harmed at all.*

**harm·less** /'hɑːmlɨs||'hɑrm-/ *adj* that cannot cause harm: *The dog seems fierce, but he's harmless.* –**harmlessly** *adv* –**harmlessness** *n* [U]

**har·mon·i·ca** /hɑː'mɒnɪkə||hɑr'mɑ-/ *n* → MOUTH-ORGAN

**har·mo·nize** ||also **-nise** *BrE* /'hɑːmənaɪz||'hɑr-/ *v* **-nized, -nizing** [I;T] **1** to sing or play (a piece of music) in HARMONY (1) **2** [*with*] to (cause to) be in agreement, esp. in style, colour, etc., with each other or something else

**har·mo·ny** /'hɑːməni||'hɑr-/ *n* **-nies 1** [C;U] notes of music combined together in a pleasant sounding way **2** [U] a state of agreement (in feelings, ideas, etc.); peacefulness: *My cat and dog live together* **in perfect harmony**. –compare DISCORD –**harmonious** /hɑː'məunɪəs||hɑr- / *adj* –**harmoniously** *adv*

**har·ness¹** /'hɑːnɨs||'hɑr-/ *n* [C *usu. sing.*; U] the bands which are used to control a horse or fasten it to a cart, or to support a baby

**harness²** *v* [T] **1** [*to*] to put a HARNESS on (esp. a horse) and/or fasten to a vehicle such as a cart **2** to use a natural force to produce useful power: *River water is harnessed to produce electricity.*

**harp** /hɑːp||hɑrp/ *n* a large musical instrument with strings running from top to bottom of an open three-cornered frame, played by stroking (STROKE¹) or PLUCKING¹ (3) the strings with the hands –**harpist** *n*

**harp on** sthg. also **harp on about** sthg.– *v prep;adv derog* [T] to talk a lot about (one's misfortunes): *My grandfather still harps on (about) the death of his youngest son.*

**har·poon** /hɑː'puːn||hɑr-/ *v,n* [T] (to strike with) a spear with a long rope, which is used for hunting large sea animals, esp. WHALES

**harp·si·chord** /'hɑːpsɪkɔːd||'hɑrpsɪkɔrd/ *n* a musical instrument used, esp. formerly, like a piano except that the strings are PLUCKED¹ (3) rather than struck

**har·row·ing** /'hærəuɪŋ/ *adj* which causes feelings of pain and worry: *To see someone killed is a very harrowing experience.*

**harsh** /hɑːʃ||hɑrʃ/ *adj* **1** unpleasant in causing pain to the senses: *a harsh light* (=too strong for the eyes)*|harsh colours|a harsh voice* –opposite **soft 2** (of people, punishments, etc.) showing cruelty or lack of kindness –**harshly** *adv* –**harshness** *n* [U]

**har·vest¹** /'hɑːvɨst||'hɑr-/ *n* **1** the act of gathering the crops: *We all helped with the harvest.* **2** the time of year when crops are picked **3** the (amount of) crops gathered: *a good harvest|a large harvest*

**harvest²** *v* [T] to gather (a crop) –compare REAP

**has** /s, z, əz, həz; *strong* hæz/ *v 3rd pers. sing. pres. tense of* HAVE

**has-been** /'· ·/ *n infml* a person or thing no longer important, fashionable, useful, etc.

**hash** /hæʃ/ *n* **1** [C;U] a meal containing meat cut up in small pieces, esp. when re-cooked **2** [S] a mixed-up affair; MESS (1) or MUDDLE¹ (esp. in the phrase **make a hash of it**) **3** [U] *infml* →HASHISH

**hash·ish** /'hæʃiːʃ, -ɪʃ/ also **hash** *infml– n* [U] a drug made from the hardened juice of the CANNABIS plant

**has·n't** /'hæzənt/ *v short for* has not: *Hasn't he finished yet?*

**hasp** /hɑːsp/ *n* a metal fastener for a box, door, etc., which is kept in place by a PADLOCK

**has·sle¹** /'hæsəl/ *n infml esp. AmE* **1** a difficult argument **2** a struggle of mind or body: *It's a real hassle to get this child to eat.*

**hassle²** *v* **-sled, -sling** [I;T] *infml esp. AmE* to cause trouble or difficulties (for)

**haste** /heɪst/ *n* [U] (too) quick movement or action: *In his haste, he forgot to put on his coat.*

**has·ten** /'heɪsən/ *v* **1** [I;T] to (cause to) move or happen faster: *She hastened home.* **2** [I +*to-v*] to be quick (to say), because the hearer may imagine something else has happened: *He told her about the accident, but hastened to add that noone was hurt.*

**hast·y** /'heɪsti/ *adj* **-ier, -iest 1** done in a hurry: *a hasty meal* (=made/eaten in a hurry) **2** too quick in acting or deciding, esp. with a bad result: *His hasty decision was a mistake.* –**hastily** *adv* –**hastiness** *n* [U]

**hat** /hæt/ *n* **1** a covering placed on top of the head –compare CAP, BONNET **2 at the drop of a hat** suddenly **3 old hat** /,·'·/ old fashioned **4 pass the hat round** to collect money, esp. to give to someone who deserves it **5 take one's hat off to (someone)** to show that one admires (someone) for an action: *I take my hat off to him for the way he arranged the party.* **6 talking through one's hat** *infml* saying something stupid

**hatch¹** /hætʃ/ *v* **1** [I;T *out*] **a** (of an egg) to break, letting the young bird out: *Three eggs have already hatched (out).* **b** to cause (an egg) to break in this way: *We hatch the eggs by keeping them in a warm place.* **2** [I *out*] (of a young bird) to break through an egg: *Three chickens have hatched (out).* **3** [T] to make (a plan or idea): *They hatched a plan to murder the king.*

**hatch²** *n* **1** (the cover used to close) an opening on a ship or aircraft through which people and things can pass **2** an opening in a wall, made esp. so that food can be passed from a kitchen to the room where people eat

**hatch·back** /'hætʃbæk/ *n* a car having a door at the back which opens upwards –see picture on page 85

**hatch·et** /'hætʃɨt/ *n* a small axe with a short handle

**hate¹** /heɪt/ *n* [U] a strong feeling of dislike: *She looked at me with hate in her eyes.* –opposite **love**

**hate²** *v* **hated, hating** [T +*to-v*/*v-ing*] **1** to have a great dislike of: *I hate violence.|The two enemies hated each other.* –opposite **love 2** *infml* to dislike: *He hates people asking him for money.|I hate (having) to tell you, but I've damaged your car.*

**hate·ful** *adj* very unpleasant to experience: *Ironing shirts is a hateful job.* –**hatefully** *adv*

**ha·tred** /'heɪtrɨd/ *n* [S;U *of, for*] the state or feeling of hating; hate: *She is full of hatred for the driver who killed her dog.* –opposite **love**

**hat·ter** /ˈhætə$^r$/ *n* a maker and/or seller of hats (esp. in the phrase **as mad as a hatter** (=completely mad))

**hat trick** /ˈ· ·/ *n* three successes of the same type coming one after the other esp. in sports, as (in football) when the same player has made three GOALS (3) in one game

**haugh·ty** /ˈhɔːti/ *adj* **-tier, -tiest** *fml derog* (of people or their acts) appearing proud; showing that one thinks other people less important than oneself –**haughtily** *adv* –**haughtiness** *n* [U]

**haul**[1] /hɔːl/ *v* [I;T *away, on, up*] to pull hard: *to haul the logs along|to haul up the fishing nets*

**haul**[2] *n* **1** [S] the act of hauling or the distance HAULed: (fig.) *It was a long haul home, carrying our bags up the hill.* **2** [C] **a** the amount of fish caught when fishing with a net **b** *infml* the amount of something gained,esp. stolen goods

**haul·age** /ˈhɔːlɪdʒ/ *n* [U] (the charge for) the business of carrying goods by road

**haunch** /hɔːntʃ/ *n* [*usu. pl.*] the fleshy part of the body between the waist and knee

**haunt**[1] /hɔːnt/ *v* [T] **1** (esp. of a dead person) to visit, usu. appearing in a strange form: *A headless man haunts the castle.* **2** [not *be +v-ing* ] to visit (a place) regularly **3** [not *be +v-ing; usu. pass.*] to be always in the thoughts of (someone): *haunted by his words*

**haunt**[2] *n* a place where someone goes regularly: *This pub is one of my favourite haunts.*

**haunt·ing** /ˈhɔːntɪŋ/ *adj* remaining in the thoughts: *a haunting memory* –**hauntingly** *adv*

**have**[1] *v*

| *present tense* *singular* | *plural* |
|---|---|
| *I* **have,** *I've* | *We* **have,** *We've* |
| *You* **have,** *you've* | *You* **have,** *you've* |
| *He/She/It* **has,** *he's/she's/it's* | *They* **have,** *they've* |
| *past tense* *singular* | *plural* |
| *I* **had,** *I'd* | *We* **had,** *we'd* |
| *You* **had,** *you'd* | *You* **had,** *you'd* |
| *He/She/It* **had** *he'd/she'd/it'd* | *They* **had,** *they'd* |
| past PARTICIPLE | **had** |
| present PARTICIPLE | **having** |
| NEGATIVE *short forms* | **haven't, hasn't, hadn't** |

For the pronunciation of these forms look them up at their place in the dictionary.

[I] (used as a helping verb with another verb) **1** (used with the past participle to form the perfect tenses of verbs): *I've/I have written a letter.|He's/He has gone to London.|Have you finished?|She said she'd been/had been there before.* **2** [*+to-v*] also **have got to**– to be forced to; must: *Do you have to go now?|I'll have to telephone later.* –see GOTTA (USAGE); see Study Notes on page 386 **3 have had it** *infml* **a** to be too old; be broken or dead: *I'm afraid the car's finally had it.* **b** to have no more hope: *We've had it–the bus left five minutes ago!*

USAGE Compare I **have** *seen that film before.* (=at some time in the past)|*I saw that film on Saturday/last night/in 1980.* (=at a particular time in the past)

**have**[2] *v* **had, having** /ˈhævɪŋ/ [T *no pass.*] **1** also **have got** *BrE*– to possess; own: *She has blue eyes.|Have you got a pencil? (BrE)/Do you have a pencil? (AmE)|This coat has no pockets.|He's got a bad cold.* –see GOTTEN (USAGE) **2** to receive or obtain: *I had a letter today.|We had the news from John.* (=John told us).|*Have some tea!* **3** to experience or enjoy: *to have breakfast|to have a swim/a wash/a fight|Have a look at this.|We're having a party/a meeting.|I had my watch stolen.* **4** [*round, over*] to ask (somebody) to one's home: *We're having some people (over/round) for drinks tonight.* **5** to allow; permit: *I won't have bad behaviour.* **6** to cause (something) to be done or to happen: *I had my hair cut.* **7** to give birth to; become the mother of: *She had her baby in hospital.* **8 have done with** to finish; put an end to **9 have it in for (someone)** *infml* to be as unkind as possible to (someone) on purpose **10 have it off/away with** *BrE infml* to have sex with **11 have/be to do with** to have a connection with: *Her job has (something) to do with looking after old people.*

**have on** *v adv* [*no pass.*] [T] **1** [not *be +v-ing*] (**have** sthg.↔ **on**) also **have got on**– to be wearing (something): *He had nothing on except a hat.* **2** [*+that*] (**have** sbdy. **on**) *BrE infml* to trick, usu. by pretending something is not true; deceive: *He was having you on (that you were late), and you believed him.* –compare PUT **on**[1] (6) **3** [not *be +v-ing*] (**have** sthg. **on**) also **have got on**– to have arranged to do: *I don't have anything on tonight/I have nothing on (for) tonight.*

**have** sthg. **out** *v adv* [T *no pass.*] **1** to get something taken out, usu. a tooth or organ of the body: *to have a tooth out/have one's* APPENDIX (1) *out* (Never say *to have out a tooth*) **2** [*with*] to settle a difficulty by talking freely or angrily: *This disagreement has gone on for too long: it's time we had it/the whole thing out!*

**have** sbdy. **up** *v adv* [T *usu. pass.*] *BrE infml* to take to court: *He was had up for dangerous driving.*

**ha·ven** /ˈheɪvən/ *n lit* a place of calm and safety: (fig.) *safe in the haven of his mother's arms*

**have·n't** /ˈhævənt/ *v short for* have not: *You've been here before, haven't you? (fml have you not?)*

**hav·oc** /ˈhævək/ *n* [U] widespread damage or confusion: *His arrival that night* **played havoc with** (=caused confused changes in) *my plans.|The wind will* **wreak havoc on** (=damage) *my garden.*

**hawk**[1] /hɔːk/ *n* a usu. large bird which catches other birds and small animals for food

**hawk**[2] *v* [T] to sell (goods) on the street or at the doors of houses, esp. while travelling from place to place: (fig.) *to hawk one's ideas around* –**hawker** *n*

**haw·thorn** /ˈhɔː-ɔːn‖-ɔrn/ *n* a tree which has white or red flowers, and red berries in autumn

**hay** /heɪ/ *n* [U] grass which has been cut and dried, esp. for cattle food –**haymaking** /ˈheɪmeɪkɪŋ/ *n* [U]

**hay fe·ver** /ˈ· ˌ··/ *n* [U] an illness rather like a bad cold, but caused by breathing in POLLEN dust from plants

**hay·stack** /ˈheɪstæk/ also **hayrick**/-rɪk/– *n* a large pile of HAY built for storing

**hay·wire** /ˈheɪwaɪəʳ/ *adj* **go haywire** (of plans, arrangements, etc.) to become confused and DISORGANIZED

**haz·ard¹** /ˈhæzəd‖-ərd/ *n* a danger: *a hazard to health/a health hazard* –**hazardous** *adj* –**hazardously** *adv* –**hazardousness** *n* [U]

**hazard²** *v* [T] *fml* to risk; put in danger: *He hazarded all his money to save the business.|I'll* **hazard a guess.** (=I'll make a guess but I may be wrong)

**haze** /heɪz/ *n* [C;U] a light mist or smoke: *a haze of cigarette smoke*

**ha·zel¹** /ˈheɪzəl/ *n* a tree which bears nuts that can be eaten

**hazel²** *n,adj* [U] (of) a light or greenish brown colour: *She has hazel eyes.*

**haz·y** /ˈheɪzi/ *adj* **-ier, -iest** misty; rather cloudy: *The mountains were hazy in the distance.*|(fig.) *I'm rather hazy* (=uncertain) *about the details of the arrangement.* –**hazily** *adv* –**haziness** *n* [U]

**H-bomb** /ˈeɪtʃ bɒm‖-bɑm/ *n* →HYDROGEN BOMB

**he¹** /i, hi; *strong* hiː/ *pron* (used as the subject of a sentence) **1** that male person or animal already mentioned: *"Where's John?" "He's gone to the cinema."* **2** that person: *Everyone should do what he thinks best.* –see ME (USAGE)

**he²** /hiː/ *n* a male person or animal: *Is your dog a he or a she?|a he-goat*

**head¹** /hed/ *n* **1** [C] the part of the body which contains the eyes, ears, nose and mouth, and the brain –see picture on page 299 **2** [*the* S] the end where this part rests: *at the head of the bed/the grave* –compare FOOT¹ (3) **3** [C] the mind or brain: *Can't you get these facts into your head?|Try not to let your* **heart** (=feelings) **rule your head.**|*It never* **entered his head** *to help me.* (=he never even thought of helping)|*He suddenly* **took it into his head** (=decided) *to learn Russian.|I haven't got much of a head for figures.* (=I'm not very good at mathematics)|We must **put our heads together** (=talk together) *and decide what to do.* **4** [C] a ruler or leader: *the head of a firm/the family|heads of state/government* **5** [C;*the* S] the part at the top or front; the most important part: *the head of the nail|Put your address at the head of the letter.|He sat at the head of the table.* **6** [*usu. pl.*] the front side of a coin which often bears a picture of the ruler's head: *"Let's* TOSS *for it."– "Heads."– "Heads it is"* (= the front fell so as to be seen), *so you win."* –compare TAILS **7** [S] **a** a person (only in the phrase **a/per head**): *It cost £3 a head to eat there.* **b** (used in counting farm animals) an animal: *three head of cattle* **8** [C] the pressure or force produced by a quantity of steam or water **9 above/over someone's head** beyond someone's understanding; too difficult **10 a: bring something to a head** to cause (an event) to reach a point where something must be done or decided **b come to a head** to reach this point **11 go to someone's head: a** to over-excite or INTOXICATE someone **b** to make someone too proud, or CONCEITED **12 have one's head in the clouds** to be impractical; not act according to the realities of life **13 head over heels: a** turning over in the air head first **b** very much; completely: *head over heels in love* **14 keep one's head** to remain calm **15 lose one's head** to act wildly or without reason because afraid, angry, confused, etc. **16 not be able to make head or tail of** *infml* to be unable to understand **17 off one's head** *infml* mad **18 -headed** having a certain type of head or hair: *curly-headed|red-headed|two-headed|empty-headed*

**head²** *v* **1** [T] to lead; be at the front of **2** [T] to be in charge of: *Who heads the government?* **3** [I;T] to (cause to) move in a certain direction: *We're heading home.* **4** [T] to strike (a ball) with the head: *He headed it into the* GOAL (2)

**head for** sthg. *v prep* [T] to move towards; go to: *Where are you heading/headed for?*|(fig.) *You're heading for an accident if you drive after drinking.* –compare ASK **for**

**head** sbdy.↔ **off** *v adv* [T] to cause to move in a different direction: *They were running towards the house, but we headed them towards the field.*

**head·ache** /ˈhedeɪk/ *n* a pain in the head: (fig.) *The problem of unemployment is a big headache for the government.* –see ACHE (USAGE)

**head·band** /ˈhedbænd/ *n* a band worn on the forehead, usu. to keep the hair back from the face

**head·dress** /ˈhed-dres/ *n* an ornamental covering for the head

**head·first** /ˈhedˈfɜːst◂‖-ɜrst/ *adj,adv* (moving or entering) with the rest of the body following the head

**head·gear** /ˈhedgɪəʳ/ *n* [C;U] (a) covering for the head

**head·ing** /ˈhedɪŋ/ *n* the words written as a title at the top of (each part of) a piece of writing

**head·land** /ˈhedlənd/ *n* a narrow piece of land running out into the sea

**head·light** /ˈhedlaɪt/ also **headlamp**/ˈhedlæmp/– *n* a powerful light fixed at the front of a vehicle, usu. one of a pair –see also SIDELIGHT (1); see picture on page 85

**head·line** /ˈhedlaɪn/ *n* **1** the heading printed in large letters above a story in a newspaper **2** [*usu. pl.*] a main point of the news, as read on radio or television

**head·long** /ˈhedlɒŋ‖-lɔŋ/ *adv,adj* **1** →HEADFIRST **2** (done) with great haste, often without thought: *He rushed headlong into marriage.*

**head·mas·ter** /ˌhedˈmɑːstəʳ‖ˈhedˌmæstər/ **headmistress** /ˌhedˈmɪstrɪ̈s‖ˈhedˌmɪstrɪ̈s/ *fem.*– *n* the teacher in charge of a school

**head-on** /ˌ· ˈ·◂/ *adv,adj* with the head or front parts meeting, usu. violently: *a head-on collision*

**head·phones** /ˈhedfəʊnz/ *n* [P] an apparatus made of two parts of metal, plastic, etc. which fits over the ears and is used to receive radio messages, etc.

**head·quar·ters** /ˈhedˌkwɔːtəz, ˌhedˈkwɔːtəz‖-ɔrtərz/ *n* **-headquarters** [+*sing./pl. v*] the office or place where the people work who control a large organization, such as the police or army: *Our firm's headquarters is/are in Geneva.*

**head·room** /ˈhed-rʊm, -ruːm/ *n* [U] space above a vehicle passing under a bridge, through a TUNNEL, etc.

**head·set** /ˈhedset/ *n esp. AmE* (a set of) HEADPHONES

**head·shrink·er** /ˈhed,ʃrɪŋkəʳ/ *n humor* →PSYCHIATRIST

**head start** /,· ˈ·/ *n* [S *over, on*] an advantage, esp. in a race: (fig.) *He has a headstart over his friends who are learning French, as his mother is French.*

**head·stone** /ˈhedstəʊn/ *n* a stone which marks the top end of a grave, usu. having the buried person's name on it; GRAVESTONE

**head·strong** /ˈhedstrɒŋ‖-strɔŋ/ *adj* (of people) determined to do what one wants against all advice

**head·way** /ˈhedweɪ/ *n* **make headway** to advance in dealing with a difficulty

**head·wind** /ˈhed,wɪnd, ,hedˈwɪnd/ *n* a wind blowing directly against one

**head·y** /ˈhedi/ *adj* **-ier, -iest 1** (of alcohol and its effects) tending to make people drunk, GIDDY, etc. (to INTOXICATE) **2** with a feeling of lightness and excitement: *heady with success*

**heal** /hi:l/ *v* [I;T *over, up*] to (cause to) become healthy, esp. to grow new skin: *His wounds are healing (over/up).*|(fig.) *Their disagreements healed (over) with time.* **–healer** *n*

**health** /helθ/ *n* [U] **1** the state of being well, without disease: *Health is more important to me than money.* –opposite **sickness 2** the condition of the body: *in poor/good health*

**health·y** /ˈhelθi/ *adj* **-ier, -iest 1** strong, not often ill; usually in good health **2** likely to produce or showing good health: *healthy seaside air|a clear healthy skin*|(fig.) *The children have a healthy* (=natural) *dislike of school.* –opposite **unhealthy –healthily** *adv* **–healthiness** *n* [U]

**heap¹** /hi:p/ *n* a pile or mass of things one on top of the other: *The books lay in a heap on the floor.*

**heap²** *v* [T *on, with, up*] to pile up in large amounts: *He heaped food on the plate.*

**hear** /hɪəʳ/ *v* **heard** /hɜːd‖hɜrd/, **hearing 1** [I;T not *be +v-ing*] to receive and understand (sounds) by using the ears: *I can't hear very well.|I heard him say so.|I can hear someone knocking.* **2** [T +(*that*); not *be+v-ing*] to be told or informed: *I heard (that) he was ill.* **3** [T] to listen with attention (esp. to a case in court): *The judge heard the case.|She heard what he had to say.* **4 won't/wouldn't hear of** refuse(s) to allow: *I won't hear of you coming in so late.* **5 Hear! Hear!** (a shout of agreement)

USAGE Compare **hear** and **listen**: To **hear** is to experience with the ears; to **listen** is to hear with attention: *I was in the garden when the telephone rang, so I didn't* **hear** *it.|We always* **listen** *to the six o'clock news on the radio.|If you* **listen** *hard, you can* **hear** *what the neighbours are saying.*

**hear about** sbdy./sthg. *v prep* [T +*v-ing*] to get to know (about): *Have you heard about Jim coming to London?|We've been hearing quite a lot about that young tennis player lately.*

**hear from** sbdy. *v prep* [T not *be +v-ing*] to receive news from (someone), usu. by letter: *I heard from her last week.|I haven't heard from him since he telephoned.*

**hear of** sbdy./sthg. *v prep* [T +*v-ing;* not *be+v-ing*] (usu. in questions, NEGATIVES², etc.) to know of (a fact/the existence of something or somebody): *Who's he?–I've never heard of him.*

**hear** sbdy. **out** *v adv* [T] to listen to (someone who is speaking) until he/she has finished: *Don't interrupt, just hear me out before you start talking.*

**hear·ing** /ˈhɪərɪŋ/ *n* **1** [U] the sense by which one hears sound: *Her hearing is getting worse. She needs a* **hearing aid.** (=a small electric machine, worn on the body, which makes sounds louder) **2** [U] the distance at which one can hear; EARSHOT: *Don't talk about it in his hearing.* (=so that he can hear) **3** [C] a chance to be heard explaining one's position: *It's a good idea, so try to get a hearing for it.* **4** [C] *law* a trial of a case before a judge

**hear·say** /ˈhɪəseɪ‖ˈhɪər-/ *n* [U] things which are said rather than proved: *I don't know if he's really leaving his job; it may only be hearsay.*

**hearse** /hɜːs‖hɜrs/ *n* a car which is used to carry a body in a COFFIN to the funeral

**heart** /hɑːt‖hɑrt/ *n* **1** [C] the organ inside the chest which controls the flow of blood by pushing it round the body **2** [S;U] this organ when thought of as the centre of the feelings, esp. kind feelings: *He seems rather fierce, but has a kind heart/he is kind* **at heart**/*his* **heart is in the right place.|Have a heart!** (=Don't be unkind to me)|I pity them **with all my heart/from the bottom of my heart.** (=with deep feeling) **3** [C] the centre: *the heart of a cabbage/of the city|Let's get to the heart of the matter.* **4** [U] courage; firmness of purpose: **Take heart** *and go on trying.|I used to dig the garden every week, but I* **lost heart** *when all the plants died.|I didn't* **have the heart to** *tell him the bad news.* **5** [C] a playing-card with one or more heart-shaped figures printed on it in red: *the Queen of Hearts* –see CARDS (USAGE) **6 after one's own heart** of the type like oneself or which one likes: *He's a man after my own heart.* **7 break someone's heart** to make someone very unhappy **8 by heart** by memory: *to know/learn by heart* **9 set one's heart on (doing) something** to want very much to have or do something **10 take (something) to heart** to feel the effect of something deeply (and take suitable action) **11 -hearted** /ˈhɑːtɪ̣d‖ˈɑr-/ having a certain type of HEART (2,4): *kind-hearted|cold-hearted*

**heart·ache** /ˈhɑːteɪk‖ˈhɑrt-/ *n* [U] deep feelings of sorrow and pain

**heart at·tack** /ˈ· ·,·/ *n* a very dangerous medical condition in which the heart suddenly stops working properly: *He died of a heart attack.*

**heart·beat** /ˈhɑːtbiːt‖ˈhɑrt-/ *n* [C;U] (the) movement of the heart as it pushes the blood

**heart·break** /ˈhɑːtbreɪk‖ˈhɑrt-/ *n* [C;U] deep sorrow

**heart·break·ing** /ˈhɑːt,breɪkɪŋ‖ˈhɑrt-/ *adj* causing great sorrow **–heartbreakingly** *adv*

**heart·brok·en** /ˈhɑːt,brəʊkən‖ˈhɑrt-/ also **broken-hearted**– *adj* (of a person) deeply hurt in the feelings; full of sorrow

**heart·burn** /ˈhɑːtbɜːn‖ˈhɑrtbɜrn/ *n* [U] a condition in which one feels an unpleasant burning in the chest, caused by INDIGESTION

**heart·en** /ˈhɑːtn‖ˈhɑr-/ [T] *fml* to encourage: *He was heartened by her kindness.* –opposite **dishearten**

**heart·felt** /ˈhɑːtfelt‖ˈhɑrt-/ *adj* deeply felt; sincere; true: *She gave him her heartfelt thanks.*

**hearth** /hɑːθ‖hɑrθ/ *n* the area around the fire in one's home, esp. the floor of the fireplace –see picture on page 355

**heart·i·ly** /'hɑːtɪli‖'hɑr-/ *adv* **1** (done) with strength, force, APPETITE, etc.: *They ate heartily.* **2** very: *I'm heartily tired/sick of your questions.*

**heart·less** /'hɑːtlɪs‖'hɑrt-/ *adj* cruel; unkind; pitiless –**heartlessly** *adv* –**heartlessness** *n* [U]

**heart·rend·ing** /'hɑːtˌrendɪŋ‖'hɑrt-/ *adj* which causes a feeling of deep sorrow or pity: *the heartrending cries of the wounded* –**heartrendingly** *adv*

**heart·strings** /'hɑːtˌstrɪŋz‖'hɑr-/ *n* [P] someone's deep feelings of love and pity

**heart-to-heart** /ˌ· · '· ◂/ *adj,n* (a talk) mentioning personal details, without hiding anything

**heart·y** /'hɑːti‖'hɑrti/ *adj* **-ier, -iest 1** WARM-HEARTED and friendly: *a hearty greeting* **2** strong and healthy (esp. in the phrase **hale and hearty**) **3** (of meals) large: *a hearty breakfast* –**heartiness** *n* [U]

**heat**[1] /hiːt/ *n* **1** [U] the quality or quantity of being warm or cold: *What is the heat of the water in the swimming pool?* **2** [S;U] hotness; WARMTH: *The heat from the fire dried their clothes.*|*I can't walk about in this heat.* (=hot weather)|(fig.) *In the* **heat of the moment/argument** *I lost my self-control.* **3** (**be**) **on heat** *BrE*||**in heat** *AmE* – (of certain female animals, e.g. dogs) (to be) in a state in which CONCEPTION (3) can occur **4** [C] a part of a race or competition whose winners compete against other winners until there is a small enough number to decide the end result

**heat**[2] *v* [I;T *up*] to (cause to) become warm or hot: *We'll heat (up) some milk for the coffee.*

**heat·ed** /'hiːtɪd/ *adj* angry or excited: *a heated argument* –**heatedly** *adv*

**heat·er** /'hiːtəʳ/ *n* a machine for heating air or water, such as those which burn gas, oil, or electricity to produce heat

**heath** /hiːθ/ *n* an open piece of wild unfarmed land where grass and other plants grow; MOOR[1] or COMMON[2] (1)

**hea·then** /'hiːðən/ *n,adj old use or humor* (of) a person who does not belong to one of the large established religions: *heathen gods* –compare PAGAN

**heath·er** /'heðəʳ/ *n* [U] a plant which grows on open windy land (MOORS) and has small usu. pink or purple flowers

**heat·ing** /'hiːtɪŋ/ *n* [U] a system for keeping rooms and buildings warm –see also CENTRAL HEATING

**heat·stroke** /'hiːtstrəʊk/ *n* [U] →SUNSTROKE

**heat wave** /'· ·/ *n* a period of unusually hot weather

**heave**[1] /hiːv/ *v* **heaved, heaving 1** [I,T] to pull and lift with effort, esp. towards oneself: *We heaved him to his feet.*|*They all heaved on the rope.* **2** [I] to rise and fall regularly: *Her chest heaved as she breathed deeply after the race.* **3** [T] *infml* to throw: *The children have just heaved a brick through my window.* **4** **heave a sigh** to let out a deep breath with a sound expressing sadness

**heave**[2] *v* **hove** /həʊv/, **heaving** [I] (esp, of a ship) to move in the stated direction or manner: *As we came into harbour another ship hove* ALONGSIDE/*into view.*

**heave to** *v adv* [I] *tech* (of a ship) to stop moving; come to rest: *The ship hove to next to ours.*

**heave**[3] *n* a pull or throw: *Just one more heave, and the stone will be in the right place.*

**heav·en** /'hevən/ *n* **1** [U] the place where God or the gods are supposed to live; place of complete happiness where the souls of good people go after death –compare HELL **2** [C *usu. pl.*] the sky: *Suddenly* **the heavens opened** *and it poured with rain.*

**heav·en·ly** /'hevənli/ *adj* [*no comp.*] **1** [A] of, from, or like heaven; in or belonging to the sky: *The sun, moon, and stars are* **heavenly bodies**. **2** *infml* wonderful: *What heavenly weather!* –compare HELLISH

**heav·en·wards** /'hevənwədz‖-ərdz/ also **heavenward** /'hevənwəd‖-ərd/ *AmE– adv* towards the sky or heaven

**heav·y** /'hevi/ *adj* **-ier, -iest 1** of a certain weight, esp. of a weight that makes carrying, moving,or lifting difficult: *The bag is too heavy for me to carry.* **2** of unusual force or amount: *heavy rain*|*a heavy blow*|*a heavy punishment*|*heavy traffic*|*A* **heavy smoker/drinker** *is one who smokes/drinks a lot or too much.*|*I'm such a* **heavy sleeper** *that the explosion didn't wake me.* **3** serious, esp. if uninteresting: *This book is heavy reading.* **4 a** feeling or showing difficulty or slowness in moving: *My head is heavy.*|*heavy movements* **b** difficult and causing tiredness: *I've had a heavy day at the office.*|*Moving that piano was heavy work.* **5** (of food) rather solid and bad for the stomach **6** (of weather) **a** still, without wind, dark, etc. **b** (at sea) stormy, with big waves **7 make heavy weather of something** *infml* to make something more difficult than it really is –opposite **light** –**heavily** *adv*: *moving/breathing/drinking heavily* –**heaviness** *n* [U]

**heavy-du·ty** /ˌ·· '·· ◂/ *adj* (of clothes, tyres, machines, oil, etc.) made to be used a lot, or strong enough for rough treatment

**heavy-hand·ed** /ˌ·· '·· ◂/ *adj* unkind or unfair in one's treatment of others; not careful in speech and action –**heavy-handedly** *adv* –**heavy-handedness** *n* [U]

**heav·y·heart·ed** /ˌhevi'hɑːtɪd ◂‖-'hɑr-/ *adj* sad –opposite **light-hearted**

**heav·y·weight** /'heviweɪt/ *n,adj* (a BOXER (1)) of the heaviest class

**He·brew** /'hiːbruː/ *adj,n* (of) the language used by the Jews, in ancient times and at present

**heck·le** /'hekəl/ *v* **-led, -ling** [I;T] to interrupt (a speaker or speech) with confusing or unfriendly remarks, esp. at a political meeting –**heckler** *n*

**hec·tare** /'hektɑːʳ, -teəʳ‖-teər/ *n* (a measure for the area of land which equals) 10,000 square metres

**hec·tic** /'hektɪk/ *adj* full of excitement and hurried movement: *a hectic day* –**hectically** *adv*

**he'd** /id, hid; *strong* hiːd/ *v short for* **1** he would: *He'd go there now if he could afford it.* **2** he had: *He'd gone.*|*He'd (got) a few minutes to spend with her.*

**hedge**[1] /hedʒ/ *n* **1** a row of bushes or small trees dividing one garden or field from another –see picture on page 297 **2** [*against*] a protection: *Buying a house is the best* **hedge against inflation**. (=protection against one's money losing its value)

**hedge**[2] *v* **hedged, hedging 1** [I;T] to make a HEDGE round (a field) **2** [I] to refuse to answer directly: *Stop hedging and answer my question!* **3 hedge one's bets** to protect oneself against loss by favouring or supporting more than one side in a competition or struggle

**hedge·hog** /ˈhedʒhɒg‖-hɔg/ *n* a small insect-eating animal which has SPINES (3) (sharp prickles) standing out from its back and is smaller than a PORCUPINE

**hedge·row** /ˈhedʒrəʊ/ *n* a row of bushes, esp. along country roads, or separating fields

**he·don·is·m** /ˈhiːdənɪzəm/ *n* [U] the idea that pleasure is the most important thing in life **–hedonist** *n* **–hedonistic** /-ˈɪstɪk / *adj*

**heed¹** /hiːd/ *v* [T] *fml* to give attention to: *She didn't heed my warning.*

**heed²** *n* [U] *fml* attention; notice: **Take heed of/pay heed to** *what I say, if you want to succeed.* **–heedful** *adj* **–heedless** *adj* [*of*]

**heel¹** /hiːl/ *n* **1** the back part of the foot –see picture on page 299 **2** the part of a shoe, sock, etc., which covers this, esp. the raised part of a shoe underneath the foot: *There's a hole in the heel of my stocking.*|*to wear high heels* (=shoes with high heels) –compare SOLE¹ (2) **3 at/on one's heels** very closely behind: *He followed (hot) on my heels.* **4 down at heel** (of a person) untidy and uncared for in appearance

**heel²** *v* [T] to put a heel on (a shoe) –compare SOLE²

**hef·ty** /ˈhefti/ *adj* **-tier, -tiest** big and/or strong: *a hefty man/meal/blow to the jaw*

**heif·er** /ˈhefəʳ/ *n* a cow which has not yet had a CALF (=a young cow)

**height** /haɪt/ *n* **1** [C;U] the quality or degree of being tall or high:*His height makes him stand out in the crowd.* **2** [C] (a point at) a fixed or measured distance above another given point: *a window at a height of ten feet above the ground*|*During the floods the river water rose to the height of the main road beside it.* –compare DEPTH (1) **3** [C] a high position or place: *We looked down from a great height to the town below.* **4** [*the* S] the main point; highest degree: *It's the height of stupidity to go sailing in this weather.*

**height·en** /ˈhaɪtn/ *v* [I;T] to (cause to) become greater in degree: *As she waited, her excitement heightened.*

**heir** /eəʳ/ **heiress** /ˈeərəs/ *fem.*– *n* [*to*] the person who has the lawful right to receive the property or title of an older member of the family who dies:*The king's eldest son is the heir to the* THRONE. (=kingdom)|*the birth of a son and heir* (=first son)

**heir·loom** /ˈeəluːm‖ˈeər-/ *n* a valuable object given by older members of a family to younger ones over many years or even several centuries

**held** /held/ *v past tense and participle of* HOLD

**hel·i·cop·ter** /ˈheləkɒptəʳ‖-kɑp-/ *n* an aircraft which is made to fly by a set of large fast-turning metal blades fixed on top of it

**hel·i·port** /ˈheləpɔːt‖-port/ *n* a HELICOPTER airport

**he·li·um** /ˈhiːlɪəm/ *n* [U] a gas that is a simple substance (ELEMENT (1)) that is lighter than air, will not burn, and is used e.g. in BALLOONS¹ (1)

**hell¹** /hel/ *n* [U] **1** (esp. in the Christian and Muslim religions) a place where the souls of the wicked are said to be punished after death: (fig.) *Driving a car in a snowstorm is real hell!* –compare HEAVEN (1) **2** *infml* (a swear word, used in anger or to strengthen an expression): *What the hell's that thing on your head?*|*That's* **a hell of** *a good car.*|*Stop telling me what to do–(you can)* **go to hell!**|*I had to run* **like hell** *to catch the bus.* **3 for the hell of it** *infml* for fun: *We went swimming at midnight just for the hell of it.* **4 give someone hell** *infml* to treat or scold (someone) very roughly in anger: *My father wasn't there when I came in late, but he gave me hell in the morning.*

**hell²** *interj infml not polite* (an expression of strong anger or disappointment): *Oh, hell! I've missed the last train.*|*Bloody hell!*

**he'll** /il, hil; *strong* hiːl/ *short for* **1** he will **2** he shall

**hell·ish** /ˈhelɪʃ/ *adj infml* terrible; very unpleasant: *The weather's been hellish recently.* –compare HEAVENLY (2)

**hel·lo** /həˈləʊ, he-/ also **hallo, hullo** *BrE– interj,n* **-los** **1** (the usual word of greeting): *Hello, John! How are you?* **2** (the word used for starting a telephone conversation): *Hello, who's speaking, please?* –compare GOODBYE **3** *BrE* (an expression of surprise): *Hello! Somebody's left their hat behind.* **4** (a call for attention to a distant person): *Hello! Is anybody there?*

**helm** /helm/ *n* the TILLER which guides a ship:(fig.) *How long has she been* **at the helm of** (=in control of) *the company?*

**hel·met** /ˈhelmət/ *n* a covering to protect the head, as worn by soldiers, motorcyclists, policemen, miners, etc.

**helms·man** /ˈhelmzmən/ *n* **-men** /mən/ a person who guides and controls, esp. when STEERing at the HELM of a boat

**help¹** /help/ *v* **1** [I;T *out*] to do something for (someone who needs something done for them); AID; ASSIST: *Please help me; I can't do it alone.*|*My father helped me (out) with money when I needed it.*|*Could you help me (to) lift this box?*|*Trade helps the development of industry.* **2** [I;T] to make better: *Crying won't help (you).*|*It won't help (you) to cry.*|*Have you got anything to help a cold?* **3** [T +*v-ing*] to avoid; prevent; change; (only in the phrase **can/can't/couldn't help**): *I couldn't help crying.*|*I can't help having big feet.*|*He never does any more work than he can help.*|**I can't help it.** (=it's not my fault)|*You've broken it now,* **it can't be helped**. (=we must accept it) **4** [T *to*] to take for (oneself), esp. dishonestly: *The money was on the table and no one was there, so he helped himself (to it).*|*"Can I have a drink?" "Help yourself!"*|**Help yourself to** *a drink.*

USAGE **Assist** is like **help** but **a** it is more formal, and **b** it suggests that the person being assisted is also doing part of the work: *I can't push the car on my own–will somebody* **help**/(*fml*) **assist** *me?* If someone is in difficulties, you **help** (not **assist**) them: *His job consists of* **helping** *old people who live alone.*|*I'm afraid I'm lost–can somebody* **help** *me?*

**help²** *n* **1** the act of helping; ASSISTANCE; AID: *If you want any help, just ask me.* **2** [C *to*] something or somebody that helps: *This machine is a great help in making cakes more quickly.* **3 Help!** Please bring help, I'm in danger

**help·ful** /ˈhelpfəl/ *adj* [*to, in*] willing to help; useful –opposite **unhelpful** **–helpfully** *adv* **–helpfulness** *n* [U]

**help·ing** /ˈhelpɪŋ/ *n* a serving of food; PORTION (3): *I'd like a second helping, I'm still hungry!*

**help·less** /ˈhelpləs/ *adj* unable to look after oneself or to act without help **–helplessly** *adv* **–helplessness** *n* [U]

**hel·ter-skel·ter¹** /ˌheltəʳ 'skeltəʳ/ *adv,adj* (done) in a great hurry; disordered/disorderly: *She went helter-skelter down the stairs.*
**helter-skelter²** *n esp. BrE* an amusement in a FAIRGROUND where one sits down and slides from the top of a tower to the bottom, moving round and round it
**hem¹** /hem/ *n* the edge of a piece of cloth when turned under and sewn down, esp. the lower edge of a skirt or dress: *This dress is too long; I must take the hem up.* (=make it shorter)
**hem²** *v* **-mm-** [T] to put a HEM on
**hem** sbdy./sthg.**in** *v adv* [T] to surround tightly; enclose: *The army was hemmed in by the enemy.*
**hem·i·sphere** /'hemə̇sfɪəʳ/ *n* **1** half a SPHERE (an object which is round like a ball) **2** a half of the earth, esp. the northern or southern half above or below the EQUATOR, or the eastern or western half
**hem·line** /'hemlaɪn/ *n* the position of the HEM; length of a dress, skirt, etc.
**hem·lock** /'hemlɒk‖-lɑk/ *n* [C;U] (a plant which produces) a poisonous drug
**he·mo·glo·bin** /ˌhi:mə'gləʊbə̇n‖'hi:məˌgləʊbə̇n/ *n* [U] red colouring matter in the blood which carries oxygen
**he·mo·phil·i·a** /ˌhi:mə'fɪlɪə/ *n* [U] a disease which shows its effects only in males and which makes the sufferer bleed for a long time after a cut –**hemophiliac** /-'fɪliæk/ *n,adj*
**hem·or·rhage** /'hemərɪdʒ/ *n* [C;U] a flow of blood, esp. a long or large and unexpected one
**hem·or·rhoid** /'hemərɔɪd/ *n* [*usu. pl.*] *tech or fml* a swollen blood vessel at the opening (ANUS) at the lower end of the bowel –see also PILES
**hemp** /hemp/ *n* [U] any of a family of plants which are used for making strong rope and a rough cloth, and some of which produce the drug CANNABIS
**hen** /hen/ *n* **1** the female bird often kept for its eggs on farms; female chicken **2** a female bird of which the male is the COCK: *a hen* PHEASANT
**hence** /hens/ *adv fml* **1** for this reason: *The town was built on the side of a hill: hence the name Hillside.* –see Study Notes on page 128 **2** from here or from now: *three days hence* –compare THENCE
**hence·forth** /ˌhens'fɔ:θ, 'hensfɔ:θ‖-orθ/ also **henceforward** /ˌhens'fɔ:wed‖-'forwərd/ – *adv fml* from now on: *I promise to behave better henceforth.*
**hench·man** /'hentʃmən/ *n* **-men** /mən/ *usu. derog* a faithful supporter, esp. of a political leader, who obeys without question, often using violence
**hen·na** /'henə/ *n* [U] a reddish-brown DYE made from a type of bush and used to colour the hair, fingernails, etc.
**hep·a·ti·tis** /ˌhepə'taɪtə̇s/ *n* [U] a disease (INFLAMMATION) of the LIVER¹ (1)
**her¹** /əʳ, həʳ; *strong* hɜ:ʳ/ *determiner* (POSSESSIVE *form of* SHE ) **1** of that female person or animal already mentioned: *Mary sat down in her chair.* **2** (used of things, esp. vehicles or countries, that are thought of as female): *the ship with all her passengers*
**her²** *pron* (*object form of* SHE): *Where is Mary? Can you see her?*|*God bless this ship and all who sail in her!* –see ME (USAGE)
**her·ald¹** /'herəld/ *n* (in former times) a person who carried messages from a ruler and gave important news to the people: (fig.) *Early flowers are heralds* (=signs) *of spring.*
**herald²** *v* [T *in*] to be a sign of something coming: *The singing of the birds heralded (in) the day.*
**her·ald·ry** /'herəldri/ *n* [U] the study and use of COATS OF ARMS –**heraldic** /he'rældɪk/ *adj*
**herb** /hɜ:b‖ɜrb, hɜrb/ *n* any of several kinds of plant which are used to make medicine or to improve the taste of food –compare SPICE –**herbal** *adj*
**her·ba·ceous** /hə'beɪʃəs‖ɜr'beɪ-, hɜr'beɪ-/ *adj* (of a plant) soft-stemmed, not woody: *We have a* **herbaceous border** (=border of herbaceous plants) *round our garden.*
**herb·al·ist** /'hɜ:bələ̇st‖'ɜr-, 'hɜr-/ *n* a person who treats disease with HERBS
**her·biv·o·rous** /hɜ:'bɪvərəs‖ɜr-, hɜr-/ *adj* (of animals) which eat grass and plants –see also CARNIVOROUS
**herd¹** /hɜ:d‖hɜrd/ *n* **1** [C +*sing./pl. v*] a group of animals of one kind which live and feed together: *a herd of elephants* **2** [C] (*in comb.*) someone who looks after a group of animals; HERDSMAN: SHEPHERD|*goatherd* **3** [C +*sing./pl. v*] *derog* people generally, thought of as acting or thinking all alike: *to follow the herd*
**herd²** *v* [I;T *into*] to (cause to) group together (as if) in a herd: *We all herded into the corner.*|*The farmer herded the cows into the field.*
**herds·man** /'hɜ:dzmən‖-ɜr-/ *n* **-men** /mən/ a man who looks after a HERD¹ (1) of animals
**here** /hɪəʳ/ *adv* **1** at, in, or to this place: *I live here.*|*Come over here.*|*It's two miles from here.*|*My friend here will help you.* **2** at this point: *Here we agree.* **3** (used for drawing attention to someone or something): *Here comes Mary.* (=I can see Mary coming)|*Here is the news . . .* –compare THERE¹ (3) **4** (used to call someone's attention): *Here! What are you doing?* **5 here and there** scattered about **6 Here goes!** *infml* Now I'm going to try something: *I've never been on a horse before–well, here goes!* **7 Here's to** (said when drinking a TOAST² (2)): *Here's to John in his new job!* **8 Here you are** Here's what you want **9 neither here nor there** not important; IRRELEVANT: *I know you want a bigger car, but that's neither here nor there; we can't afford it.*
**here·a·bouts** /ˌhɪərə'baʊts, 'hɪərəbaʊts/ also **hereabout** *AmE*– *adv* near here
**here·af·ter¹** /ˌhɪər'ɑ:ftəʳ‖-'æf-/ *adv fml or law* after this time; in the future
**hereafter²** *n* [S] the life after death
**here·by** /ˌhɪə'baɪ, 'hɪəbaɪ‖-ər-/ *adv fml or law* now; by doing or saying this: *I hereby declare her elected.*
**he·red·i·ta·ry** /hə̇'redə̇təri‖-teri/ *adj* [*no comp.*] which can be or is passed down from parent to child: *a hereditary disease*|*a hereditary* PEERAGE (2)
**he·red·i·ty** /hə̇'redə̇ti/ *n* [U] the passing on of qualities from parent to child in the cells of the body: *Some diseases are present by heredity.*
**here·in** /ˌhɪər'ɪn/ *adv fml or law* in this piece of writing
**her·e·sy** /'herə̇si/ *n* **-sies** [C;U] (the fact of holding) a (religious) belief against what is accepted

**her·e·tic** /'her$\frac{1}{3}$tɪk/ *n* a person who favours HERESY or is guilty of a heresy –**heretical** /h$\frac{1}{3}$'retikəl/ *adj*
**here·with** /ˌhɪə'wɪð‖ˌhɪər-/ *adv fml or law* with this piece of writing: *I send you herewith two copies of the contract.*
**heritage** /'her$\frac{1}{3}$tɪdʒ/ *n* [*usu. sing.*] something which is passed down over many years within a family or nation: *the country's artistic heritage* (=pictures and beautiful buildings)
**her·met·ic** /hɜː'metɪk‖hɜr-/ *adj* very tightly closed; AIRTIGHT: *A* **hermetic seal** *is used at the top of this glass bottle.* –**hermetically** *adv*
**her·mit** /'hɜːm$\frac{1}{3}$t‖'hɜr-/ *n* (esp. in former times) a person who lives alone, thinking and praying
**her·mit·age** /'hɜːm$\frac{1}{3}$tɪd·‖'hɜr-/ *n* a place where a HERMIT lives or has lived
**her·ni·a** /'hɜːnɪə‖'hɜr-/ also **rupture**– *n* [C;U] the medical condition in which an organ pushes through its covering wall, usu. when the bowel is pushed through the stomach wall
**he·ro** /'hɪərəʊ/ **heroine** /'herəʊɪn/ *fem.*– *n* **-roes 1** a person remembered or admired for (an act of) bravery, strength, or goodness **2** the most important character in a play, poem, story, etc.
**he·ro·ic** /hɪ'rəʊɪk/ *adj* **1** showing the qualities of a HERO (1): *a heroic effort* **2** *tech* concerned with heroes: *heroic poems* –**heroically** *adv*
**he·ro·ics** /hɪ'rəʊɪks/ *n* [P] speech or actions which are meant to appear grand, though they mean nothing
**her·o·in** /'herəʊɪn/ *n* a drug from MORPHINE, which is used for lessening pain, and which one can become dependent on (ADDICTed to)
**her·o·is·m** /'herəʊɪzəm/ *n* [U] great courage: *It was an act of heroism to go back into the burning building.*
**her·on** /'herən/ *n* **-ons** *or* **-on** a long-legged bird which lives near water
**her·ring** /'herɪŋ/ *n* **-ring** *or* **-rings 1** a fish which swims in large groups (SHOALS) in the sea, and is used for food **2 red herring** a fact or point of argument which draws attention away from the main point
**hers** /hɜːz‖hɜrz/ *pron* (POSSESSIVE[2] *form of* SHE) of that female person or animal already mentioned: *That's my coat and hers is over there.*
**her·self** /ə'self, hə-; *strong* hɜː-‖ər-, hər-; *strong* hɜr-/ *pron* **1** (used as the object of a verb, or after a PREPOSITION, when the same female person or animal does the action and is the object of the action): *She's proud of herself.|Sarah looked at herself in the mirror.* **2** (used to make *she,* or the name of a female person or animal, stronger): *She herself said so.|I'd like to speak to the doctor herself.*
**he's** /iz, hiz; *strong* hiːz/ *v short for* **1** he is: *He's a writer.|He's coming.* **2** (*in compound tenses*) he has: *He's got two cars.|He's had a cold.*
**hes·i·tant** /'hez$\frac{1}{3}$tənt/ *adj* showing uncertainty or slowness about deciding to act; tending to HESITATE: *She's hesitant about making new friends.* –**hesitantly** *adv* –**hesitancy** also **hesitance**– *n* [U]
**hes·i·tate** /'hez$\frac{1}{3}$teɪt/ *v* **-tated, -tating** [I + *to- v*] **1** to pause in or before an action: *He hesitated before crossing the road.|She hesitated over the choice between the two dresses.* **2** *polite* to be unwilling; find it unpleasant: *I hesitate to ask you, but will you lend me some money?* –**hesitating** *adj* –**hesitatingly** *adv* –**hesitation** /-'teən/ *n* [C;U]: *Without a moment's hesitation, she jumped into the river.|I have no hestitation in saying . . .*
**het·e·ro·ge·ne·ous** /ˌhetərəʊ'dʒiːnɪəs/ *adj* of (many) different kinds: *a heterogeneous mass of papers* –compare HOMOGENEOUS
**het·e·ro·sex·u·al** /ˌhetərə'sekʃʊəl/ *adj,n* (of or being) a person attracted to people of the other sex –compare BISEXUAL, HOMOSEXUAL –**heterosexually** *adv* –**heterosexuality** /-sek'aeti/ *n* [U]
**het up** /ˌhet 'ʌp/ *adj* [F *about*] *infml* (of people) excited; anxious: *He's het up about the examination.*
**hew** /hjuː/ *v* **hewed, hewed** *or* **hewn** /hjun/, **hewing** [I;T] *fml or lit* to cut by striking blows with an axe or other tool; HACK: *to hew down a tree*
**hex·a·gon** /'heksəgən‖-gɑn/ *n* a figure with six sides –**hexagonal** /hek'saegənəl/ *adj*
**hey** /heɪ/ *interj* (a shout used to call attention or to express surprise, interest, etc.): *Hey! Where are you going?*
**hey·day** /'heɪdeɪ/ *n* [S] the best period (of some desirable state): *In the heyday of their empire, the Romans controlled most of the western world.|In his heyday, he was a great footballer.*
**hi** /haɪ/ *interj infml* for HELLO
**hi·a·tus** /haɪ'eɪtəs/ *n* **-tus** *or* **-tuses** [*usu. sing.*] *fml* a space or GAP where something is missing
**hi·ber·nate** /'haɪbəneɪt‖-ər-/ *v* **-nated, -nating** [I] (of animals) to be or go into a sleep-like state during the winter –**hibernation** /-'neən/ *n* [U]
**hic·cup** , **hiccough** /'hɪkʌp, -kəp/ *n* (a sudden sharp sound caused by) a movement in the chest which stops the breath: *In the middle of the prayer there was a loud hiccup from my son.* –**hiccup, hiccough** *v* [I]
**hide**[1] /haɪd/ *v* **hid** /hɪd/, **hidden** /'hidn/, **hiding 1** [T] to put or keep out of sight; make or keep secret: *I hid the broken plate in the drawer.|Don't hide your feelings; say what you think.* **2** [I] to place oneself or be placed so as to be unseen: *I'll hide behind the door.*
**hide**[2] *n* an animals's skin, esp. when removed to be used for leather
**hide·bound** /'haɪdbaʊnd/ *adj* (of people) having fixed, unchangeable opinions; NARROW-MINDED
**hid·e·ous** /'hɪdɪəs/ *adj* having a terrible effect on the senses, esp. shocking to the eyes: *a hideous face/noise/wound* –see BEAUTIFUL (USAGE) –**hideously** *adv* –**hideousness** *n* [U]
**hid·ing**[1] /'haɪdɪŋ/ *n infml* a beating: *I'll* **give** you **a (good) hiding** *when we get home!*
**hiding**[2] *n* [U] **go into hiding/ be in hiding** to hide oneself/be hidden: *The escaped prisoner had been in hiding for two weeks when the police found him.*
**hi·er·ar·chy** /'haɪərɑːki‖-ɑr-/ *n* **-chies** [C;U] (an) organization of a system into higher and lower, esp. official ranks: *The government is a hierarchy.*|(fig.) *a hierarchy of moral values* –**hierarchical** /hɪə'raːkɪkəl‖-ar-/ *adj* –**hierarchically** *adv*
**hi·e·ro·glyph·ics** /ˌhaɪərə'glɪfɪks/ *n* [P] the system of writing which uses picture-like signs (=**hieroglyphs** /'haɪərəˌglɪfs/) to represent words, esp. as used in ancient Egypt
**hi-fi** /'haɪ faɪ, ˌhaɪ 'faɪ/ *n,adj* **hi-fis** [C;U] HIGH

FIDELITY (=very sensitive) apparatus for reproducing recorded sound: *When you listen to my hi-fi (set), it's like sitting in the concert hall!* –see picture on page 355

**hig·gle·dy-pig·gle·dy** /ˌhɪgəldi 'pɪgəldi/ *adj,adv infml* in disorder; mixed together without system

**high**[1] /haɪ/ *adj* **1** (not usu. of living things) having a top that is some distance, esp. a large distance above ground: *How high is it?|It's a very high building.* **2** [after *n*] measuring in height: *four metres high* **3** at a point well above the ground or above what is usual: *That shelf is too high for me; I can't reach it.*|(fig.) *the high* (=great) *cost of food|travelling at high* (=great) *speed|a high musical note|Their holiday is the* **high spot** (=something remembered with pleasure) *of the year.* **4** showing goodness; worthy of admiration: *high principles* **5** [A *no comp.*] of or concerning people of great wealth or rank: *high society/the high life* –opposite **low** (for 1,2,3,4) **6** [A *no comp.*] (of time) at the most important or mid-point of: *high summer|high noon|It's high time we went.* (=we must go now; it's getting late) **7** (of food) not fresh; spoilt by age **8** [F] *infml* **a** drunk **b** under the effects of drugs

USAGE People, and things that are narrow as well as high, are **tall** rather than **high.** Compare: *A* **high** *wall surrounds the prison.|a room with a* **high** *ceiling* and *a* **tall** *tree|a* **tall** *man.*

**high**[2] *adv* [*adv +prep/adv*] **1** to or at a high level in position, movements or sound: *They climbed high.|The plane flew high above.|The bird sang high and clearly.*|(fig.): *He's risen high in the world.* –opposite **low 2 high and dry** *infml* without help; deserted: *He took all the money and left me high and dry.* **3 high and low** everywhere: *I looked/searched high and low for it.*

**high**[3] *n* **1** [C] a high point; the highest level: *The price of food reached a new high this week.* –opposite **low 2** [C] *infml* a state of great excitement and happiness produced (as if) by a drug **3** [U] a high place, esp. heaven (only in the phrase **on high**)

**high·brow** /'haɪbraʊ/ *n,adj sometimes derog* (typical of) a person thought to show more than average knowledge of art and INTELLECTUAL interests –compare LOWBROW

**high-class** /ˌ·'·◂/ *adj* of good quality

**high com·mis·sion·er** /ˌ·:·'···/ *n* (*often caps.*) a person (like an AMBASSADOR) who represents one COMMONWEALTH country in another

**high court** /ˌ·'·◂/ *n* the most important court, which can change the decision of a lower court

**higher ed·u·ca·tion** /ˌ·· ··'··/ *n* [U] education at a university or college –compare FURTHER EDUCATION

**high fi·del·i·ty** /ˌ· ·'···◂/ also **hi-fi**– *adj* (of TAPE RECORDERS, RECORD PLAYERS, etc.) able to give out sound which represents very closely the details of the original sound before recording

**high-flown** /ˌ· '·◂/ *adj* (of language) grand-sounding, though lacking in meaning

**high-hand·ed** /ˌ· '··◂/ *adj derog* using one's power too forcefully: *a high-handed punishment* –**high-handedly** *adv* –**high-handedness** *n* [U]

**high jump** /'· ·/ *n* **1** a sport in which people jump over a bar which is raised higher and higher –see picture on page 592 **2 be for the high jump** *BrE infml* to be about to be punished: *He'll be for the high jump when they know he's used the firm's car.*

**high·land** /'haɪlənd/ *adj,n* (of) a mountainous area: *the Scottish Highlands* –compare LOWLAND

**high-lev·el** /ˌ· '··◂/ *adj* [A] (involving people) of high importance: *high-level peace talks*

**high·light**[1] /'haɪlaɪt/ *n* an important detail which stands out from the rest: *a film of the highlights of the competition*

**highlight**[2] *v* [T] to pick out (something) as an important part; throw attention onto

**high·ly** /'haɪli/ *adv* **1** (*esp. before adjectives made from verbs*) to a high degree; very: *highly skilled|highly enjoyable* **2** (very) well: *highly paid|He speaks very highly of you.*

**highly-strung** /ˌ·· '·◂/ also **high-strung**– *adj* nervous; excitable

**high-mind·ed** /ˌ· '··◂/ *adj* (of people) having high principles –**high-mindedness** *n* [U]

**High·ness** /'haɪnɨs/ *n* (a title used of or to certain royal persons): *His Highness Prince Leopold*

**high-pow·ered** /ˌ· '··◂/ *adj* showing great force (in an activity): *high-powered selling methods|a high-powered car*

**high-pres·sure** /ˌ·'··◂/ *adj* **1** (of a machine or substance) which uses or is at high pressure **2** (of an action, job, or person) carried out or working with great speed and force: *A high-pressure salesman may make you buy something you don't want.*

**high-rise** /'· ·/ *adj,n* [A;C] (a building, esp. a block of flats) with many floors (STOREYS): *She lives in a high-rise (flat).*

**high school** /'· ·/ *n* [C;U] *esp. AmE* (*caps. in names*) a SECONDARY (1) school esp. for children over age 14

**high-spir·it·ed** /ˌ·'···◂/ *adj* full of fun; adventure-loving

**high street** /'· ·/ *n BrE* (*often caps, esp. when used as or in a name*) the main street of a town

**high tea** /ˌ· '·/ *n* [U] *BrE* an early-evening meal taken instead of afternoon tea and late dinner

**high·way** /'haɪweɪ/ *n esp. AmE or law* a broad main road used esp. by traffic going from one town to another

**high·way·man** /'haɪweɪmən/ *n* **-men** /mən/ (in former times) a man who used to stop travellers on the roads and rob them of their money

**hi·jack** /'haɪdʒæk/ *v* [T] to take control of (a vehicle or aircraft) by force of arms, often for political aims –**hijacker** *n* –**hijacking, hijack** *n* [C;U]

**hike**[1] /haɪk/ *n* a long walk in the country

**hike**[2] *v* **hiked, hiking** [I] to go on a HIKE –**hiker** *n* –**hiking** *n* [U]

**hi·lar·i·ous** /hɪ'leərɪəs/ *adj* full of or causing laughter: *a hilarious film* –**hilariously** *adv*

**hi·lar·i·ty** /hɪ'lærɨti/ *n* [U] cheerfulness, expressed in laughter

**hill** /hɪl/ *n* **1** a raised part of the earth's surface, not so high as a mountain, and not usu. so bare, rocky, etc. **2** the slope of a road or path *adj* **-ier, -iest**

**hill·ock** /'hɪlək/ *n* a little hill

**hill·side** /'hɪlsaɪd/ *n* the slope of a hill, as opposed to the top **(hill top)**

**hilt** /hɪlt/ *n* the handle of a sword, or of a knife which is used as a weapon: (fig.) *She's in trouble* **up to the**

hilt. (=completely)

**him** /ɪm; *strong* hɪm/ *pron* (*object form of* HE): *Which is your brother? Is that him?|I heard him singing outside.* –see ME (USAGE)

**him·self** /ɪm'self; *strong* hɪm-/ *pron* **1** (used as the object of a verb, or after a PREPOSITION, when the same male person or animal does the action and is the object of the action): *He hurt himself.|Did he enjoy himself?|John's old enough to look after himself.*|(with general meaning) *Everyone should be able to defend himself.* **2** (used to make *he*, or the name of a male person or animal, stronger): *He himself told me.|He ate it himself.|I want the director himself, not his secretary.*

**hind** /haɪnd/ *adj* [A *no comp.*] (usu. of animals' legs) belonging to the back part –compare FORELEG

**hin·der** /'hɪndəʳ/ *v* [T] to prevent (someone from doing something or something from being done): *The noise hindered (me in) my work.*

**hind·quar·ters** /'haɪnd,kwɔːtəz‖-,kwɔrtərz/ *n* [P] the back part of an animal including the legs –compare HAUNCHES

**hin·drance** /'hɪndrəns/ *n* [*to*] something or somebody that HINDERS: *He said he'd help me do the job, but he was more of a hindrance than a help.*

**hind·sight** /'haɪndsaɪt/ *n* [U] the ability to see how and why something happened, esp. to know that it could have been prevented: *I now know with hindsight that I made a mistake* –compare FORESIGHT

**Hin·du** /'hɪnduː, hɪn'duː/ *adj,n* (of) a person whose religion is Hinduism

**Hin·du·is·m** /'hɪnduː-izəm/ *n* [U] the chief religion of India, notable esp. for its social ranks (CASTE system) and the belief that one returns after death in another form (REINCARNATION)

**hinge¹** /hɪndʒ/ *n* a metal part which joins two objects together and allows the first to swing freely, such as one joining a door to a frame, or a lid to a box: *Oil the hinges, the gate is* CREAK*ing.* (=making an unpleasant noise)

**hinge²** *v* **hinged, hinging** [T] to fix (something) on a HINGE

**hinge on/upon** sthg. *v prep* [T +*v-ing*] depend on: *Everything hinges on what we do next.*

**hint¹** /hɪnt/ *n* **1** a small or indirect suggestion: *I kept looking at my watch, but he just continued talking: he can't* **take** (=understand) **a hint. 2** a small sign: *There's a hint of summer in the air.* **3** useful advice: *helpful hints*

**hint²** *v* [I;T +*that*] to suggest indirectly: *I hinted (to him) that I was dissatisfied with his work.*

**hint at** sthg. *v prep* [T] to speak about in an indirect way: *The minister hinted at an early election.*

**hin·ter·land** /'hɪntəlænd‖-ər-/ *n* the inner part of a country, beyond the coast or the banks of an important river

**hip** /hɪp/ *n* the fleshy part of either side of the human body above the legs: *Women have rounder hips than men.* –see picture on page 299

**hip·pie, hippy** /'hɪpi/ *n* **-pies** *becoming rare* (esp. in the 1960s) a person who is (thought to be) against the standards of ordinary society, showing this esp. by having long hair, dressing in a colourful way, and (sometimes) taking drugs for pleasure

**hip·po·pot·a·mus** /,hɪpə'pɒtəməs‖-'pɑ-/ also **hippo** /'hɪpəʊ/ *infml*– *n* **-muses** *or* **-mi** /maɪ/ a large African animal with a thick body and thick hairless skin, which lives near water

**hire¹** /haɪəʳ/ *v* **hired, hiring** [T] **1** *BrE* to get the use of (something) on payment of a sum of money **2** to employ (someone) for a time for payment: *The fruit is picked by hired labourers.*

USAGE 1 In *BrE* you **hire** things for just a short time, and the owner **hires** *them* **out**: *Let's* **hire** *a car for the weekend.|I'll have to* **hire** *a suit for my wedding.* You **rent** things for a longer period: *Is that your own television, or do you* **rent** *it?* You **rent** a house or flat, and the owner **lets** *it* (**out**). But in *AmE* you **rent** all of these things, and the owner **rents** *them* **out.** 2 In *AmE* you **hire** people (=employ them), but in *BrE* people are only **hired** for a particular purpose, not for a long period; otherwise they are **appointed:** *We* **hired** *an advertising company to help us sell our new product.|We're going to* **appoint** *a new history teacher.* 3 In *BrE* and *AmE* things like buses, ships, and aircraft are not **hired** or **rented,** but **chartered.**

**hire** sbdy./sthg.↔ **out** *v adv* [T *to*] to give (one's services or the use of something) for payment: *Why don't you hire out your car to your neighbours while you're away, and earn some money?*

**hire²** *n* [U] (payment for) the act of hiring or state of being hired: *Boats for hire.|to work for hire*

**hire pur·chase** /,· '··/ *n* [U] a system of payment for goods by which one pays small sums of money regularly after receiving the goods (usually paying more than the original price) –compare CREDIT¹ (4)

**his** /ɪz; *strong* hɪz/ *determiner,pron* (POSSESSIVE *form of* HE) **1** of that male person or animal already mentioned: *John sat down in his chair.|I cleaned my shoes, and John cleaned his.* **2** of that person: *Everyone should do his best.*

**hiss** /hɪs/ *v* [I;T *at*] to make a sound like a continuous "s", esp. to show anger, disapproval, etc.: *The cat hissed as the dog came near it.|The crowd hissed (at) the speaker when he said taxes should be increased.* –**hiss** *n* : *The snake gave an angry hiss.*

**his·to·ri·an** /hɪ'stɔːrɪən‖-'sto-/ *n* a person who studies and/or writes about history

**his·tor·ic** /hɪ'stɒrɪk‖-'stɔ-, -'stɑ-/ *adj* important in history –see HISTORY (USAGE)

**his·tor·i·cal** /hɪ'stɒrɪkəl‖'stɔ-, -'stɑ-/ *adj* **1** which represents a fact/facts of history: *a historical play*/NOVEL|*We cannot be sure whether King Arthur was a historical figure.* (=whether he really existed) **2** connected with history as a study: *He gave all his historical papers to the library.* –see HISTORY (USAGE) –**historically** *adv*

**his·to·ry** /'hɪstəri/ *n* **-ries 1** [U] (the study of) events in the past, esp. events concerning the rulers and government of a country, social and trade conditions, etc.: *History is my favourite subject at school.|For the first time in our country's history, we have a woman prime minister.* **2** [C] a (written) account of history: *a short history of the last war* **3** [C] a set of events relating to a place or person: *Mr Jones has a long history of heart trouble.* **4 make history** to do something important which will be recorded and remembered

USAGE A **story** is an account of a number of connected events which may or may not have really happened. **History** is the real events of the past, and **historical** characters or events are those that have really existed or happened. A place is **historic** if it has a long **history** and an event is **historic** if it will be remembered in **history**. Compare: *a* **historic** *meeting between two great leaders|a meeting of the local* **historical** *society* (=a society concerned with history).

**his·tri·on·ic** /ˌhɪstriˈɒnɪk‖-ˈɑnɪk/ *adj* **1** concerning the theatre or acting **2** *derog* done or performed in a theatrical way; showing pretended feelings, not real ones **–histrionically** *adv*

**his·tri·on·ics** /ˌhɪstriˈɒnɪks,‖-ˈɑn-/ *n* [P] *derog* behaviour which is like a theatrical performance, with no real feelings behind it

**hit¹** /hɪt/ *v* **hit, hitting** [T] **1** to give a blow to; strike: *He hit the other man.|He hit the ball (with the* BAT*).* –see picture on page 669 **2** to (cause to) come against (something) with force: *She hit her head on the table.* **3** *infml* to reach: *We hit the main road two miles further on.|Price increases hit* (=have a bad effect on) *everyone's pocket.* (=money) **4 hit it off (with)** *infml* to have a good relationship (with): *I'm glad to see the two girls hitting it off so well.* **5 hit the roof** also **hit the ceiling** *AmE– infml* to show or express great anger

**hit on/upon** sthg. *v prep* [T] to find by lucky chance or have a good idea about: *Peter has hit upon an idea that will get us out of our difficulty.*

**hit out at** sbdy./sthg. also **hit out against** sbdy./sthg.– *v adv prep* [T] to disagree violently with and attack in words: *The newspapers are hitting out at the government's latest decision.*

**hit²** *n* **1** a blow; stroke: *He aimed a wild hit at his attacker.* **2** the act of successfully striking something aimed at: *I* SCORE*d a direct hit with my first shot.* –compare MISS² (1) **3** something, esp. a recorded song or other performance, that is very successful: *The song was a hit at once.*|(fig.) *You've* **made a hit with** *her–she likes you.*

**hit-and-run** /ˌ· · ˈ·◂/ *adj* [A] **1** (of a road accident) of a type in which the guilty driver does not stop to help **2** (of a driver) who behaves in this way

**hitch¹** /hɪtʃ/ *v* **1** [T] to fasten by hooking a rope or metal part over another object: *He hitched the horse's rope over the pole.|Another railway carriage has been hitched on.* **2** [I;T] *infml* to travel by getting (rides in other people's cars): *He hitched across Europe.|Let's hitch a ride.*

**hitch** sthg.↔ **up** *v adv* [T] **1** to pull upwards into place: *John hitched up his trousers.* **2** to fasten (to something) by HITCHing¹: *I hitched up the horses (to the cart).*

**hitch²** *n* **1** a short, sudden push or pull (up) **2** a difficulty which delays something for a while: *a slight hitch|A* **technical hitch** *prevented the lights from working.*

**hitch·hike** /ˈhɪtʃhaɪk/ *v* **-hiked, -hiking** [I] to go on a journey by getting rides in other people's cars **–hitchhiker** *n*

**hith·er** /ˈhɪðəʳ/ *adv* **1** *old use* to this place: *Come hither!* **2 hither and thither** in all directions

**hith·er·to** /ˌhɪðəˈtuː◂‖-ər-/ *adv fml* up until now

**hit-or-miss** /ˌ· · ˈ·/ *adj* which depends on chance; not planned carefully

**hive** /haɪv/ also **beehive**– *n* a place where bees live, like a small hut or box: (fig.) *What a* **hive of industry**! (=a crowded busy place)

**h'm** /m, hm/ *interj* (a sound made with the lips closed to express doubt, disagreement, or dissatisfaction)

**HMS** *abbrev. for:* His/Her MAJESTY's Ship (a title for a ship in the British Royal Navy): *HMS Belfast*

**HNC** *abbrev. for:* (in Britain) Higher National Certificate; an examination in one of many TECHNICAL subjects at the same level as GCE A-LEVEL –see also ONC

**hoard¹** /hɔːd‖hord/ *n* a (secret) store, esp. of something valuable to the owner

**hoard²** *v* [T] to store secretly in large amounts **–hoarder** *n*

**hoard·ing** /ˈhɔːdɪŋ‖ˈhor-/ *n BrE* **1** a fence round a piece of land, esp. when building is going on **2** **billboard** *AmE–* a high fence or board on which large advertisements are stuck

**hoar·frost** /ˈhɔːfrɒst‖ˈhorfrɔst/ *n* [U] white frozen drops of water, as seen on grass and plants after a cold night

**hoarse** /hɔːs‖hors/ *adj* (of a person or voice) HARSH-sounding, as during a cold –compare HUSKY **–hoarsely** *adv* **–hoarseness** *n* [U]

**hoar·y** /ˈhɔːri‖ˈhori/ *adj* **-ier, -iest** (of hair) grey or white with age

**hoax** /həʊks/ *n* a trick, esp. one which makes someone believe something which is not true, and take action upon that belief: *A telephone caller said there was a bomb in the hotel but it was just a hoax.* **–hoax** *v* [T]

**hob·ble** /ˈhɒbəl‖ˈhɑ-/ *v* **-bled, -bling** [I] to walk in an awkward way, with difficulty: *I hurt my foot, and had to hobble home.*

**hob·by** /ˈhɒbi‖ˈhɑ-/ *n* **-bies** an activity which one enjoys doing in one's free time –see RECREATION (USAGE)

**hob·by·horse** /ˈhɒbihɔːs‖ˈhɑbihɔrs/ *n* **1** a child's toy like a horse's head on a stick **2** a fixed idea to which a person keeps returning in conversation

**hob·nob** /ˈhɒbnɒb‖ˈhɑbnɑb/ *v* **-bb-** [I *with*] *sometimes derog* to have a (pleasant) social relationship, often with someone in a higher position: *I've been hobnobbing with the directors at the office party.*

**ho·bo** /ˈhəʊbəʊ/ *n* **-boes** *or* **-bos** *AmE infml* a wanderer who has no regular work; TRAMP² (1)

**hock** /hɒk‖hɑk/ *n* [C;U] (a) German white wine

**hock·ey** /ˈhɒki‖ˈhɑki/ *n* **1** *BrE*‖**field hockey** *AmE–* a game for two teams of 11 players, who use special sticks **(hockey sticks)** to hit a ball around a field in an attempt to get GOALs

**hod** /hɒd‖hɑd/ *n* a container with a long handle, used by builders' workmen for carrying bricks

**hoe¹** /həʊ/ *n* a long-handled garden tool used esp. for removing wild plants (WEEDs)

**hoe²** *v* **hoed, hoeing** [I;T] to use a HOE (on)

**hog¹** /hɒg‖hɑg, hɔg/ *n* **hogs** *or* **hog 1** *esp. AmE* a pig, esp. a fat one for eating –compare BOAR¹, SOW¹ **2** a dirty, selfish person who eats too much **3 go (the) whole hog** *infml* to do something thoroughly

**hog²** *v* **-gg-** [T] *infml* to take and keep (all of something) for oneself: *Drivers who* **hog the road** *leave no room for other cars.*

**hoist¹** /hɔɪst/ *v* [T *up*] to raise up by force, esp. when using ropes on board ship: *The sailors hoisted the flag.*

**hoist²** *n* **1** an upward push **2** an apparatus for lifting heavy goods

**hold¹** /həʊld/ *v* **held**/held/, **holding 1** [T] to keep or support with a part of the body, esp. with the hands: *The dog held the newspaper in its mouth.* –see picture on page 669 **2** [T] to put or keep (a part of the body) in the stated position: *She held the baby still.* **3** [T] to keep in position; support: *She held her hair back with a pin.*|*a roof held up by strong supports* **4** [T] to keep back or control: *The police held the angry crowd back.* **5** [T] to be able to contain: *How much water does the pan hold?*|(fig.) *Life holds many surprises.* **6** [T] to have or keep in one's possession: *He holds a half share in the business.*|*She holds the office of chairwoman.*|(fig.) *His speech held their attention/held them silent.* **7** [T] to make (something) happen: *We held a meeting on Tuesday.* **8** [T] to keep in the stated position or condition: (fig.) *We held ourselves in readiness for bad news.* **9** [T +*that*] to express one's belief (that); consider: *I hold (the view) that he's a fool.* **10** [I] to be or remain in a certain state; continue: *What he said still holds/***holds good**. (=is true)|*Can the good weather hold?*|*The bridge failed to hold and crashed into the river below.* **11 Hold it!** Stay like that; don't move! **12 hold one's breath** to stop breathing, e.g. through fear or expectation

**hold** sthg. **against** sbdy. *v prep* [T] to allow (something bad that someone has done) to have an effect on one's feelings about (this person): *We mustn't hold it against him that he has been in prison.*|*We shouldn't hold his past mistakes against him.*

**hold back** *v adv* **1** [T] (**hold** sbdy./sthg.↔ **back**) also **keep** sbdy./sthg.↔ **back**– to cause to stay in place; control: *We built banks of earth to hold back the flood waters.*|*Police held the crowds back.*|(fig.) *Jim was unable to hold back his anger any longer.* **2** [T] (**hold** sbdy.↔ **back**) to prevent the development of: *You could become a good musician, but your lack of practice is holding you back.* **3** [I;T] (=**hold** sthg.↔ **back**) to keep (something) secret: *We must have the whole story: don't hold (anything) back.*

**hold** sthg.↔ **down** *v adv* [T] **1** to keep (esp. a job): *Jim seems unable to hold down a job for more than a few weeks.* **2** to keep at a low level: *to hold prices down* –see also KEEP **down** (1)

**hold forth** *v adv* [I *on*] *often derog* to speak at length

**hold off** *v adv* [I;T (=**hold** sbdy./sthg.↔ **off**)] **1** also **keep** sbdy./sthg.↔ **off**– to (cause to) remain at a distance: *We must hold off the enemy's attack.*|*Will the rain hold off until after the game?* **2** also **put** sbdy./sthg.↔ **off**– to delay: *The leaders will hold off making a decision until Monday.*

**hold on** *v adv* [I] **1** to wait (often on the telephone); HANG **on** (2): *Could you hold on? I'll just see if he's in.* **2** to continue (in spite of difficulties); HANG **on** (3); HOLD **out** (2)

**hold onto** sthg. *v prep* [T] →HANG **onto**

**hold out** *v adv* **1** [T] (**hold out** sthg.) to offer: *I don't hold out much hope that the weather will improve.*|*She held out her hand in friendship.* **2** [I] also **hang on, hold on**– to last (in spite of difficulties); ENDURE: *The town was surrounded but the people held out until help came.*|*My old car is still holding out.*

**hold out for** sthg. *v adv prep* [T] to demand firmly and wait in order to get: *The men are still holding out for more pay.*

**hold** sthg. **over** *v adv* [T] to move to a later date: *The concert was held over until the following week because of the singer's illness.*

**hold** (sbdy.) **to** sthg. *v prep* [T] *fml* to (cause to) follow exactly or keep to: *Whatever your argument, I shall hold to my decision.*

**hold/keep** sthg.↔ **together**– *v adv* [T] to cause to remain united: *A nail holds the two pieces of wood together.*

**hold** sbdy./sthg.↔ **up** *v adv* [T] **1** to delay: *The building of the new road has been held up by bad weather.* **2** to stop in order to rob: *The criminals held up the train and took all the money.* **3** to show as an example: *Grandfather always held up his youngest son as a model of hard work.* –see also HOLDUP

**hold with** sthg. *v prep* [T] to approve of; agree with: *I don't hold with these modern ideas.*

**hold²** *n* **1** [C;U] the act of holding; GRIP² (1): **Take/get/catch hold of** *the rope, and we'll pull you up.*|**Keep hold of**/*Don't* **lose hold of** *my hand.*|(fig.) *He's* **got a good hold of** *his subject.*|*I must* **get hold of** (=find ) *some more writing paper.* **2** [C] something which can be held, esp. in climbing: *Can you find a hold for your hands so that you can pull yourself up?* –compare FOOTHOLD **3 have a hold over** to know something which gives one an influence over

**hold³** *n* the part of a ship (below DECK) where goods are stored

**hold·all** /ˈhəʊld-ɔːl/–*n* a large bag or small case for carrying clothes and articles necessary for travelling

**hold·er** /ˈhəʊldəʳ/ *n* **1** a person who has control of or possesses a place, a position, or money: *The holder of the office of chairman is responsible for arranging meetings.* –compare HOLD¹ (6) **2 -holder: a** a person who holds property; TENANT: a LEASE-*holder*/*householder* **b** something which holds or contains: *a cigarette holder*

**hold·ing** /ˈhəʊldɪŋ/ *n* something which one possesses, esp. land or SHARES¹ (2) –see also SMALLHOLDING

**hold·up** /ˈhəʊld-ʌp/ *n* **1** a delay, as of traffic **2** also **stickup** *infml*– an attempt at robbery by threatening people with a gun –see also HOLD **up** (2)

**hole¹** /həʊl/ *n* **1** an empty space within something solid: *The men have dug a hole in the road.* **2** the home of a small animal: *a rabbit hole* **3** (in GOLF) a hollow place into which the ball must be hit **4** *infml* a small unpleasant place: *His flat's a bit of a hole.* **5 pick holes in something** to say what is wrong with something, esp.when it is not really faulty

**hole²** *v* **holed, holing** [I;T] to put (a ball) in a hole in GOLF: *to hole in one* (=one stroke)

**hol·i·day¹** /ˈhɒlɨdi||ˈhɑlɨdeɪ/ *n* **1** a time of rest from work, a day (often originally of religious importance) or longer **2 on holiday/on one's holidays** having a holiday,esp. over a period of time

USAGE **Holiday** is the general *BrE* word for an official period of rest from work, which one may spend at home or visiting another place, and the general *AmE* word is **vacation**: *In this job you get four weeks'* **holiday** (*BrE*)/**vacation** (*AmE*) *a year.*|*We're going to Greece for our* **holiday(s)/vacation.** In *BrE*, **vacation** is used for the period when universities are closed: *I worked on a farm during the college* **vacation**. The period when Parliament does not meet is the **recess**. Soldiers and people employed by the government go on **leave**, and this word is also used in expressions like **sick leave** and **leave of absence.**

**holiday²** also **vacation** *AmE*– *v* [I] to have a period of holiday: *holidaying in Majorca*

**hol·i·day·mak·er** /'hɒl¹₃di,meɪkəʳ‖'hɑl¹₃deɪ-/ *n* a person on holiday –**holidaymaking** *n* [U]

**hol·i·ness** /'həʊlin¹₃s/ *n* **1** [U] the state or quality of being holy **2** (*usu. cap.*) (a title of the POPE): *Your Holiness*|*His Holiness Pope John Paul*

**hol·ler** /'hɒləʳ‖'hɑ-/ *v* [I;T *to, at*] *infml esp. AmE* to shout out: *"Let go," she hollered.* –**holler** *n*

**hol·low¹** /'hɒləʊ‖'hɑ-/ *adj* **1** having an empty space inside: *The pillars look solid, but in fact they're hollow.*|(fig.) the *hollow* (=insincere) *promises of politicians* **2** having a ringing sound like the note when an empty container is struck: *the hollow sound of a large bell* –**hollowly** *adv* –**hollowness** *n* [U]

**hollow²** *n* a space sunk into something, esp. into the ground

**hollow** sthg.↔ **out** *v adv* [T] **1** to make a hollow place in: *to hollow out a log* **2** [*of*] to make by doing this: *to hollow a* CANOE *out of a log*

**hol·ly** /'hɒli‖'hɑli/ *n* [U] a small tree with dark green shiny prickly leaves and red berries

**hol·o·caust** /'hɒləkɔːst‖'hɑ-/ *n* the loss of many lives, esp. by burning

**hol·ster** /'həʊlstəʳ/ *n* a leather holder for a PISTOL (=small hand gun),esp. one that hangs on a belt around the waist

**ho·ly** /'həʊli/ *adj* **-lier, -liest 1** connected with God and religion: *the Holy Bible*|*the holy city of Mecca/Benares* **2** (of a person or life) in the service of God and religion; pure and blameless

**hom·age** /'hɒmɪdʒ‖'hɑ-/ *n* [U] signs of great respect: *They* **paid homage to** *the king.*

**home¹** /həʊm/ *n* **1** the place where one usually lives esp. with one's family: *Nigeria is my home, but I'm living in London just now.*|*He's not* **at home** (=in the house) *now; he should be back at seven.* –see USAGE **2** a place where a thing lives, exists, etc.: *India is the home of elephants and tigers.*|*America is the home of* BASEBALL. **3** a place for the care of a group of people or animals of the same type,who do not live with a family: *a children's home* **4 be/feel at home** to be comfortable; not feel worried, esp. because one has the right skills or experience: *He's completely at home working with children.* **5 make oneself at home** to behave freely, sit where one likes, etc., as if at home –**homeless** *adj* –**homelessness** *n* [U]

USAGE We use the simple tenses of *live* (not **stay*) when talking about **home**.

**home²** *adv* **1** to or at one's home: *Is she home yet?*|*I must be getting home.* **2** to the right place: *He struck the nail home.* **3 bring home to/come home to someone** to (cause to) be fully understood by someone: *At last it's come home to me how much I owe to my parents.*

**home³** *adj* [A] **1** of, related to, or being a home, place of origin, or base of operations: *the home office of an international firm*|*Birmingham is my* **home town. 2** not foreign; DOMESTIC¹ (3): *home affairs*|*the* HOME OFFICE|*The islanders are demanding* **home rule.** (=self-government) **3** prepared, made, or done in a home: *home cooking*|**homemade** *clothes/jam*|*These* **homegrown** *apples* (=grown at home) *taste better than the ones from abroad.* **4** (of a sports match) played at the place, sports field, etc., of one's home area; *the home team*|*home games* –opposite **away²** (for **4**)

**home·com·ing** /'həʊm,kʌmɪŋ/ *n* an arrival home, esp. after long absence

**home help** /,· '·/ *n BrE* a person who is sent in by the medical and social services to do housework for someone who is ill or very old

**home in on** sthg. *v adv prep* [T] to aim exactly towards

**home·land** /'həʊmlænd, -lənd/ *n* one's native country

**home·ly** /'həʊmli/ *adj* **-lier, -liest 1** simple, not grand: *a homely meal of bread and cheese* **2** *AmE* (of a person) not good-looking –**homeliness** *n* [U]

**Home Of·fice** /'· ,··/ *n* [*the* U +*sing./pl. v*] the British government department which deals with home affairs –compare FOREIGN OFFICE

**home·sick** /'həʊm,sɪk/ *adj* feeling a great wish to be at home, when away from it –**homesickness** *n* [U]

**home·stead** /'həʊmsted, -st¹₃d/ *n* a house and land; a farm with its buildings

**home truth** /,· '·/ *n* a fact about someone which is unpleasant for him/her to know, but true

**home·ward** /'həʊmwəd‖-ərd/ *adj* going towards home: *the homeward journey* –opposite **outward** (1) –**homewards**‖also **homeward** *AmE–adv*

**home·work** /'həʊmwɜːk‖-ɜrk/ *n* [U] schoolwork, such as essays, which is done outside the classroom, esp. at home, in a library, etc –see also HOUSEWORK

**hom·i·cid·al** /,hɒm¹₃'saɪdl◂‖,hɑ-/ *adj* likely to murder

**hom·i·cide** /'hɒm¹₃saɪd‖'hɑ-/ *n fml or law* **1** [C;U] (an act of) murder **2** [C] a murderer

**hom·i·ly** /'hɒm¹₃li‖'hɑ-/ *n* **-lies** *fml* **1** →SERMON **2** *usu. derog* a long talk giving one advice on how to behave

**hom·ing** /'həʊmɪŋ/ *adj* [A] having the ability **a** (esp. of PIGEONS) to find one's way home **b** (esp.of modern weapons of war) to guide themselves onto the place they are aimed at: *a* MISSILE (1) *with a homing device*

**ho·moe·op·athy, homeo-** /,həʊmi'ɒpəθi‖-'ɑp-/ *n* [U] the practice of treating a disease by giving small amounts of a drug which, in larger amounts, would produce an illness like the disease –**homeopath** /'həʊmɪəpæθ/ *n* –**homoeopathic** /,həʊmɪə'pæθɪk/ *adj* –**homoeopathically** *adv*

**ho·mo·ge·ne·ous** /,həʊmə'dʒiːnɪəs/ *adj* formed of parts of the same kind –compare HETEROGENEOUS –**homogeneity** /,həʊmədʒ¹₃'niː¹₃ti *n* / [U] –**homogeneously** /,həʊmə'dʒiːnɪəsli/ *adv*

**ho·mo·ge·nize** ‖also **-nise** *BrE* /hə'mɒdʒənaɪz‖

-'mɑ-/ *v*-**nized, -nizing** [T] to make (the parts of a whole) become evenly spread: *homogenized milk* (=with no cream, because the fat is broken up all through the liquid)

**ho·mo·sex·u·al** /ˌheʊmə'sekʃʊəl/ *adj,n* (of or being) a person sexually attracted to people of the same sex –compare BISEXUAL, HETEROSEXUAL, LESBIAN

**hone** /həʊn/ *v* **honed, honing** [T] to sharpen (knives, swords, etc.)

**hon·est** /'ɒnɪ̣st||'ɑn-/ *adj* **1** (of people) trustworthy; not likely to lie or to cheat **2** (of actions, appearance, etc.) showing such qualities: *an honest face/opinion* –opposite **dishonest**

**hon·est·ly** /'ɒnɪ̣stli||'ɑn-/ *adv* **1** in an honest way –opposite **dishonestly 2 a** really; speaking truthfully: *I didn't tell anyone, honestly I didn't.* **b** (used for expressing strong feeling usu. mixed with disapproval): *Honestly! What a stupid thing to do!*

**hon·es·ty** /'ɒnɪ̣sti||'ɑn-/ *n* [U] the quality of being honest –opposite **dishonesty**

**hon·ey** /'hʌni/ *n* **1** [U] the sweet sticky soft material produced by bees, which is eaten on bread **2** [C] *esp. AmE* for DARLING[1]

**hon·ey·comb** /'hʌnikəʊm/ *n* a container made by bees of beeswax and consisting of six-sided cells in which honey is stored

**hon·ey·moon** /'hʌnimu:n/ *n* the holiday taken by a man and woman who have just got married –**honeymoon** *v* [I] –**honeymooner** *n*

**hon·ey·suck·le** /'hʌniˌsʌkəl/ *n* [C;U] a climbing plant with sweet-smelling yellow flowers

**honk** /hɒŋk||hɑŋk, hɔŋk/ *v,n* [I;T] (to make) the sound (like that) of a GOOSE or a car horn: *honking geese* (GOOSE)| *She honked the horn of the car.*

**hon·or·ar·y** /'ɒnərəri||'ɑnəreri/ *adj* **1** (of a rank, a university degree, etc.) given as an HONOUR, not according to the usual rules **2** (of an office or position held) without payment for one's services: *He's the honorary chairman.* –compare HONOURABLE

**hon·our**[1] *BrE*||**honor** *AmE* /'ɒnər||'ɑnər/ *n* **1** [U] great respect, often publicly expressed: *a party* **in honour of** (=to show respect to) *the visiting president* –opposite **dishonour 2** [U] high standards of character that cause one to be respected by others: *a man of honour|to fight for/to save the honour of one's country* **3** [S] something that brings pride or pleasure: *It's a great honour to have the Queen visiting our town.* **4** [C] (a title of respect for a judge): *Your/His Honour* –compare LORD[1] **5 on one's honour** in a position which would bring shame on oneself if one did not do what one has promised to: *He was (put) on his honour not to tell the secret.*

**honour**[2] *BrE*||**honor** *AmE v* [T] **1** to show respect to: *Today the Queen is honouring us with her presence.* **2** to keep (an agreement), often by making a payment: *The bank will not always honour your debts.*

**hon·our·a·ble** *BrE*||**honorable** *AmE* /'ɒnərəbəl||'ɑn-/ *adj* showing or deserving honour –opposite **dishonourable**; compare HONORARY –**honourably** *adv*

**Honourable** *BrE*||**Honorable** *AmE abbrev.* **Hon.**– *adj* [A] (a title given to the children of certain British noblemen, to judges, and various official people, including Members of Parliament): *Will the Honourable member please answer the question?*

**hon·ours** *BrE*||**honors** *AmE* /'ɒnəz||'ɑnərz/ *n* [P] **1** a specialized university UNDERGRADUATE degree, or a level gained in it: *an honours degree* **2** marks of respect, such as titles given in Britain to important people on the Queen's birthday and at New Year in the **honours list 3 (full) military honours** ceremonies at which soldiers attend, esp. to bury a great person **4 do the honours** *infml* to act as the host or hostess, as by offering drink

**hood** /hʊd/ *n* **1** a covering for the whole of the head and neck (except the face), often fastened to a coat **2** a folding cover over a car, PRAM (=baby carriage), etc. **3** *AmE* for BONNET (2)

**hood·wink** /'hʊdˌwɪŋk/ *v* [T] to trick or deceive

**hoof** /hu:f||hʊf/ *n* **hoofs** *or* **hooves** /hu:vz||hʊfs/ the hard foot of certain animals, as of the horse

**hook**[1] /hʊk/ *n* **1 a** a curved piece of metal, plastic, etc., for catching something on or hanging things on: *a fish hook|Hang your coat on the hook.* **b** a small one used with an EYE[1] (4) to fasten clothing **2** (*usu. in comb.*) a tool for cutting grass, branches, etc. **3** (in BOXING) a blow given with the elbow bent **4 be/get off the hook** to be/get out of a difficult situation

**hook**[2] *v* [T] **1** to catch (as if) with a HOOK[1] (1): *to hook a fish* **2** to hang on or fasten (as if) with a HOOK[1] (1): *Hook my dress up.|Hook the rope over that nail.*

**hooked** /hʊkt/ *adj* **1** shaped like a hook: *a hooked nose* **2** [F *on*] *infml* **a** dependent (on drugs) **b** having a great liking for and very frequently using, doing, eating, etc. –compare ADDICTED (to)

**hoo·li·gan** /'hu:lɪ̣gən/ *n* a noisy, rough person who causes trouble by fighting, breaking things, etc. –**hooliganism** *n* [U]

**hoop** /hu:p||hʊp, hu:p/ *n* a circular band of wood or metal, esp. round a barrel or used as a child's toy

**hoo·ray** /hʊ'reɪ/ *interj,n* →HURRAY

**hoot**[1] /hu:t/ *v* [I;T *at, with*] to (cause to) make a HOOT: *I hooted (my horn) at the children playing in the road.*

**hoot**[2] *n* **1** the sound made by an OWL or by a car or ship's horn **2** a shout of dislike, unpleasant laughter, etc.: *His speech was greeted with loud hoots.* **3 not care/give a hoot/two hoots** *infml* not to care at all: *He doesn't care two hoots what people think.*

**hoot·er** /'hu:tər/ *n* a SIREN (1) or whistle, esp. of the type which signals the beginning or end of work

**hoo·ver** /'hu:vər/ *n tdmk BrE* (*often cap.*) (a type of) VACUUM CLEANER –**hoover** *v* [I;T] : *Jim hoovered the carpet.*

**hooves** /hu:vz||hʊfs/ *n pl. of* HOOF

**hop**[1] /hɒp||hɑp/ *v* **-pp-** [I] **1 a** (of people) to jump on one leg –see picture on page 669 **b** (of small creatures) to jump: *The bird hopped onto my finger.* **2** [*on, in*] *infml* to get quickly onto or into: *She hopped on her bicycle/in(to) her car and rushed off.* **3 Hop it!** *BrE infml* Go away! **4 hopping mad** very angry

**hop**[2] *n* **1** an act of HOPping; jump **2** *infml* a distance travelled by a plane before landing: *It's a short hop from London to Paris.* **3 catch someone on the hop** *infml* to meet someone when he/she is unprepared

**hop**[3] *n* a tall climbing plant with flowers whose

seed-cases (**hops**) are dried and used in making beer

**hope¹** /həʊp/ *v* **hoped, hoping** [I;T +*to-v*/(*that*)/*for*] to wish and expect; desire in spite of doubts: *We're hoping to visit England this year.*|*We are hoping for some rain.*

USAGE Compare **hope** and **wish**: You can **wish** for impossible things, but you can **hope** only when the thing you want is possible: *I* **wish** *I were 20 years younger.*|*I* **hope** *you'll be better soon.* –see also WAIT¹ (USAGE)

**hope²** *n* [C;U +(*that*)/*of*] **1** the expectation of something happening as one wishes: *There's not much hope that he'll come/of him coming.* **2** a person or thing that seems likely to bring success: *Please help me–you're my only hope/last hope.* **3 hold out hope** to give reason to expect: *He can hold out no hope of succeeding.* **4 raise someone's hopes** to make someone hope for success, esp. when it is unlikely

**hope·ful** /ˈhəʊpfəl/ *adj* [+*that*] feeling or giving cause for hope: *I'm hopeful that they'll agree.*|*hopeful signs that they will agree* –**hopefulness** *n* [U]

**hope·ful·ly** /ˈhəʊpfəli/ *adv* **1** in a hopeful way **2** if our hopes succeed: *Hopefully we'll be there soon.*

USAGE This second meaning of **hopefully** is now very common, esp. in speech, but it is thought by some teachers to be incorrect.

**hope·less** /ˈhəʊpləs/ *adj* **1** showing or giving no hope: *hopeless tears*|*The doctor said John's condition was hopeless.* (=incurable) **2** *infml* useless: *Your work is hopeless.* –**hopelessly** *adv* –**hopelessness** *n* [U]

**hop·scotch** /ˈhɒpskɒtʃ‖ˈhɑpskɑtʃ/ *n* [U] a children's game in which a stone is thrown onto numbered squares and each child HOPS from one to another

**horde** /hɔːd‖hord/ *n* a large number or crowd: *A horde/Hordes of children ran over the building.* –sounds like **hoard**

**ho·ri·zon** /həˈraɪzən/ *n* the limit of one's view across the surface of the earth, where the sky seems to meet the earth or sea

**hor·i·zon·tal** /ˌhɒrəˈzɒntl‖ˌhɑrəˈzɑntl/ *adj* in a flat position, along or parallel to the ground: *Stand the table on its legs, so that the top is horizontal.* –compare VERTICAL –**horizontally** *adv*

**hor·mone** /ˈhɔːməʊn‖ˈhɔr-/ *n* any of several substances directed from organs of the body into the bloodstream so as to influence growth, development, etc.

**horn** /hɔːn‖hɔrn/ *n* **1** [C] a hard pointed growth found in a pair on the top of the heads of cattle, sheep, and goats **2** [U] the material that these growths are made of: *The knife has a horn handle.* **3** [C] an apparatus, as in a car, which gives a warning sound: *The driver blew/sounded his horn when the child stepped in front of his/her car.* –see picture on page 85 **4** [C] any of a number of musical instruments consisting of a long metal tube, usu. bent several times and played by blowing: *the French horn*|*a hunting horn*

**hor·net** /ˈhɔːnət‖ˈhɔr-/ *n* a large insect which can sting, related to the WASP

**horn·pipe** /ˈhɔːnpaɪp‖ˈhɔrn-/ *n* (the music for) a dance, esp. performed by sailors

**horn·y** /ˈhɔːni‖ˈhɔrni/ *adj* **-ier, -iest** hard and rough: *The old gardener had horny hands.*

**hor·o·scope** /ˈhɒrəskəʊp‖ˈhɑ-, ˈhɔ-/ *n* a set of ideas about someone's character, life, and future, which are gained by knowing the positions of the stars or PLANETS at the time of his birth

**hor·ren·dous** /həˈrendəs‖hɑ-, hɔ-/ *adj* really terrible; causing great fear –**horrendously** *adv*

**hor·ri·ble** /ˈhɒrəbəl‖ˈhɔ-, ˈhɑ-/ *adj* **1** causing HORROR: *a horrible accident* **2** *infml* very unkind, unpleasant, or ugly: *What a horrible dress!* –**horribly** *adv*

**hor·rid** /ˈhɒrəd‖ˈhɔ-, ˈhɑ-/ *adj* [*to*] very unpleasant or unkind; HORRIBLE (2): *Don't be so horrid (to Aunt Jane)!* –**horridly** *adv* –**horridness** *n* [U]

**hor·rif·ic** /həˈrɪfɪk‖hɔ-, hɑ-/ *adj* able to or meant to HORRIFY, shock, etc. –**horrifically** *adv*

**hor·ri·fy** /ˈhɒrəfaɪ‖ˈhɔ-, ˈhɑ-/ *v* **-fied, -fying** [T] to shock; fill with HORROR: *I was horrified at/by the news.*|*a horrifying story* –**horrifyingly** *adv*

**hor·ror** /ˈhɒrəʳ‖ˈhɔ-, ˈhɑ-/ *n* **1** [U] a feeling of great shock, fear, and dislike: *We were filled with horror at the bad news.*|*I cried out* **in horror** *as I saw the cars crash.* **2** [C] an unpleasant person: *The little horror never stops playing tricks on his parents.* **3 horror film** a film in which strange and fearful things happen, such as dead people coming to life, people turning into animals, etc.

**hors d'oeu·vre** /ˌɔː ˈdɜːv‖ˌɔr ˈdɜrv/ *n* **-d'oeuvres** /dɜːv‖dɜrvz/ *or* **-d'oeuvre** *French* any of several types of food served in small amounts at the beginning of a meal

**horse** /hɔːs‖hɔrs/ *n* **1** a large four-legged animal with hard feet (hooves(HOOF)), which people ride on and use for pulling heavy things **2** →VAULTING HORSE **3 dark horse** a person whose abilities are hidden or unknown **4 (straight) from the horse's mouth** *infml* told to one directly, from the person concerned: *"Who told you she was leaving?" "I heard it straight from the horse's mouth."* (=she herself told me) **5 put the cart before the horse** to do or put things in the wrong order

**horse·back** /ˈhɔːsbæk‖ˈhɔrs-/ *n* **1** [A] *esp. AmE* of or on the back of a horse **2 on horseback** (riding) on a horse

**horse·box** /ˈhɔːsbɒks‖ˈhɔrsbɑks/ *n* a vehicle pulled by another vehicle and used for carrying horses

**horse chest·nut** /ˌ· ˈ··‖ˈ· ˌ··/ *n* (a nut from) a large tree with white or pink flowers –compare CHESTNUT¹ (1,2)

**horse·man** /ˈhɔːsmən‖ˈhɔrs-/ **horsewoman** /-ˈwʊmən/ *fem.*– *n* **-men** /mən/ a person who rides a horse, esp. one who rides well

**horse·play** /ˈhɔːspleɪ‖ˈhɔrs-/ *n* [U] rough noisy behaviour

**horse·pow·er** /ˈhɔːsˌpaʊəʳ‖ˈhɔrs-/ *abbrev.* **HP**– *n* **horsepower** a measure of the power of an engine

**horse·rac·ing** /ˈhɔːsˌreɪsɪŋ‖ˈhɔrs-/ *n* [U] the sport of racing horses ridden by JOCKEYS, for money

**horse·rad·ish** /ˈhɔːsˌrædɪʃ‖ˈhɔrs-/ *n* a plant whose root is used to make a strong-tasting SAUCE (**horseradish sauce**) to be eaten with meat

**horse·shoe** /ˈhɔːʃ-ʃuː, ˈhɔːs-‖ˈhɔr-/ *n* **1** a curved piece of iron nailed on under a horse's foot **2** something made in this shape, believed to bring good luck

**hors·y** /ˈhɔːsi‖ˈhɔrsi/ *adj* **-ier, -iest 1** *often derog* (too) interested in horses, fond of riding, etc. **2** looking like a horse –**horsiness** *n* [U]

**hor·ti·cul·ture** /'hɔːtɪ̈ˌkʌltʃəʳ||'hɔr-/ *n* [U] the science of growing fruit, flowers, and vegetables –**horticultural** /ˌhɔːtɪ̈'kʌltʃərəl||ˌhɔr- / *adj* –**horticulturalist** *n*

**hose**[1] /həuz/ also **hosepipe** /'həuzpaɪp/– *n* [C;U] (a piece of) rubber or plastic tube used to direct water onto fires, a garden, etc.

**hose**[2] *v* **hosed, hosing** [T *down*] to use a HOSE on: *hosing the car down|to hose the garden*

**hose**[3] *n* [P] (used esp. in shops) stockings or socks

**hosiery** /'həuzɪəri, / *n* [U] socks, stockings, underclothes, etc.

**hos·pi·ta·ble** /'hɒspɪtəbəl, hɒ'spɪ- ||hɑ'spɪ-/ *adj* (of people or their acts) showing attention to the needs of others, esp. by asking them into one's home, feeding them, etc. –opposite **inhospitable** –**hospitably** *adv* –**hospitality** /hɒspɪ̈'tælɪ̈ti||'hɑ-/ *n* [U] *Mrs Brown is known for her hospitality.*

**hos·pi·tal** /'hɒspɪtl||'hɑ-/ *n* [C;U] a place where ill people stay and have treatment: *After her accident, Jane was taken to hospital/to a hospital.*

**hos·pi·tal·ize, -ise** /'hɒspɪtəl-aɪz||'hɑ-/ *v* **-ized, -izing** [T] to put (a person) into hospital: *He broke a leg and was hospitalized for a month.* –**hospitalization** /ˌhɒspɪtəl-aɪ'zeɪʃən||ˌhɑspɪtəl-ə'zeɪ- / *n* [C;U]

**host**[1] /həust/ *n* **1** a man who receives guests: *He acted as host to the visitors.*|(fig.) *the* **host country** *for the Olympic Games* **2** a person who introduces other performers, such as those on a TV show; COMPERE

**host**[2] *v* [T] to act as host at (a party, friendly meeting, etc.)

**host**[3] *n* [C +*sing./pl. v*] a large number: *A whole host of difficulties has/have arisen.*

**hos·tage** /'hɒstɪdʒ||'hɑ-/ *n* a person kept by an enemy so that the other side will do what the enemy wants: *The man with the gun* **took/held** *the child* **hostage.**

**hos·tel** /'hɒstl||'hɑ-/ *n* a building in which certain types of person can live and eat, as for students, young people working away from home, etc.: *A* **youth hostel** *is a place where esp. young people stay when they are on a walking holiday.*

**hos·tel·ry** /'hɒstəlri||'hɑ-/ *n old use or humor* a hotel

**host·ess** /'həustɪ̈s/ *n* **1** a female host **2** →AIRHOSTESS

**hos·tile** /'hɒstaɪl||'hɑstl, 'hɑstaɪl/ *adj* **1** [*to*] unfriendly; showing dislike **2** belonging to an enemy

**hos·til·i·ties** /hɒ'stɪlɪ̈tiz||hɑ-/ *n* [P] acts of fighting in war: *Hostilities have broken out between the two countries.*

**hos·til·i·ty** /hɒ'stɪlɪ̈ti||hɑ-/ *n* [U] the state of being unfriendly

**hot** /hɒt||hɑt/ *adj* **-tt- 1** having a certain degree of heat, esp. a high degree: *How hot is the water?|The water isn't hot yet.|Now the water is so hot I burnt my finger in it.*|(fig.) *hot* (=very recent) *news|hot feelings|A* **hot-blooded** *person is one who easily shows strong feelings.*|(*infml*) *She's very* **hot on** (=well-informed on and interested in) *pop music.* **2** causing a burning taste in the mouth: *Pepper makes food hot.* **3 hot air** meaningless talk or ideas **4 hot and bothered** worried by a feeling that things are going wrong **5 hot on someone's trail/track** chasing and ready to catch someone **6 hot on the heels (of)** following or happening just after **7 hot under the collar** angry or excited and ready to argue **8 not so hot** *infml* not very good; not as good as expected **9 the hot seat** *infml* a position of difficulty from which one must make important decisions

**hot·bed** /'hɒtbed||'hɑt-/ *n* a place or condition where something undesirable can exist and develop: *The city is a hotbed of crime.*

**hot-blood·ed** /ˌ· '·· ◂/ *adj* showing strong feelings; PASSIONATE –see also COLD-BLOODED

**hotch·potch** /'hɒtʃpɒtʃ||'hɑtʃpɑtʃ/ ||also **hodgepodge** /ˌhɑdʒpɑdʒ/ *AmE*– *n* [*usu. sing.*] a number of things mixed up without any sensible order of arrangement

**hot dog** /ˌ· '·||'· ·/ *n* a special sort of long red SAUSAGE in a bread ROLL[1] (2)

**ho·tel** /həu'tel/ *n* a building where people can stay in return for payment

**ho·tel·i·er** /həu'telieɪ, -lɪəʳ/ *n* a person who keeps a hotel

**hotfoot** /ˌhɒt'fut||'hɑtfut/ *v* **hotfoot it** *infml* to move fast: *We hotfooted it down the street.* –**hotfoot** *adv*

**hot·head** /'hɒthed||'hɑt-/ *n* a person who does things in haste, without thinking –**hot"headed** /ˌhɒt'hedɪ̈d◂ / *adj* –**hotheadedly** /ˌhɒt'hedɪ̈dli / *adv*

**hot·house** /'hɒthaus||'hɑt-/ *n* **-houses** /ˌhauzɪ̈z/ a warm building where flowers and delicate plants can grow; GREENHOUSE

**hot·ly** /'hɒtli||'hɑtli/ *adv* **1** in anger and with force **2** closely and eagerly: *He was* **hotly pursued** *by his dog.*

**hot·plate** /'hɒtpleɪt||'hɑt-/ *n* a metal surface, usu. on a cooking STOVE, which is heated and on which food can be cooked in a pan –see COOK (USAGE)

**hot up** *v adv* **-tt-** [I] to increase in activity which is often exciting or dangerous: *Industrial troubles are hotting up in the North.*

**hot-water bot·tle** /ˌ· '·· ˌ··/ *n* a rubber container filled with hot water which is used to warm a bed

**hound**[1] /haund/ *n* a hunting dog, esp. a foxhound

**hound**[2] *v* [T] to chase or worry continually: *The police are always hounding me.*

**hour** /auəʳ/ *n* **1** [C] any of the 24 equal periods of time into which a whole day is divided: *There are 60 minutes in an hour.|It's only an hour away.* (=it takes only an hour to travel there) **2** a time of day when a new such period starts: *He arrived* **on the hour.** (=exactly at one o'clock, two o'clock, etc.) **3** [C] a fixed point or period of time: *No one helped me* **in my hour of need.** (=when I needed help)|**Visiting hours** (=the time when one is allowed to visit) *at the hospital are 3.00 to 5.00.* **4** [C] a certain period of time: *The hours I spent with you were the happiest of my life.|I've been waiting here* **for hours.** (=for a long time) **5 after hours** /ˌ·· '·/later than the usual times of work or business **6 at all hours** (at any time) during the whole day and night **7 (at) the eleventh hour** (at) the last moment; very late **8 the small hours** the hours soon after midnight

**hour·ly** /'auəli||'auərli/ *adj,adv* (happening, appearing, etc.) every hour or once an hour

**house**[1] /haus/ *n* **houses** /'hauzɪ̈z/ **1 a** a building for people to live or work in **b** the people in such a building **2** a building for the stated purpose: *a hen house|a storehouse|the* **Houses of Parliament** (=both Britain's law-making bodies, or the buildings in which they work|*the* **House of Commons** (=the lower but more powerful law-making body, whose members are elected by the people)|*the* **House of Lords** (=the higher law-making body whose members are not elected) **3** (*cap. in names*) an important family, esp. noble or royal: *The House of Windsor is the British royal family.* **4** [*usu. sing.*] the people voting after a DEBATE: **This house** *does not support the changes made by the government.* **5** [*usu. sing.*] a theatre, or the people in it: *a full house|His jokes* **brought the house down.** (=brought loud laughter, admiration, etc., from everyone in the theatre) **6 get on like a house on fire** to become or be very good friends very easily **7 on the house** (usu. of drinks) paid for by the owner of a public house, etc.

USAGE A **house** is a building for people to live in, and is usually built on more than one level (STOREY). A **cottage** is a small, old house, esp. in the country, and a **bungalow** is a house built on only one level. A set of rooms (including a kitchen and bathroom) within a larger building is a **flat** (**apartment** *AmE*), and a small one-room flat is called a **bedsitter.** A large grand house is called a **mansion,** or (if it belongs to a king or queen) a **palace**. The place where you live is your **home,** whatever type of house it is: *After the party, we went home to our* **flat.**

**house²** /haʊz/ *v* **housed, housing** [T] to provide with a place to live

**house·boat** /'haʊsbəʊt/ *n* a boat fitted with everything necessary for living there

**house·bound** /'haʊsbaʊnd/ *adj* not able to move out of the house, esp. because of illness

**house·break·er** /'haʊs,breɪkəʳ/ *n* a thief who enters a house by force

**house·hold** /'haʊshəʊld/ *n* [C +*sing./pl. v*] all the people living together in a house: *The whole household was/were up early.*

**house·hold·er** /'haʊs,həʊldəʳ/ *n* a person who owns or is in charge of a house

**household name** /,·· '·/ also **household word**– *n* a thing or person known and spoken of by almost everybody

**house·keep·er** /'haʊs,ki:pəʳ/ *n* a person who has charge of the running of a house

**house·keep·ing** /'haʊs,ki:pɪŋ/ *n* [U] **1** work done in looking after a house and the people who live in it **2** also **housekeeping money** /'··· ,··/ – an amount of money set aside to pay for food and other things needed in the home

**house·man** /'haʊsmən/ *BrE*||**intern** *AmE*– *n* **-men** /mən/ a JUNIOR (2) doctor completing hospital training

**house·mas·ter** /'haʊs,mɑ:stəʳ||-,mæ-/ **housemistress** /-,mɪstr$\frac{1}{2}$s/ *fem.– n esp. BrE* a teacher who is in charge of a building in which children live at school

**house-proud** /'· ·/ *adj* liking to have everything in perfect order in the house and spending a lot of time on keeping it clean and tidy, perhaps too much so

**house-trained** /'· ·/ *BrE*||**housebroken**/ 'haʊs ,brəʊkən/ *AmE*– *adj* (of house pets) trained to go out of the house to empty the bowels or BLADDER

**house·warm·ing** /'haʊs,wɔ:mɪŋ||-,wɔr-/ *n* a party given for friends when one has moved into a new house

**house·wife** /'haʊs-waɪf/ *n* **-wives** /waɪvz/ a woman who works at home for her family,cleaning, cooking, etc., esp. one who does not work outside the home

**house·work** /'haʊswɜ:k||-ɜrk/ *n* [U] work done to keep the inside of a house clean and tidy –see also HOMEWORK

**hous·ing** /'haʊzɪŋ/ *n* **1** (the action of providing) places to live: *Too many people are living in bad housing.* **2** [C] protective covering, as for machinery: *the engine housing*

**housing es·tate** /'·· ·,·/ *n BrE* a group of houses and/or flats built in one place by one owner,as by a Town Council, and let or sold

**hove** /həʊv/ *v tech or humor past tense (and sometimes past participle) of* HEAVE²

**hov·el** /'hɒvəl||'hʌ-, 'hɑ-/ *n* a small dirty place to live in

**hov·er** /'hɒvəʳ||'hʌ-, 'hɑ-/ *v* [I *over, around*] **1** (of birds, certain aircraft, etc.) to stay in the air in one place **2** (of people) to wait around one place: *The children kept hovering around and interrupting me.*|(fig.) *He's hovering between life and death.*

**hov·er·craft** /'hɒvəkrɑ:ft||'hʌvərkræft, 'hɑ-/ *n* **-craft** or **-crafts** a boat which moves over land or water with a strong force of air underneath lifting it above the ground, sea, etc.: *We crossed the lake on a hovercraft/***by hovercraft.** –compare HYDROFOIL

**how¹** /haʊ/ *adv* **1** (*used in questions*) **a** in what way: *How do you spell it?* **b** in what state of health: *How is your mother?* **c** (in questions about amount or number): *How old are you?* **2** (used in expressions of feeling): *How they cried!|How difficult it is!* (compare *What a difficult book it is!*) **3 How come?** *infml* Why is it?: *How come I wasn't told?* **4 How do you do?** *polite, esp. BrE* (used when one is first introduced to someone): *"This is my wife." "How do you do?"*

**how²** *conj* the way in which; the fact that: *I remember how they laughed.*

**how·ev·er¹** /haʊ'evəʳ/ *conj* in whatever way: *However I cook eggs, she still refuses to eat them.*

**however²** *adv* **1** to whatever degree: *She always goes swimming, however cold it is.* **2** in spite of this: *It's raining hard. However, I think we should go out.|He may, however, come later.* –see Study Notes on page 128 **3** also **how ever**– (showing surprise) in what way: *However did you get here?*

**howl¹** /haʊl/ *v* [I;T] to make HOWLS²: *The wind howled in the trees.|We howled with laughter.*|(fig.) *The baby's howling.* (=weeping loudly)

**howl** sbdy.↔ **down** *v adv* [T] to make a loud disapproving noise so as to prevent (someone) from being heard

**howl²** *n* a long loud cry, esp.that made by wolves (WOLF) and dogs

**hp** *BrE abbrev. for:* HIRE PURCHASE: *We got it on hp.*

**HQ** *abbrev. for:* HEADQUARTERS: *See you back at HQ.*

**hr, hrs** *written abbrev. said as:* hour, hours

**HRH** *abbrev. for:* His/Her Royal Highness: *HRH the Prince of Wales*

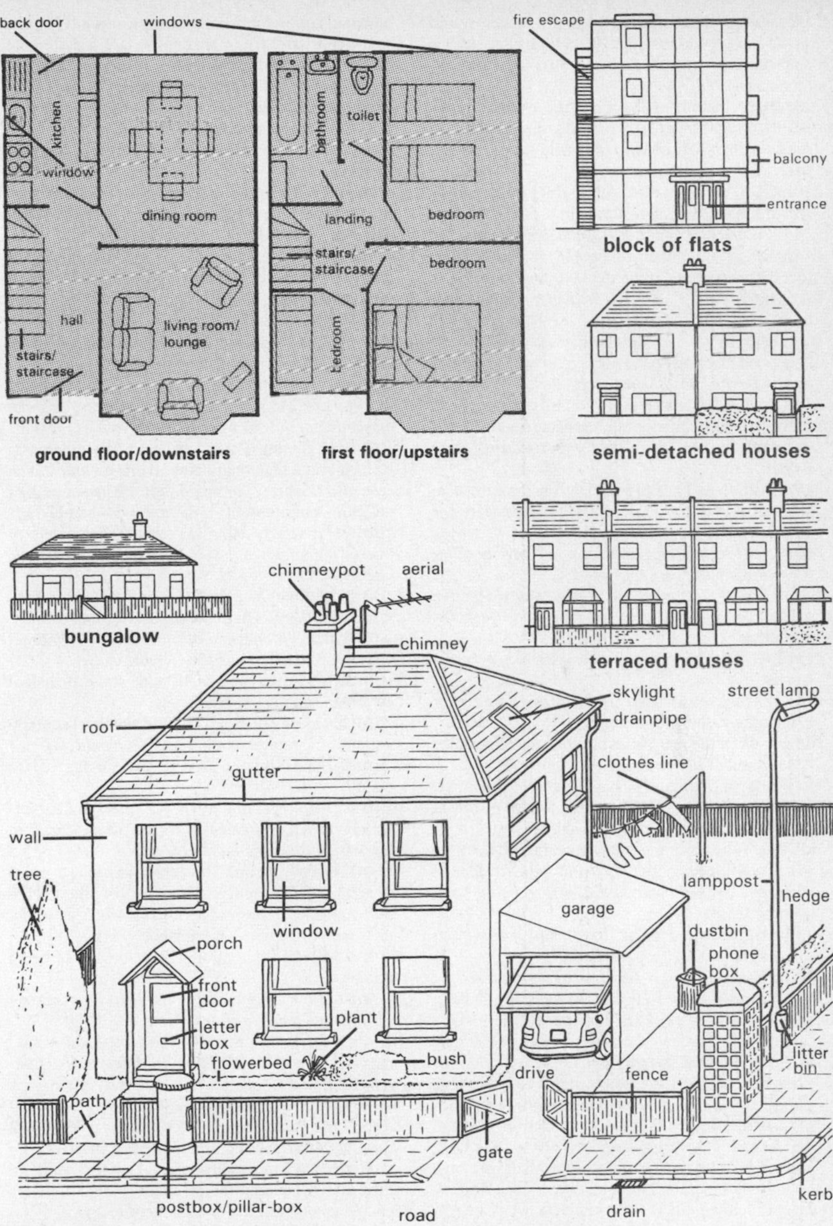


When you go into a house, you are on the **ground floor** (*BrE*)/**first floor** (*AmE*). The floor above that is the **first floor** (*BrE*)/**second floor** (*AmE*). Below the **ground floor** there is sometimes a **cellar** (a room or rooms below ground, for storing things) or a **basement** (a lower floor where people live or where things are stored).

A **door** is the entrance to a building; a **gate** is the entrance to a garden, field, road, etc.
A **hedge** is a row of bushes; a **fence** is made of wood or of metal wire; and a **wall** is usually made of brick or stone.

**hub** /hʌb/ *n* **1** the central part of a wheel, round which it turns and to which the outside edge (RIM) is connected by SPOKES[1] **2** the centre of activity or importance

**hub·bub** /ˈhʌbʌb/ *n* [S] a mixture of loud noises

**hub·cap** /ˈhʌbkæp/ *n* a metal covering over the centre of the wheel of a motor vehicle –see picture on page 85

**hud·dle[1]** /ˈhʌdl/ *v* **-dled, -dling** [I;T] to (cause to) crowd together, in a group or in a pile: *The boys huddled together under the rock to keep warm.*

**huddle[2]** *n* a number of people or things close together and not in any ordered arrangement

**hue** /hjuː/ *n fml* a colour: *The diamond shone with every hue under the sun.*

**hue and cry** /ˌ· · ˈ·/ *n* the expression of worry, anger, etc., by noisy behaviour: *They raised a (great) hue and cry against the new rule.*

**huff** /hʌf/ *n* **(in/into) a huff** (in/into) a state of bad temper when offended: *She's* **gone into a huff**/*She's* **in a huff** *because my brother didn't remember her name.*

**hug[1]** /hʌg/ *v* **-gg-** [T] **1** to hold tightly in the arms, esp. as a sign of love **2** to go along while staying near: *The boat hugged the coast.*

**hug[2]** *n* the act of hugging (HUG): *She gave her little boy a hug before he went to bed.*

**huge** /hjuːdʒ/ *adj* very big: *a huge house|The film was a huge success.* –see Study Notes on page 494 –**hugeness** *n* [U]

**huge·ly** /ˈhjuːdʒli/ *adv infml* very much: *hugely successful*

**huh** /hʌ/ *interj* (used for asking a question or for expressing surprise or disapproval)

**hulk** /hʌlk/ *n* the body of an old ship, no longer used at sea and left in disrepair

**hulk·ing** /ˈhʌlkɪŋ/ *adj* [A] big, heavy, and awkward: *We can't move that hulking great table on our own.*

**hull[1]** /hʌl/ *n* the main body of a ship

**hull[2]** *v* [T] to take the outer covering off (certain grains and seeds, esp. PEAS and beans): *Rice is gathered, cleaned, and hulled before being sold.* –compare SHELL[2] (1)

**hul·la·ba·loo** /ˈhʌləbəluː, ˌhʌləbəˈluː/ *n* **-loos** [*usu. sing.*] a lot of noise, esp. of voices

**hul·lo** /hʌˈləʊ/ *interj,n* **-los** *esp. BrE* for HELLO

**hum** /hʌm/ *v* **-mm- 1** [I] (esp. of bees ) to make a continuous BUZZ (1) **2** [I;T] (of people) to make a sound like a continuous **m**, esp. as a way of singing music with closed lips: *to hum a song* **3** [I *with*] (of work being carried out) to be active; to move fast: *Things are starting to hum (with activity).* –**hum** *n* [S]

**hu·man[1]** /ˈhjuːmən/ *adj* **1** of or concerning people: *the human voice|a newspaper story with lots of* **human interest** (=concerning someone's personal life and problems, not affairs of state, etc.) **2** showing the feelings, esp. those of kindness, which people are supposed to have: *He seems quite human when you know him.* –opposite **inhuman** (for **2**) –compare HUMANE

**human[2]** also **human being**– /ˌ·· ˈ··/ *n* a man, woman, or child, not an animal

**hu·mane** /hjuːˈmeɪn/ *adj* showing human kindness and the qualities of a civilized person –opposite **inhumane**; compare HUMAN –**humaneness** *n* [U]

**hu·man·is·m** /ˈhjuːmənɪzəm/ *n* [U] a system of beliefs concerned with the needs of man, and not with religious principles –**humanist** *n*

**hu·man·i·tar·i·an** /hjuːˌmænɪ̇ˈteərɪən/ *n,adj* (a person) concerned with trying to improve people's lives, by giving them better conditions to live in, fighting injustice, etc.

**hu·man·i·ties** /hjuːˈmænɪ̇tiz/ *n* [*the* P] studies such as literature, languages, history, etc.; the ARTS –compare the SCIENCES

**hu·man·i·ty** /hjuːˈmænɪ̇ti/ *n* [U] **1** the quality of being HUMANE or human: *a politician of great humanity* **2** human beings generally: *This new drug will help all humanity.*

**hu·man·ize** ||also **-ise** *BrE* /ˈhjuːmənaɪz/ *v* **-ized, -izing** [T] to make human or HUMANE

**hu·man·ly** /ˈhjuːmənli/ *adv* (only used in questions, NEGATIVES[2], etc.) within human powers: *It's not humanly possible to work so quickly.*

**hum·ble[1]** /ˈhʌmbəl/ *adj* **1** having a low opinion of oneself and a high opinion of others: *a humble man* –see also HUMILITY; compare PROUD **2** low in rank or position; unimportant: *a humble job* –**humbly** *adv*

**humble[2]** *v* **-bled, -bling** [T] to make (someone or oneself) humble or lower in position: *to humble one's enemy*

**hum·bug** /ˈhʌmbʌg/ *n* **1** [U] *becoming rare* nonsense **2** [C] *BrE* a hard sweet, usu. tasting of MINT[1]

**hum·drum** /ˈhʌmdrʌm/ *adj* too ordinary; without variety or change: *to lead a humdrum life*

**hu·mer·us** /ˈhjuːmərəs/ *n* the bone in the top half of the arm –sounds like **humorous**

**hu·mid** /ˈhjuːmɪ̇d/ *adj* (of air and weather) containing a lot of water VAPOUR; DAMP[2]: *a humid day*

**hu·mid·i·fy** /hjuːˈmɪdɪ̇faɪ/ *v* **-fied, -fying** [T] to make HUMID

**hu·mid·i·ty** /hjuːˈmɪdɪ̇ti/ *n* [U] the (amount of) water VAPOUR contained in the air: *It's difficult to work because of the humidity.*

**hu·mil·i·ate** /hjuːˈmɪlieɪt/ *v* **-ated, -ating** [T] to cause to feel humble or to lose the respect of others: *I felt humiliated when the teacher told the whole class that my family was poor.* –**humiliation** /-ˈeɪʃən/ *n* [C;U]

**hu·mil·i·ty** /hjuːˈmɪlɪ̇ti/ *n* [U] the quality of being humble

**hu·mor·ist** /ˈhjuːmərɪ̇st||ˈhjuː-, ˈjuː-/ *n* a person who makes jokes, esp. in writing

**hu·mor·ous** /ˈhjuːmərəs||ˈhjuː-, ˈjuː-/ *adj* funny; making people laugh: *a humorous film/remark/character in a play* –**humorously** *adv*

**hu·mour[1]** *BrE*||**humor** *AmE* /ˈhjuːməʳ||ˈhjuː-, ˈjuː-/ *n* [U] **1** the ability to be amused: *a sense of humour* **2** the quality of causing amusement: *a play with no humour in it* **3 -humoured** *BrE*||**-humored** *AmE* of the stated condition of mind: *She's always good-humoured.|He's ill-humoured today.*

**humour[2]** *BrE*||**humor** *AmE v* [T] to keep (someone) happy or calm by acceptance of (esp.) foolish wishes, behaviour, etc.: *Just humour him and he'll be quiet.*

**hump[1]** /hʌmp/ *n* a lump or round part which stands out noticeably, esp, on the back, e.g. on a camel

**hump[2]** *v* [T] *BrE infml* to carry, esp. on the back: *I humped the case upstairs.*

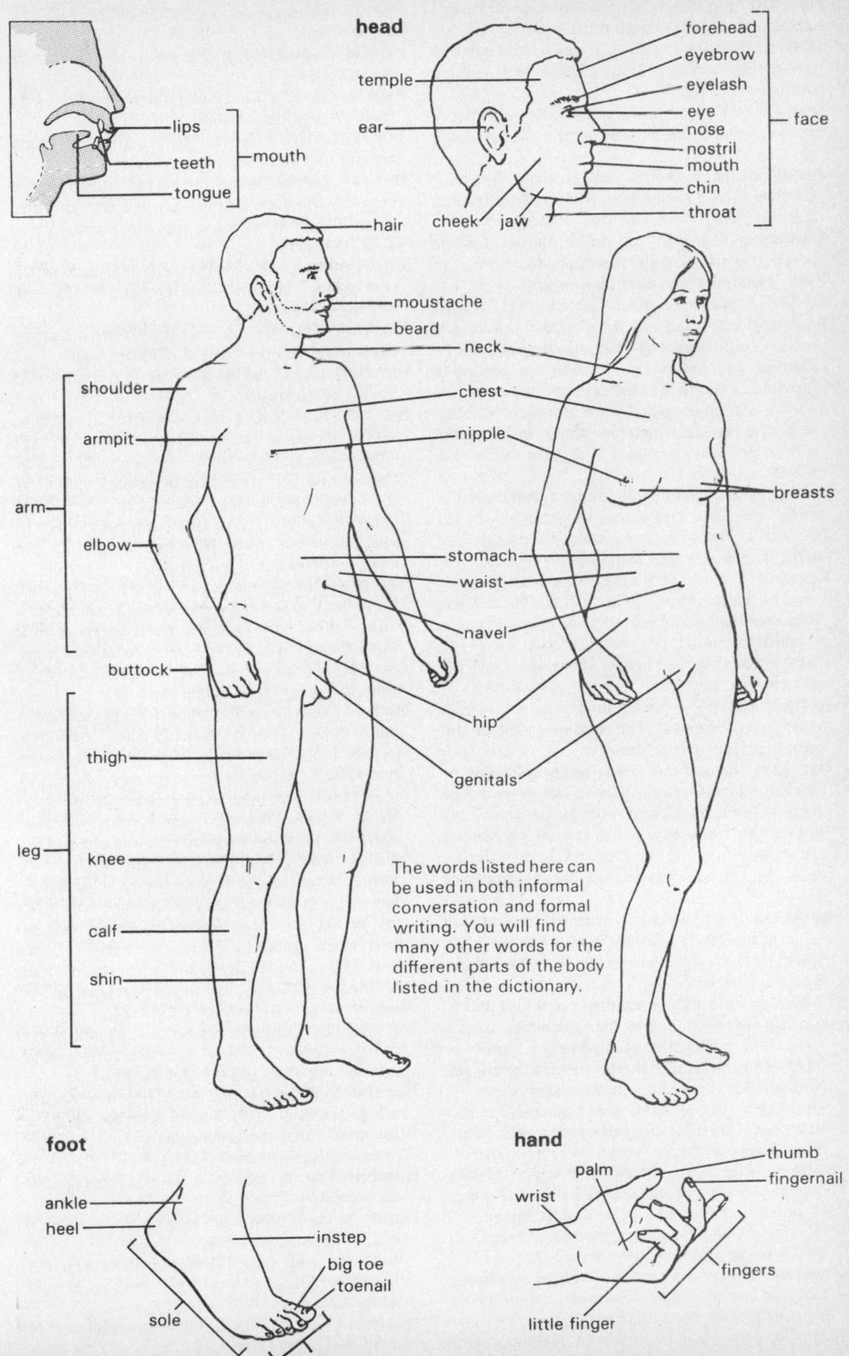


The words listed here can be used in both informal conversation and formal writing. You will find many other words for the different parts of the body listed in the dictionary.

**hu·mus** /'hjuːməs/ *n* [U] rich soil made of decayed plants, leaves, etc. –compare MULCH

**hunch¹** /hʌntʃ/ *n* [+(*that*)] an idea based on feeling rather than on reason: *I have a hunch (that) he didn't really want to go.*

**hunch²** *v* [T *up*] to pull ((part of) the body) into a rounded shape: *She sat with her shoulders hunched up.*

**hunch·back** /'hʌntʃbæk/ *n* (a person with) a back misshaped by a round lump (HUMP) **–hunchbacked** *adj*

**hun·dred** /'hʌndrəd/ *determiner,n,pron* **-dred** *or* **-dreds** (the number) 100 –see Study Notes on page 494 **–hundredth** *determiner,n,pron,adv*

USAGE 1 We say numbers like this: *326 = three* **hundred and** *twenty six. 92,804,326 = ninety two* **million,** *eight* **hundred and** *four* **thousand,** *three* **hundred and** *twenty six.* We only say **and** after **hundred. 2** Words like **hundred** and **thousand** can also be used in the plural when there is no number before them: **Hundreds** *of people attended the concert.*|**Millions** *of pounds were spent on the new school.*

**hun·dred·weight** /'hʌndrədweɪt/ (*written abbrev.* **cwt**)– **-weight** (a measure of weight equal to) (in Britain) 112 pounds, (in America) 100 pounds

**hung** /hʌŋ/ *v past tense and participle of* HANG¹

**hun·ger** /'hʌŋgəʳ/ *n* [U] **1** the wish or need for food: (fig.) *his hunger for excitement* **2** lack of food: *There is hunger in all the places where the crop was spoilt.* –compare FAMINE

**hunger for** sthg. also **hunger after** sthg.– *v prep* [T] to want very much

**hunger strike** /'·· ·/ *n* a refusal to eat as a sign of strong dissatisfaction: *The prisoners* **went on (a) hunger strike. –hunger striker** *n*

**hun·gry** /'hʌŋgri/ *adj* **-grier, -griest 1** feeling or showing hunger **2** causing hunger: *hungry work* **3 go hungry** to remain without food: *If you won't cook your own dinner, then you'll have to go hungry.* **–hungrily** *adv*

**hunk** /hʌŋk/ *n* a thick piece, esp. of food, broken or cut off

**hunt¹** /hʌnt/ *v* **1** to chase in order to catch and kill (animals and birds) either for food or for sport) **2** to search (for): *He went through the whole house hunting for his books.*

*USAGE In Britain, to go* **hunting** normally means to use dogs (HOUNDS) to chase the animal (usu. a fox), while riding a horse; the sport of killing animals or birds with a gun is called **shooting**. But in the US, the word **hunting** is used for both these sports.

**hunt** sbdy./sthg.↔ **down** also **hunt** sbdy./sthg.↔ **out**– *v adv* [T] to succeed in finding after much effort: *to hunt down a criminal*

**hunt²** *n* **1** [C] an act of hunting; *It was an exciting hunt, but the fox escaped.*|*an elephant hunt*|*Our hunt* (=search) *for a house is at last at an end.* **2** [C+*sing./pl. v*] *BrE* a group of people who regularly hunt foxes together: *to ride with the hunt*

**hunt·er** /'hʌntəʳ/ *n* a person or animal that hunts, usu. wild animals (fig.) *a fortune hunter* (=someone eagerly searching for a lot of money)

**hur·dle¹** /'hɜːdl‖-ɜr-/ *n* **1** a frame for jumping over in a race –see picture on page 592 **2** a difficulty which is to be conquered

**hurdle²** *v* **-dled, -dling** [I] to run a HURDLE¹ (1) race **–hurdler** *n*

**hurl** /hɜːl‖hɜrl/ *v* [T] to throw with force; *He hurled a brick through the window.*

**hur·ly-bur·ly** /'hɜːli ˌbɜːli‖ˌhɜrli 'bɜrli/ *n* [S;U] noisy activity: the hurly-burly of city life

**hur·ray, hooray** /hʊ'reɪ/ also **hurrah** /hʊ'rɑː/ *becoming rare– interj,n* a shout of joy or approval: *Three cheers for the losing team:* **Hip, hip, hurray!**|*We've done it! Hurray!*

**hur·ri·cane** /'hʌrəkən‖'hɜrəkeɪn/ *n* a storm with a very strong fast wind; CYCLONE or TYPHOON –see WEATHER (USAGE)

**hurricane lamp** /'··· ·/ *n* a lamp which has a strong cover to protect the flame inside from wind

**hur·ried** /'hʌrid‖'hɜrid/ *adj* done in haste: *hurried work* – **hurriedly** *adv*

**hur·ry¹** /'hʌri‖'hɜri/ *v* **-ried, -rying 1** [I;T] to (cause to) be quick in action, sometimes too quick: *Don't hurry; we're not late.*|*He hurried across the road in front of a car.* **2** [T] to send or bring quickly: *Doctors and nurses were hurried to the accident.*

**hurry up** *v adv* [I;T (=**hurry** sbdy./sthg.↔ up) to (cause to) move faster: *We'll have to hurry up (the work) in order to finish on Friday.*

**hurry²** *n* [U] **1** haste; quick activity **2** need for haste: *Don't drive so fast–there's no hurry.* **3 in a hurry: a** hastily: *You make mistakes if you do things in a hurry.* **b** eager: *I'm not in a/any hurry to change my job.* **c** *infml* (usu. *with a* NEGATIVE ²) quickly; easily: *I won't forget her kindness in a hurry.*

**hurt** /hɜːt‖hɜrt/ *v* **hurt, hurting 1** [T] to cause pain and/or damage (INJURY) to (esp. a part of the body): *He hurt his leg when he fell.*|(fig.) *My feelings were hurt when he didn't ask me to the party.* **2** [I;T] to cause (a person or other living creature) to feel pain: *My leg hurts.*|*Is that tight shoe hurting (you/your foot)?*|(fig.) *It* **won't hurt you** (=it won't be bad for you) *to miss breakfast for once.* – **hurt** *n* [U]

USAGE When **hurt** is used in the sense of bodily damage, you may be *slightly/badly/seriously* **hurt** but do not use these adverbs when speaking of unhappiness caused by someone's behaviour. Compare: *She was badly/slightly* **hurt** *when she fell from the ladder,* and *She was very/rather* **hurt** *by his unkind words.* –see WOUND² (USAGE)

**hurt·ful** /'hɜːtfəl‖'hɜrt-/ *adj* harmful; painful to the feelings: *There's no need to make such hurtful remarks.* **–hurtfully** *adj* **–hurtfulness** *n* [U]

**hur·tle** /'hɜːtl‖'hɜr-/ *v* **-tled, -tling** [I] to move or rush with great speed: *Rocks hurtled down the cliffs.*

**hus·band** /'hʌzbənd/ *n* the man to whom a woman is married –see picture on page 217

**hus·band·ry** /'hʌzbəndri/ *n* [U] *fml* farming: *animal husbandry*

**hush¹** /hʌʃ/ *v* [I;T *often in commands*] to (cause to) be silent and/or calm –compare SHUSH

**hush** sthg.↔ **up** *v adv* [T] to keep from being public knowledge: *The President tried to hush up the fact that his adviser had lied.*

**hush²** *n* [S;U] (a) silence, esp. a peaceful one: *A hush fell over the room.*

**hush-hush** /ˌ·'· ◂‖'··/ *adj infml* (of plans, arrangements, etc.) hidden, or to be hidden, from other people's knowledge; secret

**husk** /hʌsk/ *n* the dry outer covering of some friuts and seeds: *Brown bread contains the husk of wheat.*

**hus·ky**[1] /'hʌski/ *adj* **-kier, -kiest** (of a person or voice) difficult to hear and breathy, as if the throat were dry –compare HOARSE –**huskily** *adv* –**huskiness** *n* [U]

**husky**[2] *n* **-kies** a working dog with thick hair, used by ESKIMO*s* to pull SLEDGES over the snow

**hus·sy** /'hʌsi, 'hʌzi/ *n* **-sies** *old use or humor* a girl or woman who behaves in a sexually improper manner (note the phrases **brazen/shameless hussy**)

**hus·tings** /'hʌstɪŋz/ *n* [*the* P] the speeches, attempts to win votes, etc., which go on before an election

**hus·tle**[1] /'hʌsəl/ *v* **-tled, -tling** [I;T] **1** to (cause to) move fast: *I hustled the children off to school.* **2** [*into*] *esp. AmE* to persuade someone by forceful, esp. deceitful activity: *He hustled me into buying the car.*

**hustle**[2] *n* [U] hurried activity (esp. in the phrase **hustle and bustle**)

**hus·tler** /'hʌsləʳ/ *n esp. AmE* a person who HUSTLES[1] (2)

**hut** /hʌt/ *n* a small building, often made of wood, esp. one used for living in or for shelter –compare SHED[2]

**hutch** /hʌtʃ/ *n* a small box or cage with one side made of wire netting, esp. one for keeping rabbits in

**hy·a·cinth** /'haɪəsənθ/ *n* a plant with bell-shaped flowers, which grows from a BULB in spring

**hy·ae·na** /haɪ'iːnə/ *n* →HYENA

**hy·brid** /'haɪbrɪd/ *n* something, esp. an animal or plant, that is produced from parents of different breeds; CROSS[1] (7): *The hybrid from a donkey and a horse is called a* MULE.

**hy·drant** /'haɪdrənt/ *n* a water pipe in the street from which one may draw water from the public supply, esp. for putting out a fire.

**hy·draul·ic** /haɪ'drɒlɪk, -'drɔː-‖-'drɑ-, - 'drɔ-/ *adj* concerning or moved by the pressure of water or other liquids: *a hydraulic pump* –**hydraulically** *adv*

**hy·draul·ics** /haɪ'drɒlɪks, -'drɔː-‖-'drɑ-, -'drɔ/ *n* [U] the science which studies the use of water to produce power

**hy·dro·e·lec·tric** /ˌhaɪdrəʊ-ɪ'lektrɪk/ *adj* concerning or producing electricity by the power of falling water: *a hydroelectric power station* -**hydroelectrically** *adv*

**hy·dro·foil** /'haɪdrəfɔɪl/ *n* a large motorboat with legs which raise it out of the water as it moves: *to travel* **by hydrofoil** –compare HOVERCRAFT

**hy·dro·gen** /'haɪdrədʒən/ *n* [U] a gas that is a simple substance (ELEMENT (1)), without colour or smell, that is lighter than air and that burns very easily

**hydrogen bomb** /'··· ·/ also **H-bomb, fusion bomb**– *n* a very powerful type of ATOM BOMB

**hy·dro·pho·bi·a** /ˌhaɪdrə'fəʊbɪə/ *n* [U] → RABIES

**hy·dro·plane** /'haɪdrəpleɪn/ *n* a flat-bottomed motor-boat which can move very fast over the surface of water

**hy·e·na ,** **hyaena** *n* a wild dog-like animal of Africa and Asia, which eats meat and has a cry like a laugh

**hy·giene** /'haɪdʒiːn/ *n* [U] **1** the study and practice of how to keep good health, esp. by paying attention to cleanliness **2** cleanliness generally

**hy·gien·ic** /haɪ'dʒiːnɪk‖-'dʒe-, -'dʒiː-/ *adj* **1** causing or keeping good health **2** clean –opposite **unhygienic** –**hygienically** *adv*

**hymn** /hɪm/ *n* a song of praise, esp. to God, usu. one of the religious songs of the Christian church which all the people sing together during a service

**hy·per·bo·le** /haɪ'pɜːbəli‖-ɜr-/ *n* [C;U] (the use of) a form of words which makes something sound bigger, smaller, etc. than it really is; exaggeration (EXAGGERATE)

**hy·per·mar·ket** /'hɑɪpəˌmaːkɪt‖-pərˌmar-/ *n* a very large shop (large SUPERMARKET) where one may buy many types of food and other things for the home

**hy·phen** /'haɪfən/ *n* a short written or printed line (-) which can join words or SYLLABLE*s* –compare DASH[2] (3)

**hy·phen·ate** /'haɪfəneɪt/ *v* **-ated, -ating** [T] to join with a HYPHEN –**hyphenation** /-'neɪʃən/ *n* [U]

**hyp·no·sis** /hɪp'nəusɪs/ *n* [U] (the production of) a sleep-like state in which a person's mind and actions can be controlled by another person –**hypnotic** /hɪp'nɒtɪk‖-'nɑ-/ *adj* –**hypnotically** *adv*

**hyp·no·tis·m** /'hɪpnətɪzəm/ *n* [U] the practice of hypnotizing (HYPNOTIZE) someone –**hypnotist** *n*

**hyp·no·tize** ,‖also **-tise** *BrE* /'hɪpnətaɪz/ *v* **-tized, -tizing** [T] to produce HYPNOSIS in (someone)

**hy·po·chon·dri·ac** /ˌhaɪpə'kɒndriæk‖-'kɑn-/ *n* a person suffering from a state of anxiety and (unnecessary) worry about his/her health (**hypochondria**)

**hy·poc·ri·sy** /hɪ'pɒkrɪsi‖-'pɑ-/ *n* [U] the act or practice of pretending to believe, feel, or be something very different from, and usu. better than, what one actually believes, feels, or is

**hyp·o·crite** /'hɪpəkrɪt/ *n* a person who says one thing and does another, usu. something worse; one who practises HYPOCRISY: *You say you care about the poor, but you don't help them, you hypocrite!* –**hypocritical** /-'krɪtɪkəl/ *adj* –**hypocritically** *adv*

**hy·po·der·mic** /ˌhaɪpə'dɜːmɪk‖-ɜr-/ *adj,n* (of) an instrument or means of putting drugs into the body which is made to enter or INJECTed beneath the skin: *a hypodermic needle*/SYRINGE –**hypodermically** *adv*

**hy·po·ther·mi·a** /ˌhaɪpə'θɜːmɪə‖-ɜr-/ *n* [U] a medical condition in which the body temperature falls below the usual level, esp. as happens with old people who do not keep warm at home: *Every winter some old people die from hypothermia.*

**hy·poth·e·sis** /haɪ'pɒθɪsɪs‖-'pɑ-/ *n* **-ses** /siːz/ an idea which is thought suitable to explain the facts about something: *According to the government's hypothesis, the high cost of living is caused by increased wages.* –compare THEORY

**hy·po·thet·i·cal** /ˌhaɪpə'θetikəl/ *adj* supposed to be so; not yet proved to be true or known to have happened –**hypothetically** *adv*

**hys·ter·ec·to·my** /ˌhɪstə'rektəmi/ *n* [C;U] the medical operation for removing the WOMB –compare VASECTOMY

**hys·te·ri·a** /hɪ'stɪərɪə‖-'sterɪə/ *n* [U] **1** a condition of nervous excitement in which the sufferer laughs and cries uncontrollably and/or shows strange changes in behaviour or bodily state **2** wild excitement, as of a crowd of people

**hys·ter·i·cal** /hɪˈsterɪkəl/ also **hysteric** *rare– adj* **1** (of people) in a state of HYSTERIA: *The doctor slapped the hysterical child to make him calmer.* **2** (of feelings) expressed wildly, in an uncontrolled manner: *hysterical laughter* **–hysterically** *adv*

**hys·ter·ics** /hɪˈsterɪks/ *n* [P] attack(s) of HYSTERIA

# I, i

**SPELLING NOTE**

Words with the sound /aɪ/ may be spelt **e-**, like **eye.** or **ai-**, like **aisle.**

**I, i** /aɪ/ **I's, i's** *or* **Is, is 1** the 9th letter of the English alphabet **2** the ROMAN NUMERAL (number) for 1

**I** /aɪ/ *pron (used as the subject of a sentence)* the person who is speaking: *I'm not late, am I?|My husband and I are Scottish.* –see ME (USAGE)

**ice¹** /aɪs/ *n* **1** [U] water which has frozen to a solid: *There is ice on the lake in winter.|Her hands were like ice/were as cold as ice/were ice-cold.* **2** [C] *esp. BrE* a serving of ice cream: *Two ices, please.* **3 break the ice** to begin to be friendly with people one did not know before: *A few drinks will help to break the ice at the party.* **4 keep (something) on ice** to keep for later use: *It's an interesting suggestion and we'll keep it on ice.*

**ice²** *v* **iced, icing** [T] **1** to make very cold by using ice: *iced drinks* **2** to cover (a cake) with ICING

**ice over** also **ice up**– *v adv* to become covered with ice: *The lake iced over during the night.*

**ice age** /ˈ· ·/ *n* any of several periods when ice covered many northern countries

**ice·berg** /ˈaɪsbɜːg||-ɜrg/ *n* a very large piece of ice floating in the sea, most of which is below the surface

**ice·box** /ˈaɪsbɒks||-bɑks/ *n* **1** a box where food is kept cool with blocks of ice **2** *AmE* for FRIDGE

**ice cream** /ˌ· ˈ·◂||ˈ· ·/ *n* [C;U] a sweet mixture which is frozen and eaten cold, usu. containing milk or other fat products: *chocolate ice cream*

**i·ci·cle** /ˈaɪsɪkəl/ *n* a pointed stick of ice formed when water freezes as it runs or DRIPS down: *icicles hanging from the roof*

**ic·ing** /ˈaɪsɪŋ/ *n* [U] a mixture of fine powdery sugar (**icing sugar**) and liquid, used to decorate cakes

**i·con, ikon** /ˈaɪkɒn||-kɑn/ *n* an image of a holy person, used in the worship of the Eastern branches of Christianity

**ic·y** /ˈaɪsi/ *adj* **-ier, -iest 1** very cold: *My hands are icy.*|(fig.) *She gave me an icy look.* **2** covered with ice: *Icy roads are dangerous.* **–icily** *adv* **–iciness** *n* [U]

**I'd** /aɪd/ *short for*: **1** I had: *I'd gone* **2** I would: *I'd go*

**i·dea** /aɪˈdɪə/ *n* **1** [C;U] a picture in the mind: *I've got a good idea of what he wants.|Have you any idea of what I'm trying to explain?|You have* **no idea** (=you can't imagine) *how worried I was.* **2** [C] an opinion; thought: *He'll have his own ideas about that.|I've an idea* (=I think) *that he's on holiday.* **3** [C] a plan; suggestion: *I've an idea for a new book.|What a good idea! Let's do it.|She's full of good ideas.*

**i·deal¹** /aɪˈdɪəl/ *adj [no comp.]* perfect: *an ideal marriage*

**ideal²** *n* **1** a perfect example: *That's my ideal of what a house should be like.* **2** *[usu. pl.]* (a belief in) high or perfect standards: *a woman with high ideals*

**i·deal·is·m** /aɪˈdɪəlɪzəm/ *n* [U] the belief that one should live according to one's IDEALS² (2): *youthful idealism* **-idealist** *n* **–idealistic** *adj* **–idealistically** *adv*

**i·deal·ize** ||also **-ise** *BrE* /aɪˈdɪəlaɪz/ *v* **-ized, -izing** [I;T] to imagine or represent as perfect or as better than in reality: *He tends to idealize his life in the army.* **–idealization** /aɪˌdɪəlaɪˈzeɪʃən||-lə- / *n* [C;U]

**i·deal·ly** /aɪˈdɪəli/ *adv* **1** in an IDEAL¹ way: *ideally beautiful* **2** in an IDEAL¹ state of affairs: *Ideally, I would like to be a teacher, but there are no jobs.*

**i·den·ti·cal** /aɪˈdentɪkəl/ *adj [no comp.]* **1** *[with, to]* exactly alike: *Your voice is identical to hers.|***Identical twins** *look exactly alike.* **2** the same: *This is the identical hotel that we stayed in last year.* **–identically** *adv*

**i·den·ti·fi·ca·tion** /aɪˌdentǀfǀˈkeɪʃən/ *n* [U] **1** the act of IDENTIFYing or state of being identified: *identification of the dead body by the brother* **2** something (such as an official paper) which proves who one is: *His only* **means of identification** *was his passport.*

**i·den·ti·fy** /aɪˈdentǀfaɪ/ *v* **-fied, -fying** [T] to prove or show the IDENTITY of: *I identified the coat at once; it was my brother's.|I identified the criminal.*

**identify with** *v prep* [T] **1** (**identify** sbdy. **with** sthg.) to cause or consider (someone) to be connected with: *That politician is too closely identified with the former government to become a minister in ours.* **2** (**identify with** sbdy./sthg.) to feel sympathy for (someone), or feel that one shares (something): *Reading this book, we can identify with the main character's struggle.*

**i·den·ti·ty** /aɪˈdentǀti/ *n* **-ties 1** [C;U] who or what a particular person or thing is: *He had lost his* **identity card** (=a document which shows one's identity) *and was being questioned by the police.* **2** [U] sameness; exact likeness

**i·de·ol·ogy** /ˌaɪdiˈɒlədʒi||-ˈɑlə-/ *n* **-ogies** [C;U] a set of ideas, esp. if typical of a social or political group: MARXIST *ideology* **–ideological** /ˌaɪdɪəˈlɒdʒɪkəl||-ˈlɑ- / *adj* **–ideologically** *adv: Ideologically, they have many differences.* **–ideologist** /ˌaɪdiˈɒlədʒǀst||-ˈɑlə-/ *n*

**id·i·o·cy** /ˈɪdɪəsi/ *n* **-cies** [C;U] (an act of) stupidity

**id·i·om** /ˈɪdɪəm/ *n* **1** a phrase which means something different from the meanings of the separate words: *To be "hard up" is an English idiom meaning to lack money.* **2** the way of expression typical of a person or a people in their use of language: *the idiom of the young* **–idiomatic** /-ˈmætɪk/ *adj: a Frenchman who* *speaks idiomatic English*|"*To pull a face" is an idiomatic expression.* –**idiomatically** *adv*

**id·i·o·syn·cra·sy** /ˌɪdɪəˈsɪŋkrəsi/ *n* **-sies** a peculiarity of one person: *One of his idiosyncrasies is keeping pet snakes.*

**id·i·ot** /ˈɪdɪət/ *n* **1** a foolish person: *Idiot! You've dropped my watch!* **2** *old use or tech* a person of very weak mind usu. from birth –compare IMBECILE –**idiotic** /ˌɪdiˈɒtɪk‖-ˈɑ- / *adj* –**idiotically** *adv*

**i·dle**[1] /ˈaɪdl/ *adj* **1** lazy: *That boy is just* **bone idle.** (=very lazy) **2** not working: *Men are left idle when machines break down.* **3** of no use; having no result: *idle gossip/talk*|*His words were just* **idle threats;** *he can't harm us.* –**idleness** *n* [U] –**idly** *adv*

**idle**[2] *v* **-idled, -idling 1** to waste time doing nothing **2** (of an engine) to run slowly –**idler** *n*

**idle** sthg. **away** *v adv* [T] to waste (time) doing nothing: *We idled away a few hours by talking.*

**i·dol** /ˈaɪdl/ *n* an image worshipped as a god: (fig.) *The football player was the young boys' idol.*

**i·dol·a·try** /aɪˈdɒlətri‖-ˈdɑ-/ *n* [U] the worship of IDOLS –**idolatrous** *adj*

**i·dol·ize** ‖also **-ise** *BrE* /ˈaɪdəl-aɪz/ *v* **-ized, -izing** [T] to treat as an IDOL: *He idolizes his father.*

**id·yll, idyl** /ˈɪdl, ˈaɪdl‖ˈaɪdl/ *n* (a description of) a simple, happy scene, esp. in the country –**idyllic** /aɪˈdɪlɪk, ɪ-/ *adj: an idyllic scene* –**idyllically** *adv*

**i.e.** /ˌaɪ ˈiː/ *abbrev. for*: *Latin* id est (=that is to SAY[1] (6)): *females, i.e. girls and women*

**if** /ɪf/ *conj* **1** supposing that; on condition that: *If you pour oil on water, it floats.*|*We'll go if it doesn't rain/unless it rains.*|*If John were/was here, he would know what to do.*|*If he told you that, he was lying.* **2** even if; although: *a pleasant if noisy child* **3** (used after verbs like *ask, know, wonder*) whether: *Do you know if/whether she's coming?* **4** (used after words expressing feelings): *I'm sorry if she's annoyed.*|*Do you mind if I smoke?* (=May I smoke?) **5 if I were you** (used when giving advice): *If I were you I'd go home.* (=you ought to go home) **6 ifs and buts** reasons given for delay: *I don't want any ifs and buts; do it at once!*

USAGE **If** is only followed by *will/won't,* when they mean "be willing"/"be unwilling": **If** *you won't come* (=if you refuse), *I'll go alone.* Compare: **If** *it rains tomorrow, I'll go alone.* –see also AS IF, EVEN[2] (3) **if, if** ONLY[2]

**ig·loo** /ˈɪgluː/ *n* **-loos** a house made of hard icy blocks of snow, esp. as built by Eskimos

**ig·ne·ous** /ˈɪgnɪəs/ *adj tech* (of rocks) formed from LAVA

**ig·nite** /ɪgˈnaɪt/ *v* **-nited, -niting** [I;T] *fml* to (cause to) start to burn: *The liquid ignited when somebody dropped a match in it.*

**ig·ni·tion** /ɪgˈnɪʃən/ *n* **1** [C] the electrical CIRCUIT (3) which starts an engine –see picture on page 85 **2** [U] *fml* the act or action of igniting (IGNITE)

**ig·no·ble** /ɪgˈnəʊbəl/ *adj lit* not noble; dishonourable; which one should be ashamed of

**ig·no·mi·ny** /ˈɪgnəmɪni/ *n* **-nies** *fml* [C;U] (an act of) shame or dishonour –**ignominious** *adj: ignominious behaviour*|*an ignominious defeat* –**ignominiously** *adv*

**ig·no·ra·mus** /ˌɪgnəˈreɪməs/ *n* **-muses** *derog* an IGNORANT person

**ig·no·rance** /ˈɪgnərəns/ *n* [U *of*] lack of knowledge: *Ignorance of the law is no excuse.*

**ig·no·rant** /ˈɪgnərənt/ *adj* [*of*] **1** lacking knowledge: *ignorant of even the simplest facts* –see IGNORE (USAGE) **2** *infml* rude, impolite, esp. because of lack of social training

**ig·nore** /ɪgˈnɔːʳ‖ɪgˈnor/ *v* **-nored, -noring** [T] to refuse to notice; DISREGARD: *Ignore the child if he misbehaves, and he'll soon stop.*

USAGE Compare **ignore** and **be ignorant**: *He was driving very fast because he was* **ignorant** *of the fact that* (=he didn't know that) *there was a speed limit.*|*He* **ignored** *the speed limit* (=he knew about it, but paid no attention to it) *and drove very fast.*

**i·kon** /ˈaɪkɒn‖-kɑn/ *n* →ICON

**ill**[1] /ɪl/ *adj* **worse** /wɜːs‖wɜrs/, **worst** /wɜːst‖wɜrst/ **1** [F] not well in health: *She's* **seriously ill** (=very ill) *in hospital.* **2** [A] bad; harmful: *ill luck*|*He suffers from* **ill health.**|*I feel no* **ill will** (=dislike) *towards her in spite of her unkindness.* –see DISEASE (USAGE)

**ill**[2] *adv* [*no comp.*] **1** badly; unpleasantly: *to speak ill of one's neighbours*|*She seems* **ill-suited** *to this job.*|*The child has been* **ill-treated.**|He was **ill-advised** (=unwise) *to buy that old house.*|*an* **ill-fated** (=unlucky) *attempt* **2** hardly; not easily: *I can ill afford the time.*

**ill**[3] *n* [*often pl.*] a bad thing: *the ills of life*

**I'll** *v short for*: **1** I will **2** I shall

**il·le·gal** /ɪˈliːgəl/ *adj* [*no comp.*] not LEGAL; against the law: *It's illegal to park your car here.* –compare ILLEGITIMATE –**illegally** *adv*

**il·le·gal·i·ty** /ˌɪlɪˈgælɨti/ *n* **-ties 1** [U] the state of being ILLEGAL **2** [C] an act against the law

**il·le·gi·ble** /ɪˈledʒəbəl/ *adj* not LEGIBLE; which cannot be read: *illegible handwriting* –**illegibility** /ɪˌledʒəˈbɪlɨti / *n* [U] –**illegibly** *adv*

**il·le·git·i·mate** /ˌɪlɨˈdʒɪtɨmɨt/ *adj* **1** [*no comp.*] born to parents who are not married: *an illegitimate child* **2** not allowed by the rules: *an illegitimate action* –opposite **legitimate**; compare ILLEGAL –**illegitimately** *adv* –**illegitimacy** /ˌɪlɨˈdʒɪtɨməsi/ *n* [U]

**il·li·cit** /ɪˈlɪsɨt/ *adj* [*no comp.*] (done) against a law or a rule: *an illicit act*|*illicit trade in drugs* –**illicitly** *adv*

**il·lit·e·rate** /ɪˈlɪtərɨt/ *adj,n* [*no comp.*] (a person who is) not LITERATE (1); unable to read and write: *About half the population is still illiterate.*|*He's an illiterate.* –**illiteracy** /ɪˈlɪtərəsi/ *n* [U]

**ill·ness** /ˈɪlnɨs/ *n* [C;U] (a) disease; unhealthy state of the body: *A serious illness has prevented her from working for a year.* –see DISEASE (USAGE)

**il·lo·gi·cal** /ɪˈlɒdʒɪkəl‖ɪˈlɑ-/ *adj* **1** (of people or ideas) going against LOGIC **2** *infml* not sensible –opposite **logical** –**illogically** *adv*

**il·lu·mi·nate** /ɪˈluːmɨneɪt, ɪˈljuː-‖ɪˈluː-/ *v* **-nated, -nating 1** to give light to: *The room was illuminated by candles.* **2** to decorate (buildings, streets, etc.) with lights for a special occasion

**il·lu·mi·nat·ing** /ɪˈluːmɨneɪtɪŋ, ɪˈljuː-‖ɪˈluː-/ *adj* helping to explain: *an illuminating remark*

**il·lu·mi·na·tion** /ɪˌluːmɨˈneɪʃən, ɪˌljuː-‖ɪˌluː-/ *n* [U] the act of illuminating or state of being ILLUMINATED

**il·lu·mi·na·tions** /ɪˌluːmɨˈneɪʃənz, ɪˌljuː-‖ɪˌluː-/ *n* [P] the show of (coloured) lights used to make a town bright and colourful for a special occasion

**il·lu·sion** /ɪ'luːʒən/ *n* something seen wrongly, not as it really is; a false belief or idea: *The lake in the desert was just an* **optical illusion.**|*She is* **under the illusion** *that she's passed the exam, but I know she failed.*|*I* **have no illusions** *about him; I know he's a liar.*

USAGE Compare **illusion** and **delusion:** An **illusion** is usu. something that seems true to the senses, but is known to be false; a **delusion** is something which, though false, is believed to be true: *the* **illusion** *that the sun goes round the earth* (=it seems to, but we know it does not)|*man's earlier* **delusion** *that the sun went around the earth* (=people believed this really happened).

**il·lus·trate** /'ɪləstreɪt/ *v* **-trated, -trating** [T] **1** to add pictures to (something written): *an illustrated book* **2** to show the meaning of (something) by giving related examples: *His story illustrates her true generosity very clearly.*

**il·lus·tra·tion** /ˌɪlə'streɪʃən/ *n* **1** a picture, esp. in a book: *It's not a very good book, but I like the illustrations.* **2** an example which explains the meaning of something: *That's a typical illustration of his meanness.* **3 by way of illustration** as an example

**il·lus·tra·tive** /'ɪləstreɪtɪv, -strət-‖ɪ'lʌstrətɪv/ *adj* used for explaining the meaning of something: *an illustrative example* –compare ILLUSTRATE (2) **–illustratively** *adv*

**il·lus·tra·tor** /'ɪləstreɪtəʳ/ *n* a person who draws pictures, esp. for a book

**il·lus·tri·ous** /ɪ'lʌstriəs/ *adj apprec* famous; known for one's great works **–illustriously** *adv*

**I'm** /aɪm/ *short for:* I am

**im·age** /'ɪmɪdʒ/ *n* **1** a picture, esp. in the mind: *An image of a country garden came into my mind.* **2** the opinion which others have of one: *The government will have to improve its image if it wants to win the election.* **3** a copy: *He's the (very) image of his father.* **4** an object made to represent a god or person to be worshipped –compare IDOL

**im·ag·e·ry** /'ɪmɪ̣dʒəri/ *n* [U] the use of IMAGES in literature

**i·ma·gi·na·ble** /ɪ'mædʒənəbəl/ *adj* that can be imagined: *every imaginable possibility*

**i·ma·gi·na·ry** /ɪ'mædʒənəri‖-dʒɪ̣neri/ *adj* not real, but imagined: *All the characters in this book are imaginary.* –compare IMAGINATIVE

**i·ma·gi·na·tion** /ɪˌmædʒɪ̣'neɪʃən/ *n* **1** [C;U] the act of imagining or the ability to imagine: *The little boy's story shows plenty of imagination.*|*a vivid imagination* **2** [C] the mind: *The difficulties are all in your imagination.*

**i·ma·gi·na·tive** /ɪ'mædʒənətɪv/ *adj* using or having imagination: *imaginative writing*|*She is an imaginative child.* –compare: *an* **imaginative** *story*|*All the events described in this story are* **imaginary**. (=they didn't really happen) –opposite **unimaginative –imaginatively** *adv*

> **SPELLING NOTE**
> Words with the sound /aɪ/ may be spelt e-, like **eye.** or **ai-**, like **aisle.**

**i·ma·gine** /ɪ'mædʒɪ̣n/ *v* **-gined, -gining** [not *be* +*v-ing*] **1** [T +*v-ing*] to form (a picture or idea) in the mind: *Can you imagine George cooking the dinner?* **2** [T +(*that*)] to suppose or have an idea about, esp. mistakenly or without proof: *He imagines that people don't like him.*

**im·bal·ance** /ɪm'bæləns/ *n* a lack of balance or proper relationship, esp. between two qualities or between two examples of one thing: *When more males are born than females, there is a population imbalance.*

**im·be·cile** /'ɪmbəsiːl‖-səl/ *n* a person of weak mind –compare IDIOT **–imbecility** /-'sɪlɪ̣ti/ *n* [C;U]

**im·bibe** /ɪm'baɪb/ *v* **-bibed, -bibing** [I;T] *fml* to drink or take in (esp. alcohol)

**im·bue** sbdy. **with** sthg. /ɪm'bjuː/ *v prep* **-bued, -buing** [T *usu. pass.*] *fml* to fill with a strong feeling or opinion): *A President should be imbued with a sense of responsibility for the nation.*

**im·i·tate** /'ɪmɪ̣teɪt/ *v* **-tated, -tating** [T] to copy the behaviour, appearance, speech, etc., typical of (a person): *James can imitate his father's speech perfectly.* –compare IMPERSONATE, MIMIC **–imitative** /'ɪmɪ̣tətɪv‖-teɪtɪv/ *adj: imitative behaviour* **–imitator** *n*

**im·i·ta·tion** /ˌɪmɪ̣'teɪʃən/ *n* [C;U] the act or result of imitating (IMITATE): *His imitation of that singer is perfect.*|*imitation jewellery* (=a copy of the real thing)

**im·mac·u·late** /ɪ'mækjʊlɪ̣t‖- kjə-/ *adj* very clean and unspoilt: *immaculate white shoes* **–immaculately** *adv: immaculately dressed*

**im·ma·te·ri·al** /ˌɪmə'tɪəriəl/ *adj* unimportant: *When it happened is immaterial; I want to know why it happened.*

**im·ma·ture** /ˌɪmə'tʃʊəʳ‖-'tʊər/ *adj* (typical of someone who is) not MATURE; not fully formed or developed: *His foolish behaviour is very immature for a man of 30.* **–immaturely** *adv* **–immaturity** /ˌɪmə'tʃʊərɪ̣ti‖-'tʊər- / *n* [U]

**im·mea·su·ra·ble** /ɪ'meʒərəbəl/ *adj* [*no comp.*] too large to be measured: *immeasurable depths/stupidity*

**im·me·di·a·cy** /ɪ'miːdiəsi/ **also immediateness**– *n* [U] the nearness or urgent presence of something: *He did not realize the immediacy of the problem.*

**im·me·di·ate** /ɪ'miːdiət/ *adj* [*no comp.*] **1** done or needed at once: *I want an immediate reply.* **2** nearest; next: *in the immediate future*|*My immediate family consists of my son and my wife.*

**im·me·di·ate·ly**[1] /ɪ'miːdiətli/ *adv* [*adv* + *prep/adv*] at once: *I came immediately after I'd eaten.*|*Stop that, immediately!*

**immediately**[2] *conj BrE* as soon as: *I came immediately I heard the news.*

**im·me·mo·ri·al** /ˌɪmɪ̣'mɔːriəl‖-'mor-/ *adj* going back to ancient times: *People have fought wars* **from/since time immemorial.**

**im·mense** /ɪ'mens/ *adj usu. apprec* very large: *an immense palace/improvement* –see Study Notes on page 494 **–immensity** *n* [U]: *the immensity of space*

**im·mense·ly** /ɪ'mensli/ *adv apprec* very much: *I enjoyed it immensely.*

**im·merse** /ɪ'mɜːs‖-ɜrs/ *v* **-mersed, -mersing** [T *in*] to put deep under water: *He lay immersed in a hot bath.*|(fig.) *She was so immersed in her work that she* *didn't notice me.* –**immersion** /ɪ'mɜːʃən, - ʒən‖-ɜr-/ *n* [U]

**im·mer·sion heat·er** /·'·· ˌ··/ *n* an electric water heater placed in a tank which provides all the hot water for use in the home

**im·mi·grate** /'ɪmɪ̇greɪt/ *v* **-grated, -grating** [I] to come into a country to make one's life and home there –see EMIGRATE (USAGE) –**immigrant** *n* –**immigration** /- 'greɪʃən / *n* [U]: *the immigration office at the airport*

**im·mi·nence** /'ɪmɪ̇nəns/ *n* [U] the nearness of something which is going to happen: *The imminence of their exams made them work harder.*

**im·mi·nent** /'ɪmɪ̇nənt/ *adj* [*no comp.*] which is going to happen very soon –compare EMINENT, IMPENDING –**imminently** *adv*

**im·mo·bile** /ɪ'məʊbaɪl‖-bəl/ *adj* not MOBILE[1]; not able to move; unmoving –**immobility** /ˌɪməʊ'bɪlɪ̇ti / *n* [U]

**im·mo·bi·lize** ‖also **-lise** *BrE* /ɪ'məʊbɪ̇laɪz/ *v* **-lized, -lizing** [T] to make unable to move: *When its engine broke down, the car was immobilized for weeks.*

**im·mod·e·rate** /ɪ'mɒdərɪ̇t‖ɪ'mɑ-/ *adj* not MODERATE[1] (1); not (done) within sensible limits: *immoderate eating* –**immoderately** *adv*

**im·mod·est** /ɪ'mɒdɪ̇st‖ɪ'mɑ-/ *adj derog* **1** not modest; telling the good things about oneself instead of hiding them **2** likely to shock because improper or impure: *an immodest dress*|*immodest behaviour* –compare INDECENT –**immodestly** *adv* –**immodesty** *n* [U]

**im·mor·al** /ɪ'mɒrəl‖ɪ'mɔ-/ *adj* not moral; not considered good or right, esp. in sexual matters: *Using other people for one's own profit is immoral.*|*an immoral book* –see also AMORAL, MORAL –**immorally** *adv* –**immorality** /ˌɪmə'rælɪ̇ti/ *n* **-ties** [C;U]

**im·mor·tal** /ɪ'mɔːtəl‖-ɔr-/ *adj* [*no comp.*] not MORTAL; that will not die; that continues for ever: *Nobody is immortal.*|(fig.) *immortal fame* –**immortality** /ˌɪmɔː'tælɪ̇ti‖-ɔr-/ *n* [U]

**im·mor·tal·ize** ‖also **-ise** *BrE* /ɪ'mɔːtəlaɪz‖-ɔr-/ *v* **-ized, -izing** [T *in*] to give endless life or fame to (someone): *Dickens' father was immortalized for ever as Mr Micawber in "David Copperfield".*

**im·mo·va·ble** /ɪ'muːvəbəl/ *adj* which cannot be moved: (fig.) *The government is immovable on the new drinking laws.* –**immovably** *adv*

**im·mune** /ɪ'mjuːn/ *adj* **1** [*to*] unable to be harmed because of special powers in oneself: *immune to disease* **2** [*from*] protected (from): *The criminal was told he would be immune from punishment if he helped the police.* –**immunity** *n* [U]

**im·mu·nize** ‖also **-nise** *BrE* /'ɪmjʊnaɪz‖'ɪmjə-/ *v* [T] to make (someone) safe against disease by putting certain substances into the body usu. by means of a HYPODERMIC needle –see also INOCULATE –**immunization** /ˌɪmjʊnaɪ'zeɪʃən‖ˌɪmjənə- / *n* [C;U]

**im·mu·ta·ble** /ɪ'mjuːtəbəl/ *adj fml* unchangeable: *immutable laws of nature*

**imp** /ɪmp/ *n* a little devil: (fig.) *That child is a real imp.* –see also IMPISH

**im·pact** /'ɪmpækt/ *n* the force of one object hitting another: *The cup hit the wall and broke* **on impact.**| (fig.) *Her new idea made a great impact in the office.*

**im·pair** /ɪm'peər/ *v* [T] to spoil or weaken: *His hearing was impaired after the explosion.* –**impairment** *n* [U]

**im·pale** /ɪm'peɪl/ *v* **-paled, -paling** [T *on*] to run a sharp stick or weapon through (someone's body): *He fell out of the window and was impaled on the fence.*

**im·part** /ɪm'pɑːt‖-ɑrt/ *v* [T *to*] *fml* to give (qualities, knowledge, etc.): *She imparted the secret to a friend.*

**im·par·tial** /ɪm'pɑːʃəl‖-ɑr-/ *adj* [*no comp.*] fair; giving equal attention to all concerned: *an impartial judge* –opposite **biased;** see also DISINTERESTED –**impartially** *adv* –**impartiality** /ɪmˌpɑːʃi'ælɪ̇ti‖-ɑr- / *n* [U]

**im·pass·a·ble** /ɪm'pɑːsəbəl‖ɪm'pæ-/ *adj* which cannot be travelled over: *The snow has made the road impassable.* –compare IMPOSSIBLE

**im·passe** /æm'pɑːs‖'ɪmpæs/ *n* [*usu. sing.*] a point where further movement is blocked: *to reach an impasse in discussions* (=where neither side will agree)

**im·pas·sioned** /ɪm'pæʃənd/ *adj* (usu. of speech) moved by deep feelings: *an impassioned demand for the prisoners to be freed*

**im·pas·sive** /ɪm'pæsɪv/ *adj* (of people) showing or having no feelings; unusually calm –**impassively** *adv: He watched impassively as his house burned down.* –**impassivity** /ˌɪmpæ'sɪvɪ̇ti/ *n* [U]

**im·pa·tient** /ɪm'peɪʃənt/ *adj* **1** not patient; unable to wait calmly or bear the weaknesses of others: *too impatient with slow learners* **2** [F +*to-v*/*for*] eager: *impatient for his dinner* –**impatience** *n* [U +*to-v*/*for*]: *Try to control your impatience.* –**impatiently** *adv: He waited impatiently for the train to arrive.*

**im·peach** /ɪm'piːtʃ/ *v* [T] *law* to charge (esp. a public official) with a serious crime, esp. against the state –**impeachment** *n* [C;U]

**im·pec·ca·ble** /ɪm'pekəbəl/ *adj* faultless: *impeccable manners*/*behaviour* –**impeccably** *adv*

**im·pe·cu·ni·ous** /ˌɪmpɪ'kjuːnɪəs/ *adj fml, sometimes humor* having little or no money, esp. continually

**im·pede** /ɪm'piːd/ *v* **-peded, -peding** [T] *fml* to get in the way of; make (something) difficult to do: *The rescue attempt was impeded by bad weather.*

**im·ped·i·ment** /ɪm'pedɪ̇mənt/ *n* a fact or event which makes action difficult or impossible: *It's difficult to understand him because he has a speech impediment.*

**im·pel** /ɪm'pel/ *v* **-ll-** [T *in, into*] *fml* (esp. of an idea, feeling, etc.) to push (someone) forward

**im·pend·ing** /ɪm'pendɪŋ/ *adj* (usu. of something unpleasant) about to happen: *the impending examinations* –compare IMMINENT

**im·pen·e·tra·ble** /ɪm'penɪ̇trəbəl/ *adj* **1** which cannot be gone into or through: *the impenetrable forest*|(fig.) *impenetrable darkness* (=in which nothing can be seen) **2** not able to be understood or helped: *an impenetrable mystery* –see also PENETRATE

**im·per·a·tive**[1] /ɪm'perətɪv/ *adj* [+*that*] *fml* urgent; which must be done: *It's imperative that you go now.* –**imperatively** *adv*

**imperative**[2] *n tech* (an example of ) the form which

shows the use of the verb to express a command: *In "Come here!" the verb "come" is in the imperative.*

**im·per·cep·ti·ble** /ˌɪmpəˈseptəbəl‖-pər-/ *adj* not PERCEPTIBLE; unable to be noticed because of smallness or slightness: *an almost imperceptible movement in the dark* –**imperceptibility** /-əˈbɪlʲ̣ti / *n* [U] –**imperceptibly** *adv*

**im·per·fect¹** /ɪmˈpɜːfɪkt‖-ɜr-/ *adj* not perfect; faulty: *an imperfect knowledge of French* –**imperfection** /ˌɪmpəˈfekʃən‖-ər- / *n* [C;U] –**imperfectly** *adv*

**imperfect²** *n tech* (an example of) the tense of the verb which shows incomplete action in the past: *In "we were walking down the road" the verb "were walking" is in the imperfect.* –see also PERFECT¹ (5)

**im·pe·ri·al** /ɪmˈpɪərɪəl/ *adj* (*often cap.*) **1** concerning an empire or its ruler **2** (of a measure) British standard –compare IMPERIOUS –**imperially** *adv*

**im·pe·ri·al·is·m** /ɪmˈpɪərɪəlɪzəm/ *n* [U] **1** (belief in) the making of empires **2** *derog* the gaining of political and trade advantages over poorer nations by a powerful country which rules them or helps them with money –compare COLONIALISM, CAPITALISM –**imperialist** *adj,n*

**im·per·il** /ɪmˈperʲ̣l/ *v* **-ll-** *BrE*‖**-l-** *AmE* [T] to put in danger

**im·pe·ri·ous** /ɪmˈpɪərɪəs/ *adj fml* (too) commanding; expecting obedience from others: *an imperious voice* –compare IMPERIAL –**imperiously** *adv* –**imperiousness** *n* [U]

**im·per·son·al** /ɪmˈpɜːsənəl‖-ɜr-/ *adj* not showing personal feelings: *an impersonal letter|a large, impersonal organization* –**impersonally** *adv*

**im·per·so·nate** /ɪmˈpɜːsəneɪt‖-ɜr-/ *v* **-nated, -nating** [T] to pretend to be (another person) by copying his/her appearance, behaviour, etc.: *He impersonates all the well-known politicians.* –compare IMITATE, MIMIC –**impersonation** /-ˈneɪʃən / *n* [C;U] –**impersonator** *n*

**im·per·ti·nent** /ɪmˈpɜːtʲ̣nənt‖-ɜr-/ *adj* rude or not respectful, esp. to an older or more important person –compare CHEEKY –**impertinence** *n* [U] –**impertinently** *adv*

**im·per·tur·ba·ble** /ˌɪmpəˈtɜːbəbəl‖-pərˈtɜr-/ *adj* that cannot be worried; that remains calm and steady in spite of difficulties or confusion –**imperturbability** /-əˈbɪlʲ̣ti / *n* [U] –**imperturbably** *adv*

**im·per·vi·ous** /ɪmˈpɜːvɪəs‖-ɜr-/ *adj* [*to; no comp.*] **1** not allowing anything to pass through: *This material is impervious to gases and liquids.* **2** too certain in one's opinions to be changed or influenced (by): *impervious to reason/threats/criticism*

**im·pet·u·ous** /ɪmˈpetʃʊəs/ *adj* showing swift action but lack of thought: *an impetuous driver/decision* –**impetuously** *adv*

**im·pe·tus** /ˈɪmpʲ̣təs/ *n* **1** [U] the force of something moving; MOMENTUM: *The car ran down the hill under its own impetus.* **2** [C;U] (an) encouragement: *The government's plan gave fresh impetus to industry.*

**im·pi·e·ty** /ɪmˈpaɪʲ̣ti/ *n* **-ties** [C;U] (an act showing) lack of PIETY; lack of respect, esp. for religion

> **SPELLING NOTE**
> Words with the sound /aɪ/ may be spelt **e-**, like **eye.** or **ai-**, like **aisle**.

**im·pinge on** sthg. /ɪmˈpɪndʒ/ also **impinge upon** sthg.– *v prep* **-pinged, -pinging** [T] to have an effect on: *The need to see that justice is done impinges on every decision made in the courts.*

**im·pi·ous** /ˈɪmpɪəs/ *adj* lacking PIETY; showing IMPIETY –opposite **pious** –**impiously** *adv*

**imp·ish** /ˈɪmpɪʃ/ *adj* like a little devil (IMP): *an impish smile* –**impishly** *adv* –**impishness** *n* [U]

**im·plac·a·ble** /ɪmˈplækəbəl/ *adj* impossible to satisfy or PLACATE: *an implacable enemy*

**im·plant** /ɪmˈplɑːnt‖ɪmˈplænt/ *v* [T *in, into*] to fix in deeply, usu. into the body or mind

**im·ple·ment¹** /ˈɪmplʲ̣mənt/ *n* a tool or instrument: *farming/gardening implements*

**im·ple·ment²** /ˈɪmplʲ̣ment/ *v* [T] to carry out or put into practice: *The committee's suggestions will be implemented immediately.*

**im·pli·cate** /ˈɪmplʲ̣keɪt/ *v* **-cated, -cating** [T *in*] *fml* to show that (someone else) is also to blame: *The police found a letter which implicated him in the robbery.* –compare INVOLVE

**im·pli·ca·tion** /ˌɪmplʲ̣ˈkeɪʃən/ *n* **1** [U] the act of IMPLYing: *She said very little directly, but a great deal* **by implication. 2** [C] a suggestion not expressed but understood: *He smiled, but the implication was that he didn't believe me.* **3** [U] *fml* the act of implicating (IMPLICATE)

**im·pli·cit** /ɪmˈplɪsʲ̣t/ *adj* **1** [*in*] (of a statement, rule, etc.) meant though not plainly expressed; suggested: *an implicit threat|The threat was implicit in the way he looked.* –compare EXPLICIT **2** [A] unquestioning and complete: *She has implicit trust in her doctor.* –**implicitly** *adv: She trusted the doctor implicitly.*

**im·plore** /ɪmˈplɔːʳ‖-or/ *v* **-plored, -ploring** [T] to ask (someone) in a begging manner (for something or to do something): *I implore you to go now.*

**im·ply** /ɪmˈplaɪ/ *v* **-plied, -plying** [T + *that*] to express indirectly; suggest: *His manner implies that he would like to come with us.|The fact that nobody answered the telephone implies that they're not at home.* –see INFER (USAGE)

**im·po·lite** /ˌɪmpəˈlaɪt/ *adj* not polite –**impolitely** *adv* –**impoliteness** *n* [C;U]

**im·pol·i·tic** /ɪmˈpɒlʲ̣tɪk‖ɪmˈpɑ-/ *adj fml* (of an action) not POLITIC; not well-judged for one's purpose; not wise

**im·pon·de·ra·ble** /ɪmˈpɒndərəbəl‖-ˈpɑn-/ *adj* of which the importance cannot be calculated or measured exactly –**imponderable** *n* [*usu. pl.*]

**im·port¹** /ɪmˈpɔːt‖-ort/ *v* [T *from*] to bring in (something), esp. from abroad: *imported silk* –compare EXPORT¹ –**importer** *n*

**im·port²** /ˈɪmpɔːt‖-ort/ *n* **1** [C *often pl.*] something brought into a country from abroad: *Imports rose last month.* (=we imported more goods than in the month before) **2** [U] also **importation**– the act of IMPORTing: *the import of food from abroad* –compare EXPORT **3** [S] *fml* the meaning: *the import of the speech* **4** [U] *fml* IMPORTANCE: *a matter of no/great import*

**im·por·tance** /ɪmˈpɔːtəns‖-ɔr-/ *n* [U] **1** the quality or state of being important –opposite **unimportance** **2** the reason why something or someone is important: *The importance of washing one's hands is that it prevents infection.*

**im·por·tant** /ɪm'pɔːtənt‖-ɔr-/ *adj* having great effect, value, etc.: *It's important to learn to read.|a very important meeting|She's one of the most important people in the company.* –opposite **unimportant** –**importantly** *adv*

**im·por·ta·tion** /ˌɪmpɔː'teɪʃən‖-ɔr-/ *n* [C;U] the act or result of IMPORTING[1]

**im·por·tu·nate** /ɪm'pɔːtʃʊnɪ̈t‖ɪm'pɔrtʃənɪ̈t/ *adj fml* always demanding things –**importunately** *adv*

**im·por·tune** /ˌɪmpə'tjuːn‖ˌɪmpər'tuːn/ *v* **-tuned, -tuning** [T] *fml* to beg (someone) repeatedly for things or to do things

**im·pose** /ɪm'pəʊz/ *v* **-posed, -posing** [*on, upon*] **1** [T] to establish (an additional payment) officially: *A new tax has been imposed on wine.* **2** [I] to take unfair advantage, in a way that causes additional work and trouble: *Thanks for your offer of help, but I don't want to impose on you.* **3** [T] to force the acceptance of; establish: *She imposed herself as their leader.* –**imposition** /ˌɪmpə'zɪʃən/ *n* [C;U *of, on, upon*]: *It's an imposition to ask us to stay late at work.*

**im·pos·ing** /ɪm'pəʊzɪŋ/ *adj* powerful in appearance; strong or large in size: *an imposing view across the valley|an imposing building* –**imposingly** *adv*

**im·pos·si·ble** /ɪm'pɒsəbəl‖ɪm'pɑ-/ *adj* **1** [*no comp.*] not possible: *It's impossible to do all that work before tomorrow!* **2** hard to bear; very unpleasant: *His bad temper makes life impossible for all the family.|an impossible child* –compare IMPASSABLE –**impossibility** /-ə'bɪlɪ̈ti/ *n* [U] –**impossibly** *adv: (not used with verbs): impossibly difficult*

**im·pos·tor** ‖also **-ter** *AmE* /ɪm'pɒstə^r‖ɪm'pɑs-/– *n* someone who deceives by pretending to be someone else: *You're not my brother, you impostor!*

**im·po·tent** /'ɪmpətənt/ *adj* **1** [*+to-v*] lacking power to do things **2** (of a man) unable to perform the sex act –see also POTENT –**impotence** *n* [U] –**impotently** *adv*

**im·pound** /ɪm'paʊnd/ *v* [T] *fml or law* to take and shut up officially until claimed (esp. something lost or not taken care of): *If you leave your car there, the police will impound it.*

**im·pov·e·rish** /ɪm'pɒvərɪʃ‖ɪm'pɑ-/ *v* [T] to make poor

**im·prac·ti·ca·ble** /ɪm'præktɪkəbəl/ *adj* not PRACTICABLE; that cannot be used in practice: *Those new building plans are impracticable.* –**impracticability** /-ə'bɪlɪ̈ti/ *n* [U] –**impracticably** *adv*

**im·prac·ti·cal** /ɪm'præktɪkəl/ *adj* not practical; not sensible or reasonable: *He is an impractical person who can't even boil an egg.|an impractical suggestion* –**impractically** *adv* –**impracticality** /-'kælɪ̈ti/ *n* [U]

**im·preg·na·ble** /ɪm'pregnəbəl/ *adj* which cannot be entered or conquered by attack: *an impregnable castle*

**im·preg·nate** /'ɪmpregneɪt‖ɪm'preg-/ *v* **-nated, -nating** [T] **1** [*with*] to cause (a substance) to enter and spread completely through (another substance): *a new kind of furniture-cleaning cloth that's impregnated with polish* **2** *fml* to make PREGNANT (1)

**im·pre·sa·ri·o** /ˌɪmprɪ̈'sɑːriəʊ/ *n* **-os** a person who arranges performances in theatres, concert halls, etc.

**im·press** /ɪm'pres/ *v* [T] **1** to fill (someone) with admiration: *I was very impressed by/with their new house.* **2** [*on, with*] to make the importance of (something) clear to (someone); EMPHASIZE: *My father impressed on me the value of hard work.*

**im·pres·sion** /ɪm'preʃən/ *n* **1** the image or feeling a person or thing gives to someone's mind,esp. as regards its strength or quality: *a strong impression|I made a bad impression on the teacher by arriving late on my first day.|First impressions are often wrong.|What's your impression of him as a worker?|I* **got the impression***(that) they'd just had an argument.|I was* **under the impression** *that he was the head of the firm; but he wasn't.* **2** a mark left by pressure: *I saw the impression of a foot in the mud.* **3** an attempt to copy a person's appearance or behaviour, esp. when done as a theatrical performance: *He did/gave an impression of the teacher which made us all laugh.*

**im·pres·sio·na·ble** /ɪm'preʃənəbəl/ *adj* easy to influence: *The child is at an impressionable age.*

**im·pres·sion·is·m** /ɪm'preʃənɪzəm/ *n* [U] (*often cap.*) a style of painting (esp. in France, 1870–1900)which produces effects by light and colour rather than by details of form –**impressionist** *n,adj*

**im·pres·sion·is·tic** /ɪmˌpreʃə'nɪstɪk/ *adj* based on IMPRESSIONS (1) rather than on knowledge, fact, or detailed study: *an impressionistic account of what happened* –**impressionistically** *adv*

**im·pres·sive** /ɪm'presɪv/ *adj* causing admiration by giving one a feeling of size, importance, quality, etc.: *an impressive speech/speaker* –opposite **unimpressive** –**impressively** *adv* –**impressiveness** *n* [U]

**im·print** /ɪm'prɪnt/ *v* [T *on*] to print or press (a mark) on something: (fig.) *Every detail is imprinted on my mind.* –**imprint** /'ɪmprɪnt/ *n*

**im·pris·on** /ɪm'prɪzən/ *v* [T] to put in prison or keep in a place or state from which one cannot get out as one wishes –**imprisonment** *n* [U]

**im·prob·a·ble** /ɪm'prɒbəbəl‖-'prɑ-/ *adj* not probable; not likely to happen or to be true: *an improbable idea* –**improbably** *adv* –**improbability** /-ə'bɪlɪ̈ti/ *n* **-ties** [C;U]

**im·promp·tu** /ɪm'prɒmptjuː‖ɪm'prɑmptuː/ *adj,adv* (said or done) at once without preparation: *an impromptu speech* –compare IMPROVISE

**im·prop·er** /ɪm'prɒpə^r‖-'prɑ-/ *adj* **1** not suitable: *His casual style of dress was improper for a formal dinner.* **2** showing thoughts which are socially undesirable, esp. about sex: *an improper suggestion/remark* –see also PROPER (1,2) –**improperly** *adv*

**im·pro·pri·e·ty** /ˌɪmprə'praɪɪ̈ti/ *n* **-ties** *fml* **1** [U] the quality or state of being IMPROPER **2** [C] a socially undesirable act –see also PROPRIETY

**im·prove** /ɪm'pruːv/ *v* **-proved, -proving** [I;T] to (cause to) become better: *I want to improve my English.|I think your English is improving.*

**improve on/upon** sthg. *v prep* [T] to produce or be something better than; BETTER[4]: *Tom has improved on his first attempt (at drawing).*

**im·prove·ment** /ɪm'pruːvmənt/ *n* [C;U] (a sign of) the act of improving or the state of being improved: *There's been a great improvement in his work this term.|His health is showing signs of improvement.*

USAGE An **improvement** *in* something means that it has got better, but one can speak of an **improvement** *on* something, only when two things are compared: *There has been an* **improvement** *in the weather.|Today's weather is an* **improvement** *on yesterday's.*

**im·prov·i·dent** /ɪm'prɒvɨdənt‖-'prɑ-/ *adj fml* (esp. of someone who wastes money) not PROVIDENT; not preparing for the future –**improvidence** *n* [U] –**improvidently** *adv*

**im·pro·vise** /'ɪmprəvaɪz/ *v* **-vised, -vising** [I;T] to do or make (something one has not prepared for) because a sudden need has arisen: *I forgot the words of my speech, so I had to improvise.* –**improvisation** /ˌɪmprəvaɪ'zeɪʃən‖-prəvə- / *n* [C;U] –compare IMPROMPTU

**im·pru·dent** /ɪm'pru:dənt/ *adj* not PRUDENT; unwise and thoughtless (in one's actions) –**imprudence** *n* [U] –**imprudently** *adv*

**im·pu·dent** /'ɪmpjʊdənt‖-pjə-/ *adj* shamelessly bold, esp. to an older or more important person: *an impudent child/remark* –**impudence** *n* [U] –**impudently** *adv*

**im·pulse** /'ɪmpʌls/ *n* **1** [C;U] a sudden wish to do something: *She had a sudden impulse to go on holiday.|He bought the car* **on impulse. 2** [C] *tech* a single push, or a force acting for a short time in one direction along a wire, nerve, etc.: *an electrical impulse*

**im·pul·sive** /ɪm'pʌlsɪv/ *adj* having or showing a tendency to act suddenly without thinking about the suitability, results, etc., of one's acts –**impulsively** *adv* –**impulsiveness** *n* [U]

**im·pu·ni·ty** /ɪm'pju:nɨti/ *n* [U] certainty of not being punished: *He behaved badly* **with impunity** *as he knew the teacher was weak.*

**im·pure** /ɪm'pjʊəʳ/ *adj* **1** not pure; morally bad; of bad sexual habits: *impure thoughts* **2** not pure, but mixed with something else: *impure drugs*

**im·pu·ri·ty** /ɪm'pjʊərɨti/ *n* **-ties 1** [C] something mixed with something else so that it is not pure **2** [C;U] the state of not being pure, or an act showing this –see also PURITY

**im·pute** sthg. **to** sbdy./sthg. /ɪm'pju:t/ *v prep* **-puted, -puting** [T] *fml* to blame (something) on: *The police impute the rise in crime to high unemployment.* –**imputation** /ˌɪmpjʊ'teɪʃən‖-pjə-/ *n* [C;U]

**in¹** /ɪn/ *prep* **1** (shows a position surrounded by something else) contained by; so as to be contained by; not beyond: *living in a house|money in a box|to sit in a car* (but *on a bicycle*)*|to swim in the sea* (compare *to sail on the sea*)*|cows in a field|She jumped in/into the water.|We arrived in London.* (compare *we arrived at the airport.*)*|in France|an island in the Atlantic|in hospital|in prison|in church* **2** (when speaking of time) **a** during: *in January|in Spring|in 1984|in the night* (compare *at night, at 10 o'clock, on July 1st, on Saturday*)*|in the past* **b** after not more than: *It's two o'clock. I'll come in an hour.* (=at three o'clock) **3** shown or described as the subject of: *a character in a story|the people in this photograph* **4** (shows employment): *She's in politics.|a job in insurance* **5** wearing: *a girl in red/in uniform* **6** towards (a direction): *in the wrong direction|The sun was in my eyes.* (=shining directly towards them) **7** using; with: *Write it in pencil/in French.* **8** (shows the way something happens): *in public* (=publicly)*|in secret* (=secretly)*|ten feet in length* (=as to length)*|in danger|in a hurry|in reply* (=as a reply) **9** so as to be divided or arranged: *in rows|in a circle|They arrived in large numbers.* (=large numbers of them arrived) **10** (shows the larger one in a relation) per: *a slope of 1 in 3|a tax of 40p in the £* –see Study Notes on page 474

> **SPELLING NOTE**
> Words with the sound /aɪ/ may be spelt **e-**, like **eye.** or **ai-**, like **aisle**.

**in²** *adv* **1** so as to be contained or surrounded; away from the outside: *Open the bag and put the money in.|Come in!* (said when someone knocks at a door) **2** present; at home, indoors, etc.: *I'm afraid Mr Jones is out, but he'll be in soon.|The train isn't in yet.* **3** from a number of people, or from all directions to a central point: *Letters have been coming/pouring in|Papers/marks must be in by Monday.* **4 a** (of one side in a game such as cricket) BATting² (2): *Our side were in/went in to* BAT *first.*|(fig.) *The Labour party are in.* (=elected) **b** (of the ball in a game such as tennis) inside the line **5** fashionable: *Long skirts came in* (=became fashionable) *last year.* **6** (of the TIDE) close to the coast; high: *The* TIDE *is coming in now.* **7** (of a fire) lit; burning: *Is the fire still in?* –opposite **out** (for **2,4,5,6,7**) **8 day in, day out; year in, year out,** etc. day after day, year after year, etc., without change **9 in and out (of)** sometimes inside and sometimes outside: *He's been in and out of prison for years.* **10 in for** to be about to have (esp. something bad): *I'm afraid we're in for some trouble.* **11 in on** having a share in: *people who were in on* (=knew) *the secret* **12 in with** friendly with **13 the ins and outs (of something)**: the various parts and difficulties to be seen when something is looked at in detail: *the ins and outs of politics*

**in³** *adj* [A] **1** directed towards; used for sending or going in: *I took the letters from my in* TRAY. –opposite **out 2** [A] *infml* fashionable: *the in place to go*

**in·a·bil·i·ty** /ˌɪnə'bɪlɨti/ *n* [S;U +*to-v*] lack of ability; lack of power or skill: *(an) inability to work alone*

**in·ac·ces·si·ble** /ˌɪnək'sesəbəl/ *adj* [*to*] not ACCESSIBLE; which cannot be reached: *Heavy snow made the village inaccessible* (*to traffic*). –**inaccessibility** /-'bɪlɨti / *n* [U] –**inaccessibly** *adv*

**in·ac·cu·rate** /ɪn'ækjʊrɨt‖-kjə-/ *adj* not ACCURATE; not correct –**inaccurately** *adv* –**inaccuracy** *n* **-cies** [C;U]

**in·ac·tion** /ɪn'ækʃən/ *n* [U] lack of action or activity; quality or state of doing nothing

**in·ac·tive** /ɪn'æktɪv/ *adj* not active –**inactively** *adv* –**inactivity** /ˌɪnæk'tɪvɨti / *n* [U]

**in·ad·e·qua·cy** /ɪn'ædɨkwɨsi/ *n* **-cies** [C;U] (an example of) the quality or state of being INADEQUATE

**in·ad·e·quate** /ɪn'ædɨkwɨt/ *adj* [*to, for*] not ADEQUATE; not good enough in quality, ability, size, etc. (for some act): *I felt inadequate in my new job, so I left.* –**inadequately** *adv*

**in·ad·ver·tent** /ˌɪnəd'vɜ:tənt‖-ɜr-/ *adj* (done) without paying attention or by accident –**inadver-**

**tently** *adv: He inadvertently knocked over his cup of coffee.*

**in·a·li·e·na·ble** /ɪn'eɪlɪənəbəl/ *adj* [*no comp.*] which cannot be taken away: *Freedom of speech should be an* **inalienable right.**

**i·nane** /ɪ'neɪn/ *adj* empty of meaning; really stupid: *an inane remark* –**inanely** *adv* –**inanity** /ɪ'nænɪ̇ti/ *n* **-ties** [C;U]

**in·an·i·mate** /ɪn'ænɪ̇mɪ̇t/ *adj* not ANIMATE[1]; not living: *Stone is inanimate.* –compare DEAD –**inanimately** *adv* –**inanimateness** *n* [U]

**in·ap·pli·ca·ble** /ɪn'æplɪkəbəl/ *adj* not APPLICABLE; which cannot be used or is unrelated to the subject –**inapplicability** /-ə'bɪlɪ̇ti / *n* [U] –**inapplicably** *adv*

**in·ap·pro·pri·ate** /ˌɪnə'prəʊpriɪ̇t/ *adj* [*for, to*] not APPROPRIATE; not suitable: *Your short dress is inappropriate for a formal party.* –**inappropriately** *adv* –**inappropriateness** *n* [U]

**in·ar·tic·u·late** /ˌɪnɑː'tɪkjʊlɪ̇t‖ˌɪnɑr'tɪkjəl/ *adj* **1** (of speech) not ARTICULATE, not well-formed; not clearly expressed **2** (of a person) speaking unclearly, so that the intended meaning is not expressed or is hard to understand –**inarticulately** *adv*

**in·as·much as** /ˌɪnəz'mʌtʃ əz/ *conj fml* owing to the fact that; because: *Their father is also guilty, inasmuch as he knew what they were going to do.*

**in·at·ten·tion** /ˌɪnə'tenʃən/ *n* [U *to*] lack of attention

**in·at·ten·tive** /ˌɪnə'tentɪv/ *adj* [*to*] not ATTENTIVE; not giving attention: *Julia is an inattentive pupil.* –**inattentively** *adv* –**inattentiveness** *n* [U]

**in·au·di·ble** /ɪn'ɔːdəbəl/ *adj* not AUDIBLE; too quiet to be heard –**inaudibility** /ɪˌnɔːdə'bɪlɪ̇ti / *n* [U] –**inaudibly** *adv*

**in·au·gu·rate** /ɪ'nɔːgjʊreɪt‖-gjə-/ *v* **-rated, -rating** [T] **1** [*usu. pass.*] to introduce (someone important) into a new place or job by holding a special ceremony **2** to open (a new building) or start (a public affair) with a ceremony –**inaugural** *adj* [A]: *an inaugural ceremony to open the new hospital* –**inauguration** /-'reɪʃən/ *n* [C;U]

**in·aus·pi·cious** /ˌɪnɔː'spɪʃəs/ *adj* not AUSPICIOUS; seeming to show bad luck to come; not giving good hopes for the future: *an inauspicious start to the term* –**inauspiciously** *adv* –**inauspiciousness** *n* [U]

**in·born** /ˌɪn'bɔːn◂‖-ɔrn/ *adj* present from birth; part of one's nature: *Birds have an inborn ability to fly.*

**in·bred** /ˌɪn'bred◂/ *adj* **1** having become part of one's nature as a result of early training **2** (resulting from being) bred from closely related members of a family

**in·breed·ing** /'ɪnbriːdɪŋ/ *n* [U] breeding from (closely) related members of a family

**Inc** /ɪŋk/ *abbrev. for*: (in the US) INCORPORATED: *General Motors, Inc* –compare LTD

**in·cal·cu·la·ble** /ɪn'kælkjʊləbəl‖-kjə-/ *adj* which cannot be counted or measured, esp. if very great: *an incalculable risk* –**incalculably** *adv*

**in·can·des·cent** /ˌɪnkæn'desənt‖-kən-/*adj* giving a bright light when heated –**incandescence** *n* [U] –**incandescently** *adv*

**in·can·ta·tion** /ˌɪnkæn'teɪʃən/ *n* [C;U] (the saying of ) words used in magic

**in·ca·pa·ble** /ɪn'keɪpəbəl/ *adj* [*of*] not CAPABLE; not able to do something: *I'm incapable of deceiving you.* –**incapability** /-ə'bɪlɪ̇ti/ *n* [U] –**incapably** *adv*

**in·ca·pa·ci·tate** /ˌɪnkə'pæsɪ̇teɪt/ *v* **-tated, -tating** [T *for*] to make (someone) not able to do something: *He was incapacitated after the accident.*

**in·ca·pa·ci·ty** /ˌɪnkə'pæsɪ̇ti/ *n* **-ties** [S;U +*to-v*/*for*] lack of ability or power (to do something)

**in·car·ce·rate** /ɪn'kɑːsəreɪt‖-ɑr-/ *v* **-rated, -rating** [T] *fml* to imprison –**incarceration** /-'reɪʃən / *n* [U]

**in·car·nate** /ɪn'kɑːnɪ̇t‖-ɑr-/ *adj* [after *n*] in the form of a body (not a spirit or idea): *the devil incarnate|She was happiness incarnate.*

**in·car·na·tion** /ˌɪnkɑː'neɪʃən‖- ɑr-/ *n* **1** [U] the act of putting an idea, spirit, etc. into bodily form; state of being INCARNATE **2** [C] a person or thing that is the perfect example of a quality

**in·cen·di·a·ry** /ɪn'sendɪəri‖-dieri/ *adj* [A] which causes fires: *an incendiary bomb*

**in·cense**[1] /'ɪnsens/ *n* [U] a substance that gives off a sweet smell when burnt, often used in religious services

**in·cense**[2] /ɪn'sens/ *v* **-censed, -censing** [T *at*] to make (someone) very angry: *I was incensed at his rudeness.*

**in·cen·tive** /ɪn'sentɪv/ *n* [C;U +*to-v*] an encouragement to greater activity: *He's got no/little incentive to work.*

**in·cep·tion** /ɪn'sepʃən/ *n fml* the beginning: *He's worked for that company from its inception.*

**in·ces·sant** /ɪn'sesənt/ *adj* never stopping: *incessant noise* –**incessantly** *adv*

**in·cest** /'ɪnsest/ *n* [U] a sexual relationship between close relatives in a family, as between brother and sister –**incestuous** /ɪn'sestʊəs/ *adj* –**incestuously** *adv*

**inch**[1] /ɪntʃ/ *n* **1** a measure of length; 1/12 of a foot (about 0·025 metres) **2 inch by inch** by a small amount at a time

**inch**[2] *v* [I;T] to (cause to) move slowly and with difficulty in the way stated: *I inched (my way)through the narrow space between the cars.*

**in·ci·dence** /'ɪnsɪ̇dəns/ *n* [S] the rate of happening: *There's a high incidence of disease there.*

**in·ci·dent** /'ɪnsɪ̇dənt/ *n* an event, esp. one in a story: *In a recent incident two bombs exploded.*

**in·ci·den·tal** /ˌɪnsɪ̇'dentəl◂/ *adj,n* [*to*] **1** (something) happening or appearing irregularly or as a less important part of something important **2** (something, esp. a fact or detail which is) unimportant: *an incidental remark*

**in·ci·den·tal·ly** /ˌɪnsɪ̇'dentəli/ *adv* (used for adding something to what was said before, either on the same or another subject) by the WAY[1] (8): *I must go now. Incidentally, if you want that book I'll bring it next time.*

**in·cin·e·rate** /ɪn'sɪnəreɪt/ *v* **-rated, -rating** [T] *fml* to destroy (unwanted things) by burning –**incineration** /-'reɪʃən / *n* [C;U]

**in·cin·e·ra·tor** /ɪn'sɪnəreɪtə[r]/ *n* a machine for burning unwanted things

**in·cip·i·ent** /ɪn'sɪpɪənt/ *adj* [*no comp.*] *fml* at an early stage: *incipient disease*

**in·ci·sion** /ɪn'sɪʒən/ *n* [C;U] *fml* the act of cutting or a cut into something,done with a special tool for a special reason: *An incision was made into his leg.*

**in·ci·sive** /ɪn'saɪsɪv/ *adj apprec* going directly to the centre or main point of the matter that is being considered: *incisive statements* –**incisively** *adv*

**in·ci·sor** /ɪn'saɪzəʳ/ *n* any of the teeth at the front of the mouth, which have one cutting edge

**in·cite** /ɪn'saɪt/ *v* **-cited, -citing** [T] **1** to (try to) cause or encourage (someone) to a strong feeling or action: *a violent speech inciting the army to attack the government* **2** to (try to) cause or lead to (a strong feeling or action): *He was charged with inciting a* RIOT[1] (1). –**incitement** *n* [C;U]

**in·clem·ent** /ɪn'klemənt/ *adj fml* (of weather) not CLEMENT; bad, esp. cold or stormy

**in·cli·na·tion** /ˌɪnklə'neɪʃən/ *n* **1** [C;U *+to-v/to, towards*] that which one likes; liking: *You always follow your own inclinations instead of thinking of our feelings.*|*I've no inclination to be a doctor.* **2** [C] a movement from a higher to a lower place **3** [S] *fml or tech* a slope; sloping position

**in·cline**[1] /ɪn'klaɪn/ *v* **-clined, -clining 1** [I;T *+to-v/to, towards*] to encourage or cause (someone) to feel, think, etc.: *The strangeness of her story inclines me to think she is telling the truth.* –compare INCLINED (1) **2** [T] *fml* to cause to move downward

**in·cline**[2] /'ɪnklaɪn/ *n* a slope: *a steep incline*

**in·clined** /ɪn'klaɪnd/ *adj* [F *+to-v*] **1** encouraged; feeling a wish (to): *The news makes me inclined to change my mind.* –see also DISINCLINED **2** likely; tending (to): *I'm inclined to get tired easily.*

**in·clude** /ɪn'klu:d/ *v* **-cluded, -cluding** [T *+v-ing*] **1** to have as a part; contain in addition to other parts: *The price includes postage charges.* –opposite **exclude**; see COMPRISE (USAGE) **2** to put in with something else: *I included eggs on the list of things to buy.*

**in·clud·ed** /ɪn'klu:dəd/ *adj* [after *n*] INCLUDING: *Take all of us, me included.*

**in·clud·ing** /ɪn'klu:dɪŋ/ *prep* having as a part; which includes: *There are six people, including three women.* –opposite **excluding**

**in·clu·sion** /ɪn'klu:ʒən/ *n* **1** [U] the act of including or state of being included –opposite **exclusion 2** [C] something that is included

**in·clu·sive** /ɪn'klu:sɪv/ *adj* **1** containing or including everything (or many things): *an inclusive charge*|*an* **all-inclusive** *price* **2** [after *n*] (of a price or charge) including other costs that are often paid separately: *The rent is £10 inclusive of heating.*|*The rent is £10 inclusive (of everything).* **3** [after *n*] including all the numbers or dates: *Wednesday to Friday inclusive.* –see also EXCLUSIVE[1] –**inclusively** *adv*

USAGE With expressions of time, American speakers often use **through** instead of **inclusive**: *Monday to Friday* **inclusive** (*BrE*)|*Monday* **through** *Friday* (*AmE*).

**in·cog·ni·to** /ˌɪnkɒg'ni:təʊ‖ˌɪnkɑg-/ *adj,adv* [F] hiding one's IDENTITY, esp. by taking another name when one's own is well-known: *travelling incognito*

**in·co·her·ent** /ˌɪnkəʊ'hɪərənt/ *adj* not COHERENT; showing lack of suitable connections between ideas or words: *He became incoherent as the disease got worse.* –**incoherence** *n* [U] –**incoherently** *adv*

**SPELLING NOTE**

Words with the sound /aɪ/ may be spelt **e-**, like **eye**. or **ai-**, like **aisle**.

**in·come** /'ɪŋkʌm, 'ɪn-/ *n* [C;U] money which one receives regularly, usu. payment for one's work,or interest from INVESTMENTS: *(a) very small/low income* –compare EXPENDITURE; see PAY[2] (USAGE)

**in·com·ing** /'ɪnkʌmɪŋ/ *adj* [A] coming towards one; about to enter or start (to be)

**in·com·mu·ni·ca·do·** /ˌɪnkəmju:nɪ'kɑ:dəʊ/ *adv, adj* [F] (of people) kept away from people outside, and not able to give or receive messages

**in·com·pa·ra·ble** /ɪn'kɒmpərəbəl‖-'kɑm-/ *adj* [*no comp.*] too great in degree to be compared with other examples of the same type; very great: *incomparable wealth* –**incomparability** /-ə'bɪləti / *n* [U] –**incomparably** *adv: incomparably beautiful*

**in·com·pat·i·ble** /ˌɪnkəm'pætəbəl/ *adj* [*with*] not COMPATIBLE; not suitable to be together with (another thing or person/each other): *Their natures are incompatible.*|*His plan is incompatible with my intentions.* –**incompatibility** /-ə'bɪləti / *n* **-ties** [C;U] –**incompatibly** *adv*

**in·com·pe·tence** /ɪn'kɒmpətəns‖-'kɑm-/ *n* [U] lack of COMPETENCE; lack of ability and skill resulting in useless work

**in·com·pe·tent** /ɪn'kɒmpətənt‖-'kɑm-/ *adj,n* [*+to-v*] (a person who is) not COMPETENT; completely unskilful (in something): *an incompetent teacher*|*He is a total incompetent.* –**incompetently** *adv*

**in·com·plete** /ˌɪnkəm'pli:t/ *adj* not complete; not perfect –**incompletely** *adv* –**incompleteness** *n* [U]

**in·com·pre·hen·si·ble** /ɪnˌkɒmprɪ'hensəbəl‖-ˌkɑm-/ *adj* [*to*] not COMPREHENSIBLE; which cannot be understood and/or accepted –**incomprehensibility** /-ə'bɪləti/ *n* [U] *adv*

**in·com·pre·hen·sion** /ɪnˌkɒmprɪ'henʃən‖-ˌkɑm-/ *n* [U] lack of COMPREHENSION; the state of not understanding

**in·con·cei·va·ble** /ˌɪnkən'si:vəbəl/ *adj* [*to*] **1** which is too strange to be thought real: *It once seemed inconceivable (to everyone) that men should travel to the moon.* –opposite **conceivable 2** *infml* impossible; which can't happen: *He can't go on holiday alone: it's inconceivable.* –**inconceivably** *adv*

**in·con·clu·sive** /ˌɪnkən'klu:sɪv/ *adj* not CONCLUSIVE; which has not led to a decision or result: *an inconclusive discussion* –**inconclusively** *adv* –**inconclusiveness** *n* [U]

**in·con·gru·ous** /ɪn'kɒŋgruəs‖-'kɑŋ-/ *adj* [*with*] comparing strangely with what surrounds it: *The modern church looks incongruous in that old-fashioned village.* –**incongruously** *adv* –**incongruousness** *n* [U] –**incongruity** /ˌɪnkən'gru:əti/ *n* **-ties** [C;U]

**in·con·se·quen·tial** /ɪnˌkɒnsə'kwenʃəl‖-ˌkɑn-/ *adj* unimportant: *an inconsequential idea* –**inconsequentially** *adv*

**in·con·sid·e·ra·ble** /ˌɪnkən'sɪdərəbəl/ *adj* of small size or worth: *a* **not inconsiderable** (=large) *sum of money* –see also CONSIDERABLE

**in·con·sid·er·ate** /ˌɪnkən'sɪdərət/ *adj derog* not CONSIDERATE; not thinking of other people's feelings: *He's often inconsiderate to his family.* –**incon-**

siderately *adv* –inconsiderateness *n* [U]

**in·con·sis·tent** /ˌɪnkənˈsɪstənt/ *adj* **1** [*with*] (of ideas, opinions, etc.) not CONSISTENT; not agreeing with something else/one another: *Those remarks are inconsistent with what you said yesterday.* **2** likely to change: *English weather is very inconsistent; one moment it's raining and the next it's sunny.* **–inconsistently** *adv* **–inconsistency** *n* **-cies** [C;U]

**in·con·so·la·ble** /ˌɪnkənˈsəʊləbəl/ *adj* unable to be comforted because of great sorrow, or too great to be removed by comforting: *inconsolable grief* **–inconsolably** *adv: inconsolably sad*

**in·con·spic·u·ous** /ˌɪnkənˈspɪkjʊəs/ *adj* not CONSPICUOUS; not easily seen; not attracting attention **–inconspicuously** *adv* **–inconspicuousness** *n* [U]

**in·con·ti·nent** /ɪnˈkɒntɪ̣nənt‖-ˈkɑn-/ *adj* unable to control the water in the BLADDER (1), so that it is passed from the body when one does not wish to pass it **–incontinence** *n* [U]

**in·con·tro·ver·ti·ble** /ɪnˌkɒntrəˈvɜːtəbəl‖ɪnˌkɑntrəˈvɜr-/ *adj* which cannot be disproved; INDISPUTABLE **–incontrovertibly** *adv*

**in·con·ve·ni·ence¹** /ˌɪnkənˈviːnɪəns/ *n* [C;U] (an example of) a state of difficulty when things do not suit one: *It causes a lot of inconvenience when buses don't come.* –see also CONVENIENCE

**inconvenience²** *v* **-enced, -encing** [T] to make things difficult for (someone): *I hope it won't inconvenience you to drive me to the station.*

**in·con·ve·ni·ent** /ˌɪnkənˈviːnɪənt/ *adj* not CONVENIENT; causing difficulty; not what suits one: *The meeting is at an inconvenient time for me; I can't come.* **–inconveniently** *adv*

**in·cor·po·rate** /ɪnˈkɔːpəreɪt‖-ɔr-/ *v* **-rated, -rating** [T *in, into, with*] to make (something) a part of a group; include: *They incorporated his new ideas into their plans.* **–incorporation** /-ˈreɪʃən/ *n* [U]

**in·cor·po·rat·ed** /ɪnˈkɔːpəreɪtɪ̣d‖-ɔr-/ also **Inc** *abbrev.– adj* [after *n*] *fml esp. AmE* formed into a CORPORATION (2) according to law –compare LIMITED (2)

**in·cor·rect** /ˌɪnkəˈrekt/ *adj* not correct **–incorrectness** *n* [U] –compare WRONG¹ (1)

**in·cor·ri·gi·ble** /ɪnˈkɒrɪ̣dʒəbəl‖-ˈkɔ-/ *adj* (of people or behaviour) very bad and unable to be changed for the better: *She's an incorrigible liar.* **–incorrigibility** /-əˈbɪlɪ̣ti/ *n* [U] **–incorrigibly** *adv*

**in·cor·rup·ti·ble** /ˌɪnkəˈrʌptəbəl/ *adj* too honest to be improperly influenced or BRIBED –see also CORRUPT

**in·crease¹** /ɪnˈkriːs/ *v* **-creased, -creasing** [I;T] to make or become larger in amount or number: *The population of this town has increased.|They have increased the price of petrol again.* –opposite **decrease**; compare REDUCE

**in·crease²** /ˈɪŋkriːs/ *n* [C;U] a rise in amount, numbers, etc.: *Crime is* **on the increase.** (=increasing) –opposite **decrease**; compare REDUCTION

**in·creas·ing·ly** /ɪnˈkriːsɪŋli/ *adv* more and more all the time: *I'm finding it increasingly difficult to live on my wages.*

**in·cred·i·ble** /ɪnˈkredəbəl/ *adj* **1** too strange to be believed; unbelievable: *an incredible idea/story/excuse* –see also CREDIBLE **2** *infml* wonderful; unbelievably good: *She has an incredible house.* **–incredibility** /-əˈbɪlɪ̣ti/ *n* [U] **–incredibly** *adv*

**in·cred·u·lous** /ɪnˈkredjʊləs‖- dʒə-/ *adj* showing disbelief: *an incredulous look* –see also CREDULOUS **–incredulously** *adv* – **incredulity** /ˌɪnkrɪ̣ˈdjuːlɪ̣ti‖-ˈduː-/ *n* [U]

**in·cre·ment** /ˈɪŋkrɪ̣mənt/ *n* [C;U] (an) increase in money or value: *She receives a salary increment each year.* **–incremental** /-ˈmentl/ *adj*

**in·crim·i·nate** /ɪnˈkrɪmɪ̣neɪt/ *v* **-nated, -nating** [T] to cause (someone) to seem guilty of a crime or fault **–incrimination** /-ˈneɪʃən/ *n* [U]

**in·cu·bate** /ˈɪŋkjʊbeɪt‖-kjə-/ *v* **-bated, -bating** [I;T] **1** to sit on and keep (eggs) warm until the young birds come out **2** (of eggs) to be kept warm until HATCHed –compare HATCH² – **incubation** *n* [U]

**in·cu·ba·tor** /ˈɪŋkjʊbeɪtəʳ‖-kjə-/ *n* a machine for **a** keeping eggs warm until they HATCH **b** keeping alive PREMATURE (2) babies

**in·cul·cate** /ˈɪnkʌlkeɪt‖ɪnˈkʌ-/ *v* **-cated, -cating** [T *with/into*] *fml* to fix (ideas, principles, etc.) in the mind of (someone)

**in·cum·bent** //ɪnˈkʌmbənt// *adj* **1** [F *on, upon*] *fml* being the moral duty of (someone): *It's incumbent on you to advise your son before he leaves home.* **2** [A] holding the stated office: *the incumbent president*

**in·cur** /ɪnˈkɜːʳ/ *v* **-rr-** [T] to receive (some unpleasant thing) as a result of certain actions: *to incur a debt*

**in·cur·a·ble** /ɪnˈkjʊərəbəl/ *adj* that cannot be cured: *an incurable disease* **–incurability** /-əˈbɪlɪ̣ti/ *n* [U] **–incurably** *adv*

**in·cur·sion** /ɪnˈkɜːʃən, - ʒən‖ɪnˈkɜrʒən/ *n fml* a sudden attack on or entrance into a place which belongs to other people

**in·debt·ed** /ɪnˈdetɪ̣d/ *adj* [*to*] very grateful to (someone) for help given: *I'm indebted to all the people who worked so hard.* **–indebtedness** *n* [U]

**in·de·cent** /ɪnˈdiːsənt/ *adj* not DECENT (1); offensive to general standards of behaviour: *an indecent remark/joke* –compare IMMODEST (2) **–indecently** *adv: indecently dressed* **–indecency** *n* **-cies** [C;U]

**in·de·ci·sion** /ˌɪndɪˈsɪʒən/ *n* [U] lack of DECISION; uncertainty before deciding to do something, choose something, etc.: *His indecision caused him to lose the chance of a new job.*

**in·de·ci·sive** /ˌɪndɪˈsaɪsɪv/ *adj* **1** (of people) not DECISIVE; unable to make decisions **2** giving an uncertain result: *an indecisive answer/victory* **–indecisively** *adv* **–indecisiveness** *n* [U]

**in·deed** /ɪnˈdiːd/ *adv* **1** (said in answers) yes, certainly: *"Did you hear the explosion?" "Indeed I did".* **2** (used after *very* to make the meaning stronger): *very cold indeed* **3** (shows surprise and often disbelief): *"I earn $1,000 a day." "Indeed!"*

**in·de·fen·si·ble** /ˌɪndɪˈfensəbəl/ *adj* which cannot be excused or defended: *indefensible behaviour*

**in·de·fi·na·ble** /ˌɪndɪˈfaɪnəbəl/ *adj* which cannot be DEFINEd or described: *There's an indefinable air of tension in this town.* **–indefinably** *adv*

**in·def·i·nite** /ɪnˈdefənɪ̣t/ *adj* not definite; not clear; not fixed, esp. as to time: *indefinite opinions|He's away for an indefinite period (of time).* **–indefiniteness** *n* [U]

**in·def·i·nite·ly** /ɪnˈdefənɪ̣tli/ *adv* for a period of

time without a fixed end: *You can borrow the book indefinitely.*

**in·del·i·ble** /ɪn'deləbəl/ *adj* which cannot be rubbed out: *indelible ink|an indelible pencil* –**indelibly** *adv* : *an experience indelibly printed on my memory*

**in·del·i·cate** /ɪn'delǝkǝt/ *adj* not delicate; not polite or modest; rough in manners: *Her indelicate remark hurt his feelings.* –**indelicately** *adv* –**indelicacy** /ɪn'delǝkəsi / *n* **-cies** [C;U]

**in·dem·ni·fy** /ɪn'demnǝfaɪ/ *v* **-fied, -fying** [T] *against, for*] to (promise to) pay (someone) in case of loss, hurt, or damage –**indemnification** /-fǝ'keɪʃən/ *n* [C;U]

**in·dem·ni·ty** /ɪn'demnǝti/ *n* **-ties 1** [U] protection against loss, esp. in the form of a promise to pay **2** [C] payment for loss of money, goods, etc.

**in·dent** /ɪn'dent/ *v* [I;T] to start (a line of writing) further into the page than the others: *You must indent the first line of a new paragraph.*

**in·de·pen·dence** /ˌɪndǝ'pendəns/ *n* [U *from*] the quality or state of being independent; freedom: *This money gives me independence from my family.|India gained independence from Britain in 1947.*

**in·de·pen·dent** /ˌɪndǝ'pendənt◂/ *adj* **1** not governed by another country: *Zimbabwe became independent in 1980.* **2** [*of*] not needing other things or people: *She's very independent and lives all alone.* –see also DEPENDENT –**independently** *adv*

**in·de·scri·ba·ble** /ˌɪndɪs'kraɪbəbəl/ *adj* which cannot be described, e.g. because beautiful beyond belief –**indescribably** *adv*

**in·de·struc·ti·ble** /ˌɪndɪ'strʌktəbəl/ *adj* being too strong to be destroyed –**indestructibility** /-ə'bɪlǝti/ *n* [U] –**indestructibly** *adv*

**in·de·ter·mi·nate** /ˌɪndɪ'tɜːmǝnǝt‖-ɜr-/ *adj* not clearly seen as, or not fixed as, one thing or another: *Our holiday plans are still at an indeterminate stage.*

**in·dex¹** /'ɪndeks/ *n* **-dexes** *or* **-dices 1** an alphabetical list at the back of a book, on a series of cards (**index cards**) etc., of names, subjects, etc.,mentioned in it and the pages where they can be found –compare CONTENTS (2); see picture on page 415 **2** the system of numbers by which prices, costs, etc., can be compared to a former level: *the* **cost of living index**

**index²** *v* [T] to provide with or include in an INDEX¹

**index fin·ger** /'·· ˌ··/ *n* →FOREFINGER

**in·di·an** /'ɪndɪən/ *n,adj* **1** (a person) belonging to or connected with India **2** also **American Indian**– (a person) belonging to or connected with any of the original peoples of America except the Eskimos

**in·di·cate** /'ɪndǝkeɪt/ *v* **-cated, -cating 1** [T] to point at; draw attention to: *I asked him where my sister was and he indicated the shop opposite.* **2** [T +(*that*)] to show by a sign; make clear: *I indicated that his help was not welcome.* **3** [I;T +(*that*)] to show (the direction in which one is turning in a vehicle) by hand signals, lights, etc.: *He's indicating left.|Don't forget to indicate.* –**indication** /-'keɪsən/ *n* [C;U +*that/of*]: *There is every indication* (=a strong likelihood) *of a change in the weather.*

**SPELLING NOTE**

Words with the sound /aɪ/ may be spelt **e-**, like **eye.** or **ai-**, like **aisle.**

**in·dic·a·tive** /ɪn'dɪkətɪv/ *adj* [F +*that/of*] showing; suggesting: *His presence is indicative of his wish to help/that he wishes to help.* –**indicatively** *adv*

**in·di·ca·tor** /'ɪndǝkeɪtəʳ/ *n* **1** any of the lights on a car which flash to show which way it is turning –see picture on page 85 **2** a needle or pointer on a machine showing the measure of some quality

**in·di·ces** /'ɪndǝsiːz/ *n plural of* INDEX

**in·dict** /ɪn'daɪt/ *v* [T *for*] *fml* to charge (someone) formally with an offence in law –**indictable** *adj: an indictable offence* –**indictment** *n* [C;U]

**in·dif·fer·ent** /ɪn'dɪfərənt/ *adj* **1** [*to*] not interested in; not caring about or noticing: *I was so excited to see snow that I was indifferent to the cold.* **2** not very good –see DIFFERENT (USAGE) –**indifferently** *adv* –**indifference** *n* [U *to, towards*]: *He treats me with indifference.*

**in·di·ge·nous** /ɪn'dɪdʒənəs/ *adj* [*to*] *fml or tech* native; belonging (to a place) –**indigenously** *adv*

**in·di·ges·ti·ble** /ˌɪndɪ'dʒestəbəl/ *adj* (of food) not easily broken down in the stomach into substances to be used by the body –see also DIGEST¹ –**indigestibility** /-ə'bɪlǝti / *n* [U]

**in·di·ges·tion** /ˌɪndɪ'dʒestʃən/ *n* [U] illness or pain caused by the stomach being unable to deal with the food which has been eaten

**in·dig·nant** /ɪn'dɪgnənt/ *adj* [*at, over, about*] expressing or feeling surprised anger (at something which should not be so) –**indignantly** *adv*

**in·dig·na·tion** /ˌɪndɪg'neɪʃən/ *n* [U *at, over, about*] feelings of anger (against something wrong): *I expressed my indignation at being unfairly dismissed.*

**in·dig·ni·ty** /ɪn'dɪgnǝti/ *n* **-ties** [C;U] (an example of) a state which makes one feel shame or that one is on public show: *I suffered the indignity of having to say I was sorry in front of all those people.*

**in·di·rect** /ˌɪndǝ'rekt◂/ *adj* not straight; not directly connected (to or with): *The taxi driver took an indirect* ROUTE *to avoid the town centre.|The accident was an indirect result of her lack of care.|*(fig.) *an indirect answer* –opposite **direct** –**indirectly** *adv* –**indirectness** *n* [U]

**in·dis·ci·pline** /ɪn'dɪsǝplǝn/ *n* [U] lack of DISCIPLINE¹ (2); state of disorder because of lack of control

**in·dis·creet** /ˌɪndɪ'skriːt/ *adj* not DISCREET; not acting carefully and politely, esp. in the choice of what one says and does not say –**indiscreetly** *adv*

**in·dis·cre·tion** /ˌɪndɪ'skreʃən/ *n* [C;U] (an example of) the state or quality of being INDISCREET; lack of DISCRETION (1)

**in·dis·crim·i·nate** /ˌɪndɪ'skrɪmǝnǝt/ *adj* [*no comp.*] not choosing or chosen carefully: *the terrorists' indiscriminate murder of ordinary people* –**indiscriminately** *adv*

**in·di·spen·sa·ble** /ˌɪndɪ'spensəbəl/ *adj* [*to*] that is too important to live or be without: *She's become quite indispensable to the company.* –**indispensability** /-ə'bɪlǝti / *n* [U] –**indispensably** *adv*

**in·dis·posed** /ˌɪndɪ'spəuzd/ *adj fml* [F] not very well (in health): *His wife says he's indisposed, but I know he's drunk.* –compare DISPOSED –**indisposition** /ɪnˌdɪspǝ'zɪʃən/ *n* [C;U]

**in·dis·pu·ta·ble** /ˌɪndɪ'spjuːtəbəl/ *adj* being too certain to be questioned –opposite **disputable** –**indisputably** *adv*

**in·dis·tinct** /ˌɪndɪ'stɪŋkt/ *adj* not DISTINCT (2); not clear to the eye or mind or ear: *I have only an indistinct memory of my father.*|*There is a large indistinct area in the photograph.* –**indistinctly** *adv* –**indistinctness** *n* [U]

**in·dis·tin·guish·a·ble** /ˌɪndɪ'stɪngwɪʃəbəl/ *adj* [*from*] not DISTINGUISHABLE; which cannot be seen or known to be different from something else or each other: *The material is indistinguishable from real silk, but much cheaper.* –**indistinguishably** *adv*

**in·di·vid·u·al**[1] /ˌɪndɨ'vɪdʒuəl/ *adj* (*often with* each) single; particular; separate: *Each individual leaf on the tree is different.*|*Individual attention must be given to every fault in the material.*|*She wears very individual clothes.* (=different from other people's)

**individual**[2] *n* **1** a single being or member of a group, treated separately: *The rights of the individual are the most important in a free society.* **2** *infml* a person: *What a bad-tempered individual you are!*

**in·di·vid·u·al·i·ty** /ˌɪndɨˌvɪdʒʊ'ælɨti/ *n* -**ties** [S;U] the character and qualities which make someone or something different from all others –**individualist** /ˌɪndɨ'vɪdʒuəlɨst/ *n*

**in·di·vid·u·al·ly** /ˌɪndɨ'vɪdʒuəli/ *adv* one by one; separately: *Individually, the children are quite nice, but in a group they're very badly-behaved.*

**in·di·vis·i·ble** /ˌɪndɨ'vɪzəbəl/ *adj* which cannot be divided or separated into parts –**indivisibility** /-ə'bɪlɨ ti / *n* [U] –**indivisibly** *adv*

**in·doc·tri·nate** /ɪn'dɒktrɨneɪt‖ɪn'dɑk-/ *v* -**nated,** -**nating** [T *with*] *usu. derog* to put ideas into (someone's) mind: *They have those political opinions because they've been indoctrinated all their lives.* –**indoctrination** /-'neɪʃən / *n* [U]

**in·do·lent** /'ɪndələnt/ *adj fml* lazy; not liking to be active –**indolently** *adv* –**indolence** *n* [U]

**in·dom·i·ta·ble** /ɪn'dɒmɨtəbəl‖ɪn'dɑ-/ *adj fml* too strong to be discouraged: *a man of indomitable spirit* –**indomitably** *adv*

**in·door** /'ɪndɔːʳ‖'ɪndor/ *adj* [A] which is (done, used, etc.) inside a building: *indoor sports*|*indoor clothes* –opposite **outdoor**

**in·doors** /ˌɪn'dɔːz◄‖-orz◄/ *adv* to(wards), in, or into the inside of a building: *We went indoors.*|*We stayed indoors.* –opposite **outdoors**

**in·du·bi·ta·ble** /ɪn'djuːbɨtəbəl‖ɪn'duː-/ *adj fml* which cannot be doubted to be so; unquestionable –**indubitably** *adv*

**in·duce** /ɪn'djuːs‖ɪn'duːs/ *v* -**duced,** -**ducing** [T] *fml* **1** to lead (someone) (into an act) often by persuading: *I was induced to come against my will.* **2** to cause or produce: *Too much food induces sleepiness.*

**in·duce·ment** /ɪn'djuːsmənt‖ɪn'duːs-/ *n* [C;U +*to-v*] (something which provides) encouragement to do something: *I gave him money as an inducement to leave.*

**in·duc·tion** /ɪn'dʌkʃən/ *n* [U] the act or ceremony of introducing a person to a new job, organization, etc.

**in·dulge** /ɪn'dʌldʒ/ *v* -**dulged,** -**dulging** [I;T] **1** to allow (someone) to do or have what they want: *He indulges his children.* **2** [*in*] *infml* to let (oneself) have what one wants, esp. too much: *He's not really a drinker, but he indulges* (=drinks too much) *at parties.*|*I sometimes* **indulge in** *a cigarette.*

**in·dul·gence** /ɪn'dʌldʒəns/ *n* **1** [U] the habit of allowing someone to do or have what they want: *His indulgence to his children was bad for them.* **2** [C] something in which someone INDULGES: *Sweets are my only indulgence.* –**indulgent** *adj: indulgent parents* –**indulgently** *adv*

**in·dus·tri·al** /ɪn'dʌstrɪəl/ *adj* **1** of industry and the people who work in it: *industrial unrest* **2** having highly developed industries –compare: *Japan is an* **industrial** *nation.*|*The Japanese are an* **industrious** (=hard-working) *nation.* –**industrially** *adv*

**in·dus·tri·al·ist** /ɪn'dʌstrɪəlɨst/ *n* a person who is closely concerned in the system of earning profits in industry, esp. a factory owner

**in·dus·tri·al·ize** ‖also -**ise** *BrE* /ɪn'dʌstrɪəlaɪz/ *v* -**ized,** -**izing** [I;T] to (cause to) become industrially developed –**industrialization** /ɪnˌdʌstrɪəlaɪ'zeɪʃən‖ -lə- / *n* [U]

**in·dus·tri·ous** /ɪn'dʌstrɪəs/ *adj* hard-working –compare INDUSTRIAL –**industriously** *adv* –**industriousness** *n* [U]

**in·dus·try** /'ɪndəstri/ *n* -**tries** **1** [U] (the work of ) factories and large organizations generally: *The country is supported by industry.* **2** [C] a particular sort of work, usu. employing lots of people and using machinery to produce goods: *the clothing industry* **3** [U] continual hard work

**i·ne·bri·at·ed** /ɪ'niːbrieɪtɨd/ *adj fml or pomp* drunk –**inebriation** /-'eɪʃən/ *n* [U]

**in·ed·i·ble** /ɪn'edəbəl/ *adj* not EDIBLE; not suitable for eating

**in·ef·fa·ble** /ɪn'efəbəl/ *adj fml* too wonderful to be described in words: *ineffable joy* –**ineffably** *adv*

**in·ef·fec·tive** /ˌɪnɨ'fektɪv/ also **ineffectual** /ˌɪnɨ 'fektʃuəl/– *adj* not EFFECTIVE; which does not produce any result or who cannot do anything well: *an ineffectual plan/person* –compare EFFECTUAL –**ineffectively** *adv* –**ineffectiveness** *n* [U]

**in·ef·fi·cient** /ˌɪnɨ'fɪʃənt/ *adj* not EFFICIENT; that does not work well so as to produce good results quickly: *an inefficient machine*|*an inefficient secretary* –**inefficiently** *adv* –**inefficiency** *n* [U]

**in·el·e·gant** /ɪn'elɪgənt/ *adj* not ELEGANT; lacking grace; awkward –**inelegantly** *adv* –**inelegance** *n* [U]

**in·el·i·gi·ble** /ɪn'elɨdʒəbəl/ *adj* [+*to-v*/*for*] not ELIGIBLE: *He was ineligible to vote, because he didn't belong to the club.* –**ineligibility** /-ə'bɪlɨti / *n* [U]

**in·ept** /ɪ'nept/ *adj* **1** totally unable to do things: *He's inept at tennis.* **2** foolishly unsuitable: *an inept remark* –**ineptly** *adv* –**ineptitude** also **ineptness**– *n* [U]

**in·e·qual·i·ty** /ˌɪnɪ'kwɒlɨti‖-'kwa-/ *n* -**ties** [C;U] (an example of) lack of equality: *social inequality*|*There are many inequalities in the law.*

**in·ert** /ɪ'nɜːt‖-ɜrt/ *adj* [*no comp.*] **1** lacking the power or will to move: *inert matter* **2** *tech* not acting chemically with other substances: *inert gases* –**inertly** *adv*

**in·er·tia** /ɪ'nɜːʃə‖-ɜr-/ *n* [U] the force which makes a person or thing stay in the state or position which they are in

**in·es·ca·pa·ble** /ˌɪnɪs'keɪpəbəl/ *adj* which cannot be escaped from or avoided

**in·es·sen·tial** /ˌɪnɨ'senʃəl/ *adj,n* [*to*] (something which is) not ESSENTIAL; not at all necessary

**in·es·ti·ma·ble** /ɪn'estɨməbəl/ *adj* too great to be calculated; very important: *inestimable value* –see also ESTIMATE, ESTIMABLE **–inestimably** *adv*

**in·ev·i·ta·ble** /ɪ'nevɨtəbəl/ *adj* **1** which cannot be prevented from happening: *An argument was inevitable because they disliked each other so much.* **2** [A] *infml* which always happens, or is present with someone or something else **–inevitability** /-ə'bɪlɨti / *n* [U] **–inevitably** *adv*

**in·ex·act** /ˌɪnɪg'zækt/ *adj* not exact **–inexactitude** also **inexactness–** *n* [C;U]

**in·ex·cu·sa·ble** /ˌɪnɪk'skjuːzəbəl/ *adj* which is too bad to be excused: *inexcusable behaviour/lateness* –opposite **excusable –inexcusably** *adv*

**in·ex·haus·ti·ble** /ˌɪnɪg'zɔːstəbəl/ *adj* which is in such large amounts that it can never be finished **–inexhaustibly** *adv*

**in·ex·o·ra·ble** /ɪn'eksərəbəl/ *adj fml* whose actions or effects cannot be changed or prevented by one's efforts **–inexorably** *adv* **–inexorability** /- ə'bɪlɨti / *n* [U]

**in·ex·pe·di·ent** /ˌɪnɪk'spiːdɪənt/ *adj* (of acts) not EXPEDIENT[1]; not suitable or advisable **inexpedience** *n* [U]

**in·ex·pen·sive** /ˌɪnɪk'spensɪv/ *adj fml* not EXPENSIVE; cheap; low in price **–inexpensively** *adv*

**in·ex·pe·ri·ence** /ˌɪnɪk'spɪərɪəns/ *n* [U] lack of experience

**in·ex·pe·ri·enced** /ˌɪnɪk'spɪərɪənst/ *adj* (of people) not experienced; lacking the knowledge which one gains by experiencing some activity or life generally: *an inexperienced driver*

**in·ex·plic·a·ble** /ˌɪnɪk'splɪkəbəl/ *adj* not EXPLICABLE; which is too strange to be explained or understood: *The inexplicable disappearance of the woman worried everyone.* **–inexplicably** *adv*

**in·ex·pres·si·ble** /ˌɪnɪk'spresəbəl/ *adj* (of feelings) too great or too strong to be expressed in words **–inexpressibly** *adv*

**in·ex·tri·ca·ble** /ɪn'ekstrɪkəbəl, ˌɪnɪk'strɪ-/ *adj fml* which cannot be escaped from **–inextricably** *adv: Our fates are inextricably joined.*

**in·fal·li·ble** /ɪn'fæləbəl/ *adj* **1** (of people) not FALLIBLE; never making mistakes or doing anything bad **2** (of things) always having the right effect: *an infallible cure* **–infallibility** /-ə'bɪlɨti / *n* [U]

**in·fa·mous** /'ɪnfəməs/ *adj* well known for wicked behaviour: *an infamous criminal* –see FAMOUS (USAGE)

**in·fa·my** /'ɪnfəmi/ *n* **-mies** [C;U] (an example of) the quality of being INFAMOUS

**in·fan·cy** /'ɪnfənsi/ *n* [S;U] early childhood: *a happy infancy*|(fig.) *Our new plan is still only* **in its infancy.**

**in·fant** /'ɪnfənt/ *n* [A;C] a very young child: *a high rate of infant* MORTALITY|*An* **infant school** *is a school for children from about five to seven years of age.* –see CHILD (USAGE)

**SPELLING NOTE**
Words with the sound /aɪ/ may be spelt **e-**, like **eye**. or **ai-**, like **aisle**.

**in·fan·tile** /'ɪnfəntaɪl/ *adj* like, concerning, or happening to small children: *infantile illnesses*|*His behaviour is infantile* (=very foolish) *for a man of 35.*

**in·fan·try** /'ɪnfəntri/ *n* [U +*sing./pl. v*] soldiers who fight on foot: *The infantry was/were fighting bravely.* –compare CAVALRY

**in·fat·u·at·ed** /ɪn'fætʃueɪtɨd/ *adj* [*with*] (of people) filled with a strong unreasonable feeling of love for (someone) **–infatuation** /ɪnˌfætʃʊ'eɪʃən/ *n* [C;U *with*]

**in·fect** /ɪn'fekt/ *v* [T *with*] to put disease into the body of (someone): *The disease infected her eyes, and she became blind.*

**in·fec·tion** /ɪn'fekʃən/ *n* [C;U] (an example of) the state or result of being infected, or the action of infecting: *infection from impure water/by flies*|*She is suffering from a lung infection.*

**in·fec·tious** /ɪn'fekʃəs/ *adj* (of a disease) which can be spread by infection, esp. in the air: *Colds are infectious.*|(fig.) *infectious laughter* –compare CONTAGIOUS **–infectiously** *adv* **–infectiousness** *n* [U]

**in·fer** /ɪn'fɜːʳ/ *v* **-rr-** [T +(*that*)/*from*] to come to an opinion after thinking about (something): *I infer from your letter that you do not wish to see us.* **–inference** *n* [C;U]

USAGE Compare **imply** and **infer**. The speaker or writer **implies** something, and the listener or reader **infers** it: *His remarks* **implied** (=suggested indirectly) *that he hadn't enjoyed his holiday.*|*I* **inferred** *from his remarks that he hadn't enjoyed his holiday* (=this was the meaning I drew). Although **infer** is often used to mean **imply**, this is not correct.

**in·fe·ri·or**[1] /ɪn'fɪərɪəʳ/ *adj* [*to*] (of people and things) not good or less good in quality or value: *His work is inferior to mine.*|*He's so clever, he makes me feel inferior.* –opposite **superior**; see MAJOR (USAGE) **–inferiority** /ɪnˌfɪəri'ɒrɨti‖-'ɑrɨ- / *n* [U]

**inferior**[2] *n often derog* a person of lower rank, esp. in a job –compare SUPERIOR[2] (1), SUBORDINATE (1)

**in·fer·nal** /ɪn'fɜːnəl‖-ɜr-/ *adj* **1** *infml* very bad; very annoying: *Stop that infernal noise!* **2** of HELL[1] (1): *the infernal powers* **–infernally** *adv*

**in·fer·no** /ɪn'fɜːnəʊ‖-ɜr-/ *n* **-nos** a place or state that is like HELL: *The burning building became an inferno.*

**in·fer·tile** /ɪn'fɜːtaɪl‖-ɜrtəl/ *adj* not FERTILE; not able to produce young; (of land) not able to grow plants **–infertility** /ˌɪnfɜː'tɪlɨti‖-ɜr- / *n* [U]

**in·fest** /ɪn'fest/ *v* [T *with*] to cause trouble to or in, by being present in large numbers: **–infestation** /ˌɪnfe'steɪʃən / *n* [C;U]

**in·fi·del** /'ɪnfɨdl/ *n old use* (used esp. in former times by Christians and Muslims of each other) an unbeliever

**in·fi·del·i·ty** /ˌɪnfɨ'delɨti/ *n* **-ties** [C;U] (an example or act of) disloyalty or being UNFAITHFUL, esp. to one's marriage partner –see also FIDELITY

**in·fight·ing** /'ɪnfaɪtɪŋ/ *n* [U] competition and disagreement, often bitter, between close members of a group

**in·fil·trate** /'ɪnfɪltreɪt‖ɪn'fɪltreɪt, 'ɪnfɪl-/ *v* **-trated, -trating** [T *in, into*] to (cause to) go into and among (the parts or members of something), esp. quietly and with an unfriendly purpose: *to infiltrate a political party* –**infiltrator** *n* –**infiltration** /-'treɪʃən/ *n* [U]

**in·fi·nite** /'ɪnfɪnɪt/ *adj* [*no comp.*] not FINITE; without limits or end: *infinite kindness* –**infinitely** *adv: That was infinitely* (=much) *better than his last film.*

**in·fin·i·tes·i·mal** /ˌɪnfɪnɪ'tesɪməl/ *adj* [*no comp.*] very, very small –**infinitesimally** *adv*

**in·fin·i·tive** /ɪn'fɪnɪtɪv/ *n,adj tech* (of) the form of the verb that can be used after other verbs and with *to* before it (such as *go* in *I can go, I want to go,* and *It is important to go*)

**in·fin·i·ty** /ɪn'fɪnɪti/ *n* [S;U] limitless time or space: *the infinity of the universe*

**in·firm** /ɪn'fɜːm‖-ɜrm/ *adj fml* weak in body or mind, esp. from age: *old and infirm*

**in·fir·ma·ry** /ɪn'fɜːməri/ *n* **-ries** a hospital or other place where the sick are given care and treatment: *the school infirmary*

**in·fir·mi·ty** /ɪn'fɜːmɪti/ *n* **-ties** [C;U] *fml* (an example of) weakness of body or mind: *The old woman was suffering from age and infirmity.*

**in·flame** /ɪn'fleɪm/ *v* **-flamed, -flaming** [T *with*] to fill (someone) with strong feelings: *inflamed with desire/anger*

**in·flamed** /ɪn'fleɪmd/ *adj* (of a part of the body) red and swollen because hurt or diseased

**in·flam·ma·ble** /ɪn'flæməbəl/ also **flammable** *esp. AmE* or *tech*– *adj* which can be set on fire: *Petrol is highly inflammable.* –opposite **nonflammable** –compare INFLAMMATORY; see FLAMMABLE (USAGE)

**in·flam·ma·tion** /ˌɪnflə'meɪʃən/ *n* [C;U] swelling and soreness, which is often red and hot to the touch

**in·flam·ma·to·ry** /ɪn'flæmətəri‖-tori/ *adj* likely to cause strong feelings to rise, or violence to happen: *an inflammatory speech* –see also INFLAME; compare INFLAMMABLE

**in·fla·ta·ble** /ɪn'fleɪtəbəl/ *adj* which can be INFLATED for use

**in·flate** /ɪn'fleɪt/ *v* **-flated, -flating** [I;T] *fml* to (cause to) fill until swelled with air, gas, etc.; BLOW **up** (2) –opposite **deflate**

**in·flat·ed** /ɪn'fleɪtɪd/ *adj* **1** blown up (as with air): *an inflated tyre* **2** *fml* filled with pride: *He has an inflated opinion of his own importance.*

**in·fla·tion** /ɪn'fleɪʃən/ *n* [U] the condition in which prices keep rising, esp. to an undesirable degree: *The rate of inflation was 10%* (=prices rose by 10%) *last year.* –see also DEFLATE –**inflationary** *adj: the government's inflationary policies*

**in·flect** /ɪn'flekt/ *v* [I;T] *tech* **1** (of a word) to change in form at its end according to use: *The word "child" inflects differently in the plural to the word "boy".|an inflected verb|In "largest",* **-est** *is the inflection meaning "most".* **2** to cause (a word) to change in form according to use

**in·flex·i·ble** /ɪn'fleksəbəl/ *adj* not FLEXIBLE; which cannot be bent; (of people) not easily turned away from their purpose: *You'll never get him to change his mind; he's so inflexible.* –see also FLEX[1], FLEXIBLE –**inflexibility** /-ə'bɪlɪti / *n* [U] –**inflexibly** *adv*

**in·flict** sthg. **on** sbdy. /ɪn'flɪkt/ also **inflict** sthg. **upon** sbdy.– *v prep* [T] to force (something unwanted or unpleasant) on: *Don't inflict your ideas on me.*|**(fig.)** *Mary inflicted the children on her mother for the weekend.* –**infliction** *n* [C;U]

**in·flu·ence[1]** /'ɪnfluəns/ *n* **1** [C;U *over, with, on, upon*] **a** (the action of) power to gain an effect on the mind of or get results from, without asking or doing anything: *He has a strange influence over the girl.|Her influence made me a better person.|He used his influence* (=power) *to get his friend a job.* **b** a person with this power: *He's an influence for good in the club.|He is* **a good/bad influence** *on my daughter.* **2 under the influence of** in the power of; experiencing the effects of (people, things): *driving under the influence of alcohol*

**influence[2]** *v* **-enced, -encing** [T] to have an effect on; AFFECT[1]: *Don't let me influence your decision.*

**in·flu·en·tial** /ˌɪnflʊ'enʃəl/ *adj* having great influence: *an influential decision/man* –**influentially** *adv*

**in·flu·en·za** /ˌɪnflʊ'enzə/ *n* [U] *fml* or *tech* for FLU

**in·flux** /'ɪnflʌks/ *n* [*usu. sing.*] the arrival, or movement inwards, of large numbers/quantities: *There was a sudden influx of goods onto the market.*

**in·form** /ɪn'fɔːm‖-ɔrm/ *v* [T +*that/of, about*] *fml* to tell; to give information to: *I informed him (about) where to go.* –see SAY (USAGE)

**inform against/on/upon** sbdy. *v prep* [T] to tell the police, or someone in charge, about (someone who has done something wrong) –**informer** *n*

**in·for·mal** /ɪn'fɔːməl‖-ɔr-/ *adj* not formal; without ceremony: *an informal meeting|informal clothes/language* –**informality** /ˌɪnfɔː'mælɪti‖-ɔr- / *n* [U] –**informally** *adv*

**in·for·mant** /ɪn'fɔːmənt‖-ɔr-/ *n* a person who gives information

**in·for·ma·tion** /ˌɪnfə'meɪʃən‖-ər-/ *n* [U] (something which gives) knowledge in the form of facts: *The police haven't got enough information to catch the criminal.*

**in·for·ma·tive** /ɪn'fɔːmətɪv‖-ɔr-/ *adj* that tells one some useful things: *an informative television programme* –opposite **uninformative** –**informatively** *adv*

**in·formed** /ɪn'fɔːmd‖-ɔr-/ *adj* knowing things; having all the information: *well-informed|badly informed|I read the newspapers to keep myself informed about what is happening.* –opposite **uninformed**

**in·fra·red** /ˌɪnfrə'red◂/ *adj* of the heat-giving RAYS of light of longer wave-length than the red light which can be seen –compare ULTRAVIOLET

**in·fra·struc·ture** /'ɪnfrəˌstrʌktʃə[r]/ *n* the system which supports the operation of an organization: *the country's transport infrastructure* (=its roads, railways, etc.)

**in·fre·quent** /ɪn'friːkwənt/ *adj* not frequent; not (happening) often: *infrequent visits* –**infrequently** *adv* –**infrequency** *n* [U]

**in·fringe** /ɪn'frɪndʒ/ *v* **-fringed, -fringing** [T] to go against or take over (the right of another): *to* **infringe on/upon** *a nation's fishing rights at sea* –**infringement** *n* [C;U]: *Stealing is an infringement of the law.*

**in·fu·ri·ate** /ɪn'fjʊərieɪt/ *v* **-ated, -ating** [T] to make (someone) very angry

**in·fuse** /ɪn'fjuːz/ *v* **-fused, -fusing 1** [T] to put (a substance such as tea) in hot water so as to make a liquid of a certain taste **2** [*with*] to fill (someone) with a quality –**infusion** /ɪn'fjuːʒən/ *n* [C;U]: *an infusion of new ideas*

**in·ge·ni·ous** /ɪn'dʒiːnɪəs/ *adj* having or showing cleverness at making or inventing things: *an ingenious person/idea/toy* –compare: *He invented an* **ingenious** *excuse for being late.|Only the most* **ingenuous** *person would believe such a weak excuse!* –**ingeniously** *adv*

**in·ge·nu·i·ty** /ˌɪndʒ$_{\text{ə}}^{\text{I}}$'njuːˌ$_{\text{ə}}^{\text{I}}$ti‖-'nuː-/ *n* [U] skill and cleverness in making or arranging things

**in·gen·u·ous** /ɪn'dʒenjʊəs/ *adj* (of people and their acts) simple, direct, and inexperienced: *He is too ingenuous in believing what people say.* –compare INGENIOUS –**ingenuously** *adv* –**ingenuousness** *n* [U]

**in·got** /'ɪŋgət/ *n* a lump of metal in a regular shape, often brick-shaped; bar (of gold or silver)

**in·grained** /ɪn'greɪnd/ *adj* fixed deep (inside) so that it is difficult to get out or destroy: *ingrained dirt|ingrained habits*

**in·gra·ti·ate** /ɪn'greɪʃieɪt/ *v* **-ated, -ating** [T *with*] to make (oneself ) very pleasant to someone in order to gain favour: *He ingratiated himself with his employer.* –**ingratiating** *adj: an ingratiating smile* –**ingratiatingly** *adv*

**in·grat·i·tude** /ɪn'grætˌ$_{\text{ə}}^{\text{I}}$tjuːd‖-tuːd/ *n* [U] lack of GRATITUDE; ungratefulness

**in·gre·di·ent** /ɪn'griːdɪənt/ *n* one of a mixture of things from which something is made: *There's a list of the ingredients on the side of the packet.*

**in·hab·it** /ɪn'hæb$_{\text{ə}}^{\text{I}}$t/ *v* [T not *be +v-ing*] to live in –see also UNINHABITABLE –**inhabitable** *adj: an inhabitable area*

**in·hab·i·tant** /ɪn'hæb$_{\text{ə}}^{\text{I}}$tənt/ *n* a person who lives in a particular place: *inhabitants of large cities*

**in·hale** /ɪn'heɪl/ *v* **-haled, -haling** [I;T] to breathe (something) in: *He inhaled deeply.|He inhaled (smoke) deeply from his cigarette.* –opposite **exhale**

**in·her·ent** /ɪn'hɪərənt, -'he-/ *adj* [*in*] forming a natural part (of a set of qualities, a character, etc.): *The desire for freedom is inherent in us all.*

**in·her·ent·ly** /ɪn'hɪərəntli, -'he-/ *adv* in itself or oneself; by its or one's nature; as such; INTRINSICally

**in·her·it** /ɪn'her$_{\text{ə}}^{\text{I}}$t/ *v* [I;T *from*] to receive (property, a title, etc.) left by someone who has died: (fig.) *She inherited all her mother's beauty.* –see also DISINHERIT –**inheritance** *n* [C;U]

**in·hib·it** /ɪn'hɪb$_{\text{ə}}^{\text{I}}$t/ *v* [T *from*] to hold back (from something); to make INHIBITED: *His presence inhibits me.*

**in·hib·it·ed** /ɪn'hɪb$_{\text{ə}}^{\text{I}}$t$_{\text{ə}}^{\text{I}}$d/ *adj* (of people and character) unable to express what one really feels or do what one really wants: *She is too inhibited to laugh freely/to talk about sex.* –compare UNINHIBITED –**inhibitedly** *adv*

**in·hi·bi·tion** /ˌɪnh$_{\text{ə}}^{\text{I}}$'bɪʃən/ *n* [C;U] the state of, or a feeling of, being INHIBITED: *She soon loses her inhibitions when she's had two or three glasses of wine.*

**in·hos·pi·ta·ble** /ˌɪnhɒ'spɪtəbəl‖-hɑ-/ *adj* not HOSPITABLE; not showing kindness esp. not giving food and shelter in one's own home –**inhospitably** *adv*

> **SPELLING NOTE**
> Words with the sound /aɪ/ may be spelt **e-**, like **eye**. or **ai-**, like **aisle**.

**in·hu·man** /ɪn'hjuːmən/ *adj* too cruel, lacking in feelings, etc., to be worthy of human behaviour –compare INHUMANE; see also HUMAN

**in·hu·mane** /ˌɪnhjuː'meɪn/ *adj* (of people and their acts) not HUMANE; not showing human kindness: *inhumane treatment of animals* –compare INHUMAN –**inhumanely** *adv*

**in·hu·man·i·ty** /ˌɪnhjuː'mæn$_{\text{ə}}^{\text{I}}$ti/ *n* **-ties** [C;U] (an example of) lack of HUMANITY (1); the quality or state of being cruel and harming other human beings

**in·im·i·ta·ble** /ɪ'nɪm$_{\text{ə}}^{\text{I}}$təbəl/ *adj* too good for anyone else to copy with the same high quality –see also IMITATE –**inimitably** *adv*

**in·iq·ui·tous** /ɪ'nɪkw$_{\text{ə}}^{\text{I}}$təs/ *adj fml* very unjust or wicked –**iniquitously** *adv* –**iniquity** *n* **-ties** [C;U]

**i·ni·tial**[1] /ɪ'nɪʃəl/ *adj* [A *no comp.*] which is (at) the beginning of a set: *The initial talks were the base of the later agreement.* –**initially** *adv: Initially, she opposed the plan, but later she changed her mind.*

**initial**[2] *n* a large letter at the beginning of a name: *Steven Lane's initials are S.L.*

**initial**[3] *v* **-ll-** *BrE*‖**-l-** *AmE* [T] to sign one's name on (a piece of writing) by writing one's INITIALS,usu. to show approval or agreement

**i·ni·ti·ate** /ɪ'nɪʃieɪt/ *v* **-ated, -ating 1** [T] to start (something) working **2** [*into*] to introduce (someone) into a club, group, etc., esp. with a special ceremony –**initiation** /-'eɪʃən/ *n* [C;U]: *initiation into a secret society*

**i·ni·tia·tive** /ɪ'nɪʃətɪv/ *n* **1** [C] the first movement or act which starts something happening: *He* **took the initiative** *in organizing a party after his brother's wedding.* **2** [U] the ability to make decisions and take action without the help of others **3 on one's own initiative** (done) according to one's own plan and without help

**in·ject** /ɪn'dʒekt/ *v* [T *with/into*] to put (liquid) into (someone) with a special needle (SYRINGE[1]): *They are injecting him with new drugs.*|(fig.) *We hope to inject new life/interest into our work.*

**in·jec·tion** /ɪn'dʒekʃən/ *n* [C;U] the act of INJECTing, or the amount injected: *The nurse gave him an injection for/against typhoid.*

**in·ju·di·cious** /ˌɪndʒʊ'dɪʃəs/ *adj fml* (of acts) not JUDICIOUS; not wise or sensible to do; showing poor judgment –**injudiciously** *adv* –**injudiciousness** *n* [U]

**in·junc·tion** /ɪn'dʒʌŋkʃən/ *n* [ *+to-v/ +that/against*] *fml or law* a command or official order to do or not to do something

**in·jure** /'ɪndʒə^r/ *v* **-jured, -juring** [T] to hurt (a living thing): *She was injured badly in the accident.|The injured (people) were taken to hospital.* –**injurious** *adj: Smoking is injurious to health.* –see WOUND[2] (USAGE)

**in·ju·ry** /'ɪndʒəri/ *n* **-ries 1** [C;U] (an example of) harm; damage to a living thing: *insurance against injury at work|He suffered serious injuries to the arms and legs.* **2 add insult to injury** to do or say something more against someone when one has already harmed them enough

**in·jus·tice** /ɪn'dʒʌst$_{\text{ə}}^{\text{I}}$s/ *n* [C;U] **1** (an act of) not being just; unfairness –see also JUSTICE **2 do someone**

**an injustice** to judge someone in an unfair way and/or believe something bad about them which is untrue

**ink** /ɪŋk/ *n* [U] coloured liquid used esp. for writing

**ink·ling** /'ɪŋklɪŋ/ *n* [S;U *of, as to*] a possible idea or a suggestion: *He* **had no/some inkling** *of the difficulties.*

**in·laid** /ˌɪn'leɪd◂/ *adj* [*with*] having another substance set in: *wood inlaid with gold|inlaid wood*

**in·land¹** /'ɪnlənd/ *adj* [A] done or placed inside a country, not near the coast or other countries: *the inland forests|inland trade*

**in·land²** /ɪn'lænd/ *adv* [F] towards or in the heart of the country: *We walked inland.*

**in-laws** /'· ·/ *n* [P] the father and mother of the person someone has married, and also (sometimes) other relatives by marriage

**in·lay** /'ɪnleɪ/ *n* a pattern, surface, or substance set into another: *wood with an inlay of gold*

**in·let** /'ɪnlet, 'ɪnl̩ɪ̈t/ *n* **1** a narrow stretch of water reaching from a sea, lake, etc., into the land or between islands **2** a way in (for water, liquid, etc.) –see also OUTLET

**in·mate** /'ɪnmeɪt/ *n* a person living in the same room or building as others, esp. unwillingly as in a hospital or prison

**in me·mo·ri·am** /ɪn mɪ̈'mɔːrɪəm‖-'mor-/ *prep Latin* (used before the name marked on a stone above a grave) in memory of: *In Memoriam John Jones, 1871–1956.*

**inn** /ɪn/ *n* a small hotel or place where one can stay and/or drink alcohol, eat meals, etc., esp. one built many centuries ago –compare PUB

**in·nate** /ˌɪ'neɪt◂/ *adj* (of qualities) which someone was born with: *innate kindness* **–innately** *adv*

**in·ner** /'ɪnəʳ/ *adj* [A *no comp.*] **1** (placed) inside: *the inner ear|an inner room* **2** closest to the centre (and in control) of what is happening: *the inner circle of power* –compare OUTER

**in·ner·most** /'ɪnəməʊst‖-ər-/ ‖also **inmost** /'ɪn məʊst/ *BrE– adj* farthest inside: *Her innermost thoughts* –compare OUTERMOST

**in·nings** /'ɪnɪŋz/ *n* **innings** the period of time during which a cricket team or player BAT² (2)

**inn·keep·er** /'ɪnˌkiːpəʳ/ *n old use* a person who (owns and) runs an inn –see also PUBLICAN

**in·no·cent** /'ɪnəsənt/ *adj* **1** [*of*] (of people) guiltless: *He was innocent of the crime.* –opposite **guilty** **2** (of things) harmless: *innocent pleasures* **3** (of people) simple; not able to recognize evil: *a trusting innocent young child* **–innocently** *adv* **–innocence** *n* [U]

**in·noc·u·ous** /ɪ'nɒkjuəs‖ɪ'nɑk-/ *adj* (esp. of actions, statements, etc.) harmless; not intended to offend **–innocuously** *adv* **–innocuousness** *n* [U]

**in·no·va·tion** /ˌɪnə'veɪʃən/ *n* [C;U] (an example of) the introduction of something new: *The innovation of air travel during this century has made the world seem smaller.* **–innovative** /'ɪnəvətiv,-veɪtɪv/ *adj* **–innovator** *n*

**in·nu·en·do** /ˌɪnjʊ'endəʊ/ *n* **-does** *or* **-dos** [C;U] (an example of) the act of suggesting something unpleasant in words without saying it directly: *He made innuendoes about her coming home at four o'clock in the morning.*

**in·nu·me·ra·ble** /ɪ'njuːmərəbəl‖ɪ'nuː-/ *adj* [*no comp.*] too many to be counted

**i·noc·u·late** /ɪ'nɒkjʊleɪt‖ɪ'nɑkjə-/ *v* **-lated, -lating** [I;T *with/against*] to introduce a weak form of a disease into (a living body) as a protection against the disease –compare VACCINATE, INJECT **–inoculation** /-'leɪʃən / *n* [C;U]

**in·of·fen·sive** /ˌɪnə'fensɪv/ *adj* (of people and their acts) not OFFENSIVE; not causing any harm; not causing dislike in other people: *He has an inoffensive manner.* **–inoffensively** *adv* **–inoffensiveness** *n* [U]

**in·op·por·tune** /ɪn'ɒpətjuːn‖ˌɪnɑpər'tuːn/ *adj fml* not OPPORTUNE; unsuitable (for the time): *an inopportune visit/remark* **–inopportunely** *adv* **–inopportuneness** *n* [U]

**in·or·di·nate** /ɪ'nɔːdən̩ɪ̈t‖-ɔr-/ *adj fml* beyond reasonable limits: *an inordinate amount of work* **–inordinately** *adv: inordinately great demands*

**in·or·gan·ic** /ˌɪnɔː'gænɪk◂‖-ɔr-/ *adj* not ORGANIC (1); not of living material; **–inorganically** *adv*

**in·put** /'ɪnpʊt/ *n* [S;U *to*] something put in for use, esp. by a machine, such as electrical current or information for a computer –see also OUTPUT

**in·quest** /'ɪŋkwest/ *n* an official inquiry usu. to find out the cause of a sudden and unexpected death, esp. when there is a possibility of crime

**in·quire en-** /ɪn'kwaɪəʳ/ *v* **-quired, -quiring** **1** [T] to ask: *I inquired* ((*fml*) *of him*) *what he wanted/whether he would come.* **2** [I] to ask for information: *I'll inquire about the trains.|She* **inquired after** (=asked about) *my mother's health.|We* **inquired into** (=searched for information about) *his story, and found it was true.*

**in·quir·ing en-** /ɪn'kwaɪərɪŋ/, *adj* showing an interest in learning about things: *a child with an inquiring mind*

**in·quir·y en-** /ɪn'kwaɪəri‖ɪn'kwaɪəri, 'ɪŋkwəri/ *n* **-ies** [C;U] (an example of) the act of inquiring (INQUIRE): *The police are making inquiries about the crime.*

USAGE **Enquiry** and **inquiry** are almost the same, but **enquiry** is more often used for a simple request for information, and **inquiry** for a long serious study: *Thank you for your* **enquiry**/*your* **enquiries** *about my health.|a government* **inquiry** *into the dangers of smoking*

**in·qui·si·tion** /ˌɪŋkwɪ̈'zɪʃən/ *n usu. derog* an inquiry, esp. one that is carried out with little regard for the rights of the people being questioned

**in·quis·i·tive** /ɪn'kwɪzɪ̈tɪv/ *adj* (of people and their acts) trying to find out (too many) details about things and people: *Don't be so inquisitive: I'm not telling you what I did last night.* **–inquisitively** *adv* **–inquisitiveness** *n* [U]

**in·roads** /'ɪnrəʊdz/ **make inroads into/on** to take away or use up: *Teaching* **makes inroads into/on** *my free time.*

**in·sane** /ɪn'seɪn/ *adj* (of people and their acts) not SANE; mad **–insanely** *adv: insanely jealous*

**in·san·i·ta·ry** /ɪn'sænɪ̈təri‖-teri/ *adj* which is likely to harm the health by causing disease: *insanitary conditions* –see also SANITARY

**in·san·i·ty** /ɪn'sænɪ̈ti/ *n* [U] madness –opposite **sanity**

**in·sa·tia·ble** /ɪn'seɪʃəbəl/ *adj* that cannot be

satisfied: *Surely you're not still hungry; you're insatiable!* **–insatiably** *adv*

**in·scribe** /ɪn'skraɪb/ *v* **-scribed, -scribing** [T *in, into, on/with*] *fml* to write (something) by marking into (a surface); mark (a surface) with (something written, esp. a name): *She inscribed his name on the book.* **–inscription** /ɪn'skrɪpʃən/ *n*

**in·scru·ta·ble** /ɪn'skruːtəbəl/ *adj* (of people and their acts) whose meaning is hidden or hard to find out; mysterious: *an inscrutable smile* **–inscrutability** /-ə'bɪlɪ̈ti/ *n* [U] **–inscrutably** *adv*

**in·sect** /'ɪnsekt/ *n* a small creature with no bones and a hard outer covering, six legs, and a body divided into three parts, such as an ant or fly

**in·sec·ti·cide** /ɪn'sektɪ̈saɪd/ *n* [C;U] a chemical substance made to kill insects

**in·se·cure** /,ɪnsɪ'kjʊəʳ/ *adj* **1** (of people) (feeling) not SECURE[1]; afraid or unsure of oneself **2 a** not safe; which cannot support people, things, etc.: *an insecure wall* **b** unsafe; not supported: *I feel insecure on this high ladder.* **–insecurity** /,ɪnsɪ'kjʊərɪ̈ti/ *n* **-ties** [C;U] **–insecurely** *adv*

**in·sen·si·ble** /ɪn'sensəbəl/ *adj fml* **1** not conscious –compare SENSELESS (1) **2** lacking knowledge of
USAGE **Insensible** is *not* the opposite of **sensible.**

**in·sen·si·tive** /ɪn'sensɪ̈tɪv/ *adj* [*to*] **1** (of people and their acts) not SENSITIVE; not kind to others because one does not understand how they feel; TACTless: *an insensitive remark* **2** not having the feeling which is usual when one meets (a certain) experience: *insensitive to pain* **–insensitivity** /ɪn,sensɪ̈'tɪvɪ̈ti/ *n* [S;U] **–insensitively** *adv*

**in·sep·a·ra·ble** /ɪn'sepərəbəl/ *adj* [*from*] not SEPARABLE; that cannot be separated (from something else or from one another): *The two girls are inseparable friends.* **–inseparability** /-ə'bɪlɪ̈ti/ *n* [U] **–inseparably** *adv*

**in·sert** /ɪn'sɜːt‖-ɜrt/ *v* [T *in, to*] to put something inside (something else): *He inserted the key in the lock and opened the door.*

**in·ser·tion** /ɪn'sɜːʃən‖-ɜr-/ *n* [C;U] the act or action of INSERTing, or the thing inserted

**in·shore** /,ɪn'ʃɔːʳ◂‖-or/ *adv* [F] near, towards, or to the shore– see also OFFSHORE, ONSHORE **–inshore** *adj* [A]

**in·side**[1] /ɪn'saɪd◂/ *n* **1** the area within (something else); the part that is nearest to the centre, or that faces away from other people or from the open air: *paint the inside of the house* –opposite **outside 2** [*often pl.*] *infml* the stomach: *a pain in one's insides*

**in·side**[2] /ɪn'saɪd/ *prep,adv,adj* **1** within or into something: *inside the car/the house/my mouth|He opened the box and looked inside.|the inside pages of a book* –see Study Notes on page 474 **2** to or on the edge of a road: *the inside* LANE (2) (=where cars drive slowly) –opposite **outside** (for **1, 2**) **3** *infml* in less time than: *He'll be here* **inside of** *an hour.* **4** of or from the secret centre of something: *inside information* (=from someone who knows the secret truth)

> **SPELLING NOTE**
> Words with the sound /aɪ/ may be spelt **e-**, like **eye**, or **ai-**, like **aisle**.

**5 inside out** with the usual inside parts on the outside: *He put his socks on* **inside out.**

USAGE Compare **within** and **inside**: 1 Both words can express the idea of being surrounded, but **inside** is more usual in this sense; **within** is formal and only used of large areas: **inside** *the box|***within** *the prison. 2 Both words can mean "not beyond", but* **within** is more usual, and **inside** is informal: *Your shoes will be ready* **within/inside** *a week.*

**in·sid·er** /ɪn'saɪdəʳ/ *n* someone who is in a group whose membership gives him special information and/or power –see also OUTSIDER

**in·sid·i·ous** /ɪn'sɪdɪəs/ *adj* unnoticed in action but causing something very bad in the end; secretly harmful: *the insidious growth of decay* **–insidiously** *adv* **–insidiousness** *n* [U]

**in·sight** /'ɪnsaɪt/ *n* [C;U *into*] (an example of) the power of using one's mind to understand something deeply, esp. without help from outside information: *Visiting London gave me an insight into the lives of the people who live there.*

**in·sig·ni·a** /ɪn'sɪgnɪə/ *n* [P] BADGES or objects which represent the power of an official or important person, such as the crown of a king or the STRIPES of an officer

**in·sig·nif·i·cant** /,ɪnsɪg'nɪfɪkənt/ *adj* not SIGNIFICANT; not of value and/or importance **–insignificance** *n* [U] **–insignificantly** *adv*

**in·sin·cere** /,ɪnsɪn'sɪəʳ/ *adj* not sincere **–insincerity** /-'serɪ̈ti/ *n* [U]

**in·sin·u·ate** /ɪn'sɪnjʊeɪt/ *v* **-ated, -ating** [T +(*that*) /*to*] to suggest (something unpleasant) by one's behaviour or questions: *Are you insinuating that I'm not telling the truth?|an insinuating remark*

**in·sin·u·a·tion** /ɪŋ,sɪnjʊ'eɪʃən/ *n* [C;U] (an example of) the act or action of insinuating (INSINUATE): *She blamed him, not directly but by insinuation.|They made unpleasant insinuations that he might not be quite honest.* –compare IMPLICATION (2)

**in·sip·id** /ɪn'sɪpɪ̈d/ *adj* lacking a strong effect, esp. a taste: *insipid food|an insipid character* **–insipidly** *adv* **–insipidness** *n* [U]

**in·sist** /ɪn'sɪst/ *v* [I;T] **1** [+(*that*)/*on, upon*] to declare firmly (when opposed): *I insisted (to everyone) that he was wrong.|I insisted on my correctness.* **2** [+(*that*)/*to*] to order (something to happen): *I insisted on him going.|I insisted that he (should) go.|You must come with us: I insist.*

**in·sis·tence** /ɪn'sɪstəns/ *n* [U] **1** the act of INSISTing: *I did it, but only at your insistence.* **2** the quality or state of being INSISTENT (1)

**in·sis·tent** /ɪn'sɪstənt/ *adj* **1** [+(*that*)/*on, upon*] (of people) repeatedly INSISTing or making demands: *He's very insistent that he'll finish in time.|an insistent refusal* **2** (of acts) needing to be done, answered, etc.; urgent: *the insistent ringing of the telephone* **–insistently** *adv*

**in si·tu** /,ɪn 'sɪtjuː‖,ɪn 'saɪtuː/ *adv* [F] *Latin* in its original place

**in so far as** /,· · '· ·/ also **in as far as, insofar as**/,ɪnsə'fɑːr əz/– *conj* to the degree that: *I'll help you in so far as I can.*

**in·so·lent** /'ɪnsələnt/ *adj* (of people and their acts)

showing disrespectful rudeness; INSULTing –**insolently** *adv* –**insolence** *n* [U]

**in·sol·u·ble** /ɪn'sɒljʊbəl‖ɪn'sɑljə-/ ‖also **insolvable** *AmE– adj* **1** which cannot be made right, brought to a good result, or SOLVED **2** which cannot be DISSOLVED (1,2): *insoluble in water* –opposite **soluble**

**in·sol·vent** /ɪn'sɒlvənt‖ɪn'sɑl-/ *adj* not SOLVENT; not having money to pay what one owes –**insolvency** *n* [U]

**in·som·ni·a** /ɪn'sɒmnɪə‖-'sɑm-/ *n* [U] habitual inability to sleep –**insomniac** *n,adj*: *She's an insomniac; she only sleeps for two or three hours a night.*

**in·spect** /ɪn'spekt/ *v* [T] **1** to examine (the details of something) **2** to make an official visit to judge the quality of (an organization, machine, etc.)

**in·spec·tion** /ɪn'spekʃən/ *n* [C;U] (an example of) the act of INSPECTing or the state of being inspected: *a tour of inspection|I gave the radio a thorough inspection before I bought it.*

**in·spec·tor** /ɪn'spektəʳ/ *n* **1** [C] an official who INSPECTS: *A ticket inspector got on the train.* **2** [A;C] a police officer of middle rank

**in·spi·ra·tion** /ˌɪnspɪ̣'reɪʃən/ *n* **1** [C;U] (something or someone which causes) an urge to produce good and beautiful things, esp. works of art: *Dante was the inspiration for my book on Italy.* **2** [C] a good idea: *I've had an inspiration–let's go to the country.* –**inspirational** *adj*

**in·spire** /ɪn'spaɪəʳ/ *v* **-spired, -spiring** [T] **1** [+*to-v*/*to*] to encourage in (someone) the ability to act, esp. with a good result: *I was inspired to work harder.|an inspiring speech* **2** to be the force which produces (usu. a good result): *His best music was inspired by the memory of his mother.* **3** [*with*/*in*] to put (a feeling towards the subject) into (someone): *You inspire me with admiration.|He inspires hate/dislike in me.*

**in·spired** /ɪn'spaɪəd‖-ərd/ *adj* so clever as to seem to show INSPIRATION, esp. from God: *an inspired guess|She sang as if inspired.* –opposite **uninspired**

**in·sta·bil·i·ty** /ˌɪnstə'bɪlɪ̣ti/ *n* [U] lack of STABILITY; unsteadiness, esp. of character

**in·stall** /ɪn'stɔːl/ *v* [T *in*] **1** to set (an apparatus) up, ready for use: *We're installing a new heating system.* **2** to settle (someone) in an official position, esp. with ceremony: (fig.) *I installed myself in front of the fire.* –**installation** /ˌɪnstə'eɪʃən/ *n* [C;U]

**in·stal·ment** /ɪn'stɔːlmənt/ ‖also **installment** *AmE– n* **1** a single payment of a set which, in time, will complete full payment: *I shall soon pay the last instalment of my debt.* **2** a single part of a book, play, or television show which appears in regular parts until the story is completed

**in·stance** /'ɪnstəns/ *n* **1** [*of*] a single fact, event, etc., expressing a general idea; example; case: *an instance of bad behaviour* **2 for instance** for example: *You can't depend on her: for instance, she arrived late for an important meeting yesterday.* **3 in the first instance** first of all; as a beginning

**in·stant¹** /'ɪnstənt/ *n* a moment or point of time: *Not for an instant did I believe he had lied.|(At) The instant I saw him I knew he was angry.*

**instant²** *adj* [*no comp.*] **1** happening at once: *instant change* **2** [A] (of food etc.) which can be very quickly prepared for use: *instant coffee/potatoes*

**in·stan·ta·ne·ous** /ˌɪnstən'teɪnɪəs/ *adj* [*no comp.*] happening at once –**instantaneously** *adv* –**instantaneousness** *n* [U]

**in·stant·ly** /'ɪnstəntli/ *adv* [*no comp.*] at once: *The police came to my help instantly.*

**in·stead** /ɪn'sted/ *adv* **1** in place of that: *It's too wet to walk, so we'll go swimming instead.|She never studies. Instead, she plays tennis all day.* **2 instead of** in place of: *I should be at school instead of lying here in bed.|Will you go to the party instead of me?*

**in·step** /'ɪnstep/ *n* the upper surface of the foot between the toes and the ankle –see picture on page 299

**in·sti·gate** /'ɪnstɪ̣geɪt/ *v* **-gated, -gating** [T] *fml* to start (something happening, often something bad) by one's action: *He instigated the ending of free school milk.* –**instigator** *n* –**instigation** /-'geɪʃən/ *n* [U]: *We have come* **at your instigation.** (=at your suggestion)

**in·stil** /ɪn'stɪl/ ‖also **instill** *AmE– v* **-ll-** [T *in, into*] *fml* to put (ideas, feelings, etc.) into someone's mind by a continuing effort: *I instilled the need for kindness into my children.* –**instillation** /ˌɪnstɪ̣'leɪʃən / *n* [U]

**in·stinct** /'ɪnstɪŋkt/ *n* [C;U +*to-v*] the natural force in people and animals which causes certain behaviour patterns, such as nest-building, which are not based on learning or thinking: *Some animals hunt by instinct.*|(fig.) *Trust your instincts and do what you think is right.* –**instinctive** *adj*: *instinctive fear of snakes* –**instinctively** *adv*: *Instinctively, I knew she was ill.*

**in·sti·tute¹** /'ɪnstɪ̣tjuːt‖-tuːt/ *n* a society formed for a special purpose: *a scientific institute*

**institute²** *v* **-tuted, -tuting** [T] to set up for the first time (a society, rules, actions in law, etc.)

**in·sti·tu·tion** /ˌɪnstɪ̣'tjuːʃən‖-'tuː-/ *n* **1** [C] (a large building for) an organization which provides people with help, work, medical treatment, or protection, such as a school or hospital **2** [C] a habit, custom, etc., which has been in existence for a long time: *Marriage is an institution in most societies.* **3** [C;U] the act or action of instituting (INSTITUTE¹): *the institution of a new law* –**institutional** *adj*

**in·struct** /ɪn'strʌkt/ *v* [T +*that*/*to-v*] **1** to give knowledge or information to: *They instructed me in the best ways of doing the job.* **2** to give orders to: *I've been instructed to wait here until the teacher arrives.* –see ORDER² (USAGE)

**in·struc·tion** /ɪn'strʌkʃən/ *n* **1** [U] the act or action of instructing; teaching: *He's not yet trained, but still under instruction.* **2** [C *often pl.*] an order (to a person or machine), or advice on how to do something: *a book of instructions* –**instructional** *adj*

**in·struc·tive** /ɪn'strʌktɪv/ *adj* giving useful information –**instructively** *adv*

**in·struc·tor** /ɪn'strʌktəʳ/ a person who teaches an activity: *a driving instructor*

**in·stru·ment** /'ɪnstrəmənt/ *n* **1** an object used to help in work: *medical instruments* **2** also **musical instrument** /ˌ··· '···/– an object which is played to give musical sounds (such as a piano, a horn, etc.)

**in·stru·men·tal** /ˌɪnstrə'mentəl/ *adj* **1** [*in*] helpful (in); (part of) the cause of: *I was instrumental in* *catching the criminal.* **2** (of music) for instruments, not voices: *an instrumental work*

**in·sub·or·di·nate** /ˌɪnsəˈbɔːdənɪ̇t‖-ɔr-/ *adj* (of a person of lower rank, or his/her behaviour) disobedient; not showing willingness to take orders –**insubordination** /ˌɪnsəbɔːdɪ̇ˈneɪʃən‖-ɔr-/ *n* [C;U]

**in·sub·stan·tial** /ˌɪnsəbˈstænʃəl/ *adj* lacking firmness or solidity; weak or unsatisfying: *an insubstantial meal* –see also SUBSTANTIAL

**in·suf·fe·ra·ble** /ɪnˈsʌfərəbəl/ *adj* unbearable (in behaviour); too proud in manner: *insufferable rudeness|He's insufferable.* –**insufferably** *adv*

**in·suf·fi·cient** /ˌɪnsəˈfɪʃənt/ *adj* [*for*] not SUFFICIENT; not enough: *They gave insufficient help.|The food was insufficient for our needs.* –**insufficiently** *adv* –**insufficiency** *n* [S;U *of*]

**in·su·lar** /ˈɪnsjʊləʳ‖ˈɪnsələr/ *adj* narrow (in mind); interested only or mainly in a small group, country, etc. –compare PAROCHIAL (1) –**insularity** *n* [U]

**in·su·late** /ˈɪnsjʊleɪt‖ˈɪnsə-, ˈɪnʃə-/ *v* **-lated, -lating** [T *from, against*] **1** to cover (something) so as to prevent the passing of unseen forces such as electricity, heat, or sound: *Many houses could be warmer if they were insulated so that the heat is not lost.* **2** to protect (a person) from ordinary experiences: *The royal family is insulated from many of the difficulties faced by ordinary people.*

**in·su·la·tion** /ˌɪnsjʊˈleɪʃən‖ˌɪnsə-/ *n* [U] **1** the action of insulating or the state of being INSULATED (1) **2** material which INSULATES (1)

**in·sult**[1] /ɪnˈsʌlt/ *v* [T *by*] to offend, by speech or act: *an insulting remark*

**in·sult**[2] /ˈɪnsʌlt/ *n* [C;U] (an example of) speech or action which INSULTS: *He shouted insults at the boy who had kicked him.*

**in·su·pe·ra·ble** /ɪnˈsjuːpərəbəl‖ɪnˈsuː-/ *adj fml* (of something in one's way) too difficult to be conquered or passed: *insuperable difficulties*/BARRIERS –compare INSURMOUNTABLE –**insuperably** *adv*

**in·sur·ance** /ɪnˈʃʊərəns/ *n* **1** [U] (the business of making an) agreement by contract to pay money esp. in case of a misfortune (such as illness, death, or accident): *life insurance|car insurance|an* **insurance policy** (=a written contract of insurance)*|He worked in insurance.* **2** [U] money paid (by an **insurance company**) as a result of such a contract, or (to an insurance company) in order to make or keep such a contract **3** [S;U *against*] protection (against something): *I bought another lock as an additional insurance against thieves.*

**in·sure** /ɪnˈʃʊəʳ/ *v* **-sured, -suring** [T] **1** [*against*] to protect (oneself or another), esp. against loss of (money, life, goods, etc.) by INSURANCE (1): *My house is insured against fire.|I am insured.* **2** [+(*that*)] *esp. AmE* →ENSURE

USAGE Compare **insure, ensure,** and **assure:** 1 **Insure** and **assure** are both words for gaining protection through **insurance,** but **assure** is normally only used for insurance against death: *life* **assurance***|fire* **insurance** 2 **Assure** is also used more generally to mean "to make certain" and is similar to **ensure:** *I went back to the car to* **assure** *myself that I had locked it properly.|I fitted a new lock to* **ensure** *that the car would not be stolen.|My car is* **insured** *against being stolen* (=if it is stolen I will get money from the **insurance company**). 3 **Reassure** means "to comfort someone who is anxious" (not "to **assure** again"). 4 The social quality of **assurance** means that one is sure of oneself and not afraid of people: *She seems very self-***assured.**

**SPELLING NOTE**
Words with the sound /aɪ/ may be spelt **e-**, like **eye.** or **ai-**, like **aisle.**

**in·sur·gent** /ɪnˈsɜːdʒənt‖-ɜr-/ *adj,n* [A;C] (a person who is) ready to take power by or as if by force, after rising against the people who have power

**in·sur·moun·ta·ble** /ˌɪnsəˈmaʊntəbəl‖-sər-/ *adj* too large, difficult, etc., to be dealt with –compare INSUPERABLE

**in·sur·rec·tion** /ˌɪnsəˈrekʃən/ *n* [C;U] the act or occasion of rising against the people who have power, such as the government –**insurrectionist** *n*

**in·tact** /ɪnˈtækt/ *adj* [F] whole because no part has been touched or spoilt: *The fragile parcel arrived intact.* –**intactness** *n* [U]

**in·take** /ˈɪnteɪk/ *n* [S] the amount or number allowed to enter, or taken in: *the yearly intake of students*

**in·tan·gi·ble** /ɪnˈtændʒəbəl/ *adj* which by its nature cannot be known by the senses, though it can be felt: *an intangible quality|We felt an intangible presence in the room.* –see also TANGIBLE –**intangibility** /-əˈbɪlɪ̇ti/ *n* [U] –**intangibly** *adv*

**in·te·gral** /ˈɪntɪ̇grəl/ *adj* [A *no comp.*] necessary (to complete something): *an integral part of the argument*

**in·te·grate** /ˈɪntɪ̇greɪt/ *v* **-grated, -grating** [I;T *with, into*] (of members of social groups) to join in and mix with society as a whole; to cause (members of social groups) to do this: *They've lived in this country for 10 years, but have never really integrated/become integrated.|We are trying to integrate this criminal into society.* –compare SEGREGATE –**integration** /-ˈgreɪʃən/ *n* [U]

**in·te·grat·ed** /ˈɪntɪ̇greɪtɪ̇d/ *adj* showing a usu. pleasing mixture of qualities, groups, etc.: *This is an integrated school with children of different races and social classes.*

**in·teg·ri·ty** /ɪnˈtegrɪ̇ti/ *n* [U] **1** strength and firmness of character or principle; honesty that can be trusted: *a man of complete integrity* **2** *fml* state of wholeness; completeness

**in·tel·lect** /ˈɪntɪ̇lekt/ *n* [C;U] the ability to reason (rather than to feel or act)

**in·tel·lec·tual**[1] /ˌɪntɪ̇ˈlektʃʊəl/ *adj* **1** concerning the INTELLECT: *intellectual subjects* **2** able to use the INTELLECT well; showing unusual reasoning powers: *an intellectual argument* –compare SPIRITUAL[1] (1); see INTELLIGENT (USAGE) –**intellectually** *adv*

**intellectual**[2] *n* a person who works and lives by using his mind, and who is interested in activities which include thinking and understanding rather than feeling and doing

**in·tel·li·gence** /ɪnˈtelɪ̇dʒəns/ *n* [U] **1** (good) ability to learn and understand: *an intelligence test|Use your intelligence.* **2** information gathered esp. about an enemy country, or the group of people who gather it:

military intelligence

**in·tel·li·gent** /ɪn'telǀdʒənt/ *adj* having or showing powers of reasoning or understanding: *All human beings are much more intelligent than animals.|an intelligent suggestion* –opposite **unintelligent –intelligently** *adv*

USAGE Compare **intelligent** and **intellectual**: Anyone with a quick and clever mind is **intelligent**, but an **intellectual** (person) is someone who is well-educated and interested in subjects that exercise the mind. A small child, or even a dog, can be **intelligent**, but cannot be called an **intellectual**.

**in·tel·li·gi·ble** /ɪn'telǀdʒəbəl/ *adj* [*to*] (esp. of speech or writing) which can be understood –opposite **unintelligible**; compare ARTICULATE[1] (1,2) **–intelligibility** /-ə'bɪlǀti / *n* [U] **–intelligibly** *adv*

**in·tend** /ɪn'tend/ *v* [T +*to-v/that*] **1** to plan; to mean (to do): *I intended to catch the early train, but I didn't get up in time.|I intend to report you to the police.* **2** to mean to be: *The flowers were intended for you, but my mother thought they were for her.*

**in·tense** /ɪn'tens/ *adj* strong (in quality or feeling): *intense cold|intense sorrow|She is a very intense person who cares deeply about everything.* **–intensely** *adv*

**in·ten·si·fy** /ɪn'tensǀfaɪ/ *v* **-fied, -fying** [I;T] to (cause to) become more INTENSE: *Police have intensified their search for the criminal.* **–intensification** /-fɪ'keɪʃən / *n* [U]

**in·ten·si·ty** /ɪn'tensǀti/ *n* [U] the quality of being INTENSE: *The poem shows great intensity of feeling.*

**in·ten·sive** /ɪn'tensɪv/ *adj* which gives a lot of attention or action to a small amount of something/in a small amount of time: **Intensive care** *in hospitals is given to the seriously ill.* –see also EXTENSIVE **–intensively** *adv*

**in·tent**[1] /ɪn'tent/ *n* [U] **1** purpose; INTENTION: *with good intent|He entered the building* **with intent to** *steal.* **2 to all intents (and purposes)** in almost every way; very nearly

**intent**[2] *adj* [*on*] showing fixed attention (in doing or wishing to do): *an intent look|He's intent on going to France.* **–intently** *adv* **–intentness** *n* [U]

**in·ten·tion** /ɪn'tenʃən/ *n* [C;U] (an example of) a determination to act in a certain way: *I've got no intention of changing my mind.|He is full of* **good intentions,** *but can do nothing to help.*

**in·ten·tion·al** /ɪn'tenʃənəl/ *adj* (done) on purpose –opposite **unintentional –intentionally** *adv*

**in·ter** /ɪn'tɜː[r]/ *v* **-rr-** [T] *fml* to bury (a dead person) –opposite **disinter**

**in·ter·act** /ˌɪntə'rækt/ *v* [I *with, against*] to have an effect on each other or something else **–interaction** /-'rækʃən/ *n*

**in·ter·cede** /ˌɪntə'siːd‖-ər-/ *v* **-ceded, -ceding** [I *with, for*] to speak in favour of another, esp. in order to save him/her from punishment **–intercession** /-'seʃən/ *n* [C;U]

**in·ter·cept** /ˌɪntə'sept‖-ər-/ *v* [T] to stop and usu. seize (a person or thing moving from one place to another): *The parcel of drugs was intercepted by the police before it was delivered.* **–interception** /ˌɪntə'sepʃən‖-ər-/ *n* [C;U]

**in·ter·change** /'ɪntətʃeɪndʒ‖-ər-/ *n* **1** [C;U] (an example of) the act or action of putting each of (two things) in the place of the other; exchange **2** [C] (on a MOTORWAY) a system of smaller roads by which two main roads are connected

**in·ter·chan·gea·ble** /ˌɪntə'tʃeɪndʒəbəl‖-tər-/ *adj* [*with*] which can be used in place of each other/something else **–interchangeably** *adv: The two words are used interchangeably.*

**in·ter·com** /'ɪntəkɒm‖'ɪntərkɑm/ *n* a system by which one can talk through a machine to people in a near place, as used e.g. in an office by someone to speak to a secretary in an outer room

**in·ter·con·ti·nen·tal** /ˌɪntəkɒntǀ'nentəl‖-tər'kɑn-/ *adj* (used, done, connected with, etc.) different land masses (CONTINENTS): *intercontinental trade*

**in·ter·course** /'ɪntəkɔːs‖'ɪntərkors/ *n* [U] **1** →SEXUAL INTERCOURSE **2** an exchange of feelings, actions, etc., which make people know each other more closely

**in·ter·de·pen·dent** /ˌɪntədɪ'pendənt‖-ər-/ *adj* depending on each other; necessary to each other **–interdependence** *n* [U] **–interdependently** *adv*

**in·terest**[1] /'ɪntrǀst/ *n* **1** [C;U *in*] a readiness to give attention: *I have no interest in politics.|He's showing an interest in music.* **2** [U] a quality of causing attention to be given: *That's of no interest to me.* **3** [C] an activity, subject, etc., to which one gives time and attention: *Eating seems to be his only interest in life.* **4** [C;U *often pl.*] advantage, advancement, or favour: *It's* **in your interest(s)** *to put your point of view first.|Come into my office and you will hear something* **to your interest.** –compare ADVANTAGE[1] (2) **5** [U] money paid for the use of money: *He lent me the money at 6% interest.*

**interest**[2] *v* [T *in*] **1** to make (someone) feel interest: *Football doesn't interest me at all.* **2** to make (someone) want to buy, take, do something, etc.: *Can I interest you in a cup of coffee?*

**in·terest·ed** /'ɪntrǀstǀd/ *adj* **1** [+*to-v/in*] concerned; having or showing interest: *I was interested in your remark/to hear your remark.|an interested look on his face* –opposite **uninterested 2** [A] personally concerned; on whom there will be an effect; who cannot make a fair judgment from the outside: *the interested* PARTY (5) (=*tech* person) –see DISINTERESTED (USAGE) **–interestedly** *adv*

**in·terest·ing** /'ɪntrǀstɪŋ/ *adj* which takes (and keeps) one's interest: *an interesting idea* –opposite **uninteresting –interestingly** *adv*

**in·ter·fere** /ˌɪntə'fɪə[r]‖-ər-/ *v* **-fered, -fering** [I *with, in, between*] **1** to get in the way of another; block the action of another **2** *derog* to push oneself into a matter which does not concern one: *I don't like interfering old busybodies* (BUSYBODY).

USAGE Compare **interfere** *in* and **interfere** *with*: *Stop* **interfering in** *my work!* (=taking part when you are not wanted)|*This noise is* **interfering with** *my work* (=preventing me from doing it properly).

**in·ter·fer·ence** /ˌɪntə'fɪərəns‖-tər-/ *n* [U] **1** [*with*] the act or action of interfering (INTERFERE) **2** the noises and shapes which spoil the working of electrical apparatus, esp. when a radio station is difficult to listen to because of the effect of another one near to its WAVELENGTH

**in·ter·im¹** /ˈɪntərɪm/ *n* **1** the time between two events **2 in the interim** →MEANWHILE

**interim²** *adj* good enough for a limited time, but not meant to last: *The full report isn't ready yet, but you can see the interim report.*

**in·te·ri·or** /ɪnˈtɪərɪəʳ/ *adj,n* (the part which is) inside, indoors, or farthest from the edge or outside: *He went into the interior (of the country).* (=the part farthest from the coast)|*An* **interior decorator** *is a person who plans the colours and furnishings for the inside of a house.* –opposite **exterior**

**in·ter·ject** /ˌɪntəˈdʒekt‖-ər-/ *v* [I;T] *fml* to make (a sudden remark) between others

**in·ter·jec·tion** /ˌɪntəˈdʒekʃən‖-ər-/ *n fml* **1** [C] a phrase, word, or set of sounds used as a sudden remark usu. expressing surprise, anger, etc.; EXCLAMATION: *interjections such as "oh!" or "Well done!"* **2** [U] the act of INTERJECTing

**in·ter·lock** /ˌɪntəˈlɒk‖ˌɪntərˈlɑk/ *v* [I;T] to fasten or be fastened together, esp. so that movement of one part causes movement in others: *interlocking gears*

**in·ter·lop·er** /ˈɪntələupəʳ‖-tər-/ *n fml* a person found in a place, esp. among others, who has no right to be there –compare INTRUDER

**in·ter·lude** /ˈɪntəluːd‖-ər-/ *n* **1** a free period of time between activities **2** (something, esp. music, used for filling) the time (INTERVAL) between parts of a play, film, concert, etc.

**in·ter·mar·ry** /ˌɪntəˈmæri‖-ər-/ *v* **-ried, -rying** [I *with*] (of different groups of people) to marry each other –**intermarriage** *n* [U]

**in·ter·me·di·a·ry** /ˌɪntəˈmiːdɪəri‖ˌɪntərˈmiːdieri/ *n* **-ries** a person who comes between two other groups, people, etc., often so as to bring them into agreement

**in·ter·me·di·ate** /ˌɪntəˈmiːdɪət‖-ər-/ *adj* (done or happening) between two others; halfway: *an intermediate examination in English* (=not very easy nor very difficult)

**in·ter·ment** /ɪnˈtɜːmənt‖-ɜr-/ *n* [C;U] *fml* burial –see also INTER, INTERN

**in·ter·mi·na·ble** /ɪnˈtɜːmɪ̀nəbəl‖-ɜr-/ *adj* (seeming) endless: *I had interminable problems with my last car: it never worked well.* –**interminably** *adv*

**in·ter·mis·sion** /ˌɪntəˈmɪʃən‖-ər-/ *n esp. AmE* for INTERVAL (2)

**in·ter·mit·tent** /ˌɪntəˈmɪtənt‖-ər-/ *adj* happening with pauses in between; not continuous: *an intermittent fault/noise* –**intermittently** *adv*

**in·tern** /ɪnˈtɜːn‖-ɜrn/ *v* [T] to put in prison or limit the freedom of movement of (someone considered dangerous), esp. in wartime or for political reasons –compare INTERMENT –**internment** *n* [U]

**in·ter·nal** /ɪnˈtɜːnl‖-ɜr-/ *adj* **1** of or in the inside, esp. of the body: *internal damage* **2** inside a country; not foreign: *internal trade* –opposite **external** –**internally** *adv*

**internal-com·bus·tion en·gine** /ˌ·,·· ·ˈ·· ˌ··/ *n* an engine (such as a car engine) which produces power by the burning of a substance (such as petrol) inside itself

**SPELLING NOTE**

Words with the sound /aɪ/ may be spelt **e-**, like **eye.** or **ai-**, like **aisle.**

**in·ter·na·tion·al¹** /ˌɪntəˈnæʃənəl‖-tər-/ *adj* between nations; concerning more than one nation –**internationally** *adv*

**international²** *n* (a player in) an international sports match

**in·ter·play** /ˈɪntəpleɪ‖-ər-/ *n* [U] the action or effect of (two) things on each other: *the interplay of light and sound*

**in·ter·pose** /ˌɪntəˈpəuz‖-ər-/ *v* **-posed, -posing** [I;T *between, among, in*] *fml* to put, come, or say between: *She interposed a few questions into the minister's speech.*

**in·ter·pret** /ɪnˈtɜːprɪ̀t‖-ɜr-/ *v* [T] **1** to put (a language) into the words of another language usu. by talking –compare TRANSLATE (1) **2** [*as*] to understand or show the meaning of (something): *I interpret his answer as a refusal.*|*The actor interprets Shakespeare in a new way.* –see also MISINTERPRET

**in·ter·pre·ta·tion** /ɪnˌtɜːprɪ̀ˈteɪʃən‖-ɜr-/ *n* [U] the act or the result of INTERPRETing; explanation

**in·ter·pret·er** /ɪnˈtɜːprɪ̀təʳ‖-ɜr-/ *n* a person who INTERPRETs (1)

**in·ter·ro·gate** /ɪnˈterəgeɪt/ *v* **-gated, -gating** [T] to question formally for a special purpose –see ASK (USAGE) –**interrogation** /-ˈgeɪʃən/ *n* [C;U] –**interrogator** *n*

**in·ter·rog·a·tive** /ˌɪntəˈrɒgətɪv‖-ˈrɑ-/ *adj,n* (a sentence, phrase, or word) which asks a question –**interrogatively** *adv*

**in·ter·rupt** /ˌɪntəˈrʌpt/ *v* [I;T] **1** to break the flow of speech of (someone) by saying something: *Stop interrupting me; I'm trying to talk to your mother!* **2** to break the flow of (something continuous) –**interruption** /-ˈrʌpʃən/ *n* [C;U]

**in·ter·sect** /ˌɪntəˈsekt‖-ər-/ *v* [I;T] (of lines, roads, etc.) to be in such a position as to cut across (each other or something else)

**in·ter·sec·tion** /ˌɪntəˈsekʃən‖-ər-/ *n* **1** [U] the act or action of INTERSECTing **2** [C] →CROSSROADS (1)

**in·ter·sperse** /ˌɪntəˈspɜːs‖ˌɪntərˈspɜrs/ *v* **-spersed, -spersing** [T *with*] to set here and there

**in·ter·val** /ˈɪntəvəl‖-ər-/ *n* **1** a period of time between events: *There was a long interval before he replied.* **2** *BrE*‖**intermission** *AmE*– such a period of time between the parts of a play, concert, etc.: *We ate ice cream in the interval.* **3 at intervals (of)** happening regularly after equal periods of time or appearing at equal distances (of): *The bell rang at 20-minute intervals.*

**in·ter·vene** /ˌɪntəˈviːn‖-ər-/ *v* **-vened, -vening** [I] **1** [*in*] (of people) to interrupt something, esp. to prevent a bad result: *They were starting to fight when their father intervened.* **2** to happen between events: *in the intervening years* –**intervention** /-ˈvenʃən/ *n* [C;U]

**in·ter·view¹** /ˈɪntəvjuː‖-ər-/ *n* a meeting where a person is asked questions **a** to decide whether he/she can take up a job or **b** to find out about his/her actions, opinions, etc., sometimes broadcast on radio or television

**interview²** *v* [T] to ask questions of (somebody) in an INTERVIEW –**interviewer** *n*

**in·ter·weave** /ˌɪntəˈwiːv‖-ər-/ *v* **-wove** /ˈwəʊv/, **-woven** /ˈwəʊvən/, **-weaving** [T *with*] to weave together: (fig.) *Our lives are interwoven.*

**in·tes·tate** /ɪnˈtesteɪt, -stǰt/ *adj law* not having made a WILL[2] (4) which leaves one's property to named people: *He* **died intestate.**

**in·tes·tine** /ɪnˈtestǰn/ *n* the tube carrying food from the stomach; bowels **–intestinal** /ɪnˈtestǰnl/ *adj*

**in·ti·ma·cy** /ˈɪntǰməsi/ *n* [U *with*] **1** the state of being INTIMATE[1] (1,2) **2** close friendship

**in·ti·mate**[1] /ˈɪntǰmǰt/ *adj* **1** [*with*] close in (a sexual) relationship: *intimate friends|They had been intimate/***on intimate terms** *for some time.* **2** personal; private **3** detailed; resulting from close study: *an intimate knowledge of the city* **–intimately** *adv*

**in·ti·mate**[2] /ˈɪntǰmeɪt/ *v* **-mated, -mating** [T + (*that*)] *fml* to make known indirectly; suggest: *He intimated that he wanted to go.* **–intimation** /-ˈmeɪʃən/ *n* [C;U]

**in·tim·i·date** /ɪnˈtɪmǰdeɪt/ *v* **-dated, -dating** [T] to make (someone) fearful, esp. by threatening violence, because one wants them to do something **–intimidation** /-ˈdeɪʃən/ *n* [U]

**in·to** /ˈɪntə; *before consonants* ˈɪntʊ/; *strong* ˈɪntuː/ *prep* **1** so as to be in or inside: *It was raining, so they went into the house.|She jumped into the water.|He went into* (=got a job in) *business.|They worked far into the night.|You'll get into trouble.* –see Study Notes on page 474 **2** so as to be: *to translate it into French* **3** (used when dividing one number by another): *Three into six goes twice.* **4** against; so as to hit: *to run into a wall* **5** *infml* keen on; interested in: *He's given up photography now, and he's into religion and modern music.*

**in·tol·e·ra·ble** /ɪnˈtɒlərəbəl‖-ˈtɑ-/ *adj* not TOLERABLE; too difficult, painful, etc., to be borne; unbearable **–intolerably** *adv*

**in·tol·e·rant** /ɪnˈtɒlərənt‖-ˈtɑ-/ *adj* not TOLERANT; not able to accept ways of thinking and behaving which are different from one's own **–intolerantly** *adv* **–intolerance** *n* [U]

**in·to·na·tion** /ˌɪntəˈneɪʃən/ *n* [U] rise and fall in the level (PITCH[2] (3)) of the voice

**in·tox·i·cate** /ɪnˈtɒksǰkeɪt‖ɪnˈtɑk-/ *v* **-cated, -cating** [I;T] to make drunk: (fig.) *Success intoxicated him.* **–intoxication** /-ˈkeɪʃən/ *n* [U]

**in·trac·ta·ble** /ɪnˈtræktəbəl/ *adj* (of people and their acts) difficult to control **–intractability** /-əˈbɪlǰti/ *n* [U]

**in·tran·si·gent** /ɪnˈtrænsǰdʒənt/ *adj fml* (of people and their acts) showing strong ideas which cannot be changed by others' wishes –compare STUBBORN **–intransigence** *n* [U]

**in·tran·si·tive** /ɪnˈtrænsǰtɪv/ *n,adj* (a verb) which has a subject but not an object: *In this dictionary the mark* [I] *shows an intransitive verb.* –see Study Notes on page 647

**in·tra·ve·nous** /ˌɪntrəˈviːnəs/ *adj* (done) within a VEIN (=blood vessel taking blood back to the heart): *an intravenous* INJECTION **–intravenously** *adv*

**in·trep·id** /ɪnˈtrepǰd/ *adj* (of people and their acts) showing no fear **–intrepidly** *adv* **–intrepidity** /ˌɪntrəˈpɪdǰti/ *n* [U]

**in·tri·ca·cy** /ˈɪntrɪkəsi/ *n* **-cies 1** [U] the quality of being INTRICATE **2** [C] something INTRICATE

**in·tri·cate** /ˈɪntrɪkǰt/ *adj* containing many detailed parts and thus difficult to understand: *an intricate pattern/story* **–intricately** *adv*

**in·trigue**[1] /ɪnˈtriːg/ *v* **-trigued, -triguing 1** [T] to interest greatly: *Your story intrigues me.|an intriguing idea* **2** [I] to make a secret plan

**in·trigue**[2] /ˈɪntriːg, ɪnˈtriːg/ *n* [C;U] (the act or practice of making) a secret plan: *political intrigues*

**in·trin·sic** /ɪnˈtrɪnsɪk, -zɪk/ *adj* [*to, in*] being part of the nature of the stated thing: *The* **intrinsic value** *of a coin is the value of the metal it is made of.* **–intrinsically** *adv*

**in·tro·duce** /ˌɪntrəˈdjuːs‖-ˈduːs/ *v* **-duced, -ducing** [T] **1** to make known by name for the first time to each other or someone else: *I introduced John to Mary last year.|Let me introduce myself: my name is Simpson.* **2** to bring in for the first time: *Potatoes were introduced into Europe from South America.* **3** to produce the first part of (something), esp. to suggest or explain the main part: *This song introduces the most important part of the play.*

**in·tro·duc·tion** /ˌɪntrəˈdʌkʃən/ also **intro** /ˈɪntrəʊ/ *infml– n* **1** [U *of, to, into*] the act of introducing or the state of being introduced: *the introduction of a new product* **2** [C] an occasion of telling people each others' names: *Mary made the introductions and we all shook hands.* **3** [C *to*] **a** a written or spoken explanation at the beginning of a book or speech **b** a book which gives one a knowledge of the most important things before going on to advanced studies

**in·tro·duc·to·ry** /ˌɪntrəˈdʌktəri/ *adj* which INTRODUCES (3): *She made a few introductory remarks.*

**in·tro·spec·tion** /ˌɪntrəˈspekʃən/ *n* [U] the habit of looking into one's own thoughts and feelings **–introspective** *adj*

**in·tro·vert** /ˈɪntrəvɜːt‖-ɜrt/ *n* an INTROVERTED person –see also EXTROVERT

**in·tro·vert·ed** /ˈɪntrəvɜːtǰd‖-ɜr-/ *adj* concerning oneself with one's own thoughts, acts, personal life, etc., rather than spending time with others **–introversion** /ˌɪntrəˈvɜːʃən‖-ˈvɜr·ən / *n* [U]

**in·trude** /ɪnˈtruːd/ *v* **-truded, -truding** [I;T *into, on, upon*] to bring or come in when not wanted: *I don't want to intrude upon them if they're busy.*

**in·trud·er** /ɪnˈtruːdə^r/ *n* a person who has come in unasked and perhaps secretly

**in·tru·sion** /ɪnˈtruːʒən/ *n* [C;U *on*] the act or an example of intruding (INTRUDE): *The police action was an intrusion on my private life.* **–intrusive** *adj*

**in·tu·i·tion** /ˌɪntjuˈɪʃən‖-tu-/ *n* **1** [U] the power of understanding something without reasoning **2** [C +*that*] an example of this, or a piece of knowledge that results: *She had an intuition that her friend was ill.* **–intuitive** *adj* **–intuitively** *adv*

**in·un·date** /ˈɪnəndeɪt/ *v* **-dated, -dating** [T *with*] to flood over esp. in very large quantities or numbers: (fig.) *I was inundated with requests for money.* **–inundation** /-ˈdeɪʃən/ *n* [C;U]

**in·vade** /ɪnˈveɪd/ *v* **-vaded, -vading 1** [I;T] to attack and spread into so as to take control of (a country, city, etc.) **2** [I;T] to enter in large numbers: *Tourists invaded the seaside town in summer months.* **3** [T] to enter into and spoil: *to invade someone's* PRIVACY **–invader** *n*

**in·va·lid**[1] /ˈɪnvəliːd, -lǰd‖-lǰd/ *n* a person made

weak by illness: *my invalid mother*

**in·val·id²** /ɪn'vælɪ̣d/ *adj* not VALID; not correct or correctly expressed, esp. in law: *an invalid claim/ticket*

**in·val·i·date** /ɪn'vælɪ̣deɪt/ *v* **-dated, -dating** [T] to make (something) INVALID²; show that (something) is not correct –opposite **validate** –**invalidation** /-'deɪʃən / *n* [U]

**in·val·ua·ble** /ɪn'væljubəl‖-jə-/ *adj* (of qualities) too valuable for the worth to be measured: *your invaluable help* –see WORTHLESS (USAGE)

**in·var·i·a·ble** /ɪn'veərɪəbəl/ *adj* which cannot vary or change –opposite **variable** –**invariably** *adv: It's invariably* (=always) *wet when I take my holidays.*

**in·va·sion** /ɪn'veɪʒən/ *n* **1** an act of invading (INVADE) **2** the incoming or spread of something usu. harmful

**in·vec·tive** /ɪn'vektɪv/ *n* [C;U] *fml* forceful, attacking speech, used for blaming someone for something and often including swearing

**in·vent** /ɪn'vent/ *v* [T] **1** to make up, think of, or produce for the first time: *Alexander Graham Bell invented the telephone in 1876.* **2** to make up (something unreal or untrue): *The whole story was invented.*

USAGE One **discovers** something that existed before but was not known, such as a place or a fact. One **invents** something that did not exist before, such as a machine or a method.: *Who* **discovered** *America?*| *Who* **invented** *the computer?*

**in·ven·tion** /ɪn'venʃən/ *n* **1** [U] the act of inventing: *the invention of the telephone* **2** [C] something invented: *The telephone is a wonderful invention.*

**in·ven·tive** /ɪn'ventɪv/ *adj apprec* able to invent: *an inventive person/mind* –**inventively** *adv* –**inventiveness** *n* [U]

**in·ven·tor** /ɪn'ventəʳ/ *n* a person who invents something new

**in·ven·tory** /'ɪnvəntri‖-tori/ *n* **-tories** a list, esp. one of all the goods in a place

**in·verse** /'ɪnvɜːs‖-ɜrs/ *adj,n* [A;C] (something which is) opposite in order or position: *The inverse of 4/1 is* 1/4. –**inversely** *adv*

**in·vert** /ɪn'vɜːt‖-ɜrt/ *v* [T] to put in the opposite position or order, esp. upside down: *She caught the insect by inverting her cup over it.* –**inversion** *n* [C;U]

**in·ver·te·brate** /ɪn'vɜːtɪ̣brɪ̣t, -breɪt‖-ɜr-/ *adj,n tech* (a living creature) which has no SPINE (1) –see also VERTEBRATE

**inverted com·ma** /·,·· '··/ *n* **1** *BrE* for QUOTATION MARK **2 in inverted commas** used by the speaker to suggest the opposite of what has just been said: "*Her friends, in inverted commas, all disappeared when she was in trouble.*" (=so they were not really her friends) –compare SO-CALLED

**in·vest** /ɪn'vest/ *v* [I;T *in*] to use (money) to make more money out of something that will increase in value: *She invested in a house/a painting.*|(fig.) *I've invested a lot of time and effort in this plan.*

**SPELLING NOTE**
Words with the sound /aɪ/ may be spelt **e-**, like **eye.** or **ai-**, like **aisle.**

**in·ves·ti·gate** /ɪn'vestɪ̣geɪt/ *v* **-gated, -gating** [I;T] to examine carefully, or inquire about the reasons for (something), the character of (someone), etc.: *to investigate the crime* –**investigator** /ɪn'vestɪ̣geɪtəʳ / *n* –**investigation** /-'geɪʃən / *n* [C;U]

**in·ves·ti·ture** /ɪn'vestɪ̣tʃəʳ‖-tʃuəʳ/ *n* a ceremony giving someone a high rank

**in·vest·ment** /ɪn'vestmənt/ *n* **1** [U] the act or action of INVESTing **2** [C] an amount of money INVESTed: *an investment of £100 in a growing business*

**in·vet·e·rate** /ɪn'vetərɪ̣t/ *adj* [A] settled in a (bad) habit: *an inveterate* LIAR|*inveterate hatred*

**in·vid·i·ous** /ɪn'vɪdɪəs/ *adj* [A] which will make people unjustly offended or jealous –**invidiously** *adv*

**in·vi·gi·late** /ɪn'vɪdʒɪ̣leɪt/ *v* **-lated, -lating** [I;T] *BrE* to watch over (an examination or the people taking it) in order to prevent dishonesty –**invigilator** *n* –**invigilation** /-'leɪʃən / *n* [U]

**in·vig·o·rate** /ɪn'vɪgəreɪt/ *v* **-rated, -rating** [T] to give a feeling of strength and/or power to: *an invigorating swim in the lake*

**in·vin·ci·ble** /ɪn'vɪnsəbəl/ *adj* too strong to be conquered –**invincibility** /-ə'bɪlɪ̣ti / *n* [U] –**invincibly** *adj*

**in·vis·i·ble** /ɪn'vɪzəbəl/ *adj* **1** not VISIBLE; that cannot be seen; hidden from sight **2** not recorded, esp. in statements of profit and loss: *invisible earnings/*EXPORTS –**invisibility** /-əbɪlɪ̣ti/ *n* [U] –**invisibly** *adv*

**in·vi·ta·tion** /,ɪnvɪ̣'teɪʃən/ *n* **1** [C +*to-v*] an often written request to go somewhere or do something: **2** [U] the act of inviting: *entrance by invitation only*

**in·vite** /ɪn'vaɪt/ *v* **-vited, -viting** [T] **1** [*to*] to ask (somebody) to a social occasion: *She invited me to her party.*|*Why don't you invite me in (to the house)?* **2** to ask for; encourage: *I invited her to go for a walk.*|(fig.) *Some shops invite crime by making it easy to take goods.*

USAGE This word is not used when one is actually **inviting** someone. We may say "*Will you come to the party?*" and then later remark "*I* **invited** *them to the party.*"

**in·vit·ing** /ɪn'vaɪtɪŋ/ *adj* attractive: *some inviting goods in the shop window* –opposite **uninviting** –**invitingly** *adv*

**in·voice** /'ɪnvɔɪs/ *v,n* **-voiced, -voicing** [T] (to make or send) a bill for goods received

**in·voke** /ɪn'vəuk/ *v* **-voked, -voking** [T] **1** to call out to (a power, esp. God) for help **2** to request or beg for: *I invoked their help/their forgiveness.*

**in·vol·un·ta·ry** /ɪn'vɒləntəri‖ɪn'vɑlənteri/ *adj* not (done) from choice or intention; unwilled: *He gave an involuntary smile/gasp.* –see also VOLUNTARY (1) –**involuntarily** *adv*

**in·volve** /ɪn'vɒlv‖ɪn'vɑlv/ *v* **-volved, -volving** [T] **1** [*in, with*] to cause (someone) to become connected or concerned: *Don't involve other people in your mistakes.* **2** [+*v-ing*] to have as a part or result: *Taking the job involves living abroad.* –**involvement** *n* [U]

**in·volved** /ɪn'vɒlvd‖ɪn'vɑlvd/ *adj* **1** difficult to understand; COMPLICATED **2** [*with*] (of a person) closely connected in relationships and activities with others, esp. in a personal or sexual way

**in·ward** /'ɪnwəd‖-ərd/ *adj* **1** on or towards the inside

2 of the mind or spirit: *inward peace* –see also OUTWARD –**inwardly** *adv*: *inwardly happy*

**in·wards** /ˈɪnwədz‖-ər-/ also **inward** *AmE*– *adv* towards the inside –opposite **outwards**

**i·o·dine, -din** /ˈaɪədiːn‖-daɪn/ *n* [U] a simple substance (ELEMENT (1)) that is used in photography, and on wounds to prevent infection

**i·on** /ˈaɪən‖ˈaɪən, ˈaɪɑn/ *n* an atom which has been given (+) POSITIVE[1] (9) or (-) NEGATIVE[1] (3) force by the taking away or addition of an ELECTRON

**i·o·ta** /aɪˈəʊtə/ *n* [S] (only used in NEGATIVES[2], questions, etc.) a very small amount: *There's not an iota of truth in that.*

**IOU** *abbrev. for*: "I owe you"; a piece of paper saying that one owes a certain amount of money to someone else, with one's signature at the bottom: *I haven't any money; can I give you an IOU for £5?*

**IPA** *abbrev. for*: International PHONETIC Alphabet; a system of signs used for representing speech sounds: *This dictionary uses (the) IPA.*

**IQ** *abbrev. for*: INTELLIGENCE QUOTIENT; a measure of intelligence, with 100 representing the average

**IRA** *abbrev. for*: Irish REPUBLICAN Army; an illegal organization whose aim is to unite Northern and Southern Ireland by force

**i·ras·ci·ble** /ɪˈræsəbəl/ *adj* (of a person) tending to get angry –**irascibility** /-ˈbɪlǀti / *n* [U] –**irascibly** *adv*

**i·rate** /aɪˈreɪt◂/ *adj fml* angry: *an irate letter* –**irately** *adv*

**ir·i·des·cent** /ˌɪrǀˈdesənt/ *adj lit* showing changing colours as light falls on it: *iridescent soap bubbles* –**iridescence** *n* [U]

**i·ris** /ˈaɪərǀs/ *n* **1** a tall yellow or purple flower with large leaves **2** the round, coloured part of the eye

**irk** /ɜːk‖ɜrk/ *v* [T] to annoy; trouble: *It irks him to have to clean his house.*

**irk·some** /ˈɜːksəm‖ˈɜrk-/ *adj* troublesome; annoying

**i·ron**[1] /ˈaɪən‖ˈaɪərn/ *n* **1** [U] a very common and useful metal that is a simple substance (ELEMENT (1)), is used in the making of steel, and is found in very small quantities in certain foods, and in the blood **2** [C] a heavy flat-bottomed object with a handle on top, which is heated and used for making clothing and cloth smooth **3** [A] of great strength (of character); unyielding: *an iron will*

**iron**[2] *v* [T] to make (clothes) smooth with an IRON[1] (2): *I've been (doing the) ironing all day.|Would you like me to iron your shirt for you?*

**iron** sthg.↔**out** *v adv* [T] *infml* to remove or find an answer to: *to iron out the difficulties*

**Iron Cur·tain** /ˌ·· ˈ··/ *n sometimes derog* the name for the western border between the USSR (and other COMMUNIST countries) and the rest of the world, which cannot be easily crossed for purposes of trade, the exchange of information, travel, etc. (note the phrase **behind the Iron Curtain**)

**i·ron·ic** /aɪˈrɒnɪk‖aɪˈrɑ-/ also **ironical**– *adj* expressing IRONY –**ironically** *adv*: *He smiled ironically.*

**ironing board** /ˈ··· ·/ *n* a long narrow table on which clothes are spread to be made smooth (IRONED[2])

**iron lung** /ˌ·· ˈ·/ *n* a machine fitted over the body which helps a person to breathe

**i·ron·mon·ger** /ˈaɪənˌmʌŋgəʳ‖ˈaɪərnˌmʌŋ-, -ˌmɑŋ-/ *n BrE* a shopkeeper who sells HARDWARE (1), esp. metal goods

**i·ron·mon·ger·y** /ˈaɪənˌmʌŋgəri‖ˈaɪərnˌmʌŋ-, -ˌmɑŋ-/ *n* [U] *BrE* HARDWARE (1), esp. if made of metal

**i·rons** /ˈaɪənz‖ˈaɪərnz/ *n* [P] chains to keep a prisoner from moving

**i·ron·y** /ˈaɪərəni/ *n* **-ies** **1** [U] (amusing) use of words which are clearly opposite to one's meaning (as by saying "This is beautiful weather" when the weather is bad) **2** [C;U] a course of events or a condition which has the opposite result from what is expected, usu. a bad result: *life's little ironies*

**ir·ra·tion·al** /ɪˈræʃənəl/ *adj* **1** (of people and their acts) not (done by) using reason; against reasonable behaviour **2** (of living things) not RATIONAL; without power to reason –**irrationally** *adv*

**ir·rec·on·ci·la·ble** /ɪˌrekənˈsaɪləbəl/ *adj* (of people and their acts) which cannot be brought into agreement –**irreconcilably** *adv*

**ir·re·fu·ta·ble** /ˌɪrɪˈfjuːtəbəl/ *adj* too strong to be disproved: *an irrefutable argument* –see also REFUTABLE –**irrefutably** *adv*

**ir·reg·u·lar** /ɪˈregjʊləʳ‖-gjə-/ *adj* **1** (of shape) not regular; having different-sized parts; uneven; not level **2** (of time) at unevenly separated points; not equal **3** not according to the usual rules, habits, etc. **4** (in grammar) not following the usual pattern: *an irregular verb* –**irregularly** *adv* –**irregularity** /-ˈlærǀti/ *n* **-ties** [C;U]

**ir·rel·e·vance** /ɪˈrelǀvəns/ also **irrelevancy**– *n* **-cies** **1** [U] the state of being IRRELEVANT **2** [C] a remark or fact which is IRRELEVANT

**ir·rel·e·vant** /ɪˈrelǀvənt/ *adj* not RELEVANT; not having any real connection with or relation to something else: *If he can do the job well, his age is irrelevant.* (=does not matter) –compare PERTINENT –**irrelevantly** *adv*

**ir·rep·a·ra·ble** /ɪˈrepərəbəl/ *adj* which is too bad to be repaired or put right: *The flood did irreparable damage to the house.* –**irreparably** *adv*

**ir·re·place·a·ble** /ˌɪrɪˈpleɪsəbəl/ *adj* too special or unusual to be REPLACED (2)

**ir·re·pres·si·ble** /ˌɪrɪˈpresəbəl/ *adj* too strong or forceful to be held back: *irrepressible high spirits* –**irrepressibly** *adv*

**ir·re·proa·cha·ble** /ˌɪrɪˈprəʊtʃəbəl/ *adj* (of people and their acts) without blame; faultless –**irreproachably** *adv*

**ir·re·sis·ti·ble** /ˌɪrɪˈzɪstəbəl/ *adj* too strong, powerful, pleasant, etc., to be RESISTED: *an irresistible argument/force* –**irresistibly** *adv*

**ir·re·spec·tive of** /ˌɪrɪˈspektɪv əv/ *prep* without regard to: *They send information every week, irrespective of whether it's useful or not.*

**ir·re·spon·si·ble** /ˌɪrɪˈspɒnsəbəl‖-ˈspɑn-/ *adj* (of people and their acts) not RESPONSIBLE; showing lack of ability to behave carefully, think of the effect of actions on others, etc. *His behaviour was very irresponsible; he might have hurt somebody.* –**irresponsibility** /-ˈbɪlǀti / *n* [U] –**irresponsibly** *adv*

**ir·rev·e·rent** /ɪˈrevərənt/ *adj* (of people and their acts) showing lack of respect, esp. for religion

–**irreverence** *n* [U] –**irreverently** *adv*

**ir·rev·o·ca·ble** /ɪ'revəkəbəl/ *adj* that cannot be changed: *an irrevocable decision* –**irrevocably** *adv*

**ir·ri·gate** /'ɪrɨgeɪt/ *v* **-gated, -gating** [T] to supply water to (dry land) esp. by providing it with man-made streams (CANALS) –**irrigation** /-'geɪʃən / *n* [U]

**ir·ri·ta·ble** /'ɪrɨtəbəl/ *adj* easily made angry by small things –**irritability** /-ə'bɪlɨti / *n* [U] –**irritably** *adv*

**ir·ri·tant** /'ɪrɨtənt/ *n,adj* [A;C] (a substance) which IRRITATES (2)

**ir·ri·tate** /'ɪrɨteɪt/ *v* **-tated, -tating** [T] **1** to make angry or excite in an unpleasant way –see ANGRY (USAGE) **2** to make painful and sore: *Wool irritates my skin.* –**irritation** /-'teɪʃən/ *n*

**is** /s, z, əz; *strong* ɪz/ *v third person sing. present of* BE

**Is·lam** /'ɪslɑːm, 'ɪz-, ɪs'lɑːm/ *n* (the people and countries that practise) the Muslim religion, started by Mohammed –**Islamic** /ɪz'læmɪk, ɪs- / *adj*

**is·land** /'aɪlənd/ *n* **1** a piece of land surrounded by water: *Britain is an island.* **2** also **traffic island**– a raised place in the middle of the road where people crossing can wait for traffic to pass

**isle** /aɪl/ *n lit* an island

**is·n't** /'ɪzənt/ *v short for*: is not: *It's Monday, isn't it?*

**i·so·late** /'aɪsəleɪt/ *v* **-lated, -lating** [T] to keep apart or separate from others: *Several villages have been isolated by the floods.* –**isolation** /-'leɪʃən/ *n* [U]: *Living in complete isolation in the country*

**i·so·lat·ed** /'aɪsəleɪtɨd/ *adj* standing alone; the only one of its type: *an isolated farmhouse*

**is·sue**[1] /'ɪʃuː, 'ɪsjuː‖'ɪʃuː/ *n* **1** [U] the act of coming out or bringing out something: *I bought the book the day after its issue.* **2** [C] something, esp. something printed, brought or given out: *There's a new issue of Christmas stamps every year.* **3** [C] an important point: *The real issue is . . .* **4** [U +*sing./pl. v*] *old use and law* children: *He* **died without issue. 5 at issue** of importance; under consideration

**issue**[2] *v* **-sued, -suing** [T] **1** to bring out (esp. something printed and/or official) for the notice of the public **2** [*to*] to supply or provide officially: *They issued the soldiers with guns.*

**issue from** sthg. *v prep* [T] to come or result from: *His difficulties issue from his lack of knowledge.*

**isth·mus** /'ɪsməs/ *n* a narrow area of land which joins two larger land masses

**it** /ɪt/ *pron* (*used as subject or object*) **1 a** that thing, group, idea, etc., already mentioned: *"Whose coat is this?" "It's mine."|"Where's my dinner?" "The cat ate it."|The government has become very unpopular since it was elected.|They were all shouting; it* (=the shouting) *was terrible!* **b** (used of a person or animal whose sex is unknown or not thought to be important): *What a beautiful baby–is it a boy?* **2** that person: *"Who's that?" "It's me!"/"It's Harry!"/"It's the postman!"* **3** (used in statements, esp. about weather, time, or distance, as a meaningless subject or object: *It's raining.|It's Thursday.|It's 112 miles from London to Birmingham.|It's my turn.|If it weren't for the snow* (=if there were no snow) *we could climb the mountain.* **4** (used in sentences where the real subject comes later): *It's fun* **being a singer.** (=Being a singer is fun.)|It's no use **worrying.**|*It's a pity* **that you forgot.**|*It seems* **that she lost her way. 5** (used with the verb *be,* to make part of a sentence more important): *It was John who told me.* (=John told me, not Peter)|*It was yesterday that he told me.* (=not today) **6 that's it: a** there's nothing more to come: *You can have a boiled egg and that's it.* **b** that's right: *Hold the ladder for me–that's it!*

**SPELLING NOTE**

Words with the sound /aɪ/ may be spelt **e-**, like **eye.** or **ai-**, like **aisle**.

**i·tal·ics** /ɪ'tælɪks/ *n* [P;U] (the style of ) printing with small sloping letters: *This example is printed in italics.* –compare ROMAN, CAPITAL[1] (3)

**itch**[1] /ɪtʃ/ *v* **1** [I] to feel or cause soreness which makes one want to SCRATCH: *The wound itches all the time.|I itch all over.* **2** [T] *infml* to have a desire to do something soon: *I'm itching to go.*

**itch**[2] *n* **1** a sore feeling which makes one want to rub or SCRATCH the skin **2** a strong desire –**itchy** *adj* **-ier, -iest** –**itchiness** *n* [U]

**it'd** /'ɪtəd/ *short for* **1** it would: *It'd be all right if I had enough money.* **2** it had: *It'd been raining earlier that morning.*

**i·tem** /'aɪtɨm/ *n* **1** a single thing among a set or on a list **2** also **news item**– a piece of news on television or in a newspaper

**i·tem·ize** ‖also **-ise** *BrE* /'aɪtɨmaɪz/ *n* **-ized, -izing** [T] to set out all the details of (each ITEM (1)): *an itemized bill*

**i·tin·e·rant** /aɪ'tɪnərənt/ *adj* [A] travelling from place to place: *an itinerant judge*

**i·tin·e·ra·ry** /aɪ'tɪnərəri‖-nəreri/ *n* **-ries** a plan of a journey

**it'll** /'ɪtl/ *short for* **1** it will: *It'll rain.* **2** it shall

**its** /ɪts/ *determiner* (*possessive form of* IT) of that thing, animal, etc., already mentioned: *The cat drank its milk and washed its ears.*

**it's** /ɪts/ *short for* **1** it is: *It's raining.* **2** it has: *It's rained.*

**it·self** /ɪt'self/ *pron* **1** (used as the object of a verb, or after a PREPOSITION, when the same thing or creature does the action and is the object of the action): *The cat's washing itself.|The government has made itself unpopular.* **2** (used to make *it,* or the name of a thing or creature, stronger): *We won't buy new tyres when the car itself is so old.* **3 in itself** without considering the rest; as such

**ITV** *abbrev. for*: (in Britain) Independent Television; a system of broadcasting companies supported by PRIVATE (2) money: *She watched a programme on ITV.*

**IUD** *abbrev. for*: Intrauterine Device: an object placed in the childbearing organ of a woman to prevent her from having children

**I've** /aɪv/ *short for*: I have: *I've been here before.|I've got lots of time.|(esp. BrE) I've lots of time.*

**i·vo·ry** /'aɪvəri/ *n* [U] (the colour of) a hard white substance, of which elephants' TUSKS are made

**i·vy** /'aɪvi/ *n* [U] a climbing plant with shiny three- or five-pointed leaves

# J, j

**SPELLING NOTE**
Words with the sound /dʒ/, may be spelt **g-**, like **general.**

**J, j** /dʒeɪ/ **J's, j's** *or* **Js, js** the 10th letter of the English alphabet

**jab**[1] /dʒæb/ *v* **-bb-** [I;T *away, at*] to push (something pointed) with force; strike quick blows: *He jabbed his stick into the ground.*

**jab**[2] *n* **1** a sudden forceful push or blow **2** *infml* for INJECTION

**jab·ber** /ˈdʒæbəʳ/ *v* [I;T] to talk or say (something) quickly and not clearly: *I can't understand you if you keep jabbering (away) like that.* **–jabber** *n* [S;U]

**jack**[1] /dʒæk/ *n* **1** an apparatus for lifting a heavy weight, such as a car, off the ground –see JACK UP; see picture on page 85 **2** also **knave**– a playing card with a picture of a man on it: *the Jack of Hearts* –see CARDS (USAGE)

**jack**[2] *v* JACK UP

**jack·al** /ˈdʒækɔːl, -kəl‖-kəl/ *n* **-als** *or* **-al** a wild animal of the dog family

**jack·daw** /ˈdʒækdɔː/ *n* a bird of the CROW[1] family, believed to steal small bright objects

**jack·et** /ˈdʒækǝ̍t/ *n* **1** a short coat with SLEEVEs (1) –see picture on page 563 **2** the skin of a potato: *potatoes cooked in their jackets* **3** an outer cover for certain machines or engines that get very hot **4** →DUST JACKET **5** *AmE* for SLEEVE (2)

**jack-in-the-box** /ˈ·,· ·ˌ·/ *n* a children's toy which is a box from which an amusing figure jumps when the top is opened

**jack knife** /ˈ· ·/ *n* **jack knives** a usu. large folding pocket knife

**jack-knife** *v* **-knifed, - knifing** [I] (esp. of an ARTICULATED vehicle) to bend suddenly in the middle and become out of control esp. when it SKIDs

**jack-of-all-trades** /ˌ· · ˈ· ·/ *n* (*sometimes cap.*) a person who can do many different kinds of work

**jack·pot** /ˈdʒækpɒt‖-pɑt/ *n* **1** the biggest amount of money to be won in a game of cards or chance **2 hit the jackpot** *infml* to win the JACKPOT, or have a big success

**jack** sthg. ↔ **up** *v adv* [T] to lift with a JACK (1): *Jack up the car.*

**jade** /dʒeɪd/ *n* [U] (the colour of) a precious usu. green stone used in ornaments and jewellery

**ja·ded** /ˈdʒeɪdǝ̍d/ *adj* tired because of having had too much of something

**jag·ged** /ˈdʒægǝ̍d/ also **jaggy** /ˈdʒægi/– *adj* having a rough uneven edge **–jaggedly** *adv*

**jag·u·ar** /ˈdʒægjʊəʳ‖ˈdʒægwɑr/ *n* a large spotted wild cat of Central and South America

**jail**[1] ‖also **gaol** *BrE* /dʒeɪl/ *n* [C;U] a prison or place where criminals are kept as part of their punishment

**jail**[2] ‖also **gaol** *BrE v* [T] to put in JAIL

**jail·er, jailor**‖also **gaoler** *BrE* /ˈdʒeɪləʳ/ *n* a person who is in charge of a prison or prisoners

**jam**[1] /dʒæm/ *n* [U] fruit boiled and preserved in sugar and used esp. for spreading on bread

**jam**[2] *v* **-mm- 1** [T *together*] to pack or crush tightly: *I can't jam another thing into this bag.*|*The crowds jammed the streets, and no cars could pass.* **2** [T] to push forcefully and suddenly: *She jammed the top of the box down on my finger.*|*I jammed on the brakes/jammed the brakes on.* **3** [I *up*] (of parts of machines) to get stuck **4** [T] to block (radio messages) by broadcasting noise

**jam**[3] *n* **1** a mass of people or things JAMmed[2] (1) so close together that movement is difficult or impossible: *a traffic jam* **2 get into/be in a jam** *infml* to get or be in trouble

**jamb** /dʒæm/ *n* a side post of a door or window

**jam·bo·ree** /ˌdʒæmbəˈriː/ *n* a happy party or gathering, esp. of BOY SCOUTs

**jam-packed** /ˌ· ˈ·◂/ *adj* [*with*] *infml* with many people or things very close together;very CROWDED

**jan·gle** /ˈdʒæŋgəl/ *v* **-gled, -gling** [I;T] to (cause to) make a sharp unpleasant sound, as of metal striking against metal: *The bell jangled.*

**jan·i·tor** /ˈdʒænǝ̍təʳ/ *n* **1** *AmE and ScotE* for CARETAKER (1) **2** a person who guards or watches the main door of a large building, and lets people in and out –compare PORTER[1]

**Jan·u·a·ry** /ˈdʒænjʊəri‖-jʊeri/ *n* **-ries** also **Jan.** *written abbrev.*– the first month of the year

**jar**[1] /dʒɑːʳ/ *n* (the contents of) a short-necked wide-mouthed pot made of glass, stone, clay, etc.: *a* JAM[1] *jar*|*two jars of fish paste* –see picture on page 615

**jar**[2] *v* **-rr- 1** [I *on*] to make an unpleasant sound **2** [T] to give an unpleasant shock to: *The fall jarred every bone in my body.* **3** [I *with*] to go badly together: *jarring opinions/colours*

**jar**[3] *n* (something that causes) an unpleasant shock

**jar·gon** /ˈdʒɑːgən‖ˈdʒɑrgən, -gɑn/ *n* [C;U] *often derog* language that is hard to understand, esp. bezcause it is full of words known only to the members of a certain group: *computer jargon*

**jaun·dice** /ˈdʒɔːndǝ̍s‖ˈdʒɔn-, ˈdʒɑn-/ *n* [U] a disease that causes a yellowness of the skin, the white part of the eyes, etc.

**jaun·diced** /ˈdʒɔːndǝ̍st‖ˈdʒɔn-, ˈdʒɑn-/ *adj* **1** suffering from JAUNDICE **2** mistrustful; tending to judge others unfavourably: *He has rather jaundiced opinions about all these modern ideas.*

**jaunt** /dʒɔːnt‖dʒɔnt, dʒɑnt/ *v,n* [I;C *about, around*] (to go on) a short journey, usu. for pleasure

**jaun·ty** /ˈdʒɔːnti‖ˈdʒɔnti, ˈdʒɑnti/ *adj* **-tier, -tiest** (showing that one feels) satisfied with oneself and pleased with life: *a jaunty wave of the hand* **–jauntily** *adv* **–jauntiness** *n* [U]

**jav·e·lin** /'dʒævəlɨn/ *n* a light spear for throwing, esp. in sport –see picture on page 592

**jaw** /dʒɔː/ *n* one of the two bony parts of the face in which the teeth are set: *the upper/lower jaw* –see picture on page 299

**jay** /dʒeɪ/ *n* a noisy brightly-coloured bird of the CROW[1] family

**jay·walk** /'dʒeɪwɔːk/ *v* [I] to cross streets in a careless and dangerous way –**jaywalker** *n*

**jazz** /dʒæz/ *n* [U] music originated by black Americans, usu. with a strong beat and some free playing by each musician in the band

**jazz** sthg.↔ **up** *v adv* [T] *infml* to make more active, bright, or enjoyable: *to jazz up the room with some bright red curtains*

**jazz·y** /'dʒæzi/ *adj* **-ier, -iest** *infml* **1** like JAZZ music **2** attracting attention, as with bright loud colours: *a very jazzy dress* –**jazzily** *adv*

**jeal·ous** /'dʒeləs/ *adj* [*of*] *often derog* **1** wanting to keep what one has; POSSESSIVE[1] (1): *He is jealous of his possessions/of his wife's love.* **2** wanting to get what someone else has; ENVIOUS: *He is jealous of their success.* –**jealously** *adv: The dog jealously guarded its bone.*

USAGE **Jealousy** is a stronger and more unpleasant feeling than **envy.** Compare: *Peter's new job sounds very nice–I'm* **envious** */full of* **envy**/ *I* **envy** *him* (=I wish I had a job like his).|*Jane is full of* **jealousy** */is* **jealous** *of Peter* (=feels a strong dislike for him) *because she thinks she should have got the job.*

**jeal·ous·y** /'dʒeləsi/ *n* **-ies** [C;U] (a) JEALOUS feeling

**jeans** /dʒiːnz/ *n* [P] trousers made of a strong, usu. blue, cotton cloth (DENIM), worn informally –see PAIR[1] (USAGE); see picture on page 563

**jeep** /dʒiːp/ *n* a small car suitable for travelling over rough ground: *to cross the desert by jeep*

**jeer** /dʒɪəʳ/ *v* [I;T] to laugh rudely (at): *The crowd jeered (at) the prisoners.* –**jeer** *n*

**jell** /dʒel/ *v* [I] **1** also **gel**– to become firmer,like JELLY **2** also **gel** *BrE*– (of ideas, thoughts, etc.) to take a clear shape

**jel·ly** /'dʒeli/ *n* **-lies 1** [C;U] a soft food made a with GELATINE: *an orange jelly* **b** out of fruit juice boiled with sugar, so as to become clear, and used for spreading on bread: *apple jelly* –compare JAM[1] **2** [S;U] any material that is between a liquid and a solid state

**jel·ly·fish** /'dʒelifɪʃ/ *n* **-fish** *or* **-fishes** a sea creature with a body like jelly

**jem·my** /'dʒemi/ *BrE*||**jimmy** *AmE– n* **-mies** an iron bar used esp. by thieves to break open locked doors,windows, etc.

**jeop·ar·dize, -dise** /'dʒepədaɪz||-ər-/ *v* **-dized, -dizing** [T] *fml* to put in danger: *If you are rude to the boss it may jeopardize your chances of success.*

**jeop·ar·dy** /'dʒepədi||-ər-/ *n* [U] *fml* danger: *His foolish behaviour may put his whole future* **in jeopardy.**

**jerk[1]** /dʒɜːk||dʒɜrk/ *v* **1** [T] to pull suddenly: *She jerked out the knife that was stuck in the wood.* **2** [I] to move with a JERK[2] or jerks: *The bus jerked to a stop.*

**SPELLING NOTE**
Words with the sound /dʒ/, may be spelt **g-**, like **general.**

**jerk[2]** *n* a short quick pull or movement: *The knife was stuck but she pulled it out with a jerk.* –**jerky** *adj* **-ier, -iest** –**jerkily** *adv*

**jer·kin** /'dʒɜːkɨn||-ɜr-/ *n* a short coat, usu. SLEEVEless

**jerry-built** /'·· ·/ *adj derog* (esp. of houses) built quickly, cheaply, and not well

**jer·sey** /'dʒɜːzi||-ɜr-/ *n* **-seys** a tight KNITted woollen garment for the upper part of the body –see picture on page 563

**jest** /dʒest/ *v* [I] *fml* to speak without serious intention; joke –**jest** *n: He said it* **in jest.** (=as a joke) –**jesting** *adj: a jesting person/remark*

**jest·er** /'dʒestəʳ/ *n* a man kept in former times by a ruler to amuse him, tell jokes, etc.

**jet[1]** /dʒet/ *n* **1** a narrow stream of liquid, gas, etc., coming forcefully out of a small hole: *The firemen directed jets of water at the burning house.* **2** a narrow opening from which this is forced out: *Put a match to the gas jet to light the gas.* **3** an aircraft with a JET ENGINE: *travelling by jet*

**jet[2]** *v* **-tt-** [I;T *out*] to come or send out in a JET[1] (1): *The water jetted out.*

**jet[3]** *n* [U] a hard black material, used, when polished, for making ornaments

**jet-black** /ˌ· '·◄/ *adj* of the colour of JET[3]; very dark shiny black

**jet en·gine** /ˌ· '··/ *n* an engine that pushes out a stream of hot air and gases behind it, and is used for making aircraft fly

**jet-pro·pelled** /ˌ· ·'·◄/ *adj* (of a plane) pushed through the air by a JET ENGINE –**jet propulsion** *n* [U]

**jet·sam** /'dʒetsəm/ *n* see FLOTSAM AND JETSAM

**jet set** /'· ·/ *n* [U +*sing./pl. v*] rich, successful, and fashionable young people

**jet·ti·son** /'dʒetɨsən, -zən/ *v* [T] to get rid of by throwing out

**jet·ty** /'dʒeti/ *n* **-ties** a wall built out into water,used either for getting on and off ships or as a protection against the force of the waves

**Jew** /dʒuː/ *n* a member of a people, whose religion is JUDAISM, who lived in ancient times in the land of Israel, some of whom now live in the modern state of Israel and others in various countries throughout the world –**Jewish** *adj: the Jewish religion*

**jew·el** /'dʒuːəl/ *n* **1** a precious stone **2** a decoration that contains one or more of these and is worn in clothes or on the body

**jew·elled** *BrE*||**jeweled** *AmE* /'dʒuːəld/ *adj* decorated with, or having, jewels

**jew·el·ler** *BrE*||**jeweler** *AmE* /'dʒuːələʳ/ *n* a person who buys and sells jewels, watches, etc.

**jew·el·lery, -elry** /'dʒuːəlri/ *n* [U] → JEWELS (2)

**jib** /dʒɪb/ *n* a small sail

**jibe** /dʒaɪb/ *n* →GIBE

**jif·fy** /'dʒɪfi/ *n* [S] *infml* a moment: *I'll be ready* **in a jiffy.**

**jig[1]** /dʒɪg/ *n* (music for) a quick merry dance

**jig[2]** *v* **-gg- 1** [I] to dance a JIG **2** [I;T] to (cause to) move with quick short movements up and down

**jig·gle** /'dʒɪgəl/ *v* **-gled, -gling** [I;T] *infml* to (cause to) move from side to side with short quick light JERKS[2]: *Carry the cup carefully and don't jiggle it, or* *you'll spill the tea.* **-jiggly** *adj* **-jiggle** *n*

**jig·saw puz·zle** /'dʒɪgsɔː pʌzəl/ also **jigsaw**– *n* a picture stuck onto wood and cut up into many small irregular pieces to be fitted together for amusement

**jilt** /dʒɪlt/ *v* [T] to refuse to see (a lover) any more; unexpectedly refuse to marry (someone) after having promised to do so

**jin·gle¹** /'dʒɪŋgəl/ *v* **-gled, -gling** [I;T] to (cause to) sound with a JINGLE² (1): *He jingled the money in his pocket.*

**jingle²** *n* **1** a repeated sound as of small bells ringing or light metal objects striking against each other **2** a simple poem with a very regular beat, usu. of poor quality esp. as a radio or TV advertisement

**jinx¹** /dʒɪŋks/ *n* something that brings bad luck; a curse: *There seems to be a jinx on our team, because we always lose.*

**jinx²** *v* [T] *infml* to bring bad luck to

**jit·ters** /'dʒɪtəz‖-ərz/ *n* [*the* P] *infml* anxiety before an event: *I've got the jitters about that examination.* **-jittery** /'dʒɪtəri/ *adj*

**jive¹** /dʒaɪv/ *n* [U] (dancing performed to) a type of popular music with a strong regular beat

**jive²** *v* **jived, jiving** [I] to dance to JIVE music

**job** /dʒɒb‖dʒɑb/ *n* **1** regular paid employment: *He has a good job in a bank.|He's been* **out of a job** (=unemployed) *for months.* **2** a piece of work: *I've got a job for you: wash these dishes.* **3** something hard to do; difficulty: *It was/I had a (real) job to see the minister.* **4 a good/bad job** *BrE infml* a good/bad thing: *This restaurant is not cheap, so it's a good job you've brought plenty of money.* **5 just the job** *infml* exactly the thing wanted or needed **6 make the best of a bad job** to do as much or as well as possible in unfavourable conditions

USAGE What you do to earn your living is your job, your **work,** or (more formal) your **occupation**: *Do you enjoy your* **job?**|*Please state your name, age and* **occupation** *on the form.* **Post** and **position** are grander and more formal (words for a particular job): *Please send me details of the* **post/position** *which is advertised in today's paper.* A skilled job in which you use your hands is a **trade**: *She's an electrician by* **trade**. A job for which you need special training and a high level of education (such as being a Doctor or lawyer) is a **profession**. Some professions, such as teaching and nursing, are also called **vocations**, which suggests that people do them in order to help others. A **career** is a job or profession that you follow for your whole life. *Her political* **career** *began 20 years ago.* –see WORK¹ (USAGE)

**job lot** /'· ·, ˌ· '·/ *n* a group of things of different kinds, bought or sold together

**jock·ey** /'dʒɒki‖'dʒɑki/ *n* a person who rides in horse races, esp. professionally

**joc·u·lar** /'dʒɒkjʊləʳ‖'dʒɑkjələr/ *adj fml* meaning to cause laughter: *a jocular reply/person* **-jocularly** *adv* **-jocularity** /-'lærɪ̥ti / *n* [C;U]

**joc·und** /'dʒɒkənd‖'dʒɑ-/ *adj lit* merry; cheerful **-jocundity** /dʒəʊ'kʌndɪ̥ti, dʒə- / *n* [U]

**jodh·purs** /'dʒɒdpəz‖'dʒɑdpərz/ *n* [P] trousers for horse riding that are loose above the knee –see PAIR¹ (USAGE)

**jog¹** /dʒɒg‖dʒɑg/ *v* **-gg- 1** [T] to give a slight push or knock with the arm, hand, etc.: *You jogged my elbow and spoiled what I was drawing.* **2** [I] to move slowly and unsteadily: *The carriage jogged along on the rough road.* **3** [I] to run slowly and steadily: *I go jogging in the park before breakfast.* –see WALK (USAGE) **4 jog someone's memory** to make someone remember

**jog²** *n* **1** a slight shake, push, or knock **2** a slow steady run

**john** /dʒɒn‖dʒɑn/ *n AmE infml* for LAVATORY

**joie de viv·re** /ʒwɑː də 'viːvrə/ *n* [U] the joy of life

**join¹** /dʒɔɪn/ *v* **1** [I;T *to, together, up*] to come or bring together; connect (with); unite: *Join this pipe to the other one.|Join the two ends of the rope together.|Where do the two roads join (up)?|to join people in marriage* **2** [I;T *in*] to take part together (with): *Will you join me in a drink?* (=have a drink with me)|*Sarah never* **joins in,** *she always plays on her own.* **3** [T] to become a member of: *to join the army/the Labour party* **4 join forces (with)** to come together or unite for a common purpose

**join up** *v adv* [I] to offer oneself for military service

**join²** *n* a place where two things are joined together

**join·er** /'dʒɔɪnəʳ/ *n* a woodworker who makes doors, window frames, etc., inside a building –compare CARPENTER

**join·er·y** /'dʒɔɪnəri/ *n* [U] *esp. BrE* the work of a JOINER –compare CARPENTRY

**joint¹** /dʒɔɪnt/ *n* **1** a place where things (esp. bones) join **2** *BrE*‖**roast** *AmE*– a large piece of meat for cooking **3** *infml derog.* a public place, esp. one where people go for amusement **4** *infml* a cigarette containing the drug CANNABIS **5 put someone's nose out of joint** *infml* to make someone jealous by taking their place as the centre of attraction

**joint²** *adj* [A] shared by two or more people: *to take joint action|joint owners* **-jointly** *adv*

**joint³** *v* [T] **1** to provide with JOINTS¹ (1) **2** to separate (meat) into pieces at the JOINTS¹ (1)

**joist** /dʒɔɪst/ *n* one of the beams onto which a floor is fixed

**joke¹** /dʒəʊk/ *n* **1** anything said or done to cause laughter or amusement: *I was laughing because she had just told me a very funny joke.|Your bad behaviour* **is/has gone beyond a joke.** (=is/has become too serious to laugh at) **2 no joke** *infml* a serious or difficult matter: *It was no joke carrying those heavy bags.* **3 play a joke on someone** to do something to make other people laugh at someone –see also PRACTICAL JOKE

**joke²** *v* **joked, joking** [I *with, about*] to tell jokes: *You mustn't joke with him about religion.|joking remarks* **-jokingly** *adv*

**jok·er** /'dʒəʊkəʳ/ *n* **1** a person who likes to make jokes **2** an additional playing card, which in some games may have any value

**jol·ly¹** /'dʒɒli‖'dʒɑli/ *adj* **-lier, -liest** merry; happy; pleasant: *a jolly person/laugh/holiday* **-jollity** *n* [U]

**jolly²** *v* **-lied, -lying** [T] *infml* to make (someone) willing or eager (to do something); urge gently: *They jollied her into going with them.*

**jolt** /dʒəʊlt/ *v* [I;T] to (cause to) shake or be shocked: *Her angry words jolted him out of the belief that she loved him.* **-jolt** *n*

**jos·tle** /ˈdʒɒsəl‖ˈdʒɑ-/ *v* [I;T] (of a person) to knock or push against (someone): *Don't jostle (against) me.*
**jot**[1] /dʒɒt‖dʒɑt/ *n* [S] a very small amount; a bit: *not a jot of truth in it*
**jot**[2] *v* **-tt-** [T *down*] to write quickly, esp. without preparation
**jot·ter** /ˈdʒɒtəʳ‖ˈdʒɑ-/ *n* a number of pieces of paper joined together, used for writing notes on
**jour·nal** /ˈdʒɜːnəl‖-ɜr-/ *n* **1** a magazine, esp. of a society: *She's reading the British Medical Journal.* **2** →DIARY (1)
**jour·nal·is·m** /ˈdʒɜːnəl-ɪzəm‖-ɜr-/ *n* [U] the profession of producing, esp. writing for, newspapers or magazines **–journalistic** /-ˈɪstɪk/
**jour·nal·ist** /ˈdʒɜːnəl¹₃st‖-ɜr-/ *n* a person whose profession is JOURNALISM
**jour·ney**[1] /ˈdʒɜːni‖-ɜr-/ *n* **-neys** a trip of some distance, usu. by land: *He's going on/making a long journey.*|*They* **broke** (=interrupted) **their journey** *by spending the night in a hotel.* –see TRAVEL[2] (USAGE)
**journey**[2] *v* **-neyed, -neying** [I] *lit* to travel: *She's journeyed all over the world.*
**joust** /dʒaʊst/ *v* [I *with*] (in former times) to fight on horseback with LANCE*s as sport*
**jo·vi·al** /ˈdʒəʊviəl/ *adj* full of good humour; friendly: *a jovial old man/voice* **–jovially** *adv* **–joviality** /ˌdʒəʊviˈæl¹₃ti / *n* [U]
**jowl** /dʒaʊl/ *n* the lower part of the side of the face, esp. loose skin and flesh near the lower jaw
**joy** /dʒɔɪ/ *n* **1** [C;U] great happiness: *To her parents' joy, she won first prize.*|*My children are a great joy to me.* **2 for joy** because of (feeling) joy: *He jumped for joy when he opened his present.*
**joy·ful** /ˈdʒɔɪfəl/ *adj* full of joy: *a joyful person/event* **–joyfully** *adv* **–joyfulness** *n* [U]
**joy·less** /ˈdʒɔɪl¹₃s/ *adj* without joy; unhappy **–joylessness** *n* [U]
**joy·ous** /ˈdʒɔɪəs/ *adj lit* full of or causing joy: *a joyous heart/event* **–joyously** *adv* **–joyousness** *n* [U]
**joy·ride** /ˈdʒɔɪraɪd/ *n infml* a ride for pleasure in a (stolen) vehicle, often with careless driving
**joy·stick** /ˈdʒɔɪˌstɪk/ *n* a stick whose movement directs the movement of an aircraft
**JP** *n abbrev. for*: Justice of the Peace; a person who gives judgments in a less important court of law; MAGISTRATE
**jub·i·lant** /ˈdʒuːb¹₃lənt/ *adj* filled with or expressing great joy: *a jubilant person/shout* **–jubilantly** *adv* **–jubilation** /ˌdʒuːb¹₃leɪʃən/ *n* [U]
**ju·bi·lee** /ˈdʒuːb¹₃liː, ˌdʒuːb¹₃ˈliː/ *n* a period of great rejoicing, esp. to mark or remember some event
**Ju·da·is·m** /ˈdʒuːdeɪ-ɪzəm, ˈdʒuːdə-‖ˈdʒuːdə-/ *n* [U] the religion and civilization of the Jews
**jud·der** /ˈdʒʌdəʳ/ *v* [I] *BrE* (esp. of a vehicle) to shake violently; VIBRATE
**judge**[1] /dʒʌdʒ/ *v* **judged, judging** [I;T] **1** to act as a judge (in): *Who will judge the next case?* **2** [+*that*] to form or give an opinion about (someone or something): *Judge whether he's right or wrong.* –see also MISJUDGE
**judge**[2] *n* **1** [A;C] a public official who has the power to decide questions brought before a court of law: *a Judge of the High Court* **2** [C] a person who has the right to make a decision, esp. in a competition **3** [C *of*] a person who has the knowledge and experience to give valuable opinions: *She's a good judge of wine.*
**judg·ment, judgement** /ˈdʒʌdʒmənt/ *n* **1** [U] the ability to decide correctly: *I can't make that decision for you. You'll have to use your judgment.* **2** [C] an opinion: *to form a judgment* **3** [C] an official decision given by a judge or a court of law: *He* **passed** (=gave) **judgment on** *the accused man.*
**judgment day** /ˈ·· ·/ also **last judgment, day of judgment** – *n* (*often cap.*) the day when God will judge everybody
**ju·di·cial** /dʒuːˈdɪʃəl/ *adj* of a court of law, a judge, or his/her judgment –compare: *a* **judicial** *decision*|*a* **judicious** (=wise) *decision* **–judicially** *adv*
**ju·di·cia·ry** /dʒuːˈdɪʃəri‖-ʃieri, -ʃəri/ *n* **-ries** [C +*sing./pl. v*] *fml* the judges (in law) considered as one group
**ju·di·cious** /dʒuːˈdɪʃəs/ *adj* having or showing good judgment –opposite **injudicious**; compare JUDICIAL **–judiciously** *adv* **–judiciousness** *n* [U]
**ju·do** /ˈdʒuːdəʊ/ *n* [U] a type of fighting from Asia based on holding and throwing the opponent
**jug** /dʒʌg/ *BrE*‖**pitcher** *AmE*– *n* a pot for liquids with a handle and a lip for pouring –see picture on page 337
**jug·ger·naut** /ˈdʒʌgənɔːt‖-ər-/ *n BrE infml* a very large LORRY that carries loads over long distances
**jug·gle** /ˈdʒʌgəl/ *v* **-gled, -gling** [I;T *with*] **1** to keep (several objects) in the air at the same time by throwing them up quickly and catching them again **2** to do clever things (with), esp. in order to deceive from: *He went to prison for juggling his firm's accounts.* **–juggler** *n*
**juice** /dʒuːs/ *n* [C;U] **1** the liquid from fruit, vegetables, and meat: *orange juice* **2** the liquid in certain parts of the body, esp. the stomach, that helps people and animals to use (DIGEST[1]) food
**juic·y** /ˈdʒuːsi/ *adj* **-ier, -iest 1** having a lot of juice: *a juicy orange* **2** *infml* interesting, esp. because providing information about bad or improper behaviour: *I want all the juicy details.* **–juiciness** *n* [U]
**juke·box** /ˈdʒuːkbɒks‖-bɑks/ *n* a machine which plays music (or records) when a coin is put into it
**Ju·ly** /dʒʊˈlaɪ/ also **Jul.** *written abbrev.*– *n* **-lies** the seventh month of the year
**jum·ble** /ˈdʒʌmbəl/ *v* **-bled, -bling** [I;T] to mix in disorder: *Her books/thoughts (were) all jumbled (up/together).* **–jumble** *n* [S *of*]
**jumble sale** /ˈ·· ·/ *BrE*‖**rummage sale** *AmE*– *n* a sale of used articles to get money, esp. for some good work
**jum·bo** /ˈdʒʌmbəʊ/ also **jumbo-sized** /ˈ·· ·/– *adj* [A] larger than others of the same kind: *a jumbo* JET[1] (3)
**jump**[1] /dʒʌmp/ *v* **1** [I] to push oneself into the air by the force of one's legs; spring: *The horse jumped over the fence.*|*She jumped out of the window.*|(fig.) *He keeps jumping from one subject of conversation to another.* **2** [T] to spring over: *He jumped the stream.*

**SPELLING NOTE**
Words with the sound /dʒ/, may be spelt **g-**, like **general.**

–see picture on page 669 **3** [I] to make a quick sudden anxious movement: *The noise of the gun made him jump.* **4** [I] (esp. of prices and quantities) to rise suddenly and sharply: *The price of oil jumped sharply in 1973.* **5 jump the gun** to start something (like a race) too soon **6 jump the queue** to obtain an unfair advantage over others who have been waiting longer

**jump at** sthg. *v prep* [T] to be eager to accept: *She jumped at the chance to go abroad.*

**jump²** *n* **1** an act of jumping **2 be/stay one jump ahead** *infml* having an advantage over others by being in advance of them

**jump·er** /ˈdʒʌmpəʳ/ *n* **1** *BrE* a usu. woollen garment for the upper half of the body, pulled on over the head; SWEATER –see picture on page 563 **2** *AmE* a SLEEVEless dress, usu. worn over a BLOUSE

**jump·y** /ˈdʒʌmpi/ *adj* **ier, -iest** nervous: *I knew that something was going to happen, and I was very jumpy.* **–jumpily** *adv* **–jumpiness** *n* [U]

**junc·tion** /ˈdʒʌŋkʃən/ *n* an example or, usu., a place of joining, meeting, or uniting: *a railway junction where lines from all over the country meet.*

**junc·ture** /ˈdʒʌŋktʃəʳ/ *n fml* a state of affairs or point in time: **At this juncture** *in our nation's affairs, we need firm leadership.*

**June** /dʒuːn/ also **Jun.** *written abbrev.*– *n* the sixth month of the year

**jun·gle** /ˈdʒʌŋgəl/ *n* [C;U] a tropical forest too thick to walk through easily: *jungle animals/birds*

**ju·ni·or** /ˈdʒuːnɪəʳ/ *n,adj* [*to*] **1** younger: *She is junior to me.*|*You are my junior.* **2** of lower rank or position: *a junior officer/minister* –compare SENIOR[1,2]; see MAJOR (USAGE)

**Junior** *n AmE* [after *n*] the younger: *John Smith Junior is the son of John Smith.*

**junk¹** /dʒʌŋk/ *n* [U] *infml* old useless things: *What will you pay me for all this old junk?*

**junk²** *n* a flat-bottomed Chinese sailing ship

**junk·ie, junky** /ˈdʒʌŋki/ *n infml* a person who takes HEROIN as a habit

**jun·ta** /ˈdʒʌntə, ˈhʊntə/ *n* [C+sing./pl. v] *often derog* a (military) government that has come to power by force

**Ju·pi·ter** /ˈdʒuːpɨtəʳ/ *n* the largest PLANET of the group that includes the Earth, fifth in order from the sun

**jur·is·dic·tion** /ˌdʒʊərɨsˈdɪkʃən/ *n* [U] the right to use the power held by an official body, esp. a court of law: *The court can/cannot deal with this matter, as it is* **within/outside its jurisdiction.**

**ju·ris·pru·dence** /ˌdʒʊərɨsˈpruːdəns/ *n* [U] *fml* the science or knowledge of law

**ju·rist** /ˈdʒʊərɨst/ *n fml* a person with a thorough knowledge of law

**ju·ror** /ˈdʒʊərəʳ/ also **juryman** /ˈdʒʊərimən/, **jury-woman** /-ˌwʊmən/ *fem.* **-men–** *n* a member of a JURY (1)

**ju·ry** /ˈdʒʊəri/ *n* **-ries** [C +*sing./pl. v*] **1** a group of usu. 12 people chosen to decide questions of fact in a court of law: *The jury has/have decided that the prisoner is guilty.* **2** a group of people chosen to judge a competition: *the jury of the Miss World competition*

**just¹** /dʒʌst/ *adj* fair; in accordance with what is right and true: *a very just man*|*You have received a just reward/punishment.* **–justly** *adv* **–justness** *n* [U]

**just²** /dʒəst; *strong* dʒʌst/ *adv* **1** exactly at that time or place; exactly: *He was sitting just here.*|*He came just as I was leaving.*|*That's just what I wanted.* (–compare *That's not quite what I wanted.*) **2** only a little bit; almost not; hardly: *The skirt comes just below my knees.*|*I can only just lift it.* (=it is almost too heavy for me to lift) **3** only: *I don't want any dinner, just coffee.*|*Answer me, don't just stand there laughing.*|*Just listen to this!* (=used to make a command stronger) **4 just now: a** at this moment: *We're having dinner just now; come back later.* **b** a moment ago: *Paul telephoned just now; he wants some money.*

USAGE **Already**, **yet**, and **just** were formerly not used with the simple past tense when speaking of time. Expressions like: *I* **already** *saw him.*|*The bell* **just** *rang.*|*Did you eat* **yet**? are coming into *BrE* from *AmE* but some teachers do not like them.

**just about** *adv* almost; very nearly: *They had just about won the game when they had to stop playing.*

**jus·tice** /ˈdʒʌstɨs/ *n* **1** [U] the quality of being just; rightness; fairness: *The justice of these remarks was clear to everyone.* –opposite **injustice 2** [U] the action or power of the law: *to bring a criminal to justice*|*a court of justice* **3** [C] *AmE* a judge (of a law court) **4 do justice to someone/do someone justice** to treat someone in a fair way

**Justice of the Peace** /ˌ·· · · ˈ·/ *n fml* for JP

**jus·ti·fi·a·ble** /ˈdʒʌstɨfaɪəbəl/ *adj* that can be justified (JUSTIFY) –opposite **unjustifiable –justifiably** *adv*

**jus·ti·fy** /ˈdʒʌstɨfaɪ/ *v* **-fied, -fying** [T +*v-ing*/*to*] to be or give a good reason for: *How can you justify your rude behaviour?* **–justification** /-fɨˈkeɪʃən/ *n* [U] **–justified** *adj*: *Is he justified in his behaviour?*

**jute** /dʒuːt/ *n* [U] a substance from a plant used for making rope and rough cloth

**jut out** /dʒʌt/ *v adv* **-tt-** [I] to be in a position further forward than its surroundings: *The wall juts out here to allow room for the chimney.*

**ju·ve·nile¹** /ˈdʒuːvənaɪl‖-nəl, -naɪl/ *adj* of, like, by, or for young people: *juvenile books*|*a juvenile court*|*a juvenile* DELINQUENT

**juvenile²** *n fml or tech* a young person

**jux·ta·pose** /ˌdʒʌkstəˈpəʊz‖ˈdʒʌkstəpəʊz/ *v* **-posed, -posing** [T] *fml* to place side by side or close together **–juxtaposition** /ˌdʒʌkstəpəˈzɪʃən/ *n* [U]

# K, k

> **SPELLING NOTE**
> Words with the sound /k/ may be spelt **c-**, like **cool**, or **qu-**, like **queen**.

**K , k** /keɪ/ **K's, k's** *or* **Ks, ks** the 11th letter of the English alphabet

**kaf·tan** /'kæftæn||kæf'tæn/ *n* →CAFTAN

**ka·lei·do·scope** /kə'laɪdəskəʊp/ *n* a tube fitted at one end with mirrors and pieces of coloured glass which shows many coloured patterns when turned –**kaleidoscopic** /-'skɒpɪk||-'skɑ-/ *adj* –**kaleidoscopically** *adv*

**kan·ga·roo** /ˌkæŋgə'ruː◂/ *n* **-roos** an Australian animal which jumps along on its large back legs and which carries its young in a special pocket of flesh

**ka·o·lin** /'keɪəl$_{\partial}^{\text{I}}$n/ *n* [U] a fine white clay used for making cups, plates, etc., and also in medicine

**kar·at** /'kærət/ *n* →CARAT

**ka·ra·te** /kə'rɑːti/ *n* [U] an Asian style of fighting using blows with the hands and feet

**kay·ak** /'kaɪæk/ *n* a narrow covered boat esp. as used by Eskimos

**K.C.** [after *n*] *abbrev. for*: King's Counsel; (the title given, while a king is ruling, to) a British lawyer (BARRISTER) of high rank –compare Q.C.

**ke·bab** /k$_{\partial}^{\text{I}}$'bæb||k$_{\partial}^{\text{I}}$'bɑb/ *n* a dish of small pieces of meat and usu. vegetables cooked on a stick

**keel** /kiːl/ *n* **1** a bar along the bottom of a boat from which the whole frame of the boat is built up **2 on an even keel** without any sudden changes; steady; steadily

**keel o·ver** *v adv* [I] to fall over sideways: *The ship keeled over in the storm.*

**keen** /kiːn/ *adj* **1** [+*to-v*] having a strong, active interest; eager: *a keen student of politics|keen competition for the job|(BrE) keen to pass the examination|She's keen on* (=very interested in) *football/passing the examination.* **2** (of the mind, the feelings, the five senses, etc.) good, strong, quick at understanding, deeply felt, etc.: *a keen mind|a keen desire|keen sight* **3** sharp; with a fine cutting edge –**keenly** *adv* –**keenness** *n* [U]

**keep¹** /kiːp/ *v* **kept** /kept/, **keeping 1** [T] to have without the need of returning: *You can keep it; I don't need it.|I gave him £5 for the food, and told him to keep the change.* **2** [T] to have for some time or for more time: *Please keep this for me until I come back and collect it.|These old clothes are not worth keeping.* **3** [I;T +*v-ing*] to (cause to) stay, remain, or continue: *It's hard to keep warm in this cold weather.|Her illness kept her in hospital for six weeks.|He keeps (on) interrupting* (=interrupts continually)*|Keep off the grass!* (=don't walk on it)*|Try to keep out of trouble.|The work is hard, but I'll keep at it until it's finished.* **4** [T] to know (a secret) without telling: *She kept his secret for 15 years.* **5** [T] to offer regularly for sale: *That shop keeps everything you will need.* **6** [T] to make regular written records of or in: *Keep an account of what you spend.|I've always kept a* DIARY. **7** [T] to take care of and provide with food, money, etc.: *She kept her brother's children when he died.* **8** [T *from*] *fml* to guard; protect: *May God keep you (from harm)!* **9** [T] to own (and make money from): *She keeps chickens.* **10** [I] (of food) to remain fresh and fit to eat: (fig.)*"I've got something to tell you." "Won't it keep until later?"* **11** [I] to be (in the stated condition of health): *"How are you keeping?" "I'm keeping quite well."* **12** [I;T *from*] to hold back; delay or prevent: *You're late; what kept you?|I know you're busy; I won't keep you.|Can't you keep your dog from coming into my garden?* **13** [T] to fulfil: *She kept her promise/appointment.* **14 keep one's head** to remain calm **15 keep someone company** to remain with someone: *I don't want to be alone; will you keep me company?*

**keep** sthg.↔ **back** *v adv* [T] not to tell or give; WITHHOLD: *She told us most of the story, but kept back the bit about her uncle.*

**keep** sbdy./sthg.↔ **down** *v adv* [T] **1** to control; prevent from increasing: *Chemicals are used for keeping insects down.* **2** to keep in a state like slavery; OPPRESS (1)

**keep on** *v adv* **1** [I;T (=**keep on** sthg.) +*v-ing*] to continue (doing something): *Prices keep on increasing.* **2** [T] (**keep** sthg.↔ **on**) to continue to have: *I'll keep the flat on through the summer.*

**keep out** *v adv* [I;T (=**keep** sbdy./sthg.↔ **out**) *of*] to (cause to) remain outside: *Warm clothing will keep out the cold.*

**keep to** *v prep* [T] **1** (**keep to** sthg.) to move, or stay in (a certain position): *Traffic in Britain keeps to the left.|He kept to his room.* **2** (**keep to** sthg.) to limit oneself to: *keep to the subject* **3** (**keep** sthg. **to** sbdy.) to keep private to (oneself): *He kept the news to himself.|She doesn't go out much; she likes to* **keep herself to herself.**

**keep up** *v adv* **1** [T] (**keep** sthg.↔ **up**) to cause to remain high: *a belt to keep my trousers up|*(fig.) *She kept up her spirits by singing.* **2** [T] (**keep** sthg.↔ **up**) to keep in good condition: *How do you keep up this large house?* **3** [I;T] (=**keep up** sthg.) to continue: *Keep up the good work.|Will the fine weather keep up?* **4** [I;T] (=**keep** sbdy. **up**) to (cause to) remain out of bed: *I hope I'm not keeping you up.* **5** [I *with*] to remain level: *I had to run to keep up (with the girls).* **6 keep up with the Joneses** *derog* to stay level with social changes; compete with one's neighbours socially

**keep²** *n* **1** [U] (the cost of providing) necessary goods and services, esp. food and lodgings: *He doesn't do* *enough to* **earn his keep. 2** [C] a great tower of a castle

**keep·er** /'ki:pəʳ/ *n* a person who guards, protects, or looks after: *The keeper is feeding the animals.|shopkeeper|doorkeeper*

**keep·ing** /'ki:pɪŋ/ *n* [U] **1** care or charge: *Don't worry; your jewels are* **in safe keeping.** (=being guarded carefully) **2 out of/in keeping (with something)** not in/in agreement (with something): *His words are out of keeping with his actions.*

**keep·sake** /'ki:pseɪk/ *n* something, usu. small, given to be kept in memory of the giver

**keg** /keg/ *n* a small barrel

**ken·nel**[1] /'kenl/ *n* **1** a usu. small house for a dog **2** *AmE* for KENNELS

**kennel**[2] *v* **-ll-** [T] to keep or put in a KENNEL or a KENNELS

**ken·nels** /'kenlz/ *n* **kennels** a place where small animals are looked after while their owners are away

**kept** /kept/ *v past tense and participle of* KEEP

**kerb** *BrE*||**curb** *AmE* /kɜ:b||kɜrb/ *n* a line of raised stones separating the footpath from the road –see picture on page 297

**ker·chief** /'kɜ:tʃɪf||'kɜr-/ *n old use* a square piece of cloth worn (usu. by women) to cover the head, neck, etc.

**ker·nel** /'kɜ:nl||'kɜr-/ *n* the part, usu. eatable, of a nut, fruit stone, or seed inside its hard covering or shell

**ker·o·sene, -sine** /'kerəsi:n/ *n* [U] *AmE* for PARAFFIN

**kes·trel** /'kestrəl/ *n* a red-brown European bird (FALCON) which eats mice, insects, and small birds

**ketch·up** /'ketʃəp/ *n* [U] a thick red sweet liquid made from TOMATOes, used for giving a pleasant taste to food

**ket·tle** /'ketl/ *n* a metal pot with a lid, a handle, and a SPOUT (=a narrow curved mouth for pouring), used mainly for boiling water –see picture on page 337

**ket·tle·drum** /'ketldrʌm/ *n* a large metal drum, with a round curved-up bottom

**key**[1] /ki:/ *n* **keys 1** an instrument, usu. made of metal and with a special shape, used esp. for locking and unlocking a door, starting and stopping a car engine, etc. –see picture on page 85 **2** [*to*] something that explains, answers, or helps you to understand: *a key to the grammar exercises*|(fig.) *Her unhappy childhood is the key to her character.* **3** any of the parts in a writing or printing machine or musical instrument that are pressed down to make it work: *the keys of a piano/a* TYPEWRITER **4** a set of musical notes based on a particular note –sounds like **quay**

**key**[2] *v* [T *to*] to make (more) suitable: *The rate of production must be keyed to the level of buying.*

**key**[3] *adj* [A] very important; necessary for success: *She has a key position in the firm.*

**key·board** /'ki:bɔ:d||-bord/ *n* a row of KEYS[1] (3) on a musical instrument or machine: *the keyboard of a piano/a* TYPEWRITER –see picture on page 415

**keyed up** /'ki:d 'ʌp/ *adj* [about] excited or nervous: *We're all very keyed up about the examination.*

**key·hole** /'ki:həʊl/ *n* a hole for the key in a lock, a clock, etc.

**key·note** /'ki:nəʊt/ *n* [A;C] (containing) a central or the most important idea: *The keynote of her speech was that we need higher wages.*

**key ring** /'· ·/ *n* a ring or ring-shaped thing on which keys are kept

**kg.** *written abbrev. said as:* KILOGRAM(*s*)

**kha·ki** /'kɑ:ki||'kæki, 'kɑki/ *adj,n* [U] **1** a yellow-brown colour **2** cloth of this colour, esp. as worn by soldiers

**kib·butz** /kɪ'bʊts/ *n* **-zim** /sɪm/ *or* **-zes** a farm or settlement in Israel where many people live and work together

**kick**[1] /kɪk/ *v* **1** [T] to hit with the foot: *She kicked the ball.* –see picture on page 669 **2** [T] to make or SCORE by doing this: *He kicked a hole in the door.|He kicked a* GOAL. **3** [I] to move the foot or feet as if to strike a blow: *Babies kick to exercise their legs.* **4** [I] (of a gun) to move backwards forcefully when fired

**kick off** *v adv* [I] to start a game of football –see also KICKOFF

**kick** sbdy.↔ **out** *v adv* [T *of*] to remove or dismiss, esp. violently

**kick up** sthg. *v adv* [T] *infml* to cause or make (a FUSS[1] or a ROW[4]): *I know he didn't want to go, but he shouldn't have* **kicked up such a fuss/row** *about it.*

**kick**[2] *n* **1** [C] an act of kicking: *Give the door a kick to open it.* **2** [C] *infml* a strong feeling of excitement, pleasure, etc.: *She drives fast (just) for kicks.* **3** [U] *infml* power to produce an effect: *This wine has a lot of kick in it.*

**kick·off** /'kɪk-ɒf||-ɔf/ *n* the kick which begins a game of football: *The kickoff is at three o'clock today.* –see also KICK **off**

**kid**[1] /kɪd/ *n* **1** [C] *infml* a child: *There were three kids playing in the street.* **2** [A] *AmE infml* (of a brother or sister) younger: *his kid sister* **3** [C;U] (leather made from the skin of) a young goat: *a goat with two young kids*|(fig.) *Don't treat those criminals with* **kid gloves.** (=gently)

**kid**[2] *v* **-dd-** *infml* [I;T *on*] to pretend, esp. in a playful manner; deceive: *He's not really hurt: he's only kidding.*

**kid·nap** /'kɪdnæp/ *v* **-pp-**||also **-p-** *or* **-pp-** *AmE*– [T] to take (someone) away unlawfully, and often by force, in order to demand money or something else for his/her safe return –**kidnapper** *n*

**kid·ney** /'kɪdni/ *n* **-neys 1** one of the pair of human or animal organs in the lower back area, which separate waste liquid from the blood **2** one of these animal organs cooked and eaten

**kidney ma·chine** /'·· ·,·/ *n* a large machine, esp. in a hospital, that can do the work of diseased human KIDNEYS, for people who have had their kidneys removed

**kill**[1] /kɪl/ *v* **1** [I;T] to cause to die: *to kill insects/one's enemies*|(fig.) *My feet are killing me!* (=hurting very much) **2 kill time** to make free time pass by finding something to do: *While waiting for the train he killed time by reading a book.* **3 kill two birds with one stone** to get two good results from one action

USAGE **Kill** is a general word meaning to cause (anything) to die, but **murder** means to kill a person on purpose: *My uncle was* **killed** *in a plane crash.|The cold weather* **killed** *our tomato plants.|She was sent to prison for* **murdering** *her husband.* **Slaughter** and **butcher** mean to kill animals for food, but both words are also used to describe cruel or unnecessary killing of humans: *Our army was* **butchered** *by the enemy's much larger forces.|Thousands of people are needlessly* **slaughtered** *in road accidents.* To **assassinate** means to kill an important political figure: *an attempt to* **assassinate** *the President*; and to **massacre** means to kill large numbers of (esp. defenceless) people: *After their victory, the army entered the city and* **massacred** *the women and children.*

**kill** sbdy./sthg.↔ **off** *v adv* [T] to kill (living things) one at a time: *The trees were killed off by the severe winter.*

**kill²** *n* **1** [S] the bird or animal killed in hunting **2** [*the* S] the act of killing, esp. hunted birds or animals

**kill·er** /'kɪlə<sup>r</sup>/ *n infml* [A;C] a person, animal, or thing that kills: *killer* SHARKS|*This disease is a killer.*

**kill·ing¹** /'kɪlɪŋ/ *n* **make a killing** to make a large amount of money suddenly, esp. in business

**killing²** *adj* that kills or makes very tired: *This work is really killing.* –**killingly** *adv*

**kill·joy** /'kɪldʒɔɪ/ *n* a person who spoils the pleasure of other people

**kil·o·me·tre**||-**ter** *AmE* /'kɪlə,miːtə<sup>r</sup>, kɪ'lɒmɪ̣tə<sup>r</sup>|| kɪ'lɑmɪ̣tər/ *n* 1,000 metres

**kiln** /kɪln/ *n* a box-shaped heating apparatus for baking or drying: *a brick kiln*

**kil·o·gram, -gramme** /'kɪləgræm/ also **kilo** /'kiːləʊ/ *infml– n* 1,000 grams

**kil·o·watt** /'kɪləwɒt||-wɑt/ *n* 1,000 WATTS

**kilt** /kɪlt/ *n* a short skirt with many pressed folds, worn usu. by Scotsmen

**ki·mo·no** /kɪ'məʊnəʊ/ *n* **-nos** a long coatlike garment worn in Japan by women

**kin** /kɪn/ *n* [P] *old use & fml* members of one's family: *His* **next of kin** (=closest relative(s)) *were/was told of his death.* –see also KITH AND KIN; compare KINDRED

**kind¹** /kaɪnd/ *n* **1** [C *of*] a group, the members of which share certain qualities; type; sort: *We sell all kinds of hats.|Haven't you got any other kind?|that kind of book* **2** [U] nature or type: *They are different in size but not in kind.* **3 in kind: a** (of payment) using goods or natural products rather than money **b** with the same treatment: *I paid him back in kind for hitting me.* **4 kind of** *infml, esp. AmE* rather; in a certain way: *I'm feeling kind of tired.|She kind of hoped to be invited.* **5 of a kind: a** *old use* of the same sort: *They're all of a kind.* **b** of a not very good sort: *She gave us coffee of a kind, but we couldn't drink it.*

USAGE Sentences like: *Those* **kind/sort** *of parties always make me nervous* are common in speech, but are thought by teachers to be incorrect. In writing it is better to use this form: *That* **kind/sort** *always make me nervous.*

**kind²** *adj* helpful; (that shows one is) interested in the happiness or feelings of others: *She's very kind to animals.|It was very kind of you to visit me when I was ill.* –opposite **unkind**

**kin·der·gar·ten** /'kɪndəgɑːtn||-dərgɑrtn/ *n* →NURSERY SCHOOL

**SPELLING NOTE**
Words with the sound /k/ may be spelt **c-**, like **cool**, or **qu-**, like **queen**.

**kind-heart·ed** /,· '·· ◂||'· ,··/ *adj* having or showing a kind nature: *a kind-hearted person/action* –**kind-heartedly** *adv*

**kin·dle** /'kɪndl/ *v* **-dled, -dling** [I;T] to (cause to) start to burn: *The wood was wet and wouldn't kindle easily.*

**kin·dling** /'kɪndlɪŋ/ *n* [U] materials for lighting a fire, esp. dry wood, leaves, grass, etc.

**kind·ly¹** /'kaɪndli/ *adj* **-lier, -liest** pleasant; friendly: *a kindly smile|She's the kindliest/the most kindly person I have ever met.* –**kindliness** *n* [U]

**kindly²** *adv* **1** in a kind manner: *She spoke kindly to the old man.* –opposite **unkindly** **2** please: *Will you kindly pass me that book?* **3 not take kindly to** not to accept easily or willingly: *He didn't take kindly to being told how to behave.*

**kind·ness** /'kaɪndnɪ̣s/ *n* **1** [U] the quality of being kind **2** [C] a kind action: *Please have the kindness to answer this letter quickly.*

**kin·dred¹** /'kɪndrɪ̣d/ *n old use & lit* **1** [U] family relationship **2** [P] one's relatives or family. –compare KIN

**kindred²** *adj* [A] belonging to the same group; having almost the same habits, interests, etc.: *He and I are* **kindred spirits:** *we both enjoy music and football.*

**ki·net·ic** /kɪ'netɪk, kaɪ-/ *adj fml and tech* of or about movement –**kinetically** *adv*

**ki·net·ics** /kɪ'netɪks, kaɪ-/ *n* [U] the science that studies the action of force in producing or changing movement

**king** /kɪŋ/ *n* **1** [A;C *of*] (*sometimes cap.*) (the title of) the male ruler of a country, usu. the son of a former ruler **2** [C *of*] the most important member of a group **3** [C] **a** (in certain games played on a table) the most important piece **b** playing card with a picture of a king –see CARDS (USAGE), CHESS; compare QUEEN

**king·dom** /'kɪŋdəm/ *n* **1** a country governed by a king (or queen) **2** any of the three great divisions of natural objects: *the animal/vegetable/mineral kingdom*

USAGE A **kingdom** may be ruled over by a **queen**, like Britain at present.

**king·fish·er** /'kɪŋ,fɪʃə<sup>r</sup>/ *n* a small brightly-coloured bird that feeds on fish in rivers, lakes, etc.

**king·pin** /'kɪŋ,pɪn/ *n* the most important person in a group, upon whom the success of the group depends

**King's Coun·sel** /,· '··/ *n fml* for K.C.

**kink** /kɪŋk/ *n* **1** a backward turn or twist in hair, a rope, chain, pipe, etc. **2** a peculiarity of the mind or character –**kinky** *adj* **-ier, -iest**

**kins·folk** /'kɪnzfəʊk/ *n* [P] *old use* members of one's family: *He has no kinsfolk in America.*

**kins·man** /'kɪnzmən/ **kinswoman** /,wʊmən/ *fem.– n* **-men** /mən/ *old use* a relative

**ki·osk** /'kiːɒsk||-ɑsk/ *n* **1** a small open hut, such as one used for selling newspapers **2** *BrE fml* a public telephone box

**kip** /kɪp/ *v* **-pp-** [I] *BrE infml* to sleep –**kip** *n* [S;U]: *to have a kip*

**kip·per** /'kɪpə<sup>r</sup>/ *n* a salted fish (HERRING) that is cut open and preserved by being treated with smoke

**kiss¹** /kɪs/ *v* [I;T] to touch with the lips as a sign of love or as a greeting: *They kissed (each other) when they met.*

**kiss²** *n* **1** an act of kissing: *She gave him a kiss.* **2 kiss of life** *BrE* a method of preventing the death of a drowning person by breathing into his/her mouth –compare ARTIFICIAL RESPIRATION

**kit¹** /kɪt/ *n* **1** [U] *BrE* the clothes and other articles needed by a soldier, sailor, etc., or carried by a traveller: *camping kit* **2** [C] (a box for) a set of articles, esp. tools, needed for a particular purpose: *This toy aircraft is made from a kit.*(=a set of small separate pieces)

**kit²** *v* → KIT OUT

**kit bag** /'· ·/ *n BrE* a long narrow bag used by soldiers, sailors, etc., for carrying KIT (1)

**kitch·en** /'kɪtʃ½n/ *n* a room used for cooking –see also COOK; see picture on page 337

**kitch·en·ette** /,kɪtʃ½'net/ *n* a very small (part of a room used as a) kitchen

**kitchen gar·den** /,·· '··/ *n* a garden where fruit and vegetables are grown

**kite** /kaɪt/ *n* **1** a wooden or metal frame covered with paper or cloth for flying in the air, often as a plaything, at the end of a long string **2** a large bird (HAWK) that eats small birds and animals

**kith and kin** /,kɪθ ən 'kɪn/ *n* **1** [P] (friends, esp. from one's own country, and) relatives: *We may not agree with their politics, but we must remember that they are our kith and kin.* **2** [S] one of these

**kit** sbdy.↔ **out** also **kit** sbdy.↔ **up**– *v adv* **-tt-** [T *with*] to supply with necessary things: *She was all kitted out (with clothes) for the holiday.*

**kit·ten** /'kɪtn/ *n* a young cat

**kit·ten·ish** /'kɪtənɪʃ/ *adj* of or like a KITTEN; playful

**kit·ty¹** /'kɪti/ *n* a cat or KITTEN: *"Here, kitty kitty," called the little girl.*

**kitty²** *n* **-ties 1** (in some card games) a sum of money put in the centre of the table by all the players at the beginning, and taken by the winner **2** *infml* a sum of money collected by a group of people, and used for an agreed purpose

**ki·wi** /'ki:wi:/ *n* **-wis** a New Zealand bird with very short wings that cannot fly

**klep·to·ma·ni·a** /,kleptə'meɪnɪə/ *n* [U] a disease of the mind causing an uncontrollable desire to steal –**kleptomaniac** /-'meɪnɪæk/ *n*

**km.** *written abbrev. said as*: kilometre(s)

**knack** /næk/ *n* [*of*] *infml* a special skill or ability, usu. the result of practice: *He has a/the knack of making friends wherever he goes.*

**knave** /neɪv/ *n* **1** *old use* a dishonest man **2** →JACK (2) –**knavery** *n* [U]

**knead** /ni:d/ *v* [I;T] **1** to mix together and make a paste of (something, such as flour and water for making bread) by pressing with the hands **2** to press or make other movements on (a muscle or other part of the body) to cure pain, stiffness, etc.

**knee¹** /ni:/ *n* **1** the middle joint of the leg –see picture on page 299 **2** the part of a garment that covers the knee: *big holes in the knees of his old trousers* **3 go/fall on one's knees** to admit defeat and ask for mercy

**knee²** *v* **kneed, kneeing** [T *in*] to hit with the knee

**knee·cap** /'ni:kæp/ *n* the bone in front of the knee

**knee-deep** /,· '·◄/ *adj* [F *in*] deep enough to reach the knees: (fig.) *knee-deep in debt*

**kneel** /ni:l/ *v* **knelt** /nelt/‖also **kneeled** *AmE*, **kneeling** [I *down, on*] to go down or remain on the knee(s): *She knelt (down) to pray.*

**knell** /nel/ *n* the sound of a bell rung esp. for a death or funeral

**knew** /nju:‖nu:/ *v past tense of* KNOW¹

**knick·ers** /'nɪkəz‖-ərz/ *n* [P] *BrE infml* women's UNDERPANTS –see PAIR¹ (USAGE)

**knick-knack, nicknack** /'nɪk næk/ *n infml* a small ornament of any type, esp. for the house

**knife¹** /naɪf/ *n* **knives** /naɪvz/ **1** a blade fixed in a handle used for cutting as a tool or weapon –see picture on page 521 **2 have/get one's knife in someone** *infml* to treat someone as an enemy and always try to harm him/her

USAGE Note the word order in this fixed phrase: **knife and fork**

**knife²** *v* **knifed, knifing** [T *in*] to strike with a knife used as a weapon: *During the fight he was knifed in the stomach.*

**knight¹** /naɪt/ *n* **1** (in former times) a noble soldier on horseback **2** a man who has been given a title which has a rank below that of LORD¹ (2): **3** (in CHESS) a piece, usu. with a horse's head, that moves two squares forward in a straight line and one to the side

**knight²** *v* [T] to make (someone) a KNIGHT¹: *Sir George (Smith) was knighted by the Queen in 1981.*

**knight·hood** /'naɪthʊd/ *n* [C;U] the rank, title, or state of a KNIGHT¹

**knit** /nɪt/ *v* **knit** *or* **knitted, knitting** [I;T] **1** [*for*] to make (things to wear) by uniting threads into a close network by means of long needles (**knitting needles**): *I'm knitting (you) a pair of socks.* **2** [*together*] to unite or join closely: *I hope the two edges of that broken bone will knit (together) smoothly.* **3 knit one's brows** to show displeasure, worry, or deep thought by FROWNing

**knit·ting** /'nɪtɪŋ/ *n* [U] something which is being KNITted: *She keeps her knitting in a bag.*

**knit·wear** /'nɪt-weəʳ/ *n* [U] KNITted clothing: *This shop sells knitwear.*

**knives** /naɪvz/ *n pl. of* KNIFE

**knob** /nɒb‖nɑb/ *n* **1** a round lump, esp. on the surface or at the end of something: *a stick with a knob on the end|a knob of butter* **2** a round handle or control button

**knob·bly** /'nɒbli‖'nɑbli/ *BrE*‖**knobby** /'nɒbi‖'nɑbi/ *AmE*– *adj* **-blier,-bliest** having round KNOBlike lumps: *He has very thin legs and knobbly knees.*

**knock¹** /nɒk‖nɑk/ *v* **1** [I] to strike a blow; hit, usu. making a noise when doing so: *Please knock (on/at the door) before entering.* **2** [T] to hit; strike: *She knocked the cup off the table.|He knocked the fish on the head to kill it quickly.* **3** [T] *infml* to express unfavourable opinions (about someone): *Stop knocking him; he's a good singer really.*

**knock about¹/around** sthg.– *v prep* [T] *infml* to lie unnoticed in (a place): *That old thing has been knocking about the house for years.*

**knock about²/around**– *v adv infml* **1** [I] to be present or active: *"Who's that man? I've not seen him before." "Oh, he's been knocking about here for years."* **2** [I *with*] to have a relationship or be seen (with someone): *Sally's been knocking about with Jim for years.* **3** [T] (**knock** sbdy. **about**) to treat roughly: *They say he knocks his wife about.*

**knock** sthg.↔ **back** *v adv BrE infml* [T] to drink (something) quickly or in large quantities: *She knocked back 10 glasses of wine.*

**knock** sbdy./sthg.↔ **down** *v adv* [T] **1** to destroy (a building, bridge, etc.) by means of blows: *Our house is being knocked down to make way for a new road.* **2** also **knock over**– to strike (a person) to the ground (esp. with a vehicle): *Alec was knocked down by a bus yesterday.* **3** [*to*] to (cause to) reduce (a price): *I knocked him down to £3.*

**knock off** *v adv* **1** [I;T (**knock off** sthg.)+*v-ing*] *infml* to stop: *Let's knock off (work) early today.* **2** [T] (**knock** sthg.↔ **off**) to take from a total payment: *I'll knock $2 off.* **3** [T] (**knock** sthg.↔ **off**) *BrE infml* to steal from: *They knocked off the Post Office and got away with £4000.*

**knock** sbdy.↔ **out** *v adv* [T] **1** (of a drug) to cause sleep **2** (in BOXING) to make (one's opponent) lose consciousness or be unable to rise before a count of 10 seconds **3** to cause to be dismissed from a competition: *Our team was knocked out in the first part of the competition.* –see also KNOCKOUT

**knock** sthg.↔ **up** *v adv* [T] *BrE infml* to make or build in a hurry: *Can you knock up a meal for us now?*

**knock²** *n* **1** (the sound of) a blow: *a knock at the door* **2** a piece of bad luck or trouble: *He's taken/had quite a few knocks recently.*

**knock·er** /ˈnɒkəʳ‖ˈnɑkəʳ/ also **doorknocker**– *n* a metal instrument fixed to a door and used by visitors for knocking at the door

**knock-kneed** /ˌ· ˈ·◂‖ˈ· ·/ *adj* having knees that turn inwards and knock together, or at least touch, when walking (**knock-knees**)

**knock·out** /ˈnɒk-aʊt‖ˈnɑk-/ *n* **1** also **KO** *infml*– a KNOCKing out of one fighter (BOXER (2)) by another: *He won the fight by a knockout.* **2** *infml* someone (or something) causing great admiration (or surprise): *You really look a knockout in your new dress.* –see also KNOCK **out**

**knoll** /nəʊl/ *n* a small round hill

**knot¹** /nɒt‖nɑt/ *n* **1** a fastening formed by tying together the ends of pieces of string, rope, wire, etc.: *She tied her belt with a knot.* **2** a hard mass in wood where a branch joins a tree **3** a small group of people close together: *a knot of people whispering in the corner* **4** a measure of the speed of a ship, about 1,853 metres (about 6,080 feet) per hour

**knot²** *v* **-tt-** [I;T] to make a knot in or join together with a knot: *Knot the ends of the rope together.*|*This wire is too stiff to knot easily.* –opposite **unknot**

**knot·ty** /ˈnɒti‖ˈnɑti/ *adj* **-tier, -tiest** containing one or more KNOTS¹ (2)

**know¹** /nəʊ/ *v* **knew** /njuː‖nuː/, **known** /nəʊn/, **knowing 1** [I;T +(*that*); not *be* + *v-ing*] to have information in the mind: *I know he's there because I saw him.*|*I know (that) it is true.*|*He doesn't know how to do it.*|*I know what happened.*|*"He's very ill." "Yes, I know."* **2** [T] to have met and spoken to (someone) several times: *I've known Martin for years.* **3** [T] (used only in past tenses) to have seen, heard, etc.: *I've known him (to) drink twelve glasses of beer in an evening.* **4** [T *by*] to be able to recognize: *You'll know him by the colour of his hair.* **5** [T] *lit* to have experienced: *He has known much unhappiness.* **6 know a thing or two/the ropes** *infml* to have practical useful information gained from experience **7 know something backwards** to understand something perfectly **8 know one's own mind** to know what one wants **9 you know** (used for adding force to a statement): *You'll have to try harder, you know, if you want to succeed.* –see also KNOWN

USAGE Compare **know** and **learn**: To **know** is to be conscious of (a fact), to have skill in (a subject), or to have met (a person) before: I **knew** *I had passed the test.*|*She* **knows** *all about computers.*|*Do you* **know** *how to drive?* (not **Do you* **know** *to drive?*)|*"Do you* **know** *my brother?" "No, we've never met."* To learn is to get to know (a fact or subject), not a person): *I* **learnt** *that I had passed the test.*|*She's* **learning** *all about computers.*|*I'm* **learning** (*how*) *to drive.* Compare *I* **know** *how to drive* (not **am* **knowing**)

**know better** *v adv* [I *than*] to be wise or well-trained enough (not to): *She should know better than to spend all her money on chocolate.*

**know** sbdy./sthg. **from** sbdy./sthg. *v prep* [T] to be able to tell the difference between: *He doesn't know his left hand from his right.*

**know of** sbdy./sthg. *v prep* [T] **1** to have heard of or about: *Do you know of a good restaurant near here?* **2 not that I know of** not so far as I know

**know²** *n* **in the know** well-informed; having more information (about something) than most people

**know-all** /ˈ· ·/ also **know-it-all** /ˈ· · ˌ·/– *n derog* a person who behaves as if he/she knows everything

**know-how** /ˈ· ·/ *n* [U] *infml* practical ability or skill; "knowing how" to do something

**know·ing¹** /ˈnəʊɪŋ/ *adj* **1** (showing that one is) well-informed or possessing secret understanding: *a knowing person/smile/look* **2** because I know: *Knowing John, he'll be late.* (=he's always late)

**knowing²** *n* **there's no knowing** it's impossible to know: *There's no knowing what the weather will do.*

**know·ing·ly** /ˈnəʊɪŋli/ *adv* **1** in a KNOWING¹ manner **2** intentionally; with knowledge of the probable effect: *She would never knowingly hurt anyone.* –opposite **unknowingly**

**knowl·edge** /ˈnɒlɪd·‖ˈnɑ-/ *n* [S;U] **1** understanding: *a knowledge of/not much knowledge of the truth* **2** learning; that which is known: *a knowledge of/not much knowledge of French* **3** familiarity with; information about: *He has a good knowledge of London.*

**knowl·edge·a·ble** /ˈnɒlɪd·əbəl‖ˈnɑ-/ *adj* (of a person) having a good deal of knowledge; well-informed: *He's very knowledgeable about football.* –**knowledgeably** *adv*

**known¹** /nəʊn/ *adj* **1** [A] also **well-known**– generally recognized (as being something): *He's a known criminal.* **2 known as: a** generally recognized as: *She's known as a great singer.* **b** also publicly called;

**SPELLING NOTE**

Words with the sound /k/ may be spelt **c-**, like **cool**, or **qu-**, like **queen**.

Hans and his friend Peter are in the kitchen, making **something to eat**. They only want a quick **snack** and a **cup of tea**, but there weren't any clean **cups** or **plates**, so first Peter **did the washing-up**, and then put the plates on a **rack** on the **draining board**. He dried a few cups and **glasses** with a **teatowel**.
Hans has cut a couple of **slices** of bread from the loaf to **make** himself **a sandwich**. He **buttered** the bread, and then put some **slices** of cheese and tomato in the sandwich. He **pours** himself a **glass** of orange juice from the **jug**. Peter is **making the tea**. He puts some **teabags** into the **teapot**, and then pours boiling water into it from the **kettle**. Hans **helps himself** to some tea as well. Peter has his tea with milk, but Hans prefers tea with lemon.

**Questions** (Answers on page 702)

- **a** Peter needed some clean plates, so he did the .....
- **b** Hans cut two ..... of bread.
- **c** He made a cheese and tomato .....
- **d** Peter put some teabags and boiling water in the ..... to make the tea.

named: *Samuel Clemens, known as Mark Twain, became a famous American writer.* **3 make it known that . . .** *fml* to declare or cause to know that . . .:–see also UNKNOWN

**known²** *v past participle of* KNOW

**knuck·le** /ˈnʌkəl/ *n* a finger joint

**knuckle down** *v adv* **-led, -ling** [I *to*] *infml* to start working hard: *You'll really have to knuckle down (to your work) if you want to pass the examination.*

**knuckle-dust·er** /ˈ·· ˌ··/ also **brass knuckles** *AmE*– *n* a metal covering for the KNUCKLES, worn for fighting

**knuckle un·der** *v adv* [I *to*] to admit defeat; yield

**ko·a·la** /kəʊˈɑːlə/ also **koala bear** /·ˌ·· ˈ·/– *n* an Australian tree-climbing animal like a small furry bear

**Ko·ran** /kɔːˈrɑːn, kəˈrɑːn, ˈkɔːræn‖kəˈræn, -ˈrɑn, ˈkoræn/ *n* [*the* S] the holy book of the Muslims

**ko·sher** /ˈkəʊʃəʳ/ *adj* of or about food, esp. meat, which is lawful for Jews to eat

**kow·tow** /ˌkaʊˈtaʊ/ *v* [I *to*] *infml* to obey without question; be too humble (towards)

**Krem·lin** /ˈkremlən/ *n* [*the* U+*sing./pl. v*] (the group of buildings in Moscow which are the centre of) the government of the Soviet Union

**ku·dos** /ˈkjuːdɒs‖ˈkuːdɑs/ *n* [U] *BrE* honour, praise, glory, and thanks (for something done): *He got a great deal of kudos for his work at the university.*

**kung fu** /ˌkʊŋ ˈfuː/ *n* [U] a Chinese style of fighting using blows with the hands and feet, related to KARATE

**kw** *written abbrev. said as:* KILOWATT(*s*)

# L, l

**L, l** /el/ **L's, l's** *or* **Ls, ls 1** the 12th letter of the English alphabet **2** the ROMAN NUMERAL (=number) for 50

**L** *BrE written abbrev. said as:* (on an **L-plate**) learner; a driver of a car or other motor vehicle who has not passed the official driving test: *an L-driver*

**la·bel¹** /ˈleɪbəl/ *n* a piece of paper, cloth, etc. fixed to something, on which is written what it is, who owns it, etc.

**label²** *v* **-ll-** *BrE*‖**-l-** *AmE* [T] **1** to fix or tie a LABEL on: *The doctor labelled the bottle (poison/poisonous).* **2** to put into a kind or class; describe as: *His enemies labelled him a thief.*

**la·bor·a·tory** /ləˈbɒrətri‖ˈlæbrətori/ also **lab** *infml*– *n* **-tories** a building or room which contains scientific apparatus and in which a scientist works

**la·bo·ri·ous** /ləˈbɔːrɪəs‖-ˈbor-/ *adj* needing great effort: *a laborious* TASK **–laboriously** *adv* **–laboriousness** *n* [U]

**la·bour¹** *BrE*‖**labor** *AmE* /ˈleɪbəʳ/ *n* **1** [C;U] work, esp. tiring physical work, or effort **2** [U] workers, esp. those who use their hands: *skilled/unskilled labour* **3** [S;U] the act of giving birth: *She was* **in labour** *for three hours.* **4 labour of love** work done gladly and without thought of gain

**labour²** *BrE*‖**labor** *AmE v* **1** [I] to work, esp. hard **2** [I] to move or act with difficulty; struggle: *The engine was labouring.* **3** [T] to work something out in too great detail or at unnecessary length (often in the phrase **labour the point**)

**labour under** sthg. *v prep* [T] to suffer from; be troubled by: *He laboured under a misunderstanding.*

**Labour** *n,adj* (a person) supporting or connected with the LABOUR PARTY

**la·bour·er** *BrE*‖**laborer** *AmE* /ˈleɪbərəʳ/ *n* a worker whose job needs strength rather than skill

**labour ex·change** /ˈ·· ·ˌ·/ *n* (esp. formerly) JOB CENTRE

**Labour Par·ty** /ˈ·· ˌ··/ also **Labour**– *n* [U +*sing./pl. v*] a political party which tries to obtain social improvement for the less wealthy, esp. the one in Britain

**labour u·ni·on** /ˈ·· ˌ···/ *n AmE* for TRADE UNION

**Lab·ra·dor** /ˈlæbrədɔːʳ/ *n* a large black or yellow dog

**lab·y·rinth** /ˈlæbərɪnθ/ *n* a network of narrow twisting passages or paths, through which it is difficult to find one's way –compare MAZE **–labyrinthine** /ˌlæbəˈrɪnθaɪn, -θən/ *adj* [A]

**lace¹** /leɪs/ *n* **1** [C] a string or cord used for fastening something, esp. shoes **2** [U] a netlike decorative cloth made of fine thread: *lace curtains*

**lace²** *v* **laced, lacing** [T] **1** [T *up*] to draw together or fasten with a LACE¹ (1): *to lace up one's shoes* –opposite **unlace 2** [T *with*] to add a small amount of strong alcoholic drink to (weaker drink)

**la·ce·rate** /ˈlæsəreɪt/ *v* **-rated, -rating** [T] *fml* to tear (the flesh, an arm, etc.) roughly; cut: *Her face was badly lacerated by the broken glass.* **–laceration** /-ˈreɪʃən/ *n* [C;U]

**lack¹** /læk/ *v* [T] to be without; not have enough of: *We lacked food.*

**lack²** *n* [S;U] absence or need: *The plants died through/for lack of water.*

**lack·ey** /ˈlæki/ *n* **-eys** *derog* a person who behaves like a servant by obeying others without question

**lack·ing** /ˈlækɪŋ/ *adj* [F] *fml* **1** not present; missing: *Help was lacking during the storm.* **2 be lacking in** to have little of; need: *Is she lacking in courage?*

**la·con·ic** /ləˈkɒnɪk‖-ˈkɑ-/ *adj* using few words **–laconically** *adv*

**lac·quer** /ˈlækəʳ/ *v,n* [C;T;U] (to cover with) a transparent substance which forms a hard shiny surface, or makes hair stay in place; *hair lacquer*|*She lacquered the old table.* –compare VARNISH¹·²

**la·crosse** /ləˈkrɒs‖ləˈkrɔs/ *n* [U] a game played on a field by two teams, each player having a long stick with a net at the end to throw, catch, and carry the ball

**lac·tic** /ˈlæktɪk/ *adj tech* concerning or obtained from milk

**lac·y** /ˈleɪsi/ *adj* **-ier, -iest** of or like LACE¹ (2)

**lad** /læd/ *n infml* a boy; youth: *He's just a lad.*

**lad·der¹** /ˈlædəʳ/ *n* **1** a frame with steps (RUNGS), used for climbing, as up a building or the side of a ship: (fig.) *climbing the ladder of success* **2** *BrE*||**run** *AmE*– a ladder-shaped fault in a stocking

**ladder²** *v* [I;T] **a** *BrE* to cause (a stocking) to develop a ladder-shaped fault **b** *BrE*||**run** *AmE*– (of a stocking) to develop such a fault

**la·den** /'leɪdn/ *adj* [*with*] heavily loaded: *The bushes were laden with fruit.*|(fig.) *laden with sorrow*

**La·dies, -dies'** /'leɪdiz/ *BrE*||**Ladies room** /'·· ·/ *AmE*– *n* **Ladies, -dies'** a women's public LAVATORY

**la·dle¹** /'leɪdl/ *n* a large spoon with a long handle: *a soup ladle* –see picture on page 337

**ladle²** *v* **-dled, -dling** [T *into, out, out of*] to serve (food, soup, etc.) with a LADLE

**la·dy** /'leɪdi/ *n* **-dies 1** [C] *polite* a woman, esp. a woman of good social position –compare GENTLEMAN **2** [A] also **woman**– female: *a lady doctor*

**Lady** *n* **-dies** [A;C] a title put before the name of **a** a woman of noble rank **b** another title of rank or position: *Lady President*

**la·dy·bird** /'leɪdibɜːd||-ɜrd/ *n esp. BrE* a small round flying BEETLE, usu. red with black dots

**lady-in-wait·ing** /ˌ·· · '··/ *n* **ladies-in-waiting** a lady who is the servant of a queen or princess

**lag¹** /læg/ *v* **-gg-** [I *behind*] to move or develop more slowly (than others): *The children always lag behind when we go for a walk.*

**lag²** *v* [T *with*] to cover (water pipes and containers) with a special material (**lagging**) to prevent loss of heat

**la·ger** /'lɑːgəʳ/ *n* [C;U] (a drink, glass, or bottle of) a light kind of beer

**la·goon** /lə'guːn/ *n* a lake of sea water, partly or completely separated from the sea

**laid** /leɪd/ *v past tense and participle of* LAY¹

**lain** /leɪn/ *v past participle of* LIE¹

**lair** /leəʳ/ *n* the place where a wild animal hides, rests, and sleeps

**lake** /leɪk/ *n* a large mass of water surrounded by land: *We took a boat across the lake.* –compare POND

**la·ma** /'lɑːmə/ *n* a Buddhist priest of Tibet, Mongolia, etc.

**lamb¹** /læm/ *n* **1** [C] a young sheep **2** [U] the meat of a young sheep –see MEAT (USAGE)

**lamb²** *v* [I] (of sheep) to give birth to lambs

**lame¹** /leɪm/ *adj* **1** not able to walk properly as a result of some weakness in a leg or foot **2** not easily believed; weak: *He gave a lame excuse for being absent.* **–lamely** *adv* **–lameness** *n* [U]

**lame²** *v* **lamed, laming** [T] to make LAME¹ (1)

**la·ment¹** /lə'ment/ *v fml* [I;T +*v-ing*] to feel or express grief or sorrow (for or at)

**lament²** *n* **1** [*for*] a strong expression of grief or deep sorrow **2** a song or piece of music expressing sorrow, esp. for the death of somebody

**lam·en·ta·ble** /'læməntəbəl, lə'mentəbəl/ *adj* causing one to be very dissatisfied or to wish that something had not happened **–lamentably** *adv*

**lam·i·nate¹** /'læmɪ̈neɪt/ *v* **-nated, -nating** [T] to make (a strong material) by firmly joining many thin sheets of material on top of each other

**lam·i·nate²** /'læmɪ̈nɪ̈t, -neɪt/ *n* [C;U] material made by laminating (LAMINATE) sheets, e.g. of plastic

**lamp** /læmp/ *n* an apparatus for giving light, as from oil, gas, or electricity –see picture on page 355

**lam·poon** /læm'puːn/ *n* a piece of writing attacking a person, government, etc., by making them look foolish **–lampoon** *v* [T]

**lamp·post** /'læmp-pəʊst/ *n* a tall thin pillar supporting a lamp which lights a street or other public area –see picture on page 297

**lamp·shade** /'læmpʃeɪd/ *n* a cover, usu. decorative, for a lamp

**lance** /lɑːns||læns/ *n* a long spearlike weapon used by soldiers on horseback in former times

**land¹** /lænd/ *n* **1** [U] the solid dry part of the earth's surface: *She travelled over land and sea.* **2** [C] a part of the earth's surface forming a political whole; country; nation **3** [U] a part of the earth's surface all of the same natural type: *the forest lands of Norway* **4** [U] earth; soil: *He works (on) the land.* **5** [U] ground owned as property: *You are on my land.*

USAGE The earth's surface when compared with the sea is the **land**, but when compared with the sky it is the **earth**: *After a week at sea, the sailors saw* **land**.|*After a week in space, the spacecraft returned to* **earth**. An area considered as property is a piece of **land**: *the high price of* **land** *in London.* The substance in which plants grow is the **ground, earth** or **soil**. **Ground** also means the surface we walk on, but when this is indoors it is the **floor**: *The horse fell to the* **ground**.|*The plate fell to the* **floor**.

**land²** *v* **1** to come to, bring to, or put on land: *The ship landed the goods at Dover.* **2** [I] (of something moving through the air) to settle, come to rest, or fall: *The bird landed on the branch.*|*The plane landed safely.*|*The ball landed in the water.* –compare TAKE **off 3** [T] *infml* to put or arrive in a condition, place, or position: *That will land him in prison.* **4 land on one's feet: a** to have good luck **b** to come successfully out of difficulty

**land·ed** /'lændɪ̈d/ *adj* [A] owning large amounts of land: *a landed family*|*the landed gentry*

**land·ing** /'lændɪŋ/ *n* **1** the act of arriving or bringing to land: *The plane's landing was delayed because of fog.* –compare TAKEOFF **2** also **landing stage** *BrE*– a place where people and goods are landed, esp. from a ship **3** the level space or passage at the top of a set of stairs in a building –see picture on page 297

**land·la·dy** /'lændˌleɪdi/ *n* **-dies** a woman who owns and runs a small hotel (BOARDINGHOUSE): *seaside landladies* –compare LANDLORD

**land·locked** /'lændlɒkt||-lɑkt/ *adj* enclosed or almost enclosed by land: *a landlocked country, that has no port*

**land·lord** /'lændlɔːd||-ɔrd/ *n* **1** a person, esp. a man, from whom someone rents all or part of a building, land, etc. **2** a person, esp. a man, who owns or is in charge of a pub, hotel, etc. –compare LANDLADY

**land·mark** /'lændmɑːk||-ɑrk/ *n* **1** an easily recognizable object, such as a tall tree or building, by which one can tell one's position **2** something that marks an important point or change, e.g. in a person's life

**land·scape¹** /'lændskeɪp/ *n* **1** a wide view of country scenery **2** a picture of such a scene

**landscape²** *v* **-scaped, -scaping** [T] to make (the

land around new houses, factories, etc.) more like a garden
**land·slide** /'lændslaɪd/ *n* **1** a sudden fall of earth or rocks down a slope, hill, etc.: *The road was blocked by a landslide.* **2** a very large success for a person, political party, etc., in an election: *a landslide victory*
**land·slip** /'lænd,slɪp/ *n* a small LANDSLIDE (1)
**lane** /leɪn/ *n* **1 a** a narrow, often winding, road, esp. in the country **b** (part of the name of) a street in a town **2** a division **a** of a wide road, usu. marked by white lines so that fast and slow cars can stay apart **b** a running track –see picture on page 592 **3** a fixed path across the sea or through the air used regularly by ships or aircraft
**lan·guage** /'læŋgwɪdʒ/ *n* **1** [U] the system of human expression by means of words in speech or writing **2** [C] a particular system of words, as used by a people or nation: *He speaks two foreign languages.|the language of science* (=the particular words used by scientists) **3** [C;U] any system of signs, movements, etc., used to express meanings or feelings: *the language of music/mathematics|a computer language*
**language la·bor·a·tory** /'·· ·,···‖'·· ,····/ *n* a room in which people can learn languages by means of special machines, esp. TAPE RECORDERS
**lan·guid** /'læŋgwɪd/ *adj* lacking strength or will; slow and weak **–languidly** *adv*
**lan·guish** /'læŋgwɪʃ/ *v* [I] *fml or lit* **1** to be or become lacking in strength or will **2** [*in*] to experience long suffering: *to languish in prison*
**lan·guor** /'læŋgəʳ/ *n* [U] *lit* **1** tiredness of mind or body; lack of strength or will **2** pleasant or heavy stillness **–languorous** *adj* **–languorously** *adv*
**lank** /læŋk/ *adj* (of hair) straight and lifeless **–lankly** *adv* **–lankness** *n* [U]
**lank·y** /'læŋki/ *adj* **-ier, -iest** (esp. of a person) very thin and ungracefully tall **–lankily** *adv* **–lankiness** *n* [U]
**lan·tern** /'læntən‖-ərn/ *n* a container, usu. of glass and metal, that encloses the flame of a light
**lap¹** /læp/ *n* the front part of a seated person between the waist and the knees: *Come and sit on my lap.*
**lap²** *v* **-pp- 1** [I] (in racing) to race completely round the track: *Alan Jones lapped in under two minutes.* **2** [T] (in racing) to pass (another competitor) so as to be at least one LAP³ ahead of him/her
**lap³** *n* (in racing) a single journey round the track
**lap⁴** *v* **-pp- 1** [T *up*] to drink by taking up with quick movements of the tongue: *The cat lapped up the milk.* **2** [I *against*] to move or hit with little waves and soft sounds: *The sea lapped against the rocks.*
**lap** sthg.↔ **up** *v adv* **-pp-** [T] to listen eagerly to; accept without thought
**lap⁵** *n* the act or sound of LAPping⁴: *the lap of the waves*
**la·pel** /lə'pel/ *n* the part of the front of a coat (or JACKET) that is joined to the collar and folded back on each side towards the shoulders
**lapse¹** /læps/ *n* **1** a small fault, mistake, or failure in correct behaviour, esp. one that is quickly put right: *a lapse of memory* **2** a gradual passing away, esp. of time : *After a lapse of several years he came back to see us.*
**lapse²** *v* **lapsed, lapsing** [I] **1** [*into*] to sink, pass, or fall by degrees: *to lapse into silence* **2** [*from*] to fail with regard to correct behaviour, belief, etc.: *a lapsed Catholic* (=who no longer practises his/her religion) **3** (of business agreements, titles, etc.) to come to an end, esp. because of lack of use
**lar·ce·ny** /'lɑːsəni‖'lɑr-/ *n* **-nies** [C;U] *law* (an act of) stealing –compare THEFT
**larch** /lɑːtʃ‖lɑrtʃ/ *n* [C;U] (the wood of) a tall tree with bright green needle-like leaves and hard-skinned fruit (CONES)
**lard** /lɑːd‖lɑrd/ *n* [U] pig fat used in cooking
**lar·der** /'lɑːdəʳ‖'lɑr-/ *n* a cupboard or small room in a house where food is stored –compare PANTRY
**large** /lɑːdʒ‖lɑrdʒ/ *adj* **1** more than usual in size, number, or amount; big –opposite **small** –see Study Notes on page 494 **2 at large: a** (esp. of dangerous people or animals) free; uncontrolled **b** as a whole; altogether **3 as large as life** not able to be mistaken; real **–largeness** *n* [U]
**large·ly** /'lɑːdʒli‖'lɑr-/ *adv* to a great degree; chiefly: *He left his job largely because he was bored.*
**lar·gesse** ‖also **largess** *AmE* /lɑː'ʒes‖lɑr'dʒes/ *n* [U] generosity to those in need
**lar·i·at** /'lærɪət/ *n AmE* for LASSO¹
**lark¹** /lɑːk‖lɑrk/ *n infml* something done for a joke or amusement; bit of fun: *He only did it for a lark.*
**lark²** *n* a small light brown singing bird with long pointed wings, e.g. the SKYLARK
**lar·va** /'lɑːvə‖'lɑrvə/ *n* **-vae** /viː/ the wormlike young of an insect **–larval** *adj*
**lar·yn·gi·tis** /,lærɪ̇n'dʒaɪtɪ̇s/ *n* [U] a painful swollen condition of the LARYNX, which makes speech difficult
**lar·ynx** /'lærɪŋks/ also **voice box** *infml– n* **larynxes** *or* **larynges** the hollow boxlike part in the throat, in which the sounds of the voice are produced by the VOCAL CORDS
**las·civ·i·ous** /lə'sɪvɪəs/ *adj* feeling or showing uncontrolled sexual desire **–lasciviously** *adv* **–lasciviousness** *n* [U]
**la·ser** /'leɪzəʳ/ *n* an apparatus for producing a very powerful narrow beam of light, used to cut metals and other hard objects, in medical operations, etc.
**lash¹** /læʃ/ *v* **1** [T] to strike with or as if with a whip **2** [I;T *about*] to strike or move violently or suddenly: *The cat's tail lashed about angrily.* **3** [T] to tie firmly, esp. with rope: *During the storm all the boxes had to be lashed down to the ship's deck.*
**lash out** *v adv* [I *at, against*] **1** to strike or attack violently with a weapon, hand, foot, etc. **2** to attack with violent speech
**lash²** *n* **1** (a stroke given with) the thin striking part of a whip **2** a sudden or violent movement
**lass** /læs/ also **lassie** /'læsi/– *n Scot & N Eng E* a young girl or woman
**las·so¹** /lə'suː, 'læsəʊ/ also **lariat** *AmE– n* **-sos** *or* **-soes** a rope with one end that can be tightened in a circle (NOOSE), used (esp. in the US) for catching horses and cattle
**lasso²** *v* [T] to catch with a LASSO
**last¹** /lɑːst‖læst/ *n,pron* **1** [*+to-v*] the person or thing after all the others: *He was the very last to arrive.* –compare FIRST¹ **2 at (long) last** in the end; after a long time: *At long last we found out what had really happened.* **3 to the last** until the end

**last²** *determiner, adv* [*no comp.*] **1** after everything else; after the others: *George arrived last/was the last person to arrive.|This is my last £1.* (=the only remaining one) –compare FIRST² **2** on the occasion nearest in the past; most recent: *When did you last see him?|They've lived here for the last three years.* (=the three years up to this year)|*This week's class was shorter than last week's.* (not **the last week's*) –compare NEXT² (2) **3 last but not least** important, although coming at the end

**last³** *v* **1** to measure in length of time; go on; continue: *The hot weather lasted until September.* **2** [I] to remain of use, in good condition, or unweakened: *This cheap watch won't last (for) very long.*

**last·ing** /'lɑːstɪŋ||'læs-/ *adj* [A] continuing for a long time; unending: *a lasting sorrow*

**last·ly** /'lɑːstli||'læst-/ *adv* after everything else; in the end: . . . *Lastly, let me mention the help I had from my parents.* –compare FIRSTLY

**latch¹** /lætʃ/ *n* **1** a fastening for a door, gate, window, etc., worked by dropping a bar into a U-shaped space –compare BOLT¹ (2) **2** a spring lock for a house door that can be opened from the outside with a key

**latch²** *v* [I;T] to fasten or be able to be fastened with a LATCH¹ –opposite **unlatch**

**latch on** *v adv* [I *to*] *infml* to understand

**latch onto** sbdy./sthg. *v prep* [T] *infml* **1** to understand **2** to refuse to allow (someone) to go; CLING to

**late¹** /leɪt/ *adj* **1** arriving, happening, etc., after the usual, arranged, or expected time: *The train was 10 minutes late.* **2** happening towards the end of the day, life, a period, etc.: *She returned in the late afternoon.* –compare EARLY¹ **3** [A] happening only a short time ago: *Some late news has just come in.* **4** [A] who has died recently: *her late husband* **–lateness** *n* [U]

**late²** *adv* **1** after the usual, arranged, or expected time: *The bus arrived five minutes late.* **2** towards the end of a period: *The bush was planted late in the season.* –compare EARLY² **3 of late** recently

**late·ly** /'leɪtli/ *adv* in the recent past

**la·tent** /'leɪtənt/ *adj* existing but not yet noticeable or fully developed: *latent ability/talent* **–latency** *n* [U]

**lat·e·ral** /'lætərəl/ *adj* [A] *tech* of, at, from, or towards the side: *a lateral* SHOOT *on a plant*|(fig.) *a lateral idea|lateral thinking* **–laterally** *adv*

**lat·est** /'leɪtɨst/ *n* [U] *infml* the most recent news, fashion, or example

**la·tex** /'leɪteks/ *n* [U] a thick whitish liquid produced esp. by the rubber tree

**lathe** /leɪð/ *n* a machine that turns a piece of wood or metal round against a sharp tool that gives it shape

**la·ther¹** /'lɑːðəʳ||'læ-/ *n* [S;U] **a** a white mass produced by shaking a mixture of soap and water: *He put some lather on his chin, and then began to* SHAVE. **b** any mass like this (e.g. of SWEAT)

**lather²** *v* **1** [I] (esp. of soap) to produce a LATHER **2** [T] to cover with LATHER

**Lat·in** /'lætɪn/ *n,adj* **1** [U] (of) the language of the ancient Romans **2** [C] (a member) of any nation that speaks a language that comes from Latin, such as Spanish, Portuguese, Italian, or French

**Latin A·mer·i·can** /ˌ·· ·'··· ◂/ *adj* of the Spanish- or Portuguese-speaking countries of South and Central America

**lat·i·tude** /'lætɨtjuːd||-tuːd/ *n* [S;U] **1** the distance north or south of the EQUATOR measured in degrees: *The ship's latitude is 20 degrees south.* –compare LONGITUDE **2** freedom in action, opinion, expression, etc.

**lat·i·tudes** /'lætɨtjuːdz||- tuːdz/ *n* [P] an area at a certain LATITUDE

**la·trine** /lə'triːn/ *n* (esp. in camps) a hole in the ground used as a TOILET

**lat·ter** /'lætəʳ/ *adj fml* **1** [A] (*after* the, this, *or* these) nearer to the end; later: *the latter years of her life* **2** [A] the second (of two people or things just spoken of): *Of pigs and cows, the latter* (=cows) *are more valuable.|Did he walk or swim? The latter seems unlikely.* –see FORMER²

**lat·ter·ly** /'lætəli||-ər-/ *adv* recently; lately –compare FORMERLY

**lat·tice** /'lætɨs/ *n* a wooden or metal framework used as a fence, a support for climbing flowers, etc.

**lau·da·ble** /'lɔːdəbəl/ *adj fml* (esp. of behaviour, actions, etc.) deserving praise **–laudability** /-ə'bɪlɨti/ *n* [U] **–laudably** *adv*

**laugh¹** /lɑːf||læf/ *v* **1** [I *at*] to express amusement, happiness, careless disrespect, etc., by making explosive sounds with the voice, usu. while smiling: *It was so funny, I couldn't stop laughing.* **2** [T] to influence or bring to a result by laughing: *They laughed her out of the house.|He laughed himself sick.* –compare SMILE², GRIN **3 laugh in/up one's sleeve** to laugh secretly **4 no laughing matter** serious

**laugh** sthg.↔ **off/away** *v adv* [T] to cause, by laughing, to seem less or unimportant: *She bravely laughed off her pain.*

**laugh²** *n* **1** an act or sound of laughing **2 have the last laugh** to win after earlier defeats

**laugh·a·ble** /'lɑːfəbəl||'læ-/ *adj* causing laughter; funny; foolish **–laughably** *adv*

**laugh·ter** /'lɑːftəʳ||'læf-/ *n* [U] the act or sound of laughing

**launch¹** /lɔːntʃ/ *v* [T] **1** to set a (newly-built) boat into the water **2** to send (esp. a ROCKET) into the sky **3** to cause (an activity, plan, way of life, etc.) to begin: *to launch an attack/a new product* **4** [*at*] to throw with great force

**launch²** *n* [S] the act of LAUNCHING¹

**launch³** *n* a large motor boat used for carrying people on rivers, lakes, etc.

**laun·der** /'lɔːndəʳ/ *v* [T] to wash (or wash and iron) (clothes, sheets, etc.)

**laun·derette** /lɔːn'dret/ ||also **laundromat** /'lɔːndrəmæt/ *AmE*– *n* a place where the public pay to wash their clothes in machines

**laun·dry** /'lɔːndri/ *n* **-dries 1** [C] a place or business where clothes, etc., are washed and ironed **2** [U] clothes, sheets, etc., needing washing or that have just been washed

**laur·el** /'lɒrəl||'lɔ-, 'lɑ-/ *n* a small tree with smooth shiny leaves that do not fall in winter

**la·va** /'lɑːvə/ *n* [U] **1** rock in a very hot liquid state flowing from an exploding mountain (VOLCANO) **2** this material when it has become cool and turned into a grey solid

**lav·a·to·ry** /'lævətəri||-tori/ also **lav** /læv/, **loo** *BrE infml*– *n* **-ries 1** (a room containing) a large seatlike bowl connected to a pipe (DRAIN), used for getting rid of the body's waste matter **2** a special building containing a number of these rooms –compare TOILET

**lav·en·der** /ˈlævəndəʳ/ *n* [U] a plant with small strongly-smelling pale purple flowers

**lav·ish** /ˈlævɪʃ/ *adj* **1** generous or wasteful in giving or using **2** given, spent, or produced in great quantity: *lavish praise* **–lavishly** *adv* **–lavishness** *n* [U]

**lavish on** *v prep* [T] to give or spend freely, generously, or wastefully: *He lavished money/kindness on his friends.*

**law** /lɔː/ *n* **1** [C] a rule that is supported by the power of government and that governs the behaviour of members of a society: *a law against drinking and driving* **2** [*the* S] the whole body of such rules in a country: *The law forbids stealing.*|*Murder is against the law.*|**Law and order** *is necessary for a peaceful society.* **3** [U] such rules, either in total or in part, and the way in which they work: *She's studying law at university.* **4** [C] a rule of action in a sport, art, business, etc.: *the laws of tennis* **5** [C] a statement expressing what has been seen always to happen in certain conditions: *the laws of physics* **6** [*the* U +*sing.*/*pl. v*] *infml* the police or a policeman: *The law was/were there in large numbers.*

**law-a·bid·ing** /ˈ· ·ˌ··/ *adj* obeying the law

**law·ful** /ˈlɔːfəl/ *adj fml* **1** allowed by law **2** obeying the law: *lawful citizens* –opposite **unlawful** –see LEGAL (USAGE) **–lawfully** *adv* **–lawfulness** *n* [U]

**law·less** /ˈlɔːləs/ *adj fml* **1** uncontrolled; wild **2** (of a country or place) not governed by laws **–lawlessly** *adv* **–lawlessness** *n* [U]

**lawn** /lɔːn/ *n* a stretch of usu. flat ground covered with closely cut grass, esp. in a garden

**law·suit** /ˈlɔːsjuːt, -suːt‖-suːt/ also **suit**– *n* a noncriminal case in a court of law

**law·yer** /ˈlɔːjəʳ/ *n* a person (esp. a SOLICITOR) whose business it is to advise people about laws and to represent them in court

**lax** /læks/ *adj* **1** not giving attention to details or to what is correct or necessary **2** careless or lazy **3** lacking in control **–laxly** *adv* **–laxity** also **laxness– –ities** *n* [C;U]

**lax·a·tive** /ˈlæksətɪv/ *n,adj* (a medicine) that causes the bowels to empty easily

**lay**[1] /leɪ/ *v* **laid** /leɪd/, **laying 1** [T *down*] to put down so as to lie flat: *Lay your coat on the bed.*|*We've had a new carpet laid in the bedroom.* **2** [T] to set in proper order or position: **Lay the table** *for dinner.* (=place knives, forks, etc., ready for a meal) **3** [T] to cause to lie flat, settle, disappear, or cease to be active: *Her fears were soon laid (to rest).* **4** [I;T] (of birds, insects, etc.) to produce (an egg or eggs) **5** [T] to make (a statement, claim, charge, etc.) in an official way: *The police have laid a serious charge against you.* **6** [T *on*] to risk (esp. money) on the result of some happening, such as a race; BET[2]

USAGE Do not confuse **lay** [T] (**laid, laid**) with **lie** [I] (**lay, lain**). A person can **lay** his coat on the bed; when he has done this his coat is **lying** on the bed. A third verb **lie** [I] (**lied, lied**) means "to tell a **lie**".

**lay down** sthg. *v adv* [T] **1** to put down (tools, arms, etc.) as a sign that one will not use them **2** to state firmly: *to lay down the law* **3** to store (esp. wine) for future use

**lay** sthg.↔**in** *v adv* [T] to obtain and store a supply of: *We've laid in enough food for the winter.*

**lay into** sbdy. *v prep* [T] to attack with words or blows

**lay** sbdy. **low** *v adv* [T] **1** to knock down **2** to make ill: *I was laid low by a fever.*

**lay** sbdy.↔ **off** *v adv* [T] to stop employing (a worker), esp. for a period in which there is little work: *They laid us off for three months.* –compare TAKE **on**; see also LAY-OFF

**lay** sthg.↔ **on** *v adv* [T *to, for*] to supply or provide: *My father laid on the drinks for the party.*

**lay** sbdy./sthg.↔ **out** *v adv* [T] **1** to spread out or arrange **2** to plan (a building, town, garden, etc.) **3** to knock or strike (a person) down –see also LAYOUT

**lay** sbdy./sthg.↔ **up** *v adv* [T] **1** to collect and store for future use **2** [*usu. pass.*] to cause to be kept indoors or in bed with an illness: *I was laid up with a cold.* **3** to put (a boat) out of service, esp. for repairs

**lay** sthg. **waste** *v adv* [T] to make (a place) bare, esp. by violence; destroy, as in war

**lay**[2] *adj* [A] **1** of, to, or performed by people who are not in official positions within a religion **2** not having knowledge of a particular branch of learning, such as law or medicine

**lay**[3] *v past tense of* LIE[1]

**lay·a·bout** /ˈleɪəbaʊt/ *n BrE infml* a lazy person who avoids working

**lay-by** /ˈ· ·/ *n* **-bys** *BrE* a space next to a road where vehicles may park out of the way of traffic

**lay·er**[1] /ˈleɪəʳ/ *n* **1** a thickness of some material (often one of many) laid over a surface: *These seeds must be covered with a layer of earth.* **2** a person or thing that lays something: *a bricklayer*

**layer**[2] *v* [T] to make a LAYER[1] (1) of; put down in layers

**lay·man** /ˈleɪmən/ *n* **-men** /mən/ **1** a person who is not a priest in a religion **2** a LAY[2] (2) person

**lay-off** /ˈ· ·/ *n* the stopping by a business of a worker's employment at a time when there is little work –see also LAY **off**

**lay·out** /ˈleɪaʊt/ *n* **1** the planned arrangement of a town, garden, etc. **2** a drawing or plan of a building. –see also LAY **out**

**laze**[1] /leɪz/ *v* **lazed, lazing** [I;T *away, around, about*] to rest lazily; to waste (time) enjoyably: *I spent the morning just lazing (around).*

**laze**[2] *n* [S] a short period of restful and lazy inactivity

**la·zy** /ˈleɪzi/ *adj* **-zier, -ziest 1** disliking and avoiding activity or work: *He won't work: he's just too lazy!* –compare IDLE[1] **2** (esp. of periods of time) encouraging inactivity: *a lazy afternoon* **3** moving slowly: *a lazy river* **–lazily** *adv* **–laziness** *n* [U]

**lb** *written abbrev. said as*: pound (weight)

**lead**[1] /liːd/ *v* **led** /led/, **leading 1** [I;T] to bring or show the way to (a person or animal) by going in front: *She led the blind man down the stairs.*|*The horses were led into the yard.*|*You lead and we'll follow.* **2** [I;T] to be the means of reaching a place, going through an area, etc.: *This road will lead you to the town centre.*|*The path leads through the woods.* **3** [T] to persuade or influence (someone) to do something: *What led you to believe I was ill?* **4** [I;T] to direct, control, or govern (an army, a movement, a meeting, etc.) **5** [I;T] to be ahead in sports or games: *England were leading France 15–0 at half time.* **6** [T] to (cause to) experience (a kind of life): *He led a hard life.*

USAGE To **lead** is to show the way by going first, to **guide** is to show the way and explain things, and to **direct** is to explain to someone how to get to a place: *He* **led** *them down the mountain.*|*She* **guided** *the tourists round the castle.*|*Could you* **direct** *me to the station, please?* To **drive** is either to control a moving vehicle, or to make animals move forward by going behind them: **Driving** *the cattle to market.* To **steer** is to control the direction of a moving vehicle or boat.

**lead** sbdy. **on** *v adv infml* [T] to cause to believe something that is not true

**lead to** sthg. *v prep* [T +*v-ing*] to have as a result; cause: *Smoking cigarettes leads to lung disease.*

**lead up to** sthg. *v adv prep* [T] to be an introduction to: *His kindness was leading up to a request for money.*

**lead²** *n* **1** [C] a guiding suggestion or example: *We're waiting for the Prime Minister to give us a lead.*|*I'll follow your lead.* **2** [*the* S] the chief or front position: *England were* **in the lead** (=winning the game) *at half time.*|*He's* **playing the lead** (=the chief acting part) *in the new play.*|*Japan has* **taken the lead** *in car production.* (=is now producing more than anywhere else) **3** [S *of, over*] the distance, number of points, etc., by which a person or thing is in advance of another **4** [C] also **leash** *fml or tech– esp. BrE* a length of rope, leather, chain, etc., tied to a dog to control it **5** [C] an electric wire for taking the power from the supply point to an instrument or apparatus –see picture on page 337 **6** [C] a piece of information that may lead to a discovery or something being settled; CLUE: *The police have several useful leads.*

**lead³** /led/ *n* **1** [U] a soft heavy easily melted dull grey metal, used for pipes, to cover roofs, etc. **2** [C;U] a thin stick of a black substance (a kind of CARBON (1)) used in pencils: *I need a soft lead pencil.*

**lead·en** /ˈledn/ *adj* **1** of the colour of lead; dull grey: *a leaden sky* **2** dull; heavy; sad: *a leaden heart*

**lead·er** /ˈliːdəʳ/ *n* **1** a person or thing that leads or is in advance of others: *The leader (of the race) is just coming into view.* –compare WINNER **2** a person who guides or directs a group, movement, etc.: *the leader of a political party* **3** *BrE* for EDITORIAL²: *The "Times" leader said that the government was wrong.*

**lead·er·ship** /ˈliːdəʃɪp‖-ər-/ *n* [U] **1** the position of LEADER (2) **2** the qualities necessary in a LEADER (2)

**lead·ing** /ˈliːdɪŋ/ *adj* [A] **1** most important; chief; main: *She is a* **leading light** (=an important and influential person) *in the theatre.* **2** guiding, directing, or controlling: *A* **leading question** *is one formed in such a way that it suggests the desired answer.*

**leaf¹** /liːf/ *n* **leaves** /liːvz/ **1** [C] one of the usu. flat and green parts of a plant that are joined to its stem or branch **2** [C] a thin sheet of paper, esp. a page in a book **3** [U] metal, esp. gold or silver, in a very thin sheet **4** [C] part of a tabletop, usu. HINGED, that may be folded up or down to make the table bigger or smaller **5 take a leaf out of somebody's book** to follow somebody's example **6 turn over a new leaf** to begin a new course of improved behaviour, habits, etc.

**leaf²** *v* → LEAF THROUGH

**leaf·let** /ˈliːflɪ̣t/ *n* a small sheet of printed matter, usu. given free to the public

**leaf through** (sthg.) *v prep,adv* [I;T] to turn the pages of (a book, magazine, etc.) quickly without reading much

**leaf·y** /ˈliːfi/ *adj* **-ier, -iest** covered with leaves

**league** /liːg/ *n* [C +*sing./pl. v*] **1** a group of people, countries, etc., who have joined together to work for some aim **2** a group of sports clubs or players that play matches amongst themselves in competition: *Is this game a league match or a* FRIENDLY (3)? **3 in league (with)** working together, often secretly or for a bad purpose

**leak¹** /liːk/ *n* **1** a small accidental hole or crack, esp. in a container, pipe, etc., through which something flows in or out **2** the liquid, gas, etc., that escapes through such a hole: *I can smell a gas leak.* **3** an accidental or intentional spreading of news, facts, etc., that ought to be secret

**leak²** *v* **1** [I;T] to let (a liquid, gas, etc.) in or out of a LEAK¹ (1): *The bottle leaks.* **2** [I] (of a liquid, gas, etc.) to pass through a LEAK¹ (1) **3** [T *out, to*] to make known (news, facts, etc., that ought to be secret): *The politician leaked the news to the newspapers.*

**leak out** *v adv* [I] (of news, facts, etc., that ought to be secret) to become known

**leak·age** /ˈliːkɪdʒ/ *n* [U] the act or result of LEAKing² (2)

**leak·y** /ˈliːki/ *adj* **-ier, -iest** letting liquid LEAK² (2) in or out: *a leaky bucket*

**lean¹** /liːn/ *v* **leant** /lent/ *esp. BrE*‖**leaned** *esp. AmE,* **leaning 1** [I] to be in a position that is not upright; slope: *That wall leans so much it might fall over.* **2** [I] to bend (from the waist): *He leaned forward/over to hear what she said.* **3** [I;T] to rest (oneself or something) on or against something:|*She leant against the door.* –see picture on page 669

**lean on/upon** sbdy. *v prep* [T] to depend on: *to lean on my friends for help*

**lean²** *adj* **1** (of people and animals) very thin –compare FAT¹ (1) **2** (of meat) without much fat **3** producing or having little value: *This has been a lean year for business.* **–leanness** *n* [U]

**lean·ing** /ˈliːnɪŋ/ *n* [*towards*] a feeling or opinion (in favour of): *a leaning towards Socialism*

**leap¹** /liːp/ *v* **leapt** /lept/, *esp. BrE*‖ **leaped** /lept‖liːpt/ *esp. AmE* **leaping 1** [I] to jump through the air, often landing in a different place: *He leaped into the air.*|*They leapt over the stream.* **2** [T] to jump over: *He leapt the wall and ran away.* –see picture on page 669

**leap at** sthg. *v prep* [T] to accept (a chance, offer, etc.) eagerly

**leap²** *n* **1** a sudden jump, spring, or movement **2** the distance crossed by LEAPing **3** a sudden increase: *a leap in the number of births in Britain*

**leap year** /ˈ· ·/ *n* [C;U] a year, every fourth year, in which February has 29 days instead of 28 days

**learn** /lɜːn‖lɜrn/ *v* **learned** *or* **learnt** /lɜːnt‖lɜrnt/, **learning 1** [I;T +*to-v*] to gain knowledge (of) or skill (in): *The child is learning quickly.*|*I'm trying to learn French.*|*He is learning to be a dancer.*|*She is learning* *how to play the drums.* –compare TEACH **2** [T] to fix in the memory; MEMORIZE: *Learn this list of words.* **3** [I;T (*of, about*)] to become informed (of): *His mother learnt of her son's success in the newspapers.* **4 learn one's lesson** to suffer so much from doing something that one will not do it again

USAGE For the past tense and past participle, **learned** and **learnt** are equally common in *BrE,* but the usual *AmE* form is **learned.** –see KNOW[2] (USAGE)

**learn·ed** /ˈlɜːnɪ̣d‖ˈlɜr-/ *adj* having or showing much knowledge: *a learned man/book* –**learnedly** *adv*

**learn·er** /ˈlɜːnəʳ‖ˈlɜr-/ *n* a person who is learning: *She's a rather slow learner.* (=is slow at learning)|*a learner driver* (=who is learning to drive a car)

**learn·ing** /ˈlɜːnɪŋ‖ˈlɜr-/ *n* [U] deep and wide knowledge gained through study –compare KNOWLEDGE

**lease**[1] /liːs/ *n* a written agreement by which a building, piece of land, etc., is given (LET (3)) to somebody for a certain time in return for rent

**lease**[2] *v* **leased, leasing** [T *out*] to give or take the use of (land or buildings) on a LEASE

**leash** /liːʃ/ *n fml or tech* →LEAD[2] (4): *Dogs must be kept on a leash.*

**least**[1] /liːst/ *adv* (*superlative of* LITTLE) **1** in the smallest degree: *It happened just when we least expected it.*|*No one listened,* **least of all** (=especially not) *the children!* –compare MOST[1] **2 not least** *fml* partly; quite importantly: *Trade has been bad, not least because of increased costs.*

**least**[2] *determiner,pron* (*superlative of* LITTLE) **1** the smallest number or amount: *Buy the one that costs the least.*|*He's* **not in the least** (=not at all) *worried.* **2 at least: a** not less than; if not more: *They cost at least £5/£5 at least.* **b** if nothing else; anyway: *The food wasn't good, but at least it was cheap.*

**leath·er** /ˈleðəʳ/ *n* [U] treated animal skin used for making shoes, bags, etc.: *a leather coat*

**leath·er·y** /ˈleðəri/ *adj* like leather; hard and stiff

**leave**[1] /liːv/ *v* **left** /left/, **leaving 1** [I;T] to go away (from): *I hope they'll leave soon; I want to go to bed.*|*I hear (that) his brother has left home.*|*The ship is leaving for* (=to go to) *New York soon.* **2** [T] to allow to remain, esp. after going away: *The postman left a letter for us.*|*Someone has left the window open.*|*Is there any coffee left or have you drunk it all?*|*I can't deal with it now; I'll leave it until tomorrow.*|*Let's just* **leave it at that.** (=not talk or argue about it any longer) **3** [T *behind*] to fail to take or bring, esp. by accident: *Don't leave your coat (behind)!* **4** [T] to give after one's death: *I'm leaving you £500 in my* WILL[2] (4). **5** [T +*v-ing*/*with, to*] to give into the care or charge of someone: *He left his cat with us.*|*I'll leave (it to) you to buy the tickets.*|*I'll leave buying the tickets to you.* **6** [T] to cause to remain after doing a sum: *2 from 8 leaves 6.* **7 leave go/hold of** to stop holding; let go

**leave** sbdy./sthg.↔ **out** *v adv* [T *of*] to fail to put in or include: *I left out the important point.*

**leave**[2] *n* **1** [C;U] (a period of) time away from work or duty, esp. in the armed forces: *The soldiers are* **on leave.** –see HOLIDAY[1] (USAGE) **2** [U +*to-v*] *fml* permission: *Have you been given leave to swim here?* **3 take leave (of)** to say goodbye (to); go away (from)

**leaves** /liːvz/ *n pl. of* LEAF

**lech·er·ous** /ˈletʃərəs/ *adj derog* (usu. of a man) having a desire for continual sexual pleasure –**lecherously** *adv* –**lecherousness** *n* [U] –**lecher** /ˈletʃəʳ/ *n*

**lech·er·y** /ˈletʃəri/ *n* [U] *derog* continual searching for sexual pleasure

**lec·tern** /ˈlektən‖-ərn/ *n* a small sloping table for holding a book, esp. when somebody reads aloud to a group of people

**lec·ture** /ˈlektʃəʳ/ *n,v* **-tured, -turing** [C;I;T *on, about*] **1** (to give) a speech to a group of people, esp. as a method of teaching at universities **2** (to give) a long solemn scolding or warning

**lec·tur·er** /ˈlektʃərəʳ/ *n* a person who teaches or gives LECTURES at a university or college, usu. in a **lecture theatre** –compare TUTOR –**lectureship** *n*: *She's got a lectureship at Oxford.*

**led** /led/ *v past tense and participle* of LEAD[1]

**ledge** /ledʒ/ *n* **1** a narrow flat shelf, esp. one on the edge of an upright object: *He keeps some books on the window ledge, and some on a shelf on the wall.* **2** a flat shelf of rock

**led·ger** /ˈledʒəʳ/ *n* an account book recording money going in and out of a business, bank, etc.

**leech** /liːtʃ/ *n* a small wormlike creature that lives by drinking the blood of living animals

**leek** /liːk/ *n* a vegetable like the onion but with a long white fleshy stem

**leer**[1] /lɪəʳ/ *n* an unpleasant smile or sideways look expressing cruel enjoyment or thoughts of sex

**leer**[2] *v* [I *at*] to look with a LEER[1]: *He leered at the young girl.* –**leeringly** *adv*

**lee·way** /ˈliːweɪ/ *n* [C;U] additional time, space, money, etc., that allows a chance to succeed in doing something: *Ten days should be (a big) enough leeway to allow for delays.*

**left**[1] /left/ *adj* [A] **1** on or belonging to the side of the body that usu. contains the heart: *one's left arm/eye* **2** on, by, or in the direction of one's left side: *the left bank of the stream* –opposite **right**

**left**[2] *n* **1** [*the*+U] the left side or direction: *Keep to the left.* **2** [C] the left hand **3** [U +*sing./pl. v*] political parties or groups (such as those for SOCIALISM and COMMUNISM) that generally support the workers rather than the employers –opposite **right**

**left**[3] *adv* towards the left –opposite **right**

**left**[4] *v past tense and participle of* LEAVE[1]

**left-hand** /ˌ· ˈ·◂/ *adj* [A] **1** on, to, or going to the left: *the left-hand page*|*a left-hand bend* **2** of, for, with, or done by the left hand: *a left-hand stroke*

**left-hand·ed** /ˌ· ˈ··◂/ *adj* **1** using the left hand for most actions **2** made for use by a left-handed person: *left-handed scissors* –opposite **right-handed** –**left-handedly** *adv* –**left-handedness** *n* [U]

**left lug·gage of·fice** /ˌ· ˈ·· ˌ··/ *BrE*‖**baggage room** *AmE*– *n* a place, esp. in a station, where one can leave one's bags for a certain period

**left·o·vers** /ˈleftˌəʊvəz‖-ərz/ *n* [P] food remaining uneaten after a meal

**left·wards** /ˈleftwədz‖-ərdz/ *BrE*‖**leftward** *AmE*– *adv* on or towards the left –opposite **rightwards** –**leftward** *adj*

**left wing** /ˌ· ˈ· ◂/ *adj,n* [U +*sing./pl. v*] (the members) of a political party (esp. a SOCIALIST or COMMUNIST party), or of a group that favours greater political changes; LEFT² (3): *left-wing ideas* –opposite **right wing** –**left-winger** /ˌ· ˈ·· / *n*

**leg** /leg/ *n* **1** one of the limbs on which an animal walks and which support its body **2** that part of this limb above the foot –see picture on page 299 **3** the part of a garment that covers the leg: *There's a hole in your trouser leg.* **4** one of the long thin supports on which a piece of furniture stands **5** one part or stage, esp. of a journey or competition: *The last leg of the journey always seems the longest.* **6 on one's/its last legs: a** very tired **b** nearly worn out or failed **c** close to death **7 pull someone's leg** to make fun of a person in a playful way,as by making him/her believe something that is not true **8 stretch one's legs** to take a short walk, esp. when feeling stiff after sitting for a long time **9 -legged** having legs of the stated number or kind: *four-legged|sitting cross-legged*

**leg·a·cy** /ˈlegəsi/ *n* **-cies 1** money, etc., that passes to someone on the death of the owner according to his/her official written wish (WILL² (4)) **2** something passed on or left behind by someone else: (fig.) *Disease and famine are often legacies of war.*

**le·gal** /ˈliːgəl/ *adj* **1** allowed or made by law; lawful: *a legal claim* –opposite **illegal 2** [A] of, concerning, or using the law: *He took legal action to stop his neighbours making so much noise.* –**legally** *adv* –**legality** /lɪˈgælǝti/ *n* [U]

USAGE **Legal** and **lawful** both mean "allowed by the law": *Children can't buy alcohol: it's not* **legal/lawful. Legal** also means "connected with the law"; *the* **legal** *profession|Do you know your* **legal** *rights?* **Legitimate** is a similar word meaning "lawful and correct", but it can also mean "reasonable and acceptable": *You should only stay away from school if you have a* **legitimate** *reason, such as illness.*

**le·gal·ize** ||also **-ise** *BrE* /ˈliːgəlaɪz/ *v* **-ized, -izing** [T] to make legal: *Will this government legalize* CANNABIS? –**legalization** /ˌliːgəlaɪˈzeɪʃən||-gələ-/ *n* [U]

**le·ga·tion** /lɪˈgeɪʃən/ *n* [C +*sing./pl. v*] a group of government employees who represent their government in a foreign country

**le·gend** /ˈledʒənd/ *n* **1** [C] an old story about ancient times which is probably not true **2** [U] such stories collectively: *a character in legend* **3** [C] a famous person or act, esp. in a particular area of activity: *He is a legend in his own lifetime for his scientific discoveries.*

**le·gen·da·ry** /ˈledʒəndəri||-deri/ *adj* **1** of, like, or told in a LEGEND (1) **2** famous

**leg·gings** /ˈlegɪŋz/ *n* [P] an outer covering worn to protect the legs, esp. from foot to knee –see PAIR¹ (USAGE)

**leg·gy** /ˈlegi/ *adj* **-gier, -giest** (esp. of children and women, and young animals) having long legs –**legginess** *n* [U]

**le·gi·ble** /ˈledʒəbəl/ *adj* (of handwriting or print) that can be read, esp. easily –opposite **illegible** –**legibility** /-əˈbɪlǝti / *n* [U] –**legibly** *adv*

**le·gion** /ˈliːdʒən/ *n* [C +*sing./pl. v*] **1** a group of soldiers or other armed men **2** a large group of people: *a legion of admirers*

**le·gis·late** /ˈledʒǝsleɪt/ *v* **-lated, -lating** [I *for, against*] to make laws –**legislator** *n*

**le·gis·la·tion** /ˌledʒǝsˈleɪʃən/ *n* [U] **1** the act of making laws **2** a body of laws

**le·gis·la·tive** /ˈledʒǝslətɪv||-leɪtɪv/ *adj* [A] **1** of or concerning the making of laws **2** having the power and duty to make laws –**legislatively** *adv*

**le·gis·la·ture** /ˈledʒǝsleɪtʃəʳ, -lətʃəʳ/ *n* the body of people who have the power to make and change laws

**le·git·i·mate** /lǝˈdʒɪtǝmǝt/ *adj* **1** according to law; lawful or correct **2** born of parents who are lawfully married to each other –opposite **illegitimate** (for **1,2**) **3** reasonable; sensible: *They had a legitimate reason for being late.* –see LEGAL (USAGE) –**legitimately** *adv* –**legitimacy** *n* [U]

**lei·sure** /ˈleʒəʳ||ˈliː-/ *n* **1** [U] time when one is free from employment; free time: *Tennis and swimming are her leisure activities.* **2 at leisure: a** not working or busy; free **b** without hurry

**lei·sured** /ˈleʒəd||ˈliːʒərd/ *adj* having plenty of free time

**lei·sure·ly** /ˈleʒəli||ˈliːʒərli/ *adj* (done) without haste: *a leisurely walk*

**lem·on** /ˈlemən/ *n* [C;U] (a tree bearing) a fruit with a thick yellow skin and sour juice: *a lemon drink*

**lem·on·ade** /ˌleməˈneɪd/ *n* [U] **1** *BrE* a transparent drink tasting of LEMONS, containing small bubbles, to which water is not added before drinking **2** *AmE* a drink made from fresh LEMONS with sugar and water added

**lend** /lend/ *v* **lent** /lent/, **lending** [T *to*] **1** to give (someone) the possession or use of (something) for a limited time: *Can you lend me £10? I'll return it next week.|I lent her some bread; she'll bring me some more tomorrow.* –see Study Notes on page 429 **2** *fml* to add or give: *The flags lent colour to the streets.*

**length** /leŋθ/ *n* **1** [C;U] the measurement or distance from one end to the other or of the longest side of something: *The length of the room is 10 metres; it is 10 metres* **in length.**|*We walked* **the length of** *the street.* (=from one end to the other)|*The students complained about the length of the examination paper.* (=said there were too many questions) –compare BREADTH –see picture on page 592 **2** [C *of*] a piece of something, esp. of a certain length or for a particular purpose: *a length of string* **3 at length: a** after a long time; at last **b** in detail; using many words **4 go to any/great/considerable lengths** to be prepared to do anything, however dangerous, unpleasant, or wicked: *He would go to any lengths to keep his government in power.*

**length·en** /ˈleŋθən/ *v* [I;T] to make or become longer –opposite **shorten**

**length·ways** /ˈleŋθweɪz/ also **lengthwise** /-waɪz/; **longways** *adv* in the direction of the length: *Measure/fold it lengthways.*

**length·y** /ˈleŋθi/ *adj* **-ier, -iest** very long; too long –**lengthiness** *n* [U]

**le·ni·ent** /ˈliːnɪənt/ *adj* merciful in judgment; gentle: *a lenient punishment* –compare STRICT –**lenience** also **leniency** *n* [U]

**lens** /lenz/ *n* **1** a special piece of glass,curved on one or both sides, used to make glasses for the eyes, cameras, microscopes, etc. **2** a part of the eye, used to FOCUS[2] light

**lent** /lent/ *v past tense and participle of* LEND

**Lent** *n* the 40 days before EASTER, during which many Christians FAST[3]

**len·til** /ˈlentl/ *n* the small round seed of a beanlike plant, dried and used for food

**Le·o** /ˈliːəʊ/ *n* see ZODIAC

**leop·ard** /ˈlepəd‖-ərd/ **leopardess** /ˈlepədes‖-ər-/ *fem.– n* a large fierce catlike animal, yellowish with black spots, found in Africa and Southern Asia

**lep·er** /ˈlepəʳ/ *n* a person who has LEPROSY

**lep·ro·sy** /ˈleprəsi/ *n* [U] a disease in which the skin becomes rough and thick, and fingers, toes, etc., drop off **–leprous** /ˈleprəs/ *adj*

**les·bi·an** /ˈlezbɪən/ *adj,n* (of or concerning) a woman who is sexually attracted to other women –compare HOMOSEXUAL **–lesbianism** *n* [U]

**le·sion** /ˈliːʒən/ *n tech* a wound

**less**[1] /les/ *adv (comparative of* LITTLE) [*than*] **1** (*with adjectives and adverbs*) not so; to a smaller degree (than): *The next train will be less crowded than this one.* **2** (*with verbs*) not so much: *Try to shout less.|He works less than he used to.* –opposite **more**

**less**[2] *determiner,pron (comparative of* LITTLE) [*of, than*] **1** a smaller amount: *They buy less beer and fewer cigarettes now.|Can we have a bit less noise/less of that noise?*(=Be quiet!)|*It's less than a mile to the sea.* –see MORE[2] (USAGE) **2 less and less** (an amount) that continues to become smaller: *less and less work* **3 no less (than)** (expressing surprise at a large number or amount): *No less than 1000 people came.* **4 none the less** but all the same; in spite of everything; NEVERTHELESS: *I can't really afford it, but I want to buy it none the less.* **5 the less** (used to show that two things get smaller, or change, together): *The less he eats, the thinner he gets.*

**less**[3] *prep* not counting; subtracting: *You will be paid £100 less tax, so you should get about £75.*

**less·en** /ˈlesən/ *v* [I;T] to make or become less in size, importance, appearance, etc.

**less·er** /ˈlesəʳ/ *adj,adv* [A *no comp.*] *fml* (not used with *than*) not so great or so much: *the lesser of two evils|one of the lesser-known African writers*

**les·son** /ˈlesən/ *n* **1** something taught to or learned by a pupil, esp. in school; the period of time a pupil or class studies a subject: *Each history lesson lasts 40 minutes.* **2** something, e.g. an experience, from which one should learn: *His car accident* **taught him a lesson;** *he won't drive so fast again.*

**lest** /lest/ *conj fml* for fear that; in case: *I wrote down the date of his birthday lest I should forget it.*

**let** /let/ *v* **let, letting** [T] **1** to allow to do or happen: *She lets her children play in the street.|I don't smoke because my father won't let me (smoke).|He's letting his beard grow.|He let a week go by before answering the letter.|They let the prisoners go.* (=allowed them to escape) **2** must; is to: *Let each man decide for himself.|Let there be no mistake about it.|Let the line AB be equal to the line XY.* **3** *BrE* [*to, out*] to give the use of (a room, land, etc.) in return for regular payments: *This room is let (out) to a student.* –see HIRE[1] (USAGE) **4 let alone** not to mention; even less: *The baby can't even walk, let alone run.* **5 let/leave someone/something alone/be** to stop worrying someone/something; not to touch, scold, etc.: *Leave him alone: he's doing no harm.* **6 let go (of)** to stop holding: *Don't let go (of) the handle.|Let go! You're hurting my arm.* **7 let oneself go: a** to behave more freely and naturally than usual: *She really lets herself go at parties.* **b** to take less care of one's appearance than usual: *Since his wife died he's just let himself go.* **8 let someone know** to tell someone; inform: *Will you let me know if you can't come to dinner?* **9 let us: a** allow us to: *Please let us buy you a drink!* **b** also **let's**– (used when suggesting a plan that includes the person spoken to) we must/should: *Let's hurry!|Let's not go yet.*

**let** sbdy./sthg. ↔ **down** *v adv* [T] **1** to cause to be disappointed; fail to keep a promise to (someone) –see also LETDOWN **2** to make (clothes) longer –opposite **take up** (for **2**)

**let** sbdy./sthg.↔ **in** *v adv* [T] to admit; allow to enter (a house, room, etc.): *There's someone at the door; let them in, will you?|These old shoes let the rain in.*

**let** sbdy. **in for** sthg. *v adv prep* [T] to cause (esp. oneself) to have (something unwanted): *He let himself in for a lot of work when he agreed to fix that car.*

**let** sbdy. **in on** sthg. *v adv prep* [T] to allow (someone) to share (a secret)

**let** sbdy. **off**[1] (sthg.) *v adv; prep* [T] to excuse from (punishment, duty, etc.): *She let him off (doing) his homework because he was ill.|The police let him off, but warned him not to do it again.*

**let** sbdy./sthg.↔ **off**[2] *v adv* [T] **1** to cause to explode or be fired: *to let off a* FIREWORK **2** to allow to leave a vehicle

**let on** sthg.↔ *v adv* [I;T +*that/about*] *infml* to tell (a secret): *He asked me where John was, but I didn't let on.*

**let** sthg.↔ **out** *v adv* [T] **1** to express; UTTER: *He let out a cry of pain.* **2** to make (clothes) bigger –opposite **take in** (for **2**)

**let** sbdy./sthg.↔ **through** *v adv* [T] to allow to pass

**let up** *v adv* [I] to lessen; gradually cease; stop: *When will this rain let up?* –see also LETUP

**let·down** /ˈletdaʊn/ *n infml* a disappointment –see also LET **down**

**le·thal** /ˈliːθəl/ *adj* able to kill: *a lethal* DOSE (2) *of a poison*

**leth·ar·gy** /ˈleθədʒi‖-ər-/ *n* [U] state of being sleepy or unnaturally tired; lazy state of mind **–lethargic** /lɪˈθɑːdʒɪk‖-ɑr-/ *adj*

**let·ter** /ˈletəʳ/ *n* **1** [C] a written or printed message sent usu. in an envelope **2** [C] one of the signs in writing or printing that represents a speech sound **3** [S] the words of an agreement, law, etc., rather than its real or intended meaning: *be bound by the letter of the law, rather than the* SPIRIT[1] (6) *of it*

**let·ter·box** /ˈletəbɒks‖ˈletərbɑks/ *BrE*‖**mailbox** *AmE– n* **1** also **postbox**– a box in a post office, street, etc., in which letters may be posted –compare PILLAR-BOX **2** a hole in the front of a building for receiving letters –see picture on page 297

**let·ter·head** /ˈletəhed‖-ər-/ *n* the name and address of a person or business printed at the top of the owner's writing paper

**let·ter·ing** /ˈletərɪŋ/ *n* [U] letters or words written or drawn, esp. with regard to their style

**let·tuce** /ˈletɨs/ *n* [C;U] a common garden plant with large pale green leaves, used raw in SALADS –compare CABBAGE

**let-up** /ˈletʌp/ *n* [C;U] (a) stopping or lessening of activity –see also LET **up**

**leu·ke·mia** ‖ also **-kae-** *BrE* /luːˈkiːmɪə/ *n* [U] a serious disease of the blood during which a person becomes very weak and often dies

**lev·el**[1] /ˈlevəl/ *n* **1** [C;U] a position of height: *The top of this mountain is six kilometres above* **sea level**|(fig.) *The level* (=quality) *of your work is not satisfactory.*|(fig.) *The matter is being considered at ministerial level.* (=by important politicians) **2** [C] a smooth flat surface, esp. a wide area of flat ground: *You should build on the level, not on the slope.* **3** [C *of*] amount, size, or number: *The workmen have been told to increase their production level.* **4 on the level** *infml* honest(ly); truthful(ly)

**level**[2] *v* **-ll-** *BrE*‖ **-l-** *AmE* **1** [I;T *out, off*] to make or become flat and even, so that no one part is raised above the rest: *Level the ground off before you plant the seeds.*|*Prices have begun to level off.* (=stay the same after rising or falling) **2** [T] to knock or pull down to the ground: *They levelled all the old trees to make way for the road.*

**level** sthg. **at** sbdy. *v prep* [T] **1** to aim (a weapon) at **2** also **level** sthg. **against** sbdy.– to bring (a charge) against: *A serious charge was levelled at the minister.*

**level**[3] *adj* **1** having no part higher than the rest; even: *If the table top isn't level, things will roll off.* **2** [*no comp.*] equal in position or standard: *The child's head is level with his father's knee.* **3** steady and unvarying: *He gave me a level look.* **4** also **level-headed** /·· ˈ·· ◂/– calm and sensible in judgment: *She has a level head/is level-headed about money.* **5 one's level best** *infml* one's best effort; all that one can

**level**[4] *adv* so as to be level

**level cross·ing** /ˌ·· ˈ··/ *BrE*‖**grade crossing** *AmE*– *n* a place where a road and a railway cross each other, usu. protected by gates

**le·ver**[1] /ˈliːvəʳ‖ˈle-, ˈliː-/ *n* **1** a bar used for moving something heavy or stiff. One end is placed under or against the object, the middle rests on something, and the other end is pushed down **2** any part of a machine working in the same way: *Push the lever, and the machine will start.* **3** something which may be used for influencing someone

**lever**[2] *v* [T] to move (something) with a LEVER: *They levered it into position.*|(fig.) *They're trying to lever him out of his job.*

**le·ver·age** /ˈliːvərɪdʒ‖ˈle-, ˈliː-/ *n* [U] **1** the action, use, or power of a LEVER **2** power, influence, or other means of obtaining a result: *He has some leverage over the politician.*

**lev·e·ret** /ˈlevərɨt/ *n* a young HARE

**lev·i·tate** /ˈlevɨteɪt/ *v* **-tated, -tating** [I;T] to (cause to) rise and float in the air as if by magic **–levitation** /-ˈteɪʃən / *n* [U]

**lev·i·ty** /ˈlevɨti/ *n* [U] *fml or pomp* lack of seriousness

**lev·y**[1] /ˈlevi/ *n* **-ies 1** an official demand for, or collection of, a tax **2** the money collected

**levy**[2] *v* **-ied, -ying** [T *on, upon*] to demand and collect officially: *to levy a tax on tobacco*

**lewd** /luːd/ *adj* **1** wanting or thinking about sex, esp. in a manner that is not socially acceptable **2** impure; rude; OBSCENE **–lewdly** *adv* **–lewdness** *n* [U]

**lex·i·cal** /ˈleksɪkəl/ *adj tech* of or concerning words **–lexically** *adv*

**lex·i·con** /ˈleksɪkən‖-kɒn, -kən/ *n* a dictionary, esp. of an ancient language

**li·a·bil·i·ty** /ˌlaɪəˈbɪlɨti/ *n* **-ties 1** [U] the condition of being LIABLE **2** [C] something for which one is responsible, esp. by law **3** [C] the amount of debt that must be paid –compare ASSET

**li·a·ble** /ˈlaɪəbəl/ *adj* [F] **1** [*to*] often suffering from: *She is liable to bad colds.* **2** likely to, esp. from habit or tendency: *He's liable to shout when angry.* **3** [+*v-ing/for*] responsible, esp. in law, for paying for something: *He was not liable for his son's debts.*

**li·aise** /liˈeɪz/ *v* **-aised, -aising** [I *with*] to work together so that all the people working are informed about what is being done

**li·ai·son** /liˈeɪzən‖ˈlɪəzɑn, liˈeɪ-/ *n* [*with, between*] **1** a working association or connection **2** a sexual relationship between a man and a woman not married to each other

**li·ar** /ˈlaɪəʳ/ *n* a person who tells lies

**lib** /lɪb/ *n* [U] *infml* for LIBERATION (esp. in the phrases **women's lib, gay lib** (see GAY (3))

**li·bel**[1] /ˈlaɪbəl/ *n* [C;U] *law* (the making of) a written statement, picture, etc., that unfairly damages the good opinion held about a person by others –compare SLANDER[1]

**libel**[2] *v* **-ll-** *BrE*‖**-l-** *AmE* [T] to print a LIBEL against

**li·bel·lous** *BrE*‖**libelous** *AmE* /ˈlaɪbələs/ *adj* being or containing a LIBEL: *a libellous article in a newspaper* **–libellously** *adv*

**lib·e·ral**[1] /ˈlɪbərəl/ *adj* **1** willing to respect the ideas and feelings of others: *a liberal mind/thinker* **2** favouring some change, as in political or religious affairs: *The church has become more liberal in this century.* –compare REACTIONARY, RADICAL **3** favouring a wide general knowledge and wide possibilities for self-expression: *a liberal education* **4** giving or given freely and generously: *a liberal supporter of the hospital* **–liberalism** *n* [U]

**liberal**[2] *n* a person with wide understanding, who is in favour of change –compare REACTIONARY

**Liberal** *n,adj* (a person) supporting or connected with the LIBERAL PARTY

**lib·e·ral·i·ty** /ˌlɪbəˈrælɨti/ *n* [U] also **liberalness** /ˈlɪbərəlnɨs/– **1** generosity **2** broadness of mind

**lib·e·ral·ly** /ˈlɪbərəli/ *adv* generously; freely; in great amount; in large quantities

**Liberal Par·ty** /ˈ··· ˌ··/ *n* [U +*sing/pl. v*] a political party whose aims are social and industrial improvement, esp. the one in Britain

**lib·e·rate** /ˈlɪbəreɪt/ *v* **-rated, -rating** [T *from*] *fml* to set free (from control, prison, etc.): *The prisoners were liberated by the army.* **–liberator** *n*

**lib·e·rat·ed** /ˈlɪbəreɪtɨd/ *adj* having freedom of action in social and sexual matters

**lib·er·ty** /ˈlɪbəti‖-ər-/ *n* **1** [U] personal or political freedom from outside control: *People often have to fight for their liberty.* **2** [U] the chance or permission to do or use something **3 at liberty: a** free from prison, control, etc. **b** not busy; free **c** having permission or the right (to do something) **4 take liberties (with): a** to act in a rude, too friendly way (towards) **b** to make changes (in): *They took several liberties with the original story when they turned it into a film.* –compare FREEDOM

**li·bi·do** /lɪ'biːdəʊ/ *n* **-dos** *tech* the sexual urge

**Li·bra** /'liːbrə/ *n* [S] see ZODIAC

**li·brar·i·an** /laɪ'breərɪən/ *n* a person who is in charge of or helps to run a library –**librarianship** *n* [U]

**li·bra·ry** /'laɪbrəri‖- breri/ *n* **-ries 1** a building or room which contains usu. books that may be looked at or borrowed by the public (**public library**) or by members of a special group: *a record/toy library* (=containing records/toys) **2** a collection of books

**lice** /laɪs/ *n pl. of* LOUSE

**li·cence¹** ‖also **license** *AmE* /'laɪsəns/ *n* **1** [C] an official paper, card, etc., showing that permission has been given to do something, usu. for a payment: *a driving licence|a licence to sell alcohol* **2** [U] (too much) freedom of action, speech, thought, etc. –see also POETIC LICENCE

**li·cense²**, **-cence** /'laɪsəns/ *v* **-censed, -censing** [T] to give official permission to or for

**license plate** /'·· ·/ *n AmE* for NUMBERPLATE

**li·cen·tious** /laɪ'senʃəs/ *fml* behaving in a sexually uncontrolled manner –**licentiously** *adv* –**licentiousness** *n* [U]

**li·chen** /'laɪkən, 'lɪtʃən/ *n* [U] a flat spreading plant that covers the surfaces of stones and trees

**lick¹** /lɪk/ *v* [T] **1** to move the tongue across (a surface) in order to taste, clean, make wet, etc.: *to lick a postage stamp|The dog licked the dish clean.*|(fig.) *The flames licked against the building.* **2** [*up, out, off*] to take into the mouth with the tongue: *The cat licked up the milk.* **3** *infml* to defeat in a game, race, fight, etc.

**lick²** *n* **1** the act of LICKing **2** [*of*] a small amount (of cleaning, paint, etc.): *This door needs a lick of paint.*

**lic·o·rice** /'lɪkərɪs, -rɪʃ/ *n* [U] →LIQUORICE

**lid** /lɪd/ *n* **1** the piece that covers the open top of a pot, box, or other container and that lifts up or can be removed **2** →EYELID

**li·do** /'liːdəʊ, 'laɪ-/ *n* **-dos** a public swimming bath open to the air

**lie¹** /laɪ/ *v* **lay** /leɪ/, **lain** /leɪn/, **lying** /'laɪ-ɪŋ/ [I] **1** to be in a flat position on a surface: *The book is lying on the table.|He lay on the floor, reading a book.|Father is lying down* (=resting on a bed) *for a while.* **2** [*down*; not *be+v-ing*] to put the body into such a position: *I'm tired; I must lie down.* **3** to be in the stated position; be placed: *The town lies to the east of us.*|(fig.)*The decision lies with you.* (=you must make it) **4** to remain or be kept in the stated condition or position: *The machines have* **lain idle** (=been unused) *for weeks now.|Don't leave your money lying in the bank; spend it.* **5 lie low** to be in hiding or avoid being noticed –see LAY¹ (USAGE)

**lie about** *v adv* [I] to be lazy; do nothing

**lie behind** sthg. *v prep* [T] to be the reason for: *I wonder what lies behind his decision to leave.*

**lie in** *v adv* [I] *BrE* to stay in bed late in the morning –see also LIE-IN, SLEEP **in**

**lie²** *v* **lied, lying** [I] to tell a lie

**lie³** *n* an untrue statement purposely made to deceive: *to tell lies|He told her a* **white lie** *so as not to hurt her feelings.*

**lie-down** /ˌ· '·/ *n infml* a short rest, usu. on a bed

**lie-in** *n* /'· ·, ˌ· '·/ *n BrE infml* a stay in bed later than usual in the morning –see also LIE **in**

**lieu** /luː/ *n* **in lieu (of)** instead (of): *He worked on Sunday, so he took Monday off in lieu.*

**lieu·ten·ant** /lef'tenənt‖luː-/ *n* an officer of low rank in the armed forces

**life** /laɪf/ *n* **lives** /laɪvz/ **1** [U] the active force that enables (animals and plants) to continue existing: *Stones do not have life.|Is there life after death?* **2** [U] living things: *There is no life on the moon.|plant life* **3** [U] human existence: *Life isn't all fun.|You won't see life* (=all the different experiences of human existence) *if you stay at home for ever.* **4** [C] the period during which one is alive: *They have very busy lives.|I have lived in England all my life, but I will spend the rest of my life abroad.|His working life was full of accidents.* **5** [C] a person: *Several lives were lost* (=people died) *in the accident.* **6** [U] activity; movement: *There was no* **sign of life** *in the empty house.|The children are* **full of life** *this morning.* **7** [S] a person or thing that is the cause of enjoyment or activity in a group: *He was* **the life and soul of** *the party.* **8** [U] also **life imprisonment** /· ·'···/– the punishment of being put in prison for a long time which is not fixed **9** [C] also **life story** /'· ··/– a written, filmed, or other account of a person's existence; BIOGRAPHY **10 not on your life!** certainly not! **11 take one's (own)/someone's life** to kill oneself/someone –compare DEATH

**life belt** /'· ·/ *n* a belt or ring that will float, held or worn by a person who has fallen into water, to stop him/her sinking

**life·blood** /'laɪfblʌd/ *n* [U] something that gives continuing strength and force: *Trade is the lifeblood of most modern states.*

**life·boat** /'laɪfbəʊt/ *n* a boat used for saving people in danger at sea

**life·guard** /'laɪfgɑːd‖-ɑrd/ *n* a swimmer employed to help swimmers in danger –see picture on page 592

**life jack·et** /'· ˌ··/ *n* an air-filled garment that is worn round the chest to support a person in water

**life·less** /'laɪfləs/ *adj* **1** having no life; dead: *a lifeless corpse* **2** lacking strength, interest, or activity –compare LISTLESS –**lifelessly** *adv* –**lifelessness** *n* [U]

**life·like** /'laɪflaɪk/ *adj* very much like real life or a real person: *a lifelike photograph*

**life·line** /'laɪflaɪn/ *n* a rope used for saving life, esp. at sea: (fig.) *The telephone is my lifeline to the world.*

**life·long** /'laɪflɒŋ‖-lɔŋ/ *adj* [A] lasting all one's life

**life-size** /ˌ· '·◂/ also **life-sized** /ˌ· '·◂/– *adj* (of a work of art) of the same size as that which it represents

**life·time** /'laɪftaɪm/ *n* the time during which a person is alive

**lift¹** /lɪft/ *v* **1** [T *up*] to bring from a lower to a higher level: *These bags are too heavy; I can't lift them.|Stop looking at the ground; lift your head up.* –see picture on page 669 **2** [I] (esp. of clouds, mist, etc.) to move upwards and often disappear **3** [T] to bring to an end; remove: *The unpopular tax was soon lifted.* **4** [T] *infml* to steal (esp. small articles) –see also SHOPLIFT **5** [T] *infml* to take and use (other people's ideas, writings, etc.) as one's own without stating that one has done so

**lift off** *v adv* [I] (of an aircraft or space craft) to take off –see also LIFT-OFF

**lift²** *n* **1** [C] the act of lifting, rising, or raising **2** [C;U] a lifting force, such as an upward pressure of air on the wings of an aircraft **3** [C] *BrE*||**elevator** *AmE*– an apparatus in a building that moves up and down between floors and carries people or goods **4** [C] a free ride in a vehicle, esp. one given to a traveller: *Can you give me a lift into town?* **5** [S] *infml* a feeling of increased strength, higher spirits, etc.: *I was given a lift when I heard that I passed my exams.*

**lift-off** /'· ·/ also **blast-off**– *n* the start of the flight of a space vehicle –see also LIFT **off**

**lig·a·ment** /'lɪgəmənt/ *n* one of the strong bands that join bones or hold some part of the body in position: *He tore a ligament playing football.*

**light¹** /laɪt/ *n* **1** [U] the natural force that is produced by or redirected (REFLECTed) from objects and other things, so that we see them: *sunlight|firelight|I can't read in this bad light.|She worked by the light of a candle.* **2** [U] the light of the sun or the time it lasts **3** [C] something that produces light and causes other things to be seen, such as a lamp or TORCH: *Turn off the lights when you go to bed.* –see picture on page 355 **4** [C] something, such as a match or cigarette LIGHTER, that will set something else, esp. a cigarette, burning: *Can you give me a light, please?* **5** [S;U] brightness, as in the eyes, showing happiness or excitement **6** [U] the condition of being known: *Some new information has* **come to light** *about the accident.* **7** [C] the way (ASPECT) in which something or someone appears or is regarded: *The workers and the employers look at the difficulties in quite a different light.|He tried to put my actions* **in a good/bad light.** (=favourably/unfavourably) **8 in the light of** taking into account; considering **9 see the light: a** to be made public **b** to understand or accept an idea or the truth of something **c** to understand or accept a religious belief; have a SPIRITUAL experience which changes one's beliefs **10 throw/shed light on** to make clear; explain

**light²** *adj* **1** easy to see in; bright: *a light room* **2** not deep or dark in colour; pale: *light green*

**light³** *v* **lit** /lɪt/ *or* **lighted, lighting 1** [I;T *up*] to (cause to) start to burn: *He lit (up) a cigarette.|The fire won't light.* **2** [T] to give light to: *The room is lit by several lamps.* **3** [I;T *up*] to (cause to) become bright with pleasure or excitement: *Her eyes lit up when she saw me.*

USAGE Use **lit** as the past participle of **light**, except when it stands as an adjective before the noun: *He's* **lit** *a match.|The match is* **lit.**|*a* **lighted** *match.*

**light up** *v adv* **1** [I;T (=**light** sthg.↔**up**)] to give light to; make or become bright with light or colour: *The candles lit up the room.* **2** [I] *infml* to begin to smoke a cigarette or pipe

**light⁴** *adj* **1** of little weight; not heavy: *as light as air|It's very light; a child could lift it.* **2** not using or needing great effort; not powerful, severe, or serious: *A light touch is needed in playing quiet music.|a light wind|light reading/music|a light meal* (=small in amount) **3** (of sleep) from which one wakes easily; not deep **4 make light of** to treat as of little importance

**light⁵** *adv* without many possessions (LUGGAGE): *I always travel light.*

**light bulb** /'· ·/ *n* →BULB (2)

**light·en¹** /'laɪtn/ *v* [I;T] to make or become brighter or less dark –compare DARKEN

**lighten²** *v* [I;T] **1** to make or become less heavy, forceful, etc. **2** to make or become more cheerful or less troubled

**light·er** /'laɪtəʳ/ *n* **1** that which lights or sets on fire **2** also **cigarette lighter**– an instrument that produces a small flame for lighting cigarettes, pipes, or CIGARS

**light-fin·gered** /ˌ· '··◂/ *adj infml* having the habit of stealing small things

**light-head·ed** /ˌ·'··◂/ *adj* **1** unable to think clearly, as during fever or after drinking alcohol; GIDDY (1) **2** not sensible or serious; foolish –**light-headedly** *adv* –**light-headedness** *n* [U]

**light-heart·ed** /ˌ· '··◂/ *adj* cheerful; happy

**light·house** /'laɪthaus/ *n* **-houses** /ˌhauzɪ̈z/ a building with a powerful flashing light that guides ships or warns them of dangerous rocks

**light·ing** /'laɪtɪŋ/ *n* [U] **1** the act of making something give light or start burning **2** the system or apparatus that lights a room, building, etc., or the quality of the light produced: *soft* (=not very bright) *lighting in a restaurant*

**light·ly** /'laɪtli/ *adv* **1** with little weight or force; gently: *He pressed lightly on the handle.* **2** to a slight or little degree: *lightly cooked* **3** without careful thought or reasoning: *I didn't start this court action lightly, you know!* **4** without proper respect

**light·ning** /'laɪtnɪŋ/ *n* **1** [U] a powerful flash of light in the sky, usu. followed by thunder **2** [A] very quick, short, or sudden: *a lightning visit*

**light·weight** /'laɪt-weɪt/ *n,adj* **1** (a person or thing) of less than average weight **2** (a BOXER) weighing between 126 and 135 pounds –see also HEAVYWEIGHT

**light year** /'· ·/ *n* (a measure of length equal to) the distance that light travels in one year (about 6,000,000,000,000 miles)

**likable, likeable** /'laɪkəbəl/ *adj* (of a person) pleasant; attractive

**like¹** /laɪk/ *v* [T not *be* +*v-ing*] **1** [+*v-ing*] to be fond of; find pleasant: *Do you like bananas?|I've never liked her brother.|I like sailing.|How do you like my new bicycle?* –opposite **dislike 2** [+*to-v*] to wish or choose: *I'd like* (=I want) *to see you.|I'd like you to come and see me.|I don't like to ask my parents for money.|Which one would you like; the red or the blue?|Do you like milk in your coffee?* **3 I like that!** What an annoying thing!: *So you're not going to give me my money? Well, I like that!* **4 if you like** if you do not want something else: *We can go out if you like.*

USAGE When **like** means "to be fond of or enjoy", it is used on its own; when it means "to want", it is used with *would.* (Compare: I **like** *beer.* (=I'm fond of it):|*I'd* **like** (=I want) *a glass of beer.|Do you* **like** *going to the cinema?|Would you* **like** *to go to the cinema tonight?* The verb **love** is used in the same way: *I* **love** *swimming.|I'd* **love** *a swim.*

**like²** *adj* **1** the same in many ways; of the same kind: *running, swimming, and like sports|like ideas* –see also UNLIKE **2 -like: a** the same as in many ways: *lifelike* **b** typical of: *ladylike|childlike*

**like³** *prep* **1** in the same way as; of the same kind as: *Do it like this.|He was like a son to me.|When the car is painted it will look like new.* **2** typical of; showing the usual manner of: *It was (just) like her.* **3** for example: *I asked lots of people, like Mrs Jones and Dr Simpson.*

USAGE Note the difference between these uses of **like** and **as**: *He has been playing tennis* **as** *a professional for two years* (=he is a professional tennis player).|*He plays tennis* **like** *a professional* (=he is not a professional tennis player, but he plays as well as someone who is).

**like⁴** *n* [S] something which is the same or as good: *running, swimming, and the like*

**like⁵** *conj infml* **1** in the same way as: *Do it like I tell you.* **2** as if: *He acted like he owned the shop.*

**like·ly¹** /ˈlaɪkli/ *adj* **-lier, -liest 1** [+*to-v*] probable; expected: *Are we likely to arrive in time?|It seems likely that she'll pass her exams.* **2** suitable to give results: *a likely plan|He's the most likely/the likeliest of the people who've asked for the job.* –opposite **unlikely –likelihood** /ˈlaiklihud/ *n* [U *of*]

**likely²** *adv* **1** (esp. after *most, very*) probably: *They'll very likely come by car.* **2 as likely as not** probably **3 not likely!** *infml* certainly not!

**like·ness** /ˈlaɪknɪ̵s/ *n* [C;U] sameness in form: *a family likeness*

**lik·en** sbdy./sthg. **to** sbdy./sthg. /ˈlaɪkən/ *v prep* [T] *fml* to compare with: *Our little company can be likened to a big family.*

**likes** /laɪks/ *n* [P] things that one likes (usu. in the phrase **likes and dislikes**) –see also LIKING

**like·wise** /ˈlaɪk-waɪz/ *adv* [*no comp.*] **1** in the same way; the same: *John took off his shoes, so Peter did likewise.* (=they both took off their shoes) **2** also; too: *For this job you need a lot of patience; likewise you need a sense of humour.*

**lik·ing** /ˈlaɪkɪŋ/ *n* [S *for*] fondness: *to have a liking for sweets* –see also LIKES

**li·lac** /ˈlaɪlək/ *n* **1** [C] a tree with pinkish, purple, or white flowers giving a sweet smell **2** [U] a purple colour

**li·lo** /ˈlaɪləʊ/ *n* **-los** *BrE* a sort of bed made of a large plastic bag filled with air, used for lying on by the sea

**lilt** /lɪlt/ *v,n* [I;S] (to have) a regular pattern of pleasant sound: *a lilting voice/tune*

**lil·y** /ˈlɪli/ *n* **-ies** a plant usu. with large clear white flowers

**lily-liv·ered** /ˌ·· ˈ··◂/ *adj* cowardly

**limb** /lɪm/ *n* **1** a leg, arm, or wing of an animal **2** a (large) branch of a tree **3 out on a limb** alone without support, esp. in opinions or argument **4 -limbed** having limbs of the stated kind: *strong-limbed*

**lim·ber up** /ˈlɪmbəʳ/ *v adv* [I] to prepare for a race, etc. by stretching one's muscles through exercise

**lim·bo¹** /ˈlɪmbəʊ/ *n* **-bos** [C;U] a state of uncertainty: *I'm in limbo, waiting to know if I've got the job or not.*

**limbo²** *n* **-bos** a West Indian dance in which a dancer passes under a rope or bar near the floor

**lime¹** /laɪm/ *n* [U] a white substance obtained by burning a type of rock (**limestone**), used in making cement

**lime²** *n* **1** also **lime tree** /ˈ· ·/, **linden**– a tree with yellow sweet-smelling flowers **2** (a tree which bears) a small green fruit which is juicy and tastes sour

**lime·light** /ˈlaɪmlaɪt/ *n* [*the* S] a lot of attention from the public: *That politician has been* **in the limelight** *recently because of his strong opinions.*

**lim·e·rick** /ˈlɪmərɪk/ *n* a short poem with five lines, usu. humorous

**lim·it¹** /ˈlɪmɪ̵t/ *n* **1** [*of*] the farthest point or edge (of something): *the limit of one's patience|I can't walk 10 miles; I know my own limits.* –compare EDGE¹ **2 off limits (to)** *AmE* for **out of** BOUNDS (2) **3 within limits** up to a reasonable point (in amount, time, etc.)

**limit²** *v* [T *to*] to keep below or at a certain point or amount: *We must limit ourselves to an hour.*

**lim·i·ta·tion** /ˌlɪmɪ̵ˈteɪʃən/ *n* **1** [U] the fact or conditions of limiting or being limited **2** [C *usu. pl.*] a weakness of body or character which limits one's actions: *I know my limitations; I won't even try to build my own house.*

**lim·it·ed** /ˈlɪmɪ̵tɪ̵d/ *adj* **1** small in amount, power, etc., and not able to increase: *His ability to improve his work is very limited.* –opposite **unlimited 2** [A *or after n*] also **Ltd** – (of a company) having a reduced duty to pay back debts: *Longman Group Ltd*

**lim·it·ing** /ˈlɪmɪ̵tɪŋ/ *adj* which prevents improvement, increase, etc.: *A limiting* FACTOR *in the improvement of health is the lack of doctors.*

**lim·ou·sine** /ˈlɪməziːn, ˌlɪməˈziːn/ *n* an expensive car with the driver's seat separated from the back by a sheet of glass, usu. driven by a CHAUFFEUR

**limp¹** /lɪmp/ *n,v* [I;S] (to walk with) an uneven step, one foot or leg moving less well than the other: *He has/walks with a limp.*

**limp²** *adj* lacking strength or stiffness: *She went limp and fell to the ground.|This piece of card has got wet and gone limp.* **–limply** *adv* **–limpness** *n* [U]

**lim·pet** /ˈlɪmpɪ̵t/ *n* a very small sea animal with a shell, which holds on tightly to the rock where it lives

**lim·pid** /ˈlɪmpɪ̵d/ *adj lit* (esp. of liquid) clear; transparent: *eyes like limpid pools* **–limpidly** *adv*

**linc·tus** /ˈlɪŋktəs/ *n* [U] *BrE* liquid medicine to cure coughing

**lin·den** /ˈlɪndən/ *n* →LIME² (1)

**line¹** /laɪn/ *v* **lined, lining** [T (*with*)] **1** to cover the inside of something with material (e.g. a coat with light cloth or a box with paper or something soft) **2** to be an inner covering for **3 line one's pocket(s)/purse** to make money for oneself

**line²** *n* **1** a thin mark with length but no width, which can be drawn on a surface: *Can you draw a straight line?|a line drawing|*(fig.) *The old man's face is covered with lines.* (=of folded skin) **2** a long mark that acts as a limit or border: *Which of the runners was the first to cross the (finishing) line?* (=to win the race)|*The ship crossed the line* (=the EQUATOR) *at midday.|There's a very fine line between punishment and cruelty.* **3** a row: *a line of people walking into a cinema|75 lines of printed words on a page.* **4** a piece of string, wire, or cord: *a clothes line|a washing line|a fishing line* **5** a telephone connection or wire: *The lines have crossed.* (=there's a wrong connection)|*The lines went down in the storm.* **6** a railway track: *the main line from London to Leeds* **7** (*usu. in combination*) a (company that provides a) system for travelling or moving goods, esp. by sea or air: *an airline|a shipping line* **8** a direction; course: *You're standing right in the line of fire.* (=the direction in which the guns are shooting)|(fig.) *Let's try a different line of approach to the problem.|You don't have the right answer, but you're* **on the right lines.** (=following the right method, and likely to succeed) **9** a business, profession, trade, etc.: *My line is selling.|She's in the selling line.*|(fig.) *Fishing isn't really my line.* (=does not interest me) **10** a type of goods: *a new line in hats* **11** a set of people following one another in time, esp. a family: *He comes from a long line of actors.* **12 draw the line (at)** to state a limit to what one is prepared to do: *I said I'd help you to make some money, but I draw the line at stealing.* **13 in line for** being considered for and likely to get: *in line for the job* **14 in line with** in accordance with: *That isn't in line with my ideas at all.* **15 read between the lines** to find a meaning which is not actually stated: *In her letter she says she's happy, but reading between the lines I don't think she is.*

**line³** *v* **lined, lining** [T] **1** to draw or mark lines on: *lined paper|Worry lined his face.* **2** to form rows along: *The crowds lined the streets.*

**line up** *v adv* **1** [I;T (=**line** sbdy./sthg.↔**up**)] to (cause to) move into a row: *He lined up behind the others to wait his turn.* **2** [T] (**line** sbdy./sthg.↔**up**) to arrange (a show, event, etc.): *I've lined up a famous singer for the school concert.* –see also LINEUP

**lin·e·ar** /ˈlɪnɪəʳ/ *adj* **1** of or in lines: *a linear* DIAGRAM –see also LINE² (1) **2** of length: *linear measurements*

**line·man** /ˈlaɪnmən/ also **linesman**– **-men** /mən/– *n* a man whose job is to take care of railway lines or telephone wires –compare LINESMAN

**lin·en** /ˈlɪn½n/ *n* [U] **1** cloth made from FLAX **2** sheets and bedclothes, tablecloths, etc.: *to buy bed linen*

**lin·er** /ˈlaɪnəʳ/ *n* **1** a large passenger ship **2** a piece of material used inside another to protect it

**lines** /laɪnz/ *n* [P] the words learnt by an actor to be said in a play

**lines·man** /ˈlaɪnzmən/ *n* **-men** /mən/ **1** (in sport) an official who stays near the side of the playing area and decides which team has gone outside the limits, done something wrong, etc. –compare REFEREE¹; see picture on page 592 **2** →LINEMAN

**line-up** /ˈlaɪn-ʌp/ *n* [*usu. sing.*] **1** an arrangement of people or things, esp. in a line **2** a set of events, following one after the other –see also LINE **up**

**lin·ger** /ˈlɪŋgəʳ/ *v* [I *on,over*] **1** to wait for a time instead of going; delay going: *He lingered outside the school after everybody else had gone home.* **2** to be slow to disappear: *The pain lingered on for weeks.|a lingering fear, after an accident* –**lingerer** *n*

**lin·ge·rie** /ˈlænʒəriː‖ˌlɑnʒəˈreɪ, ˈlænʒəriː/ *n* [U] *fml & tech* underclothes for women

**lin·guist** /ˈlɪŋgw½st/ *n* **1** a person who studies and is good at foreign languages **2** a person who studies the science of language (LINGUISTICS)

**lin·guis·tics** /lɪŋˈgwɪstɪks/ *n* [U] the study of language in general and of particular languages –**linguistic** *adj* –**linguistically** *adv*

**lin·i·ment** /ˈlɪn½mənt/ *n* [C;U] an oily liquid to be rubbed on the skin, esp. to help soreness and stiffness of the joints

**lin·ing** /ˈlaɪnɪŋ/ *n* a piece of material covering the inner surface of a garment, box, etc.

**link¹** /lɪŋk/ *n* **1** something which connects two other parts: *Is there a link between smoking and lung diseases?| a new rail link between two towns* (=a train runs between them) **2** one ring of a chain

**link²** *v* [I;T *together, up*] to join or connect: *The road links all the new towns.|They walked with linked arms.|She was able to link up all the different pieces of information.*

**link·age** /ˈlɪŋkɪdʒ/ *n* **1** a set of LINKS **2** [S;U] the fact or way of being connected

**links** /lɪŋks/ *n* **links** [C] a piece of ground on which GOLF is played: *a golf links in the country*

**link·up** /ˈlɪŋk-ʌp/ *n* a point of joining or connection: *a road linkup|a television linkup*

**li·no·le·um** /l½ˈnəʊlɪəm/ also **lino** /ˈlaɪnəʊ/ *BrE infml*– *n* [U] a floor-covering made up of strong cloth and other substances

**lin·seed oil** /ˈlɪnsiːd ˌɔɪl/ *n* [U] an oil made from FLAX, used in some paints, inks, etc.

**lint** /lɪnt/ *n* [U] soft material used for protecting wounds

**lin·tel** /ˈlɪntl/ *n* a piece of stone or wood across the top of a window or door, forming part of the frame

**li·on** /ˈlaɪən/ **lioness** /ˈlaɪənes, -n½s/ *fem.*– *n* **lions** *or* **lion** **1** a large yellow four-footed animal of the cat family which lives mainly in Africa **2 the lion's share (of)** the greatest part (of); most (of)

**lip** /lɪp/ *n* **1 a** one of the two edges of the mouth where the skin is delicate and rather red: *He kissed her on the lips.* –see picture on page 299 **b** the ordinary skin below the nose **2** the edge (of a hollow vessel or opening): *the lip of the cup* **3 stiff upper lip** a lack of expression of feeling **4 pay lip service to** to support in words, but not in fact **5 -lipped** having lips of a certain colour, shape, etc.: *red-lipped|thin-lipped with anger*

**lip-read** /ˈlɪp riːd/ *v* [I] (usu. of people who cannot hear) to watch people's lip movements so as to understand what they are saying –**lipreading** *n* [U]

**lip·stick** /ˈlɪpˌstɪk/ *n* [C;U] (a stick-shaped mass of) material for brightening the colour of the lips

**liq·ue·fy** /ˈlɪkw½faɪ/ *v* **-fied, -fying** [I;T] to (cause to) become liquid –**liquefaction** /-ˈfækʃən/ *n* [C]

**li·queur** /lɪˈkjʊəʳ‖lɪˈkɜr/ *n* a very strong alcoholic drink which has a special, rather sweet taste

**liq·uid¹** /ˈlɪkw½d/ *n* [C;U] (a type of) substance not solid or gas, which flows and has no fixed shape: *Water is a liquid.*

**liquid²** *adj* **1** (esp. of something which is usu. solid or gas) in the form of a liquid: *liquid gold|liquid oxygen* **2** (esp. of food) soft and watery **3** (of sounds) clear and flowing, with pure notes

**liq·ui·date** /ˈlɪkw½deɪt/ *v* **-dated, -dating** [T] **1** to get rid of; destroy **2** to arrange the end of business for (a company), esp. when it has too many debts and is BANKRUPT –**liquidation** /-ˈdeɪʃən/ *n* [U]: *The company has* **gone into liquidation.** (=is BANKRUPT)

**liq·uid·ize** /ˈlɪkw½daɪz/ *v* **-ized, -izing** [T] to crush (esp. fruit or vegetables) into a liquid-like form

**liq·uid·iz·er** /ˈlɪkwədaɪzəʳ/ *n BrE* for BLENDER

**liq·uor** /ˈlɪkəʳ/ *n* [U] **1** *BrE fml or tech* alcoholic drink **2** *AmE* strong alcoholic drink, such as WHISKY

**liq·uo·rice, licorice** /ˈlɪkərɪs, -rɪʃ/ *n* [U] a sweet black substance used in medicine and sweets

**lisp¹** /lɪsp/ *v* [I;T] to speak or say with /s/ sounds which are not clear, making the /s/ seem like /θ/ **–lispingly** *adv*

**lisp²** *n* [S] the fault in speech of LISPing: *She speaks with a lisp.*

**lis·som, lissome** /ˈlɪsəm/ *adj* (of a person or the body) graceful in shape and movement **–lissomly** *adv* **–lissomness** *n* [U]

**list¹** /lɪst/ *n* a set of names of things written one after the other, so as to remember them or keep them in order: *a shopping list|He made a list of their names.*

**list²** *v* [T] to write in a list: *He listed all the things he had to do.*

**list³** *v* [I] (esp. of a ship) to lean or slope to one side **–list** *n* [S]

**lis·ten¹** /ˈlɪsən/ *v* [I *to*] to give attention in hearing: *She's listening to the radio.|Listen to the music.* –see HEAR (USAGE)

**listen in** *v adv* [I] **1** [*to*] to listen to (a broadcast on) the radio: *to listen in to the news* –see also TUNE **in 2** [*on, to*] to listen to (the conversation of) other people, esp. when one should not –compare EAVESDROP

**listen²** *n* [S] *infml* an act of listening: *Have a listen.*

**list·less** /ˈlɪstləs/ *adj* (of a person who is) lacking power of movement, activity, etc.: *Heat makes some people listless.* –compare LIFELESS **–listlessly** *adv* **–listlessness** *n* [U]

**lit** /lɪt/ *v past tense and participle of* LIGHT³

**lit·a·ny** /ˈlɪtəni/ *n* **-nies** a form of prayer in the Christian church

**li·ter** /ˈliːtəʳ/ *n AmE* for LITRE

**lit·e·ra·cy** /ˈlɪtərəsi/ *n* [U] the state of being able to read and/or write (=being LITERATE): *an adult literacy campaign* (=a movement to teach people to read) –opposite **illiteracy**

**lit·e·ral** /ˈlɪtərəl/ *adj* **1** exact: *a literal account of a conversation* **2** giving one word for each word (as in a foreign language): *a literal translation* **3** following the usual meaning of the words, without any additional meanings –compare FIGURATIVE **4** not showing much imagination: *a literal* APPROACH² (3) *to a subject* **–literalness** *n* [U]

**lit·e·ral·ly** /ˈlɪtərəli/ *adv* **1** exactly: *to do literally nothing at all* **2** (used for giving force to an adjective): *literally blue with cold* –see USAGE **3** word by word: *to translate literally* **4** according to the words and not the intention: *I took what he said literally, but he really meant something else.*

USAGE **Literally** should really be used to mean "exactly as stated". It is often used more loosely to give force to an expression, but this is thought by teachers to be incorrect. Compare: *Their house is* **literally** *10 metres from the sea* (=this is a true statement).|*He* **literally** *exploded with anger* (=he did not in fact explode).

**lit·e·ra·ry** /ˈlɪtərəri‖ˈlɪtəreri/ *adj* of, concerning, or producing literature: *a literary woman|magazine*

**lit·e·rate** /ˈlɪtərət/ *adj* **1** able to read and write **2** well-educated –opposite **illiterate**; compare NUMERATE **–literately** *adv* **–literateness** *n* [U]

**lit·e·ra·ture** /ˈlɪtərətʃəʳ‖-tʃ ʊər/ *n* **1** [U] written works which are of artistic value: *English literature* **2** *infml* printed material, esp. giving information: *Have you any literature on the new car?*

**lithe** /laɪð/ *adj* (of a person or the body) able to bend and move easily **–lithely** *adv*

**lit·i·gate** /ˈlɪtəgeɪt/ *v* **-gated, -gating** [I;T] *tech* to bring or defend (a case) in a court of law **–litigation** /-ˈgeɪʃən/ *n*

**lit·mus** /ˈlɪtməs/ *n* [U] a colouring material which turns red when touched by an acid substance and blue when touched by an ALKALI: *litmus paper*

**li·tre** *BrE*‖**-ter** *AmE* /ˈliːtəʳ/ *n* (a measure of liquid equal to) about 1¾ PINTS

**lit·ter¹** /ˈlɪtəʳ/ *n* **1** [U] things (to be) thrown away, esp. paper scattered untidily: *a litter bin/basket* –see picture on page 297 **2** [C +*sing./pl. v*] a group of young animals born at the same time to one mother, as of KITTENS

**litter²** *v* [T] to scatter; spread; cover untidily: *to litter the room with papers|papers littering the room*

**lit·tle¹** /ˈlɪtl/ *adj* **1** [A] small: *two little insects* **2** [A] short: *a little time* **3** young: *my little girl* (=daughter)|*She's too little to ride a bicycle.|my little brother/sister* (=my younger brother/sister) **4** not important: *the little things of life* –compare BIG; see SMALL (USAGE)

**little²** *adv* **less** /les/, **least** /liːst/ **1** not much: *a little known fact|She goes out very little.* –see Study Notes on page 494 **2** not at all: *They little thought that the truth would be discovered.*

**little³** *determiner, pron* **less, least 1** [U] (used without *a,* to show the smallness of the amount) not much; not enough: *I have very little (money) left.|I understood little of his speech.|It's not less than a mile* (=it's at least a mile) *to the station.|Buy the one that costs the least (money).* **2** [S *no comp.*] **a** a small amount, but at least some: *a few eggs and a little milk|May I have a little of that cake?|***b** a short time: *You'd better stay in bed for a little.* **3 a little** rather: *I was a little annoyed.* **4 little by little** gradually: *We collected enough money little by little.* **5 make little of** to treat as unimportant –see FEW (USAGE)

**little finger** /ˌ·· ˈ··/ *n* the smallest finger on the hand

**lit·ur·gy** /ˈlɪtədʒi‖-ər-/ *n* **-gies** a form of worship in the Christian church, using prayers, songs, etc., fixed patterns **–liturgical** /lɪˈtɜːdʒɪkəl‖-ɜr-/ *adj*

**liv·a·ble, liveable** /ˈlɪvəbəl/ *adj* **1** worth living; acceptable to experience **2** suitable to live in

**live¹** /lɪv/ *v* **lived, living 1** [I] to be alive; have life: *The rich live while the poor die.* **2** to continue to be alive: *His illness is so serious, he is unlikely to live.|He managed to live through two world wars.* **3** to have one's home; DWELL: *Where do you live?|I live in a flat in Liverpool.* **4** to afford what one needs: *to earn enough to live* **5** (of characters in books, plays, etc.) to seem real **6 live and let live** to accept others' behaviour; be TOLERANT

**live by** sthg. *v prep* [T] **1** [+*v-ing*] to make an income from: *He lives by stealing.* **2** to behave according to the rules of: *He lives by the book.* (=does nothing wrong)

**live** sthg.↔ **down** *v adv* [T] to cause (a bad action) to be forgotten, esp. by future good behaviour: *He was* *drunk at school–he'll never live it down.*

**live in** *v adv* [I] to sleep and eat in a house where one is employed –compare LIVE **out** (1)

**live off** sbdy./sthg. *v prep* [T] **1** to produce one's food or income from: *I live off the money from my first book.* **2** *usu. derog* to get money for one's needs from: *to live off one's parents*

**live on** sthg. *v prep* [T] to have as one's only food or income: *to live on fruit and nuts*

**live out** *v adv* **1** [I] to live in a place away from one's place of work –compare LIVE **in** **2** [T (**live out** sthg.)] to live till the end of: *Will the old man live out the month?*

**live up to** sthg. *v adv prep* [T] to keep to the high standards of: *Did the film live up to your expectations?* (=was it as good as you expected?)

**live with** sbdy./sthg. *v prep* [T] **1** *euph* to live in the same house as (someone of the opposite sex), like a married person **2** to accept (an unpleasant thing): *I don't enjoy the pain, but I can live with it.*

**live²** /laɪv/ *adj* [*no comp.*] **1** [A] alive; living: *The cat was playing with a live mouse.* –opposite **dead** **2** in a state in which it could explode: *a live bomb* **3** carrying free electricity which can shock anyone who touches it: *a live wire* **4** (of broadcasting) seen and/or heard as it happens: *It wasn't a recorded show, it was live.*

**live·li·hood** /ˈlaɪvlihʊd/ *n* the way by which one earns one's money: *I like playing in the band, but I don't do it just for fun; it's my livelihood.*

**live·ly** /ˈlaɪvli/ *adj* **-lier, -liest** **1** full of quick movement, thought, etc.: *a lively mind/song* **2** lifelike; as if real; VIVID (2): *a lively description* –**liveliness** *n* [U]

**liv·en up** /ˈlaɪvən/ *v adv* [I;T] to (cause to) become LIVELY (1)

**liv·er** /ˈlɪvəʳ/ *n* [C;U] a large organ in the body which produces BILE and cleans the blood

**liv·e·ry** /ˈlɪvəri/ *n* **-ries** uniform belonging to a particular person or group, worn by servants, or by members of the group –**liveried** *adj*

**lives** /laɪvz/ *n pl. of* LIFE

**live·stock** /ˈlaɪvstɒk‖-stɑk/ *n* [U +*sing./pl. v*] animals kept on a farm

**liv·id** /ˈlɪvɨ̣d/ *adj* **1** blue-grey, as of marks on the skin (BRUISES) after being hit **2** *infml* very angry –**lividly** *adv*

**liv·ing¹** /ˈlɪvɪŋ/ *adj* **1** alive now: *She has no living relatives.|The living are more important to us than the dead.* **2** existing in use: *a living language*

**living²** *n* **1** [C] earnings with which one buys what is necessary to life: *to* **make a living** *in industry* **2** [U] a standard one reaches in food, drink, etc.: *The* **cost of living** *increased by 10% last year.*

**living room** /ˈ·· ·/ also **sitting room** *BrE*– *n* the main room in a house where people can do things together, (usu.) apart from eating –see picture on page 355

**liz·ard** /ˈlɪzəd‖-ərd/ *n* a (usu.) small REPTILE, with a rough skin, four legs, and a long tail

**ll** *written abbrev. said as*: lines: *see ll 104-201*

**-'ll** /əl, l/ *v* short for will; shall: *He'll soon be here.*

**lla·ma** /ˈlɑːmə/ *n* **-mas** *or* **-ma** an animal of South America with thick woolly hair, sometimes used for carrying goods

**load¹** /ləʊd/ *n* **1** an amount being carried, or to be carried, esp. heavy: *a load of furniture*|(fig.) *Her grief is a heavy load to bear.* **2** the amount which a certain vehicle can carry: *a car load of people* **3** the work done by an engine, etc. **4** the power of an electricity supply **5** **loads of** also **a load of**– *infml* a large amount of; a lot of: *She's got loads of money.|That book is a load of rubbish.*

**load²** *v* **1** [I;T *up, with*] to put a load on or in (something): *Load the car (with the parcels)/the parcels into the car.* |(fig.) *They loaded me with gifts.* **2** [T] to put a CHARGE² (7) or film into (a gun or camera)

**load** sbdy./sthg.↔ **down** *v adv* [T *with*] to load with a great weight: *I was loaded down with books.*

**load·ed** /ˈləʊdɨ̣d/ *adj* **1** giving an unfair advantage: *The argument was loaded in his favour.* **2** containing a hidden trap: *a loaded question* **3** [F] *infml* having lots of money: *Let him pay; he's loaded.*

**loaf¹** /ləʊf/ *n* **loaves** /ləʊvz/ bread shaped and baked in one piece, usu. fairly large: *a loaf of bread* –compare ROLL¹ (2); see picture on page 615

**loaf²** *v* [I *about*] *infml* to waste time, esp. by not working when one should –**loafer** *n*

**loam** /ləʊm/ *n* [C;U] good soil –**loamy** *adj* **-ier, -iest**

**loan¹** /ləʊn/ *n* **1** something which is lent: *The book is a loan, not a gift.|a £1,000 loan* **2** the act of lending: *the loan of a book*

**loan²** *v* [T *to*] **1** *AmE* to give (someone) the use of; lend –see Study Notes on page 429 **2** to lend formally for a long period: *She loaned her pictures to the* MUSEUM.

**loath, loth** /ləʊθ/ *adj* [F +*to-v*] unwilling: *loath to lend money*

**loathe** /ləʊð/ *v* **loathed, loathing** [T +*v-ing*] to feel hatred or great dislike for –**loathing** *n* [C;U]

**loath·some** /ˈləʊðsəm/ *adj* which causes great dislike; very unpleasant: *the loathsome smell of burning flesh* –**loathsomely** *adv* –**loathsomeness** *n* [U]

**loaves** /ləʊvz/ *n pl. of* LOAF

**lob¹** /lɒb‖lɑb/ *v* **-bb-** [T] to send (a ball) in a LOB

**lob²** *n* (in cricket or tennis) a ball thrown or hit in a high gentle curve

**lob·by¹** /ˈlɒbi‖ˈlɑbi/ *n* **-bies** **1** [C] a hall or passage, not a room, which leads from the entrance to the rooms inside a building: *the hotel lobby* **2** [C +*sing./pl. v*] a group of people who unite for or against an action, so that those in power will change their minds: *the women's rights lobby*

**lobby²** *v* **1** [I;T] to meet (a member of parliament) in order to persuade him/her to support one's actions and needs **2** [I] to be active in making actions, plans, etc., public, so as to bring about a change of some kind

**lobe** /ləʊb/ *n* **1** also **earlobe**– the round fleshy piece at the bottom of the ear **2** *tech* any rounded division of an organ, esp. the brain and lungs

**lob·ster** /ˈlɒbstəʳ‖ˈlɑb-/ *n* [C;U] an eight-legged sea animal with a shell, the flesh of which may be eaten

**lo·cal¹** /ˈləʊkəl/ *adj* **1** of or in a certain place, esp. the place one lives in: *the/our local doctor|local news* –see TOPICAL (USAGE) **2** *tech* concerning a particular part, esp. of the body: *a local infection*

**local²** *n BrE infml* a pub near where one lives, esp. which one often drinks at

**lo·cal·i·ty** /ləʊ'kæl$^{\text{l}}_{\text{ə}}$ti/ *n* **-ties** a place or area, esp. in which something happens or has happened

**lo·cal·ize** ‖ also **-ise** *BrE* /'ləʊkəlaɪz/ *v* **-ized, -izing** [T] to keep within a small area: *to localize the pain* **–localization** /ˌləʊkəlaɪ'zeɪʃən‖-kələ-/ *n* [U]

**lo·cal·ly** /'ləʊkəli/ *adv* [*no comp.*] **1** in a local area **2** →NEARBY: *Do you live locally?*

**lo·cate** /ləʊ'keɪt‖'ləʊkeɪt/ *v* **-cated, -cating** [T] **1** to learn the position of: *We located the schools and shops as soon as we moved into the town.* **2** to fix or set in a certain place: *The house is located next to the river.*

**lo·ca·tion** /ləʊ'keɪʃən/ *n* **1** a place or position: *a suitable location for a camp* **2 on location** in a town, country, etc., to make a film

**loch** /lɒk‖lɑk/ *n ScotE* a lake

**lock¹** /lɒk‖lɑk/ *n* **1** an apparatus for closing and fastening something by means of a key: *He put new locks on the doors.* **2** a stretch of water closed off by gates, esp. on a CANAL, so that the level can be raised or lowered to move boats up or down a slope **3 lock, stock, and barrel** completely **4 under lock and key: a** safely hidden and fastened in **b** imprisoned

**lock²** *v* **1** [I;T] to fasten with a lock: *Lock the door.|The door won't lock.* **2** [T] to put in a place and lock the entrance: *to lock one's jewels in the cupboard* **3** [I] to become fixed or blocked: *I can't move the car; the wheels have locked.* **–lockable** *adj*

**lock** sthg.↔ **away** *v adv* [T] to keep safe or secret, (as) by putting in a locked place

**lock** sbdy.↔ **in** *v adv* [T] to put (esp. a person or animal) inside a place and lock the doors

**lock** sbdy.↔ **out** *v adv* [T *of*] to keep out of a place by locking the entrance –see also LOCKOUT

**lock up** *v adv* **1** [I;T (=**lock** sthg. ↔ **up**)] to make (a building) safe by locking the doors, esp. for the night **2** [T] (**lock** sbdy./sthg.↔ **up**) to put in a place of safety and lock the entrance: *People like that should be locked up!* (=in prison)

**lock³** *n* a small piece of hair: *a curly lock*

**lock·er** /'lɒkə^r‖'lɑ-/ *n* a small cupboard for keeping things in, esp. at a school where there is one for each pupil

**lock·et** /'lɒk$^{\text{l}}_{\text{ə}}$t‖'lɑ-/ *n* a small decoration for the neck, a metal case on a chain in which small pictures can be kept

**lock·out** /'lɒk-aʊt‖'lɑk-/ *n* the employers' action of not allowing people to go back to work, esp. in a factory, until they accept an agreement –see also LOCK **out**

**lo·co·mo·tive¹** /ˌləʊkə'məʊtɪv/ *adj tech* concerning or causing movement **–locomotion** /-'məʊʃən/ *n* [U]

**locomotive²** *n fml* a railway engine

**lo·cum** /'ləʊkəm/ *n* a doctor or priest doing the work of another who is away

**lo·cust** /'ləʊkəst/ *n* an insect of Asia and Africa which flies in large groups, often destroying crops

**lodge¹** /lɒdʒ‖lɑdʒ/ *v* **lodged, lodging 1** [I] to stay, usu. for a short time and paying rent: *to lodge at a friend's house/with friends* **2** [I] to live in lodgings **3** [I;T] to settle or fix firmly in a position: *A chicken bone lodged in his throat.* –see also DISLODGE **4** [T] to make (a statement) officially: *to lodge a complaint*

**lodge²** *n* **1** a small house in the GROUNDS (1) of a larger house **2** a small house for hunters, sportsmen, etc., to stay in while crossing wild country –compare CHALET (2)

**lodg·er** /'lɒdʒə^r‖'lɑ-/ *n* a person who pays rent to stay in somebody's house

**lodg·ing** /'lɒdʒɪŋ‖'lɑ-/ *n* [S;U] a place to stay for payment: *a lodging for the night|to find lodging* –compare BOARD¹ (3)

**lodg·ings** /'lɒdʒɪŋz‖'lɑ-/ *n* [P] a house where rooms are rented out: *to stay in lodgings*

**loft** /lɒft‖lɔft/ *n* a room under the roof of a building; ATTIC

**loft·y** /'lɒfti‖'lɔfti/ *adj* **-ier, -iest 1 a** of unusually high quility of thinking, feeling, etc.: *lofty aims* **b** showing belief of being better than other people: *a lofty smile* **2** *lit* high **–loftily** *adv* **–loftiness** *n* [U]

**log¹** /lɒg‖lɔg, lɑg/ *n* **1** a thick piece of wood from a tree: **2** an official written record of a journey, as in a ship, plane, etc.: *The captain described the accident in the ship's log.* **3 sleep like a log** to sleep deeply without moving

**log²** *v* **-gg-** [T] to record in a LOG¹ (2)

**lo·gan·ber·ry** /'ləʊgənbəri‖-beri/ *n* **-ries** a red fruit grown from a plant which is half BLACKBERRY and half RASPBERRY

**log·a·rith·m** /'lɒgərɪðəm‖'lɔ-, 'lɑ-/ also **log** *infml– n* a number which represents a value of another number, and which can be added to another logarithm instead of multiplying the original number **–logarithmic** /-'rɪðmɪk/ *adj*

**log·ger·heads** /'lɒgəhedz‖'lɔgər-, 'lɑ/ *n* **at loggerheads (with)** always disagreeing (with)

**lo·gic** /'lɒdʒɪk‖'lɑ-/ *n* [U] **1** the science of reasoning by formal methods **2** a way of reasoning **3** *infml* reasonable thinking: *There's no logic in spending money on useless things.* –compare LOGISTICS

**lo·gic·al** /'lɒdʒɪkəl‖'lɑ-/ *adj* **1** in accordance with the rules and science of LOGIC: *a logical argument* **2** having or showing good reasoning; sensible –opposite **illogical**; compare REASONABLE **-logically** *adv*

**lo·gis·tics** /lə'dʒɪstɪks‖ləʊ-/ *n* [P;U] the ways in which soldiers can be moved, supplied with food, etc.: *the logistics of war* –compare LOGIC **–logistic** *adj* **–logistically** *adv*

**loin·cloth** /'lɔɪnklɒθ‖-klɔθ/ *n* a loose covering for the LOINS, worn in hot countries by poor people

**loins** /lɔɪnz/ *n* [P] the lower part of the body below the waist and above the legs

**loi·ter** /'lɔɪtə^r/ *v* [I *about*} to walk about slowly with frequent stops: *The policeman watched the two men, who were loitering near the bank.* **–loiterer** *n*

**loll** /lɒl‖lɑl/ *v* **1** [I *about, around*] to be lying in a lazy loose position: *She was lolling in a chair, with her arms hanging over the sides.* **2** [I;T *out*] to (allow to) hang down loosely: *The dog's tongue lolled out.*

**lol·li·pop** /'lɒlipɒp‖'lɑlipɑp/ ‖also **lolly** *BrE– n* **1** a hard sweet made of boiled sugar set around a stick **2** anything like this, esp. frozen juice on a stick

**lollipop man** /'··· ·/ **lollipop woman** /'··· ˌ··/– *fem. n BrE* a person whose job is to stop traffic so that school children can cross, by turning towards the cars a stick with a notice on top telling them to stop

**lol·ly** /'lɒli‖'lɑli/ *n* **-lies** *BrE* for LOLLIPOP (2): *an ice lolly*

curtain
light
picture
standard lamp
ornaments
table lamp
windowsill
clock
radiator
speaker
bookcase
mantelpiece
television
stereo/hi-fi
socket
plug
video
skirting board
hearth
rug
carpet
fireplace
sofa/settee
coffee table
ashtray
cushion
armchair
(house)plant

**lone** /ləun/ *adj* [A *no comp.*] without (other) people: *a lone rider* –see ALONE (USAGE)

**lone·ly** /'ləunli/ *adj* **-lier, -liest** alone and unhappy; away from other people: *When his wife died, he was very lonely.*|*a lonely house in the country* –see ALONE (USAGE) –**loneliness** *n* [U]

**lon·er** /'ləunəʳ/ *n* a person who spends a lot of time alone, esp. by choice

**lone·some** /'ləunsəm/ *adj AmE infml* for lonely –see ALONE (USAGE)

**long¹** /lɒŋ‖lɔŋ/ *adj* **1** measuring a large amount in length, distance, or time: *long hair*|*a long journey*|*He took a long time to get here.*|*four feet long* –opposite **short 2** covering a certain distance or time: *How long was her speech?*|*It was an hour long.*|*The garden is 20 metres long and 15 metres wide.* **3 not by a long chalk** *BrE*‖**shot** *AmE infml* not at all; not nearly **4 in the long run** in the end; EVENTUALly

**long²** *adv* **1** (for) a long time: *I can't wait much longer.*|*Will you be long?* (=will it take you a long time?)|*He hasn't long been back.* (=he has only just returned) **2 as/so long as** if; on condition that: *You can go out, as long as you promise to be back before 11 o'clock.* **3 long ago** at a distant time in the past **4 no longer/(not) any longer** (used only in NEGATIVEs², questions, etc.) (not) any more; not now: *He no longer lives here.* **5 so long** *infml* goodbye

**long³** *n* **1** a long time: *I'll be back* **before long.** (=soon)|Were you there **for long?**|*It won't* **take long** *to mend the car.* **2 the long and the short of it** the general result

**long⁴** *v* [I;T +*to-v/for*] to want very much: *I'm longing to go.*|*I'm longing for him to come home.*

**long·bow** /'lɒŋbəu‖'lɔŋ-/ *n* a large powerful BOW³ made of a single curved piece of wood, for use with arrows –compare CROSSBOW

**long-dis·tance** /ˌ· '··◂/ *adj,adv* [A *no comp.*] from one point to a far point: *a long-distance runner*|*a long-distance (telephone) call*|*to telephone long-distance*

**long drink** /'· ·/ *n* a drink, e.g. beer, which usu. contains a little alcohol in a large amount of liquid –compare SHORT³ (1)

**lon·gev·i·ty** /lɒn'dʒevəti‖lɑn-, lɔn-/ *n* [U] *fml* long life

**long·hand** /'lɒŋhænd‖'lɔŋ-/ *n* [U] ordinary writing by hand, not in any shortened or machine-produced form –compare SHORTHAND

**long·ing** /'lɒŋɪŋ‖'lɔŋɪŋ/ *n,adj* [C;U *for*] (showing) a strong feeling of wanting something: *a longing for fame*|*secret longings*|*longing looks* –**longingly** *adv*

**lon·gi·tude** /'lɒndʒətjuːd‖'lɑndʒətuːd/ *n* [C;U] the position on the earth east or west of a MERIDIAN, measured in degrees –compare LATITUDE (1) –**longitudinal** /-'tjuːdənəl‖-'tuː-/ *adj*

**long jump** /'· ·/ *n* [C; *the* S] a sport in which people jump as far as possible along the ground –see picture on page 592

**long-play·ing rec·ord** /ˌ· ·· '··/ *n* →LP

**long-range** /ˌ· '·◂/ *adj* [A] covering a long distance or time: *long-range weapons*

**long·sight·ed** /ˌlɒn'saɪtəd◂‖ˌlɔŋ-/ also **farsighted** *AmE*– *adj* able to see things only when they are far away –opposite **shortsighted**; see also FARSIGHTED

**long·stand·ing** /ˌlɒŋ'stændɪŋ◂‖ˌlɔŋ-/ *adj* which has existed for a long time: *a longstanding trade agreement between two countries*

**long-term** /ˌ· '·◂/ *adj* for or in the distant future: *a long-term plan*|*No one knows what the long-term effects of new drugs will be.* –opposite **short-term**

**long wave** /ˌ· '·◂/ *n* [U] radio broadcasting on waves of 1,000 metres or more –compare SHORT WAVE

**long·ways** /'lɒŋweɪz‖'lɔŋ-/ *adv* →LENGTHWAYS

**long·wind·ed** /ˌlɒŋ'wɪndəd◂‖ˌlɔŋ-/ *adj* saying too much in a dull way: *a longwinded speech*

**loo** /luː/ *n BrE infml* for LAVATORY

**look¹** /luk/ *v* **1** [I *at, out of, away,* etc.] to turn the eyes so as to see, examine, or find something: *You are looking at this dictionary.*|*"I can't find it." "You could see it if you'd only look."*|*I looked away as the doctor put the needle in my arm.*|*He looked out of the window.* **2** to have the appearance of being (ill, well, etc.): *You look tired.*|*He looks like my brother.* **3** [T] to see and notice carefully: *Look where you're going!* **4** [I] (of a thing) to face in the stated direction: *Our house looks out on the river.* **5 look as if/look like** to seem probable that: *It looks as if we're going to miss the plane.* **6 look someone in the eye/face** to look directly and boldly at someone **7 not much to look at** not attractive

**look after** sbdy./sthg. *v prep* [T] to take care of: *Who will look after the baby?*|*I can look after myself.*|*Are you being well looked after?*

**look ahead** *v adv* [I] to plan for the future

**look around/round** *v adv* [I *for*] to search

**look at** sbdy./sthg. *v prep* [T] **1** to watch: *looking at the traffic going past the window* **2** to regard; judge: *He looks at work in a different way now he's in charge.* **3** to consider; examine: *to look carefully at a problem* **4** to remember and learn from: *Look at Mrs Jones; drink killed her!*

**look back** *v adv* [I] **1** [*to, on*] to remember **2 never look back** to have complete success: *After he won the first game, he never looked back.*

**look down on** sbdy. *v adv prep* [T] to have a low opinion of (esp. someone thought less socially important) –compare LOOK **up to**

**look for** sbdy./sthg. *v prep* [T] to try to find

**look forward to** sthg. *v adv prep* [T +*v-ing*] to expect to enjoy (something that is going to happen)

USAGE This is always followed by a noun or the *-ing* form of a verb: *I'm* **looking forward to** *seeing you next week,* not **I'm* **looking forward to** *see you.*

**look into** sthg. *v prep* [T] to examine the meaning or causes of: *There's a fault in the machine, and we're just looking into it.*

**look on¹** *v adv* [I] to watch while others take part –see also ONLOOKER

**look on²/upon** sbdy./sthg. [T *as, with*] to consider; regard: *I look on him as a friend.*

**look out** *v adv* **1** [I *for*] to take care; watch (for): *Look out! You'll crash the car!*|*Look out for Jane at the station.* **2** [T] (**look** sthg.↔**out**) to choose from one's possessions –see also LOOKOUT

**look** sthg.↔ **over** *v adv* [T] to examine quickly –compare OVERLOOK

**look round** *v adv;prep* [I;T] to look at everything,

esp. before buying: *Would you like to look round?|looking round the shops*

**look through** sthg. *v prep* [T] to examine, esp. for points to be noted

**look up** *v adv* **1** [I] to get better; improve: *Things are looking up!* **2** [T] (**look** sthg.↔ **up**) to find (information) in a book: *Look up the word in the dictionary.* **3** [T] (**look** sbdy.↔ **up**) to visit when in the same area

**look up to** sbdy. *v adv prep* [T] to respect –compare LOOK **down on**

**look²** *n* **1** an act of looking: *Have/Take a look at that!|She gave me an angry look.* (=looked angrily at me) **2** an expression on the face: *I knew she didn't like it by the look on her face.* **3** an appearance: *He has the look of a winner.*|**By the look(s) of it,** (=probably) *we shan't have much rain this month.*|*I* **don't like the look of** *that hole in the roof.*(=it suggests something bad to me) –see also LOOKS

**look³** also **look here** /ˌ· ˈ·/– *interj* (an expression, often angry, used to draw a person's attention): *Look (here), I don't mind you borrowing my car, but you ought to ask me first.*

**look·out** /ˈlʊk-aʊt/ *n* **1** [S] the act of watching or searching for: *He's* **on the lookout for** *a job.* **2** [C] **a** a place to watch from **b** a person whose duty is to watch **3** [S] *infml* a future possibility: *It's a bad lookout for us if he becomes ill.* **4 one's own lookout** *infml* one's own affair: *If the teacher finds out you've been cheating, it's your own lookout.* –see also LOOK **out**

**looks** /lʊks/ *n* [P] an attractive appearance: *He kept his (good) looks even in old age.*

**loom¹** /luːm/ *n* a frame or machine for weaving cloth

**loom²** *v* [I *up*] to come into sight in a way that seems large and unfriendly: *A figure loomed (up) out of the mist.*|(fig.) *Fear of failure* **loomed large** *in his mind.*

**loon·y** /ˈluːni/ *n,adj* **-ier, -iest** *infml* for LUNATIC

**loop¹** /luːp/ *n* the circular shape made by a piece of string, wire, rope, etc., when curved back on itself: *The loop of string makes a handle for the parcel.*|(fig.) *The aircraft made a loop in the sky.*

**loop²** *v* [I;T] **1** to make or form a LOOP **2** to fasten with a LOOP: *Loop the rope round the gate.*

**loop·hole** /ˈluːphəʊl/ *n* a way of avoiding something, esp. one provided by faults in a rule or agreement: *a loophole in the tax laws*

**loose¹** /luːs/ *adj* **1** [F *no comp.*] not fastened, tied up, shut up, etc.; free from control: *The animals broke loose and ran away.|I have one hand loose but the other is tied.* **2** [*no comp.*] not bound together: *I bought these sweets loose, not in a box.* **3** not firmly fixed; not tight: *This pole is coming loose and will soon fall over.|a loose button* **4** (of clothes) not fitting tightly **5** not exact: *a loose translation* **6** without morals: *loose living* **7 at a loose end** having nothing to do **8 let loose** to free –**loosely** *adv* –**looseness** *n* [U]

**loose²** *v* **loosed, loosing** [T] *fml or lit* to free from control; untie –compare LOOSEN

**loose³** *adv* in a loose manner; loosely

**loose⁴** *n* **on the loose** free from control, esp. of law: *a dangerous criminal on the loose*

**loos·en** /ˈluːsən/ *v* [I;T] to make or become less firm, fixed, or tight; set free; unfasten: *He loosened his collar.* –opposite **tighten**

**loosen up** *v adv* [I] to exercise the muscles ready for action: *The runners are loosening up before the race.*

**loot¹** /luːt/ *n* [U] goods stolen by thieves, soldiers, etc., in time of war or social unrest

**loot²** *v* [I;T] to take LOOT¹ (from): *Following the explosions in the town centre, crowds of people looted the shops.* –**looter** *n*

**lop** /lɒp‖lɑp/ *v* **-pp-** [T *away, off*] to cut off; remove: *to lop off branches from a tree*

**lope** /ləʊp/ *v* **loped, loping** [I] (esp. of animals) to move easily and quite fast with springing steps –**lope** *n* [S]

**lop-sid·ed** /ˌ· ˈ·· ◂/ *adj infml* having one side not balanced with the other

**loq·ua·cious** /ləʊˈkweɪʃəs/ *adj fml* talking a great deal –**loquacity** /-ləʊˈkwæsɪ̇ti/ *n* [U]

**lord¹** /lɔːd‖lɔrd/ *n* **1** a ruler or master **2** a nobleman

**lord²** *v* **lord it (over someone)** *esp. derog* to behave like a lord (to someone)

**Lord¹** *n* **1** [*the* S] God **2** [A;C] (a title of certain official people): *the Lord* MAYOR *of London*

**Lord²** *interj* an expression of surprise or worry: *Good Lord!|Oh Lord, I forgot!*

**lord·ly** /ˈlɔːdli‖-ɔr-/ *adj* **-lier, -liest** like a lord; grand

**lord·ship** /ˈlɔːdʃɪp‖-ɔr-/ *n* (the title used for) a judge, a BISHOP, or certain noblemen: *Good morning, your lordship(s).*

**lore** /lɔːʳ‖lor/ *n* [U] knowledge or old beliefs not written down: *old sea lore* –see also FOLKLORE

**lor·gnette** /lɔːˈnjet‖-ɔr-/ *n* (esp. formerly) a pair of glasses held in front of the eyes by a long handle

**lor·ry** /ˈlɒri‖ˈlɔri, ˈlɑri/ *BrE*‖ also **truck** *esp. AmE*– *n* **-ries** a large motor vehicle for carrying heavy goods

**lose** /luːz/ *v* **lost** /lɒst‖lɔst/, **losing 1** [T] to come to be without, e.g. through carelessness; fail to find: *I have lost my book.|He lost his way in the mist.* **2** [T] to (cause to) have taken away; (cause to) have no longer, as a result of time, death, or destruction: *I've lost all interest in football.|His foolish behaviour lost him his job.|She lost her parents while she was very young.* (=they died)|*He lost an eye in the accident.* **3** [I;T] to fail to win, gain, or obtain: *He lost the argument.|England lost to* (=were beaten by) *Australia.* **4** [I;T] to (cause to) have less (money) than when one started: *We lost £200 on that job.|We lost on that job.|That job lost us £200.* **5** [T] to have less of: *He's lost a lot of weight.* **6** [T] to fail to use; waste: *The doctor lost no time in getting the sick man to hospital.* **7** [T] to (cause to) fail to hear, see, or understand: *I'm sorry, you've lost me; could you explain it again?* **8** [I;T] (of a watch or clock) to work too slowly by (an amount of time): *This watch loses (50 minutes a day).* –opposite **gain** (for 4,6,8)

**lose out** *v adv* [I *on*] *infml* to make a loss; have no success: *The firm lost out on the deal.*

**los·er** /ˈluːzəʳ/ *n* a person or animal who has been defeated: *He always gets annoyed when I beat him at cards: he's a bad loser.|I'm a* **born loser.** (=I'm always defeated) –compare WINNER

**loss** /lɒs‖lɔs/ *n* **1** [U] the act or fact of losing possession (of something): *Did you report the loss of your car to the police?* **2** [C] a person, thing, or amount that is lost or taken away: *His death was a great loss to* *his friends.* **3** [C] a failure to make a profit: *The company has made a big loss/big losses this year.* **4 at a loss** confused; uncertain what to do or say **5 be a dead loss** *infml* to have no worth or use

**lost**[1] /lɒst‖lɔst/ *past tense and participle of* LOSE

**lost**[2] *adj* **1** that cannot be found: *lost keys* **2** no longer possessed: *lost youth|a lost chance* **3** [F] unable to find the way: *I* **got lost** *in the snow.* **4** [F] destroyed, killed etc.: *men lost at sea*

**lot**[1] /lɒt‖lɑt/ *n infml* **1** [C +*sing./pl. v/of*] a great quantity, number, or amount: *He has (quite) a lot of friends.|She has lots (and lots) of money.|There was lots to drink at the party.|What a lot!* –compare PLENTY; see Study Notes on page 389 **2** [*the* U +*sing./pl. v*] the whole quantity, number, or amount: *Give me the lot.|The whole lot of you are mad!* **3** [C +*sing./pl. v*] a group or amount of people or things of the same type: *Another lot of students is/are arriving soon.*

**lot**[2] *n* **1** [C] an article or articles sold together in an AUCTION sale **2** [C] *esp. AmE* an area of land used for building or parking cars on **3** [C;U] (the use of) objects of different sizes or with different marks to make a choice or decision by chance: *We* **drew/cast lots** *to decide who should go.* **4** [S] *lit* one's way of life; fate **5 a bad lot** *infml* a bad person

**lo·tion** /ˈləʊʃən/ *n* [C;U] a liquid mixture, used to make skin or hair clean and healthy

**lot·te·ry** /ˈlɒtəri‖ˈlɑ-/ *n* **-ries** a system in which many numbered tickets are sold, then a few chosen by chance, and prizes given to those who bought them –compare DRAW[2] (1), RAFFLE

**lo·tus** /ˈləʊtəs/ *n* a white or pink flower that grows, esp. in Asia, on the surface of lakes

**loud**[1] /laʊd/ *adj* **1** having or producing great strength of sound; not quiet; noisy: *loud music|a loud radio* **2** unpleasantly noisy or colourful: *loud behaviour|loud wallpaper* **–loudly** *adv* **–loudness** *n* [U]

**loud**[2] *adv* loudly; in a loud way: *Try to sing louder.*

**loud·speak·er** /ˌlaʊdˈspiːkəʳ, ˈlaʊdˌspiːkəʳ/ *n* that part of a radio, record player, etc., from which the sound comes out

**lounge**[1] /laʊndʒ/ *n* a comfortable room for sitting in, as in a house or hotel –see picture on page 297

**lounge**[2] *v* **lounged, lounging** [I *about, around*] to stand or sit in a lazy manner; pass time doing nothing

**lounge suit** /ˈ· ·/ *n* an ordinary suit for a man, as worn during the day –compare EVENING DRESS

**lour, lower** /ˈlaʊəʳ/ *v* [I *at*] *lit* to look in a bad-tempered, threatening manner; FROWN (1): (fig.) *a lowering sky before the storm*

**louse** /laʊs/ *n* **lice** /laɪs/ **1** a small insect that lives on the skin and in the hair of people and animals **2** *infml* a worthless person

**louse** sthg.↔ **up** *v adv* **loused, lousing** [T] *AmE infml* to deal unsuccessfully with; MESS UP

**lou·sy** /ˈlaʊzi/ *adj* **-sier, -siest 1** *infml* very bad, useless, etc.: *What lousy weather!* **2** [F] covered with lice (LOUSE)

**lout** /laʊt/ *n* a rough young man with bad manners **–loutish** *adj*

**love**[1] /lʌv/ *n* **1** [U] a strong feeling of fondness for a person: *a mother's love for her child|a man and a woman* **in love** (*with each other*) –opposites **hate, hatred 2** [U *of, for*] warm interest and enjoyment (in): *love of art/sport* **3** [C *of*] the object of attraction or liking: *Music was the love of his life.* **4** [C] a person who is loved: *Yes, my love.* **5** *BrE* a friendly word of address: *Hello love!* **6** [U] (in tennis) no points; NIL: *McEnroe leads 15-love.* **7 give/send somebody one's love** to send friendly greetings to **8 not for love nor money** not by any means

**love**[2] *v* **loved, loving 1** [I;T;not *be +v-ing*] to feel love, desire, or strong friendship (for): *I love my mother/husband.* **2** [T +*to-v/v-ing*] to like very much; take pleasure in: *He loves singing.|I'd love a drink.|I'd love you to come.|She loves old Humphrey Bogart films.* –opposite **hate**; see LIKE[1] (USAGE)

**love af·fair** /ˈ· ·ˌ·/ *n* an experience of (sexual) love between two people, esp. between a man and a woman

**love·ly** /ˈlʌvli/ *adj* **-lier, -liest 1** beautiful; that one loves or likes: *a lovely view of the mountains* **2** *infml* very pleasant: *a lovely meal* **–loveliness** *n* [U]

**lov·er** /ˈlʌvəʳ/ *n* **1** a person (usu. a man) who loves and/or has sex with another person outside marriage: *He is her lover; she is his mistress.* **2** a person who loves something: *an art lover*

**love·sick** /ˈlʌvˌsɪk/ *adj* sad or ill because of unreturned love

**lov·ing** /ˈlʌvɪŋ/ *adj* showing or feeling love: *a loving look* **–lovingly** *adv*

**low**[1] /ləʊ/ **1** being or reaching not far above the ground, floor, base, or bottom; not high: *a low wall/bridge/roof/shelf*|(fig.) *That comes low on the list of jobs to be done.* **2** small in size, degree, amount, worth, etc.: *a low figure|The temperature was very low yesterday.|a low price|I have a low opinion of that book.|The sugar is getting low.* (=is nearly finished) **3** [F] lacking in strength or spirit; weak or unhappy: *She's still feeling a bit low after her operation.* **4** [A] having only a small amount of a particular substance, quality, etc.: *low-fat milk* **5** not loud; soft **6** (of a musical note) deep **7** near the bottom in position or rank: *a man of low birth* **8** for a slow or the slowest speed: *Use a low* GEAR *to drive up the hill.* –opposite **high** (for **1, 2, 4, 6, 7, 8**) **–lowness** *n* [U] **9** not worthy, respectable, good, etc.: *low behaviour|a low* (=dishonest) TRICK[1] (3)

**low**[2] *adv* **1** in or to a low position, point, degree, manner, etc.: *He was bent low over a book.* **2** near the ground, floor, base, etc.; not high **3** (in music) in or with deep notes –opposite **high 4** quietly; softly

**low**[3] *n* a point, price, degree, etc., that is low: *Profits have reached a new low this month.* –opposite **high**

**low·brow** /ˈləʊbraʊ/ *n,adj usu. derog* (typical of) a person who has no interest in literature, the arts, etc. –compare HIGHBROW

**low·down** /ˈləʊdaʊn/ *n* [*the* S *on*] *infml* the plain facts or truth, esp. when not generally known

**low-down** /ˈ· ·/ *adj* [A] worthless; dishonourable: *a low-down trick*

**low·er**[1] /ˈləʊəʳ/ *adj* [A] in or being the bottom part (of something): *The bottle is on the lower shelf.* –opposite **upper**

**lower**[2] /ˈləʊəʳ/ *v* **1** [I;T] to make or become smaller in amount or degree: *Lower the price/your voice.* **2** [I;T] to move or let down: *Lower the flags.* –opposite raise (for **1,2**) **3** [T] (usu. only in NEGATIVES[2], questions, etc.) to bring (oneself) down in worth: *I wouldn't lower myself to speak to him.*

**low·er**[3] /ˈlaʊəʳ/ *v* [I] →LOUR

**lower class** /ˌ·· ˈ·◂/ *n* [C; *the* U +*sing./pl.v*] *often derog* the WORKING CLASS as regarded by those outside it –see WORKING CLASS (USAGE)

**low-key** /ˌ· ˈ·◂/ also **low-keyed**– *adj* controlled in style or quality; not loud or bright

**low·land** /ˈləʊlənd/ *n,adj* [U] (an area of land) lower than the land surrounding it: *lowland areas|the Lowlands of Scotland* –compare HIGHLAND

**low·ly** /ˈləʊli/ *adv,adj* **-lier, -liest 1** in a low position, manner, or degree: *lowly paid workers* **2** not proud; simple; humble **–lowliness** *n* [U]

**low-ly·ing** /ˌ· ˈ··◂/ *adj* (of land) not much above the level of the sea; not high

**low-pitched** /ˌ· ˈ·◂/ *adj* (of a sound) deep, low –opposite **high-pitched**

**loy·al** /ˈlɔɪəl/ *adj* true to one's friends, group, country, etc.; faithful: *a loyal supporter|He has remained loyal to the team even though they lose every game.* –opposite **disloyal –loyally** *adv* **–loyalty** *n* **-ties** [C;U]

**loy·al·ist** /ˈlɔɪəlǝ̇st/ *n* a person who remains faithful to an existing ruler or government when opposed by those who want change

**loz·enge** /ˈlɒzǝ̇ndʒ‖ˈlɑ-/ *n* a small flat sweet: *a cough lozenge*

**LP** also **long-playing record, album**– *n* a record, with recorded music, speech, etc., which plays for about 20 minutes each side –compare SINGLE[2] (2)

**L-plate** /ˈel pleɪt/ *n* (in Britain) the letter L, put on a vehicle to show that the driver is a learner

**LSD** also **acid** *infml*– *n* [U] a strong drug that causes one to see things in a strange and different way

**Ltd** *written abbrev. said as:* LIMITED (2): *M.Y. Dixon and Son, Ltd, Booksellers* –compare INC, PLC

**lu·bri·cant** /ˈluːbrɪkənt/ *n* [C;U] a substance, esp. oil, which helps parts (e.g. in a machine) to move easily

**lu·bri·cate** /ˈluːbrɪkeɪt/ *v* **-cated, -cating** [T] to make able to move easily by adding a LUBRICANT: *to lubricate the engine* **–lubrication** /-ˈkeɪʃən/ *n* [U]

**lu·cid** /ˈluːsǝ̇d/ *adj* **1** easy to understand; clear: *a lucid explanation* **2** able to express one's thoughts clearly; not confused **–lucidly** *adv* **–lucidity** /luːˈsɪdǝ̇ti/ *n* [U]

**luck** /lʌk/ *n* [U] **1** that which happens, either good or bad, to a person by, or as if by, chance; fortune: *Luck was with us and we won easily.|I've had bad luck all week.* **2** good fortune: *I wish you luck.|Give me one more kiss* **for luck. 3 be down on one's luck** to have bad luck; be without money **4 be in/out of luck** to have/not have good fortune

**luck·y** /ˈlʌki/ *adj* **-ier, -iest** having, resulting from, or bringing good luck: *a lucky man/discovery/flower* –opposite **unlucky –luckily** *adv: Luckily, she was in when I called.* **–luckiness** *n* [U]

**lu·cra·tive** /ˈluːkrətɪv/ *adj fml* producing a lot of money; profitable **–lucratively** *adv*

**lu·di·crous** /ˈluːdǝ̇krəs/ *adj* causing laughter; very foolish; RIDICULOUS: *a ludicrous suggestion*

**lug** /lʌg/ *v* **-gg-** [T] *infml* to pull or carry with great effort and difficulty

**lug·gage** /ˈlʌgɪdʒ/ *n* [U] the cases, bags, boxes, etc., of a traveller: *I've put my luggage on the train.* –see picture on page 16

**lu·gu·bri·ous** /luːˈguːbrɪəs/ *adj fml* unhappy; too sorrowful or dull: *a lugubrious face/song* **–lugubriously** *adv*

**luke·warm** /ˌluːkˈwɔːm◂‖-ɔrm/ *adj* **1** (of liquid) not very hot **2** showing hardly any interest

**lull**[1] /lʌl/ *v* [T] to cause to sleep, rest, or become less active: *The movement of the train lulled me to sleep.*

**lull**[2] *n* [S *in*] a period in which activity is less: *a lull in the fighting*

**lul·la·by** /ˈlʌləbaɪ/ *n* **-bies** a pleasant song used for causing a child to sleep

**lum·ba·go** /lʌmˈbeɪgəʊ/ *n* [U] pain in the lower back

**lum·ber**[1] /ˈlʌmbəʳ/ *v* [I] to move in a heavy awkward manner

**lumber**[2] *n* [U] **1** *esp. BrE* useless or unwanted articles stored away **2** *esp. AmE* for TIMBER (1)

**lumber**[3] *v* [T *with*] *BrE infml* to give (someone) an unwanted object, job, or responsibility: *I was lumbered with (carrying) the books.*

**lum·ber·jack** /ˈlʌmbədʒæk‖-ər-/ *n* (esp. in the US and Canada) a person whose job is to cut down trees for wood

**lu·mi·na·ry** /ˈluːmǝ̇nəri‖-neri/ *n* **-ries** *fml* a person whose mind, learning, or actions are famous and respected

**lu·mi·nous** /ˈluːmǝ̇nəs/ *adj* shining in the dark: *luminous paint* **–luminously** *adv*

**lump**[1] /lʌmp/ *n* **1** a mass of something solid with no special size or shape: *a lump of lead/clay* **2** a hard swelling on the body: *She found a lump in her left breast.* **3** a small square-sided block (of sugar): *I take one lump of sugar in my tea.* –see picture on page 449 **4 a lump in the throat** a tight sensation in the throat caused by feeling pity, sorrow, etc.

**lump**[2] *adj* **lump sum** a single undivided amount of money: *You can pay for the television either in a lump sum, or in monthly* INSTALMENTS.

**lump**[3] *v* **lump it** *infml* to accept bad conditions without complaint: *I can't afford a better car, so you'll have to* **like it or lump it.**

**lump** sthg.↔ **together** *v adv* [T] to put (two or more things) together: *The cost of these two trips can be lumped together.*

**lump·y** /ˈlʌmpi/ *adj* **-ier, -iest** having lumps: *lumpy soup*

**lu·na·cy** /ˈluːnəsi/ *n* [U] **1** madness **2** foolish or wild behaviour

**lu·nar** /ˈluːnəʳ/ *adj* of, for, or to the moon

**lunar month** /ˌ·· ˈ·/ *n* a period of 28 days (the time the moon takes to circle the earth)

**lu·na·tic** /ˈluːnətɪk/ *n,adj* (a person who is) mad, foolish, or wild

**lunch**[1] /lʌntʃ/ also **luncheon** /ˈlʌntʃən/ *fml*– *n* [C;U] a meal eaten in the middle of the day: *I'm hungry–let's have lunch.*

**lunch**[2] *v* [I] to eat LUNCH: *We're lunching with John today.*

**lunch·time** /ˈlʌntʃtaɪm/ *n* [U] the time at or during which LUNCH is eaten

**lung** /lʌŋ/ *n* either of the two breathing organs in the chest of man or certain animals

**lunge** /lʌndʒ/ *v,n* **lunged, lunging** [I *at,out*] (to make) a sudden forceful forward movement, esp. with the arm: *He lunged at me with a knife.*

**lurch¹** /lɜːtʃ‖lɜrtʃ/ *n* **leave someone in the lurch** *infml* to leave someone alone and without help when he/she is in difficulty

**lurch²** *n* a sudden, uncontrolled movement: *The boat gave a lurch sideways towards the rocks.*

**lurch³** *v* [I] to move with irregular sudden steps: *The drunken man lurched across the road.*

**lure¹** /lʊəʳ, ljʊəʳ‖lʊər/ *n* [C;S *of*] **1** something that attracts: *the lure of money* **2** something used to attract animals so that they can be caught

**lure²** *v* **lured, luring** [T] to attract; TEMPT: *She's been lured to the Middle East by the promise of high wages.*

**lu·rid** /ˈlʊərɨd, ˈljʊərɨd‖ˈlʊərɨd/ *adj* **1** unnaturally bright; strongly coloured: *a lurid picture of a sunset* **2** shocking; unpleasant: *The papers gave the lurid details of the murder.* –**luridly** *adv*

**lurk** /lɜːk‖lɜrk/ *v* [I] to wait in hiding, esp. for an evil purpose: *The murderer lurked behind the trees.*

**lus·cious** /ˈlʌʃəs/ *adj* having a very pleasant, sweet taste, smell, or appearance: *luscious fruit/wine* –**lusciously** *adv* –**lusciousness** *n* [U]

**lush** /lʌʃ/ *adj* (of plants, esp. grass) growing very well; thick and healthy

**lust** /lʌst/ *n* [C;U *for*] strong (esp. sexual) desire; eagerness to possess: *lust for power* –**lust** *v* [I *after/for*]: *lusting after power/his neighbour's daughter* –see DESIRE² (USAGE)

**lust·ful** /ˈlʌstfəl/ *adj* full of strong (sexual) desire –**lustfully** *adv*

**lus·tre** *BrE*‖**luster** *AmE* /ˈlʌstəʳ/ *n* [S;U] brightness of a polished, shiny surface –**lustrous** /ˈlʌstrəs/ *adj*: *lustrous black hair* –**lustrously** *adv*

**lust·y** /ˈlʌsti/ *adj* **-ier, -iest 1** full of strength, health, etc. **2** full of sexual desire –**lustiness** *n* [U]

**lute** /luːt/ *n* a type of old musical instrument with strings, a long neck, and a body shaped like a PEAR

**lux·u·ri·ant** /lʌgˈzjʊərɪənt, ləgˈʒʊərɪənt‖ləgˈʒʊərɪənt/ *adj* growing well, esp. in health and number: *Luxuriant forests covered the hills.* –compare LUXURIOUS –**luxuriantly** *adv* –**luxuriance** *n* [U]

**lux·u·ri·ate in** sthg. /lʌgˈzjʊərieɪt, ləgˈʒʊəri-‖ləgˈʒʊəri-/ *v prep* **-ated, -ating** [T] to enjoy oneself lazily in (doing something)

**lux·u·ri·ous** /lʌgˈzjʊərɪəs, ləgˈʒʊərɪəs‖ləgˈʒʊərɪəs/ *adj* fine and expensive; very comfortable: *a luxurious hotel* –compare LUXURIANT –**luxuriously** *adv*

**lux·u·ry** /ˈlʌkʃəri/ *n* **-ries 1** [U] great comfort, as provided by wealth: *a life of luxury|a luxury flat* **2** [C] a pleasant and often expensive thing that is not necessary: *Cream cakes are a luxury.|We can't afford to spend money on luxuries.*

**ly·chee** /ˈlaɪtʃiː/ *n* an Asian fruit with a hard shell and sweet white flesh

**ly·ing** /ˈlaɪ-ɪŋ/ *v present participle of* LIE¹ and LIE²

**lynch** /lɪntʃ/ *v* [T] (esp. of a crowd of people) to attack and kill (someone thought to be guilty of a crime), without a lawful trial

**lynx** /lɪŋks/ *n* **lynxes** *or* **lynx** a wild animal of the cat family with a short tail

**lyre** /laɪəʳ/ an ancient Greek musical instrument with strings stretched on a U-shaped frame

**lyr·ic** /ˈlɪrɪk/ *n,adj* (a short poem) like a song or expressing strong personal feelings: *lyric poetry*

**lyr·i·cal** /ˈlɪrɪkəl/ *adj* full of pleasure, strong feelings, etc. –**lyrically** *adv*

**lyr·i·cist** /ˈlɪrɨsɨst/ *n* a writer of LYRICS; songwriter

**lyr·ics** /ˈlɪrɪks/ *n* [P] the words of a song

# M, m

**M, m** /em/ **M's, m's** *or* **Ms, ms 1** the 13th letter of the English alphabet **2** the ROMAN NUMERAL (number) for 1,000

**-'m** /m/ *short for*: am: *I'm ready*

**m** *written abbrev. said as:* METRE

**MA** *abbrev. for:* Master of Arts; (a title for someone who has) a higher university degree: *Mary Jones, MA|an MA*

**ma'am** /mæm, mɑːm, məm‖mæm/ *n* **1** (a short form of MADAM) **2** *AmE* (a polite way of addressing a woman): *Yes, ma'am.*

**mac** /mæk/ *n BrE infml* for MACKINTOSH

**ma·ca·bre** /məˈkɑːbrə, -bəʳ/ *adj* causing fear, esp. because connected with death –compare GRUESOME

**mac·a·ro·ni** /ˌmækəˈrəʊni/ *n* [U] a food made from flour paste (PASTA) in the form of short thin pipes which are boiled in water –compare SPAGHETTI

**ma·caw** /məˈkɔː/ *n* a large brightly-coloured bird (PARROT) with a long tail

**mace** /meɪs/ *n* a decorative rod which is carried by an official in certain ceremonies as a sign of power

**Mach** /mæk‖mɑk/ *n* [S] the speed of an aircraft in relation to the speed of sound: *If a plane is flying at Mach 2, it is flying at twice the speed of sound.*

**ma·chet·e** /məˈtʃeɪti‖məˈʃeti, məˈtʃeti/ also **machet** /məˈtʃet, ˈmætʃɨt/ *BrE*– *n* a knife with a broad heavy blade, used for cutting and as a weapon

**ma·chine¹** /məˈʃiːn/ *n* a man-made instrument or apparatus which uses power (such as electricity) to perform work: *a sewing machine*

USAGE **Machines, appliances, tools,** and **gadgets** are all instruments for doing work. A **machine** performs work by using power, which is provided by an **engine** or **motor**: *A lot of work on farms is now done by* **machines.** Electrical **machines** used in the home (such as washing machines and FRIDGES) are often called **appliances.** A **tool** is a simpler form of **machine**, usually worked by hand, and a **gadget** is a small, useful **tool** for doing a particular job: *a shop selling spades and other garden* **tools**|*a clever little* **gadget** *for opening wine bottles.*

**machine²** *v* **-chined, -chining** [T] to make or produce by machine –**machinist** *n*

**ma·chine·gun** /mə'ʃiːngʌn/ *n* a quick-firing gun which fires continuously when the TRIGGER is pressed

**ma·chin·e·ry** /mə'ʃiːnəri/ *n* [U] **1** machines in general: *farm machinery* **2** the working parts of an apparatus **3** the operation of a system or organization: *The machinery of the law works slowly.*

**mack·e·rel** /'mækərəl/ *n* **mackerels** *or* **mackerel** [C;U] a strong-tasting sea fish which can be eaten

**mack·in·tosh** /'mækɪ̵ntɒʃ‖-tɑʃ/ also **mack, mac** /mæk/ *infml– n esp. BrE* a coat made to keep out the rain

**mac·ro·bi·ot·ic** /ˌmækrəbaɪ'ɒtɪk‖-'ɑtɪk/ *adj* concerning a type of food (esp. vegetable products grown without chemicals, etc.) which is thought to produce good health

**mad** /mæd/ *adj* **1** ill in the mind: *She went mad after the death of her son.* **2** very foolish and careless of danger: *You're mad to drive so fast!* **3** [F *about, for*] filled with strong feeling, interest, etc.: *He's mad about football.* **4** [F *at, with*] *infml* angry: *I got mad with him for being late.*|*She was* **hopping mad.** (=very angry) **5 drive someone mad** to annoy someone very much **6 like mad** *infml* very hard, fast, loud, etc.: *to work like mad*

**mad·am** /'mædəm/ *n* **1** (a polite way of addressing a woman, e.g. a customer in a shop): *Can I help you, madam?* –compare SIR **2** [*usu. sing.*] a female who likes to give orders: *She's a real little madam!*

**Madam** *n* (a formal word of address used e.g. in a business letter to a woman): *Dear Madam. . .* –compare SIR

**mad·den** /'mædn/ *v* [T] to make angry; annoy

**mad·den·ing** /'mædənɪŋ/ *adj infml* very annoying –**maddeningly** *adv*

**made**[1] /meɪd/ *v past tense and participle of* MAKE[1]

**made**[2] *adj* [F] **1** [*of*] formed: *Clouds are made (up) of water.* **2** [*for*] completely suited: *a night made for love* **3** sure of success: *When you find gold you're made.*

**mad·ly** /'mædli/ *adv* **1** as if mad: *He rushed madly out of the room.* **2** *infml* very (much): *madly in love*

**mad·man** /'mædmən/ **madwoman** /-ˌwʊmən/ *fem.– n* **-men** /mən/ a person who is mad

**mad·ness** /'mædnɪ̵s/ *n* [U] **1** the state of being mad **2** behaviour that appears mad: *It would be madness to increase taxes just before the election.*

**Ma·don·na** /mə'dɒnə‖mə'dɑ-/ *n* [C; *the* S] (a picture or figure of) Mary, the mother of Christ in the Christian religion

**mad·ri·gal** /'mædrɪgəl/ *n* a song for singers without instruments

**mael·strom** /'meɪlstrəm/ *n esp. lit* **1** a violent WHIRLPOOL **2** [*usu. sing.*] the violent, destructive force of events

**maes·tro** /'maɪstrəʊ/ *n* **-tros** a great or famous musician

**maf·i·a** /'mæfɪə‖'mɑ-, 'mæ-/ *n* [*the* S +*sing./pl. v*] an organization of (originally Sicilian) criminals who control many activities by violent means

**mag·a·zine** /ˌmægə'ziːn‖'mægəziːn/ also **mag** *infml– n* **1** a sort of book with a paper cover, which contains writing, photographs, and advertisements, usu. on a special subject or for a certain group of people, and which is printed every week or month: *a fashion magazine* **2** a storehouse or room for arms, bullets, etc. **3** the part of a gun in which bullets (CARTRIDGES) are placed before firing

**ma·gen·ta** /mə'dʒentə/ *n,adj* [U] (of) a dark purplish red colour

**mag·got** /'mægət/ *n* a wormlike creature, the young of flies or other insects, often found on meat

**ma·gic** /'mædʒɪk/ *n* [U] **1** the system of trying to control events by calling on spirits, secret forces, etc. **2** the art of a theatrical performer (CONJURER) who produces unexpected objects and results by tricks **3** a charming quality or influence –**magic** *adj* [A]: *a magic* WAND

**ma·gic·al** /'mædʒɪkəl/ *adj* of strange power, mystery, or charm:*a magical evening* –**magically** *adv*

**ma·gi·cian** /mə'dʒɪʃən/ *n* a person who practises magic; CONJURER

**ma·gis·te·ri·al** /ˌmædʒɪ̵'stɪərɪəl/ *adj* **1** *fml* having or showing the power of a master or ruler **2** [A] of or done by a MAGISTRATE

**ma·gis·trate** /'mædʒɪ̵streɪt, -strɪ̵t/ *n* an official who judges cases in the lowest law courts; JP

**mag·nan·i·mous** /mæg'nænɪ̵məs/ *adj* unusually generous towards others –**magnanimity** /ˌmægnə'nɪmɪ̵ti/ *n* [U] –**magnanimously** *adv*

**mag·nate** /'mægneɪt, -nɪ̵t/ *n* a person of wealth and power in business or industry

**mag·ne·sia** /mæg'niːʃə, -ʒə/ *n* [U] a light white powder used as a stomach medicine

**mag·ne·si·um** /mæg'niːzɪəm/ *n* [U] a silver-white metal that burns with a bright white light and is used in making FIREWORKS

**mag·net** /'mægnɪ̵t/ *n* any object, esp. a piece of iron, which can draw other (metal) objects towards it, either naturally or because of an electric current being passed through it –**magnetic** /mæg'netɪk/ *adj*: *The iron has lost its magnetic force.*|(fig.) *a magnetic person* –**magnetically** *adv*

**magnetic field** /·ˌ·· '·/ *n* the space in which the force of a MAGNET is effective

**magnetic pole** /·ˌ·· '·/ *n* either of two points near the NORTH POLE and the SOUTH POLE of the earth towards which the compass needle points

**magnetic tape** /·ˌ·· '·/ *n* [C;U] a TAPE[1] (2) on which sound or other information can be recorded

**mag·net·is·m** /'mægnɪ̵tɪzəm/ *n* [U] **1** the science of MAGNETS **2** strong personal charm

**mag·net·ize** ‖also **-ise** *BrE* /'mægnɪ̵taɪz/ *v* [T] to make into a MAGNET: *Iron can be magnetized by passing an electric current round it.*

**mag·nif·i·cent** /mæg'nɪfɪ̵sənt/ *adj* great, grand, etc.: *The royal wedding was a magnificent occasion.* –**magnificence** *n* [U] –**magnificently** *adv*

**mag·ni·fy** /'mægnɪ̵faɪ/ *v* **-fied, -fying** [T] to make (something) appear larger than it is –**magnification** /-fɪ̵'keɪʃən/ *n* [C;U]: *This* MICROSCOPE *has a magnification of eight.* (= It *makes things look eight times larger)*

**mag·ni·fy·ing glass** /'···· ·/ *n* a curved piece of glass (LENS) which makes objects seen through it look bigger

**mag·ni·tude** /'mægnɪ̵tjuːd‖-tuːd/ *n* [U] *fml* greatness of size or importance: *I had not realized the*

*magnitude of the problem.*
**mag·no·li·a** /mæg'nəʊliə/ *n* a tree with large sweet-smelling flowers
**mag·pie** /'mægpaɪ/ *n* a noisy black and white bird which likes to pick up and steal bright objects
**ma·ha·ra·ja, -jah** /ˌmɑːhə'rɑːdʒə/ *n (often cap.)* (the title of) an Indian prince
**ma·hog·a·ny** /mə'hɒgəni‖mə'hɑ-/ *n* [U] (the colour of) a dark reddish wood, used for making good furniture
**maid** /meɪd/ *n* a female servant: *a housemaid*
**maid·en¹** /'meɪdn/ also **maid**– *n lit* a girl who is not married
**maiden²** *adj* [A] **1** first; not done before: *The ship made its maiden voyage last week.* **2** (of a woman, esp. an older woman) unmarried: *a maiden aunt*
**maid·en·ly** /'meɪdnli/ *adj esp. lit* like a MAIDEN¹; sweet, modest, etc.
**maiden name** /'·· ·/ *n* the family name a woman has or had before marriage
**mail¹** /meɪl/ *n* [U] **1** the postal system: *Airmail is quicker than sea mail.*|*(AmE) It came in the mail.* **2** letters and anything else sent by post
**mail²** *v* [T *to*] *esp. AmE* for POST⁴
**mail·bag** /'meɪlbæg/ *n* a bag for carrying letters and parcels
**mail·box** /'meɪlbɒks‖-bɑks/ *n AmE* a place for collecting mail; POSTBOX
**maim** /meɪm/ *v* [T] to harm (someone) so that part of the body can no longer be used: *After the car accident she was maimed for life, and could not walk.*
**main¹** /meɪn/ *adj* [A *no comp.*] chief; most important: *a busy main road*|*the main meal of the day* –**mainly** *adv: His money comes mainly from business.*
**main²** *n* **1** [*usu. pl.*] a chief pipe or wire supplying water, gas, or electricity **2 in the main** usually; mostly
**main·land** /'meɪnlənd/ *n* [*the* S] a land mass, considered without its islands
**mains** /meɪnz/ *n* [A] supplied from a MAIN²: *mains electricity*
**main·spring** /'meɪnˌsprɪŋ/ *n* [*usu. sing.*] the chief reason behind an action: *His belief in freedom was the mainspring of his fight against slavery.*
**main·stay** /'meɪnsteɪ/ *n* [*usu. sing.; of*] someone or something which provides the chief support: *Farming is still the mainstay of this country.*
**main·stream** /'meɪnstriːm/ *n* [*the* S] the main or usual way of thinking or acting in a subject
**main·tain** /meɪn'teɪn, mən-/ *v* [T] **1** to continue to have, do, etc., as before: *He maintained his interest in football all his life.* **2** to support with money: *to maintain a family* **3** to keep in good condition; take care of: *the high cost of maintaining a house* **4** [+(*that*)/*to be*] to (continue to) argue for (an opinion): *Some people still maintain that the earth is flat.*
**main·te·nance** /'meɪntənəns/ *n* [U] **1** the act of MAINTAINing (3): *car maintenance* **2** money given to wives and/or children by a husband who does not live with them
**mai·son·ette, maisonnette** /ˌmeɪsə'net/ *n* a flat, usually on two floors, that is part of a larger house
**maize** /meɪz/ *n* [U] *esp. BrE for* CORN¹ (2)
**ma·jes·ty** /'mædʒ$\frac{1}{2}$sti/ *n* [U] greatness; a show of power, as of a king or queen –**majestic** /mə'dʒestɪk/ *adj* –**majestically** *adv*
**Majesty** *n* **-ties** (a title for speaking to or of a king or queen): *Her Majesty the Queen/Their Majesties the King and Queen opened the new school yesterday.*
**ma·jor¹** /'meɪdʒəʳ/ *adj* [A] greater when compared with others, in size, number, or importance: *The car needs major repairs.* –opposite **minor**
USAGE Although it means "of greater importance than others", **major** is not used in comparisons with *than*: *a* **major** *new book about American politics* (not **This book is* **major** *than that one*). **Minor** is used in the same way. **Superior, inferior, senior,** and **junior** can be used in comparisons, but they are followed by *to*, not *than*: *This restaurant is* **superior** *to* (not **than*) *the one we went to last week.*|*She is* **senior** *to everyone else in the company.*
**major²** *n* **1** [A;C] (*often cap.*) an officer of middle rank in an army or airforce **2** [C] *law* a person who has, in law, reached the grown-up state (in Britain, the age of 18) –compare MINOR²
**ma·jor·i·ty¹** /mə'dʒɒr$\frac{1}{2}$ti‖mə'dʒɑ-/ *n* **-ties** **1** [U +*sing./pl. v*] the greater number or amount (esp. of people): *The majority of doctors believe smoking is harmful to health.*|*At the meeting, young people were* **in the majority**. –compare MINORITY **2** [C *usu. sing.*] the difference in number between a large and smaller group: *She won by a large majority/a majority of 900 votes.* **3** [C *usu. sing.*] *law* the age when one becomes fully responsible in law for one's actions (a MAJOR² (2))
**majority²** *adj* [A] reached by agreement of most members of a group: *a majority decision*
**make¹** /meɪk/ *v* **made** /meɪd/, **making** **1** [T] to produce by work or action: *Will you make me a cup of coffee?*|*The children are making a lot of noise.*|*I'm going to make a skirt out of this material.*|*Parliament makes laws.*|*He's made his decision.* (=has decided)|*I'll make you an offer of* (=offer you) *£5 for it.*|(fig.) *She made an important discovery.* (=discovered something important) **2** [T] to put into the stated condition, position, etc.; cause to be: *Too much food made him ill.*|*I'm going to make this material into a skirt.*|*I want to make you my wife.* (=marry you) **3** [T] to force or cause (someone to do something/something to happen): *How do you make this machine work?*|*They made her wait.*|*She was made to wait for over an hour.*|*If you won't do it willingly, I'll make you (do it).* **4** [T] to tidy (a bed that has just been slept in) by straightening the sheets, pulling over the cover, etc. **5** [T] to earn (money): *He makes a lot (of money) in his job.* **6** [T] to calculate (and get as a result): *What do you make the answer to the sum?*|*What time do you make it?* **7** to add up to: *Two and two make four.* **8** to be counted as (first, second, etc.): *This makes our third party this month.* **9** [I;T] to have the qualities of (esp. something good): *This coat will make a good present for my mother.*|*This story makes good reading.* **10** [T] to arrive at or on: *We just made the train.* (=almost missed it)|*Can you make* (=attend) *the party?* **11** [T] *infml* to give the particular qualities of; complete: *The bright paint really makes the room.* **12** **make believe** to pretend: *The children are making believe that they're princes and princesses.* –see

MAKE-BELIEVE **13 make do (with something)** also **make (something) do** to use (something) even though it may not be very good or enough: *We haven't got any meat, so we'll have to make do with bread.* **14 make it** *infml* **a** to arrive in time **b** to succeed **15 make one's way** to go: *I made my way home/up the stairs.* **16 make or break** which will cause success or complete failure: *a make or break decision*

USAGE 1 Compare **do** and **make**: **Do** and **make** are used in many fixed expressions like **do** *a favour,* **make** *war*, and there is no rule about these. Usually, however, you **do** an action, and **make** something that was not there before: *to* **make** *a noise/a fire|to* **do** *the shopping/one's exercises|"What are you* **doing**?" "*Cooking.*"|"*What are you* **making**?" "*A cake.*" 2 Compare **made from** and **made of**: We use **from** when the original substance has been completely changed, and **of** when something simpler has been done and we are naming the materials used: *Paper is* **made from wood.**|*some jam* **made from** *the fruit in our garden|a bag* **made of** *leather.* 3 When **make** means to force or cause (*meaning 3*), do not use *to* before a following verb, unless the sentence is passive: *It* **made** *me cry.|He was* **made** *to walk home.*

**make for** sthg. *v prep* [T *no pass.*] **1** to move (quickly) in the direction of: *It started raining, so she made for shelter.* **2** to result in: *The large print makes for easy reading.*

**make** sthg. **of** sthg. *v prep* [T *no pass.*] to understand by: *I don't know what to make of his behaviour.* (=I can't understand it)

**make off** *v adv* [I] to escape in a hurry

**make out** *v adv* **1** [T] (**make** sbdy./sthg.↔ **out**) to see or understand with difficulty: *Can you make out what he's trying to say?* **2** [T] (**make** sthg.↔ **out**) to write in complete form: *Make the cheque out to me.* **3** [I] *infml* to succeed, in business, personal relationships, or life generally: *How did he make out after he finished school?* **4** [T +(*that*)] (**make out** sthg.) *infml* to claim or pretend, usu. falsely: *He makes out he's younger than me.* **5** [T] (**make** sbdy./sthg. **out** to be sthg.) to claim or pretend that someone, esp. oneself, is something: *He makes himself out to be very important.*

**make** sthg.↔ **over** *v adv* [T *to*] to pass over, esp. in law: *His wealth was made over to his children.*

**make up** *v adv* **1** [T] (**make** sthg.↔ **up**) to invent (a story, excuse, etc.), esp. in order to deceive **2** [I;T (=**make** sbdy. **up**)] to put special paint and powder on the face of (someone or oneself) so as to change or improve the appearance: *She makes herself up/makes up her face in the morning.* –see also MAKE-UP **3** [T] (**make** sthg.↔ **up**) to put together into a form ready for use: *Bring the sheets and make up the bed.|I'll make up a bed on the floor.* **4** [T] (**make** sthg.↔ **up**) to make (an amount or number) complete: *You must make up the money (to the right amount).* **5** [T] (**make** sthg.↔ **up**) to repay or give (an amount) in return: *You must make up what you owe before the end of the month.* **6** [I;T (=**make** sthg.↔ **up**)] to become friends again after (a quarrel): *Let's kiss and make up.*

**make up for** sthg. *v adv prep* [T +*v-ing*] to repay with something good; COMPENSATE for: *This beautiful autumn makes up for/is making up for the wet summer.|Work fast, to* **make up for lost time.**

**make up to** sbdy. *v adv prep* [T] **1** to try to gain the favour of **2 make it up to someone** to repay someone with good things in return for something: *You've been so kind. I'll make it all up to you one day.*

**make**[2] *n* **1** a type of product, esp. as produced by a particular maker: "*What make is your car?*" "*It's a Ford.*" **2 on the make** *infml & derog* searching for personal profit or gain

**make-be·lieve** /ˌ· ·'· ◂/ *n* [U] a state of pretending or the things which are pretended: *She lives in a world of make-believe.* –see also MAKE[1] (12)

**mak·er** /'meɪkəʳ/ *n* a person or firm that makes something: *My watch has gone wrong; I'm sending it back to the maker(s).|a dressmaker*

**make·shift** /'meɪkˌʃɪft/ *adj* [A] used for a time because there is nothing better: *They made a makeshift table from boxes.*

**make-up** /'· ·/ *n* **1** [C;U] powder, paint, etc., worn on the face: *Too much make-up looks unnatural.* **2** [C] the combination of qualities (in a person's character) –see also MAKE **up**

**mak·ing** /'meɪkɪŋ/ *n* **1** [U] the act or business of making something, esp. with the hands: *dressmaking|shoemaking* **2** [*the* S *of*] the cause of improvement: *Hard work will be the making of him.* –compare UNDOING

**mak·ings** /'meɪkɪŋz/ *n* [*the* P *of*] the possibility of developing (into): *He has the makings of a good doctor.*

**mal·ad·just·ed** /ˌmælə'dʒʌstɨd/ *adj* (of a person) unable to be happy or behave well in his surroundings –opposite **well-adjusted**

**mal·a·dy** /'mælədi/ *n* **-dies** *fml & lit* a disease; sick state

**ma·laise** /mə'leɪz/ *n* [C;U] a feeling of illness; lack of wellbeing: *a social malaise in the country*

**ma·lar·i·a** /mə'leərɪə/ *n* [U] a disease caused by the bite of a certain type of mosquito, in hot countries –**malarial** *adj* [A]

**mal·con·tent** /'mælkəntent‖ˌmælkən'tent/ *n* a person dissatisfied with a (political) state of affairs

**male** /meɪl/ *adj,n* **1** (of) the sex that does not give birth to young: *a male monkey* **2** (suitable to or typical of) this sex, rather than the female sex: *a male voice* –see FEMALE[2] (USAGE)

**ma·lev·o·lent** /mə'levələnt/ *adj lit* having or expressing a wish to do evil to others –opposite **benevolent** –**malevolence** *n* [U] –**malevolently** *adv*

**mal·for·ma·tion** /ˌmælfɔː'meɪʃən‖-ɔr-/ *n* [C;U] *tech* (the condition of having) a wrongly-shaped part, e.g. of the body –**malformed** /ˌmæl'fɔːmd◂‖-ɔr-/ *adj*

**mal·ice** /'mælɨs/ *n* [U] **1** the wish to hurt other people **2 bear malice** to feel continuing dislike for someone –**malicious** /mə'lɪʃəs/ *adj* –**maliciously** *adv*

**ma·lign** /mə'laɪn/ *v* [T] to express evil of, esp. wrongly: *She was maligned by the newspapers.*

**ma·lig·nant** /mə'lɪgnənt/ *adj* **1** full of hate and a strong wish to hurt: *a malignant nature* **2** *tech* (of a disease or condition) serious enough to cause death if not prevented: *a malignant growth* (TUMOUR) *on* *the body* –opposite **benign** –**malignantly** *adv* –**malignancy** *n* [U]

**ma·lin·ger** /mə'lɪŋgəʳ/ *v* [I] to avoid work by pretending to be ill –**malingerer** *n*

**mal·lard** /'mæləd‖-ərd/ *n* **mallards** *or* **mallard** a wild duck

**mal·le·a·ble** /'mælɪəbəl/ *adj* **1** (of metals) that can be made into a new shape **2** (of people) easily changed or influenced –**malleability** /-ə'bɪlɪ̈ti / *n* [U]

**mal·let** /'mælɪ̈t/ *n* a wooden hammer

**mal·nu·tri·tion** /,mælnjʊ'trɪʃən‖-nʊ-/ *n* [U] (bad health resulting from) lack of food, or the wrong sort of food –see also NUTRITION

**mal·prac·tice** /,mæl'præktɪ̈s/ *n* [C;U] (an example of) illegal activity for personal advantage, or bad treatment given by a person in a position of responsibility, e.g. a doctor or lawyer

**malt** /mɔːlt/ *n* [U] grain, usu. BARLEY, which has been specially treated and is used for making drinks, esp. beer

**mal·treat** /mæl'triːt/ *v* [T] *fml* to treat cruelly; –**maltreatment** *n* [U]

**mam·mal** /'mæməl/ *n* an animal of the type which is fed when young on its mother's milk

**mam·moth** /'mæməθ/ *n* **1** [C] a large hairy kind of elephant which lived on earth in early times **2** [A] very large: *a mammoth job*

**man**[1] /mæn/ *n* **men** /men/ **1** [C] a fully-grown human male: *men, women, and children*|*The army will make a man of you.* (=a strong courageous person) –see also WOMAN **2** [C] a human being, male or female: *All men must die.* **3** [S] human beings in general; the human race: *Man cannot live by bread alone.* **4** [C] a fully-grown male in employment or of low rank in the armed forces: *The men were not happy with the employers' offer.*|*officers and men* **5** [C] any of the objects moved by each player in a board game: CHESS *men* **6 as one man** with the agreement of everyone **7 man about town** a (rich) man who does not work but spends time at social gatherings, in clubs, theatres, etc. **8 man and wife** husband and wife **9 the man in the street** (the idea of) the average person, who represents general opinion **10 man of the world** a man with a lot of experience of life **11 to a man** every person: *They agreed to a man.* **12 -man** /mən/ **-woman** /wʊmən/ *fem.*– **a** a person who lives in a certain place: *a Frenchman* **b** a person who has a certain kind of job, skill, position, etc.: *a businessman* –see GENTLEMAN (USAGE)

USAGE Note the word order in this fixed phrase.: **men and women.**

**man**[2] *v* **-nn-** [T] to provide with men for operation: *Man the guns.*

**man**[3] *interj AmE infml* (used for expressing strong feelings, e.g. excitement, surprise, etc.)

**man·a·cle** /'mænəkəl/ *n,v* **-cled, -cling** [C;T] (to put on) a chain for fastening the hands or feet of a prisoner

**man·age** /'mænɪdʒ/ *v* **-aged, -aging 1** [T] to control or guide (esp. a business): *to manage a hotel/a house*|*She manages the money very well.* **2** [I;T +*to-v*] to succeed in dealing with (a problem): *Can you manage (to carry) the box?*|*We don't have much money, but we manage.*|*Do you think we'll manage to finish the work by Friday?* –see COULD (USAGE)

**man·age·a·ble** /'mænɪdʒəbəl/ *adj* possible to control or deal with –opposite **unmanageable**

**man·age·ment** /'mænɪdʒmənt/ *n* **1** [U] the art or practice of managing (MANAGE) something, e.g. a business or money **2** [C +*sing./pl. v*] the people in charge of a firm, industry, etc.: *The management is/are having talks with the workers.*

**man·ag·er** /'mænɪdʒəʳ/ **manageress,** /mænɪdʒə'res‖'mænɪdʒərɪ̈s/ *fem.*– *n* a person who directs the affairs of a business, a sports team, a singer, etc.: *the manager of a football team/a* POP[4] *group*|*a bank manager*|*That was a terrible meal; I'm going to complain to the manager.*

**man·a·ge·ri·al** /,mænɪ̈'dʒɪəriəl/ *adj* [A] of or concerning a MANAGER or MANAGEMENT: *a managerial position*

**man·date** /'mændeɪt/ *n* **1** the right and power given to a body of people to act according to the wishes of those who voted for it: *The government has a mandate from the people to increase taxes.* **2** a formal command given by a higher to a lower official

**man·da·to·ry** /'mændətəri‖-tori/ *adj fml* containing a command which must be obeyed

**man·di·ble** /'mændəbəl/ *n tech* a jaw which moves, usu. the lower jaw of an animal or fish

**man·do·lin** /,mændə'lɪn/ *n* a musical instrument with eight metal strings, which is rather like a LUTE

**mane** /meɪn/ *n* the long hair on the back of a horse's neck, or around the face and neck of a lion

**ma·neu·ver** /mə'nuːvəʳ/ *n,v AmE* for MANOEUVRE

**man·ga·nese** /'mæŋgəniːz/ *n* [U] a greyish white metal used in making glass, steel, etc.

**mange** /meɪndʒ/ *n* [U] a skin disease, esp. of dogs and cats –**mangy** /'meɪndʒi, 'mændʒi/ *adj* **-gier, -giest**

**man·ger** /'meɪndʒəʳ/ *n* **1** a long open container used for feeding horses and cattle **2 dog in the manger** a person who does not wish others to enjoy what he/she cannot use for his/her own enjoyment

**man·gle**[1] /'mæŋgəl/ *v* **-gled, -gling** [T] to tear or cut to pieces; crush: *After the accident the bodies were too badly mangled to be recognized.*

**mangle**[2] *n* a machine with rollers turned by a handle, between which water is pressed from clothes, sheets, etc., being passed through

**man·go** /'mæŋgəʊ/ *n* **-goes** *or* **-gos** (a tropical tree which bears) a fruit with sweet yellow-coloured flesh

**man·grove** /'mæŋgrəʊv/ *n* a tree of tropical countries which grows on muddy land (a SWAMP) and near water

**man·han·dle** /'mænhændl/ *v* **-dled, -dling** [T] to move, esp. roughly, using force: *She complained that she had been manhandled by the police.*

**man·hole** /'mænhəʊl/ *n* a covered opening in a road, through which a person can go down to repair underground pipes and wires

**man·hood** /'mænhʊd/ *n* [U] the condition or qualities of being a man: *Members of certain tribes perform special ceremonies when they reach manhood.* –see also WOMANHOOD

**ma·ni·a** /'meɪnɪə/ *n* **1** [U] *tech* a dangerous disorder of the mind **2** [C;U *for*] (a) very strong desire or interest: *a mania for (driving) fast cars*|*car mania*

**ma·ni·ac** /'meɪnɪæk/ *n* **1** a person who suffers from

MANIA (1): *a dangerous sex maniac* **2** a wild thoughtless person: *He drives like a maniac.*

**man·ic** /'mænɪk/ *adj* of or suffering from MANIA

**man·i·cure** /'mænɪ̈kjʊəʳ/ *n* [C;U] (a) treatment for the hands and fingernails,including cleaning, cutting, etc. **–manicure** *v* **-cured, -curing** [T] **–manicurist** *n*

**man·i·fest¹** /'mænɪ̈fest/ *adj fml* plain and clear to see: *Fear was manifest on his face.* **–manifestly** *adv*

**manifest²** *v* [T] *fml* to show plainly: *The disease manifests itself in yellowness of the skin and eyes.*

**man·i·fes·ta·tion** /,mænɪ̈fe'steɪʃən‖-fə-/ *n* [C;U] *fml* (an) act of showing or making clear

**man·i·fes·to** /,mænɪ̈'festəʊ/ *n* **-tos** *or* **-toes** a (written) statement making public the intentions, opinions, etc., of a political party or group

**man·i·fold¹** /'mænɪ̈fəʊld/ *adj fml* many in number and/or kind: *The problems facing the government are manifold.*

**manifold²** *n tech* a pipe with holes, to allow gases to enter or escape from an engine, e.g. in a car

**ma·nil·a, -nilla** /mə'nɪlə/ *n* [A] strong brown paper

**ma·nip·u·late** /mə'nɪpjʊleɪt‖-pjə-/ *v* **-lated, -lating** [T] **1** to handle or control skilfully: *to manipulate the controls of the machine* **2** to control and influence (someone) for one's own purpose **–manipulative** /-lətɪv‖-leɪ-/ *adj* **–manipulation** /-'leɪʃən/ *n* [C;U]

**man·kind** /,mæn'kaɪnd/ *n* [U +*sing./pl. v*] the human race, both men and women: *the worst war in the history of mankind* –see also WOMANKIND

**man·ly** /'mænli/ *adj* **-lier, -liest** having the qualities suitable to a man; strong, brave, etc.: *a manly act of courage* –compare WOMANLY **–manliness** *n* [U]

**man-made** /,· '· ◄/ *adj* **1** produced by people; not found in nature **2** (of materials) made from chemical, not natural, substances; SYNTHETIC: *Nylon is a man-made* FIBRE. –opposite **natural**

**manned** /mænd/ *adj* (of machines) having people on board: *a manned spacecraft* –opposite **unmanned**

**man·ner** /'mænəʳ/ *n* **1** [C *of; usu. sing.*] the way or style of doing something: *The sheets are usually folded in this manner.* **2** [S] a personal way of acting or behaving: *I don't like his manner; it's very rude.*|*a pleasant manner* **3 all manner of** every sort of **4 not by any manner of means** not at all

**man·ner·is·m** /'mænərɪzəm/ *n* a typical habit of behaviour, speech, etc.

**man·ners** /'mænəz‖-ərz/ *n* [P] **1** (polite) social practices or habits: *Children should be taught (good) manners.* **2 -mannered** having a certain type of manners: *good/well-mannered*|*bad/ill-mannered*

**ma·noeu·vra·ble** *BrE*‖ **maneuverable** *AmE* /mə'nuːvərəbəl/ *adj* that can be moved or directed easily **–manoeuvrability** /-ə'bɪlɪ̈ti/ *n* [U]

**ma·noeu·vre¹** *BrE*‖ **maneuver** *AmE* /mə'nuːvəʳ/ *n* **1** (a set of) planned moves of an army or of warships, e.g. for training purposes: *army manoeuvres on land* **2** a skilful move or clever trick

**manoeuvre²** *BrE*‖**maneuver** *AmE v* **-vred, -vring 1** [I;T] to (cause to) perform one or more MANOEUVRES **2** to move (skilfully) to a position: *It was difficult to manoeuvre the furniture through the door.*

**man·or** /'mænəʳ/ *n* **1** a large house with land: *a* **manor house 2** the land belonging to a nobleman (the **lord of the manor**) under the FEUDAL system

**man·pow·er** /'mæn,paʊəʳ/ *n* [U] the number of people needed for a certain type of work: *The new machines will cause a reduction in manpower.*

**man·sion** /'mænʃən/ *n* a large house, usu. belonging to a wealthy person –see HOUSE (USAGE)

**man·slaugh·ter** /'mæn,slɔːtəʳ/ *n* [U] *law* the crime of killing a person, illegally but not intentionally –compare MURDER

**man·tel·piece** /'mæntlpiːs/ also **mantelshelf** /-ʃelf/ *old use– n* the shelf above a fireplace –see picture on page 355

**man·tle** /'mæntl/ *n lit or old use* a loose outer garment; CLOAK:(fig.) *a mantle of snow on the trees*

**man·u·al¹** /'mænjʊəl/ *adj* of or using the hands: *Manual work is tiring.* **–manually** *adv*

**manual²** *n* a (small) book of information about how to do something, or use esp. a machine –compare HANDBOOK

**man·u·fac·ture¹** /,mænjʊ'fæktʃəʳ‖-jə-/ *v* **-tured, -turing** [T] to make or produce by machinery, esp. in large quantities: *manufactured goods*|*manufacturing industry* **–manufacturer** *n*

**manufacture²** *n* [U] the act of manufacturing (MANUFACTURE)

**ma·nure** /mə'njʊəʳ‖mə'nʊər/ *n* [U] waste matter from animals which is put on the land to make it produce better crops –compare FERTILIZER

**man·u·script** /'mænjʊskrɪpt‖-jə-/ *n* **1** the first copy of a book or piece of writing, esp. written by hand before being printed **2** a handwritten book, of the time before printing was invented

**man·y** /'meni/ *determiner,pron* **more** /mɔːʳ‖mɔr/, **most** /məʊst/ **1** (used without *a* to show the large size of a number): *How many letters are there in the alphabet?*|*There are (far) too many people here.*|*Not many of the children* (=Only a few of the children) *can read.*|*He bought four tickets, which was one too many.* (=he only needed three) –see Study Notes on page 494 **2 a good/great many** a large number of **3 many a man, time, etc.** many men, times, etc.: *Many a man would have run away, but he didn't.* **4 many's the time** there have been many times: *Many's the time I've remembered him.*

**map¹** /mæp/ *n* a representation or plan showing the shape and position of countries, towns, rivers, etc.: *a map of Europe/central London* –see picture on page 105

**map²** *v* **-pp-** [T] to make a map of

**map** sthg.↔**out** *v adv* [T] to plan (an event) in the future: *We spent weeks mapping out our holiday.*

**ma·ple** /'meɪpəl/ *n* a tree with many-pointed leaves, which yields a sugary liquid

**mar** /mɑːʳ/ *v* **-rr-** [T] *esp. lit* to spoil: *The big new road mars the beauty of the countryside.*

**mar·a·thon** /'mærəθən‖-θɑn/ *n* **1** [C] **a** a 26-mile running race **b** any activity that tests one's power over a long time **2** [A] very long: *a marathon speech*

**ma·raud·ing** /mə'rɔːdɪŋ/ *adj* [A] searching for something to steal, burn, or destroy: *They were attacked by marauding soldiers.* **–marauder** *n*

**mar·ble** /'mɑːbəl‖'mɑr-/ *n* **1** [A;U] a hard sort of stone used for building, SCULPTURE, etc., and usu. showing an irregular pattern of colours: *a white mar-*

*ble gravestone* **2** [C *usu. pl.*] a small hard ball of coloured glass used by children to play a game in which they roll the balls along the ground

**march**[1] /mɑːtʃ‖mɑrtʃ/ *v* **1** [I] to walk with a regular, esp. forceful, step like a soldier: *The soldiers marched along the road.*|*She was very angry and marched out (of the house).*|(fig.) *Time marches on.* –see WALK (USAGE); see picture on page 669 **2** [T] to force to walk (away): *The police marched him off to prison.* **3 Quick march!** (a command to soldiers to start marching)

**march**[2] *n* **1** [*the* U] the act of marching: *The soldiers went past on the march.*|(fig.) *the march of time* **2** [C] the distance covered while marching in a certain period of time: *It was a day's march from the city to the camp.* **3** [C] a piece of music for marching to **4** [C] marching by a large number of people from one place to another to show their opinions or dissatisfactions; DEMONSTRATION (2): *a hunger march*

**March** also **Mar.** *written abbrev.– n* the third month of the year

**mar·chio·ness** /ˌmɑːʃəˈnes‖ˈmɑrʃənɪs/ *n* the wife of a MARQUIS or the title of a noblewoman of the same rank

**mare** /meəʳ/ *n* a female horse or donkey –compare STALLION

**mar·ga·rine** /ˌmɑːdʒəˈriːn, ˌmɑːgə-‖ˈmɑrdʒərɪn/ *n* [U] a food made from animal or vegetable fats, used instead of butter on bread or in baking

**mar·gin** /ˈmɑːdʒɪn‖ˈmɑr-/ *n* **1** a space near the edge of a page: *to make notes in the margin of a book* **2** an amount above what is necessary: *He left early and caught the train by a good margin.* **3** (in business) the amount of profit: *high profit margins*

**mar·gin·al** /ˈmɑːdʒɪnl‖ˈmɑr-/ *adj* **1** of small importance or small amount: *The new law will cause a marginal increase in the cost of living.* **2** (of a place (SEAT[1] (3)) in Parliament) which may be lost or won by a small number of votes, and so pass from one party's control to that of another **–marginally** *adv*

**mar·i·gold** /ˈmærɪgəʊld/ *n* an orange flower

**mar·i·jua·na, -huana** /ˌmærɪˈwɑːnə, -ˈhwɑːnə/ also **dope, pot, grass** *infml– n* [U] a common drug made from parts of the CANNABIS plant, usu. smoked in cigarettes for pleasure –see also HASHISH

**ma·ri·na** /məˈriːnə/ *n* a small harbour for pleasure boats

**mar·i·nate** /ˈmærɪneɪt/ also **marinade** /ˈmærɪneɪd/– *v* **-nated, -nating** [T] to leave (meat or fish) in a mixture of wine, oil, SPICES, etc. before cooking

**ma·rine**[1] /məˈriːn/ *adj* [A] **1** of, near, or living in the sea: *Marine plants grow on the sea bed.* **2** of ships and sea trade: *marine insurance*

**marine**[2] *n* [A;C] a soldier who serves on a naval ship

**mar·i·ner** /ˈmærɪnəʳ/ *n lit* a sailor or seaman

**mar·i·o·nette** /ˌmærɪəˈnet/ *n* a small figure of a person, animal, etc., moved by strings or wires; sort of PUPPET

**mar·i·tal** /ˈmærɪtl/ *adj* of or concerning marriage **–maritally** *adv*

**mar·i·time** /ˈmærɪtaɪm/ *adj* [A] **1** concerning ships or the sea: *maritime law*|*a great maritime power* (=with a strong navy) **2** living or existing near the sea

**mar·jo·ram** /ˈmɑːdʒərəm‖ˈmɑr-/ *n* [U] a plant (HERB) with sweet-smelling leaves used in cooking

**mark**[1] /mɑːk‖mɑrk/ *n* **1** a spot, line, or cut that spoils the natural colour or appearance of something: *His feet left (dirty) marks all over the floor.*|(fig.) *His years in prison have left their mark on him.* **2** an object or sign serving as a guide, giving information, or showing a quality: *We followed the marks that the car had left in the grass.*|*They stood as a mark of respect when he came in.*|*a question mark*|(fig.) *He certainly* **made his mark (on** *the place) while he was here.* (=had a great influence on it) **3** a figure, letter, or sign which represents a judgment of quality in someone's work, behaviour, or performance: *The highest mark in the test was nine out of ten.*|(fig.) *I'll give him* **full marks for** *trying.* (=I think he tried very hard) **4** a particular type of a machine: *The Mark 4 gun is more powerful than the old Mark 3.* **5 On your marks, get set, go!** (used for starting a running race)

**mark**[2] *v* **1** [I;T] to make a mark on, or to receive a mark, in a way that spoils the appearance: *The hot cups have marked the table.*|*The table marks easily.*|*The disease marked her face for life.* **2** [T] to be a sign of: *The cross marks his grave.*|*Today's ceremony marks 100 years of trade between our countries.* **3** [T] to give marks (MARK[1] (3)) to: *I've got a pile of examination papers to mark.*|*The teacher marked my poem 10 out of 10.* **4 Mark my words!** You will see later I am right **5 mark time** to spend time on work, business, etc., without advancing

**mark** sthg.↔**down/up** *v adv* [T] to lower/raise (goods) in price: *These winter coats have been marked down from £45 to £25.* –see also MARKUP

**mark** sbdy./sthg.↔**out** *v adv* [T] **1** to draw lines round (an area): *They marked out the tennis court with white paint.* **2** [*for*] to show as suitable (for): *Her ability marked her out for political success.*

**mark**[3] *n* a German coin

**marked** /mɑːkt‖mɑrkt/ *adj* **1** noticeable: *He showed a marked lack of interest.* **2** [F *by*] (typically) having: *This writer's plays are marked by a gentle humour.* **3 marked man** a man who is in danger from an enemy **–markedly** /ˈmɑːkɪdli‖ˈmɑr- / *adv*

**mark·er** /ˈmɑːkəʳ‖ˈmɑr-/ *n* **1** a tool for making marks **2** an object which marks a place

**mar·ket**[1] /ˈmɑːkɪt‖ˈmɑr-/ *n* **1** a building or open place where people meet to buy and sell goods: *a cattle market* **2** a gathering of people to buy and sell on certain days at such a place: *Monday is market day.* **3** an area or country where there is a demand for goods: *They sell to foreign markets/the home market.* **4** demand for goods: *a growing market for cameras* **5 a buyer's/seller's market** a state of affairs favouring the buyer/seller: *Not many people can afford new cars just now, so it's a buyer's market.* **6 on the market** (of goods) for sale

**market**[2] *v* [T] to offer for sale: *The firm markets many types of goods.* **–marketable** *adj*

**market gar·den** /ˌ·· ˈ··/ *n esp. BrE* an area for growing vegetables and fruit for sale

**mar·ket·ing** /ˈmɑːkɪtɪŋ‖ˈmɑr-/ *n* [U] the various activities by which goods are advertised and sold

**marks·man** /ˈmɑːksmən‖ˈmɑrks-/ **markswoman** /-ˌwʊmən/ *fem.– n* **-men** /mən/ a person who can shoot well with a gun

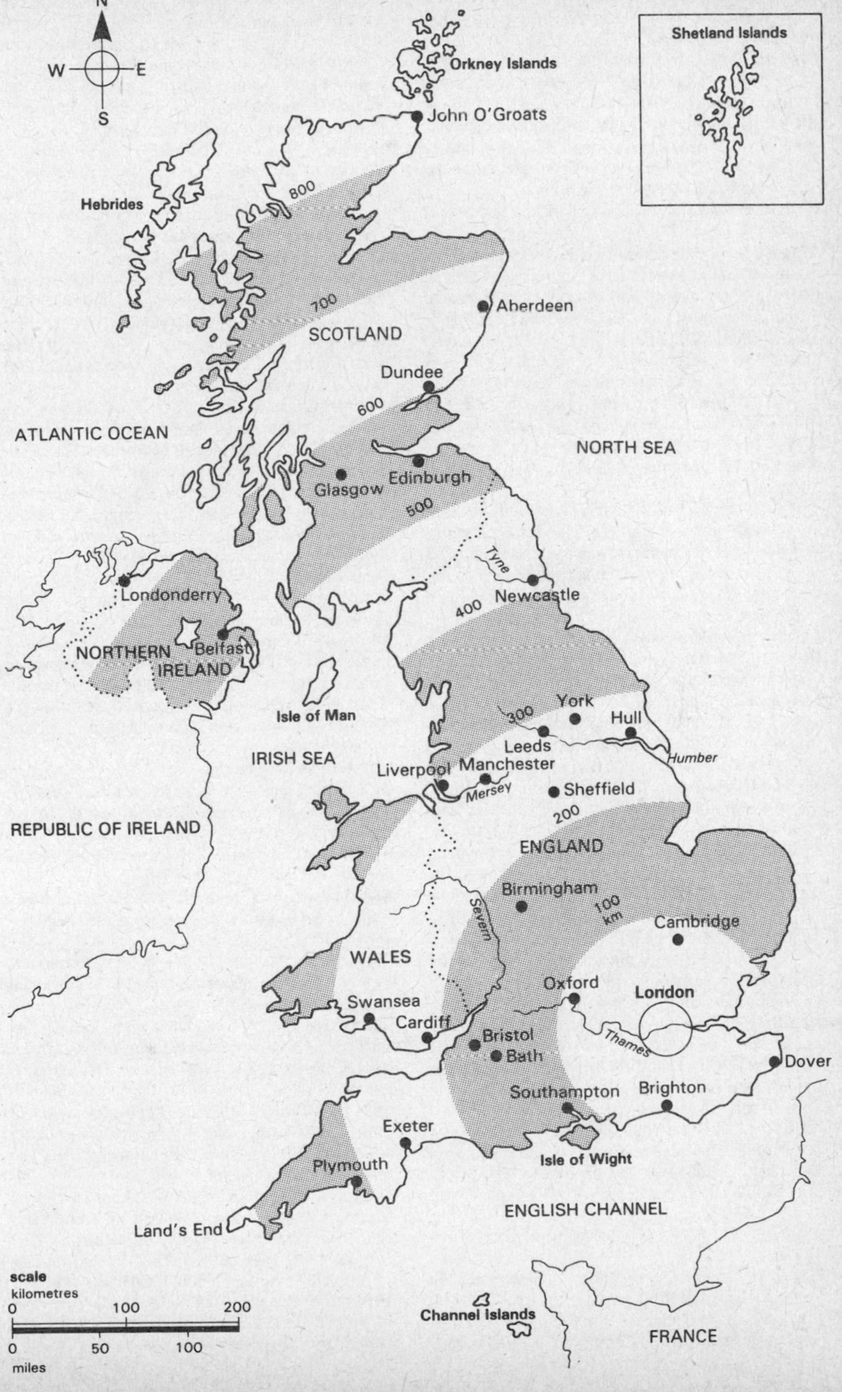
N
W
E
S
Orkney Islands
John O'Groats
Shetland Islands
Hebrides
800
700
Aberdeen
SCOTLAND
Dundee
600
ATLANTIC OCEAN
NORTH SEA
Glasgow
Edinburgh
500
Tyne
Londonderry
Newcastle
400
NORTHERN
IRELAND
Belfast
Isle of Man
300
York
Hull
Leeds
Humber
IRISH SEA
Liverpool
Manchester
Mersey
Sheffield
200
REPUBLIC OF IRELAND
ENGLAND
Birmingham
100
km
Severn
Cambridge
WALES
Oxford
London
Swansea
Cardiff
Thames
Bristol
Bath
Dover
Southampton
Brighton
Exeter
Isle of Wight
Plymouth
ENGLISH CHANNEL
Land's End
scale
kilometres
0
100
200
0
50
100
miles
Channel Islands
FRANCE

**mark·up** /'mɑːk-ʌp||'mɑrk-/ *n* the amount by which a price is raised: *a markup of 20 pence* –see also MARK² **down/up**

**mar·ma·lade** /'mɑːməleɪd||'mɑr-/ *n* [U] a sweet food which is spread on bread (JAM), made from oranges or other CITRUS fruits

**ma·roon¹** /mə'ruːn/ *v* [T] to leave (someone) alone, esp. in a place where no one lives, with no means of getting away: *The boat sank and we were marooned on a little island.* –compare ABANDON

**maroon²** *n,adj* [U] (of) a very dark red-brown colour

**mar·quee** /mɑː'kiː||mɑr-/ *n* a large tent used for outdoor public events

**mar·quis, marquess** /'mɑːkwɪ̈s||'mɑr-/ **marchioness** /ˌmɑːʃə'nes||'mɑrʃənɪ̈s/ *fem.*– *n* (the title of) a nobleman of high rank

**mar·riage** /'mærɪdʒ/ *n* [C;U] **1** the union of a man and woman by a ceremony in law: *The marriage took place in church.* **2** the state of being so united: *Her first marriage was not very happy.* (=her life with her first husband)

**mar·ria·gea·ble** /'mærɪdʒəbəl/ *adj fml* suitable to be married

**mar·ried** /'mærid/ *adj* **1** having (as) a husband or wife: *a married man*|(fig.) *He's married to his work.* (=gives it all his attention) –compare SINGLE² (4) **2** [A] of the state of marriage: *married life*

**mar·row** /'mærəʊ/ *n* **1** [U] the soft fatty substance in the hollow centre of bones **2** [C] also **squash** *AmE*– a long dark green vegetable which can grow very big

**mar·ry** /'mæri/ *v* **-ried, -rying 1** [I;T] to take (a person) in marriage: *He got married late in life.*|(fig.) *She married (into) money.* (=a rich man) **2** [T] (of a priest or official) to perform the ceremony of marriage for (two people): *An old friend married them.* **3** [T *to*] to cause to take in marriage: *She married her son to a rich woman.*

**Mars** /mɑːz||mɑrz/ *n* the PLANET fourth in order from the sun, and next to the Earth

**marsh** /mɑːʃ||mɑrʃ/ *n* [C;U] (an area of) low land that is soft and wet –**marshy** *adj* **-ier, -iest**

**mar·shal¹** /'mɑːʃəl||'mɑr-/ *n* **1** [A;C] an officer of the highest rank in certain armies and airforces **2** [C] an official who arranges a public ceremony or event **3** [A;C] (in the US) **a** an official who carries out the judgments given in a court of law **b** a chief officer of a police or fire-fighting force

**marshal²** *v* **-ll-** *BrE*||**-l-** *AmE* [T] **1** to arrange in good order: *He marshalled the facts in the speech very clearly.* **2** to lead or show the way to the correct place

**marsh·mal·low** /ˌmɑːʃ'mæləʊ||'mɑrʃmæləʊ/ *n* a type of soft round sweet

**mar·su·pi·al** /mɑː'sjuːpɪəl||mɑr'suː-/ *adj,n tech* (one) of the type of animal which carries its young in a pocket of skin (POUCH) on the mother's body

**mar·tial** /'mɑːʃəl||'mɑr-/ *adj* [A] of or concerning war, soldiers, etc.: *martial music*

**martial law** /ˌ·· '·/ *n* [U] government by the army under special laws

**Mar·tian** /'mɑːʃən||'mɑr-/ *adj,n* (a being) of the PLANET MARS, usu. in imaginary stories

**mar·tyr¹** /'mɑːtəʳ||'mɑr-/ *n* **1** a person who dies or suffers for his/her beliefs **2 make a martyr of oneself** to give up one's own wishes to help others, or in the hope of being praised

**martyr²** *v* [T] to kill or cause to suffer for a belief

**mar·tyr·dom** /'mɑːtədəm||'mɑrtər-./ *n* [U] the death or suffering of a martyr

**mar·vel¹** /'mɑːvəl||'mɑr-/ *n* a wonder; wonderful thing or example: *a marvel of science*

**marvel²** *v* **-ll-** *BrE*||**-l-** *AmE* [I;T +(*that*), *at*] to wonder; be surprised at: *We marvelled at their skill.*

**mar·vel·lous** *BrE*||**marvelous** *AmE* /'mɑːvələs||'mɑr-/ *adj* wonderful; surprisingly good: *What marvellous weather!* –**marvellously** *adv*

**Marx·is·m** /'mɑːksɪzəm/ *n* [U] the teaching of Karl Marx on which COMMUNISM is based, which explains the changes in history according to the struggle between social classes –**Marxist** *n,adj*

**mar·zi·pan** /'mɑːzɪ̈pæn||'mɑrtsɪ̈-, 'mɑrzɪ̈-/ *n* [U] a very sweet paste, of nuts, sugar, and egg, used for making some sweets and cakes

**mas·ca·ra** /mæ'skɑːrə||mæ'skærə/ *n* [U] a dark substance for colouring the EYELASHES

**mas·cot** /'mæskət||'mæskɑt/ *n* an object, animal, or person thought to bring good luck

**mas·cu·line** /'mæskjʊlɪ̈n ||-kjə-/ *adj* **1** of or having the qualities of a man **2** *tech* (in grammar) of a certain class of words: *"Drake" is the masculine form of "duck".* –compare FEMININE; see FEMALE² (USAGE) –**masculinity** /-'lɪnɪ̈ti/ *n* [U]

**mash¹** /mæʃ/ *v* [T] to crush into a soft substance: *Mash the potatoes with a fork.*

**mash²** *n* [U] *infml* MASHed¹ potatoes

**mask¹** /mɑːsk||mæsk/ *n* a covering for the face to hide or protect it: (fig.) *He hid his hatred under a mask of loyalty.* –see also GAS MASK –**masked** *adj*

**mask²** *v* [T] to cover with a MASK; hide –see also UNMASK

**mas·o·chis·m** /'mæsəkɪzəm/ *n* [U] the wish to be hurt so as to gain (esp. sexual) pleasure –compare SADISM –**masochist** *n* –**masochistic** /-'kɪstɪk/ *adj*

**ma·son** /'meɪsən/ *n* →STONEMASON

**ma·son·ry** /'meɪsənri/ *n* [U] a stone part of a building: *She was hit by a piece of falling masonry.*

**mas·que·rade¹** /ˌmæskə'reɪd/ *n* **1** a dance where people wear MASKS **2** something pretended; hiding of the truth

**masquerade²** *v* **-aded, -ading** [I *as*] to pretend (to be): *He got a free ticket to the play by masquerading as a friend of the actors.*

**mass¹** /mæs/ *n* **1** [C *of*] a solid lump, quantity, or heap, or large number: *a solid mass of rock*|(*infml*) *masses of people* **2** [U] (in science) the amount of matter in a body

**mass²** *v* [I;T] *lit* to gather together in large numbers: *Dark clouds massed, and we expected rain.*

**mass³** *adj* [A] of or for a great number of people: *a mass murderer*|*a mass meeting*

**Mass** *n* [C;U] (esp. in the ROMAN CATHOLIC church) the main religious service, based on Christ's last supper –compare COMMUNION, EUCHARIST

**mas·sa·cre¹** /'mæsəkəʳ/ *n* a killing of large numbers of people who cannot defend themselves

**massacre²** *v* **-cred, -cring** [T] to kill a large number of people: (fig.) *Their team was much better than ours, and we were massacred.* –see KILL (USAGE)

**mas·sage** /ˈmæsɑːʒ‖məˈsɑːʒ/ *n* [C;U] (an example of) treatment of the body by pressing and rubbing one's hands on it to take away pain or stiffness –**massage** *v* **-saged, -saging** [T]

**mass·es** /ˈmæsɪ̵z/ *n* [*the* P] the largest class in society; the WORKING CLASS

**mas·seur** /mæˈsɜːʳ, mə-/ **masseuse** /mæˈsɜːz, mə-/ *fem.*– *n* a person who gives MASSAGES

**mas·sive** /ˈmæsɪv/ *adj* very big; strong and powerful: *massive walls* –**massively** *adv*

**mass me·di·a** /ˌ· ˈ···/ *n* [*the* U +*sing./pl. v*] the means of giving news and opinions to large numbers of people, esp. radio, television, and the newspapers

**mass pro·duc·tion** /ˌ· ·ˈ··/ *n* [U] the making of large numbers of the same article by a fixed method –**mass-produce** *v* [T]: *cheap mass-produced furniture*

**mast** /mɑːst‖mæst/ *n* **1** a long upright pole for carrying sails on a ship **2** a flagpole –see also HALF-MAST

**mas·ter**[1] /ˈmɑːstəʳ‖ˈmæ-/ *n* **1** [*of*] **mistress** *fem.*– a man in control of people, animals, or things: *the dog's master* **2** **mistress** *fem.*–*fml* a male teacher: *The history master* **3** a man of great skill in art or work with the hands: *a master builder*/CRAFTSMAN|*a master at painting* –see also OLD MASTER

**master**[2] *adj* [A] chief; most important: *the master bedroom*

**master**[3] *v* [T] to gain control over or learn thoroughly: *It takes years to master a new language.*

**Master** *n* [A] (a title for addressing) a young boy: *Master John Smith, 4 New Road*

**mas·ter·ful** /ˈmɑːstəfəl‖ˈmæstər-/ *adj* having an ability to control others –compare MASTERLY –**masterfully** *adv*

**master key** /ˈ·· ·/ *n* a key that will open several different locks

**mas·ter·ly** /ˈmɑːstəli‖ˈmæstərli/ *adj* showing great skill: *a masterly speech* –compare MASTERFUL –**masterliness** *n* [U]

**mas·ter·mind**[1] /ˈmɑːstəmaɪnd‖ˈmæstər-/ *n* a very clever person, esp. one who is responsible for a plan: *the mastermind behind the robbery.*

**mastermind**[2] *v* [T] *infml* to plan (a course of action) cleverly: *to mastermind a crime*

**mas·ter·piece** /ˈmɑːstəpiːs‖ˈmæstər-/ *n* a piece of work, esp. art, which is the best of its type or the best a person has done

**mas·ter·y** /ˈmɑːstəri‖ˈmæ-/ *n* [U *over, of*] control (over) or skill (in): *The enemy had complete mastery of the seas, and no ships could get through.*

**mas·ti·cate** /ˈmæstɪ̵keɪt/ *v* **-cated, -cating** [I;T] *fml* to bite on and through (food); CHEW –**mastication** /-ˈkeɪʃən/ *n* [U]

**mas·tiff** /ˈmæstɪ̵f/ *n* a large powerful guard dog

**mas·tur·bate** /ˈmæstəbeɪt‖-ər-/ *v* **-bated, -bating** [I;T] to excite the sex organs (of), by handling, rubbing, etc. –**masturbation** /-ˈbeɪʃən / *n* [U]

**mat**[1] /mæt/ *n* **1** a piece of rough strong material or small RUG used for covering part of a floor **2** a small piece of material used for putting under objects on a table: *Put the hot dish down on the mat, so you don't burn the table.*

**mat**[2] →MATT

**mat·a·dor** /ˈmætədɔːʳ/ *n* the person who kills the BULL in a BULLFIGHT

**match**[1] /mætʃ/ *n* **1** [C] a game or sports event in which teams or people compete: *a football match* **2** [S *for*] a person who is equal or better in strength, ability, etc., (to another): *I'm no match for her when it comes to painting.* (=she's much better than me)|*He was very good at tennis, but* **he met his match** (=met someone who could beat him) *when he played McEnroe.* **3** [S *for*] a thing or set of things that is like or suitable to another or each other: *The hat and shoes are a perfect match.*

**match**[2] *v* **1** [I;T] to be like or suitable for use with (another or each other): *The wallpaper and paint don't match.* (each other) **2** [T *in, for*] to be or find an equal to: *This hotel can't be matched for good service and food.* **3** [T *up*] to find something like or suitable for use with: *I'm trying to match this yellow wool.* **4** **well-/ill-matched** suitable/not suitable to be with, or to compete with, each other: *a well-matched husband and wife*|*The two fighters aren't very well-matched.* (=one is much better than the other)

**match**[3] *n* a short thin stick, usu. of wood, with a substance at the end which burns when struck against a rough surface: *a box of matches*

**match·box** /ˈmætʃbɒks‖-bɑks/ *n* a small box in which matches are sold, with rough material along one or both sides on which to strike them

**match·ing** /ˈmætʃɪŋ/ *adj* [A] (esp. of colours) which are the same or suited

**match·less** /ˈmætʃlɪ̵s/ *adj fml* which has no equal in quality

**match·mak·er** /ˈmætʃˌmeɪkəʳ/ *n* a person who encourages people to marry each other

**mate**[1] /meɪt/ *n* **1** [C] a fellow workman or friend: *They are my mates/workmates/schoolmates.* **2** *BrE infml* (a way of addressing a man): *"What time is it, mate?"* **3** the rank below a ship's captain: *first mate* **4** one of a male and female pair of animals

**mate**[2] *v* **mated, mating** [I;T *with*] to become or make into a couple, esp. of animals, for the production of young: *Birds mate in the spring.*|*the* **mating season**|*They mated a horse with a donkey.*

**ma·te·ri·al**[1] /məˈtɪəriəl/ *adj* **1** of or concerning matter or substance, not spirit: *The storm did a great deal of material damage.* (=to buildings, property, etc.) **2** of the body, rather than the mind or soul: *Food is a material need.* –compare SPIRITUAL –**materially** *adv*

**material**[2] *n* **1** [C;U] anything from which something is or may be made: *Building materials are expensive.* **2** [C;U] cloth: *dress material*|*a light material* –see CLOTHES (USAGE) **3** [U *for*] knowledge of facts from which a (written) work may be produced: *She's collecting material for a book.*

**ma·te·ri·al·is·m** /məˈtɪəriəlɪzəm/ *n* [U] **1** *esp. derog* (too) great interest in the pleasures of the world, money, etc. **2** the belief that only matter exists, and that there is no world of the spirit –**materialistic** /-ˈlɪstɪk/ *adj* –**materialistically** *adv* –**materialist** *adj,n*

**ma·te·ri·al·ize** ‖also **-ise** *BrE* /məˈtɪəriəlaɪz/ *v* **-ized, -izing** [I] to take on bodily form; become real: *His hopes never materialized.*

**ma·ter·nal** /məˈtɜːnəl‖-ɜr-/ *adj* **1** of, like, or natural to a mother **2** [A] related through the mother's part of the family: *my maternal grandfather* –see also

PATERNAL –**maternally** *adv*

**ma·ter·ni·ty** /mə'tɜːnǐti‖-ɜr-/ *adj,n* [A;U] (of) motherhood or the bodily condition of becoming a mother; for women who are PREGNANT and giving birth: *a maternity dress|a maternity hospital*/WARD

**math·e·ma·ti·cian** /ˌmæθǐmə'tɪʃən/ *n* a person who studies MATHEMATICS

**math·e·mat·ics** /ˌmæθǐ'mætɪks/ also *infml* **maths** /mæθs/ *BrE*‖**math** /mæθ/ *AmE*– *n* [U] the study or science of numbers –**mathematical** *adj* –**mathematically** *adv*

**mat·i·née** /'mætǐneɪ‖ˌmætǐ'neɪ/ *n* a performance of a play or film given in the afternoon

**mat·ins, mattins** /'mætǐnz‖'mætnz/ *n* [U +*sing./pl. v*] a church service held in the morning –compare VESPERS

**ma·tri·arch** /'meɪtriɑːk‖-ɑrk/ *n* a woman who rules a family or a group of people –see also PATRIARCH –**matriarchal** /-'ɑːkəl‖-'ɑr- / *adj*

**ma·tri·ar·chy** /'meɪtriɑːki‖-ɑr-/ *n* **-chies** [C;U] (an example of) a social system in which women, not men, have power over the family and possessions –see also PATRIARCHY

**mat·ri·cide** /'mætrǐsaɪd/ *n* [C;U] (a person guilty of) the murder of his/her own mother –see also PATRICIDE

**ma·tric·u·late** /mə'trɪkjʊleɪt‖-kjə-/ *v* **-lated, -lating** [I;T] to (allow to) become a member of a university, esp. after an examination or test –**matriculation** /-'leɪʃən / *n* [C;U]

**mat·ri·mo·ny** /'mætrǐməni‖-məʊni/ *n* [U] *fml* the state of marriage –**matrimonial** /-'məʊnɪəl / *adj*

**ma·trix** /'meɪtrɪks/ *n* **matrices** /-trǐsiːz/ *or* **matrixes** *tech* **1** a hollow container (MOULD[2]) into which melted metal is poured to form a shape **2** the rock or stone in which hard stones or jewels have been formed **3** (in MATHEMATICS, science, etc.) an arrangement of numbers, figures, or signs

**ma·tron** /'meɪtrən/ *n* **1** (the title of) a woman in a hospital who has control over the nurses **2** (the title of) a woman in a school who is in charge of medicine, repair of clothes, etc. **3** *lit* an older married woman

**ma·tron·ly** /'meɪtrənli/ *adj* **1** *euph* (of a woman) rather fat –see THIN (USAGE) **2** (of a woman) having the DIGNITY of a MATRON (3)

**matt, mat**‖also **matte** *AmE* /mæt/ *adj* of a dull, not shiny, surface: *matt paint*

**mat·ted** /'mætǐd/ *adj* twisted in a thick mass: *matted hair*

**mat·ter[1]** /'mætə[r]/ *n* **1** [U] the material which makes up the world and everything in space which can be seen or touched **2** [C] a subject to which one gives attention; an affair: *There are several important matters I wish to talk to you about.|I've decided to* **let the matter drop.** (=take no further action to deal with the affair)|*Looking after 15 noisy children is* **no laughing matter.** (=is difficult) **3** [*the* S] a trouble or cause of pain, illness, etc.: **What's the matter;** *why are you crying?*|**There's nothing the matter/ Nothing's the matter with** *me.* (=nothing's wrong)|**What's the matter with** *the radio; why isn't it working?* **4** [U] written material: *I must take some suitable* **reading matter** (=books, magazines, etc.) *for the journey.* **5 a matter of: a** a little more or less than; about: *We only waited a matter of (ten) minutes.* **b** having as a part or result; needing: *Learning languages is just a matter of remembering words.* **6 a matter of course** a usual event: *When I go out of the house I lock the door* **as a matter of course. 7 a matter of life or death** something so serious that failure to do it may result in death **8 a matter of opinion** a subject on which different persons may think differently **9 as a matter of fact** really; in fact: *"I thought you wouldn't mind." "Well, as a matter of fact I don't; but you should have asked me first."* –see also MATTER-OF-FACT **10 for that matter** (*used when mentioning another possibility*) as concerns the thing mentioned: *Your mother would never allow it, and for that matter, neither would I.* **11 no matter (how, where, etc.)** it makes no difference: *I'll finish the job, no matter how long it takes.*

**matter[2]** *v* [I *to*] to be important: *It doesn't matter if I miss my train.|I don't think anybody matters to her apart from herself.*

**matter-of-fact** /ˌ·· · '·◂/ *adj* concerned with facts, not imagination or feelings; practical –see also FACT (3)

**mat·ting** /'mætɪŋ/ *n* [U] rough material for mats and for packing goods

**mat·tins** /'mætǐnz‖'mætnz/ *n* [U +*sing./pl. v*] → MATINS

**mat·tress** /'mætrǐs/ *n* a large bag of solid but yielding material for sleeping on

**ma·ture[1]** /mə'tʃʊə[r]/ *adj* **1 a** fully grown and developed **b** typical of an older person; sensible: *His child behaves in a very mature way.* –opposite **immature 2** (of cheese, wine, etc.) ready to be eaten or drunk; ripe –**maturely** *adv* –**maturity** *n* [U]

**mature[2]** *v* **-tured, -turing** [I;T] to (cause to) become MATURE: *After six years the wine will have matured.*

**maud·lin** /'mɔːdlɪn/ *adj fml* showing foolish sadness in a pitiful way: *He always becomes maudlin after he's had a few drinks.*

**maul** /mɔːl/ *v* [T *about*] **1** (esp. of animals) to hurt by tearing the flesh: *The hunter was mauled by a lion.* **2** to handle roughly or in an unwelcome way

**mau·so·le·um** /ˌmɔːsə'lɪəm/ *n* a fine stone building (TOMB) raised over a grave

**mauve** /məʊv/ *adj,n* [U] (of) a pale purple colour

**mav·e·rick** /'mævərɪk/ *n* a person, esp. a politician, who acts differently from the rest of the group

**max·im** /'mæksǐm/ *n* a rule for good and sensible behaviour, often expressed in a short saying

**max·i·mize** ‖also **-mise** *BrE* /'mæksǐmaɪz/ *v* **-mized, -mizing** [T] to increase to the greatest possible size –compare MINIMIZE

**max·i·mum** /'mæksǐməm/ *n* **-ma** /mə/ *or* **-mums 1** [C] the most, or the largest possible, quantity, number, or degree: *He smokes a maximum of 15 cigarettes a day.|The sound has reached its maximum.* (=is at its loudest) **2** [A] largest, or largest possible (in amount, degree, etc.): *maximum temperature|maximum speed* –opposite **minimum**

**may** /meɪ/ *v negative contraction* **mayn't** *BrE* [I +*to*-*v*] **1** (shows a possibility): *He may come or he may not.|"Why hasn't he come?" "He may have missed the train."* (=perhaps he has missed it)|*I may have thought that once, but I don't now.* **2** to have permission to; be allowed to: *You may come in now.|May we go home, please?* (This is now less common than **can**) –see Study Notes on page 386 **3** (used when expressing a wish): *May you live happily!* **4** **may/might as well** to have no strong reason not to: *It's late, so I may as well go to bed.* –see also CAN (USAGE), MIGHT (USAGE)

**May** *n* the 5th month of the year

**may·be** /ˈmeɪbi/ *adv* perhaps: *"Will they come?" "Maybe."*

**may·day** /ˈmeɪdeɪ/ *n* a radio signal used as a call for help from a ship or plane

**May Day** /ˈ· ·/ *n* 1st May, when political parties of the LEFT[2] hold public events

**mayn't** /meɪnt/ *v short for* may not

**may·on·naise** /ˌmeɪəˈneɪz‖ˈmeɪəneɪz/ *n* [U] a thick yellowish SAUCE made from eggs, oil, milk, etc., often used on SALADS

**mayor** /meəʳ‖ˈmeɪər/ *n* a person elected each year by a town council to be head of that city or town –**mayoral** *adj*

**mayor·ess** /ˈmeərɨ̣s‖ˈmeɪərɨ̣s/ *n* the wife of a male MAYOR, or a woman who is a MAYOR

**may·pole** /ˈmeɪpəʊl/ *n* a tall pole which can be decorated with flowers and round which people dance on **May Day** (May 1st), esp. formerly in villages

**maze** /meɪz/ *n* an arrangement of paths, often bordered with tall HEDGES[1] (1), which twist and turn, and are sometimes blocked, within an enclosed area. One tries to find the centre and then the way out again, for fun: *We were lost in the maze for several hours.*|(fig.) *a maze of narrow winding streets* –compare LABYRINTH

**MD** *abbrev. for*: Doctor of Medicine: *John Snow, MD*

**me** /mi; *strong* miː/ *pron* (*object form of* I): *Can you see me?|He bought me a drink.|He bought a drink for me.|That's me on the left of the photograph.*

USAGE **Him, her, me, us,** and **them** are used in speech after *as, than,* and *be,* but in formal writing **he, she, I, we,** and **they** are sometimes used instead: *I'm a better player than* **him**/*than* **he** ( *fml*).|*I'm not as pretty as* **her**/*as* **she** ( *fml*).|*It's* **me**!/*It is* **I** (*fml*)

**mead** /miːd/ *n* [U] an alcoholic drink made from HONEY, drunk esp. formerly in England

**mead·ow** /ˈmedəʊ/ *n* [C;U] (a field of) grassland on which cattle, sheep, etc., may feed

**mea·gre** *BrE*‖**meager** *AmE* /ˈmiːgəʳ/ *adj* not enough in quantity, quality, strength,etc.: *a meagre income* –**meagrely** *adv* –**meagreness** *n* [U]

**meal**[1] /miːl/ *n* **1** an amount of food eaten at one time: *She cooks a hot meal in the evenings.* **2** also **mealtime**– the occasion or time of eating a meal

**meal**[2] *n* [U] grain which has been crushed into a powder, esp. for flour –**mealy** *adj* **-ier, -iest**

**meal·y-mouthed** /ˌmiːli ˈmaʊðd◂/ *adj* expressing things indirectly, not plainly, esp. when something unpleasant must be said: *mealy-mouthed politicians/statements*

**mean**[1] /miːn/ *adj* **1** ungenerous; unwilling to share or help: *He's very mean with his money.* **2** unkind; nasty: *It was very mean of you not to let the children play in the snow.* **3** *esp. AmE* bad-tempered; liking to hurt: *That's a mean dog; be careful–it may bite you.* **4** *lit* (typical of a person) of low social position; humble: *a man of mean birth* **5** **no mean (something)** a very good (something): *He's no mean cook.|Running 10 miles is no mean* ACHIEVEMENT. –**meanly** *adv* –**meanness** *n* [U]

**mean**[2] *v* **meant** /ment/, **meaning** [T not *be +v-ing*] **1** [+(*that*); not *be +v-ing*] to represent (a meaning): *What does this French word mean?|The red light means "Stop".|The sign means that cars cannot enter.* **2** [+*to- v*/(*that*)] to have in mind as or for a purpose; intend: *She said Tuesday, but she meant Thursday.|I mean to go tomorrow.|Those flowers were meant for you; I meant you to have them.|I said I would help him and I meant it.* (=I am determined to do so)|*I've been meaning to ask you–how's your mother?* **3** [+*v-ing*/(*that*)] to be a sign of: *The dark clouds mean rain.|That expression on his face means (that) he's angry.|Missing the train means waiting for an hour.* (=we will have to wait) **4** [*to*] to be of importance by (a stated amount): *Her work means a lot/means everything to her.* **5** **be meant to** *esp. BrE* to have to; be supposed to: *You're meant to take your shoes off when you enter a Hindu temple.* **6** **mean business** *infml* to act with serious intentions **7** **mean well** to do or say what is intended to help, but often doesn't

**mean**[3] *n* **1** an average amount, figure, or value: *The mean of 7, 9, and 14 is found by adding them together and dividing by 3.* **2** a state, way of behaviour, etc., which is not too strong or weak, great or small, etc., but in between

**mean**[4] *adj* [A *no comp.*] (of measurements) average: *The mean yearly rainfall is 20 inches.*

**me·an·der** /miˈændəʳ/ *v* [I] **1** (of rivers and streams) to flow slowly, with many turns **2** (of people or talk) to speak or move on in a slow aimless way –**meanderingly** *adv* –**meanderings** *n* [P]

**mean·ing**[1] /ˈmiːnɪŋ/ *n* [C;U] **1** the idea which is intended to be understood: *One word can have several meanings.|What's the meaning of this?* (often said to demand an explanation of something that has angered one) **2** importance or value: *He says his life has lost its meaning (for him) since his wife died.*

**meaning**[2] *adj* [A] which gives an effect of important (hidden) meaning or thought: *a meaning look*

**mean·ing·ful** /ˈmiːnɪŋfəl/ *adj* of important meaning; containing information: *That statement is not very meaningful.|He gave her a meaningful look.* –**meaningfully** *adv* –**meaningfulness** *n* [U]

**mean·ing·less** /ˈmiːnɪŋlɨ̣s/ *adj* without meaning or purpose –**meaninglessly** *adv* –**meaninglessness** *n* [U]

**means** /miːnz/ *n* **means** **1** [C *of*] a method or way (of doing): *The quickest means of travel is by plane.|Use whatever means you can to . . .* **2** [P] money, income, or wealth, esp. large enough for comfort: *Have you the means to support a family?|a man of means* (=a rich man) **3** **by all means** certainly; please do **4** **by means of** by using: *We express our thoughts by means of words.* **5** **by no means** *fml* not at all: *I am by no means pleased with this behaviour.*

**meant** /ment/ *v past tense and participle of* MEAN[2]

**mean·time** /ˈmiːntaɪm/ *n* **in the meantime** in the time between two events: *We can't go out yet because it's raining, so let's play a game in the meantime.*

**mean·while** /ˈmiːnwaɪl/ also **meantime** *infml*– *adv* during this time; in the same period of time: *They'll be here soon. Meanwhile, let's have coffee.*

**mea·sles** /ˈmiːzəlz/ *n* [*the* U] an infectious disease in which the sufferer has a fever and small red spots on the face and body

**meas·ly** /ˈmiːzli/ *adj* **-lier, -liest** *infml* of small value, size, etc.: *a measly little gift* –**measliness** *n* [U]

**mea·su·ra·ble** /ˈmeʒərəbəl/ *adj* large enough or not too large to be reasonably measured –see also IMMEASURABLE –**measurably** *adv*: *Your work has improved measurably* (=a lot) *this year.*

**mea·sure¹** /ˈmeʒəʳ/ *n* **1** [U] a system for calculating amount, size, weight, etc.: *An* OUNCE *in liquid measure is different from an* OUNCE *in dry measure.* **2** [C] an amount in such a system: *An hour is a measure of time.* **3** [C] an instrument used for calculating amount, length, weight, etc.: *The glass is a litre measure.* –see also TAPE MEASURE **4** [S;U *of*] *fml* an amount or quality: *He has not become rich, but he has had* **a certain measure of** *success*/**some measure of** *success.* **5** [C *usu. pl.*] an action taken to gain a certain end: *The government has promised to* **take measures** *to help the unemployed.* **6 for good measure** in addition: *After I'd weighed out the apples, I put in another one for good measure.*

**measure²** *v* **-sured, -suring 1** [I;T] to find the size, length, amount, degree, etc., (of) in standard measurements: *He measured (the height of) the cupboard.* **2** [T] to show or record amount, size, length, etc.: *A clock measures time.* **3** [not *be+v-ing*] to be of a certain size: *He measures more round the waist than he used to.*

**measure** sthg.↔**out** *v adv* [T] to take a measured quantity of (something taken from a larger amount): *To make the cake, measure out 250 grams of flour and 100 grams of butter.*

**measure up** *v adv* [I *to*] to show good enough qualities (for): *He didn't measure up to the job.*

**mea·sure·ment** /ˈmeʒəmənt‖-ər-/ *n* **1** [C *usu. pl.*] a length, height, etc., found by measuring: *Which measurement shall I take first– along the room or across it?* **2** [U] the act of measuring

**meat** /miːt/ *n* [U] **1** the flesh of animals (sometimes including birds, but not including fish) which is eaten: *There's not much meat on that bone/chicken.*|*His religion forbids the eating of meat.* **2** valuable matter, ideas, etc.: *It was a clever speech, but there was no real meat in it.* –**meaty** *adj* **-ier, -iest**

USAGE The meat from some animals has a different name from the animal itself. For example, the meat from a **cow** is called **beef**, the meat from a **pig** is **pork** or **ham**, and the meat from a **calf** (a young cow) is **veal**. But the meat from a **lamb** is **lamb**, and for birds and fish the same word is used for both the meat and the creature: *Shall we have* **chicken** *or* **duck** *for dinner?*

**me·chan·ic** /mɪˈkænɪk/ *n* a person who is skilled in using, repairing, etc., machinery: *a motor/car mechanic*

**me·chan·i·cal** /mɪˈkænɪkəl/ *adj* [*no comp.*] of, connected with, moved, worked, or produced by machinery: *a mechanical digger*|(fig.) *He was asked the same question so many times that the answer became mechanical.* (=as if made by a machine) –**mechanically** *adv*

**me·chan·ics** /mɪˈkænɪks/ *n* [U] **1** the science of the action of forces on objects **2** the science of making machines **3 the mechanics of** the ways in which something works, produces results, etc.: *She has natural ability, but hasn't yet learned the mechanics of the job.* –compare TECHNIQUE

**mech·a·nis·m** /ˈmekənɪzəm/ *n* the different parts of something, esp. of a small machine, arranged together, and the action they have: *The clock doesn't go; there's something wrong with the mechanism.*|*the mechanism of the brain*|*the mechanism of local government*

**mech·a·nize** ‖also **-nise** *BrE* /ˈmekənaɪz/ *v* **-nized, -nizing** [T] to use machines for, instead of using the effort of human beings or animals: *If we can mechanize farming we can produce more crops with fewer people.* –**mechanization** /ˌmekənaɪˈzeɪʃən‖-nə- / *n* [U]

**med·al** /ˈmedl/ *n* a round flat piece of metal, or a cross, with a picture and/or words marked on it, which is usu. given to a person as an honour for an act of bravery or strength: *an Olympic gold medal*

**me·dal·li·on** /məˈdæliən/ *n* a round MEDAL like a large coin, used for decoration

**med·al·list** *BrE*‖**medalist** *AmE* /ˈmedələst/ *n* a person who has won a MEDAL, esp. in sport

**med·dle** /ˈmedl/ *v* **-dled, -dling** [I *in, with*] to interest oneself or take action (in something which is not one's concern); INTERFERE –**meddler** *n* –**meddlesome** /-səm/ *adj*: *a meddlesome old man*

**me·di·a** /ˈmiːdɪə/ *n* [U +*sing./pl. v*] the newspapers, television, and radio; MASS MEDIA: *The media have/has a lot of power today.*

**med·i·ae·val** /ˌmediˈiːvəl‖ˌmiː-/ *adj* →MEDIEVAL

**me·di·ate** /ˈmiːdieɪt/ *v* **-ated, -ating** [I;T *between*] *fml* to act or produce as a peacemaker: *The government mediated between the workers and the employers.*|*The army leaders have mediated a* CEASE-FIRE/*a settlement.* –**mediation** /-ˈeɪʃən / *n* [U] –**mediator** *n*

**med·i·cal¹** /ˈmedɪkəl/ *adj* [*no comp.*] **1** of or concerning medicine and treating the sick: *a medical student*|*a medical examination* (=of the body by a doctor) **2** of the treatment of disease by medicine rather than by operation –compare MEDICINAL; SURGICAL –**medically** *adv*

**medical²** *n infml* a medical examination (of the body): *I have to have a medical before going abroad.*

**med·i·cat·ed** /ˈmedəkeɪtəd/ *adj* including or mixed with a medical substance: *medicated* SHAMPOO

**med·i·ca·tion** /ˌmedəˈkeɪʃən/ *n* [C;U] *esp. AmE* a medical substance, esp. a drug: *It is better to sleep naturally, without taking medication.*

**me·di·ci·nal** /məˈdɪsənəl/ *adj* [*no comp.*] **1** used for medicine: *medicinal alcohol* (=not for drinking) **2** having the effect of curing, like medicine: *medicinal* HERBS –compare MEDICAL¹ –**medicinally** *adv*

**me·di·cine** /ˈmedsən‖ˈmedəsən/ *n* **1** [C;U] a substance used for treating disease, esp. a liquid which is drunk: *a bottle of medicine*|*Keep all medicines away from children.* **2** [U] the science of treating and understanding disease

**med·i·e·val, mediaeval** /ˌmediˈiːvəl‖ˌmiː-/ *adj* of the period in history between about 1100 and 1500 (the MIDDLE AGES)
**me·di·o·cre** /ˌmiːdiˈəʊkəʳ/ *adj* of not very good or bad quality or ability: *a mediocre attempt at writing a story* –**mediocrity** /ˌmiːdiˈɒkrɪ̈ti‖-ˈɑk-/ *n* [U]
**med·i·tate** /ˈmedɪ̈teɪt/ *v* **-tated, -tating** [I] **1** to fix and keep the attention on one matter, having cleared the mind of thoughts, esp. for religious reasons and/or to gain peace of mind **2** to think seriously or deeply: *He meditated for two days before deciding.*
**med·i·ta·tion** /ˌmedɪ̈ˈteɪʃən/ *n* [C;U] the act or result of meditating (MEDITATE)
**med·i·ta·tive** /ˈmedɪ̈tətɪv‖-teɪtɪv/ *adj* thoughtful; showing deep thought –**meditatively** *adv*
**me·di·um**[1] /ˈmiːdɪəm/ *n* **-dia** /dɪə/ *or* **-diums 1** a method for giving information; form of art: *He writes stories, but the theatre is his favourite medium.*|*Television can be a medium for giving information, for amusing people, and for teaching them.* –see also MASS MEDIA, MEDIA **2** a substance in which objects or living things exist, or through which a force travels; surroundings: *A fish in water is in its natural medium.*|*Sound travels through the medium of air.* **3** a middle position: *There's* **a happy medium** *between eating all the time and not eating at all.*
**medium**[2] *n* **-diums** a person who claims to have power to receive messages from the spirits of the dead
**medium**[3] *adj* [A] of middle size, amount, quality, value, etc.: *a medium-sized apple* –see Study Notes on page 494
**med·ley** /ˈmedli/ *n* **-leys 1** a piece of music made up of parts of other musical works **2** a mass or crowd (of different types) mixed together: *a medley of ideas*
**meek** /miːk/ *adj* gentle in nature; yielding to others' actions and opinions –**meekly** *adv* –**meekness** *n* [U]
**meet**[1] /miːt/ *v* **met** /met/, **meeting 1** [I;T] to come together (with), by chance or arrangement: *Let's meet for dinner.*|*I met him in the street.*|*The whole school met to hear the speech.*|*I'll drive to the station and meet her off the train.*|*The two cars met* HEAD-ON. (=had an accident) **2** [I;T] to get to know or be introduced (to) for the first time: *Come to the party and meet some new people.* **3** [I;T] to touch, (as if) naturally: *Their lips met (in a kiss).* **4** [I] to join: *The two roads meet just north of Birmingham.* **5** [T] to find or experience; MEET **with**: *She met her death in a plane crash.* **6** [T *with*] to answer, esp. in opposition: *His speech was met with cries of anger.* **7** [T] to satisfy: *Does the hotel meet your expectations?*|*This new road meets a long-felt need.* **8** [T] to pay: *Can you meet your debts?* **9 more** (in/to something) **than meets the eye** hidden facts, difficulties, or reasons (in or for something): *The job seems easy, but there's more to it than meets the eye.*

**meet up** *v adv* [I *with*] *infml* to meet, by arrangement: *Let's meet up after the play.*

**meet with** sbdy./sthg. *v prep* [T] **1** to experience or find by chance: *I met with some difficulties on the way.*|*They met with an accident on their way back.* **2** *esp AmE* to have a meeting with: *Our representatives met with several heads of state.*

**meet**[2] *n* a gathering of people, esp. (*BrE*) on horses with hunting dogs (HOUNDS) to hunt foxes or (*AmE*) for sports events
**meet·ing** /ˈmiːtɪŋ/ *n* **1** a gathering of people, esp. for a purpose: *I was late for the meeting so they started without me.* **2** the coming together of two or more people, by chance or arrangement: *Our meeting at the station was quite by chance.*
**meg·a·lo·ma·ni·a** /ˌmegələˈmeɪnɪə/ *n* [U] (the condition in which one holds) the belief that one is more important, powerful, etc., than one really is –**megalomaniac** /-ˈmeɪniæk/ *n*
**meg·a·phone** /ˈmegəfəʊn/ also **loudhailer**– *n* an instrument shaped like a horn which makes the voice louder when spoken through it, so that it can be heard over a distance –compare MICROPHONE
**meg·a·ton** /ˈmegətʌn/ a measure of force of an explosion equal to that of a million tons of TNT: *a 5-megaton atomic bomb*
**mel·an·chol·y**[1] /ˈmelənkəli‖-kɑli/ *n* [U] sadness, esp. over a period of time and not for any particular reason –**melancholic** /-ˈkɒlɪk‖-ˈkɑ-/ *adj*
**melancholy**[2] *adj* sad: *alone and feeling melancholy*|*melancholy news*
**mel·ee** /ˈmeleɪ‖ˈmeɪleɪ/ *n* [*usu. sing.*] a struggling or disorderly crowd
**mel·li·flu·ous** /mɪ̈ˈlɪfluəs/ *adj* (of words, music, or a voice) with a sweet smooth flowing sound
**mel·low**[1] /ˈmeləʊ/ *adj* **1** (of fruit and wine) sweet and ripe or MATURE, esp. after being kept for a long time **2** (of colours and surfaces) soft, warm, and smooth **3** (of people) wise and gentle through age or experience –**mellowly** *adv* –**mellowness** *n* [U]
**mellow**[2] *v* [I;T] to (cause to) become (more) MELLOW with the passing of time: *The colours mellowed as the sun went down.*|*The years have mellowed him.*
**me·lod·ic** /mɪ̈ˈlɒdɪk‖mɪ̈ˈlɑ-/ *adj* **1** [*no comp.*] of or having a MELODY **2** →MELODIOUS
**me·lo·di·ous** /mɪ̈ˈləʊdɪəs/ *adj* sweet-sounding; tuneful –**melodiously** *adv*
**mel·o·dra·ma** /ˈmelədrɑːmə/ *n* [C;U] a (type of) exciting play, full of sudden events and strong feelings: (fig.) *There was quite a melodrama when the child lost his mother in the street.*
**mel·o·dra·mat·ic** /ˌmelədrəˈmætɪk/ *adj* showing, or intended to produce, strong and excited feelings; (too) EMOTIONAL: *a melodramatic speech*
**mel·o·dy** /ˈmelədi/ *n* **-dies 1** a song or tune **2** the part which forms a clearly recognizable tune in a larger arrangement of notes
**mel·on** /ˈmelən/ *n* [C;U] a large rounded fruit, with a firm skin and juicy flesh which can be eaten
**melt** /melt/ *v* **1** [T] to cause (a solid) to become liquid: *The sun melted the snow.* **2** [I] (of a solid) to become liquid: *The ice is melting in the sun.*|(fig.) *His anger quickly melted.* (=disappeared) –compare FREEZE
USAGE The adjective **molten** means **melted,** but is used only of things that melt at a very high temperature: **molten** *rock/metal*|**melted** *chocolate/ice.*

**melt away** *v adv* [I] to disappear easily: *The opposition melted away after their leader died.*

**melt** sthg.↔**down** *v adv* [T] to make (a metal object) liquid by heating, esp. so as to use the metal again
**mem·ber** /ˈmembəʳ/ *n* [*of*] a person belonging to a

club, group, etc.: *a member of the family|a member of a political party* –opposite **non-member**
**mem·ber·ship** /'membəʃɪp‖-ər-/ *n* **1** [U] the state of being a member of a club, society, etc.: *My membership has just been renewed.* **2** [C +*sing./pl. v*] all the members of a club, society, etc.
**mem·brane** /'membreɪn/ *n* [C;U] soft thin skin in the body, covering or connecting parts of it
**me·men·to** /m$\frac{1}{ə}$'mentəʊ/ *n* **-tos** a small object which reminds one, esp. of a holiday, a friend, etc.
**mem·o** /'meməʊ/ *n* **-os** also **memorandum**– a note from one person or office to another within an organization
**mem·oirs** /'memwɑːz‖-ɑrz/ *n* [P] the story of a person's own life, esp. that of an important public figure: *The old general has started to write his memoirs.*
**mem·o·ra·ble** /'memərəbəl/ *adj* worth remembering; special in some way: *The film was memorable for* (=remembered because of) *the fine acting of the two main characters.|a memorable trip abroad* –**memorably** *adv*
**mem·o·ran·dum** /ˌmemə'rændəm/ *n* **-da** /də/ *or* **-dums** *fml* for MEMO
**me·mo·ri·al** /m$\frac{1}{ə}$'mɔːrɪəl‖m$\frac{1}{ə}$'mor-/ *n* **1** an object, such as a stone MONUMENT, in a public place in memory of a person, event, etc.: *a war memorial* **2** a custom which serves the same purpose: *The church service is a memorial to those killed in the war.*
**mem·o·rize** ‖also **-rise** *BrE* /'meməraɪz/ *v* **-rized, -rizing** [T] to learn and remember, on purpose: *He memorized the list of dates.*
**mem·o·ry** /'meməri/ *n* **-ries 1** [C;U] (an) ability to remember events and experience: *She's got a good memory for dates/faces.|He played the tune* **from memory.** (=without written music) **2** [C *of*] an example of remembering: *one of my earliest memories* **3** [S] the time during which things happened which can be remembered: *There have been two wars within the memory of my grandfather/***within living memory.** (=which can be remembered by people now alive) **4** [C] the opinion held of someone after his death: *to praise his memory* **5** the part of a computer or CALCULATOR in which information (DATA) can be stored until it is wanted
**men** /men/ *n pl. of* MAN
**men·ace**[1] /'men$\frac{1}{ə}$s/ *n* **1** [C;U *to*] something which suggests a threat or brings danger: *He spoke with menace.|The busy road outside the school is a menace.* **2** [C] *infml* a troublesome person or thing
**menace**[2] *v* **-aced, -acing** [T] *esp. fml* to threaten: *The people are being menaced by the threat of war.*
**me·nac·ing** /'men$\frac{1}{ə}$sɪŋ/ *adj* threatening: *a menacing look|Those dark clouds look rather menacing.* (=there may be a storm) –**menacingly** *adv*
**me·na·ge·rie** /m$\frac{1}{ə}$'nædʒəri/ *n* a collection of wild animals kept privately or for the public to see; zoo
**mend**[1] /mend/ *v* **1** [I;T] **a** to repair (a hole, break, fault, etc.) in (something): *I'll mend that shirt.* **b** (of something broken or worn) to be able to be repaired: *This old shoe won't mend.* **2** [I] to regain one's health: *He's mending nicely after his accident.* **3 mend one's ways** to improve one's behaviour –**mender** *n*
**mend**[2] *n* **1** a part mended after breaking or wearing; PATCH or DARN **2 on the mend** getting better after illness
**me·ni·al** /'miːnɪəl/ *adj* (of a job) humble and not interesting or important: *menial work* –**menially** *adv*
**men·o·pause** /'menəpɔːz/ also **change of life** *euph*– *n* [*the* S] the time when a woman's PERIODs (4) stop, usu. in middle age
**men·stru·al** /'menstrʊəl/ *adj* concerning a woman's PERIOD (4)
**men·stru·ate** /'menstrʊeɪt/ *v* **-ated, -ating** [I] to have a PERIOD (4) –**menstruation** /-'eɪʃən / *n* [C;U]
**men·tal** /'mentl/ *adj* [*no comp.*] **1** of the mind: *mental powers|mental illness* –compare PHYSICAL **2** [A] done only in or with the mind, esp. without the help of writing: *mental* ARITHMETIC **3** [A] concerning disorders or illness of the mind: *a mental hospital|mental treatment|a mental patient* **4** [F] *infml* mad: *Don't listen to him; he's mental.* –**mentally** *adv*
**men·tal·i·ty** /men'tæl$\frac{1}{ə}$ti/ *n* **-ties 1** [U] the abilities and powers of the mind: *of weak mentality* **2** [C] character; habits of thought: *I can't understand the mentality of people who say such things.*
**men·thol** /'menθɒl‖-θɔl, -θɑl/ *n* [U] a white substance with a MINTY[1] taste –**mentholated** *adj*
**men·tion**[1] /'menʃən/ *v* [T] **1** [+*that*] to tell about in a few words, spoken or written: *He mentioned their interest in sport/that they were interested in sport.* **2** to say the name of: *He mentioned a useful book.* **3 Don't mention it** *polite* There's no need for thanks; I'm glad to help: *"Thanks very much." "Don't mention it."* **4 not to mention (something/the fact that)** and in addition there's . . .: *They have three dogs to look after, not to mention the cat and the bird.* –see also UNMENTIONABLE
**mention**[2] *n* **1** [U] the act of mentioning: *There was no mention of our team in the newspaper.* **2** [C *usu. sing.*] a short remark about something: *The actor's wedding got a mention on television.*
**men·tor** /'mentəʳ/ *n* a person who habitually advises another
**men·u** /'menjuː/ *n* **-us** a list of dishes in a meal or to be ordered as separate meals, esp. in a restaurant –see picture on page 521
**mer·ce·na·ry**[1] /'mɜːsənəri‖'mɜrsəneri/ *n* **-ries** a soldier who fights for any country or group that pays him, not for his own country
**mercenary**[2] *adj derog* influenced by the wish to gain money or other reward
**mer·chan·dise** /'mɜːtʃəndaɪz, -daɪs‖'mɜr-/ *n* [U] things for sale; goods for trade
**mer·chant** /'mɜːtʃənt‖'mɜr-/ *n* a person who buys and sells goods, esp. in large amounts: *a coal merchant*
**merchant na·vy** /ˌ·· '··/ *n* [C +*sing./pl. v*] (the people who work on) those ships of a nation which are used in trade, not in war
**mer·ci·ful** /'mɜːsɪfəl‖'mɜr-/ *adj* showing mercy; forgiving rather than punishing: *The merciful king saved him from death.* –see also MERCILESS –**mercifully** *adv*
**mer·ci·less** /'mɜːsɪl$\frac{1}{ə}$s‖'mɜr-/ *adj* [*to*] showing no mercy; punishing rather than forgiving: *a merciless*

*judge* –see also MERCIFUL **–mercilessly** *adv* **–mercilessness** *n* [U]

**mer·cu·ri·al** /mɜː'kjʊərɪəl‖mɜr-/ *adj* [*no comp.*] quick to change: *a mercurial temper* **–mercurially** *adv*

**mer·cu·ry** /'mɜːkjʊri‖'mɜrkjəri/ also **quicksilver**– *n* [U] a heavy silver-white metal that is liquid at ordinary temperatures and is used in THERMOMETERS, BAROMETERS, etc.

**mer·cy** /'mɜːsi‖'mɜrsi/ *n* **1** [U] willingness to forgive, not to punish: *The general showed no mercy, and his prisoners were all killed.* **2** [S] a fortunate event: **It's a mercy** *the accident happened so close to the hospital.* **3 at the mercy of** powerless against: *They were lost at sea, at the mercy of wind and weather.*

**mere** /mɪəʳ/ *adj* **1** [A *no comp.*] nothing more than (a): *She lost the election by a mere 20 votes.* **2 the merest** as small or unimportant as possible: *The merest little thing makes him nervous.*

**mere·ly** /'mɪəli‖-ər-/ *adv* only . . . and nothing else: *He merely wants to know the truth.*

**merge** /mɜːdʒ‖mɜrdʒ/ *v* **merged, merging 1** [I *into*] to become lost in or part of something else/each other: *One colour merged into the other.|My friends merged into the crowd and I lost sight of them.* **2** [I;T *with*] to join together so as to become one: *The roads merge a mile ahead.|The two companies merged to become stronger.*

**merg·er** /'mɜːdʒəʳ‖'mɜr-/ *n* a joining together of two or more companies or firms

**me·rid·i·an** /mə'rɪdɪən/ *n* an imaginary line drawn from the top point of the earth (NORTH POLE) to the bottom (SOUTH POLE) over the surface of the earth, one of several used on maps to show position

**me·ringue** /mə'ræŋ/ *n* [C;U] (a light round cake made of) a mixture of sugar and the white part of eggs, beaten together

**mer·it**[1] /'mer½t/ *n* **1** [U] the quality of deserving praise, reward, etc.; personal worth: *There's little merit in passing the examination if you cheated.* **2 on its/his, etc., (own) merits** by or for its/his, etc., own qualities, good or bad, not by one's own opinions: *We must judge this plan on its own merits.*

**merit**[2] *v* [T +*v-ing*] *fml* to deserve; have a right to: *He merited all the praise they gave him.*

**mer·i·toc·ra·cy** /ˌmer½'tɒkrəsi‖-'tɑ-/ *n* **-cies** a social system which gives the highest positions to those with the most ability

**mer·i·to·ri·ous** /ˌmer½'tɔːrɪəs‖-'tor-/ *adj fml* deserving reward or praise

**mer·maid** /'mɜːmeɪd‖'mɜr-/ *n* (in stories) a young woman with the bottom half of her body like a fish's tail

**mer·ri·ment** /'merɪmənt/ *n* [U] laughter and sounds of enjoyment

**mer·ry** /'meri/ *adj* **-rier, -riest 1** cheerful; fond of laughter, fun, etc.: *a merry person|a merry smile* **2** *BrE infml* rather drunk: *We got a bit merry at the party.* **3 Merry Christmas!** Have a happy time at Christmas **–merrily** *adv* **–merriness** *n* [U]

**merry-go-round** ‖/'·· · ˌ·/ also **roundabout** *BrE*‖ **carousel** *AmE*– *n* a machine in an amusement park on which esp. children can ride round and round sitting on wooden animals

**mer·ry·mak·ing** /'meri,meɪkɪŋ/ *n* [U] *infml lit* fun and enjoyment, esp. eating, drinking, and games: *Christmas merrymaking*

**mesh**[1] /meʃ/ *n* **1** [C;U] (a piece of) material woven in a fine network with small holes between the threads: *We put some/a fine wire mesh over the chimney so that the birds wouldn't fall in.* **2** [C *usu. pl.*] the threads in such a network: *The fish were caught in the meshes of the net.*

**mesh**[2] *v* [I *with*] to connect; be held (together): *The teeth on the* GEARS *mesh as they turn round.*

**mes·mer·ize** ‖also **-ise** *BrE* /'mezməraɪz/ *v* **-ized, -izing** [T] to surprise very much, esp. so as to make speechless and unable to move: *We stood by the lake, mesmerized by the flashing colours of the fish.*

**mess** /mes/ *n* **1** [S;U] a state of disorder or untidiness; dirty material: *This room's in a mess.|The company's affairs are in a terrible mess.* **2** [C *usu. sing.*] *infml* a person whose appearance, behaviour, or thinking is in a disordered state: *You look a mess–you can't go to the office like that.* **3** [C] a place to eat for members of the armed forces: *the officers' mess* **4 make a mess of** *infml* to disorder, spoil, ruin, etc.: *This illness has made a mess of my holiday plans.*

**mess a·bout** also **mess around**– *v adv* **1** [I] to be lazy: *He spent all day Sunday just messing about.* **2** [I] to act or speak stupidly: *Stop messing about and tell me clearly what happened!* **3** [T] (**mess** sbdy. **about**) to treat badly or carelessly: *Don't mess me about; I want the money you promised me.*

**mes·sage** /'mesɪdʒ/ *n* **1** [C +*to-v/that*] a spoken or written piece of information passed from one person to another: *There's a message for you from your brother.* **2** [*the* S] the important or central idea: *the message of this book* **3 get the message** *infml* to understand what is wanted or meant

**mes·sen·ger** /'mesəndʒəʳ/ *n* a person who brings one or more messages

**mes·si·ah** /m½'saɪə/ *n* [*usu. sing.*] (*often cap.*) a new leader in a (new) religion, esp. Christ in the Christian religion

**Mes·srs** /'mesəz‖-ərz/ *abbrev.* (used chiefly in writing as the *pl.* of MR, esp.in the names of firms): *Messrs Ford and Dobson, piano repairers*

**mess** sthg.↔**up** *v adv* [T] *infml* to disorder, spoil, etc.: *Her late arrival messes up our plans.* **–mess-up** *n*

**mess·y** /'mesi/ *adj* **-ier, -iest 1** untidy **2** (causing the body to become) dirty: *It's a messy business having a tooth taken out.* **–messily** *adv* **–messiness** *n* [U]

**met** /met/ *v past tense and participle of* MEET

**me·tab·o·lis·m** /m½'tæbəlɪzəm/ *n* the chemical activities in a living thing by which it gains power (ENERGY), esp. from food

**met·al** /'metl/ *n* [C;U] any usu. solid shiny mineral substance which can be shaped by pressure and used for passing an electric current: *Copper and silver are both metals.|a metal box*

**me·tal·lic** /m½'tælɪk/ *adj* of or like metal: *metallic colours|a metallic sound*

**met·al·lur·gy** /'metəlɜːdʒi, m½'tælədʒi‖'metəlɜrdʒi/ *n* [U] the study and practice of removing metals from rocks, melting them, and using them **–metallurgist** *n*

**met·a·mor·pho·sis** /ˌmetə'mɔːfəs½s‖-ɔr-/ *n* **-ses**

/siːz/ [C;U] (a) complete change from one form to another: *A* BUTTERFLY *is produced by metamorphosis from a* CATERPILLAR.

**met·a·phor** /ˈmetəfəʳ, -fɔːʳ‖-fɔr/ *n* [C;U] (the use of) a phrase which describes one thing by stating another thing with which it can be compared (as in *the roses in her cheeks* or *The rain came down in buckets*) without using the words "as" or "like" –compare SIMILE **–metaphorical** /-ˈfɒrɪkəl‖-ˈfɔ-, -ˈfɑ-/ *adj* **–metaphorically** *adv*

**met·a·phys·ics** /ˌmetəˈfɪzɪks/ *n* [U] a branch of the study of thought (PHILOSOPHY) concerned with the science of being and knowing **–metaphysical** *adj* **–metaphysically** *adv*

**me·te·or** /ˈmiːtɪəʳ/ *n* a small piece of matter floating in space that forms a line of light if it falls into the earth's air (ATMOSPHERE)

**me·te·or·ic** /ˌmiːtiˈɒrɪk‖-ˈɔrɪk, -ˈɑrɪk/ *adj* like a METEOR, esp. in being very fast or in being bright and short-lived: *a meteoric rise to fame* **–meteorically** *adv*

**me·te·o·rite** /ˈmiːtɪəraɪt/ *n* a small METEOR that has landed on the earth without being totally burnt up

**me·te·o·rol·o·gy** /ˌmiːtɪəˈrɒlədʒi‖-ˈrɑ-/ *n* [U] the study of weather conditions **–meteorological** /ˌmiːtɪərəˈlɒdʒɪkəl‖-ˈlɑ-/ *adj* **–meteorologist** *n*

**me·ter¹** /ˈmiːtəʳ/ *n* a machine which measures the amount of something used: *a gas meter*

**meter²** *n AmE* for METRE

**meth·od** /ˈmeθəd/ *n* **1** [C] a way or manner (of doing): *new methods of building|old-fashioned teaching methods* **2** [C;U] (the use of) an orderly system or arrangement: *There's not much method in the way they do their accounts.* **3 method in one's madness** a hidden system behind disordered actions –see also METHODOLOGY

**me·thod·i·cal** /mə̇ˈθɒdɪkəl‖mə̇ˈθɑ-/ *adj* careful; using an ordered system: *a methodical person|a methodical way of doing things* **–methodically** *adv*

**Meth·o·dis·m** /ˈmeθədɪzəm/ *n* [U] the beliefs of a Christian group which follows the teachings of John Wesley **–Methodist** *adj, n*

**meth·o·dol·o·gy** /ˌmeθəˈdɒlədʒi‖-ˈdɑ-/ *n* **-gies** [C;U] *tech* the set of methods used for study or action in a particular subject, as in science or education: *a new methodology of teaching* –see also METHOD **–methodological** /ˌmeθədəˈlɒdʒɪkəl‖-ˈlɑ-/ *adj* **–methodologically** *adv*

**meth·yl·at·ed spir·its** /ˌmeθə̇leɪtə̇d ˈspɪrə̇ts/ *BrE* also **meths** /meθs/ *infml– n* [U] alcohol for burning, in lamps, heaters, etc.

**me·tic·u·lous** /mə̇ˈtɪkjʊləs‖-kjə-/ *adj* very careful, with attention to detail: *meticulous drawings|a meticulous worker* **–meticulously** *adv* **–meticulousness** *n* [U]

**me·tre¹** *BrE*‖**meter** *AmE* /ˈmiːtəʳ/ *n* (a measure of length equal to) 39·37 inches

**metre²** *BrE*‖**meter** *AmE n* [C;U] (any type of) arrangement of notes or esp. words (as in poetry) into strong and weak beats –compare RHYTHM **–metrical** /ˈmetrɪkəl/ *adj* **–metrically** *adv*

**met·ric** /ˈmetrɪk/ *adj* concerning the system of measurement (**metric system**) based on the metre and kilogram

**met·ri·ca·tion** /ˌmetrɪˈkeɪʃən/ *n* [U] the change from standards of measurement that had been used before (as, in Britain, the foot and the pound) to metres, grams, etc.

**met·ro** /ˈmetrəʊ/ *n* **-ros** [C; *the* S] (*often cap.*) an underground railway system in cities in France or various other countries: *the Leningrad Metro|Can you get there by* **metro**? –compare UNDERGROUND²

**met·ro·nome** /ˈmetrənəʊm/ *n* an instrument with an arm that moves from side to side to give the speed at which a piece of music should be played

**me·trop·o·lis** /mə̇ˈtrɒpələ̇s‖mə̇ˈtrɑ-/ *n* [C; *the* S] *fml* a chief city or the capital city of a country **–metropolitan** /ˌmetrəˈpɒlə̇tən‖-ˈpɑ-/ *adj*

**met·tle** /ˈmetl/ *n* [U] *fml often apprec* courage; the will to continue: *The runner fell, but he* **showed his mettle** *by continuing in the race.*

**mew** /mjuː/ *n, v* [C;I] →MIAOW

**mews** /mjuːz/ *n* **mews** a street in a city, where horses were once kept, now partly rebuilt for people to live in

**mez·za·nine** /ˈmezəniːn, ˈmetsə-‖ˈmezə-/ *n* a floor that comes between two other floors of a building

**mg** *written abbrev. said as:* MILLIGRAM

**mi·aow** *BrE*‖**meow** *AmE* /miˈaʊ/ *n, v* [C;I] (to make) the crying sound a cat makes

**mice** /maɪs/ *n pl. of* MOUSE

**mi·crobe** /ˈmaɪkrəʊb/ *n* a living creature that is so small that it cannot be seen without a microscope, and that may cause disease

**mi·cro·chip** /ˈmaɪkrəˌtʃɪp/ also **chip** *infml– n* a tiny set of connected ELECTRONIC parts produced as a single unit on a slice of material such as SILICON, used in computers, calculators, etc.

**mi·cro·cos·m** /ˈmaɪkrəkɒzəm‖-kɑ-/ *n* [*of*] a little self-contained world that represents all the qualities, activities, etc., of something larger

**mi·cro·fiche** /ˈmaɪkrəfiːʃ/ *n* **-fiche** *or* **-fiches** [C;U] a sheet or piece of MICROFILM

**mi·cro·film¹** /ˈmaɪkrəˌfɪlm/ *n* [C;U] (a length of) film for photographing a page, a letter, etc., in a very small size so that it can be easily stored

**microfilm²** *v* [T] to photograph (something) using MICROFILM

**mi·cro·phone** /ˈmaɪkrəfəʊn/ also **mike** *infml– n* an instrument for receiving sound waves and changing them into electrical waves, used in broadcasting or recording sound (as in radio, telephones, TAPE RECORDERS, etc.) or in making sounds louder: *He used a microphone so that everyone could hear him.* –compare MEGAPHONE; see picture on page 463

**mi·cro·pro·ces·sor** /ˌmaɪkrəʊˈprəʊsesəʳ/ *n tech* a very small computer, or part of this, which contains one or more MICROCHIPS

**mi·cro·scope** /ˈmaɪkrəskəʊp/ *n* an instrument that makes objects which are too small to be seen by the eye look larger, and so can be used for examining them –compare TELESCOPE¹

**mi·cro·scop·ic** /ˌmaɪkrəˈskɒpɪk‖-ˈskɑ-/ *adj* **1** by or as if by means of a microscope **2** *infml* very small: *It's impossible to read his microscopic handwriting.* –see Study Notes on page 494 **–microscopically** *adv*

**mi·cro·wave** /ˈmaɪkrəweɪv/ *n* an electric wave of very short length, used in sending messages by radio, in RADAR, and esp. in cooking food: *a microwave oven*

**mid·day** /ˌmɪd'deɪ◄‖'mɪd-deɪ/ *n* [U] the middle of the day; 12 o'clock NOON: *We have a meal at midday.* –compare MIDNIGHT

**mid·dle¹** /'mɪdl/ *adj* [A] in or nearly in the centre: *Ours is the middle house in that row of five.*

**middle²** *n* [*the* S] **1** the central part, point, or position: *He planted rose trees in the middle of the garden.|This bill must be paid not later than the middle of the month.* **2** *infml* the waist or the part below the waist: *He's getting fatter round the middle.* **3 in the middle of something/doing something** in the course of or busy with something/doing something

USAGE **Centre** is similar to **middle,** but it suggests an exact point: *Their house is in the* **middle** *of a field.|At the beginning of the game, the football is placed in the* **centre** *of the field.*

**middle age** /ˌ·· '·◄/ *n* [U] the years between youth and old age **–middle-aged** *adj: He's nearly 60, but he still considers himself to be middle-aged.*

**Middle Ag·es** /ˌ·· '··/ *n* [*the* P] the period in European history between about AD 1100 and 1500

**middle class** /ˌ·· '·◄/ *adj, n* [U *+sing./pl. v*] (of) the social class to which people belong who are neither very noble, wealthy, etc., nor workers with their hands –see WORKING CLASS (USAGE)

**Middle East** /ˌ·· '·◄/ also **Mid East** *AmE– n* [*the* S] the countries in Asia west of India, such as Iran, Iraq, Syria, etc., **–Middle Eastern** *adj*

**mid·dle·man** /'mɪdlmæn/ *n* **-men** /men/ a person who buys goods from a producer, and sells (at a gain) to a shopkeeper or directly to a user

**middle-of-the-road** /ˌ·· · · '·◄/ *adj* favouring ideas, esp. political ideas, that most people would agree with; not EXTREME

**mid·dling** /'mɪdəlɪŋ/ *adj infml* between large and small, good and bad, etc.; average

**midge** /mɪdʒ/ *n* a very small flying insect, like a mosquito, that bites

**midg·et** /'mɪdʒ½t/ *n* **1** [C] a very, or unusually, small person **2** [A] very small: *midget cars|midget cameras*

**Mid·lands** /'mɪdləndz/ *n* [*the* P] the central parts of England: *the industrial Midlands*

**mid·night** /'mɪdnaɪt/ *n* [U] 12 o'clock at night: *The party finished at midnight.|We went for a midnight swim.* (=in the middle of the night) –compare MIDDAY

**mid·riff** /'mɪdrɪf/ *n* the part of the human body between the chest and the waist

**mid·ship·man** /'mɪdʃɪpmən/ *n* **-men** /mən/ [A;C] a boy or young man who is being trained to become a naval officer

**midst** /mɪdst/ *n* [U] *lit or old use* the middle part or position: *the enemy* **in our midst** (=among us)

**mid·way** /ˌmɪd'weɪ◄‖'mɪdweɪ/ *adj, adv* halfway or in a middle position: *There's a small village midway between these two towns.*

**mid·week** /ˌmɪd'wiːk◄‖'mɪdwiːk/ *n, adj* [U] (happening during) the middle days of the week; Tuesday, Thursday, and esp. Wednesday

**mid·wife** /'mɪdwaɪf/ *n* **-wives** /waɪvz/ someone who has received special training to help women when they are giving birth to children

**mien** /miːn/ *n lit* a person's appearance, manner, or expression: *a thoughtful and solemn mien*

**might¹** /maɪt/ *v negative contraction* **mightn't** [I+to-*v*] **1** (shows a possibility): *He might come, but it's very unlikely.|He might have missed the train.* (=perhaps he missed it)|*I might have thought that once, but I don't believe it now.* –see USAGE **2** (used as the past of *may*): *I thought it might rain.* (=I thought *"It may rain!"*)|*They asked if they might go home.* (=They asked *"May we go home?"*) **3** *BrE* (used instead of *may,* for asking permission politely): *"Might I come in?" "Yes, you may."* –see Study Notes on page 386 **4** (used like *ought*): *You might at least say "thank you" when someone helps you.|You might have offered to help!* (=I wish you had, but you didn't)|*I might have known she'd refuse!* (=it was typical of her to refuse) **5 might well** to be likely to: *We lost the football match, but we might well have won if one of our players hadn't been hurt.* **6 might as well** MAY as well (MAY (4)): *No one will eat this food; it might just as well be thrown away.*

USAGE When it is showing a possibility, **might** sometimes suggests a smaller possibility than **may,** but often these words are used to mean the same thing: *I* **may/might** *see you tonight; I don't know yet.*

**might²** *n* [U] power; strength; force: *He tried* **with all his might** *to move the heavy rock from the road.*

**might·n't** /'maɪtənt/ *v BrE short for* might not: *They mightn't come.*

**might·y** /'maɪti/ *adj* **-ier, -iest 1** *esp. lit* having great power or strength; very great: *He struck the rock a mighty blow.* **2 high and mighty** *derog* showing too much pride and a feeling of one's own importance **–mightily** *adv*

**mi·graine** /'miːgreɪn, 'maɪ-‖'maɪ-/ *n* [C;U] a severe and repeated headache, usu. with disorder of the eyesight

**mi·grant** /'maɪgrənt/ *n* a person or animal or esp. bird that MIGRATES or is migrating: *Migrant workers move from country to country in search of work.*

**mi·grate** /maɪ'greɪt‖'maɪgreɪt/ *v* **-grated, -grating** [I *from, to*] **1** (of birds and fish) to travel regularly from one part of the world to another, according to the seasons of the year –see EMIGRATE (USAGE) **2** to move from one place to another; change one's place of living, esp. for a limited period: *Some tribes migrate with their cattle in search of fresh grass.* **–migratory** /'maɪgrətəri‖-tori/ *adj*

**mi·gra·tion** /maɪ'greɪʃən/ *n* [C;U] (an example of) the act of migrating (MIGRATE): *Scientists have studied the migration of fish over long distances.*

**mike** /maɪk/ *n infml* for MICROPHONE

**mild** /maɪld/ *adj* **1** *usu. apprec* (of a person) gentle: *He has too mild a nature to get angry, even if he has good cause.* **2** not hard or causing much discomfort or suffering; slight: *The thief was given a milder punishment than he deserved.|It's been a mild winter this year.* (=not a cold winter) –compare SEVERE **3** (of food, drink, etc.) not strong or bitter in taste: *mild cheese* **–mildness** *n* [U]

**mil·dew¹** /'mɪldjuː‖-duː/ *n* [U] a soft usu. whitish growth that forms on food, leather, plants, etc., that have been kept for a long time in warm and slightly wet conditions **–mildewy** *adj*

**mildew²** *v* [I;T] to (cause to) become covered with MILDEW: *mildewed plants*

**mild·ly** /'maɪldli/ *adv* **1** in a MILD manner: *She complained loudly to the shopkeeper, who answered her mildly.* **2** slightly: *I was only mildly interested in the story I read in the newspaper.* **3 to put it mildly** describing something as gently as possible: *The new film has not been a great success, to put it mildly.*

**mile** /maɪl/ *n* (a measure of length equal to) 1,609 metres or 1,760 yards: *He has a 10-mile drive each day to and from his work.*|*They walked for miles* (=a very long way) *without seeing another person.*|(fig.) *He was* **miles out** *in his calculations.* (=they were completely wrong)

**mile·age** /'maɪlɪdʒ/ *n* **1** [C *usu. sing.*;U] the distance that is travelled, measured in miles: *What mileage has your car done?*|*What mileage does your car do per gallon?* **2** [U] *infml* an amount of use: *The newspapers are getting a lot of mileage out of the royal wedding–there's a new story about it every day.*

**mile·om·e·ter, milometer** /maɪ'lɒmɪ̈tər‖-'lɑ-/ *n* an instrument fitted in a vehicle to record the number of miles it travels –see picture on page 85

**mile·stone** /'maɪlstəʊn/ *n* **1** a stone at the side of a road, on which is marked the number of miles to the next town **2** an important event in a person's life or in history: *The invention of the wheel was a milestone in the history of the world.*

**mi·lieu** /'mi:ljɜ:‖mi:'ljɜ:, -'ju:/ *n* **-s** or **-x** [*usu. sing.*] surroundings, esp. a person's social surroundings

**mil·i·tant¹** /'mɪlɪ̈tənt/ *adj* having or expressing a readiness to fight or use force: *A few militant members of the crowd attacked the speaker.* –compare MILITARY **–militancy** *n* [U] **–militantly** *adv*

**militant²** *n* a MILITANT person: *They say these student disorders have been caused by a few militants.*

**mil·i·ta·ry¹** /'mɪlɪ̈təri‖-teri/ *adj* [A] of, for, by, or connected with soldiers, armies, or war fought by armies: *In some countries all the young men do a year's military service.*|*combined naval and military operations*|*a military hospital* –compare MILITANT

**military²** *n* [*the* P] soldiers; the army: *The government called in the military to help the police.*

**mil·i·tate a·gainst** sthg. /'mɪlɪ̈teɪt/ *v prep* **-tated, -tating** [T +*v-ing*] to act as a reason against: *The fact that he'd been in prison militated against his chances of getting a job in a bank.*

**mi·li·tia** /mɪ̈'lɪʃə/ *n* [C +*sing.*/*pl. v*] a body of men not belonging to a regular army, but trained as soldiers to serve only in their home country: *The militia is/are sometimes used for dealing with* RIOTS.

**milk¹** /mɪlk/ *n* [U] **1** a white liquid produced by human or animal females for the feeding of their young, and (in the case of cows' and goats' milk) often drunk by human beings or made into butter and cheese: *a bottle of milk* **2** a whitish liquid or juice obtained from certain plants and trees: COCONUT *milk* **3 cry over spilt milk** to waste time being sorry about something bad that cannot be repaired or changed for the better

**milk²** *v* **1** [I;T] **a** to take milk from (a cow, goat, or other animal): *The farmer milks (the cows) twice a day.* **b** (of a cow, goat, etc.) to give milk: *This cow isn't milking very well.* **2** [T] *infml* to get money, knowledge of a secret, etc., from (someone or something) by clever or dishonest means: *The politician was too experienced to be milked by newspaper men.* (=he refused to give them any news)

**milk float** /'· ·/ *n BrE* a vehicle used by a MILKMAN for delivering milk, now usu. driven by electricity

**milk·maid** /'mɪlkmeɪd/ *n* (esp. formerly) a woman who milks cows

**milk·man** /'mɪlkmən/ *n* **-men** /mən/ a man who sells milk, esp. one who goes from house to house each day to deliver it

**milk shake** /,· '·‖'· ·/ *n* a drink of milk and usu. ice cream shaken up together and given the taste of fruit, chocolate, etc.

**milk·y** /'mɪlki/ *adj* **-ier, -iest 1** made of, containing, or like milk: *I like my coffee milky.* (=made with a lot of milk) **2** (of water or other liquids) not clear; cloudy; having a milklike appearance **–milkiness** *n* [U]

**mill¹** /mɪl/ *n* **1** (a building containing) a large machine for crushing corn or grain into flour –see also WINDMILL **2** a factory or WORKSHOP: *Cotton cloth is made in a cotton mill.* **3** a small machine, used esp. in a kitchen, in which a stated material can be crushed into powder: *a pepper mill*

**mill²** *v* [T] **1** to crush (grain) in a mill **2** to produce (flour) by this means

**mill about/around** *v adv* [I] *infml* to move without purpose in large numbers: *There were a lot of people milling about in the streets.*

**mil·len·ni·um** /mɪ'leniəm/ *n* **-nia** /nɪə/ **1** a period of 1,000 years **2 the millennium** a future age in which all people will be happy and contented

**mil·le·pede** /'mɪlɪ̈pi:d/ *n* →MILLIPEDE

**mill·er** /'mɪlər/ *n* a man who owns or works a mill that produces flour

**mil·let** /'mɪlɪ̈t/ *n* [U] the small seeds of certain grasslike plants used as food: *millet cakes*

**mil·li·gram, -gramme** /'mɪlɪ̈græm/ *n* (a measure of weight equal to) 1,000th of a gram

**mil·li·me·tre** *BrE*‖**-ter** *AmE* /'mɪlɪ̈mi:tər/ *n* (a measure of length equal to) 1,000th of a metre

**mil·li·ner** /'mɪlɪ̈nər/ *n* a person who makes and/or sells women's hats

**mil·li·ne·ry** /'mɪlɪ̈nəri‖-neri/ *n* [U] the articles made or sold by a MILLINER

**mil·lion** /'mɪljən/ *determiner,n,pron* **million** *or* **millions** (the number) 1,000,000; $10^6$ –see HUNDRED (USAGE); –see Study Notes on page 494 **–millionth** *determiner,n,pron,adv*

**mil·lion·aire** /,mɪljə'neər/ **millionairess** /-rɪ̈s/ *fem.*– *n* a person who has 1,000,000 pounds or dollars; very wealthy person

**mil·li·pede, millepede** /'mɪlɪ̈pi:d/ *n* a small creature rather like a worm, with a lot of legs

**mill·stone** /'mɪlstəʊn/ *n* a person or thing that gives someone great trouble, anxiety, etc.: *His lazy son is* **a millstone round his neck.**

**mil·om·e·ter** /maɪ'lɒmɪ̈tər‖-'lɑ-/ *n* → MILEOMETER

**mime¹** /maɪm/ *n* **1** [C;U] an act or the practice of using actions without language to show meaning: *I couldn't speak Chinese, but I showed in mime that I wanted a drink.*|*the art of mime* **2** [C] an actor who performs without using words

**mime²** *v* **mimed, miming** [I;T] to act (something) in MIME: *The actor was miming the movements of a bird.* –compare MIMIC²

**mim·e·o·graph** /ˈmɪmɪəgrɑːf‖-græf/ *v* [T] *AmE* for DUPLICATE: *a mimeographed copy*

**mim·ic¹** /ˈmɪmɪk/ *n* a person who is good at copying another's manners, speech, etc., esp. in a way that causes laughter

**mimic²** *v* **-ck-** [T] to copy the action of: *She made us all laugh by mimicking the teacher/the teacher's voice.* –compare IMITATE, MIME² –**mimicry** *n* [U]

**min·a·ret** /ˌmɪnəˈret, ˈmɪnəret/ *n* a tall thin tower on a mosque, from which Muslims are called to prayer

**mince¹** /mɪns/ *v* **minced, mincing 1** [T] to cut (esp. meat) into very small pieces **2** *derog* to walk in an unnatural way, taking little short steps **3 not to mince matters/one's words** to speak of something bad or unpleasant using plain direct language

**mince²** *n* [U] **1** *BrE* for MINCED meat **2** *AmE* for MINCEMEAT

**mince·meat** /ˈmɪns-miːt/ *n* [U] **1** a mixture of CURRANTS, dried fruit, dried orange skin, etc. (not meat) used as a sweet filling to put inside pastry **2 make mincemeat of** *infml* to defeat or destroy (a person, belief, etc.) completely

**mind¹** /maɪnd/ *n* **1** [C;U] a person's way of thinking or feeling; thoughts: *Her mind is filled with dreams of becoming a great actress.*|*She has a very quick mind.*|*A number of possibilities* **come to mind.** (=I can think of a number) **2** [U] memory: *I couldn't quite* **call** *his name* **to mind.** (=remember it)|*I'm afraid it* **went** *right* **out of my mind.** (=I forgot about it).|*I'll* **bear** *your suggestion* **in mind.** (=continue to consider it)|*You* **put** *me* **in mind of** (=remind me of) *my brother.* **3** [C] attention: **Keep your mind on** *your work.*|*You can do it if you* **put your mind to it.** (=give all your attention to it)|*She found that hard work was the best way to* **take her mind off** *her sorrow.*|*Let us now* **turn our minds to** (=begin to consider) *tomorrow's meeting.* **4** [C] intention: *Nothing was further from my mind.* (=that was not at all what I intended)|*Those boys have been stealing my apples again; I've* **got a good mind to** (=I think I may) *report them to the police.*|*If he's* **set his mind on** *doing it,* (=decided firmly to do it) *nothing will stop him.* **5** [C] opinion: *We are* **of one/of the same mind** *on this matter.* (=we both or all think the same about it)|**To my mind** (=in my opinion) *you're quite wrong.*|*John thinks we should go to Scotland for our holiday, but I'm still* **in two minds** *about it.* (=I find it difficult to make a decision) **6** [C] a person considered for his/her ability to think well: *She's among the best minds* (=cleverest people) *in the country.* **7 change one's mind** to change one's intentions or opinion: *I was going to leave tomorrow, but I've changed my mind (about him).* **8 in one's right mind** (*only used in* NEGATIVES², *questions, etc.*) altogether sensible or SANE: *No one in their right mind would buy that old car.* **9 make up one's mind** to reach a decision or firm opinion (about) **10 on one's mind** troubling one's thoughts: *She's had a lot on her mind recently.* **11 out of one's mind** mad **12 -minded** having the stated kind of mind: *strong-minded*

**mind²** *v* **1** [I;T +(*that*)/*out*] (*usu. in commands*) to be careful (of); pay close attention (to): *Mind that step; it's loose!*|*Mind you don't drop it!*|*Mind out! There's a car coming.*|*Just get on with your work; don't mind me.* (=don't pay any attention to my presence) **2** [T] to take care or charge of; look after: *Our neighbour is minding our dog while we're on holiday.* **3** [I;T +*v-ing*/*that;* not *be*/*v-ing*] (*often used with* would, *in requests, or in* NEGATIVE¹ *sentences*) to have a reason against or be opposed to (a particular thing); be troubled by or dislike: *"Would you mind if I went home early?"*|*"Which one would you like?" "I don't mind."* (=I would be pleased with either)|*Would you mind making* (=please make) *a little less noise?*|*I wouldn't mind a drink.* (=I'd like one)|*Do you mind the window (being) open?* (=that it is open) **4 mind one's own business** (*usu. in commands*) to pay attention to one's own affairs, and not to other people's **5 mind you** take this fact into account: *Grandfather spends a lot of time in bed now; mind you, he is 93!* **6 never mind** it doesn't matter; don't worry: *"We've missed the train!" "Never mind; there will be another one in ten minutes."* **7 -minder** a person whose job is to look after the thing stated: *a child-minder*

**mind·less** /ˈmaɪndlɪ̵s/ *adj derog* not having, needing, or using the power of thinking; stupid: *mindless cruelty* –**mindlessly** *adv* –**mindlessness** *n* [U]

**mine¹** /maɪn/ *pron* (POSSESSIVE form of *I*) of the person who is speaking: *That's your coat there; mine is here.*

**mine²** *n* **1** a deep hole or network of holes under the ground from which coal, gold, tin, and other mineral substances are dug: *a tin mine*|*Many men were buried underground when there was an accident at the mine.*|(fig.) *The old man was* **a mine of information** *about the village where he had lived for 50 years.* –see also COALMINE, GOLDMINE; compare QUARRY **2** a kind of bomb that is placed just below the ground or in the sea and is exploded electrically from far away or when touched, passed over, etc.

**mine³** *v* **mined, mining 1** [I;T *for*] to dig or work a MINE² (1) in (the earth): *mining for coal* **2** [T] to obtain by digging from a MINE² (1): *Tin used to be mined in the south-western part of England.* **3** [T] to put MINES² (2) in or under: *All the roads leading to the city had been mined.*

**mine·field** /ˈmaɪnfiːld/ *n* a stretch of land or water in which MINES² (2) have been placed

**min·er** /ˈmaɪnəʳ/ *n* a worker in a MINE² (1) –sounds like **minor**

**min·e·ral** /ˈmɪnərəl/ *n* any of various esp. solid substances that are formed naturally in the earth (such as stone, coal, salt, etc.), esp. as obtained from the ground for man's use

**mineral wa·ter** /ˈ··· ˌ··/ *n* [C;U] **1** water that comes from a natural spring and contains minerals, often drunk for health reasons **2** *BrE* a sweet gassy nonalcoholic drink sold in bottles

**min·gle** /ˈmɪŋgəl/ *v* **-gled, -gling** [I;T *with, together*] *esp. lit* to mix (with another thing or with people) so as to be an undivided whole: *The king mingled with the people in the streets.*

**mini** /mɪni/ *n, adj infml* (something that is) very small compared with others of its kind: *a mini(skirt)*

**min·i·a·ture** /ˈmɪnɪətʃəʳ, ˈmɪnɪ̵tʃəʳ‖ˈmɪnɪətʃʊər/ *n* **1**

[C] a very small copy or representation of anything **2** [A] (esp. of something copied or represented) very small: *The child was playing with his miniature railway.* **3** [C] a very small painting of a person

**min·i·bus** /'mɪnibʌs/ *n* a small bus with seats for between six and twelve people: *The children go to school in a minibus*/**by minibus.**

**min·i·mal** /'mɪn½məl/ *adj* of the smallest possible amount, degree, or size: *Fortunately, the storm only did minimal damage to the crops.* –**minimally** *adv*

**min·i·mize** ‖also **-mise** *BrE* /'mɪn½maɪz/ *v* **-mized, -mizing** [T] to lessen to the smallest possible amount or degree: *You can minimize the dangers of driving if you obey all the rules of the road.*|*He'd made a bad mistake, but tried to minimize its seriousness.* (=treat it as if it were not serious) –compare MAXIMIZE

**min·i·mum** /'mɪn½məm/ *n* **-ma** /mə/ *or* **-mums 1** [C] the least, or the smallest possible, quantity, number, or degree: *We will try to keep the cost of repairs down to a minimum.* **2** [A] smallest, or smallest possible (in amount, degree, etc.): *The minimum pass mark in this examination is 40 out of 100.*|*He couldn't join the police, because he was below the minimum height allowed by the rules.* –opposite **maximum**

**min·ing** /'maɪnɪŋ/ *n* [U] the action or industry of getting minerals out of the earth by digging: *coalmining*|*a mining company*

**min·is·ter** /'mɪn½stəʳ/ *n* **1** a politician who is a member of the government and is in charge of a particular government department: *the Minister of Education* **2** a priest in some branches of the Christian church –see PRIEST (USAGE)

**min·is·ter·i·al** /ˌmɪn½'stɪəriəl/ *adj* of a MINISTER (1): *ministerial duties*|*a ministerial appointment*

**minister to** sbdy. *v prep* [T] *esp. lit* to serve; perform duties to help: *ministering to the sick*

**min·is·try** /'mɪn½stri/ *n* **-tries** (*often cap.*) **1** [C] a government department led by a MINISTER (1): *The army, navy, and airforce are all controlled by the Ministry of Defence.* **2** [C] the office or position of a MINISTER (1) **3** [*the* S] the priests' profession: *Our son wants to enter the ministry.*

**mink** /mɪŋk/ *n* **minks** *or* **mink** [C;U] (the valuable brown fur of) a type of small WEASEL-like animal: *a mink coat*

**mi·nor¹** /'maɪnəʳ/ *adj* [*no comp.*] lesser or smaller in degree, size, etc.; of little importance: *He left most of his money to his sons; his daughter received only a minor share of his wealth.*|*The young actress was given a minor part in the new play.*|*a very minor illness* –sounds like **miner**; see MAJOR (USAGE)

**minor²** *n law* a person below the age (now 18 in Britain) at which he/she is fully responsible in law for his/her actions –sounds like **miner**

**mi·nor·i·ty** /maɪ'nɒr½ti‖m½'nɔ-, m½'nɑ-/ *n* **-ties 1** [C +*sing./pl. v*] the smaller number or part; a number or part that is less than half: *The nation wants peace; only a minority want/wants the war to continue.* **2** [C] a small part of a population which is different from the rest in race, religion, etc.: *a law to protect religious minorities* **3** [A] of or supported by a small, or the smaller, number of people: *Cricket is a minority sport in the US.* –compare MAJORITY

**min·ster** /'mɪnstəʳ/ *n* (now usu. part of a name) (*often cap.*) a great or important church: *Westminster*|*York Minster*

**min·strel** /'mɪnstrəl/ *n* (in the MIDDLE AGES) a musician who travelled about the country singing songs and poems

**mint¹** /mɪnt/ *n* **1** [U] a small plant whose leaves have a particular fresh smell and taste and are used in preparing drinks, making CHEWING GUM, etc. **2** [C] *infml* for PEPPERMINT: *Have one of these mints!*

**mint²** *n* **1** [C] a place in which coins and banknotes are officially made by the government **2** [S] *infml* a large amount (of money) **3 in mint condition** (of objects which people collect, such as books, postage stamps, coins, etc.) in perfect condition, as if unused

**mint³** *v* [T] to make (a coin)

**min·u·et** /ˌmɪnju'et/ *n* (a piece of music for) a type of slow graceful dance

**mi·nus¹** /'maɪnəs/ *prep* **1** made less by (the stated figure or quantity): *17 minus 5 leaves 12.* **2** being the stated number of degrees below the freezing point of water: *The temperature was minus 10 degrees.* –compare PLUS

**minus²** also **minus sign** /'·· ·/– *n* a sign (-) used for showing **a** that the stated number is less than zero **b** that the second number is to be taken away from the first –compare PLUS²

**minus³** *adj* [A] (of a number or quantity) less than zero –compare PLUS³

**min·us·cule** /'mɪnəskjuːl/ *adj* very, very small

**min·ute¹** /'mɪn½t/ *n* **1** [C] one of the 60 parts into which an hour is divided: *The train arrived at four minutes past eight.*|*It's only a few minutes' walk from here to the station.* (=a walk taking a very short time) **2** [S] *infml* a very short space of time: *I'll be ready in a minute.* (=very soon)|*"Are you ready yet?" "No, but I won't be a minute."* (=I'll be ready very soon) **3** [C] (a unit of measurement equal to) a 60th of a degree: *an angle of 80 degrees 30 minutes (80° 30').* **4 the minute (that)** as soon as: *I recognized the actor the minute (that) I saw him.* –see also MINUTES

**mi·nute²** /maɪ'njuːt‖-'nuːt/ *adj* **1** very small: *His writing is minute.* –see Study Notes on page 494 **2** giving attention to the smallest points; very careful and exact: *minute details* –**minuteness** *n* [U] –**minutely** *adv*

**min·utes** /'mɪn½ts/ *n* [P] a written record of business done, suggestions made, decisions taken, etc., at a meeting: *Before the committee started its work, the minutes of the last meeting were read out.*|*to take* (=write) *minutes*

**mir·a·cle** /'mɪrəkəl/ *n* an act or happening (usu. having a good result), that cannot be explained by the laws of nature, esp. one done by a holy person: *According to the Bible, Christ worked many miracles such as turning water into wine.*|*Doctors do their best to treat the sick, but they can't perform miracles.*|(fig.) *The teacher told me that it'd be a miracle if I passed the examination.* –**miraculous** /m½'rækjʊləs‖-kjə-/ *adj*: *The army won a miraculous victory over a much stronger enemy.* –**miraculously** *adv*: *It was a terrible explosion but, miraculously, no one was killed.*

**mi·rage** /'mɪrɑːʒ‖m½'rɑʒ/ *n* a strange effect of hot air conditions in a desert, in which objects appear which are not really there

**mir·ror¹** /ˈmɪrəʳ/ *n* a piece of glass, or other shiny or polished surface, that throws back (REFLECTS) images: *The driver saw the police car in his mirror.* –see picture on page 563

**mirror²** *v* [T] to show, as in a mirror: (fig.) *The election results mirror public opinion quite well.* (=give a true representation of it)

**mirth** /mɜːθ‖mɜrθ/ *n* [U] *esp. lit* merriness and laughter –**mirthless** *adj*

**mis·ad·ven·ture** /ˌmɪsədˈventʃəʳ/ *n* [C;U] *esp. law or lit* an accident; (event caused by) bad luck: **death by misadventure** (=accidental death)

**mis·an·throp·ic** /ˌmɪsənˈθrɒpɪk‖-ˈθrɑ-/ *adj* (of a person) who hates everybody, trusts no one, and avoids being in the company of others –compare MISOGYNIST, PHILANTHROPIST

**mis·ap·ply** /ˌmɪsəˈplaɪ/ *v* **-plied, -plying** [T] *fml* to put to a wrong use; use wrongly or for a wrong purpose –**misapplication** /ˌmɪsæplɪ̇ˈkeɪʃən/ *n* [C;U *of*]

**mis·ap·pre·hend** /ˌmɪsæprɪˈhend/ *v* [T] *fml* to understand (something) in a mistaken way: *The accident was caused by one motorist completely misapprehending the intentions of the other.* –**misapprehension** *n* [C;U +*that*]

**mis·ap·pro·pri·ate** /ˌmɪsəˈprəʊprieɪt/ *v* **-ated, -ating** [T] *fml or law* to take dishonestly and put to a wrong use: *The lawyer was sent to prison for misappropriating money placed in his care.* –**misappropriation** /-ˈeɪʃən/ *n* [C;U *of*]

**mis·be·have** /ˌmɪsbɪˈheɪv/ *v* **-haved, -having** [I;T] to behave (oneself) badly or improperly: *The pupil was punished for misbehaving (himself) in class.*

**mis·be·ha·viour** *BrE*‖**misbehavior** *AmE* /ˌmɪs bɪˈheɪvɪəʳ/ *n* [U] bad improper behaviour

**mis·cal·cu·late** /ˌmɪsˈkælkjʊleɪt‖-kjə-/ *v* **-lated, -lating** [I;T] to calculate (figures, time, etc.) wrongly; form a wrong judgment of (something): *I missed the train; I'd miscalculated the time it would take me to reach the station.* –**miscalculation** /-ˈleɪʃən/ *n* [C;U]

**mis·car·riage** /ˌmɪsˈkærɪdʒ, ˈmɪskærɪdʒ/ *n* **1** an act or case of producing lifeless young, esp. early in their development, before the proper time of birth –compare ABORTION **2 miscarriage of justice** (a) failure by the law courts to do justice, esp. as when a person who is not guilty is sent to prison

**mis·car·ry** /mɪsˈkæri/ *v* **-ried, -rying** [I] **1** (of a woman) to have a MISCARRIAGE **2** (of an intention, plan, etc.) to be unsuccessful; fail to have the intended or desired result.

**mis·cel·la·ne·ous** /ˌmɪsəˈleɪnɪəs/ *adj* of several kinds or different kinds; having a variety of sorts, qualities, etc. –**miscellaneously** *adv*

**mis·chance** /ˌmɪsˈtʃɑːns‖-ˈtʃæns/ *n* [C;U] *fml* (an example of) bad luck: *Only a serious mischance will prevent him from arriving tomorrow.*

**mis·chief** /ˈmɪstʃɪ̇f/ *n* [U] **1** bad, but not seriously bad, behaviour (esp. of children) probably causing trouble, and possibly damage: *The little boy gets into mischief easily.*|*She knew the children were* **up to some mischief** (=doing or planning something wrong), *and she found them in the garden digging up the flowers.* **2** *fml* damage or harm; wrong-doing: *The storm did a lot of mischief to the crops.* –**mischievous** /ˈmɪstʃɪ̇vəs/ *adj: One expects healthy children to be mischievous at times.* –**mischievously** *adv* –**mischievousness** *n* [U]

**mis·con·ceive** /ˌmɪskənˈsiːv/ *v* **-ceived, -ceiving** [T] to think (something) out badly and without proper consideration for what is suitable: *The government's plan for the railways is wholly misconceived.*

**mis·con·cep·tion** /ˌmɪskənˈsepʃən/ *n* [C;U] (an example of) understanding wrongly; state of being mistaken in one's understanding

**mis·con·duct** /ˌmɪsˈkɒndʌkt‖-ˈkɑn-/ *n* [U] *fml* bad behaviour, esp. improper sexual behaviour

**mis·con·struc·tion** /ˌmɪskənˈstrʌkʃən/ *n* [C;U] *fml* (an example of) mistaken understanding: *A law must be stated in the clearest language, so that it is not* **open to misconstruction.** (=so that there is no possibility that it will be wrongly understood)

**mis·con·strue** /ˌmɪskənˈstruː/ *v* **-strued, -struing** [T] *fml* to place a wrong meaning on (something said or done) –see also CONSTRUE

**mis·deed** /ˌmɪsˈdiːd/ *n fml or lit* a wrong or wicked act: *He deserved long imprisonment for his many misdeeds.*

**mis·de·mea·nour** *BrE* ‖**misdemeanor** *AmE* /ˌmɪs dɪˈmiːnəʳ/ *n* **1** a bad or improper act that is not very serious **2** *law* a crime that is less serious than, for example, stealing or murder –compare FELONY

**mis·di·rect** /ˌmɪsdɪ̇ˈrekt/ *v* [T] to direct wrongly: *I wanted to go to the station, but I was misdirected.*

**mi·ser** /ˈmaɪzəʳ/ *n derog* a person who hates spending money, and who becomes wealthy by storing it –**miserly** *adj* –**miserliness** *n* [U]

**mis·e·ra·ble** /ˈmɪzərəbəl/ *adj* **1** very unhappy: *The child is cold, hungry, and tired, so of course he's feeling miserable.* **2** very poor (in quality or amount): *a miserable failure*|*What miserable weather!* –**miserably** *adv: She failed miserably.*

**mis·e·ry** /ˈmɪzəri/ *n* [U] great unhappiness or great pain and suffering (of body or of mind): *Her baby died and, to add to her misery, her husband left her.*

**mis·fire** /ˌmɪsˈfaɪəʳ/ *v* **-fired, -firing** [I] **1** (of a gun) to fail to send out the bullet when fired **2** (of a plan, joke, etc.) to fail to have the desired or intended result

**mis·fit** /ˈmɪsˌfɪt/ *n* a person who does not fit well and happily into his/her social surroundings, or who is not suitable for the position he/she holds

**mis·for·tune** /mɪsˈfɔːtʃən‖-ɔr-/ *n* [C;U] (an example of) bad luck, often of a serious nature: *He failed in business not because of misfortune, but because of his own mistakes.*

**mis·giv·ing** /ˌmɪsˈgɪvɪŋ/ *n* [C;U] (feeling of) doubt, fear of the future, and/or distrust: *He looked with misgiving at the strange food on his plate.*|*I could see he had some misgivings about lending me his car.*

**mis·gov·ern** /ˌmɪsˈgʌvən‖-ərn/ *v* [T] to govern (a country) badly or unjustly –**misgovernment** *n* [U]

**mis·guid·ed** /mɪsˈgaɪdɪ̇d/ *adj* (of behaviour, an action, etc.) directed to wrong or foolish results; badly judged –**misguidedly** *adv*

**mis·han·dle** /ˌmɪsˈhændl/ *v* **-dled, -dling** [T] to handle or treat roughly, without skill, or insensitively: *Our company lost an important order because the directors mishandled the whole affair.*

**mis·hap** /ˈmɪshæp/ *n* an unfortunate, often slight, accident; unfortunate happening: *A mishap prevented him playing in the football match.*

**mis·in·form** /ˌmɪsɪnˈfɔːm‖-ɔrm/ *v* [T *about*] to tell (someone) something that is incorrect or untrue, either on purpose or by accident: *He charged the government with misinforming the nation.*

**mis·in·ter·pret** /ˌmɪsɪnˈtɜːprɪ̆t‖-ɜr-/ *v* [T] to put a wrong meaning on (something said, done, etc.); explain wrongly: *The driver misinterpreted the policeman's signal and turned in the wrong direction.* –**misinterpretation** /-ˈteɪʃən / *n* [C;U]

**mis·judge** /ˌmɪsˈdʒʌdʒ/ *v* **-judged, -judging** [T] to judge (a person, action, time, distance, etc.) wrongly; form a wrong opinion of: *He's honest, and you misjudge him if you think he isn't.* –**misjudgment, -judgement** *n* [C;U *of*]

**mis·lay** /mɪsˈleɪ/ *v* **-laid** /ˈleɪd/, **-laying** [T] to put (something) in a place and forget where; lose (something) in this way, often only for a short time

**mis·lead** /mɪsˈliːd/ *v* **-led** /ˈled/, **-leading** [T] to cause (someone) to form a mistaken idea or to act wrongly or mistakenly: *I was misled by the car's appearance–it looked much newer than it really was.|Don't let his friendly manner mislead you into trusting him.|a misleading description* –**misleadingly** *adv*

**mis·man·age** /ˌmɪsˈmænɪdʒ/ *v* **-aged, -aging** [T] to control or deal with (private, public, or business affairs) badly, unskilfully, etc.: *It's not surprising the company's in debt–it's been completely mismanaged.* –**mismanagement** *n* [U *of*]

**mis·no·mer** /mɪsˈnəʊməʳ/ *n* a wrong or unsuitable name: *To call it a hotel is a misnomer–it was more like a prison!*

**mi·so·gy·nist** /mɪ̆ˈsɒdʒɪ̆nɪ̆st‖mɪ̆ˈsɑ-/ *n* a person who hates women –compare MISANTHROPIC, PHILANTHROPIST

**mis·place** /ˌmɪsˈpleɪs/ *v* [T] **1** to have (good feelings) for an undeserving person or thing: *Your trust in that man is misplaced.* **2** →MISLAY: *I've misplaced my glasses again.* –**misplacement** *n* [U *of*]

**mis·print** /ˈmɪs-prɪnt/ *n* a mistake in printing

**mis·pro·nounce** /ˌmɪs-prəˈnaʊns/ *v* **-nounced, -nouncing** [T] to pronounce (a word, letter, etc.) incorrectly –**mispronunciation** /-prənʌnsiˈeɪʃən/ *n* [C;U]

**mis·quote** /ˌmɪsˈkwəʊt/ *v* **-quoted, -quoting** [T] to make a mistake in reporting (words) spoken or written by (a person): *The politician complained that the newspapers had misquoted him.* –**misquotation** /-kwəʊˈteɪʃən/ *n* [C;U]

**mis·read** /ˌmɪsˈriːd/ *v* **-read** /ˈred/, **-reading** [T] to read or understand (something) wrongly: *He misread the date on the letter; it was October 15th, not 16th.|The general misread the enemy's intentions, and didn't expect an attack.*

**mis·rep·re·sent** /ˌmɪsrepriˈzent/ *v* [T] to give intentionally an untrue explanation or description of (someone, or someone's words or actions): *The newspaper misrepresented what I had said.* –**misrepresentation** /mɪsˌreprɪzenˈteɪʃən/ *n* [C;U]

**miss¹** /mɪs/ *v* **1** [I;T +*v-ing*] to fail to hit, catch, find, meet, see, hear, etc.: *The falling rock just missed my head.|He arrived too late and missed the train.|He shot at me but missed.|I don't want to miss seeing that play on television tonight.* **2** [T +*v-ing*] to feel sorry or unhappy at the absence or loss of: *Her children have gone to Australia and she misses them very much.|I miss living in the country.|Give the beggar a coin; you won't miss it.* **3** [T] to discover the absence or loss of: *I didn't miss the key until I got home and found it wasn't in my bag.* **4 miss the boat** *infml* to lose a good chance, esp. by being too slow

**miss out** *v adv* **1** [T] (**miss** sbdy./sthg.↔**out**) to leave out; fail to put in, add, read, etc.: *Your account of the accident misses out one or two important facts.* **2** [I *on*] to lose a chance to gain advantage or enjoyment: *You really missed out by not coming to the party.*

**miss²** *n* **1** a failure to hit, catch, hold, etc., that which is aimed at: *The ball didn't quite go into the goal, but it was a* **near miss.** **2 give something a miss** *infml, esp. BrE* to not take, go to, do, etc., something: *I'm tired–I think I'll give the film a miss.*

**miss³** *n (sometimes cap.)* (a form of address used) **a** *esp. BrE* (by pupils to) a woman teacher: *Can I go home now, Miss?* **b** (by anyone to) a waitress, girl working in a shop, etc.

**Miss** *n* [A] (a title placed before the name of) an unmarried woman or a girl: *Miss Brown|The Miss Browns/the Misses Brown are sisters.* –compare MRS, MS

**mis·shap·en** /ˌmɪsˈʃeɪpən, mɪˈʃeɪ-/ *adj* badly or wrongly shaped or formed

**mis·sile** /ˈmɪsaɪl‖ˈmɪsəl/ *n* **1** an explosive weapon which can fly under its own power (ROCKET), and which can be aimed at a distant object **2** *fml* an object or a weapon thrown by hand or shot from a gun: *The angry crowd at the football match threw bottles and other missiles at the players.*

**miss·ing** /ˈmɪsɪŋ/ *adj* not to be found; not in the proper or expected place; lost: *One of the duties of the police is to try to find missing persons.|I noticed that he had a finger missing from his left hand.*

**mis·sion** /ˈmɪʃən/ *n* **1** a group of people who are sent abroad for a special reason: *a British trade mission to Russia* **2** the duty or purpose for which these people are sent: *The soldiers' mission was to attack the radio station.* **3** a place where a particular form of religion is taught, medical services are given, etc.: *They come to the mission from many miles around to see a doctor.* **4** the particular work for which one believes oneself to have been sent into the world: *Her mission in life was helping old people.*

**mis·sion·a·ry** /ˈmɪʃənəri‖-neri/ *n* **-ries** a person who is sent usu. to a foreign country, to teach and spread religion there

**mis·spell** /ˌmɪsˈspel/ *v* **-spelt** /ˈspelt/ *or* **-spelled, -spelling** [T] to spell wrongly –**misspelling** *n* [C;U]

**mis·spend** /ˌmɪsˈspend/ *v* **-spent** /ˈspent◂/, **-spending** [T] to spend (time, money, etc.) wrongly or unwisely; waste

**mist¹** /mɪst/ *n* [C;U] (an area of) clouds of very small drops of water floating in the air, near or reaching to the ground; thin FOG

**mist²** *v* [I;T *over, up*] to (cause to) be covered with MIST: *The windows misted over/up.* –see also DEMIST

**mis·take**[1] /m$\frac{1}{2}$'steɪk/ *v* **mistook** /m$\frac{1}{2}$'stʊk/, **mistaken** /m$\frac{1}{2}$'steɪkən/, **mistaking** [T] to have a wrong idea about; understand wrongly: *She doesn't speak very clearly, so I mistook what she said.|He'd mistaken the address, and gone to the wrong house.* –see also UNMISTAKABLE

**mistake** sbdy./sthg. **for** sbdy./sthg. *v prep* [T] to think wrongly that (a person or thing) is (someone or something else): *They mistook him for his brother.*

**mistake**[2] *n* a wrong thought, act, etc.; something done, said, believed, etc., as a result of wrong understanding, lack of knowledge or skill, etc.: *There were several spelling mistakes in your written work.|There must be some mistake in this bill; please add up the figures again.|She put salt into her tea* **by mistake.** –see ERROR (USAGE)

**mis·tak·en** /m$\frac{1}{2}$'steɪkən/ *adj* wrong; incorrect: *If you thought she intended to be rude, you were mistaken.|I had the mistaken idea that it would be quicker to take the train.* –**mistakenly** *adv*

**Mister** *n* [A] →MR

**mis·time** /ˌmɪs'taɪm/ *v* **-timed, -timing** [T] to do or say (something) at a wrong or unsuitable time: *The general mistimed his attack; it should have been made an hour earlier.*

**mis·tle·toe** /'mɪsəltəʊ/ *n* [U] a plant with small white berries that is often hung in rooms at Christmas time

**mis·tress** /'mɪstr$\frac{1}{2}$s/ *n* **1** a woman who is in control: *She felt she was no longer mistress in her own house when her husband's mother came to stay.|(esp. BrE) All the girls like their new English mistress.* (=teacher of English) –compare MASTER[1] **2** a woman with whom a man has a sexual relationship, usu. not a socially acceptable one: *His wife left him when she discovered he had a mistress.*

**mis·trust** /mɪs'trʌst/ *v* [T] not to trust –**mistrust** *n* [S;U *of*]: *He keeps his money at home because he has a great mistrust of banks.* –**mistrustful** *adj* [*of*]

**mist·y** /'mɪsti/ *adj* **-ier, -iest** full of or covered with MIST: *a misty morning*| (fig.) *eyes misty with tears*

**mis·un·der·stand** /ˌmɪsʌndə'stænd||- ər-/ *v* **-stood** /'stʊd/, **-standing** [not *be +v-ing*] **1** [I;T] to understand wrongly; put a wrong meaning on: *I think you misunderstood me/misunderstood what I said.* **2** [T] to fail to see or understand the true character or qualities of (someone): *My wife misunderstands me.*

**mis·un·der·stand·ing** /ˌmɪsʌndə'stændɪŋ||-ər-/ *n* **1** [C;U] (an example of) the act of putting a wrong meaning (on something); confusion: *I think there's been some/a misunderstanding: I meant that we should meet at nine in the morning, not nine at night.* **2** [C] *often euph* a disagreement less serious than a quarrel

**mis·use**[1] /ˌmɪs'juːz/ *v* **-used, -using** [T] to use (something) in a wrong way or for a wrong purpose

**mis·use**[2] /ˌmɪs'juːs/ *n* [C;U *of*] (an example of) bad, wrong, or unsuitable use: *a misuse of power.*

**mite** /maɪt/ *n* **1** a type of very small insect-like creature **2** a small child, esp. for whom one feels sorry

**mit·i·gate** /'mɪt$\frac{1}{2}$geɪt/ *v* **-gated, -gating** [T] *fml* to lessen the seriousness of (wrong or harmful action): *The judge said that nothing could mitigate the cruelty with which the mother had treated her child.|Are there any* **mitigating circumstances** *in this case?* (=conditions that lessen the seriousness of a crime) –see also UNMITIGATED –**mitigation** /-'geɪʃən / *n* [U]

**mi·tre** ||also **miter** *AmE* /'maɪtə[r]/ *n* a tall pointed hat worn by priests of high rank (BISHOPS and ARCHBISHOPS)

**mitt** /mɪt/ *n infml* **1** for MITTEN **2** *infml* a hand: *Those are my cigarettes; get your mitts off them.*

**mit·ten** /'mɪtn/ also **mitt** *infml*– *n* a garment for the hand (GLOVE) in which all four fingers are covered by one large baglike part –see PAIR (USAGE)

**mix**[1] /mɪks/ *v* **1** [I;T *up/with*] to (cause to) be combined so as to form a whole, of which the parts cannot (easily) be separated one from another: *You can't mix oil and water.| Oil and water don't mix.|Oil doesn't mix with water.|You can mix blue and yellow to produce green.* **2** [I *with*] (of a person) to be, or enjoy being in the company of others: *He mixes well with all kinds of people.*

**mix** sbdy./sthg.↔ **up** *v adv* [T] **1** [*with*] to confuse or mistake: *It's easy to mix him up with his brother; they're so alike.* **2** to put into disorder: *If you mix up those papers we shan't find the one we need quickly.* –see also MIX-UP

**mix**[2] *n* **1** [C;U] a combination of different substances, prepared to be ready, or nearly ready, for (the stated) use: *cake mix* **2** [S *of*] a group of different things, people, etc.; mixture: *There was rather a strange mix of people at the party.*

**mixed** /mɪkst/ *adj* **1** of different kinds: *I have mixed feelings about the book.*(=I like it in some ways, but not in others) **2** of or for both sexes: *a mixed school|mixed bathing*

**mixed up** /ˌ· '·◂/ *adj* **1** [F *in/with*] connected (with someone or something bad): *I'm afraid he's mixed up in some dishonest business.* **2** confused: *I'm mixed up about politics–I don't understand it.*

**mix·er** /'mɪksə[r]/ *n* **1** a machine by or in which substances are mixed: *a food mixer* –see picture on page 337 **2** a person who MIXES[1] (2) well or badly with other people: *To do this job well, you need to be a good mixer.*

**mix·ture** /'mɪkstʃə[r]/ *n* **1** [C;U] a set of substances mixed together: *This tobacco is a mixture of three different sorts.|You need some cough mixture.* (=medicine for preventing coughing) **2** [S] a combination (of things or people of different types or qualities): *I listened to his excuse with a mixture of amusement and disbelief.* **3** [U] *fml* the action of mixing or state of being mixed

**mix-up** /'· ·/ *n infml* a state of disorder, as caused by bad planning, faulty arrangements, etc.: *There was a mix-up at the station and we got on the wrong train.* –see also MIX **up**

**mm** *written abbrev. said as:* MILLIMETRES

**moan**[1] /məʊn/ *n* **1** a low sound of pain, grief, or suffering: *From time to time there was a moan (of pain) from the sick man.|*(fig.) *the moan of the wind in the trees* **2** *usu. derog* a complaint: *He's never satisfied; he always has some moan or another.*

**moan**[2] *v* [I] **1** to make the sound of a MOAN: *The sick child moaned a little, and then fell asleep.* **2** *derog* to complain; speak in a complaining voice: *Stop moan-*

ing; you really have nothing to complain about. **–moaner** *n*

**moat** /məut/ *n* a long deep hole that in former times was dug for defence round a castle, fort, etc., and was usually filled with water

**mob[1]** /mɒb‖mab/ *n often derog* a large noisy crowd, esp. one which is violent: *An angry mob gathered outside the palace.*|*mob violence*

**mob[2]** *v* **-bb-** [T] (of a group of people) to crowd around (someone) esp. because of interest or admiration: *When he left the hall after his speech, the party leader was mobbed by his supporters.*

**mo·bile[1]** /'məubaɪl‖-bəl, -biːl/ *adj* movable; able to move, or be moved, quickly and easily; not fixed in one position: *She's much more mobile* (=able to move from place to place) *now that she's bought a car.*|*a mobile home* (=a CARAVAN (1)) –see also IMMOBILE **–mobility** /məu'bɪl ̇ti/ *n* [U]

**mo·bile[2]** /'məubaɪl‖-biːl/ *n* an ornament or work of art made of small models, cards, etc., tied to wires or string and hung up so that they are moved by currents of air

**mo·bil·ize** ‖also **-ise** *BrE* /'məub ̇laɪz/ *v* **-ized, -izing** [I;T] to (cause to) gather together for a particular service or use, esp. for war: *Our country's in great danger; we must mobilize (the army).*|*He's trying to mobilize all the support/supporters he can get for his new political party.* –see also DEMOBILIZE **–mobilization, -sation** /-'zeɪʃən/ *n* [C;U]

**moc·ca·sin** /'mɒkəsɪn‖'ma-/ *n* a shoe made of soft leather –see PAIR[1] (USAGE)

**mock[1]** /mɒk‖mak/ *v* **1** [I;T] to laugh (at) or make fun (of), esp. unkindly or unfairly: *The pupil did his best, and the teacher was wrong to mock (his efforts).* **2** [T] to make fun of by copying: *He made all the other boys laugh by mocking the way the teacher spoke and walked.* **–mockingly** *adv*

**mock[2]** *adj* [A *no comp.*] not real or true; like (in appearance, taste, etc.) something real: *The army training exercises ended with a mock battle.*

**mock·e·ry** /'mɒkəri‖'ma-/ *n* **-ries 1** [U] the act or action of MOCKING (MOCK) **2** [S] something that is not what it is supposed to be: *The medical examination was a mockery; the doctor hardly looked at the child.* **3 make a mockery of** to cause to appear worthless, stupid, etc.: *His failure made a mockery of all the teacher's efforts to help him.*

**mo·dal verb** /məudl/ *n* see page 386

**mod con** /,mɒd 'kɒn‖,mad 'kan/ *n* **all mod cons** *BrE infml* (esp. in newspaper advertisements for houses) all modern conveniences (such as hot water, central heating, etc.)

**mode** /məud/ *n fml* a way of acting, behaving, speaking, writing, living,etc.: *He suddenly became wealthy, which changed his whole mode of life.*

**mod·el[1]** /'mɒdl‖'madl/ *n* **1** [A;C] a small representation or copy of something: *a model of the Eiffel Tower*|*model aircraft* **2** [C] a person, esp. a young woman, employed to wear clothes and show them to possible buyers (as in a shop, by being photographed, etc.) **3** [C] a person employed to be painted, drawn, photographed, etc. by an artist **4** [A;C] a person or thing that can serve as a perfect example or pattern, worthy to be followed or copied: *She's a model student.* **5** [C] a particular type of vehicle, weapon, machine, instrument, or garment, as made by a particular maker: *Rolls-Royce have produced a new model.*

**model[2]** *v* **-ll-** ‖**-l-** *AmE* **1** [T] to make a model of: *He modelled a ship out of bits of wood.* **2** [T] to shape (a soft substance, such as clay) into an article **3** [I] to work as a MODEL[1] (2,3) **4** [T] to wear and show (a garment) as a MODEL[1] (2): *Angela is modelling an attractive blue silk dress.*

**model** sbdy. **on/upon** sbdy. *v prep* [T] to form the character, qualities, etc., of (oneself) as a copy of (another person): *She models herself on her mother.*

**mod·e·rate[1]** /'mɒdər ̇t‖'ma-/ *adj* **1** of middle degree; neither large nor small, high nor low, fast nor slow, etc.: *At the time of the accident, the train was travelling at a moderate speed.*|*a child of only moderate ability* (=not especially clever)|*moderate wage demands* **2** not favouring political or social ideas that are very different from those of most people; not EXTREME: *moderate political opinions* –see also IMMODERATE

**mod·e·rate[2]** /'mɒdəreɪt‖'ma-/ *v* **-rated, -rating** [I;T] to make or become less in force, degree, rate, etc.; reduce: *He should moderate his language when children are present.* (=shouldn't use words not fit for them to hear)|*The wind was strong all day, but it moderated in the evening.*

**mod·e·rate[3]** /'mɒdər ̇t‖'ma-/ *n* a person whose opinions are MODERATE[1] (2) –compare EXTREMIST

**mod·e·rate·ly** /'mɒdər ̇tli‖'ma-/ *adv* [*no comp.*] to a MODERATE[1] (1) degree; not very: *a moderately successful film*

**mod·e·ra·tion** /,mɒdə'reɪʃən‖,ma-/ *n* [U] **1** the ability or quality of keeping one's desires within reasonable limits; self-control: *He showed great moderation in answering so gently the attacks made on his character.* **2 in moderation** within sensible limits: *Some people say that smoking in moderation isn't harmful to one's health.*

**mod·ern** /'mɒdn‖'madərn/ *adj* of the present time, or of the not far distant past; not ancient: *The modern history of Italy begins in 1860, when the country became united.*|*In this part of the city, you can see ancient and modern buildings next to each other.*|*modern languages* (=as opposed to Latin, Greek, etc.)|*a very modern railway station built of* CONCRETE[2] *and glass* –see NEW (USAGE) **–modernity** /mɒ'dɜːn ̇ti‖mə'dɜr-/ *n* [U]

**mod·ern·ize** ‖also **-ise** *BrE* /'mɒdənaɪz‖'madər-/ *v* **-ized, -izing** [T] to make (something) suitable for modern use, or for the needs of the present time: *The house needs modernizing: it has no bathroom or electricity.* **–modernization** /,mɒdənaɪ'zeɪʃən‖,madərnə- / *n* [C;U]

**mod·est** /'mɒd ̇st‖'ma-/ *adj* **1** *apprec* having or expressing a lower opinion than is probably deserved, of one's own abilities: *She's very modest about her success.* **2** not large in quantity, size, value, etc.: *There has been a modest rise in house prices this year.* **3** *apprec* (esp. of a woman or her clothes) avoiding or not showing anything that is improper –see also IMMODEST **–modestly** *adv*

**mod·es·ty** /'mɒd ̇sti‖'ma-/ *n* [U] *often apprec* the

quality, state, or fact of being MODEST: *His natural modesty saved him from being spoilt by success.*

**mod·i·cum** /ˈmɒdɪkəm‖ˈmɑ-/ *n* [S *of*] a small amount (of anything): *If he had a modicum of sense, he wouldn't do such a foolish thing.*

**mod·i·fi·ca·tion** /ˌmɒdǀfǀˈkeɪʃən‖ˌmɑ-/ *n* **1** [U] the act of MODIFYing or state of being modified **2** [C] a change made in something: *A few simple modifications to this plan would greatly improve it.*

**mod·i·fi·er** /ˈmɒdǀfaɪəʳ‖ˈmɑ-/ *n* (in grammar) a word that changes the meaning of another word –see Study Notes on page 389

**mod·i·fy** /ˈmɒdǀfaɪ‖ˈmɑ-/ *v* **-fied, -fying** [T] to change (a plan, an opinion, a condition, or the form or quality of something), esp. slightly **–modification** /-fǀkeɪʃən/ *n* [C;U]

**mod·ish** /ˈməʊdɪʃ/ *adj* fashionable

**mod·u·late** /ˈmɒdjʊleɪt‖ˈmɑd·ə-/ *v* **-lated, -lating** [T] *tech* to vary the strength, nature, etc., of (a sound)

**mod·ule** /ˈmɒdjuːl‖ˈmɑd·uːl/ *n* **1** a part having a standard shape and size, used in building, making furniture, etc. **2** a part of a space vehicle that can be used independently of the other parts

**mo·hair** /ˈməʊheəʳ/ *n* [U] (cloth made from) the long fine silky hair of a type of goat (**Angora goat**)

**Mo·ham·me·dan** /məʊˈhæmǀdn, mə-/ also **Muhammadan**– *adj,n* →MUSLIM

**Mo·ham·me·dan·is·m** /məʊˈhæmǀdənɪzəm, mə-/ *n* [U] the Muslim religion

**moist** /mɔɪst/ *adj* slightly wet; DAMP: *The thick steam in the room had made the walls moist.*|*eyes moist with tears* **–moistly** *adv* **–moistness** *n* [U]

**moist·en** /ˈmɔɪsən/ *v* [I;T] to make or become slightly wet

**mois·ture** /ˈmɔɪstʃəʳ/ *n* [U] water, or other liquids, in small quantities or in the form of steam or mist: *The desert air contains hardly any moisture.*

**mo·lar** /ˈməʊləʳ/ *n* any of the large teeth at the back of the mouth used for breaking up food

**mo·las·ses** /məˈlæsǀz/ *n* [U] **1** a thick dark sweet liquid produced from newly cut sugar plants **2** *AmE* for TREACLE

**mold** /məʊld/ *n,v AmE* for MOULD

**mole¹** /məʊl/ *n* a small dark brown mark on the skin

**mole²** *n* **1** a small furry almost blind animal that digs passages underground to live in **2** *BrE infml* a person who provides secret information to an enemy about an organization or company in which he/she is employed –compare SPY¹; AGENT (1)

**mol·e·cule** /ˈmɒlɪkjuːl‖ˈmɑ-/ *n* the smallest part of any substance that can exist without losing its own chemical nature, consisting of one or more atoms **–molecular** /məˈlekjʊləʳ‖-kjə-/ *adj*

**mole·hill** /ˈməʊlˌhɪl/ *n* **1** a small heap of earth made by a MOLE² (1) digging underground **2 make a mountain out of a molehill** to make an unimportant matter seem more important than it is

**mo·lest** /məˈlest/ *v* [T] **1** to annoy or attack: *A dog that molests sheep has to be killed.* **2** *euph* to attack (esp. a woman or a child) sexually **–molestation** /ˌməʊleˈsteɪʃən/ *n* [U]

**mol·li·fy** /ˈmɒlǀfaɪ‖ˈmɑ-/ *v* **-fied, -fying** [T] to make calmer: *He bought his angry wife a gift, but she refused to be mollified.* **–mollification** /ˌmɒlǀfǀˈkeɪʃən‖ˌmɑ-/ *n* [U]

**mol·lusc** ‖also **mollusk** *AmE* /ˈmɒləsk‖ˈmɑ-/ *n* any of a class of animals with soft bodies and no backbone or limbs and usu. covered with a shell: *SNAILS and OCTOPUSes are molluscs.*

**molt** /məʊlt/ *n,v AmE* for MOULT

**mol·ten** /ˈməʊltn/ *adj* (of metal or rock) turned to liquid by very great heat; melted –see MELT (USAGE)

**mom** /mɒm‖mɑm/ *n AmE* for MUM

**mo·ment** /ˈməʊmənt/ *n* **1** [C] a very short period of time: *It will only take a moment.*|*I'll be back in a moment/in a few moments.* (=very soon)|Just a moment (=wait); *I want to speak to you.* **2** [S] a particular point in time: *Just at that moment, the door opened and the teacher walked in.* **3** [C +*to-v/for; usu. sing.*] the right time for doing something: *Now is the moment to say it.* **4** [U] *fml* importance: *a matter of (the greatest) moment* **5 at any moment** at an unknown time only a little after the present: *He might come back at any moment.* **6 at the moment** at the present time; now **7 the moment (that)** just as soon as; at exactly the time when: *I recognized him the moment (that) I saw him.*

**mo·men·ta·ry** /ˈməʊməntəri‖-teri/ *adj* lasting for a very short time: *Her feeling of fear was only momentary; it soon passed.* –compare MOMENTOUS **–momentarily** *adv*: *He was momentarily unable to speak.*

**mo·men·tous** /məʊˈmentəs, mə-/ *adj* of very great importance or seriousness: *the momentous news that war had begun* –compare MOMENTARY

**mo·men·tum** /məʊˈmentəm, mə-/ *n* [U] *esp. tech* the quantity of movement in a body: *As the rock rolled down the mountainside, it gathered momentum.* (=moved faster and faster)|(fig.) *The struggle for independence is gaining momentum* (=growing stronger) *every day.*

**Mon.** *written abbrev. for:* Monday

**mon·arch** /ˈmɒnək‖ˈmɑnərk, -ɑrk/ *n* a ruler of a state (such as a king, queen, etc.) who has the right to rule by birth **–monarchic** /məˈnɑːkɪk‖məˈnɑr-/ also **monarchical**– *adj*

**mon·arch·ist** /ˈmɒnəkǀst‖ˈmɑnər-/ *n* a person in favour of the idea that kings, queens, etc., should rule, rather than elected leaders

**mon·ar·chy** /ˈmɒnəki‖ˈmɑnərki/ *n* **-chies 1** [U] rule by a king or queen **2** [C] a state ruled by a king or queen –compare REPUBLIC

**mon·as·tery** /ˈmɒnəstri‖ˈmɑnəsteri/ *n* **-teries** a building in which MONKs live –compare CONVENT

**mo·nas·tic** /məˈnæstɪk/ *adj* of monasteries (MONASTERY) or MONKs

**mo·nas·ti·cis·m** /məˈnæstǀsɪzəm/ *n* [U] the life, or way of life, of MONKs in a MONASTERY

**Mon·day** /ˈmʌndi, -deɪ/ *n* the second day of any week; the day after Sunday: *He'll arrive on Monday*|*on Monday evening.*|*She works (on) Mondays.*

**mon·e·ta·ry** /ˈmʌnǀtəri‖ˈmɑnǀteri/ *adj* of or connected with money: *The monetary system of certain countries used to be based on gold.*

**mon·ey** /ˈmʌni/ *n* [U] **1** coins or paper notes with their value printed on them, given and taken in buying and selling: *He doesn't usually carry much money on him.* (=in his pockets)|*The repairs will*

## STUDY NOTES modal verbs

### **can, may, should,** etc.

The verbs below are all MODAL verbs. They are used as helping verbs with another verb to change its meaning in some way. The lists tell you what the verbs mean, and how to use them.

| | | |
|---|---|---|
| power | *She* **can** *speak French.*<br>*I* **could** *swim when I was five.*<br>*I* **was able** *to lift the box.* | |
| permission | **Can** *we go home now, please?*<br>**Could** *I turn the radio down?*<br>*You* **may** *come in now.*<br>**Might** *I open the window?* | **can** is now the most common word. **could, may,** and **might** are more polite ways of asking for permission. |
| requests and suggestions | **Can** *you close the door, please?*<br>**Could** *you help me please?*<br>**Shall** *we go to the cinema?* | **could** is more polite than **can.** **shall** is usually used with *I* and *we.* |
| necessary | *I* **must** *go now – it's late.*<br>*Do you* **have to/Have** *you* **got to** *go?*<br>I **had to** *leave early yesterday.*<br>**Need** *I go?*<br>*What* **am** *I* **to** *do?* | |
| not necessary | *I* **didn't need to/needn't have** *put on my thick coat.*<br>*You* **needn't** *arrive until 10.30.* | **didn't need to/needn't have** means that it wasn't necessary to put my coat on, but I did. |
| right or wrong | *You* **should/ought to** *be ashamed of yourself.*<br>*I* **shouldn't have/oughtn't to** *have said that.* | **should/ought to** are used for actions which are thought to be good or right, **must/have to** for necessary actions.<br>**shouldn't/oughtn't to** are used for actions which are thought to be bad or wrong, **needn't** for unnecessary actions. |
| commands | *You* **mustn't** *tell anyone. You* **must** *keep it secret.*<br>*You* **are not to** *go. You* **are to** *stay here.* | |
| certainly/ certainly not | *You* **must** *be tired. You* **can't** *be tired.*<br>*They* **must have** *gone home. They* **can't have** *gone home.* | **can't** and **can't have** are the opposites of **must** and **must have** in this meaning. |
| future | *It* **will** *rain tomorrow.*<br>*We* **shall** *be away next week.* | **shall** is usually used only with *I* and *we*, and is becoming less common than **will.** |
| perhaps | *It* **may/might** *snow tomorrow.* | **might** makes something sound less likely than **may.** |
| past | *We* **used to** *work in the same office.*<br>*We* **would** *often go to the cinema together.* | **would** can only be used to describe a repeated action. |
| brave enough | *How* **dare** *you say that!*<br>*I* **daren't** *go there again.* | |

Here are some ways of using these modal verbs in different types of sentences:

| | with not and n't (NEGATIVES) | in a question | describing what someone said (indirect SPEECH) |
|---|---|---|---|
| can | *She* **can't/cannot** *speak French.* | **Can** *she speak French?* | *She said she* **could** *speak French.* |
| could | *I* **couldn't/could not** *swim when I was five.* | **Could** *you swim when you were five?* | *He said he* **could** *swim when he was five.* |
| may | *You* **may not/(mayn't)** *go to the party.* | **May** *I go to the party?* | *I said you* **may** *go.* |
| might | *I* **mightn't/might** *not come.* | **Might** *you come with us?* | *He said he* **might** *come.* |
| shall | *We* **shan't/shall not** *go to the cinema.* | **Shall** *we go to the cinema?* | *They said we* **should** *go to the cinema.* |
| must | *You* **mustn't/must not** *go.* | **Must** *you go now?* | *They said they* **must** *go.* |
| have to | *You* **don't/do not have to** *go.* | **Do** *you* **have to/Have** *you* **to** *go?* | *They said they* **had to** *go.* |
| need | *You* **don't need to/needn't/need not** *leave now.* | **Do** *you* **need to/Need** *you leave now?* | *They said they* **needed to** *leave.* |
| are to | *You* **aren't/are not to** *stay.* | **Are** *you* **to** *stay here?* | *They said they* **were to** *stay.* |
| should | *He* **shouldn't/should not** *go.* | **Should** *he go?* | *They said he* **should** *go.* |
| ought to | *You* **oughtn't/ought not to** *go there.* | **Ought** *you* **to** *go there?* | *They said you* **ought to** *go.* |
| will | *It* **won't/will not** *rain.* | **Will** *it rain?* | *They said it* **would** *rain.* |
| used to | *I* **didn't used to/used not to/usedn't to** *work there.* | **Did** *you* **used to/Used you to** *work there?* | *They said they* **used to** *work there.* |
| would | *I* **wouldn't/would not** *go to the cinema.* | **Would** *you go to the cinema?* | *They said they* **would** *often go to the cinema.* |
| dare | *I* **daren't/dare not** *go there.* | **Dare** *you go there?* | *They said they* **dared** *go there all the time.* |

*cost a lot of money.* **2** wealth: *Money doesn't always bring happiness.|If this old picture really is by a famous artist, we'll be* **in the money.** (=we will be wealthy) **3 one's money's worth** full value for the money one has spent: *We enjoyed the film so much that we felt we'd got our money's worth.* –see also POCKET MONEY

**mon·gol** /ˈmɒŋgəl‖ˈmɑŋ-/ *n* a person born with a weakness of the mind and a broad flattened head and face and sloping eyes

**mon·grel** /ˈmʌŋgrəl‖ˈmɑŋ-, ˈmʌŋ-/ *n* an animal, esp. a dog, whose parents were of mixed breeds or different breeds –compare PEDIGREE

**mon·i·tor¹** /ˈmɒnɪ̇təʳ‖ˈmɑ-/ *n* **1** a pupil chosen to help the teacher in various ways: *Jimmy has been made dinner money monitor.* (=he collects the money paid for school meals) **2** a person or apparatus that MONITORS²

**monitor²** *v* [T] to watch, listen to, or examine (esp. the working of a machine, or radio and television broadcasts): *We have been monitoring the enemy's radio broadcasts to try to find out their plans.*

**monk** /mʌŋk/ *n* a member of an all-male religious group that lives together in a MONASTERY –compare FRIAR, NUN –**monkish** *adj*

**mon·key** /ˈmʌŋki/ *n* **-keys 1** a small tree-climbing animal, with a long tail, and part of the class of animals most like man **2** *infml* a child who is full of annoying playfulness and tricks

**monkey nut** /ˈ·· ·/ *n BrE becoming rare* for PEANUT

**monkey wrench** /ˈ·· ·/ *n* a tool that can be ADJUSTed for holding or turning things of different widths

**mon·o** /ˈmɒnəʊ‖ˈmɑ-/ *adj* **1** using a system of sound recording, broadcasting, or receiving in which the sound appears to come from one direction only when played back: *a mono record/record player* –compare STEREO **2 mono-** one; single: *a monocycle* (=a cycle with only one wheel)

**mon·o·chrome** /ˈmɒnəkrəʊm‖ˈmɑ-/ *adj* having, using, or showing one colour only: *a monochrome television set* (=one showing black and white pictures, not coloured ones)

**mon·o·cle** /ˈmɒnəkəl‖ˈmɑ-/ *n* an apparatus like glasses, but for one eye only

**mo·nog·a·my** /məˈnɒgəmi‖məˈnɑ-/ *n* [U] the custom or practice of having only one wife or husband at one time –see also BIGAMY, POLYGAMY –**monogamous** *adj*

**mon·o·gram** /ˈmɒnəgræm‖ˈmɑ-/ *n* a figure formed of two or more letters, esp. the first letters of a person's names, often printed on writing paper, etc. –**monogrammed** *adj*

**mon·o·lith** /ˈmɒnəlɪθ‖ˈmɑ-/ *n* a large pillar made from one piece or mass of stone and standing by itself

**mon·o·lith·ic** /ˌmɒnəˈlɪθɪk‖ˌmɑ-/ *adj* **1** of or like a MONOLITH: *a monolithic building* **2** *often derog* forming a large unchangeable whole: *a monolithic system of government* –**monolithically** *adv*

**mon·o·logue** ‖also **monolog** *AmE* /ˈmɒnəlɒg‖ˈmɑnəlɔg, -lɑg/ *n* [C;U] **1** a long speech, part in a play or film, etc., spoken by one person only **2** *infml often derog* a rather long speech by one person, which prevents others from taking part in the conversation –see also DIALOGUE

**mon·o·plane** /ˈmɒnəpleɪn‖ˈmɑ-/ *n* an aircraft having a single wing on each side of it –compare BIPLANE

**mo·nop·o·lize** ‖also **-lise** *BrE* /məˈnɒpəlaɪz‖məˈnɑ-/ *v* **-lized, -lizing** [T] to have or obtain a MONOPOLY of; have or get complete unshared control of: *This company has monopolized the cigarette industry.*|(fig.) *One child monopolized the teacher's attention.* –**monopolization** /məˌnɒpəlaɪˈzeɪʃən‖məˌnɑpələ-/ *n* [U *of*]

**mo·nop·o·ly** /məˈnɒpəli‖məˈnɑ-/ *n* **-lies 1** [C] (a person, company, etc. that has) the right or power, shared with no one else, to provide a service, trade in anything, produce something, etc.: *a government monopoly* **2** [S] possession of, or control over, something, which is not shared by another or others: *He thinks he has a monopoly of brains.* (=that he alone is clever)|*A university education shouldn't be the monopoly of those whose parents are rich.*

**mon·o·rail** /ˈmɒnəʊreɪl, -nə-‖ˈmɑ-/ *n* (a train travelling on) a railway with a single rail

**mon·o·syl·lab·ic** /ˌmɒnəsɪˈlæbɪk‖ˌmɑ-/ *adj* **1** (of a word) having one SYLLABLE **2** (of speech, a remark, etc.) formed of words with one SYLLABLE; short and rather rude: *He would give only monosyllabic replies, such as "yes" and "no".*

**mon·o·syl·la·ble** /ˈmɒnəˌsɪləbəl‖ˈmɑ-/ *n* a word of one SYLLABLE: *"Can, hot, neck" are monosyllables.*

**mon·o·tone** /ˈmɒnətəʊn‖ˈmɑ-/ *n* [S] a manner of speaking or singing in which the voice continues on the same note: *to speak in a monotone*

**mo·not·o·nous** /məˈnɒtənəs‖məˈnɑ-/ *adj* having a tiring uninteresting sameness or lack of variety: *My job at the car factory is rather monotonous.* –**monotonously** *adv* –**monotony** *n* [U]

**mon·soon** /mɒnˈsuːn‖mɑn-/ *n* [C; *the* S] **1** the (period or season of) heavy rains which fall in India and neighbouring countries **2** the wind that brings these rains –see WEATHER (USAGE)

**mon·ster** /ˈmɒnstəʳ‖ˈmɑn-/ *n* **1** [A;C] an animal, plant, or thing of unusually great size or strange form: *a monster potato* **2** [C] a creature, imaginary or real, that is unnatural in shape, size, or qualities, and usu. causes fear: *a sea monster*|*Children love to hear stories about terrible monsters.* **3** [C *of*] a very evil person: *The judge told the murderer that he was a monster.*

**mon·stros·i·ty** /mɒnˈstrɒsɪ̇ti‖mɑnˈstrɑ-/ *n* **-ties** something made or built in such a way that it is, or is considered, very ugly: *Have you seen that new office building in the town centre? It's a monstrosity!*

**mon·strous** /ˈmɒnstrəs‖ˈmɑn-/ *adj* **1** of unnaturally large size, strange shape, etc. **2** shocking; DISGRACEful: *monstrous cruelty*|*Your behaviour in class is monstrous!* –**monstrously** *adv*

**month** /mʌnθ/ *n* **1** any of the 12 named divisions of the year **2** a period of about four weeks: *The baby is six months old.* –see also LUNAR MONTH

**month·ly** /ˈmʌnθli/ *adj,adv* (happening, appearing, etc.) every month or once a month: *a monthly meeting*

**mon·u·ment** /ˈmɒnjʊmənt‖ˈmɑnjə-/ *n* **1** a building, pillar, STATUE, etc., that preserves the memory of a person or event: *This pillar is a monument to all those*

## STUDY NOTES modifiers

Some adverbs, like **very**, **quite**, **rather**, etc., can be used to change the meaning of a word, phrase, or sentence. They can be used to make the meaning stronger:

*It's* **very** *hot today.* (=more than just hot)

Or they can be used to make the meaning less strong:

*It's* **fairly** *hot today.* (=less than just hot, but definitely not cold)

In the diagram below, the meanings of the groups of words get stronger as you move down the page:

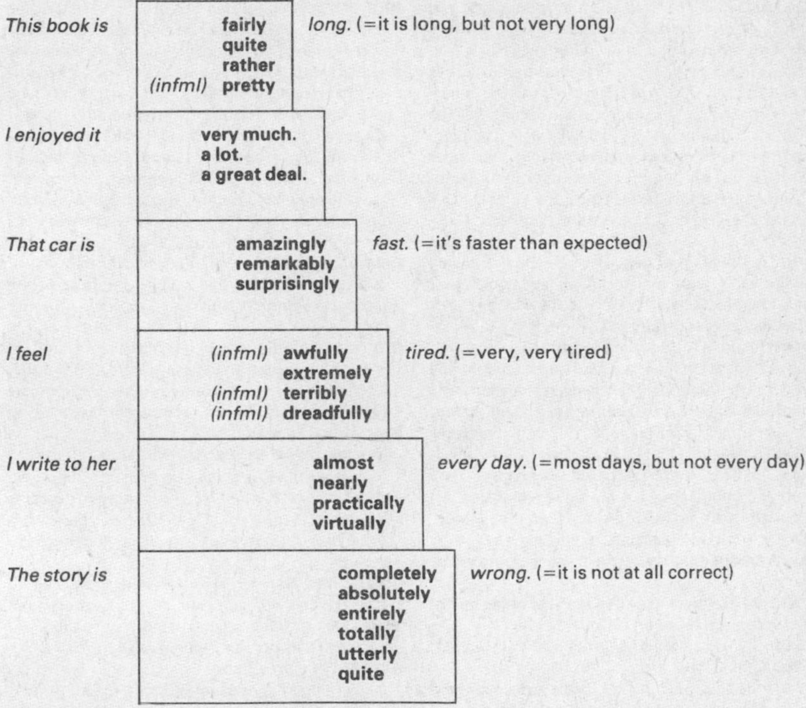

This book is
fairly
quite
rather
(infml) pretty
long. (=it is long, but not very long)
I enjoyed it
very much.
a lot.
a great deal.
That car is
amazingly
remarkably
surprisingly
fast. (=it's faster than expected)
I feel
(infml) awfully
extremely
(infml) terribly
(infml) dreadfully
tired. (=very, very tired)
I write to her
almost
nearly
practically
virtually
every day. (=most days, but not every day)
The story is
completely
absolutely
entirely
totally
utterly
quite
wrong. (=it is not at all correct)


*Note* the two different meanings of **quite**:

*The book is* **quite** *long.* (=not very long)
*The story is* **quite** *wrong.* (=completely wrong)

*Note* that the words **fairly**, **quite**, **rather**, and **pretty** can have slightly different meanings depending on the rest of the sentence:

*It's* **fairly** *warm today.* (=pleasantly warm)

but

*It's* **rather** *warm today.* (=perhaps too warm)

Look up these words in your dictionary to find some more examples of their different meanings and uses.

who died in the war.|(fig.) *That big empty office building is a monument to bad planning.* **2** an old building, etc., or what remains of it, considered worthy of preservation for its historic interest or beauty: *an ancient monument*

**mon·u·ment·al** /ˌmɒnjʊˈmentl◂‖ˌmɑnjə-/ *adj* **1** of, intended for, or having the nature of a MONUMENT (1) **2** very large, and of great and lasting worth: *The artist spent years on his monumental painting, which covered the whole roof of the church.* **3** very great in degree: *monumental stupidity*

**moo** /muː/ *n,v* [I] (to make) the noise that a cow makes

**mood**[1] /muːd/ *n* **1** [C] a state of the feelings at a particular time: *The beautiful sunny morning put him in a happy mood.*|*His moods change very quickly.*|*The teacher's in a bad mood* (=in a bad temper) *today.* **2** [C] a state of feeling in which one is bad-tempered: *Don't ask him to lend you money when he's in one of his moods.* **3** [*the* S +*to-v*/*for*] the right state of mind (for a particular activity, thing, etc.): *She was very tired, and in no mood for dancing.*

**mood**[2] *n tech* any of three groups of forms of a verb, expressing **a** a fact (INDICATIVE) **b** a command or request (IMPERATIVE[2]) **c** a condition, doubt, etc. (SUBJUNCTIVE)

**mood·y** /ˈmuːdi/ *adj* **-ier, -iest** *usu. derog* **1** having MOODS[1] (1) that change often and quickly **2** bad-tempered, angry, displeased, or unhappy, etc. **–moodily** *adv* **–moodiness** *n* [U]

**moon** /muːn/ *n* **1** [*the* S] the body which moves round the earth once every 28 days, and can be seen shining in the sky at night **2** [S] this body as it appears at a particular time: *Last night there was a full moon.* (=appearing as a full circle) **3** [C] a body that turns round a PLANET other than the earth: *Saturn has several moons.* **4 over the moon** very happy: *She's over the moon about her new baby.* **–moonless** *adj*

**moon a·bout/around** *v adv* [I] *infml* to wander about or behave in an aimless unhappy way

**moon·beam** /ˈmuːnbiːm/ *n* a beam of light from the moon

**moon·light** /ˈmuːnlaɪt/ *n* [U] the light of the moon: *The moonlight shone on the calm sea.*

**moon·lit** /ˈmuːnˌlɪt/ *adj* [A] given light by the moon: *a beautiful moonlit night*

**moor**[1] /mʊəʳ/ *n* [*often pl.*] *esp. BrE* a wide, open area of land, covered with rough grass or low bushes and not farmed because of its bad soil

**moor**[2] *v* [I;T *to*] to fasten (a ship, boat, etc.) to land, the bed of the sea, etc. by means of ropes, chains, an ANCHOR, etc.

**moor·ings** /ˈmʊərɪŋz/ *n* [P] a place where a ship or boat is MOORed: *Several ships broke away from their moorings in the storm.*

**moor·land** /ˈmʊələnd‖ˈmʊər-/ *n* [U] open country that is a MOOR[1]

**moose** /muːs/ *n* **moose** a type of large deer that lives in north America (and in northern Europe, where it is called an ELK)

**moot point** /ˌmuːt ˈpɔɪnt/ *n* an undecided point; point on which there is disagreement or doubt

**mop**[1] /mɒp‖mɑp/ *n* **1** a tool for washing floors or dishes, made of a stick with either a number of threads of thick string, or a piece of SPONGE[1] (2), fastened to one end **2** *infml* a thick usu. untidy mass (of hair)

**mop**[2] *v* **-pp-** [T] **1** to clean with, or as if with, a MOP[1] (1): *I usually mop the kitchen floor twice a week.* **2** to make dry by rubbing with something dry: *to mop one's* BROW (=forehead) *with a handkerchief*

**mop** sthg.↔ **up** *v adv* [T] to remove (unwanted liquid, dirt, etc.) with, or as if with, a MOP[1] (1): *It was you who spilt the milk; you'll have to mop it up.*

**mope** /məʊp/ *v* **moped, moping** [I] to be in low spirits, often without trying to become more cheerful

**mo·ped** /ˈməʊped/ *n* a bicycle which has a small engine, to help the rider esp.when going uphill

**mor·al**[1] /ˈmɒrəl‖ˈmɔ-/ *adj* **1** [A *no comp.*] concerning or based on the difference between right and wrong or good and evil: *a man of high moral standards*|*She refused to join the army on moral grounds.* **2** keeping exactly to what is (considered by society to be) good or acceptable in behaviour, esp. in matters of sex: *My grandfather was a very moral man; he never told a lie in his life.* –opposite **immoral 3 moral support** support given without material help; encouragement **4 moral victory** the result of a competition or argument in which the losing side feels it has proved itself to be right or just –see also AMORAL

**moral**[2] *n* a good lesson in behaviour, the right way of leading one's life, etc. that can be learnt from a story or event: *The moral of this story is that crime does not pay.*

**mo·rale** /məˈrɑːl‖məˈræl/ *n* [U] the state of mind (of a person, team, army, etc.) esp. with regard to pride, determination not to yield, etc.: *The team's morale was high after the victory.* –compare MORALS

**mor·al·ist** /ˈmɒrəlɪ̈st‖ˈmɔ-/ *n usu. derog* a person who concerns himself/herself with trying to control the MORALS of other people **–moralistic** /-ˈlɪstɪk/ *adj*

**mo·ral·i·ty** /məˈrælɪ̈ti/ *n* [U] rightness or pureness of behaviour, of an action, etc.: *One sometimes wonders if there's any morality in politics.* –opposite **immorality**

**mor·al·ize,** also **-ise** *BrE* /ˈmɒrəlaɪz‖ˈmɔ-/ *v* **-ized, -izing** [I *about, on, upon*] *usu. derog* to express one's thoughts on the rightness or wrongness of behaviour, actions, etc. **–moralizer** *n*

**mor·al·ly** /ˈmɒrəli‖ˈmɔ-/ *adv* **1** *apprec* in a MORAL[1] (2) manner –opposite **immorally 2** with regard to right or good behaviour: *What you did wasn't actually against the law, but it was morally wrong.*

**mor·als** /ˈmɒrəlz‖ˈmɔ-/ *n* [P] standards of behaviour, esp. in matters of sex: *a person of loose morals* (=bad sexual behaviour)|*In his business affairs he has no morals.* (=he acts dishonestly, etc.) –compare MORALE

**mo·rass** /məˈræs/ *n* a stretch of soft, wet, low ground that is dangerous for walking: (fig.) *The report took a long time to read because of the morass of details.*

**mor·a·to·ri·um** /ˌmɒrəˈtɔːrɪəm‖ˌmɔrəˈto-/ *n* **-ria** /rɪə/ **1** a declaration that a particular activity will be stopped or delayed for a time: *a moratorium on the building of new houses by the town council* **2** the length of such a delay

**mor·bid** /ˈmɔːbɪ̈d‖ˈmɔr-/ *adj derog* having or showing an unhealthy unnatural interest in or liking for unpleasant subjects, esp. concerning death **–morbidly** *adv* **–morbidity** /-'bɪdǝ̇ti/ *n* [U]

**more¹** /mɔːr‖mor/ *adv* (COMPARATIVE² of *many, much*) [*than*] **1** to a greater degree: *This book is more interesting than that one.*|*I sleep more in the winter.* –opposite **less 2** (with *once, no*) again: *I'll repeat the question once more.*|*The ship sank below the waves and was seen no more.* (=never again)

**more²** *determiner,pron* (COMPARATIVE² of *many, much*) [*of, than*] **1** a greater number or amount: *There are more rooms in this house than in mine.*|*As he grows older, he spends more (of his) time in bed.* –see MORE (USAGE) **2** an additional number or amount: *Have some more tea!*|*I have to write two more letters this morning.* (=besides those already written) **3 any more** any longer; now: *They don't live here any more.* **4 more and more** increasingly; (an amount) that continues to increase: *more and more difficult*|*I seem to spend more and more money on food every week!* –opposite **less and less 5 more or less** about; not exactly: *The repairs will cost £50, more or less.* **6 the more** (used to show that two things get larger, or change, together): *The more he eats, the fatter he gets.* –opposite **the less**

USAGE **More** is the opposite of both **less** (for amounts) and **fewer** (for numbers). Compare: *a few/three/many* **more** (opposite **fewer**) *friends*|*a bit/rather/much* **more** (opposite **less**) *money*

**more·o·ver** /mɔː'rǝuvǝʳ‖mo-/ *adv fml* besides what has been said: *The price is too high, and moreover, the house isn't in a suitable position.*

**morgue** /mɔːg‖mɔrg/ *n* a building in which dead bodies of unknown people are kept until it is discovered who they were –compare MORTUARY

**Mor·mon** /'mɔːmǝn‖'mɔr-/ *n* a member of a religious body originally formed in the US, and calling itself **The Church of Jesus Christ of Latter-Day Saints**

**morn** /mɔːn‖mɔrn/ *n* a morning

**morn·ing** /'mɔːnɪŋ‖'mɔr-/ *n* **1** [C;U] the first part of the day, usu. until the time when the midday meal is eaten: *I must go to the shops some time during the morning.*|*I'll see you in the morning.* (=tomorrow morning)|*I met him in town this morning.*|*He didn't get home until two o'clock in the morning.* **2** [A] of, in, or taking place in this part of the day: *an early morning cup of tea*|*the morning newspapers*

**mo·ron** /'mɔːrɒn‖'moran/ *n usu. derog* a very foolish person **–moronic** *adj* **–moronically** *adv*

**mo·rose** /mǝ'rǝus/ *adj* bad-tempered; not cheerful **–morosely** *adv* **–moroseness** *n* [U]

**mor·phine** /'mɔːfiːn‖'mɔr-/ *n* [U] a powerful drug used for stopping pain

**mor·row** *n* [*the* S] *lit* the day following today

**mor·sel** /'mɔːsǝl‖'mɔr-/ *n* a very small piece (of food): (fig.) *He hasn't a morsel of sense.*

**mor·tal¹** /'mɔːtl‖'mɔrtl/ *adj* **1** that must die; not living for ever –opposite **immortal 2** causing death: *a mortal wound* **3** [A] very great (in degree): *in mortal danger*

**mortal²** *n esp. lit* a human being (as compared with a god, a spirit, etc.): *All mortals must die.*

**mor·tal·i·ty** /mɔː'tælǝ̇ti‖mɔr-/ *n* **1** [S;U] (the rate of) the number of deaths from a certain cause, among a certain type of people, etc.: *If this disease spreads, the doctors fear that there'll be a high mortality.*|**Infant mortality** (=the rate at which deaths of babies take place) *is still very high in some countries.* **2** [U] the condition of being MORTAL¹ (1) –opposite **immortality** (for 2)

**mor·tal·ly** /'mɔːtǝli‖'mɔr-/ *adv* in a manner that causes death: *He fell to the ground, mortally wounded.*|(fig.) *She was mortally* (=greatly) *offended by your remarks.*

**mor·tar¹** /'mɔːtǝʳ‖mɔr-/ *n* **1** a heavy gun with a short barrel, firing an explosive that falls from a great height **2** a bowl made from a hard material, in which substances are crushed with a PESTLE into very small pieces or powder

**mortar²** *n* [U] a mixture of lime, sand, and water, used in building

**mort·gage¹** /'mɔːgɪd·‖'mɔr-/ *n* **1** an agreement to have money lent, esp. so as to buy a house, by which the house or land belongs to the lender until the money is repaid **2** the amount lent on a mortgage

**mortgage²** *v* **-gaged, -gaging** [T] to give the right or the claim to the ownership of (a house, land, etc.) in return for money lent for a certain period

**mor·ti·fy** /'mɔːtǝ̇faɪ‖'mɔr-/ *v* **-fied, -fying** [T] to hurt (a person's) feelings, causing shame, anger, etc.: *The teacher was mortified by his inability to answer the question.* **–mortification** /-fǝ̇'keɪʃǝn/ *n* [U]

**mor·tu·a·ry** /'mɔːtʃuǝri‖'mɔrtʃueri/ *n* **-ries** a place esp. in a hospital where a dead body is kept until the time of the funeral –compare MORGUE

**mo·sa·ic** /mǝu'zeɪ-ɪk/ *n* [C;U] (a piece of decorative work produced by) the fitting together of small pieces of coloured stone, glass, etc., so as to form a pattern or picture

**Mos·lem** /'mɒzlǝ̇m‖'maz-/ *n,adj* →MUSLIM

**mosque** /mɒsk‖mask/ *n* a building in which Muslims worship

**mos·qui·to** /mǝ'skiːtǝu/ *n* **-toes** a small flying insect that pricks the skin and then drinks blood, and can in this way cause the disease of MALARIA

**moss** /mɒs‖mɔs/ *n* [U] a small flat green or yellow flowerless plant that grows in a thick furry mass on wet soil, or on a wet surface **–mossy** *adj*

**most¹** /mǝust/ *adv* (SUPERLATIVE *of much*) **1** to the greatest degree: *the most comfortable hotel in this town*|*What annoyed me most was the way he laughed at my mistake.* –compare LEAST **2** *fml* very: *a most enjoyable party*

**most²** *determiner,pron* (SUPERLATIVE of *many, much*) [*of*] **1** the greatest number or amount: *Most people take their holidays in the summer.*|*He spends most of his time travelling.*|*She bought the one that cost the most.* –compare LEAST² (1); see Study Notes on page 494 **2 at most** not more than; if not less: *She's at most 25 years old.* –compare **at** LEAST² **3 for the most part** mainly: *Summers in the south of France are for the most part dry and sunny.* **4 make the most of** to get the best advantage from: *We've only got one day in London, so let's make the most of it and see everything.*

**most·ly** /'mǝustli/ *adv* mainly; in most cases or most of the time: *She uses her car mostly for her job.*

**MOT** *n abbrev for:* Ministry of Transport; (in Britain) a regular official examination of cars more than three years old, carried out to make sure that they are fit to be driven: *My car failed its* MOT (*test*).

**mo·tel** /məʊ'tel/ *n* a hotel specially built for travelling motorists

**moth** /mɒθ||mɔθ/ *n* a quite large winged insect, related to the BUTTERFLY, which flies mainly at night. The young of some types of moth (the **clothes-moth**) eat and make holes in clothes

**moth·ball** /'mɒθbɔːl||'mɔθ-/ *n* [*usu. pl.*] a small ball made of a strong-smelling substance, used for keeping MOTHS away from clothes

**moth-eat·en** /'· ˌ··/ *adj* (of a garment) destroyed, or partly destroyed, by MOTHS: (fig.) *a moth-eaten* (=very worn out) *old chair*

**moth·er**[1] /'mʌðə^r/ *n* **1** a female parent: *His mother and father are both doctors.|a mother hen and her young* CHICKS|*Can I borrow your car please, mother?* –see picture on page 217 **2 the/one's mother country** the country of one's birth **3 the/one's mother tongue** one's native language –**motherless** *adj*

**mother**[2] *v* [T] **1** (esp. of a woman) to care for (someone) like a mother **2** *derog* to treat (someone) with too great protectiveness and care

**moth·er·hood** /'mʌðəhʊd||-ər-/ *n* [U] the state of being a mother: *Motherhood doesn't suit her; she shouldn't have had children.* –compare FATHERHOOD

**mother-in-law** /'·· · ·/ *n* **mothers-in-law** the mother of a person's husband or wife –see picture on page 217

**moth·er·ly** /'mʌðəli||-ər-/ *adj apprec* having or showing the love, kindness, etc., of a mother –**motherliness** *n* [U]

**mother-of-pearl** /ˌ·· · '·/ *n* [U] a hard smooth variously coloured substance on the inside of certain shells, used for making decorative articles

**mother su·pe·ri·or** /ˌ·· ·'···/ *n* (*usu. caps.*) the female head of a CONVENT

**mo·tif** /məʊ'tiːf/ *n* a subject, pattern, idea, etc., forming the base on which something, esp. a work of art, is made

**mo·tion**[1] /'məʊʃən/ *n* **1** [U] the act, manner, or state of moving: *The gentle rolling motion of the ship made me feel sleepy.|Parts of the film were shown again* **in slow motion.** (=making the movements appear slower than in real life)|*Press this button to put/set the machine in motion.* (=start it working) **2** [C] a single or particular movement or way of moving: *He made a motion with his hand, as if to tell me to keep back.* **3** [C +*to-v/that*] a suggestion formally put before a meeting: *The motion to increase the club's membership charges was defeated by 15 votes to 10.* **4** [C] *esp. BrE fml* an act of emptying the bowels

**motion**[2] *v* [I;T] to direct (someone) by means of a movement, usu. with the hand: *She motioned (to) me to come into the room.*

**mo·tion·less** /'məʊʃənlɪ̈s/ *adj* without any movement; quite still: *The cat remained motionless, waiting for the mouse to come out of its hole.* –**motionlessly** *adv* –**motionlessness** *n* [U]

**mo·ti·vate** /'məʊtɪ̈veɪt/ *v* **-vated, -vating** [T] to provide (someone) with a reason or cause for doing something: *Everything she does is motivated only by a desire for money.* –**motivation** /ˌməʊtɪ̈'veɪʃən/ *n* [C;U]

**mo·tive** /'məʊtɪv/ *n* a cause of or reason for action; that which urges a person to act in a certain way: *In a case of murder, the police question everyone who might have a motive.|What do you think his motives were in buying the director a drink?* –**motiveless** *adj*

**mot·ley** /'mɒtli||'mɑtli/ *adj derog or humor* of many different kinds, classes, etc.: *a motley crowd of people*

**mo·tor**[1] /'məʊtə^r/ *n* a machine that changes power, esp. electrical power, into movement: *This car is driven by an electric motor.* –see MACHINE (USAGE)

**motor**[2] *adj* [A] **1** driven by an engine: *a motor-boat|a motor* SCOOTER|a motor MOWER **2** of, for, or concerning vehicles driven by an engine, esp. those used on roads: *the motor industry/trade|motor racing*

**motor**[3] *v* [I] *BrE* to travel by car; drive: *We motored over to Cambridge to see some friends.*

**mo·tor·car** /'məʊtəkɑː^r||-tər-/ *n BrE fml* a car

**mo·tor·cy·cle** /'məʊtəˌsaɪkəl||-tər-/ also **motorbike** *BrE infml*– *n* a large heavy bicycle driven by an engine: *to go to work* **by motorcycle** –**motorcyclist** *n*

**mo·tor·ist** /'məʊtərɪ̈st/ *n* a person who drives a car –compare PEDESTRIAN

**mo·tor·ize** ||also **-ise** *BrE* /'məʊtəraɪz/ *v* **-ized, -izing** [T] to provide (soldiers, an army, etc.) with motor vehicles

**mo·tor·way** /'məʊtəweɪ||-tər-/ *BrE*||**expressway** *AmE n* a very wide road built esp. for fast long-distance travel –see STREET (USAGE)

**mot·tled** /'mɒtld||'mɑ-/ *adj* marked irregularly with variously coloured spots or parts: *mottled leaves*

**mot·to** /'mɒtəʊ||'mɑ-/ *n* **-tos** *or* **-toes** a short sentence or a few words taken as the guiding principle of a person, a school, etc.: *The school motto is "Never lose hope".* –compare SLOGAN

**mould**[1] ||also **mold** *AmE* /məʊld/ *n* [U] **1** a soft greenish growth on bread, cheese, etc. that has been kept too long, or on objects which have been left for a long time in warm wet air **2** loose soft soil that is rich in (the stated) decayed vegetable substances: *He planted the seeds in a box filled with leaf mould.*

**mould**[2] ||also **mold** *AmE n* a hollow vessel having a particular shape, into which some soft substance is poured, so that when the substance hardens, it takes this shape: *a jelly mould shaped like a rabbit*

**mould**[3] ||also **mold** *AmE v* [T] to shape or form (something solid) esp. using a MOULD[2]: *The car body is moulded in the factory.|a figure of a man moulded out of/in clay|*(fig.) *His character has been moulded more by his experiences in life than by his education.*

**mould·y** ||also **moldy** *AmE* /'məʊldi/ *adj* **-ier, -iest** *derog* of or covered with MOULD[1] (1): *mouldy cheese|a mouldy smell* –**mouldiness** *n* [U]

**moult** ||also **molt** *AmE* /məʊlt/ *v* [I;T] (of a bird or animal) to lose or throw off (feathers, hair, or fur)

**mound** /maʊnd/ *n* [*of*] a heap (of earth, stones, etc.); small hill: (fig.) *There's a mound of papers on my desk.*

**mount**[1] /maʊnt/ *n* [A;C] *old use or (cap.) as part of a name* a mountain: *Mount Everest*

**mount**[2] *v* **1** [I;T] to get on (a horse, a bicycle, etc.): *He mounted (his horse) and rode away.* –opposite

**dismount 2** [I;T] *fml* to go up; climb: *The old lady can mount the stairs only with difficulty.* **3** [I *up*] to rise in level or increase in amount: *His debts continued to mount up.* **4** [T] to fix on a support or in a frame: *She mounted the photograph on stiff paper.* **5** [T] to prepare or begin (an attack): *The unions are getting ready to mount a powerful attack on the government.*

**mount³** *n* an animal on which one rides: *This old donkey is a good quiet mount for a child.*

**moun·tain** /'maʊntɪn/ *n* a very high hill, usu. of bare or snow-covered rock: *He looked down from the mountain to the valley below.*|(fig.) *a mountain of work*

**moun·tain·eer** /ˌmaʊntɪ'nɪəʳ/ *n* a person who climbs mountains as a sport or profession –**mountaineering** *n* [U]

**moun·tain·ous** /'maʊntɪnəs/ *adj* full of or containing mountains: *mountainous country*

**mourn** /mɔːn‖morn/ *v* [I;T *for, over*] to feel and/or show grief, esp. for the death of someone: *The old woman mourns her son's death/for her son.*

**mourn·er** /'mɔːnəʳ‖'mor-/ *n* a person who attends a funeral

**mourn·ful** /'mɔːnfəl‖'morn-/ *adj sometimes derog* sad; causing, feeling, or expressing sorrow –**mournfully** *adv* –**mournfulness** *n* [U]

**mourn·ing** /'mɔːnɪŋ‖'mor-/ *n* [U] (the expression of) grief, esp. for a death: *All the theatres and cinemas were closed, as a sign of mourning for the dead president.*

**mouse** /maʊs/ *n* **mice** /maɪs/ a small furry animal with a long tail that lives in houses and in fields: *a field mouse*|*I think we've got mice in the kitchen.*

**mousse** /muːs/ *n* [C;U] (a sweet dish made from) cream, eggs, and other substances mixed together and then frozen: *chocolate mousse*

**mous·tache** ‖also **mustache** *AmE* /mə'stɑːʃ‖'mʌstæʃ/ *n* hair growing on the upper lip –see picture on page 299

**mous·y** /'maʊsi/ *adj* **-ier, -iest 1** *often derog* (of hair) having a dull brownish-grey colour **2** *derog* (of a person, esp. a woman) unattractively plain; DRAB

**mouth¹** /maʊθ/ *n* **mouths 1** the opening on the face through which a person or animal may take food into the body and speak or make sounds –see picture on page 299 **2** an opening, entrance, or way out: *the mouth of a cave*|*the mouth of a river* (=where it joins the sea) **3 by word of mouth** by speaking and not by writing **4 down in the mouth** not cheerful; in low spirits **5 put words into someone's mouth: a** to tell someone what to say **b** *derog* to suggest or claim, falsely, that someone has said a particular thing **6 take the words out of someone's mouth** to say something that someone else was going to say, before he/she has had time or a chance to speak **7 -mouthed** *usu. derog.* having the stated way of speaking: *loud-mouthed*|*foul-mouthed*

**mouth²** /maʊð/ *v* [I;T] **1** to speak or say (something), esp. repeatedly without understanding or sincerity, or in a displeasing way: *He walked out of the room, mouthing curses.* **2** to move the lips as if speaking but without making any sound

**mouth·ful** /'maʊθfʊl/ *n* **1** [C] as much (food or drink) as fills the mouth: *I'm so full I couldn't eat another mouthful.* **2** [S] *infml, usu. humor* a big long word that one finds difficulty in saying or pronouncing: *Her name is quite a mouthful!*

**mouth·or·gan** /'maʊθˌɔːgən‖-ˌɔr-/ also **harmonica**– *n* a small musical instrument, played by being held to the mouth, moved from side to side, and blown into or sucked through

**mouth·piece** /'maʊθpiːs/ *n* **1** the part of anything (such as a musical instrument, a telephone, etc.) that is held in or near the mouth **2** [*of* ] *often derog* a person, newspaper, etc. that expresses the opinions of others: *This newspaper is the mouthpiece of the government.*

**mouth-wa·ter·ing** /'· ˌ···/ *adj* (of food) that makes one want to eat

**mo·va·ble, moveable** /'muːvəbəl/ *adj* that can be moved; not fixed in one place or position: *a chair with movable arms* –see also IMMOVABLE

**move¹** /muːv/ *v* **moved, moving 1** [I;T] to (cause to) change place or bodily position: *Please move your car; it's blocking the road.*|*Can you sit still without moving for 10 minutes?*|*He was trapped in the crashed car and could not move his legs.*|*That clever student should be moved up to a higher class.* **2** [I] to be in movement; go, walk, run, etc., esp. in a particular way: *Don't get off the train while it's still moving.*|*The dancer moves very gracefully.*|*That car is really moving!* (=travelling very fast) **3** [I] (of work, events, etc.) to advance; get nearer to an end: *Work on the new building is moving more quickly than was expected.* **4** [I] also **move house** *BrE*– to change one's place of living: *Their present house is too small, so they've decided to move./***move house. 5** [I] to lead one's life or pass one's time (esp. with or among people of a certain kind): *She moves with a lot of writers and artists.* **6** [T +*to-v*/*to*] to cause (to act from) feelings of pity, sadness, anger, admiration, etc.: *The child's suffering moved me.*|*I was very moved by her story.* –see also MOVING, UNMOVED **7** [I;T +*that*/*for*] to put forward, at a meeting (a suggestion on which arguments for and against are heard, and a decision taken,esp. by voting): *I move that we support the introduction of this law.*|*We moved for an adjournment of half an hour.*

**move along** *v adv* **1** [I] to move further towards the front or back: *The people standing in the bus moved along, to make room for others.* **2** [I;T (=**move** sbdy. **along**)] →MOVE **on** (2)

**move in** *v adv* [I] to take possession of a new home: *We've bought the house, but we can't move in until next month.*

**move off** *v adv* [I] to leave; DEPART: *The guard blew his whistle, and the train moved off.*

**move on** *v adv* **1** [I *to*] to change (to something new): *I think we've talked enough about that subject; let's move on.* **2** [I;T (=**move** sbdy. **on**)] to (order to) go away to another place or position: *The man was annoying people, so the policeman moved him on.*

**move over** *v adv* [I] to change position in order to make room for someone or something else: *Move over and let your grandmother sit down.*

**move²** *n* **1** [S] an act of moving; movement: *If you make a move, I'll shoot.* **2** [C] an act of going to a new home, office, etc. **3** [C] (in games such as CHESS) an act of taking a piece from one square and putting it on another **4** [C] a (step in a) course of action towards a particular result: *New moves to settle the disagreement between the workers and employers have ended in failure.* **5 get a move on** *infml* (*often in commands*) to hurry up

**move·ment** /ˈmuːvmənt/ *n* **1** [C;U] (an act of) moving or of being moved; (example of) activity: *Movement can be painful when you've hurt your back.|the movement of goods by road|The police are watching this man's movements* (=all his activities) *very carefully.* **2** [C +*sing./pl. v*] a group of people who make united efforts for a particular purpose: *The trade union movement works/work to obtain higher wages and better conditions.* **3** [C] a general feeling, way of thinking, acting, etc. towards something new, not directed by any particular person or group: *the movement towards equality for women* **4** [C] a main division of a musical work, esp. of a SYMPHONY **5** [C] the moving parts of a piece of machinery, esp. a clock or watch

**mov·ie** /ˈmuːvi/ *n infml esp. AmE* for FILM[1] (3)

**mov·ies** /ˈmuːviz/ *n* [*the* P] *infml esp. AmE* for CINEMA: *We're going to the movies.*

**mov·ing** /ˈmuːvɪŋ/ *adj* **1** causing strong feelings, esp. of pity: *The film was so moving that she almost wept.* **2** [A *no comp.*] that moves; not fixed: *Oil the moving parts of this machine regularly.* **–movingly** *adv*

**mow** /məʊ/ *v* **mowed, mown** /məʊn/ *or* **mowed, mowing** [I;T] to cut (grass, corn, etc.) with a MOWER or a SCYTHE

**mow** sbdy.↔**down** *v adv* [T] to kill, destroy, or knock down, esp. in great numbers: *The soldiers were mown down by fire from the enemy's guns.*

**mow·er** /ˈməʊə[r]/ *n* a machine for MOWING, esp. (a **lawnmower**) one for cutting grass

**MP** *n abbrev. for:* Member of Parliament; a person who has been elected to represent the people in a parliament, in Britain the HOUSE[1] (3) of Commons: *Michael Foot, MP|an MP*

**mpg** *written abbrev. said as:* miles per GALLON (esp. of petrol): *a car that does 35 mpg*

**mph** *written abbrev. said as:* miles per hour: *driving along at 60 mph*

**Mr** /ˈmɪstə[r]/ also **Mister**– *n* [A] **1** a title for a man who has no other title: *Mr Smith|Mr John Smith* –compare MESSRS **2** a title used when addressing certain men in official positions: *Mr Chairman* |(in the US) *Mr President*

**Mrs** /ˈmɪsɨz/ *n* [A] a title for a married woman who has no other title: *Mrs Jones |Mrs Sarah Jones* –compare MISS, MS

**Ms** /mɪz, məz/ *n* [A] a title for a woman who does not wish to call herself either "Mrs" or "Miss" –compare MISS, MRS

**MS** *n pl* **MSS** *written abbrev. said as:* MANUSCRIPT

**MSc** /ˌem es ˈsiː/ also **MS** *AmE*– *abbrev. for:* Master of Science; (a title for someone who has) a university degree which can be taken one or two years after a BSc: *Jill Smith, MSc|an MSc*

**Mt** *written abbrev. said as:* MOUNT[1]: *Mt Everest*

**much**[1] /mʌtʃ/ *adv* **more** /mɔː[r]‖mor/, **most** /məʊst/ **1** by a great degree: *much fatter than I am|much too busy|I'd much rather not.|Thank you very much.* **2** nearly; in most ways: *much the same as usual*

USAGE Use **much** with adjectives made from the PASSIVE form of verbs, in the same way as **very** is used with ordinary adjectives: *This picture is* **much** *admired/is* **very** *beautiful.*

**much**[2] *determiner,pron,n* **more, most** [U] **1** (*used in questions and* NEGATIVES[2] *and after* so *and* too, *but not usu. in simple statements*) a great amount: *not very much time|far too much work|How much does it cost?|The film has just started; we haven't missed very much.|(fml) I have much pleasure in giving you this prize.* –see Study Notes on pages 389, 494 **2 as much again** twice as much **3 I thought as much** I expected that (esp. something bad): *So they found out he's been cheating. I thought as much.* **4 make much of** to treat as important **5 much as** although: *Much as I want to, I can't come.* **6 not much of a** not a very good: *It's not much of a day for a walk.* **7 not up to much** *infml* not very good: *The film's not up to much.* **8 so much for** that is the end of: *It's raining–so much for my idea of taking a walk.* **9 this/that much** the particular amount or words: *I'll say this much, he's a good worker (although I don't like him).* **10 too much for** too hard for: *Climbing the stairs is too much for her now.*

**muck** /mʌk/ *n* [U] *infml* **1** dirt **2** waste matter dropped from animals' bodies, esp. as used for spreading on the land; MANURE **–mucky** *adj* **-ier, -iest**

**muck a·bout/around** *v adv* [I] *esp. BrE infml* to behave in a silly way: *Stop mucking about and listen to what I'm saying.*

**muck in** *v adv* [I] *infml* to join in work or activity (with others): *If we all muck in we'll soon finish the work.*

**muck** sthg.↔**up** *v adv* [T] *esp. BrE infml* to spoil or make dirty: *I've mucked up my shirt by working in the garden.*

**mu·cus** /ˈmjuːkəs/ *n* [U] a slippery liquid produced in certain parts of the body, esp. the nose

**mud** /mʌd/ *n* [U] **1** very wet earth in a sticky mass **2 one's name is mud** one is spoken badly of after causing trouble

**mud·dle**[1] /ˈmʌdl/ *n* [*usu. sing*] a state of confusion and disorder: *I was in such a muddle that I didn't know what day it was.*

**muddle**[2] *v* **-dled, -dling** [T *up*] **1** to put into disorder: *You're muddling up the papers.* **2** to confuse: *She gave me so many instructions that I got muddled (up).*

**muddle along** *v adv* [I] to continue in a confused manner, without a plan

**muddle through** *v adv* [I] to have successful results without the best methods of reaching them: *There were problems, but we muddled through somehow.*

**mud·dy**[1] /ˈmʌdi/ *adj* **-dier, -diest** covered with or containing mud: *the muddy waters of the river|Take off those muddy boots.*

**muddy**[2] *v* **-died, -dying** [T] to make dirty with mud: *Your dog's muddying the kitchen floor.*

**mud·guard** /ˈmʌdgɑːd‖-ɑrd/ *BrE*‖ **fender** *AmE n* a metal cover over the wheel of a vehicle to keep the mud from flying up

**muf·fle** /ˈmʌfəl/ *v* **-fled, -fling** [T *usu. pass.*] to make (a sound) less easily heard, esp. with a material: *muffled voices coming from the next room*

**muf·fler** /ˈmʌfləʳ/ *n* **1** *esp. old use* a SCARF worn to keep one's neck warm **2** *AmE* for SILENCER (b)

**mug¹** /mʌg/ *n* **1** (the contents of) a kind of cup with a flat bottom, straight sides, and handle, but without a SAUCER: *a mug of coffee* –see picture on page 337 **2** *BrE infml* a foolish person who is easily deceived

**mug²** *v* **-gg-** [T] to rob with violence, esp. in a dark street –**mugger** *n* –**mugging** *n* [C;U]

**mug·gy** /ˈmʌgi/ *adj* **-gier, -giest** (of weather) unpleasantly warm but not dry –**mugginess** *n* [U]

**Mu·ham·ma·dan** /mʊˈhæmədn, mə-/ *adj,n* → MUSLIM

**mul·ber·ry** /ˈmʌlbəri‖-beri/ *n* **-ries** (a tree with) a dark purple fruit which can be eaten

**mulch** /mʌltʃ/ *n* [S;U] a covering of material, often made from decaying plants, which is put over the soil to improve it –compare HUMUS

**mule** /mjuːl/ *n* the animal which is the young of a donkey and a horse

**mull** /mʌl/ *v* [T] to heat (wine or beer) with sugar, SPICES, and other things: *mulled wine*

**mull** sthg.↔ **over** *v adv; prep* [T] to think over; consider for a time: *I haven't decided what to do; I'm mulling it over.*

**mul·lah** /ˈmʌlə, ˈmʊlə/ *n* a Muslim teacher of law and religion

**mul·ti·far·i·ous** /ˌmʌltəˈfeəriəs/ *adj* [*no comp.*] of many different types: *multifarious interests* –**multifariously** *adv*

**mul·ti·lat·e·ral** /ˌmʌltɪˈlætərəl/ *adj* concerning or including more than two (usu. political) groups of people: *a multilateral agreement on world oil prices* –see also BILATERAL, UNILATERAL –**multilaterally** *adv*

**mul·ti·ple¹** /ˈmʌltəpəl/ *adj* [*no comp.*] including many different parts, types, etc.: *The driver of the crashed car received multiple injuries.* (INJURY)

**multiple²** *n* [*of*] a number which contains a smaller number an exact number of times: *3×4=12; so 12 is a multiple of 3.*

**mul·ti·pli·ca·tion** /ˌmʌltəpləˈkeɪʃən/ *n* [U] the method of combining two numbers by adding one of them to itself as many times as the other states: *2×4=8 is an example of multiplication.*

**mul·ti·pli·ci·ty** /ˌmʌltəˈplɪsəti/ *n* [S] a large number or great variety: *a multiplicity of ideas*

**mul·ti·ply** /ˈmʌltəplaɪ/ *v* [I;T] **1** [*by*] to combine by MULTIPLICATION: *to multiply 2 by 3|2 multiplied by 3 (2×3)=2+2+2.|You added when you should have multiplied.* –compare DIVIDE (3) **2** to increase: *to multiply one's chances of success|When animals have more food, they generally multiply* (=breed) *faster.*

**mul·ti·ra·cial** /ˌmʌltɪˈreɪʃəl◂/ *adj* consisting of or involving several races of people

**mul·ti·sto·rey** /ˌmʌltɪˈstɔːri◂‖-ˈstori◂/ *adj* [A] (of a building) having several levels or floors: *a multistorey office-block*

**mul·ti·tude** /ˈmʌltətjuːd‖-tuːd/ *n* **1** *fml* a large number: *A multitude of thoughts filled her mind.* **2** *old use & bibl* a large crowd

**mum** /mʌm/ *BrE*‖**mom** *AmE n infml* mother: *Can I go to the cinema please, mum?*

**mum·ble** /ˈmʌmbəl/ *v* **-bled, -bling** [I;T +*that*] to speak (words) unclearly: *The old woman mumbled a prayer.|I wish you wouldn't mumble–I can't hear what you're saying.*

**mum·mi·fy** /ˈmʌmɪfaɪ/ *v* **-fied, -fying** [T] to preserve (a dead body) as a MUMMY²

**mum·my¹** /ˈmʌmi/ *BrE*‖**mommy, momma** *AmE n* **-mies** (*used esp. by or to children*) mother: *I want my mummy!* –see also MUM

**mummy²** *n* a dead body preserved from decay by treatment with special substances

**mumps** /mʌmps/ *n* [*the* U] an infectious illness in which the GLANDs (=organs which send substances into the bloodstream) swell, particularly those around the neck and mouth

**munch** /mʌntʃ/ *v* [I;T] to eat (something) with a strong movement of the jaw, esp. making a noise: *munching an apple*

**mun·dane** /mʌnˈdeɪn/ *adj usu. derog* ordinary, with nothing exciting or unusual in it; uninteresting: *a mundane life*

**mu·ni·ci·pal** /mjuːˈnɪsəpəl‖mjʊ-/ *adj* concerning (the parts of) a town, city, etc., under its own government: *municipal buildings* –**municipally** *adv*

**mu·ni·ci·pal·i·ty** /mjuːˌnɪsəˈpæləti‖mjʊ-/ *n* **-ties** a town, city, or other small area having its own government for local affairs

**mu·nif·i·cence** /mjuːˈnɪfəsəns‖mjʊ-/ *n* [U] *fml* generosity –**munificent** *adj*

**mu·ni·tions** /mjuːˈnɪʃənz‖mjʊ-/ *n* [P] large arms for war, such as bombs, guns, etc.

**mu·ral** /ˈmjʊərəl/ *n* a painting which is painted on a wall

**mur·der¹** /ˈmɜːdəʳ‖ˈmɜr-/ *n* **1** [C;U] the crime of killing a human being intentionally: *She was found guilty of murder.|Police are still looking for the murder weapon.* **2** [U] *infml* a very difficult experience: *At last I repaired the clock, but it was murder getting the pieces back in.* –compare MANSLAUGHTER

**murder²** *v* [T] to kill illegally, and on purpose: *a murdered man* –see KILL (USAGE) –**murderer** *n*

**mur·der·ous** /ˈmɜːdərəs‖ˈmɜr-/ *adj* of, like, or suggesting murder: *murderous intentions|a murderous expression on his face* –**murderously** *adv*

**murk·y** /ˈmɜːki‖ˈmɜr-/ *adj* **-ier, -iest** dark and unpleasant: *a murky night|*(fig.) *a man with a murky past*

**mur·mur¹** /ˈmɜːməʳ‖ˈmɜr-/ *n* **1** a soft low sound: *the murmur of the stream* **2 without a murmur** without complaint

**murmur²** *v* [I;T +*that*] to make a soft sound, esp. to speak or say in a quiet voice: *a child murmuring in her sleep|As she delivered her speech, the crowd murmured their approval.*

**mus·cle** /ˈmʌsəl/ *n* **1** [C;U] (one of) the pieces of elastic material in the body which can tighten to produce movement, esp. bending of the joints: *to develop one's arm muscles by playing tennis* **2** [U] strength: *the military muscle of the big world powers* **3 not move a muscle** to stay quite still

**muscle in** *v adv* [I *on*] *infml* to force one's way into (esp.) a group activity, usu. so as to gain a share in what is produced

**mus·cu·lar** /ˈmʌskjʊləʳ‖-kjə-/ *adj* **1** of, concerning, or done by muscles: *a muscular disease* **2** having big muscles; strong-looking: *a muscular body|He's big and muscular.*

**muse** /mjuːz/ *v* **mused, musing** [I *over,* (*up*)*on*] to think deeply, forgetting about the world around one: *She sat musing for hours.*

**mu·se·um** /mjuːˈzɪəm‖mjʊ-/ *n* a building where objects are kept and usu. shown to the public because of their scientific, historical, or artistic interest

**mush** /mʌʃ/ *n* [U] a soft mass of half-liquid, half-solid material, esp. food –**mushy** *adj* **-ier, -iest**: *mushy potatoes|mushy* PEAS

**mush·room¹** /ˈmʌʃruːm, -rʊm/ *n* any of several types of plant (FUNGUS), some of which can be eaten, which grow and develop very quickly

**mushroom²** *v* [I] to grow and develop fast: *New houses have mushroomed on the edge of the town.*

**mu·sic** /ˈmjuːzɪk/ *n* [U] **1** the arrangement of sounds in pleasant patterns and tunes: *That's a beautiful piece of music.* **2** the art of doing this: *to study music|a music student* **3** a written or printed set of notes: *a sheet of music* **4 face the music** to admit to blame, responsibility, etc., and accept the results, esp. punishment or difficulty

**mu·sic·al¹** /ˈmjuːzɪkəl/ *adj* **1** [A] of, like, or producing music: *musical instruments|a rather musical way of speaking* **2** skilled in and/or fond of music: *a very musical child*

**musical²** *n* a play or film with songs and often dances

**music centre** /ˈ·· ˌ··/ *n* a piece of electrical apparatus which can play records and CASSETTES, and also contains a radio

**mu·si·cian** /mjuːˈzɪʃən‖mjʊ-/ *n* a person who performs on a musical instrument, or who writes music –compare COMPOSER

**musk** /mʌsk/ *n* [U] a strong-smelling substance used in making PERFUMES –**musky** *adj* **-ier, -iest**: *a musky smell*

**mus·ket** /ˈmʌskȷ̇t/ *n* an early type of gun

**mus·ket·eer** /ˌmʌskȷ̇ˈtɪəʳ/ *n* a soldier who was armed with a MUSKET

**Mus·lim** /ˈmʌzlȷ̇m, ˈmʊz-, ˈmʊs-/ also **Moslem, Mohammedan, Muhammadan**– *n,adj* (a person) of the religion started by Mohammed –see also ISLAM

**mus·lin** /ˈmʌzlȷ̇n/ *n* [U] a very fine thin cotton material, used (esp. formerly) for light dresses

**mus·sel** /ˈmʌsəl/ *n* a small sea animal (a MOLLUSC) living inside a black shell, whose soft body can be eaten as food

**must¹** /məst; *strong* mʌst/ *v negative contraction* **mustn't** [I +*t*~~o~~-*v*] **1** (past usu. **had to**) (used to show what it is necessary for one to do, what one ought to do, or what one is forced to do): *I must leave at six today.* (but *I had to leave at six yesterday.*)| *You mustn't tell anybody about this–it's a secret.|You must go and see that new film; you'll really enjoy it.|"Dogs must be kept on a lead"* (notice) –see Study Notes on page 386 **2** (past **must have**) to be likely or certain to: *You must feel tired after your long walk.|There's nobody here–they must have all gone home.|You must be* (=I suppose that you are) *the new English teacher.*

USAGE **1 Must** is used in two ways, expressing (1) what is necessary, and (2) what is certain or probable. For sense (1) the past is usually **had to**: ***I* had to** *get up early yesterday;* and the NEGATIVE² is either **mustn't** (=it is forbidden) or **needn't** (=it is unnecessary): *You* **mustn't** *smoke in this part of the train.|You* **needn't** *arrive at the airport until 10.30.* –see also NEED (USAGE). For sense (2) the past is **must have,** and the NEGATIVE² is **can't** (present) and **can't have** (past): *They* **must have** *got lost.* (=I'm sure they have)|*They* **can't have** *got lost.* (=I'm sure they haven't) **2 Ought to** and **should** can be used as less strong forms of **must** in both these senses. Compare: *The doctor told me I* **must** *stop smoking.|My friends told me I* **ought to/should** *stop smoking.|The game* **must have** *finished by now.* (=I'm sure it has)|*The game* **ought to/should** *have finished by now.* (=I expect it probably has)

**must²** *n* [S] something which it is necessary or very important to have or experience: *Warm clothes are a must in the mountains.*

**mus·tache** /məˈstɑːʃ‖ˈmʌstæʃ/ *n AmE* for MOUSTACHE

**mus·tard** /ˈmʌstəd‖-ərd/ *n* [U] (a yellow-flowered plant whose seeds produce) a hot-tasting powder which is mixed with water and eaten in small quantities with meat –see picture on page 521

**mus·ter** /ˈmʌstəʳ/ *v* [I;T] to gather or collect: *The* TROOPS *mustered on the hill.*

**must·n't** /ˈmʌsənt/ *v short for* must not: *You mustn't talk in class.*

**must·y** /ˈmʌsti/ *adj* **-ier, -iest** with an unpleasant smell as if old: *musty old books* –**mustiness** *n* [U]

**mu·ta·tion** /mjuːˈteɪʃən/ *n* [C;U] (an example of) the action of change in the cells of a living thing producing a new quality in the material or parts of the body

**mute¹** /mjuːt/ silent; without speech –**mutely** *adv*

**mute²** *n* a person who cannot speak

**mut·ed** /ˈmjuːtȷ̇d/ *adj* (of a sound or a colour) made softer than is usual

**mu·ti·late** /ˈmjuːtȷ̇leɪt/ *v* **-lated, -lating** [T] to damage by removing a part of: *She was mutilated in the accident and now has only one leg.| a mutilated body* –**mutilation** /-ˈleɪʃən/ *n* [C;U]

**mu·ti·neer** /ˌmjuːtȷ̇ˈnɪəʳ, -tən-/ *n* a person who takes part in a MUTINY

**mu·ti·nous** /ˈmjuːtȷ̇nəs, -tən-/ *adj* taking part in a MUTINY: (fig.) *The mutinous children refused to obey their teacher.* –**mutinously** *adv*

**mu·ti·ny¹** /ˈmjuːtȷ̇ni, -təni/ *n* **-nies** [C;U] (an example of) the act of taking power from the person in charge, esp. from a captain on a ship

**mutiny²** *v* **-nied, -nying** [I] to take part in a MUTINY

**mut·ter** /ˈmʌtəʳ/ *v* [I;T +*that*] to speak (usu. angry or complaining words) in a low voice, not easily heard: *He muttered a threat.* –**mutter** *n* [S]

**mut·ton** /ˈmʌtn/ *n* [U] the meat from a sheep –see MEAT (USAGE)

**mu·tu·al** /ˈmjuːtʃʊəl/ *adj* [*no comp.*] **1** equally so, one towards the other: *Stalin and Trotsky were mutual enemies.|their mutual dislike* (=she dislikes him and he dislikes her) **2** equally shared by each one: *mutual interests|our mutual friend* –**mutually** *adv*

**muz·zle¹** /ˈmʌzəl/ *n* **1** the front part of an animal's face, with the nose and mouth **2** the front end of a gun barrel **3** a covering round an animal's mouth, to prevent it from biting

**muzzle**[2] *v* **-zled, -zling** [T] to put a MUZZLE[1] (3) on: (fig.) *Those who know the truth have been muzzled*(=kept silent) *by those in power.*

**my** /maɪ/ *determiner* (POSSESSIVE *form of* I) **1** of the person who is speaking: *my car|my mother* **2** (used as a cry of surprise or pleasure): *My! What a clever boy!*

**my·o·pic** /maɪ'ɒpɪk, -'əʊpɪk‖-'ɑpɪk/ *adj* unable to see clearly objects which are not close; SHORT-SIGHTED

**myr·i·ad** /'mɪrɪəd/ *adj,n lit* (of) a great and varied number

**my·self** /maɪ'self/ *pron* **1** (used as the object of a verb, or after a PREPOSITION, when the person who is speaking does the action and is the object of the action): *I hurt myself.|I'm pleased with myself.*

**mys·te·ri·ous** /mɪ'stɪərɪəs/ *adj* not easily understood; full of mystery: *the mysterious disappearance of my brother|They're being very mysterious* (=not telling anyone) *about their holiday plans.* **–mysteriously** *adv* **–mysteriousness** *n* [U]

**mys·te·ry** /'mɪstəri/ *n* **-ries 1** [C] something which cannot be explained or understood: *Her death is a mystery.* **2** [U] a strange secret nature or quality: *stories full of mystery*

**mys·tic** /'mɪstɪk/ *n* a person who practises MYSTICISM

**mys·tic·al** /'mɪstɪkəl/ also **mystic**– *adj* **1** concerning MYSTICISM **2** of hidden religious power and importance **–mystically** *adv*

**mys·ti·cis·m** /'mɪst$_{\frac{1}{2}}$sɪzəm/ *n* [U] the attempt to gain, or practice of gaining, a knowledge of real truth and union with God by prayer and MEDITATION

**mys·ti·fy** /'mɪst$_{\frac{1}{2}}$faɪ/ *v* **-fied, -fying** [T] to make (someone) wonder; completely BEWILDER: *I'm completely mystified about what happened.* **–mystification** /-f$_{\frac{1}{2}}$'keɪʃən/ *n* [C;U]

**mys·tique** /mɪ'stiːk/ *n* [*usu. sing.*] a feeling of mystery or separateness which surrounds certain activities, professions, etc.: *the mystique of women*

**myth** /mɪθ/ *n* **1** [C] an ancient story, usu. containing religious or magical ideas, which may explain natural or historical events **2** [U] such stories generally: *an idea common in myth* **3** [C +*that*] a false story or idea, which may be widely believed: *the myth that men are better drivers than women*

**myth·i·cal** /'mɪθɪkəl/ *adj* [*no comp.*] **1** of or in a MYTH (1) **2** not real; imagined or invented

**my·thol·o·gy** /mɪ'θɒlədʒi‖-'θɑ-/ *n* **-gies** [C;U] (a system of beliefs contained in) MYTHS (1) **–mythological** /ˌmɪθə'lɒdʒɪkəl‖-'lɑ-/ *adj*

# N, n

**SPELLING NOTE**

Words with the sound /n/, may be spelt **kn-**, like **know**, or **pn-**, like **pneumonia.**

**N, n** /en/ **N's, n's** *or* **Ns, ns** the 14th letter of the English alphabet

**n** *written abbrev. for:* **1** noun **2** note

**N** *written abbrev. for:* North(ern)

**nab** /næb/ *v* **-bb-** [T] *infml* to seize (esp. as a thief): *He was nabbed while stealing the money.*

**nag**[1] /næg/ *v* **-gg-** [I;T +*to-v*/*at*] **1** to find fault with; try to persuade (someone) by continuous complaining: *I wish you'd stop nagging!|He's been nagging (at) me all week to mend his shirt.* **2** to worry or annoy continuously: *a nagging headache*

**nag** sbdy. **into** sthg. *v prep* [T +*v-ing*] to cause to do (something) by NAGging: *The children have nagged me into taking them to the cinema.*

**nag**[2] *n* a horse that is old or in bad condition

**nail**[1] /neɪl/ *n* **1** a thin pointed piece of metal for hammering into pieces of wood, usu. to fasten them together **2 a** → FINGERNAIL **b** *rare* → TOENAIL **3 hard as nails** *infml* without any tender feelings **4 hit the nail on the head** *infml* to do or say something exactly right

**nail**[2] *v* [T *to, on*] to fasten (as) with a nail or nails: *She nailed a sign to/on the post.*

**nail** sthg.↔ **down** *v adv* [T] **1** to fasten down, with a nail or nails: *Will you nail down that loose board in the floor?* **2** [*to*] to force (someone) to tell plans or wishes clearly: *Before they repair the car, nail them down to a price.* (=make them tell you how much it will cost)|*I can never nail her down (to anything).*

**nail·brush** /'neɪlbrʌʃ/ *n* a small stiff brush for cleaning hands, and esp. FINGERNAILS

**nail file** /'· ·/ *n* a small instrument with a rough surface for shaping FINGERNAILS

**nail var·nish** /'· ˌ··/ *BrE*‖**nail polish** *AmE* /'·ˌ··/ *n* [U] coloured or transparent liquid which dries to give a hard shiny surface, used esp. by women on their FINGERNAILS

**na·ive, naïve** /naɪ'iːv‖nɑ'iːv/ *adj* having or showing no experience (as of social rules or behaviour), esp. because one is young: *The youngest boy was laughed at for his naive remarks.|It's naive (of you) to believe he'll do what he says.* **–naively, naïvely** *adv* **–naivety, naïvety, -eté** *n* [U]

**na·ked** /'neɪk$_{\frac{1}{2}}$d/ *adj* **1** (of (a part of) a person's body) not covered by clothes: *He was naked to the waist.* (=wore nothing above his waist)|(fig.) *a naked light* (=without glass over it) **2 with the naked eye** without any instrument to help one see: *Bacteria are too small to see with the naked eye.* **–nakedly** *adv* **–nakedness** *n* [U]

**name**[1] /neɪm/ *n* **1** [C] the word(s) that someone or something is called or known by: *Her name is Mary Wilson; her first name is Mary.|What's the name of that river?|Do you know a boy* **by the name of** (=called) *David?* **2** [S] fame; the opinion others have of one: *This restaurant has a good name.|She* **made a name**

**for herself/made her name** (=became famous) *as a painter.* **3 to one's name** *infml* (esp. of money) as one's property: *He hasn't a penny to his name.*

**name²** *v* **named, naming** [T] **1** to give a name to: *They named their baby son John.* (=gave him the name John)|*She was named after* (=given the same name as) *her mother.* **2** to say what the name of (someone or something) is: *Can you name this plant?* **3** to choose or appoint: *The President named him (as) Secretary of State.*|*"How much will you sell me this for?" "Name your own price."*

**name·drop** /'neɪmdrɒp‖-drɑp/ *v* **-pp-** [I] *derog & infml* to mention famous people's names to make it seem that one knows them or their work well –**namedropper** *n* –**namedropping** *n* [U]

**name·less** /'neɪmləs/ *adj* **1** not known by name; ANONYMOUS: *the work of a nameless 13th-century poet*|*a certain person who must/shall be nameless* (=whose name I will not tell) **2** too terrible to describe or name: *guilty of nameless crimes*

**name·ly** /'neɪmli/ *adv* (and) that is (to say): *Only one person can do the job, namely you.*

**name·sake** /'neɪmseɪk/ *n* one of two or more people with the same name: *I often get letters that are addressed to my namesake down the street.*

**nan·ny** /'næni/ *n* **-nies** (esp. in rich families) a woman employed to take care of children

**nanny goat** /'·· ·/ *n* (*used esp. by or to children*) a female goat –compare BILLY GOAT

**nap¹** /næp/ *n* a short sleep, esp. during the day: *Father always takes/has a nap in the afternoon.*

**nap²** *v* **catch someone napping** *infml* to find, or take advantage of, someone offguard or not doing his/her duty

**na·palm** /'neɪpɑːm‖-pɑm, -pɑlm/ *n* [U] a jelly made from petrol, which burns fiercely and is used in bombs

**nape** /neɪp/ *n* [S] the back (of the neck)

**nap·kin** /'næpkən/ *n* **1** also **serviette**– a piece of cloth or paper used for protecting one's clothes and for cleaning one's hands and lips during a meal –see picture on page 521 **2** *BrE fml* for NAPPY

**nap·py** /'næpi/ *BrE*‖**diaper** *AmE n* **-pies** a piece of soft cloth or paper worn between the legs and around the waist of a baby

**nar·cis·sus** /nɑː'sɪsəs‖nɑr-/ *n* **-suses** *or* **-si** /saɪ/ a white or yellow spring flower, such as the DAFFODIL

**nar·cot·ic** /nɑː'kɒtɪk‖nɑr'kɑ-/ *n* [*often pl.*] a drug which in small amounts causes sleep or takes away pain, and in large amounts is harmful and habit-forming: *He was sent to prison on a narcotics charge.* (=an offence concerning selling or using these drugs) –**narcotic** *adj*

**nar·rate** /nə'reɪt‖'næreɪt, næ'reɪt, nə-/ *v* **-rated, -rating** [T] *fml* to tell (a story); describe (an event or events) in order: *Shall I narrate a strange experience of mine?* –**narration** /nə'reɪʃən‖næ-, nə-/ *n* [C;U] –**narrator** *n*

**nar·ra·tive** /'nærətɪv/ *n* [C;U] (the act or practice of telling) a story: *a narrative of last week's events* –**narrative** *adj* [*no comp.*]: *a narrative poem*

> **SPELLING NOTE**
> Words with the sound /n/, may be spelt **kn-**, like **know**, or **pn-**, like **pneumonia.**

**nar·row¹** /'nærəʊ/ *adj* **1** small from one side to the other, esp. in comparison with length or with what is usual: *a narrow street*|*The gate is too narrow for a car.* –opposite **broad**; compare WIDE **2** limited; RESTRICTED (3): *The secret is known only to a narrow group of people.*|*She has very narrow ideas about religion.* **3** only just successful: *to win by a narrow* MAJORITY|*a narrow escape* –compare CLOSE⁴ (6); see THIN (USAGE) –**narrowness** *n* [U]

**narrow²** *v* [I;T] to (cause to) decrease in width: *The river narrows here.* –compare BROADEN, WIDEN

**nar·row·ly** /'nærəʊli/ *adv* hardly; only just: *One car went too fast and narrowly missed hitting another car.*

**narrow-mind·ed** /,·· '··◂‖'·· ,··/ *adj derog* unwilling to respect the opinions (or actions) of others when different from one's own; PREJUDICED: *a narrow-minded attitude* –opposite **broadminded** –**narrowmindedness** *n* [U]

**na·sal** /'neɪzəl/ *adj* of or related to the nose: *to breathe through the nasal passage*|*a nasal* (=making sounds through the nose) *voice* –**nasally** *adv*

**nas·ty** /'nɑːsti‖'næsti/ *adj* **-tier, -tiest 1** unpleasant in manner; angry or threatening: *Who's that nasty old woman?*|*He* **turned nasty** (=started to threaten me) *when I said I couldn't pay him.* **2** very ugly or unpleasant to see, taste, smell, etc.: *cheap and nasty furniture* **3** painful; severe; dangerous: *a nasty accident with one person killed*|*a nasty cut on the head* **4** morally bad or improper; OBSCENE: *You've got a nasty mind.* –**nastily** *adv* –**nastiness** *n* [U]

**na·tion** /'neɪʃən/ *n* **1** a large group of people living in one area and usu. having an independent government: *The President spoke to the nation.* –compare COUNTRY¹ (1) **2** a large group of people with the same race and language: *the American Indian nations in the western United States* –see RACE (USAGE)

**na·tion·al¹** /'næʃənəl/ *adj* of, concerning, or belonging to a nation: *a national newspaper* (=one read everywhere in the country)| *a national holiday* (=a holiday everywhere in the country)|*The national news comes after the international news.*|*the National Theatre* –**nationally** *adv*

**national²** *n* a person, esp. someone abroad, who belongs to another, usu. stated, country: *American nationals in England* –compare CITIZEN, ALIEN

**national an·them** /,··· '··/ *n* the official song of a nation, to be sung or played on certain formal occasions

**na·tion·al·is·m** /'næʃənəlɪzəm/ *n* [U] **1** (too great) love of and pride in a country shown by its people **2** desire by a racial group (nation) to form an independent country: *Scottish nationalism*

**na·tion·al·ist** /'næʃənələst/ *adj,n* (a person) believing in NATIONALISM (2): *a Basque nationalist*|*the nationalist party in Wales*

**na·tion·al·is·tic** /,næʃənə'lɪstɪk/ *adj often derog* of or showing (too) great love of one's country: *a nationalistic election speech* –**nationalistically** *adv*

**na·tion·al·i·ty** /,næʃə'næləti/ *n* **-ties** [C;U] membership of a nation by a person: *She lives in France but has British nationality.*|*people of many different nationalities* –compare CITIZENSHIP

**na·tion·al·ize** ‖also **-ise** *BrE* /'næʃənəlaɪz/ *v* **-ized,**

-**izing** [T] (of a government) to buy or take control of (a business, industry, etc.) for the state: *The British government nationalized the railways in 1948.* –opposites **denationalize, privatize –nationalization** /ˌnæʃənəlaɪˈzeɪʃən‖-nələ-/ *n* [U]

**national park** /ˌ··· ˈ·/ *n* an area of land, usu. large, which is kept in its natural state by the government for people to visit

**national ser·vice** /ˌ··· ˈ··/ *BrE*‖**draft** *AmE n* the system of making all men (and sometimes all women) serve in the armed forces for a limited period: *Britain no longer has national service.*

**na·tion·wide** /ˌneɪʃənˈwaɪd ◂/ *adj* (used esp. in newspapers, on the radio, etc.) happening, existing, etc., over a whole country; NATIONAL[1]: *a nationwide broadcast* (=heard everywhere in the country)

**na·tive**[1] /ˈneɪtɪv/ *adj* **1** [A] belonging to or being the place of one's birth: *her native language*|*He was never popular in his native Australia.* –compare FOREIGN (1) **2** [A] (of a person) belonging to a country from birth: *native speakers of English* (=those who learn English as their first language) **3** [*to*] growing, living, found, etc., in a place: *a plant native to the eastern USA* **4** belonging to someone from birth; not learned; INNATE: *native ability*

**native**[2] *n* **1** someone who was born (in a place): *a native of New York City* **2** *often derog and becoming rare* (esp. used by Europeans about non-Europeans) one of the original people living in a place: *The government of the island treated the natives badly.*

**Na·tiv·i·ty** /nəˈtɪvǰti/ *n* the birth of Christ

**NATO** /ˈneɪtəʊ/ *n abbrev. for:* North Atlantic Treaty Organization; a group of countries (including the USA and Britain) which give military help to each other

**nat·ter** /ˈnætəʳ/ *v* [I] *BrE infml* to talk continuously about unimportant things; CHATTER: *They nattered (away) all afternoon.* –**natter** *n* [S]

**nat·ty** /ˈnæti/ *adj* **-tier, -tiest** *infml* neat in appearance; SMART[1] (1): *a very natty dresser* (=a person who dresses in a neat, fashionable style) –**nattily** *adv*

**nat·u·ral**[1] /ˈnætʃərəl/ *adj* **1** of, concerning, or being what exists or happens ordinarily in the world, esp. not caused, made, or controlled by people: *the natural mineral wealth of a country*|*death from natural causes* –compare MAN-MADE, ARTIFICIAL **2** usual; ordinary: *It's natural to feel nervous when you go to a new school.* **3** not looking or sounding different from usual; UNAFFECTED (2): *Try to look natural for your photograph.* **4** [A *to*] belonging to someone from birth; not learned: *natural charm*|*a natural musician* (=with natural musical ability) –see also UNNATURAL, SUPERNATURAL –**naturalness** *n* [U]

**natural**[2] *n* [*usu. sing.*] *infml* someone or something well suited (to a job, part in a play, etc.) or certain to succeed: *As an actor, he's a natural.*

**natural gas** /ˌ··· ˈ·/ *n* [U] gas which is taken from under the earth or sea and mainly burnt for cooking and heating

**natural his·to·ry** /ˌ··· ˈ···/ *n* [U] the study of plants, animals, and rocks

**nat·u·ral·ist** /ˈnætʃərəlǰst/ *n* a person who studies plants or animals

**nat·u·ral·ize** ‖also **-ise** *BrE* /ˈnætʃərəlaɪz/ *v* **-ized, -izing** [T] to make (a person born elsewhere) a citizen of a country: *He was naturalized after living in Britain for ten years.* –**naturalization** /ˌnætʃərəlaɪˈzeɪʃən‖-lə-/ *n* [U]

**nat·u·ral·ly** /ˈnætʃərəli‖-tʃərəli, -tʃərli/ *adv* **1** according to the nature of someone or something: *He is naturally lazy.* **2** without trying to look or sound different from usual: *He behaves naturally.* **3** of course; as expected: *"Did you win the game?" "Naturally."*|*Naturally you will be feeling tired after your long walk.*

**natural re·sourc·es** /ˌ··· ·ˈ··/ *n* [P] the land, forests, mineral wealth, etc., that a country possesses

**natural sci·ence** /ˌ··· ˈ··/ *n* [C;U] BIOLOGY, chemistry, and PHYSICS –compare SOCIAL SCIENCE

**natural se·lec·tion** /ˌ··· ·ˈ··/ *n* [U] *tech* the course of events by which only the plants and animals best suited to the conditions around them continue to live

**na·ture** /ˈneɪtʃəʳ/ *n* **1** [U] everything that exists in the world independently of human beings, such as earth and rocks, the weather, and plants and animals: *They stopped to admire the beauties of nature.* (=scenery)|*Farming on this bad land is a struggle against nature.* **2** [C;U] the qualities which make someone different from others; character: *She has a generous nature/is generous* **by nature**.|*It's (in) her nature to be generous.* **3** [S] a type; sort: *ceremonies of a solemn nature* **4 second nature** an action or ability that has become a habit, as if part of one's character: *Speaking French is second nature to him.*

**naught** /nɔːt‖nɔt, nɑt/ *n* [U] *old use & lit* nothing: *All his hopes* **came to naught** *when he failed the exam.* –compare NOUGHT

**naugh·ty** /ˈnɔːti‖ˈnɔti, ˈnɑti/ *adj* **-tier, -tiest 1** (esp. of children) bad in behaviour; not obeying a parent, teacher, set of rules, etc.: *You naughty boy! I told you not to play in the road.* –see WICKED (USAGE) **2** *euph* morally, esp. sexually, improper: *an amusing and naughty book* –**naughtily** *adv* –**naughtiness** *n* [U]

**nau·se·a** /ˈnɔːzɪə, -sɪə‖-zɪə, -ʃə/ *n* [U] a feeling of sickness and desire to VOMIT (to throw up the contents of the stomach through the mouth)

**nau·se·ate** /ˈnɔːzieɪt, -si-‖-zi, -ʒi-/ *v* **-ated, -ating** [T] to cause to feel NAUSEA: *a nauseating smell*|(fig.) *His attitude towards women really nauseates me.* –**nauseous** *adj*: *I feel a bit nauseous.*

**nau·ti·cal** /ˈnɔːtɪkəl/ *adj* of or concerning sailors, ships, or sailing –**nautically** *adv*

**nautical mile** /ˌ··· ˈ·/ *n* a measure of distance, used at sea, equal to 1,852 metres –compare KNOT[1] (4)

**na·val** /ˈneɪvəl/ *adj* of a navy or ships of war: *a naval officer*|*naval battles*

**nave** /neɪv/ *n* the long central part of a church in which the people (CONGREGATION) sit

**na·vel** /ˈneɪvəl/ *n* a small sunken place in the middle of the stomach, caused when the connection to the mother (the UMBILICAL CORD) was cut at birth –see picture on page 299

**nav·i·ga·ble** /ˈnævǰgəbəl/ *adj* (of a body of water) deep and wide enough to allow ships to travel: *This river is navigable for 200 kilometres.*

**nav·i·gate** /ˈnævǰgeɪt/ *v* **-gated, -gating** [I;T] to direct the course of (a ship, plane, etc.): *Get in the car; I'll drive if you hold the map and navigate.*

**nav·i·ga·tion** /ˌnævǰˈgeɪʃən/ *n* [U] the act, practice, or science of navigating (NAVIGATE): *Navigation is difficult on this river because of the hidden rocks.*

**nav·i·ga·tor** /'nævəgeɪtəʳ/ *n* the officer on a ship or aircraft who plans and directs its course –compare PILOT

**na·vy** /'neɪvi/ *n* **-vies 1** [C +*sing./pl. v*] the organization, including ships, people, buildings, etc., which makes up the power of a country for war at sea: *He joined the navy nearly 30 years ago.* **2** [C] the ships of war belonging to a country: *a small navy of ten ships* –see also MERCHANT NAVY

**navy blue** /,·· '·◂/ also **navy–** *adj,n* [U] very dark blue (colour)

**nay** /neɪ/ *adv lit* not only this, but also: *a bright, nay (a) blinding light* (=not only bright but blinding)

**NB** *abbrev. for: (used esp. in writing) Latin* nota bene (=note well)

**NCO** *n abbrev. for:* NON COMMISSIONED OFFICER: *He became an NCO at 18.*

**NE** *written abbrev. said as:* northeast(ern)

**near¹** /nɪəʳ/ *adj* **1** [*to*] not far; not at much distance: *the near future|Go and pick an apple from the nearest tree.|We live in the town centre, so my office is quite near.|He's one of my nearest relatives.* (=is closely related to me) –see Study Notes on page 474 **2** [A *no comp.*] **a** closer: *He stood on the near bank of the river.* –opposite **far b** *esp. BrE* for NEARSIDE **–nearness** *n* [U *to*]

USAGE **Near** and **close** are almost the same in meaning, but there are certain phrases in which one must be used and not the other. Notice: *the* **near** *future|the* **near** *distance* (not **close**); *a* **close** *friend|***close** *behind* (not **near**). **Close** cannot be used as a PREPOSITION.

**near²** *adv,prep* [*to*] not far (from): *We live near (to) the church.|Don't go too near (to) the edge of the cliff.|Remind me again nearer (to) the time of the meeting.|The bus is nowhere near as fast as/not nearly as fast as* (=much slower than) *the train.*

**near³** *v* [I;T] to come closer in distance or time (to); APPROACH¹ (1): *He got more and more nervous as the day of the examination neared.*

**near-⁴** almost: *a near-perfect performance|a near-impossible decision|a near-white colour*

**near·by** /nɪə'baɪ‖nɪər-/ *adv,adj* [*no comp.*] near; close by: *We went to a nearby town.|a football match being played nearby*

**near·ly** /'nɪəli‖'nɪərli/ *adv* [*no comp.*] almost; not far from, but not quite: *He very nearly died.|The train was nearly full.|not nearly enough money* (=far too little money) –see Study Notes on page 389

**near·side** /'nɪəsaɪd‖'nɪər-/ *adj* [A] *BrE* being on the side of a vehicle nearest to the edge of the road: *the nearside back light of a car* –opposite **offside**

**near·sight·ed** /,nɪə'saɪtəd◂‖'nɪərsaɪtəd/ *adj AmE* for SHORTSIGHTED **–nearsightedness** *n* [U]

**neat** /ni:t/ *adj* **1** in good order; showing care in appearance; tidy: *neat handwriting|He keeps his office neat and tidy.* **2** clever and effective: *a neat trick* **3** also **straight** *esp. AmE–* (of alcoholic drinks) without ice or water or other liquid: *I like my* WHISKY *neat.* **–neatly** *adv* **–neatness** *n* [U]

**SPELLING NOTE**
Words with the sound /n/, may be spelt **kn-**, like **know**, or **pn-**, like **pneumonia.**

**neb·u·lous** /'nebjʊləs‖-bjə-/ *adj* not clear; not DISTINCT (2); VAGUE: *nebulous political ideas*

**ne·ces·sar·i·ly** /'nesəsərəli, ,nesə'serəli‖,nesə'serəli/ *adv* in a way that must be so; unavoidably: *Food that looks good doesn't necessarily taste good.* (=it might taste bad)

**ne·ces·sa·ry** /'nesəsəri‖-seri/ *adj* [*to, for*] that must be; that must be had or obtained; needed: *Food is necessary for life.|Is it really necessary for me to attend the meeting?* –see also UNNECESSARY

**ne·ces·si·tate** /nə'sesəteɪt/ *v* **-tated, -tating** [T +*v-ing*] *fml* to cause a need for; make necessary: *Your mistakes necessitate doing the work again.*

**ne·ces·si·ty** /nə'sesəti/ *n* **-ties 1** [S;U +*to-v/of, for*] the condition of being necessary, needed, or unavoidable; need: *Is there any necessity for another election?|We're faced with the necessity of buying* (=we have to buy) *a new car.|He was forced* **by necessity** *to look for a job. He needed some money.* **2** [C] something that is necessary: *Food and clothing are necessities of life.* –compare LUXURY (2)

**neck¹** /nek/ *n* **1** the part of the body by which the head is joined to the shoulders –see picture on page 299 **2** the part of a garment that goes round this part of the human body: *the neck of a shirt* **3** a narrow part that sticks out from a broader part: *the neck of a bottle* **4 neck and neck** *infml* (of two horses, people, etc., in competition) equal so far; with an equal chance of winning **5 stick one's neck out** *infml* to take a risk; say or do something which may fail, be wrong, or hurt one **6 -necked** (of a piece of clothing) having a certain shape or style of neck: *a V-necked dress|an open-necked shirt* (=unbuttoned at the neck)

**neck²** *v* [I] *infml* to kiss, CARESS, etc., but without having full sexual relations

**neck·lace** /'nek-ləs/ *n* a string of jewels, BEADS, PEARLS, etc., or a chain of gold, silver, etc., worn around the neck as a decoration

**neck·line** /'nek-laɪn/ *n* the line made by the neck opening of a piece of women's clothing: *a low neckline*

**neck·tie** /'nektaɪ/ *n AmE* for TIE¹ (1)

**nec·tar** /'nektəʳ/ *n* [U] **1** (in ancient Greek and Roman literature) the drink of the gods: (fig.) *A cold beer is like nectar when you're thirsty.* **2** the sweet liquid collected by bees from flowers

**née** /neɪ/ *adv* (*used after a married woman's name and before her original family name*) formerly named: *Mrs Carol Cook née Williams*

**need¹** /ni:d/ *n* **1** [S;U *of, for*] the condition of lacking or wanting something necessary or very useful: *There is a growing need for new housing in this area.|The doctor told me I was* **in need of** *a good rest.|Take money from the bank* **as the need arises.** (=whenever it is necessary) **2** [S;U +*to-v/for*] a necessary duty; what must be done: *There's no need for you to come too.|*(fig.) *There's no need to be so rude.* (=you shouldn't be) **3** [C *usu. pl.*] *fml* something one must have: *The hotel* STAFF¹ (=workers) *will attend to all your needs/your every need.* **4** [U] *fml & euph* the state of not having enough food or money: *We are collecting money for children* **in need.** **5 if need be** if it is necessary

**need²** *v* [T+*to-v*/*v-ing;* not *be*+*v-ing*] to have a need for; want for some useful purpose; lack: *Children need milk.*|*This soup needs salt.*|*My coat needs mending/ needs to be mended.*|*I need my coat mended.*|*If I need you to come and help I'll call.*|*You don't need to come if you don't want to.* (=there is no need for you to come)

**need³** *v* NEGATIVE *contraction* **needn't** [I +~~to~~-*v;* not *be*+*v-ing*] (used as a helping verb with another verb in questions and NEGATIVES², not in simple statements) to have to: *"Need you go so soon?" "No, we needn't./Yes, we must."*|*You needn't talk so loud.* –see Study Notes on page 386

USAGE Compare: *I* **needn't have** *put on my thick coat.* (=but I did)|*I* **didn't need** *to put on my thick coat.* (=so I didn't *or* but I did) –see MUST (USAGE)

**nee·dle¹** /ˈniːdl/ *n* **1** a long pointed metal pin with a hole in one end for the thread, used in sewing **2** a thin pointed object that looks like this: *a* PINE² *needle* (=a thin leaf of this tree) **3** a thin pointed rod used in working with long threadlike pieces of wool: KNIT*ting needles* **4** (in a RECORD PLAYER) the very small pointed jewel or piece of metal which picks up the sound recorded on a record; STYLUS **5** a very thin hollow pointed tube, at the end of a HYPODERMIC SYRINGE, which is pushed into someone's skin to put a liquid (esp. medicine) into the body **6** a long thin pointer: *the needle of a compass*

**needle²** *v* **-dled, -dling** [T *about*] *infml* to annoy (someone) by repeated unkind remarks, stupid jokes, etc.; TEASE (1): *The boys always needled Jim about being fat.*

**need·less** /ˈniːdlɨs/ *adj* **1** not needed; unnecessary: *needless trouble preparing for guests who didn't come* **2 needless to say** of course; as was to be expected: *Needless to say, it rained when I left my window open.* **–needlessly** *adv*

**nee·dle·work** /ˈniːdlwɜːk‖-wɜrk/ *n* [U] work done with a NEEDLE¹ (3) by sewing or EMBROIDERing: *tired eyes from doing fine needlework*

**need·n't** /ˈniːdnt/ *v short for:* NEED³ not: *You needn't go if you don't want to.*|*I needn't have put on this thick coat.* (=but I did)

**need·y** /ˈniːdi/ *adj* **-ier, -iest** poor; without food, clothing, etc.: *a needy family*|*money to help the needy*

**ne'er** /neəʳ/ *adv lit* never: *Will he ne'er come home again?*

**ne'er-do-well** /ˈneə duː ˌwel‖ˈneər-/ *n* **-wells** *derog* a useless or lazy person

**neg·a·tive¹** /ˈnegətɪv/ *adj* **1** saying or meaning "no": *a negative answer to my request*|*negative expressions like "not at all"* –opposite **affirmative 2** without any active qualities or results: *negative advice that only tells you what not to do*|*The test for bacteria was negative.* (=none were found) **3** (of electricity) of the type that is carried by ELECTRONS **4** (of a number or quantity) less than zero: *a negative profit* (=a loss)|*If* x *is* POSITIVE¹ (5) *then* -x *is negative.* –opposite **positive** (for **2, 3, 4**) **–negatively** *adv*

**negative²** *n* **1** a word, expression, or statement saying or meaning "no": *The answer to my request was* **in the negative.**|"Never" and "not at all" are negatives. –opposite **affirmative 2** a photograph or film showing dark areas in nature as light and light areas as dark –compare POSITIVE² (3)

**ne·glect¹** /nɪˈglekt/ *v* [T] **1** [+*v-ing*] to give too little attention or care to: *neglected children*|*You've been neglecting your work.* **2** [+*to-v*] to fail (to do something), esp. because of carelessness or forgetfulness: *Don't neglect to lock the door when you leave.*

**neglect²** *n* [U] **1** the action of NEGLECTing: *the owner's neglect of repairs to his house* **2** the condition or fact of being NEGLECTed: *The garden is in a state of neglect.*

**ne·glect·ful** /nɪˈglektfəl/ *adj* in the habit of NEGLECTing things: *a mother who is neglectful of her children* **–neglectfully** *adv* **–neglectfulness** *n* [U]

**neg·li·gee** /ˈneglɨʒeɪ‖ˌneglɨˈʒeɪ/ *n* a woman's light and usu. fancy NIGHTDRESS

**neg·li·gent** /ˈneglɪdʒənt/ *adj* not taking enough care: *He's been negligent in not locking the doors as he was told to do.* **–negligently** *adv* **–negligence** *n* [U]: *The driver's negligence was the cause of the accident.*

**neg·li·gi·ble** /ˈneglɪdʒəbəl/ *adj* too slight or unimportant to be worth any attention: *The damage to my car is negligible.* **–negligibly** *adv*

**ne·go·ti·a·ble** /nɪˈgəʊʃɪəbəl, -ʃə-/ *adj* **1** that can be settled or changed by being NEGOTIATED: *a negotiable contract*|*He says his claim is not negotiable.* **2** (of a cheque or order to pay money) that can be exchanged for money **3** *infml* that can be passed through, along, etc.: *The road is only negotiable in the dry season.*

**ne·go·ti·ate** /nɪˈgəʊʃieɪt/ *v* **-ated, -ating 1** [I +*to-v*/*with*] to talk with another person or group in order to try to come to an agreement: *The trade union is negotiating with the employers to get a better contract.* **2** [T *with*] to produce (an agreement) or settle (a piece of business) in this way: *The trade union negotiated a new contract with the owner.* **3** [T] *infml* to go safely over, through, along, etc.: *Will this small car negotiate that steep hill?* **–negotiator** *n*

**ne·go·ti·a·tion** /nɪˌgəʊʃiˈeɪʃən/ *n* [C;U] an act or the action of negotiating (NEGOTIATE): *The agreement was the result of long negotiation(s).*|*the negotiation of new wage levels*|*The contract is* **under negotiation**. (=now being settled)

**Ne·gro** /ˈniːgrəʊ/ **Negress** /ˈniːgrɨs/ *fem.*– *n* **-groes** *tech or not polite* a person belonging to a dark-skinned race; BLACK person

**neigh** /neɪ/ *v,n* [I] (to make) the loud and long cry of a horse

**neigh·bour** *BrE*‖**-bor** *AmE* /ˈneɪbəʳ/ *n* a person living or located near another: *my next-door neighbour* (=the person living in the next house)|*We're neighbours now.*

**neigh·bour·hood** *BrE*‖**-borhood** *AmE* /ˈneɪbəhʊd‖-ər-/ *n* **1** [C +*sing./pl. v*] (the people living in) a small area within a larger place such as a town: *a quiet neighbourhood with good shops* **2** [S] the area around a point or place: *You'll find it* **in the neighbourhood (of** *the station)*.

**neigh·bour·ing** *BrE*‖**-boring** *AmE* /ˈneɪbərɪŋ/ *adj* [A *no comp.*] (esp. of places) near or close by: *There is a bus service for the neighbouring villages.*

**neigh·bour·ly** *BrE*‖**-borly** *AmE* /ˈneɪbəli‖-ər-/ *adj* friendly; like (that of) a good neighbour –opposite **unneighbourly –neighbourliness** *n* [U]

**nei·ther¹** /ˈnaɪðəʳ‖ˈniː-/ *determiner,pron* not one and not the other of two: *Neither road/Neither of the roads is very good.* (=they are both bad)|*They neither of them wanted to go.*|*"Will you have tea or coffee?" "Neither!"* –see also EITHER

**neither²** *conj* **1** not either: *He neither ate, drank, nor smoked.*|*Neither my father nor I were there.* –see EITHER (USAGE) **2** (*used with* NEGATIVE² *expressions*) also not: *I haven't read this book, and neither has my brother.* (=both haven't read it)|*"I can't swim!" "Neither can I!"* (=both of us are unable to swim)

USAGE Notice the word order of **Neither/Nor** *can I*, which is the same as that of a question.

**nem·e·sis** /ˈneməsəs/ *n* **-ses** /siːz/ [U] *lit* (*sometimes cap.*) just and esp. unavoidable punishment

**ne·o·lith·ic** /ˌniːəˈlɪθɪk/ *adj* (*often cap.*) of the period about 10,000 years ago when people began to settle in villages, grow crops, and keep animals –compare PALEOLITHIC

**ne·on** /ˈniːɒn‖-ɑn/ *n* [U] a chemically inactive gas that is a simple substance (ELEMENT (1)) and is present in small amounts in the air

**neon light** /ˈ·· ·/ *n* a glass tube filled with NEON which lights when an electric current goes through it, often shaped to form a sign advertising something

**neph·ew** /ˈnevjuː, ˈnef-‖ˈnef-/ *n* the son of one's (wife's or husband's) brother or sister –compare NIECE; see picture on page 217

**nep·o·tis·m** /ˈnepətɪzəm/ *n* [U] the practice of favouring one's relatives when one has power, esp. by giving them good jobs

**Nep·tune** /ˈneptjuːn‖-tuːn/ *n* the PLANET 8th in order from the sun

**nerve¹** /nɜːv‖nɜrv/ *n* **1** [C] any of the threadlike parts of the body which form a system to carry feelings and messages to and from the brain **2** [U] strength or control of mind; courage: *a man of nerve*|*I wanted to write an angry letter but I* **lost my nerve.** **3** [S;U] *derog* boldness; EFFRONTERY (1): *He's the dirtiest man I know, and he* **has the nerve** *to tell me my shoes need cleaning!*|*What a nerve!*

**nerve²** *v* **nerved, nerving** [T] *fml* to give courage to (someone, esp. oneself) –see also UNNERVE

**nerve-rack·ing** /ˈ· ˌ··/ *adj infml* difficult to do or bear calmly, esp. because dangerous: *a nerve-racking journey through the high mountains*

**nerves** /nɜːvz‖nɜrvz/ *n* [P] *infml* **1** a condition of great nervousness: *nerves before an examination.* **2** **get on someone's nerves** to make someone annoyed or bad-tempered: *That man gets on my nerves.*

**ner·vous** /ˈnɜːvəs‖ˈnɜr-/ *adj* **1** afraid; worried: *He was nervous before the plane journey.* **2** of or related to the NERVOUS SYSTEM of the body, or to the feelings: *a nervous disease* –**nervously** *adv* –**nervousness** *n* [U]

USAGE Compare **nervous**, **concerned**, and **anxious**: You can be **nervous** (=rather afraid) while something is happening, and **concerned** (=worried) about something that is happening, but **anxious** means worried about what might happen: *I didn't play well because I was too* **nervous.**|*We're rather* **concerned** *about father's health.*|*Your mother will be* **anxious** *until she hears that you're safe.*

**SPELLING NOTE**
Words with the sound /n/, may be spelt **kn-**, like **know**, or **pn-**, like **pneumonia.**

**nervous break·down** /ˌ·· ˈ··/ *n* a serious medical condition of deep worrying, anxiety, weeping, and tiredness

**nervous sys·tem** /ˈ·· ˌ··/ *n* (in people and animals) the system (=the brain, NERVES, etc.) which receives and passes on feelings and messages, etc. from inside and outside the body

**nerv·y** /ˈnɜːvi‖ˈnɜr-/ *adj* **-ier, -iest** *infml* **1** *BrE* nervous and anxious **2** *AmE* having NERVE¹ (3); BRASH

**nest¹** /nest/ *n* **1** a hollow place built or found by a bird for a home and a place to keep its eggs **2** the home of certain other animals or insects: *an ants' nest* **3** a group of like objects which fit closely into or inside one another: *a nest of tables/boxes*

**nest²** *v* [I] to build or use a nest

**nest egg** /ˈ· ·/ *n* an amount of money saved for future use

**nes·tle** /ˈnesəl/ *v* **-tled, -tling** [T *down*] to settle or lie warmly, closely, or comfortably: *She nestled her head on/against his shoulder.*

**net¹** /net/ *n* **1** [C;U] a material of strings, wires, threads, etc. twisted, tied, or woven together with regular spaces between them –compare MESH **2** [C] any of various objects made from this, such as **a** a large piece spread out under water to catch fish **b** a trap: *a* BUTTERFLY *net* **c** a length dividing the two sides of the court in tennis, BADMINTON, etc. **d** an enclosure at the back of the GOAL in football, HOCKEY, etc. –see picture on page 592

**net²** *v* **-tt-** [T] to catch (as if) in a net: *We netted three fish.*

**net³** also **nett** *BrE adj* [A or after *n*] (of an amount) when nothing further is to be subtracted: *net profit* (=after tax, rent, etc. are paid)|*net weight* (=of an object without its packet)|*This jar of coffee weighs 250 grams net.* –compare GROSS¹ (4)

**net⁴** *v* **-tt-** [T *for*] to gain as a profit: *The sale netted a fat profit for the company.* –compare GROSS²

**net·ball** /ˈnetbɔːl/ *n* [U] a women's game (related to BASKETBALL) in which teams make points by making a ball fall through one of the two high rings at the opposite ends of a court

**neth·er** /ˈneðəʳ/ *adj* [A] *lit or humor* lower; under: *the* **nether regions** (=lower parts) *of the body*

**net·ting** /ˈnetɪŋ/ *n* [U] string, wire, etc., made into a net: *a fence of wire netting*

**net·tle¹** /ˈnetl/ *n* a wild plant having leaves which may sting and make red marks on the skin

**nettle²** *v* **-tled, -tling** [T] to make (someone) angry or impatient: *I was rather nettled by his rudeness.*

**net·work** /ˈnetwɜːk‖-wɜrk/ *n* **1** a large system of lines, tubes, wires, etc., that cross or meet one another: *Britain's railway network*|*the network of blood vessels in the body* **2** a group of radio or television stations in different places using many of the same broadcasts

**neu·ro·sis** /njʊˈrəʊsəs‖nʊ-/ *n* **-ses** /siːz/ [C;U] *tech* a disorder of the mind marked by strong unreasonable ideas and feelings of fear, anxiety, etc.

**neu·rot·ic** /njʊˈrɒtɪk‖nʊˈrɑ-/ *adj* related to or suffering from NEUROSIS: *(infml) He's neurotic about getting fat!* –**neurotic** *n*

**neu·ter**[1] /ˈnjuːtəʳ‖ˈnuː-/ *adj* **1** *tech* (in grammar) in or related to a class (GENDER) of words which are neither MASCULINE nor FEMININE: *a neuter noun/ending* **2** (of plants or animals) with no or undeveloped sexual organs: *Worker bees are neuter.*

**neuter**[2] *n tech* (the class of) a NEUTER word or word form: *How do you put this adjective into the neuter?*

**neuter**[3] *v* [T *usu. pass.*] to remove part of the sex organs of (an animal) by an operation –compare CASTRATE

**neu·tral**[1] /ˈnjuːtrəl‖ˈnuː-/ *adj* **1** without any feelings on either side of a question **2** being or belonging to a country which is not fighting or helping either side in a war: *a neutral country* **3** having no qualities of the stated kind, as of something **a** very weak or colourless: *trousers of a neutral colour* **b** (in chemistry) neither an acid nor a BASE[1] (4) **c** with no electrical charge –**neutrally** *adv*

**neutral**[2] *n* **1** [U] the position of the GEARS in a car or other machine, in which no power is carried from the engine to the wheels: *When you start the engine, be sure the car is in neutral.* **2** [C] a NEUTRAL[1] (2) person or country

**neu·tral·i·ty** /njuːˈtrælǀti‖nuː-/ *n* [U] the condition or quality of being NEUTRAL[1] (2), esp. in a war

**neu·tral·ize** ‖also **-ise** *BrE* /ˈnjuːtrəlaɪz‖ˈnuː-/ *v* **-ized, -izing** [T] to cause to have no effect; destroy the qualities, force, or activity of: *to neutralize an acid with a* BASE|*High taxes will neutralize increased wages.* –compare COUNTERACT –**neutralization** /ˌnjuːtrəlaɪˈzeɪʃən‖ˌnuːtrələ- / *n* [U]

**neu·tron** /ˈnjuːtrɒn‖ˈnuːtrɑn/ *n* a very small piece of matter that helps to form the central part of an atom and carries no electricity

**neutron bomb** /ˈ··ˌ·/ *n* a type of ATOM BOMB that destroys life but which causes little damage to property

**nev·er** /ˈnevəʳ/ *adv* not ever; not at any time: *I've never been to Paris.*|*Never forget to lock the door at night.*|*Never have I met such a strange person.*

USAGE Compare **never, sometimes, often,** etc.: *Peter* **never** *arrives late*/**always** *comes on time.*|*Mary is* **rarely/hardly ever**/*(fml)* **seldom** *late; she's* **usually/nearly always** *on time.*|*Jane is* **occasionally/sometimes** *late, and Jim is* **often/frequently** *late.*

**nev·er·more** /ˌnevəˈmɔːʳ◂‖ˌnevərˈmor◂/ *adv lit* never again –compare EVERMORE

**nev·er·the·less** /ˌnevəðəˈles‖-vər-/ also **nonetheless**– *adv* in spite of that: *I can't go. Nevertheless, thank you for inviting me.* –see Study Notes on page 128

**new** /njuː‖nuː/ *adj* **1** recently begun, made, built, etc.: *a new government*|*new fashions*|*We sell new and used furniture.*|*Have you seen her new car?* **2** [A] **a** only recently found or known: *the discovery of a new star* **b** having been in the stated position only a short time: *a new member of the club* **3** [A *no comp.*] different; (an)other: *to learn a new language* **4** [A *no comp.*] just beginning to be used, etc.; fresh: *They've gone to Australia to start a new life.* **5 new to** just beginning to know about or do; still unfamiliar with: *a young clerk new to the job* **6 new-**‚newly; recently: *a newborn baby*|*a new-found friend* –**newness** *n* [U]

USAGE **New** is a general word for something that exists now but has only been in existence for a short time: *a* **new** *road/law/book.* **Recent** describes something that happened or came into existence a short time ago, and is used esp. of events: *our* **recent** *holiday*|*The* **recent** *election produced a* **new** *government.* **Modern** covers a greater period of time than **new,** and means "belonging to the present time or not too distant past": *an examination in* **modern** *history, from 1550 to 1982*|**Modern** *medical science has conquered many diseases.* **Contemporary** means "belonging to the present or the recent past", and **current** describes something that exists now, but may or may not be **new: contemporary** *art/politics*|*The government's* **current** *ideas on defence date from many years ago.* –compare OLD (USAGE)

**new·com·er** /ˈnjuːkʌməʳ‖ˈnuː-/ *n* [*to*] one who has recently come, or has begun coming: *a newcomer to the city* (=visiting or living there for the first time)|*The team is a newcomer to the competition. (=hasn't been in it before)*

**new·fan·gled** /ˌnjuːˈfæŋgəld◂‖ˌnuː-/ *adj* [A] *derog or humor* (of ideas, inventions, etc.) new and unnecessary or of no value: *We need better teachers, not newfangled ideas of education!*

**new·ly** /ˈnjuːli‖ˈnuːli/ *adv* (*used before a past participle*) recently; freshly: *a newly built house*

**new·ly·wed** /ˈnjuːliwed‖ˈnuː-/ *n* [*usu. pl.*] a man or woman recently married: *a newlywed* COUPLE

**news** /njuːz‖nuːz/ *n* [U] what is reported (esp. in newspapers and on radio and television) about a recent event or events; new information: *news of the election results*|*I heard it on the nine o'clock news.*|*Have you heard the news about Mary? She's going to have a baby.*

**news·a·gent** /ˈnjuːzˌeɪdʒənt‖ˈnuːz-/ *BrE*‖ **newsdealer** /ˈ·ˌ··/ *AmE n* (a person in charge of) a shop selling newspapers and magazines: *You can get that paper at your local newsagent's (shop).*

**news·cast·er** /ˈnjuːzkɑːstəʳ‖ˈnuːzkæ-/ also **newsreader** /-ˌriːdəʳ/ *BrE*– *n* a person who broadcasts news on radio or television

**news con·fer·ence** /ˈ· ˌ···/ *n* →PRESS CONFERENCE

**news·let·ter** /ˈnjuːzˌletəʳ‖ˈnuːz-/ *n* a small sheet of news sent regularly to a particular group of people

**news·pa·per** /ˈnjuːsˌpeɪpəʳ‖ˈnuːz-/ also **paper**– *n* **1** [C] a paper printed and sold usu. daily or weekly, with news, notices, advertisements, etc.: *an evening newspaper*|*the Sunday papers* **2** [U] paper on which these have been printed: *Wrap it up in newspaper.*

**news·print** /ˈnjuːzˌprɪnt‖ˈnuːz-/ *n* [U] *tech* a cheap paper used mostly for newspapers

**news·reel** /ˈnjuːzriːl‖ˈnuːz-/ *n* a short cinema film of news

**news·stand** /ˈnjuːzstænd‖ˈnuːz-/ *n* a table, often inside a shelter outdoors, from which newspapers, magazines, etc. are sold

**news·wor·thy** /ˈnjuːzˌwɜːði‖ˈnuːzˌwɜrði/ *adj* interesting enough to be reported as news

**newt** /njuːt‖nuːt/ *n* a small four-legged animal living both on land and in water

**New Tes·ta·ment** /ˌ· ˈ···/ *n* the second part of the

Bible, containing the earliest writings about the life of Christ –compare OLD TESTAMENT

**New World** /ˌ· ˈ·/ *n* [*the* S] North, Central, and South America; the Western HEMISPHERE

**new year** /ˌ· ˈ·/ *n* (*often caps.*) the year which has just begun or will soon begin: *Happy New Year!* (=a greeting spoken at the beginning of the year)

**New Year's Day** /ˌ· · ˈ·/ *n* (in Western countries) January 1st

**New Year's Eve** /ˌ· · ˈ·/ *n* (in Western countries) December 31st

**next**[1] /nekst/ *adj* **1** nearest; without anything coming between: *They live in the next house to ours.*|*We'll have to stop at the next petrol station.* **2** the nearest after: *If I miss this train I'll catch the next/the next one.*|*Are you coming to our next meeting?*|*I'll be on holiday next week.* (not *the next week*)|*The best way is by air; the* **next best** (=the second best) *is by train.*

**next**[2] *adv* **1** just afterwards: *What will you do next?* **2** the first time after this or that: *I'll tell you the answer when we next meet.* –compare LAST[2] (2) **3 next to: a** close beside: *sitting next to Mary* –see Study Notes on page 474 **b** almost: *He earns next to nothing.* (=very little money)

**next-door** /ˌ· ˈ·◂/ *adj* [A] in or being the next building, esp. in a row: *next-door neighbours*

**next door** /ˌ· ˈ·/ *adv* [F *to*] in or being the next building: *We live next door to a cinema.*

**next of kin** /ˌ· · ˈ·/ *n* **next of kin** *law* the person most closely related to someone: *Her next of kin was/were informed about the accident.*

**NHS** *abbrev. for:* (in Britain) National Health Service; a system of medical treatment for everyone, paid for by taxes: *an NHS hospital*

**nib** /nɪb/ *n* the pointed piece on the end of a pen, usu. metal, out of which the ink flows

**nib·ble** /ˈnɪbəl/ *v* **-bled, -bling** [I;T *away, at, on*] to take small bites (out of something): *Aren't you hungry? You're only nibbling (at) your food.*|*The mice have nibbled away part of the cheese.* **–nibble** *n*

**nice** /naɪs/ *adj* **1** *infml* good; pleasant; pleasing: *How nice of you to do that!*|*a nice day* (=with good weather)|*This soup tastes very nice.*|*How nice to see you!* (=a greeting) **2** *fml* showing or needing careful understanding; fine; delicate: *a nice difference between two meanings* **3** *derog & infml* bad; unpleasant: *Don't be so rude; that's a nice way to behave to your aunt!* **–niceness** *n* [U]

USAGE **Nice** is very commonly used in speech, but in formal writing it is better to avoid it, and use **amusing**, **beautiful**, **interesting**, etc., according to the meaning.

**nice·ly** /ˈnaɪsli/ *adv* well; in a good, pleasant, kind, or skilful way: *to smile nicely*|*The man is doing nicely* (=his condition is quite good) *in hospital after his accident.* **2** in an exact, fine, or delicate way

**ni·ce·ty** /ˈnaɪsəti/ *n* **-ties** a fine or delicate point; detail: *Let's answer the question in general: we haven't time to consider all the niceties.*

> **SPELLING NOTE**
> Words with the sound /n/, may be spelt **kn-**, like **know**, or **pn-**, like **pneumonia.**

**niche** /nɪtʃ, niːʃ/ *n* **1** a hollow place in a wall, usu. made to hold a piece of art (like a BUST or STATUE) **2 find a niche for oneself** to find a suitable place, job, position, etc.

**nick**[1] /nɪk/ *n* **1** a small (accidental) cut in a surface or edge: *not badly hurt, only nicks and cuts* **2** *BrE infml* prison: *ten years* **in the nick 3 in the nick of time** just in time: *I caught the baby in the nick of time before he fell down the stairs.*

**nick**[2] *v* [T] **1** to make or cut a NICK[1] in: *A bullet nicked his leg.* **2** *BrE infml* to steal: *He nicked my bicycle.*

**nick**[3] *n* [U] *BrE infml* bodily condition; SHAPE[1] (2): *The house was* **in good/bad nick.** (=in a good/bad state)

**nick·el** /ˈnɪkəl/ *n* **1** [U] a hard silver-white metal that is a simple substance (ELEMENT (1)) and is used in the production of other metals **2** [C] the coin of the US and Canada worth five cents: *Can you give me a* DIME *for two nickels?*

**nick·nack** /ˈnɪknæk/ *n infml* for KNICK-KNACK

**nick·name**[1] /ˈnɪkneɪm/ *n* a name used informally instead of (some)one's own name, usu. given because of one's character or as a short form of the actual name: *His real name is Mr MacDonald, but he has the nickname "Mac".*

**nickname**[2] *v* **-named, -naming** [T] to give (someone) a NICKNAME: *They nicknamed him "Fats" because of his weight.*

**nic·o·tine** /ˈnɪkətiːn/ *n* [U] a poisonous chemical contained in tobacco

**niece** /niːs/ *n* the daughter of one's (wife's or husband's) brother or sister –compare NEPHEW; see picture on page 217

**nif·ty** /ˈnɪfti/ *adj* **-tier, -tiest** *infml* very good, attractive, or effective: *a nifty little car*

**nig·gard·ly** /ˈnɪgədli‖-ər-/ *adj derog* **1** (of a person) not willing to spend money, time, etc.; STINGY **2** small or limited; MEAN[1] (1): *a niggardly offer for such a good bicycle* **–niggardliness** *n* [U]

**nig·gle** /ˈnɪgəl/ *v* **-gled, -gling** [I] **1** to pay too much attention to small details: *She niggled over every detail of the bill.* **2** to annoy or worry continually **–niggling** *adj* [A]: *a niggling doubt*

**nigh** /naɪ/ *adv,prep* **1** *lit & old use* near **2 well nigh** also **nigh on**– *dial or old use* almost: *well nigh 50 years*

**night** /naɪt/ *n* **1** [C;U] the dark part of each day, when the sun cannot be seen: *The nights are longer in winter.*|*I slept well last night.*|*Cats can see well* **at/by night.**|*She lay awake* **all night (long)**. (=from the time she went to bed until morning)|*The baby woke up twice* **in the night**.|*tomorrow night* –compare DAY **2** [C] an evening, considered as an occasion: *We saw the show on its first night.* (=at its first performance, in the evening) **3 night after night** *infml* regularly every night: *He goes out drinking night after night.* **4 night and day** also **day and night**– *infml* all the time

**night·cap** /ˈnaɪtkæp/ *n* **1** a usu. alcoholic drink taken before going to bed **2** a soft cloth cap worn in bed in former times

**night·club** /ˈnaɪtklʌb/ *n* a club open late at night where people may eat, drink, dance, and often see a show

**night·dress** /ˈnaɪtdres/ also **nightie** /ˈnaɪti/ *infml,* **nightgown** /-gaʊn/ *AmE*– *n* a piece of women's clothing like a loose dress, made to be worn in bed

**night·fall** /ˈnaɪtfɔːl/ *n* [U] the beginning of night; DUSK

**nigh·tin·gale** /ˈnaɪtɪŋgeɪl/ *n* a type of bird (THRUSH) known for its beautiful song

**night·life** /ˈnaɪtlaɪf/ *n* [U] the activity of people who go out to enjoy themselves at night in BARS[1] (5), NIGHTCLUBS, etc.

**night·ly** /ˈnaɪtli/ *adj,adv* (happening, done, used, etc.) every night: *a play performed nightly|a nightly news broadcast* –compare DAILY

**night·mare** /ˈnaɪtmeəʳ/ *n* a terrible dream **–nightmarish** *adj* **–nightmarishly** *adv*

**night school** /ˈ· ·/ *n* a school or set of classes meeting in the evening, esp. for people who have jobs during the day: *You can learn French at night school.*

**night shift** /ˈ· ·/ *n* (a period of) work done during the night, as in a factory: *He worked (on) the night shift.|a night-shift worker*

**night·time** /ˈnaɪt-taɪm/ *n* [U] the time each day when it is dark –opposite **daytime**

**night watch·man** /ˌ· ˈ··/ *n* a man with the job of guarding a building at night

**nil** /nɪl/ *n* nothing; zero: *The new machine reduced labour costs to almost nil.|Our football team won by four* GOALS (3) *to nil.*

**nim·ble** /ˈnɪmbəl/ *adj apprec* quick, light, and neat in movement; AGILE: *a nimble climber* **–nimbleness** *n* [U] **–nimbly** *adv*

**nin·com·poop** /ˈnɪŋkəmpuːp/ *n infml* a stupid person; fool

**nine** /naɪn/ *determiner,n,pron* (the number) 9

**nine·teen** /ˌnaɪnˈtiːn◂/ *determiner,n,pron* **1** (the number) 19 **2 talk nineteen to the dozen** *infml* to talk quickly and continuously **–nineteenth** *determiner,n,adv,pron*

**nine·ty** /ˈnaɪnti/ *determiner,n,pron* **-ties** (the number) 90 **–ninetieth** /ˈnaɪntiɪ̍θ/ *determiner,n,adv,pron*

**nin·ny** /ˈnɪni/ *n* **-nies** *infml & derog* a silly foolish person

**ninth** /naɪnθ/ *determiner,n,adv,pron* 9th

**nip**[1] /nɪp/ *v* **-pp- 1** [I;T] to catch in a tight sharp hold between two points or surfaces, such as between the finger and thumb: *The dog has nipped* (=has bitten) *the postman on the leg.* **2** [I *in, out, up, down, etc.*] *BrE infml* to go quickly; hurry: *I'll nip out and buy a newspaper.* **3 nip in the bud** to do harm to (something) at an early stage, esp. so as to keep from succeeding: *Her plans to go out were nipped in the bud when her mother arrived for the evening.*

**nip**[2] *n* [S] **1** a coldness: *There's a nip in the air today.* **2** the act or result of NIPping[1] (1): *I gave my fingers a nasty nip as I caught them in the door.*

**nip**[3] *n infml* a small amount of an alcoholic drink, not beer or wine: *a nip of* WHISKY

**nip·per** /ˈnɪpəʳ/ *n infml* a small child

**nip·ple** /ˈnɪpəl/ *n* **1** a dark part of the breast of a woman, through which a baby may suck milk –compare TEAT; see picture on page 299 **2** *AmE* the piece of rubber shaped like this on the end of a baby's bottle; TEAT **3** a small opening shaped like this on a machine, for oil or GREASE

**nip·py** /ˈnɪpi/ *adj* **-pier, -piest 1** having a NIP[2] (1): *a nippy morning* **2** quick in movement: *You'll have to be nippy if you want to be on time.* **–nippiness** *n* [U]

**nit**[1] /nɪt/ *n* an egg of an insect (usu. a LOUSE) that is sometimes found in people's hair

**nit**[2] *n BrE derog infml* for NITWIT

**nit·pick·ing** /ˈnɪtˌpɪkɪŋ/ *adj,n* [U] *derog infml* paying too much attention to small and unimportant points; TRIVIAL(ity): *He can't understand a general argument; he always asks nitpicking little questions.*

**ni·trate** /ˈnaɪtreɪt, -trɪ̍t/ *n* [C;U] any of several chemicals used mainly (as FERTILIZER) in improving soil for growing crops: SODIUM *nitrate*

**ni·tric ac·id** /ˌnaɪtrɪk ˈæsɪ̍d/ *n* [U] a powerful acid ($HNO_3$) which eats away (CORRODES) other materials and is used in explosives and other chemical products

**ni·tro·gen** /ˈnaɪtrədʒən/ *n* [U] a gas that is a simple substance (ELEMENT (1)), without colour or smell, that forms most of the earth's air

**ni·tro·gly·ce·rine, -rin** /ˌnaɪtrəʊˈglɪsərɪ̍n, -trə-, -riːn‖-rɪ̍n/ *n* [U] a powerful liquid explosive

**nit·wit** /ˈnɪtˌwɪt/ *n infml* a silly foolish person

**no**[1] /nəʊ/ *determiner,adv* **1** (used in an answer expressing refusal or disagreement): *"Is it raining?" "No, it's snowing."|"Will you post this letter for me?" "No, I don't want to go out."* –opposite **yes 2** not any; not at all: *There's no sugar in the bowl.|I've no time to talk to you just now.|I'm feeling no better.* (=feeling the same or worse)|(used in warnings and road signs) *No parking* (=do not park here)|*It's no distance to the station.* (=not far at all) –see Study Notes on page 494

USAGE Compare **no** and **not.** Use **no** before nouns (**no** *money*), before noun- like verbs (**no** *smoking*), before adjectives followed by a noun (**no** *thick shoes*), or before adverbs of comparison (**no** *better*). Use **not: a** before verbs, to change them to the opposite of their meaning: *I'm* **not** *coming.* **b** before **a, all, both, every, half, the,** etc. (DETERMINERS): **not** *a chance*|**not** *all of us*|**not** *enough* **c** before names (**not** *George*), adverbs (**not** *often*), prepositions (**not** *on Sunday*), and most adjectives where no noun follows (*they're* **not** *stupid*).

**no**[2] *n* [S] an answer or decision of no: *a clear no to my request for money* –opposite **yes**

**no. nos.** *written abbrev. said as:* NUMBER[1](2)

**no·bil·i·ty** /nəʊˈbɪlɪ̍ti, nə-/ *n* **1** (in certain countries) the group of people of the highest social class **2** [U] the quality or condition of being NOBLE[1]

**no·ble**[1] /ˈnəʊbəl/ *adj* **1** of high (moral) quality; deserving praise; worthy: *noble and generous feelings* –opposite **ignoble 2** of or belonging to a high social titled rank: *a woman of noble birth*

**noble**[2] *n* (esp. in FEUDAL times) a person of the highest and most powerful social class –compare COMMONER

**no·ble·man** /ˈnəʊbəlmən/ **noblewoman** /-ˌwʊmən/ *fem.– n* **-men** /mən/ a member of the NOBILITY; PEER[1] (2,3)

**no·bly** /ˈnəʊbli/ *adv* in a noble way, esp. in a way deserving of praise

**no·bod·y**[1] /ˈnəʊbədi‖-ˌbɑdi, -bədi/ also **no one**– *pron* no person; not anybody: *There's nobody* (or *there isn't anybody*) *here.|Can you help me? Nobody else* (=no other person) *can.* –compare EVERYBODY

**nobody**[2] *n* **-ies** a person of no importance: *I want to* *be famous! I'm tired of being a nobody.*

**noc·tur·nal** /nɒk'tɜːnl‖nɑk'tɜr-/ *adj fml or tech* of, happening, or active at night: *a nocturnal visit/bird* –**nocturnally** *adv*

**nod** /nɒd‖nɑd/ *v* **-dd- 1** [I;T] to bend (one's head) forward and down, esp. to show agreement or give a greeting or sign: *She nodded (her head) when she passed me in the street.|I asked her if she was ready to go and she nodded.|*(fig.) *flowers nodding in the wind* **2** [T] to show in this way: *They nodded their agreement.* **3** [I *off*] *infml* to let one's head drop in falling asleep: *I nodded off in the meeting and didn't hear what was said.* –**nod** *n*: *He greeted us with a nod (of the head).*

**nod·ule** /'nɒdjuːl‖'nɑdʒuːl/ *n tech* a small round mass or lump esp. on a plant or a person's body –**nodular** /'nɒdjʊləʳ‖'nɑdʒə-/ *adj*

**No·el** /nəʊ'el/ *n lit* (the season of) Christmas

**no-go ar·e·a** /ˌ· '· ˌ···/ *n infml* (in a city with two opposed groups of people) an area controlled by one group and dangerous for anyone else to enter

**noise** /nɔɪz/ *n* [C;U] (an) unwanted, unpleasant, or confused sound: *Try not to make a noise when you go upstairs; the baby's asleep.|There's so much noise in this restaurant I can hardly hear you talking.* –**noiseless** *adj* –**noiselessly** *adv* –**noiselessness** *n* [U]

USAGE A **sound** is anything that you hear: *the* **sound** *of voices/of music/of breaking plates.* A **voice** is the sound of a person speaking or singing: *to have a loud* **voice**. A **noise** is usually a loud unpleasant **sound**: *Stop making so much* **noise**!

**nois·y** /'nɔɪzi/ *adj* **-ier, -iest** making a lot of noise: *a noisy car |It's noisy in this office.* –**noisily** *adv* –**noisiness** *n* [U]

**no·mad** /'nəʊmæd/ *n* a member of a tribe which travels about, esp. to find grass for its animals: *the nomads of the desert* –**nomadic** /nəʊ'mædɪk/ *adj*: *nomadic tribes|a nomadic life* –**nomadically** *adv*

**no-man's-land** /'· · ˌ·/ *n* [S] the area of land between two opposing armies, belonging to neither

**nom de plume** /ˌnɒm də 'pluːm‖ˌnɑm-/ *n* **noms de plume** (*same pronunciation*) →PEN NAME

**no·men·cla·ture** /nəʊ'menklətʃəʳ, 'nəʊmənkleɪ-‖'nəʊmənkleɪ-/ *n* [C;U] *fml* a system of naming things in science, etc.:

**nom·i·nal** /'nɒmɪ̍nl‖'nɑ-/ *adj* **1** in name or form but usu. not in reality: *The old man is only the nominal head of the business; his daughter makes all the decisions.* **2** (of an amount of money) very small; NEGLIGIBLE: *sold at a nominal price* (=a very low price) –**nominally** *adv*

**nom·i·nate** /'nɒmɪ̍neɪt‖'nɑ-/ *v* **-nated, -nating** [T] **1** [*for*] to suggest or name (someone) officially for election to a position, office, honour, etc.: *I wish to nominate Jane Morrison for president of the club.* **2** [*as*] to appoint (someone) to such a position, office, etc.: *The president nominated me (as/to be) his representative at the meeting.*

**nom·i·na·tion** /ˌnɒmɪ̍'neɪʃən‖ˌnɑ-/ *n* [C;U] (an example of) the act or result of nominating or being nominated (NOMINATE): *The club agreed to all the committee's nominations.|Who will get the nomination for president?*

**SPELLING NOTE**

Words with the sound /n/, may be spelt **kn-**, like **know**, or **pn-**, like **pneumonia.**

**nom·i·na·tive**[1] /'nɒmɪ̍nətɪv, 'nɒmnə-‖'nɑ-/ *adj* showing that a word is the subject of a verb: *"We" is nominative, but "us" is accusative.*

**nominative**[2] *n tech* the CASE[1] (6) (set of forms) showing that a word is the subject of a verb: *Put this noun in(to) the nominative.*

**nom·i·nee** /ˌnɒmɪ̍'niː‖ˌnɑ-/ *n* a person who has been NOMINATED

**non·ag·gres·sion** /ˌnɒn-ə'greʃən‖ˌnɑn-/ *n* [A] not attacking: *a nonaggression agreement* (=each side promising not to attack the other) –see also AGGRESSION

**non·a·ligned** /ˌnɒn-ə'laɪnd‖ˌnɑn-/ *adj* (of a country) not supporting the actions of any particular powerful country or group of countries –see also ALIGN –**nonalignment** *n* [U]

**non·cha·lant** /'nɒnʃələnt‖ˌnɑnʃə'lɑnt/ *adj* showing calmness, and often lack of interest; COOL[1] (2): *He appeared nonchalant in court even when the judge ordered him to pay £1,000.* –**nonchalance** *n* [S;U]: *She showed a surprising nonchalance the first time she flew a plane.* –**nonchalantly** *adv*

**non·com·ba·tant** /ˌnɒn'kɒmbətənt‖ˌnɑnkəm'bætənt/ *n* a person, esp. in the armed forces (such as a CHAPLAIN), who does not take part in actual fighting: *noncombatant duty*

**non·com·mis·sioned of·fi·cer** /ˌnɒnkəˌmɪʃənd 'ɒfɪsəʳ‖ˌnɑn-, 'ɔf-, 'ɑf-/ *n* an officer of low rank in the armed forces

**non·com·mit·tal** /ˌnɒnkə'mɪtl‖ˌnɑn-/ *adj* not expressing a clear opinion or intention: *I asked him if he approved of our plan, but he was noncommittal.* –see also COMMIT (3) –**noncommittally** *adv*

**non·con·form·ist** /ˌnɒnkən'fɔːmɪ̍st‖ˌnɑnkən'fɔr-/ *adj,n* (of, concerning, or being) a person who does not follow some customary way(s) of living, acting, thinking, etc.: *nonconformist habits* –opposite **conformist** –**nonconformity, nonconformism** *n* [U]

**Nonconformist** *adj,n* (a member) of any of several Christian religious groups which have separated from the CHURCH OF ENGLAND: *a Nonconformist minister*

**non·con·trib·u·to·ry** /ˌnɒnkən'trɪbjʊtəri‖ˌnɑnkən'trɪbjətori/ *adj* [A] (of a PENSION plan) paid for by the employer only and not by the person who will receive the money (the EMPLOYEE)

**non·de·script** /'nɒndɪ̍ˌskrɪpt‖ˌnɑndɪ̍'skrɪpt/ *adj* without any strong or interesting qualities; dull: *She was wearing nondescript clothes.*

**none**[1] /nʌn/ *pron* **1** not any: *None of the money is mine.|None of my friends ever comes/come to see me.* (=I have more than two friends, but they don't come to see me. Use *neither of my friends* when there are only two)|*Even an old car is better than none at all.* –see EITHER[1](USAGE); see Study Notes on page 494 **2 none but** *fml* only **3 none other** (*shows surprise*) no one else: *It was none other than Tom! We thought he was in Africa!*

**none**[2] *adv* **1 none the** not at all; no: *My car is none the worse for* (=is no worse because of) *the accident.* **2 none too** not very: *The food is none too good here.*

**non·en·ti·ty** /nɒ'nentˌti‖nɑ-/ *n* **-ties** a person without much ability, character, or importance: *a weak government full of nonentities*

**none·the·less** /ˌnʌnðə'les◂/ *adv* in spite of that; NEVERTHELESS –see Study Notes on page 128

**non-e·vent** /ˌ· ·'·/ *n infml* a happening that is much less important, interesting, etc., than expected: *The election was a real non-event; only a few people voted.*

**non·ex·ist·ent** /nɒnɪg'zɪstənt‖nɑn-/ *adj* not existing: *This year's profits were very small; in fact, almost nonexistent.*

**non·fic·tion** /ˌnɒn'fɪkʃən‖ˌnɑn-/ *n* [U] writing that is about facts rather than imagined things; not poetry, plays, stories, or NOVELS –see also FICTION

**non·flam·ma·ble** /ˌnɒn'flæməbəl‖ˌnɑn-/ *adj* difficult or impossible to burn –opposite **inflammable** –see FLAMMABLE (USAGE)

**non·in·ter·ven·tion** /ˌnɒnˌɪntə'venʃən‖ˌnɑnˌɪntər-/ also **noninterference** /ˌnɒnˌɪntə'fɪərəns‖ˌnɑnˌɪntər-/– *n* [U] the practice by a government of taking no part in the affairs or disagreements of another country –see also INTERVENE

**non·pay·ment** /ˌnɒn'peɪmənt‖ˌnɑn-/ *n* [U *of*] failure to pay (bills, tax, etc.)

**non·plussed** /ˌnɒn'plʌst‖ˌnɑn-/ *adj* surprised; not knowing what to think or do: *The speaker was completely nonplussed by the question.*

**non·pro·lif·e·ra·tion** /ˌnɒnprəˌlɪfə'reɪʃən‖ˌnɑn-/ *n* [U] the result of keeping atomic weapons in only the same amounts and in the same countries as at the (present) time: *a nonproliferation agreement* –see also PROLIFERATE

**non·sense** /'nɒnsəns‖'nɑnsens/ *n* [U] speech, writing, thinking, behaviour, etc., that is stupid; RUBBISH[1] (2): *The government's new ideas are nonsense.|I've never heard such nonsense!|Stop that nonsense, children! Behave yourselves.*

**non·sen·si·cal** /nɒn'sensˌkəl‖nɑn-/ *adj* full of NONSENSE; foolish or ABSURD: *nonsensical opinions* **–nonsensically** *adv*

**non seq·ui·tur** /ˌnɒn 'sekwˌtə^r‖ˌnɑn-/ *n* **non sequiturs** *fml & Latin* a statement which does not follow from the facts or arguments which are given

**non·stan·dard** /ˌnɒn'stændəd◂‖ˌnɑn'stændərd◂/ *adj* (of words, expressions, pronunciations, etc.) not usually used by educated native speakers of a language

**non·start·er** *n BrE infml* a person or idea without any chance of success: *We wanted to buy a house, but that was a nonstarter: we hadn't nearly enough money.*

**non·stick** /ˌnɒn'stɪk◂‖ˌnɑn-/ *adj* [A] (of a cooking pan) having a specially treated smooth inside surface that food will not stick to

**non·stop** /ˌnɒn'stɒp◂‖ˌnɑn'stɑp◂/ *adj,adv* without a pause or interruption; without stopping: *a nonstop journey|You can now fly nonstop from London to Singapore.*

**non·vi·o·lence** /ˌnɒn'vaɪələns‖ˌnɑn-/ *n* [U] opposition without using force or violence, shown esp. by not obeying laws or orders **–nonviolent** *adj: nonviolent* PROTEST[1] **–nonviolently** *adv*

**noo·dle** /'nuːdl/ *n* [*usu. pl.*] a usu. long thin piece of a paste made from flour, water, and eggs. The pieces are boiled until soft and eaten in soups, with meat, etc.

**nook** /nʊk/ *n lit or humor* a sheltered and private place: *a shady nook in the garden*

**noon** /nuːn/ *n* 12 o'clock in the daytime; MIDDAY: *We left home at noon.|Noon is the earliest time I can come.*

**noon·day** /'nuːndeɪ/ *n lit* for MIDDAY: *the noonday sun*

**no one** /'· ·/ *pron* →NOBODY[1]

**noose** /nuːs/ *n* a ring formed by the end of a cord, rope, etc., which closes more tightly as it is pulled (esp. as used to hang a person)

**nor** /nɔː^r/ *conj* **1** (used in a list of NEGATIVES often after *neither*): *It can't be done by you nor me nor anyone.|Neither my father nor I were there.* –see EITHER[1] (USAGE) **2** (used with NEGATIVE expressions) also not; neither: *"I can't swim." "Nor can I!"* (=both of us are unable to swim) –see NEITHER (USAGE)

**norm** /nɔːm‖nɔrm/ *n* **1** a standard of proper behaviour or principle of right and wrong; rule: *social norms* **2** a usual or expected number, amount, pattern of action or behaviour, etc.; average: *The norm in this examination is 70 out of 100.*

**nor·mal** /'nɔːməl‖'nɔr-/ *adj* according to what is expected, usual, or average: *normal working hours from nine to five|Rainfall has been above/below normal this July.|a normal child* –see also ABNORMAL

**nor·mal·i·ty** /nɔː'mælˌti‖nɔr-/ also **normalcy** /'nɔːməlsi‖'nɒr-/ *AmE– n* [U] the quality or fact of being NORMAL

**nor·mal·ize** ‖also **-ise** *BrE* /'nɔːməlaɪz‖'nɔr-/ *v* **-ized, -izing** [I;T] (esp. in relations between countries) to (cause to) come back to a good or friendly state: *Relations were slow to normalize after the war.* **–normalization** /ˌnɔːməlaɪ'zeɪʃən‖ˌnɔrmələ-/ *n* [U]

**nor·mal·ly** /'nɔːməli‖'nɔr-/ *adv* **1** in a NORMAL way or to a NORMAL degree: *He was behaving normally in spite of his anxiety.* **2** in the usual conditions; ordinarily: *I normally go to bed early, but I stayed up late last night.* –see also ABNORMAL

**north[1]** /nɔːθ‖nɔrθ/ *n* [*the* S] (*often cap.*) **1** (the direction of) one of the four main points of the compass, which is on the left of a person facing the rising sun: *I'm lost: which direction is north?|a window facing the north|the north wall of a building* **2** [A] (of a wind) coming from this direction: *a cold north wind* –compare NORTHERLY **3 the North** (part of a country) lying in this direction: *There is much unemployment in the North of England.*

**north[2]** *adv (often cap.)* towards the NORTH[1](1): *to travel (further) north|The room faces North, so it's always rather cold.|Edinburgh is (a long way) north of London.*

**north·bound** /'nɔːθbaʊnd‖'nɔrθ-/ *adj* travelling towards the north: *northbound traffic*

**north·east[1]** /ˌnɔːθ'iːst◂‖ˌnɔrθ-/ *n* **1** [*the* S] (the direction of) the point of the compass which is half-way between north and east **2** (of a wind) coming from this direction: *a northeast wind* **–northeasterly** *adj*

**northeast[2]** *adv* towards the NORTH-

EAST[1] (1): *to sail northeast*

**nor·ther·ly** /ˈnɔːðəli‖ˈnɔrðərli/ *adj* **1** towards or in the north: *a northerly direction* **2** (of a wind) coming from the north: *a cold northerly wind*

**nor·thern** /ˈnɔːðən‖ˈnɔrðərn/ *adj* (*often cap.*) of or belonging to the north part of anything, esp. of the world or of a country: *The northern half of the Earth is called the Northern* HEMISPHERE.

**nor·thern·most** /ˈnɔːðənməʊst‖ˈnɔrðərn-/ *adj* furthest north: *the northernmost parts of Scotland*

**North Pole** /ˌ· ˈ·/ *n* [*the* S] (the lands around) the most northern point on the surface of the earth –see also SOUTH POLE

**north·ward** /ˈnɔːθwəd‖ˈnɔrθwərd/ *adj* going towards the north: *a northward journey* –**northwards**‖ also **northward** *AmE*– *adv*: *to sail northwards*

**north·west[1]** /ˌnɔːθˈwest◂‖ˌnɔrθ-/ *n* **1** [*the* S] (the direction of) the point of the compass which is half-way between north and west **2** (of a wind) coming from this direction –**northwesterly** *adj*

**northwest[2]** *adv* towards the NORTHWEST[1] (1): *Birmingham is northwest of London.*

**nose[1]** /nəʊz/ *n* **1** [C] the part of the face above the mouth, which is the organ of smell and through which air is breathed –see picture on page 299 **2** [C] *infml* this organ regarded as representing too great interest in things which do not concern one: *Keep your nose out of/Stop* **poking your nose into** *my affairs!* **3** [S] the sense of smell: *This dog has a good nose.*|(fig.) *A newspaper reporter must have a nose for a good story.* (=have a special ability to find one) **4** [C] the front end of something, such as a car, plane, tool, or gun **5 look down one's nose at** *infml* to have or show a low opinion of **6 pay through the nose** *infml* to pay far too much **7 put someone's nose out of joint** *infml* to make someone jealous by taking his/her place as the centre of attention **8 under someone's (very) nose** *infml* right in front of someone; quite openly: *They stole the jewels from under the (very) nose(s) of the police.* **9 -nosed** having a certain shape or kind of nose: *red-nosed*|*broken-nosed*

**nose[2]** *v* **nosed, nosing 1** [I;T] to move or push ahead slowly or carefully: *The car nosed (out) into the traffic.* **2** [I] *infml* to attempt to find out esp. things that do not concern one; search: *nosing about for information*|*Stop nosing into my affairs!*

**nose** sthg.↔ **out** *v adv* [T] *infml* to discover by close searching: *to nose out some interesting facts*

**nose·bag** /ˈnəʊzbæg/ also **feedbag** *AmE*– *n* a bag hung around a horse's head to hold its food

**nose·bleed** /ˈnəʊzbliːd/ *n* a case of bleeding from the nose: *I had a nosebleed earlier today.*

**nose·dive** /ˈnəʊzdaɪv/ *v* **-dived, -diving** [I] (of an aircraft) to drop suddenly with the nose pointing straight down: (fig.) *Profits have nosedived* (=gone down very sharply) *in the last year.* –**nosedive** *n*

**nosh** /nɒʃ‖nɑʃ/ *n* [U] *BrE infml* food: *Let's have some nosh before the film starts.*

**nos·tal·gia** /nɒˈstældʒə‖nɑ-/ *n* [U] fondness for something in the past: *I was filled with nostalgia by hearing my favourite old song.* –**nostalgic** *adj* –**nostalgically** *adv*

> **SPELLING NOTE**
> Words with the sound /n/, may be spelt **kn-**, like **know**, or **pn-**, like **pneumonia.**

**nos·tril** /ˈnɒstrəl‖ˈnɑ-/ *n* either of the two openings at the end of the nose, through which one breathes –see picture on page 299

**nos·y, nosey** /ˈnəʊzi/ *adj derog* interested in things that do not concern one; PRYING: *Our nosy neighbours are always looking in through our windows.* –**nosiness** *n* [U]

**not** /nɒt‖nɑt/ *adv shortened to* **n't** *after helping verbs* **1** (used for changing a word or expression to one with the opposite meaning): *not thirsty*|*not on Sunday*|*We're not/We aren't coming.*|*It's a cat, not a dog.*|*Not everyone likes this book.* (=some people don't like it) **2** (used in place of a whole expression): *"Will it rain?" "I hope not."* (=I hope it won't rain)|*I'll try to be there by nine, but if not, start the meeting without me.* –compare SO[1] (3) **3 not a** not even one: *"How much did this cost?" "Not a penny!"* (=nothing) **4 not that** although it is not true that: *Where were you last night? Not that I care, of course.* –see NO (USAGE)

**no·ta·ble[1]** /ˈnəʊtəbəl/ *adj* [*for*] worthy of notice; REMARKABLE; OUTSTANDING: *notable events*|*a notable lawyer* –**notability** /ˌnəʊtəˈbɪləti/ *n* [U]

**notable[2]** *n* [*usu. pl.*] a famous or important person

**no·ta·bly** /ˈnəʊtəbli/ *adv* **1** especially; particularly: *Many members were absent, notably the vice-chairman.* **2** noticeably: *notably higher sales*

**no·ta·tion** /nəʊˈteɪʃən/ *n* [C;U] (writing that uses) a set of written signs to describe the stated kinds of things: *a page covered with musical notation*

**notch[1]** /nɒtʃ‖nɑtʃ/ *n* a V-shaped cut in a surface or edge: *He cut a notch in the stick with a sharp knife.*

**notch[2]** *v* [T] **1** to make a notch in **2** [*up*] *infml* to win or record (a victory or gain): *The team notched (up) their third victory in a row.*

**note[1]** /nəʊt/ *v* **noted, noting** [T] **1** to pay attention to and remember: *Please note my new address.* **2** to write down as a record or reminder: *He* **noted down** *my new address.*

**note[2]** *n* **1** also **tone** *AmE*– (a written sign representing) a single musical sound of a particular degree of highness or lowness: *I can't sing the high notes.* **2** a quality (of voice): *a note of anger in his voice* **3** a record or reminder in writing: *Make a note of how much money you spend.*|*She takes* (=writes down) *good notes of everything that's said in class.* **4** a remark added to a piece of writing and placed outside the main part of the writing (as at the bottom of a page), esp. to give additional information **5** a short letter, usu. informal **6** also **bill** *AmE*– a piece of paper money: *a £5 note* **7 of note** *fml* of fame or importance: *She's a musician of (some/great) note.*

**note·book** /ˈnəʊtbʊk/ *n* a book in which NOTES[2] (3) may be written

**not·ed** /ˈnəʊtəd/ *adj* [*for*] well-known; famous: *a noted performer*|*a town noted for its cheeses*

**note·pa·per** /ˈnəʊtˌpeɪpə[r]/ *n* [U] paper for writing letters and NOTES[2] (5) –see also WRITING PAPER

**note·wor·thy** /ˈnəʊtˌwɜːði‖-ɜr-/ *adj* (esp. of things and events) worthy of attention; NOTABLE[1]

**noth·ing** /ˈnʌθɪŋ/ *pron* **1** not any thing; no thing:

*There's nothing in this box; it's empty.|I've got nothing to do.* **2** something of no importance: *She means nothing to me.|They* **think nothing of** *walking 20 miles.* **3 for nothing: a** for no money; free: *He gave me this bicycle for nothing.* **b** with no good result: *All her efforts were/went/counted for nothing.* **4 nothing but** only: *He's nothing but a criminal.* **5 nothing for it** no other way possible: *With the bridge destroyed, there was nothing for it; we had to swim.* **6 nothing like: a** nothing better than: *There's nothing like a cup of tea when you're thirsty.* **b** not nearly: *It's nothing like so cold today (as it was yesterday).* **7 nothing to do with** no connection with **8 to say nothing of** as well as; including: *Three people were badly hurt, to say nothing of the damage to the building.* –compare SOMETHING, EVERYTHING

**noth·ing·ness** /'nʌθɪŋnɪ̣s/ *n* [U] the state of being nothing; not being: *Is there only nothingness after death?*

**no·tice**[1] /'nəʊtɪ̣s/ *n* **1** [C;U] (a written statement giving) information, direction, warning about something that will happen or has happened, etc.: *notices of births, marriages and deaths in the local newspaper|The notice on the wall says "No smoking".|The factory is closed* **until further notice.** (=until you are informed of its reopening)|*Can you be ready* **at short notice**? (=if I tell you only a short time before)|*I* **gave in my notice** *at work today.* (=officially informed my employers that I intend to leave)|*The owners of the flat have given us six weeks' notice to leave.* (=told us we must leave in six weeks) **2** [U] attention: **Don't take any notice of** (=pay no attention to) *what they say.|His writings brought him into public notice.* **3** [C] a statement of opinion, esp. in a newspaper, about a new book, play, etc.; REVIEW[1] (2): *favourable notices in the newspapers*

**notice**[2] *v* **-ticed, -ticing** [I;T +(*that*)] to pay attention to, esp. with the eyes: *She was wearing a new dress, but he didn't even notice (it).|I noticed (that) he wasn't wearing any socks.|Did you notice where I put it?|I noticed her leave/leaving.*

**no·tice·a·ble** /'nəʊtɪ̣səbəl/ *adj* that can be noticed; worth noticing: *a noticeable drop in the amount of crime* **–noticeably** *adv: noticeably fewer people*

**notice board** /'·· ˌ·/ *BrE*||**bulletin board** *AmE*– *n* a board on a wall, which notices may be fixed to –see picture on page 105

**no·ti·fy** /'nəʊtɪ̣faɪ/ *v* **-fied, -fying** [T *of*] to tell (someone), esp. formally: *to notify the police of a crime|I'll notify my lawyer to write out the agreement.* **–notification** /-fɪ̣'keɪʃən/ *n* [C;U]

**no·tion** /'nəʊʃən/ *n* [+*that*/*of*] an idea, belief, or opinion; CONCEPTION (1): *I haven't the faintest notion (of) what you're talking about.|silly notions*

**no·to·ri·e·ty** /ˌnəʊtə'raɪəti/ *n* [U] the state of being NOTORIOUS

**no·to·ri·ous** /nəʊ'tɔːriəs, nə-||-'to-/ *adj derog* famous for something bad; widely and unfavourably known: *a notorious thief/prison|an area notorious for crime* –see FAMOUS (USAGE) **–notoriously** *adv*

**not·with·stand·ing** /ˌnɒtwɪθ'stændɪŋ, -wɪð-||ˌnɑt-/ *prep,adv fml* in spite of (this): *Notwithstanding any other agreements, we will make a new contract with the firm.|He tried to prevent the marriage but it took place notwithstanding.*

**nought** /nɔːt/ *n* **1** *BrE* (the figure) 0; zero: *0·6 is usually read "nought point six".* **2** *esp. old use & lit* nothing; NAUGHT

**noun** /naʊn/ *n* a word that is the name of a person, place, thing, quality, action, etc., and can be used as the subject or object of a verb. Nouns are marked *n* in this dictionary. –compare PRONOUN

**nour·ish** /'nʌrɪʃ||'nɜrɪʃ, 'nʌ-/ *v* [T] to cause to stay alive or grow by giving food, water, etc.: *nourishing food|a well-nourished baby* –see also UNDERNOURISH

**nour·ish·ment** /'nʌrɪʃmənt||'nɜrɪʃ-, 'nʌ-/ *n* [U] something that NOURISHes; food: *The child took no nourishment all day.*

**nov·el**[1] /'nɒvəl||'nɑ-/ *n* a long written story dealing with invented people and events: *"War and Peace", the great novel by Leo Tolstoy*

**novel**[2] *adj* new; not like anything known before: *a novel suggestion, something we hadn't tried before*

**nov·el·ist** /'nɒvəlɪ̣st||'nɑ-/ *n* a writer of NOVELs

**nov·el·ty** /'nɒvəlti||'nɑ-/ *n* **-ties 1** [U] the state or quality of being NOVEL[2] **2** [S] something new and unusual: *It was quite a novelty to meet someone like that.* **3** [C] an unusual cheap, usu. not very useful, small object: *shops full of Christmas novelties*

**No·vem·ber** /nəʊ'vembəʳ, nə-/ also **Nov.** *written abbrev.*– *n* the 11th month of the year

**nov·ice** /'nɒvɪ̣s||'nɑ-/ *n* **1** a person with no experience in a skill or subject; BEGINNER: *a novice at swimming* **2** a person who has recently joined a religious group to become a MONK OR NUN

**now**[1] /naʊ/ *adv* **1 a** at this time; at present: *We used to live in Bristol but now we live in London.|Goodbye for now.|From now on* (=starting now) *I will try to do better.* **b** at the time mentioned in a story: *He opened the door. Now the noise was very loud.* **2** (used for starting a new subject, or to warn someone or tell them what to do): *Now, let's move on to the next question.|Now then, what's happened?|Be careful, now!|Now, now, stop crying!* **3 (every) now and then/again** sometimes **4 just now: a** at this moment: *I'm busy just now, come back later.* **b** a moment ago: *He telephoned just now.* –compare THEN[1]

**now**[2] also **now that**– *conj* because something has happened: *Now (that) John's arrived, we can begin.*

**now·a·days** *adv* at the present time

**no·where** /'nəʊweəʳ/ *adv* not anywhere; in or to no place: *The book was nowhere to be found.|The poor old man has got nowhere to live.|(fml) Nowhere have I seen so many beautiful houses.|Five pounds goes nowhere now.* (=will hardly buy anything) –compare SOMEWHERE, EVERYWHERE

**nox·ious** /'nɒkʃəs||'nɑk-/ *adj fml* harmful; poisonous: *noxious chemicals in the river water*

**noz·zle** /'nɒzəl||'nɑ-/ *n* a short tube fitted to the end of a HOSE, pipe, etc., to direct and control the stream of liquid or gas coming out

**n't** /ənt/ *short for* not: *hadn't|didn't|wouldn't|isn't*

**nu·ance** /'njuːɑːns||'nuː-/ *n* a slight difference in colour, meaning, etc.: *nuances of taste which are hard to describe*

**nu·bile** /'njuːbaɪl||'nuːbəl/ *adj fml or humor* (of a girl) young and sexually attractive

**nu·cle·ar** /'njuːklɪəʳ||'nuː-/ *adj* **1** of, concerning, or using the NUCLEUS of an atom, ATOMIC ENERGY, or the ATOM BOMB: *a nuclear power station|nuclear war|nuclear* PHYSICS **2** of, concerning, or being a NUCLEUS

**nuclear dis·ar·ma·ment** /ˌ··· ·ˈ···/ *n* [U] the giving up of atomic weapons by agreement between nations

**nuclear re·ac·tor** /ˌ··· ·ˈ··/ also **reactor, atomic pile**– *n* a large machine that produces ATOMIC ENERGY

**nu·cle·us** /ˈnjuːklɪəs‖ˈnuː-/ *n* **1** an original or central point, part, or group inside a larger thing, group, organization, CELL (3), etc.: *We are the nucleus of the group.* **2** the central part of an atom, made up of NEUTRONs and PROTONs

**nude¹** /njuːd‖nuːd/ *adj* not covered by clothes; NAKED

**nude²** *n* **1** [C] (a piece of art showing) a person without clothes **2** [U] the state of being NUDE: *They went swimming* **in the nude.**

**nudge** /nʌdʒ/ *v* **nudged, nudging** [T] to touch or push gently, esp. with one's elbow: *He nudged his friend to let him know it was time to leave.* –**nudge** *n*

**nud·is·m** /ˈnjuːdɪzəm‖ˈnuː-/ *n* [U] the practice of living without clothes, esp. in a group –**nudist** *adj,n*: *a nudist camp|a nudist village*

**nu·di·ty** /ˈnjuːdɪ̈ti‖ˈnuː-/ *n* [U] the quality or state of being NUDE: *a lot of nudity in recent films*

**nug·get** /ˈnʌgɪ̈t/ *n* a small rough lump of a precious metal, found in the earth: *a gold nugget*

**nui·sance** /ˈnjuːsəns‖ˈnuː-/ *n* a person, animal, action, or thing that annoys or causes trouble: *Sit down and stop being a nuisance/making a nuisance of yourself.|What a nuisance! I've forgotten my ticket.*

**nuke** /njuːk‖nuːk/ *n,v* [C;T] *infml* (to attack with) a NUCLEAR weapon

**null and void** /ˌ· · ˈ·/ *adj fml & law* without force or effect in law: *The court ruled that the claim was null and void.*

**nul·li·fy** /ˈnʌlɪ̈faɪ/ *v* **-fied, -fying** [T] *fml* to cause or declare to have no effect (in law): *a claim nullified by the court* –**nullification** /-fɪ̈ˈkeɪʃən / *n* [U]

**numb¹** /nʌm/ *adj* [*with*] (of the body) unable to feel anything: *My hands are numb after an hour outside on such a cold day.*|(fig.) *numb with shock* –**numbly** *adv* –**numbness** *n* [U]

**numb²** *v* [T] to cause to feel nothing or no pain; make NUMB¹: *fingers numbed with cold|the numbing effect of the drug* –**numbingly** *adv*

**num·ber¹** /ˈnʌmbəʳ/ *n* **1** [C] (a written sign representing) a member of a system used in counting: *1, 2, and 3 are numbers.|Choose any number between one and ten.|What is your telephone number?* **2** [A] (usu. written No., no.) having the stated size, place in order, etc.: *We live at No. 57, Church Street.* (=our house has the number 57) **3** [C;U] (a) quantity or amount: *The number of chairs in the room is 10.|Members of the club are few in number.*|**A number of** (=several) *visitors came to the meeting.|I've told you* **any number of** (=very many) *times not to do that.|Our army was beaten by* **sheer weight of numbers**. (=by the large amount of enemy soldiers) **4** [C] a (copy of a) magazine printed at a particular time; ISSUE¹ (2): *the latest number of "Vogue" magazine* **5** [C] a piece of (popular) music **6 opposite number** *BrE infml* a person with the same position in another organization, government, etc.; COUNTERPART

USAGE Plural nouns after a number usually take a plural verb, but if you are giving an opinion about the size of the number itself, use a singular verb. Compare: *25 bottles of wine* **were** *drunk at the office party.|£25* **is** *too much to pay.* –see AMOUNT (USAGE)

**SPELLING NOTE**

Words with the sound /n/, may be spelt **kn-**, like **know**, or **pn-**, like **pneumonia.**

**number²** *v* [T] **1** to give a number to: *Number the questions (from) 1 to 10.* **2** to reach as a total; be in number: *The people at the meeting numbered several* THOUSANDs. **3** [*among, as, with*] to be included: *He is numbered among the best of modern writers.* **4 someone's days are numbered** *infml* someone cannot continue or live much longer

**num·ber·plate** /ˈnʌmbəpleɪt‖-ər-/ *BrE*‖ **license plate** *AmE n* either of the signs (usu. at the front and back ends) on a vehicle showing its official number (REGISTRATION NUMBER) –see picture on page 85

**Number Ten, No. 10** /ˌ·· ˈ·/ *n* No. 10 Downing Street; the address of the home of the British PRIME MINISTER

**nu·me·ral** /ˈnjuːmərəl‖ˈnuː-/ *adj,n* (any of the systems of signs) used for representing a number or numbers; (of) NUMBER¹ (1) –compare ROMAN NUMERALs, ARABIC NUMERALs

**nu·me·rate** /ˈnjuːmərɪ̈t‖ˈnuː-/ *adj BrE* able to do MATHEMATICS and ARITHMETIC –opposite **innumerate**; compare LITERATE –**numeracy** *n* [U]

**nu·mer·i·cal** /njuːˈmerɪkəl‖nuː-/ *adj* of, concerning, showing, or shown by numbers: *numerical ability* (=skill with numbers)|*numerical order* –**numerically** *adv*: *numerically greater*

**nu·me·rous** /ˈnjuːmərəs‖ˈnuː-/ *adj* many: *numerous reasons* –**numerously** *adv*

**nun** /nʌn/ *n* a woman member of a religious (usu. Christian) group (ORDER¹ (10)), who lives a life of service to God with others in a CONVENT –compare MONK

**nun·ne·ry** /ˈnʌnəri/ *n* **-ries** a building in which NUNs live; CONVENT –compare MONASTERY

**nup·tial** /ˈnʌpʃəl/ *adj* [A] *pomp or tech* of or concerning marriage or the marriage ceremony: *the nuptial day* –**nuptials** *n* [P]

**nurse¹** /nɜːs‖nɜrs/ *n* **1** [A;C;S] a person who is trained to take care of sick, hurt, or old people, esp. as directed by a doctor in a hospital: *a student nurse* (=a person learning to be a nurse)|*a private nurse taking care of him at home* **2** a woman employed to take care of a young child –compare NANNY

**nurse²** *v* **nursed, nursing 1** [T] to take care of as or like a nurse: *He nursed her back to health.|She spends her time nursing her old father.* **2** [I;T] to give (a baby) milk from the breast: *a nursing mother* **3** [T] to hold (esp. a bad feeling) in the mind: *She still nursed a grudge* (=kept an angry feeling) *against her old enemy.*

**nurse·maid** /ˈnɜːsmeɪd‖ˈnɜrs-/ *n* →NURSE¹ (2)

**nur·se·ry** /ˈnɜːsəri‖ˈnɜr-/ *n* **-ries 1** a place where small children are taken care of while their parents are at work, shopping, etc. –compare PLAYGROUP, CRÈCHE **2** an area where young plants and trees are grown **3** *esp. old use* a small child's bedroom or playroom in a house

**nur·se·ry·man** /'nɜːsərimən‖'nɜr-/ *n* **-men** /mən/ a person who grows plants in a NURSERY (2)

**nursery rhyme** /'··· ·/ also **Mother Goose rhyme** *AmE*– *n* a short usu. old and well-known song or poem for small children

**nursery school** /'··· ·/ also **kindergarten**– *n* a school for young children of three to five years of age: *children at nursery school*

**nurs·ing** /'nɜːsɪŋ‖'nɜr-/ *n* [U] the job of a NURSE[1] (1): *She went into nursing.* (=became a nurse)

**nursing home** /'·· ·/ *n* a usu. private establishment where old or sick people are cared for by nurses

**nur·ture** /'nɜːtʃə^r‖'nɜr-/ *v* **-tured, -turing** [T] *lit* to give care and food to: *nurtured by loving parents*

**nut** /nʌt/ *n* **1 a** a dry fruit with a seed (KERNEL) surrounded by a hard shell **b** this seed, which is eaten **2** a small piece of metal for screwing onto a BOLT **3** *infml* a person who is or seems to be unbalanced in mind; mad person **4** *infml* one's head: *You must be off your nut!* (=mad) **5 a hard/tough nut to crack** *infml* a difficult question, person, etc., to deal with

**nut·case** /'nʌtkeɪs/ *n infml & humor* a mad person; NUT (3)

**nut·crack·er** /'nʌt,krækə^r/ *n* a tool for cracking the shell of a nut: *Have we got a nut cracker/a pair of nutcrackers in the house?* –see PAIR (USAGE)

**nut·meg** /'nʌtmeg/ *n* [C;U] a seed or powder used (as a SPICE) to give a particular taste to food

**nu·tri·ent** /'njuːtriənt‖'nuː-/ *adj,n tech* (a food or chemical) providing for life and growth

**nu·tri·tion** /njuː'trɪʃən‖nuː-/ *n* [U] the action of providing or state of being provided with food; NOURISHMENT –see also MALNUTRITION

**nu·tri·tious** /njuː'trɪʃəs‖nuː-/ *adj* valuable to the body as food; NOURISHING: *nutritious food*

**nuts** /nʌts/ *adj* [F] *infml* mad; CRAZY: *I'll go nuts if I have to wait much longer.*

**nut·ty** /'nʌti/ *adj* **-tier, -tiest 1 a** tasting like nuts: *wine with a nutty taste* **b** filled with nuts: *a nutty cake* **2** *infml* mad; CRAZY **nuttiness** *n* [U]

**nuz·zle** /'nʌzəl/ *v* **-zled, -zling** [I;T *up, against*] (esp. of an animal) to rub, touch, or push with the nose: *The dog nuzzled the sleeping child.*

**NW** *written abbrev. said as:* northwest(ern)

**ny·lon** /'naɪlɒn‖-lɑn/ *n* [U] a strong man-made material made into clothes, cords, and plastics: *nylon thread/thread made of nylon|a nylon shirt*

**ny·lons** /'naɪlɒnz‖-lɑnz/ *n* [P] *becoming rare* women's nylon stockings: *a pair of nylons* –see PAIR (USAGE)

**nymph** /nɪmf/ *n* (in Greek and Roman literature) any of the less important spirits or goddesses of nature, represented as young girls

**nym·pho·ma·ni·ac** /,nɪmfə'meɪniæk/ *n,adj* (of or being) a woman who has unusually strong sexual desires

# O, o

**O , o** /əʊ/ **O's, o's** *or* **Os, os 1** the 15th letter of the English alphabet **2** (in speech) zero

**oaf** /əʊf/ *n* a stupid ungraceful person (esp. male): *You* CLUMSY *oaf!* **–oafish** *adj* **–oafishly** *adv* **–oafishness** *n* [U]

**oak** /əʊk/ *n* [C;U] (the hard wood of) a type of large tree

**OAP** *n abbrev. for:* OLD AGE PENSIONer

**oar** /ɔː^r‖or/ *n* a long pole with a wide flat blade, used for rowing a boat: *He pulled hard on the oars.* –compare PADDLE[1]

**o·a·sis** /əʊ'eɪsɪ̈s/ *n* **-ses** a place with water and plants in a desert

**oath** /əʊθ/ *n* **oaths** /əʊðz/ **1** a solemn promise: *to swear/take an oath* **2** an expression of strong feeling using religious or sexual words improperly: *oaths and* CURSES **3 be on/under oath** *law* to have made a solemn promise to tell the truth

**oat·meal** /'əʊtmiːl/ *n* [U] crushed OATS used for making cakes and breakfast food (=PORRIDGE)

**oats** /əʊts/ *n* [P] **1** a type of grain that provides food for people and animals **2**→OATMEAL **3 sow one's wild oats** to chase pleasure foolishly while still young

**ob·du·rate** /'ɒbdʒʊrɪ̈t‖'ɑbdə-/ *adj fml* unchangeable in beliefs or feelings; STUBBORN **–obdurately** *adv* **–obduracy** *n* [U]

**o·be·di·ent** /ə'biːdiənt/ *adj* doing what one is ordered to do; willing to obey: *an obedient dog* –opposite **disobedient –obediently** *adv* **–obedience** *n* [U]

**ob·e·lisk** /'ɒbəlɪsk‖'ɑ-, 'əʊ-/ *n* a tall pointed stone pillar built usu. in honour of a person or event

**o·bese** /əʊ'biːs/ *adj fml* very fat –see THIN (USAGE) **–obesity** *n* [U]

**o·bey** /əʊ'beɪ, ə-/ *v* **-beyed, -beying** [I;T] to do (what one is asked or ordered to do) by (someone): *Obey (the law/orders/your teachers) or you will be punished.* –opposite **disobey**

**o·bit·u·a·ry** /ə'bɪtʃʊəri‖-tʃʊeri/ *n* **-ries** a formal report, esp. in a newspaper, that someone has died, esp. with an account of the dead person's life

**ob·ject**[1] /'ɒbdʒɪkt‖'ɑb-/ *n* **1** a thing that can be seen or touched **2** [*of*] something that produces interest or other effect: *an object of admiration/of fear* **3** purpose; aim: *The object of his visit was to open the new hospital.* **4** *tech* a term used in grammar to describe words in a certain position. In the sentences *John gave Mary a book; John gave a book to Mary, "(to) Mary"* is the **indirect object** of the verb, and *"book"* is the **direct object** –compare SUBJECT[1] (6); see Study Notes on page 647 **5 no object** not a difficulty: *Money is no object with me.*

**ob·ject**[2] /əb'dʒekt/ *v* **1** [I *to*] to be against; feel dislike: *Do you object to smoking?* **2** [T +(*that*)] to give as an OBJECTION: *I wanted to climb the hill, but Bill objected that he was too tired.* –**objector** *n*

**ob·jec·tion** /əb'dʒekʃən/ *n* [*to*] **1** a statement or feeling of dislike, disapproval, or opposition: *to raise/voice an objection* **2** a reason or argument against

**ob·jec·tio·na·ble** /əb'dʒekʃənəbəl/ *adj* unpleasant; offensive: *objectionable people/behaviour* –**objectionably** *adv*

**ob·jec·tive**[1] /əb'dʒektɪv/ *adj* not influenced by personal feelings; existing outside one's own mind: *an objective fact* –opposite **subjective** –**objectively** *adv: Objectively (speaking), he can't possibly succeed.* –**objectivity** /ˌɒbdʒek'tɪvəti‖ˌɑb-/ *n* [U]

**objective**[2] *n* an object to be won; purpose of a plan

**ob·jet d'art** /ˌɒbʒeɪ 'dɑːʳ‖ˌɑb-/ *n* **objets d'art** (*same pronunciation*) *French* an object, usu. small, having some artistic value

**ob·li·gate** /'ɒbləgeɪt‖'ɑb-/ *v* **-gated, -gating** [T *usu. pass.*] *fml* to make (someone) feel it necessary (to do something); OBLIGE (1): *He felt obligated to visit his parents.*

**ob·li·ga·tion** /ˌɒblə'geɪʃən‖ˌɑb-/ *n* a duty; necessity: *There is no obligation to buy in this shop.*

**ob·lig·a·to·ry** /ə'blɪgətəri‖-tori/ *adj* necessary; which must be done by law, rule, etc. –compare OPTIONAL

**o·blige** /ə'blaɪdʒ/ *v* **-bliged, -bliging** [T] **1** [*usu. pass.*] to force (someone to do something): *He felt obliged to leave after such an unpleasant quarrel.* **2** *polite* to do (someone) a favour: *Could you oblige me by opening the window?* **3 (I'm) much obliged (to you)** *polite* (I'm) very grateful (to you)

**o·blig·ing** /ə'blaɪdʒɪŋ/ *adj* kind and eager to help –**obligingly** *adv*

**o·blique** /ə'bliːk/ *adj* **1** indirect: *an oblique remark* **2** in a sideways direction; sloping: *an oblique line* **3** *tech* (of an angle) more or less than 90°

**o·blit·er·ate** *v* **-ated, -ating** [T] to remove all signs of; destroy –**obliteration** /-'reɪʃən / *n* [U]

**o·bliv·i·on** /ə'blɪviən/ *n* [U] **1** the state of having forgotten; unconsciousness; OBLIVIOUSness **2** the state of being forgotten

**o·bliv·i·ous** /ə'blɪviəs/ *adj* [*to, of*] not noticing: *He was quite oblivious to the danger he was in.* –**obliviously** *adv* –**obliviousness** *n* [U]

**ob·long** /'ɒblɒŋ‖'ɑblɔŋ/ *adj,n* (a figure) with four straight sides, forming four right angles, which is longer than it is wide –compare RECTANGLE

**ob·nox·ious** /əb'nɒkʃəs‖-'nɑk-/ *adj fml* unpleasant; nasty: *an obnoxious smell/person* –**obnoxiously** *adv*

**o·boe** /'əubəu/ *n* a type of musical WIND INSTRUMENT made of wood

**ob·scene** /əb'siːn/ *adj* (esp. of ideas, books, etc., usu. about sex) nasty; offensive –**obscenely** *adv* –**obscenity** /əb'senəti/ *n* **-ties** [C;U]

**ob·scure**[1] /əb'skjʊəʳ/ *adj* **1** hard to understand; not clear: *a speech full of obscure political jokes* **2** not well known: *an obscure poet* –**obscurely** *adv* –**obscurity** *n* **-ties** [C;U]

**obscure**[2] *v* **-scured, -scuring** [T] to hide; make difficult to see: *My view was obscured by the trees.*

**ob·se·qui·ous** /əb'siːkwɪəs/ *adj fml* too eager to obey or serve; too humble: *an obsequious manner*

**ob·ser·vance** /əb'zɜːvəns‖-ɜr-/ *n* [U] *fml* behaviour in accordance with a law, ceremony, or custom: *the observance of the speed limit/of Christmas*

**ob·ser·vant** /əb'zɜːvənt‖-ɜr-/ *adj* quick at noticing things –opposite **unobservant**

**ob·ser·va·tion** /ˌɒbzə'veɪʃən‖ˌɑbzər-/ *n* **1** [C;U] action of noticing **2** [U] ability to notice things: *His powers of observation are poor.* (=he doesn't notice things) **3** [C] a remark: *He made the observation that ...* **4 under observation** being carefully watched during some period of time: *She is in hospital under observation.* (=to see if she is ill)

**ob·ser·va·to·ry** /əb'zɜːvətəri‖əb'zɜrvətori/ *n* **-ries** a place from which scientists watch the moon, stars, etc.

**ob·serve** /əb'zɜːv‖-ɜrv/ *v* **-served, -serving** [T] **1** [(*that*)] to see and notice; watch carefully: *to observe the stars|They were observed entering the bank.* **2** to act in accordance with (law or custom (esp. religious)) **3** [(*that*)] to make a remark; say

**ob·serv·er** /əb'zɜːvəʳ‖-ɜr-/ *n* **1** one who OBSERVES (1,2) **2** one who attends meetings, classes, etc., to OBSERVE (1) only, not to take part

**ob·sess** /əb'ses/ *v* [T] to fill (someone's) mind continuously: *He's obsessed by football.*

**ob·ses·sion** /əb'seʃən/ *n* [*about, with*] a fixed idea from which the mind cannot be freed –**obsessional** *adj*

**ob·ses·sive** /əb'sesɪv/ *adj* of or like an OBSESSION: *his obsessive interest in sex*

**ob·so·les·cent** /ˌɒbsə'lesənt‖ˌɑb-/ *adj* becoming OBSOLETE –**obsolescence** *n* [U]

**ob·so·lete** /'ɒbsəliːt‖ˌɑbsə'liːt/ *adj* no longer used; out of date: *obsolete machinery|*(fig.) *obsolete ideas* –see OLD (USAGE)

**ob·sta·cle** /'ɒbstəkəl‖'ɑb-/ *n* [*to*] something which stands in the way and prevents action or success: *She felt that her family was an obstacle to her work.*

**ob·stet·rics** /əb'stetrɪks/ *n* [U] the branch of medicine concerned with the birth of children –**obstetric(al)** *adj*

**ob·sti·nate** /'ɒbstənət‖'ɑb-/ *adj* not willing to change one's opinion, obey, etc.: *Don't be so obstinate!* –**obstinately** *adv* –**obstinacy** *n* [U]

**ob·struct** /əb'strʌkt/ *v* [T] **1** to block up: *to obstruct a road* **2** to put difficulties in the way of: *to obstruct a plan* –**obstruction** *n* [C;U]: *an obstruction in the road* –**obstructive** *adj* –**obstructively** *adv* –**obstructiveness** *n* [U]

**ob·tain** /əb'teɪn/ *v* [T] *more fml than* **get**– to get: *By this method, you obtain a good result.* –**obtainable** *adj*: *I'm afraid that the record you asked for is no longer obtainable.* –opposite **unobtainable**

**ob·tru·sive** /əb'truːsɪv/ *adj* very noticeable –see also UNOBTRUSIVE –**obtrusively** *adv* –**obtrusiveness** *n* [U]

**ob·tuse** /əb'tjuːs‖-'tuːs/ *adj* **1** *fml* stupid **2** *tech* (of an angle) between 90° and 180° –**obtusely** *adv* –**obtuseness** *n* [U]

**ob·vi·ous** /'ɒbvɪəs‖'ɑb-/ *adj* easy to understand;

clear; which must be recognized: *It's quite obvious that he's lying.* –**obviousness** *n* [U]

**ob·vi·ous·ly** /'ɒbviəsli||'ɑb-/ *adv* it can be easily seen (that); plainly: *Obviously, you didn't read it.* –compare APPARENTLY, EVIDENTLY

**oc·ca·sion** /ə'keɪʒən/ *n* **1** a time when something happens: *On that occasion I was not at home.* **2** a special event or ceremony: *The opening of a new school is always a great occasion.* **3 on occasion** from time to time; occasionally

**oc·ca·sion·al** /ə'keɪʒənəl/ *adj* [A] happening from time to time; not regular: *We get the occasional visitor here.* –see NEVER (USAGE) –**occasionally** *adv*

**oc·cult** /'ɒkʌlt, ə'kʌlt||ə'kʌlt, 'ɑ-/ *adj* secret; magical and mysterious; hidden from ordinary people

**oc·cu·pant** /'ɒkjʊpənt||'ɑkjə-/ *n* [*of*] *fml* a person who lives in a certain place: *Are you the occupant of this house?*

**oc·cu·pa·tion** /ˌɒkjʊ'peɪʃən||ˌɑkjə-/ *n* **1** [C] a job; employment –see JOB (USAGE) **2** [U *of*] taking possession of: *The workers' occupation of the factory lasted three weeks.*

**oc·cu·pa·tion·al** /ˌɒkjʊ'peɪʃənəl||ˌɑkjə-/ *adj* of or about an OCCUPATION (1): *For professional footballers, injuries are an* **occupational hazard**. (=a risk connected with their work) –**occupationally** *adv*

**oc·cu·pi·er** /'ɒkjʊpaɪə<sup>r</sup>||'ɑkjə-/ *n* an OCCUPANT, esp. of a house

**oc·cu·py** /'ɒkjʊpaɪ||'ɑkjə-/ *v* **-pied, -pying** [T] **1** to be in (a place): *to occupy a house/a bed/a railway carriage* **2** to fill (a certain position, space, or time): *His books occupy a lot of space.|Writing occupies a lot of his free time.* **3** to cause to spend time (doing something): *He occupied himself in/with collecting stamps.* **4** to move into and hold possession of (an enemy's country, town, etc.)

**oc·cur** /ə'kɜː<sup>r</sup>/ *v* **-rr-** [I] **1** *more fml than* **happen**– (esp. of unplanned events) to happen; take place: *Many accidents occur in the home.* **2** (esp. of something not alive) to exist: *That sound doesn't occur in his language.*

**occur to** sbdy. *v prep* [T] (of an idea) to come to (someone's) mind: *Just as I was leaving the house, it occurred to me that I had forgotten my keys.*

**oc·cur·rence** /ə'kʌrəns||ə'kɜ-/ *n* an event; happening

**o·cean** /'əʊʃən/ *n* **1** [*the* U] the great mass of salt water that covers most of the earth **2** [C] (*often cap. as part of a name*) any of the great seas into which this mass is divided: *the Pacific Ocean* –**oceanic** /ˌəʊʃi'ænɪk / *adj*

**o'clock** /ə'klɒk||ə'klɑk/ *adv* (*used with the numbers from 1 to 12 in telling time*) exactly the hour stated according to the clock: *"What time is it?" "It's 9 o'clock".*

**oc·ta·gon** /'ɒktəgən||'ɑktəgɑn/ *n tech* a flat figure with eight sides and eight angles –**octagonal** /ɒk'tægənəl / *adj*

**oc·tave** /'ɒktɪv, -teɪv||'ɑk-/ *n* a space of eight degrees between musical notes

**Oc·to·ber** /ɒk'təʊbə<sup>r</sup>||ɑk-/ also **Oct.** *written abbrev.*– *n* the 10th month of the year

**oc·to·pus** /'ɒktəpəs||'ɑk-/ *n* a deep-sea creature with eight arms (TENTACLES)

**oc·u·list** /'ɒkjʊlɪst||'ɑkjə-/ *n fml* an eye-doctor

**odd** /ɒd||ɑd/ *adj* **1** strange; unusual: *odd behaviour|an odd person* **2** [A] separated from a pair or set to which it belongs: *an odd shoe* **3** (of a number) that cannot be divided exactly by 2: *1, 3, 5, 7, etc., are odd.* –opposite **even** **4** [A] not regular; OCCASIONAL: *He does the odd job for me from time to time.|I only get the odd moment to read.* **5** [after *n*] *infml* (after numbers) with rather more: *20-odd years*

**odd·i·ty** /'ɒdɪti||'ɑ-/ *n* **-ties** a strange person, thing, etc.

**odd·ly** /'ɒdli||'ɑdli/ *adv* strangely: *Oddly enough, he didn't remember his own birthday.*

**odd·ment** /'ɒdmənt||'ɑd-/ *n* [*often pl.*] something left over or remaining

**odds** /ɒdz||ɑdz/ *n* [P] **1** the probability that something will or will not happen: *The odds are 10 to 1 that her horse will win the race.|The odds are that he will fail his examination.* **2 at odds (with)** in disagreement (with) **3 it/that makes no odds** *BrE* it/that makes no difference; has no importance

**odds and ends** /ˌ· · '·/ *n* [P] small articles without much value

**odds-on** /· '·◂/ *adj* very likely (to win): *The odds-on favourite* (=the horse that was generally expected to win) *came in last, to everyone's surprise.*

**ode** /əʊd/ *n* a usu. long poem

**o·di·ous** /'əʊdɪəs/ *adj fml* hateful; very unpleasant –**odiously** *adv*

**o·dour** *BrE*||**odor** *AmE* /'əʊdə<sup>r</sup>/ *n* a smell, esp. an unpleasant one –**odourless** *adj*

**o'er** /əʊə<sup>r</sup>/ *adv,prep lit* over

**oe·soph·a·gus, esophagus** /ɪ'sɒfəgəs||ɪ'sɑ-/ *n tech* the food tube leading down into the stomach

**of** /əv, ə; *strong* ɒv||əv, ə; *strong* ɑv/ *prep* **1** belonging to (something not alive): *the leg of the table* (but note *John's leg|the dog's leg*)|*the colour of her hair|the size of the room* **2** made from: *a dress of silk|a crown of gold* **3** containing: *a bag of potatoes* **4** (shows a part or amount): *two pounds of sugar|much of the night|the members of the team|both of us* **5 a** that is/are; being: *the City of New York|the art of painting|at the age of eight|two friends of mine|some fool of a boy* (=some foolish boy) **b** happening in or on: *the University of London|the Battle of Waterloo* **6** (of works of art or literature) **a** by: *the plays of Shakespeare* **b** about: *a picture of John* **7** in relation to; in connection with: *the king of England|a teacher of English|the time of arrival |to die of hunger|to cure someone of a disease|fond of swimming|within a mile of here* (=not more than a mile from here) **8** with; having: *a matter of no importance* **9** (shows what someone or something is or does): *the laughter of the children|How kind of John to buy the tickets.* **10 a** (used in dates): *the 27th of February* **b** *AmE* (used in telling time) before: *It's five (minutes) of two.* (=1.55) **c** during: *They always like to go there of an evening.*

**off**[1] /ɒf||ɔf/ *adv,adj* [F] **1** from or no longer in a place or position; away: *They got into the car and drove off.|The door handle fell off.|She stood a few yards off.|Catch this bus and get off* (=out of the bus) *at the station.|He took his shoes off.* (=from his feet)|*They're off!* (=the race has started)|(*fml*) *Be* off with you! (=go away)|*I'm taking Monday off.* (=away from work) **2** not lit or working: *Turn the light/*TAPS *off.*|*The TV is off.* –opposite **on 3** so as to be completely finished or no longer there: *Finish the work off before you go home.* **4** (of food) no longer good to eat or drink: *The milk is off/has gone off.* **5** not quite right; not as good as usual: *Her work has gone off lately.*|(*infml*) *I think it was a bit off, not even answering my letter!* **6** not going to happen after all: *I'm afraid the party's off.* –compare ON² (6) **7** having little or a lot of something, esp. money: *They're rather badly off.* (=they're poor)|*They're better off than we are.*|*How are you off for ..?* (=have you enough?) **8 off and on** also **on and off**– from time to time; sometimes

**off²** *prep* **1** not on; away from: *Keep off the grass.*|*He jumped off the bus.*|*She cut a piece off the loaf.* –see Study Notes on page 474 **2** (esp. of a road) turning away from (a larger one): *a narrow street off the High Street* **3** in the sea near: *an island off the coast of France* **4** no longer wanting or having something: *He's off his food.*|*The doctor took him off drugs.* –opposite **on**

**off³** *adj* [A] (of a time) **a** not as good as usual: *This is one of his off days; he usually plays better.* **b** quiet and dull: *Tickets are cheaper during the off season.*

**of·fence** *BrE*||**offense** *AmE* /ə'fens/ *n* **1** [C *against*] a wrong; crime: *Driving while drunk is a serious offence.* **2** [C;U] cause for hurt feelings: *to give/cause offence to someone*|*to take offence at something*

**of·fend** /ə'fend/ *v* **1** [T] to hurt the feelings of: *I was very offended that you forgot my birthday.* **2** [T] to cause displeasure to: *Cruelty offends many people.* **3** [I *against*] to do wrong

**of·fend·er** /ə'fendəʳ/ *n euph* a criminal

**of·fen·sive¹** /ə'fensɪv/ *adj* **1** causing offence; unpleasant: *offensive behaviour*–opposite **inoffensive 2** of or about attacking: *an offensive weapon*–opposite **defensive –offensively** *adv* **–offensiveness** *n* [U]

**offensive²** *n* **1** a continued attack **2 on the offensive** making a continued attack

**of·fer¹** /'ɒfəʳ||'ɔ-, 'ɑ-/ *v* **1** [T *to, for*] to hold out (to a person) for acceptance or refusal: *Will you offer the guests some coffee.*|*They've offered us £25,000 for the house. Shall we take it?* **2** [I;T +*to-v*] to express willingness (to do something): *She offered to help.* **3** [T *up, to*] to give (to God): *He offered (up) a prayer.*

**offer²** *n* **1** [+*to-v*/*of*] a statement offering (to do) something: *an offer of help* **2** [*of*] something which is offered: *an offer of £5* –compare OFFERING

**of·fer·ing** /'ɒfərɪŋ||'ɔ-, 'ɑ-/ *n* something offered, esp. to God

**off·hand** /ˌɒf'hænd◂||ˌɔf-/ *adv,adj* **1** careless; disrespectful: *an offhand manner* **2** at once; without time to think: *I can't give an answer offhand.* **–offhandedly** *adv* **–offhandedness** *n* [U]

**of·fice** /'ɒf⅟ₒs||'ɔ-, 'ɑ-/ *n* **1** [C] a place where business is done: *I work in an office.*|*a ticket office* **2** [C] (*usu. caps.*) a government department: *the Foreign Office* **3** [C;U] a position of responsibility or power, esp. in government: *to hold/enter/leave office*|*Our party has been in/out of office for three years.*

**of·fi·cer** /'ɒf⅟ₒsəʳ||'ɔ-, 'ɑ-/ *n* **1** a person in a position of command in the armed forces **2** a person who holds a position of some importance, esp. in government, a business, or a group: *a local government officer* **3** a policeman

USAGE **Civil servants** are people who work for the government, and an **official** is someone who works for a government or other large organization in a position of responsibility: *a meeting between* **civil servants** *from the Department of Transport and important railway* **officials**. An **officer** is usually a member of the armed forces in a position of command, or a member of the police force, but the word is sometimes used like **offical**. A **clerk** is an office worker of fairly low rank. This word is also used in *AmE* for someone who works in a shop (a **sales clerk**), but the *BrE* word is **shop assistant.**

**of·fi·cial¹** /ə'fɪʃəl/ *n* a person who holds an OFFICE (3): *a union official* –see OFFICER (USAGE)

**official²** *adj* of, about, or from a position of trust, power, and responsibility: *an official position*|*an official occasion* –Compare: *an* **official** *letter concerning my income tax*|*a rather* **officious** *letter from my neighbour, complaining about the noise from my radio* –opposite **unofficial** –compare OFFICIOUS

**of·fi·cial·ly** /ə'fɪʃəli/ *adv* **1** in an official manner **2** as (believed to have been) stated by officials: *The £ is officially worth $2.40, but I can buy it more cheaply.* –opposite **unofficially**

**of·fi·ci·ate** /ə'fɪʃieɪt/ *v* **-ated, -ating** [I *at*] to perform official duties: *Who officiated at your wedding?*

**of·fi·cious** /ə'fɪʃəs/ *adj derog* too eager to give orders or to offer advice –compare OFFICIAL² **–officiously** *adv* **–officiousness** *n* [U]

**off·ing** /'ɒfɪŋ||'ɔ-, 'ɑ-/ *n* **in the offing** about to happen

**off-li·cence** /'· ··/ *n BrE* a shop where alcohol is sold to be taken away

**off-peak** /ˌ· '·◂/ *adj* [A] **1** less busy: *Telephone charges are lower during off-peak periods.* **2** existing during less busy periods: *off-peak electricity* –compare PEAK¹ (2)

**off·set** /'ɒfset, ˌɒf'set||'ɔfset, ˌɔf'set/ *v* **-set, -setting** [T] to make up for; balance: *The cost of getting there was offset by the fact that it's a very cheap place to live.*

**off·shoot** /'ɒfʃuːt||'ɔf-/ *n* a new stem or branch: (fig.) *an offshoot of a large organization*

**off·shore** /ˌɒf'ʃɔːʳ||ˌɔf'ʃor◂/ *adv,adj* [after *n*] in the water, at a distance from the shore: *Britain's offshore oil*|*two miles offshore* –see also INSHORE, ONSHORE

**off·side** /ˌɒf'saɪd◂||ˌɔf-/ *adj,adv* **1** (in certain sports) in a position in which play is not allowed –opposite **onside 2** [A] *BrE* being on the side of a vehicle farthest from the edge of the road–opposite **nearside**

**off·spring** /'ɒfˌsprɪŋ||'ɔf-/ *n* [U] *fml or humor* a child or children; the young of an animal

**off-white** /ˌ· '·◂/ *n,adj* [U] a colour that is not quite a pure white

**oft** /ɒft||ɔft/ *adv lit* often: *oft-repeated advice*

**of·ten** /'ɒfən, 'ɒftən||'ɔ-/ *adv* **1** many times; in many cases: *"How often do you go there?" "Once a month, but I wish I could go more often."* **2 as often as not** quite often; at least half the time: *As often as not he forgets his homework.* **3 every so often** sometimes; OCCASIONALLY **4 more often than not** more than half of the time; usually: *More often than not she's late for*

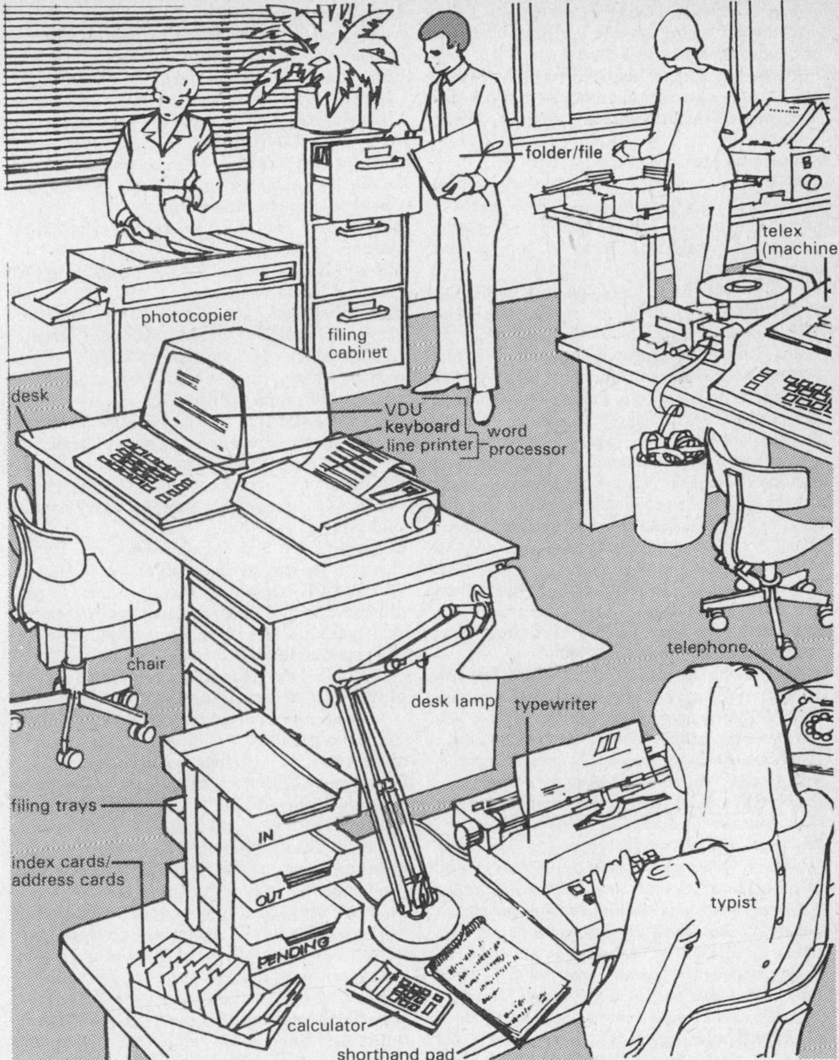


Jane works in the modern offices of a large international company. On her **desk** she has the usual **office equipment**, such as a **telephone**, a **typewriter**, and **filing trays** for letters and papers. She uses an **electric typewriter**, instead of the **manual typewriter** she used to have, and the company has just bought a **word processor**. With this machine the **typist/operator** can **type** a letter, and then see what has been typed on an **electronic screen/display**, and **correct** any mistakes before the machine types the letter. The machine can print many separate copies of a letter and put a different name and address on each one.
If she has to do some calculations, Jane uses an electronic **pocket calculator**, and there is a **photocopier** in the office for making copies of letters and other papers.
Jane normally sends letters **by post**, but if she has to send a written message quickly she uses the **telex.** This is a machine like a typewriter: a message is typed, and then another telex machine somewhere else receives the message and types it out again a few hours later.

**Questions** (Answers on page 702)

**a** Telephones, typewriters, and filing trays are examples of .......
**b** A machine for making copies is a .....
**c** We send written messages quickly by .....
**d** Usually a letter is sent by .....

*school.* –see NEVER (USAGE)

**o·gle** /ˈəʊgəl/ *v* **-gled, -gling** [I;T *at*] to look (at) with great interest, esp. sexual interest

**o·gre** /ˈəʊgəʳ/ **ogress** /ˈəʊgrɪ̈s/ *fem.*– *n* **1** (in fairy stories) a fierce creature like a very large man, who is thought to eat children **2** a person who makes others afraid

**oh** /əʊ/ *interj* (expressing surprise, fear, etc.)

**ohm** /əʊm/ *n* a measure of electrical RESISTANCE (4)

**oil**[1] /ɔɪl/ *n* [U] a fatty liquid (from animals, plants, or under the ground) used for burning, for making machines run easily, for cooking, etc.: *corn oil*|OLIVE *oil*|*engine oil*

**oil**[2] *v* [T] to put oil onto or rub oil on or into

**oil paint·ing** /ˈ· ˌ··/ *n* **1** [U] the art of painting in OILS **2** [C] a picture painted in OILS

**oil·rig** /ˈɔɪlˌrɪg/ *n* an apparatus for getting oil from underground, esp.from land that is under the sea

**oils** /ɔɪlz/ *n* [P] paints (esp. for pictures) containing oil –compare WATERCOLOUR

**oil·skin** /ˈɔɪlˌskɪn/ *n* [C;U] (a garment made of) cloth treated with oil so that water will not pass through it

**oil slick** /ˈ· ·/ *n* a thin sheet of oil floating on water, esp. as a result of an accident to an oil-carrying ship

**oil·y** /ˈɔɪli/ *adj* **-ier, -iest 1** of, about, or like oil: *an oily liquid* **2** covered with or containing oil: *oily food* **3** *derog* too polite: *I don't like his oily manner.*

**oink** /ɔɪŋk/ *v,n* [C;I] *infml* (to make) the sound that a pig makes

**oint·ment** /ˈɔɪntmənt/ *n* [C;U] a substance (often medicinal) to be rubbed on the skin

**o·kay**[1], **OK** /əʊˈkeɪ/ *adj,adv infml* [F] **1** all right: *That car goes okay now.* **2** (*asking for or expressing agreement, or giving permission*) all right; agreed; yes: *Let's go there, okay?*| *"Shall we go there?" "Okay".*

**okay**[2], **OK** *v* **okayed, okaying** [T] *infml* to approve: *Has the bank okayed your request for a loan?*

**okay**[3], **OK** *n* **okays, OK's** *infml* approval; permission: *I got the OK to leave early.*

**old** /əʊld/ *adj* **1** advanced in age; of age: *"How old is the baby?" "She's eight months old."* **2** having lived or existed for a long time: *an old man*|*old and young people*|*old and new books*|*The old* (=old people) *do not always understand young people.* **3** having been in use for a long time: *old shoes*|*an old car* **4** [A] having continued in the stated relationship for a long time: *We are old friends.* **5** [A] known for a long time: *Don't tell me the same old story again!*|*Good old John!* **6** [A] former: *He got his old job back.* **7 of old: a** long ago; in the past: *days of old* **b** since a long time ago: *I know him of old.* –compare YOUNG

USAGE 1 Note that **old,** not **young** or **new,** is used when measuring age: *a* **young** *baby*|*a* **new** *car,* but *How* **old** *is the baby?*|*How* **old** *is your car?*|*a three week* **old** *baby,* etc. 2 **Old** is a general word for great age, and **elderly** is a polite way of saying old when speaking of people: *an* **old** *church*|*an* **old/elderly** *lady.* **Venerable** is used of someone who is old and respected: *a* **venerable** *white- haired priest.* **Ancient** is the word used for the people or products of civilizations of the distant past: **ancient** *Egypt*| *an* **ancient** *Greek bowl.* **Antique** is used of things that are rare and valuable as well as old: *an* **antique** *French writing desk.* Things or ideas that are no longer suitable or useful are **antiquated,** and when something new takes their place they become **obsolete: antiquated** *beliefs/methods*|*The new computer has made this old machine* **obsolete. Old-fashioned** is like **antiquated,** but it is less *derog* and can also be used of people. –see also ELDER (USAGE), NEW (USAGE)

**old age pen·sion** /ˌ· · ˈ··/ *n* [U; *the* S] money paid regularly by the State to old people **–old age pensioner** *n* –compare SENIOR CITIZEN

**old boy** /ˌ· ˈ·/ **old girl** *fem.*– *n BrE* a former pupil of a school

**old·en** /ˈəʊldən/ *adj* [A] *lit & old use* past; long ago: **in olden days**|**in olden times**

**old-fash·ioned** /ˌ· ˈ·· ◂/ *adj* (of a type that is) no longer common: *old-fashioned ideas*|*an old-fashioned house* –see OLD (USAGE)

**old mas·ter** /ˌ· ˈ··/ *n* (a picture by) an important painter of an earlier period

**Old Tes·ta·ment** /ˌ· ˈ··· ◂/ *n* [*the* S] the first part of the Bible, containing ancient Hebrew writings about the Jews –compare NEW TESTAMENT

**old-tim·er** /ˌ· ˈ··/ *n* **1** a person who has been somewhere or done something for a long time **2** *AmE* an old man

**O lev·el** /ˈ· ˌ··/ also **ordinary level**– *n* [C;U] (the lower of the two standards of) examination in the British GCE –see also A LEVEL

**ol·i·gar·chy** /ˈɒlɪ̈gɑːki‖ˈɑlɪ̈gɑrki, ˈəʊ-/ *n* **-chies 1** [C;U] (a state which has) government or rule by a few people, (often) for their own interests **2** [C +*sing./pl. v*] the group who govern such a state

**ol·ive** /ˈɒlɪ̈v‖ˈɑ-/ *n* **1** [C] (the small egg-shaped fruit of) a tree grown in Mediterranean countries **2** [U] also **olive green** /ˌ·· ˈ· ◂/– light green

**olive branch** /ˈ·· ·/ *n* [*the* S] a sign of peace

**O·lym·pic Games** /əˌlɪmpɪk ˈgeɪmz/ also **Olympics**– *n* **Olympic Games** [C +*sing./pl. v*] an international sports event held once every four years in different countries **–Olympic** *adj* [A]

**o·me·ga** /ˈəʊmɪ̈gə‖əʊˈmegə, -ˈmiː-, -ˈmeɪ-/ *n* the last letter of the Greek alphabet (Ω, ω)

**ome·let, -lette** /ˈɒmlɪ̈t‖ˈɑm-/ *n* eggs beaten together and cooked in hot fat (by FRYING): *a cheese omelet*

**o·men** /ˈəʊmən/ *n* [*of*] a sign that something is going to happen in the future: *a good/bad omen*

**om·i·nous** /ˈɒmɪ̈nəs‖ˈɑ-/ *adj* being an OMEN, esp. of something bad: *ominous clouds* **–ominously** *adv*

**o·mis·sion** /əʊˈmɪʃən, ə-/ *n* **1** [U] the act of OMITTING or state of being omitted **2** [C] something (or someone) OMITTED

**o·mit** /əʊˈmɪt, ə-/ *v* **-tt-** [T] **1** to leave out; not include **2** [+*to-v/v-ing*] to leave undone; not do: *He omitted to tell me when he was leaving.*

**om·ni·bus** /ˈɒmnɪbəs, -ˌbʌs‖ˈɑm-/ *n* **1** a book containing several works, esp. by one writer –compare ANTHOLOGY **2** *fml & old use* for BUS

**om·nip·o·tent** /ɒmˈnɪpətənt‖ɑm-/ *adj* all-powerful **–omnipotence** *n* [U]

**om·nis·ci·ent** /ɒmˈnɪʃənt, -ˈnɪsɪənt‖ɑmˈnɪʃənt/ *adj* all-knowing; knowing everything **–omniscience** *n* [U]

**on**[1] /ɒn‖ən, ɑn/ *prep* **1** also **upon** *fml*– a touching, supported by, hanging from, or connected with: *a lamp on the table/the wall*|*a ring on my finger*|*a ball* on a string|*He cut his foot on* (=against) *a piece of glass.*|*We're not on the telephone.* (=we have no telephone) **b** towards; in the direction of: *on my right*|*an attack on the enemy* **c** at the edge of; along: *a town right on the river*|*trees on both sides of the street* **d** directly after and because of: *acting on your advice*|*On thinking about it, I decided not to go.* **e** about (a subject): *a book on India* **f** in (a large vehicle): *on the train* **g** (before words about travelling): *on my way to school* **h** directed towards: *a tax on income*|*They spent their money on beer.* **i** following continuously; AFTER[1] (2): *to suffer defeat on defeat* **2 a** (used with days, dates, and times): *on Tuesday*|*on July 1st*|*on time* (=not late or early)|*on the hour* (=exactly at two, three, etc.) (compare *in the morning, in 1984, at 6 o'clock*) **b** using; by means of: *on foot*|*on a bicycle*|*A car runs on petrol.*|*I can't afford to live on my pay.*|*I heard it on the radio.*|*talking on the telephone* **c** in a state of: *on fire*|*on sale*|*on holiday*|*on purpose* (but *by accident*) **d** working for; belonging to: *to serve on a committee*|*a job on a newspaper*|*Which side was she on in the game?* **e** *infml* paid for by: *Drinks are on me!* –see Study Notes on page 474

**on²** *adv,adj* [F] **1** continuously, instead of stopping: *He worked on (and on) all night.* **2** further; forward: *If you walk on you'll come to the church.*|*If any letters come can I send them on?* (=to your new address)|*I'll do it later on.* (=afterwards)|*to put the clock on* (=so that it shows a later time) **3** so as to be fastened or in place: *with his coat on*|*He had nothing* (=no clothes) *on.*|*The bus stopped, and we got on.* (=into the bus) **4** with the stated part in front: *The two cars crashed head on.* **5** lit; working: *Turn the light/the* TAPS *on.* –opposite **off** **6** happening or going to happen: *There's a new film on at the cinema.*|*What have you got on tomorrow?* –compare OFF[1] (6) **7 be on about/at** *infml* to keep talking (about something/to someone) in a dull or complaining way: *What's he on about now?*|*She's always on at me to* (=trying to persuade me to) *have my hair cut.* **8 not on** *infml* impossible to do: *You can't refuse now; it's just not on!* **9 on and off** also **off and on**– from time to time; sometimes

**ONC** *abbrev. for:* (in Britain) Ordinary National Certificate; an examination in a TECHNICAL subject at the same level as A LEVEL –see also HNC

**once¹** /wʌns/ *adv* **1** one time and no more: *We've met only once.*|*They go to the cinema once a week.*|*I'll help you just this once.* **2** some time ago; formerly: *He once lived in Rome.* **3 all at once** suddenly **4 at once: a** now; without delay: *Do it at once!* **b** at the same time; together: *Don't all speak at once!* **5 (just) for once** for this one time only: *For once he was telling the truth.* **6 once and for all** for the last time: *Once and for all, I won't go!* **7 once in a while** now and then; sometimes **8 once more: a** one more time **b** also **once again**– now again as before: *John's back home once more.* **9 once or twice** (only) a few times **10 once upon a time** (beginning a story for children) at some time in the past: *Once upon a time there lived a king ...*

**once²** *conj* from the moment that; when: *Once he arrives we can start.*

**once-o·ver** /ˈ· ˌ··/ *n* [*usu. sing.*] *infml* a quick look or examination: *He gave the car the once-over and decided not to buy it.*

**on·com·ing** /ˈɒnˌkʌmɪŋ‖ˈɔn-, ˈɑn-/ *adj* [A] coming towards one: *oncoming cars*

**one¹** /wʌn/ *determiner,n* **1** the number 1: *Only one person came.*|TWENTY-*one*|*one o'clock*|*page one*|*one pound 50*|*one/a litre of wine*|*one of your friends* (=a friend of yours)|*She's the one person* (=the only person) *who can do it.*|*I for one* (=this is my personal opinion) *think it's rather good.* –see HALF (USAGE) –see Study Notes on page 494 **2** a certain; some: *I saw her one day in June.*|*Come and see us one evening.* **3** the same: *They all ran in one direction.*|*She's president and secretary in one.* (=she's both) **4** (used with *another, the other,* etc.) a particular example or type (of): *He can't tell one tree from another.*|*One (of them) went North, the other went South.* **5 be all one (to)** to make no difference (to): *I don't mind which we do; it's all one (to me).* **6 one after another/after the other** singly; one by one

**one²** *pron* **1** (*pl.* **ones**) a single thing or person mentioned: *Have you any books on farming? I want to borrow one.* (=a book on farming) (compare *I want to borrow some* =some books on farming)|*There are only hard chocolates left; we've eaten all the soft ones.* **2** (*no pl.*) *fml* anybody at all; YOU (2): *One should do one's duty*/(*AmE*) *his duty.*

**one an·oth·er** /ˌ· ·ˈ··/ *pron* →EACH OTHER: *They hit one another.*|*We often stay in one another's houses.* –see EACH OTHER (USAGE)

**one-armed ban·dit** /ˌ· · ˈ··/ also **fruit machine** *BrE,* **slot machine** *AmE*– *n infml* a machine with one long handle, into which people put money to try to win more money

**one-off** /ˌ· ˈ·/ *n,adj infml* (something) done or made once only: *This car is a one-off model.*

**o·ner·ous** /ˈɒnərəs, ˈəʊ-‖ˈɑ-, ˈəʊ-/ *adj fml* difficult; heavy; troublesome: *an onerous duty* **–onerously** *adv* **–onerousness** *n* [U]

**one·self** /wʌnˈself/ *pron* **1** (used as the object of a verb, or after a PREPOSITION, when the subject is *one*): *One can't enjoy oneself if one/if he (AmE) is too tired.* **2** (used to make *one* stronger): *To do something oneself is often easier than getting someone else to do it.* **3 be oneself** to be in one's usual state of mind or body: *She was very ill yesterday but she's more herself today.*|*I'll forgive you; I know you weren't yourself when you said that.* **4 by oneself** alone; without help: *The baby can walk by himself now.*|*Do they live all by themselves in that big house?* **5 to oneself** for one's own private use; not to be shared: *I want a bedroom to myself.*

**one-sid·ed** /ˌ· ˈ··◂/ *adj* **1** seeing only one side (of a question); unfair: *a one-sided attitude* **2** with one side much stronger than the other: *a one-sided game* **–one-sidedly** *adv* **–one-sidedness** *n* [U]

**one·time** /ˈwʌntaɪm/ *adj* [A] former

**one-up·man·ship** /wʌnˈʌpmənʃɪp/ *n* [U] the art of getting an advantage over others

**one-way** /ˌ· ˈ·◂/ *adj* [A] **1** moving or allowing movement in only one direction: *one-way traffic*|*a one-way street* –compare TWO-WAY **2** *esp. AmE* →SINGLE[1] (6)

**on·go·ing** /ˈɒnˌgəʊɪŋ‖ˈɑn-/ *adj* continuing; that go(es) on

**on·ion** /'ʌnjən/ *n* [C;U] a strong-smelling round white vegetable used in cooking

**on·look·er** /'ɒn,lʊkə$^r$‖'ɔn-, 'ɑn-/ *n* a person who sees something happening without taking part in it

**on·ly¹** /'əʊnli/ *adj* [A] with no others in the same group: *the only person who wants the job|an only child* (=with no brothers or sisters)

**only²** *adv* **1** nothing more than; and nobody or nothing else: *only five minutes more|Ladies only!|not only he but the whole family|I saw him only yesterday.* (=and no longer ago)|*Don't eat it; it will only make you ill.* (=that is the only possible result) –see Study Notes on page 128 **2 if only** (expressing a wish): *If only she would come!* **3 only too** very; completely: *It's only too true.*

USAGE In writing, put **only** just before the part of the sentence that it is about: **Only** *John saw the lion.* (=no one else saw it)|*John* **only** *saw the lion.* (=he didn't shoot it)|*John saw* **only** *the lion.* (=he didn't see the tiger)

**only³** *conj* except that; but: *He wants to go, only he can't.*

**o.n.o.** *written abbrev. said as:* or near offer

**on·rush** /'ɒnrʌʃ‖'ɔn-, 'ɑn-/ *n* a strong movement forward –**onrushing** *adj* [A]

**on·set** /'ɒnset‖'ɔn-, 'ɑn-/ *n* [*the* S] the first attack or beginning (of something bad): *the onset of a fever*

**on·shore** /,ɒn'ʃɔː$^r$◂‖,ɔn'ʃor, ,ɑn-◂/ *adv,adj* on (to) or on the shore –compare OFF-SHORE

**on·side** /,ɒn'saɪd◂‖,ɔn-, ,ɑn-/ *adj,adv* not OFFSIDE (1)

**on·slaught** /'ɒnslɔːt‖'ɔn-, 'ɑn-/ *n* [*on*] a fierce attack (on): *The politician made a strong onslaught* (=attacking speech) *on the unions.*

**on·to** /'ɒntʊ, -tə‖'ɔn-, 'ɑn-/ *prep* to a position or point on: *He jumped onto/on the horse.*

**o·nus** /'əʊnəs/ *n* [*the* S *of*] duty; responsibility: *The onus of proof lies with you.*

**on·ward** /'ɒnwəd‖'ɔnwərd, 'ɑn-/ *adj* [A] forward in space or time: *the onward march of events* –**onwards**‖ also **onward** *AmE– adv*: *from breakfast onwards*

**on·yx** /'ɒnɪks‖'ɑ-/ *n* [C;U] a precious stone having bands of various colours in it

**oops** /ʊps/ *interj infml* (said when someone has fallen, dropped something, or made a mistake): *Oops! I nearly dropped my cup of tea!*

**ooze¹** /uːz/ *n* [U] mud or thick liquid, as at the bottom of a river

**ooze²** *v* **oozed, oozing 1** [I] (of liquid) to pass or flow slowly: (fig.) *Their courage oozed away.* **2** [T] to allow (liquid) to pass slowly out: *The meat oozed blood.*|(fig.) *He oozes charm.*

**o·pal** /'əʊpəl/ *n* [C;U] a precious stone which looks like milky water with colours in it

**o·paque** /əʊ'peɪk/ *adj* **1** not allowing light to pass through **2** hard to understand –compare TRANSPARENT –**opaquely** *adv* –**opaqueness, opacity** /əʊ'pæsəti/ *n* [U]

**OPEC** /'əʊpek/ *abbrev. for:* Organization of Petroleum Exporting Countries; a group of countries who produce oil (=PETROLEUM), and plan together how to sell it

**o·pen¹** /'əʊpən/ *adj* **1** not shut: *an open door|with open eyes*|(fig.) *an open mind* (=not closed to new ideas) **2** [A] not enclosed: *the open country|open fields* **3** [A] not covered: *an open boat|the open air* **4** not fastened: *an open shirt* **5** not decided: *an open question|The job is still open.* **6** not hiding anything; honest: *Let's be open with each other.* **7** ready for business: *The bank isn't open yet.* **8** that anyone can enter: *an open competition* **9 open to: a** not safe from: *This country is open to attack by an enemy.* **b** willing to receive **c** possible for –compare CLOSED

**open²** *v* **1** [I;T] to (cause to) become open: *Open your eyes.* **2** [I;T *up, out*] to (cause to) spread out or unfold: *to open a book* **3** [I;T] to (cause to) start: *The story opens with a snowstorm.|The shop opens at nine o'clock.* **4** [T] to make usable (a passage) by removing the things that are blocking it **5 open fire (at/on)** to start shooting (at) –compare CLOSE¹

USAGE One **opens** or **shuts** doors, windows, or boxes. One **turns** water or gas TAPS *on* or *off*. One **turns** or **switches** electrical things *on* or *off*.

**open out** *v adv* [I] to speak more freely

**open up** *v adv* **1** [T *to*] (**open** sthg.↔ **up**) to make possible the development of; start: *They opened the country up (to trade).* **2** [I *often in commands*] *infml* to open a door **3** [I] OPEN **out**

**open³** *n* [*the* U] **1** the outdoors: *life in the open* **2 in(to) the open** (of opinions, secrets, etc.) in(to) general knowledge

**open-air** /,·· '·◂/ *adj* [A] of or in the outdoors: *an open-air theatre* –opposite **indoor**

**open-end·ed** /,·· '··◂/ *adj* without any definite end, aim, or time limit set in advance

**o·pen·er** /'əʊpənə$^r$/ *n* a person or thing that opens something: *a bottle opener*

**open-hand·ed** /,·· '··◂/ *adj* generous –**open-handedly** *adv* –**open-handedness** *n* [U]

**o·pen·ing¹** /'əʊpənɪŋ/ *n* **1** [C;U] the act of becoming or causing to become open: *the opening of a new university* –compare CLOSURE **2** [C *in*] a hole or clear space; GAP: *an opening in the fence* **3** [C *for*] a favourable set of conditions (for): *good openings for business*

**opening²** *adj* [A] first; beginning: *her opening words* –opposite **closing**

**o·pen·ly** /'əʊpənli/ *adv* not secretly: *They talked openly about their plans.* –**openness** *n* [U]

**open-mind·ed** /,·· '··◂/ *adj* willing to consider new arguments, ideas, opinions, etc.: *open minded parents* –compare BROAD-MINDED, SMALL-MINDED –**open-mindedly** *adv*

**op·e·ra** /'ɒpərə‖'ɑ-/ *n* [C;U] (the art of making) a musical play in which many or all of the words are sung –**operatic** /,ɒpə'rætɪk‖,ɑ-/ *adj* –**operatically** *adv*

**op·e·rate** /'ɒpəreɪt‖'ɑ-/ *v* **-rated, -rating 1** [I;T] to (cause to) work: *to operate a machine/a factory|The new law doesn't operate in our favour.* **2** [I] to be in action: *That business operates in several countries.* **3** [I *on*] to cut the body in order to set right or remove a diseased part, usu. in a special room (**operating theatre**) in a hospital

**op·e·ra·tion** /,ɒpə'reɪʃən‖,ɑ-/ *n* **1** [U] (a state of) working; the way a thing works: *The operation of a new machine can be hard to learn.|When does the new law* **come into operation?** **2** [C] a thing (to be) done; an activity: *to begin operations|a difficult operation* **3**

[C *on*] the cutting of the body in order to set right or remove a diseased part: *an operation on the patient* **4** [C] an (esp. military) action; movement: *the army's operations in Northern Ireland*

**op·e·ra·tion·al** /ˌɒpəˈreɪʃənəl‖ˌɑ-/ *adj* **1** [F] (of things) in operation; ready for use: *Is the machine operational yet?* **2** [A] of or about operations: *operational costs* –compare OPERATIVE –**operationally** *adv*

**op·e·ra·tive** /ˈɒpərətɪv‖ˈɑpərə-, ˈɑpəreɪ-/ *adj* [F] (of plans, laws, etc.) in operation; producing effects –opposite **inoperative**; compare OPERATIONAL (1)

**op·e·ra·tor** /ˈɒpəreɪtəʳ‖ˈɑ-/ *n* a person who works a machine, apparatus, telephone SWITCHBOARD, etc. –see TELEPHONE (USAGE)

**oph·thal·mic** /ɒfˈθælmɪk, ɒp-‖ɑf-/ *adj tech* of the medical study and treatment of the eyes

**o·pin·ion** /əˈpɪnjən/ *n* **1** [C;U] what a person thinks about something: *What's your opinion?*|**In my opinion** *you're wrong.*|**Public opinion** *is against him.* **2** [C] professional judgment or advice: *I asked for a second opinion from another doctor.* **3 have a good/bad/high/low opinion of** to think well/badly of

**o·pin·ion·at·ed** /əˈpɪnjəneɪtǝ̍d/ *adj derog* very sure of the rightness of one's opinions

**o·pi·um** /ˈəʊpɪəm/ *n* [U] a sleep-producing drug made from the seeds of the white POPPY

**o·pos·sum** /əˈpɒsəm‖-ˈpɑ-, ˈpɑsəm/ →POSSUM

**op·po·nent** /əˈpəʊnənt/ *n* a person who takes the opposite side, esp. in playing or fighting –see also PROPONENT

**op·por·tune** /ˈɒpətjuːn‖ˌɑpərˈtuːn/ *adj* **1** (of times) right for a purpose: *an opportune moment* **2** coming at the right time: *an opportune remark* –opposite **inopportune** –**opportunely** *adv*

**op·por·tun·is·m** /ˈɒpətjuːnɪzəm‖ˌɑpərˈtuː-/ *n* [U] *derog* the taking advantage of every chance for success, sometimes at other people's cost –**opportunist** *n*

**op·por·tu·ni·ty** /ˌɒpəˈtjuːnǝ̍ti‖ˌɑpərˈtuː-/ *n* **-ties** [C;U +*to-v*/*for, of*] a favourable (OPPORTUNE) moment or occasion (for doing something): *a wonderful opportunity to go shopping*|*I* **took the opportunity** *of seeing the minister.* –see CHANCE (USAGE)

**op·pose** /əˈpəʊz/ *v* **-posed, -posing** [T] **1** to be or act against: *We opposed the building of the motorway.* **2 as opposed to** as completely different from; in CONTRAST or opposition to **3 be opposed to** to oppose: *I am opposed to that plan.* –see also PROPOSE

**op·po·site¹** /ˈɒpəzǝ̍t‖ˈɑ-/ *n* a person or thing that is as different as possible (from another): *Black and white are opposites.*|*You are nice; he is just the opposite.*

**opposite²** *adj* [*to*] **1** as different as possible from: *the opposite direction*|(fig.) *the opposite sex* **2** [F] facing: *the houses opposite*|*He sits opposite.* **3 opposite number** a person in the same job elsewhere: *She's my opposite number in the company's New York office.*

**opposite³** also **opposite to**– *prep* facing: *the houses opposite (to) ours* –see Study Notes on page 474

**op·po·si·tion** /ˌɒpəˈzɪʃən‖ˌɑ-/ *n* **1** [U *to*] the act or state of being opposed to or fighting against: *There will be a lot of opposition to that new road.* **2** [C +*sing./pl. v*] (*often cap.*) the political parties opposed to the government, esp. the most important such party: *The Opposition is/are going to vote against the government.*

**op·press** /əˈpres/ *v* [T] **1** to rule in a hard and cruel way **2** [*usu. pass.*] to cause to feel ill or sad: *I feel oppressed by/with worry.*

**op·pres·sion** /əˈpreʃən/ *n* [U] the condition of oppressing or being OPPRESSed (esp. 1)

**op·pres·sive** /əˈpresɪv/ *adj* **1** cruel; unjust **2** causing feelings of illness or sadness: *oppressive heat* –**oppressively** *adv* –**oppressiveness** *n* [U]

**op·pres·sor** /əˈpresəʳ/ *n* a person (or group) that OPPRESSES (1)

**opt for** sthg. /ɒpt‖ɑpt/ *v prep* [T] to choose (one thing) rather than any others –see also OPT OUT

**op·tic** /ˈɒptɪk‖ˈɑp-/ *adj* [A] of or belonging to the eyes: *the optic nerve*

**op·ti·cal** /ˈɒptɪkəl‖ˈɑp-/ *adj* [A] of or about the sense of sight: *optical instruments* –**optically** *adv*

**op·ti·cian** /ɒpˈtɪʃən‖ɑp-/ *n* a person who makes and sells glasses for the eyes

**op·tics** /ˈɒptɪks‖ˈɑp-/ *n* [U] the scientific study of light

**op·ti·mis·m** /ˈɒptǝ̍mɪzəm‖ˈɑp-/ *n* [U] the belief that whatever happens will be good, and that things will end well –compare PESSIMISM –**optimist** *n* –**optimistic** /-ˈmɪstɪk/ *adj* –**optimistically** *adv*

**op·ti·mum** /ˈɒptǝ̍məm‖ˈɑp-/ *adj* [A] best or most favourable: *optimum conditions for growing rice*

**op·tion** /ˈɒpʃən‖ˈɑp-/ *n* **1** [U] the freedom to choose: *You must do it; you have no option.* **2** [C] something chosen or offered for choice: *The government has two options: to reduce spending or to increase taxes.*

**op·tion·al** /ˈɒpʃənəl‖ˈɑp-/ *adj* which may be freely chosen or not chosen: *optional subjects at school* –compare OBLIGATORY –**optionally** *adv*

**opt out** *v adv* [I *of*] *infml* to choose not to take part (in something) –see also OPT FOR

**op·u·lence** /ˈɒpjʊləns‖ˈɑpjə-/ *n* [U] (a state of) very great and showy wealth –**opulent** *adj* –**opulently** *adv*

**or** /əʳ; *strong* ɔːʳ/ conj **1** (used in a list of possibilities): *Which is it, coffee or tea?*|*Either say you're sorry or get out!*|*She wants to live in London or Paris or Rome/London, Paris, or Rome.* **2** (*after a* NEGATIVE²) and not: *He never smokes or drinks.* **3** if not; otherwise: *Wear your coat or (else) you'll be cold.*|*He can't be ill or he wouldn't have come.* **4 or so** about; or more: *a minute/three minutes or so*|*five dollars or so*

**or·a·cle** /ˈɒrəkəl‖ˈɔ-, ˈɑ-/ *n* **1** *sometimes derog* a person who is thought to be very wise and able to give the best advice **2** (in ancient Greece) a place where a god was believed to answer people's questions, often in words hard to understand

**o·ral** /ˈɔːrəl‖ˈo-/ *adj* **1** spoken, not written **2** of, about, or using the mouth –**orally** *adv*

**or·ange¹** /ˈɒrǝ̍ndʒ‖ˈɔ-, ˈɑ-/ *n* a very common reddish-yellow round fruit with a bitter-sweet taste and a thick skin

**orange²** *adj,n* [U] (of) the colour of an orange

**o·rang·u·tang** /ɔːˌræŋuːˈtæŋ, -ˈtæn‖ǝ̍ˈræŋətæŋ/ also **-tan** /tæn/– *n* a large red-haired monkey with no tail

**o·ra·tion** /əˈreɪʃən, ɔː-/ *n fml* a formal and solemn public speech

**or·a·tor** /ˈɒrətəʳ‖ˈɔ-, ˈɑ-/ *n* **1** a person who delivers (makes) an ORATION **2** a good public speaker **–oratory** *n* [U]

**orb** /ɔːb‖ɔrb/ *n* a ball-like object, esp. one carried by a king or queen on formal occasions

**or·bit**[1] /ˈɔːbɨt‖ˈɔr-/ *n* the path of something moving round a heavenly body, e.g. the moon or a spacecraft moving round the earth **–orbital** /ˈɔːbɪtəl‖ˈɔr- / *adj*

**orbit**[2] *v* [I;T] to move in an ORBIT round (something)

**or·chard** /ˈɔːtʃəd‖ˈɔrtʃərd/ *n* a field where fruit trees grow

**or·ches·tra** /ˈɔːkɨstrə‖ˈɔr-/ *n* [C +*sing./pl. v*] a large group of people who play music together on stringed and other instruments: *The orchestra is/are playing well.* **–orchestral** /ɔːˈkestrəl‖ɔr-/ *adj* [A]

**or·chid** /ˈɔːkɨd‖ˈɔr-/ *n* a plant with very showy flowers

**or·dain** /ɔːˈdeɪn‖ɔr-/ *v* [T] **1** to make (someone) a priest or religious leader: *He was ordained in 1982.* **2** [+*that*] *fml* (of God, the law, etc.) to order

**or·deal** /ɔːˈdiːl, ˈɔːdiːl‖ɔrˈdiːl, ˈɔrdiːl/ *n* a difficult or painful experience

**or·der**[1] /ˈɔːdəʳ‖ˈɔr-/ *n* **1** [U] the special way in which things are arranged in connection with each other: *The words in a dictionary are shown in alphabetical order.* **2** [U] the state in which things are carefully and neatly arranged in their proper place: *Your room is very untidy; go and put it in order.* –opposite **disorder 3** [U] fitness for use or operation: *The telephone's* **out of order.** (=does not work) **4** [U] the condition in which laws and rules are obeyed: *That young teacher can't keep order in his classroom.* –opposite **disorder**; see also LAW (2) **5** [C;U +*to-v/that*] a command; direction: *You must obey my orders.*|*I have orders to search your room.* (=I have been commanded to do so)|*I'm here* **by order of** *the general.* (=he commanded me to come)|*The ship left* **under orders** *to sail to the Pacific.* (=having been commanded to do so) **6** [C] a request to supply goods: *an order for three bottles of milk to be sent to us each day* **7** [C] the goods supplied in accordance with such a request: *I'm going to collect my order from the shop.* **8** [C] a written or printed paper which allows the holder to do something, e.g. to be paid money –see also MONEY ORDER, POSTAL ORDER **9** [C +*sing./pl. v*] a society of people who lead a holy life of service according to a particular set of religious rules, esp. a group of MONKS or NUNS **10** [*the* C *of*] (*often cap. as part of a name*) a group of people who have all received special honour given for service, bravery, etc.: *a member of the Order of the Garter* **11 in order** *fml* acceptable: *It'll be quite in order for you to speak now.* **12 in order to** also **in order that** *(fml)*– with the purpose of: *We used the computer in order to save time/(fml) in order that we might save time.* –see Study Notes on page 128 **13 of/in the order of** *BrE* about; about as much or as many as: *His income is of the order of £7,000 a year.* **14 on order** asked for from the maker or supplier but not yet supplied **15 out of order** not in accordance with the rules of a formal meeting –see also ORDER[2] (3)

**order**[2] *v* **1** [T +*that*] to give an order (to or for); command: *The general has ordered an advance/ordered that the army (should) advance.* **2** [I;T] to ask for (something) to be brought, made, etc., in return for payment: *Don't forget to order a taxi.*|*I've ordered you a beer.*|*"Have you ordered yet, madam?" asked the waiter.* **3** [T] to arrange; direct: *We must order our affairs better.*

USAGE People whose position gives them the right to be obeyed can **order** or give **orders,** but **command** is usually only used in a military sense: *The doctor* **ordered** *me to rest for a week.*|*The general* **ordered/commanded** *his men to advance.* **Instruct, tell,** and **ask** are similar to **order**, but not as strong.

**order** sbdy. **about/around** *v adv* [T] to annoy by giving many orders, esp. unpleasantly

**or·dered** /ˈɔːdəd‖ˈɔrdərd/ *adj* arranged; tidy; regular: *an ordered life*

**or·der·ly**[1] /ˈɔːdəli‖ˈɔrdərli/ *adj* **1** well-arranged **2** of a tidy nature and habits **3** peaceful and well-behaved: *an orderly crowd* –opposite **disorderly –orderliness** *n* [U]

**orderly**[2] *n* **1** a soldier who attends an officer **2** an attendant in a hospital

**or·ders** /ˈɔːdəz‖ˈɔrdərz/ *n* [P] *tech* the state of being a priest or other person permitted to perform Christian services and duties (esp. in the phrase **holy orders**)

**or·din·al num·ber** /ˈɔːdɨnəl, nʌmbəʳ‖ˈɔr-/ *n* a number showing position or order in a set: *1st, 2nd, and 3rd are all ordinals.* –compare CARDINAL NUMBER

**or·di·na·ri·ly** /ˈɔːdənərɨli‖ˌɔrdənˈerɨli/ *adv* **1** in an ordinary way **2** usually: *Ordinarily, he goes by train.*

**or·di·nary** /ˈɔːdənri‖ˈɔrdəneri/ *adj* **1** not unusual; common **2 out of the ordinary** unusual; uncommon –see also EXTRAORDINARY **–ordinariness** *n* [U]

**or·di·na·tion** /ˌɔːdɨˈneɪʃən‖ˌɔr-/ *n* [C;U] the act or ceremony of ORDAINing a priest

**ore** /ɔːʳ‖or/ *n* [C;U] rock, earth, etc., from which metal can be obtained –sounds like **oar**

**or·gan** /ˈɔːgən‖ˈɔr-/ *n* **1** a part of an animal or plant that has a special purpose: *The* LIVER *is an organ and so is the heart.*|*the sexual organs* **2** an organization, usu. official, that has a special purpose: *the organs of the government* **3** a musical instrument that uses air to produce sounds, played rather like a piano and often found in churches

**or·gan·ic** /ɔːˈgænɪk‖ɔr-/ *adj* **1** [A] of living things: *organic life/chemistry/diseases* –opposite **inorganic 2** [A] made of parts with specialized purposes: *an organic system* **3** (of food) grown without the help of chemical FERTILIZERS **–organically** *adv*

**or·gan·is·m** /ˈɔːgənɪzəm‖ˈɔr-/ *n* **1** a living being **2** a whole made of specialized parts

**or·gan·ist** /ˈɔːgənɨst‖ˈɔr-/ *n* a musician who plays an ORGAN (3)

**or·gan·i·za·tion** ‖also **-sation** *BrE* /ˌɔːgənaɪˈzeɪʃən‖ˌɔrgənə-/ *n* **1** [C] a group of people with a special purpose, such as a club or business **2** [U] the arrangement or planning of parts so as to form an effective whole **–organizational** *adj* **–organizationally** *adv*

**or·gan·i·ze** ‖also **-ise** *BrE* /ˈɔːgənaɪz‖ˈɔr-/ *v* **-ized, -izing 1** [T *into*] to arrange into a good working system; make necessary arrangements for (something) **2** [I;T] *esp. AmE* for UNIONIZE **–organizer** *n*

**or·gan·ized** ‖also **-ised** *BrE* /ˈɔːgənaɪzd‖ˈɔr-/ *adj* arranged into a system that works well –opposite **disorganized**

**or·gas·m** /ˈɔːgæzəm‖ˈɔr-/ *n* [C;U] the highest point of sexual pleasure **–orgasmic** /ɔːˈgæzmɪk‖ɔr-/ *adj*

**or·gy** /ˈɔːdʒi‖ˈɔr-/ *n* **-gies** a wild party, usu. with alcohol, often with sex

**O·ri·ent** /ˈɔːrɪənt, ˈɒrɪ-‖ˈo-/ *n* [*the* S] *fml or lit* Asia; the (Far) East **–Oriental** /ˌɔːriˈentl, ˌɒ-‖ˌo-/ *n,adj*

**o·ri·en·ta·tion** /ˌɔːrɪənˈteɪʃən, ˌɒ-‖ˌo-/ *n* [C;U] a position or direction: (fig.) *a new orientation in life* –see also DISORIENTATE

**or·i·fice** /ˈɒrəfəs‖ˈɔ-, ˈɑ-/ *n fml* an opening or hole

**or·i·gin** /ˈɒrədʒən‖ˈɔ-, ˈɑ-/ *n* **1** [C;U] a starting point: *the origin of a river/of a belief|a word of unknown origin* **2** [U] parents and conditions of early life: *a woman of humble origin(s)* (=from a low social class)

**o·rig·i·nal**[1] /əˈrɪdʒənəl, -dʒənəl/ *adj* **1** [A *no comp.*] first; earliest: *The original owner of the house was the Duke of Wellington.* **2** *often apprec* new; different; unlike others: *an original idea/ invention/thinker/ painting* –opposite **unoriginal** (for **2**)

**original**[2] *n* **1** [C] (usu. of paintings) the one from which copies can be made **2** [*the* S] the language in which something was originally written: *Have you read Homer in the original?*

**o·rig·i·nal·i·ty** /əˌrɪdʒəˈnæləti/ *n* [U] *often apprec* the quality of being ORIGINAL[1] (2): *Her book shows great originality.*

**o·rig·i·nal·ly** /əˈrɪdʒənəli, -dʒənəli/ *adv* **1** in the beginning; formerly: *The family originally came from France.* **2** in a new or different way

**o·rig·i·nate** /əˈrɪdʒəneɪt/ *v* **-nated, -nating** [I;T] to (cause to) begin: *Her book originated in/from a short story.* **–orginator** *n*

**or·na·ment**[1] /ˈɔːnəmənt‖ˈɔr-/ *n* **1** [C] an object possessed because it is (thought to be) beautiful rather than because it is useful: *Their house is full of little ornaments.* –see picture on page 355 **2** [U] something which is added to make something else more beautiful

**or·na·ment**[2] /ˈɔːnəment‖ˈɔr-/ *v* [T *with*] to add ORNAMENT to

**or·na·men·tal** /ˌɔːnəˈmentəl‖ˌɔr-/ *adj* **1** providing or serving as ORNAMENT **2** *often derog* perhaps beautiful, but not really necessary **–ornamentally** *adv*

**or·nate** /ɔːˈneɪt‖ɔr-/ *adj sometimes derog* having a great deal of decoration; not simple: *an ornate style* **–ornately** *adv* **–ornateness** *n* [U]

**or·ni·thol·o·gy** /ˌɔːnəˈθɒlədʒi‖ˌɔrnəˈθɑ-/ *n* [U] the scientific study of birds **–ornithologist** *n* **–ornithological** /ˌɔːnəθəˈlɒdʒɪkəl‖ˌɔrnəθəˈlɑ-/ *adj*

**or·phan** /ˈɔːfən‖ˈɔr-/ *v,n* (to cause to be) a person (esp. a child) lacking one or usu. both parents: *She was orphaned when her parents died in a plane crash.*

**or·phan·age** /ˈɔːfənɪdʒ‖ˈɔr-/ *n* a place where ORPHAN children live

**or·tho·dox** /ˈɔːθədɒks‖ˈɔrθədɑks/ *adj* **1** generally or officially accepted: *orthodox ideas* **2** holding accepted opinions: *an orthodox Muslim* –see also UNORTHODOX **–orthodoxy** *n* [U]

**Orthodox Church** /ˌ··· ˈ·/ *n* [*the* S] any of several Christian churches esp. in eastern Europe

**or·tho·pae·dic, -pedic** *adj* [A] of the branch of medicine that deals with (the putting straight of) bones: *an orthopaedic hospital*

**Os·car** /ˈɒskər‖ˈɑs-/ *n* an American cinema prize

**os·cil·late** /ˈɒsəleɪt‖ˈɑ-/ *v* **-lated, -lating** [I] *tech* to keep on moving from side to side, between two limits or choices **–oscillation** /-ˈleɪʃən/ *n* [C;U]

**os·prey** /ˈɒspri, -preɪ‖ˈɑ-/ *n* **-preys** a large fish-eating bird

**os·ten·si·ble** /ɒˈstensəbəl‖ɑ-/ *adj* [A] (of reasons) seeming or pretended, but perhaps not really true **–ostensibly** *adv*: *He did it ostensibly for love, but really for money.*

**os·ten·ta·tion** /ˌɒstənˈteɪʃən, -ten-‖ˌɑ-/ *n* [U] *derog* unnecessary show of wealth, knowledge, etc. **–ostentatious** *adj* **–ostentatiously** *adv*

**os·tra·cize** ‖also **-cise** *BrE* /ˈɒstrəsaɪz‖ˈɑ-/ *v* **-cized, -cizing** [T] (of a group of people) to refuse to have social dealings with (another person or group of people) **–ostracism** *n* [U]

**os·trich** /ˈɒstrɪtʃ‖ˈɔ-, ˈɑ-/ *n* **-triches** *or* **-trich** a very large African bird which runs very quickly but cannot fly

**oth·er** /ˈʌðər/ *determiner,pron* **1** the second of two; the remaining (one or ones): *holding the wheel with one hand and waving with the other (one)|They live on the other side of the street.|Mary's here. Where are the others?* **2** more of the same kind: *John and two other boys* (Compare *John and two girls*)|*Some of them are red and others are brown.* **3** not the same; not this, not oneself, not one's own, etc.: *He enjoys spending other people's money.* (=not his own)| *Others may laugh at her but I like her.* **4 other than** except: *There's nobody here other than me.* **5 the other day/afternoon/evening/night** on a recent day/ afternoon/evening/night –see also EACH OTHER

USAGE **Other** is not used after **an.** The word is then **another**: *Would you like* **another**/*some* **others?**

**oth·er·wise** /ˈʌðəwaɪz‖ˈʌðər-/ *adv* **1** in a different way; differently: *I hate him and I won't pretend otherwise.* (=pretend I don't)|*We'll get there somehow, by train or otherwise.* **2** in every other way; apart from that: *The soup was cold, but otherwise the meal was good.* **3** if not: *Do it now. Otherwise, it will be too late.*

**ot·ter** /ˈɒtər‖ˈɑ-/ *n* **-ters** *or* **-ter** a swimming fish-eating animal with attractive fur

**ouch** /aʊtʃ/ *interj* (an expression of sudden pain)

**ought** /ɔːt/ *v present tense negative contraction* **oughtn't** /ˈɔːtənt/ [I +*to-v*] (used as a helping verb with another verb) **1** (to show a moral duty): *She ought to/She should look after her children better.|You ought to be ashamed of yourself.|He ought to be punished, oughtn't he?* (=someone should punish him)|*He oughtn't to have said that (but he did).|This old coat ought to be thrown away.* (=it would be sensible to throw it away) –see Study Notes on page 386 **2** (to show that something can be naturally expected): *Prices ought to come down soon.|You ought to be hungry by now.*

USAGE **Oughtn't** means that something is wrong; **needn't** means that something is unnecessary: *You* **needn't** *talk so loud; I can hear you quite well.|You* **oughtn't** *to talk so loud; you might wake the baby.*

**ounce** /aʊns/ *written abbrev.* **oz**– *n* **1** [C] (a measure of weight equal to) 1/16 of a pound; approx 28 grams **2** [S *of*] (even) a small amount: *Haven't you got an ounce of sense?*

**our** /ɑːʳ; *strong* aʊəʳ/ *determiner* (POSSESSIVE¹ (2) *form of* WE) of the people who are speaking: *our daughter|our modern world*

**Our La·dy** /ˌ· ˈ··/ *n* Mary, the mother of CHRIST

**ours** /aʊəz‖aʊərz/ *pron* (POSSESSIVE¹ (2) *form of* WE) of the people who are speaking: *This is your room, and ours* (=our room) *is next door.|Ours is/are on the table.|"a friend of ours"* (SEU S.)

**our·selves** /aʊəˈselvz‖aʊər-/ *pron* **1** (used as the object of a verb, or after a PREPOSITION, when the people who are speaking do the action and are the objects of the action): *We saw ourselves on television.|John and I have bought ourselves* (=for ourselves) *a new car.* **2** (used to make WE stronger): *We built the house ourselves.*

**oust** /aʊst/ *v* [T *from*] to force out; cause to leave

**out¹** /aʊt/ *adv,adj* [F] **1** in or to the open air or the outside: *Open the bag and take the money out.|Shut the door to keep the wind out.|He put his tongue out.|She opened the cage and let the bird out.* (=let it go free) **2** absent; away from home, one's country, etc. or from the centre or middle (of something): *I'm afraid Mr Jones is out/has gone out; he'll be in soon.|They went out to Africa.|We've given out all the tickets.* (=to everyone)|*You can wash out the dirty marks.* (=so that they won't be there)|*The fishermen came out* (=on STRIKE² (1)) *in sympathy with the sailors.|I tore my coat on a nail that was sticking out from a wall.* **3** (of a guess or sum) wrong: *The bill was £4 out.|The rise in prices put my calculations badly out.* **4 a** (of a player in cricket) no longer batting (BAT² (2)): *Sussex all out for 351* **b** (of the ball in a game such as tennis) outside the line **5** so as to be no longer fashionable: *Long skirts are out this year.* **6** (of a fire or light) no longer burning: *The fire's gone out.|Please put your cigarettes out.* **7** completely: *to clean out the room|I'm tired out.* **8** in a loud voice; aloud: *Read/Call out the names.|Out with it!* (=say it) **9** (of a flower) fully open and ripe **10** (of the TIDE) away from the coast; low: *The* TIDE *is going out now.* **11 out and about** (of someone who has been ill) able to get up and leave the house **12 out for** trying to get: *Don't trust him; he's only out for your money.* **13 out to** trying to: *Be careful: he's out to get* (=harm) *you.|They're out to win.* –compare IN²

**out of** *prep* **1** from inside; away from: *to jump out of bed|to walk out of a room|out of danger* (=safe) –see Study Notes on page 474 **2** from among: *Three out of four people choose this soap!* **3** not having; lacking: *We're nearly out of petrol.* **4** because of: *I came out of interest.* –see Study Notes on page 128 **5** (shows what something is made from): *made out of wood* **6 out of it** lonely and unhappy because one is not included in something: *I felt rather out of it in France because I can't speak French.*

**out²** *adj* [A] **1** directed outwards; used for sending or going out: *Put the letter in the out* TRAY. –opposite **in 2 out and out** complete; total: *an out-and-out lie*

**out·back** /ˈaʊtbæk/ *n* [*the* S] the part of Australia that is far away from cities

**out·bid** /aʊtˈbɪd/ *v* **-bid, -bidding** [T] to offer more than (someone else)

**out·board mo·tor** /ˌaʊtbɔːd ˈməʊtəʳ‖-bord-/ *n* a motor fixed to the back end of a small boat

**out·break** /ˈaʊtbreɪk/ *n* [*of*] a sudden appearance or beginning of something bad: *an outbreak of disease/of insects/of fighting* –compare BREAK¹ **out**

**out·burst** /ˈaʊtbɜːst‖-ɜr-/ *n* [*of*] a sudden powerful expression of feeling or activity: *outbursts of weeping/laughter/gunfire*

**out·cast** /ˈaʊtkɑːst‖-kæst/ *n,adj* (a person) forced from his/her home or deserted by his/her friends

**out·class** /aʊtˈklɑːs‖-ˈklæs/ *v* [T] to be very much better than

**out·come** /ˈaʊtkʌm/ *n* [*of* ] an effect or result

**out·crop** /ˈaʊtkrɒp‖-krɑp/ *n* a rock which stands up out of the ground

**out·cry** /ˈaʊtkraɪ/ *n* **-cries** a public show of anger: *If they try to close the railway, there'll be a great outcry.*

**out·dat·ed** /ˌaʊtˈdeɪtɪ̆d ◂/ also **out-of-date**– *adj* no longer in general use

**out·dis·tance** /aʊtˈdɪstəns/ *v* **-tanced, -tancing** [T] to go further or faster than

**out·do** /aʊtˈduː/ *v* **-did** /ˈdɪd/, **-done** /ˈdʌn/, **-doing** [T] to do or be better than: *She outdid him in running and swimming.*

**out·door** /ˌaʊtˈdɔːʳ ◂‖-ˈdor/ *adj* [A] existing, happening, done, or used in the open air: *outdoor shoes|outdoor life* –opposite **indoor**

**out·doors** /ˌaʊtˈdɔːz‖-orz/ also **out of doors**– *adv,n* [*the* S] (in) the open air –opposite **indoors**

**out·er** /ˈaʊtəʳ/ *adj* [A *no comp.*] on the outside; at a greater distance from the middle: *the outer walls|outer London* –opposite **inner**

**out·er·most** /ˈaʊtəməʊst‖-ər-/ *adj* [A] furthest outside or furthest from the middle: *the outermost stars* –compare INNERMOST

**outer space** /ˌ··ˈ·/ *n* [U] the area where the stars and other heavenly bodies are

**out·fit** /ˈaʊtˌfɪt/ *n* **1** [C] all the things, esp. clothes, needed for a particular purpose **2** [C+*sing./pl.v*] *infml* a group of people, esp. if working together

**out·flank** /aʊtˈflæŋk/ *v* [T] to go round the side of (an enemy) and attack from behind

**out·go·ing** /ˌaʊtˈgəʊɪŋ ◂/ *adj* **1** [A *no comp.*] leaving; going out; finishing a period in office: *the outgoing president* –compare INCOMING **2** having or showing eagerness to mix socially with others; friendly: *She's very outgoing.* –compare FORTHCOMING (3)

**out·go·ings** /ˈaʊtˌgəʊɪŋz/ *n* [P] amounts of money that are spent –compare INCOME

**out·ing** /ˈaʊtɪŋ/ *n* a short pleasure trip

**out·land·ish** /aʊtˈlændɪʃ/ *adj* strange and unpleasing: *What an outlandish hat!* **–outlandishly** *adv* **–outlandishness** *n* [U]

**out·last** /aʊtˈlɑːst‖-ˈlæst/ *v* [T] to last longer than

**out·law¹** /ˈaʊtlɔː/ *n* (esp. in former times) a criminal who has not been caught by the police

**outlaw²** *v* [T] **1** to declare (someone) a criminal **2** to declare (something) illegal

**out·lay** /ˈaʊtleɪ/ *n* [*on, for*] money spent for a purpose

**out·let** /'autlet, -lɪ̈t/ *n* [*for*] a way through which something (usu. a liquid or a gas) may go out: (fig.) *an outlet for his feelings* –compare INLET
**out·line**[1] /'autlaɪn/ *n* [*of*] **1** a line showing the shape (of something): *the outline of her face* **2** the main ideas or facts (of something): *an outline of history/of the main points of the talk* –**outline** *v* **-lined, -lining** [T]: *She outlined the main points of the talk.*
**out·live** /aut'lɪv/ *v* **-lived, -living** [T] to live longer than
**out·look** /'autluk/ *n* **1** a view from a particular place **2** future probabilities **3** [*on*] one's general point of view –see VIEW (USAGE)
**out·ly·ing** /'aut,laɪ-ɪŋ/ *adj* [A] far from the centre: *an outlying area of the country*
**out·ma·noeu·vre** *BrE*||**outmaneuver** *AmE* /,aut mə'nuːvəʳ/ *v* **-vred, -vring** [T] to make more effective movements than (an opponent); put in a position of disadvantage
**out·mod·ed** /aut'məudɪ̈d/ *adj* no longer in fashion or use
**out·num·ber** /aut'nʌmbəʳ/ *v* [T] to be larger in numbers than: *We were outnumbered by the enemy.*
**out-of-date** /,· · '·◂/ *adj* →OUTDATED
**out-of-the-way** /,· · · '·◂/ *adj* **1** distant; far away from people and places **2** not known by ordinary people
**out·pa·tient** /'aut,peɪʃənt/ *n* a sick person who goes to a hospital for treatment while continuing to live at home
**out·post** /'autpəust/ *n* [*of*] a group of people or settlement at some distance from the main group or settlement
**out·put** /'autput/ *n* [U] production: *an output of 10,000 tins a year* –compare INPUT
**out·rage**[1] /'autreɪdʒ/ *n* [C;U] (anger caused by) a very wrong or cruel act
**outrage**[2] *v* **-raged, -raging** [T] to offend greatly: *The closing of the hospital has outraged public opinion.*
**out·ra·geous** /aut'reɪdʒəs/ *adj* very offensive –**outrageously** *adv*
**out·right**[1] /aut'raɪt/ *adv* **1** completely: *He owns that house outright.* **2** openly: *I told him outright about it.*
**out·right**[2] /'autraɪt/ *adj* [A] complete: *an outright loss*
**out·set** /'autset/ *n* [*the* S] the beginning: *At/From the outset there was trouble.*
**out·shine** /aut'ʃaɪn/ *v* **-shone** /-'ʃɒn||-'ʃəun/, **-shining** [T] to shine more brightly than: (fig.) *She outshines* (=is much better than) *the others.*
**out·side**[1] /aut'saɪd, 'autsaɪd/ *n* [*the* S] **1** the outer part of a solid object; the part that is furthest from the centre, or that faces away: *to paint the outside of the house|This coat is cloth on the inside and fur on the outside.* –opposite **inside 2 at the (very) outside** at the most: *£100 at the outside*
**outside**[2] /'autsaɪd/ *adv,adj,prep* [*no comp.*] **1** out of or beyond something; towards or in the open air: *outside the door/the town/my experience|an outside covering|children playing outside in the street* –see Study Notes on page 474 **2** of or from elsewhere: *We can't do it ourselves; we need outside help.* **3** greater; more than: *an outside figure of £100|anything outside £100* **4** (of a chance or possibility) slight; unlikely; distant **5** away from the edge of a road: *If you want to drive fast, use the outside* LANE (2). –compare INSIDE[2]
**out·sid·er** /aut'saɪdəʳ/ *n* **1** a person who is not accepted as a member of a particular social group –compare INSIDER **2** a person or animal not considered to have a good chance to win –compare FAVOURITE[1] (3)
**out·size** /'autsaɪz/ *adj* [A] (esp. of clothing) larger than the standard sizes
**out·skirts** /'autskɜːts||-ɜr-/ *n* [P *of*] (esp. of a town) the outer areas: *They live on the outskirts of Paris.*
**out·smart** /aut'smɑːt||-ɑr-/ *v* [T] *infml* to defeat by acting more cleverly than; OUTWIT
**out·spo·ken** /aut'spəukən/ *adj* expressing openly what is thought or felt –**outspokenly** *adv* –**outspokenness** *n* [U]
**out·spread** /,aut'spred◂/ *adj* spread out flat or to full width: *with arms outspread*
**out·stand·ing** /aut'stændɪŋ/ *adj* **1** better than others; very good **2** not yet done or paid: *some work outstanding|outstanding debts* –**outstandingly** *adv*
**out·stretched** /,aut'stretʃt◂/ *adj* stretched out to full length
**out·strip** /aut'strɪp/ *v* **-pp-** [T] to do better, go faster than
**out·ward** /'autwəd||-ərd/ *adj* [A] **1** away: *the outward voyage* –opposite **homeward 2** on the outside: *outward cheerfulness* –opposite **inward**
**out·ward·ly** /'autwədli||-ər-/ *adv* seeming to be, but in reality probably not being: *only outwardly calm*
**out·wards** /'autwədz||-ər-/ also **outward** *AmE*– *adv* towards the outside –opposite **inwards**
**out·weigh** /aut'weɪ/ *v* [T] to be more important than: *My love for her outweighs everything else.*
**out·wit** /aut'wɪt/ *v* **-tt-** [T] to defeat by being cleverer than
**out·worn** /aut'wɔːn||-'worn/ *adj* (of an idea, custom, etc.) no longer useful or used –compare WORN-OUT
**o·val** /'əuvəl/ *n,adj* (anything which is) egg-shaped
**o·va·ry** /'əuvəri/ *n* **-ries** the part of a female that produces eggs
**o·va·tion** /əu'veɪʃən/ *n* a joyful expression of public approval: *a standing ovation* (=when people stand and APPLAUD)
**ov·en** /'ʌvən/ *n* a box used for cooking, baking, etc. –see COOK (USAGE)
**o·ver**[1] /'əuvəʳ/ *adv* **1** downwards from an upright position: *He pushed me and I fell over.* **2** across an edge, a distance, or an open space: *We flew over to the US.* (=across the Atlantic)|*Come and sit over here.* (=on this side of the room) **3** from one person or group to another: *He signed the money over to his son.* **4** above; more: *children of seven and over* (=older) –opposite **under 5** so that another side is shown: *Turn the page over.|dogs rolling over (and over) on the grass* **6** so as to be covered and not seen: *Let's paint it over in green.|Cover her over with a sheet.* **7** completely through; from beginning to end: *You'd better think/talk it over carefully.* **8** (showing that something is repeated): *I've told him several times over/told him over and over.* **9** remaining; not used when part has been taken: *Was there any money over?* **10** so as to be in each other's positions: *Let's change these two pictures over.* **11** too much; too:

Don't be *over anxious about it.*

**over²** *prep* **1** directly above; higher than, but not touching: *The lamp hung over/above the table.*|*The doctor leaned over the sick child.* –see Study Notes on page 474 **2** so as to cover: *He put the newspaper over his face.* **3** from side to side of, esp. by going up and then down again: *to jump over the wall/the ditch* (Compare *across the ditch*, but not **across the wall*)|*If we can't go over the mountain we must go round it.*|*The car ran over* (not **across*) *a dog and killed it.*|*to fall over* (=across the edge of) *a cliff* **4** on the far side of: *They live (just) over/across the street.* **5** in many parts of; everywhere in: *They travelled (all) over Europe.* **6** commanding; in control of: *He ruled over a large kingdom.*|*I don't want anyone over me, telling me what to do.* **7** more than; above: *over 30 books*|*children over seven* (=older than seven) **8** during: *to hold a meeting over dinner*|*Will you be at home over Christmas?* **9** by means of; using: *I don't want to say it over the telephone.*|*I heard it over the radio.* **10** on the subject of; about: *difficulties over his income tax*|*He's taking rather a long time over it.* (=in doing it) **11 over and above** as well as; besides –compare UNDER²

**over³** *adj* [F *with*] finished; ended: *I'm sorry, the party's over; it's finished.*|*At last the examinations are* **over and done with.** (=completely finished)

**over⁴** *n* (in cricket) the act of throwing (BOWLing) the ball at the hitter (BATSMAN) a particular number of times (usually six)

**o·ver·all** /ˌəuvərˈɔːl◂/ *adj,adv* [A; after *n*] **1** including everything: *the overall measurements of the room*|*The fish measured 1·7 metres overall.* **2** on the whole; generally: *Overall, prices are still rising.*

**o·ver·alls** /ˈəuvərɔːlz/ *n* [P] loose trousers often fastened over the shoulders and worn by workers over other clothes

**o·ver·arm** /ˈəuvərɑːm‖-ɑr-/ *adj,adv* (in sport) with the arm moving above the shoulder: *He threw it overarm.*|*an overarm throw* –opposite **underarm**

**o·ver·awe** /ˌəuvərˈɔː/ *v* **-awed, -awing** [T] to fill with respect and fear

**o·ver·bal·ance** /ˌəuvəˈbæləns‖-vər-/ *v* **-anced, -ancing** [I;T] to (cause to) become unbalanced and fall over

**o·ver·bear·ing** /ˌəuvəˈbeərɪŋ‖-vər-/ *adj* trying to make other people obey without regard for their ideas or feelings **–overbearingly** *adv*

**o·ver·board** /ˈəuvəbɔːd‖ˈəuvərbord/ *adv* **1** over the side of a ship or boat into the water **2 go overboard for/about** *infml* to become very attracted to

**o·ver·bur·den** /ˌəuvəˈbɜːdn‖ˌəuvərˈbɜrdn/ [T *with*] to make (someone or something) carry or do too much

**o·ver·cast** /ˌəuvəˈkɑːst◂‖ˌəuvərˈkæst◂/ *adj* dark with clouds: *an overcast sky/day*|(fig.) *Her face was overcast with sadness.*

**o·ver·charge** /ˌəuvəˈtʃɑːdʒ‖ˌəuvərˈtʃɑrdʒ/ *v* **-charged, -charging** [I;T] to charge (someone) too much: *They overcharged me (by) 25p for the food.* –opposite **undercharge**

**o·ver·coat** /ˈəuvəkəut‖-vər-/ *n* a long warm coat worn over other clothes in cold weather

**o·ver·come** /ˌəuvəˈkʌm‖-vər-/ *v* **-came** /ˈkeɪm/, **-come, -coming 1** [I;T] to fight successfully against; defeat: *to overcome the enemy* **2** [T] (usu. of feelings) to take control and influence the behaviour of (someone): *overcome by tiredness/grief*

**o·ver·com·pen·sate** /ˌəuvəˈkɒmpənseɪt, -pen-‖-vərˈkɑmpən-, -pen-/ *v* **-sated, -sating** [I *for*] to try to correct some weaknesses by taking too strong an action in the opposite direction **–overcompensation** /-ˈseɪʃən/ *n* [U]

**o·ver·crowd** /ˌəuvəˈkraud‖-vər-/ *v* [T *with*] to put or allow too many people or things in (one place)

**o·ver·do** /ˌəuvəˈduː‖-vər-/ *v* **-did** /ˈdɪd/, **-done** /ˈdʌn/, **-doing** [T] **1** to do, decorate, perform, etc., too much: *The love scenes in the play were a bit overdone.*|*I've been* **overdoing it.** (=working too much) **2** to use too much: *Don't overdo the salt.*

**o·ver·done** /ˌəuvəˈdʌn‖-vər-/ *adj* cooked too much –opposite **underdone**

**o·ver·dose** /ˈəuvədəus‖-vər-/ *n* too much of a drug: *He died by taking an overdose.*

**o·ver·draft** /ˈəuvədrɑːft‖ˈəuvərdræft/ *n* permission from a bank to OVERDRAW; the sum by which one has OVERDRAWN

**o·ver·draw** /ˌəuvəˈdrɔː‖-vər-/ *v* **-drew** /ˈdruː/, **-drawn** /ˈdrɔːn/, **-drawing** [I;T] to get a bank to pay one more money than one has in (one's account): *My account is £300 overdrawn./overdrawn by £300.*

**o·ver·due** *adj* [after *n*] **1** left unpaid too long **2** later than expected: *The train is 15 minutes overdue.*

**o·ver·es·ti·mate** /ˌəuvərˈestɪ̈meɪt/ *v* **-mated, -mating** [I;T] **1** to give too high a value for (an amount): *We overestimated the cost, so we still have some money left.* **2** to have too high an opinion of: *I think you're overestimating his abilities.* –see also UNDERESTIMATE

**o·ver·flow¹** /ˌəuvəˈfləu‖-vər-/ *v* [I;T] **1** to flow over the edges (of ): *The river overflowed (its banks).* **2** [*into*] to go beyond the limits (of): *The crowd overflowed the theatre into the street.*

**o·ver·flow²** /ˈəuvəfləu‖-vər-/ *n* **1** an act of OVERFLOWing **2** something that OVERFLOWs: *Bring a pot to catch the overflow from this pipe.* **3** a pipe or CHANNEL¹ (3) for carrying away water that is more than is needed

**o·ver·grown** /ˌəuvəˈgrəun◂‖-vər-/ *adj* [*with*] covered esp. with plants growing uncontrolled

**o·ver·hang** /ˌəuvəˈhæŋ‖-vər-/ *v* **-hung** /ˈhʌŋ/, **-hanging** [I;T] to hang over (something): *overhanging cliffs* **–overhang** /ˈ···/ *n*

**o·ver·haul** /ˌəuvəˈhɔːl‖-vər-/ *v* [T] to examine thoroughly and perhaps repair if necessary: *to overhaul a car* **–overhaul** /ˈ···/ *n*

**o·ver·head** /ˌəuvəˈhed‖-vər-/ *adv,adj* above one's head: *electricity carried by overhead wires* (=not underground)

**o·ver·heads** /ˈəuvəhedz‖-vər-/ *n* [P] money spent regularly to keep a business running: *Their office is in central London, so their overheads are very high.*

**o·ver·hear** /ˌəuvəˈhɪəʳ‖-vər-/ *v* **-heard** /ˈhɜːd‖ˈhɜrd/, **-hearing** [T] to hear (what others are saying) without their knowledge: *I overheard them talking.*

**o·ver·joyed** /ˌəuvəˈdʒɔɪd‖-vər-/ *adj* [F +*to-v/that*] very pleased; full of joy

**o·ver·land** /ˌəuvəˈlænd◂‖-vər-/ *adv,adj* across or by land and not by sea or air

**o·ver·lap¹** /ˌəuvəˈlæp‖-vər-/ *v* **-pp-** [I;T] to cover (something) partly: *Some roofs are made with overlapping* SLATES¹.|(fig.) *History and politics overlap and should be studied together.*
**o·ver·lap²** /ˈəuvəlæp‖-vər-/ *n* [C;U] the amount by which two or more things OVERLAP each other
**o·ver·leaf** /ˌəuvəˈliːf‖ˈəuvərliːf/ *adv* on the other side of the page
**o·ver·load** /ˌəuvəˈləud‖-vər-/ *v* **-loaded** *or* **-laden** /ˈleɪdən/, **-loading** [T] **1** to load too heavily **2** to cause (a machine) to work too hard, and so use too much electricity: *Don't overload the electrical system by using too many machines.*
**o·ver·look** /ˌəuvəˈluk‖-vər-/ *v* [T] **1** to have or give a view of from above: *a room overlooking the sea.* **2** to look at but not see; not notice; miss **3** to pretend not to see; forgive: *I'll overlook your lateness this time*
**o·ver·much** /ˌəuvəˈmʌtʃ◂‖-vər-/ *adv,determiner, pron* [*usu. with* NEGATIVES²] too much; very much: *He doesn't like me overmuch.*
**o·ver·night** /ˌəuvəˈnaɪt◂‖-vər-/ *adv,adj* **1** for or during the night: *an overnight journey|an overnight bag* **2** suddenly: *Byron became famous overnight.*
**o·ver·pass** /ˈəuvəpɑːs‖ˈəuvərpæs/ *n AmE* for FLYOVER
**o·ver·pop·u·lat·ed** /ˌəuvəˈpɒpjuleɪtɪ̣d‖ˌəuvər ˈpɑpjə-/ *adj* having too many people **–overpopulation** /-ˈleɪʃən/ *n* [U]
**o·ver·pow·er** /ˌəuvəˈpauəʳ‖-vər-/ *v* [T] **1** to conquer (someone) by greater power **2** → OVERCOME (1,2)
**o·ver·rate** /ˌəuvəˈreɪt/ *v* **-rated, -rating** [T] to put too great or high a value on: *I think that film has been overrated.* –see also UNDERRATE
**o·ver·ride** /ˌəuvəˈraɪd/ *v* **-rode** /ˈrəud/, **-ridden** /ˈrɪdn/, **-riding** [T] to take no notice of (another person's orders, claims, etc.)
**o·ver·rule** /ˌəuvəˈruːl/ *v* **-ruled, -ruling** [T] to decide against (someone who made) an earlier judgment: *The judge overruled us/our claim.*
**o·ver·run** /ˌəuvəˈrʌn/ *v* **-ran** /ˈræn/, **-run** /ˈrʌn/, **-running 1** [T] to spread over, usu. causing harm: *The enemy overran the conquered country.* **2** [I;T] to continue beyond (a time limit or an appointed stopping place): *Sorry I'm late; the meeting overran.*
**o·ver·seas** /ˌəuvəˈsiːz◂‖-vər-/ *adv,adj* across the sea: *They've gone to live overseas.|overseas students*
USAGE **Overseas** *students* have come to one's own country from abroad in order to study; the same idea is expressed by *students from* **overseas.** But *students* **overseas** are people studying in other countries.
**o·ver·see** /ˌəuvəˈsiː‖-vər-/ *v* **-saw** /ˈsɔː/, **-seen** /ˈsiːn/, **-seeing** [T] to watch to see that work is properly done: *to oversee the work/the workers* **–overseer** /ˈəuvəˌsɪəʳ/ *n*
**o·ver·shad·ow** /ˌəuvəˈʃædəu‖-vər-/ *v* [T] **1** to throw a shadow over **2** to make appear less important: *Her new book will overshadow all her earlier ones.*
**o·ver·shoot** /ˌəuvəˈʃuːt‖-vər-/ *v* **-shot** /ˈʃɒt‖ˈʃɑt/, **-shooting** [I;T] to go too far or beyond at a fast speed, and miss: *The train overshot the station.*
**o·ver·sight** /ˈəuvəsaɪt‖-vər-/ *n* [C;U] (an) unintended failure to notice or do something: *The mistake was the result of (an) oversight.* –see ERROR (USAGE)
**o·ver·sim·pli·fy** /ˌəuvəˈsɪmplɪ̣faɪ‖-vər-/ *v* **-fied, -fying** [I;T] to express (something) so simply that its true meaning is changed or lost **–oversimplification** /-fɪ̣ˈkeɪʃən/ *n* [C;U]
**o·ver·sleep** /ˌəuvəˈsliːp‖-vər-/ *v* **-slept** /ˈslept/, **-sleeping** [I] to sleep too long or too late
**o·ver·state** /ˌəuvəˈsteɪt‖-vər-/ *v* **-stated, -stating** [T] to state too strongly, making things appear better, worse, or more important than they really are: *She* **overstated her case,** *so we didn't believe her.* –opposite **understate**
**o·vert** /ˈəuvɜːt, əuˈvɜːt‖-ɜrt/ *adj fml* public; not secret –opposite **covert –overtly** *adv*
**o·ver·take** /ˌəuvəˈteɪk‖-vər-/ *v* **-took** /ˈtuk/, **taken** /ˈteɪkən/, **-taking** [I;T] to come up level with and pass: *A car overtook me although I was going very fast.*
**o·ver·throw** /ˌəuvəˈθrəu‖-vər-/ *v* **-threw** /ˈθruː/, **-thrown** /ˈθrəun/, **-throwing** [T] to defeat; remove from official power: *to overthrow the government* **–overthrow** /ˈ···/ *n* [*the* S]
**o·ver·time** /ˈəuvətaɪm‖-vər-/ *n,adv* [U] (time) beyond the usual time, esp. working time: *They're working overtime to finish the job quickly.*
**o·ver·ture** /ˈəuvətjuəʳ, -tʃəʳ‖-vər-/ *n* a musical introduction to a large musical piece, esp. an OPERA
**o·ver·tures** /ˈəuvətjuəz, -tʃəz‖-vər-/ *n* [P] an offer to begin to deal with someone in the hope of reaching an agreement: *to make peace overtures to the enemy*
**o·ver·turn** /ˌəuvəˈtɜːn‖ˌəuvərˈtɜrn/ *v* [I;T] to (cause to) turn over: *The boat/The lamp overturned.*
**o·ver·weight** /ˌəuvəˈweɪt◂‖-vər-/ *adj* [after *n*] weighing too much: *This parcel/person is overweight by two kilos/is two kilos overweight.|an overweight person* –compare UNDERWEIGHT; see THIN (USAGE)
**o·ver·whelm** /ˌəuvəˈwelm‖-vər-/ *v* [T] **1** to defeat or make powerless (usu. a group of people) by much greater force of numbers **2** (of feelings) to OVERCOME (2) completely and usu. suddenly
**o·ver·whelm·ing** /ˌəuvəˈwelmɪŋ‖-vər-/ *adj* very large or great; too large or great to oppose **–overwhelmingly** *adv*
**o·ver·work¹** /ˌəuvəˈwɜːk‖ˌəuvərˈwɜrk/ *v* [I;T] to (cause to) work too much
**overwork²** *n* [U] too much work; working too hard
**o·ver·wrought** /ˌəuvəˈrɔːt◂/ *adj* too nervous and excited
**ow** /au/ *interj* (an expression of sudden pain)
**owe** /əu/ *v* **owed, owing** [T] **1** [*to, for*] to have to pay: *He owes (me) £20 (for my work).* –see Study Notes on page 429 **2** [*to*] to feel grateful (to) (for): *We owe our parents a lot.*
**ow·ing** /ˈəuɪŋ/ *adj* [F or after *n*] still to be paid: *How much is owing to you?|There is still £5 owing.*
**owing to** /ˈ·· ·/ *prep* because of: *We were late, owing to the snow.* –see Study Notes on page 128
**owl** /aul/ *n* a bird that flies at night
**own¹** /əun/ *determiner,pron* **1** belonging to oneself and to nobody else: *I only borrowed the book; it's not my own.|The country has its own oil and doesn't need to buy any.|a room of your own* **2 have/get one's own back (on someone)** to succeed in doing harm (to someone) in return for harm done to oneself **3 on**

one's own by oneself; without help: *I can't carry it on my own; it's too heavy.*

**own²** *v* [T] **1** to possess (something), esp. by lawful right: *Who owns this house/this dog?* **2** [+(*that*)] *fml* to admit

**own up** *v adv* [I *to*] to admit a fault or crime: *She owned up to taking the money.*

**own·er** /ˈəʊnəʳ/ *n* a person who owns something, esp. by lawful right –**ownership** *n* [U]

**ox** /ɒks‖ɑks/ *n* **oxen** /ˈɒksən‖ˈɑk-/ a large animal of the cattle type, wild or used by man

**Ox·bridge** /ˈɒksˌbrɪdʒ‖ˈɑks-/ *n* the universities of Oxford and/or Cambridge –compare REDBRICK

**ox·ide** /ˈɒksaɪd‖ˈɑk-/ *n* [C;U] a chemical substance in which something is combined with oxygen: *iron oxide*

**ox·i·dize** ‖also **-dise** *BrE* /ˈɒksǝdaɪz‖ˈɑk-/ *v* **-dized, -dizing** [I;T] to (cause to) combine with oxygen, esp. in such a way as to make or become RUSTY –**oxidization** /ˌɒksǝdaɪˈzeɪʃən‖-də- / *n* [U]

**ox·y·gen** /ˈɒksɪdʒən‖ˈɑk-/ *n* [U] a gas present in the air, without colour, taste, or smell, but necessary for all forms of life on earth

**oy·ster** /ˈɔɪstəʳ/ *n* a flat shellfish, eaten cooked or raw, which can produce a jewel called a PEARL

**oy·ster·catch·er** /ˈɔɪstəˌkætʃəʳ‖-ər-/ *n* a seabird that catches and eats shellfish

**oz** *written abbrev. said as:* OUNCE¹ or OUNCES

**o·zone** /ˈəʊzəʊn/ *n* [U] **1** *infml* air that is pleasant to breathe, esp. near the sea **2** *tech* a type of oxygen

# P, p

**P, p** /piː/ **P's, p's** *or* **Ps, ps** the 16th letter of the English alphabet

**p¹** *abbrev. for: (BrE infml)* (new) penny/pence: *This newspaper costs 8p.* –see PENNY (USAGE)

**p²** *written abbrev. said as:* page –see also PP

**PA** *n abbrev. for:* **1** Personal Assistant (=a secretary employed to look after the affairs of one person) **2** public-address system; an electrically controlled apparatus used for making someone clearly heard by a large group of people, by means of LOUDSPEAKERS, esp. out of doors

**pace¹** /peɪs/ *n* **1** [S;U] rate or speed in walking, running, etc.: *a slow pace|The fastest runner* **set the pace** *and the others followed.|She works very fast: I can't* **keep pace with** (=work at the same speed as) *her.* **2** [C] (the distance moved in) a single step in running or walking: *The fence is ten paces from the house.* –compare STEP¹ (3) **3 put someone through his/her paces** to make someone do something as a test of his/her abilities

**pace²** *v* **paced, pacing 1** [I;T] to walk (across) with slow, regular, steady steps, esp. backwards and forwards: *The policeman paced up and down.|The lion paced the floor of its cage.* **2** [T *off, out*] to measure by taking steps of an equal and known length: *to pace out a room* **3** [T] to set the speed or rate of movement for: *She knew how fast she was running, because her trainer was pacing her on a bicycle.*

**pace·mak·er** /ˈpeɪsˌmeɪkəʳ/ *n* **1** also **pacesetter** /-ˌsetəʳ/ *AmE*– **a** a person who sets a speed that others in a race try to equal **b** a person who sets an example for others **2** a machine used to make weak or irregular heartbeats regular

**pac·i·fis·m** /ˈpæsǝfɪzəm/ *n* [U] the belief that all wars are wrong

**pac·i·fist** /ˈpæsǝfǝst/ *n* an active believer in PACIFISM; person who refuses to fight in a war because of such a belief

**pac·i·fy** /ˈpæsǝfaɪ/ *v* **-fied, -fying** [T] to make calm, quiet, and satisfied: *to pacify a crying baby* –**pacification** /-fǝˈkeɪʃən / *n* [U]

**pack¹** /pæk/ *n* **1** a number of things wrapped or tied together, or put in a case, esp. for carrying on the back: *The climber carried some food in a pack on his back.|They used* **packhorses** *to carry their food and tents across the mountains.* **2** [+*sing./pl. v*] a group of wild animals (esp. the WOLF) that hunt together, or a group of dogs trained together for hunting **3** [+*sing./pl. v*] *derog* a collection, group, etc. (esp. in the phrases **pack of thieves, pack of lies**) **4** a complete set of cards used in playing a game **5** *esp. AmE* a packet: *a pack of cigarettes*

**pack²** *v* **1** [I;T] to put (things, esp. one's belongings) into (a case, boxes, etc.) for travelling or storing: *She packed her bags and left.|I'm leaving in an hour and I haven't packed yet!|He packed some bread and cheese for his dinner.|a packed meal* –opposite **unpack 2** [T] to cover, fill, or surround closely with a protective material: *Pack some paper round the dishes in the box so that they will not break.* **3** [I;T *in, down*] to fit, crush, or push into a space: *If you pack those things down we can get more into the box.*

**pack** sbdy./sthg.↔ **in** *v adv* [T] *infml* **1** to attract in large numbers: *That film is really packing them in.* (=attracting large crowds) **2 pack it in** to cease an activity: *Pack it in; stop arguing!*

**pack** sbdy.↔ **off** *v adv* [T *to*] *infml*→BUNDLE **off**: *He packed his children off to school and then went out.*

**pack up** *v adv* [I] *infml* **1** to finish work **2** *BrE* (of a machine) to stop working

**pack·age¹** /ˈpækɪdʒ/ *n* (a parcel containing) a number of things packed or bound together:

**package²** *v* **-aged, -aging** [T *up*] to place in or tie up as a PACKAGE: *He packaged up the old clothes and put them in the cupboard.|Too much packaging increases the cost of the food we buy.*

**package deal** /ˈ·· ·/ *n infml* an agreement that includes a number of things all of which must be accepted together

**package tour** /ˈ·· ·/ *n* a completely planned holiday arranged by a company at a fixed price

**packed** /pækt/ also **packed-out** /ˌ·ˈ·/ *infml*– *adj* (of a room, building, etc.) full of people; CROWDED

**pack·er** /ˈpækəʳ/ *n* a person who PACKS² (1,2) esp. **a** food for preserving **b** the furniture, clothing, etc., of people moving from one house to another

**pack·et** /ˈpækɨt/ *n* **1** a small PACKAGE¹; a number of small things tied or put together into a small box, case, or bag: *a packet of envelopes/cigarettes* –see picture on page 615 **2** *infml* a large amount of money: *That car cost me a packet.*

**pack·ing** /ˈpækɪŋ/ *n* [U] material used in PACKing² (2)

**packing case** /ˈ·· ·/ *n* a strong wooden box in which things are packed to be stored or sent elsewhere

**pact** /pækt/ *n* a solemn agreement: *a pact of peace between the two nations*

**pad¹** /pæd/ *n* **1** anything made or filled with a soft material used to protect something, make it more comfortable, etc.: *American footballers wear shoulder-pads for protection.|Put a clean pad of cotton over the wound.* **2** a number of sheets of paper fastened together, used for writing letters, drawing pictures, etc.: *a writing pad* **3** the thick-skinned underpart of the foot of some four-footed animals **4** *infml* a house or flat

**pad²** *v* **-dd-** [T *out*] to fill with soft material in order to protect, shape, or make more comfortable: *a coat with padded shoulders*|(fig.) *I made my speech longer by padding it out with a few jokes.*

**pad³** *v* **-dd-** to walk steadily and usu. softly: *John's dog padded along beside him as he walked.*

**pad·ding** /ˈpædɪŋ/ *n* [U] material used to PAD² something

**pad·dle¹** /ˈpædl/ *n* a short pole with a wide flat blade at one or both ends, used for pushing and guiding a small boat (esp. a CANOE¹). Unlike an OAR, it is not fastened in position on the side of the boat

**paddle²** *v* **-dled, -dling** [I;T] to move (a small light boat, esp. a CANOE¹) through water, using one or more PADDLES; row gently

**paddle³** *v* **-dled, -dling** [I] *esp. BrE* (esp. of children) to walk about in water only a few inches deep –compare WADE

**paddle steam·er** /ˈ·· ˌ··/ *n* a steamship which is pushed forward by PADDLE WHEELS

**paddle wheel** /ˈ···/ *n* a large wheel fixed to the side or back of a ship, and turned by a steam-engine to make the ship move forward through the water –compare PROPELLER

**padd·ling pool** /ˈ·· ·/ *n* a small stretch of water (e.g. in a park) only a few inches deep, where children PADDLE³

**pad·dock** /ˈpædək/ *n* a small field where horses are kept and exercised, or where horses are brought together before a race so that people may see them

**pad·dy** /ˈpædi/ also **rice paddy** /ˈ· ··/, **paddy field** /ˈ·· · /– *n* **-dies** a field where rice is grown in water

**pad·lock** /ˈpædlɒk‖-lɑk/ *n* a movable lock with a U-shaped metal bar, which can be used to lock gates, bicycles, cupboards, etc. –**padlock** *v* [T]: *Did you remember to padlock the gate?*

**pa·dre** /ˈpɑːdri, -reɪ/ *n infml* a priest, esp. one in the Armed Forces; CHAPLAIN –see PRIEST (USAGE)

**pae·di·a·tri·cian** /ˌpiːdɪəˈtrɪʃən/ *n* →PEDIATRICIAN

**pae·di·at·rics** /ˌpiːdiˈætrɪks/ *n* [U] →PEDIATRICS

**pa·gan** /ˈpeɪgən/ *n* a person who is not a believer in any of the chief religions of the world –**pagan** *adj*

**page¹** /peɪdʒ/ *n* one or both sides of a sheet of paper in a book, newspaper, etc.: *This book has 256 pages.*

**page²** also **page boy** /ˈ··/– *n* **1** a boy servant in a hotel, club, etc., usu. uniformed **2** (at a wedding) a boy attendant on the BRIDE (=the woman getting married)

**page³** *v* **paged, paging** [T] (in a hotel, hospital, etc.) to call aloud for (someone who is wanted for some reason), esp. through a LOUDSPEAKER

**pag·eant** /ˈpædʒənt/ *n* a public show or ceremony, usu. out of doors, esp. **a** one in which there is a procession of people in rich dress **b** one in which historical scenes are acted

**pag·eant·ry** /ˈpædʒəntri/ *n* [U] splendid show of ceremonial grandness with people in fine dress: *the pageantry of a royal wedding*

**pa·go·da** /pəˈgəʊdə/ *n* a temple (esp. Buddhist or Hindu) built on several floors with a decorative roof at each level

**paid** /peɪd/ *v past tense and participle of* PAY¹

**paid-up** /ˌ· ˈ·◂/ *adj* having paid in full (esp. so as to continue being a member) –compare PAY¹ **up**

**pail** /peɪl/ *n* a bucket used for carrying liquids: *a milk pail* –sounds like **pale**

**pain¹** /peɪn/ *n* **1** [U] suffering; great discomfort of the body or mind: *She was in pain/crying with pain after she broke her arm.|His behaviour caused his parents a great deal of pain.* **2** [C] a feeling of suffering or discomfort in a particular part of the body –compare ACHE **3** [S] also **pain in the neck** /ˌ··· ˈ·/– *infml* a person or thing that causes annoyance or displeasure; NUISANCE: *He's a real pain.* –see also PAINS –sounds like **pane**

**pain²** *v* [T] to cause to feel pain in the mind; hurt

**pained** /peɪnd/ *adj* showing that one is displeased or hurt in one's feelings: *After they had quarrelled there was a pained silence between them.*

**pain·ful** /ˈpeɪnfəl/ *adj* causing pain: *a painful cut on my thumb* –**painfully** *adv* –**painfulness** *n* [U]

**pain·kill·er** /ˈpeɪnˌkɪləʳ/ *n* a medicine which lessens or removes pain

**pain·less** /ˈpeɪnlɨs/ *adj* causing no pain: (fig.) *The examination was quite painless.* –**painlessly** *adv*

**pains** /peɪnz/ *n* [P] trouble; effort: *We gave the taxi driver something for his pains.|The teacher* **was at (great) pains** (=took great trouble) *to make sure that we all understood.*

**pains·tak·ing** /ˈpeɪnzˌteɪkɪŋ/ *adj* careful and thorough: *painstaking care* –**painstakingly** *adv*

**paint¹** /peɪnt/ *n* [U] liquid colouring matter which can be put or spread on a surface to make it a certain colour: *a tin of green paint*|**Wet Paint** (a warning sign placed near a freshly-painted surface) –compare DYE

**paint²** *v* [I;T] **1** to put paint on (a surface): *She painted the door blue/a bright colour.* **2** to make (a picture of) (somebody or something) using paint: *Who painted this picture?*|(fig.) *Her letters paint a wonderful picture of her life in Burma.* **3 paint the town red** *infml* to go out and have a good time, usu. when celebrating (CELEBRATE) something

**paint·er** /ˈpeɪntəʳ/ *n* **1** a person whose job is painting houses, rooms, etc. **2** a person who paints pictures;

artist: *a* PORTRAIT *painter*

**paint·ing** /ˈpeɪntɪŋ/ *n* **1** [U] the art or practice of painting pictures **2** [C] a picture made in this way

**paints** /peɪnts/ *n* [P] a set of small tubes or cakes of paint of different colours, usu. in a box (**paint box**), as used by an artist: *a set of oil paints*

**paint·work** /ˈpeɪntwɜːk‖-wɜrk/ *n* [U] a painted surface, esp. of a movable object such as a car: *The paintwork was damaged when my car hit the gate.*

**pair**[1] /peəʳ/ *n* **pairs** *or* **pair 1** something made up of two parts that are alike and are joined and used together: *a pair of trousers|a pair of scissors* **2** two things that are alike or of the same kind, and are usu. used together: *a pair of shoes |a pair of Kings* (=two playing cards of the same value) **3** [+*sing./pl.v*] two people closely connected, esp. a COUPLE[1] (2): *The* **happy pair** *is/are going to Spain after their wedding.* –sounds like **pear**

USAGE Some words for two things joined together, like **trousers** and **scissors**, are used like plural nouns, but they are not thought of as having a number. So one can say *These* **trousers**/*My other* **trousers** *are dirty*, or *two more* **pairs** *of* **trousers**, but not *two **trousers**, **both* **trousers**. **Pair** is also used for things like **shoes**, which are not joined together, so that one can say *one* **shoe**, *both* **shoes**, as well as *a* **pair** *of* **shoes**. Any word in this dictionary which is followed by the note "see PAIR (USAGE)" can be used in the expression *a* **pair** *of X*. –compare BRACE, COUPLE

**pair**[2] *v* [I;T] **1** [*off, up*] to (cause to) form into one or more PAIRS[1] (2,3): *Birds often pair in the spring.|We tried to pair Jane and David off.* **2** to make, or join with somebody to make, a PAIR[1] (3)

**pair up** *v adv* [I;T (=**pair** sbdy.↔ **up**) *with*] to (cause to) join in pairs, esp. for purposes of work or sport

**pa·ja·mas** /pəˈdʒɑːməz‖-ˈdʒɑ-, -ˈdʒæ-/ *n* [P] *AmE* for PYJAMAS

**pal** /pæl/ *n infml* a close friend: *an old pal of mine* –**pally** *adj* **-lier, -liest** [F]: *The boys are very pally.*

**pal·ace** /ˈpælǝs/ *n* a large and splendid house, esp. where a king or queen officially lives: (fig.) *Her house is a palace compared to ours!* –see HOUSE (USAGE)

**pal·ais** /ˈpæleɪ; *infml* ˈpæli‖pæˈleɪ/ *n* **palais** /ˈpæleɪz‖pæˈleɪz/ *BrE* a large hall used for dancing

**pal·a·ta·ble** /ˈpælətəbəl/ *adj* **1** pleasant to taste **2** agreeable to the mind; pleasant –opposite **unpalatable**

**pal·ate** /ˈpælǝt/ *n* **1** the top part (ROOF[1] (4)) of the inside of the mouth **2** [*usu. sing.*] the ability to judge food or wine

**pa·la·tial** /pəˈleɪʃəl/ *adj* (usu. of buildings) like a palace; large and splendid: *a palatial hotel*

**pale**[1] /peɪl/ *adj* **1** (of a person's face) having less than the usual amount of colour; rather white **2** (esp. of colours) not bright; weak: *pale blue|the pale light of the moon* –compare LIGHT[2] (2), DEEP (3) –**paleness** *n* [U]

**pale**[2] *v* **paled, paling** [I] to become pale: (fig.) *All our other worries paled* (=began to seem unimportant) *beside the possibility of war.*

**pal·e·o·lith·ic** /ˌpæliəʊˈlɪθɪk‖ˌpeɪ-/ *adj* (*often cap.*) of the earliest known period of human existence (**Old Stone Age**), when people made weapons and tools of stone: *a paleolithic axe* –compare NEOLITHIC

**pal·ette** /ˈpælǝt/ *n* a board with a curved edge and a hole for the thumb, on which an artist mixes colours

**pal·ings** /ˈpeɪlɪŋz/ *n* [P] a fence made out of pointed pieces of wood

**pall**[1] /pɔːl/ *n* **1** a covering of dark cloth spread over a COFFIN (a box in which a dead body is carried and buried): (fig.) *a pall of smoke hiding the city* **2** *AmE* a COFFIN with a body inside

**pall**[2] *v* [I *on*] to become uninteresting or dull, esp. through being done, heard, etc., too often or for too long: *His interest in his new job soon began to pall.*

**pall·bear·er** /ˈpɔːlˌbeərəʳ/ *n* a person who walks beside or helps to carry a COFFIN at a funeral

**pal·lid** /ˈpælǝd/ *adj* (esp. of the face, skin, etc.) unusually or unhealthily pale; WAN: *She had a pallid look.* –**pallor** *n* [S;U]

**palm**[1] /pɑːm‖pɑm, pɑlm/ also **palm tree** /ˈ· ·/– *n* a tall tropical tree with a branchless stem and a mass of large leaves at its top: *a* DATE *palm* –see COCONUT

**palm**[2] *n* the inner surface of the hand between the base of the fingers and the wrist –see picture on page 299

**palm**[3] *v* → PALM OFF

**palm·ist** /ˈpɑːmǝst‖ˈpɑm-, ˈpɑlm-/ *n* a person who claims to be able to tell someone's future by examining the lines on his/her PALM[2] –compare FORTUNE-TELLER –**palmistry** *n* [U]

**palm** sthg.↔ **off** *v adv* [T *on, as*] *infml* to sell (or gain profit from) something by wrongly describing it; deceitfully gain acceptance for: *She tried to palm the painting off as a real Renoir.* –compare PASS[1] **off,** FOB OFF

**pal·pa·ble** /ˈpælpəbəl/ *adj fml* easily and clearly known by the senses or the mind; OBVIOUS: *a palpable lie* –**palpably** *adv*: *What you say is palpably false.*

**pal·pi·ta·tion** /ˌpælpǝˈteɪʃən/ *n* [C;U *often pl.*] an irregular or too rapid beating of the heart, caused by illness, too much effort, etc.

**pal·try** /ˈpɔːltri/ *adj* **-trier, -triest** unimportant; worthlessly small: *a paltry sum of money*

**pam·pas** /ˈpæmpəz, -pəs/ *n* [*the* P;S] the large wide treeless plains in parts of South America

**pam·per** /ˈpæmpəʳ/ *v* [T] to show too much attention to making (somebody) comfortable; treat too kindly: *a pampered cat*

**pam·phlet** /ˈpæmflǝt/ *n* a small book with paper covers which deals usu. with some matter of public interest: *a political pamphlet on education*

**pan**[1] /pæn/ *n* **1** any of various kinds of metal container used in cooking, usu. with one long handle and sometimes with a lid –see also BEDPAN, DUSTPAN, FRYING PAN, SAUCEPAN **2** the bowl of a LAVATORY (1)

**pan**[2] *v* **-nn- 1** [I;T *for*] to wash (soil or GRAVEL) in a type of SIEVE, looking for a precious metal: *panning for gold* **2** [T] *infml* to pass severe judgment on; CRITICIZE very severely

**pan**[3] *v* **-nn-** [I;T *over, round, to*] to move (a camera while filming), from side to side, up and down, back, etc.

**pan·a·ce·a** /ˌpænəˈsɪə/ *n often derog* something that is said to cure any illness, put right all troubles, etc.

**pa·nache** /pəˈnæʃ, pæ-/ *n* [U] a manner of doing things that is showy and splendid, and without any

## STUDY NOTES pairs of verbs

### **bring** and **take**

*I asked the waiter to* **bring** *me a coffee, and to* **take away** *the dirty dishes.*

**bring** means "to cause to come with one to the place where the speaker is or will be"

*They came to my party and* **brought** *me a lovely present.*

**take** means "to cause to go with one to another place"

*We went to her party and* **took** *her a present.*

Note also:

**fetch** means "to go and get from another place and bring back"

*I have to* **fetch** *the children from school at four o'clock.*

**send** means "to cause to go, without going oneself"

*I can't go to her party, but I'll* **send** *her a card.*

---

### **lend** and **borrow**

*The boy wants to* **borrow** *a pound* **from** *the girl.*
*The girl* **lends** *a pound* **to** *the boy.*

If she **lends** (also **loans** *AmE*) the money to him, it is only a **loan**. He will have to **pay back** (or **repay**) the money to her.

If he has **borrowed** the money, and has not **paid** it **back**, he **owes** her the money.

*"I've no money for my bus fare. Can I* **borrow** *a pound?/Can you* **lend** *me a pound?"*

*"OK, I'll* **lend** *you a pound, but you must* **pay** *me* **back/pay** *it* **back/give** *it* **back** *on Monday."*

---

### **say** and **tell**

**say** and **tell** are very similar in meaning, but we use them differently in sentences. We usually **say** (something), but **tell** (somebody) (something). Compare:

*I* **said** *"Be quiet!"*

*I* **told** *you to be quiet!*

*She* **said** *a few words then sat down.*

*She* **told** *(us) a very funny story.*

*He* **said** *"I'm very tired".*
*He* **said** *(that) he was very tired.*
*He* **said** *(to me) that he was tired.*

*He* **told** *me (that) he was very tired.*

Note the use of **tell** in the phrases **tell a lie, tell the truth, tell a story, tell the time.**

---

seeming difficulty
**pan·cake** /'pæŋkeɪk/ *n* a thin soft flat cake made of flour, milk, eggs, etc. (BATTER), cooked in a flat pan and eaten hot with a sweet or SAVOURY filling
**pan·da** /'pændə/ also **giant panda**– *n* **pandas** *or* **panda** a large bearlike animal with black and white fur, originally from China
**pan·de·mo·ni·um** /,pændɪ̆'məunɪəm/ *n* [U] a state of wild and noisy disorder
**pan·der to** sbdy./sthg. /'pændəʳ/ *v prep* [T] *derog* to provide something that satisfies (the low or undesirable wishes of): *a newspaper that panders to people's interest in sex*
**pane** /peɪn/ *n* a single sheet of glass for use in a frame, esp. of a window –sounds like **pain**
**pan·el¹** /'pænl/ *n* **1** a separate usu. four-sided division of the surface of a door, wall, etc., which is different in some way to the surface round it **2** a board on which controls or instruments of various kinds are fastened **3** [+*sing./pl. v*] a group of speakers who answer questions to inform or amuse the public,usu. on a radio or television show: *a panel game|What do/does the panel think?* –see also PANELLIST **4** a piece of cloth of a different colour or material, set in a dress
**panel²** *v* **-ll-** *BrE*||**-l-** *AmE* [T] to divide into or decorate with PANELS¹ (1,4): *a panelled room*
**pan·el·ling** *BrE*||**paneling** *AmE* /'pænəlɪŋ/ *n* [U] →PANELS¹ (1)
**pan·el·list** *BrE*||**panelist** *AmE* /'pænəlɪ̆st/ *n* a member of a PANEL¹ (3)
**pang** /pæŋ/ *n* a sudden sharp feeling of pain: *pangs of hunger|a pang of sadness*
**pan·ic¹** /'pænɪk/ *n* [C;U] (a state of) sudden uncontrollable fear or terror: *There was (a) panic when the fire started.*
**panic²** *v* **-ck-** [I;T *at*] to (cause to) feel PANIC: *The crowd panicked at the sound of the guns.*
**panic-strick·en** /'·· ,··/ *adj* filled with wild terror
**pan·ni·er** /'pænɪəʳ/ *n* a basket, esp. one of a pair, carried by a horse or donkey, on a bicycle, etc.
**pan·o·ra·ma** /,pænə'rɑːmə||-'ræmə/ *n* a complete view over a wide area –**panoramic** /-'ræmɪk/ *adj*: *a panoramic view of the city*
**pan·sy** /'pænzi/ *n* **-sies** a small plant with wide flat flowers
**pant¹** /pænt/ *v* [I;T] to take quick short breaths, or say (something) in this way, esp. after great effort or in great heat: *The dog panted in the heat.|She panted out the message.*
**pant²** *n* a short quick breath
**pan·the·is·m** /'pænθi-ɪzəm/ *n* [U] the religious idea that God and the universe are the same thing –**pantheist** *n*
**pan·ther** /'pænθəʳ/ *n* **panthers** *or* **panther** **1** a LEOPARD, esp. a black one **2** *AmE* for COUGAR
**pan·ties** /'pæntiz/ also **pants** *esp. BrE*– *n* [P] a short undergarment worn below the waist by women and girls; KNICKERS –see also UNDERPANTS; see PAIR (USAGE)
**pan·to·mime** /'pæntəmaɪm/ also **panto** /'pæntəu/ *infml*– *n* [C;U] a funny British play for children, based on a fairy story, and usu. produced at Christmas
**pan·try** /'pæntri/ *n* **-tries** a small room with shelves in a house, where food is kept; LARDER
**pants** /pænts/ *n* [P] **1** *BrE* for UNDERPANTS or PANTIES **2** *AmE* for trousers –see PAIR (USAGE)
**pa·pa¹** /pə'pɑː/ *n BrE* (a name for father, used formerly)
**pap·a²** /'pɑpə/ *n AmE infml* (a name for father)
**pa·pa·cy** /'peɪpəsi/ *n* [*the* S] the power and office of the POPE
**pa·pal** /'peɪpəl/ *adj* [A] of the POPE or of the PAPACY
**pa·pa·ya** /pə'paɪə/ also **pawpaw** *BrE*– *n* [C;U] (the large yellow-green fruit of) a tall tree grown in tropical countries
**pa·per¹** /'peɪpəʳ/ *n* **1** [U] material made in the form of sheets from very thin threads of wood or cloth, used for writing on, covering parcels or walls,etc.: *a sheet of paper|a paper bag/handkerchief* **2** [C] *infml* a newspaper: *Have you seen today's paper?* **3** [C] a set of printed questions used as an examination in a particular subject: *The history paper was really easy.* **4** [C] a piece of writing for specialists, often read aloud **5 on paper** as written down or printed, but not yet tested by experience: *These plans seem good on paper, but we cannot be sure they will work.*
**paper²** *v* [T] to cover (a wall or walls) with WALLPAPER: *She papered the room with green paper.*
**pa·per·back** /'peɪpəbæk||-ər-/ *n* [A;C] a book with a thin cardboard cover: *This shop only sells paperbacks.|a paperback* NOVEL¹/*a* NOVEL¹ **in paperback** –compare HARDBACK
**paper clip** /'·· ·/ *n* a small piece of curved wire used for holding sheets of paper together
**pa·pers** /'peɪpəz||-ərz/ *n* [P] pieces of paper with writing on them, esp. as used for official purposes
**pa·per·weight** /'peɪpəweɪt||-ər-/ *n* a heavy object placed on top of loose papers to keep them from being scattered
**pa·per·work** /'peɪpəwɜːk||-pərwɜrk/ *n* [U] regular work of writing reports, letters, keeping records, etc.,esp. as part of a job
**pa·pi·er-mâ·ché** /,pæpieɪ 'mæʃeɪ, ,peɪpə-||,peɪpər/ *n* [U] paper mixed with GLUE to form a soft mass, and used for making boxes, models, etc.
**pap·ri·ka** /'pæprɪkə||pə'priːkə/ *n* [U] a red powder (PEPPER) used in cooking to give a hot taste to food
**pa·py·rus** /pə'paɪərəs/ *n* **-ri,** *or* **-ruses** [U] paper made in ancient Egypt from a grasslike plant
**par** /pɑːʳ/ *n* [S] **1** a level which is equal or almost the same; PARITY: *These two things are* **on a par** *(with each other).* **2** (in the game of GOLF) the number of strokes the average player should take to hit the ball into a hole **3 below par** *infml* not in the usual or average condition (of health, activity, etc.)
**par·a·ble** /'pærəbəl/ *n* a short simple story which teaches a moral or religious lesson
**pa·rab·o·la** /pə'ræbələ/ *n* a curve like the line made by a ball when it is thrown forward in the air and falls to the ground
**par·a·chute¹** /'pærəʃuːt/ *n* an apparatus made of cloth, fastened to persons or objects dropped from aircraft in order to make them fall slowly
**parachute²** *v* **-chuted, -chuting** [I;T] to (cause to) drop from an aircraft by means of a PARACHUTE
**pa·rade¹** /pə'reɪd/ *n* **1** [C;U] (an example of) a

gathering together for the purpose of being officially looked at, or for a march or ceremony: *The soldiers are* **on parade**.|*The Olympic Games begin with a parade of all the competing nations.* **2** [C] a wide public path or street, often beside the seashore

**parade²** *v* **-raded, -rading 1** [I;T] (esp. of soldiers) to gather together in ceremonial order, for the purpose of being officially looked at, or for a march **2** [T] *often derog* to show in order to gain admiration: *He is always parading his knowledge/his wealth.*

**par·a·dise** /ˈpærədaɪs/ *n* **1** [S] (*usu. cap.*) Heaven **2** [S] (*usu. cap.*) (in the Bible) the Garden of Eden, home of Adam and Eve **3** a place of perfect happiness: (fig.) *This hotel is a sportsman's paradise.* (=has everything a sportsman needs) **4 fool's paradise** a state of great contentment for which there is no real reason and which is unlikely to last

**par·a·dox** /ˈpærədɒks‖-dɑks/ *n* **1** a statement which seems to be impossible, because it says two opposite things, but which has some truth in it: *"More haste, less speed" is a paradox.* **2** an improbable combination of opposing qualities, ideas, etc.: *It is a paradox that in such a rich country there should be so many poor people.* **–paradoxical** /ˌpærəˈdɒksɪkəl‖-ˈdɑk- / *adj* **–paradoxically** *adv*

**par·af·fin** /ˌpærəˈfɪn◂, ˈpærəfɨn/ *BrE*‖**kerosene** *AmE– n* [U] an oil made from PETROLEUM, coal, etc., burnt for heat and in lamps for light

**par·a·gon** /ˈpærəgən‖-gɑn/ *n* [*of*] a person or thing that is a perfect model to copy (often in the phrase **a paragon of virtue**)

**par·a·graph** /ˈpærəgrɑːf‖-græf/ *n* a division of a piece of writing made up of one or more sentences, of which the first word starts a new line: *Look at the third paragraph on page 23.*

**par·a·keet** /ˈpærəkiːt/ *n* a kind of small PARROT

**par·al·lel¹** /ˈpærəlel/ *adj* [*no comp.*] **1** (of lines or rows) running side by side but never getting nearer to or further away from each other: *parallel lines*|*The railway line runs parallel with/to the road.* **2** comparable (to): *My experience in this matter is parallel to yours.*

**parallel²** *n* **1** a parallel line, row, or surface **2** a comparable person or thing: *an actor* **without (a) parallel** *in the modern cinema*|*There are few parallels* (=points of likeness) *between American football and European football.* **3** also **parallel of latitude** /ˌ··· ·ˈ···/– any of a number of lines on a map drawn parallel to the EQUATOR

**parallel³** *v* **-l-** [T] to equal; match: *Her life parallels mine.* –see also UNPARALLELED

**par·al·lel·o·gram** /ˌpærəˈleləgræm/ *n tech* a flat four-sided figure with opposite sides equal and parallel

**par·a·lyse** *BrE*‖**paralyze** *AmE* /ˈpærəlaɪz/ *v* **-lysed, -lysing** [T] to make (the body muscles) unable to move: *paralysed with fear*

**pa·ral·y·sis** /pəˈrælɨsɨs/ *n* **-ses** /siːz/ [C;U] (a) loss of feeling in and control of the body muscles: *paralysis of the arm*

**par·a·lyt·ic** /ˌpærəˈlɪtɪk/ *n,adj* **1** (a person) suffering from PARALYSIS **2** causing PARALYSIS: *a paralytic* STROKE² (3) **3** *infml* (of a person) very drunk **–paralytically** *adv*

**par·a·mil·i·tary** /ˌpærəˈmɪlɨtri‖-teri/ *adj* like or used as a regular military force: *the paramilitary organizations of Northern Ireland*

**par·a·mount** /ˈpærəmaunt/ *adj* great above all others; highest in power or importance: *of paramount importance*

**par·a·noi·a** /ˌpærəˈnɔɪə/ *n* [U] a disease of the mind in which the sufferer believes that others hate him/her and are purposely mistreating him/her, or that he/she is a person of high importance **–paranoiac** /-æk/ *adj,n*

**par·a·noid** /ˈpærənɔɪd/ *adj* (as if) suffering from PARANOIA: *My father locks every door in the house as he is paranoid about being robbed.*

**par·a·pet** /ˈpærəpɨt, -pet/ *n* a low wall at the edge of a roof, bridge, etc.

**par·a·pher·na·li·a** /ˌpærəfəˈneɪlɪə‖-fər-/ *n* [U] a number of small articles of various kinds, esp. personal belongings or those needed for some skill or work: *a house full of paraphernalia*

**par·a·phrase** /ˈpærəfreɪz/ *v,n* **-phrased, -phrasing** [C;T] (to make) a re-expression of (something written or said) in words that are easier to understand

**par·a·ple·gic** /ˌpærəˈpliːdʒɪk/ *adj,n* (of or being) a person suffering from PARALYSIS of the lower part of the body

**par·a·site** /ˈpærəsaɪt/ *n* **1** a plant or animal that lives on or in another and gets food from it **2** a useless person who is supported by the wealth or efforts of other people **-parasitic** /-ˈsɪtɪk/ *adj*: *a parasitic plant* **–parasitically** *adv*

**par·a·sol** /ˈpærəsɒl‖-sɔl, -sɑl/ *n* a light cloth-covered circular frame UMBRELLA held over the head for protection from the sun

**par·a·troop·er** /ˈpærəˌtruːpəʳ/ *n* a soldier trained to drop from an aircraft using a PARACHUTE

**par·a·troops** /ˈpærətruːps/ *n* [P] a group of PARATROOPERS

**par·boil** /ˈpɑːbɔɪl‖ˈpɑr-/ *v* [T] to boil until partly cooked

**par·cel** /ˈpɑːsəl‖ˈpɑr-/ *n* **1** a thing or things wrapped in paper and tied or fastened for easy carrying, posting, etc.: *I'm taking this parcel to the post office.*|*a parcel of clothes* **2 part and parcel of** a most important part that cannot be separated from the whole of

**parcel** sthg.↔ **out** *v adv* **-ll-** *BrE*‖**-l-** *AmE* [T] to divide into parts or shares

**parcel** sthg.↔ **up** *v adv* **-ll-** *BrE*‖**-l-** *AmE* [T] to make into a PARCEL

**parch** /pɑːtʃ‖pɑrtʃ/ *v* [T] (of the sun) to make hot and dry: *I'm parched!* (=very thirsty)

**parch·ment** /ˈpɑːtʃmənt‖ˈpɑr-/ *n* [U] **1** a writing material used esp. in ancient times, made from the skin of a sheep or goat **2** a paper of good quality that looks like this material

**par·don¹** /ˈpɑːdn‖ˈpɑrdn/ *n* **1** [C;U] (an act or example of) forgiveness **2** [C] *law* an action of a court or ruler forgiving a person for an illegal act, and giving freedom from punishment **3 I beg your pardon** also **pardon me**– *polite* **a** "Please excuse me for having accidentally touched/pushed you." **b** also **pardon** *infml*– "I did not hear/understand what you said and would like you to repeat it." –see SORRY (USAGE)

**pardon²** *v* [T *for*] **1** to forgive; excuse: *We must* pardon him his little faults. **2** to give an official PARDON[1] (2) to or for

**par·don·a·ble** /'pɑːdənəbəl‖'pɑr-/ *adj* that can be pardoned –opposite **unpardonable**

**pare** /peəʳ/ *v* **pared, paring** [T] to cut away the thin outer covering, edge, or skin of: *to pare one's fingernails/an apple* –sounds like **pair**

**pare** sthg.↔ **down** *v adv* [T] to reduce (esp. a cost)

**par·ent** /'peərənt/ *n* [*often pl.*] the father or mother of a person or animal: *John and Mary have become parents.* (=They have become the father and mother of a child) –compare RELATION, RELATIVE[1] –see picture on page 217 –**parental** /pə'rentl/ *adj* [A]

**par·ent·age** /'peərəntɪdʒ/ *n* [U] origin; birth: *a child of unknown parentage*

**pa·ren·the·sis** /pə'renθ$\frac{1}{2}$s$\frac{1}{2}$s/ *n* **-ses** /siːz/ **1** [*usu. pl.*] also **bracket** *BrE*– either of a pair of small curved lines ( ), used in writing to enclose added information **2** an added explanation or thought enclosed in this way –**parenthetic** /ˌpærən'θetɪk/ also **parenthetical**– *adj*: *parenthetic remarks* –**parenthetically** *adv*

**par·ent·hood** /'peərənthʊd/ *n* [U] the state or condition of being a parent

**par ex·cel·lence** /ˌpɑːr 'eksəlɑːns‖-eksə'lɑns/ *adj* [after *n*] *French* without equal, as the best and/or most typical of its kind

**pa·ri·ah** /pə'raɪə/ *n* a person not accepted by society

**par·ish** /'pærɪʃ/ *n* an area in the care of a single priest and served by one main church: *a parish church/priest*

**pa·rish·io·ner** /pə'rɪʃənəʳ/ *n* a person living in a particular PARISH, esp. one who regularly attends the PARISH church

**par·i·ty** /'pær$\frac{1}{2}$ti/ *n* [U] the state or quality of being equal: *parity between men's and women's pay* –see also DISPARITY

**park**[1] /pɑːk‖pɑrk/ *n* **1** a large usu. grassy enclosed piece of land in a town, used by the public for pleasure and rest **2** *BrE* also **parkland**– a large enclosed stretch of land with grass, trees, etc., round a large country house –see also CAR PARK

**park**[2] *v* [I;T] to put (a car or other vehicle) somewhere for a time: *Don't park (the car) in this street.*|(fig.) *Don't park your books on my desk!* –see PARKING (USAGE)

**par·ka** /'pɑːkə‖'pɑrkə/ *n* →ANORAK

**park·ing** /'pɑːkɪŋ‖'pɑr-/ *n* [U] the leaving (parking) of a car or other vehicle in a particular place for a time

USAGE You **park** (your car) in a **car park** or **parking** place. The sign **Parking** means "Permission to **park**". It is *not* the name of a place, so you cannot ask **Where is the* **parking**?

**parking lot** /'·· ·/ *n AmE* for CAR PARK

**parking meter** /'·· ˌ··/ *n* an apparatus at the side of a street, into which one puts a coin to pay for parking a car beside it for a certain time

**park·land** /'pɑːk-lænd‖'pɑrk-/ *n* [U] *BrE* for PARK[1] (2)

**par·lance** /'pɑːləns‖'pɑr-/ *n* [U] *fml* a particular manner of speech or use of words: *In naval parlance, the left side of a ship is the* PORT *side.*

**par·lia·ment** /'pɑːləmənt‖'pɑr-/ *n* (*usu. cap.*) **1** a body of people (**Members of Parliament**) wholly or partly elected by the people of a country to make laws **2** (in the United Kingdom) the main law-making body, made up of the King or Queen, the Lords, and the elected representatives of the people: *Parliament sits* (=meets regularly) *at Westminster.* –**parliamentary** /ˌpɑːlə'mentəri‖ˌpɑr-/ *adj*

**par·lia·men·tar·i·an** /ˌpɑːləmən'teərɪən‖ˌpɑr-/ *n* a skilled and experienced member of a parliament

**par·lour** *BrE*‖**parlor** *AmE* /pɑːləʳ‖'pɑr-/ *n* **1** *esp. AmE (in comb.)* a shop for some kind of personal service or for selling a particular type of article: *an ice-cream parlour*|*a* MASSAGE *parlour* **2** *now rare* a room in a house used for receiving guests, etc.

**pa·ro·chi·al** /pə'rəʊkɪəl/ *adj* **1** (of the mind, one's interests, opinions, etc.) limited; narrow **2** of a PARISH –compare INSULAR –**parochially** *adv* –**parochialism** *n* [U]

**par·o·dy**[1] /'pærədi/ *n* **-dies** **1** [C *of*] a weak and unsuccessful copy: *a parody of justice* **2** [C;U *of, on*] (a piece of) writing or music intended to amuse by copying the style of a known writer or musician

**parody**[2] *v* **-died, -dying** [T] to make a PARODY of

**pa·role**[1] /pə'rəʊl/ *n* [U] the letting out of a person from prison, conditional upon good behaviour, before the end of the official period of imprisonment: *The prisoner was let out* **on parole.**

**parole**[2] *v* **-roled, -roling** [T] to set free on PAROLE

**par·ox·ys·m** /'pærəksɪzəm/ *n* a sudden uncontrollable explosive expression: *paroxysms of anger/laughter*

**par·quet** /'pɑːkeɪ, 'pɑːki‖pɑr'keɪ/ *n* [A;U] small flat blocks of wood fitted together in a pattern on to the floor of a room: *a parquet floor*

**par·rot** /'pærət/ *n* any of a large group of tropical birds, having a curved beak and usu. brightly coloured feathers, that can be taught to copy human speech

**par·ry**[1] /'pæri/ *v* **-ried, -rying** [T] to turn aside or keep away (an attacking blow or a weapon): (fig.) *She parried the unwelcome question skilfully.*

**parry**[2] *n* **-ries** an act of PARRYing, esp. in fencing (FENCE[2] (1))

**par·si·mo·ni·ous** /ˌpɑːs$\frac{1}{2}$'məʊnɪəs‖ˌpɑr-/ *adj fml* too careful with money; unwilling to spend –**parsimoniously** *adv* –**parsimony** /'pɑːs$\frac{1}{2}$məni‖'pɑrs$\frac{1}{2}$məʊni/ *n* [U]

**pars·ley** /'pɑːsli‖'pɑr-/ *n* [U] a small garden plant (HERB) with curly leaves, used in cooking or on uncooked foods

**pars·nip** /'pɑːsnɪp‖'pɑr-/ *n* a garden plant with a thick white or yellow root that is used as a vegetable

**par·son** /'pɑːsən‖'pɑr-/ *n* a priest who is in charge of a PARISH, usu. of the CHURCH OF ENGLAND

**par·son·age** /'pɑːsənɪdʒ‖'pɑr-/ *n* the house where a PARSON lives

**part**[1] /pɑːt‖pɑrt/ *n* **1** [C;U *of*] a piece which is less than the whole: *Which part of the town do you live in?*|*Part of the house was/Parts of the house were damaged by the fire.*|*She lived there for the greater part of* (=most of) *her life.* **2** [C] any of the pieces into which something is divided: *Cut the cake into eight equal parts.*|*I didn't like the first part of the book.* **3** [C] a necessary or important piece of a machine or other apparatus: *Do you sell car parts?* **4** [S;U] a share or duty in some activity: *Did you* **take part in/have any part in** *the meeting?|Luck* **played a part in** (=helped to cause) *his success.* **5** [C] (the words, actions of) a character in a play, film, etc.: *In the play, I take the part of a policeman.|Have you learnt your part yet?* **6** [U] a side or position in an argument: *He always takes his sister's part.* (=supports her) **7 for my part** as far as I am concerned; speaking for myself **8 for the most part** *fml* mostly; most of the time: *She is for the most part a well-behaved child.* **9 in part** in some degree; partly **10 on the part of someone** by someone; of someone: *It was a mistake on your part to meet him.*

**part²** *v* **1** [I;T] to (cause to) become separate or no longer together: *She tried to part the two fighting dogs.|If we must part, I hope we can part (as) friends.|The clouds parted, and the sun shone down.* **2** [T] to separate (hair on the head) along a line with a comb; make a PARTING¹(2) **3 part company (with): a** to end a relationship (with) **b** no longer to be together (with) **c** to disagree (with)

**part with** sthg. *v prep* [T] to give up, esp. unwillingly: *It's not easy to part with one's children.*

**part³** *adv* →PARTLY (esp. in the phrase **part . . ., part . . .**): *The medical exams are part written, part practical.*

**part⁴** *adj* [A] not complete; PARTIAL (1): *part payment*

**par·take** /pɑːˈteːk‖pɑr-/ *v* **partook** /pɑːˈtʊk‖pɑr-/, **partaken** /pɑːˈteːkən‖pɑr-/, **partaking** [I *of*] *old use or humor* to eat or drink, esp. something offered: *Will you partake of a drink with us?*

**par·tial** /ˈpɑːʃəl‖ˈpɑr-/ *adj* **1** [*no comp.*] not complete: *The play was only a partial success.* **2** favouring one person, side, etc., more than another, esp. in a way that is unfair –opposite **impartial 3** [F *to*] having a strong liking for: *I'm very partial to sweet foods.*

**par·ti·al·i·ty** /ˌpɑːʃiˈæləti‖ˌpɑr-/ *n* **1** [U] the quality or fact of being PARTIAL (2); BIAS¹ (1) –opposite **impartiality 2** [S *for*] a special liking

**par·tial·ly** /ˈpɑːʃəli‖ˈpɑr-/ *adv* **1** not completely; PARTLY: *I am partially to blame for the accident.* **2** in a PARTIAL (2) way

**par·tic·i·pant** /pɑːˈtɪsəpənt‖pɑr-/ *n* [*in*] a person who takes part or has a share in an activity or event

**par·tic·i·pate** /pɑːˈtɪsəpeɪt‖pɑr-/ *v* **-pated, -pating** [I *in* ] to take part or have a share in an activity or event –**participation** /-ˈpeɪʃən/ *n* [U]

**par·ti·ci·ple** /ˈpɑːtəsɪpəl‖ˈpɑr-/ *n* (in English grammar) either of two forms of a verb (PAST PARTICIPLE and PRESENT PARTICIPLE) which may be used in compound forms of the verb or as adjectives –**participial** *adj*

**par·ti·cle** /ˈpɑːtɪkəl‖ˈpɑr-/ *n* **1** a very small piece of matter: *dust particles floating in the sunlight*|(fig.) *There wasn't a particle of truth in what he said.* **2** (in grammar) any of several usu. short words in a sentence apart from the subject, verb, etc.: *"But, and, out, up" are used as particles in some sentences.*

**par·tic·u·lar** /pəˈtɪkjʊləʳ‖pərˈtɪkjələr/ *adj* **1** [A *no comp.*] worthy of notice; special; unusual: *There was nothing in the letter of particular importance.* **2** [A *no comp.*] single and different from others; of a certain sort: *I don't like this particular hat, but the others are quite nice.* **3** showing (too) much care or interest in small matters; hard to please: *He is very particular about his food.* **4 in particular** especially: *I noticed his eyes in particular, because they were very large.*

**par·tic·u·lar·ly** /pəˈtɪkjʊləli‖pərˈtɪkjələrli/ *adv* especially; in a way that is special and different from others: *He isn't particularly clever.*

**par·tic·u·lars** /pəˈtɪkjʊləz‖pərˈtɪkjələrz/ *n* [P *of*] the facts or details (esp. about an event): *We haven't got time to* **go into particulars** *about the accident.*

**part·ing¹** /ˈpɑːtɪŋ‖ˈpɑr-/ *n* **1** [C;U] (an example of) the action of PARTING² (1) **2** [C] also **part** *AmE*– the line on the head where the hair is PARTED² (2) **3 the parting of the ways** the point at which two people must separate, or a choice must be made

**parting²** *adj* [A] done or given at the time of PARTING² (1): *a parting kiss*

**par·ti·san, zan** /ˌpɑːtəˈzæn‖ˈpɑrtəzən, -sən/ *n* **1** a strong supporter of a party, group, plan, etc.: *a partisan speech* **2** a member of an armed group that fights in secret against an enemy that has conquered its country

**par·ti·tion¹** /pɑːˈtɪʃən‖pər-, pɑr-/ *n* **1** [U] division into two or more parts (esp. of a country) **2** [C] something that divides, esp. a thin wall in a house

**partition²** *v* [T] to divide into two or more parts

**partition** sthg.↔**off** *v adv* [T] to make (esp. a part of a room) separate by means of a PARTITION¹ (2)

**part·ly** /ˈpɑːtli‖ˈpɑr-/ *adv* in some degree but not completely: *What you say is partly true.*

**part·ner¹** /ˈpɑːtnəʳ‖ˈpɑr-/ *n* **1** a person who shares in the same activity, esp. either of two people dancing together or playing together in games such as tennis or BRIDGE³ –see picture on page 592 **2** any of the owners of a business, who share the profits and losses

**partner²** *v* [T] to act as partner to

**part·ner·ship** /ˈpɑːtnəʃɪp‖ˈpɑrtnər-/ *n* **1** [U] the state of being a partner, esp. in business: *We've been in partnership for five years.* **2** [C] a business owned by two or more partners

**part of speech** /ˌ· · ˈ·/ *n* (in grammar) any of the classes into which words are divided according to their use: *"Noun", "verb", and "adjective" are parts of speech.*

**par·took** /pɑːˈtʊk‖pɑr-/ *v past tense of* PARTAKE

**par·tridge** /ˈpɑːtrɪdʒ‖ˈpɑr-/ *n* **-tridges** *or* **-tridge** [S;U] (the meat of) a middle-size bird shot for sport and food

**part-time** /ˌ· ˈ·◂/ *adj,adv* (working or giving work) during only a part of the regular working time: *a part-time job|She works part-time.* –see also FULL-TIME

**par·ty** /ˈpɑːti‖ˈpɑrti/ *n* **-ties 1** [C] a gathering of people, usu. by invitation, for food and amusement: *to give* (=have) *a party|Did you enjoy Susie's party?|a party dress* **2** [C +*sing./pl. v*] a group of people doing something together: *A party of schoolchildren went to France.|a* **search party,** *looking for the lost child* **3** [C +*sing./pl. v*] an association of people having the same political aims, esp. as formed to try to win elections: *What is* **the party line** (=the official opinion of the party) *on nuclear weapons?* **4** [A] the system of government based on political parties: *the* *party system|party politics* **5** [C] *law* one of the people or sides in an agreement or argument –see also THIRD PARTY

**pass**[1] /pɑːs‖pæs/ *v* **1** [I;T] to reach and move beyond (a person or place): *I passed the pub on my way to the library.* **2** [I] to go forward; advance: *The road was so crowded that the car could not pass (through).|A cloud passed across the sun.* **3** [I;T] to go through or across: *No one is allowed to pass the gates of the camp.*|(fig.) *I'll let that remark pass.* (=I will not say anything about that remark)|(fig.) *Angry words passed between them.* **4** [T] to put; cause to go: *She passed the rope around the tree.* **5** [T] to give (esp. by hand): *Please pass me the salt!* **6** [I;T] (in various sports) to kick, throw, hit, etc. (esp. a ball) to a member of one's own side **7** [I;T] **a** (of time) to go by **b** to cause (time) to go by, esp. in a way that does not seem too long or dull: *She passed the time by reading a book.* **8** [I] to change: *When you melt ice, it passes from a solid to a liquid state.* **9** [I] to go from one person's control or possession to another's: *When she dies, her money will pass to her son.* **10** [I;T] to give official acceptance to (a suggested law or other formal suggestion) **11** [I;T] to succeed in (an examination): *She passed her driving test.* –opposite **fail 12** [T *as*] to accept after examination: *I can't pass this bad piece of work!* **13** [T *on, upon*] to give (a judgment, opinion, etc.) –see SENTENCE[1] **14** [T] to say: *He's always passing rude remarks about me.* **15** [I] to come to an end: *Summer passed quickly.* **16** **pass the time of day (with)** to give a greeting (to), and/or have a short conversation (with) **17 pass water** *euph* for URINATE –see PAST[1] (USAGE)

**pass away/on** *v adv* [I] *euph* (esp. of a person) to die: *She passed away in her sleep.*

**pass by** *v adv* **1** [I] to go past **2** [T] (**pass** sbdy.↔ **by**) also **pass** sbdy.↔ **over**– to pay no attention to; disregard: *You made a mistake, but I'll pass the matter by.*

**pass** sthg.↔ **down** *v adv* [T] →HAND[2] **down**

**pass for** *v prep* to be (mistakenly) accepted as: *She could pass for a much younger woman.*

**pass off** *v adv* **1** [I] to stop: *The rain passed off.* **2** [I] to take place successfully: *The meeting passed off well.* **3** [T *as*] (**pass** sbdy./sthg. **off**) to present falsely: *She passed herself off as a doctor.*

**pass on** *v adv* **1** [I] →PASS **away 2** [T] (**pass** sthg.↔ **on**) →HAND[2] **on**

**pass out** *v adv* **1** [I] to faint **2** [T] (**pass** sthg.↔ **out**) *AmE* for HAND[2] **out**; DISTRIBUTE (1)

**pass** sbdy.↔ **over**[1] *v adv* [T] →PASS **by** (2)

**pass over**[2] sthg. *v prep* [T] to try not to notice or mention: *Let us pass over his rude remarks in silence.*

**pass** sthg.↔ **up** *v adv* [T] to let go; miss: *Don't pass up a chance like that!*

**pass**[2] *n* a way by which one may go through, esp. over a range of mountains

**pass**[3] *n* **1** an act of moving past: *The aircraft made a few passes over the enemy camp, but didn't drop any bombs.* **2** a piece of printed paper which shows that one is permitted to do a certain thing, such as travel on a railway without paying, enter a building, etc. **3** a successful result in an examination –opposite **fail 4** an act of PASSING[1] (6) a ball **5** *infml* an attempt to make somebody sexually interested in one, usu. by touching, stroking, etc.: *He* **made a pass at** *her.*

**pass.** *written abbrev. said as:* PASSIVE[1] (2)

**pass·a·ble** /ˈpɑːsəbəl‖ˈpæ-/ *adj* **1** (just) good enough to be accepted; not bad **2** (of a road or river) fit to be used, crossed, etc. –opposite **impassable** (for **2**)

**pas·sage** /ˈpæsɪdʒ/ *n* **1** [C] a usu. narrow way through; opening: *a passage through the forest* **2** [U *of*] the action of going across, by, over, through, etc., in space: *The bridge is not strong enough to allow the passage of vehicles.* **3** [C] also **passageway**– a narrow connecting way, esp. inside a building; CORRIDOR **4** [U *of*] (of time) the course; onward flow **5** [S] (the cost of) a long journey by ship: *He* **worked his passage** *by doing jobs on the ship.* **6** [C] a usu. short part of a speech or a piece of writing or music

**pas·sage·way** /ˈpæsɪdʒweɪ/ →PASSAGE (3)

**pas·sé** /ˈpɑːseɪ, ˈpæseɪ‖pæˈseɪ/ *adj* [F] *derog* no longer considered modern; old-fashioned

**pas·sen·ger** /ˈpæsɪ̵ndʒəʳ, -sən-/ *n* a person, not the driver, travelling in a public or private vehicle

**pass·er-by** /ˌpɑːsəˈbaɪ‖ˌpæsər-/ *n* **passersby** /-səz-‖-sərz-/ a person who happens (by chance) to pass by a place

**pas·sing**[1] /ˈpɑːsɪŋ‖ˈpæ-/ *adj* [A *no comp.*] **1** moving or going by: *She watched the passing cars.* **2** not lasting very long: *a passing thought*

**passing**[2] *n* **in passing** in the course of a statement (esp. one about a different matter): *He mentioned in passing that he had a new car.*

**pas·sion** /ˈpæʃən/ *n* [C;U] (a) strong, deep, often uncontrollable feeling, esp. of love, hatred, or anger: *The poet expressed his burning passion for the woman he loved.*|(fig.) *He has a passion for cream cakes.*

**pas·sion·ate** /ˈpæʃənɪ̵t/ *adj* showing or filled with PASSION: *a passionate speech/woman/interest in politics* –**passionately** *adv*

**pas·sive**[1] /ˈpæsɪv/ *adj* **1** *sometimes derog* not active; influenced by outside forces but not doing anything; suffering without opposition **2** *tech* (of a verb or sentence) expressing an action which is done to the subject of a sentence: *"Was thrown" is a passive verb in "The boy was thrown from his horse".* –compare ACTIVE[1] (3) –**passively** *adv*

**passive**[2] also **passive voice**– *n* [*the* S] *tech* (in grammar) the PASSIVE[1] (2) part or forms of a verb: *"The ball was kicked by the boy" is in the passive.* –compare ACTIVE[2]

**pas·siv·i·ty** /pæˈsɪvɪ̵ti/ also **passiveness** /ˈpæsɪvnɪ̵s/– *n* [U] the state or quality of being PASSIVE[1](1)

**Pass·o·ver** /ˈpɑːsəʊvəʳ‖ˈpæs-/ *n* [C;S] (in the Jewish religion) a holiday in memory of the escape of the Jews from slavery in Egypt

**pass·port** /ˈpɑːspɔːt‖ˈpæsport/ *n* a small official book that proves the nationality of a person, and is used esp. when entering a foreign country: (fig.) *Do you think that money is a passport to happiness?* –see picture on page 16

**pass·word** /ˈpɑːswɜːd‖ˈpæswɜrd/ *n* a secret word or phrase which one has to say in order to be allowed to enter a building, camp, etc.

**past**[1] /pɑːst‖pæst/ *adj* **1** [A; after *n*] (of time) much earlier than the present: *In past years/years past they* never would have done that. –compare FUTURE[1] **2** [A; after *n*] (*with the* PERFECT[1] (5) *tenses*) (of time) a little earlier than the present; up until the time of speaking: *the past few days* **3** finished; ended: *Winter is past and spring has come.* **4** [A] former; not any longer: *She's a past president of the club.* **5** [A] (of a verb form) expressing an action or event that happened before the present moment: *the past tense*

USAGE The past participle of **pass** is **passed**, but it is not used as an adjective. Instead, use **past**, which has the same pronunciation. Compare: *This week has* **passed** *quickly.*|*the* **past** *week*

**past²** *prep* **1 a** farther than: *The hospital is about a mile past the school.* **b** up to and then beyond: *We drove past the house.* –see Study Notes on page 474 **2** beyond in time or age: *It's half past three.*|*She's past* (=older than) *eighty.* **3 past caring** in a state of no longer caring what happens: *He's been without a job so long that he's past caring.* **–past** *adv*: *A whole year went past/by.*

**past³** *n* [S] **1** (what happened in) time before the present: *In the past I have had many jobs.*|*Our country has a glorious past.* (=history) **2** the past tense

**pas·ta** /ˈpæstə‖ˈpɑ-/ *n* [U] food made, in various different shapes, from flour paste, and often covered with SAUCE and/or cheese

**paste¹** /peɪst/ *n* [C;U] **1** a thin soft mixture used for sticking paper together, or onto other surfaces **2** any soft wet mixture of powder and liquid that is easily shaped or spread: *toothpaste*|*Make a paste of flour, fat, and water.* **3** a food made by crushing solid foods into a smooth soft mass, used for spreading on bread: *meat paste*|*fish paste* –compare PÂTÉ

**paste²** *v* **pasted, pasting** [T] to stick or fasten (paper) with paste: *a notice pasted to/on the door*

**pas·tel** /ˈpæstl‖pæˈstel/ *n* (a picture drawn with) a stick of chalklike colouring matter

**pas·teur·ize** ‖also **-ise** *BrE* /ˈpɑːstʃəraɪz, -stə-/ *v* **-ized, -izing** [T] to heat (a liquid, esp. milk) in a certain way in order to destroy bacteria **–pasteurization** /ˌpæstʃəraɪˈzeɪʃən, -stə-‖-rə- / *n* [U]

**pas·tille** /pæˈstiːl/ *n* a small round hard sweet, esp. one containing a medicine for the throat

**pas·time** /ˈpɑːstaɪm‖ˈpæs-/ *n* something done to pass one's time in a pleasant way –see RECREATION (USAGE)

**past mas·ter** /ˌ· ˈ··/ *n* [*at, in, of*] a person who is very skilled (in a particular subject or action)

**pas·tor** /ˈpɑːstəʳ‖ˈpæ-/ *n* a Christian religious leader in charge of a church and its members (esp. of a NONCONFORMIST Church)

**pas·tor·al** /ˈpɑːstərəl‖ˈpæ-/ *adj* **1** of or concerning the members of a religious group, or its leader's duties towards them: *The priest/*RABBI *makes pastoral visits every Tuesday.*|*pastoral care* (=spiritual help and advice) **2** *lit* concerning simple peaceful country life: *pastoral poetry*

**past par·ti·ci·ple** /ˌ· ˈ····/ *n* (in grammar) a form of a verb which may be used (in compound forms of the verb) to express actions done or happening in the past, or sometimes as an adjective: *"Done" and "walked" are the past participles of "do" and "walk".*

**past per·fect** /ˌ· ˈ··/ *n* →PLUPERFECT

**pas·try** /ˈpeɪstri/ *n* **-tries 1** [U] a mixture of flour, fat, and milk or water, eaten when baked, used esp. to enclose other foods **2** [C] an article of food (esp. a small sweet cake) made from this

**pas·ture¹** /ˈpɑːstʃəʳ‖ˈpæs-/ *n* [C;U] (a piece of) grassy land where cattle feed

**pasture²** *v* **-tured, -turing** [T] to put (farm animals) in a PASTURE

**pas·ty¹** /ˈpæsti/ *n* **-ties** (esp. in Britain) a folded piece of pastry baked with meat in it

**past·y²** /ˈpeɪsti/ *adj* **-ier, -iest** (of the face) white and unhealthy-looking

**pat¹** /pæt/ *n* **1** a light friendly touch with the flat hand: *He gave the dog a pat.* **2** a small shaped mass of butter **3 pat on the back** *infml* an expression of praise or satisfaction for something done

**pat²** *v* **-tt-** [T] to touch gently and repeatedly, esp. with the flat hand (often to show kindness, pity, etc.): *He patted the dog.*

**patch¹** /pætʃ/ *n* **1** a (usu. small) piece of material used to cover a hole or a damaged place **2** an area on a surface that is different (being wet, rough, etc.) from the surface round it: *wet patches on the wall*|*patches of mist* **3** a (usu. small) piece of ground, esp. as used for growing vegetables: *a potato patch* **4 bad patch** *BrE* a time of trouble or misfortune **5 not a patch on** *infml* not nearly as good as

**patch²** *v* [T] to put a PATCH¹ (1) on a hole, worn place, etc. in (esp. a garment): *patched trousers*

**patch** sthg.↔ **up** *v adv* [T] **1** to mend with PATCHES (1): *to patch up an old coat*|(fig.) *The doctors patched up the soldier and sent him home.* **2** →MAKE¹ **up** (6): *to patch up a quarrel*

**patch·work** /ˈpætʃwɜːk‖-ɜrk/ *n* [A;C;U] sewn work made by joining together a number of pieces of cloth of different colours, patterns, and shapes: *a patchwork bedcover*|(fig.) *From the aircraft we could see a patchwork of fields of different shapes and colours.*

**patch·y** /ˈpætʃi/ *adj* **-ier, -iest 1** made up of, or appearing in, PATCHES¹ (2): *patchy mist* **2** *usu. derog* incomplete; uneven: *My knowledge of science is patchy.*|*The concert was patchy.* **–patchily** *adv* **–patchiness** *n* [U]

**pât·é** /ˈpæteɪ‖pɑˈteɪ, pæ-/ *n* [U] a food made by crushing solid foods (esp. LIVER) into a smooth soft mass –compare PASTE¹ (3)

**pa·tent¹** /ˈpeɪtnt, ˈpæ-‖ˈpæ-/ *adj* **1** (esp. of things that are not material) easy and plain to see; OBVIOUS **2** protected, by a PATENT², from being copied or sold by those who do not have a right to do so: *a patent lock*

**patent²** *n* a piece of writing from a government office (**Patent** /ˈpætnt/ **Office**)giving someone the right to make or sell a new invention for a certain number of years

**patent³** *v* [T] to obtain a PATENT² for –compare PATENT¹ (2)

**patent leath·er** /ˌpeɪtnt ˈleðəʳ◂‖ˌpæ-/ *n* [U] fine very shiny black leather: *patent leather shoes*

**pa·tent·ly** /ˈpeɪtntli‖ˈpæ-/ *adv derog* clearly and plainly: *a patently false statement*

**pa·ter·nal** /pəˈtɜːnl‖-ɜr-/ *adj* **1** of, like, or received from a father: *paternal love* **2** *derog* protecting people like a father but allowing them no freedom **3** related to a person through the father's side of the family: *my paternal grandmother* (=my father's mother) –compare MATERNAL –**paternally** *adv*

**pa·ter·nal·is·m** /pəˈtɜːnəl-ɪzəm‖-ɜr-/ *n* [U] *derog* the PATERNAL (2) way of controlling people, etc. –**paternalist** *n* –**paternalistic** /-ˈɪstɪk/ *adj*

**pa·ter·ni·ty** /pəˈtɜːnɪti‖-ɜr-/ *n* [U] *law* origin from the male parent

**path** /pɑːθ‖pæθ/ *n* **1** also **pathway**– a track or way made by or for people walking over the ground: *a path through the woods* –see picture on page 297 **2** an open space made to allow forward movement: *a path through the crowd* **3** a line along which something moves: *the path of an arrow*

**pa·thet·ic** /pəˈθetɪk/ *adj* **1** causing a feeling of pity or sorrow: *the child's pathetic cries of pain* **2** *derog* worthless; hopelessly unsuccessful: *He's a really pathetic actor!* –**pathetically** *adv*

**path·o·log·i·cal** /ˌpæθəˈlɒdʒɪkəl‖-ˈlɑ-/ *adj* **1** [A] *tech* of or concerning PATHOLOGY **2** *tech* caused by disease, esp. of the mind **3** *infml* unreasonable; caused by the imagination only: *a pathological fear of the dark* –**pathologically** *adv*

**pa·thol·o·gist** /pəˈθɒlədʒɪst‖-ˈθɑ-/ *n* a specialist in PATHOLOGY (esp. a doctor who examines a dead body to find out how the person has died)

**pa·thol·o·gy** /pəˈθɒlədʒi‖-ˈθɑ-/ *n* [U] *tech* the study of disease

**pa·thos** /ˈpeɪθɒs‖-θɑs/ *n* [U] *lit* the quality in speech, writing, etc., that causes a feeling of pity and sorrow

**path·way** /ˈpɑːθweɪ‖ˈpæθ-/ *n* →PATH (1)

**pa·tience** /ˈpeɪʃəns/ *n* [U] **1** the quality of being patient: *You need a lot of patience when you work here.*|*She showed great patience.* –opposite **impatience** **2** also **solitaire** *AmE*– a card game for one player

**pa·tient¹** /ˈpeɪʃənt/ *adj* having or showing the ability to bear long waiting, or anything unpleasant, calmly and without complaining –opposite **impatient** –**patiently** *adv*

**patient²** *n* a person receiving medical treatment from a doctor and/or in a hospital –see CUSTOMER (USAGE)

**pat·i·o** /ˈpætiəʊ/ *n* **-os** an open space between a house and garden, with a stone floor, used for sitting on in fine weather

**pa·tri·arch** /ˈpeɪtriɑːk‖-ɑrk/ *n* **1** an old and much-respected man –see also MATRIARCH **2** (*usu. cap.*) one of the chief BISHOPs of the eastern churches

**pa·tri·arch·y** /ˈpeɪtriɑːki‖-ɑr-/ *n* **-ies** [C;U] (an example of) a social system ruled or controlled only by men –see also MATRIARCHY –**patriarchal** /ˈpeɪtriɑːkəl‖-ɑr-/ *adj*: *a patriarchal society*

**pat·ri·cide** /ˈpætrɪsaɪd/ *n* [C;U] (a person guilty of) the murder of his/her own father –see also MATRICIDE

**pat·ri·mo·ny** /ˈpætrɪməni‖-məʊni/ *n* **-nies** [S;U] property INHERITed (=received by right of birth) from one's father, grandfather, etc. –**patrimonial** /ˌpætrɪˈməʊnɪəl/ *adj*

**pat·ri·ot** /ˈpætrɪət, -triɒt, ˈpeɪ-‖ˈpeɪtrɪət, -triɑt/ *n approv* a person who loves his/her country

**pat·ri·ot·is·m** /ˈpætrɪətɪzəm, ˈpeɪ-‖ˈpeɪ-/ *n* [U] love for and loyalty to one's country –**patriotic** /-ˈɒtɪk‖-ˈɑtɪk/ *adj* –**patriotically** *adv*

**pa·trol¹** /pəˈtrəʊl/ *n* **1** [U] the act of PATROLling²: *They're* **on patrol**. **2** [C +*sing./pl. v*] (in military use) a small group of people sent to search for the enemy, or to protect a place from the enemy

**patrol²** *v* **-ll-** [I;T] to go at regular times round (an area, building, etc.) to see that there is no trouble, that no one is trying to get in or out illegally, etc.

**pa·trol·man** /pəˈtrəʊlmən/ *n* **-men** /mən/ *AmE* a policeman who regularly PATROLs² a particular area

**pa·tron** /ˈpeɪtrən/ *n* **1** a person who uses a particular shop, hotel, etc., esp. regularly **2** [*of*] a person who supports and regularly gives money to a worthy purpose, or to another person or group of people: *a patron of the arts* –compare CUSTOMER

**pat·ron·age** /ˈpætrənɪdʒ/ *n* [U] **1** the support given by a PATRON **2** *sometimes derog* the ability to appoint people to important positions

**pat·ron·ize** ‖also **-ise** *BrE* /ˈpætrənaɪz‖ˈpeɪ-, ˈpæ-/ *v* **-ized, -izing** [T] **1** to act towards as if better or more important than: *a patronizing remark*|*a patronizing smile* **2** to be a PATRON (1) of

**patron saint** /ˌ·· ˈ·/ *n* a Christian holy man or woman of former times (SAINT), regarded as giving special protection to a particular place, activity, etc.: SAINT *Christopher is the patron saint of travellers.*

**pat·ter¹** /ˈpætəʳ/ *n,v* [I;S] (to make) the sound of something striking a hard surface lightly, quickly, and repeatedly: *the patter of rain on the window*

**patter²** *n* [U] very fast continuous amusing talk, esp. as used by a person telling jokes or doing tricks

**pat·tern¹** /ˈpætn‖ˈpætərn/ *n* **1** a regularly repeated arrangement (esp. of lines, shapes, etc., on a surface or of sounds, words, etc.): *The cloth has a pattern of red and white squares.* **2** the way in which something happens or develops: *The illness is not following its usual pattern.* **3** a shape used as a guide for making something, esp. a piece of paper used to show the shape of a part of a garment: *a dress pattern*

**pattern²** *v* [T] **1** to make a PATTERN¹ (1) on: *a patterned material* **2** to make as if according to a PATTERN¹ (3); copy exactly

**paunch** /pɔːntʃ/ *n derog or humor* a fat stomach, esp. a man's –**paunchy** *adj* –**ier, -iest**

**pau·per** /ˈpɔːpəʳ/ *n* a person who is very poor

**pause¹** /pɔːz/ *n* a short but noticeable break in activity or speech: *a pause in the conversation*

**pause²** *v* **paused, pausing** [I] to stop for a short time before continuing

**pave** /peɪv/ *v* **paved, paving** [T] to cover (a path, area, etc.) with a surface of flat stones: *a paved courtyard*|(fig.) *This agreement will* **pave the way for** (=make possible) *a lasting peace.*

**pave·ment** /ˈpeɪvmənt/ *n* **1** *BrE*‖**sidewalk** *AmE*– a hard surface or path at the side of a street for people to walk on –see picture on page 297 **2** *AmE* the hard surface of a street

**pa·vil·ion** /pəˈvɪljən/ *n* **1** *BrE* a building beside a sports field, for the use of the players and those watching the game **2** a large usu. decorative building used for public amusements or EXHIBITIONs (1), esp. one intended to be used only for a short time

**pav·ing** /ˈpeɪvɪŋ/ *n* [U] material used to PAVE a surface: *a paving stone*

**paw¹** /pɔː/ *n* an animal's foot that has nails or CLAWS

**paw²** *v* [I;T] **1** [*at*] (of an animal) to touch or try to touch with a PAW: *The dog pawed (at) the bone.* **2** [ *at,* about] *infml* (of a person) to feel or touch with the hands, esp. in a rough or sexually improper manner: *She was watching the film, but he kept pawing (at) her.*

**pawn**[1] /pɔːn/ *v* [T] to leave (something of value) with a PAWNBROKER as a promise that one will repay the money one has borrowed

**pawn**[2] *n* **1** (in CHESS) one of the eight smallest and least valuable of a player's pieces **2** an unimportant person used by somebody else for his/her own advantage

**pawn·bro·ker** /ˈpɔːnˌbrəukəʳ/ *n* a person to whom people bring valuable articles so that they may borrow money for a time

**paw·paw** /ˈpɔːpɔː/ *n* [C;U] *BrE* for PAPAYA

**pay**[1] /peɪ/ *v* **paid, paying 1** [I;T +*to-v*/ *for*] to give (money) to (someone) in return for goods bought, work done, etc.: *I paid £5 for that book/to have my radio mended.|I'll pay you £3 to clean my car.|I've already paid.* **2** [T] to settle (a bill, debt, etc.): *Have you paid the electricity bill yet?* **3** [T *in, into*] to put (money, a cheque, etc.,) into a bank account to be kept safe **4** [I;T] to be profitable to or worth the effort of (someone): *If we can't make our farm pay, we'll sell it.|a well-paid job* (=job that pays a lot of money)|*It won't pay you* (=be to your advantage) *to argue with him.|Crime doesn't pay.* **5** [I *for*] to suffer for some bad action: *I'll make him pay for being so rude to me.* **6** [T] to make or say (esp. in the phrases **pay a visit, pay a call, pay a compliment, pay one's respects**): *I'll pay you a visit next week.* **7** [T *to*] to give (one's attention): **Pay attention** *to what I'm saying.* **8 pay one's way** to pay money for things as one buys them, so as not to get into debt

**pay** sbdy./sthg.↔ **back** *v adv* [T] **1** to return what is owing: *Have I paid (you) back the £10 you lent me?* –see Study Notes on page 429 **2** to return bad treatment, rudeness, etc. to (someone who has done something wrong to oneself): *I'll pay you back for what you did to me!*

**pay off** *v adv* **1** [T] (**pay** sthg.↔ **off**) to pay the whole of (a debt) **2** [T] (**pay** sbdy.↔ **off**) to pay and dismiss from a job **3** [I] to be successful: *Our plan certainly paid off; it was a great idea.* –see also PAYOFF

**pay** sthg.↔ **out** *v adv* [T] **1** to lift and slowly give out (a rope) **2** to give (money) in return for goods or services: *I paid out a lot of money for that car.*

**pay up** *v adv* [I] to pay a debt in full, often unwillingly –compare PAID-UP

**pay**[2] [U] **1** money received for work: *He gets his pay each Thursday.* **2 in the pay of** *derog* employed by: *This man is in the pay of the enemy.*

USAGE **Pay** is a general word for the money you receive from work, but **income** means any money you receive, whether from work or from INVESTMENTS, rents, etc.: *Have you any* **income** *apart from your pay?* **Remuneration** is like **pay**, but much more formal. A **salary** is paid monthly into the bank (esp. to professional people) and **wages** are paid weekly in cash (esp. to people who work with their hands). Money paid for certain professional services (e.g. to a lawyer) is a **fee**.

**pay·a·ble** /ˈpeɪəbəl/ *adj* [F] that may or must be paid: *This bill is payable now.|Your cheque should be made payable to "John Smith".* (=this name should be written on the cheque)

**pay·day** /ˈpeɪdeɪ/ *n* [C;S] the day on which wages are (to be) paid

**PAYE** *abbrev. for: BrE* pay as you earn; a system by which income tax is taken away from wages before the wages are paid

**pay·ee** /peɪˈiː/ *n tech* a person to whom money is or should be paid

**pay·ment** /ˈpeɪmənt/ *n* **1** [U] the act of PAYing[1](1,2): *Here is a cheque in payment of my account.* –see also NONPAYMENT **2** [C] an amount of money (to be) paid

**pay·off** /ˈpeɪɒf‖-ɔf/ *n* [*the* S] *infml* **1** the act or time of paying wages, debts, etc. **2** punishment; RETRIBUTION –see also PAY[1] **off**

**pay pack·et** /ˈ· ˌ··/ *BrE*‖**pay envelope** /ˈ· ˌ···/ *AmE*– *n* an envelope containing wages, given to an employed person each week

**pay·roll** /ˈpeɪrəul/ *n* **1** [C] a list of workers employed by a company and the amount of wages each person is to be paid **2** [S] the total amount of wages paid in a particular company

**P.C.** *abbrev. for: BrE* Police Constable; a male member of the police force having the lowest rank: *P.C. Johnson|Two P.C.s were attacked.* –see also W.P.C.

**PE** *n abbrev for:* PHYSICAL (3) education; PHYSICAL TRAINING

**pea** /piː/ *n* a round green seed, used for food

**peace** /piːs/ *n* **1** [S;U] a condition or period in which there is no war **2** [*the* S] a state of freedom from disorder within a country, with the citizens living according to the law: *We should all* **keep the peace. 3** [U] calmness; quietness; freedom from anxiety: *Please let me do my work in peace.|All I want is some* **peace and quiet.**|*peace of mind* –sounds like **piece**

**peace·a·ble** /ˈpiːsəbəl/ *adj* disliking argument or quarrelling –**peaceably** *adv*

**peace·ful** /ˈpiːsfəl/ *adj* **1** quiet; untroubled: *a peaceful day* **2** liking peace: *peaceful nations* –**peacefully** *adv* –**peacefulness** *n* [U]

**peace·time** /ˈpiːstaɪm/ *n* [U] a time when a nation is not at war –opposite **wartime**

**peach** /piːtʃ/ *n* **1** [C] a round fruit with soft yellowish-red skin and sweet juicy flesh, and a large seed in its centre **2** [U] the colour of the skin of this fruit; yellowish-red

**pea·cock** /ˈpiːkɒk‖-kɑk/ *n* **-cocks** *or* **-cock** a large male bird famous for its long beautiful tail feathers

**pea·hen** /ˈpiːhen/ *n* a large brownish bird, the female PEACOCK

**peak**[1] /piːk/ *n* **1** a sharply pointed mountain top: *The (mountain) peaks are covered with snow all the year.* **2** the highest point or level of a varying amount, rate, etc.: *Sales have reached a new peak.|peak hour traffic* –compare OFF-PEAK **3** the flat curved part of a cap which sticks out in front above the eyes

**peak**[2] *v* [I] to reach a PEAK[1] (2)

**peaked** /piːkt/ *adj* [A] having a PEAK[1](3)

**peal**[1] /piːl/ *n* **1** the sound of the loud ringing of bells **2** a loud long sound or number of sounds one after the other: *a peal of thunder* –sounds like **peel**

**peal**[2] *v* [I;T *out*] to (cause to) ring out or sound loudly –sounds like **peel**

**pea·nut** /ˈpiːnʌt/ also **groundnut**– *n* a nut which

grows in a shell under the ground, and can be eaten

**pea·nut but·ter** /ˌ·· ˈ··/ *n* [U] a soft substance made of crushed PEANUTS , usu. eaten on bread

**pear** /peəʳ/ *n* a sweet juicy fruit, narrow at the stem end and wide at the other –sounds like **pair**

**pearl** /pɜːl||pɜrl/ *n* **1** [C] a small hard round white mass formed inside the shell of OYSTERS, very valuable as a jewel **2** [U] the colour of this; silvery-white **3** [A;U] →MOTHER-OF-PEARL

**pearl·y** /ˈpɜːli||ˈpɜrli/ *adj* **-ier, -iest** like or decorated with PEARLS (1): *pearly teeth|a pale pearly grey*

**peas·ant** /ˈpezənt/ *n* **1** (now used usu. of developing countries or former times) a person who works on the land, esp. one who owns or rents a small piece of land **2** *derog* a person without education or manners

**peas·ant·ry** /ˈpezəntri/ *n* [*the* U +*sing./pl. v*] all the PEASANTS (1) of a particular country

**peat** /piːt/ *n* [U] partly decayed vegetable matter which takes the place of ordinary soil in certain areas, and is used for burning instead of coal –**peaty** *adj* **-ier, -iest**

**peb·ble** /ˈpebəl/ *n* a small roundish smooth stone found esp. on the seashore or on a riverbed

**peck**[1] /pek/ *v* **1** [I;T *at*] (of birds) to strike (at something) with the beak: *That bird tried to peck me.*|(fig.)*You're only pecking at your food: what's wrong?* **2** [T] *infml* to kiss in a hurry or without much feeling

**peck**[2] *n* **1** a stroke or mark made by PECKING[1](1) **2** *infml* a hurried kiss

**peck·ish** /ˈpekɪʃ/ *adj* [F] *BrE infml* hungry

**pe·cu·li·ar** /pɪˈkjuːlɪəʳ/ *adj* **1** strange; unusual (esp. in a troubling or displeasing way): *This food has a peculiar taste; do you think it's all right?* **2** [F *to*] belonging only (to a particular person, place, etc.): *This style of cooking is peculiar to the South-West of the country.*

**pe·cu·li·ar·i·ty** /pɪˌkjuːliˈærǝ̇ti/ *n* **-ties 1** [U] the quality of being PECULIAR **2** [C] something which is PECULIAR: *One of the peculiarities of her behaviour is that she shouts instead of talking.*

**pe·cu·li·ar·ly** /pɪˈkjuːlɪəli||-ər-/ *adv* **1** especially; more than usually: *This question is peculiarly difficult.* **2** strangely

**pe·cu·ni·a·ry** /pɪˈkjuːnɪəri||-nieri/ *adj fml & pomp* connected with or consisting of money

**ped·a·go·gy** /ˈpedəgɒdʒi||-gəʊ-/ *n* [U] *fml* the study of ways of teaching –**pedagogic** /ˌpedəˈgɒdʒɪk||-ˈgɑ-, -ˈgəʊ-/ *adj*

**ped·al**[1] /ˈpedl/ *n* a kind of bar which is part of a machine and can be pressed with the foot in order to control the working of the machine: *One of the pedals has come off my bicycle.*| *the brake pedal*

**pedal**[2] *v* **-ll-** *BrE*|| **-l-** *AmE* [I;T] to move (esp. a bicycle) along by using PEDALS[1]: *She pedalled the bicycle up the hill.*|*I was just pedalling along.*

**ped·ant** /ˈpednt/ *n derog* a person whose attention to detail is too great –**pedantic** /pǝ̇ˈdæntɪk/ *adj*: *a pedantic teacher*

**ped·dle** /ˈpedl/ *v* **-dled, -dling** [I;T] to try to sell (small goods) by going from place to place: *She went to prison for peddling drugs.*

**ped·es·tal** /ˈpedǝ̇stl/ *n* **1** the base on which a pillar or STATUE stands **2 put/set somebody on a pedestal** to consider somebody better, nobler, etc., than oneself or others

**pe·des·tri·an**[1] /pǝ̇ˈdestrɪən/ *n* a person walking (esp. in a street used by cars) –compare MOTORIST

**pedestrian**[2] *adj* not interesting or unusual; lacking in imagination: *He was rather a pedestrian student.*

**pedestrian cross·ing** /·ˌ··· ˈ··/ *n* a special place for PEDESTRIANS to cross the road

**pe·di·a·tri·cian, paediatrician** /ˌpiːdɪəˈtrɪʃən/ *n* a doctor who specializes in PEDIATRICS

**pe·di·at·rics, paediatrics** /ˌpiːdiˈætrɪks/ *n* [U] the branch of medicine concerned with children and their diseases

**ped·i·gree** /ˈpedǝ̇griː/ *n* **1** [A] (of animals, esp. dogs) descended from a recorded (and usu. specially chosen) family, and therefore of high quality **2** [C;U] (a set of) people (or animals) from whom a person (or animal) is descended: *a dog of unknown pedigree* –compare THOROUGHBRED, MONGREL

**ped·lar** also **peddler** /ˈpedləʳ/– *n* a person who goes from place to place trying to sell small articles: *a drug pedlar*

**pee**[1] /piː/ *v* [I] *infml* for URINATE

**pee**[2] *n* [S;U] *infml* an act or result of urinating (URINATE): *I think I'll go for/have a pee.*

**peek**[1] /piːk/ *v* [I *at*] *infml* to look (at something) quickly, esp. when one should not: *He just had time to peek into the room before the door closed.* –sounds like **peak**; compare PEEP[1], PEER[2]

**peek**[2] *n* [S] *infml* an act of PEEKing –sounds like **peak**

**peel**[1] /piːl/ *v* **1** [T] to remove the outer covering from (a fruit, vegetable, etc.): *a machine that peels potatoes* **2** [T *off*] to remove (the outer covering) from something: *Peel the skin off (the banana).*|*They peeled off their clothes and jumped into the water.* **3** [I] (of an outer covering or surface) to come off, esp. in small pieces: *My skin always peels when I've been in the sun.*|*The paint was peeling (off the walls).*

**peel**[2] *n* [U] the outer covering, esp. of those fruits and vegetables which one usu. PEELS[1] (1) before eating: *orange/apple peel* –compare RIND

**peel·ings** /ˈpiːlɪŋz/ *n* [P] parts PEELED[1] (1) off (esp. from potatoes)

**peep**[1] /piːp/ *v* [I *at*] to look quickly and secretly: *His hands were covering his face, but I could see him peeping through his fingers.* –compare PEEK[1], PEER[2]

**peep**[2] *n* [S *at*] *infml* a short, incomplete, and perhaps secret look: *He took a peep through the door.*

**peep**[3] *n* [S] a weak high sound as made by a young bird or a mouse: (fig.) *I don't want to hear a peep* (=even the smallest sound) *out of you.*

**peer**[1] /pɪəʳ/ *n* **1** an equal in rank, age, quality, etc.: *The opinion of his peers/his peer group is more important to him than his parents' ideas.* –see also PEERLESS **2** (in Britain) a member of any of five noble ranks (BARON, VISCOUNT, EARL, MARQUIS, and DUKE) **3** (in Britain) a person who has the right to sit in the HOUSE[1] (2) of Lords: **a life peer** (=one given this rank but not allowed to pass it on at death) –see also PEERESS

**peer**[2] *v* [I *at*] to look very carefully or hard, esp. as if not able to see well: *She peered through the mist, trying to find the right path.*|*He peered at me over the top of his glasses.* –compare PEEK[1], PEEP[1]

**peer·age** /ˈpɪərɪdʒ/ *n* [C;U] **1** the whole body of PEERS[1] (2,3) **2** the rank of a PEER[1] (2,3): *After ten years in the government she was given a peerage.*

**peer·ess** /ˈpɪərəs/ *n* **1** a female PEER[1] (3) **2** the wife of a PEER[1] (3)

**peer·less** /ˈpɪələs‖ˈpɪər-/ *adj fml* without an equal; better than any other –see also PEER[1] (1)

**peeve** /piːv/ *v* **peeved, peeving** [T *usu. pass.*] *infml* to annoy

**peev·ish** /ˈpiːvɪʃ/ *adj* bad-tempered; easily annoyed by unimportant things –**peevishly** *adv* –**peevishness** *n* [U]

**peg[1]** /peg/ *n* **1** a short piece of wood, metal, etc., used for fastening things, hanging things on, etc.: *Hang your coat on the peg in the hall.*|*First hammer the* **tent pegs** *into the ground, then tie the ropes onto them.* **2** also **clothespeg** *BrE*‖**clothespin** *AmE*– an instrument like this for hanging washed clothes on a line to dry **3 off the peg** (of clothes) not specially made to fit a particular person's measurements: *Off-the-peg clothes are usually cheaper than clothes made-to-measure.* (MEASURE[1] (7)) **4 square peg in a round hole** a person who is not suited to the position or group in which he/she is placed **5 take somebody down a peg (or two)** *infml* to show somebody that he/she is not as important as he/she thought he/she was

**peg[2]** *v* **-gg-** [T] **1** to fasten with a PEG[1] (1,2): *Peg the clothes (out) on the line to dry.* **2** to fix or hold (prices, wages, etc.) at a certain level

**peg out** *v adv* [I] *infml BrE* to die

**pe·jo·ra·tive** /pəˈdʒɒrətɪv‖-ˈdʒɔ-, -ˈdʒɑ-/ *n,adj fml* (a word, phrase, etc.) that suggests that somebody or something is bad or worthless: *"Mean" is a more pejorative word than "economical".*

**pe·kin·ese** /ˌpiːkəˈniːz/ *n* a small dog with long silky hair

**pel·i·can** /ˈpelɪkən/ *n* a large water bird which catches fish and stores them in a long baglike part under its beak

**pel·let** /ˈpelət/ *n* **1** a small ball of any soft material made by or as if by rolling between the fingers **2** a small ball of metal made to be fired from a gun

**pel·met** /ˈpelmət/ *n* a narrow piece of wood or cloth above a window that hides the rod on which curtains hang

**pelt[1]** /pelt/ *n* the skin of a dead animal, esp. with the fur still on it

**pelt[2]** *v* **1** [T *with*] to attack by throwing things at: *He pelted us with stones.* **2** [I *down*] (of rain) to fall heavily and continuously: *It's pelting (down)!* **3** [I] to run very fast: *They pelted down the hill.*

**pelt[3]** *n* **(at) full pelt** as fast as possible

**pel·vis** /ˈpelvəs/ *n* the bowl-shaped frame of bones at the base of the backbone (SPINE (1)) –**pelvic** *adj*

**pen[1]** /pen/ *n* an instrument for writing or drawing with ink, such as a BALLPOINT, FOUNTAIN PEN, or FELT-TIP PEN –see picture on page 105

**pen[2]** *n* a small piece of land enclosed by a fence, used esp. for keeping animals in

**pen[3]** *v* **-nn-** [T] *pomp* to write: *to pen some poetry*

**pen[4]** *v* **-nn-** [T *up, in*] to shut (animals) in a PEN[2]: (fig.) *I'm tired of being penned (up) in the office all day.*

**pe·nal** /ˈpiːnl/ *adj* [*no comp.*] **1** of punishment (by law): *penal laws*|**penal servitude** (=imprisonment in which one also has to do hard work) **2** for which one may be punished by law: *a penal offence*

**pe·nal·ize** ‖also **-ise** *BrE* /ˈpiːnəl-aɪz‖ˈpiːnəl-, ˈpenəl-/ *v* **-ized, -izing** [T *for*] **1** to punish, sometimes unfairly **2** (in sports) to punish (a player's action) by giving an advantage to the other team: *Their team was penalized for intentionally wasting time.*

**pen·al·ty** /ˈpenlti/ *n* **-ties 1** the punishment for breaking a law, rule, or agreement in law: *She has* **paid the penalty** *for her crimes.*|(fig.) *One of the penalties of fame is that people point at you in the street.* **2** something (such as a number of years in prison or an amount of money to be paid) that is ordered as a punishment: *Fishing in this river is forbidden; penalty £5.* **3** (in sports) a disadvantage suffered by a player or team for breaking a rule: *We were given a* **penalty (kick)** (=a free kick at the GOAL) *after one of our players was hit.* –see picture on page 592

**pen·ance** /ˈpenəns/ *n* [U] self-punishment suffered, esp. for religions reasons, to show that one is sorry for having done wrong

**pence** /pens/ *BrE pl. of* PENNY –see also TWOPENCE, SIXPENCE; see PENNY (USAGE)

**pen·chant** /ˈpɒnʃɒn, ˈpentʃənt‖ˈpentʃənt/ *n* [*for*] *French* a strong liking

**pen·cil[1]** /ˈpensəl/ *n* a narrow pointed instrument, usu. wooden, containing a thin stick of a black substance or coloured material, used for writing, drawing, or (an **eyebrow pencil**) for darkening the EYEBROWS –see picture on page 105

**pencil[2]** *v* **-ll-** *BrE*‖**-l-** *AmE* [T] to draw, write, or mark with a PENCIL[1]

**pen·dant, -dent** /ˈpendənt/ *n* a hanging piece of jewellery, esp. a chain worn round the neck with a small decorative object hanging from it

**pend·ing[1]** /ˈpendɪŋ/ *prep* until: *This matter must wait pending her return from Europe.*

**pending[2]** *adj* [F *no comp.*] waiting to be decided or settled

**pen·du·lous** /ˈpendjʊləs‖-dʒə-/ *adj fml* hanging down loosely so as to swing freely: *pendulous breasts*

**pen·du·lum** /ˈpendjʊləm‖-dʒə-/ *n* a weight hanging from a fixed point so as to swing freely, esp. as used to control the working of a clock

**pen·e·trate** /ˈpenətreɪt/ *v* **-trated, -trating 1** [I;T *through, into*] to enter, cut, or force a way (into or through something): *The knife penetrated his stomach.*|*The rain penetrated through to his skin.* **2** [T] to understand: *to penetrate the mystery of the atom* –see also IMPENETRABLE –**penetrable** /-trəbəl/ *adj* –**penetrability** /-ˈbɪləti/ *n* [U]

**pen·e·trat·ing** /ˈpenətreɪtɪŋ/ *adj* **1** (of the eye, questions, etc.) sharp and searching **2** (of a person, the mind, etc.) able to understand clearly and deeply **3** (of sounds) sharp and loud: *a penetrating voice* –**penetratingly** *adv*

**pen·e·tra·tion** /ˌpenəˈtreɪʃən/ *n* [U] **1** the act or action of penetrating (PENETRATE) **2** the ability to understand quickly and clearly

**pen friend** /ˈ· ·/ *BrE*‖**pen pal** *AmE*– *n* a person, esp. in a foreign country, whom one has come to know by the friendly exchange of letters

**pen·guin** /ˈpeŋgwən/ *n* a large black-and-white

flightless seabird of esp. the ANTARCTIC

**pen·i·cil·lin** /ˌpenᵊˈsɪlᵊn/ *n* [U] a substance used as a medicine to destroy certain bacteria in people and animals

**pe·nin·su·la** /pᵊˈnɪnsjʊlə||-sələ/ *n* a piece of land almost completely surrounded by water: *Italy is a peninsula.* –**peninsular** *adj*

**pe·nis** /ˈpiːnᵊs/ *n* **-nises** *or* **-nes** /niːz/ the outer sex organ of males

**pen·i·tent** /ˈpenᵊtənt/ *adj fml* feeling or showing sorrow for having done wrong, with the intention not to do so again –opposite **impenitent** –**penitently** *adv* –**penitence** *n* [U]

**pen·i·ten·tia·ry** /ˌpenᵊˈtenʃəri/ *n* **-ries** a prison, esp. in the US

**pen·knife** /ˈpen-naɪf/ *n* **-knives** /naɪvz/ a small knife with usu. two folding blades, usu. carried in the pocket

**pen name** /ˈ· ·/ *n* a name used by a writer instead of his/her real name –see also PSEUDONYM

**pen·nant** /ˈpenənt/ *n* a long narrow pointed flag, esp. as used by schools, sports teams, etc., or on ships for signalling

**pen·ni·less** /ˈpenɪlᵊs/ *adj* having no money

**pen·ny** /ˈpeni/ *n* **pennies** *or* **pence** /pens/ *BrE or* **p** *BrE infml* **1** [C] also **copper, p** *BrE infml*– (in Great Britain after 1971) a small copper and tin (BRONZE) coin, 100 of which make a pound **2** [C] also **copper** *BrE infml*– (in Great Britain before 1971) a BRONZE coin, 12 of which made a shilling; 1d **3** [C] (in the US and Canada) (a coin worth) a cent **4** [S] (*used in* NEGATIVE[1] *sentences*) a small amount of money: *The journey won't cost you a penny if you come in my car.* **5 in for a penny, in for a pound** if something has been begun it should be finished whatever the cost may be **6 spend a penny** *euph* for URINATE **7 the penny dropped/has dropped** *BrE infml* the meaning (of something said) was at last understood **8 -penny** having the value of a certain number of pennies: *a threepenny stamp*

USAGE For the plural, use **pennies** to mean the coins themselves, and **pence** or **p** for an amount of money: *She had several coins in her pocket, but no* **pennies.**|It only cost a few **pence**/*30* **pence**/*five* **p.**

**pen pal** /ˈ· ·/ *n AmE* for PEN FRIEND

**pen·sion**[1] /ˈpenʃən/ *n* an amount of money paid regularly (esp. by a government or a company) to someone who no longer works, esp. because of old age or illness –see also OLD AGE PENSION

**pension**[2] *v* →PENSION OFF

**pen·sion·a·ble** /ˈpenʃənəbəl/ *adj* giving one the right to receive a PENSION: *a man of pensionable age*

**pen·sion·er** /ˈpenʃənəʳ/ *n* a person who is receiving a PENSION

**pension** sbdy.↔ **off** *v adv* [T] to dismiss from work but continue to pay a PENSION to

**pen·sive** /ˈpensɪv/ *adj* deeply, perhaps sadly, thoughtful: *The woman in this painting has a pensive smile.* –**pensively** *adv* –**pensiveness** *n* [U]

**pen·ta·gon** /ˈpentəgən||-gɑn/ *n* a flat shape with five sides and five angles –**pentagonal** /penˈtægənl/ *adj*

**Pentagon** *n* [*the* S] (the chief officers working in) the building in Washington from which the armed forces of the US are directed

**pen·ta·gram** /ˈpentəgræm/ *n* a five-pointed star, used as a magic sign

**pen·tath·lon** /penˈtæθlən/ *n* a sports event in which those taking part have to compete in five different sports (running, swimming, riding, shooting, and fencing (FENCE[2] (1))

**pent·house** /ˈpenthaus/ *n* a desirable small house or set of rooms built on top of a tall building

**pent up** /ˌ· ˈ·◂/ *adj* shut up within narrow limits: *I don't like being pent up in the house all the time.*|(fig.) *pent-up feelings*

**pe·nul·ti·mate** /pɪˈnʌltᵊmᵊt/ *adj* [A] next to the last: *November is the penultimate month of the year.*

**peo·ple**[1] /ˈpiːpəl/ *n* **1** [P] persons in general; persons other than oneself: *Were there many people at the meeting?|If you do that, people will start to talk (about your behaviour).|People who live in the south of England speak in a different way from people who live in the north.* **2** [*the* P] all the persons in a society, esp. those who do not have special rank or position: *a politician who was loved by the (common) people* **3** [C] a race; nation: *The Chinese are a hard-working people.|the peoples of Africa* **4** [P] the persons from whom one is descended and to whom one is related: *His people have lived in this valley for over 200 years.* **5 go to the people** (of a political leader) to hold an election or REFERENDUM in order to gain the approval of the PEOPLE[1] (2) for a government or a plan –see PERSON, RACE (USAGE)

**people**[2] *v* **-pled, -pling** [T] *fml* to fill with PEOPLE[1] (1): *a desert peopled only by wandering tribes*

**pep** /pep/ *n* [U] *infml* keen activity and forcefulness; VIGOUR

**pep·per**[1] /ˈpepəʳ/ *n* **1** [U] a hot-tasting powder made from the crushed seeds of certain plants, used for making food taste better –see picture on page 521 **2** [C] also **capsicum** *tech*– a large round, or long and narrow, red or green fruit, sometimes with a hot taste, used as a vegetable –**peppery** *adj*

**pepper**[2] *v* [T] **1** to add or give the taste of PEPPER[1] (1) to (food) **2** [*with*] to hit repeatedly (esp. with shots or with small but annoying things)

**pep·per·mint** /ˈpepəˌmɪnt||-ər-/ *n* **1** [U] a MINT[1] (1) plant with a special strong taste, used esp. in making sweets and medicine **2** [C] also **mint**– a sweet with this taste

**pep pill** /ˈ· ·/ *n infml* a PILL (1) taken to make one quicker in thought and action for a short time

**pep talk** /ˈ· ·/ *n infml* a talk intended to make people work harder, more quickly, etc.

**per** /pəʳ; *strong* pɜːʳ/ *prep* for each: *apples costing 30 pence per pound|Our charge is £6 per hour/an hour.|My rent is £600* **per annum.** (=per year)

**per·am·bu·la·tor** /pəˈræmbjʊleɪtəʳ||-bjə-/ *n fml* for PRAM

**per·ceive** /pəˈsiːv||pər-/ *v* **-ceived, -ceiving** [T +(*that*)] *fml* to have or come to have knowledge of (something) through one of the senses (esp. sight) or through the mind; see: *She cannot perceive the difference between red and green.|We perceived that we were unwelcome and left.* –**perceivable** *adj*

USAGE Compare **perceive** and **conceive**: You **perceive** (=become conscious of) something that already exists. You **conceive** (=form in the mind) a completely new idea: *We* **perceived** *that the teacher was angry with us.*|*She* **conceived** *a bold plan of escape.*

**per cent** /· '·/ *adv,n* (one part) in or for each 100; %: *The restaurant has a service charge of ten per cent (10%).*|(fig.) *I am 100 per cent in agreement with you.* (=totally in agreement)

**per·cen·tage** /pə'sentɪdʒ‖pər-/ *n* [*usu. sing.*] an amount stated as if it is part of a whole which is 100; PROPORTION (3): *What percentage of people die of this disease every year?*

**per·cep·ti·ble** /pə'septəbəl‖pər-/ *adj fml* able to be PERCEIVEd; noticeable –opposite **imperceptible** –**perceptibly** *adv*

**per·cep·tion** /pə'sepʃən‖pər-/ *n* **1** [U] also **perceptiveness**– the ability to PERCEIVE; keen natural understanding: *a woman of great perception* **2** [C] a result of perceiving (PERCEIVE); something noticed and understood: *my sudden perception of the difficulty*

**per·cep·tive** /pə'septɪv‖pər-/ *adj* quick to notice and understand –compare SENSITIVE –**perceptively** *adv* –**perceptiveness** *n* [U]

**perch¹** /pɜːtʃ‖pɜrtʃ/ *n* **1** a branch, rod, etc., where a bird rests **2** a high position in which a person or building is placed: *From our perch up there on top of the cliff we can see the whole town.*

**perch²** *v* **1** [I] (of a bird) to come to rest from flying: *The birds perched on the telephone wires.* **2** [I;T] to (cause to) go into or be in the stated position (esp. unsafely, or on something narrow or high): *She perched (herself) on a tall chair.*|*a house perched on the edge of the cliffs*

**perch³** *n* **perch** *or* **perches** a lake and river fish with prickly FINS, used as food

**per·co·late** /'pɜːkəleɪt‖'pɜr-/ *v* **-lated, -lating 1** [I *through*] (of liquid) to pass slowly (through a material having small holes or GAPS in it): (fig.) *News from the war percolated through to us very slowly.* **2** [T] also **perk** *infml*– to make (coffee) in a special pot by the slow passing of hot water through crushed coffee beans –**percolation** /-'leɪʃən/ *n* [C;U]

**per·co·la·tor** /'pɜːkəleɪtəʳ‖'pɜr-/ *n* a pot in which coffee is PERCOLATED (2)

**per·cus·sion** /pə'kʌʃən‖pər-/ *n* **1** [U] the forceful striking together of two (usu. hard) objects **2** [U +*sing./pl. v*] musical instruments that are played by being struck, esp. as a division of a band (**percussion section**): *The drum is a percussion instrument.*

**per·cus·sion·ist** /pə'kʌʃənɪst‖pər-/ *n* a person who plays PERCUSSION (2) instruments

**pe·remp·to·ry** /pə'remptəri/ *adj fml* (of a person, his/her manner, etc.) showing an expectation of being obeyed at once and without question; impolitely quick and unfriendly –**peremptorily** *adv*

**pe·ren·ni·al¹** /pə'renɪəl/ *adj* **1** lasting forever or for a long time; CONSTANT: *Politics provides a perennial subject of argument.* **2** (of a plant) living for more than two years –**perennially** *adv*

**perennial²** *n* a PERENNIAL¹ (2) plant

**per·fect¹** /'pɜːfɪkt‖'pɜr-/ *adj* **1** complete, with nothing missing, spoilt, etc.: *She still has a perfect set of teeth.* **2** of the very best possible kind, degree, or standard: *The weather during our holiday was perfect.*|*a perfect crime* (=one in which the criminal is never discovered) **3** suitable and satisfying in every way: *This big house is perfect for our large family.* **4** [A] *often infml* complete; thorough: *a perfect stranger* **5** [A] *tech* (of verb forms, tenses, etc.) concerning a period of time up to and including the present (**present perfect**), past (**past perfect**), or future (**future perfect**) (as in "*She has gone*", "*She had gone*", "*She will have gone*") –see also IMPERFECT²

**per·fect²** /pə'fekt‖pər-/ *v* [T] to make perfect: *He went to Germany to perfect his German.*

**per·fec·tion** /pə'fekʃən‖pər-/ *n* [U] **1** the state or quality of being perfect: *The meat was cooked* **to perfection.** –opposite **imperfection 2** the act of developing completely or making perfect: *The perfection of this new medical treatment may take several years.* **3** the perfect example: *As an actress, she is perfection itself.*

**per·fec·tion·ist** /pə'fekʃənɪst‖pər-/ *n sometimes derog* a person who is not satisfied with anything that is not PERFECT¹: *It takes him hours to cook a simple meal because he's such a perfectionist.*

**per·fect·ly** /'pɜːfɪktli‖'pɜr-/ *adv* **1** in a perfect way: *She speaks French perfectly.* –opposite **imperfectly 2** very; completely: *The walls must be perfectly clean before you paint them.*

**per·fid·i·ous** /pə'fɪdɪəs‖pər-/ *adj fml & lit* disloyal; TREACHEROUS (1) –**perfidiously** *adv*

**per·fi·dy** /'pɜːfɪdi‖'pɜr-/ *n* **-dies** [C;U] *fml & lit* (an example of) disloyalty; TREACHERY

**per·fo·rate** /'pɜːfəreɪt‖'pɜr-/ *v* **-rated, -rating** [T] to make a hole or holes through (something) such as paper –**perforation** /,pɜːfə'reɪʃən‖,pɜr-/ *n* [U;C *often pl.*]: *perforations between postage stamps*

**per·form** /pə'fɔːm‖pər'fɔrm/ *v* **1** [T] to do; carry out (a piece of work, an order, etc.): *The doctor performed the operation.*|*Who will perform the marriage ceremony for them?* **2** [I;T] to give, act or show (a play, a part in a play, a piece of music, etc.) esp. before the public: *What play will be performed tonight?*|*She will be performing at the piano.* **3** [I] to work or carry out an activity (in the stated way): *This car performs well/badly on long journeys.*

**per·form·ance** /pə'fɔːməns‖pər'fɔr-/ *n* **1** [C;U] the action of PERFORMING (1,2), or an action PERFORMED (1,2): *Our football team's performance has been excellent this year.*|*His performance of/as Othello was terrible.*|*The band will give two more performances before leaving Britain.* **2** [U] (of people or machines) the ability to do something, esp. needing skill: *The car's performance on corners needs to be improved.*

**per·form·er** /pə'fɔːməʳ‖pər'fɔr-/ *n* a person (or thing) that PERFORMS (2), esp. an actor, musician, etc. –compare SPECTATOR

**per·fume¹** /'pɜːfjuːm‖pər'fjuːm/ also **scent**– *n* [C;U] **1** a sweet or pleasant smell, as of flowers **2** sweet-smelling liquid, often made from flowers, for use esp. on a woman's face, wrists, and body

**per·fume²** /pə'fjuːm‖pər-/ *v* **-fumed, -fuming** [T] **1** *fml or lit* to fill with PERFUME¹ (1): *roses perfuming the air* **2** to put PERFUME¹ (2) on: *a perfumed handkerchief*

**per·func·to·ry** /pə'fʌŋktəri‖pər-/ *adj fml* done hastily and without thought, interest, or care –**perfunctorily** *adv* –**perfunctoriness** *n* [U]

**per·haps** /pə'hæps‖pər-/ *adv* **1** it may be; possibly: *Perhaps it'll rain.*|*"Will he come?" "Perhaps not."* **2** (used when asking for something politely): *Perhaps you could help me ..?* (=please help me)

**per·il** /'perɨl/ *n fml* **1** [U] danger, esp. of being harmed or killed **2** [C] something that causes danger **3 at one's peril** (used when advising someone not to do something) with the near certainty of meeting great danger

**per·il·ous** /'perɨləs/ *adj fml* dangerous; risky –**perilously** *adv*

**pe·rim·e·ter** /pə'rɪmɨtə^r/ *n* the border round any closed flat figure or special area of ground, esp. a camp or airfield: *The perimeter of the airfield is protected by guard-dogs.*|*a perimeter fence*

**pe·ri·od** /'pɪərɪəd/ *n* **1** a stretch of time with a beginning and an end, but not always of measured length: *There were long periods when we had no news of him.*|*Tomorrow's weather will be dry with sunny periods.* **2** a particular stretch of time in the development of a person, a civilization, the earth, an illness, etc.: *the Victorian period of English history*|*a play about the French Revolution, with all the actors wearing period clothes* (=clothes of that period) **3** a division of a school day; lesson: *a history period* **4** also **menstrual period** *fml*– a monthly flow of blood from the body of a woman –see also MENSTRUATE

**pe·ri·od·ic** /ˌpɪəri'ɒdɪk‖-'ɑ-/ also **periodical**– *adj* happening occasionally, usu. at regular times: *periodic attacks of fever* –**periodically** *adv*

**pe·ri·od·i·cal** /ˌpɪəri'ɒdɪkəl‖-'ɑ-/ *n* a magazine which appears at regular times (e.g. every month)

**per·i·pa·tet·ic** /ˌperɨpə'tetɪk/ *adj fml or tech* travelling about; going from place to place

**pe·riph·e·ral** /pə'rɪfərəl/ *adj* **1** of slight importance by comparison; not central: *matters of peripheral interest* **2** of or connected with a PERIPHERY –**peripherally** *adv*

**pe·riph·e·ry** /pə'rɪfəri/ *n* -**ries** *fml* [*usu. sing.*] a line or area enclosing something; outside edge: *the periphery of the town*

**per·i·scope** /'perɨskəʊp/ *n* a long tube with mirrors fitted in it so that people who are lower down (esp. in SUBMARINES) can see what is above them

**per·ish** /'perɪʃ/ *v* **1** [I] (in writing, and esp. in newspapers) to die, esp. in a terrible or sudden way; be completely destroyed: *Almost a hundred people perished in the hotel fire last night.* **2** [I;T] *BrE* to (cause to) decay or lose natural qualities: *The oil has perished the car tyres.*

**per·ish·a·ble** /'perɪʃəbəl/ *adj* (of food) that quickly decays –opposite **nonperishable** –**perishables** *n* [P]

**per·ish·ing** /'perɪʃɪŋ/ *adj BrE infml* (of weather) very cold: *It's really perishing (cold) this morning!*

**per·jure** /'pɜːdʒə^r‖'pɜr-/ *v* -**jured**, -**juring**: **perjure oneself** to tell a lie on purpose after promising solemnly to tell the truth (esp. in a court of law)

**per·jur·er** /'pɜːdʒərə^r‖'pɜr-/ *n* a person who PERJURES himself/herself

**per·ju·ry** /'pɜːdʒəri‖'pɜr-/ *n* [U] the act of perjuring oneself (PERJURE)

**perk**[1] /pɜːk‖pɜrk/ also **perquisite** *fml*– *n* [*usu. pl.*] *infml* money and goods (or non-material advantage) that one gets regularly from one's work apart from pay: *One of the perks of this job is that you don't have to work on Tuesdays.*

**perk**[2] *v* [I;T] *infml* for PERCOLATE (2)

**perk up** *v adv* [I;T (=**perk** sbdy.↔**up**)] *infml* to (cause to) become more cheerful, show interest, etc.

**perk·y** /'pɜːki‖'pɜrki/ *adj* -**ier**, -**iest** boldly cheerful; full of life and interest –**perkily** *adv* –**perkiness** *n* [U]

**perm**[1] /pɜːm‖pɜrm/ *BrE*‖**permanent** *AmE,* also **permanent wave** *fml*– *n infml* waves or curls put into hair by chemical treatment so that they will last for several months

**perm**[2] *v* [T] *BrE infml* to give a PERM to

**per·ma·nence** /'pɜːmənəns‖'pɜr-/ *n* [U] the state of being PERMANENT –opposite **impermanence**

**per·ma·nent** /'pɜːmənənt‖'pɜr-/ *adj* lasting or intended to last for a long time or for ever: *a permanent job/address* –compare TEMPORARY –**permanently** *adv*

**per·me·ate** /'pɜːmieɪt‖'pɜr-/ *v* -**ated**, -**ating** [I;T *through*] *more fml than* **pass through**– to pass through or into every part of (something): *Water permeated through the cracks in the wall.*|*A strong desire for political change permeated the country.* –**permeation** /-'eɪʃən/ *n* [U]

**per·mis·si·ble** /pə'mɪsəbəl‖pər-/ *adj* allowed; permitted

**per·mis·sion** /pə'mɪʃən‖pər-/ *n* [U +*to-v*] an act of PERMITting[1]; agreement; CONSENT: *We asked his permission to use the car.*|*Did she give you permission?*

**per·mis·sive** /pə'mɪsɪv‖pər-/ *adj often derog* allowing a great deal of, or too much, freedom, esp. in sexual matters (often in the phrase **the permissive society**) –**permissively** *adv* –**permissiveness** *n* [U]

**per·mit**[1] /pə'mɪt‖pər-/ *v* -**tt**- *more fml than* **allow**– **1** [T +*to-v*/*v-ing*] to allow: *I cannot permit this to happen.*|*The rules of the club do not permit smoking.* **2** [I] to make it possible (for a stated thing to happen): *I will come in June if my health permits.*|*weather permitting* (=if the weather is good enough to allow it) **3** [T] also **permit of** *fml*– to allow as possible; admit: *The facts permit (of) no other explanation.*

**per·mit**[2] /'pɜːmɪt‖'pɜr-/ *n* an official written statement giving one the right to do something: *You can't work here without a permit.*

**per·mu·ta·tion** /ˌpɜːmjʊ'teɪʃən‖ˌpɜr-/ *n* [C;U] (esp. in MATHEMATICS) (the act of) changing the order of a set of things arranged in a group: *The six possible permutations of ABC are, ABC, ACB, BCA, BAC, CAB, and CBA.*

**per·ni·cious** /pə'nɪʃəs‖pər-/ *adj fml* very harmful; having an evil effect –**perniciously** *adv* –**perniciousness** *n* [U]

**per·nick·e·ty** /pə'nɪkɨti‖pər-/ *adj infml & often derog* worrying (too much) about small things; FUSSY

**per·ox·ide** /pə'rɒksaɪd‖-'rɑk-/ also **hydrogen peroxide** *fml*– *n* [U] *infml* a chemical liquid used to take the colour out of dark hair and to kill bacteria

**per·pen·dic·u·lar** /ˌpɜːpən'dɪkjʊlə^r‖ˌpɜrpən'dɪkjələr/ *adj* **1** exactly upright; not leaning to one side **2** [*to*] (of a line or surface) at an angle of 90 degrees to a line or surface –**perpendicularly** *adv*

**per·pe·trate** /'pɜːpɨtreɪt‖'pɜr-/ *v* -**trated**, -**trating** [T] *fml or humor* to be guilty of; do; COMMIT (1) (something wrong or criminal) –**perpetration** /-'treɪʃən/ *n* [U] –**perpetrator** *n*

**per·pet·u·al** /pəˈpetʃuəl‖pər-/ *adj* **1** lasting for ever or for a long time: *the perpetual snows on the mountains* **2** *often derog* happening often or uninterruptedly: *his perpetual complaints* **–perpetually** *adv*

**per·pet·u·ate** /pəˈpetʃueɪt‖pər-/ *v* **-ated, -ating** [T] to preserve; cause to be continued or remembered **–perpetuation** /-ˈeɪʃən/ *n* [U]

**per·pe·tu·i·ty** /ˌpɜːpʒˈtjuːʒti‖ˌpɜrpʒˈtuː-/ *n* [U] *fml* **in perpetuity** for a time without end: *The land was given to them in perpetuity.*

**per·plex** /pəˈpleks‖pər-/ *v* [T] to cause to feel confused and troubled by being difficult to understand or answer **–perplexed** *adj*: *They looked perplexed when I told them that their parents had gone.* **–perplexedly** /-ʒdli/ *adv*

**per·plex·i·ty** /pəˈpleksʒti‖pər-/ *n* [U] the state of being PERPLEXed

**per·qui·site** /ˈpɜːkwʒzɪt‖ˈpɜr-/ *n fml* for PERK[1]

**per se** /ˌpɜː ˈseɪ‖ˌpɜr ˈsiː, ˌpɜr ˈseɪ, ˌpeər ˈseɪ/ *adv Latin fml* considered alone and not in connection with other things

**per·se·cute** /ˈpɜːsɪkjuːt‖ˈpɜr-/ *v* **-cuted, -cuting** [T] to treat cruelly; cause to suffer (esp. for religious or political beliefs) **–persecution** /-ˈkjuːʃən/ *n* [C;U] **–persecutor** *n*

**per·se·ver·ance** /ˌpɜːsʒˈvɪərəns‖ˌpɜr-/ *n* [U] continual steady effort made to fulfil some aim

**per·se·vere** /ˌpɜːsʒˈvɪəʳ‖ˌpɜr-/ *v* **-vered, -vering** [I *at, in, with*] to continue firmly in spite of difficulties **–persevering** *adj*

**per·sist** /pəˈsɪst‖pər-/ *v* [I] **1** [*with, in*] to continue firmly (and perhaps unreasonably) in spite of opposition or warning: *If you persist in breaking the law you will go to prison.* **2** to continue to exist: *The cold weather will persist for the rest of the week.*

**per·sis·tent** /pəˈsɪstənt‖pər-/ *adj often derog* **1** continuing in a habit or course of action, esp. in spite of opposition or warning: *a persistent thief|your persistent attempts to annoy me* **2** continuing to exist, happen, or appear for a long time, esp. for longer than is usual or desirable: *a persistent cough* **–persistence** *n* [U] **–persistently** *adv*

**per·son** /ˈpɜːsən‖ˈpɜr-/ *n* **1** [C] a human being: *You're just the person I wanted to see.* **2** [C] *sometimes derog* a human being, esp. somebody unknown or not named –see USAGE **3** [C;U] (in grammar) any of the three special forms of verbs or PRONOUNS that show the speaker (**first person**), the one spoken to (**second person**),or the human being or thing spoken about (**third person**) **4 in person** personally: *I can't come* **in person,** *but I'm sending my secretary.*

USAGE The usual plural of **person** is **people**: *Only one* **person**/*A lot of* **people** *replied to our advertisement.* **Persons** is formal, and often used in official writings, notices, etc.: *He was murdered by a* **person** *or* **persons** *unknown.*

**per·so·na** /pəˈsəunə‖pər-/ *n* (in PSYCHOLOGY) the outward character a person takes on in order to persuade other people (and himself/herself) that he/she is a particular type of person

**per·son·a·ble** /ˈpɜːsənəbəl‖ˈpɜr-/ *adj* attractive in appearance or character

**per·son·age** /ˈpɜːsənɪdʒ‖ˈpɜr-/ *n fml or pomp* a famous or important person

**per·son·al** /ˈpɜːsənəl‖ˈpɜr-/ *adj* **1** concerning, belonging to, or for the use of a particular person; private: *father's personal chair|a letter marked "Personal"* **2** done or made directly by a particular person, not by a representative: *The minister made a personal visit to the scene of the fighting.* **3** of the body or appearance: *Personal cleanliness is important for health.* **4** (of remarks) directed against (the appearance or character of) a particular person: *I told them not to make personal remarks about him.* **5** (in grammar) showing the PERSON (3) –see also IMPERSONAL, PERSONAL PRONOUN

**personal col·umn** /ˈ··· ˌ··/ *n* a part of a newspaper that gives or asks for messages, news, etc., about particular persons

**per·son·al·i·ty** /ˌpɜːsəˈnælʒti‖ˌpɜr-/ *n* **-ties 1** [C;U] the qualities that make up the whole nature or character of a particular person: *He has a weak personality.* **2** [U] unusual, strong, exciting character: *She has a lot of personality.* **3** [C] a person who is well known to the public or to people connected with some particular activity: *a television personality*

**per·son·al·ize** ‖also **-ise** *BrE* /ˈpɜːsənəlaɪz‖ˈpɜr-/ *v* **-ized, -izing 1** [I;T] *often derog* to change so as to be concerned with personal matters or relationships rather than with facts: *Let's not personalize (this argument).* **2** [T] to make PERSONAL (1), esp. by adding one's address or one's name: *personalized handkerchiefs*

**per·son·al·ly** /ˈpɜːsənəli‖ˈpɜr-/ *adv* **1** directly and not through somebody acting for one: *He is personally in charge of all the arrangements.* **2** speaking for oneself only; as far as oneself is concerned: *She said she didn't like it, but personally I thought it was very good.* **3** as a person; not considered for any qualities that are not PERSONAL (1): *Personally she may be very charming, but is she a good doctor?* **4** as directed against oneself in a PERSONAL (4) way: *Don't take my remarks about your plan personally.*

**personal pro·noun** /ˌ··· ˈ··/ *n* a word standing for a noun (PRONOUN) and used for showing the speaker, the one spoken to, or the one spoken of: *"I", "you", and "they" are personal pronouns.*

**per·son·i·fy** /pəˈsɒnʒfaɪ‖pərˈsɑ-/ *v* **-fied, -fying** [T] to be a (perfect) example of; be the living form of (some quality) **–personification** /-fʒˈkeɪʃən/ *n* [C;U]: *Although she is poor, she is* **the personification of** (=a perfect example of) *generosity.*

**per·son·nel** /ˌpɜːsəˈnel‖ˌpɜr-/ *n* [P] all the people employed by a company, in the armed forces, etc.: *army personnel|The company needs new personnel.*

**per·spec·tive** /pəˈspektɪv‖pər-/ *n* **1** [U] (the rules governing) the art of drawing solid objects on a flat surface so that they give a natural effect of depth, distance, and solidity (esp. in the phrase **in perspective, out of perspective**): *The picture looks strange because it has no perspective.|The objects in the background are out of perspective.* **2** [C;U] the way in which a matter is judged, so that background, future possible problems, etc., are taken into consideration: *We must look at the problem* **in perspective/in its proper perspective.** **3** [C *of*] a view, esp. one stretching far into the distance: (fig.) *a perspective of our country's history*

**per·spex** /ˈpɜːspeks‖ˈpɜr-/ *n* [U] *tdmk* (*sometimes cap.*) a strong plastic material that can be used instead of glass

**per·spi·ca·cious** /ˌpɜːspɪˈkeɪʃəs‖ˌpɜr-/ *adj fml or humor* having or showing keen judgment and understanding –**perspicacity** /-ˈkæsəti/ *n* [U]

**per·spi·ra·tion** /ˌpɜːspəˈreɪʃən‖ˌpɜr-/ *n* [U] *euph* for SWEAT[1] (1)

**per·spire** /pəˈspaɪəʳ‖pər-/ *v* **-spired, -spiring** [I] *euph* for SWEAT[1] (1)

**per·suade** /pəˈsweɪd‖pər-/ *v* **-suaded, -suading 1** [*into, out of*] to cause to do something by reasoning, arguing, begging, etc.: *Try to persuade him to come with us.|They persuaded us into/out of going* (=to go/not to go) *to the party.* –see also DISSUADE **2** to cause to feel certain; CONVINCE: *She was not persuaded of the truth of his statement.* –see CONVINCE (USAGE)

**per·sua·sion** /pəˈsweɪʒən‖pər-/ *n* **1** [U] the act of persuading (PERSUADE) **2** [U] the ability to influence others **3** [C] (a group holding) a particular belief: *people of different political persuasions*

**per·sua·sive** /pəˈsweɪsɪv‖pər-/ *adj* having the power to influence others to believe or do what one wishes –**persuasively** *adv* –**persuasiveness** *n* [U]

**pert** /pɜːt‖pɜrt/ *adj* slightly disrespectful in a bold and rather amusing way –**pertly** *adv* –**pertness** *n* [U]

**per·tain to** sthg. /pəˈteɪn‖pər-/ *v prep* [T] *fml* to belong to or have a connection with

**per·ti·na·cious** /ˌpɜːtəˈneɪʃəs‖ˌpɜr-/ *adj fml* determined; STUBBORN –**pertinacity** /-ˈnæsəti/ *n* [U]

**per·ti·nent** /ˈpɜːtənənt‖ˈpɜr-/ *adj* [*to*] *fml* connected directly (with something that is being considered); RELEVANT: *several pertinent questions* –opposite **irrelevant** –**pertinently** *adv*

**per·turb** /pəˈtɜːb‖pərˈtɜrb/ *v* [T] *fml* to cause to worry; put into a state of disorder

**pe·ruse** /pəˈruːz/ *v* **-rused, -rusing** [T] *fml or humor* to read through carefully –**perusal** /pəˈruːzəl/ *n* [C;U]

**per·vade** /pəˈveɪd‖pər-/ *v* **-vaded, -vading** [T] *fml or lit* (of smells and of ideas, feelings, etc.) to spread through every part of: *The smell of cooking pervaded the room.*

**per·va·sive** /pəˈveɪsɪv‖pər-/ *adj sometimes derog* of a kind that will probably or easily PERVADE; widespread: *the pervasive influence of television* –**pervasively** *adv* –**pervasiveness** *n* [U]

**per·verse** /pəˈvɜːs‖pərˈvɜrs/ *adj* (of people, actions, etc.) purposely continuing in what is wrong, unreasonable, or against the wishes of others: *We all wanted to go tomorrow, but he had to be perverse, and chose to go today.* –**perversely** *adv* –**perversity** also **perverseness**– *n* **-ties** [C;U]

**per·ver·sion** /pəˈvɜːʃən, -ʒən‖pərˈvɜrʒən/ *n* **1** [U] the action of PERVERTING[1] **2** [C] a PERVERTED[1] form (of what is true, reasonable, considered to be natural, etc.): *a sexual perversion*

**per·vert**[1] /pəˈvɜːt‖pərˈvɜrt/ *v* [T] **1** to turn (someone) away from what is right and natural, esp. to influence in the direction of (what are considered) unnatural sexual habits **2** to use for a bad purpose: *Scientific knowledge was perverted to help cause destruction and war.|To* **pervert the course of justice** *is to prevent justice being done.*

**per·vert**[2] /ˈpɜːvɜːt‖ˈpɜrvɜrt/ *n derog* a person whose sexual behaviour is not (considered) natural

**pe·se·ta** /pəˈseɪtə (*Spanish* peˈseta)/ *n* a Spanish coin, on which the Spanish money system is based

**pes·si·mis·m** /ˈpesəmɪzəm/ *n* [U] the habit of thinking that whatever happens will be bad –see also OPTIMISM –**pessimist** *n*: *A few pessimists think we will lose the election, but most of us are sure we will win.* –**pessimistic** *adj* –**pessimistically** *adv*

**pest** /pest/ *n* **1** a usu. small animal or insect that harms or destroys food supplies **2** *infml* an annoying person or thing

**pes·ter** /ˈpestəʳ/ *v* [I;T *for, with*] to annoy (somebody) continually, esp. with demands: *They pestered us for money.|My son has been pestering me to take him with me.*

**pes·ti·cide** /ˈpestəsaɪd/ *n* [C;U] a chemical substance used to kill PESTS (1)

**pes·ti·lence** /ˈpestələns/ *n* [C;U] *esp. old use* a disease that causes death and spreads quickly to large numbers of people

**pes·tle** /ˈpesəl, ˈpestl/ *n* an instrument with a heavy rounded end, used for crushing substances in a special bowl (MORTAR)

**pet**[1] /pet/ *n* [A;C] **1** an animal kept in the home as a companion: *a pet dog|She keeps a monkey as a pet.* **2** a person (esp. a child) or thing specially favoured above others: *She is the teacher's pet.*|(fig.) *Politicians are my* **pet hate**. (=thing I dislike most)

**pet**[2] *v* **-tt- 1** [T] to touch kindly with the hands, showing love **2** [I;T] *infml* to kiss and touch (another or each other) in sexual play

**pet·al** /ˈpetl/ *n* any of the (usu. coloured) leaflike divisions of a flower

**pe·ter out** /ˈpiːtəʳ/ *v adv* [I] to come gradually to an end

**pe·tite** /pəˈtiːt/ *adj apprec* (of a woman, her appearance, etc.) small and neat

**pe·ti·tion**[1] /pəˈtɪʃən/ *n* (a paper containing) a request or demand made to a government or other body, usu. signed by many people: *a petition against the closure of the local railway line*

**petition**[2] *v* [I;T +*to-v*/*for*] to make a PETITION or request to: *The people petitioned (the government) to be allowed to return to their island.*

**pet·ri·fy** /ˈpetrəfaɪ/ *v* **-fied, -fying 1** [T] *infml* to put into a state of great shock or fear: *I was so petrified by the face at the window that I couldn't move.* **2** [I;T] to turn into stone: *the Petrified Forest in Arizona*

**pet·ro·chem·i·cal** /ˌpetrəˈkemɪkəl/ *n* a chemical substance obtained from PETROLEUM or natural gas

**pet·rol** /ˈpetrəl/ *BrE*‖**gas, gasoline** *AmE*– *n* [U] a liquid obtained from PETROLEUM, used esp. for producing power in the engines of cars, aircraft, etc.: *We can fill (the car) up with petrol at the petrol station.*

**pe·tro·le·um** /pəˈtrəulɪəm/ *n* [U] a mineral oil obtained from below the surface of the earth, and used to produce PETROL, PARAFFIN, and various chemical substances

**petroleum jel·ly** /·ˌ··· ˈ··/ *n* [U] a solid substance made from PETROLEUM, used esp. as a medicine for the skin

**petrol sta·tion** /ˈ·· ˌ··/ *n BrE* for FILLING STATION

**pet·ti·coat** /'petikəut/ *n* a skirt worn by women as an undergarment

**pet·ty** /'peti/ *adj* **-tier, -tiest 1** (by comparison) unimportant: *petty difficulties* **2** *derog* having or showing a mind that is narrow and ungenerous: *petty acts of unkindness* **–pettily** *adv* **–pettiness** *n* [C;U]

**petty cash** /ˌ·· '·/ *n* [U] an amount of money kept ready in an office for making small payments

**petty of·fi·cer** /ˌ·· '···◂/ *n* [A;C] a NONCOMMISSIONED OFFICER in the navy

**pet·u·lant** /'petʃulənt||-tʃə-/ *adj* showing childish bad temper over unimportant things, or for no reason at all **–petulantly** *adv* **–petulance** *n* [U]

**pew** /pju:/ *n* **1** a long seat (BENCH (1)) for people to sit on in church **2** *humor* a seat (esp. in the phrase **take a pew**)

**pew·ter** /'pju:tə^r/ *n* [U] (dishes and vessels made from) a greyish metal made by mixing lead and tin

**PG** *n,adj* [A;C] *abbrev. for:* parental guidance; (a film) which may in parts be unsuitable for children –compare U

**pha·lanx** /'fælæŋks||'feɪ-/ *n* **-lanxes** *or* **-langes** /fə'lændʒi:z/ [C +*sing./pl. v*] **1** (in ancient Greece) a group of soldiers packed closely together for better protection **2** any group of people packed closely together for attack or defence

**phal·lus** /'fæləs/ *n* an image of the male sex organ (PENIS), esp. as used as a sign of sexual power **–phallic** *adj*

**phan·tom** /'fæntəm/ *n* a shadowy likeness of a dead person; GHOST

**pha·raoh** /'feərəu/ *n* [A;C] (*often cap.*) (the title of) the ruler of ancient Egypt

**phar·ma·ceu·ti·cal** /ˌfɑ:mə'sju:tɪkəl||ˌfɑrmə'su:-/ *adj* [A] connected with (the making of) medicine: *a pharmaceutical company*

**phar·ma·cist** /'fɑ:məsɪ̈st||'fɑr-/ *BrE*||**druggist** *AmE– n fml* a person who prepares and sells medicine; CHEMIST (2)

**phar·ma·col·o·gy** /ˌfɑ:mə'kɒlədʒi||ˌfɑrmə'kɑ-/ *n* [U] the scientific study of medicines and drugs **–pharmacologist** *n*

**phar·ma·cy** /'fɑ:məsi||'fɑr-/ *BrE*||**drugstore** *AmE– n* **-cies 1** [U] the making and/or giving out of medicine **2** [C] a shop where medicines are sold; CHEMIST'*s* (2) shop –compare DISPENSARY

**phase¹** /feɪz/ *n* **1** a stage of development: *a dangerous phase in relations between the two nations*|*Most children* **go through a phase** *of opposing all their parents' wishes.* **2** any of a number of changes in the appearance of the moon or a PLANET as seen from the earth at different times: *the phases of the moon*

**phase²** *v* **phased, phasing** [T] to plan or arrange in separate PHASES¹ (1): *The introduction of the metric system in Britain is being phased.* (=done in stages)

**phase sthg.↔ in/out** *v adv* [T] to introduce/remove in stages or gradually

**PhD** /ˌpi: eɪtʃ 'di:/ *n abbrev. for:* (a person who has gained) an advanced university degree

**pheas·ant** /'fezənt/ *n* **pheasant** *or* **pheasants** [C;U] (the meat of) a large long-tailed bird hunted for food

**phe·nom·e·nal** /fɪ'nɒmɪ̈nəl||-'nɑ-/ *adj* very unusual; scarcely believable: *phenomenal strength* **–phenomenally** *adv*

**phe·nom·e·non** /fɪ'nɒmɪ̈nən||fɪ'nɑmɪ̈nɑn, -nən/ *n* **-na** /nə/ **1** a fact or event in nature (or society), esp. one that is unusual and/or of scientific interest: *the phenomena of nature* **2** a very unusual person, thing, event, etc.

**phew, whew** /fju:/ *interj* (the sound of) a quick short whistling breath, either in or out, expressing gladness, tiredness, or shock

**phi·al** /'faɪəl/ ||also **vial** /'vaɪəl/ *AmE n* a small bottle, esp. one of liquid medicine

**phi·lan·thro·pist** /fɪ̈'lænθrəpɪ̈st/ *n* a person who is kind and helpful to those who are poor or in trouble, esp. by making generous gifts of money

**phi·lan·thro·py** /fɪ̈'lænθrəpi/ *n* [U] a feeling of kindness and love for all people, esp. as shown in an active way by giving help **–philanthropic** /ˌfɪlən'θrɒpɪk||-'θrɑ-/ *adj*

**phi·lat·e·ly** /fɪ̈'lætəli/ *n* [U] *tech* stamp-collecting **–philatelist** *n*

**phil·is·tine** /'fɪlɪ̈staɪn||-sti:n/ *n derog* a person who has no understanding of, or interest in, art, music, beautiful things, etc.

**phi·lol·o·gy** /fɪ̈'lɒlədʒi||-'lɑ-/ *n* [U] *tech* the science of the nature and development of words, language, or a particular language **–philologist** *n*

**phi·los·o·pher** /fɪ̈'lɒsəfə^r||-'lɑ-/ *n* **1** a person who studies (and sometimes teaches) PHILOSOPHY (1) **2** a person who has formed a PHILOSOPHY (2)

**phil·o·soph·i·cal** /ˌfɪlə'sɒfɪkəl||-'sɑ-/ also **philosophic** /ˌfɪlə'sɒfɪk||-'sɑ-/– *adj* **1** accepting (esp. difficulty or unhappiness) with calmness and quiet courage **2** of or concerning PHILOSOPHY (1): *the philosophical writings of Sartre* **–philosophically** *adv*

**phi·los·o·phize** ||also **-phise** *BrE* /fɪ̈'lɒsəfaɪz||-'lɑ-/ *v* **-phized, -phizing** [I *about*] to think, talk, or write like a PHILOSOPHER

**phi·los·o·phy** /fɪ̈'lɒsəfi||-'lɑ-/ *n* **-phies 1** [U] the study of the nature and meaning of existence, reality, knowledge, goodness, etc. **2** [C] any of various systems of thought having this as its base: *the philosophy of Aristotle*|(fig.) *Eat, drink, and be merry; that's my philosophy!* (=my rule for living)

**phlegm** /flem/ *n* [U] **1** the thick jelly-like substance produced in the nose and throat (esp. when one has a cold); yellow or green MUCUS **2** calmness; lack of excitement

**phleg·mat·ic** /fleg'mætɪk/ *adj fml* calm and unexcitable **–phlegmatically** *adv*

**pho·bi·a** /'fəubɪə/ *n* a strong and usu. unreasonable fear and dislike: *He has a phobia about water.*

**phoe·nix** /'fi:nɪks/ *n* an imaginary bird of ancient times, believed to burn itself at the end of its life and be born again from the ashes

**phone¹** /fəun/ *n* a telephone

**phone²** *v* **phoned, phoning** [I;T +*to-v*/*up*] to telephone: *Phone me (up) when you arrive at the station.*|*He phoned (me) to say he couldn't come.* –see TELEPHONE (USAGE)

**phone-in** /'· ·/ *BrE*||**call-in** *AmE– n* a radio or television PROGRAMME (2) during which telephoned questions, statements, etc., from the public are broadcast

**pho·net·ic** /fə'netɪk/ *adj* **1** of or concerning the sounds of human speech **2** using signs to represent the actual sounds of speech: *This dictionary uses a phonetic alphabet as a guide to pronunciation.* –**phonetically** *adv*

**pho·net·ics** /fə'netɪks/ *n* [U] *tech* the study and science of speech sounds

**pho·ney, phony** /'fəuni/ *adj* **-nier, -niest** *infml derog* pretended; false –**phoney, phony** *n*: *He's a phoney!*

**phos·pho·res·cence** /ˌfɒsfə'resəns‖ˌfɑs-/ *n* [U] the giving out of light with little or no heat –**phosphorescent** *adj*

**phos·pho·rus** /'fɒsfərəs‖'fɑs-/ *n* [U] a poisonous yellowish waxlike simple substance (ELEMENT (1)) that shines faintly in the dark and starts to burn when brought out into the air

**pho·to** /'fəutəu/ *n* **-tos** *infml* a photograph

**pho·to·cop·i·er** /'fəutəuˌkɒpɪə[r]‖-təˌkɑ-/ *n* a machine that makes photocopies (PHOTOCOPY) –see picture on page 415

**pho·to·cop·y** /'fəutəuˌkɒpi‖-təˌkɑpi/ *v,n* **-ied, -ying: -ies** [C;T] (to make) a photographic copy of a letter, drawing, etc. –compare XEROX

**pho·to·e·lec·tric cell** /ˌfəutəu-ɪˌlektrɪk 'sel/ *n* an instrument by which light is made to start an electrical apparatus working

**photo fin·ish** /ˌ·· '··/ *n* the end of a race in which the leaders finish so close together that a photograph has to be taken to show which is the winner

**pho·to·gen·ic** /ˌfəutəu'dʒenɪk, ˌfəutə-/ *adj* (esp. of people) having an appearance that looks pleasing or effective when photographed

**pho·to·graph**[1] /'fəutəgrɑːf‖-græf/ also **photo, picture** *infml*– *n* a picture obtained by using a camera and film sensitive to light: *Have you seen John's photograph in the newspaper?* (=a photograph of John)|*He* **took a photograph of** *the child.*

**photograph**[2] *v* [T] to take a photograph of

**pho·tog·ra·pher** /fə'tɒgrəfə[r]‖-'tɑ-/ *n* a person who takes photographs, esp. as a business or an art

**pho·to·graph·ic** /ˌfəutə'græfɪk/ *adj* [A] concerning, got by, or used in producing photographs –**photographically** *adv*

**pho·tog·ra·phy** /fə'tɒgrəfi‖-'tɑ-/ *n* [U] the art or business of producing photographs

**pho·to·stat** /'fəutəstæt/ *n,v* **-tt-** [T] *tdmk* (*sometimes cap.*) →PHOTOCOPY

**phras·al verb** /ˌfreɪzəl 'vɜːb‖'vɜrb/ *n* a small group of words that acts like a verb and consists usu. of a verb with an adverb and/or a PREPOSITION: *"Run out" and "use up" are phrasal verbs.* –see Study Notes opposite

**phrase**[1] /freɪz/ *n* **1** (in grammar) a small group of words without a FINITE verb, forming part of a sentence: *"Walking along the road" and "a packet of cigarettes" are phrases.* –compare SENTENCE, CLAUSE **2** a short expression, esp. one that is clever and very suited to what is meant

**phrase**[2] *v* **phrased, phrasing** [T] to express in (particular) words: *a politely phrased refusal*

**phrase·book** /'freɪzbuk/ *n* a book giving and explaining phrases of a particular (foreign) language, for people to use when they go abroad

**phra·se·ol·o·gy** /ˌfreɪzi'ɒlədʒi‖-'ɑ-/ *n* [U] *fml* the way in which words are chosen, arranged, and/or used: *scientific phraseology*

**phys·i·cal** /'fɪzɪkəl/ *adj* **1** of or concerning material things (as opposed to things of the mind, spirit, etc.): *the physical world* –compare MENTAL, SPIRITUAL **2** of or according to the laws of nature: *Is there a physical explanation for these strange happenings?* **3** of or concerning the body **4** [A] concerning the natural formation of the earth's surface: *physical* GEOGRAPHY **5** [A] (of certain sciences) of the branch that is connected with PHYSICS: *physical chemistry*

**phys·i·cally** /'fɪzɪkli/ *adv* **1** according to the laws of nature: *It's* **physically impossible** *to work so fast.* **2** with regard to the body: *He is physically fit, but mentally* (=with regard to the mind) *rather confused.*

**physical train·ing** /ˌ··· '··/ also **physical education** /ˌ··· ··'··/, **PT, PE** *abbrev. infml*– *n* [U] development of the body by games, exercises, etc., esp. in schools –compare GYM (2)

**phy·si·cian** /fɪ'zɪʃən/ *n* a doctor, esp. one who treats diseases with medicines (as opposed to a doctor who performs operations (SURGEON))

**phys·i·cist** /'fɪzɪsɪst/ *n* a person who studies PHYSICS

**phys·ics** /'fɪzɪks/ *n* [U] a science concerned with the study of matter and natural forces (such as light, heat, movement, etc.)

**phys·i·ol·o·gy** /ˌfɪzi'ɒlədʒi‖-'ɑ-/ *n* [U] a science concerned with the study of how the bodies of living things, and their various parts, work –**physiologist** *n* –**physiological** /ˌfɪzɪə'lɒdʒɪkəl‖-'lɑ-/ *adj*

**phys·i·o·ther·a·py** /ˌfɪziəu'θerəpi/ *n* [U] the use of exercises, rubbing, heat, etc., in the treatment of disease, broken limbs, etc. –**physiotherapist** *n*

**phy·sique** /fɪ'ziːk/ *n* the form and character of a human body –see BODY (USAGE)

**pi** /paɪ/ *n* (in GEOMETRY) a Greek letter (Π, π) used for representing the fixed RATIO of the CIRCUMFERENCE of a circle to its DIAMETER: *Pi equals about 22/7 or 3·14159.*

**pi·a·nist** /'pɪənɪst, 'pjɑː-‖pi'ænɪst, 'pɪə-/ *n* a person who plays the piano

**pi·an·o** /pi'ænəu/ also **pianoforte** /piˌænəu'fɔːti‖-fort-/ *fml*– *n* **-os** a large musical instrument, played by pressing narrow black or white bars (KEYS[1] (3)) which cause small hammers to hit wire strings

**pic·co·lo** /'pɪkələu/ *n* **-los** a small musical instrument that looks like a FLUTE but plays higher notes

**pick**[1] /pɪk/ *v* [T] **1** to choose: *He picked the biggest cake he could find.* **2** to pull or break off (part of a plant) by the stem from a tree or plant; gather: *He picked her a rose.*|*They've gone fruit-picking today.* **3** to take up or remove, usu. with the fingers or a pointed instrument, esp. separately or bit by bit: *picking the meat from a bone* **4** to remove unwanted pieces from, esp. with a finger or a pointed instrument: *Don't pick your nose!* **5** to make with or as with a pointed instrument (usu. in the phrase **pick a hole/holes in**) **6** *AmE* for PLUCK[1] (3) **7** to bring about intentionally (usu. in the phrase **pick a fight/quarrel with someone**) **8** to steal or take from, esp. in small amounts: *It's easy to have your pocket picked in a big crowd.*|*He's good at picking people's brains.* (=getting people to say what their ideas are, esp. so that he can use them for himself) **9** to unlock (a lock) with any instrument other than a key, esp. secretly and for a bad purpose: *They picked the lock and entered*

## STUDY NOTES phrasal verbs

Verbs like **give up**, **look after**, and **put up with** are important because they are very common in English. They are often thought to be difficult, but this dictionary makes it very easy for you to understand what they mean and how to use them.

**give up**, **look after**, and **put up with** do not mean the same as **give**, **look**, and **put**. For example, to **give** something **up** means "to stop having or doing something".

The dictionary helps you to learn the meaning of these PHRASAL VERBS by listing them under the main verb, so that they can be easily found. So **give up** is listed under **give**, after the meanings of the main verb:

> **give** *v* [T] to cause (someone) to have, receive, or own (something): *She gave him a book for his birthday.|Give me the bags while you open the door.*
> **give up** *v adv* [T] to stop having or doing: *The doctor told me to give up smoking.|I gave that idea up a long time ago.*

The entry for **give up** tells you that it means "to stop having or doing". This means that instead of saying:

*I* **stopped** *playing football after I left school.*

you could say:

*I* **gave up** *playing football after I left school.*

Phrasal verbs, just like main verbs, can be INTRANSITIVE or TRANSITIVE (see Study Notes on page 647). If they are intransitive, they are shown like this:

> **get by** *v adv* [I] to be able to continue one's way of life: *She can't get by on so little money.*

When they are transitive, this means that they must be followed by a noun or noun phrase (direct OBJECT). Transitive phrasal verbs are shown like this:

> **bring off** *v adv* [T] to succeed in doing (something difficult): *It was a very difficult job but Anne was able to bring it off successfully.*

Phrasal verbs are made up of a verb and a PREPOSITION, or a verb and an adverb, or both. This means that direct objects can sometimes follow the verb, and sometimes follow the preposition or adverb.

To help you to use phrasal verbs correctly, this dictionary actually shows you where the object goes, using the words:
sbdy. (=somebody)
sthg. (=something)

> **look up to** sbdy. *v prep* [T] to respect

this means that the object is a person, and that it can only follow the preposition:

*He always* **looked up to** *his older brother*

> **push** sbdy. **around** *v adv* [T] to treat roughly and unfairly, esp. in order to force obedience

this means that the object is a person, and that it can only follow the verb:

*That big boy* **pushes** everybody else **around.**
*Don't* **push** me **around**!

> **make** sthg. ↔ **up** *v adv* [T] to invent (a story, excuse, etc.)

this means that the object is a thing, in this case a story, excuse, etc, and the ↔ means that it can follow either the verb or the adverb:

*He* **made up** a story *for the children.*
*He* **made** a story **up** *for the children.*

But note that PRONOUNS *always* follow the verb.

*He* **made** it **up.**

> **acquaint** sbdy. **with** sthg. *v prep* [T] to tell; make known to

this means that the phrasal verb has two objects. The first object is a person, and follows the verb, the second object is a thing, and follows the preposition:

*I* **acquainted** him **with** the facts.

> **put** sthg. **down to** sbdy./sthg. *v adv prep* [T] to state that (something) is caused by (something else)

this means that the phrasal verb has two objects; a thing that follows the verb, and a person or a thing that follows **to** (not the adverb **down**):

*I* **put** his mistake **down to** his bad memory.
*I* **put** all the trouble **down to** Jean.

the house. **10 pick and choose** to choose very carefully, considering each choice for a long time **11 pick holes in** *usu. derog* to find fault with; find the weak points in

**pick at** sthg. *v prep* [T] to eat (a meal) with little effort or interest: *to pick at one's dinner*

**pick** sbdy./sthg.↔ **off** *v adv* [T] to shoot (people or animals) one by one, by taking careful aim

**pick on** sbdy. *v prep* [T] *infml* to choose, esp. for punishment or blame: *Why pick on me?*

**pick** sbdy./sthg.↔ **out** *v adv* [T] **1** to choose **2** to see clearly among others: *He picked out his sister in the crowd.*

**pick up** *v adv* **1** [T] (**pick** sbdy./sthg.↔ **up**) to take hold of and lift up: *Pick up the box by the handles.* –see picture on page 669 **2** [T] (**pick** sthg.↔ **up**) to gather together; collect: *Please pick up all your toys when you've finished playing.* **3** [I] to improve: *Trade is picking up again.* **4** [T] (**pick** sthg.↔ **up**) to gain; get: *Where did you pick up that book/your excellent English?* **5** [I;T (**pick** sthg.↔ **up**)] to (cause to) start again: *to pick up (the conversation) where we left off* **6** [T] (**pick** sbdy./sthg.↔ **up**) to collect; arrange to go and get: *Pick me up at the hotel.|I'm going to pick up my coat from the cleaner's.* **7** [T] (**pick** sbdy./sthg.↔ **up**) to collect in a vehicle **8** [T] (**pick** sbdy.↔ **up**) *infml* to become friendly with during a short meeting, usu. with sexual intentions: *I didn't like him: he was just trying to pick me up.* **9** [T] (**pick** sbdy.↔ **up**) to catch (a criminal): *The bank robbers have been picked up at the airport.* **10** [T] (**pick** sthg.↔ **up**) to be able to hear or receive (on a radio): *We picked up signals for help from the burning plane.* **11** [T] (**pick** sbdy. **up**) to raise (oneself) after a fall or failure: *Pick yourself up!* –see also PICK-UP

**pick²** *n* [U] **1** choice: *Which one do you want–***take your pick! 2** the best (of many) (esp. in the phrase **the pick of**)

**pick³** *n* **1** a sharp pointed, usu. small instrument: *an ice pick|a* TOOTHPICK **2** *infml* for PICKAXE

**pick·axe** ||also **-ax** *AmE* /ˈpɪk-æks/ *n* a large tool with a wooden handle fitted into a curved iron bar with two sharp points, used for breaking up roads, rock, etc.

**pick·er** /ˈpɪkəʳ/ *n* a person or instrument that gathers: *The cotton pickers want more money.*

**pick·et¹** /ˈpɪkᵻt/ *n* **1** a person placed at the entrance to a factory, shop, etc., to prevent anyone (esp. other workers) from going in during a STRIKE² **2** a soldier or group of soldiers with the special job of guarding a camp

**picket²** *v* [I;T] to surround or guard with or as PICKETS¹: *The workers picketed the factory (gates).*

**pick·le¹** /ˈpɪkəl/ *n* **1** [U] a liquid (esp. VINEGAR or salt water) used to preserve meat or esp. vegetables **2** [C;U] a (piece or pieces of) vegetable preserved in this **3 in a pickle** *infml* in a difficult position or condition

**pickle²** *v* **-led, -ling** [T] to preserve (food) in PICKLE¹ (1)

**pick·led** /ˈpɪkəld/ *adj* **1** (of food) which has been PICKLED²: *pickled onions* **2** [F] *infml* drunk

**pick-me-up** /ˈ· ·,·/ *n infml* something, esp. a drink or a medicine, that makes one feel stronger and more cheerful

**pick·pock·et** /ˈpɪk,pɒkᵻt||-,pɑk-/ *n* a person who steals things from people's pockets, esp. in a crowd –see THIEF (USAGE)

**pick-up** /ˈ· ·/ *n* **1** an act of PICKing **up 2** the part of a record-player which receives and plays the sound from a record **3** a light VAN having an open body with low sides

**pic·nic¹** /ˈpɪknɪk/ *n* a pleasure trip in which (cold) food is taken to be eaten somewhere outdoors: *They went on/for a picnic in the country.|Let's take a picnic with us!* (=the food itself)

**picnic²** *v* **-ck-** [I] to go on or have a PICNIC

**pic·to·ri·al** /pɪkˈtɔːrɪəl||-ˈto-/ *adj* having, or expressed in, PICTURES¹ (1) **–pictorially** *adv*

**pic·ture¹** /ˈpɪktʃəʳ/ *n* **1** [C] a painting or drawing: *Draw a picture of that tree.* –see picture on page 355 **2** [C] a photograph: *May I take your picture?* (=a picture of you) **3** [S] a person or thing that is beautiful to look at: *This garden is a picture in the summer.* **4** [S] the perfect example: *That baby is* **the picture of** *health.* **5** [C *usu. sing.*] what is seen on a television set or at the cinema: *You can't get a clear picture on this set.* **6** [C *usu. sing.*] an image in the mind, esp. an exact once produced by a skilful description: *This book gives a good picture of life in England 200 years ago.* **7** [C] a cinema film: *There's a good picture this week.* –see PICTURES

**picture²** *v* **-tured, -turing** [T] **1** to imagine: *I can't quite picture myself as a mother.* **2** to paint or draw so as to give an idea of: *The artist pictured him as a boy.*

**pic·tures** /ˈpɪktʃəz||-ərz/ *BrE*||**movies** *AmE*– *n* [*the* P] *infml* the cinema: *to go to the pictures*

**pic·tur·esque** /,pɪktʃəˈresk/ *adj* **1** charming or interesting enough to be made into a picture **2** (of language) unusually clear, strong, and descriptive

**pid·dling** /ˈpɪdlɪŋ/ *adj derog* small and unimportant

**pid·gin** /ˈpɪdʒᵻn/ *n* [C;U] a language which is a mixture of two or more other languages –compare CREOLE

**pie** /paɪ/ *n* [C;U] **1** a pastry case filled with meat or fruit, baked usu. in a deep dish (**pie dish**): *an apple pie|a meat pie|Have some more pie.* –compare TART **2 have a finger in every pie** to concern oneself with or be connected with different matters **3 pie in the sky** *infml* a hopeful plan or suggestion that has not been, or has little chance of being, put into effect

**pie·bald** /ˈpaɪbɔːld/ *adj,n* (a horse) coloured with large black and white shapes (PATCHES)

**piece** /piːs/ *n* **1** a bit, such as: **a** a part (of anything solid) which is separated, broken, or marked off from a larger or whole body: *a piece of land|He tore off a small piece of paper.|*(fig.) *Let me give you a piece of advice.* –see picture on page 449 **b** a single object that is an example of a kind or class, or that forms part of a set: *a piece of paper* (=a whole sheet)*|a piece of furniture* **2 a** any of many parts made to be fitted together: *You buy the table in four pieces which you put together.* **b** an object or person forming part of a set: *an 80-piece band* (=a group of musicians with 80 players or instruments) **3** one of a set of small objects or figures used in playing certain board games, esp. CHESS **4** an example of something made or done, esp. of a stated quality: *This watch is a*

Sometimes it is difficult to know which word you should use when you mean "a small part or piece of something". This diagram will help you find the right word.

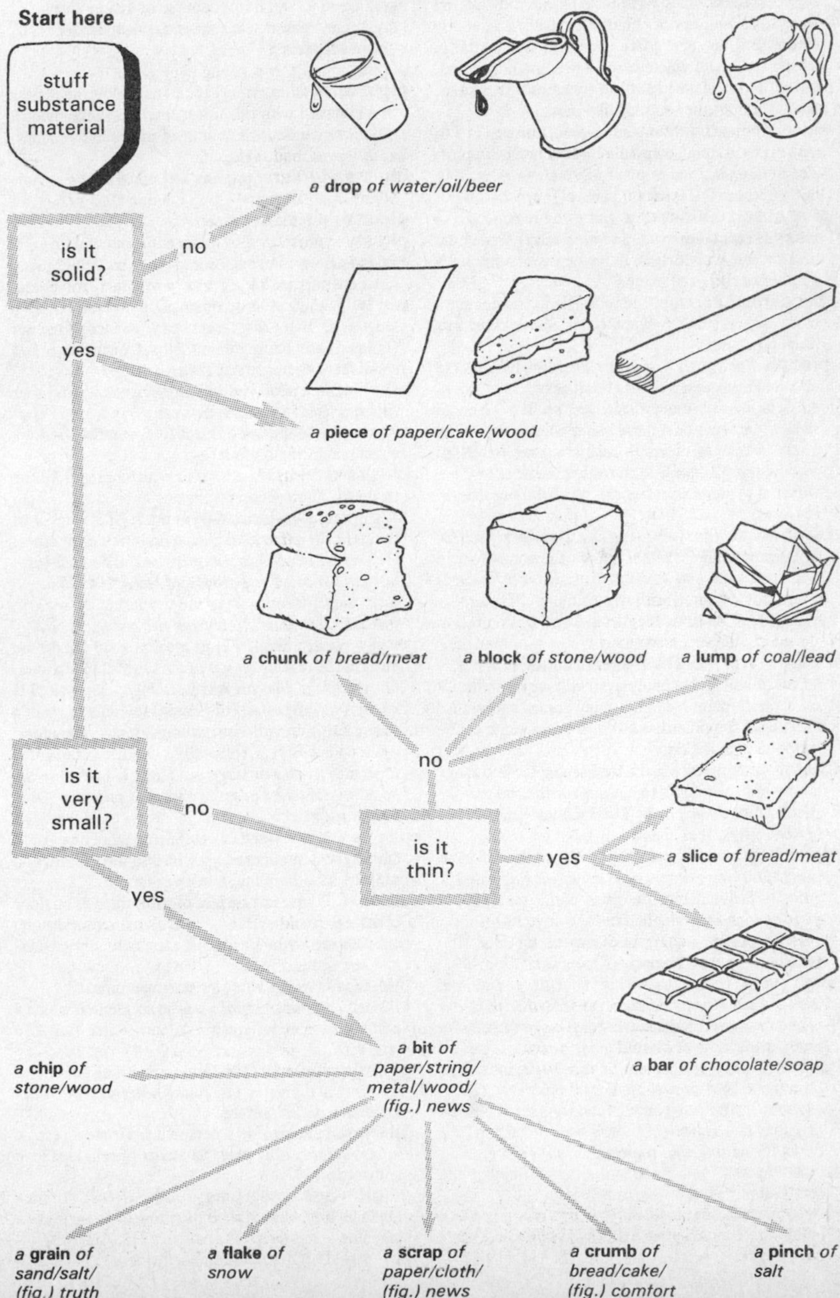

fine piece of work.|a quiet piece of music|Did you see the piece in the newspaper about Mrs. Smith's accident? **5** *BrE* a coin: *a 50-pence piece* **6 a piece of cake** *infml* something very easy to do **7 give somebody a piece of one's mind** to tell somebody angrily what one thinks of him/her; scold somebody severely **8 in one piece** *infml* **a** (of a thing) undamaged; still whole **b** (of a person) unharmed, esp. after an accident **9 piece by piece** one by one; one part at a time –sounds like **peace**

**piece** sthg.↔ **together** *v adv* **pieced, piecing** [T] **1** to make (esp. a story) complete by adding part to part: *The policeman tried to piece together the facts.* **2** to put together (the separate parts of)

**pi·èce de ré·sis·tance** /piː,es də reziː'stɒns/ *n* **pièces de résistance** (*same pronunciation*) *French* the best or most important thing or event, among a number of things or events

**piece·meal** /'piːsmiːl/ *adj,adv* (done, made, etc.) bit by bit; only one part at a time: *The building was assembled piecemeal.*

**piec·es** /'piːs$\frac{1}{2}$z/ *n* **1 go (all) to pieces** to lose the ability to think or act clearly because of fear, sorrow, etc. **2 in pieces** broken; destroyed **3 pull to pieces** to show to be ineffective: *She pulled their argument to pieces.* **4 take to pieces** to (cause to) separate into parts: *Take this engine to pieces and see what's wrong with it.* **5 to pieces** into (small) bits: *It fell to pieces in my hand.*

**piece·work** /'piːswɜːk‖-wɜrk/ *n* [U] work paid for by the amount done rather than by the hours worked

**pied** /paɪd/ *adj* [A] (esp. of certain types of bird) irregularly coloured with two or more colours

**pier** /pɪəʳ/ *n* **1** a bridgelike framework built out into the sea at which boats can stop to take in or land their passengers or goods **2** a framework like this at places where people go for holidays, with small buildings on it where people can eat, play games and amuse themselves **3** a pillar used to support a bridge or the roof of a high building

**pierce** /pɪəs‖pɪərs/ *v* **pierced, piercing** [I;T] to make a hole in or through (something) with a point: *The needle pierced her finger.*|*The knife pierced the rubber ball.*|(fig.) *A sudden cry pierced the silence.*

**pierc·ing** /'pɪəsɪŋ‖'pɪər-/ *adj* **1** very sharp, esp. in an unpleasant way: *a piercing cry*|*a piercing wind* **2** going to the centre or the main point; searching: *a piercing look* –**piercingly** *adv*

**pi·e·ty** /'paɪəti/ *n* [U] deep respect for God and religion –opposite **impiety**

**pig** /pɪg/ *n* **1** a fat, usu. pink, short-legged animal kept on farms for food –see MEAT (USAGE) **2** *derog* a bad-mannered person who eats too much: *John really* **made a pig of himself** *at the party.*

**pi·geon** /'pɪd3$\frac{1}{2}$n/ *n* **pigeons** *or* **pigeon** (the meat of) a quite large light-grey short-legged bird

**pi·geon·hole** /'pɪd3$\frac{1}{2}$nhəʊl/ *n* one of a set of boxlike divisions in a frame (e.g. on a wall or on top of a desk) for putting esp. papers in

**pigeon-toed** /,·· '·◂/ *adj* (of a person) having the feet pointing inwards

**pig·gy·back** /'pɪgibæk/ *adj,adv,n* (a ride given to a child who is) carried in a sitting position on one's back

**pig·gy·bank** /'pɪgibæŋk/ *n* a small container, usu. in the shape of a pig, used by children for saving coins

**pig·head·ed** /,pɪg'hed$\frac{1}{2}$d◂/ *adj derog* determinedly holding to an opinion or course of action in spite of argument, reason, etc.; STUBBORN –**pigheadedly** *adv* –**pigheadedness** *n* [U]

**pig·let** /'pɪgl$\frac{1}{2}$t/ *n* a young pig

**pig·ment** /'pɪgmənt/ *n* **1** [C;U] (a) colouring matter that is mixed with oil, water, etc., to make paint **2** [U] natural colouring matter of plants and animals, as in leaves, hair, skin, etc.

**pig·men·ta·tion** /,pɪgmən'teɪʃən/ *n* [U] the colouring of living things

**pig·my** /'pɪgmi/ *n* →PYGMY

**pig·sty** /'pɪgstaɪ/ also **pigpen** /'pɪgpen/ *AmE*– *n* **-sties 1** also **sty**– an enclosure with a small building in it, where pigs are kept **2** *infml* a very dirty room, etc.

**pig·tail** /'pɪgteɪl/ *n* (worn esp. by young girls) a length of hair that has been twisted together (PLAITed) and hangs down the back of the neck and shoulders –compare PONYTAIL

**pike¹** /paɪk/ *n* **pike** *or* **pikes** a large fish that eats other fish and lives in rivers and lakes

**pike²** *n* a long-handled spear formerly used by soldiers fighting on foot

**pil·chard** /'pɪltʃəd‖-ərd/ *n* a small sea fish like the HERRING, often preserved in tins as food

**pile¹** /paɪl/ *n* **1** a heap, esp. as made of a number of things of the same kind placed on top of each other: *We put the newspapers in piles on the floor.* **2** [*usu. pl.*] *infml* a lot: *I've got piles of work to do today.* **3** [*usu. sing.*] *infml* a very large amount of money; fortune: *She made a pile from her acting.*

**pile²** *v* **piled, piling 1** [T] to make a PILE¹ (1) of: *He piled the boxes one on top of the other.* **2** [T] to load, fill, or cover: *The cart was piled high with fruit.* **3** [I *in(to)*, *out (of)*] *infml* (of people) to come or go in a (disorderly) crowd: *Everyone piled into the room.*

**pile up** *v adv* [I;T (**pile** sthg.↔ **up**)] to (cause to) form into a mass or large quantity: *We piled up the boxes outside the house.*|*My work is piling up.* –see also PILE-UP

**pile³** *n* a heavy wooden, metal, or stonelike (CONCRETE²) post hammered upright into the ground as a support for a building, a bridge, etc.

**pile⁴** *n* [C;U] the soft surface of short threads on floor coverings (CARPETS) and some cloths (esp. VELVET)

**pile driv·er** /' ·,··/ *n* a machine for hammering PILES³ into the ground

**piles** /paɪlz/ *n* [P] *infml* for HEMORRHOIDS

**pile-up** /'paɪlʌp/ *n infml* a traffic accident in which a number of vehicles crash into each other –see also PILE **up**

**pil·fer** /'pɪlfəʳ/ *v* [I;T] to steal (something small or a lot of small things): *a boy found pilfering from other children's desks* –**pilferer** *n*

**pil·grim** /'pɪlgr$\frac{1}{2}$m/ *n* a person who travels (esp. a long way) to a holy place as an act of religious love and respect

**pil·grim·age** /'pɪlgr$\frac{1}{2}$mɪd3/ *n* [C;U] (a) journey made by a PILGRIM: *Aziz is planning to* **go on/make a pilgrimage** *to Mecca.* –see TRAVEL (USAGE)

**pill** /pɪl/ *n* **1** [C] a medicine in the shape of a small, hard ball which is swallowed **2** [*the* S] (*often cap.*) a PILL (1) taken regularly by women as a means of birth control: *She is* **on the pill**. (=taking the pill regularly)

**pil·lage¹** /ˈpɪlɪdʒ/ *n* [U] *old use* the act of pillaging (PILLAGE[2]); PLUNDER

**pillage²** *v* **-laged, -laging** [T] *old use* to steal things violently from (a place taken in war); PLUNDER

**pil·lar** /ˈpɪləʳ/ *n* **1** a tall upright usu. round post made of stone used as a support or decoration **2** [*of*] something in the shape of this: *a pillar of smoke* **3** [*of*] an important member and active supporter: *She has been a pillar of the church all her life.*

**pillar-box** /ˈ·· ·/ also **postbox**– *n BrE* a round pillar-shaped box in the street, into which letters are posted –see also LETTERBOX –see picture on page 297

**pil·li·on** /ˈpɪlɪən/ *n* a seat for a second person on a motorcycle, placed behind the driver

**pil·low** /ˈpɪləʊ/ *n* a cloth bag longer than it is wide, filled with soft material, used for supporting the head in bed

**pil·low·case** /ˈpɪləʊkeɪs/ also **pillow slip** /ˈ·· ·/– *n* a washable cloth covering for a PILLOW

**pi·lot¹** /ˈpaɪlət/ *n* **1** a person who flies an aircraft **2** a person with a special knowledge of a particular stretch of water, who is employed to go on board and guide ships that use it

**pilot²** *v* [T] **1** to act as PILOT of (an aircraft or ship) **2** to help and guide: *She piloted the old man through the crowd to his seat.*

**pilot³** *adj* [A] serving as a trial for something: *We're doing a pilot study to see if this product will sell well.*

**pilot light** /ˈ·· ·/ *n* a small gas flame kept burning all the time, used for lighting larger gas burners when the gas in them is turned on

**pimp** /pɪmp/ *n* a man who provides a woman (PROSTITUTE) for the satisfying of someone's sexual desires

**pim·ple** /ˈpɪmpəl/ *n* a small raised diseased spot on the skin –**pimply** *adj*: *pimply skin*

**pin¹** /pɪn/ *n* **1** a short thin piece of metal that looks like a small nail, used for fastening together pieces of cloth, paper, etc. **2** a thin piece of metal, pointed at one end and with a decoration at the other, used esp. as a form of jewellery **3** a short piece of wood or metal used as a support, for fastening things together, etc.; PEG

**pin²** *v* **-nn-** [T] **1** to fasten or join with a pin or pins –opposite **unpin 2** to keep in one position: *In the accident, he was pinned under the car.*

**pin** sbdy./sthg.↔ **down** *v adv* [T] **1** to fasten down; prevent from moving **2** to make give clear details, make a firm decision, etc.; NAIL **down** (2): *I won't pin you down to a particular day: come any day.*

**pin** sthg. **on** sbdy./sthg. *v prep* [T] to fix (guilt, etc.) on: *Don't try to pin the blame on me!*

**pin·a·fore** /ˈpɪnəfɔːʳ‖-for/ *n* **1** a loose garment that does not cover the arms or back, worn over a dress to keep it clean **2** also **pinafore dress** /ˈ··· ·/– a dress that does not cover the arms, and under which a BLOUSE or other garment is worn

**pin·cers** /ˈpɪnsəz‖-ərz/ *n* [P] **1** a tool made of two crossed pieces of metal and used for holding tightly and pulling small things, such as a nail from wood –compare PLIERS; see PAIR (USAGE) **2** the horny CLAWS of certain shellfish, used for seizing food

**pinch¹** /pɪntʃ/ *v* **1** [I;T] to press (esp. a person's flesh) tightly between two hard surfaces, or between the thumb and a finger, accidentally or on purpose: *He pinched her arm.* **2** [I] to give pain by being too tight: *Don't buy the shoes if they pinch.* **3** [T] *infml* to take without permission; steal: *My car's been pinched!*

**pinch²** *n* **1** an act of PINCHing[1] (1) **2** an amount that can be picked up between the thumb and a finger: *a pinch of salt* –see picture on page 449 **3 at a pinch** *BrE*‖**in a pinch** *AmE*– if necessary **4 feel the pinch** to be in difficulties because of lack of money

**pinched** /pɪntʃt/ *adj* [F *with*] (of the face) thin or tired-looking: *pinched with cold/anxiety*

**pin·cush·ion** /ˈpɪn,kʊʃən/ *n* a filled bag like a small CUSHION into which PINS[1] (1) are stuck until they are needed

**pine¹** /paɪn/ *v* **pined, pining** [I] **1** [*away*] to become thin and lose strength and health slowly, through disease or esp. grief **2** [+*to-v*/*for*] to have a strong but esp. unfulfillable desire

**pine²** *n* **1** [C] also **pinetree** /ˈpaɪntriː/– a tall tree with woody fruits (**pinecones**) and thin sharp leaves (**pine needles**) that do not drop off in winter, found esp. in colder parts of the world **2** [U] the white or yellowish soft wood of this tree

**pine·ap·ple** /ˈpaɪnæpəl/ *n* [C;U] (the sweet yellow flesh of) a large dark yellow tropical fruit with a mass of stiff leaves on top: *tinned pineapple*

**ping** /pɪŋ/ *v,n* [I;S] (to make) a short sharp ringing sound, e.g. by hitting a glass with something hard

**ping-pong** /ˈ· ·/ *n* [U] *infml* for TABLE TENNIS

**pinion** /ˈpɪnɪən/ *v* [T] *fml* to prevent the movement of (a person or animal) by holding or tying up the limbs

**pink¹** /pɪŋk/ *n,adj* [U] **1** pale red **2 in the pink (of condition/health)** *usu. humor* in perfect health; very well

**pink²** *v* [I] (of a car engine) to make high knocking sounds as a result of not working properly

**pink·ish** /ˈpɪŋkɪʃ/ *adj* slightly PINK[1]

**pin·na·cle** /ˈpɪnəkəl/ *n* **1** a pointed stone decoration built on a roof, esp.in old churches and castles **2** a thin tall pointed rock or rocky mountain top **3** the highest point or degree: *the pinnacle of one's success*

**pin·point** /ˈpɪnpɔɪnt/ *v* [T] **1** to find or describe the exact nature or cause of **2** to show the exact position of

**pin·prick** /ˈpɪn,prɪk/ *n* a small mark made (as if) by a pin

**pins and nee·dles** /,· · ˈ··/ *n* [P] *infml* slight continuous pricking feelings in a part of the body (esp. a limb) to which the supply of blood is returning

**pin·stripe** /ˈpɪnstraɪp/ *n* any of a number of thin (usu. white) lines repeated at regular spaces along (usu. dark) cloth to form a pattern: *Some businessmen wear pinstripe suits.* –**pinstriped** *adj*

**pint** /paɪnt/ *n* **1** a measure for liquids, equal to about 0.57 of a litre; half a QUART **2** *infml* a drink of beer of this amount

**pin·up** /ˈpɪnʌp/ *n* a picture of an attractive person, such as a popular singer, a woman wearing no clothes, etc., esp. as stuck up on a wall

**pi·o·neer¹** /ˌpaɪəˈnɪəʳ/ *n* **1** one of the first settlers in a new or unknown land **2** a person who does something first and so prepares the way for others: *a pioneer of operations on the human heart*
**pioneer²** *v* [T] to begin or help in the early development of
**pi·ous** /ˈpaɪəs/ *adj* showing and feeling deep respect for God and religion –opposite **impious** –**piously** *adv*
**pip¹** /pɪp/ *n* a small fruit seed, esp. of an apple, orange, etc.
**pip²** *n* a short high-sounding note, esp. as given on the radio to show the exact time, or as used in the operation of telephones: *Don't put any money into the telephone until you hear the pips.*
**pip³** *v* **-pp-** *BrE infml* **pipped at the post** just beaten at the end of some struggle
**pipe¹** /paɪp/ *n* **1** a tube used for carrying liquids and gas: *a hot-water pipe* **2** a small tube with a bowl-like container at one end, used for smoking tobacco: *He lit his pipe.* **3 a** a simple tubelike musical instrument, played by blowing **b** any of the tubelike metal parts through which air is forced in an ORGAN (3)
**pipe²** *v* **piped, piping 1** [T *into, to*] to carry (esp. liquid or gas) through PIPES¹ (1) **2** [I;T] to play (music) on a PIPE¹ (3a) or on BAGPIPES
**pipe down** *v adv* [I] *infml* to stop talking; be quiet
**pipe up** *v adv* [I] *infml* to begin to speak or sing, esp. in a high voice
**piped mu·sic** /ˌ·ˈ··/ also **canned music**– *n* [U] *derog* quiet recorded music played continuously in a public place, such as a shop or restaurant
**pipe dream** /ˈ· ·/ *n* an impossible hope, plan, idea, etc.
**pipe·line** /ˈpaɪp-laɪn/ *n* **1** a long line of PIPES¹ (1), often underground, for carrying liquids or gas **2 in the pipeline** on the way
**pip·er** /ˈpaɪpəʳ/ *n* a musician who plays on a PIPE¹ (3a), or esp. on BAGPIPES
**pipes** /paɪps/ *n* [P] *infml* for BAGPIPES
**pip·ing¹** /ˈpaɪpɪŋ/ *n* [U] **1** a number or system of PIPES¹ (1); pipes in general **2** the act or art of playing on a PIPE¹(3a) or BAGPIPES
**piping²** *adv* **piping hot** (esp. of liquids or food) very hot: *piping hot soup*
**pi·quant** /ˈpiːkənt/ *adj fml* **1** having a pleasant sharp taste **2** pleasantly interesting and exciting to the mind –**piquancy** *n* [U] –**piquantly** *adv*
**pique¹** /piːk/ *n* [U] a feeling of displeasure, esp. caused by the hurting of one's pride: *He left* **in a fit of pique.**
**pique²** *v* **piqued, piquing** [T *usu. pass.*] to make angry by hurting the pride
**pi·ra·cy** /ˈpaɪərəsi/ *n* [U] **1** robbery by PIRATES¹ (1) **2** the action of pirating (PIRATE²)
**pi·ra·nha** /pɪ̆ˈrɑːnjə, -nə/ *n* a fierce South American meat-eating river fish
**pi·rate¹** /ˈpaɪərət/ *n* **1** (esp. formerly) a person who sails the seas stopping and robbing ships **2** a person who uses the work of other people without permission, e.g. one who prints and sells a book without permission to do so –**piratical** /paɪˈrætɪkəl, pɪ̆-/ *adj*
**pirate²** *v* **-rated, -rating** [T] to make and sell (a book, newly invented article, etc.) without permission, when the right to do so belongs to someone else
**pir·ou·ette¹** /ˌpɪruˈet/ *n* a very fast turn made on the front part of one foot, esp. as done by a BALLET dancer
**pirouette²** *v* **-etted, -etting** [I] to dance one or more PIROUETTES
**Pis·ces** /ˈpaɪsiːz/ *n* **-ces** see ZODIAC
**piss¹** /pɪs/ *v taboo* **1** [I] →URINATE **2** [*it* I] to rain heavily: *It's really pissing down!*
**piss²** *n* [U] *taboo* for URINE
**pissed** /pɪst/ *adj* [F] *taboo* drunk
**pis·ta·chi·o** /pɪ̆ˈstɑːʃiəʊ‖pɪ̆ˈstæ-/ *n* **-os** a small pleasant-tasting green nut
**pis·tol** /ˈpɪstl/ *n* a small gun held and fired in one hand
**pis·ton** /ˈpɪstn/ *n* (in pumps and engines) a solid pipe-shaped piece of metal that fits tightly into a tube (CYLINDER (2)) in which it moves up and down by pressure or explosion, and so gives movement to other parts of the machine
**pit¹** /pɪt/ *n* **1** a large natural or man-made hole in the ground: *The children were playing in the sandpit.* **2** a deep hole dug in the ground to get materials, esp. coal, out: *He worked all his life down the pit.* **3** [*usu. pl.*] (in motor racing) a place beside a track where cars can come during a race to be quickly examined and repaired **4** a natural hollow in the surface of a living thing (esp. in the phrase **pit of the stomach** =the hollow place just below the bones of the chest, esp. thought of as being the place where fear is felt) –see also ARMPIT **5** [*usu. pl.*] a small hollow mark or place in the surface of something, esp.as left on the face after certain diseases, esp. SMALLPOX **6** also **orchestra pit**– the space below and in front of a theatre stage where musicians sit and play during a (musical) play **7 the pits** *infml* the worst possible example of something: *That new film is the pits!*
**pit²** *v* **-tt-** [T] to mark with PITS¹ (5): *a pitted face*
**pit³** *n AmE* for STONE¹ (3) –compare PIP¹
**pit⁴** *v* **-tt-** [T] *AmE* for STONE² (2)
**pit** sbdy./sthg. **against** sbdy./sthg. *v prep* [T] to match or set against, in a fight, competition, struggle, etc.
**pit-a-pat** /ˈ··ˌ·/ also **pitter-patter**– *adv,adj,n* [*the* S] *infml* (making or having) the sound or movement of a number of quick light beats: *His heart went pit-a-pat.|the pitter-patter of rain*
**pitch¹** /pɪtʃ/ *v* **1** [I;T] to set up (a tent, camp, etc.) in position on open ground, esp. for a certain time only –opposite **strike 2** [I;T] (in the game of BASEBALL) **a** to aim and throw (a ball) **b** to be a PITCHER² **3** [T] to set the degree of highness or lowness of (a sound, music, etc.) **4** [T] to give a particular feeling or expression to (something said or written): *He pitched his speech so that even the children could understand.* **5** [I;T] to (cause to) fall heavily or suddenly forwards or outwards: *His foot caught in a rock and he pitched forwards.* **6** [I] (of a ship or aircraft) to move along with the back and front going up and down independently –compare ROLL² (6)
**pitch in** *v adv* [I] *infml* to start to work or eat eagerly
**pitch²** *n* **1** [C] *BrE*‖**field** *AmE*– (in sport) a special marked-out area of ground on which football, HOCKEY, NETBALL, etc., are played –see picture on page 592 **2** [C] a place in some public area, such as a

street or market, where somebody regularly tries to gain money from people who are passing, e.g. by performing, selling small articles, etc. **3** [C] the degree of highness or lowness of a musical note or speaking voice **4** [S] a degree; level: *a high pitch of excitement* **5** [C;S;U] (esp. in building) amount or degree of slope: *the pitch of the roof* **6** [S] (of a ship or aircraft) a backward and forward movement; the action of PITCHing[1] (6) –compare ROLL[2] (6) **7** [C] (in BASEBALL) the way or act of PITCHing[1] (2a) a ball **8** [C] *infml* a salesman's special way of talking about the goods he is trying to sell: *He has a very clever* **sales pitch.**

**pitch³** *n* [U] a black substance that is melted into a sticky material used for making hard protective coverings, or for putting between cracks (esp. in a ship) to stop water coming through

**pitch-black** /ˌ· '·◂/ also **pitch-dark**– *adj* very dark; difficult to see in –**pitch-blackness** *n* [U]

**pitched bat·tle** /ˌ· '··/ *n* (in former times) a battle between complete forces or armies with positions already prepared –compare SKIRMISH

**pitch·er¹** /'pɪtʃəʳ/ *n* **1** a large container for holding and pouring liquids, usu. made of clay **2** *AmE* for JUG

**pitcher²** *n* (in BASEBALL) a player who throws the ball towards the player who is BATting[2] (1)

**pitch·fork** /'pɪtʃfɔːk‖-fɔrk/ *n* a long-handled farm tool with two curved metal points at one end, used esp. in lifting dried cut grass (HAY)

**pit·e·ous** /'pɪtɪəs/ *adj* causing or intended to cause pity: *a piteous cry* –**piteously** *adv*

**pit·fall** /'pɪtfɔːl/ *n* an unexpected danger or difficulty; mistake that may easily be made: *There are many pitfalls for young people today.*

**pith** /pɪθ/ *n* [U] **1** a soft white substance that fills the stems of certain plants and trees **2** a white material just under the skin of oranges and other fruit of the same type

**pit·head** /'pɪt-hed/ *n* the entrance to a coal mine

**pith·y** /'pɪθi/ *adj* **-ier, -iest 1** of, like, or having much PITH (1,2) **2** (of something said or written) strongly stated without wasting any words –**pithily** *adv* –**pithiness** *n* [U]

**pit·i·a·ble** /'pɪtɪəbəl/ *adj* worthy of pity –**pitiably** *adv*

**pit·i·ful** /'pɪtɪfəl/ *adj* **1** causing or deserving pity: *a pitiful sight* **2** *derog* not worthy or deserving respect; worthless: *my pitiful attempts to sing* –**pitifully** *adv*

**pit·i·less** /'pɪtɪl[i]s/ *adj* showing no pity; merciless; severe: *a pitiless king who made all his people suffer*|(fig.) *a cold and pitiless wind blowing from the north* –**pitilessly** *adv* –**pitilessness** *n* [U]

**pit·tance** /'pɪtəns/ *n* [*usu. sing.*] a very small ungenerous amount of pay

**pit·ter-pat·ter** /'pɪtəʳ ˌpætəʳ/ *adv,adj,n* [*the* S] →PIT-A-PAT

**pit·y¹** /'pɪti/ *n* **1** [U] sorrow for the suffering or unhappiness of others: *I helped the old man* **out of pity** **2** [S] a sad or inconvenient state of affairs: **What a pity**, *you have to leave!* **3 have/take pity on (someone)** to help (someone) as a result of feeling PITY[1] (1)

**pity²** *v* **-ied, -ying** [T] **1** to feel PITY[1] (1) for **2** *derog* to consider to be PITIFUL (2): *I pity you if you can't answer such a simple question!*

**piv·ot¹** /'pɪvət/ *n* a fixed central point or pin on which something turns

**pivot²** *v* [I *on*] to turn round on or as if on a PIVOT: (fig.) *The whole war pivoted on* (=depended on) *a single battle.*

**pix·ie, pixy** /'pɪksi/ *n* **-ies** a small fairy believed to like playing tricks on people

**piz·za** /'piːtsə/ *n* [C;U] a round flat piece of bread DOUGH or pastry baked with a mixture of cheese, TOMATOes, etc., on top

**pl.** *written abbrev. said as:* plural

**plac·ard** /'plækɑːd‖-ərd/ *n* a large printed or written notice or advertisement

**pla·cate** /plə'keɪt‖'pleɪkeɪt/ *v* **-cated, -cating** [T] to cause to stop feeling angry –**placatory** /plə'keɪtəri, 'plækə-‖'pleɪkətori/ *adj: his placatory words*

**place¹** /pleɪs/ *n* **1** [C] a particular part of space or position in space: *This is the place where the accident happened.*|*I think this is the best place to put the clock.*|(fig.) *Sport never had a place in his life.* (=was not important to him) **2** [C] a particular spot or area on a surface: *I've got a sore place in the middle of my back.* **3** [C] a particular part of the earth's surface, town, etc.: *Moscow is a very cold place in winter.* **4** [C] a proper or usual position or occasion: *Put it back in its place.*|*A business meeting isn't the place in which to talk about private affairs.*|*Electric trains have* **taken the place of** (=are used instead of) *steam trains in Britain.* **5** [C] a building, room, or piece of land used for a stated purpose: *cinemas and other places of amusement*|*a marketplace* **6** [C] a position in relation to a set of other things: *She finished in second place in the race.* (=was the second to finish)|*Please* **keep my place** *in the* QUEUE (=line of waiting people) *until I come back.*|*I've* **lost my place** *in my book.* (=I can't find the page that I was reading) **7** [C] the position of a figure in a row of figures, to the right of a decimal point: *1.222 is written to three decimal places.* **8** [*the* S] a numbered point in an argument, explanation, etc.: **In the first place** *I don't want to go, and* **in the second place** *I can't afford to.* **9** a seat: *empty places on the bus* **10** [C *usu. sing.*] a position of employment, in a team, etc.: *a place at university* **11** [C] social position; rank: *The minister said that there was* CORRUPTION **in high places.** (=among people of high rank and influence)|*That remark really* **put** *him* **in his place.** (=reminded him that he is not as important as he would like to be) **12** [S] duty; what one should or must do: *It's not your place to tell me what to do.* **13** [C] *infml* a house; home: *Come over to my place tomorrow.* **14 in/out of place**: **a** in/not in the proper position **b** suitable/unsuitable **15 in place of** instead of **16 take place** to happen: *When did this take place?* –see HAPPEN (USAGE)

USAGE **Room** [U] and **place** [C] both mean free space that can be used for a purpose; but **place** is used for a single particular piece of space, while **room** means space in general: "*Is there any* **room** *for me to sit down in here?*" "*Yes, there's a* **place** *in the corner.*"|*This is the* **place** *where we keep the coal.*|*There's no* **room** *for any more coal in here.*

**place²** *v* **placed, placing** [T] **1** to put in a certain position: *He placed the book on the shelf.*|(fig.) *You* place me in a difficult position.|(fig.) *I place a great deal of importance on grammar.* (=consider it to be very important) **2** to pass to a person, firm, etc., who can do the needed action: *I* **placed an order** *with them for 500 pairs of shoes.* **3** [*usu. pass.*] to declare that (a thing or person) has achieved a (stated) position among others: *I would place her among the best singers in Britain.*|*She was placed second.* (=finished the race in second place) **4** to remember fully the name of, or where one last saw or heard, someone or something: *I can't quite place that man.*

**plac·id** /'plæsɪ̈d/ *adj* **1** (of people or animals) quiet; not easily angered or excited **2** (of things) calm; peaceful –**placidly** *adv*

**pla·gia·ris·m** /'pleɪdʒərɪzəm/ *n* **1** [U] the action of plagiarizing (PLAGIARIZE) **2** [C] an idea, story, etc., that is PLAGIARIZED –**plagiarist** *n*

**pla·gia·rize** ||also **-rise** *BrE* /'pleɪdʒəraɪz/ *v* **-rized, -rizing** [I;T] to take (words, ideas, etc.) from someone else's work and use as one's own without admitting one has done so

**plague**[1] /pleɪg/ *n* **1** [C; *the* S;U] a quick-spreading quick-killing disease, esp. a particular one that produces high fever and swellings on the body **2** [C] a widespread, uncontrollable, and harmful mass or number of something: *a plague of rats*

**plague**[2] *v* **plagued, plaguing** [T] to annoy by doing some repeated action: *They plagued him with questions.*

**plaice** /pleɪs/ *n* **plaice** [C;U] a European flat fish used for food –sounds like **place**

**plaid** /plæd/ *n* [C;U] (a long piece of) woollen cloth, often with a special coloured pattern (TARTAN), esp. as worn over the shoulder by Scottish people

**plain**[1] /pleɪn/ *n* a large stretch of flat land: *the Great Plains of the US* –sounds like **plane**

**plain**[2] *adj* **1** clear; easy to see, hear, or understand: *His meaning is plain.* **2** simple; without decoration or pattern: *plain food*|*plain paper* (=paper with nothing on it) **3** *euph esp. old use* (esp. of a woman) not pretty or good-looking; rather ugly –see BEAUTIFUL (USAGE) **4** (of a person or what he/she says) direct and honest; expressing exactly what is meant; FRANK: *plain language* –**plainness** *n* [U]

**plain**[3] *n* [U] *tech* a simple stitch in KNITting –compare PURL

**plain-clothes** /ˌ· '·◂/ *adj* (of a policeman) wearing ordinary clothes while working, rather than a uniform

**plain·ly** /'pleɪnli/ *adv* in a PLAIN[2] (1,2,4) manner; as is plain: *She was plainly very unhappy.*

**plain sail·ing** /ˌ· '··/ *n* [U] a course of action that is simple and free from trouble

**plain·spo·ken** /ˌpleɪn'spəukən◂/ *adj* direct in the use of words, often in a rude way –compare OUTSPOKEN

**plain·tiff** /'pleɪntɪ̈f/ *n law* a person who brings a charge against somebody (DEFENDANT) in a court of law

**plain·tive** /'pleɪntɪv/ *adj* **1** expressing suffering and a desire for pity: *the plaintive cries of the dog shut in the kitchen* **2** expressing gentle sadness: *a plaintive old song* –**plaintively** *adv* –**plaintiveness** *n* [U]

**plait**[1] /plæt||pleɪt/ *BrE*||**braid** *AmE*– *n* a length of something, esp. hair, made by PLAITing[2]

**plait**[2] *BrE*||**braid** *AmE*– *v* to pass or twist three or more lengths of (hair, dried stems of grass, etc.) over and under each other to form one ropelike length

**plan**[1] /plæn/ *n* **1** a (carefully considered) arrangement for carrying out some future activity: *Have you made any plans for tomorrow night?* **2** a line drawing (often one of a set) showing something (such as a building, room, or piece of machinery) as it might be seen from above: *a street-plan of London*|*Have you seen the plans for the new library?* **3 go according to plan** to happen as planned, without any difficulties

**plan**[2] *v* **-nn- 1** [I;T +*to-v*/*for, on, ahead*] to make a plan for (something): *We've been planning this visit for months.*|*She never plans (ahead)–she doesn't like too much organization.*|*I'd planned on doing*/*I'd planned to do some work this afternoon.* **2** [T] to make drawings, models, or other representations of (something to be built or made)

**plane**[1] /pleɪn/ *n* a tool with a blade that takes very thin pieces off wooden surfaces to make them smooth –sounds like **plain**

**plane**[2] *v* **planed, planing** [I;T] to use a PLANE[1] on (something)

**plane**[3] *n* **1** (in GEOMETRY) a flat or level surface **2** a level; standard: *Let's keep the conversation on a friendly plane.* **3** *infml* for AEROPLANE

**plan·et** /'plænɪ̈t/ *n* a large body in space that moves round a star, esp. round the sun: *The Earth is a planet.*|*the planet Mars* –**planetary** /'plænɪ̈təri||-teri/ *adj* [A]: *planetary movements*

**plan·e·tar·i·um** /ˌplænɪ̈'teərɪəm/ *n* **-riums** *or* **-ria** /rɪə/ a building containing an apparatus that throws spots of light onto the inside of a curved roof to show an image of the movements of planets and stars

**plane tree** /'· ·/ also **plane**– *n* a broad-leaved wide-spreading tree that commonly grows in towns

**plank**[1] /plæŋk/ *n* **1** a long, usu. heavy, flat narrow piece of wood: *a small bridge made of planks* **2** a main principle of a political party's stated group of aims: *The party's main plank is reducing taxes.*

**plank**[2] *v* [T *with*] to cover with PLANKS[1] (1)

**plank·ton** /'plæŋktən/ *n* [U] the very small forms of plant and animal life that live in water (esp. the sea) and are eaten as food by many fish

**plan·ner** /'plænəʳ/ *n* a person who plans, esp. who plans the way in which towns are to develop: *a town planner*

**plant**[1] /plɑːnt||plænt/ *v* **1** [I;T] to put (plants or seeds) in the ground to grow: *April is the best time to plant.* **2** [T *with*] to supply (a place) with seeds or growing plants: *We're planting a small garden.*|*The hillside was planted with trees.* **3** [T *on*] *infml* to hide (esp. stolen goods) on a person so that he/she will seem guilty: *Those drugs aren't mine–the police planted them on me!* **4** [T] to fix or place firmly or with force: *He planted himself in a chair by the fire.*

**plant** sthg.↔ **out** *v adv* [T] to place (plants) in enough room for growth

**plant**[2] *n* **1** a living thing that has leaves and roots, and grows usu. in earth, esp. the kind smaller than trees: *All plants need water and light.*|*a tomato plant* –see picture on page 297 **2 a** a machine; apparatus: *a small* **power plant** *for electricity* **b** a factory: *a* new chemical plant

**plan·ta·tion** /plæn'teɪʃən, plɑːn-||plæn-/ *n* **1** a large piece of land, esp. in hot countries, on which crops such as tea, sugar, and rubber are grown: *a rubber plantation* **2** a large group of growing trees planted esp. to produce wood

**plant·er** /'plɑːntəʳ||'plæn-/ *n* a person who owns or is in charge of a PLANTATION (1): *a tea planter*

**plaque** /plæk/ *n* **1** [C] a flat metal or stone plate with writing on it, fixed to a wall in memory of a person or event, or as a decoration **2** [U] *tech* a substance that forms on teeth in the mouth, and in which bacteria live and breed

**plas·ma** /'plæzmə/ *n* [U] the liquid part of blood

**plas·ter¹** /'plɑːstəʳ||'plæ-/ *n* **1** [U] a pastelike mixture of lime, water, sand, etc., which hardens when dry and is used, esp. on walls, to give a smooth surface **2** [C;U] also **sticking plaster**– *BrE* (a thin band of) sticky material put on the skin to protect small wounds **3 in plaster** in a PLASTER CAST (2)

**plaster²** *v* [T] **1** [*over*] to put wet PLASTER¹ (1) on; cover with plaster: *These rough places on the wall could be plastered over.* **2** [*with/on*] to spread (something), perhaps too thickly, on: *They plastered the wall with signs.|They plastered signs on the wall.*

**plaster cast** /ˌ·· '·, '·· ·/ *n* **1** a copy of a stone or metal figure (STATUE) made from PLASTER OF PARIS **2** a case made from PLASTER OF PARIS, placed round a part of the body to protect or support a broken bone

**plas·tered** /'plɑːstəd||'plæstərd/ *adj* [F] *humor* drunk

**plas·ter·er** /'plɑːstərəʳ||'plæ-/ *n* a person whose job is to PLASTER² (1) esp. walls

**plaster of Par·is** /ˌplɑːstər əv 'pærɨs||ˌplæ-/ *n* [U] a quick-drying whitish paste made of a chalklike powder mixed with water, used for PLASTER CASTS, in decorative building work, etc.

**plas·tic¹** /'plæstɪk/ *n* [C;U] a light man-made material produced chemically from oil or coal, which is shaped when soft, keeps its shape when hard and is used to make different objects: *a plastic spoon|The spoon is plastic.|Plastics are often used today.*

**plastic²** *adj* **1** (of a substance) easily formed into various shapes by pressing **2** [A] *fml* connected with the art of shaping forms in clay, stone, wood, etc. (esp.in the phrase **the plastic arts**)

**plas·ti·cine** /'plæstɨsiːn/ *n* [U] *tdmk, esp. BrE* (*sometimes cap.*) a soft claylike substance made in many different colours, used by young children for making small models, shapes, etc.

**plas·tic·i·ty** /plæs'tɪsɨti/ *n* [U] the state or quality of being PLASTIC² (1)

**plas·tics** /'plæstɪks/ *n* [U] the science of producing PLASTIC¹ materials

**plastic sur·ge·ry** /ˌ·· '···/ *n* [U] the repairing or improving of damaged or badly shaped parts of the body

**plate¹** /pleɪt/ *n* **1** [C] **a** a flat, usu. round dish with a slightly raised edge from which food is eaten or served: *a dinner plate|a paper plate*–see picture on page 521 **b** also **plateful** /'pleɪtfʊl/– the amount of food that this will hold: *a plate of meat* **2** [U] common metal with a thin covering of gold or silver: *gold plate* **3** [U] metal articles, usu. made of gold or silver, as used at meals or in services at church: *the church plate* **4** [C] a picture in a book, printed on different paper from the written part and often coloured **5** [C *usu. sing.*] **a** also **dental plate**– a thin piece of pink plastic shaped to fit inside a person's mouth, into which false teeth are fixed **b** also **denture** *fml*– a set of false teeth fixed into this **6** [C] (*often in comb.*) a flat, thin, usu. large piece of metal, glass, etc., for use in building, in parts of machinery, as a protection, etc. **7** [C] a small sheet of metal, usu. brass, fixed to the entrance to an office, bearing the name of the person who works there, or of a firm **8** [*the* S] a collection of money taken in church: *The plate was more than £10.* **9 hand/give somebody something on a plate** *infml* to hand/give somebody something desirable, too willingly and easily **10 have (a lot/too much,** etc.**) on one's plate** *infml* to have (a lot of/too much, etc. work or things to do) to deal with at a certain moment

**plate²** *v* **plated, plating** [T *with*] to cover (a metal article) thinly with another metal, esp. gold, silver, or tin: *The ring wasn't solid gold–it was only gold-plated.*

**plat·eau** /'plætəʊ||plæ'təʊ/ *n* **-eaus** *or* **-eaux** /təʊ/ **1** a large stretch of level land much higher than the land around it **2** a state in which an activity ceases developing: *sales have now reached a plateau*

**plate glass** /ˌ· '·◄/ *n* [U] fine clear glass made in large, quite thick sheets for use esp. in shop windows –**plate-glass** *adj* [A]

**plat·form** /'plætfɔːm||-fɔrm/ *n* **1** a raised floor of boards for speakers, performers, etc.: *She spoke from the platform.|Please speak to the platform.* (=to the people on the platform) **2** a raised flat surface built along the side of the track at a railway station for travellers getting on or off a train: *The Liverpool train is now at Platform One.* –see picture on page 501 **3** [*usu. sing.*] the main ideas and aims of a political party, esp. as stated before an election: *The party's platform is reducing taxes.*

**plat·ing** /'pleɪtɪŋ/ *n* [U] a thin covering of metal put on by plating (PLATE²)

**plat·i·num** /'plætɨnəm/ *n* [U] expensive greyish-white metal that is a simple substance (ELEMENT (1)) and is used esp. in very valuable jewellery: *a platinum ring|This ring is (of) platinum.*

**plat·i·tude** /'plætɨtjuːd||-tuːd/ *n derog* a statement that is true but not new, interesting, or clever: *He seems to have no original ideas; his speech was full of platitudes.* –compare CLICHÉ –**platitudinous** /ˌplætɨ'tjuːdɨnəs||-'tuː-/ *adj*

**pla·ton·ic** /plə'tɒnɪk||-'tɑ-/ *adj* (of love or friendship between two people) only of the mind and spirit; not sexual –**platonically** *adv*

**pla·toon** /plə'tuːn/ *n* [C +*sing./pl. v*] a small body of soldiers which is part of a COMPANY (5) and is commanded by a LIEUTENANT

**plat·ter** /'plætəʳ/ *n esp. AmE* a large flat dish used for serving food, esp. meat

**plat·y·pus** /'plætɨpəs/ also **duck-billed platypus**– *n* a small furry Australian animal (MAMMAL) that lays eggs and has a beak like a duck's, but gives milk to its young

**plau·dit** /'plɔːdɨt/ *n fml* [*usu. pl.*] a show of pleased approval: *the plaudits of the* CRITICS

**plau·si·ble** /'plɔːzəbəl/ *adj* **1** (of a statement, argument, etc.) seeming to be true or reasonable: *Your explanation sounds plausible; I think I believe it.* –opposite **implausible** –compare FEASIBLE **2** (of a person) skilled in producing (seemingly) reasonable statements which may not be true: *a plausible liar* –**plausibly** *adv* –**plausibility** /-ə'bɪlɨti/ *n* [U]

**play**[1] /pleɪ/ *n* **1** [U] activity for amusement only, esp. among the young: *the children* **at play** **2** [C] (a performance of) a piece of writing to be acted in a theatre or on TV: *I saw two plays last month.*|*I've just read a wonderful new play; it's going to be put on* (=performed) *next year.* **3** [U] the action in a sport: *I enjoyed the cricket match; it was a good day's play.* **4** [U] freedom of movement given by slight looseness: *Give the rope some play.*|(fig.) *He gave free play to his feelings and shouted angrily.* **5** [U] action; effect; use: *She had to* **bring** *all her experience* **into play** *to do the job.* **6** [U] quick, not lasting movement: *the play of sunshine and shadow among the trees* **7 in/out of play** (of the ball in football, etc.) in a position where the rules allow it to be played

**play**[2] *v* **1** [I] (esp. of children) to do things that are enjoyable and interesting, esp. including running and jumping and using toys: *a child playing with his toys* **2** [I;T] to take part in (a sport or game) (against): *Shall we play cards?*|*England are playing France at football tomorrow.* **3** [T] to strike and send (a ball), esp. in the stated way: *She played that ball very well.* **4** [T] to plan and carry out for one's own amusement or gain: *They played a joke on her.*|(fig.) *I thought my eyes must be playing tricks on me.* (=deceiving me) **5** [I;T] to produce esp. musical sounds (from or of): *The radio was playing very loudly.*|*She plays the piano well.* **6** [T] (of an actor) to perform: *The part of Hamlet was played by Laurence Olivier.* **7** [I;T] to place (a playing card) face upwards on the table **8** to pretend to be: *He played dead.* **9** [I] to move lightly and irregularly: *A smile played across her lips.* **10** [I;T] to direct or be directed, esp. continuously: *The fireman played the* HOSE *onto the burning house.* **11 play for time** to cause delay, in order to gain time **12 play hard to get** to pretend one is not sexually interested in someone, in order to make him or her become more interested in oneself **13 play into someone's hands** to act in a way that gives someone an advantage over one **14 play it by ear** *infml* to act as things develop, rather than making plans in advance **15 play (it) safe** to act so as to try to avoid a misfortune **16 play one's cards right** to use well the chances, conditions, etc., that one has **17 play the fool** to act foolishly **18 play the game** to be fair, honest, and honourable **19 play with fire** to take great risks

**play at** sthg. *v prep* [T +*v-ing*] →PLAY[2] (8)

**play** sthg.↔ **back** *v adv* [T] to go through and listen to (something that has just been recorded on a machine)

**play** sthg.↔ **down** *v adv* [T] to cause to seem less important

**play** sbdy./sthg.↔ **off** *v adv* [T *against*] to set in opposition, esp. for one's own advantage: *She played one friend off against the other.* –see also PLAY-OFF

**play on/upon** sthg. *v prep* [T] to try to increase or strengthen (esp. the feelings of others) for one's own advantage: *I played on his generosity and in the end he agreed to lend me his car.*

**play** (sbdy.) **up** *v adv* [I;T] *infml* to cause trouble or suffering to: *My bad leg is playing (me) up.*

**play-act** /'· ·/ *v* [I] to pretend; behave with an unreal show of feeling –**play-acting** *n* [U]

**play·boy** /'pleɪbɔɪ/ *n* a wealthy young man who lives mainly for pleasure

**play·er** /'pleɪəʳ/ *n* **1** a person taking part in a game or sport –see picture on page 592 **2** *esp. old use* an actor

**play·ful** /'pleɪfəl/ *adj* **1** gaily active; full of fun: *a playful little dog* **2** not intended seriously: *a playful kiss on the cheek* –**playfully** *adv* –**playfulness** *n* [U]

**play·ground** /'pleɪgraʊnd/ *n* a piece of ground kept for children to play on, esp. at a school

**play·group** /'pleɪgruːp/ *n* a kind of informal school for very young children (esp. of three to five years old) –compare NURSERY, CRÈCHE

**play·house** /'pleɪhaʊs/ *n* **-houses** /ˌhaʊzɨz/ (*usu. cap. as part of a name*) a theatre

**playing card** /'·· ·/ *n fml* for CARD[3] (1)

**play·mate** /'pleɪmeɪt/ also **playfellow** /'pleɪˌfeləʊ/– *n fml* a companion who shares in children's play

**play-off** /'· ·/ *n* a second match played to decide a winner, when the first has not –see also PLAY **off**

**play on words** /ˌ· · '·/ *n* **plays on words** →PUN[1]

**play·pen** /'pleɪpen/ *n* a frame enclosed by bars or a net for a small child to play safely in

**play·room** /'pleɪrʊm, -ruːm/ *n* a room set aside for children's play

**play·thing** /'pleɪˌθɪŋ/ *n* **1** a toy **2** a person who is treated lightly and without consideration by another

**play·time** /'pleɪtaɪm/ *n* a (short) period of time, esp. at a school, when children can go out to play

**play·wright** /'pleɪraɪt/ *n* a writer of plays

**plc** *abbrev for*: public limited company: *S. Pearson plc* –compare LTD

**plea** /pliː/ *n* **1** [C *for*] *fml* an eager or serious request: *a plea for forgiveness* **2** [*the* S] *fml* an excuse: *He did not attend the dinner; his plea was that he was too busy to come.* **3** [C *of*] *law* a statement by a person in a court of law, saying whether or not he/she is guilty of a charge: *a plea of guilty/not guilty*

**plead** /pliːd/ *v* **pleaded** *or* **plead**||also **pled** /pled/ *AmE,* **pleading 1** [I *with*] to make continual and deeply felt requests: *He pleaded (with her) until she agreed to do as he wished.* **2** [T] to give as an excuse for an action: *I'm sorry I didn't answer your letter; I can only plead forgetfulness.* **3** [I] *law* to answer a charge in court: *The girl charged with murder was said to be mad and* **unfit to plead.** **4** [I;T] *law* to declare in official language that one is (in a state of): *She pleaded guilty/not guilty.*|*He pleaded* INSANITY.

**pleas·ant** /'plezənt/ *adj* **1** pleasing to the senses, feelings, or mind; enjoyable: *the pleasant smell of flowers*|*It's* (=the weather is) *usually pleasant here in August.* **2** (esp. of people) likeable; friendly: *a pleasant woman*|*He made an effort to be pleasant.* –opposite **unpleasant** –**pleasantly** *adv*

**pleas·ant·ry** /'plezəntri/ *n* **-ries** a light amusing remark; pleasant joke

**please**[1] /pliːz/ *v* **pleased, pleasing 1** [I;T] to make (someone) happy; give pleasure (to): *You can't please everybody.|Do it to please me.|The man in the shop is always eager to please (everybody).* –opposite **displease 2** [I] (*not as the main verb of a sentence*) to choose; like: *Come and stay as long as you please.* **3 if you please** *fml* (used to give force after a request) PLEASE²: *Come this way, if you please.* **4 please yourself** *infml* do as you wish, it doesn't matter to me

**please²** *interj* (used when asking politely for something): *A cup of tea, please.|Please be quiet.|"More coffee?" "Please."* (=yes please)

**pleased** /pliːzd/ *adj* feeling or showing satisfaction or happiness: *I'm very pleased you've decided to come.|She looked pleased.|I'm pleased with your work.|He was looking very* **pleased with himself,** *so I knew he had passed his driving test.* –opposite **displeased**

**pleas·ing** /ˈpliːzɪŋ/ *adj* giving pleasure or satisfaction: *a pleasing result to our talks* **–pleasingly** *adv*

**plea·sur·a·ble** /ˈpleʒərəbəl/ *adj fml* enjoyable; pleasant **–pleasurably** *adv*

**plea·sure** /ˈpleʒəʳ/ *n* **1** [U] the feeling of happiness or satisfaction resulting from an experience that one likes: *He listened with pleasure to the beautiful music.|It gives me no pleasure to have to tell you this.|He* **took great pleasure in** (=greatly enjoyed) *telling me that my team had lost.* –opposite **displeasure 2** [C] a cause of happiness, enjoyment, or satisfaction: *It's been a pleasure to talk to you.|She has few pleasures in life* **3** [U] enjoyment; RECREATION: *Are you here on business or just for pleasure?* **4** [S] *polite* something that one is pleased to do (esp. in the phrase **a/my/our pleasure**): *"Thank you for helping me." "My pleasure./It was a pleasure."*

**pleat¹** /pliːt/ *v* to make PLEATS² in: *a pleated skirt*

**pleat²** *n* a specially pressed narrow fold in cloth

**ple·be·ian** /plɪˈbiːən/ *n,adj derog* (a member) of the lower social classes: *plebeian habits*

**pleb·is·cite** /ˈplebɪ̇sɪ̇t‖-saɪt/ *n* a direct vote of the people of a nation on a matter of national importance: *to hold a plebiscite on* DIVORCE*|It was decided* **by plebiscite.** –compare REFERENDUM

**plec·trum** /ˈplektrəm/ *n* a small thin piece of wood, plastic, etc., used for playing certain stringed instruments such as the GUITAR

**pled** /pled/ *v AmE past tense and participle of* PLEAD

**pledge¹** /pledʒ/ *n* **1** [C] something given or received as a sign of faithful love or friendship: *Take this ring as a pledge of our friendship.* **2** [C] something valuable left with someone else as proof that one will fulfil an agreement **3** [C;U] a solemn promise or agreement: *It was told me under pledge of secrecy.*

**pledge²** *v* **pledged, pledging** [T] *fml* **1** [+*to-v/that*] to make a solemn promise or agreement: *They have pledged that they will always remain faithful to each other.* **2** [*to*] to bind (someone) with a solemn promise: *She was pledged to secrecy.*

**ple·na·ry** /ˈpliːnəri/ *adj fml* **1** (of power of government) complete; without limit **2** (of a meeting) attended by all who have the lawful right to attend

**plen·i·po·ten·tia·ry** /ˌplenɪ̇pəˈtenʃəri‖-ʃieri/ *n,adj* **-ries** (a person) having full power to act in all matters, as a representative of one's government, esp. in a foreign country

**plen·te·ous** /ˈplentɪəs/ *adj lit* for PLENTIFUL

**plen·ti·ful** /ˈplentɪfəl/ *adj* existing in quantities or numbers that are (more than) enough: *The camp has a plentiful supply of food.* **–plentifully** *adv*

**plen·ty** /ˈplenti/ *n* [U +*sing./pl. v*] as much or as many as one needs; enough: *plenty of money|£100 is plenty.|There are plenty more chairs in here.|He gave them plenty to eat.|Don't get any more sugar: we've got plenty.* –compare LOT¹

**pleth·o·ra** /ˈpleθərə/ *n* [S *of*] *fml or humor* an amount or supply much greater than is needed

**pli·a·ble** /ˈplaɪəbəl/ also **pliant** /ˈplaɪənt/– *adj* **1** easily bent without breaking **2** easily influenced; yielding to the wishes and commands of others **–pliability** /ˌplaɪəˈbɪlɪ̇ti/, **pliancy** *n* [U]

**pli·ers** /ˈplaɪəz‖-ərz/ *n* [P] a small tool made of two crossed pieces of metal with long flat jaws at one end, used to bend small things or to bend and cut wire –compare PINCERS; see PAIR (USAGE)

**plight** /plaɪt/ *n* [*usu. sing.*] a (bad, serious, or sorrowful) condition or state: *The poor girl was in a terrible plight.|the plight of homeless children*

**plim·soll** /ˈplɪmsəl, -səʊl/ *BrE*‖**sneaker** *AmE*– *n* [*usu. pl.*] a light shoe with a top made of heavy cloth and a flat rubber bottom, used esp. for games and sports –see PAIR (USAGE); see picture on page 563

**plinth** /plɪnθ/ *n* a square block, usu. of stone, serving as the base of a pillar or STATUE

**plod** /plɒd‖plɑd/ *v* **-dd-** [I] **1** to walk slowly, esp. with difficulty and great effort: *The old man plods along, hardly able to lift each foot.* **2** [*esp. away* (*at*)] to work steadily, esp. at something uninteresting: *He plodded away (at the work) all night.*

**plod·der** /ˈplɒdəʳ‖ˈplɑ-/ *n* a slow, not very clever, but steady worker who often succeeds in the end

**plonk¹** /plɒŋk‖plɑŋk, plɔŋk/ *n,adv* [*adv +prep/adv;* S] *infml* (with) a hollow sound as of something dropping or falling onto a metal object: *I heard a plonk, and saw that the box had fallen off the table.|The box fell plonk on the floor.*

**plonk²** *v* [T] *infml* to put down heavily or with force: *She plonked herself in the chair and refused to move.*

**plonk³** *n* [U] *infml esp. BrE & AustrE* cheap wine

**plop** /plɒp‖plɑp/ *v,n,adv* [*adv +prep/adv;* S] *infml* (to fall with) a sound as of something dropping smoothly into liquid: *The stone plopped into the stream.|There was a loud plop as the bag fell to the floor and burst.|The soap fell plop into the bath.*

**plot¹** /plɒt‖plɑt/ *n* **1** a small marked or measured piece of ground for building or growing things: *a building plot|I grow potatoes on my little plot of land.* **2** the set of connected events on which a story, play, film, etc., is based **3** a secret plan to do something usu. against a person, needing combined action by several people: *a plot to kill the Queen*

**plot²** *v* **-tt- 1** [I;T+*to-v*] to plan together secretly: *They're plotting against him.|They're plotting to kill him/plotting his murder/plotting how to murder him.* **2** [T] to mark (the position of a moving aircraft or ship) on a map **3** [T] to express or represent by means of pictures or a map **4** [T] to make (a line or curve showing certain stated facts) by marking on paper marked with small squares: *to plot (a line showing) the increase in sales this year* **–plotter** *n* [*usu. pl.*]

**plough¹** ‖also **plow** *AmE* /plaʊ/ *n* **1** a farming tool with a heavy cutting blade drawn by a motor vehicle or animal(s) and used to break up and turn over the earth, esp. before seeds are planted **2** any tool or machine that works like this –see also SNOWPLOUGH

**plough²** ‖also **plow** *AmE v* **1** [I;T] to break up or turn over (land) with a PLOUGH¹ (1): *Farmers plough (their fields) in autumn or spring.* **2** [I] to force a way or make a track: *The great ship ploughed across the ocean.*|(fig.) *He ploughed through the book to the end.* (=the book was very dull or difficult)

**plough** sthg.↔ **back** *v adv* [T] to put (money earned) back into a business so as to develop and EXPAND the business

**ploy** /plɔɪ/ *n* **ploys** *infml* a way of behaving in order to gain some advantage: *His ploy is to pretend to be ill.*

**pluck¹** /plʌk/ *v* **1** [T] to pull the feathers off (a dead hen, duck, etc., being prepared for cooking) **2** [T *out, from, off*] to pull sharply; pick: *to pluck out the grey hairs*|(*lit*) *He plucked a rose/an apple.* **3** [I;T *at*] also **pick** *AmE*– to play a stringed musical instrument by pulling (the strings)

**pluck up** *v adv* **pluck up (one's) courage** to show bravery in spite of (one's) fears: *He could not pluck up enough courage to ask her to marry him.*

**pluck²** *n* [U] courage and will: *Mountain climbers need a lot of pluck.*

**pluck·y** /ˈplʌki/ *adj* **-ier, -iest** brave and determined –**pluckily** *adv*

**plug¹** /plʌg/ *n* **1** a small piece of rubber, wood, metal, etc., used for blocking a hole, esp. in a pipe: *She pulled the plug out of the bath and the water ran out.* **2** a small plastic object with two or three metal pins which are pushed into an electric power point (SOCKET) to obtain power for an electrical apparatus –see picture on page 355 **3** *infml* a favourable opinion, esp. given on radio or television, about a record, book, etc., meant to make people want to buy the thing spoken of

**plug²** *v* **-gg-** [T] **1** to block, close, or fill up with a PLUG¹ (1): *Use this to plug the hole in your boat.* –opposite **unplug 2** *infml* to advertise (something) by repeatedly mentioning: *He's been plugging his new book on the radio.*

**plug** sthg.↔ **in** *v adv* [T] to connect to a supply of electricity

**plum** /plʌm/ *n* **1** [C] a sweet smooth-skinned fleshy fruit, usu. dark red or yellow, with a single hard seed (STONE) **2** [U] a dark reddish-blue colour **3** [A;C] *infml* something very desirable: *a plum job*

**plum·age** /ˈpluːmɪdʒ/ *n* [U] a bird's covering of feathers

**plumb¹** /plʌm/ *n* a mass of lead tied to the end of a string (**plumb line**), used to find out the depth of water or whether a wall is built exactly upright

**plumb²** *v* [T] **1** to (try to) find out the meaning of: *plumbing the deep mysteries of the mind* **2 plumb the depths (of)** to reach the lowest point (of): *to plumb the depths of unhappiness*

**plumb·er** /ˈplʌməʳ/ *n* a person whose job is to fit and repair water pipes, esp. in a building

**plumb·ing** /ˈplʌmɪŋ/ *n* [U] **1** all the pipes, containers for storing water, etc., in a building: *an old house with noisy plumbing* **2** the work of a PLUMBER

**plume** /pluːm/ *n* a feather, esp. a large or showy one: (fig.) *a plume of smoke*

**plum·met** /ˈplʌmɪ̈t/ *v* [I *down*] to fall steeply or suddenly: *Prices have plummeted.* –compare ROCKET²

**plump** /plʌmp/ *adj usu. apprec* (of people, animals, or parts of the body) pleasantly fat; nicely rounded: *a plump baby* –see THIN (USAGE) –**plumpness** *n* [U]

**plump for** sthg. *v prep* [T+*v-ing*] *infml* to decide in favour of: *We plumped for the red car.*

**plump** sthg.↔ **up** *v adv* [T] to make (esp. bed coverings) rounded and soft by shaking

**plun·der¹** /ˈplʌndəʳ/ *v* [I;T] to seize (goods) illegally or by force from (people or a place), esp. in time of war: *They plundered the helpless town.*

**plunder²** *n* [U] goods seized by PLUNDERing

**plunge¹** /plʌndʒ/ *v* **plunged, plunging 1** [I;T] to (cause to) move or be thrown suddenly forwards and/or downwards: *The car stopped suddenly and he plunged forward.*|(fig.) *Prices have plunged.* (=become suddenly lower) **2** [I] (of the neck of a woman's garment) to have a low curve or V-shape that shows a quite large area of the chest: *a plunging* NECKLINE

**plunge into** *v prep* [T] **1** (**plunge** (sthg.) **into** sbdy./sthg.) to push or rush suddenly or violently into the depths or thickness of: *He plunged into the water.*|*She plunged the knife into his back.* **2** (**plunge** sbdy./sthg. **into** sthg.) to cause to feel or be in a state of: *The room was plunged into darkness.*

**plunge²** *n* [S] **1** an act of plunging (PLUNGE), esp. head first into water **2** *infml* **take the plunge** to decide upon and perform an act determinedly, after having delayed through anxiety or uncertainty

**plung·er** /ˈplʌndʒəʳ/ *n* a rubber cup on the end of a handle, used for unblocking pipes by means of SUCTION

**plu·per·fect** /pluːˈpɜːfɪkt‖-ɜr-/ *adj,n* (a tense) that expresses an action completed before a particular time in the past (stated or understood), and is formed in English with *had* and a past participle

**plu·ral** /ˈplʊərəl/ *adj,n* (a form, or a word in a form) that expresses more than one: *"Dogs" is a plural noun.*|*"Children" is the plural of "child"* –compare SINGULAR

**plus¹** /plʌs/ *prep* with the addition of (the stated figure or quantity): *3 plus 6 is 9* (3+6=9).|*It costs a pound, plus ten pence for postage.* (=the total spent is £1.10) –compare MINUS

**plus²** also **plus sign** /ˈ· ·/– *n* a sign (+) showing that two or more numbers are to be added together, or that a number is greater than zero –compare MINUS²

**plus³** *adj* **1** [A] (of a number or quantity) greater than zero: *a plus quantity* –compare MINUS³ **2** [after *n*] and above (a stated number): *All the children here are 12 plus.* (=are 12 years old or older)

**plush** /plʌʃ/ *adj* [A] *infml* splendid and expensive: *the town's plush new cinema*

**Plu·to** /ˈpluːtəʊ/ *n* the PLANET 9th in order from the sun, the most distant of the group that includes the Earth

**plu·to·crat** /ˈpluːtəkræt/ *n* a person who has power because of his/her wealth –**plutocratic** /-ˈkrætɪk/ *adj*

**plu·to·ni·um** /pluːˈtəuniəm/ *n* [U] a man-made simple substance (ELEMENT (1)) that is used esp. in the production of atomic power

**ply**[1] /plaɪ/ *v* **plied, plying 1** [I;T *between*] (of taxis, buses, and esp. boats) to travel regularly (in or on): *This ship plies between London and Australia.* **2** [T] *lit* to work (regularly) at (a trade): *The newspaper-seller* **plies his trade** *in the streets.*

**ply** sbdy. **with** sthg. *v prep* [T] to keep supplying with (esp. food, drink, or questions)

**ply**[2] *n* [U] a measure of the thickness of woollen thread, rope, PLYWOOD, etc., according to the number of single threads or sheets of material it is made from: *This is four-ply wool.*|*three-ply wood*

**ply·wood** /ˈplaɪwud/ *n* [U] strong board made of several thin sheets of wood stuck together

**p.m.** /ˌpiː ˈem/ *abbrev. for: Latin* post meridiem (=after midday) (used after numbers expressing time): *He caught the 5 p.m. (train) from Manchester.* –opposite **a.m.**

**P M** *abbrev. for:* (*infml esp. BrE*) PRIME MINISTER

**pneu·mat·ic** /njuːˈmætɪk‖nu-/ *adj* **1** worked by air pressure: *a pneumatic* DRILL[2] (1) **2** containing air: *a pneumatic tyre* –**pneumatically** *adv*

**pneu·mo·ni·a** /njuːˈməuniə‖nu-/ *n* [U] a serious disease of the lungs with INFLAMMATION and difficulty in breathing

**P O** *written abbrev. said as:* **1** POST OFFICE **2** POSTAL ORDER

**poach**[1] /pəutʃ/ *v* [T] to cook (esp. eggs or fish) in gently boiling water or other liquid: *poached eggs*

**poach**[2] *v* [I;T *for, on*] **1** to catch or shoot (animals, birds, or fish) without permission on private land: *poaching (for) rabbits* **2** to take or use unfairly (a position or idea belonging to someone else) –**poacher** *n*

**P O Box** /ˌpi əu ˈbɒks◂‖-ˈbaks/ also **Post Office Box** *fml– n* a numbered box in a post office, to which a person's mail can be sent: *For further details, write to (PO) Box 179.*

**pock·et**[1] /ˈpɒk$\frac{1}{ə}$t‖ˈpak$\frac{1}{ə}$t/ *n* **1** [C] a small flat cloth bag sewn into or onto a garment, for keeping small articles in: *The policeman wanted to know what was in my pockets.* –see picture on page 563 **2** [C] a container made by fitting a piece of cloth, net, etc., into the inside of a case or a car door, onto the back of an aircraft seat, etc. **3** [C *of*] a small area or group that exists separated from others like it: *pockets of mist*|*There are pockets of unemployment in the industrial areas.* **4** [A] small enough to be carried in the pocket: *a pocket camera* **5 be/live in each other's pockets** *infml* (of two people) to be together too much **6 out of pocket** *BrE* having spent money without any good result: *After the accident with my new car, I was £500 out of pocket.*

**pocket**[2] *v* [T] **1** to put into one's POCKET[1] (1) **2** to take (money or something small) for one's own use, esp. dishonestly: *He pocketed the money for the children.*

**pock·et·book** /ˈpɒk$\frac{1}{ə}$tbuk‖ˈpa-/ *n AmE* a woman's HANDBAG or PURSE[1] (1,2), esp. one without a shoulder STRAP

**pock·et·ful** /ˈpɒk$\frac{1}{ə}$tful‖ˈpa-/ *n* [*of*] the amount that a POCKET[2] (1) will hold

**pocket mon·ey** /ˈ·· ˌ··/ *BrE*‖**allowance** *AmE– n* [U] money given weekly to a child by his/her parents

**pock·mark** /ˈpɒkmaːk‖ˈpakmark/ *n* a hollow mark left on the skin where a raised spot has been –**pockmarked** *adj*

**pod**[1] /pɒd‖pad/ *n* a long narrow seed vessel of various plants, esp. beans and PEAS: *a* PEA *pod*

**pod**[2] *v* **-dd-** [T] to take (beans, PEAS, etc.) from the POD before cooking

**podg·y** /ˈpɒd·i‖ˈpa-/ also **pudgy**– *adj* **-ier, -iest** *infml* (of a person or part of the body) short and fat –**podginess** *n* [U]

**po·di·um** /ˈpəudiəm/ *n* **-diums** *or* **-dia** /dɪə/ a raised part of a floor, or a large movable block, for a performer, speaker, musical CONDUCTOR, etc., to stand on

**po·em** /ˈpəu$\frac{1}{ə}$m/ *n* a piece of writing, arranged in patterns of lines and of sounds, usu. expressing in IMAGINATIVE language some thought, feeling, or human experience

**po·et** /ˈpəu$\frac{1}{ə}$t/ *n* a person who writes poems

**po·et·ic** /pəuˈetɪk/ also **poetical**– *adj* of, like, or connected with poets or poetry –**poetically** *adv*

**poetic jus·tice** /·ˌ·· ˈ··/ *n* [U] perfect justice, by which wrong-doers are justly punished

**poetic li·cence** /·ˌ·· ˈ··/ *n* [U] the freedom allowed by custom in the writing of poetry to change facts, not to obey the usual rules of grammar, etc.

**po·et·ry** /ˈpəu$\frac{1}{ə}$tri/ *n* [U] **1** the art of a poet **2** poems in general: *a book of poetry* **3** *apprec* a quality of beauty, grace, and deep feeling: *the poetry of Nureyev's movements* –compare PROSE

**poi·gnant** /ˈpɔɪnjənt/ *adj* producing a sharp feeling of sadness or pity: *poignant memories of my childhood* –**poignantly** *adv* –**poignancy** *n* [U]

**point**[1] /pɔɪnt/ *n* **1** [C *of*] a sharp end: *the point of a needle* **2** [C] a position in space or time; a particular place, moment, or state: *The bus stops at four or five points along this road.*|*It was* **at that point** (=moment) *that I saw him leave.*|*I've* **come to the point** *where I can't listen to her any longer.* **3** [C] a scoring (SCORE) system used in deciding who is the winner in various sports and games: *We won the* RUGBY *game by 12 points to 3.* **4** [C] also **decimal point**– a sign (·) used for separating a whole number from any following decimals: *When we read out 4·23 we say "four point two three".* **5** [C;U] a degree of temperature: *Heat the water till it reaches* **boiling point. 6** [C] a single particular idea, fact, or part of an argument or statement: *There are two or three points in your speech that I didn't understand.*|*You've got a point there.* (=What you have said may well be right) **7** [*the* S;U] the idea contained in something said or done, which gives meaning to the whole: *I didn't* **see the point of** *his last remark.*|*I* **missed the point.** *What did he mean?*|*I* **take your point.** (=I understand your suggestion)|**That's not the point.** (=not really important to or connected with the main thing being talked about)|*I'm in a hurry, so* **come/get to the point.** (=speak about the most important or urgent matter)|*The fact that he's your brother is* **beside the point.** (=has nothing to do with the main subject) **8** [C] a noticeable quality or ability of someone or something: *Work isn't her strong point.* **9** [U] purpose; use: *There's not much point in repairing that* old car. **10** [C] also **power point**– *esp. BrE* a small plastic or metal container, usu. fixed in a wall, into which a PLUG[1] (2) can be fitted so as to connect an electrical apparatus to the supply of electricity; SOCKET **11** [U] the dangerous end of a weapon, considered as a means of having power or influence over someone: *He forced his prisoner* **at gun point/at the point of** *a gun to stand against the wall.* **12** [C] (*often cap., as part of name*) a piece of land with a sharp end that stretches out into the sea **13** [C] (in GEOMETRY) an imaginary spot or place that has position but no size **14** [C] also **cardinal point, compass point, point of the compass**– any of the 32 marks on a compass, 11° 15′ apart, that show direction **15 at the point of** just before: *at the point of death* **16 in point** which proves or is an example of the subject under consideration: *What happened to us on holiday is* **a case in point. 17 on the point of** just starting to; just about to **18 point of no return** a point in doing something at which it becomes clear that if one continues one will not be able to stop **19 point of order** a matter connected with the proper running of an official meeting **20 point of view** a way of considering or judging a thing, person, event, etc.: *Look at it from my point of view.* (=see how it has an effect on me) **21 to the point of** so as to be almost: *Her manner of speaking is direct to the point of rudeness.* **22 when it comes/came to the point** when the moment for action or decision comes/came

**point²** *v* **1** [I *at, to*] to hold out a finger, a stick, etc., in order to show direction or position or to cause someone to look: *She pointed at him and said, "He's the thief!"|He pointed to the house on the corner and said, "That's where I live."* **2** [T *at, towards*] to aim, direct, or turn: *He pointed his gun at her and fired.* **3** [T] to fill in and make smooth the spaces between the bricks of (a wall, house, etc.) with MORTAR or cement **4 point the finger at** *infml* to hold (someone) up to public blame; ACCUSE

**point** sbdy./sthg.↔ **out** *v adv* [T +*that/to*] to draw attention to: *He pointed her out to me.|May I point out that if we don't leave now we shall miss the bus?*

**point to/towards** sthg. *v prep* [T] to suggest the strong possibility of; be a sign of

**point-blank** /ˌ·ˈ·◂/ *adj,adv* **1** (fired) from a very close position: *He fired at the animal point-blank.* **2** (in a way that is) forceful and direct: *a point-blank refusal|He refused point-blank.*

**point·ed** /ˈpɔɪntɪ̣d/ *adj* **1** shaped to a point at one end: *long pointed fingernails* **2** (of something said or done) directed, in a noticeable and often unfriendly way, at a particular person or group: *She looked at the clock in a pointed way, so I understood that it was time to leave.* **–pointedly** *adv*

**point·er** /ˈpɔɪntəʳ/ *n* **1** a stick used by someone to point at things on a large map, board, etc. **2** a small needlelike piece of metal that points to the numbers on a measuring apparatus **3** a type of hunting dog **4** a useful suggestion or piece of advice

**point·less** /ˈpɔɪntlɪ̣s/ *adj* **1** *often derog* meaningless **2** useless; unnecessary **–pointlessly** *adv* **–pointlessness** *n* [U]

**points** /pɔɪnts/ *BrE*‖**switches** *AmE*– *n* [P] a pair of short RAILS² (2) that can be moved to allow a train to change track

**poise¹** /pɔɪz/ *v* **poised, poising** [T] to hold or place lightly in a position in which it is difficult to remain steady: *He poised the glass on the edge of the shelf.*

**poise²** *n* [U] **1** good judgment, self-control, and a quiet belief in one's abilities **2** the way of holding one's head or body: *the dancer's beautiful poise*

**poised** /pɔɪzd/ *adj* **1** [F] in a state of balance: *poised between life and death* **2** [F +*to- v/for*] in a state of readiness to act or move: *poised for action* **3** *apprec* having POISE² (1)

**poi·son¹** /ˈpɔɪzən/ *n* [C;U] (a) substance that harms or kills if a living animal or plant takes it in: *He tried to kill himself by taking poison.*

**poison²** *v* [T] **1** to give poison to; harm or kill with poison: *We decided to kill the rats by poisoning them.* **2** to put poison into or onto (something): *a poisoned arrow* **3** to influence (someone's behaviour, mind, etc.) in a harmful or evil way: *She tried to poison her husband's mind against his first wife.* **–poisoner** *n*

**poi·son·ous** /ˈpɔɪzənəs/ *adj* containing, or having the effects of, poison: *poisonous snakes/berries|This medicine is poisonous.*|(fig.) *poisonous* (=evil, nasty) *ideas* **–poisonously** *adv*

**poke¹** /pəuk/ *v* **poked, poking** [I;T] **1** to push sharply out of or through an opening: *His elbow was poking through his torn shirt* SLEEVE.|*She poked her head round the corner.* **2** to push (a pointed thing) into (someone or something): *You nearly poked me (in the eye) with your pencil.* **3 poke fun at** to make jokes against **4 poke one's nose into something** *infml* to enquire into something that does not concern one

**poke about** *v adv* [I] *infml* to search: *She poked about in her bag for her ticket.*

**poke²** *n* an act of poking (POKE¹ (2)) with something pointed

**pok·er¹** /ˈpəukəʳ/ *n* a thin metal rod used to move the wood or coal in a fire in order to make it burn better

**po·ker²** *n* [U] a card game usu. played for money

**pok·y** /ˈpəuki/ *adj* **-ier, -iest** *infml* (of a place) uncomfortably small: *a poky little house*

**po·lar** /ˈpəuləʳ/ *adj* [A] of, near, like, or coming from lands near the North or South POLES

**polar bear** /ˌ·· ˈ·/ *n* **bears** *or* **bear** a large white bear that lives near the NORTH POLE

**po·lar·i·ty** /pəˈlærɪ̣ti/ *n* **-ties** [C;U] the state of having or developing two opposite qualities: *a growing polarity between the government and the trade unions*

**po·lar·ize** ‖also **-ise** *BrE* /ˈpəuləraɪz/ *v* **-ized, -izing** [I;T] to (cause to) gather about two opposite points: *The government's actions have polarized society into two classes.|Society has polarized into two classes.* **–polarization, -isation** /-raɪˈzeɪʃən‖-rə-/ *n* [C;U]

**Po·lar·oid** /ˈpəulərɔɪd/ *n tdmk* **1** [U] a material used in the glass in SUNGLASSES, car windows, etc. to make light shine less brightly through it **2** [C] a camera that produces a finished photograph only seconds after the picture has been taken

**pole¹** /pəul/ *n* a long usu. thin round stick or post: *a flagpole|a beanpole* (=for supporting climbing bean plants)|*telegraph poles beside the railway line*

**pole²** *n* **1** either end of an imaginary straight line (AXIS) around which a solid round mass turns, esp. **a**

(the lands around) the most northern and southern points on the surface of the earth **b** the two points in the sky to the north and south around which stars seem to turn –see also MAGNETIC POLE, NORTH POLE, SOUTH POLE **2** either of the points at the ends of a MAGNET **3** either of the two points at which wires may be fixed onto an electricity-storing apparatus (BATTERY) –the **negative pole** and the **positive pole** **4** **poles apart** widely separated; having no shared quality, idea, etc.

**pole star** /ˈ· ·/ also North Star /ˌ· ˈ·/– *n* [S] *(often cap.)* the rather bright star that is nearest to the centre of the heavens (NORTH POLE) in the northern part of the world

**pole vault** /ˈ· ·/ *n* (the sport of making) a jump over a high raised bar, the jumper using a long pole to lift himself –see picture on page 592 **–pole-vault** *v* [I]

**po·lice¹** /pəˈliːs/ *n* [*the* P] an official body of men and women whose duty is to protect people and property, to make sure that everyone obeys the law, to catch criminals, etc.: *The police have caught the murderer.|the police force|a police car*

**police²** *v* **-liced, -licing** [T] to keep order in (a place) by or as if using police: *The town is well policed.*

**po·lice·man** /pəˈliːsmən/ also **police officer** /·ˈ· ˌ···/– *n* **-men** /mən/ a male member of a police force

**police state** /·ˈ· ·/ *n derog* a country in which most activities of the citizens are controlled by (secret) political police

**police sta·tion** /·ˈ· ˌ··/ *n* the local office of the police in a town, part of a city, etc.

**po·lice·wom·an** /pəˈliːsˌwʊmən/ *n* **-women** /ˌwɪmɪ̈n/ [A;C] a female police officer

**pol·i·cy¹** /ˈpɒlɪ̈si/ *n* **-cies** [C;U] a plan or course of action in directing affairs, esp. as chosen by a political party, government, business company, etc.: *One of the party's policies is to control public spending.|government policy*

**policy²** *n* a written statement of the details of an agreement with an insurance company

**po·li·o** /ˈpəʊliəʊ/ also **poliomyelitis** /ˌpəʊliəʊ maɪəˈlaɪtɪ̈s/ *tech*– *n* [U] a serious infectious disease of the nerves in the backbone (SPINE), often resulting in a lasting loss of the power to move certain muscles (PARALYSIS)

**pol·ish¹** /ˈpɒlɪʃ‖ˈpɑ-/ *v* **1** [I;T *up*] to make or become smooth and shiny by continual rubbing: *Polish your shoes with a brush.|Silver polishes easily with this special cloth.* **2** [T] to make (a speech, piece of writing, performance, etc.) as perfect as possible: *The musicians gave a very polished performance.*

**polish** sthg.↔ **off** *v adv* [T] *infml* to finish (food, work, etc.)

**polish²** *n* **1** [C;U] a liquid, powder, paste, etc., used in polishing a surface: *a tin of shoe polish* **2** [S] a smooth shiny surface produced by rubbing: *That hot plate will spoil the polish on this table.* **3** [U] *apprec* fine quality or perfection (of manners, education, etc.)

**po·lite** /pəˈlaɪt/ *adj* having or showing good manners, consideration for others, and/or correct social behaviour: *What polite well-behaved children!* –opposite **impolite** **–politely** *adv* **–politeness** *n* [U]

**pol·i·tic** /ˈpɒlɪtɪ̈k‖ˈpɑ-/ *adj fml* **1** (of behaviour or actions) well-judged with regard to one's own advantage: *a politic decision* –opposite **impolitic** **2** (of a person) skilful in acting to obtain a desired result

**po·lit·i·cal** /pəˈlɪtɪkəl/ *adj* **1** of or concerning politics and/or government: *a political party|the loss of political freedoms|They are political prisoners, in prison because of their political beliefs.* –opposite **nonpolitical** **2** very interested in or active in politics: *The students in this university are very political.* –opposite **apolitical** **–politically** *adv*

**pol·i·ti·cian** /ˌpɒlɪ̈ˈtɪʃən‖ˌpɑ-/ *n* a person whose business is politics, esp. a member of a parliament

**pol·i·tics** /ˈpɒlɪ̈tɪks‖ˈpɑ-/ *n* **1** [U +*sing./pl. v*] the art, science, or business of government: *Tom is studying politics at university.|She takes an active part in local politics.|Politics has/have never interested me.* **2** [P] political opinions: *What are your politics?*

**pol·ka** /ˈpɒlkə, ˈpəʊlkə/ *n* (a piece of music for) a quick simple dance for people in pairs

**poll¹** /pəʊl/ *n* **1** [C] the giving of votes at an election: *The result of the poll won't be known until midnight.* **2** [C] also **opinion poll**– a questioning of a number of people chosen by chance, to find out the general opinion about something or someone **3** [S] the number of votes recorded at an election: *a heavy poll* (=with a large number of people voting)

**poll²** *v* [T] to receive (a stated number of votes) at an election: *She polled 10,542 votes.*

**pol·len** /ˈpɒlən‖ˈpɑ-/ *n* [U] fine yellow dust on the male part of a flower that causes other flowers to produce seeds when it is carried to them

**pollen count** /ˈ·· ·/ *n* a measure of the amount of POLLEN floating in the air

**pol·li·nate** /ˈpɒlɪ̈neɪt‖ˈpɑ-/ *v* **-nated, -nating** [T] to cause (a flower or plant) to be able to produce seeds by bringing POLLEN **–pollination** /-ˈneɪʃən/ *n* [U]

**poll·ing** /ˈpəʊlɪŋ/ *n* [U] the giving of votes at an election; voting

**polling booth** /ˈ·· ·/ *n esp. BrE* a place inside a building used for voting (**polling station**) where a person records his/her vote secretly

**pol·lut·ant** /pəˈluːtənt/ *n* [C;U] a substance or thing that POLLUTES

**pol·lute** /pəˈluːt/ *v* **-luted, -luting** [T] to make (air, water, soil, etc.) dangerously impure or unfit for use: *The river has been polluted by factory waste.*

**pol·lu·tion** /pəˈluːʃən/ *n* [U] **1** the action of polluting (POLLUTE) **2** a substance or other thing that POLLUTES: *There's a lot of pollution in the air here.*

**po·lo** /ˈpəʊləʊ/ *n* [U] a ball game played between two teams of players on horseback with long-handled wooden hammers

**polo neck** /ˈ·· ·/ *n* a high round rolled collar, usu. woollen: *a polo-neck* SWEATER

**pol·ter·geist** /ˈpɒltəgaɪst‖ˈpəʊltər-/ *n* a spirit that is said to make noises, throw objects about a room, etc.

**pol·y** /ˈpɒli‖ˈpɑli/ *n* **-ys** *BrE infml* for POLYTECHNIC

**pol·y·es·ter** /ˈpɒliestəʳ, ˌpɒliˈestəʳ‖ˈpɑliestər/ *n* [U] a man-made material used esp. to make cloth for garments: *a shirt made of polyester and cotton*

**pol·y·eth·y·lene** /ˌpɒliˈeθəliːn‖ˌpɑ-/ *n* [U] *AmE* for POLYTHENE

**po·lyg·a·my** /pə'lɪgəmi/ *n* [U] the custom or practice of having more than one wife at the same time –compare MONOGAMY, BIGAMY –**polygamist** *n* –**polygamous** *adj*: *a polygamous society*

**pol·y·gon** /'pɒlɪgən‖'pɑlɪgɑn/ *n* (in GEOMETRY) a figure on a flat surface having five or more straight sides

**pol·y·sty·rene** /,pɒlɪ'staɪəriːn‖,pɑ-/ *n* [U] a light plastic, used esp. for making containers

**pol·y·tech·nic** /,pɒlɪ'teknɪk‖,pɑ-/ also **poly** *infml– n* (esp. in Britain) a place of higher education providing training in many arts and esp.trades connected with skills and machines

**pol·y·thene** /'pɒlɪθiːn‖'pɑ-/ *BrE*‖also **polyethylene** *AmE– n* [U] a plastic not easily damaged by water or chemicals, used esp. as a protective covering, for making household articles, etc.: *a polythene bag*

**pom·e·gran·ate** /'pɒmɪgrænɪt‖'pʌmɪgrænɪt, 'pɑm-/ *n* a round fruit containing a mass of small seeds in a red juicy flesh

**pomp** /pɒmp‖pɑmp/ *n* [U] grand solemn ceremonial show, esp. on some public or official occasion

**pom·pom** /'pɒmpɒm‖'pɑmpɑm/ *n* a small ball made of bits of wool worn as a decoration on garments

**pom·pous** /'pɒmpəs‖'pɑm-/ *adj derog* foolishly solemn and self-important: *pompous language|a pompous official* –**pomposity** /pɒm'pɒsɪti‖pɑm'pɑ-/ also **pompousness**– *n* [U] –**pompously** *adv*

**pon·cho** /'pɒntʃəu‖'pɑn-/ *n* **-chos** a garment consisting of a single long wide piece of usu. thick woollen cloth with a hole in the middle for the head

**pond** /pɒnd‖pɑnd/ *n* an area of still water smaller than a lake: *a duck pond in the park*

**pon·der** /'pɒndəʳ‖'pɑn-/ *v* [I;T *on, over*] *fml* to spend time in considering (a fact, difficulty, etc.): *When I asked her advice, she pondered (the matter) and then told me not to go.*

**pon·der·ous** /'pɒndərəs‖'pɑn-/ *adj fml* slow and awkward because of size and weight: (fig.) *a ponderous style of writing* –**ponderously** *adv* –**ponderousness** *n* [U]

**pong** /pɒŋ‖pɑŋ/ *v,n* [I] *BrE infml* (to make) an unpleasant smell

**pon·tiff** /'pɒntɪf‖'pɑn-/ *n* [*the* S *usu.cap.*] (in various religions) a chief priest, esp. the POPE

**pon·tif·i·cate** /pɒn'tɪfɪkeɪt‖pɑn-/ *v* **-cated, -cating** [I *about, on*] *usu. derog* to speak or write as if one's own judgment is the only correct one

**pon·toon¹** /pɒn'tuːn‖pɑn-/ *n* any of a number of flat-bottomed boats fastened together side by side to support a floating bridge (**pontoon bridge**) across a river

**pontoon²** *BrE*‖**twenty-one** *AmE– n* [U] a card game, usu. played for money

**po·ny** /'pəuni/ *n* **-nies** a small horse

**po·ny·tail** /'pəuniteɪl/ *n* a bunch of hair tied high at the back of the head –compare PIGTAIL

**poo·dle** /'puːdl/ *n* a type of dog with thick curling hair, usu. cut in special shapes

**poof** /puːf, pʊf/ *n BrE derog infml* a male HOMOSEXUAL

**pooh** /puː/ *interj* **1** (said when smelling something unpleasant) **2** *derog* (said to show disbelief or disapproval at a suggestion, idea, etc.)

**pooh-pooh** /,· '·/ *v* [T] *infml* to treat as not worthy of consideration: *They pooh-poohed the idea.*

**pool¹** /puːl/ *n* **1** a small area of still water in a hollow place, usu. naturally formed: *After the rain, there were little pools of water on the ground.* **2** [*of*] a small amount of any liquid on a surface: *She was lying in a pool of blood.* **3** →SWIMMING POOL

**pool²** *n* **1** [C] a common supply of money, goods, workers, etc., which may be used by a number of people: *Our firm has a car pool, so if I need a car there's always one there.|A* **typing pool** *is a group of* TYPISTS, *in one large office, who do all the typing for a company.* **2** [U] a type of American BILLIARDS: *to shoot pool* (=to play pool) –compare SNOOKER

**pool³** *v* [T] to combine; share: *If we pool our ideas, we may be able to produce a really good plan.*

**pools** /puːlz/ *n* also **football pools** *fml–* [*the* P] an arrangement (esp. in Britain) by which people risk (BET) small amounts of money on the results of certain football matches

**poop** /puːp/ *n tech* the back end of a ship

**poor** /puəʳ/ *adj* **1** having very little money and therefore a low standard of living: *He was too poor to buy shoes for his family.|The government's plan will hurt the poor.* –opposite **rich 2** below the usual standard; low in quality: *in poor health|a poor crop of beans* **3** [A *no comp.*] deserving or causing pity: *The poor old man had lost both his sons in the war.*

**poor·ly¹** /'puəli‖'puərli/ *adv* badly; not well: *poorly dressed/paid*

**poorly²** *adj* [F] *BrE* ill: *She feels poorly today.*

**poor·ness** /'puənɪs‖puər-/ *n* [U *of*] a low standard; lack of a desired quality: *the poorness of the quality in this car* –compare POVERTY

**pop¹** /pɒp‖pɑp/ *v* **-pp- 1** [I;T] to (cause to) make a short sharp explosive sound: *When he pulled the* CORK *out of the bottle, it popped.* **2** [I] *infml* to spring: *The child's eyes almost popped out of her head with excitement.* **3** [I;T] *infml* to go, come, or put suddenly, quickly, etc.: *I've just popped in to return your book.|I'm afraid she's just popped out for a few minutes.|He popped his head round the door.* **4 pop the question (to)** *infml* to make an offer of marriage (to); PROPOSE (3) (to)

**pop²** *n* **1** [C] a sound like that of a slight explosion: *When he opened the bottle it went pop.* **2** [U] *infml* a sweet drink containing a harmless gas; LEMONADE (1)

**pop³** *n AmE infml* father: *Can I borrow the car, pop?*

**pop⁴** *n* [U] modern popular music, esp. as favoured by younger people: *I prefer* CLASSICAL (2) *music to pop (music).|a pop group* (=a group of people who sing and play pop music) –compare ROCK ²

**pop⁵** *written abbrev. said as:* **1** population **2** popularly

**pop·corn** /'pɒpkɔːn‖'pɑpkɔrn/ *n* [U] grains of corn that have been swollen and burst by heat, usu. eaten with salt and butter

**pope** /pəup/ *n* [A;C] (*often cap.*) the head of the ROMAN CATHOLIC Church: *the election of a new pope|Pope John Paul*

**pop·lar** *n* [C;U] (the wood of) a very tall straight thin tree

**pop·py** /'pɒpi‖'pɑpi/ *n* **-pies** a plant with showy esp. red flowers

**pop·u·lace** /'pɒpjuləs‖'pɑpjə-/ *n* [U +*sing./pl.v*]

Sue was hoping to go to a **pop concert** at the weekend to see a famous **pop group**. She phoned the theatre **box office** to **book** tickets **in advance**, but they told her that the concert was already **fully booked/sold out**: there were no **seats** left. "But there may be some **cancellations** (=tickets brought back because they weren't wanted) which you can buy **at the door**," she was told.

Sue meets her friend in the **foyer** on the night of the concert, and they are able to buy two tickets. Sue buys a **programme** to read about the group. At the entrance to the **auditorium** their tickets are looked at and torn in half to show that they have been used. As they go into the hall they see that the lights have **gone down** and the band is already **on stage**.

*fml* all the common people of a country: *The populace no longer supports/support the government.*

**pop·u·lar** /'pɒpjʊlə^r^||'pɑpjə-/ *adj* **1** favoured by many people; well liked: *a popular song|She's very popular with her pupils.* –opposite **unpopular 2** [A] *sometimes derog* suited to the understanding, liking, or needs of the general public: *The popular newspapers take a great interest in the Royal Family.* **3** [A *no comp.*] *fml* of or for the general public: *popular opinion|the popular vote*

**pop·u·lar·i·ty** /ˌpɒpjʊ'lærəti||ˌpɑpjə-/ *n* [U] the quality or state of being well liked, favoured, or admired –opposite **unpopularity**

**pop·u·lar·ize** ||also **-ise** *BrE* /'pɒpjʊləraɪz||'pɑpjə-/ *v* **-ized, -izing** [T] **1** to make (something difficult) easily understandable to ordinary people by a simple explanation **2** to make (something new) generally known and used –**popularization** /-raɪ'zeɪʃən||-rə-/ *n* [C;U]

**pop·u·lar·ly** /'pɒpjʊləli||'pɑpjələrli/ *adv* generally; by most people: *It's popularly believed that town life is unhealthy.*

**pop·u·late** /'pɒpjʊleɪt||'pɑpjə-/ *v* **-lated, -lating** [T *often pass.*] (of a group) to settle or live in (a particular area): *a thickly-populated area|North America was mainly populated by new settlers from abroad.*

**pop·u·la·tion** /ˌpɒpjʊ'leɪʃən||ˌpɑpjə-/ *n* [C;U *of*] the (number of) people living in an area, country, etc.: *What was the population of Europe in 1900?*

**pop·u·lous** /'pɒpjʊləs||'pɑpjə-/ *adj* (of a place) having a large population, esp. when compared with size

**porce·lain** /'pɔːslən||'porsələn/ *n* [U] (cups, dishes, etc. made of) thin shiny material of very fine quality, which is produced by baking a clay mixture

**porch** /pɔːtʃ||portʃ/ *n* **1** a built-out roofed entrance to a house or church –see picture on page 297 **2** *AmE* for VERANDA

**por·cu·pine** /'pɔːkjʊpaɪn||'porkjə-/ *n* a short-legged animal that has very long stiff prickles (QUILLS) all over its back and sides. It is larger than a HEDGEHOG.

**pore** /pɔː^r^||por/ *n* a very small opening (esp. in the skin) through which liquids (esp. SWEAT[1]) may pass

**pore o·ver** sthg. *v prep* **pored, poring** [T] to study or give close attention to (usu. something written or printed)

**pork** /pɔːk||pork/ *n* [U] meat from pigs –compare BACON, HAM; see MEAT (USAGE)

**porn** /pɔːn||pɔrn/ *n* [U] *infml* for PORNOGRAPHY

**por·nog·ra·phy** /pɔː'nɒgrəfi||pɔr'nɑg-/ also **porn** *infml*– *n* [U] **1** the treatment of sexual subjects in pictures or writing in a way that is meant to cause sexual excitement **2** books, photographs, etc., containing this –**pornographer** *n* –**pornographic** /ˌpɔːnə'græfɪk||ˌpɔr-/ *adj*

**po·rous** /'pɔːrəs||'po-/ *adj* allowing liquid to pass slowly through: *porous soil|This clay pot is porous.* –opposite **nonporous**

**por·poise** /'pɔːpəs||'pɔr-/ *n* a large fishlike sea animal that swims about in groups –compare DOLPHIN

**por·ridge** /'pɒrɪdʒ||'pɑ-, 'pɔ-/ *n* [U] a breakfast food made by boiling crushed grain (OATMEAL) in milk or water

**port[1]** /pɔːt||port/ *n* **1** (a) harbour: *There is only one port along this rocky coast.|We reached port by evening.* **2** a town with a harbour: *England has many ports.|Our next* **port of call** (=the next place at which the ship will stop) *is Lisbon.*

**port[2]** *n* [S] the left side of a ship or aircraft as one faces forward: *The damaged ship was leaning to port.|on the port side* –compare STARBOARD

**port[3]** *n* [U] strong usu. sweet Portuguese wine usu. drunk after a meal –compare SHERRY

**por·ta·ble** /'pɔːtəbəl||'por-/ *adj* that can be (easily) carried or moved; quite small and light: *a portable television*

**por·tal** /'pɔːtl||'portl/ *n fml or lit* a (very grand) door or entrance to a building

**port·cul·lis** /pɔːt'kʌləs||port-/ *n* (in old castles, forts, etc.) a strong gatelike framework hung above an entrance and lowered as a protection against attack

**por·tend** /pɔː'tend||por-/ *v* [T] *fml* to be a sign or warning of (a future undesirable event): *black clouds portending a storm*

**por·tent** /'pɔːtent||'por-/ *n fml or lit* a (wonderful or terrible) sign or warning, esp. of something strange or undesirable: *portents of war*

**por·ten·tous** /pɔː'tentəs||por-/ *adj fml or lit* that warns or FORETELLS (of evil happenings); threatening –compare OMINOUS

**por·ter[1]** /'pɔːtə^r^||'por-/ *n esp. BrE* a man in charge of the entrance to a hotel, school, hospital, etc.

**porter[2]** *n* a person employed to carry travellers' bags, esp. at railway stations, airports, etc. –see picture on page 501

**port·fo·li·o** /pɔːt'fəʊliəʊ||port-/ *n* **-os 1** a large flat case like a very large book cover, for carrying drawings, business papers, etc. **2** the office and duties of a (particular) minister of state: *the portfolio of foreign affairs*

**port·hole** /'pɔːthəʊl||'port-/ *n* a small usu. circular window along the side of a ship or aircraft

**por·ti·co** /'pɔːtɪkəʊ||'por-/ *n* **-coes** *or* **-cos** a grand entrance to a building, consisting of a roof supported by pillars

**por·tion** /'pɔːʃən||'por-/ *n* [*of*] **1** a part separated or cut off: *passengers travelling in the front portion of the train* **2** a share: *A portion of the blame for the accident must be borne by the driver.* **3** a quantity of food for one person as served in a restaurant

**portion** sthg.↔ **out** *v adv* [T *among, between*] to share

**port·ly** /'pɔːtli||'por-/ *adj* **-lier, -liest** *euph or humor* (of a grown-up person, often rather old) round and fat: *a portly old man* –**portliness** *n* [U]

**port·man·teau** /pɔːt'mæntəʊ||port-/ *n* **-teaus** *or* **-teaux** /təʊz/ a large travelling case for clothes, esp. one that opens out in the middle into two equal parts

**por·trait** /'pɔːtrət||'por-/ *n* [*of*] **1** a painting, drawing, or photograph of a real person: *a portrait of the Royal Family* **2** a lifelike written description

**por·trai·ture** /'pɔːtrətʃə^r^||'por-/ *n* [U] the art of making PORTRAITS (esp.1)

**por·tray** /pɔː'treɪ||por-/ *v* **-trayed, -traying** [T] **1** to represent (someone or something) in painting, in a book, etc., esp. according to one's own ideas or so as to produce a certain effect: *Her book portrays the king as a cruel man.* **2** to act the part of (a particular character) in a play –**portrayal** *n* [C;U]

**pose¹** /pəʊz/ *v* **posed, posing 1** [I;T *for*] to (cause to) sit or stand in a particular effective position, esp. for a photograph, painting, etc.: *After the wedding we all posed for a photograph.* **2** [T] to set; offer for consideration: *You've posed us an awkward question.*|*This new law poses several problems for farmers.*

**pose as** sbdy. *v prep* [I] to pretend to be: *The prisoner posed as a prison officer in order to escape.*

**pose²** *n* **1** a position of the body, esp. as taken up to produce an effect in art: *I stood in various poses while I was photographed.* **2** *derog* an unnatural way of behaving which is intended to produce an effect

**posh** /pɒʃ‖pɑʃ/ *adj infml derog or apprec* for, or typical of, people of high social rank: *a posh hotel*|*She has a rather posh way of speaking.*

**po·si·tion¹** /pəˈzɪʃən/ *n* **1** [C;U] the place where someone or something is or should be: *We can find our position by looking at this map.*|*One of the chairs is* **out of position.**|*Put it back* **in position. 2** [C;U *in*] a particular place or rank in a group: *She's in top position in the class.* **3** [C *usu. sing.*] a condition or state: *By telling her that, you've put me in a very difficult position.*|*In the company's present position, they cannot afford to offer higher wages.*|*I'd like to help you, but I'm afraid I'm not* **in a position to** *do so.* (=I can't) **4** [C] the way or manner in which someone or something is placed or moves, stands, sits, etc.: *He had to work in a most uncomfortable position under the car.* **5** [C] a job; employment: *She's got a good position in an oil company.* –see JOB (USAGE)

**position²** *v* [T] to put in the stated or proper POSITION¹ (1): *He positioned himself by the entrance.*

**pos·i·tive¹** /ˈpɒzətɪv‖ˈpɑ-/ *adj* **1** allowing no room for doubt; DEFINITE: *We still don't have a positive answer as to how he died.*|*a positive refusal* **2** [F+(*that*)/*of*] (of a person) having no doubt about something; sure: *Are you positive he's the man you saw yesterday?* **3** effective; actually helpful: *Don't just watch me give me some positive advice!*|*positive thinking* **4** [*no comp.*] (in grammar) of or being the simple form of an adjective or adverb, which expresses no COMPARISON –compare COMPARATIVE², SUPERLATIVE¹ **5** [*no comp.*] (in MATHEMATICS) (of a number or quantity) greater than zero **6** [*no comp.*] (of a photograph) having light and dark areas as they are in nature, not the other way around **7** [*no comp.*] (of a medical test) showing signs of disease **8** [A *no comp.*] *infml (used for giving force to a noun)* complete; real: *It was a positive delight to hear her sing so beautifully.* –compare NEGATIVE

**positive²** *n* **1** (in grammar) the POSITIVE¹ (4) degree or form of an adjective or adverb: *The positive of "prettiest" is "pretty".* **2** (in MATHEMATICS) a quantity greater than zero **3** a POSITIVE¹ (6) photograph –compare NEGATIVE

**pos·i·tive·ly** /ˈpɒzətɪvli‖ˈpɑ-/ *adv* **1** (as if) with certainty: *He said quite positively that he would come.* **2** *infml* (*used for adding force to an expression*) really; indeed: *She's not just pretty-she's positively beautiful!* –compare POSITIVE¹ (8)

**pos·sess** /pəˈzes/ *v* [T not *be +v-ing*] **1** *fml* to own; have: *They asked me if I possessed a gun.* **2** (of a feeling or idea) to influence (someone) so completely as to control or direct actions: *What possessed you* (=caused you) *to act so strangely?*

**pos·sessed** /pəˈzest/ *adj fml or lit* wildly mad, (as if) controlled by an evil spirit: *She waved the knife at me and screamed, as if possessed.*

**pos·ses·sion** /pəˈzeʃən/ *n* **1** [U *of*] ownership: *She was found* **in possession of** *dangerous drugs.*|*The soldiers* **took possession of** (=seized) *the enemy's fort.* **2** [C *often pl.*] a piece of personal property: *I lost all my possessions in the war.*

**pos·ses·sive¹** /pəˈzesɪv/ *adj* **1** *derog* unwilling to share (something one owns, someone's attention, etc.) with other people **2** (in grammar) of or being a word that shows ownership or connection: *"My" and "its" are possessive adjectives.* –compare GENITIVE –**possessively** *adv* –**possessiveness** *n* [U]

**possessive²** *n* a POSSESSIVE¹ (2) word or form: *"Hers" is the possessive of "she".*

**pos·ses·sor** /pəˈzesəʳ/ *n fml* an owner: *He is the fortunate possessor of a fine singing voice.*

**pos·si·bil·i·ty** /ˌpɒsəˈbɪləti‖ˌpɑ-/ *n* **-ties 1** [S;U +*that*/*of*] the state or fact of being possible; a (degree of) likelihood: *Police are considering the possibility that the fire was started intentionally.*|*Is there any possibility that you'll be able to come tomorrow?* **2** [C] something that is possible: *The general would not accept that defeat was a possibility.*|*Your product* **has possibilities**; *with our help it could be a great success.* –see also IMPOSSIBLE

**pos·si·ble** /ˈpɒsəbəl‖ˈpɑ-/ *adj* **1** that can exist, happen, or be done: *It's no longer possible to find a cheap flat in central London.*|*I'll help you* **if possible.** (=if it is possible)|*Try to finish the job* **as soon as possible.** –opposite **impossible 2** that may or may not be, happen, or be expected: *It is possible but not probable that I shall go there next week.* **3** acceptable; suitable: *one of many possible answers*

**pos·si·bly** /ˈpɒsəbli‖ˈpɑ-/ *adv* **1** in accordance with what is POSSIBLE: *I'll do all I possibly can.*|*You can't possibly walk 20 miles in an hour.* **2** perhaps: *"Will you be here tomorrow?" "Possibly."*

**post¹** /pəʊst/ *n* **1** a strong upright pole or bar made of wood, metal, etc., usu. fixed into the ground: *The fence was made of posts joined together with wire.*|*a gate post*|*a signpost* **2** [*the* S] the starting or finishing place in a race, esp. a horse race: *My uncle's horse was* **first past the post.**|*the* **finishing post**

**post²** *v* [T] **1** to make public or show by fixing to a wall, board, post, etc.: *The names of the members of the team will be posted (up) today.* **2** [T *usu. pass.*] to make known (as being) by putting up a notice: *The ship was posted missing.*

**post³** *BrE*‖also **mail** *esp. AmE*– *n* **1** [U] the official system for carrying letters, parcels, etc., from the sender to the receiver: *He sent the parcel* **by post. 2** [*the* S;U] (a single official collection or delivery of) letters, parcels, etc.: *Has the afternoon post arrived?*|*Has any post come for me today?*|*Please reply* **by return of post** (*BrE*)‖**by return mail** (*AmE*). (=by the next official collection)

**post⁴** *BrE*‖**mail** *AmE*– *v* [T] **1** to take (a letter, parcel, etc.) to a post office or put into a collection box for sending: *Did you post that letter I gave you* yesterday? **2 keep someone posted** to continue to give someone all the latest news about something

**post**[5] *n* **1** a job: *The post was advertised in today's newspaper.* –see JOB (USAGE) **2** a special place of duty, esp. on guard or on watch: *The soldiers must be at their posts by 8.30.* **3** a small distant fort, camp, etc., at which a body of soldiers is kept

**post**[6] *v* [T] **1** to place (soldiers etc.) on duty in a special place: *Post a guard outside the palace.* **2** [*usu.pass.*] *esp. BrE* to send (someone) to a particular place on duty, to work, etc.: *Smith has been posted to Hong Kong.*

**post·age** /ˈpəʊstɪdʒ/ *n* [U] the charge for carrying a letter, parcel, etc., by post

**postage stamp** /ˈ·· ·/ *n fml* for STAMP[2] (1)

**post·al** /ˈpəʊstl/ *adj* [A] connected with the public letter service: *Postal charges have risen again.*

**postal or·der** /ˈ·· ˌ··/ *BrE*‖**money order** *AmE*– *n* a small piece of paper that can be bought from a post office, and sent to someone who can take it to a post office and exchange it for a stated amount of money

**post·box** /ˈpəʊstbɒks‖-baks/ also **letterbox** *BrE*‖ **mailbox** *AmE*– *n BrE* an official box into which letters are put for sending by post –see also PILLAR-BOX –see picture on page 297

**post·card** /ˈpəʊstkaːd‖-kard/ *n* a card on which a message may be sent by post, sometimes having a picture on one side (a **picture postcard**)

**post·code** /ˈpəʊstkəʊd/ *BrE*‖**zip code** *AmE*– *n* a group of letters and numbers that can be added to the address on letters so that they may be delivered more quickly

**post·date** /ˌpəʊstˈdeɪt/ *v* **-dated, -dating** [T] to write on (a letter, cheque, etc.) a date later than the date of writing: *a postdated cheque* –see also BACKDATE

**post·er** /ˈpəʊstəʳ/ *n* a large printed notice or (coloured) drawing to be put up in a public place or in a private room

**pos·te·ri·or** /pɒˈstɪərɪəʳ‖pa-/ *n* **1** *humor* the part of the body a person sits on; BUTTOCKS **2** *usu tech* nearer the back –opposite **anterior**

**pos·ter·i·ty** /pɒˈsterəti‖pa-/ *n* [U] *fml* people who will be born and live after one's own time

**post·grad·u·ate** /ˌpəʊstˈgrædjʊət‖-ˈgrædʒʊət/ also **graduate** *AmE*– *n,adj* (a person doing studies that are) done at a university after one has received one's first degree

**post·haste** /ˌpəʊstˈheɪst/ *adv lit* at very great speed; in a great hurry

**post·hu·mous** /ˈpɒstjʊməs‖ˈpastʃə-/ *adj* coming after one's death: *posthumous fame* –**posthumously** *adv*: *His last book was published posthumously.*

**post·man** /ˈpəʊstmən/ *BrE*‖**mailman** *AmE*– *n* **-men** /mən/ a man employed to collect and deliver letters, parcels, etc.

**post·mark** /ˈpəʊstmaːk‖-mark/ *n* an official mark made on letters, parcels, etc., usu. over the stamp, showing when and from where they are sent –**postmark** *v* [T *usu.pass.*]: *The parcel was postmarked Brighton.*

**post·mas·ter** /ˈpəʊstˌmaːstəʳ‖-ˌmæ-/ **postmistress** /-ˈmɪstrəs/ *fem.*– *n* a person officially in charge of a post office

**post·mor·tem** /ˌpəʊstˈmɔːtəm‖-ˈmɔr-/ *n Latin* an examination of a dead body to discover the cause of death; AUTOPSY: (fig.) *There will have to be a postmortem on the company's bad sales results.*

**post·na·tal** /ˌpəʊstˈneɪtl/ *adj* [A] *tech* of or for the time after a birth

**post of·fice** /ˈ· ˌ··/ *n* a building, office, shop, etc., which deals with the post and certain other government business such as (in Britain) telephone bills

**post·pone** /pəusˈpəun/ *v* **-poned, -poning** [T +*v-ing*/*until, to*] to delay; move to some later time; DEFER: *We're postponing our holiday until August.* –**postponement** *n* [C;U]

**post·script** /ˈpəʊstˌskrɪpt/ also **P.S.** *infml*– *n* a short addition to a letter, below the place where one has signed one's name

**pos·tu·late** /ˈpɒstjʊleɪt‖ˈpastʃə-/ *v* **-lated, -lating** [T +*that*] *fml* to accept (something that has not been proved) as true, as a base for reasoning

**pos·ture**[1] /ˈpɒstʃəʳ‖ˈpas-/ *n* **1** [U] the general way of holding the body: *Only humans have a natural upright posture.* **2** [C] a fixed bodily position

**posture**[2] *v* **-tured, -turing** [I] *often derog* to place oneself in a fixed bodily position, esp. in order to make other people admire one

**post·war** /ˌpəʊstˈwɔːʳ◂/ *adj* [A] belonging to the time after a war

**po·sy** /ˈpəʊzi/ *n* **-sies** a small bunch of flowers

**pot**[1] /pɒt‖pat/ *n* **1** [C] a round vessel of baked clay, metal, glass, etc., used for containing liquids or solids and esp. for cooking: *a pot of paint*|*a teapot* –see picture on page 337 **2** [C *of*] also **potful** /ˈpɒtfʊl‖ˈpat-/– the amount that a POT[1] (1) will hold: *A pot of tea for two, please.* **3** [C] a round vessel for liquid and solid body waste, usu. used in the bedroom by an old or sick person, or by a small child, and kept under the bed **4** [C *usu. pl.*] *infml* a large amount (of money): *They're very rich; they've got pots of money.* **5** [C] *infml* for POTSHOT **6** [U] *infml* for MARIJUANA **7 go to pot** *infml* to become ruined or worthless, esp. from lack of care **8 take pot luck** to take what is offered, without choice

**pot**[2] *v* **-tt-** [T] **1** to put (a young plant) in a pot filled with earth **2** to shoot and kill, esp. for food or sport

**po·tas·si·um** /pəˈtæsɪəm/ *n* [U] a silver-white soft easily melted metal that is a simple substance (ELEMENT (1))

**po·ta·to** /pəˈteɪtəʊ/ *n* **-toes** [C;U] a roundish root vegetable with a thin brown or yellowish skin, that is cooked and served in many different ways: *baked potatoes* –see also CHIP[1] (3)

**potato chip** /·ˈ·· ·/ also **chip**– *n AmE & AustrE* for CRISP[2]

**pot·bel·ly** /ˈpɒtˌbeli‖ˈpat-/ *n* **-lies** *often derog or humor* a large rounded noticeable stomach

**po·tent** /ˈpəʊtənt/ *adj fml* (of medicines, drugs, drinks, etc.) having a strong and/or rapid effect on the body or mind: (fig.) *a potent* (=effective) *argument* –see also IMPOTENT

**po·ten·tate** /ˈpeʊtənteɪt/ *n* (esp. in former times) a ruler with direct power over his/her people, not limited by a law-making body

**po·ten·tial**[1] /pəˈtenʃəl/ *adj* [*no comp.*] existing in possibility; not at present active or developed, but able to become so: *Every seed is a potential plant.*|*a* potential leader **–potentially** *adv*

**potential²** *n* [U] (the degree of) possibility for developing or being developed: *a new invention with a big sales potential*

**pot·hole** /ˈpɒthəʊl‖ˈpɑt-/ *n* **1** a deep round hole in the surface of rock by which water enters and flows underground, often through a cave **2** a hole in the surface of a road caused by traffic or bad weather

**pot·hol·ing** /ˈpɒtˌhəʊlɪŋ‖ˈpɑt-/ *n* [U] the sport of climbing down inside POTHOLES (1) **–potholer** *n*

**po·tion** /ˈpəʊʃən/ *n lit* a single drink of a liquid mixture, intended as medicine, poison, or a magic charm: *a sleeping/love potion*

**pot·shot** /ˈpɒt-ʃɒt‖ˈpɑt-ʃɑt/ *n infml* a carelessly aimed shot: *I took a potshot at the rabbit, but missed.*

**pot·ted** /ˈpɒtɪ̈d‖ˈpɑ-/ *adj* [A] (of meat, fish, or chicken) made into a paste and preserved in a pot, for eating when spread on bread

**pot·ter** /ˈpɒtəʳ‖ˈpɑ-/ *n* a person who makes pots, dishes, etc., out of baked clay, esp. by hand

**potter a·bout** *v adv* [I] *infml* to spend time in activities that demand little effort: *I spent the afternoon pottering about in the garden.*

**pot·ter·y** /ˈpɒtəri‖ˈpɑ-/ *n* [U] **1** the work of a POTTER **2** (objects made out of) baked clay

**pot·ty¹** /ˈpɒti‖ˈpɑti/ *adj* **-tier, -tiest** *BrE infml* **1** silly; slightly mad: *That noise is driving me potty.* **2** [F *about*] having a strong uncontrolled interest in or admiration for: *He's just potty about her!*

**potty²** *n* **-ties** a POT¹ (3) for children, now usu. made of plastic

**pouch** /paʊtʃ/ *n* **1** a small leather bag, esp. to hold tobacco or (formerly) gunpowder **2** a pocket of skin, esp. one in the lower half of the body, in which certain animals (MARSUPIALS) carry their young

**pouf, pouffe** /puːf/ *n* a low soft drum-shaped object, used as a seat

**poul·tice** /ˈpəʊltɪ̈s/ *n* a soft heated wet mass of any of various substances, spread on a thin cloth and laid against the skin to lessen pain, swelling, etc.

**poul·try** /ˈpəʊltri/ *n* **1** [P] farmyard birds, such as hens, ducks, etc., kept for supplying eggs and meat **2** [U] hens, ducks, etc., considered as meat: *Poultry is rather cheap now.*

**pounce** /paʊns/ *v* **pounced, pouncing** [I *at, on, upon*] to fly down or spring suddenly in order to seize something: *The cat pounced on the bird.*|(fig.) *The policeman pounced on the thief.*

**pound¹** /paʊnd/ *n* **1** [C] a standard measure of weight equal to ·454 kilograms: *Sugar is sold by the pound.*|*Two pounds of apples, please.* **2** [C; *the* S] also **pound sterling** *fml*– the British standard of money, divided into 100 pence: *Five pounds is usually written "£5".*|*a five-pound note*|*Recently, the pound has* **grown stronger against** (=has increased its value in relation to) *the dollar.* **3** [C] the standard of money in several countries: *the Egyptian pound* **4** **-pounder** something weighing a certain number of pounds: *I went fishing and caught a five-pounder.*

**pound²** *v* **1** [T *up*] to crush into a soft mass or powder by striking repeatedly with a heavy object: *This machine pounds the stones into a powder.* **2** [I;T *away, against, at, on*] to strike or beat repeatedly, heavily, and noisily: *The stormy waves pounded against the rocks.*|*My heart pounded with excitement.*

**pound³** *n* a place where lost dogs and cats, or cars that have been illegally parked, are kept by the police until claimed

**pour** /pɔːʳ‖por/ *v* **1** [I;T *away, in, out*] to (cause to) flow steadily and rapidly: *Blood poured from the wound.*|*Shall I pour you another cup of tea?*|(fig.) *The government has been pouring money into the steel industry recently.* **2** [*it* I *down*] to rain hard and steadily: *It's pouring (down).*|*in the pouring rain* –see WEATHER (USAGE)

**pour** sthg.↔ **out** *v adv* [T] to tell (a story, news, one's troubles, etc.) freely and with feeling

**pout** /paʊt/ *v* [I;T] to show childish bad temper and displeasure by pushing (the lips) forward **–pout** *n*

**pov·er·ty** /ˈpɒvəti‖ˈpɑvərti/ *n* [U] the state of being very poor: *Poverty prevented the boy from continuing his education.*

**poverty-strick·en** /ˈ··· ˌ··/ *adj* very poor indeed

**P O W** *abbrev. for:* PRISONER OF WAR: *a POW camp*

**pow·der¹** /ˈpaʊdəʳ/ *n* [C;U] (a kind of) substance in the form of very fine dry grains: *He stepped on the piece of chalk and crushed it to powder.*|*a packet of soap powder*|*face powder* (=a type of COSMETIC¹)

**powder²** *v* [T] to put POWDER (esp. face powder or TALCUM POWDER) on: *John powdered the baby after its bath.*

**pow·dered** /ˈpaʊdəd‖-ərd/ *adj* produced or dried in the form of powder: *powdered milk*

**powder room** /ˈ·· ·/ *n euph* a women's public LAVATORY in a hotel, restaurant, etc.

**pow·der·y** /ˈpaʊdəri/ *adj* like or easily broken into powder: *powdery snow*

**pow·er¹** /ˈpaʊəʳ/ *n* **1** [C;U +*to-v*/*of*] what one can do; ability: *Man is the only animal that has the power of speech.*|*She claims to have the power to see into the future.*|*He did everything in his power* (=all he could) *to help her.*|*When he wrote this book, he was at the height of his powers as a writer.* **2** [U] force; strength: *You can really feel the power of the sun here.*|*a nation's sea power* (=the strength of its navy) **3** [U] force that may be used for doing work, driving a machine, or producing electricity: *Mills used to depend on wind power or water power.*|*The damaged ship was able to reach port* **under her own power**. –see HORSEPOWER, MANPOWER **4** [U] control over others: *the power of the government*|*He wants power as well as money.*|*Which political party is* **in power** *now?* (=which one is the government party?) **5** [C +*to-v*] right to act, given by law or official position: *The police have special powers to deal with this state of affairs.* **6** [C] a person, group, nation, etc., that has influence or control: *a meeting of world powers* (=the strongest nations in the world)|(fig.) *No power on earth can make me do what I don't want to.* **7** [C] (in MATHEMATICS) the number of times that an amount is to be multiplied by itself: *The amount 2 to the power of 3 is written* $2^3$, *and means* 2×2×2. **8** [U] a measure of the degree to which a microscope, TELESCOPE, etc. is able to make things seen through it look larger **9** [S *of*] *infml* a large amount; great deal: *Your visit did me* **a power of good. 10 the powers that be** *often humor* the people in high official positions who make decisions that have an effect on one's life

**11 -powered** using or producing a certain type or amount of POWER (3): *a low-powered engine|a gas-powered heating system*

**power²** *v* **1** [T *usu.pass*] to supply power to (esp. a moving machine): *powered by electricity* **2** *infml* to move or travel powerfully and at speed

**pow·er·ful** /'pauəfəl||-ər-/ *adj* **1** having great power; very strong; full of force: *a powerful swimmer|a meeting of the world's most powerful nations|The ship is driven by two powerful motors.* **2** having a strong effect: *The minister made a powerful speech.|a powerful drug* **–powerfully** *adv*: *He's very powerfully built.* (=has a big strong body)

**pow·er·less** /'pauəl¦əs||'pauər-/ *adj* [+*to-v*] lacking power or strength; weak; unable: *The car went out of control, and the driver was powerless to stop it.* **–powerlessly** *adv* **–powerlessness** *n* [U]

**power point** /'·· ·/ *n BrE* for POINT¹ (14)

**power sta·tion** /'·· ,··/ also **power plant** *AmE*– *n* a large building in which electricity is made

**pp** *written abbrev. said as:* pages: *see pp 15-37* –see also P²

**PR** *abbrev. for:* PUBLIC RELATIONS

**prac·ti·ca·ble** /'præktɪkəbəl/ *adj* that can be successfully used or acted upon (though not yet tried): *Is it practicable to grow crops on this dry land?* –opposite **impracticable** **–practicably** *adv* **–practicability** /-ə'bɪl¦əti/ *n* [U]

USAGE Do not confuse **practicable** and **practical**. Although they can sometime mean the same thing (a **practicable/practical** plan or suggestion is one that will work), **practicable** is never used of people and only rarely of objects.

**prac·ti·cal¹** /'præktɪkəl/ *adj* **1** concerned with action, practice, or actual conditions and results, rather than with ideas: *She has studied medicine at university, but has not had much practical experience of hospital work.* **2** effective or convenient in actual use; suited to actual conditions: *a very practical little table that folds up out of the way when not needed* **3** *often apprec* sensible; clever at doing things and dealing with difficulties: *a very practical woman* –opposite **impractical** (for **2,3**) –see PRACTICABLE (USAGE) **–practicality** /- 'kæl¦əti/ *n* **-ties** [C;U]: *I'm not sure about the practicality of that suggestion.*

**practical²** *n infml* a PRACTICAL¹ (1) lesson, test, or examination, as in science: *a chemistry practical*

**practical joke** /,··· '·/ *n* a trick played upon one person to give amusement to others

**prac·ti·cal·ly** /'præktɪkəli/ *adv* **1** usefully; suitably **2** very nearly; almost: *The holidays are practically over; there's only one day left.* –see Study Notes on page 389

**prac·tice** ||also **-tise** *AmE* /'prækt¦əs/ *n* **1** [C;U] (a) (regularly) repeated performance or exercise in order to gain skill in an activity: *It takes a lot of practice to be really good at this sport.|a football practice|teaching practice|I'm* **out of practice** *at playing the piano.* (=unable to play well because of lack of practice) **2** [U] the actual doing of something: *It sounded a good idea, but* **in practice** *it didn't work.|We must now put our plans into practice.* –compare THEORY (2) **3** [C;U] *fml* something that is regularly or habitually done: *It was her practice to have dinner at six o'clock.* –see HABIT (USAGE) **4** [C] the business of a doctor or lawyer: *He has a practice in London.*

**prac·tise** ||also **-tice** *AmE* /'prækt¦əs/ *v* **- tised, -tising** **1** [I;T+*v-ing*] to do (an action) or perform on (a musical instrument) regularly or repeatedly in order to gain skill: *She's been practising the piano for nearly an hour.* **2** [T] to act in accordance with, esp. habitually: *They were prevented from practising their religion.|a practising Jew|(fml.) We must learn to practise* ECONOMY. (=avoid spending money) **3** [I;T] to do the work of a doctor or lawyer: *She practises medicine/practises as a doctor.|She's a practising doctor.* **4 practise what one preaches** to do oneself what one is always telling others to do

**prac·tised** ||also **- ticed** *AmE* /'prækt¦əst/ *adj* skilled through practice: *a practised cheat|thoroughly practised in the art of singing*

**prac·ti·tion·er** /præk'tɪʃənəʳ/ *n* a person who works in a profession, esp. a doctor or lawyer: *medical practitioners* –see GENERAL PRACTITIONER

**prag·mat·ic** /præg'mætɪk/ *adj* dealing with matters in the way that seems best under the actual conditions, rather than following a rule or PRINCIPLE; practical **–pragmatically** *adv*

**prag·ma·tis·m** /'prægmətɪzəm/ *n* [U] PRAGMATIC thinking or way of considering things

**prai·rie** /'preəri/ *n* (esp. in North America) a wide treeless grassy plain

**praise¹** /preɪz/ *v* **praised, praising** [T *for*] **1** to speak favourably and with admiration of **2** *fml or lit* to offer thanks and honour to (God), esp. in song in a church service

**praise²** *n* [U] **1** expression of admiration: *The new film has received a lot of praise.|a book* **in praise of** *country life* **2** *fml or lit* glory; worship: *Let us give praise to God.* **3 sing the praises of** to praise (too) eagerly: *He's always singing his own praises.* (=praising himself)

**praise·wor·thy** /'preɪzwɜːði||-ɜr-/ *adj apprec* deserving praise **–praiseworthiness** *n* [U]

**pram** /præm/ *BrE*||also **perambulator** *fml,* also **baby carriage** *AmE*– *n* a four-wheeled carriage, pushed by hand, for a baby

**prance** /prɑːns||præns/ *v* **pranced, prancing** [I] (of a horse) to jump high or move quickly by raising the front legs and springing forwards on the back legs: (fig.) *The children pranced about with delight.*

**prank** /præŋk/ *n* a playful but foolish trick, not intended to harm: *a schoolboy prank*

**prat·tle¹** /'prætl/ *v* **-tled, -tling** [I *on, about*] *usu. derog.* to talk meaninglessly and continually in a childish way: *He prattled on about his job.*

**prattle²** *n* [U] *infml often derog* childish or unimportant talk

**prawn** /prɔːn/ *n esp. BrE* a small pink ten-legged sea animal, good for food, larger than a SHRIMP

**pray** /preɪ/ *v* **prayed, praying** [I;T +*to-v/that/for, to*] to speak, often silently, to God (or gods), showing love, giving thanks, or asking for (something): *They went to the mosque to pray.|I will pray to God for your safety.|(infml) The cricket match is on Saturday, so we're praying for* (=strongly hoping for) *a fine day.*

**prayer** /preəʳ/ *n* **1** [U] the act of praying to God or gods: *They believe that prayer can bring peace to the world.* **2** [C] a solemn request made to God or gods: *Her prayer was answered and her parents came home safely.* **3** [C *usu. pl.*] a daily religious service among a group of people, mainly concerned with praying: *school prayers*

**prayer book** /'· ·/ *n* a book containing prayers for use in church

**preach** /pri:tʃ/ *v* **1** [I;T +*that/to*] to give (a religious talk (SERMON)) esp. as part of a service in church: *Christ preached to large crowds.* **2** [T] to advise or urge others to accept (something that one believes in): *She's always preaching the value of fresh air.* **3** [I *at*] *derog* to offer (unwanted advice on matters of right and wrong): *My sister has been preaching at me again about my bad behaviour.* –**preacher** *n*

**pre·am·ble** /'pri:æmbəl/ *n fml or derog* a statement at the beginning of a speech or piece of writing, giving its reason and purpose

**pre·ar·range** /ˌpri:ə'reɪndʒ/ *v* **-ranged, -ranging** [T] to arrange in advance: *at a prearranged signal*

**pre·car·i·ous** /prɪ'keərɪəs/ *adj* unsafe; not firm or steady: *The climber had only a precarious hold on the slippery rock.*|*The position of the company is still precarious.* –**precariously** *adv* –**precariousness** *n* [U]

**pre·cau·tion** /prɪ'kɔ:ʃən/ *n* an action done in order to avoid possible known danger, discomfort, etc.: *We* **took precautions** *against illness.* –**precautionary** *adj*

**pre·cede** /prɪ'si:d/ *v* **-ceded, -ceding** [I;T] *fml* to come or go (just) in front (of): *The minister's statement preceded* (=came before) *the Queen's speech.* –compare SUCCEED (2) –**preceding** *adj* [A]: *I remember the war but not the preceding years.*

**pre·ce·dence** /'pres$\frac{1}{2}$dəns/ *n* [U] (the right to) a particular place before others, esp. because of importance: *The ruler* **has/takes precedence over** *all others in the country.*|*Let us deal with the questions* **in order of precedence.** (=the most important one being answered first)

**pre·ce·dent** /'pres$\frac{1}{2}$dənt/ *n* [C;U] (the use of) a former action or case that acts as an example or rule for present action: *When he made the judgment, the judge had to follow the precedent which had been established in 1920.*|*The judgment* **set a new precedent.**

**pre·cept** /'pri:sept/ *n* a guiding rule on which behaviour, a way of thought or action, etc., is based

**pre·cinct** /'pri:sɪŋkt/ *n* **1** [*of; usu.pl.*] the space, often enclosed by walls, that surrounds an important building or group of buildings: *It's quiet within the precincts of the old college.* **2** a part of a town planned for, or limited to, a special use: *a new shopping precinct* (=an area containing only shops)|*a* PEDESTRIAN *precinct* (=an area in a town where motor traffic is not allowed) **3** *AmE* a division of a town or city for election or police purposes

**pre·cincts** /'pri:sɪŋkts/ *n* [P *of*] *fml* neighbourhood; area around (a town or other place): *The precincts of the port are full of people when the ships come in.*

**pre·cious**[1] /'preʃəs/ *adj* of great value: *a precious jewel*|*That old toy is John's most precious* (=most dearly loved) *possession.*

**precious**[2] *adv infml* very (esp. in the phrases **precious little/few**)

**precious met·al** /ˌ·· '··/ *n* [C;U] a rare and valuable metal, such as gold or silver

**precious stone** /ˌ·· '·/ also **stone**– *n* a rare and valuable jewel, such as a diamond, EMERALD, etc. –compare SEMIPRECIOUS

**pre·ci·pice** /'pres$\frac{1}{2}$p$\frac{1}{2}$s/ *n* a steep or almost upright side of a high rock, mountain, or cliff

**pre·cip·i·tate**[1] /pr$\frac{1}{2}$'sɪp$\frac{1}{2}$teɪt/ *v* **-tated, -tating** **1** [T] *fml* to hasten the coming of (an unwanted event): *Falling sales precipitated the failure of the company.* **2** [I;T] (in chemistry) to (cause to) separate from a liquid because of chemical action

**pre·cip·i·tate**[2] /pr$\frac{1}{2}$'sɪp$\frac{1}{2}$t$\frac{1}{2}$t/ *n* [C;U] (in chemistry) a solid substance that has been separated from a liquid by chemical action

**precipitate**[3] /pr$\frac{1}{2}$'sɪp$\frac{1}{2}$t$\frac{1}{2}$t/ *adj fml* wildly hasty; acting or done without care or thought –compare PRECIPITOUS –**precipitately** *adv*

**pre·cip·i·ta·tion** /pr$\frac{1}{2}$ˌsɪp$\frac{1}{2}$'teɪʃən/ *n* [U] **1** *fml* unwise haste **2** *tech* (amount of ) rain, snow, etc. **3** (in chemistry) the act of precipitating (PRECIPITATE[1] (2))

**pre·cip·i·tous** /pr$\frac{1}{2}$'sɪp$\frac{1}{2}$təs/ *adj* dangerously steep –compare PRECIPITATE[3]

**pré·cis** /'preɪsi:‖preɪ'si:/ *n* **précis** /'preɪsi:z‖preɪ'si:z/ a shortened form of a speech or piece of writing, giving only the main points

**pre·cise** /prɪ'saɪs/ *adj* **1** exact (in form, detail, measurements, time, etc.): *very precise calculations*|*Our train leaves at about half past ten, or,* **to be precise,** *10.33.* **2** careful and correct in regard to the smallest details –opposite **imprecise** –**preciseness** *n* [U]

**pre·cise·ly** /prɪ'saɪsli/ *adv* **1** exactly: *The train leaves at 10 o'clock precisely.* **2** yes, that is correct; you are right: *"So you think we ought to wait until autumn?" "Precisely."*

**pre·ci·sion** /prɪ'sɪʒən/ *n* **1** [U] also **preciseness**– exactness: *She doesn't express her thoughts with precision, so people often misunderstand her.* –opposite **imprecision** **2** [A] used for producing very exact results: *precision instruments*

**pre·clude** /prɪ'klu:d/ *v* **-cluded, -cluding** [T +*v-ing/from*] *fml* to prevent: *We try to preclude any possibility of misunderstanding.* –**preclusion** /prɪ 'klu:ʒən / *n* [U]

**pre·co·cious** /prɪ'kəʊʃəs/ *adj sometimes derog* (of a young person or his/her abilities) showing unusually early development of mind or body –**precociously** *adv* –**precociousness** *n* [U] –**precocity** /prɪ'kɒs$\frac{1}{2}$ti‖-'kɑ-/ *n* [U]

**pre·con·ceived** /ˌpri:kən'si:vd/ *adj* (of an idea, opinion, etc.) formed in advance, without (enough) knowledge or experience –**preconception** /-kən'sepʃən/ *n*: *Most of my preconceptions about John were proved wrong when I actually met him.*

**pre·cur·sor** /prɪ'kɜ:səʳ‖-'kɜr-/ *n* [*of*] *fml* a person or thing that comes before and is a sign or earlier type of one that is to follow: *The precursor of the modern car was a horseless carriage with a petrol engine.*

**pred·a·tor** /'predətəʳ/ *n* a PREDATORY (1) animal

**pred·a·to·ry** /ˈpredətəri‖-tori/ *adj* **1** (esp.of a wild animal) living by killing and eating other animals **2** concerned with or living (as if) by robbery and seizing the property of others: *predatory tribes*|(fig.) *This town is full of predatory hotel keepers!*

**pre·de·ces·sor** /ˈpriːdəsesəʳ‖ˈpre-/ *n* **1** a person who held an (official) position before someone else: *Our new doctor is much younger than his predecessor.* **2** something formerly used, but which has now been changed for something else: *This government seems to me no better than any of its predecessors.*

**pre·des·ti·na·tion** /prɪˌdestəˈneɪʃən, ˌpriːdes-/ *n* [U] the belief that God or fate has decided everything that will happen, and that no human effort can change things –compare FREE WILL

**pre·des·tine** /prɪˈdestən/ *v* **-tined, -tining** [T] *fml* to fix, as if by God or fate, the future of: *He felt that he was predestined to lead his country to freedom.*

**pre·de·ter·mine** /ˌpriːdɪˈtɜːmən‖-ɜr-/ *v* **-mined, -mining** [T *usu.pass.*] to fix unchangeably from the beginning: *The colour of a person's hair is often predetermined by that of his parents.*

**pre·dic·a·ment** /prɪˈdɪkəmənt/ *n* a difficult or unpleasant state of affairs in which one must make a difficult choice

**pred·i·cate** /ˈpredɪkət/ *n* the part of a sentence which makes a statement about the subject: *In "Fishes swim" and "She is an artist", "swim" and "is an artist" are predicates.*

**pre·dic·a·tive** /prɪˈdɪkətɪv‖ˈpredəkeɪ-/ *adj* (of an adjective, noun, or phrase) coming after the noun being described or after the verb of which the noun is the subject: *In "He is alive", "alive" is a predicative adjective.* –compare ATTRIBUTIVE

**pre·dict** /prɪˈdɪkt/ *v* [T +(*that*)] to see or describe (a future happening) in advance as a result of knowledge, experience, reason, etc.: *She predicted that he would marry a doctor.* –compare FORECAST

**pre·dic·ta·ble** /prɪˈdɪktəbəl/ *adj* that can be PREDICTed –opposite **unpredictable** –**predictably** *adv*

**pre·dic·tion** /prɪˈdɪkʃən/ *n* **1** [C +*that*] something that is PREDICTED **2** [U] the act of PREDICTing

**pre·di·lec·tion** /ˌpriːdɪˈlekʃən‖ˌpredlˈek-/ *n* [*for*] a special liking that has become a habit: *Charles has always had a predilection for red-haired women.*

**pre·dis·pose** /ˌpriːdɪˈspəuz/ *v* **-posed, -posing** [T *to*] *fml* to influence (someone) in the stated way: *I have heard nothing that predisposes me to dislike her.*|*His weak chest predisposes him to illness.*

**pre·dis·po·si·tion** /ˌpriːdɪspəˈzɪʃən/ *n fml* [*to*] a state of body or mind that is favourable (to something, often something bad)

**pre·dom·i·nant** /prɪˈdɒmənənt‖-ˈdɑ-/ *adj* [*over*] most powerful, noticeable, or important: *Bright red was the predominant colour in the room.* –**predominance** *n* [S;U]

**pre·dom·i·nant·ly** /prɪˈdɒmənəntli‖-ˈdɑ-/ *adv* mostly; mainly: *The votes were predominantly in favour of the government.*

**pre·dom·i·nate** /prɪˈdɒməneɪt‖-ˈdɑ-/ *v* **-nated, -nating** [I *over*] to be greater or greatest in numbers, force, influence, etc.

**pre·em·i·nent** /priːˈemənənt/ *adj usu. apprec* above all others in the possession of some (usu. good) quality, ability, or main activity –**preeminence** *n* [U] –**preeminently** *adv*

**pre·empt** /priːˈempt/ *v* [T] to cause to have no influence or force by means of taking action in advance: *The council found that their traffic plans had been preempted by a government decision.*

**preen** /priːn/ *v* [I;T] (of a bird) to clean or smooth (itself or its feathers) with the beak: (fig.) *John stood preening himself in front of the mirror.*

**pre·fab** /ˈpriːfæb‖ˌpriːˈfæb/ *n infml* a small prefabricated house

**pre·fab·ri·cate** /priːˈfæbrɪkeɪt/ *v* **-cated, -cating** [T] to make (the parts of a building, ship, etc.) in a factory ready for fitting together in any place chosen for building –**prefabricated** *adj* –**prefabrication** /-ˈkeɪʃən/ *n* [U]

**pref·ace**[1] /ˈprefəs/ *n* [*to*] an introduction to a book or speech –compare FOREWORD

**preface**[2] *v* **-aced, -acing** [T *with, by*] to provide with a PREFACE[1]: *He prefaced his speech with an amusing story.*

**pre·fect** /ˈpriːfekt/ *n* **1** (in some British schools) an older pupil given certain powers and duties with regard to keeping order over other pupils **2** (*sometimes cap.*) (in certain countries today) a public officer or judge with duties in government, the police, or the army: *the Prefect of Police of Paris*

**pre·fer** /prɪˈfɜːʳ/ *v* **-rr-** [T] **1** [+*to-v*/*v-ing*/*to*] to choose (one thing or action) rather than another; like better: *I prefer dogs to cats.*|*"Would you like meat or fish?" "I'd prefer meat, please."*|*Would you prefer me to come on Monday?* **2** [*against*] *law* to put forward for official consideration or action according to law (esp. in the phrases **prefer charges/a charge**)

**pref·e·ra·ble** /ˈprefərəbəl/ *adj* [*to; no comp.*] better (esp. because more suitable); to be PREFERred: *Anything is preferable to having them with us for the whole week!* –**preferably** *adv*

**pref·e·rence** /ˈprefərəns/ *n* **1** [C;U *for, to*] (a) desire or liking (for one thing rather than another): *They've always had a preference for taking their holidays abroad.* (=rather than in their own country)|*I'd choose the small car in preference to the larger one.* **2** [U] special favour or consideration shown to a person, group, etc.: *In considering people for the job, we give preference to those with some experience.*

**pref·e·ren·tial** /ˌprefəˈrenʃəl/ *adj* [A] of, giving, receiving, or showing PREFERENCE (2): *The minister admitted that he gave* **preferential treatment** *to people from his own party.*

**pre·fix** /ˈpriːfɪks/ *n* (in grammar) a word or part of a word that is placed at the beginning of another word and that changes its meaning or use: *"Re-" (meaning "again") is a prefix in "refill".* –compare SUFFIX

**preg·nan·cy** /ˈpregnənsi/ *n* **-cies** [C;U] (an example of) the condition of being PREGNANT (1)

**preg·nant** /ˈpregnənt/ *adj* **1** (of a woman or female animal) having an unborn child or unborn young in the body: *How long has she been pregnant?*|*She is five months pregnant.* **2** [A] full of important but unexpressed meaning: *His words were followed by a pregnant pause.*

**pre·hen·sile** /prɪ'hensaɪl‖-səl/ *adj tech* (of a part of the body) able to curl round, seize, and hold things: *a monkey hanging from the tree by its prehensile tail*

**pre·his·tor·ic** /ˌpriːhɪ'stɒrɪk‖-'stɔ-, -'stɑ-/ *adj* of or belonging to a time before recorded history: *prehistoric man|prehistoric burial grounds* **–prehistory** /priː'hɪstəri/ *n* [U]

**pre·judge** /ˌpriː'dʒʌdʒ/ *v* **-judged, -judging** [T] to form an (unfavourable) opinion about (someone or something) before knowing or examining all the facts **–prejudgment, -judgement** *n* [C;U]

**prej·u·dice[1]** /'predʒədɪs/ *n* [C;U] (an example of) unfair and often unfavourable feeling or opinion not based on reason or enough knowledge: *a new law to discourage* **racial prejudice** (=prejudice against members of other races)|*a prejudice against women drivers*

**prejudice[2]** *v* **-diced, -dicing** [T] **1** [*against, in favour of*] to cause (someone or someone's mind) to have a PREJUDICE[1]; influence: *He is prejudiced against French wine because he is Italian.* **2** to weaken; harm (someone's case, expectations, etc.): *Your bad spelling may prejudice your chances of getting this job.*

**prej·u·diced** /'predʒədɪst/ *adj usu. derog* feeling or showing PREJUDICE[1]; unfair –opposite **unprejudiced**

**prej·u·di·cial** /ˌpredʒʊ'dɪʃəl, -dʒə-/ *adj* [F *to*] *fml* harmful: *Too much smoking is prejudicial to health.*

**prel·ate** /'prelɪt/ *n* a priest of high rank, esp. a BISHOP or someone with a higher rank

**pre·lim·i·na·ry[1]** /prɪ'lɪmɪnəri‖-neri/ *n* **-ries** [*usu. pl.*] a preparation; PRELIMINARY[2] act or arrangement: *There are a lot of preliminaries to be gone through before you can visit China.*

**preliminary[2]** *adj* [A] coming before and introducing or preparing for something more important: *The students take a preliminary test in March, and the main examination in July.*

**prel·ude** /'preljuːd/ *n* [*to; usu.sing.*] **1** something that comes before and acts as an introduction to something more important: *The fighting in the streets may be a prelude to more serious trouble.* **2** a short piece of music that introduces a large musical work

**pre·mar·i·tal** /priː'mærɪtəl/ *adj* happening or existing before marriage: *premarital sex* **–premaritally** *adv*

**pre·ma·ture** /'prematʃəʳ, -tʃʊəʳ, ˌpremə'tʃʊəʳ‖ˌpriːmə'tʊər/ *adj* developing, happening, or coming before the natural or propertime: *his premature death at the age of 32|The baby was two months premature.* (=born two months earlier than expected)|*I think your attack on the new law is a bit premature, as we do not yet know all the details.* **–prematurely** *adv*

**pre·med·i·tat·ed** /priː'medɪteɪtɪd‖prɪ-/ *adj* intentional; done on purpose; planned: *premeditated murder*

**premier[1]** *n* [A;C] (*often cap.*) the head of the government (PRIME MINISTER) in certain countries: *a meeting between the Irish Premier and the President of France* **–premiership** *n*

**prem·i·er[2]** /'premɪəʳ‖prɪ'mɪər/ *adj* [A] *fml* first (in position or importance): *Britain's premier university*

**prem·i·ere, -ère** /'premɪeəʳ‖prɪ'mɪər/ *n* the first public performance of a play or a cinema film

**prem·ise** ‖also **-iss** *BrE* /'premɪs/ *n* [C +*that*] *fml* a statement or idea on which reasoning is based: *The lawyer based his argument on the premise that people are innocent until they are proved to be guilty.*

**prem·is·es** /'premɪsɪz/ *n* [P] a building with any surrounding land, considered as a particular piece of property: *business premises|Food bought in this shop may not be eaten* **on the premises.** (=must be taken away before being eaten)

**pre·mi·um** /'priːmɪəm/ *n* **1** a sum of money paid (regularly) to an insurance company to protect oneself against some risk of loss or damage **2 at a premium** rare or difficult to obtain, and therefore worth more than usual: *During the holiday months of July and August, hotel rooms are at a premium.*

**pre·mo·ni·tion** /ˌpremə'nɪʃən, ˌpriː-/ *n* [C +*that/of*] a feeling that something (esp. something unpleasant) is going to happen; forewarning: *The day before her accident, she had a premonition of danger.*

**pre·mon·i·to·ry** /prɪ'mɒnɪtəri‖-'mɑnɪtori/ *adj fml* giving a warning

**pre·na·tal** /ˌpriː'neɪtl/ *adj tech esp. AmE* for ANTENATAL

**pre·oc·cu·pa·tion** /priːˌɒkjʊ'peɪʃən‖-ˌɑkjə-/ *n* **1** [U] the state of being PREOCCUPIED: *his preoccupation with his health* **2** [C] a matter which takes up all one's attention

**pre·oc·cu·pied** /priː'ɒkjʊpaɪd‖-'ɑkjə-/ *adj* with the mind fixed on something else (esp. something worrying); inattentive to present matters: *You were too preoccupied to recognize me in the street yesterday.*

**pre·oc·cu·py** /priː'ɒkjʊpaɪ‖-'ɑkjə-/ *v* **-pied, -pying** [T] to fill the thoughts of (someone) almost completely, esp. so that not enough attention is given to other (present) matters

**prep** /prep/ also **preparation** *fml*– *n* [U] *BrE infml* studying and getting ready for lessons; HOMEWORK

**prep·a·ra·tion** /ˌprepə'reɪʃən/ *n* **1** [U] the act of preparing: *He didn't do enough preparation for his examination.|Plans for the new school are now* **in preparation.** (=being prepared) **2** [C *for; usu. pl.*] an arrangement (for a future event): *Preparations for the queen's visit are almost complete.* **3** [C] something that is made ready for use by mixing a number of (chemical) substances: *a new preparation for cleaning metal*

**pre·par·a·to·ry** /prɪ'pærətəri‖-tori/ *adj* [A] **1** done in order to get ready for something **2 preparatory to** *prep fml* before; as a preparation for

**preparatory school** /·'···· ·/ also **prep school** *infml*– *n* (esp. in Britain) a private school where young pupils are made ready to attend a higher school (esp.a PUBLIC SCHOOL)

**pre·pare** /prɪ'peəʳ/ *v* **-pared, -paring 1** [I;T +*to-v*/*for*] to get ready; make ready: *First prepare the rice by washing it, then cook it in boiling water.|They are busy preparing to go on holiday.|Will you help me prepare for* (=get everything ready for) *the party?* **2** [T *for*] to accustom (someone or someone's mind) to some (new) idea, event, or condition: *He prepared himself for/to accept defeat.*

**pre·pared** /prɪ'peəd‖-ərd/ *adj* [*no comp.*] **1** got ready in advance: *The chairman read out a prepared statement.* –opposite **unprepared 2** [F +*to-v*] willing:

*I'm not prepared to listen to your weak excuses.*

**pre·pay** /ˌpriːˈpeɪ/ *v* **-paid** /ˈpeɪd/, **-paying** [T] to pay for (something) in advance

**pre·pon·de·rance** /prɪˈpɒndərəns‖-ˈpɑn-/ *n* [S;U *of*] *fml* the quality or state of being greater in amount, number, etc. **–preponderant** *adj* **–preponderantly** *adv*

**prep·o·si·tion** /ˌprepəˈzɪʃən/ *n* a word used with a noun or PRONOUN to show its connection with another word: *In "He walked into the house" and "She succeeded by working hard", "into" and "by" are prepositions.* **–prepositional** *adj* : *"In bed" and "on top" are prepositional phrases.*

**pre·pos·sess·ing** /ˌpriːpəˈzesɪŋ/ *adj fml* (of a person or a quality of his/her character) very pleasing; charming –opposite **unprepossessing**

**pre·pos·ter·ous** /prɪˈpɒstərəs‖-ˈpɑs-/ *adj* completely unreasonable or improbable; ABSURD: *That's a preposterous idea!* **–preposterously** *adv*

**prep school** /ˈ· ·/ *n* [C;U] *infml* for PREPARATORY SCHOOL

**pre·req·ui·site** /priːˈrekwəzət/ *n,adj fml* [*to, for*] (something) that is necessary before something else can happen or be done: *Before starting, the company's approval is a prerequisite.*

**pre·rog·a·tive** /prɪˈrɒgətɪv‖-ˈrɑ-/ *n fml* [*usu. sing.*] a special right belonging to someone by rank, position, or nature: *A ruler may use his prerogative of mercy towards a criminal.*

**pres·age** /ˈpresɪdʒ, prəˈseɪdʒ/ *v* **-aged, -aging** [T not *be+v-ing*] *lit* to be a warning of; FORETELL

**Pres·by·te·ri·an** /ˌprezbəˈtɪəriən/ *n,adj* (a member) of a PROTESTANT Church governed by a body of official people all of equal rank, as in Scotland

**pres·by·ter·y** /ˈprezbətəri/ *n* **-ies 1** (in the PRESBYTERIAN Church) a local court or ruling body **2** (in the ROMAN CATHOLIC Church) the house in which a priest lives

**pre·scribe** /prɪˈskraɪb/ *v* **-scribed, -scribing** [I;T *for*] **1** to order the use of (something, esp. a medicine or treatment): *The doctor prescribed a medicine for the child's stomach pains.* **2** *fml* (of a person or body that has the right to do so) to state (what must be done in certain conditions): *What punishment does the law prescribe for this crime?*

**pre·scrip·tion** /prɪˈskrɪpʃən/ *n* **1** [U] the act of prescribing (PRESCRIBE) **2** [C] something that is PRESCRIBED: (fig.) *What's your prescription for a happy marriage?* **3** [C] (a written order describing) a particular medicine or treatment ordered by a doctor: *Take this prescription to your local* CHEMIST*'s.*

**pres·ence** /ˈprezəns/ *n* [U] **1** (the fact or state of) being present: *She was so quiet that her presence was hardly noticed.|Your presence is requested at the meeting on Thursday.* –opposite **absence 2** [U] personal appearance and manner, as having a strong effect on others **3 in the presence of someone** also **in someone's presence**– close enough to be seen or heard by someone **4 presence of mind** the ability to act calmly, quickly, and wisely in conditions of sudden danger or surprise: *When the fire started, John had the presence of mind to turn off the gas.*

**pres·ent**[1] /ˈprezənt/ *n* a gift: *They unwrapped their Christmas presents.*

**pre·sent**[2] /prɪˈzent/ *v* [T] *more fml than* **give**– **1** to give (something) away, esp. at a ceremonial occasion: *He presented a silver cup to the winner/presented the winner with a silver cup.* **2** (of non-material things) to be the cause of; give: *Money presents no difficulty to us.* **3** to offer (esp. in the phrases **present one's apologies/compliments/respects,** etc.) **4** to offer for consideration or bring to someone's attention: *The committee is presenting its report next week.* **5** to provide for the public to see in a theatre, cinema, etc.: *The theatre company is presenting "Hamlet" next week.* **6** *fml* to introduce (someone) esp. to someone of higher rank: *May I present Mr. Smith (to you)?* **7** to introduce and take part in (a television or radio show)

**pres·ent**[3] /ˈprezənt/ *adj* **1** [F] in the place talked of or understood: *How many people were present at the meeting?* –opposite **absent 2** [A] existing or being considered now: *What is your present address?* **3** [A] (of a tense or a form of a verb) expressing an existing state or action: *"He wants" and "they are coming" are examples of verbs in present tenses.*

**present**[4] /ˈprezənt/ *n* **1** [*the* S] the PRESENT[3](2) time: *We learn from the past, experience the present, and hope for success in the future.* **2** [C] the PRESENT[3](3) tense **3 at present** at this time; now **4 for the present** now but not necessarily in the future

**pre·sen·ta·ble** /prɪˈzentəbəl/ *adj* fit to be shown, heard, etc., in public; fit to be seen and judged –opposite **unpresentable –presentably** *adv*

**pre·sen·ta·tion** /ˌprezənˈteɪʃən‖ˌpriːzen-, -zən-/ *n* **1** [C;U *of*] the act or action of PRESENTING[2] something: *The presentation of prizes will begin at three o'clock.* **2** [U *of*] the way in which something is said, offered, shown, explained, etc., to others

**pres·ent-day** /ˌprezənt ˈdeɪ◂/ *adj* [A] modern; existing now: *present-day prices*

**pres·ent·ly** /ˈprezəntli/ *adv* **1** soon: *The doctor will be here presently.* **2** *esp. AmE* at present; now: *The doctor is presently writing a book.*

**present par·ti·ci·ple** /ˌ·· ˈ····/ *n* (in grammar) a form of a verb which ends in *-ing* and may be used in compound forms of the verb to express actions done or happening in the past, present, or future, or sometimes as an adjective: *In the sentence "I'm going", "going" is a present participle.*

**pres·er·va·tion** /ˌprezəˈveɪʃən‖-zər-/ *n* [U] **1** [*of*] the act or action of preserving (PRESERVE): *The police are responsible for the preservation of law and order.* **2** the state of being or remaining in (a stated) condition after a long time: *The old building is in a good state of preservation except for the wooden floors.*

**pre·ser·va·tive** /prɪˈzɜːvətɪv‖-ɜr-/ *n,adj* [C;U] (a usu. chemical substance) that can be used to PRESERVE[1] (3) foods

**pre·serve**[1] /prɪˈzɜːv‖-ɜrv/ *v* **-served, -serving** [T] **1** to keep (someone or something) alive, safe from destruction, etc.: *The Town Council spent a lot of money to preserve the old castle.* **2** to cause (a condition) to last; keep unchanged: *It is the duty of the police to preserve public order.* **3** to keep (something, esp. food) in good condition for a long time by some special treatment: *preserved fruit* –compare CONSERVE[1]

**preserve²** *n* **1** [C *usu. pl.*; U] *more fml than* **jam**– a substance made from fruit boiled in sugar, used esp. for spreading on bread; JAM **2** [C] a stretch of land or water kept for private hunting or fishing **3** [C] something considered to belong to or be for the use of only a certain person or limited number of people: *She considers the arranging of flowers in the church to be her own preserve.*

**pre·side** /prɪ'zaɪd/ *v* **-sided, -siding** [I *at*] to be in charge; lead: *the presiding officer at the election*

**preside over** sthg. *v prep* [T] to direct (a committee or other formal group of people): *The meeting was presided over by a minister.*

**pres·i·den·cy** /'prezǝdǝnsi/ *n* **-cies 1** [*of*] the office of president: *Roosevelt was elected four times to the presidency of the US.* **2** the length of time a person is president

**pres·i·dent** /'prezǝdǝnt/ *n* **1** [C;A] (*often cap.*) the head of government in many modern states that do not have a king or queen: *the President of France|President Reagan* **2** [C] (*sometimes cap.*) the head of a club or society, some universities or colleges, some government departments, etc.: *the President of the Board of Trade/of Corpus Christi College* **3** [C] *AmE* (*sometimes cap.*) the head of a business company, firm, bank, etc. **–presidential** *adj* [A]

**press¹** /pres/ *v* **1** [I;T] to push firmly and steadily: *Press this button to start the engine.* **2** [T] to direct weight or force on (something) in order to crush, flatten, pack tightly, or get juice out: *To make wine, first you must press the* GRAPES.*|pressed flowers* **3** [T] to give (clothes) a smooth surface and a sharp fold by using a hot iron **4** [T] to hold firmly as a sign of friendship, love, pity, etc.: *He pressed my hand warmly when we met.* **5** [I;T] to continue to force (an attack, hurried action, etc.) on (someone): *We must hurry,* **time is pressing.** (=there is not much time) **6** [T] to continue to demand or ask for: *She pressed her guest to stay a little longer.*

**press on/forward** *fml*– *v adv* [I *with*] to continue; advance with courage or without delay: *Let's press on with our work.*

**press²** *n* **1** [*the* U +*sing./pl.v*] (writers and reporters for) newspapers and magazines in general (often including the news-gathering services of radio and television): *the power of the press|a press photographer|The press have/has been invited to a meeting to hear the minister's intentions.* **2** [S] an act of pushing steadily against something **3** [S] treatment given by newspapers in general when reporting about a person or event: *The play had a good press.* (=the newspapers said it was good) **4** [C] →PRINTING PRESS **5** [C] (*usu. cap.*) a business for printing (and sometimes also for selling) books, magazines, etc.: *the University Press* **6** [C] an act of smoothing a garment with a hot iron **7** [C] a machine used for pressing **8 go to press** (of a newspaper for any particular day) to start being printed

**press con·fer·ence** /'· ,···/ also **news conference**– *n* a meeting arranged by an important person to which news reporters are invited to listen to a statement or to ask questions

**press cut·ting** /'· ,··/ *n* a short notice, picture, etc., cut out of a newspaper or magazine

**pressed** /prest/ *adj* [F *for*] having hardly enough (of ): *I'm* **pressed for time** *this morning so I'll see you in the afternoon.*

**press·gang¹** /'presgæŋ/ *n* (in former times) a band of sailors under an officer, employed to seize men for service in the navy

**pressgang²** *v* [T *into*] *infml* to force (someone) to do something unwillingly

**press·ing** /'presɪŋ/ *adj* demanding or needing attention, action, etc., now: *pressing business matters*

**press·man** /'presmæn/ *n* **-men** /men/ *BrE infml* a newspaper reporter

**press-stud** /'· ·/ also **snap fastener** *AmE*– *n* a small metal fastener for a garment, in which one part is pressed into a hollow in another

**press-up** /'· ·/ *BrE*||**push-up** *AmE*– *n* a form of exercise in which one lies face down on the ground and pushes one's body up with one's arms

**pres·sure¹** /'preʃǝʳ/ *n* **1** [U *of*] the action of pressing with force or weight: *The pressure of the water turns this wheel, and this is used to make electric power.* **2** [C;U] the strength of this force: *These air containers will burst at high pressures.* **3** [C;U] the (force of the) weight of the air: *Low pressure often brings rain.* **4** [U] forcible influence: *We* **put pressure on** *the government to change this law.|He only agreed to leave the country* **under pressure.** (=after being forcibly persuaded to do so) **5** [U *of*] the conditions of work, a style of living, etc. which cause anxiety and difficulty: *The pressure of work was too great for him.* –see also BLOOD PRESSURE, HIGH-PRESSURE

**pressure²** *v* **-sured, -suring** [T *into*] *esp. AmE* for PRESSURIZE(1)

**pressure cook·er** /'·· ,··/ *n* a tightly covered metal cooking pot in which food can be cooked very quickly by the pressure of hot steam

**pressure group** /'·· ·/ *n* [C +*sing./pl. v*] a group of people that actively tries to influence public opinion and government action, usu. for its own advantage

**pres·sur·ize** ||also **-ise** *BrE* /'preʃǝraɪz/ *v* **-ized, -izing** [T] **1** also **pressure** *esp. AmE*– to (try to) make (someone) do something by means of forceful demands or influence: *They have pressurized the farmers into producing more milk.* **2** to control the air pressure inside (an aircraft) so that the pressure does not become much lower than that on earth: *a pressurized* CABIN (3)

**pres·tige** /pre'sti:ʒ/ *n* [U] general respect or admiration felt for someone or something by reason of rank, proved high quality, etc.: *The old universities of Oxford and Cambridge still have a lot of prestige.*

**pres·ti·gious** /pre'stɪdʒǝs||-'sti:-, -'stɪ-/ *adj usu. apprec* having or bringing PRESTIGE

**pre·su·ma·bly** /prɪ'zju:mǝbli||-'zu:-/ *adv* probably; it may reasonably be supposed that: *Presumably the bad weather has delayed the train.*

**pre·sume** /prɪ'zju:m||-'zu:m/ *v* **-sumed, -suming 1** [I;T +(*that*)] to take (something) as true without direct proof; suppose: *From the way they talked I presumed they were married.* **2** [I +*to-v*] *fml* to dare to do something which one has no right to do: *Are you presuming to tell me how to drive my car?*

**presume upon/on** sthg. *v prep* [T] *fml* to make a

## STUDY NOTES prepositions

In the picture you can see:

1 – a woman going **into** the supermarket to do her shopping, and a man coming **out of** the supermarket. He is carrying two bags of shopping.

2 – a girl walking **across** the road. She is going **to** the supermarket too.

3 – some people getting **off** the bus. A young man is waiting to get **on** the bus.

4 – someone looking **out of** the bus window.

5 – some children running **along** the street.

6 – a woman with a pram walking **past** the supermarket.

7 – a man and woman walking **towards** the bus.

8 – another man walking **away from** the bus.

9 – a woman walking **through** the door of the cafe. Her child is pointing **to/towards/in the direction of** the bus.

10 – a man walking **round** the corner from the car park.

11 – a woman going **up** the steps **into** the library. A man is coming **down** the steps **from** the library with some books.

12 – a café **next to** a greengrocer's. The greengrocer's is **between** the café and the bank.

13 – a greengrocer's with a "For Sale" notice on the wall **above/over** the door.

14 – a bank **near** the café.

15 – a boy and a girl **inside** the café having a cup of coffee. They have left their bicycles **outside** the cafe.

16 – a car waiting **at** the pedestrian crossing. A man is sitting **in** the car. In the picture on the other page you can see some people **on** the bus.

17 – a boy **on** a bicycle **behind** the car.

18 – some people crossing the road **in front of** the car.

19 – a bus stop **opposite** the supermarket.

20 – a bank with some people waiting **by** the door for it to open.

21 – a man leaning **against** the wall of the bank, **below/under** the sign.

wrong use of (someone's kindness) by asking for help, etc.

**pre·sump·tion** /prɪ'zʌmpʃən/ *n* **1** [C +*that*] an act of supposing: *Your presumption that I would agree with your plan is false.* **2** [U] improper boldness that shows too high an opinion of oneself

**pre·sump·tu·ous** /prɪ'zʌmptʃuəs/ *adj derog* showing too much boldness towards others as a result of having too high an opinion of oneself –**presumptuously** *adv*

**pre·sup·pose** /ˌpriːsə'pəuz/ *v* **-posed, -posing** [T +*that*] to suppose or take to be true; ASSUME –**presupposition** /-sʌpə'zɪʃən/ *n* [C;U +*that*]: *Your judgment of the case is based on the presupposition that the witness is telling the truth.*

**pre·tence** ||also **-tense** *AmE* /prɪ'tens||'priːtens/ *n* [S;U] **1** a false appearance, reason, or show intended to deceive or as a game: *She isn't really ill; it's only pretence.|The guests didn't like the food, but they* **made a pretence of** *eating some of it.* **2 false pretences** *law* acts intended to deceive (esp. in the phrase **by/under false pretences**)

**pre·tend** /prɪ'tend/ *v* [I;T +*to-v*/(*that*)] **1** to give an appearance of (something that is not true), with the intention of deceiving: *She pretended she didn't know me when I passed her in the street.|He pretended to be reading.|She wasn't really crying; she was only pretending.* **2** (usu. of a child) to imagine as a game: *Let's pretend we're on the moon!*

**pre·tend·er** /prɪ'tendəʳ/ *n* [*to*] a person who makes a (doubtful or unproved) claim to some high position, such as to be the rightful king

**pre·ten·sion** /prɪ'tenʃən/ *n* **1** [C *often pl.*] a claim to possess skill, qualities, etc.: *I make no pretensions to skill as an artist, but I enjoy painting.* **2** [U] *fml* the quality of being PRETENTIOUS

**pre·ten·tious** /prɪ'tenʃəs/ *adj* claiming (in an unpleasing way) importance that one does not possess: *a pretentious film* –opposite **unpretentious** –**pretentiously** *adv* –**pretentiousness** *n* [U]

**pre·text** /'priːtekst/ *n* a reason given for an action in order to hide the real intention; excuse: *He came to the house* **under/on the pretext of** *seeing Mr Smith, but he really wanted to see me.* –see EXCUSE (USAGE)

**pret·ty**[1] /'prɪti/ *adj* **-tier, -tiest 1** (esp. of a woman, a child, or a small fine thing) pleasing or nice to look at, listen to, etc.; charming but not beautiful or grand: *She looks much prettier with long hair than with short hair.|What a pretty little garden!* –see BEAUTIFUL (USAGE) **2 sitting pretty** *infml* (of a person) in a favourable position or condition –**prettily** *adv* –**prettiness** *n* [U]

**pretty**[2] *adv* **1** rather; quite but not completely: *pretty comfortable|pretty cold* –see Study Notes on page 389 **2 pretty much** also **pretty well**– almost: *pretty much the same|pretty well impossible*

**pre·vail** /prɪ'veɪl/ *v* [I] *fml* **1** [*against, over*] to gain control or victory; win a fight: *Justice has prevailed; the guilty man has been punished.* **2** [*among, in*] to (continue to) exist or be widespread: *A belief in magic still prevails among some tribes.*

**prevail upon/on** sbdy. *v prep* [T] *fml* to persuade: *Can I prevail upon you to stay a little longer?*

**pre·vail·ing** /prɪ'veɪlɪŋ/ *adj* [A *no comp.*] **1** (of a wind) that blows over an area most of the time **2** most common or general (in some place or at some time): *He wore his hair in the prevailing fashion.*

**prev·a·lent** /'prevələnt/ *adj* [*among, in*] *fml* existing commonly, generally, or widely (in some place or at some time): *Eye diseases are prevalent in some tropical countries.* –**prevalence** *n* [U *of*]

**pre·var·i·cate** /prɪ'værɪkeɪt/ *v* **-cated, -cating** [I] *fml* to try to hide the truth by not answering questions clearly or completely truthfully –**prevarication** /-'keɪʃən/ *n* [C;U]

**pre·vent** /prɪ'vent/ *v* [T *from*] *more fml than* **stop**– to keep (something) from happening or stop (someone) from doing something: *How can we prevent this disease (from) spreading?* –**preventable** *adj*

**pre·ven·tion** /prɪ'venʃən/ [U *of*] the act or action of PREVENTING: *the prevention of crime*

**pre·ven·tive** /prɪ'ventɪv/ also **preventative** /-tətɪv/– *n, adj* (something that is) intended to prevent something, esp. illness

**pre·view** /'priːvjuː/ *n* [*of*] a private showing of paintings, a cinema film, etc., before they are shown to the general public

**pre·vi·ous** /'priːvɪəs/ *adj* [A *no comp.*] **1** happening, coming, or being earlier in time or order: *He has had no previous experience of this kind of work.* **2 previous to** *prep fml* before; PRIOR **to** –**previously** *adv*: *I hadn't seen him previously.*

**pre·war** /ˌpriː'wɔːʳ◂/ *adj* [A] belonging to the time before a war

**prey** /preɪ/ *n* [U] **1** an animal that is hunted and eaten by another animal **2** a way of life based on killing and eating other animals (in the phrases **beast/bird of prey**): *A tiger is a beast of prey.*

**prey on/upon** sbdy./sthg. *v prep* [T] **1** (of an animal) to hunt and eat as PREY: *Cats prey on birds and mice.* **2** (of sorrow, troubles, etc.) to trouble greatly: *This problem has been preying on my mind* (=troubling me) *all day.*

**price**[1] /praɪs/ *n* **1** an amount of money that must be paid to buy something: *What is the price of this suit?|House prices are getting higher/rising/going up.|*(fig.) *Isn't bad health a high price to pay for the pleasure of drinking?* **2 at a price** for a lot of money: *You can buy excellent wine here–at a price.* **3 not at any price** not under any conditions, even if favourable –see COST (USAGE)

**price**[2] *v* **priced, pricing** [T] **1** to fix the price of: *highly priced goods* **2** to mark (goods in a shop) with a price **3 price oneself out of the market** to make one's prices so high that people are unwilling to buy one's goods or services: *The photographer priced himself out of the market by charging so much.*

**price·less** /'praɪsləs/ *adj* **1** of very great value; of worth too great to be described or calculated: *a priceless collection of paintings* –see WORTHLESS (USAGE) **2** *infml* very funny or laughably foolish: *You look priceless in those big trousers!*

**pric·ey, pricy** /'praɪsi/ *adj* **-ier, -iest** *BrE infml* dear in price; expensive: *Houses are pricey in this area.*

**prick**[1] /prɪk/ *n* **1** a small sharp pain: *She felt a sharp prick when the needle went into her finger.* **2** a small mark or hole made by pricking

**prick**[2] *v* **1** [T *with, on, in*] to make a very small hole or holes in the skin or surface of (something or oneself) with a sharp-pointed object: *She pricked herself with a needle.* **2** [I;T] to (cause to) feel a sensation of light sharp pain on the skin: *The leaves of this plant can prick you.*|(fig.) *Her conscience pricked her.*

**prick up** *v adv* **prick up one's ears** (esp. of an animal) to raise the ears so as to listen attentively: *He pricked up his ears* (=began to listen) *when they started to talk about him.*

**prick·le**[1] /'prɪkəl/ *n* a small sharp-pointed growth on the skin of some plants or animals: A PORCUPINE *is covered with prickles.*

**prickle**[2] *v* **-led, -ling** [I;T] to give or feel a pricking sensation: *Woollen clothes often prickle my skin.*

**prick·ly** /'prɪkli/ *adj* **-lier, -liest 1** covered with prickles: *prickly bushes* **2** that gives a pricking sensation

**pride** /praɪd/ *n* **1** [U] (a feeling of) satisfaction and pleasure in what one can do or has done, or in someone or something connected with oneself: *They* **take** *great* **pride in** *their daughter, who is now a famous scientist.* **2** [U] self-respect: *I think you hurt his pride by laughing at the way he speaks English.* **3** [U] *derog* too high an opinion of oneself because of one's rank, wealth, abilities, etc. **4** [*the* S] the most valuable person or thing: *This fine picture is* **the pride of** *my collection.*|*It is my* **pride and joy.** (=something that is greatly valued)

**pride** sbdy. **on/upon** sthg. *v prep* [T] to be pleased and satisfied with (oneself) about: *She prided herself on her ability to speak eight languages.*

**priest** /pri:st/ *n* **1** (in the Christian Church, esp. in the ROMAN CATHOLIC Church) a specially trained person, usu. a man, who performs various religious duties and ceremonies for a group of worshippers **2 priestess** *fem.*– a specially-trained person with related duties and responsibilities in certain non-Christian religions

USAGE **Priest** is a general word for someone who is in charge of the religious worship of a group of Christian people, but the word is used esp. in the ROMAN CATHOLIC Church. A **priest** in the CHURCH OF ENGLAND is called a **clergyman**, and in the NONCONFORMIST Churches the usual word is **minister**. A **priest** who is responsible for the religious needs of a large organization (such as a university or hospital) is a **chaplain** or (in the armed forces) a **padre**.

**priest·hood** /'pri:sthʊd/ *n* [*the* U] the office, position, or rank of a priest

**prig** /prɪg/ *n derog* a person who believes himself/herself morally better than others –**priggish** *adj* –**priggishness** *n* [U]

**prim** /prɪm/ *adj* **-mm-** *usu. derog* having a stiff self-controlled manner; easily shocked by anything improper or rude: *She's much too* **prim and proper** *to enjoy such a rude joke.* –**primly** *adv* –**primness** *n* [U]

**pri·ma·cy** /'praɪməsi/ *n* [U *of*] *fml* the state or quality of being first in rank, importance, position, etc.

**pri·ma don·na** /,pri:mə 'dɒnə‖-'dɑnə/ *n* **1** the leading woman singer in (an) OPERA **2** *derog* an excitable self-important person

**pri·mae·val** /praɪ'mi:vəl/ *adj* →PRIMEVAL

**pri·ma·ri·ly** /'praɪmərəli‖praɪ'merəli/ *adv* mainly; chiefly: *We do sell paintings here, but this is primarily a furniture shop.*

**pri·ma·ry**[1] /'praɪməri‖-meri/ *adj* **1** chief; main: *of primary importance* **2** [A] (of education or a school) for children between five and 11 years old –compare SECONDARY (1), ELEMENTARY (2)

**primary**[2] *n* **-ries** (esp. in the US) an election at which the members of a political party vote for the person that they would like to see as their party's choice (CANDIDATE) for a political office

**primary col·our** /,··· '··/ *n* any of three colours (red, yellow, and blue) from which all other colours can be made by mixing

**pri·mate**[1] /'praɪmeɪt/ *n* a member of the most highly developed group of breast-feeding animals (MAMMALS), which includes man, monkeys, and related animals

**pri·mate**[2] /'praɪmǝ̇t/ *n* (*often cap.*) a priest of the highest rank; ARCHBISHOP

**prime**[1] /praɪm/ *n* [S] the state or time of (someone's or something's) greatest perfection, strength, or activity: *Many young soldiers were cut off* **in their prime.** (=killed in battle while still young)

**prime**[2] *adj* [A *no comp.*] **1** first in time, rank, or importance; chief: *a matter of prime importance* **2** of the very best quality or kind: *a prime joint of* BEEF

**prime**[3] *v* **primed, priming** [T] to prepare **a** (a machine) for working by filling with water, oil, etc. **b** (a surface) for painting by covering with a thickness of paint, oil, etc.: (fig.) *It was a difficult case, but the man on trial had been carefully primed* (=instructed in advance) *by his lawyer.*

**prime min·is·ter** /,· '···/ also **P M** *infml*– *n* (*often caps.*) the chief minister and leader of the government in Britain and many other countries

**prime num·ber** /,· '··/ *n tech* a number that can be divided exactly only by itself and the number one: *23 is a prime number.*

**prim·er** /'praɪmər/ *n* [C;U] a paint or other substance spread over the bare surfaceof wood before the main painting

**pri·me·val**, **-mae-** /praɪ'mi:vəl/ *adj* [*no comp.*] of the earliest period of the earth's existence; very ancient: *primeval forests*

**prim·i·tive** /'prɪmǝ̇tɪv/ *adj* **1** [A] of or belonging to the earliest stage of development, esp. of life or of man: *Primitive man made tools from sharp stones and animal bones.*|*primitive art on the walls of caves* **2** simple; roughly made or done; not greatly developed or improved: *Small seashells have sometimes been used as a primitive kind of money.* –**primitively** *adv* –**primitiveness** *n* [U]

**prim·rose** /'prɪmrəʊz/ *n* **1** [C] a common wild plant or its light yellow spring flowers **2** [U] also **primrose yellow** /,·· '··/– a light yellow colour

**prince** /prɪns/ *n* [A;C] (*often cap.*) **1** a son or other near male relation of a king or queen: *Prince Edward is the Queen's youngest son.* **2** a ruler of a usu. small country or state: *Prince Rainier of Monaco*

**prince·ly** /'prɪnsli/ *adj* **1** of or belonging to a PRINCE **2** fine; splendid; generous: *a princely gift*

**prin·cess** /,prɪn'ses◂‖'prɪnsəs/ *n* [A;C] (*often cap.*) **1** a daughter or other near female relation of a king or queen **2** the wife of a PRINCE

**prin·ci·pal**[1] /ˈprɪnsəpəl/ *adj* [A *no comp.*] chief; main; most important; of highest rank: *the principal character in the story* –compare PRINCIPLE

**principal**[2] *n* **1** [C] (*often cap.*) the head of some universities, colleges, and schools **2** [S] a sum of money lent, on which interest is paid **3** [C *often pl.*] a leading performer in a play, group of musicians, etc. –compare PRINCIPLE

**prin·ci·pal·i·ty** /ˌprɪnsəˈpæləti/ *n* **-ties** a country that a PRINCE (2) rules

**prin·ci·pally** /ˈprɪnsəpli/ *adv* chiefly; mostly: *Although he's a lawyer, he's principally employed in controlling a large business.*

**prin·ci·ple** /ˈprɪnsəpəl/ *n* [C +*that/of*] **1** a general truth or belief that is used as a base for reasoning or action: *One of the principles of this dictionary is that explanations should be in simple language.|They agreed to the plan* **in principle,** (=regarding the main idea) *but there were several details they didn't like.* **2** a law of nature, esp. as governing the making or working of a machine, apparatus, etc.: *A bicycle and a motorcycle are built on the same principle, though the force that moves them is different.* **3 on principle** because of settled fixed beliefs: *I refuse to go there, on principle.* –compare PRINCIPAL

**prin·ci·ples** /ˈprɪnsəpəlz/ *n* [P] **1** the general rules on which a skill, science, etc., is based: *the principles of cooking* **2** high personal standards of what is right and wrong, used as a guide to behaviour: *a man without principles*

**print**[1] /prɪnt/ *n* **1** [C] a mark made on a surface showing the shape, pattern, etc., of the thing pressed into it: *a* FOOTPRINT|(fig.) *Sorrow had left its print on her face.* **2** [U] letters, words, or language in printed form: *I can't read small print without my glasses.|I wouldn't have believed it if I hadn't seen it* **in print.** (=in a book, newspaper, etc.) **3** [C] a photograph printed on paper **4** [C] a picture printed from a small sheet of metal **5 in/out of print** (of a book) that can still/no longer be obtained from the printer

**print**[2] *v* **1** [I;T] to press (letters or pictures) onto (esp. paper) by using shapes covered with ink or paint: *The last line on this page hasn't been properly printed.|This machine can print 60 pages a minute.* **2** [I;T] to make (a book, magazine, etc.) by pressing letters or pictures onto paper: *This firm prints a lot of educational books.* **3** [T] to cause to be included in or produced as a book, newspaper, etc.: *All today's newspapers have printed the minister's speech in full.* **4** [T] to make or copy (a photograph) on paper sensitive to light, from a specially treated sheet of photographic film **5** [I;T] to write without joining the letters: *Please print your name and address here.*

**print·er** /ˈprɪntəʳ/ *n* a person who owns or works in a printing business

**print·ing** /ˈprɪntɪŋ/ *n* [U] the act or art of PRINTING[2] (esp.2)

**printing press** /ˈ·· ·/ also **press**– *n* a machine that prints books, newspapers, etc.

**print·out** /ˈprɪntˌaʊt/ *n* [C;U] a printed record produced by a computer

**pri·or**[1] /ˈpraɪəʳ/ *adj* [A *no comp.*] **1** earlier; coming or planned before: *I was unable to attend the wedding because of* **a prior engagement. 2** more important; coming first in importance: *I stopped playing football because my work had a prior claim on my time.* **3 prior to** *prep fml* before: *The contract will be signed prior to the ceremony.*

**prior**[2] **prioress** /ˈpraɪərəs/ *fem.*– *n* [A;C] the head of a PRIORY

**pri·or·i·ty** /praɪˈɒrəti‖-ˈɔr-/ *n* **-ties 1** [U] the state or right of being first in position or earlier in time: *The badly wounded* **have/take priority** *for medical attention* **over** *others.* **2** [C] something that needs attention, consideration, service, etc., before others: *The government should try to* **get its priorities right.** (=deal with what is most important first)

**pri·o·ry** /ˈpraɪəri/ *n* **-ries** *(often cap.)* a Christian religious house or group of men (MONKS) or women (NUNS) living together, which is smaller and less important than an ABBEY

**prise** /praɪz/ *v* **prised, prising** [T] *esp. BrE* for PRIZE[4]

**pris·m** /ˈprɪzəm/ *n* **1** (in GEOMETRY) a solid figure with a flat base and parallel upright edges **2** a transparent three-sided block, usu. made of glass, that breaks up white light into different colours

**pris·on** /ˈprɪzən/ *n* **1** a large (state) building where criminals are kept locked up as a punishment: *The thief was sent to prison for a year.* **2** a place or condition in which one is shut up or feels a loss of freedom: *Tom hates school; it's a prison to him.*

**pris·on·er** /ˈprɪzənəʳ/ *n* **1** a person kept in a prison for some crime or while waiting to be tried: *The prisoners were trying to escape.|He was* **taken prisoner** *by enemy soldiers.|They* **kept/held** *him* **prisoner** *for three months.* **2** a person or animal (seized and) held with limited freedom of movement

**prisoner of war** /ˌ··· · ˈ·/ also **POW** *infml*– *n* a member of the armed forces caught by the enemy during a war and kept as a prisoner

**priv·a·cy** /ˈprɪvəsi, ˈpraɪ-‖ˈpraɪ-/ *n* [U] the state of being away from the presence, notice, or activities of others: *There's not much privacy in these flats because of the large windows.*

**pri·vate**[1] /ˈpraɪvət/ *adj* **1** intended only for oneself or a chosen group; not shared with everyone in general: *You shouldn't read people's private letters.|Don't repeat what I told you to anyone; it's private.* –compare PUBLIC **2** not connected with or paid for by the government, public service, etc.: *a private hospital* **3** not connected with one's business, work, rank, etc.; unofficial: *a private visit* **4** quiet; without lots of people: *Is there a private corner where we can sit and talk by ourselves?* **5 in private** without other people listening or watching –**privately** *adv*

**private**[2] *n* [A;C] *(often cap.)* a soldier of the lowest rank

**private en·ter·prise** /ˌ·· ˈ···/ *n* [U] →CAPITALISM

**private school** /ˌ·· ˈ·/ *n* a school, not supported by government money, where education must be paid for –compare PUBLIC SCHOOL

**pri·va·tion** /praɪˈveɪʃən/ *n* [C;U] *fml* (a) lack of the necessary things or the main comforts of life: *Everyone suffers privations during a war.*

**pri·va·tize** /ˈpraɪvətaɪz/ *v* (of a central government) to sell a state-owned company or industry to private owners –compare NATIONALIZE –**privatization** /ˌpraɪvətaɪˈzeɪʃən/ *n* [U]

**priv·et** /ˈprɪvɨ̞t/ *n* [U] a bush with leaves that stay green all the year, often grown in gardens to form a HEDGE[1] (1)

**priv·i·lege** /ˈprɪvɨ̞lɪdʒ/ *n* **1** [C;U] (a) special right or advantage limited to one person or a few (fortunate) people of a particular kind: *Education is a privilege in many countries.* **2** [S] a special favour; advantage that gives one great pleasure: *He's a fine musician; it's a privilege to hear him play.* –**privileged** *adj*: *We are privileged tonight to have as our main speaker the Foreign Minister of France.*

**priv·y** /ˈprɪvi/ *adj* [F *to*] *fml* sharing secret knowledge (of)

**prize**[1] /praɪz/ *n* something of value given to someone who is successful in a game, race, competition, etc., or given for some deed that is admired: *Her beautiful roses won* **first prize** *at the flower show.*

**prize**[2] *adj* [A] **1** that has gained a PRIZE[1]: *prize cattle|a prize rose* **2** *infml & humor* worthy of a PRIZE[1] for quality, size, etc.: *That hen has produced a prize egg, bigger than any I've ever seen.* **3** given as a PRIZE[1]: *prize money*

**prize**[3] *v* **prized, prizing** [T] to value highly: *The boy's bicycle was his most prized possession.*

**prize**[4], **prise** *v* **prized, prizing** [T] →PRY[2]: *With a long iron bar we prized the top off the box.*

**pro**[1] /prəʊ/ *n* **pros** [*usu. pl.*] an argument or reason in favour (of something): *We should hear all the* **pros and cons** *of the matter before we make a decision.*

**pro**[2] *n* **pros** *infml* for PROFESSIONAL: *a football pro*

**PRO** *n infml* for PUBLIC RELATIONS officer

**prob·a·bil·i·ty** /ˌprɒbəˈbɪlɨ̞ti‖ˌprɑ-/ *n* **-ties 1** [U] the state or quality of being probable **2** [U +*that/of*] likelihood: *There's little probability of reaching London tonight.*|**In all probability** (=almost certainly) *we shall be late.* **3** [C +*that/of*] a probable event or result: *War is a real probability in the world today.* –opposite **improbability** (for **1,2,3**) **4** [C +*that/of*] (in MATHEMATICS) the chance of an event happening, expressed as a calculation based on known numbers

**prob·a·ble** /ˈprɒbəbəl‖ˈprɑ-/ *adj* that has a good chance of being true or correct; likely: *It's possible that it will rain, but with such a blue sky it doesn't seem probable.*|*a probable result* –opposite **improbable** –**probably** *adv*: *The train has probably left.*

**pro·ba·tion** /prəˈbeɪʃən‖prəʊ-/ *n* [U] **1** (the time of) the testing of a person's character, behaviour, abilities, etc., esp. for a job, to be a member of some society, etc. (esp. in the phrase **on probation**) **2** *law* the system of allowing a law-breaker to go free and unpunished if he/she will promise to behave well (esp. in the phrase **on probation**) –**probationary** *adj*

**pro·ba·tion·er** /prəˈbeɪʃənəʳ‖prəʊ-/ *n* a person who is on PROBATION

**probation of·fi·cer** /·ˈ·· ˌ···/ *n* a person whose job is to watch, advise, and help law-breakers who are put on PROBATION (2)

**probe**[1] /prəʊb/ *n* **1** a long thin metal instrument, usu. with a rounded end, esp. one used to search the inside of a wound, a hole in a tooth, etc. **2** also **space probe**– an apparatus sent into the sky to examine conditions in outer space **3** (esp. in newspapers) a careful and thorough inquiry or examination

**probe**[2] *v* **probed, probing** [I;T *into*] to search with a PROBE[1]: (fig.) *She tried to probe* (=search into) *my mind and discover what I was thinking.*

**pro·bi·ty** /ˈprəʊbɨ̞ti/ *n* [U] *fml* perfect honesty

**prob·lem** /ˈprɒblɨ̞m‖ˈprɑ-/ *n* **1** a (serious) difficulty that needs attention and thought: *the unemployment problem in this area* **2** a question (esp. connected with numbers, facts, etc.) for consideration or for which an answer is needed: *The little boy can already do simple problems in* ARITHMETIC.

**prob·lem·at·ic** /ˌprɒblɨ̞ˈmætɪk‖ˌprɑ-/ also **problematical**– *adj* doubtful; not settled: *The future of our business is problematic.* –**problematically** *adv*

**pro·bos·cis** /prəˈbɒsɨ̞s‖-ˈbɑ-/ *n* **-cises** *or* **-cides** /-sɪdiːz/ *tech* **1** the long movable nose of certain animals, esp. the elephant **2** a long tubelike part of the mouth of some insects

**pro·ce·dure** /prəˈsiːdʒəʳ/ *n* [C;U] a set of actions necessary for doing something properly: *Writing a cheque is quite a simple procedure.* –compare PROCESS[1] –**procedural** *adj*

**pro·ceed** /prəˈsiːd/ *v* [I] **1** [+*to-v*/*with*] to begin and continue (some course of action): *Tell us your name and then proceed with your story.*|*As soon as he came in he proceeded to tell us all his troubles.* **2** [*with*] *fml* to continue (after stopping): *Don't let me stop you; proceed with your work.* **3** *fml* to advance; move along a course: *Do not proceed across a main road without first looking to the right and the left.*

**pro·ceed·ings** /prəˈsiːdɪŋz/ *n* [P] **1** an action taken in law (esp. in the phrases **start/take (legal) proceedings**) **2** (undesirable or illegal) happenings

**pro·ceeds** /ˈprəʊsiːdz/ *n* [P] money gained from the sale of something, or as the result of some activity for getting money

**pro·cess**[1] /ˈprəʊses‖ˈprɑ-/ *n* **1** [C] any continued set of natural actions over which man has little control: *the process of breathing*|*Coal was formed out of dead forests by chemical processes.* **2** [C] a continued set of actions performed intentionally in order to reach some result: *the process of learning to read* **3** [U] course; time during which something is still being done: *The firm is now* **in the process of** *moving the machines to a new factory.* **4** [C] a particular system or treatment of materials used esp. in producing goods –compare PROCEDURE

**process**[2] *v* [T] **1** to treat by a particular PROCESS[1](4): *processed cheese*|*One has to process a photographic film to print pictures from it.* **2** to put (facts, numbers, etc.) into a computer for examination

**pro·ces·sion** /prəˈseʃən/ *n* **1** [C] a line of people, vehicles, etc., moving forward in an orderly, often ceremonial, way **2** [U] a continuous onward movement of people or things: *The workers marched* **in procession** *to the minister's office.*

**pro·ces·sion·al** /prəˈseʃənəl/ *adj* [A] connected with or used in a solemn religious procession: *a processional march*

**pro·claim** /prəˈkleɪm‖prəʊ-/ *v* [T +*that*] **1** *fml* to make known publicly; declare officially: *The ringing bells proclaimed the news of the birth of the prince.*|*A national holiday was proclaimed.* **2** *lit* to show clearly: *His* ACCENT *proclaimed that he was American.*

**proc·la·ma·tion** /ˌprɒklə'meɪʃən‖ˌprɑ-/ *n* **1** [C] an official public statement: *a royal proclamation* **2** [U] the action of PROCLAIMING

**pro·cras·ti·nate** /prə'kræstʲəneɪt/ *v* **-nated, -nating** [I] *fml* to delay repeatedly and without good reason in doing some necessary act **–procrastination** /-'neɪʃən/ *n* [U]

**pro·cre·ate** /'prəʊkrieɪt/ *v* **-ated, -ating** [I;T] *fml or tech* to produce or give life to (young) **–procreation** /-'eɪʃən/ *n* [U]

**pro·cure** /prə'kjʊə^r‖prəʊ-/ *v* **-cured, -curing 1** [T *for*] *fml* to obtain, esp. by effort or careful attention **2** [I;T *for*] to provide (a woman) for someone else's sexual satisfaction

**prod** /prɒd‖prɑd/ *v* **-dd-** [I;T *at, with*] to push or press (something or someone) with a pointed object; POKE(2): (fig.) *John is lazy; he won't do any work if he's not prodded into it.* (=urged to do it) **–prod** *n*

**prod·i·gal** /'prɒdɪgəl‖'prɑ-/ *adj fml* carelessly wasteful, esp. of money **–prodigality** /-'gælʲəti/ *n* [U] **–prodigally** *adv*

**pro·di·gious** /prə'dɪdʒəs/ *adj* wonderful, esp. because of size, amount, or quality; very great: *a prodigious memory* **–prodigiously** *adv*

**prod·i·gy** /'prɒdɪdʒi‖'prɑ-/ *n* **-gies** something unusual and wonderful, esp. a person who has unusual and very noticeable abilities: *a* **child prodigy** (=an unusually clever child)

**pro·duce**¹ /prə'djuːs‖-'duːs/ *v* **-duced, -ducing 1** [T] to show, bring out, or offer for examination or consideration: *Can you produce any proof of your date of birth?* **2** [T] to grow or supply: *Canada produces good wheat.* **3** [T] to give birth to (young):(fig.) *the finest writer our country has ever produced* **4** [I;T] to make (something, esp. goods) from materials: *Gas can be produced from coal.* **5** [T] to cause; have as a result or effect: *Gordon's jokes produced a great deal of laughter.* **6** [T] to prepare in all details and bring before the public:*The book/play was badly produced.* –see PRODUCTION (USAGE)

**prod·uce**² /'prɒdjuːs‖'prɑduːs/ *n* [U] something that has been produced by growing or farming:*The wine bottle was marked "Produce of Spain".* –see PRODUCTION (USAGE)

**pro·duc·er** /prə'djuːsə^r‖-'duː-/ *n* **1** a person or company that produces goods, foods, or materials **2** a person who has general control esp. of the money for a play, film, or broadcast, but who does not direct the actors –compare DIRECTOR, IMPRESARIO

**prod·uct** /'prɒdʌkt‖'prɑ-/ *n* **1** something useful produced by growth or from the ground, or made in a factory: *Fruit and gold are important products of South Africa.* –see PRODUCTION (USAGE) **2** something that is produced as a result of thought, will, planning, conditions, etc.: *Criminals are sometimes the product of bad homes.* **3** (in MATHEMATICS) the number got by multiplying two or more numbers: *The product of 3 multiplied by 2 multiplied by 6 is 36.*

**pro·duc·tion** /prə'dʌkʃən/ *n* **1** [U *of*] the act of producing (PRODUCE¹ (1,2,4)): *Entrance is permitted only on production of a ticket.|the production of cloth by hand* **2** [U] the amount produced: *Production of iron has increased in the last few weeks.* **3** [C;U] (the act of producing) a play, film, or broadcast: *This new theatre is becoming known for its good productions.* –see also MASS PRODUCTION

USAGE Compare **produce** (*n*), **product**, and **production**: Things **produced** on a farm are **produce**; things **produced** by industry are **products**; and plays, films, etc., **produced** for the theatre, television, etc., are **productions**: *The market sells a variety of fresh* **produce**.|*The company's* **products** *include washing machines and radios.*|*a new* **production** *of "Hamlet".*

**pro·duc·tive** /prə'dʌktɪv/ *adj* **1** that produces well or much: *a very productive writer/meeting* **2** [F *of*] causing or producing (a result): *It was a very long meeting, but it wasn't productive (of any important decisions).* –opposite **unproductive –productively** *adv*

**pro·duc·tiv·i·ty** /ˌprɒdʌk'tɪvʲəti, -dək-‖ˌprɑ-/ *n* [U] the (measured) ability to grow things or the (calculated) rate of making goods

**Prof.** *written abbrev. said as:* PROFESSOR

**profane**¹ /prə'feɪn/ *adj fml* having or showing disrespect for God or for holy things: *To smoke in a church or mosque would be a profane act.* –compare BLASPHEMOUS; see also SACRED **–profanely** *adv*

**profane**² *v* **-faned, -faning** [T] *fml* to treat (esp. something holy) disrespectfully

**pro·fan·i·ty** /prə'fænʲəti/ *n* **-ties** [C;U] *fml* (an example of) PROFANEness –compare OBSCENITY

**pro·fess** /prə'fes/ *v* [T] **1** *fml* to declare plainly (some personal feeling, belief, etc.): *She professed a belief in God.* **2** to claim (often falsely): *I don't profess to know anything about poetry.* **–professed** *adj* [A]: *a professed Muslim*

**pro·fes·sion** /prə'feʃən/ *n* **1** [C] a form of employment, esp. one that is respected in society and is possible only after training (such as law, medicine, and the Church): *He is a lawyer* **by profession. 2** [U +*sing./pl.v*] the whole body of people in a particular profession: *The teaching profession claim(s) to be badly paid.* **3** [C *of*] *fml* a declaration (of one's belief, opinion, or feeling) –see JOB (USAGE)

**pro·fes·sion·al**¹ /prə'feʃənəl/ *adj* **1** [A *no comp.*] working in one of the professions: *A doctor is a professional man.* **2** *usu. apprec* showing or using the qualities of training of a member of a profession: *The magician performed his tricks with professional skill.|professional standards* –see also UNPROFESSIONAL **3** [*no comp.*] doing for money what others do for enjoyment: *a professional painter* –compare AMATEUR (1) **4** [*no comp.*] done by people who are paid: *professional football* –compare AMATEUR (1) **–professionally** *adv*

**professional**² *n* **1** a person who earns money by practising a particular skill or sport: *He has just* **turned** (=become a) **professional. 2** *apprec* a person who has great experience and high professional standards: *She's a real professional.* –compare AMATEUR (2)

**pro·fes·sion·al·is·m** /prə'feʃənəlɪzəm/ *n* [U] **1** the behaviour, skill, or qualities shown by a PROFESSIONAL¹ (1) person **2** *apprec* the quality of being a PROFESSIONAL² (2)

**pro·fes·sor** /prə'fesə^r/ *n* **1** [A;C;U] *BrE* (the title of) a teacher of the highest rank in a university department: *Professor Ward|a history professor/a professor of history* **2** [A;C] *AmE* a teacher at a university or college –**professorial** /ˌprɒfəˈsɔːriəl‖ˌprɑfəˈsor-/ *adj*

**prof·fer** /ˈprɒfəʳ‖ˈprɑ-/ *v* [T *to*] *fml* to offer: *He refused the proffered drink.*

**pro·fi·cient** /prəˈfɪʃənt/ *adj* [*at, in*] thoroughly skilled: *She is proficient at/in swimming.* –**proficiently** *adv* –**proficiency** *n* [U *at, in*]

**pro·file** /ˈprəʊfaɪl/ *n* **1** [C;U] a side view, esp. of someone's head: *He drew her* **in profile.** **2** [C] a short description, esp. of a person's life and character, as given on television or in a newspaper **3 keep a low profile** to avoid drawing attention to oneself or one's actions

**prof·it¹** /ˈprɒfɨt‖ˈprɑ-/ *n* **1** [C;U] money gain; money gained by business: *He sold his house* **at a profit** (=sold it for more than it had cost him); *he* **made a profit** *of £1,000 on the sale.* –opposite **loss 2** [U] *fml* advantage gained from some action: *reading for profit and pleasure*

**profit²** *v* [T] *fml or old use* (of a thing) to be of use or advantage to (someone or something): *It will profit you nothing* (=will not help you) *to do that.*

**profit by/from** sthg. *v prep* [T +*v-ing*] to learn or gain advantage from: *to profit by others' mistakes*

**prof·i·ta·ble** /ˈprɒfɨtəbəl‖ˈprɑ-/ *adj* useful; resulting in gain (of money): *a profitable company* –opposite **unprofitable** –**profitably** *adv*

**pro·fi·teer** /ˌprɒfɨˈtɪəʳ‖ˌprɑ-/ *v* [I] *derog* to make unfairly large profits –**profiteer** *n*

**profit mar·gin** /ˈ·· ˌ··/ *n* the difference between the cost of production and the selling price

**prof·li·gate** /ˈprɒflɨgɨt‖ˈprɑ-/ *adj fml* **1** [*of*] (of a person or spending of money) carelessly and boldly wasteful **2** wicked; shamelessly immoral –**profligacy** *n* [U] *fml* –**profligate** *n*

**pro·found** /prəˈfaʊnd/ *adj more fml than* **deep**– **1** [A] deep; complete: *a profound silence|the profound depths of the ocean* **2** *often apprec* having or showing thorough knowledge and deep understanding: *a profound thinker|a profound mind.* –**profoundly** *adv*: *I am profoundly* (=very) *grateful.*

**pro·fun·di·ty** /prəˈfʌndɨti/ *n* **-ties** [C;U] *more fml than* **depth**– depth or thoroughness, esp. of mind or feeling

**pro·fuse** /prəˈfjuːs/ *adj* [F *in, of*] (too) freely produced or poured out: *Her head was covered with a profuse mass of curls.|profuse tears|She was profuse in her thanks.* –**profusely** *adv* –**profusion** /prəˈfjuːʒən/ *n* [S;U]: *There is a profusion of flowers in the garden in summer; flowers grow there* **in profusion.**

**prog·e·ny** /ˈprɒdʒɨni‖ˈprɑ-/ *n* [U +*sing./pl.v*] *tech or lit, sometimes humor* children (of a person) or the young (of an animal): *Her* NUMEROUS *progeny was/were all asleep.*

**prog·no·sis** /prɒgˈnəʊsɨs‖prɑg-/ *n* **-ses** /siːz/ *tech* a doctor's opinion, based on medical experience, of what course a disease will probably take –compare DIAGNOSIS

**pro·gram¹** /ˈprəʊgræm/ *n* **1** a plan of the operations to be performed by a computer when dealing with a set of facts **2** *AmE* for PROGRAMME

**program²** *v* **-mm-** *or* **-m-** [T] **1** to supply (a computer) with a plan of the operations to be performed: *Please program the computer to give me more information.* **2** *AmE* for PROGRAMME

**pro·gramme¹** *BrE*‖**-gram** *AmE* /ˈprəʊgræm/ *n* **1** a list of performers or things to be performed at a concert, a theatre, a sports competition, etc. –see picture on page 463 **2** a complete show or performance: *What is your favourite television programme?* **3** a fixed plan of what one is going to do: *a new political programme intended to win votes*

**programme²** *BrE*‖**-gram** *AmE* *v* **-mm-** [T] to plan or arrange: *The central heating system is programmed to start working at six o'clock each morning.*

**pro·gram·mer, programer** /ˈprəʊgræməʳ/ *n* a person who prepares a PROGRAM¹ for a computer

**pro·gress¹** /ˈprəʊgres‖ˈprɑ-/ *n* [U] **1** advance; journey onward: *The ship made slow progress through the rough sea.|Please do not enter while a lesson is* **in progress.** (=continuing) **2** continual improvement or development: *Jane is still sick in hospital, but she's* **making progress.** (=is getting better)

**pro·gress²** /prəˈgres/ *v* [I] **1** to advance: *The year is progressing; it will soon be autumn.* **2** to improve; develop (favourably): *Mary is progressing in the art of cooking* –compare REGRESS

**pro·gres·sion** /prəˈgreʃən/ *n* [S;U] (the action of) PROGRESSing², esp. by stages

**pro·gres·sive** /prəˈgresɪv/ *adj* **1** [*no comp.*] moving forward continuously or by stages **2** that favours or uses new ideas: *This is a very progressive firm that uses the most modern systems.* –**progressively** *adv*: *It got progressively worse/better.*

**pro·hib·it** /prəˈhɪbɨt‖prəʊ-/ *v* [T +*v-ing/from*] *fml* **1** to forbid by law or rule: *Smoking in this railway carriage is prohibited.* **2** to prevent; make impossible

**pro·hi·bi·tion** /ˌprəʊhɨˈbɪʃən/ *n* **1** [U *of*] the act of PROHIBITing (1) **2** [C *against*] *fml* an order forbidding something

**pro·hib·i·tive** /prəˈhɪbɨtɪv‖prəʊ-/ *adj* preventing the use or misuse of something: *The government has put a prohibitive tax* (=higher than anyone can pay) *on foreign goods.* –**prohibitively** *adv*: *prohibitively* EXPENSIVE

**proj·ect¹** /ˈprɒdʒekt‖ˈprɑ-/ *n* (a plan for) work or activity of any kind: *The government has begun a project at the port to increase the size of the harbour.*

**pro·ject²** /prəˈdʒekt/ *v* **1** [I;T] to (cause to) stand out beyond an edge or surface: *His ears project noticeably.* **2** [T] to (aim and) throw through the air with force **3** [T *into, onto*] to cause (heat, sound, light, or shadow) to be directed into space or onto a surface: *A singer must learn to project his voice so as to be heard in a large hall.* **4** [T] to consider as a possible thing to do; plan: *our projected visit to Australia*

**pro·jec·tile** /prəˈdʒektaɪl‖-tl/ *n* an object or weapon that shoots or is shot forward, esp. from a gun

**pro·jec·tion** /prəˈdʒekʃən/ *n* **1** [U *of*] the act of PROJECTing² **2** [C *of*] something that has been PROJECTed² (3) or PROJECTS² (1)

**pro·jec·tion·ist** /prəˈdʒekʃənɨst/ *n* a person who works a PROJECTOR, esp. in a cinema

**pro·jec·tor** /prəˈdʒektəʳ/ *n* an apparatus for PROJECTing² (3) films or pictures onto a surface

**pro·le·tar·i·an** /ˌprəʊlɨˈteəriən/ *n, adj often derog* (a member) of the PROLETARIAT

**pro·le·tar·i·at** /ˌprəʊlǝ̍ˈteəriət/ *n* [U +*sing./pl.v*] the class of (esp. unskilled) workers who have to work for wages: *The industrial proletariat* –compare BOURGEOISIE

**pro·lif·e·rate** /prəˈlɪfəreɪt/ *v* **-rated, -rating** [I] to increase rapidly in numbers –see also NONPROLIFERATION –**proliferation** /-reɪʃən/ *n* [S;U *of*]

**pro·lif·ic** /prəˈlɪfɪk/ *adj fml* producing many or much: *a prolific writer* –**prolifically** *adv*

**pro·logue** *BrE*‖**prolog** *AmE* /ˈprəʊlɒg‖-lɔg, -lɑg/ *n* [*to*] *(sometimes cap.)* an introduction to a play, long poem, etc. –compare EPILOGUE

**pro·long** /prəˈlɒŋ‖-ˈlɔŋ/ *v* [T] to make longer; LENGTHEN: *He prolonged his visit by two weeks.* –**prolongation** /ˌprəʊlɒŋˈgeɪʃən‖-ɔŋ-/ *n* [C;U *of*]

**pro·longed** /prəˈlɒŋd‖-ˈlɔŋd/ *adj* continuing for a long time: *a prolonged absence*

**prom·e·nade¹** /ˌprɒməˈnɑːd◂, ˈprɒmənɑːd‖ˌprɑm əˈneɪd/ *n* **1** also **prom** *BrE infml*– a wide path beside a road along the coast in a holiday town **2** *fml* an unhurried walk or ride for pleasure or exercise

**promenade²** *v* **-naded, -nading** [I;T] *fml* to walk slowly to and fro along (a place, street, etc.)

**prom·i·nent** /ˈprɒmǝ̍nənt‖ˈprɑ-/ *adj* **1** standing out (beyond a surface): *her prominent teeth* **2** [*in*] of great ability, fame, etc.: *a prominent politician* **3** noticeable or easily seen –**prominently** *adv* –**prominence** *n* [C;U]: *He is* **coming into prominence** *as an artist.*

**pro·mis·cu·ous** /prəˈmɪskjuəs/ *adj derog* not limited to one sexual partner: *a promiscuous young person/life* –**promiscuously** *adv* –**promiscuity** /ˌprɒm ǝ̍ˈskjuːǝ̍ti‖ˌprɑ-/ also **promiscuousness**– *n* [U]

**prom·ise¹** /ˈprɒmǝ̍s‖ˈprɑ-/ *n* **1** [C +*to-v/that/of*] a statement, which someone else has a right to believe and depend on, that one will or will not do something, give something, etc.: *If you* **make a promise** *you should keep it; you ought not to* **break a promise.** **2** [S;U *of*] (signs or reasons for) expectation or hope (of something good): *The boy is* **showing** *great* **promise** *as a cricketer.*

**promise²** *v* **-ised, -ising** [I;T] **1** [+*to-v/(that)*] to make a promise to do or give (something) or that (something) shall be done: *I promise to return your bicycle in good condition.*|*"She's not coming tonight." "But she promised!"* |*I've* **promised** *this book* **to** *Susan.* **2** [+*to-v*] to cause one to expect or hope for (something); to give PROMISE¹(2): *It promises to be a fine day.*

**prom·is·ing** /ˈprɒmǝ̍sɪŋ‖ˈprɑ-/ *adj apprec* full of PROMISE¹ (2); showing signs of advance towards success –opposite **unpromising** –**promisingly** *adv*

**prom·on·to·ry** /ˈprɒməntəri‖ˈprɑməntori/ *n* **-ries** a high point of land stretching out into the sea

**pro·mote** /prəˈməʊt/ *v* **-moted, -moting** [T] **1** [*to*] to advance (someone) in position or rank: *The young army officer was promoted captain/promoted to the rank of captain.* –opposite **demote** **2** to help actively in forming, arranging, or encouraging (a business, concert, play, etc.): *How can we promote the sales of this product?*

**pro·mot·er** /prəˈməʊtəʳ/ *n* a person who PROMOTES (2) activities or people

**pro·mo·tion** /prəˈməʊʃən/ *n* [C;U *of*] **1** (an) advancement in rank or position: *There are good chances of promotion in this firm.* –opposite **demotion** **2** (an) action to help something develop or succeed (esp. publicly): *This year's sales promotions haven't been very successful.*

**prompt¹** /prɒmpt‖prɑmpt/ *v* **1** [T] to cause or urge: *Hunger prompted him to steal.* **2** [I;T] to remind (an actor) of the next words in a speech

**prompt²** *adj* [F] done, given, or acting quickly, at once, or at the right time: *Prompt payment of bills greatly helps our company.*|*This worker is always prompt in his duties.* –**promptly** *adv* When he called me a thief I promptly hit him. –**promptness** *n* [U]

**prompt³** *adv infml* exactly (in regard to time): *The performance will start at seven o'clock prompt.*

**prompt·er** /ˈprɒmptəʳ‖ˈprɑmp-/ *n* a person who PROMPTS¹ (2) actors who forget their words

**prone** /prəʊn/ *adj* **1** [F +*to-v/to*] likely to suffer (usu. something unpleasant or unwanted): *He's very prone to colds in winter.*|*Mary's always falling over; she's* **accident-prone.** **2** (of a person or position) stretched out flat with the face and front of the body downwards –compare SUPINE

**prong** /prɒŋ‖prɔŋ/ *n* **1** a thin sharp-pointed piece or part esp. of a fork **2** **-pronged: a** having a certain number of prongs: *a four-pronged fork* **b** (of an attack) coming from a certain number of directions at the same time: *a two-pronged attack*

**pro·noun** /ˈprəʊnaʊn/ *n* (in grammar) a word that is used in place of a noun or a noun phrase: *Instead of saying "the man came" you can use a pronoun and say "he came".*

**pro·nounce** /prəˈnaʊns/ *v* **-nounced, -nouncing** **1** [I;T] to make the sound of (a letter, a word, etc.): *In the word "knew", the "k" is not pronounced; the word is pronounced without the "k".* **2** [T +*that*] *fml* to declare (officially): *Everyone pronounced the dinner to be very good.*|*The priest pronounced them man and wife.*

**pro·nounced** /prəˈnaʊnst/ *adj* very strong or noticeable: *He has very pronounced ideas on everything.*|*a pronounced* LIMP

**pro·nounce·ment** /prəˈnaʊnsmənt/ *n* [+*that/on, upon*] a (solemn or official) declaration or statement

**pro·nun·ci·a·tion** /prəˌnʌnsiˈeɪʃən/ *n* **1** [U] the way in which something is pronounced **2** [S;U] a particular person's way of pronouncing

**proof¹** /pruːf/ *n* **1** [C;U +*that/of*] (a) way of showing that something is true: *There is no proof that he was here.* **2** [C] a test or trial: *A soldier's courage is* **put to the proof** *in battle.* **3** [C;U] a test copy made of something printed, so that mistakes can be put right before the proper printing is done **4** [U after *n*] the standard of strength of some kinds of alcoholic drink: *This* GIN *is 15 per cent proof.* –see PROVE

**proof²** *adj* **1** [F *against*] giving or having protection against something harmful or unwanted:|*a waterproof coat*|*a soundproof room*|(fig.) *His courage is proof against* (=not influenced by) *the greatest pain.* **2** [after *n*] (of certain types of alcoholic drink) of the stated alcoholic strength in comparison with some standard: *In the US,* WHISKEY *of 90 proof is 45% alcohol.*

**prop**[1] /prɒp‖prɑp/ *n* a support placed to hold up something heavy: *She uses a* **clothes prop** *to prevent the washing on her clothes line from touching the ground.*|(fig) *Her daughter was a prop to* (=supported) *her during her illness.*

**prop**[2] *v* **-pp-** [T *up*] to support or keep in position: *Prop the gate open with a brick.*|*He propped his bicycle* (*up*) *against the fence.*

**prop**[3] also **property** *fml*– *n* [*usu. pl.*] any small article that is used on the stage in the acting of a play

**prop·a·gan·da** /ˌprɒpəˈgændə‖ˌprɑ-/ *n* [U] *often derog* ideas, false or true information, etc. spread about officially, esp. by a government: *The government produced much political propaganda.*

**prop·a·gate** /ˈprɒpəgeɪt‖ˈprɑ-/ *v* **-gated, -gating 1** [I] (of living things) to increase in number by producing young: *Most plants propagate by seed.* **2** [T] to cause to have descendants: *Insects propagate themselves by means of eggs.* **3** [T] to cause to spread to a great number of people: *The political party started the newspaper to propagate its ideas.* –**propagator** *n* –**propagation** /-ˈgeɪʃən/ *n* [U *of*]

**pro·pel** /prəˈpel/ *v* [T] to move, drive, or push forward: *The wind propels a sailing boat.*

**pro·pel·ler** /prəˈpeləʳ/ *n* two or more blades fixed to a central bar that is turned at high speed by an engine, used for driving a ship or aircraft

**pro·pen·si·ty** /prəˈpensɪ̈ti/ *n* **-ties** [+*to-v*/*for, to, towards*] *fml* a natural tendency towards a particular (usu. undesirable) kind of behaviour: *a propensity for complaining*|*a propensity to sudden anger*

**prop·er** /ˈprɒpəʳ‖ˈprɑ-/ *adj* **1** [A *no comp.*] right; suitable; correct: *The child is too ill to be nursed at home; she needs proper medical attention at a hospital.*|*These pages aren't in their proper order; page 22 comes after page 26.* **2** *sometimes derog* paying great attention to what is considered correct in society: *I don't consider that short dress to be proper for going to church in.* –see also IMPROPER **3** [A] *infml* real; actual: *The little boy wanted a proper dog as a pet, not a toy dog.* **4** [after *n, no comp.*] itself; in its actual, most limited meaning: *Many people call themselves Londoners though they live outside, not in the city proper.*

**prop·er·ly** /ˈprɒpəli‖ˈprɑpərli/ *adv* **1** suitably; correctly: *I'm learning German, but I still can't speak it properly.* –see also IMPROPER **2** really; actually; exactly: *I'm not, properly speaking, a nurse, as I haven't been trained, but I've looked after many sick people.*

**proper noun** /ˌ·· ˈ·/ also **proper name**– *n* (in grammar) a name used for a single particular thing or person, and spelt with a CAPITAL[2] (2) letter: *"James", "London", and "China" are proper nouns.* –see also COMMON NOUN

**prop·er·ty** /ˈprɒpəti‖ˈprɑpərti/ *n* **-ties 1** [U] something which is owned: possession(s): *The police found some stolen property hidden in the thief's house.* **2** [U] land, buildings, or both together: *The city is growing and property in the centre is becoming more valuable.* **3** [C] a building, piece of land, or both together: *Several properties in this street are to be let.* **4** [C *of*] a quality, power, or effect that belongs naturally to something: *Many plants have medicinal properties.* **5** [C *usu. pl.*] *fml* for PROP[3]

**proph·e·cy** /ˈprɒfɪ̈si‖ˈprɑ-/ *n* **-cies 1** [U] the foreseeing and foretelling of future events **2** [C+*that*] a statement telling something that is to happen in the future: *The teacher's prophecy that the boy would become famous was later fulfilled.*

**proph·e·sy** /ˈprɒfɪ̈saɪ‖ˈprɑ-/ *v* **-sied, -sying** [I;T +*that*] to give (a warning, statement about some future event, etc.): *I wouldn't like to prophesy who will win the election.*

**proph·et** /ˈprɒfɪ̈t‖ˈprɑ-/ *n* **1** (in the Christian, Jewish, and Muslim religions) a man who believes that he is directed by God to make known and explain God's will and/or to lead or teach a religion **2** **prophetess** /ˈprofɪ̈tes‖ˈprɑfɪ̈təs/ *fem.*– an important thinker, poet, etc., who introduces and teaches some new idea **3** **prophet of doom** *derog* a person who is always foretelling ruin, destruction, misfortune, etc.

**pro·phet·ic** /prəˈfetɪk/ also **prophetical**– *adj* **1** [*of*] correctly telling of things that will happen in the future **2** of or like a PROPHET (2) –**prophetically** *adv*

**pro·pi·ti·ate** /prəˈpɪʃieɪt/ *v* **-ated, -ating** [T] *fml* to win the favour of (someone who is angry or unfriendly) by some pleasing act –**propitiation** /-ˈeɪʃən/ *n* [U *for, of*]

**pro·pi·tious** /prəˈpɪʃəs/ *adj* [*for, to*] *fml* advantageous; favourable –**propitiously** *adv*

**pro·po·nent** /prəˈpəʊnənt/ *n* [*of*] a person who argues in favour of something –see also OPPONENT

**pro·por·tion** /prəˈpɔːʃən‖-ˈpor-/ *n* **1** [U] the correct relationship between the size, position, and shape of the different parts of a whole: *This drawing isn't* **in proportion;** *the car is larger than the house.* –opposite **disproportion 2** [C;U *of*] the compared relationship between two things in regard to size, importance, etc.: *The proportion of boys to girls in our school is 2 to 3.*|*Are you paid* **in proportion to** (=according to) *the number of hours you work?* **3** [C *of*] a part or share (as measured in amount and compared with the whole): *"What proportion of your wages do you spend on rent?" "About a quarter."* **4** **in/out of proportion** (not) according to real importance; (not) sensibly: *When one is angry one often does not see things* **in proportion. 5 sense of proportion** ability to judge what matters, without being influenced by personal feeling

**pro·por·tion·al** /prəˈpɔːʃənəl‖-ˈpor-/ *adj* **1** concerning PROPORTION (2) **2** [*to*] in (correct) PROPORTION (2): *His pay is proportional to the amount of work he does.* –opposite **disproportional** (for 2) –**proportionally** *adv*

**pro·por·tion·ate** /prəˈpɔːʃənɪ̈t‖-ˈpor-/ *adj* [*to*] in the right PROPORTION (1,2) –opposite **disproportionate** –**proportionately** *adv*

**pro·pos·al** /prəˈpəʊzəl/ *n* **1** [+*to-v*/*at*/*for, often pl.*] a plan or suggestion: *peace proposals* **2** [*of*] an offer of marriage –compare PROPOSITION[1] (3) **3** [+*to-v*/*that*/*of*] the act of proposing (PROPOSE)

**pro·pose** /prəˈpəʊz/ *v* **-posed, -posing 1** [T +*to-v*/(*that*)/*as, for*] to suggest; put forward for consideration: *I propose resting for half an hour.*|*I propose that we have a rest.* **2** [T +*to- v*] to intend: *I propose to go to London on Tuesday.* **3** [I;T *to*] (usu. of a man) to make an offer of (marriage)

**prop·o·si·tion**[1] /ˌprɒpəˈzɪʃən‖ˌprɑ-/ *n* **1** [+*that*] a statement in which an opinion or judgment is expressed **2** a suggested business offer or arrangement: *He* **made me a proposition** *concerning the sale of my car.* **3** *euph* an offer to have sex with someone –compare PROPOSAL (2)

**proposition**[2] *v* [T] *infml* to make (someone) a PROPOSITION[1] (3): *She was angry when he propositioned her*

**pro·pound** /prəˈpaʊnd/ *v* [T] *fml* to put forward as a question or matter for consideration

**pro·pri·e·ta·ry** /prəˈpraɪətəri‖-teri/ *adj* [A] privately owned or controlled

**pro·pri·e·ties** /prəˈpraɪətiz/ *n* [*the* P] *fml* the rules of proper social behaviour

**pro·pri·e·tor** /prəˈpraɪətəʳ/ **proprietress** /-trɪ̵s/ *fem.*– *n esp. fml* an owner (esp. of a business, etc.): *I wasn't satisfied with our treatment at that hotel, so I shall complain to the proprietor.*

**pro·pri·e·ty** /prəˈpraɪəti/ *n* [U] *fml* **1** rightness of social or moral behaviour: *You can trust John to behave with perfect propriety.* **2** fitness; rightness: *I doubt the propriety of making a public statement before we have studied the official reports.* –see also IMPROPRIETY

**pro·pul·sion** /prəˈpʌlʃən/ *n* [U] *tech* force that drives (PROPELS) something, esp. a vehicle, forward: *This aircraft works by* JET *propulsion.* (=it has JET engines)

**pro·sa·ic** /prəʊˈzeɪ-ɪk, prə-/ *adj* dull; uninteresting: *a prosaic job/article* –**prosaically** *adv*

**pro·scribe** /prəʊˈskraɪb/ *v* **-scribed, -scribing** [T] *fml* to forbid (esp. something dangerous or harmful), esp. by law –**proscription** /prəʊˈskrɪpʃən, prə-/ *n* [C;U]

**prose** /prəʊz/ *n* [C;U] written language in the form used in conversation: *Newspaper articles are written in prose.* –compare POETRY

**pros·e·cute** /ˈprɒsɪkjuːt‖ˈprɑ-/ *v* **-cuted, -cuting** [I;T *for*] to bring a criminal charge against (someone) in a court of law: *He was prosecuted for stealing.*

**pros·e·cu·tion** /ˌprɒsɪˈkjuːʃən‖ˌprɑ-/ *n* **1** [C;U] (an example of) prosecuting or being PROSECUTEd by law **2** [U +*sing./pl. v*] the group of people who bring a criminal charge against someone in court: *The prosecution is/are coming into court.*|*A famous lawyer has been asked to appear* **for the prosecution.** –compare DEFENCE

**pros·e·cu·tor** /ˈprɒsɪkjuːtəʳ‖ˈprɑ-/ *n* the person (often a lawyer) who PROSECUTEs another –see PUBLIC PROSECUTOR

**pros·pect**[1] /ˈprɒspekt‖ˈprɑ-/ *n* **1** [C;U *of*] (a) reasonable hope or chance (of something happening): *There's not much prospect of my being able to come.*|*a job with excellent prospects* (=chances of future success) **2** [S;U *of*] something which is probable: *She doesn't like the prospect of having to live alone.* **3** [C *usu. sing.*] *fml* a wide or distant view: *From the top of the hill there's a beautiful prospect over the valley.* –see VIEW (USAGE)

**pros·pect**[2] /prəˈspekt‖ˈprɑspekt/ *v* [I;T *for*] to examine (land, an area, etc.) in order to find gold, silver, oil, etc. –**prospector** *n*

**pro·spec·tive** /prəˈspektɪv/ *adj* expected; probable; intended: *a prospective buyer for the house*

**pro·spec·tus** /prəˈspektəs/ *n* a printed statement giving details of a university, a new business, etc.

**pros·per** /ˈprɒspəʳ‖ˈprɑ-/ *v* [I] to become successful

**pro·sper·i·ty** /prɒˈsperɪ̵ti‖prɑ-/ *n* [U] good fortune and success, esp. in money matters

**pros·per·ous** /ˈprɒspərəs‖ˈprɑ-/ *adj* successful; rich –**prosperously** *adv*

**pros·ti·tute**[1] /ˈprɒstɪ̵tjuːt‖ˈprɑstɪ̵tuːt/ **male prostitute** *masc.*– *n* a person, esp. a woman, who earns money by having sex with a person who will pay for it –**prostitution** /-tjuːʃən/ *n* [U *of*]

**prostitute**[2] *v* **-tuted, -tuting** [T] *fml* **1** to hire (oneself) as a PROSTITUTE[1] **2** to put to a dishonourable use, for money: *He prostituted his abilities by acting in television advertisements.*

**pros·trate**[1] /ˈprɒstreɪt‖ˈprɑ-/ *adj* **1** lying flat, with the face to the ground –compare PRONE (2) **2** having lost all strength, courage, and ability to act, as a result of some experience: *She was prostrate with grief.* –**prostration** /-streɪʃən/ *n* [C;U]

**pros·trate**[2] /prɒˈstreɪt‖ˈprɑstreɪt/ *v* **-trated, -trating** [T] **1** to put in a PROSTRATE[1] (1) position **2** [*usu. pass.*] to cause to be PROSTRATE[1] (2): *a prostrating illness*

**pro·tag·o·nist** /prəʊˈtægənɪ̵st/ *n* **1** [*of*] a supporter or leader of some (new) idea or purpose: *Mrs Pankhurst was one of the chief protagonists of women's rights.* **2** the chief character in a play or story

**pro·tect** /prəˈtekt/ *v* [T *against, from*] to keep safe, by guarding or covering: *He raised his arm to protect his face from the blow.* –**protector** *n*

**pro·tec·tion** /prəˈtekʃən/ *n* **1** [U *against, for*] the act of protecting or state of being protected: *A thin coat gives little protection against the cold.* **2** [S] a person or thing that protects

**pro·tec·tive** /prəˈtektɪv/ *adj* **1** [A] that gives protection: *protective clothing* **2** [*towards*] wishing to protect –**protectiveness** *n* [U]

**pro·tec·tor·ate** /prəˈtektərɪ̵t/ *n* a country controlled and protected by a more powerful nation

**prot·é·gé** /ˈprɒtɪ̵ʒeɪ‖ˈprəʊ-/ **protégée** *fem.* (*same pronunciation*)– *n* a person who is guided and helped by someone of influence or power

**pro·tein** /ˈprəʊtiːn/ *n* [C;U] any of many substances (present in such foods as meat and eggs) that help to build up the body and keep it healthy

**pro·test**[1] /ˈprəʊtest/ *n* [C;U] **1** (a) complaint or strong spoken expression of dissatisfaction, disagreement, opposition, etc. *They refused to buy meat,* **in protest. 2 under protest** unwillingly

**pro·test**[2] /prəˈtest/ *v* **1** [I *about, against, at*] to express one's disagreement, feeling of unfairness, annoyance, etc.: *They protested about the bad food at the hotel.*|*They protested to the owner.* **2** [T+*that*] to declare, esp. in complaint or opposition: *We urged her to come to the party with us, but she protested that she was too tired.* –**protester** *n*

**Prot·es·tant** /ˈprɒtɪ̵stənt‖ˈprɑ-/ *n,adj* (a member) of a part of the Christian church that separated from the ROMAN CATHOLIC Church in the 16th century –**Protestantism** *n* [U]

**prot·es·ta·tion** /ˌprɒtɪ̵ˈsteɪʃən, ˌprəʊ-‖ˌprɑ-, prəʊ-/ *n* [+*that/of*] *fml* a (solemn) declaration, esp.

against opposition: *The meeting ended with protestations of friendship from everyone.*

**pro·to·col** /'prəutəkɒl||-kɔl/ *n* [U] the system of fixed rules and accepted behaviour used esp. by representatives of governments on official occasions

**pro·ton** /'prəutɒn||-tɑn/ *n* a very small piece of matter with a POSITIVE electrical charge that helps to form the central part of an atom

**pro·to·type** /'prəutətaɪp/ *n* [*of*] the first form of anything, from which all later (improved) forms develop: *the prototype of a new car*

**pro·trac·ted** *adj* lasting a long time esp. longer than expected: *a protracted argument*

**pro·trac·tor** /prə'træktə^r||prəu-/ *n* an instrument usu. in the form of a half-circle, used for measuring and drawing angles

**pro·trude** /prə'tru:d||prəu-/ *v* **-truded, -truding** [I;T] *fml* to (cause to) stick out: *The policeman saw a gun protruding from the man's pocket.*|*protruding teeth* –**protrusion** /prə'tru:ʒən||prəu-/ *n* [C;U *of*]

**pro·tu·ber·ance** /prə'tju:bərəns||prəu'tu:-/ *n fml* a swelling: *protuberances on the flower's stem*

**proud** /praud/ *adj* **1** *apprec* having and showing self-respect –compare HUMBLE[1] (2) **2** *derog* having too high an opinion of oneself: *He's too proud to be seen in public with his poorly-dressed mother.* **3** [+*to-v*/*that*/*of*] having or expressing personal satisfaction and pleasure in something: *Tom is very proud of his new car.*|*Our football team feels proud that it has won every match this year.* **4** [A] splendid; noble; grand; glorious: *this proud and great university* **5 do (someone) proud** to treat someone, esp. a guest, splendidly –see PRIDE –**proudly** *adv*

**prove** /pru:v/ *v* **proved, proved** or **proven** /'pru:vən/, esp. *AmE* **proving 1** [T +*that*/*to*] to give proof of; show to be true: *He has proved his courage in battle.*|*The marks of the prisoner's fingers on the gun proved that he was the guilty man.* –see also DISPROVE **2** [I;T] to show in the course of time or experience, etc., to be of the quality stated: *He proved himself to be an amusing companion.*|*My advice proved to be wrong.* –see also PROOF[1]

**prov·en** /'pru:vən; *Scot* 'prəuvən/ also **proved**– *adj* [A] *apprec* that has been tested and shown to be true: *a man of proven ability* –opposite **unproven**

**prov·erb** /'prɒvɜ:b||'prɑvɜrb/ *n* a short well-known saying usu. in popular language: *"Don't put all your eggs in one basket" is a proverb.*

**pro·ver·bi·al** /prə'vɜ:bɪəl||-ɜr-/ *adj* **1** of, concerning, or like a PROVERB: *the proverbial eggs in the basket* **2** very widely known and spoken of; undoubted: *His generosity is proverbial.* –**proverbially** *adv*

**pro·vide** /prə'vaɪd/ *v* **-vided, -viding** [T] **1** [*for*/*with*] to supply (something needed or useful): *That hotel provides good meals.* **2** [+*that*] (of a law, rule, agreement, etc.) to state a special arrangement that must be fulfilled: *The law provides that valuable ancient buildings must be preserved by the government.*

**provide for** sbdy. *v prep* [T] to support; supply with the necessary things of life: *He has a wife and five children to provide for.*

**pro·vid·ed** /prə'vaɪdɪ̵d/ also **provided that, providing, providing that** /·'·· ·/– *conj* if and only if; on condition that: *I will go, (always) provided/providing (that) you go too.*

**prov·i·dence** /'prɒvɪ̵dəns||'prɑ-/ *n* [S;U] a special event showing God's care or the kindness of fate (often in the phrase **divine providence**): *It seemed like providence that the doctor happened to be passing just at the time of the accident.*

**prov·i·dent** /'prɒvɪ̵dənt||'prɑ-/ *adj* (careful in) providing for future needs, esp. by saving or storing –opposite **improvident** –**providently** *adv*

**prov·i·den·tial** /ˌprɒvɪ̵'denʃəl||ˌprɑ-/ *adj fml* happening just when needed; lucky –**providentially** *adv*

**prov·ince** /'prɒvɪ̵ns||'prɑ-/ *n* **1** [C] one of the main divisions of some countries (and formerly of some empires) that forms a separate whole for purposes of government control **2** [U] a branch of thought, knowledge, or study: *Chinese art is outside my province.* (it is something I know nothing about)

**prov·inc·es** /'prɒvɪ̵nsɪ̵z||'prɑ-/ *n* [P] the parts of a country that are distant from the main city: *The film is now being shown in the provinces.*

**pro·vin·cial**[1] /prə'vɪnʃəl/ *n* a PROVINCIAL[2] (esp. 2) person

**provincial**[2] *adj* **1** [A] of a PROVINCE (1), or the PROVINCES **2** *often derog* having or showing the old-fashioned manners, opinions, customs, etc., regarded (esp. in former times) as typical of people of the PROVINCES –**provincially** *adv*

**pro·vi·sion**[1] /prə'vɪʒən/ *n* **1** [U *of*] the act of providing: *The provision of a new library has been of great advantage to the students.* **2** [U *against, for*] preparation (for future needs): *They spend all their money and* **make no provision for** *the future.* **3** [C +*that*] a condition in an agreement or law; PROVISO: *He made provisions for his children.*

**provision**[2] *v* [T *for*] to provide with food and other supplies in large quantities

**pro·vi·sion·al** /prə'vɪʒənəl/ *adj* for the present time only, with the probability of being changed –compare TEMPORARY –**provisionally** *adv*

**pro·vi·sions** /prə'vɪʒənz/ *n* [P] food supplies

**pro·vi·so** /prə'vaɪzəu/ *n* **-sos** [C +*that*] something added that limits the conditions in which an agreement will be accepted, esp. in business matters: *I've agreed to do the work, with the proviso that I'll be paid before I do it.* –compare PROVISION

**prov·o·ca·tion** /ˌprɒvə'keɪʃən||ˌprɑ-/ *n* **1** [U] the act of provoking or state of being PROVOKED **2** [C] something that PROVOKES: *the provocations of teaching a class of badly-behaved children*

**pro·voc·a·tive** /prə'vɒkətɪv||-'vɑ-/ *adj* causing argument, anger, or (sexual) interest: *a provocative speech*|*a provocative dress* –**provocatively** *adv*

**pro·voke** /prə'vəuk/ *v* **-voked, -voking** [T] **1** to make angry or bad-tempered: *That dog is very dangerous when provoked.* **2** to cause (a feeling or action): *Her rudeness provoked me to strike her.*

**pro·vok·ing** /prə'vəukɪŋ/ *adj usu. fml* annoying –**provokingly** *adv*

**prow** /prau/ *n esp. lit* the pointed front part of a ship or boat; BOW[5]

**prow·ess** /'prauɪ̵s/ *n* [U *as, at, in*] *fml or lit* unusual ability or skill: *He shows great prowess at acting.*

**prowl**[1] /praul/ *v* [I] (esp. of an animal looking for food, or of a thief) to move about quietly trying not to be seen or heard: *I woke in the middle of the night and heard someone prowling about* (=a **prowler**) *in the garden.*

**prowl²** *n* [S] *infml* an act of PROWLing¹: *a lion* **on the prowl,** *looking for food*

**prox·im·i·ty** /prɒk'sɪmɨti||prɑk-/ *n* [U *to*] *fml* **1** nearness **2 in the proximity of** *fml* near

**prox·y** /'prɒksi||'prɑksi/ *n* **-ies** (a person having) the right to act for or represent another person, esp. as a voter at an election: *to vote* **by proxy**

**prude** /pru:d/ *n derog* a person who makes a show of being easily shocked and does not do or say anything supposed to be impure **–prudish** *adj* **–prudishly** *adv* **–prudishness** *n* [U]

**pru·dent** /'pru:dənt/ *adj* sensible and wise; careful: *It's prudent to wear a thick coat when the weather is cold.* –opposite **imprudent –prudently** *adv* **–prudence** *n* [U]: *John showed prudence in obeying his angry father.*

**prud·er·y** /'pru:dəri/ *n* [U] *derog* the behaviour of a PRUDE

**prune¹** /pru:n/ *n* a dried PLUM

**prune²** *v* **pruned, pruning** [T] [*back*] to cut off or shorten some of the branches of (a tree or bush) in order to improve the shape and growth

**pry¹** /praɪ/ *v* **pried, prying** [I *into*] to try to find out about someone else's private affairs: *Stop prying: you shouldn't read my letters!*|*prying newspaper reporters*

**pry²** also **prize–** *v* [T] to move, lift, or break with a tool or metal bar: *I couldn't pry the cover off this wooden box without breaking it.*

**P.S.** *n infml abbrev. for:* POSTSCRIPT: . . . *Yours sincerely, J. Smith. P.S. I shan't be able to come before Thursday.*

**psalm** /sɑ:m||sɑm, sɑlm/ *n* a song or poem in praise of God, esp. one of the collection of Psalms in the Bible

**pseud** /sju:d||su:d/ *n BrE infml* a person who acts as though he is better than others in knowledge, social position, etc., but is seen not to be

**pseu·do·nym** /'sju:dənɪm||'su:dənɪm/ *n* an invented name used, esp. by a writer of books, in place of the real name: *Eric Blair wrote* **under the pseudonym of** *George Orwell.*

**psy·che** /'saɪki/ *n* [ *usu. sing.* ] *tech or fml* the human mind, soul, or spirit

**psy·che·del·ic** /ˌsaɪkɨ'delɪk/ *adj* **1** (of a mind-influencing drug) having the effect of making the senses seem keener than in reality **2** (of a form of art) producing an effect on the brain by means of strong patterns of noise, colour, lines, moving lights, etc.

**psy·chi·a·trist** /saɪ'kaɪətrɨst||sə-/ *n* a doctor trained in PSYCHIATRY

**psy·chi·a·try** /saɪ'kaɪətri||sə-/ *n* [U] the study and treatment of diseases of the mind **–psychiatric** /ˌsɑɪkiætrɪk/ *adj*: *a psychiatric hospital*

**psy·chic** /'saɪkɪk/ also **psychical–** *adj* **1** concerning the mind or soul: *psychic disorders* **2** concerning the truth of strange happenings not explained by scientists, such as the power to see into the future **–psychically** *adv*

**psy·cho·an·a·lyse** ||also **-lyze** *AmE* /ˌsaɪkəʊ'ænəlaɪz/ *v* **-lysed, -lysing** [T] to treat by PSYCHOANALYSIS

**psy·cho·a·nal·y·sis** /ˌsaɪkəʊ-ə'nælɨsɨs/ *n* [U] a way of treating certain disorders of the mind by examination of the sufferer's past life, dreams, etc., in an effort to find past experiences that may be causing the illness

**psy·cho·an·a·lyst** /ˌsaɪkəʊ'ænəlɨst/ also **analyst** *AmE– n* a person who is trained in PSYCHOANALYSIS

**psy·cho·log·i·cal** /ˌsaɪkə'lɒdʒɪkəl||-'lɑ-/ *adj* **1** of or connected with the way that the mind works: *There must be some psychological explanation for his bad health.* **2** [A] using PSYCHOLOGY: *psychological tests* **–psychologically** *adv*

**psy·chol·o·gist** /saɪ'kɒlədʒɨst||-'kɑ-/ *n* a person who is trained in PSYCHOLOGY

**psy·chol·o·gy** /saɪ'kɒlədʒi||-'kɑ-/ *n* **-gies 1** [U] the study or science of the mind and the way it works **2** [C;U] *infml* the mind and character of a particular person or group: *I can't understand that man's psychology.*

**psy·cho·path** /'saɪkəpæθ/ *n tech* a person who has a serious disorder of character that may cause violent or criminal behaviour **–psychopathic** /-'pæθɪk / *adj*

**psy·cho·sis** /saɪ'kəʊsɨs/ *n* [C;U] *tech* a serious disorder of the mind that may produce character changes

**psy·cho·so·mat·ic** /ˌsaɪkəʊsə'mætɪk||-kəse-/ *n tech* (of an illness) caused by fear or anxiety rather than by a bodily disorder **–psychosomatically** *adv*

**psy·cho·ther·a·py** /ˌsaɪkəʊ'θerəpi/ *n* [U] *tech* treatment of disorders of the mind using PSYCHOLOGY rather than drugs, etc. **–psychotherapist** *n*

**psy·chot·ic** /saɪ'kɒtɪk||-'kɑ-/ *n,adj tech* (of or being) a person suffering from PSYCHOSIS

**P T** *infml abbrev. for*: PHYSICAL TRAINING

**PTO** *BrE abbrev. for*: (written at the bottom of a page) please turn over; look at the next page

**pub** /pʌb/ also **public house** *BrE fml– n* (esp. in Britain) a building (not a club or hotel) where alcohol may be bought and drunk during fixed hours –compare BAR¹ (5)

**pu·ber·ty** /'pju:bəti||-ər-/ *n* the stage of change in the human body from childhood to the grown-up state in which it is possible to produce children

**pu·bic** /'pju:bɪk/ *adj* [A] of or near the sexual organs: *pubic hair*

**pub·lic¹** /'pʌblɪk/ *adj* **1** of, for, or concerning people in general; not private: *a public library*|*public gardens.*|**Public opinion** (=what most people think or believe) *was against the old political system.*|*Smoking is not allowed in public places.* **2** known to all or to many: *The news was not* **made public** *for several days.* **3 in the public eye** often seen in public or on television, or mentioned in newspapers **–publicly** *adv*

**public²** *n* [*the* U *+sing./pl. v*] **1** people in general: *The town gardens are open to the public* **2** a group in society considered for its interest in a particular person, activity,etc.: *the singer pleases his public by singing its/their favourite songs* **3 in public** in the presence of other people –opposite **in private**

**pub·li·can** /'pʌblɪkən/ *n BrE* a person who runs a PUB

**pub·li·ca·tion** /ˌpʌblɨ'keɪʃən/ *n* **1** [U *of*] the act of making something known to the public: *the publica-*

tion of the results of the election **2** [U] the offering for sale to the public of something printed: *The book is ready for publication.* **3** [C] something PUBLISHed (1), such as a book or magazine

**public bar** /ˌ·· ˈ·/ *n BrE* a room in a pub, hotel, etc., that is plainly furnished, and where the cheapest prices are charged for drinks –compare SALOON BAR

**public con·ve·ni·ences** /ˌ·· ·ˈ····/ also **conveniences**– *n BrE* [P] public TOILETS provided by local government

**pub·li·cist** /ˈpʌblˌsˌst/ *n* a person whose business is to bring something to the attention of the public, esp. products for sale

**pub·lic·i·ty** /pʌˈblɪsˌti/ *n* [U] **1** public notice or attention: *The film star's marriage got a lot of publicity.* **2** the business of bringing someone or something to (favourable) public notice, esp. for purposes of gain

**pub·li·cize, -cise** /ˈpʌblˌsaɪz/ *v* **-cized, -cizing** [T] to bring to public notice or attention

**public re·la·tions** /ˌ·· ·ˈ··/ also **PR**– *n* [P] the relations between an organization and the general public, which must be kept friendly: *If we plant flowers in front of the factory it will be good (for) public relations.*

**public school** /ˌ·· ˈ·/ *n* **1** *BrE* a private SECONDARY school for children who usu. live as well as study there **2** *AmE* a free local PRIMARY school for children who study there but live at home –compare PRIVATE SCHOOL

**public spir·it·ed** /ˌ·· ˈ···/ *adj apprec* showing willingness and the desire to serve people and do what is helpful for all

**pub·lish** /ˈpʌblɪʃ/ *v* **1** [I;T] (of a business firm) to choose, arrange, have printed, and offer for sale to the public (a book, magazine, newspaper, etc.) **2** [T] to make known generally: *News of the ruler's death was not published for several days.*

**pub·lish·er** /ˈpʌblɪʃəʳ/ *n* a person or firm whose business is to PUBLISH (1) books, newspapers, etc., or (sometimes) to make and sell records

**pub·lish·ing** /ˈpʌblɪʃɪŋ/ *n* [U] the business or profession of preparing and offering books, newspapers, etc., for sale

**puce** /pjuːs/ *n,adj* [U] (of) a dark brownish purple colour

**puck** /pʌk/ *n* a hard flat circular piece of rubber used instead of a ball in the game of ice HOCKEY

**puck·er** /ˈpʌkəʳ/ *v* [I;T *up*] to tighten into (unwanted) folds: *to pucker (up) one's lips* **–pucker** *n*

**pud·ding** /ˈpʊdɪŋ/ *n* [C;U] **1** *BrE* the sweet dish in a meal, served after meat or fish; DESSERT: *What's for pudding?* –compare SWEET **2** a usu. solid dish based on pastry, rice,eggs, etc., usu. served hot: *an apple pudding|a* STEAK *and* KIDNEY *pudding|a rice pudding*

**pud·dle** /ˈpʌdl/ *n* a small amount of rainwater lying in a hollow place in the ground

**pu·er·ile** /ˈpjʊəraɪl‖-rəl/ *adj fml* fit only for children; silly **–puerility** /-ˈrɪlˌti/ *n* **-ties** [C;U]

**puff¹** /pʌf/ *v* **1** [I] to breathe rapidly and with effort, usu. during or after hurried movement: *He puffed up the steep slope.* **2** [I;T *away, at, on*] to (cause to) blow out repeatedly, esp. in small amounts: *Don't puff cigarette smoke in my face.* **3** [I] to move while sending out little clouds of smoke: *The railway train puffed into the station.*

**puff out** *v adv* [I;T (=**puff** sthg.↔**out**) *with*] to (cause to) enlarge, esp. with air: *The bird puffed out its feathers.*

**puff up** *v adv* [I;T (=**puff** sthg.↔**up**) *with, usu. pass.*] to (cause to) swell

**puff²** *n* **1** an act of PUFFing¹ (1,2): *He took a puff at his cigarette.* **2** a sudden short rush of air, smoke, etc.: *a puff of wind* –compare GUST **3** a hollow piece of light pastry (**puff pastry**) that is filled with a soft (usu. sweet) mixture: *a cream puff*

**puf·fin** /ˈpʌfˌn/ *n* a North Atlantic seabird that has a very large brightly coloured beak

**puff·y** /ˈpʌfi/ *adj* **-ier, -iest** rather swollen **–puffiness** *n* [U]

**pug** /pʌg/ *n* a small short-haired dog with a wide flat face and a turned-up nose

**pug·na·cious** /pʌgˈneɪʃəs/ *adj fml* fond of quarrelling and fighting: *pugnacious people/behaviour* **–pugnaciously** *adv* **–pugnacity** /-ˈnæsˌti/ *n* [U] *fml*

**puke** /pjuːk/ *v* **puked, puking** [I;T] *infml* to be sick; VOMIT *n* [U]

**pull¹** /pʊl/ *v* **1** [I;T] to move (something) along behind one while moving: *The train is pulled by a powerful engine.|Help me move this piano: you pull and I'll push.* –see picture on page 669 **2** [I;T *up, on, at, out*] to move (someone or something) towards oneself, sometimes with force: *He pulled his chair up to the table.|He pulled his socks on.|The cupboard door is stuck and I can't pull it open.|The child pulled (at) its mother's coat.* **3** [T] to draw or press towards one in order to cause an apparatus to work: *To fire the gun, pull the* TRIGGER. **4** [T *in*] to attract: *The football match pulled in great crowds.|He's not popular enough to pull many votes at the election.* **5** [I] (of an apparatus) to move when drawn or pressed towards one: *The handle pulls so easily that a child could open the door.* **6** [T] to bring out (a small weapon) ready for use: *He* **pulled a gun on** *me.* (=took out a gun and aimed it at me) **7 pull a face** to make an expression with the face to show rude amusement, disagreement, dislike, etc. **8 pull a fast one (on)** *infml* to get the advantage (over) by a trick **9 pull one's weight** to do one's full share of work **10 pull to pieces** to say or show that (something or someone) is bad or worthless by pointing out the weak points or faults

**pull away** *v adv* [I *from*] (esp. of a road vehicle) to start to move off: *He jumped onto the bus just as it was pulling away.*

**pull** sthg.↔**down** *v adv* [T] to destroy (something built): *They are pulling down the houses in the street.*

**pull in** *v adv* **1** [I] (of a train) to arrive at a station **2** [I] also **pull over**– (of a vehicle or boat) to move to one side (and stop) **3** [T] (**pull** sthg.↔**in**) *infml* to earn (a lot of money)

**pull off** *v adv* **1** [T] (**pull** sthg.↔**off**) *infml* to succeed in (a difficult attempt): *The trick looked impossible, but she pulled it off.* **2** [I] to drive a vehicle onto the side of the road –compare PULL **in** (2), PULL **over**

**pull out** *v adv* **1** [I] (of a train) to leave a station **2** [I;T (=**pull** sbdy.↔**out**) *of*] to (cause to) leave a place or time of trouble: *The army pulled out of the area.*

**pull over** *v adv* [I;T (=**pull** sthg.↔**over**)] to direct or move (one's vehicle) over to one side of the road –compare PULL **in** (2), PULL **off** (2)

**pull through** *v adv* [I;T (=**pull** sbdy. **through**)] **1** to (cause to) live in spite of illness or wounds –see also BRING **through 2** to (help to) succeed in spite of difficulties: *Margaret had difficulty with her work for the examinations, but her teacher pulled her through.*

**pull together** *v adv* **1** [I] (of a group of people) to work so as to help a common effort **2** [T *no pass.*] (**pull** sbdy. **together**) to control the feelings of (oneself): *Stop acting like a baby!* **Pull yourself together!**

**pull up** *v adv* [I;T (=**pull** sthg. **up**)] to (cause to) come to a stop: *The car pulled up outside the station.*

**pull²** *n* **1** [C;U] (an act of) pulling: *Give the rope a pull.* (=pull it)|*the moon's pull on the sea* **2** [U] *infml* special influence; (unfair) personal advantage **3** [C] a rope, handle, etc., used for pulling something or causing something to act by pulling: *a bellpull*

**pul·let** /ˈpulɨ̣t/ *n* a young hen during its first year of laying eggs

**pul·ley** /ˈpuli/ *n* **-leys** an apparatus consisting of a wheel over which a rope or chain can be moved, used for lifting heavy things

**pull·o·ver** /ˈpulˌəuvəʳ/ *n n* a woollen garment for the top half of the body, that has no fastenings and is pulled on over the head –compare SWEATER, JUMPER –see picture on page 563

**pul·mo·na·ry** /ˈpʌlmənəri‖ˈpulmәneri, ˈpʌl-/ *adj* [A] *tech* of, concerning, or having an effect on the lungs

**pulp¹** /pʌlp/ *n* **1** [S;U] a soft almost liquid mass, such as the soft inside part of many fruits or vegetables: *A banana is mainly pulp, except for its skin.*|*You've boiled these vegetables too long; you've boiled them to a pulp.* **2** [U] wood or other vegetable materials softened and used for making paper

**pulp²** *v* [I;T] to (cause to) become PULP¹

**pul·pit** /ˈpulpɪt/ *n* a small raised enclosure of wood or stone in a church, from which the priest addresses the worshippers

**pul·sate** /pʌlˈseɪt‖ˈpʌlseɪt/ *v* **-sated, -sating** [I *with*] **1** to shake very regularly **2** →PULSE² **–pulsation** /-ˈseɪʃən/ *n* [C;U]

**pulse¹** /pʌls/ *n* [*usu. sing.*] the regular beating of blood in the main blood vessels carrying blood from the heart, esp. as felt by a doctor at the wrist: *The doctor* **felt/took** *the woman's* **pulse.** (=counted the number of beats per minute)

**pulse²** *v* **pulsed, pulsing** [I *through, with*] to beat steadily as the heart does: *He could feel the blood pulsing through his body.*|*pulsing with excitement*

**pulse³** *n* [C;U] (the seeds of) beans, PEAS, LENTILS, etc., used as food

**pul·ver·ize** ‖also **-ise** *BrE* /ˈpʌlvəraɪz/ *v* **-ized, -izing** **1** [I;T] to (cause to) become a fine powder or dust by crushing **2** [T] *infml* to defeat thoroughly

**pu·ma** /ˈpjuːmə/ *n* **pumas** *or* **puma** →COUGAR

**pum·ice** /ˈpʌmɨ̣s/ also **pumice stone** /ˈ·· ·/– *n* [U] a very light, silver-grey rock, used for cleaning and for rubbing surfaces smooth

**pum·mel** /ˈpʌməl/ also **pommel** *AmE v* **-ll-** *BrE*‖**-l-** *AmE* [T] to hit repeatedly, esp. with the closed hand

**pump¹** /pʌmp/ *n* **1** [C] a machine for forcing liquids, air, or gas into or out of something: *The heart is a kind of natural pump that moves the blood around the body.*|*a water pump*|*a petrol pump*|*a bicycle pump* **2** [S] an act of PUMPing²

**pump²** *v* **1** [I;T] to (cause to) empty or fill with a liquid or gas by means of a PUMP¹ (1): *He pumped up his car tyres.*|*They had pumped the well dry, and could get no more water.*|*His heart was pumping fast.* **2** [T] *infml* to ask (someone) questions in the hope of finding out something that one wants to know

**pump·kin** /ˈpʌmpkɨ̣n/ *n* [C;U] (a plant with) a very large dark yellow roundish fruit that grows on the ground

**pun¹** /pʌn/ also **play on words**– *n* an amusing use of a word or phrase that has two meanings, or of words having the same sound but different meanings: *He made the following pun: "Seven days without water make one weak".* (=week)

**pun²** *v* **-nn-** [I *on, upon*] to make PUNS¹: *He punned on the likeness of "weak" and "week".*

**punch¹** /pʌntʃ/ *v* **1** [I;T] to strike (someone or something) hard with the closed hand (FIST): *He punched the man in the chest/on the nose.* –see picture on page 669 **2** [T *in*] to make (a hole) in (something) using a PUNCH³

**punch²** *n* **1** [C *in, on*] a quick strong blow made with the closed hand (FIST): *I'd like to give that man a punch on the nose.* **2** [U] *apprec* forcefulness; effective power: *His speech lacked punch.*

**punch³** *n* a steel tool for cutting holes: *a ticket punch*

**punch⁴** *n* [U] a drink made from fruit juice, wine, sugar, water, etc.

**punch line** /ˈ· ·/ *n* [*usu. sing.*] the last few words of a joke or story, that give meaning to the whole and cause amusement or surprise

**punch-up** /ˈ· ·/ *n BrE infml* a fight

**punc·til·i·ous** /pʌŋkˈtɪliəs/ *adj fml, usu. apprec* very exact and particular about details, esp. of behaviour **–punctiliously** *adv* **–punctiliousness** *n* [U]

**punc·tu·al** /ˈpʌŋktʃuəl/ *adj* not late; happening, doing something, etc., at the exact time: *She's never punctual in answering letters; she's always late.* **–punctuality** /-ˈælɨ̣ti/ *n* [U] **–punctually** *adv*

**punc·tu·ate** /ˈpʌŋktʃueɪt/ *v* **-ated, -ating** [T] **1** to divide (written matter) into sentences, phrases, etc., by means of PUNCTUATION MARKS **2** [*usu. pass.*] to interrupt repeatedly: *The football game was punctuated by the cheers of supporters.*

**punc·tu·a·tion** *n* [U] (the marks used in) punctuating (PUNCTUATE (1)) a piece of writing

**punctuation mark** /ˌ··ˈ·· ·/ *n* any sign used in punctuating (PUNCTUATE (1)), such as a COMMA (,), a FULL STOP (.), a QUESTION MARK (?), etc.

**punc·ture¹** /ˈpʌŋktʃəʳ/ *n* a small hole made with a sharp point through a soft surface, esp. a tyre: *I'm sorry I'm late: My car had a puncture.*

**puncture²** *v* **-tured, -turing** [I;T] to make or get a PUNCTURE¹: *The child's rubber ball punctured when it fell on a prickly bush.*|*He is in hospital, suffering from a punctured lung.*

**pun·dit** /ˈpʌndɨ̣t/ *n often humor* a person of knowledge (in a particular subject): *political pundits*

**pun·gent** /ˈpʌndʒənt/ *adj* having a strong, sharp, stinging taste or smell: (fig.) *pungent* (=sharp) *remarks* **–pungently** *adv* **–pungency** *n* [U]

**pun·ish** /ˈpʌnɪʃ/ *v* [T] **1** [*for*] to cause (someone) to suffer for (a fault or crime): *Motorists should be punished severely for dangerous driving.*|*Dangerous driving should be severely punished.* **2** to deal roughly with (an opponent), esp. by taking advantage of a weakness

**pun·ish·a·ble** /ˈpʌnɪʃəbəl/ *adj* [*by, for*] that may be punished by law: *Murder is punishable by death in some countries.*

**pun·ish·ing** /ˈpʌnɪʃɪŋ/ *adj infml* that makes one thoroughly tired and weak: *a long and punishing climb* **–punishingly** *adv*

**pun·ish·ment** /ˈpʌnɪʃmənt/ *n* **1** [U] the act of punishing or condition of being punished: *The boy accepted his punishment without complaining.* **2** [C] a way in which a person is punished: *A good judge will try to make the punishment fit the crime.*

**pu·ni·tive** /ˈpjuːnətɪv/ *adj* **1** intended as punishment **2** very severe: *punitive taxes* –compare PUTATIVE **–punitively** *adv*

**punk** /pʌŋk/ *adj* [A] (in Britain since the 1970s) of a movement among certain young people who are opposed to the values of money-based society and who express this esp. in loud, often violent music (**punk rock**)

**pun·net** /ˈpʌnət/ *n esp. BrE* a small square basket in which soft fruits are sold

**punt** /pʌnt/ *n,v* [C;I] (to go for a journey by) a long narrow flat-bottomed river boat, moved by someone pushing a long pole against the bottom of the river

**punt·er** /ˈpʌntəʳ/ *n BrE infml* a person who risks money (GAMBLES) on the result of esp. a horse race

**pu·ny** /ˈpjuːni/ *adj* **-nier, -niest** *derog* small and weak; poorly developed: *puny little arms and legs*

**pup** /pʌp/ *n* **1** a young SEAL[1] (1) or OTTER **2** →PUPPY

**pu·pa** /ˈpjuːpə/ *n* **-pas** *or* **-pae** /piː/ an insect in the middle stage of its development, contained in and protected by a covering –compare CHRYSALIS, COCOON

**pu·pil**[1] /ˈpjuːpəl/ *n* a person, esp. a child, who is being taught: –see picture on page 105

**pupil**[2] *n* the small black round opening in the middle of the coloured part of the eye, through which light passes

**pup·pet** /ˈpʌpət/ *n* **1** [C] a toylike jointed wooden or cloth figure of a person or animal, that is made to move by someone pulling wires or strings that are fixed to it –compare MARIONETTE **2** [C] also **glove puppet**– a toylike cloth figure of a person or animal, moved by putting the hand inside it **3** [A] *often derog* not independent, but controlled by someone else: *a puppet government*

**pup·pe·teer** /ˌpʌpəˈtɪəʳ/ *n* a person who performs with PUPPETS (1,2)

**pup·py** /ˈpʌpi/ also **pup**– *n* **-pies** a young dog

**pur·chase**[1] /ˈpɜːtʃəs‖ˈpɜr-/ *v* **-chased, -chasing** [T *for*] *fml or tech* to buy: *to purchase a new house*

**purchase**[2] *n fml* **1** [U] buying: *He gave his son some money for the purchase of his school books.* **2** [C *often pl.*] **a** an act of buying: *She* **made** *several* **purchases** *in the dress shop.* **b** an article that has just been bought

**pur·chas·er** /ˈpɜːtʃəsəʳ‖ˈpɜr-/ *n tech* a person who buys goods from another

**pure** /pjʊəʳ/ *adj* **1** not mixed with any other substance, esp. dirt or other harmful matter: *pure silver*|*The air by the sea is pure and healthy.* **2** free from evil: *a pure young girl* –see also IMPURE **3** clear; not mixed: *a cloudless sky of the purest blue*|*pure young voices* **4** [A] *infml* complete; thorough; only: *By pure chance he found the rare book he needed in a little shop.* **5** [A] (of an art or branch of study) considered only for its own nature as a skill or exercise of the mind, separate from any use that might be made of it: *pure science* –compare APPLIED

**pu·ree** /ˈpjʊəreɪ‖pjʊˈreɪ/ *n,v* **-reed, -reeing** [C;U;T] (to prepare) food boiled to a soft half-liquid mass and rubbed through a fine wire frame: *an apple puree*

**pure·ly** /ˈpjʊəli‖ˈpjʊərli/ *adv* completely; wholly; only: *I helped him purely out of friendship.*

**pur·ga·tive** /ˈpɜːgətɪv‖ˈpɜr-/ *n,adj* (a medicine) that causes the bowels to empty: *a purgative effect*

**pur·ga·to·ry** /ˈpɜːgətəri‖ˈpɜrgətori/ *n* **-ries** **1** [U] (*often cap.*) (esp. according to the ROMAN CATHOLIC religion) a state or place in which the soul of a dead person must be made pure by suffering for wrong-doing on earth, until it is fit to enter Heaven **2** [C;U] *often humor* a place, state, or time of suffering

**purge**[1] /pɜːdʒ‖pɜrdʒ/ *v* **purged, purging** [T *from, of*] **1** to make clean and free from (something evil or impure): *Try to purge your spirit (of hatred).*|*The people wished to purge their* SINS. **2** to get rid of (an unwanted person) in (a state, political party, group, etc.) by unjust or forceful means **3** to clear (waste matter) from (the bowels) by means of medicine

**purge**[2] *n* an act or set of actions intended to get rid of unwanted members of a (political) group, suddenly, often unjustly, and often by force: *The new president carried out a purge of disloyal army officers.*

**pu·ri·fy** /ˈpjʊərəfaɪ/ *v* **-fied, -fying** [T *of*] to make PURE (esp.1,3): *This salt has been purified for use in medicine.* **–purification** /-fəˈkeɪʃən/ *n* [U *of*]

**pur·ist** /ˈpjʊərəst/ *n* a person who is always (too) careful to practise the correct way of doing something, esp. in matters of grammar, use of words, etc.

**pu·ri·tan** /ˈpjʊərətn/ *adj,n usu. derog* (of, like, or being) a person who has rather hard fixed standards of behaviour and self-control, and thinks pleasure is unnecessary or wrong **–puritanical** /-tænɪkəl/ *adj*: *a puritanical father* **–puritanically** *adv*

**pu·ri·ty** /ˈpjʊərəti/ *n* [U] the quality or state of being pure –see also IMPURITY

**purl** /pɜːl‖pɜrl/ *n* [U] *tech* a simple stitch in KNITTING **–purl** *v*

**pur·loin** /pɜːˈlɔɪn, ˈpɜːlɔɪn‖-ɜr-/ *v* [T] *fml* to steal (esp. something of small value)

**pur·ple** /ˈpɜːpəl‖ˈpɜr-/ *adj,n* (of) a dark colour made of a mixture of red and blue –compare VIOLET (2)

**pur·port**[1] /pɜːˈpɔːt‖pɜrˈport/ *v* [T+*to-v*] to have an (intended) appearance of being: *He purports to be a rich businessman, but I don't believe him.*

**pur·port**[2] *n* [U *of*] *fml* the general meaning or intention (of someone's words or actions): *The purport of the message seemed to be this:...*

**pur·pose** /ˈpɜːpəs‖ˈpɜr-/ *n* **1** [C] an intention or

plan; reason for an action: *Did you come to London* **for the purpose of** *seeing your family, or for business purposes?|It wasn't an accident; you did it* **on purpose.** (=intentionally) –see Study Notes on page 128 **2** [C] use; effect; result: *Don't waste your money; put it to some good purpose.|I haven't got a pen, but a pencil will* **answer/serve the same purpose.** (=will do what is needed) **3** [U] steady determined following of an aim; willpower

**purpose-built** /ˌ·· '·◂/ *adj BrE* specially made for a particular purpose: *We live in a purpose-built flat, not a* CONVERSION.

**pur·pose·ful** /'pɜːpəsfəl‖'pɜr-/ *adj* directed towards a special purpose –**purposefully** *adv*

**pur·pose·less** /'pɜːpəsl$\frac{1}{\partial}$s‖'pɜr-/ *adj* aimless; meaningless –**purposelessly** *adv*

**pur·pose·ly** /'pɜːpəsli‖'pɜr-/ *adv* intentionally: *I purposely came today, as I knew you'd be in.*

**purr** /pɜːʳ/ *v,n* [C;I] (to make) a low continuous sound produced in the throat by a pleased cat: (fig.) *The big car purred along the road.*

**purse¹** /pɜːs‖pɜrs/ *n* **1** a small flattish leather or plastic bag used, esp. by women, for carrying money –compare WALLET **2** *AmE* a woman's HANDBAG, esp. one without a shoulder STRAP; POCKETBOOK

**purse²** *v* **pursed, pursing** [T] to draw (esp. the lips) together in little folds: *She pursed her lips with dislike.*

**purs·er** /'pɜːsəʳ‖'pɜr-/ *n* an officer on a ship who keeps the ship's accounts and is also in charge of the travellers' rooms, comfort, etc.

**pur·sue** /pə'sjuː‖pər'suː/ *v* **-sued, -suing** [T] **1** *more fml than* **chase**– to follow, esp. in order to catch, kill, or defeat: *The police are pursuing an escaped prisoner.|The travellers were pursued by beggars.* **2** to continue (steadily) with; be busy with: *He is pursuing his studies at the university.*

**pur·su·er** /pə'sjuːəʳ‖pər'suːər/ *n* a person or animal that PURSUES (1): *The deer ran faster than its pursuers.*

**pur·suit** /pə'sjuːt‖pər'suːt/ *n* **1** [U] the act of pursuing (PURSUE) someone or something: *The police car raced through the streets* **in pursuit of** *another car.* **2** [C] any activity to which one gives one's time, whether as work or for pleasure: *One of the boy's favourite pursuits is stamp collecting.*

**pur·vey** /pɜː'veɪ‖pɜr-/ *v* **-veyed, -veying** [T *to*] *fml or tech* to supply (food or other needed goods) as a trade –**purveyor** *n* [*of, to*]

**pus** /pʌs/ *n* [U] a thick yellowish liquid produced in an infected wound or poisoned part of the body

**push¹** /pʊʃ/ *v* **1** [I;T] to use sudden or steady pressure in order to move (someone or something) forward, away from oneself, or to a different position: *He pushed me and I fell into the water.|Don't push: wait before you get on the bus.|You push and I'll pull.* –see picture on page 669 **2** [I;T] to make (one's way) by doing this: *She pushed past me.|He pushed his way through the crowd.* **3** [T] to try to force (someone) to do something by continual urging: *If you push him too hard, he may make mistakes in his work.|My friends are all pushing me to enter politics.* **4** [I;T] *infml* to force (someone or something) on the notice of others, as a means of success: *The company are pushing their new product.* (=advertising it widely) **5** [T] *infml* to sell (illegal drugs) **6 push one's luck** to take an increasing risk

**push** sbdy. **around** *v adv* [T] *infml* to treat roughly and unfairly, esp. in order to force obedience

push in *v adv* [I] *infml* to interrupt rudely

**push off** *v adv* [I] *infml* to go away: *What are you doing in this garden? Push off at once!*

**push on** *v adv* [I] to hurry: *We're late; we must push on.*

**push** sbdy./sthg. **through** (sthg.) *v adv; prep* [T] to force to be successful (in): *push the student through (the examination)*

**push²** *n* **1** [C] an act of pushing: *They gave the car a push* (=pushed it) *to start it.* **2** [C] a planned attack and advance of great strength by an army **3** [U] *infml* active will to succeed, esp. by forcing oneself and one's wishes on others **4** [*the* S] *infml* dismissal from one's job: *He* **got/was given the push.** –compare PULL²

**push·bike** /'pʊʃbaɪk/ *n BrE infml* for BICYCLE

**push·chair** /'pʊʃ-tʃeəʳ/ *BrE*‖**stroller** *AmE*– *n* a small folding chair on wheels for pushing a small child about

**pushed** /pʊʃt/ *adj* [F] *infml* **1** [*for*] having difficulty in finding enough (money, time, etc.): *I'm always rather pushed for money at the end of the month.* **2** having no free time; busy: *I'd like to stop for a longer talk, but I'm rather pushed today.*

**push·er** /'pʊʃəʳ/ *n infml* a person who sells illegal drugs

**push·o·ver** /'pʊʃˌəʊvəʳ/ *n* [C;S] *infml* something that is very easy to do or win: *The examination was a pushover: I knew all the answers.*

**push-up** /'· ·/ *n AmE* for PRESS-UP

**push·y** /'pʊʃi/ also **pushing**– *adj* **-ier, -iest** *usu. derog* too active and forceful in getting things done, esp. for one's own advantage

**pus·sy** /'pʊsi/ also **puss, pussycat**– *n* **-sies** *infml* (a word used for calling) a cat

**pus·tule** /'pʌstjuːl‖-tʃuːl/ *n tech* a small raised spot on the skin containing poisonous matter

**put¹** /pʊt/ *v* **put, putting** [T] **1** to move, place, lay, or fix in, on, or to a stated place: *Put the chair nearer the fire.|You put too much salt in this food.|She picked it up, then quickly put it down.|He put the children to bed.|*(fig.) *Let's* **put an end to** *this nonsense.* (=stop it)|*Everyone* **puts the blame on** *me.* (=blames me)|The murderer was **put to death.** (=killed) –see picture on page 669 **2** to cause to be: *He put his books in order.|"You've made a mistake." "I'll* **put it right** *at once."* **3** to give expression to; say: *She is –how shall I put it? –not exactly fat, but rather well- built.* **4** to write down: *Put your name at the top of the page.* **5** to throw (a heavy metal ball (SHOT (5))) as a form of sporting competition **6 put paid to** *BrE* to ruin; finish completely: *His accident has put paid to his chances of taking part in the race.*

**put** sthg.↔**about** *v adv* [T +*that*] *infml* to spread (bad or false news): *"It's being put about that she was secretly married." "Who put that lie about?"*

**put** sthg.↔**across/over** *v adv* [T] to cause to be understood; explain: *I'm not putting my meaning across very well.*

**put** sthg.↔**aside** *v adv* [T] to save (money, etc.), usu. for a special purpose: *He has a little money put aside for a holiday.* –compare PUT **away** (2), PUT **by**

**put** sthg.↔**away** *v adv* [T] **1** to remove to a place where it is usually stored: *Put the books away neatly in the cupboard.* **2** also **put** sthg.↔**by**– to save (esp. money) for later use –compare PUT **aside**

**put** sthg.↔**back** *v adv* [T] **1** to cause to show an earlier time: *put the clocks back* –compare PUT **forward** (2) **2** to delay: *The fire in the factory has put back production.*

**put** sthg.↔**by** *v adv* [T] →PUT **away** (2)

**put** sbdy./sthg.↔**down** *v adv* [T] **1** to control; defeat: *put down the opposition* **2** *infml* to make feel humble **3** to kill (an animal) esp. because of old age or illness

**put** sbdy. **down for** sthg. *v adv prep* [T] to put (someone's name) on a waiting list for a race, a school, etc.

**put** sthg. **down to** sbdy./sthg. *v adv prep* [T] to state that (something) is caused by (something else): *I put his bad temper down to his recent illness.*

**put** sbdy./sthg. **forward** *v adv* [T] **1** to offer: *May I put your name forward as a possible chairman of the committee?* **2** to cause to show a later time: *put the clocks forward* –compare PUT **back**(1)

**put in** *v adv* **1** [I *at*] (of a ship) to enter a port: *The ship puts in at Bombay* **2** [T] (**put** sthg.↔**in**) to make or send (a request or claim): *If the goods were damaged in the post, you can put in a claim to the post office.* **3** [T] (**put** sthg.↔**in**) to do or spend, esp. for a purpose: *put in an hour's work* –see INPUT

**put in for** sthg. *v adv prep* [T] to make a formal request for; APPLY (1) for: *They've put in for more money.*

**put into** *v prep* [T] **1** (**put** sthg. **into** sthg.) to add to: *Put more effort into your work!* **2** (**put into** sthg.) (of a ship) to enter (a port): *The boat had to put into Sydney for supplies.*

**put** sbdy./sthg.↔**off**[1] *v adv* [T] **1** [+*v-ing*/*till, until*] to move to a later date; delay; *I feel ill; I'll have to put off my visit/put off going till next month.*|*We've invited them to dinner, but we shall have to put them off because the baby's sick.* **2** to make excuses to (someone) in order to avoid a duty: *I put him off with a promise to pay him next week.* **3 a** to discourage: *The speaker was trying to make a serious point, but people kept putting him off by shouting.* **b** to cause to feel dislike: *His bad manners put her (right) off.* **4**→TURN **off** (1) –opposite **put on**

**put** sbdy. **off**[2] sthg. *v prep*[T] to discourage from: *Don't talk, it puts him off his game.*|*The smell put me off eating*

**put** sbdy./sthg.↔**on**[1] *v adv* [T] **1** to cover (part of) the body with (esp. clothing): *She put her hat and coat on.*|*He put on his glasses to read the letter.* –opposite **take off** –see DRESS (USAGE) **2** to pretend to have (an opinion, quality, etc.): *She's not really ill; she puts it on in order to gain attention.* **3** to increase: *to put on speed*|*She has put on weight.* **4** to perform (a play, show, etc.) on a stage. **5** to provide: *So many people wanted to go to the match that another train had to be put on.* **6** *AmE infml* to play a trick on; deceive –compare HAVE **on 7** →TURN **on** (1): *Put on the light*|*the radio.* –opposite **put off**

**put** sthg. **on**[2] sthg. *v prep* [T] **1** to add (a quantity) to: *The war put at least £50,000,000 on the taxes.* **2** to risk (money) on; BET[2]

**put** sbdy. **onto** sthg. *v prep* [T] *infml* to give information about: *I can't advise you in this matter, but I can put you onto a good lawyer.*

**put out** *v adv* [T] **1** (**put** sthg.↔**out**) to make stop burning: *She put the light/the fire out.* **2** (**put** sbdy. **out**) to trouble or annoy: *She was so put out by the man's rudeness that she didn't know what to say.*|*Will it put you out if I bring another guest?* **3** (**put** sthg.↔**out**) to broadcast or print: *The government will put out a new statement next week.* **4 put oneself out** to take trouble: *She never puts herself out to help people.*

**put** sthg.↔**over** *v adv* [T]→PUT **across**: *The speaker didn't put his ideas over clearly enough.*

**put through**[1] *v adv* [T] **1** put sbdy. **through**) [*to*] to connect (a telephone caller) by telephone: *Can you put me through to this number?* **2** (**put** sthg.↔**through**) to complete (a piece of business) successfully

**put** sbdy. **through**[2] sthg. *v prep* [T] to cause to experience: *You've put him through a lot of pain.*

**put to** *v prep* [T] **1** (**put** sbdy./sthg. **to** sbdy.) to ask (a question) of or make (an offer) to **2** (**put** sbdy./sthg. **to** sthg.) to test by using the stated means: *Let's put the matter to a vote.* **3** (**put** sbdy. **to** sthg.) to cause to be in (a certain place or condition): *She put the child to bed.* **4 be (hard) put to it to (do something)** to find it difficult to (do something): *You'd be hard put to it to make it more cheaply.*

**put together** *v adv* [T] **1** (**put** sthg. **together**) to form; make a group of: *He put a team together.* **2** [*usu. pass.*] to combine: *His share was more than all the others' put together.*|*They* **put their heads together** (=combined ideas) *for an answer.*

**put up** *v adv* [T] **1** (**put** sthg.↔**up**) to raise: *to put up a tent* **2** (**put** sthg.↔**up**) to put in a public place: *put up a notice* –opposite **take down 3** (**put** sthg.↔**up**) to increase (a price) **4** (**put** sbdy.↔**up**) to provide food and lodging for: *I'm afraid I can't put you up; you'll have to go to a hotel.* **5** (**put up** sthg.) to offer, show, make, or give, esp. in a struggle: *What a coward; he didn't put up much of a fight!* **6** (**put** sthg. **up**) to offer for sale: *She's putting her house up (for sale).*

**put** sbdy. **up to** sthg. *v adv prep* [T] to give the idea of (doing esp. something bad): *Who put you up to this trick?*

**put up with** sbdy./sthg. *v adv prep* [T] to suffer without complaining: *I can't put up with your rudeness any more; leave the room.*|*That woman has a lot to put up with.* (=has many troubles to bear)

**put**[2] *adj* **stay put** *infml* to remain where placed: *The lid won't stay put; it keeps falling off.*

**pu·ta·tive** /ˈpjuːtətɪv/ *adj* [A] *fml* generally accepted or supposed to be: *his putative relations* –compare PUNITIVE

**pu·tre·fy** /ˈpjuːtrɪ̈faɪ/ *v* **-fied, -fying** [I;T] *more fml than* **rot**– to decay; (cause to) become PUTRID –**putrifaction** /-ˈfækʃən/ *n* [U] *fml or tech*

**pu·trid** /pjuːtrɪ̈d/ *adj* (esp. of an animal or plant substance) very decayed and bad-smelling

**putt** /pʌt/ *v* [I;T] (in the game of GOLF) to strike (the ball) gently along the ground towards or into the hole –**putt** *n*

**put·ty** /ˈpʌti/ *n* [U] a soft oily paste, used esp. in fixing glass to window frames

**put-up·on** /ˈ· ·,·/ *adj* [F] (of a person) used for someone else's advantage: *The way his neighbour always borrows things from him makes him feel put-upon.*

**puz·zle¹** /ˈpʌzəl/ *v* **-zled, -zling 1** [T *often pass.*] to cause (someone) difficulty in the effort to explain or understand: *The woman's illness puzzled the doctor; he couldn't find the cause.* **2** [I *about,over,as to*] to make a great effort of the mind in order to understand or find the answer to a difficult question: *He was puzzling over the old map* –**puzzled** *adj*: *I'm puzzled about what to do next.*

**puzzle²** *n* **1** a game, toy, or apparatus in which parts must be fitted together correctly, intended to amuse or exercise the mind: *a* CROSSWORD *puzzle|a book of puzzles|a* JIGSAW PUZZLE **2** [*usu. sing.*] something that one cannot understand or explain

**PVC** *n* [U] a type of plastic: *PVC film|This coat is (made of) PVC.*

**pyg·my, pigmy** /ˈpɪgmi/ *n* **-mies 1** a member of a race of very small people **2** any person or animal of much less than usual height

**py·ja·mas** *BrE*||**pajamas** *AmE* /pəˈdʒɑːməz||-ˈdʒæ-, -ˈdʒɑ-/ *n* [P] a soft loose-fitting pair of trousers and short coat worn in bed, esp. by men –see PAIR¹ (USAGE)

**py·lon** /ˈpaɪlən||-lɑn, -lən/ *n* a tall framework of steel bars used for supporting wires that carry electricity over land

**pyr·a·mid** /ˈpɪrəmɪd/ *n* **1** (in GEOMETRY) a solid figure with a flat usu. square base and straight flat three-angled sides that slope upwards to meet at a point **2** (*often cap.*) a very large ancient stone building in the shape of this, used formerly, esp. in Egypt, as the burial place of a king

**pyre** /paɪəʳ/ *n* a high mass of wood for the ceremonial burning of a dead body

**py·thon** /ˈpaɪθən||-θɑn, -θən/ *n* a large non-poisonous tropical snake that kills animals for food by winding round them and crushing them

# Q, q

**Q , q** /kjuː/ **Q's, q's** *or* **Qs, qs** the 17th letter of the English alphabet

**Q.C. also Queen's Counsel** *fml*– *n* [after *n*] (the title given, while a queen is ruling, to) a British lawyer (BARRISTER) of high rank: *Sir John Smithers, Q.C.* –compare K.C.

**quack¹** /kwæk/ *v,n* [C;I] (to make) the sound that ducks make

**quack²** *n* a person dishonestly claiming to have medical knowledge or skills: *a quack doctor*

**quad¹** /kwɒd||kwɑd/ **also quadrangle** /kwɒdræŋgəl||ˈkwɑ-/ *fml*– *n BrE* a square open area with buildings around it, esp. in a school or college

**quad²** *n infml* for QUADRUPLET

**quad·rant** /ˈkwɒdrənt||ˈkwɑ-/ *n* **1** a quarter of a circle **2** an instrument for measuring angles

**quad·ru·ped** /ˈkwɒdrʊped||ˈkwɑdrə-/ *n tech* a four-footed creature –compare BIPED

**quad·ru·ple¹** /ˈkwɒdrʊpəl, kwɒˈdruː-||kwɑˈdruː-/ *v* **-pled, -pling 1** [T] to multiply (a number or amount) by four **2** [I] to become four times as great

**quadruple²** *predeterminer,n,adv* [U] *fml* (an amount which is) four times as big as something mentioned or usual: *quadruple the amount of profit*

**quad·ru·plet** /ˈkwɒdrʊplɪ̈t||kwɑˈdrʌp-/ also **quad** *infml*– *n* [*usu. pl.*] one of four children born of the same mother at the same time

**quag·mire** /ˈkwægmaɪəʳ, ˈkwɒg-||ˈkwæg-/ *n* a large area of soft wet ground; BOG

**quail¹** /kweɪl/ *n* **quail** *or* **quails** [C;U] (meat of) a type of small bird, highly regarded as food

**quail²** *v* [I *with, at*] to be afraid; tremble: *He quailed (with fear) at the thought of telling her the bad news.*

**quaint** /kweɪnt/ *adj* unusual and attractive, esp. because old: *a quaint old village* –**quaintly** *adv* –**quaintness** *n* [U]

**quake¹** /kweɪk/ *v* **quaked, quaking** [I *with, at*] to shake; tremble: *to quake with fear*

**quake²** *n infml* for EARTHQUAKE

**Quak·er** /ˈkweɪkəʳ/ *n,adj* (a member) of a Christian religious group which opposes violence

**qual·i·fi·ca·tion** /ˌkwɒlɪ̈fɪ̈ˈkeɪʃən||ˌkwɑ-/ *n* **1** a proof that one has gained a certain degree of knowledge or completed a course of training in a particular field: *a medical qualification* **2** [+ *to-v/for*] An ability or quality which makes someone suitable for a particular job: *She has the right qualifications for the job.* **3** [+ *that*] something that limits the force of a statement: *We support the plan, but with the qualification that it should be done more cheaply.*

**qual·i·fied** /ˈkwɒlɪ̈faɪd||ˈkwɑ-/ *adj* **1** [+*to-v/for*] having suitable knowledge, ability, or experience, esp. for a job: *He's not qualified to teach young children.* **2** limited: *He gave qualified agreement.*

**qual·i·fy** /ˈkwɒlɪ̈faɪ||ˈkwɑ-/ *v* **-fied, -fying 1** [I;T +*to-v*] to (cause to) reach a necessary standard of ability or performance, or to gain a QUALIFICATION (1): *This test will qualify you to fly an aircraft.|Will our team qualify for the second* ROUND⁴ (1) *of the competition?* **2** [T] to limit the force or meaning of (something stated): *I'd like to qualify my last remark.*

**qual·i·ta·tive** /ˈkwɒlɪ̈tətɪv||ˈkwɑlɪ̈teɪ-/ *adj* of or about quality: *a qualitative judgment* –compare QUANTITATIVE –**qualitatively** *adv*

**qual·i·ty** /ˈkwɒlɪ̈ti||ˈkwɑ-/ *n* **-ties 1** [C;U] a (high) degree of goodness: *material of low/poor quality|an actor of real quality* (=a very good actor) **2** [C] something typical of a person or material: *Sympathy is his best quality.|She shows qualities of leadership.*

**qualm** /kwɑːm‖kwɑm, kwalm/ *n* [*about*] an uncomfortable feeling of uncertainty, esp. as to whether something is right: *He* **had no qualms about** *cheating the tax collectors.*

**quan·da·ry** /ˈkwɒndəri‖ˈkwɑn-/ *n* **-ries** [*about, over*] a feeling of not knowing what to do: *I was* **in a quandary** *about whether to go.*

**quan·ti·fy** /ˈkwɒntɪ̣faɪ‖ˈkwɑn-/ *v* **-fied, -fying** [T] *fml* to measure (an amount or quantity) **–quantifiable** *adj* **–quantification** /-tɪ̣fɪ̣ˈkeɪʃən/ *n* [U]

**quan·ti·ta·tive** /ˈkwɒntɪ̣tətɪv‖ˈkwɑntɪ̣teɪ-/ *adj* of or about quantity –compare QUALITATIVE **–quantitatively** *adv*

**quan·ti·ty** /ˈkwɒntɪ̣ti‖ˈkwɑn-/ *n* **-ties 1** [U] a measurable property of something: *The food was enough in quantity* (=there was plenty of it), *but not very good in quality.* **2** [C] an amount or number: *Police found a large quantity of illegal drugs.* **3 an unknown quantity** something or someone whose true nature or value is not yet known

**quar·an·tine**[1] /ˈkwɒrəntiːn‖ˈkwɑ-/ *n* [S;U] a period of time when a person or animal that may be carrying disease is kept separate from others so that the disease cannot spread: *Animals entering Britain from abroad are put in quarantine for six months.*

**quarantine**[2] *v* **-tined, -tining** [T] to put in QUARANTINE[1]

**quar·rel**[1] /ˈkwɒrəl‖ˈkwɔ-, ˈkwɑ-/ *n* **1** [*with*] an angry argument **2** [*with,* only used in NEGATIVES[2], questions, etc.] a cause for disagreement: *I have no quarrel with what the minister says.*

**quarrel**[2] *v* **-ll-** *BrE*‖**-l-** *AmE* [I *about, over, with*] to have an angry argument: *She quarrelled (about politics) with George.*

**quar·rel·some** /ˈkwɒrəlsəm‖ˈkwɔ-,ˈkwɑ-/ *adj* (of a person) likely to argue; often arguing

**quar·ry**[1] /ˈkwɒri‖ˈkwɔ-, ˈkwɑ-/ *n* **-ries** a place on the surface of the earth from which stone, sand, etc. are dug out –compare MINE[2] (1)

**quarry**[2] *v* **-ried, -rying** [I;T] to dig out (stone, sand, etc.) from a QUARRY[1]

**quarry**[3] *n* [S] the person or animal that one is hunting

**quart** /kwɔːt‖kwɔrt/ *n* a measure for liquids which is 1/4 of a GALLON; two PINTS

**quar·ter**[1] /ˈkwɔːtə^r‖ˈkwɔr-/ *n* **1** a 4th part of a whole: *a quarter of a mile|A quarter* (=1/4 of a pound) *of sweets please.* **2** 15 minutes before or after the hour: *It's (a) quarter past 10.* (=10.15)|*(a) quarter to 10 (BrE)/of 10 (AmE)* (=9.45)|*in three quarters of an hour* (=45 minutes) **3** a period of three months, used esp. for making payments **4** (in the US and Canada) a coin worth 25 cents (=1/4 of a dollar) **5** a place or person(s) from which something comes or may be expected: *Help is arriving from all quarters.* **6** a part of a town, often typical of certain people: *the artists' quarter* **7 at close quarters** near together –see also QUARTERS

**quarter**[2] *v* [T] **1** to cut or divide into four parts **2** to provide lodgings for (esp. soldiers)

**quar·ter·fi·nal** /ˌkwɔːtəˈfaɪnl‖-ər-/ *n* any of four matches in a competition of which the winners will play in the two SEMIFINAL matches

**quar·ter·ly** /ˈkwɔːtəli‖ˈkwɔrtər-/ *adj,adv* (happening, appearing, etc.) every three months

**quar·ter·mas·ter** /ˈkwɔːtəˌmɑːstə^r‖ˈkwɔrtərˌmæ-/ *n* a military officer in charge of provisions

**quar·ters** /ˈkwɔːtəz‖ˈkwɔrtərz/ *n* [P] lodgings: **Married quarters** *are houses where soldiers live with their families.*

**quar·tet** /kwɔːˈtet‖kwɔr-/ *n* (a piece of music written for) four people playing instruments or singing together

**quartz** /kwɔːts‖kwɔrts/ *n* [U] a hard mineral substance, now used in making very exact watches and clocks

**quash** /kwɒʃ‖kwɑʃ, kwɔʃ/ *v* [T] **1** to officially refuse to accept: *The high court judge quashed the decision of the lower court.* **2** → SUPPRESS

**qua·ver** /ˈkweɪvə^r/ *v* [I] (of a voice) to shake **–quaver** *n* **–quavery** *adj*

**quay** /kiː/ *n* a place where boats can stop to load and unload, usu. built of stone and part of a harbour -sounds like **key**

**quea·sy** /ˈkwiːzi/ *adj* **-sier, -siest** having the feeling that one is going to be sick (VOMIT): *I felt a little queasy on the ship.* **–queasily** *adv* **–queasiness** *n* [U]

**queen** /kwiːn/ *n* **1** [A;C] (the title of) **a** a female ruler of a country: *Queen Elizabeth the Second of England* **b** the wife of a king **2** [C] the winning female in a competition: *a beauty queen* **3** [C] the large leading female insect of a group: *the queen ant/bee* **4** [C] any of the four playing cards with a picture of a female ruler, ranking next in value after the king: *the queen of hearts* –see CARDS (USAGE)

**queen moth·er** /ˌ· ˈ··/ *n* the mother of a ruler

**Queen's Coun·sel** /ˌ· ˈ··/ *n fml* for Q.C.

**queen's ev·i·dence** /ˌ· ˈ···/ also **king's evidence** *BrE*‖ **state's evidence** *AmE*– *n* **turn queen's evidence** (of a criminal) to give information in a court of law against other criminals, esp. in order to receive less punishment oneself

**queer**[1] /kwɪə^r/ *adj* **1** strange; ODD: *What a queer story!* **2** *infml* not well: *I'm feeling a little queer; I think I'll go home.* **3** *infml derog* for HOMOSEXUAL **–queerly** *adv* **–queerness** *n* [U]

**queer**[2] *n infml derog* a male HOMOSEXUAL

**quell** /kwel/ *v* [T] to stop; SUPPRESS: *"Minister Quells Attempt to Defeat Government"* (title in newspaper)

**quench** /kwentʃ/ *v* [T *with, in*] to take away the force of (flames, desire, etc.) esp. with water: *to quench one's thirst with a glass of water*

**quer·u·lous** /ˈkwerʊləs/ *adj fml derog* complaining **–querulously** *adv* **–querulousness** *n* [U]

**que·ry**[1] /ˈkwɪəri/ *n* **-ries** a question or doubt: *to* **raise** *a few* **queries**

**query**[2] *v* **-ried, -rying** [T] to express a doubt about: *Nobody would query her ability.|to query a point*

**quest** /kwest/ *n* [*of, for*] *esp. lit* a search; an attempt to find: *the long quest for a cure for the disease|They travelled* **in quest of** *gold.*

**ques·tion**[1] /ˈkwestʃən/ *n* **1** [C] a sentence or phrase which asks for information: *I asked you a question and you didn't answer.|The question is: how was he killed?* **2** [C] a difficulty or matter to be settled; PROBLEM (1): *It's a question of finding enough time.* **3** [C;U] (a) doubt: *There was some question as to his*

## STUDY NOTES quantity

### countable nouns

**apple** and **chair** are both COUNTABLE nouns because they are things we can count; there can be more than one of them:

*an apple* *three apples* *a chair* *two chairs*

These nouns can be used in the plural and can be used with **a** or **an** when they are singular.

In the dictionary, [C] means countable, and [U] means uncountable. If a noun does not have a [C] or a [U] printed by it, this means that it is always countable.

### uncountable nouns

**sand** and **water** are UNCOUNTABLE nouns, because they are substances which cannot be counted:

*water* *sand*

These nouns are not usually used in the plural.

There are some nouns, like **love** and **beauty** (ABSTRACT nouns) which cannot be counted because they are not physical things like apples and chairs. These are uncountable nouns too.

For more information on countable and uncountable nouns and on singular and plural nouns turn to page **20a**.

---

### **more** and **less**

The lists below show you which words to use with [C] and [U] nouns to show quantity. They answer questions like *How many?* and *How much?*

**How many?**
(use with [C] nouns)

**every, all**
**Every** *student*/**All** *the students came to the meeting.*

**most**
**Most** *of my friends came to the party.*

**many**
**Many** *people walk to school every day.*

**some, several**
**Some** *of these apples taste sour.*|*Several people were waiting for the bus.*

**not many, only a few, few**
*There are* **not many**/**only a few** *tickets left.*|*There are* **few** *children in this area.*

**not . . . any, no, none**
*He could***n't** *answer* **any** *of the exam questions.*|*There are* **no** *eggs left;* **none** *at all.*

all

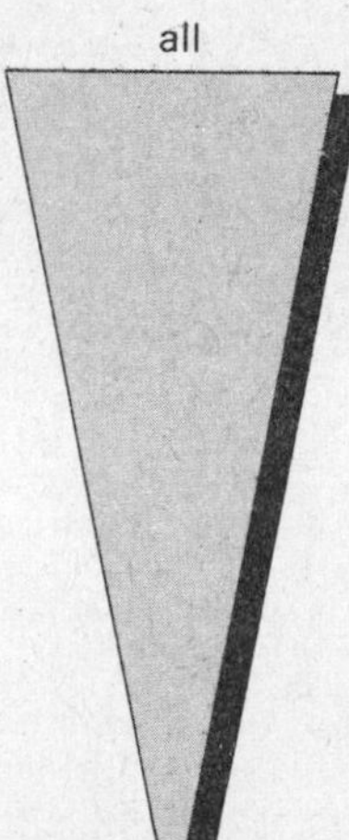

none

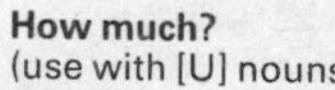

**How much?**
(use with [U] nouns)

**all**
*He ate* **all** *the bread.*

**most**
*He spends* **most** *of his time reading.*

**much**
**Much** *of what you say is true.*

**some**
*There's* **some** *bread in the cupboard.*

**a little, not much, little**
*There's only* **a little**/**not much** *room left.*|*Hurry up! There's* **little** *time.*

**not . . . any, no, none**
*He did***n't** *give me* **any** *help.*|*There is* **no** *petrol in the car;* **none** *at all.*

**some** and **any**

**any** is usually used instead of **some** in questions and sentences with *not:*

*Have you got* **any** *eggs*/*milk?*
*No, I haven't got* **any** *eggs*/*milk.*

It is also possible to use **some** in a question, especially when you expect the answer to be *yes:*

*Have you got* **some** *eggs*/*milk, please?*
*Would you like* **some** *more coffee?*

---

### nouns that are both countable and uncountable

Some nouns, like **light** and **coffee**, can be [C] (countable) in one meaning and [U] (uncountable) in another. When they are [C] they can become plural; when they are [U] they cannot. For example:

[U] *the* **light** *of the sun*

[C] *Turn on the* **lights**.

[U] *a jar of* **coffee**

[C] *Three* **coffees** *please*.

### plural and singular nouns

Some nouns, like **scissors**, are used only in the plural, i.e. they take a plural verb. These nouns are marked [P] in the dictionary:

> **scissors** *n* [P] two sharp blades with handles at one end with holes for the fingers, fastened at the centre so that they open in the shape of the letter X and cut when they close: *These scissors are very sharp.|a pair of scissors*

Some nouns, like **babble**, are usually used only in the singular. These nouns are used with **a** or **an**, and are marked [S] in the dictionary:

> **babble** *n* [S] a confused sound of many people talking at the same time: *A babble of voices was all I could hear.*

---

### **number** and **size**

The lists below show you how to use these words to show quantity in numbers and in size. Quantity in numbers answers the question *How many?* and quantity in size answers the question *How big?*

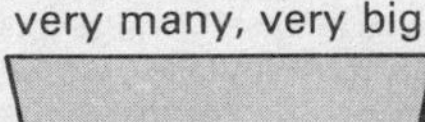


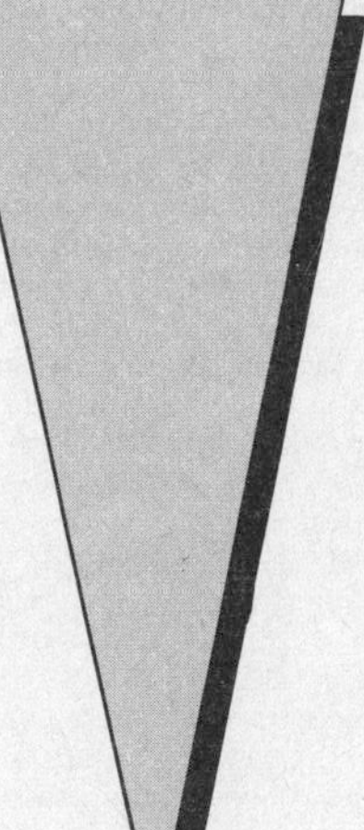

very few, very small

**How many?**

**billions**
*There are* **billions** *of stars in the sky.*

**millions**
**Millions** *of people watched the football match on television.*

**thousands**
*Their new car cost* **thousands** *of pounds.*

**hundreds**
*There were* **hundreds** *of people on the beach.*

**dozens**
*There were* **dozens** *of people waiting in the queue.*

**one or two**
*Only* **one or two** *of my friends noticed that I'd had my hair cut.*

**How big?**

**vast, huge, enormous, gigantic, colossal, immense**
*China is a* **vast/huge/enormous** *country.|There is a* **gigantic/colossal/immense** *new building in the centre of the city.*

**big, large, great big**
*There was a* **big/large/great big** *box on the floor.*

**average/medium**
*She is about* **average** *height.|The room is* **medium** *sized.*

**little, small**
*He was a* **little** *man – thin and not very tall.|She carried a* **small** *bag in her hand.*

**tiny**
*There was a* **tiny** *insect on the flower.*

**minute, microscopic**
*I can't read his* **minute/microscopic** *writing.*

honesty. **4 call (something) in/into question** to raise doubts about (something): *His honesty was called into question.* **5 in question** under consideration; being talked about: *That is not the point in question.* **6 out of the question** impossible: *You can't go to the wedding in that old shirt; it's out of the question.* **7 there's no question about/that** there's no doubt about that **8 there's no question of** there's no possibility of

**question²** *v* [T] **1** [*about*] to ask (someone) a question/questions **2** to raise doubts about: *I would never question her honesty.* –see ASK (USAGE)

**ques·tion·a·ble** /'kwestʃənəbəl/ *adj* that may be QUESTIONed² (2); perhaps not true, right, or honest: *a questionable idea* **–questionably** *adv*

**question mark** /'·· ·/ *n* the mark used at the end of a sentence that asks a question (?)

**ques·tion·naire** /ˌkwestʃə'neəʳ, ˌkes-/ *n* a piece of paper, usu. given to several people, showing a set of questions to be answered in order to provide information

**queue¹** /kju:/ *n BrE* a line of people, cars, etc., waiting to move, to get on a vehicle, or to enter a building: *a long queue outside the cinema/at the bus stop* –see picture on page 16

**queue²** *v* **queued, queuing** [I *up, for*] *BrE* to form or join a line while waiting: *We queued (up) for the bus.|We queued for hours.*

**quib·ble** /'kwɪbəl/ *v* **-bled, -bling** [I *about, over, with*] to argue about small points: *Don't quibble over the money; pay her what she asks.* **–quibble** *n* **–quibbling** *adj*

**quick¹** /kwɪk/ *adj* **1** [+*to-v/about,at,with*] swift; soon finished: *a quick drink|a quick answer|She's quick to learn/quick at learning.* **2** easily showing anger (in the phrases **a quick temper, quick-tempered**) **–quickly** *adv* **–quickness** *n* [U]

**quick²** *n* [*the* U] the flesh to which the fingernails and toenails are joined: (fig.) *He* **cut me to the quick** (=hurt me deeply) *with that unkind remark.*

**quick³** *adv* **1** quickly: *Come quick; something terrible has happened!* **2** (in comb.): *a quick-acting medicine*

**quick·en** /'kwɪkən/ *v* [I;T] to (cause to) become quick

**quick·sand** /'kwɪksænd/ *n* [C;U] wet sand which sucks in anyone or anything that tries to cross it

**quick·step** /'kwɪkstep/ *n* (music for) a dance with swift steps

**quick-wit·ted** /ˌ· '·· ◂/ *adj* clever; quick to understand and act

**quid** /kwɪd/ *n* **quid** *BrE infml* a pound (in money); £1: *She earns at least 200 quid a week.*

**qui·es·cent** /kwaɪ'esənt/ *adj fml* at rest; in a state of inactivity, esp. one that will not last **–quiescence** *n* **–quiescently** *adv*

**quiet¹** /'kwaɪət/ *adj* **1** with little noise: *a quiet voice* –compare LOUD¹ (1) **2** without unwanted activity or excitement; calm; untroubled: *a quiet life* **3** not making oneself noticed by activity: *The children are quiet today.* **–quietly** *adv* **–quietness** *n* [U]

**qui·et²** *n* [U] **1** state of being quiet; quietness: *an evening of* **peace and quiet 2 on the quiet** *infml* without telling anyone; secretly

**qui·et·en** /'kwaɪətn/ *BrE*‖**quiet** *AmE*– *v* [I;T *down*] to (cause to) become QUIET¹: *The children quickly quietened down.|I quietened his fears.*

**quill** /kwɪl/ *n* **1** (a former type of pen made from) a bird's long stiff feather **2** a sharp prickle on some animals, such as the PORCUPINE

**quilt** /kwɪlt/ *n* a cloth cover for a bed filled with soft warm material

**quilt·ed** /'kwɪltɨd/ *adj* made with cloth containing soft material and with stitching across it

**quince** /kwɪns/ *n* a hard fruit related to the apple, used esp. in jelly

**quin·ine** /'kwɪni:n‖'kwaɪnaɪn/ *n* [U] a drug used for treating fevers, esp. MALARIA

**quin·tes·sence** /kwɪn'tesəns/ *n fml* the perfect type or example: *John is* **the quintessence of** *good manners.* **–quintessential** /ˌkwɪntɨ'senʃəl/ *adj* **–quintessentially** *adv*

**quin·tet** /kwɪn'tet/ *n* (a piece of music written for) five people playing instruments or singing together

**quin·tu·plet** /'kwɪntjʊplɨt, kwɪn'tju:p-‖kwɪn'tʌp-/ *n* [*usu. pl.*] one of five children born of the same mother at the same time

**quip** /kwɪp/ *v,n* **-pp-** [C;I] (to make) a clever and amusing remark

**quirk** /kwɜ:k‖kwɜrk/ *n* **1** a strange happening or accident: *By some quirk of fate the two of us were on the same train.* **2** (a tendency to) a strange type of behaviour: *an unusual quirk in his character*

**quit** /kwɪt/ *v* **quitted** *or* **quit** *BrE*‖**quit** *AmE*, **quitting** [I;T +*v-ing*] *infml* to stop (doing something) and leave: *I've quit my job.|I've quit working.|"I quit!"*

**quite** /kwaɪt/ *predeterminer,adv* **1** [*adv* +*adv/adj/prep*] completely; perfectly: *quite different|quite the best shop|Are you quite sure?|not quite ready* **2** to some degree; rather: *quite small|quite a lot of people|It was quite good, but not perfect.* –see Study Notes on page 389 **3** *esp. BrE (used as an answer)* I agree; that's true: *"He behaved very badly." "Quite (so)."* **4 quite something** *infml* unusual, esp. unusually good: *It's quite something to be made a government minister at the age of 29.*

**quits** /kwɪts/ *adj* [F *with*] *infml* back on an even level with someone after an argument, after repaying money which is owed, etc.: *Now we're quits.|I'm quits with him.|Give him £1 and* **call it quits.** (=agree that the argument is settled)

**quiv·er¹** /'kwɪvəʳ/ *v* [I *with,at*] to tremble a little: *I quivered (with fear) at the sound.|a quivering movement* **–quiver** *n: a quiver of excitement*

**quiver²** *n* a container for arrows which is carried on the back

**quix·ot·ic** /kwɪk'sɒtɪk‖-'sɑ-/ *adj* trying to do the impossible, often for others, while oneself running into danger **–quixotically** *adv*

**quiz¹** /kwɪz/ *n* **-zz-** a competition or game where questions are put

**quiz²** *v* **-zz-** [T *about*] to ask questions of (someone), esp. repeatedly: *He quizzed me about where I'd been last night.*

**quiz·zi·cal** /'kwɪzɪkəl/ *adj* suggesting the idea **a** that one knows something and/or is laughing at the other person **b** that one is asking a question without saying anything: *a quizzical smile/*GLANCE² (1) **–quizzically** *adv*

**quoit** /kwɔɪt, kɔɪt/ *n* a ring to be thrown over a small upright post in a game (**quoits**)

**quo·rum** /'kwɔːrəm||'kworəm/ *n fml* a stated number of people, without whom a meeting cannot be held

**quo·ta** /'kwəutə/ *n* a number or amount allowed according to official limits: *The quota of students the university is allowed to accept has been reduced.*

**quo·ta·ble** /'kwəutəbəl/ *adj* worthy of being QUOTED

**quo·ta·tion** /kwəu'teɪʃən/ *n* **1** [U] the act of quoting (QUOTE) **2** [C] also **quote** *infml*– a sentence or phrase taken from a work of literature and repeated **3** [C] also **quote** *infml*– the calculated cost of a piece of work: *He gave me a quotation for mending the roof.* (=he told me how much it would cost)

**quotation mark** /·'·· ·/ *n* either of a pair of marks (" ") (' ') showing the beginning and end of words QUOTED

**quote** /kwəut/ *v* **quoted, quoting 1** [I;T *from*] to repeat in speech or writing the words of (a book or writer): *He quotes (from) the Bible to support his beliefs.* **2** [T] to mention (an example) to give force to one's arguments: *She quoted me several examples.* **3** [T *to*] to offer a price, (esp. for work to be done): *The price they quoted was very low.*

**quo·tient** /'kwəuʃənt/ *n* a number which is the result when one number is divided by another

# R, r

**SPELLING NOTE**
Words with the sound /r/ may be spelt **wr-**, like **wrong.**

**R , r** /ɑːʳ/ **R's, r's** *or* **Rs, rs 1** the 18th letter of the English alphabet **2 the three R's** reading, writing, and ARITHMETIC, thought to form the beginning of a child's education

**R** *abbrev for*: royal, as in R.A.F.

**rab·bi** /'ræbaɪ/ *n* **-bis** (the title of) a Jewish religious leader and teacher of Jewish law

**rab·bit¹** /'ræbɪ̵t/ *n* [C;U] (the fur or meat of) a common small long-eared animal of the HARE family that lives in a hole (BURROW) in the ground

**rabbit²** *v* **-tt-** *BrE*||**-t-** *AmE* [I *on*] *infml derog* to talk continuously in a dull and esp. complaining way: *He keeps rabbitting (on) about his health.*

**rab·ble** /'ræbəl/ *n* a disordered crowd of noisy people

**rabble-rous·ing** /'·· ,··/ *adj* [A] (of a speaker or speech) exciting the mass of the people to hatred and violence: *a rabble-rousing speech*

**rab·id** /'ræbɪ̵d/ *adj* **1** suffering from RABIES **2** [A] *derog* (of a person or his/her opinions) showing violent or unreasoning keenness: *a rabid* TORY

**ra·bies** /'reɪbiːz/ also **hydrophobia** *fml*– *n* [U] a disease of certain animals, including humans, passed on by the bite of an infected animal, esp. a dog, and causing madness and death

**rac·coon** ||also **racoon** *BrE* /rə'kuːn, ræ-||ræ-/ *n* [C;U] (the thick fur of) a small meat-eating North American animal with a long tail

**race¹** /reɪs/ *n* [*against, between, with*] a competition in speed: *to have/lose/win a race|a race against time*

**race²** *v* **raced, racing 1** [I;T] to compete in a race (against): *She's a very good swimmer and often races.|I'll race you to the end of the road.* **2** [I;T] to (cause to) go very fast: *We raced the sick woman to hospital.|*(fig.) *The holidays raced by.* **3** [T] to cause (an animal or vehicle) to run a race: *My horse has hurt his foot so I can't race him.* –see WALK (USAGE) **4** [I] (of an engine) to work too fast

**race³** *n* **1** [C] one of the divisions of human beings, each having certain bodily characteristics: *the black/white/brown races* **2** [C] a group of people with the same history, language, customs, etc.: *the German race* **3** [C] a (stated) type of creature: *the human race* (=people in general) **4** [A] of or between races (RACE³ (1)): *race relations*

USAGE **Race, nation, state,** and **tribe** are all words for large groups into which human beings may be divided. The largest of these groups is a **race**, and this word is used of people of the same colour and/or physical type. A **nation** is a group of people (smaller than a **race**) who have a common history and language, and usually live in the same place. Unlike **race** and **nation**, a **state** is a political division and can mean either an independent country or one of the partly-independent divisions in a country like the US: *The German* **nation** *is divided into two* **states**, *East Germany and West Germany.|the Indian* **nations** *of N. America|the modern* **states** *of Africa|the* **State** *of Texas.* A **tribe** is a social group, smaller than a **nation**, which has the same customs and beliefs, and often the same language: *a* **tribe** *of hunters living in the Amazon forest*

**race·course** /'reɪs-kɔːs||-kors/ *n* a track round which horses race

**rac·es** /'reɪsɪ̵z/ *n* [*the* P] an occasion when horse races are held at a RACECOURSE: *a day at the races*

**race·track** /'reɪs-træk/ *n* a course round which runners, cars, etc., race

**ra·cial** /'reɪʃəl/ *adj* connected with (one's own) RACE³ (1): *racial pride/hatred/type*

**ra·cial·ly** /'reɪʃəli/ *adv* from the point of view of RACE³ (1): *Racially, the two nations are the same.*

**rac·ing** /'reɪsɪŋ/ *n* [A] used for racing in competitions: *a racing car|a racing* PIGEON

**rac·ism** /'reɪsɪzəm/ also **racialism** /'reɪʃəlɪzəm/– *n* [U] *derog* political and social practices based on the belief that one race is the best

**ra·cist** /'reɪsɪ̵st/ also **racialist** 'reɪʃəlɪst/– *adj,n* (of or about) a person who believes that his/her own race is the best

**rack¹** /ræk/ *n* **1** [C] a framework with bars, hooks,

etc., for holding things: *He washed the dishes and put them in the plate rack to dry.*|*a* LUGGAGE *rack on a train* –see picture on page 615 **2** [*the* S] an instrument of TORTURE consisting of a frame on which people used to be stretched by turning its wheels

**rack²** *v* [T] to cause great pain: *a racking headache*|*He was racked with pain/by doubts.*

**rack³** **wrack** *n* [U] **rack and ruin** the ruined state caused by lack of care: *The house went to/is in rack and ruin.*

**rack·et¹, racquet** /'rækǝt/ *n* an instrument consisting of a network usu. of nylon stretched in a frame with a handle, used for hitting the ball in games such as tennis –see picture on page 592

**racket²** *n infml* **1** [S] a loud noise: *Stop making such a racket! I can't sleep.* **2** a dishonest way of getting money, e.g. by threatening or cheating people

**rack·e·teer** /ˌrækǝ'tɪǝʳ/ *n derog* someone who works a RACKET² (2)

**rac·on·teur** /ˌrækɒn'tɜːʳ||ˌrækɑn-/ *n* someone good at telling stories

**ra·coon** /rǝ'kuːn, ræ-||ræ-/ *n BrE* for RACCOON

**rac·y** /'reɪsi/ *adj* **-ier, -iest** (of speech or writing) amusing, full of life and perhaps dealing with sex: *racy stories* **–racily** *adv* **–raciness** *n*

**ra·dar** /'reɪdɑːʳ/ *n* [U] a method of finding the position of solid objects by receiving radio waves seen on a glass plate (SCREEN)

**ra·di·ance** /'reɪdɪǝns/ *n* [U] the quality of being RADIANT (1,2)

**ra·di·ant** /'reɪdɪǝnt/ *adj* **1** [A] sending out light or heat in all directions; shining: *the radiant sun* **2** [*with*] (of a person or his/her appearance) showing love and happiness: *her radiant face* **3** [A] *tech* sent out by RADIATION: *radiant heat* **–radiantly** *adv*

**ra·di·ate** /'reɪdieɪt/ *v* **-ated, -ating** [T] to send out (light or heat): (fig.) *She radiated happiness.*

**radiate from** sthg. *v prep* [T *no pass.*] to come out or spread in all directions from: *a system of roads radiating from the town centre*

**ra·di·a·tion** /ˌreɪdi'eɪʃǝn/ *n* **1** [U] the radiating (RADIATE) of heat, light, etc. **2** [C] something which is radiated: *This apparatus produces harmful radiations.* **3** [U] → RADIOACTIVITY: *atomic radiation*

**ra·di·a·tor** /'reɪdieɪtǝʳ/ *n* **1** an apparatus, esp. one consisting of pipes with steam or hot water passing through them, used for heating buildings –see picture on page 355 **2** an apparatus which keeps the engine of a motor vehicle cool

**rad·i·cal¹** /'rædɪkǝl/ *adj* **1** (of changes) thorough and complete: *The government made radical improvements to the tax system.* **2** (of a person or his opinions) in favour of thorough and complete political change –compare REACTIONARY **–radically** *adv*

**radical²** *n* a person who wishes to make rapid and thorough social and political changes **–radicalism** *n* [U]

**rad·i·i** /'reɪdiaɪ/ *n pl. of* RADIUS

**ra·di·o¹** /'reɪdiǝʊ/ *n* **-os** **1** [C] an apparatus made to receive sounds broadcast through the air by means of electrical waves: *a transistor radio*|*I heard the election results* **on the radio.** –see picture on page 85 **2** [U] the sending or receiving of sounds through the air by electrical waves: *The police talked to each other by radio.* **3** [U] the radio broadcasting industry: *Her first job was in radio.*

> **SPELLING NOTE**
> Words with the sound /r/ may be spelt **wr-**, like **wrong.**

**radio²** *v* **-oed, -oing** [I;T] to send (a message) by radio: *The ship radioed for help.*

**ra·di·o·ac·tiv·i·ty** /ˌreɪdiǝʊæk'tɪvǝti/ *n* [U] the quality, harmful to living things, that some simple substances (ELEMENTS) have of giving out force (ENERGY (2)) by the breaking up of atoms **–radioactive** /-'æktɪv/ *adj*: radioactive waste

**ra·di·og·ra·phy** /ˌreɪdi'ɒgrǝfi||-'ɑg-/ *n* [U] the taking of photographs made with short waves (X-RAYS), usu. for medical reasons **–radiographer** *n*

**ra·di·o·ther·a·py** /ˌreɪdiǝʊ'θerǝpi/ *n* [U] the treatment of diseases by RADIOACTIVITY or X-RAYS

**rad·ish** /'rædɪʃ/ *n* a small vegetable whose red or white hot-tasting root is eaten raw in SALADS

**ra·di·um** /'reɪdiǝm/ *n* [U] a rare shining white metal that is a simple substance (ELEMENT), has a high level of RADIOACTIVITY, and is used in the treatment of certain diseases, esp. CANCER

**ra·di·us** /'reɪdiǝs/ *n* **-dii** /diaɪ/ **1** (the line marking) the distance from the centre of a circle or SPHERE (1) to its edge or surface –compare DIAMETER **2** a circular area measured from its centre point: *He lives somewhere within a ten-mile radius of the town.*

**R.A.F.** /ˌɑːr eɪ 'ef, *infml* ræf/ *n* (in Britain) *abbrev. for*: Royal Air Force: *Join the R.A.F.*

**raf·fi·a** /'ræfɪǝ/ *n* [U] the soft string-like substance from the leaf stems of a PALM tree, used for making hats, baskets, etc.

**raf·fle¹** /'ræfǝl/ *n* a way of making money, esp. for charity, by selling numbered tickets of which one is chosen by chance to win a prize: *He won a car in the raffle.* –compare DRAW² (1), LOTTERY

**raffle²** *v* **-fled, -fling** [T *off*] to offer as the prize in a RAFFLE

**raft** /rɑːft||ræft/ *n* **1** a type of flat boat made by fixing together large pieces of wood **2** also **life raft**– a small boat made of rubber and filled with air, for the use of passengers on a sinking ship or crashed plane

**raf·ter** /'rɑːftǝʳ||'ræf-/ *n* one of the large sloping esp. wooden beams that hold up a roof

**rag¹** /ræg/ *n* **1** [C;U] (a small piece of) old cloth: *He cleaned the machine with an oily rag/a piece of oily rag.* **2** [C] an old worn-out garment: *The beggar was dressed in rags.* **3** [C] *infml derog* a newspaper of low quality: *Why are you reading that rag?*

**rag²** *v* **-gg-** [T] to play rough tricks on or make fun of; TEASE: *They ragged him about his big ears.*

**rag³** *n BrE* an amusing procession of college students through the streets on a special day in the year (**rag day**), collecting money for CHARITY (2)

**rag·a·muf·fin** /'rægǝˌmʌfǝn/ *n lit* a dirty young child in torn clothes

**rag·bag** /'rægbæg/ *n often derog* a confused mixture: *His argument is a ragbag of disconnected facts.*

**rage¹** /reɪdʒ/ *n* **1** [C;U] (a state of) wild uncontrollable anger: *The child wept with rage.*|*He* **flies into a rage** *every time I mention money.* –see ANGRY

(USAGE) **2** [C] *infml* a very popular fashion: *Short hair is* **(all) the rage** (=very fashionable) *now.*

**rage²** *v* **raged, raging** [I] **1** [*against, at*] to be in a RAGE¹ (1) **2** to be full of violent force: *The battle raged.|a raging headache|The disease raged through the city.*

**rag·ged** /ˈrægɨd/ *adj* **1** old and torn: *a ragged shirt* **2** dressed in old torn clothes: *a ragged boy* **3** (of work) unfinished and imperfect: *a ragged performance* **–raggedly** *adv* **–raggedness** *n* [U]

**rag·time** /ˈrægtaɪm/ *n* [U] a type of music of black US origin, popular in the 1920s: *a ragtime band*

**raid¹** /reɪd/ *n* [*on*] **1** a quick attack on an enemy position: *to make a raid on the enemy coast|an* **air raid** (=an attack by aircraft) **2** an unexpected visit by the police, in search of criminals or illegal goods: *a police raid on the house looking for drugs.*

**raid²** *v* [I;T] to visit or attack (a place) on a RAID: *raid a house* **–raider** *n*

**rail¹** /reɪl/ *n* **1** [C] a fixed bar, esp. one to hang things on or for protection: *Keep your hand on the rail as you climb the steps.|a clothes rail* **2** [C] one of the pair of metal bars fixed to the ground, along which a train runs: *Passengers must not cross the rails.*|(fig.) *Jane* **has gone** *slightly* **off the rails** (=become disordered in mind) *since the accident.* –see picture on page 501 **3** [A] connected with the railway: *send it by rail* (=by train)

**rail²** *v* [I *against, at*] *fml* to complain angrily: *railing against the latest tax increases*

**rail·ing** /ˈreɪlɪŋ/ *n* [*often pl.*] one of a set of RAILS¹ (1) making up a fence: *He leant on the railings.*

**rail·road** /ˈreɪlrəʊd/ *v* [T] **1** to hurry (someone) unfairly: *The workers were railroaded into signing the agreement.* **2** to pass (a law) or carry out (a plan) quickly in spite of opposition: *The chairman railroaded the plan through the committee.*

**rail·way** /ˈreɪlweɪ/ *BrE*‖**railroad** *AmE*– *n* (a system, including engines, stations, etc. of) track for trains

**rai·ment** /ˈreɪmənt/ *n* [U] *lit* clothes

**rain¹** /reɪn/ *n* **1** [U] water falling in separate drops from the clouds: *The rain fell continuously.|She went out in the rain without a coat.*|**It looks like rain.** (=as if there will be rain). –compare DEW **2** [S] a thick fall of anything: *a rain of bombs* **3 as right as rain** *infml* in perfect health: *Jane's been ill, but she's as right as rain now.* –see WEATHER (USAGE)

**rain²** *v* **1** [*it* I] (of rain) to fall: *It's raining.|It began to rain hard.* **2** [I;T *down*] to (cause to) fall like rain: *Tears rained down her cheeks.|Their rich uncle rained gifts upon the children.* **3 rain cats and dogs** to rain very heavily

**rain** sthg.↔ **off** *v adv* [T] *infml* to cause to stop because of rain: *The game was rained off.*

**rain·bow** /ˈreɪnbəʊ/ *n* an arch of different colours that sometimes appears in the sky after rain

**rain·coat** /ˈreɪnkəʊt/ *n* a light coat worn to keep the wearer dry when it rains

**rain·drop** /ˈreɪndrɒp‖-drɑp/ *n* a single drop of rain

**rain·fall** /ˈreɪnfɔːl/ *n* [C;U] the amount of rain, HAIL, or snow that falls in an area in a certain time

**rain for·est** /ˈ· ˌ··/ *n* a wet tropical forest with tall trees growing thickly together

**rains** /reɪnz/ *n* [*the* P]→MONSOON (1): *The rains have started early this year.*

**rain·y** /ˈreɪni/ *adj* **-ier, -iest** having a lot of rain: *a very rainy day/place*|(fig.) *Save your money* **for a rainy day**. (=for a time when you need it)

**raise¹** /reɪz/ *v* **raised, raising** [T] **1** to lift, push, or move upwards: *to raise the lid of a box|raise one's hat|She raised her finger to her lips as a sign for silence.|The car raised a cloud of dust as it rushed past.|He raised the fallen child to its feet.* (=helped it to stand) **2** to make higher in amount, degree, size, etc.: *to raise the rent/the temperature/someone's pay* –opposite **lower** (for 1, 2) **3** to collect together: *to raise an army|We couldn't raise enough money for a holiday.* **4** to produce, cause to grow or increase, and look after (living things); BRING **up** (1) (children): *raise a family|raise horses* **5** to mention or put forward (a subject): *There's an important point I want to raise.* **6 a** to make (a noise): *The men raised a cheer.* **b** to cause people to make (a noise) or have (feelings): *Her joke raised a laugh.|His long absence raised doubts/fears about his safety.* **7 raise hell/the roof** *infml* to become very angry: *Mother will raise hell if you wake the baby.* –see RISE (USAGE)

**raise²** *n AmE* for RISE² (4)

**rai·sin** /ˈreɪzən/ *n* a sweet dried fruit (GRAPE) used in cakes, etc.

**raj** /rɑːdʒ/ *n* [*the* S] (a period of) rule, esp. British rule in India: *The days of the (British) raj are ended.*

**ra·jah, raja** /ˈrɑːdʒə/ *n* [C;S] (the title of) an Indian ruler

**rake¹** /reɪk/ *n* a tool consisting of a row of teeth at the end of a long handle, used for making the soil level, gathering up dead leaves, etc.

**rake²** *v* **raked, raking 1** [I;T] to make (a place) level with a RAKE¹: *Rake the garden paths (smooth).* **2** [T *together, up*] to collect with a RAKE¹: *Rake up the dead leaves.* **3** [I *about, around*] to search carefully by turning over a mass: *She raked about/around among her papers to see if she could find it.*

**rake** sthg.↔ **in** *v adv* [T] *infml* to earn or gain (a lot of money): *He must be raking in £500 a week!*

**rake** sthg.↔ **up** *v adv* [T] *infml* **1** to remember and talk about (something that should be forgotten): *Please don't rake up that old quarrel again.* **2** to collect together, esp. with difficulty: *to rake up enough money for the rent*

**rake³** *n old use* a man who has led a wild life with regard to drink and women

**rake-off** /ˈ· ·/ *n* a (usu. dishonest) share of profits: *The taxi-driver gets a rake-off from the night club.*

**rak·ish** /ˈreɪkɪʃ/ *adj* bold and wild like (that of) a RAKE³: *lead a rakish life|She wore her hat at a rakish angle.* (=sideways on her head) **–rakishly** *adv* **–rakishness** *n* [U]

**ral·ly¹** /ˈræli/ *v* **-lied, -lying 1** [I;T] to come or bring together (again) for a shared purpose: *The whole nation rallied to the government.|The leader rallied his tired soldiers and they drove the enemy back.* **2** [I] to recover from illness or unhappiness: *He soon rallied from the shock of his father's death.*

**rally round** *v adv* [I] *infml* (esp. of a group) to come to someone's help at a time of difficulty: *Her friends all rallied round when she was ill.*

**rally²** *n* **-lies 1** a large (esp. political) public meeting **2** a motor race over public roads **3** (in tennis) a long struggle to gain a point, with each player hitting the ball again and again

**ram**[1] /ræm/ *n* **1** a fully-grown male sheep –compare EWE **2** → BATTERING RAM **3** any machine that repeatedly drops or pushes a weight onto or into something

**ram**[2] *v* **-mm-** [T] **1** to run into (something) very hard: *His car rammed the wall.* **2** [*down*] to force into place with heavy pressure: *He rammed down the soil round the newly planted bush.*|(fig.) *Father keeps ramming it down my throat* (=forcing the idea on me) *that I should become a doctor.*

**Ram·a·dan** /ˈræmədæn, -dɑːn, ˌ··ˈ·/ *n* the 9th month of the Muslim year, during which no food or drink may be taken between sunrise and sunset

**ram·ble**[1] /ˈræmbəl/ *v* **-bled, -bling** [I] **1** [*about*] to go on a RAMBLE[2] **2** [*about*] to talk or write in an aimless disordered way: *The old man rambled on (about his youth).* –**rambling** *n* [U]

**ramble**[2] *n* a (long) walk for enjoyment, often in the country: *go for/on a ramble through the woods*

**ram·bler** /ˈræmbləʳ/ *n* a person that RAMBLES[1] (1)

**ram·bling** /ˈræmblɪŋ/ *adj* **1** (of speech or writing) disordered and wandering: *a long and very rambling letter* **2** (of houses, streets, etc.) of irregular shape; twisting and winding **3** (of a plant) growing loosely in all directions: *a rambling rose*

**ram·i·fi·ca·tion** /ˌræmǝ̵̇fǝ̵̇ˈkeɪʃən/ *n fml* **1** a branch of a system with many parts: *the many ramifications of a railway system* **2** [*usu.pl.*] one of a large number of results that follow from an action or decision; CONSEQUENCE

**ramp** /ræmp/ *n* a man-made slope that connects two levels: *Drive the car up the ramp.*

**ram·page** /ræmˈpeɪdʒ, ˈræmpeɪdʒ/ *v* **-paged, -paging** [I] to rush about wildly or angrily: *The elephants rampaged through the forest.* –**rampage** *n* [*the* S]: *football crowds* **on the rampage**

**ram·pant** /ˈræmpənt/ *adj* (of crime, disease, beliefs, etc.) widespread and impossible to control: *Sickness was rampant in the country.* –**rampantly** *adv*

**ram·part** /ˈræmpɑːt‖-ɑrt/ *n* [*usu. pl.*] a wide bank of earth built to protect a fort or city

**ram·rod** /ˈræmrɒd‖-rɑd/ *n* a stick for pushing the gunpowder into or cleaning a gun

**ram·shack·le** /ˈræmʃækəl/ *adj* (of a building or vehicle) badly made or needing repair; falling to pieces: *a ramshackle old house*

**ran** /ræn/ *v past tense of* RUN

**ranch** /rɑːntʃ‖ræntʃ/ *n* (in the western US and Canada) a very large farm, esp. one where sheep, cattle, or horses are produced

**ranch·er** /ˈrɑːntʃəʳ‖ˈræn-/ *n* a person who owns or works on a RANCH

**ran·cid** /ˈrænsǝ̵̇d/ *adj* (of oily food or its taste or smell) not fresh: *rancid butter*|*a rancid taste*

**ran·cour** *BrE*‖**rancor** *AmE* /ˈræŋkəʳ/ *n* [U] *fml* a feeling of bitter, unforgiving spite and hatred –**rancorous** *adj* –**rancorously** *adv*

> **SPELLING NOTE**
> Words with the sound /r/ may be spelt **wr-**, like **wrong.**

**rand** /rænd/ *n* **rand** the standard unit of money of South Africa, divided into 100 cents

**ran·dom**[1] /ˈrændəm/ *adj* [A] made or done aimlessly, without any plan: *a random choice*|*a random sample of people* (=people chosen in such a way that anyone is equally likely to be chosen) –**randomly** *adv* –**randomness** *n* [U]

**random**[2] *n* **at random** aimlessly; without any plan: *The travellers at the airport were searched at random.*

**rand·y** /ˈrændi/ *adj* **-ier, -iest** *infml* (of a person or his/her feelings) full of sexual desire –**randiness** *n* [U]

**rang** /ræŋ/ *v past tense of* RING

**range**[1] /reɪndʒ/ *n* **1** [C] a connected line of mountains, hills, etc.: *a mountain range* **2** [C] an area where shooting is practised, or where MISSILEs (1) are tested: *a firing range* **3** [C] (in N. America) a wide stretch of grassy land where cattle feed **4** [U] the distance at which one can see or hear: *Shout as soon as she comes within range.* **5** [S;U] the distance that a gun can fire: *He shot the rabbit at short/close/long range.*|*What's the range of this gun?* **6** [S] the measurable limits between which something varies: *a country with a wide range of temperature*|*people in the £6000–£8000 income range* **7** [C] a set of different objects of the same kind, esp. for sale in a shop: *Come and see our range of gardening tools.*

**range**[2] *v* **ranged, ranging 1** [I not *be +v-ing*] to vary between limits; reach from one limit to another: *The children's ages range from 5 to 15/between 5 and 15.* **2** [I;T *through,over; no pass.*] *esp. lit* to wander freely (through, over): *We ranged (over) the hills and valleys.*|*Our conversation ranged over* (=included) *many subjects.* **3** [T] to put in position; arrange: *She ranged the goods neatly in the shop window.*

**rang·er** /ˈreɪndʒəʳ/ *n* **1** the keeper of a forest **2** (in N. America) a policeman on horseback in a country area

**rank**[1] /ræŋk/ *n* **1** [C;U] (a) degree of value, ability, importance, etc., in a group: *the rank of general*|*He's above me in rank.* **2** [C;U] (high) social position: *people of all ranks* **3** [C] a line of people, esp. soldiers, or things: *Taxis stand in a (taxi) rank waiting to be hired.*|(fig.) *the ranks* (=the large group) *of the unemployed* **4 rank and file** the ordinary people in an organization as opposed to the leaders

**rank**[2] *v* **1** [I;T *as,among*] to be or put (in a certain class): *This town ranks (high) among the English beauty spots.*

**rank**[3] *adj* **1** (of a plant) too thick and widespread: *rank grass* **2** (of smell or taste) very strong and unpleasant: *rank tobacco* **3** [A] (esp. of bad things) complete: *a rank beginner at the job* –**rankly** *adv* –**rankness** *n* [U]

**ran·kle** /ˈræŋkəl/ *v* **-kled, -kling** [I] to continue to be remembered with bitterness and anger: *His rudeness to me still rankles.*

**ran·sack** /ˈrænsæk/ *v* [T] to search through and rob: *Enemy soldiers ransacked the town.*|(fig.) *She ransacked her pockets for the keys.*

**ran·som** /ˈrænsəm/ *n* (a sum of money paid for) the freeing of a prisoner: *They took away* (KIDNAPped) *the boy and* **held** *him* **to ransom**. (=kept him prisoner so as to demand payment) –**ransom** *v* [T]

**rant** /rænt/ *v* [I *on*] to talk in a loud excited way: *The priest ranted on about the devil and all his works.*

Anna and Michael **took a taxi** to the **station** to **catch their train** to Exeter. They arrived just **in time**: the train is **due to leave** in a few minutes. They don't need to go to the **ticket/booking office**, because they bought their tickets yesterday, and **reserved** two **seats** to be sure of getting somewhere to sit.
At the **ticket barrier**, they show their tickets to the **ticket collector**, who **clips** them to show that they have been used. On the **platform** Anna looks for a **porter** to help them with their **luggage**. They find their seats in the first **compartment** in the **carriage** next to the **buffet*** **car**. They put their **cases** on the **luggage rack** as the train **moves off**.
During the journey a **ticket inspector** comes to look at each passenger's ticket. Anna asks him if they have to **change** (**trains**). The inspector tells her it's an **express** (**train**) and it goes **direct** to Exeter (=so they don't have to change).
The train **pulls into** the station exactly **on time** (=it isn't early or late), and the passengers **get off**.

*See the pronunciation guide in the dictionary for how you say this word.

**Questions** (Answers on page 702)

What is the word or expression for:

- **a** the place where you buy your ticket
- **b** the man who looks at the tickets on the train
- **c** the place where you can buy drinks
- **d** not early or late

**rap**[1] /ræp/ *n* **1** (the sound of) a quick light blow: *to hear a rap on the door* **2 take the rap (for)** *infml* to receive the punishment (for someone else's crime)
**rap**[2] *v* **-pp-** [I;T *at, on*] to strike quickly and lightly: *someone rapping loudly at the door/on the table*
**ra·pa·cious** /rəˈpeɪʃəs/ *adj fml* taking everything one can, esp. by force: *a rapacious band of robbers* **–rapaciously** *adv* **–rapaciousness** *n* [U] **–rapacity** /rəˈpæsɪ̈ti/ *n* [U].
**rape**[1] /reɪp/ *v* **raped, raping** [T] to have sex with (a woman) against her will
**rape**[2] *n* [C;U] **1** (a case of) the act and crime of raping (RAPE[1]): *He was sent to prison for rape.* **2** *fml* spoiling: *the rape of our beautiful forests*
**rape**[3] *n* [U] a European plant grown as animal food and for oil
**rap·id**[1] /ˈræpɪ̈d/ *adj* quick-moving; fast: *The improvement was rapid.*|*to ask questions in rapid* SUCCESSION|*The school promised rapid results* **–rapidity** /rəˈpɪdɪ̈ti/ *n* [U] **–rapidly** *adv*
**rapid**[2] *n* [*usu. pl.*] a part of a river where the water moves very fast over rocks
**ra·pi·er** /ˈreɪpɪəʳ/ *n* a long sharp thin sword
**rap·ist** /ˈreɪpɪ̈st/ *n* a man guilty of RAPE[2] (1)
**rap·port** /ræˈpɔː‖-or/ *n* [U *between, with*] close agreement and understanding: *to have/feel/develop rapport with someone*
**rap·proche·ment** /ræˈprɒʃmɑ̃, ræˈprəʊʃ-‖ˌræ prəʊʃˈmɑ̃/ *n fml* a coming together again in friendship of former enemies: *At last there are signs of a rapprochement between our two countries.*
**rapt** /ræpt/ *adj* giving one's whole mind (to): *rapt attention* **–raptly** *adv* **–raptness** *n* [U]
**rap·ture** /ˈræptʃəʳ/ *n* [P;U] *fml* great joy and delight: *He* **went into raptures** (=became full of joy) *at/about the news.* **–rapturous** *adj* **–rapturously** *adv*
**rare**[1] /reəʳ/ *adj* **1** unusual; not common: *a rare event*|*It's very rare for him to be late.* **2** (esp. of air) thin; light: *the rare air of the mountains* **–rareness** [U]
USAGE Uncommon and perhaps valuable things are **rare**: *a* **rare** *bird/coin.* Common useful things that we have not got enough of are **scarce**: *Potatoes were* **scarce** *last winter.* We can use **rare**, but not **scarce**, about time: *one of my* **rare** (=not happening often) *visits to Paris.*
**rare**[2] *adj* (of meat, esp. STEAK) lightly cooked –compare WELL-DONE
**rar·e·fied** /ˈreərɪ̈faɪd/ *adj* **1** (of air in high places) light; thin, with less oxygen than usual **2** *humor* very high or grand: *He moves in very rarefied circles; his friends are all lords.*
**rare·ly** /ˈreəli‖ˈreərli/ *adv* not often: *I have rarely seen such a beautiful sunset.* –compare SCARCELY; see NEVER (USAGE)
**rar·ing** /ˈreərɪŋ/ *adj* [F +*to-v*] *infml* very eager: *The children were* **raring to go.** (=eager to start)
**rar·i·ty** /ˈreərɪ̈ti/ **-ties 1** [U] the quality of being RARE[1] (1) **2** [C] something uncommon: *This type of flower is becoming a rarity.*

**SPELLING NOTE**
Words with the sound /r/ may be spelt **wr-**, like **wrong.**

**ras·cal** /ˈrɑːskəl‖ˈræs-/ *n* **1** a dishonest person **2** *humor* a person, esp. a child, who misbehaves: *You little rascal! Where have you hidden my shoes?*
**rash**[1] /ræʃ/ *adj* foolishly bold; not thinking enough of the results: *a rash decision*|*I agreed* **in a rash moment** **–rashly** *adv* **–rashness** *n* [U]
**rash**[2] *n* [S] a set of red spots on the face and/or body, caused by illness: *He* **came out in** (=become covered with) **a rash** *today.*|(fig.) *a rash of complaints* (=large number)
**rash·er** /ˈræʃəʳ/ *n* a thin piece of BACON: *a few rashers (of* BACON*) for breakfast*
**rasp** /rɑːsp‖ræsp/ *v* [T] **1** to rub, producing a sensation of roughness: *The cat's tongue rasped my hand.*|(fig.) *His loud voice rasped (on)* (=had an annoying effect on) *my nerves.* **2** to say in a rough voice
**rasp·ber·ry** /ˈrɑːzbəri‖ˈræzberi/ *n* **-ries 1** a soft sweet red berry (or its bush): *raspberries and cream* **2** *infml* a rude sound made by putting one's tongue out and blowing
**rat**[1] /ræt/ *n* **1** a long-tailed animal (RODENT) related to but larger than the mouse **2** *infml* a low worthless disloyal man: *But you promised to help us, you rat!* **3 smell a rat** *infml* to guess that something wrong is happening
**rat**[2] *v* **-tt-** [I *on*] *infml* to act in a disloyal way; break a promise: *They said they'd help but they've ratted (on us).*
**ratch·et** /ˈrætʃɪ̈t/ *n* a toothed wheel or bar provided with a piece of metal that fits between its teeth so as to allow movement in one direction but not the other
**rate**[1] /reɪt/ *n* **1** [C *of*] a value, cost, speed, etc., measured by its relation to some other amount: *to travel at the rate of 100 km an hour*|*The* **birth rate** *is the number of births compared to the number of the people.*|*to drive at a steady rate* **2** [C] a charge or payment fixed according to a standard scale: *They're demanding higher rates of pay.* **3** [C *usu. pl.*] (in Britain) a local tax paid by owners of buildings (**ratepayers**) for locally provided services **4** [A] of the (numbered) quality: *a* **first-rate** (=very good) *performer* **5 at any rate** in any case; whatever happens **6 at this/that rate** if events continue in the same way as now/then: *At this rate we won't be able to afford a holiday.* **7 rate of exchange** the relationship between the money of two countries
**rate**[2] *v* **rated, rating** [T] **1** to consider; set a value on: *I rate her highly as a poet.* **2** [*usu. pass.*] *BrE* to fix a RATE[1] (3) on (a building): *a house rated at £500*
**ra·tea·ble value, ratable** /ˈreɪtəbəl/ *n.* a value given to a building for the purpose of calculating the RATES[1] (3) to be charged: *What's the rateable value of this shop?*
**ra·ther** /ˈrɑːðəʳ‖ˈræðər/ *predeterminer, adv* **1** to some degree; QUITE (2): *a rather cold day*|*rather a cold day*|*driving rather fast*|*These shoes are rather too big.*|*It rather surprised me.* –see Study Notes on page 389 **2** more willingly: *I'd rather play tennis than swim.*|*"Have a drink?" "No thanks, I would rather/sooner not."* **3** more truly: *He ran rather than walked.*|*He came home very late last night, or rather very early this morning.* **4** *esp. BrE infml (used as an*

*answer)* Yes, certainly!: *"Would you like a swim?" "Rather."*

USAGE **Fairly** *cold weather* or *driving* **fairly** *fast* mean "cold enough", "fast enough", but **rather** *cold*, **rather** *fast* may mean "too cold", "too fast".

**rat·i·fy** /'rætǐfaɪ/ *v* **-fied, -fying** [T] *fml* to make official by signing (a written agreement): *The heads of the two governments met to ratify the* TREATY. **–ratification** /-fǐ'keɪʃən/ *n* [U]

**rat·ing¹** /'reɪtɪŋ/ *n* **1** the position of popularity given to a record, a radio or television show, etc.: *This song's been getting very good ratings.* **2** [C] (in the British navy) a sailor who is not an officer **3** [C] the business responsibility that a person or firm is thought to have: *She has a good* CREDIT¹ (6) *rating, so she can borrow a lot of money.*

**ra·ti·o** /'reɪʃiəʊ‖'reɪʃəʊ/ *n* **-os** a figure showing the number of times one quantity contains another: *The ratio of 10 to 5 is 2 to 1.*|*We divided it in the ratio 2:1.* –compare PROPORTION

**ra·tion¹** /'ræʃən‖'ræ-, 'reɪ-/ *n* a share (of food, petrol, etc.) allowed to one person for a period, esp. during a war, or a period of short supply

**ration²** *v* [T] **1** [*to*] to limit (someone) to a fixed RATION¹: *She rationed them to two eggs a week.* **2** to limit and control (supplies): *They had to ration petrol during the war.*

**ration** sthg.↔ **out** *v adv* [T] to give out (supplies) in RATIONS¹: *He rationed out the water to the sailors.*

**ra·tion·al** /'ræʃənəl/ *adj* **1** (of people) able to reason **2** (of ideas and behaviour) sensible; according to reason: *a rational explanation* –opposite **irrational** **–rationally** *adv* **–rationality** /-'nælǐti/ *n* [U]

**ra·tio·nale** /ˌræʃə'nɑːl‖-'næl/ *n* [C;U] *fml* the reason(s) on which a system or practice is based

**ra·tion·al·ize** ‖also **-ise** *BrE* /'ræʃənəlaɪz/ *v* **- ized, -izing 1** [I;T] to find reasons for (one's own unreasonable behaviour or opinions): *If you rationalize your fears, you can understand them better.* **2** [T] *BrE* to improve (a method or system) and make it less wasteful: *to rationalize the organization of the firm* **–rationalization** /-laɪ'zeɪʃən, - lǝ-/ *n* [C;U]

**rat race** /'· ·/ *n* [*the* S] *infml* the endless competition for success in business: *Paul got so tired of the rat race that he stopped working.*

**rat·tle¹** /'rætl/ *v* **-tled, -tling 1** [I;T] to (cause to) make a lot of quick little noises: *The beggar rattled the coins in his tin.* **2** [T] *infml* to make nervous or anxious: *Keep calm –don't get rattled.*

**rattle/reel** sthg.↔ **off**– *v adv* [T] to repeat quickly and easily from memory: *He rattled off the poem.*

**rattle on/away**– *v adv* [I] to talk quickly and continuously: *He kept rattling on about his holidays.*

**rattle through** sthg. *v prep* [T] to perform quickly: *to rattle through his speech/her work*

**rattle²** *n* [C;S] (a toy or instrument that makes) a rattling noise (RATTLE¹ (1)): *The baby was playing with his rattle.*|*the rattle of milk bottles*

**rattle·snake** /'rætlsneɪk/ ‖**also rattler** *AmE*– *n* a poisonous American snake that makes a rattling noise (RATTLE¹ (1))with its tail

**rat·ty** /'ræti/ *adj* **-tier, -tiest 1** *BrE infml* annoyed: *Father got a bit ratty when I broke those plates.* **2** of or like a rat

**rau·cous** /'rɔːkəs/ *adj* (of voices) rough and unpleasant: **–raucously** *adv* **–raucousness** *n* [U]

**raunch·y** /'rɔːntʃi/ *adj* **-ier, -iest** *AmE infml* having or showing a strong desire for sex **–raunchiness** *n* [U]

**rav·age** /'rævɪdʒ/ *v* **-aged, -aging** [T] **1** to ruin: *crops ravaged by storms* **2** to rob (an area) with violence: *The conquering army ravaged the country.*

**rav·ag·es** /'rævɪdʒǐz/ *n* [P *of*] the destroying effects: *the ravages of fire/war*

**rave** /reɪv/ *v* **raved, raving** [I *about, against, at*] to talk wildly as if mad: *He raved all night in his fever.*

**rave about** sbdy./sthg. *v prep* [T] *infml* to speak about with (too) great admiration: *Everybody raved about the new singer.*

**ra·ven** /'reɪvən/ *n* [A;C] (the colour of) a large shiny black bird with a deep unmusical voice (CROAK)

**rav·e·nous** /'rævənəs/ *adj* very hungry **–ravenously** *adv*

**rave-up** /'· ·/ *n infml* a very wild party

**ra·vine** /rə'viːn/ *n* a deep narrow valley with steep sides –see VALLEY (USAGE)

**rav·ing** /'reɪvɪŋ/ *adj,adv infml* talking wildly: *a raving madman*|*He's raving (mad).* **–ravings** *n* [P]: *the ravings of a madman/of the sick man*

**rav·i·o·li** /ˌrævi'əʊli/ *n* [U] small cases of flour paste (PASTA) filled with meat and boiled –compare SPAGHETTI, MACARONI

**rav·ish** /'rævɪʃ/ *v* [T] **1** *lit* to RAPE **2** [*by, with; usu. pass*] to fill with delight: *ravished by her beauty*

**rav·ish·ing** /'rævɪʃɪŋ/ *adj* very beautiful; causing great delight: *a ravishing sight* **–ravishingly** *adv*

**raw** /rɔː/ *adj* **1** (of food) not cooked: *raw vegetables* **2** in the natural state: *raw silk/cotton*|**Raw materials** *are the natural substances from which industrial products are made.* **3** (of a person) not yet trained; not experienced: *a raw* RECRUIT *who has just joined the army* **4** (of a part of the skin) painful; sore: *hands raw with cold* **5** (of weather) cold and wet: *a raw winter day* **6 raw deal** *infml* unfair or cruel treatment: *to have/get (rather) a raw deal* **–rawly** *adv* **–rawness** *n* [U]

**ray** /reɪ/ *n* [*of*] a narrow beam (of heat, light, etc.): *the sun's rays*|*an* X-RAY *photograph*|(fig.) *a ray* (=a small bit) *of hope*

**ray·on** /'reɪɒn‖-ɑn/ *n* [U] a smooth silk-like material made from wool or cotton (CELLULOSE)

**raze** /reɪz/ *v* **razed, razing** [T] *fml* to flatten (buildings, towns, etc.): *a bomb attack that* **razed** *the city* **to the ground**

**ra·zor** /'reɪzəʳ/ *n* a sharp sometimes electric instrument for removing hair, esp. the hair that grows on a man's face –see also SAFETY RAZOR

**R.C.** *n abbrev. for*: ROMAN CATHOLIC

**Rd** *written abbrev. said as*: Road

**re** /riː/ *prep* [U] (esp. in business letters) on the subject of; with regard to: *re your enquiry of the 19th October*

**re** /əʳ/ *short for*: are: *We're ready but they're not.*

**reach¹** /riːtʃ/ *v* **1** [T] to arrive at; get to: *They reached London on Thursday.*|*to reach the end of the book*|*The news only reached me yesterday.*|*My income reached five figures* (=at least £10,000) *last year.*|(fig.) *He doesn't allow the problems of other people to reach* (=have an effect on) *him.* **2** [I] to stretch out a hand or arm for some purpose: *The shopkeeper reached for a packet of tea.* **3** [I;T] to be able to touch (something) by stretching out a hand or arm: *"Can you reach that apple on the tree?" "I'm not tall enough to reach (it)."* **4** [I;T] (of things or places) to be big enough to touch; stretch out as far as: *The ladder won't quite reach (as far as) the window.|The garden reaches down to the lake.*|(fig.) *His influence hasn't reached the capital yet.* **5** [T] to get or give by stretching out a hand or arm: *Reach down the box from the cupboard.* **6** [T] to get a message to; CONTACT[2]: *She can always be reached by the office telephone.*

**reach** sthg. **out** *v adv* [T] *(no pass.)* to stretch out (a hand or arm): *She reached out a hand and took the book.*

**reach²** *n* **1** [U *of*] the distance that one can touch by stretching, or that one can travel: *The bottle was within/beyond reach.* (=he could/could not reach it)|*to live within easy reach of the shops* **2** [S] the length of one's arm: *He has a longer reach than I have so he can climb better.* **3** [C] a straight stretch of water between two bends in a river: *the upper reaches of the river*

**re·act** /ri'ækt/ *v* [I] **1** [*to,against*] to act in reply; to behave differently as a result: *How did he react to your suggestion?|He reacted against his father's influence by running away.* **2** [*with, on*] *tech* (of a substance) to change when mixed with or brought together with another: *An acid can react with a* BASE[1] (4) *to form a salt.*

**re·ac·tion** /ri'ækʃən/ *n* **1** [C *to*] a case or way of REACTING: *What was your reaction to the news?* **2** [U] *fml derog* the quality of being REACTIONARY: *The* REVOLUTION *was defeated by the forces of reaction.* **4** [C;U] *tech* (a) change caused in a chemical substance by the action of another

**re·ac·tion·a·ry** /ri'ækʃənəri‖-ʃəneri/ *adj,n derog* (a person) strongly opposed to social or political change –compare RADICAL[1]

**re·ac·tiv·ate** /ri'ækt̍ʒveɪt/ *v* **-ated, -ating** [T] to cause (esp. machinery) to become active again

**re·ac·tor** /ri'æktəʳ/ *n* → NUCLEAR REACTOR

**read¹** /riːd/ *v* **read** /red/, **reading 1** [I;T] to look at and understand (something printed or written): *The child is learning to read.|She reads well for a six-year-old.|I often read a book at night.|to read music|to read a map|I can read French but I can't speak it.*|(fig.) *I can read your thoughts (from your face).* **2** [I;T +*that*] to get (the stated information) from print or writing: *I read about the murder/read the account of the murder in the paper.|I read that the new director was a woman.* **3** [I not *be +v-ing*] (of something written) to have (the stated form or meaning) or give (the stated idea): *Her letters always read well|The name reads "Benson" not "Fenton".|His letter reads as follows . . .* **4** [I;T] to say (printed or written words) to others: *He read the children a story.|The teacher read (the poem) aloud to the class.|She read out the football results.* **5** [T] (of measuring instruments) to show: *The* THERMOMETER *reads 33 degrees.* **6** [T] to study (a subject) at university: *Helen's reading History/Law at Oxford.* **7 read between the lines** to find a meaning that is not expressed: *If you read between the lines, this letter is really a request for money.* **8 take something as read** to accept something to be true or satisfactory, without any need to consider it further: *We can take his ability as read, but will he be interested in doing the job?* **9 -read**: **a** (of a person) having a stated amount of knowledge gained from books: *a well-read woman* **b** (of a book, newspaper, etc.) read by a stated number of people: *a little-read* NOVEL

**SPELLING NOTE**
Words with the sound /r/ may be spelt **wr-**, like **wrong.**

**read** sthg. **into** sthg. *v prep* [T] to believe (something) to be meant though not expressed by (something else): *Don't read more into her letter than she intended.*

**read** (sthg.↔) **up** *v adv* [I;T *on*] *infml* to study (a subject) thoroughly: *to read up (on) the tax laws*

**read²** *n* [S] *BrE infml* an act or period of reading: *Can I have a read of your paper?*

**rea·da·ble** /'riːdəbəl/ *adj* **1** interesting or easy to read **2** → LEGIBLE **–readability** /-də'bɪl̍ʒti / *n* [U]

**re·ad·dress** /ˌriːə'dres/ also **redirect**– *v* [T *to*] to write a different address on (a letter): *Readdress my letters (to the new house).*

**read·er** /'riːdəʳ/ *n* a person who reads (a certain thing or in a certain way): *Are you a fast reader?|the readers of a newspaper*

**read·er·ship** /'riːdəʃɪp‖-ər-/ *n* [S] the number or type of READERS of a newspaper or magazine: *a readership of 500,000*

**read·i·ly** /'red̍ʒli/ *adv* **1** willingly: *He readily promised to help.* **2** with no difficulty: *They can readily be bought anywhere.*

**read·i·ness** /'redin̍ʒs/ *n* **1** [S;U +*to-v*] (a) willingness: *(a) readiness to learn* **2** [*in* U] the state of being ready: *Everything is* **in readiness for** *the party.*

**read·ing** /'riːdɪŋ/ *n* **1** [U] the act or practice of reading: *Children learn reading and writing at school.* **2** [C *of*] an opinion about the meaning of something: *My reading of the law is that we needn't pay.* **3** [C] a figure shown by a measuring instrument: *What are the temperature readings for this machine?* **4** [U] something to be read: *suitable reading for children* **5** [A] for reading: *the reading room at the library|a reading lamp*

**re·ad·just** /ˌriːə'dʒʌst/ *v* [I;T *to*] to get or put back into the proper state or position: *to readjust (oneself) to school life after the holidays* **–readjustment** *n* [C;U] *: a period of readjustment*

**read·y¹** /'redi/ *adj* **-ier, -iest 1** [F +*to-v/for*] prepared and fit (for use): *Is breakfast ready?|The letters are ready for the post/ready to be signed.|They* **made ready** (=prepared) *for the attack.* **2** [F +*to-v*] willing: *She's always ready to help.* **3** [A] (of mental abilities) quick: *a ready understanding of difficult problems*

**ready²** *interj BrE* **Ready, steady, go!** also **on your mark(s), get set, go!**– (used when telling people to begin a race)

**ready³** *adv (used before a past participle)* in advance: *a ready-cooked dinner*

**ready-made** /ˌ·· '·◂/ *adj* (esp. of clothes) not made

specially for the buyer; able to be worn at once: *a ready-made suit*

**real** /rɪəl/ *adj* actually existing; true not false: *Is your ring real gold?|a story of real life* –**realness** *n* [U]

**real es·tate** /'· ·,·/ *n* [U] *fml & law* property in land and houses

**re·a·lis·m** /'rɪəlɪzəm/ *n* [U] determination to face facts and deal with them practically, without being influenced by feelings –**realist** *n*

**re·a·lis·tic** /rɪə'lɪstɪk/ *adj* **1** showing REALISM (1): *Our income has got smaller, so we must be realistic and sell our car.* –opposite **unrealistic 2** (of art or literature) life-like: *a realistic drawing* –**realistically** *adv*

**re·al·i·ty** /ri'æləti/ *n* **-ties 1** [U] the quality or state of being real; real existence: *She believes in the reality of God.|Everyone liked the stranger, but* **in reality** (=in actual fact) *he was a criminal.* **2** [C;U] something or everything that is real: *His dream of marrying Jean became a reality.|to escape from reality*

**re·a·li·za·tion, -sation** /,rɪəlaɪ'zeɪʃən‖-lə-/ *n* **1** [S; *the* U +*that/of*] (an experience of) understanding and believing: *the full realization that he was guilty* **2** [*the* U *of*] the becoming real (of a hope or plan): *the realization of my hopes*

**re·a·lize** ‖also **-lise** *BrE* /'rɪəlaɪz/ *v* **-lized, -lizing** [T] **1** [+(*that*)] to understand and believe (a fact): *He didn't realize he was wrong.|I didn't realize how late it was.* **2** to make real (a hope or purpose); CARRY **out:** *She realized her intention of becoming an actress.* **3** *fml* to get (money) by selling property: *The house* (=the selling of it) *realized a profit.*

**real·ly** /'rɪəli/ *adv* **1** in fact; truly: *Did he really say that?|I really don't/I don't really want any more.|It's really rather a nice picture.|You should really have asked me first.* **2** thoroughly: *It's really cold today.|a really cold day|I really hate him.* **3** (shows interest or slight displeasure): *"I collect rare coins." "Really?"|Well, really! What a nasty thing to do!*

**realm** /relm/ *n* **1** (*often cap.*) *lit & law* a kingdom: *the defence of the Realm* **2** a world; area of activity: *the realm of science|within the realms of possibility*

**ream** /ri:m/ *n* **1** a measure for sheets of paper **a** (in Britain) 480 sheets **b** (in the US) 500 sheets **2** *infml* a lot (of writing): *She wrote reams of notes.*

**reap** /ri:p/ *v* [I;T] to cut and gather (a crop of grain): (fig.) *to reap a reward/a profit* –compare SOW, HARVEST

**reap·er** /'ri:pər/ *n* a person or machine that REAPS

**re·ap·pear** /,ri:ə'pɪər/ *v* [I] to appear again after an absence –**reappearance** *n* [U]

**re·ap·prais·al** /,ri:ə'preɪzəl/ *n fml* [C;U] (a new judgment formed by) examining something again to see whether one should change one's opinion of it: *Our relations with Japan needed (a) reappraisal.*

**rear¹** /rɪər/ *v* **1** [T] to care for until fully grown: *to rear a family* –compare RAISE¹ (esp. 4) **2** [I] (of a four-legged animal) to rise upright on the back legs **3** [T] to lift up (one's head, etc.); *The lion reared its head.|*(fig.) *A problem has just* **reared its ugly head.** (=just appeared)

**rear²** *n* **1** [U] the back: *a garden at the rear of the house|a rear window* –compare FRONT **2** [C] *euph* the part of the body on which one sits; BUTTOCKS **3 bring up the rear** to come last (as in a procession)

**re·arm** /ri:'ɑ:m‖-'ɑrm/ *v* [I;T *with*] to provide (oneself or others) with weapons again, or with new weapons: *to rearm the country with modern* MISSILES –compare DISARM –**rearmament** *n* [U]

**re·ar·range** /,ri:ə'reɪndʒ/ *v* **-ranged, -ranging** [T] to put into a different order: *Let's rearrange (the furniture in) the room.* –**rearrangement** *n* [C;U]

**rea·son¹** /'ri:zən/ *n* **1** [C;U +*to-v/that*] the cause of an event; the explanation or excuse for an action: *The reason for the flood was all that heavy rain.|The reason that/why he died was lack of medical care|There is/We have reason to believe that she was murdered.|What is your reason for wanting to enter the country?|He thinks,* **with reason** (=rightly), *that I don't like him.* **2** [U] the power to think, understand, and form opinions: *People are different from animals because they possess the power of reason.* **3** [U] good sense: *Why won't you* **listen to reason?** (=be persuaded by advice) **4 anything within reason** anything that is not too much to expect: *He'll do anything within reason for me, but he won't break the law.* **5 it stands to reason** it is clear to all sensible people: *It stands to reason that he won't go if we don't pay him.*

USAGE 1 Some people think a sentence such as *The* **reason** *for my absence was* **because** *I was ill* is bad English. It is better to say: *The* **reason** *for my absence was* **that** *I was ill.* 2 Compare **cause** and **reason.** A **cause** is something that produces a result; a **reason** is something that explains or excuses an action: *The* **cause** *of the accident was the fact that he was driving too fast.|The* **reason** *why he was driving so fast was that he was late for an important meeting* –see EXCUSE (USAGE)

**reason²** *v* **1** [I] to use one's REASON¹ (2): *She can reason very clearly.* **2** [T +*that*] to form or give an opinion based on REASON¹ (2) (that): *I reasoned that she did not answer my letter because she was angry.*

**reason with** sbdy. *v prep* [T] to try to persuade by fair argument: *You should reason with the child instead of just telling him to obey.*

**rea·so·na·ble** /'ri:zənəbəl/ *adj* **1** sensible: *a perfectly reasonable thing to do* –opposite **unreasonable**; compare LOGICAL **2** (esp. of prices) fair; not too much: *a reasonable price* –**reasonableness** *n* [U]

**rea·son·a·bly** /'ri:zənəbli/ *adv* **1** sensibly **2** fairly; rather: *The car is in reasonably good order.*

**rea·soned** /'ri:zənd/ *adj* [A] (of a statement, argument, etc.,) clearly thought out; based on reason: *a (well-)reasoned statement*

**rea·son·ing** /'ri:zənɪŋ/ *n* [U] the use of one's REASON¹ (2): *Your reasoning was quite correct.*

**re·as·sure** /,ri:ə'ʃʊər/ *v* **-sured, -suring** [T *about*] to make free from fear or worry: *The doctor reassured the sick man (about his health).* –**reassurance** /,ri:ə'ʃʊərəns/ *n* [C;U] –**reassuringly** *adv*

**re·bate** /'ri:beɪt/ *n* an official return of part of a payment: *I want to claim a 5% rebate on my tax.* –compare DISCOUNT

**reb·el¹** /'rebəl/ *n* a person who REBELS: *She became a rebel when her father was put in prison.|a rebel army*

**re·bel²** /rɪ'bel/ *v* **-ll-** [I *against*] to oppose or fight (against anyone in power): *The people have rebelled against their foreign rulers.|Most children rebel* against school rules.

**re·bel·lion** /rɪ'beljən/ *n* [C;U] an act or the state of REBELling –compare REVOLUTION (1)

**re·bel·lious** /rɪ'beljəs/ *adj* (seeming) disobedient and hard to control: *rebellious behaviour* **–rebelliously** *adv* **–rebelliousness** *n* [U]

**re·birth** /ˌriː'bɜːθ‖-ɜrθ/ *n* [S] *fml* a renewal of life; change of spirit: *the rebirth of learning in the Western world*

**re·born** /ˌriː'bɔːn‖-ɔrn/ *adj* [F] *fml or lit* as if born again: *Our hopes of success were reborn.*

**re·bound[1]** /rɪ'baʊnd/ *v* [I] to fly back after hitting something: *The ball rebounded from the wall and I caught it.*|(fig.) *His lies rebounded on* (=had an unexpected effect on) *himself because nobody trusted him any more.*

**re·bound[2]** /'riːbaʊnd/ *n* **on the rebound: a** while REBOUNDing[1]: *to catch the ball on the rebound* **b** as a quick action in reply to failure in a relationship: *to marry a different person on the rebound*

**re·buff** /rɪ'bʌf/ *n fml* a rough or cruel answer given to someone who is trying to be friendly or is asking for help: *He met with/suffered a rebuff.* **–rebuff** *v* [T] : *She rebuffed all my offers of friendship.*

**re·build** /ˌriː'bɪld/ *v* **-built,** /bɪlt/, **building** [T] to build again or build new parts to

**re·buke** /rɪ'bjuːk/ *v* **-buked, -buking** [T] *fml* to give a short (esp. official) scolding to: *The police were rebuked by the judge for the way they had acted.* **–rebuke** *n*

**re·but** /rɪ'bʌt/ *v* **-tt-** [T] *fml* to prove the falsity of (a statement or charge); REFUTE **–rebuttal** *n*

**re·cal·ci·trant** /rɪ'kælsɪ̣trənt/ *adj,n fml* (a person) that refuses to obey or be controlled, even after being punished: *recalcitrant behaviour* **–recalcitrance** *n* [U]

**re·call[1]** /rɪ'kɔːl/ *v* **1** [T +*v-ing*/*that*; not *be* +*v-ing*] to remember: *I can't recall seeing him* **2** [T *from,to*] to call or take back: *The government recalled the general after he lost the battle.*|*The makers have recalled a lot of cars that were unsafe.*

**re·call[2]** /rɪ'kɔːl‖rɪ'kɔl,'riːkɔl/ *n* **1** [S;U] (a) call to return: *the recall of the general from abroad* **2** [U] the power to remember something learned or experienced: *Mary has* **total recall** *and never forgets anything.*

**re·cant** /rɪ'kænt/ *v* [I;T] *fml* to say publicly that one no longer holds (a former political or religious belief): *She recanted (her faith) and became a Christian.* **–recantation** /riːkæn'teɪʃən/ *n* [C;U]

**re·ca·pit·u·late** /ˌriːkə'pɪtʃʊleɪt‖-tʃə-/ also **recap** /'riːkæp/ *infml*– *v* **-lated, -lating** [I;T] to repeat (the chief points of something that has been said): *He recapitulated the main points of the speech.* **–recapitulation** /ˌriːkəpɪtʃʊ'leɪʃən‖-tʃə-/ *n* [C;U]

**re·cap·ture** /riː'kæptʃə^r/ *v* **-tured, -turing** [T] **1** to CAPTURE[2] (1,2) again: *The police recaptured the escaped criminal.* **2** *lit* to bring back into the mind: *a book that recaptures the happiness of youth*

> **SPELLING NOTE**
> Words with the sound /r/ may be spelt **wr-**, like **wrong.**

**re·cede** /rɪ'siːd/ *v* **-ceded, -ceding** [I *from*] **1** (of things) to move back or away: *His hair is beginning to recede (from his forehead).* **2** to slope backwards: *a receding chin*

**re·ceipt** /rɪ'siːt/ *n* **1** [C] a written statement that one has received money: *Ask him to give you a receipt when you pay the bill.* **2** [U *of*] *fml* the event of receiving: **On receipt of** (=when he receives) *your instructions, he will send the goods.*

**re·ceipts** /rɪ'siːts/ *n* [P] the money received from a business: *The receipts have increased since last year.*

**re·ceive** /rɪ'siːv/ *v* **-ceived, -ceiving 1** *more fml than* **get**– [T] to get: *to receive a letter/a lot of attention* **2** [I;T] *fml* to accept as a visitor or member; welcome: *He was received into the Church.* **3 on the receiving end (of)** *infml* suffering (unpleasant actions done to one): *We were on the receiving end of several complaints.*

**re·ceiv·er** /rɪ'siːvə^r/ *n* **1** [C] the part of a telephone that is held to one's ear –see TELEPHONE (USAGE) **2** [C] a radio or television set **3** [*the* S] (in British law) the person officially appointed to take charge of the affairs of a BANKRUPT[1] (1): *His business has failed and is* **in the hands of the receiver**. **4** [C] a person who deals in stolen property

**re·cent** /'riːsənt/ *adj* having happened or come into existence only a short time ago: *recent history* –see NEW (USAGE) **–recentness** *n* [U]

**re·cent·ly** /'riːsəntli/ *adv* not long ago; lately: *I've only recently begun to learn French.*

**re·cep·ta·cle** /rɪ'septəkəl/ *n tech or fml* a container

**re·cep·tion** /rɪ'sepʃən/ *n* **1** [C] an act of receiving; welcome: *to get a very friendly reception* **2** [C] a large formal party: *a wedding reception* **3** [U] the office, desk, or department that receives visitors to a hotel or large organization: *Leave your key at reception.* **4** [U] the quality of radio or television signals: *Radio reception isn't very good here.*

**re·cep·tion·ist** /rɪ'sepʃənɪ̣st/ *n* a person who welcomes or deals with people arriving in a hotel, visiting a doctor, etc.

**re·cep·tive** /rɪ'septɪv/ *adj* [*of,to*] (of a person or his/her mind) willing to consider new ideas: *He's not very receptive to my suggestions.* **–receptively** *adv* **–receptiveness** *n* [U]

**re·cess** /rɪ'ses‖'riːses/ *n* **1** [C;U] a pause for rest during the working day or year: *Parliament is* **in recess** *now.* –see HOLIDAY (USAGE) **2** [C] a space in the wall of a room for shelves, cupboards, etc; ALCOVE **3** [C *often pl.*] *lit* a secret inner part of a place

**re·ces·sion** /rɪ'seʃən/ *n* a period of reduced business activity; SLUMP[2](1)

**re·ci·pe** /'resɪ̣pi/ *n* [*for*] a set of instructions for cooking a dish: *a recipe for making chocolate cake*|*to follow a recipe*|*a recipe book*|(fig.) *a recipe for a happy marriage*

**re·cip·i·ent** /rɪ'sɪpiənt/ *n* [*of*] *fml* a person who receives something

**re·cip·ro·cal** /rɪ'sɪprəkəl/ *adj fml* given and received in return; MUTUAL: *a reciprocal trade agreement between two nations* **–reciprocally** *adv*

**re·cip·ro·cate** /rɪ'sɪprəkeɪt/ *v* **-cated, -cating** *fml* [I;T] to give or do (something) in return: *They invited us to their party, and we reciprocated (their* *invitation).* **–reciprocation** /-'keɪʃən/ *n* [U]

**re·cit·al** /rɪ'saɪtl/ *n* **1** a performance of poetry or esp. music, given by one performer or written by one writer: *to give a piano recital* **2** *fml* an account; report: *He gave us a long recital of his experiences.*

**re·cite** /rɪ'saɪt/ *v* **-cited, -citing** **1** [I;T] to say (something learned) aloud from memory, esp. as a public performance: *I don't like reciting poetry in public.* **2** [T] to give a list of: *He recited a list of his complaints.* **–recitation** /ˌresɪ'teɪʃən/ *n* [C;U]

**reck·less** /'rekləs/ *adj* [*of*] (of a person or behaviour) too hasty; not caring about danger: *reckless driving* **–recklessly** *adv* **–recklessness** *n* [U]

**reck·on** /'rekən/ *v* [T] **1** [+ *to-v/among, as*] to consider; regard: *She is reckoned (to be) a very good politician.|I reckon him as a friend/among my friends.* **2** [+(*that*)] *infml* to guess; suppose: *I reckon (that) he'll come soon.|How much do you reckon (that) she earns?* **3** to calculate; add up (an amount, cost, etc.): *My pay is reckoned from the 1st of the month.|She reckoned up the cost.*

**reckon on** sthg. *v prep* [T +*v-ing*] to expect; BANK **on:** *We didn't reckon on seeing him.*

**reckon with** sbdy./sthg. *v prep* [T] **1** to have to deal with: *If they try to dismiss you, they'll have the union to reckon with.* **2 to be reckoned with** to be taken into account seriously as a possible opponent, danger, etc.: *a woman to be reckoned with*

**reckon without** sbdy./sthg. *v prep* [T] to fail to consider: *When he decided to change his job he reckoned without the difficulty of selling his house.*

**reck·on·ing** /'rekənɪŋ/ *n* [U] **1** the act of calculating: *By my reckoning, it must be 60 kilometres from here to the coast.* **2 day of reckoning** the time when one must suffer for a mistake

**re·claim** /rɪ'kleɪm/ *v* [T *from*] **1** to claim the return of: *I want to reclaim some of the tax I paid last year.* **2** to make (land) fit for use: *to reclaim land from the sea* **3** to obtain (useful materials) from a waste product: *to reclaim valuable metal from old cars* **–reclamation** /ˌrekləˈmeɪʃən/ *n* [U]

**re·cline** /rɪ'klaɪn/ *v* **-clined, -clining** [I;T *against,on*] to lie back or down; be or put oneself in a position of rest: *recline on the bed|in a reclining position*

**re·cluse** /rɪ'kluːs||'rekluːs/ *n* a person who purposely lives alone away from the world –compare HERMIT

**rec·og·ni·tion** /ˌrekəg'nɪʃən/ *n* [S;U] **1** the act of recognizing: *Please accept this cheque* **in recognition of/as a recognition of** *all your help.* **2 change beyond/out of all recognition** to change so as to be impossible to recognize: *Illness and age had changed her out of all recognition.*

**rec·og·nize** ||also **-nise** *BrE* /'rekəgnaɪz/ *v* **-nized, -nizing** [T] **1** to know and remember (someone or something one has seen before): *I recognized Mary in the photograph.* **2** [*as*] to accept as being lawful or real, or as having value: *They refused to recognize our new government.|a recognized method of teaching English* **3** [+*that*] to see clearly; be prepared to agree: *I recognize that she is the best worker we have.* **4** to show official gratefulness for: *The government recognized his services by making him a lord.* **–recognizable** *adj* **–recognizably** *adv*

**re·coil** /rɪ'kɔɪl/ *v* [I] **1** [*from*] to draw back suddenly in fear or dislike: *She recoiled from her attacker.* **2** (of a gun) to spring back when fired **–recoil** /'riːkɔɪl, rɪ'kɔɪl/ *n* [S;U]

**rec·ol·lect** /ˌrekə'lekt/ *v* to remember (something formerly known): *Do you recollect her name?*

**rec·ol·lec·tion** /ˌrekə'lekʃən/ *n* **1** [U] the power or action of remembering the past **2** [C] something in one's memory of the past: *I have a vague recollection of living in the country when I was very young.*

**rec·om·mend** /ˌrekə'mend/ *v* **1** [T *as,for*] to make a favourable judgment of; praise: *Can you recommend a good dictionary (to me)?|They recommended him for the job/as a good lawyer.* **2** [T +*v-ing/that*] to advise or suggest: *I recommend that you inquire about the job.* **3** [T *to*] (of a quality) to make (someone or something) attractive: *This hotel has nothing to recommend it (to travellers) except cheapness.*

**rec·om·men·da·tion** /ˌrekəmen'deɪʃən/ *n* **1** [U] advice; the act of RECOMMENDing (1,2): *They bought the car on his recommendation.* **2** [C] a letter or statement that RECOMMENDs (1) (esp. someone for a job)

**rec·om·pense**[1] /'rekəmpens/ *v* **-pensed, -pensing** [T *for*] *fml* to give a RECOMPENSE[2] to

**recompense**[2] *n* [S;U *for*] *fml* (a) reward or payment for trouble or suffering: *They received £500 in recompense for the damage to their house.* –compare COMPENSATION

**rec·on·cile** /'rekənsaɪl/ *v* **-ciled, -ciling** [T *with*] **1** to make peace between: *They quarrelled but now they're completely reconciled.* **2** to find agreement between (two seemingly opposing actions or ideas): *How do you reconcile your political principles with your religious beliefs?* **–reconcilable** *adj*

**reconcile** sbdy. **to** sthg. *v prep* [T] to cause (someone) to accept (something unwanted or unpleasant): *He never became reconciled to the loss of his wife.*

**rec·on·cil·i·a·tion** /ˌrekənsɪli'eɪʃən/ *n* [S;U] (a) peace-making: *There was no hope of a reconciliation between the two families.*

**re·con·di·tion** /ˌriːkən'dɪʃən/ *v* [T] to repair and bring back into working order: *a reconditioned engine*

**re·con·nais·sance** /rɪ'kɒnəsəns||rɪ'kɑ-/ *n* [C;U] (an) act of reconnoitring (RECONNOITRE)

**re·con·noi·tre** ||also **-ter** *AmE* /ˌrekə'nɔɪtə<sup>r</sup>||ˌriː-/ *v* **-tred, -tring** [I;T] to go near (the place where an enemy is) in order to find out the enemy's numbers, position, etc.

**re·con·sid·er** /ˌriːkən'sɪdə<sup>r</sup>/ *v* [I;T] to think again and change one's mind about (a subject): *Won't you reconsider your decision to leave the club?* **–reconsideration** /-'reɪʃən / *n* [U]

**re·con·sti·tute** /riː'kɒnstɪtjuːt||riː'kɑnstɪtuːt/ *v* [T] **1** to bring back into existence, usu. in a changed form: *We decided to reconstitute the committee under a new chairman.* **2** to bring back (dried food) into its original condition by adding water: *to reconstitute milk powder|reconstituted potato*

**re·con·struct** /ˌriːkən'strʌkt/ *v* [T] **1** to rebuild after destruction or damage **2** to build up a complete description or picture of (something only partly known): *to reconstruct a crime from known facts*

–**reconstruction** /ˌriːkənˈstrʌkʃən / *n* [C;U]: *a reconstruction of the events before the crime*

**re·cord**[1] /rɪˈkɔːd‖-ɔrd/ *v* **1** [T] to write down so that it will be known: *to record the events of the past* **2** [I;T] to preserve (sound or a television broadcast) so that it can be heard and/or seen again: *The broadcast was recorded, not* LIVE[2] (4).|*She has recorded several songs.* **3** [T] (of an instrument) to show by measuring: *The* THERMOMETER *recorded a temperature of 28 degrees.*

**rec·ord**[2] /ˈrekɔːd‖-ərd/ *n* **1** a written statement of facts, amounts, events, etc.: *Keep a record of how much you spend.* **2** the known facts about someone's past behaviour: *She has a long criminal record.* **3** the best yet done; the highest/lowest figure ever reached: *to break/make/establish a record for long-distance swimming* **4** a circular piece of plastic on which sound is stored: *Have you heard my new record?* **5 off the record** *infml* unofficial(ly): *He told us off the record that the firm was doing badly this year.* **6 on record** (of facts or events) (ever) recorded: *the coldest winter on record*|*She is on record as having said that she opposed high taxation.*

**rec·ord**[3] /ˈrekɔːd‖-ərd/ *adj* [A] more, faster, better, etc., than ever before: *a record crop of corn*|*finished in record time*

**record-break·ing** /ˈ·· ˌ··/ *adj* (usu. in sport) that goes beyond the former RECORD[2] (3): *a record-breaking speed*

**recorded de·liv·er·y** /·ˌ·· ·ˈ···/ *n* [U] *BrE* the method of sending mail, by which proof that it has been delivered is obtained

**re·cord·er** /rɪˈkɔːdə<sup>r</sup>‖-ɔr-/ *n* **1** a wooden musical instrument like a whistle **2** → TAPE RECORDER

**re·cord·ing** /rɪˈkɔːdɪŋ‖-ɔr-/ *n* (esp. in broadcasting) a performance, speech, etc., that has been RECORDed[1] (2)

**record play·er** /ˈ·· ˌ··/ ‖**also phonograph** *AmE*– *n* an instrument which can turn the information stored on a RECORD[2] (4) back into the original sounds, music, etc.

**re·count**[1] /rɪˈkaʊnt/ *v* [T] *fml* to tell (a story): *She recounted the story of her travels across Asia.*

**re·count**[2] /ˌriːˈkaʊnt/ *v* [T] to count again: *They had to recount the votes.*

**re·count**[3] /ˈriːkaʊnt/ *n* a second or new count, esp. of votes

**re·coup** /rɪˈkuːp/ *v* [T] to regain (esp. money); get back: *I shall recoup my travelling* EXPENSES *from my employers.*

**re·course** /rɪˈkɔːs‖ˈriːkors/ *n* [U] a means of help: *The sick man* **had recourse to** (=made use of) *drugs to lessen his pain.* –compare RESORT (2); see RESOURCE (USAGE)

**re·cov·er** /rɪˈkʌvə<sup>r</sup>/ *v* **1** [T] to get back (something lost or taken away): *The police recovered the stolen jewellery.*| *She recovered consciousness soon after the accident.* **2** [I *from*] to return to the proper state of health, strength, ability, etc.: *The country has not yet recovered from the war.* –**recoverable** *adj*

**SPELLING NOTE**
Words with the sound /r/ may be spelt **wr-**, like **wrong.**

**re-cov·er** /ˌriːˈkʌvə<sup>r</sup>/ *v* [T] to put a new cover on

**re·cov·er·y** /rɪˈkʌvəri/ *n* **1** [U *of*] RECOVERing or being RECOVERED (1): *the recovery of the stolen jewels* **2** [S *from*] RECOVERing (2): *She made a quick recovery from her illness, and was soon back at work.*

**re-cre·ate** /ˌriːkriˈeɪt/ *v* **-ated,-ating** [T] to make again: *to recreate the past in one's imagination*

**rec·re·a·tion** /ˌrekriˈeɪʃən/ *n* [C;U] (a form of) amusement: *His only recreations are drinking beer and working in the garden.* –**recreational** *adj*

USAGE **Sport** is a form of **recreation** needing physical effort and usually played according to rules. A **game** may be either an example of this, or an activity in which people compete with each other using their brains. An important public **game** is a **match:** *I'm not really interested in* **sport**.|*My favourite* **sports** *are cricket and football.*|Let's have *a* **game** *of tennis/cards.*|*Have you got a ticket for the football* **match** *on Saturday?* A **hobby** is a form of **recreation** which people often do on their own, not in order to compete: *Her* **hobbies** *are gardening, stamp-collecting, and playing the piano.*

**re·crim·i·nate** /rɪˈkrɪmɪneɪt/ *v* **-nated, -nating** [I *against*] to blame a person who has treated one badly –**recriminatory** /-nətəri‖-tori / *adj* **-recrimination** /-ˈneɪʃən/ *n* [C;U]: *Let's make friends, instead of wasting our time on recrimination(s).*

**re·cruit**[1] /rɪˈkruːt/ *n* [*to*] a new member (esp. of the armed forces): *New recruits are always welcome.*

**recruit**[2] *v* **1** [I] to find RECRUITs: *a recruiting drive* (=special effort to recruit) *for the army* **2** [T] to get (someone) as a RECRUIT: *to recruit some new members* –**recruitment** *n* [U]

**rec·tan·gle** /ˈrektæŋgəl/ *n tech* a shape with four straight sides forming four RIGHT ANGLEs –compare SQUARE[1] (1), OBLONG

**rec·tan·gu·lar** /rekˈtæŋgjʊlə<sup>r</sup>‖-gjə-/ *adj tech* in the shape of a RECTANGLE

**rec·ti·fy** /ˈrektɪfaɪ/ *v* **-fied, -fying** [T] *fml* to put right: *Would you rectify the mistakes in my bill?* –**rectification** /-fɪˈkeɪʃən/ *n* [C;U]

**rec·tor** /ˈrektə<sup>r</sup>/ *n (the title of)* **1** (in the CHURCH OF ENGLAND) the priest in charge of a PARISH **2** the head of certain colleges and schools

**rec·to·ry** /ˈrektəri/ *n* **-ries** the house where a RECTOR (1) lives

**rec·tum** /ˈrektəm/ *n* **-tums** *or* **-ta** /tə/ *tech* the lowest end of the large bowel, from which solid waste matter passes to the ANUS

**re·cum·bent** /rɪˈkʌmbənt/ *adj fml* lying down: *a recumbent figure on the bed*

**re·cu·pe·rate** /rɪˈkjuːpəreɪt, -ˈkuː-/ *v* **-rated, -rating** [I] to get well again after illness: *You'll soon recuperate; all you need is a good holiday.* –**recuperation** /-ˈreɪʃən / *n* [U]

**re·cur** /rɪˈkɜː<sup>r</sup>/ *v* **-rr-** [I] to happen again, or more than once: *If the pain recurs, take this medicine.* –**recurrence** /rɪˈkʌrəns‖-ˈkɜr-/ *n* [U] –**recurrent** *adj* –**recurrently** *adv*

**re·cy·cle** /ˌriːˈsaɪkəl/ *v* **-cled, -cling** [T] to treat (a used substance) so that it is fit to use again: *The glass from bottles can be recycled.*|*a bag made of recycled paper*

**red**[1] /red/ *adj* **1** of the colour of blood: *Let's paint the door red.* **2** (of hair) of a bright brownish orange or copper colour **3** (of the human skin or lips) pink: *to turn red with shame or anger* –**redness** *n* [U]

**red**[2] *n* **1** [C;U] (a) red colour **2** [U] red clothes: *dressed in red* **3 in the red** in debt: *Your account is in the red.* –opposite **in the black 4 see red** to become angry suddenly and lose control of oneself

**Red**[1] *adj often derog* →COMMUNIST

**Red**[2] *n derog* a COMMUNIST

**red-blood·ed** /ˌ· '··◂/ *adj apprec* (of a person, behaviour, etc.) bold and strong: *a red-blooded young man*

**red·brick** /'redˌbrɪk/ *n* (*often cap.*) any English university started in the late 19th century in a city outside London –compare OXBRIDGE

**red car·pet** /ˌ· '··/ *n* [A;S] a special ceremonial welcome to a guest: *They gave him red-carpet treatment.*

**Red Cross** /ˌ· '·/ *n* [*the* U +*sing./pl.v*] an international Christian organization that looks after sick and wounded people

**red·cur·rant** /ˌred'kʌrənt◂‖-'kɜr-/ *n* a small red berry or the bush on which it grows

**red·den** /'redn/ *v* [I;T] to (cause to) turn red: *She reddened (with* EMBARRASSment*) when they praised her so much.|The sunset reddened the clouds.*

**red·dish** /'redɪʃ/ *adj* slightly red

**re·deem** /rɪ'diːm/ *v* [T] **1** *fml* to buy or gain the freedom of: *to redeem someone from* SIN **2** [*from*] to buy back (what was PAWNed or MORTGAGED) **3** to carry out; fulfil: *to redeem one's promise* **4 redeeming feature** a single good point in a person or thing that is bad in all other ways: *His only redeeming feature is his sense of humour.* –**redeemable** *adj*

**re·demp·tion** /rɪ'dempʃən/ *n* [U] **1** REDEEMing or being REDEEMed **2 beyond/past redemption** *fml* too evil to be REDEEMed (1)

**re·de·ploy** /ˌriːdɪ'plɔɪ/ *v* to rearrange (soldiers, workers, etc.) in a more effective way –**redeployment** *n* [U]

**red-hand·ed** /ˌ· '··◂/ *adj* [F] in the act of doing something wrong: *They* **caught** *the thief* **red-handed** *while he was just putting the diamonds in his pocket.*

**red·head** /'redhed/ *n infml* a woman with RED[1](2) hair: *He married a beautiful redhead.*

**red-hot** /ˌ· '·◂/ *adj* (of metal) so hot that it shines red

**Red In·di·an** /ˌ· '···/ *n not polite* → INDIAN (2)

**re·di·rect** /ˌriːdaɪ'rekt, -dʒ-/ *v* [T] → READDRESS

**red-let·ter** /ˌ· '··/ *n* **a red-letter day** a specially happy day that will be remembered: *It was a red-letter day for us when Paul came home from the war.*

**re·do** /riː'duː/ *v* **-did** /'dɪd/, **-done** /'dʌn/, *3rd person sing. present tense* **-does** /'dʌz/, **-doing** [T] to do again: *to redo a piece of work/one's hair*

**red·o·lent** /'redələnt/ *adj* [F +*of*] *fml* smelling of; or making one think of: *an old house redolent of mystery* –**redolence** *n* [U]

**re·doub·le** /riː'dʌbəl/ *v* **-led, -ling** [I;T] to (cause to) increase greatly: *The police redoubled their efforts to find the missing child.*

**re·doub·ta·ble** /rɪ'daʊtəbəl/ *adj lit & humor* greatly respected and feared: *a redoubtable opponent*

**re·dress**[1] /rɪ'dres/ *v* [T] *fml* **1** to put right (a wrong, injustice, etc.) **2 redress the balance** to make things equal again

**re·dress**[2] /rɪ'dres‖'riːdres/ *n fml* satisfaction or payment for a wrong that has been done: *You must* SEEK *redress in the law courts for the damage to your car.*

**red tape** /ˌ· '·/ *n* [U] detailed, often unnecessary rules that delay (esp. government) business

**re·duce** /rɪ'djuːs‖rɪ'duːs/ *v* **-duced, -ducing 1** [T *from, to*] to make smaller, cheaper, etc.: *I bought this shirt because it was reduced (from £3 to £2).|He won't reduce the rent of our house.* –compare INCREASE **2** [I] *infml* (of a person) to lose weight on purpose –**reducible** *adj*

**reduce** sbdy./sthg. **to** sthg. *v prep* [T] **1** to bring (something) to (a smaller size or simpler form): *The fire reduced the forest to a few trees.|We can reduce his statement to three simple facts.* **2** [*usu. pass.*] to bring (esp. someone) to (a weaker or less favourable state): *She was reduced to begging for her living.* **3 reduce someone to tears** to make someone cry

**re·duc·tion** /rɪ'dʌkʃən/ *n* [C;U] making or becoming smaller; the amount taken off in making something smaller: *some/a slight reduction in the price of food|price reductions* –compare INCREASE

**re·dun·dan·cy** /rɪ'dʌndənsi/ *n* **-cies** [C;U] (a case of) being REDUNDANT: *The government action will cause a lot of redundancy/many redundancies among coalminers.|A big redundancy payment* (=made to a worker who has become REDUNDANT)

**re·dun·dant** /rɪ'dʌndənt/ *adj* (esp. of a worker) not needed; more than is necessary: *Seventy men at the factory were* **made redundant** (=dismissed and not replaced) *because there was no work for them to do.|In the sentence "She lives alone by herself", the word "alone" is redundant.* –**redundantly** *adv*

**reed** /riːd/ *n* **1** a grasslike plant that grows in wet places **2** (in a musical instrument) a thin piece of wood or metal that produces sound by shaking (VIBRATION) when air is blown over it

**reef** /riːf/ *n* a line of sharp rocks or bank of sand on or near the surface of the sea: *The ship was wrecked on a reef.*

**reef knot** /'· ·/ *n* a double knot that will not come undone easily

**reek** /riːk/ *n* [S] a strong unpleasant smell: *a reek of tobacco and beer*

**reek of** sthg. *v prep* [T *no pass.*] to smell strongly and unpleasantly of: (fig.) *The sale of that house reeks of dishonesty.*

**reel**[1] /riːl/ *n* a round object on which a length of sewing thread, wire, cinema film, fishing line, recording TAPE[1] (2), etc., is wound –compare BOBBIN

**reel**[2] *v* [T *in, off, etc.*] to move by winding: *to reel in the fishing line*

**reel** sthg.↔ **off** *v adv* [T] → RATTLE **off**

**reel**[3] *v* [I] to (seem to) move unsteadily: *He came reeling up the street, drunk.|The room reeled before my eyes and I became unconscious.|When I hit him he reeled (back) and almost fell.*

**re·en·try** /riː'entri/ *n* **-tries** [C;U] (an act of) entering again: *The spacecraft made a successful reentry into the earth's* ATMOSPHERE.

**re·fec·to·ry** /rɪ'fektəri/ *n* **-ries** (in schools, colleges, etc.) a large hall in which meals are served

**ref·er·ee**[1] /ˌrefəˈriː/ *n* **1** also **ref** *infml*– a judge in charge of some games –see USAGE **2** a person who provides a REFERENCE (3)

USAGE **Referee** is used in connection with **basketball, billiards, boxing, football, hockey, rugby,** and **wrestling. Umpire** is used in connection with **badminton, baseball, cricket, swimming, tennis,** and **volleyball.** –see picture on page 592

**referee**[2] *v* **-eed, -eeing** [I;T] to act as REFEREE[1] (1) for (a game): *John will referee (the football match).*

**ref·er·ence** /ˈrefərəns/ *n* **1** [C;U *to*] (an example of) mentioning: *In the conversation, Janet kept making nasty references to me.* **2** [C;U *to*] (an example of) looking at something for information: *Use this dictionary for easy reference.* **3** [C] a piece of written information about someone's character, ability, etc., esp. when he or she is looking for employment: *When you look for a job, good references will help you.* –see also TESTIMONIAL **4 in/with reference to** *fml* in connection with

**reference book** /ˈ···· ·/ *n* a book that is looked at for information, e.g. a dictionary

**ref·e·ren·dum** /ˌrefəˈrendəm/ *n* **-da** /də/ *or* **-dums** a direct vote by all the people of a nation or area on some particular political question: *to decide the question by holding a referendum* –compare PLEBISCITE

**re·fer to** /rɪˈfɜːʳ/ *v prep* [T] **1** (**refer to** sbdy./sthg.) to mention; speak about: *Which companies was she referring to when she talked about competing firms?* **2** (**refer to** sthg.) to look at for information: *If you don't know what this means, refer to the dictionary.* **3** (**refer to** sbdy./sthg.) to concern; be directed towards: *The new law does not refer to land used for farming.* **4** (**refer** sbdy./sthg. **to** sbdy.) to send to (someone else) for decision or action: *The shop referred the complaint (back) to the manager.*

**re·fill**[1] /ˌriːˈfɪl/ *v* [T] to fill again: *I'll refill my cigarette lighter with gas.*

**re·fill**[2] /ˈriːfɪl/ *n* (a container holding) a quantity of ink, petrol, etc., to REFILL[1] something

**re·fine** /rɪˈfaɪn/ *v* **-fined, -fining** [T] to make pure: *Oil must be refined before it can be used.*

**re·fined** /rɪˈfaɪnd/ *adj* **1** made pure: *refined oil* **2** (of a person, behaviour, etc.) having, showing, or intending to show education and gentleness of manners: *a refined way of speaking* –opposite **unrefined**

**re·fine·ment** /rɪˈfaɪnmənt/ *n* **1** [C *on*] a useful addition or improvement: *The new car has many new refinements such as a radio.* **2** [U] the act of making pure: *the refinement of sugar* **3** [U] the quality of being REFINED (2): *a woman of great refinement*

**re·fin·e·ry** /rɪˈfaɪnəri/ *n* **-ries** a building and apparatus for refining (REFINE) metals, oil, or sugar: *a sugar refinery*

**re·flect** /rɪˈflekt/ *v* **1** [T] to throw back (heat, light, sound, or an image): *The mirror reflected my face.* **2** [T] to express; give an idea of: *Does the letter reflect your real opinions?* **3** [I;T +*that/on*] to think carefully: *I have been reflecting on what you said.*

> **SPELLING NOTE**
> Words with the sound /r/ may be spelt **wr-**, like **wrong.**

**reflect on** sbdy./sthg. *v prep* [T] **1** (of an action or event)to cause to be seen or considered in a particular, usu. unfavourable way: *The latest unemployment figures reflect badly on the government's policies.*

**re·flec·tion** /rɪˈflekʃən/ *n* **1** [C] an image REFLECTed (1) in a mirror or polished surface: *We looked at our reflections in the lake.* **2** [U] the REFLECTing (1) of heat, light, sound, or an image: *The moon looks bright because of the reflection of light.* **3** [C;U] (a) deep and careful thought: *his reflections on Indian politics*|**On reflection,** *he agreed to the plan.*

**re·flec·tor** /rɪˈflektəʳ/ *n* a surface that REFLECTs (1) light –see picture on page 85

**re·flex** /ˈriːfleks/ *n* an unintentional movement that is made in reply to some outside influence: *The doctor hit my knee with a hammer to test my reflexes.*|*I can't help closing my eyes when I see a bright light–it's a* **reflex action.**

**re·flex·ive** /rɪˈfleksɪv/ *n,adj* (a word) showing that the action in the sentence has its effect on the person or thing that does the action: *In "He cut himself", "himself" is a* **reflexive pronoun.**

**re·form**[1] /rɪˈfɔːm‖-ɔrm/ *v* [I;T] to (cause to) improve; make or become right: *Harry has completely reformed/is a completely reformed character now–he's stopped taking drugs.* **–reformer** *n*

**reform**[2] *n* [C;U] (an) action that improves conditions or effectiveness, removes unfairness, etc.: *social reforms*|*a reform of the tax system*

**ref·or·ma·tion** /ˌrefəˈmeɪʃən‖-fər-/ *n* [C;U] (an) improvement; REFORMING[1] or being reformed: *a complete reformation in Harry's character*

**Reformation** *n* [*the* S] the religious movement in Europe in the 16th century leading to the establishment of the PROTESTANT churches

**re·fract** /rɪˈfrækt/ *v* [T] (of water, glass, etc.) to cause (light) to change direction when passing through at an angle **–refraction** *n* [U]: *Refraction makes a straight stick look bent if it is partly in water.*

**re·frain**[1] /rɪˈfreɪn/ *v* [I *from*] to hold oneself back from doing something: *Please refrain from smoking.*

**refrain**[2] *n* a part of a song that is repeated, esp. at the end of each VERSE: *They all sang the refrain.*

**re·fresh** /rɪˈfreʃ/ *v* [T] to cause to feel fresh or active again: *A hot bath will refresh you.*|*He refreshed himself with a glass of beer.*|*I looked at the map to* **refresh my memory** *of* (=help me remember) *the road.*

**refresher course** /·ˈ·· ·/ *n* a training course given to a group of members of the same profession to bring their knowledge up to date: *to hold/attend a refresher course on modern teaching methods*

**re·fresh·ing** /rɪˈfreʃɪŋ/ *adj* **1** producing a feeling of comfort and new strength: *a refreshing sleep* **2** pleasantly new and interesting: *It's refreshing to talk to such a truthful person.* **–refreshingly** *adv*

**re·fresh·ment** /rɪˈfreʃmənt/ *n* [*often pl.*] food and drink, esp. provided at a meeting, public event, etc.: *Refreshments will be served after the meeting.*

**re·fri·ge·rate** /rɪˈfrɪdʒəreɪt/ *v* **-rated, -rating** [T] to make (food, liquid, etc.) cold, as a way of preserving; freeze: *refrigerated meat/beer* **–refrigeration** /-ˈreɪʃən/ *n* [U]

**re·fri·ge·ra·tor** /rɪˈfrɪdʒəreɪtəʳ/ *n* fml for FRIDGE

**re·fu·el** /ˌriːˈfjuːəl/ *v* **-ll-** *BrE*‖**-l-** *AmE* [I;T] to (cause to) fill up again with FUEL: *The aircraft refuelled at Cairo.*

**ref·uge** /ˈrefjuːdʒ/ *n* [C;U] (a place that provides) protection or shelter from danger: *a mountain refuge for climbers|They* **took refuge** (=found shelter) *under a tree.*

**ref·u·gee** /ˌrefjʊˈdʒiː/ *n* a person who has been driven from his/her country for political reasons or during a war

**re·fund**[1] /rɪˈfʌnd/ *v* [T] to give (money) as a REFUND[2]: *They refunded (us) our money.*

**re·fund**[2] /ˈriːfʌnd/ *n* [C;U] (a) repayment: *to demand a refund on unsatisfactory goods*

**re·fus·al** /rɪˈfjuːzəl/ *n* [C;U +*to-v*] (a case of) refusing: *My offer to buy the house met with* (=was answered with) *a cold refusal.*

**re·fuse**[1] /rɪˈfjuːz/ *v* **-fused, -fusing** [I;T +*to-v*] not to accept or do or give: *She refused to marry him.|She refused his offer.* –opposite **accept**

USAGE **Refuse, reject, decline,** and **turn down** are all used to show failure to agree to an offer or request, but they are not exactly the same. **Decline** suggests a polite refusal (esp. of an offer or invitation) but **refuse** is less polite and suggests more firmness: *I'm afraid I must* **decline** *your invitation/***decline** *to answer that question.|The prisoner* **refused** *to give his name.|They've* **refused** *(us) permission to build on this land.* **Turn down** is similar to **refuse:** *I wrote to them about the job, but they* **turned** *me* **down. Reject** suggests a complete refusal to consider (an offer or suggestion) or to accept (a person): *The railway workers have* **rejected** *the government's pay offer.|He feels* **rejected** *by society.*

**ref·use**[2] /ˈrefjuːs/ *n* [U] *fml* waste material: *kitchen refuse*

**re·fute** /rɪˈfjuːt/ *v* **-futed, -futing** [T] to prove to be wrong: *I refuted him/his argument easily.|to refute the claim that the world is flat* –see also IRREFUTABLE **–refutation** /ˌrefjʊˈteɪʃən/ *n* [C;U]

**re·gain** /rɪˈgeɪn/ *v* [T] to get or win (something) back: *to regain one's health* **2** *lit* to reach (a place) again

**re·gal** /ˈriːgəl/ *adj* very splendid; of, like, or suitable for a king or queen: *a regal old lady* **–regally** *adv*

**re·gale** sbdy. **with** sthg. /rɪˈgeɪl/ *v prep* **- galed, -galing** [T] to give enjoyment to (oneself or another) with: *He regaled us with some stories about his youth.*

**re·ga·li·a** /rɪˈgeɪlɪə/ *n* [U] ceremonial clothes and decorations, esp. those used at official ceremonies: *a* MAYOR*'s regalia*

**re·gard**[1] /rɪˈgɑːd||-ɑrd/ *n* [U] **1** respect: *I hold her in high/low/the greatest regard.* **2** [*for, to*] respectful attention: *You have no regard for my feelings!* **3 in/with regard to** →REGARDING

**regard**[2] *v* [T] **1** [*as, with*] to consider: *I have always regarded him highly/with the greatest admiration.|I regard him as my friend.* **2** *fml* to look at: *She regarded him thoughtfully.*

**re·gard·ing** /rɪˈgɑːdɪŋ||-ɑr-/ also **as regards, re–** *prep fml* (esp. in business letters) on the subject of; in connection with: *Regarding your recent enquiry . . .*

**re·gard·less** /rɪˈgɑːdl$\frac{1}{3}$s||-ɑr-/ *adv infml* whatever may happen: *Get the money, regardless!*

**regardless of** *prep* without worrying about: *They decorated the house regardless of the cost.*

**re·gards** /rɪˈgɑːdz||-ɑr-/ *n* [P] good wishes: *Give him my (best) regards.*

**re·gat·ta** /rɪˈgætə/ *n* a meeting for races between rowing or sailing boats

**re·gen·cy** /ˈriːdʒənsi/ *n* [U] (the period of) government by a REGENT

**re·gent** /ˈriːdʒənt/ *n* (*often cap.*) a person who governs in place of a king or ruling queen who is ill, absent, or still a child **–regent** *adj* [after *n*]: *the Prince Regent*

**reg·gae** /ˈregeɪ/ *n* [U] (*often cap.*) a type of popular music from the West Indies with a strong, continually repeated BEAT[2] (2)

**re·gime** /reɪˈdʒiːm/ *n* a particular (type of) government: *The country is under a military regime.*

**re·gi·ment**[1] /ˈredʒ$\frac{1}{3}$mənt/ *n* [C +*sing./pl. v*] a large military group, commanded by a COLONEL: *His regiment is/are going abroad.***–regimental** /-ˈmentl/ *adj* [A]: *the regimental band*

**re·gi·ment**[2] /ˈredʒ$\frac{1}{3}$ment/ *v* [T] *derog* to control (people) firmly: *a very regimented school* **–regimentation** /ˌredʒ$\frac{1}{3}$menˈteɪʃən||-mən-/ *n* [U]

**re·gion** /ˈriːdʒən/ *n* **1** a fairly large area or part without exact boundaries: *the southern region of England|a pain in the region of the heart* **2 in the region of** about: *It will cost in the region of £200.* **–regional** *adj* **–regionally** *adv*

**re·gis·ter**[1] /ˈredʒ$\frac{1}{3}$stə[r]/ *n* **1** (a book containing) a record or list: *to keep a register of births and deaths|The teacher can't find his school attendance register.* –see also CASH REGISTER **2** *tech* the range of a human voice or musical instrument

**register**[2] *v* **1** [T] to put into an official list or record: *to register the birth of a baby* **2** [I] to enter one's name on a list: *to register at a hotel/as an elector* **3** [T] to show; record: *The* THERMOMETER *registered 35°C.|She/Her face registered anxiety.* **4** [T] to send by REGISTERED POST: *a registered letter*

**registered post** /ˌ··· ˈ·/ *BrE*||**registered mail** *AmE*– *n* [U] a postal service which, for an additional charge, protects the sender of a valuable letter or parcel against loss

**register of·fice** /ˈ··· ˌ··/ also **registry office**– *n* an office where marriages can legally take place and where births, marriages, and deaths are recorded

**re·gis·trar** /ˌredʒ$\frac{1}{3}$ˈstrɑː[r]◄||ˈredʒ$\frac{1}{3}$strɑr/ *n* a keeper of official records, esp. in a REGISTER OFFICE

**re·gis·tra·tion** /ˌredʒ$\frac{1}{3}$ˈstreɪʃən/ *n* [U] the act of REGISTERING[2] (1,2)

**registration num·ber** /··ˈ·· ˌ··/ *n* the official set of numbers and letters that must be shown on the front and back of a car

**re·gis·try** /ˈredʒ$\frac{1}{3}$stri/ *n* **-tries** a place where records are kept

**re·gress** /rɪˈgres/ *v* [I] to return to an earlier, less developed state –see also PROGRESS **–regression** *n* [U]

**re·gret**[1] /rɪˈgret/ *v* **-tt-** [T +*v-ing/that*] to feel upset or be sorry about (a sad fact or event):|*We've always regretted selling the farm.|She regrets that she can't come.|(fml)* **We regret to inform you** (=we are sorry to say) *that you owe the bank £1000.*

**regret**[2] *n* [U] unhappiness (at the loss of something, at a sad event, etc.): *They said goodbye with great* *regret.*|*He said he* **had no regrets** *about leaving the university.* –**regretful** *adj* –**regretfully** *adv*

**re·gret·ta·ble** /rɪ'gretəbəl/ *adj* that one should feel sorry about: *His behaviour at the party was most regrettable.* –**regrettably** *adv: regrettably drunk*

**re·group** /ˌriː'gruːp/ *v* [I,T] to (cause to) form into new groups or into groups again

**reg·u·lar**[1] /'regjʊləʳ‖-gjə-/ *adj* **1** happening, coming, doing something, again and again with the same length of time between each occasion: *They could hear the regular* TICK *of the clock.*|*a regular customer*|*regular working hours* **2** happening every time: *regular attendance at church* –opposite **irregular 3** not varying: *You must drive at a regular speed if you want to save petrol.* **4** [A *no comp.*] professional; not just employed for a time: *the regular army* **5** evenly shaped: *He has regular* FEATURES. (=of the face) **6** [A *no comp.*] *infml* complete; thorough: *That child is a regular actor–when he cries, he's only pretending.*

**regular**[2] *n* **1** *infml* a REGULAR[1] (1) visitor, customer, etc. **2** a soldier who is a member of an army kept by a country all the time

**reg·u·lar·i·ty** /ˌregjʊ'lærǰti‖-jə-/ *n* [U] the quality of being REGULAR[1]

**reg·u·lar·ly** /'regjʊləli‖-jələrli/ *adv* at REGULAR[1] (1) times: *Take the medicine regularly three times a day.*

**reg·u·late** /'regjʊleɪt‖-gjə-/ *v* **-lated, -lating** [T] to control or put into correct order: *to regulate one's habits/the amount of petrol entering the engine*

**reg·u·la·tion** /ˌregjʊ'leɪʃən‖-gjə-/ *n* **1** [C] an esp. official rule or order: *regulations governing the sale of guns* **2** [U] control; bringing of order: *the regulation of public spending*

**re·gur·gi·tate** /rɪ'gɜːdʒǰteɪt‖-ɜr-/ *v* **-tated, -tating** [T] *fml* to pour (food already swallowed) out again from the mouth –**regurgitation** /-'teɪʃən / *n* [U]

**re·ha·bil·i·tate** /ˌriːhə'bɪlǰteɪt/ *v* **-tated, -tating** [T] **1** to make able to live an ordinary life again, as by training: *to rehabilitate criminals* **2** to put back into good condition: *to rehabilitate old houses* –**rehabilitation** /-'teɪʃən/ *n* [U]

**re·hash** /riː'hæʃ/ *v* [T] *infml* to use (the same ideas) again in a new form which is not really different or better: *a politician who keeps rehashing the same old speech* –**rehash** /'riːhæʃ/ *n*

**re·hears·al** /rɪ'hɜːsəl‖-ɜr-/ *n* [C;U] the act or an occasion of rehearsing (REHEARSE): *The play needed many rehearsals.*|*At a* **dress rehearsal** *the actors wear the clothes they will wear in the performance.*

**re·hearse** /rɪ'hɜːs‖- ɜrs/ *v* **-hearsed, -hearsing** [I;T] to practise (something) for later performance: *The actors were rehearsing (a play) in the theatre.*

**re·house** /ˌriː'haʊz/ *v* **-housed, -housing** [T] to put (someone) into a new or better house: *a plan to rehouse poor people in better homes*

**reign**[1] /reɪn/ *n* a period of REIGNing: *during the reign of King George*

**reign**[2] *v* [I *over*] **1** to be the king or queen **2** *lit* to exist: *Silence reigned once more after the thunder.*

> **SPELLING NOTE**
> Words with the sound /r/ may be spelt **wr-**, like **wrong.**

**re·im·burse** /ˌriːǰm'bɜːs‖-ɜrs/ *v fml* to pay (money) back to (a spender): *We will reimburse you (for) the money you spent.* –**reimbursement** *n* [U]

**rein** /reɪn/ *n* **1** a long narrow band usu. of leather, by which a horse (or sometimes a small child) is controlled and guided **2 give (free) rein to** to give freedom to (feelings or desires): *to give free rein to one's imagination* **3 keep a tight rein on** to control firmly

**re·in·car·nate** /ˌriːɪn'kɑːneɪt, ˌ···'·‖-ɑr-/ *v* **-nated, -nating** [T *as; usu. pass.*] to cause to return to life in a new body, after death: *I believe I will be reincarnated as a snake.*

**re·in·car·na·tion** /ˌriːɪnkɑː'neɪʃən‖-ɑr-/ *n* **1** [U] the act or fact of being REINCARNATED: *Buddhists believe in reincarnation* **2** [C] the creature that results

**rein·deer** /'reɪndɪəʳ/ *n* **reindeer** a type of large deer with long branching horns

**re·in·force** /ˌriːǰn'fɔːs‖-'fors/ *v* **-forced, -forcing** [T] to strengthen by adding esp. materials or people: *to reinforce a coat by sewing pieces of leather on the elbows*|*to reinforce an army* –**reinforcement** *n*: *This roof needs reinforcement.*

**re·in·force·ments** /ˌriːǰn'fɔːsmənts‖-'fors-/ *n* [P] more people sent to REINFORCE an army

**re·in·state** /ˌriːǰn'steɪt/ *v* **-stated, -stating** [T *as, in*] to put back into a position formerly held: *He was dismissed, but was later reinstated (as a toolmaker/in his former job).* –**reinstatement** *n* [C;U]

**re·it·e·rate** /riː'ɪtəreɪt/ *v* **-rated, -rating** [T] to repeat several times: *The miners have reiterated their demands for more money.* –**reiteration** /-'reɪʃən/ *n* [C;U]

**re·ject**[1] /rɪ'dʒekt/ *v* [T] **1** to refuse to accept: *She rejected my suggestion.* **2** to throw away as useless or imperfect: *to choose the good apples and reject the bad ones* –see REFUSE (USAGE)

**re·ject**[2] /'riːdʒekt/ *n* something REJECTed[1] (2)

**re·jec·tion** /rɪ'dʒekʃən/ *n* [C;U] (an example of) REJECTing or being rejected: *I was annoyed at her rejection of my offer.*

**re·joice** /rɪ'dʒɔɪs/ *v* **-joiced, -joicing** [I;T *+to-v/that*] *fml & lit* to feel or show great joy: *to rejoice at/over good news*

**re·joic·ing** /rɪ'dʒɔɪsɪŋ/ *n* [U] *fml* great joy, esp. shown by a number of people

**re·join·der** /rɪ'dʒɔɪndəʳ/ *n* an answer, esp. a rude one

**re·ju·ve·nate** /rɪ'dʒuːvəneɪt/ *v* **-nated, -nating** [T *often pass.*] to make young again: *The mountain air will rejuvenate you.* –**rejuvenation** /- 'neɪʃən / *n* [U]

**re·lapse** *v* **-lapsed, -lapsing** [I *into*] to fall back (into a bad state of health or way of life) after an improvement; return: *He relapsed into his old bad habits.* –**relapse** /'riːlæps, rɪ'læps/ *n: He can't return to work because he's had a relapse.*

**re·late** /rɪ'leɪt/ *v* **-lated, -lating** [T] *fml* **1** to tell (a story) **2** to see or show a connection between: *I can't relate those two ideas.*

**relate to** *v prep* [T] **1** (**relate** sthg. **to/with** sthg.) to connect (one thing) with (another): *I can't relate what he does to what he says.* **2** (**relate to** sbdy./sthg.) →REFER TO(3)

**re·lat·ed** /rɪ'leɪtǰd/ *adj* [*by, to*] connected; of the same family or kind: *We are related by marriage.|banking and related matters*

**re·la·tion** /rɪ'leɪʃən/ *n* **1** [C] a member of one's family: *to invite all your relations to stay at Christmas* **2** [U] also **relationship**– connection: *the relation between wages and prices*

**re·la·tions** /rɪ'leɪʃənz/ *n* [P *between, with*] way of treating and thinking of each other: *to have/establish friendly relations with someone*

**re·la·tion·ship** /rɪ'leɪʃənʃɪp/ *n* [C;U] **1** family or personal connection: *My relationship with my boyfriend has lasted six months now.|the relationship between the police and the local people* **2** →RELATION (2)

**rel·a·tive**[1] /'relətɪv/ *n fml* for RELATION (1): *My uncle is my closest relative.*

**relative**[2] *adj* compared to each other or to something else: *the relative costs of building in stone and brick|After his money troubles, he's now living in relative comfort.* –compare ABSOLUTE

**rel·a·tive·ly** /'relətɪvli/ *adv* quite; when compared to others of the same kind: *She walks relatively fast for a small child.*

**relative pro·noun** /ˌ··· '··/ *n tech* a word like *who, which*, or *that: In "The man who lives next door is a doctor", "who" is a relative pronoun.*

**rel·a·tiv·i·ty** /ˌrelə'tɪvəti/ *n* [U] (*often cap.*) the relationship between time, size, and mass, which are said to change with increased speed: *Einstein's* THEORY *of relativity*

**re·lax** /rɪ'læks/ *v* **1** [I;T] to make or become less active or worried: *Sit down and relax!|The music will help to relax you.* **2** [I;T] to make or become less stiff or tight: *His muscles relaxed.* –compare TENSE[3] **3** [T] to make (effort or control) less severe: *You must not relax your control for a moment.*

**re·lax·a·tion** /ˌri:læk'seɪʃən/ *n* **1** [C;U] (something done for) rest and amusement: *Playing the piano is one of his favourite relaxations.* **2** [U] the act of RELAXing or condition of being RELAXed: *the relaxation of controls on government spending*

**re·lay**[1] /'ri:leɪ/ *n* [C;U] **1** one part of a team or organization, that takes its turn in keeping an activity going continuously, a new group taking the place of the first one: *groups of men working* **in/by relay(s)** *to clear the blocked railway line|A* **relay (race)** *is a race in which each member of each team runs part of the distance.* **2** a system or apparatus that receives and passes on messages by telephone, radio, etc.: *a broadcast from America by relay*

**re·lay**[2] /'ri:leɪ/ *v* [T] to send out by RELAY[1] (2): *to relay a broadcast*

**re·lease**[1] /rɪ'li:s/ *v* **-leased, -leasing** [T] **1** [*from*] to set free; allow to come out: *to release a prisoner from prison|to release the* HANDBRAKE *of a car* **2** to allow **a** (a new film or record) to be shown or bought publicly **b** (a news story or piece of government information) to be made known: *The new trade figures have just been released.*

**release**[2] *n* **1** [S;U *from*] a setting free: *After his release from prison he came home.* **2** [C] a letter or message that sets free: *The governor of the prison signed the release.* **3** something such as a new film or piece of information that has been RELEASED[1] (2): *The new release is at our local cinema.* **4 on general release** (of a film) able to be seen at all the cinemas in an area

**rel·e·gate** /'reləgeɪt/ *v* **-gated, -gating** [T *to*] to put into a lower or worse position: *to relegate the old furniture to the children's room|Everyone was surprised when the football team was relegated (to a lower division).*

**re·lent** /rɪ'lent/ *v* [I] to have or show pity; become less cruel: *At first she threatened to dismiss us all, but later she relented.*

**re·lent·less** /rɪ'lentləs/ *adj* without pity: *a relentless enemy* **–relentlessly** *adv: He beat the dog relentlessly.*

**rel·e·vant** /'reləvənt/ *adj* [F *to*] connected with the subject: *His nationality isn't relevant to whether he's a good lawyer/isn't a relevant point.* –opposite **irrelevant –relevance** *n* [U *to*]: *What you say has no relevance to what we're talking about.* **–relevantly** *adv*

**re·li·a·ble** /rɪ'laɪəbəl/ *adj* able to be trusted; dependable: *She may forget to come–she's not very reliable.|a reliable pair of boots* –opposite **unreliable –reliability** /-ə'bɪləti/ *n* [U] **–reliably** *adv: I am reliably informed that he takes drugs.*

**re·li·ant** /rɪ'laɪənt/ *adj* [F *on*] depending on; RELYing ON: *Our country should not be so reliant on the oil it produces.* –compare SELF-RELIANT **–reliance** *n* [U *on*]

**rel·ic** /'relɪk/ *n* **1** a part of the body or clothing of a holy person which is kept and respected after his/her death **2** something old that reminds us of the past: *This stone axe is a relic of ancient times.*

**re·lief** /rɪ'li:f/ *n* **1** [S;U] (a) feeling of comfort at the ending of anxiety, fear, or pain: *a drug for the relief of pain|You're safe! What a relief!* **2** [U] help for people in trouble: *The government sent relief* (=money, food, clothes) *to the people who lost their homes in the flood.* **3** [C +*sing./pl.v*] a person or group taking from another the responsibility for a duty: *The relief for the military guard is/are expected soon.|a relief driver* **4** [C;U] (a shape or) decoration which stands out above the rest of the surface it is on

**re·lieve** /rɪ'li:v/ *v* **-lieved, -lieving** [T] **1** to lessen (pain or trouble): *a drug that relieves headaches* **2** to take a duty from (someone) as a RELIEF (3): *The guard will be relieved at midnight.* **3** to give variety to; make more interesting: *to relieve a dull evening with a little dancing*

**relieve** sbdy. **of** sthg. *v prep* [T] to take from (someone) (something heavy to carry or hard to do): *Let me relieve you of that heavy parcel.*

**re·lieved** /rɪ'li:vd/ *adj* [F +*to-v*/(*that*)] given RELIEF (1): *Your mother will be very relieved (to hear that you are safe).*

**re·li·gion** /rɪ'lɪdʒən/ *n* [C;U] (a particular system of) belief in one or more gods, esp. the belief that he/she/they made the world and can control it

**re·li·gious** /rɪ'lɪdʒəs/ *adj* [A] **1** of or concerning religion: *a religious service* **2** (of a person or behaviour) obeying the rules of a religion very carefully: *a very religious man* **3** performing duties very carefully, as a matter of conscience

**re·li·gious·ly** /rɪ'lɪdʒəsli/ *adv* faithfully and regularly: *He washes the floor religiously every morning.*

**re·lin·quish** /rɪ'lɪŋkwɪʃ/ *v* [T] *fml* to give up; yield:

*He relinquished his claim to the land.*

**rel·ish**[1] /ˈrelɪʃ/ *n* **1** [U] (a great deal of) enjoyment, esp. of food; pleasure: *He drank the wine with relish.* **2** [C;U] (a) substance eaten with a meal, such as PICKLES or SAUCE, to add taste and interest

**relish**[2] *v* [T +*v-ing*] to enjoy; be pleased with: *John won't relish having to wash all those dishes.*

**re·live** /ˌriːˈlɪv/ *v* **-lived, -living** [T] to experience again in the imagination: *to relive one's childhood*

**re·lo·cate** /ˌriːləʊˈkeɪt‖riːˈləʊkeɪt/ *v* **-cated, -cating** [I;T] to move to or set up in a new place: *The factory has been relocated.* –**relocation** /-ˈkeɪʃən/ *n* [U]

**re·luc·tant** /rɪˈlʌktənt/ *adj* [F +*to-v*] unwilling, and therefore perhaps slow to act: *to give a reluctant promise|He was very reluctant to help.* –**reluctance** *n* [S;U] –**reluctantly** *adv*

**re·ly on** sbdy./sthg. /rɪˈlaɪ/ also **rely upon** sbdy./sthg.– *v prep* **-lied, -lying** [T +*v-ing*] to trust (esp. that something will happen or someone will do something): *You can't rely on the weather.|Don't rely on the bank lending you the money* (=perhaps they won't)|*You can rely on me (to help you).*

**re·main** /rɪˈmeɪn/ *v* **1** [I] to stay or be left behind after others have gone: *Of the seven brothers only four now remain; the rest are dead.* **2** to continue to be (in an unchanged state): *Peter became a judge but John remained a fisherman.* –see STAY (USAGE)

**re·main·der** /rɪˈmeɪndəʳ/ *n* [*the* U +*sing./pl.v*] what is left over; the rest: *The remainder of the books are in the box.|The remainder is in the box.*

**re·mains** /rɪˈmeɪnz/ *n* [P] **1** [*of*] parts which are left: *the remains of dinner/of an old castle* **2** *fml* a dead body: *His remains lie in the churchyard.*

**re·make** /ˌriːˈmeɪk/ *v* **-made, -making** [T] to make (esp. a film) again –**remake** /ˈriːmeɪk/ *n*

**re·mand** /rɪˈmɑːnd‖rɪˈmænd/ *v* [T *usu.pass.*] to send back to prison from a court of law, to be tried later (often in the phrase **remanded in custody**) –**remand** *n* [C;U]: *He's* **on remand**. (=in prison waiting for a *trial)*

**re·mark**[1] /rɪˈmɑːk‖-ɑrk/ *v* [T +*that*] to say, esp. something which one has just noticed; give as an opinion: *He remarked that it was getting late.*

**remark on** sthg. **also remark upon** sthg.– *v prep* [T] to say or write something about: *Everyone remarked loudly on his absence.*

**remark**[2] *n* [*about,on*] a spoken or written opinion; COMMENT[1]: *to make/pass rude remarks about her appearance*

**re·mar·ka·ble** /rɪˈmɑːkəbəl‖-ɑr-/ *adj* worth speaking of; unusual or noticeable: *a most remarkable sunset* –**remarkably** *adv*: *a remarkably fine day* –see Study Notes on page 389

**re·me·di·al** /rɪˈmiːdɪəl/ *adj* [*no comp.*] curing or helping; providing a REMEDY: *to do remedial exercises for a weak back* –**remedially** *adv*

**rem·e·dy**[1] /ˈremədi/ *n* **-dies** [C;U *for*] a cure: *Alcohol is the best remedy for colds.*

**remedy**[2] *v* **-died, -dying** [T] to put or make right (anything bad): *to remedy an injustice/ a fault/a loss*

**SPELLING NOTE**

Words with the sound /r/ may be spelt **wr-**, like **wrong.**

**re·mem·ber** /rɪˈmembəʳ/ *v* **1** [I;T +*v-ing*/(*that*)] to keep in the memory; call back into the mind: *Certainly I posted your letter–I remember posting it.|I can't remember how to get there/where she lives/what happened then.* **2** [I;T +*to-v*] to take care not to forget: *Remember to post my letter!* –opposite **forget** (for 1,2) **3** [T] *often euph* to give money or a present to: *She always remembers me at Christmas.*

**remember** sbdy. **to** sbdy. *v prep* [T] *infml* to send greetings from (someone) to: *Please remember me to your mother.*

USAGE Note the difference between **remember** +*v-ing* and **remember** +*to-v*: *I* **remember** *locking the door as I left the house* (=I locked it and can call this event to mind).|*I* **remembered** *to lock the door as I left the house* (=I took care not to forget to do this).

**re·mem·brance** /rɪˈmembrəns/ *n* **1** [C;U *of*] the state or act of remembering: *a church service in remembrance of those killed in the war* –see MEMORY **2** [C *of*] something kept or given to remind one: *He gave me his photograph as a remembrance (of him).*

**re·mind** /rɪˈmaɪnd/ *v* [T +*that/of*] to tell or cause (someone) to remember (a fact, or to do something): *Remind me to write to Mother.|She reminded me that I hadn't written to Mother.|I've forgotten how to do this; will you remind me?|The sight of the clock reminded me that I was late.*

**remind** sbdy. **of** sbdy./sthg. *v prep* [T] to cause to remember (someone or something) by seeming the same: *This hotel reminds me of the one we stayed in last year.*

**re·mind·er** /rɪˈmaɪndəʳ/ *n* something, esp. a letter, to make one remember: *He hadn't paid the bill, so the shop sent him a reminder.*

**rem·i·nisce** /ˌreməˈnɪs/ *v* **-nisced, -niscing** [I] to talk pleasantly about the past: *The old friends reminisced (about their youth).* –**reminiscence** *n* [C;U]

**rem·i·nis·cent** /ˌreməˈnɪsənt/ *adj* [F *of*] that reminds one of; like: *This hotel is reminiscent of the one we stayed in last year.|a taste reminiscent of chicken*

**re·miss** /rɪˈmɪs/ *adj* [F] *fml* careless, esp. about a duty: *It was remiss of me not to answer your letter.*

**re·mis·sion** /rɪˈmɪʃən/ *n* **1** [U] the act of REMITting (1) **2** [C;U] (a) lessening of the time a person has to stay in prison: *The prisoner was given six months' remission for good behaviour.*

**re·mit** /rɪˈmɪt/ *v* **-tt-** *fml* **1** [T] to free someone from (a debt or punishment) **2** [I;T] to send (money) by post: *to remit a cheque*

**re·mit·tance** /rɪˈmɪtəns/ *n* an amount of money REMITted (2)

**rem·nant** /ˈremnənt/ *n* **1** a part that remains: *the remnants of a feast* **2** a small piece of cloth left over from a larger piece and sold cheap: *a remnant sale*

**rem·on·strate** /ˈremənstreɪt‖rɪˈmɑn-/ *v* **-strated, -strating** [I *against,with*] *fml* to complain; express disapproval: *to remonstrate with him* (=complain to him) *about his behaviour* –**remonstrance** /rɪˈmɒnstrəns‖-ˈmɑn-/ *n* [C;U]

**re·morse** /rɪˈmɔːs‖-ɔrs/ *n* sorrow for having done wrong: *He felt/He was filled with remorse after hitting the child.* –**remorseful** *adj* –**remorsefully** *adv* –**remorseless** *adj* –**remorselessly** *adv*

**re·mote** /rɪˈməʊt/ *adj [from]* **1** distant in space, time, or manner: *remote stars|the remote future|a remote village|Her manner was polite but remote.* (=not friendly) **2** widely separated; not close: *The connection between these two ideas is very remote.* **3** (esp. of a chance or possibility) slight: *I haven't the remotest idea what you mean.* **–remoteness** *n* [U]

**remote con·trol** /ˌ·· ·ˈ·/ *n* [U] a system for controlling machinery from a distance by radio signals

**re·mote·ly** /rɪˈməʊtli/ *adv* to a very small degree

**re·mov·al** /rɪˈmuːvəl/ *n* [C;U] (an) act of removing

**removal van** /·ˈ·· ·/ also **pantechnicon** *BrE*, **moving van**– *n BrE* a large covered vehicle (VAN) used for moving furniture

**re·move** /rɪˈmuːv/ *v* **-moved, -moving 1** [T *from*] to take away (from a place); get rid of: *Remove your hat.|to remove a child from a class|to remove mud from your shoes* **2** [T *from*] *fml* to dismiss: *That officer must be removed (from his position).* **3** [I *from,to*] *fml* to go to live or work in another place: *Our office has removed to Bristol from London.* **4** **removed from** distant from: *What you say now is far removed from what you said before.* **5** **-remover** a chemical for cleaning off the stated (unwanted) substance: *paint-remover*

**re·mu·ne·rate** /rɪˈmjuːnəreɪt/ *v* **-rated, -rating** [T *for*] *fml* to reward; pay (someone) for work or trouble **–remuneration** /-ˈreɪʃən / *n* [S;U]: *to receive (a small) remuneration –see* PAY (USAGE)

**re·mu·ne·ra·tive** /rɪˈmjuːnərətɪv‖-reɪtɪv/ *adj fml* (of work) well-paid; profitable

**Re·nais·sance** /rɪˈneɪsəns‖ˌrenəˈsans/ *n* the period in Europe between the 15th and 17th centuries, when the art, literature, and ideas of ancient Greece were discovered again and widely studied

**rend** /rend/ *v* **rent** /rent/‖also **rended** *AmE*, **rending** [T *apart*] *lit* to divide by force; split: (fig.) *A terrible cry rent the air.*

**ren·der** /ˈrendəʳ/ *v* [T] *fml* **1** to give (esp. help): *You have rendered me a service.* **2** to cause to be: *His illness rendered him unfit for service in the army.* **3** to perform: *to render the song beautifully*

**ren·der·ing** /ˈrendərɪŋ/ *n* [*of*] a performance (of a play or piece of music): *a splendid rendering of the song*

**ren·dez·vous** /ˈrɒndɪvuː, -deɪ-‖ˈrɑn- *n* **-vous** /vuːz/ **1** an arrangement to meet at a certain time and place **2** the place (and time) chosen for meeting **3** a popular place for people to meet: *This club is a rendezvous for writers.* **–rendezvous** *v* **-voused, -vousing** [I] *tech*: *The two spacecraft rendezvoused successfully.*

**ren·di·tion** /renˈdɪʃən/ *n* [*of*] → RENDERING

**ren·e·gade** /ˈrenɪgeɪd/ *n derog* a person who deserts one country or belief to join another; TRAITOR

**re·new** /rɪˈnjuː‖rɪˈnuː/ *v* [T] **1** to give new life and freshness to: *I came back from my holiday with renewed strength.* **2** to replace (something old) with something new of the same kind: *to renew one's library ticket* **3** to repeat (an action): *In the morning the enemy renewed their attack.* **–renewal** *n* [C;U]

**re·new·a·ble** /rɪˈnjuːəbəl‖rɪˈnuː-/ *adj* that can or must be RENEWed (2): *a renewable ticket*

**re·nounce** /rɪˈnaʊns/ *v* **-nounced, -nouncing** [T] *more fml than* **give up – 1** to give up (esp. a claim): *He renounced his claim to the property.* **2** to say formally that one has no more connection with: *He renounced his religion and became a Muslim.*

**ren·o·vate** /ˈrenəveɪt/ *v* **-vated, -vating** [T] to repair; put back into good condition: *to renovate an old house* **–renovation** /-ˈveɪʃən/ *n* [C;U]

**re·nown** /rɪˈnaʊn/ *n* [U] fame: *a painter of some renown/of great/high renown* **–renowned** *adj*: *renowned as an inventor|renowned for his inventions*

**rent¹** /rent/ *n* [C;U] (a sum of) money paid regularly for the use of a room, building, television set, piece of land, etc.: *They* LET (3) *the house to a young man at a rent of £50 a week.|to pay a high/low rent|to pay more/less rent*

**rent²** *v* [T] **1** [*from*] to pay rent for the use of: *I rent a room from Mrs Jones.* **2** to allow to be used in return for rent; LET (3): *to rent (out) a room to a student* **3** *esp. AmE* to pay money for the use of (a car, boat, etc.) for a short time; HIRE: *to rent a suit* –see HIRE (USAGE)

**rent³** *n* a large tear (as if) in cloth

**rent⁴** *v past tense & participle of* REND

**rent·al** /ˈrentl/ *n fml* a sum of money fixed to be paid as rent: *to pay the television rental*

**rent-free** /ˌ·ˈ·◂/ *adv,adj* (used) without payment of rent: *to live rent-free|a rent-free flat*

**re·nun·ci·a·tion** /rɪˌnʌnsiˈeɪʃən/ *n* [C;U] a case or the act of renouncing (RENOUNCE (1))

**re·or·gan·ize** **-ise** /riːˈɔːgənaɪz‖-ˈɔr-/ *v* **-ized, -izing** [I;T] to ORGANIZE (something) again, esp. so as to be more effective **–reorganization** /-naɪˈzeɪʃən‖-nɪ-/ *n* [U]

**rep¹** /rep/ *n infml* a salesman: *the company rep*

**rep²** *n infml* a REPERTORY (1) theatre or company: *the local rep*

**re·paid** /rɪˈpeɪd/ *v past tense & participle of* REPAY

**re·pair¹** /rɪˈpeəʳ/ *v* [T] **1** to mend (something worn or broken): *to repair a broken watch/a road/old shoes* **2** *fml* to put right (a wrong, mistake, etc): *How can I repair the wrong I have done her?* see also IRREPARABLE **–repairable** *adj* **–repairer** *n*

**repair²** *n* **1** [*usu. pl.*] an act or result of mending: *to carry out the repairs to my damaged car* **2** **in (a) good/bad (state of) repair** in good/bad condition

**rep·a·ra·tion** /ˌrepəˈreɪʃən/ *n* [U] *fml* repayment for loss or wrong

**rep·ar·tee** /ˌrepɑːˈtiː‖ˌrepərˈtiː/ *n* [U] (the ability to make) quick amusing answers in conversation: *I enjoy listening to their* WITTY *repartee.*

**re·past** /rɪˈpɑːst‖rɪˈpæst/ *n fml* a meal

**re·pat·ri·ate** /riːˈpætrieɪt‖riːˈpeɪ-/ *v* **-ated, -ating** [T] to bring or send (someone) back to his/her own country **–repatriation** /- ˈeɪʃən / *n* [U]

**re·pay** /rɪˈpeɪ/ *v* **-paid** /ˈpeɪd/, **-paying** [T] **1** to return what is owed; pay back: *When will you repay me the £5 I lent you?* –see Study Notes on page 429 **2** [*by,for,with*] to reward: *How can I ever repay you for your kindness?*

**re·pay·a·ble** /rɪˈpeɪəbəl/ *adj* (of money) that can or must be paid back: *The debt is repayable in 30 days.*

**re·pay·ment** /rɪˈpeɪmənt/ *n* [C;U] the action of paying back; something paid back: *a/some small repayment for all you have done|The repayments of the* *loan are spread over 25 years.*

**re·peal** /rɪ'piːl/ *v* [T] to put an official end to (a law): *to repeal a property law* –**repeal** *n* [U]

**re·peat**[1] /rɪ'piːt/ *v* **1** [T *that*] to say or do again: *to repeat a word/a mistake* **2** [T] to say (something heard or learnt) to others: *Don't repeat what I told you.* **3 not bear repeating** (of words) to be too bad to say again **4 repeat oneself** to say or be the same thing again and again: *History seems to be repeating itself.*

**repeat**[2] *n* a performance shown or broadcast a second time: *I wish we could see more new programmes on television, not repeats all the time.*

**re·peat·ed** /rɪ'piːtɨd/ *adj* [A] done again and again: *repeated failure* –**repeatedly** *adv*

**re·pel** /rɪ'pel/ *v* **-ll-** [T] **1** to drive back (as if) by force: *to repel an attack* **2** to cause feelings of dislike in

**re·pel·lent**[1] /rɪ'pelənt/ *adj* causing great dislike; nasty: *repellent behaviour*

**repellent**[2] *n* [C;U] (a) substance that drives something, esp. insects, away: *a mosquito repellent*

**re·pent** /rɪ'pent/ *v* [I;T +*v-ing/of*] *fml* to be sorry for (wrongdoing): *He repented (of) his wickedness.* –**repentance** *n* [U] –**repentant** *adj*: *her repentant face*

**re·per·cus·sion** /ˌriːpə'kʌʃən‖ˌriːpər-/ *n* a far-reaching effect, esp. one of many (of some action or event): *The president's death had unexpected repercussions.*

**rep·er·toire** /'repətwɑːʳ‖-ər-/ *n* the collection of plays, pieces of music, etc., that a performer or theatre company can perform: (fig.) *He has a large repertoire of funny stories.*

**rep·er·to·ry** /'repətəri‖'repartori/ also **rep** *infml*– *n* [U] the practice of performing several plays, with the same actors and in the same theatre, one after the other on different days: *a repertory theatre/company*

**rep·e·ti·tion** /ˌrepɨ'tɪʃən/ *n* [C;U] the act of REPEATing[1] (1) or something repeated: *This accident is a repetition of one that happened here three weeks ago.*

**rep·e·ti·tious** /ˌrepɨ'tɪʃəs/ **also repetitive** /rɨ'petɨtɪv/ *adj derog* containing parts that are said or done too many times: *a repetitious speech*

**re·place** /rɪ'pleɪs/ *v* **-placed, -placing** [T] **1** to put (something) back in the right place: *He replaced the book on the shelf.* **2** to take the place of: *George has replaced Edward as captain of the team.* **3** [*with, by*] to change (one person or thing) for another, often better, newer, etc.: *We've replaced the old adding machine with a computer.|You'll have to replace those tyres: they're badly worn.* –**replaceable** *adj*

USAGE Compare **replace** and **displace**: Like the second sense of **replace, displace** can mean "to fill and take the place of", but when it is used of people it usually suggests sadness, anger, or lack of justice: *The old adding machine has been* **replaced** *by a modern computer.|It's most unfair that I should be* **displaced** *by a younger person.*

**re·place·ment** /rɪ'pleɪsmənt/ *n* **1** [U] the act of replacing (REPLACE (3)) **2** [C] someone or something that REPLACES (2): *We need a replacement for the secretary who left.*

**SPELLING NOTE**
Words with the sound /r/ may be spelt **wr-**, like **wrong.**

**re·play** /ˌriː'pleɪ/ *v* **-played, -playing** [T] to play (esp. a match) again: *The teams finished level, so they'll replay the match on Wednesday.* –**replay** /'riːpleɪ/ *n*

**re·plen·ish** /rɪ'plenɪʃ/ *v* [T] to fill up again; bring (a supply) back to its proper level: *to replenish the food cupboard/our supplies* –**replenishment** *n* [U]

**re·plete** /rɪ'pliːt/ *adj* [F *with*] *fml* completely full, esp. of food: *It was a big meal and we all felt replete.*

**rep·li·ca** /'replɪkə/ *n* a close copy, e.g. of a painting or other work of art

**re·ply**[1] /rɪ'plaɪ/ *v* **-plied, -plying** [I;T +*that/to*] *more fml than* **answer**– to answer; say or do as an answer: *"Did you forget to do it?" I asked. "Of course not," she replied.| Have you replied to his letter?* –see ANSWER (USAGE)

**reply**[2] *n* **-plies** [C;U] an act of replying: *What did you say* **in reply to** *his suggestion?*

**re·port**[1] /rɪ'pɔːt‖-ort/ *n* **1** [C] an account or description of events, experiences, business records etc.: *a newspaper report|a company report for the year* **2** [C] *fml* the noise of an explosion or shot: *a loud report* **3** [C;U] (a piece of) talk that spreads without official support; RUMOUR **4** [C] → SCHOOL REPORT

**report**[2] *v* **1** [I;T +*v-ing/that/on*] to tell of; provide information (about); give or write an account of: *They reported the appearance of a new star/that they had seen a new star.|She has been reporting on the war in the Middle East.* **2** [I *for,to*] to go somewhere and say that one is there (and ready for work or duty): *They report for work at 8.00 a.m.* **3** [T *for,to*] to make a complaint about: *He reported the boy (to the head teacher) (for making a noise).*

**re·port·er** /rɪ'pɔːtəʳ‖-'por-/ *n* a person who writes about news for a newspaper, or for radio or television –compare JOURNALIST

**re·pose** /rɪ'pəʊz/ *n* [U] *fml* rest; quiet sleep; calm: *in repose* –**repose** *v* **-posed, -posing** [I;T]

**rep·re·hen·si·ble** /ˌreprɪ'hensəbəl/ *adj* (of a person or behaviour) deserving to be blamed –**reprehensibly** *adv*

**rep·re·sent** /ˌreprɪ'zent/ *v* [T] **1** to show; be a sign or picture of; stand for: *This painting represents a storm at sea.|The red lines on the map represent railways.* **2** to act or speak officially for (another person or people): *He represents the people of Bradford in Parliament.|to represent one's fellow-workers at the union meeting* **3** [+*to-v/as*] to describe, perhaps falsely, (someone or something)(as): *She represents herself as a supporter of the union.*

**rep·re·sen·ta·tion** /ˌreprɪzen'teɪʃən/ *n* **1** [U] the act of REPRESENTing (2) or the condition of being REPRESENTED (2): *They demanded political representation.* **2** [C *of*] something that REPRESENTS (1): *This painting is a representation of a storm at sea.*

**rep·re·sen·ta·tive**[1] /ˌreprɪ'zentətɪv/ *adj* **1** [*of*] typical; being an example (of what others are like): *Are your opinions representative of those of the other students?* –opposite **unrepresentative** **2** (of a system of government) in which the people and their opinions are REPRESENTED (2)

**representative**[2] *n* [*of*] a person acting in place of or in the interests of one or more others: *They sent a representative to the meeting.|She is our local repre-*

*sentative in Parliament* –see also SALESMAN

**re·press** /rɪ'pres/ *v* [T] to control or hold back (natural feelings, actions, etc.): *I could not repress my laughter.* **–repressed** *adj*: *a repressed desire* **–repression** *n* [U]: *the repression of political opposition.*

**re·pres·sive** /rɪ'presɪv/ *adj derog* (of a law or other kind of control) hard and cruel: *a repressive political system that allows no freedom*

**re·prieve¹** /rɪ'pri:v/ *v* **-prieved, -prieving** [T] to give a REPRIEVE² to: *to reprieve the prisoner*|(fig.) *I was expecting to lose my job but I've been reprieved.*

**reprieve²** *n* an official order delaying the punishment of a prisoner who was to die: *to* GRANT² (1) *him a reprieve*

**rep·ri·mand** /'reprɪma:nd/ *v* [T] to scold officially and severely **–reprimand** *n* [C;U]: *to receive a reprimand*

**re·print¹** /ˌri:'prɪnt/ *v* [T] to print (a book) again when supplies have run out

**re·print²** /'ri:ˌprɪnt/ *n* a REPRINTed book –compare EDITION

**re·pri·sal** /rɪ'praɪzəl/ *n* [C;U] (an act of) punishing others for harm done to oneself: *to drop bombs on an enemy village in reprisal/as a reprisal*

**re·proach¹** /rɪ'prəʊtʃ/ *n* **1** [U] blame: *She gave me a look of reproach.*|*His manners are* **above/beyond reproach.** (=perfect) **2** [C] a word or words of blame: *When he came home drunk he was greeted with loud reproaches.* **–reproachful** *adj* **–reproachfully** *adv*

**reproach²** *v* [T *for, with*] to blame (someone), not angrily but sadly: *He reproached her for being lazy.*

**rep·ro·bate** /'reprəbeɪt/ *adj,n usu. humor* (a person) of bad character

**re·pro·duce** /ˌri:prə'dju:s‖-'du:s/ *v* **-duced, -ducing** [I;T] **1** to produce the young of (oneself or one's own kind): *Some tropical fish reproduce (themselves) by laying eggs.* **2** to produce a copy (of): *a painting that reproduces every detail of the scene*

**re·pro·duc·tion** /ˌri:prə'dʌkʃən/ *n* **1** [U] the act or method of producing young **2** [U] copying: *The quality of reproduction isn't very good on this recording.* **3** [C] a copy, esp. of a work of art: *a cheap reproduction of a great painting* **–reproductive** *adj* [A]: *the female reproductive system*

**re·prove** /rɪ'pru:v/ *v* **-proved, -proving** [T *for*] *fml* to scold for bad behaviour: *to reprove a child (for staying out late)* **–reproof** /rɪ'pru:f/ *n* [C;U] **–reproving** *adj*: *a reproving voice* **–reprovingly** *adv*

**rep·tile** /'reptaɪl‖'reptl/ *n* a rough-skinned creature whose blood changes temperature according to the temperature around it: *Snakes and* LIZARDS *are reptiles.* **–reptilian** /-'tɪlɪən/ *adj*

**re·pub·lic** /rɪ'pʌblɪk/ *n* a nation, usu. governed by elected representatives, whose head of state is a president –compare MONARCHY

**re·pub·li·can¹** /rɪ'pʌblɪkən/ *adj* [*no comp.*] belonging to or favouring a REPUBLIC: *a republican system of government*|*republican ideas*

**republican²** *n* a person who believes in a REPUBLICAN government

**Republican** *n,adj* (a member or supporter) of the **Republican party**, one of the two largest political parties of the US –compare DEMOCRAT

**re·pu·di·ate** /rɪ'pju:dieɪt/ *v* **-ated, -ating** [T] to refuse to accept or recognize: *to repudiate offers of friendship*|*He repudiated the suggestion that he had told a lie.* **–repudiation** /-'eɪʃən/ *n* [U]

**re·pug·nance** /rɪ'pʌgnəns/ *n* [S;U *to*] a feeling of strong dislike: *She turned away from him in repugnance.* **–repugnant** *adj*

**re·pulse** /rɪ'pʌls/ *v* **-pulsed, -pulsing** [T] **1** to drive back (an enemy attack); REPEL **2** to refuse coldly (an offer of friendship) **–repulse** *n*

**re·pul·sion** /rɪ'pʌlʃən/ *n* **1** [S;U] strong dislike and fear: *He looked with repulsion at the dead body.* **2** [U] *tech* the force by which bodies drive each other away –opposite **attraction** **–repulsive** *adj*: *a repulsive smell*|*repulsive forces* **–repulsively** *adv* **–repulsiveness** *n* [U]

**rep·u·ta·ble** /'repjʊtəbəl‖-pjə-/ *adj* respectable; well spoken of: *a reputable firm of builders* –opposite **disreputable** **–reputably** *adv*

**rep·u·ta·tion** /repjʊ'teɪʃən‖-pjə-/ *n* [S;U] **1** (an) opinion held by others (about someone or something); the degree to which one is well thought of: *The restaurant has a good reputation.*|*He has the reputation of being a coward.*|*If this matter becomes known, it will ruin your reputation.* –compare CHARACTER (2), CHARACTERISTIC **2 live up to one's reputation** to behave in the way people have come to expect

**re·pute** /rɪ'pju:t/ *n* [U] *fml* **1** →REPUTATION: *a man of low* (=bad) *repute* **2** good REPUTATION: *a hotel of (some) repute*

**re·put·ed** /rɪ'pju:tɪ̣d/ *adj* [A;F +*to-v*] generally supposed (to be); considered (as): *the reputed father of her baby*|*She is reputed to be rich.* **–reputedly** *adv*

**re·quest¹** /rɪ'kwest/ *n* **1** a polite demand: *a request for help* **2** [C] something that has been asked for: *Do they play requests on this radio show?* (=records that have been asked for by listeners) **3 at someone's request** because someone asked: *I bought it at the request of my father.* **4 on request** when asked for: *Buses stop here on request.*

**request²** *v* [T +*that/of*] *more fml than* **ask**– to demand politely: *The judge requested silence.*

**req·ui·em** /'rekwɪəm, 'rekwiem/ *n* (a piece of music for) a Christian ceremony (MASS) for the soul of a person who has just died

**re·quire** /rɪ'kwaɪəʳ/ *v* **-quired, -quiring 1** [T +*v-ing/that*] *more fml than* **need**– to need: *This suggestion requires careful thought.*|*His health requires that he should go to bed early.* **2** [T +*that*] *fml* to demand; order, expecting obedience: *All passengers are required to show their tickets.*

**re·quire·ment** /rɪ'kwaɪəmənt‖-ər-/ *n more fml than* **need**– **1** something needed or demanded: *This shop can supply all your requirements.* **2 meet someone's requirements** to do or be what someone REQUIRES

**req·ui·site** /'rekwɪ̣zɪ̣t/ *n,adj* [*for*] (something) needed for a purpose: *sports requisites*|*Have you got the requisite stamp on your passport?*

**req·ui·si·tion** /ˌrekwɪ̣'zɪʃən/ *n* [C;U *for, on*] (a) formal demand, esp. by the army: *The soldiers made a requisition on the village for horses.* **–requisition** *v* [T]: *The army requisitioned the stores of petrol.*

**res·cue¹** /'reskju:/ *v* **-cued, -cuing** [T *from*] to save from harm or danger; set free: *to rescue a man from drowning/a cat from a high tree* –**rescuer** *n*

**rescue²** *n* an act of rescuing (RESCUE¹): *A rescue team are trying to reach the trapped miners.|Jean couldn't do her school work, but her mother* **came to her rescue.** (=helped her)

**re·search¹** /rɪ'sɜ:tʃ, 'ri:sɜ:tʃ‖-ɜr-/ *n* [C;U] (an) advanced and detailed study of a subject, so as to learn new facts: *research students/workers|to do some research/carry out some researches on diseases of the blood*

**research²** *v* [I;T] to do RESEARCH¹ (on or for): *to research a subject|We've been researching for three years with no result.* –**researcher** *n*

**re·sem·ble** /rɪ'zembəl/ *v* **-bled, -bling** [T *in*] to look or be like: *She resembles her sister in appearance but not in character.* –**resemblance** *n* [C;U *between*]: *There's a strong resemblance between the two sisters.*

**re·sent** /rɪ'zent/ *v* [T +*v-ing*] to feel angry or bitter at: *He resents being called a fool.* –**resentful** *adj*: *to give him a resentful look* –**resentfully** *adv*

**re·sent·ment** /rɪ'zentmənt/ *n* [U] the feeling of RESENTing bad treatment: *I don't bear you any resentment.* (=I don't feel angry with you)

**res·er·va·tion** /ˌrezə'veɪʃən‖-ər-/ *n* **1** [C;U +*that*] a doubt in one's mind: *I have some reservations about the truth of his story.|I accept your offer* **without reservation(s).** (=with no uncertainty) **2** [C] (in the US) a piece of land set apart for N. American Indians to live in **3** [C] → BOOKING: *Have you made the reservations for our holiday?*

**re·serve¹** /rɪ'zɜ:v‖-ɜrv/ *v* **-served, -serving** [T] **1** to keep for a special purpose: *These seats are reserved for old people.* **2** → BOOK² (1): *to reserve a seat on the plane*

**reserve²** *n* **1** [C *of*] a store (of something) kept for future use: *to keep a reserve/some reserves of food* **2** [C] the military force that a country keeps for use if needed: *to call out the reserve(s)* **3** [C] a piece of land RESERVED for a (stated) purpose: *a nature reserve* **4** [U] (of a person or character) the quality of being RESERVED (1): *the well-known reserve of the Scots* **5** [C] a player whose job is to play in a team game in place of any member who cannot play because of injury, etc. **6 in reserve** ready for use if needed: *We always keep some money in reserve*

**re·served** /rɪ'zɜ:vd‖-ɜr-/ *adj* **1** (of a person) not liking to talk about oneself or one's feelings; SHY **2** having been RESERVED¹ (2): *reserved seats*

**res·er·voir** /'rezəvwɑ:ʳ‖-ərvɑr, -vɔr/ *n* a place where liquid is stored, esp. a man-made lake to provide water for a city

**re·shuf·fle** /ri:'ʃʌfəl, '···/ *n* a changing around of the positions of people employed in an organization –**reshuffle** /rɪ:'ʃʌfəl/ *v* **-fled, -fling** [I;T]

**re·side** /rɪ'zaɪd/ *v* **-sided, -siding** [I] *fml* to have one's home; live: *to reside abroad*

**res·i·dence** /'rez⅟ədəns/ *n* **1** [C] *fml* the place where one lives; a house **2** [U] the state of residing (RESIDE): *They took up residence in Jamaica.* **3 in residence** actually living in a place: *The students are not in residence* (=not at the university) *during the holidays.*

> **SPELLING NOTE**
> Words with the sound /r/ may be spelt **wr-**, like **wrong.**

**res·i·dent¹** /'rez⅟ədənt/ *adj* [*in*] living in a place: *a resident doctor* (=living in the hospital)

**resident²** *n* a person who lives in or is staying in a place, not a visitor: *This hotel serves meals to residents only.*

**res·i·den·tial** /ˌrez⅟ə'denʃəl/ *adj* (of part of a town) consisting of private houses, without offices or factories

**re·sid·u·al** /rɪ'zɪdʒʊəl/ *adj* remaining; left over

**res·i·due** /'rez⅟ədju:‖-du:/ *n* [*usu. sing.*] *tech* what is left, esp. after chemical treatment

**re·sign** /rɪ'zaɪn/ *v* [I;T *from*] **1** to leave (a job or position): *to resign from a committee|to resign one's post* **2 resign oneself to** to accept (something unpleasant) without complaint: *You must resign yourselves to waiting a bit longer.* –see also RESIGNED

**res·ig·na·tion** /ˌrezɪg'neɪʃən/ *n* **1** [C;U] (an act of) RESIGNING (1) **2** [C] a written statement to inform that one intends to RESIGN (1): *to hand in/send in my resignation* **3** [U] the state of being RESIGNED: *to accept one's fate with resignation*

**re·signed** /rɪ'zaɪnd/ *adj* [*to*] accepting something unpleasant without complaint: *He seemed resigned (to his mother's death).* –**resignedly** /-n⅟ədli/ *adv*

**re·sil·i·ent** /rɪ'zɪlɪənt/ *adj* **1** (of a substance) able to spring back to the former shape when pressure is removed: *Rubber is more resilient than wood.* **2** (of living things) strong enough to recover from difficulty, disease, etc.: *a resilient character* –**resilience** *n* [S;U]: *Rubber has more resilience than wood.* –**resiliently** *adv*

**res·in** /'rez⅟ən/ *n* **1** [U] a thick sticky liquid from certain trees such as the FIR **2** [C] any of various man-made plastic substances, used in industry –**resinous** *adj*

**re·sist** /rɪ'zɪst/ *v* [T +*v-ing*] **1** to oppose; stand or fight against (force): *to resist an enemy attack|The government are resisting the nurses' pay demands.* **2** to remain unchanged or unharmed by: *the power to resist disease* **3** [*usu. neg.*] to force oneself not to yield to or accept: *I can't resist chocolate cake.| She could hardly resist laughing.* –**resistible** *adj* –opposite **irresistible**

**re·sist·ance** /rɪ'zɪstəns/ *n* **1** [S;U] (an act of) RESISTing (1) opposition: *The committee put up a lot of resistance to the chairman's plan.* **2** [U] the (stated) force opposed to anything moving: *wind resistance to an aircraft* **3** [U] the ability (of a living body) to RESIST (2) disease: *Mary has great powers of resistance and will get well quickly.* **4** [U] the power of a substance to RESIST (2) the passing through it of an electric current

**re·sis·tant** /rɪ'zɪstənt/ *adj* [*to*] having or showing RESISTANCE (3) (to): *resistant to disease*

**res·o·lute** /'rezəlu:t/ *adj* (of a person or his character) firm; determined in purpose –**resolutely** *adv* –**resoluteness** *n* [U]

**res·o·lu·tion** /ˌrezə'lu:ʃən/ *n* **1** [U] the quality of being RESOLUTE: *You should show more resolution.* **2**

[U *of*] the action of resolving (RESOLVE[1] (1)): *The lawyer's advice led to the resolution of all our difficulties.* **3** [C +*to-v*] a formal decision made by a group vote: *At the meeting, there was a resolution for/against building a new library.* **4** [C +*to-v*] a determined decision to do or stop doing something: *my New Year resolution* (=one made on January 1st for the year ahead) *to stop smoking* –compare RESOLVE[2] (1)

**re·solve[1]** /rɪ'zɒlv‖rɪ'zɑlv, rɪ'zɔlv/ *v* **-solved, -solving** **1** [T] to settle or clear up (a difficulty): *There weren't enough beds, but the matter was resolved by making George sleep on the floor.* **2** [I;T +*to-v/that*] to decide; make a determined decision: *to resolve to work hard/that one will work hard* **3** [I;T +*to-v/that*] (of a committee or public body) to make a RESOLUTION (3) (that): *Parliament has resolved that . . .*

**resolve[2]** *n* [C +*to-v*] *fml* **1** [C +*to-v*]→RESOLUTION (4) **2** [U] →RESOLUTION (1)

**res·o·nant** /'rezənənt/ *adj* (of a sound) deep, full, clear, and continuing: *the resonant note of a bell* **–resonance** *n* [U]: *the bell-like resonance of his voice* **–resonantly** *adv* **–resonate** *v* **-nated, -nating** [I]

**re·sort** /rɪ'zɔːt‖-ɔrt/ *n* **1** [C] a holiday place, or place considered good for the health: *a health/mountain resort* **2** [U *to*] the action of RESORTING TO: *to pass the examination without resort to cheating* –compare RECOURSE; see RESOURCE (USAGE) **3 as a/in the last resort** if everything else fails: *In the last resort we can always sleep in the car for a night.*

**resort to** sthg. *v prep* [T +*v-ing*] to turn to (often something bad) for help: *She resorted to stealing when she had no more money.*

**re·sound** /rɪ'zaʊnd/ *v* **1** [I *through, throughout*] (of a sound) to be loudly and clearly heard: *Their laughter resounded through the hall.* **2** [I *with*] (of a place) to be filled (with sound): *The hall resounded with laughter.*

**re·sound·ing** /rɪ'zaʊndɪŋ/ *adj* [A] **1** (of a sound) loud and clear; ECHOing[2] (1): *a resounding crash* **2** very great: *a resounding success* **–resoundingly** *adv*

**re·source** /rɪ'zɔːs, -'sɔːs‖-ors/ *n* **1** [*usu. pl.*] a possession (esp. of a country) in the form of wealth or goods: *a country rich in* **natural resources** (=minerals, oil, etc.) **2** a means of comfort or help: *Religion is her only resource now.* **3 leave someone to his/her own resources** to let someone pass the time as he/she wishes

USAGE **Resort, recourse,** and **resource** can all mean something that is used to gain a result when everything else has failed, but they are each used in different phrases: *to have* **resort/recourse** *to violence|in the last* **resort**|*as a last* **resource.**

**re·source·ful** /rɪ'zɔːsfəl, -'sɔːs-‖-ors-/ *adj apprec* (of a person) good at finding a way round difficulties **–resourcefully** *adv* **–resourcefulness** *n* [U]

**re·spect[1]** /rɪ'spekt/ *n* **1** [S;U *for*] admiration; feeling of honour: *He is held in the greatest respect by all his students.* –opposite **disrespect** –compare SELF-RESPECT **2** [U *for, to*] attention (to); care (for); *to have no respect for the speed limit/for human life* **3** [C] a detail; point: *The new job is better paid, but in some respects less interesting.* **4 with respect to** *fml* concerning: *I am writing with respect to your recent letter.*

**respect[2]** *v* [T] **1** to feel RESPECT[1] (1) for: *The teacher feels that her students don't respect her.* **2** to show RESPECT[1] (2) for: *I promise to respect your wishes.*

**re·spec·ta·ble** /rɪ'spektəbəl/ *adj* **1** showing or having standards acceptable to society: *It's not respectable to be drunk in the street.*|*to put on a clean shirt and look respectable* **2** quite good; enough in amount or quality: *a respectable income* **–respectability** /-ə'bɪlɪ̣ti/ *n* [U] **–respectably** *adv*

**re·spect·ful** /rɪ'spektfəl/ *adj* [*to*] feeling or showing RESPECT[1] (1) (to): *The crowd waited in respectful silence for the great man to speak.* –opposite **disrespectful –respectfully** *adv*

**re·spec·tive** /rɪ'spektɪv/ *adj* [A] of or for each one; particular and separate: *They went home to their respective houses.*

**re·spec·tive·ly** /rɪ'spektɪvli/ *adv* each separately in the order mentioned: *The nurses and the miners received pay rises of 8% and 12% respectively.*

**re·spects** /rɪ'spekts/ *n* [P] polite formal greetings: *Give my respects to your wife.*

**res·pi·ra·tion** /ˌrespɪ̣'reɪʃən/ *n* [U] *fml & tech* the action of breathing: *Respiration is difficult at great heights.* –see also ARTIFICIAL RESPIRATION

**res·pi·ra·tor** /'respɪ̣reɪtər/ *n* an apparatus that is worn over the nose and mouth, to help people to breathe

**re·spi·ra·to·ry** /rɪ'spɪrətəri, 'respɪ̣reɪtəri, rɪ'spaɪərə-‖'respərətori,/ *adj* [A] connected with breathing: *respiratory diseases*

**res·pite** /'respɪt, -paɪt‖-pɪt/ *n* [C;U *from; usu. sing.*] (a short period of) pause or rest, during a time of effort, pain, or trouble: *without (a moment's) respite*

**re·splen·dent** /rɪ'splendənt/ *adj* bright and shining; splendid: (fig.) *George arrived, resplendent in a new white suit.* **–resplendence** *n* [U] **–resplendently** *adv*

**re·spond** /rɪ'spɒnd‖rɪ'spɑnd/ *v* **1** [I;T *to*] *more fml than* **answer**– to answer; *They still haven't responded to my letter.* –see ANSWER (USAGE) **2** [I *by, to, with*] to act in answer: *He responded (to my suggestion) with a laugh/by laughing.*

**respond to** sthg. *v prep* [T *no pass.*] (esp. of a disease) to get better as a result of; REACT favourably to: *The disease failed to respond to drugs.*

**re·sponse** /rɪ'spɒns‖rɪ'spɑns/ *n more fml than* **answer**– [C;U *to*] (an action as) an answer: *He made/gave no response (to my question).*|*There was no response.*|*in respect to your request*|*a favourable response to their pay demands*

**re·spon·si·bil·i·ty** /rɪˌspɒnsə'bɪlɪ̣ti‖rɪˌspɑn-/ *n* **-ties 1** [U *for, to*] the condition of being RESPONSIBLE (1): *I take full responsibility for breaking the window.* **2** [U] the quality of being RESPONSIBLE (2,3): *a position of great responsibility in the Government* **3** [C] something for which one is RESPONSIBLE (1): *a woman with many responsibilities*

**re·spon·si·ble** /rɪ'spɒnsəbəl‖rɪ'spɑn-/ *adj* **1** [F *for, to*] having the duty of looking after someone or something, so that one can be blamed (by the stated person) if things go wrong: *I am responsible to the director for making sure that the company is profitable.* **2** sensible and trustworthy: *You can leave the children with him–he's very responsible.* –opposite

**irresponsible 3** (of a job) needing a trustworthy person to do it **4 be responsible for** to be the cause of: *Who is responsible for breaking the mirror?*

**re·spon·si·bly** /rɪ'spɒnsəbli‖rɪ'spɑn-/ *adv* in a RESPONSIBLE (2) way: *I'll trust you to behave responsibly while I'm out.* –opposite **irresponsibly**

**re·spon·sive** /rɪ'spɒnsɪv‖rɪ'spɑn-/ *adj* [*to*] answering readily with words or feelings: *responsive to kindness.*| *a responsive smile* –opposite **unresponsive** –**responsively** *adv* –**responsiveness** *n* [U]

**rest¹** /rest/ *n* **1** [C;U *from*] (a period of) freedom from action or anything tiring: *I'm tired: let's take/have a rest.*|*to get a good night's rest* (=sleep)|*Sunday is my rest day.*|*The machine is* **at rest**. (=not moving)|*The car rolled down the hill and* **came to rest** *at the bottom.* **2** [C] a support (for the stated thing): *an armrest*|*a headrest*|*Use this shelf as a rest for your camera.* **3 set someone's mind/fears at rest** to free someone from anxiety

**rest²** *v* **1** [I;T] to (allow to) take a REST¹ (1): *I always rest for an hour after dinner.*|*Sit down and rest your feet.* **2** [T *against,on*] to lean or support: *Rest your bicycle against the wall.* **3** [I] to lie buried: *Let him rest in peace.*|(fig.) *Let the argument rest there.* **4** [I] to stop being active: *The police promised not to rest until all the criminals were caught.* |*I shall not rest* (=have peace of mind) *until this matter is settled.* **5 rest assured** to be certain: *Rest assured/You can rest assured that we will do all we can.*

**rest on** sbdy./sthg. also **rest upon** sbdy./sthg. *v prep* [I] **1** to lean on; be supported by: *The bridge rests on stone arches.*|(fig.) *Your argument rests on a statement that can't be proved.* **2** (of sight or the eyes) to be directed towards: *His eyes rested on the peaceful valley below.*

**rest with** sbdy. *v prep* [T *no pass.*] to be the responsibility of: *The decision rests with you.*

**rest³** *n* [U +*sing./pl. v*] what is left; the ones that still remain: *We'll eat some of the fish now and keep the rest (of it) for dinner.*|*He's only got one shirt, because all the rest (of them) are being washed.*|*John is English and the rest of us are Welsh.*

**res·tau·rant** /'restərã, -rɒnt‖-rənt, -rɑnt/ *n* a place where meals are sold and eaten –compare CAFE –see picture opposite

**res·tau·ra·teur** /ˌrestərə'tɜːʳ/ *n* the owner of a restaurant, esp. one who runs it himself/herself

**rest·ful** /'restfəl/ *adj* peaceful; giving one a feeling of REST¹ (1) –**restfully** *adv* –**restfulness** *n* [U]

**res·ti·tu·tion** /ˌrestɪ'tjuːʃən‖-'tuːʃən/ *n* [U *of*] *fml* the act of returning something lost or stolen to its owner, or of paying for damage: *to make restitution (of something, to someone)*

**res·tive** /'restɪv/ *adj* unwilling or unable to keep still: *a restive horse* –**restively** *adv*

**rest·less** /'restləs/ *adj* never quiet; always moving about: *We spent a very restless night.* –**restlessly** *adv* –**restlessness** *n* [U]

**re·sto·ra·tive** /rɪ'stɔːrətɪv‖-'sto-/ *n,adj fml* (a food, medicine, etc) that brings back health and strength

**SPELLING NOTE**
Words with the sound /r/ may be spelt **wr-**, like **wrong.**

**re·store** /rɪ'stɔːʳ‖rɪ'stor/ *v* **-stored, -storing** [T] **1** [*to*] to give or bring back: *to restore stolen property*|*to call in the army to restore law and order*|*I feel quite restored (to health) after my holiday.*|*The Labour Party was restored to power at the election.* **2** to put (old buildings, furniture, or works of art) back into the original state –**restoration** /ˌrestə'reɪʃən/ *n* [C;U]: *the restoration of public order after a time of violence*|*the restoration of a painting*

**re·strain** /rɪ'streɪn/ *v* [T *from*] to control; prevent (from doing something): *If you can't restrain your dog (from biting people) you must lock him up.*

**re·strained** /rɪ'streɪnd/ *adj* calm and controlled; not showing strong feelings –opposite **unrestrained**

**re·straint** /rɪ'streɪnt/ *n* **1** [U] *apprec* the quality of being RESTRAINED or RESTRAINing oneself: *I think you showed great restraint in not hitting him after what he said.* **2** [C] *often derog* something that limits or RESTRAINS: *He hates the restraints of life in a small town.*

**re·strict** /rɪ'strɪkt/ *v* [T *to*] to keep within limits: *I restrict myself to (smoking) two cigarettes a day.* –**restriction** *n* [C;U]: *to be allowed to drink without restriction*|*the many restrictions of army life*

**re·strict·ed** /rɪ'strɪktɪd/ *adj* **1** [*no comp.*] controlled, esp. by law: *The sale of alcohol is restricted in Britain.* **2** [to] for a particular purpose, or for the use of a particular group only: *a restricted area, where only the army are allowed to go* **3** limited: *restricted space in a small house*

**re·stric·tive** *adj often derog* that RESTRICTS: *He finds the job too restrictive.* –**restrictively** *adv*

**rest room** /'· ·/ *n AmE* a public LAVATORY (2), in a hotel, restaurant, etc.

**re·sult¹** /rɪ'zʌlt/ *v* [I *from*] to happen as an effect or RESULT² (1): *His illness resulted from eating bad food.*

**result in** sthg. *v prep* [T +*v-ing; no pass.*] to have as a RESULT² (1); cause: *The accident resulted in the death of two passengers/in two passengers dying.*

**result²** *n* **1** [C;U] what happens because of an action or event: *His illness is a/the result of (eating) bad food.*| *Your hard work is beginning to show results.* (=have a noticeable effect)|*He was late* **as a result of** (=because of) *the snow.* –see Study Notes on page 128 **2** [C *usu. pl.*] (the news of) a person's or team's success or failure in an examination, sports match, etc.: *I heard the football results on the radio* **3** [C] the answer to a sum

**re·sul·tant** /rɪ'zʌltənt/ *adj* [A] happening as an effect: *The drivers all sounded their horns and the resultant noise was unbearable.*

**re·sume** /rɪ'zjuːm‖rɪ'zuːm/ *v* **-sumed, -suming** *fml* **1** [I;T +*v-ing*] to begin (something, or doing something) again after a pause: *We'll stop now and resume (working) at two o'clock.* **2** [T] to take again: *to resume one's seat* –**resumption** /rɪ'zʌmpʃən/ *n* [U]: *the resumption of business after a holiday*

**ré·su·mé** /'rezjʊmeɪ, 'reɪ- ‖ˌrezʊ'meɪ/ *n* →SUMMARY

**re·sur·gence** /rɪ'sɜːdʒəns‖-ɜr-/ *n* [S;U] a return to power, life, and activity: *(a) resurgence of nationalist feeling* –**resurgent** *adj* [A]

**res·ur·rect** /ˌrezə'rekt/ *v* [T] to bring back into use, fashion, or attention: *to resurrect an old custom*

**res·ur·rec·tion** /ˌrezə'rekʃən/ *n* **1** [U] renewal (of

Robert and Maria have decided to **eat out** instead of cooking a meal **at home**. They went into a cheap **restaurant**, and now they are reading the **menu** and waiting to **be served**. After the **waitress** has finished **clearing** another table, she comes to **take their order**.
Robert: I'd like **fish and chips**, please.
Maria: And I think I'll have a cheese **salad**.
Waitress: Would you like to **order** a drink?
Maria: No, thank you.
Waitress: What would you like for **dessert**?
Robert: Nothing, thank you – just two **coffees**.

When they finish their coffee they pay the **bill**, leaving a small **tip** for the waitress when they go.

**Questions** (Answers on page 702)

**a** We looked at the . . . . . and decided what to eat.
**b** The waitress came and took our . . . . .
**c** After the meal, the waitress gave us the . . . . . and we paid her.
**d** Money you leave for the waitress is called a . . . . .

life, hope, etc.) **2** [*the S*] (*often cap.*) (in Christian belief) the rising of Christ from his grave

**re·sus·ci·tate** /rɪˈsʌsǐteɪt/ *v* **-tated, -tating** [T] to bring (a person) back to life: *to try to resuscitate a drowned man* **–resuscitation** /-ˈteɪʃən / *n* [U]

**re·tail¹** /ˈriːteɪl/ *n* [U] the sale of goods in shops to CUSTOMERS, for their own use, not for resale: *the retail of goods|retail prices* –compare WHOLESALE

**retail²** *adv* by RETAIL¹; from a RETAILER: *to buy it retail* –compare WHOLESALE

**re·tail·er** /ˈriːteɪləʳ/ *n* someone who sells things by RETAIL¹; shopkeeper

**re·tain** /rɪˈteɪn/ *v* [T] to keep possession of; avoid losing: *In spite of all his troubles he retained his sense of humour.|retain a lot of facts in one's memory* –see also RETENTION

**re·tal·i·ate** /rɪˈtælieɪt/ *v* **-ated, -ating** [I *against,by*] to pay back evil with evil: *Mary kicked Susan, and Susan retaliated (by biting her).* **–retaliation** /-ˈeɪʃən / *n* [U]

**re·tard** /rɪˈtɑːd‖-ɑrd/ *v* [T] *esp. fml or tech* to make slow; cause to happen later or more slowly: *Cold weather retards the growth of the crops.*

**re·tard·ed** /rɪˈtɑːdǐd‖-ɑr-/ *adj* (of a child) slower in development, esp. mentally, than others

**retch** /retʃ/ *v* [I] to try to be sick (VOMIT) but without success

**re·ten·tion** /rɪˈtenʃən/ *n* [U] the state or action of RETAINing: *the retention of facts in the mind* **–retentive** *adj: He has a very retentive memory.* **–retentively** *adv* **–retentiveness** *n* [U]

**re·think** /ˌriːˈθɪŋk/ *v* **-thought** /θɔːt/, **-thinking** [I;T] to think again; reconsider (a subject): *We'd better rethink the whole plan* **–rethink** /ˈriːθɪŋk / *n* [S]

**ret·i·cent** /ˈretǐsənt/ *adj* (of a person or behaviour) silent; not saying as much as is known or felt: *a reticent manner* **–reticence** *n* [U] **–reticently** *adv*

**ret·i·na** /ˈretǐnə/ *n* **-nas** *or* **-nae** /aɪ/ the light-sensitive area of nerve-endings at the back of the eye

**ret·i·nue** /ˈretɪnjuː‖-nuː/ *n* [C *+sing./pl. v*] a group of servants and followers travelling with an important person: *The President's retinue is/are arriving the day before he does.*

**re·tire** /rɪˈtaɪəʳ/ *v* **-tired, -tiring 1** [I;T] to (cause to) stop working at one's job, profession, etc., usu. because of age: *My father retired at the age of 60.* **2** [I *from,to*] to go away or back: *The ministers retired to make their decision.* **3** [I] *fml* to go to bed

**re·tired** /rɪˈtaɪəd‖-ərd/ *adj* (of a person) having stopped working, usu. because of age: *My father is retired/is a retired doctor.*

**re·tire·ment** /rɪˈtaɪəmənt‖-ər-/ *n* **1** [C;U] a case or the act of retiring (RETIRE (1)): *He was given a gold watch on his retirement.* **2** [U] the period after one has RETIRED (1): *He enjoyed his retirement.*

**re·tir·ing** /rɪˈtaɪərɪŋ/ *adj* **1** avoiding the company of others: *He has a retiring nature and hates parties.* **2** [A] at which one RETIRES (1): *What's the* **retiring age** *for miners?*

> **SPELLING NOTE**
> Words with the sound /r/ may be spelt **wr-**, like **wrong.**

**re·tort** /rɪˈtɔːt‖-ɔrt/ *v,n* [C;T *+that*] (to make) a quick, usu. angry or amusing answer: *He retorted that it was all my fault.* –see ANSWER (USAGE)

**re·trace** /rɪˈtreɪs, riː-/ *v* **-traced, -tracing** [T] to go over again; go back over: *She* **retraced her steps** (=went back) *to try to find her lost ring.*

**re·tract** /rɪˈtrækt/ *v* [I;T] **1** to admit that (something one said earlier) should not have been said: *The politician retracted his statement.* **2** to (cause to) draw back or in: *A cat can retract its* CLAWS, *but a dog can't.* **–retractable** *adj* **–retraction** *n* [C;U]

**re·treat¹** /rɪˈtriːt/ *v* [I *from,to*] (esp. of an army) to move away; go back, esp. when forced to do so: *The army was forced to retreat* –compare ADVANCE¹ (1)

**retreat²** *n* **1** [C;U *from,to*] (an act of) RETREATing: *Napoleon's retreat from Moscow* **2** [S] a military signal for RETREATing: *to* **sound the retreat** *by beating a drum* **3** [C] a place into which one can go for peace and safety

**re·tri·al** /ˌriːˈtraɪəl/ *n* an act of trying a law case again: *to demand a retrial*

**ret·ri·bu·tion** /ˌretrǐˈbjuːʃən/ *n* [S;U *for*] *fml* (a) deserved punishment: *Do evil actions bring retribution after death?*

**re·trieve** /rɪˈtriːv/ *v* **-trieved, -trieving** [T *from*] to regain; find and bring back: *I ran back to retrieve the bag I had left in the train.|to retrieve information from a computer system* **–retrieval** *n* [U]

**ret·ro·grade** /ˈretrəgreɪd/ *adj* moving back towards an earlier and worse state

**ret·ro·gress** /ˌretrəˈgres/ *v* [I *to*] *esp. fml or tech* to go back (to an earlier and worse state) **–retrogression** *n* [U]

**ret·ro·spect** /ˈretrəspekt/ *n* [U] the act of looking back towards the past: *One's school life seems happier* **in retrospect** *than it really was.*

**re·tro·spec·tive** /ˌretrəˈspektɪv/ *adj* concerned with the past: *retrospective thoughts*

**re·turn¹** /rɪˈtɜːn‖-ɜrn/ *v* **1** [I *from, to*] to come or go back: *to return home|to return to London|What time does your husband return (from work)?|Let's return to the subject of my holiday.* **2** [T] to give, put, or send back: *Don't forget to return (me) my keys.|We returned the empty bottles (to the shop).|He returned the gun to his pocket.* **3** [I] to happen again: *Spring will soon return.* **4** [T *usu. pass.*] to elect (someone) as a Member of Parliament or to a political position **5** [T] to state officially, esp. in answer to a demand: *He returned his earnings as £6,000 on the tax declaration.|The* JURY *returned a* VERDICT (=gave a judgment) *of "Not Guilty".* **6 return a favour** to do a kind action in return for another

**return²** *n* **1** [C;U *from,to*] the act or an example of RETURNing¹ (1): *We look forward to your return (from China).|On his return he found her asleep.* **2** [U] the act of RETURNing¹ (2) something: *The library are demanding the return of the books.* **3** [C *of*] a case of happening again: *the return of spring* **4** [C *often pl.*] a profit: *These shares bring in a good return/good returns.* **5** [C] an official statement or set of figures RETURNed¹ (5) **6** [C] a RETURN³ ticket **7 by return (of post)** by the next post **8 in return (for)** in exchange (for); in payment (for): *He gave her some roses in return for her kindness.*

**return³** *BrE*‖ **round-trip** *AmE– adj* (of a ticket or its cost) for a trip from one place to another and back again: *The price is £1 single and £1.80 return.* –compare SINGLE² (1)

**re·tur·na·ble** /rɪˈtɜːnəbəl‖-ɜr-/ *adj* that must or can be given or sent back: *returnable bottles*

**re·u·ni·on** /riːˈjuːnɪən/ *n* **1** [U] the state of being together again **2** [C] a meeting of friends after a separation: *a reunion of old students of the college*

**re·u·nite** /ˌriːjuːˈnaɪt/ *v* **-nited, -niting** [I;T *with*] to (cause to) come or join together again: *After the war, the soldiers were reunited with their families.*

**rev¹** /rev/ *n infml* for REVOLUTION (4)

**rev²** *v* **-vv-** [T *up*] *infml* to increase the speed of (an engine): *Don't rev (up) your engine so loudly.*

**Rev** *written abbrev said as:* REVEREND: *the Rev D. Macleod*

**re·val·ue** /riːˈvæljuː/ *v* **-ued, -uing** to increase the exchange value of (a country's money) –see also DEVALUATION **–revaluation** /-ˈeɪʃən/ *n* [C;U]

**re·veal** /rɪˈviːl/ *v* [T] **1** to allow to be seen: *The curtains opened, to reveal a darkened stage.* **2** [+ *that*] to make known: *She suddenly revealed (the fact) that she was not married.*

**re·veal·ing** /rɪˈviːlɪŋ/ *adj* allowing something to be seen or known: *a very revealing dress*

**re·veil·le** /rɪˈvæli‖ˈrevəli/ *n* [S] music played as a signal to waken soldiers in the morning

**rev·el** /ˈrevəl/ *v* **-ll-** *BrE*‖**-l-** *AmE* [I] *old use or humor* to pass the time in dancing, feasting, etc.: *They were drinking and revelling all night.* **–reveller** *BrE*‖ **reveler** *AmE n*

**revel in** sthg. *v prep* [T + *v-ing*] to enjoy greatly: *She revels in hearing about my difficulties.*

**rev·e·la·tion** /ˌrevəˈleɪʃən/ *n* **1** [U *of*] the making known (of something secret) **2** [C] a (surprising) fact that is made known: *We listened to her strange revelations about her past.*

**rev·el·ry** /ˈrevəlri/ *n* [U] wild noisy dancing and feasting; REVELling

**re·venge¹** /rɪˈvendʒ/ *v* **-venged, -venging** [T] **1** to do something in REVENGE² for (some harm done to oneself): *to revenge an injustice* **2** to do something in REVENGE² for harm done to: *Hamlet revenged his dead father.* (=killed the man who killed him)

USAGE **Revenge** and **avenge** are very similar in meaning, but to **avenge** or **take vengeance** suggests the idea of correcting an injustice, while to **revenge** or **take revenge** suggests satisfying the desire to harm someone who has harmed you.

**revenge²** *n* [S;U *for, on*] (a) punishment given to someone in return for harm done to oneself: *The village was bombed* **in revenge for** *protecting enemy soldiers.*

**rev·e·nue** /ˈrevənjuː‖-nuː/ *n* [U] income, esp. that which the government receives as tax

**re·ver·be·rate** /rɪˈvɜːbəreɪt‖-ɜr-/ *v* **-rated, -rating** [I] (of sound) to be thrown back again and again: ECHO repeatedly: *The thunder reverberated across the valley.* **–reverberation** /-ˈreɪʃən/ *n* [C;U]

**re·vere** /rɪˈvɪəʳ/ *v* **-vered, -vering** [T] *fml* to give great respect and admiration to: *She revered her father all her life.*

**Rev·e·rend** /ˈrevərənd/ *n* [A;S] *adv* a title of respect for a Christian priest *(The) Reverend Donald Jones*

**rev·e·rent** /ˈrevərənt/ *adj* having or showing a feeling of great respect or admiration –opposite **irreverent –reverence** *n* [S;U *for*] **–reverently** *adv*

**rev·e·rie** /ˈrevəri/ *n* [C;U *about*] (a state of) pleasant thoughts and dreams while awake

**re·vers·al** /rɪˈvɜːsəl‖-ɜr-/ *n* [C;U *of*] (a case of) being REVERSED²: *He suffered a reversal of fortune and lost all his money.*

**re·verse¹** /rɪˈvɜːs‖-ɜrs/ *adj* [A] opposite in position; back; being the REVERSE³: *the reverse side of the cloth*|*Please read the names on the list* **in reverse order**. (=from the end to the beginning)

**reverse²** *v* **-versed, -versing 1** [I;T] to (cause to) go backwards: *He reversed the car through the gate.*| *The car reversed through the gate.* **2** [T] to change (a decision or judgment) to the opposite: *He reversed the court's judgment and set the prisoner free.* **3** [T] to change round (proper order or positions): *Today we'll reverse the usual order of the lesson* **4 reverse the charges** also **call collect** *AmE*–to make a telephone call to be paid for by the person receiving it **–reversible** *adj: This coat is reversible–you can wear it inside out.*

**reverse³** *n* **1** [*the* U *of*] the opposite: *He did the reverse of what we expected: instead of being angry, he bought us a drink.* **2** [U] also **reverse gear**– the position of the controls that causes backward movement, esp. in a car: *Put the car into reverse.*

**re·vert to** sbdy./sthg. /rɪˈvɜːt‖-ɜrt/ *v prep* [T] **1** [+*v-ing*] to go back to (a former condition, habit, subject of conversation): *He's stopped taking drugs now, but he may revert to taking them again.*|*After the settlers left, the area soon reverted to desert.* **2** *law* (of property) to go back to (an owner) **–reversion** *n* [U *to*]: *reversion to bad habits*

**re·view¹** /rɪˈvjuː/ *n* **1** an act of REVIEWing² (1): *After a careful review of political events he decided not to vote at all.* **2** a magazine or newspaper article giving judgments on a new book, play, television show, etc. **3** a show of the armed forces, in the presence of a king or queen or an important general: *a naval review* **4 be/come under review** to be/start to be considered with a view to possible changes: *The company's wage system is coming under review.*

**review²** *v* **1** [T] to consider and judge (an event or state of affairs); go over again in the mind: *The committee is reviewing its decision.* **2** [I;T] to write a REVIEW¹ (2) of (a play, book, etc.): *The play was well reviewed* (=was praised) *in all the newspapers.*

**re·view·er** /rɪˈvjuːəʳ/ *n* a person who REVIEWS² (2) plays, books, etc.

**re·vile** /rɪˈvaɪl/ *v* **-viled, -viling** [T] *fml* to curse; speak very strongly and angrily to or of

**re·vise** /rɪˈvaɪz/ *v* **-vised, -vising 1** [T] to read through (a piece of writing) carefully, making improvements and putting mistakes right **2** [T] to change (opinions, intentions, etc.) because of new information or more thought **3** [I;T] *BrE* to study again (lessons already learnt) in preparation for an examination

**re·vi·sion** /rɪˈvɪʒən/ *n* **1** [C;U] (an act of) revising (REVISE¹ (1)) **2** [C] a piece of writing that has been REVISED¹ (1) **3** [U] *BrE* the work of studying again lessons already learnt: *revision for the examination*

**re·vi·tal·ize** ||also **-ise** *BrE* /riː'vaɪtəl-aɪz/ *v* **-ized, -izing** [T] to put new strength or power into **–revitalization** /-'zeɪʃən/ *n* [U]

**re·vi·val** /rɪ'vaɪvəl/ *n* **1** [C;U *of*] (a) rebirth or renewal; reviving or being REVIVED: *a revival of interest in old films* **2** [C] a new performance of an old play after many years

**re·vive** /rɪ'vaɪv/ *v* **-vived, -viving** [I;T] **1** to make or become conscious or healthy again: *That rose will revive if you water it.* **2** to bring or come back into use or existence: *to revive an old custom*

**re·voke** /rɪ'vəʊk/ *v* **-voked, -voking** [T] to put an end to (a law, decision, permission, etc.); CANCEL

**re·volt**[1] /rɪ'vəʊlt/ *v* **1** [I *against*] to act violently against those in power: *The people revolted against the military government.* **2** [T] to shock; cause (someone) to feel violent dislike and sickness: *Such cruelty revolted him.* –see also REVULSION; compare DISGUST

**revolt**[2] *n* [C;U *against*] (an example of) the act of REVOLTing[1] (1): *a nation* **in (a state of) revolt**

**re·volt·ing** /rɪ'vəʊltɪŋ/ *adj* very nasty and unpleasant: *a revolting smell of bad eggs* **–revoltingly** *adv*

**rev·o·lu·tion** /ˌrevə'luːʃən/ *n* **1** [C;U] (a time of) great social change, esp. the changing of a ruler and/or political system by force: *the Russian revolution* **2** [C *in*] a complete change (in ways of thinking or acting): *The invention of air travel caused a revolution in our way of living|the computer revolution* **3** [C;U] (one complete) circular movement round a fixed point: *The earth makes one revolution round the sun each year.* **4** [C] also **rev** *infml*–(in a machine) one complete circular movement on a central point, as of a wheel: *a speed of 100 revolutions per minute* –see also REVOLVE

**rev·o·lu·tion·a·ry**[1] /ˌrevə'luːʃənəri||-ʃəneri/ *adj* **1** [A *no comp.*] connected with (a) REVOLUTION (1): *a revolutionary leader* **2** completely new and different; being or causing a REVOLUTION (2): *a revolutionary new way of growing rice*

**revolutionary**[2] *n* **-ries** a person who favours or joins in a REVOLUTION (1)

**rev·o·lu·tion·ize** ||also **-ise** *BrE* /ˌrevə'luːʃənaɪz/ *v* **-ized, -izing** [T] to cause a complete change in; cause a REVOLUTION (2) in: *The discovery of the new drug has revolutionized the treatment of many diseases.*

**re·volve** /rɪ'vɒlv||rɪ'vɑlv/ *v* **-volved, -volving** [I;T *on, round*] to (cause to) spin round (on or around a central point); make REVOLUTIONs (4): *The wheels began to revolve slowly.|The Earth revolves round the sun once a year.|revolving doors*

**revolve around** sbdy./sthg. *v prep* [T not *be* + *v-ing; no pass.*] to have as a centre or main subject: *A baby's life revolves mainly around its mother and father.*

**re·volv·er** /rɪ'vɒlvə^r||rɪ'vɑl-/ *n* a type of small gun (PISTOL)

**re·vue** /rɪ'vjuː/ *n* a light theatrical show with songs, dances, and jokes, esp. about the events and fashions of the present time

**SPELLING NOTE**
Words with the sound /r/ may be spelt **wr-**, like **wrong.**

**re·vul·sion** /rɪ'vʌlʃən/ *n* [S;U *against*] (a) feeling of being shocked and REVOLTed[1] (2): *We looked away in revulsion from the scene of the accident.*

**re·ward**[1] /rɪ'wɔːd||-ɔrd/ *v* [T *for,with*] to give a REWARD to (someone): *He rewarded the boy (for bringing back the lost dog).|How can I reward you for all your help?*

**reward**[2] *n* [C;U *for*] (something given or gained as) return for work or service: *She got nothing* **in reward** *(for her kindness).|The police are offering a reward of £1,000 for information about the robbery.*

**re·ward·ing** /rɪ'wɔːdɪŋ||-ɔr-/ *adj* (of an experience or action) worth doing or having; WORTHWHILE: *a rewarding job* –opposite **unrewarding**

**re·wire** /ˌriː'waɪə^r/ *v* **-wired, -wiring** [T] to put new electric wires into (a building)

**re·write** /ˌriː'raɪt/ *v* **-wrote** /'rəʊt/, **-written** /-'rɪtn/, **-writing** [T] to write again in a different, esp. more suitable, way

**rhap·so·dy** /'ræpsədi/ *n* **-dies** [*about,over*] an expression of (too) great praise and wild excitement

**rhet·o·ric** /'retərɪk/ *n* [U] **1** the art of speaking or writing so as to persuade people effectively **2** *derog* speech or writing that sounds fine and important, but is really insincere or without meaning **–rhetorical** /rɪ'tɒrɪkəl||-'tɔ-, -'tɑ- / *adj* [A] **–rhetorically** *adv*

**rhetorical ques·tion** /-ˌ··· '··/ *n* a question asked only for effect, and not expecting any answer

**rheu·mat·ic** /ruːmætɪk/ *adj* connected with or having RHEUMATISM: *a rheumatic condition of the joints|a rheumatic old woman*

**rheu·ma·tis·m** /'ruːmətɪzəm/ *n* [U] a disease causing pain and stiffness in the joints or muscles

**rhi·no·ce·ros** /raɪ'nɒsərəs||-'nɑ-/ also **rhino** /raɪnəʊ/ *infml– n* **rhinoceros** *or* **rhinoceroses** a large, heavy, thick-skinned animal of Africa or Asia, with either one or two horns on its nose

**rho·do·den·dron** /ˌrəʊdə'dendrən/ *n* a bush that is grown for its large bright flowers, and keeps its leaves in winter (is EVERGREEN)

**rhu·barb** /'ruːbɑːb||-ɑrb/ *n* [U] a broad-leaved garden plant whose thick juicy stems are boiled with sugar and eaten

**rhyme**[1] /raɪm/ *n* **1** [C] a word that RHYMEs[2] *with another: "Bold" and "cold" are rhymes.* **2** [U] the use of words that RHYME[2] in poetry: *Shakespeare sometimes wrote in rhyme.* **3** [C] a short and not serious piece of writing, using words that RHYME[2] **4 rhyme or reason** (only used in NEGATIVEs[2], questions, etc.) any sense or meaning: *There doesn't seem to be (any) rhyme or reason in his actions–is he mad?*

**rhyme**[2] *v* **rhymed, rhyming** [I *with*; not *be* + *v-ing*] (of words or lines of poetry) to end with the same sound (as another word, or as each other): *"House" rhymes with "mouse".|This poem doesn't rhyme*

**rhyth·m** /'rɪðəm/ *n* [C;U] (a) regular, repeated pattern of sounds or movements in speech, dancing, music, etc.: *the exciting rhythms of African drum music*|(fig.) *the rhythm of the seasons*

**rhyth·mic** /'rɪðmɪk/ *adj* having RHYTHM: *the rhythmic beating of one's heart* **–rhythmically** *adv*

**rib**[1] /rɪb/ *n* one of the 12 pairs of bones running round the chest of a man or animal, from the SPINE (1) to where they join at the front

**rib²** *v* **-bb-** [T] *infml* to make fun of (someone) in a friendly way: *He is ribbed by his friends.*

**rib·ald** /'rɪbəld/ *adj* humorously rude and disrespectful: *ribald jokes|ribald soldiers* **–ribaldry** *n* [U]

**rib·bon** /'rɪbən/ *n* [C;U] (a piece of) silk or other cloth woven in a long narrow band and used for tying the hair, for decoration, etc.: *red ribbons in her hair|a black* TYPEWRITER *ribbon*

**rib cage** /'· ·/ *n* the wall of RIBS that encloses and protects the lungs

**rice** /raɪs/ *n* [U] (the seeds of) a food grain grown in wet tropical places, esp. in India and China: *Would you like rice with your meat?|***Rice pudding** *is a sweet dish made by baking rice with milk and sugar.*

**rich** /rɪtʃ/ *adj* **1** (of a person) wealthy; possessing a lot of money or property **2** [F *in*] containing a lot of a certain thing: *This fish is rich in oil.* **3** (of possessions) expensive, valuable, and beautiful: *rich silk/furniture* **4** (of food) containing a lot of cream, sugar, eggs, etc.; heavy; *a very rich Christmas cake* **5** (of land) good for growing crops in: *rich soil* **6** (of a sound or colour) deep and strong: *the rich notes of the church* ORGAN (3)*|a rich dark red* –opposite **poor** (for 1,5) **–richness** *n* [U]

**rich·es** /'rɪtʃ$\frac{1}{2}$z/ *n* [P] *lit* wealth: *All his riches are no good to him if he is so ill.*

**rich·ly** /'rɪtʃli/ *adv* splendidly; in a large quantity: *a queen's dress richly decorated with jewels*

**rick** /rɪk/ *n* a large pile of wheat stems (STRAW) or dried grass (HAY), that stands out in a field

**rick·et·y** /'rɪk$\frac{1}{2}$ti/ *adj* weakly joined and likely to break: *a rickety old cart*

**rick·shaw, -sha** /'rɪkʃɔː/ *n* a small vehicle used in East Asia for carrying one or two passengers and powered by a man either pulling or cycling.

**ric·o·chet** *v* **-cheted** /ʃeɪd/, **-cheting** /-ʃeɪ-ɪŋ/ [I *off*] (of a stone, bullet, etc.) to change direction when it hits a surface at an angle: *The bullet ricocheted off the bridge.*

**rid** /rɪd/ *v* see RID OF

**rid·dance** /'rɪdəns/ *n* **Good riddance!** (said when one is glad that someone or something has gone) –see also RID OF

**rid·dle** /'rɪdl/ *n* a difficult and amusing question to which one must guess the answer: (fig.) *Robert's character is a complete riddle* (=mystery) *to me.*

**riddle** sbdy./sthg. **with** sthg. *v prep* **-dled, -dling** [T *often pass.*] to make full of (holes): *The tent's riddled with holes.|Don't move or I'll riddle you with bullets!*

**ride¹** /raɪd/ *v* **rode** /rəʊd/, **ridden** /'rɪdn/, **riding 1** [I;T] to travel along, sitting on and controlling (a horse, or other animal, a bicycle, or a motorcycle): *Can you ride a bicycle?|We rode across the fields.|He got on his bicycle and rode off down the road.|The king rode on an elephant.|Alison is learning to ride.* (=ride a horse) –compare DRIVE **2** [I *in*] to travel in a vehicle not controlled by oneself: *She gets sick when she rides in a bus.*

**ride** sthg.↔ **out** *v adv* [T] to come safely through (bad weather, trouble, difficult times, etc.): *to ride out the storm/the* RECESSION

**ride up** *v adv* [I] (of clothing) to move upwards or out of place: *Her skirt rides up when she sits down.*

**ride²** *n* **1** a journey on an animal, in a vehicle, etc., esp. for pleasure: *Shall we go for a ride in the car?* –compare DRIVE **2 take someone for a ride** *infml* to deceive someone

**rid·er** /'raɪdəʳ/ *n* a person who rides esp. a horse

**ridge** /rɪd·/ *n* a long narrow raised part of any surface, such as the top of a range of mountains or of a sloping roof where the two sloping surfaces meet: *He walked along the mountain ridge*

**rid·i·cule¹** /'rɪd$\frac{1}{2}$kjuːl/ *n* [U] unkind laughter; being made fun of: *His behaviour deserves ridicule rather than blame.*

**ridicule²** *v* **-culed, -culing** [T] to laugh unkindly at; make unkind fun of: *They all ridiculed the idea.*

**ri·dic·u·lous** /rɪ'dɪkjʊləs||-kjə-/ *adj derog* silly; deserving RIDICULE¹: *She looks ridiculous in those tight trousers.* **–ridiculously** *adv*: *The examination was ridiculously easy.* **–ridiculousness** *n* [U]

**rid·ing** /'raɪdɪŋ/ *n* [U] the skill or exercise of travelling on a horse: *a riding lesson*

**rid** sbdy./sthg. **of** sbdy./sthg. /rɪd/ *v prep* **rid of** *or* **ridded of, rid of, ridding of** [T] **1** to make free of: *They swore that they would rid the country of its military rulers.|He's gone, and I'm glad to be rid of him.* (=to be free of him again) **2 get rid of: a** to free oneself from (something unwanted): *Try to* **get rid of** *your nasty cold.* **b** to drive, throw, or give away or destroy: *How can I* **get rid of** *the flies in the kitchen?*

**rife** /raɪf/ *adj* [F] *esp. lit* **1** (of bad things) widespread; common: *Disease and violence were rife in the city.* **2** [*with*] full (of bad things): *The city was rife with disease and violence.*

**ri·fle¹** /'raɪfəl/ *n* a long-barrelled gun fired from the shoulder

**rifle²** *v* **-fled, -fling** [T *of*] to search through and steal everything valuable out of (a place): *Somebody has been rifling my drawers.*

**rift** /rɪft/ *n* [*between, in*] *fml & lit* a crack; narrow opening made by breaking: *a rift in the clouds|*(fig.) *a rift between two friends*

**rig¹** /rɪg/ *v* **-gg-** [T] to provide (a ship) with the necessary ropes, sails, etc. : *a fully-rigged vessel*

**rig** sthg.↔ **up** *v adv* [T] *infml* to put together for a short time out of materials easily found: *Let's try to rig up some sort of shelter.*

**rig²** *n* **1** the way a ship's sails are arranged: *Judging by its rig, I'd say it was a fishing boat.* **2** a piece of apparatus (for the stated purpose): *an* OILRIG

**rig³** *v* **-gg-** [T] to arrange (an event) dishonestly for one's own advantage: *They complained that the election had been rigged.*

**rig·ging** /'rɪgɪŋ/ *n* [*the* U] all the ropes and sails on a ship: *The ship lost most of her rigging in the storm.*

**right¹** /raɪt/ *adj* **1** [A] on or belonging to the side of the body that does not contain the heart: *Most people write with their right hand.* **2** [A] on, by, or in the direction of this side: *a right turn, not a left turn*

**right²** *n* **1** [U] the RIGHT¹ (2) side or direction: *Take the turning on the right.* **2** [U +*sing.pl. v*] (*often cap.*) political parties or groups (such as the CONSERVATIVE or REPUBLICAN parties) that favour fewer political changes and less State control, and generally support the employers or those in official positions rather than the workers: *The right oppose(s) the new* *taxes.*|*the far Right* –opposite **left**

**right**[3] *adj* **1** [F +*to-v*] just; morally good: *I'll try to do whatever is right.*|*It's not right to tell lies.*|*I was right in reporting/right to report the matter to the police.* **2** correct; true: *Is that the right time?*|*"Is this Piccadilly Circus?" "Yes, that's right."* –opposite **wrong** (for 1,2) **3 put right** also **set right– a** to put into the correct position: *Put the picture right–it's not straight.*|*Put the clock right.* (=make it show the correct time) **b** also **put straight–** to give correct information to (someone who has a wrong opinion), often rather sharply: *He thought it was Thursday, but I put him right.* **4 right enough** also **sure enough–** as was expected: *I told him to come, and right enough he arrived the next morning.* **5 Right you are!** also **Right oh!** –Yes; I will; I agree: *"Shut the window, please." "Right you are!"* **–rightness** *n* [U]

**right**[4] *n* **1** [U] what is RIGHT[3] (1): *She's old enough to know the difference between right and wrong.* **2** [S;U *of,to*] (a) morally just or lawful claim: *She has a right/has no right to say that.*|*She has a right/the right to half your money.*|*She is British* **by right of** *marriage.* **3 in one's own right** because of a personal claim that does not depend on anyone else: *Elizabeth II is queen of England in her own right.* (=not because she is married to a king) **4 in the right** having justice on one's side –opposite **in the wrong** –see also RIGHTS

**right**[5] *adv* **1** towards the RIGHT[2] (1): *He turned right.* –opposite **left 2** [*adv* +*adv/prep*] completely; directly: *right now*|*right in the middle*|*right/straight after breakfast*|*right/straight in front of you*|*Go right back to the beginning.* **3** properly; correctly: *to guess right*|*Did I do it right?* –opposite **wrong 4** (in answer to a suggestion or plan) Yes; I will; ALL RIGHT: *"Come tomorrow." "Right. What time?"* **5 right away** at once; without delay

**right**[6] *v* [T] to put (something) right or upright again: *The cat righted itself during the fall, and landed on its feet.*

**right an·gle** /ˈ· ˌ··/ *n* an angle of 90 degrees, as at any of the four corners of a square **–right-angled** *adj*

**right·eous** /ˈraɪtʃəs/ *adj* [*no comp.*] *lit & bibl* **1** (doing what is) lawful and morally good: *"I never drink or smoke," he said in a righteous voice.* **2** (of feelings) having good or just cause: *righteous anger* **–righteously** *adv* **–righteousness** *n* [U]

**right·ful** /ˈraɪtfəl/ *adj* [A] lawful; according to a just claim: *Who is the rightful owner of this car?* **–rightfully** *adv* **–rightfulness** *n* [U]

**right-hand** /ˌ· ˈ·◂/ *adj* [A] **1** on or to the right side: *Take a right-hand turn.* –opposite **left-hand 2 right-hand man** a person's most useful and valuable helper

**right-hand·ed** /ˌ· ˈ··◂/ *adj* using the right hand for most actions rather than the left: *Most people are right-handed.* –opposite **left-handed**

**right·ly** /ˈraɪtli/ *adv* correctly; truly; justly: *He believed,* **rightly or wrongly**, that she was guilty.

> **SPELLING NOTE**
> Words with the sound /r/ may be spelt **wr-**, like **wrong.**

**right of way** /ˌ· · ˈ·/ *n* **rights of way 1** [C] *law* a right to follow a path across someone else's land: *We have a right of way across his field.* **2** [*the* U] the right of traffic to drive, cross, pass, etc., before other vehicles: *It's our right of way at this turning.*

**rights** /raɪts/ *n* [P] **1** the political, social, etc., advantages to which someone has a just claim, morally or in law: *to fight for women's rights* **2 by rights** in justice; if things were done properly: *I shouldn't by rights be working so late.* **3 set/put someone/something to rights** to make someone/something just, healthy, correct, etc.: *We need to put/set the country to rights again.* **4 within one's rights** not going beyond one's just claims: *You'd be quite within your rights to refuse to work on Sunday.*

**right wing** /ˌ· ˈ·◂/ *adj,n* [U +*sing. pl.v*] (the members) of a political party (esp. a CONSERVATIVE or REPUBLICAN party) or group, favouring fewer political changes, CAPITALISM, etc.: *a right wing politician*|*The right wing of the party is/are opposed to this plan.* –opposite **left wing**; compare FASCIST, RIGHT[2] (3)

**ri·gid** /ˈrɪdʒɨd/ *adj* stiff; not easy to bend: *a tent supported on a rigid framework*|*She was rigid with fear.*|(fig.) *He's very rigid in his ideas on marriage.* **–rigidly** *adv* **–rigidity** /rɪˈdʒɪdɨti/ *n* [U]

**rig·ma·role** /ˈrɪgmərəul/ *n* [S;U] *infml derog* a long confused story or a long set of actions that must be performed but seem to have little purpose: *He had to go through the usual rigmarole of signing legal papers in order to complete the business deal.*

**rig·or mor·tis** /ˌrɪgə ˈmɔːtɨs, ˌraɪgɔː-‖ˌrɪgər/ *n* [U] *Latin* the stiffening of the muscles after death

**rig·or·ous** /ˈrɪgərəs/ *adj* **1** careful and thorough: *The doctor gave him a rigorous examination.* **2** severe; painful: *the rigorous hardships of the journey* **–rigorously** *adv*

**rig·our** *BrE* **rigor** *AmE* /ˈrɪgə^r/ *n* [U] **1** hardness; lack of mercy: *He deserves to be punished with the full rigour of the law.* **2** severe conditions: *the rigour(s) of a Canadian winter*

**rile** /raɪl/ *v* **riled, riling** [T] *infml* to annoy; make angry: *It riles me when he won't stop whistling.* –see ANGRY (USAGE)

**rim** /rɪm/ *n* **1** the outside edge or border of esp. a round or circular object: *the rim of a cup/of a wheel* **2 -rimmed** having a rim or rims of: *horn-rimmed glasses* **–rimless** *adj*: *She wore rimless glasses.*

**rind** /raɪnd/ *n* [U] the thick, sometimes hard, outer covering of certain foods or fruits, esp. of the LEMON: *a piece of* LEMON *rind*|*cheese rind*

USAGE Although the skin of the orange is of this type, it is called **peel**

**ring**[1] /rɪŋ/ *n* **1** [C] a circular band, esp. one of gold, silver, etc. worn on the finger: *She wears a wedding ring to show that she's married.*|*the rings of the* PLANET *Saturn* | *A key ring is for carrying keys on.* **2** [C] a circular line, mark, or arrangement: *children dancing in a ring*|*count the rings of a tree when it is cut across*|*the ring of a cooker* –see picture on page 337 **3** [*the* S] any closed-in central space where performances take place, as in a CIRCUS (2) or for BOXING **4** [C] a group of people who work together, esp. dishonestly, to control business affairs for their own advantage: *a drug ring* **5 make/run rings round someone** to do things much better and faster than someone

**ring²** *v* [T *with*] to make, put, or form a ring round: *Police ringed the building.*

**ring³** *v* **rang** /ræŋ/, **rung** /rʌŋ/, **ringing 1** [T] to cause (a bell) to sound: *The cyclist rang his bell loudly.|Ring the bell for* (=to call) *your secretary.* **2** [I] (of a bell, telephone, etc.) to sound: *The telephone's ringing.|The doorbell rang loudly.* **3** [I *for*] to ring a bell as a sign that one wants something: *She rang for a drink.* **4** [I *with*] (of the ears) to be filled with a continuous sound: *The crash really made my ears ring.* **5** *BrE*‖ **call** *AmE*–[I;T *up*] to telephone (someone): *Please ring (up) the doctor.|I'll ring you (back)* (=telephone you again)|*I wonder when mother will ring?* –see TELEPHONE (USAGE) **6 ring a bell** *infml* to remind one of something **7 ring false/true** to sound untrue/true: *It was a clever excuse, but it didn't really ring true.* **8 ring the changes (on)** to introduce variety (in): *You can wear the shirt with trousers, or ring the changes and wear it with a dress.*

**ring off** *v adv* [I] *BrE* to end a telephone conversation: *I'd better ring off now–the baby's crying.*

**ring out** *v adv* [I] (of a voice, bell, etc.) to sound loudly and clearly: *A loud shot rang out.*

**ring up** sthg. *v adv* [T] to record (money paid) on a CASH REGISTER

**ring⁴** *n* **1** [C;S] (an act of making) a sound of or like a bell: *He gave several loud rings at the door.|the ring of horseshoes on the street* **2** [S] a quality: *Her story had* **a ring of truth** *about it.* **3 give someone a ring** to telephone someone: *I'll give you a ring tonight.* –see TELEPHONE (USAGE)

**ring·lead·er** /ˈrɪŋˌliːdəʳ/ *n* a person who leads others to do wrong or make trouble –see also RING¹ (4)

**ring·let** /ˈrɪŋlɨt/ *n* a long hanging curl of hair

**ring·mas·ter** /ˈrɪŋˌmɑːstəʳ‖-ˌmæ-/ *n* a person, esp. a man, whose job is directing performances in the CIRCUS (2) ring

**ring road** /ˈ· ·/ *BrE*‖**beltway** *AmE*– *n* a road that goes round the edge of a large town so that traffic need not pass through the centre

**ring·side** /ˈrɪŋsaɪd/ *adj, n* [A; *the* S] (at) the edge of a RING¹ (3) where things are happening: *We had* **ringside seats** *for the big fight, and saw it all.*

**rink** /rɪŋk/ *n* a specially prepared surface, either of ice, for skating (SKATE), or of any hard material, for roller-skating (ROLLER SKATE)

**rinse¹** /rɪns/ *v* **rinsed, rinsing** [T *out*] **1** to wash (esp. clothes) in clean water so as to take away soap, dirt, etc.: *I'll just rinse (out) these shirts.|Rinse your mouth (out).* **2** to wash (soap, dirt, etc.) out (of something) with clean water: *Rinse the soap out of this shirt.*

**rinse²** *n* **1** [C] an act of rinsing (RINSE¹): *Give the shirts at least three rinses.* **2** [C;U] (a) liquid for colouring the hair: *a (bottle of) blue rinse*

**ri·ot¹** /ˈraɪət/ *n* **1** [C] a scene of noisy, uncontrolled, often violent behaviour by a usu. large disorderly crowd of people: *The army was called in to* PUT **down** (1) *a riot.|The football supporters* **ran riot** (=became violent and uncontrollable) *after the defeat of their team.* **2** [S] *infml* a very funny and successful occasion or person: *I hear the new show is a riot–let's go and see it!*

**riot²** *v* [I] to take part in a RIOT¹ (1): *The crowds are rioting for more pay/rioting against the Government.* –**rioter** *n*

**ri·ot·ous** /ˈraɪətəs/ *adj* **1** (of people or behaviour) wild and disorderly: *a riotous crowd* **2** *apprec* (of an occasion) noisy and exciting: *They spent a riotous night drinking and singing.* –**riotously** *adv*

**rip¹** /rɪp/ *v* **-pp-** [I;T] to tear or be torn quickly and violently: *The sail ripped under the force of the wind.|He ripped the cloth with his knife.|I ripped the letter open.|He ripped the curtains to/into pieces.*

**rip** sbdy.sthg.↔ **off** *v adv* [T] *infml* **1** to charge (someone) too much: *They really ripped us off at that hotel.* **2** to steal: *Someone's ripped off my car!* –see also RIP-OFF

**rip** sthg.↔ **up** *v adv* [T] to tear violently into pieces: *Angrily, she ripped the letter up.*

**rip²** *n* a long tear or cut: *a rip in the material*

**RIP** *abbrev. for*: rest in peace (written on gravestones)

**rip·cord** /ˈrɪpkɔːd‖-kɔrd/ *n* the cord that one pulls to open a PARACHUTE after jumping from an aircraft

**ripe** /raɪp/ *adj* **1** (of fruit and crops) fully grown and ready to be eaten: *a field of ripe corn* **2** (esp. of cheese) old enough to be eaten **3** [F *for; no comp.*] ready or suitable (for): *land ripe for industrial development|I won't tell her the news until* **the time is ripe.** –**ripeness** *n*

**rip·en** /ˈraɪpən/ *v* [I;T] to make or become ripe: *The sun ripens the corn.|The corn ripens in the sun.*

**rip-off** /ˈ· ·/ *n infml* an act of charging too much –see also RIP¹ **off**

**rip·ple¹** /ˈrɪpəl/ *v* **-pled, -pling 1** [I;T] to (cause to) move in RIPPLES² (1): *The wind rippled the surface of the cornfield.* **2** [I] to make a sound like gently running water: *a rippling stream*

**ripple²** *n* **1** [C] a very small wave; gentle waving movement: *ripples on a pool when the wind blows* **2** [S] a sound of or like gently running water: *I heard the ripple of the stream.*

**rise¹** /raɪz/ *v* **rose** /rəʊz/, **risen** /ˈrɪzən/, **rising** [I] **1** to go up; get higher: *The river is rising after the rains.|Smoke rose from the factory chimneys.|Her voice rose higher and higher with excitement.|The price of bread has risen by 15%.|The road rises steeply from the village.|He rose to an important position in the firm.|My spirits rose* (=I became happier) *when I heard the news.* –opposite **fall 2** (of the sun, moon, or stars) to come up; appear above the horizon: *The sun rises in the east.* –opposite **set 3** *fml* to get out of bed; get up: *She rises before it is light.* **4** also **arise** *fml*–to stand up from lying, kneeling, or sitting: *She rose to greet her guests.* **5** to show above the surroundings: *trees rising over the roof-tops* **6** (of wind or storms) to get stronger **7** (of a river) to begin: *The River Rhine rises in Switzerland.* **8** to come up to the surface of a liquid: *The fish are rising; perhaps we'll catch one.* **9 rise again** also **rise from the dead**–to come back to life after being dead **10 rise to the occasion** to show that one can deal with a difficult matter: *When the unexpected guests came, we rose to the occasion by making a meal.*

USAGE Do not confuse **rise**, which is always [I] and means "to go up to a higher position," and **raise**, which is always [T] and means "to move someone or something to a higher position" :*They* **raised** *the curtain and the play began.*|*The curtain* **rose** *and the play began.* **Arise** can mean the same as **rise,** but this is very formal; its usual meaning is "to come into being": *A problem has* **arisen** *with the new computer.*

**rise against** sbdy./sthg. *v prep* [T] to REBEL against (rule or rulers); begin to oppose: *The people rose (up) against their leaders.*

**rise**[2] *n* **1** [C *in*] an increase (in price, amount, temperature, etc.): *a rise in the cost of living* **2** [U] the act of growing greater or more powerful: *the rise and fall of the Roman Empire* **3** [C] an upward slope; small hill **4** [C] *BrE*‖**raise** *AmE*– an increase in wages: *We all got a £6-a-week rise last month.* **5 give rise to** to be the cause of; lead to (esp. bad things): *Unhealthy conditions* **give rise to** *disease.*

**risk**[1] /rɪsk/ *n* **1** [C;S;U] a danger: *There's some/a great/no risk of fire.*|*The disease is spreading, and all young children are* **at risk.** ( =in danger)|*You have to take/***run** *a lot of* **risks** (=do dangerous things) *in my job.* **2** [C] (in insurance) (a person or thing that is) a danger: *I'm afraid I'm a poor risk for life insurance–my health is so bad.*|*to* INSURE *it for all risks* **3 at one's own risk** agreeing to bear any loss or danger: *"Anyone swimming in this lake does so* **at his own risk**". (notice) **4 at the risk of** with danger of: *He saved my life at the risk of losing his own.*

**risk**[2] *v* [T] **1** to place in danger: *to risk one's health* **2** [+*v-ing*] to take the chance of: *He risked his parents' anger by marrying me.* **3 risk one's neck** to endanger one's life

**risk·y** /ˈrɪski/ *adj* **-ier, -iest** (esp. of an action) dangerous: *You drove too fast round that corner–it was a risky thing to do.* **–riskily** *adv* **–riskiness** *n* [U]

**ri·sot·to** /rɪˈzɒtəʊ‖-sɔ-/ *n* **-tos** [C;U] (a) food made of rice cooked with cheese, onions, chicken, etc.

**ris·qué** /ˈrɪskeɪ‖rɪˈskeɪ/ *adj* (of a joke, story, etc.) slightly rude; concerned with sex

**ris·sole** /ˈrɪsəʊl/ *n* a small round flat mass of cut-up meat (or fish), cooked in hot fat

**rite** /raɪt/ *n* a form of behaviour with a fixed pattern, usu. for a religious purpose: *funeral rites* –sounds like **right**

**rit·u·al** *n* [C;U] one or more ceremonies or customary acts which are often repeated in the same form: *the ritual of morning prayers in school*|*Christian ritual* (=the form of church service)|*(humor) She went through her usual ritual of making sure all the doors were locked.* **–ritual** *adj: ritual dancing* **–ritually** *adv*

**ri·val**[1] /ˈraɪvəl/ *n* [*for,in*] a person with whom one competes: *Bob and I were rivals for the job.*

**rival**[2] *adj* [A] competing: *a rival company*

**rival**[3] *v* **-ll-** *BrE*‖**-l-** *AmE* [T] to equal; be as good as: *Ships can't rival aircraft for speed.* –see also UNRIVALLED

**ri·val·ry** /ˈraɪvəlri/ *n* **-ries** [C;U *in,with*] competition; (a case of) being RIVALS[1]: *the many rivalries of office life*|*fierce rivalry between the two companies*

**SPELLING NOTE**
Words with the sound /r/ may be spelt **wr-**, like **wrong.**

**riv·er** /ˈrɪvəʳ/ *n* a wide natural stream of water flowing between banks into a lake, into another wider stream, or into the sea: *to go swimming in the river/sailing on the river*|*the river Amazon* –compare STREAM[1]

**riv·er·bed** /ˈrɪvəbed‖-ər-/ *n* the ground over which a river flows between its banks

**riv·er·side** /ˈrɪvəsaɪd‖-ər-/ *n* [A;S] the land on or near the banks of a river: *to tie up the boat by the riverside*|*a riverside hotel*

**riv·et**[1] /ˈrɪvɪ̵t/ *n* a metal pin for fastening together metal plates (as when building a ship)

**rivet**[2] *v* [T] **1** to fasten with RIVETS[1] **2** to attract and hold (someone's attention) strongly: *The strange sound riveted the attention of a passing policeman.*

**riv·et·ing** /ˈrɪvɪ̵tɪŋ/ *adj* very interesting; holding one's attention: *a riveting book*

**ri·vi·e·ra** /ˌrɪviˈeərə/ *n* a warm stretch of coast that is popular with holidaymakers: *the French Riviera*

**RN** *abbrev. for*: Royal Navy (=the British navy): *Captain Brown, RN*

**road** /rəʊd/ *n* a smooth prepared track along which wheeled vehicles can travel: *It takes three hours by train and four* **by road**. (=driving)| |*You must teach the children about* **road safety**.|*I must stop and rest, I've been* **on the road** (=travelling) *for twelve hours.*|*My address is 21 Princess Road.* –see STREET (USAGE); –see picture on page 297

**road·block** /ˈrəʊdblɒk‖-blɑk/ *n* a bar or other object(s) placed across a road, esp. by the police, to stop traffic

**road·side** /ˈrəʊdsaɪd/ *n adj* (at or near) the edge of the road: *We ate our meal by the roadside/at a roadside restaurant.*

**road·way** /ˈrəʊdweɪ/ *n* [S] the middle part of a road where vehicles drive: *Don't stop on the roadway; go to the side.* –compare FOOTPATH, PAVEMENT

**road works** /ˈrəʊdwɜːks‖-ɜr-/ *n* [P] (often seen on a warning sign for motorists) road repairs being carried out

**road·wor·thy** /ˈrəʊdˌwɜːði‖-ɜr-/ *adj* (of a vehicle) in a fit condition to be driven on the road –opposite **unroadworthy –roadworthiness** *n* [U]

**roam** /rəʊm/ *v* [I;T] to wander with no very clear aim (through, around, etc.): *to roam the hills*|*roaming from place to place*

**roar**[1] /rɔːʳ‖rɔr/ *v* **1** [I] to give a deep loud continuing sound: *The lion/The football crowd roared.*|*The car roared past* **2** [I;T +*that/out*] to say or express with a deep loud continuing sound: *He* **roared with laughter/pain/anger.**

**roar**[2] *n* a deep loud continuing sound: *the roar of an angry lion/of a football crowd*|*roars of laughter*

**roar·ing** /ˈrɔːrɪŋ‖ˈrɔrɪŋ/ *adv* very (great): *He came home* **roaring drunk.**|*The film was a* **roaring success.**|*The new restaurant is* **doing a roaring trade.** (= doing very good business)

**roast**[1] /rəʊst/ *v* [I;T] to cook or be cooked by dry heat, either in front of an open fire or in a hot box (OVEN): *to roast a chicken*|*roasted coffee beans*|*The meat is roasting nicely.* –see COOK (USAGE)

**roast**[2] *n* **1** [C] a large piece of ROASTED[1] meat: *We had a roast for dinner.* **2** [A] ROASTED[1]: *roast potatoes*

**roast·ing** /'rəustɪŋ/ *adj,adv* [*no comp.*] very (hot): *a roasting (hot) summer day*

**rob** /rɒb‖rɑb/ *v* **-bb-** [I;T *of*] to take the property of (a person or organization) illegally: *to rob a bank* –see THIEF (USAGE)

**rob·ber** /'rɒbəʳ‖'rɑ-/ *n* a person who robs: *a band/a* GANG *of robbers* –see THIEF (USAGE)

**rob·ber·y** /'rɒbəri‖'rɑ-/ *n* **-ies** [C;U] **1** (an example of) the crime of taking someone else's property; robbing: *He was charged with robbery.* **2 daylight robbery** *infml* charging too much money: *£2 for a beer? It's daylight robbery!*

**robe¹** /rəub/ *n* a long flowing garment **a** for informal occasions: *a bath robe* **b** for official or ceremonial occasions: *a judge's black robes*

**robe²** *v* **robed, robing** [I;T *in*] to dress in ROBES; put on a ROBE: *the king and queen robed in red*

**rob·in** /'rɒbᵻn‖'rɑ-/ *n* a small brown European bird with a red breast

**ro·bot** /'rəubɒt‖-bɑt, -bət/ *n* a machine that can move and do some of the work of a person: *Some of the work in the car factory is now done by robots.*

**ro·bust** *adj* having or showing good health and strength: *a robust baby|a robust company* –**robustly** *adv* –**robustness** *n* [U]

**rock¹** /rɒk‖rɑk/ *v* [I;T] to (cause to) move regularly backwards and forwards or from side to side: *She rocked the child in her arms.|The boat rocked (to and fro) on the water.* **2** [T] to cause great shock and surprise to: *The news of the President's murder rocked the nation.*

**rock²** *n* **1** [U] stone forming part of the earth's surface: *a passage cut through (the) solid rock* **2** [C] a large piece or mass of stone: *danger from falling rocks|ships driven onto the rocks by a storm* **3** [U] (in Britain) a hard sticky kind of sweet made in long round bars: *a stick of (Brighton) rock* **4 on the rocks: a** (of alcoholic drinks) with ice: WHISKY *on the rocks* **b** (esp. of a marriage) in difficulties

**rock³** *n* [U] → ROCK 'N' ROLL

**rock and roll** /ˌ· · '·/ *n* [U] → ROCK 'N' ROLL

**rock bot·tom** /ˌ· '··◂/ *n* [U] (esp. of prices) the lowest point; the bottom: *rock bottom prices.*

**rock·er** /'rɒkəʳ‖'rɑ-/ *n* **1** one of the curved pieces of wood underneath a ROCKING CHAIR, ROCKING HORSE, or CRADLE¹ (1) **2** *AmE* for ROCKING CHAIR **3 off one's rocker** *infml* mad

**rock·e·ry** /'rɒkəri‖'rɑ-/ also **rock garden**– *n* **-ries** a (part of a) garden laid out as a heap of rocks with low-growing plants growing between them

**rock·et¹** /'rɒkᵻt‖'rɑ-/ *n* **1** a tube-shaped apparatus driven by burning gases, used for space travel, and to power bombs or MISSILES (1) **2** a model of this, packed with gunpowder and used as a FIREWORK

**rocket²** *v* [I *up*] (esp. of levels, amounts, etc.) to rise quickly and suddenly: *rocketing prices* –compare PLUMMET

**rock·ing chair** /'rɒkɪŋ tʃeəʳ‖'rɑ-/ ‖ also **rocker** *AmE*– *n* a chair fitted with ROCKERS (1)

**rocking horse** /'·· ·/ *n* a wooden horse fitted with ROCKERS (1), for a child to ride on

**rock 'n' roll** /ˌrɒk ən 'rəul‖ˌrɑk-/ also **rock, rock and roll** *n* [U] popular modern dance music with a strong, loud beat, which usu. repeats the same few phrases and is played on electric instruments

**rock·y** /'rɒki‖'rɑki/ *adj* **-ier, -iest** full of, made of, or like rock: *a rocky path* –**rockiness** *n* [U]

**rod** /rɒd‖rɑd/ *n* a long thin stiff pole or bar of wood, metal, or plastic: *to go fishing with rod and line*

**rode** /rəud/ *v past tense of* RIDE

**ro·dent** /'rəudənt/ *n* a member of the family of small plant-eating animals with strong sharp teeth, that includes rats, mice, and rabbits

**ro·de·o** /rəu'deɪ-əu, 'rəudi-əu/ *n* **-os** in the western US, a public performance at which COWBOYS ride wild horses, catch cattle with ropes, etc.

**roe** /rəu/ *n* [C;U] (a) mass of eggs or male seed (SPERM) in a fish, often eaten as food –sounds like **row**

**rogue** /rəug/ *n becoming rare* **1** a very dishonest person, esp. a man: *Don't buy a used car from that rogue.* **2** *humor* a boy who likes playing tricks: *You little rogue–where are my shoes?*

**rogu·ish** /'rəugɪʃ/ *adj becoming rare* (typical of a person) who is playful and fond of playing tricks: *a roguish smile* –**roguishly** *adv* **roguishness** *n* [U]

**role** /rəul/ *n* the part taken by someone in life or in any activity, esp. the part of some particular actor in a play: *Olivier played the role of Hamlet.|to fulfil her role as a mother* –see also TITLE ROLE

**roll¹** /rəul/ *n* **1** [*of*] a piece of the stated material that has been rolled into a tube: *a roll of film/of cloth* **2** a small long or round loaf for one person: *breakfast rolls|a cheese roll* (=a roll cut and filled with cheese) **3** (*often cap.*) an official list of names: *The teacher* **called the roll.** (=read the list aloud to see if everyone was there)

**roll²** *v* **1** [I;T] to move by turning over and over, or from side to side: *The ball rolled into the hole.|The dog rolled over onto its back.|We rolled the barrels of oil onto the ship.* **2** [I] to move steadily and smoothly along (as if) on wheels: *The train rolled slowly into the station.|The clouds are rolling away.* **3** [T *up*] to form into a tube or other stated shape by curling round and round: *He rolled up the map.|She rolled the clay into a ball.|Please roll me a cigarette.* –opposite **unroll 4** [I] (of a ship) to swing from side to side with the movement of the waves –compare PITCH¹ (6) **5** [T] to make (flat) by pressing with a ROLLER (1) or ROLLING PIN: *Roll the pastry as flat as you can.* **6** [I] to make a long deep sound like that of a lot of quick strokes: *The thunder/drums rolled.* **7** [I;T] (of the eyes) to move round and round

**roll by** *v adv* [I] to go steadily past: *The years rolled by.*

**roll in** sthg. *v prep* [T *no pass.*] to have plenty of (money): *She's rolling in money.*

**roll** sthg.↔ **out** *v adv* [T] to spread (a piece of material) out flat and thin by pressing with a ROLLER (1) or a ROLLING PIN: *roll out the pastry* –compare ROLL² (5)

**roll up** *v adv* **1** [T] (**roll** sthg.↔ **up**) to roll (SLEEVES (1)) *up one's arms; roll (trousers) up one's legs* **2** [I] *infml* to arrive (in any unacceptable way): *She rolled up an hour late.* **3** [I] (used esp. in commands, when asking people to come inside and see a show at a* CIRCUS (2), FAIR³ (1), etc.) to come in: *Roll up, roll up, to see the lions.*

**roll³** *n* **1** [S] a long deep sound as of a lot of quick strokes: *a roll of thunder/of drums* **2** [C] a rolling movement, over and over or to and fro sideways: *the slow roll of a ship on the rough sea*
**roll call** /'· ·/ *n* [U] the time or act of reading out a list of names to see who is there
**roll·er** /'rəʊləʳ/ *n* **1** a tube-shaped piece of wood, metal, hard rubber, etc., that rolls over and over, as used **a** in a machine, for crushing, pressing, printing, etc. **b** for smoothing the surface of grass or roads **c** for moving heavy things that have no wheels: *They pushed the boat down to the water on rollers.* **d** for shaping: *She curls her hair with rollers.* **2** a rod round which something is rolled up: *a big map on a roller*
**roller blind** /'·· ·/ *n BrE* a kind of curtain (BLIND³) that rolls up and down over a window –compare SHADE¹ (2)
**roller coast·er** /'·· ,··/ *n* a kind of small railway with sharp slopes and curves, popular in amusement parks
**roller skate** *n* [*usu. pl.*] a wheeled frame for fitting under a shoe, or a shoe with wheels fixed on, allowing the wearer to move quickly on a road or smooth surface –**roller-skate** *v* **-skated, -skating** [I]
**roll·ing** /'rəʊlɪŋ/ *adj* [A] (of land) rising and falling in long gentle slopes: *a rolling plain*
**rolling pin** /'·· ·/ *n* a tube-shaped piece of wood or other material, for spreading pastry out flat and thin before cooking
**rolling stock** /'·· ·/ *n* [U] everything on wheels that belongs to a railway, such as engines and carriages
**Roman** *n,adj* (a citizen) of the ancient empire or the city of Rome
**Roman Cath·o·lic** /,·· '···/ *adj, n* (a member) of the branch of the Christian religion (the **Roman Catholic Church**) whose leader (POPE) rules from Rome: *Her family are Roman Catholic/are all Roman Catholics.*
**ro·mance** /rəʊ'mæns, rə-/ *n* **1** [C] a story of love, adventure, strange happenings, etc., often set in a distant time or place: *a romance about a king who married a beggar girl* **2** [U] the quality that such stories have; the quality in the human mind that hopes for such experiences in real life: *the romance of life in the Wild West* **3** [C] a love affair: *I think he is having a little romance with Julia.*
**Roman nu·me·ral** /,·· '···/ *n* any of a set of signs, originally used in ancient Rome and sometimes now, for numbers, for example I, II, III, IV, V, etc. –compare ARABIC NUMERAL
**ro·man·tic¹** /rəʊ'mæntɪk, rə-/ *adj* **1** belonging to or suggesting ROMANCE¹: *a very romantic love story* **2** *sometimes derog* fanciful; not practical: *She has romantic ideas about being an actress.* –**romantically** *adv*
**romantic²** *n* ROMANTIC¹ (2) person: *He was a romantic who went off to the South Seas to paint pictures.*
**ro·man·ti·cize** ||also **-ise** *BrE* /rəʊ'mæntɪsaɪz, rə-/ *v* **-cized, -cizing** [I;T] to make (something) seem more interesting or ROMANTIC¹ (2) than it really is: *Keep to the facts and stop romanticizing!|He romanticizes his past.*

> **SPELLING NOTE**
> Words with the sound /r/ may be spelt **wr-**, like **wrong.**

**Ro·ma·ny** /'rəʊməni||'ra-/ *n* **-nies** **1** [C] →GIPSY **2** [A;U] of or related to the GIPSY people or their language
**romp** /rɒmp||ramp/ *v* [I *about,around*] to play noisily and roughly with a lot of running and jumping: *children romping about in the garden* –**romp** *n*
**romp·ers** /'rɒmpəz||'rampərz/ *n* [P] a one-piece garment for babies combining a top and short trouser-like bottom: *a pair of rompers* –see PAIR (USAGE)
**roof¹** /ruːf/ *n* **1** the outside covering on top of a building, closed vehicle, tent, etc.: *The rain's coming in–we must mend the roof.* –compare CEILING –see picture on page 297 **2** a house; home: *She and I can't live* **under the same roof.** **3 a/no roof over one's head** somewhere/nowhere to live **4 roof of the/one's mouth** the bony upper part of the inside of the mouth; PALATE
**roof²** *v* [T *with*] to put a roof on: *a house roofed with lead*
**roof·ing** /'ruːfɪŋ/ *n* [U] material for making or covering roofs
**roof rack** /'· ·/ *n BrE* a metal frame fixed on top of a car roof, for carrying things
**rook** /rʊk/ *n* a large black European bird like a CROW
**room** /ruːm, rʊm/ *n* **1** [C] a division of a building, with its own walls, floor, and CEILING: *I want a double room* (=for two people) *with a view.|a bedroom|a sitting-room* **2** [U +*to-v*] space that could be filled, or that is enough for any purpose: *There's no room to move.|Move along and* **make room for** *me!|A piano* **takes up** *a lot of* **room.**|(fig.) *He needs room* (=a chance) *to develop his skill as a painter.* **3** [U *for*] **a** need for: *There's plenty of room for improvement in his work.* **b** reason for: *There's no room for doubt.* –see PLACE (USAGE) **4 -roomed** having a certain number or size of rooms: *a six-roomed house* –**roomful** *n* [*of*]: *a roomful of noisy children*
**room·mate** /'ruːm,meɪt, 'rʊm-/ *n* a person with whom one shares a lodging
**room ser·vice** /'· ,··/ *n* [U] a service provided by a hotel, by which food, drink, etc., are sent up to a person's room
**room·y** /'ruːmi/ *adj* **-ier, -iest** with plenty of space: *a roomy house/cupboard/car* –**roominess** *n* [U]
**roost** *v* [I] (of a bird) to sit and sleep for the night
**roost·er** /'ruːstəʳ/ *n esp. AmE* for COCK
**root¹** /ruːt/ *n* **1** [*often pl.*] the part of a plant that grows down into the soil in search of food and water: **2** the part of a tooth, hair, or organ that holds it to the rest of the body **3** the origin; cause; central part or base: *Let's get to/get at the root of this matter.* **4** *tech* (in MATHEMATICS) a number that when multiplied by itself a stated number of times gives another stated number: *3 is the* **square root** *of 9.* (3×3=9)|*3 is the* **cube root** *of 27* (3×3×3=27) **5 take/strike root** (of plants or ideas) to become established and begin to grow –see also ROOTS
**root²** *v* [I;T] to (cause to) form roots: *Try to root this plant in the garden.|Do roses root easily?*
**root** sbdy./sthg.↔ **out** *v adv* [T] to get rid of completely (someone or something bad); destroy: *This*

*disease could easily be rooted out.*

**root³** *v* [I *about,around,for*] to search (for something) by turning things over: *Who's been rooting about among my papers?*

**root crop** /'· ·/ *n* a crop that is grown for its roots, such as CARROTS

**root·ed** /'ru:t$\frac{1}{2}$d/ *adj* [F *to*] fixed (as if by roots): *He stood rooted (to the spot).*| *a deeply-rooted fear*

**root·less** /'ru:tl$\frac{1}{2}$s/ *adj* homeless and without ROOTS –**rootlessness** *n* [U]

**roots** /ru:ts/ *n* [P] the feeling of belonging by origin to one particular place: *Her roots are in Scotland.*

**rope¹** /rəup/ *n* **1** [C;U] (a piece of) strong thick cord made by twisting –compare STRING¹ **2 know the ropes** to know from experience the rules and customs in a place or activity: *I've done this before so I know the ropes; shall I show you how to do it?*

**rope²** *v* **roped, roping** [T *up*] to tie up with a rope: *roped chests of tea*

**rope** sbdy.↔ **in** *v adv* [T] *infml* to persuade to help in one's plans or join an activity: *I've been roped in to help sell the tickets.*

**rope** sthg.↔ **off** *v adv* [T] to separate (an area) from the rest with ropes: *They've roped off one end of the room.*

**rope lad·der** /'· ˌ··/ *n* a ladder made of two long ropes connected by cross pieces of wood, rope, or metal

**ro·sa·ry** /'rəuzəri/ *n* **-ries** (esp. in the ROMAN CATHOLIC religion) a set of prayers or the string of BEADS (=small decorative balls) used to count them

**rose¹** /rəuz/ **1** (the brightly-coloured, sweet-smelling flower of) a bush with strong prickly stems and divided leaves **2** [A] (of) a colour from pink to a deep purplish red **3 a bed of roses** a very pleasant state to be in

**rose²** *v past tense of* RISE

**ro·sé** /'rəuzeɪ‖rəu'zeɪ/ *n* [U] a type of light pink wine: *a glass of rosé*

**rose·ma·ry** /'rəuzməri‖-meri/ *n* [U] a low bush whose sweet-smelling leaves are used in cooking

**ro·sette** /rəu'zet/ *n* a bunch of narrow silk bands (RIBBONS) made up in the form of a rose and usu. worn as a sign of something: *The winner of the competition was given a red rosette.*

**ros·ter** /'rɒstə^r‖'rɑ-/ *n* a list of people's names that shows when it is each person's turn to do a certain job –compare ROTA

**ros·trum** /'rɒstrəm‖'rɑ-/ *n* **-trums** *or* **-tra** /trə/ a raised place (PLATFORM) for a public speaker, CONDUCTOR (1), etc.: *the teacher on his rostrum*

**ros·y** /'rəuzi/ *adj* **-ier, -iest 1** (esp. of the human skin) healthily pink: *rosy cheeks* **2** (esp. of the future) giving hope: *Things don't look very rosy at my firm; I'm looking for another job.* –**rosiness** *n* [U]

**rot¹** /rɒt‖rɑt/ *v* **-tt-** [I;T] to (cause to) decay: *The rain has rotted the roof beams.*.|(fig.) *They left him to rot in prison for 20 years.* –see also ROTTEN

**rot²** *n* [U] **1** (the action of) decay: *an old hollow tree full of rot*|(fig.) *How can we* **stop the rot** *in our society?* **2** *BrE infml* foolish remarks or ideas: *Don't talk rot!*

**ro·ta** /'rəutə/ *n BrE* (a list showing) an arrangement for people to take turns to do a job; ROSTER: *a rota for parents to drive children to school*

**ro·ta·ry** /'rəutəri/ *adj* (of movement) turning round a fixed point, like a wheel

**ro·tate** /rəu'teɪt‖'rəuteɪt/ *v* **-tated, -tating** [I;T] **1** to (cause to) turn round a fixed point: *The earth rotates once every 24 hours.*|*You can rotate the wheel with your hand.* **2** to (cause to) take turns or come round in regular order: *to rotate the crops*

**ro·ta·tion** /rəu'teɪʃən/ *n* **1** [U] the action of rotating (ROTATE): *the rotation of the earth*|*The seasons follow each other* **in rotation**. (=coming round one after the other) **2** [C] one complete turn round a fixed point: *to make ten rotations a second*

**ro·tis·ser·ie** /rəu'tɪsəri/ *n* an apparatus for cooking meat by turning it over and over on a bar (SPIT² (1)), over direct heat

**ro·tor** /'rəutə^r/ *n* a part of a machine that ROTATES (1), esp. the system of blades that raise a HELICOPTER into the air

**rot·ten** /'rɒtn‖'rɑtn/ *adj* **1** decayed; gone bad: *rotten eggs*|*a rotten branch* **2** bad; unkind; *What a rotten thing to do to her!* –**rottenness** *n* [U]

**ro·tund** /rəu'tʌnd/ *adj fml or humor* (of a person) fat and round –**rotundity** *n* [S;]

**rou·ble** /'ru:bəl/ *n* (a coin or note worth) the standard amount in the money system of the USSR

**rouge** /ru:·/ *n* [U] a red substance used for colouring the cheeks

**rough¹** /rʌf/ *adj* **1** having an uneven surface; not smooth: *The rough road made the car shake.*|*A cat's tongue is rough.* **2** not gentle, tender, or polite; using force: *a rough voice*|*Play nicely and don't be rough!* **3** not delicate or comfortable; simple: *Life was rough in the American West in the last century.* **4** (of weather, the sea, or a sea journey) stormy and violent; not calm **5** [*no comp.*] (of plans, calculations, etc.) not (yet) in detail or the finished form; not exact: *a rough drawing*|*Do your calculations on rough paper* ( =for rough work).|*I've a rough idea where it is.* **6** *infml* unfortunate and perhaps unfair: *She's been having a rough time recently.*|*It's a bit* **rough on** (=unfortunate for) *him, having to do two people's work.* **7 rough and ready** simple and without comfort –**roughness** *n* [U]

**rough²** *n* [U] **1** the uneven ground with long grass on a GOLF course **2 in rough** in an incomplete or undetailed form: *Draw it in rough first.* **3 take the rough with the smooth** to accept bad things as well as good things without complaining

**rough³** *v* **rough it** *infml* to live in a simple and not very comfortable way

**rough⁴** *adv* **1** in ROUGH¹ (3) conditions, esp. out of doors: *The old man* **slept rough** *for several weeks.* **2** in a ROUGH¹ (2) way: *Those boys certainly play rough!*

**rough·age** /'rʌfɪdʒ/ *n* [U] coarse matter contained in food, that helps the bowels to work

**rough·en** /'rʌfən/ *v* [I;T] to make or become rough: *Before painting the wood, roughen the surface with* SANDPAPER.

**rough·ly** /'rʌfli/ *adv* **1** in a rough manner: *He pushed her roughly away.* **2** about; more or less: *There were roughly 200 people there.*

**rou·lette** /ru:'let/ *n* [U] a game of chance in which a small ball is spun round a moving wheel and falls into a hole marked with a number

**round**[1] /raʊnd/ *adj* **1** circular: *a round plate* **2** shaped like a ball; SPHERICAL: *The Earth is round, not flat.* **3** (of parts of the body) fat and curved: *the child's round red cheeks* **4** [A] (of numbers) complete; and not less: *a round dozen* **5 in round figures** (of numbers) not exactly, but to the nearest 10, 100, 1,000, etc.: *The car cost £9,878–that's £10,000 in round figures.*

**round**[2] ||also **around** *AmE– adv* **1** moving in a circle; measured in a circle: *The wheels went round and round.|a tree three metres round|He works* **all (the) year round.**(=during the whole year) **2** on all sides; in a circular position: *The children gathered round to hear the story.* **3** here and there; about: *They travel round together.* **4** to a particular place: *They invited us round* (=to their house) *for tea.* **5** so as to face the other way; so as to face a certain way: *Turn the picture round to face the wall.|He's got his hat on* **the wrong way round.** (=the back of his hat is at the front) **6 round about** a little bit more or less than; about: *I live round about ten miles from here.* **7 the other way round** in the opposite order: *The dog didn't bite the boy. It was the other way round–the boy bit the dog!*

**round**[3] ||also **around** *AmE– prep* **1** (shows movement or position in a circle with a centre): *The earth goes round the sun.|They danced round (and round) the tree.|We sat round the table.* **2** into all parts of; all over (a place): *He showed us round the castle.* **3** so as to get past; not going straight but changing direction: *He disappeared round the corner.* –see Study Notes on page 474

**round**[4] *n* **1** [*of*] a number or set (of events): *a continual round of parties|a second round of wage claims* (=by trade unions for their members)|*We won the first round* (=set of matches) *of the Football Cup.* **2** a regular journey to a number of houses, offices, etc., in a town: *In the morning I do a paper/milk round.* (=deliver newspapers/milk to houses)|*The policeman made his daily rounds of the village.* **3** a share given out to everyone present: *I'll buy you all a round of drinks!* **4 a** (in GOLF) a complete game including all the holes **b** (in BOXING) one of the periods of fighting in a match, separated by short rests: *He was knocked out in the second round.* **5** one single shot: *He fired round after round.|I've only got two rounds left.* (=bullets for two shots) **6** a complete piece cut off the end (of a loaf of bread): *He ate six rounds of bread and butter!* **7** a type of song for three or four voices, in which each sings the same tune, one starting a line after another has just finished it

**round**[5] *v* **1** [T] to travel round: *She rounded the corner at 95 miles per hour.* **2** [I;T] to make or become round: *round one's lips to whistle|The child's eyes rounded with excitement.*

**round** sthg.↔ **off** *v adv* [T *by, with*] to end suitably and satisfactorily: *We rounded off the evening with a hot drink/by singing a song.*

**round** sbdy./sthg.↔ **up** *v adv* [T] **1** [*to*] to change (an exact figure) to the next highest whole number: *round up 49·5p to 50p* **2** to gather together (scattered things, people, or animals, esp. cattle): *Round up a few friends to help you!*

**SPELLING NOTE**
Words with the sound /r/ may be spelt **wr-**, like **wrong.**

**round·a·bout**[1] /'raʊndəbaʊt/ *n* **1** *BrE* ||**(traffic) circle** *AmE–* a central space at a road crossing, which makes cars go in a circle round it **2** *BrE* for MERRY-GO-ROUND

**roundabout**[2] *adj* (of the way to somewhere) indirect; not the shortest: (fig.) *I heard the news in a roundabout way.*

**roun·ders** /'raʊndəz||-ərz/ *n* [U] a British ball game like BASEBALL, usu. played by children, in which a player hits the ball and then runs round the edge of a square area

**round-eyed** /ˌ· '·◂/ *adj* with the eyes wide open, as in surprise or wonder

**round-shoul·dered** /ˌ· '··◂/ *adj* with bent shoulders; with a back that is not upright

**round-trip** /ˌ· '·◂/ *adj AmE* for RETURN[3]: *a round-trip ticket*

**round trip** *n* a journey to a place and back again

**rouse** /raʊz/ *v* **roused, rousing** [T *from, out of*] to waken: *He's very hard to rouse in the morning.*|(fig.) *The speaker roused the audience to anger.*

**rous·ing** /'raʊzɪŋ/ *adj* that makes people excited: *a very rousing speech about freedom*

**rout** /raʊt/ *v* [T] to defeat completely and drive away: *They routed the enemy.* **–rout** *n*

**route**[1] /ruːt||ruːt, raʊt/ *n* a way planned or followed from one place to another: *the shortest route from London to Edinburgh* –sounds like **root**

**route**[2] *v* **routed, routing** [T *by, through*] to send by a particular ROUTE[1]: *They routed the goods through Italy/by way of Germany.*

**rou·tine**[1] /ruː'tiːn/ *n* [C;U] the regular fixed ordinary way of working or doing things: *Please do it according to routine.|These two babies have quite different daily routines.*

**routine**[2] *adj* [A] regular; not unusual: *a routine medical examination|a routine job* **–routinely** *adv*

**rove** /rəʊv/ *v* **roved, roving** [I;T] to wander; move continually (around): *to rove the seas in search of adventure*

**rov·er** /'rəʊvə^r/ *n lit* a wanderer

**row**[1] /rəʊ/ *v* [I;T] **1** to move (a boat) through the water with OARS (=long poles with flat ends) **2** to travel or carry in this way: *He rowed (the travellers) across the lake.*

**row**[2] /rəʊ/ *n* [*of*] a neat line (of people or things) side by side: *a row of houses/of cups on a shelf|Children standing hand in hand in a row.* (=side by side) *a row of seats* –see picture on page 463

**row**[3] /raʊ/ *n infml* **1** [C] a noisy quarrel, sometimes with violent actions: *He had a row with his wife.* **2** [S] a noise: *Stop making such a row; I can't sleep!*

**row**[4] /raʊ/ *v* [I *with*] *infml* to quarrel, often noisily or violently: *They always row about money.*

**row·an** /'rəʊən, 'raʊən/ also **mountain ash** – *n* a small tree of the rose family with bright red berries

**row·dy** /'raʊdi/ *adj* **-dier, -diest** noisy and rough: *a rowdy evening in the pub| rowdy behaviour/children* **–rowdily** *adv* **–rowdiness** *n* [U]

**row·ing boat** /'·· ˌ·/ also **rowboat** *AmE– n* a small

boat that is moved through the water with OARs (=long poles with flat ends)

**roy·al** /'rɔɪəl/ *adj* [A] for, belonging to, or connected with a king or queen: *the royal palaces|the Royal Navy|the royal family* –**royally** *adv*

**Royal High·ness** /ˌ·· '··/ *n* (the words used when speaking to or of) a prince or princess: *Thank you very much, Your Royal Highness.|His Royal Highness, Prince Charles*

**roy·al·ist** /'rɔɪəlɪ̇st/ *adj,n* (typical of) someone who supports a king or queen or the idea that a country should be ruled by one

**roy·al·ty** /'rɔɪəlti/ *n* **-ties 1** [U] royal power and rank **2** [U +*sing./pl. v*] people of the royal family: *The flag is only raised when royalty is/are present.* **3** [C] a payment made to a writer of a book, piece of music, etc. as part of the profit from selling that work: *The writer gets a 5% royalty on each copy of his book.*

**RPM** *abbrev. for:* REVOLUTIONs (4) per minute, a measure of engine speed

**RSVP** *abbrev. for: French* répondez s'il vous plaît; please reply (written on invitations)

**rub**[1] /rʌb/ *v* **-bb- 1** [T *with, together*] to slide (one surface) with pressure to and fro or round and round against (another); put (something) on a surface in this way: *She rubbed the window (with a cloth).|He rubbed his hands (together) to warm them with pleasure.|Rub salt into the meat before cooking it.* **2** [I *against, on*) (of a surface) to slide in this way (against on another): *This tyre seems badly worn; it must be rubbing against/on something.*

**rub** sbdy./sthg.↔ **down** *v adv* [T] to dry or make smooth by rubbing: *rubbing herself down after a swim|Rub the door down before you paint it.*

**rub** sthg.**in** *v adv* [T] **1** to make (liquid) go into a surface by rubbing: *Rub the polish well in.* **2 rub it in** *infml* to keep talking about something that another person wants to forget: *"You have been late for school every day." "I know; don't rub it in!"*

**rub off** *v adv* [I *on,onto*] to come off a surface (onto another) by rubbing: (fig.) *I hope that some of her good qualities will rub off onto you.*

**rub** sthg.↔ **out** *v adv* [T] *BrE* to remove (esp. pencil writing) with a piece of rubber: *to rub out a word*

**rub** sthg. ↔ **up** *v adv* [T] **1** to polish by rubbing **2 rub someone up the wrong way** to annoy someone

**rub**[2] *n* [S] an act of rubbing: *Give the table a good rub with this polish.*

**rub·ber** /'rʌbəʳ/ *n* **1** [U] a substance, made either from the juice of a tropical tree or chemically, which keeps out water and springs back into position when stretched **2** [C] *esp. BrE* a piece of this substance used for removing pencil marks; ERASER –see picture on page 105

**rubber band** /ˌ·· '·/ *n* a thin circular piece of rubber used for fastening things together: *Put a rubber band round your hair/round this bunch of flowers.*

**rub·ber·y** /'rʌbəri/ *adj often derog* strong and springy like rubber: *The meat's a bit rubbery–you didn't cook it for long enough!*

**rub·bish**[1] /'rʌbɪʃ/ *n* [U] **1** waste material to be thrown away: *to burn the rubbish|a rubbish heap* **2** silly remarks; nonsense: *He's talking rubbish.*

**rubbish**[2] *interj* How silly!

**rub·bish·y** /'rʌbɪʃi/ *adj infml* worthless and silly: *a rubbishy love story*

**rub·ble** /'rʌbəl/ *n* [U] (a mass of) broken stones or bricks: *After the bombing her house was just a heap of rubble.*

**ru·bel·la** /ru:'belə/ *n* [U] *tech* for GERMAN MEASLES

**ru·ble** /'ru:bəl/ *n* → ROUBLE

**ru·by** /'ru:bi/ *n* **-bies** [A;C] (the colour of) a deep red precious stone: *a ruby ring|ruby wine*

**ruck·sack** /'rʌksæk/ *n* a bag fastened to the shoulders, used by climbers and walkers to carry their belongings

**rud·der** /'rʌdəʳ/ *n* a wooden or metal blade at the back of a ship or aircraft that swings to and fro to control the direction

**rud·dy** /'rʌdi/ *adj* **-dier, -diest** (of the face) pink and healthy-looking: *ruddy cheeks* –**ruddiness** *n* [U]

**rude** /ru:d/ *adj* **1** (of a person or behaviour) not at all polite: *It's rude to tell someone you don't like them.|Don't be so rude to your father.* **2** [A] simple and roughly made: *a rude hut* **3** [A] sudden and violent: *a rude shock* **4** improper, concerned with sex: *a rude story* –**rudeness** *n* [U] –**rudely** *adv*

**ru·di·men·ta·ry** /ˌru:dɪ̇'mentəri/ *adj* (of facts, knowledge, etc.) simple; coming or learnt first: *a rudimentary knowledge of chemistry*

**ru·di·ments** /'ru:dɪ̇mənts/ *n* [P] the RUDIMENTARY parts (of a subject): *to learn the rudiments of grammar/of Italian*

**rue** /ru:/ *v* **rued, ruing** [T +*v-ing*] *old use & humor* to be sorry about (something one has done or not done): *I rue never having been to university.|She'll* **rue the day** (=She'll always be sorry that) *she married him.*

**rue·ful** /'ru:fəl/ *adj* feeling or showing that one RUEs something: *a rueful smile* –**ruefully** *adv*

**ruff** /rʌf/ *n* **1** a kind of stiff white collar worn in Europe in the 16th century **2** a ring of hair or feathers round the neck of an animal or bird –sounds like **rough**

**ruf·fi·an** /'rʌfɪən/ *n becoming rare* a bad, perhaps violent, man: *He was attacked by a band of ruffians.*

**ruf·fle**[1] /'rʌfəl/ *v* **-fled, -fling 1** [T *up*] to move the smooth surface of; make uneven: *The bird ruffled (up) its feathers.* **2** [I;T] to make or become rather angry: *Don't get so ruffled.*

**ruffle**[2] *n* a band of cloth sewn in folds as a decoration round the neck or wrists of a garment; FRILL

**rug** /rʌg/ *n* **1** a thick usu. woollen floor mat, smaller than a CARPET[1] (2) –see picture on page 355 **2** a large warm woollen covering to wrap round oneself when travelling

**rug·by** /'rʌgbi/ also **rugby football** /ˌ·· '··/ *infml,* **rugger** /'rʌgəʳ/– *n* [U] *(sometimes cap.)* a type of football played with an oval ball, by two teams of either 13 men (**rugby league**) or 15 men (**rugby union**)

**rug·ged** /'rʌgɪ̇d/ *adj* (of a thing) large, rough, and strong-looking: *rugged hills* –**ruggedly** *adv* –**ruggedness** *n* [U]

**ru·in**[1] /'ru:ɪ̇n/ *n* **1** [U] (the cause of) destruction and decay: *an ancient temple which has fallen into ruin|Drink was your father's ruin and it will be the ruin of you too!* **2** [C] a RUINed[2] (1) building

**ruin²** *v* [T] **1** to destroy or spoil (completely): *an ancient ruined city|She poured water all over my painting and ruined it.* **2** to cause total loss of money to: *I was ruined by that law case.*

**ru·in·ous** /ˈruːənəs/ *adj* causing destruction or total loss of money: *The cost will be ruinous.|a ruinous war* –**ruinously** *adv*

**ru·ins** /ˈruːənz/ *n* [P] the remains of an old building or buildings: *the ruins of an ancient castle|The castle is now* **in ruins.**

**rule¹** /ruːl/ *n* **1** [C +*that*] **a** a principle or order which guides behaviour, says how things are to be done, etc.: *It's against the rules to pick up the ball.|We have a rule that the loser of the game buys/that the loser should buy everyone a drink.* **b** the usual way that something happens: *the rules of grammar* **2** [U] power to RULE² (1); time or manner of ruling: *Their country is under foreign rule.* (=governed by foreigners)|*Her rule lasted 20 years.|the rule of law* **3** [C]→RULER (2): *a two-foot rule* **4 as a rule** usually; generally **5 rules and regulations** small annoying RULES¹ (1) usu. in large numbers: *You must obey all the rules and regulations about car insurance.*

USAGE When speaking of scientific facts it is usual to call them **laws** rather than **rules:** *the* **law** *that oil floats on water.*

**rule²** *v* **ruled, ruling 1** [I;T *over*]to have and use the highest form of power over (a country, people, etc.) esp. as a king/queen or government:*The king ruled (the country/the people) for 30 years.* **2** [I;T +*that/on, against*] (esp. in law) to make and state an official decision:*The judge ruled that he could visit his children at weekends.* –compare RULING¹ **3 be ruled by** to be influenced or controlled by: *Don't let yourself be ruled by your feelings in this matter.*

**rule** sbdy./sthg.↔ **out** *v adv* [T] not to consider; EXCLUDE (2): *We can't* **rule out the possibility** *that he'll change his mind.*

**rul·er** /ˈruːləʳ/ *n* **1** a person who RULES² (1) **2** a long narrow flat piece of hard material with straight edges, marked with inches or CENTIMETRES, and used for measuring things or for drawing straight lines: *a 12-inch ruler* –see picture on page 105

**rul·ing¹** /ˈruːlɪŋ/ *n* [C +*that/on*] an official decision: *The judge has made/given several rulings on these matters.* –compare RULE² (2)

**ruling²** *adj* [A] most powerful: *His garden is his ruling* PASSION (4). (=his main interest)

**rum** /rʌm/ *n* [U] a strong alcoholic drink made from the juice of the sugar CANE (=plant)

**rum·ble** /ˈrʌmbəl/ *v* **-bled, -bling** [I] to make or move with a deep continuous rolling sound: *The thunder rumbled in the distance.|The heavy cart rumbled down the rough street.* –**rumble** *n* [S]

**ru·mi·nant** /ˈruːmənənt/ *adj,n* (an animal) that RUMINATES (2): *The cow is a ruminant.*

**ru·mi·nate** /ˈruːməneɪt/ *v* **-nated, -nating** [I] **1** [*about,over*] (of a person) to think deeply: *He ruminated over the problem.* **2** (of cattle, deer, etc.) to bring back food from the stomach and CHEW it (=bite it over and over again) –**rumination** /-ˈneɪʃən/ *n* [U]

**SPELLING NOTE**
Words with the sound /r/ may be spelt **wr-**, like **wrong.**

**rum·mage** /ˈrʌmɪdʒ/ *v* **-maged, -maging** [I *about,through,among*] to turn things over while trying to find something: *Who's been rummaging about among my papers?* –**rummage** *n* [S *about,around*]

**rum·my** /ˈrʌmi/ *n* [U] a simple card game for two or more players, played with two sets (PACKS) of cards

**ru·mour** *BrE*‖ **rumor** *AmE* /ˈruːməʳ/ *n* **1** [U] unofficial news; common talk, perhaps untrue: **Rumour has it** *that he's found a new job.* **2** [C +*that/about,of*] a story that reaches one through this: *All kinds of strange rumours about Jean are going around.* –compare GOSSIP

**ru·moured** *BrE*‖ **rumored** *AmE* /ˈruːməd‖-ərd/ *adj* [F +*to-v that*] reported unofficially and perhaps untruly: *It's rumoured that she's getting married.|She is rumoured to be getting married.*

**rump** /rʌmp/ *n* the part of an animal at the back just above the legs

**rum·ple** /ˈrʌmpəl/ *v* **-pled, -pling** [T] to disarrange (hair, clothes, etc.); make untidy: *her rumpled dress*

**rum·pus** /ˈrʌmpəs/ *n* [S] *infml* a noisy argument, quarrel, or disagreement: *to* **kick up** (make) **a rumpus**

**run¹** /rʌn/ *v* **ran** /ræn/, **run** /rʌn/, **running 1** [I] to move on one's legs at a speed faster than walking: *I had to run to catch the bus.|The children came running when she called them.|He ran a mile in four minutes.* –see picture on page 669 **2** [T] to cause to take part in a race: *He's running his horse in the 2.30 race.* **3** [I;T] to (cause to) move quickly: *A thought ran through my mind.|Could you* **run your eyes over** *the list of figures?* (=look at it quickly)|*The car ran down the hill out of control.* **4** [I;T] to (cause to) work or be in operation: *Don't touch the engine while it's running.|This machine runs on/by electricity.*|(fig.) *Is everything running smoothly at the office?* **5** [I not *be* +*v-ing*] to pass; stretch; continue: *The road runs along the river bank.* **6** [I;T] to (cause to) travel as arranged: *This bus doesn't run on Sundays.* **7** [I] (of a liquid) to flow: *to wash in running water* **8** [I] to pour out liquid: *Your nose is running.|The well has run dry.* **9** [T] to cause (liquid) to flow (into): *Run the water till it gets hot.|Please run me a bath.* **10** [I] to (melt and) spread by the action of heat or water: *The butter will run if you put it near the fire.|The colours of your shirt ran when I washed it.* **11** [I *against,for,in*] *esp. AmE* to be or become a CANDIDATE (=a person trying to get elected) in an election; compete (for an office, against someone else) in this way; STAND¹ (10): *He ran for President in the election.* **12** [I] to continue in operation, performance, etc.: *Her play ran in New York for 18 months.|My car insurance has two months to run.* **13** [T] *infml* to take (somebody or something) to somewhere in a vehicle: *Can I run you home?* **14** [T] to control; be in charge of and cause to work: *His parents run a small hotel.|Who runs this firm?|I can't afford to run* (=own and drive) *a car.* **15 run into the ground** to tire (oneself or someone else) out with hard work **16 run short: a** to use almost all one has and not have enough left: *We've run short of oil.* **b** also **run low**–to become less than enough: *Time is running short.*

**run after** sbdy./sthg. *v prep* [T] **1** to chase: *a dog running after rabbits* **2** *infml* to try to gain the attention and company of: *He's always running after women.*

**run along** *v adv* [I *often in commands*] *infml (used esp. to children)* to leave; go away: *Run along now, all of you! I'm busy.*

**run around** *v adv* [I] to go about in company (with, together): *Her husband found out that she'd been running around with another man.*

**run away** *v adv* [I *from*] to escape by running: *She hit the child and he ran away.* –see also RUNAWAY

**run away/off with** sbdy./sthg. *v adv prep* [T] **1** to carry off; gain control of: *Don't let your temper run away with you.* **2** to go away with (someone of the opposite sex): *He ran away with his teacher's wife.* **3** to steal: *He's run away with all my jewels.*

**run down** *v adv* **1** [T] (**run** sbdy./sthg.↔ **down**) to knock down and hurt (a person or animal) with one's vehicle –compare RUN **into** (1), RUN **over** (2) **2** [T] (**run** sbdy./sthg.↔ **down**) to chase and catch (a person or animal): *to run down a criminal* **3** [T] (**run** sbdy./sthg.↔ **down**) to speak of without respect; DISPARAGE: *She's jealous of your success; that's why she's always running you down.* **4** [I] (esp. of a clock, or of an electric BATTERY) to lose power and stop working, e.g. because it needs winding up: (fig.) *an industry that is running down* –see also RUN-DOWN

**run** sbdy./sthg. **in** *v adv* [T] **1** to bring (an engine) slowly into full use: *I'm running my new car in.* **2** *infml* (of the police) to catch (a criminal); ARREST[1] (1): *He was run in for possessing drugs.*

**run into** sbdy./sthg. *v prep* **1** [T] **a** to cause (a vehicle) to meet (something) with force: *to run one's car into a tree* **b** (of a vehicle) to meet (something) with force: *to run into a lamp-post* –compare RUN **down**, RUN **over 2** [T] also **run to**– to add up to; reach (a length or amount): *a debt running into thousands of pounds* **3** [T] *infml* to meet (someone) by chance

**run off with** sbdy./sthg. *v adv prep* [T] → RUN **away with**

**run out** *v adv* [I] to come to an end, or have no more: *Have you nearly finished? Time is running out.*|*Can you give me a cigarette? I've run out.*

**run out of** sthg. *v adv prep* [T] to use all one's supply of; have no more of: *We're running out of time.*|*to run out of petrol*

**run over** *v adv* **1** [I] (of liquids or their containers) to overflow: *The water/The cup ran over.* **2** [T] (**run** sbdy./sthg.↔ **over**) (of a vehicle or its driver) to knock down and pass over the top of: *He was run over by a bus.*|*The bus ran him over/ran over him.* –compare RUN **into** (1), RUN **down** (1)

**run through** *v prep* [T] **1** (**run through** sthg.) also **run over** – to repeat for practice: *Let's run through the first scene again.* **2** (**run through** sthg.) to read or examine quickly: *I'll just run through this list of figures.* **3** (**run** sthg. **through** sthg.) to pass or draw right through: *She ran her fingers through her hair.*

**run to** sthg. *v prep* [T not *be* +*v-ing*] to be enough, or have enough, to pay for: *My wages won't run to a car.*|*We can't run to a holiday this year.*

**run** sthg.↔ **up** *v adv* [T] **1** to raise (a flag): *They ran up the national flag on the queen's birthday.* **2** to cause (one's bills or debts) to grow: *She ran up a large bill for all her new clothes.* –see also RUN-UP

**run[2]** *n* **1** [C] an act of RUNning[1] (1): *He went for a run before breakfast.*|*a five-mile run* **2** [C *usu. sing.*] a short pleasure journey: *Let's go for a run in the car.* **3** [C] a journey esp. by train: *It's a 55-minute run from London to Brighton.* **4** [S] a continuous set of performances of a play, film, etc.: *The play had a run of three months.* **5** [S *of*] a continuous set of similar events: *I've had a run of bad luck recently.* **6** [S *on*] eager buying or selling: *There's been a great run on beer in this hot weather.*|*a run on the £* (=selling pounds in the money market) **7** [C] a usu. enclosed area where the stated animals are kept: *a chicken run* **8** [C] a sloping course for the stated downhill sport: *a* SKI-*run* **9** [C] in cricket, a point won by two players running from one WICKET to the other, passing each other on the way **10 a (good) run for one's money** *infml* **a** plenty of opposition in a competition **b** good results for money spent or effort made: *He died at 92: I think he had a good run for his money.* **11 in the long run** after enough time; in the end: *It'll be cheaper in the long run to build it in stone.* **12 on the run** trying to escape or to hide, esp. from the police **13 the common/ordinary run (of)** the usual sort (of) **14 the run of (a place)** the freedom to visit or use (a place): *He's given our children the run of his garden.*

**run·a·way** /ˈrʌnəweɪ/ *adj* [A] **1** out of control: *a runaway horse*|(fig.) *a runaway success* (=a very great success) **2** having escaped by running: *a runaway child* –see also RUN **away** –**run-away** *n*

**run-down[1]** /ˈ· ·/ *n* a detailed report of a set of events, business results, etc.: *He gave me a run-down on everything that had happened while I was away.*

**run-down[2]** /ˌ· ˈ·◂/ *adj* in poor health or condition: *You need a holiday; you look a bit run-down.*|*an old run-down hotel* –see also RUN **down** (4)

**rung[1]** /rʌŋ/ *n* one of the cross-bars that form the steps of a ladder

**rung[2]** *v past participle of* RING[3]

**run·ner** /ˈrʌnə^r/ *n* **1** a person who runs, esp. in a race or as a sport: *only six runners in the race*|*a long-distance runner* **2** one of the two thin blades on which a SLEDGE (=wheel-less carriage) slides over the snow

**runner bean** /ˌ·· ˈ·/ *BrE*‖**string bean** *AmE*– *n* a climbing bean with long green PODs (=seed containers) which are eaten as food

**runner-up** /ˌ·· ˈ·/ *n* **runners-up** *or* **runner-ups** the person or team that comes second in a race or competition

**run·ning[1]** /ˈrʌnɪŋ/ *n* **1** [U] the act or sport of running **2 in/out of the running** with some/no hope of winning: *Charles is still* **in the running** *for the new job.*

**running[2]** *adj* [A] **1** (of water) flowing, esp. (from TAPs[1] (1)): *This hotel has hot and cold running water in every room.* **2** done while one is running along: *a running jump/fight/kick* **3** continuous: *He has a* **running battle** *with his wife.*|*A* **running commentary** *is an account of a (sports) event given by a broadcaster while it is actually happening.* **4** (of money) spent or needed to keep something working: *The* **running costs** *of that big car must be very high.* **5** for or concerned with running as a sport: *running shoes* **6** providing liquid: *a running nose* **7 in running order** (of a machine) working properly

**running**[3] *adv (after a plural noun with a number*) one after the other without a break: *She won the prize three times running.*

**run·ny** /'rʌni/ *adj* **-nier, -niest** *infml* **1** more liquid than is usual or expected: *runny butter* **2** (of the nose or eyes) producing liquid, as when one has a cold

**run-of-the-mill** /ˌ· · · '· ◂/ *adj often derog* ordinary; not special or exciting: *a run-of-the-mill job*

**run-up** /'· ·/ *n* [*the* S] (the activities in) the period of time leading up to an event: *during the run-up to the election* –see also RUN **up**

**run·way** /'rʌnweɪ/ *n* a specially prepared hard surface, on which aircraft land and TAKE **off** (=leave the ground)

**ru·pee** /ruː'piː/ *n* (a note or coin worth) a standard measure of money in India, Pakistan, Sri Lanka, etc.

**rup·ture**[1] /'rʌptʃəʳ/ *n* **1** [C;U] (a) sudden breaking apart or bursting: *the rupture of a blood vessel* **2** [C] → HERNIA

**rupture**[2] *v* **-tured, -turing 1** [I;T] to break or burst: *He'll rupture a muscle if he goes on dancing like that!* **2** [T] to give (oneself) a HERNIA: *She ruptured herself lifting a heavy weight.*

**ru·ral** /'rʊərəl/ *adj* of or like the COUNTRYSIDE; concerning country or village life: *people living in rural areas* –compare URBAN, RUSTIC **–rurally** *adv*

**ruse** /ruːz‖ruːs, ruːz/ *n* a trick to deceive an opponent: *The fox pretended to be dead as a ruse to confuse the hunters.*

**rush**[1] /rʌʃ/ *v* **1** [I;T] to (make someone or something) hurry or act quickly: *There's plenty of time; we needn't rush.|They rushed up the stairs.|Let me think about it and don't rush me.* **2** [T] to attack suddenly and all together: *Perhaps if we all rush him at once he'll drop his gun.* **3 rush someone off his/her feet** to make someone hurry too much or work too hard: *I've been rushed off my feet all day at the office and I'm tired.*

**rush**[2] *n* **1** [C] a sudden rapid hasty movement **2** [S;U +*to-v*] (too much) haste: *We needn't leave yet; what's all the rush?| the rush* (= hurried demand) *for tickets for the football match* **3** [U]a period of great and hurried activity: *I hate shopping during the Christmas rush when everyone's buying presents.*

**rush**[3] *n* a grasslike water plant whose long thin hollow stems are often dried and made into mats, baskets, etc.

**rush hour** /'· ·/ *n* either of the two periods in the day when people are travelling to and from work in a city and the streets are crowded: *I try to get to work before the rush hour starts.*

**rusk** /rʌsk/ *n* a kind of hard dry BISCUIT given to babies

**rus·set** /'rʌsɨ̣t/ *n,adj* [S;U] *esp. lit* (of) a reddish brown or golden brown colour

**Rus·sian** /'rʌʃən/ *adj,n* (of or related to) **a** the language and people of Russia **b** the chief language, people, and state of the USSR: *the Russian language|Do you speak Russian?|Our neighbour is Russian/a Russian.*

**rust**[1] /rʌst/ *n* [U] **1** the reddish brown surface that forms on iron and some other metals when attacked by water and air see also RUSTY **2** the colour of this: *a rust-coloured dress*

**rust**[2] *v* [I;T] to (cause to) become covered with RUST[1] (1): *The lock has rusted and needs oil.*

**rus·tic**[1] /'rʌstɪk/ *adj often apprec* **1** connected with or suitable for the country; RURAL: *The village has a certain rustic charm.* **2** simple and rough, esp. as compared to (that of) the town: *their rustic way of speaking* –compare URBAN, RURAL

**rustic**[2] *n often derog* a person from the country, esp. a farm worker

**rus·tle**[1] /'rʌsəl/ *v* **-tled,-tling 1** [I;T] **a** (of paper, dry leaves, silk, etc.) to make slight sounds when moved or rubbed together: *Her long silk skirt rustled as she walked.* **b** to cause to make these sounds: *Stop rustling that newspaper!* **2** [T] *AmE* to steal (cattle or horses that are left loose in open country)

**rustle** sthg.↔ **up** *v adv* [T *for*] to find a supply of; collect or prepare quickly: *I'll try and rustle up something to eat.*

**rustle**[2] *n* [S] a sound of rustling (RUSTLE[1] (1)): *We heard a rustle of leaves.*

**rus·tler** /'rʌsləʳ/ *n AmE* a cattle thief; person who RUSTLES[1] (2)

**rust·y** /'rʌsti/ *adj* **-ier, -iest 1** covered with RUST[1] (1): *a rusty nail* **2** [F] (of one's knowledge of a subject) mostly forgotten: *My French is rusty* **–rustiness** *n* [U]

**rut** /rʌt/ *n* **1** a deep narrow track left in soft ground by a wheel: *The farm carts have worn ruts in this field.* **2 be in/get into a rut** to be in/get into a fixed and dull way of life

**ruth·less** /'ruːθlɨ̣s/ *adj* (of a person or behaviour) showing no human feelings; without pity: *a ruthless enemy* **–ruthlessly** *adv* **–ruthlessness** *n* [U]

**rye** /raɪ/ *n* [U] a grass plant grown in cold countries for its grain, used for making flour: *rye bread*

# S, s

**SPELLING NOTE**

Words with the sound /s/ may be spelt **c-**, like **city**, or **ps-**, like **psychology.**

**S, s** /es/ **S's, s's** *or* **Ss, ss** the 19th letter of the English alphabet

**S** *written abbrev. said as*: south(ern)

**-'s** /z, s/ *v short for:* **1** is: *What's that?* **2** has: *He's gone.* **3** us (only in the phrase **let's**)

USAGE The short forms of **am, are, had, has, is, will,** and **would** are not used at the end of the sentence: *I'm not coming but they* **are.**|*They're not coming but I* **am.**|*She's wondering where he* **is.**

**Sab·bath** /'sæbəθ/ *n* [S] **1** the 7th day of the week; Saturday, kept as a day of rest and worship by Jews and some Christians **2** Sunday, kept as such a day by most Christian churches

**sab·bat·i·cal** /sə'bætɪkəl/ *adj,n* (of) a period, allowed with pay, in which one may leave one's place of work to travel and study: *Mary is away* **on sabbatical/on sabbatical leave** *this term.*

**sa·ble** /'seɪbəl/ *n* [C;U] (the dark fur of) a small animal of northern Europe and Asia

**sab·o·tage**[1] /'sæbətɑːʒ/ *n* [U] intentional damage, usu. carried out secretly, to machines, buildings, etc., to weaken a business or a country

**sabotage**[2] *v* **-taged, -taging** [T] to practise SABOTAGE[1] on

**sab·o·teur** /ˌsæbə'tɜːʳ/ *n* a person who practises SABOTAGE[1]

**sa·bre** *BrE*||**saber** *AmE* /'seɪbəʳ/ *n* a heavy military sword, or a sword like this used in FENCING[1] –compare FOIL[2]

**sac** /sæk/ *n tech* a part shaped like a bag inside a plant or animal, usu. containing a particular liquid

**sac·cha·rin** /'sækərɨn/ *n* [U] a very sweet-tasting chemical used instead of sugar

**sac·cha·rine** /'sækəriːn/ *adj* very, esp. unpleasantly sweet

**sach·et** /'sæʃeɪ||sæ'ʃeɪ/ *n* a small usu. plastic bag holding a small amount of liquid (e.g. SHAMPOO) to be used all at one time

**sack**[1] /sæk/ *n* **1** [C] a large bag, usu. of strong cloth or leather, used for carrying flour, coal, grain, etc.: *two sacks of potatoes*|*Coal costs £4 a sack.* **2** [S] the taking away of one's job by an employer: *If you're late again, he'll give you the sack/you'll get the sack.*

**sack**[2] *v* [T] (of an employer) to take away the job of; dismiss

**sack**[3] *v* [T] (of an army in former times) to rob and destroy (a conquered city); PLUNDER[1]

**sac·ra·ment** /'sækrəmənt/ *n* an important Christian ceremony (e.g. BAPTISM or marriage) **–sacramental** /-'mentl / *adj*

**sa·cred** /'seɪkrɨd/ *adj* **1** [A] belonging to or concerning religion: *sacred music*|*sacred history* **2** holy by connection with God or gods: *sacred writings* **3** serious, solemn, and important in the way religious things are: *a sacred promise*|*a sacred duty* **–sacredly** *adv* **–sacredness** *n* [U]

**sac·ri·fice**[1] /'sækrɨfaɪs/ *n* [C;U] **1** (an) offering to God or a god, esp. of an animal by killing it in a ceremony **2** a/the loss or giving up of something of value, esp. for something thought to be of greater value: *She made a lot of sacrifices for her children.*

**sacrifice**[2] *v* **-ficed, -ficing 1** [I;T] to make an offering of (something) as a SACRIFICE[1] (1) **2** [T] to give up or lose, esp. for some purpose or belief: *She sacrificed her job because of her political ideas.*

**sac·ri·fi·cial** /ˌsækrɨ'fɪʃəl/ *adj* of or being (a) SACRIFICE[1] (1): *a sacrificial lamb* **–sacrificially** *adv*

**sac·ri·lege** /'sækrɨlɪdʒ/ *n* [C;U] (an act of) treating a holy thing without respect: (fig.) *I think it would be a sacrilege to destroy this beautiful old building.* **–sacrilegious** /-'lɪdʒəs/ *adj* **–sacrilegiously** *adv*

**sac·ro·sanct** /'sækrəsæŋkt/ *adj often derog or humor* too holy or important to be allowed to suffer any harm or disrespect: *My weekends are sacrosanct–I never work then.*

**sad** /sæd/ *adj* **1** unhappy; feeling or causing grief or sorrow: *The news of his death made me very sad.*|*a sad day for our team* **2** [A] deserving blame or pity; bad: *The old car is in a sad state.*|*It's* **a sad state of affairs** *when children aren't taught to read properly.*–**sadly** *adv* **–sadness** *n* [U]

**sad·den** /'sædn/ *v* [I;T] to make or become sad: *We were saddened by the death of our friend.*

**sad·dle**[1] /'sædl/ *n* **1** a usu. leather seat made to fit over the back of a horse, camel, etc. **2** a seat on a bicycle, motorcycle, etc. **3** a piece of meat from the back of a sheep or deer: *a saddle of lamb*

**saddle**[2] *v* **-dled, -dling** [T] **1** [*up*] to put a SADDLE on (an animal): *She saddled (up) her horse and rode away.* **2** [*with, upon*] to give (someone) something unpleasant, unwanted, or troublesome: *He's saddled with a large house which he can't sell.*

**saddle up** *v adv* [I]to put a SADDLE on a horse

**sad·dle·bag** /'sædlbæg/ *n* a bag on a horse, bicycle, motorcycle, etc., fixed behind, across, or below the SADDLE

**sa·dis·m** /'seɪdɪzəm/ *n* [U] unnatural fondness for cruelty to other people, sometimes as a way of getting sexual pleasure –compare MASOCHISM **–sadist** *n* **–sadistic** /sə'dɪstɪk/ *adj* **–sadistically** *adv*

**s.a.e.** *written abbrev. said as*: stamped addressed envelope

**sa·fa·ri** /sə'fɑːri/ *n* a trip through wild country, esp. in East Africa, hunting or photographing big animals: *to go* **on safari**

**safe**[1] /seɪf/ *adj* **1** [F *from*] out of danger; not threatened by harm; protected: *safe from attack*|*As soon as the animals were in their cages, we were safe.*|*Your money will be* **as safe as houses** (=perfectly safe) *with me.* **2** [F] not hurt; unharmed: *We found the children* **safe and sound** (=completely unharmed) *after their dangerous adventure.* **3** [*for*] not allowing danger or harm: *Is this a safe place to swim?* –opposite **unsafe 4** not likely to cause risk or disagreement: *It's safe to say that crime will continue at a high rate this year.* **–safely** *adv* **–safeness** *n* [U]

**safe**[2] *n* **1** a box or cupboard with thick metal sides and a lock used for protecting valuable things from thieves **2** a food cupboard: *a meat safe*

**safe-de·pos·it** /ˌ· ·'··/ *n* [U] safe storing of small valuable objects, usu. in small boxes (**safe-deposit boxes**) in a special room in a bank

**safe·guard** /'seɪfgɑːd||-gɑrd/ *v,n* [C;T *against*] (to be) a means of protection (for): *The new law contains safeguards against the misuse of government power.*

**safe·keep·ing** /ˌseɪf'kiːpɪŋ/ *n* [U] the action or state of protection from harm for things of value: *Put your important papers in the bank for safekeeping.*

**safe·ty** /'seɪfti/ *n* [U] the condition of being safe; freedom from danger, harm, or risk: *My main concern is for the safety of my family.*|*She led the children to a place of safety.*|*The safety of the ship is the* *captain's responsibility.*

**safety belt** /'·· ·/ *n* → SEAT BELT

**safety cur·tain** /'·· ,··/ *n* a theatre curtain which will not burn, and which may be lowered in front of the stage

**safety match** /'·· ·/ *n* a match which can be lighted only when rubbed along a special surface on its box

**safety pin** /'·· ·/ *n* a wire pin which is bent so that its point is covered when the pin is being used

**safety ra·zor** /'·· ,··/ *n* a RAZOR with a cover over its blade, to protect the skin from being cut

**safety valve** /'·· ·/ *n* a part of a machine which allows gas, steam, etc., to escape when the pressure becomes too great: (fig.) *I think that sport can be a safety valve for people's violent feelings.*

**saf·fron** /'sæfrən/ *n* [U] **1** powder of a deep orange colour used for colouring and for giving a special taste to food **2** an orange-yellow colour

**sag** /sæg/ *v* **-gg-** [I *down*] to sink or bend downwards, esp. from the usual or correct position: *The branch sagged (down) under the weight of the apples.*| (fig.) *My spirits sagged* (=I became less happy) *when I saw all the work I had to do.*

**sa·ga** /'sɑːgə/ *n* a long story about the brave and exciting actions of a distant time in history: (fig.) *He told me the saga* (=long dull story) *of his illness.*

**sa·ga·cious** /sə'geɪʃəs/ *adj lit* wise **–sagaciously** *adv* **–sagacity** /sə'gæsɪ̣ti / *n* [U]

**sage¹** /seɪdʒ/ *n,adj* (a person, esp. an old man, who is) wise as a result of long thinking and experience **–sagely** *adv*

**sage²** *n* [U] a type of MINT¹ used in cooking

**Sa·git·tar·i·us** /ˌsædʒɪ̣'teəriəs/ *n* see ZODIAC

**sa·go** /'seɪgəʊ/ *n* [U] a white food substance used for making sweet dishes with milk

**sahib** /sɑːb‖'sɑ-ɪb/ *n* [C; after *n*] *Ind & PakE (usu. cap.)* (used in India as a title of respect for males): *Jones Sahib|Yes, Sahib.*

**said¹** /sed/ *v past tense and participle of* SAY

**said²** *adj* [*the* A] *fml* the particular (person, thing, etc.) spoken of before: *John James Smith is charged with stealing.|The said John Smith was seen leaving the shop at the times stated.*

**sail¹** /seɪl/ *n* **1** [C;U] a piece of strong cloth fixed in position on a ship to move it through the water by the force of the wind: to HOIST *the sails* (=raise them into position)|*a ship* **in full sail** (=with all its sails spread) **2** [S] a short trip, usu. for pleasure, in a boat with these: *Let's go for a sail this afternoon.* **3** [C] **set sail** to begin a trip at sea

**sail²** *v* **1** [I;T] **a** (of a ship) to travel on the water: *to watch the ships sail by* **b** to command or direct (a ship) on the water: *The captain sailed the ship through the passage.* **2** [I] to travel by ship: *We sailed across the Atlantic.* **3** [I] to begin a voyage: *Our ship sails tomorrow (for New York).* **4** [I] to move smoothly or easily: *She sailed through the examination.* (=she passed easily)

**sail·ing** /'seɪlɪŋ/ *n* [U] **1** the skill of directing the course of a ship **2** the sport of riding in or directing a small boat with sails

> **SPELLING NOTE**
> Words with the sound /s/ may be spelt **c-**, like **city**, or **ps-**, like **psychology**.

**sail·or** /'seɪlə^r/ *n* **1** a person with a job on a ship, esp. one who is not a ship's officer **2** a member of a navy

**saint** /seɪnt/ *n* **1** a person officially recognized after death as specially holy and worthy of formal honour in the Christian church **2** *infml* a very good and completely unselfish person: *She must be a real saint to stay married to that awful man.* **–sainthood** *n* [U]

**Saint** /sənt; *strong* seɪnt/ *n* [A] (a title before a SAINT'*s* (1) name): *Saint Joan of Arc*

**saint·ly** /'seɪntli/ *adj* **-lier, -liest** of or like a SAINT: *a saintly man/life* **–saintliness** *n* [U]

**sake** /seɪk/ *n* **1 for the sake of: a** for the good of: *Do it for my sake.* (=to please me) **b** for the purpose of: *He's just talking for the sake of hearing his own voice.* **2 for God's/goodness/pity('s) sake** *infml* **a** (used when asking strongly for something): *For goodness sake, don't tell him!* **b** (shows annoyance): *What's the matter now, for God's sake?*

**sa·la·cious** /sə'leɪʃəs/ *adj fml* sexually improper or shocking; OBSCENE: *a salacious newspaper article about a schoolgirl and a priest* **–salaciously** *adv*

**sal·ad** /'sæləd/ *n* [C;U] a mixture of usu. uncooked vegetables served cold, sometimes with other (stated) foods added: *a green salad* (=mostly LETTUCE)|*a cheese/chicken salad*

**sa·la·mi** /sə'lɑːmi/ *n* [U] a large SAUSAGE with a strong salty taste, often eaten cold

**sal·a·ried** /'sælərid/ *adj* having a SALARY, as opposed to wages: *salaried workers|a salaried job*

**sal·a·ry** /'sæləri/ *n* **-ries** [C;U] fixed regular pay each month for a job, esp. for workers of higher rank: *a high/good salary* –see PAY (USAGE)

**sale** /seɪl/ *n* **1** an act of selling; contract or agreement exchanging something for money: *The sale of my house hasn't been easy.|I hope I'll make the sale today.* **2** a special offering of goods at lower prices than usual: *I got this hat cheap at a/in the sale.|regular price £3, sale price £1.49* –see also JUMBLE SALE **3** →AUCTION: *a furniture sale* **4** the total amount sold of something offered to be sold: *We're hoping for a large sale of our new product.|sales figures* (=the number sold) **5 for sale** offered to be sold, esp. by a private owner: *The sign on the house says "For Sale".* **6 on sale** offered to be sold, esp. in a shop: *The new car is now on sale.*

**sales** /seɪlz/ *adj* [A] of, for, or related to selling: *the sales department of a company|the sales director*

**sales·clerk** /'seɪlzklɑːk‖-klɜrk/ *n AmE* for SHOP ASSISTANT

**sales·man** /'seɪlzmən/ **saleswoman** /wʊmən/ *fem.*– *n* **-men** /mən/ a person whose job is to sell goods either in a shop, or directly to businesses, homes, etc.

**sa·li·ent** /'seɪliənt/ *adj fml* most noticeable or important: *the salient points of the speech*

**sa·line** /'seɪlaɪn/ *adj* of, related to, or containing salt

**sa·li·va** /sə'laɪvə/ *n* [U] the natural watery liquid produced in the mouth **–salivary** /sə'laɪvəri‖'sælɪ̣veri/ *adj: the salivary* GLANDS

**sal·i·vate** /'sælɪ̣veɪt/ *v* **-vated, -vating** [I] to produce SALIVA in the mouth, esp. at the sight or thought of food **–salivation** /-'veɪʃən/ *n* [U]

**sal·low** /sæləʊ/ *adj* (of the skin) yellow and unhealthy-looking –**sallowness** *n* [U]
**salm·on** /'sæmən/ *n* **salmon** *or* **salmons** [C;U] a large fish with silvery skin and yellowish-pink flesh eaten as food: *a salmon-pink dress*
**sal·on** /'sælɒn‖sə'lɑn/ *n* a business concerned with hair care, beauty treatment, etc.: *a beauty salon*
**sa·loon** /sə'lu:n/ *n* **1** also **saloon car** *BrE*‖**sedan** *AmE*– a car for four to six passengers, with a roof, closed sides, and windows **2** →SALOON BAR **3** (typically in the American wild west) a large public drinking place
**saloon bar** /·'· ·/ also **saloon, lounge bar**– *n BrE* a comfortably furnished room in a pub, where drinks cost more than in the PUBLIC BAR
**salt**[1] /sɔ:lt/ *n* **1** [U] a very common white solid with many uses, esp. in cooking to improve the taste of food: *The vegetables need more salt.*|*Please pass the salt.* –see picture on page 521 **2** [C] *tech* a chemical substance which may be formed by the combining of an acid and a BASE[1](4) or metal **3** [C] **old salt** an old, experienced sailor **4 rub salt in someone's wound(s)** to make someone's sorrow, pain, etc., even worse **5 the salt of the earth** *pomp* a person or people regarded as admirable and dependable **6 take something with a grain/pinch of salt** to accept that something is probably completely untrue
**salt**[2] *v* [T] to add salt to; put salt on: *Have you salted the vegetables?*
**salt** sthg.↔**away** *v adv* [T] *infml* to save (esp. money) for the future
**salt**[3] *adj* **1** containing, full of, or tasting of salt; salty: *salt water* **2** [A] formed by salty water: *a salt lake* –see also SALTY
**salt·cel·lar** /'sɔlt,selə^r/ *n* a container for salt, used at meals
**salt·wa·ter** /,sɔ:lt'wɔ:tə^r/ *adj* [A] being or belonging to salty water or sea water: *saltwater fish* –opposite **freshwater**
**salt·y** /'sɔ:lti/ *adj* **-ier, -iest** of, containing, or tasting of salt: *This soup's too salty.* –**saltiness** *n* [U]
**sa·lu·bri·ous** /sə'lu:brɪəs/ *adj fml or lit* favourable to good health; WHOLESOME: *They live in a very salubrious area.* –**salubriousness** *n* [U]
**sal·u·ta·ry** /'sæljʊtəri‖-jəteri/ *adj* causing improvement or a good effect: *The accident was a salutary experience: I'll never drink and drive again.*
**sal·u·ta·tion** /,sælju'teɪʃən‖-ljə-/ *n* [C;U] *fml* (an) expression of greeting by words or action
**sa·lute**[1] /sə'lu:t/ *v* **-luted, -luting 1** [I;T] to make a SALUTE[2] (1a) (to): *to salute an officer* **2** [T] *esp. lit* to greet, esp. with words or a sign: *He saluted his friend.*
**salute**[2] *n* **1** [C] a military sign of recognition, such as **a** a raising of the right hand to the forehead **b** a ceremonial firing of guns or lowering of flags **2** [C;U] *lit* a greeting; SALUTATION **3 take the salute** (of a person of high rank) to stand while being SALUTED[1] (1a) by soldiers marching past
**sal·vage**[1] /'sælvɪdʒ/ *n* [U] **1** the act of saving things from destruction, esp. of saving a wrecked ship or its goods from the sea **2** property saved from being destroyed: *a sale of salvage from the wreck*
**salvage**[2] *v* **-vaged, -vaging** [T] to save (goods or property) from loss or damage: *We were unable to salvage anything when the factory burnt down.*
**sal·va·tion** /sæl'veɪʃən/ *n* [U] **1** (esp. in the Christian religion) the saving or state of being saved from SIN **2** *fml* something that saves or preserves from loss, ruin, or failure: *After so much dry weather, this rain has been the farmers' salvation.*
**Salvation Ar·my** /·,·· '··/ *n* [S] a Christian organization that has military uniforms and ranks, and is best known for its help to poor people
**salve**[1] /sɑ:v, sælv‖sæv/ *n* [C;U] (an) oily paste (OINTMENT) for putting on a cut, wound, etc.
**salve**[2] *v* **salved, salving** [T] *lit* to make (esp. feelings) less painful; SOOTHE: *He tried to* **salve his conscience** *with excuses, but he knew he was doing wrong.*
**sal·ver** /'sælvə^r/ *n* a fine metal plate, esp. of silver, for serving food, drink, etc., formally
**sal·vo** /'sælvəʊ/ *n* **-vos** *or* **-voes** [*of*] a firing of several guns at once, in a ceremony or in battle
**Sa·mar·i·tan** /sə'mærɪ̈tn/ *n* **good Samaritan** a person who gives help to someone in need
**sam·ba** /'sæmbə/ *n* a fast dance of Brazilian origin
**same**[1] /seɪm/ *adj* [*the, this, that, these, those* +*adj*] **1** not changed or different; not another: *Father sits in the same chair every evening.*|*You've made the same mistakes as last time/that you made last time.* **2** alike in every way: *Men and women should get the same pay for doing the same jobs.* **3 one and the same** exactly the same **4 same here** *infml* the same with me; me too: *"I think I ate too much." "Same here. I did too".*
**same**[2] *pron* **1** the same thing, person, etc.: *All the newspapers say the same.*|*Thanks for helping me: I'll do the same for you sometime.* **2 same to you!** *infml* (in answer to a greeting or sometimes an angry wish) I wish you the same thing: *"Happy Christmas" "Same to you!"*
**same·ness** /'seɪmnɪ̈s/ *n* [U] the state of being (almost) the same; very close likeness: *His books all have a certain sameness about them.*
**sam·ple**[1] /'sɑ:mpəl‖'sæm-/ *n,adj* (being) a small part representing the whole; typical small quantity, thing, etc.: *The nurse took a sample of my blood/a blood sample for tests.*|*Here are some sample questions from last year's examination.*
**sample**[2] *v* **-pled, -pling** [T] **1** to take and examine a SAMPLE[1] of; test: *She sampled the wine before giving it to the others.* **2** to get to know about by experience; TRY **out:** *to sample the pleasures of country life*
**sam·u·rai** /'sæmʊraɪ/ *n* **-rai** *or* **-rais** a military nobleman in Japan in former times
**san·a·to·ri·um** /,sænə'tɔ:rɪəm‖-'tor-/ ‖also **sanitorium, sanatarium** *AmE*– *n* **-iums** *or* **-ia** /ɪə/ a kind of hospital for sick people who are getting better and need treatment, rest, etc.
**sanc·ti·fy** /'sæŋktɪ̈faɪ/ *v* **-fied, -fying** [T] *fml* to make holy: *The priest sanctified the church with a special ceremony.* –**sanctification** /-fɪ̈'keɪʃən/ *n* [U]
**sanc·ti·mo·ni·ous** /,sæŋktɪ̈'məʊnɪəs/ *adj derog* making a show of being religious; pretending to be holy: *sanctimonious behaviour* –**sanctimoniously** *adv* –**sanctimoniousness** *n* [U]
**sanc·tion**[1] /'sæŋkʃən/ *n* **1** [U] *fml* permission or approval: *The minister acts with the sanction of Parliament.* **2** [C] an action taken against a person or

esp. a country that has broken a law or rule: *We have established sanctions forbidding anyone to trade with that country* . **3** [C] something that forces people to keep a rule or standard: *a moral sanction*

**sanction²** *v* [T] *fml* to accept, approve, or permit

**sanc·ti·ty** /'sæŋktɨti/ *n* [U] holiness: *the sanctity of a formal promise*

**sanc·tu·a·ry** /'sæŋktʃuəri‖-tʃueri/ *n* **-ries 1** [C] the part of a Christian religious building considered most holy **2** [C;U] (a place of) protection or safety from harm, esp. for a person escaping from officers of the law **3** [C] an area for birds or animals where they may not be hunted

**sand¹** /sænd/ *n* [U] the small loose grains of material found on beaches and in deserts, used for making cement, glass, etc.

**sand²** *v* [T] **1** [*down*] to make smoother by rubbing, usu. with SANDPAPER **2** to put sand on: *The roads were sanded during the cold weather.*

**san·dal** /'sændl/ *n* a light open-sided shoe worn in warm weather –see picture on page 563

**san·dal·wood** /'sændlwud/ *n* [U] **1** a hard yellowish sweet-smelling Asian wood **2** a brown colour

**sand·bank** /'sændbæŋk/ *n* a bank of sand in a river, harbour, etc.

**sand·cas·tle** /'sænd,kɑːsəl‖-,kæ-/ *n* a small model, esp. of a castle, built in sand by children

**sand dune** /'· ·/ *n* → DUNE

**sand·pa·per** /'sænd,peɪpəʳ/ *v,n* [T;U] (to rub with) paper covered on one side with sand or hard grainy material, used for making rough surfaces smoother

**sand·pit** /'sænd,pɪt/ *n BrE* a box, or place in the ground, containing sand for children to play in

**sand·stone** /'sændstəun/ *n* [U] soft rock formed by sand fixed in a natural cement

**sand·storm** /'sændstɔːm‖-ɔrm/ *n* a windstorm in which sand is blown about in a desert

**sand·wich¹** /'sænwɪdʒ‖'sændwɪtʃ, 'sænwɪtʃ/ *n* two pieces of bread with some other (stated) food between them, eaten with the hands: *a cheese sandwich*

**sandwich²** *v* [T *in, between*] to put tightly in between two other things: *a piece of plastic sandwiched between two pieces of glass*

**sandwich board** /'·· ·/ *n* a pair of advertising signs for hanging at the front and back of a person who walks about in public

**sandwich course** /'·· ·/ *n BrE* a course of study in an industrial or professional subject which includes periods spent in working for a company

**sand·y** /'sændi/ *adj* **-ier, -iest 1** containing or full of sand **2** (esp. of hair) yellowish-brown in colour, like sand –**sandiness** *n* [U]

**sane** /seɪn/ *adj* **1** healthy in mind; not mad –opposite **insane 2** based on or showing good reasonable thinking; sensible: *a sane education system* –**sanely** *adv*

**sang** /sæŋ/ *v past tense of* SING

**sang·froid** /,sɒŋ'frwɑː‖,sɔŋ'frwɑː (*Fr* sɑ̃frwa)/ *n* [U] *French* calm courage; self-control

> **SPELLING NOTE**
> Words with the sound /s/, may be spelt **c-**, like **city**, or **ps-**, like **psychology.**

**san·guine** /'sæŋgwɨn/ *adj fml* expecting the best; showing OPTIMISM: *a person of sanguine temper*

**san·i·ta·ry** /'sænɨtəri‖-teri/ *adj* **1** of or concerning health, esp. the treatment or removal of waste, dirt, or infection **2** clean; free from danger to health: *sanitary conditions* –see also INSANITARY

**sanitary tow·el** /'···· ,··/ ‖also **sanitary napkin** *AmE*– *n* soft paper worn between a woman's legs during her PERIOD¹ (4) to take up the flow from the WOMB

**san·i·ta·tion** /,sænɨ'teɪʃən/ *n* [U] means for protecting public health, esp. by the removing and treatment of waste

**san·i·to·ri·um** /,sænɨ'tɔːrɪəm‖-'tor-/ *n* **-iums** *or* **-ia** /ɪə/ *AmE* for SANATORIUM

**san·i·ty** /'sænɨti/ *n* [U] the quality of being SANE –opposite **insanity**

**sank** /sæŋk/ *v past tense of* SINK¹

**San·ta Claus** /'sæntə klɔːz‖'sænti klɔz, 'sæntə-/ ‖ also **Father Christmas** *BrE*– *n* an imaginary old man believed by children to bring presents at Christmas

**sap¹** /sæp/ *n* [U] the watery juice carrying food through a plant

**sap²** *v* **-pp-** [T] to weaken or destroy, esp. over a long time: *Her long illness gradually sapped her strength.*

**sap·ling** /'sæplɪŋ/ *n* a young tree

**sap·phire** /'sæfaɪəʳ/ *n* [C;U] a precious stone of a transparent bright blue colour

**sar·cas·m** /'sɑːkæzəm‖'sɑr-/ *n* [U] speaking or writing using expressions which clearly mean the opposite to what is felt: *"It was a good idea to tell my motheryoudidn'tlikeherdress," shesaidwithsarcasm.*

**sar·cas·tic** /sɑː'kæstɪk‖sɑr-/ *adj* using or marked by SARCASM: *a sarcastic remark* –**sarcastically** *adv*

**sar·dine** /sɑː'diːn‖sɑr-/ *n* **1** a young small fish, e.g. the PILCHARD, esp. as food preserved in oil **2 like sardines** *infml* packed, crowded, etc., very tightly together

**sar·don·ic** /sɑː'dɒnɪk‖sɑr'dɑnɪk/ *adj* SCORNFUL –**sardonically** *adv*

**sa·ri** /'sɑːri/ *n* a length of light cloth wrapped around the body, worn esp. by Hindu women

**sa·rong** /sə'rɒŋ‖sə'rɔŋ, sə'rɑŋ/ *n* a loose skirt worn by Malayan women and men

**sash¹** /sæʃ/ *n* a length of cloth worn round the waist, or (usu. as a mark of honour) over one shoulder

**sash²** *n* a frame into which sheets of glass are fixed to form part of a window, door, etc.

**sash win·dow** /'· ,··/ *n* a window of two SASHES² which opens by sliding one up or down –compare CASEMENT WINDOW

**sat** /sæt/ *v past tense and participle of* SIT

**Sa·tan** /'seɪtn/ *n* the devil

**sa·tan·ic** /sə'tænɪk/ *adj* very cruel, evil, or wicked; FIENDISH –**satanically** *adv*

**satch·el** /'sætʃəl/ *n* a small bag, usu. with a band for carrying over the shoulder: *a school satchel* –see picture on page 16

**sate** /seɪt/ *v* **sated, sating** [T *usu. pass.*] *fml* to satisfy with more than enough of something: *I've been eating these sweets all morning and I'm completely sated.*

**sat·el·lite** /'sætɨlaɪt/ *n* **1** a heavenly body or man-made object which moves around a larger one (a PLANET): *The broadcast came from America* **by**

satellite. **2** something, esp. a country, that depends on the power of another

**sa·ti·ate** /'seɪʃieɪt/ *v* **-ated, -ating** [T *usu. pass*] to satisfy fully, esp. too fully

**sat·in** /'sætɪn/ *adj,n* [U] (made of) a kind of very fine shiny smooth silk cloth

**sat·in·y** /'sætɪni/ also **satin**– *adj* very pleasantly smooth, shiny, and soft, like satin: *satiny skin*

**sat·ire** /'sætaɪəʳ/ *n* [C;U *on*] (a work of) literature, etc., intended to show the foolishness of something in an amusing way: *a satire on the government*

**sa·tir·i·cal** /sə'tɪrɪkəl/ also **sa·tir·ic**– *adj* being or using SATIRE –**satirically** *adv*

**sat·ir·ize,** ‖also **-ise** *BrE* /'sætɪraɪz/ *v* **-ized, -izing** [T] to use SATIRE against: *a book satirizing the military government*

**sat·is·fac·tion** /ˌsætɪs'fækʃən/ *n* **1** [C;U] (something that causes) contentment or pleasure: *I always get a feeling of satisfaction from doing the job properly.* –opposite **dissatisfaction 2** [U] *fml* fulfilment of a need, desire, etc.: *satisfaction of public demand* **3** [U] *fml* condition of being certain: *It's been proved* **to my satisfaction** (=I am fully persuaded) *that you're telling the truth.*

**sat·is·fac·to·ry** /ˌsætɪs'fæktəri/ *adj* good enough; pleasing: *Of all the radios he tried, only one was satisfactory.|Sales are very satisfactory this month.* –opposite **unsatisfactory** –**satisfactorily** *adv*

**sat·is·fy** /'sætɪsfaɪ/ *v* **-fied, -fying** [T] **1** to make (someone) happy; please: *She told me that she was not satisfied with my examination results.|Some people are very hard to satisfy.* –opposite **dissatisfy 2** to be or give enough for; fulfil (a need, desire, etc.): *You can't vote until you have satisfied all the formal conditions.* **3** [*that/of*] to cause to believe fully: *Are you satisfied that he is telling the truth?*

**sat·is·fy·ing** /'sætɪsfaɪ-ɪŋ/ *adj* giving satisfaction: *a satisfying meal/job* –**satisfyingly** *adv*

**sat·u·rate** /'sætʃəreɪt/ *v* **-rated, -rating** [T *with*] **1** to make completely wet; SOAK[1] (2): *The blood had saturated his shirt.* **2** to fill completely: *It's hard to get a teaching job now; the* MARKET[1] (4) *is saturated.* (=there are too many teachers and not enough jobs) –**saturation** /-'reɪʃən / *n* [U]

**Sat·ur·day** /'sætədi, -deɪ‖-ər-/ *n* the 7th and last day of the week; day before Sunday: *She arrived (on) Saturday (morning).|We do our shopping on Saturdays.*

**Sat·urn** /'sætən‖-ərn/ *n* the PLANET which is 6th in order from the sun and is surrounded by large rings

**sauce** /sɔːs/ *n* **1** [C;U] a thick, usu. cooked liquid put on or eaten with food: TOMATO *sauce|a white sauce for fish |ice cream with chocolate sauce* –see picture on page 521 **2** [U] *infml* disrespectful (but often harmless) talk, as to a parent, teacher, etc.: *That's enough of your sauce, my boy!*

**sauce·pan** /'sɔːspən/ *n* a deep usu. round metal cooking pot with a handle and usu. a lid –see picture on page 337

**sau·cer** /'sɔːsəʳ/ *n* a small plate with edges curving up, for putting a cup on –see picture on page 521

**sauc·y** /'sɔːsi/ ‖also **sassy** *AmE*– *adj* **-ier, -iest** *infml* disrespectful, or producing sexual interest, in an amusing way –**saucily** *adv* –**sauciness** *n* [U]

**sau·na** /'sɔːnə‖'saʊnə/ also **sauna bath**– *n* (a room or building for) a Finnish type of bath in steam

**saun·ter** /'sɔːntəʳ/ *v* [I] to walk in an unhurried way –**saunter** *n* [S]

**saus·age** /'sɒsɪdʒ‖'sɔ-/ *n* [C;U] a thin edible tube of animal skin filled with meat, bread, SPICES, etc.: *Would you prefer sausages or* BACON *with your eggs?*

**sausage roll** /ˌ·· '·/ *n* a small piece of SAUSAGE meat in a covering of pastry

**sau·té**[1] /'səʊteɪ‖səʊ'teɪ/ *n* a SAUTéed[2] dish: *a sauté of potatoes and onions|sauté potatoes*

**sauté**[2] *v* **-téed** *or* **-téd, -téeing** *or* **-téing** [T] to cook quickly in a little hot oil or fat: *Sauté the onions for five minutes.*

**sav·age**[1] /'sævɪdʒ/ *adj* **1** forcefully cruel or violent; fierce; FEROCIOUS: *a savage dog|savage anger|a savage attack in the newspapers* **2** [A] uncivilized: *savage people* –**savagely** *adv* –**savageness** *n* [U]

**savage**[2] *n* an uncivilized person

**savage**[3] *v* **-aged, -aging** [T] (esp. of an animal) to attack and bite fiercely: *savaged by a mad dog*

**sav·ag·e·ry** /'sævɪdʒəri/ *n* **-ries** [C;U] (an act of) SAVAGE[1] (1) behaviour: *He beat the dog with great savagery.|the savageries of war*

**sa·van·na, -nah** /sə'vænə/ *n* [C;U] (an open flat area of) grassy land in a warm country

**save**[1] /seɪv/ *v* **1** [T *from*] to make safe from danger: *Help! Save me!|He saved his friend from falling.* **2** [I;T *up, for*] to keep (esp. money) for later use: *Children should learn to save.|We're saving (up) for a new car.|She saved her strength for the last minutes of the race.* **3** [T *+v-ing/from*] to make unnecessary (for): *Will you go to the shop for me? It'll save (me) going into town.|a labour-saving machine* **4** [T] (of a football player, esp. a GOALKEEPER) to stop one's opponents from getting (a GOAL)

**save on** sthg. *v prep* [T] to avoid the waste of: *If we all go in one car, we'll save on petrol.*

**save**[2] *n* (in football) a quick action by the GOALKEEPER which prevents the opponents scoring (SCORE[2]) a GOAL

**save**[3] also **saving**– *prep lit & old use* leaving out; except: *He answered all the questions save one.*

**sav·er** /'seɪvəʳ/ *n* **1** something that prevents loss or waste: *a time-saver* **2** a person who saves money

**sav·ing** /'seɪvɪŋ/ *adj* [A] that makes good or acceptable in spite of weakness, faults, etc.; REDEEMING (4): *The film's* **saving grace** (=the one good thing that makes it acceptable) *is the beautiful photography.*

**sav·ings** /'seɪvɪŋz/ *n* [P] money saved, esp. in a bank

**savings account** /'·· ·ˌ·/ *n* a bank account which earns higher INTEREST[1] (5) than a DEPOSIT ACCOUNT

**sa·viour** *BrE*‖**savior** *AmE* /'seɪvɪəʳ/ *n* **1** [C] a person or thing that saves from danger or loss: *She was her country's saviour during the war.* **2** [S] (*usu. cap.*) (in the Christian religion) Jesus Christ

**sa·vour**[1] *BrE*‖**savor** *AmE* /'seɪvəʳ/ *n* [S;U] a taste or smell: *This soup has a savour of fish.*

**savour**[2] *BrE*‖**savor** *AmE* *v* [T] to enjoy, as by tasting, slowly and purposefully: *She drank the wine slowly, savouring every drop.*

**sa·vour·y**[1] *BrE*‖**savory** *AmE* /'seɪvəri/ *adj BrE* (of food) not sweet; having the taste of meat, cheese, vegetables, etc.

**savoury[2]** *BrE*‖**savory** *AmE n* **-ies** a small salty dish

**saw[1]** /sɔː/ *n* a hand- or power-driven tool with a row of sharp tooth-like points for cutting hard materials|*an electric saw*

**saw[2]** *v* **sawed, sawn**‖also **sawed** *AmE,* **sawing 1** [I;T *up, off, etc.*] to cut with a SAW: *He sawed the logs up into little pieces.|The tree was nearly sawn through.|She sawed off a dead branch.* **2** [I *at*] to move one's hand, a knife, etc., backwards and forwards, (as if) cutting with a SAW: *He sawed at the loaf of bread with his knife.*

**saw[3]** *v past tense of* SEE

**saw·dust** /ˈsɔːdʌst/ *n* [U] dust or very small pieces of wood made by a SAW in cutting

**Sax·on** /ˈsæksən/ *adj* of or concerning a people of north Germany who conquered and settled in England in the 5th century –see also ANGLO-SAXON

**sax·o·phone** /ˈsæksəfəun/ also **sax** *infml– n* a metal musical wind instrument usu. used in JAZZ and dance music **–saxophonist** /sækˈsɒfənɪ̈st‖ˈsæksəfəunɪ̈st/ *n*

**say[1]** /seɪ/ *v* **said** /sed/, **saying,** *3rd person sing. present tense* **says** /sez/ **1** [T] to pronounce (a sound, word, etc.): *"I'd like another drink," he said.|Have you said your prayers?|So I* **said to myself.** (=thought) *"I wonder what she means".* **2** [I;T +(*that*)] to express (a thought, intention, etc.) in words: *He said he would like another drink.|Don't believe anything he says.|Who can say how it happened?|"Will we win?" "I can't say."* (=I don't know)|*My watch says* (=shows) *5.30.* –see Study Notes on page 429 **3** [T +(*that*) (*usu. in commands*)] to suppose; ASSUME (1): *Say your plan fails: then what do we do?* **4 I say** *BrE infml* (used as an expression of surprise, or for calling someone's attention) **5 it goes without saying** of course; clearly: *It goes without saying that our plans depend on the weather.* **6 that is to say** also **i.e.** *abbrev.–* in other words; expressed another (more exact) way **7 they say** people say; it's usually thought **8 to say nothing of** as well as; including: *three people hurt, to say nothing of the damage to the building* **9 you don't say (so)!** *infml* (an expression of surprise or disbelief)

USAGE Compare **say, tell, inform, speak,** and **talk:** 1 **Say** is nearly always [T] and can only have words (not a person) as its object: *He* **said** *"I'm tired".|He* **said** *(that) he was tired.|He* **said** *a few words then sat down.* **Tell** is nearly always [T] and can have one object or two: words, or a person, or both: *He* **told** *us (that) he was tired.| He* **told** *(us) a funny story.* **Inform** *(fml)* is always [T] and its object is always a person: *He* **informed** *us that he was tired.* Of all these words, only **say** can be used with the actual words spoken, and only **tell** can be used for commands: *He* **said** *"Open the door".|He* **told** *me to open the door.* 2 **Speak** and **talk** are usually [I]. They are very close in meaning, but **talk** sometimes gives the idea of a conversation, rather than of a single person making statements: *We* **talked** *for hours (about politics).|The director* **spoke** *to us about the company's plans.* **Speak** and **talk** are sometimes [T], but can never have a person as their object: *Do you* **speak** *French?|You're* **talking** *nonsense!*

**SPELLING NOTE**
Words with the sound /s/, may be spelt **c-**, like **city**, or **ps-**, like **psychology.**

**say[2]** *n* [S;U] **1** (a) power or right of (sharing in) decision: *The unions had no say in the new pay agreement.* **2 have one's say** to have the chance to say something, esp. to express one's opinion

**say·ing** /ˈseɪ-ɪŋ/ *n* a well-known wise statement; PROVERB: *As they say "There's no smoke without fire."*

**scab** /skæb/ *n* **1** a hard mass of dried blood which forms over a cut or wound **2** *derog infml* a worker who does the work of one who is on STRIKE[2] (1); BLACKLEG

**scab·bard** /ˈskæbəd‖-ərd/ *n* a leather or metal tube enclosing the blade of a sword, knife, etc.

**scab·by** /ˈskæbi/ *adj* **-bier, -biest** covered with SCABS[1] (1)

**scaf·fold** /ˈskæfəld, -fəuld/ *n* **1** a framework round a house being built, for workmen to stand on **2** a raised stage for the killing of criminals (esp. in former times) by hanging

**scaf·fold·ing** /ˈskæfəldɪŋ/ *n* [U] poles and boards used in a system of SCAFFOLDS (1)

**scald[1]** /skɔːld/ *v* [T] **1** to burn with hot liquid: *He scalded his tongue on/with the hot coffee.|They were scalded by steam from the burst pipe.* **2** to heat (a liquid, e.g. milk) almost to the point of boiling

**scald[2]** *n* a skin burn from hot liquid or steam

**scald·ing** /ˈskɔːldɪŋ/ *adj* boiling or nearly boiling: **scalding hot** *water*

**scale[1]** /skeɪl/ *n* **1** a pair of pans for weighing an object by comparing it with a known weight: *a scale used for weighing gold* –see PAIR (USAGE) **2** [*often pl.*] any weighing machine: *bathroom scales* –see picture on page 615

**scale[2]** *n* **1** [C] a set of numbers or standards for measuring or comparing: *wind forces measured on a standard scale* **2** [C] a set of marks, esp. numbers, on an instrument at exactly fixed distances apart, used for measuring: *a ruler with a metric scale* **3** [C] a set of numbers comparing measurements on a map or model with actual measurements: *a scale of 1 inch to the mile|a scale of 1:25 000|a* **scale model/drawing** (=made according to a scale)|*a large-/small-scale map* **4** [C;U] size, esp. in relation to other things or to what is usual: *a large-scale business |business on a large scale* **5** [C] a set of musical notes in upward or downward order : *the scale of A* (=with the note A for its base) **6 to scale** according to a fixed rule for reducing the size of something in a drawing, model, etc.: *The house was drawn to scale, except one part which was* **out of scale.**

**scale[3]** *n* **1** [C] one of the small stiff pieces forming the outer body covering of fish, snakes, etc. **2** [U] greyish material forming inside hot water pipes, pots in which water is boiled, etc. –see also FUR (3)

**scale[4]** *v* **scaled, scaling** [T] **1** to climb up: *scale a wall/ladder* **2** to increase or reduce, esp. by a fixed rate: *Income tax is scaled according to how much you earn.*

**scal·lop,** scol- /ˈskɒləp‖ˈskɑ-/ *n* **1** an edible sea animal (a MOLLUSC) which has a pair of rounded shells **2** one of a row of small curves forming an edge or pattern: *a dress with scallops around the neck*

**scal·ly·wag** /'skæliwæg/ *n usu. humor* a trouble-making or dishonest person, esp. a child; RASCAL

**scalp¹** /skælp/ *n* the skin on the top of the human head, where hair grows

**scalp²** *v* [T] (esp. of American Indians in former times) to cut off the SCALP¹ of (a dead enemy) as a mark of victory

**scal·pel** /'skælpəl/ *n* a small sharp knife used by doctors in operations

**scal·y** /'skeɪli/ *adj* **-ier, -iest** covered with SCALES³ –**scaliness** *n* [U]

**scamp** /skæmp/ *n* a trouble-making but usu. playful child

**scam·per** /'skæmpəʳ/ *v* [I] to run quickly and usu. playfully: *The mouse scampered into its hole.*

**scam·pi** /'skæmpi/ *n* [U] *BrE* (a dish made from) large PRAWNS

**scan** /skæn/ *v* **-nn-** [T] **1** to examine closely, esp. in search: *He was scanning the sky for planes.* **2** to look at quickly without careful reading: *to scan the list of names*

**scan·dal** /'skændl/ *n* **1** [C;U] (something which causes) a public feeling that something is not proper: *The news about the minister's private life caused a scandal.*|(fig.) *The price of petrol is a scandal!* **2** [U] true or false talk which brings shame on another: *I'm not interested in scandal about the neighbours!*

**scan·dal·ize,**||also **-ise** *BrE* /'skændəl-aɪz/ *v* **-ized, -izing** [T] to offend (someone's) feelings of what is right or proper

**scan·dal·ous** /'skændələs/ *adj* offensive to feelings of what is right or proper: *scandalous behaviour* –**scandalously** *adv*

**Scan·di·na·vi·an** /ˌskænd$\frac{1}{3}$'neɪvɪən/ *adj* of or concerning the people or languages of Denmark, Finland, Norway, Sweden, and Iceland

**scant** /skænt/ *adj* hardly enough: *He paid scant attention to what was said.*

**scant·y** /'skænti/ *adj* **-ier, -iest** hardly big enough; almost too small, few, etc.: *a scanty breakfast* –**scantily** *adv* –**scantiness** *n* [U]

**scape·goat** /'skeɪpgəʊt/ *n* a person or thing taking the blame for the fault of others

**scar¹** /skɑːʳ/ *n* a mark remaining on the skin from a wound, cut, etc.: (fig.) *a country showing the scars of recent war*

**scar²** *v* **-rr-** [T] to mark with a SCAR

**scarce** /skeəs||skeərs/ *adj* not much or many; hard to find; not PLENTIFUL: *Good fruit is scarce in winter, and costs a lot.* –compare COMMON; see RARE (USAGE)

**scarce·ly** /'skeəsli||-ər-/ *adv* hardly; almost not; BARELY (2): *She spoke scarcely a word.* –compare RARELY

**scar·ci·ty** /'skeəs$\frac{1}{3}$ti||-ər-/ *n* **-ties** [C;U *of*] a state of being SCARCE; lack: *scarcities of all kinds of goods*

**scare¹** /skeəʳ/ *v* **scared, scaring 1** [I;T] **a** to cause sudden fear to; FRIGHTEN: *Don't let the noise scare you: it's only the wind.* **b** to become afraid: *a woman who doesn't scare easily* **2** [T *off, away*] to cause to go by making afraid: *He made a noise and scared off the animals.*|*The high price is scaring away possible buyers.*

**scare²** *n* [S] a sudden feeling of fear: *What a scare you gave me, appearing suddenly in the dark!*

**scare³** *adj* [A] intended to cause fear: *scare stories about war, printed in the newspapers*

**scare·crow** /'skeəkrəʊ||-ər-/ *n* an object in the shape of a person, set up in a field to keep birds away from crops

**scared** /skeəd||skeərd/ *adj* [+*to-v/that*] afraid or made anxious: *Why won't you come on the trip? Are you scared?*|*I'm scared to fly in a plane. I'm scared that it might crash.*|*I was* **scared stiff/out of my wits/to death** *by the dog.*

**scarf** /skɑːf||skɑrf/ *n* **scarfs** *or* **scarves** a piece of cloth for wearing round the neck, head, or shoulders for protection against the cold or for decoration

**scar·let** /'skɑːl$\frac{1}{3}$t||-ɑr-/ *adj,n* [U] (of) a very bright red colour

**scarlet fever** /ˌ·· '··/ *n* [U] a serious disease marked by a painful throat and red spots on the skin

**scar·y** /'skeəri/ *adj* **-ier, -iest** *infml* causing fear: *a scary dark street*|*a scary story*

**scath·ing** /'skeɪðɪŋ/ *adj* bitterly cruel in judgment: *scathing remarks* –**scathingly** *adv*

**scat·ter** /'skætəʳ/ *v* **1** [I;T] **a** to cause (a group) to separate widely: *The gunshot scattered the birds.* **b** (of a group) to separate widely: *The birds scattered.* **2** [T *with, on, over*] to spread widely by throwing: *to scatter seed on the field/scatter the field with seed*|(fig.) *He scatters money about as if he were rich.*

**scat·ter·brain** /'skætəbreɪn||-ər-/ *n infml* a likeable but careless or forgetful person –**scatterbrained** *adj*

**scat·ty** /'skæti/ *adj* **-tier, -tiest** *BrE infml* slightly mad or SCATTERBRAINED –**scattiness** *n* [U]

**scav·enge** /'skæv$\frac{1}{3}$ndʒ/ *v* **-enged, -enging** [I;T] to search for (usable objects) among waste: *homeless dogs scavenging for food* –compare SCROUNGE

**scav·eng·er** /'skæv$\frac{1}{3}$ndʒəʳ/ *n* **1** a creature (such as the VULTURE or JACKAL) which feeds on waste or decaying flesh **2** a person who SCAVENGES

**sce·na·ri·o** /s$\frac{1}{3}$'nɑːriəʊ||-'næ-, -'ne-/ *n* **-os** a description of a possible course of action or events or of the story of a film, play, etc.

**scene** /siːn/ *n* **1** [C] **a** (in a play) any of the divisions, often within an ACT² (3), during which there is no change of place or time **b** (in a film, broadcast, etc.) a single period of action in one place **2** [C] a view of a place: *a beautiful scene from our hotel window*|*a street scene* **3** [C] a place where something happens: *the scene of the crime* **4** [C] an event full of action, excitement, etc. regarded as like something in a play or film: *angry scenes in Parliament* **5** [C] a show of anger or feelings, esp. between two people in public: *Why did you* **make a scene** *in the restaurant?* **6** [S] *infml* an area of activity: *He knows a lot about the pop music scene.* **7 behind the scenes** out of sight; secretly: *decisions made behind the scenes, without public knowledge* **8 set the scene** to prepare; make ready: *The unjust peace agreement set the scene for another war.* –see VIEW (USAGE)

**sce·ne·ry** /'siːnəri/ *n* [U] **1** the set of painted backgrounds used on a theatre stage **2** natural surroundings, esp. in beautiful and open country –see VIEW (USAGE)

**sce·nic** /ˈsiːnɪk/ *adj* of, concerning, or showing natural SCENERY (2): *a scenic route along the coast* **–scenically** *adv*

**scent**[1] /sent/ *n* **1** [C] a smell, esp. **a** as left by a hunted animal **b** a particular usu. pleasant smell: *the scent of roses* **2** [U] *BrE*→PERFUME **3** [S] a way to the discovery; TRACK[1] (1): *a scientist who thinks she's* **on the scent** *of a cure for heart disease* –sounds like **sent**

**scent**[2] *v* [T] **1** (esp. of animals) to smell, esp. to learn the presence of by smelling: (fig.) *She scented danger.* **2** [*usu. pass.*] to fill with a SCENT[1] (1b): *the air, scented with spring flowers*

**scep·tic** *BrE*‖**skeptic** *AmE* /ˈskeptɪk/ *n* a SCEPTICAL person, esp. about the claims made by a religion, a political party, etc.

**scep·ti·cal** *BrE*‖**skeptical** *AmE* /ˈskeptɪkəl/ *adj* [*of, about*] (habitually) unwilling to believe; doubting: *I'm sceptical of/about the weather improving.* **–sceptically** *adv* **–scepticism** *BrE*‖**skepticism** *AmE n* [S;U]

**scep·tre** *BrE*‖**scepter** *AmE* /ˈseptəʳ/ *n* a short rod carried by a ruler as a sign of power

**sched·ule**[1] /ˈʃedjuːl‖ˈskedʒʊl, -dʒəl/ *n* **1** a timetable of things to be done, dealt with, etc.; PROGRAMME[1] (3): *a factory production schedule* **2** a formal list, such as **a** a list of prices **b** *AmE* a timetable of trains, buses, etc. **3 ahead of/on/behind schedule** before/at/after the planned time

**schedule**[2] *v* **-uled, -uling** [T] **1** [*for*] to plan for a certain future time: *The meeting is scheduled to take place next week.* **2** [*usu. pass.*] to put (a flight, train, etc.) into a regular timetable: *Are you going by a scheduled flight or by* CHARTER[1] (2)?

**scheme**[1] /skiːm/ *n* **1** a plan, system, or general arrangement; *a health insurance scheme* **2** a clever dishonest plan: *a scheme to escape taxes*

**scheme**[2] *v* **schemed, scheming** [I +*to-v*] to make clever dishonest plans; PLOT[2] (4) **–schemer** *n*

**schis·m** /ˈsɪzəm, ˈskɪzəm/ *n* [C;U] (a) separation between parts originally of the same group, esp. in the Christian church

**schiz·oid** /ˈskɪtsɔɪd/ *adj tech* of or like SCHIZOPHRENIA

**schiz·o·phre·ni·a** /ˌskɪtsəʊˈfriːnɪə, -sə-/ *n* [U] *tech* a disorder of the mind causing a person to draw away from other people into a life in the imagination only

**schiz·o·phren·ic** /ˌskɪtsəʊˈfrenɪk, -sə-/ *adj,n tech* (typical of) a person with SCHIZOPHRENIA

**schol·ar** /ˈskɒləʳ‖ˈskɑ-/ *n* **1** a person with great knowledge of a subject; LEARNED person **2** the holder of a SCHOLARSHIP (1)

**schol·ar·ly** /ˈskɒləli‖ˈskɑlərli/ *adj* concerned with or based on serious detailed study; of or like a SCHOLAR (1)

**schol·ar·ship** /ˈskɒləʃɪp‖ˈskɑlər-/ *n* **1** [C] a sum of money given to a student by an official body, to pay (partly) for a course of study **2** [U] the knowledge, work, or method of SCHOLARS (1); exact and serious study: *Her book is a fine piece of scholarship.*

> **SPELLING NOTE**
> Words with the sound /s/, may be spelt **c-**, like **city**, or **ps-**, like **psychology.**

**scho·las·tic** /skəˈlæstɪk/ *adj* [A] of or concerning schools and teaching

**school**[1] /skuːl/ *n* **1** [C;U] (study at) a place of education for children: *a* PRIMARY/SECONDARY *school|new schools built by the government|She walked home after school.* **2** [C +*sing.pl. v*] the students (and teachers) at such a place: *The whole school were/was sorry when she left.* **3** [C;U] an establishment for teaching a particular subject, skill, etc.: *She goes to (an) art school.*|NIGHT SCHOOL **4** [C] (in certain universities) a department concerned with a particular subject: *the School of Law* **5** [C] a group of people with the same methods, opinions, style of painting, etc.: *Rembrandt and his school|There are different* **schools of thought** *on this problem.* **6** [C;U] *AmE* for UNIVERSITY

**school**[2] *v* [T *in*] to teach, train, or bring under control: *well schooled in obedience*

**school**[3] *n* [*of*] a large group of one kind of fish or certain sea animals swimming together

**school·boy** /ˈskuːlbɔɪ/ **schoolgirl** /-gɜːl‖-gɜrl/ *fem.*– *n* a boy attending school

**school·ing** /ˈskuːlɪŋ/ *n* [U] education or attendance at school: *He had only five years of schooling.*

**school·mas·ter** /ˈskuːlˌmɑːstəʳ‖-ˌmæ-/ **schoolmistress** /-ˌmɪstrɨs/ *fem.*– *n BrE* a male teacher at a school

**school re·port** /ˌ· ·ˈ·/ also **report** *BrE*‖**report card** *AmE*– *n* a written statement by teachers about a child's work at school

**schoo·ner** /ˈskuːnəʳ/ *n* **1** a fast sailing ship **2** a large tall drinking glass, esp. for SHERRY

**sci·ence** /ˈsaɪəns/ *n* **1** [U] (the study of) knowledge which depends on testing facts and stating general natural laws **2** [C;U] a branch of such knowledge, esp. **a** any of the branches usu. studied at universities, such as PHYSICS, BIOLOGY, chemistry, and ENGINEERING (**the sciences**): *studying a science subject* –compare ARTS; see also NATURAL SCIENCE **b** anything which may be studied exactly: *the science of cooking|military science* –see also SOCIAL SCIENCE

**science fic·tion** /ˌ·· ˈ··/ also **sci-fi** *infml*– *n* [U] stories about imaginary developments in science and their effect on life

**sci·en·tif·ic** /ˌsaɪənˈtɪfɪk/ *adj* **1** [A *no comp.*] of, being, or concerning science: *The microscope is a scientific instrument.* **2** needing or showing exact knowledge, skill, or use of a system: *She has a very scientific method of dealing with political problems.* –opposite **unscientific** (for 2) **–scientifically** *adv*

**sci·en·tist** /ˈsaɪəntɨst/ *n* a person who works in a science, esp. PHYSICS, chemistry, or BIOLOGY

**scim·i·tar** /ˈsɪmɨtəʳ/ *n* a curved sword that is sharp on the outer edge, formerly used in the Middle East

**scin·til·lating** /ˈsɪntɨleɪtɪŋ/ *adj* (esp. of speech) full of interest; quick and clever

**scis·sors** /ˈsɪzəz‖-ərz/ *n* [P] two sharp blades with handles at one end with holes for the fingers, fastened at the centre so that they open in the shape of the letter X and cut when they close: *These scissors are very sharp.|a pair of scissors* –compare SHEARS; see PAIR (USAGE)

**scoff**[1] /skɒf‖skɔf, skɑf/ *v* [I *at*] to speak or act

disrespectfully; laugh unkindly (at); RIDICULE²: *I told them my ideas but they scoffed at them.* –**scoffer** *n*
**scoff²** *v* [T] *infml* to eat eagerly and fast: *The dog always scoffs its food.*
**scold** /skəʊld/ *v* [I;T] to speak in an angry and complaining way (to), esp. to blame: *The child was scolded by its mother.* –**scolding** *n* [C;U]
**scol·lop** /'skɒləp‖'skɑ-/ *n* → SCALLOP
**scone** /skɒn, skəʊn‖skəʊn, skɑn/ ‖also **biscuit** *AmE*– *n* a soft round breadlike cake of a size for one person
**scoop¹** /sku:p/ *n* **1** a container for moving liquids or loose soft materials: *a measuring scoop|two scoops of ice-cream* **2** a report made by a newspaper before any other newspapers –compare EXCLUSIVE
**scoop²** *v* [T] **1** [*up, out, out of*] to take up or out, (as if) with a SCOOP¹ (1): *to scoop up a handful of sand|to scoop some sugar out of the bag* **2** (of a newspaper) to make a news report before (another newspaper)
**scoot** /sku:t/ *v* [I] *infml* to run quickly
**scoot·er** /'sku:təʳ/ *n* **1** also **motor scooter**– a small motorcycle, with a covering over the engine at the back **2** a child's vehicle with two small wheels, an upright handle fixed to the front wheel, and a narrow board for one foot, pushed by the other foot touching the ground
**scope** /skəʊp/ *n* [U] **1** the limits of a question, subject, etc.: *The committee was not interested in people's private lives–this subject was outside the scope of their inquiry.* **2** [*for*] chance for action or thought: *There's not much scope for* INITIATIVE *in this job.*
**scorch** /skɔ:tʃ‖-ɔr-/ *v* **1** [I;T] to burn so as to change a thing's colour, taste, or feeling but not completely destroy it: *to scorch a shirt with an iron that's too hot*|(fig.) *fields scorched by the sun* **2** [I] *infml* to travel very fast: *The car scorched down the road.*
**scorch·er** /'skɔ:tʃəʳ‖-ɔr-/ *n* [S] *infml* a very hot day
**scorch·ing** /'skɔ:tʃɪŋ‖-ɔr-/ *adj,adv* (in a way) that SCORCHES: *scorching heat|a scorching hot day*
**score¹** /skɔ:ʳ‖skor/ *n* **1** the number of points, GOALS (3), etc., gained in a game, sport, competition, examination, etc.: *The score stood at/was 2 to 1 at half time.*|*a high/low score in the end of term test.* **2 a** a written copy of a piece of music, esp. for a large group of performers: *a full score* (=showing all the parts in separate lines on the page) **b** the music for a film or play: *There were some good songs in that film; who wrote the score?* **3** [*usu. sing.*] a reason; account: *We have enough money; don't worry* **on that score. 4** an old disagreement or hurt kept in mind; GRUDGE² (1): *I've* **got a score to settle** *with him.* (=I want to make sure he is punished) **5 know the score** *infml* to understand the true and usu. unfavourable facts of a matter
**score²** *v* **scored, scoring 1** [I;T] to gain (points, GOALS (3), etc.) in a sport, game, competition, examination, etc.: *He scored three points/times in the last half of the game.*|*She scored the highest marks in the exam.* **2** [I] to record the SCORE¹ (1) of a sports match as it is played: *Who will score for us?* **3** [T] to mark or cut one or more lines on, (as) with a sharp instrument: *Score the paper to make it easy to fold.* **4** [I;T *off, against, over*] to make (a clever and successful point), esp. in an argument against someone: *I hate conversations where people try to score (points) off each other.* **5** [I;T] to gain or win (a success, victory, prize, etc.): *This writer has scored again with another popular book.*

**score** sthg.↔**out/through** *v adv* [T] *fml* to draw a line through (written words) to show that they should not be read; CROSS **out**
**score³** *determiner, n* **score** *or* **scores 1** *becoming rare* (a group of) 20: *threescore or three score* (=60) **2 scores (of)** large numbers (of): *scores of people, perhaps 80 or more*
**score·board** /'skɔ:bɔ:d‖'skorbord/ *n* a board on which the SCORE¹ (1) of a game is recorded as it is played
**scor·er** /'skɔ:rəʳ‖'skorər/ *n* **1** a person who keeps the SCORE¹ (1) of a sports match as it is played **2** a player who scores points, GOALS (3), etc.
**scorn¹** /skɔ:n‖skɔrn/ *n* [U] strong, usu. angry disrespect; CONTEMPT : *He* **poured scorn on** *my suggestion.* –**scornful** *adj* –**scornfully** *adv*
**scorn²** *v* [T + *to-v/v-ing*] to refuse to accept or consider, esp because of SCORN¹ or pride: *She scorned our offers of help.*
**Scor·pi·o** /'skɔ:piəʊ‖-ɔr-/ *n* see ZODIAC
**scor·pi·on** /'skɔ:pɪən‖-ɔr-/ *n* a tropical insect with a curving tail which stings poisonously
**scotch** /skɒtʃ‖skɑtʃ/ *v* [T] to put an end to: *to scotch a false story by explaining the true facts*
**Scotch** *n* [C;U] also *fml* **Scotch whisky** – (a glass of) a strong alcoholic drink (WHISKY) made in Scotland
**scotch tape** /ˌ· '·, '· ·/ *n,v AmE tdmk* → SELLOTAPE
**scot-free** /ˌ· '·/ *adj* [F] *infml* without harm or punishment: *The thief got away scot-free.*
**Scot·land Yard** /ˌskɒtlənd 'jɑ:d‖ˌskɑtlənd 'jɑrd/ *n* [U +*sing.pl. v*] (the main office of) the London police
**Scot·tish** /'skɒtɪʃ‖'skɑtɪʃ/ also **Scots** /skɒts‖skɑts/– *adj* of, being, concerning, or typical of Scotland
USAGE **Scots** is less common than **Scottish,** and is usually only used of people: *a well-known* **Scots/Scottish** *actor|the* **Scottish** *islands.* **Scotch** is normally only used of the products of Scotland: **Scotch** *wool*/BEEF/WHISKY. **Scots** is usu. used only of people (*a* **Scots** *lawyer| a* **Scottish** *plant*).
**scoun·drel** /'skaʊndrəl/ *n* a wicked selfish person; VILLAIN
**scour¹** /skaʊəʳ/ *v* [T *for*] to go through (an area) thoroughly in search of someone or something: *The police scoured the area looking for the lost child.*
**scour²** *v* [T] **1** [*down, out, off*] to clean (a surface) by hard rubbing with a rough material: *scour out a dirty pan|scour off the dirt from the floor* **2** [*out*] (of water) to form by wearing away
**scour·er** /'skaʊərəʳ/ *n* a tool, esp. a small ball of plastic wire, for cleaning cooking pots and pans
**scourge** /skɜ:dʒ‖-ɜr-/ *n* a cause of great harm or suffering: *the scourge of war*
**scout¹** /skaʊt/ *v* [I *around, about, for*] to go looking for something: *He scouted around for a shop that was open late.*
**scout²** *n* **1** [C] a soldier sent out to search for information about the land, the enemy, etc. **2** [C] → BOY SCOUT **3** [S] an act of SCOUTING¹: *He had a scout round*

*to see what he could find.*

**scowl**[1] /skaʊl/ *v* to make a SCOWL[2]; FROWN[1] (1) angrily

**scowl**[2] *n* an angry threatening expression of the face; angry FROWN

**scrab·ble** /ˈskræbəl/ *v* **-bled, -bling** [I *about*] to move wildly and quickly (as if) looking for something

**scrag·gy** /ˈskrægi/ *adj* **-gier, -giest** thin and bony: *a scraggy-looking dog*

**scram** /skræm/ *v* **-mm-** [I *usu. in commands*] *infml* to go away fast; run away: *You're not wanted here, so scram!*

**scram·ble**[1] /ˈskræmbəl/ *v* **-bled, -bling 1** [I] to move or climb quickly, esp. over a rough or steep surface: *I scrambled up the rock.* **2** [I +*to-v*/*for*] to struggle with others eagerly or in a disorderly way: *people scrambling for shelter/scrambling to get out of the way* **3** [T] to mix the white and yellow parts of (eggs) together while cooking them: *scrambled eggs*

**scramble**[2] *n* [S] **1** an act of moving or climbing over a rough surface: *It's quite a scramble to get to the top of the hill.* **2** an eager and disorderly struggle: *a scramble for the best seats*

**scrap**[1] /skræp/ *n* **1** [C] a small piece; bit: *a scrap of paper|scraps of news/food* –see picture on page 449 **2** [A;U] material which cannot be used for its original purpose but which may still have some value: *scrap metal* –see also SCRAPS

**scrap**[2] *v* **-pp-** [T] to get rid of as no longer useful or wanted; DISCARD

**scrap**[3] *n infml* a usu. sudden, not serious, fight or quarrel: *It wasn't a real fight, just a scrap.*

**scrap**[4] *v* **-pp-** [I *with*] *infml* to quarrel or fight

**scrap·book** /ˈskræpbʊk/ *n* a book of empty pages in which a collection of photographs, newspaper articles, etc., is fastened

**scrape**[1] /skreɪp/ *v* **scraped, scraping 1** [T] to remove (material) from a surface by repeated rubbing or by pulling an edge firmly across it: *I scraped the skin off the vegetables with a knife.* **2** [T *down*] to clean or make (a surface) smooth in this way: *She scraped the door (down) before painting it again.* **3** [I;T *on, against*] to (cause to) rub roughly: *He scraped* (=hurt) *his knee when he fell.* **4** [I *along, by, through*] **a** to live with only just enough money: *scraping by on very small wages* **b** to succeed by doing work of the lowest acceptable quality: *She just scraped through* (=passed) *the examination by one mark.*

**scrape** sthg.↔**up/together**– *v adv* [T] to gather (a total, esp. of money) with difficulty by putting small amounts together

**scrape**[2] *n* **1** an act or sound of scraping (SCRAPE) **2** a slight wound made by scraping (SCRAPE): *He suffered a few cuts and scrapes.*

**scrap heap** /ˈ· ·/ *n* **1** [C] a pile of waste material, esp. metal **2** [*the* S] an imaginary place where unwanted things, people, or ideas go: *Put that plan on the scrap heap: it'll never work.*

**SPELLING NOTE**
Words with the sound **/s/**, may be spelt **c-**, like **city**, or **ps-**, like **psychology.**

**scrap·py** /ˈskræpi/ *adj* **-pier, -piest** made of disconnected bits; not well arranged or planned: *a scrappy, badly-written report*

**scraps** /skræps/ *n* [P] pieces of food not eaten at a meal, and thrown away: *Feed the scraps to the pig.*

**scratch**[1] /skrætʃ/ *v* **1** [I;T] to rub and tear or mark (a surface) with something pointed or rough, e.g. CLAWS or FINGERNAILS: *Be careful of the cat: it'll scratch (you)!|The table top is scratched.|a dog scratching at the door to be let in|She scratched her elbow on a nail.* **2** [T] to remove or mark in this way: *He scratched his name on the wall with a knife.* **3** [I;T] to rub (a part of the body) lightly to stop ITCHing[1] (1): *The cat likes to be scratched behind its ears.|He scratched his arm where he had been bitten by an insect.* **4** [I;T] to remove (oneself, a horse, etc.) from a race or competition before it starts: *The horse (was) scratched on the day of the race.* **5 scratch the surface** to deal with only the beginning of a matter or only a few of many cases

**scratch**[2] *n* **1** [C] a mark or sore place made by SCRATCHing[1] (1): *a scratch on the table top|He got a few cuts and scratches in the accident.* **2** [C] a sound made by SCRATCHing[1] (1): *The recording was spoiled by scratches.* **3** [S] an act of SCRATCHing[1] (3): *a dog* **having a scratch** (=scratching itself) **4** [A] made or put together in a hurry using whatever could be found: *a scratch football team* **5 from scratch** *infml* starting from the beginning or with nothing **6 up to scratch** *infml* at or to a good enough standard: *The piano player was not up to scratch.*

**scratch·y** /ˈskrætʃi/ *adj* **-ier, -iest** (of a recording) spoilt by SCRATCHes[2] (2) –**scratchiness** *n* [U]

**scrawl**[1] /skrɔːl/ *v* [T] to write in a careless, hurried, or awkward way

**scrawl**[2] *n* [*usu. sing.*] something written awkwardly, or fast and carelessly: *Her handwriting is a scrawl.*

**scraw·ny** /ˈskrɔːni/ *adj* **-nier, -niest** *derog* (of people or animals) without much flesh on the bones; thin: *a scrawny little man/dog*

**scream**[1] /skriːm/ *v* **1** [I] to cry out loudly on a high note, in fear, pain, excitement, or sometimes laughter: *The man was screaming with pain.|to scream for help|I screamed with laughter at the joke.* **2** [T +*that*/*out*] to express in this way: *He screamed (out) a warning to us.*

**scream**[2] *n* **1** [C] a loud sharp cry expressing pain, fear, excitement, or sometimes laughter: *We heard a terrible scream.|*(fig.) *the scream of the electric saw as it cut the log* **2** [S] *infml* a very funny person, or thing: *She thought it was a scream when I fell off my chair.*

**scree** /skriː/ *n* [U] a mass of small broken rocks on the side of a mountain

**screech** /skriːtʃ/ *v* [I;T] (of people, animals, or machinery) to give out an unpleasant high sharp sound, as in terror or pain: *birds screeching in the trees|*(fig.) *The car screeched to a stop.* –**screech** *n: a screech of brakes*

**screed** /skriːd/ *n* a long and usu. dull speech or piece of writing

**screen**[1] /skriːn/ *n* **1** [C] an upright frame used as a small movable wall for dividing a room, protecting people from view, from cold air, etc: *They put a screen around his bed so that the doctor could ex-*

*amine him.*|*Put the window screens up to keep the flies out.* **2** [C] something that protects, shelters, or hides: *a screen of trees to keep out the wind*|(fig.) *His job at the bank was just a screen for his life as a spy.* **3** [C] a surface on which a cinema film is shown: *She first appeared on the screen* (=acted in her first film) *ten years ago.* **4** [S] the cinema industry: *a play written for the screen* (=to be shown as a film)|*a* **screen test** (=test of one's ability to act in films) **5** [C] the front glass surface of an electrical instrument, esp. a television, on which pictures or information appear

**screen²** *v* [T] **1** [*from*] to shelter or protect from light, wind, etc.: *He screened his eyes with his hand.* **2** [*off, from*] to hide from view, (as) with a SCREEN (1): *Her face was screened by a tree.*|*Part of the room was screened off.* **3** to test (people) to see whether they are loyal, suitable for a job, etc.: *100 carefully screened people were invited to meet the President.* **4** to show (a cinema film): *a new film, first screened only last month*

**screen·play** /'skri:npleɪ/ *n* a story written for a film

**screw¹** /skru:/ *n* **1** a type of usu. metal fastener similar to a nail but having a raised circular edge (THREAD¹ (4)) so that it holds firmly when fastened into a material by turning (usu. with a SCREWDRIVER) –compare BOLT¹ (1), NAIL¹ (1), **2**→ PROPELLER **3 have a screw loose** *humor* to be slightly mad

**screw²** *v* **1** [T] to fasten with one or more screws: *The table legs are screwed to the floor.* **2** [I;T] **a** to turn or tighten (a screw or something that moves in the same way): *Screw the two pipes together end to end.*|*Screw the lid on tightly.* **b** (of such a thing) to turn or tighten: *The two pieces screw together easily.* –see also UNSCREW **3** [T *out of*] *infml* to get by forcing or by dishonest means: *He screwed the others out of their share of the money.* **4** [I;T] *taboo* to have sex (with someone) **5 have one's head screwed on (right)** to be sensible; do nothing foolish

**screw** sthg.↔**up** *v adv* [T] **1** *infml* to ruin: *The bad weather screwed up our holiday.* **2** to twist **a** a part of the face, esp. to express disapproval or uncertainty: *She screwed up her eyes in the bright light.* **b** (paper or cloth) carelessly or to make a ball **3 screw up one's courage** to stop oneself from being afraid: *He screwed up his courage and asked for more money.*

**screw·driv·er** /'skru:ˌdraɪvəʳ/ *n* a tool with a narrow blade at one end, which turns SCREWS into and out of their places

**screw·y** /'skru:i/ *adj* **-ier, -iest** *infml* seeming strange, and often funny or annoying; CRAZY (1,2): *He's a bit screwy.*

**scrib·ble¹** /'skrɪbəl/ *v* **-bled, -bling 1** [I;T] to write (meaningless marks): *The child can't write yet but she loves to scribble with a pencil.* **2** [T] to write carelessly or in a hurry: *He scribbled me a note.*

**scribble²** *n* **1** [C] a meaningless written mark: *scribbles on the wall* **2** [S;U] (a piece of) hasty careless writing: *His writing is nothing but (a) scribble.*

**scribe** /skraɪb/ *n* a person employed to copy things in writing, esp. in times before the invention of printing

**scrimp** /skrɪmp/ *v* **scrimp and save** to save (money) slowly and with difficulty, esp. by living poorly: *She had to scrimp and save to pay for her holiday.*

**script** /skrɪpt/ *n* **1** [C;U] the set of letters used in writing a language; ALPHABET: *words printed in Arabic script* **2** [U] writing done by hand, esp. with the letters or words joined **3** [C] the written form of a speech, play, or broadcast

**scrip·tur·al** /'skrɪptʃərəl/ *adj* according to a holy writing, esp. the Bible

**scrip·ture** /'skrɪptʃəʳ/ *n* [C;U] *(often cap.)* holy writings, esp. the Bible

**script·writ·er** /'skrɪptˌraɪtəʳ/ *n* a writer of SCRIPTS (3)

**scroll** /skrəul/ *n* a long straight piece of skin or paper with writing on it, that can be rolled up, esp. as used formerly

**scrooge** /skru:dʒ/ *n infml & derog (sometimes cap.)* → MISER

**scro·tum** /'skrəutəm/ *n* **-ta** /tə/ *or* **-tums** *tech* the bag of flesh holding the TESTICLES of male animals

**scrounge** /skraundʒ/ *v* **scrounged, scrounging** [I;T *off*] *often derog* to get (money or whatever else one needs), without work or payment or by persuading others: *He's always scrounging off his friends.*|*Can I scrounge a cigarette off you?* –**scrounger** *n*

**scrub¹** /skrʌb/ *v* **-bb- 1** [I;T] to clean by hard rubbing, e.g. with a stiff brush: *He scrubbed the floor clean.* **2** [T] to cause not to happen; CANCEL (1): *We've scrubbed our holiday plans this year.*

**scrub²** *n* [S] an act of SCRUBbing¹ (1): *Give that floor a good hard scrub.*

**scrub³** *n* [A;U] low-growing bushes and short trees growing in poor soil

**scruff** /skrʌf/ *n* **the scruff of the neck** the flesh at the back of the neck: *caught/grabbed by the scruff of the neck*

**scruf·fy** /'skrʌfi/ *adj* **-fier, -fiest** dirty and untidy; SHABBY: *a scruffy hotel/boy*

**scrum** /skrʌm/ also **scrummage** /'skrʌmɪdʒ/ *fml* – *n* (in RUGBY) a group formed at certain times in the game by the front players of both teams pushing against each other

**scrump·tious** /'skrʌmpʃəs/ *adj infml* (esp. of food) very good; DELICIOUS

**scru·ple** /'skru:pəl/ *n* **1** [C] a moral principle which keeps one from doing something wrong: *a man with no scruples* **2** [U] the desire to do what is right; conscience: *He acted wrongly and without scruple.*

**scru·pu·lous** /'skru:pjuləs‖-pjə-/ *adj* **1** correct even in the smallest detail; exact; PAINSTAKING: *The nurse treated him with the most scrupulous care.* **2** carefully doing only what is right; exactly honest; CONSCIENTIOUS: *She is very scrupulous in her business activities; everybody trusts her.* –opposite **unscrupulous** (for 2) –**scrupulously** *adv* –**scrupulousness** *n* [U]

**scru·ti·nize** ‖also **-ise** *BrE* /'skru:tənaɪz/ *v* **-nized, -nizing** [T] to give SCRUTINY to; examine closely: *She scrutinized his work carefully before allowing him to send it out.*

**scru·ti·ny** /'skru:təni/ *n* [U] careful and thorough examination: *She* SUBJECTED³ *his work to close scrutiny.*

**scud** /skʌd/ *v* **-dd-** [I] *lit* (esp. of clouds and ships) to move along quickly as if driven: *Clouds* *scudded across the sky.*

**scuff** /skʌf/ *v* [T *up*] to make a rough mark on the smooth surface of (shoes, a floor, etc.); SCRAPE[1] (3): *The floor was badly scuffed where they had been dancing.*

**scull**[1] /skʌl/ *n* a small light racing boat for one person rowing with a pair of light OARS

**scull**[2] *v* [I;T] to row (a SCULL[1])

**scul·le·ry** /'skʌləri/ *n* **-ries** a room in large or older houses, for washing and keeping dishes, pots, etc.

**sculp·tor** /'skʌlptəʳ/ *n* an artist who does SCULPTURE

**sculp·ture**[1] /'skʌlptʃəʳ/ *n* **1** [U] the art of shaping figures (e.g. people or things) out of stone, wood, metal, etc.: *to study sculpture in art school* **2** [C;U] (a piece of) work produced by this art

**sculpture**[2] also **sculpt** /skʌlpt/ *v* **-tured, -turing** [I;T] to make (esp. works of SCULPTURE) by shaping: *sculptured pillars*

**scum** /skʌm/ *n* **1** [S;U] a filmy covering of impure material on the surface of a liquid **2** [U *+sing.pl. v*] *derog* worthless evil people: *He says people who* TORTURE *other people are* **the scum of the earth.** (=the worst people in the world) **–scummy** *adj* **-mier, -miest**

**scup·per** /'skʌpəʳ/ *v* [T] *BrE infml* to ruin: *He scuppered our plans by not giving us his support.*

**scurf** /skɜːf‖skɜrf/ *n* [U] small dry loose bits of dead skin esp. in the hair **–scurfy** *adj*

**scur·ri·lous** /'skʌrɨləs/ *adj* making or containing very rude, improper, or evil statements: *a scurrilous attack in the newspapers* **–scurrilously** *adv* **–scurrilousness** [U]

**scur·ry**[1] /'skʌri/ *v* **-ried, -rying** [I] to move quickly with short steps; hurry: *The mouse scurried away.*

**scurry**[2] *n* [S] a movement or esp. sound of SCURRYing: *I heard the scurry of feet in the hall.*

**scut·tle**[1] /'skʌtl/ *v* **-tled, -tling** [T] to sink (a ship, esp. one's own) by making holes in the bottom of it

**scuttle**[2] *v* [I] to run with short quick steps, esp. to escape; SCURRY: *The children scuttled off/away when they saw the policeman.*

**scythe**[1] /saɪð/ *n* a long-handled tool with a curving blade for cutting long grass

**scythe**[2] *v* **scythed, scything** [I;T *down, off*] to cut (grass) with a SCYTHE

**SE** *written abbrev. said as:* southeast(ern)

**sea** /siː/ *n* **1** [C; U] the great body of salty water that covers much of the earth's surface; ocean: *boats sailing on the sea|Most of the earth is covered by sea.|sea water|sea travel| (a) seacoast|We went* **by sea**, *not by air.* **2** [C] a large body of salty water smaller than an ocean, or enclosed by land: *the Red Sea|the Mediterranean Sea* **3** [S *of*] a large mass or quantity: *The actor looked out from the stage onto a sea of faces.* **4** [C] movement of waves on water: *The ship ran into strong winds and heavy seas.* **5 at sea** *infml* as if lost; not understanding; BEWILDERed: *He felt completely at sea in his new school.*

> **SPELLING NOTE**
> Words with the sound /s/, may be spelt **c-**, like **city**, or **ps-**, like **psychology.**

**sea·bed** /'siːbed/ *n* [S] the land at the bottom of the sea

**sea·far·ing** /'siːˌfeərɪŋ/ *adj* [A] *esp. lit* having strong connections with the sea and sailing: *a seafaring nation*

**sea·food** /'siːfuːd/ *n* [U] fish and fishlike animals (esp. SHELLFISH) from the sea which can be eaten

**sea·front** /'siːfrʌnt/ *n* [C;U] the part of a coastal town that is on the edge of the sea, often with a broad path along it for holiday visitors

**sea·gull** /'siːgʌl/ *n* → GULL

**sea·horse** /'siːhɔːs‖-hɔrs/ *n* a very small fish with a neck and head that look like those of a horse

**seal**[1] /siːl/ *v* [T] **1** to fix a SEAL[2] (1) onto: *an official statement signed and sealed* **2** [*up, down*] to fasten or close with a SEAL[2] (2,3) or a tight cover or band of something: *She sealed the parcel (shut) with sticky* TAPE.|(fig.) **My lips are sealed;** *I won't tell you.* **3** to make certain, formal, or solemn: *They sealed their agreement by shaking hands.*

**seal** sbdy./sthg.↔**in** *v adv* [T] to keep inside without a chance to escape: *Cook the meat quickly at first to seal in the juices.|The door closed behind us and sealed us in the dark room.*

**seal** sthg.↔**off** *v adv* [T] to close tightly so as not to allow entrance or escape: *Police sealed off the street.*

**seal**[2] *n* **1** the official mark of a government, company, etc., fixed to some formal and official writings: *This letter carries the royal seal.*|(fig.) *The new car has my* **seal of approval.** (=I think it is very good) **2** a small piece of paper, wax, or wire, fastened across an opening to protect it: *The seal on this bottle is broken.* **3** a tight connection on a machine, for keeping a gas or liquid in or out: *The seal has worn and the machine is losing oil.*

**seal**[3] *n* **seals** *or* **seal** a large fish-eating sea animal with broad flat limbs (FLIPPERs) suitable for swimming

**seal·ing wax** /'·· ·/ *n* [U] a usu. red solid substance, which melts and then hardens quickly and is used for fixing SEALs[2] (1)

**sea li·on** /'· ˌ··/ *n* **sea lions** *or* **sea lion** a large SEAL[3] of the Pacific Ocean

**seam** /siːm/ *n* **1** a line of stitches joining two pieces of cloth, leather, etc. **2** the line where two edges meet: *seamless stockings* (=with no join) **3** a narrow band of mineral between masses of other rocks: *a coal seam*

**sea·man** /'siːmən/ *n* **-men** /mən/ a member of a navy, or a sailor on a ship, who is not an officer

**sea·man·ship** /'siːmənʃɪp/ *n* [U] the skill of handling a ship and directing its course

**seam·stress** /'siːmstrɨs/ *n* a woman whose job is sewing

**seam·y** /'siːmi/ *adj* **-ier, -iest** bad; unpleasant: *the seamy side of city life* **–seaminess** *n* [U]

**sé·ance** /'seɪɑ̃s, 'seɪɔns‖'seɪɑns (*Fr sẽs*)/ *n French* a meeting where people try to talk to or receive messages from dead people

**sea·plane** /'siːpleɪn/ *n* an aircraft which takes off from and lands on water

**sea·port** /'siːpɔːt‖-port/ *n* a town with a harbour used by large ships

**sear** /sɪəʳ/ *v* [T] **1** to burn with a sudden powerful heat: *searing pain* **2** to cook the outside of (a piece of meat) quickly

**search**[1] /sɜːtʃ‖sɜrtʃ/ *v* [I;T *for*] to look through or examine (a place or person) thoroughly or carefully to try to find something: *The police searched the woods for the lost child.*|*She searched (through) her pockets for a cigarette.*|*Scientists are still searching for a cure to the common cold.* **–searcher** *n*

**search**[2] *n* [C *for*] an act of searching: *a search for the lost child*|*birds flying south* **in search of** *winter sun*

**search·ing** /ˈsɜːtʃɪŋ‖ˈsɜr-/ *adj* sharp and thorough; anxious to discover the truth: *She gave me a searching look.* **–searchingly** *adv*

**search·light** /ˈsɜːtʃlaɪt‖ˈsɜr-/ *n* a large usu. movable light with a powerful beam, used when searching for aircraft in the sky, missing or escaped people, etc. –compare FLOODLIGHT

**search par·ty** /ˈ· ˌ··/ *n* **-ties** [C *+sing./pl.v*] a group of people searching, esp. for a lost person

**sea·shell** /ˈsiːʃel/ *n* a shell of a small sea animal

**sea·shore** /ˈsiːʃɔː‖-ʃor/ *n* [U] land along the edge of the sea, usu. sand or rocks –see SHORE (USAGE)

**sea·sick** /ˈsiːˌsɪk/ *adj* feeling sick because of the movement of a ship on water **–seasickness** *n* [U]

**sea·side** /ˈsiːsaɪd/ *n* [*the* S] *BrE* the edge of the sea, esp. as a holiday place: *a seaside town*|*a holiday at/by the seaside* –see SHORE (USAGE)

**sea·son**[1] /ˈsiːzən/ *n* **1** a period of time each year, e.g. **a** spring, summer, autumn, or winter **b** marked by weather or particular activities: *the rainy season*|*the football season*|*My* **season ticket** *means that I can travel any number of times during the stated period.* **2 in season: a** (of fresh foods) at the time when they are usually ready for eating: *Fruit is cheapest in season.* –opposite **out of season b** (of certain female animals) on HEAT[1] (3) **c** (of animals) permitted to be hunted at the time: *You can fish in the* **open season,** *but not in the* **close season.**

**season**[2] *v* [T] **1** [*with*] to give special taste to (a food) by adding salt, pepper, a SPICE, etc. **2** to make (wood) hard and fit for use by gradual drying: *seasoned wood furniture*

**sea·so·na·ble** /ˈsiːzənəbəl/ *adj* suitable or typical for the time of year: *seasonable weather* **–seasonably** *adv*

**sea·son·al** /ˈsiːzənəl/ *adj* happening or active only at a particular season: *seasonal employment at a holiday camp*

**sea·soned** /ˈsiːzənd/ *adj* with a great deal of experience in the stated activity: *a seasoned traveller/news reporter*

**sea·son·ing** /ˈsiːzənɪŋ/ *n* [C;U] something that SEASONS food

**seat**[1] /siːt/ *n* **1** a place for sitting: *Using all our chairs we'll have seats for ten people.*|*the front/back seat of a car*|*tickets for good seats at the theatre* –see picture on page 463 **2** the part on which one sits: *The seat of the chair is broken.*|*The seat of my trousers is worn.* **3** a place as a member of an official body: *to win/lose a seat in parliament in an election* **4** [*of*] a place where a particular activity happens: *a famous university and* **seat of learning 5 take/have a seat** please sit down

**seat**[2] *v* [T] **1** to cause or help to sit: *He seated himself near the window.*|*(fml) Please be seated.* (=sit down) –see also UNSEAT **2** (of a room, table, etc.) to have room for seats for: *a large hall which seats 1,000* –see SIT (USAGE)

**seat belt** /ˈ· ·/ also **safety belt**– *n* a fixed belt fastened around a person in a car or plane to protect him/her from sudden movement, esp. in an accident –see picture on page 85

**seat·ing** /ˈsiːtɪŋ/ *n* [U] provision of seats: *Do we have enough seating for the guests?*

**sea ur·chin** /ˈ· ˌ··/ *n* a small ball-shaped sea animal that has a hard shell with many sharp points

**sea·weed** /ˈsiːwiːd/ *n* [U] a usu. dark green plant growing in the sea

**sea·wor·thy** /ˈsiːwɜːði‖-ɜr-/ *adj* (of a ship) in good condition for a sea voyage **–seaworthiness** *n* [U]

**sec·a·teurs** /ˈsekətɜːz‖ˌsekəˈtɜrz/ *n* [P] *BrE* strong scissors for cutting parts off garden plants –see PAIR[1] (USAGE)

**se·cede** /sɪˈsiːd/ *v* **-ceded, -ceding** [I *from*] *fml* to officially leave a group or organization, esp. because of disagreement **–secession** /sɪˈseʃən/ *n* [U]

**se·clud·ed** /sɪˈkluːdɪ̈d/ *adj* very quiet and private: *a secluded country house*

**se·clu·sion** /sɪˈkluːʒən/ *n* [U] the state of being SECLUDED: *The famous actor now lives in seclusion.*

**sec·ond**[1] /ˈsekənd/ *determiner,adv,n,pron* **1** 2nd **2** [C] an imperfect article that is sold at a lower price: *If you want to buy dishes cheaply, you can get factory seconds.* **3** [C] a person who helps another, esp. in a BOXING match or DUEL[1] (1) **4 second to none** *infml* the best: *As a tennis player Ann is second to none.*

**second**[2] *n* **1** a length of time equal to 1/60 of a minute **2** a measure of an angle to 1/3600 of a degree (or 1/60 of a MINUTE[1] (3))

**second**[3] *v* [T] to support (a formal suggestion (MOTION[1] (3)) at a meeting so that argument or voting may follow: *"Will anyone second this motion?" "I second it, Mr Chairman."* **–seconder** *n*

**se·cond**[4] /sɪˈkɒnd‖sɪˈkɑnd/ *v* [T] *BrE fml* to move (someone) to a special duty, usu. for a limited time: *Mr Adams was ill, so someone else was seconded to do his work.* **–secondment** *n* [C;U]

**sec·ond·a·ry** /ˈsekəndəri‖-deri/ *adj* **1** (of education or a school) for children over 11 years old: *secondary schools/teachers* –compare PRIMARY (2) **2** developing from something earlier or original: *a secondary infection caused by a cold* **3** [*to*] of second rank, value, importance, etc.: *a matter of secondary importance*

**secondary mod·ern** /ˌ···· ˈ··/ *n* (esp. formerly) a SECONDARY school which does not prepare students for university or further study

**second-class** /ˌ·· ˈ·◂/ *adj* **1** regarded as below a standard; INFERIOR: *He regards women as second-class citizens.* **2** being SECOND-CLASS: *a second-class railway carriage/letter* –compare FIRST-CLASS **–second-class** *adv: travelling second-class*

**second class** *n* [U] **1** a class of mail for letters delivered slower than FIRST CLASS **2** the ordinary type of seating or living arrangements on a train or boat

**second-de·gree** /ˌ·· ·ˈ·◂/ *adj* of the next to the most serious kind: *second-degree murder*|*second-degree burns*

**second-hand**[1] /ˌ·· ˈ·◂/ *adj,adv* **1** used by an earlier owner; not new: *a second-hand car*|*I got this book second-hand.* **2** passed on from someone else: *It was* *a second-hand report, based on what others had told him.* –see also HAND[2] (10), FIRSTHAND

**second-hand[2]** *adj* [A] dealing in SECOND-HAND[1] goods: *a second-hand shop*

**second na·ture** /ˌ·· ˈ··/ *n* [U] a very firmly fixed habit: *It's second nature for him to think of others.*

**second-rate** /ˌ·· ˈ·◂/ *adj* of less than the best quality; INFERIOR[1]: *a second-rate film/actor* –see also FIRST-RATE

**se·cre·cy** /ˈsiːkrɨsi/ *n* [U] **1** the practice of keeping secrets: *Secrecy is important to our plans.* **2** the state of being kept secret

**se·cret[1]** /ˈsiːkrɨt/ *adj* [*from*] kept from the view or knowledge of others: *secret plans|These plans must be kept secret (from the enemy).|a secret meeting place in the forest|Adrian is a secret admirer of Helen, though he has never spoken to her.* **–secretly** *adv*

**secret[2]** *n* **1** something kept hidden or known only to a few: *Our relationship must remain a secret.|Can you* **keep** (=not tell) **a secret?**|*The meeting was held* **in secret. 2** something unexplained; mystery: *What is the secret of your success?* (=how do you do it?)

**secret a·gent** /ˌ·· ˈ··/ *n* a person gathering information secretly, esp. for a foreign government; SPY

**sec·re·tar·i·al** /ˌsekrəˈteəriəl/ *adj* of or concerning the work of a secretary: *secretarial college*

**sec·re·tar·i·at** /ˌsekrəˈteəriət/ *n* an official department with a high-ranking government officer as its head: *the United Nations Secretariat in New York*

**sec·re·ta·ry** /ˈsekretəri‖-teri/ *n* **-ries 1** a person with the job of preparing letters, arranging meetings, etc., for another: *a job as* **private secretary** *to the company chairman* **2** a minister or other high-ranking government officer: *the Home/Foreign Secretary|the First Secretary at the* EMBASSY **3** an officer of an organization who keeps records, writes official letters, etc.: *a union secretary*

**se·crete[1]** /sɪˈkriːt/ *v* **-creted, -creting** [T] (esp. of an animal or plant organ) to produce (a usu. liquid substance)

**secrete[2]** *v* [T] to put into a hidden place; hide

**se·cre·tion** /sɪˈkriːʃən/ *n* **1** [C;U] (the production of) usu. liquid material by part of a plant or animal **2** [U] the act of hiding something

**se·cre·tive** /ˈsiːkrɨtɪv, sɪˈkriːtɪv/ *adj* fond of keeping secrets **–secretively** *adv* **–secretiveness** *n* [U]

**secret ser·vice** /ˌ·· ˈ··/ *n* [*the* S] a government department dealing with spying (SPY[1] (2))

**sect** /sekt/ *n* a group of people sometimes within a larger group, having a special set of (esp. religious) beliefs

**sec·tar·i·an** /sekˈteəriən/ *adj* resulting from division into SECTS: *sectarian differences|sectarian violence* **–sectarianism** *n* [U]

**sec·tion[1]** /ˈsekʃən/ *n* **1** [C] a separate part of a larger object, place, group, etc.: *the business section of a city|the brass section* (=those who play brass instruments) *of a band|a bookcase which comes apart into sections|signals controlling each section of railway track* **2** [C] a representation of something as if it were cut from top to bottom and looked at from the side –compare ELEVATION (3), PLAN[1] (2)

> **SPELLING NOTE**
> Words with the sound /s/, may be spelt **c-**, like **city**, or **ps-**, like **psychology.**

**section[2]** *v* [T] **1** to divide into SECTIONS **2** to cut or show a SECTION[1] (2) from **–sectional** *adj: sectional furniture|a sectional drawing*

**sec·tor** /ˈsektəʳ/ *n* **1** a part of an area of activity, esp. of business: *employment in the public and private sectors* (=those controlled by the government, and by private business)|*the banking sector* **2** an area of military operation: *the British sector in Berlin*

**sec·u·lar** /ˈsekjʊləʳ‖-kjə-/ *adj* not connected with a church; not religious: *secular music*

**se·cure[1]** /sɪˈkjʊəʳ/ *adj* **1** [*from, against*] safe; protected against danger or risk: *a secure job* (=not likely to be lost) **2** closed, firm, or tight enough for safety: *Make the windows secure before leaving the house.* **3** having no doubt or anxiety: CONFIDENT: *The child felt secure near its parents.*–opposite **insecure** (for 1,3) **–securely** *adv*

**secure[2]** *v* **-cured, -curing** [T] **1** [*for*] *fml* to get, esp. as the result of effort: *He's secured himself a good job.* **2** to fasten tightly: *They secured the windows as the storm began.* **3** [*from, against*] to make safe: *The soldiers secured the camp against attack.*

**se·cu·ri·ty** /sɪˈkjʊərɨti/ *n* [U] **1** (something that provides) the state of being or feeling SECURE: *the security of a happy home* **2** valuable property promised to a lender of money in case repayment is not made: *He used his house as security to borrow the money.* **3** protection against lawbreaking, violence, etc.: *For security reasons the visitors were searched.|Security was tight during the President's visit.*

**se·dan** /sɪˈdæn/ *n AmE* for SALOON (1)

**se·date[1]** /sɪˈdeɪt/ *adj* not easily troubled; calm; quiet: *a sedate old lady* **–sedately** *adv* **–sedateness** *n* [U]

**sedate[2]** *v* **-dated, -dating** [T] to make sleepy or calm, esp. with a SEDATIVE **–sedation** *n* [U]: *He's* **under sedation** *and resting quietly in bed.*

**sed·a·tive** /ˈsedətɪv/ *adj,n* (a drug) causing sleep: *The doctor gave him a sedative to help him sleep.*

**sed·en·ta·ry** /ˈsedəntəri‖-teri/ *adj fml* used to or performed while sitting: *sedentary jobs/workers*

**sed·i·ment** /ˈsedɨmənt/ *n* [S;U] solid material that settles to the bottom of a liquid: *(a) brown sediment in the bottom of the coffee cup*

**se·di·tion** /sɪˈdɪʃən/ *n* [U] *fml* speaking, writing, or action intended to make people disobey a government **–seditious** *adj*: *a seditious speech/speaker*

**se·duce** /sɪˈdjuːs/ *v* **-duced, -ducing** [T] **1** to persuade (usu. someone young and without sexual experience) to have sex with one **2** to cause or persuade (someone) to do something wrong by making it seem attractive; ENTICE: *The warm weather seduced me away from my studies.* **–seducer** *n* **–seduction** /sɪˈdʌkʃən/ *n* [C;U]

**se·duc·tive** /sɪˈdʌktɪv/ *adj* having qualities likely to SEDUCE; very desirable or attractive: *her seductive voice|a seductive offer of higher pay* **–seductively** *adv* **–seductiveness** *n* [U]

**see[1]** /siː/ *v* **saw** /sɔː/, **seen** /siːn/, **seeing 1** [I not *be +v-ing*] to use the eyes; have or use the power of sight: *It was so dark he could hardly see (to do his work).|He doesn't see very well in his right eye.* **2** [T +*(that);* not *be +v-ing*] to get sight of; notice, examine, or recognize by looking: *I looked for her but I couldn't see her in the crowd.|I saw the train come/coming into the station.|Can you see where I put my glasses?|He saw his dog killed by the car.*|(fig.) *You and I have seen* (=experienced) *some good times together.*|(fig.) *This old house has* **seen better days**. (=is in bad condition) **3** [I;T +*(that)*; not *be + v-ing*] to understand: *"Do you see what I mean?" "Yes; now I see."|I can't see why you don't like it.* **4** [I;T] to find out or decide: *Will you see if Adam wants his tea yet?|"Can I go and stay with my friends?" "We'll see."* (=we'll decide later) **5** [T +*(that)*; not *be +v-ing*] to make sure; take care: *See that you're ready at eight o'clock.* **6** [T +*v-ing*; not *be +v-ing*] to form a picture in the mind of; imagine: *I can't see her lending me any money.* (I'm suro she won't) **7** [T] to visit, call upon, or meet: *Come and see me tomorrow.|The doctor can't see you yet; he's seeing someone else at the moment.|We haven't* **seen much of** *you lately.* (=we haven't been together) **8** [T] to go with; ACCOMPANY (1): *I'll see you home.* **9 let me see** (used for expressing a pause for thought): *"Do you know this book?" "Let me see . . . Yes, now I do."* **10 see fit to** to decide to **11 see one's way to** to feel able to **12 see red** to be very angry **13 see stars** to see flashes of light, esp. as the result of being hit on the head **14 see the back/last of** *infml* to be finished with; have no further association with: *I'll be glad to see the back of him.* **15 see the light**: **a** to understand or accept an idea or the truth of something **b** to have a religious experience which changes one's belief **c** to be born or come to exist **16 see things** to think that one sees something that is not there: *I must be seeing things; I can't believe they've got another new car!* **17 So I see** What you say is already clear or easy to see: *"I'm afraid I'm a bit late." "So I see."*

USAGE Compare **see, look,** and **watch**: To see is to experience with the eyes; to **look** is to use the eyes on purpose and with attention; and to **watch** is to look at something in which there is movement: *The ball was going so fast that I didn't* **see it.|You can see** *John in the photograph among the crowd.|The children are watching television/ the football match.*

**see about** sthg. *v prep* [T +*v-ing*] to make arrangements for; take action about: *It's time for me to see about dinner/to see about cooking dinner.*

**see** sbdy./sthg. **off** *v adv* [T] **1** to go to the airport, station, etc., with (someone who is beginning a trip): *He saw his friend off at the bus station.* **2** to cause to go away; chase away: *He wouldn't leave, so our dog saw him off.*

**see** sbdy./sthg.↔**out** *v adv* [T] **1** to last until the end of: *Will our supplies see the winter out?* **2** to go to the door with (someone who is leaving): *I'll see you out.*

**see through**[1] sbdy./sthg. *v prep* [T] to recognize the truth about (an excuse, false statement, etc.)

**see** sbdy. **through**[2] (sthg.) *v adv;prep* [T] to provide for until the end of(a time or difficulty): *enough money to see him through (a year abroad)*

**see to** sbdy./sthg. *v prep* [T +*v-ing*] to attend to; take care of: *Will you see to the children?*

**see**[2] *n* the office of, or area governed by, a BISHOP –compare DIOCESE

**seed**[1] /siːd/ *n* **1** [C;U] the part of some plants that may grow into a new plant: *a bag of grass seed* **2** [C] something from which growth begins; GERM (2): *seeds of future trouble* **3** a SEEDed[2] (3) player in a competition **–seedless** *adj: a seedless orange*

**seed**[2] *v* **1** [I] (of a plant) to grow and produce seed **2** [T] to remove seeds from (fruit) **3** [T] to place (esp. a tennis player at the start of a competition) in order of likelihood to win: *a seeded player*

**seed·ling** /ˈsiːdlɪŋ/ *n* a young plant grown from a seed

**seed·y** /ˈsiːdi/ *adj* **-ier, -iest 1** having an untidy, worn-out appearance: *a rather seedy and unpleasant part of the town* **2** full of seeds: *a seedy orange* **3** slightly unwell **–seedily** *adv* **–seediness** *n* [U]

**see·ing** /siːɪŋ/ also **seeing that** /ˈ·· ·/, **seeing as** *infml– conj* as it is true that: *Seeing (that) she's old enough to get married, I don't think you can stop her.*

**seek** /siːk/ *v* **sought** /sɔːt/, **seeking 1** [I;T *after, for, out*] *fml* to make a search (for); try to find or get (something): *He sought out his friend in the crowd.|to seek (after) the truth|seek public office* **2** [T] *fml* to ask for; go to request: *You should seek advice from your lawyer.* **3** [T +*to-v*] *lit* to try; make an attempt: *They sought to punish him for his crime but he escaped.* **–seeker** *n*

**seem** /siːm/ *v* [not *be +v-ing*] **1** [+*to-v*] to give the idea or effect of being; appear: *She always seems (to be) sad.|There seems (to be) every hope that business will get better.* **2** [+*(that)*] to appear to be true: *It seems (as if) there will be an election soon.*

**seem·ing** /ˈsiːmɪŋ/ *adj* [A] that seems to be, but perhaps is not real: *a seeming piece of good luck which later led to all kinds of trouble*

**seem·ing·ly** /ˈsiːmɪŋli/ *adv* as far as one can tell; EVIDENTly: *Seemingly there is nothing we can do.*

**seem·ly** /ˈsiːmli/ *adj* **-lier, -liest** (esp. of behaviour) pleasing by being suitable to an occasion or to social standards –opposite **unseemly –seemliness** *n* [U]

**seen** /siːn/ *v past participle of* SEE[1]

**seep** /siːp/ *v* [I] (of a liquid) to flow slowly through small openings in a material; OOZE[2]: *Water had seeped into the house through the walls.* **–seepage** *n* [S;U]

**see·saw**[1] /ˈsiːsɔː/ *n* a board balanced in the middle for children to sit on at opposite ends so that when one end goes up the other goes down, used for fun

**seesaw**[2] *v* [I] to move up and down: *seesawing prices*

**seethe** /siːð/ *v* **seethed, seething** [I] **1** (of a liquid) to move about as if boiling **2** to be very excited or angry: *a country seething with political unrest*

**seg·ment**[1] /ˈsegmənt/ *n* any of the parts into which something may be divided; SECTION[1] (1): *a dish of orange segments*

**segment**[2] /segˈment/ *v* [I;T] to (cause to) divide into SEGMENTS[1] **–segmentation** /ˌsegmənˈteɪʃən/ *n* [S;U]

**seg·re·gate** /ˈsegrɪgeɪt/ *v* **-gated, -gating** [T] to separate from the rest of a social group: *Boys and girls are segregated in this school.* –compare INTEGRATE

**seg·re·ga·tion** /ˌsegrɪˈgeɪʃən/ *n* [U] the separation of esp. a social or racial group from others, e.g. by laws against using the same schools, hotels, buses, etc. –opposite **integration**; compare APARTHEID

**seis·mic** /ˈsaɪzmɪk/ *adj tech* of or caused by EARTHQUAKES

**seize** /siːz/ *v* **seized, seizing** [T] **1** to take hold of eagerly and forcefully; GRAB: *He seized my hand.|She seized (hold of) the child.|*(fig.) *She seized (on) the chance of a trip abroad.* **2** to take control of by official order or by force: *The weapons were seized by the police.|(fig.) She was seized by a desire to be a singer.*

**seize up** *v adv* [I] *BrE* (of part of a machine) to become stuck and stop working; JAM² (3)

**sei·zure** /ˈsiːʒəʳ/ *n* **1** [U] the act of seizing (SEIZE): *The courts ordered the seizure of all her property.* **2** [C] a sudden attack of an illness: *a heart seizure*

**sel·dom** /ˈseldəm/ *adv* not often; rarely: *He very seldom eats any breakfast.|He seldom, if ever, reads a book.* –see NEVER (USAGE)

**se·lect¹** /sɪ̈ˈlekt/ *v* [T] to choose: *He selected a shirt to match his suit.*

**select²** *adj* **1** [A] carefully chosen: *A select group of people were invited to the first performance.* **2** limited to certain members; EXCLUSIVE¹ (1): *a select club*

**se·lec·tion** /sɪ̈ˈlekʃən/ *n* **1** [C;U] the act of SELECTing, or a thing selected: *the selection of a football team* **2** [C] a collection, e.g. of goods for sale: *The shop has a fine selection of cheeses.*

**se·lec·tive** /sɪ̈ˈlektɪv/ *adj* **1** careful in choosing: *He is always very selective when he chooses his suits.* **2** concerning only certain articles; not general: *selective controls on goods brought into the country for sale* –**selectively** *adv* –**selectiveness** *n* [U]

**se·lec·tor** /sɪ̈ˈlektəʳ/ *n* a person or instrument that SELECTS, esp. a member of a committee choosing a sports team

**self** /self/ *n* **selves** /selvz/ **1** [C;U] a person with his/her own nature, character, abilities, etc.: *Knowledge of self increases as one gets older.* **2** [C] a typical part of one's mental or physical nature: *back to her old self after a long illness*

**self-ad·dressed** /ˌ· ·ˈ·◂/ *adj* addressed for return to the sender: *a self-addressed envelope*

**self-as·sur·ance** /ˌ· ·ˈ··/ *n* [U] sure belief in one's own abilities; SELF-CONFIDENCE –**self-assured** *adj*

**self-cen·tred** /ˌ· ˈ··◂/ *adj* interested only in oneself; selfish

**self-con·fessed** /ˌ· ·ˈ·◂/ *adj* [A] admitted by oneself to be the stated kind of person; AVOWED: *a self-confessed drug taker* –see also CONFESSED

**self-con·fi·dence** /ˌ· ˈ···/ *n* [U] belief in one's own power to do things successfully –**self-confident** *adj*

**self-con·scious** /ˌ· ˈ··◂/ *adj* nervous and uncomfortable about oneself as seen by others –**self-consciously** *adv* –**self-consciousness** *n* [U]

**self-con·tained** /ˌ· ·ˈ·◂/ *adj* complete in itself; having no part shared with anything else: *a self-contained flat*

**SPELLING NOTE**

Words with the sound /s/, may be spelt **c-**, like **city**, or **ps-**, like **psychology**.

**self-con·trol** /ˌ· ·ˈ·/ *n* [U] control over one's feelings: *She never loses her self-control, even when things keep going badly.* –**self-controlled** *n*

**self-de·feat·ing** /ˌ· ·ˈ··◂/ *adj* having the effect of preventing its own success: *a self-defeating plan*

**self-de·fence** /ˌ· ·ˈ·/ *n* [U] the act or skill of defending oneself: *He shot the man* **in self-defence**. (=only to protect himself)

**self-de·ni·al** /ˌ· ·ˈ··/ *n* [U] the habit of not allowing oneself pleasures

**self-de·ter·min·a·tion** /ˌ· ···ˈ··/ *n* [U] the right of the people of a place to make a free decision about the form of their government, esp. whether or not to be independent of another country

**self-dis·ci·pline** /ˌ· ˈ···/ *n* [U] the training of oneself to control one's emotions and desires

**self-ef·fac·ing** /ˌ· ·ˈ··◂/ *adj* keeping oneself from attracting attention; modest

**self-em·ployed** /ˌ· ·ˈ·◂/ *adj* earning money from one's own business and not as pay from an employer

**self-ev·i·dent** /ˌ· ˈ···◂/ *adj* plainly true without need of proof: *Her intelligence is self-evident.*

**self-ex·plan·a·to·ry** /ˌ· ·ˈ····/ *adj* (esp. of speaking or writing) explaining itself; needing no further explanation

**self-gov·ern·ment** /ˌ· ˈ···/ *n* [U] government without outside control; independence

**self-im·port·ance** /ˌ· ·ˈ··/ *n* [U] too high an opinion of one's own importance –**self-important** *adj*: *a self-important little man who tells others what to do*

**self-im·posed** /ˌ· ·ˈ·◂/ *adj* (of a duty, etc.) that one has forced oneself to accept: *a self-imposed limit of three cigarettes a day*

**self-in·dul·gence** /ˌ· ·ˈ··/ *n* [U] the too easy allowance of pleasure or comfort to oneself –**self-indulgent** *adj*

**self-in·terest** /ˌ· ˈ··/ *n* [U] concern for what is best for oneself: *I don't really like my rich uncle, but I'm always friendly to him out of self-interest.*

**self·ish** /ˈselfɪʃ/ *adj* concerned only with one's own advantage without care for others: *a selfish boy|to act for purely selfish reasons* –opposite **unselfish** –**selfishly** *adv* –**selfishness** *n* [U]

**self·less** /ˈselflɪ̈s/ *adj* completely unselfish –**selflessly** *adv* –**selflessness** *n* [U]

**self-made** /ˌ· ˈ·◂/ *adj* raised to success and wealth by one's own efforts alone: *a self-made man*

**self-pit·y** /ˌ· ˈ··/ *n* [U] too great pity for one's own sorrows or troubles

**self-pos·sessed** *adj* having firm control over one's own feelings and actions, esp. in difficult or unexpected conditions; calm –**self-possession** *n* [U]

**self-pres·er·va·tion** /ˌ· ··ˈ··/ *n* [U] the natural tendency to keep oneself from death or harm

**self-re·li·ant** /ˌ· ·ˈ··/ *adj* able to act without depending on the help of others –**self-reliance** *n* [U]

**self-re·spect** /ˌ· ·ˈ·/ *n* [U] proper pride in oneself; the feeling that one need not be ashamed of oneself

**self-right·eous** /ˌ· ˈ··/ *adj* too proud of one's own rightness or goodness –**self-righteously** *adv* –**self-righteousness** *n* [U]

**self-sac·ri·fice** /ˌ· ˈ···/ *n* [U] the giving up of one's pleasure or interests in favour of others or of a worthier purpose –**self-sacrificing** *adj*

**self-sat·is·fied** /ˌ· ˈ···/ *adj* too pleased with oneself; SMUG; COMPLACENT –**self-satisfaction** *n* [U]

**self-seek·ing** /ˌ· ˈ··◂/ *n,adj* [U] (action) that works only for one's own advantage: *a self-seeking politician*

**self-serv·ice** /ˌ· ˈ··◂/ *adj,n* [U] (working by) the system in which buyers collect what they want and then pay at a special desk: *a self-service petrol station/restaurant*

**self-styled** /ˌ· ˈ·◂/ *adj* [A] *usu. derog* given the stated title by oneself, usu. without any right to it: *a self-styled "doctor" who has no qualifications*

**self-suf·fi·cient** /ˌ· ·ˈ··◂/ *adj* [*in*] able to provide for one's needs without outside help: *Britain is now self-sufficient in oil.* –**self-sufficiency** *n* [U]

**sell** /sel/ *v* **sold** /səʊld/, **selling 1** [I;T *to*] to give (property or goods) in exchange for money: *I sold my car to my friend for £500.|I sold my friend my car for £500.|I went to the market to buy, not to sell. Do you sell cigarettes in this shop?* –compare BUY[1] **2** [I *at, for*] to be bought; get buyers; gain a sale: *This newspaper is selling for/at 20p.|The tickets cost too much and sold badly/wouldn't sell.* **3** [T] to help or cause to be bought: *Bad news sells newspapers.* **4** [T *on, to*] *infml* to persuade (someone) to accept a product, idea, etc.: *I'm completely sold on this new machine; it saves so much time!|What a stupid excuse! You'll never sell that to anyone!* **5 sell oneself: a** to make oneself or one's ideas seem attractive to others **b** to give up one's principles for money or other gain

**sell** sthg.↔**off** *v adv* [T] to get rid of (goods) by selling, usu. cheaply: *They're selling off their furniture because they're moving to Australia.*

**sell** (sbdy./sthg.)↔**out** *v adv* [I;T] **1** [*of*] to sell all of (what was for sale): *The concert is sold out.|We've sold out of milk.* **2** to be disloyal to (one's principles or friends), esp. for money: *He sold out (his artistic standards) and now writes for money.* –see also SELL-OUT

**sell** (sthg.) **up** *v adv* [I;T] to sell (something, esp. a business) completely: *They sold up and went to live in Cornwall.*

**sell·er** /ˈselə^r/ *n* **1** a person who sells–compare BUYER **2** a product with the stated amount of sales: *Her new book is already a best-seller.* (=very many copies have been sold)

**sel·lo·tape** /ˈseləteɪp, ˈseləʊ-/ **scotch tape** *AmE tdmk– n* [U] *tdmk* (*often cap.*) sticky thin clear material sold in rolls, for sticking paper, etc.

**sell-out** /ˈ· ·/ *n* **1** a performance, sports match, etc., for which all tickets are sold **2** an act of disloyalty to one's principles or friends; BETRAYAL –see also SELL **out** (2)

**selves** /selvz/ *n pl. of* SELF

**se·man·tics** /sɪˈmæntɪks/ *n* [U] the study of the meanings of words –**semantic** *adj*

**sem·a·phore** /ˈseməfɔː^r‖-for/ *n* [U] a system of sending messages, using two flags held one in each hand

**sem·blance** /ˈsembləns/ *n* [S] an appearance; outward form: *a semblance of peace*

**se·men** /ˈsiːmən/ *n* [U] the liquid produced by the male sex organs, carrying SPERM

**se·mes·ter** /sɨˈmestə^r/ *n* either of the two periods into which a year at universities, usu. in the US, is divided –compare TERM

**sem·i·cir·cle** /ˈsemɪˌsɜːkəl‖-ɜr-/ *n* half a circle –**semicircular** /-ˈsɜːkjʊlə^r‖-ˈsɜrkjələr/ *adj*

**sem·i·co·lon** /ˌsemɪˈkəʊlən‖ˈsemɪˌkəʊlən/ *n* the mark (;) used to separate different parts of a list and independent parts of a sentence

**sem·i·de·tached** /ˌsemɪdɪˈtætʃt/ *adj,n* (being) one of a pair of joined houses –see picture on page 297

**sem·i·fi·nal** /ˌsemɪˈfaɪnl◂‖ˈsemɪˌfaɪnl/ *n* (in sport) one of a pair or set of matches whose winners then compete against one another to decide the winner of the whole competition

**sem·i·nar** /ˈsemɨnɑː^r/ *n* a small class of usu. advanced students studying with a teacher

**sem·i·na·ry** /ˈsemɨnəri‖-neri/ *n* **-ries** a college for training priests

**sem·i·pre·cious** /ˌsemɪˈpreʃəs◂/ *adj* (of a jewel, stone, etc.) of lower value than a PRECIOUS STONE

**Se·mit·ic** /sɨˈmɪtɪk/ *adj* **1** of the Jews, Arabs, and various other peoples in ancient times –compare ANTI-SEMITISM **2** Jewish

**sem·o·li·na** /ˌseməˈliːnə/ *n* [U] hard grains of crushed wheat used in making certain food: *semolina* PUDDING (2)

**sen·ate** /ˈsenɨt/ *n* [C +*sing./pl. v*] (*usu. cap.*) **1** the smaller (UPPER) of the two law-making groups (HOUSES[1] (2)) in some countries such as the US: *The Senate has/have voted to support the President's defence plans.* –compare CONGRESS **2** the governing council at some universities

**sen·a·tor** /ˈsenətə^r/ *n* [A;C] (*often cap.*) a member of a SENATE (1)

**send** /send/ *v* **sent,** /sent/ **sending 1** [T *to*] to cause or order (a person or thing) to go somewhere without going there oneself: *If you need money I'll send it to you/I'll send you some.|He was sent (by his mother) to buy some milk.* –see Study Notes on page 429 **2** [I *for*] to cause a message, request, or order to go out: *Send for a doctor!* **3** [T] to cause to be in a particular state: *The news sent the family into great excitement.* **4** [T] to cause to move quickly and uncontrollably: *The explosion sent glass flying everywhere.* **5** [I;T] (of a radio or the person using it) to TRANSMIT: *The ship's radio sent out signals for help.*

**send away/off** *v adv* **1** [T] (**send** sbdy.↔**away**) to send to another place: *He sent his son away/off to school in Germany.* **2** [I *for*] to order goods to be sent by post: *I sent away for some rare books.*

**send** sbdy./sthg.↔**down** *v adv* [T] **1** to cause to go down: *Bad news sent market prices down.* **2** *BrE* to dismiss (a student) from university for bad behaviour

**send off** *v adv* **1** [T] (**send** sthg.↔**off**) to post (a letter, parcel, etc.) **2** [T] (**send** sbdy.↔**off**) *BrE* (in sport) to cause (a player) to leave the field because of a serious breaking of the rules or bad behaviour **3** [I;T] (=**send** sbdy.↔**off**) *for*] →SEND **away** –see also SEND-OFF

**send** sthg.↔**out** *v adv* [T] to send from a central point: *to send out invitations/orders*

**send** sbdy./sthg. **up** *v adv* [T] **1** to cause to go up: *a fire sending up smoke into the air* **2** *BrE* to copy the funny or silly qualities, actions, etc. of (a person, etc.); make fun of

**send-off** /ˈ· ·/ *n* a usu. planned show of good wishes at the start of a trip, new business, etc.: *We were given a great send-off at the airport.* –see also SEND **off**

**se·nile** /ˈsiːnaɪl/ *adj* weak in body or in mind because of old age **–senility** /s½ˈnɪl½ti/ *n* [U]

**se·ni·or¹** /ˈsiːnɪəʳ/ *n* a person who is older or higher in rank than another

**senior²** *adj* **1** [F *to; no comp.*] older or of higher rank: *He is senior to me.* **2** of high rank: *a meeting of the most senior army officers* –compare JUNIOR

**Senior** *n* [after *n*] *esp. AmE* the older: *John Smith Senior* –compare JUNIOR; see MAJOR (USAGE)

**senior cit·i·zen** /ˌ··· ˈ···/ *n* an old person, esp. one over the age of 60 or 65 –compare PENSIONER

**se·ni·or·i·ty** /ˌsiːniˈɒr½ti‖ˈɔ-, -ˈɑ-/ *n* [U] the quality of being SENIOR² (1) in rank or age

**sen·sa·tion** /senˈseɪʃən/ *n* **1** [C;U] (a) direct feeling coming from the senses: *He could feel no sensation in his arm.* **2** [C] a general feeling in the mind or body: *The train had stopped, but I had the sensation that it was still moving.* **3** [C] (a cause of) a state of excited interest: *The discovery was/caused a great sensation.*

**sen·sa·tion·al** /senˈseɪʃənəl/ *adj* **1** causing or intended to cause excited interest: *a sensational murder* **2** *infml* wonderful; very good or exciting: *You won? That's sensational!* **–sensationally** *adv*

**sen·sa·tion·al·is·m** /senˈseɪʃənəlɪzəm/ *n* [U] *usu. derog* the intentional producing of excitement or shock, e.g. by books, magazines, etc., of low quality

**sense¹** /sens/ *n* **1** [S;U] (a) power to understand and make judgments about something: *a sense of values/direction|a successful man with good business sense* –see SENSIBLE (USAGE) **2** [S] a feeling, esp. one that is hard to describe exactly: *a sense of fear|a sense that someone was standing behind him* **3** [U] good and esp. practical understanding and judgment: *Haven't you got enough sense to come in out of the rain?* –see also COMMON SENSE; see SENSIBLE (USAGE) **4** [C *of*] any of the five SENSES (1): *to lose one's sense of smell/taste* **5** [C] a meaning: *"man" in its broadest sense, meaning both men and women* **6 in a sense** in one way of speaking; partly: *You are right in a sense, but you don't know all the facts.* **7 make sense**: **a** to have a clear meaning: *No matter how you read it, this sentence doesn't make (any) sense.|I can't* **make sense of** (=understand) *it.* **b** to be a wise course of action: *It makes sense to take care of your health.* **8 talk sense** *infml* to speak reasonably **9 there's no sense in** *infml* there's no good reason for: *There's no sense in going by boat when the plane is just as cheap and much quicker.*

**sense²** *v* **sensed, sensing** [T *that*] to have a feeling, without being told directly, of: *The horse sensed danger and stopped.*

**sense·less** /ˈsensl½s/ *adj* **1** in a sleeplike state, as after a blow on the head; unconscious –compare INSENSIBLE **2** foolish; purposeless: *senseless violence* **–senselessly** *adv* **–senselessness** *n* [U]

**SPELLING NOTE**

Words with the sound /s/, may be spelt **c-**, like **city**, or **ps-**, like **psychology.**

**sens·es** /ˈsens½z/ *n* [P] **1** the five natural powers of sight, hearing, feeling, tasting, and smelling, which give a person or animal feelings and information about the outside world **2** one's powers of (reasonable) thinking: *Are you mad? Have you* **taken leave of your senses?**

**sen·si·bil·i·ty** /ˌsensəˈbɪl½ti/ *n* **-ties** [C;U] *fml* (a) tender or delicate feeling: *She plays the piano with great sensibility.* –see SENSIBLE (USAGE)

**sen·si·ble** /ˈsensəbəl/ *adj* **1** reasonable; having or showing good sense: *a sensible child/plan/idea* **2** *fml* noticeable; that can be sensed **–sensibly** *adv*

USAGE **Sensible**, in its usual meaning of "reasonable and practical", concerns your ability to understand and make judgements (your **sense¹** (3)). But **sensibility**, which is not related to this meaning of **sensible**, concerns your ability to experience delicate feelings, and it is closer to **sensitive**: a **sensitive** person has great **sensibility** and is quick to enjoy or suffer.

**sen·si·tive** /ˈsens½tɪv/ *adj* **1** [*to*] quick to show or feel the effect of something: *sensitive to cold/pain|light-sensitive photographic paper* **2** showing delicate feelings or judgment: *a sensitive performance/actor* –opposite **insensitive** **3** *sometimes derog* easily offended **4** dealing with secret government work: *sensitive official papers* **–sensitively** *adv* –see SENSIBLE (USAGE) **–sensitivity** /- ˈtɪv½ti/ also **sensitiveness** *n* [U]

**sen·so·ry** /ˈsensəri/ *adj* of, the bodily senses: *sensory* PERCEPTION

**sen·su·al** /ˈsenʃuəl/ *adj* **1** *sometimes derog* interested in giving pleasure to one's own body, e.g. by sex, food, and drink –compare SENSUOUS **2** of, or seen, felt, etc. by the senses: *sensual experiences*

**sen·su·ous** /ˈsenʃuəs/ *adj* of, or causing pleasant feelings of the senses: *sensuous music* –compare SENSUAL **–sensuously** *adv* **–sensuousness** *n* [U]

**sent** /sent/ *v past tense and participle of* SEND

**sen·tence¹** /ˈsentəns/ *n* **1** (in grammar) a group of words that forms a statement, command, EXCLAMATION, or question, usu. contains a subject and a verb, and (in writing) begins with a capital letter and ends with one of the marks . ! ? The following are all sentences: *"Sing the song again." "How well he sings!" "Who sang at the concert last night?"* –compare CLAUSE, PHRASE **2** a punishment for a criminal found guilty in court: *The sentence was ten years (in prison).|the death sentence|The judge* **gave/passed/pronounced sentence on** *him.*

**sentence²** *v* **-tenced, -tencing** [T *to*] (of a judge or court) to give a punishment to: *He was sentenced to three years in prison.*

**sen·ti·ment** /ˈsent½mənt/ *n* [C;U] **1** (a) tender or fine feeling of pity, love, sadness, etc.: *There's no place for sentiment in business!* **2** (a) thought or judgment arising from feeling: *strong public sentiment on the question of unemployment*

**sen·ti·ment·al** /ˌsent½ˈmentl/ *adj* **1** having or coming from tender feelings rather than reasonable or practical ones: *We keep the old clock for sentimental reasons; it was a present from my father.* **2** showing too much of such feelings, esp. of a weak or silly kind: *sentimental love stories* **–sentimentally** *adv* **–sentimentality** /men'tæl½ti/ *n* [U] *often derog*

**sen·ti·nel** /'sentɪnəl/ *n lit & old use* a guard; SENTRY

**sen·try** /'sentri/ *n* **-tries** a soldier standing as a guard

**sep·a·ra·ble** /'sepərəbəl/ *adj* that can be separated –opposite **inseparable**

**sep·a·rate¹** /'sepəreɪt/ *v* **-rated, -rating 1** [I;T *from, into*] to set or move apart: *Separate the two pipes by unscrewing them.*|*The teacher separated the children into two groups/separated the boys from the girls.* **2** [T] to keep apart; mark a division between: *two towns separated by a river* **3** [I;T *up, into*] to break or divide up into parts **4** [I] (of a husband and wife) to live apart, esp. by a formal agreement

**sep·a·rate²** /'sepər½t/ *adj* **1** not the same; different: *This word has three separate meanings.* **2** [A] not shared with another; INDIVIDUAL: *We have separate rooms.* **3** [F *from*] apart: *Keep the boys separate from the girls.* **–separateness** *n* [U] **–separately** *adv*

**sep·a·ra·tion** /ˌsepə'reɪʃən/ *n* **1** [C;U] (a) breaking or coming apart **2** [C;U *from*] (a time of) being or living apart: *He was unhappy because of his separation from his mother.* **3** [C] *law* a formal agreement by a husband and wife to live apart –compare DIVORCE

**sep·a·rat·ist** /'sepərətɪst/ *n* a member of a group that wants to become separate from a larger political or religious body

**se·pi·a** /'si:pɪə/ *n* [U] (the colour of) a brown paint or ink: *an old sepia photograph*

**Sep·tem·ber** /sep'tembəʳ/ also **Sept.** *written abbrev– n* the 9th month of the year

**sep·tic** /'septɪk/ *adj* infected by disease bacteria

**sep·ul·chre** *BrE*‖ **-cher** *AmE* /'sepəlkəʳ/ *n old use & bibl* a burial place; TOMB **–sepulchral** /s½'pʌlkrəl/ *adj*

**se·quel** /'si:kwəl/ *n* **1** [*to*] something that follows something else, esp. as a result **2** a story, film, etc., which continues the action of an earlier one

**se·quence** /'si:kwəns/ *n* **1** [C] a group of things arranged in an order, esp. following one another in time: *a sequence of historical plays by Shakespeare* **2** [U] the order in which things or events follow one another; SUCCESSION: *Please keep the cards in sequence; don't mix them up.*|*The* **sequence of events** *on the night of the murder still isn't known.*

**se·quin** /'si:kw½n/ *n* a very small round shiny piece of metal or plastic sewn onto a piece of clothing for decoration

**ser·e·nade¹** /ˌser½'neɪd/ *n* a song or other music sung or played in the open air at night, esp. to a woman by a lover

**serenade²** *v* **-naded, -nading** [T] to sing or play a SERENADE¹ to

**se·rene** /s½'ri:n/ *adj* completely calm and peaceful: *a serene summer night*|*a serene trust in God* **–serenely** *adv* **–serenity** /s½'renəti / *n* [U]

**serf** /sɜ:f‖sɜrf/ *n* a person, not quite a slave, forced to stay and work on his/her master's land, esp. in a FEUDAL system

**serf·dom** /'sɜ:fdəm‖'sɜr-/ *n* [U] the state or fact of being a SERF

**serge** /sɜ:dʒ‖sɜrdʒ/ *n* [U] a type of strong cloth used esp. for suits, coats, and dresses

**ser·geant** /'sɑ:dʒənt‖'sɑr-/ *n* [A;C] **1** a NONCOMMISSIONED OFFICER of upper rank in the army or airforce **2** a police officer with next to the lowest rank

**sergeant ma·jor** /ˌ·· '·· ◂/ *n* [A;C] an officer of low rank in an army

**se·ri·al¹** /'sɪərɪəl/ *adj* of, happening or arranged in a SERIES or row of things in order: *the serial number of a bank note* **-serially** *adv*

**serial²** *n* a written or broadcast story appearing in parts at fixed times: *a radio serial*

**se·ri·al·ize** ‖also **-ise** *BrE* /'sɪərɪəlaɪz/ *v* **-ized, -izing** [T] to print or broadcast (a book already written) as a SERIAL² **–serialization** /- laɪ'zeɪʃən‖-lə-/ *n* [C;U]

**se·ries** /'sɪəri:z/ *n* **series** a group of things of the same kind, coming one after another in order: *a television series* (=a series of shows on television) *about modern art*|*After a series of unsuccessful attempts, he has at last passed his driving test.*|*The British team will be playing a series of matches in Australia this winter.*

**se·ri·ous** /'sɪərɪəs/ *adj* **1** solemn; not joking or cheerful; GRAVE²: *a serious expression on her face*|*Do you think he is serious about leaving his wife?* (=does he really intend to do it?) **2** not slight: *serious damage*|*serious crime* **3** of an important kind; needing great skill or thought: *a serious artist/piece of art* **–seriousness** *n* [U]

**se·ri·ous·ly** /'sɪərɪəsli/ *adv* **1** in a serious way: *to study music seriously*|*seriously wounded* **2 take (someone/something) seriously** to treat (someone or something) as important or true and deserving thought and attention, or belief

**ser·mon** /'sɜ:mən‖'sɜr-/ *n* **1** a talk given (PREACHED) as part of a church service **2** *infml* a (too) long and solemn warning or piece of advice

**ser·pent** /'sɜ:pənt‖'sɜr-/ *n lit* a snake

**ser·rat·ed** /s½'reɪt½d, se-/*adj* having a row of connected V-shapes like teeth (as on a saw): *a serrated edge*|*a serrated knife*

**se·rum** /'sɪərəm/ *n* **-rums** *or* **-ra** /rə/ [C;U] (a) liquid containing disease-fighting substances and prepared for putting into a person's or animal's blood –compare VACCINE

**ser·vant** /'sɜ:vənt‖'sɜr-/ *n* **1** a person who is paid to work for another in the other's house: *They have two servants: a cook and a gardener.* **2** [*of*] *fml* a person used for the service or purposes of another: *A politician should be a servant of the people.* –see also CIVIL SERVANT

**serve¹** /sɜ:v‖sɜrv/ *v* **served, serving 1** [I;T *as, in, on, under*] to work or do a useful job (for): *He served in the army/on the committee.*|*They served under the king.* **2** [T *with*] to provide with something necessary or useful: *A pipe serves all the houses with water.* **3** [I;T *as, for*] to be suitable for (a purpose): *One room had to serve as/for both bedroom and living room.*|*I haven't got a hammer, but this stone should serve (my purpose).* **4** [I;T *with*] to offer (food) for eating: *Please serve the coffee now.*|*What time is breakfast served in this hotel?* **5** [T] (of a person in a shop) to attend to (a customer): *Are you being served?* (=Is someone else attending to you?) **6** [T] to spend (a period of time) in prison: *He served ten years/a long sentence for his crime.*|*He* **served time** (=was in prison) *for murder.* **7** [I;T] (in tennis,

VOLLEYBALL, etc.) to begin play by striking (the ball) to the opponent **8** [T] *law* to deliver (an official order to appear in court) to (someone): *serve a* SUMMONS *on him/him (with) a summons* **9 serve someone right** *infml* to be a suitable punishment for someone: *After all you've eaten it'll serve you right if you feel ill.*

**serve**[2] *n* →SERVICE[1] (7)

**serv·er** /'sɜːvəʳ‖'sɜr-/ *n* something used in serving food, esp. a specially shaped tool for putting a particular kind of food onto a plate

**ser·vice**[1] /'sɜːv̍əs‖'sɜr-/ *n* **1** [U] attention to buyers in a shop or to guests in a hotel, restaurant, etc.: *The service in this place is slow/bad. We waited ten minutes for service.* **2** [C *usu. pl.*] *fml* an act or job done for someone: *You may need the services of a lawyer.* **3** [U] work or duty done for someone: *He died* **in the service** *of his country.* **4** a regular examination of a machine to keep it in good condition *Take your car for a service/for regular services.* **5** [C;U] a business or organization doing useful work or supplying a need: *Is there any railway service here on Sundays?|a postal service* **6** [C] a fixed form of public worship; a religious ceremony: *Our church has three services each Sunday.* **7** [C] *esp. BrE* a government department: *the* CIVIL SERVICE **8** [C;U] (duty in) any of the armed forces: *He saw active service in in the last war.* **9** [C] an act or manner of serving (SERVE[1] (7)) in tennis: *He has a good fast service.* **10** [C] the dishes, tools, etc., needed to serve a stated meal: *a silver tea service* **11** [A;U] (something for the use of) people working in a place, esp. servants in a house: *a service entrance|She was* **in service** (=worked as a servant) *all her life.* **12 at your service** *polite or pomp* willing to do what you command: *If you need any help, I am at your service.* **13 of service** useful; helpful: *(polite) Can I be of service to you?* –compare DISSERVICE

**service**[2] *v* **-viced, -vicing** [T] to repair or put in good condition: *to service the car*

**ser·vi·cea·ble** /'sɜːv̍əsəbəl‖'sɜr-/ *adj* that can be used; fit for (long or hard) use: *serviceable shoes*

**ser·vice·man** /'sɜːv̍əsmən‖'sɜr-/ *n* **-men** /mən, men/ a male member of the army, navy, etc.

**service sta·tion** /'·· ˌ··/ *n esp. AmE* a place (GARAGE) that repairs motor vehicles and may also sell petrol –compare FILLING STATION

**ser·vi·ette** /ˌsɜːvi'et‖ˌsɜr-/ *n BrE* a table NAPKIN (1)

**ser·vile** /'sɜːvaɪl‖'sɜrvəl, -vaɪl/ *adj derog* behaving like a slave; allowing complete control by another: *servile obedience* **–servility** /sə'vɪl̍əti/ *n* [U]

**ser·vi·tude** /'sɜːv̍ətjuːd‖'sɜrv̍ətuːd/ *n* [U *to*] *lit* the condition of a slave or of one who is forced to obey another: *a life of servitude to the enemy conquerors*

**ses·sion** /'seʃən/ *n* **1** a formal meeting of an organization, esp. a law-making body or court: *The next session of Parliament will begin in November.|This court is now* **in session.** **2** *esp. AmE* one of the parts of the year when teaching is given at a university **3** a meeting or period of time used esp. by a group for a particular purpose: *a dancing session*

**SPELLING NOTE**

Words with the sound /s/, may be spelt **c-**, like **city**, or **ps-**, like **psychology.**

**set**[1] /set/ *v* **set, setting 1** [T] to put so as to stay in a place: *Set your heavy load down here.*|(fig.) *His great ability sets him apart* (=makes him clearly different) *from the others.* **2** [T] to put into order for use: *Set the table for dinner.* (=put the plates, glasses, etc., on it) **3** [T] to fix or establish (a rule, time, standard, number, etc.): *The price has been set at £1000.|He set a land speed record.* **4** [T] to fix firmly (a part of the body, esp. to show one's feelings): *The child has* **set his heart** *on it.* (=wants it very much)|*I've* **set my mind** *on it.* (=firmly decided on it) **5** [I] (esp. of the sun) to pass downwards out of sight: *In the winter the sun sets early.* –opposite **rise 6** [T] to cause to be: *I opened the cage and set the bird free.* **7** [T] to cause to start: *Your remarks have set me thinking.* **8** [T] to give (a piece of work) for (someone) to do: *Who set the examination?|He set the class (some exercises).* **9** [T *usu. pass.*] to give a particular SETTING (3) to: *The book is set in 17th-century Spain.* **10** [T] to write music for (words): *Has the poem ever been set (to music)?* **11** [T *in/with*] to fix (a precious stone) into (a piece of jewellery): *set a diamond in a ring|a ring set with three diamonds* **12** [I;T] **a** to put (a broken bone or limb) into a fixed position so that it will mend **b** (of a broken bone or limb) to become joined in a fixed position **13** [I] (of a liquid, paste, jelly, etc.) to become solid **14** [T] to arrange (hair) when wet to give the desired style when dry **15 set foot in/on** to enter; visit: *Nobody has ever set foot on that island.* **16 set light/fire/a match to** to cause (something) to burn in the stated way **17 set someone's teeth on edge** to give someone the unpleasant sensation caused by certain acid tastes or high sounds **18 set store by** to feel to be of the stated amount of importance: *I set great store by your support.* **19 set the pace** to fix the speed for others to follow **20 set to rights** to make just, healthy, correct, etc.: *This medicine will set you to rights.* **21 set to work** to start working

**set about** sthg. *v prep* [T+*v-ing*] to begin to do; start: *She set about complaining as soon as she arrived.*

**set** sbdy./sthg. **against** sbdy/sthg. *v prep* [T] **1** to balance (one thing) against (something opposite); subtract from: *Some business losses can be set against taxes.* **2** to cause to oppose: *a war which set family against family*

**set** sthg.↔**aside** *v adv* [T] **1** also **set by**– to save for a special purpose: *She set aside a little money each week.* **2** to pay no attention to: *Setting aside what I think, what would you like to do?*

**set back** *v adv* [T] **1** (**set** sthg.↔**back**) to place at a distance behind something: *a house set 15 metres back from the road* **2** (**set** sthg.↔**back**) to make late: *The bad weather will set back our building plans (by three weeks).* **3** (**set** sbdy. **back** sthg.) *infml* to cost (someone) (a large amount of money): *That new car set me back quite a lot.* –see also SETBACK

**set** sbdy./sthg.↔**down** *v adv* [T] **1** to write; make a record of: *I have set down everything that happened, as I remember it.* **2** *BrE* (of a vehicle or its driver) to stop and let (a passenger) get out: *The bus sets the children down just outside the school.*

**set in** *v adv* [I] (of a disease, unfavourable weather, etc.) to begin and (probably) continue: *Winter sets in* early in the north.

**set off** *v adv* **1** [I] also **set out**– to begin a journey: *She set off on a trip across Europe.* **2** [T] (**set** sthg.↔**off**) to cause to explode: *The bomb could be set off at any time.* **3** [T] (**set off** sthg.) to cause (sudden activity): *The discovery of gold in California set off a rush to get there.* **4** [T] (**set** sthg.↔**off**) to make (one thing) look better by putting it near something different: *a white belt to set off her blue dress*

**set on** *v prep* [T] **1** (**set on** sbdy.) also **set upon**– (esp. of a group) to attack: *He was set on by robbers.* **2** (**set** sbdy/sthg. **on** sbdy.) to cause to attack or chase: *If you come to my house again, I'll set the dog on you!*

**set out** *v adv* **1** [I *from, for*] → SET **off** (1) **2** [I +*to-v*] to begin a course of action: *He set out to paint the whole house but finished only the front.* **3** [T] (**set** sthg.↔**out**) also **set forth** *fml or pomp*– to explain in order, esp. in writing: *The reasons for my decision are set out in my report.* **4** [T] (**set** sthg.↔**out**) to arrange or spread out in order: *The meal was set out on a long table.*

**set** sthg.↔**up** *v adv* [T] **1** to raise into position: *Roadblocks were set up by the police to catch the escaped prisoner.* **2** to establish (an organization, business, etc.): *The council set up a committee to enquire into local unemployment.*

**set** (sbdy.) **up as** sthg. *v adv prep* [T] to establish (oneself or someone else) in business as: *He set (himself) up as a house painter and soon became successful.* –see also **set up** SHOP[1]

**set**[2] *adj* **1** fixed; arranged: *I have to study at set hours each day.*|*a set book* (=that must be studied for an examination) **2** (of part of the body, manner, state of mind, etc.) fixed in position; unmoving: *set opinions* **3** [F *on,upon*] determined; of a fixed intention: *I can't stop you if you're set on going.* **4** [F +*to-v*/*for*] ready; prepared: *I was (all) set to leave the house when the telephone rang.*

**set**[3] *n* **1** [C] a group of naturally connected things that belong together: *a set of gardening tools*|*a 21-piece tea set* (=cups, plates, teapot, etc.) **2** [C] an apparatus for receiving television or radio signals: *a television set*|*Is your set* (=television) *working?* **3** [C] scenery for a play, film, etc.: *a stage set*|*Everyone must be on the set* (=the place where the film is made) *by eight o'clock.* **4** [C] a group of games in a tennis match **5** [*the* S] a position of part of the body: *the set of her shoulders*

**set·back** /ˈsetbæk/ *n* a return to a less good position: *She seemed better after her illness but then she had a sudden setback.* –see also SET **back**

**set·square** /ˈsetskweəʳ/ *BrE*‖ **triangle** *AmE*– *n* a flat three-sided plate used for drawing straight lines and angles exactly

**set·tee** /seˈtiː/ *n* a long seat for more than one person, with a back and usu. arms; SOFA –see picture on page 355

**set·ter** /ˈsetəʳ/ *n* **1** a long-haired dog often trained to point out the positions of animals for shooting **2** a person or thing that sets: *a trendsetter*|*a typesetter*

**set·ting** /ˈsetɪŋ/ *n* **1** [U] the action of a person or thing that sets: *the setting of the sun* **2** [C] the way or position in which something, esp. an instrument, is set: *This machine has two settings, fast and slow.* **3** [C] a set of surroundings; background: *a beautiful setting for a holiday*|*Our story has its setting in ancient Rome.*|*a diamond in a gold setting*

**set·tle** /ˈsetl/ **-tled, -tling 1** [I;T] to go and live (in): *They got married and settled in Manchester.* **2** [I;T] to (place so as to) stay and be comfortable: *He settled himself in his chair.* **3** [I;T] to (cause to) go downwards: *A bird settled* (=came down and landed) *on the branch.*|*Shake the bag to settle the sugar in it.* **4** [I;T] to make or become quiet, calm, still, etc.: *This medicine should settle your nerves.*|*Settle down, children; stop running about!* **5** [I;T +*that*/*on,upon*] to make the last arrangements (about); decide: *That's settled; we'll do it tomorrow!*|*We've settled on Wales* (=decided to go there) *for our holiday, but we haven't settled when to go.* **6** [I;T] to end (an argument, esp. in law); bring (a matter) to an agreement: *They settled their quarrel in a friendly way.*|*The two companies* **settled out of court**. (=ended their argument without going to a court of law) **7** [T] to pay (a bill or money claimed)

**settle down** *v adv* **1** [I;T (=**settle** sbdy. **down**)] to (cause to) sit comfortably: *She settled (herself) down in a chair with a book.* **2** [I] to establish a home and live a quiet life: *I want to get married and settle down.* **3** [I] to become used to a way of life, job, etc.: *He soon settled down in his new school.* –see also SETTLE (4)

**settle for** sthg. *v prep* [T] to accept (something less than hoped for): *I want £500 for my car and I won't settle for less.*

**settle in** *v adv* [I;T (=**settle** sbdy. **in**)] to (help to) get used to a new home, job, etc.: *It was the first time she had left home, so it took her a while to settle in.*

**settle up** *v adv* [I *with*] to pay what is owed: *to settle up with the waiter after a meal*

**set·tled** /ˈsetld/ *adj* unlikely to change; fixed: *settled weather/habits* –opposite **unsettled**

**set·tle·ment** /ˈsetlmənt/ *n* **1** [C] a small village in an area with few people: *a settlement on the edge of the desert* **2** [U] the movement of a new population into a place to live there: *the settlement of the American West* **3** [C] an agreement or decision ending an argument, question, etc.: *the settlement of the law case* **4** [C] a payment of money claimed: *a settlement of a bill*

**set·tler** /ˈsetləʳ/ *n* one of a new population, usu. in an area with few people: *early settlers in Australia*

**set-up** /ˈ· ·/ *n* [S] an arrangement or organization: *What's the set-up in this office?* –see also SET **up** (2)

**sev·en** /ˈsevən/ *determiner,n,pron* (the number) 7 –**seventh** *determiner,n,pron,adv*

**sev·en·teen** /ˌsevənˈtiːn◂/ *determiner,n,pron* (the number) 17 –**seventeenth** *determiner,n,pron,adv*

**sev·en·ty** /ˈsevənti/ *determiner,n,pron* **-ties** (the number) 70 –**seventieth** *determiner,n,pron,adv*

**sev·er** /ˈsevəʳ/ *v more fml than* **cut** *or* **break**– **1** [T *from*] to cut; divide, esp. into two parts: *His arm was severed from his body in the accident.*|*a severed* ARTERY **2** [I] to break: *The rope severed and he fell.*

**sev·e·ral**[1] /ˈsevərəl/ *determiner,pron* a few but not many; some: *several visits to London*|*several hundred people*|*Several of the apples are bad.* –see Study Notes on page 494

**several**[2] *adj* [A] *fml & lit* separate; different; RESPECtive: *They shook hands and went their several ways.*

**sev·er·ance** /ˈsevərəns/ *n* [C;U] the/an act or result of SEVERING: *(a) severance of relations between the two countries*

**se·vere** /sə̇ˈvɪəʳ/ *adj* **1** not kind or gentle in treatment; STERN; STRICT (1): *a severe look on her face|severe military rules* **2** very harmful or painful: *severe pain|the severest winter for ten years* –compare MILD (2) **3** plain; without decoration; AUSTERE: *severe beauty* **–severely** *adv* **–severity** /ˈ-verə̇ti/ **-ties** *n* [C;U]

**sew** /səʊ/ *v* **sewed, sewn**||also **sewed** *AmE*, **sewing** [I;T] to join or fasten (cloth, leather, etc.) by stitches made with thread; make or mend with needle and thread: *Would you sew on this button/sew this button onto my shirt?|Who taught you how to sew?*

**sew** sthg.↔**up** *v adv* [T] **1** to close or repair by sewing **2** *infml* to put into one's control; determine or settle: *The People's Party have got the election sewn up; they're sure to win.* **–sewing** *n* [U]: *I used to hate sewing before we got a* **sewing machine.**

**sew·age** /ˈsjuːɪdʒ, ˈsuː-||ˈsuː-/ *n* [U] the waste material and water carried in SEWERS

**sew·er** /ˈsjuːəʳ, ˈsuːəʳ||ˈsuːər/ *n* a man-made passage or large pipe under the ground for carrying away water and waste material

**sex** /seks/ *n* **1** [U] the condition of being either male or female: *In the space marked "sex", put an "M" for male or an "F" for female.* **2** [C] the set of all male or all female creatures: *a member of the opposite sex* **3** [A] connected with the bodily system of producing children: *sex organs* **4** [U] SEXUAL INTERCOURSE or activity connected with this act: *Do you think sex outside marriage is wrong?|There's a lot of sex and violence in this film.*

**sex·is·m** /ˈseksɪzəm/ *n* [U] the opinion that women are less able in most ways than men

**sex·ist** /ˈseksə̇st/ *adj,n* (a person) showing SEXISM: *I'm tired of his sexist jokes about women drivers!*

**sex·less** /ˈseksləs/ *adj* **1** sexually uninteresting; not SEXY **2** not male or female; NEUTER[1] (2)

**sex·tant** /ˈsekstənt/ *n* an instrument used on a ship or aircraft to calculate its position

**sex·u·al** *adj* of sex or the sexes: *sexual* REPRODUCTION –see EROTIC (USAGE) **–sexually** *adv*

**sexual in·ter·course** /ˌ··· ˈ···/ also **intercourse**– *n* [U] the bodily act between two animals or people in which the male sex organ enters the female

**sex·u·al·i·ty** /ˌsekʃʊˈælə̇ti, -sjʊ-||ˌsekʃʊ-/ *n* [U] fondness for, or interest in, sexual activity

**sex·y** /ˈseksi/ *adj* **-ier, -iest** exciting in a sexual way: *sexy clothes* –see EROTIC (USAGE) **–sexily** *adv*

**SF** *abbrev. for:* SCIENCE FICTION

**Sgt** *written abbrev. said as:* SERGEANT

**sh**, **s, Sh** /ʃ/ *interj* (used for demanding silence or less noise): *Sh! You'll wake the baby!*

**shab·by** /ˈʃæbi/ *adj* **-bier, -biest 1** (esp. of clothes) appearing poor because of long wear; (of people) poorly dressed: *a shabby old coat* –compare SCRUFFY **2** ungenerous or not worthy; unfair; MEAN[1] (1,2): *What a shabby trick, making me walk home!* **–shabbily** *adv* **–shabbiness** *n* [U]

**SPELLING NOTE**
Words with the sound /ʃ/ may be spelt **ch-**, like **chauffeur.**

**shack** /ʃæk/ *n* a small roughly built house; hut

**shack·le**[1] /ˈʃækəl/ *n* **1** a band for fastening around the wrist or ankle of an animal, prisoner, etc. to prevent movement **2** [*usu. pl.*] something that prevents freedom of action or expression: *bound by the shackles of out-of-date beliefs*

**shackle**[2] *v* **-led, -ling** [T] to bind (as if) with SHACKLES: *hands shackled together|shackled by old customs*

**shade**[1] /ʃeɪd/ *n* **1** [U] shelter from direct light, esp. from sunlight outdoors, made by something blocking it: *sitting in the shade of a tree* **2** [C] something that keeps out light or its full brightness: *a lampshade|a green eyeshade* **3** [C] a degree of colour: *a lighter shade of blue* **4** [C] a slight difference in degree; NUANCE: *a word with several shades of meaning* **5** [C] a little bit: *a shade too loud*

USAGE **Shade** is any area sheltered from the sun. a **shadow** is a clear shape made by the **shade** of a particular person or thing. Compare: *The trees in the garden provide plenty of* **shade.**|*The dog saw its* **shadow** *on the grass.*

**shade**[2] *v* **shaded, shading** [T] **1** to shelter from direct light or heat: *She shaded her eyes from the sun with her hand.* **2** [*in*] to represent the effect of shade or shadow on (an object in a picture): *to shade in the background of a drawing*

**shad·ow**[1] /ˈʃædəʊ/ *n* **1** [C;U] is blocked by something: *As the sun set, the shadows became larger.|The tree* CAST (=produced) *its shadow on the wall.|His shadow followed him along the road.* (=because the sun was in front of him) **2** [C] a form from which the real substance has gone: *After his illness he was only a shadow of his former self.* **3** [S] (used only in NEGATIVES[2], questions, etc.) a slightest bit; TRACE[2] (2): *not a shadow of doubt*

**shadow**[2] *v* [T] **1** to make a shadow on; darken (as) with a shadow **2** to follow and watch closely, esp. secretly: *She was shadowed by the police.*

**shad·ow cab·i·net** /ˈ·· ˌ···/ *n* [*the* S] (esp.) in Britain) the leading politicians of the opposition party in Parliament, who each study the work of a particular government department

**shad·ow·y** /ˈʃædəʊi/ *adj* **-ier, -iest 1** hard to see or know about clearly; not DISTINCT (2): *a shadowy and little-known historical figure* **2** full of shade; in shadow: *the shadowy depths of the forest*

**shad·y** /ˈʃeɪdi/ *adj* **-ier, -iest 1** in or producing shade: *shady trees* **2** *infml* not very honest: *a shady politician*

**shaft** /ʃɑːft||ʃæft/ *n* **1** the long handle of a spear, hammer, axe, etc. **2** one of the pair of poles that an animal is fastened between to pull a vehicle **3** a bar which turns, or around which a belt or wheel turns, to pass power through a machine: *a* PROPELLER *shaft* **4** a beam of light: *a shaft of sunlight* **5** a long passage, usu. up and down or sloping: *a mine shaft|a lift shaft*

**shag** /ʃæg/ *n* [U] rough strong tobacco

**shag·gy** /ˈʃægi/ *adj* **-gier, -giest** consisting of or covered with long, rough hair: *a shaggy beard/dog/coat* **–shagginess** *n* [U]

**shake**[1] /ʃeɪk/ *v* **shook**/ʃʊk/, **shaken, shaking 1** [I;T] to (cause to) move quickly up and down and to and fro: *The explosion shook the house.|The house shook.|She was shaking with laughter/ anger/ fear.|Shake the bottle before use.|She shook the sand from her shoes.* (=removed it by shaking) **2** [I;T] to take and hold (someone's right hand) in one's own, as a sign of greeting, goodbye, or agreement: *They* **shook hands** *(with each other).* **3** [T *up*] to trouble the mind or feelings of; upset: *She was shaken (up) by the news.* **4 shake one's head** to move one's head from side to side to answer "no"

**shake** sbdy./sthg.↔**off** *v adv* [T] to get rid of; escape from: *I just can't shake this cold off.*

**shake** sthg.↔**out** *v adv* [T] to open or spread with a shaking movement: *He shook out the dirty mat.*

**shake** sthg.↔**up** *v adv* [T] **1** to rearrange; make changes in (an organization): *The new chairman will shake up the company.* –see also SHAKE-UP **2** to mix by shaking

**shake²** *n* an action of shaking: *She answered "no" with a shake of the head.*

**shake-up** /ˈ· ·/ *n* a rearrangement of an organization: *a government shake-up with three ministers losing their jobs* –see also SHAKE **up**

**shak·y** /ˈʃeɪki/ *adj* **-ier, -iest 1** shaking or unsteady, e.g. from nervousness or weakness **2** not solid or firm; undependable: *an unsafe shaky ladder|shaky in her beliefs* **–shakily** *adv* **–shakiness** *n* [U]

**shale** /ʃeɪl/ *n* [U] soft rock which naturally divides into thin sheets

**shall** /ʃəl; *strong* ʃæl/ *v negative contraction* **shan't** [I + ~~to~~-*v*] **1** (used with *I* and *we* to show the future): *We shall* (but *They will*) *be away next week.|I shall* (but *He will*) *have finished the book by Friday.* **2** *fml* (used with *you, he, she, it, they* to show a promise, command, or law): *It shall be done as you wish.|This law shall have effect in Scotland.* **3** (used, esp. with *I* and *we*, in questions or offers that ask the hearer to decide): *Shall I* (=Do you want me to) *open the window?* –see also SHOULD, WILL –see Study Notes on page 386

USAGE In ordinary modern speech **will,** or the short form **'ll,** is used more often than **shall** in the first and second meanings; but in the third meaning, **shall** is always used.

**shal·lot** /ʃəˈlɒt‖ʃəˈlɑt/ *n* a small onion-like vegetable

**shal·low** /ˈʃæləʊ/ *adj* **1** not deep; not far from top to bottom: *the shallow end of the swimming pool* **2** lacking deep or serious thinking; SUPERFICIAL: *a shallow thinker* **–shallowly** *adv* **–shallowness** *n* [U]

**sham¹** /ʃæm/ *n* **1** [S] something false pretending to be the real thing; piece of deceit: *The agreement was a sham; nobody intended to keep to it.* **2** [A] not real; copying the real thing: *sham jewellery*

**sham²** *v* **-mm-** [I;T] to put on the false appearance of (some disease, condition, etc.): *He isn't really ill; he's shamming.*

**sham·ble** /ˈʃæmbəl/ *v* **-bled, -bling** [I] to walk awkwardly, dragging the feet: *shambling along the street*

**sham·bles** /ˈʃæmbəlz/ *n* [S] *infml* a scene of great disorder; MESS¹ (1): *After the party the house was a shambles.*

**shame¹** /ʃeɪm/ *n* **1** [U] the painful feeling of one's own guilt, wrongness, or failure or that of a close friend, relative, etc.: *I feel no shame for my action.|I was filled with shame when I remembered how badly I'd behaved at the party.* **2** [U] loss of honour; DISGRACE: *Your bad behaviour brings shame on the whole school.* **3** [S] an unfortunate state of affairs; something that ought not to be: **What a shame** *that it rained on the day of your garden party!* **4 put someone/something to shame** to show someone/something to be less good by comparison: *Your beautiful garden puts my few little flowers to shame.*

**shame²** *v* **shamed, shaming** [T] to bring dishonour to; DISGRACE: *He shamed his family by being sent to prison.*

**shame·faced** /ˌʃeɪmˈfeɪst◂/ *adj* showing suitable shame **–shamefacedly** *adv*

**shame·ful** /ˈʃeɪmfəl/ *adj* deserving blame; which one ought to be ashamed of **–shamefully** *adv*

**shame·less** /ˈʃeɪmlǝs/ *adj* **1** (of a person) unable to feel shame: *an immodest and shameless person* **2** done without shame; INDECENT: *shameless disloyalty* **–shamelessly** *adv*

**sham·poo¹** /ʃæmˈpuː/ *n* **-poos 1** [C;U] a usu. liquid soaplike product used for washing the hair, CARPETS, etc.: *creamy shampoo for dry hair* **2** [C] an act of SHAMPOOing²

**shampoo²** *v* **-pooed, -pooing, -poos** [T] to wash with SHAMPOO¹

**sham·rock** /ˈʃæmrɒk‖-rɑk/ [C;U] a type of CLOVER with three leaves on each stem, used as the national sign of Ireland

**shan·dy** /ˈʃændi/ *n* **-dies** [C;U] *BrE* a drink made from a mixture of beer and GINGER ALE or LEMONADE (1)

**shan't** /ʃɑːnt‖ʃænt/ *v short for:* shall not: *Shall I go, or shan't I?*

**shan·ty¹** /ˈʃænti/ *n* **-ties** a small roughly built usu. wooden house; SHACK

**shanty², chanty** *n* **- ties** a song formerly sung by sailors

**shape¹** /ʃeɪp/ *n* **1** [C;U] the appearance or form of something: *a cake in the shape of a heart|We saw a shape through the mist but we couldn't see who it was.|What shape will future society have?* **2** [U] *infml* state or condition: *He's taking lots of exercise to* **get into shape.** (=develop a good physical condition)|*Our garden is in good shape.* **3 take shape²** to begin to be or look like the finished form: *ideas taking shape in his mind* **–shapeless** *adj*

**shape** *v* **shaped, shaping 1** [T] to make or influence the form of: *The bird shaped its nest from mud and sticks/shaped mud and sticks into a nest.|My time at school shaped my future.* **2** [I] to develop well or in the stated way: *How is the new job shaping (up)?*

**shaped** /ʃeɪpt/ *adj* having a certain shape: *a cloud shaped like a camel|a heart-shaped cake*

**shape·ly** /ˈʃeɪpli/ *adj* **-ier, -iest** (esp. of a woman's body) having a good-looking shape **–shapeliness** *n* [U]

**share¹** /ʃeəʳ/ *n* **1** [S] the part belonging or owed to, or done by, a person: *If you want a share in/of the pay, you'll have to do your share of the work.* **2** [A;C] any of the equal parts into which the ownership of a company may be divided: *She owns 50 shares in the business.|a* DIVIDEND (1) *of 50 pence per share|Share prices rose yesterday.*

**share**[2] *v* **shared, sharing 1** [I;T *with,among,between*] to use, pay, have, etc., with others: *We haven't enough books for everyone; some of you will have to share.|Everyone in the house shares the bathroom.|He's sure we'll win the match, but I don't share his faith in the team.|Children should be taught to share (their toys).* **2** [T *out,among,between*] to divide and give out in shares: *His property was shared (out) between his children.* **3 share and share alike** *infml* to have an equal share in everything –**sharer** *n*

**share·hold·er** /'ʃeə,həʊldər||'ʃeər-/ *BrE*||**stockholder** *AmE*– *n* an owner of shares in a business

**shark** /ʃɑːk||ʃɑrk/ *n* **1** a large, dangerous fish with sharp teeth **2** *infml* a person clever at getting money from others in dishonest ways

**sharp**[1] /ʃɑːp||ʃɑrp/ *adj* **1** having a thin cutting edge or a fine point: *a sharp knife/needle/nail* –opposite **blunt 2** quick and sensitive: *a sharp mind|sharp eyes* **3** causing a sensation like that of cutting, biting, or stinging: *a sharp wind|a sharp taste|a sharp pain* **4** not rounded: *a sharp nose* **5** having a quick change in direction; sudden: *a sharp right turn|a sharp rise/fall in prices* **6** clear in shape or detail; DISTINCT (2): *a sharp photographic image* **7** quick and strong: *a sharp blow on the head* **8** (of words) intended to hurt; angry: *a sharp scolding* **9** [after *n*] (of a note in music) raised by ½ TONE (5) (in the phrases **F sharp, C sharp**, etc.) –compare FLAT[1] (6) **10** clever to the point of dishonesty: *The firm is well-known for* **sharp practice.** –**sharply** *adv* **sharpness** *n* [U]

**sharp**[2] *adv* [after *n*] exactly at the stated time: *The meeting starts at three o'clock sharp.*

**sharp·en** /'ʃɑːpən||'ʃɑr-/ *v* [I;T] to make or become sharp: *to sharpen a pencil/knife*

**sharp·en·er** /'ʃɑːpənər, 'ʃɑːpnər||'ʃɑr-/ *n* a machine or tool for SHARPENing

**shat·ter** /'ʃætər/ *v* **1** [I;T] to (cause to) break suddenly into small pieces; SMASH: *A stone shattered the window; the glass shattered.*|(fig.) *Hopes of reaching an agreement were shattered today.* **2** [T *usu. pass.*] *BrE infml* to make very tired and weak: *I feel completely shattered after that run up the hill.*

**shave**[1] /ʃeɪv/ *v* **shaved, shaving 1** [I;T *off*] to cut off (hair or beard) from (one's face, etc.) with a RAZOR: *I've shaved off my beard.|I cut myself while I was shaving.|Do you shave your legs?* **2** [T *off*] to cut off (very thin pieces) from (a surface): *She shaved the bottom of the door to make it close properly.* **3 -shaven** having been SHAVED: *a clean-shaven face* (=with no beard)

**shave**[2] *n* **1** an act or result of shaving (SHAVE) **2 a close/narrow shave** *infml* a narrow escape

**shav·er** /'ʃeɪvər/ *n* a tool for shaving (SHAVE), esp. an electric RAZOR

**shav·ing** /'ʃeɪvɪŋ/ *n* **1** [U] the act of closely cutting off hair **2** [C *usu. pl.*] a very thin piece cut from a surface with a sharp blade: *wood shavings made with a* PLANE[1]

**shawl** /ʃɔːl/ *n* a piece of cloth for wearing over a woman's head and shoulders or wrapping round a baby

**SPELLING NOTE**
Words with the sound /ʃ/ may be spelt **ch-**, like **chauffeur.**

**she**[1] /ʃi; *strong* ʃiː/ pron (used as the subject of a sentence) **1** that female person or animal already mentioned: *That's an intelligent woman. Who is she?* **2** (used of things, esp. countries and certain vehicles, that are thought of as female): *The ship has come in, but she will leave in ten minutes.*

**she**[2] *n* a female person or animal: *Is your dog a he or a she?|a she-goat*

**sheaf** /ʃiːf/ *n* **sheaves 1** a bunch of grain plants tied together **2** [*of*] a handful of long or thin things laid or tied together; BUNDLE[1] (1): *a sheaf of notes*

**shear** /ʃɪər/ *v* **sheared, sheared** *or* **shorn** /ʃɔːn||ʃorn/, **shearing 1** [T] to cut off wool from (sheep) **2** [T] *esp. lit* to cut off hair from: *He looked strange with his closely shorn head.* **3** [I *off*] *tech* (esp. of thin rods, pins, etc.) to break in two under a sideways force

**shears** /ʃɪəz||ʃɪərz/ *n* [P] large heavy scissors, used e.g. for cutting grass –see PAIR (USAGE)

**sheath** /ʃiːθ/ **sheaths** /ʃiːðz/ **1** a closefitting case for a knife or sword blade **2** a rubber covering worn over a man's sex organ when having sex, used as a means of birth control; CONDOM

**sheathe** /ʃiːð/ *v* **sheathed, sheathing** [T] to put into a SHEATH (1)

**shed**[1] /ʃed/ *n* a lightly built usu. wooden building, usu. for storing things: *a toolshed/cattle shed*

**shed**[2] *v* **shed, shedding** [T] **1** to cause to flow out: *He shed tears of sorrow.|arguments which* **shed** *new* **light on** *the question* (=make it clearer)|*They wanted to bring down the government, but without* **shedding blood**. (=without causing death) –see also BLOODSHED **2** (of a plant or animal) to throw off naturally: *trees shedding their leaves in autumn|Some snakes shed their skin each year.*

**she'd** /ʃid; *strong* ʃiːd/ *short for:* **1** she would **2** she had

**sheen** /ʃiːn/ *n* [S;U] (a) brightness on a surface: *hair with a beautiful sheen*

**sheep** /ʃiːp/ *n* **sheep 1** a grass-eating animal that is kept for its wool and its meat –compare RAM, EWE; see MEAT (USAGE) **2 black sheep** an unsatisfactory member of a group: *After he had been in prison Peter was regarded as the black sheep of the family.* **3 the sheep and the goats** those who are good, able, successful, etc., and those who are not: *a hard examination, intended to separate the sheep from the goats*

**sheep·dog** /'ʃiːpdɒg||-dɔg/ *n* a dog trained to drive sheep and keep them together

**sheep·ish** /'ʃiːpɪʃ/ *adj* slightly ashamed and afraid of others: *a sheepish smile* –**sheepishly** *adv* –**sheepishness** *n* [U]

**sheer**[1] /ʃɪər/ *adj* **1** [A] pure; unmixed with anything else; nothing but: *He won by sheer luck/determination.* **2** very steep; straight up and down: *a sheer cliff* **3** very thin and almost transparent: *ladies' sheer stockings*

**sheer**[2] *adv* straight up or down: *a sheer cliff*

**sheer**[3] *v* [I *off,away*] to turn (as if) to avoid hitting something; change direction quickly: *The boat came close to the rocks and then sheered away.*

**sheet** /ʃiːt/ *n* **1** a large piece of cloth used in a pair on a bed: *We change the sheets every week.* **2** a piece of paper: *a sheet of newspaper* **3** a broad stretch or piece of something thin: *a sheet of ice over the lake*|**sheet metal** (=metal in sheets) **4** a moving or powerful wide mass: *sheets of rain*

**sheikh**, **sheik** /ʃeɪk||ʃiːk/ *n* [A;C] **1** an Arab chief or prince **2** a Muslim religious leader or teacher

**shelf** /ʃelf/ *n* **shelves** /ʃəlvz/ **1** a flat long and narrow board fixed against a wall or in a frame, for placing things on: *a book-shelf*|*some new shelves for the kitchen* **2** something with a shape like one of these, esp. a narrow surface (LEDGE) of rock

**shell**[1] /ʃel/ *n* **1** [C;U] a hard covering of an animal, egg, fruit, nut, or seed: *The seashore was covered with shells.*|*a* SNAIL *shell*|*a nutshell*|*some pieces of eggshell* –see also SEASHELL **2** [C] the outside frame of a building **3** [C] an explosive for firing from a large gun: *shells bursting all around* –compare BULLET

**shell**[2] *v* **1** [T] to remove from a natural shell or POD: *to shell* PEAS **2** [I;T] to fire SHELLS[1] (3) (at): *The enemy lines were weakened by shelling.*

**shell out** (sthg.) *v adv* [I;T] *infml* to pay (money): *He wouldn't shell out for his share of the meal.*

**she'll** /ʃil; *strong* ʃiːl/ *short for:* **1** she will: *She'll come if she can.* **2** she shall

**shell·fish** /ˈʃelˌfɪʃ/ *n* **shellfish** [C;U] any animal without a SPINE (1) that lives in water and has a shell: *The lobster is a shellfish.*

**shel·ter**[1] /ˈʃeltəʳ/ *n* **1** [U] protection, esp. from the weather: *In the storm I* **took shelter** *under a tree.* **2** [C] a building or enclosure offering protection: *a bus shelter* (=roofed enclosure at a bus stop)

**shelter**[2] *v* **1** [T *from*] to give shelter to: *to shelter a plant from the sun*|*sheltering the homeless* **2** [I *from*] to find shelter: *In the rain people were sheltering in the doorways of shops.*

**shel·tered** /ˈʃeltəd||-ərd/ *adj* protected from harm, risk or unpleasant realities: *a sheltered life*

**shelve** /ʃelv/ *v* **shelved, shelving** **1** [T] to put on a shelf; arrange on shelves **2** [T] to put aside (usu. a plan) until a later time: *We've shelved our holiday plans.* **3** [I *down,up*] (of land) to slope gradually

**shelv·ing** /ˈʃelvɪŋ/ *n* [U] (material for) shelves

**shep·herd**[1] /ˈʃepəd||-ərd/ *n* a man or boy who takes care of sheep in the fields

**shepherd**[2] *v* [T] to lead or take care of like sheep: *We shepherded the children into the bus.*

**shep·herd·ess** /ˈʃepədes||-ərdǝ̇s/ *n* (esp. in poetry and art) a woman or girl who takes care of sheep in the fields

**sher·bet** /ˈʃɜːbət||ˈʃɜr-/ *n* [U] *BrE* sweet powder for adding to water to make a drink, esp. for children

**sher·iff** /ˈʃerǝ̇f/ *n* [A;C] (in the US) an elected officer responsible for public order

**sher·ry** /ˈʃeri/ *n* **-ries** [C;U] strong wine from Spain, often drunk in Britain before a meal –compare PORT[3]

**she's** /ʃiz; *strong* ʃiːz/ *short for:* **1** she is: *She's working in an office.* **2** she has: *She's got a new job.*

**shew** /ʃəʊ/ *v* **shewed, shewn, shewing** *now rare* for SHOW[1]

**shield**[1] /ʃiːld/ *n* **1** a broad piece of metal, wood, etc. carried by soldiers in former times as a protection from arrows or blows **2** a representation of this used for a BADGE, etc. **3** a protective cover, esp. on a machine: *The spacecraft was fitted with a heat-shield*

**shield**[2] *v* [T *from*] to protect or hide from harm or danger: *She lied to the police to shield her friend.*

**shift**[1] /ʃɪft/ *v* [I;T] to change in position or direction; move from one place to another: *We shifted the books next door.*|*The wind shifted to the west.*|(fig.) *Don't try to shift the blame onto me!*|(*infml*) *Shift that box will you; it's in my way.*

**shift**[2] *n* **1** [C] a change in position, direction, or character; *a shift in the wind/in political opinion* **2** [C +*sing./pl.v*] (a group of workers for) a period of work in a factory, etc.: *I work on the day/night shift.*|*The night shift is/are arriving now.*|*shift work*

**shift·less** /ˈʃɪftləs/ *adj* lazy and without purpose –**shiftlessly** *adv* –**shiftlessness** *n* [U]

**shift·y** /ˈʃɪfti/ *adj* **-ier, -iest** looking dishonest; not to be trusted –**shiftily** *adv*

**shil·ling** /ˈʃɪlɪŋ/ *n* **1** an amount of money used in Britain until 1971: *One shilling = 12 (old) pence = $^1/_{20}$ of £1.* **2** an amount of money in some African countries, equal to 100 cents

**shim·mer** /ˈʃɪməʳ/ *v* [I] to shine with a soft trembling light: *water shimmering in the moonlight* –**shimmer** *n* [U]

**shin**[1] /ʃɪn/ *n* the bony front part of the leg between the knee and ankle –see picture on page 299

**shin**[2] ||also **shinny** *AmE*– *v* **-nn-** [I *up, down*] to climb (a tree, pole, etc.) quickly and easily, using the hands and legs: *She shinned up the tree.*

**shine**[1] /ʃaɪn/ *v* **shone**/ʃɒn||ʃəʊn/, **shining** **1** [I] to give off light; look bright: *a fine morning with the sun shining (down)*|*The car shone in the sun.*|(fig.) *She's a good student generally, but sports are where she really shines.* (=shows special ability) **2** [T] to direct (a lamp, etc.): *Shine your torch here.*

**shine**[2] *v* **shined, shining** [T] to polish; make bright by rubbing: *Shine your shoes before going out.*

**shine**[3] *n* [S] **1** brightness; shining quality: *The wooden surface had a beautiful shine.* **2** an act of polishing: *These shoes need a shine.* **3 (come) rain or shine** in good or bad weather; whatever happens: *I promise we'll be there, rain or shine.*

**shin·gle** /ˈʃɪŋgəl/ *n* [U] small rough rounded pieces of stone, larger than GRAVEL, lying in masses along a seashore –**shingly** *adj* **-glier, -gliest**

**shin·ny** /ˈʃɪni/ *v* **-nied, -nying** *AmE* for SHIN[2]

**shin·y** /ˈʃaɪni/ *adj* **-ier, -iest** (esp. of a smooth surface) looking as if polished; bright: *a shiny new coin* –**shininess** *n* [U]

**ship**[1] /ʃɪp/ *n* **1** a large boat for carrying people or goods on the sea: *life on board ship*|*We went on a ship/***by ship.** **2** *infml* a large aircraft or spacecraft

**ship**[2] *v* **-pp-** [T] **1** to carry or send by ship: *I'm flying to America but my car is being shipped.* **2 ship water** (of a boat) to take in water over the side

**ship·ment** /ˈʃɪpmənt/ *n* **1** [C] a load of goods sent together: *A large shipment of grain has just arrived.* **2** [U] the action of sending, carrying, and delivering goods: *articles lost in shipment*

**ship·per** /ˈʃɪpəʳ/ *n* a dealer who sends and delivers goods: *wine shippers*

**ship·ping** /ˈʃɪpɪŋ/ *n* [U] **1** ship traffic; ships as a group **2** the sending and delivery of something: *a shipping charge* (=charge for shipping) *of £1*

**ship·shape** /ˈʃɪpʃeɪp/ *adj* clean and neat; in good order

**ship·wreck**[1] /ˈʃɪp-rek/ *n* [C;U] a/the destruction of a ship, by hitting rocks or sinking

**shipwreck**[2] *v* [T] to cause to suffer SHIPWRECK: *sailors shipwrecked on an island*

**ship·yard** /ˈʃɪp-jɑːd‖-jɑrd/ *n* a place where ships are built or repaired

**shire** /ʃaɪəʳ/ *n old use* → COUNTY

**shirk** /ʃɜːk‖ʃɜrk/ *v* [I;T +*v-ing*] to avoid (something unpleasant) because of laziness, etc.: *We mustn't shirk our cleaning job.|to shirk one's responsibilities* –**shirker** *n*

**shirt** /ʃɜːt‖ʃɜrt/ *n* a piece of clothing for the upper part of the body, usu. of light cloth with a collar and SLEEVES –compare SWEATSHIRT –see picture opposite

**shirt·sleeves** *n* [P] **in one's shirtsleeves** wearing nothing over one's shirt: *On hot days the men in the office work in their shirtsleeves.*

**shirt·y** /ˈʃɜːti‖ˈʃɜr-/ *adj* **-ier, -iest** *infml* bad- tempered; angry and rude

**shiv·er**[1] /ˈʃɪvəʳ/ *v* [I] (esp. of people) to shake, as from cold or fear; tremble: *It was so cold that we were all shivering.* –**shivery** *adj* **-ier, -iest**

**shiver**[2] *n* a feeling of SHIVERing[1]: *That strange noise* **sends shivers (up and) down my spine**. (=my back)

**shoal**[1] /ʃəʊl/ *n* a bank of sand not far below the surface of the water, making it dangerous to boats

**shoal**[2] *n* [C +*sing./pl. v, of*] a large group of fish swimming together: (fig.) *People arrived in shoals.*

**shock**[1] /ʃɒk‖ʃɑk/ *n* **1** [C;U] (the state caused by) something unexpected and usu. very unpleasant: *The bad news left us all speechless from shock.|His death came as a great shock.* **2** [C;U] (a) violent force, as from a hard blow, crash, explosion, etc.: *The shock of the explosion was felt far away.* **3** [C;U] the sudden violent effect of electricity passing through the body **4** [U] *tech* weakness after physical damage to the body: *She is still in shock after her accident.*

**shock**[2] *v* [T] to cause unpleasant or angry surprise: *I was shocked by his sudden death/his rudeness.*

**shock·ing** /ˈʃɒkɪŋ‖ˈʃɑ-/ *adj* **1** very improper, wrong, or sad: *a shocking accident* **2** very bad though not evil: *What a shocking waste of time!* –**shockingly** *adv*

**shock·proof** /ˈʃɒkpruːf‖ˈʃɑk-/ *adj* (esp. of a watch) not easily damaged by being dropped, hit, etc.

**shod** /ʃɒd‖ʃɑd/ *adj lit* wearing shoes: *poor badly-shod children*

**shod·dy** /ˈʃɒdi‖ˈʃɑdi/ *adj* **-dier, -diest 1** made or done cheaply and badly: *shoddy workmanship* **2** ungenerous or not worthy; dishonourable: *a shoddy trick* –**shoddily** *adv* –**shoddiness** *n* [U]

**shoe** /ʃuː/ *n* **1** an outer covering for the human foot, usu. of leather and having a hard base (**sole**) and a support (**heel**) under the heel of the foot: *to put on/take off one's shoes* –compare BOOT[1] (1), SANDAL, SLIPPER –see picture opposite **2** → HORSESHOE **3 in someone's shoes** in someone's position; experiencing what another has to experience: *I'm glad I'm not in his shoes!*

> **SPELLING NOTE**
> Words with the sound /ʃ/ may be spelt **ch-**, like **chauffeur.**

**shoe·horn** /ˈʃuːhɔːn‖-hɔrn/ *n* a curved piece of metal or plastic for putting inside the back of a shoe when putting it on, to help the foot go in easily

**shoe·lace** /ˈʃuːleɪs/ *n* a thin cord or piece of leather used to tie the front parts of a shoe together

**shoe·string** /ˈʃuːˌstrɪŋ/ *n* **1** *AmE* for SHOELACE **2 on a shoestring** on a very small amount of money: *He started his business on a shoestring and built it up.*

**shone** /ʃɒn‖ʃəʊn/ *v past tense and participle of* SHINE[1]

**shoo**[1] /ʃuː/ *interj* (said, usu. not angrily, to animals or small children) go away!

**shoo**[2] [T] **shooed, shooing** to drive away (as if) by saying "SHOO": *He shooed the children away.*

**shook** /ʃʊk/ *v past tense of* SHAKE

**shoot**[1] /ʃuːt/ *v* **shot** /ʃɒt‖ʃɑt/, **shooting 1** [I;T] to fire (a weapon): *I'm coming out with my hands up; don't shoot!|He shot at a bird, but missed it.* (Compare *He shot a bird and killed it.*) **2** [T] to send or fire (a bullet, arrow, etc.) from a weapon: *I shot an arrow at the wall.* **3** [T] to hit, wound, or kill with a gun: *He shot a bird.|He was shot three times in the arm.|She shot him dead.|They shot their way out of prison.|He goes to Scotland every year to shoot wild duck.* (=for sport) **4** [I;T] to send or come out quickly or suddenly: *She shot him an angry look.|Blood shot out of the wound.* **5** [I] to go fast or suddenly: *He shot past me in his fast car.|Pain shot through his arm.* **6** [I] to win a point in a game by kicking or throwing a ball: *in a good position to shoot* **7** [I;T] to make a photograph or film (of): *This film was shot in California.* **8** [T] to pass quickly by or along: *a boat shooting the* RAPIDS –see FIRE (USAGE), HUNT (USAGE)

**shoot** sbdy./sthg.↔**down** *v adv* [T] **1** to bring down and destroy (an aircraft) by shooting **2** *infml* to say "no" firmly to (a person or idea): *another idea shot down by the chairman*

**shoot out** *v adv* [I;T(=**shoot** sthg.↔**out**] to (cause to) come out suddenly: *The snake shot out its tongue.|Its tongue shot out.*

**shoot up** *v adv* [I] to go upwards, increase, or grow quickly: *Prices have shot up lately.*

**shoot**[2] *n* **1** a new growth from a plant, esp. a young stem and leaves **2** an occasion for shooting (esp. animals): *a weekend shoot*

**shooting star** /ˌ·· ˈ·/ also **falling star**– *n* a METEOR from space which burns brightly as it passes through the earth's air

**shooting stick** /ˈ·· ·/ *n* a pointed walking-stick with a top which opens out to form a seat, for sitting outdoors

**shop**[1] /ʃɒp‖ʃɑp/ *n* **1** *BrE*‖**store** *AmE*– a room or building where goods are regularly kept and sold: *the local village shop|The shops in town close at 5.30.|a bookshop* –see picture opposite **2** a place where things are made or repaired; WORKSHOP: *a repair shop* **3 set up shop** to start in business: *He's set up shop as a lawyer in town.* **4 talk shop** to talk about one's work, esp. on a social occasion

**shop**[2] *v* **-pp-** [I *for*] to visit shops in order to buy; buy goods: *Did you* **go shopping** *today?|I was shopping for some new clothes, but I couldn't find anything.*

Jane is looking for a new coat. She sees one that she likes on a **rack**.
Jane: Excuse me, I'd like to **try on** this coat.
Assistant: Certainly. I think it will **fit** you – it's about your size.
Jane: I'll try it on, then. Oh dear, it's too small. The **sleeves** are too short and it's a bit **tight**. The colour doesn't **go with** (=look nice with) my shoes, either. I think **I'll leave it**, thank you.
Jane goes to look at some dresses **in the sale** (a period when goods are sold at a lower price).
Jane: I'll take this dress, but I haven't got any **cash on me**. Do you take **credit cards**?
Assistant: No, but we do accept cheques if you have a **banker's card/cheque card**.
Jane: Good, then I'll **pay by cheque**

–see CUSTOMER (USAGE) –**shopper** *n*

**shop around** *v adv* [I] to compare prices in different shops: *We shopped around for a new car.*

**shop as·sis·tant** /ˈ· ·ˌ··/ *BrE*‖**salesclerk** *AmE*– *n* a person who serves buyers in a shop

**shop floor** /ˌ· ˈ·◂/ *n* [*the* S] (the place of work of) ordinary workers: *What does the shop floor think about the rise in pay?*

**shop·keep·er** /ˈʃɒpˌkiːpəʳ‖ˈʃɑp-/ *BrE*‖**storekeeper** *AmE*– *n* a person, usu . the owner, in charge of a small shop

**shop·lift** /ˈʃɒpˌlɪft‖ˈʃɑp-/ *v* [I;T] to take (goods) from a shop without paying –see THIEF (USAGE) –**shoplifter** *n*

**shop·soiled** /ˈʃɒpsɔɪld‖ˈʃɑp-/ *adj BrE* slightly damaged or dirty from being in a shop for a long time

**shop stew·ard** /ˌ· ˈ··/ *n* a trade union officer elected by union members in a particular place of work

**shore**[1] /ʃɔːʳ‖ʃor/ *n* [C;U] the land along the edge of a large stretch of water: *to walk along the shore|to see a boat about a mile from/off the shore|The sailors got into trouble while they were on shore.* (=on land) –see also ASHORE

USAGE The land along the edge of a river is the **bank**, and the land along the edge of the sea or a lake is the **shore.Coast** is used for the whole area bordering the sea. Compare: *We walked along the* **shore**.|*My parents live on the south* **coast** (=near the sea, but not necessarily right on the edge). When considered as a place of enjoyment, the **coast** is called the **seaside**, and the part of the shore that is covered by sand or smooth stones is called the **beach:** *We're taking the children to the* **seaside** *on Saturday.*|*We spent the whole day lying on the* **beach.**

**shore**[2] *v* [T *up*] to strengthen or give support to (something weak or in danger of failing): *government action to shore up farm prices*

**shorn** /ʃɔːn‖ʃorn/ *v past participle of* SHEAR

**short**[1] /ʃɔːt‖ʃort/ *adj* **1** not far from one end to the other; little in distance or length (opposite **long**) or in height (opposite **tall**): *It's only a short way/distance from here.*|*He's a short man, shorter than his wife.* **2** lasting only a little time: *a short visit of only half an hour|only a short time ago|I've got a short memory.* **3** not having or being enough: *"I'm short of money this week; can you lend me some?" "Sorry; I'm rather short myself."*|*These goods are in short supply; the price will be high.*|*I need £1 but I'm 5p short; I've only got 95p.*|*Our car broke down only two miles short of where we wanted to go.* **4** rudely impatient: *I'm sorry I was short with you; I ought to have answered your question more politely.*|*He's very* **short-tempered.** (=becomes angry easily) **5** [A] (of a drink) of a kind (such as SPIRITS[1] (7)) usu. served in a small glass –compare LONG DRINK **6 for short** as a shorter way of saying the same name: *My name is Alexander, "Al" for short.* **7 in short** to put it into a few words; all I mean is: *You can't make me! I won't do it! In short–no!* **8 short and sweet** *infml* not wasting words or time; short and direct in expression **9 short for** a shorter form of, or way of saying: *The usual word "pub" is short for "public house".* **10 short of: a** up to but not including: *threats of every action short of war* **b** except for; without: *There's no way to cross the river, short of swimming.* –**shortness** *n* [U]

**short**[2] *adv* suddenly; ABRUPTly (1): *The driver stopped short when the child ran into the street.*

**short**[3] *n* **1** a drink of strong alcohol, such as WHISKY or RUM –compare LONG DRINK **2** → SHORT CIRCUIT

**short·age** /ˈʃɔːtɪdʒ‖ˈʃɔr-/ *n* [C;U *of*] a condition of having less than needed; an amount lacking: *food shortages during the war|a shortage of water*

**short·bread** /ˈʃɔːtbred‖ˈʃɔrt-/ *n* [U] a thin hard sweet BISCUIT made with a lot of butter

**short·cake** /ˈʃɔːtkeɪk‖ˈʃɔrt-/ *n* [U] **1** *BrE* thick SHORTBREAD **2** *AmE* cake over which sweetened fruit is poured: *strawberry shortcake*

**short-change** /ˌ· ˈ·/ *v* [T] to give back less than enough money (CHANGE[2] (4)) to (a buyer)

**short-cir·cuit** /ˌ· ˈ··/ *v* [I;T] to (cause to) have a SHORT CIRCUIT

**short circuit** *n* a faulty electrical connection that usu. puts the power supply out of operation

**short·com·ing** /ˈʃɔːtˌkʌmɪŋ‖ˈʃɔrt-/ *n* [*usu. pl.*] a fault; DEFECT: *a man with many shortcomings*

**short cut** /ˌ· ˈ·, ˈ· ·‖ˈ· ·/ *n* a quicker more direct way

**short·en** /ˈʃɔːtn‖ˈʃɔrtn/ *v* [I;T] to make or become shorter: *She shortened the dress.* –opposite **lengthen**

**short·fall** /ˈʃɔːtfɔːl‖ˈʃɔrt-/ *n* an amount lacking to reach the amount needed or expected: *There will be a shortfall in wheat supplies this year.*

**short·hand** /ˈʃɔːthænd‖ˈʃɔrt/ *n* [U] rapid writing in a system using signs or shorter forms for letters, words, etc.: *The secretary made notes in shorthand.* –compare LONGHAND

**short-list** /ˈ· ·/ *v* [T] *BrE* to put on a SHORT LIST

**short list** *n BrE* a list of the few most suitable people for a job, chosen from all those people who want that job

**short-lived** /ˌ· ˈ·◂/ *adj* lasting only a short time

**short·ly** /ˈʃɔːtli‖ˈʃɔrt-/ *adv* **1** soon; in a little time: *Mr Jones will be back shortly.* **2** impatiently; not politely: *He answered rather shortly; I thought he was quite rude.*

**shorts** /ʃɔːts‖ʃɔrts/ *n* [P] **1** trousers ending at or above the knees, worn in playing games, by children, etc. **2** *AmE* men's short UNDERPANTS –see PAIR (USAGE)

**short·sight·ed** /ˌʃɔːtˈsaɪtɪ̣d◂‖ˌʃɔrt-/ *adj* **1** *BrE*‖**nearsighted** *AmE*– unable to see things clearly if they are not close to the eyes –opposite **longsighted 2** not considering what is likely to happen in the future: *It's very shortsighted not to spend money on repairing your house.* –opposite **farsighted** –**shortsightedly** *adv* –**shortsightedness** *n* [U]

**short-term** /ˌ· ˈ·◂/ *adj* concerning a short period of time; in or for the near future: *short-term planning/borrowing* –opposite **long-term**

**short wave** /ˌ· ˈ·◂/ *n* [U] radio broadcasting or receiving on waves of less than 60 metres in length

**shot**[1] /ʃɒt‖ʃɑt/ *n* **1** [C] an action of shooting a weapon: *He fired three shots.*|*He was wounded by a shot in the leg.* **2** [C] a kick, throw, etc., of a ball intended to win a point: *His shot went to the right of the goal.* **3** [C] a person who shoots with the stated degree of skill: *She's a good/poor shot.* **4** [C] a chance or attempt to do something; TRY[2] (1); GO[2] (2): *It's not easy but I'd like to have a shot at it.*|*Looking* for her in the library was a **long shot** (=an attempt unlikely to succeed); *I had no idea where she was.* **5** [C] a sending up of a spacecraft or ROCKET: *a moon shot* (=for a voyage to the moon) **6** [U] nonexplosive metal balls for shooting from some kinds of guns, esp. CANNONs in former times and SHOTGUNs **7** [C] a photograph or a short continuous action in a film: *fashion shots|an action shot* **8** [C] *infml* a taking of a drug into the bloodstream through a needle; INJECTION: *a shot of PENICILLIN* **9** [C] *infml* a small drink (esp. of WHISKY) all swallowed at once **10** a heavy metal ball which is thrown as a sport (**putting the shot**) –see picture on page 592 **11 big shot** *derog* an important person **12 like a shot** *infml* quickly and eagerly: *He accepted the offer like a shot.* **13 shot in the arm** *infml* something which acts to bring back a better, more active condition: *The big sale was a shot in the arm to the failing company.* **14 shot in the dark** *infml* a wild guess unsupported by arguments

**shot²** *adj* woven in different colours, giving a changing effect of colour: *a dress of shot silk*

**shot³** *v past tense and participle of* SHOOT

**shot·gun** /ˈʃɒtɡʌn‖ˈʃɑt-/ *n* a gun which fires a quantity of small metal balls (SHOT¹ (6)) and is used esp. for shooting birds

**should** /ʃəd; *strong* ʃʊd/ *v negative contraction* **shouldn't** [I+ ~~to~~-v] **1 a** ought to: *you should be ashamed of yourself.|He shouldn't have/oughtn't to have said that.* (=he said it but it was bad to do so)|*I should write a letter this evening, but I want to watch television.* **b** (to show that something can be naturally expected): *They should be/ought to be here soon.* –see Study Notes on page 386 **2 a** (in reported speech with a past verb) shall: *I thought I should succeed.* (=I thought "I shall succeed".) **b** (used instead of *shall* in "if" sentences with a past tense verb): *I should* (but *She would*) *be surprised if he came.|I should stay out of trouble if I were you.* (=You ought to . . .) **c** (used after *that* in certain expressions of feeling: *It's odd that you should mention that.|They demanded that John should go./(AmE* also) *that John go.* **d** *fml* (used in "if" sentences about what is possible in the future): *If I should die, you would get the money.|Should any visitors call,* (=if they call) *tell them I'm busy.* **3 I should have thought** *esp. BrE* (shows surprise): *20 degrees? I should have thought it was colder than that.* **4 I should like** I want: *I should like to ask a question.* –see LIKE (USAGE) **5 I should think** I believe: *"Can you come?" "Yes, I should think so."*

**shoul·der¹** /ˈʃəʊldəʳ/ *n* **1** the part of the body at each side of the neck where the arms are connected: *If you stand on my shoulders you will be able to see over the wall.* –see picture on page 299 **2** the part of a garment that covers this part of the body **3** something like this part of the body in shape, such as a slope on a mountain near the top, or the outward curve on a bottle below the neck **4 head and shoulders above** very much better than: *This book stands/is head and shoulders above all others.* **5 shoulder to shoulder** side by side; close together

**shoulder²** *v* [T] **1** to place (a load) on the shoulder(s): (fig.) *to shoulder the responsibility of high political office* **2** to push with the shoulders: *He shouldered his way to the front of the crowd.*

**shoulder blade** /ˈ·· ·/ *n* either of the two flat bones on each side of the upper back

**should·n't** /ˈʃʊdnt/ *v short for:* should not: *You shouldn't laugh at him.*

**shout¹** /ʃaʊt/ *v* [I;T +(*that*)/*out*] to speak or say very loudly *I can hear you; there's no need to shout.|"Help!" he shouted.|He shouted for help.*

**shout** sbdy.↔**down** *v adv* [T] to prevent (a speaker) from being heard, by shouting: *The crowd shouted down the unpopular speaker.*

**shout²** *n* a loud cry or call: *a warning shout*

**shove¹** /ʃʌv/ *v* **shoved, shoving** [I;T] to push, esp. in a rough careless way: *There was a lot of* **pushing and shoving** *to get on the bus.|Shove the chair into the corner, would you?*

**shove** sbdy. **around** *v adv* [T] *infml* for PUSH **around**

**shove off** *v adv* [I] **1** (of a boat or a person in it) to leave the shore **2** [*in commands*] *infml* Go away!: *Shove off! I'm busy.*

**shove²** *n* a strong push: *Give it a shove!*

**shov·el¹** /ˈʃʌvəl/ *n* **1** a usu. long-handled tool with a broad blade for lifting and moving loose material –compare SPADE **2** a part like this on a digging or earth-moving machine

**shovel²** *v* **-ll-** *BrE*‖**-l-** *AmE* [I;T] to move, make, or work (as if) with a SHOVEL: *He shovelled a path through the snow.*

**show¹** /ʃəʊ/ *v* **showed, shown**‖also **showed** *AmE*, **showing 1** a[T] to allow or cause to be seen: *Let me show you my holiday photographs.|The painting shows a girl holding a baby.* **2** [I] to appear; be able to be seen: *That spot of dirt won't show.|*(fig.) *She did very little work on this report, and it shows!* (=it is very clear to see) **3** [T] to go with and guide: *May I show you to your seat?|The visitors were* **shown round/over** *the castle.* **4** [T +(*that*)] to prove or make clear (to): *His remarks showed he didn't understand.|Will you show me how to use this machine?|This report shows the accident to have been the driver's fault.* **5** [I;T] (esp. of a film) to be offered at present: *"What's showing at the cinema?"* **6** [T] to cause to be felt in one's actions: *They showed their enemies no mercy.* **7 it (all) goes to show** *infml* it proves the point: *It all goes to show that crime doesn't pay.* **8 show one's face** to appear before people: *I'm surprised he dared to show his face here after his behaviour last week.* **9 show one's hand** to make one's power or intentions clear **10 to show for** as a profit or reward from: *He's got nothing to show for his life's work except a lot of memories.*

**show** sbdy. **around/round** sthg. *v prep; adv* [T] to be a guide to (someone) on a first visit to (a place): *Before you start work I'll show you around the office.*

**show off** *v adv* [I] to behave so as to try to get people to admire one, one's abilities, etc.: *Don't look at him! He's just showing off!* –see also SHOW-OFF

**show** sbdy. **over** sthg. *v prep* [T] to guide (someone)

**SPELLING NOTE**

Words with the sound /ʃ/ may be spelt **ch-**, like **chauffeur.**

through (esp. an interesting building or a house for sale)

**show up** *v adv* **1** [I;T(=**show** sthg.↔**up**)] to (cause to) be easily seen: *This bright sunlight really shows up the cracks in the wall.* **2** [T] (**show** sbdy./sthg.↔**up**) to make known the esp. unpleasant truth about **3** [I] *infml* to arrive; be present: *Did everybody show up for the party?* **4** [T] (**show** sbdy.↔**up**) *esp. BrE* to make (someone) feel ashamed: *My husband always shows me up at parties; he always gets drunk.*

**show²** *n* **1** [C] a performance, esp. in a theatre or on radio or television: *What television shows do you usually watch?* **2** [C] a collection of things for the public to look at; EXHIBITION (1): *a cat/flower/car show* **3** [S] a showing: *The army put on a show of strength.* (=showed their strength openly)|*The vote was taken by* **a show of hands**. (=decided by counting the raised hands of voters) **4** [S] an outward appearance, as opposed to what is really true, happening, etc.: *I made a show of interest, but I really didn't care about what he was saying.* **5** [U] grandness; splendid appearance or ceremony **6** [S] *infml* an organization or activity: *He's in charge of the whole show.* **7 on show** being shown to the public

**show busi·ness** /'· ˌ··/ also **show biz** *infml*– *n* [U] the business of performing; the job of people who work in films, the theatre, etc.

**show·down** /'ʃəʊdaʊn/ *n infml* a settlement of a disagreement in an open direct way

**show·er¹** /'ʃaʊəʳ/ *n* **1** a short-lasting fall of rain or snow: *Some showers are expected this afternoon.* –see WEATHER (USAGE) **2** a fall of many small things or drops of liquid: *The bucket fell over, sending a shower of water into the street.* **3 a** a washing of the body by standing under running water: *to take/have a shower* **b** an apparatus for this

**shower²** *v* **1** [I;T] to pour down in SHOWERs (on): *Nuts showered down from the tree.*|(fig.) *They showered her with gifts.* **2** [I] to take a SHOWER¹ (3a)

**show·er·y** /'ʃaʊəri/ *adj* (e.g. of weather) bringing rain from time to time but not for long

**show·ing** /'ʃəʊɪŋ/ *n* **1** [C] an act of putting on view: *a showing of new fashions* **2** [S] a record of success or quality; performance: *a poor showing by the local team*

**show jump·ing** /'· ˌ··/ *n* [U] a horseriding competition judged on ability in jumping a course of fences –**show jumper** *n*

**show·man** /'ʃəʊmən/ *n* **-men** /mən/ **1** a person whose business is producing plays, musical shows, etc. **2** a person who always behaves as if performing for others

**shown** /ʃəʊn/ *v past participle of* SHOW¹

**show-off** /'· ·/ *n infml* a person who SHOWs¹ **off**

**show·room** /'ʃəʊrʊm, -ruːm/ *n* a large room where examples of goods for sale may be looked at

**show·y** /'ʃəʊi/ *adj* **-ier, -iest** too colourful, bright, attention-getting, etc. –**showily** *adv*

**shrank** /ʃræŋk/ *v past tense of* SHRINK

> **SPELLING NOTE**
> Words with the sound /ʃ/ may be spelt **ch-**, like **chauffeur.**

**shrap·nel** /'ʃræpnəl/ *n* [U] metal scattered in small pieces from an exploding bomb or SHELL¹ (3)

**shred¹** /ʃred/ *n* **1** [C] a small narrow piece torn or roughly cut off: *His coat was torn to shreds.* **2** [S] (used in NEGATIVEs² (1), questions, etc.) a smallest piece; bit: *There isn't a shred of truth in his story.*

**shred²** *v* **-dd-** [T] to cut or tear into SHREDs: *shredded* CABBAGE

**shrew** /ʃruː/ *n* **1** a small mouselike animal **2** a bad-tempered scolding woman

**shrewd** /ʃruːd/ *adj* **1** clever in judgment: *a shrewd lawyer who knows all the tricks* **2** well-reasoned and likely to be right: *a shrewd guess* –**shrewdly** *adv* –**shrewdness** *n* [U]

**shrew·ish** /'ʃruːɪʃ/ *adj* typical of a bad-tempered woman (SHREW (2)) –**shrewishly** *adv*

**shriek¹** /ʃriːk/ *v* [I;T] to cry out with a high sound; SCREECH: *"Help!" she shrieked.*|*They were all shrieking with laughter.*

**shriek²** *n* a wild high cry (e.g. of pain or terror)

**shrill** /ʃrɪl/ *adj* (of a sound) high and sounding sharp; PIERCING: *a shrill whistle* –**shrilly** /'ʃrɪl-li, 'ʃrɪli/ *adv* –**shrillness** *n* [U]

**shrimp** /ʃrimp/ *n* **shrimp** *or* **shrimps 1** a small sea creature with long legs and a fanlike tail –compare PRAWN, SCAMPI **2** *derog* a small person

**shrine** /ʃraɪn/ *n* a place for worship; place held in respect for its religious or other connections

**shrink** /ʃrɪŋk/ *v* **shrank** /ʃræŋk/ *or* **shrunk** /ʃrʌŋk/, **shrunk** *or* **shrunken** /'ʃrʌŋkən/, **shrinking 1** [I;T] to (cause to) become smaller, as from the effect of heat or water: *Washing wool in hot water will make it shrink.*|(fig.) *The number of students has shrunk.* **2** [I] to move back and away: *The dog shrank into a corner.*

**shrink from** sthg. *v prep* [T +*v-ing*] to be afraid of; avoid because of fear; RECOIL (1) from: *He shrank from (the thought of) having to kill anyone.*

**shrink·age** /'ʃrɪŋkɪdʒ/ *n* [U] the act or amount of SHRINKing (1); loss in size: *As a result of shrinkage, the shirt is now too small to wear.*

**shriv·el** /'ʃrivəl/ *v* **-ll-** *BrE*‖ **-l-** *AmE* [I;T*up*] to (cause to) dry out and become smaller by twisting into small folds: *plants shrivelling (up) in the dry heat*

**shroud¹** /ʃraʊd/ *n* **1** the cloth for covering a dead body at burial **2** something that covers and hides: *A shroud of secrecy hangs over/surrounds the plan.*

**shroud²** *v* [T *usu. pass.*] to cover and hide: *hills shrouded in mist*|*a mystery shrouded in uncertainty*

**shrub** /ʃrʌb/ *n* a low bush

**shrub·be·ry** /'ʃrʌbəri/ *n* **-ries** [C;U] (part of a garden planted with) SHRUBs forming a mass or group

**shrug** /ʃrʌg/ *v* **-gg-** [I;T] to raise (one's shoulders), esp. as an expression of doubt, lack of interest, etc.: *He shrugged (his shoulders), saying he didn't know and didn't care.* –**shrug** *n: She answered with a shrug.*

**shrug** sthg. **off** *v adv* [T] to treat as unimportant or easily dealt with: *She just shrugs off her troubles.*

**shud·der¹** /'ʃʌdəʳ/ *v* [I +*to-v/at*] to shake uncontrollably for a moment, as from fear or strong dislike; tremble: *He shuddered at the sight of the dead body.*|(fig.) *I shudder to think what your father will say when he sees this broken window.*

**shudder²** *n* an act of SHUDDERing: *He gave a*

shudder in the cold.

**shuf·fle¹** /'ʃʌfəl/ *v* **-fled, -fling 1** [I;T] to mix up the order of (playing cards): *It's your turn to shuffle.*|(fig.) *shuffling papers around on his desk* **2** [I] to walk slowly without lifting one's feet: *The old woman shuffled across the room.*

**shuffle²** *n* **1** [S] a slow dragging walk **2** [C] an act of shuffling (SHUFFLE¹ (1)) cards **3** [C] → SHAKE-UP: *a shuffle of government ministers*

**shun** /ʃʌn/ *v* **-nn-** [T + *v-ing*] to avoid; keep away from: *He was shunned by society.*|*We shunned seeing other people.*

**shunt** /ʃʌnt/ *v* **1** [T] to move (a railway train or carriage) from one track to another, esp. to a SIDING **2** [I] (of a railway train or carriage) to move in this way: (fig.) *Smith has been shunted to a smaller office.*

**shush** /ʃʊʃ/ *v* **1** [I *in commands*] to become quiet; HUSH: *Shush! somebody might hear us.* **2** [T] to tell to be quiet, e.g. by saying "SH"

**shut** /ʃʌt/ *v* **shut, shutting 1** [I;T] to put or go into a covered, blocked, or folded-together position; close: *Shut the gate so that the dog can't get out.*|*He shut his eyes and tried to sleep.*|*She shut the book.*|*The doors shut, and the train moved off.* **2** [T] to keep or hold by closing: *He shut himself in his room to think.*|*She shut her skirt in the door and tore it.* **3** [I;T] to stop in operation; SHUT **down**: *The shops shut at 5.30.*|*He lost his job when they shut the factory.* –see OPEN (USAGE)

**shut** sbdy.↔**away** *v adv* [T] to keep guarded away from others; ISOLATE: *She shut herself away in her country house.*

**shut** (sthg.↔)**down** *v adv* [I;T] (of a business or factory) to stop operation, esp. for a long time: *The hotel shuts down in winter.* –see also SHUTDOWN

**shut** sthg.↔**off** *v adv* [T] **1** to cause to stop in flow or operation, usu. by turning a handle or pressing a button: *They shut off the gas before going on holiday.* **2** to keep separate or away: *a valley shut off by mountains from the rest of the world*

**shut·down** /'ʃʌtdaʊn/ *n* a stopping of work, e.g. in a factory because of a labour quarrel, holiday, lack of demand, etc. –see also SHUT **down**

**shut·ter¹** /'ʃʌtə^r/ *n* **1** one of a pair of wooden or metal covers that can be closed in front of the outside of a window –compare BLIND³ (2) **2** a part of a camera which opens for a very short time to let light fall on the film

**shutter²** *v* [T] to close with SHUTTERS¹ (1): *an empty town, with all the shops shuttered and the people gone*

**shut·tle¹** /'ʃʌtl/ *n* a regular service to and fro by air, bus, etc.: *There is a shuttle (bus service) between the town centre and the station.*|*a space shuttle* (=a spacecraft that can make regular trips to space)

**shuttle²** *v* **-tled, -tling** [I;T] to move to and fro often or regularly

**shut·tle·cock** /'ʃʌtlkɒk‖-kɑk/ *n* a small light object which is hit across a net in the game of BADMINTON

**shy¹** /ʃaɪ/ *adj* **shyer** *or* **shier, shyest** *or* **shiest 1** not bold; nervous in the company of others; BASHFUL: *When the children met the Queen, they were too shy to speak.*|*a shy smile* **2** (of animals) unwilling to come near people **3 once bitten, twice shy** *infml* a person who has been tricked will be more careful in the future **4 -shy** afraid of; not liking: *She's camera-shy and hates being photographed.*|*He's not ill; he's just work-shy.* **–shyly** *adv* **–shyness** *n* [U]

**shy²** *v* **shied, shying** [I] **1** [*at*] (of a horse) to make a sudden movement, e.g. from fear: *The horse shied at the loud noise.* **2** [*off, away*] to avoid something unpleasant, as by moving aside: *They shied away from buying the house when they learnt the price.*

**sib·ling** /'sɪblɪŋ/ *n fml* a brother or sister

**sic** /sɪk/ *adv Latin* (usu. in BRACKETS¹ (2) after a word in writing) written in this wrong way intentionally; not my mistake: *The writer tells us that the war lasted from 939* (sic) *to 1945!*

**sick** /sɪk/ *adj* **1** not well; ill; having a disease: *visiting my sick uncle in hospital*|*a sick cow*|*The sick and wounded were allowed to go free.* –see DISEASE (USAGE) **2** [F] upset in the stomach so as to want to throw up what is in it; NAUSEATED: *He began to feel sick when the ship started to move.* **3** [F *of*] tired of; having too much of: *I'm sick of listening to your complaints; be quiet!* **4** unnaturally cruel; MORBID: *a sick joke/mind* **5** [A] for illness: *sick pay*|*sick leave* **6 be sick** to throw up what is in the stomach; VOMIT: *He was sick twice before he could leave the room.* **7 make someone sick** *infml* to be strongly displeasing to someone: *You make me sick!* **8 -sick** feeling sick from the stated kind of travel: *carsick*|*seasick*

**sick·en** /'sɪkən/ *v* **1** [T] to cause strong feelings of dislike in; NAUSEATE: *a sickening sight* **2** [I *for*] to become ill; show signs of a disease: *The animal began to sicken and soon died.*

**sick·ly** /'sɪkli/ *adj* **-lier, -liest 1** often ill; weak and unhealthy: *a sickly child*|*a sickly-looking plant* **2** unpleasantly weak or pale: *His face was a sickly yellow.* **3** causing a sick feeling: *a sickly smell*

**sick·ness** /'sɪkn½s/ *n* **1** [C;U] the condition of being ill; an illness or disease: *absence owing to sickness* –compare HEALTH **2** [U] the condition of feeling sick; NAUSEA: *He suffers from carsickness.*

**sick pay** /'· ·/ *n* [U] pay for time spent away from a job during illness

**sick·room** /'sɪk-rʊm, -ru:m/ *n* a room where someone lies ill in bed

**side¹** /saɪd/ *n* **1** an upright surface of something, not the top, bottom, front, or back: *The front door is locked; we'll have to go around to the side of the house.*|*The sides of the bowl were beautifully painted.*|*The house was on the side of the hill/on the hillside.* **2** any of the flat surfaces of something: *A cube has six sides.* **3** an edge or border: *A square has four equal sides.*|*I sat on the side of the road/on the roadside.* **4** either of the two surfaces of a thin flat object: *Write on only one side of the paper.* **5** a part, place, or division according to a real or imaginary central line: *the left/right side of his face*|*Cars drive on the left side of the road in England.* **6** the right or left part of the body, esp. from the shoulder to the top of the leg: *I've got a pain in my left side.* **7** the place next to something or someone: *On one side of the window was a mirror, and on the other a painting.*|*His daughter walked by his side.*|*During her illness he never left her side.* **8** a part to be considered, usu. in opposition to another: *Try to look at all sides of the problem.*|*a new side to his character* **9** (a group which holds) a position in a quarrel, war, etc.: *In most wars neither side wins.*|*Whose side are you on; mine or hers?*|*I never* **take sides**. (=support one side against the other) **10** [C +*sing.pl. v*] a sports team: *Our side is/are winning.* **11** the part of a line of a family that is related to a particular person: *He's Scottish on his mother's side.* **12 on the short/easy/low etc. side** rather too short/easy/low etc.: *I like the house but I think the price is on the high side.* **13 on the side** as a (sometimes dishonest) additional activity: *He's a teacher, but he makes a little money on the side by repairing cars in his free time.* –see also SIDELINE **14 put on/to one side** to take out of consideration for the present; keep for possible use later **15 side by side** next to one another: *They lined up side by side for the photograph.* **16 -sided** having a certain number or kind of sides: *an eight-sided coin*

**side**[2] *adj* [A] **1** at, from, towards, etc., the side: *a side door* **2** besides the main or regular thing: *Certain drugs have harmful side effects.*|*We must keep to the main point and not talk about* **side issues**.|*The main dish was meat, with various vegetables as side dishes.*

**side**[3] *v* **sided, siding** [I *with, against*] to support one party in a quarrel, fight, etc., against another: *Frank sided with David in the argument.*

**side·board** /'saɪdbɔːd‖-bord/ *n* a piece of DINING ROOM furniture like a low cupboard, used to hold dishes, glasses, etc.

**side·boards** /'saɪdbɔːdz‖-bordz/ *BrE*‖**sideburns** /-bɜːnz‖-bɜrnz/ *AmE*– *n* [P] growths of hair on the sides of a man's face, esp. when worn long

**side·car** /'saɪdkɑːʳ/ *n* a usu. enclosed seat fastened to the side of a motorcycle to hold a passenger

**side ef·fect** /'· ·,·/ *n* an effect in addition to the intended one: *medicines sometimes have unpleasant side effects.*

**side·light** /'saɪdlaɪt/ *n* **1** either of a pair of small lamps fixed on either side of the front of a vehicle –see also HEADLIGHT –see picture on page 85 **2** a piece of interesting though not very important information: *The book gives some interesting sidelights on the history of the war.*

**side·line** /'saɪdlaɪn/ *n* **1** an activity in addition to one's regular job: *Jane's a doctor, but she does a bit of writing as a sideline.* –compare **on the** SIDE[1] (12) **2** a line marking the side edge of a football field, tennis court, etc. –see picture on page 592

**side·long** /'saɪdlɒŋ‖-lɔŋ/ *adv,adj* directed sideways: *a sidelong blow/smile*

**side·show** /'saɪdʃəʊ/ *n* **1** a separate small show at a fair or CIRCUS (1), usu. with some amusement or game **2** a usu. amusing activity beside a more serious main one

**side·step** /'saɪdstep/ *v* **-pp-** [I;T] **1** to take a step to the side to avoid (e.g. a blow) **2** to avoid (an unwelcome question, duty, etc.): *to sidestep a problem*

**side street** /'· ·/ *n* a narrow less important street, esp. one that meets a main street –compare BACK STREET

**SPELLING NOTE**

Words with the sound /s/ may be spelt **c-**, like **city**, or **ps-**, like **psychology.**

**side·track** /'saɪdtræk/ *v* [T] to cause (someone) to leave one subject or activity and follow another usu. less important one: *The children were sidetracked by the television and didn't do their homework.*

**side·walk** /'saɪdwɔːk/ *n AmE* for PAVEMENT (1)

**side·ways** /'saɪdweɪz/ *adv,adj* to or towards one side: *to step sideways*|*a sideways jump*

**sid·ing** /'saɪdɪŋ/ *n* a short railway track connected to a main track, used for carriages not in use, etc.

**si·dle** /'saɪdl/ *v* [I *up*] to walk secretively or nervously, as if one is ready to turn and go the other way: *He sidled up to the stranger and tried to sell him the stolen ring.*

**siege** /siːdʒ/ *n* an operation by an army surrounding a defended place to force it to yield, usu. by preventing any supplies from reaching it.

**si·er·ra** /si'erə/ *n* a row, range, or area of sharply-pointed mountains

**si·es·ta** /si'estə/ *n* a short sleep after the midday meal, as is the custom in hot countries

**sieve**[1] /sɪv/ *n* **1** a tool of wire or plastic net on a frame, used for separating large from small solid bits, or solid things from liquid **2 head/memory like a sieve** *infml* a mind that forgets quickly

**sieve**[2] *v* **sieved, sieving** [T] to put through a SIEVE; separate using a sieve: *Sieve the flour before using it.*

**sift** /sɪft/ *v* [I;T] **1** to put (something) through a SIEVE or net **2** [*through*] to make a close examination of (things in a mass or group): *He sifted through his papers to find the lost letter.*

**sigh**[1] /saɪ/ *v* [I] **1** to let out a deep breath slowly and with a sound expressing tiredness, sadness, etc. **2** *lit* (of the wind) to make a sound like this

**sigh**[2] *n* an act or sound of SIGHing: *We all* **heaved** (=made) **a sigh** *of* RELIEF.

**sight**[1] /saɪt/ *n* **1** the power of seeing; EYESIGHT: *Our dog lost his sight in a road accident.* **2** [U] presence in one's view; the range of what can be seen: *He never lets his children out of his sight.*|*The house is hidden from sight by a row of trees.*|*The boat was within sight of land.*|*Keep out of sight!.*|(fig.) *Peace is now in sight.* (=near) **3** [C] something that is seen: *the familiar sight of the postman going along the street* **4** [C *usu. pl.*] something worth seeing: *the sights of London.* –see also SIGHTSEEING **5** [S] something which looks very bad or laughable: *What a sight you are, with paint all over your clothes!* **6** [C *often pl.*] a part of an instrument or weapon which guides the eye in aiming **7** [S] *infml* a lot: *That meal was a sight better than the last one I ate here.*|*She earns a sight more than I do.* **8 at first sight** at the first time of seeing or meeting: *love at first sight* **9 catch sight of** to see for a moment: *I caught sight of her hurrying away.* **10 lose sight of** to stop seeing or being conscious of: *We mustn't lose sight of* (=forget) *our aim.*

**sight**[2] *v* [T] to get a view of, esp. after looking for some time; see for the first time: *Several rare birds have been sighted in this area.* –**sighting** *n*

**sight·ed** /'saɪt½d/ *adj* (of a person) able to see; not blind

**sight·see·ing** /'saɪtsiːɪŋ/ *n* [U] going about as a tourist and visiting places of interest: *We spent a few days sightseeing in Athens.* –**sightseer** *n*

**sign**[1] /saɪn/ *n* **1** a standard mark; something which is seen and represents a known meaning; SYMBOL: *Written music uses lots of signs.* **2** [+ *to-v*] a movement of the body intended to express a meaning; signal: *She put her finger to her lips as a sign to be quiet.* **3** a board or notice giving information, warning, etc.: *Pay attention to the traffic/road signs.* **4** something that shows the presence or coming of something else: *All the signs are that business will get better.|Swollen ankles can be a sign of heart disease.* **5** also **sign of the zodiac**– any of the 12 divisions of the year represented by groups of stars: *What sign were you born under?*

**sign**[2] *v* **1** [I;T] to write (one's name) on (a paper, etc.), esp. for official purposes: *She signed her name on the cheque/signed the cheque.* **2** [I;T *to*] to make a movement as a sign to (someone); signal **3** [I;T +*to-v*] to SIGN **up/on**: *The football team has signed two new players.*

**sign** sthg.↔**away** *v adv* [T] to give up formally (ownership, a claim, a right, etc.), by signing a paper: *He signed away his share in the property.*

**sign for** sthg. *v prep* [T] to sign one's name to show that one has received; formally accept: *The postman asked me to sign for the letter.*

**sign in** *v adv* [I] to record one's name when arriving –opposite **sign out**

**sign on** *v adv* **1** [I;T (=**sign** sbdy.↔**on**)] to (cause to) join a working force by signing a paper; ENLIST (1) **2** [I] to state officially that one is unemployed

**sign out** *v adv* [I] to record one's name when leaving –opposite **sign in**

**sign up** *v adv* [I;T (=**sign** sbdy. ↔**up**) +*to-v*] to (cause to) sign an agreement to take part in something, or to take a job; ENLIST (1): *I've signed up (to take a course) at the local college.*

**sig·nal**[1] /ˈsɪgnəl/ *n* **1** a sound or action understood to give a message: *A red lamp is often a danger signal.|smoke signals|When I look at my watch, it's a signal for us to leave.* **2** a railway apparatus, usu. with coloured lights, near the track to direct train drivers **3**→ TRAFFIC LIGHTS **4** a sound or image sent by radio or television waves: *a strong/weak television signal*

**signal**[2] *v* **-ll-** *BrE*||**-l-** *AmE* **1** [I *to, for*] to give a signal: *She was signalling wildly, waving her arms.* **2** [I;T +*to-v/that*] to express, warn, or tell by a signal or signals: *The policeman signalled (to) the traffic to move forward.|The thief signalled (his friend) that the police were coming.* **3** [T] to be a sign of; MARK[2]: *The defeat signalled the end of the war.*

**signal**[3] *adj* [A] *fml* very clear or very great; OUTSTANDING (1): *a signal failure* **–signally** *adv*

**sig·na·to·ry** /ˈsɪgnətəri||-tori/ *n* **-ries** *fml* any of the people or countries that sign an agreement, esp. one between nations

**sig·na·ture** /ˈsɪgnətʃəʳ/ *n* a person's name written by his/her own hand, at the end of a letter, cheque, official paper, etc.

**sig·nif·i·cance** /sɪgˈnɪfɪkəns/ *n* [S;U] importance; meaning; value: *an industry of great significance to the country* –opposite **insignificance**

**sig·nif·i·cant** /sɪgˈnɪfɪkənt/ *adj* **1** of noticeable importance: *a significant increase in crime* –opposite **insignificant** **2** having a special meaning: *a significant smile* **–significantly** *adv*

**sig·ni·fy** /ˈsɪgnǝ̍faɪ/ *v* **-fied, -fying** *fml* **1** [T +*that*] to be a sign of; mean: *A fever usually signifies that there is something wrong with the body.* **2** [I;T] to express (esp. an opinion) by an action: *They signified their agreement by raising their hands.*

**sign lan·guage** /ˈ· ˌ··/ *n* [U] a system of hand movements for expressing meanings, as used by the DEAF (1) and DUMB (1), by some American Indians, etc.

**sign of the zo·di·ac** /ˌ· · · ˈ···/ *n* see ZODIAC

**sign·post** /ˈsaɪnpəust/ *n* a sign showing directions and distances, e.g. next to a road

**si·lage** /ˈsaɪlɪdʒ/ *n* [U] grass or other plants cut and stored in a SILO (1) for cattle food

**si·lence**[1] /ˈsaɪləns/ *n* [U] **1** absence of sound; stillness: *nothing but silence in the empty house|The silence was broken by a loud cry.* **2** the state of not speaking or making a noise: *She received the bad news in silence.* **3** failure to mention a particular thing: *government silence on the matter*

**silence**[2] *v* **-lenced, -lencing** [T] **1** to cause to stop making a noise: *We silenced the enemy guns.* **2** to force to stop expressing opinions, etc.: *The judge silenced them by putting them in prison.*

**si·lenc·er** /ˈsaɪlənsəʳ/ *n* an apparatus for reducing noise, esp. a part of a petrol engine which fits onto the pipe (**exhaust pipe**) where burnt gases come out

**si·lent** /ˈsaɪlənt/ *adj* **1** not speaking; not using spoken expression: *a silent prayer|silent reading|a silent film* (=one with no sound) **2** free from noise; quiet: *the silent hours of the night* **3** (of a letter in a word) not having a sound; not pronounced: *silent "k" in "know"* **–silently** *adv*

**sil·hou·ette**[1] /ˌsɪluːˈet/ *n* **1** a picture of something in solid black against a background; shadow-like shape of something, esp. of a person seen from the side: *His silhouette appeared on the curtain.* **2 in silhouette** as a dark shape against a light background

**silhouette**[2] *v* **-etted, -etting** [T *usu. pass.*] to cause to appear as a SILHOUETTE

**sil·i·con** /ˈsɪlɪkən/ *n* [U] a simple substance (ELEMENT (1)) that is nonmetallic and found in nature in great quantities

**silicon chip** /ˌ··· ˈ·/ *n* →MICROPROCESSOR

**silk** /sɪlk/ *n* [U] fine thread which is produced by a kind of insect (SILKWORM) and made into cloth: *a dress of the finest silk*

**silk·en** /ˈsɪlkən/ *adj lit* **1** soft, smooth, or shiny like silk; SILKY: *silken hair* **2** made of silk: *silken garments*

**silk·worm** /ˈsɪlkwɜːm||-wɜrm/ *n* an insect (CATERPILLAR) which produces a COCOON of silk

**silk·y** /ˈsɪlki/ *adj* **-ier, -iest** like silk; soft, smooth, or shiny: *the cat's fine silky fur* **–silkiness** *n* [U]

**sill** /sɪl/ *n* the flat piece at the base of an opening or frame, esp. a WINDOWSILL

**sil·ly** /ˈsɪli/ *adj* **-lier, -liest** foolish; laughable; not serious or sensible: *It's silly to go out in the rain if you don't have to.*

**si·lo** /ˈsaɪləu/ *n* **-los** **1** a usu. round tower on a farm for storing SILAGE **2** an underground base from which a ROCKET may be fired

**silt** /sɪlt/ *n* [U] loose sand, mud, etc., carried in running water and then dropped at the entrance to a harbour, etc.

**silt up** *v adv* [I;T (=**silt** sthg.↔**up**)] to fill or become filled with SILT

**sil·ver**[1] /'sɪlvəʳ/ *n* [U] **1** a soft whitish precious metal that is a simple substance (ELEMENT), can be brightly polished, and is used esp. in jewellery and coins **2** coins made of silver or a similar metal: *Could you give me £1 in silver, please?* **3** spoons, forks, dishes, etc., for the table, made of silver or a similar metal

**silver**[2] *adj* **1** made of silver: *Is your ring silver?* **2** like silver in colour: *a silver-haired old man*

**silver birch** /ˌ·· '·/ *n* the common white BIRCH tree

**silver pa·per** /ˌ·· '·· ◂/ also **silver foil**– *n* [U] paper with one bright metallic surface, as used in packets for cigarettes, food, etc.

**sil·ver·smith** /'sɪlvəˌsmɪθ‖-ər-/ *n* a maker of jewellery, etc., in silver

**sil·ver·y** /'sɪlvəri/ *adj* **1** like silver in shine and colour **2** having a pleasant metallic sound

**sim·i·lar** /'sɪmələʳ, 'sɪmɪləʳ/ *adj* like or alike; of the same kind: *bread, cake, and other similar foods|We have similar opinions* –**similarly** *adv*

**sim·i·lar·i·ty** /ˌsɪm$\frac{1}{5}$'lær$\frac{1}{5}$ti/ *n* **-ties 1** [U] the quality of being alike: *How much similarity is there between the two religions?* **2** [C] a point of likeness

**sim·i·le** /'sɪm$\frac{1}{5}$li/ *n* an expression comparing two things, using the words *like* or *as*: *"As white as snow" is a simile.* –compare METAPHOR

**sim·mer**[1] /'sɪməʳ/ *v* [I;T] to (cause to) cook gently in liquid at just below boiling point: *Let the soup simmer.*|(fig.) *simmering with anger/excitement* –see COOK (USAGE)

**simmer down** *v adv* [I] to become calmer; control one's excitement: *Simmer down and stop crying!*

**simmer**[2] *n* [S] a heat just below boiling

**sim·per** /'sɪmpəʳ/ *v* [I] to smile in a silly unnatural way –**simperingly** *adv* –**simper** *n*

**sim·ple** /'sɪmpəl/ *adj* **1** not decorated; plain: *simple but well-prepared food|buildings in a simple style* **2** easy to understand or do; not difficult: *a simple explanation* **3** of the ordinary kind, without special qualities, etc.; not COMPLICATED: *A knife is one of the simplest of tools.|a simple case of stealing* **4** not mixed with anything else; pure: *the simple truth* **5** easily tricked; foolish: *You may be joking, but he's simple enough to believe you.*

**sim·ple·ton** /'sɪmpəltən/ *n now rare* a weak-minded trusting person

**sim·pli·ci·ty** /sɪm'plɪs$\frac{1}{5}$ti/ *n* [U] the state of being simple: *a beautiful simplicity of style|He believes everything with childlike simplicity.*

**sim·pli·fy** /'sɪmpl$\frac{1}{5}$faɪ/ *v* **-fied, -fying** [T] to make plainer, easier, or less full of detail: *Try to simplify your explanation for the children.* –see also OVERSIMPLIFY; compare COMPLICATE –**simplification** /-f$\frac{1}{5}$'keɪʃən/ *n* [U]

**sim·ply** /'sɪmpli/ *adv* **1** in a simple way; easily, clearly, or naturally **2** just; only: *I don't like driving; I do it simply to get to work.* **3** really; very (much): *simply wonderful*

> **SPELLING NOTE**
> Words with the sound /s/ may be spelt **c-**, like **city**, or **ps-**, like **psychology.**

**sim·u·late** /'sɪmjʊleɪt‖-mjə-/ *v* **-lated, -lating** [T] *fml* to give the effect or appearance of; IMITATE: *He shook a sheet of metal to simulate the noise of thunder.* –**simulation** /-'leɪʃən/ *n* [C;U]

**sim·u·lat·ed** /'sɪmjʊleɪt$\frac{1}{5}$d‖-mjə-/ *adj* made to look, feel, etc., like the real thing: *simulated fur*

**sim·ul·ta·ne·ous** /ˌsɪməl'teɪnɪəs‖ˌsaɪ-/ *adj* happening at the same moment: *a flash of lightning and a simultaneous crash of thunder* –**simultaneously** *adv*

**sin**[1] /sɪn/ *n* **1** [C;U] (an example of) disobedience to God; the breaking of holy law: *the sin of pride|to* **commit a sin** –compare CRIME **2** [C] *esp. humor* something that should not be done: *He thinks it's a sin to stay in bed after eight o'clock.*

**sin**[2] *v* **-nn-** [I *against*] to break God's laws; do wrong

**since**[1] /sɪns/ *adv, prep,conj* (with the present tense, or with *have* or *had*) between a point in the past and now: *It's a long time since our last holiday.|Her husband died ten years ago but she's since remarried.|We've been friends (ever) since we left school.|Since leaving Paris, we've visited Brussels and Amsterdam.*–see AGO (USAGE)

**since**[2] *conj* as it is true that: *Since you can't answer the question, I'll ask someone else.* –see Study Notes on page 128

USAGE **Since** and **seeing (that)** are similar to **because** but can only be used of facts that are known to be true: **Since/Seeing that** *you're always late for work* (=this is fact), *I've decided to dismiss you.* But they could not be used in a question like: *Did he lose his job* **because** *he was always late?* (=was that the reason?)

**sin·cere** /sɪn'sɪəʳ/ *adj* having or showing no deceit or falseness; real, true, or honest: *a sincere admiration of his qualities* –opposite **insincere**

**sin·cere·ly** /sɪn'sɪəli‖-ər-/ *adv* in a sincere way; truly: *I sincerely hope that you will be well again soon.* **Yours sincerely** used at the end of a letter, before the signature, addressed to someone by name: *Dear Jane/Ms Anson... Yours sincerely...* –compare FAITHFULLY, TRULY

**sin·cer·i·ty** /sɪn'ser$\frac{1}{5}$ti/ *n* [U] the quality of being sincere; honesty –opposite **insincerity**

**si·ne·cure** /'saɪnɪkjʊəʳ, 'sɪn-/ *n* an easy, well-paid job

**sin·ew** /'sɪnjuː/ *n* [C;U] a strong cord in the body connecting a muscle to a bone; TENDON

**sin·ew·y** /'sɪnjuːi/ *adj* **1** (of meat) containing SINEW; not easy to cut or eat **2** having strong muscles

**sin·ful** /'sɪnfəl/ *adj* **1** wicked **2** *infml* shameful; seriously wrong or bad –**sinfully** *adv* –**sinfulness** *n* [U]

**sing** /sɪŋ/ *v* **sang**/sæŋ/, **sung**/sʌŋ/, **singing 1** [I;T *to, for*] to produce (music, songs, etc.) with the voice: *Birds sing loudest in the early morning.|The children were singing Christmas songs.|I'll try and sing the baby to sleep.* (=make him sleep by singing) **2** [I] to make or be filled with a ringing sound: *My ears are still singing from the noise.* **3** [I;T *of*] *lit* to tell about, or praise in poetry: *Poets sang the king's praises; they sang of his brave deeds.* –**singer** *n*

**sing out** (sthg.) *v adv* [I;T] to sing or call loudly

**sing.** *written abbrev. said as:* singular

**singe** /sɪndʒ/ *v* **singed, singeing** [T] **1** to burn off the ends from (hair, threads, etc.): *He got too near the* fire and singed his beard. **2** to burn lightly on the surface; SCORCH[1] (1): *The iron singed the shirt.*

**sing·ing** /ˈsɪŋɪŋ/ *n* [U] the art or sound of singing: *to study singing|a poor singing voice*

**sin·gle**[1] /ˈsɪŋgəl/ *adj* **1** [A] only one: *A single tree gave shade from the sun.|His single aim was to make money* **2** having only one part; not double or MULTIPLE[1]: *For strong sewing use double, not single thread.* **3** [A] separate; considered by itself: *There's no need to write down every single word I say.* **4** unmarried **5** [A] for only one person: *a single bed* –compare DOUBLE[1] (2) **6** [A] *BrE* ‖ **one-way** *AmE*– (of a ticket) for a trip from one place to another but not back again –opposite (for sense **6**) **return**

**single**[2] *n* **1** *BrE* a SINGLE[1] (6) ticket: *Two singles to London, please.* –compare RETURN[3] **2** a record with only one short song on each side –compare LP

**single-deck·er** /ˌ·· ˈ·· ◂/ *n* a bus with seats on only one level –compare DOUBLE-DECKER

**single file** /ˌ·· ˈ·/ *n, adv* (moving in) a line of people, vehicles, etc., one behind another

**single-hand·ed** /ˌ·· ˈ·· ◂/ *adj,adv* done by one person; without help from others: *a single-handed sailing voyage|He rebuilt his house single-handed.*

**single-mind·ed** /ˌ·· ˈ·· ◂/ *adj* with one clear purpose –**single-mindedly** *adv* [U] –**single-mindedness** *n* [U]

**single** sbdy./sthg. **out** *v adv* **-gled, -gling** [T *for*] to choose from a group, esp. for special treatment: *He was singled out for punishment.*

**sin·gles** /ˈsɪŋgəlz/ *n* **singles** a match, esp. of tennis, with one player against one other –compare DOUBLES

**sin·glet** /ˈsɪŋglɪ̆t/ *n BrE* a man's garment without SLEEVES worn as a shirt when playing some sports

**sin·gly** /ˈsɪŋgli/ *adv* separately; one by one

**sing·song** /ˈsɪŋsɒŋ‖-sɔŋ/ *n* **1** [A;S] a repeated rising and falling of the voice in speaking: *to talk in a singsong (voice)* **2** [C] *BrE* an informal party for singing songs

**sin·gu·lar**[1] /ˈsɪŋgjʊləʳ‖-gjə-/ *adj* **1** (in grammar) of the form representing only one thing: *The noun "mouse" is singular; it is the singular form of "mice".* –compare PLURAL **2** *fml* unusual: *a woman of singular beauty* –**singularity** *n* –**ties** [C;U]

**singular**[2] *n* (a word in) a form representing only one: *"Trousers" has no singular.*

**sin·gu·lar·ly** /ˈsɪŋgjʊləli‖-gjələrli/ *adv fml* particularly; very: *a singularly beautiful woman*

**sin·is·ter** /ˈsɪnɪ̆stəʳ/ *adj* threatening evil: *a sinister look on his face|a sinister-looking crack in the roof*

**sink**[1] /sɪŋk/ *v* **sank** /sæŋk/‖also **sunk** /sʌŋk/ *AmE*, **sunk**‖also **sunken** /sʌŋkən/ *AmE*, **sinking** **1** [I;T] to (cause to) go down below a surface, or to the bottom of water: *This rubber ball won't sink; it floats.|They sank the ship with bombs.|The moon sank below the hills.|This lack of money will sink our plans.* (=make them fail) **2** [I] to go down in number, strength, value, etc.: *The population of the village is slowly sinking.|He's sinking* (=losing strength) *fast and won't live much longer.* **3** [I] to fall, e.g. from lack of strength: *He fainted and sank to the ground.* **4** [T] to dig out or force into the earth: *to sink a well/a mine* SHAFT (5) **5** [T *in, into*] to put (money, labour, etc.) into; INVEST: *I've sunk all my money into buying a new house.* –**sinkable** *adj*

**sink in** *v adv* [I] **1** to become fully understood: *The lesson has sunk in; he won't make the same mistake again.* **2** to enter a solid through the surface: *If the ink sinks in it'll be hard to remove it.*

**sink** (sthg.) **into** sthg. *v prep* [T] to put, force, or go below or into: *The dog sank its teeth into the meat.*

**sink**[2] *n* **1** a large basin in a kitchen, for washing pots, vegetables, etc. –see picture on page 337 **2** *AmE* for WASHBASIN

**sin·ner** /ˈsɪnəʳ/ *n* a person who SINs; one who has disobeyed God

**sin·u·ous** /ˈsɪnjʊəs/ *adj fml* twisting like a snake; full of curves: *a sinuous road through the mountains*

**si·nus** /ˈsaɪnəs/ *n* any of the air-filled spaces in the bones of the face that have an opening into the nose

**sip**[1] /sɪp/ *v* **-pp-** [I;T *at*] to drink, taking only a little at a time: *She sipped politely at her drink.*

**sip**[2] *n* a very small amount of a drink

**si·phon**[1], **syphon** /ˈsaɪfən/ *n* **1** a tube bent so that a liquid is drawn upwards and then downwards through it to a lower level **2** a kind of bottle for holding SODA WATER

**siphon**[2], **syphon** *v* [T *off, out*] to take away by means of a SIPHON[1] (1): *to siphon (out) petrol from a tank*

**sir** /səʳ; *strong* sɜːʳ/ *n* (a respectful address to an older man or one of higher rank, to a male buyer in a shop, etc.): *Thank you, sir.|"Can we go home now, sir?" asked the schoolchildren.*

**Sir** *n* **1** [A] (a title used before the name of a KNIGHT[1] (1) or BARONET): *Sir Harold Wilson|Sir Harold* **2** (used at the beginning of a formal letter): *Dear Sir, ....* –compare MADAM

**sire**[1] /ˈsaɪəʳ/ *n old use* (a form of address to a king)

**sire**[2] *v* [T] **sired, siring** (esp. of a horse) to be the father of: *This horse has sired several race winners.*

**si·ren** /ˈsaɪərən/ *n* **1** an apparatus for making a loud warning sound, used on ships, police cars, etc. **2** a dangerous beautiful woman

**sir·loin** /ˈsɜːlɔɪn‖ˈsɜr-/ also **sirloin steak**– *n* [C;U] (a piece of) meat from cattle (BEEF) cut from the best part of the lower back

**sis·sy**, **cissy** /ˈsɪsi/ *n,adj* **-sies** *infml* (a boy who looks or acts) like a girl; (one who seems) silly and unmanly

**sis·ter** /ˈsɪstəʳ/ *n* **1** [C] a female relative with the same parents: *Joan and Mary are sisters.|Joan is Mary's sister.* –see picture on page 217 **2** [A] (of women or things considered female) in the same group; fellow: *a sister ship* **3** [A;C] *BrE* (a title for) a nurse in charge of a department (WARD) of a hospital: *Sister Brown|the night sister* **4** [A;C] (a title for) a woman member of a religious group, esp. a NUN: *Sister Mary Grace|a Christian sister* –compare BROTHER –**sisterly** *adj*

**sis·ter·hood** /ˈsɪstəhʊd‖-ər-/ *n* **1** [U] a sisterly relationship between women **2** [C +*sing./pl. v*] a society of women leading a religious life –compare BROTHERHOOD

**sister-in-law** /ˈ··· ˌ·/ *n* **sisters-in-law** **1** the sister of one's husband or wife **2** the wife of one's brother **3** the wife of the brother of one's husband or wife –compare BROTHER-IN-LAW –see picture on page 217

**sit** /sɪt/ *v* **sat**/sæt/, **sitting** **1** [I] to rest in a position with the upper body upright and supported at the bottom of the back, e.g. on a chair or other seat: *He sat at his desk working.*|*sitting by the fire* –see picture on page 669 **2** [I;T *down*] to (cause to) go into this position; (cause to) take a seat: *Sit down please, children.*|*She sat the baby (down) on the grass.* –compare STAND **3** [I] (of an animal or bird) to be in or go into a position with the tail end of the body resting on a surface **4** [I] to lie; rest; have a place: *books sitting on the shelf*|*a village sitting on the hill* **5** [I *on*] to have a position in an official body: *He sits on several committees.* **6** [I] (of an official body) to have a meeting: *The court sat until all the arguments had been heard.* **7** [I;T *for*] *BrE* to take (a written examination): *to sit (for)* one's A LEVELS **8 sit tight** *infml* to keep in the same position; not move: *If your car breaks down, sit tight and wait for the police.*

USAGE 1 You **sit** *at* a table or desk; *on* a chair, a SOFA, a bicycle, or the ground; *in* a car, a garden or an armchair. 2 Do not confuse **sit** [I], and **seat** [T], which means "to provide a seat or seats for": *He* **sat** *near the front of the hall.*|*This hall will* **seat** *500 people.* A third verb, **set** [T], can mean "to place in a sitting position": *He* **set** *the child on his knee*

**sit about/around**– *v adv* [I] *infml* to do nothing, esp. while waiting or while others act

**sit back** *v adv* [I] to take no more active part; rest: *to sit back and enjoy the results of hard work*

**sit in** *v adv* [I] **1** [*for,as*] to take another's regular place, e.g. in a meeting or office job: *The president is ill so the secretary is sitting in for her at the meeting.* **2** to take part in a SIT-IN

**sit on** sthg. *v prep* [T] *infml* to delay taking action on: *He's been sitting on my letter for months.*

**sit** sthg.↔**out** *v adv* [T] **1** to remain seated during (a dance); not take part in **2** also **sit through**– to stay until the end of (a performance), esp. without enjoyment

**sit up** *v adv* **1** [I;T (=**sit** sbdy. **up**)] to (help to) rise to a sitting position: *The loud noise made her sit up in bed.*|*She sat the old man up in bed.* **2** [I *for*] to stay up late; not go to bed: *Don't sit up (for me) if I'm late.*

**si·tar** /ˈsɪtɑːʳ, sɪˈtɑːʳ/ *n* a N Indian stringed musical instrument

**site¹** /saɪt/ *n* **1** a place where something of special interest existed or happened: *the site of the Battle of Waterloo* **2** a piece of ground for building on: *the site of a planned new town*

**site²** *v* **sited, siting** [T *usu. pass.*] to place on a SITE¹ (2); LOCATE (2): *a beautifully sited house*

**sit-in** /ˈ· ·/ *n* a method of expressing dissatisfaction and anger in which a group of people enter a public place, stop its usual business, and refuse to leave: *There's a sit-in at the local hospital because the government is trying to close it.* –see also SIT **in**

**sit·ting¹** /ˈsɪtɪŋ/ *n* **1** a period of time spent seated in a chair: *I read the book in/at a single sitting.* **2** a serving of a meal for a number of people at one time: *two sittings for dinner, one at seven and one at eight* **3** a meeting of an official body; SESSION (1)

> **SPELLING NOTE**
> Words with the sound /s/ may be spelt **c-**, like **city**, or **ps-**, like **psychology.**

**sitting²** *adj* [A] **1** that now has a seat on an official body, such as Parliament: *the sitting member for this area* **2** *BrE* that now lives in a place: *a sitting* TENANT

**sitting room** /ˈ·· ·/ *n esp. BrE* for LIVING ROOM

**sit·u·at·ed** /ˈsɪtʃueɪtᵻd/ *adj* [F] in a particular place; LOCATED (2)

**sit·u·a·tion** /ˌsɪtʃuˈeɪʃən/ *n* **1** a position or condition at the moment; state of affairs: *the political situation* **2** *fml* a job: *the "Situations Vacant" advertisements in the newspaper*

**six** /sɪks/ *determiner,n,pron* **1** (the number) 6 **2 at sixes and sevens** *infml* confused or undecided **–sixth** *determiner,n,pron,adv*

**six·pence** /ˈsɪkspəns/ *n* [C;U] (in Britain until 1971) (a coin worth) the sum of six pennies; 6d

**six·teen** /ˌsɪkˈstiːn◂/ *determiner,n,pron* (the number) 16 **–sixteenth** *determiner,n,pron,adv*

**sixth form** /ˈ· ·/ *n* [C +*sing.pl. v*] the highest level in a British school; the group of students preparing to take A LEVELS

**sixth sense** /ˌ· ˈ·/ *n* [S] an ability to see or know that does not come from the five senses; INTUITION

**six·ty** /ˈsɪksti/ *determiner,n,pron* **-ties** (the number) 60 **–sixtieth** *determiner,n,pron,adv*

**siz·a·ble**, **sizeable** /ˈsaɪzəbəl/ *adj* rather large; CONSIDERABLE: *a sizeable income*

**size** /saɪz/ *n* **1** [C;U] (a degree of) bigness or smallness: *What's the size of your back garden?*|*rocks of all sizes* **2** [U] bigness: *The company is able to keep its prices down simply because of its size.* **3** [C] any of a set of measures in which objects such as clothes are made: *I take a size 44 shoe.*|*What size bottle would you like? The small size is 25p and the large size is 45p.* **4 -sized** also **-size**– of a certain size or number: *small-sized*|*a good-sized* (=large) *crowd*

**size** sbdy./sthg.↔**up** *v adv* **sized, sizing** [T] to form an opinion about; get an idea of: *to size up the goods for sale*

**siz·zle** /ˈsɪzəl/ *v* **-zled, -zling** [I] to make a sound as of food cooking in hot fat: *meat sizzling in the pan*

**skate¹** /skeɪt/ *n* **1** also **ice skate**– either of a pair of metal blades fitted to the bottom of shoes for moving swiftly on ice **2**→ ROLLER SKATE **3 get/put one's skates on** *infml* to hurry

**skate²** *v* **skated, skating** [I] to move on SKATES: *to skate across the lake*|*to go skating* **–skater** *n*

**skate over/round** sthg.– *v prep* [T] to avoid treating seriously; GLOSS OVER

**skate³** *n* **skate** *or* **skates** [C;U] a large flat sea fish

**skein** /skeɪn/ *n* [*of*] a loosely wound length of thread or YARN (1)

**skel·e·ton** /ˈskelᵻtn/ *n* **1** [C] the framework of bones in a human or animal body **2** [C] something forming a framework: *the steel skeleton of a tall building* **3** [A] enough to keep an operation going, and no more: *a skeleton rail service*

**skep·tic** /ˈskeptɪk/ *n AmE* for SCEPTIC

**sketch¹** /sketʃ/ *n* **1** a rough drawing: *Rembrandt's sketches for his paintings* **2** a short description in words: *a sketch of life in the 1890s* **3** a short informal usu. humorous piece of acting

**sketch²** *v* **1** [I;T] to draw SKETCHES¹ (1) or make a sketch of **2** [T *in,out*] to describe roughly with few details: *to sketch in/out the main points of our plan*

**sketch·y** /ˈsketʃi/ *adj* **-ier, -iest** not thorough or complete; without details; rough: *a sketchy memory* –**sketchily** *adv* –**sketchiness** *n* [U]
**skew·er**[1] /ˈskjuːəʳ/ *n* a long wooden or metal pin for holding pieces of meat together while cooking
**skewer**[2] *v* [T] to fasten or make a hole through, esp. with a SKEWER[1]: *Skewer the chicken before cooking.*
**ski**[1] /skiː/ *n* **skis** either of a pair of long thin narrow pieces of wood, plastic, or metal, fastened to a boot and used for travelling on snow
**ski**[2] *v* **skied, skiing** [I] to go on SKIS: *to go skiing|to ski down a hill* –see also WATER SKIING –**skier** *n*
**skid**[1] /skɪd/ *v* **-dd-** [I] (of a vehicle or a wheel) to slip sideways out of control
**skid**[2] *n* an act or path of SKIDding: *The car went into a skid|skid marks on the road*
**skiff** /skɪf/ *n* a small light boat for rowing or sailing by one person
**skil·ful** *BrE*||**skillful** *AmE* /ˈskɪlfəl/ *adj* having or showing skill –**skilfully** *adv*
**skill** /skɪl/ *n* [C;U] practical knowledge and power; (an) ability to do something (well): *a pilot of great skill|Reading and writing are different skills.* –see GENIUS (USAGE)
**skilled** /skɪld/ *adj* [*in*] having or needing skill: *a skilled job/electrician* –opposite **unskilled**
**skil·let** /ˈskɪlɪ̆t/ *n AmE* for FRYING PAN
**skim** /skɪm/ *v* **-mm- 1** [T *off*] to remove (floating fat or solids) from the surface of a liquid: *to skim (off) the cream from the milk* **2** [I;T *through*] to read quickly to get the main ideas; SCAN[1] (2) **3** [I; T] to (cause to) move swiftly over (a surface): *to skim stones over a lake|birds skimming over the waves*
**skimp** /skɪmp/ *v* [I;T *on*] to spend, or use less (of) than is really needed: *to skimp on food to save money*
**skimp·y** /ˈskɪmpi/ *adj* **-ier, -iest** not being enough; almost too small: *a skimpy meal/dress* –**skimpily** *adv* –**skimpiness** *n* [U]
**skin**[1] /skɪn/ *n* **1** [U] the natural outer covering of an animal or human body, from which hair may grow: *a skin disease|Babies have soft skin.* **2** [C;U] this part of an animal body used as leather, fur, etc.: *a sheep-skin coat* **3** [C] a natural outer covering of some fruits and vegetables; PEEL: *banana skins* **4** [C;U] the solid surface that forms over some liquids: *Paint in a tin forms a skin when the lid is left off.* **5 by the skin of one's teeth** *infml* narrowly; only just: *We caught the train by the skin of our teeth.* **6 –skinned** having a certain type or colour of skin: *pale-skinned|smooth-skinned* –see also THICK-SKINNED
**skin**[2] *v* **-nn-** [T] to remove the skin from: *to skin a rabbit/an onion*
**skin-deep** /ˌ· ˈ·◂/ *adj* not deep or lasting: *Their differences of opinion are only skin-deep.*
**skin-dive** /ˈ· ·/ *v* **-dived, -diving** [I] to swim under water without heavy breathing apparatus or a protective suit: *to go skin-diving* –compare FROGMAN –**skin diver** *n* –**skin diving** *n* [U]
**skin·flint** /ˈskɪnˌflɪnt/ *n derog* a person who is not generous; MISER
**skin·head** /ˈskɪnhed/ *n* (in Britain) a youth (usu. a boy) with his hair cut very short
**skin·ny** /ˈskɪni/ *adj* **-nier, -niest** *derog* thin; without much flesh –see THIN (USAGE)
**skint** /skɪnt/ *adj* [F] *BrE infml* completely without money; BROKE[1]
**skin-tight** /ˌ· ˈ·◂/ *adj* (of clothes) fitting tightly against the body
**skip**[1] /skɪp/ *v* **-pp- 1** [I] to move in a light dancing way, with quick steps and jumps: *The little boy skipped along at his mother's side.* –see picture on page 669 **2** [I] to move in no fixed order: *The speaker kept skipping from one subject to another.* **3** [I;T] to pass over or leave out: *to skip (over) the uninteresting parts of a book|to skip a meeting/a meal* **4** [I] to jump over a rope passed repeatedly beneath one's feet, as a game
**skip**[2] *n* a light quick stepping and jumping movement
**skip**[3] *n BrE* a builder's large metal container for old bricks, wood, etc., to be taken away
**skip·per** /ˈskɪpəʳ/ *n infml* a captain of a ship, sports team, etc. –**skipper** *v* [T] *Smith skippered the team.*
**skir·mish**[1] /ˈskɜːmɪʃ||-ɜr-/ *n* **1** a fight between small groups of soldiers, ships, etc. –compare FIXED BATTLE **2** a slight exchange of arguments between opponents
**skirmish**[2] *v* [I *with*] to fight in a SKIRMISH[1]
**skirt**[1] /skɜːt||skɜrt/ *n* **1** a woman's outer garment that fits around the waist and hangs down –see picture on page 563 **2** a part of a coat or dress that hangs below the waist
**skirt**[2] *v* [T] to be or go around the outside of: *a road skirting the town*|(fig.) *Her speech skirted* (=avoided) *all the really important questions.*
**skirting board** /ˈ·· ·/ *n* [C;U] *BrE* (a) board fixed along the base of a wall where it meets the floor of a room –see picture on page 355
**skit** /skɪt/ *n* [*on*] a short humorous acted-out scene, often copying and making fun of something
**skit·tle** /ˈskɪtl/ *n* a bottle-shaped object used in SKITTLES
**skit·tles** /ˈskɪtlz/ *n* [U] an English game in which a player tries to knock down SKITTLEs by throwing a ball at them
**skive** /skaɪv/ *v* **skived, skiving** [I *off*] *BrE infml* to avoid work, often by staying out of the way of others who are working –**skiver** *n*
**skiv·vy** /ˈskɪvi/ *n* **-vies** *BrE derog* a servant who does only the unpleasant jobs in a house
**skulk** /skʌlk/ *v* [I] to move about secretly, through fear or for some evil purpose
**skull** /skʌl/ *n* **1** the bone of the head which encloses the brain **2 skull and crossbones** a sign for death or danger, used esp. on PIRATE[1] (1) flags in former times
**skull·cap** /ˈskʌlkæp/ *n* a simple closefitting cap for the top of the head
**skunk** /skʌŋk/ *n* a small black and white N American animal which gives out an unpleasant strong-smelling liquid when attacked
**sky** /skaɪ/ *n* **skies 1** [C;U] the upper air; the space above the earth: *The sky turned dark as the storm came near.|a bit of blue sky between the clouds|sunny skies* –compare HEAVEN **2 The sky's the limit** *infml* There is no upper limit
**sky blue** /ˌ· ˈ·◂/ *n* [U] the pleasant bright blue colour of a clear sunny sky –**skyblue** *adj*
**sky-high** /ˌ· ˈ·◂/ *adv,adj infml* very high; to a very high level: *Prices have gone sky-high.*

**sky·lark** /ˈskaɪlɑːk‖-lɑrk/ *n* small bird (LARK) that sings as it flies up

**sky·light** /ˈskaɪlaɪt/ *n* a window in a roof –see picture on page 297

**sky·scrap·er** /ˈskaɪˌskreɪpəʳ/ *n* a very tall city building

**slab** /slæb/ *n* a thick flat piece of metal, stone, food, etc.: *a slab of cake/cheese/cement*

**slack**[1] /slæk/ *adj* **1** (of a rope, wire, etc.) not pulled tight –compare TAUT **2** not firm; weak; loose: *slack laws/control* **3** not busy or active: *Business is slack just now.* **4** not properly careful or attentive: *You've been slack in your work recently.* **–slackly** *adv* **–slackness** *n* [U]

**slack**[2] *v* [I] to be lazy; avoid work or not work quickly enough: *You're always slacking!* **–slacker** *n*

**slack**[3] *n* [U] the part of a rope, wire, etc., that hangs loose: *Pull the rope tight to* **take up/in the slack**. (=make the rope tighter)

**slack·en** /ˈslækən/ *v* [I;T *off, up*] to make or become SLACK[1]; reduce in activity, force, or tightness: *The train slackened speed.|Slacken (up) the tent ropes before it rains.* –compare TIGHTEN

**slacks** /slæks/ *n* [P] trousers, esp. of an informal kind –see PAIR (USAGE)

**slag** /slæg/ *n* [U] waste material left when metal is separated from its natural rock

**slain** /sleɪn/ *v past participle of* SLAY

**slake** /sleɪk/ *v* **slaked, slaking** [T] *fml* to satisfy (thirst) with a drink; QUENCH

**slam**[1] /slæm/ *v* **-mm- 1** [I;T] to shut loudly and violently: *Please don't slam the door.|The door slammed (shut).* **2** [T] to push, move, etc., quickly and violently: *He slammed the papers down on the desk and angrily walked out.* **3** [T] (used in newspapers) to attack with words: *"Minister slams Local Government Spending."*

**slam**[2] *n* [S] the act or loud noise of a door closing violently: *He shut the door with a slam.*

**slan·der**[1] /ˈslɑːndəʳ‖ˈslæn-/ *n* [C;U] (the offence of making) an intentionally false spoken report, story, etc., which unfairly damages the good opinion held about a person by others –compare LIBEL

**slander**[2] *v* [T] to speak SLANDER against; harm by making a false statement **–slanderous** *adj*

**slang** /slæŋ/ *n* [U] language that is not usu. acceptable in serious speech or writing; very informal words and expressions, often as used by a particular group: *Slang often goes in and out of fashion quickly.|schoolboy/criminal slang|* "SKINT" *and* "BROKE" *are slang words for "having no money"*.

**slant**[1] /slɑːnt‖slænt/ *v* **1** [I;T] to put or be at an angle; (cause to) SLOPE: *The roof slants upwards from left to right.* **2** [T] to express (facts, a report, etc.) in a way favourable to a particular opinion: *The newspaper report was slanted towards the unions.*

**slant**[2] *n* **1** [S] a SLANTing direction or position: *a steep upward slant|a line drawn at/on a slant* **2** [C] a particular way of looking at or expressing (news or facts): *an interesting new slant on the presidential elections*

**SPELLING NOTE**
Words with the sound /s/ may be spelt **c-**, like **city**, or **ps-**, like **psychology**.

**slap**[1] /slæp/ *n* a quick blow with the flat part of the hand: *She gave him a slap on the cheek.*

**slap**[2] *v* **-pp-** [T] **1** to strike quickly with the flat part of the hand: *to slap someone on the face/slap someone's face* –see picture on page 669 **2** to place thickly, roughly, or carelessly: *to slap paint on a wall*

**slap**[3] *adv* [*adv* + *prep*] *infml* directly; right; SMACK[3]: *The car ran slap into the shop window.*

**slap·dash** /ˈslæpdæʃ/ *adj* careless and hurried: *a slapdash piece of work*

**slap·stick** /ˈslæpˌstɪk/ *n* [U] humorous acting (COMEDY) that depends on fast action and simple jokes

**slap-up** /ˈ· ·/ *adj* [A] *BrE infml* (of food) fine and esp. fancy: *a slap-up meal*

**slash**[1] /slæʃ/ *v* **1** [I;T *at*] to cut with long sweeping violent strokes: *The cinema seats had been slashed.* **2** [T] to reduce (an amount, price, etc.) steeply: *"This week only– prices slashed!"* (shop advertisement)

**slash**[2] *n* **1** a long sweeping cut or blow **2** a straight cut making an opening in a garment

**slat** /slæt/ *n* a thin flat piece of wood, plastic, etc., esp. in furniture or VENETIAN BLINDS **–slatted** *adj*

**slate**[1] /sleɪt/ *n* **1** [U] heavy rock easily split into flat thin pieces **2** [C] a small piece of this used for covering a roof **3** [C] an imaginary record of past mistakes, disagreements, etc.: *Let's forget our quarrel and start again with* **a clean slate.**

**slate**[2] *v* **slated, slating** [T] to cover (a roof) with SLATES[1] (2)

**slaugh·ter**[1] /ˈslɔːtəʳ/ *n* [U] **1** the killing of many people or animals, esp. cruelly or wrongly; MASSACRE **2** the killing of animals for meat

**slaughter**[2] *v* [T] **1** to kill (esp. many people) cruelly or wrongly; MASSACRE: *people needlessly slaughtered* **2** to kill (animals) for food; BUTCHER –see KILL (USAGE) **3** *infml* to defeat severely in a game

**slaugh·ter·house** /ˈslɔːtəhaʊs‖-ər-/ also **abattoir**– *n* a building where animals are killed for meat

**slave**[1] /sleɪv/ *n* **1** a person owned in law by another; servant without personal freedom **2** [*of, to*] a person completely in the control of another person or thing: *a slave to fashion/drink*

**slave**[2] *v* **slaved, slaving** [I *away*] to work like a slave; work hard: *I've been slaving away in the office.*

**slave driv·er** /ˈ· ˌ··/ *n infml* a person who makes other people work very hard

**slav·er** /ˈslævəʳ/ *v* [I] to let liquid (SALIVA) come out of the mouth; DROOL

**sla·ve·ry** /ˈsleɪvəri/ *n* [U] **1** the system of having slaves **2** the condition of being a slave

**Sla·vic** /ˈslɑːvɪk, ˈslæ-/ also **Slavonic** /sləˈvɒnɪk‖-ˈvɑ-/– *adj* of or concerning the E European people (**Slavs**), including Russians, Czechs, Poles, Yugoslavs, etc.

**slav·ish** /ˈsleɪvɪʃ/ *adj* **1** slavelike; showing complete dependence on others **2** copying or copied very closely from something else; not fresh or changed: *a slavish translation* **–slavishly** *adv*

**slay** /sleɪ/ *v* **slew** /sluː/, **slain** /sleɪn/, **slaying** *esp. AmE or lit* to kill violently; murder **–slayer** *n*

**slea·zy** /ˈsliːzi/ *adj* **-zier, -ziest** cheap, dirty, and poor-looking: *a sleazy hotel* **–sleaziness** *n* [U]

**sled** /sled/ *n,v* → SLEDGE

**sledge¹** sled·/ *n* a vehicle for sliding along snow or ice, used in play and sport or for carrying heavy loads –compare SLEIGH

**sledge²** *v* **sledged, sledging 1** [I] *BrE* to go down slopes on a SLEDGE¹: *to* **go sledging 2** [I;T] *AmE* to travel or carry on a SLEDGE¹

**sledge·ham·mer** /ˈsled·ˌhæməʳ/ *n* a large heavy hammer used to drive in posts, break stones, etc.

**sleek** /sliːk/ *adj* **1** (esp. of hair or fur) smooth and shining, as from good health and care **2** (too) neat or fashionable in appearance –**sleekness** *n* [U]

**sleep¹** /sliːp/ *n* [S;U] **1** (a period of) the natural resting state of unconsciousness of the body: *I haven't had enough sleep.|I need a good (night's) sleep.* **2 get to sleep** to succeed in sleeping: *I couldn't get to sleep last night.* **3 go to sleep** to begin to sleep; fall asleep **4 put to sleep: a** *euph* to kill (a suffering animal) mercifully **b** *infml* to make (a person) unconscious, e.g. for an operation

**sleep²** *v* **slept** /slept/, **sleeping 1** [I] to rest in sleep: *He likes to sleep for an hour in the afternoon.|I didn't sleep well last night.* **2** [T] to provide beds or sleeping-places for (a number of people): *The back seat of the car folds down to sleep two.*

**sleep in** *v adv* [I] **1** to sleep late in the morning: *I slept in and missed an important meeting.* –compare LIE¹ **in 2** to sleep at one's place of work: *a big house with two servants who slept in*

**sleep** sthg.↔**off** *v adv* [T] *v* to get rid of the effect of by sleeping: *to sleep off a big dinner*

**sleep on** sthg. *v prep* [T] to delay deciding on (a question) until the next day; spend a night considering

**sleep through** sthg. *v prep* [T] not to wake up during; be asleep and miss hearing, seeing, etc.

**sleep together** *v adv* [I] *euph* (of two people) to have sex

**sleep with** sbdy. *v prep* [T] *euph* to have sex with

**sleep·er** /ˈsliːpəʳ/ *n* **1** a person sleeping: *a heavy sleeper* (=difficult to wake up) **2** *BrE*‖**tie** *AmE*– a heavy piece of wood, metal, etc., supporting a railway track –see picture on page 501 **3** a train with beds

**sleeping bag** /ˈ·· ·/ *n* a large warm bag for sleeping in, e.g. when camping

**sleeping pill** /ˈ·· ·/ also **sleeping tablet**– *n* a PILL which helps a person to sleep

**sleep·less** /ˈsliːpləs/ *adj* **1** not providing sleep: *a sleepless night* **2** esp. *lit* not able to sleep: *He lay sleepless on his bed.* –**sleeplessness** *n* [U]

**sleep·walk·er** /ˈsliːpˌwɔːkəʳ/ *n v* a person who walks about while asleep –**sleepwalking** *n* [U]

**sleep·y** /ˈsliːpi/ *adj* **-ier, -iest 1** tired and ready for sleep **2** quiet; inactive or slow-moving: *a sleepy country town* –**sleepily** *adv* –**sleepiness** *n* [U]

**sleet¹** /sliːt/ *n* [U] partly frozen rain –see WEATHER (USAGE) –**sleety** *adj* **-ier, -iest**

**sleet²** *v* [*it* +I] (of SLEET) to fall

**sleeve** /sliːv/ *n* **1** a part of a garment for covering an arm: *a dress with short/long sleeves* –see picture on page 563 **2** *BrE* ‖ **jacket** *AmE*– a stiff envelope for keeping a GRAMOPHONE record in **3 have/keep something up one's sleeve** to keep something secret for use at the right time in the future **4 -sleeved** having sleeves of a certain length or shape: *a short-sleeved shirt* –**sleeveless** *adj*

**sleigh** /sleɪ/ *n* a vehicle which slides along snow and is pulled by a horse –compare SLEDGE

**sleight of hand** /ˌslaɪt əv ˈhænd/ *n* [U] skill and quickness of the hands in doing tricks

**slen·der** /ˈslendəʳ/ *n* **1** delicately or gracefully thin; SLIM: *a slender woman/tree* –see THIN (USAGE) **2** slight; hardly enough: *only the slenderest chance of success* –**slenderness** *n* [U]

**slept** /slept/ *v past tense & participle of* SLEEP

**sleuth** /sluːθ/ *n humor* for DETECTIVE

**slew¹** *BrE*‖**slue** *AmE* /sluː/ *v* [I;T *round, around*] to (cause to) turn violently –compare SWERVE

**slew²** *v past tense of* SLAY

**slice¹** /slaɪs/ *n* **1** [*of*] a thin flat piece cut from something: *a slice of bread|Cut the cake into slices.*|(fig.) *The workers are hoping for a slice* (=a share) *of the company's profits.* –see picture on page 449 **2** a kitchen tool for lifting and serving pieces of food **3** (in sports like GOLF and tennis) a shot which makes the ball move away from a straight course

**slice²** *v* **sliced, slicing 1** [T *up*] to cut into SLICES¹ (1): *to slice up a cake|A loaf of sliced bread, please.* **2** [I;T *into*] to cut with a knife: *He sliced (into) his fingers by accident.* **3** [I;T] to hit (a ball) with a SLICE¹ (3)

**slick¹** /slɪk/ *adj* **1** clever or effective, but often not honest: *a slick salesman* **2** spoken too easily to be right or true: *slick excuses* –**slickly** *adv* –**slickness** *n* [U]

**slick²** *n* → OIL SLICK

**slick** sthg.↔**down** *v adv* [T] to make (esp. hair) flat and shiny with water, oil, etc.

**slide¹** /slaɪd/ *v* **slid** /slɪd/, **sliding 1** [I;T] to (cause to) go smoothly over a surface: *He slid along the ice.|He slid his glass across the table.* **2** [I] to go silently and unnoticed; slip: *She slid out of the room when no one was looking.* **3 let something slide** *infml* to pay no attention to something, esp. though laziness

**slide²** *n* **1** a slipping movement over a surface: *The car went into a slide on the ice.* **2** an apparatus for sliding down: *a children's playground slide* **3** a fall; downward turn: *a rockslide* (=a sudden fall of rocks down a hill)|*to stop the slide in living standards* **4** a piece of film in a frame for passing light through to show a picture: *They showed slides of their holiday.|a slide show* **5** a small glass plate to put an object on for seeing under a microscope **6** also **hair slide**– a small fastener used to keep a girl's hair in place

**sliding scale** /ˌ·· ˈ·/ *n* a system of pay, taxes, etc., calculated by rates which may vary according to changing conditions

**slight¹** /slaɪt/ *adj* **1** small in degree; not considerable: *a slight pain/improvement* **2** not strong-looking; thin and delicate: *a rather slight old lady* **3 in the slightest** (only used in NEGATIVES¹ (1), questions, etc.) at all: *"Do you mind if I open the window?" "Not in the slightest: please do."* –**slightness** *n* [U]

**slight²** *v* [T] to treat without respect, or as if unimportant –**slightingly** *adv*

**slight³** *n* a SLIGHTing act; INSULT: *He took it as a slight when nobody noticed him..*

**slight·ly** /ˈslaɪtli/ *adv* **1** to a small degree; a little: *slightly drunk* **2** in a SLIGHT¹ (2) way

**slim[1]** /slɪm/ *adj* **-mm- 1** (esp. of people) attractively thin; not fat –see THIN (USAGE) **2** of hope, probability, etc.) poor; slight: *Our chances of winning are slim.* **–slimness** *n* [U]

**slim[2]** *v* **-mm-** [I] to make oneself SLIM[1] (1); get thinner: *I don't want any cake; I'm slimming/trying to slim.* **–slimmer** *n* **–slimming** *n* [U]

**slime** /slaɪm/ *n* [U] nasty, bad-smelling mud or sticky liquid

**slim·y** /ˈslaɪmi/ *adj* **-ier, -iest 1** like, being, or covered with SLIME; unpleasantly slippery **2** insincerely humble: *a slimy manner* **–sliminess** *n* [U]

**sling[1]** /slɪŋ/ *v* **slung** /slʌŋ/, **slinging** [T] **1** to throw, esp. carelessly or with effort: *He slung his coat over his shoulder.|The noisy children were slung out of the class.* **2** to move or hang with a rope, etc.: *The line of flags was slung up between two trees.*

**sling[2]** *n* **1** a piece of cloth for hanging from the neck to support a damaged arm or hand **2** a length of cord with a piece of leather in the middle, for throwing stones

**slink** /slɪŋk/ *v* **slunk**/slʌŋk/, **slinking** [I] to move quietly and secretly, as if ashamed: *to slink away*

**slip[1]** /slɪp/ *v* **-pp- 1** [I] to slide out of place or fall by sliding: *The old lady slipped and fell on the ice.|The hammer slipped and hit my fingers instead of the nail.* **2** [I;T] to move smoothly, secretly, or unnoticed: *She slipped into/out of the room when no one was looking.|As the years slipped by/past, I thought less about her.* **3** [I;T] to put on or take off (a garment): *Slip into/Slip on some old clothes, and come and help me in the garden.* **4** [I] to get worse or lower: *He has slipped in my opinion since I found out more about him.|Standards are slipping in this hotel.* **5** [T] to give secretly: *He slipped the waiter £1 to get a good table.* **6 let slip: a** to fail to take (a chance, offer, etc.) **b** to say without intending **7 slip a disc** to get a SLIPPED DISC **8 slip one's mind** to be forgotten or unnoticed: *I'm sorry I forgot your birthday; it completely slipped my mind.*

**slip up** *v adv* [I] to make a slight mistake: *The secretary slipped up and the letter was never sent.* –see also SLIP-UP

**slip[2]** *n* **1** an act of slipping or sliding **2** a usu. slight mistake: *"Too" was a* **slip of the pen;** *I meant to write "to".* –see ERROR (USAGE) **3** a woman's undergarment like a short dress not covering the arms or neck –see also GYMSLIP **4** → SLIPWAY **5 give someone the slip** *infml* to escape from someone, esp. someone who is chasing one

**slip[3]** *n* **1** a small piece of paper **2 slip of a boy/girl** *becoming rare* a small thin boy or girl

**slip·knot** /ˈslɪpnɒt‖-nɑt/ *n* a knot that can be tightened round something by pulling one of its ends

**slipped disc** /ˌ· ˈ·/ *n* [S] a painful displacement of one of the connecting parts in the human back

**slip·per** /ˈslɪpəʳ/ *n* a light shoe with the top made of soft material, worn indoors: *a pair of slippers*

**slip·per·y** /ˈslɪpəri/ *adj* **-ier, -iest 1** difficult to hold or to stand on, drive on, etc., without slipping: *a slippery road* **2** *infml* not to be trusted; SHIFTY: *a slippery character* **–slipperiness** *n* [U]

> **SPELLING NOTE**
> Words with the sound /s/ may be spelt **c-**, like **city**, or **ps-**, like **psychology.**

**slip road** /ˈ· ·/ *n BrE* a road for driving onto or off a MOTORWAY

**slip·shod** /ˈslɪpʃɒd‖-ʃɑd/ *adj* careless; not exact or thorough: *a slipshod piece of work*

**slip-up** /ˈ· ·/ *n* a slight mistake –see also SLIP[1] **up**

**slip·way** /ˈslɪpweɪ/ *n* also **slip**– a sloping track for moving ships into or out of water

**slit[1]** /slɪt/ *v* **slit, slitting** [T] to make a SLIT[2] in; make a cut along: *to slit an envelope (open) with a knife* –compare SLOT[1] (1)

**slit[2]** *n* a narrow cut or opening

**slith·er** /ˈslɪðəʳ/ *v* [I] **1** to move in a slipping or twisting way like a snake **2** to slide unsteadily: *She slithered across the ice.*

**sliv·er** /ˈslɪvəʳ/ *n* [*of*] a small thin sharp piece cut or torn off: *a sliver of glass from the broken window*

**slob** /slɒb‖slɑb/ *n infml* a rude, lazy, or carelessly-dressed person

**slob·ber** /ˈslɒbəʳ‖ˈslɑ-/ *v* [I;T] to let (liquid) fall from the lips: *a dog slobbering at the sight of food*

**slog[1]** /slɒg‖slɑg/ *v* **-gg-** *BrE* [I] to do hard dull work: *to slog away at a job* **–slogger** *n*

**slog[2]** *n BrE* [S;U] (a time or course of) hard dull work without stopping: *School is a hard slog.*

**slo·gan** /ˈsləʊgən/ *n* a short phrase expressing a usu. political or advertising message –compare MOTTO

**sloop** /sluːp/ *n* **1** a kind of small sailing ship **2** a small armed ship such as a CUTTER (1)

**slop** /slɒp‖slɑp/ *v* **-pp- 1** [T] to cause some of (a liquid) to go over the side of a container; SPILL (1) **2** [I] (of a liquid) to do this: *Some of the soup slopped over the edge of the bowl.*

**slope[1]** /sləʊp/ *v* **sloped, sloping** [I] to lie in a direction neither straight up nor straight across; be at an angle: *a sloping roof|The road slopes up/down slightly at this point.*

**slope off** *v adv* [I] *BrE infml* to go away secretly, esp. to escape or avoid work

**slope[2]** *n* **1** a surface that slopes: *to climb a steep slope|a* SKI *slope* **2** a degree of sloping; a measure of an angle from a level direction: *a slope of 30 degrees*

**slop·py** /ˈslɒpi‖ˈslɑpi/ *adj* **-pier, -piest 1** (e.g. of clothes) loose, informal, and careless- or dirty-looking **2** not careful or thorough enough: *a sloppy piece of writing* **3** silly in showing feelings; SENTIMENTAL **–sloppily** *adv* **–sloppiness** *n* [U]

**slops** /slɒps‖slɑps/ *n* [P] food waste, esp. for feeding to animals

**slosh** /slɒʃ‖slɑʃ/ *v* [I] **1** to go through water or mud: *sloshing along in our rubber boots* **2** (of liquid) to move about against the sides of a container

**slot[1]** /slɒt‖slɑt/ *n* **1** a long straight narrow opening, esp. in a machine or tool: *to put a coin in the slot* –compare SLIT **2** *infml* a place in a list, system, etc.: *The 7 o'clock slot on the radio is usually filled with a news broadcast.*

**slot[2]** *v* **-tt-** [T] **1** to cut a SLOT[1] (1) in **2** [*in, into*] *BrE* to put into a SLOT[1] (2); find a place for: *I'm going to try to slot in some reading on my holiday.*

**sloth** /sləʊθ/ *n* **1** [U] *esp. lit* unwillingness to work; laziness **2** [C] a slow-moving animal of S America

**sloth·ful** /ˈsləʊθfəl/ *adj lit* unwilling to work or be active; lazy –**slothfully** *adv* –**slothfulness** *n* [U]
**slot ma·chine** /ˈ· ·ˌ·/ *n* **1** *BrE* a machine for selling drinks, cigarettes, etc.; VENDING MACHINE **2** *AmE* for ONE-ARMED BANDIT
**slouch**[1] /slaʊtʃ/ *n* [S] a tired-looking round-shouldered way of standing or walking
**slouch**[2] *v* [I] to stand or walk with a SLOUCH[1]
**slough** sthg.↔ **off** /slʌf/ *v adv* [T] (esp. of a snake) to throw off (dead outer skin)
**slov·en·ly** /ˈslʌvənli/ *adj* untidy; not clean or orderly: *slovenly people/work* –**slovenliness** *n* [U]
**slow**[1] /sləʊ/ *adj* **1** [z+*to-v*] not moving or acting quickly; having less than a usual or average speed: *slow music/poison|a slow train/walk|The government was slow to act on the committee's report.* (=took a long time) –compare FAST **2** not quick in understanding; dull in mind **3** [F or after *n*] (of a clock) showing a time that is earlier than the true time: *The clock is two minutes slow.* –opposite **fast** –**slowly** *adv* –**slowness** *n* [U]
**slow**[2] *adv* slowly
USAGE **Slowly** is the usual adverb. **Slow** (*adv.*) is rarely used except in comb.: **slow**-*moving traffic.* But its comparative and SUPERLATIVE (2) forms **slower** and **slowest** are just as common as *more* **slowly** and *most* **slowly**. *John ran* **slower**/*more* **slowly** *than the others and missed the train.*
**slow**[3] *v* [I;T *up, down*] to make or become slower: *The train slowed as it went around the curve.| Business slows up/down in summer.*
**slow·coach** /ˈsləʊkəʊtʃ/ *n BrE infml* a person who moves or works too slowly
**slow mo·tion** /ˌ· ˈ··/ *n* [U] action which takes place at a much slower speed than in real life, esp. as shown in films
**sludge** /slʌd·/ *n* [U] **1** thick mud **2** dirty waste oil in an engine
**slue** /sluː/ *v* **slued, sluing** [I;T *round, around*] *AmE* for SLEW[1]
**slug**[1] /slʌg/ *n* a small limbless creature, related to the SNAIL but with no shell
**slug**[2] *n* a lump or piece of metal, esp. a bullet
**slug**[3] *v* **-gg-** [T] *AmE infml* to strike with a heavy blow
**slug·gish** /ˈslʌgɪʃ/ *adj* slow-moving; not very active or quick: *a sluggish stream|feeling rather sluggish in the heat of the day* –**sluggishly** *adv* –**sluggishness** *n* [U]
**sluice**[1] /sluːs/ *n* a passage for water with an opening (**sluice gate**) through which the flow can be controlled
**sluice**[2] *v* **sluiced, sluicing** [T *out, down*] to wash with floods of water: *to sluice out the cowshed*
**slum** /slʌm/ *n infml* **1** [*often pl.*] a city area of poor living conditions and dirty unrepaired buildings **2** *infml* a very untidy place –**slummy** *adj* **-ier, -iest**
**slum·ber** /ˈslʌmbəʳ/ *n,v* [C;U;I] *lit* (to be in) a state of sleep: *waking from her slumber(s)*
**slump**[1] /slʌmp/ *v* [I] **1** to sink down; fall heavily or in a heap: *He slumped into his chair.* **2** to go down in number or strength: *Sales have slumped recently.*
**slump**[2] *n* a time of seriously bad business conditions and high unemployment; DEPRESSION (2)
**slung** /slʌŋ/ *v past tense & participle of* SLING
**slunk** /slʌŋk/ *v past tense & participle of* SLINK
**slur**[1] /slɜːʳ/ *v* **-rr-** [T] to pronounce (a sound or word) unclearly, as when drunk
**slur**[2] *n* **1** [S] a SLURRING[1] way of speaking **2** [C] an unfair damaging remark: *a slur on his good name*
**slurp** /slɜːp‖slɜrp/ *v* [I;T] *infml* to eat (soft food) or drink noisily: *children slurping their milk*
**slush** /slʌʃ/ *n* [U] **1** partly melted snow **2** literature, films, etc., concerned with silly love stories –**slushy** *adj*– **-ier, -iest**
**slut** /slʌt/ *n derog* **1** a woman who acts immodestly or immorally **2** an untidy lazy woman –**sluttish** *adj*
**sly** /slaɪ/ *adj* **slier** *or* **slyer, sliest** *or* **slyest 1** clever in deceiving; CRAFTY: *a sly old fox* **2 on the sly** secretly –**slyly** *adv* –**slyness** *n* [U]
**smack**[1] /smæk/ *v* [T] **1** to strike loudly, with the flat part of the hand: *The mother smacked the child* **2** to open and close (one's lips) noisily
**smack of** sthg. *v prep* [T] to have a taste or suggestion of: *a plan that smacks of disloyalty*
**smack**[2] *n* (the sound of) a quick loud forceful blow: *If you don't stop making that noise, you'll get a smack!|The book hit the floor with a loud smack.*
**smack**[3] *adv* [*adv + prep*] *infml* with force: *to run smack into a wall*
**smack**[4] *n* a small sailing boat used for fishing
**small**[1] /smɔːl/ *adj* **1** not large; of less than average size, weight, importance, etc.: *a book written for small children|The girl is small for her age.|The Indian elephant is smaller than the African elephant.| You made one or two small mistakes, but otherwise your work was good.* –see Study Notes on page 494 **2** [A] doing only a limited amount of a business or activity: *to be a small businessman* (=own a small business) **3** [A] very little; slight: *She had small hope of success.|You've been eating far too much;* **small wonder** *you're getting fat.* (=it's not surprising) –**smallness** *n* [U]
USAGE **Small** and **little** both mean "of less than average size, weight, importance, etc." but **little** often has the added meaning of fondness: *a nice little dog|a poor little child*, or of dislike: *Silly little fool!*
**small**[2] *adv* in a small manner: *He writes so small I can't read it.*
**small change** /ˌ· ˈ·/ *n* [U] money in coins of small value
**small·hold·ing** /ˈsmɔːlˌhəʊldɪŋ/ *n BrE* a piece of land farmed by one person, smaller than an ordinary farm –**smallholder** *n*
**small hours** /ˈ· ·/ *n* [*the* P] the early morning hours just after midnight
**small-mind·ed** /ˌ· ˈ··◄/ *adj* having narrow selfish interests; unwilling to listen to others –compare OPEN-MINDED, BROADMINDED –**small-mindedness** *n* [U]
**small·pox** /ˈsmɔːlpɒks‖-pɑks/ *n* [U] a serious infectious disease until recent times, causing spots which left marks on the skin
**small talk** /ˈ· ·/ *n* [U] light conversation on unimportant subjects
**small-time** /ˌ· ˈ·◄/ *adj* limited in activity, ability, etc.; unimportant: *a small-time criminal*
**smarm·y** /ˈsmɑːmi‖-ɑr-/ *adj* **-ier, -iest** *BrE infml* unpleasantly and falsely polite
**smart**[1] /smɑːt‖smɑrt/ *adj* **1** *esp. BrE* neat and stylish

in appearance: *a smart new shirt* **2** *esp. AmE* good or quick in thinking; clever **3** quick and forceful: *a smart blow* **4** used by fashionable people: *a smart restaurant* **–smartly** *adv* **–smartness** *n* [U]

**smart²** *v* [I] **1** to cause or feel a painful stinging sensation, usu. not lasting long: *His knee was smarting.* **2** [*over, under*] to be hurt in one's feelings: *She was still smarting over his unkind words.*

**smart·en up** /ˈsmɑːtn‖-ɑr-/ *v adv* [I;T (=**smarten** sbdy./sthg.↔**up**)] to make or become good-looking, neat, or stylish: *They smartened up the office.*

**smash¹** /smæʃ/ *v* [I;T] **1** [*up*] to (cause to) break into pieces violently: *to smash a window|The dish smashed on the floor.|to smash (up) one's car* **2** to go, drive, or hit forcefully against something solid; crash: *He smashed his foot through the door.*

**smash²** *n* **1** a powerful blow: *a smash that sent his opponent to the floor* **2** (the noise of) a violent breaking: *the smash of glasses breaking* **3** also **smash hit**– a very successful new play, film, etc.; HIT² (3): *a new musical smash* **4** a hard downward attacking shot, esp. in tennis **5** → SMASH-UP

**smash·er** /ˈsmæʃəʳ/ *n infml* a person or thing that is very fine

**smash·ing** /ˈsmæʃɪŋ/ *adj BrE infml* wonderful; excellent: *We had a smashing holiday.*

**smash-up** /ˈ· ·/ *n* a road or railway accident: *a five-car smash-up*

**smat·ter·ing** /ˈsmætərɪŋ/ *n* [S *of*] a small amount of knowledge: *I know a smattering of Italian.*

**smear¹** /smɪəʳ/ *n* **1** a mark made by SMEARing² **2** a charge made intentionally to try to turn public feelings against someone: *a* **smear campaign** *against the leader of the opposition party*

**smear²** *v* **1** [T] to cause (a sticky or oily material) to spread across: *Prepare the dish by smearing butter on it/by smearing it with butter.* **2** [I] (of such material) to do this: *Be careful: the paint may smear.*

**smell¹** /smel/ *v* **smelt** *esp. BrE*‖**smelled** *esp. AmE* **smelling 1** [I] to have or use the sense of the nose: *an old dog who can hardly smell any longer* **2** [T +*v -ing*/(*that*)] to notice, examine, or recognize by this sense: *to smell cooking|I could smell that the milk wasn't fresh.|He can always smell when rain is coming.|*(fig.) *I could smell trouble.* **3** [I *of, like*] to have a particular smell: *a sweet-smelling flower* **4** [I *of*] to have an unpleasant smell: *This meat smells.*

**smell** sbdy./sthg.↔**out** *v adv* [T] to find (as if) by smelling: *to smell out a news story*

**smell²** *n* **1** [U] the power of using the nose: *dogs that track by smell alone* **2** [C] a quality that has an effect on the nose: *Some flowers have strong smells.|a smell of coffee* **3** [S] an act of SMELLing¹ (2) something: *Have a smell of this wine; is it all right?*

**smell·y** /ˈsmeli/ *adj* **-ier, -iest** unpleasant-smelling **–smelliness** *n* [U]

**smelt¹** /smelt/ *v* [T] to melt (metal-containing earth (ORE)) so as to separate and remove the metal

**smelt²** *v past tense & participle of* SMELL

> **SPELLING NOTE**
> Words with the sound /s/ may be spelt **c-**, like **city**, or **ps-**, like **psychology.**

**smile¹** /smaɪl/ *n* an expression of the face with the mouth turned up at the ends and the eyes bright, that usu. expresses amusement, happiness, approval, etc.

USAGE A **smile** is an expression of the face showing amusement or happiness. A **grin** is a very wide **smile** which shows the teeth, and a **leer** is an unpleasant **smile** suggesting cruelty, thoughts of sex, etc. When you **laugh,** you produce explosive sounds with the voice at the same time as **smiling.** A loud **laugh** is a **guffaw** (*rare*) and a quiet **laugh** is a **chuckle.** To **giggle** is to laugh repeatedly and in an uncontrollable manner. All these words can be used both as nouns and as verbs.

**smile²** *v* **smiled, smiling 1** [I] to have or make a smile: *The children were smiling happily.|He smiled at me.* **2** [T] to express with a smile: *She smiled a greeting.* **3** [I *on*] to act or look favourably: *The weather smiled on us; it was a fine day.* **–smilingly** *adv*

**smirk** /smɜːk‖smɜrk/ *v,n* [C;I] (to make) a silly satisfied smile

**smite** /smaɪt/ *v* **smote** /sməʊt/, **smitten** /ˈsmɪtn/‖ also **smote** *AmE,* **smiting** [T] **1** *old use & lit* to strike hard: *He smote his enemy with his sword.* **2** [*usu. pass.*] to have a powerful sudden effect on: *smitten by/with sadness*

**smith** /smɪθ/ *n* **1** a worker in metal: *a blacksmith|a goldsmith* **2** a maker: *a gunsmith*

**smith·e·reens** /ˌsmɪðəˈriːnz/ *n* **(in)to smithereens** *infml* into very small bits: *The glass was smashed to smithereens.*

**smith·y** /ˈsmɪði‖-θi, -ði/ *n* **-ies** a BLACKSMITH'*s* place of work

**smock** /smɒk‖smɑk/ *n* a loose shirtlike garment usu. worn by women

**smog** /smɒg‖smɑg, smɔg/ *n* [U] the unhealthy mixture of FOG¹, smoke, and vehicle waste gases in the air in some large cities

**smoke¹** /sməʊk/ *n* **1** [U] gas that can be seen in the air and is usu. given off by burning: *smoke from a chimney|the smell of tobacco smoke* **2** [C] **a** an act of smoking: *a short smoke on his pipe* **b** *infml* something (esp. a cigarette) for smoking **3 go up in smoke** to end without results, esp. suddenly **–smokeless** *adj*

**smoke²** *v* **smoked, smoking 1** [I;T] to breathe in smoke from (esp. tobacco, as in cigarettes): *Do you mind if I smoke?|She smokes 20 cigarettes a day.* **2** [I] to send out smoke: *smoking chimneys* **3** [T] to preserve and give a special taste to (meat, fish, etc.) by hanging it in smoke **4** [T] to darken with smoke, esp. by allowing smoke to settle on a surface: *smoked glass*

**smoke** sbdy./sthg.↔**out** *v adv* [T] to fill a place with smoke to force (a person, animal, etc.) to come out from hiding

**smok·er** /ˈsməʊkəʳ/ *n* **1** a person who smokes **2** a railway carriage where smoking is allowed –opposite **non-smoker**

**smoke·screen** /ˈsməʊkskriːn/ *n* **1** a cloud of smoke made to hide an activity from enemy sight **2** something which hides one's real intentions

**smok·y** /ˈsməʊki/ *adj* **-ier, -iest 1** filled with or producing smoke: *a smoky fire/room* **2** with the taste or appearance of smoke: *a smoky mist|smoky-tasting fish* **–smokiness** *n* [U]

**smol·der** /sməʊldəʳ/ *v AmE* for SMOULDER

**smooth¹** /smuːð/ *adj* **1** having an even surface; not rough: *The sea looks calm and smooth.|a baby's smooth skin|a smooth road* **2** even in movement without sudden changes: *to bring a car to a smooth stop* **3** (of a liquid mixture) without lumps; evenly thick: *Beat the mixture until smooth.* **4** (of a taste) not bitter or sour; pleasant in the mouth: *a smooth taste* **5** too pleasant or polite in manner: *a smooth salesman* **–smoothly** *adv* **–smoothness** *n* [U]

**smooth²** *v* [T] **1** [*out, down*] to make smooth: *to smooth out a tablecloth|* (fig.) *This agreement will smooth the way for peace.* **2** [*away*] to remove (roughness) from a surface

**smooth** sthg.↔**over** *v adv* [T] to make (difficulties) seem unimportant: *to smooth over the bad feelings*

**smote** /sməʊt/ *v past tense of* SMITE

**smoth·er** /smʌðəʳ/ *v* **1** [I;T] to die or kill from lack of air; SUFFOCATE: *a baby smothered in bed|to smother a fire|*(fig.) *They smothered all opposition.* **2** [T] to cover thickly: *smothered in kisses*

**smoul·der** ||**smol-** *AmE–* /ˈsməʊldəʳ/ *v* [I] **1** to burn slowly without a flame **2** to have violent feelings that are kept from being expressed; (of such feelings) to exist without being expressed: *smouldering anger*

**smudge¹** /smʌd·/ *v* **smudged, smudging** [I;T] to make or become dirty with a mark of rubbing: *He smudged the ink with his hand.*

**smudge²** *n* a dirty mark **–smudgy** *adj* **–-ier, -iest**

**smug** /smʌg/ *adj* **-gg-** too pleased with oneself **–smugly** *adv* **–smugness** *n* [U]

**smug·gle** /ˈsmʌgəl/ *v* **-gled, -gling** [T] to take (esp. goods) from one country to another illegally: *It's a serious crime to smuggle drugs into Britain.* **–smuggler** *n* **–smuggling** *n* [U]

**smut** /smʌt/ *n* **1** [C;U] (a small piece of) dirt or SOOT that makes dark marks **2** [U] morally offensive books, stories, etc.

**smut·ty** /ˈsmʌti/ *adj* **-tier, -tiest** morally improper: *a smutty joke/book* **–smuttily** *adv* **–smuttiness** *n* [U]

**snack** /snæk/ *n* an amount of food smaller than a meal; something eaten informally between meals

**snack bar** /ˈ· ·/ *n* an informal public eating place that serves SNACKS

**snag** /snæg/ *n* **1** a hidden or unexpected difficulty **2** a pulled thread in cloth, esp. in a stocking

**snail** /sneɪl/ *n* **1** a small animal (MOLLUSC) with a soft body, no limbs, and a hard shell on its back **2 snail's pace** a very slow speed

**snake¹** /sneɪk/ *n* a cold-blooded animal (REPTILE) with a long limbless body, a fork-shaped tongue, and often a poisonous bite

**snake²** *v* **snaked, snaking** [I;T] to move in a twisting way: *a train snaking (its way) through the mountains*

**snake charm·er** /ˈ· ˌ··/ *n* a person who controls snakes, usu. by playing music, as a public amusement

**snakes and lad·ders** /ˌ· · ˈ··/ *n* [U] a board game in which players may move pieces upwards and forwards or are forced to move downwards and backwards

**snap¹** /snæp/ *v* **-pp- 1** [I *at*] to (try to) close the jaws quickly: *The dog snapped at my ankles.* **2** [I;T] to (cause to) break suddenly off or in two: *The branch snapped under all the snow.|*(fig.) *After waiting an hour, my patience snapped and I went home.* **3** [I;T] to move so as to cause a sound of SNAPping¹ (1,2): *The lid snapped shut.* **4** [I;T *at*] to say or speak quickly, usu. in an annoyed way: *"You're late!", she snapped (at me).* **5** [T] *infml* to photograph; take a SNAPSHOT of **6 snap one's fingers** to make a noise by moving the second finger quickly along the thumb **7 snap out of it** *infml* to free oneself quickly from a bad state of mind

**snap** sthg.↔**up** *v adv* [T] to take or buy quickly and eagerly: *to snap up a bargain* (=buy goods at a cheap price)

**snap²** *n* **1** [C] an act or sound of SNAPping¹: *He called the waiter with a snap of his fingers.* **2** [C] *infml* for SNAPSHOT **3** [C] any of several kinds of sweet BISCUITS (1) **4** [U] (in Britain) a type of card game

**snap³** *adj* [A] done quickly and without warning or long consideration: *a snap decision*

**snap·py** /ˈsnæpi/ *adj* **-pier, -piest 1** → LIVELY (1): *snappy conversation* **2** stylish; fashionable: *a snappy dresser* (=a person who wears stylish clothes) **3 Make it snappy!** *infml* Hurry up!

**snap·shot** /ˈsnæpʃɒt||-ʃɑt/ *n* an informal picture taken with a hand-held camera

**snare¹** /sneəʳ/ *n* a trap for catching an animal, esp. by means of a rope

**snare²** *v* **snared, snaring** [T] to catch (as if) in a SNARE¹: *to snare a rabbit*

**snarl¹** /snɑːl||snɑrl/ *v* [I] (of an animal) to make a low angry sound while showing the teeth: *a snarling dog|*(fig.) *The old man snarled angrily at the children.*

**snarl²** *n* an act or sound of SNARLing¹; angry GROWL

**snarl³** *v* [T *up; usu. pass.*] to make confused or difficult; TANGLE: *snarled (up) traffic*

**snarl-up** /ˈ· ·/ *n* a confused state, esp of traffic

**snatch¹** /snætʃ/ *v* [T] to get hold of hastily and forcefully: *The thief snatched her handbag and ran.* **–snatcher** *n*

**snatch at** sthg. *v prep* [T] to try to SNATCH; make every effort to get: *to snatch at a chance*

**snatch²** *n* **1** an act of SNATCHing¹ (at) something: *He made a brave snatch at victory but failed.* **2** a short and incomplete period of something: *to sleep in snatches|a snatch of music*

**sneak¹** /sniːk/ *v* [I;T] to go or take quietly and secretly: *to sneak past a guard|to sneak around to the back door|I sneaked a look at the plans on her desk.*

**sneak up** *v adv* [I *on*] to come quietly and secretly near: *Don't sneak up on/behind me like that!*

**sneak²** *n* a person who should not be trusted, esp. one who gives information about others to people in power

**sneak·er** /ˈsniːkəʳ/ *n AmE* a cloth shoe with a rubber bottom, worn informally or for sports: *a pair of sneakers*

**sneak·ing** /ˈsniːkɪŋ/ *adj* [A] **1** secret; not expressed, as if shameful: *a sneaking desire to eat a cake* **2** (of a feeling or belief) not proved but probably right: *a sneaking suspicion that the plan won't work*

**sneak·y** /ˈsniːki/ *adj* **-ier, -iest** acting or done secretly and deceitfully **–sneakiness** *n* [U]

**sneer¹** /snɪəʳ/ *v* [I] **1** to express proud dislike and disrespect by a kind of unpleasant one-sided smile **2**

[*at*] to behave as if something is not worthy of serious notice: *Don't sneer at their religion.* **–sneeringly** *adv*

**sneer²** *n* a SNEERing look or remark

**sneeze** /sniːz/ *v,n* **sneezed, sneezing** [C;I] (to produce) a sudden uncontrolled burst of air out of the nose and mouth: *The dust made him sneeze.*

**snick·er** /ˈsnɪkəʳ/ *v,n* [C;I] *AmE* for SNIGGER

**snide** /snaɪd/ *adj* amusing, but in a way that is intended to hurt the feelings; MEAN¹ (2): *a snide remark* **–snidely** *adv* **–snideness** *n* [U]

**sniff¹** /snɪf/ *v* **1** [I *at*] to draw air into the nose with a sound, esp. in short repeated actions **2** [I;T *at*] to do this to discover a smell (in or on): *dogs sniffing (at) the ground*

**sniff at** sthg. *v prep* [T] to refuse proudly: *You shouldn't sniff at such a good offer.*

**sniff²** *n* an act or sound of SNIFFing

**snif·fle** /ˈsnɪfəl/ also **snuffle**– *v* **-fled, -fling** [I] to SNIFF repeatedly, as when one is crying or has a cold

**snig·ger¹** /ˈsnɪgəʳ/ also **snicker** *AmE*– *v* [I *at*] to laugh quietly or secretly in a disrespectful way

**snigger²** also **snicker** *AmE*– *n* an act or sound of SNIGGERing

**snip¹** /snɪp/ *n* **1** [C] a short quick cut with scissors: *make a snip in the cloth* **2** [S] *BrE infml* an attractive and surprisingly cheap article for sale; BARGAIN¹ (2)

**snip²** *v* **-pp-** [T] to cut with scissors, esp. in short quick strokes: *to snip off the corner of a packet|snip a hole in the paper*

**snipe** /snaɪp/ *v* **sniped, sniping** [I *at*] **1** to shoot from a hidden position at unprotected people **2** to attack in a nasty way **–sniper** *n*

**snip·pet** /ˈsnɪpɪ̣t/ *n* [*of*] a small bit of something usu. nonmaterial: *a snippet of poetry*

**sniv·el** /ˈsnɪvəl/ *v* **-ll-** *BrE*‖ **-l-** *AmE* [I] to act or speak in a weak complaining way: *If you fail, don't come snivelling back to me.* **–sniveller** *n*

**snob** /snɒb‖snɑb/ *n* **1** a person who dislikes those he/she feels to be of lower social class, and admires people of a higher social class **2** a person who is too proud of having special knowledge in a subject: *a musical snob who likes only Mozart* **–snobbish** *adj* **–snobbishly** *adv* **–snobbishness** *n* [U]

**snob·be·ry** /ˈsnɒbəri‖ˈsnɑb-/ *n* [U] the behaviour of a SNOB

**snoo·ker¹** /ˈsnuːkəʳ‖ˈsnʊ-/ *n* [U] a game like BILLIARDS, played on a special table with 15 red balls and seven balls of other colours

**snooker²** *v* [T] *infml* to put into a difficult position; trap or trick

**snoop** /snuːp/ *v* [I] to look into, or concern oneself with other people's property or activities without permission: *I caught him snooping (around) in my office.* **–snooper** *n*

**snoot·y** /ˈsnuːti/ *adj* **-ier, -iest** *infml* proudly rude; SUPERCILIOUS: *a snooty attitude* **–snootily** *adv* **–snootiness** *n* [U]

**snooze** /snuːz/ *v,n* **snoozed, snoozing** [I;S] *infml* (to have) a short sleep; DOZE

> **SPELLING NOTE**
> Words with the sound /s/ may be spelt **c-**, like **city**, or **ps-**, like **psychology.**

**snore¹** /snɔːʳ‖snor/ *v* **snored, snoring** [I] to breathe noisily through the nose and mouth while asleep

**snore²** *n* a noisy way of breathing when asleep: *His snores woke her up.*

**snor·kel** /ˈsnɔːkəl‖-ɔr-/ *n* an air tube that can rise above the surface of water, allowing a swimmer under water to breathe

**snort** /snɔːt‖snɔrt/ *v* [I] to make a rough noise by blowing air down the nose, sometimes to express anger or impatience **–snort** *n*

**snout** /snaʊt/ *n* the long nose of any of various animals (such as pigs)

**snow¹** /snəʊ/ *n* **1** [U] water frozen into small flat white bits (FLAKEs) that fall like rain in cold weather and cover the ground thickly **2** [C] a fall of snow –see WEATHER (USAGE)

**snow²** *v* [*it*+I] (of snow) to fall: *Look! It's snowing.*

**snow·ball¹** /ˈsnəʊbɔːl/ *n* a ball pressed together from snow, as thrown at each other by children

**snowball²** *v* [I] to grow bigger at a faster and faster rate: *The effect of rising prices has snowballed.*

**snow·bound** /ˈsnəʊbaʊnd/ *adj* blocked or kept indoors by heavy snow

**snow·drift** /ˈsnəʊˌdrɪft/ *n* a deep bank of snow formed by the wind

**snow·drop** /ˈsnəʊdrɒp‖-drɑp/ *n* a small white European flower which appears in the early spring

**snowed in** /· ˈ·/ *adj* **1** unable to travel because of snow: *We were snowed in* (=could not leave home) *for three days last winter.* **2** also **snowed up**– impossible for people to travel in or out because of snow: *The village was snowed in twice last year.*

**snowed under** /· ˈ··/ *adj* having more work than one can easily deal with, esp. in a short time: *I'm completely snowed under with work.*

**snow·fall** /ˈsnəʊfɔːl/ *n* **1** [C] a fall of snow **2** [S;U] the amount of snow that falls: *an average snowfall of five inches per year*

**snow·flake** /ˈsnəʊfleɪk/ *n* one of the small flat bits of frozen water which fall as snow

**snow·man** /ˈsnəʊmæn/ *n* **-men** /men/ a figure of a man made out of snow, esp. by children

**snow·plough** *BrE*‖**-plow** *AmE* /ˈsnəʊplaʊ/ *n* an apparatus or vehicle for pushing snow off roads or railways

**snow·storm** /ˈsnəʊstɔːm‖-ɔrm/ *n* a very heavy fall of snow, esp. blown by strong winds

**snow-white** /ˌ· ˈ·◂/ *adj* as white as snow; pure white

**snow·y** /ˈsnəʊi/ *adj* **-ier, -iest 1** full of snow or snowing: *snowy weather* **2** pure white: *snowy (white) hair* **–snowiness** *n* [U]

**snub¹** /snʌb/ *v* **-bb-** [T] to treat rudely, by paying no attention: *I greeted her as we passed in the street, but she just snubbed me.*

**snub²** *n* an act of SNUBbing

**snub³** *adj* [A] (of a nose) short and flat at the end

**snuff** /snʌf/ *n* [U] tobacco made into powder for breathing into the nose

**snuf·fle** /ˈsnʌfəl/ *v, n* [C;I] → SNIFFLE

**snuff** sthg.↔ **out** *v adv* [T] to put out (a candle flame) by pressing

**snug** /snʌg/ *adj* **-gg- 1** warm and comfortable; COSY: *a snug little room|lying snug in bed* **2** (of clothes) fitting closely –**snugly** *adv* –**snugness** *n* [U]

**snug·gle** /'snʌgəl/ *v* **-gled, -gling** [I *up, down*] to settle into a warm comfortable position; NESTLE: *Snuggle up to me and I'll keep you warm.*

**so**[1] /səʊ/ *adv* **1** to such a degree: *He was so fat that he couldn't get through the hole.|He held his hands a little way apart, and said "The fish was so long".|I'm so glad* (=very glad) *you could come!|You mustn't worry so.*|(used like *as*, in NEGATIVE[2] (1) comparisons) *She doesn't run so fast as she used to.* –see AS (USAGE) **2** in this way; in that way: *First you turn on the engine, so .|It so happens that we have the same birthday.|He keeps all his papers* **just/exactly so**. (=tidily arranged) **3** (used in place of something stated already): *He hopes he'll win and I hope so too.|Are you married?* **If so,** (=if that is true) *give your wife's name.|"Is it true she's got a new job?" "So she says."|He's very young, but* **even so** (=even though that is true) *he ought to know better.|"Is it interesting?" "Yes,* **more so** (=more interesting) *than I expected."* –compare NOT (2) –see Study Notes on page 128 **4** (followed by *be, have, do*, or a verb like *will, can*, or *should*, and then its subject) also: *I'd like another drink, and so would John.|"Ann can play the piano". "So can I!"* (compare *"Ann can't play the piano." "Nor can I."* (=I, also, can't play the piano)) **5** (followed by *there* or a pronoun subject and then *be, have, do*, or a verb like *will, can*, or *should*) indeed: *"There's a fly in your coffee." "So there is!"|"Look, your wife has just come in." "So she has!"* **6 and so on/forth** and other things of that kind: *pots, pans, dishes, and so on* **7 so as to** in order to: *The test questions are kept secret, so as to prevent cheating.|He did it so as not to be caught.* **8 So long!** *infml* Goodbye!

**so**[2] *conj* **1** with the result that; therefore: *It was dark, so I couldn't see what was happening.|I had a headache so I went to bed.* **2** [*that*] with the purpose that: *I packed him a little food so/so that he wouldn't be hungry.* –see Study Notes on page 128 **3 So what?** *infml* Why should I care?

**so**[3] *adj* [F] true: *You know very well that just isn't so.|Is that really so?*

**soak**[1] /səʊk/ *v* [I;T] **1** [*in*] to (cause to) remain in a liquid: *Leave the dirty clothes to soak.* **2** [*in, into, through*] (of a liquid) to enter (a solid) through its surface: *The ink had soaked through the thin paper.*

**soak** sthg.↔**up** *v adv* [T] to draw in (a liquid) through a surface: *The carpet soaked up the blood.*

**soak**[2] *n* an act or state of SOAKing (1)

**soaked** /səʊkt/ *adj* [F] thoroughly wet, e.g. from rain: *You're soaked! Take off those wet clothes!*

**soak·ing** /'səʊkɪŋ/ *adv,adj* very (wet): *My coat's soaking/soaking wet.*

**so-and-so** /'· · ˌ·/ *n* **so-and-sos 1** [U] someone or something; a certain one not named: *a list of people, with so-and-so saying he'll give £5, so-and-so £2, etc.* **2** [C] *euph* (used instead of a stronger word) a rude, wicked, etc., person: *That so-and-so who mended my watch charged me £20!*

**soap**[1] /səʊp/ *n* [U] a product made from fat and used with water for washing: *a* **bar/cake of soap**|*soap powder* –compare DETERGENT –**soapy** *adj* **-ier, -iest**: *soapy water|a cheese with a rather soapy taste*

**soap**[2] *v* [T] to rub soap on or over: *I was just soaping myself in the bath when the telephone rang.*

**soap op·e·ra** /'· ˌ···/ *n* a continuing television or radio story (SERIAL[2]) about the lives and problems of its imaginary characters

**soar** /sɔːʳ||sor/ *v* [I] **1** *lit* to fly; go fast or high on wings: *birds soaring over the hills* **2** to rise far or fast: *The temperature soared to 35°C.|soaring prices|The cliffs soar 500 ft into the air.*

**sob** /sɒb||sɑb/ *v* **-bb-** [I] to breathe while weeping, in sudden short bursts: *a little boy sobbing in the corner|She sobbed herself to sleep.* (=wept until she fell asleep) –**sob** *n: "Don't be so nasty to me!" she said with a sob.*

**so·ber**[1] /'səʊbəʳ/ *adj* **1** in control of oneself; not drunk **2** thoughtful, serious, or solemn –**soberly** *adv* –**sobriety** /sə'braɪəti/ *n* [U]

**sober**[2] *v* [I;T] to make or become serious or thoughtful: *Her illness had a sobering effect on her.*

**sober up** *v adv* [I;T (=**sober** sbdy. **up**)] to make or become SOBER[1] (1); get or be no longer drunk: *I hope this coffee sobers him up.*

**so-called** /ˌ· '·◂/ *adj* [A] improperly or falsely named: *so-called Christians who show no love to anyone*

**soc·cer** /'sɒkəʳ||'sɑ-/ also **football, Association Football** *BrE*– *n* [U] a football game between two teams of eleven players using a round ball which is kicked but not handled

**so·cia·ble** /'səʊʃəbəl/ fond of being with other people; friendly –opposite **unsociable** –**sociability** /-ʃə'bɪlˌʃti/ *n* [U] –**sociably** *adv*

**so·cial** /'səʊʃəl/ *adj* **1** of or concerning human society or its organization: *opinions on various social questions* **2** based on rank in society: *people of different social classes* **3** shared with friends: *We have an active social life.* (=We spend a lot of time meeting friends, etc.) **4** forming groups or living together by nature: *social insects such as ants* –see also ANTISOCIAL –**socially** *adv*

**so·cial·is·m** /'səʊʃəlɪzəm/ *n* [U] a belief or system (sometimes considered to include COMMUNISM) aiming at the establishment of a society in which every person is equal

**so·cial·ist**[1] /'səʊʃəlˌʃst/ *n* **1** a believer in SOCIALISM **2** (*usu. cap.*) a member of a SOCIALIST political party

**socialist**[2] *adj* of, concerning, or following SOCIALISM: *socialist principles*

**so·cial·ize** ||also **-ise** *BrE* /'səʊʃəl-aɪz/ *v* **-ized, -izing** [I *with*] to spend time with other people in a friendly way: *I enjoy socializing after work.*

**social sci·ence** /ˌ·· '··||'·· ˌ··/ also **social studies**– *n* [C;U] (a branch of) the study of people in society, usu. including history, politics, ECONOMICS, SOCIOLOGY, and ANTHROPOLOGY –see also NATURAL SCIENCE

**social se·cu·ri·ty** /ˌ·· ·'···/ *BrE*||**welfare** *AmE*– *n* [U] government money paid to people who are without jobs, old, ill, etc.

**social serv·ice** /ˌ·· '··||'·· ˌ··/ *n BrE* any of the services provided by a government, e.g. medical care, police, or the collection of waste

**social work** /'·· ·/ *n* [U] work done by government or private organizations to improve bad social conditions –**social worker** *n*

**so·ci·e·ty** /sə'saɪɨti/ *n* **-ties 1** [C;U] a large group of people with shared customs, laws, etc.: *a history of ancient society* **2** [U] people living together, considered as a whole: *Society has a right to expect obedience to the law.* **3** [C] an organization of people with similar aims, interests, etc.; club: *a film society* **4** [U] *fml* the companionship of others: *the society of one's friends* **5** [U] the fashionable people in an area: *a society occasion|London society*

**so·ci·ol·o·gy** /ˌsəʊsi'ɒlədʒi, ˌsəʊʃi-‖-'ɑlə-/ *n* [U] the scientific study of societies and human behaviour **–sociological** /-ə'lɒdʒɪkəl‖-'lɑ-/ *adj* **–sociologist** *n*

**sock** /sɒk‖sɑk/ *n* **1** a soft covering for the foot and lower part of the leg, usu. worn inside a shoe –compare STOCKING –see picture on page 563 **2 pull one's socks up** *BrE infml* to try to improve oneself

**sock·et** /'sɒkɨt‖'sɑ-/ *n* an opening, hollow place, or machine part into which something fits: *eye sockets|to fit an electric light bulb into a socket* –see picture on page 355

**sod** /sɒd‖sɑd/ *n* [C;U] (a piece of) earth with grass and roots growing in it

**so·da** /səʊdə/ *n* [U] **1** → SODA WATER **2** *AmE* for POP[2] (2): *a bottle of orange soda*

**soda wa·ter** /'·· ˌ··/ *n* [U] water filled with gas (CARBON DIOXIDE): *Whisky and soda (water), please.*

**sod·den** /'sɒdn‖'sɑdn/ *adj* heavy with wetness

**so·di·um** /'səʊdɪəm/ *n* [U] a silver-white metal that is a simple substance (ELEMENT (1)), found only in combination with other substances

**so·fa** /'səʊfə/ *n* a comfortable seat wide enough for two or three people to sit on –see picture on page 355

**soft** /sɒft‖sɔft/ *adj* **1** not firm against pressure; not hard or stiff: *a soft chair/bed|soft snow|a book with a soft cover* **2** smooth and delicate to the touch: *a baby's soft skin* **3** restful and pleasant to the senses, esp. the eyes: *soft lights|soft colours* –opposite **harsh 4** quiet; not loud: *soft music* **5** *infml* easily persuaded; weak: *You're too soft with him.* **6** (of a drink) containing no alcohol **7** (of water) without certain minerals; allowing soap to act easily: *We're lucky that the local water is quite soft.* **8** not of the worst, or most harmful or kind: *soft drugs like* CANNABIS –opposite **hard** (for 1, 2, 5, 7, 8) **9** *infml* foolish or mad: *Have you gone soft in the head?* **10 have a soft spot for** to be fond of **–softly** *adv* **–softness** *n* [U]

**soft-boiled** /ˌ· '·◂/ *adj* (of an egg) boiled not long enough for the inside to become solid –see also HARD-BOILED

**soft·en** /'sɒfən‖'sɔ-/ *v* [I;T *up*] to make or become soft, gentle, less stiff, or less severe: *a cream for softening dry skin.* –opposite **harden**

**soft·heart·ed** /ˌsɒft'hɑːtɨd◂‖ˌsɔft'hɑr-/ *adj* having tender feelings; easily moved to pity –opposite **hard-hearted –softheartedness** *n* [U]

**soft-spok·en** /ˌ· '··◂/ *adj* having a gentle voice

**soft·ware** /'sɒftweəʳ‖'sɔft-/ *n* the MAGNETIC TAPES, PROGRAMS, etc that make a computer work –compare HARDWARE

**SPELLING NOTE**

Words with the sound /**s**/ may be spelt **c-**, like **city**, or **ps-**, like **psychology.**

**soft·wood** /'sɒftwʊd‖'sɔft-/ *n* [U] wood from EVERGREEN trees that is easy to cut –opposite **hardwood**

**sog·gy** /'sɒgi‖'sɑgi/ *adj* **-gier, -giest** heavy or lacking firmness as a result of wetness: *soggy ground after the heavy rain|If you boil the vegetables too long, they'll go soggy.* **–soggily** *adv* **–sogginess** *n* [U]

**soil[1]** /sɔɪl/ *n* [U] the top covering of the earth in which plants grow; ground: *rich/sandy soil* –see LAND (USAGE)

**soil[2]** *v* [T] to make dirty: *a soiled shirt collar*

**sol·ace** /'sɒlɨs‖'sɑ-/ *n* [C;U] (something that provides) comfort in grief or anxiety

**so·lar** /'səʊləʳ/ *adj* of, from, or concerning the sun or the sun's light: *solar time|a solar heating system* –compare LUNAR

**solar sys·tem** /'·· ˌ··/ *n* **1** [*the* S] the sun together with the bodies (PLANETS) going around it **2** [C] such a system around another star

**sold** /səʊld/ *v past tense & participle of* SELL

**solder[1]** /'sɒldəʳ,səʊl-‖'sɑdər/ *n* [U] soft metal used when melted for joining other metal surfaces

**solder[2]** *v* [T] to join or repair with SOLDER: *to solder two wires together*

**sol·dier** /'səʊldʒəʳ/ *n* a member of an army, esp. one who is not an officer

**soldier on** *v adv* [I] *BrE* to continue working in spite of difficulties: *He cut his finger, but bravely soldiered on and finished the job.*

**sole[1]** /səʊl/ *n* **1** the bottom surface of the foot –see picture on page 299 **2** the part of a sock, shoe, etc., covering this, esp. not including the heel

**sole[2]** *v* **soled, soling** [T] to put a SOLE[1] (2) on (a shoe): *to have one's shoes soled* –compare HEEL[2]

**sole[3]** *n* **sole** *or* **soles** [C;U] a flat fish often eaten as food

**sole[4]** *adj* [A] **1** only: *The* **sole survivor** (the one person still alive ) *of the crash* **2** belonging to one person and no other; unshared: *My sole responsibility*

**sole·ly** /'səʊl-li/ *adv* not including others; only

**sol·emn** /'sɒləm‖'sɑ-/ *adj* **1** serious: *a solemn moment* **2** of the grandest, most formal kind: *a solemn wedding* **–solemnly** *adv*

**so·lem·ni·ty** /sə'lemnɨti/ *n* **-ties 1** [U] the quality of being solemn **2** [C *usu. pl.*] a formal act proper for a solemn event: *all the solemnities of the occasion*

**sol·em·nize** ‖also **-nise** *BrE* /'sɒləmnaɪz‖'sɑ-/ *v* **-nized, -nizing** [T] *lit or fml* to perform a formal religious ceremony of (esp. marriage) **–solemnization** /-naɪ'zeɪʃən‖-nə-/ *n* [U]

**so·li·cit** /sə'lɪsɨt/ *v* **1** [I;T *for*] to ask for (money, help, a favour, etc.): *Beggars are not allowed to solicit in public places.|to solicit votes* **2** [I] to offer oneself for sex for pay, esp. in public: *The police charged her with soliciting.*

**so·lic·i·tor** /sə'lɪsɨtəʳ/ *n* (esp. in England) a lawyer who gives advice, appears in lower courts, and prepares cases for a BARRISTER to argue in a high court

**so·lic·i·tous** /sə'lɪsɨtəs/ *adj* [*about, of, for*] *fml* anxious to help; carefully interested **–solicitously** *adv* **–solicitousness** *n* [U]

**sol·id[1]** /'sɒlɨd‖'sɑ-/ *adj* **1** not needing a container to hold its shape; not liquid or gas: *The milk had frozen solid.* **2** having an inside filled up; not hollow: *solid rubber tyres* **3** made of material tight together: *solid rock* **4** without spaces or breaks; CONTINUOUS; *I waited for three solid hours.* **5** of good quality; firm and well made: *solid furniture|a solid old house built 100 years ago* **6** [A] completely of one material without mixture of others: *a solid gold watch* **7** *tech* having length, width, and height: *A* SPHERE *is a solid figure.* **–solidly** *adv* **–solidity** /sə'lɪdȷ̵ti/ *n* [U]

**solid²** *n* **1** a SOLID¹ (1) object; something that does not flow: *Water becomes a solid when it freezes.* **2** an object with length, width, and height **3** [*usu. pl.*] an article of non-liquid food: *He cannot eat solids.*

**sol·i·dar·i·ty** /ˌsɒlȷ̵'dærȷ̵ti‖ˌsɑ-/ *n* [U] loyalty and agreement of interests, aims, or standards among a group

**so·lid·i·fy** /sə'lɪdȷ̵faɪ/ *v* **-fied, -fying** [I;T] to make or become solid, hard, or firm: *If you leave it in a cool place, the jelly will solidify.* **–solidification** /-fȷ̵'keɪʃən/ *n* [U]

**so·lil·o·quy** /sə'lɪləkwi/ *n* **-quies** a speech made to oneself alone, esp. in a play

**sol·i·ta·ry** /'sɒlȷ̵təri‖'sɑlȷ̵teri/ *adj* **1** (fond of being) alone: *He's a rather solitary young man.* **2** in a lonely place **3** [A] (used in NEGATIVES² (1)), questions, etc. single; SOLE⁴: *Can you give me one solitary piece of proof for what you say?* –see ALONE (USAGE) **–solitarily** *adv*

**sol·i·tude** /'sɒlȷ̵tjuːd‖'sɑlȷ̵tuːd/ *n* [U] the quality or state of being alone and away from other people

**so·lo¹** /'səʊləʊ/ *n* **-los** a piece of music played or sung by one person –compare DUET

**solo²** *adj,adv* without a companion: *my first solo flight* (=flying a plane by myself)|*Have you ever flown solo?*|*a good solo voice* (=suitable for singing alone)

**so·lo·ist** /'səʊləʊȷ̵st/ *n* a performer of a musical SOLO¹

**sol·stice** /'sɒlstȷ̵s‖'sɑl-/ *n* either the shortest day in the year (the **winter solstice,** December 22 in the northern half of the world) or the longest day in the year (the **summer solstice,** June 22 in the northern half of the world) –compare EQUINOX

**sol·u·ble** /'sɒljʊbəl‖'sɑljə-/ *adj* [*in*] that can be DISSOLVED (1): *Salt is soluble in water.* –opposite **insoluble –solubility** /-'bɪlȷ̵ti/ *n* [U]

**so·lu·tion** /sə'luːʃən/ *n* **1** [C] an answer to a difficulty or problem: *It's difficult to find a solution to this question.* **2** [C;U] (a) liquid containing a solid or gas mixed into it: *a sugar solution* (=sugar in water)

**solve** /'sɒlv‖'sɑlv, sɔlv/ *v* **solved, solving** [T] to find an answer to or way of dealing with: *to solve a problem* **–solvable** *adj*

**sol·vent¹** /'sɒlvənt‖'sɑl-, 'sɔl-/ *adj* having enough money to pay all that is owed; not in debt –opposite **insolvent –solvency** *n* [U]

**solvent²** *n* [C;U] (a) liquid able to DISSOLVE (1) a solid substance: *Alcohol and petrol are solvents.*

**som·bre** *BrE*‖**-ber** *AmE* /'sɒmbəʳ‖'sɑm-/ *adj* **1** sadly serious; GLOOMY (2) **2** (esp. of colours) dark: *a sombre business suit* **–sombrely** *adv* **–sombreness** *n* [U]

**some¹** /sʌm/ *determiner,pron* **1** a certain amount or number (of): *Some parts of the country are very mountainous.*|*He asked for money and I gave him some.* (compare *but I didn't give him any*).|*Some of those stories* (=not all) *are very good.*|*The fire went on for some time* (=quite a long time) *before it was brought under control.* **2** an unknown (one): *There must be some reason for what he did.* **3 some ... or (an)other** not a particular one; a person or thing that is not stated exactly: *I read it in some book or other.*|*I met him somewhere or other.*|*Somebody or other will have to go.*

USAGE In NEGATIVE² (1) statements, **any** or **no** are used instead of **some**: *I haven't* **any** *socks.*|*I have* **no** socks. If **some**, **somebody**, etc., are used in questions, it means that we think the answer will be "yes", but if **any, anybody,** etc. are used, we do not know what the answer will be: *Is there* **something** *to eat?* (=I can smell food)|*Is there* **anything** *to eat?* (=I'm hungry!)

**some²** /səm; *strong* sʌm/ *determiner* (used like *a, an*) a little; a few: *I saw some boys* (or *a boy*) *I knew.*|*Would you like some tea* (or *a cup of tea*)? –see Study Notes on page 494

**some·bod·y** /'sʌmbɒdi‖-bɑdi/ also **someone**– *pron* a person; some person but not a particular or known one: *There's somebody on the telephone for you.*|*You'd better ask someone to help you.* –see EVERYBODY, SOME (USAGE)

**some·day** /'sʌmdeɪ/ *adv* at some future time: *Perhaps someday I'll be rich.*

**some·how** /'sʌmhaʊ/ *adv* in some way not yet known: *We'll get the money somehow.*|*The book has somehow disappeared.*

**som·er·sault** /'sʌməsɔːlt‖-ər-/ *v,n* [C;I] (to do) a rolling backward or forward movement in which the feet go over the head before the body returns upright –compare CARTWHEEL

**some·thing** /'sʌmθɪŋ/ *pron* **1** some unknown thing; a certain thing: *I think I dropped something.*|*I was looking for something cheaper.* –see SOME (USAGE) **2** a thing of some value; a thing better than nothing: *At least we didn't lose any money. That's something!*|*You can't get something for nothing.* (=a profit without any risk or effort) –compare NOTHING **3 or something** (used when the speaker is not sure): *He said the hole had been made by a mouse or something.* **4 something like: a** rather like: *shaped something like a potato* **b** *BrE infml* about: *something like 1,000 people* **5 something to do with** (having) a connection with: *His job has something to do with oil.* –see also SOME¹ (3) ... **or (an)other**

**some·time¹** /'sʌmtaɪm/ *adv* at some uncertain time: *We'll go there sometime next summer.*|*Our house was built sometime around 1905.*

**sometime²** *adj* [A] *fml* having been once; former: *the sometime chairman of British Rail*

**some·times** /'sʌmtaɪmz/ *adv* [*no comp.*] now and then, but not very often: *Sometimes he comes by train and sometimes by car.* (=he comes either by train or by car) –see NEVER (USAGE)

**some·what** /'sʌmwɒt‖-wɑt/ *adv* **1** a little; rather: *somewhat cold weather*|*It somewhat surprised me.*

**some·where** /'sʌmweəʳ/ also **someplace** *AmE*– *adv* **1** in or to some place: *He's somewhere in the garden.*|*I don't like this restaurant; let's go some-*

where else. –see SOME[1] (USAGE)

**son** /sʌn/ *n* **1** someone's male child –compare DAUGHTER –see picture on page 217 **2** (used by an older man to a much younger man or boy): *What's your name, son?*

**so·na·ta** /sə'nɑːtə/ *n* a piece of music for one or two instruments, one of which is a piano

**song** /sɒŋ‖sɔŋ/ *n* **1** [C] a usu. short piece of music with words for singing: *a lovesong/*FOLK*song|That's my favourite song.* **2** [U] the act or art of singing: *She suddenly* **burst into song.** (=started singing) **3** [C;U] the music-like sound of a bird

**song·bird** /'sɒŋbɜːd‖'sɔŋbɜrd/ *n* a bird that can sing well

**son·ic** /'sɒnɪk‖'sɑ-/ *adj* of or concerning sound waves

**son-in-law** /'· · ,·/ *n* **sons-in-law** the husband of one's daughter –compare DAUGHTER-IN-LAW –see picture on page 217

**son·net** /'sɒnᵻt‖'sɑ-/ *n* a 14-line poem with a formal pattern of line endings (RHYMES[1] (2))

**so·nor·ous** /'sɒnərəs, sə'nɔːrəs‖sə'norəs/ *adj fml* having a pleasantly full loud sound: *a sonorous bell/voice* **–sonorously** *adv*

**soon** /suːn/ *adv* **1** [*adv* + *adv/adj/prep*] before long; within a short time: *soon after the party* |**The sooner** *you do it, the better.*|*He got married as soon as he left university.*|**No sooner had we sat down** *than* (=the moment we sat down) *we had to get up again.* –see HARDLY (USAGE) **2** (with *as, than*) willingly: *I'd sooner/rather die than marry you!*|*"Will you dance?" "I'd just as soon not, if you don't mind".* **3 sooner or later** at some time certainly; if not soon then later: *Don't worry; she'll get here sooner or later.*

**soot** /sʊt/ *n* [U] black powder produced by burning **–sooty** *adj* **-ier, -iest**

**soothe** /suːð/ *v* **soothed, soothing** [T] **1** to make less angry or anxious; comfort or calm: *A nice cup of tea will soothe your nerves.*|*soothing words* **2** to make less painful: *soothing medicine* **–soothingly** *adv*

**so·phis·ti·cat·ed** /sə'fɪstᵻkeɪtᵻd/ *adj* **1** having or showing signs of experience in social life and behaviour; no longer natural or simple: *sophisticated tastes* –opposite **unsophisticated 2** not easily understood; COMPLICATED: *sophisticated machinery/arguments* **–sophistication** *n* [U]

**sop·o·rif·ic** /,sɒpə'rɪfɪk‖,sɑ-/ *adj* causing one to fall asleep: *a soporific drug/speech* **–soporifically** *adv*

**sop·ping** /'sɒpɪŋ‖'sɑ-/ *adv,adj infml* very (wet): *Our clothes are sopping/sopping wet.*

**sop·py** /'sɒpi‖'sɑpi/ *adj* **-pier, -piest** *BrE infml* (of a person, story, etc.) too full of tender feelings like sorrow and love; SENTIMENTAL (2)

**so·pra·no** /sə'prɑːnəʊ‖-'præ-/ *n* **-nos** (a person with) a singing voice in the highest usual range, above ALTO **–soprano** *adj*

**sor·cer·er** /'sɔːsərə[r]‖'sɔr-/ **sorceress** *fem.– n* a person believed to do magic by using the power of evil spirits **–sorcery** *n* [U]

> **SPELLING NOTE**
> Words with the sound **/s/** may be spelt **c-**, like **city**, or **ps-**, like **psychology.**

**sor·did** /'sɔːdᵻd‖'sɔr-/ *adj* **1** unpleasant and shameful: *a sordid attempt to cheat his brother* **2** very dirty and poor: *a rather sordid little house.* **–sordidly** *adv* **–sordidness** *n* [U]

**sore**[1] /sɔː[r]‖sor/ *adj* **1** painful or aching from a wound, infection, or hard use: *a sore throat from a cold|My feet are sore from all that running yesterday.* **2** [A] likely to cause offence: *Don't joke about his weight; it's rather a* **sore point** *with him.* **–soreness** *n* [U]

**sore**[2] *n* a painful usu. infected place on the body

**sore·ly** /'sɔːli‖'sorli/ also **sore** *old use– adv* severely or painfully; greatly: *John's in hospital and he's sorely missed by the family.*

**sor·row**[1] /'sɒrəʊ‖'sɑ-, 'sɔ-/ *n* [C;U *over, at, for*] (a cause of) unhappiness; sadness; grief: *sorrow at the death of a friend|the joys and sorrows of life|He expressed his sorrow for what he had done.* **–sorrowful** *adj* **–sorrowfully** *adv*

**sorrow**[2] *v* [I *over, at, for*] *lit* to feel or express sorrow; grieve: *sorrowing for his lost youth*

**sor·ry**[1] /'sɒri‖'sɑri, 'sɔri/ *adj* **-rier,-riest 1** [F +*to-v*/(*that*)] grieved; sad: *I'm sorry to say that we have failed.*|*I was sorry to hear your bad news.* **2** [+ (*that*) *for, about*] unhappy at one's past actions: *If you're really sorry, I'll forgive you.*|*I'm sorry I broke your pen.* **3** [F] (used for expressing polite refusal, disagreement, etc.): *(I'm) sorry but you can't bring your dog in here.* **4** [A] causing pity mixed with disapproval: *He was a sorry sight in his dirty old clothes.* **5 be/feel sorry for** to feel pity towards: *I feel sorry for whoever marries him!*

USAGE Compare the following uses of **sorry: a** *"My mother is very ill." "I'm* **sorry.**" (=very sad to hear that) **b** *"You're standing on my foot." "(I'm)* **sorry!**" (=I didn't realize I was doing it). **c** *"You're standing on my foot."* **"Sorry?"** (=What did you say?) American speakers usually say **Excuse me** in senses **b** and **c. Pardon/***I beg your* **pardon** could also be used in sense **c** but are more formal.

**sorry**[2] *interj* **1** (used for expressing polite refusal, disagreement, etc.): *Sorry; you can't come in.* **2** *BrE* (used for asking someone to repeat something): *"I'm cold." "Sorry?" "I said, I'm cold."*

**sort**[1] /sɔːt‖sɔrt/ *n* **1** [*of*] a group of people, things, etc., all sharing certain qualities; type; kind: *What sort of food do you like best?*|*people of all sorts|all sorts of people* –see KIND **2** [*usu. sing.*] *infml* a person: *She's* **not such a bad sort** (=quite a nice person) **3 of sorts** of a poor or doubtful kind: *It's a painting of sorts, but not a very good one.* **4 out of sorts** feeling unwell or annoyed **5 sort of** *infml* rather; in a way: *I sort of thought you might say that.*

**sort**[2] *v* [I;T *through, over, out*] to put (things) in order; place according to kind, rank, etc.: *a job sorting letters in the Post Office|Can you sort these clothes into two piles, please?* **–sorter** *n*

**sort** sthg.↔**out** *v adv* [T] **1** [*from*] to separate from a mass: *Will you sort out the papers to be thrown away, and put the rest back?* **2** *BrE* to put in order; put right: *a silly quarrel that's now been sorted out*

**sor·tie** /'sɔːti‖'sɔrti/ *n* **1** a short attack made by an army from a position of defence **2** a short trip into an unfamiliar or unfriendly place: (fig.) *His first sortie into the world of film-making wasn't very successful.*

**SOS** *n* an international signal calling for help, used esp. by ships in trouble

**so-so** /ˈ· ·/ *adj,adv infml* not very bad(ly) and not very good/well: *Business is only so-so.*

**sot·to vo·ce** /ˌsɒtəʊ ˈvəʊtʃi‖ˌsɑ-/ *adv* in a soft voice so that other people cannot hear

**souf·flé** /ˈsuːfleɪ‖suːˈfleɪ/ *n* [C;U] a light airy dish made from eggs, flour, milk, and often cheese

**sought** /sɔːt/ *n past tense & participle of* SEEK

**soul** /səʊl/ *n* **1** [C] the part of a person that is not the body and is thought not to die: *She's dead, but her soul's in heaven.* **2** [U] an attractive quality of sincerity and deep feeling: *The performance was lacking in soul.* **3** [C] a person: *Don't tell this to a soul.*|*She's a dear old soul.* **4** [U] → SOUL MUSIC: *a soul group* **5 keep body and soul together** to have just enough money, food, etc., to live **6 the life and soul of** the most active or important part of: *He's the life and soul of any party.* **7 the soul of** a fine example of: *Your son is the soul of charm.*

**soul-des·troy·ing** /ˈ· ·ˌ··/ *adj* very uninteresting: *a soul-destroying job making screws*

**soul·ful** /ˈsəʊlfəl/ *adj* full of feeling; expressing deep feeling: *a soulful look/song* **–soulfully** *adv* **–soulfulness** *n* [U]

**soul·less** /ˈsəʊl-lɨs/ *adj* having no warm or friendly human qualities: *a big soulless office building*

**soul mu·sic** /ˈ· ˌ··/ *n* [U] a type of popular music supposed to show feelings strongly and directly

**sound**[1] /saʊnd/ *n* **1** [C;U] what can be heard; (something that causes) a sensation in the ear: *to hear the sound of voices*|*strange sounds from the next room*|*Sound travels* (in **sound waves**) *at 1,100 feet per second* –see NOISE (USAGE) **2** [S] an idea produced by something read or heard: *From the sound of it, I'd say the matter was serious.* **–soundless** *adj* **–soundlessly** *adv*

**sound**[2] *v* **1** [I not *be +v-ing*] to seem when heard: *Your idea sounds (like) a good one.*|*Does this sentence sound right?* **2** [I;T] to (cause to) make a sound: *Sound your horn to warn other drivers.*

**sound off** *v adv* [I *on, about*] *usu.derog* to express an opinion freely and forcefully: *He's always sounding off about the behaviour of young people.*

**sound** sbdy.↔**out** *v adv* [T *on, about*] to try to find out the opinion or intentions of

**sound**[3] *adj* **1** in good condition; without disease or damage: *in sound health* –opposite **unsound** **2** solid; firm; strong: *the company's sound performance* **3** based on truth or good judgment; not likely to be wrong: *sound advice/judgment* **4** (of sleep) deep and untroubled **–soundly** *adv* **–soundness** *n* [U]

**sound**[4] *adv* SOUNDLY[3] (4) (esp. in the phrase **sound asleep**)

**sound**[5] *n* a water passage connecting two larger bodies of water and wider than a STRAIT

**sound ef·fects** /ˈ· ·ˌ·/ *n* [P] sounds produced to give the effect of the natural sounds (such as thunder or breaking glass) needed in a broadcast or film

**sound·proof**[1] /ˈsaʊndpruːf/ *adj* keeping sound from getting in or out

**soundproof**[2] *v* [T] to make SOUNDPROOF: *a soundproofed room*

**sound·track** /ˈsaʊndtræk/ *n* the recorded music from a film

**soup** /suːp/ *n* [U] liquid cooked food containing small pieces of meat, fish, or vegetables

**soup** sthg.↔**up** *v adv* [T] *infml* to increase the power of (a car or engine)

**sour**[1] /saʊəʳ/ *adj* **1** having the taste that is not bitter, salty, or sweet, and is produced esp. by acids: *sour green apples* **2** having the taste of chemical action by bacteria (FERMENTATION): *This milk has gone sour; it has a sour taste.* **3** bad-tempered; unsmiling: *He gave me a sour look.* **–sourly** *adv* **–sourness** *n* [U]

**sour**[2] *v* [I;T] to make or become sour: (fig.) *The argument soured relations between us.*

**source** /sɔːs‖sors/ *n* **1** [*of*] a place from which something comes: *to find the source of the engine trouble*|*Have you any other source of income apart from your job?* **2** the place where a stream of water starts: *Where is the source of the River Thames?* –compare SPRING[2] (1)

**south**[1] /saʊθ/ *adv* (*often cap.*) towards the south: *to travel south*|*Africa is south of Spain.*

**south**[2] *n* [*the* S] (*often cap.*) **1** one of the four main points of the compass, on the right of a person facing the rising sun **2** the part of a country which is further south than the rest: *The South of England is warmer than the North.*

**south·bound** /ˈsaʊθbaʊnd/ *adj* travelling towards the south: *To get to Oxford Circus, take the southbound train.*

**south·east**[1] /ˌsaʊθˈiːst◂/ *adv (often cap.)* towards the southeast: *windows facing southeast*

**southeast**[2] *n* [*the* S] (*often cap.*) (the direction of) the point of the compass that is halfway between south and east

**south·east·er·ly** /ˌsaʊθˈiːstəli‖-ər-/ *adj* **1** towards the southeast: *in a southeasterly direction* **2** (of a wind) coming from the southeast

**south·east·ern** /ˌsaʊθˈiːstən‖-ərn/ *adj (often cap.)* of or belonging to the southeast part, esp. of a country

**south·east·ward** /ˌsaʊθˈiːstwəd‖-ərd/ *adj fml* going towards the southeast **–southeastwards**‖also **southeastward** *AmE– adv*

**south·er·ly** /ˈsʌðəli‖-ər-/ *adj* **1** towards the south **2** (of a wind) coming from the south: *warm southerly winds*

**south·ern** /ˈsʌðən‖-ərn/ *adj (often cap.)* of or belonging to the south part, esp. of the world or a country: *the southern US*|*the warm southern sun*

**South·ern·er** /ˈsʌðənəʳ‖-ər-/ *n* a person who lives in or comes from the southern part of a country

**south·ern·most** /ˈsʌðənməʊst‖-ər-/ *adj fml* furthest south

**South Pole** /ˌ· ˈ·/ *n* [*the* S] (the lands around) the most southern point on the surface of the earth –see also NORTH POLE

**south·ward** /ˈsaʊθwəd‖-ərd/ *adj* going towards the south **–southwards**‖also **southward** *AmE– adv*

**south·west**[1] /ˌsaʊθˈwest◂/ *adv (often cap.)* towards the southwest: *to sail southwest*

**south·west**[2] *n* [*the* S] *(often cap.)* (the direction of) the point of the compass which is halfway between south and west

**south·west·er·ly** /ˌsauθ'westəli‖-ərli/ *adj* **1** towards or in the southwest **2** (of a wind) coming from the southwest

**south·west·ern** *adj* (*often cap.*) of or belonging to the southwest part, esp. of a country

**south·west·ward** /ˌsauθ'westwəd‖- ərd/ *adj* going towards the southwest –**southwestwards**‖ also **southwestward** *AmE– adv*

**sou·ve·nir** /ˌsuːvə'nɪəʳ, 'suːvənɪəʳ/ *n* an object kept as a reminder of an event, trip, place, etc.: *I bought this bag as a souvenir of my visit to London.*

**sou'west·er** /sau'westəʳ/ *n* a hat of shiny material (OILSKIN) worn esp. by sailors in storms

**sove·reign¹** /'sɒvrɪ̵n‖'sɑv-/ *n* **1** a ruler such as a king or queen **2** a former British gold coin worth £1

**sovereign²** *adj* **1** in control of a country; ruling: *Sovereign power must lie with the people.* **2** (of a country) independent and self-governing –**sovereignty** *n* [U]

**So·vi·et** *adj* of or concerning the USSR (the **Soviet Union**) or its people

**sow¹** /sau/ *n* a fully grown female pig –compare BOAR (1), HOG¹ (1)

**sow²** /səu/ *v* **sowed, sown** *or* **sowed, sowing** [I;T *with/on*] to plant or scatter (seeds) on (a piece of ground): *to sow grass/to sow a field with grass* –compare REAP

**soy·a bean** /'sɔɪə ˌbiːn/ also **soybean**– *n* (the bean of) a widely-grown plant which produces oil

**spa** /spɑː/ *n* a place with a spring of mineral water where people come for cures of various diseases

**space¹** /speɪs/ *n* **1** [C;U] something measurable in length, width, or depth; room: *Is there enough space at the table for 10 people?|Keep some space between you and the car ahead.|a parking space|a town with some open space* (=land not built on) *near the centre|Six people have been killed on this road in the space of a year.* (=during this length of time) **2** [U] that which surrounds all objects and continues outwards in all directions: *He didn't see me; he was just looking out into space.* **3** [U] what is outside the earth's air; where other heavenly bodies move: *to travel through space|a space station|in outer space*

**space²** *v* **spaced, spacing** [T *out*] to place apart; arrange with spaces between: *Space the desks two metres apart so that the pupils can't cheat.*

**space·craft** /'speɪs-krɑːft‖-kræft/ *n* **spacecraft** a vehicle able to travel in SPACE¹ (3)

**space·ship** /'speɪsˌʃɪp/ *n* (esp. in stories) a spacecraft for carrying people

**spa·cious** /'speɪʃəs/ *adj* having a lot of room; ROOMY: *a spacious office* –**spaciousness** *n* [U]

**spade¹** /speɪd/ *n* **1** a tool like a SHOVEL but with a blade to push into the ground, for digging earth **2 call a spade a spade** *infml* to speak the plain truth

**spade²** *n* a playing card with one or more figures shaped like a black pointed leaf printed on it: *the six of spades* –see CARDS (USAGE)

**spa·ghet·ti** /spə'geti/ *n* [U] an Italian food of flour paste (PASTA) in long strings –compare MACARONI

**SPELLING NOTE**

Words with the sound /s/, may be spelt **c-**, like **city**, or **ps-**, like **psychology.**

**span¹** /spæn/ *n* **1** a stretch between two limits, esp. in time: *over a span of three years* **2** a length of time over which something continues or works well: *a short memory span* **3** the length of a bridge, arch, etc., between supports –see also WINGSPAN

**span²** *v* **-nn- A** [T] to form a bridge over; stretch over: *A bridge spanned the stream.*|(fig.) *His life spanned eighty years.*

**span·gle** /'spæŋgəl/ *n* a small piece of shiny metal sewn in large numbers esp. on dresses; SEQUIN

**span·iel** /'spænjəl/ *n* a small short-legged dog with long ears and long wavy hair

**spank** /spæŋk/ *v* [T] to strike (esp. a child) with the open hand, esp. on the BUTTOCKS –**spank** *n* –**spanking** *n*: *If you don't stop that noise, you'll get a spanking!*

**span·ner** /'spænəʳ/ *BrE*‖**wrench** *AmE– n* a metal hand tool with jaws or a hollow end, for fitting over and twisting screwed parts (NUTS (2))

**spar¹** /spɑːʳ/ *n* a thick pole, esp. one used on a ship to support sails or ropes –compare MAST

**spar²** *v* **-rr-** [I *with*] **1** to BOX³ without hitting hard, as in practice (between **sparring partners**) **2** to exchange words as if fighting or competing

**spare¹** /speəʳ/ *v* **spared, sparing** [T] **1** to afford to give: *Can you spare me five minutes?|We're so busy that no one can be spared for any other work.* **2** *esp. old use* to treat with mercy; not harm: *Take my money but spare my life!* **3** to keep from giving (someone) (something unnecessary): *Spare me the details; just tell me about what they decided.* **4**(only used in NEGATIVEs² (1) questions, etc.) to keep from using, spending, etc.: *No expense* (=money) *was spared in preparing the food.*

**spare²** *adj* **1** not in use but kept for use: *a spare tyre/bedroom* **2** not needed for use; free: *something to do in her spare time|Have you got a spare minute?* **3** rather thin; LEAN² (1): *her spare figure*

**spare³** *n* a second object of the same kind that is kept for possible use: *This tyre is damaged. Have you got a spare?*

**spar·ing** /'speərɪŋ/ *adj* [*in, of*] using or giving little; FRUGAL (1) –opposite **unsparing** –**sparingly** *adv*: *Use this paint sparingly–it's expensive!*

**spark¹** /spɑːk‖spɑrk/ *n* **1** a small bit of burning material thrown out by a fire or by the striking together of two hard objects **2** a flash of light produced by electricity passing across a space **3** [*of*] a very small but important bit, esp. of a quality: *a spark of cleverness/politeness*

**spark²** *v* [I] to produce SPARKs (1) or a SPARK (2)

**spark** sthg.↔**off** *v adv* [T] *BrE* to lead to; be the direct cause of: *What sparked off the quarrel?*

**spar·kle** /'spɑːkəl‖'spɑr-/ *v* **-kled, -kling** [I] **1** to shine in small flashes: *a diamond that sparkled in the sunlight*|(fig) *a sparkling* (=a bright and lively) *conversation* **2** (of a drink) to give off gas in small bubbles: *sparkling wine* –compare STILL¹ (3) –**sparkle** *n* [C;U]

**spark plug** /'· ·/ also **sparking plug** *BrE– n* the part which makes an electric SPARK¹ (2) in a petrol engine

**spar·row** /'spærəu/ *n* a small brownish bird very common in many parts of the world

**sparse** /spɑːs‖spɑrs/ *adj* scattered; thin or few: *lots* of bare *floor and only sparse furniture* **–sparsely** *adv* **–sparseness** *n* [U]

**spar·tan** /ˈspɑːtn‖-ɑr-/ *adj* simple and without attention to comfort; severe: *a rather spartan meal of meat and boiled potatoes*

**spas·m** /ˈspæzəm/ *n* **1** a sudden uncontrolled tightening of muscles **2** [*of*] a sudden violent effort, feeling, or act; FIT[3]: *spasms of grief/ laughter/ coughing*

**spas·mod·ic** /spæzˈmɒdɪk‖-ˈmɑ-/ *adj* **1** of or like a SPASM: *spasmodic pain* **2** not continuous; irregular; with pauses between: *the government's spasmodic attempts to deal with the problem* **–spasmodically** *adv*

**spas·tic** /ˈspæstɪk/ *n,adj* (a person) suffering from a disease in which some parts of the body will not move because the muscles stay tightened

**spat** /spæt/ *v past tense & participle of* SPIT

**spate** /speɪt/ *n* [S *of*] *BrE* a large number or amount: *a spate of accidents on a dangerous stretch of road*

**spa·tial** /ˈspeɪʃəl/ *adj fml* of, concerning, or being in space **–spatially** *adv*

**spat·ter** /ˈspætəʳ/ *v* [I;T *withon*] to cause (drops of liquid) to scatter on: *The car spattered my clothes with mud/spattered mud on my clothes.|A little oil spattered on the wall.*

**spat·u·la** /ˈspætjʊlə‖-tʃələ/ *n* a tool with a wide flat blade, for spreading, mixing, or lifting soft substances

**spawn¹** /spɔːn/ *v* **1** [I;T] (of fishes and FROGS, etc.) to lay (eggs) in large quantities together **2** [T] to produce in large numbers: *The computer industry has spawned hundreds of new companies.*

**spawn²** *n* [U] the eggs of water animals like fishes and FROGS

**speak** /spiːk/ *v* **spoke** /spəʊk/, **spoken**/ˈspəʊkən/, **speaking 1** [I] to say things; talk: *I'd like to speak to/with you about my idea.|I was so shocked I could hardly speak.|After their quarrel, they're still not speaking (to each other)/not* **on speaking terms**. (=willing to talk and be polite to each other) –see SAY (USAGE) **2** [T] to express or say: *Are you speaking the truth?* **3** [T] to be able to talk in (a language): *Do you speak English?| a French-speaking secretary.* **4** [I] to make a speech: *I've invited her to speak on American politics.* **5** [I] to express thoughts, ideas, etc., in some other way than by talk: *Actions speak louder than words.|Everything at the party spoke of careful planning.* **6 so to speak** as one might say; rather **7 speak one's mind** to express one's thoughts directly: *He always speaks his mind, so many people think he's rude.* **8 to speak of** (only used in NEGATIVES² (1), questions, etc.) worth mentioning; of much value or amount: *There's been no rain to speak of, only a few drops.*

**speak for** sbdy./sthg. *v prep* [T] **1** to express the thoughts, opinions, etc., of: *a powerless group with no one to speak for them* **2** to get the right to (something) in advance; RESERVE¹

**speak out** *v adv* [I] to speak boldly, freely, and plainly: *The newspapers are afraid to speak out against the government.*

**speak up** *v adv* [I] **1** to speak more loudly: *Speak up, please; I can't hear you.* **2**→ SPEAK **out**: *She spoke up in defence of her beliefs.*

**speak·er** /ˈspiːkəʳ/ *n* **1** a person making a speech: *an interesting speaker* **2** a person who speaks a language: *a speaker of English* **3** a LOUDSPEAKER, esp. one used in a STEREO system –see picture on page 355

**spear¹** /spɪəʳ/ *n* a pole with a sharp point at one end used formerly for throwing as a weapon

**spear²** *v* [T] to make a hole in or catch (as) with the point of a spear; IMPALE

**spear·head** /ˈspɪəhed‖ˈspɪər-/ *v,n* [C;T] (to be) the leader of (an attack); (be) a leading force: *The attack on slavery was spearheaded by William Wilberforce.*

**spear·mint** /ˈspɪəˌmɪnt‖ˈspɪər-/ *n* [U] a common MINT plant used for its fresh taste, e.g. in CHEWING GUM

**spe·cial¹** /ˈspeʃəl/ *adj* of a particular kind; not ordinary or usual: *A special train was provided for the football supporters.|a special friend of mine|As it's a special occasion, let's have a bottle of wine with our dinner.*

**special²** *n* something that is not of the regular or ordinary kind: *a two-hour television special*

**spe·cial·ist** /ˈspeʃəlɪ̇st/ *n* [*in*] a person who has special knowledge or training in a field of work or study: *a heart specialist|a specialist in coins.*

**spe·ci·al·i·ty** /ˌspeʃiˈælɪ̇ti/ ‖also **specialty** /ˈspeʃəlti/ *AmE*– *n* **-ties 1** a special field of work or study: *Her speciality is Greek poetry.* **2** [*of*] a particularly fine product: *Fish is the restaurant's speciality.*

**spe·cial·ize** ‖also **-ise** *BrE* /ˈspeʃəlaɪz/ *v* **-ized, -izing** [I *in*] to limit one's study, business, etc., to particular things or subjects: *a doctor who specializes in tropical diseases* – **specialization** /-laɪˈzeɪʃən‖-lə-/ *n*

**spe·cial·ized** ‖also **-ised** *BrE* /ˈspeʃəlaɪzd/ *adj* developed for a particular use or concerning a particular subject; *specialized tools/knowledge*

**spe·cial·ly** /ˈspeʃəli/ *adv* **1** for one particular purpose: *I made a cake specially for you.* **2** → ESPECIALLY: *It's not specially hot today.*

**spe·cies** /ˈspiːʃiːz/ *n* **-cies** [*of*] a group of plants or animals of the same kind, which are alike in all important ways and can breed together –compare GENUS

**specific** /spɪ̇ˈsɪfɪk/ *adj* **1** detailed and exact: *You say that your factory is in England. Can you be a bit more specific?* **2** [A] particular; certain; fixed: *a specific tool for each job* **–specificity** *n* [U] **–specifically** *adv: They told us specifically to avoid the main road.|a book written specifically for children*

**spe·ci·fi·ca·tion** /ˌspesɪ̇fɪ̇ˈkeɪʃən/ *n* **1** [C *usu. pl.*] any of the parts of a detailed plan or set of descriptions or directions: *According to the radio's specifications, this wire should go into that hole.* **2** [U *of*] the action of SPECIFYing

**spe·ci·fy** /ˈspesɪ̇faɪ/ *v* **-fied, -fying** [T] to mention exactly; choose or name: *Please specify when you will be away/the dates of your absence.*

**spe·ci·men** /ˈspesɪ̇mən/ *n* **1** a single typical thing or example: *a fine specimen of a mountain lion* **2** a piece or amount of something to be shown, tested, etc.: *The doctor will need a specimen of your blood.*

**spe·cious** /ˈspiːʃəs/ *adj fml* seeming right or correct but not so in fact: *a specious argument* **–speciously** *adv* **–speciousness** *n* [U]

**speck** /spek/ *n* [*of*] a small spot or mark: *a speck of dirt in my eye*

**speck·le** /'spekəl/ *n* a small coloured mark, esp. one of a large number –**speckled** *adj*: *speckled bird's eggs*

**spec·ta·cle** /'spektəkəl/ *n* **1** a grand public show or scene **2** a silly sight; something to laugh at: *to make a spectacle of oneself*

**spec·ta·cles** /'spektəkəlz/ also **specs** *infml*– *n more fml than* **glasses** [P] glasses to help a person to see: *I can't read the newspaper without my spectacles.* –see PAIR (USAGE)

**spec·tac·u·lar**[1] /spek'tækjʊləʳ‖-jə-/ *adj* grandly unusual; attracting excited notice –opposite **unspectacular** –**spectacularly** *adv*

**spectacular**[2] *n* a SPECTACULAR[1] entertainment: *a television spectacular with lots of famous stars*

**spec·ta·tor** /spek'teɪtəʳ‖'spekteɪtər/ *n* a person who watches (esp. an event or sport) without taking part –see picture on page 592

**spec·tre** ‖-**ter** *AmE* /'spektəʳ/ *n* a spirit without a body; GHOST[1] (1)

**spec·trum** /'spektrəm/ *n* -**tra**/trə/ **1** the set of bands of coloured light into which a beam of white light may be separated **2** a range of any of various kinds of waves: *a radio/sound spectrum*|(fig.) *the spectrum of opinion*

**spec·u·late** /'spekjʊleɪt‖-jə-/ *v* -**lated,** -**lating 1** [I;T +(*that*)] to think (about a matter) without facts that would lead to a firm result: *We can only speculate about the future.* **2** [I *in*] to buy or deal in goods, SHARES[1] (2), etc., in the hope of a large profit: *speculating in gold mines* –**speculator** *n* –**speculation** *n* [C;U]: *What you say is pure speculation.* (=only a guess)

**spec·u·la·tive** /'spekjʊlətɪv‖-jə-/ *adj* based on speculation (SPECULATE): *a speculative guess/sale* –**speculatively** *adv*

**speech** /spiːtʃ/ *n* **1** [U] the act or power of speaking; spoken language: *Only humans have the power of speech.* **2** [U] a way of speaking: *By your speech I can tell you're from Liverpool.* **3** [C] an act of speaking formally to a group of listeners: *to give/make a speech*|*The speech was reported in the newspapers.* **4** **direct/indirect speech**: *"He said he was hungry." is an example of indirect speech. In direct speech his actual words were "I'm hungry."*

**speech·less** /'spiːtʃlɪ̈s/ *adj* [*with*] unable for the moment to speak because of strong feeling, shock, etc.: *speechless with anger* –**speechlessly** *adv* –**speechlessness** *n* [U]

**speed**[1] /spiːd/ *n* **1** [C] rate of movement: *a speed of 55 kilometres per hour*|*to move along at a slow speed*|*to keep within/exceed the* **speed limit** (=the fastest speed allowed by law on a road) **2** [U] swift movement: *They won because of their speed with the ball.*|*The car was travelling* **at speed**. (=very fast)

**speed**[2] *v* **sped** /sped/‖also **speeded** *AmE*, **speeding** [I]**1** to (cause to) go quickly: *We saw a car speeding away.*|*The time sped quickly by.* **2** to break the speed limit: *Was I really speeding, officer?*

**speed up** *v adv* [I;T (=**speed** sthg.↔**up**)] to (cause to) go faster: *The director wants us to speed up production of the new car.*

**speed·boat** /'spiːdbəʊt/ *n* a small power-driven boat built for high speed

**speed·om·e·ter** /spɪ'dɒmɪ̈təʳ, 'spiːdɒ-‖-'dɑ-/ also **speedo** *BrE infml*– *n* an instrument in a vehicle for telling its speed –see picture on page 85

**speed·way** /'spiːdweɪ/ *n* -**ways** [C;U] (a track for) a type of motorcycle racing

**speed·y** /'spiːdi/ *adj* -**ier,** -**iest** going, working, or passing fast; quick; swift: *a speedy journey* –**speedily** *adv* –**speediness** *n* [U]

**spell**[1] /spel/ *v* **spelt** (*esp. BrE*) **spelled** (*esp. AmE*), **spelling 1** [T *with*] to name in order the letters of (a word): *My name is spelt S-M-Y-T-H.* **2** [I] to form words from letters: *to learn to spell* **3** [T *no pass.*] (of letters in order) to form (a word): *B-O-O-K spells "book".* **4** [T] to mean: *This vote spells defeat for the government.* –**speller** *n*

**spell** sthg.↔**out** *v adv* [T] **1** to explain in a very detailed way: *to spell out the government's plans in a newspaper article* **2** to write or say (a word) letter by letter

**spell**[2] *n* (magic words used to produce) a condition caused by or as if by magical power

**spell**[3] *n* an unbroken period of time: *a spell of work abroad*

**spell·bound** /'spelbaʊnd/ *adj* [F] with the attention held as if by magic: *The children sat spellbound as the old man told his story.*

**spell·ing** /'spelɪŋ/ *n* [C;U] the way of forming words from letters: *Her spelling has improved.*|*English and American spellings of some words are different.*

**spend** /spend/ *v* **spent, spending 1** [I;T *on, for*] to give out (esp. money) in payment: *to spend £4,000 for/on a new car*|*cuts in government spending* **2** [T *in*] to pass or use (time): *Come and spend the weekend with us.*|*to spend three years in prison* **3** [T] *lit* to wear out or use completely: *The storm soon spent its force.*

**spend·thrift** /'spend,θrɪft/ *n* a person who spends money wastefully

**spent** /spent/ *adj* **1** already used; no longer for use: *spent bullets/matches* **2** worn out; very tired

**sperm** /spɜːm‖spɜrm/ *n* **sperm** *or* **sperms 1** [C] a cell produced by the sex organs of a male animal, which is able to unite with the female egg to produce new life **2** [U] the liquid from the male sex organs in which these swim; SEMEN

**spew** /spjuː/ *v* [I;T] **1** to send or come out in a flood: **2** [*up*] *infml* for VOMIT[2]

**sphere** /sfɪəʳ/ *n* **1** a round figure in space; ball-shaped mass **2** an area of existence, action, etc.: *His main* **sphere of influence** *is the world of banking.*

**spher·i·cal** /'sferɪkəl/ *adj* having the form of a SPHERE (1)

**sphinx** /sfɪŋks/ *n* an ancient Egyptian image of a lion with a human head

**spice**[1] /spaɪs/ *n* **1** [C;U] a vegetable product used esp. in the form of powder for giving a taste to other foods –compare HERB **2** [S;U] interest or excitement: *a few good stories to add spice to the speech*

**spice**[2] *v* **spiced, spicing** [T *up, with*] to add SPICE[1] to

**SPELLING NOTE**

Words with the sound /s/, may be spelt **c-**, like **city**, or **ps-**, like **psychology**.

**spick-and-span** /ˌspɪk ən ˈspæn/ *adj* clean and bright; like new

**spic·y** /ˈspaɪsi/ *adj* **-ier, -iest 1** containing or tasting of SPICE[1] (1): *I don't like spicy food.* **2** exciting and perhaps slightly improper or rude: *spicy stories*

**spi·der** /ˈspaɪdəʳ/ *n* a small eight-legged creature which makes silk threads, usu. into nets for catching insects

**spi·der·y** /ˈspaɪdəri/ *adj* **-ier, -iest** long and thin like a SPIDER'*s* legs: *the old lady's spidery writing*

**spike**[1] /spaɪk/ *n* a usu. long piece of metal with a point at one end: *spikes along the top of a fence|spikes on the bottom of running shoes*–**spiky** *adj* **-ier, -iest** *infml: spiky hair*

**spike**[2] *v* **spiked, spiking** [T] to fix with SPIKES[1]; drive SPIKES into

**spill** /spɪl/ *v* **spilled** *or* **spilt, spilling 1** [I;T] to (cause to) pour out accidentally, e.g. over the edge of a container: *My hand slipped and I spilt my drink on my leg.*|(fig.) *The crowd spilt over* (=spread) *from the church into the streets.* **2 spill the beans** *infml* to tell a secret too soon or to the wrong person

**spin**[1] /spɪn/ *v* **spun** /spʌn/, **spinning** [I;T] **1** to make (thread) by twisting (cotton, wool, etc.): *to spin thread|to spin wool into thread*|(fig.) *to* **spin a yarn** (=to tell a story) **2** to (cause to) turn round and round fast; WHIRL[1]: *to spin a* TOP[4]|*I spun round to see who had spoken.*

**spin** sthg.↔**out** *v adv* [T] to make longer, esp. unnecessarily; stretch: *to spin out a story*

**spin**[2] *n* **1** [C] an act of spinning **2** [S] a short trip for pleasure: *Come for a spin in my car.*

**spin·ach** /ˈspɪnɪdʒ, -ɪtʃ‖-ɪtʃ/ *n* [U] a vegetable with broad green leaves

**spin·al** /ˈspaɪnl/ *adj* of, for, or concerning the SPINE (1): *spinal disease*

**spin·dle** /ˈspɪndl/ *n* **1** a round pointed rod used for twisting the thread in spinning **2** a machine part round which something turns

**spin·dly** /ˈspɪndli/ *adj* **-dlier, -dliest** long, thin, and weak-looking: *a young horse with spindly legs*

**spin-dry** /ˌ·ˈ·/ *v* **-dried, -drying** [T] to remove water from (wet clothes) in a machine (**spin dryer**), that spins round and round fast

**spine** /spaɪn/ *n* **1** also **spinal column, backbone**– the row of bones down the centre of the back of humans and some animals **2** the end of a book where the pages are fastened together **3** a stiff sharp-pointed plant or animal part; prickle

**spine·less** /ˈspaɪnlɨs/ *adj* **1** lacking courage, esp. in dealing with others: *He's too spineless to ask for more money.* **2** (of an animal) having no SPINE (1) –**spinelessly** *adv* –**spinelessness** *n* [U]

**spin·ney** /ˈspɪni/ *n* **-neys** *BrE* a small area full of trees and low plants

**spinning wheel** /ˈ·· ·/ *n* a small machine used esp. formerly for spinning thread

**spin-off** /ˈ· ·/ *n* a useful product or result besides the main one

**spin·ster** /ˈspɪnstəʳ/ *n sometimes derog* an unmarried woman, esp. an older one –compare BACHELOR

**spi·ral**[1] /ˈspaɪərəl/ *n* a curve winding round a central point and moving continuously either towards the centre or upwards: *a spiral watch-spring|a spiral staircase*

**spiral**[2] *v* **-ll-** *BrE* ‖**-l-** *AmE* [I] to move in a SPIRAL[1]; rise or fall in a winding way: *The damaged plane spiralled towards the earth.|spiralling prices*

**spire** /spaɪəʳ/ *n* a tower rising steeply to a point, as on a church

**spir·it**[1] /ˈspɪrɨt/ *n* **1** [C] a person's soul or mind: *His spirit was troubled.|I can't come to your wedding, but I'll be there* **in spirit.** (=I'll think about you on the day)|*The religious leader is now dead but his spirit lives on in the work of others.* **2** [C] a being without a body, such as a GHOST[1] (1): *evil spirits* **3** [*the* S *of*] the central quality or force of something that makes it special: *the 17th-century spirit of enquiry* **4** [U] force, effort, or excitement shown: *a horse with spirit|They always lose because they have no* **team spirit.** (=no feeling of loyalty to the team) **5** [S] an intention or feeling in the mind; ATTITUDE (1): *You should take my remarks in the right spirit, without offence.|He came to the party, but didn't really* **enter into the spirit** *of it.* (=didn't try to enjoy it) **6** [*the* S *of*] the real intended meaning of a law, rule, etc., rather than what it actually says: *Judges often try to apply the spirit of the law.* –opposite **letter 7** [C *usu. pl.*] a strong alcoholic drink, such as WHISKY or BRANDY, produced by DISTILLing: *I prefer spirits to beer.*

**spirit**[2] *v* [T *away, off*] to take in a secret mysterious way: *The actress was spirited away secretly in a car.*

**spir·it·ed** /ˈspɪrɨtɨd/ *adj* **1** active and excited; ANIMATED: *a spirited quarrel/defence* **2 -spirited** having a certain kind of temper or feeling: HIGH-SPIRITED|PUBLIC-SPIRITED

**spirit lev·el** /ˈ·· ˌ··/ also **level** *AmE*– *n* a tool for testing whether a surface is level

**spir·its** /ˈspɪrɨts/ *n* [P] the cheerful or sad state of one's mind: *in high spirits* (=cheerful)

**spir·i·tu·al**[1] /ˈspɪrɨtʃuəl/ *adj* **1** nonmaterial; of the nature of spirit: *one's spiritual nature*–compare MENTAL, PHYSICAL **2** religious; holy: *spiritual songs|an adviser in spiritual matters* –**spiritually** *adv*

**spiritual**[2] *n* a religious song sung originally by the black peoples of the US

**spir·i·tual·is·m** /ˈspɪrɨtʃulɪzəm/ *n* [U] the belief that dead people may send messages to living people usu. through a person (MEDIUM[2]) with special powers –**spiritualist** *n*

**spit**[1] /spɪt/ *v* **spat**/spæt/‖also **spit** *AmE,* **spitting** [I;T *out, up*] to force (liquid) from the mouth: *to spit on the ground.*|(fig.) *She angrily spat out her answer.*

**spit**[2] *n* [U] the liquid in the mouth; SALIVA

**spit**[3] *n* **1** a thin pointed rod for sticking meat onto, for cooking over a fire **2** a small usu. sandy point of land running out into a stretch of water

**spite**[1] /spaɪt/ *n* [U] **1** unreasonable dislike for and desire to annoy another person: *I'm sure he took my parking space just* **out of/from spite. 2 in spite of** taking no notice of; although something is true: *I went out in spite of the rain.* –see Study Notes on page 128 –**spiteful** *adj* –**spitefully** *adv* –**spitefulness** [U]

**spite**[2] *v* **spited, spiting** [T] to treat with SPITE[1]; annoy intentionally: *He did it to spite me.*

**spit·tle** /ˈspɪtl/ *n* [U] → SPIT[2]; SALIVA

**splash**[1] /splæʃ/ *v* [I;T] **1 a** (of a liquid) to fall or strike noisily, in drops, waves, etc.: *The rain splashed on the window.* **b** to cause (a liquid) to do this; throw a liquid (at): *children splashing water in the bath|He splashed his face with cold water.* **2** [*out*] *BrE* to spend (money) freely: *I splashed out and bought two records.*

**splash²** *n* **1** a SPLASHing¹ act, movement, or noise: *I fell into the water with a splash.* **2** a mark made by SPLASHing¹: *a splash of paint on the floor*

**splat** /splæt/ *n,adv* [S; *adv + prep*] (with) a noise of something wet hitting a surface

**splay** /spleɪ/ *v* **splayed, splaying** [I;T *out*] to (cause to) spread out or become larger at one end

**splen·did** /'splendɪ̇d/ *adj* **1** grand in appearance; glorious: *a splendid golden crown* **2** very fine; excellent: *a splendid example of stupidity|You've passed the examination? Splendid!* **–splendidly** *adv*

**splen·dour** ‖**-dor** *AmE* /'splendəʳ/ *n* [U] grand beauty: *the splendour of the high distant mountains*

**splice** /splaɪs/ *v* **spliced, splicing** [T *to, together*] to fasten end to end, by weaving (ropes), sticking (pieces of film), etc.: *The recording tape's broken; can you splice these two bits together?*

**splint** /splɪnt/ *n* a flat piece of wood, metal, etc., used for keeping a broken bone in position

**splin·ter¹** /'splɪntəʳ/ *n* **1** [C] a small needle-like piece broken off something: *to get a splinter in one's finger* **2** [A] a group that has separated from a larger body: *They left the party and formed a* **splinter group.**

**splinter²** *v* [I;T] to (cause to) break into small needle-like pieces

**split¹** /splɪt/ *v* **split, splitting 1** [I;T] to (cause to) divide along a length, esp. by a blow or tear: *This soft wood splits easily.|His coat had split down the back.* –see BREAK (USAGE) **2** [I;T *up, into*] to divide into separate often opposing parts or groups: *We split (up) into two groups.|The book is split up into 12* CHAPTERS.*|The vote split the Labour Party.|to split the atom* **3** [T] to divide among people; share: *I'll come with you, and we'll split the cost of the petrol.* **4** [I *up, with*] to end a friendship, marriage, etc.: *Did you know that John and Mary had split up?* (=that their marriage had ended)

**split²** *n* **1** a cut or break made by splitting: *to mend a split in my trousers* **2** a division or separation within a group: *a split in the Labour Party*

**split-lev·el** /ˌ· '·· ◂/ *adj* (of a building) having floors at different heights in different parts

**split sec·ond** /ˌ· '·· ◂/ *n* a small part of a second; moment **–split-second** *adj*

**split·ting** /'splɪtɪŋ/ *adj* (esp. of a headache) very painful

**splut·ter¹** /'splʌtəʳ/ *n* a wet SPITting¹ noise

**splutter²** *v* **1** [I;T] to say or talk quickly and as if confused: *"But-but..." he spluttered.* **2** [I] to make a wet SPITting¹ noise

**spoil¹** /spɔɪl/ *v* **spoiled** *or* **spoilt, spoiling 1** [T] to make useless; ruin: *The visit was spoilt by an argument.|He spoiled the soup by putting too much salt in it.* **2** [I] to decay or lose goodness: *The fruit has spoilt in the hot sun.* **3** [T] to treat very or too well: *Spoil yourself! Have another chocolate.|a spoilt and selfish child who has had too much attention*

**SPELLING NOTE**
Words with the sound /s/, may be spelt **c-**, like **city**, or **ps-**, like **psychology.**

**spoil²** *n* [C;U] things taken without payment, as by an army or by thieves: *to divide up the spoil(s)*

**spoil·sport** /'spɔɪlspɔːt‖-ort/ *n* a person who puts an end to someone else's fun

**spoke¹** /spəʊk/ *n* any of the bars which connect the outer ring of a wheel to the centre, as on a bicycle

**spoke²** *v past tense of* SPEAK

**spok·en** /'spəʊkən/ *v* **1** *past participle of* SPEAK **2** **-spoken** speaking in a certain way: *well-spoken*

**spokes·man** /'spəʊksmən/ **spokeswoman** *fem.*, also **spokesperson**– *n* **-men** /mən, men/, a person chosen to speak for a group officially

**sponge¹** /spʌndʒ/ *n* **1** [C] a simple sea creature which grows a soft rubber-like frame full of small holes **2** [C;U] a piece of this animal's frame or of rubber or plastic like it, used for washing the body, etc. **3** [C;U] *BrE* for SPONGE CAKE

**sponge²** *v* **sponged, sponging 1** [T *off, down*] to clean with a wet cloth or SPONGE¹ (2): *to sponge down the car* **2** [T] to remove (liquid) in this way: *to sponge blood from a wound* **3** [I *on, from*] *derog* to get money, meals, etc., free by taking advantage of another's good nature **–sponger** *n*

**sponge cake** /'· ·/ *n* [C;U] (a) light cake made from eggs, sugar, and flour

**spong·y** /'spʌndʒi/ *adj* **-ier, -iest** like a SPONGE¹ (1); soft and wet: *The grass is spongy after the rain.* **–sponginess** *n* [U]

**spon·sor¹** /'spɒnsəʳ‖'spɑn-/ *n* **1** a person who takes responsibility for a person or thing: *the sponsor of a* BILL¹ (2) *in Parliament* **2** a business which pays for a show, sports event, etc., usu. in return for advertising **–sponsorship** *n* [U]

**sponsor²** *v* [T] to act as SPONSOR for: *The cricket match is being sponsored by a cigarette company.*

**spon·ta·ne·ous** /spɒn'teɪnɪəs‖spɑn-/ *adj* produced from natural feelings or causes; unplanned: *a spontaneous cheer from the crowd* **–spontaneously** *adv* **–spontaneity** /ˌspɒntə'neɪəti, -'niː-‖ˌspɑn-/ *n* [U]

**spoof** /spuːf/ *n* a funny untrue copy or description; PARODY¹ (1): *a magazine spoof of university life*

**spook** /spuːk/ *n infml* a spirit; GHOST¹ (1)

**spook·y** /'spuːki/ *adj* **-ier, -iest** *infml* causing fear in a strange way; EERIE: *a spooky old house*

**spool** /spuːl/ *n* **1** a wheel for winding wire, camera film, etc., round **2** *AmE* for REEL¹

**spoon¹** /spuːn/ *n* **1** a tool for mixing, serving, and eating food: *a silver/wooden spoon|a* TEASPOON –see picture on page 337 **2** → SPOONFUL: *two spoons of sugar*

**spoon²** *v* [T *up, out*] to take up or move with a spoon: *Spoon (out) the mixture into glasses.*

**spoon-feed** /'· ·/ *v* **-fed, -feeding** [T] **1** to feed (esp. a baby) with a spoon **2** to teach (people) in very easy lessons

**spoon·ful** /'spuːnfʊl/ *n* **spoonfuls** *or* **spoonsful** the amount that a spoon will hold: *a spoonful of sugar*

**spo·rad·ic** /spə'rædɪk/ *adj* happening irregularly: *sporadic fighting* **–sporadically** *adv*

**spore** /spɔːʳ‖spor/ *n* a very small seedlike cell produced by some plants, which is able to develop into a new plant

**spor·ran** /ˈspɒrən‖ˈspɔ-, ˈspɑ-/ *n* a fur-covered bag worn as a PURSE[1] (1) in front of a KILT

**sport¹** /spɔːt‖sport/ *n* **1** [C;U] a game or activity done for physical exercise and pleasure: *Do you think football is an exciting sport?|I've never been very keen on sport.* –see RECREATION (USAGE) –see picture on page 592 **2** [C] a person who accepts defeat or a joke without becoming angry or upset: *You're a sport to laugh at the trick we played on you.*

**sport²** *v* [T] to wear publicly: *He was sporting a moustache.*

**sport·ing** /ˈspɔːtɪŋ‖ˈspor-/ *adj* **1** [A] of or concerning outdoor sports: *a painter of sporting scenes* **2** fair-minded and generous, esp. in sports: *a sporting attitude* –opposite **unsporting 3** offering a fair risk: *a sporting chance of winning* **–sportingly** *adv*

**sports** /spɔːts‖sports/ *n* **1** [P] *BrE* a meeting at which people compete in running, jumping, etc. (ATHLETICS): *The school sports* **2** [A] of, for, or connected with sports: *the sports page of the paper*

**sports car** /ˈ· ·/ *n* a low usu. open fast car

**sports·jacket** *BrE*‖**sport jacket** *AmE* /ˈ· ··/ *n* an informal men's JACKET

**sports·man** /ˈspɔːtsmən‖ˈspor-/ **sportswoman** *fem.*– *n* **-men** /mən/ **1** a person who plays sports **2** a good SPORT[1] (2)

**sports·man·like** /ˈspɔːtsmənlaɪk‖ˈspor-/ *adj* showing good SPORTSMANSHIP

**sports·man·ship** /ˈspɔːtsmənʃɪp‖ˈspor-/ *n* [U] a spirit of fair play and graceful winning and losing

**spot¹** /spɒt‖spɑt/ *n* **1** [C] a usu. round part or area different from the main surface, e.g. in colour: *a white dress with blue spots* **2** [C] a particular place: *Spain is our favourite holiday spot.|Wherever she's needed she's quickly* **on the spot**. (=at the place of action) **3** [C] a dirty mark: *to clean off ink spots with soap and water* **4** [C] *euph* for PIMPLE **5** [S] a difficult position; FIX[2] (1): *Could you lend me some money–I'm in a bit of a spot.* **6** [S] *BrE infml* a little bit; small amount: *a spot of tea* **7** [A] limited to a few times or places: *We needn't test everyone; we'll just make spot* CHECKS[1] (1).

**spot²** *v* **-tt-** [T] **1** to pick out with the eye; recognize: *to spot a friend in a crowd* **2** to mark with spots: *white cloth spotted with green|a spotted dog*

**spot·less** /ˈspɒtlǝ̣s‖ˈspɑt-/ *adj* completely clean: *a spotless house|*(fig.) *a spotless* REPUTATION **–spotlessly** *adv* **–spotlessness** *n* [U]

**spot·light¹** /ˈspɒtlaɪt‖ˈspɑt-/ *n* **1** [C] a lamp with a narrow beam that can be directed, used esp. in theatres –see picture on page 463 **2** [*the* S] public attention: *in the spotlight*

**spotlight²** *v* **-lit** *or* **-lighted, -lighting** [T] to direct attention to, (as if) with a SPOTLIGHT: *an article spotlighting the difficulties of school-leavers*

**spot·ter** /ˈspɒtəʳ‖ˈspɑ-/ *n* a person who keeps watch for a particular thing: *a train spotter*

**spot·ty** /ˈspɒti‖ˈspɑti/ *adj* **-tier, -tiest** *BrE infml* having spots on one's face

**spouse** /spaʊs, spaʊz/ *n law* a husband or wife

**spout¹** /spaʊt/ *v* **1** [I;T *out*] to throw or come out in a forceful stream: *a well spouting oil* **2** [T] to pour out in a stream of words: *She spouted on and on.*

**spout²** *n* an opening from which liquid comes out, such as a tube or pipe: *the spout of a teapot*

**sprain** /spreɪn/ *v* [T] to damage (a joint in the body) by sudden twisting: *to sprain one's ankle* –compare STRAIN **–sprain** *n: a nasty sprain of the ankle*

**sprang** /spræŋ/ *v past tense of* SPRING[1]

**sprawl** /sprɔːl/ *v* **1** [I;T *out*] to stretch out (oneself or one's limbs) awkwardly in lying or sitting: *She sprawled (herself) out in a comfortable chair.* **2** [I *out*] to spread ungracefully: *The city sprawls for miles in each direction.* **–sprawl** *n*

**spray¹** *n* **1** [U] water in very small drops blown from the sea, a waterfall, etc.: *We parked the car by the sea and it got covered in spray.* **2** [C;U] (a can or other container holding) liquid to be SPRAYED[2] out under pressure: *spray paint| insect spray* (=to kill insects)

**spray²** *v* [I;T *with/on*] to scatter or be scattered in small drops under pressure: *to spray paint on a wall|*(fig.) *sprayed with bullets.*

**spray³** *n* (an arrangement of flowers, jewels, etc., in the shape of) a small branch with its leaves and flowers

**spray·er** /ˈspreɪəʳ/ *n* a person or apparatus that SPRAYS[2] out a liquid

**spread¹** /spred/ *v* **spread, spreading 1** [I;T *out*] to (cause to) open, reach, or stretch out; make or become longer, broader, wider, etc.: *a ship with sails spread|The fire/The news soon spread through the town.* **2** [I *over, for*] to cover a large area or period of time: *His interests now spread over several subjects.* **3** [T *with/on*] to put (a covering) on: *to spread butter on bread/spread a piece of bread with butter* **4** [T *over*] to scatter, share, or divide over an area, period of time, etc.; DISTRIBUTE: *to spread the cost over three years* **5** [I;T] to make or become widely known: *Don't spread the news around!*

**spread²** *n* **1** [S] the act or action of spreading: *the spread of a disease/the city* **2** [C *usu. sing.*] a distance, range, or time of spreading: *a tree with a spread of 100 feet|a spread of interests* **3** [C] a newspaper or magazine article or advertisement usu. running across one or more pages: *a two-page spread* **4** [C] a large or grand meal: *Our host had a fine spread waiting for us.* **5** [C;U] a soft food for spreading on bread: *a cheese spread*

**spread-ea·gle** /ˌ· ˈ··‖ˈ· ˌ··/ *v* **-gled, -gling** [I;T *usu. pass.*] to put or go into a position with arms and legs spread out: *to lie spread-eagled on the bed*

**spree** /spriː/ *n* a time of free and wild fun, spending, drinking, etc.

**sprig** /sprɪg/ *n* a small end of a stem or branch with leaves: *soup with a sprig of* PARSLEY

**spright·ly** /ˈspraɪtli/ *adj* **-lier, -liest** cheerful and active; LIVELY (1): *a sprightly dance/old man* **–sprightliness** *n* [U]

**spring¹** /sprɪŋ/ *v* **sprang** /spræŋ/‖also **sprung** /sprʌŋ/ *AmE,* **sprung, springing 1** [I] to jump; BOUND[5] (1): *She sprang to her feet/sprang over the wall.* **2** [I *up*] to happen or appear quickly from nothing; arise: *A wind suddenly sprang up.|Towns sprang up in the desert when gold was found there.* **3** [I;T] to open or close with a SPRING[2] (3): *The box sprang open when I touched the button.* **4** [T *on*] to produce as a surprise: *to spring a surprise party on someone* **5 spring a leak**

## swimming

diving board
shallow end
swimmers
width
length
pool
deep end
lifeguard
springboard

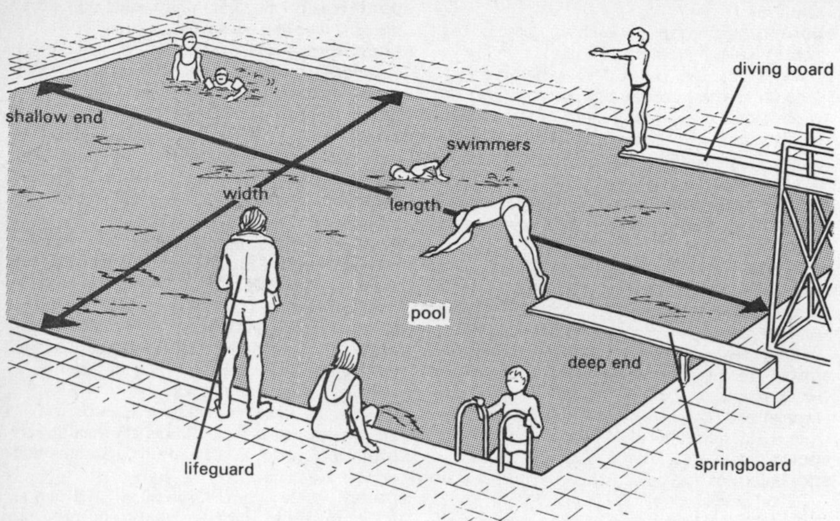

## football

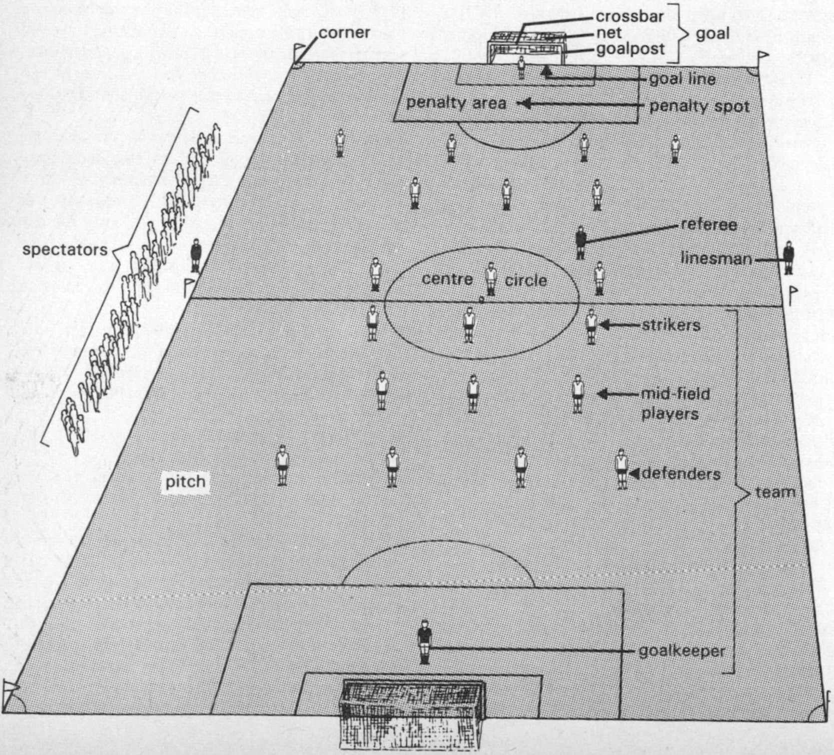

crossbar
net
goalpost
goal
corner
goal line
penalty area
penalty spot
referee
spectators
linesman
centre circle
strikers
mid-field players
defenders
team
pitch
goalkeeper

## tennis

partners
net
player
ball
racket
court
umpire
baseline
sideline

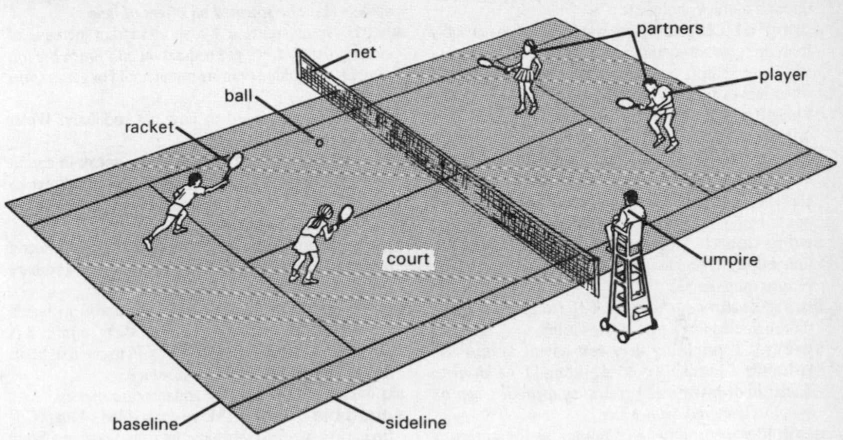

## athletics

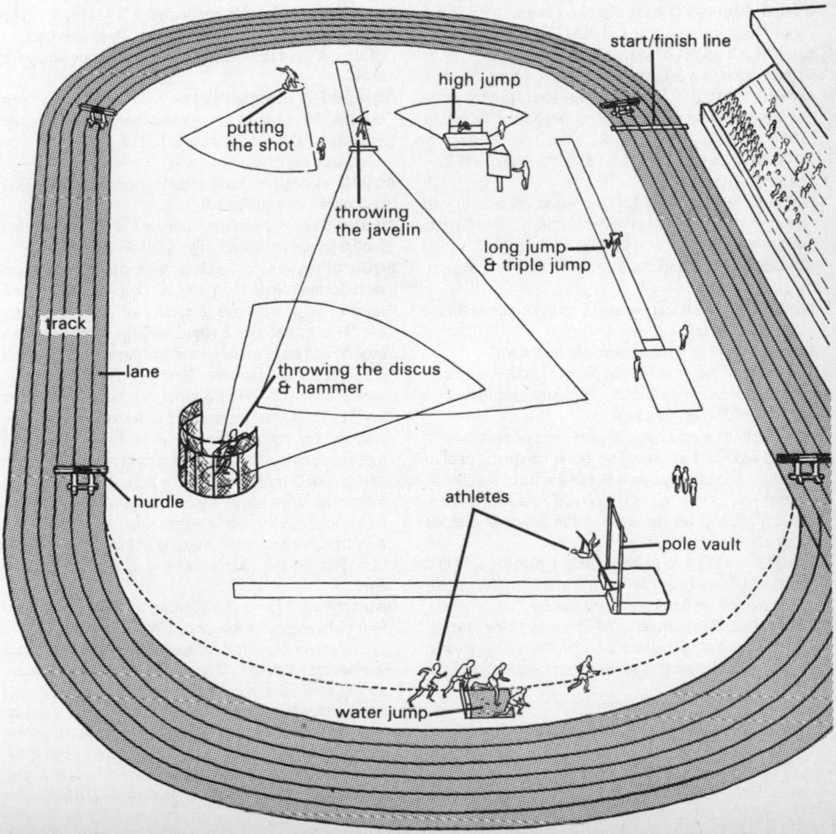

start/finish line
high jump
putting
the shot
throwing
the javelin
long jump
& triple jump
track
lane
throwing the discus
& hammer
hurdle
athletes
pole vault
water jump

(of a ship, container, etc.) to begin to let liquid through a crack, hole, etc.

**spring²** *n* **1** [C] a place where water comes up naturally from the ground –compare SOURCE (2) **2** [C] (*often cap.*) the season between winter and summer in which leaves and flowers appear **3** [C] an object, usu. a length of metal wound around, which returns to its original shape after being pushed, pulled, etc.: *a watch-spring|What an uncomfortable chair! It needs new springs.* **4** [U] the quality of this object; elasticity: *not much spring in this old bed* **5** [C] an act of springing: *The cat made a spring at the mouse.*

**spring·board** /ˈsprɪŋbɔːd‖-bord/ *n* a board for jumping off to give height to a DIVE² (1) or jump –see picture on page 592

**spring-clean** /ˌ·ˈ·◂/ *v,n* [I;T;S] (to give a place) a thorough cleaning, esp. in the spring

**spring·y** /ˈsprɪŋi/ *adj* **-ier, -iest** having SPRING² (4)

**sprin·kle** /ˈsprɪŋkəl/ *v* **-kled, -kling** [T *with/on*] to scatter in drops or small grains: *to sprinkle water on the grass/the grass with water*

**sprin·kler** /ˈsprɪŋkləʳ/ *n* an apparatus for scattering drops of water: *a garden sprinkler|a sprinkler system in a building for protection against fire*

**sprin·kling** /ˈsprɪnklɪŋ/ *n* [*of*] a small scattered group or amount: *a sprinkling of snow/of new faces*

**sprint¹** /sprɪnt/ *v* [I] to run at one's fastest speed for a short distance –see WALK (USAGE) **–sprinter** *n*

**sprint²** *n* **1** an act of SPRINTING **2** a short race

**sprite** /spraɪt/ *n* a fairy, esp. a playful one

**sprout¹** /spraʊt/ *v* [I;T *from, up*] to (cause to) grow or send up new growth: *leaves beginning to sprout from trees*

**sprout²** *n* **1** a new growth on a plant; SHOOT² (1) **2**→ BRUSSELS SPROUT

**spruce¹** /spruːs/ *n* [C;U] (the wood of) a tree with short needle-shaped leaves found in northern parts of the world

**spruce²** *adj* tidy and clean; SMART¹ (1) **–sprucely** *adv: sprucely dressed*

**spruce³** *v* **spruced, sprucing** [T *up*] to make SPRUCE²: *to spruce oneself (up) for a party*

**sprung** /sprʌŋ/ *v past participle of* SPRING¹

**spry** /spraɪ/ *adj* (esp. of old people) active; quick in movement: *a spry old lady* –compare SPRIGHTLY

**spud** /spʌd/ *n infml* a potato

**spun** /spʌn/ *v past tense & participle of* SPIN¹

**spur¹** /spɜːʳ/ *n* **1** a pointed object worn on the heel of a rider's boot to urge on a horse **2** a force leading to action; INCENTIVE: *news which will be a spur to continued effort* **3 on the spur of the moment** without preparation or planning

**spur²** *v* **-rr-** [T] **1** to prick (a horse) with SPURS¹ (1) **2** [+*to-v/on*] to urge to faster action or greater effort: *She spurred on her team to try harder.*

**spu·ri·ous** /ˈspjʊəriəs/ *adj* **1** like something else but false: *a spurious signature* **2** bad in reasoning; wrong: *a spurious argument* **–spuriously** *adv* **–spuriousness** *n* [U]

> **SPELLING NOTE**
> Words with the sound /s/, may be spelt **c-**, like **city**, or **ps-**, like **psychology**.

**spurn** /spɜːn‖spɜrn/ *v* [T] to refuse with angry pride; SCORN² (1): *She spurned all offers of help.*

**spurt¹** /spɜːt‖spɜrt/ *n* **1** a short sudden increase of effort; BURST²: *Let's* **put a spurt on** *and finish the job tonight.* **2** a sudden pouring out of liquid or gas: *a spurt of blood*

**spurt²** *v* [I *out, from*] to flow out suddenly: *Water spurted from the broken pipe.*

**sput·ter** /ˈspʌtəʳ/ *v* **1** [I;T] to say or speak in confusion; SPLUTTER² (1) **2** [I] to make repeated soft explosive sounds: *The car's engine sputtered for a moment and then died.* **–sputter** *n*

**spy¹** /spaɪ/ *n* **spies** a person employed to find out secret information, as from an enemy or company –compare MOLE² (2), AGENT (1)

**spy²** *v* **spied, spying 1** [I *into, on, upon*] to watch secretly: *He's always spying into others' affairs* **2** [I *on, upon*] to act as a SPY¹ **3** [T] *esp. lit* to catch sight of: *She spied a horse in the far distance.*

**sq** *written abbrev. said as*: square: *6 sq metres*

**squab·ble** /ˈskwɒbəl‖ˈskwɑ-/ *v,n* **-bled, -bling** [C;I] (to have) a quarrel over something unimportant: *What are you children squabbling about now?*

**squad** /skwɒd‖skwɑd/ *n* [C +*sing./pl. v*] a group of people working as a team: *The bomb squad*

**squad car** /ˈ· ·/ *n AmE* for POLICE CAR

**squad·ron** /ˈskwɒdrən‖ˈskwɑ-/ *n* [C +*sing./pl. v*] a large group of soldiers with TANKS (2), of warships, or of aircraft in an airforce: *The squadron is/are ready for duty.*

**squal·id** /ˈskwɒlɪ̵d‖ˈskwɑ-/ *adj* very dirty and uncared-for: *squalid living conditions* **–squalidly** *adv* **–squalor** /ˈskwɒləʳ‖skwɑ-/ *n* [U]: *a part of the city now sunk into squalor*

**squall** /skwɔːl/ *n* a sudden strong wind often bringing rain or snow **–squally** *adj*

**squan·der** /ˈskwɒndəʳ‖ˈskwɑn-/ *v* [T] to spend foolishly; use up wastefully: *squandered money*

**square¹** /skweəʳ/ *n* **1** a shape with four straight equal sides forming four right angles: *Draw a square with sides of 10 centimetres.|a square of cloth* –compare RECTANGLE, OBLONG **2** (the buildings surrounding) a broad open place at the meeting of streets: *The market is held in the town square.|He lives in Norfolk Square.* –see STREET (USAGE) **3** a number equal to another number multiplied by itself: *16 is the square of 4.* –see also SQUARE ROOT **4** a straight-edged often L-shaped tool for drawing and measuring right angles –see also SETSQUARE **5** *infml now rare* a person who does not follow the latest ideas, styles, etc.: *Don't ask her advice about clothes; she's a real square!* **6 square one** *BrE* the very beginning; starting point: *All my papers were lost in the fire, so now I'm* **back to square one**.

**square²** *adj* **1** [*no comp.*] having four equal sides and four right angles: *A handkerchief is usually square.|a square tower* **2** (nearly) forming a right angle: *a square jaw|square shoulders* **3** level: *That shelf isn't square on the wall; can you straighten it?* **4** [A *no comp.*] being a measurement of area equal to that of a square with sides of a particular length: *144 square inches equals 1 square foot.* **5** [after *n; no comp.*] being the stated length on all four sides: *The room is 6 metres square.* **6** [F *no comp.*] paid and settled: *Our* account is all *square*. **7** [F *no comp*.] equal in points; TIED[2] (3): *The teams are* **all square** *at one match each.* **8** *infml now rare* of or like a SQUARE[1] (5); old-fashioned **9 square deal** fair and honest treatment: *I don't think I'm getting a square deal at that garage*. –see also FAIR[2] (2) **10 square meal** a good satisfying meal **–squarely** *adv* **–squareness** *n* [U]

**square³** *v* **squared, squaring 1** [T] to make square: *He squared off the end of the piece of wood.|She refused; squaring her shoulders.* **2** [T] to mark squares on: *squared paper* **3** [T *usu. pass.*] to multiply (a number) by itself once: *2 squared equals 4*. (written $2^2=4$) **4** [I;T *with*] to (cause to) fit a particular explanation or standard: *His statement doesn't square with the facts.* **5** [T] to pay or pay for; settle: *I squared my account at the store.*

**square up** *v adv* [I] *infml* to settle a bill; *Let's square up; how much is the bill?*

**square⁴** also **squarely**– *adv* [*adv* + *prep*] *infml* directly; with nothing in the way: *He looked her square in the eye.*

**square root** /ˌ· ˈ·/ *n* the number not less than 0 which when multiplied by itself equals a particular number: *3 is the square root of 9*. (because 3x3=9) –see also SQUARE[1] (3)

**squash¹** /skwɒʃ‖skwɑʃ, skwɔʃ/ *v* **1** [I;T] to force or be forced into a flat shape or a small space: *I sat on my hat and squashed it.|May I squash in next to you?* **2** [T] to force into silence or inactivity: *squashed by an unkind remark*

**squash²** *n* **1** [S] a crowd of people in a small space: *a squash in the train* **2** [U] a game played in a walled court with RACKETS[1] and a rubber ball **3** [U] *BrE* a sweet fruit drink: *a glass of orange squash*

**squat¹** /skwɒt‖skwɑt/ *v* **-tt-** [I] **1** to sit on a surface with one's legs drawn fully up or under the body, esp. balancing on the front of the feet –see picture on page 669 **2** to live in a place without permission; be a SQUATTER

**squat²** *adj* ungracefully short or low and thick: *an ugly squat building*

**squat·ter** /ˈskwɒtəʳ‖ˈskwɑ-/ *n* a person who lives in an empty building without permission

**squaw** /skwɔː/ *n* an American Indian woman

**squawk** /skwɔːk/ *n,v* [C;I] (to make) a loud rough-sounding cry, esp. as made by birds

**squeak** /skwiːk/ *n,v* [C;I] (to make) a very high but not loud sound: *a squeaking door|the squeak of a mouse* **–squeaky** *adj* **-ier, -iest**: *a squeaky voice*

**squeal** /skwiːl/ *n,v* [C;I] (to make) a long very high sound or cry: *squealing tyres/pigs|squeals of delight from the children*

**squeam·ish** /ˈskwiːmɪʃ/ *adj* easily shocked; unable to stand unpleasantness: *It's a violent film, so don't go if you're squeamish.* **–squeamishly** *adv* **–squeamishness** *n* [U]

**squeeze¹** /skwiːz/ *v* **squeezed, squeezing 1** [T] to press together; COMPRESS[1] (1): *to squeeze an orange|to squeeze out a wet cloth* **2** [I;T] to fit by forcing, CROWDing, or pressing: *The car was full but I squeezed in anyway.* **3** [T *from, out of*] to force out by pressure: *to squeeze toothpaste out of a tube*

**squeeze²** *n* **1** [C] an act of pressing in from opposite sides or around: *She gave his hand a gentle squeeze.* **2** [C] a small amount SQUEEZED[1] (3) out: *a squeeze of lemon* **3** [S] a condition of CROWDing or pressing: *There's room for one more, but it'll be a squeeze.* **4** [C] a situation in which there is a lack of certain things, of money to borrow, etc. *a* CREDIT[1] (4) *squeeze*

**squelch** /skweltʃ/ *n,v* [C;I] (to make) a sound of partly liquid material being pressed down, e.g. when stepping through mud

**squid** /skwɪd/ *n* **squids** *or* **squid** a sea creature with 10 arms at one end of a long body

**squig·gle** /ˈskwɪgəl/ *n infml* a short wavy or twisting line: *Her writing is just squiggles.* **–squiggly** *adj*

**squint¹** /skwɪnt/ *v* [I] **1** to look with almost closed eyes, as at a bright light **2** [not *be* +*v-ing*] to have a SQUINT[2]

**squint²** *n* a disorder of the eye muscles causing the eyes to look in two different directions

**squire** /skwaɪəʳ/ *n* (esp. formerly) the main landowner in an English country area

**squirm** /skwɜːm‖-ɜrm/ *v* [I] to twist the body about, as from discomfort or nervousness: *questions that made him squirm*

**squir·rel** /ˈskwɪrəl‖ˈskwɜrəl/ *n* a small four-legged animal with a long furry tail that climbs trees and eats nuts

**squirt¹** /skwɜːt‖-ɜrt/ *v* **1** [I;T] to force or be forced out in a thin stream: *to squirt oil into a lock|water squirting out from a hole in the pipe* **2** [T *with*] to hit with a stream of liquid: *I was squirted with water.*

**squirt²** *n* **1** a quick thin stream; JET[1] (1) **2** *infml derog* a young unimportant person

**Ssh** /ʃ/ *interj* → SH

**St** *n written abbrev. said as:* **1** [after *n*] Street: *Regent St* **2** [A] SAINT: *St Andrew*

**stab¹** /stæb/ *n* **1** a blow or wound made with a pointed weapon: *a stab in the chest* **2** a sudden painful feeling; PANG: *a stab of guilt* **3 have a stab at** to try: *Have a stab at (answering) question 3.*

**stab²** *v* **-bb-** [I;T *at*] to strike forcefully with a pointed weapon: *Julius Caesar was stabbed to death.*

**stab·bing** /ˈstæbɪŋ/ *adj* (esp. of pain) sharp and sudden

**sta·bil·i·ty** /stəˈbɪlə̇ti/ *n* [U] the state of being STABLE[3]: *the stability of their marriage* –opposite **instability**

**sta·bil·ize** ‖also **-ise** *BrE* /ˈsteɪbə̇laɪz/ *v* **-ized, -izing** [I;T] to make or become firm or steady: *The price of coffee has been rising and falling, but has now stabilized.* **–stabilization** /-laɪˈzeɪʃən‖-lə-/ *n* [U]

**sta·bil·iz·er**‖also **-iser** *BrE* /ˈsteɪbə̇laɪzəʳ/ *n* an apparatus or chemical that STABILIZEs something: *The ship's stabilizers keep it steady in bad weather.*

**sta·ble¹** /ˈsteɪbəl/ *n* [*often pl.*] **1** a building for keeping and feeding horses in **2** a group of racing horses with one owner

**stable²** *v* **-bled, -bling** [T] to put in a STABLE[1] (1)

**stable³** *adj* not easily moved, upset, or changed; firm: *a stable chair/government/character* –opposite **unstable –stably** *adv*

**stack¹** /stæk/ *n* [*of*] **1** an orderly pile: *a stack of papers/dishes* **2** *infml* a large amount or number: *stacks of work to do*

**stack²** *v* [I;T *up*] to make into a neat pile; arrange in a STACK: *The chairs were neatly stacked at the back of the hall.*

**sta·di·um** /'steɪdɪəm/ *n* **-ums** *or* **-a** /dɪə/ a large sports ground with rows of seats built around a sports field

**staff¹** /stɑːf‖stæf/ *n* [C +*sing./pl. v*] the group of workers who do the work of an organization: *The school's teaching staff is/are excellent.|a staff of 15|She's* **on the staff of** *the new university.*

**staff²** *v* [T *with*] to supply with STAFF; provide the workers for: *a hospital staffed with 20 doctors*

**staff³** *n* a thick stick used as a support or as a mark of office

**stag** /stæg/ *n* **stags** *or* **stag 1** a fully grown male deer **2 stag party** a party for men only, esp. just before a man gets married

**stage¹** /steɪdʒ/ *n* **1** [C] a period in a course of events: *The plan is still in its early stages/at an early stage.* **2** [C] a part of a journey: *We travelled by (easy) stages, stopping often along the way.* **3** [C] the raised floor on which plays are performed in a theatre: *The actor was* **on stage** *for hours.* –see picture on page 463 **4** [*the* S] work in the theatre: *When she was five years old, she decided that she wanted to go on the stage.* (=become an actress)

**stage²** *v* **staged, staging** [T] **1** to perform or arrange for public show; put on: *to stage an art show/a football match* **2** to cause to happen, esp. for public effect: *to stage a one-day* STRIKE² (1)

**stage·coach** /'steɪdʒkəʊtʃ/ *n* (in former times) a horse-drawn closed vehicle carrying passengers: *to travel* **by stagecoach**

**stage fright** /'· ·/ *n* [U] nervousness felt when performing in public

**stage man·ag·er** /'· ˌ···/ *n* a person in charge of a theatre stage during a performance

**stag·ger¹** /'stægəʳ/ *v* **1** [I] to move unsteadily on one's feet: *a drunk man staggering across the street* **2** [T] to arrange not to come at the same time: *The schools in this area have staggered holidays*

**stagger²** *n* an unsteady movement of a person having difficulty walking: *She gave a stagger as she began to feel faint.*

**stag·ger·ing** /'stægərɪŋ/ *adj* almost unbelievable; very surprising: *a staggering rise in the cost of petrol* **–staggeringly** *adv*

**stag·ing** /'steɪdʒɪŋ/ *n* [C;U] the action or art of producing a play: *a new staging of "Hamlet"*

**stag·nant** /'stægnənt/ *adj* (of water) not flowing or moving, and often bad-smelling: (fig.) *Business is stagnant at the moment.* (=inactive) **–stagnantly** *adv*

**stag·nate** /stæg'neɪt‖'stægneɪt/ *v* **-nated, -nating** [I] to become STAGNANT; stop moving or developing **–stagnation** /-'neɪʃən/ *n* [U]

**staid** /steɪd/ *adj* serious and dull by habit; unadventurous **–staidly** *adv* **–staidness** *n* [U]

**stain¹** /steɪn/ *v* [I;T] **1** to change the colour of, in a way that is lasting: *teeth stained by years of smoking|stained* (=coloured) *glass windows in a church* **2** to darken using chemicals: *stained wood*

**SPELLING NOTE**

Words with the sound /s/, may be spelt **c-**, like **city**, or **ps-**, like **psychology.**

**stain²** *n* [C;U] **1** a STAINed place or spot: *bloodstains on my shirt|(lit) the stain upon his honour* **2** a chemical for darkening esp. wood

**stain·less** /'steɪnl¦ɜs/ *adj* not easily attacked by air and water (=by RUST): *a set of stainless steel knives*

**stair** /steəʳ/ *n* **1** [A;C] → STAIRS: *a stair* CARPET **2** [C] a step in a set of stairs

**stair·case** /'steəkeɪs‖-ər-/ also **stairway**– *n* a set of stairs with its supports and side parts –see picture on page 297

**stairs** /steəz‖-ərz/ *n* [P] a fixed length of steps built for going from one level to another, esp. inside a building: *to go up and down the stairs|a* **flight of stairs** –see also DOWNSTAIRS, UPSTAIRS –see picture on page 297

**stake¹** /steɪk/ *n* **1** [C] a pointed piece of wood for driving into the ground as a mark, for holding a rope, etc. **2** [*the* S] (in former times) a post to which a person was tied in order to be killed by burning **3** [C] something that may be gained or lost; INTEREST¹ (5): *Profit-sharing gives workers a stake in their company.|He lost his stake* (=money he had STAKED²) *when the horse finished last.* **4 at stake** at risk

**stake²** *v* **staked, staking** [T] to risk (esp. money) on a result; BET: *I've staked all my hopes on you.*

**stal·ac·tite** /'stæləktaɪt‖stə'læktaɪt/ *n* a sharp downward-pointing part of a cave roof like an ICICLE, formed over a long time by water dropping from the roof –compare STALAGMITE

**stal·ag·mite** /'stæləgmaɪt‖stə''ægmaɪt/ *n* an upward-pointing part of a cave floor formed by drops from a STALACTITE and often joining it to form a solid pillar

**stale** /steɪl/ *adj* no longer fresh: *bits of stale bread for the birds*|(fig.) *stale jokes* **–staleness** *n* [C;U]

**stale·mate** /'steɪlmeɪt/ *n* [C;U] **1** (in the game of CHESS) a position from which neither player can win **2** a condition in which neither side in a quarrel, argument, etc., seems able to move or gain an advantage

**stalk¹** /stɔːk/ *v* **1** [T] to hunt (esp. an animal) by following it quietly and staying hidden: *to stalk a criminal* **2** [I] to walk stiffly and proudly: *She was so angry with him that she stalked out of the house.*

**stalk²** *n* the main part of a plant supporting its leaves, fruits, or flowers; stem

**stall¹** /stɔːl/ *n* **1** an indoor enclosure, e.g. in a BARN or STABLE, for one animal: *cattle in their stalls* **2** *esp. BrE* a table or small open-fronted shop in a public place: *a market stall|a station bookstall*

**stall²** *v* **1** [I] *infml* to delay: *Stop stalling and answer my question!* **2** [I;T] **a** (of an engine) to stop through lack of power or speed: *The car/engine stalled on the hill.* **b** to cause or force (an engine) to do this

**stal·li·on** /'stælɪən/ *n* a fully-grown male horse –compare MARE

**stalls** /stɔːlz/ *n* [P] *BrE* the seats on the main level of a cinema or theatre –see picture on page 463

**stal·wart¹** /'stɔːlwət‖-ərt/ *adj* strong and unmoving in body, mind, purpose, etc.: *a stalwart supporter/fighter* **–stalwartly** *adv* **–stalwartness** *n* [U]

**stalwart²** *n* a firm follower, esp. of a political party

**sta·men** /'steɪmən/ *n tech* the male

POLLEN-producing part of a flower

**stam·i·na** /'stæm$\frac{1}{2}$nə/ *n* [U] the strength of body or mind to fight tiredness, illness, etc.; power to keep going: *You need great stamina to run the 10,000 metres race.*

**stam·mer¹** /'stæmə^r/ *v* [I;T] to speak or say with pauses and repeated sounds, either habitually or because of excitement, fear, etc.: *She stammers when she feels nervous.|He stammered his thanks.* –compare STUTTER –**stammerer** *n*

**stammer²** *n* [*usu. sing.*] the fault of STAMMERing in speech

**stamp¹** /stæmp/ *v* **1** [I;T *on*] to put (the feet) down hard: *She was stamping about keeping her feet warm.|He stamped his foot angrily.* **2** [T *with/on*] to mark (a pattern, sign, letters, etc.) by pressing: *This machine stamps the date on all letters/stamps all letters with the date.* **3** [T] to stick a stamp onto: *Has this letter been stamped?*

**stamp** sthg.↔**out** *v adv* [T] to put an end to completely; ERADICATE: *to stamp out a disease*

**stamp²** *n* **1** also **postage stamp** *fml*– a small piece of paper for sticking on a piece of mail, on certain official papers, etc. **2** (a mark made by) an instrument or tool for printing onto a surface: *The stamp in the library book shows it must be returned tomorrow.*|(fig.) *His words have the stamp of truth.* **3** an act of stamping, e.g. with the foot

**stam·pede¹** /stæm'pi:d/ *n* a sudden rush of fearful animals: (fig.) *a stampede to buy gold*

**stampede²** *v* **-peded, -peding** [I;T *into*] to drive or go in a disorderly or unreasonable rush: *We mustn't be stampeded into doing anything foolish.*

**stance** /stɑ:ns‖stæns/ *n* **1** a way of standing, esp. in various sports **2** a way of thinking; ATTITUDE (1)

**stand¹** /stænd/ *v* **stood** /stʊd/, **standing 1** [I] to support oneself upright on one's feet: *I couldn't get a seat on the bus, so I had to stand.* –compare SIT **2** [I;T *up*] to (cause to) rise to a position of doing this: *He stood (up) when the lady entered the room.|He stood the child on the wall so that she could see.* **3** [I] to be in or take a particular position like this: *Stand back and let the man through.*|(fig.) *Stand firm; don't let them change your opinion.* **4** [I] to be in height: *The building stands over 200 feet high.* **5** [I;T] to be, put, or rest upright or on a base: *Few houses were left standing after the bomb hit.|Stand the ladder against the wall.* **6** [I +*to-v*] to be in a particular condition: *My bank account stands at £550.|If this new law is passed, we stand to lose* (=will be in a position to lose) *a lot of money.* **7** [I] to remain unmoving or unchanged: *The machinery has been* **standing idle** (=unused) *for months. |Leave the mixture of liquids to stand overnight.|My offer of help still stands.* **8** [T +*v-ing*/not *be*+*v-ing*] (usu. used in NEGATIVES², questions, etc.) to accept successfully; bear: *I can't stand getting up early.|This work will hardly stand close examination.|He seems to like me but I can't* **stand the sight of** *him.* –see BEAR (USAGE) **9** [T] to pay the cost of (something) for: *Let me stand you dinner.* **10** [I *for*] *BrE*‖**run** *AmE*– to put oneself forward to be elected; be a CANDIDATE: *She's going to stand for Parliament.* **11 stand a chance** to have a chance: *You don't stand a chance of getting the job!* **12 standing on one's head** *infml* with great ease: *I could do that job standing on my head.* **13 stand on one's hands/head** to support oneself on the hands/head and hands, with the feet in the air **14 stand on one's own (two) feet/legs** to be able to live without help from others **15 stand something on its head** to change or upset something violently: *It was a discovery which stood the whole of chemistry on its head.* **16 it stands to reason** it is clear to all sensible people; it is OBVIOUS **17 stand trial** to be tried in court

**stand by¹** sbdy./sthg. *v prep* [T] to support; be loyal to: *I'll stand by my promise to you.*

**stand by²** *v adv* [I] **1** to remain inactive: *How can you stand by and watch the country go to ruin?* **2** (esp. in radio and military use) to stay ready: *Stand by to receive a message/to fire.* –see also STANDBY

**stand down** *v adv* [I] to yield one's position in a competition or election: *He stood down in favour of the other candidate.*

**stand for** sthg. *v prep* [T] **1** to be a sign or short form of; represent; mean: *What does* "PTO" *stand for?* **2** to have as a principle; support: *Before we elect her to Parliament, we want to know what she stands for.* **3**[+ *v-ing*] (used in NEGATIVE² sentences) to accept; PUT **up with:** *I won't stand for such treatment!*

**stand in** *v adv* [I *for*] to act as a STAND-IN: *She's standing in for him while he's on holiday.*

**stand out** *v adv* [I] **1** to have an easily-seen shape, colour, etc.: *The road sign is easy to read; the words stand out well.* **2** to be much better or the best; *She stood out as the best in the class.*

**stand up** *v adv* [I *to, under*] to stay in good condition after hard use: *a good floor wax that will stand up to continual passing to and fro*

**stand up for** sbdy./sthg. *v adv prep* [T] to defend against attack: *You must stand up for your rights!*

**stand²** *n* **1** a strong effort of defence: *In February 1916 the French Army made a stand at Verdun.* **2** a clear, publicly-stated position: *If he wants my vote he'll have to* **take a stand** *on the question of East-West relations.* **3** a piece of furniture for putting something on: *a hatstand|music stand* (for holding sheets of music) **4** a small often outdoor shop or place for showing things; STALL¹ (2): *a newsstand* (=selling newspapers) **5** [*usu.pl.*] an open-fronted building at a sports ground with rows of seats or standing space rising behind each other: *He kicked the ball into the stands.* **6** *AmE* for WITNESS BOX: *Will the next witness take the stand?*

**stan·dard¹** /'stændəd‖-ərd/ *n* **1** something used, accepted, or officially fixed as a measure of quality, purity, weight, etc.: *a teacher who sets high standards for his pupils|Your recent work hasn't been up to standard.* (=has been below an acceptable level)|*The government has an official standard for the purity of silver.* **2** a ceremonial flag: *the royal standard*

**standard²** *adj* **1** ordinary; not rare or special: *These nails come in three standard sizes.* **2** [A] generally recognized as correct or acceptable: *It's one of the standard books on the subject.|standard spelling/pronunciation* –compare NONSTANDARD, SUBSTANDARD

**stan·dard·ize** ‖also **-ise** *BrE* /'stændədaɪz‖-ər-/ *v*

-**ized, -izing** [T] to make alike in every case: *a system of standardized road signs* –**standardization** /-daɪˈzeɪʃən‖-də-/ *n* [U]

**standard lamp** /ˈ·· ·/ *n BrE* a lamp on a tall base which stands on the floor –see picture on page 355

**standard of liv·ing** /ˌ··· ˈ··/ also **living standard**– *n* the degree of wealth and comfort in everyday life that a person, country, etc., has: *a rapid rise in the country's standard of living*

**stand·by** /ˈstændbaɪ/ *n* -**bys** a person or thing that is kept ready to be used: *If the electricity fails, the hospital has a standby power apparatus.|The police are* **on standby.**|*They bought two cheap standby tickets for Rome.* (=they had to wait and see if any seats were available) –see also STAND **by**[2]

**stand-in** /ˈ· ·/ *n* a person who takes the place or job of another for a time –see also STAND **in**

**stand·ing**[1] /ˈstændɪŋ/ *adj* [A] remaining; kept in use or force: *We have a standing invitation; we can visit them whenever we like.|a standing army|Do you pay your bills by* **standing order?** (=an order to pay a fixed amount from a bank account every month, year, etc.)

**standing**[2] *n* [U] **1** rank; position in a system, organization, or list: *a lawyer of high standing* **2** continuance; time during which something has kept on; DURATION: *friends of* **long standing**

**stand·off·ish** /stændˈɒfɪʃ‖-ˈɔfɪʃ/ *adj* rather unfriendly; coldly formal –**standoffishly** *adv* –**standoffishness** *n* [U]

**stand·point** /ˈstændpɔɪnt/ *n* a position from which things are seen and opinions formed; POINT[1] (20) of view

**stand·still** /ˈstændˌstɪl/ *n* [S] a condition of no movement or activity; stop: *a car at a standstill*

**stank** /stæŋk/ *v past tense of* STINK

**stan·za** /ˈstænzə/ *n* a group of lines forming a division of a poem

**sta·ple**[1] /ˈsteɪpəl/ *n* **1** a small bit of thin wire which is driven through sheets of paper to hold them together **2** a small U-shaped piece of metal for holding e.g. electrical wires in place

**staple**[2] *v* -**pled, -pling** [T] to fasten with STAPLES

**staple**[3] *n* **1** something, esp. a food, that forms the most important part: *a staple diet of vegetables* **2** a main product: *the staples among British farm products*

**sta·pler** /ˈsteɪpləʳ/ *n* a hand instrument for driving STAPLES[1] into paper

**star**[1] /stɑːʳ/ *n* **1** a brightly-burning heavenly body of great size, esp. one very far away **2** *infml* any heavenly body, such as a PLANET, that appears as a bright point in the sky –see SHOOTING STAR **3** a five or more pointed figure, e.g. for wearing as a mark of office, rank, etc., or as a sign to show quality: *He only stays at five star* (=the best) *hotels.* **4** [*usu. pl.*] a heavenly body regarding as determining one's fate: *She was born under an unlucky star.* **5** a famous or very skilful performer: *a film/football star* **6** → ASTERISK **7 see stars** to see flashes of light, esp. as a result of being hit on the head –**starless** *adj*

**SPELLING NOTE**
Words with the sound /s/, may be spelt **c-**, like **city**, or **ps-**, like **psychology.**

**star**[2] *v* -**rr- 1** [T] to mark with one or more stars (ASTERISKS) **2** [I;T *in*] to have or appear as a main performer: *an old film starring Charlie Chaplin|Humphrey Bogart starred in this film.*

**star·board** /ˈstɑːbəd‖ˈstɑrbərd/ *n* [S] the right side of a ship or aircraft as one faces forward –compare PORT[2]

**starch**[1] /stɑːtʃ‖-ɑr-/ *n* **1** [C;U] (a white tasteless substance forming an important part of) a food such as grain, rice, beans, and potatoes **2** [U] a product made from this for stiffening cloth

**starch**[2] *v* [T] to stiffen with STARCH[1] (2): *to starch a shirt*

**starch·y** /ˈstɑːtʃi‖ˈstɑr-/ *adj* -**ier, -iest 1** full of, or like, STARCH[1]: *starchy foods* **2** *infml* stiffly correct and formal

**star·dom** /ˈstɑːdəm‖ˈstɑr-/ *n* [U] the position of a famous performer

**stare** /steəʳ/ *v* **stared, staring** [I;T *at*] to look fixedly (at) with wide-open eyes, as in wonder, fear, anger, or deep thought: *It's rude to stare (at other people).|He sat staring into space, thinking.* –**stare** *n*: *She gave him a long cool stare.*

**stare** sbdy. **out** *v adv* [T] to make (a person or animal) look away under the power of a long steady look

**star·fish** /ˈstɑːˌfɪʃ‖ˈstɑr-/ *n* **starfish** *or* **starfishes** a flat sea animal with five arms forming a star shape

**stark**[1] /stɑːk‖stɑrk/ *adj* **1** hard, bare, or severe in appearance: *the stark shape of rocks against the sky* **2** [A] pure; complete; UTTER: *stark madness* –**starkly** *adv*

**stark**[2] *adv* **stark naked** *infml* completely NAKED

**star·let** /ˈstɑːlɪ̵t‖ˈstɑr-/ *n* a young actress who has had some success, but who is not yet very famous

**star·light** /ˈstɑ-ləɪt‖ˈstɑr-/ *n* [U] the light given by the stars

**star·ling** /ˈstɑːlɪŋ‖ˈstɑr-/ *n* a common greenish-black European bird

**star·ry** /ˈstɑːri/ *adj* -**rier, -riest** filled with stars: *a starry winter sky*

**starry-eyed** /ˌ·· ˈ·◂/ *adj* full of unreasonable hopes

**Stars and Stripes** /ˌ· · ˈ·/ *n AmE pomp* the flag of the US

**star-stud·ded** /ˈ· ˌ··/ *adj infml* filled with famous performers: *a star-studded cast in tonight's show*

**start**[1] /stɑːt‖stɑrt/ *v* **1** [I;T *up*] to bring or come into being; begin: *How did the trouble start?|I'm trying to start up a swimming club* **2** [I;T +*to-v/v-ing*] to put into or go into activity, operation, etc.: *It's started to rain/started raining.|If everyone is ready we can start.|I can't start the car.* (=the car's engine)| *I can't get the fire started.* (=can't light the fire)|*The film starts in ten minutes; hurry up!* –compare STOP[1] **3** [I *off, out, for*] to begin a journey: *It's a long trip; we'll have to* **start out/off** *early and* **start back** *for home in the afternoon.* **4** [I *at, from*] to go from a particular point; have a beginning or lower limit: *The railway line starts from Moscow and goes all the way to Siberia.|Prices start at £5.* **5** [T] to begin using: *Start each page on the second line.* **6** [I *at*] to make a quick uncontrolled movement, as from sudden surprise; be STARTLEd: *The touch on his shoulder made him start.* **7 to start with** also **for a start**– (used before the first in a list of facts, reasons, etc.). *It won't work; to start with, it's a bad idea, and secondly it'll cost too much.*

USAGE 1 Both **start** and **begin** are used in the patterns [T +*to-v*] and [T +*v-ing* ] with the same meaning; but the [T +*to-v*] pattern is better **a** if **begin** or **start are** themselves in the *-ing* form: *I think it's* **beginning/starting** *to rain*; or **b** if the verb that follows concerns one's feelings, ideas, etc.: *I began to realize that he was right.*|*I* **started** *to wonder if .....* –compare STOP (USAGE) 2 **Begin** cannot be used instead of **start** in the following meanings: *We* **started** *(out) for London* (=began our journey)|*They've* **started** (=brought into existence) *a new political party.*|*I can't* **start** *the car/The car won't* **start.** (=begin working). **Commence** is used like **begin**, but is very formal.

**start**[2] *n* **1** [C] an act or place of starting: *It's getting late; we must* **make a start**. (=begin)|*The runners lined up at the start.* **2** [C] the beginning of something: *The start of the film was dull* –compare FINISH **3** [C *usu. sing.*] a sudden uncontrolled movement, e.g. of surprise: *I woke up with a start.* **4** [C;U] the amount by which someone is ahead of someone else: *The thieves have had (a) three days' start on/over the police*

**start·er** /'stɑːtəʳ||'stɑr-/ *n* **1** a person, horse, car, etc., in a race or match at the start **2** a person who gives the signal for a race to begin **3** an apparatus for starting an engine –compare BEGINNER

**start·le** /'stɑːtl||'stɑrtl/ *v* **-led, -ling** [T] to cause to jump with sudden surprise: *The noise startled me*

**starv·a·tion** /stɑː'veɪʃən||stɑr-/ *n* [U] suffering or death from lack of food

**starve** /stɑːv||stɑrv/ *v* **starved, starving** [I;T] to (cause to) die or suffer from lack of food: *They starved to death in the desert.*|*He's starving himself trying to lose weight.*|(fig.) *The engine was starved of petrol.*

**state**[1] /steɪt/ *n* **1** [C] a condition in which a person or thing is: *the state of one's health*|*a happy state of mind* **2** [C;U] (*often cap.*) a country or its government: *Should industry be controlled by the state?*|*state-owned railways*|*state secrets* –see RACE (USAGE) **3** [A;U] the formality and ceremony connected with high-level government: *the visiting President was received in state.*|*a state occasion* **4** [C] (*often cap.*) any of the smaller partly self- governing parts making up certain nations: *the 50 states of the US* **5** [C] *infml* a very nervous or excited condition: *He* **got into a state** *before the examination began.* **6 lie in state** (of a dead body) to be placed in a public place so that people may honour it

**state**[2] *v* **stated, stating** [T] *fml* **1** [+(*that*)] to say, express, or put into words: *This book states the case for women's rights very clearly.* **2** to set in advance; name: *Theatre tickets must be used on the stated date.*

USAGE To **state** something is to express it formally in writing or speech: *The witness* **stated** *that she had never seen Mr Brown before.*|*The notice* **states** *clearly that dogs are not allowed.* **Declare** is similar, but is mainly used of spoken statements, esp. of an official kind: *The minister* **declared** *her intention of joining the new political party.* To **announce** something is to make it publicly known for the first time, but not necessarily in a formal way: She came in and **announced** that she was expecting a baby. To **assert** suggests making a very forceful statement about something, and to **affirm** suggests stating something in order to remove doubts that others may have; both words are rather formal: *He* **asserted** *his belief that the plan would fail.*|*We didn't believe her at first, but she* **affirmed** *that she was telling the truth.*

**state·ly** /'steɪtli/ *adj* **-lier, -liest** formal and grand in style or size: *a* **stately home** –**stateliness** *n* [U]

**state·ment** /'steɪtmənt/ *n* **1** something that is stated; a formal declaration: *the witness's statement* **2** a list showing amounts of money paid, received, owing, etc., and their total: *a bank statement*

**States** /steɪts/ *n infml* the US: *a holiday in the States*

**states·man** /'steɪtsmən/ *n* **-men** /mən/ a political leader, esp. one who is respected as being wise and fair-minded –**statesmanship** *n* [U]

**stat·ic** /'stætɪk/ *adj* **1** not moving or changing: *static prices* **2** (of electricity) not flowing in a current: *static electricity in some people's hair*

**sta·tion**[1] /'steɪʃən/ *n* **1** also **depot** *AmE*– a building on a railway or bus line where passengers or goods are taken on: *a station hotel/waiting room* –see picture on page 501 **2** a building that is a centre for a particular service: *a police/fire/petrol station* **3** a company or apparatus that broadcasts on television or radio: *I can't get* (=hear) *many foreign stations on this little radio.* **4** a usu. small military establishment: *a naval station*

**station**[2] *v* [T] to put into a place; POST[6] (1): *Guards were stationed around the prison.*

**sta·tion·a·ry** /'steɪʃənəri||-neri/ *adj* standing still; not moving: *a stationary car*

**sta·tion·er** /'steɪʃənəʳ/ *n* a person or shop that sells STATIONERY

**sta·tion·er·y** /'steɪʃənəri||-neri/ *n* [U] materials for writing; paper, ink, pencils, etc.

**station wag·on** /'·· ,··/ *n AmE* for ESTATE CAR

**stat·is·ti·cian** /,stæt½s'tɪʃən/ *n* a person who works with STATISTICS

**sta·tis·tics** /stə'tɪstɪks/ *n* [P;U] (the science which deals with) collected numbers representing facts or measurements: *These statistics show deaths per 1,000 of population.* –**statistical** *adj* –**statistically** *adv*

**stat·ue** /'stætʃuː/ *n* a likeness esp. of a person or animal, made in stone, metal, etc.

**stat·u·esque** /,stætʃʊ'esk/ *adj* like a STATUE; calmly and grandly beautiful

**stat·u·ette** /,stætʃʊ'et/ *n* a very small STATUE

**stat·ure** /'stætʃəʳ/ *n* [U] *fml* **1** a person's natural height **2** quality or position gained by proved worth: *a woman of (high) stature, respected by others*

**sta·tus** /'steɪtəs/ *n* **-tuses 1** [C;U] position in law or in relation to others: *What's your status in this country? Are you a citizen?* **2** [U] recognition and respect by others: *Her famous name gave her status in the group.*

**status quo** /,steɪtəs 'kwəʊ/ *n* [*the* S] *Latin* the existing state of affairs

**stat·ute** /'stætʃuːt/ *n fml* a written law

**stat·u·to·ry** /ˈstætʃʊtəri‖-tʃətori/ *adj fml* fixed by STATUTE: *statutory control of wages*

**staunch**[1] /stɔːntʃ‖stɔntʃ, stɑntʃ/ *adj* dependably loyal; firm: *a staunch friend* –**staunchly** *adv* –**staunchness** *n* [U]

**staunch**[2] ‖also **stanch** *AmE*– *v* [T] to stop the flow of (esp. blood)

**stave** sthg.↔ **off** /steɪv/ *v adv* **staved, staving** [T] to keep away; keep back for a time: *enough food to stave off hunger*

**stay**[1] /steɪ/ *v* **1** [I] to remain; continue to be: *I stayed late at the party last night.|Can you stay for/to dinner, or must you go?|Don't turn here; stay on the same road.|Please stay seated.|The men* **stayed out on strike** (=did not go to work because of a disagreement with their employer) *for a week.|We want to stay ahead of the others.* **2** [I] to live in a place for a while; be a visitor or guest: *My wife's mother is staying with us.|to stay the night at a hotel* **3** [T] to last or continue for the whole length of: *to* **stay the course** *in a race* **4 stay put** to remain in one place; not move: *We stayed put by the fire all day.*

USAGE **Remain** is similar to **stay,** but it is more formal and it cannot be used instead of **stay** in sense (2): *We* **stayed** (not **remained**) *at the Savoy Hotel.*

**stay on** *v adv* [I] to remain after the usual or expected time for leaving: *He is 65 next month but is staying on as chairman.*

**stay**[2] *n* **1** [C] a usu. limited time of living in a place: *a short stay in hospital* **2** [C;U] a delay ordered by a judge: *The prisoner was given a stay of* EXECUTION. (=the judgment was not carried out)

**stead·fast** /ˈstedfɑːst‖-fæst/ *adj* faithful; steadily loyal: *steadfast support* –**steadfastly** *adv*

**stead·y**[1] /ˈstedi/ *adj* **-ier, -iest 1** firm; sure in position or movement: *a steady hand/steady nerves* **2** moving or developing evenly; regular: *a steady growth in industry|a steady east wind* –opposite **unsteady** (for **1, 2**) **3** not changing; STABLE: *a steady income/job* –**steadily** *adv* –**steadiness** *n*

**steady**[2] *v* **-ied, -ying** [I;T] to make or become steady, regular, or less changing: *She started to fall, then steadied herself.|A cup of tea will steady your nerves.*

**steak** /steɪk/ *n* [C;U] a flat piece of meat, esp. BEEF, or fish: *Two steaks, please.* –compare CHOP[2]

**steal** /stiːl/ *v* **stole**/stəʊ/, **stolen, stealing 1** [I;T] to take (what belongs to another) without any right: *She used to steal money from her father's drawer|*(fig.) *to steal a kiss* (=to kiss someone quickly, without permission) **2** [I] to move secretly and quietly: *He stole out of the house without anyone seeing him.* **3 steal the show** to get all the attention expected by someone else at a public event –see THIEF (USAGE)

**stealth** /stelθ/ *n* [U] the action of acting secretly or unseen: *She took the money* **by stealth** –**stealthy** *adj* **-ier, -iest** –**stealthily** *adv*

**steam**[1] /stiːm/ *n* [U] **1** water in the state of a gas, as produced by boiling **2** such a gas used under pressure to produce power: *In this country we no longer use steam trains/trains powered by steam.* **3** strong feelings or energy, kept in by self-control: *I was so angry I* **let off steam** *by shouting at the dog.* **4 under one's/it's own steam** by one's/its own power or effort

**SPELLING NOTE**
Words with the sound /s/, may be spelt **c-**, like **city**, or **ps-**, like **psychology.**

**steam**[2] /stiːm/ *v* **1** [I] to send out steam: *steaming hot coffee* **2** [I] to travel by steam power: *The ship steamed into the harbour.* **3** [T] to cook in steam: *a steamed pudding* **4** [T] to use steam on, esp. for unsticking or softening: *to steam open a letter*

**steam up** *v adv* [I;T (=**steam** sthg.↔**up**)] to cover or be covered with steam: *Her glasses (became) steamed up when she came into the warm room.*

**steam·er** /ˈstiːmər/ *n* → STEAMSHIP

**steam·roll·er**[1] /ˈstiːmˌrəʊlər/ *n* a heavy machine with very wide wheels for flattening road surfaces

**steamroller**[2] *v* [T] *infml* to crush or force using very great power or pressure: *He was steamrollered into signing the agreement.*

**steam·ship** /ˈstiːmˌʃɪp/ *n* a large non-naval ship driven by steam power

**steed** /stiːd/ *n lit* a horse for riding

**steel**[1] /stiːl/ *n* [U] iron in a hard strong form containing some CARBON and sometimes other metals, and used for making knives, machines, etc.

**steel**[2] *v* [T] to harden (oneself) enough to do something: *He steeled himself to speak to the chairman.*

**steel·works** /ˈstiːlwɜːks‖-ɜrks/ *n* **steelworks** a factory where steel is made

**steel·y** /ˈstiːli/ *adj* **-ier, -iest** like steel, esp. in colour or hardness: *steely blue eyes|steely determination*

**steep**[1] /stiːp/ *adj* **1** rising or falling quickly or at a large angle: *a steep hill|a steep rise in prices* **2** *infml* (of a demand) unreasonable; too much: *£500 for that car is a bit steep.* –**steeply** *adv* –**steepness** *n* [U]

**steep**[2] *v* [I;T] to leave or be left in a liquid, for softening, cleaning, etc.; SOAK

**stee·ple** /ˈstiːpəl/ *n* a church tower with the top rising to a point (SPIRE)

**stee·ple·chase** /ˈstiːpəltʃeɪs/ *n* a race for people or horses, with a series of jumps to be made during the run

**stee·ple·jack** /ˈstiːpəldʒæk/ *n* a person whose work is building or repairing tall chimneys, STEEPLES, etc.

**steer**[1] /stɪər/ *v* [I;T] **1** to direct the course of (e.g. a ship or vehicle): *to steer a car round a corner|to steer a conversation onto a favourite subject* –see LEAD (USAGE) **2 steer clear of** to keep away from; avoid

**steer**[2] *n* a male animal of the cattle family (ox) with its sexual organs removed, esp. a young one raised for its meat –compare BULLOCK

**steering wheel** /ˈ·· ·/ *n* the wheel which one turns to control a car's or ship's direction of movement –see picture on page 85

**stel·lar** /ˈstelər/ *adj tech* of or concerning the stars

**stem**[1] /stem/ *n* **1** the central part of a plant above the ground, from which the leaves grow, or the smaller part which supports a leaf or flower **2** any narrow upright part which supports another: *the stem of a wine glass* **3 -stemmed** having a certain kind of stem: *a smooth-stemmed plant|a long-stemmed glass*

**stem**[2] *v* **-mm-** [T] to stop (a flow of liquid): *to stem the flow of blood from the wound*

**stem from** sthg. *v prep* [T +*v-ing*] to have as origin: *Her interest in books stems from her childhood.*

**stench** /stentʃ/ *n fml* a strong bad smell

**sten·cil¹** /ˈstensəl/ *n* a piece of paper, metal, etc., in which patterns or letters have been cut

**stencil²** *v* **-ll-** *BrE*‖**-l-** *AmE* [T] to copy by using a STENCIL

**step¹** /step/ *n* **1** the act of putting one foot in front of the other in order to move along: *Take two steps forward and two steps back.* **2** the sound this makes –compare FOOTSTEP **3** the distance between the feet when stepping: *The door is three steps away.*|*It's just a step* (=a short distance) *from my house to his.* –compare PACE¹ (2) **4** a flat edge, esp. in a set of surfaces each higher than the other, on which the foot is placed for climbing up and down; stair, RUNG of a ladder, etc.: *Mind the step outside the door.*|*She was standing on the church steps.*|*A* **flight of steps** *led up to the house.* **5** an act, esp. in a set of actions: *Our first step must be a pay rise then we must improve conditions.*|*We must* **take steps** (=take action) *to help them.* **6** a movement of the feet in dancing: *a fast step* **7 in step/out of step** (esp. of soldiers) stepping with the left and right leg at the same time as/a different time than the others **8 step by step** gradually **9 watch one's step** *infml* to behave or act carefully

**step²** *v* **-pp-** [I] **1** [*on*] to put one foot down usu. in front of the other, in order to move along: *to step forward/aside*|*She stepped on a loose stone and twisted her ankle.* **2** to walk: *Step into the house while you're waiting.* **3 step out of line** to act differently from others or from what is expected

**step down/aside** *v adv* [I] → STAND **down**

**step in** *v adv* [I] to enter an argument, plan, etc., between other people by saying or doing something: *Mother stepped in and forbade me to go camping.*

**step up** sthg.↔*v adv* [T] *infml* to increase (an amount of something) in size or speed: *to step up the work*

**step·lad·der** /ˈstepˌlædəʳ/ *n* a short ladder with a folding support behind it

**steppe** /step/ *n* a large area of land without trees, esp. in the Soviet Union

**stepping-stone** /ˈ·· ·/ *n* **1** one of a row of large stones, which one walks on to cross a river **2** a way of improving one's position: *This job is a stepping-stone to a better one.*

**steps** /steps/ *n* [P] *BrE* for STEPLADDER –see PAIR (USAGE)

**ster·e·o¹** /ˈsteriəʊ, ˈstɪər-/ also **stereo set**– *n* **-os** a record player which gives out sound from two places by means of two LOUDSPEAKERS –see picture on page 355

**stereo²** also **stereophonic** *fml*– *adj* which gives out, or is given out as, sound coming from two different places: *a stereo recording* –compare MONO

**ster·e·o·type¹** /ˈsterɪətaɪp/ *n* a fixed pattern which represents a type of person or event: *He's the stereotype of an army officer.*

**stereotype²** *v* **-typed, -typing** [T] to think of (a thing or person) as an example of a general type: *She has a stereotyped view of teachers, believing that they are all as bad as hers were.*

**ster·ile** /ˈsteraɪl‖-rəl/ *adj* **1** (of living things) unable to produce young –compare FERTILE **2** made free from all GERMS and bacteria: *a sterile room in a hospital* **–sterility** /stəˈrɪlɨti / *n* [U]

**ster·il·ize** ‖also **-ise** *BrE* /ˈsterɨlaɪz/ *v* **- ized, -izing** [T] to make STERILE (1,2) **–sterilization** /laɪˈzeɪʃən‖-lə-/ *n* [U]

**ster·ling¹** /ˈstɜːlɪŋ‖-ɜr-/ *n* [U; after *n*] *tech* the type of money used in Britain, based on the pound (£): *The value of sterling has risen.*|*the pound sterling*

**sterling²** *adj* [A] **1** *tech* (of gold and esp. silver) of standard value **2** of good true qualities: *a sterling helper*

**stern¹** /stɜːn‖stɜrn/ *adj* **1** showing firmness towards others' behaviour: *a stern teacher* **2** difficult to bear: *a stern punishment* **–sternly** *adv* **–sternness** *n* [U]

**stern²** *n* the back end of a ship –compare BOW⁵

**steth·o·scope** /ˈsteθəskəʊp/ *n* a medical instrument which fits into a doctor's ears, used for listening to the heart, the breathing, etc.

**ste·ve·dore** /ˈstiːvɨdɔːʳ‖-dor/ *BrE*‖**longshoreman** *AmE*– *n* a person whose job is loading and unloading ships; DOCKER

**stew¹** /stjuː‖stuː/ *n* [C;U] a meal of meat, vegetables, etc., cooked together in liquid –see COOK (USAGE)

**stew²** *v* [I;T] **1** to cook (something) slowly and gently in liquid **2 stew in one's own juice** *infml* to be left to suffer as a result of one's own actions

**stew·ard** /ˈstjuːəd‖ˈstuːərd/ *n* **1** a man who serves passengers on a ship or plane **2** one of the people who arrange a public event such as a horse race

**stew·ard·ess** /ˌstjuːəˈdes‖ˈstuːərdɨs/ *n* a woman who serves passengers on a plane or ship

**stick¹** /stɪk/ *n* **1** a usu. small thin piece of wood **2** a thin rod of wood used for a special purpose: *a walking stick* **3** [*of*] a thin rod of any material: *a stick of* ROCK (=a hard kind of sweet)|*a stick of* CELERY **4 get the wrong end of the stick** *infml* to misunderstand

**stick²** *v* **stuck** /stʌk/, **sticking 1** [T] to push (a pointed object) into or through something: *Don't stick pins into the chair!* **2** [I;T] to (cause to) be fixed with a sticky substance: *Stick a stamp on the letter.* **3** [I] to become or remain fixed: *The paper's sticking to my hand/has stuck on my hand.*|*The door has stuck.* **4** [T] *infml* to put: *He stuck a flower in his buttonhole.* **5** [T +*v-ing*] (used in NEGATIVES², questions, etc.) *infml* to bear; stand: *I can't stick his voice.* –compare STAND¹ (8) **6 stick one's neck out** *infml* to take a risk: *A politician supporting an unpopular law is sticking his neck out: he may lose the next election.*

**stick around** *v adv* [I] *infml* to stay or wait in a place

**stick at** sthg. *v prep* [T] **1** to continue to work hard at: *to stick at the job* **2** to refuse to do (something wrong): *a criminal who would* **stick at nothing**

**stick by** sbdy./sthg. *v prep* [T] *infml* to continue to support: *to stick by a friend*

**stick out** *v adv* **1** [I;T (=**stick** sthg.↔**out**)] to (cause to) be positioned beyond the rest: *Her ears stick out.* **2** [I] *infml* to be clearly seen: *It* **sticks out a mile** *that we aren't welcome here.*

**stick to** sthg. *v prep* [T] to refuse to leave or change: *to stick to one's plans*

**stick together** *v adv* [I] *infml* (of two or more people) to stay loyal to each other: *The two brothers have always stuck together.*

**stick up for** sbdy./sthg. *v adv prep* [T] *infml* to

defend by words or actions: *When they hit you, stick up for yourself instead of crying.*

**stick·er** /ˈstɪkəʳ/ *n* a small piece of sticky paper with a picture or message on: *political stickers*

**stick-in-the-mud** /ˈ· · · ˌ·/ *n* **-muds** *infml* a person who will not change or accept new things

**stick·ler** /ˈstɪkləʳ/ *n* [*for*] a person who thinks a particular quality is very important: *She's a stickler for the truth.*

**stick·y** /ˈstɪki/ *adj* **-ier, -iest 1** made of or containing material which can stick to anything else: *sticky sweets|His fingers are sticky with jam.* **2 (come to/meet) a sticky end** *infml* (to suffer) ruin, dishonour, death, etc. **–stickily** *adv* **–stickiness** *n* [U]

**stiff**[1] /stɪf/ *adj* **1** not easily bent: *stiff paper|Shoes are stiff when they're new.* **2** painful when moving or moved: *stiff aching muscles* **3** in an almost solid state; firm: *Beat the mixture until it is stiff.* **4** formal; not friendly: *a stiff smile* **5** [A] *infml* (of a drink of strong alcohol) large and without water or other liquid added: *a stiff whisky* **6** difficult to do: *a stiff examination* **–stiffly** *adv* **–stiffness** *n* [U]

**stiff**[2] *adv infml* **1 bore someone stiff** to make someone very tired with dull talk **2 scare someone stiff** to make someone terribly afraid

**stiff·en** /ˈstɪfən/ *v* [I;T] to make or become STIFF[1] (1,2,4) *a shirt with a stiffened collar*

**sti·fle** /ˈstaɪfəl/ *v* **-fled, -fling** [T] to cause difficulty in breathing properly: (fig.) *a stifling hot day|It was an uninteresting conversation and I had to stifle* (=keep back) *a* YAWN.

**stig·ma** /ˈstɪgmə/ *n* **-mas** a sign of shame; feeling of being ashamed: *a stigma about asking for money.*

**stile** /staɪl/ *n* an arrangement of steps which must be climbed to cross a fence or wall outdoors

**still**[1] /stɪl/ *adj* **1** not moving: *Keep still while I fasten your shoe.* **2** quiet or silent: *The room was still at the end of the speech.* **3** (of drinks) not containing bubbles: *still orange (juice)* –compare SPARKLE (2) **–stillness** *n* [U]

**still**[2] *v* [T] *lit* to make quiet or calm: *The food stilled the baby's cries.*

**still**[3] *n* [S] *lit* quietness or calm: *the still of the evening*

**still**[4] *adv* [*no comp.*] **1** at a particular time; even later than expected: *Are you still here? You should have gone home hours ago.|"Have you finished your dinner yet?" "No I still haven't finished it".* **2** even so; in spite of that: *We knew he was unlikely to win, but it's still unfair that he didn't get a higher mark.|It's raining. Still, we must go out.* –see Study Notes on page 128 **3** (used for making comparisons stronger): *It's cold now, but it'll be still/even colder at night.|The first question is difficult, the second is more difficult and the third is still/even more difficult.*

**still·born** /ˈstɪlbɔːn, ˌstɪlˈbɔːn||-ɔrn/ *adj* born dead **–stillbirth** /ˈstɪlbɜːθ/ *n* [C;U]

**stilt** /stɪlt/ *n* one of a pair of poles, with supporting pieces for the foot, which can allow the user to walk raised above the ground

**stilt·ed** /ˈstɪltɨd/ *adj* (of a style of writing or speaking) very formal and unnatural

**SPELLING NOTE**

Words with the sound /s/, may be spelt **c-**, like **city**, or **ps-**, like **psychology.**

**stim·u·lant** /ˈstɪmjʊlənt||-jə-/ *n* **1** anything taken into the body, usu. a drug, which increases activity for a time **2** anything (e.g. praise) which encourages more activity

**stim·u·late** /ˈstɪmjʊleɪt||-jə-/ *v* **-lated, -lating** [T] **1** to excite (the body or mind): *Exercise stimulates the body.* **2** to encourage: *She was stimulated into new efforts.* **–stimulation** /-ˈeɪʃən/ *n* [U]

**stim·u·lus** /ˈstɪmjʊləs||-jə-/ *n* **-li** /liː/ something which is the cause of activity: *Light is a stimulus to growth in plants.*

**sting**[1] /stɪŋ/ *v* **stung** /stʌŋ/, **stinging** [I;T] **1** to (cause to) feel a sharp pain: *My eyes are stinging from the smoke.|The smoke is stinging my eyes.* **2** to prick with or have a STING[2]: *An insect stung me*

**sting**[2] *n* **1** a sharp organ used as a weapon by some animals, often poisonous **2** a pain-producing substance on a plant's surface: NETTLE*s have a sting.* **3** a sharp pain, esp. caused by a plant or insect

**stin·gy** /ˈstɪndʒi/ *adj* **-gier, -giest** *infml* unwilling to give, esp. money: *a stingy person* **–stinginess** *n* [U]

**stink** /stɪŋk/ *v,n* **stank** /stæŋk/ *or* **stunk** /stʌŋk/, **stunk, stinking** [I *of*] (to give) a strong bad smell: *a stink of fish*

**stint**[1] /stɪnt/ *v* [T *of*] to give too small an amount (of): *Don't stint yourself; take all you want.*

**stint**[2] *n* a fixed amount, esp. of work: *doing a stint in the army*

**stip·ple** /ˈstɪpəl/ *v* **-pled, -pling** [I;T] to draw or paint by using dots

**stip·u·late** /ˈstɪpjʊleɪt||-jə-/ *v* **-lated, -lating** [T +*(that)*] to demand as a condition

**stip·u·la·tion** /ˌstɪpjʊˈleɪʃən||-jə-/ *n* a condition of agreement: *She agreed, but with several stipulations.*

**stir**[1] /stɜːʳ/ *v* **-rr- 1** [T] to move around and mix (esp. liquid) e.g. with a spoon: *He stirred his coffee.* **2** [I;T] to (cause to) move from a position: *She stirred in her sleep.|The wind stirred her hair.* **3** [T] to excite (people's feelings): *The story stirred her sympathy.|stirring music*

**stir up** sthg. *v adv* [T] to cause (trouble): *Don't stir up trouble unnecessarily.*

**stir**[2] *n* **1** [C] an act of STIRRing[1]: *Give the mixture a stir.* **2** [S] public excitement: *The news* **caused** *quite* **a stir**.

**stir·rup** /ˈstɪrəp||ˈstɜ-/ *n* a metal piece for the rider's foot to go in, hanging from the sides of a horse's SADDLE

**stitch**[1] /stɪtʃ/ *n* **1** [C] a movement of a needle and thread through cloth in sewing: *to put a stitch in a shirt* **2** [C] a turn of the wool round the needle in KNITting: *to drop* (=lose) *a stitch* **3** [C] the piece of thread or wool seen in place after the completion of such a movement: *a short/loose stitch* **4** [U] a particular style of sewing or KNITting: *feather stitch in sewing* **5** [S] a sharp pain in the side, esp. caused by running **6 in stitches** *infml* laughing helplessly

**stitch**[2] *v* [I;T] to sew: *Will you stitch a button on this shirt?*

**stoat** /stəʊt/ *n* a small brown furry animal that eats other animals –compare ERMINE

**stock**[1] /stɒk||stɑk/ *n* **1** [C *of*] a supply of something for use: *the country's stocks of coal|a good stock* (=a lot) *of food in the house* **2** [U] (supply of) goods for sale: *How much stock is there in the shop ?|"Have you any blue shirts* **in stock?**" *"No, they're/we're* **out of stock.**" (=we have none for sale) **3** [C;U] money lent to a government or company at a fixed rate of interest: *stocks and* SHARES|*government stock* **4** [U] farm animals, esp. cattle; LIVESTOCK **5** [U] a liquid made from the juices of meat, vegetables, etc., used in cooking **6** [U] a family line, esp. of the stated sort: *a man of farming stock* **7** [C] a piece of wood used as a support or handle, e.g. for a gun or tool **8 take stock (of)** to consider the state of things so as to take a decision: *He took stock of his situation and decided he needed a holiday.* –compare STOCKTAKING

**stock²** *v* [T] **1** to keep supplies of: *They stock all types of shoes.* **2** to supply: *a shop well stocked with goods*

**stock up** *v* [I *with*] to collect a full store of goods: *We must stock up with food for the holiday.*

**stock·ade** /stɒ'keɪd||sta-/ *n* a fence of upright pieces of wood (STAKES) built for defence

**stock·brok·er** /'stɒk,brəʊkə^r||'stak-/ *n* a person whose job is buying and selling STOCKS¹ (3) and SHARES¹ (2)

**stock ex·change** /'· ·,·/ also **stock market**– *n* [*the* S] (*usu. caps.*) the place where STOCKS¹ (3) and SHARES¹ (2) are bought and sold

**stock·ing** /'stɒkɪŋ||'sta-/ *n* a close-fitting, usu. nylon, covering for a woman's foot and leg –compare SOCK, TIGHTS; see PAIR (USAGE)

**stock·ist** /'stɒkəst||'sta-/ *n* a person or firm that keeps certain goods for sale: *a stockist of shirts*

**stock·pile** /'stɒkpaɪl||'stak-/ *v,n* **-piled, -piling** [T] (to keep) a large store of materials for future use

**stock-still** /,· '·◂/ *adv* without the slightest movement: *She stood stock-still and listened.*

**stock·tak·ing** /'stɒk,teɪkɪŋ||'stak-/ *n* [U] the making of a list of goods held in a business

**stock·y** /'stɒki||'sta-/ *adj* **-ier, -iest** thick, short, and strong in body –**stockily** *adv* –**stockiness** *n* [U]

**stodg·y** /'stɒdʒi||'sta/ *adj* **-ier, -iest 1** (of food) thick, heavy, and sticky **2** dull and difficult: *a stodgy book*

**sto·ic·al** /'stəʊɪkəl/ also **stoic**– *adj* patient when suffering –**stoic** *n* –**stoically** *adv* –**stoicism** *n* [U]: *to bear all one's misfortunes with stoicism*

**stoke** /stəʊk/ *v* **stoked, stoking** [T *up*] to fill (an enclosed fire) with material (FUEL) which is burned to give heat, power, etc.: *to stoke up the fire with coal*

**stole¹** /stəʊl/ *n* a long straight piece of material worn on the shoulders by women, esp. for a social occasion

**stole²** *v past tense of* STEAL

**sto·len** /'stəʊlən/ *v past participle of* STEAL

**stol·id** /'stɒləd||'sta-/ *adj* showing no excitement –**stolidly** *adv*

**stom·ach¹** /'stʌmək/ *n* a baglike organ in the body where food is DIGESTED (=broken down for use by the body) after being eaten –see picture on page 299

**stomach²** *v* [T] (used only in NEGATIVES², questions, etc.) to accept without displeasure: *I can't stomach his jokes.*

**stom·ach·ache** /'stʌmək-eɪk/ *n* [C;U] (a) continuing pain in the ABDOMEN: *I've got (a) stomachache!* –see ACHE (USAGE)

**stomp** /stɒmp||stamp, stɔmp/ *v* [I] *infml* to walk or dance with a heavy step: *stomping up the stairs*

**stone¹** /stəʊn/ *n* **1** [C] a piece of rock, esp. not very large, either of natural shape or cut out specially for building **2** [U] solid mineral material; a type of rock: *sandstone|limestone|a stone surface* **3** [C] a single hard seed inside some fruits, such as the CHERRY, PLUM, and PEACH **4** [C] →PRECIOUS STONE **5** [C] →GRAVESTONE –see also HAILSTONE, MILLSTONE, STEPPING-STONE **6 leave no stone unturned** to try every way possible (of doing) **7 stone's throw** a short distance: *The station is only a stone's throw away.*

**stone²** *v* **stoned, stoning** [T] **1** to throw stones at (someone), esp. as a punishment: *The criminal was stoned to death.* **2** to take the seeds or STONES¹ (3) out of (fruit): *stoned peaches*

**stone³** *n* **stone** *or* **stones** (in Britain) (a measure of weight equal to) 14 pounds (lbs): *He weighs 13 stone(s).|a 20-stone man*

**stoned** /stəʊnd/ *adj* [F] *infml* **1** excited by the use of drugs **2** very drunk

**stone·ma·son** /'stəʊn,meɪsən/ also **mason**– *n* a person whose job is cutting stone into shape for building

**stone·ware** /'stəʊnweə^r/ *n* [U] pots and other vessels made from a special hard clay that contains a hard stone (FLINT)

**stone·work** /'stəʊnwɜːk||-ɜrk/ *n* [U] the parts of a building made of stone

**ston·y** /'stəʊni/ *adj* **-ier, -iest 1** containing or covered with stones: *stony ground* **2** cruel; showing no pity or feeling: *a stony heart* –**stonily** *adv*

**stood** /stʊd/ *v past participle & tense of* STAND

**stool** /stuːl/ *n* **1** a seat without a supporting part for the back or arms: *a piano stool* –see picture on page 337 **2** *fml & tech* a piece of solid waste matter passed from the body

**stoop** /stuːp/ *v* [I;T] to bend (the head and shoulders) forwards and down –**stoop** *n* [S]: *an old woman with a stoop*

**stoop to** sthg. *v prep* [T +*v-ing*] to fall to a low standard of behaviour by (doing): *I wouldn't stoop to stealing money.*

**stop¹** /stɒp||stap/ *v* **-pp- 1** [I;T +*v-ing*] to (cause to) cease moving or continuing an activity: *We stopped working at teatime.|Do the buses stop* (=so that people can get on/off) *at the market?|He held out his hand to stop the bus.* (=as a signal)|*Stop making such a noise.* **2** [I;T] to (cause to) end: *I wish the rain would stop.* –compare START¹ **3** [T] to prevent: *I'm going and you can't stop me.|You must stop her telling such lies.* **4** [I] to remain; stay: *I have to stop in tonight.* (=not go out)|*We invited him to tea and he stopped for supper!* **5** [T *up*] to block: *There's something inside stopping (up) the pipe.* **6** [T] to prevent from being given or paid: *The bank stopped (payment of) his cheque because he had no money in his account.* **7 stop short of** to decide against (a strong action): *She wouldn't stop short of stealing if she thought it would help her children.* –**stoppable** *adj* [*no comp.*]

**stop off** *v adv* [I *at*] *infml* to make a short visit to a place while making a journey somewhere else: *We need some matches; we'll stop off when we see a shop.*

**stop²** *n* **1** an act of stopping or the state of being stopped: *We had to make a few stops on the way.* **2** a place on a road where buses or other public vehicles stop for passengers: *a bus stop* **3** a dot used as a mark of PUNCTUATION, esp. a FULL STOP **4** an object which prevents movement: *a doorstop* **5** a set of pipes on an ORGAN (3) with a movable part to provide a certain type of notes **6 pull all the stops out** to do everything possible to complete an effect or action

**stop·cock** /'stɒpkɒk‖'stɑpkɑk/ *n* a VALVE or TAP which controls the flow of water in a pipe

**stop·gap** /'stɒpgæp‖'stɑp-/ *n* something or someone that fills a need for a time: *a stopgap secretary*

**stop·o·ver** /'stɒp,əʊvər‖'stɑp-/ *n* a short stay between parts of a journey, e.g. a long plane journey

**stop·page** /'stɒpɪdʒ‖'stɑ-/ *n* **1** a blocked state which stops movement, as in a waste pipe or a pipe in the body **2** the act of stopping something, esp. work or pay

**stop·per** /'stɒpər‖'stɑ-/ *n* an object which fits in and closes the opening to a bottle or JAR

**stop press** /,· '· ◂/ *n* [*the* S] the last news added to a newspaper after the main part has been printed

**stop·watch** /'stɒpwɒtʃ‖'stɑpwɑtʃ, -wɔtʃ/ *n* a watch which can be stopped and started at any time, so that the time taken by an action can be measured exactly

**stor·age** /'stɔːrɪdʒ‖'stor-/ *n* [U] **1** the act of storing: *storage space* **2** a place for storing goods: *Her furniture is* **in storage** *while she finds a new house.*

**store**[1] /stɔːr‖stor/ *v* **stored, storing** [T *in, up*] to keep somewhere for future use: *to store food in the cupboard|to store one's furniture in a* WAREHOUSE

**store**[2] *n* **1** [*of*] a supply for future use: *a store of coal* **2** a large building in which articles are stored; WAREHOUSE **3** a large shop: *a furniture store* **4** *AmE* for SHOP: *the local village store* **5 in store** about to happen: *There's a shock in store for him.* **6 set . . . store by** to feel to be of (the stated amount of) importance: *He sets great store by her.*

**store·house** /'stɔːhaʊs‖'stor-/ *n* **-houses** /haʊzɪ̇z/ → STORE[2] (2)

**store·room** /'stɔːrʊm, -ruːm‖'sto-/ *n* a room where goods are kept till needed

**sto·rey** *BrE*‖**story** *AmE* /'stɔːri‖'sto-/ *n* **1** a floor or level in a building: *There are three storeys including the ground floor.* **2 -storeyed** *BrE*‖**-storied** *AmE* having a certain number of STOREYS: *a six-storeyed block of flats*

**stork** /stɔːk‖stɔrk/ *n* a large usu. white bird, with a long beak, neck, and legs, which walks in water looking for food

**storm**[1] /stɔːm‖stɔrm/ *n* a rough weather condition with wind, rain, etc.: *a thunderstorm|a snowstorm|a sandstorm* –see WEATHER (USAGE)

**storm**[2] *v* **1** [T] to attack with sudden violence: *to storm the city* **2** [I *at*] to show violent anger: *He stormed about the house, breaking things.*

**storm·y** /'stɔːmi‖-ɔr-/ *adj* **-ier, -iest 1** having storms: *a stormy day* **2** noisy and angry: *a stormy quarrel*

**sto·ry** /'stɔːri‖'stori/ *n* **-ries 1** an account of events, real or imagined **2** *infml (used by and to children)* a lie (esp. in the phrase **to tell stories**) –see also TALL STORY **3** (material for) an article in a newspaper, magazine, etc.: *This event will be a good story for the paper.* –see HISTORY (USAGE)

> **SPELLING NOTE**
> Words with the sound /s/, may be spelt **c-**, like **city**, or **ps-**, like **psychology**.

**stout**[1] /staʊt/ *adj* **1** rather fat and heavy: *He became stout as he grew older.* **2** strong; thick: *He cut a stout stick to help him walk.* **3** [A] brave; determined: *a stout supporter of the team* **–stoutly** *adv* **–stoutness** *n* [U]

**stout**[2] *n* [U] a strong dark beer

**stout·heart·ed** /,staʊt'hɑːtɪ̇d ◂‖-ɑr-/ *adj lit* brave; of a firm character

**stove** /stəʊv/ *n* an enclosed apparatus for cooking or heating which works by burning coal, oil, etc., or by electricity –compare COOKER, HEATER, FIRE[1] (3)

**stow** /stəʊ/ *v* [T *away*] to put away or pack, esp. for some time: *to stow goods (away) in boxes*

**stow·a·way** /'stəʊəweɪ/ *n* a person who hides on a ship or plane to get a free journey

**strad·dle** /'strædl/ *v* **-dled, -dling** [T] to sit or stand with the legs on either side of: *to straddle a horse*

**strag·gle** /'strægəl/ *v* **-gled, -gling** [I] **1** to move or spread untidily, without ordered shape: *straggling branches/houses* **2** to fall away from the main group while walking or marching **–straggler** *n*

**strag·gly** /'strægəli/ *adj* **-glier, -gliest** growing or spreading out in an untidy shape: *straggly hair*

**straight**[1] /streɪt/ *adj* **1** not bent or curved: *a straight line|She has straight, not curly hair.* **2** level or upright: *Put the mirror straight.|Put the pole up straight.* **3** honest; truthful: *a straight answer* –compare LEVEL, BENT **4** [F] correct: *Just to* **put the record straight**, *this is what really happened.* **5** (of alcohol) without added water: *a straight whisky|to drink whisky straight* –compare NEAT (3) **6** serious: *a straight play|It was difficult to keep a straight face when he fell over the dog.* **–straightness** *n* [U]

**straight**[2] *adv* [*adv* + *adv/prep*] **1** in a straight line: *Sit up straight.|straight down the road|straight/right in front of you* **2** directly: *Go straight home.|straight/right after breakfast*

**straight**[3] *n* a straight part, esp. on a race track: *The cars crashed on the straight.*

**straight·a·way** /,streɪtə'weɪ/ *adv* at once

**straight·en** /'streɪtn/ *v* [I;T *up, out*] to make or become straight, level, or tidy: *Straighten your hat.*

**straighten** sthg.↔**out** *v adv* [T] to remove the confusions or difficulties in: *to straighten out one's business affairs*

**straighten up** *v adv* [I] to get up from a bent-over position

**straight·for·ward** /,streɪt'fɔːwəd‖-'fɔrwərd/ *adj* simple and honest; without hidden meanings **–straightforwardly** *adv*

**strain**[1] /streɪn/ *n* **1** [C] a breed or type of plant or animal: *This strain of wheat can grow during a cold spring.* **2** [S] *lit* a way of using words: *Her letters were written in a happy strain.* **3** [C] *lit* a tune; notes of music: *the strains of a well-known song*

**strain**[2] *v* **1** [I;T *at*] to stretch or pull tightly: *He strained at the rope and the boat moved.* **2** [I;T] to make great efforts (with): *to strain to hear|straining to understand|She strained her ears to hear.* **3** [T] to damage or weaken (a part of the body): *to strain a* *muscle* **4** [I *against*] to press oneself closely: *She strained against the ropes which tied her.* **5** [T] *fml* to force beyond acceptable or truthful limits: *to strain the truth* **6** [T] to separate (a liquid from a solid) by pouring through a narrow space, esp. the fine holes in a STRAINER: *to strain the vegetables*

**strain**[3] *n* **1** [C;U] (the force causing) the condition of being STRAINED[2] (1): *The rope broke under the strain.* **2** [C *on*] a fact or state which tests the powers, esp. of mind and body: *The additional work put a great strain on him.* **3** [U] a state of TENSION (2): *She's under a lot of strain at the moment; her child's very ill.* **4** [C;U] damage to a part of the body caused by too great effort: *heart strain* –compare SPRAIN

**strained** /streɪnd/ *adj* **1** not natural in behaviour; unfriendly: *His manner was strained.* **2** nervous or tired: *a strained face at the end of the day*

**strain·er** /ˈstreɪnəʳ/ *n* an instrument for separating solids from liquids, such as a SIEVE, a COLANDER, or a FILTER[1] (1)

**strait** /streɪt/ *n* [*usu. pl.*] (*often cap. as part of a name*) a narrow passage of water connecting two seas: *the Straits of Dover*

**strait·jack·et** /ˈstreɪtˌdʒækɪ̈t/ *n* a garment which holds the arms down, preventing a madman from violent movement

**strait·laced** /ˌstreɪtˈleɪst◂/ *adj derog* having severe ideas about morals

**straits** /streɪts/ *n* [P] a difficult position in life: *Now that Father's lost his job, we're* **in serious straits**.

**strand** /strænd/ *n* [*of*] a single piece or thread: *Many strands are twisted together to form a rope.*

**strand·ed** /ˈstrændɪ̈d/ *adj* in a helpless position; unable to get away: *a whale stranded on the shore|stranded in the middle of the traffic*

**strange** /streɪndʒ/ *adj* **1** hard to accept or understand; surprising: *It's strange you've never met him.* **2** not known before; unfamiliar: *He stood in a strange street.* –**strangely** *adv*: *Strangely, I've never seen that television show before.* –**strangeness** *n* [U]

**strang·er** /ˈstreɪndʒəʳ/ *n* **1** a person who is unfamiliar: *Don't talk to strangers!* **2** a person in an unfamiliar place: *I'm a stranger here. Can you tell me where the station is?* –compare FOREIGNER

**stran·gle** /ˈstræŋgəl/ *v* **-gled, -gling** [T] to kill by pressing on the throat–**strangulation** /-gjʊˈleɪʃən‖-gjə-/ *n* [U]: *Death was caused by strangulation.*

**stran·gle·hold** /ˈstræŋgəlhəʊld/ *n* a strong hold round the neck: (fig.) *the stranglehold of large firms on industry*

**strap**[1] /stræp/ *n* a strong narrow band of material, such as leather, used as a fastening: *a watch strap*

**strap**[2] *v* **-pp-** [T] **1** to fasten in place with STRAPS: *to strap a bag onto one's back* **2** to beat with a STRAP

**strap·ping** /ˈstræpɪŋ/ *adj* [A] big and strong: *a fine, strapping man*

**stra·ta** /ˈstrɑːtə‖ˈstreɪtə/ *n pl. of* STRATUM

**strat·a·gem** /ˈstrætədʒəm/ *n* a trick to deceive an enemy

**stra·te·gic** /strəˈtiːdʒɪk/ also **strategical**– *adj* done for reasons of STRATEGY: *a strategic decision* –**strategically** *adv*

**strat·e·gy** /ˈstrætɪ̈dʒi/ *n* **-gies** **1** [U] the art of planning a war: *a general who was a master of strategy* –compare TACTICS **2** [C;U] (a piece of) skilful planning –**strategist** *n*

**strat·i·fy** /ˈstrætɪ̈faɪ/ *v* **-fied, -fying** [I;T] to arrange or become arranged in separate levels or strata (STRATUM): *a stratified society|stratified rock* –**stratification** /-fɪ̈ˈkeɪʃən/ *n* [U]

**strat·os·phere** /ˈstrætəsfɪəʳ/ *n* [*the* S] the outer part of the air which surrounds the earth, starting at about ten kilometres above the earth –compare ATMOSPHERE

**stra·tum** /ˈstrɑːtəm‖ˈstreɪ-/ *n* **-ta** /tə/ **1** a band of rock of a certain kind **2** a level of people in society; social class: *There are several social strata in the town.*

**straw** /strɔː/ *n* **1** [U] dried stems of grain plants, such as wheat, used for animals to sleep on, for making baskets, mats, etc. **2** [C] **a** one stem of wheat, rice, etc. **b** a thin paper or plastic tube for sucking up liquid –see picture on page 521 **3 the last straw** an addition to a set of troubles which makes them too much to bear

**straw·ber·ry** /ˈstrɔːbəri‖-beri, -bəri/ *n* **-ries** a plant which grows near the ground, or its red juicy fruit

**stray**[1] /streɪ/ *v* **strayed, straying** [I] to wander away: *Our dog strayed from home.*|(fig.) *Her thoughts strayed from the subject.*

**stray**[2] *n* **strays** an animal lost from its home

**stray**[3] *adj* [A] **1** lost from home: *stray cats* **2** met or happening by chance: *hit by a stray shot*

**streak**[1] /striːk/ *n* [*of*] **1** a thin line or band: *streaks of grey in her black hair*|(fig.) *a streak of cruelty in his character* **2 be on a winning/losing streak** to have repeated success/failure for a period

**streak**[2] *v* **1** [I] to move very fast: *The cat streaked across the road with the dog behind it.* **2** [T] to cover with STREAKS[1] (1): *a face streaked with dirt*

**streak·y** /ˈstriːki/ *adj* **-ier, -iest** marked with STREAKS[1] (1): *streaky bacon* (=with lines of fat among the meat)

**stream**[1] /striːm/ *n* **1** a natural flow of water, usu. smaller than a river: *(fig.) a stream of people* **2** [*usu. sing.*] (the direction of) a current of water: (fig.) *He went against the stream (of public opinion).* –see also DOWNSTREAM, UPSTREAM **3** *BrE* (in schools) a level of ability within a group of pupils of the same age: *She's in the top stream.*

**stream**[2] *v* **1** [I] to flow fast and strong; pour out: *The pipe broke and water streamed onto the floor.*|(fig.) *They streamed out of the cinema.* **2** [I *out*] to float in the air: *The wind caught her hair, and it streamed out behind her.* **3** [T] *BrE* to group in STREAMS[1] (3): *The pupils are streamed into four ability groups.*

**stream·er** /ˈstriːməʳ/ *n* a long narrow flag, piece of paper, or BANNER, used for decorating buildings at a time of public enjoyment

**stream·line** /ˈstriːmlaɪn/ *v* **-lined, -lining** [T] to form into a smooth shape which moves easily through water or air: *a streamlined racing car*|(fig.) *to streamline a business* (=to make it more effective)

**street** /striːt/ *n* **1** a road with houses or other town buildings on one or both sides: *101 Oxford Street, London* **2 streets ahead of** *infml* much better than **3 up one's street** in one's area of interest or activity: *Gardening is right up his street.*

USAGE A **street** is in the middle of a town, and a **road** is usually in the country. The **way** to a place is either **a** the direction, and the instructions needed for getting there: *Can you tell me the* **way** *to Buckingham Palace?* or **b** one's journey from one place to another: *A funny thing happened to me on my* **way** *to the theatre!*

**street·car** /ˈstriːtkɑːʳ/ *n AmE* for TRAM

**strength** /streŋθ, strenθ/ *n* [U] **1** the quality or degree of being strong: *He hasn't got enough strength to get out of bed.|strength of character|I bought it* **on the strength of** (=because of) *his advice.* **2** something providing strength or power: *His knowledge of the subject is the strength of his argument.* –compare WEAKNESS **3** force measured in numbers: *They came* **in strength** (=a lot of them came) *to see the fight.*

**strength·en** /ˈstreŋθən, ˈstrenθən/ *v* [I;T] to make or become stronger: *to strengthen a fence|The wind strengthened during the night.* –compare WEAKEN

**stren·u·ous** /ˈstrenjuəs/ *adj* **1** needing great effort: *a strenuous day* **2** showing great activity: *a strenuous supporter of women's rights* **–strenuously** *adv* **–strenuousness** *n* [U]

**stress¹** /stres/ *n* [C;U] **1** force or pressure caused by difficulties in life: *He's under stress because he has too much work to do.* **2** force of weight caused by something heavy: *The vehicles passing over put stress on the material of the bridge.* **3** the degree of force put on a part of a word: *In "under", the main stress is on "un".*

**stress²** *v* [T] to give importance to (a matter): *She stressed the need for careful spending.*

**stress mark** /ˈ· ·/ *n* a mark (/ˈorˌ/) to show that STRESS¹ (3) falls on a certain part of a word

**stretch¹** /stretʃ/ *v* **1** [I;T] to make or become wider or longer: *My wool coat stretched when I washed it.|Rubber bands stretch.* (=are elastic)|(fig.) *You are stretching my patience to the limit.* **2** [I] to spread out: *The sea stretched (out) as far as I could see.* **3** [I;T *out*] to straighten (the limbs or body) to full length: *He stretched (himself) out in front of the fire.* –see picture on page 669 **4 stretch one's legs** to have a walk, esp. after sitting for a time

**stretch²** *n* **1** [C] an act of stretching, esp. the body **2** [U] the (degree of) ability to increase in length or width: *stretch socks* **3** [C] a level area of land or water: *a wide stretch of road|the finishing stretch (in a race)* **4** [C *of*] a continuous period of time: *a stretch of ten years abroad|They had to stand for hours* **at a stretch**. (=without stopping)

**stretch·er** /ˈstretʃəʳ/ *n* a framework on which a sick person can be carried

**strew** /struː/ *v* **strewed, strewn** /struːn/ *or* **strewed, strewing** [T *on, over, with*] to scatter: *There were papers strewn all over the floor.*

**strick·en** /ˈstrɪkən/ *adj* experiencing the effects of trouble, illness, etc.: *stricken by debts|grief-stricken*

**strict** /strɪkt/ *adj* **1** severe, esp. in rules of behaviour: *They are very strict with their children.* –compare LENIENT **2 a** exact: *a strict interpretation of the rules* **b** complete: *strict secrecy* **–strictly** *adv* **–strictness** *n* [U]

> **SPELLING NOTE**
> Words with the sound /s/, may be spelt **c-**, like **city**, or **ps-**, like **psychology**.

**stric·ture** /ˈstrɪktʃəʳ/ *n fml* an expression of blame: *the strictures of the public on the private lives of the famous*

**stride¹** /straɪd/ *v* **strode** /strəʊd/, **stridden** /ˈstrɪdən/, **striding** [I] to walk with long steps or cross with one long step: *He strode over the stream.*

**stride²** *n* **1** a long step in walking **2 make great strides** to improve or do well **3 take (something) in one's stride** to accept and deal with easily: *She took her father's death in her stride.* –see WALK (USAGE)

**stri·dent** /ˈstraɪdənt/ *adj* with a hard sharp sound or voice: *a strident speaker/voice* **–stridently** *adv*

**strife** /straɪf/ *n* [U] trouble between people: *family/political strife*

**strike¹** /straɪk/ *v* **struck** /strʌk/, **struck**||also **stricken** /ˈstrɪkən/ *AmE*, **striking 1** [I;T] *more fml than* **hit**– to hit: *She struck him in the face.|He struck out at his attackers.|The army struck* (=attacked) *at dawn.*|(fig.)*We must strike a blow for freedom.* **2** [T] to make or put into action by hitting: *He struck a light.* (=by lighting a match) .|*The clock struck 12.* (=12 o'clock)|(fig.) *We should be able to* **strike a bargain**. (=reach an agreement)|*It's difficult to* **strike a balance** (=be fair to everybody) **3** [T] to have an effect on; AFFECT with: *How does the room strike you?* (=what do you think of it?)|*That strikes me as a good idea.* (=I think it is good) |*They were* **struck dumb** *with fear.|The noise struck terror into their hearts|The whole village was struck down by a strange illness.* **4** [T] to come suddenly to the mind of: *If a better idea strikes you, let me know.|It strikes me* (=I think) *that we should stay here for the night.* **5** [I] to stop working because of disagreement: *The union struck for better working conditions.* **6** [T] to discover (a material or place): *They struck oil under the sea.* **7** [I *off, out*] to start going: *They struck off on a new course.|He struck out* (=began to swim) *towards the shore.|After he'd worked for his father for years, he decided to* **strike out on his own**. (=to start to work for himself) **8** [T] to lower (sails, a flag, or a tent): *The army* **struck camp** (=took down their tents) *and moved on.* –compare PITCH¹ (1) **9 strike it rich** *infml* to find sudden wealth **10 strike while the iron's hot** to use a favourable occasion as soon as it comes, without losing time **11 within striking distance** very near –see also STRICKEN

**strike** sbdy.↔**off** *v adv* [T] to dismiss (someone) from a professional body by removing his/her name from an official list

**strike up** *v adv* **1** [I;T (=**strike up** sthg.)] to begin playing **2** [T *with*] (**strike up** sthg.) to start to make (a friendship): *They struck up a friendship*

**strike²** *n* **1** a time when no work is done because of disagreement, e.g. over pay or working conditions: *The workers* **went on strike 2** success in finding esp. a mineral in the the earth: *an oil strike*

**strik·er** /ˈstraɪkəʳ/ *n* **1** a person on STRIKE² (1) **2** one of the attacking players in esp. a football team –see picture on page 592

**strik·ing** /ˈstraɪkɪŋ/ *adj* which draws the attention: *a very striking woman|a striking idea* **–strikingly** *adv*

**string¹** /strɪŋ/ *n* **1** [C;U] (a) thin cord: *pictures hung on string* –compare ROPE **2** [C] a thin piece of material stretched across a musical instrument (a **stringed**

**instrument**), to give sound –see also STRINGS **3** [C *of*] a set (of things) connected together on a thread: *a string of* BEADS|(fig.) *a string of complaints* **4 no strings attached** (esp. of an agreement) with no limiting conditions **5 pull strings** to use influence, esp. secretly: *He pulled a few strings to get that job.*

**string²** *v* **strung** /strʌŋ/, **stringing** [T] **1** to put one or more STRINGS¹ (2) on (a musical instrument) **2** to thread (BEADS) on a string: (fig.) *to string phrases/words together* **3 highly strung** (of a person) very sensitive, easily excited, etc.

**string** sbdy. **along** *v adv infml* [T] to encourage (someone's) hopes deceitfully: *He will never be paid the money they promised him; they're just stringing him along.*

**string** sthg.↔**out** *v adv* [I;T] to spread (something) out in a line: *He strung out the washing to dry.*

**string** sthg.↔**up** *v adv* [T] to hang (something) high: *They strung up coloured lights round the room.*

**string bean** /ˌ· ˈ·/ *n AmE* for RUNNER BEAN

**strin·gent** /ˈstrɪndʒənt/ *adj* (of rules) severe; which must be obeyed –**stringently** *adv* –**stringency** *n* [U]: *the stringency of wartime rules*

**strings** /strɪŋz/ *n* [P] the set of (players with) instruments with STRINGS¹ (2) in an ORCHESTRA

**string·y** /ˈstrɪŋi/ *adj* **-ier, -iest** having very thin flesh or muscle: *a stringy body/arm* –**stringiness** *n* [U]

**strip¹** /strɪp/ *v* **-pp- 1** [T *off*] to remove (the covering or parts of): *Elephants strip the leaves off/from trees.*| *They stripped the shirt from his back.* **2** [I;T *off*] to undress: *He stripped off and jumped into the water.*

**strip²** *n* **1** [*of*] a narrow piece: *a strip of land/paper* **2** the clothes of a particular colour worn by a team in football: *a blue and white strip*

**strip car·toon** /ˌ· ·ˈ·/ *n BrE* for COMIC STRIP

**stripe** /straɪp/ *n* a band of colour, among one or more other colours: *Tigers have orange fur with black stripes.* –**striped** *adj*

**strip·per** /ˈstrɪpəʳ/ *n infml* a STRIPTEASE performer

**strip·tease** /ˈstrɪptiːz, ˌstrɪpˈtiːz/ also **strip show**– *n* [C;U] (a) removal of clothes by a person, esp. a woman, performed as a show

**strip·y** /ˈstraɪpi/ *adj* **-ier, -iest** covered in STRIPES of colour: *a stripy pattern*

**strive** /straɪv/ *v* **strove** /strəʊv/, **striven** /ˈstrɪvən/‖also **strived** *AmE,* **striving** [I +*to-v/for, against*] to struggle hard (to get or conquer): *She strove for recognition as an artist*

**strode** /strəʊd/ *v past tense of* STRIDE

**stroke¹** /strəʊk/ *v* **stroked, stroking** [T] to pass the hand over gently, esp. for pleasure: *The cat likes being stroked.*

**stroke²** *n* **1** [C] a blow, esp. with (the edge of) a weapon: *a stroke of the whip* **2** [S *of*] an unexpected piece (of luck) **3** [C] a sudden illness in part of the brain which can cause loss of movement in parts of the body

**stroll** /strəʊl/ *v* [I] to walk, esp. slowly, for pleasure –**stroll** *n* [*usu. sing.*]: *to go for a stroll*

**strong** /strɒŋ‖strɔŋ/ *adj* **1** having (a degree of) power, esp. of the body: *She is not very strong after her illness.* **2** not easily broken, spoilt, or changed: *strong beliefs|a strong argument|Languages are her* **strong point**. (=something she does well) **3** [after *n*] of a certain number: *Our club is 50 strong.* **4** (esp. of drinks) having a lot of the material which gives taste: *The tea is too strong.* –compare WEAK (3) **5 (still) going strong** active, esp. when old: *The old clock is still going strong.* –**strongly** *adv*

**strong·box** /ˈstrɒŋbɒks‖ˈstrɔŋbɑks/ *n* a usu. metal box or SAFE² (1) for keeping valuable things

**strong·hold** /ˈstrɒŋhəʊld‖ˈstrɔŋ-/ *n* **1** a fort **2** a place where an activity is common: *The village is a stronghold of old customs.*

**strong lan·guage** /ˌ· ˈ··/ *n* [U] *euph* swearing; curses

**strong-mind·ed** /ˌ· ˈ··◂/ *adj* firm in beliefs, wishes, etc. –**strong-mindedness** *n* [U]

**strong room** /ˈ· ·/ *n* a room, e.g. in a bank, with a special thick door and walls, where valuable objects can be kept

**strove** /strəʊv/ *v past tense of* STRIVE

**struck** /strʌk/ *v past tense & participle of* STRIKE

**struc·tur·al** /ˈstrʌktʃərəl/ *adj* of or concerning STRUCTURE, esp. of a building: *a structural fault* –**structurally** *adv*

**struc·ture¹** /ˈstrʌktʃəʳ/ *n* **1** [U *of*] the way in which parts are formed into a whole: *the structure of the brain/a sentence* **2** [C] anything formed of many parts, esp. a building: *a tall structure*

**structure²** *v* **-tured, -turing** [T] to arrange (esp. ideas) into a whole form: *to structure one's argument*

**strug·gle¹** /ˈstrʌgəl/ *v* **-gled, -gling** [I] to make violent movements, esp. when fighting against a person or thing: (fig.) *They struggled against* POVERTY. (=lack of money)

**struggle²** *n* a hard fight or bodily effort: *the struggle between the two teams*

**strum** /strʌm/ *v* **-mm-** [I;T *on*] to play a stringed instrument (STRING¹ (2)) informally, esp. without skill: *strumming (on) a* GUITAR

**strung** /strʌŋ/ *v past tense & participle of* STRING

**strut¹** /strʌt/ *v* **-tt-** [I] to walk in a proud strong way, trying to look important

**strut²** *n* a piece of wood or metal holding the weight of a part of a building, an aircraft, etc.

**stub¹** /stʌb/ *n* **1** a short end, esp. of a cigarette or pencil **2** the piece of a cheque or ticket left as a record after use

**stub²** *v* **-bb-** [T] to hurt (one's toe) by hitting it against something

**stub** sthg.↔**out** *v adv* [T] to stop (a cigarette) from burning by pressing the end against something

**stub·ble** /ˈstʌbəl/ *n* [U] short stiff pieces of something which grows, esp. a short beard or the remains of wheat after being cut –**stubbly** *adv* **-blier, -bliest**

**stub·born** /ˈstʌbən‖-ərn/ *adj* determined; with a strong will –**stubbornly** *adv* –**stubbornness** *n* [U]

**stub·by** /ˈstʌbi/ *adj* **-bier, -biest** short and thick: *his stubby fingers*

**stuck¹** /stʌk/ *adj* [F] **1** unable to move or be moved; fixed in place: *The door's stuck.*|(fig.) *If the bank won't lend us the money we'll be stuck.* **2** fixed by sticky material: *a bit of paper stuck to my shoe* –see also UNSTUCK

**stuck²** *v past tense & participle of* STICK

**stuck-up** /ˌ· ˈ·◂/ *adj infml* proud in manner: *too stuck-up to speak to his old friends*

**stud¹** /stʌd/ *n* a number of horses or other animals kept for breeding

**stud²** *n* **1** a fastener used instead of a button and buttonhole, esp. one with two separate parts which are pressed together (**press stud**) **2** a nail or similar object standing out from a flat-topped surface, used for decoration, to mark off road sections, etc.

**stud³** *v* **-dd-** [T] to cover with (something like) STUDS²: *a star-studded sky*

**stu·dent** /ˈstjuːdənt‖ˈstuː-/ *n* **1** [A;C] a person who is studying at a place of education or training: *a history student|a student teacher* –see picture on page 105 **2** [*of*] a person with a stated interest: *a student of human nature*

**stud·ied** /ˈstʌdid/ *adj fml* carefully considered before being expressed: *a studied remark*

**stu·di·o** /ˈstjuːdiəʊ‖ˈstuː-/ *n* **-os 1** a workroom for a painter, photographer, etc. **2** a room from which broadcasts are made: *a television studio* **3** a place where cinema films are made: *Pinewood studios*

**stu·di·ous** /ˈstjuːdɪəs‖ˈstuː-/ *adj* **1** eager to study; studying hard **2** *fml* careful: *to pay studious attention to detail* –**studiously** *adv* –**studiousness** *n* [U]

**stud·y¹** /ˈstʌdi/ *n* **-ies 1** [U] the act of studying **2** [C;U] a subject studied: *to give time to one's studies* **3** [C] a thorough enquiry into, esp. including a piece of writing on, a particular subject: *a study of Shakespeare's plays* **4** [C] a room used for studying

**study²** *v* **studied, studying 1** [I;T] to spend time in learning (a subject): *She studies French.* **2** [T] to examine carefully: *She studied the report.*

**stuff¹** /stʌf/ *n* [U] **1** material of any sort, of which something is made: *What's this strange stuff on the floor?* **2** *infml* things in a mass; matter: *I can't carry all my stuff in this bag.* **3 do one's stuff** *infml* to show one's ability as expected

**stuff²** *v* [T] **1** [*with/into*] to push (a substance) into; fill with a substance: *to stuff a shoe with newspaper/stuff the newspaper into the shoe|(infml) He stuffed himself with food.* **2** to fill the skin of (a dead animal), to make it look real: *a stuffed elephant* **3** to put STUFFING (2) inside: *to stuff a chicken*

**stuff·ing** /ˈstʌfɪŋ/ *n* [U] **1** material used as a filling for something: *to use feathers as stuffing* **2** *BrE*‖ **dressing** *AmE*– a special mixture of foods placed inside a bird or piece of meat before cooking to improve the taste

**stuff·y** /ˈstʌfi/ *adj* **-ier, -iest 1** having air which is not fresh: *a stuffy room* **2** (of ideas or manners) formal and old-fashioned –**stuffily** *adv* –**stuffiness** *n* [U]

**stum·ble** /ˈstʌmbəl/ *v* **-bled, -bling** [I] **1** to catch the foot on the ground while moving along and start to fall: *She stumbled and fell.* **2** to stop or make mistakes in speaking or reading aloud: *She stumbled at/over the long word.* –**stumble** *n*

**stumble across/on** sbdy./sthg. *v prep* [T] to meet or discover by chance

**stumbling block** /ˈ·· ·/ *n* something which prevents action: *It's a good plan, but the opposition of the local people may be a stumbling block.*

> **SPELLING NOTE**
> Words with the sound /s/, may be spelt **c-**, like **city**, or **ps-**, like **psychology**.

**stump¹** /stʌmp/ *n* **1** the part of something left after the rest has been cut down, cut off, or worn down: *a tree stump|the stump of a tooth/pencil* **2** (in cricket) one of the three upright pieces of wood at which the ball is thrown

**stump²** *v* **1** [I] to move heavily: *He stumped angrily up the stairs.* **2** [T] *infml* to cause (someone) to be unable to reply; BAFFLE: *Her question stumped him*

**stump·y** /ˈstʌmpi/ *adj* **-ier, -iest** short and thick in body

**stun** /stʌn/ *v* **-nn-** [T] **1** to make unconscious by hitting the head **2** to shock or surprise greatly: *I was completely stunned by his refusal to help.*

**stung** /stʌŋ/ *v past tense & participle of* STING

**stunk** /stʌŋk/ *v past tense of* STINK

**stun·ning** /ˈstʌnɪŋ/ *adj* very attractive; delightful; beautiful –**stunningly** *adv*

**stunt¹** /stʌnt/ *v* [T] to prevent (full growth) (of): *Lack of food may stunt the growth.*

**stunt²** *n* **1** an act of bodily skill, often dangerous: *In the film he had to drive a car into the sea, and other dangerous stunts.* **2** an action done in order to gain attention: *an advertising stunt*

**stunt man** /ˈ· ·/ **stuntwoman** *fem.*– *n* a person who does dangerous acts in a film so that the actor does not have to take risks

**stu·pe·fy** /ˈstjuːpə̇faɪ‖ˈstuː-/ *v* **-fied, -fying** [T] *fml* to make unable to think; surprise very much –**stupefaction** /-ˈfækʃən / *n* [U]

**stu·pen·dous** /stjuːˈpendəs‖stuː-/ *adj* surprisingly great: *a stupendous success* –**stupendously** *adv*

**stu·pid** /ˈstjuːpə̇d‖ˈstuː-/ *adj* silly or foolish: *a stupid person* –**stupidly** *adv* –**stupidity** /-ˈpɪdə̇ti / *n*

**stu·por** /ˈstjuːpəʳ‖ˈstuː-/ *n* a state in which one cannot think or use the senses: *in a* DRUNKEN *stupor*

**stur·dy** /ˈstɜːdi‖-ɜr-/ *adj* **-dier, -diest** strong and firm, esp. in body –**sturdily** *adv* –**sturdiness** *n* [U]

**stut·ter** /ˈstʌtəʳ/ *v* [I] to speak with difficulty in producing sounds, esp. habitually holding back the first consonant –compare STAMMER –**stutter** *n* –**stutterer** *n*

**sty¹** /staɪ/ *n* **sties** → PIGSTY (1)

**sty², stye** *n* an infected swollen place on the eyelid

**style¹** /staɪl/ *n* **1** [C;U] a general way of doing something: *the modern style of building|a formal style of writing|a hair style* **2** [C] fashion, esp. in clothes: *the style of the 30s* **3** [U] high quality of social behaviour, appearance, or manners: *She gives dinner parties* **in style,** (=in a grand way) *with the best food and wine.* **4 -style**: **a** in the manner of a certain person, place, etc.: *He wears his hair long, hippie-style.|I like my hamburgers cooked American-style.* **b** like a certain thing in appearance only: *a leather-style case*

**style²** *v* **styled, styling** [T] to form in a certain pattern, shape, etc.: *The dress is carefully styled.*

**styl·ish** /ˈstaɪlɪʃ/ *adj* fashionable –**stylishly** *adv* –**stylishness** *n* [U]

**styl·ist** /ˈstaɪlə̇st/ *n* a person who is concerned with styles of appearance: *a hair stylist*

**styl·is·tic** /staɪˈlɪstɪk/ *adj fml* of or concerning style, esp. in writing or art –**stylistically** *adv*

**styl·ize** ‖also **-ise** *BrE* /ˈstaɪlaɪz/ *v* **-ized, -izing** [T] *fml* (in art or description) to present in a fixed, often unnatural style

**sty·lus** /'staɪləs/ *n* **-luses** *or* **-li** /-liː/ the needle-like instrument in a RECORD PLAYER that picks up the sound signals from a record

**suave** /swɑːv/ *adj* having very good smooth manners which sometimes hide bad character –**suavely** *adv*

**sub** /sʌb/ *n infml* **1** → SUBSCRIPTION (1) **2** → SUBMARINE[1]

**sub·com·mit·tee** /'sʌbkəˌmɪti/ *n* [C +*sing./pl.v*] a smaller group formed from a larger committee to deal with a certain matter in more detail: *The subcommittee has/have decided . . .*

**sub·con·scious**[1] /sʌb'kɒnʃəs‖-'kɑn-/ *adj* (of thoughts, feelings, etc.) present at a hidden level of the mind –see CONSCIOUS (USAGE) –**subconsciously** *adv*

**subconscious**[2] also **unconscious**– *n* [*the* S] the hidden level of the mind and the thoughts that happen there

**sub·con·ti·nent** /ˌsʌb'kɒntənənt‖-'kɑn-/ *n* a large mass of land not quite large enough to be called a CONTINENT: *the Indian subcontinent*

**sub·di·vide** /ˌsʌbdə'vaɪd/ *v* **-vided, -viding** [I;T] to divide (something that is already divided) into smaller parts –**subdivision** /-də'vɪʒən/ *n* [U]

**sub·due** /səb'djuː‖-'duː/ *v* **-dued, -duing** [T] to gain control of; conquer: *Napoleon subdued most of Europe.|She tried to subdue her anger.*

**sub·dued** /səb'djuːd‖-'duːd/ *adj* **1** gentle; reduced in strength of light, sound, etc.: *subdued lighting|a subdued voice* **2** unnaturally quiet in behaviour

**sub·hu·man** /sʌb'hjuːmən/ *adj* of less than human qualities: *subhuman behaviour*

**sub·ject**[1] /'sʌbdʒɪkt/ *n* **1** a person owing loyalty to a certain state or royal ruler: *a subject of the King* –compare CITIZEN **2** something being considered or dealt with: *Don't change the subject; answer the question.|The subject of the painting is the Battle of Waterloo.|a book on the subject of insects* **3** a branch of knowledge studied as part of one's education: *She's taking six subjects in her examinations.* **4** a person or animal used in an EXPERIMENT: *an experiment to discover the effects of smoking, with mice as the subjects* **5** *tech* (in grammar) the noun, PRONOUN, etc., which is most closely related to the verb in forming a sentence: *In the sentence "Mary hit John", "Mary" is the subject of the sentence.* –compare OBJECT[1] (4)

**subject**[2] *adj* **1** [*to*] governed by someone or something else; not independent: *a subject race|subject to the law* **2** [F *to*] likely or tending (to have): *The arrangements are subject to change.*

**sub·jec·tive** /səb'dʒektɪv/ *adj* **1** influenced by personal feelings: *This is a very subjective judgment of her abilities.* **2** existing only in the mind; imaginary: *a subjective image of water in the desert*–see also OBJECTIVE –**subjectively** *adv* –**subjectivity** /ˌsʌbdʒek'tɪvəti/ *n* [U]

**subject to**[1] **subject** sbdy. **to** sthg. /səb'dʒekt tə, tʊ, tuː (*as for* **to**)/ *v prep* [T *often pass.*] to cause to experience or suffer: *The man was subjected to questioning by the police.*

**subject to**[2] /'sʌbdʒɪkt/ *prep* depending on: *Our plans are subject to the weather.*

**sub·ju·gate** /'sʌbdʒʊgeɪt‖-dʒə-/ *v* **-gated, -gating** [T] to conquer and take power over: *a subjugated people* –**subjugation** /-'geɪʃən/ *n* [U]

**sub·junc·tive** /səb'dʒʌŋktɪv/ *adj,n* (being or concerning) a special form (MOOD[2]) of the verb used in certain languages to express doubt, wishes, a dependent verb, etc.: *In the sentence "If I were you I would complain to the director", "were" and "would" are subjunctives.*

**sub·let** /sʌb'let/ *v* **-tt-** [I;T] (of a person who rents property from its owner) to rent part of a property to someone else: *He rents the house and sublets a room to a friend.*

**sub·lime** /sə'blaɪm/ *adj* very noble or wonderful; causing pride, joy, etc. –**sublimely** *adv*

**sub·ma·rine**[1] /'sʌbməriːn, ˌsʌbmə'riːn/ also **sub** *infml*– *n* a ship, esp. a warship, which can stay under water

**submarine**[2] *adj tech* growing or being under or in the sea: *submarine plant life|a submarine pipeline*

**sub·merge** /səb'mɜːdʒ‖-ɜr-/ *v* **-merged, -merging** [I;T] to (cause to) go under the surface of water: *The submarine submerged, then rose to the surface.|dangerous submerged rocks*

**sub·mis·sion** /səb'mɪʃən/ *n* **1** [U *to*] the acceptance of someone else's power; obedience: *his submission to his father's wishes* **2** [C] *fml* a suggestion

**sub·mis·sive** /səb'mɪsɪv/ *adj* gentle and willing to obey orders –**submissively** *adv* –**submissiveness** *n* [U]

**sub·mit** /səb'mɪt/ *v* **-tt- 1** [I;T *to*] to yield (oneself); agree to obey: *to submit (oneself) to another's wishes* **2** [T] to offer for consideration: *to submit new plans*

**sub·nor·mal** /ˌsʌb'nɔːməl‖-ɔr-/ *adj* less than is usual, esp. in power of the mind: *He was born subnormal and will never learn to speak.*

**sub·or·di·nate**[1] /sə'bɔːdənət‖-ɔr-/ *n,adj* [*to*] *fml* (a person) of a lower rank or position –compare INFERIOR

**sub·or·din·ate**[2] /sə'bɔːdəneɪt‖-ɔr-/ *v* **-ated, -ating** *fml* to put in a position of less importance: *He subordinated his own wishes to those of the group.* –**subordination** /-'neɪʃən/ *n* [U]

**sub·scribe** /səb'skraɪb/ *v* **-scribed, -scribing 1** [I *to*] to pay regularly in order to receive a magazine, newspaper, etc. for a period of time **2** [I;T *to*] to give (money) with other people in support of some good aim: *She subscribes to an animal protection society.*

**subscribe to** sthg. *v prep.* [T +*v-ing*] *fml* to agree with; approve of: *I can't subscribe to unnecessary killing.*

**sub·scrib·er** /səb'skraɪbə[r]/ *n* **1** a person who SUBSCRIBES **2** a person who pays for the use of a service over a period of time: *a telephone subscriber*

**sub·scrip·tion** /səb'skrɪpʃən/ *n* **1** [C] an amount of money given, esp. regularly, to a society or for a magazine, etc. **2** [U] the act of subscribing (SUBSCRIBE): *The library was paid for by public subscription.*

**sub·se·quent** /'sʌbsəkwənt/ *adj* [A;F *to*] *fml* coming after something else, sometimes as a result of it: *We made plans for a visit, but subsequent difficulties with the car prevented it.* –**subsequently** *adv*

**sub·ser·vi·ent** /səb'sɜːvɪənt‖-ɜr-/ *adj* [*to*] habitually willing to do what others want –**subserviently** *adv* –**subservience** *n* [U]

**sub·side** /səb'saɪd/ *v* **-sided, -siding** [I] **1** (of a building, land, etc.) to sink gradually further into the ground **2** (of bad weather conditions) to become less severe or forceful: |(fig.) *His anger quickly subsided.*

**sub·si·dence** /səb'saɪdəns, 'sʌbsədəns/ *n* [C;U] (an example of) the fact of subsiding (SUBSIDE (1)); the sinking of land or buildings

**sub·sid·i·a·ry** /səb'sɪdɪəri‖-dieri/ *n,adj* **-ries** [*to, of*] (something which is) connected but of second importance to the main company, plan, work, etc.

**sub·si·dize** ‖also **-dise** *BrE* /'sʌbsədaɪz/ *v* **-dized, -dizing** [T] (of governments, large organizations, etc.) to pay part of the costs of (something) for (someone): *Should public transport be subsidized?* **–subsidization** /-daɪ'zeɪʃən‖-də-/ *n* [U]

**sub·si·dy** /'sʌbsədi/ *n* **-dies** money paid, esp. by the government to an organization, to make prices lower, goods cheaper, etc.

**sub·sist** /səb'sɪst/ *v* [I *on*] to stay alive when having small amounts of money or food: *They subsisted on bread and water/on £20 a week.* **–subsistence** *n* [U]: *to live* **at subsistence level** (=with just enough food to stay alive)

**sub·son·ic** /ˌsʌb'sɒnɪk‖-'sɑ-/ *adj* (flying at a speed) below the speed of sound: *subsonic aircraft* –see also SUPERSONIC

**sub·stance** /'sʌbstəns/ *n* **1** [C] a material; type of matter: *Salt is a useful substance.* **2** [*the* S;U] the important part; the real meaning: *The substance of what he said was that he was against the idea.*

**sub·stan·dard** /ˌsʌb'stændəd‖-ərd/ *adj* not good enough; unacceptable: *substandard work/clothing* –see also STANDARD²

**sub·stan·tial** /səb'stænʃəl/ *adj* **1** solid; strongly made: *a substantial desk* **2** large enough to be noticeable; of some size or value: *substantial improvements|a substantial amount of money* –see also INSUBSTANTIAL

**sub·stan·tial·ly** /səb'stænʃəli/ *adv* quite a lot: *to help substantially*

**sub·stan·ti·ate** /səb'stænʃieɪt/ *v* **-ated, -ating** [T] *fml* to prove the truth of: *Can you substantiate your claim?* **–substantiation** /-ʃi'eɪʃən/ *n* [U]

**sub·sti·tute¹** /'sʌbstətjuːt‖-tuːt/ *n* [*for*] a person or thing acting in place of another: *She is the doctor's substitute during holiday times.*

**substitute²** *v* **-tuted, -tuting 1** [T *for*] to put (something or someone) in place of another: *We substituted rice for potatoes.* **2** [I *for*] to act as a SUBSTITUTE; be used instead of: *She substituted for the worker who was ill.* **–substitution** /'tjuːʃən‖-'tuː-/ *n* [C;U]

**sub·ter·fuge** /'sʌbtəfjuːdʒ‖-ər-/ *n* [C;U] (deceit by) a trick or dishonest way of doing something

**sub·ter·ra·ne·an** /ˌsʌbtə'reɪnɪən/ *adj* underground: *subterranean rivers*

**sub·ti·tles** /'sʌbˌtaɪtlz/ *n* [P] words printed over a film in a foreign language to translate what is being SAID: *a French film with English subtitles* –compare dub²

**SPELLING NOTE**
Words with the sound /s/, may be spelt **c-**, like **city**, or **ps-**, like **psychology**.

**sub·tle** /'sʌtl/ *adj* **-tler, -tlest 1** delicate, hardly noticeable, and usu. pleasant: *a subtle taste|subtle differences in meaning* **2** very clever, esp. in deceiving: *a subtle advertisement* **–subtly** *adv*

**sub·tle·ty** /'sʌtəlti/ *n* **1** [U] the quality of being SUBTLE: *the subtlety of her argument* **2** [C] a SUBTLE idea or detail

**sub·tract** /səb'trækt/ *v* [T *from*] **–subtraction** *n* [C;U]

**sub·urb** /'sʌbɜːb‖-ɜrb/ *n* [*often pl.*] an outer area of a town or city, usu. where people live rather than work: *a suburb of London|I live in the suburbs.*

**sub·ur·bi·a** /sə'bɜːbɪə‖-ɜr-/ *n* [U] *often derog* the SUBURBS

**sub·ver·sive** /səb'vɜːsɪv‖-ɜr-/ *adj* which tries to destroy those in power: *The new party has subversive ideas.* **–subversively** *adv* **–subversiveness** *n* [U]

**sub·vert** /səb'vɜːt‖-ɜrt/ *v* [T] *fml* to try to destroy the power and influence of (esp. a governing body) **–subversion** /-'vɜːʃən‖-ɜr- / *n* [U]

**sub·way** /'sʌbweɪ/ *n* **1** [C] a path under a road or railway **2** [C;*the* S] *AmE* an underground railway: *It's quicker to go* **by subway**. –compare UNDERGROUND

**suc·ceed** /sək'siːd/ *v* **1** [I *in*] to gain a purpose or reach an aim; do well: *She succeeded the second time she took the examination.* –compare FAIL¹; see COULD (USAGE) **2** [T] to follow after, take the place of: *Mr. Smith succeeded Mr. Jones as our teacher.*

**suc·cess** /sək'ses/ *n* **1** [U] the act of SUCCEEDing (1) in something **2** [C] a person or thing that SUCCEEDs (1)

**suc·cess·ful** /sək'sesfəl/ *adj* having succeeded; having gained an aim: *a successful businesswoman* –opposite **unsuccessful –successfully** *adv*

**suc·ces·sion** /sək'seʃən/ *n* **1** [U] the fact of following one after the other: *His words came out in quick succession.* **2** [C *of*] a set of people or things following on one after the other: *a succession of rainy days* **3** [U] the act or right of SUCCEEDing (2) someone in a position

**suc·ces·sive** /sək'sesɪv/ *adj* following one after the other: *two visits on successive days* **–successively** *adv*

**suc·ces·sor** /sək'sesəʳ/ *n* a person or thing that comes after another: *the chairman's successor*

**suc·cinct** /sək'sɪŋkt/ *adj* clearly expressed in few words **–succinctly** *adv* **–succinctness** *n* [U]

**suc·cour** *BrE*‖**-cor** *AmE* /'sʌkəʳ/ *n,v* [U;T] *fml & lit* (to provide with) help given in difficulty

**suc·cu·lent** /'sʌkjʊlənt‖-kjə-/ *adj apprec* juicy: *a succulent fruit/piece of meat* **–succulence** *n* [U]

**suc·cumb** /sə'kʌm/ *v* [I *to*] *fml* to yield: *He succumbed to persuasion.*

**such** /sʌtʃ/ *predeterminer,determiner,pron* **1** so great; so good, bad, or unusual: *Don't be such a fool!|He told us such funny stories that we all laughed.|He wrote to her every day, such was his love for her.* **2** of the same kind; of that kind: *chairs, tables, and all such furniture|He said "Get out!" or some such remark.|They're dirty and untidy; I can't understand such people.|You can borrow my old car, such as it is.* (=it's not a very good car) **3 such as** (used before an example): *people such as my*

sister|*animals such as horses, cattle, and deer*
USAGE Compare **such** and **so** in these examples: *It was* **such** *an interesting meeting*. (=the meeting was **so** interesting)|*There were* **such** *a lot of people*. (=there were **so** many people)|*It was* **such** *a shock*. (=it was **so** *shocking*)

**such·like** /ˈsʌtʃlaɪk/ *pron,adj* [A] *infml* (things) of that kind: *tennis, cricket, and suchlike* (sports)

**suck** /sʌk/ *v* **1** [I;T] to draw (liquid) into the mouth by using the lips and muscles at the side of the mouth: *to suck milk through a straw* **2** [I;T *at*] to eat (something) by holding it in the mouth and melting it: *sucking (away at) a sweet*|(fig.) *The baby was sucking its thumb*. **3** [T] to pull into a position by SUCTION: *current sucked them under the water*. –**suck** *n*

**suck·er** /ˈsʌkəʳ/ *n* **1** a person or thing that sucks **2** something which sticks to a surface by SUCTION: *You stick this hook to the wall with a sucker.*|*Flies have suckers on their feet.* **3** a new growth from the root or lower stem of a plant **4** *infml* a foolish person who is easily cheated

**suck·le** /ˈsʌkəl/ *v* **-led, -ling** [I;T] (esp. of animals) to feed (the young) with milk from the mother's breast –see also NURSE² (2)

**suc·tion** /ˈsʌkʃən/ *n* [U] the act of drawing air or liquid away so that **a** another gas or liquid enters or **b** a solid sticks to another surface, because of the pressure of the air outside: *We'll get the water out with a* **suction pump**.

**sud·den** /ˈsʌdn/ *adj* **1** happening quickly and unexpectedly: *a sudden illness* **2 all of a sudden** unexpectedly –**suddenly** *adv* –**suddenness** *n* [U]

**suds** /sʌdz/ also **soapsuds**– *n* [P] the bubbles formed by soap when mixed with water

**sue** /suː, sjuː‖suː/ *v* **sued, suing** [I;T *for*] to bring a claim in law against (someone): *The minister says that the newspaper story about him is completely untrue, and that he intends to sue* (*the person who wrote it*).

**suede, suède** /sweɪd/ *n* [U] soft leather with a rough surface: *suede shoes*

**su·et** /ˈsuːət, ˈsjuːət‖ˈsuː-/ *n* [U] hard fat used in cooking, made from the KIDNEYS of an animal

**suf·fer** /ˈsʌfəʳ/ *v* **1** [I] to experience pain or difficulty: *He suffered terribly all through his illness.* **2** [T] to experience (something painful): *The army suffered heavy losses* (=many soldiers were killed) *in the battle.* **3** [I] to grow worse; lessen in quality: *He drank a lot and his work suffered.*

**suffer from** sthg. *v prep* [T] to experience (something unpleasant, e.g. an illness), esp. over a period of time: *My mother suffers from backache.*

**suf·fer·ance** /ˈsʌfərəns/ *n* **on sufferance** with permission, though not welcomed

**suf·fer·er** /ˈsʌfərəʳ/ *n* a person who suffers, esp. from a stated illness: *headache sufferers*

**suf·fer·ing** /ˈsʌfərɪŋ/ *n* [C;U] (an experience of) pain or difficulty: *suffering during the war*

**suf·fice** /səˈfaɪs/ *v* **-ficed, -ficing** [I *for*; not *be +v-ing*] *fml* to be enough: *Her income suffices for her needs.*

**suf·fi·cien·cy** /səˈfɪʃənsi/ *n* [S *of*] *fml* a supply which is enough –opposite **insufficiency**

**suf·fi·cient** /səˈfɪʃənt/ *adj* enough: *£20 should be sufficient for a new pair of shoes.* –opposite **insufficient**

**suf·fix** /ˈsʌfɪks/ *n* (in grammar) a word or part of a word that is placed at the end of another word and that changes its meaning or use –compare PREFIX

**suf·fo·cate** /ˈsʌfəkeɪt/ *v* **-cated, -cating** [I;T] to (cause to) die because of lack of air –**suffocation** /-ˈkeɪʃən / *n* [U]

**suf·fra·gette** /ˌsʌfrəˈdʒet/ *n* (in Britain in the early 20th century) a woman who was a member of a group which tried to gain **suffrage** (=the right to vote) for women

**sug·ar¹** /ˈʃʊgəʳ/ *n* [U] a sweet substance obtained from plants (esp. **sugarcane** and **sugar beet**) and used in food: *I take sugar in tea, but not in coffee.*

**sugar²** *v* [T] to put sugar in: *to sugar one's tea*

**sug·ar·y** /ˈʃʊgəri/ *adj* **1** containing sugar **2** too sweet, nice, kind, etc.

**sug·gest** /səˈdʒest‖səgˈdʒest/ *v* [T] **1** [+*v-ing*/(*that*)] to say or write (an idea to be considered): *I suggest finishing now*/(*that*) *we finish now.* **2** [+(*that*)] to give signs (of): *Her expression suggested anger*/(*that*) *she was angry.*

**sug·ges·ti·ble** /səˈdʒestəbəl‖səg-/ *adj* easily influenced: *a suggestible child*|*She's at a suggestible age.*

**sug·ges·tion** /səˈdʒestʃən‖səg-/ *n* **1** [C +(*that*)] something suggested: *The teacher made some suggestions to prepare us for the examination.* **2** [U] the act of suggesting: *I went there on your suggestion.* **3** [C *of*] a slight sign: *a suggestion of a smile*

**sug·ges·tive** /səˈdʒestɪv‖səg-/ *adj* which suggests thoughts of sex: *a suggestive remark* –**suggestively** *adv*

**su·i·cid·al** /ˌsuːəˈsaɪdl, ˌsjuː-‖ˌsuː-/ *adj* **1** with a tendency to SUICIDE: *feeling suicidal* **2** likely to lead to death or destruction: *a suicidal attempt to climb a dangerous mountain* –**suicidally** *adv*

**su·i·cide** /ˈsuːəsaɪd, ˈsjuː-‖ˈsuː-/ *n* **1** [U] the act of killing oneself: *to* **commit suicide** **2** [C] an example of this

**suit¹** /suːt, sjuːt‖suːt/ *n* **1 a** a set of outer clothes made of the same material, usu. including a short coat (JACKET) with trousers or skirt –see picture on page 563 **b** a set of clothes for a special purpose: *a bathing suit* **2** one of the four sets of cards used in games –see CARDS (USAGE) **3** → LAWSUIT **4 follow suit** to do the same as someone else has

**suit²** *v* **1** [I;T] to satisfy or please; be convenient for: *It's a small house but it suits us*/*our needs.* **2** [T] to match or look right with: *That colour doesn't suit him.* **3 be suited (to/for)** to be fit, suitable, or of the right kind (for): *He wasn't suited to*/*for the job and left after three months.*| *Tom and Jane are very well suited (for each other).* **4 suit oneself** *infml* to do what one likes: *"The others are going out, but I think I'll stay at home." "Suit yourself."*

**sui·ta·ble** /ˈsuːtəbəl, ˈsjuː-‖ˈsuː-/ *adj* [*for*] fit (for a purpose); right; convenient: *Is she suitable for the job?* –opposite **unsuitable** –**suitably** *adv*

**suit·case** /ˈsuːtkeɪs, ˈsjuːt-‖ˈsuːt-/ *n* a flat box for carrying clothes and possessions when travelling –see also CASE²; –see picture on page 16

**suite** /swiːt/ *n* **1** [*of*] a set of rooms, esp. in a hotel **2** [*of*] a set of furniture, esp. a SETTEE and two chairs (**three-piece suite**) **3** a piece of music with several loosely connected parts

**sul·tor** /ˈsuːtəʳ, ˈsjuː-‖ˈsuː-/ *n old use* a man wishing to marry a woman

**sulk** /sʌlk/ *v* [I] to show lasting annoyance, esp. silently and for slight cause **–sulky** *adj* **-ier, -iest –sulkily** *adv* **–sulkiness** *n* [U]

**sul·len** /ˈsʌlən/ *adj* **1** silently showing dislike and lack of cheerfulness: *a sullen face* **2** dark and unpleasant: *a sullen sky* **–sullenly** *adv* **–sullenness** *n* [U]

**sul·phur** *BrE*‖**sulfur** *AmE* /ˈsʌlfəʳ/ *n* [U] a simple substance (ELEMENT (1)) that is found as a light yellow powder

**sul·tan** /ˈsʌltən/ *n* a Muslim ruler, as formerly in Turkey

**sul·ta·na** /sʊlˈtɑːnə‖-ˈtænə/ *n* a small seedless RAISIN (dried fruit) used in baking

**sul·try** /ˈsʌltri/ *adj* **-trier, -triest 1** (of weather) hot, airless, and uncomfortable **2** causing strong sexual attraction: *a sultry smile* **–sultriness** *n* [U]

**sum** /sʌm/ *n* **1** [C] a usu. simple calculation, such as adding or dividing: *learning to do sums at school* **2** an amount: *I've spent a large sum/large sums of money on repairing the car.* **3** [*the* S *of*] the total produced when numbers, amounts, etc., are added together: *The sum of 6 and 4 is 10.*

**sum·mar·ize** ‖also **-ise** *BrE* /ˈsʌməraɪz/ *v* **-ized, -izing** [T] to make or give a SUMMARY of (something longer) –see also SUM UP

**sum·ma·ry¹** /ˈsʌməri/ *n* **-ries** [*of*] a short account giving the main points

**summary²** *adj fml* done at once, esp. (of punishments) without considering mercy: *summary dismissal*/EXECUTION (1)

**sum·mer** /ˈsʌməʳ/ *n* [C;U] the season between spring and autumn when the sun is hot: *warm summer weather|the hottest summer for 20 years* **–summery** *adj: warm and summery|a summery dress*

**sum·mer·house** /ˈsʌməhaʊs‖-ər-/ *n* a small building in a garden, with seats in the shade

**sum·mer·time** /ˈsʌmətaɪm‖-ər-/ *n* [*the* U] the season of summer; the time of hot weather

**summing-up** /ˌ·· ˈ·/ *n* **summings-up** a SUMMARY¹, esp. spoken by a judge at the end of a court case –see also SUM UP

**sum·mit** /ˈsʌm¹̣t/ *n* **1** [C *of*] the top, esp. the highest part of a mountain: (fig.) *She has now reached the summit of her* AMBITIONS. **2** [A;C] (a meeting) between heads of state

**sum·mon** /ˈsʌmən/ *v* [T *to*] *fml* to give an official order (to come, do, etc.): *to be summoned (in)to the presence of the Queen*

**summon** sthg.↔**up** *v adv* [T] to draw (a quality) out of oneself, esp. with an effort: *She summoned up all her strength and pushed open the door.*

**sum·mons¹** /ˈsʌmənz/ *n* an order to appear in a court of law: *They* **served a summons** *on her.*

> **SPELLING NOTE**
> Words with the sound /s/, may be spelt **c-**, like **city**, or **ps-**, like **psychology**.

**summons²** *v* [T] to give a SUMMONS to; order to appear in court

**sump·tu·ous** /ˈsʌmptʃuəs/ *adj* expensive and grand: *a sumptuous feast* **–sumptuously** *adv* **–sumptuousness** *n* [U]

**sum up** *v adv* **-mm- 1** [I;T (=**sum** sthg.↔**up**)] to give the main points of (a report, a meeting, etc.); SUMMARIZE –see also SUMMING-UP **2** [T] (**sum** sbdy./sthg. ⟷ **up**) to consider and judge quickly: *to sum up the problem*

**sun¹** /sʌn/ *n* **1** [*the* S] the burning star in the sky, from which the earth receives light and heat **2** [*the* S;U] light and heat from the sun: *to sit in the sun* **3** [C] a star round which PLANETS may turn

**sun²** *v* **-nn-** [T] to place (oneself) in sunlight: *She was sunning herself in the garden.*

**sun·bathe** /ˈsʌnbeɪð/ *v* **-bathed, -bathing** [I] to sit or lie in strong sunlight in order to make the body brown **–sunbather** *n*

**sun·beam** /ˈsʌnbiːm/ *n* a beam of sunlight

**sun·burn** /ˈsʌnbɜːn‖-ɜrn/ *n* [U] (the condition of having) sore skin after experiencing too much strong sunlight **–sunburnt** *adj*

**sun·dae** /ˈsʌndeɪ‖-di/ *n* a dish made from ice cream with fruit, sweet-tasting juice, etc.

**Sun·day** /ˈsʌndi, -deɪ/ *n* the first day of the week; the day between Saturday and Monday: *She'll arrive (on) Sunday.*

**Sunday school** /ˈ·· ·/ *n* [C;U] religious teaching for children on a Sunday

**sun·dial** /ˈsʌndaɪəl/ *n* an apparatus, used esp. in former times, which shows the time according to where the shadow of a pointer falls

**sun·down** /ˈsʌndaʊn/ *n* [S] →SUNSET

**sun·dry** /ˈsʌndri/ *adj* [A] various: *books, pens, and sundry other articles*

**sun·flow·er** /ˈsʌnˌflaʊəʳ/ *n* a plant with a large yellow flower, and seeds used to make cooking oil

**sung** /sʌŋ/ *v past participle of* SING

**sun·glass·es** /ˈsʌnˌglɑːs¹̣z‖-ˌglæ-/ *n* [P] glasses with dark glass in them to protect the eyes from the sun –see PAIR (USAGE)

**sunk** /sʌŋk/ *v past participle of* SINK

**sunk·en** /ˈsʌŋkən/ *adj* **1** which has (been) sunk: *a sunken ship* **2** hollow; having fallen lower than the surrounding surface: *sunken eyes*

**sun·lamp** /ˈsʌnlæmp/ also **sunray lamp**– *n* a lamp which gives out light like that which comes from the sun, used to cure some skin diseases

**sun·light** /ˈsʌnlaɪt/ *n* [U] natural light from the sun

**sun·lit** /ˈsʌnˌlɪt/ *adj* brightly lit by the sun

**sun·ny** /ˈsʌni/ *adj* **-nier, -niest 1** having bright sunlight: *a sunny room/day* **2** cheerful: *a sunny smile* **–sunnily** *adv* **–sunniness** *n* [U]

**sun·rise** /ˈsʌnraɪz/ *n* [C;U] the time when the sun appears after the night

**sun·set** /ˈsʌnset/ *n* [C;U] the time when the sun disappears as night begins: *a beautiful sunset*

**sun·shade** /ˈsʌnʃeɪd/ *n* →PARASOL

**sun·shine** /ˈsʌnʃaɪn/ *n* [U] strong sunlight: *I was sitting in the garden, enjoying the sunshine.*

**sun·stroke** /ˈsʌnstrəʊk/ also **heatstroke**– *n* [U] an illness caused by the effects of too much strong sunlight

**sun·tan** /'sʌntæn/ also **tan**– *n* the brownness of the skin after the effects of sunshine –**suntanned** *adj*

**su·per** /'suːpəʳ, 'sjuː-‖'suː-/ *adj infml* wonderful

**su·per·an·nu·at·ed** /ˌsuːpər'ænjueɪt̬ɪ̈d, ˌsjuː-‖ ˌsuː-/ *adj fml* **1** too old for work **2** old-fashioned

**su·per·an·nu·a·tion** /ˌsuːpərænju'eɪʃən, ˌsjuː-‖ ˌsuː-/ *n* [U] *fml* money paid as a PENSION, esp. from one's former place of work

**su·perb** /suː'pɜːb, sjuː-‖suː'pɜrb/ *adj* excellent; wonderful: *The food was superb.* –**superbly** *adv*

**su·per·charg·er** /'suːpəˌtʃɑːdʒər, 'sjuː-‖ 'suːpərˌtʃar-/ *n* an apparatus for producing more power from an engine by forcing more air into the place where the FUEL, such as petrol, burns –**supercharge** *v* **-charged, -charging** [T]

**su·per·cil·i·ous** *adj derog* (as if) thinking others of little importance; HAUGHTY –**superciliously** *adv* –**superciliousness** *n* [U]

**su·per·fi·cial** /ˌsuːpə'fɪʃəl, ˌsjuː-‖ˌsuːpər-/ *adj* **1** on the surface; not deep *a superficial crack in the wall* **2** *often derog* not serious or searching in thought, ideas, etc.: *a superficial knowledge* –**superficiality** *n* [U] –**superficially** *adv*

**su·per·flu·ous** /suː'pɜːfluəs, sjuː-‖suː'pɜr-/ *adj* more than is necessary; not needed or wanted –**superfluously** *adv* –**superfluousness** *n* [U]

**su·per·hu·man** /ˌsuːpə'hjuːmən, ˌsjuː-‖ˌsuːpər 'hjuː-/ *adj* seeming beyond human powers: *superhuman strength/patience*

**su·per·im·pose** /ˌsuːpərɪm'pəuz, ˌsjuː-‖ˌsuː-/ *v* **-posed, -posing** [T *on*] to put (one thing) over something else: *to superimpose one film image on another*

**su·per·in·tend** /ˌsuːpərɪn'tend, ˌsjuː-‖ˌsuː-/ *v* [T] to be in charge of and direct; SUPERVISE

**su·per·in·tend·ent** /ˌsuːpərɪn'tendənt, ˌsjuː-‖ ˌsuː-/ *n* **1** a person in charge of some work, building, etc. **2** a British police officer of middle rank

**su·pe·ri·or**[1] /suː'pɪərɪəʳ, sjuː-‖sʊ-/ *adj* **1** [A] of higher rank or class: *I'll report you to your superior officer!* –see MAJOR (USAGE) **2** of high quality: *superior wool* –opposite **inferior** (for **1,2**) **3** *derog* (as if) thinking oneself better than others: *a superior smile* –**superiority** /-ri'ɒrɪ̈ti‖-ri'ɔ-,-'ɑ-/ *n* [U]

**superior**[2] *n* **1** a person of higher rank, esp. in a job: *I'll have to ask my superiors about that.* –compare INFERIOR[2] **2** [after *n*] (*usu. cap.*) (a title for) the head of a religious group: *Mother Superior*

**su·per·la·tive**[1] /suː'pɜːlətɪv, sjuː-‖sʊ'pɜr-/ *n* **1** [*the* S] the highest degree of comparison of an adjective or adverb: *"Good" becomes "best" in the superlative.* **2** [C] a word in this form –see Study Notes on page 119 –**superlatively** *adv*

**superlative**[2] *adj fml* best; greatest: *of superlative quality*

**su·per·man** /'suːpəmæn, 'sjuː-‖'suːpər-/ *n* **-men** /men/ (in stories) a man with powers of mind and body much greater than others'

**su·per·mar·ket** /'suːpəˌmɑːkɪ̈t, 'sjuː-‖'suːpər ˌmɑrkɪ̈t/ *n* a large shop where one serves oneself with food and other goods –see picture on page 615

**su·per·nat·u·ral** /ˌsuːpə'nætʃərəl, ˌsjuː-‖ˌsuːpər-/ *adj* not explained by natural laws but by the powers of gods, magic, etc.: *supernatural powers* –compare UNNATURAL –**supernaturally** *adv*

**su·per·sede** /ˌsuːpə'siːd, ˌsjuː- ‖ˌsuːpər-/ *v* **-seded, -seding** [T] to take the place of as an improvement: *His job was superseded by a computer*

**su·per·son·ic** /ˌsuːpə'sɒnɪk, ˌsjuː-‖ˌsuːpər'sɑ-/ *adj* (flying at a speed) above the speed of sound: *a supersonic aircraft* –see also SUBSONIC

**su·per·star** /'suːpəstɑːʳ, 'sjuː-‖'suːpər-/ *n* an unusually famous performer, esp. a popular musician or a film actor

**su·per·sti·tion** /ˌsuːpə'stɪʃən, ˌsjuː-‖ˌsuːpər-/ *n* [C;U *that*] (a) belief which is not based on reason but on magic or old ideas: *It's a common superstition that black cats are unlucky.*

**su·per·sti·tious** /ˌsuːpə'stɪʃəs, ˌsjuː-‖ˌsuːpər-/ *adj* strongly influenced by SUPERSTITION –**superstitiously** *adv*

**su·per·struc·ture** /'suːpəˌstrʌktʃəʳ, 'sjuː-‖'suː pər-/ *n* an arrangement of parts (e.g. the upper parts of a ship) built up on top of the rest

**su·per·vise** /'suːpəvaɪz, 'sjuː-‖'suːpər-/ *v* **-vised, -vising** [I;T] to keep watch over (work and workers) as the person in charge –**supervision** /-'vɪʒən/ *n* [U]: *The work was done under my supervision.* –**supervisor** *n* –**supervisory** *adj*

**su·pine** /'suːpaɪn, 'sjuː-‖suː'paɪn/ *adj fml* lying on one's back looking upwards –compare PRONE (2)

**sup·per** /'sʌpəʳ/ *n* [C;U] the last meal of the day, taken in the evening

**sup·plant** /sə'plɑːnt‖sə'plænt/ *v* [T] *fml* to take the place of, esp. unfairly or improperly: *The President was supplanted by a political rival.*

**sup·ple** /'sʌpəl/ *adj* bending or moving easily, esp. in the joints of the body –**suppleness** *n* [U]

**sup·ple·ment**[1] /'sʌplɪ̈mənt/ *n* an additional amount of something, e.g. a separate part of a newspaper

**sup·ple·ment**[2] /'sʌplɪ̈ment/ *v* [T *by, with*] to make additions to: *He supplements his wages from the factory by working as a gardener at weekends.*

**sup·ple·men·ta·ry** /ˌsʌplɪ̈'mentəri/ *adj* [*to*] additional: *a supplementary electricity supply*

**sup·pli·cate** /'sʌplɪ̈keɪt/ *v* **-cated, -cating** [I;T *for*] *fml or lit* to beg (someone), esp. for help –**supplication** /-'keɪʃən/ *n* [C;U]

**sup·pli·er** /sə'plaɪəʳ/ *n* a person or firm that supplies something, esp. goods

**sup·plies** /sə'plaɪz/ *n* [P] necessary materials for daily life, esp. for a group of people over a period of time –see also SUPPLY[2]

**sup·ply**[1] /sə'plaɪ/ *v* **-plied, -plying** [T] **1** [*to*] to give (something that is needed): *The government supplies free books to schools.* **2** [*with*] to give things to (a person) for use: *We were supplied with a uniform.*

**supply**[2] *n* **-plies 1** [C;U] (a) system of supplying: *difficulties with the food/water supply* **2** [C] an amount: *a large supply of food* –see also SUPPLIES **3** [U] the rate at which an amount is provided: *The supply of electricity is limited in the mornings.* **4 in short supply** scarce

**supply and de·mand** /·ˌ· · ·'·/ *n* [U] the balance between the amount of goods for sale and that amount that is needed, esp. as this affects prices

**sup·port**[1] /sə'pɔːt‖-ort/ *v* [T] **1** to bear the weight of: *Do you think those shelves can support so many* *books?* **2** to provide money for (a person) to live on: *She has a large family to support.* **3** to approve of and encourage: *to support the workers' demand for higher wages* **4** to be loyal to, esp. by attending matches or performances: *Which football team do you support?* **5** to strengthen (an idea, opinion, etc.); be in favour of: *The popularity of the new party supports the idea that people want a change.*

**support²** *n* **1** [U] the act of SUPPORTing: *We are staying away from work* **in support of** *our demands.* **2** [C] something which bears the weight of something else: *the supports of the bridge* **3** [U] money to live: *a person with no means of support* **4** [U] encouragement and help: *Thank you for your support.*

**sup·port·er** /sə'pɔːtəʳ‖-or-/ *n* a person who loyally supports (an activity), defends (a principle), etc.: *a supporter of women's rights/of Liverpool football club*

**sup·pose¹** /sə'pəuz/ *v* **-posed, -posing** [T + *(that)* not *be* + *v-ing*] **1** to consider as probable: *I suppose he's gone home.|I suppose she won't agree/I don't suppose she'll agree.* **2** to believe: *I suppose you're right.|He was commonly supposed (to be) dead.* **3 be supposed to: a** to be expected, because of duty, law, etc., to: *Everyone is supposed to wear a seat belt in the car.|You're not supposed to smoke in here.* (=you are not allowed to) **b** *infml* to be generally considered to be: *I haven't seen it myself, but it is supposed to be a really good film.*

**suppose²** also **supposing**– *conj* **1** if; what will happen if: *Suppose it rains, what shall we do?* **2** (used in making a suggestion): *Suppose we wait a while.*

**sup·pos·ed·ly** /sə'pəuzɪ̣dli/ *adv* as believed; as it appears: *Supposedly, she's a rich woman.*

**sup·po·si·tion** /ˌsʌpə'zɪʃən/ *n* **1** [U + *(that)*] the act of supposing (SUPPOSE¹ (1)) or guessing: *His belief that things will improve is pure supposition.* (=is based only on guessing) **2** [C] a guess: *My supposition is that he stole the money.*

**sup·press** /sə'pres/ *v* [T] **1** to crush (esp. an action or state) by force: *Opposition to the government was quickly suppressed.|to suppress one's feelings of anger* **2** to prevent from appearing: *to suppress the truth/a smile* –**suppression** *n* [U]

**su·prem·a·cy** /sə'preməsi/ *n* [U] the state of being SUPREME: *Russia's naval supremacy*

**su·preme** /suː'priːm, sjuː-, sə-‖sʊ-, suː-/ *adj* **1** highest in position, esp. of power: *the supreme command|The matter will have to be decided by the* **Supreme Court**. (=the highest law court in many countries) **2** highest in degree: *supreme happiness/courage* –**supremely** *adv*

**sur·charge** /'sɜːtʃɑːdʒ‖'sɜrtʃɑrdʒ/ *n* an amount charged in addition to the usual amount

**sure¹** /ʃʊəʳ/ *adj* **1** [F + *(that)*] having no doubt: *I think so, but I'm not sure.|Are you quite sure this is the right bus?|I'm not sure whether he's telling the truth.* –opposite **unsure** **2** [F + *to-v*] certain (to happen): *It's a really good film; you're sure to enjoy it.* **3** to be trusted: *One thing is sure; he can't have gone far.|Those black clouds are a sure sign it's going to rain.* **4 make sure of something/that: a** to find out for certain: *I'll just make sure (that) the car's locked.* **b** to arrange so: *Make sure you get here before midnight.* **5 sure of oneself** believing in one's own abilities, actions, etc. –**sureness** *n* [U]

USAGE 1 **Certain** is like **sure**, but suggests a stronger idea of really knowing something to be true: *I'm* **certain** *she won't be at the party* (=it is impossible that she will be there) *because she's on holiday in Spain.|I'm* **sure** (=I strongly believe that) *she won't be at the party because she's very busy.* There is a similar difference between **certainly** and **surely.** 2 In the pattern **sure** + *that,* the subject must be a person. Compare: *I am* **certain/sure** *that they'll lose the election.|It is* **certain** (not ***sure**) *that they'll lose....*

**SPELLING NOTE**
Words with the sound /s/, may be spelt **c-**, like **city**, or **ps-**, like **psychology**.

**sure²** *adv* **1** *esp. AmE infml* certainly: *Sure I will.|She sure is tall.* **2 for sure** certainly so: *She won't lend you any money, and that's for sure.*

**sure·ly** /'ʃʊəli‖'ʃʊərli/ *adv* **1** with certainty: *slowly but surely* **2** I believe or hope: *Surely you remember him?|You know him, surely?* **3** *esp. AmE* of course

**sur·e·ty** /'ʃʊərɪ̣ti/ *n* **-ties** [C;U] money given to make sure that a person will appear in court –see also BAIL

**surf¹** /sɜːf‖sɜrf/ *n* [U] the white water (FOAM) formed by waves when they break on rocks, etc.

**surf²** *v* [I] to ride as a sport over breaking waves near the shore, on a special narrow board (a **surfboard**) –**surfer** *n*

**sur·face¹** /'sɜːfɪ̣s‖'sɜr-/ **1** [C] the outer part: *the earth's surface|the surface of the table* **2** [C] the top of a body of liquid: *A wave broke across the surface of the pool.* **3** [*the* S] what is easily seen, not the main (hidden) part: *He seems quiet* **on the surface**, *but he's very different when you get to know him.*

**surface²** *v* **-faced, -facing** **1** [I] to come to the surface of water: *fish surfacing to catch insects|*(fig.) *old arguments surfacing again* **2** [T] to cover (e.g. a road) with hard material

**surface³** *adj* (of post) travelling by land and sea: *Surface mail takes longer than* AIRMAIL.

**sur·feit** /'sɜːfɪ̣t‖'sɜr-/ *n* [*of; usu. sing.*] *old use or humor* too large an amount, esp. of food

**surge¹** /sɜːdʒ‖sɜrdʒ/ *n* [*usu. sing.*] a powerful forward movement, of or like a wave: *a surge of people/electric current|*(fig.) *a surge of anger*

**surge²** *v* **surged, surging** [I] **1** to move in or like powerful waves: *The crowd surged* **2** [*up*] (of a feeling) to arise powerfully: *Anger surged (up) within her.*

**sur·geon** /'sɜːdʒən‖'sɜr-/ *n* a doctor whose job is to practise SURGERY (1)

**sur·ge·ry** /'sɜːdʒəri‖'sɜr-/ *n* **-ries** **1** [U] the performing of medical operations: *Your condition is serious; you will need surgery.* (=you must have an operation) **2** [C] *BrE* a place where doctors (or DENTISTS) give people advice on their health, etc.

**sur·gi·cal** /'sɜːdʒɪkəl‖'sɜr-/ *adj* [A] of, by, or for SURGERY (1): *a surgical knife* –compare MEDICAL

**sur·ly** /'sɜːli‖'sɜrli/ *adj* **-lier, -liest** angry, bad-mannered, etc.: *a surly fellow/look*

**sur·mise** /sə'maɪz‖sər-/ *v* **-mised, -mising** [I;T

Bob **does his shopping** during his lunch hour. After a quick lunch, he goes to the **supermarket** in the new **shopping centre**. He walks around putting the things he needs in a **basket**. He always writes a **shopping list** of things he needs to buy, but he often forgets to look at it. When he looks for some coffee on the **shelves**, he can't find any: an **assistant** tells him they have **run out of** coffee. When he has finished his shopping, he has to **join a queue** at the **check-out**. When it's his turn to pay, he asks the **cashier** for a plastic **carrier bag.** She checks the **prices** on the items and **rings** them **up** on the **cash register/till.** Then she tells him the **total**, and he **pays cash**. She gives him the **receipt** and his **change.** As he is putting his change away he finds his shopping list, still in his pocket.

+*that*] *fml* to suppose as a reasonable guess: *From his letter I surmised that he was unhappy.* –**surmise** *n*

**sur·mount** /sə'maʊnt‖sər-/ *v* [T] *fml* to conquer (esp. difficulties) –**surmountable** *adj*

**sur·name** /'sɜːneɪm‖'sɜr-/ *n* one's family name: *Alan Smith's surname is Smith.* –see also FIRST NAME

**sur·pass** /sə'pɑːs‖sər'pæs/ *v* [T] *fml* to go beyond, in amount or degree: *to surpass all expectation*

**sur·plus** /'sɜːpləs‖'sɜr-/ *n,adj* (an amount) more than what is needed or used: *Mexico has a large surplus of oil*

**sur·prise**[1] /sə'praɪz‖sər-/ *n* **1** [U] the feeling caused by an unexpected event **2** [A;C] an unexpected event: *It was a pleasant surprise to see him again.|a surprise meeting* **3 take by surprise** to happen when unexpected: *When he offered me the job it took me by surprise/I was quite taken by surprise.*

**surprise**[2] *v* **-prised, -prising** [T] **1** to cause surprise to: *The taste surprised him; it was not as he had imagined it.|I was surprised to hear that his wife had left him.* **2** to come on or attack when unprepared: *They surprised us with a visit.*

**sur·pris·ing** /sə'praɪzɪŋ‖sər-/ *adj* causing surprise: *It's not surprising that they lost the game.* –**surprisingly** *adv* –see Study Notes on page 389

**sur·real·is·m** /sə'rɪəlɪzəm/ *n* [U] a modern dreamlike type of art and literature in which the artist connects unrelated images and objects –**surrealist** *adj,n*

**sur·real·is·tic** /səˌrɪə'lɪstɪk/ *adj* **1** of a strange dreamlike quality **2** (as if) concerning SURREALISM

**sur·ren·der**[1] /sə'rendə^r/ *v* **1** [I;T *to*] to yield as a sign of defeat: *to surrender (oneself/one's army) to the enemy* **2** [T] *fml* to give up possession of: *I surrender my claim to the money.* –compare GIVE **up**

**surrender**[2] *n* [U] the act of SURRENDERing

**sur·rep·ti·tious** /ˌsʌrəp'tɪʃəs/ *adj* done, gained, etc., secretly: *a surreptitious kiss* –**surreptitiously** *adv* –**surreptitiousness** *n* [U]

**sur·round**[1] /sə'raʊnd/ *v* [T *by*] to be or go around on every side: *The prison is surrounded by a high wall.|(fig.) surrounded by comforts*

**surround**[2] *n* an edge, esp. decorative

**sur·round·ing** /sə'raʊndɪŋ/ *adj* [A] around and nearby: *in the surrounding area*

**sur·round·ings** /sə'raʊndɪŋz/ *n* [P] everything that surrounds a place or person, esp. as it affects the quality of life: *She grew up in comfortable surroundings.* –see ENVIRONMENT (USAGE)

**sur·veil·lance** /sɜː'veɪləns‖sɜr-/ *n* [U] a close watch kept on someone, esp. someone believed to have criminal intentions: *The police have been keeping him* **under surveillance**.

**sur·vey**[1] /sə'veɪ‖sər-/ *v* **-veyed, -veying** [T] **1** to look at (a person, place, etc.) as a whole: *to survey the view* **2** to examine the condition of (a building): *Has the house been properly surveyed?* **3** to make a map of (an area of land): *to survey the east coast*

**sur·vey**[2] /'sɜːveɪ‖'sɜr-/ *n* **1** a general view or examination (of a place or condition): *a survey of public opinion* **2** an examination of a house, esp. for someone who may buy it: *Make sure you get a thorough survey.* **3** the making of a map

**SPELLING NOTE**

Words with the sound /s/, may be spelt **c-**, like **city**, or **ps-**, like **psychology**.

**sur·vey·or** /sə'veɪə^r‖sər-/ *n* a person whose job is to SURVEY[1] (2,3) buildings or land

**sur·viv·al** /sə'vaɪvəl‖sər-/ *n* **1** [U] the fact or likelihood of surviving (SURVIVE): *hopes of survival* **2** [C] something which has continued to exist from an earlier time: *That fashion is a survival from the 1970s.*

**sur·vive** /sə'vaɪv‖sər- / *v* **-vived, -viving** [I;T] to continue to live (after): *Her parents died in the accident, but she survived.|She survived the accident.*

**sur·vi·vor** /sə'vaɪvə^r‖sər-/ *n* a person who has continued to live after coming close to death

**sus·cep·ti·ble** /sə'septəbəl/ *adj* [*to*] **1** easily influenced: *susceptible to suggestion* **2** [F] likely to suffer (from): *susceptible to the cold* –**susceptibility** /-tə'bɪlɪ̵ti / *n* [U *to*]

**sus·pect**[1] /sə'spekt/ *v* [T not *be* +*v-ing*] **1** [+(*that*)] to believe to exist or be true; think likely: *We suspect that he is lost* **2** [*of*] to believe to be guilty: *They suspect him of murder.* **3** to be doubtful about the value of: *I suspect his* MOTIVES.

**sus·pect**[2] /'sʌspekt/ *n* a person who is SUSPECTED[1] (2) of guilt, esp. in a crime

**suspect**[3] *adj* of uncertain truth, quality, etc.: *That is a rather suspect answer; I don't believe it.*

**sus·pend** /sə'spend/ *v* [T] **1** [*from*] to hang from above: *to suspend a rope from a tree* **2** [*usu. pass.*] to hold still in liquid or air: *dust suspended in the sunlight* **3** to delay or stop for a period of time: *to suspend punishment* **4** to prevent from belonging to a group, etc., for a time, usu. because of misbehaviour: *She was suspended from school.*

**sus·pend·er** /sə'spendə^r/ *n* a fastener hanging down from an undergarment to hold a woman's stockings up

**sus·pend·ers** /sə'spendəz‖-ərz/ *n* [P] *AmE* for BRACES –see PAIR (USAGE)

**sus·pense** /sə'spens/ *n* [U] a state of uncertain expectation: *We waited in suspense.*

**sus·pen·sion** /sə'spenʃən/ *n* **1** [U] the act of SUSPENDing or state of being suspended **2** [C;U] the apparatus fixed to the wheels of a car, etc., to lessen the effects of rough road surfaces

**sus·pi·cion** /sə'spɪʃən/ *n* **1** [U] **a** the act of SUSPECTing[1] or state of being suspected: *She is* **under suspicion of** *murder.* **b** lack of trust: *She always treated us with suspicion.* **2** [C +(*that*)] **a** a feeling of SUSPECTing[1]: *I have a suspicion that he's right.* **b** a belief about someone's guilt: *The police have their suspicions about who killed him.* **3** [S *of*] a slight amount (of something seen, heard, tasted, etc.)

**sus·pi·cious** /sə'spɪʃəs/ *adj* **1** [*of*] SUSPECTing[1] guilt; not trusting: *She was suspicious of us/our intentions.|The man's strange behaviour made the police suspicious.* **2** making people think one is guilty: *He is a suspicious character.* (=person) –**suspiciously** *adv*

**sus·tain** /sə'steɪn/ *v* [T] **1** to keep strong; strengthen: *The meal sustained us through the day.* **2** to keep (in existence) over a long period: *She owes her success to sustained hard work.|He couldn't sus-*

tain his interest. **3** to suffer (pain, etc.): *They sustained severe injuries in the accident.*

**sus·te·nance** /'sʌstənəns/ *n* [U] *fml* **1** the ability of food to keep people strong **2** food which does this

**SW** *written abbrev. said as:* southwest(ern)

**swab**[1] /swɒb‖swɑb/ *n* (a piece of material which will hold) liquid to be tested for infection

**swab**[2] *v* **-bb-** [T *down*] to clean (esp. the floors (DECKS) of a ship)

**swag·ger**[1] /'swægər/ *v* [I] to walk with a proud swinging movement: *He swaggered down the street after winning the fight.* **–swaggerer** *n* **–swaggeringly** *adv*

**swagger**[2] *n* [S] a proud manner of walking

**swal·low**[1] /'swɒləʊ‖'swɑ-/ *v* **1** [T] to move (food or drink) down the throat from the mouth: *to swallow a mouthful of bread/soup* **2** [I] to make the same movement of the throat, esp. as a sign of nervousness: *He swallowed, and walked into the examination room.* **3** [T] *infml* to accept or believe: *What s stupid excuse–he'll never swallow that!*

**swallow** sbdy./sthg.↔**up** *v adv* [T] to take in, causing to disappear: *Higher living costs have swallowed up our pay rise.*

**swallow**[2] *n* an act of swallowing

**swallow**[3] *n* a small bird with pointed wings and a double-pointed tail

**swam** /swæm/ *v past tense of* SWIM

**swamp**[1] /swɒmp‖swɑmp, swɔmp/ *n* [C;U] (an area of) soft wet land; (a) BOG: *The land is dangerous; it's mainly swamp.* **–swampy** *adj* **-ier, -iest**

**swamp**[2] *v* [T] to fill with water, esp. causing to sink: (fig.) *We were swamped with work after the holiday.*

**swan** /swɒn‖swɑn/ *n* a large white bird with a long neck, which lives on rivers and lakes: *A young swan is called a* **cygnet.**

**swank** /swæŋk/ *v* [I] *infml* to act or speak in an unpleasantly proud way

**swank·y** /'swæŋki/ *adj* **-ier, -iest** *infml* very fashionable or expensive: *a really swanky party*

**swap**[1], **swop** /swɒp‖swɑp/ *v* **-pp-** [I;T] *infml* to exchange (goods or positions): *I swapped my car for/with his.*

**swap**[2], **swop** *n* [*usu. sing.*] *infml* an exchange: *to do a swap*

**swarm**[1] /swɔːm‖swɔrm/ *n* [C +*sing./pl. v*] a large group (of insects, esp. bees) moving in a mass: (fig.) *a swarm of tourists*

**swarm**[2] *v* [I] to move in a crowd: *As the fire spread, people came swarming out of the building.*

**swarm with** sbdy./sthg. *v prep* [T] to be full of (moving crowds of people, insects, etc.): *The place swarmed with tourists.*

**swar·thy** /'swɔːði‖-ɔr-/ *adj* **-thier, -thiest** (of a person) having a fairly dark skin

**swat**[1] /swɒt‖swɑt/ *v* **-tt-** [T] to hit (an insect) with a flat object, esp. so as to kill it

**swat**[2] *n* an act of SWATting

**swathe** /sweɪð‖swɑð, swɔð, sweɪð/ *v* **swathed, swathing** [T *in*] *lit or fml* to wrap round in cloth: (fig.) *hills swathed in mist*

**sway**[1] /sweɪ/ *v* **swayed, swaying 1** [I;T] to (cause to) swing from side to side: *The trees swayed in the wind.* **2** [T] to influence: *When choosing a job don't be swayed just by promises of high earnings.*

**sway**[2] *n* [U] **1** SWAYing movement: *The sway of the ship* **2** *old use & lit* power to rule: *Caesar's sway*

**swear** /sweər/ *v* **swore** /swɔːr‖swor/, **sworn** /swɔːn‖sworn/, **swearing 1** [I *at*] to curse; use bad language: *Stop swearing in front of the children.* **2** [T +*to-v*/(*that*)] to state or promise formally or by an OATH (1): *He swore to obey/he would obey the king.*|(*infml*) *Peter says he was there, but I swear I never saw him.* **3** [T *to*] to cause to take an OATH (1): *I've been sworn to secrecy.*

**swear by** sthg. *v prep* [T +*v-ing*] *infml* to trust in: *He swears by taking a cold bath every morning, and says he has never been ill.*

**swear** sbdy.↔**in** *v adv* [T] to cause to take an OATH (1) of loyalty: *The new President was sworn in.*

**swear·word** /'sweəwɜːd‖'sweərwɜrd/ *n* a word used in SWEARing (1)

**sweat**[1] /swet/ *n* **1** [U] also **perspiration**– liquid which comes out from the body through the skin to cool it: *I was covered in sweat after playing football.* **2** [S] an anxious state: *in a sweat* **3** [S] *infml* hard work

**sweat**[2] *v* [I] **1** to have SWEAT[1] (1) coming out through the skin: *sweating in the heat/with fear* **2** to work very hard, esp. for little money

**sweat·er** /'swetər/ *n* a heavy woollen garment for the top of the body; JUMPER

**sweat·shirt** /'swet-ʃɜːt‖-ɜrt/ *n* a loose cotton garment with long SLEEVES, for the upper part of the body –see picture on page 563

**sweat·y** /'sweti/ *adj* **-ier, -iest 1** covered in or smelly with SWEAT[1] (1): *sweaty feet* **2** unpleasantly hot; causing one to SWEAT[2]: *sweaty weather/work*

**swede** /swiːd/ *n* [C;U] a round yellow vegetable like a TURNIP

**sweep**[1] /swiːp/ *v* **swept** /swept/, **sweeping 1** [T] to clean or remove by brushing: *He swept the floor.* –compare BRUSH[2] **2** [I;T] to move quickly and powerfully (all over): *The crowd swept through the gates.*|*A storm swept (over) the country.*|(fig.) *The new dance swept the country.* (=was soon popular everywhere) **3** [I;T] to be or move in a curve across (an area): *The hills sweep round the hidden valley.* **4** [I] (of a person) to move (away) in a proud firm manner: *She swept angrily from the room.* **5 sweep someone off his/her feet: a** to cause someone to fall suddenly in love with one **b** to persuade someone completely and suddenly

**sweep** (sthg.↔)**up** *v adv* [I;T] to collect and remove (a mess) by sweeping the floor

**sweep**[2] *n* **1** an act of sweeping: *This room needs a good sweep.* **2** a swinging movement, as of the arm: *with a sweep of his sword* **3** [*usu. sing.*] a long curved line or area of country: *the long sweep of the distant hills*|(fig.) *the broad sweep of her argument* (=covering all parts of the subject) **4** → SWEEPSTAKE **5** *infml* for CHIMNEYSWEEP **6 clean sweep: a** a complete removal or change: *to make a clean sweep of all the old ideas* **b** a complete victory: *It's a clean sweep for Germany; they finished first, second, and third in the race.*

**sweep·er** /'swiːpər/ *n* a person or thing that sweeps: *a road-sweeper*

**sweep·ing** /'swiːpɪŋ/ *adj* **1** including many things: *sweeping changes* **2** too general: *a sweeping statement*

**sweep·stake** /'swi:psteɪk/ *n* a form of betting (BET[2]), usu. on a horserace, in which several people take part

**sweet[1]** /swi:t/ *adj* **1** having a taste like that of sugar: *a sweet apple|sweet wine|This tea is too sweet* (=contains too much sugar) –opposite **bitter 2** pleasant to the senses: *sweet music|the sweet smell of flowers* **3** (esp. of small or young things) charming; lovable: *Your little boy looks very sweet in his new coat.* **4** gentle or attractive in manner: *a sweet temper/smile* **–sweetly** *adv* **–sweetness** *n* [U]

**sweet[2]** *n BrE* **1** [C] a small piece of sweet substance, e.g. chocolate, eaten for pleasure –compare CANDY **2** [C;U] (a dish of) sweet food served at the end of a meal –compare PUDDING, DESSERT

**sweet corn** /'· ·/ *n* [U] *BrE* for CORN[1] (2)

**sweet·en** /'swi:tn/ *v* **1** [I;T] to make or become sweeter: *I don't like my coffee sweetened.* **2** [T] *infml* to give presents to, in order to persuade: *We sweetened him with the promise of a toy and he stopped crying.*

**sweet·en·er** /'swi:tənə^r/ *n* a substance used instead of sugar to make food and drink taste sweet

**sweet·heart** /'swi:thɑ:t‖-hɑrt/ *n becoming rare* (a word used to address) a person whom one loves

**sweet pea** /ˌ· '·‖'· ·/ *n* a climbing plant with sweet-smelling flowers

**swell[1]** /swel/ *v* **swelled, swollen** /'swəulən/ *or* **swelled, swelling 1** [I *up*] to increase in fullness and roundness: *Her ankle swelled (up) after the fall.*|(fig.) *His heart swelled with pride as he watched his daughter win the race.* –see also SWOLLEN **2** [I;T *out*] to fill, giving a round shape: *The wind swelled (out) the sails.|The sails swelled out in the wind.*

**swell[2]** *n* [S] **1** the movement of large stretches of the sea up and down, without separate waves **2** an increase of sound

**swell[3]** *adj AmE infml* very good; of good quality: *a swell teacher*

**swell·ing** /'swelɪŋ/ *n* a swollen place on the body: *a nasty swelling on my foot*

**swel·ter·ing** /'sweltərɪŋ/ *adj infml* very hot: *Open the window: it's sweltering in here!*

**swept** /swept/ *v past tense & participle of* SWEEP

**swerve[1]** /swɜ:v‖swɜrv/ *v* **swerved, swerving 1** [I] to turn suddenly to one side: *The car swerved to avoid the dog.* **2** [I;T *from*] to (cause to) change from a course or purpose: *Nothing will swerve him from his aims.*

**swerve[2]** *n* a swerving movement (SWERVE[1] (1)): *a sudden swerve to the left*

**swift[1]** /swɪft/ *adj* [+*to-v*] *more fml than* **quick**– rapid; quick in action: *a swift runner|He was swift to take offence.* **–swiftly** *adv* **–swiftness** *n* [U]

**swift[2]** *n* a small bird with long wings, similar to a SWALLOW[2]

**swig** /swɪg/ *v* **-gg-** [T] *infml* to drink, esp. in large mouthfuls **–swig** *n: a swig of beer*

**swill[1]** /swɪl/ *v* [T *out, down*] to wash by pouring large amounts of water: *to swill the yard*

**SPELLING NOTE**

Words with the sound /s/, may be spelt **c-**, like **city**, or **ps-**, like **psychology**.

**swill[2]** *n* **1** [U] pig food, mostly uneaten human food in partly liquid form **2** [S] an act of SWILLing[1]

**swim[1]** /swɪm/ *v* **swam** /swæm/, **swum** /swʌm/, **swimming 1** [I] to move through water by moving the limbs and/or tail: *We're all going swimming.|Some snakes can swim.* **2** [T] to cross or complete (a distance) by doing this: *to swim a river/100 metres* **3** [I *with, in*] to be full of or covered with liquid: *soup swimming with fat* **4** [I] to cause one to feel DIZZY (1); seem to spin round: *I was tired and my head was swimming.* **–swimmer** *n* –see picture on page 592

**swim[2]** *n* an act or occasion of swimming: *Let's go for a swim!*

**swim·ming** /'swɪmɪŋ/ *n* [U] the act or sport of those who swim

**swimming bath** /'·· ·/ also **swimming baths**– *n BrE* a public SWIMMING POOL, usu. indoors –see also BATHS; see BATH (USAGE)

**swimming cos·tume** /'·· ˌ··/ also **swimsuit**– *n* →BATHING SUIT

**swimming pool** /'·· ·/ *n* a special pool for swimming in –see picture on page 592

**swimming trunks** /'·· ·/ *n* [P] a man's garment worn for swimming –see PAIR (USAGE)

**swin·dle[1]** /'swɪndl/ *v* **-dled, -dling** [T *out of*] to cheat (someone), esp. getting money illegally: *He's swindled me out of £100!* **–swindler** *n*

**swindle[2]** *n* an act of swindling (SWINDLE): *a tax swindle*

**swine** /swaɪn/ *n* **swine 1** *old use or tech* a pig: *swine fever* **2** *infml* a nasty unpleasant person

**swing[1]** /swɪŋ/ *v* **swung** /swʌŋ/, **swinging 1** [I;T] to (cause to) move backwards and forwards or round and round, from a fixed point; (cause to) move in a curve: *The sign was swinging in the wind.|The children were swinging on a rope.|The door swung open/shut.|He swung his arm and hit me in the face.* **2** [I] to turn quickly: *He swung round and said: "Why are you following me?"|The car swung into the car park and nearly hit me.*|(fig.) *Public opinion is swinging against the government.* **3** [I] to walk rapidly and actively with light steps: *swinging gaily down the street* **4** [I] *infml* to have or play with a pleasing exciting beat: *That music/That band really swings.*

**swing[2]** *n* **1** [C;U] an act or the manner of swinging: *with a swing of his arms* **2** [C] (a ride on) a seat hanging on ropes or chains, on which one moves backwards and forwards: *The children are playing on the swings in the park.* **3** [C] a noticeable change: *a big swing in public opinion* **4 in full swing** (of a party, event, work, etc.) at the most active part

**swinge·ing** /'swɪndʒɪŋ/ *adj* (esp. of arrangements concerning money) very great in force, degree, etc.: *swingeing cuts* (=reductions) *in public spending*

**swing·ing** /'swɪŋɪŋ/ *adj* active, fashionably modern, and full of life: *a swinging party* **–swingingly** *adv* **–swinger** *n*

**swipe[1]** /swaɪp/ *n* a sweeping stroke or blow: *He* **took a swipe at** *me.*

**swipe[2]** *v* **swiped, swiping 1** [I;T *at*] to (try to) hit forcefully, esp. with a swing of the arm: *He swiped at the ball, but missed it.* **2** [T] *infml* to steal

**swirl[1]** /swɜ:l‖swɜrl/ *v* [I] to move with twisting turns:

*The water swirled about his feet.*

**swirl²** *n* **1** a SWIRLing movement: *She danced with a swirl of her skirt.* **2** a twisting mass (of water, dust, etc.): *swirls of smoke*

**swish¹** /swɪʃ/ *v* **1** [I;T] to (cause to) cut through the air making a sharp whistling noise: *to swish a whip|the cow's swishing tail* **2** [I] (esp. of clothes) to make a soft sound in movement: *swishing silk* **–swish** *n*

**swish²** *adj infml* fashionable and expensive: *a very swish restaurant*

**switch¹** /swɪtʃ/ *n* **1** an apparatus for stopping an electric current from flowing **2** a complete change, esp. unexpected: *a sudden switch in our plans* **3** a small thin stick **4** *AmE* for POINTS

**switch²** *v* [I;T] **1** to change or exchange: *They switched positions.|He got tired of teaching and switched to painting.* **2** [*to*] to move or change by a SWITCH¹ (1): *She switched the lights from green to red.*

**switch off** *v adv* **1** [I;T (=**switch** sthg.↔**off**)] to turn off (an electric light or apparatus) by means of a SWITCH¹ (1) –see OPEN (USAGE) **2** [I] *infml* to stop listening: *He switches off when you try to talk to him.*

**switch** (sthg.↔) **on** *v adv* [I;T] to turn on (an electric light or apparatus) by means of a SWITCH¹ (1) –see OPEN (USAGE)

**switch over** *v adv* [I] **1** [*to, from*] to change completely: *to switch over to the opposite political party* **2** to change from one radio or television CHANNEL to another

**switch·board** /ˈswɪtʃbɔːd‖-bord/ *n* a central board which connects different telephone lines, e.g. within a company

**swiv·el** /ˈswɪvəl/ *v* **-ll-** *BrE*‖**-l-** *AmE* [I;T *round*] to (cause to) turn round; PIVOT²: *a swivelling chair|She swivelled round as I came into the room.*

**swol·len¹** /ˈswəʊlən/ *adj* **1** having got bigger, often because of water or air inside: *a swollen foot* **2** [A] too great or proud: *a swollen opinion of oneself*

**swollen²** *v past participle of* SWELL¹

**swoon** /swuːn/ *v* [I] *esp. old use* to lose consciousness; FAINT² **–swoon** *n*

**swoop¹** /swuːp/ *v* [I] to descend sharply, esp. in attack: *The bird swooped to catch the mouse.*|(fig.) *The policemen swooped on the thieves.*

**swoop²** *n* a SWOOPing action **2 at one fell swoop** all at the same time

**swop** /swɒp‖swɑp/ *v,n* →SWAP

**sword** /sɔːd‖sord/ *n* **1** a weapon with a long sharp steel blade, used esp. in former times **2 cross swords (with)** to be opposed (to), esp. in argument

**sword·fish** /ˈsɔːdˌfɪʃ‖-or-/ *n* **swordfish** *or* **swordfishes** a large fish with a long sword-like upper jaw

**swords·man** /ˈsɔːdzmən‖-or-/ *n* **-men** /mən/ a skilled fighter with a sword

**swore** /swɔːʳ‖swor/ *v past tense of* SWEAR

**sworn¹** /swɔːn‖sworn/ *adj* [A] complete, and with no possibility of changing: *sworn enemies*

**sworn²** *v past participle of* SWEAR

**swot¹** /swɒt‖swɑt/ *n BrE infml usu. derog* a person who works (too) hard at his studies

**swot²** *BrE*‖**grind** *AmE*– *v* **-tt-** [I *up*] *infml* to study hard

**swum** /swʌm/ *v past participle of* SWIM

**swung** /swʌŋ/ *v past tense & participle of* SWING

**syc·a·more** /ˈsɪkəmɔːʳ‖-mor/ *n* [C;U] (the hard wood of) any of several types of tree, esp. (in Europe) the MAPLE

**syc·o·phant** /ˈsɪkəfənt/ *n derog* a person who tries too much to please (FLATTERS) those in positions of power, so as to gain advantage for himself **–sycophantic** /-ˈfæntɪk/ *adj*

**syl·la·ble** /ˈsɪləbəl/ *n* a (part of a) word which contains a vowel sound: *There are two syllables in "window": "win" and "dow".*

**syl·la·bus** /ˈsɪləbəs/ *n* **-buses** *or* **-bi** /bi, baɪ/ an arrangement of subjects for study, esp. a course of studies leading to an examination

**sym·bol** /ˈsɪmbəl/ *n* **1** [*of*] a sign or object which represents a person, idea, etc.: *a good luck symbol* –compare EMBLEM **2** a letter or figure, often one belonging to an official system, which expresses a sound, chemical substance, etc.: *"$H_2O$" is the symbol for water.*

**sym·bol·ic** /sɪmˈbɒlɪk‖-ˈbɑ-/ also **symbolical**– *adj* [*of*] of, as, or using a SYMBOL: *The Christian ceremony of* BAPTISM *is a symbolic act.* **–symbolically** *adv*

**sym·bol·is·m** /ˈsɪmbəlɪzəm/ *n* [U] the use of SYMBOLs, esp. in literature, painting, film, etc.

**sym·bol·ize** ‖also **-ise** *BrE* /ˈsɪmbəlaɪz/ *v* **-ized, -izing** [T] to represent by SYMBOLs; be a symbol of: *A wedding ring symbolizes the union of the two partners.* **–symbolization** /-laɪˈzeɪʃən‖-lə-/ *n* [U]

**sym·met·ri·cal** /sɪˈmetrɪkəl/ also **symmetric**– *adj* having both sides exactly alike –opposite **asymmetric –symmetrically** *adv*

**sym·me·try** /ˈsɪm¦tri/ *n* [U] (the pleasing effect resulting from) exact likeness between the opposite sides of something

**sym·pa·thet·ic** /ˌsɪmpəˈθetɪk/ *adj* [*to*] feeling or showing sympathy: *She was sympathetic to my ideas.* –opposite **unsympathetic –sympathetically** *adv*

**sym·pa·thies** /ˈsɪmpəθiz/ *n* [P] feelings of support: *Although I pity him, my sympathies are with his family.*

**sym·pa·thize** ‖also **-thise** *BrE* /ˈsɪmpəθaɪz/ *v* **-thized, -thizing** [I *with*] to feel or show sympathy or approval: *It's hard to sympathize with her political opinions.* **–sympathizer** *n*

**sym·pa·thy** /ˈsɪmpəθi/ *n* [U] **1** (the expression of) pity for the sufferings of other people: *She pressed his hand in sympathy.|I didn't get much sympathy from the doctor when I told her about my illness.* **2** agreement in or understanding of the feelings of others: *I have a lot of sympathy for his opinions.*

**sym·pho·ny** /ˈsɪmfəni/ *n* **-nies** a piece of music for a large group of instruments (ORCHESTRA), usu. having four parts (MOVEMENTS) **–symphonic** /sɪmˈfɒnɪk‖-ˈfɑ-/ *adj*

**symp·tom** /ˈsɪmptəm/ *n* [*of*] an outward sign of an inward, often bad, condition: *Yellowness of the eyes is one of the symptoms of* JAUNDICE.|*His attempt to kill himself is a symptom of his unhappiness.* **–symptomatic** /-ˈmætɪk/ *adj* [*of*]

**syn·a·gogue** /ˈsɪnəgɒg‖-gɑg/ *n* a place where Jews meet for religious worship

**syn·chro·nize** ||also **-nise** *BrE* /ˈsɪŋkrənaɪz/ *v* **-nized, -nizing 1** [T] to set (clocks and watches) to show the same time **2** [I;T] to (cause to) happen at the same speed **–synchronization** /-naɪˈzeɪʃən||-nə-/ *n* [U]

**syn·di·cate¹** /ˈsɪndɪkɨ̥t/ *n* [C +*sing./pl. v*] a group of firms or people combined together for a particular purpose, usu. business: *A syndicate of businessmen*

**syn·di·cate²** /ˈsɪndɨ̥keɪt/ *v* **-cated, -cating** [I;T] to form into a SYNDICATE **–syndication** /-ˈkeɪʃən / *n* [U]

**syn·drome** /ˈsɪndrəʊm/ *n* a set of qualities, happenings, SYMPTOMS, etc., typical of a general condition

**syn·od** /ˈsɪnəd/ *n* an important meeting of church members to make decisions on church matters

**syn·o·nym** /ˈsɪnənɪm/ *n tech* a word with the same meaning as another word: *"Sad" and "unhappy" are synonyms.* –opposite **antonym**

**sy·non·y·mous** /sɨ̥ˈnɒnɨ̥məs||-ˈnɑ-/ *adj* [*with*] having the same or nearly the same meaning (as): *Being a woman is synonymous with being a second-class citizen, in her opinion.* **–synonymously** *adv*

**sy·nop·sis** /sɨ̥ˈnɒpsɨ̥s||-ˈnɑp-/ *n* **-ses** /siːz/ a short account of something longer, e.g. the story of a film, play, or book

**syn·tax** /ˈsɪntæks/ *n* [U] the rules of grammar which are used for ordering and connecting words in a sentence **–syntactic** /-ˈtaktɪk/ *adj* **–syntactically** *adv*

**syn·the·sis** /ˈsɪnθɨ̥sɨ̥s/ *n* **-ses** /siːz/ [C;U] (something made by) the combining of separate things, ideas, etc., into a complete whole: *the synthesis of rubber* –compare ANALYSIS

**syn·the·size** ||also **-sise** *BrE* /ˈsɪnθɨ̥saɪz/ *v* **-sized, -sizing** [T] to make up or produce by combining parts; (esp.) to make something similar to a natural product by combining chemicals: *to synthesize a drug*

**syn·thet·ic** /sɪnˈθetɪk/ *adj* not naturally produced; ARTIFICIAL (1); produced by synthesizing (SYNTHESIZE): *synthetic tobacco* **–synthetically** *adv*

**syph·i·lis** /ˈsɪfəlɨ̥s/ *n* [U] a serious VENEREAL DISEASE

**sy·phon** /ˈsaɪfən/ *n,v* →SIPHON

**sy·ringe¹** /sɨ̥ˈrɪndʒ/ *n* a pipe used in science and medicine, into which liquid can be sucked and from which it can be pushed out, esp. through a needle, to put drugs into the body

**syringe²** *v* **-ringed, -ringing** [T] to treat or clean (a diseased part, wound, etc.) using a SYRINGE

**syr·up** /ˈsɪrəp||ˈsɜ-, ˈsɪ-/ *n* [U] **1** thick sweet liquid, esp. sugar and water: *Tinned fruit usually has a lot of syrup with it.* **2** medicine in the form of a thick sweet liquid

**syr·up·y** /ˈsɪrəpi||ˈsɜ-, ˈsɪ-/ *adj* **1** like or containing SYRUP **2** too sweet; SENTIMENTAL (2) –compare SUGARY

**sys·tem** /ˈsɪstɨ̥m/ *n* **1** [C] a group of related parts working together: *the postal system|This drug has an effect on your whole system.* (=the way your body works) **2** [C *of*] an ordered set of ideas, methods, or ways of working: *What are the differences between the American and British systems of government?|She has a special system for winning money on horse races.* **3** [U] orderly methods: *You need some system in your life if you want to succeed.*

**sys·te·mat·ic** /ˌsɪstɨ̥ˈmætɪk/ *adj apprec* based on a regular plan or fixed method; thorough: *a systematic search of the room* **–systematically** *adv*

**sys·te·ma·tize** ||also **-tise** *BrE* /ˈsɪstɨ̥mətaɪz/ *v* **-tized, -tizing** to arrange into a system or by a set method **–systematization** /-ˈzeɪʃən/ *n* [U]

# T, t

**T, t** /tiː/ **T's, t's** *or* **Ts, ts 1** the 20th letter of the English alphabet **2 to a T** *infml* exactly; perfectly: *The dress fits her to a T.* –see also T-SHIRT

**ta** /tɑː/ *interj BrE infml* thank you

**tab** /tæb/ *n* **1** a small piece of cloth, paper, etc., fixed to something, e.g. to help in handling, or as a sign of what it is: *Hang your coat up by the tab on the collar.|I sewed tabs with my name on in all my school clothes.* **2** *esp. AmE infml* a bill **3 keep tabs/a tab on** *infml* to watch closely: *Keep tabs on your spending.*

**tab·by** /ˈtæbi/ *n* **-bies** a cat with dark bands on its fur, esp. a female cat

**tab·er·nac·le** /ˈtæbənækəl||-ər-/ *n* a movable framework of wood, used formerly in worship by the Jews

**ta·ble¹** /ˈteɪbəl/ *n* **1** [C] a piece of furniture with a flat top supported by one or more upright legs: *a kitchen table|At the restaurant, we asked for a table for two.* –see picture on page 521 **2** [A] made to be placed and used on such a piece of furniture: *a table lamp* **3** [S] the food served at a meal: *to choose from the cold table in a restaurant* **4** [C] a printed or written collection of figures, facts, or information, arranged in orderly rows across and down the page: *a bus timetable|There is a table of contents at the front of this dictionary.* **5 at table** during a meal: *It is bad manners to blow your nose at table.* **6 turn the tables (on someone)** to seize a position of strength from someone, after having been in a position of weakness

**table²** *v* **-bled, -bling** [T] *BrE* to suggest (a matter, report, etc.) for consideration by a committee, Parliament, etc.: *to table an* AMENDMENT

**ta·ble·cloth** /ˈteɪbəlklɒθ||-klɔθ/ *n* a cloth for covering a table, esp. during a meal

**ta·ble d'hôte** /ˌtɑːbəl ˈdəʊt (*Fr* tabl dot)/ *n* [A] *French* (of a complete meal in a hotel or restaurant) served at a fixed price –compare A LA CARTE

**ta·ble·spoon** /ˈteɪbəlspuːn/ *n* **1** a large spoon used for serving food **2** also **tablespoonful**– the amount held by this

**tab·let** /ˈtæblɨ̥t/ *n* **1** a small round solid piece of medicine; a PILL: *The doctor told me to take two tablets before every meal,* **2** a large flat block, esp. one of stone or metal with words cut into it

**table ten·nis** /ˈ·· ˌ··/ also **ping-pong** *infml*– *n* [U] a game played on a table by two or four players who use BATS to hit a small ball to each other across a net

**tab·loid** /ˈtæblɔɪd/ *n* a newspaper with rather small pages, many pictures, and little serious news

**ta·boo** /təˈbuː, tæˈbuː/ *n* **-boos** [C;U] (an act, subject, etc. forbidden by) a feeling of strong religious or social disapproval: *a taboo against sex before marriage* **–taboo** *adj: Certain rude words are taboo in general conversation.*

**tab·u·late** /ˈtæbjʊleɪt‖-bjə-/ *v* **-lated, -lating** [T] to arrange (facts, figures, etc.) in the form of a table or list **–tabular** /ˈtæbjʊləʳ‖-bjə-/ *adj: The information is shown in tabular form.* **–tabulation** /-ˈleɪʃən/ *n* [U]

**ta·cit** /ˈtæsʲɪt/ *adj* [A] expressed or understood without being put into words: *a tacit agreement* **–tacitly** *adv*

**ta·ci·turn** /ˈtæsʲɪtɜːn‖-ɜrn/ *adj fml* usually silent; not liking to say a lot **–taciturnity** /-ˈtɜːnʲɪti‖-ˈtɜr-/ *n* [U] **–taciturnly** *adv*

**tack**[1] /tæk/ *n* **1** [C] a small nail with a sharp point and flat head: *He hammered a tack into the wall to hang a picture.* **2** [C;U] (a change in) the direction of a sailing ship as shown by the position of its sails: *The captain ordered a change of tack.*|(fig.) *If you can't persuade him, try a new tack and offer him money.* **3** [C] a long loose stitch used for fastening pieces of cloth together before sewing them properly

**tack**[2] *v* **1** [T] to fasten to a solid surface with a TACK[1] (1): *She tacked a notice to the board.* **2** [I] to change the course of a sailing ship **3** [T] to sew (cloth) with long loose stitches: *Tack the pieces of cloth together before sewing them properly.*

**tack** sthg.**↔on** *v adv* [T *to*] *infml* to add to the end of a speech, book, etc.: *She tacked a few words on to the letter her sister had written.*

**tack·le**[1] /ˈtækəl/ *n* **1** [C] (in football or RUGBY) an act of stopping, or trying to stop, an opponent who has the ball **2** [U] the equipment used in some sports: *Don't forget to bring your fishing tackle.* **3** [C;U] a system of ropes and wheels (PULLEYS) for working a ship's sails, raising heavy weights, etc.

**tackle**[2] *v* **-led, -ling 1** [T] to take action in order to deal with: *How can we tackle this problem?* **2** [I;T] (in football or RUGBY) to (try to) take the ball away from (an opponent) **3** [T] *infml* to seize and attack: *The robber tried to run away but a man tackled him.*

**tack·y** /ˈtæki/ *adj* **-ier, -iest** sticky: *The paint is still tacky so don't touch it.*

**tact** /tækt/ *n* [U] the ability to do or say the right thing at the right time, and to avoid offending people; skill in dealing with people: *A minister of foreign affairs has to have tact.* **–tactful** *adj* **–tactfully** *adv* **–tactless** *adj* **–tactlessly** *adv* **–tactlessness** *n* [U]

**tac·tic** /ˈtæktɪk/ *n* a means of getting a desired result: *clever tactics*

**tac·tic·al** /ˈtæktɪkəl/ *adj* of or related to a TACTIC or TACTICS: *a tactical decision* **–tactically** *adv*

**tac·tics** /ˈtæktɪks/ *n* [U +*sing./pl v*] the art of arranging military forces so as to gain success in battle: (fig.) *clever tactics for winning a game/election* –compare STRATEGY (1)

**tac·tile** /ˈtæktaɪl‖ˈtæktl/ *adj tech* of the sense of touch; felt by touch: *a tactile sensation*

**tad·pole** /ˈtædpəʊl/ *n* a small black water creature that grows into a FROG or TOAD

**tag**[1] /tæg/ *n* **1** a small piece of paper, material, etc., fixed to something to give information about it: *a name/price tag* **2** a phrase or sentence spoken (too) often

**tag**[2] *v* **-gg- 1** [T] to fasten a TAG[1] (1) to (something) **2** [T *on, onto, to*] to fix (something) onto something else: *He tagged a request for money to the end of his letter.* **3** [I *along, on*] *infml* to follow or go with someone: *a child tagging along behind its mother*|*If you're going to the park, do you mind if I tag along?*

**tag**[3] *n* [U] a children's game in which one player chases and tries to touch the others

**tail**[1] /teɪl/ *n* **1** the movable long growth at the back of a creature's body: *a dog's tail* **2** anything like this in appearance or position: *the tails of a coat*|*a* COMET*'s tail*|*the tail* (=back end) *of a plane/a procession*|*the* **tail end** (=last part) *of the film* –see picture on page 16 **3** the side of a coin which does not have the head of a ruler on it (esp. in the phrase **heads or tails**) –compare HEAD[1] (6) **4** [C] *infml* a person employed to watch and follow someone: *The police have got a tail on the criminal.* **5 turn tail** to run away **6 -tailed** having a certain kind of tail: *long-tailed*|*bushy-tailed* **–tailless** *adj*

**tail**[2] *v* [T] *infml* to follow closely behind (someone): *The police have been tailing me.*

**tail off/away** *v adv* [I] to lessen in quantity, strength, or quality: *His voice tailed off as his courage failed.*

**tai·lor**[1] /ˈteɪləʳ/ *n* a person who makes outer garments, esp. for men

**tailor**[2] *v* [I;T] to make (an outer garment) by cutting and sewing cloth, esp. to fit a particular person: (fig.) *We can tailor our insurance to meet your needs.*

**tailor-made** /ˌ·· ˈ·◂/ *adj* [*for*] (of clothes) made specially to fit the wearer: *a tailor-made suit*|(fig.) *This job is tailor-made for John.* –see also READY-MADE

**tails** /teɪlz/ *n* [P] a man's formal evening coat with the lower back part divided into two: *The men wore tails at the wedding.*

**taint**[1] /teɪnt/ *v* [T] to infect or make morally impure; spoil: *His good name has been tainted by dishonesty.*

**taint**[2] *n* [S;U *of*] *fml* (a) slight touch of decay, infection, or evil influence: *a taint of madness*

**take**[1] /teɪk/ *v* **took** /tʊk/, **taken** /ˈteɪkən/, **taking** [T] **1** to get; have; use: *We're going to take* (=buy or rent) *a flat in London.*|*Do you take the bus or the train when you go home?*|*Let's take a walk.*|*Take a seat.*|*Did you take your medicine?* **2** to obtain; receive; accept: *I won't take less than £1,000 for my car.*|*Why should I take the blame?*|*You never take my advice.*|*I don't think it will work, but I'll* **take a chance** *and try it.*|*This machine only takes five-pence coins.* (=it will work only if you put five-pence coins into it)|*This bottle takes* (=has room for) *a litre.* **3** to get possession of; gain; seize; win: *The city was taken by the enemy.*|*Jane took second place in the race.* **4** to hold with the hands: *She took his arm and led him across the road.* **5** to remove from someone's possession, by stealing or by mistake: *Who has taken my pen?* **6** to remove; subtract. *If you take 5 from 12 you* get 7. **7** to copy from an original, with changes: *This play was taken from a book by Dickens.* **8** to carry from one place to another: *We usually take the children to school in the car.*|*Take your aunt a cup of tea, please.*|(fig.) *Her ability took her to the top of her profession.* –see Study Notes on page 429 **9** to need: *That takes some believing!* (=is hard to believe)|*It takes a lot of money to buy a house like that.*|*It took me four hours to drive there.*|*The journey from Brighton to London takes 55 minutes.* **10** to record: *The policeman took my name and address.*|*I had my picture taken.* (=I was photographed)|*The nurse took my temperature.* (=with a THERMOMETER) **11** to understand; think; suppose: *I took his smile to mean yes/as meaning yes.*|*I take it you agree.* (=I ASSUME you agree)|*Do you take me for a fool?* (=Do you think I am a fool?) **12** to act towards in a stated way: *I always take your suggestions seriously.* **13** to do; perform; put into effect: *The government took these measures to deal with unemployment.*|*Are you willing to take* (=swear) *the oath?* **14** to cause to become: *She was taken ill and had to go to hospital.* **15 take for granted: a** to accept (a fact, an action, etc.) without questioning if it is true or will happen: *I just took it for granted that you knew.* **b** to treat (a person) without consideration or kindness: *He never thanks you for your help; he just takes you for granted.* **16 take it from me** also **take my word for it**– believe me when I say: *You can take it from me that he won't help you.* **17 take one's time (over): a** to use as much time as is necessary; not hurry **b** to take more time than is reasonable **18 take place** to happen **19 take the law into one's own hands** to correct a wrong by acting alone, rather than by informing the police **20 take the rough with the smooth** to accept bad things as well as good things, without complaining

**take** sbdy. **aback** *v adv* [T] to surprise and confuse: *I was rather taken aback by his rudeness.*

**take after** sbdy. *v prep* [T] to look or behave like (an older relative): *Mary takes after her mother; she's always cheerful.*

**take** sthg.↔**apart** *v adv* [T] to separate (a small machine) into pieces: *He took the watch apart to mend it.* –compare TAKE **down**

**take** sbdy./sthg.↔**back** *v adv* [T] **1** to admit that one was wrong in (what one said): *I'm sorry I was rude; I take back what I said.* –compare WITHDRAW (2) **2** to agree to receive back (something or someone): *The shop will take the toy back if it breaks.*|*If my husband leaves me, I won't take him back.*

**take** sthg.↔**down** *v adv* [T] **1** to separate (a large machine or article) into pieces: *to take down a dangerous bridge* –compare TAKE **apart,** PUT **up 2** to make a record of: *She took down my phone number.*

**take** sbdy./sthg.↔**in** *v adv* [T] **1** to provide a home for (a person): *He had nowhere to live, so we took him in.* **2** to include: *This is the total cost of the holiday, taking in everything.* **3** to make (clothes) narrower: *The dress was too big, so I took it in.* –compare LET **out** (1) **4** to understand: *I didn't take in what you were saying.* **5** to deceive: *Don't be taken in by his promises.*

**take off** *v adv* **1** [T] (**take** sthg.↔**off**) to remove (esp. clothes): *Take your coat off.* –compare PUT **on 2** [I] (esp. of a plane) to rise into the air –compare LAND[2] (2) **3** [T] (**take** sbdy.↔**off**) *infml* to copy (someone's speech or manners): *to take off members of the royal family* –compare IMPERSONATE, MIMIC[2]; see also TAKEOFF

**take on** *v adv* [T] **1** (**take** sbdy.↔**on**) to start to employ: *The firm took on a new clerk.* –compare LAY **off 2** (**take on** sthg.) to begin to have (a quality or appearance): *His face took on a new expression.* **3** (**take** sbdy.↔**on**) to start a fight with: *Why don't you take on someone your own size?* **4** (**take** sthg. ↔**on**) to accept (responsibility): *Don't take on too much work.*

**take** sbdy./sthg.↔**out** *v adv* [T] **1** to remove from inside: *to have a tooth taken out* **2** to go somewhere with (a person): *I'm taking the children out to the theatre tonight.* **3** to obtain officially: *Have you taken out insurance yet?* **4 take someone out of himself/herself** to amuse or interest someone who is feeling unhappy or unwell **5 take it out of someone** *infml* to use all someone's strength: *The long journey really took it out of mother.*

**take** sthg. **out on** sbdy. *v adv prep* [T] *infml* to express (one's feelings) by making (someone else) suffer: *It's not my fault that you've had a bad day; don't take it out on me.*

**take** (sthg.↔)**over** *v adv* [I;T] to gain control over or responsibility for: *Our chairman has left, so Peter will take over (his job).* –see also TAKEOVER

**take to** sbdy./sthg. *v prep* [T] **1** to feel an immediate liking for: *Jean took to Paul as soon as they met.* **2** [+*v-ing*] to begin as a practice, habit, etc.: *John's taken to drinking a lot.* **3** to go to for rest, escape, etc.: *Father's ill, so he has taken to his bed.*

**take** sbdy./sthg.↔**up** *v adv* [T] **1** [+*v-ing*] to begin to do; interest oneself in: *John took up writing poetry while at school.* **2** to fill; use: *The work took up the whole of Sunday.*|*books taking up space* **3** to continue: *I'll take up the story where I finished yesterday.* **4** [*with*] to complain or ask about: *I will take this matter up with a lawyer.* **5** [*on*] to accept the offer of (a person): *Can I take you up on your offer of a meal?* **6 taken up (with)** very busy (with): *He can't help; he's too taken up with his own problems.*

**take up with** sbdy. *v adv prep* [T] *infml* to become friendly with

**take**[2] *n* **1** [*usu. sing.*] *infml* the amount of money taken by a business, thief, etc. **2** a scene that is photographed for a film

**take·a·way** /ˈteɪkəweɪ/ *BrE*‖**carryout** *AmE*– *adj,n* [A;C] (from) a shop from which cooked meals are taken away to be eaten: *a takeaway meal*

**take·off** /ˈteɪk-ɒf‖-ɔf/ *n* **1** [C;U] the beginning of a flight, e.g. when a plane rises from the ground: *a smooth takeoff*|*Takeoff is at 12 o'clock.* –compare LANDING (1) **2** [C] *infml* an amusing copy of someone's behaviour: *a funny takeoff of leading politicians* –see also TAKE[1] **off** (2)

**take·over** /ˈteɪkˌəʊvəʳ/ *n* an act of gaining control, esp. of a business company, by buying most of its shares –see also TAKE[1] **over**

**tak·ings** /ˈteɪkɪŋz/ *n* [P] receipts of money, esp. by a shop: *to count the day's takings*

**tal·cum pow·der** /ˈtælkəm ˌpaʊdəʳ/ also **talc**– *n* [U] very fine powder which is put on the body to dry it, or make it smell nice

**tale** /teɪl/ *n* **1** a story: *a tale of adventure* **2** a false or unkind account: *Children shouldn't tell tales.*

**tal·ent** /ˈtælənt/ *n* [C;U *for*] (a) special natural ability or skill: *a talent for drawing|artistic talent* –see GENIUS (USAGE) –**talented** *adj: a very talented actor*

**tal·is·man** /ˈtælɪ̈zmən/ *n* **-mans** an object which is believed to have magic powers of protection

**talk**[1] /tɔːk/ *v* **1** [I] to speak; produce human words: *Human beings can talk; animals can't.|I want to talk to you about something.|She's talking to her father.* **2** [I] to express thoughts as if by speech: *People who cannot speak can talk by using signs.* **3** [T] to express in words: *Talk sense!* **4** [T] to be able to speak (a language): *to talk French* –see also SAY (USAGE)

**talk down to** sbdy. *v adv prep* [T] to speak to (someone) in a way that makes one seem more important, more clever, etc

**talk** sbdy. **into** sthg. *v prep* [T] to persuade (someone) to do (something): *She talked me into buying her car.* –compare TALK[1] **out of**

**talk** sbdy. **out of** sthg. *v adv prep* [T] **1** to persuade (someone) not to do (something): *She talked him out of killing himself.* –compare TALK[1] **into 2 talk one's way out of** to escape from (trouble) by talking

**talk** sthg.↔**over** *v adv* [T *with*] to speak about thoroughly: *I want to talk this over with you.*

**talk** sbdy. **round** *v adv* [T *to*] to persuade (someone) to change his/her mind: *She opposed the idea at first, but we talked her round.*

**talk**[2] *n* **1** [C *with*] a conversation: *I met Mrs Jones at the shops and had a long talk with her.* **2** [C *on, about*] an informal speech: *a talk on modern films* **3** [U] a particular way of speech or conversation: *baby talk* **4** [U] empty or meaningless speech: *His threats were just talk. Don't worry!* –see also TALKS

**talk·a·tive** /ˈtɔːkətɪv/ *adj* liking to talk a lot –**talkativeness** *n* [U]

**talk·er** /ˈtɔːkəʳ/ *n* a person who talks: *He's a great talker–no one else could say a word.*

**talking-to** /ˈ·· ·/ *n* **-tos** *infml* a scolding

**talks** /tɔːks/ *n* [P] a formal exchange of opinions and views: *The two presidents met for talks.|peace talks*

**tall** /tɔːl/ *adj* **1** having a greater than average height: *a tall man/building/tree* **2** [after *n*] having the stated height: *four feet tall* –see HIGH (USAGE) –**tallness** *n*

**tall or·der** /ˌ· ˈ··/ *n* a request that is unreasonably difficult to perform

**tal·low** /ˈtæləʊ/ *n* [U] hard animal fat used for making candles

**tall sto·ry** /ˌ· ˈ··/ *n* a story that is difficult to believe

**tal·ly**[1] /ˈtæli/ *n* **-lies** an account; record of points; SCORE

**tally**[2] *v* **-lied, -lying** [I;T *with*] to (cause to) agree or equal exactly: *Your figures don't tally with mine.*

**tal·on** /ˈtælən/ *n* a sharp curved nail on the feet of some hunting birds

**tam·bou·rine** /ˌtæmbəˈriːn/ *n* a circular frame with a skin stretched over it, with small metal plates round the edge, which is shaken or beaten to make a musical sound

**tame**[1] /teɪm/ *adj* **1** not fierce or wild; trained to live with people: *a tame animal* **2** *infml* dull; unexciting: *a tame football match* –**tamely** *adv* –**tameness** *n* [U]

**tame**[2] *v* **tamed, taming** [T] to train (something wild or dangerous, esp. an animal) to obey –compare DOMESTICATE –**tamable** *or* **tameable** *adj* –**tamer** *n*

**tam·per with** sthg. /ˈtæmpəʳ/ *v prep* [T] to make changes in (something) without permission: *My car wouldn't start after he tampered with it.*

**tam·pon** /ˈtæmpɒn‖-pɑn/ *n* a mass of cotton fitted into a woman's sex organ to take in (ABSORB) the monthly bleeding

**tan**[1] /tæn/ *v* **-nn- 1** [T] to change (animal skin) into leather by a special treatment **2** [I;T] to make or become brown, esp. by sunlight: *Janet tanned quickly in the sun.*

**tan**[2] *n* **1** [U] a yellowish brown colour: *These shoes are tan, not dark brown.* **2** [C] →SUNTAN

**tan·dem** /ˈtændəm/ *n* a bicycle built for two riders sitting one behind the other

**tang** /tæŋ/ *n* [*usu.sing.*] a strong taste or smell: *the tang of the sea air* –**tangy** *adj* **-ier, -iest**

**tan·gent** /ˈtændʒənt/ *n* **1** a straight line touching a curve but not cutting across it **2 go off at a tangent** *infml* to change suddenly from one course of action, thought, etc., to another –**tangential** /-ˈdʒenʃəl/ *adj* –**tangentially** *adv*

**tan·ge·rine** /ˌtændʒəˈriːn‖ˈtændʒəriːn/ *n* [C;U] (the colour of) a small sweet orange with a loose skin

**tan·gi·ble** /ˈtændʒəbəl/ *adj* **1** that can be felt by touch –opposite **intangible 2** clear and certain; real: *tangible proof* –**tangibility** /-dʒəˈbɪlɪ̈ti/ *n* [U] –**tangibly** *adv*

**tan·gle**[1] /ˈtæŋgəl/ *v* **-gled, -gling** [I;T] to make or become a mass of disordered and twisted threads: *Your hair's so tangled that I can't comb it.*|(fig.) *tangled thoughts* –opposite **untangle**

**tangle with** sbdy. *v prep* [T] *infml* to quarrel or argue with

**tangle**[2] *n* a confused mass or disordered state of hair, thread, etc.: *wool in a tangle*

**tan·go** /ˈtæŋgəʊ/ *n* **-gos** [C;U] (music for) a spirited dance of Spanish American origin –**tango** *v* [I]

**tank** /tæŋk/ *n* **1** a large container for storing liquid or gas: *the petrol tank of a car|a fish tank* **2** a large, heavy, armoured vehicle with a gun, which moves on metal belts

**tan·kard** /ˈtæŋkəd‖-ərd/ *n* a large drinking cup, usu. with a handle and lid

**tank·er** /ˈtæŋkəʳ/ *n* a ship or road vehicle built for carrying large quantities of gas or liquid

**tan·noy** /ˈtænɔɪ/ *n* **-noys** *BrE tdmk* a system of broadcasting to the public by means of LOUDSPEAKERS

**tan·ta·lize** ‖also **-lise** *BrE* /ˈtæntl-aɪz/ *v* **-lized, -lizing** [T] to raise the hopes of by keeping something strongly desired just out of reach: *a tantalizing smell of food*

**tan·ta·mount** /ˈtæntəmaʊnt/ *adj* [F *to*] equal in value, force, or effect: *Your answer is tantamount to a refusal.*

**tan·trum** /ˈtæntrəm/ *n* a sudden uncontrolled attack of anger

**tap**[1] /tæp/ *BrE*‖**faucet** *AmE*– *n* **1** an apparatus for letting out liquid or gas from a pipe, barrel, etc. –see picture on page 337 **2 on tap: a** (of beer) from a barrel

**b** ready for use when needed: *plenty of information on tap*

**tap²** *v* **-pp-** [T] **1** to open (a barrel) so as to draw off liquid **2** to use or draw from: *to tap the nation's natural mineral wealth* **3** to listen to (telephone conversations) through a secret telephone connection

**tap³** *v* **-pp-** [I;T *on*] to strike (the hand, foot, etc.) lightly against something: *The teacher tapped her fingers on the desk impatiently* **–tap** *n: a tap on the shoulder*

**tap danc·ing** /'· ,··/ *n* [U] dancing in which the dancer beats time to music with his/her feet, wearing special shoes

**tape¹** /teɪp/ *n* **1** [C;U] (a length of) narrow material, used e.g. for tying up parcels **2 a** [C;U] (a) MAGNETIC band on which sound can be recorded **b** [C] also **tape recording**– a length of this on which sound has been recorded: *some tapes of her songs*

**tape²** *v* **taped, taping 1** [I;T] also **tape-record** /'··,·/– to record (sound) on TAPE¹ (2) by using a TAPE RECORDER **2** [T *up*] to fasten or tie (a parcel, packet, etc.) with TAPE¹ (1)

**tape deck** /'· ·/ *n* the apparatus in a TAPE RECORDER that records and plays back sound

**tape mea·sure** /'· ,··/ *n* a narrow band of cloth or steel, marked with divisions of length, used for measuring

**ta·per¹** /'teɪpəʳ/ *v* [I;T *off*] to (cause to) become gradually narrower towards one end: *The stick tapered off to a point.*

**taper²** *n* a very long thin candle

**tape re·cord·er** /'· ·,··/ *n* an apparatus which can record and play back sound on TAPE¹ (2)

**tap·es·try** /'tæp¹₃stri/ *n* **-tries** [C;U] (a piece of) heavy cloth on which a picture, pattern, etc., is woven: *a beautiful tapestry on the wall*

**tape·worm** /'teɪpwɜːm‖-wɜrm/ *n* a long flat worm that lives in the bowels of people and animals

**tap·i·o·ca** /,tæpi'əʊkə/ *n* [U] small hard white grains of food made from the roots of a tropical plant (CASSAVA)

**tap·pet** /'tæp¹₃t/ *n* a part of the VALVE (1) system of an engine

**tar¹** /tɑːʳ/ *n* [U] a black substance, thick and sticky when hot and hard when cold, used for making roads, preserving wood, etc.

**tar²** *v* **-rr-** [I;T] to cover with TAR: *to tar a road*

**ta·ran·tu·la** /tə'ræntjʊlə‖-tʃələ/ *n* a large hairy poisonous SPIDER

**tar·dy** /'tɑːdi‖'tɑrdi/ *adj* **-dier, -diest** *fml or lit* slow in acting or happening **–tardily** *adv* **–tardiness** *n* [U]

**tar·get** /'tɑːg¹₃t‖'tɑr-/ *n* **1** anything fired at, esp. a round board with circles on it, used in shooting practice **2** [*of*] a person or thing that people blame or laugh at: *He is the target of many jokes.* **3** a total or object which one desires to reach: *My target is to save £5 a week.*

**tar·iff** /'tær¹₃f/ *n* **1** a list of fixed prices charged by a hotel, restaurant, etc. **2** a tax collected by a government, usu. on goods coming into a country

**tar·mac** /'tɑːmæk‖'tɑr-/ also **tarmacadam** *fml*– n [U] (an area covered with) a mixture of TAR¹ and small stones used for making roads **–tarmac** *adj*

**tar·nish** /'tɑːnɪʃ‖'tɑr-/ *v* [I;T] to make or become dull, discoloured, or less bright: *tarnished brass*|(fig.) *tarnished honour* **–tarnish** *n* [U]

**tar·ot** /'tærəʊ/ *n* (a set of) 22 cards used for telling the future

**tar·pau·lin** /tɑː'pɔːl¹₃n‖tɑr-/ *n* [C;U] (a sheet or cover of) heavy cloth covered with TAR¹ so that water will not pass through

**tar·ra·gon** /'tærəgən/ *n* [U] (the leaves of) a plant used for giving a special taste to food

**tar·ry** /'tæri/ *v* **-ried, -rying** [I] *old use & lit* to stay in a place; delay

**tart¹** /tɑːt‖tɑrt/ *n* [C;U] (an) open JAM or fruit PIE; circle of pastry cooked with fruit or JAM on it

**tart²** *adj* **1** sharp to the taste; not sweet **2** bitter; using SARCASM **–tartly** *adv* **–tartness** *n* [U]

**tar·tan** *n* **1** [U] Scottish woollen cloth woven with bands of different colours crossing each other **2** [C] a special pattern on this cloth, used as the sign of a particular Scottish CLAN

**tar·tar** *n* a fierce person with a violent temper

**tartar sauce, tartare sauce** /tɑː,tɑː 'sɔːs‖'tɑrtəʳ sɔs/ *n* [U] a thick SAUCE (1) eaten with fish

**task** /tɑːsk‖tæsk/ *n* **1** a piece of esp. hard work to be done; duty: *the task of sweeping the floors*|*She finds looking after her old father a difficult task.* **2 take someone to task** to scold someone severely

**task force** /'· ·/ *n* [C +*sing./pl. v*] a military force or a group of police, sent to a place for a special purpose

**task·mas·ter** /'tɑːsk,mɑːstəʳ‖'tæsk,mæstər/ *n* a person who gives jobs, esp. hard and unpleasant ones, to other people: *He is a hard taskmaster.*

**tas·sel** /'tæsəl/ *n* a bunch of threads tied into a round ball at one end and hung on clothes, curtains, etc. for decoration **–tasselled** *BrE*‖**tasseled** *AmE adj*

**taste¹** /teɪst/ *v* **tasted, tasting 1** [T] to test the TASTE² (1) of (food or drink) by taking a little into the mouth: *I always taste the wine before allowing the waiter to fill my glass.* **2** [T] to experience the TASTE² (1) of: *I've got a cold so I can't taste what I'm eating.* **3** [I] to have a particular TASTE² (1): *These oranges taste nice.*|*This soup tastes of chicken.*

**taste²** *n* **1** [C;U] the sensation of saltiness, sweetness, bitterness, etc., that is produced when food or drink is put in the mouth: *Sugar has a sweet taste.*|*This cake has no/very little taste.*|*I've got a cold, so I've lost my sense of taste.* **2** [C] a small quantity of food or drink: *I had a taste of the soup to see if it was nice.*|(fig.) *a taste* (=short experience) *of freedom* **3** [C;U] the ability to enjoy and judge beauty, art, music, etc.: *a taste for music*|*She has good taste in clothes.*

**taste·ful** /'teɪstfəl/ *adj* having or showing good TASTE² (3) **–tastefully** *adv* **–tastefulness** *n* [U]

**taste·less** /'teɪstləs/ *adj* **1** having no TASTE² (1) **2** having or showing poor TASTE² (3): *tasteless furniture* **–tastelessly** *adv* **–tastelessness** *n* [U]

**tast·er** /'teɪstəʳ/ *n* a person whose job is testing the quality of food and drink by tasting them

**tast·y** /'teɪsti/ *adj* **-ier, -iest** having a pleasant taste: *a tasty meal* **–tastily** *adv*

**ta-ta** /tæ'tɑː/ *interj infml* goodbye

**tat·tered** /'tætəd‖-ərd/ *adj* old and torn

**tat·ters** /'tætəz‖-ərz/ *n* [P] old, torn clothing or bits of cloth: *His shirt was* **in tatters**.

**tat·too¹** /tæ'tuː, tə'tuː/ *v* [T] to make (a picture,

message, etc.) on (the skin) by pricking it with a pin and then pouring coloured DYEs in: *A heart was tattooed on his chest.|He wants his hand tattooed.*

**tat·too²** *n* **-toos** a picture, message, etc. made by TATTOOing

**tattoo³** *n* **-toos 1** a rapid beating of drums played as a signal **2** an outdoor military show with music, usu. at night: *the Edinburgh tattoo*

**tat·ty** /'tæti/ *adj* **-tier, -tiest** *infml* untidy or in poor condition: *tatty clothes* **–tattily** *adv* **–tattiness** *n* [U]

**taught** /tɔːt/ *v past tense & participle of* TEACH

**taunt** /tɔːnt/ *v* [T] to try to make (someone) angry or unhappy by making unkind remarks: *They taunted him for being afraid of water.* **–tauntingly** *adv* **–taunt** *n* [*often pl.*]: *cruel taunts about his dead father*

**Tau·rus** /'tɔːrəs/ *n* see ZODIAC

**taut** /tɔːt/ *adj* **1** tightly drawn; stretched tight: *taut muscles* –compare SLACK **2** showing signs of anxiety: *a taut expression on her face* **–tautly** *adv* **–tautness** *n* [U]

**tau·tol·o·gy** /tɔː'tɒlədʒi‖tɔː'tɑ-/ *n* **-gies** [C;U] (an) unnecessary repeating of the same idea in different words (as in *He sat alone by himself.*) **–tautological** /-tə'lɒdʒɪkəl‖- 'lɑ- / *adj*

**tav·ern** /'tævən‖-ərn/ *n old use* a pub

**taw·dry** /'tɔːdri/ *adj* **-drier, -driest** cheaply showy; lacking good TASTE² (3) **–tawdriness** *n* [U]

**taw·ny** /'tɔːni/ *adj* **-nier, -niest** brownish yellow

**tax¹** /tæks/ *v* **1** [T] to charge a tax on: *Tobacco is taxed heavily in Britain.|Why don't we tax the rich more heavily?* **2** [I;T] to make heavy demands (on); tire: *a long taxing journey|to tax one's patience* **–taxable** *adj*

**tax²** *n* [C;U] (a sum of) money paid to the government according to income, property, goods bought, etc.: *The government have increased the taxes on petrol and beer.| Half of my wages go in income tax.*

**tax·a·tion** /tæk'seɪʃən/ *n* [U] the act of taxing; money raised from taxes: *We must increase taxation if we are to spend more on the health service.*

**tax-free** /,·'·◂/ *adj,adv* free from taxation: *tax-free income|You can live on this little island tax-free.*

**tax·i¹** /'tæksi/ also **taxicab** *fml*, **cab**– *n* a car and driver which may be hired by the public: *I came* **by taxi**.

**taxi²** *v* **-ied, -iing** *or* **-ying** [I] (of a plane) to move along the ground before taking off

**tax·i·der·my** /'tæksɨdɜːmi‖-ɜr-/ *n* [U] the art of preserving and filling the skins of dead animals, so that they look like the living creature **–taxidermist** *n*

**taxi rank** /'·· ·/ also **taxi stand, cabstand** *AmE*– *n* a place where taxis wait to be hired

**TB** *abbrev. for*: TUBERCULOSIS

**tea** /tiː/ *n* **1** [U] the dried leaves of a bush grown in Asia: *a packet of tea* **2** [C;U] a hot brown drink made by pouring boiling water onto these leaves: *a cup of tea with milk and sugar|Give me two teas* (=cups of tea) *and a coffee, please.* **3** [C;U] a small meal, usu. served in the afternoon with a cup of TEA (2): *What are we having for tea today?* **4** [U] a medicinal drink made like tea: HERB *tea* **5 one's cup of tea** *infml* the sort of thing one likes: *Tennis isn't my cup of tea.*

**tea·bag** /'tiːbæg/ *n* a small bag with tea leaves inside, put into boiling water to make tea

**tea cad·dy** /'· ,··/ *n* **-dies** a small box, tin, etc., in which tea is kept

**teach** /tiːtʃ/ *v* **taught** /tɔːt/, **teaching** [I;T +*that/v-ing/to*] to give (someone) training or lessons in (a particular subject, skill, etc.): *She teaches my son history.|Mary teaches politics to university students.|My religion teaches that war is wrong.|He taught the boys (to play) cricket.|I taught them what to do.|Teach me how to swim.|She taught (me) singing|My husband teaches at a local school.* –compare LEARN

**teach·er** /'tiːtʃə^r/ *n* a person who teaches, esp. as a profession: *a history/music teacher* –see picture on page 105

**teach·ing** /'tiːtʃɪŋ/ *n* **1** [U] the work of a teacher **2** [C;U] something that is taught: *to follow Christ's teaching/teachings|the teachings of Freud*

**tea co·sy** /'· ,··/ *n* **-sies** a thick covering put over a teapot to keep it hot

**tea·cup** /'tiːkʌp/ *n* **1** a cup in which tea is served **2 storm in a teacup** a lot of trouble over something unimportant

**teak** /tiːk/ *n* [C;U] a large tree or its very hard wood used for making furniture, ships, etc.

**tea·leaf** /'tiːliːf/ *n* **-leaves** /liːvz/ one of the small pieces of leaf used for making tea

**team** /tiːm/ *n* [C +*sing./pl. v*] **1** a group of people who work, act, or esp. play together: *The school cricket team was/were winning.|Football is a team game.* –see picture on page 592 **2** two or more animals pulling the same vehicle: *a team of oxen/horses*

**team spir·it** /'· ,··/ *n* [U] the feeling of loyalty among members of a team working effectively together

**team up** *v adv* [I *with*] to work together; combine: *I teamed up with Jane to do the job.*

**team·work** /'tiːmwɜːk‖-wɜrk/ *n* [U] the ability of a group to work well together

**tea·pot** /'tiːpɒt‖'tiːpɑt/ *n* a vessel with a handle and a SPOUT (=bent pouring pipe), from which tea is served –see picture on page 337

**tear¹** /tɪə^r/ *n* a drop of liquid that flows from the eye during pain or sadness: *to* **burst into tears** (=suddenly start crying)|*He was* **in tears**. (=crying)

**tear²** /teə^r/ *v* **tore** /tɔː^r‖tor/, **torn** /tɔːn‖torn/, **tearing 1** [T] to pull apart or into pieces by force, esp. so as to leave irregular edges: *Why did you tear the cloth instead of cutting it with scissors?|an old torn dress|He tore a hole in his trousers climbing over the wall.* **2** [T *away, off, out, up*] to remove by force: *Our roof was torn off in the storm.*|(fig.) *The film was so interesting that I couldn't tear myself away.* **3** [I] to become torn (TEAR² (1)): *This material tears easily.* **4** [I] to move excitedly with great speed: *The children tore noisily down the street.|I'm* **in a tearing hurry**. (=a great hurry) **5 tear a strip off someone** *infml* to scold someone severely

**tear** sthg.↔**down** *v adv* [T] to pull down (esp. a building); destroy

**tear into** sbdy. *v prep* [T *no passive*] to attack violently, esp. with words

**tear** sthg.↔**up** *v adv* [T] to destroy completely by tearing: *He tore up her letter angrily.*

**tear³** /teə^r/ *n* a torn (TEAR² (1)) place in cloth, paper, etc.

**tear·a·way** /'teərəweɪ/ *n infml* a noisy, violent youth

**tear·drop** /'tɪədrɒp‖'tɪərdrɑp/ *n* a single TEAR¹

**tear·ful** /ˈtɪəfəl‖ˈtɪər-/ *adj* crying; weeping, or likely to weep –**tearfully** *adv* –**tearfulness** *n* [U]

**tea·room** /ˈtiːruːm, -rʊm/ *n* a restaurant where tea and light meals are served

**tease** /tiːz/ *v* **teased, teasing** [I;T] **1** to make unkind jokes about or laugh unkindly at (a person): *At school, they teased me because I was fat.* **2** to annoy (an animal) on purpose: *Stop teasing the cat!*

**teas·er** /ˈtiːzəʳ/ *n infml* **1** a difficult question **2** also **tease**– a person who likes to TEASE (1)

**tea·spoon** /ˈtiːspuːn/ *n* **1** a small spoon used for mixing sugar into tea, coffee, etc. **2** also **teaspoonful**– the amount held by this

**teat** /tiːt/ *n* **1** a rubber object with a hole in it, fixed to a bottle for a baby to suck **2** a NIPPLE (1), usu. of an animal

**tea·time** /ˈtiːtaɪm/ *n* [U] the time in the afternoon when tea is served

**tea tow·el** /ˈ· ˌ··/ also **dish towel** *AmE*– *n* a cloth for drying cups, plates, etc., after washing them –see picture on page 337

**tech·ni·cal** /ˈteknɪkəl/ *adj* **1** of or related to a particular subject, esp. a practical or scientific one: *This law book is full of technical words–I can't understand it.* **2** having or providing special knowledge in such a subject: *technical workers|a technical college* –**technically** *adv*

**technical college** also **tech** *infml*– *n* (esp. in Britain) a college providing courses in practical subjects art, social studies, etc., for students who have left school –compare POLYTECHNIC

**tech·ni·cal·i·ty** /ˌteknǝˈkælǝti/ *n* **-ties** a small detail or rule: *a technicality in the law*

**tech·ni·cian** /tekˈnɪʃən/ *n* a skilled worker in esp. a scientific or industrial subject

**tech·nique** /tekˈniːk/ *n* [C;U] (a) way of doing some specialist activity or artistic work: *perfect piano technique|different techniques of photography*

**tech·nol·o·gy** /tekˈnɒlədʒi‖-ˈnɑ-/ *n* **-gies** [C;U] the branch of knowledge dealing with scientific and industrial methods and their practical use in industry –**technologist** *n* –**technological** /ˌteknəˈlɒdʒɪkəl‖-ˈlɑ-/ *adj: The development of the steam engine was a great technological advance.* –**technologically** *adv*

**ted·dy bear** /ˈtedi beəʳ/ also **teddy**– *n* a toy bear filled with soft material

**te·di·ous** /ˈtiːdɪəs/ *adj* long, tiring, and uninteresting; dull: *a tedious book/speaker* –**tediously** *adv* –**tediousness** *n* [U]

**te·di·um** /ˈtiːdɪəm/ *n* [U] TEDIOUSNESS

**tee** /tiː/ *n* (in GOLF) (the area surrounding) the small nail-shaped object from which the player first hits the ball

**teem**[1] /tiːm/ *v* [I *with*] *esp. lit* to be or have present in large numbers: *a river teeming with fish*

**teem**[2] *v* [I] *infml* to rain very heavily: *The rain teemed down for hours.|It's teeming (with rain).*

**teen·age** /ˈtiːneɪdʒ/ also **teenaged**– *adj* [A] of, for, or being a TEENAGER: *teenage fashions|a teenage boy*

**teen·ag·er** /ˈtiːneɪdʒəʳ/ *n* a young person of between 13 and 19 years old –see CHILD (USAGE)

**teens** /tiːnz/ *n* [P] the period of one's life from the age of 13 to 19: *She's in her teens.*

**tee shirt** /ˈtiː ʃɜːt‖-ʃɜrt/ *n* →T-SHIRT

**tee·ter** /ˈtiːtəʳ/ *v* [I *on*] to stand or move in an unsteady way: *to teeter along in high shoes*

**teeth** /tiːθ/ *n* [P] **1** *plural of* TOOTH –see picture on page 299 **2 armed to the teeth** very heavily armed

**teethe** /tiːð/ *v* **teethed, teething** [I] (of babies) to grow teeth

**tee·to·tal** /ˌtiːˈtəʊtl◂/ *adj* never drinking alcohol –**teetotaller** *BrE*‖**teetotaler** *AmE n*

**tel·e·com·mu·ni·ca·tions** /ˌtelikəmjuːnǝˈkeɪʃənz/ *n* [P] the receiving or sending of messages by telephone, television, telegraph, or radio

**tel·e·gram** /ˈtelǝgræm/ *n* [C;U] a message sent by telegraph

**tel·e·graph**[1] /ˈtelǝgrɑːf‖-græf/ *n* [U] a method of sending messages along wire by electric signals: *The news was sent by telegraph.*

**telegraph**[2] *v* [I;T +(*that*)/*to*] to send by TELEGRAPH: *They telegraphed us to come.* –**telegraphic** /-ˈgræfɪk/ *adj: telegraphic apparatus* –**telegraphically** *adv*

**telegraph pole** /ˈ··· ·/ also **telegraph post**– *n* a pole for supporting telephone and telegraph wires

**te·lep·a·thy** /tǝˈlepəθi/ *n* [U] the sending of thoughts from one person's mind to another's without the ordinary use of the senses –**telepathic** /ˌtelǝˈpæθɪk/ *adj* –**telepathically** *adv*

**tel·e·phone**[1] /ˈtelǝfəʊn/ also **phone** *infml*– *n* an apparatus which sends sounds, esp. speech, over long distances by electrical means: *He told me the news by telephone|She's* **on the telephone** (=talking to someone by means of the telephone) *at the moment.* –see picture on page 415

USAGE **Telephone** can be used as a noun or a verb, and so can the short form **phone**. If you want to **telephone** your mother (or **call** her, **ring** her, **give** her **a ring**), you **dial** her (**phone**) **number**, which can be found in the **directory**. If it is a long-distance call, you may have to ask the **operator** to connect you. The phone will **ring**, and if your mother is at home she will **answer** it by picking up the **receiver**, If she is busy she may ask you to **call back** later; if she doesn't want to speak to you, she may **hang up** (=replace the receiver); or if she is already **on the phone** when you call her, her number is **engaged** (**busy** *AmE*). A telephone in a public place is a **phone box** or **call box**.

**telephone**[2] also **phone**– *v* **-phoned, -phoning** [I;T] **1** [*to*] to speak (a message) to (someone) by telephone: *I telephoned your aunt the news.|Did you telephone Bob?|I telephoned mother to come.|You can telephone your order (through) to the shop.* **2** to (try to) reach (a place or person) by telephone: *You can't telephone London direct from here.*

**telephone ex·change** /ˈ··· ·ˌ·/ *n* a place where telephone connections are made

**te·leph·o·nist** /tǝˈlefənǝst/ *n* a person who works at a TELEPHONE EXCHANGE

**tel·e·pho·to lens** /ˌtelǝfəʊtəʊ ˈlenz/ *n* a LENS that allows a camera to take clear enlarged pictures of distant objects

**tel·e·scope**[1] /ˈtelǝskəʊp/ *n* a tubelike scientific instrument which makes distant objects appear nearer and larger –compare MICROSCOPE

**telescope**[2] *v* **-scoped, -scoping** [I;T] to make or become shorter by one part sliding over another: *The instrument telescopes so as to fit into this small box.|In the film, the story of his childhood is* *telescoped into a few short scenes.*

**tel·e·scop·ic** /ˌtel$\frac{1}{2}$'skɒpɪk‖-'skɑ-/ *adj* **1** of, like, or seen through a TELESCOPE[1]: *a telescopic* LENS*/picture of the moon* **2** made of parts that slide over one another to make the whole shorter

**tel·e·vise** /'tel$\frac{1}{2}$vaɪz/ *v* **-vised, -vising** [T] to broadcast by television: *The tennis match will be televised.*

**tel·e·vi·sion** /'tel$\frac{1}{2}$ˌvɪʒən, ˌtel$\frac{1}{2}$'vɪʒən/ also **telly, TV** *infml*– *n* **1** [C] also **television set**– a boxlike apparatus for receiving pictures and sound –see picture on page 355 **2** [U] the method of broadcasting pictures and sound by means of electrical waves; the news, plays, advertisements, etc., shown in this way: *watching television|What's* **on (the) television** *tonight?|Jean works* **in television**. (=the industry of television broadcasting)

**tel·ex**[1] /'teleks/ *n* **1** [U] (an international service providing) telegraphic method of sending printed messages –see picture on page 415 **2** [C] a message sent in this way: *A telex has just arrived from Hong Kong.*

**telex**[2] *v* [I;T +(*that*)/*to*] to send (a message) to (a person, place, etc.) by TELEX[1] (1): *Telex Paris that prices have increased.|Telex him to come.*

**tell** /tel/ *v* **told** /təʊld/, **telling 1** [T +(*that*)/*to*] to make (something) known in words to (someone); express in words; speak: *Did you tell Aunt Joan the news?|John told us he'd seen you in town.|Can you tell me what time the party starts?|Are you telling me the truth?* –see Study Notes on page 429 **2** [T+*to-v*/(*that*)] to warn; advise: *I told you David would want a drink.|I told you not to buy that old car.|I told you so!* **3** [T] to order; direct: *Do you think children should do as they're told?|I told you to get here early, so why are you late?* **4** [T] to show; make known: *This light tells you if the machine is on or off.* **5** [I;T +(*that*)/*whether, if, from*] to know for certain; recognize: *It was so dark I couldn't tell it was you.|I can't tell if it's him or not.|"Which team will win?" "Who can tell?"* **6** [I] to be noticeable; have an effect: *In the last stage of the race, her tiredness began to tell (on her).* **7** [I] to speak someone's secret to someone else: *If I whisper you my secret will you promise not to tell?* **8 tell the time** to read the time from a clock or watch –see ORDER (USAGE)

**tell** sbdy.↔**off** *v adv* [T] *infml* to scold

**tell on** sbdy./sthg. *v prep* [T] **1** also **tell upon** sbdy./sthg. *fml*– to have a bad effect on: *All those late nights are telling on your work.* **2** *infml* (*used esp. by children*) to inform against: *I missed the lesson and John told on me.*

**tell·er** /'teləʳ/ *n* **1** a person employed to receive and pay out money in a bank **2** a person who counts votes at an election

**tell·ing** /'telɪŋ/ *adj* **1** very effective: *a telling argument* **2** that shows one's feelings or opinions: *a telling remark*

**tell·tale**[1] /'telteɪl/ *n infml* a person who informs about other people's secrets, wrong actions, etc.

**telltale**[2] *adj* [A] that makes a fact known: *the telltale look of jealousy in his eyes*

**tel·ly** /'teli/ *n* [C;U] *BrE infml* for TELEVISION

**te·me·ri·ty** /t$\frac{1}{2}$'mer$\frac{1}{2}$ti/ *n* [U] *fml* foolish boldness; RASHness: *He had the temerity to ask for higher wages after only a day's work.*

**tem·per**[1] /'tempəʳ/ *n* **1** [C] a particular state or condition of the mind: *Jean's in a bad temper.* (=angry)|*She has a sweet temper.* (=is calm by nature) **2** [C;U] an angry state of mind: *John's in a temper today.* **3 fly/get into a temper** to become angry suddenly **4 keep one's temper** to stay calm **5 lose one's temper** to become angry **6 -tempered** having a certain kind of temper or nature: *bad-tempered*

**temper**[2] *v* [T] **1** *tech* to harden and strengthen (esp. metal): *Steel is tempered by heating and then cooling it.* **2** *fml* to soften; make less severe: *justice tempered with mercy*

**tem·pe·ra·ment** /'tempərəmənt/ *n* [C;U] a person's nature; one's usual way of thinking or acting: *an excitable temperament*

**tem·pe·ra·men·tal** /ˌtempərə'mentl/ *adj* **1** having frequent changes of temper: *The actor was so temperamental that people refused to work with him.* **2** caused by one's nature: *a temperamental dislike of sports* –**temperamentally** *adv*

**tem·pe·rance** /'tempərəns/ *n* [U] **1** self-control; being TEMPERATE (1) **2** total avoidance of alcoholic drinks

**tem·pe·rate** /'tempər$\frac{1}{2}$t/ *adj* **1** practising or showing self-control: *temperate behaviour* **2** (of parts of the world) free from very high or very low temperatures: *a temperate* CLIMATE (=weather conditions)

**tem·pe·ra·ture** /'tempərətʃəʳ/ *n* [C;U *in, of*] **1** the degree of heat or coldness: *a change of temperature* **2 have/run a temperature** to have a higher bodily temperature than usual **3 take someone's temperature** to measure the temperature of someone's body with a THERMOMETER

**tem·pest** /'temp$\frac{1}{2}$st/ *n lit* a violent storm –**tempestuous** /tem'pestʃuəs/ *adj: the tempestuous sea/wind*|(fig.) *a tempestuous meeting* –**tempestuously** *adv* –**tempestuousness** *n* [U]

**tem·ple**[1] /'tempəl/ *n* a building for public worship in certain religions: *a Buddhist temple*

**temple**[2] *n* one of the flat places on each side of the forehead –see picture on page 299

**tem·po** /'tempəʊ/ *n* [*usu. sing.*] the speed at which music is played: (fig.) *the fast tempo of city life*

**tem·po·ral** /'tempərəl/ *adj fml* **1** of or related to material affairs, as opposed to SPIRITUAL religious affairs: *the temporal power of the state* **2** *tech* of or limited by time: *"When" is a temporal* CONJUNCTION.

**tem·po·ra·ry** /'tempərəri, -pəri‖-pəreri/ *adj* lasting only for a limited time: *a temporary holiday job* –compare PERMANENT –**temporarily** /'tempərər$\frac{1}{2}$li‖ˌtempə'rer$\frac{1}{2}$li/ *adv: I was temporarily delayed.* –**temporariness** /'tempərərin$\frac{1}{2}$s‖-pəreri-/ *n* [U]

**tempt** /tempt/ *v* [T] **1** to (try to) persuade (someone) to do something bad: *He tried to tempt me to cheat in the examination.|to tempt him with money* **2** to attract: *a tempting offer|The warm sun tempted us to go out.* –**tempter** (**temptress** *fem.*) *n* –**temptingly** *adv*

**temp·ta·tion** /temp'teɪʃən/ *n* [+*to-v*] **1** [U] the act of TEMPTing or the state of being tempted: *the temptation to smoke a cigarette* **2** [C] something that attracts or tempts: *the temptations of a big city*

**ten** /ten/ *determiner,n,pron* (the number) 10 –**tenth** *determiner,n,pron,adv*

**ten·a·ble** /ˈtenəbəl/ *adj fml* **1** that can be defended: *not a tenable argument* –opposite **untenable 2** [F *for*] (of an office, position, etc.) that can be held by somebody: *How long is the post tenable (for)?*

**te·na·cious** /tə̇ˈneɪʃəs/ *adj* firm and unyielding: *a tenacious defence of the government's policy* **–tenaciously** *adv* **–tenaciousness** *n* [U] **–tenacity** /-ˈnæsə̇ti / *n* [U]

**ten·an·cy** /ˈtenənsi/ *n* **-cies** [C;U] (the length of time during which a person can have) the use of a room, land, building, etc., for which rent has been paid: *a tenancy agreement which will last for six months*

**ten·ant** /ˈtenənt/ *n* a person who pays rent for the use of a room, building, land, etc.

**tend**[1] /tend/ *v* [I] **1** [+*to-v*] to be likely (to do something); have a tendency: *Janet tends to talk quickly.|It tends to rain a lot here.* **2** to move or develop in a certain direction: *Prices are tending upwards.*

**tend**[2] *v* [T] *more fml than* **look after**– to take care of; look after: *She tended her husband lovingly during his illness.|a farmer tending his sheep*

**ten·den·cy** /ˈtendənsi/ *n* **-cies** [+*to-v*/*towards*] a natural likelihood: *This town has a tendency to rain.*

**ten·der**[1] /ˈtendəʳ/ *adj* **1** soft; easy to bite through: *tender meat* –opposite **tough 2** sore; easily hurt: *His wound is still tender.* **3** gentle and loving: *a tender heart* **4** [A] *lit* young; inexperienced: *a child of tender years* **–tenderly** *adv* **–tenderness** *n* [U]

**tender**[2] *n* a vehicle carrying coal, pulled behind a railway engine, esp. formerly

**tender**[3] *n* a statement of the price one would charge for doing a job

**tender**[4] *v* [T] *fml* to offer; present: *"Passengers must tender the exact amount of money."* (notice on a bus)|*The minister tendered his* RESIGNATION (3).

**tender for** sthg. *v prep* [T] to make a formal offer to do (a piece of work) at a certain price

**ten·der·heart·ed** /ˌtendəˈhɑːtə̇d◂‖-dərˈhɑr-/ *adj* easily moved to love, pity, or sorrow **–tenderheartedly** *adv*

**ten·don** /ˈtendən/ *n* a thick strong cord that connects a muscle to a bone

**ten·dril** /ˈtendrə̇l/ *n* a thin curling stem of a climbing plant

**ten·e·ment** /ˈtenə̇mənt/ *n* also **tenement house**– a large building divided into flats, esp. in the poorer areas of a city

**ten·et** /ˈtenə̇t/ *n fml* a principle or belief: *the tenets of our Church*

**ten·nis** /ˈtenə̇s/ *n* [U] a game played between two people (**singles**) or two pairs of people (**doubles**) who use RACKETS to hit a small ball backwards and forwards across a low net on a specially marked area (a **tennis court**): *Would you like a game of tennis?|a tennis ball*

**ten·or** /ˈtenəʳ/ *n* **1** [C;U] (a man with) the highest natural male singing voice –compare BASS[3] (1) **2** [C] an instrument with the same range of notes as this **3** [C *usu. sing.*] *fml* the general meaning: *I understood the tenor of his speech but not the details.*

**ten·pin bowl·ing** /ˌtenpɪnˈbəulɪŋ/ *BrE*‖**tenpins** *AmE*– *n* [U] → BOWLING

**tense**[1] /tens/ *n* [C;U] any of the forms of a verb that show the time of the action or state expressed: *"I am" is present tense, "I was" is past tense, "I will be" is future tense.*

**tense**[2] *adj* **1** stretched tight; stiff: *tense muscles/nerves* **2** nervous; anxious: *a tense period of waiting* **–tensely** *adv* **–tenseness** *n* [U]

**tense**[3] *v* **tensed, tensing** [I;T *up*] to make or become TENSE[2] –compare RELAX (2)

**ten·sion** /ˈtenʃən/ *n* **1** [U] the degree of tightness of a wire, rope, etc.: *If the tension of this string is increased it will break.* **2** [C;U] (a feeling of) nervous anxiety, worry, or pressure: *I am suffering from nervous tension.|the tensions of life in a big city* **3** [U] electric power: *Danger! High tension wires.*

**tent** /tent/ *n* a movable shelter made of cloth supported by poles and ropes: *Before it got dark the campers* PITCH*ed* (=put up) *their tent in a field.*

**ten·ta·cle** /ˈtentə̇kəl/ *n* a long snakelike boneless limb on certain creatures, used for moving, seizing, touching, etc.: *the tentacles of an octopus*

**ten·ta·tive** /ˈtentətɪv/ *adj* made or done only as a suggestion; not certain: *Our plans are only tentative.* **–tentatively** *adv* **–tentativeness** *n* [U]

**ten·ter·hooks** /ˈtentəhuks‖-ər-/ *n* **on tenterhooks** in a state of anxious expectation

**ten·u·ous** /ˈtenjuəs/ *adj* very thin; not strong: *a tenuous connection between the film and the book on which it is based* **–tenuously** *adv* **–tenuousness** *n* [U]

**ten·ure** /ˈtenjəʳ, -juəʳ/ *n* [U] *fml* **1** the right of holding land or a job: *the tenure of an office|conditions of tenure* **2** the length of time one holds office

**te·pee** /ˈtiːpiː/ *n* a round tent of the type used by North American Indians

**tep·id** /ˈtepə̇d/ *adj* (esp. of liquid) only slightly warm: (fig.) *a rather tepid welcome* **–tepidity** /teˈpɪdə̇ti/ *n* **–tepidly** *adv*

**term**[1] /tɜːm‖tɜrm/ *n* **1** [C;U *in, of, during*] one of the periods of time into which the school or university year is divided: *the summer term|During term, we have examinations.* **2** [C] a fixed period of time: *a term of office* **3** [C] a word or expression, esp. one used in a particular activity, profession, etc.: *a medical term* **4 in the long/short term** over a long/short period of time: *In the short term we will lose money, but in the long term we will make a profit.* –see also TERMS

**term**[2] *v* [T] to name; call: *The chairman of this parliament is termed the "Speaker".*

**ter·mi·nal**[1] /ˈtɜːmə̇nəl‖ˈtɜr-/ *adj* **1** of, having, or being an illness that will cause death: *terminal patients* (=people who are dying) **2** of or at the end of something **–terminally** *adv*

**terminal**[2] *n* **1** a bus station in the centre of a town, esp. for passengers going to or arriving from an airport **2** a point at which connections can be made to an electric system (CIRCUIT (3)) or messages passed to or from a computer

**ter·mi·nate** /ˈtɜːmə̇neɪt‖ˈtɜr-/ *v* **-nated, -nating** [I;T] *more fml than* **end**– to bring or come to an end: *to terminate a contract* **–termination** /-ˈneɪʃən / *n* [C;U]

**ter·mi·nol·o·gy** /ˌtɜːmə̇ˈnɒlədʒi‖ˌtɜrmə̇ˈnɑ-/ *n* **-gies** [C;U] (a system of) specialized words and expressions used in a particular science, profession, or activity: *I don't understand scientific terminology.*

–**terminological** /-nəˈlɒdʒɪkəl/ *adj* –**terminologically** *adv*

**ter·mi·nus** /ˈtɜːmɪnəs‖ˈtɜr-/ *n* **-ni** /naɪ/ *or* **-nuses** the last station or stop on a railway or bus line

**ter·mite** /ˈtɜːmaɪt‖ˈtɜr-/ *n* an antlike tropical insect that destroys wood, and builds hills of earth

**terms** /tɜːmz‖tɜrmz/ *n* [P] **1** the conditions of an agreement, contract, etc.: *The terms of the agreement are quite clear.* **2** conditions of payment, prices, etc.: *We sell furniture at very reasonable terms.* **3 come to terms with** to accept (something unpleasant): *He seems to have come to terms with losing his sight.* **4 in no uncertain terms** clearly and usu. angrily: *He told me in no uncertain terms to go away.* **5 in terms of/in . . . terms** with regard to: *In terms of property, we're quite rich.* **6 on good/bad/friendly/equal terms** having a good, bad, etc. relationship: *Now that I'm no longer working for him, we can meet on equal terms.* **7 on speaking terms** friendly enough to speak: *After their argument they weren't on speaking terms.* **8 think in terms of** to consider: *We're thinking in terms of moving house.*

**terms of ref·e·rence** /ˌ· · ˈ···/ *n* [P] the subject(s) to which a discussion or enquiry has been limited: *This problem is outside the committee's terms of reference.*

**ter·race** /ˈterɪs/ *n* **1** a row of houses joined to each other –see picture on page 297 **2** one of the wide steps on which watchers stand at a football match **3** a flat area cut from a slope: *The trees grew in terraces on the side of the mountain.* –**terrace** *v* **-raced, -racing** [T]: *The hillside was terraced.*

**ter·ra·cot·ta** /ˌterəˈkɒtə‖-ˈkɑ-/ *n* [U] (articles made from) hard reddish brown baked clay

**ter·ra fir·ma** /ˌterə ˈfɜːmə‖-ˈfɜr-/ *n* [U] *Latin, pomp* dry land: *After the rough sea voyage we were glad to reach terra firma.*

**ter·rain** /teˈreɪn, tɪ-/ *n* [C;U] a stretch of land considered esp. with regard to its physical character: *rocky terrain*

**ter·ra·pin** /ˈterəpɪn/ *n* **terrapin** *or* **terrapins** a small water TURTLE

**ter·res·tri·al** /tɪˈrestrɪəl/ *adj* **1** of or related to the earth, rather than the moon, space, etc. **2** of or living on land, rather than in water: *a terrestrial animal* –**terrestrially** *adv*

**ter·ri·ble** /ˈterəbəl/ *adj* **1** very severe indeed: *a terrible war/accident* **2** *infml* very bad indeed: *a terrible play*

**ter·ri·bly** /ˈterəbli/ *adv* **1** very badly, severely, etc.: *The army suffered terribly.* **2** *infml* very: *I've been terribly worried about you.* –see Study Notes on page 389

**ter·ri·er** /ˈterɪəʳ/ *n* a small dog originally used for hunting

**ter·rif·ic** /təˈrɪfɪk/ *adj infml* **1** very good; enjoyable; excellent: *a terrific party* **2** very great: *She drove at a terrific speed.*

**ter·rif·i·cally** /təˈrɪfɪkli/ *adv infml* very: *It's terrifically cold today.*

**ter·ri·fy** /ˈterɪfaɪ/ *v* **-fied, -fying** [T] to fill with terror or fear: *Heights terrify me!*

**ter·ri·to·ry** /ˈterɪtəri‖-tori/ *n* **-ries** [C;U] **1** (an area of) land, esp. ruled by one government: *We travelled through unknown territory.* **2** (an) area regarded by a person, animal, group, etc., as belonging to it alone: *animals fighting for their territory* –**territorial** *adj: a country's territorial possessions*

**ter·ror** /ˈterəʳ/ *n* **1** [C;U] (a cause of) great fear: *They ran from the enemy in terror.|the terrors of war* **2** [C] *infml* an annoying person: *Your son's a real terror!*

**ter·ror·is·m** /ˈterərɪzəm/ *n* [U] the illegal use of (threats of) violence to obtain political demands –**terrorist** *adj,n: Terrorists were responsible for the bomb explosion.*

**ter·ror·ize** ‖also **-ise** *BrE* /ˈterəraɪz/ *v* **-ized, -izing** [T] to fill (someone) with terror

**terror-strick·en** /ˈ·· ˌ··/ also **terror-struck**– *adj* filled with great terror

**terse** /tɜːs‖tɜrs/ *adj* (of a speaker or speech) short; using few words –**tersely** *adv* –**terseness** *n* [U]

**ter·tia·ry** /ˈtɜːʃəri‖ˈtɜrʃieri, -ʃəri/ *adj fml* third in place, degree, or rank: *tertiary education* (=at university, etc., following SECONDARY education)

**test**[1] /test/ *n* **1** a number of questions, jobs, etc., set to measure someone's ability or knowledge; short examination: *a history test|I've passed my driving test.* **2** a practical examination or trial: *Before buying the car I went for a test drive.|atom bomb tests* **3** something used as a standard when judging: *Employers will use this agreement as a test for future wage claims.* **4 put something to the test** to find out the qualities of something by using it in certain conditions –**tester** *n*

**test**[2] *v* **1** [T] to examine by means of a test: *I must have my eyes tested.* **2** [T] to be a difficult test for: *These wet roads really test a car's tyres.* **3** [I;T] to search by means of tests: *testing (the ground) for oil*

**tes·ta·ment** /ˈtestəmənt/ *n fml* →WILL[2] (4) (esp. in the phrase **last will and testament**) –see also OLD TESTAMENT, NEW TESTAMENT

**test case** /ˈ· ·/ *n* a case in a court of law which establishes a particular principle, which is then used as a standard for other cases

**tes·ti·cle** /ˈtestɪkəl/ *n* one of the two round SPERM-producing organs in the male, below the PENIS

**tes·ti·fy** /ˈtestɪfaɪ/ *v* **-fied, -fying** [I;T +(*that*)/ *against, for, to*] to make a solemn statement; bear witness: *The teacher testified to the pupil's ability.|He testified that he'd seen the robbery.*

**tes·ti·mo·ni·al** /ˌtestɪˈməʊnɪəl/ *n* **1** a formal written statement of a person's character, ability, etc. –see REFERENCE (3) **2** something given or done to show thanks

**tes·ti·mo·ny** /ˈtestɪməni‖-məʊni/ *n* **-nies** [C;U] a formal statement, as made by a witness in a court of law

**test match** /ˈ· ·/ also **test**– *n* a cricket or RUGBY match played between teams of different countries

**test pi·lot** /ˈ· ˌ··/ a pilot who flies new aircraft in order to test them

**test tube** /ˈ· ·/ *n* a small tube of thin glass, closed at one end, used in scientific tests

**tes·ty** /ˈtesti/ *adj* **-tier, -tiest** impatient; easily annoyed –**testily** *adv* –**testiness** *n* [U]

**tet·a·nus** /ˈtetənəs/ also **lockjaw** *infml*– *n* [U] a serious disease caused by infection in a cut or wound which stiffens the muscles, esp. of the jaw

**tête-à-tête** /ˌtet ɑː 'tet, ˌtet ə 'tet/ *adv* (of two people) together in private: *They had dinner tête-à-tête.* –**tête-à-tête** *n: The two women had a tête-à-tête* (=private conversation) *in the corner.*

**teth·er** /'teðəʳ/ *n* **1** a rope or chain to which an animal is tied **2 at the end of one's tether** unable to suffer any more –**tether** *v* [T]: *a dog tethered to a post*

**text** /tekst/ *n* **1** [C;U] the words in a book as opposed to notes, pictures, etc.: *Children's books often have more pictures than text.* **2** [C] the original words or printed form of a speech, article, book, etc.: *The full text of the minister's speech will be printed in tomorrows papers.* **3** [C] a sentence from the Bible to be talked about esp. by a priest in a SERMON –**textual** *adj*

**text·book** /'tekstbuk/ also **coursebook**– *n* a standard printed book for the study of a subject, esp. used in schools –see picture on page 105

**tex·tile** /'tekstaɪl/ *n* any material made by weaving: *a textile factory|silk and cotton textiles*

**tex·ture** /'tekstʃəʳ/ *n* [C;U] **1** the degree of roughness or smoothness, coarseness or fineness, of a surface, as felt by touch: *the smooth texture of silk* **2 -textured** having a certain kind of TEXTURE: *coarse-textured cloth|fine-textured skin*

**than** /ðən; *strong* ðæn/ *conj,prep* (used in comparisons, to show a difference): *She's older than me/than I am.|They arrived earlier than usual.|more than a week|less than £100* –see ME, HARDLY (USAGE), DIFFERENT (USAGE 1)

**thank** /θæŋk/ *v* [T *for*] **1** to express gratefulness to (someone); give thanks to: *The old lady thanked me for helping her.* –see also THANK YOU **2 have (oneself) to thank** to be responsible for something bad: *You've only got yourself to thank for the accident.* (=it's your own fault) **3 thank God/goodness/heaven** (an expression of pleasure at the end of anxiety: *Thank God my son's alive!*

**thank·ful** /'θæŋkfəl/ *adj* [+*to-v/that*] glad that something good has happened: *I was thankful to be/that I was free* –**thankfully** *adv* –**thankfulness** *n* [U]

**thank·less** /'θæŋkləs/ *adj* **1** not feeling or showing thanks **2** not rewarded with thanks: *a thankless job* –**thanklessly** *adv* –**thanklessness** *n* [U]

**thanks** /θæŋks/ *n* [P] **1** words expressing gratefulness: *Give thanks to God.|to return a borrowed book with thanks* **2 thanks to** because of: *Thanks to your stupidity, we lost the game.*

**thanks·giv·ing** /ˌθæŋks'gɪvɪŋ◂/ *n* [C;U] (an) expression of gratefulness, esp. to God

**Thanksgiving** also **Thanksgiving Day**– *n* a holiday in the U.S. on which God is thanked for the year's crops

**thank·you** /'θæŋkjuː/ *n* an expression of thanks: *a special thankyou for all your help*

**thank you** /'· ·/ also **thanks** *infml*– *interj* (used politely to mean) I am grateful to you: *Thank you for the present.|"Would you like a cup of tea?" "No, thank you."*

USAGE If one is offered something that one does not want, one replies *"No,* **thank you.**" A reply of "**Thank you**" means that one wants it: *"Have a drink!"* "**Thank you.** *Tea, please."*

**that¹** /ðæt/ *determiner,pron* **those** /ðəuz/ **1** the one or amount stated; the one that is further in place, time, or thought: *You look in this box here, and I'll look in that box over there.|That's my sister there.|Who told you that?/that story?|Look at that!|We had tea, and after that,* (=then) *we went home.| Don't look at me like that* (=in the way you just did) *it wasn't my fault!* **2 that's that** that settles the matter: *You can't go, and that's that.* –compare THIS¹

**that²** /ðæt/ *adv infml* so; as much as that: *I don't like him all that much.*

**that³** /ðət; *strong* ðæt/ conj **1** (introduces various kinds of CLAUSE. It is often left out.): *It's true (that) she's French.|I believe (that) you want to go home.|He was so rude (that) she refused to speak to him.|I saw him on the day (that)* (=when) *he arrived.|There's no proof (that) she was there.* **2** [U] **a** (*used as a subject*) who or which: *It was George who/(that) told me.|Did you see the letter that/which came today?* –see USAGE 1 **b** *(used as object. It is often left out)* whom or which: *Did you get the books (that/which) I sent you?|Here's the man (that/whom) I was telling you about.*

USAGE 1 **That³** (2) can be used instead of **who** or **which,** and is particularly useful when you are talking about both people and things: *the people and machines* **that** *produce the nation's wealth.* 2 **That** cannot be used instead of **who** or **which** when they add more information to the sentence: *He broke his leg,* **which** (not***that**) *was very sad.* (=and this was very sad)|*This is my father,* **who** (not ***that**) *lives in Glasgow.* But compare: *Which of my brothers did you meet –the one* **who/that** *lives in Glasgow or the one* **who/that** *lives in Leeds?*

**thatch** /θætʃ/ *n* [U] roof covering made of STRAW, REEDS, etc. –**thatched** *adj: Our house has a thatched roof.|a thatched house*

**thaw** /θɔː/ *v* **1** [I;T *out*] to (cause to) increase in temperature and so become liquid or soft: *The snow is thawing.|In the mountains, it doesn't thaw in summer.* (=the snow and ice do not melt) –compare FREEZE **2** [I] (of a person) to become friendlier, less formal, etc. –**thaw** *n: There was a thaw in the spring.* (=a warmer period when snow and ice melted)

**the¹** /ðə, ði; *strong* ðiː/ *definite article,determiner* **1** (used before singular and plural nouns, when it is clearly understood who or what is meant): *We have a cat and two dogs. The cat* (=our cat) *is black and the dogs* (=our dogs) *are white.|The sun* (=there is only one sun) *is shining.|The sky is blue.|Take these letters to the post office.* (=there is only one post office near here, and you know where it is)|*the Queen of Denmark* (=Denmark has only one queen)|*I spoke to her on the telephone.|For our holidays we went to the South of France.* **2** (used as part of some names): *the Rhine|the Atlantic|the Alps* **3** (used before an adjective to make it into a noun): *the poor* (=poor people)|*the old* (=old people)|*The English* (=English people) *drink a lot of beer.|I can't do the impossible.* (=things that are impossible) **4** (used before a singular noun to make it general): *The lion is a wild animal.* (=lions are wild animals) **5** (used before names of musical instruments): *She plays the piano.* **6** (used before names of measures) each: *This cloth is sold by the metre.|paid by the hour* **7** (used before the plural of 20, 30, 40, etc., to show a period of 10 years): *In the 30s* (=from 1930 to 1939) *there was a lot of unemployment.*

USAGE 1 With certain words, **the** is not used except when there is something else before or after the noun that tells us which one or what kind is meant. This is true of **a** nouns such as *music, history, time, beauty, work* (=ABSTRACT nouns). We say *Life is difficult* but **The** *life of a writer is difficult.* **b** nouns such as *wine, silk, coal, gold, sugar* (=[U] nouns). Compare: *She gave us beer and cheese; I drank* **the** *beer but I didn't eat* **the** *cheese.* **c** names of times, after *at, by, on*: *at sunset|by night|onMonday* (but *on* **the** *Monday after Christmas,* because *after Christmas* tells us which Monday is meant). 2 **The** is not used **a** with most names of diseases: *He's got* SMALLPOX. **b** in many expressions about organizations and means of travelling: *by car|at school|in bed|in prison* **c** in expressions like: *He became President.|They appointed her captain.* **d** when someone is directly addressed: *Come here, doctor!* **e** with **man** or **woman** in meaning 4; *Man is related to the monkey.*

**the²** *adv* **1** (used in comparisons, to show that two things happen together): *The more he eats, the fatter he gets.* **2** (used in comparisons, to show that something or someone is better, worse, etc., than before): *He's had a holiday, and looks (all) the better for it.* **3** (showing that something or someone is more than any other): *Of all her children, Mary is the cleverest/the most sensible.*

**the·at·re** *BrE*‖ **-ter** *AmE* /'θɪətəʳ/ *n* **1** [C] a place for the performance of plays: *London's theatres* **2** [U] the work of people who write or act in plays: *I'm interested in the theatre.* **3** [C] also **operating theatre**– a special room in a hospital, where operations are done **4** [C] a scene of important military events: *the Pacific theatre of World War Two*

**the·at·ri·cal** /θi'ætrɪkəl/ *adj* **1** of or for the theatre: *a theatrical company* **2** (of behaviour) showy; not natural **–theatrically** *adv*

**thee** /ði:/ *pron old use* (*object form of* THOU) you

**theft** /θeft/ *n* [C;U] (an example of) the act of stealing

**their** /ðəʳ; *strong* ðeəʳ/ *determiner* (*possessive form of* THEY) of those people, animals, or things already mentioned: *They washed their faces.*

**theirs** /ðeəz‖ðeərz/ *pron* (*possessive form of* THEY) of those people, animals, or things already mentioned: *I do my work and the others do theirs.* –see also OF (6)

**them** /ðəm; *strong* ðem/ *pron* (*object form of* THEY): *Where are my shoes? I can't find them.|What have you done with them?|He bought them drinks.*

**theme** /θi:m/ *n* **1** the subject of a talk or piece of writing **2** a tune on which a piece of music is based

**theme song** /'· ·/ also **theme tune**– *n* a song or tune played at the beginning and end of, and sometimes during, a television programme, film, etc.

**them·selves** /ðəm'selvz/ *pron* **1** (used as the object of a verb, or after a PREPOSITION, when the same people, animals, or things do the action and are the objects of the action): *The children are enjoying themselves.|They're pleased with themselves.* **2** (used to make *they*, or the name of a group of people or things, stronger): *They built the house themselves.*

**then¹** /ðen/ *adv* **1** at that time: *We lived in the country then.|Will we still be alive then?|I'll be married by then.|From then on,* (=starting then) *he worked harder.* **2** next; afterwards: *Let's have a drink and then go home.* **3** in that case; therefore: *If you want to go home, then go.* **4** besides; and also: *You must ask John to the party, and then there's Paul too.* **5 but then** however: *He lost the race, but then he never really expected to win.*

**then²** *adj* [A] at that time in the past: *the then president of the country*

**thence** /ðens/ *adv fml* from there: *We can fly to London and thence to Paris.* –see also HENCE

**the·o·lo·gian** /θɪə'ləudʒən/ *n* a person who has studied THEOLOGY

**the·ol·o·gy** /θi'ɒlədʒi‖θi'ɑ-/ *n* [U] the study of religion and of God **–theological** /θɪə'lɒdʒɪkəl‖-'lɑ-/ *adj* **–theologically** *adv*

**the·o·rem** /'θɪərəm/ *n tech* (esp. in MATHEMATICS) a statement that can be shown to be true by reasoning

**the·o·rize** ‖also **-rise** *BrE* /'θɪəraɪz/ *v* **-rized, -rizing** [I *about, on*] *fml* to form a THEORY (1) or theories

**the·o·ry** /'θɪəri/ *n* **-ries 1** [C +(*that*)] a reasoned argument, intended to explain a fact or event; idea that has not yet been proved to be true: *the theory that man is descended from monkeys* **2** [U] the general principles of a science or art as opposed to its practice: *The plans are good* **in theory**, *but they won't work in practice.* **–theoretical** /ˌθɪə'retɪkəl/ also **theoretic**– *adj: a theoretical possibility* **–theoretically** *adv: Theoretically it's my job, but in fact I don't do it.* **–theorist** *n*

**ther·a·peu·tic** /ˌθerə'pju:tɪk/ *adj* of or related to the treating or curing of a disease: *a therapeutic exercise*

**ther·a·py** /'θerəpi/ *n* [U] the treatment of illnesses of the mind or body, esp. without drugs or operations: OCCUPATIONAL *therapy*|RADIO *therapy|physiotherapy* **–therapist** *n: a speech therapist*

**there¹** /ðeəʳ/ *adv* **1** to, at, or in that place: *I live there.|Go over there.|It's cold out there.* **2** at that point: *I read to the bottom of the page and decided to stop there.* **3** (used for drawing attention to someone or something): *There goes John.* (=I can see John going past) –compare HERE **4** (used for comforting someone or for expressing satisfaction, encouragement, victory, etc.): *There, there, stop crying.|There, I told you I was right.* **5 there and then** also **then and there**– at that time and place: *There and then he asked her to marry him.* **6 There you are: a** There is what you wanted **b** I told you so: *There you are. I said he would fall.*

**there²** /ðeəʳ, ðəʳ/ *pron* (used to show that someone or something exists or happens): *There's a cat on the roof.|There are some letters for you.|There was a knock on the door.|Is there a telephone near here?*

**there·a·bouts** /ˌðeərə'bauts/ also **thereabout** *AmE*– *adv* near that place, time, number, etc.: *a boy of six or thereabouts*

**there·af·ter** /ðeə'rɑ:ftəʳ‖-'ræf-/ *adv fml* after that; afterwards: *Thereafter we heard no more about it.*

**there·by** /ðeə'baɪ, 'ðeəbaɪ‖-ər-/ *adv fml or law* by that means; by doing or saying that: *He became a citizen, thereby gaining the right to vote.*

**there·fore** /'ðeəfɔ:ʳ‖'ðeər-/ *adv* for that reason; so: *I don't know much about China, therefore I can't ad-*

*vise you about it.* –see Study Notes on page 128

**there·in** /ðeə'rɪn/ *adv fml or law* in that: *She would never marry him and therein lay the cause of his unhappiness.*

**there·of** /ðeə'rɒv‖-'rɑv/ *adv fml or law* of that; of it

**there·to** /ðeə'tuː‖ðeər'tuː/ *adv fml or law* to that; to it: *He read a letter and signed his name thereto.*

**there·up·on** /ˌðeərə'pɒn, 'ðeərəpɒn‖-pɔn, -pɑn/ *adv fml* because of that; at that moment: *He thereupon asked her to marry him.*

**therm** /θɜːm‖θɜrm/ *n* a measurement of heat used in Britain, esp. for measuring an amount of gas used

**ther·mal** /'θɜːməl‖'θɜr-/ *adj* of, producing, or caused by heat: *thermal springs* (=hot-water springs)

**ther·mo·me·ter** /θə'mɒmᵻtəʳ‖θər'mɑ-/ *n* an instrument for measuring and showing temperature

**ther·mos** /'θɜːməs‖'θɜr-/ *n tdmk* →FLASK (3)

**ther·mo·stat** /'θɜːməstæt‖'θɜr-/ *n* an apparatus that can be set to keep a particular level of temperature in a room, apparatus, etc.

**the·sau·rus** /θɪ'sɔːrəs, 'θesərəs/ *n* a book of words put in lists according to their meaning

**these** /ðiːz/ *determiner,pron plural of* THIS[1]

**the·sis** /'θiːsᵻs/ *n* **-ses** /siːz/ a long piece of writing done for a higher (POSTGRADUATE) university degree

**they** /ðeɪ/ *pron* (used as the subject of a sentence) **1** those people, animals, or things already mentioned: *John and Mary are here; they come every week.|Take these books: they might be useful.* **2** people; everyone: *They say prices will increase.|They* (=the people in power) *still haven't repaired the road.*

**they'd** /ðeɪd/ *short for:* **1** they had: *If only they'd been here.* **2** they would: *They'd never believe you.*

**they'll** /ðeɪl/ *short for:* **1** they will **2** they shall

**they're** /ðəʳ; *strong* ðeəʳ, ðeɪəʳ/ *short for:* they are

**they've** /ðeɪv/ *short for:* they have

**thick**[1] /θɪk/ *adj* **1** having a large distance between opposite surfaces; not thin: *a thick board/book|thick wire* **2** [after *n*] measuring in depth or width: *ice five centimetres thick* **3** (of liquid) not flowing easily: *thick soup* **4** [F *with*] full of; covered with: *The air was thick with smoke.* **5** (of a voice) not clear in sound: *thick-voiced |a thick* ACCENT[1] (1) **6** closely packed together; DENSE (1,2): *a thick forest|thick mist* **7** *infml* (of a person) stupid **8 as thick as thieves** *infml* very friendly **–thick** *adv: The flowers grow thickest here.|Results are now coming in* **thick and fast.** (=quickly and in great numbers) **–thickly** *adv*

**thick**[2] *n* [S] **1** the part, place, time, etc. of greatest activity: **in the thick of** *the fight/the traffic* **2 through thick and thin** through both good and bad times

**thick·en** /'θɪkən/ *v* [I;T] to make or become thick: *Thicken the soup by adding flour.|*(fig.) *The* PLOT[1] (2) *thickened.* (=the story became more confusing)

**thick·et** /'θɪkᵻt/ *n* a thick growth of bushes and small trees

**thick·ness** /'θɪknᵻs/ *n* [C;U] the state or degree of being thick: *The beam has a thickness of 4 cm.*

**thick·set** /ˌθɪk'set◂/ *adj* having a short broad body

**thick-skinned** /ˌ· '·◂/ *adj sometimes derog* insensitive; not worried by disapproval

**thief** /θiːf/ *n* **thieves** a person who steals

USAGE **Thief** is a general word for a person who steals. A **thief** who takes things from shops without paying is a **shoplifter**, and someone who **steals** from people in the street is a **pickpocket. Burglars** and **housebreakers** both steal from houses, but a burglar usually steals at night. A **robber** is more violent and steals from banks, people, etc. One **steals** things but one **burgles** places: *My wedding ring was* **stolen** *when the house was* **burgled**. One **robs** people or places (of things): *They* **robbed** *the bank and* **stole** *£50,000.|He knocked me down and* **robbed** *me of my watch.*

**thieve** /θiːv/ *v* **thieved, thieving** [I] to steal things; act as a thief

**thigh** /θaɪ/ *n* the top part of the human leg between the knee and the HIP –see picture on page 299

**thim·ble** /'θɪmbəl/ *n* a small hard cap put over the finger that pushes the needle when sewing

**thin**[1] /θɪn/ *adj* **-nn- 1** having a small distance between opposite surfaces; not thick: *a thin board|thin ice|a thin shirt* **2** having little fat on the body; not fat: *She looked thin after her illness.* –see USAGE **3** (of a liquid) watery; flowing easily: *thin soup* **4** widely separated; not DENSE (1,2): *Your hair's getting very thin.|thin mist* **5** lacking in strength; weak: *thin high musical notes|a thin excuse* **6 thin on the ground** *infml* scarce **–thin** *adv: Don't cut the bread so thin.* **–thinly** *adv: Spread the butter thinly.* **–thinness** *n* [U]

USAGE 1 **Thin** is a general word to describe people who have little or no fat on their bodies. If someone is thin in a pleasant way, we say they are **slim** or (less common) **slender**, but if they are too thin they are **skinny** (*infml*), **underweight,** or (worst of all) **emaciated**: *I wish I was as* **slim** *as you!|She looks very* **thin/skinny/underweight** *after her illness./The prisoners were* **emaciated**. The opposite of **thin** in this sense is **fat**, but this is not very polite. **Plump**, overweight, **chubby** (esp. of babies), and **matronly** (only of older women) are all more polite ways of saying the same thing. A person who is very fat is **obese**. 2 Things that are long and **thin**, in the sense of having a short distance from one side to another, are **narrow** (opposite **wide**): *a* **narrow** *road|a* **narrow** *room.* 3 **Fine** is used to describe things that are **thin,** when one is giving the idea of careful sensitive work: *She drew with a* **fine** *pen.|***fine** *silk thread* –opposite **thick**

**thin**[2] *v* **-nn-** [I;T *out*] to make or become thin or less DENSE (1,2): *to thin out* (=separate) *the plants*

**thine**[1] /ðaɪn/ *pron old use, bibl, or lit* (*possessive form of* THOU) that/those belonging to THEE; yours

**thine**[2] *determiner old use, bibl, or lit* (*before a vowel or* h) THY

**thing** /θɪŋ/ *n* **1** [C] any material object; an object that is not named: *What do you use this thing for?|My daughter enjoys making things out of clay.|I haven't got a thing* (=any suitable garment) *to wear.|It's so dark I can't see a thing.* (=anything) **2** [C] a remark, subject, or idea: *What a nasty thing to say!|There's one more thing I want to say.|He says the first thing that comes into his head.* **3** [C] an act; deed: *What's the next thing we have to do?|I expect great things from you, son!|The first thing is for you to talk to your teacher.* (=that is what you should do first) **4** [C] a creature; person, animal, etc.: *There wasn't a living thing in the woods.* **5** [S] *infml* something necessary or desirable: *Cold beer is just the thing on a hot day.* **6** [S] *infml* an activity very satisfying to one personally:

*Everyone should be free to* **do their own thing**. **7 for one thing** (used for introducing a reason): *For one thing it costs too much, and for another it's the wrong colour.* **8 have a thing about** *infml* to have a strong like or dislike for **9 it's a good thing** it's lucky: *It's a good thing George can't hear us!*

**thing·a·ma·jig, thingumajig** /ˈθɪŋəmədʒɪg/ also **thingamabob, thingummy**– *n infml* a person or thing whose name one has forgotten: *a new thingamajig for opening bottles*

**things** /θɪŋz/ *n* [P] **1** one's personal possessions; belongings: *Pack your things. We're going.* **2** the general state of affairs: *Things are getting worse.*

**think** /θɪŋk/ *v* **thought** /θɔ:t/, **thinking 1** [I;T *about*] to use the power of reason; use the mind to form opinions; have (a thought): *Do you still think in English when you're speaking French?|Can animals think?|Think hard before you answer the question.|Think* (=consider the matter carefully) *before you accept his offer!|thinking great thoughts|What are you thinking about?| thinking people* (=those who use their reason) **2** [T +(*that*)] to believe; consider: *I think he's wrong, don't you?|Who do you think murdered the old lady?|He thinks himself a great poet.|"Do you think it will rain?" "Yes, I think so./No, I don't think so."* **3** [T] (*used after* cannot *and* could not *and in the infinitive after* try, want, *etc.*) to remember: *I can't think what his name is.|I'm trying to think how to get there.* **4** [I;T +(*that*)] to expect: *We didn't think we'd be this late.|I thought as much.* (used when one has heard some news, to mean "that's just what I expected") **5** [I] to direct the mind in a particular way: *to think big* **6 think aloud** to speak one's thoughts as they come **7 think twice** to think very carefully about something –**thinker** *n: Bertrand Russell, one of the great thinkers of our age* –**think** *n* [S *about*] *infml: I'll have a think about this.*

**think of** sbdy./sthg. *v prep* [T +*v-ing*] **1** also **think about** sbdy./sthg.– to consider; have in one's mind: *We're thinking of going to France for our holidays.* **2** also **think about** sbdy./sthg.– to have as an opinion about: *What do you think of this plan?* **3** (*used after* cannot *and* could not *and in the infinitive after* try, want, *etc.*) to remember: *I can't think of his name.* **4** to suggest: *I thought of the idea first.* **5 not think much of** to have a low opinion of **6 think better of** to decide against: *I was going to go, but I thought better of it.* **7 think highly/well/little/poorly** etc. **of someone** or **something** to have a good/bad etc. opinion of someone or something **8 think nothing of** to regard as usual or easy: *She thinks nothing of walking ten miles.* **9 think nothing of it** do not thank me for it

**think** sthg.↔**out** also **think** sthg.↔**through** *AmE– v adv* [T] to consider carefully and in detail (a plan, problem, etc.)

**think** sthg.↔**over** *v adv* [T] to consider carefully: *It's a good offer, but I must think it over.*

**think** sthg.↔**up** *v adv* [T] to invent (esp. an idea): *to think up a plan/an excuse*

**think·ing** /ˈθɪŋkɪŋ/ *n* [U] **1** the act of using one's mind to produce thoughts **2** opinion; judgment; thought: *What's your thinking on this matter?*

**thin·ner** /ˈθɪnəʳ/ *n* [U] a liquid added to paint to make it spread more easily

**thin-skinned** /ˌ· ˈ·◂/ *adj sometimes derog* sensitive; easily offended

**third** /θɜ:d‖θɜrd/ *determiner,adv,n,pron* 3rd

**third par·ty** /ˌ· ˈ··◂/ *n tech* **1** a person in a law case who is not one of the two main people concerned **2** a person not named in an insurance agreement but protected by the insurance in the event of an accident

**third-rate** /ˌ· ˈ·◂/ *adj* of very poor quality

**Third World** /ˌ· ˈ·◂/ *n* the industrially less developed countries of the world, esp. in Asia and Africa

**thirst** /θɜ:st‖θɜrst/ *n* **1** [C;S;U] the need to drink; desire for drink: *Running five miles gave him a thirst.* **2** [S *for*] a strong desire: *the thirst for power*

**thirst for/after** sthg. *v prep* [T] *lit* to have a strong desire for: *Our people thirst for independence.*

**thirst·y** /ˈθɜ:sti‖ˈθɜr-/ *adj* **-ier, -iest 1** feeling or causing thirst: *I feel thirsty.* **2** [F *for*] having a strong desire for: *She was thirsty for power.* –**thirstily** *adv*

**thir·teen** /ˌθɜ:ˈti:n◂‖ˌθɜr-/ *determiner,n,pron* (the number) 13 –**thirteenth** *determiner,n,pron,adv*

**thir·ty** /ˈθɜ:ti‖ˈθɜrti/ *determiner,n,pron* **-ties** (the number) 30 –**thirtieth** *determiner,n,pron,adv*

**this**[1] /ðɪs/ *determiner,pron* **these** /ði:z/ **1** the one or amount (going to be) stated; the one that is near in place, time, or thought: *Who told you this story/this?|You look in this box here, and I'll look in that box over there.|I saw Mrs Jones this morning.* (=earlier today)|*Do it like this.* (=in the way I'm showing you) **2** *infml* (used in stories) a certain: *This man came up to me in the street . . .*

**this**[2] *adv infml* so; as much as this: *I've never been out this late before.|Cut off about this much thread . . .*

**this·tle** /ˈθɪsəl/ *n* a wild plant with prickly leaves and usu. purple flowers

**thith·er** /ˈðɪðəʳ‖ˈθɪðər/ *adv old use* to that place; in that direction –see also HITHER

**thong** /θɒŋ‖θɔŋ/ *n* a narrow length of leather used as a fastening, whip, etc.

**tho·rax** /ˈθɔ:ræks‖ˈθo-/ *n* **-races** /rəsi:z/ *or* **-raxes** *tech* a main part of the body in animals between the neck and ABDOMEN; chest

**thorn** /θɔ:n‖θɔrn/ *n* **1** [C] a sharp pointed prickle growing on a plant: *the thorns on a rose bush* **2** [C;U] (*usu. in comb.*) a bush, plant, or tree having such prickles: *a* HAWTHORN **3 thorn in one's flesh/side** a continual cause of annoyance –**thorny** *adj* **-ier, -iest**: (fig.) *a thorny* (=difficult) *question* –**thorniness** *n* [U]

**thor·ough** /ˈθʌrə‖ˈθʌrəʊ, ˈθʌrə/ *adj* [A] complete and careful: *a thorough search|a thorough worker* –**thoroughly** *adv: After a hard day's work I feel thoroughly tired.* –**thoroughness** *n* [U]

**thor·ough·bred** /ˈθʌrəbred‖ˈθʌrəʊ-, ˈθʌrə-/ *adj,n* (an animal, esp. a horse) of pure breed

**thor·ough·fare** /ˈθʌrəfeəʳ‖ˈθʌrəʌ-, ˈθʌrə-/ *n* a road for public traffic: *a busy thoroughfare*

**those** /ðəʊz/ *determiner,pron plural of* THAT: *Will those* (=the people) *who want to join the club please sign here?*

**thou** /ðaʊ/ *pron old use or bibl* (*used as the subject of a sentence with special old forms of verbs*) the person to whom one is speaking; you: *"Thou shall not kill."*

**though**[1] /ðəʊ/ *conj* **1** in spite of the fact that; even if:

*Though/Even though it's hard work, I enjoy it.* –see Study Notes on page 128 **2 as though** as if: *He behaves as though he were rich.* –see also ALTHOUGH

**though²** *adv* in spite of everything; however: *It's hard work. I enjoy it, though.*

**thought¹** /θɔːt/ *n* **1** [U] the act or way of thinking; consideration: *She sat, deep in thought.|ancient Greek thought* (=way of thinking)|*Give the matter plenty of thought.|Without thought for her own safety, she jumped into the river to save him.* **2** [C;U] something that is thought; (an) idea, opinion, etc.: *What are your thoughts on the subject?* **3** [U *of*] intention: *I had no thought of annoying you.* **4 second thought** a thought that a past decision may not be correct: *I said I wouldn't go; but* **on second thoughts** *I think I will.*

**thought²** *v past tense & participle of* THINK

**thought·ful** /ˈθɔːtfəl/ *adj* **1** thinking deeply: *The girl looked thoughtful and sad.* **2** paying attention to the feelings of other people: *It was very thoughtful of you to visit me.* –**thoughtfully** *adv* –**thoughtfulness** *n* [U]

**thought·less** /ˈθɔːtləs/ *adj* careless; selfish: *How thoughtless of you to forget my birthday.* –**thoughtlessly** *adv* –**thoughtlessness** *n* [U]

**thought-out** /ˌ· ˈ·◂/ *adj* produced after the stated consideration: *a well thought-out plan*

**thou·sand** /ˈθaʊzənd/ *determiner,n,pron* **-sand** *or* **-sands** (the number) 1,000 –see Study Notes on page 494 –**thousandth** *determiner,n,pron,adv*

**thrash** /θræʃ/ *v* **1** [T] to beat with a whip or stick **2** [T] to defeat thoroughly **3** [I *about*] to move wildly about: *The fish thrashed about in the net.*

**thrash** sthg.↔**out** *v adv* [T] to reach agreement about (a problem) or produce (a decision) by much talk and consideration: *After a long argument we thrashed out a plan.*

**thrash·ing** /ˈθræʃɪŋ/ *n* a severe beating or defeat

**thread¹** /θred/ *n* **1** [C;U] (a length of) very fine cord, used in sewing or weaving: *cotton/nylon thread*|(fig.) *His life* **hangs by a thread**. (=is in very great danger) **2** [C] a line of reasoning in an argument or story: *to lose the thread of one's argument* **3** [C] a raised line around the outside of a screw

**thread²** *v* [T] to pass a thread through: *to thread a needle with cotton|to thread buttons on a string*|(fig.) *I threaded my way through the crowd.*

**thread·bare** /ˈθredbeəʳ/ *adj* (of cloth, clothes, etc.) worn thin; very worn and old

**threat** /θret/ *n* **1** [C;U] a warning that one is going to hurt, punish, etc.: *a threat to kill me* **2** [C *to, of; usu. sing.*] a (sign of) possible danger: *The clouds brought a threat of rain.*

**threat·en** /ˈθretn/ *v* **1** [I;T +*to-v/with*] to express or be a threat to: *I was threatened with dismissal if I didn't obey.|a threatening letter|She threatened to murder me.|Noisy traffic threatens our peaceful way of life.* **2** [T] to give warning of (something bad): *The black clouds threatened rain.* –**threateningly** *adv*

**three** /θriː/ *determiner,n,pron* (the number) 3

**three-di·men·sion·al** /ˌ· ·ˈ··· ◂/ *adj* having length, depth, and height

**three-quar·ter** /ˌ· ˈ··◂/ *adj* consisting of three FOURTHS (¾) of the whole: *a three-quarter length coat*

**thresh** /θreʃ/ *v* [I;T] to separate the grain from (corn, wheat, etc.) usu. with a machine –**thresher** *n*

**thresh·old** /ˈθreʃhəʊld, -ʃəʊld/ *n* **1** a piece of wood or stone fixed beneath the door into a house **2** [*usu. sing.*] the place or point of beginning: *Scientists are now* **on the threshold of** *a new discovery.*

**threw** /θruː/ *v past tense of* THROW

**thrice** /θraɪs/ *predeterminer,adv old use* three times

**thrift** /θrɪft/ *n* [U] wise careful use of money and goods –**thrifty** *adj* **-ier, -iest**: *a thrifty housewife/meal* –**thriftily** *adv*

**thrill¹** /θrɪl/ *v* [I;T *at, to*] to (cause to) feel a THRILL² or thrills: *a thrilling story* –**thrillingly** *adv*

**thrill²** *n* (something producing) a sudden very strong feeling of excitement, pleasure, or fear: *Meeting the famous footballer was a great thrill for the children.*

**thrill·er** /ˈθrɪləʳ/ *n* a book, play, or film that tells a very exciting story, esp. of crime and violence

**thrive** /θraɪv/ *v* **throve** /θrəʊv/ *or* **thrived, thrived** *or* **thriven** /ˈθrivən/, **thriving** [I *on*] to develop well and be healthy; be successful: *a thriving business*

**throat** /θrəʊt/ *n* **1** the passage from the back of the mouth down inside the neck: *a sore throat* **2** the front of the neck –see picture on page 299

**throat·y** /ˈθrəʊti/ *adj* **-ier, -iest** having a low rough sound: *a throaty laugh*

**throb** /θrɒb‖θrɑb/ *v* **-bb-** [I] to beat strongly and rapidly: *My heart was throbbing with excitement.* –**throb** *n: the throb of machinery*

**throes** /θrəʊz/ *n* [P] **1** *esp. lit* severe pains (esp. in the phrase **death throes**) **2 in the throes of** struggling with: *a country in the throes of war*

**throm·bo·sis** /θrɒmˈbəʊsəs‖θrɑm-/ *n* **-ses** /siːz/ [C;U] the condition of having a blood CLOT in a blood vessel

**throne** /θrəʊn/ *n* **1** [C] the ceremonial chair of a king, queen, etc. **2** [S] the rank or office of a king or queen

**throng¹** /θrɒŋ‖θrɔŋ/ *n* [C +*sing./pl. v*] a large crowd of people: *A throng of people is/are here.*

**throng²** *v* [I;T] to go (as if) in a crowd: *People thronged to see the play.*

**throt·tle¹** /ˈθrɒtl‖ˈθrɑtl/ *v* **-tled, -tling** [T] to seize (someone) tightly by the throat and so stop his/her breathing; STRANGLE

**throttle²** *n* a part of a pipe (VALVE) that opens and closes to control the flow of liquid into an engine

**through¹** /θruː/ *prep* **1** into at one side, and out at the other: *Water flows through this pipe.|We couldn't see through the mist.|She drove straight through the town.* **2** by way of; by means of: *She climbed in through the window.|I got this book through the library* –see Study Notes on page 474. **3** because of: *The war was lost through bad organization.* **4** past: *I drove through a red light.* (=a set of TRAFFIC LIGHTS showing "Stop")|*Did you get through* (=Did you pass) *your examination?* **5** to or at the end of: *I don't think the old man will live through the night.|I've read through the report.* **6** all over; among the parts of: *We travelled through France and Belgium.|I searched through all my papers.*

**through²** *adv* **1** in at one side and out at the other: *I opened the gate and let them through.* **2** all the way from beginning to end: *She read the letter through.|Does this train go right through to London?* **3** to a successful end: *I failed the examination, but she* got through. (=passed) **4** *BrE* connected by telephone: *"Can you put me through to Mr Jones?" "You're through now."* **5** [*with*] *infml* to or at the end; finished: *Are you through yet?|I'm through with alcohol.* (=I won't drink any more) **6 through and through** completely; in every way

**through³** *adj* [A] going all the way from one end to the other: *a through train|a through road*

**through·out** /θruːˈaʊt/ *adv* **1** in every part: *The house is painted throughout.* **2** from beginning to end: *The prince remained loyal throughout.* **–throughout** *prep: throughout the country/night*

**throw¹** /θrəʊ/ *v* **threw** /θruː/, **thrown** /θrəʊn/, **throwing 1** [I;T] to send through the air by a sudden movement or straightening of the arm: *She threw the ball 50 metres.* –see picture on page 669 **2** [T] to move or put suddenly, or with force: *The two fighters threw themselves at each other.|His words threw us all into confusion.* **3** [T] to cause to fall off: *The horse threw him.* **4** [T] to move (a SWITCH, handle, etc.) in order to connect or disconnect parts of a machine **5** [T] to make (one's voice) appear to come from somewhere other than one's mouth **6** [T] to shape (an object) out of wet clay when making POTTERY **7** [T] *infml* to arrange or give (a party, dinner, etc.) **8** [T] *infml* to confuse; shock: *His behaviour really threw me.* **9 throw a fit** to have a sudden attack of uncontrolled temper **10 throw oneself at someone: a** to rush violently towards someone **b** to attempt forcefully to win the love of someone **11 throw oneself into** to work very busily at **–thrower** *n*

**throw** sthg.↔ **away** *v adv* [T] to lose by foolishness: *He threw away the chance of a good job.*

**throw** sthg.↔ **in** *v adv* [T] *infml* to supply in addition, without increasing the price: *The room costs fifteen pounds a night, with breakfast thrown in.*

**throw** sbdy./sthg.↔ **off** *v adv* [T] to free oneself from: *to throw off a cold*

**throw** sthg.↔ **open** *v adv* [T *to*] to allow people to enter: *We threw the house open for the party.*

**throw** sbdy./sthg.↔ **out** *v adv* [T] **1** to refuse to accept: *The committee threw out my suggestions.* **2** to dismiss; force to leave: *The teacher threw me out for making too much noise.*

**throw** sbdy.↔ **over** *v adv* [T] to end a relationship with

**throw** sbdy./sthg.↔ **together** *v adv* [T] **1** to make hastily: *I just threw the meal together.* **2** to bring together: *Chance threw us together at a party.*

**throw up** *v adv* **1** [T] (**throw** sthg.↔ **up**) to stop doing: *to throw up a job* **2** [I] *infml* for VOMIT

**throw²** *n* **1** an act of throwing **2** the distance to which something is thrown: *a throw of 100 metres*

**thru** /θruː/ *adv,adj,prep AmE infml* for through

**thrush** /θrʌʃ/ *n* a small bird with a brownish back and spotted breast

**thrust** /θrʌst/ *v* **thrust, thrusting 1** [T] to push forcefully and suddenly: *We thrust our way through the crowd.* **2** [I *at*] to make a sudden forward stroke with a sword, knife, etc. **–thrust** *n* [C;U]

**thud** /θʌd/ *n* a dull sound caused by a heavy object striking something soft: *He fell to the floor with a thud.* **–thud** *v* **-dd-** [I]

**thug** /θʌg/ *n* a violent criminal

**thumb¹** /θʌm/ *n* **1** the short thick finger which is set apart from the other four –see picture on page 299 **2 stick out like a sore thumb** *infml* to seem out of place **3 thumbs up** (an expression of satisfaction, victory, or approval) **4 under somebody's thumb** *infml* under the control or influence of someone

**thumb²** *v* [I;T] **1** *infml* to ask for (a free ride) from passing motorists by holding out one's thumb; HITCHHIKE: *to thumb a lift to London* **2** [*through*] to look through (a book) quickly

**thumb·nail** /ˈθʌmneɪl/ *n* **1** [C] the hard flat piece at the end of the thumb **2** [A] small; short: *a thumbnail sketch*

**thumb·tack** /ˈθʌmtæk/ *n AmE* for DRAWING PIN

**thump¹** /θʌmp/ *v* [I;T] to strike with a heavy blow: *I'll thump you on the nose!*

**thump²** *n* (the dull sound of) a heavy blow

**thun·der¹** /ˈθʌndəʳ/ *n* [U] the loud explosive noise that follows a flash of lightning: (fig.) *the thunder of distant guns* **–thunderous** *adj: (fig.) thunderous* (=very loud) APPLAUSE **–thunderously** *adv*

USAGE Note the word order in this fixed phrase: **thunder and lightning.**

**thunder²** *v* **1** [I] to produce thunder: (fig.) *The guns thundered in the distance.* **2** to shout loudly: *"Get out!" he thundered.*

**thun·der·bolt** /ˈθʌndəbəʊlt‖-dər-/ *n* a flash of lightning, with thunder

**thun·der·clap** /ˈθʌndəklæp‖-ər-/ *n* a single loud crash of thunder

**thun·der·storm** /ˈθʌndəstɔːm‖-dərstɔrm/ *n* a storm of heavy rain with thunder and lightning

**thun·der·struck** /ˈθʌndəstrʌk‖-ər-/ *adj* [F] very surprised indeed

**thun·der·y** /ˈθʌndəri/ *adj* (of the weather) giving signs that thunder is likely

**Thurs·day** /ˈθɜːzdi, -deɪ‖ˈθɜr-/ the 5th day of the week: *He'll arrive (on) Thursday.|I'm always in on Thursday evenings.|(esp. AmE) She works Thursdays.*

**thus** /ðʌs/ *adv fml* **1** in this way: *We hope the new machine will work faster, thus reducing our costs.* **2** with this result –see Study Notes on page 128 **3 thus far** up until now

**thwart** /θwɔːt‖θwɔrt/ *v* [T] to oppose successfully: *My plans were thwarted by the weather.*

**thy** /ðaɪ/ *determiner old use (possessive form of* THOU) belonging to THEE; your

**thyme** /taɪm/ *n* [U] (the dried leaves of) a plant, used for giving a special taste to food

**thy·roid** /ˈθaɪrɔɪd/ also **thyroid gland**– *n* an organ in the neck that controls growth and activity

**ti·a·ra** /tiˈɑːrə/ *n* a piece of jewellery like a small crown, esp. as worn on the head by women on formal occasions

**tic** /tɪk/ *n* a sudden movement of the muscles, esp. in the face, usu. caused by a nervous illness

**tick¹** /tɪk/ *n* **1** the short regularly repeated sound of a clock or watch **2** *BrE*‖**check** *AmE*– a mark (✓) put against an answer, name on a list, etc., to show that it is correct, that the person is present, etc. **3** *BrE infml* a moment: *I'll be there in a tick.*

**tick²** *v* **1** [I] (of a clock, watch, etc.) to make a regularly repeated short sound **2** [T *off*] *BrE*‖**check** *AmE*– to mark (an answer, name, etc.) with a TICK¹

(2), to show that it is correct

**tick** sbdy.↔**off** *v adv* [T] *infml* to scold: *He ticked me off because I was late.* –**ticking off** *n* **tickings off**

**tick over** *v adv* [I] to continue working at a slow steady rate: *The car's engine was ticking over.*

**tick**[3] *n* a very small insect-like creature that fixes itself to animals and sucks their blood

**tick**[4] *n* [U] *infml* for CREDIT[1] (4): *Can I have these shoes* **on tick** *until I get paid?*

**tick·et** /'tɪk$\frac{1}{2}$t/ *n* **1** a printed piece of paper or card which shows that a person has paid for a journey on a bus, entrance into a cinema, etc.: *a bus/train/cinema ticket|Entrance to the theatre is* **by ticket** *only.* **2** a piece of card or paper that shows the price, size, etc., of an object for sale **3** a printed notice of an offence against the driving laws: *If you park there, you might get a (parking) ticket.*

**tick·le**[1] /'tɪkəl/ *v* **-led, -ling 1** [T] to touch (someone's body) lightly to produce laughter or nervous excitement **2** [I;T] to give or feel a sensation of nervous excitement: *These rough sheets tickle.* **3** [T] to delight or amuse

**tickle**[2] *n* [C;U] (an) act or feeling of tickling (TICKLE[1] (1,2))

**tick·lish** /'tɪklɪʃ/ *adj* **1** (of a (part of a) person) sensitive to tickling **2** (of a problem, etc.) difficult: *a ticklish question*

**tid·al** /'taɪdl/ *adj* of, having, or related to the TIDE (1): *tidal currents|a* **tidal wave** (=very large dangerous ocean wave)

**tid·bit** /'tɪd,bɪt/ *n AmE* for TITBIT

**tide** /taɪd/ *n* **1** [C] (a current caused by) the regular rise and fall of the seas: *The sea comes right up to the cliffs when the tide is in.*|(fig.) *the tide of public opinion* **2** [U] *old use* time; season: *Christmastide*

**tide·mark** /'taɪdmɑːk‖-mɑrk/ *n* the highest point reached by a TIDE (1) on the shore

**tide** sbdy. **over** (sthg.) *v adv; prep* **tided, tiding** [T] to help (someone) through (a difficult period): *Can you lend me ten pounds, to tide me over this week?*

**tid·ings** /'taɪdɪŋz/ *n* [P] *old use* news

**ti·dy**[1] /'taɪdi/ *adj* **-dier, -diest 1** (liking things to be) neatly arranged: *a tidy room/person* **2** *infml* quite large: *a tidy income* –**tidily** *adv* –**tidiness** *n* [U]

**tidy**[2] *v* **-died, -dying** [I;T *up*] to make neat

**tie**[1] /taɪ/ *n* **1** also **necktie** *AmE*– a band of cloth worn round the neck and tied in a knot at the front –see also BOW TIE; see picture on page 563 **2** a cord, string, etc., used for fastening something **3** something that unites; BOND (1): *family ties|ties of friendship* **4** something that limits one's freedom: *Young children can be a tie.* **5** an equality of results, votes, etc.: *The result of the election was a tie.* –compare DRAW[1] (6)

**tie**[2] *v* **tied, tying 1** [I;T *up*] to fasten or be fastened with a cord, string, band, etc.: *to tie up a parcel|Tie your shoelaces.|My dress ties (up) at the back.|to tie a dog to a fence* **2** [T] to make (a knot or BOW[3] (3)): *to tie a knot* **3** [I *with, for*] to be equal in a competition: *to tie for second place*

**tie** sbdy. **down** *v adv* [T] **1** to limit the freedom of: *She feels her job is tying her down.* **2** [*to*] to force to take a particular position, make a decision, etc.

**tie in** *v adv* [I *with*] to be in agreement with: *This story doesn't tie in with the facts.* –see also TIE **up**

**tie** sthg.↔**up** *v adv* [T] **1** [*in*] to limit the free use of (money, property, etc.) by certain conditions **2** [*with*] to connect: *The police are trying to tie up his escape from prison with the murder.* –compare TIE[2] **in 3 tied up** very busy

**tier** /tɪəʳ/ *n* any of a number of levels, esp. of seats, rising one behind or above another: *Their wedding cake had three tiers.*

**tiff** /tɪf/ *n* a slight quarrel: *a lovers' tiff*

**ti·ger** /'taɪgəʳ/ **tigress** *fem.*– *n* a large fierce Asian wild cat that has yellow fur with black bands

**tight**[1] /taɪt/ *adj* **1** fitting (too) closely; leaving no free room or time: *tight shoes|a tight* SCHEDULE **2** closely fastened; firmly fixed in place: *This drawer is so tight I can't open it.| Is this roof completely watertight?* **3** fully stretched: *Pull the thread tight.* **4** (of money) difficult to obtain **5** *infml* drunk **6** *infml* not generous with money **7 in a tight corner/spot** in a difficult position –**tightly** *adv* –**tightness** *n* [U]

**tight**[2] *adv* **1** closely; firmly; tightly: *She held him tight and kissed him.* **2 sit tight** to stay where one is

**tight·en** /'taɪtn/ *v* [I;T *up*] to make or become tighter: *The government are tightening up (on)* (=becoming firmer about) *the driving laws.* –compare LOOSEN, SLACKEN

**tight·fist·ed** /,taɪt'fɪst$\frac{1}{2}$d◂/ also **tight**– *adj infml* very ungenerous with money

**tight·rope** /'taɪt-rəʊp/ *n* a tightly stretched rope or wire, high above the ground, on which performers walk and do tricks

**tights** /taɪts/ *n* [P] a close-fitting garment worn esp. by women, and made of thin material covering the legs and lower part of the body –see PAIR (USAGE)

**ti·gress** /'taɪgr$\frac{1}{2}$s/ *n* a female tiger

**tile**[1] /taɪl/ *n* a thin piece of baked clay or plastic, metal, etc. used for covering roofs, walls, floors, etc.

**tile**[2] *v* **tiled, tiling** [T] to cover (a roof, floor, wall, etc.) with TILES: *to tile a roof|a tiled floor*

**till**[1] /tɪl/ *prep,conj* →UNTIL –see INCLUSIVE (USAGE)

**till**[2] *n* a drawer where money is kept in a shop

**till**[3] /tɪl, tl/ *v* [T] *old use* to cultivate (the ground)

**til·ler** /'tɪləʳ/ *n* a long handle fastened to the RUDDER of a boat, to turn it

**tilt**[1] /tɪlt/ *v* [I;T] to (cause to) slope by raising one end

**tilt**[2] *n* **1** a slope: *She wore her hat at a tilt.* **2 (at) full tilt** *infml* at full speed

**tim·ber** /'tɪmbəʳ/ *n* **1** [U] wood or growing trees to be used for building **2** [C] a wooden beam

**time**[1] /taɪm/ *n* **1** [U] a continuous measurable quantity from the past, through the present, and into the future; the passing of minutes, days, months, and years: *The universe exists in space and time.|***In time** (=after a certain period) *you'll forget him.|Only* **time will tell** *if you're right.|The men are working* **against time** *to finish the bridge.* (=it must be finished soon and there is still much to do) **2** [S;U] a period of a certain usu. stated length, e.g. between two events or for the completion of an action: *Learning English takes quite a long time.|Take more time and care over your work.|I don't have much time,* (=I am in a hurry) *so tell me quickly.|She stays in* **all the time**. (=She never goes out)*|I'll be back in no time.* (=very soon) **3** [U] a system of measuring time: *British Summer Time* **4** the period in which an action is completed, esp. a performance in a race: *Her time was just under four minutes.* **5** [S;U] a particular point in the day stated in hours, minutes, and sometimes seconds: *"What's the time?" "It's one o'clock."|"What time's John coming to tea?" "Four o'clock."|This clock* **keeps good time**. (=works correctly) **6** [S;U] a particular moment or occasion: *It's time to go to bed.|***Closing time** *at this pub is eleven o'clock.|He's in a good temper, so* **now's the time** *to tell him you've crashed his car.|They arrived* **ahead of time**. (=early)|*I told you* **at the time** (=when the thing we are talking about happened) *that I thought you were being foolish.|He comes here* **from time to time**. (=occasionally)|*Do the trains ever run* **on time** (=at the right time) *here?|The people came in* **two at a time.** (=in groups of two)|*I've told you* **time after time/time and again** (=repeatedly) *not to do that.* **7** [C *often plural*] a period: *in ancient times|in Queen Victoria's time|We had a good time* (=enjoyed ourselves) *at the party.|a writer who is* **ahead of her time** (=has ideas too modern or original for the period in which she lives)|**At one time** (=formerly) *I used to like her, but not any more.|He lived* **for a time** (=for a short period) *in Spain.* **8** [U] the rate of speed of a piece of music: *You* **beat time** *and I'll play.|The players at the back aren't* **keeping time**. **9 at the same time** in spite of this; yet: *He can be very rude, but at the same time I can't help liking him.* **10 for the time being** for a limited period: *I'll let you keep the book for the time being, but I'll want it back next week.* **11 have no time for** *infml* to dislike **12 have the time of one's life** to have a very enjoyable experience **13 in good time: a** at the right time **b** early enough **14 in one's own good time** *infml* when one is ready and not before **15 in time** early enough: *We must make sure we arrive in time to get a good seat.*

USAGE To **spend** time suggests using it in a sensible or useful way, but to **pass** time gives the idea of too much time that must be filled: *We* **spent** *the day painting the outside of the house.|How do you* **pass** *the time now that you're no longer working?* To **waste** time suggests that it has been badly used: *We* **wasted** *an hour trying to find a parking place!*

**time²** *v* **timed, timing** [T] **1** [*usu. passive*] to set the time at which (something) happens or is to happen: *The bell is timed to ring at six o'clock.|She timed her visit well, and arrived at the right moment.* **2** to record the speed of or time taken by: *We timed our journey: it took us two hours.*

**time bomb** /'· ·/ *n* a bomb that can be set to explode at a particular time

**time-hon·oured** /'· ,··/ *adj* respected because of age or long use: *a time-honoured custom*

**time·keep·er** /'taɪm,kiːpəʳ/ *n* a person who records the time of competitors in a race, work done by others, etc.

**time lag** /'· ·/ also **lag**– *n* the period of time in between two connected events

**time·less** /'taɪmlɨs/ *adj* lasting for ever; not changed by time: *the timeless beauty of the stars* **–timelessly** *adv* **–timelessness** *n* [U]

**time lim·it** /'· ,··/ *n* a period of time within which something must be done

**time·ly** /'taɪmli/ *adj* **-lier, -liest** happening at just the right time: *a timely warning*

**tim·er** /'taɪməʳ/ *n* a person or machine that records time

**times¹** /taɪmz/ *prep* multiplied by: *3 times 3=9 is usually written 3×3=9.*

**times²** *n* [P] **1** the present time: *a sign of the times* **2** occasions on which something was done: *I played cricket five times last week.* **3 at times** sometimes **4 behind the times** old-fashioned **5 for old times' sake** because of happy times in the past **6 move with the times** to change one's own ideas, methods, etc. at the same rate as changing fashions, social customs, etc.

**time·ta·ble** /'taɪm,teɪbəl/ *n* a table of the times at which buses and trains arrive and leave, classes in a school or college take place, etc. **–timetable** *v* **-bled, -bling** [T *for usu. passive*]: *The meeting was timetabled to begin at two o'clock.*

**time·worn** /'taɪmwɔːn‖-worn/ *adj lit* showing signs of decay through age

**tim·id** /'tɪmɨd/ *adj* fearful; lacking courage **–timidity** /tɪ'mɪdɨti/ *n* [U] **–timidly** *adv*

**tim·ing** /'taɪmɪŋ/ *n* [U] (judgment in) the arrangement and control of events, actions, etc.: *a dancer with perfect timing*

**tim·o·rous** /'tɪmərəs/ *adj fml* afraid; nervous **–timorously** *adv*

**tim·pa·ni** /'tɪmpəni/ *n* [U +*sing./pl. v*] a set of KETTLEDRUMS: *The timpani is/are too loud.* **–timpanist** *n*

**tin¹** /tɪn/ *n* **1** [U] a soft whitish metal that is a simple substance (ELEMENT (1)), used to cover (PLATE) metal objects with a protective shiny surface **2** [C] also **can** *esp. AmE*– a small metal box or container: *a tin of beans/tobacco* –see picture on page 615

**tin²** also **can** *esp. AmE*– *v* **-nn-** [T] to preserve (esp. food) by packing it in tins: *tinned fruit/meat*

**tin³** *adj* made of tin

**tinc·ture** /'tɪŋktʃəʳ/ *n* [C;U] a medical substance mixed with alcohol

**tin·der** /'tɪndəʳ/ *n* [U] *fml* any material that catches fire easily: *The plants are as dry as tinder.*

**tin·foil** /'tɪnfɔɪl/ *n* [U] a very thin bendable sheet of shiny metal, used as a protective wrapping, esp. for food

**tinge** /tɪndʒ/ *v* **tinged, tingeing** *or* **tinging** [T] to give a small amount of a colour to: *black hair tinged with grey|*(fig.) *Her admiration for him was tinged with jealousy.* **–tinge** *n* [S *of*]: *a tinge of sadness in her voice*

**tin·gle** /'tɪŋgəl/ *v* **-gled, -gling** [I] to feel a slight prickly sensation: *My fingers tingled with the cold.* **–tingle** *n* [S]: (fig.) *a tingle of fear/excitement*

**tin·ker¹** /'tɪŋkəʳ/ *n* a person who travels from place to place mending metal pots, pans, etc.

**tinker²** *v* [I *with*] to try to repair something without useful results: *Don't tinker with my television.*

**tin·kle** /'tɪŋkəl/ *v* **-kled, -kling** [I;T] to (cause to) make light ringing sounds: *The bell tinkled as he opened the shop door.* **–tinkle** *n* [*usu. sing.*]: *the tinkle of glasses*

**tin·ny** /'tɪni/ *adj* **-nier, -niest 1** of, like, or containing tin **2** having a thin metallic sound: *a tinny bell*

**tin o·pen·er** *BrE*‖**can opener** *AmE*– /'· ,···/ *n* a tool for opening tins –see picture on page 337

**tin·sel** /'tɪnsəl/ *n* [U] thin sheets or threads of shiny material used for decoration, esp. at Christmas

**tint** /tɪnt/ *n* a pale or delicate shade of a colour –**tint** *v* [T]: *She tinted her hair red.* (=gave her hair a slight red colour)

**ti·ny** /'taɪni/ *adj* **-nier, -niest** very small indeed –see Study Notes on page 494

**tip**[1] /tɪp/ *n* **1** the usu. pointed end of something: *the tip of one's nose/fingers* **2** a small end, cap, or point: *I only smoke cigarettes with tips.* **3 have (something) on the tip of one's tongue** to be about to remember (a name, word, etc.) –**tip** *v* **-pp-** [T]: *tipped cigarettes*

**tip**[2] *v* **-pp- 1** [I;T] to (cause to) lean at an angle: *The child tipped the plate and the cake fell off it.* **2** [I;T *over, up*] to (cause to) fall over: *I'm sorry I tipped the bottle over.* **3** [T] to pour (a substance) from one container into another: *She tipped the water into the basin.* **4** [T] to throw or leave (unwanted articles) somewhere

**tip**[3] *n* a place where unwanted waste is left

**tip**[4] *v* **-pp-** [I;T] to give a small amount of money to (a waiter, etc.) as thanks for a service performed –**tip** *n: I gave the taxi driver a large tip for being so helpful.*

**tip**[5] *n* [*on*] a helpful piece of advice: *tips on cookery*

**tip** sbdy.↔**off** *v adv* [T +*that/about*] to give secret information or a warning to: *The police were tipped off that the criminals were planning to rob the bank* **–tip-off** /'··/ *n: The police were given a tip-off.*

**tip·ple** /'tɪpəl/ *n* [*usu. sing.*] *infml* an alcoholic drink: *What's your favourite tipple?*

**tip·ster** /'tɪpstə^r/ *n* a person who gives advice about the likely winners of horse and dog races

**tip·sy** /'tɪpsi/ *adj* **-sier, -siest** slightly drunk –**tipsily** *adv* –**tipsiness** *n* [U]

**tip·toe**[1] /'tɪptəʊ/ *n* **on tiptoe** on one's toes with the rest of the feet raised above the ground

**tiptoe**[2] *v* [I] to walk on TIPTOE –see picture on page 669

**ti·rade** /taɪ'reɪd, tɪ̇-||'taɪreɪd, tɪ̇'reɪd/ *n* a long scolding speech

**tire**[1] /taɪə^r/ *v* **tired, tiring** [I;T *of*] to make or become tired: *a tiring day|She never tires of talking.*

**tire** sbdy.↔**out** *v adv* [T] to make completely tired: *The children tired me out.|I'm* **tired out** *so I'll go to bed.*

**tire**[2] *n AmE* for TYRE

**tired** /taɪəd||taɪərd/ *adj* **1** needing to rest or sleep **2** [F *of*] no longer interested in; annoyed with: *I'm tired of your stupid remarks.* –**tiredly** *adv* –**tiredness** *n* [U]

**tire·less** /'taɪəlɪ̇s||'taɪər-/ *adj* never getting tired: *a tireless worker* –**tirelessly** *adv*

**tire·some** /'taɪəsəm||'taɪər-/ *adj* annoying: *a tiresome child* –**tiresomely** *adv*

**tis·sue** /'tɪʃuː, -sjuː||-ʃuː/ *n* **1** [U] animal or plant cells, esp. those that make up a particular organ: *lung tissue|leaf tissue* **2** [C;U] (a piece of) soft thin paper

**tit**[1] /tɪt/ *n infml* **1** →BREAST[1] (1) **2** →NIPPLE (1)

**tit**[2] *n* a small European bird: *a blue tit*

**tit·bit** /'tɪt'bɪt/ *BrE*||**tidbit** *AmE– n* a small piece of particularly nice food: (fig.) *a titbit of news*

**tit for tat** /ˌ· · '·/ *n infml* something unpleasant done in return for something unpleasant one has suffered

**tit·il·late** /'tɪtɪ̇leɪt/ *v* **-lated, -lating** [T] to excite pleasantly: *titillating news* –**titillation** /'leɪʃən/ *n* [U]

**tit·i·vate** /'tɪtɪ̇veɪt/ *v* **-vated, -vating** [I;T] *infml* to make (esp. oneself) pretty or tidy

**ti·tle** /'taɪtl/ *n* **1** [C] a name given to a book, painting, play, etc.: *The title of the play is "Hamlet".* **2** [C] a word or name, such as "Mr", "Lady", "Doctor", "General", etc., used before a person's name as a sign of rank, profession, etc. **3** [S;U *to*] *tech* the lawful right to ownership or possession: *Has he any title to this land?*

**ti·tled** /'taɪtld/ *adj* having a noble title, such as "Lord"

**title deed** /'·· ·/ *n* a paper showing a person's right of ownership of property

**title role** /'·· ·/ *n* the chief part (ROLE) in a play, after which the play is named

**tit·ter** /'tɪtə^r/ *v* [I] to laugh quietly in a nervous or silly way –**titter** *n*

**tit·tle-tat·tle** /'tɪtl ˌtætl/ *n* [U] *infml* for GOSSIP[1] (1)

**tit·u·lar** /'tɪtʃʊlə^r||-tʃə-/ *adj* holding a title but not having the duties or power of office:

**T-junc·tion** /'tiː ˌdʒʌŋkʃən/ *n* a place where two roads join in the shape of a T

**to**[1] /tə, tʊ; *strong* tuː/ *prep* **1** going in the direction of; towards: *the road to London|She threw the ball to me.* (=for me to catch it. *She threw the stone at me* means that she wanted to hurt me.) –see Study Notes on page 474 **2** as far as; so as to reach: *We went to London.|The traffic lights changed to green.|Count from 1 to 20.|They stayed here from Monday to/till Friday.|ten to twelve feet of water* (=between ten and twelve) **3** (used with words about sending, giving, or belonging): *I'm writing a letter/writing to John.|She wants a room to herself.* **4** touching or facing: *The paper stuck to the wall.|sitting with my back to/towards the engine* **5** in connection with: *kind to animals|the key to the door|They live* **next door to** *me.* **6** (used with words about addition): *Add 2 to 4.* **7** also **of** *AmE–* (of the clock) before: *It's five (minutes) to four.* (=03.55. **Till** is not used here.) **8** per; in each: *There are 100 pence to the £.*

**to**[2] *adv* **1** into consciousness: *After he hit his head, he didn't* **come to** *for half an hour.* **2** so as to be shut: *The wind blew the door to.* **3 close/near to** really close: *He doesn't seem so young when you see him close to.*

**to**[3] (**to** can be used before a verb to show it is in the INFINITIVE) **1** (after certain verbs): *He wants to go.|You ought to understand.* **2** (describing what someone asked, advised, warned, etc.) **a**: *He told them to shoot.* (=He said "Shoot!") **b** (after *how, what, when, where, whether, which, who, whom, whose*): *Tell me where to go!|He wondered what to do.* **3** (after some nouns): *They made an attempt to land.* **4** (after some adjectives): *I'm sorry to hear it.* **5** (when using a verb like a noun): *To wear boots would be safest.|It would be safest to wear boots.* **6** (when speaking of purpose): *He said it to annoy her/so as to annoy her.|I want some scissors to cut my nails with/***in order to** *cut my nails.|There were plenty of things to eat.* –see Study Notes on page 128 **7** (with *too* and *enough*, when speaking of result): *He's too fat to dance.*

USAGE In general, it is a good idea to avoid putting any other word between **to** and the verb that follows it, as in *He tried* **to** *quietly leave the room.* This is called a **split infinitive**. But sometimes there is no other way to arrange the sentence, as in *Your job is* to *really understand these children.*

**toad** /təʊd/ *n* an animal like a large FROG (1)

**toad·stool** /'təʊdstu:l/ *n* a fleshy, usu. poisonous plant (FUNGUS) that looks like the MUSHROOM

**to-and-fro** /ˌ· · '·/ *adj* forwards and backwards or from side to side: *a to-and-fro movement* –**to and fro** *adv: The teacher walked to and fro in front of the class.*

**toast**[1] /təʊst/ *n* **1** [U] bread made brown by being heated **2** [C] a call on other people to drink and wish for someone's success and happiness: *to drink a toast to the newly married pair* **3** [*the* S] the person or thing in whose honour this is done

**toast**[2] *v* [T] **1** to make (bread, cheese, etc.) brown by holding it close to heat: (fig.) *to toast* (=warm) *one's feet by the fire* –see COOK (USAGE) **2** to drink and wish for the success and happiness of (someone)

**toast·er** /'təʊstəʳ/ *n* an electric apparatus for TOASTing[2] (1) bread –see picture on page 337

**to·bac·co** /tə'bækəʊ/ *n* [U] a plant or its large leaves, prepared for smoking in cigarettes, pipes, etc.

**to·bac·co·nist** /tə'bækənɪ̥st/ *n* a person who sells tobacco, cigarettes, etc.

**to·bog·gan** /tə'bɒgən‖-'bɑ-/ *n* a board curved up at the front, for carrying people over snow, esp. down slopes –**toboggan** *v* [I]: *children tobogganing in the snow*

**to·day** /tə'deɪ/ *adv,n* **1** (on) this present day: *Today's my birthday!|Are we going shopping today?* **2** (at) this present time; now: *the young people of today|People travel more today than they used to.*

**tod·dle** /'tɒdl‖'tɑdl/ *v* **-dled, -dling** [I *about*] to walk with short unsteady steps, as a small child does

**tod·dler** /'tɒdləʳ‖'tɑd-/ *n* a child who has just learnt to walk –see CHILD (USAGE)

**to-do** /tə 'du:/ *n* [*usu. sing.*] *infml* a state of excited confusion: *What a to-do about nothing!*

**toe**[1] /təʊ/ *n* **1** one of the five parts at the end of each foot –compare FINGER[1] –see picture on page 299 **2 on one's toes** ready for action

**toe**[2] *v* **-toed, toeing** [T] **toe the line** to obey orders

**toe·nail** /'təʊneɪl/ *n* one of the hard flat pieces at the end of the toes –see picture on page 299

**tof·fee, toffy** /'tɒfi‖'tɑfi/ also **taffy** *AmE*– *n* [C;U] (a piece of) a hard brown sweet made by boiling sugar and butter

**to·ga** /'təʊgə/ *n* a loose outer garment worn by the ancient Romans

**to·geth·er** /tə'geðəʳ/ *adv* **1** into one group; so as to be joined: *The people gathered together.|Tie the ends together.|Add these numbers together.* **2** with one another: *We went to school together.* **3** at the same time: *Why do all the bills seem to come together?* **4** *infml* (of a person) very much in control of his/her life, actions, EMOTIONs, etc., very well ORGANISED: *I admire Jane; she's a really together person.* **5 together with** as well as; in addition to: *He sent her some roses, together with a nice letter.*

**to·geth·er·ness** /tə'geðənɪ̥s‖-ðər-/ *n* [U] a feeling of being united with other people; friendliness

**tog·gle** /'tɒgəl‖'tɑ-/ *n* a small shaped bar of wood used as a button

**togs** /tɒgz‖tɑgz, tɔgz/ *n* [P] *infml* clothes

**tog** sbdy. **up** /tɒg‖tɑg, tɔg/ also **tog** sbdy. **out**– *v adv* **-gg-** [T *in*] *infml* to dress in specially nice clothes

**toil** /tɔɪl/ *v* [I] *fml or lit* **1** to work hard and untiringly **2** to move with tiredness, difficulty, or pain: *The slaves toiled up the hill pulling the heavy blocks.* –**toil** *n* [U]

**toi·let** /'tɔɪlɪ̥t/ *n* **1** [C] (a room with) a large seatlike bowl connected to a pipe (DRAIN), used for getting rid of the body's waste matter; LAVATORY –see picture on page 297 **2** [U] *fml* the act of washing, dressing oneself, and taking care of one's appearance

**toilet pa·per** /'·· ˌ··/ *n* [U] thin paper for cleaning the body when waste matter has been passed from it

**toi·let·ries** /'tɔɪlɪ̥triz/ *n* [P] articles or substances used in dressing, washing, etc.

**toilet roll** /'·· ·/ *n* a rolled-up length of TOILET PAPER

**toilet wa·ter** /'·· ˌ··/ *n* [U] a pleasant-smelling but not very strong PERFUME

**to·ken** /'təʊkən/ *n* **1** [A;C] a sign or reminder; small part meant to represent something greater: *a token payment|a token* STRIKE[2] **2** [C] a piece of metal, card, etc. used instead of money, for a particular purpose: *a book token* (=card that one can exchange for a book or books)

**told** /təʊld/ *v past tense & participle of* TELL

**tol·e·ra·ble** /'tɒlərəbəl‖'tɑ-/ *adj* fairly good; that can be TOLERATED –see also INTOLERABLE –**tolerably** *adv*

**tol·e·rance** /'tɒlərəns‖'tɑ-/ *n* **1** [C;U *of, to*] the ability to suffer pain, hardship, etc., without being damaged: *He has no tolerance to cold.* **2** [U] also **toleration**– the quality of allowing people to behave in a way that may not please one, without becoming annoyed

**tol·e·rate** /'tɒləreɪt‖'tɑ-/ *v* **-rated, -rating** [T] to allow (something one does not like) to be practised or done: *I can't tolerate bad manners.* –see BEAR (USAGE) –**tolerant** *adj* –**tolerantly** *adv*

**tol·e·ra·tion** /ˌtɒlə'reɪʃən‖ˌtɑ-/ *n* [U] →TOLERANCE (2)

**toll**[1] /təʊl/ *n* **1** a tax paid to use a road, bridge, etc. **2** [*usu. sing.*] the cost in health, life, etc., from something: *the death toll from road accidents|Years of worry have* **taken their toll** *on him.*

**toll**[2] *v* [I;T] to ring (a bell) slowly and repeatedly –**toll** *n* [S]: *the toll of the bell*

**toll·gate** /'təʊlgeɪt/ *n* a gate at which a TOLL[1] (1) must be paid

**tom·a·hawk** /'tɒməhɔ:k‖'tɑ-/ *n* a small light axe used by North American Indians

**to·ma·to** /tə'mɑ:təʊ‖-'meɪ-/ *n* **-toes 1** [C;U] (a) soft red fruit eaten as a vegetable **2** [C] the plant on which this fruit grows

**tomb** /tu:m/ *n* a grave, esp. a large decorated one

**tom·boy** /'tɒmbɔɪ‖'tɑm-/ *n* **-boys** a spirited young girl who likes to be rough and noisy –**tomboyish** *adj*

**tomb·stone** /'tu:mstəʊn/ *n* →GRAVESTONE

**tom·cat** /'tɒmkæt‖'tɑm-/ also **tom** *infml*– *n* a male cat

**tome** /təʊm/ *n lit or humor* a large book

**tom·fool·e·ry** /tɒm'fu:ləri‖tɑm-/ *n* [U] foolish behaviour

**to·mor·row** /tə'mɒrəʊ‖'mɔ-, -'mɑ-/ *adv,n* **1** (on) the day after today: *We're going to a party tomorrow.|tomorrow night* –compare YESTERDAY **2** (in) the future: *tomorrow's world*

**tom-tom** /'tɒm tɒm||'tɑm tɑm/ *n* a long narrow drum, beaten with the hands

**ton** /tʌn/ *n* **tons** *or* **ton 1** a measurement of weight equal in Britain to 2,240 pounds and in the US to 2,000 pounds **2** also **tonne, metric ton**– a measurement of weight equal to one thousand kilos **3** a measurement of the size of a ship or the amount of goods it can carrry **4** [*of*] *infml* a very large quantity or weight: *I bought tons of food.*

**tone** /təʊn/ *n* **1** [C] a sound, esp. of a musical instrument or singing voice, considered with regard to its quality **2** [C] a particular quality of the voice; manner of expression: *to speak in low tones*|*I don't like your tone (of voice).* **3** [C] a variety of a colour: *a picture painted in tones of blue* **4** [U] the general quality: *the tone of our neighbourhood* **5** [C] also **step** *AmE– tech* a fixed separation between musical notes in a SCALE[2] (5): *There is a tone between B and C sharp; B and C are half a tone apart.* –**tonal** *adj*

**tone-deaf** /ˌ· '·◄/ *adj* unable to tell the difference between musical notes

**tone** sthg.↔**down** *v adv* **toned, toning** [T] to reduce the violence or force of: *You must tone down your language; stop swearing.*

**tone in** *v adv* **toned, toning** [I *with*] to match: *Your hat and shoes tone in well with your dress.*

**tone·less** /'təʊnlɨs/ *adj* lacking colour and spirit; lifeless: *a toneless voice* –**tonelessly** *adv*

**tone** sbdy./sthg.↔**up** *v adv* [T] to make stronger, more healthy, etc.: *Swimming is the best way to tone up your body.*

**tongs** /tɒŋz||tɑŋz, tɔŋz/ *n* [P] an instrument with two movable arms, used for holding or lifting: *She used the tongs to add coal to the fire.* –see PAIR (USAGE)

**tongue** /tʌŋ/ *n* **1** [C] the movable fleshy organ in the mouth, used for tasting, producing speech, etc. –see picture on page 299 **2** [C;U] this organ taken from an animal such as the ox, used as food **3** [C] an object like a TONGUE (1) in shape or purpose, such as the piece of material under the LACES in a shoe **4** [C] a spoken language: *My native tongue is English.* **5 hold one's tongue** (*usu. in commands*) to remain silent **6 (with) (one's) tongue in (one's) cheek** *infml* saying or doing something one does not seriously mean **7 -tongued: a** having a certain kind of tongue: *a fork-tongued snake* **b** having a certain way of speaking: *sharp-tongued*

**tongue-tied** /'· ·/ *adj* unable to speak freely, e.g. through nervousness

**tongue twist·er** /'· ˌ··/ *n* a word or phrase difficult to speak quickly

**ton·ic** /'tɒnɪk||'tɑ-/ *n* anything which increases health or strength: *Country air is a good tonic.*|*The doctor gave me a special tonic.* (=medicine) –**tonic** *adj*

**tonic wa·ter** /'·· ˌ··/ also **tonic**– [U] gassy water made bitter with QUININE, often added to alcoholic drinks: *a gin and tonic*

**to·night** /tə'naɪt/ *adv,n* (on) this present night, or the one after today: *What's on television tonight?*

**ton·nage** /'tʌnɪdʒ/ *n* [U] **1** the amount of goods a ship can carry, or its size, expressed in TONS (3) **2** the total shipping of a navy, port, or country, expressed in TONS (3)

**tonne** /tʌn/ *n* **tonnes** *or* **tonne** →TON (2)

**ton·sil** /'tɒnsəl||'tɑn-/ *n* one of two small organs at the sides of the throat near the back of the tongue

**ton·sil·li·tis, tonsilitis** /ˌtɒnsɨ'laɪtɨs||ˌtɑn-/ *n* [U] a disease of the TONSILS

**too** /tuː/ *adv* **1** [+ *to-v*] more than enough; more than is good: *You're going too fast, slow down!*|*This dress is too small* (=not big enough) *for me.*|*It's too cold to go swimming.*|*He wasn't too pleased.* (=he was rather annoyed) **2** also; as well: *I can dance; I can sing, too.* (Compare *I can't dance; I can't sing, either.*) –see Study Notes on page 128

USAGE One can say *The day is* **too** *hot* or *It's* **too** *hot a day* (notice the word order); but **too** cannot be used in the pattern **too** + adjective + noun, so one cannot say **a* **too** *hot day.*

**took** /tʊk/ *v past tense of* TAKE[1]

**tool** /tuːl/ *n* **1** any instrument such as an axe, hammer, spade, etc., for doing special jobs –see MACHINE (USAGE) **2** a person unfairly used by another for the other person's own purposes **3 down tools** *infml* to stop working

**toot** /tuːt/ *v* [I;T] to (cause to) make a short warning sound as with a horn, whistle, etc.: *The car drivers tooted their horns.* –**toot** *n*

**tooth** /tuːθ/ *n* **teeth** /tiːθ/ **1** one of the small hard bony objects in the mouth, used for biting and tearing food –see picture on page 299 **2** any of the pointed parts that stand out from a comb, SAW, etc. **3 long in the tooth** *infml* old **4 sweet tooth** a liking for food which is sweet and sugary **5 tooth and nail** very violently: *to fight tooth and nail* –see also TEETH

**tooth·ache** /'tuːθ-eɪk/ *n* [C;U] (a) pain in a tooth –see ACHE (USAGE)

**tooth·brush** /'tuːθbrʌʃ/ *n* a small brush used for cleaning the teeth

**tooth·paste** /'tuːθpeɪst/ *n* [U] a substance used for cleaning the teeth

**tooth·pick** /'tuːθˌpɪk/ *n* a small pointed piece of wood used for removing food stuck between the teeth

**top[1]** /tɒp||tɑp/ *n* **1** [A;C] the highest or upper part: *the top of the page/hill*|*The mountain tops were hidden in mist.*|*They live on the top floor.*|*the top* (=upper surface) *of my desk*|*the table top* **2** [*the* S *of*] the best or most important position: *He started life at the bottom and worked his way to the top.* –compare BOTTOM **3** [C] a cover: *I can't unscrew the top of this bottle.* **4** [C] a garment worn on the upper part of the body **5 at the top of (one's) voice** as loudly as possible **6 at top speed** very fast **7 get on top of** *infml* to be too much for: *This work is getting on top of me.* **8 on top (of)** in addition (to): *He lost his job and on top of that his wife left him.*

**top[2]** *adj* at the top; first or best: *Fred is our top man.*|(*BrE*) *top of the class*

**top[3]** *v* **-pp-** [T] **1** to form or be a top for: *a cake topped with cream* **2** to be higher, better, or more than **3** to remove the top from (a vegetable, fruit, etc.) **4 top the bill** to be the chief actor or actress in a play

**top** sthg.↔**up** *v adv* [T *with*] to fill (a partly empty container) with liquid: *Let me top up your glass.*

**top[4]** *n* a child's toy that spins and balances on its point

**to·paz** /'təʊpæz/ *n* [C;U] (a precious stone cut from) a transparent yellowish mineral

**top·coat** /ˈtɒpkəʊt‖ˈtɑp-/ *n* →OVERCOAT
**top dog** /ˌ· ˈ·/ *n infml* the person in the most important position
**top hat** /ˌ· ˈ·/ *n* a man's formal tall silk hat
**top-heav·y** /ˌ· ˈ··◂/ *adj* [F] not properly balanced because of too much weight at the top
**top·ic** /ˈtɒpɪk‖ˈtɑ-/ *n* a subject for conversation, talk, writing, etc.
**top·ic·al** /ˈtɒpɪkəl‖ˈtɑ-/ *adj* of, related to, or being a subject of present interest: *Recent events have made this film very topical.* –**topically** *adv*
USAGE **Topical** has the same connection with time as **local** has with place: *a book of great* **topical** *interest* (=interesting now but not always)|*a book of great* **local** *interest* (=interesting here but not everywhere).
**top·less** /ˈtɒpləs‖ˈtɑp-/ *adj* (of a woman or a garment) leaving the breasts bare
**top·most** /ˈtɒpməʊst‖ˈtɑp-/ *adj* highest
**to·pog·ra·phy** /təˈpɒgrəfi‖-ˈpɑ-/ *n* [U] (the science of describing or mapping) the character of a place, esp. as regards the shape and height of the land –**topographer** *n* –**topographical** /ˌtɒpəˈgræfɪkəl‖ˌtɑ-/ *adj* –**topographically** *adv*
**top·ping** /ˈtɒpɪŋ‖ˈtɑ-/ *n* [C;U] something put on top of food: *cream topping*
**top·ple** /ˈtɒpəl‖ˈtɑ-/ *v* **-pled, -pling** [I;T *over*] to make or become unsteady and fall down: (fig.) *The government was toppled by the army.*
**top-se·cret** /ˌ· ˈ··◂/ *adj* to be kept very secret
**top·sy-tur·vy** /ˌtɒpsi ˈtɜːvi◂‖ˌtɑpsi ˈtɜrvi◂/ *adv,adj* in a state of confusion
**torch** /tɔːtʃ‖tɔrtʃ/ *n* **1** also **flashlight** *AmE*– a small electric light carried in the hand **2** a mass of burning material tied to a stick and carried to give light **3** *AmE* for BLOWLAMP
**torch·light** /ˈtɔːtʃlaɪt‖ˈtɔr-/ *n* [U] light produced by TORCHES (1,2): *a torchlight procession*
**tore** /tɔːʳ‖tor/ *v past tense of* TEAR²
**to·re·a·dor** /ˈtɒrɪədɔːʳ‖ˈto-, ˈtɑ-/ *n* one of the men who takes part in a Spanish BULLFIGHT riding on a horse
**tor·ment¹** /ˈtɔːment‖ˈtɔr-/ *n* [C;U] (a cause of) very great pain or suffering: *He was* **in torment** *after the operation.*|*to suffer torments*|*That child is a torment to his parents.*
**tor·ment²** /tɔːˈment‖tɔr-/ *v* [T] to cause to suffer pain –**tormentor** *n*
**torn¹** /tɔːn‖torn/ *adj* [*apart, between*] divided by opposing forces: *torn between two desires*
**torn²** *v past participle of* TEAR²
**tor·na·do** /tɔːˈneɪdəʊ‖tɔr-/ *n* **-does** *or* **-dos** a very violent wind that spins at great speeds
**tor·pe·do** /tɔːˈpiːdəʊ‖tɔr-/ *n* **-does** a long explosive shell, driven along under the sea by its own motors, used to destroy ships –**torpedo** *v* [T]
**tor·pid** /ˈtɔːpəd‖ˈtɔr-/ *adj fml* inactive; slow: *a torpid mind* –**torpidly** *adv* –**torpor** /ˈtɔːpeʳ‖ˈtɔr- / *n* [U]
**tor·rent** /ˈtɒrənt‖ˈtɔ-, ˈtɑ-/ *n* a violently rushing stream: *The rain fell* **in torrents**.|(fig.) *a torrent of bad language* –**torrential** /tɒˈrenʃəl‖tɔ- / *adj: torrential rain*
**tor·rid** /ˈtɒrəd‖ˈtɔ-, ˈtɑ-/ *adj* **1** very hot: *torrid weather* **2** concerning strong uncontrolled feelings: *a torrid story of sex and violence* –**torridly** *adv*
**tor·sion** /ˈtɔːʃən‖ˈtɔr-/ *n* [U] *tech* twisting or turning; being twisted or turned
**tor·so** /ˈtɔːsəʊ‖ˈtɔr-/ *n* **-sos** the human body without the head and limbs; TRUNK (2)
**tor·toise** /ˈtɔːtəs‖ˈtɔr-/ *n* a slow-moving land animal with a hard shell –compare TURTLE
**tor·toise·shell** /ˈtɔːtəsʃel, ˈtɔːtəʃel‖ˈtɔr-/ *n* [U] (the colour of) the hard brown and yellow shell of the TORTOISE or TURTLE, used for making combs, boxes, etc.
**tor·tu·ous** /ˈtɔːtʃuəs‖ˈtɔr-/ *adj* **1** twisted; winding **2** not direct; DEVIOUS or deceiving: *a tortuous argument* –**tortuously** *adv* –**tortuousness** *n* [U]
**tor·ture¹** /ˈtɔːtʃəʳ‖ˈtɔr-/ *n* **1** [U] the causing of severe pain, done out of cruelty, to find out information, etc. **2** [C;U] (a) severe pain or suffering: *the tortures of jealousy*
**torture²** *v* **-tured, -turing** [T] to cause great pain to (a person or animal) out of cruelty, as a punishment, etc.: *The prisoner was tortured to make him admit to the crime.* –**torturer** *n*
**To·ry** /ˈtɔːri‖ˈtori/ *n,adj* **-ries** (a member) (of) the British CONSERVATIVE party: *Tory principles*
**toss** /tɒs‖tɔs/ *v* **1** [T *to*] to throw: *to toss a ball* **2** [I;T *about*] to (cause to) move about rapidly: *The boat was tossed about in the stormy sea.*|*He tossed about in his sleep.*|*The horse tossed its head back.* **3** [T] to mix lightly: *to toss a* SALAD **4** [I;T *up, for*] to throw (a coin) to decide something according to which side lands face upwards: *There's only one sweet and two of us, so let's toss (up) for it.* –**toss** *n* [C;S]: *Our team won the toss so we play first.*
**toss** sthg.↔**off** *v adv* [T] to produce quickly with little effort: *She tossed off a few suggestions.*
**toss-up** /ˈ· ·/ *n* [S] *infml* an even chance: *It's a toss-up between the two of them as to who will get the job.*
**tot¹** /tɒt‖tɑt/ *n* **1** a very small child: **a tiny tot** **2** a small amount of a strong alcoholic drink: *a tot of rum/whisky*
**tot²** *v* →TOT UP
**to·tal¹** /ˈtəʊtl/ *adj* complete; whole: *the total population of Britain* –**totally** *adv: I totally agree with you.* –see Study Notes on page 389
**total²** *n* a number or quantity obtained by adding; complete amount: *A total of two hundred people visited the castle.*|**In total**, *there were two hundred visitors.*
**total³** *v* **-ll-** *BrE*‖**-l-** *AmE* [T] to equal a total of; add up to: *Your debts total one thousand pounds.*
**to·tal·i·tar·i·an** /təʊˌtæləˈteərɪən/ *adj* of or being a political system in which one political group controls everything and does not allow opposition parties to exist
**to·tal·i·ty** /təʊˈtæləti/ *n* [U] *fml* completeness
**tote** /təʊt/ *v* **toted, toting** [T] *infml* to carry
**to·tem** /ˈtəʊtəm/ *n* (a representation of) an animal, plant, or object thought to have a close relationship with the family group: *The North American Indians used to make* **totem poles**. (=tall poles with totems painted onto them)
**tot·ter** /ˈtɒtəʳ‖ˈtɑ-/ *v* [I] to move or walk in an unsteady way: *The old lady tottered down the stairs.*

**tot·ter·y** /ˈtɒtəri‖ˈtɑ-/ *adj* unsteady; shaky

**tot** sthg.↔**up** /tɒt‖tɑt/ *v adv* **-tt-** [T] to add up (figures, money, etc.)

**tou·can** /ˈtuːkən, -kæn/ *n* a brightly coloured tropical bird with a large beak

**touch**[1] /tʌtʃ/ *v* **1** [I;T] to be not separated from (something) by any space: *Stand close together so that your shoulders are touching.|The branches hung down and touched the water.* **2** [I;T] to feel or press with a part of the body, esp. the hands or fingers: *Visitors are asked not to touch the paintings.|You can look, but you mustn't touch.|He touched the bell and a servant appeared.*|(fig.) *In his talk he* **touched on** (=mentioned shortly) *the state of affairs in Africa.* **3** [T *usu. negative*] to take action concerning; handle; use: *He swore he'd never touch a drink* (=drink alcohol) *again.|He put away the book he was writing and didn't touch it again for years.|You haven't touched* (=eaten) *your food; I hope you're not ill.* **4** [T *usu. negative*] to compare with; be equal to: *No one can touch the Swiss at making watches.* **5** [T] to cause to feel pity: *His sad story so touched me/my heart that I nearly cried.|a touching story* **6 touch wood** to touch something made of wood in order to turn away bad luck **–touchable** *adj*

**touch down** *v adv* [I] **1** (of a plane) to land **2** (in RUGBY) to press the ball to the ground behind one's opponent's GOAL in order to win a TRY[2] (2) **–touchdown** *n*

**touch off** sthg. *v adv* [T] to cause to explode: (fig.) *His stupid remarks touched off a fight.*

**touch** sthg.↔**up** *v adv* [T] to improve by making small changes or additions

**touch**[2] *n* **1** [U] the sense by which a material object is known to be hard, smooth, rough, cold, hot, etc.: *A cat's fur is soft to the touch.* (=feels soft) **2** [C] an act of touching: *He felt the touch of her hand on his shoulder.* **3** [U] connection so as to receive information: *I'm trying to* **get in touch with** *my brother.|Please write; it would be nice to* **keep in touch**/*I don't want us to* **lose touch**.|*I'd like to go back to teaching, but I'm* **out of touch** *with my subject now.*|(fig.) *I think you've* **lost touch with** *reality.* **4** [S *of*] a slight amount: *This soup needs a touch more salt.* **5** [C] a slight added detail that improves or completes something: *I'm just putting* **the finishing touches** *to the cake.* **6** [S;U] skill, esp. in artistic performance: *He's lost another game–do you think he's* **losing his touch?** **7** [U] (in SOCCER and RUGBY) the area of ground outside the field of play

**touch-and-go** /ˌ· · ˈ·◂/ *adj* risky; of uncertain result: *It was touch-and-go whether he would get there in time.*

**touched** /tʌtʃt/ *adj* [F] **1** feeling grateful: *I was very touched by their present.* **2** *infml* slightly mad

**touch·stone** /ˈtʌtʃstəʊn/ *n* anything used as a test or standard; CRITERION

**touch·y** /ˈtʌtʃi/ *adj* **-ier, -iest** easily offended; too sensitive **–touchily** *adv* **–touchiness** *n* [U]

**tough**[1] /tʌf/ *adj* **1** strong; not easily weakened: *These mountain sheep are very tough.|***as tough as old boots** (=very tough) **2** difficult to cut or eat: *tough meat* –opposite **tender 3** difficult to do; demanding effort: *a tough job* **4** rough; hard: *The government will get tough with people who avoid paying taxes.* **5** *infml* too bad; unfortunate: *Tough luck!* **–toughly** *adv* **–toughness** *n* [U]

**tough**[2] *n infml* a rough violent person, esp. a criminal

**tough·en** /ˈtʌfən/ *v* [I;T *up*] to make or become TOUGH[1]

**tou·pee** /ˈtuːpeɪ‖tuːˈpeɪ/ *n* a piece of false hair that fits over a place on a man's head where the hair no longer grows

**tour**[1] /tʊəʳ/ *n* **1** [*round*] a journey during which several places are visited: *a tour round Europe|The National Theatre is* **on tour** *in the North.* **2** [*round*] a short trip to or through a place: *We went on a guided tour round the castle.* **3** [*in*] a period of duty at a single place or job, esp. abroad

**tour**[2] *v* [I;T *round*] to visit as a tourist: *We're touring (round) Italy for our holidays.|a touring holiday*

**tour de force** /ˌtʊə də ˈfɔːs‖ˌtʊər də ˈfors/ *n* [S] a show of strength or skill

**tour·is·m** /ˈtʊərɪzəm/ *n* [U] **1** the business of providing holidays for tourists **2** the practice of travelling for pleasure on holiday

**tour·ist** /ˈtʊərɪ̵st/ *n* a person travelling for pleasure: *a cheap tourist hotel*

**tour·na·ment** /ˈtʊənəmənt, ˈtɔː-‖ˈtɜr-, ˈtʊər-/ *n* **1** a number of competitions between players, played until the most skilful wins: *a tennis tournament* **2** (in former times) a competition of courage and skill between noble soldiers (KNIGHTS) fighting with weapons

**tour·ni·quet** /ˈtʊənɪkeɪ, ˈtɔː-‖ˈtɜrnɪkɪ̵t, *n* anything, esp. a band of cloth, twisted tightly round a limb to stop bleeding

**tou·sle** /ˈtaʊzəl/ *v* **-sled, -sling** [T] to disarrange (esp. the hair); make untidy

**tout**[1] /taʊt/ *v* [I *for*] to try to persuade people to buy one's goods, use one's services, etc.: *touting for business*

**tout**[2] *n* a person who TOUTS: *A* **ticket tout** *offered me a two pound ticket for ten pounds.*

**tow**[1] /təʊ/ *v* [T] to pull (a vehicle) along by a rope or chain

**tow**[2] *n* [C;U] **1** an act of TOWING or the state of being TOWED: *a vehicle* **on tow** (=being towed) **2 in tow** *infml* following closely behind

**to·wards** /təˈwɔːdz‖tordz/ also **toward** *esp. AmE*– *prep* **1** in the direction of: *She was walking towards town when I met her.|He stood with his back towards me.* –see Study Notes on page 474 **2** not long before: *Towards the end of the afternoon it began to rain.* **3** in relation to: *What are his feelings towards us?* **4** for part payment of: *We save £5 a week towards our holiday.*

**tow·el**[1] /ˈtaʊəl/ *n* a piece of cloth or paper used for drying wet things

**towel**[2] *v* **-ll-** *BrE*‖**-l-** *AmE* [T] to rub or dry with a TOWEL

**tow·el·ling** *BrE*‖**toweling** *AmE* /ˈtaʊəlɪŋ/ *n* [U] thickish cloth, used for making esp. TOWELS[1]

**tow·er**[1] /ˈtaʊəʳ/ *n* a tall building standing alone or forming part of a castle, church, etc.: *the Tower of London|the Eiffel Tower|a radio/television tower*

**tower**[2] *v* [I *above, over*] to be very tall, esp. in relation to the surroundings: *The mountains towered* *over the town in the valley.|towering trees*

**tower block** /'·· ·/ *n* a tall block of flats or offices

**town** /taʊn/ *n* **1** [C] a large group of houses and other buildings where people live and work –compare CITY, VILLAGE **2** [S] the business or shopping centre of such a place: *We went to (the) town to do some shopping today.|I was* **in town** *on business last week.* **3** [C +*sing./pl.v*] the people who live in a TOWN (1): *The whole town is/are in agreement about the plan.* **4** [S] (life in) TOWNS (1) and cities in general: *I like the town better than the country.|to leave the country for the town* **5 go to town** *infml* to act freely, esp. by spending a lot of money **6 (out) on the town** *infml* enjoying oneself, esp. at night

**town coun·cil** /ˌ· '··/ *n* [C +*sing./pl.v*] *BrE* an elected governing body of a town

**town hall** /ˌ· '·/ *n* a building used for a town's local government offices and public meetings

**town·ship** /'taʊnʃɪp/ *n* (in South Africa) a place where nonwhite citizens live

**towns·peo·ple** /'taunzˌpiːpəl/ also **townsfolk**– *n* [*the* P] the people who live in a town

**tox·ic** /'tɒksɪk‖'tɑk-/ *adj* poisonous: *a toxic drug|toxic waste from a factory* **–toxicity** /-'sɪsɪ̣ti/ *n* [U]

**tox·i·col·o·gy** /ˌtɒksɪ'kɒlədʒi‖ˌtɑksɪ'kɑ-/ *n* [U] the scientific and medical study of poisons **–toxicologist** *n*

**tox·in** /'tɒksə̣n‖'tɑk-/ *n* a poison produced by bacteria in a plant or animal body

**toy** /tɔɪ/ *n* [A;C] **1** an object for children to play with: *a toy soldier* **2** (being) a small breed of dog

**toy with** sthg. *v prep* [T] to play with purposelessly: (fig.) *He toyed with* (=considered, but not seriously) *the idea of changing his job.*

**trace**¹ /treɪs/ *v* **traced, tracing** [T] **1** to follow the course, line, history, development, etc. of: *The criminal was traced to London.|His family can trace its history back to the tenth century.|I can't trace* (=find) *the letter you sent me.* **2** to copy the lines or shape of (a drawing, map, etc.) using transparent paper (**tracing paper**) **–traceable** *adj*

**trace**² *n* **1** [C;U] a mark or sign showing the former presence or passing of something or someone: *The police found no trace of the man.|lost without trace* **2** [C] a very small amount of something: *traces of poison in the dead man's blood*

**trac·ing** /'treɪsɪŋ/ *n* a copy of a map, drawing, etc., made by tracing (TRACE¹ (2))

**track**¹ /træk/ *n* **1** a line or number of marks left by a person, animal, vehicle, etc., that has passed before: *We followed the fox's tracks.|The police are* **on his track** (=following him) **2** a rough path or road: *a bicycle track* **3** the metal lines on which a train runs –see picture on page 501 **4** a course specially prepared for racing: *a racetrack* –see picture on page 592 **5** one of the pieces of music on a long-playing record or TAPE¹ (2) **6 in one's tracks** *infml* where one is; suddenly: *He stopped in his tracks when he saw her.* **7 keep/lose track (of)** to keep/not keep oneself informed about a person, state of affairs, etc. **8 off the beaten track** not well-known or often visited **9 on the right/wrong track** thinking or working correctly/incorrectly **10 a one-track mind** *infml* a tendency to give all one's attention to one subject

**track**² *v* [T] to follow the track of something or someone **–tracker** *n*: *The police used tracker dogs to find the criminal.*

**track** sbdy./sthg.↔**down** *v adv* [T] to find by hunting or searching

**track·suit** /'træksuːt/ *n* a warm loose-fitting suit worn by people when training for sport

**tract**¹ /trækt/ *n* a short article, esp. about a religious or moral subject

**tract**² *n* **1** a wide stretch of land **2** *tech* a system of related organs, with one purpose

**trac·ta·ble** /'træktəbəl/ *adj fml* easily controlled **–tractability** /-tə'bɪlɪ̣ti/ *n* [U]

**trac·tion** /'trækʃən/ *n* [U] (the power used for) pulling a heavy load over a surface: *steam traction*

**traction en·gine** /'·· ˌ··/ *n* a large steam-powered vehicle, used esp. formerly for pulling heavy loads

**trac·tor** /'træktəʳ/ *n* a motor vehicle with large wheels and thick tyres used for pulling farm machinery or other heavy objects

**trade**¹ /treɪd/ *n* **1** [U] the business of buying and selling goods: *a trade agreement between England and France* **2** [C] a particular business or industry: *He works in the cotton/tourist trade.* **3** [C] a job, esp. one needing special skills: *the trade of a printer|He's a printer* **by trade**. **4** [S] an amount of business: *The shop* **does a good/bad trade** *on Saturdays.* –see JOB (USAGE)

**trade**² *v* **traded, trading 1** [I *in, with*] to carry on trade: *He trades in meat.|to trade with another country* **2** [T *for*] to buy, sell, or exchange: *They traded their clothes for food.*

**trade** sthg.↔**in** *v adv* [T *for*] to give in part payment for something new: *to trade an old car in for a new one* **–trade-in** *n*

**trade·mark** /'treɪdmɑːk‖-mɑrk/ *n* a special mark or name for a product, which can not be used by any other producer

**trade name** /'· ·/ also **brand name**– *n* a name given to a particular product, by which it may be recognized among those made by other producers

**trad·er** /'treɪdəʳ/ *n* a person who buys and sells goods

**trades·man** /'trəɪdzmən/ *n* **-men** /mən/ a person who buys and sells goods, esp. a shopkeeper

**trade un·i·on** /ˌ· '···/ also **trades union** *BrE*‖**labor union** *AmE*– *n* an organization of workers to represent their interests and deal as a group with employers **–trade unionism** *n* [U] **–trade unionist** *n*

**trade wind** /'· ·/ *n* a tropical wind that blows towards the EQUATOR (=the imaginary line running round the middle of the earth)

**trading post** /'·· ·/ *n* →POST⁵ (2)

**tra·di·tion** /trə'dɪʃən/ *n* **1** [U] the passing down of opinions, beliefs, practices, customs, etc., from the past to the present **2** [C] an opinion, belief, custom, etc., passed down in this way: *It is a tradition that women get married in long white dresses.* **–traditional** *adj* **–traditionally** *adv*

**traf·fic** /'træfɪk/ *n* [U] **1** moving vehicles in roads or streets, ships in the seas, planes in the sky, etc. –compare CIRCULATION (2) **2** trade; buying and selling: *the unlawful traffic in drugs*

**traffic in** sthg. *v prep* **-ck-** [T *with*] to carry on trade, esp. of an illegal kind, in (the stated goods): *trafficking in stolen goods* **–trafficker** *n* [*in*]

**traffic lights** /'·· ·/ *n* [P] coloured lights used for controlling and directing traffic on roads

**tra·ge·dy** /'trædʒ½di/ *n* **-dies 1** [C] a serious play that ends sadly: *Shakespeare's "Hamlet" is a very famous tragedy.* **2** [U] these plays considered as a group –compare COMEDY **3** [C;U] a terrible, unhappy, or unfortunate event: *It was a tragedy that she died so young.*

**tra·gic** /'trædʒɪk/ *adj* **1** [A] of or related to TRAGEDY (2): *a tragic actress* –compare COMIC[1] (2) **2** very sad, unfortunate, etc.: *a tragic accident*|*(infml) It was tragic when our football team lost the match.* **–tragically** *adv*

**trail[1]** /treɪl/ *v* **1** [I;T *along, behind*] to drag or be dragged behind: *The child was trailing a toy car on a string.*|*Her long skirt was trailing (along) behind her.* **2** [T] to follow the tracks of: *The hunters trailed the elephant for hours.* **3** [I *along, behind*] to walk tiredly: *The defeated army trailed back to camp.* **4** [I] (of a plant) to grow over or along the ground

**trail[2]** *n* **1** the track or smell of a person or animal **2** a path across rough country **3** a stream of dust, smoke, etc., behind something moving

**trail·er** /'treɪləʳ/ *n* **1** a vehicle pulled by another vehicle: *a car pulling a boat on a trailer* **2** an advertisement for a new film, showing small parts of it **3** *AmE* for CARAVAN (1)

**train[1]** /treɪn/ *n* **1** a line of connected railway carriages drawn by an engine: *to travel* **by train 2** a long line of moving people, vehicles, or animals **3** a part of the back of a long dress that spreads over the ground **4** a chain of related events, thoughts, etc.: *The noise interrupted my* **train of thought**.

**train[2]** *v* **1** [I;T +*to-v*/*for*] to give or be given teaching and practice in a profession or skill: *to train soldiers to fight*|*She is training to be a doctor.*|*He spends two hours a day training for the race.* **2** [T *on, upon*] to aim (a gun or HOSEPIPE, for example) at something or someone **3** [T] to direct the growth of (a plant) **–trainable** *adj* **–trainer** *n*

**train·ee** /treɪ'niː/ *n* a person who is being trained

**train·ing** /'treɪnɪŋ/ *n* [S;U] **1** the act of TRAINING[2] (1) or being trained; instruction: *to* **go into training** *for a match* **2 in/out of training** in/not in a good healthy condition for a sport, test of skill, etc.

**trait** /treɪt/ *n* a particular quality of someone or something; CHARACTERISTIC: *Generosity is her best trait.*

**trai·tor** *n* a person who is disloyal, esp. to his/her country **–traitorous** *adj esp. lit* **–traitorously** *adv*

**tra·jec·to·ry** /trə'dʒektəri/ *n* **-ries** *tech* the curved path of an object fired through the air: *the trajectory of a bullet*

**tram** /træm/ also **tramcar** *BrE*‖**streetcar** *AmE*– *n* a public vehicle, driven by electricity, that runs along metal lines set in the road

**tramp[1]** /træmp/ *v* **1** [I] to walk with firm heavy steps **2** [I;T] to walk steadily through or over: *They tramped (through) the woods all day.*

**tramp[2]** *n* **1** [C] a person with no home or job, who wanders from place to place **2** [S] the sound of heavy walking: *the tramp of the soldiers' feet on the road* **3** [C] a long walk **4** [C] *esp. AmE* an immoral woman

**tram·ple** /træmpəl/ *v* **-pled, -pling** [I;T *down, on, over, upon*] to step heavily with the feet (on); crush: (fig.) *to trample on someone's feelings*

**tram·po·line** /'træmpəliːn‖ˌtræmpə'liːn/ *n* an apparatus consisting of a sheet of material held to a metal frame by springs, on which ACROBATS and GYMNASTS jump up and down

**trance** /trɑːns‖træns/ *n* a sleeplike condition of the mind (esp. in the phrase **in a trance**)

**tran·quil** /'træŋkw½l/ *adj* calm; quiet; peaceful: *a tranquil lake/smile* **–tranquillity** *BrE*‖**tranquility** *AmE* /-'kwɪl½ti/ *n* [U] **–tranquilly** *adv*

**tran·quil·lize** also **-lise** *BrE*‖ **-quilize** *AmE* /'træŋkw½laɪz/ *v* **-lized, -lizing** [T] to make calm

**tran·quil·liz·er** also **-liser** *BrE*‖**-quilizer** *AmE* /'træŋkw½laɪzəʳ/ *n* a drug used for reducing nervous anxiety and making a person calm

**trans·act** /træn'zækt/ *v* [T] to carry (a piece of business, etc.) through to an agreement

**trans·ac·tion** /træn'zækʃən/ *n* **1** [U] the act of TRANSACTing **2** [C] something transacted; a piece of business

**trans·at·lan·tic** /ˌtrænzət'læntɪk/ *adj* connecting or concerning countries on both sides of the Atlantic ocean: *a translantic agreement*|*a transatlantic flight*

**tran·scend** /træn'send/ *v* [T] *lit* to go or be above or beyond: *The size of the universe transcends our imagination.* **–transcendence** also **transcendency**– *n* [U]

**tran·scen·den·tal** /ˌtrænsen'dentl/ *adj* going beyond human knowledge, thought, belief, and experience: *transcendental* MEDITATION

**trans·con·ti·nen·tal** /ˌtrænzkɒnt½'nentl, ˌtræns-‖ -kɑn-/ *adj* crossing a CONTINENT

**tran·scribe** /træn'skraɪb/ *v* **-scribed, -scribing** [T] **1** to make a full copy of (esp. notes or recorded matter) **2** [*for*] to arrange (a piece of music) for an instrument or voice other than the original **–transcription** /-'skrɪpʃən / *n* [C;U]

**tran·script** /'trænskrɪpt/ *n* a written or printed copy; something TRANSCRIBED

**trans·fer[1]** /træns'fɜːʳ/ *v* **-rr- 1** [I;T] to (cause to) move from one place, job, vehicle, etc., to another: *The office was transferred from Belfast to Dublin.*|*He is hoping to transfer/be transferred to another team.* **2** [T] to give the ownership of (property) to another person **–transferable** *adj* **–transference** /'trænsfərəns‖træns'fɜr- / *n* [U]

**trans·fer[2]** /'trænsfɜːʳ/ *n* **1** [C;U] (an example of) the act of TRANSFERring: *He wants a transfer to another team.* **2** [C] a drawing, pattern, etc., for sticking or printing onto a surface: *a Mickey Mouse transfer*

**trans·fig·ure** /træns'fɪgəʳ‖-gjər/ *v* **-ured, -uring** [T] to change in appearance and make glorious: *transfigured with joy* **–transfiguration** /-'reɪʃən / *n* [C;U]

**trans·fix** /træns'fɪks/ *v* [T *with; usu. passive*] to make unable to move or think because of terror, powerful interest, etc.

**trans·form** /træns'fɔːm‖-fɔrm/ *v* [T] to change completely in form, appearance, or nature: *to transform heat into power* **–transformation** /-fə'meɪʃən‖-fər-/ *n* [C;U]

**trans·form·er** /træns'fɔːməʳ‖-ɔr-/ *n* an apparatus for changing electrical force (VOLTAGE)

**trans·fu·sion** /træns'fjuːʒən/ *n* [C;U] (a case of) putting the blood of one person into the body of another: *The driver had to have a blood transfusion after the accident.* **–transfuse** *v* **-fused, -fusing** [T]

**trans·gress** /trænz'gres||træns-/ *v* [T] *fml* **1** to go beyond (a proper limit) **2** to break (a law, agreement, etc.) **–transgression** *n* [C;U] **–transgressor** *n*

**tran·si·ent** /'trænzıənt||'trænʃənt/ also **transitory**– *adj* lasting for only a short time **–transience** *n* [U]

**tran·sis·tor** /træn'zıstəʳ, -'sıstəʳ/ *n* **1** a small electrical apparatus, esp. used in radios, televisions, etc. –compare VALVE **2** also **transistor radio**– a radio that has these instead of VALVES

**tran·sit** /'trænsɪ̵t, -zɪ̵t/ *n* [U] the act of moving people or goods from one place to another: *His letter must have got lost* **in transit**.

**tran·si·tion** /træn'zıʃən, -'sı-/ *n* [C;U] (an act of) changing or passing from one state, subject, or place to another: *We hope there will be a peaceful transition to the new system.* **–transitional** *adj: a transitional period* **–transitionally** *adv*

**tran·si·tive** /'trænsɪ̵tıv, -zɪ̵-/ *adj,n* (a verb) that takes a direct OBJECT: *In this dictionary the mark [T] shows a transitive verb.* –see Study Notes on page 647

**trans·late** /trænz'leıt, træns-/ *v* **-lated, -lating** [I;T] to change (speech or writing) from one language into another: *The book was translated from French into English.* **–translation** *n* [C;U]: *I've only read Tolstoy's books* **in translation**. **–translator** *n*

**trans·lu·cent** /trænz'lu:sənt||træns-/ *adj* not transparent but clear enough to allow light to pass through **–translucence** also **translucency**– *n* [U]

**trans·mis·sion** /trænz'mıʃən||træns-/ *n* **1** [U] the act of TRANSMITting or of being transmitted **2** [C] something broadcast by television or radio **3** [C] the parts of a vehicle that carry power from the engine to its wheels

**trans·mit** /trænz'mıt||træns-/ *v* **-tt- 1** [I;T] to send out (electric signals, messages, news, etc.); broadcast **2** [T] to send or carry from one person, place, or thing to another: *to transmit a disease*

**trans·mit·ter** /trænz'mıtəʳ||træns-/ *n* **1** an apparatus that sends out radio or television signals **2** someone or something that TRANSMITS

**trans·par·en·cy** /træn'spærənsi, -'speər-/ *n* **-cies 1** [C] a piece of photographic film, on which a picture can be seen when light is passed through **2** [U] the state of being transparent

**trans·par·ent** /træn'spærənt, -'speər-/ *adj* that can be seen through: *Glass is transparent.|Her silk dress was almost transparent.*|(fig.) *a transparent* (=clear) *meaning* –compare OPAQUE **–transparently** *adv*

**tran·spire** /træn'spaıəʳ/ *v* **-spired, -spiring** [I] **1** [+ *that*] (of an event, secret, etc.) to become gradually known: *It later transpired that he had lied about the money.* **2** *infml* to happen: *Let's wait and see what transpires.*

USAGE **Transpire,** meaning "to happen", is thought by some teachers to be incorrect.

**trans·plant¹** /træns'plɑ:nt||-'plænt/ *v* [T] **1** to move (a plant) from one place and plant it in another **2** to move (an organ, piece of skin, hair, etc.) from one part of the body to another or from one person to another: *to transplant a heart* **–transplantation** /-plɑ:n'teıʃən||-plæn- / *n* [U]

**trans·plant²** /'trænsplɑ:nt||-plænt/ *n* **1** something TRANSPLANTed **2** an act or operation of TRANSPLANTing¹ (2): *to do a heart transplant*

**trans·port¹** /'trænspɔ:t||-ort/ *n* **1** [U] also **transportation** *AmE*– the act of TRANSPORTing² (1) or of being transported: *The transport of goods by air is very expensive.* **2** [U] also **transportation** *AmE*– a means or system of carrying passengers or goods from one place to another: *a public transport system|I'd like to go to the concert, but I've no transport.* (=method of getting there) **3** [C] a ship or aircraft for carrying soldiers or supplies

USAGE 1 You **ride** a horse, bicycle, or anything else that you sit on with your legs hanging down. You **drive** (=control and guide) a car or any other wheeled vehicle that you sit inside, and your passengers are **riding** in it or being **driven.** The person in control of a train or bus **drives** it, the person in control of a plane **flies** (FLY) or **pilots** it, and on a boat the person in control **sails** or **pilots** it. –see also LEAD (USAGE) 2 You **get on(to)** anything you **ride,** and later **get off** it or *(fml)* **dismount** from it; you **get on(to)** a bus or train and later **get off** it or *(fml)* **alight** from it; you **get on/off** a boat or *(fml)* **embark/disembark**; you **get on** or **board** a plane, and later **get off** it; and you **get into** and **out of** a car or taxi. 3 Notice the pattern [**by** + U], which can be used with all forms of transport: *You can go from the airport to the town centre* **by** *car,* **by** *taxi,* **by** *bus, or even* **by** HELICOPTER.

**trans·port²** /træn'spɔ:t||-ort/ *v* [T] **1** to carry (goods, people, etc.) from one place to another **2** (in former times) to send (a criminal) to a distant land as a punishment **–transportable** *adj*

**trans·port·er** /træn'spɔ:təʳ||-or-/ *n* a long vehicle on which a number of cars can be carried

**trans·pose** /træn'spəuz/ *v* **-posed, -posing** [T] **1** to change the order or position of (two or more things): *to transpose the letters of a word* **2** to change the KEY¹ (4) of (a piece of music) **–transposition** /-pə'zıʃən/ *n*

**trans·verse** /trænz'vɜ:s||træns'vɜrs/ *adj* lying or placed across: *a transverse beam* **–transversely** *adv*

**trans·ves·tite** /trænz'vestaıt||træns-/ *adj,n* (of or being) a person who likes to wear the clothes of the opposite sex **–transvestism** *n* [U]

**trap¹** /træp/ *n* **1** an apparatus for catching and holding animals: *a mouse caught in a trap* **2** a plan for deceiving and tricking a person **3** a light two-wheeled vehicle pulled by a horse **4** *infml* a mouth: *Keep your trap shut!* (=be quiet)

**trap²** *v* **-pp-** [T *for, into*] to catch in a trap or by a trick: *He trapped me into admitting I had done it.*

**trap·door** /'træpdɔ:ʳ||-dor/ *n* a small door covering an opening in a floor or roof

**tra·peze** /trə'pi:z/ *n* a short bar hung high above the ground from two ropes, used by ACROBATS and GYMNASTS

**trap·per** /'træpəʳ/ *n* a person who traps wild animals, esp. for their fur

**trap·pings** /'træpıŋz/ *n* [P] articles of dress or decoration, esp. as a sign of rank: *He wore all the trappings of high office.*

**trash** /træʃ/ *n* [U] **1** something worthless or of low quality **2** *AmE* for RUBBISH (1)

**trash·can** /'træʃkæn/ *n AmE* for DUSTBIN

**trash·y** /ˈtræʃi/ *adj* **-ier, -iest** worthless: *trashy ideas/books* –**trashiness** *n* [U]
**trau·ma** /ˈtrɔːmə, ˈtraʊmə/ *n* **-mas** *or* **-mata** /mətə/ damage to the mind caused by a sudden shock
**trau·mat·ic** /trɔːˈmætɪk/ *adj* (of an experience) deeply shocking –**traumatically** *adv*
**trav·el**[1] /ˈtrævəl/ *v* **-ll-** *BrE*‖**-l-** *AmE* **1** [I] to go from place to place; make a journey: *to travel round the world for a year*|(fig.) *His mind travelled back to* (=he remembered) *his childhood.* **2** [I;T] to pass, go, or move through (a place or distance): *How fast does light travel?*|*The news travelled fast.* **3 travel light** to travel without much LUGGAGE
**travel**[2] *n* [U] the act of travelling
USAGE Although **travel** (verb) is a general word for going from one place to another, the nouns **travel** [U] and **travels** [P] usually suggest travelling for long distances and long periods of time: *He came home after years of foreign* **travel**.|*She wrote a book about her* **travels** *in South America.* **A journey** is the time spent and the distance covered in going from one place to another: *I go to work by train, and the* **journey** *takes 40 minutes.*|*an uncomfortable* **journey** *in a crowded train.* **Voyage** is similar, but is used mainly of sea journeys (or sometimes journeys in space), and a journey by plane is a **flight**: *Take some books to read on the* **journey/voyage/flight**. A journey made for religious reasons is a **pilgrimage**, and a difficult and dangerous journey made by a group of people for a special purpose is an **expedition**: *a* **pilgrimage** *to Mecca*|*Scott's famous* **expedition** *to the South Pole*
**travel a·gen·cy** /ˈ·· ˌ···/ also **travel bureau**– *n* **-cies** a business that arranges people's holidays and journeys
**travel a·gent** /ˈ·· ˌ··/ *n* a person who owns or works in a TRAVEL AGENCY
**trav·el·ler** *BrE*‖**traveler** *AmE* /ˈtrævələʳ/ *n* a person on a journey
**traveller's cheque** /ˈ··· ˌ·/ *n* a cheque sold by a bank to a person intending to travel abroad, exchangeable at most banks for the money of the particular country
**trav·els** *n* [P] travelling; journeys –see TRAVEL (USAGE)
**tra·verse** /ˈtrævɜːs‖trəˈvɜrs/ *v* **-versed, -versing** [T] *fml* to pass across, over, or through
**trav·es·ty** /ˈtrævəsti/ *n* **-ties** a copy, account, or example of something that completely misrepresents it: *His trial was a travesty of justice.*
**trawl**[1] /trɔːl/ *v* [I;T] to fish with a TRAWL[2]
**trawl**[2] *n* a large wide-mouthed fishing net that is drawn along the sea bottom
**trawl·er** /ˈtrɔːləʳ/ *n* a fishing vessel that uses a TRAWL[2]
**tray** /treɪ/ *n* **trays** a flat piece of wood or metal with raised edges, used for carrying small articles: *a tray/trayful of glasses* –see picture on page 521
**treach·e·rous** /ˈtretʃərəs/ *adj* **1** disloyal; deceitful **2** dangerous: *treacherous currents* –**treacherously** *adv*
**treach·e·ry** /ˈtretʃəri/ *n* **1** [U] disloyalty; deceit; unfaithfulness; falseness –compare TREASON **2** [C *usu. pl.*] a TREACHEROUS (1) action
**trea·cle** /ˈtriːkəl/ *BrE*‖**molasses** *AmE*– *n* [U] a thick sticky dark liquid made from sugar
**tread**[1] /tred/ *v* **trod** /trɒd‖trɑd/, **trodden** /ˈtrɒdn‖ˈtrɑ-/ *or* **trod, treading 1** [I *on*] to walk or step: *Don't tread on the flowers!* **2** [T] to walk on, over, or along: *Every day he trod the same path to school.* **3** [T] to press firmly with the feet: *They crush the juice out of the fruit by treading it.* **4 tread on somebody's toes** to offend somebody **5 tread water** to stay upright in deep water with the head above the surface, by moving the legs
**tread**[2] *n* **1** [S] the act, manner, or sound of walking: *a noisy tread* **2** [C;U] the raised pattern on a tyre **3** [C] the part of a stair on which the foot is placed
**trea·dle** /ˈtredl/ *n* an apparatus worked by the feet to drive a machine: *the treadle of a sewing machine*
**trea·son** /ˈtriːzən/ *n* [U] (the crime of) disloyalty to one's country –compare TREACHERY –**treasonable** also **treasonous**– *adj: a treasonable crime against the state* –**treasonably** *adv*
**trea·sure**[1] /ˈtreʒəʳ/ *n* **1** [U] wealth in the form of gold, silver, jewels, etc. **2** [C] a very valuable object: *the nation's art treasures*
**treasure**[2] *v* **-sured, -suring** [T] to keep or regard as precious: *a treasured memory*
**trea·sur·er** /ˈtreʒərəʳ/ *n* a person in charge of the money belonging to a club, organization, etc.
**treasure trove** /ˈ·· ·/ *n* [U] valuable objects found hidden in the ground and claimed by no one
**trea·su·ry** *n* [*the* U +*sing./pl. v*] (*usu. cap.*) the government department that controls and spends public money –compare EXCHEQUER
**treat**[1] /triːt/ *v* [T] **1** to act or behave towards: *She treats us as/like children.* **2** to deal with; handle; consider: *This glass must be treated with care.*|*He treated the idea as a joke.* **3** to try to cure by medical means: *to treat a disease* **4** to buy or give (someone) something especially pleasant: *He treated himself to a holiday in Spain.* **5** to put (a substance) through a chemical or industrial action in order to change it: *The car has been specially treated against* RUST. –**treatable** *adj*
**treat**[2] *n* something that gives pleasure, esp. when unexpected: *It's a great treat for her to go to London.*|*This is* **my treat**. (=I will pay for everything)
**trea·tise** /ˈtriːtəs, -təz/ *n* [*on*] a serious book or article that examines a particular subject
**treat·ment** /ˈtriːtmənt/ *n* [C;U] the act, manner, or method of treating someone or something: *He's gone to hospital for special treatment.*
**treat·y** /ˈtriːti/ *n* **-ties** a formal agreement, esp. between countries
**treb·le**[1] /ˈtrebəl/ *n* **1** [C] (a person with or a musical part for) a high singing voice **2** [U] the upper half of the whole range of musical notes –compare BASS[3]
**treble**[2] *adv,adj* **1** in three parts; three together –see also TRIPLE[2] **2** (of a voice or musical instrument) high in sound: *to sing treble* –compare BASS[2]
**treble**[3] *predeterminer* three times: *He earns treble my wages.*|*The house is worth treble what they paid for it.*
**treble**[4] *v* **-led, -ling** [I;T] to make or become three times as great–see also TRIPLE[1]
**tree** /triː/ *n* a tall plant with a wooden trunk and branches: *an apple tree*|*the trees in the wood* –see picture on page 297 –**treeless** *adj*
**trek** /trek/ *v* **-kk-** [I] to make a long hard journey, esp.

## STUDY NOTES verbs

### transitive verbs

**like** and **thank** are both TRANSITIVE verbs. This means that they must be followed by a noun or noun phrase as a DIRECT OBJECT. If you take away the direct object the sentence no longer makes sense. So we can say:

*Anne* **likes** *apples.*
*They* **thanked** *Mrs Jones.*

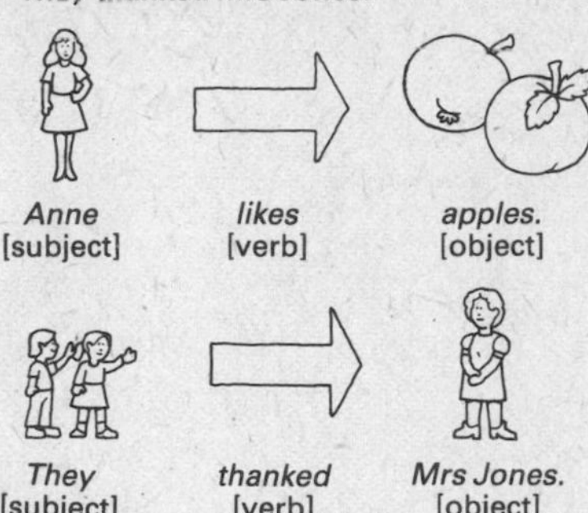

*Anne* [subject] *likes* [verb] *apples.* [object]

*They* [subject] *thanked* [verb] *Mrs Jones.* [object]

In the dictionary, transitive verbs are shown like this [T]:

> **thank** *v* [T] to give thanks to; express gratefulness to: *The old lady thanked me for helping her.*

### intransitive verbs

**rise** and **arrive** are both INTRANSITIVE verbs. This means that their meaning is complete without a direct object. So we can say:

*The family* **arrived.**
*The sun* **rose.**

*The family* [subject] *arrived.* [verb]

*The sun* [subject] *rose.* [verb]

In the dictionary, intransitive verbs are shown like this [I].

> **rise** *v* [I] (of the sun, moon, or stars) to come up; appear above the horizon: *The sun rises in the east.*

We can add other nouns to both [T] (transitive) and [I] (intransitive) verbs, but these are not direct objects:

*They thanked Mrs Jones for the presents.* *The sun rises every morning.*

---

Many verbs, like **speak** and **stop**, can be both [T] (transitive) and [I] (intransitive). These verbs look like this in the dictionary:

> **speak** *v* **1** [I] to say things; talk: *I'd like to speak to you about my essay.* **2** [T] to be able to talk in a language: *I'm learning to speak French.*

> **stop** *v* [I;T] to (cause to) cease moving or continuing an activity: *Do the buses stop at the market?* | *The driver stopped the bus and let the people get off.*

---

Some verbs, like **become**, do not have an [I] or a [T] after them. These verbs must be followed by another word for their meaning to be complete, but the word can be a noun or an adjective or an adverb. These nouns, adjectives, and adverbs always tell us something about the subject of a sentence. For example:

> **become** *v* to start to be; come to be: *He became a teacher.* | *The weather became warmer.*

Other verbs like **become** are **appear, be, feel, look, remain,** and **seem.** –see SEEM (USAGE)

---

43–960

on foot –**trek** *n: a long trek through the mountains*

**trel·lis** /ˈtrelɨs/ *n* [C;U] (a) light upright wooden framework, esp. used as a support for climbing plants

**trem·ble** /ˈtrembəl/ *v* **-bled, -bling** [I] **1** to shake uncontrollably: *to tremble with fear/cold/excitement|The whole house trembled as the train went by.* **2** [+*to-v/for*] to feel fear or anxiety: *I tremble to think what will happen.* –**tremble** *n* [S] *infml: He was* **all of a tremble**. (=trembling) –**tremblingly** *adv*

**tre·men·dous** /trɪˈmendəs/ *adj* **1** very great in size, amount, or degree: *to travel at a tremendous speed|a tremendous explosion* **2** wonderful: *We went to a tremendous party last night.* –**tremendously** *adv*

**trem·or** /ˈtreməʳ/ *n* a shaking movement: *an earth tremor* (=small EARTHQUAKE)*|a tremor of fear*

**trem·u·lous** /ˈtremjʊləs‖-mjə-/ *adj* slightly shaking; nervous: *a tremulous voice* –**tremulously** *adv* –**tremulousness** *n* [U]

**trench** /trentʃ/ *n* a long narrow hole cut in the ground; ditch

**trend** /trend/ *n* **1** a general direction; tendency: *the trend of rising unemployment|the latest trends* (=fashions) *in women's clothes* **2** **set the trend** to start or popularize a fashion

**trend·set·ter** /ˈtrend,setəʳ/ *n infml* a person who starts or popularizes a particular style or fashion

**trend·y** /ˈtrendi/ *adj* **-ier, -iest** *infml, sometimes derog* very fashionable: *a trendy dress/girl* –**trendiness** *n* [U]

**trep·i·da·tion** /ˌtrepɨˈdeɪʃən/ *n* [U] *fml* a state of anxiety: *in fear and trepidation*

**tres·pass¹** /ˈtrespəs, -pæs/ *v* [I] to go onto privately-owned land without permission –**trespasser** *n*

**trespass on/upon** sthg. *v prep* [T] *fml* to make too much use of: *It would be trespassing upon their generosity to accept any more.*

**trespass²** *n* [C;U] (an example of) the act of TRESPASSing

**tress·es** /ˈtresɨz/ *n* [P] *lit* a woman's long hair

**tres·tle** /ˈtresəl/ *n* a wooden beam fixed to a pair of legs, used esp. as a support for a table (**trestle table**)

**tri·al** /ˈtraɪəl/ *n* **1** [C;U] (an act of) hearing and judging a person or case in a court: *He is* **on trial**. (=being tried in a court of law) **2** [C;U] (an act of) testing to find quality, value, usefulness, etc.: *a trial period|She took the car* **on trial**. (=for a short time, to test it) **3** [C] a cause of worry or trouble: *That child is a trial to his parents.* **4** **stand trial** to be tried in court **5** **trial and error** a way of getting satisfactory results by trying several methods and learning from one's mistakes: *learning to cook by trial and error*

**tri·an·gle** /ˈtraɪæŋgəl/ *n* **1** a flat figure with three straight sides and three angles **2** a small three-sided musical instrument made of steel, played by being struck with a steel rod –**triangular** /-ˈæŋgjʊləʳ‖-gjə-/ *adj: a triangular piece of land*

**tribe** /traɪb/ *n* [C +*sing./pl. v*] a group of people of the same race, beliefs, language, etc., under the leadership of a chief or chiefs: *American Indian tribes* –see RACE (USAGE) –**tribal** *adj* –**tribalism** *n* [U]: *the tribalism* (=the importance of tribal feeling) *of Africa*

**tribes·man** /ˈtraɪbzmən/ *n* **-men** /mən/ a (male) member of a tribe

**trib·u·la·tion** /ˌtrɪbjʊˈleɪʃən‖-bjə-/ *n* [C;U] *fml* (a cause of) trouble, grief, and suffering: *the trials and tribulations of modern life*

**tri·bu·nal** /traɪˈbjuːnəl/ *n* [C +*sing./pl.v*] a court of people officially appointed to deal with special matters: *The* **rent tribunal** reduced my rent.

**tri·bu·ta·ry** /ˈtrɪbjʊtəri‖-bjəteri/ *n* **-ries** a stream or river that flows into a larger stream or river: *the tributaries of the Rhine*

**trib·ute** /ˈtrɪbjuːt/ *n* [C;U] **1** something done, said, or given to show respect or admiration for someone: *We* **pay tribute** *to his courage.* **2** (a) payment made by one ruler or country to another as the price of peace, protection, etc.

**trice** /traɪs/ *n* **in a trice** *infml* in the shortest possible time

**trick¹** /trɪk/ *n* **1** an act needing special skill, esp. done to confuse or amuse: *magic tricks|No one understood how I did the card trick.* **2** a special skill: *John taught me the trick of opening a bottle of wine properly.* **3** something done to deceive or make someone look stupid: *The children loved to* **play tricks on** *their teacher.* **4** the cards played or won in one TURN² (5) of a game of cards –see CARDS (USAGE) **5** **do the trick** *infml* to fulfil one's purpose: *This medicine ought to do the trick.* (=cure the disease)

**trick²** *adj* [A] *infml* **1** made for playing tricks: *a trick spoon that melts in hot liquid* **2** full of hidden difficulties: *a trick question*

**trick³** *v* [T *into*] to cheat (someone): *She tricked me into paying for her meal at the restaurant.*

**trick·e·ry** /ˈtrɪkəri/ *n* [U] the use of tricks to deceive or cheat

**trick·le** /ˈtrɪkəl/ *v* **-led, -ling** [I] to flow in drops or in a thin stream: *Blood trickled down his face.* –**trickle** *n* [S]: (fig.)a trickle of customers

**trick·ster** /ˈtrɪkstəʳ/ *n* a person who deceives or cheats people

**trick·y** /ˈtrɪki/ *adj* **-ier, -iest** **1** (of work, a state of affairs, etc.) difficult to handle or deal with; delicate **2** (of a person or actions) clever and deceitful; SLY: *a tricky politician* –**trickiness** *n* [U]

**tri·cy·cle** /ˈtraɪsɪkəl/ *n* a bicycle with three wheels, two at the back and one at the front, used esp. by children

**tri·dent** /ˈtraɪdənt/ *n* a forklike instrument or weapon with three points

**tried¹** /traɪd/ *adj* found to be good by testing: *a tried method*

**tried²** *v past tense & participle of* TRY¹

**tri·fle** /ˈtraɪfəl/ *n* **1** [C] a thing of little value or slight importance: *wasting one's money on trifles* **2** [C;U] (esp. in Britain) a dish of cakes with fruit, jelly, and cream or CUSTARD **3** **a trifle** to some degree; rather

**trifle with** sbdy./sthg. *v prep* [T] to treat without seriousness or respect: *The general is not a man to be trifled with.*

**tri·fling** /ˈtraɪflɪŋ/ *adj* of little importance or value

**trig·ger¹** /ˈtrɪgəʳ/ *n* the small tongue of metal pressed by the finger to fire a gun

**trigger²** *v* [T *off*] to start (esp. a chain of events): *Price increases trigger off demands* *for wage increases.*

**trig·o·nom·e·try** /ˌtrɪgəˈnɒmɪ̇tri‖-ˈnɑ-/ *n* the branch of MATHEMATICS (=the science of numbers) that deals with the relationship between the sides and angles of TRIANGLE*s* (=three-sided figures)

**tril·by** /ˈtrɪlbi/ *n* **-bies** *esp. BrE* a man's soft FELT hat

**trill** /trɪl/ *n* (a sound like) the rapid repeating of two musical notes –**trill** *v* [I;T]: *trilling birds*

**tril·o·gy** /ˈtrɪlədʒi/ *n* **-gies** a group of three related books, plays, etc.

**trim**[1] /trɪm/ *v* **-mm-** [T] **1** [*off*] to make neat, even, or tidy by cutting: *to have one's hair trimmed|to trim off loose threads* **2** [*with*] to decorate: *a coat trimmed with fur* **3** to reduce: *to trim one's costs* **4** to move (a sail) into the desired position

**trim**[2] *adj* tidy; neat in appearance: *a trim figure/garden* –**trimly** *adv*

**trim**[3] *n* **1** [S] an act of cutting: *to give one's hair a trim* **2** [U] proper condition; fitness: *The team was* **in (good) trim** *for the match.*

**tri·mes·ter** /traɪˈmestəʳ/ *n AmE* a TERM of three months at a school or college

**trim·ming** /ˈtrɪmɪŋ/ *n* [*usu. pl.*] something used for TRIMMING[1] (2); a pleasant addition: *duck served with all the trimmings* (=vegetables, potatoes, etc.)

**trin·ket** /ˈtrɪŋkɪ̇t/ *n* a small piece of jewellery of low value

**tri·o** /ˈtriːəʊ/ *n* **-os 1** [C +*sing./pl.v*] a group of three people, esp. musicians: *A trio is/are playing tonight.* **2** [C] a piece of music written for three performers

**trip**[1] /trɪp/ *v* **-pp- 1** [I;T *over, up*] to (cause to) catch one's foot and lose one's balance: *He tripped over a root and fell.|The boy put his leg out to trip the teacher (up).* **2** [I,T *up*] to (cause to) make a mistake: *The lawyer always tries to trip witnesses up.* **3** [I] to move or dance with quick light steps: *The girl tripped lightly down the path.*

**trip**[2] *n* **1** a usu. short journey from one place to another: *a trip to Europe|a business trip|a day trip* (=journey for pleasure lasting just one day) *to the country* **2** a fall; act of tripping

**tri·par·tite** /traɪˈpɑːtaɪt‖-ˈɑr-/ *adj* **1** having three parts **2** (of an agreement) agreed on by three parties

**tripe** /traɪp/ *n* [U] **1** the wall of the stomach of the cow or ox, eaten as food **2** *infml* worthless or stupid talk, writing, etc.: *Why do you read such tripe?*

**trip·le**[1] /ˈtrɪpəl/ *v* **-led, -ling** [I;T] to (cause to) grow to three times the amount –see also TREBLE[4]

**triple**[2] *adj* **1** having three parts **2** three times repeated: *a triple dose* (=amount) *of medicine* –see also TREBLE[2]

**triple jump** /ˈ·· ·/ *n* [*the* S] an ATHLETICS event in which the competitors take a hop, a step, and then a jump –see picture on page 592

**trip·let** /ˈtrɪplɪ̇t/ *n* any of three children born of the same mother at the same time

**trip·li·cate** /ˈtrɪplɪ̇kɪ̇t/ *adj* consisting of three parts that are exactly alike: *triplicate copies of the contract* –**triplicate** *n: The contract has been written* **in triplicate**.

**tri·pod** /ˈtraɪpɒd‖-pɑd/ *n* a three-legged support, e.g. for a camera

**trip·per** /ˈtrɪpəʳ/ *n esp. BrE, often derog* a person on a pleasure trip

**trite** /traɪt/ *adj* (of remarks, ideas, etc.) too often used to be meaningful or effective –**tritely** *adv* –**triteness** *n* [U]

**tri·umph**[1] /ˈtraɪəmf, -ʌmf/ *n* [C;U] (the joy caused by) a complete victory or success: *a triumph over the enemy|shouts of triumph* –**triumphant** *adj* –**triumphantly** *adv*

**triumph**[2] *v* [I] [*over*] to be victorious (over): *to triumph over all one's difficulties*

**tri·um·phal** /traɪˈʌmfəl/ *adj* of, related to, or marking a TRIUMPH[1]: *a triumphal arch*

**triv·i·a** /ˈtrɪviə/ *n* [P] unimportant or useless things; TRIFLE*s* (1)

**triv·i·al** /ˈtrɪviəl/ *adj* of little importance: *Why do you get angry over such trivial matters?* –**trivially** *adv* –**triviality** /-iˈælɪ̇ti/ *n* **-ties** [C;U]

**trod** /trɒd‖trɑd/ *v past tense & participle of* TREAD[1]

**trod·den** /ˈtrɒdn‖ˈtrɑdn/ *v past participle of* TREAD[1]

**troll** /trəʊl/ *n* (in ancient Scandinavian stories) one of a race of friendly or evil beings, living in caves or hills

**trol·ley** /ˈtrɒli‖ˈtrɑli/ *n* **-leys 1** any of various small low carts or vehicles, esp. one pushed by hand –see picture on page 615 **2** *esp. BrE* a small table on wheels (CASTER*s*) from which food and drinks are served

**trol·ley·bus** /ˈtrɒlibʌs‖ˈtrɑ-/ *n* a bus that draws power from electric wires running above it

**trom·bone** /trɒmˈbəʊn‖trɑm-/ *n* a large brass musical instrument with a long sliding tube –**trombonist** *n*

**troop**[1] /truːp/ *n* [C +*sing./pl. v*] **1** a band of people or animals: *a troop of monkeys/children* **2** a body of soldiers, esp. on horses or in armoured vehicles

**troop**[2] *v* [I] to move together in a group: *Everyone trooped into the meeting.*

**troop·er** /ˈtruːpəʳ/ *n* [A;C] (the title of) a soldier of the lowest rank, esp. in the CAVALRY

**troops** /truːps/ *n* [P] soldiers

**tro·phy** /ˈtrəʊfi/ *n* **-phies 1** a prize given for winning a race, competition, etc. **2** something taken after much effort, esp. in war or hunting: *to hang the lion's head on the wall as a trophy*

**trop·ic** /ˈtrɒpɪk‖ˈtrɑ-/ *n* one of the two imaginary lines (lines of LATITUDE) drawn around the world at about 23½° north (**the tropic of Cancer**) and south (**the tropic of Capricorn**) of the imaginary line round the middle of the world (EQUATOR) –**tropics** *n* [*the* P] the hot area of the world between these lines

**trop·i·cal** /ˈtrɒpɪkəl‖ˈtrɑ-/ *adj* **1** of, related to, or living in the tropics: *tropical flowers|the tropical sun* **2** very hot: *tropical weather* –**tropically** *adv*

**trot**[1] /trɒt‖trɑt/ *n* [S] **1** (of a horse) a fairly quick movement between a walk and a GALLOP **2** a fairly fast human speed between a walk and a run **3 on the trot** *infml* one after another: *to win three games on the trot*

**trot**[2] *v* **-tt-** [I;T] to (cause to) move at a TROT

**trot·ter** /ˈtrɒtəʳ‖ˈtrɑ-/ *n* [C;U] (a) pig's foot used as food

**trou·ba·dour** /ˈtruːbədɔːʳ, -dʊəʳ‖-doʳ, -dʊər/ *n* a travelling singer and poet in former times

**troub·le**[1] /ˈtrʌbəl/ *v* **-led, -ling 1** [T] to make anxious, nervous, worried, etc.: *You look troubled; what's worrying you?* **2** [I;T +*to-v/for*] (esp. in polite expressions) to cause inconvenience to (someone else or oneself): *I'm sorry to trouble you, but can you tell me the time?|Don't trouble to write when I'm* gone.|*May I trouble you for the salt?* (=please pass it to me) **3** [T] to cause (someone) pain as a disease does: *He's been troubled with a bad back for years.*

**trouble²** *n* **1** [C;U] (a) difficulty, worry, anxiety, annoyance, etc.: *to have trouble getting the car started*|*Paying rent is the least of my troubles at present.* **2** [U *with*] danger; risk; a difficulty or dangerous state of affairs: *The little boy was* **in trouble** *so I swam out to save him.*|*He told a lie rather than* **get into trouble**. (=be blamed for doing wrong) **3** [S;U] (an) inconvenience; effort: *I hope we've not put you to any trouble.*|*We must thank him for* **taking the trouble** (=causing himself work) *to cook us a meal.* **4** [C;U] (an example of) political or social disorder: *There's been a lot of trouble in this country in the past year.* **5** [S *with*] a bad point; fault: *The trouble with you is that you're stupid.* **6** [U] (a) medical condition; illness: *heart/back trouble* **7 ask/look for trouble** to behave so as to cause difficulty or danger for oneself

**troub·le·mak·er** /ˈtrʌbəlˌmeɪkəʳ/ *n* a person who habitually causes trouble

**troub·le·shoot·er** /ˈtrʌbəlˌʃuːtəʳ/ *n* a person employed to find and remove causes of trouble, usu. in an organization

**troub·le·some** /ˈtrʌbəlsəm/ *adj* causing trouble or anxiety: *a troublesome child*

**trough** /trɒf‖trɔf/ *n* **1** a long narrow boxlike container, esp. for holding water or food for animals **2** a long narrow hollow area, e.g. between two waves; DEPRESSION **3** *tech* (in METEOROLOGY) an area of lower pressure between two areas of high pressure

**troupe** /truːp/ *n* [C +*sing./pl. v*] a group of singers, actors, dancers, etc.

**trou·sers** /ˈtraʊzəz‖-ərz/ *n* [P] an outer garment covering the body from the waist down, with two parts each fitting a leg –see picture on page 563 **–trouser** *adj* [A]: *a trouser factory*|*a trouser leg* –see PAIR (USAGE)

**trous·seau** /ˈtruːsəʊ, truːˈsəʊ/ *n* **-seaux** *or* **-seaus** /səʊz/ the personal possessions, esp. clothes, that a woman brings with her when she marries

**trout** /traʊt/ *n* **trout** [C;U] (the flesh of) a fish with darkish spots on its brown skin, used for food

**trow·el** /ˈtraʊəl/ *n* **1** a tool with a flat blade for spreading cement, PLASTER, etc. **2** a small spade-like garden tool with a curved blade

**tru·ant** /ˈtruːənt/ *n* a pupil who purposely stays away from school without permission: *Anyone who* **plays truant** *will be punished.* **–truancy** *n* [U]

**truce** /truːs/ *n* (an agreement between two enemies for) the stopping of fighting for esp. a long period –compare CEASE-FIRE

**truck** /trʌk/ *n* **1** *esp. AmE* for LORRY: *Heavy trucks aren't allowed to cross this bridge.*|*The goods were taken to the harbour* **by truck**. **2** *BrE* an open railway vehicle for carrying goods: *coal trucks*

**truc·u·lent** /ˈtrʌkjʊlənt‖-kjə-/ *adj* fierce; always willing to quarrel or attack **–truculence** *n* [U] **–truculently** *adv*

**trudge¹** /trʌdʒ/ *v* **trudged, trudging** [I] to walk with heavy steps, slowly and with effort: *to trudge through deep snow*

**trudge²** *n* a long tiring walk

**true** /truː/ *adj* **truer, truest 1** in accordance with fact or reality; actual: *a true story*|*Is the news true?*|*Is it true you're going away?*|*The book is very* **true to life**. (=like actual life) **2** real; sincere: *true love* **3** [*to*] faithful; loyal: *a true friend*|*to stay true to one's principles* **4** exact: *a true copy* **5** correctly fitted or placed: *If the door's not exactly true it won't close properly.* **6 come true** to happen just as one wished, expected, dreamt, etc. **7 true to type** behaving or acting just as one would expect

**true-life** /ˌ·ˈ·◂/ *adj* [A] based on fact: *a true-life adventure story*

**truf·fle** /ˈtrʌfəl/ *n* **1** a fleshy FUNGUS that grows underground and is highly regarded as a food **2** a soft sweet

**tru·is·m** /ˈtruːɪzəm/ *n* a statement that is so clearly true that there is no need to mention it

**tru·ly** /ˈtruːli/ *adv* **1** exactly: *He is not truly stupid, but he is lazy.* **2** really: *I am truly grateful to you.* **3 yours truly** (used at the end of a formal letter before the signature) –compare FAITHFULLY, SINCERELY

**trump¹** /trʌmp/ *n* **1** (in card games) any card of a SUIT chosen to be of higher rank than the other SUITS: (fig.) *Then, he* **played his trump card** (=used an important advantage at the last minute) *and brought in a witness.* **2 turn/come up trumps** to behave in a generous or helpful way, esp. unexpectedly

**trump²** *v* [T] to beat (a card) by playing a TRUMP

**trump up** sthg. *v adv* [T] to invent (a false reason, story, etc.) in order to harm someone else: *He was sent to prison on a trumped-up charge.*

**trum·pet¹** /ˈtrʌmp₃ᵗt/ *n* **1** a brass wind instrument, played by pressing three buttons in various combinations **2** a loud cry, esp. of an elephant

**trumpet²** *v* [I] **1** to play a TRUMPET¹ (1) **2** (esp. ot an elephant) to make a loud sound **–trumpeter** *n*

**trun·cate** /trʌŋˈkeɪt‖ˈtrʌŋkeɪt/ *v* **-cated, -cating** [T] *fml* to shorten (something) by cutting a part or end off it: (fig.) *a truncated report*

**trun·cheon** /ˈtrʌntʃən/ *n* a short thick stick carried as a weapon by policemen

**trun·dle** /ˈtrʌndl/ *v* **-dled, -dling** [I;T] to (cause to) move heavily on wheels: *to trundle a cart along the street*

**trunk** /trʌŋk/ *n* **1** the thick main stem of a tree **2** the human body apart from the head and limbs **3** a large box in which clothes or belongings are stored or packed for travel **4** the very long nose of an elephant **5** *AmE* for BOOT¹ (2)

**trunk call** /ˈ· ·/ *BrE*‖**long distance call** *AmE*– *n* a telephone call made over a long distance

**trunk road** /ˈ· ·/ *n* a main road

**trunks** /trʌŋks/ *n* [P] a short trouser-like garment worn by men, esp. for swimming –see PAIR (USAGE)

**truss¹** /trʌs/ *v* [T *up*] to tie up firmly with cord, rope, etc.: *to truss (up) a chicken before cooking it*

**truss²** *n* **1** a framework of beams built to support a roof, bridge, etc. **2** a special belt worn to support muscles in a case of HERNIA

**trust¹** /trʌst/ *n* **1** [U *in*] firm belief in the honesty or worth of someone or something; faith: *It took the teacher a long time to gain the children's trust.* (=it was a long time before they trusted him) **2** [U] responsibility: *a position of trust* **3** [U] care; keeping: *After their parents' death the children were put in my trust.* **4** [C;U] (an arrangement for) the holding and controlling of property for someone else: *money* **held in trust** *for a child|to set up a trust* **5 take on trust** to accept without proof

**trust²** *v* **1** [T] to believe in the honesty and worth of; have faith in: *Don't trust him, he's dishonest.* **2** [I;T +(*that*)] to hope: *I trust you enjoyed yourself.*

**trust in** sbdy./sthg. *v prep* [T] to have faith in

**trust·ee** /trʌs'tiː/ *n* a person or firm that holds and controls property for someone else

**trust·ful** /'trʌstfəl/ also **trusting**– *adj* (too) ready to trust others: *the trustful nature of a small child* –**trustfully** *adv* –**trustfulness** *n* [U]

**trust·wor·thy** /'trʌstˌwɜːðiǁ-ɜr-/ *adj* worthy of trust; dependable –**trustworthiness** *n* [U]

**trust·y** /'trʌsti/ *adj* **-ier, -iest** *old use or humor* faithful: *My trusty old car will get us home safely.*

**truth** /truːθ/ *n* **truths** /truːðz/ **1** [U] that which is true; the true facts: *You must always tell the truth.* **2** [U] the quality of being true: *I don't doubt the truth of his information.* **3** [C] a fact or principle accepted as true: *the truths of science* **4 in truth** in fact; really

**truth·ful** /'truːθfəl/ *adj* **1** (of a statement, account, etc.) true: *a truthful account of what happened* **2** (of a person) who habitually tells the truth: *a truthful boy* –**truthfully** *adv* –**truthfulness** *n* [U]

**try¹** /traɪ/ *v* **tried, trying 1** [T +*v-ing/out*] to test by use and experience: *Have you tried this new soap?|It seems a good idea; I'll try it out.* **2** [I;T +*to-v*] to attempt: *I don't think I can do it but I'll try.|Please try to come.* **3** [T] to attempt to open (a door, window, etc.): *I think the door's locked but I'll try it just to find out.* **4** [T] to examine (a person thought guilty or a case) in a court of law: *They're going to try him for murder.* **5** [T] to test (someone's patience); annoy: *I've had a very trying time at work today.*

USAGE Note the difference between *He* **tried** *to climb the mountain.* (but he couldn't)|*He* **tried** *climbing the mountain.* (he climbed it, to see what it was like)

**try** sthg.↔**on** *v adv* [T] to put on (a garment, hat, shoe, etc.) to see if it fits

**try²** *n* **tries 1** an attempt: *Let me have a try.* **2** (in RUGBY) points won by putting the ball down behind the opposing team's GOALS (2)

**tsar, czar, tzar** /zɑːʳ, tsɑːʳ/ **tsarina, czarina, tzarina** *fem.*– *n* [A;C] the ruler of Russia before 1917

**tset·se fly, tzetze fly** /'tetsi flaɪ, 'tsetsi-, 'setsi-/ *n* a blood-sucking African fly that causes disease

**T-shirt, tee shirt** /'tiː ʃɜːtǁ-ʃɜrt/ *n* a close-fitting collarless garment, with short arms, for the upper body –see picture on page 563

**tsp** *written abbrev. said as:* TEASPOON: *one tsp of salt*

**tub** /tʌb/ *n* **1** a large round usu. wooden vessel, for packing, storing, washing, etc. **2** *infml* a bath **3** a small round esp. plastic container for food –see picture on page 615

**tu·ba** /'tjuːbəǁ'tuːbə/ *n* a large brass wind instrument that produces low notes

**tub·by** /'tʌbi/ *adj* **-bier, -biest** *infml* short and fat

**tube** /tjuːbǁtuːb/ *n* **1** [C] a hollow round pipe of metal, glass, rubber, etc., used esp. for holding liquids **2** [C] a small soft metal container, fitted with a cap, for holding TOOTHPASTE, paint, etc. –see picture on page 615 **3** [C] any hollow pipe or organ in the body **4** [S] *BrE* (*sometimes cap.*) → UNDERGROUND²: *to travel on the tube/by tube* **5** [C] → CATHODE RAY TUBE

**tu·ber** /'tjuːbəʳǁ'tuː-/ *n* a fleshy swollen underground stem, such as the potato

**tu·ber·cu·lo·sis** /tjuːˌbɜːkjʊ'ləʊsǀsǁtuːˌbɜrkjə-/ *n* [U] a serious infectious disease that usu. attacks the lungs –**tubercular** *adj*

**tub·ing** /'tjuːbɪŋǁ'tuː-/ *n* [U] metal, plastic, etc., in the form of a tube

**tu·bu·lar** /'tjuːbjʊləʳǁ'tuːbjə-/ *adj* of, being, or made of a tube or tubes: *chairs with tubular metal frames*

**T.U.C.** /ˌtiː juː 'siː/ *abbrev. for:* Trades Union Congress; the association of British trade unions –compare CBI

**tuck¹** /tʌk/ *v* [T] to put into a desired or convenient position: *Tuck your shirt into your trousers.|He had a book tucked under his arm.*

**tuck** sthg.↔**away** *v adv* [T] to put in a safe or hidden place: *She's got a lot of money tucked away.*

**tuck in** *v adv* **1** [I] to eat eagerly **2** [T] (**tuck** sbdy. **in**) → TUCK **up**

**tuck** sbdy. **up/in** *v adv* [T *in*] to make (someone) comfortable in bed by pulling the bed clothes tight

**tuck²** *n* **1** [C] a flat fold of material sewn into a garment **2** [U] *BrE* food, esp. cakes, sweets, etc., as eaten by school children: *a tuck shop*

**Tues·day** /'tjuːzdiǁ'tuːz-/ *n* the third day of the week: *He'll arrive (on) Tuesday.|I have a music lesson on Tuesdays.|(esp. AmE) She works Tuesdays.|He arrived on a Tuesday.*

**tuft** /tʌft/ *n v* [*of*] a bunch (of hair, feathers, grass, etc.) –**tufted** *adj*

**tug¹** /tʌg/ *v* [I;T *at*] to pull hard with force or much effort: *The child tugged at my arm to attract my attention.*

**tug²** *n* a sudden strong pull

**tug·boat** /'tʌgbəʊt/ also **tug**– *n* a small powerful boat used for guiding large vessels into or out of harbours, etc.

**tug-of-war** /ˌ· · '·/ *n* [C;U] a test of strength in which two teams pull against each other on a rope

**tu·i·tion** /tjuː'ɪʃənǁtuː-/ *n* [U] *more fml than* **teaching**– instruction; teaching

**tu·lip** /'tjuːlǀpǁ'tuː-/ *n* a garden plant that grows from a BULB, or its large colourful cup-shaped flowers

**tum·ble¹** /'tʌmbəl/ *v* **-bled, -bling** [I] **1** to fall or roll over suddenly, helplessly, or in disorder: *to tumble down the stairs|The children tumbled off the bus at the park.* **2** *infml* to understand suddenly: *It was a long time before she tumbled (to what I meant).*

**tumble²** *n* a fall

**tum·bler** /'tʌmbləʳ/ *n* a drinking glass with no handle or stem

**tum·my** /'tʌmi/ *n* **-mies** *infml* stomach: *a tummy ache*

**tu·mour** *BrE*ǁ**tumor** *AmE* /'tjuːməʳǁ'tuː-/ *n* a mass of diseased cells in the body

**tu·mult** /'tjuːmʌltǁ'tuː-/ *n* [C;U] *fml* (a state of) confused noise and excitement –**tumultuous** *adj: a tumultuous welcome* –**tumultuously** *adv*

**tu·na** /ˈtjuːnə‖ˈtuːnə/ also **tunny**– *n* **tuna** *or* **tunas** [C;U] (the flesh of) a large sea fish, used for food: *a tin of tuna fish*

**tun·dra** /ˈtʌndrə/ *n* [*the* S;U] a cold treeless plain in the far north of Europe, Asia, and North America

**tune**[1] /tjuːn‖tuːn/ *n* **1** an arrangement of musical sounds: *Do you know the tune to this song?* **2 in/out of tune**: **a** at/not at the correct musical level (PITCH[1] (3)): *The piano is out of tune.* **b** in/not in agreement or sympathy: *His ideas were in tune with mine.* **3 change one's tune** to change one's opinion, behaviour, etc. **4 to the tune of** to the amount of: *We were robbed to the tune of fifty pounds.*

**tune**[2] *v* **tuned, tuning** [T *up*] **1** to set (a musical instrument) at the proper musical level (PITCH[1] (3)) **2** to put (an engine) in good working order

**tune in** *v adv* [I;T *to*] to set (a radio) to receive broadcasts from a particular radio station: *We always tune in at 10 o'clock to hear the news.*

**tune·ful** /ˈtjuːnfəl‖ˈtuːn-/ *adj* having a pleasing tune; pleasant to listen to –**tunefully** *adv*

**tune·less** /ˈtjuːnləs‖ˈtuːn-/ *adj* unmusical; unpleasant to listen to –**tunelessly** *adv*

**tun·er** /ˈtjuːnəʳ‖ˈtuː-/ *n* **1** the part of a radio or television that changes the signals into sound and/or pictures **2** a person who TUNES[2] (1) musical instruments

**tu·nic** /ˈtjuːnɪk‖ˈtuː-/ *n* **1** a loose armless outer garment **2** a short coat worn by policemen, soldiers, etc., as part of a uniform

**tuning fork** /ˈ·· ·/ *n* a small steel instrument that produces a fixed musical note when struck, used in tuning (TUNE[2] (1)) musical instruments

**tun·nel**[1] /ˈtʌnl/ *n* an underground or underwater passage (for a road, railway, etc.) through or under a hill, town, etc.

**tunnel**[2] *v* **-ll-** *BrE*‖**-l-** *AmE* [I] to make a TUNNEL under or through (a hill, river, etc.)

**tup·pence** /ˈtʌpəns/ *n BrE infml* for TWOPENCE

**tur·ban** /ˈtɜːbən‖ˈtɜr-/ *n* **1** a man's head-covering of Muslim origin, consisting of a long length of cloth wound round the head **2** a woman's small tight-fitting hat

**tur·bine** /ˈtɜːbaɪn‖ˈtɜrbᵻn, -baɪn/ *n* an engine or motor driven by the pressure of a liquid or gas

**tur·bo·charg·er** /ˈtɜːbəʊˌtʃɑːdʒəʳ‖ˈtɜr-/ also **turbo** *infml*– *n* a SUPERCHARGER, driven by waste gas (EXHAUST) from an engine –**turbocharge** *v* **-charged, -charging** [T]: *My car has been turbocharged* (=a turbocharger has been fitted) *so it's very powerful.*

**tur·bot** /ˈtɜːbɒt, -bət‖ˈtɜrbət/ *n* [C;U] (the flesh of) a large fish with a flat diamond-shaped body, used for food

**tur·bu·lence** /ˈtɜːbjʊləns‖ˈtɜrbjə-/ *n* [U] **1** the state of being TURBULENT **2** irregular and violent movement of the air: *turbulence during a plane flight*

**tur·bu·lent** /ˈtɜːbjʊlənt‖ˈtɜrbjə-/ *adj* violent; disorderly; uncontrolled; stormy: *turbulent weather/winds|a turbulent period of history*

**tu·reen** /tjʊˈriːn‖təˈriːn/ *n* a large deep dish with a lid, from which soup is served

**turf**[1] /tɜːf‖tɜrf/ *n* **turfs** *or* **turves** /tɜːvz‖tɜrvz/ **1** [C;U] (a piece of) the surface of the soil with grass growing in it **2** [*the* S] horseracing

**turf**[2] *v* [T] to cover (a piece of land) with TURF[1] (1)

**turf** sbdy.↔**out** *v adv* [T] *infml* to throw out: *He was turfed out of his house for not paying the rent.*

**turf ac·coun·tant** /ˈ· ·ˌ··/ *n* → BOOKMAKER

**tur·gid** /ˈtɜːdʒᵻd‖ˈtɜr-/ *adj* (of language or style) too solemn and self-important –**turgidly** *adv* –**turgidity** /tɜːˈdʒɪdᵻti‖tɜr-/ *n* [U]

**tur·key** /ˈtɜːki‖ˈtɜrki/ *n* **-keys** [C;U] (the flesh of) a large bird bred for its meat which is used as food, esp. at Christmas

**Turkish bath** /ˌ·· ˈ·/ *n* a steam bath and MASSAGE

**tur·moil** /ˈtɜːmɔɪl‖ˈtɜr-/ *n* [S;U] a state of confusion, excitement, and trouble: *The town was* **in turmoil**.

**turn**[1] /tɜːn‖tɜrn/ *v* **1** [I;T] to (cause to) go round: *The wheel turned slowly.|She turned the key in the lock.|to turn the pages of a book* **2** [I *round*] to bend round; look round: *He turned and waved.* **3** [T] to go around: *The car turned the corner.* **4** [I;T] to (cause to) change direction: *She turned the car into the narrow street.|The car turned into the hotel entrance.|Turn right here and then left at the end of the street.|The police turned* (=pointed) *their guns at the robbers.|*(fig.)*Her condition has turned for the worse.|*(fig.)*He has turned to crime.* (=become a criminal)|(fig.) *We must now turn our attention to the coming elections.* **5** [T *in, down, back*] to fold: *He turned the corner of the page down so that he could find his place.* **6** [I;T] to (cause to) become (different): *He claimed to have invented a substance to turn iron into gold.|In 50 years this place has turned from a little village into a large town.|The heat has turned the grass brown.|He turns nasty if you laugh at him.|The heat has turned the milk.* (=made it sour)|*Don't let all this praise* **turn your head**. (=make you proud) **7** [T not *be +v-ing*] to become; reach; pass (a certain age, time, amount, etc.): *He has turned 40.* (=he is older than 40)|*It's just turned three o'clock.* (=is just after three o'clock) **8** [T *away, out*] to cause to go; send; drive: *My father would turn me out if he knew I took drugs.* **9 turn one's hand to** to begin to practise (a skill) **10 turn one's stomach** to make one feel sick

**turn** (sbdy.) **against** sbdy./sthg. *v prep* [T] to make or become opposed to or an enemy of

**turn away** *v adv* **1** [I] to refuse to look at something or someone **2** [T] (**turn** sbdy.↔**away**) to refuse to admit: *We were turned away from the restaurant because we weren't properly dressed.*

**turn back** *v adv* [I;T (=**turn** sbdy.↔**back**)] *v* to (cause to) return in the direction from which one has come: *We had to turn back because the road was blocked by snow.*

**turn** sbdy./sthg.↔**down** *v adv* [T] **1** to lessen the force, strength, loudness, etc., of (a radio, heating system, etc.): *Turn that radio down at once!* **2** to refuse (a request, person, etc.): *to turn down an offer*

**turn in** *v adv* **1** [I] *infml* to go to bed **2** [T] (**turn** sbdy./sthg.↔**in/over**) to deliver to the police

**turn off** *v adv* **1** [T] (**turn** sthg.↔**off**) to stop a flow of (water, gas, electricity, etc.): *Turn off the television!* **2** [I;T (=**turn off** sthg.)] to leave (one road) for another: *We turned off at Birmingham.* **3** [T] (**turn** sbdy. **off**) *infml* to (cause to) dislike: *He really turns me off.*

**turn on** *v adv* [T] **1** (**turn** sthg.↔**on**) to cause (water, gas, electricity, etc.) to flow: *He turned on the light.*| (fig.) *She turns on her charm whenever she wants anything.* –see OPEN (USAGE) **2** (**turn on** sbdy.) to attack (someone) suddenly **3** (**turn** sbdy. **on**) *infml* to excite or interest (a person), esp. sexually

**turn out** *v adv* **1** [T] (**turn** sthg.↔**out**) to stop (a light, heating apparatus, etc.) **2** [I] to come out or gather as for a meeting, public event, etc.: *Crowds turned out for the procession.* –compare TURNOUT **3** [T] (**turn** sthg.↔**out**) to produce: *This factory can turn out a hundred cars a day.* **4** [I +*to-v*] to happen to be in the end: *His statement turned out to be false.*

**turn over** *v adv* **1** [T] (**turn** sthg.↔**over**) to think about; consider: *to turn an idea over in one's mind* **2** [I] (of an engine) to run at the lowest speed **3** [T *to*] →TURN **in** (2) –compare TURNOVER

**turn to** sbdy./sthg. *v prep* [T] **1** to go to for help **2** to look at (the stated page) in a book

**turn up** *v adv* **1** [T] (**turn** sthg.↔**up**) to find: *to turn up new information* **2** [I] to be found: *The missing bag turned up, completely empty, in the river.* **3** [T] (**turn** sthg.↔**up**) to shorten (a garment) –compare TURN-UP **4** [I] to arrive: *She turns up late for everything.*|*Don't worry, something will turn up.* (=happen) **5** [T] (**turn** sthg.↔**up**) to increase the force, strength, loudness, etc., of (a radio, heating system, etc.) by using controls

**turn²** *n* **1** [C] an act of turning; single movement completely round a fixed point: *a couple of turns of the handle* **2** [C] a change of direction: *a turn in the road/river*|*Take* (=follow) *the second turn on the right.* –compare TURNING **3** [S] a movement or development in direction: *I'm afraid there's been* **a turn for the worse**. (=things have become worse)|*How do you explain this strange* **turn of events**? (=this strange happening)|*a turn* (=change) *in government thinking* **4** [*the* S *of*] a point of change in time: *at the turn of the century*|*the turn of the hour* **5** [C +*to-v*] a rightful chance or duty to do something: *It's my turn to drive next.*|*You've missed your turn so you'll have to wait.*|*We* **took turns** *at driving the car.* (=first she did it, then I did it, then she, etc.)|*Would you like a turn (to play)?*|*We visited the old lady* **in turn**. (=one after the other)|*I hope I haven't spoken* **out of turn**? (=spoken when I should have remained silent) **6** [C] *infml* an attack of illness: *He had one of his funny turns again last night.* **7** [S] *infml* a shock: *Seeing you gave us quite a turn.* **8** [C] (a person who gives) a usu. short performance esp. in a theatre, circus, show, etc.: *a* COMEDY (=amusing) *turn*|*the star turn* **9 a good turn** a useful or helpful action: *He did me a good turn when he sold me his car cheaply.* **10 to a turn** (esp. of food) perfectly cooked: *This meat's* **done to a turn**.

**turn·coat** /ˈtɜːnkəʊt‖ˈtɜrn-/ *n derog* a person who changes his principles, or loyalty esp. to a political party

**turn·ing** /ˈtɜːnɪŋ‖ˈtɜr-/ *n* a place where one road branches off from another: *You'll find a public telephone down the first turning on the left.* –compare TURN² (2)

**turning point** /ˈ·· ·/ *n* a moment of important change: *a turning point in history*

**tur·nip** /ˈtɜːnɪ̵p‖ˈtɜr-/ *n* [C;U] (a plant with) a large yellowish root used for food

**turn·out** /ˈtɜːnaʊt‖ˈtɜrn-/ *n* [*usu. sing.*] the number of people who come out to attend a meeting, vote, etc.: *a big turnout at the election* –compare TURN **out** (2)

**turn·o·ver** /ˈtɜːn,əʊvəʳ‖ˈtɜrn-/ *n* [S] the money value of sales in a business, or the number of workers who leave, etc., during a particular period: *a turnover of £5,000 a week* –compare TURN **over**

**turn·stile** /ˈtɜːnstaɪl‖ˈtɜrn-/ *n* a small gate with four arms, on a central post, which allows people to pass one at a time, usu. after payment

**turn·ta·ble** /ˈtɜːn,teɪbəl‖ˈtɜrn-/ *n* the round spinning surface on which a record is played

**turn-up** /ˈ· ·/ *BrE*‖**cuff** *AmE*– *n* a narrow band of cloth turned upwards at the bottom of a trouser leg –compare TURN **up** (3)

**tur·pen·tine** /ˈtɜːpəntaɪn‖ˈtɜr-/ also **turps** /tɜːps‖tɜrps/ *infml*– *n* [U] a thin oil, used for thinning or removing paint

**tur·quoise** /ˈtɜːkwɔɪz, -kwɑːz‖ˈtɜrkwɔɪz/ *adj,n* [U] (the colour of) a bluish-green precious mineral

**tur·ret** /ˈtʌrɪ̵t/ *n* **1** a small tower, usu. at a corner of a larger building **2** (on a TANK (2), plane, etc.) a low heavily-armoured steel DOME, with guns on it –**turreted** *adj*

**tur·tle** /ˈtɜːtl‖ˈtɜrtl/ *n* **turtles** *or* **turtle** a COLD-BLOODED (1) animal that lives esp. in water, with a soft body covered by a hard horny shell –compare TORTOISE

**tur·tle·neck** /ˈtɜːtlnek‖ˈtɜr-/ *n esp. AmE* for POLO NECK

**tusk** /tʌsk/ *n* a very long pointed tooth, usu. one of a pair, that comes out near the mouth in certain animals such as the elephant

**tus·sle** /ˈtʌsəl/ *v* **-sled, -sling** [T *with*] *infml* to fight roughly without weapons; struggle roughly –**tussle** *n*

**tut** *interj* the sound of /tʌt/, used for expressing slight disapproval or annoyance: *Tut (tut)! I've got some chalk on my coat.*

**tu·tor** /ˈtjuːtəʳ‖ˈtuː-/ *n* **1** a teacher who gives private instruction to a single pupil or a very small class **2** (in British universities) a teacher who directs the studies of a number of students –compare LECTURER –**tutor** *v* [I;T *in*]

**tu·to·ri·al¹** /tjuːˈtɔːrɪəl‖tuːˈtorɪəl/ *adj* of or related to a TUTOR or his duties

**tutorial²** *n* (esp. in British universities) a lesson given to a very small class –compare SEMINAR, LECTURE

**tux·e·do** /tʌkˈsiːdəʊ/ also **tux** *infml*– *n* **-dos** *AmE* for DINNER JACKET

**TV** *abbrev. for*: television

**twad·dle** /ˈtwɒdl‖ˈtwɑdl/ *n* [U] *infml* foolish talk or writing; nonsense

**twang** /twæŋ/ *n* **1** a quick ringing sound such as that made by pulling then freeing a very tight string **2** a quality of speech, in which the voice sounds as though it is coming through the nose

**'twas** /twɒz‖twɑz/ *short for* (*old use or lit*) it was

**tweak** /twiːk/ *v* [T] to seize, pull, and twist (the ear or nose) with a sudden movement –**tweak** *n*

**tweed** /twiːd/ *n* [U] a coarse woollen cloth: *a tweed suit*

**tweet** /twiːt/ *v,n* [C;I] (to make) the short weak high

noise of a small bird; CHIRP

**twee·zers** /ˈtwiːzəz‖-ərz/ *n* [P] a small metal tool with two parts, esp. used for picking up or pulling out small objects –see PAIR (USAGE)

**twelve** /twelv/ *determiner,n,pron* (the number) 12 –**twelfth** /twelfθ, twelθ/ *determiner,adv,n,pron*

**twen·ty** /ˈtwenti/ *determiner,n,pron* (the number) 20 –**twentieth** *determiner,n,pron,adv*

**twenty-one** /ˌ·· ˈ·◂/ *determiner,n,pron*(thenumber) 21

**twice** /twaɪs/ *predeterminer,adv* two times: *I've read the book twice.|I work twice as hard as you.|He eats twice what you eat/twice the amount that you eat.*

**twid·dle** /ˈtwɪdl/ *v* **-dled, -dling** [T] to move (the fingers) or play with (something) aimlessly: *He just sat there, twiddling his fingers.*

**twig** /twɪg/ *n* a small thin woody stem growing from a branch –**twiggy** *adj*

**twi·light** /ˈtwaɪlaɪt/ *n* [U] the time when night is about to become day or (more usually) when day is about to become night –compare DUSK

**twill** /twɪl/ *n* [U] strong woven cotton cloth

**twin** /twɪn/ *n* **1** either of two children born of the same mother at the same time: *Jean and John are twins.|my twin sister* **2** either of two people or things closely connected or very like each other: *twin towns|twin beds* (=two single beds in a room)

**twine¹** /twaɪn/ *n* [U] strong cord or string made by twisting threads together

**twine²** *v* **twined, twining** [I;T] to twist; wind

**twinge** /twɪndʒ/ *n* a sudden sharp pain: (fig.) *a twinge of conscience*

**twin·kle** /ˈtwɪŋkəl/ *v* **-kled, -kling** [I *with*] to shine with an unsteady light: *stars twinkling in the sky|Her eyes twinkled* (=were bright) *with amusement.* –**twinkle** *n* [S]: *a twinkle of delight in his eyes*

**twin·kling** /ˈtwɪŋklɪŋ/ *n* [S] a moment: **in the twinkling of an eye** (=very short time)

**twirl** /twɜːl‖twɜrl/ *v* [I;T] to (cause to) turn round and round quickly; (cause to) spin –**twirl** *n*

**twist¹** /twɪst/ *v* **1** [T *round, together*] to wind: *She twisted her hair round her fingers to make it curl.* **2** [T] to turn: *Twist the handle and the box will open.|I twisted my foot.* (=hurt it by turning it sharply) **3** [I;T] to (cause to) change shape; bend: *The child twisted the wire|to twist* (=bend and break) *an apple off a branch|*(fig.)*He twisted my words* (=changed the meaning of what I said) *to make me look guilty.*

**twist²** *n* **1** [C] an act of twisting **2** [C;U] something, such as thread, rope, etc., made by twisting two or more lengths together **3** [C] a bend: *a road with a lot of twists* **4** [C] an unexpected change or development: *a strange twist of fate* –**twisty** *adj* **-ier, -iest**

**twist·er** /ˈtwɪstəʳ/ *n* a dishonest person who cheats other people

**twit** /twɪt/ *n infml* a stupid fool

**twitch¹** /twɪtʃ/ *v* [I;T] **1** to (cause to) move suddenly and quickly: *The horse twitched its ears.* **2** [*at*] to give a sudden quick pull to (something): *I felt someone twitch at my coat.*

**twitch²** *n* **1** a repeated short sudden movement of a muscle, done without conscious control –compare TIC **2** a sudden quick pull

**twit·ter** /ˈtwɪtəʳ/ *v* [I] **1** (of a bird) to make a number of short rapid sounds **2** [*on, about*] (of a person) to talk quickly and nervously: *He's always twittering on.* –**twitter** *n* [S;U]: *the twitter of birds*

**two** /tuː/ *determiner,n,pron* **1** (the number) 2 –compare SECOND; see Study Notes on page 494 **2 in two** into two parts: *Cut it in two.*

**two-faced** /ˌtuːˈfeɪst◂/ *adj* deceitful; insincere

**two·pence, tuppence** /ˈtʌpəns‖ˈtʌpəns, ˈtuːpens/ *n* [C;U] *BrE* **1** (a British coin worth) two pence **2 not care twopence** *infml* not to care at all

**two·penny, tuppenny** /ˈtʌpəni‖ˈtʌpəni, ˈtuːpeni/ *adj BrE* costing two pence: *a twopenny ticket*

**two-piece** /ˌ· ˈ·◂/ *adj* [A] consisting of two matching parts: *a two-piece suit*

**two·some** /ˈtuːsəm/ *n* [*usu. sing.*] *infml* a group of two people or things

**two-way** /ˌ· ˈ·◂/ *adj* moving or allowing movement in both directions: *a two-way street|two-way traffic*

**ty·coon** /taɪˈkuːn/ *n* a businessman or industrialist with great wealth and power

**ty·ing** /taɪ-ɪŋ/ *v pres. participle of* TIE²

**type¹** /taɪp/ *n* **1** [C] a particular kind, class, or group; group or class of people or things very like each other: *What type of plant is this?|She's the type of person that I admire.* **2** [C;U] (one of the) small blocks of metal or wood with the shapes of letters on them, used in printing **3** [U] printed words

**type²** *v* **typed, typing** [I;T] to write (something) with a TYPEWRITER

**type·cast** /ˈtaɪpkɑːst‖-kæst/ *v* **-cast, -casting** [T] to repeatedly give (an actor) the same kind of part: *He was typecast as a criminal because of his face.*

**type·face** /ˈtaɪpfeɪs/ *n* the size and style of the letters used in printing

**type·writ·er** /ˈtaɪpˌraɪtəʳ/ *n* a machine that prints letters by means of keys which are struck by the fingers –see picture on page 415

**ty·phoid** /ˈtaɪfɔɪd/ also **typhoid fever**– *n* an infectious disease causing fever and often death, caused by bacteria in food or drink

**ty·phoon** /taɪˈfuːn/ *n* a very violent tropical storm

**ty·phus** /ˈtaɪfəs/ [U] an infectious disease, carried by lice (LOUSE) and FLEAS, that causes severe fever

**typ·i·cal** /ˈtɪpɪkəl/ *adj* [*of*] combining and showing the main signs of a particular kind, group, or class: *a typical eighteenth-century church|It was typical of him to arrive so late.* –**typically** *adv*

**typ·i·fy** /ˈtɪpəfaɪ/ *v* **-fied, -fying** [T] to serve as a typical example of: *He typifies the Englishman abroad.*

**typ·ist** /ˈtaɪpəst/ *n* a secretary employed mainly for typing (TYPE²) letters –see picture on page 415

**tyr·an·nize**‖also **-nise** *BrE* /ˈtɪrənaɪz/ *v* **-nized, -nizing** [I;T] to use power over (a person, country, people, etc.) with unjust cruelty

**tyr·an·ny** /ˈtɪrəni/ *n* [U] **1** the use of cruel or unjust power to rule a person or country **2** government by a cruel ruler with complete power –**tyrannical** /təˈrænɪkəl/ *adj* –**tyrannically** *adv*

**ty·rant** /ˈtaɪərənt/ *n* a person with complete power, who rules cruelly and unjustly

**tyre** *BrE*‖**tire** *AmE* /taɪəʳ/ *n* a thick rubber band, solid or filled with air, that fits round a wheel: *a car tyre* –see picture on page 85

**tzar** /zɑːʳ, tsɑːʳ/ *n* [A;C] → TSAR

# U, u

**U, u** /juː/ **U's, u's** *or* **Us, us,** the 21st letter of the English alphabet

**U** *n,adj* [A;C] (in Britain) (a film) that is suitable for people of any age: *The film "Bambi" is a U.* –compare PG

**u·biq·ui·tous** /juː'bɪkwɨtəs/ *adj fml* appearing, happening, done, etc., everywhere

**ud·der** /'ʌdəʳ/ *n* the bag-like organ of a cow, female goat, etc., from which milk is produced

**UFO** /'juːfəʊ, ˌjuː ef 'əʊ/ *n* **UFO's** *abbrev. for:* unidentified (IDENTIFY) flying object; a spacecraft thought to come from another world in space

**ugh** /ʊx, ʌg/ *interj* (an expression of dislike): *Ugh! This medicine tastes nasty.*

**ug·ly** /'ʌgli/ *adj* **-lier, -liest 1** unpleasant to see: *an ugly face|Some parts of the city are rather ugly.* **2** very unpleasant: *An ugly scene developed in the crowd when a group of boys started fighting.| an ugly temper* see BEAUTIFUL (USAGE) **–ugliness** *n* [U]

**UHF** also **ultrahigh frequency** *fml*– *n* [U] (the sending out of radio waves at) the rate of 300,000,000 to 3,000,000,000 times per second, producing excellent sound quality –see also VHF

**UK** *n abbrev. for:* United Kingdom (of Great Britain and Northern Ireland)

**u·ku·le·le** /ˌjuːkə'leɪli/ *n* a musical instrument like a small GUITAR

**ul·cer** /'ʌlsəʳ/ *n* a rough place on the skin or inside the body which may bleed or produce poisonous matter: *a stomach ulcer|mouth ulcers*

**ul·te·ri·or** /ʌl'tɪərɪəʳ/ *adj* hidden or kept secret, esp. because bad: *He has an* **ulterior motive** *for seeing her: he's going to ask for some money.*

**ul·ti·mate** /'ʌltɨmɨt/ *adj* [A] **1** (the) last; being at the end or happening in the end: *The ultimate responsibility lies with the President.* **2** *infml* greatest or best: *This is the ultimate in modern science.*

**ul·ti·mate·ly** /'ʌltɨmɨtli/ *adv* in the end: *Ultimately the President makes all decisions.*

**ul·ti·ma·tum** /ˌʌltɨ'meɪtəm/ *n* **-tums** *or* **-ta** /tə/ a statement of something that must be done under a threat of force: *They gave us an ultimatum to pay the money back in five days, or they would take us to court.*

**ul·tra·ma·rine** /ˌʌltrəmə'riːn/ *adj,n* [U] (of) a very bright blue colour

**ul·tra·son·ic** /ˌʌltrə'sɒnɪk||-'sɑ-/ *adj* (of sound waves) beyond the range of human hearing

**ul·tra·vi·o·let** /ˌʌltrə'vaɪəlɨt/ *adj* (of light) beyond the purple end of the SPECTRUM and unable to be seen by human beings: *ultraviolet* RAYS –compare INFRARED

**um·bil·i·cal cord** /ʌmˌbɪlɪkəl 'kɔːd||-'kɔrd/ *n* the tube of flesh which joins the young to the mother before birth, and through which the young is fed

**um·brage** /'ʌmbrɪdʒ/ *n* **take umbrage** to show that one's feelings have been hurt

**um·brel·la** /ʌm'brelə/ *n* **1** an arrangement of cloth over a folding frame with a handle, used for keeping rain off the head **2** a protecting power: *a country under the umbrella of the United Nations*

**um·pire¹** /'ʌmpaɪəʳ/ *n* a judge in charge of a game such as cricket, tennis, etc. –see REFEREE (USAGE); see picture on page 592

**umpire²** *v* **-pired, -piring** [I;T] to act as an UMPIRE

**ump·teen** /ˌʌmp'tiːn◂/ *determiner,pron infml* a large number (of): *I've seen that film umpteen times.* **–umpteenth** *n,determiner: That's the umpteenth time I've told you not to do that!*

**UN** *n abbrev. for:* United Nations

**un·a·bashed** /ˌʌnə'bæʃt◂/ *adj* not ashamed, esp. when something unusual or EMBARRASSing happens

**un·a·bat·ed** /ˌʌnə'beɪtɨd/ *adj* (of a wind, a person's strength, etc.) without losing force: *The storm continued unabated.* –see also ABATE

**un·a·ble** /ʌn'eɪbəl/ *adj* [F +*to-v*] not able; without the power, knowledge, time, etc., to do something: *I'd like to go, but I'm unable to.* –compare INABILITY

**un·a·bridged** /ˌʌnə'brɪdʒd◂/ *adj* (esp. of something written) not ABRIDGED; not shortened

**un·ac·com·pa·nied** /ˌʌnə'kʌmpənid◂/ *adj* **1** not accompanied (ACCOMPANY); without someone or something else going with one: *Children unaccompanied by an* ADULT (=a grown-up person) *will not be admitted.* **2** without music as ACCOMPANIMENT: *an unaccompanied song*

**un·ac·coun·ta·ble** /ˌʌnə'kaʊntəbəl/ *adj* surprising; not easily explained: *unaccountable behaviour* –see also ACCOUNT **for –unaccountably** *adv*

**un·a·dul·te·rat·ed** /ˌʌnə'dʌltəreɪtɨd/ *adj* **1** (esp. of food) not mixed with impure substances **2** [A] complete; UTTER: *unadulterated nonsense*

**un·af·fect·ed** /ˌʌnə'fektɨd/ *adj* **1** not AFFECTED (1): *People in the south of the country were unaffected by the lack of petrol.* **2** not AFFECTED; natural in behaviour or character: *unaffected joy*

**u·nan·i·mous** /juː'nænɨməs/ *adj* (of people) all agreeing; (of decisions) made with everyone agreeing: *The vote was unanimous* **–unanimously** *adv* **–unanimity** /'juːnə'nɪmɨti/ *n* [U]

**un·ap·proa·cha·ble** /ˌʌnə'prəʊtʃəbəl◂/ *adj* (of a person) difficult to talk to; not seeming to encourage friendliness

**un·armed** /ˌʌn'ɑːmd◂||-'ɑr-/ *adj* without weapons

**un·as·sum·ing** /ˌʌnə'sjuːmɪŋ◂, -'suː-||-'suː-/ *adj* not showing a wish to be noticed; quiet in manner

**un·at·tached** /ˌʌnə'tætʃt◂/ *adj* **1** not connected **2** not married or ENGAGED (3)

**un·at·tend·ed** /ˌʌnə'tendɨd◂/ *adj* alone; without people present or in charge: *Your car will be damaged if you leave it unattended here.*

**un·a·wares** /ˌʌnə'weəz||-'weərz/ *adv* **1** unintentionally or without noticing **2 take someone unawares** to surprise someone

**un·bal·anced** /ˌʌnˈbælənst/ *adj* (of a person, his/her character, etc.) slightly mad: *He became a bit unbalanced after his wife died.*
**un·bear·a·ble** /ʌnˈbeərəbəl/ *adj* too bad to be borne: *unbearable heat* –**unbearably** *adv*
**un·be·lie·va·ble** /ˌʌnbɨˈliːvəbəl/ *adj* very surprising: *It's unbelievable how many children she has!* –**unbelievably** *adv*
**un·bend** /ʌnˈbend/ *v* **-bent** /bent/, **-bending** [I] to behave in an informal manner, esp. when usu. formal; RELAX: *She was very formal at first, but then she unbent a little and told a joke.*
**un·bend·ing** /ʌnˈbendɪŋ/ *adj* refusing to change opinions, decisions, etc.
**un·born** /ˌʌnˈbɔːn◂‖-ɔrn/ *adj* not yet born
**un·bound·ed** /ʌnˈbaʊndɨd/ *adj* limitless; far-reaching: *unbounded joy*
**un·bri·dled** /ʌnˈbraɪdld/ *adj esp.lit* not controlled: *unbridled anger*
**un·bur·den** /ˌʌnˈbɜːdn‖-ɜr-/ *v* [T *of*] to free (oneself, one's mind, etc.) by talking about a secret trouble: *She unburdened herself (of her secret) to me.*
**un·but·ton** /ˌʌnˈbʌtn/ *v* [T] to unfasten the buttons of
**un·called-for** /ʌnˈkɔːld fɔːʳ/ *adj* not deserved or right: *Such rudeness is quite uncalled-for.*
**un·can·ny** /ʌnˈkæni/ *adj* **-nier, -niest** mysterious; not natural or usual: *There was an uncanny silence before we heard the strange voice.* –**uncannily** *adv*
**un·cared-for** /ʌnˈkeəd fɔːʳ‖-ˈkeərd-/ *adj* not well looked after: *uncared-for clothes*
**un·ce·re·mo·ni·ous** /ˌʌnserɨˈməʊnɪəs/ *adj* **1** informal: *an unceremonious but sincere welcome* **2** not done politely; rudely quick: *She finished the meal with unceremonious haste.* –**unceremoniously** *adv* –**unceremoniousness** *n* [U]
**un·cer·tain** /ʌnˈsɜːtn‖-ɜr-/ *adj* **1** [F] not certain; doubtful: *I'm uncertain about how to get there.* **2** undecided or unable to decide: *Our holiday plans are still uncertain.* **3** changeable: *uncertain weather* –**uncertainly** *adv* –**uncertainty** *n* **-ties** [C;U]
**un·char·i·ta·ble** /ʌnˈtʃærɨtəbəl/ *adj* not kind or fair in judging others: *an uncharitable remark*
**un·chart·ed** /ʌnˈtʃɑːtɨd‖-ɑr-/ *adj lit* (of a place) not known well enough for records, esp. maps, to be made: *the uncharted forests of Brazil*
**un·checked** /ˌʌnˈtʃekt◂/ *adj* not prevented from moving, developing, etc.; not CHECKED[2] (3): *The disease spread unchecked.*
**un·cle** /ˈʌŋkəl/ *n* [A;C] *(often cap.)* the brother of one's father or mother, or the husband of one's aunt: *He's my uncle.|Take me swimming, Uncle (Jack)!* –see picture on page 217
**un·clean** /ˌʌnˈkliːn◂/ *adj* not clean; not considered pure, esp. in a religious way: *In ancient times* LEPERS *were thought unclean.*
**Uncle Sam** /ˌ·· ˈ·/ *n infml* the US
**un·com·for·ta·ble** /ʌnˈkʌmftəbəl/ *adj* not comfortable: *an uncomfortable chair*|(fig.) *I felt uncomfortable* (=EMBARRASSed) *when John and Jane started arguing with each other.* –**uncomfortably** *adv*
**un·com·mit·ted** /ˌʌnkəˈmɪtɨd◂/ *adj* [*to*] not COMMITTED; not having given loyalty to any one thing, group, belief, etc.: *She will join the club later, but at the moment wants to remain uncommitted.*
**un·com·mon·ly** /ʌnˈkɒmənli‖-ˈkɑ-/ *adv fml & old use* very; unusually: *That's uncommonly kind of you.*
**un·com·pro·mis·ing** /ʌnˈkɒmprəmaɪzɪŋ‖-ˈkɑm-/ *adj* refusing to change ideas or decisions –**uncompromisingly** *adv*
**un·con·cerned** /ˌʌnkənˈsɜːnd‖-ɜr-/ *adj* [*about*] not CONCERNED; not worried or anxious: *She must have hurt herself, but she seemed quite unconcerned.* –**unconcernedly** /-nɨdli/ *adv*
**un·con·di·tion·al** /ˌʌnkənˈdɪʃənəl/ *adj* not limited by any conditions: *unconditional freedom/surrender* –**unconditionally** *adv*
**un·con·scious**[1] /ʌnˈkɒnʃəs‖-ˈkɑn-/ *adj* **1** having lost consciousness: *She hit her head and was unconscious for several minutes.* **2** not intentional: *unconscious rudeness* –see CONSCIOUS (USAGE) –**unconsciously** *adv* –**unconsciousness** *n* [U]
**unconscious**[2] *n* → SUBCONSCIOUS
**un·cork** /ʌnˈkɔːk‖-ɔrk/ *v* [T] to open (esp. a bottle) by removing the CORK[1] (2)
**un·count·a·ble** /ˈʌnkaʊntəbəl/ *adj* that cannot be counted: *An* **uncountable noun** *is marked* [U] *in this dictionary.* –opposite **countable**; see Study Notes on page 494
**un·couth** /ʌnˈkuːθ/ *adj* not having good manners; rough in speech and ways: *an uncouth young man*
**un·cov·er** /ʌnˈkʌvəʳ/ *v* [T] to remove a covering from: (fig.) *The police have uncovered a plan to shoot the President.*
**un·crit·i·cal** /ʌnˈkrɪtɪkəl/ *adj* [*of*] not CRITICAL; not making any judgments; (unwisely) accepting, without deciding if good or bad –**uncritically** *adv*
**unc·tu·ous** /ˈʌŋktʃuəs/ *adj fml* too smooth in speech; showing insincere kindness, interest, etc. –**unctuously** *adv* –**unctuousness** *n* [U]
**un·cut** /ˌʌnˈkʌt◂/ *adj* **1** (of a film or story) not cut; not made shorter **2** (of a diamond or precious stone) not shaped for use in jewellery, etc.
**un·daunt·ed** /ʌnˈdɔːntɨd/ *adj* not at all discouraged by danger or difficulty; bold
**un·de·cid·ed** /ˌʌndɪˈsaɪdɨd/ *adj* **1** in doubt: *I'm undecided about where to go for my holidays.* **2** without any decision or result being reached: *The match was left undecided.*
**un·de·ni·a·ble** /ˌʌndɪˈnaɪəbəl/ *adj* clearly and certainly so, in existence, etc.: *His skill is undeniable, but he works too slowly.* –**undeniably** *adv*
**un·der**[1] /ˈʌndəʳ/ *adv* in or to a lower place; below: *children of seven and under* (=younger)
**under**[2] *prep* **1** directly below; covered by: *to breathe under water|The insect crept under the door.|What are you wearing under your coat?* –see picture on page 474 **2** less than; below: *under £5|children under seven* (=younger than seven) –opposite **over 3** working for; controlled by: *She has three secretaries under her.* **4** during the rule of: *Spain under Franco* **5** in the class of (a heading): *Iron comes under "Metals" in the list.* **6** (used to express various states or conditions): *under/in the* CIRCUMSTANCES*|under the influence of alcohol|The matter is still under discussion* (=being talked about.|*I am under contract so I must finish the job.|I was* **under the impression** (=I thought) *that he was honest.|to work under great difficulties* **7 under age**

too young in law, esp. for drinking alcohol, entering certain public places alone, driving a car, etc. **8** **under cover (of)** hidden or sheltered (by): *They escaped under cover of darkness.* –compare BELOW, BENEATH

**un·der·arm** /ˈʌndərɑːm‖-ɑrm/ *adj,adv* **1** (in sport) (done) with the hand not moving above the shoulder –opposite **overarm** **2** *euph* of the ARMPIT

**un·der·car·riage** /ˈʌndəˌkærɪdʒ‖-ər-/ *n* the wheels of an aircraft

**und·er·charge** /ˌʌndəˈtʃɑːdʒ‖ˌʌndərˈtʃɑrdʒ/ *v* **-charged, -charging** [I;T] to take too small an amount of money from (someone); charge too little –see also OVERCHARGE

**un·der·clothes** /ˈʌndəkləuðz, -kləuz‖-dər-/ also **underclothing** [U]– *n* [P] → UNDERWEAR

**un·der·coat** /ˈʌndəkəut‖-dər-/ *n* a covering of paint put onto a surface as a base for a top covering of paint

**un·der·cov·er** /ˌʌndəˈkʌvəʳ◂‖-dər-/ *adj* acting or done secretly, esp. as a SPY: *an undercover agent*

**un·der·cur·rent** /ˈʌndəˌkʌrənt‖-dər-/ *n* a hidden current of water beneath the surface: (fig.) *An undercurrent of violence could be felt as you walked around the town.*

**un·der·cut** /ˌʌndəˈkʌt‖-ər-/ *v* **-cut, -cutting** [T] to sell goods or services more cheaply than (a competitor)

**un·der·dog** /ˈʌndədɒg‖ˈʌndərdɔg/ *n* **1** a person, country, etc., which is expected to lose in a competition with another **2** a poor weak person, country, etc. that is always treated badly by others

**un·der·done** /ˌʌndəˈdʌn◂‖-ər-/ *adj* not completely cooked –see also OVERDONE

**un·der·es·ti·mate** /ˌʌndərˈestəmeɪt/ *v* **-mated, -mating** [I;T] to have too low an opinion of the degree or number of: *I underestimated the cost of the journey, and now have no money left.* –see also OVERESTIMATE

**un·der·foot** /ˌʌndəˈfʊt‖-ər-/ *adv* below one's feet; for walking on: *The ground was stony underfoot.*

**un·der·go** /ˌʌndəˈgəu‖-dər-/ *v* **-went** /ˈwent/, **-gone** /ˈgɒn‖ˈgɔn/, **-going** [T] to experience (esp. suffering or difficulty): *She is undergoing treatment at the hospital.*

**un·der·grad·u·ate** /ˌʌndəˈgrædʒuət‖-ər-/ also **undergrad** /ˈʌndəgræd‖-ər-/ *infml*– *n* a university student who has not yet taken his/her first degree –see also GRADUATE

**un·der·ground¹** /ˈʌndəgraund‖-ər-/ *adj* **1** below the surface of the earth: *an underground passage* **2** secret; representing a political view which is not acceptable to the government: *an underground newspaper* –**underground** /ˌ··ˈ·/ *adv*

**underground²** also **tube** *BrE*‖**subway** *AmE*– *n* a railway system in which the trains run in passages under the surface of the ground: *We travelled across London on the underground.*|*We went* **by underground**. –compare METRO

**un·der·growth** /ˈʌndəgrəuθ‖-dər-/ *n* [U] bushes, tall plants, etc., growing around and under trees: *to hide in the undergrowth*

**un·der·hand** /ˌʌndəˈhænd◂‖-ər-/ also **underhanded**– *adj* dishonest, esp. secretly: *He got the money in a very underhand manner.*

**un·der·lie** /ˌʌndəˈlaɪ‖-ər-/ *v* **-lay** /ˈleɪ/, **-lain** /leɪn/, **-lying** [T] (of feelings and qualities) to form a (hidden) explanation of: *Does some personal difficulty underlie his lack of interest in work?*

**un·der·line** /ˌʌndəˈlaɪn‖-ər-/ also **underscore**– *v* **-lined, -lining** [T] to mark (one or more words) by drawing a line underneath, esp. to show importance or to give force: (fig.)*The accident at the factory underlines* (=shows the importance of) *the need for better safety standards.*

**un·der·manned** /ˌʌndəˈmænd‖-ər-/ *adj* →UNDERSTAFFED –see also MAN²

**un·der·men·tioned** /ˌʌndəˈmenʃənd◂‖-ər-/ *adj* [A] *fml* mentioned later in the same piece of writing

**un·der·mine** /ˌʌndəˈmaɪn‖-ər-/ *v* **-mined, -mining** [T] to wear away (something) from beneath, removing support: *The house is unsafe since the* FOUNDATIONS *were undermined by floods.*|*Illness undermined his strength.*

**un·der·neath¹** /ˌʌndəˈniːθ‖-ər-/ *prep,adv* under; below: *The insect crept underneath the door.*|*She wore a coat with a dress underneath.*

**underneath²** *n* [S] the lower part of something; bottom surface: *the underneath of the table*

**un·der·nour·ish** /ˌʌndəˈnʌrɪʃ‖-ər-/ *v* [T] to feed with too little or bad quality food, causing lack of growth –see also NOURISH –**undernourishment** *n* [U]

**un·der·pants** /ˈʌndəpænts‖-ər-/ *n* [P] short underclothes for men or women, covering the lower part of the body –see PAIR (USAGE)

**un·der·pass** /ˈʌndəpɑːs‖ˈʌndərpæs/ *n* a road or (esp.) a path for walkers (SUBWAY) that goes under another road

**un·der·priv·i·leged** /ˌʌndəˈprɪvəlɪdʒd‖-dər-/ *adj* (of people) not having the advantages of other people

**un·der·rate** /ˌʌndəˈreɪt/ *v* **-rated, -rating** [T] to have too low an opinion of (ability, strength, etc.): *We underrated his powers as a speaker.* –see also OVERRATE

**un·der·score** /ˌʌndəˈskɔːʳ‖ˌʌndərˈskor/ *v* **-scored, -scoring** [T] → UNDERLINE

**un·der·shirt** /ˈʌndəʃɜːt‖ˈʌndərʃɜrt/ *n AmE* for VEST

**un·der·side** /ˈʌndəsaɪd‖-ər-/ *n* the part underneath; lower side or surface: *the underside of a car*

**un·der·signed** /ˈʌndəsaɪnd‖-ər-/ *adj* **the undersigned** the person(s) whose signature(s) is/are lower on the paper: *The undersigned (persons) wish to be considered for election: John Smith, Joe Brown, Mary Jones.*

**un·der·sized** /ˌʌndəˈsaɪzd◂‖-ər-/ also **undersize**– *adj* too small or smaller than usual

**un·der·staffed** /ˌʌndəˈstɑːft‖ˌʌndərˈstæft/ also **undermanned**– *adj* having too few workers: *The office is understaffed since the secretary left.*

**un·der·stand** /ˌʌndəˈstænd‖-ər-/ *v* **-stood** /ˈstʊd/, **-standing** [not *be* +*v-ing*] **1** [I;T] to know or get the meaning of (something): *Do you understand (this idea)?*|*I can't understand modern art.* **2** [T] to know or feel closely the nature of (a person, feelings, etc.): *I understand how you feel.* **3** [T +(*that*)] *fml or polite* to have been informed; have found out (a fact): *I understand you're coming to work for us.* **4** [T

+(*that*)] to take or judge (as the meaning): *By "children" it's understood (that) they mean people under 14.|We understood them to mean that they would wait for us.* **5 make oneself understood** to make one's meaning clear to others, esp. in speech –**understandable** *adj* –**understandably** *adv: He was understandably upset when he lost the game.*

**un·der·stand·ing** /ˌʌndəˈstændɪŋ‖-ər-/ *n* **1** [C;U] the act of understanding; power to judge: *According to my understanding of the letter, he owes you money.* **2** [S;U] sympathy: *There is (a) deep understanding between them.* **3** [C] a private, not formal, agreement: *We have come to an understanding.* (=reached an agreement)

**un·der·state** /ˌʌndəˈsteɪt‖-ər-/ *v* **-stated, -stating** [T] to cause (something) to seem less important than it is: *They understated the problem.* –see also OVERSTATE

**un·der·state·ment** /ˈʌndəˌsteɪtmənt‖-dər-/ *n* (a) statement which is not strong enough: *To say the film was bad is an understatement.*

**un·der·stud·y** /ˈʌndəˌstʌdi‖-ər-/ *n* **-ies** an actor who learns an important part in a play so as to take the place of the person who plays that part, if necessary

**un·der·take** /ˌʌndəˈteɪk‖-ər-/ *v* **-took** /ˈtʊk/, **-taken** /ˈteɪkən/, **-taking** [T] **1** to take up (a position); start on (work): *She undertook responsibility for the changes.* **2** [+*to-v*(*that*)] to promise or agree: *She undertook to pay back the money within six months.*

**un·der·tak·er** /ˈʌndəteɪkəʳ‖-dər-/ *n* a person whose job it is to arrange funerals

**un·der·tak·ing** /ˌʌndəˈteɪkɪŋ‖ˈʌndərteɪ-/ *n* **1** a piece of work, or something needing effort: *To start a new farm is rather a large undertaking.* **2** [+*to-v*(*that*)] a promise: *I want a firm undertaking that you won't be late again.*

**un·der·tone** /ˈʌndətəʊn‖-dər-/ *n* a quiet voice: *He spoke in an undertone.*

**un·der·wa·ter** /ˌʌndəˈwɔːtəʳ◂‖-dər-/ *adj,adv* (used, done, etc.) below the surface of the water: *an underwater camera|They swam underwater.*

**un·der·wear** /ˈʌndəweəʳ‖-dər-/ also **underclothes** [P], **underclothing**– *n* [U] the clothes worn next to the body under other clothes, such as VESTS, UNDERPANTS, BRAS, etc.

**un·der·weight** /ˌʌndəˈweɪt◂‖-ər-/ *adj* [after *n*] weighing too little: *He is several pounds underweight.* –see also OVERWEIGHT; see THIN (USAGE)

**un·der·went** /ˌʌndəˈwent‖-ər-/ *v past tense of* UNDERGO

**un·der·world** /ˈʌndəwɜːld‖ˈʌndərwɜrld/ *n* **1** (*usu. cap.*) (in ancient stories) the place where the spirits of the dead live **2** the criminal world

**un·de·si·ra·ble**[1] /ˌʌndɪˈzaɪərəbəl/ *adj fml* not DESIRABLE; unpleasant; not wanted –**undesirability** /-rəˈbɪlɪ̥ti/ *n* [U]

**undesirable**[2] *n* a person not wanted or liked by other people

**un·de·vel·oped** /ˌʌndɪˈveləpt/ *adj* (usu. of a place) not DEVELOPed; in its natural state, esp. not having industry, mining, modern farming, etc.

**un·dis·tin·guished** /ˌʌndɪˈstɪŋgwɪʃt◂/ *adj* not DISTINGUISHED; ordinary; not excellent: *an undistinguished performance/writer*

**un·di·vid·ed** /ˌʌndɪˈvaɪdɪ̥d◂/ *adj* complete: *to give one's* **undivided attention**

**un·do** /ʌnˈduː/ *v* **-did** /ˈdɪd/, **-done**/ˈdʌn/, **-doing** [T] **1** to unfasten (what is tied or wrapped): *to undo the string round a parcel|He undid the parcel.* –see also UNDONE, DO **up** (1,3) **2** to remove the effects of: *The sudden fire undid months of hard work.*

**un·do·ing** /ʌnˈduːɪŋ/ *n* [S] the cause of ruin, failure, etc.: *Our attempt to climb higher was our undoing: we fell off the rock.* –compare MAKING

**un·done** /ˌʌnˈdʌn◂/ *adj* **1** [F] unfastened or loose: *Your button has come undone.* **2** not done

**un·doubt·ed** /ʌnˈdaʊtɪ̥d/ *adj* known for certain to be (so): *his undoubted wealth* –**undoubtedly** *adv*: *That is undoubtedly true.*

**un·dreamed-of** /ʌnˈdriːmd əv, -ɒv‖- əv, -ɑv/ also **undreamt-of** /ʌnˈdrempt əv, -ɒv‖- əv, -ɑv/– *adj* [A] better than could have been imagined: *undreamed-of happiness/wealth*

**un·dress** /ʌnˈdres/ *v* **1** [I] to take one's clothes off: *The doctor asked me to undress.|I (got) undressed and went to bed.* **2** [T] to take the clothes off (someone): *He undressed the baby and put her in the bath.*

**un·due** /ˌʌnˈdjuː◂‖-ˈduː◂/ *adj* [A] too much; not suitable: *with undue haste*

**un·du·late** /ˈʌndjʊleɪt‖-dʒə-/ *v* **-lated, -lating** [I] to move or lie like waves rising and falling: *undulating hills* –**undulation** *n* [C;U]

**un·du·ly** /ʌnˈdjuːli‖-ˈduː-/ *adv* too much (so); very: *not unduly worried|not worried unduly*

**un·earth** /ʌnˈɜːθ‖-ˈɜrθ/ *v* [T] to dig up: *to unearth a box buried under a tree*|(fig.) *to unearth a secret*

**un·earth·ly** /ʌnˈɜːθli‖-ˈɜr-/ *adj* **1** not natural; GHOSTLY: *to feel an unearthly presence in the room* **2** *infml* (of time) very inconvenient, esp. because too early or late: *What an unearthly time of night to call!*

**un·eas·y** /ʌnˈiːzi/ *adj* **-ier, -iest** not comfortable, esp. because worried or anxious: *uneasy about the future* –**uneasily** *adv* –**uneasiness, unease** *n* [U]

**un·e·co·nom·ic** /ˌʌniːkəˈnɒmɪk, ˌʌnekə-‖-ˈnɑ-/ also **uneconomical**– *adj* not producing profit; wasteful: *an uneconomic use of time* –compare ECONOMICAL –**uneconomically** *adv*

**un·ed·u·cat·ed** /ʌnˈedʒʊkeɪtɪ̥d‖-dʒə-/ *adj* not EDUCATED; showing a lack of (good) education: *uneducated speech*

**un·em·ployed** /ˌʌnɪmˈplɔɪd/ *adj* not having a job: *There are many unemployed workers in this town.*

**un·em·ploy·ment** /ˌʌnɪmˈplɔɪmənt/ *n* [U] **1** a lack of jobs for a large number of people in a society: *Unemployment became worse as factories closed.* **2** the condition of lacking a job

**un·en·light·ened** /ˌʌnɪnˈlaɪtənd/ *adj* not ENLIGHTENed; not having knowledge, sometimes because uneducated; IGNORANT

**un·en·vi·a·ble** /ʌnˈenvɪəbəl/ *adj* unpleasant; not to be wished for: *The policeman had the unenviable job of telling the woman that her husband was dead.*

**un·e·qual** /ʌnˈiːkwəl/ *adj* **1** [*in, to*] not of equal size, value, etc.: *unequal amounts|unequal in size* **2** [F *to*] (of a person) not having enough strength, ability, etc.: *He was unequal to the job.* –**unequally** *adv*

**un·e·qualled** *BrE*‖**unequaled** *AmE* /ʌnˈːkwəld/ *adj* the greatest possible: *unequalled courage*

**un·e·quiv·o·cal** /ˌʌnɪˈkwɪvəkəl/ *adj* not EQUIVOCAL (1); totally clear in meaning –**unequivocally** *adv*

**un·er·ring** /ʌnˈɜːrɪŋ/ *adj* without making a mistake: *unerring judgment/aim* –**unerringly** *adv*

**un·e·ven** /ʌnˈiːvən/ *adj* **1** not smooth or even: *Her hair has been badly cut and the ends are uneven.* **2** of varying quality: *a rather uneven* (=sometimes bad) *piece of writing* –**unevenly** *adv* –**unevenness** *n* [U]

**un·fail·ing** /ʌnˈfeɪlɪŋ/ *adj* (esp. of something good) never ceasing to be (so): *with unfailing interest/courage* –**unfailingly** *adv*

**un·faith·ful** /ʌnˈfeɪθfəl/ *adj* [*to*] not FAITHFUL (3); disloyal to one's marriage partner or lover by having a sexual relationship with another person

**un·fath·o·ma·ble** /ʌnˈfæðəməbəl/ *adj* which cannot be understood: *an unfathomable mystery* –**unfathomably** *adv*

**un·fa·vou·ra·ble** *BrE*‖**unfavorable** *AmE* /ʌnˈfeɪvərəbəl/ *adj* not favourable; not good: *unfavourable weather|I've been hearing unfavourable reports about your work.* –**unfavourably** *adv*

**un·feel·ing** /ʌnˈfiːlɪŋ/ *adj* cruel; not sympathetic towards others: *an unfeeling* ATTITUDE *towards other people* –**unfeelingly** *adv*

**un·flag·ging** /ʌnˈflægɪŋ/ *adj* without tiring or stopping: *an unflagging interest in the job*

**un·flinch·ing** /ʌnˈflɪntʃɪŋ/ *adj* fearless; firm: *unflinching courage* –**unflinchingly** *adv*

**un·fold** /ʌnˈfəʊld/ *v* **1** [T] to open from a folded position: *She opened the envelope, took out the letter, and unfolded it.* **2** [I;T] to make or become clear, more fully known, etc.: *The story unfolds slowly.*

**un·fore·seen** /ˌʌnfɔːˈsiːn◂‖-for-/ *adj* not FORESEEN; unexpected: *unforeseen delays*

**un·for·get·ta·ble** /ˌʌnfəˈgetəbəl‖-fər-/ *adj* (of an experience) too good or bad to be forgotten: *an unforgettable day* –**unforgettably** *adv*

**un·for·tu·nate¹** /ʌnˈfɔːtʃʊnɨt‖-ˈfɔrtʃə-/ *adj* **1** not FORTUNATE; unlucky: *an unfortunate accident/man* **2** unsuitable: *an unfortunate remark*

**unfortunate²** *n sometimes pomp* an unlucky person, esp. one who has no social advantages, no home, etc.

**un·for·tu·nate·ly** /ʌnˈfɔːtʃʊnɨtli‖-ˈfɔrtʃə-/ *adv* I am afraid that . . .: *Unfortunately, we arrived too late to catch the plane.* –compare FORTUNATELY

**un·found·ed** /ʌnˈfaʊndɨd/ *adj* not supported by facts; without base: *Your fears were unfounded.*

**un·furl** /ʌnˈfɜːl‖-ɜrl/ *v* [T] to unroll and open (a flag, sail, etc.)

**un·gain·ly** /ʌnˈgeɪnli/ *adj* not graceful; awkward in movement; CLUMSY –**ungainliness** *n* [U]

**un·gov·er·na·ble** /ʌnˈgʌvənəbəl‖-vər-/ *adj fml* uncontrollable: *an ungovernable temper* –see also GOVERN (2)

**un·gra·cious** /ʌnˈgreɪʃəs/ *adj* not GRACIOUS; not polite: *an ungracious refusal* –**ungraciously** *adv*

**un·grate·ful** /ʌnˈgreɪtfəl/ *adj* not grateful –**ungratefully** *adv*

**un·guard·ed** /ʌnˈgɑːdɨd‖-ɑr-/ *adj* careless over what is made known: *An unguarded remark let everyone know his secret.*

**un·hap·pi·ly** /ʌnˈhæpɨli/ *adv* **1** in an unhappy way **2** *fml* for UNFORTUNATELY: *Unhappily, we never saw her again.*

**un·hap·py** /ʌnˈhæpi/ *adj* **-pier, -piest 1** not happy **2** *fml* unsuitable: *His unhappy choice of words hurt many people's feelings.* –**unhappiness** *n* [U]

**un·health·y** /ʌnˈhelθi/ *adj* **-ier, -iest 1** not generally in good health **2** not likely to give good health: *unhealthy weather conditions* **3** unnatural: *an unhealthy interest in death* –**unhealthily** *adv* –**unhealthiness** *n* [U]

**un·heard** /ˈʌnˈhɜːd◂‖-ɜrd/ *adj* not listened to: *Her complaints* **went unheard**.

**unheard-of** /-ˈ- -/ *adj* very strange and unusual: *It's unheard-of to pass the examination so young.*

**un·hinge** /ʌnˈhɪndʒ/ *v* **-hinged, -hinging** [T] to drive (a person) mad; to cause (the mind) to become UNBALANCED: *The terrible experience unhinged him/his mind.*

**un·hook** /ʌnˈhʊk/ [T] **1** to remove from a hook: *to unhook the meat* **2** to unfasten the hooks of: *to unhook a dress*

**u·ni·corn** *n* an imaginary horselike animal with one horn growing forwards from its forehead

**un·i·den·ti·fied** /ˌʌnaɪˈdentɨfaɪd/ *adj* whose name, nature, or origin has not been found: *An unidentified man shot the President.* –see also UFO

**uniform¹** /ˈjuːnɨfɔːm‖-ɔrm/ *n* [C;U] a certain type of clothing which all members of a group wear, esp. in the army, a school, or the police: *a policeman's uniform|school uniform* –**uniformed** *adj: Two policemen came to the door: one was uniformed, and the other was in plain clothes.* (=not wearing a uniform)

**u·ni·form²** *adj* with every part the same; regular: *a uniform colour* –**uniformity** /-ˈfɔːmɨti‖-ɔr-/ *n* [U] –**uniformly** *adv*

**u·ni·fy** /ˈjuːnɨfaɪ/ *v* **-fied, -fying** [T] **1** to make (parts) into one (whole): *Spain was unified in the 16th century.* **2** to make all the same: *to unify the systems* –**unification** /juːnɨfɨˈkeɪʃən/ *n* [U]

**u·ni·lat·e·ral** /ˌjuːnɨˈlætərəl/ *adj* done by or having an effect on only one of the groups in an agreement: *unilateral* DISARMAMENT –compare BILATERAL, MULTILATERAL

**un·im·pea·cha·ble** /ˌʌnɪmˈpiːtʃəbəl/ *adj fml* blameless; that cannot be doubted: *an unimpeachable character/witness*

**un·in·formed** /ˌʌnɪnˈfɔːmd◂‖-ɔr-/ *adj* not informed; (done) without enough knowledge

**un·in·hab·i·ta·ble** /ˌʌnɪnˈhæbɨtəbəl/ *adj* not HABITABLE; unfit to be lived in

**un·in·hib·it·ed** /ˌʌnɪnˈhɪbɨtɨd/ *adj* free in action and behaviour, esp. doing and saying what one likes –see also INHIBITED –**uninhibitedly** *adv*

**un·in·te·rest·ed** /ʌnˈɪntrɨstɨd/ *adj* [*in*] not interested –see DISINTERESTED (USAGE)

**un·in·ter·rupt·ed** /ˌʌnɪntəˈrʌptɨd/ *adj* continuous –**uninterruptedly** *adv*

**u·ni·on** /ˈjuːnɪən/ *n* **1** [U] the act of joining or state of being joined into one: *the union of two people in marriage* **2** [C] (*often cap.*) a group of countries or states joined together: *the Soviet Union* **3** [C +*sing./pl. v*] a club or society, esp. a TRADE UNION: *Do you belong to a union?|The Students' Union is/are holding elections today.* **4** [C;U] *fml* (a) marriage: *a union blessed by the Church*

**u·ni·on·ize** ||also **-ise** *BrE* /'juːnɪənaɪz/||also **organize** esp. *AmE*– *v* **-ized, -izing** [I;T] to (cause to) form a TRADE UNION –**unionization** /-'zeɪʃən/ *n* [U]

**Union Jack** /ˌ··· '·/ *n* the national flag of Great Britain

**u·nique** /juː'niːk/ *adj* **1** [*no comp.*] being the only one of its type: *This stamp is unique; there are no others like it.* **2** *infml* unusual: *That's a rather unique dress.* –**uniquely** *adv* –**uniqueness** *n* [U]

USAGE Although **unique** is often used to mean "unusual" this is thought by many people to be incorrect.

**u·ni·sex** /'juːnəseks/ *adj infml* (usu. of clothes) which can be used by both male and female: *a unisex hairdresser* (=for both men and women)

**u·ni·son** /'juːnəsən, -zən/ *n* **in unison: a** in perfect agreement **b** together

**u·nit** /'juːnət/ *n* **1** a thing or group regarded as being a complete whole: *an army unit|The family is a small social unit.|a unit of housing* (=a house, flat, etc.) **2** an amount or quantity taken as a standard of measurement: *The pound is the unit of money in Britain.* **3** a piece of furniture, storage apparatus, etc., which can be fitted with others of the same type: *a kitchen unit* **4 a** the smallest whole number; the number 1 **b** any whole number less than 10

**U·ni·tar·i·an** /ˌjuːnə'teərɪən/ *adj,n* (a member) of a branch of the Christian church which does not believe in the **Trinity** (the union of the three forms of God)

**u·nite** /juː'naɪt/ *v* **-nited, -niting 1** [I;T] to join together into one: *The threat of a foreign attack united the government and its opponents.* **2** to act together for a purpose: *They united (in their attempts) to form a club.*

**u·nit·ed** /juː'naɪtəd/ *adj* **1** joined in a state of love, agreement, etc.: *a very united family* **2** [A] with everyone concerned having the same aim: *to make a united effort* **3** [A] (*cap. in names*) joined in a political organization: *the United Nations* –**unitedly** *adv*

**u·ni·ty** /'juːnəti/ *n* [S;U] (a) state of being united: *a new unity between different branches of the church|The argument spoilt their former unity.*

**u·ni·ver·sal** /ˌjuːnə'vɜːsəl◂||-ɜr-/ *adj* **1** concerning all members of a group: *There was universal agreement.* **2** for all people or every purpose; widespread: *a subject of universal interest* –**universality** /-'sæləti/ *n* [U] –**universally** *adv*

**u·ni·verse** /'juːnəvɜːs||-ɜrs/ *n* (*often cap.*) all space and the matter which exists in it: *Did God make the universe?*

**u·ni·ver·si·ty** /ˌjuːnə'vɜːsəti◂||-ɜr-/ *n* **-ties** [C;U] a place of education at the highest level, where degrees are given: *I spent three years at university.|a university* LECTURER (=teacher)

**un·kempt** /ˌʌn'kempt◂/ *adj* (esp. of hair) untidy

**un·kind** /ˌʌn'kaɪnd◂/ *adj* not kind; cruel or thoughtless –**unkindly** *adv* –**unkindness** *n* [C;U]

**un·known** /ˌʌn'nəʊn◂/ *n,adj* (a person or thing) whose name, value, or origin is not known: *an unknown quantity*

**un·law·ful** /ʌn'lɔːfəl/ *adj* against the law: *an unlawful action* –opposite **lawful** –**unlawfully** *adv*

**un·leash** /ʌn'liːʃ/ *v* [T] to set free (a dog) from a LEAD[2] (4): (fig.) *She unleashed her anger on us.*

**un·leav·ened** /ʌn'levənd/ *adj* (of bread) made without YEAST, and therefore flat and unrisen

**un·less** /ʌn'les, ən-/ *conj* if not; except if: *I'll go unless he telephones.|Don't leave the building unless I tell you to.*

**un·like** /ˌʌn'laɪk/ *adj,prep* [F] not like; different: *She's very unlike her mother; they're completely unlike.|It's unlike him to be late; he's usually on time.*

**un·like·ly** /ʌn'laɪkli/ *adj* [+*to-v*] not likely; improbable: *He may come, but it's very unlikely.|They're unlikely to marry.|It seems unlikely that they'll come.* –**unlikeliness** also **unlikelihood**– *n* [U]

**un·load** /ʌn'ləʊd/ *v* **1** [T] to remove (a load) from (something): *to unload the books/the car* **2** [I;T] to have (a load) removed: *The train is unloading at the moment.* **3** [I;T] to remove the CHARGE[2] (6) from (a gun) or film from (a camera)

**un·lock** /ʌn'lɒk||-lɑk/ *v* [T] to unfasten the lock of: *She unlocked the door and then opened it.*

**un·looked-for** /ʌn'lʊkt fɔːʳ/ *adj lit* unexpected

**un·loose** /ʌn'luːs/ *v* **-loosed, -loosing** [T] *lit* to set free

**un·loos·en** /ʌn'luːsən/ *v* [T] to loosen: *He sat down and unloosened his belt.*

**un·luck·y** /ˌʌn'ʌki/ *adj* **-ier, -iest** not lucky: *He's very unlucky; he never wins anything.|She was unlucky enough to break her leg on the first day of her holiday.*

**un·made** /ˌʌn'meɪd◂/ *adj* (of a bed) not made ready for sleeping

**un·mask** /ʌn'mɑːsk||-'mæsk/ *v* [T] to show the hidden truth about: *to unmask the thief*

**un·men·tio·na·ble** /ʌn'menʃənəbəl/ *adj* too unpleasant to be spoken of (MENTIONED)

**un·mis·ta·ka·ble** /ˌʌnmə'steɪkəbəl/ *adj* clearly recognizable; that cannot be thought to be otherwise (MISTAKEN): *Jim's unmistakable voice* –**unmistakably** *adv*

**un·mit·i·gat·ed** /ʌn'mɪtəgeɪtəd/ *adj* [A] in every way bad; not lessened or excused in any way (MITIGATED): *He is an unmitigated liar!*

**un·moved** /ʌn'muːvd/ *adj* **1** not feeling pity; not MOVED[1] (6) **2** not worried; calm

**un·nat·u·ral** /ˌʌn'nætʃərəl/ *adj* **1** not natural; unusual: *Her hair is an unnatural colour.* **2** against ordinary ways of behaving: *unnatural sexual practices* –compare SUPERNATURAL –**unnaturally** *adv*

**un·ne·ces·sa·ry** /ʌn'nesəsəri||-seri/ *adj* not necessary or wanted; additional to what is needed or expected: *That was an unnecessary remark.* –**unnecessarily** /ʌn'nesəsərəli||ˌʌn-nesə'serəli/ *adv: unnecessarily rude*

**un·nerve** /ˌʌn'nɜːv||-ɜrv/ *v* **-nerved, -nerving** [T] to take away the courage of: *The accident unnerved him and he hasn't driven since.* –see also NERVE[2]

**un·ob·tru·sive** /ˌʌnəb'truːsɪv/ *adj* not easily seen or noticed: *He's a quiet unobtrusive student, but always does well in the examinations.* –see also OBTRUSIVE –**unobtrusively** *adv* –**unobtrusiveness** *n* [U]

**un·of·fi·cial** /ˌʌnə'fɪʃəl◂/ *adj* not official; informal: *an unofficial meeting|an unofficial* STRIKE[2] (1) –**unofficially** *adv*

**un·or·tho·dox** /ʌn'ɔːθədɒks||ʌn'ɔrθədɑks/ *adj* not

ORTHODOX; not according to usual beliefs, methods, etc.: *He has an unorthodox style of playing tennis, but he usually wins.*

**un·pack** /ʌn'pæk/ *v* [I;T] to remove (possessions) from (a container): *I'm just going to unpack (my clothes/my case).*

**un·par·al·leled** /ʌn'pærəleld/ *adj* too great to be equalled: *an unparalleled success* –see also PARALLEL[3]

**un·pick** /ʌn'pɪk/ *v* [T] to take out (the stitches) from (material)

**un·pleas·ant** /ʌn'plezənt/ *adj* not pleasant; causing dislike; not enjoyable; unkind: *unpleasant smells/weather|She was rather unpleasant to me.* –**unpleasantly** *adv* –**unpleasantness** *n* [U]

**un·pre·ce·dent·ed** /ʌn'presɪ̇dentɪ̇d/ *adj* never having happened before: *unprecedented rainfall/price increases*

**un·pre·ten·tious** /ˌʌnprɪ'tenʃəs/ *adj* not showing signs of wealth, importance, etc.: *an unpretentious little house* –**unpretentiously** *adv* –**unpretentiousness** *n* [U]

**un·prin·ci·pled** /ʌn'prɪnsɪ̇pəld/ *adj* (done) without regard to usual standards of honourable behaviour: *He is totally unprincipled in money matters, you can't trust him.*

**un·prin·ta·ble** /ʌn'prɪntəbəl/ *adj* (of words) unacceptable for printing, usu. because offensive

**un·pro·fes·sion·al** /ˌʌnprə'feʃənəl/ *adj* (esp. of behaviour) not suitable in a certain profession or activity, esp. because bad in some way –**unprofessionally** *adv*

**un·pro·voked** /ˌʌnprə'vəukt◂/ *adj* (esp. of a bad action) not caused by another action: *The boys' attack on the old woman was quite unprovoked.*

**un·qual·i·fied** /ʌn'kwɒlɪ̇faɪd‖-'kwɑ-/ *adj* **1** [+*to-v*] not having suitable knowledge or QUALIFICATIONS: *I am unqualified to talk on this subject.* **2** not limited: *an unqualified success* (=very successful)

**un·ques·tio·na·ble** /ʌn'kwestʃənəbəl/ *adj* which cannot be QUESTIONED[2] (2); certain –**unquestionably** *adv: She is unquestionably our best player.*

**un·rav·el** /ʌn'rævəl/ *v* **-ll-** *BrE*‖**-l-** *AmE* **1** [I;T] to cause (threads, cloth, etc.) to become separated or unwoven **b** (of threads, cloth, etc.) to become separated or unwoven **2** [T] to make clear (a mystery)

**un·real** /ˌʌn'rɪəl◂/ *adj* (of an experience) seeming imaginary or unlike reality

**un·rea·so·na·ble** /ʌn'riːzənəbəl/ *adj* **1** unfair in demands; not sensible or showing reason **2** (of prices, costs, etc.) too great –**unreasonably** *adv* –**unreasonableness** *n* [U]

**un·rea·son·ing** /ʌn'riːzənɪŋ/ *adj* not using the power of reason: *unreasoning anger*

**un·re·lent·ing** /ˌʌnrɪ'lentɪŋ/ *adj* continuous; without decreasing in power: *a week of unrelenting activity* –compare RELENTLESS –**unrelentingly** *adv*

**un·re·lieved** /ˌʌnrɪ'liːvd◂/ *adj* continuous or complete: *unrelieved anxiety/sadness*

**un·re·mit·ting** /ˌʌnrɪ'mɪtɪŋ◂/ *adj* never stopping: *unremitting activity*

**un·re·quit·ed** /ˌʌnrɪ'kwaɪtɪ̇d◂/ *adj fml* not given in return (esp. in the phrase **unrequited love**)

**un·re·served** /ˌʌnrɪ'zɜːvd◂‖-ɜr-/ *adj* without limits or RESERVATIONS: *You have my unreserved admiration.* –**unreservedly** /-vɪ̇dli/ *adv*

**un·rest** /ʌn'rest/ *n* [U] dissatisfaction, esp. socially: *Unemployment causes social unrest.*

**un·re·strained** /ˌʌnrɪ'streɪnd◂/ *adj* not held back or reduced: *unrestrained anger/violence*

**un·ri·valled** *BrE*‖**unrivaled** *AmE* /ʌn'raɪvəld/ *adj* unequalled; very good: *an unrivalled footballer*

**un·roll** /ʌn'rəul/ *v* [I;T] to open from a rolled position: *They unrolled the cloth onto the table.*

**un·ru·ly** /ʌn'ruːli/ *adj* **-lier, -liest** wild in behaviour; uncontrollable: *unruly children* –**unruliness** *n* [U]

**un·said** /ʌn'sed/ *adj* (thought of but) not spoken: *She left her ideas unsaid.*

**un·sa·vour·y** *BrE*‖**unsavory** *AmE* /ʌn'seɪvəri/ *adj* unpleasant or unacceptable in moral values: *an unsavoury character* (=person)

**un·scathed** /ʌn'skeɪðd/ *adj* not harmed: *He walked away from the accident completely unscathed.*

**un·screw** /ʌn'skruː/ *v* [T] **1** to remove the screw(s) from (something) **2** to undo by twisting: *I can't unscrew (the top of) this bottle.*

**un·scru·pu·lous** /ʌn'skruːpjʊləs‖-pjə-/ *adj* not caring about honesty and fairness: *unscrupulous business methods* –opposite **scrupulous** –**unscrupulously** *adv* –**unscrupulousness** *n* [U]

**un·seat** /ʌn'siːt/ *v* [T] to remove from a position of power, e.g. a seat in Parliament

**un·seem·ly** /ʌn'siːmli/ *adj esp. old use* not suitable (in behaviour) –opposite **seemly** –**unseemliness** *n* [U]

**un·set·tle** /ʌn'setl/ *v* **-tled, -tling** [T] **1** to make less calm, more dissatisfied, etc.: *The sudden changes unsettled her.* **2** to cause illness to (esp. the stomach): *Foreign food always unsettles me/my stomach.*

**un·set·tled** /ˌʌn'setld◂/ *adj* (of weather) not settled; changeable

**un·sha·kea·ble, -kable** /ʌn'ʃeɪkəbəl/ *adj* firm (in belief): *an unshakeable belief in God*

**un·sight·ly** /ʌn'saɪtli/ *adj* not pleasant to look at; ugly: *an unsightly* SCAR –**unsightliness** *n* [U]

**un·skilled** /ˌʌn'skɪld◂/ *adj* **1** not trained for a particular type of job: *unskilled workers* **2** not needing special skill: *an unskilled job*

**un·so·phis·ti·cat·ed** /ˌʌnsə'fɪstɪ̇keɪtɪ̇d◂/ *adj* not SOPHISTICATED; simple in likes, dislikes, etc.; inexperienced in the world and social life

**un·sound** /ˌʌn'saund◂/ *adj* **1** not healthy, strong, or SOUND[3]: *The roof of the building is unsound.* **2** (of ideas) not having a firm base in fact

**un·spar·ing** /ʌn'speərɪŋ/ *adj* holding nothing back, esp. money or help: *unsparing loyalty* –**unsparingly** *adv*

**un·spea·ka·ble** /ʌn'spiːkəbəl/ *adj* terrible: *unspeakable pain* –**unspeakably** *adv*

**un·stuck** /ˌʌn'stʌk◂/ *adj* **come unstuck** to go wrong; be unsuccessful: *He/His plans came unstuck.*

**un·stud·ied** /ˌʌn'stʌdɪ̇d/ *adj fml* natural; without effort: *unstudied grace*

**un·swerv·ing** /ʌn'swɜːvɪŋ‖-ɜr-/ *adj* firm in purpose, esp. loyal

**un·tan·gle** /ˌʌn'tæŋgəl/ *v* **-gled, -gling** [T] to remove TANGLES from; make free from twisted parts: *Can you untangle these wires?*

**un·tapped** /ˌʌn'tæpt◂/ *adj* not used or drawn from: *The sea is an untapped supply of* ENERGY (3).

**un·ten·a·ble** /ʌn'tenəbəl/ *adj* (esp. of a belief or argument) which cannot be defended
**un·thin·ka·ble** /ʌn'θɪŋkəbəl/ *adj* which one cannot believe has happened or cannot wish to happen: *Failure at this late stage is unthinkable.*
**un·think·ing** /ʌn'θɪŋkɪŋ/ *adj* careless; done or said without considering the effect; THOUGHTLESS –**unthinkingly** *adv*
**un·ti·dy** /ˌʌn'taɪdi/ *adj* **-dier, -diest** not tidy; not neatly arranged: *an untidy room*
**un·tie** /ʌn'taɪ/ *v* **-tied, -tying** [T] to undo (a knot or something tied): *Untie the string/the dog.*
**un·til** /ʌn'tɪl, ən-/ also **till**– *prep,conj* up to the time when; up to as late as: *Wait until tomorrow.|We won't start until* (=before) *Bob comes.|Keep driving straight on until you get to the hospital, then turn left.*
**un·time·ly** /ʌn'taɪmli/ *adj fml* **1** happening too soon: *The accident put an untimely end to the party.* **2** not suitable for the occasion –**untimeliness** *n* [U]
**un·tir·ing** /ʌn'taɪərɪŋ/ *adj* not showing tiredness, esp. in spite of hard work –**untiringly** *adv*
**un·to** /'ʌntuː/ *prep old use & bibl* to
**un·told** /ˌʌn'təʊld◂/ *adj* **1** too great to be counted; limitless: *untold wealth* **2** not told or expressed: *an untold story*
**un·to·ward** /ˌʌntə'wɔːd‖ˌʌn'tord/ *adj fml* unfortunate; not wanted: *an untoward event*
**un·truth** /ʌn'truːθ, 'ʌntruːθ/ *n fml euph* a lie
**un·truth·ful** /ʌn'truːθfəl/ *adj* not truthful; lying, esp. habitually: *an untruthful boy* –**untruthfully** *adv*
**un·used¹** /ˌʌn'juːzd◂/ *adj* not having been used: *Put away the unused plates and cups.*
**un·used²** /ˌʌn'juːst/ *adj* [F *to*] not accustomed: *He's unused to flying, so he was nervous in the plane.*
**un·u·su·al** /ʌn'juːʒʊəl,-ʒəl/ *adj* not usual; rare; not common; interesting because different from others: *an unusual amount of rain|an unusual face*
**un·u·su·al·ly** /ʌn'juːʒʊəli,-ʒəli/ *adv* **1** in an unusual way **2** very; more than is common: *He's unusually fond of chocolate.*
**un·veil** /ˌʌn'veɪl/ *v* [I;T] to remove a VEIL or covering (from): *They unveiled the plaque to open the new school.*
**un·war·rant·ed** /ʌn'wɒrəntɪ̣d/ *adj* (done) without good reason; not with just cause
**un·well** /ʌn'wel/ *adj* [F] not well; ill, esp. for a short time
**un·wiel·dy** /ʌn'wiːldi/ *adj* awkward to move, esp. because it is large, heavy, etc.: *a large, unwieldy box*
**un·wind** /ʌn'waɪnd/ *v* **-wound** /'waʊnd/, **-winding 1** [I;T] **a** to undo (something wound round): *He unwound the wool from the ball.* **b** (of something wound round) to become undone **2** [I] *infml* for RELAX
**un·wit·ting** /ˌʌn'wɪtɪŋ◂/ *adj* [A] not knowing or intended: *unwitting rudeness* –**unwittingly** *adv*
**un·zip** /ˌʌn'zɪp/ *v* **-pp-** [T] to open by undoing a ZIP (fastener)
**up¹** /ʌp/ *adv* **1** from below towards a higher place; away from the floor, the ground, or the bottom: *Can you lift that box up onto the shelf for me?|We swam a long way under water and then came up for air.|The sleeping dog jumped up when it saw its master.|It gets hot after the sun has come up.* (=appeared above the horizon. The sun comes *out* from behind a cloud.) **2** in a high place: *flying 10,000 metres up in the air* **3** into an upright or raised position: *Stand up when the teacher comes in!|He turned his collar up to keep his neck dry.|They're putting up* (=building) *a new house.* **4** out of bed: *to get up early|to stay up late* **5** towards or in the north: *travelling up to Scotland from London* **6** (showing a higher level or better condition): *Production has gone up this year.* (=we have produced more) **7** along; towards the person speaking: *He came up to me and asked my name.* **8** (showing more noise, strength, activity, etc.): *Please turn the radio up.*|**Speak up!** *I can't hear you.* **9** (so as to be) completely finished: *The money's all used up.|Eat up your vegetables.|Time's up!* **10** into parts or pieces: *to tear up a newspaper|They divided up the money.* **11** firmly; tightly; safely: *to tie up a parcel|He nailed up the door so they couldn't open it.* **12** so as to be together: *Please add up these numbers.|to collect up the fallen apples* **13** on top (in phrases like **right side up, wrong end up**) **14 up against** having to face: *to come up against a problem/a difficulty|We're really* **up against it** (=in difficulties) *now.* **15 up and down: a** higher and lower: *to jump up and down* **b** backwards and forwards: *to walk up and down* –compare DOWN
**up²** *adj* [*no comp.*] **1** [A] directed or going up: *the up train* **2** (of a road) being repaired: *"Road Up"* (on a sign) **3 up and about** out of bed: *She's not very ill; she'll soon be up and about again.* **4** *infml* **What's up?** What's the matter? **5 up to: a** busy with; doing something bad: *What are the children up to?* **b** good enough for; clever enough for: *Michael's not really up to that job.|My German isn't up to translating that letter.|Do you feel up to going out?* (=well enough to go out) **c** the duty or responsibility of: *It's up to him to do it.|It's up to you (to decide) whether to go or not.*
**up³** *prep* **1** to or in a higher place in; upwards by way of: *He ran up the hill.|The water got up my nose.|His office is up those stairs.* –see Study Notes on page 474 **2** along; to or at the far end of: *They live just up the road.* **3** against the direction of (the current of a river) –opposite **down 4 up and down: a** higher and lower on: *climbing up and down a ladder* **b** backwards and forwards along: *His eyes moved up and down the rows of people.*
**up⁴** *v* **-pp-** *infml* **1** [T] to raise; increase: *to up the price of petrol* **2** [I not *be* +*v-ing*] to get or jump up (and): *He upped and left.*
**up-and-com·ing** /ˌ· · '·· ◂/ *adj* [A] showing signs of being about to succeed, usu. in a profession, work, etc. : *an up-and-coming actress*
**up·braid** /ˌʌp'breɪd/ *v* [T] *fml or old use* to scold
**up·bring·ing** /'ʌpbrɪŋɪŋ/ *n* [S] (a way of) training and caring for a child: *He has had a good upbringing.* –see also BRING **up**
**up·date** /ˌʌp'deɪt/ *v* **-dated, -dating** [T] to make more modern or UP TO DATE
**up·end** /ʌp'end/ *v* [T] to cause to stand on end: *We'll have to upend the cupboard to get it through the door.*
**up·grade** /ˌʌp'greɪd/ *v* **-graded, -grading** [T] to give a higher position to (esp. an employed person) opposite **downgrade**
**up·heav·al** /ʌp'hiːvəl/ *n* [C;U] (a) great change and movement: *all the upheaval of moving house*

**up·hill** /ˌʌp'hɪl/ *adj,adv* on an upward slope: *walking uphill* –opposite **downhill**

**up·hold** /ˌʌp'həʊld/ *v* **-held** /'held/, **-holding** [T] **1** to support; prevent from being weakened or taken away: *to uphold the right to free speech* **2** to declare to be right; CONFIRM: *The judge upheld the lower court's decision.* –**upholder** *n*

**up·hol·ster** /ʌp'həʊlstəʳ/ *v* [T] to fit (a chair) with soft coverings over filling material (PADDING) –**upholsterer** *n*

**up·hol·ster·y** /ʌp'həʊlstəri/ *n* [U] (the making of) CARPETS, curtains, soft chairs, etc.

**up·keep** /'ʌpkiːp/ *n* [U *of*] the act or cost of keeping something repaired and in order: *We can no longer afford the upkeep of a large house.*

**up·land** /'ʌplənd/ *n* the higher land in an area: *the upland areas of the country*

**up·lift** /ˌʌp'lɪft/ *v* [T] to encourage cheerful or holy feelings in: *uplifting words*

**up·on** /ə'pɒn‖ə'pɑn/ *prep fml* for ON¹ (1)

**up·per¹** /'ʌpəʳ/ *adj* [A] **1** in a higher position or rank (than something lower): *Passengers may smoke on the upper floor of the bus.*|*The House of Lords is the* **Upper House** *of the British Parliament.* **2 have/get the upper hand** to have or get control

**upper²** *n* the top part of a shoe or boot above the HEEL and SOLE

**upper class** /ˌ·· '·◂/ *adj,n* [*the* U+*sing./pl. v.*] (of) a small social class whose members belong to a few old, sometimes noble, and usu. very rich families: *upper-class attitudes* –see also MIDDLE CLASS, WORKING CLASS; see WORKING CLASS (USAGE)

**up·per·cut** /'ʌpəkʌt‖-ər-/ *n* (in BOXING) a blow with the hand moving upwards to the opponent's chin

**up·per·most** /'ʌpəməʊst‖-pər-/ *adv,adj* in the highest or strongest position: *uppermost in my mind . . .* (=what I think about most)

**up·right¹** /'ʌp-raɪt/ *adj* **1** (standing) straight up, esp. habitually: *a tall upright young man* **2** honest, fair, responsible, etc.: *an upright citizen*

**upright²** *adv* straight up; not bent

**up·ris·ing** /'ʌpˌraɪzɪŋ/ *n* an esp. small REVOLT against esp. a government by the ordinary people of a country

**up·roar** /'ʌp-rɔːʳ‖'ʌp-ror/ *n* [S;U] confused noisy activity, esp. shouts

**up·root** /ˌʌp'ruːt/ *v* [T] to tear up by the roots: (fig.) *to uproot oneself and move abroad*

**ups and downs** /ˌ·· '·/ *n* [P] good and bad periods: *Life is full of ups and downs.*

**up·set¹** /ʌp'set/ *v* **-set, -setting** [T] **1** to knock over, causing confusion: *to upset a cup full of coffee*|(fig.) *Her plans were upset by the change in the weather.* **2** *to cause to worry, not be calm, etc.: His violent temper upset the children.* **3** to make ill in the stomach: *The foreign food upset me/my stomach.*

**up·set²** /ˌʌp'set◂/ *adj* **1** [F] worried; feeling unhappy about something **2** slightly ill: *an upset stomach*

**up·set³** /'ʌpset/ *n* **1** [C;U] the act of upsetting, or state of being in confusion: *a complete upset of our plans* **2** [C] a slight illness, usu. of the stomach: *a stomach upset*

**up·shot** /'ʌpʃɒt‖'ʌpʃɑt/ *n* [S] the result in the end; OUTCOME: *The two leaders talked for several hours, and the upshot was a new peace agreement.*

**up·side down** /ˌʌpsaɪd 'daʊn/ *adv* **1** in a position with the top turned to the bottom **2** in disorder

**up·stage¹** /ˌʌp'steɪdʒ/ *adv* towards the back of the stage in the theatre

**upstage²** /ʌp'steɪdʒ/ *v* **-staged, -staging** [T] to take attention away from (someone else) for oneself

**up·stairs** /ˌʌp'steəz◂‖-ərz/ *adv,adj* [A;F] at, to, or on the upper floor(s) of a building: *He ran upstairs.*|*an upstairs bedroom* –see also DOWNSTAIRS; see picture on page 297 –**upstairs** *n*

**up·start** /'ʌpstɑːt‖-ɑrt/ *n derog* a person who has risen too suddenly or unexpectedly to a high position

**up·stream** /ˌʌp'striːm◂/ *adv,adj* (moving) against the current, stream, etc. –opposite **downstream**

**up·surge** /'ʌpsɜːdʒ‖-ɜr-/ *n* [*of*] a sudden appearance of anger, feeling, etc.: *an upsurge of joy*

**up·tight** /'ʌptaɪt, ʌp'taɪt/ *adj infml* very worried, nervous, etc.

**up to date** /ˌ· · '·◂/ *adj* **1** modern **2 bring someone/something up to date** to tell someone/include in something the latest information

**up·ward** /'ʌpwəd‖-ərd/ *adj* [A] going up: *an upward movement of prices* –opposite **downward**

**up·wards** /'ʌpwədz‖-ər-‖/ also **upward** *AmE*– *adv* going up **2** with a particular side facing up: *He lay face upwards.* –see also DOWNWARDS

**u·ra·ni·um** /jʊ'reɪnɪəm/ *n* [U] a heavy white metal that is a simple substance (ELEMENT (1)) and gives out RADIOACTIVITY

**U·ra·nus** /jʊ'reɪnəs, 'jʊərənəs/ *n* the PLANET seventh in order from the sun

**ur·ban** /'ɜːbən‖'ɜr-/ *adj* [A] of a town or city: *urban life*

**ur·bane** /ɜː'beɪn‖ɜr-/ *adj* (of a person or his/her behaviour) smoothly polite –**urbanely** *adv* –**urbanity** *n* [U]

**ur·chin** /'ɜːtʃɪ̇n‖'ɜr-/ *n* a small dirty untidy child, esp. a boy: *a street urchin*

**urge¹** /ɜːdʒ‖ɜrdʒ/ *v* **urged, urging** [T] **1** [*on*] to drive or force (forward); encourage: *to urge the team on* **2** to beg or strongly persuade: *They urged us to go with them.* **3** [*on*] to tell of with force; STRESS: *She urged on us the need for speed.*

**urge²** *n* [+*to-v*] a strong wish or need: *powerful sexual urges*| *She felt the/an urge to hit him.*

**ur·gent** /'ɜːdʒənt‖'ɜr-/ *adj* very important and needing to be dealt with quickly or first: *It's not urgent; it can wait till tomorrow.* –**urgently** *adv* –**urgency** *n* [U]

**u·ri·nal** *n* a men's LAVATORY for urinating (URINATE)

**u·ri·nate** /'jʊərɪ̇neɪt/ *v* **-nated, -nating** [I] to pass URINE from the body

**u·rine** /'jʊərɪ̇n/ *n* [U] liquid waste material, passed from the body

**urn** /ɜːn‖ɜrn/ *n* **1** a large container in which tea or coffee may be heated and kept **2** a large container (VASE), esp. one in which the ashes of a dead person are kept

**us** /əs, s; *strong* ʌs/ *pron* (*object form of* WE): *Did he see us?*|*That house is too small for us.*

**US** *n abbrev. for:* **1** also **USA**– the United States (of America) **2** of the United States: *the US navy*

**us·age** /'juːzɪdʒ, 'juːsɪdʒ/ *n* **1** [U] the way of using something; the type or degree of use **2** [C;U] the generally accepted way of using a language

**use**[1] /juːs/ *n* **1** [U] the act of using or state of being used: *Do you approve of the use of guns by the police?* **2** [U] the ability or right to use something: *He lost the use of both legs in the accident.*|*to be given the use of the library* **3** [C;U] the purpose or reason for using something: *a machine with many uses* **4** [U] the usefulness or advantage given by something: *Is this book any use?*|*What's the use of worrying?* **5 in use** being used

**use**[2] /juːz/ *v* **used, using** [T] **1** to employ for a purpose; put to use: *a pan used for cooking eggs*|*The company now uses a computer to do all its accounts.* **2** to finish; CONSUME (2): *All the paper has been used.*|*The car's using too much oil.* **3** *derog* to treat (someone) with consideration only for one's own advantage **–usable** *adj* **–user** *n*

**use** sthg.↔**up** *v adv* [T] to finish completely

**use**[3] /juːs/ *v* **used** /juːst/, *BrE negative short forms* **usedn't, usen't** /'juːsənt/ [I +*to-v*] (used in the past tense only, to show that something happened always or regularly): *I used to go swimming on Saturdays but now I don't.*|*He didn't use to/used not to like fish, but now he does.*|*It used to be thought that the earth was flat.*|*He doesn't work here now, but he used to.*|*Didn't she use to live in Coventry?* –see Study Notes on page 386

USAGE 1 **Used to** and **would** are both used of things that happened always or regularly in the past, but **would** is not used at the beginning of a story: *We* **used to** *swim every day when we were children. We* **would** *run down to the lake and jump in . . .* 2 The usual question form of **used to** is *Did(n't) she* **use/used to**, but **Used/Usen't** *she* **to** are also possible. In the NEGATIVE[2], *She* **used** *not* **to/usen't to** and *She didn't* **used/use to** are all possible, but *She never* **used to,** which expresses the same idea, is probably more common.

**used**[1] /juːzd/ *adj* (usu. of goods) which has already had an owner; SECOND-HAND: *used cars*

**used**[2] /juːst/ *adj* [F *to*] accustomed: *to get used to English food*|*I'm not used to getting up so early.* –opposite **unused**

**use·ful** /'juːsfəl/ *adj* **1** effective in use: *a useful idea* **2** helpful: *She's a useful person to have around.* **–usefulness** [U]

**use·less** /'juːsləs/ *adj* not of any use **–uselessly** *adv* **–uselessness** *n* [U]

**ush·er**[1] /'ʌʃəʳ/ *n* a person who shows people to their seats on an important occasion, e.g. in church at weddings

**usher**[2] *v* [T *in, out*] *fml* to bring (in): *She ushered him into the room.*

**ush·er·ette** /ˌʌʃə'ret/ *n* a woman or girl who works in a cinema, showing people to their seats

**USSR** *abbrev. for:* Union of Soviet Socialist Republics (Soviet Union)

**usu.** *adv written abbrev. said as:* usually

**u·su·al** /'juːʒuəl, 'juːʒəl/ *adj* **1** happening most often; customary: *We will meet at the usual time.* –see also UNUSUAL **2 as usual** as generally has happened before: *As usual, he arrived last.*

**u·su·al·ly** /'juːʒuəli, 'juːʒəli/ *adv* often; generally: *I'm not usually so late.*|*I'm not late, usually.* –see NEVER (USAGE)

**u·surp** /juː'zɜːp‖-ɜrp/ *v* [T] *fml* to seize for oneself (power or position), esp. illegally **–usurper** *n*

**u·su·ry** /'juːʒəri/ *n* [U] *derog* the practice of lending money to be paid back at a high rate of interest

**u·ten·sil** /juː'tensəl/ *n fml or tech* an object for use in a particular way, esp. a tool: *kitchen utensils* –see picture on page 337

**u·te·rus** /'juːtərəs/ *n* **-ri** /ri, raɪ/ *or* **-ruses** *tech* for WOMB

**u·til·i·ty** /juː'tɪləti/ *n* **-ties 1** [U] the degree of usefulness **2** [C] any useful service for the public, such as the bus service, a water supply, etc.

**u·til·ize**‖also **-ise** *BrE* /'juːtəlaɪz/ *v* **-ized, -izing** [T] *fml* to make (good) use of; use: *to utilize one's abilities* **–utilizable** *adj* **–utilization** /-'zeɪʃən/ *n* [U]

**ut·most** /'ʌtməust/ also **uttermost** *lit– adj,n* [A] (effort) of the greatest degree: *with her utmost strength*|*to do one's utmost* (=make the greatest possible effort)

**u·to·pi·a** /juː'təupɪə/ *n* (*often cap.*) an imaginary perfect society **–utopian** *adj*

**ut·ter**[1] /'ʌtəʳ/ *adj* [A] complete: *It's an utter mystery.*|*He's an utter fool.* **–utterly** *adv* –see Study Notes on page 389

**utter**[2] *v* [T] to speak (sound), esp. for a short time: *to utter a cry*|*He uttered a few words.*

**ut·ter·ance** /'ʌtərəns/ *n fml or tech* **1** [U] the act of speaking **2** [C] something spoken

**U-turn** /'juː tɜːn‖-ɜr-/ *n* a turning movement in a car, taking one back in the direction one came from: (fig.) *a U-turn in government plans*

# V, v

**V, v** /viː/ **V's, v's** *or* **Vs, vs 1** the 22nd letter of the English alphabet **2** the ROMAN NUMERAL (number) for 5

**v** *written abbrev. said as:* verb

**V**[1] *n* a thing or part shaped like the letter V: *She cut the material out in a V.*

**V**[2] *written abbrev. said as*: VOLT

**v.** also **vs.**– *abbrev for:* (esp. in sport) versus (against): *the England v. Australia cricket match*

**va·can·cy** /'veɪkənsi/ *n* **-cies 1** [C] an unfilled place, such as a hotel room that is not being used **2** [C] an unfilled job in a factory, office, etc.: *We've only got vacancies for metal workers at present.* **3** [U] the state of being VACANT (3)

**va·cant** /ˈveɪkənt/ *adj* **1** (of a house, room, seat, space, etc.) not being used or lived in **2** (of a job) not at present filled: *The job was advertised in the "Situations Vacant" part of the newspaper.* **3** showing lack of active or serious thought: *a vacant expression on his face* –**vacantly** *adv: He stared vacantly into space.*

**va·cate** /vəˈkeɪt, veɪ-‖ˈveɪkeɪt/ *v* **-cated, -cating** [T] to move out of; stop using or living in: *You must vacate the hotel room by Friday.*

**va·ca·tion** /vəˈkeɪʃən‖veɪˈkeɪʃən/ *n* **1** *BrE* one of the periods of holiday when universities are closed: *The college is* **on vacation**. **2** any period of holiday: *Where did you go for your vacation?* –see HOLIDAY (USAGE) –**vacation** *v* [I] *AmE*

**vac·cin·ate** /ˈvæksɪneɪt/ *v* **-ated, -ating** [T *against*] to introduce VACCINE into the body of (someone), as a protection against a disease –**vaccination** /-ˈneɪʃən/ *n* [C;U *against*]

**vac·cine** /ˈvæksiːn‖vækˈsiːn/ *n* [C;U] a poisonous substance (containing a VIRUS) used for protecting people against diseases

**vac·il·late** /ˈvæsɪleɪt/ *v* **-lated, -lating** [I *between*] to be continually changing from one opinion or feeling to another; be uncertain of what action to take –**vacillation** /-ˈleɪʃən / *n* [C;U]

**vac·u·ous** /ˈvækjuəs/ *adj fml* foolish, esp. in showing no sign of ideas, thought, or feeling: *a vacuous expression* –**vacuously** *adv*

**vac·u·um**[1] /ˈvækjuəm/ *n* a space that is completely empty of all gas, esp. from which all air has been taken away: (fig.) *Her death left a vacuum* (=emptiness) *in his life.*

**vacuum**[2] *v* [I;T] *infml* to clean (a house, room, floor, etc.) using a VACUUM CLEANER

**vacuum clean·er** /ˈ··· ˌ··/ also **hoover** *infml, tdmk*– *n* an apparatus which cleans floor coverings by drawing up the dirt from them in air

**vacuum flask** /ˈ··· ·/ *n* → FLASK (3)

**vag·a·bond** /ˈvægəbɒnd‖-bɑnd/ *n old use* a usu. lazy or worthless person who lives an irregular or wandering life –compare VAGRANT

**va·ga·ry** /ˈveɪgəri/ *n* **-ries** [*often pl.*] an unusual or purposeless idea, act, or thought: *the vagaries of love*

**va·gi·na** /vəˈdʒaɪnə/ *n* the passage which leads from the outer sex organs of women or female animals, to the organ (WOMB) in which young are formed –**vaginal** /vəˈdʒaɪnl‖ˈvædʒɪnl/ *adj*

**va·grant**[1] /ˈveɪgrənt/ *n* a person who lives a wandering life with no steady home or work –compare VAGABOND –**vagrancy** *n* [U]

**vagrant**[2] *adj* [A] going from place to place with no fixed purpose: *a vagrant life*

**vague** /veɪg/ *adj* **1** not clearly seen, described, expressed, felt, or understood: *the vague shapes of animals in the mist|a vague description* **2** not expressing oneself clearly: *The policeman was rather vague when I asked him how to get to the station.* –**vaguely** *adv* –**vagueness** *n* [U]

**vain** /veɪn/ *adj* **1** full of self-admiration; thinking too highly of one's appearance, abilities, etc. **2** without result; useless: *a vain attempt to climb the mountain* **3 in vain** uselessly; without success: *We tried in vain to make him change his mind.* –**vainly** *adv*

**val·ance** /ˈvæləns/ *n* **1** a narrow length of cloth hanging as a border from the frame of a bed to the floor **2** *AmE* for PELMET

**vale** /veɪl/ *n* (as part of a place name or in poetry) a broad low valley: *the Vale of Evesham* –sounds like **veil**

**val·en·tine** /ˈvæləntaɪn/ *n* (*often cap.*) a greeting card sent to a lover on **Saint Valentine's Day** (February 14th)

**val·et** /ˈvælɪt, ˈvæleɪ/ *n* **1** a man's personal male servant, who looks after his clothes, etc. **2** a person who cleans and presses the clothes of people staying in a hotel

**val·i·ant** /ˈvælɪənt/ *adj fml or lit* (of a person or act) very brave, esp. in war; HEROIC –**valiantly** *adv*

**val·id** /ˈvælɪd/ *adj* **1** (of a reason, argument, etc.) having a strong firm base; that can be defended: *He had a valid excuse for arriving late at work.* **2** that can be used legally: *a train ticket valid for three months* –opposite **invalid** **3** *law* written or done in a proper manner so that a court of law would agree with it –**validity** /vəˈlɪdɪti/ *n* [U *of*]: *The judge did not question the validity of my statement.* –**validly** *adv*

**val·i·date** /ˈvælɪdeɪt/ *v* **-dated, -dating** [T] *fml* to make VALID: *She validated the agreement by signing it.* –**validation** /-ˈdeɪʃən/ *n* [C;U]

**va·lise** /vəˈliːz‖vəˈliːs/ *n becoming rare* a small bag used while travelling, esp. for carrying clothes

**val·ley** /ˈvæli/ *n* **-leys** the land lying between two lines of hills or mountains, often with a river running through it

USAGE A deep narrow mountain **valley** with steep sides is a **ravine** or **gorge**, or (if it is very large) a **canyon**.

**val·our** *BrE*‖**valor** *AmE* /ˈvælə^r/ *n* [U] *fml or lit* great bravery, esp. in war

**val·u·a·ble** /ˈvæljuəbəl‖ˈvæljəbəl/ *adj* **1** worth a lot of money: *a valuable diamond* **2** very useful: *valuable help* –see WORTHLESS (USAGE)

**val·u·a·bles** /ˈvæljuəbəlz‖-jə-/ *n* [P] things (such as pieces of jewellery) that are worth a lot of money: *You should put your valuables in the bank.*

**val·u·a·tion** /ˌvæljuˈeɪʃən/ *n* **1** [U;C *of*] the action of calculating how much money something is worth: *The company's business is the valuation of property/making valuations of property.* **2** [C *of*] a value or price (esp. of land or property) decided upon in this way: *a valuation of £7,000*

**val·ue**[1] /ˈvæljuː/ *n* **1** [U] the degree of usefulness of something: *You'll find this map of great value/of little value in helping you to get round London.|The government sets a higher value on defence* (=considers it more important) *than on education.* **2** [C;U] the worth of something in money or as compared with other goods for which it might be changed: *Because of continual price increases, the value of the pound has fallen in recent years.|I bought this old painting for £10, but its real value must be about £500.|The thieves took some clothes and a few books, but nothing of great value.* **3** [U] worth compared with the amount paid: *We offer the best value in London: only four pounds for a meal with wine and coffee!|You always get value for money at that shop.* (=the goods are always worth the price charged) –see also VALUES; see COST, WORTHLESS (USAGE) –**valueless** *adj*

**value²** *v* **-ued, -uing** [T] **1** to calculate the value, price, or worth of (something): *He valued the house and its contents at £25,000.* **2** to consider to be of great worth: *I've always valued your friendship.*

**value-ad·ded tax** /ˌ·· '·· ·‖ˌ·· ·· '·/ *n* [U] → VAT

**val·u·er** /'væljuəʳ/ *n* a person whose work is to decide how much money things are worth

**val·ues** /'væljuːz/ *n* [P] standards; people's ideas about the worth of certain qualities: *moral values*

**valve** /vælv/ *n* **1** a doorlike part of a pipe, which controls the flow of liquid, air, gas, etc., through the pipe: *You put air into a bicycle tyre through the valve.|The valves of the heart allow the blood to pass in one direction only.* **2** also **tube** *AmE*– a closed glass tube with no air in it, used for controlling a flow of electricity, as (esp. formerly) in radio or television

**vam·pire** /'væmpaɪəʳ/ *n* an evil spirit which is believed to live in a dead body and suck the blood of sleeping people

**van** /væn/ *n* **1** a covered road vehicle for carrying goods and sometimes people: *a baker's van|a police van* –compare LORRY **2** *BrE* a covered railway carriage for goods and sometimes people: *the guard's van*

**van·dal** /'vændl/ *n* a person who intentionally damages or destroys beautiful or useful things: *All the seat-covers on the train had been torn by vandals.*

**van·dal·is·m** /'vændəl-ɪzəm/ *n* [U] intentional, needless, and usu. widespread damage and destruction, esp. of public property

**van·dal·ize**‖also **-ise** *BrE* /'vændəl-aɪz/ *v* **-ized, -izing** [T] to damage or destroy (esp. a piece of public property) intentionally: *The public telephone has been vandalized.*

**vane** /veɪn/ *n* a bladelike part of certain machines, which has a flat surface that makes it possible to use the force of wind or water as the driving power: *the vanes of a* PROPELLER –sounds like **vein**

**van·guard** /'væŋgɑːd‖-ɑrd/ *n* **1** [C +*sing./pl.v*] the soldiers marching at the front of an army, or sent on ahead to protect it against surprise attack: *The vanguard is/are under attack.* **2** [*the* U] the leading part of any kind of advancement in human affairs: *In the modern world the scientists are* **in the vanguard of** *all industrial development.*

**va·nil·la** /və'nɪlə/ *n* [U] a substance obtained from a tropical plant, used for improving the taste of certain sweet foods: *vanilla ice cream*

**van·ish** /'vænɪʃ/ *v* [I] **1** to disappear: *With a wave of his hand, the magician made the rabbit vanish.* **2** to cease to exist: *Many types of animal have now vanished from the earth.*

**van·i·ty** /'vænˌ̍ti/ *n* [U] the quality of being too proud of oneself or one's appearance, abilities, etc.

**van·quish** /'væŋkwɪʃ/ *v* [T] *lit* to conquer; defeat completely

**va·por·ize**‖also **-ise** *BrE* /'veɪpəraɪz/ *v* **-ized, -izing** [I;T] to (cause to) change into VAPOUR (1,2): *Water vaporizes when boiled.*

**va·pour** *BrE*‖**vapor** *AmE* /'veɪpəʳ/ *n* **1** [C;U] a gaslike form of a liquid (such as mist or steam): *A cloud is a mass of vapour in the sky.* **2** [U] *tech* the gas to which the stated liquid or solid can be changed by the action of heat: *water vapour*

**var·i·a·ble¹** /'veərɪəbəl/ *adj* **1** likely to change; not staying the same; not steady: *variable winds* **2** that can be intentionally varied –**variability** /-ə'bɪlˌ̍ti/ *n* [U] –**variably** *adv*

**variable²** *n usu. tech* something (such as temperature) which can vary in quantity or size: *The time of the journey depends on a number of variables, such as the amount of traffic on the road.*

**var·i·ance** /'veərɪəns/ *n* **at variance (with)** in opposition (to); not in agreement (with)

**var·i·ant¹** /'veərɪənt/ *adj* [A *no comp.*] different; varying: *variant spellings*

**variant²** *n* a different form, esp. of a word or phrase: *"Favor" is the American variant of the British "favour".*

**var·i·a·tion** /ˌveəri'eɪʃən/ *n* [C;U] (an example or degree of) the action of varying: *price variations*

**var·i·cose veins** /'værˌ̍kəʊs/ *n* a medical condition in which the blood vessels (esp. of the leg) have become greatly swollen

**var·ied** /'veərid/ *adj* **1** of different kinds: *Opinions on the play were varied.* **2** not staying the same; changing: *to lead a varied life*

**var·ie·gat·ed** /'veərɪəgeɪtˌ̍d/ *adj* (esp. of a flower or leaf) marked irregularly in spots, lines, masses, etc., of different colours –**variegation** /-'geɪʃən/ *n* [U]

**va·ri·e·ty** /və'raɪəti/ *n* **-ties 1** [U] the state of varying; difference of condition or quality: *My last job lacked variety; I was doing the same things all the time.* **2** [S *of*] a group or collection containing different sorts of the same thing or people: *Everyone arrived late at the party, for a variety of reasons.* **3** [C] a type which is different from others in a group: *That farmer is always looking for new varieties of wheat.* **4** [U] a theatre or television show including singing, dancing, acts of skill, etc.: *a variety show*

**var·i·ous** /'veərɪəs/ *adj* [A] **1** different: *There are various ways of cooking an egg.* **2** several; a number of: *Various people said they had seen the accident.* –see DIFFERENT (USAGE) –**variously** *adv*: *The depth of this cave has been variously calculated at from 200 metres to 500 metres.*

**var·nish¹** /'vɑːnɪʃ‖'vɑr-/ *n* **1** [C;U] (a) liquid which, when brushed onto articles made esp. of wood, gives a clear hard shiny surface **2** [*the* S] the shiny appearance produced by using this substance: *Hot plates may spoil the varnish on a table.* –compare LACQUER

**varnish²** *v* [T] to cover with VARNISH: *to varnish a table/one's fingernails*

**var·y** /'veəri/ *v* **-ied, -ying** [I;T] to be, make, or become different: *Opinions on this matter vary.|She varies her dress as fashion changes.|Her health varies from good to rather weak.*

**vase** /vɑːz‖veɪs, veɪz/ *n* a glass or clay container, used esp. to put flowers in

**va·sec·to·my** /və'sektəmi/ *n* **-mies** [C;U] (an operation for) removing a man's ability to become a father by cutting the small tube that carries the male seeds (SPERM)

**vast** /vɑːst‖væst/ *adj* very large and wide; great in size or amount: *vast spaces* –see Study Notes on page 494 –**vastness** *n* [U]

**vast·ly** /'vɑːstli‖'væstli/ *adv* very greatly: *His piano* *playing has vastly improved since last year.*

**vat** /væt/ *n* a very large barrel or container for holding liquids (such as WHISKY, DYE, etc.), esp. when they are being made

**VAT** /ˌviː eɪ ˈtiː, væt/ *n* [U] (in Britain and some other European countries) a tax (**value-added tax**) added to the price of an article, and paid by the buyer to the seller, who then pays it to the government

**vault**[1] /vɔːlt/ *n* **1** an underground room in which the bodies of the dead are placed, or in which valuable things are stored **2** a roof or CEILING formed, as in most churches, by a number of arches

**vault**[2] *v* [I;T] to jump over (something) in one movement using the hands or a pole to gain more height: *to vault over a gate|to polevault*

**vault**[3] *n* a jump made by VAULTING[2] –see also POLE VAULT

**vaulting horse** /ˈ·· ·/ also **horse**– *n* a wooden apparatus which people can VAULT[2] over for exercise

**VD** *n* [U] → VENEREAL DISEASE

**VDU** *n abbrev. for* visual display unit; an apparatus with a SCREEN[1] (5) which shows writing or information from a computer or a WORD PROCESSOR –see picture on page 415

**'ve** /v, əv/ *v short for* have: *We've finished.*

**veal** /viːl/ *n* [U] meat from the young of a cow (CALF) –see MEAT (USAGE)

**veer** /vɪəʳ/ *v* [I] to turn or change direction: *The car was out of control and suddenly veered across the road.|The conversation veered to food.*

**vege·ta·ble** /ˈvedʒtəbəl/ *n* a (part of a) plant that is grown for food: *meat and vegetables|We grow many different vegetables: potatoes, onions, beans, etc.*

**veg·e·tar·i·an** /ˌvedʒᵻˈteərɪən/ *n* a person who does not eat meat or fish, but only vegetables, grains, fruit, etc. **–vegetarian** *adj: a vegetarian restaurant/meal* **–vegetarianism** *n* [U]

**veg·e·tate** /ˈvedʒᵻteɪt/ *v* **-tated, -tating** [I] to live a dull life without interests or social activity

**veg·e·ta·tion** /ˌvedʒᵻˈteɪʃən/ *n* [U] plants in general: *the vegetation of the tropical forest*

**ve·he·ment** /ˈvɪəmənt/ *adj* fiercely strong; violent: *She made a vehement attack on the government's actions.* **–vehemently** *adv* **–vehemence** *n* [U]

**ve·hi·cle** /ˈviːᵻkəl/ *n* **1** something in or on which people or goods can be carried, esp. along roads (such as a bicycle, car, cart, or bus) **2** *fml* something by means of which something else can be passed on or spread: *Television has become an important vehicle for spreading political ideas.*

**ve·hic·u·lar** /viːˈhɪkjʊləʳ‖-kjə-/ *adj fml* concerning vehicles on roads: *vehicular traffic*

**veil**[1] /veɪl/ *n* **1** [C] a covering of fine cloth or net for the head or face, worn esp. by women, sometimes for religious reasons **2** [S *of*] something which covers or hides something else: *a veil of mist*|(fig.) *No one knew what the army was doing; there was a veil of secrecy over their activities.*

**veil**[2] *v* [T] to cover with a VEIL

**veiled** /veɪld/ *adj* **1** wearing a VEIL[1] (1) **2** hidden; expressed indirectly: *veiled threats*

**vein** /veɪn/ *n* **1** [C] a tube that carries blood from any part of the body to the heart –compare ARTERY **2** [C] one of a system of thin lines which run in a pattern through leaves and the wings of certain insects **3** [S] a style or MOOD: *speaking in a serious vein|a number of jokes all in the same vein* **4** [C] a crack in rock, filled with useful metal: *a vein of silver* –compare SEAM (3)

**ve·loc·i·ty** /vᵻˈlɒsᵻti‖vᵻˈlɑ-/ *n* **-ties** [C;U] *tech* (a) speed in a certain direction; rate of movement

**ve·lour, velours** /vəˈlʊəʳ/ *n* [U] a heavy cloth made from silk, cotton, etc., with a soft slightly furry surface

**vel·vet** /ˈvelvᵻt/ *n* [U] a fine closely-woven cloth made esp. of silk but also of nylon, cotton, etc., with a short soft furry surface on one side only

**vel·vet·y** /ˈvelvᵻti/ *adj* like VELVET; very soft

**ve·nal** /ˈviːnl/ *adj fml* **1** (of a person) acting unfairly or wrongly, in return for money or other reward: *venal judges* **2** (of an action) done, not for the proper or honest reasons, but for money **–venality** /-ˈnælᵻti/ *n* [U] **–venally** *adv*

**ven·det·ta** /venˈdetə/ *n* a long-lasting and violent quarrel between families

**vending ma·chine** /ˈ·· ·ˌ·/ *n* a machine from which cigarettes, drinks, stamps, etc., can be obtained by putting a coin into it

**vend·or, -er** /ˈvendəʳ/ *n* **1** a seller of small articles that can be carried about or pushed on a cart: *a fruit vendor* **2** *law* the seller of a house, land, etc.

**ve·neer** /vᵻˈnɪəʳ/ *n* **1** [C;U] a thin covering of good quality wood forming the outer surface of an article made of a cheaper material **2** [S *of*] an outer appearance which hides the unpleasant reality

**ven·e·ra·ble** /ˈvenərəbəl/ *adj* (of an old person or thing) considered to deserve great respect or honour, because of character, religious or historical importance, etc. –see OLD (USAGE)

**ven·e·rate** /ˈvenəreɪt/ *v* **-rated, -rating** [T] *fml* to treat with great respect and honour, and sometimes worship **–veneration** /-ˈreɪʃən / *n* [U]

**ve·ne·re·al dis·ease** /vᵻˈnɪərɪəl/ also **VD**– *n* [C;U] (a type of) disease passed from one person to another during sexual activity

**ve·ne·tian blind** /vᵻˈniːʃən/ *n* [*usu. pl.*] a covering for the inside of a window, made of long thin flat bars of metal, plastic, or wood, fixed to strings so that it can be raised or lowered, or turned to let in or shut out light and air

**ven·geance** /ˈvendʒəns/ *n* [U] **1** severe harm or damage done to another person as a punishment for harm he/she has done to oneself, one's family, etc.: *He* **took vengeance on** *the murderer.* –see also REVENGE **2 with a vengeance** *infml* to a high degree; with greater force than is usual: *The wind's blowing with a vengeance.*

**venge·ful** /ˈvendʒfəl/ *adj lit* showing a fierce desire to punish a person for the harm he/she has done to oneself **–vengefully** *adv*

**ven·i·son** /ˈvenᵻsən/ *n* [U] the flesh of a deer as food –see MEAT (USAGE)

**ven·om** /ˈvenəm/ *n* [U] **1** liquid poison which certain snakes, insects, and other creatures use in biting or stinging **2** great hatred: *Her remarks about him were full of venom.* **–venomous** *adj* **–venomously** *adv*

**vent**[1] /vent/ *v* [T *on*] to give expression to (one's feelings): *He vented his anger on us.*

**vent²** *n* **1** a hole, opening, or pipe by which gases, smoke, air, or liquid can enter or escape from an enclosed space **2** a long narrow straight opening at the bottom of a coat, at the sides or back **3 give vent to** to express freely (a strong feeling): *He gave vent to his anger by shouting at the children.*

**ven·ti·late** /ˈventɪ̥leɪt‖-tl-eɪt/ *v* **-lated, -lating** [T] to allow fresh air to enter (a room, building, etc.): *a smoky, badly-ventilated bar*

**ven·ti·la·tion** /ˌventɪ̥ˈleɪʃən‖-tlˈeɪ-/ *n* [U] (the system that is used for) the passing into and around a room, building, etc., of fresh air: *The workers complained about the factory's lack of ventilation.*

**ven·ti·la·tor** /ˈventɪ̥leɪtəʳ‖-tl-eɪ-/ *n* any arrangement or apparatus for the ventilating (VENTILATE) of a room, building, etc.

**ven·tril·o·quis·m** /venˈtrɪləkwɪzəm/ *n* [U] the art of speaking or singing without moving the lips or jaws, so that the sound seems to come from somewhere else **–ventriloquist** *n*

**ven·ture¹** /ˈventʃəʳ/ *v* **-tured, -turing 1** [I;T +*to-v*] to risk going somewhere or doing something dangerous: *Don't venture too near the edge of the well; you might fall in.* **2** [T +*to-v*] to take the risk of saying (something that may be opposed or considered foolish): *I venture to say that men will live on the moon.*|*to venture a suggestion*

**venture²** *n* an attempt; course of action (esp. in business) of which the result is uncertain

USAGE **Venture** (noun or verb) suggests some risk to one's life or money: *a business* **venture**|*Nobody* **ventured** (=dared) *to speak to the angry king.* An **adventure** is an exciting experience, which may or may not be dangerous as well. The plural **adventures** is often used in the title of a story about the exciting activities of a particular character: "*The* **Adventures** *of Sinbad the Sailor*".

**ven·ue** /ˈvenjuː/ *n* a meeting place arranged for some purpose or activity: *The venue of the big match is the football ground at Wembley.*

**Ve·nus** /ˈviːnəs/ *n* the PLANET second in order from the sun, and next to the earth

**ve·ran·da, -dah** /vəˈrændə/ also **porch** *AmE*– *n* an addition to a house, built out from the walls, esp. at ground level, having a floor and a roof (usu. supported by pillars) but no outside wall: *to sit in the shade on the veranda* –compare BALCONY

**verb** /vɜːb‖vɜrb/ *n* a word or phrase that tells what someone or something is, does, or experiences: *In "She is tired" and "He wrote a letter", "is" and "wrote" are verbs.*

**verb·al** /ˈvɜːbəl‖ˈvɜr-/ *adj* **1** spoken, not written: *a verbal agreement* **2** connected with words and their use: *verbal skill* –compare VERBOSE

**verb·al·ize**‖also **-ise** *BrE* /ˈvɜːbəl-aɪz‖ˈvɜr-/ *v* **-ized, -izing** [I;T] *fml* to express (something) in words

**verb·al·ly** /ˈvɜbəl-i‖ˈvɜr-/ *adv* in spoken words and not in writing

**verbal noun** /ˌ·· ˈ·/ also **gerund**– *n* a noun which describes an action or experience and ends in *-ing* like a PRESENT PARTICIPLE: *"Building" is a verbal noun in "The building of the bridge was slow work", but not in "The bank was a tall building".*

**ver·ba·tim** /vɜːˈbeɪtɪ̥m‖vɜr-/ *adj,adv* repeating the actual words exactly: *His memory was so good that he could repeat many Shakespeare plays verbatim.*

**ver·bi·age** /ˈvɜːbi-ɪdʒ‖ˈvɜr-/ *n* [U] too many unnecessary words in speech or writing

**ver·bose** /vɜːˈbəus‖vɜr-/ *adj fml* using too many words: *Your report is twice as long as it needs to be: it's too verbose.* –compare VERBAL **–verbosely** *adv* **–verbosity** /-ˈbɒsɪ̥ti‖-ˈba-/ *n* [U]

**ver·dant** /ˈvɜːdənt‖ˈvɜr-/ *adj lit* green with freshly growing plants or grass: *the verdant fields*

**ver·dict** /ˈvɜːdɪkt‖ˈvɜr-/ *n* **1** the official decision made by a JURY in a court of law, at the end of a trial: *Members of the* JURY, *what is your verdict? Guilty, or not guilty?* **2** *infml* a statement of (carefully considered) opinion: *The general verdict was that people had enjoyed the film.*

**verge** /vɜːdʒ‖vɜrdʒ/ *n* the edge or border of a road, path, etc.: *a grass verge*|(fig.) *She was* **on the verge of** (=very near to) *tears.*

**verge on/upon** sthg. *v prep* **verged, verging** [T] to be near to (the stated quality or condition): *His strange behaviour sometimes verges on madness.*

**ver·i·fy** /ˈverɪ̥faɪ/ *v* **-fied, -fying** [T +*that*] to make sure that (a fact, statement, etc.) is true: *The police are verifying the prisoner's statement by questioning witnesses.* **–verifiable** *adj* **–verification** /-fɪ̥ˈkeɪʃən/ *n* [U]

**ver·i·si·mil·i·tude** /ˌverɪ̥sɪ̥ˈmɪlɪ̥tjuːd‖-tuːd/ *n* [U] *fml* the quality of seeming to be true; likeness to reality

**ver·i·ta·ble** /ˈverɪ̥təbəl/ *adj* [A] (used to give force to an expression) that may be described as; real: *The meal was a veritable feast.* **–veritably** *adv*

**ver·mil·i·on** /vəˈmɪlɪən‖vər-/ *adj,n* [U] bright reddish-orange (colour)

**ver·min** /ˈvɜːmɪ̥n‖ˈvɜr-/ *n* [U +*sing./pl.v*] **1** any usu. small animal or bird that causes damage and is difficult to control: *To a farmer a rabbit is vermin because it eats young plants.* **2** any kind of unpleasant biting insect (such as a FLEA, LOUSE, etc.) that lives on the body of man or animals: *Vermin is/are found in large numbers on many animals.* **–verminous** *adj*

**ver·mouth** /ˈvɜːməθ‖vərˈmuːθ/ *n* [U] a drink made from wine with the addition of bitter or strong-tasting substances from roots and HERBS

**ver·nac·u·lar** /vəˈnækjuləʳ‖vərˈnækjələr/ *adj,n* (using) the native spoken language of a country or area: *In some churches, they speak Latin, but in others they use the vernacular.*

**ver·ru·ca** /vəˈruːkə/ *n* a small hard often infectious growth on the skin, usu. on the bottom of the feet

**ver·sa·tile** /ˈvɜːsətaɪl‖ˈvɜrsətl/ *adj* **1** having many different kinds of skill or ability: *He's a very versatile performer; he can act, sing, dance, and play the piano.* **2** having many different uses: *Nylon is a versatile material.* **–versatility** /-ˈtɪlɪ̥ti/ *n* [U]

**verse** /vɜːs‖vɜrs/ *n* **1** [U] written language in the form of poetry: *Not all verse is great poetry.*|*comic verse* –see also BLANK VERSE **2** [C] a set of lines which forms one part of a poem or song: *He read three verses of the poem.* **3** [C] one of the (groups of) sentences that together form one numbered division (CHAPTER) of one of the books of the Bible

**versed** /vɜːst‖vɜrst/ *adj* [F *in*] possessing a thorough

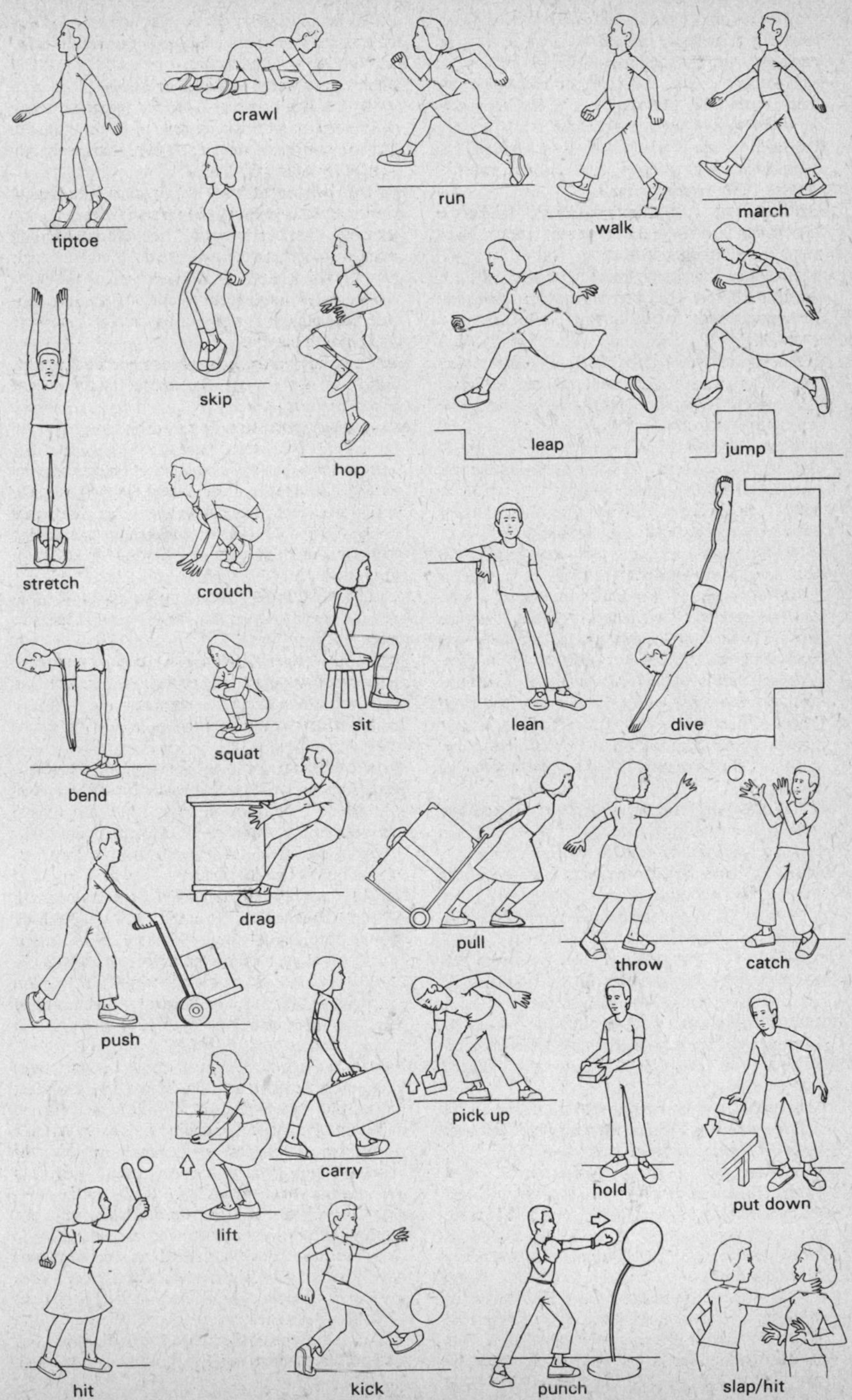
tiptoe
crawl
run
walk
march
skip
hop
leap
jump
stretch
crouch
sit
lean
dive
bend
squat
drag
pull
throw
catch
push
lift
carry
pick up
hold
put down
hit
kick
punch
slap/hit

knowledge (of a subject, an art, etc.); experienced (esp. in the phrase **well versed in**)

**ver·sion** /ˈvɜːʃən‖ˈvɜrʒən/ *n* [*of*] **1** one person's account of an event: *The two newspapers gave different versions of what happened.* **2** a slightly different form, copy, or style of an article: *This dress is a cheaper version of the one we saw in the shop.* **3** a translation: *the King James Version of the Bible*

**ver·sus** /ˈvɜːsəs‖ˈvɜr-/ *prep* → v.

**ver·te·bra** /ˈvɜːtəbrə‖ˈvɜr-/ *n* **-brae** /braɪ, bri/ one of the small hollow bones down the centre of the back which form the SPINE (1)

**ver·te·brate** /ˈvɜːtəbrət, -breɪt‖ˈvɜr-/ *adj,n tech* (an animal, bird, fish, etc.) which has a SPINE –see also INVERTEBRATE

**ver·ti·cal** /ˈvɜːtɪkəl‖ˈvɜr-/ *adj* (of an object, line, or surface) forming an angle of 90 degrees with the level ground, or with a straight line in a figure; upright: *The northern side of the mountain is almost vertical.* –compare HORIZONTAL –**vertically** *adv*

**ver·ti·go** /ˈvɜːtɪgəʊ‖ˈvɜr-/ *n* [U] a feeling of great unsteadiness, sickness, or faintness, caused usu. by looking down from a great height

**verve** /vɜːv‖vɜrv/ *n* [U] life, force, and eager enjoyment: *playing the piano with great verve*

**ve·ry**[1] /ˈveri/ *adv* **1** especially; to a great degree: *It's very warm today.|a very good cake|a very exciting book|The traffic in the town centre moves very slowly.|Thank you very much.* –see Study Notes on page 389 **2** (used with SUPERLATIVE[1] (2) adjectives, or words like *same, own, first, last,* to make them stronger): *the very best film I've seen this year|There have been three accidents in this very same place.|my very own boat* **3 very well** (in answer to a suggestion, request, or plan) all right (but I don't particularly want to): *"Please come home early." "Very well, if I must."*

USAGE One says **very** *big* or *the* **very** *biggest,* but **much** *bigger.*

**very**[2] *adj* [A] (*used for giving force to an expression*) actual: *This is the very pen the writer used.* |*I'll go this very minute.* (=at once)|*I found it at the very bottom of the box.*|*The very walls* (=Even the walls) *of the old city are full of history.*

**very high fre·quen·cy** /ˌ·· · ˈ···/ *n* [U] → VHF

**ves·pers** /ˈvespəz‖-ərz/ *n* [U] (in some divisions of the Christian church) the evening service

**ves·sel** /ˈvesəl/ *n fml* **1** a usu. round container, such as a glass, pot, bucket, or barrel, used esp. for holding liquids: *a drinking vessel* **2** a ship or large boat: *a fishing vessel* –see also BLOOD VESSEL

**vest** /vest/ *n* **1** *BrE*‖**undershirt** *AmE*– a short undergarment, usu. without coverings for the arms, worn on the upper part of the body **2** *AmE* for WAISTCOAT

**vested in·terest** /ˌ·· ˈ··/ *n often derog* a personal reason for doing or continuing something, because one gains advantage from it: *The tobacco companies have a vested interest in claiming that cigarette smoking isn't harmful.*

**ves·ti·bule** /ˈvestəbjuːl/ *n fml* a wide passage or small room just inside the outer door of a (public) building; entrance hall

**ves·tige** /ˈvestɪdʒ/ *n* [*of*] the very small slight remains (of something): *the last vestiges of Inca civilization|There's not a vestige* (=not the slightest bit) *of truth in his statement.*

**vest** sthg. **in** sbdy. *v prep* [T *usu. pass.*] *fml* to give legally (a right or power) to (a person or group): *The right to make new laws is vested in the government.*

**vest·ment** /ˈvestmənt/ *n* [*often pl.*] *fml* a ceremonial garment, esp. as worn by priests for church services

**ves·try** /ˈvestri/ *n* **-tries** a room in a church a where the priest and church singers put on their ceremonial garments or **b** which is used for prayer meetings, church business, etc.

**vet**[1] /vet/ also **veterinary surgeon** /ˈ····· ˌ··/ *fml BrE*‖**veterinarian** /ˌvetərəˈneəriən/ *AmE*– *n* a trained animal doctor

**vet**[2] *v* **-tt-** [T] *infml* to examine carefully for correctness, past record, etc.: *New policemen are carefully vetted.*

**vet·e·ran** /ˈvetərən/ *n,adj* [A;C] **1** [*of*] (a person) who in the past has had long experience, esp. in war: *Grandfather is a veteran (soldier) of the First World War.*|*At the age of 12 the boy was already a veteran traveller, having been all over the world with his father.* **2** (a thing) that has grown old with long use: *Every year a race is held in England for veteran cars.* (=those made before 1916) –compare VINTAGE[1] (3)

**vet·e·ri·na·ry** /ˈvetərənəri‖-neri/ *adj* [A] connected with the medical care and treatment of sick animals: *veterinary science* –see also VET[1]

**ve·to**[1] /ˈviːtəʊ/ *n* **-toes 1** [C;U] (esp. in politics) the official power to refuse permission for an action, or to forbid something to be done: *to exercise one's veto* **2** [C *on*] a refusal to give permission for something; act of forbidding something completely

**veto**[2] *v* **-toed, -toing** [T] to prevent or forbid (some action); refuse to allow (something): *The minister's plan to reduce defence spending was vetoed by the president.*

**vex** /veks/ *v* [T] *esp. old use* to displease (someone); cause (someone) to feel angry or bad-tempered –**vexation** /-ˈseɪʃən/ *n* [C;U]

**VHF** *n* [U] very high FREQUENCY (2); (the sending out of radio waves at) the rate of 30,000,000 to 300,000,000 times per second: *This radio station broadcasts only on VHF.*|*a VHF radio* –see also UHF

**vi·a** /ˈvaɪə‖ˈvɪə/ *prep* travelling or sent through (a place) on the way: *We flew to Athens via Paris and Rome.*|(*infml*) *I sent a message to Mary via her sister.*

**vi·a·ble** /ˈvaɪəbəl/ *adj* able to succeed in operation: *This plan wouldn't be viable in practice.* –**viability** /-ˈbɪləti/ *n* [U] –**viably** *adv*

**vi·a·duct** /ˈvaɪədʌkt/ *n* a long high bridge which carries a road or railway line across a valley

**vi·brant** /ˈvaɪbrənt/ *adj* **1** alive; forceful; powerful and exciting: *a city vibrant with life* **2** (of colour or light) pleasantly bright and strong –**vibrantly** *adv*

**vi·brate** /vaɪˈbreɪt‖ˈvaɪbreɪt/ *v* **-brated, -brating** [I;T] to (cause to) shake continuously and very rapidly with a fine slight movement: *Tom's heavy footsteps upstairs make the old house vibrate.*

**vi·bra·tion** /vaɪˈbreɪʃən/ *n* [C;U] (a) slight continuous shaky movement: *You can feel the vibrations when a plane flies over our house.*

**vic·ar** /ˈvɪkəʳ/ *n* (in the CHURCH OF ENGLAND) a priest in charge of a church and the area (PARISH) belonging to it

**vic·ar·age** /ˈvɪkərɪdʒ/ *n* a VICAR's house

**vi·car·i·ous** /vɪˈkeərɪəs‖vaɪ-/ *adj* experienced by the imagination through watching or reading about other people; indirect: *He gets vicarious pleasure by going to watch films about sex.* **–vicariously** *adv*

**vice¹** /vaɪs/ *n* **1** [C;U] (any particular kind of) evil living, esp. in sexual practices, taking of harmful drugs, etc.: *There is a lot of vice in our cities.* **2** [C;U] (an example of) wickedness of character –opposite **virtue 3** [C] *infml, often humor* a bad habit: *Smoking is my only vice.*

**vice²** *BrE*‖**vise** *AmE n* a tool with metal jaws, used for holding a piece of wood or metal firmly in place so that it can be worked on

**vice·roy** /ˈvaɪsrɔɪ/ *n* a king's or queen's representative ruling for him/her in another country: *When Britain ruled India, the British king was represented there by a viceroy.*

**vice ver·sa** /ˌvaɪs ˈvɜːsə, ˌvaɪsi-‖-ɜr-/ *adv* in the opposite way from that just stated: *When she wants to go out, he wants to stay in, and vice versa.* (=when he wants to go out, she wants to stay in)

**vi·cin·i·ty** /vəˈsɪnəti/ *n* [U] the surroundings; neighbourhood: *Are there any shops in this vicinity/in the vicinity of your house?*

**vi·cious** /ˈvɪʃəs/ *adj* **1** cruel; having or showing hate and the desire to hurt: *He gave the dog a vicious blow with his stick.* **2** dangerous; able or likely to cause severe hurt: *a vicious-looking knife* **3 vicious circle** a set of events in which cause and effect follow each other in a circular pattern: *"Crime leads to prison, which leads to unemployment, which leads to crime. It's a vicious circle."* **–viciously** *adv* **–viciousness** *n* [U]

**vic·tim** /ˈvɪktəm/ *n* [*of*] a person, animal, or thing that suffers pain, harm, etc., as a result of other people's actions, or of illness, bad luck, etc.: *Four people were killed in the explosion, but police have not yet named the victims.*

**vic·tim·ize**‖also **-ise** *BrE* /ˈvɪktəmaɪz/ *v* **-ized, -izing** [T] to cause (someone) to suffer unfairly: *victimized because of one's views* **–victimization** /-ˈzeɪʃən/ *n* [U]

**vic·tor** /ˈvɪktəʳ/ *n fml or lit* a winner in a battle, race, game, or other kind of struggle

**Vic·to·ri·an** /vɪkˈtɔːrɪən‖-ˈto-/ *adj,n* **1** (any British person) of or living in the time when Queen Victoria ruled (1837–1901): *Victorian furniture|Florence Nightingale was a famous Victorian.* **2** like the middle-class society in the time of Queen Victoria; very respectable and religious in a formal way: *His opinions about sex are very Victorian.*

**vic·to·ry** /ˈvɪktəri/ *n* **-ries** [C;U *in, over*] (an) act of winning or state of having won (in war or in any kind of struggle): *The officers led their men to victory in battle.|The hockey team had a string of victories* (=a number of wins) *last season.* –opposite **defeat –victorious** *adj: the victorious team* **–victoriously** *adv*

**vict·uals** /ˈvɪtlz/ *n* [P] *old use* food and drink

**vid·e·o¹** /ˈvɪdiəʊ/ *adj* [A] **1** connected with or used in the showing of pictures by television: *a video* DISPLAY *system* –compare AUDIO **2** using VIDEOTAPE¹: *a video recording*

**video²** also **videotape recorder** *fml*– *n* an instrument which records pictures and sound using VIDEOTAPE¹: *I'm going to record that television play on my video.* –see picture on page 355

**vid·e·o·tape¹** /ˈvɪdiəʊteɪp/ *n* [U] a long narrow band of MAGNETic material on which television pictures (and sound) are recorded

**videotape²** *v* **-taped, -taping** [T] to record (a television show) on VIDEOTAPE

**vie** /vaɪ/ *v* **vied, vying** [I *with, for*] to compete (against someone) (for something): *They are vying (with each other) for the lead.*

**view¹** /vjuː/ *n* **1** [U] ability to see or be seen from a particular place; sight: *My view of the harbour was blocked by the new building.|The valley was hidden from view in the mist.|When we reached the top of the mountain, we came in view of* (=were able to see) *a wide plain below/a wide plain came into view.* (=was able to be seen) **2** [C *of*] (a picture or photograph of) something seen from a particular place, esp. a stretch of pleasant country: *There's a view of the river from my window.* **3** [S *of*] a special chance to see someone or something: *If you stand here you'll get a better view of the procession.* **4** [C] a personal opinion, belief, idea, etc., about something: *In my view, he's a fool.|What are your views on free education?* **5 in view of** considering; taking into consideration: *In view of his age, the police have decided not to* PROSECUTE. **6 keep something in view** to remember something as a possibility or for future consideration if a favourable chance comes **7 on view** being shown to the public: *Our new range of cars is now on view.* **8 take a dim/poor view of** *infml* to think unfavourably about **9 with a view to doing something** with the aim of; in order to do something: *He put a new roof on his house with a view to increasing its value.*

USAGE 1 Compare **scenery**, **scene**, and **view**: The general appearance of the country, considered for its beauty, is **scenery**: *the beautiful* **scenery** *of the English Lakes.* A **view** is the part of the **scenery** that can be seen from one place: *There's a fine* **view** *of the mountains from our hotel window.* **Scene** can mean the same as **view**, but a **scene** is more likely to include people and movement: *a happy* **scene** *of children playing in the garden.* 2 Like **view**, **prospect** and **outlook** also describe what you see when you look from a particular place. But all three words have common fig. meanings. **View** in this sense is like **opinion**, and what is expected to happen in the future is the **outlook** or **prospect**: *What are your* **views** *on the present government?|Trade's bad, and the* **outlook** *for next year is even worse.|The* **prospect** *of the coming examinations made us all nervous.*

**view²** *v* [T] **1** *esp. tech* to examine; look at thoroughly: *Several possible buyers have come to view the house.* **2** to consider; regard; think about: *He viewed his son's absence from school very badly.* (=did not approve of it)|*How do you view this matter?* (=What is your opinion about it?)

**view·er** /ˈvjuːəʳ/ *n* a person watching television

**view·point** /ˈvjuːpɔɪnt/ *n* → POINT OF VIEW

**vig·il** /ˈvɪdʒəl/ *n* [C;U] (an act of) remaining watchful for some purpose (e.g. on guard, in prayer, or looking after sick people), esp. during the night (esp. in the phrases **keep vigil, all-night vigil**)

**vig·i·lant** /ˈvɪdʒəˌlənt/ *adj fml* continually watchful or on guard –**vigilance** *n* [U] –**vigilantly** *adv*

**vig·i·lan·te** /ˌvɪdʒəˈlænti/ *n esp. derog* a member of an unofficial organization which keeps order and punishes crime in an area where an official body either does not exist or does not work properly

**vig·our** *BrE*‖**vigor** *AmE* /ˈvɪgəʳ/ *n* [U] forcefulness; strength shown in power of action –**vigorous** *adj: a vigorous speech* –**vigorously** *adv*

**vile** /vaɪl/ *adj* hateful; shameful; evil; low and worthless: *Would you be so vile as to steal a coat from a blind man?* **2** *infml* very bad or unpleasant: *This food is vile!* –**vilely** *adv* –**vileness** *n* [U]

**vil·i·fy** /ˈvɪləfaɪ/ *v* **-fied, -fying** [T] *fml* to say bad things about; abuse –**vilification** /-fəˈkeɪʃən/ *n* [U]

**vil·la** /ˈvɪlə/ *n* a pleasant house with a garden, esp. one in the country or used for holidays: *We're renting a villa in the south of France for the summer holidays.*

**vil·lage** /ˈvɪlɪdʒ/ *n* a collection of houses and other buildings (such as a church, pub, school, and one or more shops) in a country area, smaller than a town: *the village schoolmaster*|*The whole village* (=all the people in the village) *went to the baker's funeral.*

**vil·lag·er** /ˈvɪlɪdʒəʳ/ *n* a person who lives in a village

**vil·lain** /ˈvɪlən/ *n* **1** (esp. in old plays, films, and stories) a wicked man, esp. the main bad character: *The villain carried off the young girl and tied her to the railway line.* –opposite **hero 2** *BrE infml* a criminal –**villainous** *adj*

**vil·lain·y** /ˈvɪləni/ *n* [U] *esp. lit* wicked behaviour

**vin·ai·grette** /ˌvɪnəˈgret, ˌvɪneɪ-/ *n* [U] a sharp-tasting mixture of oil, VINEGAR, salt, pepper, etc., served with some cold dishes of meat, fish, vegetables and SALAD

**vin·di·cate** /ˈvɪndəkeɪt/ *v* **-cated, -cating** [T] to prove to be true or right; free from blame: *The government's actions have been vindicated by the improvement in living standards.* –**vindication** /-ˈkeɪʃən/ *n* [S;U *of*]

**vin·dic·tive** /vɪnˈdɪktɪv/ *adj* showing the desire to harm someone who has harmed oneself –**vindictively** *adv* –**vindictiveness** *n* [U]

**vine** /vaɪn/ *n* **1** a climbing plant that produces bunches of juicy green or purple fruit (GRAPES) **2** any creeping or climbing plant (such as the IVY, the CUCUMBER, etc.)

**vin·e·gar** /ˈvɪnɪgəʳ/ *n* [U] an acid-tasting liquid made usu. from MALT or sour wine, used in preserving or adding taste to food

**vine·yard** /ˈvɪnjəd‖-jərd/ *n* a piece of land planted with VINES (1) for wine production

**vin·tage¹** /ˈvɪntɪdʒ/ *adj* [A] **1** (of wines) made in a year when the VINTAGE² produced wines of high quality **2** produced in a time famous for high quality and lasting value: *a vintage silent film*|*a vintage tennis performance by Connors* **3** (of a car) made between 1916 and 1930 –compare VETERAN (2)

**vintage²** *n* (a fine wine produced from) the gathering of GRAPES in a particular year: *The vintage was earlier than usual this year.*|*a good vintage*

**vi·nyl** /ˈvaɪnəl/ *n* [U;C] firm bendable plastic used instead of leather, rubber, wood, etc.

**vi·o·la** /viˈəʊlə/ *n* a stringed musical instrument, like the VIOLIN but a little larger

**vi·o·late** /ˈvaɪəleɪt/ *v* **-lated, -lating** [T] **1** to disregard or act against (a promise, etc.): *The country violated the international agreement.* **2** *esp. lit* to break, spoil, or destroy (something that ought to be respected): *to violate a grave* **3** *lit or euph* to have sex with (a woman) by force; RAPE –compare DEFILE –**violation** /-ˈleɪʃən/ *n* [C;U]: *a violation of the recent agreement*

**vi·o·lence** /ˈvaɪələns/ *n* [U] **1** very great force in action or feeling: *The wind blew with great violence.* **2** use of bodily force to hurt or harm: *The police used unnecessary violence on the crowd.*|*robbery with violence*

**vi·o·lent** /ˈvaɪələnt/ *adj* using, showing, or produced by great damaging force: *The madman was violent and had to be locked up.*|*a violent storm*|*She was in a violent temper.*|*a violent death* –**violently** *adv*

**vi·o·let** /ˈvaɪələt/ *n,adj* **1** [C] a small plant with sweet-smelling dark purplish-blue flowers **2** [U] (having) a purplish-blue colour

**vi·o·lin** /ˌvaɪəˈlɪn/ *n* a four-stringed musical instrument, supported between the left shoulder and the chin and played by drawing a BOW³ (2) across the strings –**violinist** *n*

**vi·o·lon·cel·lo** /ˌvaɪələnˈtʃeləʊ/ *n* **-los** *fml* for CELLO

**VIP** *n infml* a very important person; person of great influence or fame: *The airport VIP lounge*

**vi·per** /ˈvaɪpəʳ/ *n* a small poisonous snake

**vir·gin¹** /ˈvɜːdʒən‖ˈvɜr-/ *n* a person (esp. a woman or girl) who has never had sexual relations with a member of the opposite sex –**virginal** *adj*

**virgin²** *adj* **1** [A] without sexual experience **2** fresh; unspoiled: *no footmarks on the virgin snow*

**vir·gin·i·ty** /vɜːˈdʒɪnəti‖vɜr-/ *n* [U] the state of being a VIRGIN¹: *She was 19 when she* **lost her virginity**. (=had sex with a man for the first time)

**Virgin Mar·y** /ˌ·· ˈ··/ *n* (in the Christian religion) Mary, the mother of Christ

**Vir·go** /ˈvɜːgəʊ‖ˈvɜr-/ *n* see ZODIAC

**vir·ile** /ˈvɪraɪl‖ˈvɪrəl/ *adj usu. apprec* (of a man) having strong and manly qualities, esp. in matters of sex: *a virile young sportsman*

**vi·ril·i·ty** /vəˈrɪləti/ *n* [U] *usu. apprec* male sexual power; manly qualities

**vir·tu·al** /ˈvɜːtʃuəl‖ˈvɜr-/ *adj* [A] almost what is stated; in fact though not in name: *The king was so much under the influence of his wife that she was the virtual ruler of the country.*

**vir·tu·al·ly** /ˈvɜːtʃuəli‖ˈvɜr-/ *adv* almost; very nearly: *The dinner's virtually ready.* –see Study Notes on page 389

**vir·tue** /ˈvɜːtʃuː‖ˈvɜr-/ *n* **1** [U] goodness, nobleness, and worth of character: *a man of the highest virtue* –opposite **vice 2** [C] any good quality of character or behaviour: *the virtues of loyalty, courage, and truthfulness* **3** [C;U] (an) advantage: *One of the virtues of this material is that it's easily washable.* **4 by virtue of** as a result of; by means of: *She became a British citizen by virtue of her marriage to an Englishman.*

**vir·tu·o·so** /ˌvɜːtʃuˈəʊzəʊ‖ˌvɜrtʃuˈəʊsəʊ/ *n* **-sos** a very skilful performer in one of the arts, esp. music

–**virtuosity** *n* [U]

**vir·tu·ous** /'vɜːtʃuəs‖'vɜr-/ *adj* possessing, showing, or practising VIRTUE(*s*) (1,2) –**virtuously** *adv*

**vir·u·lent** /'vɪrulənt‖'vɪrə-/ *adj* **1** (of a poison, a disease caused by bacteria, etc.) very powerful, quick-acting, and dangerous to life or health **2** (of a feeling or its expression) very bitter; full of hatred –**virulence** *n* –**virulently** *adv*

**vi·rus** /'vaɪərəs/ *n* a living thing even smaller than bacteria which causes infectious disease in the body, in plants, etc.: *virus infections* –compare GERM

**vi·sa** /'viːzə/ *n* an official mark put onto a PASSPORT giving a foreigner permission to enter, pass through, or leave a particular country: *Do Americans need a visa to visit Britain?*

**vis·age** /'vɪzɪdʒ/ *n lit* the human face, esp. with regard to its expression or appearance

**vis-à-vis** /ˌviːz ɑː 'viː, ˌviːz ə 'viː/ *prep fml or pomp* with regard to; when compared to: *This year's profits show an improvement vis-à-vis last year's.*

**vis·count** /'vaɪkaunt/ **viscountess** *fem.*– *n* [A;C] *(often cap.)* (the title of) a British nobleman next in rank below an EARL

**vis·cous** /'vɪskəs/ *adj* (of a liquid) thick and sticky; that does not flow easily –**viscosity** /-'kɒsəti‖-'ka-/ *n* [U]

**vis·i·bil·i·ty** /ˌvɪzə'bɪləti/ *n* [U] (esp. in official weather reports) the degree of clearness with which objects can be seen according to the weather: *We had a splendid view of the mountains because of the very good visibility.*|*The mist was so thick that visibility was down to only ten metres.* (=you could only see up to a distance of ten metres)

**vis·i·ble** /'vɪzəbəl/ *adj* that can be seen; noticeable to the eye –opposite **invisible** –**visibly** *adv: He was visibly anxious about the examination.*

**vi·sion** /'vɪʒən/ *n* **1** [U] the ability to see: *I've had my eyes tested and the report says that my vision is perfect.* **2** [U] power of imagination and expression; wisdom in understanding the true meaning of facts, esp. with regard to the future: *a man of vision*|*We need someone with real vision to lead the party.* **3** [C *of*] something that is without bodily reality, seen (as) in a dream, in the imagination, or as a religious experience: *a vision of God*|*He has a clear vision of the future he wants for his children.*|(fig.) *There was so much traffic on the way to the airport that I* **had visions of** *missing the plane.* (=I thought I would miss it)

**vi·sion·a·ry[1]** /'vɪʒənəri‖-neri/ *adj* **1** *apprec* having or showing VISION (2) **2** fanciful; existing in the mind only and unlikely to happen

**visionary[2]** *n* **-ries** a person whose aims are noble or excellent but impractical

**vis·it[1]** /'vɪzət/ *v* **1** [I;T] to go and spend time in (a place) or with (a person): *While we're in Europe we ought to visit Holland.*|*Aunt Jane usually visits us for two or three weeks in the spring.*|*When we were in London we visited the Tower twice.*|*Visiting hours in the hospital* (=the times when sick people may be visited) *are from 4.30 to 6.00.* **2** [T] to go to (a place) in order to make an official examination: *The school was visited by the education officer.*

**visit** sthg. **on** sbdy. *v prep* [T] *fml or bibl* to direct (one's anger, a punishment, etc.) against: *God has visited his anger on us.*

**visit[2]** *n* an act or time of visiting: *He makes several business visits to America every year.*|*We've just had a visit from the police.* (=the police have visited us)|*I think you should* **pay a visit to** *the doctor*/**pay** *the doctor* **a visit** *about your arm.*

**vis·i·ta·tion** /ˌvɪzə'teɪʃən/ *n* [*by, of*] a formal visit by someone in charge (esp. by a high official person to discover whether things are in good order)

**vis·it·or** /'vɪzətə^r/ *n* [*to*] a person who visits: *Visitors to the castle are asked not to take photographs.*|*Visitors to a place of interest or hotel often write their names in a* **visitors book**.

**vi·sor** /'vaɪzə^r/ *n* **1** the part of a HELMET which protects the face **2** the front part of a cap

**vis·ta** /'vɪstə/ *n* a distant view, to which the eye is directed between narrow limits, e.g. by rows of trees

**vi·su·al** /'vɪʒuəl/ *adj* gained by or connected with seeing: *Visual knowledge of a place of battle helps a general to plan his attack.*|*The* **visual arts** *are painting, dancing, etc., as opposed to music and literature.* –**visually** *adv: visually pleasing*

**visual aid** /ˌ··'·/ *n* an object that can be looked at (such as a picture, map, or film) used for helping people to learn

**vi·su·al·ize** ‖also **-ise** *BrE* /'vɪʒuəlaɪz/ *v* **-ized, -izing** [T +*v-ing*/*as*] to form a picture of (something or someone) in the mind; imagine: *He described the place and I tried to visualize it.*|*Can you visualize living there?* –**visualization** /-'zeɪʃən/ *n* [U]

**vi·tal** /'vaɪtl/ *adj* **1** [*to, for*] very necessary; of the greatest importance: *This point is vital to my argument.*|*Your support is vital for the success of my plan.*|*He was lucky that the bullet hadn't entered a* **vital organ**. (=one which is necessary for life) **2** full of life and force: *Their leader's vital and cheerful manner filled his men with courage.* **3 vital statistics: a** *infml* the measurements of a woman's body round the chest, waist, and HIPS **b** certain official facts about people's lives, esp. their births, marriages, and deaths

**vi·tal·i·ty** /vaɪ'tæləti/ *n* [U] lively forcefulness of character or manner: *His singing lacks vitality.*

**vi·tal·ly** /'vaɪtl-i/ *adv* in the highest possible degree: *It is vitally important to switch off the electricity before attempting to repair the television.*

**vit·a·min** /'vɪtəmən, 'vaɪ-‖'vaɪ-/ *n* any one of several chemical substances which are present in certain foods, and are important for growth and good health: *This type of bread has added vitamins.*|*Oranges contain vitamin C.*

**vi·ti·ate** /'vɪʃieɪt/ *v* **-ated, -ating** [T] *fml* to spoil; harm the quality of: *The report is vitiated by continual spelling mistakes.*

**vit·re·ous** /'vɪtriəs/ *adj tech* of or like glass: *Vitreous rocks are hard and shiny.*|*vitreous* CHINA

**vit·ri·ol·ic** /ˌvɪtri'ɒlɪk‖-'ɑlɪk/ *adj* (of a feeling or its expression) bitter and violent: *vitriolic remarks*

**vi·va·cious** /və'veɪʃəs/ *adj* (esp. of a woman) full of life and high spirits –**vivaciously** *adv* –**vivacity** /-'væsəti/ *n* [U] –**vivaciousness** *n* [U]

**viv·id** /'vɪvəd/ *adj* **1** (of light or colour) bright and strong: *a vivid flash of lightning*|*vivid red hair* **2** that produces sharp clear pictures in the mind; lifelike: *a child with a vivid imagination|a vivid description* **–vividly** *adv* **–vividness** *n* [U]

**viv·i·sec·tion** /ˌvɪvə̍ˈsekʃən/ *n* [U] the practice of performing operations on living animals, esp. in order to increase medical knowledge

**vix·en** /ˈvɪksən/ *n* a female fox

**viz.** /vɪz/ *adv* that is to say: *On most English farms you'll find only four kinds of animal, viz. horses, sheep, cattle, and pigs.*

USAGE Usually read aloud as "NAMELY".

**vo·cab·u·la·ry** /vəˈkæbjʊləri, vəʊ-‖-bjəleri/ *n* **-ries** **1** all the words known to a particular person, or used in a particular kind of work, etc.: *Our baby's got a vocabulary of about ten words.|the vocabulary of the lawcourts* **2** a list of words, usu. in alphabetical order and with explanations of their meanings, less complete than a dictionary

**vo·cal** /ˈvəʊkəl/ *adj* **1** [A] connected with or produced by or for the voice: *The tongue is one of the vocal organs.|vocal music* **2** *infml* expressing oneself freely and noisily in words: *a very vocal meeting* **–vocally** *adv*

**vocal cords, vocal chords** /ˈ·· ·, ˌ·· ˈ·/ *n* [P] thin bands of muscle at the upper end of a person's air passage (WINDPIPE) that produce sound

**vo·cal·ist** /ˈvəʊkələ̍st/ *n* a singer of popular songs, esp. one who sings with a band

**vo·ca·tion** /vəʊˈkeɪʃən/ *n* **1** [S;U *for*] a particular fitness or ability (for a certain kind of work, esp. of a worthy kind): *She's a good doctor because she has a real vocation for looking after the sick.* **2** [C] a job, esp. a worthy one for which one has a VOCATION (1): *Teaching children is more than just a way of making money: it's a vocation.* **3** [S] a special call from God to be a priest, MONK, etc. –see JOB (USAGE)

**vo·ca·tion·al** /vəʊˈkeɪʃənəl/ *adj* preparing for a particular type of job: *vocational training for pilots*

**vo·cif·er·ous** /vəˈsɪfərəs, vəʊ-‖vəʊ-/ *adj fml* noisy in the expression of one's feelings: *vociferous demands* **–vociferously** *adv* **–vociferousness** *n* [U]

**vod·ka** /ˈvɒdkə‖ˈvɑdkə/ *n* [U] a strong, colourless, and almost tasteless alcoholic drink, first made in Russia and Poland

**vogue** /vəʊg/ *n* the fashion or custom at a certain time: *High boots were the vogue for women last year.*|**in vogue/out of vogue** (=fashionable/not fashionable)

**voice¹** /vɔɪs/ *n* **1** [C;U] the sound(s) produced by humans in speaking and singing: *He had such a bad cold he lost his voice.|She lowered her voice.* (=spoke quietly)|*We could hear the children's voices in the garden.|a good voice for singing/a good singing voice|He* **gave voice to** (=expressed) *his opinions.* **2** [U] (the expressing of) an opinion: *The crowd was large, but they were all* **of one voice.** (=they all said the same thing)|(fig.)*He was very angry at first but in the end the* **voice of reason** *won.* **3** [C *usu. sing.*] *tech* the form of the verb which shows whether the subject of a sentence acts (**active voice**) or is acted on (**passive voice**) **4 at the top of one's voice** very loudly **5 raise one's voice: a** to speak louder **b** to speak loudly and angrily (to someone): *Don't raise your voice to me.* **6 -voiced** having a voice of the stated kind: *loud-voiced|soft-voiced|sweet-voiced*

**voice²** *v* **voiced, voicing** [T] to express in words, esp. forcefully: *The chairman voiced all our feelings.*

**void¹** /vɔɪd/ *adj* **1** [F *of*] *fml* empty (of); without; lacking: *That part of the town is completely void of interest for visitors.* –see also DEVOID **2** *esp. law* (of any kind of official agreement) having no value or effect from the beginning: *An agreement signed by a child is void.* –see also NULL AND VOID

**void²** *n* [S] an empty space, esp. the space around our world and beyond the stars: *A ball of fire seemed to fall out of the void, disappearing before it reached the earth.*|(fig.)*The child's death left a painful void in his parents' lives.*

**vol** *n abbrev. said as:* VOLUME (1)

**vol·a·tile** /ˈvɒlətaɪl‖ˈvɑlətl/ *adj* **1** (of a person or his/her character) quickly-changing and undependable **2** (of a liquid or oil) easily changing into a gas: *Petrol is volatile.* **–volatility** /-ˈtɪlə̍ti / *n* [U]

**vol-au-vent** /ˌvɒl əʊ ˈvɑ̃‖ˌvɑl- (*Fr* vɔlovɑ̃)/ *n French* a small pastry case filled with meat, chicken, etc.

**vol·ca·no** /vɒlˈkeɪnəʊ‖vɑl-/ *n* **-noes** *or* **-nos** a mountain with a large opening (CRATER) at the top through which melting rock (LAVA), steam, gases, etc., escape from time to time with explosive force from inside the earth: *An* **active volcano** *may explode at any time.|An* **extinct volcano** *has ceased to be able to explode.* **–volcanic** /-ˈkænɪk/ *adj: volcanic rocks/activity*

**vole** /vəʊl/ *n* a small short-tailed animal of the rat and mouse family, which lives in fields, woods, banks of rivers, etc.: *a water vole*

**vo·li·tion** /vəˈlɪʃən‖vəʊ-, və-/ *n* [U] *fml* the act of using one's will in choosing a course of action: *I didn't ask him to go; he went* **of his own volition.**

**vol·ley** /ˈvɒli‖ˈvɑli/ *n* **-leys** **1** a number of shots, arrows, stones, etc., fired or thrown at the same time: *a volley of shots was heard*|(fig.) *a volley of curses* **2** (esp. in tennis) a hitting of a ball which has not touched the ground first

**vol·ley·ball** /ˈvɒlibɔːl‖ˈvɑ-/ *n* [U] a game in which a large ball is struck by hand across a net without being allowed to touch the ground

**volt** /vəʊlt/ *n* a standard measure of electrical force used in causing a flow of electrical current along wires

**volt·age** /ˈvəʊltɪdʒ/ *n* [C;U] electrical force measured in VOLTS

**volte-face** /ˌvɒlt ˈfɑːs‖ˌvɔlt-/ *n* [*usu. sing.*] *esp. fml* a change to a completely opposite opinion or course of action: *to do/make a volte-face*

**vol·u·ble** /ˈvɒljʊbəl‖ˈvɑljə-/ *adj often derog* talking with a great flow of words: *a voluble speaker* **–volubility** /-ˈbɪlə̍ti / *n* [U] **–volubly** *adv*

**vol·ume** /ˈvɒljuːm‖ˈvɑljəm/ *n* **1** [U] (degree of) loudness of sound: *The television is too loud; turn the volume down.* **2** [U *of*] size or quantity thought of as measurement of the space filled by something: *The volume of this container is 100,000* CUBIC *metres.* **3** [C] a book, esp. one of a set of the same kind: *We have a set of Dickens' works in 24 volumes.* **4** [C;U] *esp. tech* amount produced by some kind of (industrial) activity: *The volume of passenger travel on the railways is increasing again.*

**vo·lu·mi·nous** /və'luːmɨnəs, və'ljuː-‖və'luː-/ *adj* **1** (of a garment) very loose and full; using much cloth: *a voluminous skirt* **2** containing or able to hold a lot: *a voluminous suitcase* –**voluminously** *adv*

**vol·un·ta·ry** /'vɒləntəri‖'vɑlənteri/ *adj* **1** (of a person or an action) acting or done willingly, without payment and without being forced: *He made a voluntary statement to the police.|At election time the party needs a lot of voluntary helpers.* **2** [A] controlled or supported by people who give their money, services, etc., free: *Many social services are still provided by voluntary organizations.* –**voluntarily** *adv: He made the promise quite voluntarily.*

**vol·un·teer**[1] /ˌvɒlən'tɪəʳ‖ˌvɑ-/ *n* a person who VOLUNTEERS[2] (1,2): *This work costs us nothing; it's all done by volunteers.*

**volunteer**[2] *v* **1** [I +*to-v*] to offer one's services or help without payment; offer (to do something), esp. when others are unwilling: *He volunteered to help me move.* **2** [I +*to-v/for*] to offer to join the armed forces of one's own free will **3** [T] to tell (something) without being asked: *My friend volunteered an interesting piece of news.*

**vo·lup·tu·ous** /və'lʌptʃuəs/ *adj* (esp. connected with women) that suggests or expresses sexual pleasure: *voluptuous movements|a voluptuous mouth.* –**voluptuously** *adv* –**voluptuousness** *n* [U]

**vom·it**[1] /'vɒmɨt‖'vɑ-/ *v* [I;T] to throw up (the contents of the stomach) through the mouth; be sick: *He ate so much that he vomited.*

**vomit**[2] *n* [U] food or other matter that has been VOMITed

**voo·doo** /'vuːduː/ *n* [U] *(often cap.)* (esp. in the West Indies) a set of magical beliefs and practices, used as a form of religion

**vo·ra·cious** /və'reɪʃəs, vɒ-‖vɔ-, və-/ *adj fml* eating or desiring large quantities of food: *Pigs are voracious eaters.*|(fig.) *She's a voracious reader.* –**voracity** *n* [U] /-'ræsɨti/ –**voraciously** *adv*

**vor·tex** /'vɔːteks‖'vɔr-/ *n* **-texes** *or* **-tices** /-tɨsiːz/ *esp. lit* a circular moving mass of anything, esp. water or wind, which causes objects to be drawn into its hollow centre, as in a WHIRLPOOL or WHIRLWIND

**vote**[1] /vəʊt/ *n* **1** [C] an act of making a choice or decision on a matter by means of voting: *Since there is some disagreement on this matter, let's* **take a vote** *on it/let's* **put it to the vote.** **2** [C] a choice or decision as expressed by voting: *There were 15 votes in favour of my suggestion, and 23 against.|She will certainly not get my vote* (=I will not vote for her) *at the next election.|You must* **cast** (=record) **your vote** *before eight o'clock tonight.* **3** [S] the whole number of such choices made by a particular set of people: *the Irish/Jewish vote* **4** [*the* S] the right to vote in political elections: *In Britain, people get the vote at the age of 18.* **5 vote of thanks** a public expression of thanks: *We proposed a vote of thanks to the speaker for his talk.*

**vote**[2] *v* **voted, voting 1** [I +*to-v/(that)/for, against, on*] to express one's choice officially from among the possibilities offered (by marking a piece of paper, raising one's hand at a meeting, etc.): *You're too young to vote.|Did you vote for Mrs Thatcher in the last election?|The railway workers have voted to go back to work.|The sign said "Vote Labour".* (=vote for this party)|(fig. *infml*) *I vote we go home.* (=let's go home) –compare ELECT **2** [T] to agree, by a vote, to provide (something): *Parliament has voted the town a large sum of money for a new road.* **3** [T] *infml* to agree as the general opinion: *The party was voted a success.*

**vot·er** /'vəʊtəʳ/ *n* a person who is voting

**vouch·er** /'vaʊtʃəʳ/ *n BrE* a kind of ticket that may be used instead of money for a particular purpose: *a travel voucher|Some firms give their workers luncheon vouchers, which they can use to buy a meal.*

**vouch for** sbdy./sthg. /vaʊtʃ/ *v prep* [T] **1** to declare one's belief in (someone or something), from one's own personal experience or knowledge: *I've read this report carefully and I can vouch for its accuracy.* **2** to take responsibility for (someone's future behaviour)

**vow**[1] /vaʊ/ *n* a solemn promise: *All the men* **took/made a vow** *of loyalty to their leader.*

**vow**[2] *v* [T +*to-v/(that)*] to declare or swear solemnly (that one will do something): *He vowed to kill his wife's lover.|When young John was caught stealing he vowed he'd never do it again.*

**vow·el** /'vaʊəl/ *n* **1** a human speech sound in which the breath is let out without any stop or any closing of the air passage in the mouth: *The simple vowel sounds of British English are represented in this dictionary by* /iː, ɪ, e, æ, ɑː, ɒ, ɔː, ʊ, uː, ʌ, ɜː, ə/. **2** a letter used for representing any of these: *The vowels in the English alphabet are* a, e, i, o, u, *and sometimes* y. –compare CONSONANT, DIPHTHONG

**voy·age**[1] /'vɔɪ-ɪdʒ/ *n* a long journey made by boat or ship (or in space): *a voyage from England to India*

**voyage**[2] *v* **-aged, -aging** [I] *lit or fml* to make a long journey by sea –see TRAVEL (USAGE)

**vs.** /'vɜːsəs‖'vɜr-/ *AmE* for v.

**vul·gar** /'vʌlgəʳ/ *adj* **1** very rude, low, or bad-mannered; going against the accepted standards of polite society: *the children's vulgar language|Putting food into one's mouth with a knife is considered vulgar in England.* **2** showing a lack of fine feeling or good judgment in the choice of what is beautiful: *vulgar furniture* –**vulgarly** *adv*

**vul·gar·i·ty** /vʌl'gærɨti/ *n* **-ties 1** [U] the quality of being VULGAR **2** [C *often pl.*] VULGAR speech or action

**vul·ne·ra·ble** /'vʌlnərəbəl/ *adj* [*to*] easily harmed, hurt, or attacked; sensitive: *We're in a vulnerable position here, with the enemy on the hill above us.|The young girl looked very vulnerable.* –**vulnerability** /-rə'bɪlɨti/ *n* [U *to*] –**vulnerably** *adv*

**vul·ture** /'vʌltʃəʳ/ *n* a large ugly tropical bird with almost featherless head and neck, which feeds on dead animals

**vy·ing** /'vaɪ-ɪŋ/ *v pres. participle of* VIE

# W, w

**W, w** /ˈdʌbəljuː/ **W's, w's** *or* **Ws, ws** the 23rd letter of the English alphabet

**W** *written abbrev. said as*: **a** west(ern) **b** WATT

**wad** /wɒd‖wɑd/ *n* [*of*] **1** a thick collection of things, such as pieces of paper, folded, pressed, or fastened together: *a wad of bank notes* **2** a thick soft mass of material used for filling an empty space, hole, etc.: *wads of cotton in one's ears to keep out noise*

**wad·dle** /ˈwɒdl‖ˈwɑdl/ *v* **-dled, -dling** [I *along*] to walk with short steps, moving one's body from one side to the other, like a duck –**waddle** *n*

**wade** /weɪd/ *v* **waded, wading** [I *across, into, through*] to walk through water: *We had to wade across the river, and the water came up to our knees.* –compare PADDLE[3]

**wade through** sthg. *v prep* [T] *infml* to finish (something long or unpleasant) with effort: *I waded through that long report at last.*

**wa·fer** /ˈweɪfəʳ/ *n* **1** a very thin BISCUIT eaten esp. with ice cream **2** a thin round piece of bread used in the Christian religious ceremony of Holy COMMUNION

**waf·fle¹** /ˈwɒfəl‖ˈwɑ-/ *n* a large light sweet cake, common in America

**waffle²** *v* **-fled, -fling** [I *on*] *BrE infml* to talk nonsense in words that sound good: *Stop waffling and answer the question!* –**waffle** *n* [U]

**waft** /wɑːft, wɒft‖wɑft, wæft/ *v* [I;T] *esp. lit* to (cause to) move lightly (as if) on wind or waves: *Cooking smells wafted along the hall.*

**wag** /wæg/ *v* **-gg-** [I;T] (esp. of a dog) to shake (its tail) quickly and repeatedly from side to side: *The dog wagged its tail when it saw us.* –compare WAGGLE –**wag** *n*

**wage¹** /weɪdʒ/ *n* [A;S] wages: *a weekly wage of £120|The company's wage bill is over a million pounds a year.*

**wage²** *v* [T] *fml* to begin and continue (a struggle of some kind): *to* **wage war**|*The police are waging a war on/against crime in the city.*

**wa·ger** /ˈweɪdʒəʳ/ *v* [T +(*that*)] *fml* to BET³ –**wager** *n*

**wag·es** /ˈweɪdʒ½z/ *n* [P] a payment for labour or services, usu. received daily or weekly –see PAY (USAGE)

**wag·gle** /ˈwægəl/ *v* **-gled, -gling** [I;T] to (cause to) move frequently from side to side: *Can you waggle your ears?* –compare WAG –**waggle** *n* [S]

**wag·gon** *BrE*‖**wagon** *AmE* /ˈwægən/ *n* **1** a strong four-wheeled road vehicle, mainly for heavy loads, drawn by horses or oxen: *He takes his fruit to market by wagon/on a wagon.* **2** *BrE* a railway goods vehicle, esp. one with an open top

**waif** *n esp. lit* an uncared-for or homeless child: *a pitiful little waif*

**wail** /weɪl/ *v* [I;T +*that/with*] to cry out (something) with a long sound suggesting grief or pain: *The wind wailed in the chimney all night.|"You've taken my apple," he wailed.* –**wail** *n: the wails of a lost child*

**waist** /weɪst/ *n* (the part of a garment that goes round) the narrow part of the human body just above the legs and HIPS: *What do you measure round the waist?|It's a nice skirt, but too big round the waist.* –see picture on page 299

**waist·coat** /ˈweɪskəʊt, ˈweskət‖ˈweskət‖/ also **vest** *AmE*– *n* a close-fitting garment without arms worn esp. under the JACKET (short coat) of a three-piece suit

**waist·line** /ˈweɪstlaɪn/ *n* a line measured round the waist at its narrowest part: *Your waistline is getting bigger.*

**wait¹** /weɪt/ *v* [I +*to-v/for, about, around*] **1** to stay somewhere without doing anything until somebody or something comes or something happens: *We waited and waited.|We waited 20 minutes (for a bus).|We're waiting anxiously to hear the examination results.|Try not to keep her waiting.|"What's for dinner?" "Wait and see."* (=Wait, and you'll soon know the answer)|(fig.) *The business can wait until after dinner.* **2 wait at table** to serve meals, esp. as a regular job

USAGE Compare **wait** and **expect**. To **wait** suggests staying in the same place and/or taking no action until something happens: *I spent an hour* **waiting** *for a bus.|We can't start the meeting yet, we're* **waiting** *for John (to arrive).* If you **expect** something, you think it will probably happen, arrive, etc., whether you want it to or not: *I'm* **expecting** *a big telephone bill this month.|We were* **expecting** *12 guests* (=we thought 12 would come), *but only seven came.* –see also HOPE (USAGE)

**wait on/upon** sbdy. *v prep* [T] **1** *esp. old use* to attend as a servant **2 wait on someone hand and foot** to serve someone very humbly: *Don't expect me to wait on you hand and foot; make your own breakfast!*

**wait up** *v adv* [I *for*] *infml* to delay going to bed: *Don't wait up (for me): I shall be home very late.*

**wait²** *n* **1** an act or period of waiting: *We had a long wait for a bus.* **2 lie in wait (for someone)** to hide, waiting to attack (someone): *The robbers were lying in wait for me as I came out of the bank.*

**wait·er** /ˈweɪtəʳ/ **waitress** /-tr½s/ *fem.*– *n* a person who serves food at the tables in a restaurant –see picture on page 521

**waiting list** /ˈ·· ·/ *n* a list of people who want something (such as theatre tickets or a job): *There's a long waiting list of people who want telephones.*

**waiting room** /ˈ·· ·/ *n* a room for people who are waiting, e.g. to see a doctor

**waive** /weɪv/ *v* **waived, waiving** [T] *fml* to give up willingly (a right, a rule, etc.): *We cannot waive this rule except in case of illness.* –sounds like **wave**

**wake¹** /weɪk/ *v* **woke** /wəʊk/ *or* **waked, woken**

/ˈwəʊkən/ *or* **waked**, **waking** [I;T *up*] **1** to (cause to) cease to sleep: *I woke (up) at eight o'clock.*|*The children woke us up.*|(fig.) *The company has only just woken up to* (=become conscious of) *computers.* **2 Wake up** *infml* Listen!; Pay attention!

USAGE **Waken**, **awake**, and **awaken** can all be used in the patterns [I] and [T], though **awake** is usually [I] and **waken/awaken** are usually [T]. But **wake** (*up*) is the most common and least formal word in both patterns.

**wake²** *n* (esp. in Ireland) a gathering to watch and grieve over a dead person on the night before the burial

**wake³** *n* a track or path, esp. one left by a ship in water: (fig.) *disease* **in the wake of** (=as a result of) *the war*

**wake·ful** /ˈweɪkfəl/ *adj* not able to sleep; sleepless: *a wakeful night* –**wakefully** *adv* –**wakefulness** *n* [U]

**wak·en** /ˈweɪkən/ *v* [I;T *up*] *fml* to (cause to) wake: *We were wakened by a loud noise.*

**wak·ing** /ˈweɪkɪŋ/ *adj* [A] of the time when one is awake: *She spends all her waking hours working.*

**walk¹** /wɔːk/ *v* **1** [I;T] to (cause to) move at a walk: *Do you walk to work, or do you come by bus?*|*to walk (for) ten miles*|*She likes walking.* –see picture on page 669 **2** [T] to pass over, through, or along on foot: *tired out after walking the streets of London all day*|*to walk a* TIGHTROPE **3** [T] to take (an animal) for a walk; exercise: *He's walking the dog.* **4** [T] to go on foot with (someone), usu. to a stated place: *I'll walk you to the bus stop.*

USAGE **walk** is the usual word for moving on foot at a normal speed: *Do you* **walk** *to work, or do you go by bus?* To **amble** or **stroll** is to walk in an easy, unhurried way, esp. for pleasure. To **stride** is to walk purposefully with long steps, and to **march** is to walk with forceful regular steps as soldiers do. **Run** is the general word for moving quickly on one's legs. **Race, dash,** and **sprint** all suggest running very fast for a short distance: *I* **raced/dashed/sprinted** *down the road to catch the bus.* To **jog** is to run in a steady unhurried way as a form of exercise: *She goes* **jogging** *every morning.*

**walk into** sthg. *v prep* [T] to meet through carelessness: *He walked right into the trap.*

**walk off/away with** sthg. *v adv prep* [T] *infml* **1** to steal: *Someone's walked off with my bicycle.* **2** to win easily: *She walked off with first prize.*

**walk out** *v adv* [I *of*] to go on STRIKE² (1) –**walkout** *n: There's been an unofficial walkout at the car factory.*

**walk out on** sbdy. *v adv prep* [T] *infml* to leave suddenly, esp. in a time of trouble; desert: *He walked out on his wife and family.*

**walk over** sbdy. *v prep* [T] *infml* to treat badly: *His wife walks (all) over him.* –see also WALKOVER

**walk²** *n* **1** (of people and creatures) a natural and unhurried way of moving on foot from one place to another **2** a (usu. short) journey on foot: *Let's go for / have/take a short walk.*|*The station's just a ten-minute walk from here.* **3** a place, path, or course for walking: *There is a beautiful walk along the river.* (=beside the river)

**walk·ie-talk·ie** /ˌwɔːki ˈtɔːki/ *n infml* a two-way radio that can be carried, allowing one to talk as well as listen

**walking stick** /ˈ·· ·/ *n* a stick used by someone to support himself/herself while walking

**walk·o·ver** /ˈwɔːkˌəʊvəʳ/ *n infml* an easy victory –see also WALK **over**

**wall¹** /wɔːl/ *n* **1** an upright dividing surface (esp. of stone or brick) intended for defence or safety, or for enclosing something: *a garden surrounded by stone walls*|*the city wall of London*|(fig.) *a wall of fire/wall of silence* **2** the side of a building or a room: *Hang that picture on the wall.* –see picture on page 297 **3 bang/run one's head against a (brick) wall** *infml* to try to do something difficult with very little hope of success **4 with one's back to the wall** fighting with no way of escape

**wall²** *v* [T *in, up*] to provide, close with, or surround with a wall: *an old walled town in Portugal*

**wall** sthg.↔**off** *v adv* [T *from*] to separate with one or more walls: *This part of the house is walled off.*

**wal·la·by** /ˈwɒləbi‖ˈwɑ-/ *n* **-bies** *or* **-by** a KANGAROO of small to middle size

**wall·chart** /ˈwɔːltʃɑːt‖ˈwɑ-/ *n* a CHART¹ (1) containing information, used esp. as a teaching aid in a classroom –see picture on page 105

**wal·let** /ˈwɒlɨt‖ˈwɑ-/ *n* a small flat leather case which can usu. be folded, for holding paper money, tickets, etc., usu. carried by a man in his pocket

**wal·lop** /ˈwɒləp‖ˈwɑ-/ *v* [T] *infml* to hit with force: *to wallop someone* –**wallop** *n: He hit the floor with a wallop.*

**wal·low** /ˈwɒləʊ‖ˈwɑ-/ *v* [I *in*] to move or roll about happily in deep mud, dirt, water, etc.: *Pigs enjoy wallowing in mud.*|(fig.) *wallowing in self-pity/her success* –**wallow** *n* [*in*]: *a wallow in the mud*

**wall·pa·per** /ˈwɔːlˌpeɪpəʳ/ *n* [U] decorative paper to cover the walls of a room –**wallpaper** *v* [I;T]: *We've decided to wallpaper the bedroom.*

**wal·nut** /ˈwɔːlnʌt/ *n* **1** [C] an edible nut with a round rough shell **2** [C;U] the tree that produces these nuts, or its wood

**wal·rus** /ˈwɔːlrəs‖ˈwɔl-, ˈwɑl-/ *n* **-ruses** *or* **-rus** a large SEAL-like sea-animal with two long teeth (TUSKS) standing out from the face

**waltz¹** /wɔːls‖wɔlts/ *n* (music for) a slow social dance for a man and a woman: *a waltz by Strauss*

**waltz²** *v* [I;T] to (cause to) dance a WALTZ: *Can you waltz?*|*He waltzed her across the room.*

**wan** /wɒn‖wɑn/ *adj esp. lit* appearing ill, weak, and tired: *a wan smile* –**wanly** *adv* –**wanness** *n* [U]

**wand** /wɒnd‖wɑnd/ *n* a thin stick used by a person who does magic tricks: *He waved his magic wand and pulled a rabbit out of the hat.*

**wan·der** /ˈwɒndəʳ‖ˈwɑn-/ *v* **1** [I;T *about*] to move about (an area) without a fixed course, aim, or purpose: *The lost child was wandering (about) the streets.*|(fig.) *His mind began to wander.* (=to become confused) **2** [I *off*] to move away (from the main idea): *Don't wander off the point.* –**wanderer** *n*

**wan·der·lust** /ˈwɒndəlʌst‖ˈwɑndər-/ *n* [S;U] a strong desire not to stay in one place

**wane¹** /weɪn/ *v* **waned, waning** [I] to become gradually smaller or less after being full or complete: *The moon* WAXES³ **and wanes** *every month.*

**wane²** *n* **on the wane** becoming smaller, weaker, or less: *The government's popularity is on the wane.*
**wan·gle** /ˈwæŋgəl/ *v* **-gled, -gling** [T] *infml* to get (something) from someone, esp. by cleverness or a trick: *I wangled an invitation (out of George).*
**wan·na** /ˈwɒnə,ˈwɔnə‖ˈwanə,ˈwɔnə/ **1** want to **2** want a
USAGE **Want to** and **want a** are sometimes pronounced in this way. They may be written **wanna** in stories to show an informal way of speaking: *I don't wanna go.* (=I don't want to go.)|*Wanna drink?* (=Do you want a drink?)
**want¹** /wɒnt‖wɔnt, wɑnt/ *v* [not *be +v-ing*] **1** [T *+to-v*] to have a strong desire to or for; feel a strong desire to have: *I want a drink.*|*I want to have a drink.*|*What do you want for your birthday?* (=What present would you like?) **2** [T *+v-ing*] to need: *The house wants painting.* **3** [T *+to-v*] ought: *You want to see a doctor about your cough.* **4** [T] to wish or demand the presence of: *I wasn't wanted at the office, so I left.* **5** [T *usu. pass.*] (esp. of the police) to hunt or look for in order to catch: *He is wanted for murder.*|*He is a wanted man.* **6** [I] to lack enough food, clothing, shelter, etc.: *You shall never want while I have any money left.*
**want for** sthg. *v prep* [T *usu. in* NEGATIVES²] *fml* (of a person) to lack: *Their children have never wanted for anything.* (=have always had everything they need)
**want²** *n* **1** [S;U] lack, absence, or need: *The plants died* **for/from want of** *water.*|*I'll take this one for want of a better.* **2** [U] severe lack of things necessary to life: *How terrible to live* **in want!**
**want·ing** /ˈwɒntɪŋ‖ˈwɔn-, ˈwɑn-/ *adj* **be found (to be) wanting (in)** to be considered not good enough, strong enough, or full enough (of)
**wan·ton** /ˈwɒntən‖ˈwɔn-, ˈwɑn-/ *adj* **1** *lit* wild and full of fun: *wanton behaviour* **2** having no just cause or no good reason: *wanton cruelty* **–wantonly** *adv*
**wants** /wɒnts‖wɔnts, wɑnts/ *n* [P] needs: *My wants are few and are soon satisfied.*
**war¹** /wɔːʳ/ *n* [C;U] **1** (an example or period of) armed fighting between nations, esp. for a long period: *He fought in both World Wars.*|*Is war necessary?*|*a prisoner of war*|*Those two countries have been* **at war** *(with each other) for a long time.*|*There were many battles before the war was finally over.* **2** a struggle between opposing forces or for a particular purpose: *class war*|*to* **wage war on/against** *disease* **3 (having) been in the wars** *infml* (having) been hurt or damaged: *Your car looks as if it's been in the wars!*
**war²** *v* **-rr-** [I *with, against, for*] *lit* to take part in or direct a war: *a warring country*
**war·ble** /ˈwɔːbəl‖ˈwɔr-/ *v* **-bled, -bling** [I;T] (esp. of birds) to sing with a clear, continuous, yet varied note **–warble** *n* [*the* S *of*]
**ward** /wɔːd‖wɔrd/ *n* **1** a division of a hospital, esp. a large room usu. for people all needing treatment of the same kind: *the heart ward of a teaching hospital* **2** a division of a city, esp. for political purposes: *Which ward does she represent on the council?* **3** a person, esp. a child, who is under the protection of another person or of a law court (=is a **ward of court**) –compare GUARDIAN
**war dance** /ˈ· ·/ *n* a dance performed esp. by tribes in preparation for battle or after a victory
**war·den** /ˈwɔːdn‖ˈwɔrdn/ *n* **1** a person who looks after a place (and people): *the warden of an old people's home* **2** an official who helps to see that certain laws are obeyed: *A* **traffic warden** *sees that all cars are properly parked.* **3** *AmE* the head of a prison; GOVERNOR
**ward·er** /ˈwɔːdəʳ‖ˈwɔr-/ *n BrE* a prison guard
**ward off** sthg. *v adv* [T] protect oneself against (a blow, a danger, a cold, etc.): *Brushing your teeth regularly helps to ward off tooth decay.*
**war·drobe** /ˈwɔːdrəub‖ˈwɔr-/ *n* **1** a cupboard or large upright box, with a door, in which one hangs up clothes **2** a collection of clothes (esp. of one person or for one activity): *a new summer wardrobe*
**ware·house** /ˈweəhaus‖ˈweər-/ *n* **-houses** /hauzɪ̈z/ a building for storing things, esp. to be sold or before being moved
**wares** /weəz‖weərz/ *n* [P] *lit* articles for sale, usu. not in a shop: *The baker travelled round the town selling his wares.*
**war·fare** /ˈwɔːfeər‖ˈwɔr-/ *n* [U] (type of) war: *chemical warfare*
**war·head** /ˈwɔːhed‖ˈwɔr-/ *n* the explosive front end of a bomb or esp. MISSILE
**war·i·ly** /ˈweərɪ̈li/ *adv* see WARY **–wariness** *n* [U]
**war·like** /ˈwɔːlaɪk‖ˈwɔr-/ *adj* ready for war or liking war: *a warlike appearance/nation*
**warm¹** /wɔːm‖wɔrm/ *adj* **1** having or giving a pleasant feeling of heat: *warm milk*|*a warm fire*|*a warm sunny day* **2** able to keep in heat or keep out cold: *warm clothes* **3** showing or marked by strong feeling, esp. good feeling: *warm support for the local team*|*a warm welcome* **4** giving a pleasant feeling of cheerfulness or friendliness: *warm colours*|*a warm voice* –compare COOL **5** [F] (esp. in children's games) near a hidden object, the right answer to a question, etc.: *You're getting warm: you've nearly found the answer!* –opposite **cool** or **cold** **–warmly** *adv: He greeted me warmly.* **–warmness** *n* [U]
**warm²** *v* [I;T] to make or become warm: *They warmed their hands/themselves by the fire.*|*a warming fire/drink*|*The soup is warming in the pot over the fire.* –compare COOL
**warm to/towards** sbdy./sthg. *v prep* [T] *infml* to begin to like or be interested in: *The more he spoke, the more he warmed to his subject.*
**warm up** *v adv* [I;T (=**warm** sbdy./sthg.↔**up**)] **1** to make or become warm: *Come and warm yourself up by the fire.*|*The room soon warmed up.* **2** to make or become ready for action or performance: *The singers are warming up before the concert.*|*Let's warm up the car engine a bit before we start.* **–warm-up** /ˈ··/ *n*
**warm³** *n* [S] **1** [*the*] a warm place, state, or condition: *Come into the warm, out of the cold.* **2** the act of making oneself warm
**warm-blood·ed** /ˌ· ˈ··◂/ *adj tech* (of birds, MAMMALS, etc.) able to keep the temperature of the body high whether the outside temperature is high or low –see also COLD-BLOODED
**warm-heart·ed** /ˌ· ˈ··◂/ *adj* having or showing warm friendly feelings –see also COLD-HEARTED **–warm-heartedness** *n* [U]
**war·mon·ger** /ˈwɔːˌmʌŋgəʳ‖ˈwɔrˌmʌŋ-, -ˌmɑŋ-/ *n*

derog a person who encourages war

**warmth** /wɔːmθ‖wɔrmθ/ *n* [U] the state or quality of being warm: *the warmth of the fire/of his feelings*

**warn** /wɔːn‖wɔrn/ *v* [I;T +*that/of, against*] to tell of something bad that may happen; tell of how to prevent something bad: *The morning paper warned (us) of serious delays at the airport.|Drivers have been warned to avoid the roads through the city centre.|He warned the firm that profits would be low that year.|a red warning light on a car*

**warn·ing** /ˈwɔːnɪŋ‖ˈwɔr-/ *n* **1** [C;U +*to-v/of*] the act of warning or the state of being warned: *They attacked without warning.|a warning not to go there* **2** [C +*to-v/of*] something that warns: *Let that be a warning to you.|The accident served as a warning of what may happen.*

**warp¹** /wɔːp‖wɔrp/ *n* [S] **1** a twist out of a true level or straight line: *There's a warp in this table top.* **2** [*the*] *tech* threads running along the length of cloth –compare WEFT

**warp²** *v* [I;T] to (cause to) turn or twist out of shape: *A record warps if it gets too hot.*|(fig.) *the warped mind of a violent killer*

**war·path** /ˈwɔːpɑːθ‖ˈwɔrpæθ/ *n* **on the warpath** starting to fight or struggle: *Those politicians are on the warpath for higher taxes again.*

**war·rant¹** /ˈwɒrənt‖ˈwɔ-, ˈwɑ-/ *n* an official written order, esp. allowing the police to take certain action: *You can't search my house without a* **search warrant**.

**warrant²** *v* [T] **1** [+*v-ing*] to cause (an action) to appear right or reasonable: *Her small income does not warrant her taking a long holiday.* –see also UNWARRANTED **2** [+(*that*)] *infml old use* to declare as if certain: *I'll warrant (you) (that) he's not there!*

**war·ran·ty** /ˈwɒrənti‖ˈwɔ-, ˈwɑ-/ *n* **-ties** [C;U] *tech* a written GUARANTEE: *We'll repair your car without charging because it's still* **under warranty**.

**war·ren** /ˈwɒrən‖ˈwɔ-, ˈwɑ-/ *n* **1** a system of underground passages in which a number of rabbits live –compare BURROW **2** *usu. derog* a place in which too many people live, or in which one gets lost easily: *a warren of narrow old streets*

**war·ri·or** /ˈwɒrɪəʳ‖ˈwɔ-, ˈwɑ-/ *n lit* a soldier or experienced fighter

**war·ship** /ˈwɔːˌʃɪp‖ˈwɔr-/ *n* a naval ship used for war, esp. one armed with guns

**wart** /wɔːt‖wɔrt/ *n* a small hard ugly swelling on the skin, esp. of the face or hands

**war·time** /ˈwɔːtaɪm‖ˈwɔr-/ *n* [U] a period during which a war is going on –opposite **peacetime**

**war·y** /ˈweəri/ *adj* **-ier, -iest** [*of*] careful; looking out for danger: *Our dog is rather wary of strangers.* **–warily** *adv* **–wariness** *n* [U]

**was** /wəz; *strong* wɒz‖wəz; *strong* wɑz/ *v past tense of* BE, 1st and 3rd person singular: *I/he was*

**wash¹** /wɒʃ‖wɔʃ, wɑʃ/ *v* **1** [T *down, off, out, with*] to clean with liquid: *to wash clothes/one's car/one's hands/oneself (with soap and water)* **2** [I *with*] to clean oneself or a part of one's body with liquid: *I always wash before dinner.* **3** [I] to bear cleaning with liquid without damage: *These clothes wash well.* **4** [I;T *against, over*] to flow over or against (something) continually: *The waves washed (against/over) the shore.* **5** [T *away, off*] to cause to be carried by liquid: *The waves washed him into the sea.* **6** [I *used in* NEGATIVE¹ (1) *sentences*] *infml* to be believed: *His story just won't wash (with me).* **7 wash one's hands of** *infml* to refuse to be responsible for: *I wash my hands of you and all your wild ideas!*

**wash** sthg.↔**down** *v adv* [T] **1** to clean with a lot of water: *to wash down the car/the walls* **2** [*with*] to swallow (food or medicine) with the help of liquid: *Wash the dry cake down with tea.*

**wash out** *v adv* **1** [I;T (=**wash** sthg.↔**out**) *of*] to remove or be removed by washing: *Was she able to wash the dirty mark out (of her coat)?* **2** [T (**wash** sthg.↔**out**)] to prevent or destroy by water, esp. rain: *The cricket match was washed out (by rain).* –see also WASHOUT

**wash up** *v adv infml* **1** [I] *BrE* to wash the dishes, knives, forks, etc. after a meal: *Who's going to wash up tonight, then?* –see also WASHING-UP **2** [I] *AmE* to wash one's face and hands **3** [T] (**wash** sbdy./sthg.↔ **up**) (of waves) to bring in to the shore: *The sea washed up the body of the drowned sailor.*

**wash²** *n* **1** [S] the act or an action of washing or being washed: *Go upstairs and have a wash.|Give the car a good wash.* **2** [*the* S] things to be washed, or being washed; LAUNDRY (2): *I've got no clean shirts; they're all* **in the wash**. –see also WASHING **3** [S;U] a movement of water (usu. caused by the passing of a boat) –compare WAKE³ **4** [C;U] the liquid with which something is washed or coloured: *He rinses his mouth out with mouthwash.*

**wash·a·ble** /ˈwɒʃəbəl‖ˈwɔ-, ˈwɑ-/ *adj* that can be washed without damage: *washable cotton*

**wash·ba·sin** /ˈwɒʃˌbeɪsən‖ˈwɔʃ-, ˈwɑʃ-/ ‖also **washbowl** *AmE*– *n* a large fixed basin for water for washing the hands and face, esp. in a bathroom compare SINK²

**washed-out** /ˌ· ˈ·◂/ *adj* very tired: *She felt washed-out after working all night.|You look washed-out!*

**wash·er** /ˈwɒʃəʳ‖ˈwɔ-, ˈwɑ-/ *n* **1** a person or machine that washes **2** a ring of metal, rubber, etc., between a NUT (2) and BOLT, or between two pipes, to make a better, tighter joint **3** → WASHING MACHINE

**wash·ing** /ˈwɒʃɪŋ‖ˈwɔ-, ˈwɑ-/ *n* [U] things (esp. clothes) washed or to be washed: *Hang the washing out to dry.* –see also WASH² (2)

**washing ma·chine** /ˈ·· ·ˌ·/ *n* a machine for washing clothes –see picture on page 337

**washing-up** /ˌ·· ˈ·/ *n* [U] *BrE infml* (the act of washing) dirty dishes, plates, etc. left after a meal: *I'll do the washing-up!* –see also WASH **up** (1)

**wash·out** /ˈwɒʃ-aut‖ˈwɔʃ-, ˈwɑʃ-/ *n infml* a failure: *The plan was a washout after all, and cost us a lot of money.* –see also WASH **out** (2)

**wash·room** /ˈwɒʃrum, -ruːm‖ˈwɔʃ-, ˈwɑʃ-/ *n AmE euph* for LAVATORY

**was·n't** /ˈwɒzənt‖ˈwɑ-/ *short for* was not: *I wasn't at school yesterday because I was ill.*

**wasp** /wɒsp‖wɑsp, wɔsp/ *n* a flying stinging insect related to the bee, which is usu. coloured yellow and black

**wast·age** /ˈweɪstɪdʒ/ *n* [S;U] wasting; something wasted: *A quarter of the goods were damaged: that's a wastage of 25%.*

**waste**[1] /weɪst/ *n* **1** [S;U] loss, wrong use, or lack of full use: *These new weapons are a waste of money.*|*The meeting was a complete waste of time.* (=nothing was done or decided)|*Don't let all this good food* **go to waste!** **2** [U] used, damaged, or unwanted matter: *A lot of poisonous waste from the chemical works goes into the river.*|*Waste from the body passes out from the bowels.* –compare LAY WASTE, REFUSE[2] **3** [C] *often lit* an unused or useless stretch of land or water: *No crops will grow on these stony wastes.*|*the Arctic wastes*

**waste**[2] *v* **wasted, wasting** [I;T] **1** [*on*] to use wrongly, not use, or use too much of: *I've wasted a lot of money on that car.*|*Don't waste electricity: turn off the lights when you go out.* –see TIME (USAGE) **2** [*away*] to (cause to) lose flesh, strength, etc., slowly: *He became ill and began to waste away.*

**waste**[3] *adj* [A] **1** (esp. of areas of land) empty; not productive; ruined or destroyed: *waste land* **2** got rid of as worthless or damaged: *waste material/paper* **3** used for holding or carrying away what is worthless or no longer wanted: *waste pipes*

**waste·ful** /ˈweɪstfəl/ *adj* tending to waste or marked by waste: *wasteful habits* **–wastefully** *adv* **–wastefulness** *n* [U]

**waste·pa·per bas·ket** /ˌweɪstˈpeɪpəʳ ˌbɑːskɪ̵̀t, ˈweɪstˌpeɪpəʳ||ˈweɪstˌpeɪpər ˌbæ-/|| also **wastebasket** *AmE*– *n* a container for used or unnecessary material (esp. paper) in a house or office

**watch**[1] /wɒtʃ||wɑtʃ, wɔtʃ/ *v* **1** [I;T] to look at (some activity or event): *Do you often watch television?*|*They watched the car go past.* –see SEE (USAGE) **2** [T +*to-v*/*for*] to look for; expect and wait (for): *She watched (for) a chance to cross the road.*|*She watched to see what I would do.* **3** [T +(*that*)] to take care of, be careful with, or pay attention to: *I'll watch the baby.*|*Watch that the milk doesn't boil over.*|*Watch what you say when you talk to the general.* **4** [T] to attend carefully to (someone or someone's action): *Watch Jim.*|*Watch Jim do/doing it.*|*Watch how to do this.* **5 Watch it!** *infml* Be careful! : *Watch it when you handle the glasses!* **–watcher** *n*

**watch out** *v adv* [I] *infml* (esp. in giving orders) to take care: *Watch out! There's a car coming.*

**watch over** sbdy./sthg. *v adv* [T] to guard and protect; take care of

**watch**[2] *n* **1** [C] a small clock to be worn or carried: *a wristwatch*|*My watch has stopped.* **2** [S] one or more people ordered to watch a place or a person: *In spite of the watch on the house, the thief escaped.* **3** [C;U] (sailors who have to be on duty during) a period of two or four hours at sea: *You'll be on the first watch tonight.*|*Who's on watch now?* **4 keep (a) close/careful watch on** to fix one's attention on, carefully: *The government is keeping (a) close watch on rising prices.*

**watch·dog** /ˈwɒtʃdɒg||ˈwɑtʃdɔg, ˈwɔtʃ-/ *n* **1** a fierce dog kept to guard property **2** a person or group that tries to guard against bad or dishonest behaviour: *a government watchdog on television advertisements*

**watch·ful** /ˈwɒtʃfəl||ˈwɑtʃ-, ˈwɔtʃ-/ *adj* [*for*] careful to notice things: *She was watchful for any sign of activity in the empty house.* **–watchfully** *adv* **–watchfulness** *n* [U]

**watch·mak·er** /ˈwɒtʃˌmeɪkəʳ||ˈwɑtʃ-, ˈwɔtʃ-/ *n* a person who makes or repairs watches or clocks

**watch·man** /ˈwɒtʃmən||ˈwɑtʃ-, ˈwɔtʃ-/ *n* **-men** /mən/ a guard, esp. of a building: *Call the* **night watchman** *if there is any trouble tonight.*

**watch·word** /ˈwɒtʃwɜːd||ˈwɑtʃwərd, ˈwɔtʃ-/ *n* a word or phrase used as a sign of recognition among members of a group; PASSWORD

**wa·ter**[1] /ˈwɔːtəʳ||ˈwɔ-, ˈwɑ-/ *n* [U] **1** the most common liquid, which falls from the sky as rain, forms rivers, lakes, and seas, and is drunk by people and animals: *The prisoner was given only bread and water.*|*The hotel has hot and cold water in all the bedrooms.*|*After all the rain, most of the town was* **under water**.|*The goods came* **by water**, (=by boat) *not by air.* **2 above water** *infml* out of difficulty: *We don't make much money, but we are able to* **keep our heads above water**. (=we have enough money for our needs) **3 in/into hot water** *infml* in/into trouble: *We'll get into hot water if the teacher hears about this.* **4 throw cold water on** *infml* to speak against; point out difficulties in (a plan, idea, etc.) esp. in an unhelpful way –see also WATERS

**water**[2] *v* **1** [T] to pour water on (plants or land): *It's very dry: we must water the garden.* **2** [I] (esp. of the eyes or mouth) to form or let out a liquid like water: *My eyes watered when I cut the onions.*|*The sight of the food made my mouth water.*

**water** sthg.↔**down** *v adv* [T *often pass.*] to weaken (a liquid) by adding water: *This beer has been watered down!*|(fig.) *a watered-down statement*

**wa·ter·borne** /ˈwɔːtəbɔːn||ˈwɔtərborn, ˈwɑ-/ *adj* supported or carried by water: *waterborne trade/diseases*

**water butt** /ˈ·· ·/ *n* a barrel for collecting rainwater from the roof

**water clos·et** /ˈ·· ˌ··/ *n fml* for WC

**wa·ter·col·our** *BrE* ||**-color** *AmE* /ˈwɔːtəˌkʌ[illegible] ˈwɔtər-, ˈwɑ-/ *n* [C;U] (a picture painted with) p[illegible] mixed with water: *She mostly paints in watercol*[illegible] –compare OILS

**wa·ter·cress** /ˈwɔːtəkres||ˈwɔtər-, ˈwɑ-/ *n* [illegible] hot-tasting plant grown in water and used a[illegible] esp. in SALADS

**wa·ter·fall** /ˈwɔːtəfɔːl||ˈwɔtər-, ˈwɑ-/ *n* wat[illegible] straight down over rocks, sometimes fro[illegible] height

**wa·ter·front** /ˈwɔːtəfrʌnt||ˈwɔtər-, ˈw[illegible] *sing.*] land near a stretch of water, esp. [illegible] a port: *to walk along the waterfront*

**wa·ter·hole** /ˈwɔːtəhəʊl||ˈwɔtər-, ˈw[illegible] area of water in dry country, where [illegible] to drink

**watering can** /ˈ··· ·/ *n* a container [illegible] for watering garden plants

**wa·ter·logged** /ˈwɔːtəlɒgd||ˈ[illegible] -lɑgd/ *adj* (of land or a floating o[illegible] *The boat became so waterlogge*[illegible] *ground was waterlogged.*

**water main** /ˈ·· ·/ *n* a large un[illegible] ing a supply of water

**wa·ter·mark** /ˈwɔːtəmɑːk||ˈ[illegible] mark made on paper by the [illegible] is held up to the light

**wa·ter·mel·on** /ˈwɔːtəˌmelən‖ˈwɔtər-, ˈwɑ-/ *n* [C;U] a large round fruit with juicy red flesh and black seeds

**water po·lo** /ˈ·· ˌ··/ *n* [U] a game played by two teams of swimmers with a ball in a pool

**wa·ter·proof** /ˈwɔːtəpruːf‖ˈwɔtər-, ˈwɑ-/ *adj,n* (something, such as an outer garment) which does not allow water to go through: *Put on your waterproof (coat) before you go out in the rain.|Is the tent waterproof?*

**wa·ters** /ˈwɔːtəz‖ˈwɔtərz, ˈwɑ-/ *n* [P] **1** sea near (or belonging to) the stated country: *fishing in Icelandic waters* **2** the water of the stated river, lake, etc.: *This is where the waters of the Amazon flow out into the sea.*

**wa·ter·shed** /ˈwɔːtəʃed‖ˈwɔtər-, ˈwɑ-/ *n* **1** the high land separating two river systems **2** the point of an important change from one state of affairs to another: *Leaving her first job was a watershed in her life.*

**wa·ter·side** /ˈwɔːtəsaɪd‖ˈwɔtər-, ˈwɑ-/ *n* [*the* S] the edge of a natural body of water

**water ski·ing** /ˈ·· ˌ··/ *n* [U] the sport in which one travels over water on SKIS, pulled by a boat: *to go water skiing*

**wa·ter·tight** /ˈwɔːtətaɪt‖ˈwɔtər-, ˈwɑ-/ *adj* **1** through which no water can go: *a watertight box* **2** allowing or having no mistakes: *a watertight argument/ plan/ excuse*

**wa·ter·way** /ˈwɔːtəweɪ‖ˈwɔtər-, ˈwɑ-/ *n* a stretch of water up which a ship can go, such as part of a river: *Canals and rivers form the* **inland waterways** *of a country.*

**wa·ter·works** /ˈwɔːtəwɜːks‖ˈwɔtərwɜrks, ˈwɑ-/ *n* [P] buildings, pipes, and supplies of water forming a public water system: *He has a job at the waterworks.*

**wa·ter·y** /ˈwɔːtəri‖ˈwɔ-, ˈwɑ-/ *adj* **1** containing (too much) water: *watery soup* **2** very pale in colour: *walls painted a watery yellow colour*

**watt** /wɒt‖wɑt/ *n* a measure of electrical power: *A* KILOWATT *is 1000 watts.*

**wave¹** /weɪv/ *v* **waved, waving 1** [I;T *at*] to move (one's hand, or something held in the hand) as a signal, esp. in greeting: *The children waved their flags as the Queen passed.|They're waving (at us).|They waved goodbye.|The policeman waved the traffic on.* (=signalled to the drivers to move) **2** [I] to move in the air, backwards and forwards or up and down: *The trees waved in the wind.* **3** [I;T] to (cause to) lie in regular curves: *I had my hair waved.*

**wave** sthg.↔**aside** *v adv* [T] to push aside without giving attention to (esp. ideas, suggestions, etc.): *He waved aside my offer of help.*

**wave²** *n* **1** the movement of the hand in waving: *The President gave the crowd a wave.* **2** one of a number of raised lines of water on the surface, esp. of the sea: *In bad weather, the waves are very large.* **3** an evenly curved part of the hair: *natural waves in her hair* –compare CURL **4** a suddenly rising and increasing feeling, way of behaviour, etc.: *the recent wave of violence* –see also HEAT WAVE **5** a form in which some forms of ENERGY (2), such as light and sound, move: *radio waves*

**wave band** /ˈ· ·/ *n* a set of sound waves of similar lengths: *Radio 2 can be heard on the long wave band.*

**wave·length** /ˈweɪvleŋθ/ *n* **1** a radio signal sent out on radio WAVES² (5) that are a particular distance apart: (fig.) *You and I are* **on different wavelengths.** (=have completely different beliefs, ways of thinking, etc.) **2** the distance between one wave² (5) and another

**wa·ver** /ˈweɪvəʳ/ *v* [I *between*] to be unsteady or uncertain: *He wavered before deciding.*

**wav·y** /ˈweɪvi/ *adj* **-ier, -iest** having regular curves: *wavy hair* –**waviness** *n* [U]

**wax¹** /wæks/ *n* [U] a solid material made of fats or oils, which changes to a thick liquid when melted by heat: *a wax candle|wax in the ears* (=a natural substance) –see also BEESWAX

**wax²** *v* [T] to put wax on, esp. as a polish: *to wax the floor*

**wax³** *v* [I] (esp. of the moon) to grow –compare WANE

**wax·works** /ˈwækswɜːks‖-wɜrks/ *n* **waxworks** a place where one can see models of human beings made in wax: *Madame Tussaud's is a famous waxworks in London.*

**way¹** /weɪ/ *n* **1** [C] the (right) road(s), path(s), etc., to follow in order to reach a place: *Is this the way out?|Please show me the way to the shops.|If you* **lose your way**, *ask a policeman.|Move* **out of my way** *so I can pass.*|(fig.) *Nothing must* **stand in the way of** (=prevent) *our plans.|I met him* **on the way** *home.* (=as I was going home)|*There is a* **right of way** *across this field* (=we are allowed to walk across it) –see USAGE **2** [C] a direction: *Which way is the house from here?|Come this way.* **3** [S] the distance to be travelled in order to reach a place or point: *We're a long way from home.|Christmas is still a long way off.* **4** [C +*to-v*/(*that*)] a manner or method: *a funny way of laughing|What is the best way to do it?|Those two girls do their hair in the same way.|She hasn't got a job but she has* **ways and means** *of getting money.* **5** [U] forward movement: *The car broke down and I had to* **make my way** *on foot.*|(fig.) *The party got* **under way** (=started) *at nine o'clock.* **6** [C] a degree or point: *In many ways yours is a better plan.|In a way I can see what you mean, though I disagree with you.* **7** [C] (part of the name of) a road or path: *Oxford Way* –see STREET (USAGE) **8 by the way** (used to introduce a new subject in speech) in addition **9 by way of: a** by going through: *You can get to Harlow by way of London.* **b** with the intention of: *By way of introducing himself he showed me his card.* **10 get one's own way** to do or get what one wants, in spite of others **11 give way** to yield: *We refused to give way to their demands.* **12 have it both ways** to gain advantage from opposing opinions or actions: *Do you want to pass your examinations or just have a good time? You can't have it both ways!* **13 under way** moving forward: *Work on the new bridge is now under way.*

USAGE Compare **in the way** and **on the way**: *I couldn't get through the gate because your car was* **in the way**. (=blocking the entrance)|*I saw the accident* **on the way** *to work.* (=while I was going to work)

**way²** *adv* [*adv+adv*] *esp. AmE* far: *The film was made way back in 1929.|We're way behind with our work.*

**way·far·er** /ˈweɪˌfeərəʳ/ *n old use & lit* a traveller on foot –compare PEDESTRIAN

**way·lay** /weɪˈleɪ/ *v* **-laid** /ˈleɪd/, **-laying** [T] to stop (a person going somewhere) for a special purpose: *She waylaid me after the lesson and asked where I had been the week before.*

**way-out** /ˌ· ˈ·◂/ *adj infml* unusually good, strange, or modern

**way·side** /ˈweɪsaɪd/ *n* [*the* S] the side of the road: *They stopped by the wayside to rest.*

**way·ward** /ˈweɪwəd‖-ərd/ *adj* changeable and not easy to guide (in character): *a wayward son*

**WC** also **water closet** *fml*– *n* a LAVATORY which is emptied by a flow of water

**we** /wi; *strong* wiː/ *pron (used as the subject of a sentence)* the people who are speaking; I and one or more others: *Shall we* (=you and I) *sit together, Mary?|May we* (=I and the others) *go now, sir?*

**weak** /wiːk/ *adj* **1** not strong; not strong enough to work or last properly: *I still feel a bit weak after my illness.|The shelf's too weak to hold all those books.|a weak heart|weak eyes|*(fig.) *She's good at history, but rather weak at French.* **2** not strong in character: *The teacher's so weak that the children do what they like.* –see also WEAK-KNEED **3** containing too much water: *weak soup/tea* **–weakly** *adv*

**weak·en** /ˈwiːkən/ *v* [I;T] to (cause to) become weak, esp. in health or character: *The illness weakened her heart.|a country weakened by war and disease|She asked so many times that in the end we weakened and let her go.* –compare STRENGTHEN

**weak-kneed** /ˌ· ˈ·◂/ *adj* habitually afraid and nervous; cowardly

**weak·ling** /ˈwiːk-lɪŋ/ *n* a person lacking strength in body or character

**weak·ness** /ˈwiːknɪ̇s/ *n* **1** [U] the state of being weak, esp. in mind, body, or character **2** [C] a fault; weak part: *The cost of your plan is its main weakness.|Drinking is his weakness.* –compare STRENGTH **3** [C *for*] a strong liking, esp. for something which is bad for one: *a weakness for chocolate*

**weal** /wiːl/ *n* a mark on the skin, as from a stroke of a whip; WELT: *The dog was covered in weals.* –sounds like **wheel**

**wealth** /welθ/ *n* **1** [U] (a large amount of) money and possessions: *her great wealth|a man of wealth* **2** [S *of*] a large number: *a wealth of examples*

**wealth·y** /ˈwelθi/ *adj* **-ier, -iest** (of a person) rich **–wealthily** *adv*

**wean** /wiːn/ *v* [T] to accustom (a young child or animal) to food instead of mother's milk: *Most babies are weaned by the time they are one.|*(fig.) *How can we wean him from getting drunk every night?*

**weap·on** /ˈwepən/ *n* a tool for harming or killing in attack or defence: *guns, bombs, gas, and other weapons*

**wear¹** /weəʳ/ *v* **wore** /wɔːʳ‖wor/, **worn** /wɔːn‖worn/, **wearing 1** [T] to have (esp. clothes) on the body: *He's wearing a new coat.|Does your brother wear glasses?|She's wearing her diamonds.* (=jewellery) –compare HAVE **on**; see DRESS¹ (USAGE) **2** [T] to have (a particular expression on the face): *She wore an angry expression.* **3** [I;T] to reduce or be reduced by continued use: *I liked this shirt, but the collar has worn.|The water has worn the rocks (down).|The noise wore her nerves (to nothing).* **4** [T] to produce by wear, use, rubbing, etc.: *You've worn a hole in your sock.|The villagers had worn a path through the fields.* **5** [T] to last in the stated condition: (fig.) *Considering his age, he has worn well.* (=still looks young) **–wearable** *adj*

**wear away** *v adv* [I;T (=**wear** sthg.↔**away**)] to (cause to) disappear by use, rubbing, etc.: *In the last hundred years, the wind has worn the rocks away.*

**wear** sbdy./sthg. **down** *v adv* [T] to reduce the strength or size of: *We wore down their opposition after several hours' argument.*

**wear off** *v adv* [I] to be reduced until it disappears: *The pain is wearing off.*

**wear on** *v adv* [I] to pass slowly (in time): *The meeting wore on all afternoon.*

**wear out** *v adv* **1** [I;T (=**wear** sthg.↔**out**)] also **wear through**– to (cause to) be reduced to nothing or a useless state by use: *Her shoes wore out quickly.|worn-out old shoes* **2** [T] (**wear** sbdy.↔ **out**) to tire greatly: *If you don't stop working you'll wear yourself out.* –see also WORN-OUT

**wear²** *n* [U] **1** use which reduces the material: *This mat has had a lot of wear.|I spent all evening at the party, but the next day I was* **none the worse for wear**. (=still fresh and active) **2** damage from use: *These shoes I bought last week are already showing signs of wear/***wear and tear**. **3** the quality of lasting in use: *There's still some wear in these tyres.*

**wear³** *n* [U] (used esp. in business) clothes of the stated type, or for the stated purpose: *men's wear|sports wear|holiday wear*

**wear·ing** /ˈweərɪŋ/ *adj* tiring: *She's very wearing when she talks on and on.|It's a very wearing job.* –see also HARDWEARING

**wear·i·some** /ˈwɪərisəm/ *adj* which makes one feel tired and BORED⁴: *a wearisome day*

**wear·y¹** /ˈwɪəri/ *adj* **-ier, -iest** [*of*] tired: *You look weary.|a weary smile* **–wearily** *adv* **–weariness** *n* [U]

**weary²** *v* **-ied, -ying** [I;T *with, of*] to (cause to) become WEARY: *He soon wearied of* (=grew tired of) *his job on the farm.*

**wea·sel** /ˈwiːzəl/ *n* a small thin furry animal which can kill other small animals

**weath·er¹** /ˈweðəʳ/ *n* [U] **1** the condition of wind, rain, sunshine, snow, etc., at a certain time or over a period of time: *good weather|What will the weather be like tomorrow?* **2 make heavy weather of** to make (something) seem difficult for oneself **3 under the weather** not very well or happy

USAGE 1 **Wind** is a general word for a moving current of air. A **breeze** is a pleasant gentle wind; a **gust** is a sudden strong rush of **air**; and a **gale** is a very strong wind: *There's a nice* **breeze** *down by the sea.|A* **gust** *of wind blew the door shut.|Our chimney was blown down in a* **gale**. 2 **Rain** is water falling from the clouds; icy, partly frozen rain is called **sleet**; hard frozen drops of rain are called **hail**; and frozen rain falling in soft white pieces is **snow**. 3 If it is raining heavily, we say it is **pouring** (*down*), if only very lightly, it is **drizzling** (DRIZZLE). 4 A **shower** is a fall of rain (or snow) that does not last long. A heavy fall of rain, together with strong winds and (sometimes) thunder and lightning, is a **storm**. A **blizzard** is a severe snowstorm, and a **hurricane** is a storm with very high winds. The yearly season of rainy weather in some tropical countries is called the **monsoon**.

**weather²** *v* **1** [T] to pass safely through (a storm or difficulty): *The ship weathered the storm, and arrived safely.|The examination was difficult but I think I weathered it quite well.* **2** [I;T] to change or be changed by being open to the air and weather: *Rocks weather until they are worn away.*

**weather-beat·en** /'·· ,··/ *adj* marked or damaged by the wind, sun, etc.: *a weather-beaten* (=brown and lined) *face*

**weath·er·cock** /'weðəkɒk||-ərkɑk/ also **weather vane**– *n* a small metal apparatus, often shaped like a cock and fixed to the top of a building, which is blown round by the wind and so shows its direction

**weather fore·cast** /'·· ,··/ *n* a description of weather conditions as they are expected to be by people whose job is to study them (METEOROLOGY)

**weath·er·man** /'weðəmæn||-ər-/ *n* **-men** /men/ a person who makes WEATHER FORECASTs, as on television and the radio

**weave¹** /wi:v/ *v* **wove** /wəuv/, **woven** /'wəuvən/, **weaving 1** [I] to form threads into material by crossing one thread under and over a set of longer threads stretched out on a LOOM: *Do you know how to weave?* **2** [T] to make by doing this: *to weave a mat*|(fig. *lit*) *He wove an interesting story from a few facts in a history book.*

**weave²** *n* the way in which a material is woven and the pattern formed by this: *a loose/fine weave*

**weave³** *v* **weaved, weaving** [I;T] to move along, turning and changing direction frequently: *weaving in and out between the cars|He weaved his way through the crowd.*

**weav·er** /'wi:vəʳ/ *n* a person whose job is to weave cloth

**web** /web/ *n* **1** a net of thin threads spun (SPIN) by some insects, esp. SPIDERs, to trap other insects **2** a detailed arrangement or network: *a web of deceit* (=a set of lies)

**webbed** /webd/ *adj* having skin between the toes, as on a duck's foot: *webbed feet*

**web-foot·ed** /,· '··◂/ also **web-toed**– *adj* having WEBBED feet: *Ducks are web-footed.*

**wed** /wed/ *v* **wedded** *or* **wed, wedding** [I;T not *be* +*v-ing*] *lit* to marry: *They were wed in the spring.*

**we'd** /wid; *strong* wi:d/ *short for* **1** we had **2** we would

**wed·ding** /'wedɪŋ/ *n* a marriage ceremony, esp. with a party or meal after a church service: *Have you been invited to their wedding?* –compare MARRIAGE

**wedding ring** /'·· ·/ *n* a usu. gold ring, used in the marriage ceremony and worn to show that one is married

**wedge¹** /wedʒ/ *n* **1** a V-shaped piece of wood, one end being thin and the other quite wide, used e.g. for holding a door open: *Put a wedge under the door so that it will stay open.* **2** something shaped like this: *shoes with wedge heels* **3 thin end of the wedge** something which seems unimportant but will open the way for more serious things of a similar kind: *If we let the children stay up late tonight, it'll be the thin end of the wedge.*

**wedge²** *v* **wedged, wedging** [T] to fix firmly with a WEDGE: *Wedge the door (open/shut).*|(fig.) *The people sitting close to me wedged me in/into the corner.*

**wed·lock** /'wedlɒk||-lɑk/ *n* [U] *old use* **1** the state of being married **2 born out of wedlock** born of unmarried parents; ILLEGITIMATE

**Wednes·day** /'wenzdi,-deɪ/ *n* the fourth day of the week; day between Tuesday and Thursday: *He'll arrive (on) Wednesday/on Wednesday afternoon.*| *She works (on)* Wednesdays.

**wee** /wi:/ *adj ScotE* very small: *a wee child*

**weed¹** /wi:d/ *n* **1** an unwanted wild plant: *The garden's full of weeds.* **2** *derog* a weak-bodied person, esp. a very thin one

**weed²** *v* [I;T] to remove WEEDs¹ (1) (from): *to weed the garden|to weed the grass out of/from the rose garden*

**weed** sbdy./sthg.↔**out** *v adv* [T] to get rid of (things or people that are not wanted): *He weeded out the books he no longer needed.*

**weed·y** /'wi:di/ *adj* **-ier, -iest** *infml* weak in body: *a weedy young man*

**week** /wi:k/ *n* **1** a period of seven days (and nights), esp. from Sunday to Saturday: *The flight to Accra goes twice a week.|I'll see you next week.* **2** also **working week**– the period of time during which one works, as in a factory or office: *She works a 60-hour week.|The five-day week is usual in most firms.* **3 (the stated day) week** also **a week on (the stated day)** *BrE*– a week after (the stated day): *She's coming on Sunday week/a week on Sunday.|tomorrow week* **4 week in, week out** without change or rest

**week·day** /'wi:kdeɪ/ *n* a day of the week **a** not Saturday or Sunday: *I only work on weekdays, not on Saturday or Sunday.* **b** not Sunday

**week·end** /,wi:k'end, 'wi:kend||'wi:kend/ *n* Saturday and Sunday, esp. when considered a holiday

**week·ly¹** /'wi:kli/ *adj,adv* (happening or appearing) once a week or every week: *a weekly visit/magazine*

**weekly²** *n* **-lies** a magazine or newspaper which appears once a week

**weep** /wi:p/ *v* **wept** /wept/, **weeping** [I;T *over*] *fml or lit* to let fall (tears) from the eyes: *They wept over their failure.|I could weep when I think of all the money we've lost.* –compare CRY

**weep·y** /'wi:pi/ *adj* **-ier, -iest** *infml* tending to cry: *not very well, and feeling weepy*

**weft** /weft/ *n* the threads of a material woven across the downward set of threads –compare WARP¹ (2)

**weigh** /weɪ/ *v* [T] **1** to find the weight of, esp. by a machine: *to weigh oneself* **2** to have a certain weight: *It weighs six kilos.|I weigh less than I used to.* **3** to consider or compare carefully: *He weighed the ideas in his mind.* **4 weigh anchor** to raise an ANCHOR

**weigh** sbdy./sthg. **down** *v adv* [T *with*] to make heavy (with a load): *I was weighed down with the shopping.*|(fig.) *weighed down with responsibilities*

**weigh on** sbdy./sthg. *v prep* [T] to cause worry to: *His lack of money weighed on his mind.*

**weigh** sthg.↔**out** *v adv* [T] to measure in amounts by weight: *I weighed out half a kilo of flour and added it to the mixture.*

**weigh** sbdy./sthg.↔**up** *v adv* [T] to (try to) understand; form an opinion about: *I can't weigh him up.*

**weight¹** /weɪt/ *n* **1** [U] the heaviness of anything, esp. as measured by a certain system; amount which something weighs: *two kilos in weight|What's the weight of your bag?|to* **put on/lose weight** (=to become heavier/lighter)|*She is* **under/over weight**. (=too light/too heavy) **2** [C] a piece of metal of a standard heaviness, which can be balanced against a substance to measure equal heaviness of that substance: *a one-kilo weight* **3** [C] a usu. heavy object, esp. one used for holding something down: *a paperweight|You shouldn't lift heavy weights after an operation.*|(fig.) *The loss of the money is a weight on my mind.* (=a worry) **4** [U] value or importance: *Don't worry what he thinks; his opinion doesn't* **carry much weight**. **5 pull one's weight** to join in work or activity equally with others **6 throw one's weight about/around** to give orders to others, because one thinks oneself important

**weight²** *v* [T *with*] to put a weight on or add a heavy material to: *a weighted fishing net*

**weight** sbdy./sthg.↔**down** *v adv* [T *with; usu.pass.*] to load heavily; WEIGH **down**: *weighted down with shopping*

**weight·ed** /ˈweɪtɪ̠d/ *adj* [F *towards, against*] giving advantage: *The system of elections is weighted in favour of the main political parties.*

**weight·ing** /ˈweɪtɪŋ/ *n* [S;U] *BrE* something additional, esp. additional pay given because of the high cost of living in a certain area: *They got a London weighting of £600 a year.*

**weight·less** /ˈweɪtlɪ̠s/ *adj* having no weight, as when in space –**weightlessness** *n* [U]

**weight lift·ing** /ˈ· ˌ··/ *n* [U] the sport of lifting specially shaped weights above the head –**weight lifter** *n*

**weight·y** /ˈweɪti/ *adj* **-ier, -iest** important and serious: *a weighty problem/argument* –**weightily** *adv* –**weightiness** *n* [U]

**weir** /wɪəʳ/ *n* a wall across a river, stopping or controlling the flow of the water above it

**weird** /wɪəd‖wɪərd/ *adj* **1** strange; unnatural **2** *infml* unusual and not sensible or acceptable: *He has some weird ideas.* –**weirdly** *adv* –**weirdness** *n* [U]

**wel·come¹** /ˈwelkəm/ *interj* [*to*] (an expression of pleasure at someone's arrival or return): *Welcome home/back!|Welcome to England.*

**welcome²** *v* **-comed, -coming** [T] to meet or greet, esp. with pleasure: *The Queen welcomed the President when he arrived.|They welcomed him with flowers.|a welcoming smile|*(fig.) *They welcomed the idea/my suggestion.* (=they were pleased with it)

**welcome³** *adj* **1** acceptable and wanted: *a welcome suggestion|You are always welcome at my house.|a welcome change* **2** [F *+to-v/to*] allowed freely (to have), sometimes because not wanted: *He's coming to visit you? You're welcome to him!|You're welcome to try, but you won't succeed.* **3 You're welcome** (a polite expression when thanked for something): *"Thank you!" "You're welcome."* **4 make (someone) welcome** to receive (a guest) with friendliness

**welcome⁴** *n* a greeting: *They gave us* **a warm welcome.**

**weld** /weld/ *v* [I;T *to, together*] **a** to join (usu. metals) by pressing or melting them together when hot **b** (of metals) to become joined in this way –**weld** *n*

**weld·er** /ˈweldəʳ/ *n* a person whose job is to make WELDed joints

**wel·fare** /ˈwelfeəʳ/ *n* [U] well-being; comfort and good health: *We're thinking only of his welfare: we want him to be happy in his new school.|She's in* **welfare work**: *she helps people who have no jobs, family problems, etc.*

**welfare state** /ˌ·· ˈ·‖ˈ·· ·/ *n* (a country with) a system of government-provided health care, unemployment pay, etc.

**well¹** /wel/ *n* **1** a place where water comes from underground: *to find a well in the desert|well water* **2** a hole like this through which oil is drawn from underground **3** an enclosed space in a building running straight up and down, e.g. for a LIFT² (3) to travel in, or around which stairs turn: *the stairwell*

**well²** *v* [I *out, up*] (of liquid) to rise and flow (from): *Blood welled (out) from the cut.|Tears welled (up) in her eyes.*

**well³** *adv* **better** /ˈbetəʳ/, **best** /best/ **1** in a good way; kindly, satisfactorily, etc.: *She paints very well.|a well-dressed young man| They speak well of him at school.|The business is doing well.* (=succeeding)|*She did well* (=gained a good profit) *out of the sale of her house.* **2** thoroughly: *Wash it well before you dry it.* **3** [*adv + prep/adv*] very much: *I can't reach it; it's well above my head.|He arrived well within the time.* **4** justly; suitably: *I couldn't very well say no.|You did well to tell him.|You may well ask!* (=we are all wondering) **5 as well: a** in addition; also; too: *I'm going to London, and John's going as well.* –see Study Notes on page 128 **b** with as good a result: *We might (just) as well have stayed at home.* **6 as well as** in addition to: *I'm learning French as well as English.* –see Study Notes on page 128 **7 just as well** (as a reply) There's no harm done; There's no loss: *"I was too late to see the film." "Just as well: it wasn't very good".* **8 pretty well** almost: *The work is pretty well finished.* **9 well and truly** completely: *George is well and truly drunk.* **10 Well done!** (said when someone has been successful): *You've passed your examination. Well done!* **11 well out of** lucky to be free from (an affair): *It's lucky you left before the trouble started; you were well out of it.* **12 well up in** knowing a great deal about: *well up in the latest fashions*

**well⁴** *interj* **1** (used for showing surprise, doubt, acceptance, etc.): *She's got a new job. Well, well!|Well, what a surprise.|Well, all right, I agree.* **2** (used when continuing a story): *Well, then she said . . .* **3 Oh well!** (used for showing cheerfulness when something bad has happened): *"Oh well, I mustn't complain; it isn't so bad."*

**well⁵** *adj* **better, best** [F] **1** healthy: *I'm not feeling very well.|She was ill for a month but she's nearly well now.* **2** right; in an acceptable state: *to make sure that all is well* **3 It's all very well** (shows dissatisfaction): *It's all very well (for you) to say you're sorry, but I've been waiting here for two hours!*

**we'll** /wil; *strong* wiːl/ *v short for* **1** we will **2** we shall

**well-ad·vised** /ˌ· ·ˈ· ◂/ *adj* sensible: *You would be well-advised to see the doctor about that pain.*

**well-bal·anced** /ˌ· ˈ·· ◂/ *adj* **1** (of people and their characters) sensible and not controlled by unreasonable feelings **2** (of food) containing the right amounts of what is good for the body: **a well-balanced diet**

**well-be·ing** /ˌwelˈbiːɪŋ ◂‖ˈwelˌbiːɪŋ/ *n* [U] personal and bodily comfort, esp. good health: *The warm summer weather always gives me a sense of wellbeing.*

**well-bred** /ˌ· ˈ·◂/ *adj* well-behaved and polite: *a well-bred voice*

**well-done** /ˌ· ˈ·◂/ *adj* (of food, esp. meat) cooked for a longer rather than shorter period of time –compare RARE[2]

**well-earned** /ˌ· ˈ·◂/ *adj* much deserved: *a well-earned rest after so much hard work*

**well-found·ed** /ˌ· ˈ·· ◂/ *adj* based on facts: *My fears that we would lose the game were well-founded.*

**well-groomed** /ˌ· ˈ·◂/ *adj* having a very neat clean appearance: *a well-groomed young person*

**well-heeled** /ˌ· ˈ·◂/ *adj infml* rich

**well-in·formed** /ˌ· ·ˈ·◂/ *adj* knowing a lot about several subjects or a particular subject

**wel·ling·ton** /ˈwelɪŋtən/ also **wellington boot**– *n* a rubber boot which keeps water from the feet and lower part of the legs

**well-in·ten·tioned** /ˌ· ·ˈ··◂/ also **well-meaning**– *adj* acting in the hope of good results, though often failing: *It was a well-intentioned effort to help.*

**well-known** /ˌ· ˈ·◂/ *adj* known by many people: *a well-known fact* –see FAMOUS (USAGE)

**well-mean·ing** /ˌ· ˈ··◂/ *adj* →WELL-INTENTIONED: *a well-meaning person/effort*

**well-nigh** /ˈ· ·/ *adv fml* almost: *well-nigh impossible*

**well-off** /ˌ· ˈ·◂/ *adj* **1** [F *for*] rich: *They're very well-off.*|(fig.) *We're well-off for space* (=we have plenty of space) *in our new house.* **2 you don't know when you're well off** you're more fortunate than you know

**well-read** /ˌ· ˈ·◂/ *adj* having read many books and gained much useful information

**well-spok·en** /ˌ· ˈ··◂/ *adj* having a socially acceptable way of speaking esp. typical of educated people

**well-thought-of** /ˌ· ˈ· ·◂/ *adj* (of a person) liked and admired generally

**well-timed** /ˌ· ˈ·◂/ *adj* said or done at the most suitable time: *well-timed advice*

**well-to-do** /ˌ· · ˈ·◂/ *adj infml* rich

**well-tried** /ˌ· ˈ·◂/ *adj* often used before and known to work well: *well-tried methods*

**well-wish·er** /ˈ· ˌ··/ *n* a person giving good wishes to another, esp. on a special occasion

**well-worn** /ˌ· ˈ·◂/ *adj* (of phrases) with little meaning, because over-used

**Welsh** /welʃ/ *adj* of Wales, its people, or their language

**welt** /welt/ a raised mark on the skin e.g. from a stroke of a whip; WEAL

**wel·ter** /ˈweltəʳ/ *n* [S] a disordered mixture: *a welter of confused ideas*

**wench** /wentʃ/ *n old use* a girl, esp. in the country

**wend** /wend/ *v lit* **wend one's way** to move or travel over a distance, esp. slowly

**went** /went/ *v past tense of* GO

**wept** /wept/ *v past tense and participle of* WEEP

**were** /wəʳ; *strong* wɜːʳ/ *v negative short form* **weren't** /wɜːnt‖ˈwɜrənt, wɜrnt/ *past tense of* BE

**we're** /wɪəʳ; *strong* wiːəʳ/ *short for:* we are

**were·wolf** /ˈweəwulf, ˈwɪə-‖ˈweər-, ˈwɪər-/ *n* **-wolves** (in stories) a man who sometimes turns into a WOLF

**west**[1] /west/ *adv* (*often cap.*) towards the west: *to travel west*|*She sat facing West, watching the sun go down.*

**west**[2] *n* (*often cap.*) [*the* S] one of the four main points of the compass, which is on the left of a person facing north: *the west door of the church*|*The sun sets in the west.*

**West** *n* [*the* S] **1** the western part of the world, esp. western Europe and the United States: *Leaders from the West are having peace talks in Moscow.* **2** the part of a country which is further west than the rest

**west·bound** /ˈwestbaund/ *adj* travelling towards the west: *the westbound train*

**West End** /ˌ· ˈ·◂/ *n* [*the* S] the western part of central London, where the shops, theatres, etc., are: *West-End shops*

**west·er·ly** /ˈwestəli‖-ərli/ *adj* **1** [A] towards or in the west: *in a westerly direction* **2** (of a wind) coming from the west: *a westerly wind* –compare WESTWARD

**west·ern**[1] /ˈwestən‖-ərn/ *adj* (*often cap.*) of or belonging to the west part of the world or of a country: *the Western nations*

**western**[2] *n* (*often cap.*) a story, usu. on a film, about life in the West of the US in the past

**West In·di·an** /ˌ· ˈ···/ *adj* of or from the West Indies: *West Indian cooking*

**west·ward** /ˈwestwəd‖-ərd/ *adj* going towards the west: *a westward journey* –compare WESTERLY –**westwards** *BrE*‖**westward** *AmE adv: They travelled westwards.*

**wet**[1] /wet/ *adj* **1** covered with liquid; not dry: *I can't go out till my hair's dry; it's still wet from being washed.*|*wet ground*|*wet paint* (=still sticky)|*Don't go out, you'll get* **wet through**. (=completely wet) **2** rainy: *wet weather*|*We can't go out, it's too wet.* **3** *infml derog* of a person lacking in strength of mind: *Don't be so wet! You can do it, if you try!* **4 wet blanket** *derog* a person who discourages others, prevents them enjoying themselves, etc. –**wetness** *n* [U]

**wet**[2] *n* [*the* S] rainy weather: *Don't go out in the wet.*

**wet**[3] *v* **wet** *or* **wetted, wetting** [T] **1** to cause to be wet: *Wet the cloth and clean the table with it.* **2 wet the bed** to pass water from the body in bed, because of a loss of control while asleep

**we've** /wiv; *strong* wiːv/ *short for:* we have

**whack**[1] /wæk/ *v* [T] to hit with a noisy blow

**whack**[2] *n* **1** (the noise made by) a hard blow **2** [*usu.sing.*] *infml* a (fair or equal) share: *Have you all had your whack?*

**whacked** /wækt/ *adj* [F] *infml* very tired: *I'm completely whacked.*

**whack·ing**[1] /ˈwækɪŋ/ *adj infml* very (big): *They live in a whacking great house in Hollywood.*

**whacking**[2] *n* a beating

**whale** /weɪl/ *n* **1** a very large animal which lives in the sea, and looks like a fish but is a MAMMAL: *The Blue Whale is the world's biggest living animal.* **2 whale of a time** *infml* a very enjoyable time

**whal·ing** /'weɪlɪŋ/ *n* [U] the hunting of WHALES to produce oil and other materials

**wharf** /wɔːf||wɔrf/ *n* **wharfs** *or* **wharves** /wɔːvz||wɔrvz/ a place where ships can be tied up to unload goods –compare DOCK

**what** /wɒt||wɑt, wʌt/ *predeterminer,determiner,pron* **1** (used in questions about an unknown thing, person, or kind of thing/person): *What are you doing?|What colour is it?|What time will you come?|"I got up at four o'clock." "What did you say?" "You did what?" "What?"* (Some people think "*What?*" is not very polite here. Compare PARDON[1] (3).)|*"What do you do?" "I'm a teacher."* **2** the thing or things that: *She told me what to do.|I know what you mean.|Show me what you bought.|I gave her what books* (=the books that) *I had.* **3** (shows surprise): *What a strange thing to say!|What a pity!* (compare *How sad!*)|*What beautiful weather!* **4 what for?** *infml* why?: *"I'm going to Paris." "What for?"* –see also FOR[1] (2) **5 what have you** *infml* anything (else) like that: *In his pocket I found a handkerchief, string, old sweets, and what have you.* **6 what if?** what will happen if?: *What if we move the picture over here?|What if she doesn't come?* **7 what is/was something like?** (used when asking for a description): *"What's the new teacher like?" "He's got a red beard."|"What's it like, being an actor?"* **8 what's his/her/its name** also **what d'you call him/her/it**– *infml* (used when speaking of a person or thing whose name one cannot remember): *Mary's gone out with what's his name: you know, the boy with the red car.* **9 what the . . .?** *infml* (used with various words to show anger or surprise) what: *What the devil are you doing?|What the* HELL *does he want?* **10 what with** because of (esp. something bad): *What with all this work and so little sleep, I don't think I can do this job much longer.* –see WHICH (USAGE)

**what·ev·er**[1] /wɒ'tevəʳ||wɑ-, wʌ-/ also **whatsoever** /ˌwɒtsəʊ'evəʳ||ˌwɑt-, ˌwʌt-/ *lit– determiner,pron* **1** any(thing) at all that: *Goats eat whatever (food) they can find.* **2** no matter what: *Whatever you do, don't keep him waiting!*

**whatever**[2] *pron* **1** *infml* anything (else) like that: *Anyone seen carrying bags, boxes, or whatever, was stopped by the police.* **2** (*showing surprise*) what?: *Look at that strange animal! Whatever is it?* **3** it doesn't matter what: *"Do you want to got to the cinema, or the pool, or out for a meal?" "Whatever!"* –see EVER (USAGE)

**whatever**[3] also **whatsoever**– *adj* [after *n*] (*used in* NEGATIVES[2] (1), *questions, etc.*) at all: *I have no money whatsoever.*

**wheat** /wiːt/ *n* [U] a plant or its grain, from which flour is made: *a field of wheat*

**whee·dle** /'wiːdl/ *v* **-dled, -dling** [I;T] to persuade (someone) to do what one wants by pleasant but insincere behaviour and words

**wheedle** sthg. **out** *v adv* [T *of*] to obtain from someone by insincerely pleasant persuading: *He wheedled five pounds out of his father.*

**wheel**[1] /wiːl/ *n* **1** [C] a circular object with an outer frame which turns around an inner part (HUB), used for making vehicles move, driving machinery, etc. **2** [*the* S] the STEERING WHEEL of a car or guiding wheel of a ship: *I'm rather tired; will you* **take the wheel?** (=drive instead of me) **3 -wheeler** a vehicle with the stated number of wheels: *a three-wheeler (car)*

**wheel**[2] *v* **1** [T] to move ((something on) a wheeled object): *The nurse wheeled the table up to the bed.* **2** [I *around, round*] to turn suddenly: *I called him as he was running away and he wheeled round and looked at me.* **3** [I] (of birds) to fly round and round in circles: GULLS *wheeling over the sea*

**wheel·bar·row** /'wiːlˌbærəʊ/ also **barrow**– *n* a small cart with one wheel at the front, two legs, and two handles at the back for pushing

**wheel·base** /'wiːlbeɪs/ *n* the distance between the front and back AXLES on a vehicle

**wheel·chair** /'wiːltʃeəʳ/ *n* a chair with large wheels used by a person who cannot walk

**wheeze** /wiːz/ *v* **wheezed, wheezing** [I] to make a noisy whistling sound e.g. when breathing with difficulty: *a wheezing old man* **–wheeze** *n*

**wheez·y** /'wiːzi/ *adj* **-ier, -iest** that WHEEZES, esp. habitually: *a wheezy old bicycle pump* **–wheezily** *adv*

**whelk** /welk/ *n* a sea animal which lives in a shell, and is sometimes used as food

**when**[1] /wen/ *adv,conj* **1** at what time?; at the time that: *When will they come?|She'll tell us when to open it.|I jumped up when she called.* **2** considering that; although; as: *I can't tell you anything when you won't listen.|Why do you want a new job when you've got such a good one already?* –see HARDLY (USAGE)

**when**[2] *pron* (*in questions*) what time: **Since when** *has he had a beard?*

**whence** /wens/ *adv old use* (from) where; (from) which: *They returned to the land (from) whence they came.*

**when·ev·er** /we'nevəʳ/ *adv,conj* **1** at whatever time: *Whenever we see him, we speak to him.|Come whenever you like.* **2** (*showing surprise*) at what time?: *Whenever did you have time to do it?* –see EVER (USAGE)

**where**[1] /weəʳ/ *adv,conj* at or to what place?; at or to the place that: *Where do you live?|the office where I work|I asked her where to put it.|Sit where you like.*

**where**[2] *pron* what place: *Where do you come from?*

**where·a·bouts**[1] /ˌweərə'baʊts◂||'weərəbaʊts/ *adv,conj* where?; near what place?: *Whereabouts did I leave my bag?*

**where·a·bouts**[2] /'weərəbaʊts/ *n* [U +*sing./pl. v*] the place where someone or something is: *The escaped prisoner's whereabouts is/are still unknown.*

**where·as** /weə'ræz/ *conj* (shows an opposite) but; although: *They want a house, whereas we would rather live in a flat.*

**where·by** /weə'baɪ||weər-/ *adv fml* by which: *a law whereby all children receive free education*

**where·in** /weə'rɪn/ *adv,conj fml* in what; in which

**where·of** /weə'rɒv||weə'rʌv, -'rɑv/ *adv,conj fml* of what; of which

**where·so·ever** /ˌweəsəʊ'evəʳ||'weərsəʊˌevər/ *conj,adv lit* for WHEREVER (1)

**where·u·pon** /ˌweərə'pɒn||'weərəpɑn, -pɔn/ *conj fml* after which: *He saw me coming, whereupon he ran off in the other direction.*

**wher·ev·er** /weə'revəʳ/ *adv,conj* **1** to or at whatever place: *Wherever you go, I go too.|Sleep wherever you* *like.* **2** (showing surprise) to or at what place?: *Wherever have you been?* –see EVER (USAGE)

**where·with·al** /ˈweəwɪðɔːl‖-ər-/ *n* [*the* S +*to-v*] the necessary means, esp. money (to do something): *I'd like a new car but I haven't the wherewithal (to pay for it).*

**whet** /wet/ *v* **-tt-** [T] **1** *fml* to sharpen: *She whetted the knife on the stone.* **2 whet someone's appetite** to make someone wish for more: *Going to France for a week has whetted her appetite.* –sounds like **wet**

**wheth·er** /ˈweðəʳ/ *conj* **1** (shows a choice between possibilities): *He asked me whether/if she was coming.* (=He asked: "Is she coming?")|*I'll find out whether/if she's ready.*|*He wondered whether to go or not.*|*Tell me whether or not you like it.* **2** (shows that it does not matter which is chosen): *I'll go, whether you come with me or not.* (=I'll go whatever happens)|*Whether you like it or not, I'm going.*

**whew** /hjuː/ *interj* → PHEW

**whey** /weɪ/ *n* [U] the watery part of sour milk after the solid part has been removed –see also CURD

**which** /wɪtʃ/ *determiner,pron* **1** (used in questions, when a choice is to be made): *Which shoes shall I wear, the red ones or the brown ones?*|*Which of these books is yours?* **2** (shows what thing or things is/are meant): *Did you see the letter which/that came today?*|*This is the book which/that I told you about.* **3** (used esp. in written language, after a COMMA, to add more information to a sentence) **a** (about a thing or things): *The train, which takes only two hours to get there, is quicker than the bus, which takes three.* **b** (about the first part of the sentence): *She said she'd been waiting for half an hour, which was true.* (=she had in fact been waiting for half an hour)

USAGE Compare **which** and **what**: 1 **Which** is used when a choice must be made. **What** is used in questions about something unknown: **What** *colour do you want?*|**Which** *colour do you want, red or blue?* 2 **Which** can be followed by *of*, but **what** cannot: **Which** *of the films did you like best?* –see WHO, THAT (USAGE)

**which·ev·er** /wɪˈtʃevəʳ/ *determiner,pron* **1** any (one) of the set that: *Take whichever seat you like.* **2** no matter which: *It has the same result, whichever way you do it.* **3** (showing surprise) which?: *Whichever did you choose?*

**whiff** /wɪf/ *n* [S *of*] a short-lasting smell or movement of air: *Something good must be cooking; I got a whiff of it through the window.*

**while¹** /waɪl/ *n* [S] **1** a length of time, esp. a short one: *Just wait for a while and then I'll help you.* **2 worth one's/someone's while** worth one's/someone's time and trouble: *Do you think it's worth our while waiting for a bus, or shall we just walk?*|*If you join our firm, we'll* **make it worth your while**. (=we'll pay you well) –see also WORTHWHILE

**while²** ‖also **whilst** /waɪlst/ *BrE*– *conj* **1** during the time that: *They arrived while we were having dinner.*|*While she read, I cooked the dinner.* **2** although; WHEREAS: *Their country has plenty of oil, while ours has none.*

**while** sthg.↔**away, wile away** *v adv* **whiled, whiling** [T] to pass (time) lazily: *to while away the hours thinking of the holidays*

**whim** /wɪm/ *n* a sudden idea or wish, often not reasonable: *a sudden whim to buy a cream cake*

**whim·per** /ˈwɪmpəʳ/ *v* **1** [I] (esp. of a creature that is afraid) to make small weak cries **2** [I;T] to speak or say in a small trembling voice: *"Don't hurt me!" he whimpered.* –**whimper** *n: a whimper of pain/fear*

**whim·si·cal** /ˈwɪmzɪkəl/ *adj* fanciful; with strange ideas –**whimsically** *adv*

**whine** /waɪn/ *v* **whined, whining** [I] **1** to make a high sad cry: *The dog whined outside the door.* **2** to complain in an unnecessarily sad voice: *Stop whining, child!* –**whine** *n:* (fig.) *the whine of an aircraft engine*

**whin·ny** /ˈwɪni/ *v* **-nied, -nying** [I] to make a gentle sound which horses make –**whinny** *n* **-nies**

**whip¹** /wɪp/ *n* **1** a long piece of rope or leather fastened to a handle, used for hitting animals or people **2** a sweet food made of beaten eggs and other foods whipped together **3** a member of Parliament who is responsible for making other members of his/her party attend at voting time

**whip²** *v* **-pp-** **1** [T] to beat with a WHIP¹ (1) **2** [I;T] to move (something) quickly: *He whipped out his gun.*|*The wind whipped* (=moved quickly and fiercely) *across the plain.* **3** [T] to beat until stiff (esp. cream or the white part of eggs): *whipped cream* –compare WHISK² (2), BEAT¹ (2)

**whip** sthg.↔**up** *v adv* [T] **1** to cause (feelings) to rise, become stronger, etc.: *to whip up support for the government* **2** to make quickly: *to whip up a meal*

**whip·ping** /ˈwɪpɪŋ/ *n* a beating, esp. as a punishment

**whip-round** /ˈ· ·/ *n BrE infml* a collection of money among a group of people, e.g. in a place of work, to give to one member: *We're having a whip-round for old Fred, who's leaving the firm.*

**whirl¹** /wɜːl‖wɜrl/ *v* [I;T] to (cause to) move round and round very fast: *the whirling dancers*|*The leaves were picked up by the wind and whirled into the air.* –compare SPIN¹ (2)

**whirl²** *n* **1** [S] the act or sensation of WHIRLing: *My head's* **in a whirl** (=confused); *I must sit down and think.* **2** [C] very fast confused movement or activity: *a whirl of social activity*

**whirl·pool** /ˈwɜːlpuːl‖ˈwɜrl-/ *n* a place with circular currents of water in a sea or river, which can draw objects into it: *The floating sticks were sucked into the whirlpool.*

**whirl·wind** /ˈwɜːlˌwɪnd‖ˈwɜrl-/ *n* a tall pipe-shaped body of air moving rapidly in a circle: *A whirlwind destroyed the town.*

**whirr** *BrE*‖**whir** *AmE* /wɜːʳ/ *v* **-rr-** [I] to make a regular sound like something turning, or moving up and down, very quickly: *the whirring sound of an insect's wings* –**whirr** *n*

**whisk¹** /wɪsk/ *n* **1** [*usu. sing.*] a quick movement, esp. to brush something off: *with a whisk of his hand* **2** a small hand-held tool for beating eggs, whipping cream, etc.: *an egg whisk*

**whisk²** *v* [T] **1** to move or remove quickly: *The horse was whisking its tail to brush the flies off its back.*|*She whisked the cups away.*|*She whisked him (off) home.* **2** to beat (esp. eggs), esp. with a WHISK¹ (2)

**whis·ker** /ˈwɪskəʳ/ *n* [*usu. pl.*] one of the long stiff hairs that grow near the mouth of a cat, rat, etc.

**whis·kers** /ˈwɪskəz‖-ərz/ *n* [P] hair growing on the

sides of a man's face –compare BEARD

**whis·key** /ˈwɪski/ *n* **-keys** [C;U] WHISKY made in Ireland or the US

**whis·ky** /ˈwɪski/ *n* **-kies** [C;U] (a glass of) a strong alcoholic drink (SPIRIT[1] (7)) made from MALTED grain, such as BARLEY, produced esp. in Scotland: *a bottle of whisky|Two whiskies, please.*

**whis·per[1]** /ˈwɪspəʳ/ *v* [I;T] to speak (words) very quietly, using the breath but not the voice: *The children were whispering in the corner.*|(fig.) *the wind whispering in the roof*

**whisper[2]** *n* whispered words: *She said it* **in a whisper.**|(fig.) *the whisper of the wind*

**whist** /wɪst/ *n* [U] a card game for two pairs of players

**whis·tle[1]** /ˈwɪsəl/ *n* **1** a simple musical instrument for making a high sound by passing air or steam through: *The* REFEREE *blew his whistle, and the game stopped.* **2** the high sound made by passing air or steam through a small tube-shaped instrument, a mouth, or a beak: *He gave a loud whistle of surprise.*

**whistle[2]** *v* **-tled, -tling 1** [I] to make a WHISTLE[1] (2), esp. with the mouth, so as to make music or to attract attention: *He whistled to me from the other side of the street.*|(fig.) *The wind whistled round them.* **2** [T] to produce (music) by doing this: *He whistled a popular tune.*

**Whit** /wɪt/ *n* → WHITSUN: *the Whit weekend*

**white[1]** /waɪt/ *adj* **1 a** of the colour of snow and milk: *white paint|white hair* (=when one is very old) **b** pale in colour: *white wine|white-faced with fear* **2** (of a person) of a pale-skinned race –compare BLACK[1] (3), FAIR[1] (4) **3** (of coffee) with milk or cream –opposite **black** –**whiteness** *n* [U]

**white[2]** *n* **1** [U] the colour which is white **2** [C] a person of a pale-skinned race: *There were both whites and blacks at the meeting.* **3** [C] the white part of the eye **4** [C;U] the part of an egg which is colourless, but white after cooking: *Beat three egg whites until stiff.*

**white-col·lar** /ˌ· ˈ·· ◂/ *adj* [A] not of the people who work with their hands; of office workers, indoor workers, etc.: *a white-collar job* –see also BLUE-COLLAR

**White·hall** /ˈwaɪthɔːl, ˌwaɪtˈhɔːl/ *n* [U +*sing./pl. v*] the British government (esp. the government departments rather than the members of Parliament): *What action has/have Whitehall taken on this matter?*

**White House** /ˈ· ·/ *n* the official home in Washington of the President of the United States

**whit·en** /ˈwaɪtn/ *v* [I;T] to (cause to) become (more) white: *I must whiten my tennis shoes.*

**white pa·per** /ˌ· ˈ··/ *n* (in Britain) an official government report on a certain subject: *a new white paper on education*

**white·wash[1]** /ˈwaɪtwɒʃ‖-wɔʃ, -wɑʃ/ *n* [U] **1** a white liquid mixture made from lime, used esp. for painting walls **2** an attempt to hide something wrong: *What he said was just whitewash to hide his mistake.*

**whitewash[2]** *v* [T] **1** to cover with WHITEWASH[1] (1): *whitewashing the farm buildings* **2** to try to hide (something wrong)

**whith·er** /ˈwɪðəʳ/ *adv,conj old use* **1** to which (place): *the place whither* (=to which) *he went* –compare WHENCE **2** to what place?: *Whither goes he?* (=Where is he going?)

**whi·ting** /ˈwaɪtɪŋ/ *n* **-tings** *or* **-ting** a sea fish used for food

**Whit·sun** /ˈwɪtsən/ also **Whit**– *n* (the public holiday, or the whole week including) the seventh Sunday after Easter

**whit·tle** /ˈwɪtl/ *v* **-tled, -tling** [T *down, away*] to cut (wood) to a smaller size by taking off small thin pieces: *whittling down a piece of wood*|(fig.) *Lack of sleep whittled his strength away.*

**whiz, whizz** /wɪz/ *v* **-zz-** [I] *infml* to move very fast, often with a noisy sound: *Cars were whizzing past.*

**whiz kid** /ˈ· ·/ *n infml* a clever person who moves ahead in life very quickly

**who** /huː/ *pron* (*used esp. as the subject of a verb*) **1** (*used in questions*) what person or people?: *Who's at the door?|Who are they?|Who won the race?* **2** (shows what person or people is/are meant): *The woman who/that wrote this letter works in a hospital.|Do you know the people who/that live here?|A postman is a man who/that delivers letters.* **3** (used esp. in written language, after a COMMA, to add more information about a person or people): *This is my father, who lives in Glasgow.* (=and he lives in Glasgow)

USAGE Except in very formal language, **who** can be used instead of **whom** as an object in questions: **Who** *did you see?*|**Who** *was she dancing with?* –see THAT (USAGE)

**WHO** *n abbrev. for*: the World Health Organization; an international organization which aims to improve the health of people throughout the world

**whoa** /wəʊ, həʊ/ *interj* (a call to a horse to) stop

**who'd** /huːd/ *short for* **1** who had **2** who would

**who·ev·er** /huːˈevəʳ/ *pron* **1** anybody at all that: *I'll take whoever wants to go.* **2** no matter who: *Whoever it is, I don't want to see them/him.* **3** *(showing surprise)* who?: *Whoever can that be at the door?*

**whole[1]** /həʊl/ *adj* **1** not spoilt or divided: *a tin of whole* PEACHES (=not cut in half)|*to swallow it whole* (=without breaking it up in the mouth) **2** [A] not less than (a); all (the): *I spent the whole day in bed.|the whole truth|He drank a whole bottle of wine.*

**whole[2]** *n* [*usu. sing.*] **1** [*of*] the complete amount, thing, etc.: *The whole of the morning was wasted.|We can't treat the group* **as a whole**, *but singly.* **2** the sum of the parts: *Two halves make a whole.* **3 on the whole** generally; mostly: *On the whole, I like it.*

**whole-heart·ed** /ˌ· ˈ·· ◂/ *adj* with all one's ability, sincerity, etc.: *to give one's whole-hearted attention/sympathy* –**wholeheartedly** *adv*

**whole·meal** /ˈhəʊlmiːl‖/ also **whole wheat** *AmE*– *adj* [A] made without removing the covering of the grain: *wholemeal flour|wholemeal bread* (=a type of brown bread)

**whole·sale[1]** /ˈhəʊlseɪl/ *n* [U] the business of selling goods in large quantities, esp. to shopkeepers –compare RETAIL[2]

**wholesale[2]** *adj,adv* **1** of or concerned in selling in large quantities esp. for selling again: *a wholesale wine dealer* –compare RETAIL[2] **2** in too large, unlimited numbers: *wholesale* SLAUGHTER

**whole·sal·er** /ˈhəʊlˌseɪləʳ/ *n* a businessman who sells WHOLESALE[2] (2) goods

**whole·some** /'həulsəm/ *adj* **1** good for the body: *wholesome food* **2** good in effect, esp. morally: *a wholesome film* –**wholesomeness** *n* [U]

**who'll** /huːl/ *short for:* who will

**whol·ly** /'həul-li/ *adv* completely: *not wholly to blame for the accident*

**whom** /huːm/ *pron* (the object form of WHO, used esp. in formal speech or writing): *Whom did you see?|I met a woman whom I know.|The minister, to whom I spoke recently, agrees.* –see WHO, THAT (USAGE)

**whoop** /wuːp, huːp/ *v,n* [I;C] (to make) a loud cry, as of joy

**whop·per** /'wɒpə<sup>r</sup>||'wɑ-/ *n infml* **1** a big thing: *Did you catch that fish? What a whopper!* **2** a big lie: *He told a real whopper to excuse his lateness.*

**whore** /hɔːʳ||hor/ *n old use & bibl* for PROSTITUTE

**who're** /'huːəʳ/ *short for:* who are

**whorl** /wɜːl||wɜrl/ *n* the shape which a line makes when going round in a SPIRAL, e.g. in some seashells

**who's** /huːz/ *short for* **1** who is: *Who's he talking about?* **2** who has: *Who's he brought to dinner?* **3** *infml* who does: *Who's he mean?*

**whose** /huːz/ *determiner,pron* **1** (used in questions) of whom?: *Whose house is this?|Whose is that car?* **2** of whom: *That's the man whose house was burned down.* **3** of which: *a minister whose ideas are not popular*

**who·so·ev·er** /ˌhuːsəu'evəʳ/ *pron old use* for WHOEVER (1,2)

**who've** /huːv/ *short for:* who have: *people who've been there|Who've you been staying with?*

**why** /waɪ/ *adv,conj* **1** for what reason: *Why did you do it?|They asked him why he was so dirty.|Is there a reason why you can't come?|I see why it won't work.* –see Study Notes on page 128 **2 Why not** (making a suggestion): *Why not go by bus?*

**wick** /wɪk/ *n* **1** a piece of twisted thread in a candle, which burns as the wax melts **2** a piece of material in an oil lamp which draws up oil while burning

**wick·ed** /'wɪk$\frac{1}{5}$d/ *adj* very bad; evil: *a wicked man|*(fig.) *a wicked waste of money* –**wickedly** *adv* –**wickedness** *n* [U]

USAGE **Wicked** and **evil** are very strong words for people or acts that are seriously morally wrong: *a* **wicked/evil** *murderer.* Disobedient children are usually called **naughty** or, if one finds their bad behaviour rather amusing, **mischievous.**

**wick·er·work** /'wɪkəwɜːk||'wɪkərwɜrk/ also **wicker**– *n* [A;U] any example(s) of objects produced by weaving TWIGS, REEDS, etc.: *wicker(work) furniture*

**wick·et** /'wɪk$\frac{1}{5}$t/ *n* (in cricket) **a** either of two sets of three sticks (STUMPS[1] (2)), at which the ball is thrown (BOWLed[2] (1)) **b** also **pitch**– the stretch of grass between these two sets –see CRICKET (USAGE)

**wide**[1] /waɪd/ *adj* **1** large from side to side or edge to edge: *The skirt's too wide.|The gate isn't wide enough for me to drive the car through.* **2** [after *n*] measuring from side to side: *The garden is eight metres long and six metres wide.* **3** covering a large space or range of things: *over the wide seas|wide interests* –compare NARROW[1] **3** also **wide open**– fully open: *wide eyes*

**wide**[2] *adv* **1** completely (open), esp. the mouth: *open wide/wide open|wide-eyed with surprise|wide-awake* (=fully awake) **2** [*of*] (in sport) far away from the right point: *The ball went wide (of the* GOAL (2)).

**wide·ly** /'waɪdli/ *adv* **1** over a wide space or range of things: *widely known|It's widely believed* (=by many people) *that the government will lose the election.* **2** to a large degree: *widely different*

**wid·en** /'waɪdn/ *v* [I;T] to make or become (wide or) wider: *to widen a road* –compare NARROW[2]

**wide·spread** /'waɪdspred/ *adj* found, placed, etc., in many places: *a widespread disease/belief*

**wid·ow** /'wɪdəu/ *n* a woman whose husband has died, and who has not married again

**wid·owed** /'wɪdəud/ *adj* left alone after the death of one's husband/wife

**wid·ow·er** /'wɪdəuəʳ/ *n* a man whose wife has died, and who has not married again

**width** /wɪdθ/ *n* size from side to side: *The garden is six metres in width.* –see picture on page 592 **2** [C] a piece of material of the full width, as it was woven: *We need four widths of curtain material to cover the window.*

**wield** /wiːld/ *v* [T] to control the action of: *She wields a lot of influence.|(old use & lit) to wield a weapon*

**wife** /waɪf/ *n* **wives** /waɪvz/ the woman to whom a man is married: *My wife is a company director.|the President and his wife* –compare HUSBAND; see picture on page 217

**wife·ly** /'waɪfli/ *adj esp. old use* having or showing the good qualities of a wife

**wig** /wɪg/ *n* an arrangement of false hair to make a covering for the head: *The actress wore a black wig over her* BLOND *hair.|Judges wear wigs in court.*

**wig·gle** /'wɪgəl/ *v* **-gled, -gling** [I;T] to (cause to) move in small esp. side to side movements: *to wiggle one's toes* –**wiggle** *n* [S]: *She walks with a wiggle.*

**wig·wam** /'wɪgwæm||-wɑm/ *n* a tent of the type used by some North American Indians

**wild**[1] /waɪld/ *adj* **1** usu. living in natural conditions or having natural qualities; not TAME or CULTIVATED: *a wild animal/flower|the wild hills* **2** not CIVILIZED; SAVAGE: *wild tribes* **3** having or showing strong feelings, esp. of anger: *He looked wild with anger.* **4** (of natural forces) violent; strong: *a wild wind* **5** having or showing lack of thought or control: *a wild guess* (=without knowing any facts)|*a wild throw* **6** [F *about*] having a great (sometimes unreasonable) liking (for): *She's wild about racing cars.* –**wildness** *n* [U]

**wild**[2] *n* [*the* C;S] natural areas full of animals and plants, with few people: *The lion escaped and returned to the wild.|lost in the wilds (of an unknown country)*

**wild**[3] *adv* **run wild** to behave as one likes, without control

**wild·cat** /'waɪldkæt/ *adj* [A] (in industry) happening unofficially and unexpectedly: *wildcat* STRIKES[2] (1)

**wil·der·ness** /'wɪldən$\frac{1}{5}$s||-dər-/ *n* **1** [*the* S] *old use & bibl* an area of land with little life, esp. a desert **2** [C *of*] an unchanging empty stretch of land, water, etc.: *in a wilderness of houses*

**wild·fire** /'waɪldfaɪəʳ/ *n* **like wildfire** very fast: *The news spread/went round like wildfire.*

**wild·fowl** /'waɪldfaul/ *n* [P] birds that are shot for sport, esp. waterbirds

**wild-goose chase** /ˌ· ˈ· ·/ *n* **(lead someone) a wild-goose chase** (to cause someone) a useless search

**wild·life** /ˈwaɪldlaɪf/ *n* [U] animals (and plants) which live in a wild state: *a wildlife park*

**wild·ly** /ˈwaɪldli/ *adv* in a wild way: *He ran wildly down the street.|His answer was wildly wrong.* (=very greatly wrong)

**wiles** /waɪlz/ *n* [P] tricks; deceitful PERSUASION: *She was tricked by the salesman's wiles.*

**wil·ful** *BrE*||**willful** *AmE* /ˈwɪlfəl/ *adj* **1** having the intention of doing what one likes, in spite of other people: *a wilful child|wilful behaviour* **2** [A] done on purpose: *wilful misbehaviour|wilful damage to the farmer's crops* –**wilfully** *adv* –**wilfulness** *n* [U]

**will**[1] /wɪl/ *v negative short form* **won't** [I +~~to~~-v] **1** (used to show the future): *They say that it will rain tomorrow.* –see Study Notes on page 386 **2** to be willing to; be ready to: *I won't go!|We can't find anyone who will take the job.|The door won't shut.|Will you have some tea?* (used when offering something politely) **3** (used when asking someone to do something): *Will you telephone me later please?|Shut the door, will you?|You won't tell him, will you?* (=I hope not) **4** (shows what always happens): *Accidents will happen.|Oil will float on water.|He will ask silly questions.* **5** (used like **can**, to show what is possible): *This car will hold six people.* **6** (used like **must**, to show what is likely): *That will be the postman at the door now.* –see also WOULD; see SHALL (USAGE)

**will**[2] *n* **1** [C;U] the power in the mind to choose one's actions: *Free will makes us able to choose our way of life.* **2** [C;U] intention or power to make things happen: *the will to live|He didn't have the will to change.* **3** [U] what is wished or intended (by the stated person): *Her death is God's will.* **4** [C] the written wishes of a person in regard to sharing his/her property among other people after his/her death: *Have you made your will yet?|I was left £1,000 in my grandfather's will.* **5 at will** as one wishes **6 -willed** having a certain kind of WILL[2] (1): *a weak-willed man*

**will**[3] *v* [T] **1** [+(*that*)] to make or intend (to happen) esp. by power of the mind: *We willed him to stop, but he just drove past.* **2** [*to*] *law* to leave (possessions or money) in a WILL[2] (4) to be given after one's death

**will·ing** /ˈwɪlɪŋ/ *adj* [+*to-v*] ready (to do something): *Are you willing to help?|a willing helper* –**willingly** *adv* –**willingness** *n* [U +*to-v*]

**wil·low** /ˈwɪləʊ/ *n* [C;U] (the wood from) a tree which grows near water, with long thin branches

**wil·low·y** /ˈwɪləʊi/ *adj* pleasantly thin and graceful: *a girl with a willowy figure*

**will·pow·er** /ˈwɪlˌpaʊəʳ/ *n* [U] strength of WILL[2] (1): *He hasn't the willpower to stop eating so much.*

**wil·ly-nil·ly** /ˌwɪli ˈnɪli/ *adv* regardless of whether (generally) wanted or not: *They introduced the new laws willy-nilly.*

**wilt** /wɪlt/ *v* [I] (of a plant) to become less fresh and start to die: *The flowers are wilting for lack of water.|* (fig.) *I'm wilting* (=becoming weak) *in this heat.* –compare WITHER

**wil·y** /ˈwaɪli/ *adj* **-ier, -iest** clever in tricks, esp. for getting what one wants: *a wily fox* –see also WILES –**wiliness** *n* [U]

**win**[1] /wɪn/ *v* **won** /wʌn/, **winning 1** [I;T] to be the best or first in (a struggle, competition, or race): *She won the race.|Who won?|Who won the election?|to win at cards|the winning team* **2** [T] to be given (something) as the result of success in a competition, race, or game of chance: *She won a prize/cup/£100.|I won £20 at cards.* **3** [T] to gain (for oneself) by effort or ability: *By her hard work she won a place for herself/won herself a place in the school team.*

USAGE Compare **win**, **earn**, and **gain**. To **win** is to be successful in (a contest, a war, a game, etc.) and perhaps to receive (a prize) as a result: *Who is going to* **win** *the election?|She* **won** *£1000 in a competition.* If you work for money (or any other reward), you **earn** it, and this also suggests that you deserve what you have worked for: *You've been working hard and you've* **earned** (=you deserve) *a rest.|She* **earns** *£1000 a month.* To **gain** is to obtain (something useful and desirable) and, unlike **win** and **earn**, it is not used in connection with money: *By reducing prices, we* **gained** *an advantage over our opponents.|She* **gained** *experience while working for the newspaper.*

*win* sbdy.↔**over/round** *v adv* [T *to*] to gain the support of (someone), often by persuading: *He disagreed, but we won him round to our point of view.*

**win**[2] *n* (esp. in sport) a victory or success: *three wins and two defeats*

**wince** /wɪns/ *v* **winced, wincing** [I *at*] to close one's eyes, move suddenly, etc., (as if) drawing away from something unpleasant: *I could see him wince when I told him how much the repairs would cost.* –compare JUMP[1] (3), START[1] (6)

**winch** /wɪntʃ/ *v,n* [T;C] (to move by) a machine for pulling up heavy objects by means of a turning part: *They winched the car out of the ditch.|They used a winch to lift the car.*

**wind**[1] /wɪnd/ *n* **1** [C;U] strongly moving air: *high/strong/heavy winds|We couldn't play tennis because there was too much wind.* –compare BREEZE, AIR; see WEATHER (USAGE) **2** [U] breath or breathing: *He couldn't get his wind* (=could not breathe properly) *after his run.* –compare WINDPIPE **3** [U] (the condition of having) air or gas in the stomach: *You get wind when you eat too quickly.* **4 get wind of** *infml* to hear about, esp. accidentally or unofficially: *If anyone gets wind of our plans, we'll be in trouble.* **5 (something) in the wind** (something secret) about to happen/being done **6 it's an ill wind (that blows nobody any good)** even bad things may have some good results **7 put/get the wind up** *infml* to make/become afraid or anxious

**wind**[2] /wɪnd/ *v* [T] to cause to be breathless: *He hit him in the stomach and winded him.*

**wind**[3] /waɪnd/ *v* **wound** /waʊnd/, **winding 1** [T *round*] to wrap around several times: *The nurse wound a bandage round my wounded arm.* **2** [T *up*] to tighten the working parts by turning: *to wind a clock* **3** [T] to move by turning (a handle): *to wind down the car window* **4** [I;T] to follow or take a course with many twists and turns: *He wound his way through the trees.|The river winds through the country.*

**wind down** *v adv* [I] **1** (of a clock or watch) to work more slowly before at last stopping **2** (of a person) to rest until calmer, after work or excitement: *He went on holiday to wind down.*

**wind** sbdy.↔**up** to cause (someone) to become excited or annoyed

**wind up** *v adv* **1** [I;T (=**wind** sthg.↔**up**) *with*] to come to, or bring to, an end: *to wind up the evening with a drink|to wind up a company* **2** [I] *infml* to put oneself (in a certain state or place), accidentally: *You'll wind up in prison if you go on behaving like that.* –compare END **up**

**wind·bag** /'wɪndbæg/ *n infml* a person who talks too much, esp. about dull things

**wind·break** /'wɪndbreɪk/ *n* a fence, wall, line of trees, etc., which stops the wind coming through with its full force

**wind·fall** /'wɪndfɔːl/ *n* **1** a piece of fruit blown down off a tree: *These apples are windfalls, but they're good.* **2** an unexpected lucky gift, esp. money: *a windfall of £100 from a distant relative|His win at the races gave him a windfall of £100.*

**wind·ing** /'waɪndɪŋ/ *adj* (esp. of a road, river, path, etc.) of a twisting turning shape: *They followed a winding road through the country.|a winding old staircase* –see WIND[3] (4)

**wind in·stru·ment** /'wɪnd ˌɪnstrʊmənt/ *n* any musical instrument played when air is blown through it

**wind·mill** /'wɪndˌmɪl/ *n* a building containing a machine that crushes corn, provides electricity, pumps water, etc., and is driven by large esp. wooden sails which are turned round by the wind

**win·dow** /'wɪndəʊ/ *n* a (usu.) glass opening, esp. in the wall of a building, in a car, etc., to let in light and air and which one can see through: *the front window|a car window* –see picture on page 297

**window dress·ing** /'·· ˌ··/ *n* [U] the art or practice of arranging goods in a shop window to attract people (fig.) *The new government tax reductions are only window dressing.* –**window dresser** *n*

**win·dow·pane** /'wɪndəʊpeɪn/ *n* one whole piece of glass in a window

**window-shop·ping** /'·· ··/ *n* [U] looking at the goods shown in shop windows without necessarily intending to buy: *to go window- shopping*

**win·dow·sill** /'wɪndəʊˌsɪl/ ||also **windowledge** /'wɪndəʊˌledʒ/ *BrE– n* the flat shelf formed by the wood or stone below a window –see picture on page 355

**wind·pipe** /'wɪndpaɪp/ *n* the tube which forms an air passage from the throat to the top of the lungs

**wind·screen** /'wɪndskriːn/ *BrE*||**windshield** /-ʃiːld/ *AmE– n* the piece of glass across the front of a car, lorry, etc., which the driver looks through –see picture on page 85

**windscreen wip·er** /'·· ˌ··/ also **wiper**– *n* a movable arm which clears rain from the WINDSCREEN of a car –see picture on page 85

**wind·sock** /'wɪndsɒk||-sɑk/ *n* a tube-like piece of material, fastened to a pole at airports, which shows the direction of the wind

**wind·swept** /'wɪndswept/ *adj* **1** (of country) usu. flat and open to frequent strong winds: *a bare windswept plain* **2** (as if) blown into an untidy state: *a windswept appearance*

**wind·y** /'wɪndi/ *adj* **-ier, -iest** with a lot of wind: *a windy day* –**windily** *adv* –**windiness** *n* [U]

**wine** /waɪn/ *n* [C;U] (an) alcoholic drink made from GRAPES or other fruit: *a glass of wine|the wines of Alsace|apple wine*

**wing**[1] /wɪŋ/ *n* **1** one of the limbs by which a bird or insect flies **2** one of the parts standing out from the side of a plane which support it in flight –see picture on page 16 **3** one of the parts of a car which cover the wheel –see picture on page 85 **4** any part of an object or group which stands out from the side: *the west wing of the house* **5** (in sport) the position or player on the far right or left of the field **6** a group representing certain views within a political party: *Which wing of the party is she on?* –see also LEFT WING, RIGHT WING **7 under someone's wing** being protected, helped, etc., by someone: *to take the new pupils under one's wing*

**wing**[2] *v* [I;T] *lit* to fly (as if) on wings

**wing com·mand·er** /'· ·ˌ··/ *n* an officer of middle rank in the Royal Air Force

**wings** /wɪŋz/ *n* [P] (either of) the sides of a stage, where an actor is hidden from view: *She stood watching* **in the wings**. –see picture on page 463

**wing·span** /'wɪŋspæn/ *n* the distance from the end of one wing to the end of the other, when both are stretched out –see also SPAN[1] (3)

**wink**[1] /wɪŋk/ *v* [I] **1** [*at*] to close and open one eye rapidly, usu. as a signal between people, esp. of amusement: *He winked at her, and she knew he was only pretending to be angry.* **2** (of a light) to flash on and off: *The car winked before turning.*

**wink**[2] *n* **1** [C] a WINKing movement **2** [S *only in* NEGATIVE[1] *sentences*] (used of sleep) a short time: *I didn't sleep a wink/get a wink of sleep.*

**win·kle** /'wɪŋkəl/ *n* a small sea animal that lives in a shell and is eaten as food

**winkle** sbdy./sthg. **out** *v adv* **-kled, -kling** [T *of*] *infml* to get or remove by force or hard work: *At last I winkled the truth out of him.*

**win·ner** /'wɪnə[r]/ *n* a person or animal that has won or is thought likely to win –compare LOSER; LEADER

**win·ning** /'wɪnɪŋ/ *adj* which attract(s): *winning ways|a winning smile*

**win·nings** /'wɪnɪŋz/ *n* [P] money which has been won in a game, by BETting[2] (1) on a (horse) race, etc.

**win·some** /'wɪnsəm/ *adj old use* nice-looking; attractive: *a winsome appearance*

**win·ter**[1] /'wɪntə[r]/ *n* [C;U] the coldest season, between autumn and spring: *I go on holiday in winter.|a cold winter|winter sports* (=on snow or ice)

**winter**[2] *v* [I *in*] to spend the winter: *to winter in a warm country*

**win·ter·time** /'wɪntətaɪm||-ər-/ *n* [*the* U] the winter season: *Heating bills are highest in (the) wintertime.*

**win·try** /'wɪntri/ also **wintery**– *adj* like winter, esp. cold or snowy: *wintry clouds|a wintry scene*

**wipe**[1] /waɪp/ *v* **wiped, wiping** [T] **1** to pass a cloth or other material against (something) to remove dirt, liquid, etc.: *Wipe your feet/shoes (on the mat).|Wipe the table.* **2** [*away, off*] to remove by doing this: *to* wipe the tears away

**wipe** sbdy./sthg.↔**out** *v adv* [T] to destroy all of: *The enemy wiped out the whole nation.*

**wipe up** *v adv* **1** [T] (**wipe** sthg.↔**up**) to remove (liquid/dirt SPILLed or dropped) with a cloth: *Wipe up that mess!* **2** [I;T (=**wipe** sthg. ↔**up**)] to dry (dishes, plates, etc., that have been washed) with a cloth: *If I wash the dishes will you wipe up?*

**wipe²** *n* a wiping (WIPE¹) movement: *Give your nose a good wipe.*

**wip·er** /ˈwaɪpəʳ/ *n* → WINDSCREEN WIPER

**wire¹** /waɪəʳ/ *n* **1** [C;U] (a piece of) thin metal like a thread: *a wire fence|They tied his hands with wire.*|BARBED *wire* |*The string wasn't strong enough, so we used wire.* **2** [C] metal like this used for carrying electricity from one place to another **3** *infml, esp. AmE* a telegram

**wire²** *v* **wired, wiring** [T] **1** [*up*] to connect up wires in (something), esp. in an electrical system: *to wire (up) a house/to re-wire it* **2** [+*that*] to send a telegram to: *He wired me (about) the results of the examination.*

**wire·less** /ˈwaɪələ̇s‖ˈwaɪər-/ *n* [C;U] *BrE, becoming rare* for RADIO

**wire net·ting** /ˌ· ˈ··/ *n* a material made of wires woven together into a network, used esp. as a fence

**wir·ing** /ˈwaɪərɪŋ/ *n* [*the* U] the arrangement of the wired electrical system in a building: *good wiring|This old wiring needs replacing.*

**wir·y** /ˈwaɪəri/ *adj* **-ier, -iest** rather thin, with strong muscles: *a wiry body* **–wiriness** *n* [U]

**wis·dom** /ˈwɪzdəm/ *n* [U] the quality of being wise: *to have/show great wisdom*

**wisdom tooth** /ˈ··· ·/ *n* (in humans) one of the four large back teeth, which do not usu. appear until the rest of the body has stopped growing

**wise** /waɪz/ *adj usu. fml & polite* **1** having or showing good sense, cleverness, the ability to understand what happens and decide on the right action: *a wise man/decision|It was wise of you to leave.* **2 none the wiser** knowing no more, after being told: *I was none the wiser after he'd explained everything.* **–wisely** *adv*

**wise·crack** /ˈwaɪzkræk/ *v,n* [T;C] *infml* (to make) a joking remark or reply

**wise guy** /ˈ· ·/ *n infml* a person who thinks he knows more than others

**wish¹** /wɪʃ/ *v* [not *be* +*ving*] **1** [T +*that*] to want (what is at present impossible): *I wish the weather wasn't so cold.|I wish I could fly.* **2** [I *for*] to want and try to cause a particular thing: *You have everything you could wish for.* **3** [T] to hope that (someone) has (something): *We wish you a merry Christmas/good luck/a safe journey.* **4** [I;T] *polite* to want: *Do you wish me to come back later?* –see HOPE (USAGE)

**wish** sbdy./sthg. **on** sbdy. *v prep* [T] [*usu. in questions or in* NEGATIVE¹ *sentences*] to hope that someone else should have: *She's a difficult person; I wouldn't wish her on my worst enemy.*

**wish²** *n* **1** [+*to-v*] a feeling of wanting, esp. what at present is impossible: *a wish to see the world|a wish for peace* **2** a desire for and attempt to make a particular thing happen, esp. by magic (esp. in the phrase **make a wish**) **3** what is wished for: *his last wish* (=before death)

**wish·bone** /ˈwɪʃbəʊn/ *n* a V-shaped bone in a cooked chicken or other farm bird

**wishful think·ing** /ˌ·· ˈ··/ *n* [U] acting as though something is true or will happen because one would like it to be: *He says he's sure to get a job when he leaves university, but it may be just wishful thinking.*

**wish·y-wash·y** /ˈwɪʃi ˌwɒʃi‖-ˌwɔʃi, -ˌwaʃi/ *adj derog* without strength; weak: *wishy-washy ideas*

**wisp** /wɪsp/ *n* [*of*] **1** a small separate piece: *a wisp of hair|wisps of grass* **2** a small thin twisting bit (of smoke or steam)

**wist·ful** /ˈwɪstfəl/ *adj* having or showing a wish which may not be satisfied, or thoughts of past happiness which may not return: *to look wistful* **–wistfully** *adv* **–wistfulness** *n* [U]

**wit** /wɪt/ *n* **1** [C;U] (a person who has) the ability to say things which are both clever and amusing: *conversation full of wit|Oscar Wilde was a famous wit.* –see also WITTY **2** [U] power of thought; INTELLIGENCE: *He hadn't the wit to say no.* **3 at one's wits end** made too worried by difficulties to know what to do next **4 have/keep one's wits about one** to be ready to act sensibly: *You need your wits about you when you're driving.* **5 -witted** having the stated type of ability or understanding: *quick-witted|dim-witted* (=stupid)

**witch** /wɪtʃ/ *n* a woman who has, or is believed to have, magic powers –compare WIZARD

**witch·craft** /ˈwɪtʃkrɑːft‖-kræft/ *n* [U] the practice of magic to make things (esp. bad things) happen

**witch·doc·tor** /ˈwɪtʃˌdɒktəʳ‖-ˌdɑk-/ *n* a man in an undeveloped society who is believed to have magical powers

**witch-hunt** /ˈ· ·/ *n* a search for people whose political views are disliked, so that they may be made to suffer, removed from power, etc.

**with** /wɪð, wɪθ/ *prep* **1** among or including; in the presence of: *staying with* (=at the house of) *a friend|Mix the flour with some milk.|Leave your dog with me.|Connect this wire with that one.* (=so that they are joined) **2** having; showing: *a book with a green cover|They fought with courage.* –opposite **without 3** by means of; using: *to eat with a spoon|Cut it with the scissors.|What will you buy with the money?|This photograph was taken with a cheap camera.* **4** (shows the idea of covering, filling, or containing): *covered with dirt|I filled it with sugar.|made with eggs* **5** in support of; in favour of: *to vote with the government|I agree with every word.|You're either with me or against me.* **6** in the same direction as: *to sail with the wind* **7** at the same time and rate as: *The wine improves with age.* **8** (used in comparisons): *to compare chalk with cheese|level with the street* **9** against: *Stop fighting with your brother.* **10** (shows separation from): *to break with the past* **11** in spite of: *With all his faults, I still like him.* **12** because of: *singing with joy|grass wet with rain|With John away,* (=John is away) *we've got more room.* **13** concerning; in the case of: *in love with him|Be patient with them.|What's the matter with your foot?* **14** (used in exclamations expressing a wish or command): *On with the dance!* (=let the dancing continue)|*Down with school!|Off to bed with you!* (=Go to bed!)

**with·draw** /wɪðˈdrɔː, wɪθ-/ *v* **-drew** /ˈdruː/, **-drawn**

/'drɔːn/, **-drawing 1** [I;T *from*] to (cause to) move away or back: *to withdraw the army|The army withdrew.* **2** [T *from*] to take away or back: *to withdraw £5 from a bank account*|(fig.) *to withdraw a remark* –compare DEPOSIT¹ (2) **3** [I;T *from*] to (cause to) not take part in: *He withdrew (his horse) from the race.*

**with·draw·al** /wɪð'drɔːəl, wɪθ-/ *n* [C;U] (an example of) the act of WITHDRAWing or state of being WITHDRAWN

**with·drawn** /wɪð'drɔːn, wɪθ-/ *adj* habitually quiet and concerned with one's own thoughts

**with·er** /'wɪðəʳ/ *v* [I;T *away*] (of a plant) to make or become reduced in size, colour, etc.: *The cold withered the leaves.*|(fig.) *withered hopes|The flowers withered in the cold.* –compare WILT

**with·er·ing** /'wɪðərɪŋ/ *adj* (of an expression or remark) which causes one to be silent and/or uncertain: *a withering look* **–witheringly** *adv*

**with·hold** /wɪð'həuld, wɪθ-/ *v* **-held** /'held/, **-holding** [T *from*] to keep (back) on purpose: *to withhold information*

**with·in** /wɪ'ðɪn‖wɪ'ðɪn, wɪ'θɪn/ *adv,prep* **1** *fml* inside: *within the castle|"This Building To Be Sold. Enquire Within"* (on a notice) **2** not beyond; not more than: *They'll arrive within an/the hour.|to keep within the law* (=not break it) –see INSIDE (USAGE)

**with·out** /wɪ'ðaut‖wɪ'ðaut, wɪ'θaut/ *adv,prep* **1** not having: *to go out without a coat|We couldn't have done it without Mary.|There's no milk, so drink your tea without.* **2** (*before* -ing *verbs*) not: *He left without telling me.|Can you wash it without breaking it?*

**with·stand** /wɪð'stænd, wɪθ-/ *v* **-stood** /'stud/, **-standing** [T] to oppose without yielding; RESIST: *to withstand an attack|Children's furniture must withstand kicks and blows.*

**wit·ness¹** /'wɪtn¦s/ *n* **1** [*of*] also **eyewitness**– a person who is present when something happens: *There were no witnesses when the accident happened.* **2** a person who tells in a court of law what he saw happen, what he knows about someone, etc. **3** [*to*] a person who signs an official paper to show that he has seen the maker sign it: *a witness to the* WILL² (4) **4** [*to*] a sign or proof (of): *The success of the show* **bears witness to** *our good planning.*

**witness²** *v* [T] **1** to be present at the time of and see: *She witnessed the accident.* **2** to be present as a WITNESS¹ (3) at the making of: *to witness the signature*

**witness box** /'·· ·/ *BrE*‖**witness stand** /'·· ·/ *AmE*– *n* the raised area where witnesses stand in court when being questioned

**wit·ti·cis·m** /'wɪt¦sɪzəm/ *n* a WITTY remark

**wit·ty** /'wɪti/ *adj* **-tier, -tiest** having or showing a clever mind and amusing way of expressing thoughts: *a witty remark* **–wittily** *adv* **–wittiness** *n* [U]

**wives** /waɪvz/ *n pl. of* WIFE

**wiz·ard** /'wɪzəd‖-ərd/ *n* **1** (esp. in stories) a man who has magic powers –compare WITCH **2** a person with unusual abilities of a certain kind: *He's a wizard at playing the piano.*

**wiz·ened** /'wɪzənd/ *adj* (as if) dried up, with lines in the skin: *wizened apples|a wizened old lady*

**wk** *written abbrev. for:* week

**wob·ble** /'wɒbəl‖'wɑ-/ *v* **-bled, -bling** [I;T] to move unsteadily from one direction to another: *The table's wobbling.|You're making the table wobble/wobbling the table.* **–wobble** *n: a wobble in her voice*

**wob·bly** /'wɒbli‖'wɑ-/ *adj* **-blier, -bliest** tending to WOBBLE: *wobbly handwriting*

**woe** /wəu/ *n* [C;U] *esp. old use* (something causing) great sorrow: *a tale of woe* (=a story of misfortune)|*He told her all his woes.*

**woe·be·gone** /'wəubɪgɒn‖-gɔn, -gɑn/ *adj* very sad in appearance

**woe·ful** /'wəufəl/ *adj* **1** very sad: *woeful eyes* **2** which makes one sorry: *a woeful lack of understanding* **–woefully** *adv*

**woke** /wəuk/ *v past tense of* WAKE

**wok·en** /'wəukən/ *v past participle of* WAKE

**wolf¹** /wulf/ *n* **wolves** /wulvz/ **1** a wild animal of the dog family which hunts other animals in a group (PACK¹ (2)) **2** *derog* a man who always seeks women for sex only **–wolfish** *adj*

**wolf²** *v* [T *down*] to eat quickly, in large amounts: *He wolfed his meal.*

**wom·an** /'wumən/ *n* **women** /'wɪm¦n/ **1** a fully grown human female: *Is your doctor a man or a woman?* **2** women in general **3** [A] female: *women workers* –compare LADY, MAN; see GENTLEMAN (USAGE)

**wom·an·hood** /'wumənhud/ *n* [U] the condition or qualities of being a woman –see also MANHOOD

**wom·an·ish** /'wumənɪʃ/ *adj usu. derog* (of a man) like a woman in character, behaviour, appearance, etc.: *a womanish walk* –compare EFFEMINATE

**wom·an·ize** ‖also **-ise** *BrE* /'wumənaɪz/ *v* **-ized, -izing** [I] (of men) to habitually spend time with many women, esp. in order to have sexual relationships **–womanizer** *n*

**wom·an·kind** /'wumənkaɪnd/ *n* women considered together as one body –see also MANKIND

**wom·an·ly** /'wumənli/ *adj* having or showing the qualities thought suitable to a woman: *She showed a womanly concern for their health.* –compare MANLY **–womanliness** *n* [U]

**womb** /wuːm/ *n* the female sex organ of a MAMMAL where her young develop before they are born

**wom·en·folk** /'wɪm¦nfəuk/ *n* [P] *old use or humor infml* women

**won** /wʌn/ *v past tense and past participle of* WIN

**won·der¹** /'wʌndəʳ/ *v* **1** [I *about*] to express a wish to know: *I wonder if she knows we're here.|I wonder why they didn't arrive.|I wonder what really happened.* **2** [I;T +*that/at*] to be surprised and want to know (why): *I wonder at his rudeness.|I wonder (that) he can come here after what happened.*

USAGE Compare **wonder** (in the second meaning) and **admire**: You can **wonder** *at* (=be very much surprised by) both good and bad things, but you **admire** only good things (=look at them with pleasure and respect), without any feelings of surprise: *Arriving in New York, she* **wondered** *at the tall buildings and crowded streets.|She* **admired** *the fine shops and beautiful buildings.*

**wonder²** *n* **1** (something which causes) a feeling of strangeness, surprise, and admiration: *They were filled with wonder at the new waterfall.|The temple of Diana was one of the seven* **Wonders of the World** *in* ancient times. **2** [C] a wonderful act or producer of such acts: (*infml*) *She's a wonder, the way she arranges everything.* **3 It's a/no wonder (that)** It's (not) surprising: *It's a wonder you recognized him.* **4 work wonders** to bring unexpectedly good results: *This new cleaner works wonders.*

**wonder**[3] *adj* [A] which is unusually good of its kind: *wonder drugs*

**won·der·ful** /ˈwʌndəfəl‖-dər-/ *adj* unusually good: *wonderful news* –**wonderfully** *adv*

**won·ky** /ˈwɒŋki‖ˈwɑŋki/ *adj* **-kier, -kiest** *BrE infml* not steady: *That table's a bit wonky!*

**wont** /wəunt‖wont/ *n* [S] *fml* a habit or custom: *He spoke for too long, as is his wont.*

**won't** /wəunt/ *short for* will not: *I won't go!*

**woo** /wuː/ *v* **wooed, wooing** [T] **1** *old use* (of a man) to pay attention to (a woman one hopes to marry) –compare COURT[2] (3) **2** to make efforts to gain (the support of): *to woo the voters before an election*

**wood** /wud/ *n* **1** [U] the material of which trees are made, which is cut and dried in various forms for burning, making paper or furniture, etc.: *Put some more wood on the fire.*|*Most doors are made of wood.* **2** [C] a place where trees grow, smaller than a forest: *a walk in the wood(s)* **3 can't see the wood for the trees** missing the general meaning of something because of paying too much attention to its details

**wood·cut·ter** /ˈwudˌkʌtəʳ/ *n* (esp. in fairy stories) a man whose job is to cut down trees

**wood·ed** /ˈwudɪ̵d/ *adj* having woods; covered with growing trees: *wooded hills*

**wood·en** /ˈwudn/ *adj* **1** made of wood **2** stiff; unbending: *wooden movements* –**woodenly** *adv*

**wood·land** /ˈwudlənd, -lænd/ *n* [U] wooded country: *large areas of woodland*|*woodland birds*

**wood·peck·er** /ˈwudˌpekəʳ/ *n* a bird with a long beak, which can make holes in the wood of trees and pull out insects

**wood·wind** /ˈwudˌwɪnd/ *n* [U +*sing./pl. v*] (the players of) the set of (wooden) instruments in an ORCHESTRA which are played by blowing: *The woodwind is/are too loud.*

**wood·work** /ˈwudwɜːk‖-wɜrk/ *n* [U] **1** (the skill of making) wooden objects, esp. furniture; CARPENTRY **2** the parts of a house that are made of wood: *a mouse behind/in the woodwork*

**wood·worm** /ˈwudwɜːm‖-wɜrm/ *n* **-worm** *or* **-worms** [C;U] (damage done by) the small soft wormlike young (LARVA) of certain BEETLEs, which make holes in wood

**wood·y** /ˈwudi/ *adj* **-ier, -iest 1** of or with woods: *a woody valley* **2** of or like wood: *a woody plant*

**woof** /wuf/ *n,interj infml* (a word used for describing the sound (BARK) made by a dog)

**wool** /wul/ *n* [U] **1** the soft thick hair which sheep and some goats have **2** thick thread or cloth made from this: KNITting *wool*|*a wool suit* –compare WORSTED **3** soft material from plants, such as cotton before it is spun: *cotton wool* **4 pull the wool over someone's eyes** to trick someone or hide the facts from him/her

**wool·len** ‖also **woolen** *AmE* /ˈwulən/ *adj* made of wool: *a woollen coat*

**wool·lens** ‖also **woolens** *AmE* /ˈwulənz/ *n* [P] garments made of wool, esp. KNITted –see also WOOLLY[2]

**wool·ly**[1] /ˈwuli/ *adj* **-lier, -liest 1** of or like wool: *woolly socks* **2** (of thoughts) not clear in the mind: *His ideas are a bit woolly.*

**woolly**[2] *n* **-lies** [*usu. pl.*] *infml* a garment made of wool, esp. KNITted: *winter woollies*

**woolly-head·ed** /ˌ·· ˈ·· ◂/ *adj* tending not to think clearly or have sensible ideas

**woo·zy** /ˈwuːzi/ *adj* **-zier, -ziest** *infml* unsteady; DIZZY

**word**[1] /wɜːd‖wɜrd/ *n* **1** [C] (a written representation of) one or more sounds which can be spoken to represent an idea, object, action, etc.: *What is the French word for "hello"?*|*I know the tune but not the words.*|*Tell me what happened* **in your own words.** (=not repeating what somebody else said)|**Words fail me!** (=I'm too surprised/shocked to say anything)|*He told me what happened,* **word for word.** (=repeating everything that was said) **2** [S] the shortest (type of) statement: *Don't say a word to anybody.*|*I don't believe a word of it.*|*He never has a good word to say for me.* (=is always expressing disapproval of me) **3** [C] a short speech or conversation: *Can I have a few words/a word with you?*|*a word or two of advice* **4** [U +*that*] a message or news: *My friend* **sent word** *that he was well.* **5** [S +(*that*)] a promise: **I give you my word** *(of honour) I won't tell your secret.*|*He always* **keeps his word.**|*She said she wouldn't do it, and she was* **as good as her word.** (=she didn't do it) **6** [C *usu. sing.*] an order: *When I give the word, start writing.* **7 from the word go** from the beginning **8 have words (with)** *euph* to argue angrily (with) **9 (get) a word in edgeways** (*used in* NEGATIVEs[2], *questions, etc.*) (to make) a remark made in spite of others who are speaking all the time: *He talks so much that no one else can get a word in edgeways.* **10 in other words** expressing the same thing in different words; which is the same as saying **11 (not) in so many words** (not) expressed with that meaning but only suggested: *"Did she say she liked him?" "Not in so many words, (but . . .)"*

**word**[2] *v* [T] to express in words: *He worded the explanation well.*|*a carefully-worded letter*

**word·ing** /ˈwɜːdɪŋ‖ˈwɜr-/ *n* [S] the words chosen to express something: *the wording of the contract*

**word-per·fect** /ˌ· ˈ··/ *BrE*‖**letter-perfect** *AmE*– *adj* having or showing correctness in repeating every word: *Her speech was word-perfect.*

**word pro·ces·sor** /ˈwɜːd ˌprəusesəʳ‖ˈwɜrd ˌpro-/ *n* a machine like a TYPEWRITER, that contains a small computer and that has a SCREEN[1] (5). Writing appears on the screen and can be changed or corrected before it is printed on paper. –see also VDU; see picture on page 415

**word·y** /ˈwɜːdi‖ˈwɜrdi/ *adj* **-ier, -iest** using or containing too many words: *a wordy explanation* –compare VERBOSE

**wore** /wɔːʳ‖wor/ *v past tense of* WEAR

**work**[1] /wɜːk‖wɜrk/ *n* **1** [U] activity which uses effort, esp. with a special purpose, not for amusement: *Digging in the garden is hard work.*|*There are men* **at work** *mending the road.*|*The repairman* **set to work on** *the television.* (=began to repair it) **2** [U] what one is working on: *I'm taking some work home from* the office this evening.|*Bring your work out into the garden with us.* **3** [U] (the nature or place of) a job or business: *What work do you do?|She got home very late from work.|Are you allowed to smoke at work?|My husband is* **out of work**. (=has no job) **4** [U] what is produced by work, esp. of the hands: *This mat is my own work.* (=I made it) **5** [C *usu. pl.*] a work of art; object produced by painting, writing, etc.: *the works of Shakespeare* (=plays and poems) –see also WORKS **6 have one's work cut out** to have something difficult to do, esp. in the time allowed: *You'll have your work cut out to finish that job by tomorrow!* **7 make short work of** to finish quickly and easily

USAGE This is a general word that can be used of activities of the mind and of the body. Both **labour** and **toil** can sometimes be used instead, but both of these express the idea of tiring and unpleasant effort. –see JOB (USAGE)

**work²** *v* **1** [I;T] to (cause to) be active or use effort or power: *She's been working in the garden all afternoon.|I'm working on a new book.* (=writing one)|*She worked hard at her lessons.|This machine works by/on electricity.|I think the teacher works us too hard.* (=we have to work too hard)|*Press the button that works the machine.* **2** [I;T] to be employed: *My mother works in an office.|He worked his way through college.* (=did jobs because he didn't have a GRANT²) **3** [I] to be active in the proper way, without failing: *Does this light work?|I don't think your plan will work.* (=succeed) **4** [I;T] to (cause to) reach a state or position by small movements: *The screw worked loose and the door fell off the cupboard.|Work the brush into the corner.|He gradually worked his way to the front of the crowd.*|(fig.) *He worked himself into a temper.* **5** [T] to produce (an effect): *I think a long holiday would work wonders for your health.* **6 work to rule** to obey exactly the rules of one's work in such a way that one causes inconvenience to others, in order to give force to a claim for more money, shorter working hours, etc. –see also WORK-TO-RULE

USAGE Although almost everyone works, expressions like **worker**, **workman**, and *out of* **work** are used particularly of people who work with their hands. –see also WORKING CLASS

**work** sthg.↔**off** *v adv* [T] to remove, by work or activity: *to work off one's anger|to work off a debt*

**work out** *v adv* **1** [T] (**work** sthg.↔**out**) to calculate the answer to: *to work out a sum* **2** [I] to have an answer which can be calculated: *The sum doesn't work out.|The cost works out at £6 a night.* **3** [I;T (=**work** sthg. **out**)] to (cause to) have a good result: *Things will work themselves out.|I hope the new job works out for you.* **4** [I] *infml* to exercise: *to work out in the* GYMNASIUM –see also WORKOUT

**work up** *v adv* **1** [T] (**work** sbdy.↔**up**) to excite the feelings, esp. anger, tears, etc., of (esp. oneself): *The politician worked the crowd up.* –see also WORKED UP **2** [I;T (=**work** sthg.↔**up**) *to*] to develop (towards): *She's working up to what she wants to say.|I've worked up a thirst while playing tennis.*

**work·bench** /ˈwɜːkbentʃ‖ˈwɜrk-/ *n* (a table with) a hard surface for working on with tools: *a* CARPENTER *at his workbench*

**work·book** /ˈwɜːkbʊk‖ˈwɜrk-/ *n* a school book with questions and exercises. The answers are usually written in the book by the student. –see picture on page 105

**work·day** /ˈwɜːkdeɪ‖ˈwɜrk-/ also **working day**– *n* **1** a day which is not a holiday **2** the amount of time during which one works each day

**worked up** /ˌ· ˈ·◂/ *adj* [F] very excited; showing strong feelings, esp. when worried: *That child* **gets worked up** *about going to school.* –see WORK² **up** (1)

**work·er** /ˈwɜːkəʳ‖ˈwɜr-/ *n* **1** a person or animal which works **2** a hard worker: *She's a real worker; she gets twice as much done as anybody else.* **3** also **working man** /ˌ·· ˈ·/– a person who works with his hands rather than his mind; WORKING CLASS person: *a factory worker*

**work force** /ˈ· ·/ *n* [S] the people who work in industry generally, considered as a group: *the work force of this country|a work force of 250*

**work·ing** /ˈwɜːkɪŋ‖ˈwɜr-/ *adj* [A] **1** concerning or including work: *The visiting minister had a working breakfast with the President.* **2** who works with the hands: *a working man* –see also WORKMAN **3** (of time) spent in work: *the working day/week* **4** used in work, business, etc.: *a working tool|***in working order** (=in a state of working well)

**working class** /ˌ·· ˈ·◂/ *n,adj* [C *+sing./pl.v; often pl. with sing. meaning*] (of) the social class to which people belong who work with their hands: *a working-class home|"The working class is/The working classes are getting angry about unemployment", she said.* –compare MIDDLE CLASS, UPPER CLASS

USAGE **Working class** can be used in any of the following patterns: 1 Sing. with sing./pl. v: *The* **working class** *doesn't/don't support this political party.* 2 Pl. with sing. meaning: *The* **working classes** *are getting angry about unemployment.* 3 As an adj: *This is a* **working-class** *area.|Most of the people in this area are* **working-class**. **Lower class**, **middle class**, and **upper class** can all be used in the same ways.

**working knowl·edge** /ˌ·· ˈ··/ *n* [S] enough practical knowledge to do something: *She has a working knowledge of car engines and can do most repairs.*

**working par·ty** /ˈ·· ˌ··/ *n* a committee which examines a particular subject and reports what it finds

**work·ings** /ˈwɜːkɪŋz‖ˈwɜr-/ *n* [P] the way in which something works or acts: *I shall never understand the workings of an engine.*

**work·man** /ˈwɜːkmən‖ˈwɜrk-/ *n* **-men** /mən/ a man who works with his hands, esp. in a particular skill or trade: *The workmen fixed the water system.*

**work·man·like** /ˈwɜːkmənlaɪk‖ˈwɜrk-/ *adj* having or showing the qualities of a good workman: *workmanlike methods*

**work·man·ship** /ˈwɜːkmənʃɪp‖ˈwɜrk-/ *n* [U] (signs of) skill in making things: *good workmanship*

**work·out** /ˈwɜːkaʊt‖ˈwɜr-/ *n infml* a period of bodily exercise and training, esp. for a sport –see also WORK² **out** (4)

**works¹** /wɜːks‖wɜrks/ *n* [*the* P] the moving parts (of a machine)

**works²** *n* **works** an industrial place of work; factory: *a gas works|the works* CANTEEN

**work·shop** /ˈwɜːkʃɒp‖ˈwɜrkʃɑp/ *n* a room or place, as in a factory or business, where things are produced, repairs are done, etc.

**work-shy** /ˈ· ·/ *adj derog* not liking work and trying to avoid it: *He's not ill: he's just workshy!*

**work·top** /ˈwɜːktɒp‖ˈwɜrktɑp/ *n* a flat surface on top of a piece of kitchen furniture, used for preparing food, etc.

**work-to-rule** /ˌ· · ˈ·/ *n* a form of working which causes activity to become slower, because (sometimes unnecessary) attention is paid to every point in the rules –compare GO-SLOW, WORK[2] (6)

**world** /wɜːld‖wɜrld/ *n* **1** [*the* S] the body in space on which we live; the earth: *He's the richest man in the world.|the Second World War* (=between many countries of the world) **2** [C] a PLANET or star system, esp. one which may contain life: *a strange creature from another world* **3** [*the* S] a particular part of the earth or of life on earth: *the Third World* (=the poorer countries)|*the animal world* (=animals and their lives) **4** [*the* S] a particular area of human activity: *the world of football* **5** [*the* S] people in general; everyone: *The whole world knows about it.* **6** [*the* S] human life (and its affairs): *He's very young and inexperienced, and doesn't know about* **the ways of the world.**|*She has* **brought** *four children* **into the world.** (=given birth to four children) **7** [S *of*] a large number or amount: *The medicine did me a/the world of good.|The new fire makes a world of difference: I'm much warmer now.* **8 for all the world as if/like** exactly as if/like **9 (have) the best of both worlds** (to have) the advantages which each choice offers, without having to choose between them **10 in the world** (in a question expressing surprise): *What in the world* (=whatever) *are you doing?* **11 not for the world** certainly not: *I wouldn't hurt her for the world.* **12 out of this world** *infml* unusually good; wonderful **13 worlds apart** completely different: *Their ways of life are worlds apart.*

**world-class** /ˌ· ˈ·◂/ *adj* among the best in the world: *a world-class footballer*

**world·ly** /ˈwɜːldli‖ˈwɜr-/ *adj* **-lier, -liest 1** [A; *no comp.*] of the material world: *all my worldly goods* **2** concerned with the ways of society, esp. social advantage; not SPIRITUAL –**worldliness** *n* [U]

**worldly-wise** /ˌ·· ˈ·◂‖ˈ·· ·/ *adj* experienced in the ways of people

**world pow·er** /ˌ· ˈ··/ *n* an important nation whose trade, politics, etc., have an international effect

**world·wide** /ˌwɜːldˈwaɪd◂‖ˌwɜr-/ *adj,adv* in or over all the world: *worldwide sales*

**worm**[1] /wɜːm‖wɜrm/ *n* **1** a small thin tube-like creature with no backbone or limbs, esp. the one which lives in and moves through earth (**earthworm**): *The dog has worms.* (=which live inside the body) **2** a person who is thought worthless, cowardly, etc.

**worm**[2] *v* [T] **1** [*in, into*] to move by twisting or effort: *He wormed himself through the opening.*|(fig.) *He* **wormed his way** *into her heart.* **2** to remove living worms from the body of, esp. by chemical means

**worm** sthg. **out** *v adv* [T *of*] to obtain (information) by questioning, esp. over a period of time: *I wormed the secret out (of them).*

**worn** /wɔːn‖worn/ *v past participle of* WEAR[1]

**worn-out** /ˌ· ˈ·◂/ *adj* **1** completely finished by continued use: *worn-out shoes* –see also OUTWORN **2** [F] very tired: *She was worn-out after three sleepless nights.* –see also WEAR **out**

**wor·ried** /ˈwʌrid‖ˈwɜrid/ *adj* [*about*] anxious: *a worried look* –**worriedly** *adv*

**wor·ry**[1] /ˈwʌri‖ˈwɜri/ *v* **-ried, -rying 1** [I;T *about, over*] to be or make anxious: *It worries me that he's working so hard.|a very worrying state of affairs|Worrying about your health can make you ill.|Don't worry!* **2** [T] (esp. of a dog) to chase and bite (an animal): *The dog was found worrying sheep, and had to be shot.*

**worry**[2] *n* **-ries** [C;U] (a cause of) a feeling of anxiety: *Money is just one of our worries.* (=there are others)

**worse**[1] /wɜːs‖wɜrs/ *adj* **1** (COMPARATIVE[2] *of* BAD) lower in quality; more bad; less good: *worse weather than last week|I'm better at history than Jean, but worse at French.|He may be late. Worse still, he may not come at all.* **2** [F] (COMPARATIVE[2] *of* ILL) more ill: *At least, he's no worse.* –compare BETTER[1] **3 none the worse (for)** not harmed (by): *He's none the worse for his fall from the window.*

**worse**[2] *adv* (COMPARATIVE[2] *of* BADLY) **1** in a worse way: *You're behaving worse than an animal.* **2** to a worse degree; more: *It's hurting worse than before.* –compare BETTER[2]

**worse**[3] *n* [U] **1** something worse: *I thought that what happened was bad enough, but worse was to follow.* –compare BETTER[3] **2 a change for the worse** a bad change

**wors·en** /ˈwɜːsən‖ˈwɜr-/ *v* [I;T] to (cause to) become worse: *The rain has worsened our difficulties.* –compare BETTER[4]

**wor·ship**[1] /ˈwɜːʃɪp‖ˈwɜr-/ *n* [U] **1** (the act of showing) great respect, admiration, etc., esp. to God or a god: *They joined in worship together.* **2** a religious service: *They attended worship.*

**worship**[2] *v* **-pp-** *BrE*‖**-p-** *AmE* **1** [I;T *at*] to show great respect, admiration, etc.: (fig.)*He worships the very ground she walks on.* **2** [I] to attend a church service: *to worship regularly* –**worshipper** *n*

**Worship** *n* **your/his Worship** *BrE* (a title of respect used to/of certain official people such as a MAGISTRATE or a MAYOR)

**worst**[1] /wɜːst‖wɜrst/ *adj* (SUPERLATIVE[2] *of* BAD) [A] the lowest in quality; the most bad: *This is the worst accident for years.|the worst driver I know* –compare BEST

**worst**[2] *adv* (SUPERLATIVE[2] *of* BADLY) in the worst way; most badly: *Who suffered worst?|the worst-dressed man* –compare BEST

**worst**[3] *n* [*the* S] **1** the most bad thing or part; the greatest degree of badness: *I've seen bad work, but this is the worst.|The worst of it is that I could have prevented the accident.|Tell me the worst!* (=the worst part of the news) –compare BEST **2 at (the) worst** if the worst happens; if one thinks of it in the worst way: *He's a fool at (the) best, and at (the) worst he's a criminal.* **3 do one's worst** to do as much harm as one can (esp. when not much harm can be done): *Let the enemy do his worst; we are ready for him.* **4 get the worst of (it)** to be defeated in: *John got the worst of the argument.* **5 if the worst comes to the**

**worst** if the worst difficulties happen; if there is no better way: *If the worst comes to the worst and the car won't start, we can always go by bus.*

**wor·sted** /ˈwʊstɪ̈d/ *n* [U] wool cloth: *a worsted suit* –compare WOOL (2)

**worth**[1] /wɜːθ‖wɜrθ/ *prep* **1** of the value of: *This house is worth a lot of money.* **2** having possessions amounting to: *She's worth £1,000,000.* **3** good enough for; deserving: *a film worth seeing.|Don't lock the door; it isn't worth the trouble/worth it.|It's worth making an effort to look well-dressed.*

**worth**[2] *n* [U] value: *property of little or no worth*

**worth·less** /ˈwɜːθlɪ̈s‖ˈwɜrθ-/ *adj* **1** of no value: *a worthless action* **2** (of a person) of bad character: *a worthless member of society*

USAGE Things of great value are **valuable**, and very **valuable** things are **priceless**: *a* **priceless** *16th century Chinese plate.* **Invaluable** is similar in meaning, but is used of qualities rather than things: *Your help has been* **invaluable**: *we couldn't have done the job without you.* Things of little or no value are **valueless** or **worthless**.

**worth·while** /ˌwɜːθˈwaɪl◂‖ˌwɜr-/ *adj* worth doing; worth the trouble taken: *We had a long wait, but it was worthwhile because we got the tickets.*

**wor·thy** /ˈwɜːði‖ˈwɜrði/ *adj* **-thier, -thiest 1** [A;F +*to-v/of*] deserving: *worthy of help/dislike|a worthy winner|not worthy to be chosen* **2** *esp. old use* to be admired, respected, etc.: *a worthy man* **3 -worthy: a** fit or safe to travel in or on: *This boat isn't seaworthy: it may sink.* **b** deserving: *a praiseworthy action|a newsworthy event* **–worthily** *adv* **–worthiness** *n* [U]

**would** /wʊd/ *v negative short form* **wouldn't** [I +~~to~~-v] **1 a** (describing WILL in the past): *They said it would be fine.* (=They said: "It will be fine") **b** (used instead of WILL with a past tense verb): *They couldn't find anyone who would* (=who was willing to) *take the job.|She would be surprised if he came.* **2 a** (*shows what always happened*) used to: *We used to work in the same office. We would often have coffee together.* –see Study Notes on page 386; see USE[3] (USAGE) **b** (shows that one is annoyed at something usual or typical): *That's exactly like him: he would lose the key!* **3 would you** (used when politely asking someone to do something): *Would you please lend me your pencil?* –see LIKE[3] (USAGE)

**wound**[1] /wuːnd/ *n* a damaged place in the body, usu. a hole or tear through the skin, esp. done on purpose by a weapon: *only a flesh wound* (=not deep)|(fig.) *a wound to her pride*

**wound**[2] /wuːnd/ *v* [T] to cause a wound to: *The shot wounded his arm.|She wounded him in the arm.*

USAGE People get **wounded** in war or fighting, and **injured** in accidents. Both words are more serious than **hurt**: *He was seriously* **wounded** *by an enemy bullet.|They were badly* **injured** *when their car hit a tree.|I* **hurt** *my foot when I dropped the hammer on it.*

**wound**[3] /waʊnd/ *v past tense and participle of* WIND[3]

**wove** /wəʊv/ *v past tense of* WEAVE

**wov·en** /ˈwəʊvən/ *v past participle of* WEAVE

**wow** /waʊ/ *interj infml* (an expression of surprise and admiration): *Wow! Look at her new car!*

**W.P.C.** *abbrev. for: BrE* Woman Police Constable; a female member of the police force having the lowest rank –see also P.C.

**wran·gle** /ˈræŋgəl/ *v,n* **-gled, -gling** [I *with*] (to have) an angry or noisy argument

**wrap**[1] /ræp/ *v* [T] **-pp- 1** [*up, in*] to cover (in a material folded around): *I wrapped the book in brown paper before I posted it.|They wrapped my new shoes in the shop.* **2** [(*a*)*round*] to fold (a material) over: *I wrapped the* RUG (2) *around the sick man's legs to keep him warm.*

**wrap up** *v adv* [I] **1** to wear warm clothes: *In cold weather you should wrap up well.* **2 wrapped up in** giving complete love or attention to: *He's so wrapped up in her, he can't see her faults.*

**wrap**[2] *n becoming rare* a garment or piece of material which is used as a covering, esp. a SCARF, SHAWL, or RUG (2)

**wrap·per** /ˈræpəʳ/ *n* a piece of paper which forms a loose cover on a book

**wrap·ping** /ˈræpɪŋ/ *n* [C;U] material used for folding round and covering something: *wrapping paper around a present*

**wrath** /rɒθ‖ræθ/ *n* [U] *lit* great anger: *the wrath of God* **–wrathful** *adj* **–wrathfully** *adv*

**wreak** /riːk/ *v* [T *on*] *esp. lit* to do (violence) or express (strong feelings) in violence: *to wreak* VENGEANCE *(on someone)*

**wreath** /riːθ/ *n* **1** an arrangement of flowers or leaves, esp. in a circle, esp. one given at a funeral –compare GARLAND **2** a curl of smoke, mist, gas, etc.

**wreathe** /riːð/ *v* **wreathed, wreathing** [T *in*] *lit* to circle round and cover completely: *Mist wreathed the hilltops.*|(fig.) *She/Her face was wreathed in smiles.*

**wreck**[1] /rek/ *n* **1** [C] a ship lost at sea or (partly) destroyed on rocks: *the wreck of the Mary Dere* –see also SHIPWRECK **2** [C;U] (a person or thing in) the state of being ruined or destroyed: *He's a complete wreck after his illness.*

**wreck**[2] *v* [T] to destroy: *The ship was wrecked on the rocks.|The weather wrecked our plans.*

**wreck·age** /ˈrekɪdʒ/ *n* [U *of*] the broken parts of a destroyed thing: *the wreckage of old ships*

**wren** /ren/ *n* a very small bird which sings

**wrench**[1] /rentʃ/ *v* [T] **1** to pull hard with a twisting or turning movement: *He closed the door so hard that he wrenched the handle off.* **2** to twist and damage (a joint of the body): *to wrench one's ankle*

**wrench**[2] *n* **1** an act of twisting and pulling **2** painful grief at a separation: *the wrench of leaving one's family* **3 a** *AmE* for SPANNER **b** *BrE* a SPANNER with jaws whose distance apart may be changed

**wrest** /rest/ *v* [T *from, out of*] *fml* to pull (away) violently: *She wrested it from his hands.*|(fig.) *to wrest the truth out of someone*

**wres·tle** /ˈresəl/ *v* **-tled, -tling 1** [I *with*] to fight by holding and throwing the body: *She wrestled with her attacker.*|(fig.) *wrestling with a difficult examination paper* **2** [I;T] to fight (someone) like this as a sport (**wrestling**) –compare BOX[3] **–wrestler** *n*

**wretch** /retʃ/ *n* **1** a poor or unhappy person: *unlucky wretches with no homes* **2** a person or animal disliked and thought bad and useless **–wretched** /-ɪ̈d/ *adj: feeling wretched after an illness|You wretched child!* **–wretchedly** *adv* **–wretchedness** *n* [U]

**wrig·gle**[1] /ˈrɪgəl/ *v* **-gled, -gling** [I;T] to twist (a part of the body) from side to side: *He wriggled uncomfortably on the hard chair.*|(fig.) *You're to blame, so don't try to* **wriggle out of** *it.* (=escape from it)

**wriggle²** *n* a wriggling (WRIGGLE) movement

**wring¹** /rɪŋ/ *v* **wrung** /rʌŋ/, **wringing** [T] **1 a** to twist (esp. the neck, causing death) **b** to press hard on; SQUEEZE: *He wrung his hands in sorrow.* **2** [*out, from*] **a** to twist and/or press (wet clothes) to remove water: *Wring those wet things out.* **b** to press (water) from clothes: *Wring the water out (of the cloth).*|(fig.) *They wrung the truth out of me in the end.* **3 wringing wet** very wet –sounds like **ring**

**wring²** *n* an act of WRINGing

**wring·er** /ˈrɪŋəʳ/ *n* a machine with rollers between which water is pressed from clothes, sheets, etc.

**wrin·kle¹** /ˈrɪŋkəl/ *n* a line in something which is folded or crushed, esp. on the skin when a person is old –**wrinkly** *adj* **-klier, -kliest**

**wrinkle²** *v* **-kled, -kling** [I;T *up*] to (cause to) form into lines, folds, etc.: *He wrinkled (up) his nose at the bad smell.*|*the wrinkled face of the old man*

**wrist** /rɪst/ *n* the joint between the hand and the lower part of the arm –see picture on page 299

**wrist·watch** /ˈrɪstwɒtʃ‖-wɑtʃ, -wɔtʃ/ *n* a watch made to be fastened on the wrist with a band (STRAP)

**writ** /rɪt/ *n* an official paper given in law to tell someone (not) to do a particular thing

**write** /raɪt/ *v* **wrote** /rəʊt/, **written** /ˈrɪtn/, **writing 1** [I;T] to make (marks that represent letters or words) by using esp. a pen or pencil on paper: *The children are learning to write.*|*Write the address on the envelope.* **2** [T] to express and record in this way: *to write a report/a book* **3** [I;T] to be a writer of (books, plays, etc.): *She writes for the stage.* **4** [I;T +*to-v/v-ing/that/to*] to produce and send (a letter): *He writes me a letter every day, but I don't* **write back** (=reply) *very often.*|*I wish he would write more often.*

**write** sthg.↔**down** *v adv* [T] to record in writing (esp. what has been said): *Write your idea down while it's clear in your mind.*

**write in** *v adv* [I *for*] to send a letter to a firm, asking for something or giving an opinion: *We wrote in for a free book, but the firm never replied.*

**write off** *v adv* **1** [T *as*] (**write** sbdy./sthg.↔**off**) to regard as being lost, having failed, etc.: *We'll just have to write our plans off if we can't find the money for them.*|*The newspapers wrote him off as a failure.* –see also WRITE-OFF **2** [I *for*] to write to a firm, esp. to buy something: *She wrote off for the book, because the shop didn't have it.*

**write** sthg.↔**out** *v adv* [T] **1** to write in full: *to write out a report* **2** to write (something official): *to write out a cheque/receipt*

**write** sthg.↔**up** *v adv* [T] to write (again) in a complete and useful form: *to write up one's notes* –see also WRITE-UP

**write-off** /ˈ· ·/ *n* something which is completely ruined: *The car was a write-off after the accident.* –see also WRITE **off** (1)

**writ·er** /ˈraɪtəʳ/ *n* a person who writes, esp. as a job

**write-up** /ˈ· ·/ *n infml* a written report, esp. one giving a judgment, as of goods or a play: *a good write-up in the local newspaper* –see also WRITE **up**

**writhe** /raɪð/ *v* **writhed, writhing** [I] to twist the body, as when in great pain: *writhing with/in pain*

**writ·ing** /ˈraɪtɪŋ/ *n* **1** [U] the activity of writing, esp. books: *Writing is a difficult way of earning a living.* **2** [U] handwriting: *I can't read the doctor's writing.* **3** [C;U] written work or form: *Put that down in writing.*|*Darwin's scientific writings*

**writing pa·per** /ˈ·· ˌ··/ also **notepaper**– *n* [U] smooth, good quality paper for writing letters on

**writ·ten** /ˈrɪtn/ *v past participle of* WRITE

**wrong¹** /rɒŋ‖rɔŋ/ *adj* **1** not correct: *the wrong answer*|*The clock's wrong; it's later than the time it shows.*|*This is the wrong time* (=not a suitable time) *to ask for a pay rise.* **2** [F] evil; against moral standards: *Telling lies is wrong/It's wrong to tell lies.* –opposite **right** –**wrongly** *adv*

**wrong²** *adv* **1** wrongly: *You've spelt the word wrong.* –opposite **right 2 get it wrong** to misunderstand **3 go wrong: a** to make a mistake: *The sum isn't right but I can't see where I went wrong.* **b** to end badly: *After five years, their marriage suddenly went wrong.* **c** to stop working properly: *The car's gone wrong.*|*Something's* **gone wrong with** *the car.*

**wrong³** *n* **1** [U] what is not morally right or correct: *to know right from wrong* –opposite **right 2** [C] *fml* any seriously bad or unjust action: *He did you a terrible wrong.* **3 in the wrong** mistaken or deserving blame: *Which of the two drivers was in the wrong?*

**wrong⁴** *v* [T] to be unfair to or cause difficulty, pain, etc., to: *I wronged him by saying he had lied.*

**wrong·do·ing** /ˈrɒŋˌduːɪŋ‖ˌrɔŋˈduːɪŋ/ *n* [U] (an example of) bad, evil, or illegal behaviour –**wrongdoer** *n*

**wrong·ful** /ˈrɒŋfəl‖ˈrɔŋ-/ *adj* unjust; unlawful: *wrongful imprisonment* –**wrongfully** *adv*

**wrote** /rəʊt/ *v past tense of* WRITE

**wrought** /rɔːt/ *adj old use & lit* made or done: *carefully wrought works of literature*|*wrought by hand*

**wrought i·ron** /ˌ· ˈ·· ◂/ *n* [U] iron shaped into a useful form or pleasing pattern: *a wrought-iron gate*

**wrung** /rʌŋ/ *v past tense and participle of* WRING

**wry** /raɪ/ *adj* **wrier, wriest** showing dislike, lack of pleasure, etc.: *a wry face* (=expression)/*smile* –**wryly** *adv*

# X, x

**X, x** /eks/ **X's, x's** *or* **Xs, xs** **1** the 24th letter of the English alphabet **2** the ROMAN NUMERAL (number) for 10

**x** *n* (in MATHEMATICS) a quantity that is unknown until a calculation has been made: *If 3x=6, x=2.*

**xen·o·pho·bi·a** /ˌzenəˈfəʊbɪə/ *n* [U] unreasonable fear and dislike of foreigners or strangers **–xenophobic** *adj*

**xe·rox** /ˈzɪərɒks, ˈze-‖ˈzɪərɑks, ˈziː-/ *v,n* [I;T] *tdmk* (*often cap.*) (to make) a photographic copy of (something printed or written) on a special electric copying machine; PHOTOCOPY

**X·mas** /ˈkrɪsməs, ˈeksməs/ *n infml* Christmas

**x-ray** /ˈeks reɪ/ *v* [T] (*often cap.*) to photograph, examine, or treat by means of X-RAYS: *They x-rayed her leg to find out if the bone was broken.*

**X-ray** *n* **1** [*usu. pl.*] a powerful unseen beam of light which can pass through substances that are not transparent, and which is used esp. for photographing medical conditions inside the body **2** a photograph taken using this

**xy·lo·phone** /ˈzaɪləfəʊn/ *n* a musical instrument made up of a set of flat wooden bars which produce musical notes when struck with small wooden hammers

# Y, y

**SPELLING NOTE**
Words with the sound /j/ may be spelt **u-**, like **use**, or **eu-**, like **Europe.**

**Y, y** /waɪ/ **Y's, y's** *or* **Ys, ys** the 25th letter of the English alphabet

**yacht** /jɒt‖jɑt/ *n* **1** a sailing boat, esp. one used for pleasure –compare DINGHY **2** a large, often motor-driven boat used for pleasure

**yacht·ing** /ˈjɒtɪŋ‖ˈjɑtɪŋ/ *n* [U] (the act of) sailing, travelling, or racing in a YACHT: *She went yachting.*

**yak** /jæk/ *n* a long-haired ox of central Asia

**yam** /jæm/ *n* a tropical climbing plant whose root is eaten as a vegetable

**yank** /jæŋk/ *v* [I;T] *infml* to pull suddenly and sharply: *He yanked (on) the rope.* **–yank** *n*

**Yank** also **Yankee**– *n infml* a citizen of the United States of America

**yap** /jæp/ *v* **-pp-** [I] (esp. of dogs) to make short sharp excited noises (sharp BARKS) **–yap** *n*

**yard¹** /jɑːd‖jɑrd/ *n* a measure of length that is a little less than a METRE; three feet; 36 inches

**yard²** *n* **1** an enclosed or partly enclosed area next to a building or group of buildings **2** *AmE* for BACKYARD (2) **3** an enclosed area used for a particular business: *shipyard|coalyard*

**yard·stick** /ˈjɑːdˌstɪk‖ˈjɑrd-/ *n* a standard of measurement or comparison: *Is money the only yardstick of success?*

**yarn** /jɑːn‖jɑrn/ *n* **1** [U] thread, e.g. of wool or cotton **2** [C] *infml* a long and sometimes untrue story: *He would often* **spin (us) a yarn** *about his adventures.*

**yawn** /jɔːn/ *v* [I] **1** to open the mouth wide and breathe in deeply, as when tired or uninterested **2** to be or become wide open: *a yawning hole* **–yawn** *n: I gave a loud yawn, but he just kept on talking.*

**yd** *written abbrev. said as:* YARD(*s*)¹

**ye** /jiː/ *pron old use* you

**yeah** /jeə/ *adv infml* yes

**year** /jɪəʳ, jɜːʳ‖jɪər/ *n* **1** also **calendar year**– a period of 365 or 366 days divided into 12 months beginning on January 1st and ending on December 31st –see also LEAP YEAR **2** a period of 365 days measured from any point: *I arrived here two years ago today.* **3** a period of (about) a year in the life of an organization: *We take our examinations at the end of the school year.* **4 all the year round** during the whole year

**year·ling** /ˈjɪəlɪŋ, ˈjɜː-‖ˈjɪər-/ *n* an animal, esp. a young horse, between one and two years old

**year·ly** /ˈjɪəli, ˈjɜː-‖ˈjɪərli/ *adj,adv* [A] (happening, appearing, etc.) every year or once a year

**yearn** /jɜːn‖jɜrn/ *v* [I +*to-v*/*for*] *esp. lit* to have a strong, loving, or sad desire: *They yearned to return home.|He yearned for her presence/for her to come home.* **–yearning** *n* [C;U]

**yeast** /jiːst/ *n* [U] a form of very small plant life that is used in making bread, and for producing alcohol in beer and wine **–yeasty** *adj: a yeasty taste*

**yell** /jel/ *v* [I;T *at, out*] to say, shout, or cry loudly: *He yelled (out) orders.|Don't yell at me!* **–yell** *n*

**yel·low** /ˈjeləʊ/ *adj,n* [U] (of) a colour like that of butter, gold, or the middle part (YOLK) of an egg **–yellow** *v* [I;T]: *That paper has yellowed with age.*

**yelp** /jelp/ *v,n* [I] (to make) a short sharp high cry, as of pain or excitement: *The dog yelped/gave a yelp when I hit it.*

**yen¹** /jen/ *n* **yen** the standard amount (UNIT) of money in Japan

**yen²** *n* [S +*to-v*/*for*] a strong desire: *a yen for travel*

**yes** /jes/ *adv* (used as an answer expressing agreement or willingness): *"Are you ready?" "Yes, I* *am.*"|"*Close the door.*" "*Yes, sir.*" –opposite **no**

**yes-man** /ˈjes mæn/ *n derog* a person who always agrees with his/her employer, leader, etc.

**yes·ter·day** /ˈjestədi, -deɪ‖-ər-/ *adv,n* **1** (on) the day before today: *I saw her at yesterday's meeting.*|*She came to tea yesterday/yesterday afternoon.* –compare TOMORROW **2** (of) a short time ago: *the fashions of yesterday*

**yet**[1] /jet/ *adv* **1** (*used only in questions and* NEGATIVES[2]) by a particular time; even sooner than expected; already: *Has John arrived yet?*|*She hasn't answered yet.*|*John hasn't done much work yet, but Anne has already finished.*|*He hasn't telephoned as yet.* (=up till now) **2** in the future; in spite of the way things seem now: *We may win yet.*|*The plan may even yet succeed.* **3** even; still: *yet another reason*|*a yet worse mistake*

**yet**[2] *conj* even so; but: *strange yet true*|*She's a funny girl, yet you can't help liking her.* –see Study Notes on page 128

**yew** /juː/ *n* [C;U] (the wood of) a tree with small dark green leaves and small red berries

**yield** /jiːld/ *v* **1** [I;T] to give; produce: *His business yields big profits.* **2** [I;T *to*] to give up control (of); SURRENDER: *We were forced to yield (our position to the enemy).* **3** [I] to bend, break, etc., because of a strong force: (fig.)*The government will yield under pressure from the army.*

**yip·pee** /jɪˈpiː‖ˈjɪpi/ *interj infml* (a cry of delight, happiness, success, etc.)

**yo·del** /ˈjəudl/ *v* **-ll-** *BrE*‖**-l-** *AmE* [I;T] to sing (a song) with many rapid changes between the natural voice and a very high voice –**yodel** *n*

**yo·ga** /ˈjəugə/ *n* [U] a Hindu system of exercises to free the self from the body, will, and mind

**yog·hurt, yogurt, yoghourt** /ˈjɒgət‖ˈjəugərt/ *n* [U] milk that has turned thick and slightly acid through the action of certain bacteria and is eaten, not drunk

**yo·gi** /ˈjəugi/ *n* a person who teaches YOGA

**yoke**[1] /jəuk/ *n* **1** a wooden bar used for joining together two animals, esp. oxen, in order to pull heavy farm vehicles, etc. **2** a frame fitted across a person's shoulders for carrying two equal loads –sounds like **yolk**

**yoke**[2] *v* **yoked, yoking** [T *together*] to join (as if) with a YOKE: *Yoke the oxen together.* –sounds like **yolk**

**yo·kel** /ˈjəukəl/ *n humor or derog* a simple or foolish country person

**yolk** /jəuk‖jəuk, jelk/ *n* [C;U] the yellow central part of an egg –compare WHITE[2] (4)

**yon·der** /ˈjɒndəʳ‖ˈjɑn-/ also **yon**– *adj,adv* [A; after *n*] *lit or old use* over there: *He has walked to yonder hill.*

**you** /jə, jʊ; *strong* juː/ *pron (used as subject or object)* **1** the person or people being spoken to: *You are my only friend.*|*You must all listen carefully.*|*You fool!* **2** a person; anyone: *You can't trust him.* (=it's impossible to trust him) –compare ONE[2] (2)

**you'd** /jəd, jʊd; *strong* juːd/ *short for* **1** you had **2** you would

**you'll** /jəl, jʊl; *strong* juːl/ *short for* **1** you will **2** you shall

**young**[1] /jʌŋ/ *adj* **younger** /-gəʳ/, **youngest** /-gəst/ **1** in an early stage of life or development; recently born or begun: *a young person/country* **2** of, for, concerning, or having the qualities of a young person: *a young manner* –compare OLD –**youngish** /-ɪʃ/ *adj*

**young**[2] *n* [P] **1** [*the*] young people considered as a group **2** young animals: *The lion fought to protect her young.*

**young·ster** /ˈjʌŋstəʳ/ *n* a young person, esp. a boy

**your** /jəʳ; *strong* jɔːʳ‖jər; *strong* jʊər, jor/ *determiner* (POSSESSIVE[1] (2) *form of* YOU) of the person or people being spoken to: *Your hands are dirty.*|*You must all come and bring your husbands.*

**you're** /jəʳ; *strong* jɔːʳ‖jər; *strong* jʊər, jor/ *short for:* you are

**yours** /jɔːz‖jʊərz, jorz/ *pron* **1** (POSSESSIVE[1] (2) *form of* YOU) of the person or people being spoken to: *This is our room, and yours* (=your room) *is down the passage.* **2** (*usu. cap.*) (written at the end of a letter): **Yours/Yours faithfully/Yours sincerely**, *John Brown*

**your·self** /jəˈself‖jər-/ *pron* **-selves** /ˈselvz/ **1** (used as the object of a verb, or after a preposition, when the person being spoken to does the action and is the object of the action): *You'll hurt yourself.*|*Buy yourself some shoes.* (=for yourself) **2** (used to make YOU stronger): *You and Mary will have to carry it (by) yourselves.*

**youth** /juːθ/ *n* **youths** /juːðz‖juːðz, juːθs/ **1** [U] the period of being young; early life **2** [C] *often derog* a young person, esp. a young male: *A group of youths caused the trouble.* –see CHILD (USAGE) **3** [*the* U +*sing./pl. v of*] young men and women considered as a group: *the youth of the country*

**youth·ful** /ˈjuːθfəl/ *adj* **1** of or having the qualities of youth: *youthful* ENTHUSIASM **2** young –**youthfully** *adv* –**youthfulness** *n* [U]

**you've** /jev; *strong* juːv/ *short for* you have

**yule** /juːl/ *n rare* (*sometimes cap.*) Christmas

**yule·tide** /ˈjuːltaɪd/ *n esp. lit or pomp* (*sometimes cap.*) Christmas: *Yuletide greetings*

# Z, z

**Z, z** /zed‖ziː/ **Z's, z's** *or* **Zs, zs** the 26th and last letter of the English alphabet

**za·ny** /ˈzeɪni/ *adj* **-nier, -niest** foolish in an amusing way: *She made us all laugh with her zany tricks.*

**zeal** /ziːl/ *n* [U] eagerness; keenness: *She shows great zeal for knowledge.*

**zeal·ous** /ˈzeləs/ *adj* [+*to-v*/*for, in*] *more fml than* **keen**– eager; keen: *zealous for fame/in doing his duty/to succeed* –**zealously** *adv* –**zealousness** *n* [U]

**ze·bra** /ˈziːbrə, ˈze-‖ˈziːbrə/ *n* **-bras** *or* **-bra** a horse-like African wild animal with broad dark brown and white lines all over the body

**zebra cross·ing** /ˌ·· ˈ··/ *n* (in Britain) a place on a busy street, painted with black and white lines to show that people have the right to walk across there

**zen·ith** /ˈzenǀθ‖ˈziː-/ *n* [*usu. sing*] the highest point, e.g. of hope or fortune: *Rome's power reached its zenith under the emperor Trajan.*

**zep·pe·lin** /ˈzepəlɪn/ *n* a large AIRSHIP used by the Germans in World War I

**ze·ro** /ˈzɪərəʊ‖ˈziːrəʊ/ *n* **-ros** *or* **-roes 1** the name of the sign 0 and of the number it stands for **2** the point between + and − on a scale; on the CENTIGRADE scale, the temperature at which water freezes: *It was five below zero last night.*

USAGE In saying a number, **zero** is generally used for 0 in scientific matters. In daily life, American speakers may use it in speech where a British speaker would say NOUGHT, O, or NIL.

**zest** /zest/ *n* [S;U] (a feeling of) eager excitement: *She entered into the work with zest/with a zest.*

**zig·zag**[1] /ˈzɪgzæg/ *n* a line shaped like a row of z's: *to go in a zigzag|a zigzag path*

**zigzag**[2] *v* **-gg-** [I] to go in a ZIGZAG

**zinc** /zɪŋk/ [U] a bluish-white metal that is a simple substance (ELEMENT[1]) used in the production of other metals

**Zi·on·is·m** /ˈzaɪənɪzəm/ *n* a national movement of Jewish people to establish and strengthen an independent state of Israel **–Zionist** *n*

**zip**[1] /zɪp/ *v* **-pp- 1** [T] *BrE* to open or close with a ZIP[2]: *He zipped the bag open/shut.* **2** [I] to make the sound of something moving quickly through the air: *The bullet zipped past my head.*

**zip** sbdy./sthg.↔**up** *v adv* [T] *BrE* to fasten (a person into something) with a ZIP[2]: *Will you zip me up/zip up my dress?* -opposite **unzip**

**zip**[2] also **zip fastener** /ˌ· ˈ···/ *BrE*‖**zipper** /ˈzɪpəʳ/ *AmE– n* a fastener made of two sets of metal or plastic teeth and a sliding piece that draws them together, used esp. on clothes

**zip code** /ˈ· ·/ *n AmE* for POSTCODE

**zo·di·ac** /ˈzəʊdiæk/ *n* **1** [*the* S] an imaginary belt through space along which the sun, the moon, and the nearest heavenly bodies (PLANETS) appear to travel and which is divided into 12 equal parts (SIGNS) **2** [C] a circular representation of this with pictures and names for each part (SIGN), Aquarius, Pisces, Aries, Taurus, Gemini, Cancer, Leo, Virgo, Libra, Scorpio, Sagittarius and Capricorn, esp. as used by people who believe in the influence of the stars on one's character and fate

**zone** /zəʊn/ *n* a division or area marked off from others by particular qualities: *a war/danger zone|a* US *postal zone*

**zoo** /zuː/ also **zoological gardens** [P] *fml– n* **zoos** a park where many kinds of living animals are kept for show

**zo·ol·o·gy** /zəʊˈɒlədʒi, zʊˈɒ-‖-ˈɑl-/ *n* [U] the scientific study of animals, and of where and how they live **–zoological** /-əˈlɒdʒɪkəl‖-ˈla-/ *adj* **–zoologist** *n*

**zoom**[1] /zuːm/ *v* [I] **1** (of an aircraft) to go quickly upwards **2** *infml* (of a driver or vehicle) to go quickly: *Jack zoomed past in his car.* **3** [*in, out*] (of a cinema camera) to move quickly between a distant and a close-up view: *The camera zoomed in on the child.*

**zoom**[2] *n* [S] (the deep low sound of) the upward flight of an aircraft

# Answer Key

**Exercise 1**
arm – bend – car – date – end – fight

**Exercise 2**
under – visit – wind – Xmas – yellow – zoo

**Exercise 3**
ice – iceberg – ice cream – icicle
absent – absently – absent-minded – absolute
allowable – alloy – all right – all-round
power – powerless – power point – power station

**Exercise 4**
act – act out – act up – actual – add – add up – addition

**Exercise 5**
judgment – generalize – enrol

**Exercise 6**
*BrE:* theatre – rumour
*AmE:* theater – rumor

**Exercise 7**
With /iː/ as in team: field – key – people – scene – sheep – team
With /e/ as in bed: bed – bread – bury – friend – said
With /ɒ/ as in pot: cough – pot – watch
With /uː/ as in do: blue – boot – do – group – move – shoe

**Exercise 8**
abil ity – ad van tage – after noon – af terwards

**Exercise 9**
The number of the students at the school will increase next year.
There will be an increase in the number of students next year.
This card will permit you to enter the building.
You need a permit to enter the building.

**Exercise 10**
2. shorter
3. close together
4. a door
5. hens and ducks
6. a bachelor
7. pain or fear
8. children or an old car
9. a newly born child
10. houses or rooms

**Exercise 11**
1. able (2) 2. account (7) 3. reason (3) 4. moon (4)

**Exercise 12**
Words that you could use in a school essay: begin – look for – succinct – television – wrong

**Exercise 13**
There was an election after the President was assassinated/killed.
The boy was killed in a car accident.

**Exercise 14**
Please bring some wine when you come to the party.
Next week my father is going to take my young sister to the cinema.

**Exercise 15**
**a** fit
**b** sale
**c** try

**Exercise 16**
agree – disagree; adaptable – unadaptable; allow – disallow; adequate – inadequate; relevant – irrelevant; inflate – deflate; logical – illogical; mature – immature

**Exercise 17**
The market was very busy and there was a lot of activity.
My brother wanted to buy a car so he asked for my advice.

**Exercise 18**
That huge building is over 200 feet high.
My little brother is afraid of dogs.
He burned his hand because he didn't know that the pan was hot.

**Exercise 19**
attack (attacks) – apple (apples) – adventure (adventures)

**Exercise 20**
donkeys – tomatoes – oxen – mice – cars – fish *or* fishes

**Exercise 21**
These sentences are complete: *The storm abated. The train arrived.*
The others must have an object. There are many possible ways of completing the sentences; and these are only some suggestions: *He abandoned the search. They amazed the audience.*

**Exercise 22**
awake (awoke) – choose (chosen) – drink (drank) – ride (rode)

**Exercise 23**
abscond from – abstain from – adapt to – apply for

**Exercise 24**
playing – to go – smoking – to see

**Exercise 25**
look after somebody *or* something – push somebody around – reckon on something – call on somebody – throw something around

## Answers to picture questions

**Airport**
a check-in b boarding c Departure d Duty-Free e (boarding) Gate

**Kitchen**
a washing-up b slices c sandwich d teapot

**Office**
a office equipment b photocopier c telex d post

**Train**
a ticket/booking office b ticket inspector c buffet car d on time

**Restaurant**
a menu b order c bill d tip

# Word building

## Word beginnings

**a-**[1] /ə/ (*makes adjectives and adverbs*) **asleep** sleeping | **alive** living

**a-**[2] /eɪ, æ, ə/ not: **atypical** not typical

**aero-** /ˈeərəʊ/ relating to air: **aerodynamics** the study of forces on a body moving through air

**Afro-** /ˈæfrəʊ/ relating to Africa: **Afro-Asian** relating to both Africa and Asia

**ambi-** /ˈæmbɪ, æmˈbɪ/ both; double: **ambiguous** having more than one possible meaning; unclear | **ambidextrous** able to use both hands equally well

**Anglo-** /ˈæŋgləʊ/ relating to England: **Anglo-American** relating to both England and America

**ante-** /ˈæntɪ/ before: **antenatal** relating to the time before birth –compare **post-**

**anti-** /ˈæntiʸ, ˈæntɪ, ˈæntaɪ/ **1** having a feeling or opinion against: **antinuclear** opposing the use of nuclear weapons and power –compare **pro- 2** opposite to or of: **anticlimax** a much less satisfying end (CLIMAX) than expected | **anticlockwise** in the opposite direction to the movement of the hands of a clock **3** preventing or acting against: **antifreeze** a liquid put into water in a car to stop it from freezing

**arch-** /ɑːtʃ, ɑːk/ chief; first: **archbishop** a chief bishop

**astro-** /əˈstrɑ, ˈæstrəʊ, ˈæstrə/ relating to the stars, planets, and space: **astronomy** the study of the planets and stars

**audi-, audio-,** /ˈɔːdi/ /ˈɔːdi-əʊ/ relating to sound and hearing: **audiovisual** using or relating to both sound and sight

**auto-** /ɔːtəʊ, ɔːtə/ **1** self: **autobiography** a book about one's own life written by oneself **2** without help: **automatic** working by itself without human operation

**be-** /bɪ/ (*makes verbs*) to make; become; treat as: **belittle** to say that a person or thing is small or unimportant

**bi-** /baɪ/ two; twice: **biplane** a plane with two wings | **bilingual** able to speak two languages equally well | **biweekly** happening once every two weeks, or twice a week

**bio-** /ˈbaɪəʊ, baɪˈɒ/ relating to life and living things: **biochemistry** the scientific study of the chemistry of living things | **biodegradable** able to be broken down into harmless products by the action of living things

**by-** /baɪ/ **1** less important: **by-product** something formed in addition to the main product **2** near: **bypass** a road near a city or town so that drivers can go around it rather than through it

**cent-, centi** /sent/ /ˈsentə̥/ 100; 100th: **Centigrade** a scale of temperature in which water boils at 100° | **centimetre** a measurement of length = 0.01 metres

**co-** /kəʊ/ together; with: **co-worker** a person with whom one works

**contra-** /ˈkɒntrə/ opposite; against: **contradict** to say the opposite of (a statement, opinion, etc)

**counter-** /ˈkaʊntəʳ/ opposite; against: **counter-revolution** a movement opposing a revolution | **counterattack** an attack opposing another attack

**de-** /diː, dɪ/ the reverse or opposite of: **de-emphasize** to make less important | **devalue** to make (the value of something such as a currency) less

**deca-, dec-** /ˈdekə/ /dek/ ten: **decade** a period of ten years

**deci-** /desə̥/ a tenth part: **decilitre** 0.1 litres

**dis-** /dɪs/ **1** the opposite of: **discontented** not happy; not contented | **disagree** to have a different opinion; not agree **2** to reverse; remove: **disconnect** to remove a connection of (something, esp. something electrical)

**en-, em-** /ɪn/ /ə̥m; *strong* em/ (*makes verbs*) **1** to put in, on, or around: **encase** to cover completely (as) with a case | **enclose** to put a wall or fence around **2** to make; cause to be: **enlarge** to make larger | **empower** to give (someone) the right or power to do something

**equi-** /ˌekwə̥, ˌiːkwə̥/ equal: **equidistant** equally distant | **equivalent** (of amount, number, etc.) same; equal

**Euro-** /ˈjʊərəʊ/ European: **Eurovision** an organisation for exchanging television and radio programmes in Europe

**ex-** /eks/ no longer being; former: **ex-husband** a man who was a woman's husband, but who is now DIVORCED from her

**extra-** /ˈekstrə/ beyond; outside: **extrasensory** beyond the five sense of sight, smell, sound, taste and touch

**fore-** /fɔːʳ/ **1** earlier; before: **foresee** to guess what is going to happen in the future **2** placed in front of; before; front part of: **forearm** the front part of the arm, below the elbow | **forefront** the most forward place

**geo-** /ˈdʒiːəʊ/ relating to the earth: **geology** the study of the materials (soil, rocks, etc.) which make up the earth | **geography** the study of the seas, rivers, towns, etc., on the surface of the earth

**hecto-** /ˈhektəʊ/ 100: **hectolitre** 100 litres

**hetero-** /ˈhetərə, -rəʊ/ other; different: **heterogeneous** of (many) different kinds | **heterosexual** attracted to people of the opposite sex –compare **homo-**

**homo-** /ˈhəʊməʊ, ˈhɒmə-/ same; like: **homogeneous** formed of parts of the same kind | **homosexual** attracted to people of the same sex –compare **hetero-**

**hyper-** /ˈhaɪpəʳ/ above or too (much): **hypercritical** too critical

**in-** /ɪn/ **1** also **il-** /ɪl/, **im-** /ɪm/, **ir-** /ɪr/ not: **inexact** not exact **2** in; into; on: **inset** something put in as an addition into something else

USAGE **in-** meaning "not" usually changes to **il-** before *l*: **illegal** not legal; **im-** before *b*, *m*, or *p*: **imbalance** lack of balance | **immobile** not mobile | **impatient** not patient; **ir-** before *r*: **irregular** not regular or even; not usual

**inter-** /ˈɪntəʳ/ between; among: **international** having to do with more than one nation | **intermarriage** marriage between members of different groups, families, etc.

**intra-**, **intro-** /ˌɪntrə/ /ˌɪntrəʊ/ inside: **introspection** looking into one's own thoughts and feelings | **intravenous** inside a VEIN

**kilo-** /ˈkɪlə/ 1,000: **kilogram** 1,000 grams; **kilometre** 1,000 metres

**macro-** /ˈmækrəʊ/ large; great: **macroeconomics** the study of the economics of a country or countries

**mal-** /mæl/ bad; wrong: **malformation** the condition of being shaped wrongly **malfunction** a fault in the operation of a machine

**mega-** /ˈmegə/ million: **megawatt** 1,000,000 WATTS (units of electric power)

**micro-** /ˈmaɪkrəʊ/ **1** very small: **microcomputer** a very small computer **2** a millionth: **microsecond** a millionth (0.000 000 1) of a second

**mid-** /mɪd/ middle: **midpoint** a point at or near the center or middle | **midway** halfway or in a middle position

**milli-** /ˈmɪlɪ̵/ a thousandth: **milligram** 1,000th (=0.001) of a gram (a measurement of weight) | **millimeter** 1,000th (=0.001) of a meter (a measurement of length)

**mis-** /mɪs/ **1** bad; wrong: **misspelling** a wrong spelling | **misjudge** to have a wrong opinion of **2** the opposite of: **mistrust** not to trust

**mono-** /ˈmɒnəʊ/ one; single: **monorail** a railway with only one rail | **monopoly** a situation where only one person or group sells a particular thing, produces something, etc. | **monosyllabic** (of a word) having one syllable

**multi-** /ˈmʌltɪ̵/ many; more than one: **multi-coloured** having many colours | **multistorey** (of a building) having many levels or floors

**neo-** /ˈniːəʊ, ˈniːə/ new; a later kind of: **neoclassical** a new or later kind of classical style: *the neoclassical architecture of America*

**non-** /nɒn/ not: **nonstop** without stopping before the end | **nonpayment** not having paid: *He is in trouble for nonpayment of his taxes.*

**out-** /aʊt/ **1** outside: **outdoors** in the open air **2** more than; beyond: **outgrow** to grow too big for: *The girl has outgrown her clothes.*

**over-** /ˈəʊvəʳ/ **1** too much: **overexcited** too excited | **overpopulation** the condition of having too many people (in a country) **2** across; above: **overland** across or by land

**photo-** /ˈfəʊtəʊ/ **1** light: **photoelectric cell** an instrument which starts an electrical apparatus working by means of light **2** photography: **photocopy** (to make) an exact copy of (a letter, drawing, etc.) using a special machine

**post-** /pəʊst/ after; later than: **postwar** belonging to the time after a war | **postpone** to put off to a later time

**pre-** /priː/ before: **prewar** before a war | **preschool** relating to children who are too young to go to school

**pro-** /prəʊ/ in favour of: **pro-education** in favour of education –compare **anti-**

**pseudo-** /ˈsjuːdəʊ, ˈsuː-/ not real; false: **pseudonym** a false name, used esp. by a writer of books | **pseudomodern** seeming to be (but not) modern

**psych-, psycho-** /saɪk/ /ˈsaɪkəʊ/ relating to the mind: **psychotherapy** the treatment of disorders of the mind | **psychology** the study of the mind and of behaviour

**quadr-, quadri-** /ˈkwɒdr/ /ˈkwɒdrɪ̵/ four: **quadrilateral** (a figure) with four sides

**quasi-** /ˈkwɑːzi/ seeming or like: **quasiscientific** seeming to be scientific

**quin-** /kwɪn/ five: **quintet** (music for) five players or singers together

**re-** /riː, rɪ/ again: **remake** to make (esp. a film) again | **rethink** to think about again

USAGE When **re-** means "again", it is pronounced /riː/. In other words beginning with **re-**, it is usually pronounced /rɪ/ (or /riː/ before a vowel). Compare **recover** (–to get better) /rɪˈkʌvəʳ/ and **re-cover** (–to cover again) /ˌriːˈkʌvəʳ/

**self-** /self/ of or by oneself, independent: **self-explanatory** that explains itself | **self-control** control of oneself | **self-employed** working for oneself

**semi-** /ˈsemɪ/ **1** half: **semicircle** half a circle **2** partly: **semisolid** partly solid and partly liquid | a **semi-detached** *house* a house partly joined to another house by one shared wall

**sub-** /sʌb/ **1** under: **submarine** a ship which can travel under water **2** a smaller part of: **subregion** a small part of a region **3** less than: **subhuman** having less than human qualities

**super-** /ˈsuːpəʳ, ˈsjuː-/ greater or more than: **supersonic** faster than the speed of sound | **superstar** a very famous and popular performer

**tele-** /ˈteli/ at or over a long distance: **telescope** an instrument for looking at objects that are far away | **telephone** an electrical apparatus for talking to other people a long distance away

**thermo-** /ˈθɜːməʊ/ heat: **thermometer** an instrument for measuring temperature | **thermodynamics** the study of the relationship between heat and mechanical energy

**trans-** /træns, trænz/ **1** across; on the other side of: **transatlantic** crossing, on the other side of, or concerning countries on both sides of the Atlantic **2** change: **transform** to change completely in form, appearance, or nature

**tri-** /traɪ/ three: **triangle** a flat figure with three straight sides

**ultra-** /ˈʌltrə/ **1** beyond: **ultrasonic** (of sound waves) beyond the range of human hearing **2** very; excessively: **ultramodern** very modern | **ultramarine** a very bright blue colour

**un-** /ʌn/ **1** (*makes adjectives and adverbs*) not: **uncomfortable** not comfortable | **unhappy** not happy | **unwashed** not washed **2** (*makes verbs*) to make the opposite of; reverse: **undress** to take one's clothes off | **unlock** to unfasten the lock of | **untie** to undo (a knot or something tied)

**vice-** /vaɪs/ next in rank or importance: **vice-president** the person next in official rank below a president: *the Vice-President of the United States*

# Word endings

**-ability, -ibility** /əˈbɪl ̥ti/ (*makes nouns from adjectives ending in* **-able, -ible**) **flexibility** the quality of being flexible (= easy to bend or change) | **reliability** the quality of being reliable; able to be trusted

**-able, -ible** /əbəl/ (*makes adjectives*) **1** able to be ...ed: **washable** able to be washed | **drinkable** that can be drunk **2** showing or having: **knowledgeable** having a good deal of knowledge | **reasonable** showing or having reason or good sense

**-age** /ɪdʒ/ (*makes nouns*) **baggage** all the bags and containers with which a person travels | **storage** a place for storing goods | **passage** the action of going across, by, over, etc.

**-al, -ial** /əl, əl/ /ɪəl/ **1** (*makes adjectives*) **political** of or concerning politics **2** (*makes nouns*) **arrival** the act of arriving | **refusal** the act of refusing

**-an, -ian, -ean** /ən/ /ɪən/ **1** (*makes adjectives and nouns from names of places or people*) **American** a person belonging to or connected with America | **Christian** a person who believes in the teachings of Jesus Christ **2** (*makes adjectives*) **Dickensian** of or like Dickens or his books **3** (*makes nouns from words ending in* **-ic**, **-ics**, *and* **-y**) **historian** a person who studies and/or writes about history

**-ance, -ence** /əns/ (*makes nouns*) **1 importance** the quality or state of being important | **patience** the quality of being patient **2** an example of: **performance** an act of PERFORMing in a play, film, etc.

**-ant, -ent** /ənt/ **1** (*makes adjectives*) **pleasant** pleasing to the senses, feelings, or mind | **different** unlike; not of the same kind **2** (*makes nouns*) **servant** a person who works for another in the other's house | **student** a person who is studying at a school, college, etc. | **disinfectant** a chemical used to DISINFECT | **deodorant** a substance that removes unpleasant smells (ODOURS)

**-ar** /əʳ, ɑːʳ/ **1** (*makes nouns*) see -ER² **2** (*makes adjectives*) **muscular** having big muscles; strong-looking

**-arian** /eərɪən/ (*makes nouns and adjectives*) **vegetarian** someone who does not eat meat or fish | **librarian** a person who is in charge of or helps to run a library

**-ary** /əri/ **1** (*makes nouns*) a person or thing connected with or a place for: **library** a building or room which contains books that can be read and usually borrowed **2** (*makes adjectives*) **customary** established by custom; usual

**-ate** / ̥t, eɪt/ **1** (*makes adjectives*) showing; full of: **considerate** showing consideration for **2** (*makes verbs*) to act as; cause to become: **activate** to cause to be active | **regulate** to bring order or method to; make REGULAR **3** (*makes nouns*) a group of people: **electorate** all the people in a place or country who can vote

**-ation** /ˈeɪʃən/ (*makes nouns*) **declaration** an act of declaring | **hesitation** an act of hesitating (= pausing in or before an action) | **exploration** the act or an action of exploring (EXPLORE) (= to travel to a place for the purpose of discovery)

**-ative** /ətɪv/ (*makes adjectives*) **imaginative** using or having imagination | **talkative** liking to talk a lot

**-ator** /eɪtəʳ/ (*makes nouns*) a person or thing that does something: **narrator** a person who NARRATES | **generator** a machine which makes energy, usu. electricity

**-cide** /saɪd/ (*makes nouns*) kill: **suicide** the act of killing oneself | **insecticide** a chemical substance made to kill insects

**-cracy** /krəsi/ (*makes nouns*) a government or class characterized by ...: **democracy** a government that is DEMOCRATIC; government by elected representatives of the people

**-cy** /si/ (*makes nouns*) **accuracy** the quality of being ACCURATE (= exact and correct)

**-d** /d, ̥d, t / see -ED

**-dom** /dəm/ (*makes nouns*) **1** the state of being (something): **boredom** the state of being BORED (= uninterested because of something dull) **2 kingdom** the country rules by a king or queen: *the United Kingdom*

**-ean** /ɪən/ see -AN

**-ed, -d** /d, ɪd, t/ **1** (*makes regular past tenses and past participles*) *we* **laughed** | *I have* **waited** | *a man* **wanted** *by the police* **2** (*makes adjectives*) *a* **bearded** *man* (= a man with a beard) | *a long-***tailed** *cat*

**-ee** /iː/ (*makes nouns*) **1** somebody to whom something is done: **employee** a person who is employed | **trainee** a person who is being trained | **refugee** a person who has been driven from his/her country **2** somebody who is or does something: **absentee** a person who is absent from work, etc.

**-eer** /ɪəʳ/ (*makes nouns*) a person who does an activity: **mountaineer** a person who climbs mountains | **profiteer** someone who makes large profits in times of war or difficulty

**-en** /ən/ **1** (*makes adjectives*) made of: **golden** of or like gold | **wooden** made of wood **2** (*makes verbs*) to cause to be or to have: **darken** to make or become dark: *The sky darkened after sunset.* | **soften** to make or become soft

**-ent** /ənt/ see -ANT

**-er¹, -r** /əʳ/ (*makes the comparative of short adjectives and adverbs*) **hotter** more hot | **safer** more safe –see Study Notes on page 135

**-er², -ar, -or, -r** /əʳ/ (*makes nouns*) **1** a person who does an activity: **footballer** a person who plays football | **teacher** a person who teaches | **liar** a person who tells lies | **actor** a person who acts | **writer** a person who writes **2** a person who lives in (a place): **Londoner** a person who lives in London | **villager** a person who lives in a village **3** a thing that: **cooker** an apparatus on which food is cooked under direct heat | **heater** a machine for heating air, water, etc.

**-ery, -ry** /əri/ (*makes nouns*) **1** the art of or quality of: **cookery** the art of cooking | **bravery** the quality of being brave **2** a place where something is done: **bakery** a place where bread is baked and/or sold

**-es** / ̥z/ see -S

**-ese** /iːz/ (*makes adjectives and nouns*) relating to a country, its language or people, or a style: **Japanese** of or relating to the people, language, or country of Japan | **journalese** in the style of the language used in newspapers

**-esque** /esk/ having a manner or style like: **picturesque** looking like a picture: *a picturesque old village*

**-ess** / ̥s/ female: **actress** a woman who acts in plays and films | **lioness** a female lion

**-est, -st** / ̥st/ (*makes the superlative of many short adjectives and adverbs*) **highest** the most high: *Mount Everest is the highest mountain in the world.* | **hottest** the most hot: *the hottest day of the year* –see Study Notes on page 135

**-ette** /et/ (*makes nouns*) small: **kitchenette** a small kitchen

**-fold** /fəʊld/ (*makes adjectives*) times; multiplied by: **fourfold** four times (an amount)

**-ful**[1] /fəl/ (*makes adjectives*) **delightful** causing delight; highly pleasing | **painful** causing pain

**-ful**[2] /fʊl/ (*makes nouns*) the amount that a container holds: **cupful** the amount held by a cup | **spoonful** the amount held by a spoon

**-fy** /faɪ/ see -IFY

**-hood** /hʊd/ (*makes nouns*) the state or period of being: **childhood** the time or condition of being a child | **womanhood** the state or period of being a woman

**-ial** /ɪəl/ see -AL

**-ian** /ɪən/ see -AN

**-ibility** /ə'bɪlᵻti/ see -ABILITY

**-ible** /əbəl/ see -ABLE

**-ic** /ɪk/ (*makes adjectives*) **poetic** of, like, or connected with poets or poetry –see -ICAL (USAGE)

**-ical** /ɪkəl/ (*makes adjectives*) connected with: **historical** connected with history

USAGE Some pairs of words ending in **-ic** and **-ical** have different meanings. For example, **historic** means 'having a long history' or 'being remembered in history,' but **historical** means 'something that happened in the past' or 'relating to the study of history.'

**-ics** /ɪks/ (*makes nouns*) a science or particular activity: **economics** the scientific study of the way industry and trade produce and use wealth | **athletics** the sport of exercising the body by running, jumping, etc.

**-ie** /i/ see Y (2)

**-ify, -fy** /ᵻ,faɪ/ /faɪ/ (*makes verbs*) to make or become: **purify** to make pure | **simplify** to make simple | **clarify** to make clearer or easier to understand

**-ing** /ɪŋ/ **1** (*makes the present participle of verbs*) *she's* **sleeping** | *I'm* **waiting** *for you.* **2** (*makes nouns from verbs*) **Running** *keeps you healthy.* | *a* **sleeping** *pill* (= a pill to make a person sleep) | *a beautiful* **painting** | **Painting** *is fun.*

**-ise** /aɪz/ see -IZE

**-ish** /ɪʃ/ (*makes adjectives*) **1** relating to a country, its language, or people: **British** of Britain | **Swedish** of Sweden **2** like; typical of: **childish** (*often derog*) of or typical of a child | **foolish** like a fool; without good sense; stupid | **3** rather: **reddish** slightly red | **smallish** rather small **4** approximately: **fortyish** about forty | **sixish** at about 6 o'clock

**-ism** /ɪzəm/ (*makes nouns*) **1** the ideas, principles, or teaching of: **socialism** a belief in equality and in public ownership | **Buddhism** a religion of east and central Asia, based on the teachings of the Buddha **2** a practice or activity: **terrorism** the practice of using violence to obtain political demands **3** a quality or characteristic: **heroism** the quality of being a HERO (= someone who acts with great courage)

**-ist** /ᵻst/ **1** (*makes nouns and adjectives*) a follower of a movement: **socialist** a person who believes in SOCIALISM **2** (*makes nouns*) someone who studies, produces, plays, or operates: **guitarist** someone who plays the guitar | **pianist** someone who plays the piano | **machinist** a person who operates a machine | **linguist** someone who studies language | **novelist** someone who writes NOVELS

**-ite** /aɪt/ (*makes nouns and adjectives*) a follower of a movement: **Trotskyite** a supporter of Trotsky's ideas

**-ity, -ty** /ᵻti/ /ti/ (*makes nouns*) the quality or an example of: *It was an act of* **stupidity** *to drive so fast.* | **cruelty** *to animals*

**-ive** /ɪv/ (*makes adjectives*) having a tendency, character, or quality: **creative** creating new ideas and things | **descriptive** that describes | **explosive** that can explode

**-ize, -ise** /aɪz/ (*makes verbs*) **popularize** to make popular | **legalize** to make legal | **criticize** to find fault with; judge severely

USAGE Both **-ize** and **-ise** are used in British English, but only **-ize** is generally used in American English.

**-less** /ləs/ (*makes adjectives*) **1** without: **hopeless** without hope | **painless** causing no pain | **careless** without taking care | **powerless** without power or strength **2** that never ...s; that cannot be ...ed: **tireless** never getting tired | **countless** that cannot be counted

**-let** /lᵻt/ (*makes nouns*) small: **booklet** a small book, usually with paper covers | **piglet** a young pig

**-like** /laɪk/ (*makes adjectives*) like or similar to: **childlike** of or typical of a child

**-logy, -ology** /lədʒi/ 'ɒlədʒi/ (*makes nouns*) the science or study of: **geology** the study of the materials which make up the earth | **sociology** the scientific study of societies and human groups

**-ly** /li/ **1** (*makes adverbs from adjectives*) *Please drive* **carefully.** | *The man was walking very* **slowly. 2** (*makes adjectives and adverbs*) happening regularly: **hourly** happening every hour | **daily** happening each day **3** (*makes adjectives*) having the manner of: **motherly** having or showing the love, kindness, etc., of a mother **4** (*makes adverbs*) from a particular point of view: *Some people didn't like the film, but* **personally** *I thought it was very good.*

**-ment** /mənt/ (*makes nouns from verbs*) **1** the act or result of: **government** the act or method of ruling a country | **encirclement** the action or result of making a circle around something | **development** the action or result of developing **2** the condition of: **confinement** the state of being CONFINED (enclosed within limits); the time during which a woman about to give birth has to stay in bed

**-most** /məʊst/ (*makes the superlative of some adjectives and adverbs*) most: **topmost** nearest the top | **northernmost** nearest the north

**-ness** /nᵻs/ (*makes nouns*) **goodness** the quality of being good | **loudness** the quality of being loud

**-ology** /ɒlədʒi/ see -LOGY

**-or** /əʳ/ see -ER

**-ory** /əri/ **1** (*makes adjectives*) **satisfactory** causing SATISFACTION; good enough **2** (*makes nouns*) place or thing used for: **observatory** a place where scientists look at stars, etc.

**-ous** /əs/ (*makes adjectives*) **dangerous** able to or likely to cause danger | **spacious** having a lot of space

**-phile** /faɪl/ (*makes nouns*) a person who is attracted to: **Anglophile** a person who likes England

**-philia** /'fɪliə/ (*makes nouns*) love of: **Anglophilia** a love of England –compare **-phobia**

**-phobia** /'fəʊbɪə/ (*makes nouns*) very strong fear or dislike: **Anglophobia** a dislike of England | **claustrophobia** a fear of being in a closed space –compare **-philia**

**-ry** /ri/ see -ERY

**-s, -es** /z, s, ᵻz/ **1** (*makes the plural of nouns*) *one* **cat**, three **cats** | *one* **glass**, *two* **glasses 2** (*makes the third person singular of the present tense of verbs*) *she* **sings** | *He* **likes** *reading.* | *He* **watches** *television.*

**-ship** /ʃɪp/ (*makes nouns*) **1** the state or condition of having or being: **friendship**: *the condition of having a friendly relationship* | **partnership**: the state of being a partner, esp. in business. **2** skill; craft: **scholarship** the knowledge, work or method of SCHOLARS | **workmanship** skill in making things | **musicianship** skill in performing or judging music

**-some** /səm/ **1** (*makes nouns*) **twosome** a group of two people or things **2** (*makes adjectives*) causing; producing: **fearsome** causing fear | **troublesome** causing trouble

**-ster** /stəʳ/ (*makes nouns*) a person who does an activity or who is of a certain group: **youngster** a young person

**-th** /θ/ (*makes adjectives from numbers, except for those ending in 1, 2, or 3*) **sixth** | **hundredth** | **fortieth**

**-ty** /ti/ see -ITY

**-ule** /ju:l/ a small kind of: **globule** a drop of liquid

**-ure** /jəʳ/ (*makes nouns from verbs*) **closure** the act of closing | **failure** lack of success; failing

**-ward, -wards** /wəd/ /wədz/ (*makes adjectives and adverbs*) in the direction of: **backward** directed toward the back, the beginning, or the past | **homeward** going toward home

**-ware** /weər/ (*makes nouns*): **hardware** metal goods for the home and garden, such as pans, tools, etc. | **ironware** goods made from iron

**-ways** /weɪz/ see -WISE

**-wise, -ways** /waɪz, weɪz/ **1** (*makes adjectives and adverbs*) in the manner or direction of: **lengthways** in the direction of the length | **clockwise** in the direction in which the hands of a clock move **2** (*often infml*) (*makes adverbs*) with regard to: **moneywise** with regard to money: *I'm having a lot of problems moneywise.*

**-y** /i/ **1** (*makes nouns*) **jealousy** a JEALOUS feeling | **sympathy** pity for the suffering of another **2** also **-ie** – (*infml*) (*makes nouns*) names for people: **granny** grandmother | **Jamie** James **3** (*makes nouns*) names for animals, used esp. by small children: **doggy** dog **4** (*makes adjectives*) **noisy** making a lot of noise | **sunny** having bright sunlight

# List of irregular verbs

The list below shows those verbs that have irregular past tense, PAST PARTICIPLE, or PRESENT PARTICIPLE forms.
(–see Dictionary Skills Workbook page 22a)

The INFINITIVE form is shown first, e.g. **begin**
2 = past tense, e.g. *As I was walking home it* **began** *to rain.*
3 = past participle, e.g. *It* **had** *already* **begun** *to rain before I left home.*
4 = present participle, e.g. *It* **is** *just* **beginning** *to rain now.*
The number 2/3 means that the past tense and past participle are the same form. The pronunciation of each form is shown at its own place in the dictionary.

abide[1] 2/3 abided 4 abiding
abide[2] 2 abode 3 abided 4 abiding
arise 2 arose 3 arisen 4 arising
awake 2 awoke *or* awaked
3 awaked *or* awoken 4 awaking
be –see BE
bear 2 bore 3 borne 4 bearing
beat 2 beat 3 beaten *or* beat 4 beating
become 2 became 3 become 4 becoming
befall 2 befell 3 befallen 4 befalling
begin 2 began 3 begun 4 beginning
behold 2/3 beheld 4 beholding
bend 2/3 bent 4 bending
bereave 2/3 bereaved *or* bereft 4 bereaving
beseech 2/3 besought *or* beseeched 4 beseeching
beset 2/3 beset 4 besetting
bet 2/3 bet *or* betted 4 betting
bid[1] 2/3 bid 4 bidding
bid[3] 2 bade *or* bid 3 bidden *or* bid 4 bidding
bide 2 bode *or* bided 3 bided 4 biding
bind 2/3 bound 4 binding
bite 2 bit 3 bitten 4 biting
bleed 2/3 bled 4 bleeding
bless 2/3 blessed *or* blest 4 blessing
blow 2 blew 3 blown 4 blowing
break 2 broke 3 broken 4 breaking
breed 2/3 bred 4 breeding
bring 2/3 brought 4 bringing
broadcast 2/3 broadcast || *also* broadcasted *AmE*
4 broadcasting
build 2/3 built 4 building
burn 2/3 burnt *or* burned 4 burning
burst 2/3 burst 4 bursting
buy 2/3 bought 4 buying
cast 2/3 cast 4 casting
catch 2/3 caught 4 catching
chide 2 chided *or* chid
3 chid *or* chidden || *also* chidded *AmE*
4 chiding
choose 2 chose 3 chosen 4 choosing
cleave 2 cleaved *or* cleft *or* clove
3 cleaved *or* cleft *or* cloven 4 cleaving
cling 2/3 clung 4 clinging
clothe 2 clothed || *also* clad *AmE*
3 clad || *also* clothed *AmE* 4 clothing
come 2 came 3 come 4 coming
cost 2/3 cost 4 costing
creep 2/3 crept 4 creeping
cut 2/3 cut 4 cutting
dare 2/3 dared 4 daring
deal 2/3 dealt 4 dealing
dig 2/3 dug 4 digging
dive 2 dived || *also* dove *AmE* 3 dived 4 diving
do –see DO
draw 2 drew 3 drawn 4 drawing
dream 2/3 dreamed *or* dreamt 4 dreaming
drink 2 drank 3 drunk 4 drinking
drive 2 drove 3 driven 4 driving
dwell 2/3 dwelt *or* dwelled 4 dwelling
eat 2 ate 3 eaten 4 eating
fall 2 fell 3 fallen 4 falling
feed 2/3 fed 4 feeding
feel 2/3 felt 4 feeling
fight 2/3 fought 4 fighting
find 2/3 found 4 finding
flee 2/3 fled 4 fleeing
fling 2/3 flung 4 flinging
fly 2 flew 3 flown 4 flying
forbear 2 forbore 3 forborne 4 forbearing
forbid 2 forbade *or* forbad
3 forbidden *or* forbid 4 forbidding
forecast 2/3 forecast *or* forecasted 4 forecasting
foresee 2 foresaw 3 foreseen 4 foreseeing
foretell 2/3 foretold 4 foretelling
forget 2 forgot 3 forgotten 4 forgetting
forgive 2 forgave 3 forgiven 4 forgiving
forsake 2 forsook 3 forsaken 4 forsaking
forswear 2 forswore 3 forsworn 4 forswearing
freeze 2 froze 3 frozen 4 freezing
get 2 got 3 got *esp. BrE* || gotten *AmE* 4 getting
gild 2/3 gilded *or* gilt 4 gilding
give 2 gave 3 given 4 giving
go 2 went 3 gone 4 going
grind 2/3 ground 4 grinding
grow 2 grew 3 grown 4 growing
hang[1] 2/3 hung 4 hanging
hang[2] 2/3 hanged 4 hanging
have –see HAVE
hear 2/3 heard 4 hearing
heave[1] 2/3 heaved 4 heaving
heave[2] 2/3 hove 4 heaving
hew 2 hewed 3 hewed *or* hewn 4 hewing
hide 2 hid 3 hidden 4 hiding
hit 2/3 hit 4 hitting
hold 2/3 held 4 holding
hurt 2/3 hurt 4 hurting
keep 2/3 kept 4 keeping
kneel 2/3 knelt || *also* kneeled *AmE* 4 kneeling
knit 2/3 knit *or* knitted 4 knitting
know 2 knew 3 known 4 knowing
lay 2/3 laid 4 laying
lead 2/3 led 4 leading
lean 2/3 leant *esp. BrE*|| leaned *esp. AmE*
4 leaning
leap 2/3 leapt *esp. BrE*|| leaped *esp. AmE*
4 leaping
learn 2/3 learned *or* learnt 4 learning
leave 2/3 left 4 leaving
lend 2/3 lent 4 lending
let 2/3 let 4 letting
lie[1] 2 lay 3 lain 4 lying
lie[2] 2/3 lied 4 lying
light 2/3 lit *or* lighted 4 lighting
lose 2/3 lost 4 losing

make 2/3 made 4 making
mean 2/3 meant 4 meaning
meet 2/3 met 4 meeting
mislay 2/3 mislaid 4 mislaying
mislead 2/3 misled 4 misleading
misspell 2/3 misspelt *or* misspelled 4 misspelling
misspend 2/3 misspent 4 misspending
mistake 2 mistook 3 mistaken 4 mistaking
misunderstand
2/3 misunderstood 4 misunderstanding
mow 2 mowed 3 mown *or* mowed 4 mowing
outbid 2 outbid
3 outbid || *also* outbidden *AmE* 4 outbidding
outdo 2 outdid 3 outdone 4 outdoing
outshine 2/3 outshone 4 outshining
overcome 2 overcame 3 overcome 4 overcoming
overdo 2 overdid 3 overdone 4 overdoing
overhang 2/3 overhung 4 overhanging
overhear 2/3 overheard 4 overhearing
override 2 overrode 3 overridden 4 overriding
overrun 2 overran 3 overrun 4 overrunning
oversee 2 oversaw 3 overseen 4 overseeing
overshoot 2/3 overshot 4 overshooting
oversleep 2/3 overslept 4 oversleeping
overtake 2 overtook 3 overtaken 4 overtaking
overthrow 2 overthrew
3 overthrown 4 overthrowing
partake 2 partook 3 partaken 4 partaking
pay 2/3 paid 4 paying
prove 2 proved 3 proved *or* proven 4 proving
put 2/3 put 4 putting
quit 2/3 quit 3 quit *or* quitted 4 quitting
read 2/3 read 4 reading
rebuild 2/3 rebuilt 4 rebuilding
redo 2 redid 3 redone 4 redoing
relay 2/3 relayed 4 relaying
remake 2/3 remade 4 remaking
rend 2/3 rent || *also* rended *AmE* 4 rending
repay 2/3 repaid 4 repaying
rewrite 2 rewrote 3 rewritten 4 rewriting
rid 2 rid *or* ridded 3 rid 4 ridding
ride 2 rode 3 ridden 4 riding
ring[2] 2/3 ringed 4 ringing
ring[3] 2 rang 3 rung 4 ringing
rise 2 rose 3 risen 4 rising
run 2 ran 3 run 4 running
saw 2 sawed 3 sawn || *also* sawed *AmE* 4 sawing
say 2/3 said 4 saying
see 2 saw 3 seen 4 seeing
seek 2/3 sought 4 seeking
sell 2/3 sold 4 selling
send 2/3 sent 4 sending
set 2/3 set 4 setting
sew 2 sewed 3 sewn || *also* sewed *AmE* 4 sewing
shake 2 shook 3 shaken 4 shaking
shave 2/3 shaved 4 shaving
shear 2 sheared 3 sheared *or* shorn 4 shearing
shed 2/3 shed 4 shedding
shine[1] 2/3 shone 4 shining
shine[2] 2/3 shined 4 shining
shoot 2/3 shot 4 shooting
show 2 showed 3 shown || *also* showed *AmE*
4 showing
shrink 2 shrank *or* shrunk
3 shrunk *or* shrunken 4 shrinking
shut 2/3 shut 4 shutting
sing 2 sang 3 sung 4 singing
sink 2 sank || *also* sunk *AmE*
3 sunk || *also* sunken *AmE* 4 sinking
sit 2/3 sat 4 sitting
slay 2 slew 3 slain 4 slaying
sleep 2/3 slept 4 sleeping
slide 2/3 slid 4 sliding
sling 2/3 slung 4 slinging
slink 2/3 slunk 4 slinking
slit 2/3 slit 4 slitting
smell 2/3 smelt *esp. BrE* || smelled *esp. AmE*
4 smelling
smite 2 smote
3 smitten || *also* smote *AmE* 4 smiting
sow 2 sowed 3 sown *or* sowed 4 sowing
speak 2 spoke 3 spoken 4 speaking
speed 2/3 sped || *also* speeded *AmE* 4 speeding
spell 2/3 spelt *esp. BrE* || spelled *esp. AmE*
4 spelling
spend 2/3 spent 4 spending
spill 2/3 spilled *or* spilt 4 spilling
spin 2/3 spun 4 spinning
spit 2/3 spat || *also* spit *AmE* 4 spitting
split 2/3 split 4 splitting
spoil 2/3 spoiled *or* spoilt 4 spoiling
spread 2/3 spread 4 spreading
spring 2 sprang || *also* sprung *AmE*
3 sprung 4 springing
stand 2/3 stood 4 standing
steal 2 stole 3 stolen 4 stealing
stick 2/3 stuck 4 sticking
sting 2/3 stung 4 stinging
stink 2 stank *or* stunk 3 stunk 4 stinking
strew 2 strewed 3 strewn *or* strewed 4 strewing
stride 2 strode 3 stridden 4 striding
strike 2 struck
3 struck || *also* stricken *AmE* 4 striking
string 2/3 strung 4 stringing
strive 2 strove
3 striven || *also* strived *AmE* 4 striving
swear 2 swore 3 sworn 4 swearing
sweep 2/3 swept 4 sweeping
swell 2 swelled 3 swollen *or* swelled 4 swelling
swim 2 swam 3 swum 4 swimming
swing 2/3 swung 4 swinging
take 2 took 3 taken 4 taking
teach 2/3 taught 4 teaching
tear 2 tore 3 torn 4 tearing
tell 2/3 told 4 telling
think 2/3 thought 4 thinking
thrive 2 throve *or* thrived
3 thrived *or* thriven 4 thriving
throw 2 threw 3 thrown 4 throwing
thrust 2/3 thrust 4 thrusting
tread 2 trod 3 trodden *or* trod 4 treading
unbend 2/3 unbent 4 unbending
undergo 2 underwent 3 undergone 4 undergoing
understand 2/3 understood 4 understanding
undertake 2 undertook
3 undertaken 4 undertaking
undo 2 undid 3 undone 4 undoing
unwind 2/3 unwound 4 unwinding
uphold 2/3 upheld 4 upholding
upset 2/3 upset 4 upsetting
wake 2 woke *or* waked
3 woken *or* waked 4 waking
waylay 2/3 waylaid 4 waylaying
wear 2 wore 3 worn 4 wearing
weave[1] 2 wove 3 woven 4 weaving
weave[3] 2/3 weaved 4 weaving
wed 2/3 wedded *or* wed 4 wedding
weep 2/3 wept 4 weeping
wet 2/3 wet *or* wetted 4 wetting
win 2/3 won 4 winning
wind[2] 2/3 winded 4 winding
wind[3] 2/3 wound 4 winding
withdraw 2 withdrew 3 withdrawn 4 withdrawing
withhold 2/3 withheld 4 withholding
withstand 2/3 withstood 4 withstanding
wring 2/3 wrung 4 wringing
write 2 wrote 3 written 4 writing

# Sound/pronunciation

The symbols used to show pronunciation in this dictionary are those of the International Phonetic Alphabet (IPA), and are the same as those used in the *Longman Dictionary of Contemporary English*, and in the *English Pronouncing Dictionary* by Professor A. C. Gimson (Dent, 14th Edition, 1977). We use these symbols to show both British and American pronunciations.

**British pronunciation** The type of British speech described in this dictionary is called Received Pronunciation, or RP. It is the speech of some educated English speakers, especially in the south of England, and is the type of British English pronunciation that is most commonly taught to students of English.

**American pronunciation** The type of American English described in this dictionary is one of the more common forms of American English.

The pronunciation of many words is the same in both British and American English. Whenever they are different, we show the American pronunciation following the British one, after the sign ||, like this:

**pot** /pɒt||pɑt/

This means that the British pronunciation is /pɒt/, and the American pronunciation is /pɑt/.

When the British and American pronunciations are very similar, we show the part of the American pronunciation that is different. For example:

**abnormal** /æb'nɔːməl||-'nɔr-/

This means that the British pronunciation is /æb'nɔːməl/ and the American pronunciation is /æb'nɔrməl/.

**Abbreviations** Abbreviations, like **BA** and **EEC** are usually pronounced by saying the letters one at a time: /biː eɪ/, and /iː iː siː/, so we do not show pronunciations for them.

Some abbreviations, however, like **NATO**, are pronounced as though they were a word:

**NATO** /'neɪtəʊ/

Some abbreviations, like **VAT**, are sometimes pronounced by saying the individual letters, and sometimes as though they were a word, so we show both pronunciations:

**VAT** /viː eɪ tiː; væt/

**Strong and weak forms** Many common words, like **am**, **of**, **to**, etc., can be pronounced in more than one way:

**am** /m, əm; *strong* æm/

This means that **am** is usually pronounced /m/ and /əm/ in conversation:

*I'm* /aɪm/ *going to the shops.*

*I am* /əm/ *going soon.*

But when **am** is used at the end of a sentence, or when it is stressed, we use the strong form /æm/:

*Who's going to the shops? I am* /æm/.

**Special signs**

/ə/ means that the sound /ə/ may be pronounced, or may be left out. For example: **memory** /'meməri/ may be pronounced /'meməri/ or /'memri/.

/ɪ̵ ə/ means that some speakers use the sound /ə/ and some use the sound /ɪ/. For example: **possible** /'pɒsɪ̵əbəl/ may be pronounced /'pɒsəbəl/ or /'pɒsɪbəl/.

/i/ at the end of a word means that British speakers usually say /ɪ/, while American speakers usually say /iː/. For example: **happy** /'hæpi/ is pronounced /'hæpɪ/ in British English, and /'hæpiː/ in American English.

/ʳ/ at the end of a word means that in American English the /r/ sound is usually pronounced, while in British English it is pronounced only when the next word begins with a vowel sound. For example: **far** /fɑːʳ/ is usually pronounced /fɑː/ in British English, but **far away** would be pronounced /fɑːrə'weɪ/.

/'/ shows that the SYLLABLE after this sign is said with more force or STRESS (main stress) than the other syllables in the word. For example: **able** /'eɪbəl/ is pronounced able, with the main stress on the first syllable, and **ability** /ə'bɪlɪ̵əti/ is pronounced ability, with the main stress on the second syllable.

/ˌ/ shows that the syllable after this sign is said with some stress, but not as much as main stress. For example: **agriculture** /'ægrɪˌkʌltʃəʳ/ is pronounced agriculture, with the main stress on the first syllable, and less stress (secondary stress) on the third syllable.

/◄/ shows stress shift. The main stress of some adjectives and nouns changes when they are used before another noun. For example: **independent** /ˌɪndɪ̵ə'pendənt◄/ means that we say: *She is very independent.* but: *an independent woman.*

/·'· ·/ When an entry is made up of two words, like **alarm clock**, with the pronunciations shown at **alarm** and **clock**, we do not repeat it at **alarm clock**. Instead we show you how the phrase **alarm clock** is stressed by using a dot for each syllable /·/, and the stress marks /'/ and /ˌ/. For example: **alarm clock** /·'· ·/ means that the main stress is put on the second syllable of **alarm**: alarm clock.

/-/ A hyphen has two uses. In **nighttime** /'naɪt-taɪm/ it is used to show that the /t/ sound is pronounced twice. In **mosaic** /məʊ'zeɪ-ɪk/ it is used to show that there are two separate vowel sounds in the middle of the word, /eɪ/ and /ɪ/.

The hyphen is also used to show that part of a pronunciation is repeated. For example: **absurd** /əb'sɜːd, -'zɜːd/ means that there are two possible pronunciations for **absurd**: /əb'sɜːd/ and /əb'zɜːd/.

## Short forms used in the dictionary

| | |
|---|---|
| *abbrev.* | ABBREVIATION |
| *adj* | adjective |
| *adv* | adverb |
| *AmE* | American English |
| & | and |
| *apprec* | APPRECIATIVE (2) |
| *bibl* | biblical |
| *BrE* | British English |
| *cap.* | CAPITAL[1] (3) |
| *comb.* | combining/ combination |
| *comp.* | COMPARATIVE[2] |
| *conj* | CONJUNCTION |
| *derog* | DEROGATORY |
| *dial* | DIALECT |
| E | East |
| *Eng* | England/English |
| esp. | especially |
| etc. | and so on |
| *euph* | euphemistic (EUPHEMISM) |
| *fem.* | FEMININE (2) |
| fig. | FIGURATIVE |
| *fml* | formal |
| *humor* | humorous |
| *infml* | informal |
| *interj* | INTERJECTION (1) |
| *lit* | LITERARY |
| *masc.* | MASCULINE (2) |
| *n* | noun |
| N | North |
| *obs* | OBSOLETE |
| *pass.* | PASSIVE[2] |
| *pl.* | plural |
| *pomp* | POMPOUS |
| *prep* | PREPOSITION |
| *pron* | PRONOUN |
| S | South |
| SEU S. | Survey of English Usage (spoken) |
| SEU W. | Survey of English Usage (written) |
| *sing.* | singular |
| *tdmk* | TRADEMARK |
| *tech* | TECHNICAL (2) |
| US | United States |
| usu. | usually |
| *v* | verb |
| W | West |

## Grammar codes

[A] ATTRIBUTIVE; an adjective or noun that is used before the noun that it is describing: *a* **main** *road* | *a* **trouser** *leg*

[C] COUNTABLE; a noun that can be counted, and that has a plural form: *This is a* **dictionary**. | *There are many* **dictionaries** *in the library*.

[F] PREDICATIVE; an adjective or adverb that is used only following the noun that it is describing, or following the verbs **be** and **seem**: *That car is three years* **old**. | *He was* **asleep**.

[I] INTRANSITIVE; a verb that has no OBJECT: *They all* **came** *yesterday*.

[P] plural; a noun that is used with a plural verb, and that has no singular noun form: *These* **trousers** *are too tight*.

[S] singular; a noun that is used only in the singular, and that has no plural form: *There was a* **babble** *of voices*.

[T] TRANSITIVE; a verb that has a DIRECT OBJECT: *She* **rides** *a bicycle to school*.

[U] UNCOUNTABLE; a noun that cannot be counted, and that has no plural form: *We drink* **milk** *with our dinner*. | *There is not much* **milk** *left*. | *I found some* **information** *about the town*.

[*no comp.*] shows that an adjective or adverb does not have a COMPARATIVE[2] or a SUPERLATIVE[1] form with **-er** or **-est**, and that it cannot be used with **more** and **most**.

[+*that*] shows that a word can be followed by a CLAUSE beginning with **that**: *He* **read** *that oil prices were going down*.

[+(*that*)] shows that a word can be followed by a CLAUSE beginning with **that**. You don't have to write the word **that**: *He* **knew** *he would be late for work*.

[+*to-v*] shows that a word can be followed by an INFINITIVE verb with **to**: *I* **want** *to leave early today*.

[+~~*to*~~-*v*] shows that a verb can be followed by an INFINITIVE verb without **to**: *I* **saw** *him leave early today*.

[+*v-ing*] shows that a verb can be followed by another verb in the **-ing** form: *I* **like** *playing football*.

[not *be*+*v-ing*] shows that a verb cannot be used in the **-ing** form after the verb **be**.

[+*sing.*/*pl.* v] shows that a noun represents a group. In the singular it may be followed by either a singular or a plural verb: *The football* **team** *is/are playing tonight*. In the plural it must be followed by a plural verb.

[after *n*] shows that an adjective, adverb, or noun can follow a noun: *a piece of wood three inches* **thick**

[*adv*+*adv/prep*] shows that an adverb can be followed by another adverb or by a PREPOSITION: *They live* **far** *away*. | *We could see* **far** *into the distance*.